W9-DFW-341

# ☛ THE COMPLETE Crossword WordFinder ☚

# THE COMPLETE Crossword WordFinder

Compiled and Edited by

Diane Emerson Spino

G. P. Putnam's Sons
New York

G. P. Putnam's Sons
*Publishers Since 1838*
A member of Penguin Putnam Inc.
200 Madison Avenue
New York, NY 10016


Published simultaneously in Canada

Library of Congress Cataloging-in-Publication Data
Spino, Diane.
The complete crossword wordfinder /
compiled and edited by Diane Emerson Spino
p. cm.
ISBN 0-399-14343-2
1. Crossword puzzles—Glossaries, vocabularies, etc. I. Title.
GV1507.C7S63 1997 97-10341 CIP
793.73′2′03—dc21

Printed in the United States of America
1 3 5 7 9 10 8 6 4 2

*Book design by Deborah Kerner*

# CONTENTS

# INTRODUCTION

This word finder will assist you in locating potential solutions to word puzzles. You can use it for crosswords, *Wheel of Fortune* word puzzles, cryptoquotes, and Scrabble. The words are sorted first according to length and then alphabetically according to the first letter, then the second letter, and so forth.

Section 1 of this book contains dictionary words. These are nouns, verbs, adjectives, and other parts of speech, as well as nonpunctuated words, including abbreviations. Prefixes and suffixes that are not stand-alone words are excluded, as are multiword phrases that are defined exclusively as phrases. Plurals of words that are formed by adding *s* or *es* are excluded, but irregular plurals are included. Irregular past-tense verb forms verse are treated similarly.

Section 2 contains nonpunctuated names of famous people. Because crossword puzzle solutions do not use punctuation or spaces, these elements are omitted here. The names listed include famous people in anthropology, archaeology, astronomy, biology, chemistry, earth science, mathematics, medicine, physics, and technology from 600 B.C. to the present, as well as Academy Award winners, U.S. presidents, Nobel Prize winners, Grammy Hall of Famers, Pulitzer Prize winners, modern prolific inventors, and others. (References appear in the bibliography.)

Section 3 contains geographical names, and includes lists of countries, states, their two-letter abbreviations, and their capital cities. At the end of this section is an alphabetical listing of major bodies of water: oceans, seas, lakes, straits, gulfs, bays, sounds, and channels.

## How to Look Up Words

**STEP 1.** Determine the word length by counting the number of letters in the unknown word.

**STEP 2.** Try to determine at least one of the letters in the unknown word, and its position. Count the number of letters in the unknown word from left to right, up to and including the known letter.

**STEP 3.** Look in the Contents for the section that contains words of the same *length* as the unknown word. Turn to that section in the text.

**STEP 4.** Look within the section for the list containing words *sorted according to the same letter position* as that of your known letter.

**STEP 5.** View the columns of words vertically until the known letter, in its correct position, is located.

**STEP 6.** Continue to view the columns of words vertically until the last word containing the known letter, in its correct position, is located. (The letter on which the sort is being made appears in **bold** in the text.)

**STEP 7.** The words located in steps 5 and 6 contain the potential solutions for the word sought in the puzzle.

## Helpful Hint

If you discover an extremely large number of possible solutions to your query, try to identify another letter in the unknown word, narrowing down the potential solutions. You can search the sorts for words that meet both criteria; or you can follow steps 2 through 7 using the new letter. For example, there are many potential solutions for words ending in *e*. In such situations, try to identify a consonant or other letter through which to locate a word.

# 2 LETTER WORDS

**1st Letter**

AA AB AC AD AF AG AK AL AM AN AO AP AR AS AT AU AV AX AZ BA BB BC BD BE BF BG BI BK BL BM BN BO BP BR BS BU BV BX BY CA CB CC CD CE

CF CG CH CI CJ CK CL CM CN CO CP CQ CR CS CT CU CW CZ DA DB DC DD DE DF DG DJ DK DN DO DP DR DS DU DV DX DZ EA ED EE EG EL EM EQ ES ET EU

EW EX FB FD FE FF FL FM FN FO FP FR FT FY GA GB GD GE GI GK GM GO GP GQ GR GT GU HA HB HC HD HE HF HG HH HI HJ HL HM HO HP HQ HR HS HT HV

IA IB IC ID IE IF IL IN IP IQ IR IS IT IV IW JD JG JN JO JP JR JV KC KD KG KM KN KO KP KR KS KT KV KW KY LA LB LC LD LF LG LH LI LK LL LM

LN LO LP LR LS LT LU LV LZ MA MB MC MD ME MF MG MI MK ML MM MN MO MP MR MS MT MV MY NA NB NC ND NE NF NG NH NI NJ NL NM NO NP NS NT NU NV

NW NY NZ OB OD OE OF OG OH OK OM ON OP OR OS OT OX OZ PA PB PC PD PE PF PG PH PI PK PL PM PN PO PP PQ PR PS PT PU PW PX QC QD QM QR QT QU

QV QY RA RB RC RD RE RF RH RI RM RN RR RS RT RU RW SA SB SC SD SE SF SG SH SI SJ SL SM SN SO SP SQ SR SS ST SV SW SX TA TB TC TD TE TH TI

TK TL TM TN TO TP TR TV TX UH UK UN UP US UT UV UW UX VA VB VC VD VF VG VI VL VP VS VT VV WA WB WC WE WH WI WK WL WO WT WV WW WY XD XE XI

XL XN XT XU YB YD YE YR YT ZN ZR

**2nd Letter**

AA BA CA DA EA GA HA IA LA MA NA PA RA SA TA VA WA AB BB CB DB FB GB HB IB LB MB NB OB PB

RB SB TB VB WB YB AC BC CC DC HC IC KC LC MC NC PC QC RC SC TC VC WC AD BD CD DD ED FD GD HD ID JD KD LD MD ND OD PD QD RD SD TD VD XD YD

BE CE DE EE FE GE HE IE ME NE OE PE RE SE TE WE XE YE AF BF CF DF FF HF IF LF MF NF OF PF RF SF VF AG BG CG DG EG HG JG KG LG MG NG OG PG

SG VG CH HH LH NH OH PH RH SH TH UH WH BI CI GI HI LI MI NI PI RI SI TI VI WI XI CJ DJ HJ NJ SJ AK BK CK DK GK LK MK OK PK TK UK WK AL BL

CL EL FL HL IL LL ML NL PL SL TL VL WL XL AM BM CM EM FM GM HM KM LM MM NM OM PM QM RM SM TM AN BN CN DN FN IN JN KN LN MN ON PN RN SN TN

UN XN ZN AO BO CO DO FO GO HO JO KO LO MO NO PO SO TO WO AP BP CP DP FP GP HP IP JP KP LP MP NP OP PP SP TP UP VP CQ EQ GQ HQ IQ PQ SQ AR

BR CR DR FR GR HR IR JR KR LR MR OR PR QR RR SR TR YR ZR AS BS CS DS ES HS IS KS LS MS NS OS PS RS SS US VS AT CT ET FT GT HT IT KT LT MT

NT OT PT QT RT ST UT VT WT XT YT AU BU CU DU EU GU LU NU PU QU RU XU AV BV DV HV IV JV KV LV MV NV QV SV TV UV VV WV CW EW IW KW NW PW RW

SW UW WW AX BX DX EX OX PX SX TX UX BY FY KY MY NY QY WY AZ CZ DZ LZ NZ OZ

# 3 LETTER WORDS

**1st Letter**

AAA ABA ABC ABL ABM ABP ABR ABS ACC ACE ACK ACT ADA ADC ADD ADJ ADM ADO ADV ADZ AEC AEF AEQ AET AFB AFC AFR AFT AGE AGO AGR AGT AID AIL AIM AIR AKA AKC ALA ALC ALD ALE ALG ALK ALL ALP ALT AMA AMB

AMP AMT ANC AND ANN ANS ANT ANY APB APE API APL APO APP APR APT ARC ARE ARK ARM ARR ART ARV ASC ASH ASK ASP ASS ASV ATE ATL ATM ATN ATP ATT AUD AUG AUK AUS AUX AVE AVG AVO AWE AWK AWL AWN AYE BAD BAG BAL

BAN BAR BAT BAY BBA BBB BBC BBL BBS BCD BCS BDL BED BEE BEF BEG BET BEY BFA BHD BIB BID BIG BIN BIT BKG BKS BKT BLK BLT BMP BMR BOA BOB BOG BOO BOP BOQ BOR BOT BOW BOX BOY BPL BPS BRA BRO BSA BSC BTU BUD

BUG BUM BUN BUR BUS BUT BUY BWI BYE CAB CAD CAF CAL CAM CAN CAP CAR CAT CAV CAW CAY CBC CBS CBW CCC CCW CDR CEN CFI CGA CGS CHG CHM CIA CID CIE CIF CIR CIT CIV CLD CLK CLO CLR CLU CML CMS CNO CNS COB COD

COG COL COM CON COO COP COR COS COT COW COY CPA CPD CPL CPO CPS CPT CPU CRC CRT CRY CSA CSM CST CTG CTN CTR CUA CUB CUD CUE CUM CUP CUR CUT CWO CWT CYC CYL CYO DAB DAC DAD DAM DAN DAR DAT DAU DAY DBL DDE

DDS DDT DEB DEC DEF DEG DEL DEM DEN DEP DER DET DEV DEW DFC DFM DIA DID DIE DIF DIG DIL DIM DIN DIP DIR DIV DLL DLO DMA DMD DMZ DNA DOA DOB DOC DOE DOG DOL DOM DON DOS DOT DOZ DPI DPT DRY DSC DSM DSO DSP

DST DTE DUB DUD DUE DUG DUN DUO DUP DVM DWT DYE EAR EAT EBB ECG ECM EDP EDT EEG EEL EFF EFT EGA EGG EGO EHF EKE EKG ELF ELK ELL ELM EMF EMP EMS EMU ENC END ENE ENG ENL ENS ENV EOM EON EPH EPS ERA ERE ERR

ESD ESE ESP ESQ EST ETA ETC ETD ETV ETY EUR EVA EVE EVG EWE EXC EXE EXP EXT EYE FAA FAC FAD FAG FAH FAN FAO FAR FAS FAT FAX FAY FBI FCC FCP FCY FDA FEB FEC FED FEE FEM FEN FET FEW FEY FEZ FHA FIB FIE FIG

FIN FIO FIR FIT FIX FLU FLY FOB FOC FOE FOG FOP FOR FOS FOT FOX FPC FPM FPO FPS FRI FRO FRS FRT FRY FTC FTP FUN FUR FUT FWD FYI GAB GAD GAG GAL GAO GAP GAR GAS GAW GAY GAZ GCA GCT GEL GEM GEN GER GET GHQ

GIE GIF GIG GIN GMC GMT GNP GNU GOB GOD GOO GOP GOT GOV GPF GPO GRO GSA GTD GUI GUM GUN GUT GUY GYM GYP HAB HAD HAG HAM HAP HAS HAT HAW HAY HBM HCL HEB HEM HEN HEP HER HEW HEX HGT HHD HIE HIM HIP HIS HIT

HMS HOB HOD HOE HOG HON HOP HOR HOS HOT HOW HRH HSB HST HUB HUD HUE HUG HUM HUN HUT HVY HWY HYP IBM ICC ICE ICJ ICY IDE IGY IHP IHS ILK ILL ILS IMF IMP INC IND INF INI INK INN INP INS INT INV ION IOU IPS

IRA IRE IRK IRQ IRS ISA ISL ISM ISO ISR ITS IUD IVY IWW JAB JAG JAM JAN JAP JAR JAS JAW JAY JCC JCL JCS JCT JER JET JEW JIB JIG JOB JOG JOT JOY JRC JUG JUL JUN JUT JUV KEG KEN KEY KIA KID KIN KIP KIT KJV

KKK LAB LAC LAD LAG LAM LAN LAP LAT LAW LAX LAY LCD LCL LCM LDG LEA LED LEE LEG LEI LEK LEM LET LEU LEV LGK LHD LIB LID LIE LIN LIP LIQ LIT LLB LLD LNG LOB LOG LOP LOQ LOT LOW LOX LPG LPI LPN LSD LSS LTC

LTD LTG LTL LTR LUB LUG LYE MAC MAD MAG MAJ MAL MAN MAP MAR MAT MAW MAX MAY MBA MDA MED MEG MEM MEN MER MET MEV MEW MEX MFA MFD MFG MFM MFR MGR MGT MHZ MIA MIC MID MIL MIN MIS MIX MKS MLD MME MNP MOB MOD

MOL MOM MON MOO MOP MOT MOW MPC MPG MPH MRS MSD MSG MSL MSS MST MTG MUD MUG MUM MUN MUS MVP MVS NAB NAG NAH NAK NAP NAS NAT NAV NAY NBC NBS NCE NCO NCV NEB NEE NEG NEH NEI NES NET NEV NEW NFS NGK NHI NIB

NIL NIP NIT NIX NNE NNW NOD NOH NOM NOR NOS NOT NOV NOW NPN NSA NSC NSF NSW NTH NTP NUB NUM NUN NUT NWT NYC OAF OAK OAR OAS OAT OBI OBJ OBL OBS OBV OCR OCS OCT ODD ODE OED OEM OEO OES OFF OFM OFS OFT OHM

| OIL | PIC | QID | RTE | SON | THE | VAR | WOO | DAT | MAC | TAG | PBX | DDS | HEB | REA | MFA |
|---|---|---|---|---|---|---|---|---|---|---|---|---|---|---|---|
| OJT | PIE | QLD | RUB | SOP | THY | VAT | WOW | DAU | MAD | TAM | RBC | DDT | HEM | REC | MFD |
| OLD | PIF | QMC | RUE | SOS | TIA | VAX | WPM | DAY | MAG | TAN | RBI | EDP | HEN | RED | MFG |
| OLE | PIG | QMG | RUG | SOT | TIC | VDT | WPN | EAR | MAJ | TAP | SBA | EDT | HEP | REF | MFM |
| ONE | PIN | QTO | RUM | SOW | TID | VEL | WRY | EAT | MAL | TAR | TBA | FDA | HER | REG | MFR |
| ONT | PIP | QTY | RUN | SOX | TIE | VEN | WSW | FAA | MAN | TAT | TBS | IDE | HEW | REL | NFS |
| OOP | PIS | QUE | RUT | SOY | TIM | VET | WWW | FAC | MAP | TAW | WBC | LDG | HEX | REM | OFF |
| OPE | PIT | RAD | RWY | SPA | TIN | VEX | XGA | FAD | MAR | TAX | ACC | MDA | JER | REP | OFM |
| OPP | PIX | RAF | RYE | SPP | TIP | VFD | YAK | FAG | MAT | UAR | ACE | ODD | JET | REQ | OFS |
| OPT | PKG | RAG | SAA | SPY | TIT | VFW | YAM | FAH | MAW | VAL | ACK | ODE | JEW | RES | OFT |
| ORB | PKT | RAM | SAC | SRO | TKT | VGA | YAP | FAN | MAX | VAN | ACT | PDA | KEG | RET | PFC |
| ORD | PLY | RAN | SAD | SSA | TLC | VHF | YAW | FAO | MAY | VAR | BCD | PDD | KEN | REV | PFD |
| ORE | PMK | RAP | SAG | SSE | TMO | VIA | YEA | FAR | NAB | VAT | BCS | PDQ | KEY | REX | RFD |
| ORG | PMT | RAT | SAM | SSG | TNC | VIC | YEN | FAS | NAG | VAX | CCC | PDT | LEA | SEA | RFI |
| OSB | PNP | RAW | SAP | SSP | TNG | VIE | YES | FAT | NAH | WAC | CCW | QDA | LED | SEC | SFC |
| OSF | POC | RAY | SAT | SSR | TNT | VIL | YET | FAX | NAK | WAD | ECG | TDY | LEE | SEE | UFO |
| OSI | POD | RBC | SAW | SSS | TOE | VIM | YEW | FAY | NAP | WAF | ECM | VDT | LEG | SEL | VFD |
| OTS | POE | RBI | SAY | SST | TOG | VIP | YOB | GAB | NAS | WAG | FCC | AEC | LEI | SEM | VFW |
| OUR | POI | RCT | SBA | SSW | TOM | VIS | YON | GAD | NAT | WAN | FCP | AEF | LEK | SEN | AGE |
| OUT | POL | REA | SCH | STA | TON | VIZ | YOU | GAG | NAV | WAR | FCY | AEQ | LEM | SEP | AGO |
| OVA | POP | REC | SCI | STD | TOO | VLB | ZAP | GAL | NAY | WAS | GCA | AET | LET | SEQ | AGR |
| OWE | POR | RED | SEA | STE | TOP | VOA | ZED | GAO | OAF | WAV | GCT | BED | LEU | SER | AGT |
| OWL | POS | REF | SEC | STG | TOR | VOC | ZEN | GAP | OAK | WAX | HCL | BEE | LEV | SET | CGA |
| OWN | POT | REG | SEE | STK | TOT | VOL | ZIP | GAR | OAR | WAY | ICC | BEF | MED | SEW | CGS |
| PAC | POW | REL | SEL | STP | TOW | VOU | ZOO | GAS | OAS | YAK | ICE | BEG | MEG | SEX | EGA |
| PAD | POX | REM | SEM | STY | TOY | VOW | ZPG | GAW | OAT | YAM | ICJ | BET | MEM | TEA | EGG |
| PAL | PPC | REP | SEN | SUB | TPK | VSS |  | GAY | PAC | YAP | ICY | BEY | MEN | TEE | EGO |
| PAM | PPD | REQ | SEP | SUE | TRY | WAC |  | GAZ | PAD | YAW | JCC | CEN | MER | TEL | HGT |
| PAN | PPM | RES | SEQ | SUM | TSP | WAD |  | HAB | PAL | ZAP | JCL | DEB | MET | TEN | IGY |
| PAP | PPT | RET | SER | SUN | TSR | WAF | 2ND | HAD | PAM | ABA | JCS | DEC | MEV | TER | LGK |
| PAR | PRF | REV | SET | SUP | TTL | WAG | LETTER | HAG | PAN | ABC | JCT | DEF | MEW | TEX | MGR |
| PAS | PRN | REX | SEW | SVC | TUB | WAN | AAA | HAM | PAP | ABL | LCD | DEG | MEX | VEL | MGT |
| PAT | PRO | RFD | SEX | SWA | TUG | WAR | BAD | HAP | PAR | ABM | LCL | DEL | NEB | VEN | NGK |
| PAW | PRP | RFI | SFC | SYL | TUN | WAS | BAG | HAS | PAS | ABP | LCM | DEM | NEE | VET | RGB |
| PAY | PRY | RGB | SGD | SYM | TVA | WAV | BAL | HAT | PAT | ABR | NCE | DEN | NEG | VEX | SGD |
| PBX | PSG | RIB | SGT | SYN | TWO | WAX | BAN | HAW | PAW | ABS | NCO | DEP | NEH | WEB | SGT |
| PCI | PSI | RID | SHE | TAB | TWP | WAY | BAR | HAY | PAY | BBA | NCV | DER | NEI | WED | VGA |
| PCT | PST | RIG | SHT | TAC | TWX | WBC | BAT | JAB | RAD | BBB | OCR | DET | NES | WEE | XGA |
| PCX | PTA | RIM | SHY | TAG | UAR | WEB | BAY | JAG | RAF | BBC | OCS | DEV | NET | WEN | BHD |
| PDA | PTE | RIP | SIC | TAM | UFO | WED | CAB | JAM | RAG | BBL | OCT | DEW | NEV | WET | CHG |
| PDD | PTG | RIV | SIG | TAN | UHF | WEE | CAD | JAN | RAM | BBS | PCI | EEG | NEW | YEA | CHM |
| PDQ | PTO | RLL | SIN | TAP | ULT | WEN | CAF | JAP | RAN | CBC | PCT | EEL | OED | YEN | EHF |
| PDT | PTV | RNA | SIP | TAR | UMT | WET | CAL | JAR | RAP | CBS | PCX | FEB | OEM | YES | FHA |
| PEA | PUB | RND | SIR | TAT | UPI | WHF | CAM | JAS | RAT | CBW | RCT | FEC | OEO | YET | GHQ |
| PEG | PUG | ROB | SIT | TAW | URL | WHO | CAN | JAW | RAW | DBL | SCH | FED | OES | YEW | HHD |
| PEI | PUL | ROD | SIX | TAX | URN | WHS | CAP | JAY | RAY | EBB | SCI | FEE | PEA | ZED | IHP |
| PEL | PUN | ROE | SJD | TBA | USA | WHY | CAR | LAB | SAA | FBI | ADA | FEM | PEG | ZEN | IHS |
| PEN | PUP | ROG | SKI | TBS | USE | WID | CAT | LAC | SAC | HBM | ADC | FEN | PEI | AFB | LHD |
| PEP | PUS | ROM | SKT | TDY | USM | WIG | CAV | LAD | SAD | IBM | ADD | FET | PEL | AFC | MHZ |
| PER | PUT | ROT | SKY | TEA | USN | WIN | CAW | LAG | SAG | MBA | ADJ | FEW | PEN | AFR | NHI |
| PET | PVT | ROW | SLD | TEE | USO | WIS | CAY | LAM | SAM | NBC | ADM | FEY | PEP | AFT | OHM |
| PEW | PYA | RPG | SLY | TEL | USP | WIT | DAB | LAN | SAP | NBS | ADO | FEZ | PER | BFA | PHD |
| PFC | PYX | RPM | SMA | TEN | USS | WMK | DAC | LAP | SAT | OBI | ADV | GEL | PET | CFI | PHR |
| PFD | QDA | RPN | SOB | TER | USU | WNW | DAD | LAT | SAW | OBJ | ADZ | GEM | PEW | DFC | PHS |
| PHD | QED | RPO | SOC | TEX | UTE | WOE | DAM | LAW | SAY | OBL | BDL | GEN | QED | DFM | SHE |
| PHR | QEF | RPS | SOD | THC | VAL | WOK | DAN | LAX | TAB | OBS | CDR | GER | QEF | EFF | SHT |
| PHS | QEI | RSV | SOL | THD | VAN | WON | DAR | LAY | TAC | OBV | DDE | GET | QEI | EFT | SHY |

| | | | | | | | | | | | | | | | |
|---|---|---|---|---|---|---|---|---|---|---|---|---|---|---|---|
| THC | KID | VIE | LLB | ENV | DON | NOS | ZOO | ARE | DSP | ATP | CUD | RUE | CYL | MIA | LLB |
| THD | KIN | VIL | LLD | GNP | DOS | NOT | APB | ARK | DST | ATT | CUE | RUG | CYO | NSA | LOB |
| THE | KIP | VIM | MLD | GNU | DOT | NOV | APE | ARM | ESD | BTU | CUM | RUM | DYE | OVA | LUB |
| THY | KIT | VIP | OLD | INC | DOZ | NOW | API | ARR | ESE | CTG | CUP | RUN | EYE | PDA | MOB |
| UHF | LIB | VIS | OLE | IND | EOM | OOP | APL | ART | ESP | CTN | CUR | RUT | FYI | PEA | NAB |
| VHF | LID | VIZ | PLY | INF | EON | POC | APO | ARV | ESQ | CTR | CUT | SUB | GYM | PTA | NEB |
| WHF | LIE | WID | QLD | INI | FOB | POD | APP | BRA | EST | DTE | DUB | SUE | GYP | PYA | NIB |
| WHO | LIN | WIG | RLL | INK | FOC | POE | APR | BRO | GSA | ETA | DUD | SUM | HYP | QDA | NUB |
| WHS | LIP | WIN | SLD | INN | FOE | POI | APT | CRC | HSB | ETC | DUE | SUN | LYE | REA | ORB |
| WHY | LIQ | WIS | SLY | INP | FOG | POL | BPL | CRT | HST | ETD | DUG | SUP | NYC | RNA | OSB |
| AID | LIT | WIT | TLC | INS | FOP | POP | BPS | CRY | ISA | ETV | DUN | TUB | PYA | SAA | PUB |
| AIL | MIA | ZIP | ULT | INT | FOR | POR | CPA | DRY | ISL | ETY | DUO | TUG | PYX | SBA | RGB |
| AIM | MIC | KJV | VLB | INV | FOS | POS | CPD | ERA | ISM | FTC | DUP | TUN | RYE | SEA | RIB |
| AIR | MID | OJT | AMA | LNG | FOT | POT | CPL | ERE | ISO | FTP | EUR | AVE | SYL | SMA | ROB |
| BIB | MIL | SJD | AMB | MNP | FOX | POW | CPO | ERR | ISR | GTD | FUN | AVG | SYM | SPA | RUB |
| BID | MIN | AKA | AMP | NNE | GOB | POX | CPS | FRI | LSD | ITS | FUR | AVO | SYN | SSA | SOB |
| BIG | MIS | AKC | AMT | NNW | GOD | ROB | CPT | FRO | LSS | LTC | FUT | DVM | | STA | SUB |
| BIN | MIX | BKG | BMP | ONE | GOO | ROD | CPU | FRS | MSD | LTD | GUI | EVA | | SWA | TAB |
| BIT | NIB | BKS | BMR | ONT | GOP | ROE | DPI | FRT | MSG | LTG | GUM | EVE | | TBA | TUB |
| CIA | NIL | BKT | CML | PNP | GOT | ROG | DPT | FRY | MSL | LTL | GUN | EVG | 3RD LETTER | TEA | VLB |
| CID | NIP | EKE | CMS | RNA | GOV | ROM | EPH | GRO | MSS | LTR | GUT | HVY | | TIA | WEB |
| CIE | NIT | EKG | DMA | RND | HOB | ROT | EPS | HRH | MST | MTG | GUY | IVY | AAA | TVA | YOB |
| CIF | NIX | KKK | DMD | TNC | HOD | ROW | FPC | IRA | NSA | NTH | HUB | MVP | ABA | USA | ABC |
| CIR | OIL | MKS | DMZ | TNG | HOE | SOB | FPM | IRE | NSC | NTP | HUD | MVS | ADA | VGA | ACC |
| CIT | PIC | PKG | EMF | TNT | HOG | SOC | FPO | IRK | NSF | OTS | HUE | OVA | AKA | VIA | ADC |
| CIV | PIE | PKT | EMP | WNW | HON | SOD | FPS | IRQ | NSW | PTA | HUG | PVT | ALA | VOA | AEC |
| DIA | PIF | SKI | EMS | BOA | HOP | SOL | GPF | IRS | OSB | PTE | HUM | SVC | AMA | XGA | AFC |
| DID | PIG | SKT | EMU | BOB | HOR | SON | GPO | JRC | OSF | PTG | HUN | TVA | BBA | YEA | AKC |
| DIE | PIN | SKY | GMC | BOG | HOS | SOP | IPS | MRS | OSI | PTO | HUT | AWE | BFA | AFB | ALC |
| DIF | PIP | TKT | GMT | BOO | HOT | SOS | LPG | ORB | PSG | PTV | IUD | AWK | BOA | AMB | ANC |
| DIG | PIS | ALA | HMS | BOP | HOW | SOT | LPI | ORD | PSI | QTO | JUG | AWL | BRA | APB | ARC |
| DIL | PIT | ALC | IMF | BOQ | ION | SOW | LPN | ORE | PST | QTY | JUL | AWN | BSA | BBB | ASC |
| DIM | PIX | ALD | IMP | BOR | IOU | SOX | MPC | ORG | RSV | RTE | JUN | BWI | CGA | BIB | BBC |
| DIN | QID | ALE | MME | BOT | JOB | SOY | MPG | PRF | SSA | STA | JUT | CWO | CIA | BOB | BSC |
| DIP | RIB | ALG | PMK | BOW | JOG | TOE | MPH | PRN | SSE | STD | JUV | CWT | CPA | CAB | CBC |
| DIR | RID | ALK | PMT | BOX | JOT | TOG | NPN | PRO | SSG | STE | LUB | DWT | CSA | COB | CCC |
| DIV | RIG | ALL | QMC | BOY | JOY | TOM | OPE | PRP | SSP | STG | LUG | EWE | CUA | CUB | CRC |
| FIB | RIM | ALP | QMG | COB | LOB | TON | OPP | PRY | SSR | STK | MUD | FWD | DIA | DAB | CYC |
| FIE | RIP | ALT | SMA | COD | LOG | TOO | OPT | SRO | SSS | STP | MUG | HWY | DMA | DEB | DAC |
| FIG | RIV | BLK | TMO | COG | LOP | TOP | PPC | TRY | SST | STY | MUM | IWW | DNA | DOB | DEC |
| FIN | SIC | BLT | UMT | COL | LOQ | TOR | PPD | URL | SSW | TTL | MUN | NWT | DOA | DUB | DFC |
| FIO | SIG | CLD | WMK | COM | LOT | TOT | PPM | URN | TSP | UTE | MUS | OWE | EGA | EBB | DOC |
| FIR | SIN | CLK | ANC | CON | LOW | TOW | PPT | WRY | TSR | AUD | NUB | OWL | ERA | FEB | DSC |
| FIT | SIP | CLO | AND | COO | LOX | TOY | RPG | ASC | USA | AUG | NUM | OWN | ETA | FIB | ENC |
| FIX | SIR | CLR | ANN | COP | MOB | VOA | RPM | ASH | USE | AUK | NUN | RWY | EVA | FOB | ETC |
| GIE | SIT | CLU | ANS | COR | MOD | VOC | RPN | ASK | USM | AUS | NUT | SWA | FAA | GAB | EXC |
| GIF | SIX | DLL | ANT | COS | MOL | VOL | RPO | ASP | USN | AUX | OUR | TWO | FDA | GOB | FAC |
| GIG | TIA | DLO | ANY | COT | MOM | VOU | RPS | ASS | USO | BUD | OUT | TWP | FHA | HAB | FCC |
| GIN | TIC | ELF | CNO | COW | MON | VOW | SPA | ASV | USP | BUG | PUB | TWX | GCA | HEB | FEC |
| HIE | TID | ELK | CNS | COY | MOO | WOE | SPP | BSA | USS | BUM | PUG | WWW | GSA | HOB | FOC |
| HIM | TIE | ELL | DNA | DOA | MOP | WOK | SPY | BSC | USU | BUN | PUL | EXC | IRA | HSB | FPC |
| HIP | TIM | ELM | ENC | DOB | MOT | WON | TPK | CSA | VSS | BUR | PUN | EXE | ISA | HUB | FTC |
| HIS | TIN | FLU | END | DOC | MOW | WOO | UPI | CSM | WSW | BUS | PUP | EXP | KIA | JAB | GMC |
| HIT | TIP | FLY | ENE | DOE | NOD | WOW | WPM | CST | ATE | BUT | PUS | EXT | LEA | JIB | ICC |
| JIB | TIT | ILK | ENG | DOG | NOH | YOB | WPN | DSC | ATL | BUY | PUT | AYE | MBA | JOB | INC |
| JIG | VIA | ILL | ENL | DOL | NOM | YON | ZPG | DSM | ATM | CUA | QUE | BYE | MDA | LAB | JCC |
| KIA | VIC | ILS | ENS | DOM | NOR | YOU | ARC | DSO | ATN | CUB | RUB | CYC | MFA | LIB | JRC |

| | | | | | | | | | | | | | | | |
|---|---|---|---|---|---|---|---|---|---|---|---|---|---|---|---|
| LAC | FWD | WED | ROE | DEG | STG | INK | PUL | OFM | MEN | GAO | LAP | BMR | BPS | TBS | HGT |
| LTC | GAD | WID | RTE | DIG | TAG | IRK | REL | OHM | MIN | GOO | LIP | BOR | BUS | USS | HIT |
| MAC | GOD | ZED | RUE | DOG | TNG | KKK | RLL | PAM | MON | GPO | LOP | BUR | CBS | VIS | HOT |
| MIC | GTD | ACE | RYE | DUG | TOG | LEK | SEL | PPM | MUN | GRO | MAP | CAR | CGS | VSS | HST |
| MPC | HAD | AGE | SEE | ECG | TUG | LGK | SOL | RAM | NPN | ISO | MNP | CDR | CMS | WAS | HUT |
| NBC | HHD | ALE | SHE | EEG | WAG | NAK | SYL | REM | NUN | MOO | MOP | CIR | CNS | WHS | INT |
| NSC | HOD | APE | SSE | EGG | WIG | NGK | TEL | RIM | OWN | NCO | MVP | CLR | COS | WIS | JCT |
| NYC | HUD | ARE | STE | EKG | ZPG | OAK | TTL | ROM | PAN | OEO | NAP | COR | CPS | YES | JET |
| PAC | IND | ATE | SUE | ENG | ASH | PMK | URL | RPM | PEN | PRO | NIP | CTR | DDS | ACT | JOT |
| PFC | IUD | AVE | TEE | EVG | EPH | STK | VAL | RUM | PIN | PTO | NTP | CUR | DOS | AET | JUT |
| PIC | KID | AWE | THE | FAG | FAH | TPK | VEL | SAM | PRN | QTO | OOP | DAR | EMS | AFT | KIT |
| POC | LAD | AYE | TIE | FIG | HRH | WMK | VIL | SEM | PUN | RPO | OPP | DER | ENS | AGT | LAT |
| PPC | LCD | BEE | TOE | FOG | MPH | WOK | VOL | SUM | RAN | SRO | PAP | DIR | EPS | ALT | LET |
| QMC | LED | BYE | USE | GAG | NAH | YAK | ABM | SYM | RPN | TMO | PEP | EAR | FAS | AMT | LIT |
| RBC | LHD | CIE | UTE | GIG | NEH | ABL | ADM | TAM | RUN | TOO | PIP | ERR | FOS | ANT | LOT |
| REC | LID | CUE | VIE | HAG | NOH | AIL | AIM | TIM | SEN | TWO | PNP | EUR | FPS | APT | MAT |
| SAC | LLD | DDE | WEE | HOG | NTH | ALL | ARM | TOM | SIN | UFO | POP | FAR | FRS | ART | MET |
| SEC | LSD | DIE | WOE | HUG | SCH | APL | ATM | USM | SON | USO | PRP | FIR | GAS | ATT | MGT |
| SFC | LTD | DOE | AEF | JAG | API | ATL | BUM | VIM | SUN | WHO | PUP | FOR | HAS | BAT | MOT |
| SIC | MAD | DTE | BEF | JIG | BWI | AWL | CAM | WPM | SYN | WOO | RAP | FUR | HIS | BET | MST |
| SOC | MED | DUE | CAF | JOG | CFI | BAL | CHM | YAM | TAN | ZOO | REP | GAR | HMS | BIT | NAT |
| SVC | MFD | DYE | CIF | JUG | DPI | BBL | COM | ANN | TEN | ABP | RIP | GER | HOS | BKT | NET |
| TAC | MID | EKE | DEF | KEG | FBI | BDL | CSM | ATN | TIN | ALP | SAP | HER | IHS | BLT | NIT |
| THC | MLD | ENE | DIF | LAG | FRI | BPL | CUM | AWN | TON | AMP | SEP | HOR | ILS | BOT | NOT |
| TIC | MOD | ERE | EFF | LDG | FYI | CAL | DAM | BAN | TUN | APP | SIP | ISR | INS | BUT | NUT |
| TLC | MSD | ESE | EHF | LEG | GUI | CML | DEM | BIN | URN | ASP | SOP | JAR | IPS | CAT | NWT |
| TNC | MUD | EVE | ELF | LNG | INI | COL | DFM | BUN | USN | ATP | SPP | JER | IRS | CIT | OAT |
| VIC | NOD | EWE | EMF | LOG | LEI | CPL | DIM | CAN | VAN | BMP | SSP | LTR | ITS | COT | OCT |
| VOC | ODD | EXE | GIF | LPG | LPI | CYL | DOM | CEN | VEN | BOP | STP | MAR | JAS | CPT | OFT |
| WAC | OED | EYE | GPF | LTG | NEI | DBL | DSM | CON | WAN | CAP | SUP | MER | JCS | CRT | OJT |
| WBC | OLD | FEE | IMF | LUG | NHI | DEL | DVM | CTN | WEN | COP | TAP | MFR | LSS | CST | ONT |
| ADD | ORD | FIE | INF | MAG | OBI | DIL | ECM | DAN | WIN | CUP | TIP | MGR | MIS | CUT | OPT |
| AID | PAD | FOE | NSF | MEG | OSI | DLL | ELM | DEN | WON | DEP | TOP | NOR | MKS | CWT | OUT |
| ALD | PDD | GIE | OAF | MFG | PCI | DOL | EOM | DIN | WPN | DIP | TSP | OAR | MRS | DAT | PAT |
| AND | PFD | HIE | OFF | MPG | PEI | EEL | FEM | DON | YEN | DSP | TWP | OCR | MSS | DDT | PCT |
| AUD | PHD | HOE | OSF | MSG | POI | ELL | FPM | DUN | YON | DUP | USP | OUR | MUS | DET | PDT |
| BAD | POD | HUE | PIF | MTG | PSI | ENL | GEM | EON | ZEN | EDP | VIP | PAR | MVS | DOT | PET |
| BCD | PPD | ICE | PRF | MUG | QEI | GAL | GUM | FAN | ADO | EMP | YAP | PER | NAS | DPT | PIT |
| BED | QED | IDE | QEF | NAG | RBI | GEL | GYM | FEN | AGO | ESP | ZAP | PHR | NBS | DST | PKT |
| BHD | QID | IRE | RAF | NEG | RFI | HCL | HAM | FIN | APO | EXP | ZIP | POR | NES | DWT | PMT |
| BID | QLD | LEE | REF | ORG | SCI | ILL | HBM | FUN | AVO | FCP | AEQ | SER | NFS | EAT | POT |
| BUD | RAD | LIE | UHF | PEG | SKI | ISL | HEM | GEN | BOO | FOP | BOQ | SIR | NOS | EDT | PPT |
| CAD | RED | LYE | VHF | PIG | UPI | JCL | HIM | GIN | BRO | FTP | ESQ | SSR | OAS | EFT | PST |
| CID | RFD | MME | WAF | PKG | ADJ | JUL | HUM | GUN | CLO | GAP | GHQ | TAR | OBS | EST | PUT |
| CLD | RID | NCE | WHF | PSG | ICJ | LCL | IBM | HEN | CNO | GNP | IRQ | TER | OCS | EXT | PVT |
| COD | RND | NEE | ALG | PTG | MAJ | LTL | ISM | HON | COO | GOP | LIQ | TOR | OES | FAT | RAT |
| CPD | ROD | NNE | AUG | PUG | OBJ | MAL | JAM | HUN | CPO | GYP | LOQ | TSR | OFS | FET | RCT |
| CUD | SAD | ODE | AVG | QMG | ACK | MIL | LAM | INN | CWO | HAP | PDQ | UAR | OTS | FIT | RET |
| DAD | SGD | OLE | BAG | RAG | ALK | MOL | LCM | ION | CYO | HEP | REQ | VAR | PAS | FOT | ROT |
| DID | SJD | ONE | BEG | REG | ARK | MSL | LEM | JAN | DLO | HIP | SEQ | WAR | PHS | FRT | RUT |
| DMD | SLD | OPE | BIG | RIG | ASK | NIL | MEM | JUN | DSO | HOP | ABR | ABS | PIS | FUT | SAT |
| DUD | SOD | ORE | BKG | ROG | AUK | OBL | MFM | KEN | DUO | HYP | AFR | ANS | POS | GCT | SET |
| END | STD | OWE | BOG | RPG | AWK | OIL | MOM | KIN | EGO | IHP | AGR | ASS | PUS | GET | SGT |
| ESD | THD | PIE | BUG | RUG | BLK | OWL | MUM | LAN | FAO | IMP | AIR | AUS | RES | GMT | SHT |
| ETD | TID | POE | CHG | SAG | CLK | PAL | NOM | LIN | FIO | INP | APR | BBS | RPS | GOT | SIT |
| FAD | VFD | PTE | COG | SIG | ELK | PEL | NUM | LPN | FPO | JAP | ARR | BCS | SOS | GUT | SKT |
| FED | WAD | QUE | CTG | SSG | ILK | POL | OEM | MAN | FRO | KIP | BAR | BKS | SSS | HAT | SOT |

SST
TAT
TIT
TKT
TNT
TOT
ULT
UMT
VAT
VDT
VET
WET
WIT
YET
BTU
CLU
CPU
DAU
EMU
FLU
GNU
IOU
LEU
USU
VOU
YOU
ADV
ARV
ASV
CAV
CIV
DEV
DIV
ENV
ETV
GOV
INV
JUV
KJV
LEV
MEV
NAV
NCV
NEV
NOV
OBV
PTV
REV
RIV
RSV
WAV
BOW
CAW
CBW
CCW
COW
DEW
FEW
GAW
HAW
HEW
HOW
IWW
JAW
JEW
LAW
LOW
MAW
MEW
MOW
NEW
NNW
NOW
NSW
PAW
PEW
POW
RAW
ROW
SAW
SEW
SOW
SSW
TAW
TOW
VFW
VOW
WNW
WOW
WSW
WWW
YAW
YEW
AUX
BOX
FAX
FIX
FOX
HEX
LAX
LOX
MAX
MEX
MIX
NIX
PBX
PCX
PIX
POX
PYX
REX
SEX
SIX
SOX
TAX
TEX
TWX
VAX
VEX
WAX
ANY
BAY
BEY
BOY
BUY
CAY
COY
CRY
DAY
DRY
ETY
FAY
FCY
FEY
FLY
FRY
GAY
GUY
HAY
HVY
HWY
ICY
IGY
IVY
JAY
JOY
KEY
LAY
MAY
NAY
PAY
PLY
PRY
QTY
RAY
RWY
SAY
SHY
SKY
SLY
SOY
SPY
STY
TDY
THY
TOY
TRY
WAY
WHY
WRY
ADZ
DMZ
DOZ
FEZ
GAZ
MHZ
VIZ

# 4 LETTER WORDS

**1st Letter**

ABBE
ABBR
ABED
ABET
ABLE
ABUT
ACAD
ACCT
ACHE
ACHY
ACID
ACME
ACNE
ACRE
ACTG
ACTH
ADDN
ADVT
AEON
AERO
AERY
AFAR
AFFT
AFRO
AGAR
AGCY
AGED
AGOG
AGUE
AHOY
AIDE
AINU
AIRY
AJAR
AKIN
ALEE
ALGA
ALLY
ALMS
ALOE
ALSO
ALTA
ALTO
ALUM
AMAH
AMDT
AMEN
AMER
AMID
AMMO
AMOK
ANAL
ANAT
ANEW
ANKH
ANON
ANSI
ANTE
ANTI
ANUS
APEX
APPL
APPT
APSE
AQUA
ARAB
ARCH
AREA
ARIA
ARID
ARIZ
ARMY
ARTY
ARUM
ASHY
ASIC
ASPI
ASSN
ASSR
ASST
ATOM
ATOP
ATTN
ATTY
AULD
AUNT
AURA
AUTH
AUTO
AVDP
AVER
AVID
AVOW
AWAY
AWOL
AWRY
AXIS
AXLE
AYAH
BABE
BABY
BACK
BADE
BAHT
BAIL
BAIT
BAKE
BALD
BALE
BALK
BALL
BALM
BAND
BANE
BANG
BANK
BARB
BARD
BARE
BARK
BARN
BART
BASE
BASH
BASK
BASS
BAST
BATE
BATH
BAUD
BAWD
BAWL
BDRM
BEAD
BEAK
BEAM
BEAN
BEAR
BEAT
BEAU
BECK
BEEF
BEEN
BEER
BEET
BELG
BELL
BELT
BEND
BENT
BERG
BEST
BEVY
BIAS
BIDE
BIER
BIKE
BILE
BILK
BILL
BIND
BIOG
BIOL
BIOS
BIRD
BITE
BKGD
BLAB
BLDG
BLDR
BLEW
BLIP
BLOB
BLOC
BLOT
BLOW
BLUE
BLUR
BLVD
BOAR
BOAT
BOCK
BODE
BODY
BOER
BOIL
BOLA
BOLD
BOLE
BOLL
BOLO
BOLT
BOMB
BOND
BONE
BOOK
BOOM
BOON
BOOR
BOOT
BORE
BORN
BOSH
BOSS
BOTH
BOUT
BOWL
BPOE
BRAD
BRAE
BRAG
BRAN
BRAT
BRAY
BREW
BRIG
BRIM
BRIO
BRIT
BROS
BROW
BSKT
BTRY
BUBO
BUCK
BUFF
BULB
BULK
BULL
BUMP
BUNG
BUNK
BUNT
BUOY
BURL
BURN
BURP
BURR
BURY
BUSH
BUSS
BUST
BUSY
BUTT
BUZZ
BYTE
CAFE
CAGE
CAKE
CALC
CALF
CALK
CALL
CALM
CAME
CAMP
CANC
CANE
CANT
CAPE
CAPS
CAPT
CARD
CARE
CARP
CART
CASE
CASH
CASK
CAST
CATV
CAUL
CAVE
CAVY
CCTV
CEDE
CEDI
CELL
CELT
CENT
CERT
CHAM
CHAP
CHAR
CHAT
CHEF
CHEM
CHEW
CHIC
CHIN
CHIP
CHIT
CHON
CHOP
CHOW
CHUB
CHUG
CHUM
CIAO
CICS
CISC
CITE
CITY
CLAD
CLAM
CLAN
CLAP
CLAW
CLAY
CLEF
CLEW
CLIP
CLOD
CLOG
CLOP
CLOT
CLOY
CLUB
CLUE
CMDG
CMDR
CMYK
COAL
COAT
COAX
COCK
COCO
CODA
CODE
COED
COHO
COIF
COIL
COIN
COKE
COLA
COLD
COLL
COLO
COLT
COMA
COMB
COME
COML
COMM
COMP
COMR
CONC
CONE
CONF
CONG
CONJ
CONK
CONN
CONS
CONT
CONY
COOK
COOL
COON
COOP
COOT
COPE
COPY
CORD
CORE
CORK
CORM
CORN
CORP
CORR
COST
COSY
COTE
COUP
COVE
COWL
COZY
CPFF
CPOM
CPOS
CRAB
CRAG
CRAM
CREE
CREW
CRIB
CRIT
CROP
CROW
CRUX
CSSR
CTRL
CUBE
CUFF
CUKE
CULL
CULT
CURB
CURD
CURE
CURL
CURT
CUSP
CUTE
CYAN
CYME
CYST
CZAR
DACE
DADA
DAFT
DAIS
DALE
DAME
DAMN
DAMP
DANE
DANK
DARE
DARK
DARN
DART
DASH
DATA
DATE
DAUB
DAWN
DAZE
DEAD
DEAF
DEAL
DEAN
DEAR
DEBT
DECK
DEED
DEEM
DEEP
DEER
DEFT
DEFY
DELE
DELI
DELL
DELY
DENT
DENY
DEPR
DEPT
DESK
DEUT
DHOW
DIAG
DIAL
DICE
DICT
DIDO
DIET
DIKE
DILL
DIME
DINE
DINT
DIRE
DIRK
DIRT
DISC
DISH
DISK
DIST
DIVA
DIVE
DOCK
DODO
DOER
DOES
DOFF
DOGE
DOLE
DOLL
DOLT
DOME
DONA
DONE
DONG
DOOM
DOOR
DOPA
DOPE
DORM
DORY
DOSE
DOTE
DOUR
DOVE
DOWN
DOZE
DRAB
DRAG
DRAM
DRAW
DRAY
DREG
DREW
DRIP
DROP
DRUB
DRUG
DRUM
DUAL
DUCK
DUCT
DUDE
DUEL
DUET
DUKE
DULL
DULY
DUMA
DUMB
DUMP
DUNE
DUNG
DUNK
DUPE
DUSK
DUST
DUTY
DYKE
EACH
EARL
EARN
EASE
EAST
EASY
ECCL
ECHO
ECOL
ECON
ECRU
ECUA
EDAM
EDDY
EDEN
EDGE
EDGY
EDIT
EDUC
EGIS
EISA
ELAN
ELEC
ELEM
ELSE
EMER
EMIR
EMIT
ENCY
ENGR
ENVY
EPEE
EPIC
ERGO
ERIE
ERST
ESDI
ESPY
ESTH
ETCH
EVAP
EVEN
EVER
EVIL
EWER
EXAM
EXCH
EXEC
EXIT
EXOD
EXOR
EXPO
EXPT
EZEK
FACE
FACT
FADE
FADM
FAIL
FAIN
FAIR
FAKE
FALL
FAME
FANE
FANG
FARE
FARM
FAST
FATE
FATH
FAUN
FAWN
FAZE
FDIC
FEAR
FEAT
FEDN
FEED
FEEL
FEET
FELL
FELT
FEND
FEPC
FERN
FETE
FEUD
FIAT
FICA
FIDO
FIEF
FIFE
FIFO
FILE
FILL
FILM
FILS
FIND
FINE
FINK
FINN
FIRE
FIRM
FISH
FIST
FIVE
FIZZ
FLAB
FLAG
FLAK
FLAP
FLAT
FLAW
FLAX
FLAY
FLEA
FLEE
FLEM
FLEW
FLEX
FLIP
FLIT
FLOE
FLOG
FLOP
FLOW
FLUB
FLUE
FLUX
FOAL

FOAM FOGY FOIL FOLD FOLK FOND FONT FOOD FOOL FOOT FORA FORD FORE FORK FORM FORT FOUL FOUR FOWL FOXY FRAY FREE FREQ FRET FROG FROM FRWY FUEL FULL FUME FUND FUNK FURL FURY FUSE FUSS FUZE FUZZ FWTW GAEL GAFF GAGE GAIN GAIT GALA GALE GALL GALV GAME GAMY GANG GAOL GAPE GARB GASH GASP GATE

GATT GAUD GAVE GAWK GAZE GEAR GELD GENE GENL GENS GENT GEOG GEOL GEOM GERM GHAT GIBE GIFT GILD GILL GILT GIRD GIRL GIST GIVE GLAD GLEE GLEN GLIB GLOB GLOP GLOW GLUE GLUM GLUT GNAT GNAW GOAD GOAL GOAT GOLD GOLF GONE GONG GOOD GOOF GOON GORE GORY GOTH GOUT GOVT GOWN GRAB GRAD GRAM GRAY

GREP GREW GREY GRID GRIM GRIN GRIP GRIT GROG GROT GROW GRUB GULF GULL GULP GURU GUSH GUST GYRO GYVE HACK HAFT HAIL HAIR HAKE HALE HALF HALL HALO HALT HAND HANG HANK HARD HARE HARK HARM HARP HART HASH HASP HATE HAUL HAVE HAWK HAZE HAZY HDBK HDKF HDWE HEAD HEAL HEAP HEAR HEAT HEED HEEL

HEFT HEIR HELD HELL HELM HELP HEME HEMP HERB HERD HERE HERO HERS HGWY HICK HIDE HIGH HIKE HILL HILT HIND HINT HIRE HISS HIST HIVE HOAX HOBO HOCK HOKE HOLD HOLE HOLY HOME HOMO HONE HONK HOOD HOOF HOOK HOOP HOOT HOPE HOPI HORN HORT HOSE HOSP HOST HOUR HOVE HOWL HRZN HTML HTTP HUFF HUGE

HULA HULK HULL HUMP HUNG HUNK HUNT HURL HURT HUSH HUSK HYMN HYPE HYPO IAMB IBEX IBIS ICBM ICKY ICON IDEA IDEM IDES IDLE IDOL IFFY IKON IMHO IMIT INCA INCH INCL INCR INFL INFO INRI INSP INST INTL INTO IOOF IOTA IRBM IRIS IRON ISDN ISLE ITAL ITCH ITEM IWAY JACK JADE JAIL JAMB JAPE JAZZ

JEEP JEER JEHU JELL JERK JESS JEST JIBE JILT JINX JIVE JOHN JOIN JOKE JOLT JOSH JOSS JOUR JOWL JPEG JUDG JUDO JULY JUMP JUNC JUNE JUNK JURY JUST JUTE KALE KAME KANA KANS KART KAYO KBPS KEEL KEEN KEEP KELP KELT KENO KEPI KERB KERF KHAN KICK KILL KILN KILO KILT KIND KINE KING KINK KIRK

KISS KITE KITH KIWI KNEE KNEW KNIT KNOB KNOT KNOW KOBO KOCH KOOK KUDO KYAT LACE LACK LADY LAID LAIN LAIR LAKE LAMA LAMB LAME LAMP LAND LANE LANG LANK LAPP LARD LARK LASH LASS LAST LATE LATH LAUD LAVA LAVE LAWN LAZE LAZY LCDR LCPL LEAD LEAF LEAK LEAL LEAN LEAP LECT LEEK LEER LEES LEFT

LEND LENS LENT LESS LEST LETT LEVY LEWD LIAR LICE LICK LIDO LIED LIEF LIEN LIEU LIFE LIFO LIFT LIKE LILT LILY LIMB LIME LIMN LIMP LINE LING LINK LINT LION LIRA LISP LIST LITH LIVE LOAD LOAF LOAM LOAN LOBE LOCH LOCK LOCO LODE LOFT LOGE LOGO LOGY LOIN LOLL LOND LONE LONG LOOK LOOM LOON

LOOP LOOT LOPE LORD LORE LORN LOSE LOSS LOST LOTH LOUD LOUR LOUT LOVE LTJG LUAU LUBE LUCK LUFF LULL LUMP LUNG LURE LURK LUSH LUST LUTE LYNX LYRE MACE MACH MADE MAGI MAID MAIL MAIM MAIN MAKE MALE MALL MALT MAMA MANE MANX MANY MARE MARK MARL MARS MART MASC MASH MASK MASS MAST MATE MATH

MATT MAUL MAXI MAYA MAZE MCGA MCPO MDNT MDSE MEAD MEAL MEAN MEAS MEAT MECH MEED MEEK MEET MELD MELT MEMO MEND MENU MEOW MERE MESA MESH MESS METE MEWS MICA MICE MICH MIDI MIEN MIFF MIKE MILD MILE MILK MILL MILT MIME MIND MINE MINI MINK MINN MINT MINX MIPS MIRE MISC MISS MIST MITE MITT

MIXT MKTG MLLE MOAN MOAT MOCK MODE MOIL MOLD MOLE MOLL MOLT MOLY MONK MONO MONT MOOD MOON MOOR MOOT MOPE MORE MORN MOSS MOST MOTE MOTH MOUE MOVE MPEG MSEC MSGR MSGT MTBF MTGE MUCH MUCK MUFF MULE MULL MURK MUSE MUSH MUSK MUSS MUST MUTE MUTT MYNA MYTH NAIF NAIL NAME NAND NANO NAPE NARC

NARD NASA NATL NATO NAUT NAVE NAVY NAZI NDEA NEAP NEAR NEAT NECK NEED NEON NEST NETH NEUT NEWS NEWT NEXT NFLD NICA NICE NICK NIGH NINE NISI NLRB NODE NOEL NOES NONE NOOK NOON NOPE NORM NORW NOSE NOSY NOTE NOUN NOVA NUDE NULL NUMB NUTS OATH OBEY OBIT OBOE ODDS ODOR OGLE OGRE OINK OKLA

OKRA OLEO OLIO OMEN OMIT ONCE ONLY ONTO ONUS ONYX OOZE OPAL OPEN OPER OPUS ORAL ORCH OREG ORGY ORIG OURS OUST OUZO OVAL OVEN OVER OVUM PACE PACK PACT PAGE PAID PAIL PAIN PAIR PALE PALL PALM PANE PANG PANT PAPA PARA PARD PARE PARK PART PASS PAST PATE PATH PAVE PAWL PAWN PAYT PEAK PEAL

PEAR PEAT PECK PEEK PEEL PEEN PEEP PEER PEKE PELF PELT PENN PENT PEON PERF PERH PERK PERM PERP PERS PERT PESO PEST PHIL PHON PHYS PICA PICE PICK PICO PIED PIER PIES PIKE PILE PILL PIMP PINE PING PINK PINT PINX PIPE PITH PITY PKWY PLAN PLAT PLAY PLEA PLOD PLOP PLOT PLOW PLOY PLUG PLUM

PLUS PNXT POCK POCO POEM POET POKE POKY POLE POLL POLO POMP POND PONE PONY POOL POOP POOR POPE PORE PORK PORT POSE POSH POSS POST POSY POUR POUT PPTN PRAM PRAY PREC PRED PREF PREM PREP PRES PREV PREY PRIG PRIM PRIN PROB PROC PROD PROF PROM PRON PROP PROS PROT PROV PROW PUBL PUCK PUFF

PUKE PULE PULL PULP PUMA PUMP PUNK PUNT PUNY PUPA PURE PURL PURR PUSH PUSS PUTT PYRE QUAD QUAI QUAY QUID QUIP QUIT QUIZ QUOT RAAF RACE RACK RACY RADM RAFT RAGA RAGE RAID RAIL RAIN RAJA RAKE RAMP RAND RANG RANI RANK RANT RAPE RAPT RARE RASH RASP RATE RAVE RAZE RAZZ RCAF RCMP READ REAL

REAM REAP REAR RECD RECT REDO REED REEF REEK REEL REFL REFR REGT REIN RELY REND RENT REPL REPT RESP REST RETD REXX RHEA RIAL RICE RICH RICK RIDE RIEL RIFE RIFF RIFT RILE RILL RIME RIND RING RINK RIOT RIPE RISC RISE RISK RITE RIVE ROAD ROAM ROAN ROAR ROBE ROCK RODE ROIL ROLE ROLL ROMP

ROOD ROOF ROOK ROOM ROOT ROPE ROSE ROSY ROTC ROTE ROUE ROUT ROVE RSVP RSWC RTFM RUBY RUDE RUFF RUIN RULE RUMP RUNE RUNG RUNT RUSE RUSH RUSK RUSS RUST RYFM SACK SAFE SAGA SAGE SAGO SAID SAIL SAKE SALE SALT SAME SAND SANE SANG SANK SANS SARI SASH SASK SATE SAVE SCAB SCAD SCAN SCAR SCIL

SCOT SCOW SCPO SCSI SCUD SCUM SEAL SEAM SEAR SEAT SECT SECY SEED SEEK SEEM SEEP SEER SELF SELL SEND SENE SENT SEPN SEPT SEQQ SERA SERB SERE SERF SERG SERV SEXY SGML SHAD SHAG SHAH SHAK SHAM SHED SHEW SHIM SHIN SHIP SHIV SHOE SHOP SHOT SHOW SHPT SHTG SHUN SHUT SICK SIDE SIFT SIGH SIGN

SIKH SILK SILL SILO SILT SINE SING SINK SIRE SITE SIZE SKAG SKEW SKID SKIM SKIN SKIP SKIT SLAB SLAG SLAM SLAN SLAP SLAT SLAV SLAW SLAY SLED SLEW SLIM SLIP SLIT SLOB SLOE SLOP SLOT SLOW SLUE SLUG SLUM SLUR SLUT SMAJ SMOG SMTP SMUG SMUT SNAG SNAP SNIP SNOB SNOW SNUB SNUG SOAK SOAP SOAR

SOCK SODA SOFA SOFT SOIL SOLD SOLE SOLN SOLO SOME SONG SOON SOOT SOPH SORB SORE SORT SOUL SOUP SOUR SPAN SPAR SPAT SPAY SPCA SPCC SPEC SPEW SPIN SPIT SPOT SPRY SPUD SPUN SPUR STAB STAG STAR STAT STAY STBD STEM STEP STER STEW STIR STOL STOP STOW STUB STUD STUN SUBJ SUCH SUCK SUDS SUET

SUFF SUIT SULK SUNG SUNK SUPP SUPT SURE SURF SURG SURV SVGA SVGS SWAB SWAG SWAM SWAN SWAP SWAT SWAY SWED SWIG SWIM SWUM SYNC SYST TACH TACK TACO TACT TAIL TAKA TAKE TALA TALC TALE TALK TALL TAME TAMP TANG TANK TAPE TAPS TARE TARN TARO TART TASK TAUT TAXI TEAK TEAL TEAM TEAR TEAT TECH

TEEM TEEN TELL TEMP TEND TENN TENT TERM TERN TERR TEST TEXT THAI THAN THAT THAW THEE THEM THEN THEW THEY THIN THIS THOU THUD THUG THUS TICK TIDE TIDY TIER TIFF TILE TILL TILT TIME TINE TINT TINY TIRE TNPK TOAD TOGA TOGS TOIL TOKE TOLD TOLE TOLL TOMB TOME TONE TONG TOOK TOOL TOOT TOPE

TOPS TORE TORN TORR TORT TORY TOSS TOTE TOUR TOUT TOWN TRAM TRAP TRAY TREE TREK TREY TRIB TRIG TRIM TRIO TRIP TROD TROT TROW TROY TRUE TSAR TSGT TUBA TUBE TUCK TUES TUFA TUFF TUFT TUNA TUNE TURF TURK TURN TUSK TWIG TWIN TWIT TYKE TYPE TYPO TYRO TZAR UGLY ULNA UNDO UNIT UNIV UNIX UNTO

UPON URDU UREA URGE URIC USAF USCG USDA USED USES USIA USMC USSR UUCP VADM VAIL VAIN VALE VAMP VANE VARY VASE VAST VEAL VEDA VEEP VEER VEIL VEIN VELD VEND VENT VERB VERT VERY VESA VEST VETO VIAL VICE VIDE VIEW VILE VINE VIOL VISA VISE VITA VIVA VLSI VOID VOLE VOLT VOTE VTOL VULG WADE

WADI WAFT WAGE WAIF WAIL WAIN WAIT WAKE WALE WALK WALL WAND WANE WANT WARD WARE WARM WARN WARP WART WARY WASH WASP WATS WATT WAVE WAVY WAXY WCTU WEAK WEAL WEAN WEAR WEED WEEK WEEN WEEP WEFT WEIR WELD WELL WELT WEND WENT WEPT WERE WEST WHAT WHEN WHET WHEY WHIG WHIM WHIP WHIR WHIT WHIZ

WHOM
WICK
WIDE
WIFE
WILD
WILE
WILL
WILT
WILY
WIND
WINE
WING
WINK
WINO
WIPE
WIRE
WIRY
WISD
WISE
WISH
WISP
WITH
WIVE
WOAD
WOKE
WOLD
WOLF
WOMB
WONT
WOOD
WOOF
WOOL
WORD
WORE
WORK
WORM
WORN
WORT
WOVE
WRAP
WREN
WRIT
WRNT
XMAS
XNTY
YANK
YARD
YARN
YAWL
YAWN
YAWP
YAWS
YEAR
YEGG
YELL
YELP
YETI
YMCA
YMHA
YMMV
YOGA
YOGI
YOKE
YOLK
YORE
YOUR
YOWL
YOYO
YRBK
YUAN
YULE
YURT
YWCA
YWHA
ZANY
ZEAL
ZEBU
ZECH
ZEPH
ZERO
ZEST
ZINC
ZING
ZION
ZONE
ZOOL
ZOOM
ZUNI

## 2ND LETTER

BABE
BABY
BACK
BADE
BAHT
BAIL
BAIT
BAKE
BALD
BALE
BALK
BALL
BALM
BAND
BANE
BANG
BANK
BARB
BARD
BARE
BARK
BARN
BART
BASE
BASH
BASK
BASS
BAST
BATE
BATH
BAUD
BAWD
BAWL
CAFE
CAGE
CAKE
CALC
CALF
CALK
CALL
CALM
CAME
CAMP
CANC
CANE
CANT
CAPE
CAPS
CAPT
CARD
CARE
CARP
CART
CASE
CASH
CASK
CAST
CATV
CAUL
CAVE
CAVY
DACE
DADA
DAFT
DAIS
DALE
DAME
DAMN
DAMP
DANE
DANK
DARE
DARK
DARN
DART
DASH
DATA
DATE
DAUB
DAWN
DAZE
EACH
EARL
EARN
EASE
EAST
EASY
FACE
FACT
FADE
FADM
FAIL
FAIN
FAIR
FAKE
FALL
FAME
FANE
FANG
FARE
FARM
FAST
FATE
FATH
FAUN
FAWN
FAZE
GAEL
GAFF
GAGE
GAIN
GAIT
GALA
GALE
GALL
GALV
GAME
GAMY
GANG
GAOL
GAPE
GARB
GASH
GASP
GATE
GATT
GAUD
GAVE
GAWK
GAZE
HACK
HAFT
HAIL
HAIR
HAKE
HALE
HALF
HALL
HALO
HALT
HAND
HANG
HANK
HARD
HARE
HARK
HARM
HARP
HART
HASH
HASP
HATE
HAUL
HAVE
HAWK
HAZE
HAZY
IAMB
JACK
JADE
JAIL
JAMB
JAPE
JAZZ
KALE
KAME
KANA
KANS
KART
KAYO
LACE
LACK
LADY
LAID
LAIN
LAIR
LAKE
LAMA
LAMB
LAME
LAMP
LAND
LANE
LANG
LANK
LAPP
LARD
LARK
LASH
LASS
LAST
LATE
LATH
LAUD
LAVA
LAVE
LAWN
LAZE
LAZY
MACE
MACH
MADE
MAGI
MAID
MAIL
MAIM
MAIN
MAKE
MALE
MALL
MALT
MAMA
MANE
MANX
MANY
MARE
MARK
MARL
MARS
MART
MASC
MASH
MASK
MASS
MAST
MATE
MATH
MATT
MAUL
MAXI
MAYA
MAZE
NAIF
NAIL
NAME
NAND
NANO
NAPE
NARC
NARD
NASA
NATL
NATO
NAUT
NAVE
NAVY
NAZI
OATH
PACE
PACK
PACT
PAGE
PAID
PAIL
PAIN
PAIR
PALE
PALL
PALM
PANE
PANG
PANT
PAPA
PARA
PARD
PARE
PARK
PART
PASS
PAST
PATE
PATH
PAVE
PAWL
PAWN
PAYT
RAAF
RACE
RACK
RACY
RADM
RAFT
RAGA
RAGE
RAID
RAIL
RAIN
RAJA
RAKE
RAMP
RAND
RANG
RANI
RANK
RANT
RAPE
RAPT
RARE
RASH
RASP
RATE
RAVE
RAZE
RAZZ
SACK
SAFE
SAGA
SAGE
SAGO
SAID
SAIL
SAKE
SALE
SALT
SAME
SAND
SANE
SANG
SANK
SANS
SARI
SASH
SASK
SATE
SAVE
TACH
TACK
TACO
TACT
TAIL
TAKA
TAKE
TALA
TALC
TALE
TALK
TALL
TAME
TAMP
TANG
TANK
TAPE
TAPS
TARE
TARN
TARO
TART
TASK
TAUT
TAXI
VADM
VAIL
VAIN
VALE
VAMP
VANE
VARY
VASE
VAST
WADE
WADI
WAFT
WAGE
WAIF
WAIL
WAIN
WAIT
WAKE
WALE
WALK
WALL
WAND
WANE
WANT
WARD
WARE
WARM
WARN
WARP
WART
WARY
WASH
WASP
WATS
WATT
WAVE
WAVY
WAXY
YANK
YARD
YARN
YAWL
YAWN
YAWP
YAWS
ZANY
ABBE
ABBR
ABED
ABET
ABLE
ABUT
IBEX
IBIS
KBPS
OBEY
OBIT
OBOE
ACAD
ACCT
ACHE
ACHY
ACID
ACME
ACNE
ACRE
ACTG
ACTH
CCTV
ECCL
ECHO
ECOL
ECON
ECRU
ECUA
ICBM
ICKY
ICON
LCDR
LCPL
MCGA
MCPO
RCAF
RCMP
SCAB
SCAD
SCAN
SCAR
SCIL
SCOT
SCOW
SCPO
SCSI
SCUD
SCUM
WCTU
ADDN
ADVT
BDRM
EDAM
EDDY
EDEN
EDGE
EDGY
EDIT
EDUC
FDIC
HDBK
HDKF
HDWE
IDEA
IDEM
IDES
IDLE
IDOL
MDNT
MDSE
NDEA
ODDS
ODOR
AEON
AERO
AERY
BEAD
BEAK
BEAM
BEAN
BEAR
BEAT
BEAU
BECK
BEEF
BEEN
BEER
BEET
BELG
BELL
BELT
BEND
BENT
BERG
BEST
BEVY
CEDE
CEDI
CELL
CELT
CENT
CERT
DEAD
DEAF
DEAL
DEAN
DEAR
DEBT
DECK
DEED
DEEM
DEEP
DEER
DEFT
DEFY
DELE
DELI
DELL
DELY
DENT
DENY
DEPR
DEPT
DESK
DEUT
FEAR
FEAT
FEDN
FEED
FEEL
FEET
FELL
FELT
FEND
FEPC
FERN
FETE
FEUD
GEAR
GELD
GENE
GENL
GENS
GENT
GEOG
GEOL
GEOM
GERM
HEAD
HEAL
HEAP
HEAR
HEAT
HEED
HEEL
HEFT
HEIR
HELD
HELL
HELM
HELP
HEME
HEMP
HERB
HERD
HERE
HERO
HERS
JEEP
JEER
JEHU
JELL
JERK
JESS
JEST
KEEL
KEEN
KEEP
KELP
KELT
KENO
KEPI
KERB
KERF
LEAD
LEAF
LEAK
LEAL
LEAN
LEAP
LECT
LEEK
LEER
LEES
LEFT
LEND
LENS
LENT
LESS
LEST
LETT
LEVY
LEWD
MEAD
MEAL
MEAN
MEAS
MEAT
MECH
MEED
MEEK
MEET
MELD
MELT
MEMO
MEND
MENU
MEOW
MERE
MESA
MESH
MESS
METE
MEWS
NEAP
NEAR
NEAT
NECK
NEED
NEON
NEST
NETH
NEUT
NEWS
NEWT
NEXT
PEAK
PEAL
PEAR
PEAT
PECK
PEEK
PEEL
PEEN
PEEP
PEER
PEKE
PELF
PELT
PENN
PENT

PEON
PERF
PERH
PERK
PERM
PERP
PERS
PERT
PESO
PEST
READ
REAL
REAM
REAP
REAR
RECD
RECT
REDO
REED
REEF
REEK
REEL
REFL
REFR
REGT
REIN
RELY
REND
RENT
REPL
REPT
RESP
REST
RETD
REXX
SEAL
SEAM
SEAR
SEAT
SECT
SECY
SEED
SEEK
SEEM
SEEP
SEER
SELF
SELL
SEND
SENE
SENT
SEPN
SEPT
SEQQ
SERA
SERB
SERE

SERF
SERG
SERV
SEXY
TEAK
TEAL
TEAM
TEAR
TEAT
TECH
TEEM
TEEN
TELL
TEMP
TEND
TENN
TENT
TERM
TERN
TERR
TEST
TEXT
VEAL
VEDA
VEEP
VEER
VEIL
VEIN
VELD
VEND
VENT
VERB
VERT
VERY
VESA
VEST
VETO
WEAK
WEAL
WEAN
WEAR
WEED
WEEK
WEEN
WEEP
WEFT
WEIR
WELD
WELL
WELT
WEND
WENT
WEPT
WERE
WEST
YEAR
YEGG

YELL
YELP
YETI
ZEAL
ZEBU
ZECH
ZEPH
ZERO
ZEST
AFAR
AFFT
AFRO
IFFY
NFLD
AGAR
AGCY
AGED
AGOG
AGUE
EGIS
HGWY
OGLE
OGRE
SGML
UGLY
AHOY
CHAM
CHAP
CHAR
CHAT
CHEF
CHEM
CHEW
CHIC
CHIN
CHIP
CHIT
CHON
CHOP
CHOW
CHUB
CHUG
CHUM
DHOW
GHAT
KHAN
PHIL
PHON
PHYS
RHEA
SHAD
SHAG
SHAH
SHAK
SHAM
SHED
SHEW

SHIM
SHIN
SHIP
SHIV
SHOE
SHOP
SHOT
SHOW
SHPT
SHTG
SHUN
SHUT
THAI
THAN
THAT
THAW
THEE
THEM
THEN
THEW
THEY
THIN
THIS
THOU
THUD
THUG
THUS
WHAT
WHEN
WHET
WHEY
WHIG
WHIM
WHIP
WHIR
WHIT
WHIZ
WHOM
AIDE
AINU
AIRY
BIAS
BIDE
BIER
BIKE
BILE
BILK
BILL
BIND
BIOG
BIOL
BIOS
BIRD
BITE
CIAO
CICS
CISC

CITE
CITY
DIAG
DIAL
DICE
DICT
DIDO
DIET
DIKE
DILL
DIME
DINE
DINT
DIRE
DIRK
DIRT
DISC
DISH
DISK
DIST
DIVA
DIVE
EISA
FIAT
FICA
FIDO
FIEF
FIFE
FIFO
FILE
FILL
FILM
FILS
FIND
FINE
FINK
FINN
FIRE
FIRM
FISH
FIST
FIVE
FIZZ
GIBE
GIFT
GILD
GILL
GILT
GIRD
GIRL
GIST
GIVE
HICK
HIDE
HIGH
HIKE
HILL

HILT
HIND
HINT
HIRE
HISS
HIST
HIVE
JIBE
JILT
JINX
JIVE
KICK
KILL
KILN
KILO
KILT
KIND
KINE
KING
KINK
KIRK
KISS
KITE
KITH
KIWI
LIAR
LICE
LICK
LIDO
LIED
LIEF
LIEN
LIEU
LIFE
LIFO
LIFT
LIKE
LILT
LILY
LIMB
LIME
LIMN
LIMP
LINE
LING
LINK
LINT
LION
LIRA
LISP
LIST
LITH
LIVE
MICA
MICE
MICH
MIDI

MIEN
MIFF
MIKE
MILD
MILE
MILK
MILL
MILT
MIME
MIND
MINE
MINI
MINK
MINN
MINT
MINX
MIPS
MIRE
MISC
MISS
MIST
MITE
MITT
MIXT
NICA
NICE
NICK
NIGH
NINE
NISI
OINK
PICA
PICE
PICK
PICO
PIED
PIER
PIES
PIKE
PILE
PILL
PIMP
PINE
PING
PINK
PINT
PINX
PIPE
PITH
PITY
RIAL
RICE
RICH
RICK
RIDE
RIEL
RIFE

RIFF
RIFT
RILE
RILL
RIME
RIND
RING
RINK
RIOT
RIPE
RISC
RISE
RISK
RITE
RIVE
SICK
SIDE
SIFT
SIGH
SIGN
SIKH
SILK
SILL
SILO
SILT
SINE
SING
SINK
SIRE
SITE
SIZE
TICK
TIDE
TIDY
TIER
TIFF
TILE
TILL
TILT
TIME
TINE
TINT
TINY
TIRE
VIAL
VICE
VIDE
VIEW
VILE
VINE
VIOL
VISA
VISE
VITA
VIVA
WICK
WIDE

WIFE
WILD
WILE
WILL
WILT
WILY
WIND
WINE
WING
WINK
WINO
WIPE
WIRE
WIRY
WISD
WISE
WISH
WISP
WITH
WIVE
ZINC
ZING
ZION
AJAR
AKIN
BKGD
IKON
MKTG
OKLA
OKRA
PKWY
SKAG
SKEW
SKID
SKIM
SKIN
SKIP
SKIT
ALEE
ALGA
ALLY
ALMS
ALOE
ALSO
ALTA
ALTO
ALUM
BLAB
BLDG
BLDR
BLEW
BLIP
BLOB
BLOC
BLOT
BLOW
BLUE

BLUR
BLVD
CLAD
CLAM
CLAN
CLAP
CLAW
CLAY
CLEF
CLEW
CLIP
CLOD
CLOG
CLOP
CLOT
CLOY
CLUB
CLUE
ELAN
ELEC
ELEM
ELSE
FLAB
FLAG
FLAK
FLAP
FLAT
FLAW
FLAX
FLAY
FLEA
FLEE
FLEM
FLEW
FLEX
FLIP
FLIT
FLOE
FLOG
FLOP
FLOW
FLUB
FLUE
FLUX
GLAD
GLEE
GLEN
GLIB
GLOB
GLOP
GLOW
GLUE
GLUM
GLUT
MLLE
NLRB
OLEO

OLIO
PLAN
PLAT
PLAY
PLEA
PLOD
PLOP
PLOT
PLOW
PLOY
PLUG
PLUM
PLUS
SLAB
SLAG
SLAM
SLAN
SLAP
SLAT
SLAV
SLAW
SLAY
SLED
SLEW
SLIM
SLIP
SLIT
SLOB
SLOE
SLOP
SLOT
SLOW
SLUE
SLUG
SLUM
SLUR
SLUT
ULNA
VLSI
AMAH
AMDT
AMEN
AMER
AMID
AMMO
AMOK
CMDG
CMDR
CMYK
EMER
EMIR
EMIT
IMHO
IMIT
OMEN
OMIT
SMAJ

SMOG
SMTP
SMUG
SMUT
XMAS
YMCA
YMHA
YMMV
ANAL
ANAT
ANEW
ANKH
ANON
ANSI
ANTE
ANTI
ANUS
ENCY
ENGR
ENVY
GNAT
GNAW
INCA
INCH
INCL
INCR
INFL
INFO
INRI
INSP
INST
INTL
INTO
KNEE
KNEW
KNIT
KNOB
KNOT
KNOW
ONCE
ONLY
ONTO
ONUS
ONYX
PNXT
SNAG
SNAP
SNIP
SNOB
SNOW
SNUB
SNUG
TNPK
UNDO
UNIT
UNIV
UNIX

UNTO
XNTY
BOAR
BOAT
BOCK
BODE
BODY
BOER
BOIL
BOLA
BOLD
BOLE
BOLL
BOLO
BOLT
BOMB
BOND
BONE
BOOK
BOOM
BOON
BOOR
BOOT
BORE
BORN
BOSH
BOSS
BOTH
BOUT
BOWL
COAL
COAT
COAX
COCK
COCO
CODA
CODE
COED
COHO
COIF
COIL
COIN
COKE
COLA
COLD
COLL
COLO
COLT
COMA
COMB
COME
COML
COMM
COMP
COMR
CONC
CONE

| | | | | | | | | | | | | |
|---|---|---|---|---|---|---|---|---|---|---|---|---|
| CONF | FOIL | HOUR | MOLE | POSS | TOLD | BPOE | CRIB | PREM | MSEC | BULB | FUSE | MUTE |
| CONG | FOLD | HOVE | MOLL | POST | TOLE | CPFF | CRIT | PREP | MSGR | BULK | FUSS | MUTT |
| CONJ | FOLK | HOWL | MOLT | POSY | TOLL | CPOM | CROP | PRES | MSGT | BULL | FUZE | NUDE |
| CONK | FOND | IOOF | MOLY | POUR | TOMB | CPOS | CROW | PREV | RSVP | BUMP | FUZZ | NULL |
| CONN | FONT | IOTA | MONK | POUT | TOME | EPEE | CRUX | PREY | RSWC | BUNG | GULF | NUMB |
| CONS | FOOD | JOHN | MONO | ROAD | TONE | EPIC | DRAB | PRIG | TSAR | BUNK | GULL | NUTS |
| CONT | FOOL | JOIN | MONT | ROAM | TONG | JPEG | DRAG | PRIM | TSGT | BUNT | GULP | OURS |
| CONY | FOOT | JOKE | MOOD | ROAN | TOOK | MPEG | DRAM | PRIN | USAF | BUOY | GURU | OUST |
| COOK | FORA | JOLT | MOON | ROAR | TOOL | OPAL | DRAW | PROB | USCG | BURL | GUSH | OUZO |
| COOL | FORD | JOSH | MOOR | ROBE | TOOT | OPEN | DRAY | PROC | USDA | BURN | GUST | PUBL |
| COON | FORE | JOSS | MOOT | ROCK | TOPE | OPER | DREG | PROD | USED | BURP | HUFF | PUCK |
| COOP | FORK | JOUR | MOPE | RODE | TOPS | OPUS | DREW | PROF | USES | BURR | HUGE | PUFF |
| COOT | FORM | JOWL | MORE | ROIL | TORE | PPTN | DRIP | PROM | USIA | BURY | HULA | PUKE |
| COPE | FORT | KOBO | MORN | ROLE | TORN | SPAN | DROP | PRON | USMC | BUSH | HULK | PULE |
| COPY | FOUL | KOCH | MOSS | ROLL | TORR | SPAR | DRUB | PROP | USSR | BUSS | HULL | PULL |
| CORD | FOUR | KOOK | MOST | ROMP | TORT | SPAT | DRUG | PROS | ATOM | BUST | HUMP | PULP |
| CORE | FOWL | LOAD | MOTE | ROOD | TORY | SPAY | DRUM | PROT | ATOP | BUSY | HUNG | PUMA |
| CORK | FOXY | LOAF | MOTH | ROOF | TOSS | SPCA | ERGO | PROV | ATTN | BUTT | HUNK | PUMP |
| CORM | GOAD | LOAM | MOUE | ROOK | TOTE | SPCC | ERIE | PROW | ATTY | BUZZ | HUNT | PUNK |
| CORN | GOAL | LOAN | MOVE | ROOM | TOUR | SPEC | ERST | TRAM | BTRY | CUBE | HURL | PUNT |
| CORP | GOAT | LOBE | NODE | ROOT | TOUT | SPEW | FRAY | TRAP | CTRL | CUFF | HURT | PUNY |
| CORR | GOLD | LOCH | NOEL | ROPE | TOWN | SPIN | FREE | TRAY | ETCH | CUKE | HUSH | PUPA |
| COST | GOLF | LOCK | NOES | ROSE | VOID | SPIT | FREQ | TREE | HTML | CULL | HUSK | PURE |
| COSY | GONE | LOCO | NONE | ROSY | VOLE | SPOT | FRET | TREK | HTTP | CULT | JUDG | PURL |
| COTE | GONG | LODE | NOOK | ROTC | VOLT | SPRY | FROG | TREY | ITAL | CURB | JUDO | PURR |
| COUP | GOOD | LOFT | NOON | ROTE | VOTE | SPUD | FROM | TRIB | ITCH | CURD | JULY | PUSH |
| COVE | GOOF | LOGE | NOPE | ROUE | WOAD | SPUN | FRWY | TRIG | ITEM | CURE | JUMP | PUSS |
| COWL | GOON | LOGO | NORM | ROUT | WOKE | SPUR | GRAB | TRIM | LTJG | CURL | JUNC | PUTT |
| COZY | GORE | LOGY | NORW | ROVE | WOLD | UPON | GRAD | TRIO | MTBF | CURT | JUNE | QUAD |
| DOCK | GORY | LOIN | NOSE | SOAK | WOLF | AQUA | GRAM | TRIP | MTGE | CUSP | JUNK | QUAI |
| DODO | GOTH | LOLL | NOSY | SOAP | WOMB | ARAB | GRAY | TROD | RTFM | CUTE | JURY | QUAY |
| DOER | GOUT | LOND | NOTE | SOAR | WONT | ARCH | GREP | TROT | STAB | DUAL | JUST | QUID |
| DOES | GOVT | LONE | NOUN | SOCK | WOOD | AREA | GREW | TROW | STAG | DUCK | JUTE | QUIP |
| DOFF | GOWN | LONG | NOVA | SODA | WOOF | ARIA | GREY | TROY | STAR | DUCT | KUDO | QUIT |
| DOGE | HOAX | LOOK | OOZE | SOFA | WOOL | ARID | GRID | TRUE | STAT | DUDE | LUAU | QUIZ |
| DOLE | HOBO | LOOM | POCK | SOFT | WORD | ARIZ | GRIM | URDU | STAY | DUEL | LUBE | QUOT |
| DOLL | HOCK | LOON | POCO | SOIL | WORE | ARMY | GRIN | UREA | STBD | DUET | LUCK | RUBY |
| DOLT | HOKE | LOOP | POEM | SOLD | WORK | ARTY | GRIP | URGE | STEM | DUKE | LUFF | RUDE |
| DOME | HOLD | LOOT | POET | SOLE | WORM | ARUM | GRIT | URIC | STEP | DULL | LULL | RUFF |
| DONA | HOLE | LOPE | POKE | SOLN | WORN | BRAD | GROG | WRAP | STER | DULY | LUMP | RUIN |
| DONE | HOLY | LORD | POKY | SOLO | WORT | BRAE | GROT | WREN | STEW | DUMA | LUNG | RULE |
| DONG | HOME | LORE | POLE | SOME | WOVE | BRAG | GROW | WRIT | STIR | DUMB | LURE | RUMP |
| DOOM | HOMO | LORN | POLL | SONG | YOGA | BRAN | GRUB | WRNT | STOL | DUMP | LURK | RUNE |
| DOOR | HONE | LOSE | POLO | SOON | YOGI | BRAT | HRZN | YRBK | STOP | DUNE | LUSH | RUNG |
| DOPA | HONK | LOSS | POMP | SOOT | YOKE | BRAY | IRBM | ASHY | STOW | DUNG | LUST | RUNT |
| DOPE | HOOD | LOST | POND | SOPH | YOLK | BREW | IRIS | ASIC | STUB | DUNK | LUTE | RUSE |
| DORM | HOOF | LOTH | PONE | SORB | YORE | BRIG | IRON | ASPI | STUD | DUPE | MUCH | RUSH |
| DORY | HOOK | LOUD | PONY | SORE | YOUR | BRIM | ORAL | ASSN | STUN | DUSK | MUCK | RUSK |
| DOSE | HOOP | LOUR | POOL | SORT | YOWL | BRIO | ORCH | ASSR | VTOL | DUST | MUFF | RUSS |
| DOTE | HOOT | LOUT | POOP | SOUL | YOYO | BRIT | OREG | ASST | AULD | DUTY | MULE | RUST |
| DOUR | HOPE | LOVE | POOR | SOUP | ZONE | BROS | ORGY | BSKT | AUNT | FUEL | MULL | SUBJ |
| DOVE | HOPI | MOAN | POPE | SOUR | ZOOL | BROW | ORIG | CSSR | AURA | FULL | MURK | SUCH |
| DOWN | HORN | MOAT | PORE | TOAD | ZOOM | CRAB | PRAM | ESDI | AUTH | FUME | MUSE | SUCK |
| DOZE | HORT | MOCK | PORK | TOGA | APEX | CRAG | PRAY | ESPY | AUTO | FUND | MUSH | SUDS |
| FOAL | HOSE | MODE | PORT | TOGS | APPL | CRAM | PREC | ESTH | BUBO | FUNK | MUSK | SUET |
| FOAM | HOSP | MOIL | POSE | TOIL | APPT | CREE | PRED | ISDN | BUCK | FURL | MUSS | SUFF |
| FOGY | HOST | MOLD | POSH | TOKE | APSE | CREW | PREF | ISLE | BUFF | FURY | MUST | SUIT |

SULK
SUNG
SUNK
SUPP
SUPT
SURE
SURF
SURG
SURV
TUBA
TUBE
TUCK
TUES
TUFA
TUFF
TUFT
TUNA
TUNE
TURF
TURK
TURN
TUSK
UUCP
VULG
YUAN
YULE
YURT
ZUNI
AVDP
AVER
AVID
AVOW
EVAP
EVEN
EVER
EVIL
OVAL
OVEN
OVER
OVUM
SVGA
SVGS
AWAY
AWOL
AWRY
EWER
FWTW
IWAY
SWAB
SWAG
SWAM
SWAN
SWAP
SWAT
SWAY
SWED
SWIG

SWIM
SWUM
TWIG
TWIN
TWIT
YWCA
YWHA
AXIS
AXLE
EXAM
EXCH
EXEC
EXIT
EXOD
EXOR
EXPO
EXPT
AYAH
BYTE
CYAN
CYME
CYST
DYKE
GYRO
GYVE
HYMN
HYPE
HYPO
KYAT
LYNX
LYRE
MYNA
MYTH
PYRE
RYFM
SYNC
SYST
TYKE
TYPE
TYPO
TYRO
CZAR
EZEK
TZAR

**3rd Letter**

ACAD
AFAR
AGAR
AJAR
AMAH
ANAL
ANAT
ARAB

AWAY
AYAH
BEAD
BEAK
BEAM
BEAN
BEAR
BEAT
BEAU
BIAS
BLAB
BOAR
BOAT
BRAD
BRAE
BRAG
BRAN
BRAT
BRAY
CHAM
CHAP
CHAR
CHAT
CIAO
CLAD
CLAM
CLAN
CLAP
CLAW
CLAY
COAL
COAT
COAX
CRAB
CRAG
CRAM
CYAN
CZAR
DEAD
DEAF
DEAL
DEAN
DEAR
DIAG
DIAL
DRAB
DRAG
DRAM
DRAW
DRAY
DUAL
EDAM
ELAN
EVAP
EXAM
FEAR
FEAT

FIAT
FLAB
FLAG
FLAK
FLAP
FLAT
FLAW
FLAX
FLAY
FOAL
FOAM
FRAY
GEAR
GHAT
GLAD
GNAT
GNAW
GOAD
GOAL
GOAT
GRAB
GRAD
GRAM
GRAY
HEAD
HEAL
HEAP
HEAR
HEAT
HOAX
ITAL
IWAY
KHAN
KYAT
LEAD
LEAF
LEAK
LEAL
LEAN
LEAP
LIAR
LOAD
LOAF
LOAM
LOAN
LUAU
MEAD
MEAL
MEAN
MEAS
MEAT
MOAN
MOAT
NEAP
NEAR
NEAT
OPAL

ORAL
OVAL
PEAK
PEAL
PEAR
PEAT
PLAN
PLAT
PLAY
PRAM
PRAY
QUAD
QUAI
QUAY
RAAF
RCAF
READ
REAL
REAM
REAP
REAR
RIAL
ROAD
ROAM
ROAN
ROAR
SCAB
SCAD
SCAN
SCAR
SEAL
SEAM
SEAR
SEAT
SHAD
SHAG
SHAH
SHAK
SHAM
SKAG
SLAB
SLAG
SLAM
SLAN
SLAP
SLAT
SLAV
SLAW
SLAY
SMAJ
SNAG
SNAP
SOAK
SOAP
SOAR
SPAN
SPAR

SPAT
SPAY
STAB
STAG
STAR
STAT
STAY
SWAB
SWAG
SWAM
SWAN
SWAP
SWAT
SWAY
TEAK
TEAL
TEAM
TEAR
TEAT
THAI
THAN
THAT
THAW
TOAD
TRAM
TRAP
TRAY
TSAR
TZAR
USAF
VEAL
VIAL
WEAK
WEAL
WEAN
WEAR
WHAT
WOAD
WRAP
XMAS
YEAR
YUAN
ZEAL
ABBE
ABBR
BABE
BABY
BUBO
CUBE
DEBT
GIBE
HDBK
HOBO
ICBM
IRBM
JIBE
KOBO

LOBE
LUBE
MTBF
PUBL
ROBE
RUBY
STBD
SUBJ
TUBA
TUBE
YRBK
ZEBU
ACCT
AGCY
ARCH
BACK
BECK
BOCK
BUCK
CICS
COCK
COCO
DACE
DECK
DICE
DICT
DOCK
DUCK
DUCT
EACH
ECCL
ENCY
ETCH
EXCH
FACE
FACT
FICA
HACK
HICK
HOCK
INCA
INCH
INCL
INCR
ITCH
JACK
KICK
KOCH
LACE
LACK
LECT
LICE
LICK
LOCH
LOCK
LOCO
LUCK

MACE
MACH
MECH
MICA
MICE
MICH
MOCK
MUCH
MUCK
NECK
NICA
NICE
NICK
ONCE
ORCH
PACE
PACK
PACT
PECK
PICA
PICE
PICK
PICO
POCK
POCO
PUCK
RACE
RACK
RACY
RECD
RECT
RICE
RICH
RICK
ROCK
SACK
SECT
SECY
SICK
SOCK
SPCA
SPCC
SUCH
SUCK
TACH
TACK
TACO
TACT
TECH
TICK
TUCK
USCG
UUCP
VICE
WICK
YMCA
YWCA

ZECH
ADDN
AIDE
AMDT
AVDP
BADE
BIDE
BLDG
BLDR
BODE
BODY
CEDE
CEDI
CMDG
CMDR
CODA
CODE
DADA
DIDO
DODO
DUDE
EDDY
ESDI
FADE
FADM
FEDN
FIDO
HIDE
ISDN
JADE
JUDG
JUDO
KUDO
LADY
LCDR
LIDO
LODE
MADE
MIDI
MODE
NODE
NUDE
ODDS
RADM
REDO
RIDE
RODE
RUDE
SIDE
SODA
SUDS
TIDE
TIDY
UNDO
URDU
USDA
VADM

VEDA
VIDE
WADE
WADI
WIDE
ABED
ABET
AGED
ALEE
AMEN
AMER
ANEW
APEX
AREA
AVER
BEEF
BEEN
BEER
BEET
BIER
BLEW
BOER
BREW
CHEF
CHEM
CHEW
CLEF
CLEW
COED
CREE
CREW
DEED
DEEM
DEEP
DEER
DIET
DOER
DOES
DREG
DREW
DUEL
DUET
EDEN
ELEC
ELEM
EMER
EPEE
EVEN
EVER
EWER
EXEC
EZEK
FEED
FEEL
FEET
FIEF
FLEA

FLEE
FLEM
FLEW
FLEX
FREE
FREQ
FRET
FUEL
GAEL
GLEE
GLEN
GREP
GREW
GREY
HEED
HEEL
IBEX
IDEA
IDEM
IDES
ITEM
JEEP
JEER
JPEG
KEEL
KEEN
KEEP
KNEE
KNEW
LEEK
LEER
LEES
LIED
LIEF
LIEN
LIEU
MEED
MEEK
MEET
MIEN
MPEG
MSEC
NDEA
NEED
NOEL
NOES
OBEY
OLEO
OMEN
OPEN
OPER
OREG
OVEN
OVER
PEEK
PEEL
PEEN

PEEP
PEER
PIED
PIER
PIES
PLEA
POEM
POET
PREC
PRED
PREF
PREM
PREP
PRES
PREV
PREY
REED
REEF
REEK
REEL
RHEA
RIEL
SEED
SEEK
SEEM
SEEP
SEER
SHED
SHEW
SKEW
SLED
SLEW
SPEC
SPEW
STEM
STEP
STER
STEW
SUET
SWED
TEEM
TEEN
THEE
THEM
THEN
THEW
THEY
TIER
TREE
TREK
TREY
TUES
UREA
USED
USES
VEEP
VEER

VIEW
WEED
WEEK
WEEN
WEEP
WHEN
WHET
WHEY
WREN
AFFT
BUFF
CAFE
CPFF
CUFF
DAFT
DEFT
DEFY
DOFF
FIFE
FIFO
GAFF
GIFT
HAFT
HEFT
HUFF
IFFY
INFL
INFO
LEFT
LIFE
LIFO
LIFT
LOFT
LUFF
MIFF
MUFF
PUFF
RAFT
REFL
REFR
RIFE
RIFF
RIFT
RTFM
RUFF
RYFM
SAFE
SIFT
SOFA
SOFT
SUFF
TIFF
TUFA
TUFF
TUFT
WAFT
WEFT

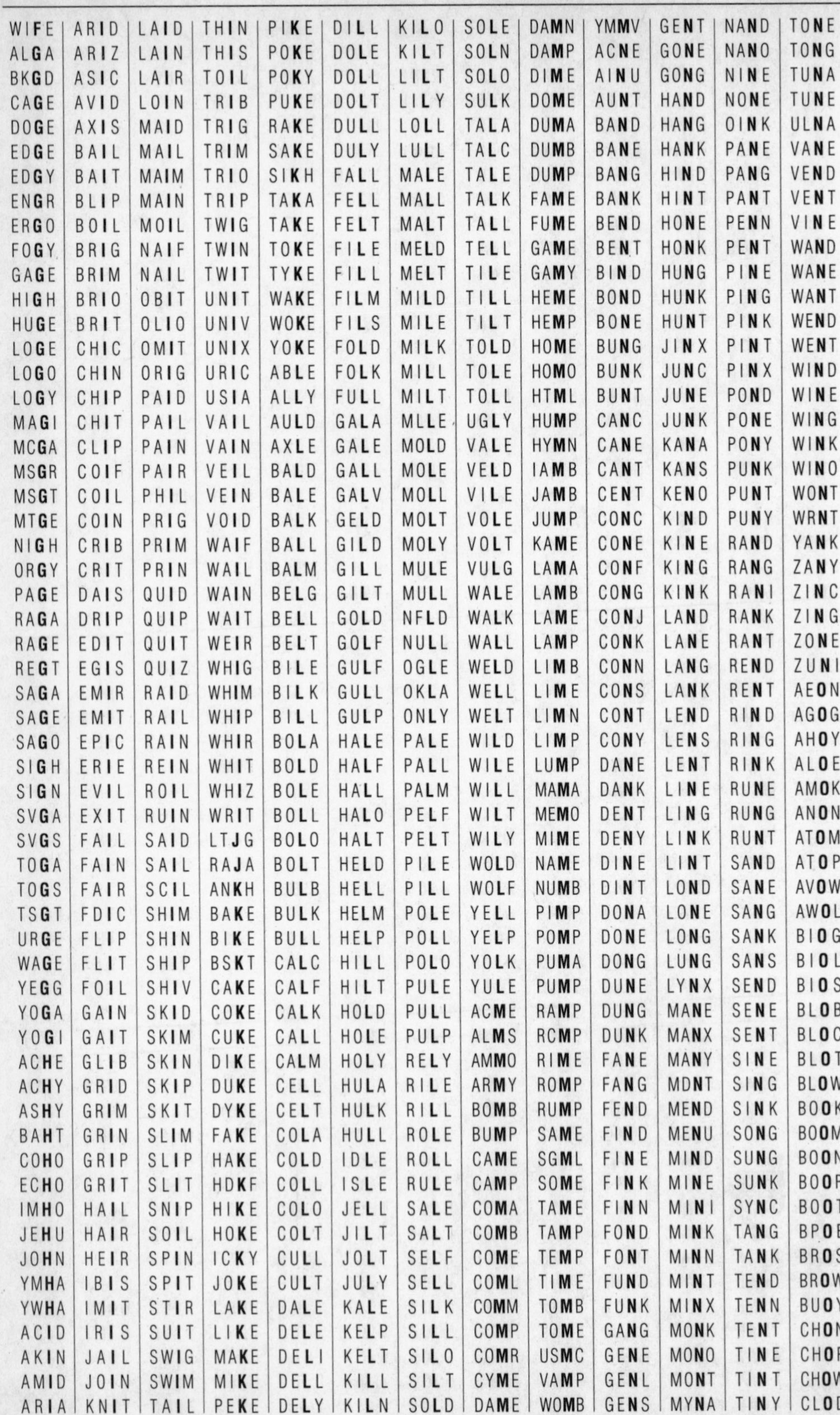

| WIFE | ARID | LAID | THIN | PIKE | DILL | KILO | SOLE | DAMN | YMMV | GENT | NAND | TONE |
|---|---|---|---|---|---|---|---|---|---|---|---|---|
| ALGA | ARIZ | LAIN | THIS | POKE | DOLE | KILT | SOLN | DAMP | ACNE | GONE | NANO | TONG |
| BKGD | ASIC | LAIR | TOIL | POKY | DOLL | LILT | SOLO | DIME | AINU | GONG | NINE | TUNA |
| CAGE | AVID | LOIN | TRIB | PUKE | DOLT | LILY | SULK | DOME | AUNT | HAND | NONE | TUNE |
| DOGE | AXIS | MAID | TRIG | RAKE | DULL | LOLL | TALA | DUMA | BAND | HANG | OINK | ULNA |
| EDGE | BAIL | MAIL | TRIM | SAKE | DULY | LULL | TALC | DUMB | BANE | HANK | PANE | VANE |
| EDGY | BAIT | MAIM | TRIO | SIKH | FALL | MALE | TALE | DUMP | BANG | HIND | PANG | VEND |
| ENGR | BLIP | MAIN | TRIP | TAKA | FELL | MALL | TALK | FAME | BANK | HINT | PANT | VENT |
| ERGO | BOIL | MOIL | TWIG | TAKE | FELT | MALT | TALL | FUME | BEND | HONE | PENN | VINE |
| FOGY | BRIG | NAIF | TWIN | TOKE | FILE | MELD | TELL | GAME | BENT | HONK | PENT | WAND |
| GAGE | BRIM | NAIL | TWIT | TYKE | FILL | MELT | TILE | GAMY | BIND | HUNG | PINE | WANE |
| HIGH | BRIO | OBIT | UNIT | WAKE | FILM | MILD | TILL | HEME | BOND | HUNK | PING | WANT |
| HUGE | BRIT | OLIO | UNIV | WOKE | FILS | MILE | TILT | HEMP | BONE | HUNT | PINK | WEND |
| LOGE | CHIC | OMIT | UNIX | YOKE | FOLD | MILK | TOLD | HOME | BUNG | JINX | PINT | WENT |
| LOGO | CHIN | ORIG | URIC | ABLE | FOLK | MILL | TOLE | HOMO | BUNK | JUNC | PINX | WIND |
| LOGY | CHIP | PAID | USIA | ALLY | FULL | MILT | TOLL | HTML | BUNT | JUNE | POND | WINE |
| MAGI | CHIT | PAIL | VAIL | AULD | GALA | MLLE | UGLY | HUMP | CANC | JUNK | PONE | WING |
| MCGA | CLIP | PAIN | VAIN | AXLE | GALE | MOLD | VALE | HYMN | CANE | KANA | PONY | WINK |
| MSGR | COIF | PAIR | VEIL | BALD | GALL | MOLE | VELD | IAMB | CANT | KANS | PUNK | WINO |
| MSGT | COIL | PHIL | VEIN | BALE | GALV | MOLL | VILE | JAMB | CENT | KENO | PUNT | WONT |
| MTGE | COIN | PRIG | VOID | BALK | GELD | MOLT | VOLE | JUMP | CONC | KIND | PUNY | WRNT |
| NIGH | CRIB | PRIM | WAIF | BALL | GILD | MOLY | VOLT | KAME | CONE | KINE | RAND | YANK |
| ORGY | CRIT | PRIN | WAIL | BALM | GILL | MULE | VULG | LAMA | CONF | KING | RANG | ZANY |
| PAGE | DAIS | QUID | WAIN | BELG | GILT | MULL | WALE | LAMB | CONG | KINK | RANI | ZINC |
| RAGA | DRIP | QUIP | WAIT | BELL | GOLD | NFLD | WALK | LAME | CONJ | LAND | RANK | ZING |
| RAGE | EDIT | QUIT | WEIR | BELT | GOLF | NULL | WALL | LAMP | CONK | LANE | RANT | ZONE |
| REGT | EGIS | QUIZ | WHIG | BILE | GULF | OGLE | WELD | LIMB | CONN | LANG | REND | ZUNI |
| SAGA | EMIR | RAID | WHIM | BILK | GULL | OKLA | WELL | LIME | CONS | LANK | RENT | AEON |
| SAGE | EMIT | RAIL | WHIP | BILL | GULP | ONLY | WELT | LIMN | CONT | LEND | RIND | AGOG |
| SAGO | EPIC | RAIN | WHIR | BOLA | HALE | PALE | WILD | LIMP | CONY | LENS | RING | AHOY |
| SIGH | ERIE | REIN | WHIT | BOLD | HALF | PALL | WILE | LUMP | DANE | LENT | RINK | ALOE |
| SIGN | EVIL | ROIL | WHIZ | BOLE | HALL | PALM | WILL | MAMA | DANK | LINE | RUNE | AMOK |
| SVGA | EXIT | RUIN | WRIT | BOLL | HALO | PELF | WILT | MEMO | DENT | LING | RUNG | ANON |
| SVGS | FAIL | SAID | LTJG | BOLO | HALT | PELT | WILY | MIME | DENY | LINK | RUNT | ATOM |
| TOGA | FAIN | SAIL | RAJA | BOLT | HELD | PILE | WOLD | NAME | DINE | LINT | SAND | ATOP |
| TOGS | FAIR | SCIL | ANKH | BULB | HELL | PILL | WOLF | NUMB | DINT | LOND | SANE | AVOW |
| TSGT | FDIC | SHIM | BAKE | BULK | HELM | POLE | YELL | PIMP | DONA | LONE | SANG | AWOL |
| URGE | FLIP | SHIN | BIKE | BULL | HELP | POLL | YELP | POMP | DONE | LONG | SANK | BIOG |
| WAGE | FLIT | SHIP | BSKT | CALC | HILL | POLO | YOLK | PUMA | DONG | LUNG | SANS | BIOL |
| YEGG | FOIL | SHIV | CAKE | CALF | HILT | PULE | YULE | PUMP | DUNE | LYNX | SEND | BIOS |
| YOGA | GAIN | SKID | COKE | CALK | HOLD | PULL | ACME | RAMP | DUNG | MANE | SENE | BLOB |
| YOGI | GAIT | SKIM | CUKE | CALL | HOLE | PULP | ALMS | RCMP | DUNK | MANX | SENT | BLOC |
| ACHE | GLIB | SKIN | DIKE | CALM | HOLY | RELY | AMMO | RIME | FANE | MANY | SINE | BLOT |
| ACHY | GRID | SKIP | DUKE | CELL | HULA | RILE | ARMY | ROMP | FANG | MDNT | SING | BLOW |
| ASHY | GRIM | SKIT | DYKE | CELT | HULK | RILL | BOMB | RUMP | FEND | MEND | SINK | BOOK |
| BAHT | GRIN | SLIM | FAKE | COLA | HULL | ROLE | BUMP | SAME | FIND | MENU | SONG | BOOM |
| COHO | GRIP | SLIP | HAKE | COLD | IDLE | ROLL | CAME | SGML | FINE | MIND | SUNG | BOON |
| ECHO | GRIT | SLIT | HDKF | COLL | ISLE | RULE | CAMP | SOME | FINK | MINE | SUNK | BOOR |
| IMHO | HAIL | SNIP | HIKE | COLO | JELL | SALE | COMA | TAME | FINN | MINI | SYNC | BOOT |
| JEHU | HAIR | SOIL | HOKE | COLT | JILT | SALT | COMB | TAMP | FOND | MINK | TANG | BPOE |
| JOHN | HEIR | SPIN | ICKY | CULL | JOLT | SELF | COME | TEMP | FONT | MINN | TANK | BROS |
| YMHA | IBIS | SPIT | JOKE | CULT | JULY | SELL | COML | TIME | FUND | MINT | TEND | BROW |
| YWHA | IMIT | STIR | LAKE | DALE | KALE | SILK | COMM | TOMB | FUNK | MINX | TENN | BUOY |
| ACID | IRIS | SUIT | LIKE | DELE | KELP | SILL | COMP | TOME | GANG | MONK | TENT | CHON |
| AKIN | JAIL | SWIG | MAKE | DELI | KELT | SILO | COMR | USMC | GENE | MONO | TINE | CHOP |
| AMID | JOIN | SWIM | MIKE | DELL | KILL | SILT | CYME | VAMP | GENL | MONT | TINT | CHOW |
| ARIA | KNIT | TAIL | PEKE | DELY | KILN | SOLD | DAME | WOMB | GENS | MYNA | TINY | CLOD |

CLOG
CLOP
CLOT
CLOY
COOK
COOL
COON
COOP
COOT
CPOM
CPOS
CROP
CROW
DHOW
DOOM
DOOR
DROP
ECOL
ECON
EXOD
EXOR
FLOE
FLOG
FLOP
FLOW
FOOD
FOOL
FOOT
FROG
FROM
GAOL
GEOG
GEOL
GEOM
GLOB
GLOP
GLOW
GOOD
GOOF
GOON
GROG
GROT
GROW
HOOD
HOOF
HOOK
HOOP
HOOT
ICON
IDOL
IKON
IOOF
IRON
KNOB
KNOT
KNOW
KOOK

LION
LOOK
LOOM
LOON
LOOP
LOOT
MEOW
MOOD
MOON
MOOR
MOOT
NEON
NOOK
NOON
OBOE
ODOR
PEON
PHON
PLOD
PLOP
PLOT
PLOW
PLOY
POOL
POOP
POOR
PROB
PROC
PROD
PROF
PROM
PRON
PROP
PROS
PROT
PROV
PROW
QUOT
RIOT
ROOD
ROOF
ROOK
ROOM
ROOT
SCOT
SCOW
SHOE
SHOP
SHOT
SHOW
SLOB
SLOE
SLOP
SLOT
SLOW
SMOG
SNOB

SNOW
SOON
SOOT
SPOT
STOL
STOP
STOW
THOU
TOOK
TOOL
TOOT
TROD
TROT
TROW
TROY
UPON
VIOL
VTOL
WHOM
WOOD
WOOF
WOOL
ZION
ZOOL
ZOOM
APPL
APPT
ASPI
CAPE
CAPS
CAPT
COPE
COPY
DEPR
DEPT
DOPA
DOPE
DUPE
ESPY
EXPO
EXPT
FEPC
GAPE
HOPE
HOPI
HYPE
HYPO
JAPE
KBPS
KEPI
LAPP
LCPL
LOPE
MCPO
MIPS
MOPE
NAPE

NOPE
PAPA
PIPE
POPE
PUPA
RAPE
RAPT
REPL
REPT
RIPE
ROPE
SCPO
SEPN
SEPT
SHPT
SOPH
SUPP
SUPT
TAPE
TAPS
TNPK
TOPE
TOPS
TYPE
TYPO
WEPT
WIPE
ZEPH
SEQQ
ACRE
AERO
AERY
AFRO
AIRY
AURA
AWRY
BARB
BARD
BARE
BARK
BARN
BART
BDRM
BERG
BIRD
BORE
BORN
BTRY
BURL
BURN
BURP
BURR
BURY
CARD
CARE
CARP
CART

CERT
CORD
CORE
CORK
CORM
CORN
CORP
CORR
CTRL
CURB
CURD
CURE
CURL
CURT
DARE
DARK
DARN
DART
DIRE
DIRK
DIRT
DORM
DORY
EARL
EARN
ECRU
FARE
FARM
FERN
FIRE
FIRM
FORA
FORD
FORE
FORK
FORM
FORT
FURL
FURY
GARB
GERM
GIRD
GIRL
GORE
GORY
GURU
GYRO
HARD
HARE
HARK
HARM
HARP
HART
HERB
HERD
HERE
HERO

HERS
HIRE
HORN
HORT
HURL
HURT
INRI
JERK
JURY
KART
KERB
KERF
KIRK
LARD
LARK
LIRA
LORD
LORE
LORN
LURE
LURK
LYRE
MARE
MARK
MARL
MARS
MART
MERE
MIRE
MORE
MORN
MURK
NARC
NARD
NLRB
NORM
NORW
OGRE
OKRA
OURS
PARA
PARD
PARE
PARK
PART
PERF
PERH
PERK
PERM
PERP
PERS
PERT
PORE
PORK
PORT
PURE
PURL

PURR
PYRE
RARE
SARI
SERA
SERB
SERE
SERF
SERG
SERV
SIRE
SORB
SORE
SORT
SPRY
SURE
SURF
SURG
SURV
TARE
TARN
TARO
TART
TERM
TERN
TERR
TIRE
TORE
TORN
TORR
TORT
TORY
TURF
TURK
TURN
TYRO
VARY
VERB
VERT
VERY
WARD
WARE
WARM
WARN
WARP
WART
WARY
WERE
WIRE
WIRY
WORD
WORE
WORK
WORM
WORN
WORT
YARD

YARN
YORE
YURT
ZERO
ALSO
ANSI
APSE
ASSN
ASSR
ASST
BASE
BASH
BASK
BASS
BAST
BEST
BOSH
BOSS
BUSH
BUSS
BUST
BUSY
CASE
CASH
CASK
CAST
CISC
COST
COSY
CSSR
CUSP
CYST
DASH
DESK
DISC
DISH
DISK
DIST
DOSE
DUSK
DUST
EASE
EAST
EASY
EISA
ELSE
ERST
FAST
FISH
FIST
FUSE
FUSS
GASH
GASP
GIST
GUSH
GUST

HASH
HASP
HISS
HIST
HOSE
HOSP
HOST
HUSH
HUSK
INSP
INST
JESS
JEST
JOSH
JOSS
JUST
KISS
LASH
LASS
LAST
LESS
LEST
LISP
LIST
LOSE
LOSS
LOST
LUSH
LUST
MASC
MASH
MASK
MASS
MAST
MDSE
MESA
MESH
MESS
MISC
MISS
MIST
MOSS
MOST
MUSE
MUSH
MUSK
MUSS
MUST
NASA
NEST
NISI
NOSE
NOSY
OUST
PASS
PAST
PESO

PEST
POSE
POSH
POSS
POST
POSY
PUSH
PUSS
RASH
RASP
RESP
REST
RISC
RISE
RISK
ROSE
ROSY
RUSE
RUSH
RUSK
RUSS
RUST
SASH
SASK
SCSI
SYST
TASK
TEST
TOSS
TUSK
USSR
VASE
VAST
VESA
VEST
VISA
VISE
VLSI
WASH
WASP
WEST
WISD
WISE
WISH
WISP
ZEST
ACTG
ACTH
ALTA
ALTO
ANTE
ANTI
ARTY
ATTN
ATTY
AUTH
AUTO

BATE
BATH
BITE
BOTH
BUTT
BYTE
CATV
CCTV
CITE
CITY
COTE
CUTE
DATA
DATE
DOTE
DUTY
ESTH
FATE
FATH
FETE
FWTW
GATE
GATT
GOTH
HATE
HTTP
INTL
INTO
IOTA
JUTE
KITE
KITH
LATE
LATH
LETT
LITH
LOTH
LUTE
MATE
MATH
MATT
METE
MITE
MITT
MKTG
MOTE
MOTH
MUTE
MUTT
MYTH
NATL
NATO
NETH
NOTE
NUTS
OATH
ONTO

PATE
PATH
PITH
PITY
PPTN
PUTT
RATE
RETD
RITE
ROTC
ROTE
SATE
SHTG
SITE
SMTP
TOTE
UNTO
VETO
VITA
VOTE
WATS
WATT
WCTU
WITH
XNTY
YETI
ABUT
AGUE
ALUM
ANUS
AQUA
ARUM
BAUD
BLUE
BLUR
BOUT
CAUL
CHUB
CHUG
CHUM
CLUB
CLUE
COUP
CRUX
DAUB
DEUT
DOUR
DRUB
DRUG
DRUM
ECUA
EDUC
FAUN
FEUD
FLUB
FLUE
FLUX

FOUL
FOUR
GAUD
GLUE
GLUM
GLUT
GOUT
GRUB
HAUL
HOUR
JOUR
LAUD
LOUD
LOUR
LOUT
MAUL
MOUE
NAUT
NEUT
NOUN
ONUS
OPUS
OVUM
PLUG
PLUM
PLUS
POUR
POUT
ROUE
ROUT
SCUD
SCUM
SHUN
SHUT
SLUE
SLUG
SLUM
SLUR
SLUT
SMUG
SMUT
SNUB
SNUG
SOUL
SOUP
SOUR
SPUD
SPUN
SPUR
STUB
STUD
STUN
SWUM
TAUT
THUD
THUG
THUS

| TOUR | HOWL | **4th Letter** | SPCA | SLAB | BEND | LORD | VOID | CITE | FETE | JOKE | MOUE | RIME |
|---|---|---|---|---|---|---|---|---|---|---|---|---|
| TOUT | JOWL | | SVGA | SLOB | BIND | LOUD | WAND | CLUE | FIFE | JUNE | MOVE | RIPE |
| TRUE | KIWI | ALGA | TAKA | SNOB | BIRD | MAID | WARD | CODE | FILE | JUTE | MTGE | RISE |
| YOUR | LAWN | ALTA | TALA | SNUB | BKGD | MEAD | WEED | COKE | FINE | KALE | MULE | RITE |
| ADVT | LEWD | AQUA | TOGA | SORB | BLVD | MEED | WELD | COME | FIRE | KAME | MUSE | RIVE |
| BEVY | MEWS | AREA | TUBA | STAB | BOLD | MELD | WEND | CONE | FIVE | KINE | MUTE | ROBE |
| BLVD | NEWS | ARIA | TUFA | STUB | BOND | MEND | WILD | COPE | FLEE | KITE | NAME | RODE |
| CAVE | NEWT | AURA | TUNA | SWAB | BRAD | MILD | WIND | CORE | FLOE | KNEE | NAPE | ROLE |
| CAVY | PAWL | BOLA | ULNA | TOMB | CARD | MIND | WISD | COTE | FLUE | LACE | NAVE | ROPE |
| COVE | PAWN | CODA | UREA | TRIB | CLAD | MOLD | WOAD | COVE | FORE | LAKE | NICE | ROSE |
| DIVA | PKWY | COLA | USDA | VERB | CLOD | MOOD | WOLD | CREE | FREE | LAME | NINE | ROTE |
| DIVE | RSWC | COMA | USIA | WOMB | COED | NAND | WOOD | CUBE | FUME | LANE | NODE | ROUE |
| DOVE | TOWN | DADA | VEDA | ASIC | COLD | NARD | WORD | CUKE | FUSE | LATE | NONE | ROVE |
| ENVY | YAWL | DATA | VESA | BLOC | CORD | NEED | YARD | CURE | FUZE | LAVE | NOPE | RUDE |
| FIVE | YAWN | DIVA | VISA | CALC | CURD | NFLD | ABBE | CUTE | GAGE | LAZE | NOSE | RULE |
| GAVE | YAWP | DONA | VITA | CANC | DEAD | PAID | ABLE | CYME | GALE | LICE | NOTE | RUNE |
| GIVE | YAWS | DOPA | VIVA | CHIC | DEED | PARD | ACHE | DACE | GAME | LIFE | NUDE | RUSE |
| GOVT | YOWL | DUMA | YMCA | CISC | EXOD | PIED | ACME | DALE | GAPE | LIKE | OBOE | SAFE |
| GYVE | FOXY | ECUA | YMHA | CONC | FEED | PLOD | ACNE | DAME | GATE | LIME | OGLE | SAGE |
| HAVE | MAXI | EISA | YOGA | DISC | FEND | POND | ACRE | DANE | GAVE | LINE | OGRE | SAKE |
| HIVE | MIXT | FICA | YWCA | EDUC | FEUD | PRED | AGUE | DARE | GAZE | LIVE | ONCE | SALE |
| HOVE | NEXT | FLEA | YWHA | ELEC | FIND | PROD | AIDE | DATE | GENE | LOBE | OOZE | SAME |
| JIVE | PNXT | FORA | ARAB | EPIC | FOLD | QUAD | ALEE | DAZE | GIBE | LODE | PACE | SANE |
| LAVA | REXX | GALA | BARB | EXEC | FOND | QUID | ALOE | DELE | GIVE | LOGE | PAGE | SATE |
| LAVE | SEXY | HULA | BLAB | FDIC | FOOD | RAID | ANTE | DICE | GLEE | LONE | PALE | SAVE |
| LEVY | TAXI | IDEA | BLOB | FEPC | FORD | RAND | APSE | DIKE | GLUE | LOPE | PANE | SENE |
| LIVE | TEXT | INCA | BOMB | JUNC | FUND | READ | AXLE | DIME | GONE | LORE | PARE | SERE |
| LOVE | WAXY | IOTA | BULB | MASC | GAUD | RECD | BABE | DINE | GORE | LOSE | PATE | SHOE |
| MOVE | CMYK | KANA | CHUB | MISC | GELD | REED | BADE | DIRE | GYVE | LOVE | PAVE | SIDE |
| NAVE | KAYO | LAMA | CLUB | MSEC | GILD | REND | BAKE | DIVE | HAKE | LUBE | PEKE | SINE |
| NAVY | MAYA | LAVA | COMB | NARC | GIRD | RETD | BALE | DOGE | HALE | LURE | PICE | SIRE |
| NOVA | ONYX | LIRA | CRAB | PREC | GLAD | RIND | BANE | DOLE | HARE | LUTE | PIKE | SITE |
| PAVE | PAYT | MAMA | CRIB | PROC | GOAD | ROAD | BARE | DOME | HATE | LYRE | PILE | SIZE |
| RAVE | PHYS | MAYA | CURB | RISC | GOLD | ROOD | BASE | DONE | HAVE | MACE | PINE | SLOE |
| RIVE | YOYO | MCGA | DAUB | ROTC | GOOD | SAID | BATE | DOPE | HAZE | MADE | PIPE | SLUE |
| ROVE | BUZZ | MESA | DRAB | RSWC | GRAD | SAND | BIDE | DOSE | HDWE | MAKE | POKE | SOLE |
| RSVP | COZY | MICA | DRUB | SPCC | GRID | SCAD | BIKE | DOTE | HEME | MALE | POLE | SOME |
| SAVE | DAZE | MYNA | DUMB | SPEC | HAND | SCUD | BILE | DOVE | HERE | MANE | PONE | SORE |
| VIVA | DOZE | NASA | FLAB | SYNC | HARD | SEED | BITE | DOZE | HIDE | MARE | POPE | SURE |
| WAVE | FAZE | NDEA | FLUB | TALC | HEAD | SEND | BLUE | DUDE | HIKE | MATE | PORE | TAKE |
| WAVY | FIZZ | NICA | GARB | URIC | HEED | SHAD | BODE | DUKE | HIRE | MAZE | POSE | TALE |
| WIVE | FUZE | NOVA | GLIB | USMC | HELD | SHED | BOLE | DUNE | HIVE | MDSE | PUKE | TAME |
| WOVE | FUZZ | OKLA | GLOB | ZINC | HERD | SKID | BONE | DUPE | HOKE | MERE | PULE | TAPE |
| BAWD | GAZE | OKRA | GRAB | ABED | HIND | SLED | BORE | DYKE | HOLE | METE | PURE | TARE |
| BAWL | HAZE | PAPA | GRUB | ACAD | HOLD | SOLD | BPOE | EASE | HOME | MICE | PYRE | THEE |
| BOWL | HAZY | PARA | HERB | ACID | HOOD | SPUD | BRAE | EDGE | HONE | MIKE | RACE | TIDE |
| COWL | HRZN | PICA | IAMB | AGED | KIND | STBD | BYTE | ELSE | HOPE | MILE | RAGE | TILE |
| DAWN | JAZZ | PLEA | JAMB | AMID | LAID | STUD | CAFE | EPEE | HOSE | MIME | RAKE | TIME |
| DOWN | LAZE | PUMA | KERB | ARID | LAND | SWED | CAGE | ERIE | HOVE | MINE | RAPE | TINE |
| FAWN | LAZY | PUPA | KNOB | AULD | LARD | TEND | CAKE | FACE | HUGE | MIRE | RARE | TIRE |
| FOWL | MAZE | RAGA | LAMB | AVID | LAUD | THUD | CAME | FADE | HYPE | MITE | RATE | TOKE |
| FRWY | NAZI | RAJA | LIMB | BALD | LEAD | TOAD | CANE | FAKE | IDLE | MLLE | RAVE | TOLE |
| GAWK | OOZE | RHEA | NLRB | BAND | LEND | TOLD | CAPE | FAME | ISLE | MODE | RAZE | TOME |
| GOWN | OUZO | SAGA | NUMB | BARD | LEWD | TROD | CARE | FANE | JADE | MOLE | RICE | TONE |
| HAWK | RAZE | SERA | PROB | BAUD | LIED | USED | CASE | FARE | JAPE | MOPE | RIDE | TOPE |
| HDWE | RAZZ | SODA | SCAB | BAWD | LOAD | VELD | CAVE | FATE | JIBE | MORE | RIFE | TORE |
| HGWY | SIZE | SOFA | SERB | BEAD | LOND | VEND | CEDE | FAZE | JIVE | MOTE | RILE | TOTE |

TREE
TRUE
TUBE
TUNE
TYKE
TYPE
URGE
VALE
VANE
VASE
VICE
VIDE
VILE
VINE
VISE
VOLE
VOTE
WADE
WAGE
WAKE
WALE
WANE
WARE
WAVE
WERE
WIDE
WIFE
WILE
WINE
WIPE
WIRE
WISE
WIVE
WOKE
WORE
WOVE
YOKE
YORE
YULE
ZONE
BEEF
BUFF
CALF
CHEF
CLEF
COIF
CONF
CPFF
CUFF
DEAF
DOFF
FIEF
GAFF
GOLF
GOOF
GULF
HALF

HDKF
HOOF
HUFF
IOOF
KERF
LEAF
LIEF
LOAF
LUFF
MIFF
MTBF
MUFF
NAIF
PELF
PERF
PREF
PROF
PUFF
RAAF
RCAF
REEF
RIFF
ROOF
RUFF
SELF
SERF
SUFF
SURF
TIFF
TUFF
TURF
USAF
WAIF
WOLF
WOOF
ACTG
AGOG
BANG
BELG
BERG
BIOG
BLDG
BRAG
BRIG
BUNG
CHUG
CLOG
CMDG
CONG
CRAG
DIAG
DONG
DRAG
DREG
DRUG
DUNG
FANG

FLAG
FLOG
FROG
GANG
GEOG
GONG
GROG
HANG
HUNG
JPEG
JUDG
KING
LANG
LING
LONG
LTJG
LUNG
MKTG
MPEG
OREG
ORIG
PANG
PING
PLUG
PRIG
RANG
RING
RUNG
SANG
SERG
SHAG
SHTG
SING
SKAG
SLAG
SLUG
SMOG
SMUG
SNAG
SNUG
SONG
STAG
SUNG
SURG
SWAG
SWIG
TANG
THUG
TONG
TRIG
TWIG
USCG
VULG
WHIG
WING
YEGG
ZING

ACTH
AMAH
ANKH
ARCH
AUTH
AYAH
BASH
BATH
BOSH
BOTH
BUSH
CASH
DASH
DISH
EACH
ESTH
ETCH
EXCH
FATH
FISH
GASH
GOTH
GUSH
HASH
HIGH
HUSH
INCH
ITCH
JOSH
KITH
KOCH
LASH
LATH
LITH
LOCH
LOTH
LUSH
MACH
MASH
MATH
MECH
MESH
MICH
MOTH
MUCH
MUSH
MYTH
NETH
NIGH
OATH
ORCH
PATH
PERH
PITH
POSH
PUSH
RASH

RICH
RUSH
SASH
SHAH
SIGH
SIKH
SOPH
SUCH
TACH
TECH
WASH
WISH
WITH
ZECH
ZEPH
ANSI
ANTI
ASPI
CEDI
DELI
ESDI
HOPI
INRI
KEPI
KIWI
MAGI
MAXI
MIDI
MINI
NAZI
NISI
QUAI
RANI
SARI
SCSI
TAXI
THAI
VLSI
WADI
YETI
YOGI
ZUNI
CONJ
SMAJ
SUBJ
AMOK
BACK
BALK
BANK
BARK
BASK
BEAK
BECK
BILK
BOCK
BOOK
BUCK

BULK
BUNK
CALK
CASK
CMYK
COCK
CONK
COOK
CORK
DANK
DARK
DECK
DESK
DIRK
DISK
DOCK
DUCK
DUNK
DUSK
EZEK
FINK
FLAK
FOLK
FORK
FUNK
GAWK
HACK
HANK
HARK
HAWK
HDBK
HICK
HOCK
HONK
HOOK
HULK
HUNK
HUSK
JACK
JERK
JUNK
KICK
KINK
KIRK
KOOK
LACK
LANK
LARK
LEAK
LEEK
LICK
LINK
LOCK
LOOK
LUCK
LURK
MARK

MASK
MEEK
MILK
MINK
MOCK
MONK
MUCK
MURK
MUSK
NECK
NICK
NOOK
OINK
PACK
PARK
PEAK
PECK
PEEK
PERK
PICK
PINK
POCK
PORK
PUCK
PUNK
RACK
RANK
REEK
RICK
RINK
RISK
ROCK
ROOK
RUSK
SACK
SANK
SASK
SEEK
SHAK
SICK
SILK
SINK
SOAK
SOCK
SUCK
SULK
SUNK
TACK
TALK
TANK
TASK
TEAK
TICK
TNPK
TOOK
TREK
TUCK

TURK
TUSK
WALK
WEAK
WEEK
WICK
WINK
WORK
YANK
YOLK
YRBK
ANAL
APPL
AWOL
BAIL
BALL
BAWL
BELL
BILL
BIOL
BOIL
BOLL
BOWL
BULL
BURL
CALL
CAUL
CELL
COAL
COIL
COLL
COML
COOL
COWL
CTRL
CULL
CURL
DEAL
DELL
DIAL
DILL
DOLL
DUAL
DUEL
DULL
EARL
ECCL
ECOL
EVIL
FAIL
FALL
FEEL
FELL
FILL
FOAL
FOIL
FOOL

FOUL
FOWL
FUEL
FULL
FURL
GAEL
GALL
GAOL
GENL
GEOL
GILL
GIRL
GOAL
GULL
HAIL
HALL
HAUL
HEAL
HEEL
HELL
HILL
HOWL
HTML
HULL
HURL
IDOL
INCL
INFL
INTL
ITAL
JAIL
JELL
JOWL
KEEL
KILL
LCPL
LEAL
LOLL
LULL
MAIL
MALL
MARL
MAUL
MEAL
MILL
MOIL
MOLL
MULL
NAIL
NATL
NOEL
NULL
OPAL
ORAL
OVAL
PAIL
PALL

PAWL
PEAL
PEEL
PHIL
PILL
POLL
POOL
PUBL
PULL
PURL
RAIL
REAL
REEL
REFL
REPL
RIAL
RIEL
RILL
ROIL
ROLL
SAIL
SCIL
SEAL
SELL
SGML
SILL
SOIL
SOUL
STOL
TAIL
TALL
TEAL
TELL
TILL
TOIL
TOLL
TOOL
VAIL
VEAL
VEIL
VIAL
VIOL
VTOL
WAIL
WALL
WEAL
WELL
WILL
WOOL
YAWL
YELL
YOWL
ZEAL
ZOOL
ALUM
ARUM
ATOM

BALM
BDRM
BEAM
BOOM
BRIM
CALM
CHAM
CHEM
CHUM
CLAM
COMM
CORM
CPOM
CRAM
DEEM
DOOM
DORM
DRAM
DRUM
EDAM
ELEM
EXAM
FADM
FARM
FILM
FIRM
FLEM
FOAM
FORM
FROM
GEOM
GERM
GLUM
GRAM
GRIM
HARM
HELM
ICBM
IDEM
IRBM
ITEM
LOAM
LOOM
MAIM
NORM
OVUM
PALM
PERM
PLUM
POEM
PRAM
PREM
PRIM
PROM
RADM
REAM
ROAM

ROOM
RTFM
RYFM
SCUM
SEAM
SEEM
SHAM
SHIM
SKIM
SLAM
SLIM
SLUM
STEM
SWAM
SWIM
SWUM
TEAM
TEEM
TERM
THEM
TRAM
TRIM
VADM
WARM
WHIM
WHOM
WORM
ZOOM
ADDN
AEON
AKIN
AMEN
ANON
ASSN
ATTN
BARN
BEAN
BEEN
BOON
BORN
BRAN
BURN
CHIN
CHON
CLAN
COIN
CONN
COON
CORN
CYAN
DAMN
DARN
DAWN
DEAN
DOWN
EARN
ECON

EDEN
ELAN
EVEN
FAIN
FAUN
FAWN
FEDN
FERN
FINN
GAIN
GLEN
GOON
GOWN
GRIN
HORN
HRZN
HYMN
ICON
IKON
IRON
ISDN
JOHN
JOIN
KEEN
KHAN
KILN
LAIN
LAWN
LEAN
LIEN
LIMN
LION
LOAN
LOIN
LOON
LORN
MAIN
MEAN
MIEN
MINN
MOAN
MOON
MORN
NEON
NOON
NOUN
OMEN
OPEN
OVEN
PAIN
PAWN
PEEN
PENN
PEON
PHON
PLAN
PPTN

| | | | | | | | | | | | | |
|---|---|---|---|---|---|---|---|---|---|---|---|---|
| PRIN | COLO | AVDP | PLOP | BEER | ROAR | LENS | BEAT | FACT | LEST | POST | THAT | UNIV |
| PRON | DIDO | BLIP | POMP | BIER | SCAR | LESS | BEET | FAST | LETT | POUT | TILT | YMMV |
| RAIN | DODO | BUMP | POOP | BLDR | SEAR | LOSS | BELT | FEAT | LIFT | PROT | TINT | ANEW |
| REIN | ECHO | BURP | PREP | BLUR | SEER | MARS | BENT | FEET | LILT | PUNT | TOOT | AVOW |
| ROAN | ERGO | CAMP | PROP | BOAR | SLUR | MASS | BEST | FELT | LINT | PUTT | TORT | BLEW |
| RUIN | EXPO | CARP | PULP | BOER | SOAR | MEAS | BLOT | FIAT | LIST | QUIT | TOUT | BLOW |
| SCAN | FIDO | CHAP | PUMP | BOOR | SOUR | MESS | BOAT | FIST | LOFT | QUOT | TROT | BREW |
| SEPN | FIFO | CHIP | QUIP | BURR | SPAR | MEWS | BOLT | FLAT | LOOT | RAFT | TSGT | BROW |
| SHIN | GYRO | CHOP | RAMP | CHAR | SPUR | MIPS | BOOT | FLIT | LOST | RANT | TUFT | CHEW |
| SHUN | HALO | CLAP | RASP | CMDR | STAR | MISS | BOUT | FONT | LOUT | RAPT | TWIT | CHOW |
| SIGN | HERO | CLIP | RCMP | COMR | STER | MOSS | BRAT | FOOT | LUST | RECT | UNIT | CLAW |
| SKIN | HOBO | CLOP | REAP | CORR | STIR | MUSS | BRIT | FORT | MALT | REGT | VAST | CLEW |
| SLAN | HOMO | COMP | RESP | CSSR | TEAR | NEWS | BSKT | FRET | MART | RENT | VENT | CREW |
| SOLN | HYPO | COOP | ROMP | CZAR | TERR | NOES | BUNT | GAIT | MAST | REPT | VERT | CROW |
| SOON | IMHO | CORP | RSVP | DEAR | TIER | NUTS | BUST | GATT | MATT | REST | VEST | DHOW |
| SPAN | INFO | COUP | RUMP | DEER | TORR | ODDS | BUTT | GENT | MDNT | RIFT | VOLT | DRAW |
| SPIN | INTO | CROP | SEEP | DEPR | TOUR | ONUS | CANT | GHAT | MEAT | RIOT | WAFT | DREW |
| SPUN | JUDO | CUSP | SHIP | DOER | TSAR | OPUS | CAPT | GIFT | MEET | ROOT | WAIT | FLAW |
| STUN | KAYO | DAMP | SHOP | DOOR | TZAR | OURS | CART | GILT | MELT | ROUT | WANT | FLEW |
| SWAN | KENO | DEEP | SKIP | DOUR | USSR | PASS | CAST | GIST | MILT | RUNT | WART | FLOW |
| TARN | KILO | DRIP | SLAP | EMER | VEER | PERS | CELT | GLUT | MINT | RUST | WATT | FWTW |
| TEEN | KOBO | DROP | SLIP | EMIR | WEAR | PHYS | CENT | GNAT | MIST | SALT | WEFT | GLOW |
| TENN | KUDO | DUMP | SLOP | ENGR | WEIR | PIES | CERT | GOAT | MITT | SCOT | WELT | GNAW |
| TERN | LIDO | EVAP | SMTP | EVER | WHIR | PLUS | CHAT | GOUT | MIXT | SEAT | WENT | GREW |
| THAN | LIFO | FLAP | SNAP | EWER | YEAR | POSS | CHIT | GOVT | MOAT | SECT | WEPT | GROW |
| THEN | LOCO | FLIP | SNIP | EXOR | YOUR | PRES | CLOT | GRIT | MOLT | SENT | WEST | KNEW |
| THIN | LOGO | FLOP | SOAP | FAIR | ALMS | PROS | COAT | GROT | MONT | SEPT | WHAT | KNOW |
| TORN | MCPO | GASP | SOUP | FEAR | ANUS | PUSS | COLT | GUST | MOOT | SHOT | WHET | MEOW |
| TOWN | MEMO | GLOP | STEP | FOUR | AXIS | RUSS | CONT | HAFT | MOST | SHPT | WHIT | NORW |
| TURN | MONO | GREP | STOP | GEAR | BASS | SANS | COOT | HALT | MSGT | SHUT | WILT | PLOW |
| TWIN | NANO | GRIP | SUPP | HAIR | BIAS | SUDS | COST | HART | MUST | SIFT | WONT | PROW |
| UPON | NATO | GULP | SWAP | HEAR | BIOS | SVGS | CRIT | HEAT | MUTT | SILT | WORT | SCOW |
| VAIN | OLEO | HARP | TAMP | HEIR | BOSS | TAPS | CULT | HEFT | NAUT | SKIT | WRIT | SHEW |
| VEIN | OLIO | HASP | TEMP | HOUR | BROS | THIS | CURT | HILT | NEAT | SLAT | WRNT | SHOW |
| WAIN | ONTO | HEAP | TRAP | INCR | BUSS | THUS | CYST | HINT | NEST | SLIT | YURT | SKEW |
| WARN | OUZO | HELP | TRIP | JEER | CAPS | TOGS | DAFT | HIST | NEUT | SLOT | ZEST | SLAW |
| WEAN | PESO | HEMP | UUCP | JOUR | CICS | TOPS | DART | HOOT | NEWT | SLUT | AINU | SLEW |
| WEEN | PICO | HOOP | VAMP | LAIR | CONS | TOSS | DEBT | HORT | NEXT | SMUT | BEAU | SLOW |
| WHEN | POCO | HOSP | VEEP | LCDR | CPOS | TUES | DEFT | HOST | OBIT | SOFT | ECRU | SNOW |
| WORN | POLO | HTTP | WARP | LEER | DAIS | USES | DENT | HUNT | OMIT | SOOT | GURU | SPEW |
| WREN | REDO | HUMP | WASP | LIAR | DOES | WATS | DEPT | HURT | OUST | SORT | JEHU | STEW |
| YARN | SAGO | INSP | WEEP | LOUR | EGIS | XMAS | DEUT | IMIT | PACT | SPAT | LIEU | STOW |
| YAWN | SCPO | JEEP | WHIP | MOOR | FILS | YAWS | DICT | INST | PANT | SPIT | LUAU | THAW |
| YUAN | SILO | JUMP | WISP | MSGR | FUSS | ABET | DIET | JEST | PART | SPOT | MENU | THEW |
| ZION | SOLO | KEEP | WRAP | NEAR | GENS | ABUT | DINT | JILT | PAST | STAT | THOU | TROW |
| AERO | TACO | KELP | YAWP | ODOR | HERS | ACCT | DIRT | JOLT | PAYT | SUET | URDU | VIEW |
| AFRO | TARO | LAMP | YELP | OPER | HISS | ADVT | DIST | JUST | PEAT | SUIT | WCTU | APEX |
| ALSO | TRIO | LAPP | FREQ | OVER | IBIS | AFFT | DOLT | KART | PELT | SUPT | ZEBU | COAX |
| ALTO | TYPO | LEAP | SEQQ | PAIR | IDES | AMDT | DUCT | KELT | PENT | SWAT | CATV | CRUX |
| AMMO | TYRO | LIMP | ABBR | PEAR | IRIS | ANAT | DUET | KILT | PERT | SYST | CCTV | FLAX |
| AUTO | UNDO | LISP | AFAR | PEER | JESS | APPT | DUST | KNIT | PEST | TACT | GALV | FLEX |
| BOLO | UNTO | LOOP | AGAR | PIER | JOSS | ASST | EAST | KNOT | PINT | TART | PREV | FLUX |
| BRIO | VETO | LUMP | AJAR | POOR | KANS | AUNT | EDIT | KYAT | PLAT | TAUT | PROV | HOAX |
| BUBO | WINO | NEAP | AMER | POUR | KBPS | BAHT | EMIT | LAST | PLOT | TEAT | SERV | IBEX |
| CIAO | YOYO | PEEP | ASSR | PURR | KISS | BAIT | ERST | LECT | PNXT | TENT | SHIV | JINX |
| COCO | ZERO | PERP | AVER | REAR | LASS | BART | EXIT | LEFT | POET | TEST | SLAV | LYNX |
| COHO | ATOP | PIMP | BEAR | REFR | LEES | BAST | EXPT | LENT | PORT | TEXT | SURV | MANX |

| | | |
|---|---|---|
| MIN**X** | HGW**Y** | XNT**Y** |
| ONY**X** | HOL**Y** | ZAN**Y** |
| PIN**X** | ICK**Y** | ARI**Z** |
| REX**X** | IFF**Y** | BUZ**Z** |
| UNI**X** | IWA**Y** | FIZ**Z** |
| ACH**Y** | JUL**Y** | FUZ**Z** |
| AER**Y** | JUR**Y** | JAZ**Z** |
| AGC**Y** | LAD**Y** | QUI**Z** |
| AHO**Y** | LAZ**Y** | RAZ**Z** |
| AIR**Y** | LEV**Y** | WHI**Z** |
| ALL**Y** | LIL**Y** | |
| ARM**Y** | LOG**Y** | |
| ART**Y** | MAN**Y** | |
| ASH**Y** | MOL**Y** | |
| ATT**Y** | NAV**Y** | |
| AWA**Y** | NOS**Y** | |
| AWR**Y** | OBE**Y** | |
| BAB**Y** | ONL**Y** | |
| BEV**Y** | ORG**Y** | |
| BOD**Y** | PIT**Y** | |
| BRA**Y** | PKW**Y** | |
| BTR**Y** | PLA**Y** | |
| BUO**Y** | PLO**Y** | |
| BUR**Y** | POK**Y** | |
| BUS**Y** | PON**Y** | |
| CAV**Y** | POS**Y** | |
| CIT**Y** | PRA**Y** | |
| CLA**Y** | PRE**Y** | |
| CLO**Y** | PUN**Y** | |
| CON**Y** | QUA**Y** | |
| COP**Y** | RAC**Y** | |
| COS**Y** | REL**Y** | |
| COZ**Y** | ROS**Y** | |
| DEF**Y** | RUB**Y** | |
| DEL**Y** | SEC**Y** | |
| DEN**Y** | SEX**Y** | |
| DOR**Y** | SLA**Y** | |
| DRA**Y** | SPA**Y** | |
| DUL**Y** | SPR**Y** | |
| DUT**Y** | STA**Y** | |
| EAS**Y** | SWA**Y** | |
| EDD**Y** | THE**Y** | |
| EDG**Y** | TID**Y** | |
| ENC**Y** | TIN**Y** | |
| ENV**Y** | TOR**Y** | |
| ESP**Y** | TRA**Y** | |
| FLA**Y** | TRE**Y** | |
| FOG**Y** | TRO**Y** | |
| FOX**Y** | UGL**Y** | |
| FRA**Y** | VAR**Y** | |
| FRW**Y** | VER**Y** | |
| FUR**Y** | WAR**Y** | |
| GAM**Y** | WAV**Y** | |
| GOR**Y** | WAX**Y** | |
| GRA**Y** | WHE**Y** | |
| GRE**Y** | WIL**Y** | |
| HAZ**Y** | WIR**Y** | |

# 5
# LETTER WORDS

**1st Letter**

ABACK
ABAFT
ABASE
ABASH
ABATE
ABBEY
ABBOT
ABEAM
ABHOR
ABIDE
ABODE
ABORT
ABOUT
ABOVE
ABSTR
ABUSE
ABYSM
ABYSS
ACORN
ACRID
ACTOR
ACUTE
ADAGE
ADAPT
ADDER
ADDLE
ADDNL
ADEPT
ADIEU
ADIOS
ADMAN
ADMIN
ADMIT
ADMIX
ADOBE
ADOPT
ADORE
ADORN
ADULT
AEGIS
AERIE
AFAIK
AFAIR
AFFIX
AFIRE
AFOOT
AFTER
AGAIN
AGAPE

AGATE
AGAVE
AGENT
AGILE
AGLOW
AGONY
AGORA
AGREE
AHEAD
AISLE
ALARM
ALBUM
ALDER
ALERT
ALGOL
ALIAS
ALIBI
ALIEN
ALIGN
ALIKE
ALIVE
ALKYD
ALLAH
ALLAY
ALLEY
ALLOT
ALLOW
ALLOY
ALOFT
ALOHA
ALONE
ALONG
ALOOF
ALOUD
ALTAR
ALTER
AMAIN
AMASS
AMAZE
AMBER
AMBLE
AMEBA
AMEND
AMISS
AMITY
AMONG
AMOUR
AMPLE
AMPUL
AMUCK
AMUSE

ANENT
ANGEL
ANGER
ANGLE
ANGLO
ANGRY
ANGST
ANGUS
ANION
ANISE
ANKLE
ANNEX
ANNOY
ANNUL
ANODE
ANTIC
ANVIL
AORTA
APACE
APART
APEAK
APHID
APHIS
APORT
APPLE
APPLY
APRIL
APRON
ARBOR
ARDOR
ARENA
ARGON
ARGOT
ARGUE
ARISE
ARITH
ARMOR
AROMA
ARRAS
ARRAY
ARROW
ARSON
ARYAN
ASCII
ASCOT
ASHEN
ASIAN
ASIDE
ASKEW
ASPEN
ASPIC

ASSAY
ASSET
ASSOC
ASTER
ASTIR
ATILT
ATLAS
ATOLL
ATONE
ATTAR
ATTIC
AUDIO
AUDIT
AUGER
AUGHT
AUGUR
AURAL
AURAR
AUXIN
AVAIL
AVAST
AVERT
AVGAS
AVIAN
AVOID
AWAIT
AWAKE
AWARD
AWARE
AWASH
AWFUL
AXIAL
AXIOM
AZTEC
AZURE
BABEL
BACON
BADGE
BAGEL
BAGGY
BAIRN
BAIZA
BAIZE
BALKY
BALMY
BALSA
BANAL
BANDY
BANJO
BANNS
BANTU

BARGE
BARON
BASAL
BASIC
BASIL
BASIN
BASIS
BASSO
BASTE
BATCH
BATHE
BATIK
BATON
BATTY
BAWDY
BAYOU
BEACH
BEANO
BEARD
BEAST
BEDEW
BEECH
BEEFY
BEFIT
BEFOG
BEGET
BEGIN
BEGUM
BEIGE
BEING
BELAY
BELCH
BELIE
BELLE
BELLS
BELLY
BELOW
BENCH
BENNY
BERET
BERRY
BERTH
BERYL
BESET
BESOM
BESOT
BETEL
BEVEL
BEZEL
BHANG
BIBLE

BIDDY
BIDET
BIGHT
BIGOT
BILGE
BILLY
BINGE
BINGO
BIPED
BIRCH
BIRTH
BISON
BITCH
BLACK
BLADE
BLAIN
BLAME
BLAND
BLANK
BLARE
BLASE
BLAST
BLAZE
BLEAK
BLEAR
BLEAT
BLEED
BLEND
BLESS
BLIMP
BLIND
BLINK
BLISS
BLITZ
BLOAT
BLOCK
BLOND
BLOOD
BLOOM
BLOWY
BLUES
BLUET
BLUFF
BLUNT
BLURB
BLURT
BLUSH
BOARD
BOAST
BOBBY
BOGEY

BOGUS
BOLUS
BONER
BONGO
BONNY
BONUS
BONZE
BOOBY
BOOST
BOOTH
BOOTY
BOOZE
BORAX
BORNE
BORON
BOSKY
BOSOM
BOSUN
BOTCH
BOUGH
BOULE
BOUND
BOURN
BOWEL
BOWER
BOXER
BRACE
BRACT
BRAID
BRAIN
BRAKE
BRAND
BRASH
BRASS
BRAVE
BRAVO
BRAWL
BRAWN
BRAZE
BREAD
BREAK
BREAM
BREED
BRIAR
BRIBE
BRICK
BRIDE
BRIEF
BRIER
BRINE
BRING

BRINK
BRISK
BROAD
BROIL
BROKE
BROOD
BROOK
BROOM
BROTH
BROWN
BRUIN
BRUIT
BRUNT
BRUSH
BRUTE
BUDDY
BUDGE
BUGGY
BUGLE
BUILD
BULGE
BULKY
BULLY
BUNCH
BUNCO
BUNNY
BURGH
BURLY
BURRO
BURST
BUSBY
BUTTE
BUTUT
BUXOM
BYLAW
BYWAY
CABAL
CABBY
CABIN
CABLE
CACAO
CACHE
CADDY
CADET
CADGE
CADRE
CAGEY
CAIRN
CAJUN
CALIF
CALLA

CALVE
CALYX
CAMEL
CAMEO
CANAL
CANDY
CANNA
CANNY
CANOE
CANON
CANTO
CAPER
CAPON
CARAT
CARET
CARGO
CARNY
CAROL
CAROM
CARRY
CARVE
CASTE
CATCH
CATER
CATTY
CAULK
CAUSE
CAVIL
CCITT
CEASE
CECUM
CEDAR
CELLO
CHAFE
CHAFF
CHAIN
CHAIR
CHALK
CHAMP
CHANT
CHAOS
CHAPS
CHARD
CHARM
CHART
CHARY
CHASE
CHASM
CHEAP
CHEAT
CHECK

CHEEK
CHEEP
CHEER
CHELA
CHERT
CHESS
CHEST
CHEWY
CHIAO
CHICK
CHIDE
CHIEF
CHILD
CHILI
CHILL
CHIME
CHIMP
CHINA
CHINE
CHINK
CHINO
CHIRP
CHIVE
CHOCK
CHOIR
CHOKE
CHOMP
CHOPS
CHORD
CHORE
CHOSE
CHRON
CHUCK
CHUMP
CHUNK
CHURL
CHURN
CHUTE
CIDER
CIGAR
CINCH
CIRCA
CIVET
CIVIC
CIVIL
CLACK
CLAIM
CLAMP
CLANG
CLANK
CLASH

CLASP
CLASS
CLEAN
CLEAR
CLEAT
CLEFT
CLERK
CLICK
CLIFF
CLIMB
CLIME
CLING
CLINK
CLOAK
CLOCK
CLONE
CLOSE
CLOTH
CLOUD
CLOUT
CLOVE
CLOWN
CLUCK
CLUMP
CLUNG
CMSGT
COACH
COAST
COBOL
COBRA
COCKY
COCOA
CODEC
CODEX
COLIC
COLON
COLOR
COMBO
COMDG
COMDR
COMDT
COMER
COMET
COMFY
COMIC
COMMA
COMMO
CONCH
CONEY
CONGA
CONIC

CONST
CONTD
CONTG
CONTR
COPRA
COPSE
CORAL
CORNY
CORPS
COUCH
COUGH
COULD
COUNT
COUPE
COURT
COVEN
COVER
COVET
COVEY
COWER
COYPU
COZEN
CRACK
CRAFT
CRAMP
CRANE
CRANK
CRAPE
CRAPS
CRASH
CRASS
CRATE
CRAVE
CRAWL
CRAZE
CRAZY
CREAK
CREAM
CREDO
CREED
CREEK
CREEL
CREEP
CREME
CREPE
CRESC
CRESS
CREST
CRICK
CRIER
CRIME

CRIMP
CRISP
CROAK
CROCK
CRONE
CRONY
CROOK
CROON
CROSS
CROUP
CROWD
CROWN
CRUDE
CRUEL
CRUET
CRUMB
CRUSE
CRUSH
CRUST
CRYPT
CRYST
CUBAN
CUBIC
CUBIT
CUPID
CURIA
CURIO
CURRY
CURSE
CURVE
CUTUP
CYCLE
CYNIC
CZECH
DACHA
DADDY
DAFFY
DAILY
DAIRY
DAISY
DALLY
DANCE
DANDY
DATED
DATUM
DAUNT
DAVIT
DEATH
DEBAR
DEBIT
DEBUG
DEBUT
DECAL
DECAY
DECOR
DECOY
DECRY

DEFER
DEFOG
DEGAS
DEICE
DEIFY
DEIGN
DEISM
DEITY
DELAY
DELFT
DELTA
DELVE
DEMON
DEMUR
DENIM
DENSE
DEPOT
DEPTH
DERBY
DERIV
DETER
DEUCE
DEVIL
DIARY
DIGIT
DINAR
DINER
DINGO
DINGY
DINKY
DIODE
DIRGE
DIRTY
DISCO
DISTN
DISTR
DITCH
DITTO
DITTY
DIVAN
DIVOT
DIZZY
DLITT
DODGE
DOGGY
DOGIE
DOGMA
DOILY
DOLLY
DOLOR
DONOR
DONUT
DOPEY
DOUBT
DOUGH
DOUSE
DOWDY

DOWEL
DOWER
DOWNY
DOWRY
DOWSE
DOYEN
DOZEN
DRAFT
DRAIN
DRAKE
DRAMA
DRANK
DRAPE
DRAWL
DREAD
DREAM
DREAR
DRESS
DRIER
DRIFT
DRILL
DRILY
DRINK
DRIVE
DROLL
DRONE
DROOL
DROOP
DROSS
DROVE
DROWN
DRUID
DRUNK
DRUPE
DRYAD
DRYER
DUCAL
DUCAT
DUCHY
DUMMY
DUMPS
DUMPY
DUNCE
DUPLE
DUSKY
DUTCH
DWARF
DWELL
DYING
EAGER
EAGLE
EARED
EARLY
EARTH
EASEL
EAVES
EBONY

ECLAT
EDEMA
EDICT
EDLIN
EDUCE
EERIE
EGRET
EIDER
EIGHT
EJECT
ELAND
ELATE
ELBOW
ELDER
ELECT
ELEGY
ELIDE
ELITE
ELOPE
ELUDE
ELVER
ELVES
EMAIL
EMBED
EMBER
EMCEE
EMEND
EMERY
EMOTE
EMPTY
ENACT
ENDOW
ENDUE
ENEMA
ENEMY
ENIAC
ENJOY
ENNUI
ENSUE
ENTER
ENTOM
ENTRY
ENVOI
ENVOY
EPOCH
EPOXY
EPROM
EPSON
EQUAL
EQUIP
EQUIV
ERASE
ERECT
ERGOT
ERISA
ERODE
ERROR

ERUPT
ESSAY
ESTER
ETHER
ETHOS
ETHYL
ETUDE
EVADE
EVENT
EVERY
EVICT
EVOKE
EXACT
EXALT
EXCEL
EXERT
EXILE
EXIST
EXPEL
EXPTL
EXTOL
EXTRA
EXUDE
EXULT
EXURB
EYRIE
EYRIR
FABLE
FACET
FAGOT
FAINT
FAIRY
FAITH
FAKIR
FALSE
FANCY
FARCE
FATAL
FATED
FATTY
FAULT
FAUNA
FAVOR
FEAST
FEAZE
FECES
FEIGN
FEINT
FELLY
FELON
FEMUR
FENCE
FERAL
FERRY
FETAL
FETCH
FETID

FETUS
FEVER
FEWER
FIBER
FICHE
FICHU
FIELD
FIEND
FIERY
FIFTH
FIFTY
FIGHT
FILAR
FILCH
FILLY
FILTH
FINAL
FINCH
FINIS
FINNY
FIORD
FIRST
FIRTH
FISHY
FIXED
FJORD
FLAIL
FLAIR
FLAKE
FLAME
FLANK
FLARE
FLASH
FLASK
FLECK
FLEER
FLEET
FLESH
FLICK
FLIED
FLIER
FLING
FLINT
FLIRT
FLOAT
FLOCK
FLOOD
FLOOR
FLORA
FLOSS
FLOUR
FLOUT
FLOWN
FLUFF
FLUID
FLUKE
FLUME

FLUNG
FLUNK
FLUSH
FLUTE
FLYBY
FLYER
FOCUS
FOEHN
FOIST
FOLIO
FOLLY
FORAY
FORCE
FORGE
FORGO
FORTE
FORTH
FORTY
FORUM
FOUND
FOUNT
FOXED
FOYER
FRAIL
FRAME
FRANC
FRANK
FRAUD
FREAK
FRESH
FRIAR
FRILL
FRISK
FRIZZ
FROCK
FROND
FRONT
FROST
FROTH
FROWN
FROZE
FRUIT
FRYER
FSLIC
FUDGE
FUGUE
FULLY
FUNKY
FUNNY
FUROR
FURRY
FURZE
FUSEE
FUSSY
FUSTY
FUZZY
GABBY

GABLE
GAFFE
GAILY
GAMIN
GAMMA
GAMUT
GANTT
GAUDY
GAUGE
GAUNT
GAUSS
GAUZE
GAVEL
GAWKY
GEESE
GELID
GENIE
GENRE
GENUS
GEODE
GETUP
GHOST
GHOUL
GIANT
GIDDY
GIMPY
GIPSY
GIRTH
GIVEN
GIZMO
GLAND
GLANS
GLARE
GLASS
GLAZE
GLEAM
GLEAN
GLEBE
GLIDE
GLINT
GLOAT
GLOBE
GLOOM
GLORY
GLOSS
GLOVE
GLOZE
GLYPH
GNARL
GNASH
GNOME
GODLY
GONAD
GONER
GOODY
GOOFY
GOOSE

GORGE
GORSE
GOUDA
GOUGE
GOURD
GRACE
GRADE
GRAFT
GRAIL
GRAIN
GRAND
GRANT
GRAPE
GRAPH
GRASP
GRASS
GRATE
GRAVE
GRAVY
GRAZE
GREAT
GREBE
GREED
GREEK
GREEN
GREET
GRIEF
GRILL
GRIME
GRIND
GRIPE
GRIST
GRITS
GROAN
GROAT
GROIN
GROOM
GROPE
GROSS
GROSZ
GROUP
GROUT
GROVE
GROWL
GRUEL
GRUFF
GRUNT
GUANO
GUARD
GUAVA
GUESS
GUEST
GUIDE
GUILD
GUILE
GUILT
GUISE

GULCH
GULLY
GUMBO
GUNNY
GUPPY
GUSHY
GUSTO
GUTTY
GUYOT
GYPSY
HABIT
HADES
HAIKU
HAIRY
HAJJI
HALER
HALLO
HALVE
HANDY
HAOLE
HAPLY
HAPPY
HARDY
HAREM
HARPY
HARRY
HARSH
HASTE
HATCH
HAUNT
HAVEN
HAVOC
HAYES
HAZEL
HEADY
HEART
HEATH
HEAVE
HEAVY
HEDGE
HEFTY
HEIST
HELIX
HELLO
HELOT
HELVE
HENCE
HENNA
HERON
HERTZ
HINDI
HINGE
HITCH
HIVES
HOARD
HOARY
HOBBY

HOGAN
HOIST
HOKUM
HOLLO
HOLLY
HOMER
HOMEY
HONEY
HONOR
HOOEY
HORDE
HORSE
HOTEL
HOUND
HOURI
HOUSE
HOVEL
HOVER
HUMAN
HUMID
HUMOR
HUMUS
HUNCH
HURON
HURRY
HUSKY
HUSSY
HUTCH
HYDRA
HYDRO
HYENA
HYING
HYMEN
ICHOR
ICING
ICTUS
IDEAL
IDIOM
IDIOT
IDYLL
IGLOO
ILEUM
IMAGE
IMAGO
IMBED
IMBUE
IMPEL
IMPER
IMPLY
INANE
INCOG
INCUR
INCUS
INDEF
INDEX
INDIC
INDUE

INEPT
INERT
INFER
INGLE
INGOT
INLAY
INLET
INNER
INPUT
INSET
INSOL
INSTR
INTEL
INTER
INURE
INURN
IRAQI
IRATE
IRISH
IRONY
IRREG
ISLAM
ISLET
ISSUE
IVORY
JABOT
JADED
JALAP
JAPAN
JAUNT
JAZZY
JEANS
JELLY
JENNY
JETTY
JEWEL
JEWRY
JIFFY
JIHAD
JIMMY
JOINT
JOIST
JOKER
JOLLY
JOULE
JOUST
JUDGE
JUICE
JUICY
JULEP
JUMBO
JUMPY
JUNCO
JUNTA
JUNTO
JUROR
KABOB

KANJI
KAPOK
KAPUT
KARAT
KARMA
KARST
KAYAK
KAZOO
KEBAB
KEDGE
KETCH
KHAKI
KIOSK
KIOWA
KITTY
KLUGE
KNACK
KNAVE
KNEAD
KNEEL
KNELL
KNIFE
KNISH
KNOCK
KNOLL
KNOUT
KNURL
KOALA
KOOKY
KORAN
KRAAL
KRAUT
KRONA
KRONE
KUDOS
KULAK
KURUS
LABEL
LABOR
LADEN
LADLE
LAGER
LAIRD
LAITY
LAMIA
LANAI
LANCE
LANKY
LAPEL
LAPIN
LAPSE
LARCH
LARGE
LARGO
LARVA
LASER
LASSO

LATCH
LATEX
LATHE
LATIN
LAUGH
LAYER
LAZAR
LEACH
LEARN
LEASE
LEASH
LEAST
LEAVE
LEDGE
LEECH
LEERY
LEGAL
LEGGY
LEGIS
LEGIT
LEMON
LEMUR
LEONE
LEPER
LETUP
LEVEE
LEVEL
LEVER
LIBEL
LICIT
LIEGE
LIEUT
LIFER
LIGHT
LIKEN
LILAC
LIMBO
LIMIT
LINEN
LINER
LINGO
LINKS
LISLE
LISTS
LITER
LITHE
LIVEN
LIVER
LIVES
LIVID
LLAMA
LLANO
LOATH
LOBBY
LOCAL
LOCUS
LODGE

LOESS
LOFTY
LOGIC
LONER
LOONY
LOOSE
LORRY
LOTUS
LOUSE
LOUSY
LOWER
LOWLY
LOYAL
LUCID
LUCKY
LUCRE
LUNAR
LUNCH
LUNGE
LURCH
LURID
LUSTY
LYING
LYMPH
LYNCH
LYRIC
MACAW
MACRO
MADAM
MAFIA
MAGIC
MAGMA
MAIZE
MAJOR
MALAY
MAMBO
MANES
MANGE
MANGO
MANIA
MANIC
MANLY
MANNA
MANOR
MANSE
MANTA
MANUF
MAORI
MAPLE
MARCH
MARGE
MARRY
MARSH
MASER
MASON
MATCH
MATZO

MAUVE
MAVEN
MAVIS
MAXIM
MAYBE
MAYOR
MCCOY
MECCA
MEDAL
MEDIA
MEDIC
MELEE
MELON
MERCY
MERGE
MERIT
MERRY
METAL
METER
METRE
METRO
MIAMI
MICRO
MIDDY
MIDGE
MIDST
MIGHT
MILCH
MIMIC
MINCE
MINIM
MINOR
MINUS
MIRTH
MISER
MISTY
MITER
MIXER
MLLES
MODEL
MODEM
MODIF
MOGUL
MOIRE
MOIST
MOLAR
MONEY
MONGO
MONTH
MOODY
MOOSE
MORAL
MORAY
MOREL
MORES
MORON
MOSEY

MOTEL
MOTET
MOTIF
MOTOR
MOTTO
MOULD
MOULT
MOUND
MOUNT
MOURN
MOUSE
MOUSY
MOUTH
MOVER
MOVIE
MUCUS
MUFTI
MUGGY
MULCH
MULCT
MUMMY
MUMPS
MUNCH
MURAL
MUSHY
MUSIC
MUSTY
MYRRH
NAACP
NABOB
NACRE
NADIR
NAIAD
NAIRA
NAIVE
NAKED
NARIS
NASAL
NASTY
NATAL
NATTY
NAVAL
NAVEL
NEEDS
NEEDY
NEGRO
NEGUS
NEIGH
NERVE
NERVY
NEVER
NEVUS
NEWEL
NEWLY
NEWSY
NEXUS
NGWEE

NICAD
NICHE
NIECE
NIFTY
NIGHT
NINNY
NIPPY
NISEI
NITER
NITRO
NOBLE
NODDY
NOHOW
NOISE
NOISY
NOMAD
NONCE
NONES
NOOSE
NORSE
NORTH
NOTCH
NOTED
NOVEL
NOWAY
NUDGE
NUMIS
NURSE
NUTTY
NYLON
NYMPH
OAKUM
OASIS
OBESE
OCCAS
OCCUR
OCEAN
OCHER
OCTAL
OCTET
ODIUM
OFFAL
OFFER
OFTEN
OLDEN
OLDIE
OLIVE
OMAHA
ONION
ONSET
OPERA
OPINE
OPIUM
OPTIC
ORATE
ORBIT
ORDER

ORGAN
ORIEL
ORRIS
OSAGE
OSIER
OTHER
OTTER
OUGHT
OUNCE
OUTDO
OUTER
OUTGO
OUTRE
OVARY
OVATE
OVERT
OVOID
OVULE
OWING
OWLET
OXBOW
OXIDE
OZONE
PACER
PADDY
PADRE
PAEAN
PAGAN
PAINT
PAISA
PALMY
PALSY
PAMPA
PANDA
PANEL
PANIC
PANSY
PANTS
PAPAL
PAPAW
PAPER
PARCH
PARKA
PARRY
PARSE
PARTY
PASHA
PASSE
PASTA
PASTE
PASTY
PATCH
PATEN
PATIO
PATSY
PATTY
PAUSE

PEACE
PEACH
PEARL
PECAN
PEDAL
PEEVE
PEKOE
PENAL
PENCE
PENIS
PENNI
PENNY
PEONY
PERCH
PERIL
PESKY
PETAL
PETER
PETTY
PEWEE
PHAGE
PHARM
PHASE
PHIAL
PHLOX
PHONE
PHONO
PHONY
PHOTO
PIANO
PICKY
PICOT
PIECE
PIETY
PIGMY
PIKER
PILAF
PILES
PILOT
PINCH
PINON
PINTO
PINUP
PIOUS
PIQUE
PITCH
PITHY
PITON
PIVOT
PIXEL
PIXIE
PIZZA
PLACE
PLAID
PLAIN
PLAIT
PLANE

PLANK
PLANT
PLASH
PLATE
PLATY
PLAYA
PLAZA
PLEAD
PLEAT
PLEBE
PLEBS
PLUCK
PLUMB
PLUME
PLUMP
PLUNK
PLUSH
PLUTO
POACH
POESY
POILU
POINT
POISE
POKER
POLAR
POLIO
POLIT
POLKA
POLYP
POOCH
POPPY
PORCH
POSER
POSIT
POSSE
POUCH
POULT
POUND
POWER
PRANK
PRATE
PRAWN
PREEN
PRESS
PRICE
PRICK
PRIDE
PRIME
PRIMP
PRINK
PRINT
PRIOR
PRISM
PRIVY
PRIZE
PROBE
PROEM

PRONE
PRONG
PROOF
PROSE
PROSY
PROUD
PROVE
PROWL
PROXY
PRUDE
PRUNE
PSALM
PSEUD
PSYCH
PUBES
PUBIC
PUBIS
PUDGY
PUKKA
PULSE
PUNCH
PUPIL
PUPPY
PUREE
PURGE
PURIM
PURSE
PUSHY
PUSSY
PUTTY
PYGMY
PYLON
QUACK
QUAFF
QUAIL
QUAKE
QUALM
QUART
QUASH
QUASI
QUEAN
QUEEN
QUEER
QUELL
QUERY
QUEST
QUEUE
QUICK
QUIET
QUILL
QUILT
QUINT
QUIRE
QUIRK
QUIRT
QUITE
QUITS

QUOIT
QUOTA
QUOTE
QUOTH
QURSH
RABBI
RABID
RADAR
RADII
RADIO
RADIX
RADON
RAISE
RALLY
RAMIE
RANCH
RANGE
RANGY
RAPID
RATIO
RATTY
RAVEL
RAVEN
RAYON
RAZOR
REACH
REACT
READY
REALM
REBEL
REBUS
REBUT
RECAP
RECIP
RECTO
RECUR
REEVE
REFER
REGAL
REIGN
RELAX
RELAY
RELIC
RELIG
REMIT
RENAL
RENEW
REPAY
REPEL
REPLY
RERUN
RESIN
RETCH
REVEL
REVUE
RHEUM
RHINO

RHYME
RIDER
RIDGE
RIFLE
RIGHT
RIGID
RIGOR
RINSE
RIPEN
RISER
RIVAL
RIVER
RIVET
RIYAL
RNZAF
ROACH
ROAST
ROBIN
ROBOT
RODEO
ROGER
ROGUE
ROMAN
ROOST
ROSIN
ROTOR
ROUGE
ROUGH
ROUND
ROUSE
ROUTE
ROWDY
ROWEL
ROYAL
RUBLE
RUDDY
RUGBY
RULER
RUMBA
RUMMY
RUMOR
RUNNY
RUPEE
RURAL
SABER
SABLE
SAINT
SALAD
SALLY
SALON
SALVE
SALVO
SANIT
SAPPY
SASSY
SATAN
SATIN

SATYR
SAUCE
SAUCY
SAUNA
SAUTE
SAVOR
SAVVY
SCALD
SCALE
SCALP
SCAMP
SCAND
SCANF
SCANT
SCARE
SCARF
SCARP
SCENE
SCENT
SCION
SCOFF
SCOLD
SCONE
SCOOP
SCOOT
SCOPE
SCORE
SCORN
SCOTS
SCOUR
SCOUT
SCOWL
SCRAM
SCRAP
SCREW
SCRIM
SCRIP
SCROD
SCRUB
SCUBA
SCUFF
SCULL
SCURF
SEAMY
SEATO
SEDAN
SEDGE
SEEDY
SEINE
SEISM
SEIZE
SEMEN
SENGI
SENNA
SENSE
SENTI
SEPAL

SEPIA
SERGE
SERIF
SERUM
SERVE
SERVO
SETUP
SEVEN
SEVER
SEWER
SHACK
SHADE
SHAFT
SHAKE
SHAKY
SHALE
SHALL
SHAME
SHANK
SHAPE
SHARD
SHARE
SHARK
SHARP
SHAVE
SHAWL
SHEAF
SHEAR
SHEEN
SHEEP
SHEER
SHEET
SHELF
SHELL
SHIER
SHIFT
SHILL
SHINE
SHINY
SHIPT
SHIRE
SHIRK
SHIRR
SHIRT
SHOAL
SHOAT
SHOCK
SHONE
SHOOK
SHOOT
SHORE
SHORN
SHORT
SHOUT
SHOVE
SHOWY
SHRED

SHREW
SHRUB
SHRUG
SHUCK
SHUNT
SIBYL
SIDLE
SIEGE
SIEVE
SIGHT
SIGMA
SILLY
SINCE
SINEW
SINGE
SINUS
SIOUX
SIREN
SIRUP
SISAL
SISSY
SITAR
SIXTY
SKATE
SKEET
SKEIN
SKIFF
SKILL
SKIMP
SKIRT
SKULK
SKULL
SKUNK
SLACK
SLAIN
SLAKE
SLANG
SLANT
SLASH
SLATE
SLAVE
SLEEK
SLEEP
SLEET
SLICE
SLICK
SLIDE
SLIER
SLIME
SLING
SLINK
SLOOP
SLOPE
SLOSH
SLOTH
SLUMP
SLUNG

SLUNK
SLURP
SLUSH
SMACK
SMALL
SMART
SMASH
SMEAR
SMELL
SMELT
SMILE
SMIRK
SMITE
SMITH
SMOCK
SMOKE
SMOTE
SMSGT
SNACK
SNAIL
SNAKE
SNARE
SNARL
SNEAK
SNEER
SNIDE
SNIFF
SNIPE
SNIPS
SNOOP
SNORE
SNORT
SNOUT
SNOWY
SNUCK
SNUFF
SOBER
SOGGY
SOLAR
SOLID
SOLON
SOLVE
SONAR
SONIC
SOOTH
SORRY
SOUGH
SOUND
SOUPY
SOUSE
SOUTH
SPACE
SPADE
SPANK
SPARC
SPARE
SPARK

SPASM
SPATE
SPAWN
SPEAK
SPEAR
SPECK
SPEED
SPELL
SPEND
SPENT
SPERM
SPICE
SPIEL
SPIKE
SPILL
SPINE
SPIRE
SPIRT
SPITE
SPLAY
SPLIT
SPOIL
SPOKE
SPOOF
SPOOK
SPOOL
SPOON
SPOOR
SPORE
SPORT
SPOUT
SPRAT
SPRAY
SPREE
SPRIG
SPUME
SPUNK
SPURN
SPURT
SQUAB
SQUAD
SQUAT
SQUAW
SQUIB
SQUID
STACK
STAFF
STAGE
STAID
STAIN
STAIR
STAKE
STALE
STALK
STALL
STAMP
STAND

STANK
STARE
STARK
START
STASH
STATE
STAVE
STEAD
STEAK
STEAL
STEAM
STEED
STEEL
STEEP
STEER
STEIN
STERE
STERN
STICK
STIFF
STILE
STILL
STILT
STING
STINK
STINT
STOAT
STOCK
STOIC
STOKE
STOLE
STOMP
STONE
STOOD
STOOL
STOOP
STORE
STORK
STORM
STORY
STOUT
STOVE
STRAP
STRAW
STRAY
STREW
STRIA
STRIP
STROP
STRUM
STRUT
STUCK
STUDY
STUFF
STUMP
STUNG
STUNK

STUNT
STYLE
SUAVE
SUCRE
SUEDE
SUGAR
SUITE
SULFA
SULKY
SULLY
SUMAC
SUNUP
SUPER
SUPRA
SUPVR
SURGE
SURLY
SWAGE
SWAIN
SWAMI
SWAMP
SWANK
SWARD
SWARM
SWART
SWASH
SWATH
SWEAR
SWEAT
SWEDE
SWEEP
SWEET
SWELL
SWEPT
SWIFT
SWILL
SWINE
SWING
SWIPE
SWIRL
SWISH
SWISS
SWITZ
SWOON
SWOOP
SWORD
SWORE
SWORN
SWUNG
SYLPH
SYNOD
SYRUP
SYSOP
TABBY
TABLE
TABOO
TABOR

TACIT
TACKY
TAFFY
TAIGA
TAINT
TALER
TALLY
TALON
TALUS
TANGO
TANSY
TAPER
TAPIR
TARDY
TAROT
TARRY
TASTE
TASTY
TAUNT
TAUPE
TAWNY
TEACH
TEASE
TEENS
TEENY
TEETH
TELEG
TELEX
TEMPO
TEMPT
TENET
TENON
TENOR
TENSE
TEPEE
TEPID
TERRY
TERSE
TESTY
THANE
THANK
THEAT
THEFT
THEGN
THEIR
THEME
THEOL
THERE
THERM
THESE
THESS
THICK
THIEF
THIGH
THINE
THING
THINK

THIRD
THOLE
THONG
THORN
THORP
THOSE
THREE
THREW
THROB
THROE
THROW
THRUM
THUMB
THUMP
THURS
THYME
TIARA
TIBIA
TICAL
TIGER
TIGHT
TILDE
TILTH
TIMES
TIMID
TINCT
TINGE
TINNY
TIPSY
TIRED
TITAN
TITHE
TITLE
TIZZY
TOADY
TOAST
TODAY
TODDY
TOKAY
TOKEN
TONER
TONGS
TONIC
TOOTH
TOPAZ
TOPER
TOPIC
TOPOG
TOQUE
TORAH
TORCH
TORSO
TOTAL
TOTEM
TOUCH
TOUGH
TOWEL

TOWER
TOXIC
TOXIN
TRACE
TRACK
TRACT
TRADE
TRAIL
TRAIN
TRAIT
TRAMP
TRANS
TRAPS
TRASH
TRAWL
TREAD
TREAS
TREAT
TREND
TRESS
TRIAD
TRIAL
TRIBE
TRICE
TRICK
TRIED
TRILL
TRINE
TRIPE
TRITE
TROLL
TROMP
TROOP
TROPE
TROTH
TROUT
TRUCE
TRUCK
TRUMP
TRUNK
TRUSS
TRUST
TRUTH
TRYST
TUBER
TULIP
TULLE
TUMID
TUMMY
TUMOR
TUNIC
TUNNY
TUQUE
TURBO
TURPS
TUTOR
TWAIN

TWANG
TWEAK
TWEED
TWEEN
TWEET
TWICE
TWILL
TWINE
TWIRL
TWIST
TWIXT
TYING
UDDER
UKASE
ULCER
ULTRA
UMBEL
UMBER
UMBRA
UMIAK
UNARM
UNBAR
UNCAP
UNCLE
UNCUT
UNDER
UNDUE
UNFIT
UNFIX
UNIFY
UNION
UNITE
UNITY
UNMAN
UNPEG
UNPIN
UNRWA
UNSAY
UNTIE
UNTIL
UNZIP
UPEND
UPPER
UPSET
URBAN
URINE
USAGE
USHER
USUAL
USURP
USURY
UTILE
UTTER
UVULA
VAGUE
VALET
VALID

VALOR
VALSE
VALUE
VALVE
VAPID
VAPOR
VARIA
VASTY
VATIC
VAULT
VAUNT
VEERY
VELAR
VELUM
VENAL
VENOM
VENUE
VENUS
VERGE
VERSE
VERSO
VERST
VERVE
VETCH
VIAND
VIBES
VICAR
VIDEO
VIGIL
VIGOR
VILLA
VINYL
VIOLA
VIPER
VIRAL
VIREO
VIRTU
VIRUS
VISIT
VISOR
VISTA
VITAL
VIVID
VIXEN
VIZOR
VOCAB
VOCAL
VODKA
VOGUE
VOICE
VOILE
VOMIT
VOUCH
VOWEL
VULVA
VYING
WACKY

WADER
WAFER
WAGER
WAGON
WAHOO
WAIST
WAIVE
WAKEN
WALTZ
WASHY
WASTE
WATCH
WATER
WAVER
WAXEN
WEALD
WEARY
WEAVE
WEDGE
WEEDY
WEENY
WEEPY
WEIGH
WEIRD
WELCH
WELSH
WENCH
WHACK
WHALE
WHARF
WHEAL
WHEAT
WHEEL
WHELK
WHELM
WHELP
WHERE
WHICH
WHIFF
WHILE
WHINE
WHIRL
WHISH
WHISK
WHIST
WHITE
WHOLE
WHOOP
WHORE
WHORL
WHOSE
WHOSO
WHSLE
WIDEN
WIDOW
WIDTH
WIELD

WIGHT
WINCE
WINCH
WINDY
WITCH
WITHE
WITHY
WITTY
WIVES
WOKEN
WOMAN
WOODY
WOOZY
WORDY
WORLD
WORRY
WORSE
WORST
WORTH
WOULD
WOUND
WOVEN
WRACK
WRATH
WREAK
WRECK
WREST
WRING
WRIST
WRITE
WRONG
WROTE
WROTH
WRUNG
WURST
XCOPY
XEBEC
XENON
XERIC
XYLEM
YACHT
YAHOO
YEARN
YEAST
YIELD
YODEL
YOKEL
YOUNG
YOURS
YOUTH
YUCCA
YUMMY
ZAIRE
ZEBRA
ZIPPY
ZLOTY
ZONAL

**2ND LETTER**

BABEL
BACON
BADGE
BAGEL
BAGGY
BAIRN
BAIZA
BAIZE
BALKY
BALMY
BALSA
BANAL
BANDY
BANJO
BANNS
BANTU
BARGE
BARON
BASAL
BASIC
BASIL
BASIN
BASIS
BASSO
BASTE
BATCH
BATHE
BATIK
BATON
BATTY
BAWDY
BAYOU
CABAL
CABBY
CABIN
CABLE
CACAO
CACHE
CADDY
CADET
CADGE
CADRE
CAGEY
CAIRN
CAJUN
CALIF
CALLA
CALVE
CALYX
CAMEL
CAMEO
CANAL
CANDY
CANNA
CANNY

CANOE
CANON
CANTO
CAPER
CAPON
CARAT
CARET
CARGO
CARNY
CAROL
CAROM
CARRY
CARVE
CASTE
CATCH
CATER
CATTY
CAULK
CAUSE
CAVIL
DACHA
DADDY
DAFFY
DAILY
DAIRY
DAISY
DALLY
DANCE
DANDY
DATED
DATUM
DAUNT
DAVIT
EAGER
EAGLE
EARED
EARLY
EARTH
EASEL
EAVES
FABLE
FACET
FAGOT
FAINT
FAIRY
FAITH
FAKIR
FALSE
FANCY
FARCE
FATAL
FATED
FATTY
FAULT
FAUNA
FAVOR
GABBY

GABLE
GAFFE
GAILY
GAMIN
GAMMA
GAMUT
GANTT
GAUDY
GAUGE
GAUNT
GAUSS
GAUZE
GAVEL
GAWKY
HABIT
HADES
HAIKU
HAIRY
HAJJI
HALER
HALLO
HALVE
HANDY
HAOLE
HAPLY
HAPPY
HARDY
HAREM
HARPY
HARRY
HARSH
HASTE
HATCH
HAUNT
HAVEN
HAVOC
HAYES
HAZEL
JABOT
JADED
JALAP
JAPAN
JAUNT
JAZZY
KABOB
KANJI
KAPOK
KAPUT
KARAT
KARMA
KARST
KAYAK
KAZOO
LABEL
LABOR
LADEN
LADLE

LAGER
LAIRD
LAITY
LAMIA
LANAI
LANCE
LANKY
LAPEL
LAPIN
LAPSE
LARCH
LARGE
LARGO
LARVA
LASER
LASSO
LATCH
LATEX
LATHE
LATIN
LAUGH
LAYER
LAZAR
MACAW
MACRO
MADAM
MAFIA
MAGIC
MAGMA
MAIZE
MAJOR
MALAY
MAMBO
MANES
MANGE
MANGO
MANIA
MANIC
MANLY
MANNA
MANOR
MANSE
MANTA
MANUF
MAORI
MAPLE
MARCH
MARGE
MARRY
MARSH
MASER
MASON
MATCH
MATZO
MAUVE
MAVEN
MAVIS

MAXIM
MAYBE
MAYOR
NAACP
NABOB
NACRE
NADIR
NAIAD
NAIRA
NAIVE
NAKED
NARIS
NASAL
NASTY
NATAL
NATTY
NAVAL
NAVEL
OAKUM
OASIS
PACER
PADDY
PADRE
PAEAN
PAGAN
PAINT
PAISA
PALMY
PALSY
PAMPA
PANDA
PANEL
PANIC
PANSY
PANTS
PAPAL
PAPAW
PAPER
PARCH
PARKA
PARRY
PARSE
PARTY
PASHA
PASSE
PASTA
PASTE
PASTY
PATCH
PATEN
PATIO
PATSY
PATTY
PAUSE
RABBI
RABID
RADAR

RADII
RADIO
RADIX
RADON
RAISE
RALLY
RAMIE
RANCH
RANGE
RANGY
RAPID
RATIO
RATTY
RAVEL
RAVEN
RAYON
RAZOR
SABER
SABLE
SAINT
SALAD
SALLY
SALON
SALVE
SALVO
SANIT
SAPPY
SASSY
SATAN
SATIN
SATYR
SAUCE
SAUCY
SAUNA
SAUTE
SAVOR
SAVVY
TABBY
TABLE
TABOO
TABOR
TACIT
TACKY
TAFFY
TAIGA
TAINT
TALER
TALLY
TALON
TALUS
TANGO
TANSY
TAPER
TAPIR
TARDY
TAROT
TARRY

TASTE
TASTY
TAUNT
TAUPE
TAWNY
VAGUE
VALET
VALID
VALOR
VALSE
VALUE
VALVE
VAPID
VAPOR
VARIA
VASTY
VATIC
VAULT
VAUNT
WACKY
WADER
WAFER
WAGER
WAGON
WAHOO
WAIST
WAIVE
WAKEN
WALTZ
WASHY
WASTE
WATCH
WATER
WAVER
WAXEN
YACHT
YAHOO
ZAIRE
ABACK
ABAFT
ABASE
ABASH
ABATE
ABBEY
ABBOT
ABEAM
ABHOR
ABIDE
ABODE
ABORT
ABOUT
ABOVE
ABSTR
ABUSE
ABYSM
ABYSS
EBONY

OBESE
ACORN
ACRID
ACTOR
ACUTE
CCITT
ECLAT
ICHOR
ICING
ICTUS
MCCOY
OCCAS
OCCUR
OCEAN
OCHER
OCTAL
OCTET
SCALD
SCALE
SCALP
SCAMP
SCAND
SCANF
SCANT
SCARE
SCARF
SCARP
SCENE
SCENT
SCION
SCOFF
SCOLD
SCONE
SCOOP
SCOOT
SCOPE
SCORE
SCORN
SCOTS
SCOUR
SCOUT
SCOWL
SCRAM
SCRAP
SCREW
SCRIM
SCRIP
SCROD
SCRUB
SCUBA
SCUFF
SCULL
SCURF
XCOPY
ADAGE
ADAPT
ADDER

ADDLE
ADDNL
ADEPT
ADIEU
ADIOS
ADMAN
ADMIN
ADMIT
ADMIX
ADOBE
ADOPT
ADORE
ADORN
ADULT
EDEMA
EDICT
EDLIN
EDUCE
IDEAL
IDIOM
IDIOT
IDYLL
ODIUM
UDDER
AEGIS
AERIE
BEACH
BEANO
BEARD
BEAST
BEDEW
BEECH
BEEFY
BEFIT
BEFOG
BEGET
BEGIN
BEGUM
BEIGE
BEING
BELAY
BELCH
BELIE
BELLE
BELLS
BELLY
BELOW
BENCH
BENNY
BERET
BERRY
BERTH
BERYL
BESET
BESOM
BESOT
BETEL

BEVEL
BEZEL
CEASE
CECUM
CEDAR
CELLO
DEATH
DEBAR
DEBIT
DEBUG
DEBUT
DECAL
DECAY
DECOR
DECOY
DECRY
DEFER
DEFOG
DEGAS
DEICE
DEIFY
DEIGN
DEISM
DEITY
DELAY
DELFT
DELTA
DELVE
DEMON
DEMUR
DENIM
DENSE
DEPOT
DEPTH
DERBY
DERIV
DETER
DEUCE
DEVIL
EERIE
FEAST
FEAZE
FECES
FEIGN
FEINT
FELLY
FELON
FEMUR
FENCE
FERAL
FERRY
FETAL
FETCH
FETID
FETUS
FEVER
FEWER

GEESE
GELID
GENIE
GENRE
GENUS
GEODE
GETUP
HEADY
HEART
HEATH
HEAVE
HEAVY
HEDGE
HEFTY
HEIST
HELIX
HELLO
HELOT
HELVE
HENCE
HENNA
HERON
HERTZ
JEANS
JELLY
JENNY
JETTY
JEWEL
JEWRY
KEBAB
KEDGE
KETCH
LEACH
LEARN
LEASE
LEASH
LEAST
LEAVE
LEDGE
LEECH
LEERY
LEGAL
LEGGY
LEGIS
LEGIT
LEMON
LEMUR
LEONE
LEPER
LETUP
LEVEE
LEVEL
LEVER
MECCA
MEDAL
MEDIA
MEDIC

MELEE
MELON
MERCY
MERGE
MERIT
MERRY
METAL
METER
METRE
METRO
NEEDS
NEEDY
NEGRO
NEGUS
NEIGH
NERVE
NERVY
NEVER
NEVUS
NEWEL
NEWLY
NEWSY
NEXUS
PEACE
PEACH
PEARL
PECAN
PEDAL
PEEVE
PEKOE
PENAL
PENCE
PENIS
PENNI
PENNY
PEONY
PERCH
PERIL
PESKY
PETAL
PETER
PETTY
PEWEE
REACH
REACT
READY
REALM
REBEL
REBUS
REBUT
RECAP
RECIP
RECTO
RECUR
REEVE
REFER
REGAL

REIGN
RELAX
RELAY
RELIC
RELIG
REMIT
RENAL
RENEW
REPAY
REPEL
REPLY
RERUN
RESIN
RETCH
REVEL
REVUE
SEAMY
SEATO
SEDAN
SEDGE
SEEDY
SEINE
SEISM
SEIZE
SEMEN
SENGI
SENNA
SENSE
SENTI
SEPAL
SEPIA
SERGE
SERIF
SERUM
SERVE
SERVO
SETUP
SEVEN
SEVER
SEWER
TEACH
TEASE
TEENS
TEENY
TEETH
TELEG
TELEX
TEMPO
TEMPT
TENET
TENON
TENOR
TENSE
TEPEE
TEPID
TERRY
TERSE

TESTY
VEERY
VELAR
VELUM
VENAL
VENOM
VENUE
VENUS
VERGE
VERSE
VERSO
VERST
VERVE
VETCH
WEALD
WEARY
WEAVE
WEDGE
WEEDY
WEENY
WEEPY
WEIGH
WEIRD
WELCH
WELSH
WENCH
XEBEC
XENON
XERIC
YEARN
YEAST
ZEBRA
AFAIK
AFAIR
AFFIX
AFIRE
AFOOT
AFTER
OFFAL
OFFER
OFTEN
AGAIN
AGAPE
AGATE
AGAVE
AGENT
AGILE
AGLOW
AGONY
AGORA
AGREE
EGRET
IGLOO
NGWEE
AHEAD
BHANG
CHAFE

CHAFF
CHAIN
CHAIR
CHALK
CHAMP
CHANT
CHAOS
CHAPS
CHARD
CHARM
CHART
CHARY
CHASE
CHASM
CHEAP
CHEAT
CHECK
CHEEK
CHEEP
CHEER
CHELA
CHERT
CHESS
CHEST
CHEWY
CHIAO
CHICK
CHIDE
CHIEF
CHILD
CHILI
CHILL
CHIME
CHIMP
CHINA
CHINE
CHINK
CHINO
CHIRP
CHIVE
CHOCK
CHOIR
CHOKE
CHOMP
CHOPS
CHORD
CHORE
CHOSE
CHRON
CHUCK
CHUMP
CHUNK
CHURL
CHURN
CHUTE
GHOST
GHOUL

KHAKI
PHAGE
PHARM
PHASE
PHIAL
PHLOX
PHONE
PHONO
PHONY
PHOTO
RHEUM
RHINO
RHYME
SHACK
SHADE
SHAFT
SHAKE
SHAKY
SHALE
SHALL
SHAME
SHANK
SHAPE
SHARD
SHARE
SHARK
SHARP
SHAVE
SHAWL
SHEAF
SHEAR
SHEEN
SHEEP
SHEER
SHEET
SHELF
SHELL
SHIER
SHIFT
SHILL
SHINE
SHINY
SHIPT
SHIRE
SHIRK
SHIRR
SHIRT
SHOAL
SHOAT
SHOCK
SHONE
SHOOK
SHOOT
SHORE
SHORN
SHORT
SHOUT

SHOVE
SHOWY
SHRED
SHREW
SHRUB
SHRUG
SHUCK
SHUNT
THANE
THANK
THEAT
THEFT
THEGN
THEIR
THEME
THEOL
THERE
THERM
THESE
THESS
THICK
THIEF
THIGH
THINE
THING
THINK
THIRD
THOLE
THONG
THORN
THORP
THOSE
THREE
THREW
THROB
THROE
THROW
THRUM
THUMB
THUMP
THURS
THYME
WHACK
WHALE
WHARF
WHEAL
WHEAT
WHEEL
WHELK
WHELM
WHELP
WHERE
WHICH
WHIFF
WHILE
WHINE
WHIRL

WHISH
WHISK
WHIST
WHITE
WHOLE
WHOOP
WHORE
WHORL
WHOSE
WHOSO
WHSLE
AISLE
BIBLE
BIDDY
BIDET
BIGHT
BIGOT
BILGE
BILLY
BINGE
BINGO
BIPED
BIRCH
BIRTH
BISON
BITCH
CIDER
CIGAR
CINCH
CIRCA
CIVET
CIVIC
CIVIL
DIARY
DIGIT
DINAR
DINER
DINGO
DINGY
DINKY
DIODE
DIRGE
DIRTY
DISCO
DISTN
DISTR
DITCH
DITTO
DITTY
DIVAN
DIVOT
DIZZY
EIDER
EIGHT
FIBER
FICHE
FICHU

FIELD
FIEND
FIERY
FIFTH
FIFTY
FIGHT
FILAR
FILCH
FILLY
FILTH
FINAL
FINCH
FINIS
FINNY
FIORD
FIRST
FIRTH
FISHY
FIXED
GIANT
GIDDY
GIMPY
GIPSY
GIRTH
GIVEN
GIZMO
HINDI
HINGE
HITCH
HIVES
JIFFY
JIHAD
JIMMY
KIOSK
KIOWA
KITTY
LIBEL
LICIT
LIEGE
LIEUT
LIFER
LIGHT
LIKEN
LILAC
LIMBO
LIMIT
LINEN
LINER
LINGO
LINKS
LISLE
LISTS
LITER
LITHE
LIVEN
LIVER
LIVES

LIVID
MIAMI
MICRO
MIDDY
MIDGE
MIDST
MIGHT
MILCH
MIMIC
MINCE
MINIM
MINOR
MINUS
MIRTH
MISER
MISTY
MITER
MIXER
NICAD
NICHE
NIECE
NIFTY
NIGHT
NINNY
NIPPY
NISEI
NITER
NITRO
PIANO
PICKY
PICOT
PIECE
PIETY
PIGMY
PIKER
PILAF
PILES
PILOT
PINCH
PINON
PINTO
PINUP
PIOUS
PIQUE
PITCH
PITHY
PITON
PIVOT
PIXEL
PIXIE
PIZZA
RIDER
RIDGE
RIFLE
RIGHT
RIGID
RIGOR

RINSE
RIPEN
RISER
RIVAL
RIVER
RIVET
RIYAL
SIBYL
SIDLE
SIEGE
SIEVE
SIGHT
SIGMA
SILLY
SINCE
SINEW
SINGE
SINUS
SIOUX
SIREN
SIRUP
SISAL
SISSY
SITAR
SIXTY
TIARA
TIBIA
TICAL
TIGER
TIGHT
TILDE
TILTH
TIMES
TIMID
TINCT
TINGE
TINNY
TIPSY
TIRED
TITAN
TITHE
TITLE
TIZZY
VIAND
VIBES
VICAR
VIDEO
VIGIL
VIGOR
VILLA
VINYL
VIOLA
VIPER
VIRAL
VIREO
VIRTU
VIRUS

VISIT
VISOR
VISTA
VITAL
VIVID
VIXEN
VIZOR
WIDEN
WIDOW
WIDTH
WIELD
WIGHT
WINCE
WINCH
WINDY
WITCH
WITHE
WITHY
WITTY
WIVES
YIELD
ZIPPY
EJECT
FJORD
SKATE
SKEET
SKEIN
SKIFF
SKILL
SKIMP
SKIRT
SKULK
SKULL
SKUNK
UKASE
ALARM
ALBUM
ALDER
ALERT
ALGOL
ALIAS
ALIBI
ALIEN
ALIGN
ALIKE
ALIVE
ALKYD
ALLAH
ALLAY
ALLEY
ALLOT
ALLOW
ALLOY
ALOFT
ALOHA
ALONE
ALONG

ALOOF
ALOUD
ALTAR
ALTER
BLACK
BLADE
BLAIN
BLAME
BLAND
BLANK
BLARE
BLASE
BLAST
BLAZE
BLEAK
BLEAR
BLEAT
BLEED
BLEND
BLESS
BLIMP
BLIND
BLINK
BLISS
BLITZ
BLOAT
BLOCK
BLOND
BLOOD
BLOOM
BLOWY
BLUES
BLUET
BLUFF
BLUNT
BLURB
BLURT
BLUSH
CLACK
CLAIM
CLAMP
CLANG
CLANK
CLASH
CLASP
CLASS
CLEAN
CLEAR
CLEAT
CLEFT
CLERK
CLICK
CLIFF
CLIMB
CLIME
CLING
CLINK

CLOAK
CLOCK
CLONE
CLOSE
CLOTH
CLOUD
CLOUT
CLOVE
CLOWN
CLUCK
CLUMP
CLUNG
DLITT
ELAND
ELATE
ELBOW
ELDER
ELECT
ELEGY
ELIDE
ELITE
ELOPE
ELUDE
ELVER
ELVES
FLAIL
FLAIR
FLAKE
FLAME
FLANK
FLARE
FLASH
FLASK
FLECK
FLEER
FLEET
FLESH
FLICK
FLIED
FLIER
FLING
FLINT
FLIRT
FLOAT
FLOCK
FLOOD
FLOOR
FLORA
FLOSS
FLOUR
FLOUT
FLOWN
FLUFF
FLUID
FLUKE
FLUME
FLUNG

FLUNK
FLUSH
FLUTE
FLYBY
FLYER
GLAND
GLANS
GLARE
GLASS
GLAZE
GLEAM
GLEAN
GLEBE
GLIDE
GLINT
GLOAT
GLOBE
GLOOM
GLORY
GLOSS
GLOVE
GLOZE
GLYPH
ILEUM
KLUGE
LLAMA
LLANO
MLLES
OLDEN
OLDIE
OLIVE
PLACE
PLAID
PLAIN
PLAIT
PLANE
PLANK
PLANT
PLASH
PLATE
PLATY
PLAYA
PLAZA
PLEAD
PLEAT
PLEBE
PLEBS
PLUCK
PLUMB
PLUME
PLUMP
PLUNK
PLUSH
PLUTO
SLACK
SLAIN
SLAKE

SLANG
SLANT
SLASH
SLATE
SLAVE
SLEEK
SLEEP
SLEET
SLICE
SLICK
SLIDE
SLIER
SLIME
SLING
SLINK
SLOOP
SLOPE
SLOSH
SLOTH
SLUMP
SLUNG
SLUNK
SLURP
SLUSH
ULCER
ULTRA
ZLOTY
AMAIN
AMASS
AMAZE
AMBER
AMBLE
AMEBA
AMEND
AMISS
AMITY
AMONG
AMOUR
AMPLE
AMPUL
AMUCK
AMUSE
CMSGT
EMAIL
EMBED
EMBER
EMCEE
EMEND
EMERY
EMOTE
EMPTY
IMAGE
IMAGO
IMBED
IMBUE
IMPEL
IMPER

IMPLY
OMAHA
SMACK
SMALL
SMART
SMASH
SMEAR
SMELL
SMELT
SMILE
SMIRK
SMITE
SMITH
SMOCK
SMOKE
SMOTE
SMSGT
UMBEL
UMBER
UMBRA
UMIAK
ANENT
ANGEL
ANGER
ANGLE
ANGLO
ANGRY
ANGST
ANGUS
ANION
ANISE
ANKLE
ANNEX
ANNOY
ANNUL
ANODE
ANTIC
ANVIL
ENACT
ENDOW
ENDUE
ENEMA
ENEMY
ENIAC
ENJOY
ENNUI
ENSUE
ENTER
ENTOM
ENTRY
ENVOI
ENVOY
GNARL
GNASH
GNOME
INANE
INCOG

INCUR
INCUS
INDEF
INDEX
INDIC
INDUE
INEPT
INERT
INFER
INGLE
INGOT
INLAY
INLET
INNER
INPUT
INSET
INSOL
INSTR
INTEL
INTER
INURE
INURN
KNACK
KNAVE
KNEAD
KNEEL
KNELL
KNIFE
KNISH
KNOCK
KNOLL
KNOUT
KNURL
ONION
ONSET
RNZAF
SNACK
SNAIL
SNAKE
SNARE
SNARL
SNEAK
SNEER
SNIDE
SNIFF
SNIPE
SNIPS
SNOOP
SNORE
SNORT
SNOUT
SNOWY
SNUCK
SNUFF
UNARM
UNBAR
UNCAP

UNCLE
UNCUT
UNDER
UNDUE
UNFIT
UNFIX
UNIFY
UNION
UNITE
UNITY
UNMAN
UNPEG
UNPIN
UNRWA
UNSAY
UNTIE
UNTIL
UNZIP
AORTA
BOARD
BOAST
BOBBY
BOGEY
BOGUS
BOLUS
BONER
BONGO
BONNY
BONUS
BONZE
BOOBY
BOOST
BOOTH
BOOTY
BOOZE
BORAX
BORNE
BORON
BOSKY
BOSOM
BOSUN
BOTCH
BOUGH
BOULE
BOUND
BOURN
BOWEL
BOWER
BOXER
COACH
COAST
COBOL
COBRA
COCKY
COCOA
CODEC
CODEX

COLIC
COLON
COLOR
COMBO
COMDG
COMDR
COMDT
COMER
COMET
COMFY
COMIC
COMMA
COMMO
CONCH
CONEY
CONGA
CONIC
CONST
CONTD
CONTG
CONTR
COPRA
COPSE
CORAL
CORNY
CORPS
COUCH
COUGH
COULD
COUNT
COUPE
COURT
COVEN
COVER
COVET
COVEY
COWER
COYPU
COZEN
DODGE
DOGGY
DOGIE
DOGMA
DOILY
DOLLY
DOLOR
DONOR
DONUT
DOPEY
DOUBT
DOUGH
DOUSE
DOWDY
DOWEL
DOWER
DOWNY
DOWRY

DOWSE
DOYEN
DOZEN
FOCUS
FOEHN
FOIST
FOLIO
FOLLY
FORAY
FORCE
FORGE
FORGO
FORTE
FORTH
FORTY
FORUM
FOUND
FOUNT
FOXED
FOYER
GODLY
GONAD
GONER
GOODY
GOOFY
GOOSE
GORGE
GORSE
GOUDA
GOUGE
GOURD
HOARD
HOARY
HOBBY
HOGAN
HOIST
HOKUM
HOLLO
HOLLY
HOMER
HOMEY
HONEY
HONOR
HOOEY
HORDE
HORSE
HOTEL
HOUND
HOURI
HOUSE
HOVEL
HOVER
JOINT
JOIST
JOKER
JOLLY
JOULE

JOUST
KOALA
KOOKY
KORAN
LOATH
LOBBY
LOCAL
LOCUS
LODGE
LOESS
LOFTY
LOGIC
LONER
LOONY
LOOSE
LORRY
LOTUS
LOUSE
LOUSY
LOWER
LOWLY
LOYAL
MODEL
MODEM
MODIF
MOGUL
MOIRE
MOIST
MOLAR
MONEY
MONGO
MONTH
MOODY
MOOSE
MORAL
MORAY
MOREL
MORES
MORON
MOSEY
MOTEL
MOTET
MOTIF
MOTOR
MOTTO
MOULD
MOULT
MOUND
MOUNT
MOURN
MOUSE
MOUSY
MOUTH
MOVER
MOVIE
NOBLE
NODDY

NOHOW
NOISE
NOISY
NOMAD
NONCE
NONES
NOOSE
NORSE
NORTH
NOTCH
NOTED
NOVEL
NOWAY
POACH
POESY
POILU
POINT
POISE
POKER
POLAR
POLIO
POLIT
POLKA
POLYP
POOCH
POPPY
PORCH
POSER
POSIT
POSSE
POUCH
POULT
POUND
POWER
ROACH
ROAST
ROBIN
ROBOT
RODEO
ROGER
ROGUE
ROMAN
ROOST
ROSIN
ROTOR
ROUGE
ROUGH
ROUND
ROUSE
ROUTE
ROWDY
ROWEL
ROYAL
SOBER
SOGGY
SOLAR
SOLID

SOLON
SOLVE
SONAR
SONIC
SOOTH
SORRY
SOUGH
SOUND
SOUPY
SOUSE
SOUTH
TOADY
TOAST
TODAY
TODDY
TOKAY
TOKEN
TONER
TONGS
TONIC
TOOTH
TOPAZ
TOPER
TOPIC
TOPOG
TOQUE
TORAH
TORCH
TORSO
TOTAL
TOTEM
TOUCH
TOUGH
TOWEL
TOWER
TOXIC
TOXIN
VOCAB
VOCAL
VODKA
VOGUE
VOICE
VOILE
VOMIT
VOUCH
VOWEL
WOKEN
WOMAN
WOODY
WOOZY
WORDY
WORLD
WORRY
WORSE
WORST
WORTH
WOULD

WOUND
WOVEN
YODEL
YOKEL
YOUNG
YOURS
YOUTH
ZONAL
APACE
APART
APEAK
APHID
APHIS
APORT
APPLE
APPLY
APRIL
APRON
EPOCH
EPOXY
EPROM
EPSON
OPERA
OPINE
OPIUM
OPTIC
SPACE
SPADE
SPANK
SPARC
SPARE
SPARK
SPASM
SPATE
SPAWN
SPEAK
SPEAR
SPECK
SPEED
SPELL
SPEND
SPENT
SPERM
SPICE
SPIEL
SPIKE
SPILL
SPINE
SPIRE
SPIRT
SPITE
SPLAY
SPLIT
SPOIL
SPOKE
SPOOF
SPOOK
SPOOL
SPOON
SPOOR
SPORE
SPORT
SPOUT
SPRAT
SPRAY
SPREE
SPRIG
SPUME
SPUNK
SPURN
SPURT
UPEND
UPPER
UPSET
EQUAL
EQUIP
EQUIV
SQUAB
SQUAD
SQUAT
SQUAW
SQUIB
SQUID
ARBOR
ARDOR
ARENA
ARGON
ARGOT
ARGUE
ARISE
ARITH
ARMOR
AROMA
ARRAS
ARRAY
ARROW
ARSON
ARYAN
BRACE
BRACT
BRAID
BRAIN
BRAKE
BRAND
BRASH
BRASS
BRAVE
BRAVO
BRAWL
BRAWN
BRAZE
BREAD
BREAK
BREAM
BREED
BRIAR
BRIBE
BRICK
BRIDE
BRIEF
BRIER
BRINE
BRING
BRINK
BRISK
BROAD
BROIL
BROKE
BROOD
BROOK
BROOM
BROTH
BROWN
BRUIN
BRUIT
BRUNT
BRUSH
BRUTE
CRACK
CRAFT
CRAMP
CRANE
CRANK
CRAPE
CRAPS
CRASH
CRASS
CRATE
CRAVE
CRAWL
CRAZE
CRAZY
CREAK
CREAM
CREDO
CREED
CREEK
CREEL
CREEP
CREME
CREPE
CRESC
CRESS
CREST
CRICK
CRIER
CRIME
CRIMP
CRISP
CROAK
CROCK
CRONE
CRONY
CROOK
CROON
CROSS
CROUP
CROWD
CROWN
CRUDE
CRUEL
CRUET
CRUMB
CRUSE
CRUSH
CRUST
CRYPT
CRYST
DRAFT
DRAIN
DRAKE
DRAMA
DRANK
DRAPE
DRAWL
DREAD
DREAM
DREAR
DRESS
DRIER
DRIFT
DRILL
DRILY
DRINK
DRIVE
DROLL
DRONE
DROOL
DROOP
DROSS
DROVE
DROWN
DRUID
DRUNK
DRUPE
DRYAD
DRYER
ERASE
ERECT
ERGOT
ERISA
ERODE
ERROR
ERUPT
FRAIL
FRAME
FRANC
FRANK
FRAUD
FREAK
FRESH
FRIAR
FRILL
FRISK
FRIZZ
FROCK
FROND
FRONT
FROST
FROTH
FROWN
FROZE
FRUIT
FRYER
GRACE
GRADE
GRAFT
GRAIL
GRAIN
GRAND
GRANT
GRAPE
GRAPH
GRASP
GRASS
GRATE
GRAVE
GRAVY
GRAZE
GREAT
GREBE
GREED
GREEK
GREEN
GREET
GRIEF
GRILL
GRIME
GRIND
GRIPE
GRIST
GRITS
GROAN
GROAT
GROIN
GROOM
GROPE
GROSS
GROSZ
GROUP
GROUT
GROVE
GROWL
GRUEL
GRUFF
GRUNT
IRAQI
IRATE
IRISH
IRONY
IRREG
KRAAL
KRAUT
KRONA
KRONE
ORATE
ORBIT
ORDER
ORGAN
ORIEL
ORRIS
PRANK
PRATE
PRAWN
PREEN
PRESS
PRICE
PRICK
PRIDE
PRIME
PRIMP
PRINK
PRINT
PRIOR
PRISM
PRIVY
PRIZE
PROBE
PROEM
PRONE
PRONG
PROOF
PROSE
PROSY
PROUD
PROVE
PROWL
PROXY
PRUDE
PRUNE
TRACE
TRACK
TRACT
TRADE
TRAIL
TRAIN
TRAIT
TRAMP
TRANS
TRAPS
TRASH
TRAWL
TREAD
TREAS
TREAT
TREND
TRESS
TRIAD
TRIAL
TRIBE
TRICE
TRICK
TRIED
TRILL
TRINE
TRIPE
TRITE
TROLL
TROMP
TROOP
TROPE
TROTH
TROUT
TRUCE
TRUCK
TRUMP
TRUNK
TRUSS
TRUST
TRUTH
TRYST
URBAN
URINE
WRACK
WRATH
WREAK
WRECK
WREST
WRING
WRIST
WRITE
WRONG
WROTE
WROTH
WRUNG
ASCII
ASCOT
ASHEN
ASIAN
ASIDE
ASKEW
ASPEN
ASPIC
ASSAY
ASSET
ASSOC
ASTER
ASTIR
ESSAY
ESTER
FSLIC
ISLAM
ISLET
ISSUE
OSAGE
OSIER
PSALM
PSEUD
PSYCH
USAGE
USHER
USUAL
USURP
USURY
ATILT
ATLAS
ATOLL
ATONE
ATTAR
ATTIC
ETHER
ETHOS
ETHYL
ETUDE
OTHER
OTTER
STACK
STAFF
STAGE
STAID
STAIN
STAIR
STAKE
STALE
STALK
STALL
STAMP
STAND
STANK
STARE
STARK
START
STASH
STATE
STAVE
STEAD
STEAK
STEAL
STEAM
STEED
STEEL
STEEP
STEER
STEIN
STERE
STERN
STICK
STIFF
STILE
STILL
STILT
STING
STINK
STINT
STOAT
STOCK
STOIC
STOKE
STOLE
STOMP
STONE
STOOD
STOOL
STOOP
STORE
STORK
STORM
STORY
STOUT
STOVE
STRAP
STRAW
STRAY
STREW
STRIA
STRIP
STROP
STRUM
STRUT
STUCK
STUDY
STUFF
STUMP
STUNG
STUNK
STUNT
STYLE
UTILE
UTTER
AUDIO
AUDIT
AUGER
AUGHT
AUGUR
AURAL
AURAR
AUXIN
BUDDY
BUDGE
BUGGY
BUGLE
BUILD
BULGE
BULKY
BULLY
BUNCH
BUNCO
BUNNY
BURGH
BURLY
BURRO
BURST
BUSBY
BUTTE
BUTUT
BUXOM
CUBAN
CUBIC
CUBIT
CUPID
CURIA
CURIO
CURRY
CURSE
CURVE
CUTUP
DUCAL
DUCAT
DUCHY
DUMMY
DUMPS
DUMPY
DUNCE
DUPLE
DUSKY
DUTCH
FUDGE
FUGUE
FULLY
FUNKY
FUNNY
FUROR
FURRY
FURZE
FUSEE
FUSSY
FUSTY
FUZZY
GUANO
GUARD
GUAVA
GUESS
GUEST
GUIDE
GUILD
GUILE
GUILT
GUISE
GULCH
GULLY
GUMBO
GUNNY
GUPPY
GUSHY
GUSTO
GUTTY
GUYOT
HUMAN
HUMID
HUMOR
HUMUS
HUNCH
HURON
HURRY
HUSKY
HUSSY
HUTCH
JUDGE
JUICE
JUICY
JULEP
JUMBO
JUMPY
JUNCO
JUNTA
JUNTO
JUROR
KUDOS
KULAK
KURUS
LUCID
LUCKY
LUCRE
LUNAR
LUNCH
LUNGE
LURCH
LURID
LUSTY
MUCUS
MUFTI
MUGGY
MULCH
MULCT
MUMMY
MUMPS
MUNCH
MURAL
MUSHY
MUSIC
MUSTY
NUDGE
NUMIS
NURSE
NUTTY
OUGHT
OUNCE
OUTDO
OUTER
OUTGO
OUTRE
PUBES
PUBIC
PUBIS
PUDGY
PUKKA
PULSE
PUNCH
PUPIL
PUPPY
PUREE
PURGE
PURIM
PURSE
PUSHY
PUSSY
PUTTY
QUACK
QUAFF
QUAIL
QUAKE
QUALM
QUART
QUASH
QUASI
QUEAN
QUEEN
QUEER
QUELL
QUERY
QUEST
QUEUE
QUICK
QUIET
QUILL
QUILT
QUINT
QUIRE
QUIRK
QUIRT
QUITE
QUITS
QUOIT
QUOTA
QUOTE
QUOTH
QURSH
RUBLE
RUDDY
RUGBY
RULER
RUMBA
RUMMY
RUMOR

RUNNY
RUPEE
RURAL
SUAVE
SUCRE
SUEDE
SUGAR
SUITE
SULFA
SULKY
SULLY
SUMAC
SUNUP
SUPER
SUPRA
SUPVR
SURGE
SURLY
TUBER
TULIP
TULLE
TUMID
TUMMY
TUMOR
TUNIC
TUNNY
TUQUE
TURBO
TURPS
TUTOR
VULVA
WURST
YUCCA
YUMMY
AVAIL
AVAST
AVERT
AVGAS
AVIAN
AVOID
EVADE
EVENT
EVERY
EVICT
EVOKE
IVORY
OVARY
OVATE
OVERT
OVOID
OVULE
UVULA
AWAIT
AWAKE
AWARD
AWARE
AWASH

AWFUL
DWARF
DWELL
OWING
OWLET
SWAGE
SWAIN
SWAMI
SWAMP
SWANK
SWARD
SWARM
SWART
SWASH
SWATH
SWEAR
SWEAT
SWEDE
SWEEP
SWEET
SWELL
SWEPT
SWIFT
SWILL
SWINE
SWING
SWIPE
SWIRL
SWISH
SWISS
SWITZ
SWOON
SWOOP
SWORD
SWORE
SWORN
SWUNG
TWAIN
TWANG
TWEAK
TWEED
TWEEN
TWEET
TWICE
TWILL
TWINE
TWIRL
TWIST
TWIXT
AXIAL
AXIOM
EXACT
EXALT
EXCEL
EXERT
EXILE
EXIST

EXPEL
EXPTL
EXTOL
EXTRA
EXUDE
EXULT
EXURB
OXBOW
OXIDE
BYLAW
BYWAY
CYCLE
CYNIC
DYING
EYRIE
EYRIR
GYPSY
HYDRA
HYDRO
HYENA
HYING
HYMEN
LYING
LYMPH
LYNCH
LYRIC
MYRRH
NYLON
NYMPH
PYGMY
PYLON
SYLPH
SYNOD
SYRUP
SYSOP
TYING
VYING
XYLEM
AZTEC
AZURE
CZECH
OZONE

## 3RD LETTER

ABACK
ABAFT
ABASE
ABASH
ABATE
ADAGE
ADAPT
AFAIK
AFAIR
AGAIN

AGAPE
AGATE
AGAVE
ALARM
AMAIN
AMASS
AMAZE
APACE
APART
AVAIL
AVAST
AWAIT
AWAKE
AWARD
AWARE
AWASH
BEACH
BEANO
BEARD
BEAST
BHANG
BLACK
BLADE
BLAIN
BLAME
BLAND
BLANK
BLARE
BLASE
BLAST
BLAZE
BOARD
BOAST
BRACE
BRACT
BRAID
BRAIN
BRAKE
BRAND
BRASH
BRASS
BRAVE
BRAVO
BRAWL
BRAWN
BRAZE
CEASE
CHAFE
CHAFF
CHAIN
CHAIR
CHALK
CHAMP
CHANT
CHAOS
CHAPS
CHARD

CHARM
CHART
CHARY
CHASE
CHASM
CLACK
CLAIM
CLAMP
CLANG
CLANK
CLASH
CLASP
CLASS
COACH
COAST
CRACK
CRAFT
CRAMP
CRANE
CRANK
CRAPE
CRAPS
CRASH
CRASS
CRATE
CRAVE
CRAWL
CRAZE
CRAZY
DEATH
DIARY
DRAFT
DRAIN
DRAKE
DRAMA
DRANK
DRAPE
DRAWL
DWARF
ELAND
ELATE
EMAIL
ENACT
ERASE
EVADE
EXACT
EXALT
FEAST
FEAZE
FLAIL
FLAIR
FLAKE
FLAME
FLANK
FLARE
FLASH
FLASK

FRAIL
FRAME
FRANC
FRANK
FRAUD
GIANT
GLAND
GLANS
GLARE
GLASS
GLAZE
GNARL
GNASH
GRACE
GRADE
GRAFT
GRAIL
GRAIN
GRAND
GRANT
GRAPE
GRAPH
GRASP
GRASS
GRATE
GRAVE
GRAVY
GRAZE
GUANO
GUARD
GUAVA
HEADY
HEART
HEATH
HEAVE
HEAVY
HOARD
HOARY
IMAGE
IMAGO
INANE
IRAQI
IRATE
JEANS
KHAKI
KNACK
KNAVE
KOALA
KRAAL
KRAUT
LEACH
LEARN
LEASE
LEASH
LEAST
LEAVE
LLAMA

LLANO
LOATH
MIAMI
NAACP
OMAHA
ORATE
OSAGE
OVARY
OVATE
PEACE
PEACH
PEARL
PHAGE
PHARM
PHASE
PIANO
PLACE
PLAID
PLAIN
PLAIT
PLANE
PLANK
PLANT
PLASH
PLATE
PLATY
PLAYA
PLAZA
POACH
PRANK
PRATE
PRAWN
PSALM
QUACK
QUAFF
QUAIL
QUAKE
QUALM
QUART
QUASH
QUASI
REACH
REACT
READY
REALM
ROACH
ROAST
SCALD
SCALE
SCALP
SCAMP
SCAND
SCANF
SCANT
SCARE
SCARF
SCARP

SEAMY
SEATO
SHACK
SHADE
SHAFT
SHAKE
SHAKY
SHALE
SHALL
SHAME
SHANK
SHAPE
SHARD
SHARE
SHARK
SHARP
SHAVE
SHAWL
SKATE
SLACK
SLAIN
SLAKE
SLANG
SLANT
SLASH
SLATE
SLAVE
SMACK
SMALL
SMART
SMASH
SNACK
SNAIL
SNAKE
SNARE
SNARL
SPACE
SPADE
SPANK
SPARC
SPARE
SPARK
SPASM
SPATE
SPAWN
STACK
STAFF
STAGE
STAID
STAIN
STAIR
STAKE
STALE
STALK
STALL
STAMP
STAND

STANK
STARE
STARK
START
STASH
STATE
STAVE
SUAVE
SWAGE
SWAIN
SWAMI
SWAMP
SWANK
SWARD
SWARM
SWART
SWASH
SWATH
TEACH
TEASE
THANE
THANK
TIARA
TOADY
TOAST
TRACE
TRACK
TRACT
TRADE
TRAIL
TRAIN
TRAIT
TRAMP
TRANS
TRAPS
TRASH
TRAWL
TWAIN
TWANG
UKASE
UNARM
USAGE
VIAND
WEALD
WEARY
WEAVE
WHACK
WHALE
WHARF
WRACK
WRATH
YEARN
YEAST
ABBEY
ABBOT
ALBUM
AMBER

AMBLE
ARBOR
BABEL
BIBLE
BOBBY
CABAL
CABBY
CABIN
CABLE
COBOL
COBRA
CUBAN
CUBIC
CUBIT
DEBAR
DEBIT
DEBUG
DEBUT
ELBOW
EMBED
EMBER
FABLE
FIBER
GABBY
GABLE
HABIT
HOBBY
IMBED
IMBUE
JABOT
KABOB
KEBAB
LABEL
LABOR
LIBEL
LOBBY
NABOB
NOBLE
ORBIT
OXBOW
PUBES
PUBIC
PUBIS
RABBI
RABID
REBEL
REBUS
REBUT
ROBIN
ROBOT
RUBLE
SABER
SABLE
SIBYL
SOBER
TABBY
TABLE

TABOO
TABOR
TIBIA
TUBER
UMBEL
UMBER
UMBRA
UNBAR
URBAN
VIBES
XEBEC
ZEBRA
ASCII
ASCOT
BACON
CACAO
CACHE
CECUM
COCKY
COCOA
CYCLE
DACHA
DECAL
DECAY
DECOR
DECOY
DECRY
DUCAL
DUCAT
DUCHY
EMCEE
EXCEL
FACET
FECES
FICHE
FICHU
FOCUS
INCOG
INCUR
INCUS
LICIT
LOCAL
LOCUS
LUCID
LUCKY
LUCRE
MACAW
MACRO
MCCOY
MECCA
MICRO
MUCUS
NACRE
NICAD
NICHE
OCCAS
OCCUR

PACER
PECAN
PICKY
PICOT
RECAP
RECIP
RECTO
RECUR
SUCRE
TACIT
TACKY
TICAL
ULCER
UNCAP
UNCLE
UNCUT
VICAR
VOCAB
VOCAL
WACKY
YACHT
YUCCA
ADDER
ADDLE
ADDNL
ALDER
ARDOR
AUDIO
AUDIT
BADGE
BEDEW
BIDDY
BIDET
BUDDY
BUDGE
CADDY
CADET
CADGE
CADRE
CEDAR
CIDER
CODEC
CODEX
DADDY
DODGE
EIDER
ELDER
ENDOW
ENDUE
FUDGE
GIDDY
GODLY
HADES
HEDGE
HYDRA
HYDRO
INDEF

INDEX
INDIC
INDUE
JADED
JUDGE
KEDGE
KUDOS
LADEN
LADLE
LEDGE
LODGE
MADAM
MEDAL
MEDIA
MEDIC
MIDDY
MIDGE
MIDST
MODEL
MODEM
MODIF
NADIR
NODDY
NUDGE
OLDEN
OLDIE
ORDER
PADDY
PADRE
PEDAL
PUDGY
RADAR
RADII
RADIO
RADIX
RADON
RIDER
RIDGE
RODEO
RUDDY
SEDAN
SEDGE
SIDLE
TODAY
TODDY
UDDER
UNDER
UNDUE
VIDEO
VODKA
WADER
WEDGE
WIDEN
WIDOW
WIDTH
YODEL
ABEAM
ADEPT
AGENT
AHEAD
ALERT
AMEBA
AMEND
ANENT
APEAK
ARENA
AVERT
BEECH
BEEFY
BLEAK
BLEAR
BLEAT
BLEED
BLEND
BLESS
BREAD
BREAK
BREAM
BREED
CHEAP
CHEAT
CHECK
CHEEK
CHEEP
CHEER
CHELA
CHERT
CHESS
CHEST
CHEWY
CLEAN
CLEAR
CLEAT
CLEFT
CLERK
CREAK
CREAM
CREDO
CREED
CREEK
CREEL
CREEP
CREME
CREPE
CRESC
CRESS
CREST
CZECH
DREAD
DREAM
DREAR
DRESS
DWELL
EDEMA
EJECT
ELECT
ELEGY
EMEND
EMERY
ENEMA
ENEMY
ERECT
EVENT
EVERY
EXERT
FIELD
FIEND
FIERY
FLECK
FLEER
FLEET
FLESH
FOEHN
FREAK
FRESH
GEESE
GLEAM
GLEAN
GLEBE
GREAT
GREBE
GREED
GREEK
GREEN
GREET
GUESS
GUEST
HYENA
IDEAL
ILEUM
INEPT
INERT
KNEAD
KNEEL
KNELL
LEECH
LEERY
LIEGE
LIEUT
LOESS
NEEDS
NEEDY
NIECE
OBESE
OCEAN
OPERA
OVERT
PAEAN
PEEVE
PIECE
PIETY
PLEAD
PLEAT
PLEBE
PLEBS
POESY
PREEN
PRESS
PSEUD
QUEAN
QUEEN
QUEER
QUELL
QUERY
QUEST
QUEUE
REEVE
RHEUM
SCENE
SCENT
SEEDY
SHEAF
SHEAR
SHEEN
SHEEP
SHEER
SHEET
SHELF
SHELL
SIEGE
SIEVE
SKEET
SKEIN
SLEEK
SLEEP
SLEET
SMEAR
SMELL
SMELT
SNEAK
SNEER
SPEAK
SPEAR
SPECK
SPEED
SPELL
SPEND
SPENT
SPERM
STEAD
STEAK
STEAL
STEAM
STEED
STEEL
STEEP
STEER
STEIN
STERE
STERN
SUEDE
SWEAR
SWEAT
SWEDE
SWEEP
SWEET
SWELL
SWEPT
TEENS
TEENY
TEETH
THEAT
THEFT
THEGN
THEIR
THEME
THEOL
THERE
THERM
THESE
THESS
TREAD
TREAS
TREAT
TREND
TRESS
TWEAK
TWEED
TWEEN
TWEET
UPEND
VEERY
WEEDY
WEENY
WEEPY
WHEAL
WHEAT
WHEEL
WHELK
WHELM
WHELP
WHERE
WIELD
WREAK
WRECK
WREST
YIELD
AFFIX
AWFUL
BEFIT
BEFOG
DAFFY
DEFER
DEFOG
FIFTH
FIFTY
GAFFE
HEFTY
INFER
JIFFY
LIFER
LOFTY
MAFIA
MUFTI
NIFTY
OFFAL
OFFER
REFER
RIFLE
TAFFY
UNFIT
UNFIX
WAFER
AEGIS
ALGOL
ANGEL
ANGER
ANGLE
ANGLO
ANGRY
ANGST
ANGUS
ARGON
ARGOT
ARGUE
AUGER
AUGHT
AUGUR
AVGAS
BAGEL
BAGGY
BEGET
BEGIN
BEGUM
BIGHT
BIGOT
BOGEY
BOGUS
BUGGY
BUGLE
CAGEY
CIGAR
DEGAS
DIGIT
DOGGY
DOGIE
DOGMA
EAGER
EAGLE
EIGHT
ERGOT
FAGOT
FIGHT
FUGUE
HOGAN
INGLE
INGOT
LAGER
LEGAL
LEGGY
LEGIS
LEGIT
LIGHT
LOGIC
MAGIC
MAGMA
MIGHT
MOGUL
MUGGY
NEGRO
NEGUS
NIGHT
ORGAN
OUGHT
PAGAN
PIGMY
PYGMY
REGAL
RIGHT
RIGID
RIGOR
ROGER
ROGUE
RUGBY
SIGHT
SIGMA
SOGGY
SUGAR
TIGER
TIGHT
VAGUE
VIGIL
VIGOR
VOGUE
WAGER
WAGON
WIGHT
ABHOR
APHID
APHIS
ASHEN
ETHER
ETHOS
ETHYL
ICHOR
JIHAD
NOHOW
OCHER
OTHER
USHER
WAHOO
YAHOO
ABIDE
ADIEU
ADIOS
AFIRE
AGILE
ALIAS
ALIBI
ALIEN
ALIGN
ALIKE
ALIVE
AMISS
AMITY
ANION
ANISE
ARISE
ARITH
ASIAN
ASIDE
ATILT
AVIAN
AXIAL
AXIOM
BAIRN
BAIZA
BAIZE
BEIGE
BEING
BLIMP
BLIND
BLINK
BLISS
BLITZ
BRIAR
BRIBE
BRICK
BRIDE
BRIEF
BRIER
BRINE
BRING
BRINK
BRISK
BUILD
CAIRN
CCITT
CHIAO
CHICK
CHIDE
CHIEF
CHILD
CHILI
CHILL
CHIME
CHIMP
CHINA
CHINE
CHINK
CHINO
CHIRP
CHIVE
CLICK
CLIFF
CLIMB
CLIME
CLING
CLINK
CRICK
CRIER
CRIME
CRIMP
CRISP
DAILY
DAIRY
DAISY
DEICE
DEIFY
DEIGN
DEISM
DEITY
DLITT
DOILY
DRIER
DRIFT
DRILL
DRILY
DRINK
DRIVE
DYING
EDICT
ELIDE
ELITE
ENIAC
ERISA
EVICT
EXILE
EXIST
FAINT
FAIRY
FAITH
FEIGN
FEINT
FLICK
FLIED
FLIER
FLING
FLINT
FLIRT
FOIST
FRIAR
FRILL
FRISK
FRIZZ
GAILY
GLIDE
GLINT
GRIEF
GRILL
GRIME
GRIND
GRIPE
GRIST
GRITS
GUIDE
GUILD
GUILE
GUILT
GUISE
HAIKU
HAIRY
HEIST
HOIST
HYING
ICING
IDIOM
IDIOT
IRISH
JOINT
JOIST
JUICE
JUICY
KNIFE
KNISH
LAIRD
LAITY
LYING
MAIZE
MOIRE
MOIST
NAIAD
NAIRA
NAIVE
NEIGH
NOISE
NOISY
ODIUM
OLIVE
ONION
OPINE
OPIUM
ORIEL
OSIER
OWING
OXIDE
PAINT
PAISA
PHIAL
POILU
POINT
POISE
PRICE
PRICK
PRIDE
PRIME
PRIMP
PRINK
PRINT
PRIOR
PRISM
PRIVY
PRIZE
QUICK
QUIET
QUILL
QUILT
QUINT
QUIRE
QUIRK
QUIRT
QUITE
QUITS
RAISE
REIGN
RHINO
SAINT
SCION
SEINE
SEISM
SEIZE
SHIER
SHIFT
SHILL
SHINE
SHINY
SHIPT
SHIRE
SHIRK
SHIRR
SHIRT
SKIFF
SKILL
SKIMP
SKIRT
SLICE
SLICK
SLIDE
SLIER
SLIME
SLING
SLINK
SMILE
SMIRK
SMITE
SMITH
SNIDE
SNIFF
SNIPE
SNIPS
SPICE
SPIEL
SPIKE
SPILL
SPINE
SPIRE
SPIRT
SPITE
STICK
STIFF
STILE
STILL
STILT
STING
STINK
STINT
SUITE
SWIFT
SWILL
SWINE
SWING
SWIPE
SWIRL
SWISH
SWISS
SWITZ
TAIGA
TAINT
THICK
THIEF
THIGH
THINE
THING
THINK
THIRD
TRIAD
TRIAL
TRIBE
TRICE
TRICK
TRIED
TRILL
TRINE
TRIPE
TRITE
TWICE
TWILL
TWINE
TWIRL
TWIST
TWIXT
TYING
UMIAK
UNIFY

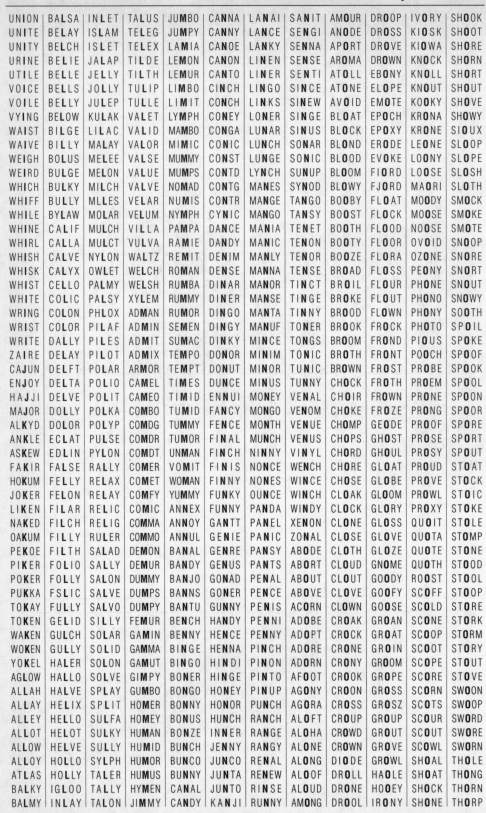

| UNION | BALSA | INLET | TALUS | JUMBO | CANNA | LANAI | SANIT | AMOUR | DROOP | IVORY | SHOOK |
|---|---|---|---|---|---|---|---|---|---|---|---|
| UNITE | BELAY | ISLAM | TELEG | JUMPY | CANNY | LANCE | SENGI | ANODE | DROSS | KIOSK | SHOOT |
| UNITY | BELCH | ISLET | TELEX | LAMIA | CANOE | LANKY | SENNA | APORT | DROVE | KIOWA | SHORE |
| URINE | BELIE | JALAP | TILDE | LEMON | CANON | LINEN | SENSE | AROMA | DROWN | KNOCK | SHORN |
| UTILE | BELLE | JELLY | TILTH | LEMUR | CANTO | LINER | SENTI | ATOLL | EBONY | KNOLL | SHORT |
| VOICE | BELLS | JOLLY | TULIP | LIMBO | CINCH | LINGO | SINCE | ATONE | ELOPE | KNOUT | SHOUT |
| VOILE | BELLY | JULEP | TULLE | LIMIT | CONCH | LINKS | SINEW | AVOID | EMOTE | KOOKY | SHOVE |
| VYING | BELOW | KULAK | VALET | LYMPH | CONEY | LONER | SINGE | BLOAT | EPOCH | KRONA | SHOWY |
| WAIST | BILGE | LILAC | VALID | MAMBO | CONGA | LUNAR | SINUS | BLOCK | EPOXY | KRONE | SIOUX |
| WAIVE | BILLY | MALAY | VALOR | MIMIC | CONIC | LUNCH | SONAR | BLOND | ERODE | LEONE | SLOOP |
| WEIGH | BOLUS | MELEE | VALSE | MUMMY | CONST | LUNGE | SONIC | BLOOD | EVOKE | LOONY | SLOPE |
| WEIRD | BULGE | MELON | VALUE | MUMPS | CONTD | LYNCH | SUNUP | BLOOM | FIORD | LOOSE | SLOSH |
| WHICH | BULKY | MILCH | VALVE | NOMAD | CONTG | MANES | SYNOD | BLOWY | FJORD | MAORI | SLOTH |
| WHIFF | BULLY | MLLES | VELAR | NUMIS | CONTR | MANGE | TANGO | BOOBY | FLOAT | MOODY | SMOCK |
| WHILE | BYLAW | MOLAR | VELUM | NYMPH | CYNIC | MANGO | TANSY | BOOST | FLOCK | MOOSE | SMOKE |
| WHINE | CALIF | MULCH | VILLA | PAMPA | DANCE | MANIA | TENET | BOOTH | FLOOD | NOOSE | SMOTE |
| WHIRL | CALLA | MULCT | VULVA | RAMIE | DANDY | MANIC | TENON | BOOTY | FLOOR | OVOID | SNOOP |
| WHISH | CALVE | NYLON | WALTZ | REMIT | DENIM | MANLY | TENOR | BOOZE | FLORA | OZONE | SNORE |
| WHISK | CALYX | OWLET | WELCH | ROMAN | DENSE | MANNA | TENSE | BROAD | FLOSS | PEONY | SNORT |
| WHIST | CELLO | PALMY | WELSH | RUMBA | DINAR | MANOR | TINCT | BROIL | FLOUR | PHONE | SNOUT |
| WHITE | COLIC | PALSY | XYLEM | RUMMY | DINER | MANSE | TINGE | BROKE | FLOUT | PHONO | SNOWY |
| WRING | COLON | PHLOX | ADMAN | RUMOR | DINGO | MANTA | TINNY | BROOD | FLOWN | PHONY | SOOTH |
| WRIST | COLOR | PILAF | ADMIN | SEMEN | DINGY | MANUF | TONER | BROOK | FROCK | PHOTO | SPOIL |
| WRITE | DALLY | PILES | ADMIT | SUMAC | DINKY | MINCE | TONGS | BROOM | FROND | PIOUS | SPOKE |
| ZAIRE | DELAY | PILOT | ADMIX | TEMPO | DONOR | MINIM | TONIC | BROTH | FRONT | POOCH | SPOOF |
| CAJUN | DELFT | POLAR | ARMOR | TEMPT | DONUT | MINOR | TUNIC | BROWN | FROST | PROBE | SPOOK |
| ENJOY | DELTA | POLIO | CAMEL | TIMES | DUNCE | MINUS | TUNNY | CHOCK | FROTH | PROEM | SPOOL |
| HAJJI | DELVE | POLIT | CAMEO | TIMID | ENNUI | MONEY | VENAL | CHOIR | FROWN | PRONE | SPOON |
| MAJOR | DOLLY | POLKA | COMBO | TUMID | FANCY | MONGO | VENOM | CHOKE | FROZE | PRONG | SPOOR |
| ALKYD | DOLOR | POLYP | COMDG | TUMMY | FENCE | MONTH | VENUE | CHOMP | GEODE | PROOF | SPORE |
| ANKLE | ECLAT | PULSE | COMDR | TUMOR | FINAL | MUNCH | VENUS | CHOPS | GHOST | PROSE | SPORT |
| ASKEW | EDLIN | PYLON | COMDT | UNMAN | FINCH | NINNY | VINYL | CHORD | GHOUL | PROSY | SPOUT |
| FAKIR | FALSE | RALLY | COMER | VOMIT | FINIS | NONCE | WENCH | CHORE | GLOAT | PROUD | STOAT |
| HOKUM | FELLY | RELAX | COMET | WOMAN | FINNY | NONES | WINCE | CHOSE | GLOBE | PROVE | STOCK |
| JOKER | FELON | RELAY | COMFY | YUMMY | FUNKY | OUNCE | WINCH | CLOAK | GLOOM | PROWL | STOIC |
| LIKEN | FILAR | RELIC | COMIC | ANNEX | FUNNY | PANDA | WINDY | CLOCK | GLORY | PROXY | STOKE |
| NAKED | FILCH | RELIG | COMMA | ANNOY | GANTT | PANEL | XENON | CLONE | GLOSS | QUOIT | STOLE |
| OAKUM | FILLY | RULER | COMMO | ANNUL | GENIE | PANIC | ZONAL | CLOSE | GLOVE | QUOTA | STOMP |
| PEKOE | FILTH | SALAD | DEMON | BANAL | GENRE | PANSY | ABODE | CLOTH | GLOZE | QUOTE | STONE |
| PIKER | FOLIO | SALLY | DEMUR | BANDY | GENUS | PANTS | ABORT | CLOUD | GNOME | QUOTH | STOOD |
| POKER | FOLLY | SALON | DUMMY | BANJO | GONAD | PENAL | ABOUT | CLOUT | GOODY | ROOST | STOOL |
| PUKKA | FSLIC | SALVE | DUMPS | BANNS | GONER | PENCE | ABOVE | CLOVE | GOOFY | SCOFF | STOOP |
| TOKAY | FULLY | SALVO | DUMPY | BANTU | GUNNY | PENIS | ACORN | CLOWN | GOOSE | SCOLD | STORE |
| TOKEN | GELID | SILLY | FEMUR | BENCH | HANDY | PENNI | ADOBE | CROAK | GROAN | SCONE | STORK |
| WAKEN | GULCH | SOLAR | GAMIN | BENNY | HENCE | PENNY | ADOPT | CROCK | GROAT | SCOOP | STORM |
| WOKEN | GULLY | SOLID | GAMMA | BINGE | HENNA | PINCH | ADORE | CRONE | GROIN | SCOOT | STORY |
| YOKEL | HALER | SOLON | GAMUT | BINGO | HINDI | PINON | ADORN | CRONY | GROOM | SCOPE | STOUT |
| AGLOW | HALLO | SOLVE | GIMPY | BONER | HINGE | PINTO | AFOOT | CROOK | GROPE | SCORE | STOVE |
| ALLAH | HALVE | SPLAY | GUMBO | BONGO | HONEY | PINUP | AGONY | CROON | GROSS | SCORN | SWOON |
| ALLAY | HELIX | SPLIT | HOMER | BONNY | HONOR | PUNCH | AGORA | CROSS | GROSZ | SCOTS | SWOOP |
| ALLEY | HELLO | SULFA | HOMEY | BONUS | HUNCH | RANCH | ALOFT | CROUP | GROUP | SCOUR | SWORD |
| ALLOT | HELOT | SULKY | HUMAN | BONZE | INNER | RANGE | ALOHA | CROWD | GROUT | SCOUT | SWORE |
| ALLOW | HELVE | SULLY | HUMID | BUNCH | JENNY | RANGY | ALONE | CROWN | GROVE | SCOWL | SWORN |
| ALLOY | HOLLO | SYLPH | HUMOR | BUNCO | JUNCO | RENAL | ALONG | DIODE | GROWL | SHOAL | THOLE |
| ATLAS | HOLLY | TALER | HUMUS | BUNNY | JUNTA | RENEW | ALOOF | DROLL | HAOLE | SHOAT | THONG |
| BALKY | IGLOO | TALLY | HYMEN | CANAL | JUNTO | RINSE | ALOUD | DRONE | HOOEY | SHOCK | THORN |
| BALMY | INLAY | TALON | JIMMY | CANDY | KANJI | RUNNY | AMONG | DROOL | IRONY | SHONE | THORP |

THOSE
TOOTH
TROLL
TROMP
TROOP
TROPE
TROTH
TROUT
VIOLA
WHOLE
WHOOP
WHORE
WHORL
WHOSE
WHOSO
WOODY
WOOZY
WRONG
WROTE
WROTH
XCOPY
ZLOTY
AMPLE
AMPUL
APPLE
APPLY
ASPEN
ASPIC
BIPED
CAPER
CAPON
COPRA
COPSE
CUPID
DEPOT
DEPTH
DOPEY
DUPLE
EMPTY
EXPEL
EXPTL
GIPSY
GUPPY
GYPSY
HAPLY
HAPPY
IMPEL
IMPER
IMPLY
INPUT
JAPAN
KAPOK
KAPUT
LAPEL
LAPIN
LAPSE
LEPER

MAPLE
NIPPY
PAPAL
PAPAW
PAPER
POPPY
PUPIL
PUPPY
RAPID
REPAY
REPEL
REPLY
RIPEN
RUPEE
SAPPY
SEPAL
SEPIA
SUPER
SUPRA
SUPVR
TAPER
TAPIR
TEPEE
TEPID
TIPSY
TOPAZ
TOPER
TOPIC
TOPOG
UNPEG
UNPIN
UPPER
VAPID
VAPOR
VIPER
ZIPPY
PIQUE
TOQUE
TUQUE
ACRID
AERIE
AGREE
AORTA
APRIL
APRON
ARRAS
ARRAY
ARROW
AURAL
AURAR
BARGE
BARON
BERET
BERRY
BERTH
BERYL
BIRCH

BIRTH
BORAX
BORNE
BORON
BURGH
BURLY
BURRO
BURST
CARAT
CARET
CARGO
CARNY
CAROL
CAROM
CARRY
CARVE
CHRON
CIRCA
CORAL
CORNY
CORPS
CURIA
CURIO
CURRY
CURSE
CURVE
DERBY
DERIV
DIRGE
DIRTY
EARED
EARLY
EARTH
EERIE
EGRET
EPROM
ERROR
EYRIE
EYRIR
FARCE
FERAL
FERRY
FIRST
FIRTH
FORAY
FORCE
FORGE
FORGO
FORTE
FORTH
FORTY
FORUM
FUROR
FURRY
FURZE
GIRTH
GORGE

GORSE
HARDY
HAREM
HARPY
HARRY
HARSH
HERON
HERTZ
HORDE
HORSE
HURON
HURRY
IRREG
JUROR
KARAT
KARMA
KARST
KORAN
KURUS
LARCH
LARGE
LARGO
LARVA
LORRY
LURCH
LURID
LYRIC
MARCH
MARGE
MARRY
MARSH
MERCY
MERGE
MERIT
MERRY
MIRTH
MORAL
MORAY
MOREL
MORES
MORON
MURAL
MYRRH
NARIS
NERVE
NERVY
NORSE
NORTH
NURSE
ORRIS
PARCH
PARKA
PARRY
PARSE
PARTY
PERCH
PERIL

PORCH
PUREE
PURGE
PURIM
PURSE
QURSH
RERUN
RURAL
SCRAM
SCRAP
SCREW
SCRIM
SCRIP
SCROD
SCRUB
SERGE
SERIF
SERUM
SERVE
SERVO
SHRED
SHREW
SHRUB
SHRUG
SIREN
SIRUP
SORRY
SPRAT
SPRAY
SPREE
SPRIG
STRAP
STRAW
STRAY
STREW
STRIA
STRIP
STROP
STRUM
STRUT
SURGE
SURLY
SYRUP
TARDY
TAROT
TARRY
TERRY
TERSE
THREE
THREW
THROB
THROE
THROW
THRUM
TIRED
TORAH
TORCH

TORSO
TURBO
TURPS
UNRWA
VARIA
VERGE
VERSE
VERSO
VERST
VERVE
VIRAL
VIREO
VIRTU
VIRUS
WORDY
WORLD
WORRY
WORSE
WORST
WORTH
WURST
XERIC
ABSTR
AISLE
ARSON
ASSAY
ASSET
ASSOC
BASAL
BASIC
BASIL
BASIN
BASIS
BASSO
BASTE
BESET
BESOM
BESOT
BISON
BOSKY
BOSOM
BOSUN
BUSBY
CASTE
CMSGT
DISCO
DISTN
DISTR
DUSKY
EASEL
ENSUE
EPSON
ESSAY
FISHY
FUSEE
FUSSY
FUSTY

GUSHY
GUSTO
HASTE
HUSKY
HUSSY
INSET
INSOL
INSTR
ISSUE
LASER
LASSO
LISLE
LISTS
LUSTY
MASER
MASON
MISER
MISTY
MOSEY
MUSHY
MUSIC
MUSTY
NASAL
NASTY
NISEI
OASIS
ONSET
PASHA
PASSE
PASTA
PASTE
PASTY
PESKY
POSER
POSIT
POSSE
PUSHY
PUSSY
RESIN
RISER
ROSIN
SASSY
SISAL
SISSY
SMSGT
SYSOP
TASTE
TASTY
TESTY
UNSAY
UPSET
VASTY
VISIT
VISOR
VISTA
WASHY
WASTE

WHSLE
ACTOR
AFTER
ALTAR
ALTER
ANTIC
ASTER
ASTIR
ATTAR
ATTIC
AZTEC
BATCH
BATHE
BATIK
BATON
BATTY
BETEL
BITCH
BOTCH
BUTTE
BUTUT
CATCH
CATER
CATTY
CUTUP
DATED
DATUM
DETER
DITCH
DITTO
DITTY
DUTCH
ENTER
ENTOM
ENTRY
ESTER
EXTOL
EXTRA
FATAL
FATED
FATTY
FETAL
FETCH
FETID
FETUS
GETUP
GUTTY
HATCH
HITCH
HOTEL
HUTCH
ICTUS
INTEL
INTER
JETTY
KETCH
KITTY

LATCH
LATEX
LATHE
LATIN
LETUP
LITER
LITHE
LOTUS
MATCH
MATZO
METAL
METER
METRE
METRO
MITER
MOTEL
MOTET
MOTIF
MOTOR
MOTTO
NATAL
NATTY
NITER
NITRO
NOTCH
NOTED
NUTTY
OCTAL
OCTET
OFTEN
OPTIC
OTTER
OUTDO
OUTER
OUTGO
OUTRE
PATCH
PATEN
PATIO
PATSY
PATTY
PETAL
PETER
PETTY
PITCH
PITHY
PITON
PUTTY
RATIO
RATTY
RETCH
ROTOR
SATAN
SATIN
SATYR
SETUP
SITAR

TITAN
TITHE
TITLE
TOTAL
TOTEM
TUTOR
ULTRA
UNTIE
UNTIL
UTTER
VATIC
VETCH
VITAL
WATCH
WATER
WITCH
WITHE
WITHY
WITTY
ABUSE
ACUTE
ADULT
AMUCK
AMUSE
AZURE
BLUES
BLUET
BLUFF
BLUNT
BLURB
BLURT
BLUSH
BOUGH
BOULE
BOUND
BOURN
BRUIN
BRUIT
BRUNT
BRUSH
BRUTE
CAULK
CAUSE
CHUCK
CHUMP
CHUNK
CHURL
CHURN
CHUTE
CLUCK
CLUMP
CLUNG
COUCH
COUGH
COULD
COUNT
COUPE

COURT
CRUDE
CRUEL
CRUET
CRUMB
CRUSE
CRUSH
CRUST
DAUNT
DEUCE
DOUBT
DOUGH
DOUSE
DRUID
DRUNK
DRUPE
EDUCE
ELUDE
EQUAL
EQUIP
EQUIV
ERUPT
ETUDE
EXUDE
EXULT
EXURB
FAULT
FAUNA
FLUFF
FLUID
FLUKE
FLUME
FLUNG
FLUNK
FLUSH
FLUTE
FOUND
FOUNT
FRUIT
GAUDY
GAUGE
GAUNT
GAUSS
GAUZE
GOUDA
GOUGE
GOURD
GRUEL
GRUFF
GRUNT
HAUNT
HOUND
HOURI
HOUSE
INURE
INURN
JAUNT

JOULE
JOUST
KLUGE
KNURL
LAUGH
LOUSE
LOUSY
MAUVE
MOULD
MOULT
MOUND
MOUNT
MOURN
MOUSE
MOUSY
MOUTH
OVULE
PAUSE
PLUCK
PLUMB
PLUME
PLUMP
PLUNK
PLUSH
PLUTO
POUCH
POULT
POUND
PRUDE
PRUNE
ROUGE
ROUGH
ROUND
ROUSE
ROUTE
SAUCE
SAUCY
SAUNA
SAUTE
SCUBA
SCUFF
SCULL
SCURF
SHUCK
SHUNT
SKULK
SKULL
SKUNK
SLUMP
SLUNG
SLUNK
SLURP
SLUSH
SNUCK
SNUFF
SOUGH
SOUND

SOUPY
SOUSE
SOUTH
SPUME
SPUNK
SPURN
SPURT
SQUAB
SQUAD
SQUAT
SQUAW
SQUIB
SQUID
STUCK
STUDY
STUFF
STUMP
STUNG
STUNK
STUNT
SWUNG
TAUNT
TAUPE
THUMB
THUMP
THURS
TOUCH
TOUGH
TRUCE
TRUCK
TRUMP
TRUNK
TRUSS
TRUST
TRUTH
USUAL
USURP
USURY
UVULA
VAULT
VAUNT
VOUCH
WOULD
WOUND
WRUNG
YOUNG
YOURS
YOUTH
ANVIL
BEVEL
CAVIL
CIVET
CIVIC
CIVIL
COVEN
COVER
COVET

COVEY
DAVIT
DEVIL
DIVAN
DIVOT
EAVES
ELVER
ELVES
ENVOI
ENVOY
FAVOR
FEVER
GAVEL
GIVEN
HAVEN
HAVOC
HIVES
HOVEL
HOVER
LEVEE
LEVEL
LEVER
LIVEN
LIVER
LIVES
LIVID
MAVEN
MAVIS
MOVER
MOVIE
NAVAL
NAVEL
NEVER
NEVUS
NOVEL
PIVOT
RAVEL
RAVEN
REVEL
REVUE
RIVAL
RIVER
RIVET
SAVOR
SAVVY
SEVEN
SEVER
VIVID
WAVER
WIVES
WOVEN
BAWDY
BOWEL
BOWER
BYWAY
COWER
DOWDY

DOWEL
DOWER
DOWNY
DOWRY
DOWSE
FEWER
GAWKY
JEWEL
JEWRY
LOWER
LOWLY
NEWEL
NEWLY
NEWSY
NGWEE
NOWAY
PEWEE
POWER
ROWDY
ROWEL
SEWER
TAWNY
TOWEL
TOWER
VOWEL
AUXIN
BOXER
BUXOM
FIXED
FOXED
MAXIM
MIXER
NEXUS
PIXEL
PIXIE
SIXTY
TOXIC
TOXIN
VIXEN
WAXEN
ABYSM
ABYSS
ARYAN
BAYOU
COYPU
CRYPT
CRYST
DOYEN
DRYAD
DRYER
FLYBY
FLYER
FOYER
FRYER
GLYPH
GUYOT
HAYES

IDYLL
KAYAK
LAYER
LOYAL
MAYBE
MAYOR
PSYCH
RAYON
RHYME
RIYAL
ROYAL
STYLE
THYME
TRYST
BEZEL
COZEN
DIZZY
DOZEN
FUZZY
GIZMO
HAZEL
JAZZY
KAZOO
LAZAR
PIZZA
RAZOR
RNZAF
TIZZY
UNZIP
VIZOR

## 4TH LETTER

ABEAM
ADMAN
AHEAD
ALIAS
ALLAH
ALLAY
ALTAR
APEAK
ARRAS
ARRAY
ARYAN
ASIAN
ASSAY
ATLAS
ATTAR
AURAL
AURAR
AVGAS
AVIAN
AXIAL
BANAL
BASAL

BELAY
BLEAK
BLEAR
BLEAT
BLOAT
BORAX
BREAD
BREAK
BREAM
BRIAR
BROAD
BYLAW
BYWAY
CABAL
CACAO
CANAL
CARAT
CEDAR
CHEAP
CHEAT
CHIAO
CIGAR
CLEAN
CLEAR
CLEAT
CLOAK
CORAL
CREAK
CREAM
CROAK
CUBAN
DEBAR
DECAL
DECAY
DEGAS
DELAY
DINAR
DIVAN
DREAD
DREAM
DREAR
DRYAD
DUCAL
DUCAT
ECLAT
ENIAC
EQUAL
ESSAY
FATAL
FERAL
FETAL
FILAR
FINAL
FLOAT
FORAY
FREAK
FRIAR

GLEAM
GLEAN
GLOAT
GONAD
GREAT
GROAN
GROAT
HOGAN
HUMAN
IDEAL
INLAY
ISLAM
JALAP
JAPAN
JIHAD
KARAT
KAYAK
KEBAB
KNEAD
KORAN
KRAAL
KULAK
LANAI
LAZAR
LEGAL
LILAC
LOCAL
LOYAL
LUNAR
MACAW
MADAM
MALAY
MEDAL
METAL
MOLAR
MORAL
MORAY
MURAL
NAIAD
NASAL
NATAL
NAVAL
NICAD
NOMAD
NOWAY
OCCAS
OCEAN
OCTAL
OFFAL
ORGAN
PAEAN
PAGAN
PAPAL
PAPAW
PECAN
PEDAL
PENAL

PETAL
PHIAL
PILAF
PLEAD
PLEAT
POLAR
QUEAN
RADAR
RECAP
REGAL
RELAX
RELAY
RENAL
REPAY
RIVAL
RIYAL
RNZAF
ROMAN
ROYAL
RURAL
SALAD
SATAN
SCRAM
SCRAP
SEDAN
SEPAL
SHEAF
SHEAR
SHOAL
SHOAT
SISAL
SITAR
SMEAR
SNEAK
SOLAR
SONAR
SPEAK
SPEAR
SPLAY
SPRAT
SPRAY
SQUAB
SQUAD
SQUAT
SQUAW
STEAD
STEAK
STEAL
STEAM
STOAT
STRAP
STRAW
STRAY
SUGAR
SUMAC
SWEAR
SWEAT

THEAT
TICAL
TITAN
TODAY
TOKAY
TOPAZ
TORAH
TOTAL
TREAD
TREAS
TREAT
TRIAD
TRIAL
TWEAK
UMIAK
UNBAR
UNCAP
UNMAN
UNSAY
URBAN
USUAL
VELAR
VENAL
VICAR
VIRAL
VITAL
VOCAB
VOCAL
WHEAL
WHEAT
WOMAN
WREAK
ZONAL
ADOBE
ALIBI
AMEBA
BOBBY
BOOBY
BRIBE
BUSBY
CABBY
COMBO
DERBY
DOUBT
FLYBY
GABBY
GLEBE
GLOBE
GREBE
GUMBO
HOBBY
JUMBO
LIMBO
LOBBY
MAMBO
MAYBE
PLEBE

PLEBS
PROBE
RABBI
RUGBY
RUMBA
SCUBA
TABBY
TRIBE
TURBO
ABACK
AMUCK
APACE
BATCH
BEACH
BEECH
BELCH
BENCH
BIRCH
BITCH
BLACK
BLOCK
BOTCH
BRACE
BRACT
BRICK
BUNCH
BUNCO
CATCH
CHECK
CHICK
CHOCK
CHUCK
CINCH
CIRCA
CLACK
CLICK
CLOCK
CLUCK
COACH
CONCH
COUCH
CRACK
CRICK
CROCK
CZECH
DANCE
DEICE
DEUCE
DISCO
DITCH
DUNCE
DUTCH
EDICT
EDUCE
EJECT
ELECT
ENACT

EPOCH
ERECT
EVICT
EXACT
FANCY
FARCE
FENCE
FETCH
FILCH
FINCH
FLECK
FLICK
FLOCK
FORCE
FROCK
GRACE
GULCH
HATCH
HENCE
HITCH
HUNCH
HUTCH
JUICE
JUICY
JUNCO
KETCH
KNACK
KNOCK
LANCE
LARCH
LATCH
LEACH
LEECH
LUNCH
LURCH
LYNCH
MARCH
MATCH
MECCA
MERCY
MILCH
MINCE
MULCH
MULCT
MUNCH
NAACP
NIECE
NONCE
NOTCH
OUNCE
PARCH
PATCH
PEACE
PEACH
PENCE
PERCH
PIECE

PINCH
PITCH
PLACE
PLUCK
POACH
POOCH
PORCH
POUCH
PRICE
PRICK
PSYCH
PUNCH
QUACK
QUICK
RANCH
REACH
REACT
RETCH
ROACH
SAUCE
SAUCY
SHACK
SHOCK
SHUCK
SINCE
SLACK
SLICE
SLICK
SMACK
SMOCK
SNACK
SNUCK
SPACE
SPECK
SPICE
STACK
STICK
STOCK
STUCK
TEACH
THICK
TINCT
TORCH
TOUCH
TRACE
TRACK
TRACT
TRICE
TRICK
TRUCE
TRUCK
TWICE
VETCH
VOICE
VOUCH
WATCH
WELCH

WENCH
WHACK
WHICH
WINCE
WINCH
WITCH
WRACK
WRECK
YUCCA
ABIDE
ABODE
ANODE
ASIDE
BANDY
BAWDY
BIDDY
BLADE
BRIDE
BUDDY
CADDY
CANDY
CHIDE
COMDG
COMDR
COMDT
CREDO
CRUDE
DADDY
DANDY
DIODE
DOWDY
ELIDE
ELUDE
ERODE
ETUDE
EVADE
EXUDE
GAUDY
GEODE
GIDDY
GLIDE
GOODY
GOUDA
GRADE
GUIDE
HANDY
HARDY
HEADY
HINDI
HORDE
MIDDY
MOODY
NEEDS
NEEDY
NODDY
OUTDO
OXIDE

| PADDY | BLUET | ELDER | INLET | NISEI | SEVEN | UNDER | SNIFF | LEGGY | FIGHT | BEGIN | GROIN |
|---|---|---|---|---|---|---|---|---|---|---|---|
| PANDA | BOGEY | ELVER | INNER | NITER | SEVER | UNPEG | SNUFF | LIEGE | FISHY | BELIE | HABIT |
| PRIDE | BONER | ELVES | INSET | NONES | SEWER | UPPER | STAFF | LINGO | FOEHN | BLAIN | HELIX |
| PRUDE | BOWEL | EMBED | INTEL | NOTED | SHEEN | UPSET | STIFF | LODGE | GUSHY | BRAID | HUMID |
| READY | BOWER | EMBER | INTER | NOVEL | SHEEP | USHER | STUFF | LUNGE | LATHE | BRAIN | INDIC |
| ROWDY | BOXER | EMCEE | IRREG | OCHER | SHEER | UTTER | SULFA | MANGE | LIGHT | BROIL | LAMIA |
| RUDDY | BREED | ENTER | ISLET | OCTET | SHEET | VALET | SWIFT | MANGO | LITHE | BRUIN | LAPIN |
| SEEDY | BRIEF | ESTER | JADED | OFFER | SHIER | VIBES | TAFFY | MARGE | MIGHT | BRUIT | LATIN |
| SHADE | BRIER | ETHER | JEWEL | OFTEN | SHRED | VIDEO | THEFT | MERGE | MUSHY | CABIN | LEGIS |
| SLIDE | CADET | EXCEL | JOKER | OLDEN | SHREW | VIPER | UNIFY | MIDGE | NICHE | CALIF | LEGIT |
| SNIDE | CAGEY | EXPEL | JULEP | ONSET | SINEW | VIREO | WHIFF | MONGO | NIGHT | CAVIL | LICIT |
| SPADE | CAMEL | FACET | KNEEL | ORDER | SIREN | VIXEN | ADAGE | MUGGY | OMAHA | CHAIN | LIMIT |
| STUDY | CAMEO | FATED | LABEL | ORIEL | SKEET | VOWEL | ALIGN | NEIGH | OUGHT | CHAIR | LIVID |
| SUEDE | CAPER | FECES | LADEN | OSIER | SLEEK | WADER | BADGE | NUDGE | PASHA | CHOIR | LOGIC |
| SWEDE | CARET | FEVER | LAGER | OTHER | SLEEP | WAFER | BAGGY | OSAGE | PITHY | CIVIC | LUCID |
| TARDY | CATER | FEWER | LAPEL | OTTER | SLEET | WAGER | BARGE | OUTGO | PUSHY | CIVIL | LURID |
| TILDE | CHEEK | FIBER | LASER | OUTER | SLIER | WAKEN | BEIGE | PHAGE | RIGHT | CLAIM | LYRIC |
| TOADY | CHEEP | FIXED | LATEX | OWLET | SNEER | WATER | BILGE | PUDGY | SIGHT | COLIC | MAFIA |
| TODDY | CHEER | FLEER | LAYER | PACER | SOBER | WAVER | BINGE | PURGE | TIGHT | COMIC | MAGIC |
| TRADE | CHIEF | FLEET | LEPER | PANEL | SPEED | WAXEN | BINGO | RANGE | TITHE | CONIC | MANIA |
| WEEDY | CIDER | FLIED | LEVEE | PAPER | SPIEL | WHEEL | BONGO | RANGY | WASHY | CUBIC | MANIC |
| WINDY | CIVET | FLIER | LEVEL | PATEN | SPREE | WIDEN | BOUGH | REIGN | WIGHT | CUBIT | MAVIS |
| WOODY | CODEC | FLYER | LEVER | PETER | STEED | WIVES | BUDGE | RIDGE | WITHE | CUPID | MAXIM |
| WORDY | CODEX | FOXED | LIBEL | PEWEE | STEEL | WOKEN | BUGGY | ROUGE | WITHY | CURIA | MEDIA |
| ABBEY | COMER | FOYER | LIFER | PIKER | STEEP | WOVEN | BULGE | ROUGH | YACHT | CURIO | MEDIC |
| ADDER | COMET | FRYER | LIKEN | PILES | STEER | XEBEC | BURGH | SEDGE | ACRID | CYNIC | MERIT |
| ADIEU | CONEY | FUSEE | LINEN | PIXEL | STREW | XYLEM | CADGE | SENGI | ADMIN | DAVIT | MIMIC |
| AFTER | COVEN | GAVEL | LINER | POKER | SUPER | YODEL | CARGO | SERGE | ADMIT | DEBIT | MINIM |
| AGREE | COVER | GIVEN | LITER | POSER | SWEEP | YOKEL | CMSGT | SIEGE | ADMIX | DENIM | MODIF |
| ALDER | COVET | GONER | LIVEN | POWER | SWEET | ABAFT | CONGA | SINGE | AEGIS | DERIV | MOTIF |
| ALIEN | COVEY | GREED | LIVER | PREEN | TALER | ALOFT | COUGH | SMSGT | AERIE | DEVIL | MOVIE |
| ALLEY | COWER | GREEK | LIVES | PROEM | TAPER | BEEFY | DEIGN | SOGGY | AFAIK | DIGIT | MUSIC |
| ALTER | COZEN | GREEN | LONER | PUBES | TELEG | BLUFF | DINGO | SOUGH | AFAIR | DOGIE | NADIR |
| AMBER | CREED | GREET | LOWER | PUREE | TELEX | CHAFE | DINGY | STAGE | AFFIX | DRAIN | NARIS |
| ANGEL | CREEK | GRIEF | MANES | QUEEN | TENET | CHAFF | DIRGE | SURGE | AGAIN | DRUID | NUMIS |
| ANGER | CREEL | GRUEL | MASER | QUEER | TEPEE | CLEFT | DODGE | SWAGE | AMAIN | EDLIN | OASIS |
| ANNEX | CREEP | HADES | MAVEN | QUIET | THIEF | CLIFF | DOGGY | TAIGA | ANTIC | EERIE | OLDIE |
| ASHEN | CRIER | HALER | MELEE | RAVEL | THREE | COMFY | DOUGH | TANGO | ANVIL | EMAIL | OPTIC |
| ASKEW | CRUEL | HAREM | METER | RAVEN | THREW | CRAFT | ELEGY | THEGN | APHID | EQUIP | ORBIT |
| ASPEN | CRUET | HAVEN | MISER | REBEL | TIGER | DAFFY | FEIGN | THIGH | APHIS | EQUIV | ORRIS |
| ASSET | DATED | HAYES | MITER | REFER | TIMES | DEIFY | FORGE | TINGE | APRIL | EYRIE | OVOID |
| ASTER | DEFER | HAZEL | MIXER | RENEW | TIRED | DELFT | FORGO | TONGS | ASCII | EYRIR | PANIC |
| AUGER | DETER | HIVES | MLLES | REPEL | TOKEN | DRAFT | FUDGE | TOUGH | ASPIC | FAKIR | PATIO |
| AZTEC | DINER | HOMER | MODEL | REVEL | TONER | DRIFT | GAUGE | USAGE | ASTIR | FETID | PENIS |
| BABEL | DOPEY | HOMEY | MODEM | RIDER | TOPER | FLUFF | GORGE | VERGE | ATTIC | FINIS | PERIL |
| BAGEL | DOWEL | HONEY | MONEY | RIPEN | TOTEM | GAFFE | GOUGE | WEDGE | AUDIO | FLAIL | PIXIE |
| BEDEW | DOWER | HOOEY | MOREL | RISER | TOWEL | GOOFY | HEDGE | WEIGH | AUDIT | FLAIR | PLAID |
| BEGET | DOYEN | HOTEL | MORES | RIVER | TOWER | GRAFT | HINGE | ALOHA | AUXIN | FLUID | PLAIN |
| BERET | DOZEN | HOVEL | MOSEY | RIVET | TRIED | GRUFF | IMAGE | AUGHT | AVAIL | FOLIO | PLAIT |
| BESET | DRIER | HOVER | MOTEL | RODEO | TUBER | JIFFY | IMAGO | BATHE | AVOID | FRAIL | POLIO |
| BETEL | DRYER | HYMEN | MOTET | ROGER | TWEED | KNIFE | JUDGE | BIGHT | AWAIT | FRUIT | POLIT |
| BEVEL | EAGER | IMBED | MOVER | ROWEL | TWEEN | QUAFF | KEDGE | CACHE | BASIC | FSLIC | POSIT |
| BEZEL | EARED | IMPEL | NAKED | RULER | TWEET | SCOFF | KLUGE | DACHA | BASIL | GAMIN | PUBIC |
| BIDET | EASEL | IMPER | NAVEL | RUPEE | UDDER | SCUFF | LARGE | DUCHY | BASIN | GELID | PUBIS |
| BIPED | EAVES | INDEF | NEVER | SABER | ULCER | SHAFT | LARGO | EIGHT | BASIS | GENIE | PUPIL |
| BLEED | EGRET | INDEX | NEWEL | SCREW | UMBEL | SHIFT | LAUGH | FICHE | BATIK | GRAIL | PURIM |
| BLUES | EIDER | INFER | NGWEE | SEMEN | UMBER | SKIFF | LEDGE | FICHU | BEFIT | GRAIN | QUAIL |

| | | | | | | | | | | | |
|---|---|---|---|---|---|---|---|---|---|---|---|
| QUOIT | UNFIT | SULKY | FOLLY | SHELF | CHAMP | SWAMP | COUNT | KRONE | SLUNK | AGLOW | DONOR |
| RABID | UNFIX | TACKY | FRILL | SHELL | CHIME | THEME | CRANE | LEONE | SOUND | ALGOL | DROOL |
| RADII | UNPIN | VODKA | FULLY | SHILL | CHIMP | THUMB | CRANK | LLANO | SPANK | ALLOT | DROOP |
| RADIO | UNTIE | WACKY | GABLE | SIDLE | CHOMP | THUMP | CRONE | LOONY | SPEND | ALLOW | ELBOW |
| RADIX | UNTIL | ADDLE | GAILY | SILLY | CHUMP | THYME | CRONY | LYING | SPENT | ALLOY | ENDOW |
| RAMIE | UNZIP | ADULT | GODLY | SKILL | CLAMP | TRAMP | DAUNT | MANNA | SPINE | ALOOF | ENJOY |
| RAPID | VALID | AGILE | GRILL | SKULK | CLIMB | TROMP | DOWNY | MOUND | SPUNK | ANION | ENTOM |
| RATIO | VAPID | AISLE | GUILD | SKULL | CLIME | TRUMP | DRANK | MOUNT | STAND | ANNOY | ENVOI |
| RECIP | VARIA | AMBLE | GUILE | SMALL | CLUMP | TUMMY | DRINK | NINNY | STANK | APRON | ENVOY |
| RELIC | VATIC | AMPLE | GUILT | SMELL | COMMA | YUMMY | DRONE | OPINE | STING | ARBOR | EPROM |
| RELIG | VIGIL | ANGLE | GULLY | SMELT | COMMO | ADDNL | DRUNK | OWING | STINK | ARDOR | EPSON |
| REMIT | VISIT | ANGLO | HALLO | SMILE | CRAMP | AGENT | DYING | OZONE | STINT | ARGON | ERGOT |
| RESIN | VIVID | ANKLE | HAOLE | SPELL | CREME | AGONY | EBONY | PAINT | STONE | ARGOT | ERROR |
| RIGID | VOMIT | APPLE | HAPLY | SPILL | CRIME | ALONE | ELAND | PENNI | STUNG | ARMOR | ETHOS |
| ROBIN | XERIC | APPLY | HELLO | STALE | CRIMP | ALONG | EMEND | PENNY | STUNK | ARROW | EXTOL |
| ROSIN | BANJO | ATILT | HOLLO | STALK | CRUMB | AMEND | EVENT | PEONY | STUNT | ARSON | FAGOT |
| SANIT | HAJJI | ATOLL | HOLLY | STALL | DOGMA | AMONG | FAINT | PHONE | SWANK | ASCOT | FAVOR |
| SATIN | KANJI | BELLE | IDYLL | STILE | DRAMA | ANENT | FAUNA | PHONO | SWINE | ASSOC | FELON |
| SCRIM | ALIKE | BELLS | IMPLY | STILL | DUMMY | ARENA | FEINT | PHONY | SWING | AXIOM | FLOOD |
| SCRIP | AWAKE | BELLY | INGLE | STILT | EDEMA | ATONE | FIEND | PIANO | SWUNG | BACON | FLOOR |
| SEPIA | BALKY | BIBLE | JELLY | STOLE | ENEMA | BANNS | FINNY | PLANE | TAINT | BARON | FUROR |
| SERIF | BOSKY | BILLY | JOLLY | STYLE | ENEMY | BEANO | FLANK | PLANK | TAUNT | BATON | GLOOM |
| SKEIN | BRAKE | BOULE | JOULE | SULLY | FLAME | BEING | FLING | PLANT | TAWNY | BAYOU | GROOM |
| SLAIN | BROKE | BUGLE | KNELL | SURLY | FLUME | BENNY | FLINT | PLUNK | TEENS | BEFOG | GUYOT |
| SNAIL | BULKY | BUILD | KNOLL | SWELL | FRAME | BHANG | FLUNG | POINT | TEENY | BELOW | HAVOC |
| SOLID | CHOKE | BULLY | KOALA | SWILL | GAMMA | BLAND | FLUNK | POUND | THANE | BESOM | HELOT |
| SONIC | COCKY | BURLY | LADLE | TABLE | GIZMO | BLANK | FOUND | PRANK | THANK | BESOT | HERON |
| SPLIT | DINKY | CABLE | LISLE | TALLY | GNOME | BLEND | FOUNT | PRINK | THINE | BIGOT | HONOR |
| SPOIL | DRAKE | CALLA | LOWLY | THOLE | GRIME | BLIND | FRANC | PRINT | THING | BISON | HUMOR |
| SPRIG | DUSKY | CAULK | MANLY | TITLE | JIMMY | BLINK | FRANK | PRONE | THINK | BLOOD | HURON |
| SQUIB | EVOKE | CELLO | MAPLE | TRILL | KARMA | BLOND | FROND | PRONG | THONG | BLOOM | ICHOR |
| SQUID | FLAKE | CHALK | MOULD | TROLL | LLAMA | BLUNT | FRONT | PRUNE | TINNY | BORON | IDIOM |
| STAID | FLUKE | CHELA | MOULT | TULLE | MAGMA | BONNY | FUNNY | QUINT | TRANS | BOSOM | IDIOT |
| STAIN | FUNKY | CHILD | NEWLY | TWILL | MIAMI | BORNE | GAUNT | RHINO | TREND | BROOD | IGLOO |
| STAIR | GAWKY | CHILI | NOBLE | UNCLE | MUMMY | BOUND | GIANT | ROUND | TRINE | BROOK | INCOG |
| STEIN | HAIKU | CHILL | OVULE | UTILE | PALMY | BRAND | GLAND | RUNNY | TRUNK | BROOM | INGOT |
| STOIC | HUSKY | COULD | POILU | UVULA | PIGMY | BRINE | GLANS | SAINT | TUNNY | BUXOM | INSOL |
| STRIA | KHAKI | CYCLE | POULT | VAULT | PLUMB | BRING | GLINT | SAUNA | TWANG | CANOE | JABOT |
| STRIP | KOOKY | DAILY | PSALM | VILLA | PLUME | BRINK | GRAND | SCAND | TWINE | CANON | JUROR |
| SWAIN | LANKY | DALLY | QUALM | VIOLA | PLUMP | BRUNT | GRANT | SCANF | TYING | CAPON | KABOB |
| TACIT | LINKS | DOILY | QUELL | VOILE | PRIME | BUNNY | GRIND | SCANT | UPEND | CAROL | KAPOK |
| TAPIR | LUCKY | DOLLY | QUILL | WEALD | PRIMP | CANNA | GRUNT | SCENE | URINE | CAROM | KAZOO |
| TEPID | PARKA | DRILL | QUILT | WHALE | PYGMY | CANNY | GUANO | SCENT | VAUNT | CHAOS | KUDOS |
| THEIR | PESKY | DRILY | RALLY | WHELK | RHYME | CARNY | GUNNY | SCONE | VIAND | CHRON | LABOR |
| TIBIA | PICKY | DROLL | REALM | WHELM | RUMMY | CHANT | HAUNT | SEINE | VYING | COBOL | LEMON |
| TIMID | POLKA | DUPLE | REPLY | WHELP | SCAMP | CHINA | HENNA | SENNA | WEENY | COCOA | MAJOR |
| TONIC | PUKKA | DWELL | RIFLE | WHILE | SEAMY | CHINE | HOUND | SHANK | WHINE | COLON | MANOR |
| TOPIC | QUAKE | EAGLE | RUBLE | WHOLE | SHAME | CHINK | HYENA | SHINE | WOUND | COLOR | MASON |
| TOXIC | SHAKE | EARLY | SABLE | WHSLE | SIGMA | CHINO | HYING | SHINY | WRING | CROOK | MAYOR |
| TOXIN | SHAKY | EXALT | SALLY | WIELD | SKIMP | CHUNK | ICING | SHONE | WRONG | CROON | MCCOY |
| TRAIL | SLAKE | EXILE | SCALD | WORLD | SLIME | CLANG | INANE | SHUNT | WRUNG | DECOR | MELON |
| TRAIN | SMOKE | EXULT | SCALE | WOULD | SLUMP | CLANK | IRONY | SKUNK | YOUNG | DECOY | MINOR |
| TRAIT | SNAKE | FABLE | SCALP | YIELD | SPUME | CLING | JAUNT | SLANG | ABBOT | DEFOG | MORON |
| TULIP | SPIKE | FAULT | SCOLD | AROMA | STAMP | CLINK | JEANS | SLANT | ABHOR | DEMON | MOTOR |
| TUMID | SPOKE | FELLY | SCULL | BALMY | STOMP | CLONE | JENNY | SLING | ACTOR | DEPOT | NABOB |
| TUNIC | STAKE | FIELD | SHALE | BLAME | STUMP | CLUNG | JOINT | SLINK | ADIOS | DIVOT | NOHOW |
| TWAIN | STOKE | FILLY | SHALL | BLIMP | SWAMI | CORNY | KRONA | SLUNG | AFOOT | DOLOR | NYLON |

ONION
OXBOW
PEKOE
PHLOX
PICOT
PILOT
PINON
PITON
PIVOT
PRIOR
PROOF
PYLON
RADON
RAYON
RAZOR
RIGOR
ROBOT
ROTOR
RUMOR
SALON
SAVOR
SCION
SCOOP
SCOOT
SCROD
SHOOK
SHOOT
SLOOP
SNOOP
SOLON
SPOOF
SPOOK
SPOOL
SPOON
SPOOR
STOOD
STOOL
STOOP
STROP
SWOON
SWOOP
SYNOD
SYSOP
TABOO
TABOR
TALON
TAROT
TENON
TENOR
THEOL
THROB
THROE
THROW
TOPOG
TROOP
TUMOR
TUTOR

UNION
VALOR
VAPOR
VENOM
VIGOR
VISOR
VIZOR
WAGON
WAHOO
WHOOP
WIDOW
XENON
YAHOO
ADAPT
ADEPT
ADOPT
AGAPE
CHAPS
CHOPS
CORPS
COUPE
COYPU
CRAPE
CRAPS
CREPE
CRYPT
DRAPE
DRUPE
DUMPS
DUMPY
ELOPE
ERUPT
GIMPY
GLYPH
GRAPE
GRAPH
GRIPE
GROPE
GUPPY
HAPPY
HARPY
INEPT
JUMPY
LYMPH
MUMPS
NIPPY
NYMPH
PAMPA
POPPY
PUPPY
SAPPY
SCOPE
SHAPE
SHIPT
SLOPE
SNIPE
SNIPS

SOUPY
SWEPT
SWIPE
SYLPH
TAUPE
TEMPO
TEMPT
TRAPS
TRIPE
TROPE
TURPS
WEEPY
XCOPY
ZIPPY
IRAQI
ABORT
ACORN
ADORE
ADORN
AFIRE
AGORA
ALARM
ALERT
ANGRY
APART
APORT
AVERT
AWARD
AWARE
AZURE
BAIRN
BEARD
BERRY
BLARE
BLURB
BLURT
BOARD
BOURN
BURRO
CADRE
CAIRN
CARRY
CHARD
CHARM
CHART
CHARY
CHERT
CHIRP
CHORD
CHORE
CHURL
CHURN
CLERK
COBRA
COPRA
COURT
CURRY

DAIRY
DECRY
DIARY
DOWRY
DWARF
EMERY
ENTRY
EVERY
EXERT
EXTRA
EXURB
FAIRY
FERRY
FIERY
FIORD
FJORD
FLARE
FLIRT
FLORA
FURRY
GENRE
GLARE
GLORY
GNARL
GOURD
GUARD
HAIRY
HARRY
HEART
HOARD
HOARY
HOURI
HURRY
HYDRA
HYDRO
INERT
INURE
INURN
IVORY
JEWRY
KNURL
LAIRD
LEARN
LEERY
LORRY
LUCRE
MACRO
MAORI
MARRY
MERRY
METRE
METRO
MICRO
MOIRE
MOURN
MYRRH
NACRE

NAIRA
NEGRO
NITRO
OPERA
OUTRE
OVARY
OVERT
PADRE
PARRY
PEARL
PHARM
QUART
QUERY
QUIRE
QUIRK
QUIRT
SCARE
SCARF
SCARP
SCORE
SCORN
SCURF
SHARD
SHARE
SHARK
SHARP
SHIRE
SHIRK
SHIRR
SHIRT
SHORE
SHORN
SHORT
SKIRT
SLURP
SMART
SMIRK
SNARE
SNARL
SNORE
SNORT
SORRY
SPARC
SPARE
SPARK
SPERM
SPIRE
SPIRT
SPORE
SPORT
SPURN
SPURT
STARE
STARK
START
STERE
STERN

STORE
STORK
STORM
STORY
SUCRE
SUPRA
SWARD
SWARM
SWART
SWIRL
SWORD
SWORE
SWORN
TARRY
TERRY
THERE
THERM
THIRD
THORN
THORP
THURS
TIARA
TWIRL
ULTRA
UMBRA
UNARM
USURP
USURY
VEERY
WEARY
WEIRD
WHARF
WHERE
WHIRL
WHORE
WHORL
WORRY
YEARN
YOURS
ZAIRE
ZEBRA
ABASE
ABASH
ABUSE
ABYSM
ABYSS
AMASS
AMISS
AMUSE
ANGST
ANISE
ARISE
AVAST
AWASH
BALSA
BASSO
BEAST

BLASE
BLAST
BLESS
BLISS
BLUSH
BOAST
BOOST
BRASH
BRASS
BRISK
BRUSH
BURST
CAUSE
CEASE
CHASE
CHASM
CHESS
CHEST
CHOSE
CLASH
CLASP
CLASS
CLOSE
COAST
CONST
COPSE
CRASH
CRASS
CRESC
CRESS
CREST
CRISP
CROSS
CRUSE
CRUSH
CRUST
CRYST
CURSE
DAISY
DEISM
DENSE
DOUSE
DOWSE
DRESS
DROSS
ERASE
ERISA
EXIST
FALSE
FEAST
FIRST
FLASH
FLASK
FLESH
FLOSS
FLUSH
FOIST

FRESH
FRISK
FROST
FUSSY
GAUSS
GEESE
GHOST
GIPSY
GLASS
GLOSS
GNASH
GOOSE
GORSE
GRASP
GRASS
GRIST
GROSS
GROSZ
GUESS
GUEST
GUISE
GYPSY
HARSH
HEIST
HOIST
HORSE
HOUSE
HUSSY
IRISH
JOIST
JOUST
KARST
KIOSK
KNISH
LAPSE
LASSO
LEASE
LEASH
LEAST
LOESS
LOOSE
LOUSE
LOUSY
MANSE
MARSH
MIDST
MOIST
MOOSE
MOUSE
MOUSY
NEWSY
NOISE
NOISY
NOOSE
NORSE
NURSE
OBESE

PAISA
PALSY
PANSY
PARSE
PASSE
PATSY
PAUSE
PHASE
PLASH
PLUSH
POESY
POISE
POSSE
PRESS
PRISM
PROSE
PROSY
PULSE
PURSE
PUSSY
QUASH
QUASI
QUEST
QURSH
RAISE
RINSE
ROAST
ROOST
ROUSE
SASSY
SEISM
SENSE
SISSY
SLASH
SLOSH
SLUSH
SMASH
SOUSE
SPASM
STASH
SWASH
SWISH
SWISS
TANSY
TEASE
TENSE
TERSE
THESE
THESS
THOSE
TIPSY
TOAST
TORSO
TRASH
TRESS
TRUSS
TRUST

TRYST
TWIST
UKASE
VALSE
VERSE
VERSO
VERST
WAIST
WELSH
WHISH
WHISK
WHIST
WHOSE
WHOSO
WORSE
WORST
WREST
WRIST
WURST
YEAST
ABATE
ABSTR
ACUTE
AGATE
AMITY
AORTA
ARITH
BANTU
BASTE
BATTY
BERTH
BIRTH
BLITZ
BOOTH
BOOTY
BROTH
BRUTE
BUTTE
CANTO
CASTE
CATTY
CCITT
CHUTE
CLOTH
CONTD
CONTG
CONTR
CRATE
DEATH
DEITY
DELTA
DEPTH
DIRTY
DISTN
DISTR
DITTO
DITTY

DLITT
EARTH
ELATE
ELITE
EMOTE
EMPTY
EXPTL
FAITH
FATTY
FIFTH
FIFTY
FILTH
FIRTH
FLUTE
FORTE
FORTH
FORTY
FROTH
FUSTY
GANTT
GIRTH
GRATE
GRITS
GUSTO
GUTTY
HASTE
HEATH
HEFTY
HERTZ
INSTR
IRATE
JETTY
JUNTA
JUNTO
KITTY
LAITY
LISTS
LOATH
LOFTY
LUSTY
MANTA
MIRTH
MISTY
MONTH
MOTTO
MOUTH
MUFTI
MUSTY
NASTY
NATTY
NIFTY
NORTH
NUTTY
ORATE
OVATE
PANTS
PARTY

PASTA
PASTE
PASTY
PATTY
PETTY
PHOTO
PIETY
PINTO
PLATE
PLATY
PLUTO
PRATE
PUTTY
QUITE
QUITS
QUOTA
QUOTE
QUOTH
RATTY
RECTO
ROUTE
SAUTE
SCOTS
SEATO
SENTI
SIXTY
SKATE
SLATE
SLOTH
SMITE
SMITH
SMOTE
SOOTH
SOUTH
SPATE
SPITE
STATE
SUITE
SWATH
SWITZ
TASTE
TASTY
TEETH
TESTY
TILTH
TOOTH
TRITE
TROTH
TRUTH
UNITE
UNITY
VASTY
VIRTU
VISTA
WALTZ
WASTE
WHITE

WIDTH
WITTY
WORTH
WRATH
WRITE
WROTE
WROTH
YOUTH
ZLOTY
ABOUT
ALBUM
ALOUD
AMOUR
AMPUL
ANGUS
ANNUL
ARGUE
AUGUR
AWFUL
BEGUM
BOGUS
BOLUS
BONUS
BOSUN
BUTUT
CAJUN
CECUM
CLOUD
CLOUT
CROUP
CUTUP
DATUM
DEBUG
DEBUT
DEMUR
DONUT
ENDUE
ENNUI
ENSUE
FEMUR
FETUS
FLOUR
FLOUT
FOCUS
FORUM
FRAUD
FUGUE
GAMUT
GENUS
GETUP
GHOUL
GROUP
GROUT
HOKUM
HUMUS
ICTUS
ILEUM
IMBUE
INCUR
INCUS
INDUE
INPUT
ISSUE
KAPUT
KNOUT
KRAUT
KURUS
LEMUR
LETUP
LIEUT
LOCUS
LOTUS
MANUF
MINUS
MOGUL
MUCUS
NEGUS
NEVUS
NEXUS
OAKUM
OCCUR
ODIUM
OPIUM
PINUP
PIOUS
PIQUE
PROUD
PSEUD
QUEUE
REBUS
REBUT
RECUR
RERUN
REVUE
RHEUM
ROGUE
SCOUR
SCOUT
SCRUB
SERUM
SETUP
SHOUT
SHRUB
SHRUG
SINUS
SIOUX
SIRUP
SNOUT
SPOUT
STOUT
STRUM
STRUT
SUNUP
SYRUP
TALUS
THRUM
TOQUE
TROUT
TUQUE
UNCUT
UNDUE
VAGUE
VALUE
VELUM
VENUE
VENUS
VIRUS
VOGUE
ABOVE
AGAVE
ALIVE
BRAVE
BRAVO
CALVE
CARVE
CHIVE
CLOVE
CRAVE
CURVE
DELVE
DRIVE
DROVE
GLOVE
GRAVE
GRAVY
GROVE
GUAVA
HALVE
HEAVE
HEAVY
HELVE
KNAVE
LARVA
LEAVE
MAUVE
NAIVE
NERVE
NERVY
OLIVE
PEEVE
PRIVY
PROVE
REEVE
SALVE
SALVO
SAVVY
SERVE
SERVO
SHAVE
SHOVE
SIEVE
SLAVE
SOLVE
STAVE
STOVE
SUAVE
SUPVR
VALVE
VERVE
VULVA
WAIVE
WEAVE
BLOWY
BRAWL
BRAWN
BROWN
CHEWY
CLOWN
CRAWL
CROWD
CROWN
DRAWL
DROWN
FLOWN
FROWN
GROWL
KIOWA
PRAWN
PROWL
SCOWL
SHAWL
SHOWY
SNOWY
SPAWN
TRAWL
UNRWA
EPOXY
PROXY
TWIXT
ALKYD
BERYL
CALYX
ETHYL
PLAYA
POLYP
SATYR
SIBYL
VINYL
AMAZE
BAIZA
BAIZE
BLAZE
BONZE
BOOZE
BRAZE
CRAZE
CRAZY
DIZZY
FEAZE
FRIZZ
FROZE
FURZE
FUZZY
GAUZE
GLAZE
GLOZE
GRAZE
JAZZY
MAIZE
MATZO
PIZZA
PLAZA
PRIZE
SEIZE
TIZZY
WOOZY

**5th Letter**

AGORA
ALOHA
AMEBA
AORTA
ARENA
AROMA
BAIZA
BALSA
CALLA
CANNA
CHELA
CHINA
CIRCA
COBRA
COCOA
COMMA
CONGA
COPRA
CURIA
DACHA
DELTA
DOGMA
DRAMA
EDEMA
ENEMA
ERISA
EXTRA
FAUNA
FLORA
GAMMA
GOUDA
GUAVA
HENNA
HYDRA
HYENA
JUNTA
KARMA
KIOWA
KOALA
KRONA
LAMIA
LARVA
LLAMA
MAFIA
MAGMA
MANIA
MANNA
MANTA
MECCA
MEDIA
NAIRA
OMAHA
OPERA
PAISA
PAMPA
PANDA
PARKA
PASHA
PASTA
PIZZA
PLAYA
PLAZA
POLKA
PUKKA
QUOTA
RUMBA
SAUNA
SCUBA
SENNA
SEPIA
SIGMA
STRIA
SULFA
SUPRA
TAIGA
TIARA
TIBIA
ULTRA
UMBRA
UNRWA
UVULA
VARIA
VILLA
VIOLA
VISTA
VODKA
VULVA
YUCCA
ZEBRA
BLURB
CLIMB
CRUMB
EXURB
KABOB
KEBAB
NABOB
PLUMB
SCRUB
SHRUB
SQUAB
SQUIB
THROB
THUMB
VOCAB
ANTIC
ASPIC
ASSOC
ATTIC
AZTEC
BASIC
CIVIC
CODEC
COLIC
COMIC
CONIC
CRESC
CUBIC
CYNIC
ENIAC
FRANC
FSLIC
HAVOC
INDIC
LILAC
LOGIC
LYRIC
MAGIC
MANIC
MEDIC
MIMIC
MUSIC
OPTIC
PANIC
PUBIC
RELIC
SONIC
SPARC
STOIC
SUMAC
TONIC
TOPIC
TOXIC
TUNIC
VATIC
XEBEC
XERIC
ACRID
AHEAD
ALKYD
ALOUD
AMEND
APHID
AVOID
AWARD
BEARD
BIPED
BLAND
BLEED
BLEND
BLIND
BLOND
BLOOD
BOARD
BOUND
BRAID
BRAND
BREAD
BREED
BROAD
BROOD
BUILD
CHARD
CHILD
CHORD
CLOUD
CONTD
COULD
CREED
CROWD
CUPID
DATED
DREAD
DRUID
DRYAD
EARED
ELAND
EMBED
EMEND
FATED
FETID
FIELD
FIEND
FIORD
FIXED
FJORD
FLIED
FLOOD
FLUID
FOUND
FOXED
FRAUD
FROND
GELID
GLAND
GONAD
GOURD
GRAND
GREED
GRIND
GUARD
GUILD
HOARD
HOUND
HUMID
IMBED
JADED
JIHAD
KNEAD
LAIRD
LIVID
LUCID
LURID
MOULD
MOUND
NAIAD
NAKED
NICAD
NOMAD
NOTED
OVOID
PLAID
PLEAD
POUND
PROUD
PSEUD
RABID
RAPID
RIGID
ROUND
SALAD
SCALD
SCAND
SCOLD
SCROD
SHARD
SHRED
SOLID
SOUND
SPEED
SPEND
SQUAD
SQUID
STAID
STAND
STEAD
STEED
STOOD
SWARD
SWORD
SYNOD
TEPID
THIRD
TIMID
TIRED
TREAD
TREND
TRIAD
TRIED
TUMID
TWEED
UPEND
VALID
VAPID
VIAND
VIVID
WEALD
WEIRD
WIELD
WORLD
WOULD
WOUND
YIELD
ABASE
ABATE
ABIDE
ABODE
ABOVE
ABUSE
ACUTE
ADAGE
ADDLE
ADOBE
ADORE
AERIE
AFIRE
AGAPE
AGATE
AGAVE
AGILE
AGREE
AISLE
ALIKE
ALIVE
ALONE
AMAZE
AMBLE
AMPLE
AMUSE
ANGLE
ANISE
ANKLE
ANODE
APACE
APPLE
ARGUE
ARISE
ASIDE
ATONE
AWAKE
AWARE
AZURE
BADGE
BAIZE
BARGE
BASTE
BATHE
BEIGE
BELIE
BELLE
BIBLE
BILGE
BINGE
BLADE
BLAME
BLARE
BLASE
BLAZE
BONZE
BOOZE
BORNE
BOULE
BRACE
BRAKE
BRAVE
BRAZE
BRIBE
BRIDE
BRINE
BROKE
BRUTE
BUDGE
BUGLE
BULGE
BUTTE
CABLE
CACHE
CADGE
CADRE
CALVE
CANOE
CARVE
CASTE
CAUSE
CEASE
CHAFE
CHASE
CHIDE
CHIME
CHINE
CHIVE
CHOKE
CHORE
CHOSE
CHUTE
CLIME
CLONE
CLOSE
CLOVE
COPSE
COUPE
CRANE
CRAPE
CRATE
CRAVE
CRAZE
CREME
CREPE
CRIME
CRONE
CRUDE
CRUSE
CURSE
CURVE
CYCLE
DANCE
DEICE
DELVE
DENSE
DEUCE
DIODE
DIRGE
DODGE
DOGIE
DOUSE
DOWSE
DRAKE
DRAPE
DRIVE
DRONE
DROVE
DRUPE
DUNCE
DUPLE
EAGLE
EDUCE
EERIE
ELATE
ELIDE
ELITE
ELOPE
ELUDE
EMCEE
EMOTE
ENDUE
ENSUE
ERASE
ERODE
ETUDE
EVADE
EVOKE
EXILE
EXUDE
EYRIE

FABLE
FALSE
FARCE
FEAZE
FENCE
FICHE
FLAKE
FLAME
FLARE
FLUKE
FLUME
FLUTE
FORCE
FORGE
FORTE
FRAME
FROZE
FUDGE
FUGUE
FURZE
FUSEE
GABLE
GAFFE
GAUGE
GAUZE
GEESE
GENIE
GENRE
GEODE
GLARE
GLAZE
GLEBE
GLIDE
GLOBE
GLOVE
GLOZE
GNOME
GOOSE
GORGE
GORSE
GOUGE
GRACE
GRADE
GRAPE
GRATE
GRAVE
GRAZE
GREBE
GRIME
GRIPE
GROPE
GROVE
GUIDE
GUILE
GUISE
HALVE
HAOLE

HASTE
HEAVE
HEDGE
HELVE
HENCE
HINGE
HORDE
HORSE
HOUSE
IMAGE
IMBUE
INANE
INDUE
INGLE
INURE
IRATE
ISSUE
JOULE
JUDGE
JUICE
KEDGE
KLUGE
KNAVE
KNIFE
KRONE
LADLE
LANCE
LAPSE
LARGE
LATHE
LEASE
LEAVE
LEDGE
LEONE
LEVEE
LIEGE
LISLE
LITHE
LODGE
LOOSE
LOUSE
LUCRE
LUNGE
MAIZE
MANGE
MANSE
MAPLE
MARGE
MAUVE
MAYBE
MELEE
MERGE
METRE
MIDGE
MINCE
MOIRE
MOOSE

MOUSE
MOVIE
NACRE
NAIVE
NERVE
NGWEE
NICHE
NIECE
NOBLE
NOISE
NONCE
NOOSE
NORSE
NUDGE
NURSE
OBESE
OLDIE
OLIVE
OPINE
ORATE
OSAGE
OUNCE
OUTRE
OVATE
OVULE
OXIDE
OZONE
PADRE
PARSE
PASSE
PASTE
PAUSE
PEACE
PEEVE
PEKOE
PENCE
PEWEE
PHAGE
PHASE
PHONE
PIECE
PIQUE
PIXIE
PLACE
PLANE
PLATE
PLEBE
PLUME
POISE
POSSE
PRATE
PRICE
PRIDE
PRIME
PRIZE
PROBE
PRONE

PROSE
PROVE
PRUDE
PRUNE
PULSE
PUREE
PURGE
PURSE
QUAKE
QUEUE
QUIRE
QUITE
QUOTE
RAISE
RAMIE
RANGE
REEVE
REVUE
RHYME
RIDGE
RIFLE
RINSE
ROGUE
ROUGE
ROUSE
ROUTE
RUBLE
RUPEE
SABLE
SALVE
SAUCE
SAUTE
SCALE
SCARE
SCENE
SCONE
SCOPE
SCORE
SEDGE
SEINE
SEIZE
SENSE
SERGE
SERVE
SHADE
SHAKE
SHALE
SHAME
SHAPE
SHARE
SHAVE
SHINE
SHIRE
SHONE
SHORE
SHOVE
SIDLE

SIEGE
SIEVE
SINCE
SINGE
SKATE
SLAKE
SLATE
SLAVE
SLICE
SLIDE
SLIME
SLOPE
SMILE
SMITE
SMOKE
SMOTE
SNAKE
SNARE
SNIDE
SNIPE
SNORE
SOLVE
SOUSE
SPACE
SPADE
SPARE
SPATE
SPICE
SPIKE
SPINE
SPIRE
SPITE
SPOKE
SPORE
SPREE
SPUME
STAGE
STAKE
STALE
STARE
STATE
STAVE
STERE
STILE
STOKE
STOLE
STONE
STORE
STOVE
STYLE
SUAVE
SUCRE
SUEDE
SUITE
SURGE
SWAGE
SWEDE

SWINE
SWIPE
SWORE
TABLE
TASTE
TAUPE
TEASE
TENSE
TEPEE
TERSE
THANE
THEME
THERE
THESE
THINE
THOLE
THOSE
THREE
THROE
THYME
TILDE
TINGE
TITHE
TITLE
TOQUE
TRACE
TRADE
TRIBE
TRICE
TRINE
TRIPE
TRITE
TROPE
TRUCE
TULLE
TUQUE
TWICE
TWINE
UKASE
UNCLE
UNDUE
UNITE
UNTIE
URINE
USAGE
UTILE
VAGUE
VALSE
VALUE
VALVE
VENUE
VERGE
VERSE
VERVE
VOGUE
VOICE
VOILE

WAIVE
WASTE
WEAVE
WEDGE
WHALE
WHERE
WHILE
WHINE
WHITE
WHOLE
WHORE
WHOSE
WHSLE
WINCE
WITHE
WORSE
WRITE
WROTE
ZAIRE
ALOOF
BLUFF
BRIEF
CALIF
CHAFF
CHIEF
CLIFF
DWARF
FLUFF
GRIEF
GRUFF
INDEF
MANUF
MODIF
MOTIF
PILAF
PROOF
QUAFF
RNZAF
SCANF
SCARF
SCOFF
SCUFF
SCURF
SERIF
SHEAF
SHELF
SKIFF
SNIFF
SNUFF
SPOOF
STAFF
STIFF
STUFF
THIEF
WHARF
WHIFF
ALONG

AMONG
BEFOG
BEING
BHANG
BRING
CLANG
CLING
CLUNG
COMDG
CONTG
DEBUG
DEFOG
DYING
FLING
FLUNG
HYING
ICING
INCOG
IRREG
LYING
OWING
PRONG
RELIG
SHRUG
SLANG
SLING
SLUNG
SPRIG
STING
STUNG
SWING
SWUNG
TELEG
THING
THONG
TOPOG
TWANG
TYING
UNPEG
VYING
WRING
WRONG
WRUNG
YOUNG
ABASH
ALLAH
ARITH
AWASH
BATCH
BEACH
BEECH
BELCH
BENCH
BERTH
BIRCH
BIRTH
BITCH

BLUSH
BOOTH
BOTCH
BOUGH
BRASH
BROTH
BRUSH
BUNCH
BURGH
CATCH
CINCH
CLASH
CLOTH
COACH
CONCH
COUCH
COUGH
CRASH
CRUSH
CZECH
DEATH
DEPTH
DITCH
DOUGH
DUTCH
EARTH
EPOCH
FAITH
FETCH
FIFTH
FILCH
FILTH
FINCH
FIRTH
FLASH
FLESH
FLUSH
FORTH
FRESH
FROTH
GIRTH
GLYPH
GNASH
GRAPH
GULCH
HARSH
HATCH
HEATH
HITCH
HUNCH
HUTCH
IRISH
KETCH
KNISH
LARCH
LATCH
LAUGH

LEACH
LEASH
LEECH
LOATH
LUNCH
LURCH
LYMPH
LYNCH
MARCH
MARSH
MATCH
MILCH
MIRTH
MONTH
MOUTH
MULCH
MUNCH
MYRRH
NEIGH
NORTH
NOTCH
NYMPH
PARCH
PATCH
PEACH
PERCH
PINCH
PITCH
PLASH
PLUSH
POACH
POOCH
PORCH
POUCH
PSYCH
PUNCH
QUASH
QUOTH
QURSH
RANCH
REACH
RETCH
ROACH
ROUGH
SLASH
SLOSH
SLOTH
SLUSH
SMASH
SMITH
SOOTH
SOUGH
SOUTH
STASH
SWASH
SWATH
SWISH

SYLPH
TEACH
TEETH
THIGH
TILTH
TOOTH
TORAH
TORCH
TOUCH
TOUGH
TRASH
TROTH
TRUTH
VETCH
VOUCH
WATCH
WEIGH
WELCH
WELSH
WENCH
WHICH
WHISH
WIDTH
WINCH
WITCH
WORTH
WRATH
WROTH
YOUTH
ALIBI
ASCII
CHILI
ENNUI
ENVOI
HAJJI
HINDI
HOURI
IRAQI
KANJI
KHAKI
LANAI
MAORI
MIAMI
MUFTI
NISEI
PENNI
QUASI
RABBI
RADII
SENGI
SENTI
SWAMI
ABACK
AFAIK
AMUCK
APEAK
BATIK

BLACK
BLANK
BLEAK
BLINK
BLOCK
BREAK
BRICK
BRINK
BRISK
BROOK
CAULK
CHALK
CHECK
CHEEK
CHICK
CHINK
CHOCK
CHUCK
CHUNK
CLACK
CLANK
CLERK
CLICK
CLINK
CLOAK
CLOCK
CLUCK
CRACK
CRANK
CREAK
CREEK
CRICK
CROAK
CROCK
CROOK
DRANK
DRINK
DRUNK
FLANK
FLASK
FLECK
FLICK
FLOCK
FLUNK
FRANK
FREAK
FRISK
FROCK
GREEK
KAPOK
KAYAK
KIOSK
KNACK
KNOCK
KULAK
PLANK
PLUCK

PLUN**K**
PRAN**K**
PRIC**K**
PRIN**K**
QUAC**K**
QUIC**K**
QUIR**K**
SHAC**K**
SHAN**K**
SHAR**K**
SHIR**K**
SHOC**K**
SHOO**K**
SHUC**K**
SKUL**K**
SKUN**K**
SLAC**K**
SLEE**K**
SLIC**K**
SLIN**K**
SLUN**K**
SMAC**K**
SMIR**K**
SMOC**K**
SNAC**K**
SNEA**K**
SNUC**K**
SPAN**K**
SPAR**K**
SPEA**K**
SPEC**K**
SPOO**K**
SPUN**K**
STAC**K**
STAL**K**
STAN**K**
STAR**K**
STEA**K**
STIC**K**
STIN**K**
STOC**K**
STOR**K**
STUC**K**
STUN**K**
SWAN**K**
THAN**K**
THIC**K**
THIN**K**
TRAC**K**
TRIC**K**
TRUC**K**
TRUN**K**
TWEA**K**
UMIA**K**
WHAC**K**
WHEL**K**
WHIS**K**

WRAC**K**
WREA**K**
WREC**K**
ADDN**L**
ALGO**L**
AMPU**L**
ANGE**L**
ANNU**L**
ANVI**L**
APRI**L**
ATOL**L**
AURA**L**
AVAI**L**
AWFU**L**
AXIA**L**
BABE**L**
BAGE**L**
BANA**L**
BASA**L**
BASI**L**
BERY**L**
BETE**L**
BEVE**L**
BEZE**L**
BOWE**L**
BRAW**L**
BROI**L**
CABA**L**
CAME**L**
CANA**L**
CARO**L**
CAVI**L**
CHIL**L**
CHUR**L**
CIVI**L**
COBO**L**
CORA**L**
CRAW**L**
CREE**L**
CRUE**L**
DECA**L**
DEVI**L**
DOWE**L**
DRAW**L**
DRIL**L**
DROL**L**
DROO**L**
DUCA**L**
DWEL**L**
EASE**L**
EMAI**L**
EQUA**L**
ETHY**L**
EXCE**L**
EXPE**L**
EXPT**L**
EXTO**L**

FATA**L**
FERA**L**
FETA**L**
FINA**L**
FLAI**L**
FRAI**L**
FRIL**L**
GAVE**L**
GHOU**L**
GNAR**L**
GRAI**L**
GRIL**L**
GROW**L**
GRUE**L**
HAZE**L**
HOTE**L**
HOVE**L**
IDEA**L**
IDYL**L**
IMPE**L**
INSO**L**
INTE**L**
JEWE**L**
KNEE**L**
KNEL**L**
KNOL**L**
KNUR**L**
KRAA**L**
LABE**L**
LAPE**L**
LEGA**L**
LEVE**L**
LIBE**L**
LOCA**L**
LOYA**L**
MEDA**L**
META**L**
MODE**L**
MOGU**L**
MORA**L**
MORE**L**
MOTE**L**
MURA**L**
NASA**L**
NATA**L**
NAVA**L**
NAVE**L**
NEWE**L**
NOVE**L**
OCTA**L**
OFFA**L**
ORIE**L**
PANE**L**
PAPA**L**
PEAR**L**
PEDA**L**
PENA**L**

PERI**L**
PETA**L**
PHIA**L**
PIXE**L**
PROW**L**
PUPI**L**
QUAI**L**
QUEL**L**
QUIL**L**
RAVE**L**
REBE**L**
REGA**L**
RENA**L**
REPE**L**
REVE**L**
RIVA**L**
RIYA**L**
ROWE**L**
ROYA**L**
RURA**L**
SCOW**L**
SCUL**L**
SEPA**L**
SHAL**L**
SHAW**L**
SHEL**L**
SHIL**L**
SHOA**L**
SIBY**L**
SISA**L**
SKIL**L**
SKUL**L**
SMAL**L**
SMEL**L**
SNAI**L**
SNAR**L**
SPEL**L**
SPIE**L**
SPIL**L**
SPOI**L**
SPOO**L**
STAL**L**
STEA**L**
STEE**L**
STIL**L**
STOO**L**
SWEL**L**
SWIL**L**
SWIR**L**
THEO**L**
TICA**L**
TOTA**L**
TOWE**L**
TRAI**L**
TRAW**L**
TRIA**L**
TRIL**L**

TROL**L**
TWIL**L**
TWIR**L**
UMBE**L**
UNTI**L**
USUA**L**
VENA**L**
VIGI**L**
VINY**L**
VIRA**L**
VITA**L**
VOCA**L**
VOWE**L**
WHEA**L**
WHEE**L**
WHIR**L**
WHOR**L**
YODE**L**
YOKE**L**
ZONA**L**
ABEA**M**
ABYS**M**
ALAR**M**
ALBU**M**
AXIO**M**
BEGU**M**
BESO**M**
BLOO**M**
BOSO**M**
BREA**M**
BROO**M**
BUXO**M**
CARO**M**
CECU**M**
CHAR**M**
CHAS**M**
CLAI**M**
CREA**M**
DATU**M**
DEIS**M**
DENI**M**
DREA**M**
ENTO**M**
EPRO**M**
FORU**M**
GLEA**M**
GLOO**M**
GROO**M**
HARE**M**
HOKU**M**
IDIO**M**
ILEU**M**
ISLA**M**
MADA**M**
MAXI**M**
MINI**M**
MODE**M**

OAKU**M**
ODIU**M**
OPIU**M**
PHAR**M**
PRIS**M**
PROE**M**
PSAL**M**
PURI**M**
QUAL**M**
REAL**M**
RHEU**M**
SCRA**M**
SCRI**M**
SEIS**M**
SERU**M**
SPAS**M**
SPER**M**
STEA**M**
STOR**M**
STRU**M**
SWAR**M**
THER**M**
THRU**M**
TOTE**M**
UNAR**M**
VELU**M**
VENO**M**
WHEL**M**
XYLE**M**
ACOR**N**
ADMA**N**
ADMI**N**
ADOR**N**
AGAI**N**
ALIE**N**
ALIG**N**
AMAI**N**
ANIO**N**
APRO**N**
ARGO**N**
ARSO**N**
ARYA**N**
ASHE**N**
ASIA**N**
ASPE**N**
AUXI**N**
AVIA**N**
BACO**N**
BAIR**N**
BARO**N**
BASI**N**
BATO**N**
BEGI**N**
BISO**N**
BLAI**N**
BORO**N**
BOSU**N**

BOUR**N**
BRAI**N**
BRAW**N**
BROW**N**
BRUI**N**
CABI**N**
CAIR**N**
CAJU**N**
CANO**N**
CAPO**N**
CHAI**N**
CHRO**N**
CHUR**N**
CLEA**N**
CLOW**N**
COLO**N**
COVE**N**
COZE**N**
CROO**N**
CROW**N**
CUBA**N**
DEIG**N**
DEMO**N**
DIST**N**
DIVA**N**
DOYE**N**
DOZE**N**
DRAI**N**
DROW**N**
EDLI**N**
EPSO**N**
FEIG**N**
FELO**N**
FLOW**N**
FOEH**N**
FROW**N**
GAMI**N**
GIVE**N**
GLEA**N**
GRAI**N**
GREE**N**
GROA**N**
GROI**N**
HAVE**N**
HERO**N**
HOGA**N**
HUMA**N**
HURO**N**
HYME**N**
INUR**N**
JAPA**N**
KORA**N**
LADE**N**
LAPI**N**
LATI**N**
LEAR**N**
LEMO**N**

LIKE**N**
LINE**N**
LIVE**N**
MASO**N**
MAVE**N**
MELO**N**
MORO**N**
MOUR**N**
NYLO**N**
OCEA**N**
OFTE**N**
OLDE**N**
ONIO**N**
ORGA**N**
PAEA**N**
PAGA**N**
PATE**N**
PECA**N**
PINO**N**
PITO**N**
PLAI**N**
PRAW**N**
PREE**N**
PYLO**N**
QUEA**N**
QUEE**N**
RADO**N**
RAVE**N**
RAYO**N**
REIG**N**
RERU**N**
RESI**N**
RIPE**N**
ROBI**N**
ROMA**N**
ROSI**N**
SALO**N**
SATA**N**
SATI**N**
SCIO**N**
SCOR**N**
SEDA**N**
SEME**N**
SEVE**N**
SHEE**N**
SHOR**N**
SIRE**N**
SKEI**N**
SLAI**N**
SOLO**N**
SPAW**N**
SPOO**N**
SPUR**N**
STAI**N**
STEI**N**
STER**N**
SWAI**N**

SWOO**N**
SWOR**N**
TALO**N**
TENO**N**
THEG**N**
THOR**N**
TITA**N**
TOKE**N**
TOXI**N**
TRAI**N**
TWAI**N**
TWEE**N**
UNIO**N**
UNMA**N**
UNPI**N**
URBA**N**
VIXE**N**
WAGO**N**
WAKE**N**
WAXE**N**
WIDE**N**
WOKE**N**
WOMA**N**
WOVE**N**
XENO**N**
YEAR**N**
ANGL**O**
AUDI**O**
BANJ**O**
BASS**O**
BEAN**O**
BING**O**
BONG**O**
BRAV**O**
BUNC**O**
BURR**O**
CACA**O**
CAME**O**
CANT**O**
CARG**O**
CELL**O**
CHIA**O**
CHIN**O**
COMB**O**
COMM**O**
CRED**O**
CURI**O**
DING**O**
DISC**O**
DITT**O**
FOLI**O**
FORG**O**
GIZM**O**
GUAN**O**
GUMB**O**
GUST**O**
HALL**O**

HELL**O**
HOLL**O**
HYDR**O**
IGLO**O**
IMAG**O**
JUMB**O**
JUNC**O**
JUNT**O**
KAZO**O**
LARG**O**
LASS**O**
LIMB**O**
LING**O**
LLAN**O**
MACR**O**
MAMB**O**
MANG**O**
MATZ**O**
METR**O**
MICR**O**
MONG**O**
MOTT**O**
NEGR**O**
NITR**O**
OUTD**O**
OUTG**O**
PATI**O**
PHON**O**
PHOT**O**
PIAN**O**
PINT**O**
PLUT**O**
POLI**O**
RADI**O**
RATI**O**
RECT**O**
RHIN**O**
RODE**O**
SALV**O**
SEAT**O**
SERV**O**
TABO**O**
TANG**O**
TEMP**O**
TORS**O**
TURB**O**
VERS**O**
VIDE**O**
VIRE**O**
WAHO**O**
WHOS**O**
YAHO**O**
BLIM**P**
CHAM**P**
CHEA**P**
CHEE**P**
CHIM**P**

CHIR**P**
CHOM**P**
CHUM**P**
CLAM**P**
CLAS**P**
CLUM**P**
CRAM**P**
CREE**P**
CRIM**P**
CRIS**P**
CROU**P**
CUTU**P**
DROO**P**
EQUI**P**
GETU**P**
GRAS**P**
GROU**P**
JALA**P**
JULE**P**
LETU**P**
NAAC**P**
PINU**P**
PLUM**P**
POLY**P**
PRIM**P**
RECA**P**
RECI**P**
SCAL**P**
SCAM**P**
SCAR**P**
SCOO**P**
SCRA**P**
SCRI**P**
SETU**P**
SHAR**P**
SHEE**P**
SIRU**P**
SKIM**P**
SLEE**P**
SLOO**P**
SLUM**P**
SLUR**P**
SNOO**P**
STAM**P**
STEE**P**
STOM**P**
STOO**P**
STRA**P**
STRI**P**
STRO**P**
STUM**P**
SUNU**P**
SWAM**P**
SWEE**P**
SWOO**P**
SYRU**P**
SYSO**P**

THOR**P**
THUM**P**
TRAM**P**
TROM**P**
TROO**P**
TRUM**P**
TULI**P**
UNCA**P**
UNZI**P**
USUR**P**
WHEL**P**
WHOO**P**
ABHO**R**
ABST**R**
ACTO**R**
ADDE**R**
AFAI**R**
AFTE**R**
ALDE**R**
ALTA**R**
ALTE**R**
AMBE**R**
AMOU**R**
ANGE**R**
ARBO**R**
ARDO**R**
ARMO**R**
ASTE**R**
ASTI**R**
ATTA**R**
AUGE**R**
AUGU**R**
AURA**R**
BLEA**R**
BONE**R**
BOWE**R**
BOXE**R**
BRIA**R**
BRIE**R**
CAPE**R**
CATE**R**
CEDA**R**
CHAI**R**
CHEE**R**
CHOI**R**
CIDE**R**
CIGA**R**
CLEA**R**
COLO**R**
COMD**R**
COME**R**
CONT**R**
COVE**R**
COWE**R**
CRIE**R**
DEBA**R**
DECO**R**

DEFER DEMUR DETER DINAR DINER DISTR DOLOR DONOR DOWER DREAR DRIER DRYER EAGER EIDER ELDER ELVER EMBER ENTER ERROR ESTER ETHER EYRIR FAKIR FAVOR FEMUR FEVER FEWER FIBER FILAR FLAIR FLEER FLIER FLOOR FLOUR FLYER FOYER FRIAR FRYER FUROR GONER HALER HOMER HONOR HOVER HUMOR ICHOR IMPER INCUR INFER INNER INSTR INTER JOKER JUROR LABOR LAGER LASER

LAYER LAZAR LEMUR LEPER LEVER LIFER LINER LITER LIVER LONER LOWER LUNAR MAJOR MANOR MASER MAYOR METER MINOR MISER MITER MIXER MOLAR MOTOR MOVER NADIR NEVER NITER OCCUR OCHER OFFER ORDER OSIER OTHER OTTER OUTER PACER PAPER PETER PIKER POKER POLAR POSER POWER PRIOR QUEER RADAR RAZOR RECUR REFER RIDER RIGOR RISER RIVER ROGER ROTOR RULER RUMOR

SABER SATYR SAVOR SCOUR SEVER SEWER SHEAR SHEER SHIER SHIRR SITAR SLIER SMEAR SNEER SOBER SOLAR SONAR SPEAR SPOOR STAIR STEER SUGAR SUPER SUPVR SWEAR TABOR TALER TAPER TAPIR TENOR THEIR TIGER TONER TOPER TOWER TUBER TUMOR TUTOR UDDER ULCER UMBER UNBAR UNDER UPPER USHER UTTER VALOR VAPOR VELAR VICAR VIGOR VIPER VISOR VIZOR WADER WAFER WAGER

WATER WAVER ABYSS ADIOS AEGIS ALIAS AMASS AMISS ANGUS APHIS ARRAS ATLAS AVGAS BANNS BASIS BELLS BLESS BLISS BLUES BOGUS BOLUS BONUS BRASS CHAOS CHAPS CHESS CHOPS CLASS CORPS CRAPS CRASS CRESS CROSS DEGAS DRESS DROSS DUMPS EAVES ELVES ETHOS FECES FETUS FINIS FLOSS FOCUS GAUSS GENUS GLANS GLASS GLOSS GRASS GRITS GROSS GUESS HADES HAYES HIVES

HUMUS ICTUS INCUS JEANS KUDOS KURUS LEGIS LINKS LISTS LIVES LOCUS LOESS LOTUS MANES MAVIS MINUS MLLES MORES MUCUS MUMPS NARIS NEEDS NEGUS NEVUS NEXUS NONES NUMIS OASIS OCCAS ORRIS PANTS PENIS PILES PIOUS PLEBS PRESS PUBES PUBIS QUITS REBUS SCOTS SINUS SNIPS SWISS TALUS TEENS THESS THURS TIMES TONGS TRANS TRAPS TREAS TRESS TRUSS TURPS VENUS

VIBES VIRUS WIVES YOURS ABAFT ABBOT ABORT ABOUT ADAPT ADEPT ADMIT ADOPT ADULT AFOOT AGENT ALERT ALLOT ALOFT ANENT ANGST APART APORT ARGOT ASCOT ASSET ATILT AUDIT AUGHT AVAST AVERT AWAIT BEAST BEFIT BEGET BERET BESET BESOT BIDET BIGHT BIGOT BLAST BLEAT BLOAT BLUET BLUNT BLURT BOAST BOOST BRACT BRUIT BRUNT BURST BUTUT CADET CARAT CARET CCITT

CHANT CHART CHEAT CHERT CHEST CIVET CLEAT CLEFT CLOUT CMSGT COAST COMDT COMET CONST COUNT COURT COVET CRAFT CREST CRUET CRUST CRYPT CRYST CUBIT DAUNT DAVIT DEBIT DEBUT DELFT DEPOT DIGIT DIVOT DLITT DONUT DOUBT DRAFT DRIFT DUCAT ECLAT EDICT EGRET EIGHT EJECT ELECT ENACT ERECT ERGOT ERUPT EVENT EVICT EXACT EXALT EXERT EXIST EXULT FACET FAGOT

FAINT FAULT FEAST FEINT FIGHT FIRST FLEET FLINT FLIRT FLOAT FLOUT FOIST FOUNT FRONT FROST FRUIT GAMUT GANTT GAUNT GHOST GIANT GLINT GLOAT GRAFT GRANT GREAT GREET GRIST GROAT GROUT GRUNT GUEST GUILT GUYOT HABIT HAUNT HEART HEIST HELOT HOIST IDIOT INEPT INERT INGOT INLET INPUT INSET ISLET JABOT JAUNT JOINT JOIST JOUST KAPUT KARAT KARST KNOUT

KRAUT LEAST LEGIT LICIT LIEUT LIGHT LIMIT MERIT MIDST MIGHT MOIST MOTET MOULT MOUNT MULCT NIGHT OCTET ONSET ORBIT OUGHT OVERT OWLET PAINT PICOT PILOT PIVOT PLAIT PLANT PLEAT POINT POLIT POSIT POULT PRINT QUART QUEST QUIET QUILT QUINT QUIRT QUOIT REACT REBUT REMIT RIGHT RIVET ROAST ROBOT ROOST SAINT SANIT SCANT SCENT SCOOT SCOUT SHAFT SHEET

SHIFT SHIPT SHIRT SHOAT SHOOT SHORT SHOUT SHUNT SIGHT SKEET SKIRT SLANT SLEET SMART SMELT SMSGT SNORT SNOUT SPENT SPIRT SPLIT SPORT SPOUT SPRAT SPURT SQUAT START STILT STINT STOAT STOUT STRUT STUNT SWART SWEAT SWEET SWEPT SWIFT TACIT TAINT TAROT TAUNT TEMPT TENET THEAT THEFT TIGHT TINCT TOAST TRACT TRAIT TREAT TROUT TRUST TRYST TWEET TWIST

TWIXT UNCUT UNFIT UPSET VALET VAULT VAUNT VERST VISIT VOMIT WAIST WHEAT WHIST WIGHT WORST WREST WRIST WURST YACHT YEAST ADIEU BANTU BAYOU COYPU FICHU HAIKU POILU VIRTU DERIV EQUIV AGLOW ALLOW ARROW ASKEW BEDEW BELOW BYLAW ELBOW ENDOW MACAW NOHOW OXBOW PAPAW RENEW SCREW SHREW SINEW SQUAW STRAW STREW THREW THROW WIDOW ADMIX AFFIX ANNEX BORAX

CALYX CODEX HELIX INDEX LATEX PHLOX RADIX RELAX SIOUX TELEX UNFIX ABBEY AGONY ALLAY ALLEY ALLOY AMITY ANGRY ANNOY APPLY ARRAY ASSAY BAGGY BALKY BALMY BANDY BATTY BAWDY BEEFY BELAY BELLY BENNY BERRY BIDDY BILLY BLOWY BOBBY BOGEY BONNY BOOBY BOOTY BOSKY BUDDY BUGGY BULKY BULLY BUNNY BURLY BUSBY BYWAY CABBY CADDY CAGEY CANDY CANNY CARNY CARRY

CATTY
CHARY
CHEWY
COCKY
COMFY
CONEY
CORNY
COVEY
CRAZY
CRONY
CURRY
DADDY
DAFFY
DAILY
DAIRY
DAISY
DALLY
DANDY
DECAY
DECOY
DECRY
DEIFY
DEITY
DELAY
DERBY
DIARY
DINGY
DINKY
DIRTY
DITTY
DIZZY
DOGGY
DOILY
DOLLY
DOPEY
DOWDY
DOWNY
DOWRY
DRILY
DUCHY
DUMMY
DUMPY
DUSKY
EARLY
EBONY
ELEGY
EMERY
EMPTY
ENEMY
ENJOY
ENTRY
ENVOY
EPOXY
ESSAY
EVERY
FAIRY
FANCY

FATTY
FELLY
FERRY
FIERY
FIFTY
FILLY
FINNY
FISHY
FLYBY
FOLLY
FORAY
FORTY
FULLY
FUNKY
FUNNY
FURRY
FUSSY
FUSTY
FUZZY
GABBY
GAILY
GAUDY
GAWKY
GIDDY
GIMPY
GIPSY
GLORY
GODLY
GOODY
GOOFY
GRAVY
GULLY
GUNNY
GUPPY
GUSHY
GUTTY
GYPSY
HAIRY
HANDY
HAPLY
HAPPY
HARDY
HARPY
HARRY
HEADY
HEAVY
HEFTY
HOARY
HOBBY
HOLLY
HOMEY
HONEY
HOOEY
HURRY
HUSKY
HUSSY
IMPLY

INLAY
IRONY
IVORY
JAZZY
JELLY
JENNY
JETTY
JEWRY
JIFFY
JIMMY
JOLLY
JUICY
JUMPY
KITTY
KOOKY
LAITY
LANKY
LEERY
LEGGY
LOBBY
LOFTY
LOONY
LORRY
LOUSY
LOWLY
LUCKY
LUSTY
MALAY
MANLY
MARRY
MCCOY
MERCY
MERRY
MIDDY
MISTY
MONEY
MOODY
MORAY
MOSEY
MOUSY
MUGGY
MUMMY
MUSHY
MUSTY
NASTY
NATTY
NEEDY
NERVY
NEWLY
NEWSY
NIFTY
NINNY
NIPPY
NODDY
NOISY
NOWAY
NUTTY

OVARY
PADDY
PALMY
PALSY
PANSY
PARRY
PARTY
PASTY
PATSY
PATTY
PENNY
PEONY
PESKY
PETTY
PHONY
PICKY
PIETY
PIGMY
PITHY
PLATY
POESY
POPPY
PRIVY
PROSY
PROXY
PUDGY
PUPPY
PUSHY
PUSSY
PUTTY
PYGMY
QUERY
RALLY
RANGY
RATTY
READY
RELAY
REPAY
REPLY
ROWDY
RUDDY
RUGBY
RUMMY
RUNNY
SALLY
SAPPY
SASSY
SAUCY
SAVVY
SEAMY
SEEDY
SHAKY
SHINY
SHOWY
SILLY
SISSY
SIXTY

SNOWY
SOGGY
SORRY
SOUPY
SPLAY
SPRAY
STORY
STRAY
STUDY
SULKY
SULLY
SURLY
TABBY
TACKY
TAFFY
TALLY
TANSY
TARDY
TARRY
TASTY
TAWNY
TEENY
TERRY
TESTY
TINNY
TIPSY
TIZZY
TOADY
TODAY
TODDY
TOKAY
TUMMY
TUNNY
UNIFY
UNITY
UNSAY
USURY
VASTY
VEERY
WACKY
WASHY
WEARY
WEEDY
WEENY
WEEPY
WINDY
WITHY
WITTY
WOODY
WOOZY
WORDY
WORRY
XCOPY
YUMMY
ZIPPY
ZLOTY
BLITZ

FRIZZ
GROSZ
HERTZ
SWITZ
TOPAZ
WALTZ

# 6 LETTER WORDS

1st Letter

ABACUS
ABATIS
ABBACY
ABBESS
ABDUCT
ABJECT
ABJURE
ABLAZE
ABLOOM
ABNAKI
ABOARD
ABOUND
ABRADE
ABROAD
ABRUPT
ABSENT
ABSORB
ABSURD
ACACIA
ACCEDE
ACCENT
ACCEPT
ACCESS
ACCORD
ACCOST
ACCRUE
ACCUSE
ACETIC
ACQUIT
ACROSS
ACTING
ACTION
ACTIVE
ACTUAL
ACUITY
ACUMEN
ADAGIO
ADDEND
ADDICT
ADDUCE
ADHERE
ADJOIN
ADJURE
ADJUST
ADMIRE
ADRIFT
ADROIT
ADSORB
ADVENT
ADVERB
ADVERT
ADVICE
ADVISE
AERATE
AERIAL
AFFAIR
AFFECT
AFFIRM
AFFORD
AFFRAY
AFGHAN
AFIELD
AFLAME
AFLOAT
AFRAID
AFRESH
AGENCY
AGENDA
AGHAST
AGLEAM
AIDMAN
AIRMAN
AIRWAY
AKIMBO
ALBEIT
ALBINO
ALCOVE
ALIGHT
ALKALI
ALLEGE
ALLIED
ALLUDE
ALLURE
ALMOND
ALMOST
ALPACA
ALPINE
ALTAIR
ALUMNA
ALWAYS
AMAZON
AMBUSH
AMENDS
AMERCE
AMOEBA
AMORAL
AMOUNT
AMPERE
AMULET
AMVETS
ANADEM
ANALOG
ANCHOR
ANEMIA
ANGINA
ANGORA
ANIMAL
ANIMUS
ANKLET
ANNALS
ANNEAL
ANNUAL
ANOINT
ANSWER
ANTHEM
ANTHER
ANTLER
ANTRUM
ANYHOW
ANYONE
ANYWAY
APACHE
APATHY
APERCU
APIARY
APICAL
APIECE
APLOMB
APOGEE
APPALL
APPEAL
APPEAR
APPEND
APPLET
APPROX
ARABIC
ARABLE
ARCADE
ARCANE
ARCCOS
ARCHON
ARCNET
ARCSIN
ARCTAN
ARCTIC
ARDENT
ARGENT
ARGOSY
ARGYLE
ARIGHT
ARMADA
ARMFUL
ARMLET
ARMORY
ARMPIT
ARNICA
AROUND
AROUSE
ARRANT
ARREST
ARRIVE
ARROYO
ARTERY
ARTFUL
ARTIST
ASCEND
ASCENT
ASHLAR
ASHORE
ASHRAM
ASLANT
ASLEEP
ASPECT
ASPIRE
ASSAIL
ASSENT
ASSERT
ASSESS
ASSIGN
ASSIST
ASSIZE
ASSORT
ASSUME
ASSURE
ASTERN
ASTHMA
ASTRAL
ASTRAY
ASTROL
ASTRON
ASTUTE
ASYLUM
ATOMIC
ATONAL
ATRIUM
ATTACH
ATTACK
ATTAIN
ATTEND
ATTEST
ATTIRE
ATTRIB
ATTUNE
AUBURN
AUGURY
AUGUST
AURORA
AUTHOR
AUTISM
AUTUMN
AVATAR
AVAUNT
AVENGE
AVENUE
AVERSE
AVIARY
AVOCET
AVOUCH
AWAKEN
AWEARY
AWEIGH
AWHILE
AWHIRL
AWNING
AZALEA
BABBLE
BABOON
BACKER
BACKUP
BADGER
BAFFLE
BAGMAN
BAGNIO
BAKERY
BALBOA
BALEEN
BALLAD
BALLET
BALLOT
BALSAM
BAMBOO
BANANA
BANDED
BANDIT
BANGLE
BANISH
BANNER
BANTAM
BANTER
BANYAN
BANZAI
BAOBAB
BARBER
BARELY
BARFLY
BARIUM
BARKER
BARLEY
BARRED
BARREL
BARREN
BARRIO
BARROW
BARTER
BASALT
BASKET
BASQUE
BATEAU
BATHOS
BATMAN
BATTEN
BATTER
BATTLE
BAUBLE
BAZAAR
BEACON
BEADLE
BEAGLE
BEAKER
BEANIE
BEAUTY
BEAVER
BECALM
BECKON
BECOME
BEDAUB
BEDBUG
BEDECK
BEDLAM
BEDPAN
BEETLE
BEFALL
BEFORE
BEFOUL
BEGGAR
BEGONE
BEHALF
BEHAVE
BEHEAD
BEHEST
BEHIND
BEHOLD
BEHOOF
BELDAM
BELFRY
BELIEF
BELIKE
BELLOW
BELONG
BELUGA
BEMIRE
BEMOAN
BEMUSE
BENDER
BENIGN
BENUMB
BENZOL
BERATE
BERBER
BEREFT
BESEEM
BESIDE
BESTIR
BESTOW
BETAKE
BETHEL
BETIDE
BETRAY
BETTER
BETTOR
BEWAIL
BEWARE
BEYOND
BICEPS
BICKER
BIGAMY
BIGWIG
BIKINI
BILLET
BILLOW
BINARY
BINHEX
BIOPSY
BIOTIC
BIOTIN
BIRDIE
BISECT
BISHOP
BISQUE
BISTRO
BITING
BITNET
BITTER
BLANCH
BLAZER
BLAZON
BLEACH
BLEARY
BLENCH
BLIGHT
BLITHE
BLOTCH
BLOUSE
BLOWSY
BLOWUP
BLUING
BLUISH
BOATER
BOBBIN
BOBBLE
BOBCAT
BOCCIE
BODICE
BODILY
BODKIN
BOGGLE
BOILER
BOLERO
BOMBER
BONBON
BONITO
BONNET
BONSAI
BOODLE
BOOKIE
BOOTEE
BORATE
BORDER
BOREAL
BORROW
BOTANY
BOTHER
BOTTLE
BOTTOM
BOUGHT
BOUNCE
BOUNTY
BOURSE
BOVINE
BOWLEG
BOWLER
BOWMAN
BOXCAR
BOXING
BRAISE
BRANCH
BRANDY
BRAZEN
BREACH
BREAST
BREATH
BREECH
BREEZE
BREVET
BRIDAL
BRIDGE
BRIDLE
BRIGHT
BRITON
BROACH
BROGAN
BROGUE
BROKEN
BROKER
BRONCO
BRONZE
BROOCH
BROWSE
BRUISE
BRUNCH
BRUNET
BRUTAL
BUBBLE
BUCKET
BUCKLE
BUDGET
BUDGIE
BUFFER
BUFFET
BULBUL
BULLET
BUMMER
BUMPER
BUNDLE
BUNGLE
BUNION
BUNKER
BUNKUM
BUQSHA
BURDEN
BUREAU
BURGEE
BURGLE
BURIAL
BURLAP
BURNER
BURROW
BURSAR
BUSBOY
BUSHED
BUSHEL
BUSILY
BUSKIN
BUSTLE
BUTANE
BUTLER
BUTTER
BUTTON
BUZZER
BYGONE
BYPASS
BYPATH
BYPLAY
BYWORD
CABALA
CABANA
CACHET
CACKLE
CACTUS
CADDIE
CAECUM
CAESAR
CAFTAN
CAHOOT
CAIMAN
CAJOLE
CALCIC
CALICO
CALIPH
CALLOW
CALLUS
CALVES
CAMBER
CAMERA
CAMPER
CAMPUS
CANAPE
CANARD
CANARY
CANCAN
CANCEL
CANCER
CANDID
CANDLE
CANDOR
CANINE
CANKER
CANNED

**C**ANNON
**C**ANNOT
**C**ANOPY
**C**ANTER
**C**ANTLE
**C**ANTON
**C**ANTOR
**C**ANVAS
**C**ANYON
**C**APFUL
**C**APTOR
**C**ARAFE
**C**ARBON
**C**ARBOY
**C**AREEN
**C**AREER
**C**ARESS
**C**ARHOP
**C**ARIES
**C**ARNAL
**C**ARPAL
**C**ARPEL
**C**ARPET
**C**ARREL
**C**ARROT
**C**ARTEL
**C**ARTON
**C**ARTOP
**C**ASABA
**C**ASEIN
**C**ASHEW
**C**ASING
**C**ASINO
**C**ASKET
**C**ASQUE
**C**ASSIA
**C**ASTER
**C**ASTLE
**C**ASUAL
**C**ATCHY
**C**ATGUT
**C**ATION
**C**ATKIN
**C**ATNAP
**C**ATNIP
**C**ATSUP
**C**ATTLE
**C**AUCUS
**C**AUDAL
**C**AUGHT
**C**AUSAL
**C**AVEAT
**C**AVERN
**C**AVIAR
**C**AVITY
**C**AVORT
**C**AYMAN
**C**AYUGA
**C**AYUSE
**C**ELERY
**C**ELLAR
**C**EMENT
**C**ENSER
**C**ENSOR
**C**ENSUS
**C**ENTER
**C**ENTRE
**C**EREAL
**C**EREUS
**C**ERISE
**C**ERIUM
**C**ERMET
**C**ERVIX
**C**ESIUM
**C**HAFER
**C**HAISE
**C**HALET
**C**HANCE
**C**HANCY
**C**HANGE
**C**HAPEL
**C**HARGE
**C**HASER
**C**HASTE
**C**HATTY
**C**HAUNT
**C**HEEKY
**C**HEERY
**C**HEESE
**C**HEQUE
**C**HERRY
**C**HERUB
**C**HICHI
**C**HICLE
**C**HILLY
**C**HINTZ
**C**HISEL
**C**HITIN
**C**HOICE
**C**HOKER
**C**HOLER
**C**HOOSE
**C**HOOSY
**C**HOPPY
**C**HORAL
**C**HOREA
**C**HORUS
**C**HOSEN
**C**HRISM
**C**HRIST
**C**HROME
**C**HROMO
**C**HUBBY
**C**HUKKA
**C**HUMMY
**C**HUNKY
**C**HURCH
**C**ICADA
**C**ILIUM
**C**INDER
**C**INEMA
**C**IPHER
**C**IRCLE
**C**IRCUS
**C**IRQUE
**C**IRRUS
**C**ITIFY
**C**ITRON
**C**ITRUS
**C**IVICS
**C**LAMMY
**C**LAMOR
**C**LAQUE
**C**LARET
**C**LASSY
**C**LAUSE
**C**LEAVE
**C**LENCH
**C**LERGY
**C**LERIC
**C**LEVER
**C**LEVIS
**C**LICHE
**C**LIENT
**C**LIMAX
**C**LINCH
**C**LINIC
**C**LIQUE
**C**LOCHE
**C**LOSET
**C**LOTHE
**C**LOVEN
**C**LOVER
**C**LUMSY
**C**LUTCH
**C**OARSE
**C**OBALT
**C**OBBLE
**C**OBWEB
**C**OCCUS
**C**OCCYX
**C**OCKLE
**C**OCOON
**C**ODDLE
**C**ODGER
**C**ODIFY
**C**OERCE
**C**OEVAL
**C**OFFEE
**C**OFFER
**C**OFFIN
**C**OGENT
**C**OGNAC
**C**OHEIR
**C**OHERE
**C**OHORT
**C**OITUS
**C**OLLAR
**C**OLLAT
**C**OLLIE
**C**OLLOQ
**C**OLONY
**C**OLUMN
**C**OMBAT
**C**OMBER
**C**OMDEX
**C**OMEDY
**C**OMELY
**C**OMFIT
**C**OMING
**C**OMITY
**C**OMMIT
**C**OMMON
**C**OMPAQ
**C**OMPAR
**C**OMPEL
**C**OMPLY
**C**ONCUR
**C**ONDOM
**C**ONDOR
**C**ONFAB
**C**ONFED
**C**ONFER
**C**ONSOL
**C**ONSTR
**C**ONSUL
**C**ONVEX
**C**ONVEY
**C**ONVOY
**C**OOKIE
**C**OOLER
**C**OOLIE
**C**OOPER
**C**OOTIE
**C**OPIER
**C**OPING
**C**OPPER
**C**OPTER
**C**OPULA
**C**OQUET
**C**ORBEL
**C**ORDON
**C**ORNEA
**C**ORNER
**C**ORNET
**C**ORONA
**C**ORPSE
**C**ORPUS
**C**ORRAL
**C**ORSET
**C**ORTEX
**C**ORYZA
**C**OSINE
**C**OSMIC
**C**OSMOS
**C**OSTLY
**C**OTTER
**C**OTTON
**C**OUGAR
**C**OULEE
**C**OUNTY
**C**OUPLE
**C**OUPON
**C**OURSE
**C**OUSIN
**C**OVERT
**C**OWARD
**C**OWBOY
**C**OWMAN
**C**OWPOX
**C**OYOTE
**C**RABBY
**C**RADLE
**C**RAFTY
**C**RANKY
**C**RANNY
**C**RATER
**C**RATON
**C**RAVAT
**C**RAVEN
**C**RAYON
**C**REASE
**C**REATE
**C**RECHE
**C**REDIT
**C**REEPY
**C**REOLE
**C**RETIN
**C**REWEL
**C**RINGE
**C**RISIS
**C**RITIC
**C**ROCUS
**C**ROTCH
**C**ROUCH
**C**RUISE
**C**RUMMY
**C**RUNCH
**C**RUTCH
**C**UBISM
**C**UCKOO
**C**UDDLE
**C**UDGEL
**C**UESTA
**C**UMBER
**C**UNNER
**C**UPOLA
**C**URATE
**C**URDLE
**C**URFEW
**C**URIUM
**C**URLEW
**C**URSOR
**C**URTSY
**C**URVET
**C**USPID
**C**USTOM
**C**UTLER
**C**UTLET
**C**UTOFF
**C**UTOUT
**C**UTTER
**C**YGNET
**C**YMBAL
**D**ABBLE
**D**ACTYL
**D**AEMON
**D**AGGER
**D**AHLIA
**D**AINTY
**D**AKOTA
**D**ALASI
**D**AMAGE
**D**AMASK
**D**AMPEN
**D**AMPER
**D**AMSEL
**D**AMSON
**D**ANDER
**D**ANDLE
**D**ANGER
**D**ANGLE
**D**ANISH
**D**APPER
**D**APPLE
**D**ARING
**D**ARKEN
**D**ARNEL
**D**ARTER
**D**ASHER
**D**ATIVE
**D**AWDLE
**D**AYBED
**D**AZZLE
**D**EACON
**D**EADEN
**D**EADLY
**D**EAFEN
**D**EARTH
**D**EBARK
**D**EBASE
**D**EBATE
**D**EBRIS
**D**EBTOR
**D**EBUNK
**D**ECADE
**D**ECAMP
**D**ECANT
**D**ECEIT
**D**ECENT
**D**ECIDE
**D**ECODE
**D**ECREE
**D**EDUCE
**D**EDUCT
**D**EEJAY
**D**EEPEN
**D**EFACE
**D**EFAME
**D**EFEAT
**D**EFECT
**D**EFEND
**D**EFILE
**D**EFINE
**D**EFORM
**D**EFRAY
**D**EFUSE
**D**EGREE
**D**EHORN
**D**ELETE
**D**ELUDE
**D**ELUGE
**D**ELUXE
**D**EMAND
**D**EMEAN
**D**EMISE
**D**EMODE
**D**EMOTE
**D**EMURE
**D**ENGUE
**D**ENIAL
**D**ENIER
**D**ENOTE
**D**ENTAL
**D**ENTIN
**D**ENUDE
**D**EODAR
**D**EPART
**D**EPEND
**D**EPICT
**D**EPLOY
**D**EPORT
**D**EPOSE
**D**EPUTE
**D**EPUTY
**D**ERAIL
**D**ERIDE
**D**ERIVE
**D**ERMAL
**D**ERMIS
**D**ERRIS
**D**ESALT
**D**ESCRY
**D**ESERT
**D**ESIGN
**D**ESIRE
**D**ESIST
**D**ESKEW
**D**ESPOT
**D**ETACH
**D**ETAIL
**D**ETAIN
**D**ETECT
**D**ETEST
**D**ETOUR
**D**EVICE
**D**EVISE
**D**EVOID
**D**EVOIR
**D**EVOTE
**D**EVOUR
**D**EVOUT
**D**EWLAP
**D**IADEM
**D**IAPER
**D**IATOM
**D**IBBLE
**D**ICKER
**D**ICKEY
**D**ICTUM
**D**IESEL
**D**IFFER
**D**IGEST
**D**ILATE
**D**ILUTE
**D**IMITY
**D**IMMER
**D**IMPLE
**D**INGHY
**D**INGLE
**D**INGUS
**D**INNER
**D**IPPER
**D**IRECT
**D**IRHAM
**D**IRNDL
**D**ISARM
**D**ISBAR
**D**ISCUS
**D**ISHED
**D**ISMAL
**D**ISMAY
**D**ISOWN
**D**ISPEL
**D**ISTAL
**D**ISUSE
**D**ITHER
**D**IVERS
**D**IVERT
**D**IVEST
**D**IVIDE
**D**IVINE
**D**OBBIN
**D**OCENT
**D**OCILE
**D**OCKET
**D**OCTOR
**D**ODDER
**D**OGGED
**D**OGLEG
**D**OINGS
**D**OLLAR
**D**OLLOP
**D**OLMEN
**D**OMAIN
**D**OMINO
**D**ONATE
**D**ONKEY
**D**OODAD
**D**OODLE
**D**OPANT
**D**ORMER
**D**ORSAL
**D**OTAGE
**D**OTARD
**D**OTTLE
**D**OUBLE
**D**OUBLY
**D**OUCHE
**D**OWNER
**D**RAFTY
**D**RAGON
**D**RAPER
**D**RAWER
**D**REARY
**D**REDGE
**D**RENCH
**D**RESSY
**D**RIVEL
**D**RIVER
**D**ROGUE
**D**ROPSY
**D**ROVER
**D**ROWSE
**D**ROWSY
**D**RUDGE
**D**UBBIN
**D**UENDE
**D**UENNA
**D**UFFER
**D**UGOUT
**D**ULCET
**D**UMDUM
**D**UPLEX
**D**URESS
**D**URING
**D**USTER
**D**YBBUK
**D**YNAMO
**E**AGLET
**E**ARTHY
**E**ARWAX
**E**ARWIG
**E**ASTER
**E**ATERY
**E**BCDIC
**E**CCLES
**E**CCLUS
**E**CLAIR
**E**CZEMA
**E**DGING
**E**DIBLE
**E**EPROM
**E**FFACE
**E**FFECT
**E**FFETE
**E**FFIGY
**E**FFORT
**E**GGNOG
**E**GOISM
**E**GRESS
**E**IGHTY
**E**ITHER
**E**LAPSE
**E**LDEST
**E**LEVEN
**E**LICIT
**E**LIXIR
**E**MBALM
**E**MBANK
**E**MBARK
**E**MBLEM
**E**MBODY
**E**MBOSS
**E**MBRYO
**E**MERGE
**E**METIC
**E**MIGRE
**E**MPIRE
**E**MPLOY
**E**NABLE
**E**NAMEL
**E**NAMOR
**E**NCAMP
**E**NCASE
**E**NCODE
**E**NCORE
**E**NCYST
**E**NDEAR
**E**NDING

ENDIVE
ENDRIN
ENDURE
ENERGY
ENFOLD
ENGAGE
ENGINE
ENGRAM
ENGULF
ENIGMA
ENISLE
ENJOIN
ENLIST
ENMESH
ENMITY
ENOUGH
ENRAGE
ENRICH
ENROLL
ENSIGN
ENSILE
ENSURE
ENTAIL
ENTICE
ENTIRE
ENTITY
ENTOMB
ENTRAP
ENTREE
ENZYME
EOLIAN
EQUATE
EQUINE
EQUITY
ERBIUM
ERMINE
EROTIC
ERRAND
ERRANT
ERRATA
ERSATZ
ESCAPE
ESCHEW
ESCORT
ESCROW
ESCUDO
ESKIMO
ESPRIT
ESTATE
ESTEEM
ETHANE
ETHICS
ETHNIC
ETHNOL
EUCHRE
EULOGY
EUNUCH
EUREKA
EVINCE
EVOLVE
EXCEED
EXCEPT
EXCESS
EXCISE
EXCITE
EXCUSE
EXEMPT
EXHALE
EXHORT
EXHUME
EXODUS
EXOTIC
EXPAND
EXPECT
EXPEND
EXPERT
EXPIRE
EXPORT
EXPOSE
EXTANT
EXTEND
EXTENT
EXTERN
EXTORT
EYELET
EYELID
FABIAN
FABLED
FABRIC
FACADE
FACIAL
FACILE
FACING
FACTOR
FACULA
FAECAL
FAERIE
FAGGOT
FAILLE
FAIRLY
FALCON
FALLOW
FALTER
FAMILY
FAMINE
FAMISH
FAMOUS
FARINA
FARROW
FASTEN
FATHER
FATHOM
FATTEN
FAUCES
FAUCET
FAVOUR
FEALTY
FECUND
FEDORA
FEEBLE
FEELER
FELINE
FELLAH
FELLOW
FELONY
FEMALE
FENDER
FENIAN
FENNEL
FERRET
FERRIC
FERULE
FERVID
FERVOR
FESTAL
FESTER
FETISH
FETTER
FETTLE
FEUDAL
FIANCE
FIASCO
FIBRIL
FIBRIN
FIBULA
FICKLE
FIDDLE
FIDGET
FIERCE
FIESTA
FIGURE
FILIAL
FILING
FILLER
FILLET
FILLIP
FILTER
FINALE
FINDER
FINERY
FINGER
FINIAL
FINISH
FINITE
FISCAL
FISHER
FITFUL
FIXITY
FIZZLE
FLABBY
FLACON
FLAGON
FLANGE
FLASHY
FLATUS
FLAUNT
FLAVOR
FLAXEN
FLEECE
FLESHY
FLIGHT
FLIMSY
FLINCH
FLITCH
FLOOZY
FLOPPY
FLORAL
FLORID
FLORIN
FLOSSY
FLOWER
FLUENT
FLUFFY
FLUNKY
FLURRY
FLYWAY
FODDER
FOEMAN
FOETAL
FOIBLE
FOLDER
FOLKSY
FOLLOW
FOMENT
FONDLE
FONDUE
FOOTED
FORAGE
FORBID
FOREGO
FOREST
FORGET
FORINT
FORKED
FORMAL
FORMAT
FORMER
FOSSIL
FOSTER
FOUGHT
FOURTH
FRACAS
FRAPPE
FREEZE
FRENCH
FRENZY
FRESCO
FRIARY
FRIDAY
FRIEND
FRIEZE
FRIGHT
FRIGID
FRINGE
FRISKY
FROLIC
FROWSY
FROZEN
FRUGAL
FRUITY
FRUMPY
FUDDLE
FUHRER
FUMBLE
FUNGUS
FUNNEL
FURORE
FURROW
FUSION
FUTILE
FUTURE
GABBLE
GABBRO
GADFLY
GADGET
GAELIC
GAFFER
GAGGLE
GAIETY
GAITER
GALAXY
GALENA
GALLEY
GALLIC
GALLON
GALLOP
GALORE
GALOSH
GAMBIT
GAMBLE
GAMBOL
GAMETE
GAMINE
GAMMER
GAMMON
GANDER
GANNET
GANTRY
GARAGE
GARBLE
GARCON
GARDEN
GARGLE
GARISH
GARLIC
GARNER
GARNET
GARRET
GARTER
GASKET
GATHER
GAUCHE
GAUCHO
GAYETY
GAZEBO
GEEZER
GEISHA
GENDER
GENERA
GENIAL
GENIUS
GENTLE
GENTRY
GERBIL
GERMAN
GERUND
GEWGAW
GEYSER
GHETTO
GIBBER
GIBBET
GIBBON
GIBSON
GIFTED
GIGGLE
GIGOLO
GIMBAL
GIMLET
GINGER
GINKGO
GIRDER
GIRDLE
GLANCE
GLIDER
GLITCH
GLOBAL
GLOSSY
GLOWER
GLUTEN
GNEISS
GOALIE
GOATEE
GOBBET
GOBBLE
GOBLET
GOBLIN
GODSON
GOGGLE
GOITER
GOLDEN
GOOBER
GOODLY
GOPHER
GOSPEL
GOSSIP
GOTHIC
GOTTEN
GOURDE
GOVERN
GRABEN
GRADER
GRAINY
GRANGE
GRATIS
GRAVEL
GRAVID
GRAYED
GREASE
GRIEVE
GRILLE
GRIPPE
GRISLY
GROCER
GROGGY
GROOVE
GROOVY
GROTTO
GROUCH
GROUND
GROUSE
GROVEL
GROWTH
GRUBBY
GRUDGE
GRUMPY
GUFFAW
GUIDON
GUILTY
GUINEA
GUITAR
GULDEN
GULLET
GUNMAN
GUNNER
GURGLE
GURKHA
GUSHER
GUSSET
GUTTER
GUZZLE
GYPSUM
GYRATE
HACKER
HACKIE
HACKLE
HAGGIS
HAGGLE
HAIRDO
HALALA
HALITE
HALLOW
HALTER
HALVES
HAMLET
HAMMER
HAMPER
HANDLE
HANGAR
HANKER
HANSEL
HANSOM
HAPPEN
HARASS
HARBOR
HARDEN
HARDLY
HARKEN
HARLOT
HARROW
HASSLE
HASTEN
HATBOX
HATRED
HATTER
HAUNCH
HAWKER
HAWSER
HAYMOW
HAZARD
HEALTH
HEARSE
HEARTH
HEARTY
HEAVEN
HEBREW
HECKLE
HECTIC
HECTOR
HEGIRA
HEIFER
HEIGHT
HELIUM
HELMET
HEPCAT
HERALD
HEREBY
HEREIN
HEREOF
HEREON
HERESY
HERETO
HERMIT
HERNIA
HEROIN
HERPES
HEYDAY
HIATUS
HICCUP
HIJACK
HINDER
HIPPED
HIPPIE
HITHER
HOAGIE
HOARSE
HOBBLE
HOBNOB
HOCKEY
HOLDUP
HOLLER
HOLLOW
HOMAGE
HOMELY
HOMILY
HOMINY
HONEST
HONOUR
HOODOO
HOOKAH
HOOKER
HOOKUP
HOOPLA
HOPPER
HORNET
HORRID
HORROR
HORSEY
HOSTEL
HOTBED
HOTBOX
HOWDAH
HOWLER
HOYDEN
HUBBUB
HUBCAP
HUBRIS
HUDDLE
HUMANE
HUMBLE
HUMBUG
HUMOUR
HUNGER
HUNKER
HURDLE
HURRAH
HURTLE
HUSSAR
HUSTLE
HUZZAH
HYAENA
HYBRID
HYPHEN
HYSSOP
IBIDEM
ICEBOX
ICEMAN
ICICLE
IDIOCY
IGNITE
IGNORE
IGUANA
ILLUME
ILLUST
IMBIBE
IMBRUE
IMMUNE
IMMURE
IMPACT
IMPAIR
IMPALA
IMPALE
IMPART
IMPEDE
IMPEND
IMPERF
IMPISH
IMPORT
IMPOSE
IMPOST
IMPUGN
IMPURE
IMPUTE
INBORN
INBRED
INCASE
INCEST
INCISE
INCITE
INCOME
INDEED
INDENT
INDIAN
INDICT
INDIGO
INDITE
INDIUM
INDOOR
INDUCE
INDUCT
INFAMY
INFANT
INFECT
INFEST
INFIRM
INFLOW
INFLUX
INFOLD
INFORM
INFUSE
INGEST

INHALE
INHERE
INHUME
INJECT
INJURE
INJURY
INKJET
INLAID
INLAND
INMATE
INMOST
INNATE
INNING
INROAD
INRUSH
INSANE
INSEAM
INSECT
INSERT
INSIDE
INSIST
INSOLE
INSTEP
INSULT
INSURE
INTACT
INTAKE
INTEND
INTENT
INTERJ
INTERN
INTONE
INTROD
INTUIT
INVADE
INVENT
INVERT
INVEST
INVITE
INVOKE
INWARD
IODIDE
IODINE
IODIZE
IONIZE
IPECAC
IRENIC
IRONIC
IRRUPT
ISLAND
ISOBAR
ISOMER
ITALIC
ITSELF
JABBER
JACKAL
JACKET
JAGGED
JAGUAR
JAILER
JALOPY
JANGLE
JARGON
JASPER
JAUNTY
JAYCEE
JAYGEE
JAYVEE
JEJUNE
JENNET
JERKIN
JERSEY
JESTER
JETSAM
JIGGER
JIGGLE
JIGSAW
JINGLE
JITNEY
JOBBER
JOCKEY
JOCOSE
JOCUND
JOGGLE
JOHNNY
JOINER
JOSTLE
JOUNCE
JOVIAL
JOYFUL
JOYOUS
JUDAIC
JUGGLE
JUICER
JUJUBE
JUMBLE
JUMPER
JUNGLE
JUNIOR
JUNKER
JUNKET
JUNKIE
JURIST
KABUKI
KAISER
KAOLIN
KARATE
KEGLER
KELVIN
KENNEL
KERMIT
KERNEL
KETTLE
KIBBLE
KIBOSH
KIDNAP
KIDNEY
KILTER
KIMONO
KINDLE
KINDLY
KIPPER
KIRTLE
KISMET
KISSER
KITSCH
KITTEN
KLATCH
KNIGHT
KOBOLD
KOPECK
KOREAN
KORUNA
KOSHER
KOWTOW
KWACHA
LABIAL
LABILE
LABIUM
LABOUR
LACKEY
LACTIC
LACUNA
LADDER
LADDIE
LADING
LAGOON
LAMENT
LAMINA
LANCER
LANCET
LANDAU
LANDED
LANDER
LAPDOG
LAPPET
LAPTOP
LARDER
LARIAT
LARYNX
LASCAR
LASSIE
LATENT
LATHER
LATTER
LAUNCH
LAUREL
LAVAGE
LAVISH
LAWFUL
LAWMAN
LAWYER
LAYMAN
LAYOFF
LAYOUT
LEADEN
LEADER
LEAFED
LEAGUE
LEAVED
LEAVEN
LEAVES
LECTOR
LEDGER
LEEWAY
LEGACY
LEGATE
LEGATO
LEGEND
LEGION
LEGMAN
LEGUME
LENGTH
LENITY
LENTIL
LEPTON
LESION
LESSEE
LESSEN
LESSER
LESSON
LESSOR
LETHAL
LETTER
LEVITY
LIABLE
LIBIDO
LIBYAN
LICHEE
LICHEN
LIGATE
LIGHTS
LIKELY
LIKING
LIKUTA
LIMBER
LIMPET
LIMPID
LINAGE
LINDEN
LINEAL
LINEAR
LINEUP
LINGER
LINING
LINKED
LINKUP
LINNET
LINTEL
LIQUID
LIQUOR
LISTEN
LITANY
LITCHI
LITMUS
LITTER
LITTLE
LIVELY
LIVERY
LIVING
LIZARD
LOADED
LOADER
LOATHE
LOBULE
LOCALE
LOCATE
LOCKER
LOCKET
LOCKUP
LOCUST
LODGER
LOGGIA
LOGJAM
LOITER
LONELY
LOOPER
LOOSEN
LORDLY
LOTION
LOUNGE
LOUVER
LOVELY
LOVING
LOWERY
LUBBER
LUCENT
LUMBAR
LUMBER
LUMMOX
LUNACY
LUPINE
LUSTER
LUXURY
LYCEUM
MACAPP
MACRON
MADAME
MADCAP
MADDEN
MADDER
MADMAN
MADRAS
MAENAD
MAGGOT
MAGNET
MAGPIE
MAGYAR
MAHOUT
MAIDEN
MAILED
MAKEUP
MAKUTA
MALADY
MALIAN
MALICE
MALIGN
MALLET
MALLOW
MAMMAL
MAMMON
MANAGE
MANANA
MANEGE
MANFUL
MANGER
MANGLE
MANIAC
MANIOC
MANNED
MANNER
MANQUE
MANTEL
MANTIS
MANTLE
MANTRA
MANUAL
MANURE
MAOISM
MARACA
MARAUD
MARBLE
MARCEL
MARGIN
MARINA
MARINE
MARKED
MARKET
MARKKA
MARKUP
MARLIN
MARMOT
MAROON
MARROW
MARTEN
MARTIN
MARTYR
MARVEL
MASCON
MASCOT
MASQUE
MASSIF
MASTER
MASTIC
MATINS
MATRIX
MATRON
MATTER
MATURE
MAYFLY
MAYHEM
MEADOW
MEAGER
MEASLY
MEDDLE
MEDIAL
MEDIAN
MEDICO
MEDIUM
MEDLEY
MEGOHM
MELLOW
MELODY
MEMBER
MEMOIR
MEMORY
MENACE
MENAGE
MENIAL
MENINX
MENSES
MENTAL
MENTOR
MERCER
MERGER
MERINO
MERMAN
MESCAL
MESSRS
METEOR
METHOD
METHYL
METIER
METRIC
METTLE
MIASMA
MICMAC
MICRON
MIDAIR
MIDDAY
MIDDEN
MIDDLE
MIDGET
MIDWAY
MIGHTY
MIKADO
MILDEW
MILIEU
MILLER
MILLET
MIMOSA
MINDED
MINGLE
MINION
MINNOW
MINUET
MINUTE
MIRAGE
MIRROR
MISCUE
MISERY
MISFIT
MISHAP
MISLAY
MISSAL
MISTER
MISUSE
MITTEN
MIZZEN
MOBILE
MODERN
MODEST
MODIFY
MODISH
MODULE
MOHAIR
MOHAWK
MOIETY
MOLDER
MOLEST
MOLTEN
MOMENT
MONDAY
MONGER
MONISM
MONKEY
MONODY
MOPPET
MORALE
MORBID
MORGAN
MORGUE
MORMON
MOROSE
MORRIS
MORROW
MORSEL
MORTAL
MORTAR
MOSAIC
MOSLEM
MOSQUE
MOSTLY
MOTHER
MOTILE
MOTION
MOTIVE
MOTLEY
MOTTLE
MOUSER
MOUSSE
MOUTON
MSCDEX
MUDDLE
MUFFIN
MUFFLE
MUKLUK
MULLET
MUMBLE
MUMMER
MURDER
MURMUR
MUSCLE
MUSEUM
MUSKEG
MUSKET
MUSLIM
MUSLIN
MUSSEL
MUSTER
MUTANT
MUTATE
MUTINY
MUTTER
MUTTON
MUTUAL
MUUMUU
MUZZLE
MYOPIA
MYRIAD
MYRTLE
MYSELF
MYSTIC
NAMELY
NAPALM
NAPERY
NAPKIN
NARROW
NATION
NATIVE
NATURE
NAUGHT
NAUSEA
NAUTCH
NAVAHO
NEARBY
NEBULA
NECTAR
NEEDLE
NEGATE
NELSON
NEPHEW
NEREID
NESTLE
NETHER
NETTLE
NEURAL
NEUROL
NEURON
NEUTER
NEWTON
NIACIN
NIBBLE
NICETY
NICKEL
NICKER
NIMBLE
NIMBUS
NIMROD
NINETY
NIPPER
NIPPLE
NITRIC
NITWIT
NOBODY
NODDLE
NODULE
NOGGIN
NONAGE
NONCOM
NONFAT
NOODLE
NORDIC
NORMAL
NORMAN
NORTON
NOTICE
NOTIFY
NOTION
NOUGAT
NOUGHT
NOVELL
NOVENA
NOVICE
NOWISE
NOZZLE
NUANCE
NUBBIN
NUBBLE
NUBILE
NUDISM
NUGGET
NUMBER
NUNCIO
NUTMEG
NUTRIA
NUZZLE
OBJECT
OBLATE
OBLIGE

OBLONG
OBSESS
OBTAIN
OBTUSE
OCCULT
OCCUPY
OCELOT
OCTANE
OCTAVE
OCTAVO
OCULAR
ODDITY
ODIOUS
OEUVRE
OFFEND
OFFICE
OFFING
OFFISH
OFFSET
OJIBWA
OMELET
ONEIDA
ONRUSH
ONWARD
OODLES
OOLITE
OPAQUE
OPIATE
OPPOSE
OPTICS
OPTION
ORACLE
ORANGE
ORATOR
ORCHID
ORDAIN
ORDEAL
ORDURE
ORGASM
ORIENT
ORIGIN
ORIOLE
ORISON
ORMOLU
ORNATE
ORNERY
ORNITH
ORPHAN
OSMIUM
OSPREY
OSSIFY
OSTLER
OTIOSE
OTTAWA
OUSTER
OUTBID
OUTCRY
OUTFIT
OUTFOX
OUTGUN
OUTING
OUTLAW
OUTLAY
OUTLET
OUTPUT
OUTRUN
OUTSET
OUTWIT
OVERDO
OVERLY
OXFORD
OXYGEN
OYSTER
PACIFY
PACKER
PACKET
PADDLE
PAGODA
PAIUTE
PALACE
PALATE
PALEON
PALING
PALLET
PALLID
PALLOR
PALMER
PALTER
PALTRY
PAMPER
PANAMA
PANDER
PANTIE
PANTRY
PAPACY
PAPAIN
PAPAYA
PAPIST
PAPULE
PARADE
PARCEL
PARDON
PARENT
PARIAH
PARING
PARISH
PARITY
PARLAY
PARLEY
PARLOR
PARODY
PAROLE
PARROT
PARSEC
PARSON
PARTLY
PASCAL
PASSEL
PASSIM
PASTEL
PASTOR
PASTRY
PATACA
PATENT
PATHOS
PATINA
PATOIS
PATROL
PATRON
PATTER
PAUNCH
PAUPER
PAVING
PAWNEE
PAWPAW
PAYOFF
PCMCIA
PEAHEN
PEAKED
PEANUT
PEBBLE
PECTIN
PEDANT
PEDDLE
PEEWEE
PELAGE
PELLET
PELVIS
PENCIL
PENMAN
PENNON
PENURY
PEOPLE
PEPPER
PEPSIN
PEPTIC
PEQUOT
PERIOD
PERISH
PERMIT
PERSON
PERUKE
PERUSE
PESETA
PESEWA
PESTER
PESTLE
PETARD
PETITE
PETREL
PETROL
PEWTER
PEYOTE
PHAROS
PHENOL
PHILOS
PHLEGM
PHLOEM
PHOBIA
PHOEBE
PHONIC
PHOTOG
PHOTON
PHRASE
PHYLUM
PHYSIC
PIAZZA
PICKAX
PICKET
PICKLE
PICKUP
PICNIC
PIDDLE
PIDGIN
PIERCE
PIFFLE
PIGEON
PIGLET
PIGNUT
PIGPEN
PIGSTY
PILFER
PILING
PILLAR
PILLOW
PIMPLE
PINCER
PINEAL
PINION
PINKIE
PIPING
PIPKIN
PIPPIN
PIQUET
PIRACY
PIRATE
PISTIL
PISTOL
PISTON
PLACER
PLACID
PLAGUE
PLAINT
PLANET
PLAQUE
PLASMA
PLATEN
PLEASE
PLEDGE
PLENTY
PLENUM
PLEXUS
PLIANT
PLIERS
PLIGHT
PLINTH
PLOVER
PLUCKY
PLUNGE
PLURAL
PLUTON
POCKET
PODIUM
POETRY
POGROM
POISON
POLDER
POLEAX
POLICE
POLICY
POLISH
POLITE
POLITY
POLLEN
POMADE
POMMEL
POMPON
PONCHO
PONDER
PONGEE
POODLE
POPGUN
POPLAR
POPLIN
POPPER
PORKER
POROUS
PORTAL
PORTER
PORTLY
POSEUR
POSSUM
POSTAL
POSTER
POTAGE
POTASH
POTATO
POTBOY
POTEEN
POTENT
POTHER
POTION
POTPIE
POTTER
POUNCE
POWDER
POWWOW
PRAISE
PRANCE
PRAYER
PREACH
PRECIS
PREFAB
PREFER
PREFIX
PRELIM
PREMED
PREMIX
PREPAY
PRESET
PRESTO
PRETTY
PREWAR
PRIEST
PRIMAL
PRIMER
PRINCE
PRINTF
PRIORY
PRISON
PRISSY
PRIVET
PROFIT
PROLIX
PROLOG
PROMPT
PRONTO
PROPEL
PROPER
PROTON
PSEUDO
PSYCHE
PSYCHO
PUBLIC
PUCKER
PUDDLE
PUEBLO
PUFFIN
PULLET
PULLEY
PULPIT
PULSAR
PUMICE
PUMMEL
PUNDIT
PUNISH
PUNKIN
PUPPET
PURDAH
PURIFY
PURINE
PURISM
PURITY
PURPLE
PURSER
PURSUE
PURVEY
PUSHER
PUTOUT
PUTRID
PUTSCH
PUTTEE
PUTTER
PUZZLE
PYRITE
PYTHON
QBASIC
QINTAR
QIVIUT
QUAHOG
QUAINT
QUAKER
QUARRY
QUARTO
QUARTZ
QUASAR
QUAVER
QUEASY
QUENCH
QUINCE
QUINSY
QUIVER
QUORUM
RABBET
RABBIT
RABBLE
RABIES
RACEME
RACISM
RACKET
RADIAL
RADIAN
RADISH
RADIUM
RADIUS
RAFFIA
RAFFLE
RAFTER
RAGGED
RAGLAN
RAGOUT
RAISIN
RAKISH
RAMBLE
RAMIFY
RAMROD
RANCHO
RANCID
RANCOR
RANDOM
RANGER
RANKLE
RANSOM
RAPIER
RAPINE
RAPPEN
RAREFY
RARING
RASCAL
RASHER
RASTER
RATHER
RATIFY
RATING
RATION
RATTAN
RATTER
RATTLE
RAVAGE
RAVINE
RAVISH
REALLY
REALTY
REAMER
REASON
REBATE
REBORN
REBUFF
REBUKE
RECALL
RECANT
RECEDE
RECENT
RECESS
RECIPE
RECITE
RECKON
RECOIL
RECORD
RECOUP
RECTAL
RECTOR
RECTUM
REDACT
REDCAP
REDDEN
REDEEM
REDUCE
REEFER
REFILL
REFINE
REFLEX
REFLUX
REFORM
REFRIG
REFUGE
REFUND
REFUSE
REFUTE
REGAIN
REGALE
REGARD
REGENT
REGIME
REGION
REGNAL
REGRET
REHASH
REJECT
REJOIN
RELATE
RELENT
RELICT
RELIEF
RELISH
RELIVE
REMAIN
REMAND
REMARK
REMEDY
REMIND
REMISS
REMORA
REMOTE
REMOVE
RENDER
RENEGE
RENNET
RENNIN
RENOWN
RENTAL
REPAIR
REPAST
REPEAL
REPEAT
REPENT
REPINE
REPLAY
REPORT
REPOSE
REPUTE
RESALE
RESCUE
RESENT
RESIDE
RESIGN
RESIST
RESORT
RESULT
RESUME
RETAIL
RETAIN
RETAKE
RETARD
RETINA
RETIRE
RETORT
RETURN
REVAMP
REVEAL
REVERB
REVERE
REVERS
REVERT
REVIEW
REVILE
REVISE
REVIVE
REVOKE
REVOLT
REWARD
RHYTHM
RIBALD
RIBAND
RIBBON
RICHES
RIDDEN
RIDDLE
RIGGER
RINGER
RIPPLE
RIPSAW
RISQUE
RITUAL
RLOGIN
ROBBER
ROBUST
ROCKER
ROCKET
RODENT
ROLLER
ROMANO
ROMPER
ROOKIE
ROSARY
ROSTER
ROTARY
ROTATE
ROTTEN
ROTUND
ROUBLE
RUBBER
RUBBLE
RUBRIC
RUCKUS
RUDDER
RUFFLE
RUGGED
RUMBLE
RUMPLE

RUMPUS
RUNLET
RUNNEL
RUNNER
RUNOFF
RUNWAY
RUPIAH
RUSSET
RUSTIC
RUSTLE
SACHEM
SACHET
SACRED
SACRUM
SADDEN
SADDLE
SADISM
SAFARI
SAFETY
SAILOR
SALAAM
SALAMI
SALARY
SALINE
SALIVA
SALLOW
SALMON
SALOON
SALUTE
SALVER
SAMPAN
SAMPLE
SANDAL
SANITY
SARONG
SASHAY
SATANG
SATEEN
SATIRE
SATRAP
SATURN
SAUCER
SAVAGE
SAVANT
SAVIOR
SAYING
SCAMPI
SCANTY
SCARAB
SCARCE
SCHEME
SCHISM
SCHIST
SCHOOL
SCHUSS
SCONCE
SCORCH

SCORIA
SCOTCH
SCRAPE
SCRAWL
SCREAM
SCREEN
SCREWY
SCRIBE
SCRIMP
SCRIPT
SCROLL
SCRUFF
SCULPT
SCURRY
SCURVY
SCUZZY
SCYTHE
SEABED
SEALER
SEAMAN
SEANCE
SEARCH
SEASON
SEAWAY
SECEDE
SECOND
SECRET
SECTOR
SECURE
SEDATE
SEDUCE
SEEMLY
SEESAW
SEETHE
SELDOM
SELECT
SELVES
SEMITE
SENATE
SENECA
SENILE
SENIOR
SENITI
SENSOR
SENTRY
SEPSIS
SEPTIC
SEQUEL
SEQUIN
SERAPE
SERAPH
SERENE
SERIAL
SERIES
SERMON
SERVER
SESAME

SETTEE
SETTER
SETTLE
SEVERE
SEWAGE
SEWING
SEXISM
SEXPOT
SEXTET
SEXTON
SEXUAL
SHABBY
SHADOW
SHAGGY
SHAKER
SHAMAN
SHANTY
SHAVER
SHAVES
SHEATH
SHEAVE
SHEIKH
SHELVE
SHERRY
SHIELD
SHIEST
SHIFTY
SHIMMY
SHINER
SHINNY
SHINTO
SHIVER
SHODDY
SHOULD
SHOVEL
SHOWER
SHREWD
SHRIEK
SHRIFT
SHRIKE
SHRILL
SHRIMP
SHRINE
SHRINK
SHRIVE
SHROUD
SICKEN
SICKLE
SIDING
SIERRA
SIESTA
SIGILL
SIGNAL
SIGNET
SILAGE
SILENT
SILICA

SILVER
SIMIAN
SIMILE
SIMMER
SIMONY
SIMPER
SIMPLE
SINFUL
SINGLE
SINKER
SIPHON
SISTER
SIZZLE
SKETCH
SKEWER
SKIMPY
SKINNY
SKYCAP
SLALOM
SLAVER
SLAVIC
SLEAZY
SLEDGE
SLEEPY
SLEEVE
SLEIGH
SLEUTH
SLIDER
SLIEST
SLIGHT
SLIPUP
SLIVER
SLOGAN
SLOPPY
SLOUCH
SLOUGH
SLOVEN
SLUDGE
SLUICE
SLURRY
SMILAX
SMIRCH
SMITHY
SMOOCH
SMOOTH
SMUDGE
SMUTCH
SNATCH
SNEEZE
SNIPPY
SNITCH
SNIVEL
SNOBOL
SNOOTY
SNOOZE
SOCCER
SOCIAL

SOCIOL
SOCKET
SODDEN
SODIUM
SODOMY
SOEVER
SOFTEN
SOIGNE
SOIREE
SOLACE
SOLDER
SOLEMN
SOMBER
SONATA
SONNET
SOOTHE
SORDID
SORREL
SORROW
SORTIE
SOUGHT
SOURCE
SOVIET
SPADIX
SPARSE
SPATHE
SPAVIN
SPECIE
SPECIF
SPEECH
SPHERE
SPHINX
SPIDER
SPIGOT
SPINAL
SPINEL
SPINET
SPIRAL
SPIREA
SPIRIT
SPLASH
SPLEEN
SPLICE
SPLINE
SPLINT
SPOKEN
SPONGE
SPOTTY
SPOUSE
SPRAIN
SPRAWL
SPREAD
SPRING
SPRINT
SPRITE
SPROUT
SPRUCE

SPRUNG
SPURGE
SPUTUM
SQUALL
SQUARE
SQUASH
SQUAWK
SQUEAK
SQUEAL
SQUINT
SQUIRE
SQUIRM
SQUIRT
STABLE
STAMEN
STANCE
STANCH
STANZA
STAPES
STAPLE
STARCH
STARVE
STATIC
STATUE
STATUS
STAVES
STEADY
STENCH
STEPPE
STEREO
STICKY
STIFLE
STIGMA
STINGY
STITCH
STOCKY
STODGY
STOLEN
STOLID
STOLON
STONED
STOOGE
STRAFE
STRAIN
STRAIT
STRAND
STREAK
STREAM
STREET
STRESS
STRICT
STRIDE
STRIFE
STRIKE
STRING
STRIPE
STRIVE

STROBE
STRODE
STROKE
STROLL
STRONG
STROVE
STRUCK
STRUNG
STUBBY
STUCCO
STUDIO
STUFFY
STUPID
STUPOR
STURDY
STYLUS
STYMIE
SUBDUE
SUBLET
SUBMIT
SUBORN
SUBSET
SUBTLE
SUBURB
SUBWAY
SUCCOR
SUCKER
SUCKLE
SUDDEN
SUFFER
SUFFIX
SUITOR
SULFUR
SULLEN
SULTAN
SULTRY
SUMMER
SUMMIT
SUMMON
SUNDAE
SUNDAY
SUNDER
SUNDRY
SUNKEN
SUNLIT
SUNSET
SUNTAN
SUPERB
SUPINE
SUPPER
SUPPLE
SUPPLY
SURETY
SURREY
SURTAX
SURVEY
SUTURE

SVELTE
SWATCH
SWATHE
SWERVE
SWITCH
SWIVEL
SYLVAN
SYMBOL
SYNTAX
SYPHON
SYSTEM
TABLET
TACKLE
TACTIC
TAILOR
TAKING
TALENT
TALLOW
TALMUD
TAMALE
TAMPER
TAMPON
TANDEM
TANGLE
TANKER
TANNER
TANNIN
TAOISM
TAPPET
TARGET
TARIFF
TARPON
TARSUS
TARTAN
TARTAR
TASSEL
TATTER
TATTLE
TATTOO
TAUGHT
TAVERN
TAWDRY
TEACUP
TEAPOT
TEASEL
TEDIUM
TEEPEE
TEETER
TEETHE
TELLER
TELNET
TEMPER
TEMPLE
TENANT
TENDER
TENDON
TENNIS

TENPIN
TENURE
TEREDO
TERROR
TESTER
TESTIS
TETCHY
TETHER
THANKS
THATCH
THEIRS
THEISM
THENCE
THEORY
THESIS
THIEVE
THIRST
THIRTY
THORAX
THOUGH
THRALL
THRASH
THREAD
THREAT
THRESH
THRICE
THRIFT
THRILL
THRIVE
THROAT
THRONE
THRONG
THROVE
THRUSH
THRUST
THWACK
THWART
THYMUS
TICKER
TICKET
TICKLE
TIDBIT
TIFFIN
TIGHTS
TILLER
TIMBER
TIMBRE
TIMELY
TINDER
TINGLE
TINKER
TINKLE
TINSEL
TIPPET
TIPPLE
TIPTOE
TIRADE

TISSUE
TITBIT
TITLED
TITTER
TITTLE
TOCSIN
TODDLE
TOFFEE
TOGGLE
TOILET
TOMATO
TOMBOY
TOMCAT
TOMTIT
TONGUE
TONSIL
TOOTHY
TOPPLE
TORERO
TORPID
TORPOR
TORQUE
TORRID
TOTTER
TOUCAN
TOUCHE
TOUCHY
TOUPEE
TOUSLE
TOWARD
TOWHEE
TRADER
TRAGIC
TRANCE
TRANSL
TRANSP
TRAUMA
TRAVEL
TREATY
TREBLE
TREMOR
TRENCH
TREPAN
TRIAGE
TRICKY
TRIFLE
TRIODE
TRIPLE
TRIPLY
TRIPOD
TRITON
TRIUNE
TRIVET
TRIVIA
TROCHE
TROIKA
TROJAN

TROPHY
TROPIC
TROUGH
TROUPE
TROWEL
TRUANT
TRUDGE
TRUISM
TRUSTY
TRYING
TSETSE
TUBING
TUBULE
TUCKER
TUGRIK
TUMBLE
TUMULT
TUNDRA
TUNNEL
TURBAN
TURBID
TURBOT
TUREEN
TURGID
TURING
TURKEY
TURNER
TURNIP
TURRET
TURTLE
TURVES
TUSKER
TUSSLE
TUXEDO
TWEEDY
TWELVE
TWENTY
TWINGE
TWITCH
TYCOON
TYPHUS
TYPIFY
TYPIST
TYRANT
ULLAGE
ULSTER
ULTIMO
ULTRIX
UMPIRE
UNABLE
UNBEND
UNBIND
UNBOLT
UNBORN
UNCIAL
UNCLAD
UNCLOG
UNCOIL
UNCORK
UNCURL
UNDIES
UNDULY
UNEASY
UNESCO
UNEVEN
UNFAIR
UNFOLD
UNFURL
UNGIRD
UNHAND
UNHOLY
UNHOOK
UNICEF
UNIQUE
UNISEX
UNISON
UNITED
UNJUST
UNKIND
UNLACE
UNLADE
UNLESS
UNLIKE
UNLOAD
UNLOCK
UNMASK
UNMEET
UNMOOR
UNPACK
UNPILE
UNPLUG
UNREAD
UNREAL
UNREEL
UNREST
UNRIPE
UNROBE
UNROLL
UNROOF
UNRULY
UNSEAL
UNSEAT
UNSHIP
UNSHOD
UNSNAP
UNSTOP
UNSUNG
UNTOLD
UNTRUE
UNTUNE
UNUSED
UNVEIL
UNWELL
UNWEPT
UNWIND
UNWISE
UNWRAP
UNYOKE
UPBEAT
UPDATE
UPHILL
UPHOLD
UPKEEP
UPLAND
UPLIFT
UPLOAD
UPMOST
UPPISH
UPPITY
UPREAR
UPROAR
UPROOT
UPRUSH
UPSHOT
UPSIDE
UPTAKE
UPTOWN
UPTURN
UPWARD
UPWELL
UPWIND
URACIL
URANIC
URANUS
URBANE
URCHIN
UREMIA
URETER
URGENT
URINAL
URSINE
USABLE
USEFUL
USENET
USURER
UTERUS
UTMOST
UTOPIA
VACANT
VACATE
VACUUM
VAGARY
VAGINA
VAGROM
VALISE
VALLEY
VALUED
VANDAL
VANISH
VANITY
VAPORY
VARIED
VARLET
VASSAL
VECTOR
VELLUM
VELOUR
VELVET
VENDEE
VENDER
VENDOR
VENEER
VENIAL
VENIRE
VENOUS
VERBAL
VERGER
VERIFY
VERILY
VERITY
VERMIN
VERNAL
VERSED
VERSUS
VERTEX
VESPER
VESSEL
VESTAL
VESTEE
VESTRY
VIABLE
VICTIM
VICTOR
VICUNA
VIKING
VILIFY
VILLUS
VINOUS
VIOLET
VIOLIN
VIRAGO
VIRGIN
VIRILE
VIRION
VIRTUE
VISAGE
VISCID
VISCUS
VISION
VISUAL
VITALS
VIVACE
VIVIFY
VIZARD
VIZIER
VOICED
VOLLEY
VOLUME
VOLUTE
VOODOO
VORTEX
VOTARY
VOTIVE
VOYAGE
VOYEUR
VULGAR
WABBLE
WADDLE
WAFFLE
WAGGLE
WAHINE
WAITER
WAIVER
WALLET
WALLOP
WALLOW
WALNUT
WALRUS
WAMBLE
WAMPUM
WANDER
WANGLE
WANTON
WAPITI
WARBLE
WARDEN
WARDER
WARMTH
WARREN
WASHER
WATERY
WATTLE
WAYLAY
WEAKEN
WEAKLY
WEALTH
WEAPON
WEASEL
WEBBED
WEEKLY
WEEVIL
WEIGHT
WELKIN
WELTER
WESKIT
WETHER
WHALER
WHAMMY
WHEEZE
WHEEZY
WHENCE
WHERRY
WHILOM
WHILST
WHIMSY
WHINNY
WHITEN
WHOLLY
WICKED
WICKER
WICKET
WIENER
WIGGLE
WIGGLY
WIGLET
WIGWAG
WIGWAM
WILLOW
WIMBLE
WIMPLE
WINDER
WINDOW
WINDUP
WINGED
WINKER
WINKLE
WINNER
WINNOW
WINTER
WINTRY
WIRING
WISDOM
WITHAL
WITHER
WITHIN
WITTED
WIZARD
WOBBLE
WOEFUL
WOMBAT
WONDER
WONTED
WOODED
WOODEN
WOODSY
WOOFER
WOOLEN
WOOLLY
WORKER
WORSEN
WORTHY
WRAITH
WRASSE
WREATH
WRENCH
WRETCH
WRITER
WRITHE
XMODEM
YAHWEH
YAMMER
YANKEE
YANQUI
YARROW
YEARLY
YEASTY
YELLOW
YEOMAN
YMODEM
YOGURT
YONDER
ZEALOT
ZENANA
ZENITH
ZEPHYR
ZIGZAG
ZINNIA
ZIPPER
ZIRCON
ZITHER
ZMODEM
ZODIAC
ZOMBIE
ZONKED
ZOUAVE
ZOUNDS
ZOYSIA
ZYGOTE

## 2nd Letter

BABBLE
BABOON
BACKER
BACKUP
BADGER
BAFFLE
BAGMAN
BAGNIO
BAKERY
BALBOA
BALEEN
BALLAD
BALLET
BALLOT
BALSAM
BAMBOO
BANANA
BANDED
BANDIT
BANGLE
BANISH
BANNER
BANTAM
BANTER
BANYAN
BANZAI
BAOBAB
BARBER
BARELY
BARFLY
BARIUM
BARKER
BARLEY
BARRED
BARREL
BARREN
BARRIO
BARROW
BARTER
BASALT
BASKET
BASQUE
BATEAU
BATHOS
BATMAN
BATTEN
BATTER
BATTLE
BAUBLE
BAZAAR
CABALA
CABANA
CACHET
CACKLE
CACTUS
CADDIE
CAECUM
CAESAR
CAFTAN
CAHOOT
CAIMAN
CAJOLE
CALCIC
CALICO
CALIPH
CALLOW
CALLUS
CALVES
CAMBER
CAMERA
CAMPER
CAMPUS
CANAPE
CANARD
CANARY
CANCAN
CANCEL
CANCER
CANDID
CANDLE
CANDOR
CANINE
CANKER
CANNED
CANNON
CANNOT
CANOPY
CANTER
CANTLE
CANTON
CANTOR
CANVAS
CANYON
CAPFUL
CAPTOR
CARAFE
CARBON
CARBOY
CAREEN
CAREER
CARESS
CARHOP
CARIES
CARNAL
CARPAL
CARPEL
CARPET
CARREL
CARROT
CARTEL
CARTON
CARTOP
CASABA
CASEIN
CASHEW
CASING
CASINO
CASKET
CASQUE
CASSIA
CASTER
CASTLE
CASUAL
CATCHY
CATGUT
CATION
CATKIN
CATNAP
CATNIP
CATSUP
CATTLE
CAUCUS
CAUDAL
CAUGHT
CAUSAL
CAVEAT
CAVERN
CAVIAR
CAVITY
CAVORT
CAYMAN
CAYUGA
CAYUSE
DABBLE
DACTYL
DAEMON
DAGGER
DAHLIA
DAINTY
DAKOTA
DALASI
DAMAGE
DAMASK
DAMPEN
DAMPER
DAMSEL
DAMSON
DANDER
DANDLE
DANGER
DANGLE
DANISH
DAPPER
DAPPLE
DARING
DARKEN
DARNEL
DARTER
DASHER
DATIVE
DAWDLE
DAYBED
DAZZLE
EAGLET
EARTHY
EARWAX
EARWIG
EASTER
EATERY
FABIAN
FABLED
FABRIC
FACADE
FACIAL
FACILE
FACING
FACTOR
FACULA
FAECAL
FAERIE
FAGGOT
FAILLE
FAIRLY
FALCON
FALLOW
FALTER
FAMILY

FAMINE
FAMISH
FAMOUS
FARINA
FARROW
FASTEN
FATHER
FATHOM
FATTEN
FAUCES
FAUCET
FAVOUR
GABBLE
GABBRO
GADFLY
GADGET
GAELIC
GAFFER
GAGGLE
GAIETY
GAITER
GALAXY
GALENA
GALLEY
GALLIC
GALLON
GALLOP
GALORE
GALOSH
GAMBIT
GAMBLE
GAMBOL
GAMETE
GAMINE
GAMMER
GAMMON
GANDER
GANNET
GANTRY
GARAGE
GARBLE
GARCON
GARDEN
GARGLE
GARISH
GARLIC
GARNER
GARNET
GARRET
GARTER
GASKET
GATHER
GAUCHE
GAUCHO
GAYETY
GAZEBO
HACKER
HACKIE
HACKLE
HAGGIS
HAGGLE
HAIRDO
HALALA
HALITE
HALLOW
HALTER
HALVES
HAMLET
HAMMER
HAMPER
HANDLE
HANGAR
HANKER
HANSEL
HANSOM
HAPPEN
HARASS
HARBOR
HARDEN
HARDLY
HARKEN
HARLOT
HARROW
HASSLE
HASTEN
HATBOX
HATRED
HATTER
HAUNCH
HAWKER
HAWSER
HAYMOW
HAZARD
JABBER
JACKAL
JACKET
JAGGED
JAGUAR
JAILER
JALOPY
JANGLE
JARGON
JASPER
JAUNTY
JAYCEE
JAYGEE
JAYVEE
KABUKI
KAISER
KAOLIN
KARATE
LABIAL
LABILE
LABIUM
LABOUR
LACKEY
LACTIC
LACUNA
LADDER
LADDIE
LADING
LAGOON
LAMENT
LAMINA
LANCER
LANCET
LANDAU
LANDED
LANDER
LAPDOG
LAPPET
LAPTOP
LARDER
LARIAT
LARYNX
LASCAR
LASSIE
LATENT
LATHER
LATTER
LAUNCH
LAUREL
LAVAGE
LAVISH
LAWFUL
LAWMAN
LAWYER
LAYMAN
LAYOFF
LAYOUT
MACAPP
MACRON
MADAME
MADCAP
MADDEN
MADDER
MADMAN
MADRAS
MAENAD
MAGGOT
MAGNET
MAGPIE
MAGYAR
MAHOUT
MAIDEN
MAILED
MAKEUP
MAKUTA
MALADY
MALIAN
MALICE
MALIGN
MALLET
MALLOW
MAMMAL
MAMMON
MANAGE
MANANA
MANEGE
MANFUL
MANGER
MANGLE
MANIAC
MANIOC
MANNED
MANNER
MANQUE
MANTEL
MANTIS
MANTLE
MANTRA
MANUAL
MANURE
MAOISM
MARACA
MARAUD
MARBLE
MARCEL
MARGIN
MARINA
MARINE
MARKED
MARKET
MARKKA
MARKUP
MARLIN
MARMOT
MAROON
MARROW
MARTEN
MARTIN
MARTYR
MARVEL
MASCON
MASCOT
MASQUE
MASSIF
MASTER
MASTIC
MATINS
MATRIX
MATRON
MATTER
MATURE
MAYFLY
MAYHEM
NAMELY
NAPALM
NAPERY
NAPKIN
NARROW
NATION
NATIVE
NATURE
NAUGHT
NAUSEA
NAUTCH
NAVAHO
PACIFY
PACKER
PACKET
PADDLE
PAGODA
PAIUTE
PALACE
PALATE
PALEON
PALING
PALLET
PALLID
PALLOR
PALMER
PALTER
PALTRY
PAMPER
PANAMA
PANDER
PANTIE
PANTRY
PAPACY
PAPAIN
PAPAYA
PAPIST
PAPULE
PARADE
PARCEL
PARDON
PARENT
PARIAH
PARING
PARISH
PARITY
PARLAY
PARLEY
PARLOR
PARODY
PAROLE
PARROT
PARSEC
PARSON
PARTLY
PASCAL
PASSEL
PASSIM
PASTEL
PASTOR
PASTRY
PATACA
PATENT
PATHOS
PATINA
PATOIS
PATROL
PATRON
PATTER
PAUNCH
PAUPER
PAVING
PAWNEE
PAWPAW
PAYOFF
RABBET
RABBIT
RABBLE
RABIES
RACEME
RACISM
RACKET
RADIAL
RADIAN
RADISH
RADIUM
RADIUS
RAFFIA
RAFFLE
RAFTER
RAGGED
RAGLAN
RAGOUT
RAISIN
RAKISH
RAMBLE
RAMIFY
RAMROD
RANCHO
RANCID
RANCOR
RANDOM
RANGER
RANKLE
RANSOM
RAPIER
RAPINE
RAPPEN
RAREFY
RARING
RASCAL
RASHER
RASTER
RATHER
RATIFY
RATING
RATION
RATTAN
RATTER
RATTLE
RAVAGE
RAVINE
RAVISH
SACHEM
SACHET
SACRED
SACRUM
SADDEN
SADDLE
SADISM
SAFARI
SAFETY
SAILOR
SALAAM
SALAMI
SALARY
SALINE
SALIVA
SALLOW
SALMON
SALOON
SALUTE
SALVER
SAMPAN
SAMPLE
SANDAL
SANITY
SARONG
SASHAY
SATANG
SATEEN
SATIRE
SATRAP
SATURN
SAUCER
SAVAGE
SAVANT
SAVIOR
SAYING
TABLET
TACKLE
TACTIC
TAILOR
TAKING
TALENT
TALLOW
TALMUD
TAMALE
TAMPER
TAMPON
TANDEM
TANGLE
TANKER
TANNER
TANNIN
TAOISM
TAPPET
TARGET
TARIFF
TARPON
TARSUS
TARTAN
TARTAR
TASSEL
TATTER
TATTLE
TATTOO
TAUGHT
TAVERN
TAWDRY
VACANT
VACATE
VACUUM
VAGARY
VAGINA
VAGROM
VALISE
VALLEY
VALUED
VANDAL
VANISH
VANITY
VAPORY
VARIED
VARLET
VASSAL
WABBLE
WADDLE
WAFFLE
WAGGLE
WAHINE
WAITER
WAIVER
WALLET
WALLOP
WALLOW
WALNUT
WALRUS
WAMBLE
WAMPUM
WANDER
WANGLE
WANTON
WAPITI
WARBLE
WARDEN
WARDER
WARMTH
WARREN
WASHER
WATERY
WATTLE
WAYLAY
YAHWEH
YAMMER
YANKEE
YANQUI
YARROW
ABACUS
ABATIS
ABBACY
ABBESS
ABDUCT
ABJECT
ABJURE
ABLAZE
ABLOOM
ABNAKI
ABOARD
ABOUND
ABRADE
ABROAD
ABRUPT
ABSENT
ABSORB
ABSURD
EBCDIC
IBIDEM
OBJECT
OBLATE
OBLIGE
OBLONG
OBSESS
OBTAIN
OBTUSE
QBASIC
ACACIA
ACCEDE
ACCENT
ACCEPT
ACCESS
ACCORD
ACCOST
ACCRUE
ACCUSE
ACETIC
ACQUIT
ACROSS
ACTING
ACTION
ACTIVE
ACTUAL
ACUITY
ACUMEN
ECCLES
ECCLUS
ECLAIR
ECZEMA
ICEBOX
ICEMAN
ICICLE
OCCULT
OCCUPY
OCELOT
OCTANE
OCTAVE
OCTAVO
OCULAR
PCMCIA
SCAMPI
SCANTY
SCARAB
SCARCE
SCHEME
SCHISM
SCHIST
SCHOOL
SCHUSS
SCONCE
SCORCH
SCORIA
SCOTCH
SCRAPE
SCRAWL
SCREAM
SCREEN
SCREWY
SCRIBE
SCRIMP
SCRIPT
SCROLL
SCRUFF
SCULPT
SCURRY
SCURVY
SCUZZY
SCYTHE
ADAGIO
ADDEND
ADDICT
ADDUCE
ADHERE
ADJOIN
ADJURE
ADJUST
ADMIRE
ADRIFT
ADROIT
ADSORB
ADVENT
ADVERB
ADVERT
ADVICE
ADVISE

EDGING
EDIBLE
IDIOCY
ODDITY
ODIOUS
AERATE
AERIAL
BEACON
BEADLE
BEAGLE
BEAKER
BEANIE
BEAUTY
BEAVER
BECALM
BECKON
BECOME
BEDAUB
BEDBUG
BEDECK
BEDLAM
BEDPAN
BEETLE
BEFALL
BEFORE
BEFOUL
BEGGAR
BEGONE
BEHALF
BEHAVE
BEHEAD
BEHEST
BEHIND
BEHOLD
BEHOOF
BELDAM
BELFRY
BELIEF
BELIKE
BELLOW
BELONG
BELUGA
BEMIRE
BEMOAN
BEMUSE
BENDER
BENIGN
BENUMB
BENZOL
BERATE
BERBER
BEREFT
BESEEM
BESIDE
BESTIR
BESTOW
BETAKE
BETHEL
BETIDE
BETRAY
BETTER
BETTOR
BEWAIL
BEWARE
BEYOND
CELERY
CELLAR
CEMENT
CENSER
CENSOR
CENSUS
CENTER
CENTRE
CEREAL
CEREUS
CERISE
CERIUM
CERMET
CERVIX
CESIUM
DEACON
DEADEN
DEADLY
DEAFEN
DEARTH
DEBARK
DEBASE
DEBATE
DEBRIS
DEBTOR
DEBUNK
DECADE
DECAMP
DECANT
DECEIT
DECENT
DECIDE
DECODE
DECREE
DEDUCE
DEDUCT
DEEJAY
DEEPEN
DEFACE
DEFAME
DEFEAT
DEFECT
DEFEND
DEFILE
DEFINE
DEFORM
DEFRAY
DEFUSE
DEGREE
DEHORN
DELETE
DELUDE
DELUGE
DELUXE
DEMAND
DEMEAN
DEMISE
DEMODE
DEMOTE
DEMURE
DENGUE
DENIAL
DENIER
DENOTE
DENTAL
DENTIN
DENUDE
DEODAR
DEPART
DEPEND
DEPICT
DEPLOY
DEPORT
DEPOSE
DEPUTE
DEPUTY
DERAIL
DERIDE
DERIVE
DERMAL
DERMIS
DERRIS
DESALT
DESCRY
DESERT
DESIGN
DESIRE
DESIST
DESKEW
DESPOT
DETACH
DETAIL
DETAIN
DETECT
DETEST
DETOUR
DEVICE
DEVISE
DEVOID
DEVOIR
DEVOTE
DEVOUR
DEVOUT
DEWLAP
EEPROM
FEALTY
FECUND
FEDORA
FEEBLE
FEELER
FELINE
FELLAH
FELLOW
FELONY
FEMALE
FENDER
FENIAN
FENNEL
FERRET
FERRIC
FERULE
FERVID
FERVOR
FESTAL
FESTER
FETISH
FETTER
FETTLE
FEUDAL
GEEZER
GEISHA
GENDER
GENERA
GENIAL
GENIUS
GENTLE
GENTRY
GERBIL
GERMAN
GERUND
GEWGAW
GEYSER
HEALTH
HEARSE
HEARTH
HEARTY
HEAVEN
HEBREW
HECKLE
HECTIC
HECTOR
HEGIRA
HEIFER
HEIGHT
HELIUM
HELMET
HEPCAT
HERALD
HEREBY
HEREIN
HEREOF
HEREON
HERESY
HERETO
HERMIT
HERNIA
HEROIN
HERPES
HEYDAY
JEJUNE
JENNET
JERKIN
JERSEY
JESTER
JETSAM
KEGLER
KELVIN
KENNEL
KERMIT
KERNEL
KETTLE
LEADEN
LEADER
LEAFED
LEAGUE
LEAVED
LEAVEN
LEAVES
LECTOR
LEDGER
LEEWAY
LEGACY
LEGATE
LEGATO
LEGEND
LEGION
LEGMAN
LEGUME
LENGTH
LENITY
LENTIL
LEPTON
LESION
LESSEE
LESSEN
LESSER
LESSON
LESSOR
LETHAL
LETTER
LEVITY
MEADOW
MEAGER
MEASLY
MEDDLE
MEDIAL
MEDIAN
MEDICO
MEDIUM
MEDLEY
MEGOHM
MELLOW
MELODY
MEMBER
MEMOIR
MEMORY
MENACE
MENAGE
MENIAL
MENINX
MENSES
MENTAL
MENTOR
MERCER
MERGER
MERINO
MERMAN
MESCAL
MESSRS
METEOR
METHOD
METHYL
METIER
METRIC
METTLE
NEARBY
NEBULA
NECTAR
NEEDLE
NEGATE
NELSON
NEPHEW
NEREID
NESTLE
NETHER
NETTLE
NEURAL
NEUROL
NEURON
NEUTER
NEWTON
OEUVRE
PEAHEN
PEAKED
PEANUT
PEBBLE
PECTIN
PEDANT
PEDDLE
PEEWEE
PELAGE
PELLET
PELVIS
PENCIL
PENMAN
PENNON
PENURY
PEOPLE
PEPPER
PEPSIN
PEPTIC
PEQUOT
PERIOD
PERISH
PERMIT
PERSON
PERUKE
PERUSE
PESETA
PESEWA
PESTER
PESTLE
PETARD
PETITE
PETREL
PETROL
PEWTER
PEYOTE
REALLY
REALTY
REAMER
REASON
REBATE
REBORN
REBUFF
REBUKE
RECALL
RECANT
RECEDE
RECENT
RECESS
RECIPE
RECITE
RECKON
RECOIL
RECORD
RECOUP
RECTAL
RECTOR
RECTUM
REDACT
REDCAP
REDDEN
REDEEM
REDUCE
REEFER
REFILL
REFINE
REFLEX
REFLUX
REFORM
REFRIG
REFUGE
REFUND
REFUSE
REFUTE
REGAIN
REGALE
REGARD
REGENT
REGIME
REGION
REGNAL
REGRET
REHASH
REJECT
REJOIN
RELATE
RELENT
RELICT
RELIEF
RELISH
RELIVE
REMAIN
REMAND
REMARK
REMEDY
REMIND
REMISS
REMORA
REMOTE
REMOVE
RENDER
RENEGE
RENNET
RENNIN
RENOWN
RENTAL
REPAIR
REPAST
REPEAL
REPEAT
REPENT
REPINE
REPLAY
REPORT
REPOSE
REPUTE
RESALE
RESCUE
RESENT
RESIDE
RESIGN
RESIST
RESORT
RESULT
RESUME
RETAIL
RETAIN
RETAKE
RETARD
RETINA
RETIRE
RETORT
RETURN
REVAMP
REVEAL
REVERB
REVERE
REVERS
REVERT
REVIEW
REVILE
REVISE
REVIVE
REVOKE
REVOLT
REWARD
SEABED
SEALER
SEAMAN
SEANCE
SEARCH
SEASON
SEAWAY
SECEDE
SECOND
SECRET
SECTOR
SECURE
SEDATE
SEDUCE
SEEMLY
SEESAW
SEETHE
SELDOM
SELECT
SELVES
SEMITE
SENATE
SENECA
SENILE
SENIOR
SENITI
SENSOR
SENTRY
SEPSIS
SEPTIC
SEQUEL
SEQUIN
SERAPE
SERAPH
SERENE
SERIAL
SERIES
SERMON
SERVER
SESAME
SETTEE
SETTER
SETTLE
SEVERE
SEWAGE
SEWING
SEXISM
SEXPOT
SEXTET
SEXTON
SEXUAL
TEACUP
TEAPOT
TEASEL
TEDIUM
TEEPEE
TEETER
TEETHE
TELLER
TELNET
TEMPER
TEMPLE
TENANT
TENDER
TENDON
TENNIS
TENPIN
TENURE
TEREDO
TERROR
TESTER
TESTIS
TETCHY
TETHER
VECTOR
VELLUM
VELOUR
VELVET
VENDEE
VENDER
VENDOR
VENEER
VENIAL
VENIRE
VENOUS
VERBAL
VERGER
VERIFY
VERILY
VERITY
VERMIN
VERNAL
VERSED
VERSUS
VERTEX
VESPER
VESSEL

VESTAL
VESTEE
VESTRY
WEAKEN
WEAKLY
WEALTH
WEAPON
WEASEL
WEBBED
WEEKLY
WEEVIL
WEIGHT
WELKIN
WELTER
WESKIT
WETHER
YEARLY
YEASTY
YELLOW
YEOMAN
ZEALOT
ZENANA
ZENITH
ZEPHYR
AFFAIR
AFFECT
AFFIRM
AFFORD
AFFRAY
AFGHAN
AFIELD
AFLAME
AFLOAT
AFRAID
AFRESH
EFFACE
EFFECT
EFFETE
EFFIGY
EFFORT
OFFEND
OFFICE
OFFING
OFFISH
OFFSET
AGENCY
AGENDA
AGHAST
AGLEAM
EGGNOG
EGOISM
EGRESS
IGNITE
IGNORE
IGUANA
CHAFER
CHAISE
CHALET
CHANCE
CHANCY
CHANGE
CHAPEL
CHARGE
CHASER
CHASTE
CHATTY
CHAUNT
CHEEKY
CHEERY
CHEESE
CHEQUE
CHERRY
CHERUB
CHICHI
CHICLE
CHILLY
CHINTZ
CHISEL
CHITIN
CHOICE
CHOKER
CHOLER
CHOOSE
CHOOSY
CHOPPY
CHORAL
CHOREA
CHORUS
CHOSEN
CHRISM
CHRIST
CHROME
CHROMO
CHUBBY
CHUKKA
CHUMMY
CHUNKY
CHURCH
GHETTO
PHAROS
PHENOL
PHILOS
PHLEGM
PHLOEM
PHOBIA
PHOEBE
PHONIC
PHOTOG
PHOTON
PHRASE
PHYLUM
PHYSIC
RHYTHM
SHABBY
SHADOW
SHAGGY
SHAKER
SHAMAN
SHANTY
SHAVER
SHAVES
SHEATH
SHEAVE
SHEIKH
SHELVE
SHERRY
SHIELD
SHIEST
SHIFTY
SHIMMY
SHINER
SHINNY
SHINTO
SHIVER
SHODDY
SHOULD
SHOVEL
SHOWER
SHREWD
SHRIEK
SHRIFT
SHRIKE
SHRILL
SHRIMP
SHRINE
SHRINK
SHRIVE
SHROUD
THANKS
THATCH
THEIRS
THEISM
THENCE
THEORY
THESIS
THIEVE
THIRST
THIRTY
THORAX
THOUGH
THRALL
THRASH
THREAD
THREAT
THRESH
THRICE
THRIFT
THRILL
THRIVE
THROAT
THRONE
THRONG
THROVE
THRUSH
THRUST
THWACK
THWART
THYMUS
WHALER
WHAMMY
WHEEZE
WHEEZY
WHENCE
WHERRY
WHILOM
WHILST
WHIMSY
WHINNY
WHITEN
WHOLLY
AIDMAN
AIRMAN
AIRWAY
BICEPS
BICKER
BIGAMY
BIGWIG
BIKINI
BILLET
BILLOW
BINARY
BINHEX
BIOPSY
BIOTIC
BIOTIN
BIRDIE
BISECT
BISHOP
BISQUE
BISTRO
BITING
BITNET
BITTER
CICADA
CILIUM
CINDER
CINEMA
CIPHER
CIRCLE
CIRCUS
CIRQUE
CIRRUS
CITIFY
CITRON
CITRUS
CIVICS
DIADEM
DIAPER
DIATOM
DIBBLE
DICKER
DICKEY
DICTUM
DIESEL
DIFFER
DIGEST
DILATE
DILUTE
DIMITY
DIMMER
DIMPLE
DINGHY
DINGLE
DINGUS
DINNER
DIPPER
DIRECT
DIRHAM
DIRNDL
DISARM
DISBAR
DISCUS
DISHED
DISMAL
DISMAY
DISOWN
DISPEL
DISTAL
DISUSE
DITHER
DIVERS
DIVERT
DIVEST
DIVIDE
DIVINE
EIGHTY
EITHER
FIANCE
FIASCO
FIBRIL
FIBRIN
FIBULA
FICKLE
FIDDLE
FIDGET
FIERCE
FIESTA
FIGURE
FILIAL
FILING
FILLER
FILLET
FILLIP
FILTER
FINALE
FINDER
FINERY
FINGER
FINIAL
FINISH
FINITE
FISCAL
FISHER
FITFUL
FIXITY
FIZZLE
GIBBER
GIBBET
GIBBON
GIBSON
GIFTED
GIGGLE
GIGOLO
GIMBAL
GIMLET
GINGER
GINKGO
GIRDER
GIRDLE
HIATUS
HICCUP
HIJACK
HINDER
HIPPED
HIPPIE
HITHER
JIGGER
JIGGLE
JIGSAW
JINGLE
JITNEY
KIBBLE
KIBOSH
KIDNAP
KIDNEY
KILTER
KIMONO
KINDLE
KINDLY
KIPPER
KIRTLE
KISMET
KISSER
KITSCH
KITTEN
LIABLE
LIBIDO
LIBYAN
LICHEE
LICHEN
LIGATE
LIGHTS
LIKELY
LIKING
LIKUTA
LIMBER
LIMPET
LIMPID
LINAGE
LINDEN
LINEAL
LINEAR
LINEUP
LINGER
LINING
LINKED
LINKUP
LINNET
LINTEL
LIQUID
LIQUOR
LISTEN
LITANY
LITCHI
LITMUS
LITTER
LITTLE
LIVELY
LIVERY
LIVING
LIZARD
MIASMA
MICMAC
MICRON
MIDAIR
MIDDAY
MIDDEN
MIDDLE
MIDGET
MIDWAY
MIGHTY
MIKADO
MILDEW
MILIEU
MILLER
MILLET
MIMOSA
MINDED
MINGLE
MINION
MINNOW
MINUET
MINUTE
MIRAGE
MIRROR
MISCUE
MISERY
MISFIT
MISHAP
MISLAY
MISSAL
MISTER
MISUSE
MITTEN
MIZZEN
NIACIN
NIBBLE
NICETY
NICKEL
NICKER
NIMBLE
NIMBUS
NIMROD
NINETY
NIPPER
NIPPLE
NITRIC
NITWIT
PIAZZA
PICKAX
PICKET
PICKLE
PICKUP
PICNIC
PIDDLE
PIDGIN
PIERCE
PIFFLE
PIGEON
PIGLET
PIGNUT
PIGPEN
PIGSTY
PILFER
PILING
PILLAR
PILLOW
PIMPLE
PINCER
PINEAL
PINION
PINKIE
PIPING
PIPKIN
PIPPIN
PIQUET
PIRACY
PIRATE
PISTIL
PISTOL
PISTON
QINTAR
QIVIUT
RIBALD
RIBAND
RIBBON
RICHES
RIDDEN
RIDDLE
RIGGER
RINGER
RIPPLE
RIPSAW
RISQUE
RITUAL
SICKEN
SICKLE
SIDING
SIERRA
SIESTA
SIGILL
SIGNAL
SIGNET
SILAGE
SILENT
SILICA
SILVER
SIMIAN
SIMILE
SIMMER
SIMONY
SIMPER
SIMPLE
SINFUL
SINGLE
SINKER
SIPHON
SISTER
SIZZLE
TICKER
TICKET
TICKLE
TIDBIT
TIFFIN
TIGHTS
TILLER
TIMBER
TIMBRE
TIMELY
TINDER
TINGLE
TINKER
TINKLE
TINSEL
TIPPET
TIPPLE
TIPTOE
TIRADE
TISSUE
TITBIT
TITLED
TITTER
TITTLE
VIABLE
VICTIM
VICTOR
VICUNA
VIKING
VILIFY
VILLUS
VINOUS
VIOLET
VIOLIN
VIRAGO
VIRGIN
VIRILE
VIRION
VIRTUE
VISAGE
VISCID
VISCUS
VISION
VISUAL
VITALS
VIVACE
VIVIFY
VIZARD
VIZIER
WICKED
WICKER
WICKET
WIENER
WIGGLE
WIGGLY
WIGLET
WIGWAG
WIGWAM
WILLOW
WIMBLE
WIMPLE
WINDER
WINDOW
WINDUP
WINGED
WINKER
WINKLE
WINNER
WINNOW
WINTER
WINTRY
WIRING
WISDOM
WITHAL
WITHER
WITHIN
WITTED
WIZARD
ZIGZAG
ZINNIA
ZIPPER

ZIRCON
ZITHER
OJIBWA
AKIMBO
SKETCH
SKEWER
SKIMPY
SKINNY
SKYCAP
ALBEIT
ALBINO
ALCOVE
ALIGHT
ALKALI
ALLEGE
ALLIED
ALLUDE
ALLURE
ALMOND
ALMOST
ALPACA
ALPINE
ALTAIR
ALUMNA
ALWAYS
BLANCH
BLAZER
BLAZON
BLEACH
BLEARY
BLENCH
BLIGHT
BLITHE
BLOTCH
BLOUSE
BLOWSY
BLOWUP
BLUING
BLUISH
CLAMMY
CLAMOR
CLAQUE
CLARET
CLASSY
CLAUSE
CLEAVE
CLENCH
CLERGY
CLERIC
CLEVER
CLEVIS
CLICHE
CLIENT
CLIMAX
CLINCH
CLINIC
CLIQUE

CLOCHE
CLOSET
CLOTHE
CLOVEN
CLOVER
CLUMSY
CLUTCH
ELAPSE
ELDEST
ELEVEN
ELICIT
ELIXIR
FLABBY
FLACON
FLAGON
FLANGE
FLASHY
FLATUS
FLAUNT
FLAVOR
FLAXEN
FLEECE
FLESHY
FLIGHT
FLIMSY
FLINCH
FLITCH
FLOOZY
FLOPPY
FLORAL
FLORID
FLORIN
FLOSSY
FLOWER
FLUENT
FLUFFY
FLUNKY
FLURRY
FLYWAY
GLANCE
GLIDER
GLITCH
GLOBAL
GLOSSY
GLOWER
GLUTEN
ILLUME
ILLUST
KLATCH
PLACER
PLACID
PLAGUE
PLAINT
PLANET
PLAQUE
PLASMA
PLATEN

PLEASE
PLEDGE
PLENTY
PLENUM
PLEXUS
PLIANT
PLIERS
PLIGHT
PLINTH
PLOVER
PLUCKY
PLUNGE
PLURAL
PLUTON
RLOGIN
SLALOM
SLAVER
SLAVIC
SLEAZY
SLEDGE
SLEEPY
SLEEVE
SLEIGH
SLEUTH
SLIDER
SLIEST
SLIGHT
SLIPUP
SLIVER
SLOGAN
SLOPPY
SLOUCH
SLOUGH
SLOVEN
SLUDGE
SLUICE
SLURRY
ULLAGE
ULSTER
ULTIMO
ULTRIX
AMAZON
AMBUSH
AMENDS
AMERCE
AMOEBA
AMORAL
AMOUNT
AMPERE
AMULET
AMVETS
EMBALM
EMBANK
EMBARK
EMBLEM
EMBODY
EMBOSS

EMBRYO
EMERGE
EMETIC
EMIGRE
EMPIRE
EMPLOY
IMBIBE
IMBRUE
IMMUNE
IMMURE
IMPACT
IMPAIR
IMPALA
IMPALE
IMPART
IMPEDE
IMPEND
IMPERF
IMPISH
IMPORT
IMPOSE
IMPOST
IMPUGN
IMPURE
IMPUTE
OMELET
SMILAX
SMIRCH
SMITHY
SMOOCH
SMOOTH
SMUDGE
SMUTCH
UMPIRE
XMODEM
YMODEM
ZMODEM
ANADEM
ANALOG
ANCHOR
ANEMIA
ANGINA
ANGORA
ANIMAL
ANIMUS
ANKLET
ANNALS
ANNEAL
ANNUAL
ANOINT
ANSWER
ANTHEM
ANTHER
ANTLER
ANTRUM
ANYHOW
ANYONE

ANYWAY
ENABLE
ENAMEL
ENAMOR
ENCAMP
ENCASE
ENCODE
ENCORE
ENCYST
ENDEAR
ENDING
ENDIVE
ENDRIN
ENDURE
ENDURO
ENERGY
ENFOLD
ENGAGE
ENGINE
ENGRAM
ENGULF
ENIGMA
ENISLE
ENJOIN
ENLIST
ENMESH
ENMITY
ENOUGH
ENRAGE
ENRICH
ENROLL
ENSIGN
ENSILE
ENSURE
ENTAIL
ENTICE
ENTIRE
ENTITY
ENTOMB
ENTRAP
ENTREE
ENZYME
GNEISS
INBORN
INBRED
INCASE
INCEST
INCISE
INCITE
INCOME
INDEED
INDENT
INDIAN
INDICT
INDIGO
INDITE
INDIUM

INDOOR
INDUCE
INDUCT
INFAMY
INFANT
INFECT
INFEST
INFIRM
INFLOW
INFLUX
INFOLD
INFORM
INFUSE
INGEST
INHALE
INHERE
INHUME
INJECT
INJURE
INJURY
INKJET
INLAID
INLAND
INMATE
INMOST
INNATE
INNING
INROAD
INRUSH
INSANE
INSEAM
INSECT
INSERT
INSIDE
INSIST
INSOLE
INSTEP
INSULT
INSURE
INTACT
INTAKE
INTEND
INTENT
INTERJ
INTERN
INTONE
INTROD
INTUIT
INVADE
INVENT
INVERT
INVEST
INVITE
INVOKE
INWARD
KNIGHT
ONEIDA

ONRUSH
ONWARD
SNATCH
SNEEZE
SNIPPY
SNITCH
SNIVEL
SNOBOL
SNOOTY
SNOOZE
UNABLE
UNBEND
UNBIND
UNBOLT
UNBORN
UNCIAL
UNCLAD
UNCLOG
UNCOIL
UNCORK
UNCURL
UNDIES
UNDULY
UNEASY
UNESCO
UNEVEN
UNFAIR
UNFOLD
UNFURL
UNGIRD
UNHAND
UNHOLY
UNHOOK
UNICEF
UNIQUE
UNISEX
UNISON
UNITED
UNJUST
UNKIND
UNLACE
UNLADE
UNLESS
UNLIKE
UNLOAD
UNLOCK
UNMASK
UNMEET
UNMOOR
UNPACK
UNPILE
UNPLUG
UNREAD
UNREAL
UNREEL
UNREST
UNRIPE

UNROBE
UNROLL
UNROOF
UNRULY
UNSEAL
UNSEAT
UNSHIP
UNSHOD
UNSNAP
UNSTOP
UNSUNG
UNTOLD
UNTRUE
UNTUNE
UNUSED
UNVEIL
UNWELL
UNWEPT
UNWIND
UNWISE
UNWRAP
UNYOKE
BOATER
BOBBIN
BOBBLE
BOBCAT
BOCCIE
BODICE
BODILY
BODKIN
BOGGLE
BOILER
BOLERO
BOMBER
BONBON
BONITO
BONNET
BONSAI
BOODLE
BOOKIE
BOOTEE
BORATE
BORDER
BOREAL
BORROW
BOTANY
BOTHER
BOTTLE
BOTTOM
BOUGHT
BOUNCE
BOUNTY
BOURSE
BOVINE
BOWLEG
BOWLER
BOWMAN

BOXCAR
BOXING
COARSE
COBALT
COBBLE
COBWEB
COCCUS
COCCYX
COCKLE
COCOON
CODDLE
CODGER
CODIFY
COERCE
COEVAL
COFFEE
COFFER
COFFIN
COGENT
COGNAC
COHEIR
COHERE
COHORT
COITUS
COLLAR
COLLAT
COLLIE
COLLOQ
COLONY
COLUMN
COMBAT
COMBER
COMDEX
COMEDY
COMELY
COMFIT
COMING
COMITY
COMMIT
COMMON
COMPAQ
COMPAR
COMPEL
COMPLY
CONCUR
CONDOM
CONDOR
CONFAB
CONFED
CONFER
CONSOL
CONSTR
CONSUL
CONVEX
CONVEY
CONVOY
COOKIE

COOLER
COOLIE
COOPER
COOTIE
COPIER
COPING
COPPER
COPTER
COPULA
COQUET
CORBEL
CORDON
CORNEA
CORNER
CORNET
CORONA
CORPSE
CORPUS
CORRAL
CORSET
CORTEX
CORYZA
COSINE
COSMIC
COSMOS
COSTLY
COTTER
COTTON
COUGAR
COULEE
COUNTY
COUPLE
COUPON
COURSE
COUSIN
COVERT
COWARD
COWBOY
COWMAN
COWPOX
COYOTE
DOBBIN
DOCENT
DOCILE
DOCKET
DOCTOR
DODDER
DOGGED
DOGLEG
DOINGS
DOLLAR
DOLLOP
DOLMEN
DOMAIN
DOMINO
DONATE
DONKEY

DOODAD
DOODLE
DOPANT
DORMER
DORSAL
DOTAGE
DOTARD
DOTTLE
DOUBLE
DOUBLY
DOUCHE
DOWNER
EOLIAN
FODDER
FOEMAN
FOETAL
FOIBLE
FOLDER
FOLKSY
FOLLOW
FOMENT
FONDLE
FONDUE
FOOTED
FORAGE
FORBID
FOREGO
FOREST
FORGET
FORINT
FORKED
FORMAL
FORMAT
FORMER
FOSSIL
FOSTER
FOUGHT
FOURTH
GOALIE
GOATEE
GOBBET
GOBBLE
GOBLET
GOBLIN
GODSON
GOGGLE
GOITER
GOLDEN
GOOBER
GOODLY
GOPHER
GOSPEL
GOSSIP
GOTHIC
GOTTEN
GOURDE
GOVERN

HOAGIE
HOARSE
HOBBLE
HOBNOB
HOCKEY
HOLDUP
HOLLER
HOLLOW
HOMAGE
HOMELY
HOMILY
HOMINY
HONEST
HONOUR
HOODOO
HOOKAH
HOOKER
HOOKUP
HOOPLA
HOPPER
HORNET
HORRID
HORROR
HORSEY
HOSTEL
HOTBED
HOTBOX
HOWDAH
HOWLER
HOYDEN
IODIDE
IODINE
IODIZE
IONIZE
JOBBER
JOCKEY
JOCOSE
JOCUND
JOGGLE
JOHNNY
JOINER
JOSTLE
JOUNCE
JOVIAL
JOYFUL
JOYOUS
KOBOLD
KOPECK
KOREAN
KORUNA
KOSHER
KOWTOW
LOADED
LOADER
LOATHE
LOBULE
LOCALE

LOCATE
LOCKER
LOCKET
LOCKUP
LOCUST
LODGER
LOGGIA
LOGJAM
LOITER
LONELY
LOOPER
LOOSEN
LORDLY
LOTION
LOUNGE
LOUVER
LOVELY
LOVING
LOWERY
MOBILE
MODERN
MODEST
MODIFY
MODISH
MODULE
MOHAIR
MOHAWK
MOIETY
MOLDER
MOLEST
MOLTEN
MOMENT
MONDAY
MONGER
MONISM
MONKEY
MONODY
MOPPET
MORALE
MORBID
MORGAN
MORGUE
MORMON
MOROSE
MORRIS
MORROW
MORSEL
MORTAL
MORTAR
MOSAIC
MOSLEM
MOSQUE
MOSTLY
MOTHER
MOTILE
MOTION
MOTIVE

MOTLEY
MOTTLE
MOUSER
MOUSSE
MOUTON
NOBODY
NODDLE
NODULE
NOGGIN
NONAGE
NONCOM
NONFAT
NOODLE
NORDIC
NORMAL
NORMAN
NORTON
NOTICE
NOTIFY
NOTION
NOUGAT
NOUGHT
NOVELL
NOVENA
NOVICE
NOWISE
NOZZLE
OODLES
OOLITE
POCKET
PODIUM
POETRY
POGROM
POISON
POLDER
POLEAX
POLICE
POLICY
POLISH
POLITE
POLITY
POLLEN
POMADE
POMMEL
POMPON
PONCHO
PONDER
PONGEE
POODLE
POPGUN
POPLAR
POPLIN
POPPER
PORKER
POROUS
PORTAL
PORTER

PORTLY
POSEUR
POSSUM
POSTAL
POSTER
POTAGE
POTASH
POTATO
POTBOY
POTEEN
POTENT
POTHER
POTION
POTPIE
POTTER
POUNCE
POWDER
POWWOW
ROBBER
ROBUST
ROCKER
ROCKET
RODENT
ROLLER
ROMANO
ROMPER
ROOKIE
ROSARY
ROSTER
ROTARY
ROTATE
ROTTEN
ROTUND
ROUBLE
SOCCER
SOCIAL
SOCIOL
SOCKET
SODDEN
SODIUM
SODOMY
SOEVER
SOFTEN
SOIGNE
SOIREE
SOLACE
SOLDER
SOLEMN
SOMBER
SONATA
SONNET
SOOTHE
SORDID
SORREL
SORROW
SORTIE
SOUGHT

SOURCE
SOVIET
TOCSIN
TODDLE
TOFFEE
TOGGLE
TOILET
TOMATO
TOMBOY
TOMCAT
TOMTIT
TONGUE
TONSIL
TOOTHY
TOPPLE
TORERO
TORPID
TORPOR
TORQUE
TORRID
TOTTER
TOUCAN
TOUCHE
TOUCHY
TOUPEE
TOUSLE
TOWARD
TOWHEE
VOICED
VOLLEY
VOLUME
VOLUTE
VOODOO
VORTEX
VOTARY
VOTIVE
VOYAGE
VOYEUR
WOBBLE
WOEFUL
WOMBAT
WONDER
WONTED
WOODED
WOODEN
WOODSY
WOOFER
WOOLEN
WOOLLY
WORKER
WORSEN
WORTHY
YOGURT
YONDER
ZODIAC
ZOMBIE
ZONKED

ZOUAVE
ZOUNDS
ZOYSIA
APACHE
APATHY
APERCU
APIARY
APICAL
APIECE
APLOMB
APOGEE
APPALL
APPEAL
APPEAR
APPEND
APPLET
APPROX
IPECAC
OPAQUE
OPIATE
OPPOSE
OPTICS
OPTION
SPADIX
SPARSE
SPATHE
SPAVIN
SPECIE
SPECIF
SPEECH
SPHERE
SPHINX
SPIDER
SPIGOT
SPINAL
SPINEL
SPINET
SPIRAL
SPIREA
SPIRIT
SPLASH
SPLEEN
SPLICE
SPLINE
SPLINT
SPOKEN
SPONGE
SPOTTY
SPOUSE
SPRAIN
SPRAWL
SPREAD
SPRING
SPRINT
SPRITE
SPROUT
SPRUCE

SPRUNG
SPURGE
SPUTUM
UPBEAT
UPDATE
UPHILL
UPHOLD
UPKEEP
UPLAND
UPLIFT
UPLOAD
UPMOST
UPPISH
UPPITY
UPREAR
UPROAR
UPROOT
UPRUSH
UPSHOT
UPSIDE
UPTAKE
UPTOWN
UPTURN
UPWARD
UPWELL
UPWIND
EQUATE
EQUINE
EQUITY
SQUALL
SQUARE
SQUASH
SQUAWK
SQUEAK
SQUEAL
SQUINT
SQUIRE
SQUIRM
SQUIRT
ARABIC
ARABLE
ARCADE
ARCANE
ARCCOS
ARCHON
ARCNET
ARCSIN
ARCTAN
ARCTIC
ARDENT
ARGENT
ARGOSY
ARGYLE
ARIGHT
ARMADA
ARMFUL
ARMLET

ARMORY
ARMPIT
ARNICA
AROUND
AROUSE
ARRANT
ARREST
ARRIVE
ARROYO
ARTERY
ARTFUL
ARTIST
BRAISE
BRANCH
BRANDY
BRAZEN
BREACH
BREAST
BREATH
BREECH
BREEZE
BREVET
BRIDAL
BRIDGE
BRIDLE
BRIGHT
BRITON
BROACH
BROGAN
BROGUE
BROKEN
BROKER
BRONCO
BRONZE
BROOCH
BROWSE
BRUISE
BRUNCH
BRUNET
BRUTAL
CRABBY
CRADLE
CRAFTY
CRANKY
CRANNY
CRATER
CRATON
CRAVAT
CRAVEN
CRAYON
CREASE
CREATE
CRECHE
CREDIT
CREEPY
CREOLE
CRETIN

CREWEL
CRINGE
CRISIS
CRITIC
CROCUS
CROTCH
CROUCH
CRUISE
CRUMMY
CRUNCH
CRUTCH
DRAFTY
DRAGON
DRAPER
DRAWER
DREARY
DREDGE
DRENCH
DRESSY
DRIVEL
DRIVER
DROGUE
DROPSY
DROVER
DROWSE
DROWSY
DRUDGE
ERBIUM
ERMINE
EROTIC
ERRAND
ERRANT
ERRATA
ERSATZ
FRACAS
FRAPPE
FREEZE
FRENCH
FRENZY
FRESCO
FRIARY
FRIDAY
FRIEND
FRIEZE
FRIGHT
FRIGID
FRINGE
FRISKY
FROLIC
FROWSY
FROZEN
FRUGAL
FRUITY
FRUMPY
GRABEN
GRADER
GRAINY

GRANGE
GRATIS
GRAVEL
GRAVID
GRAYED
GREASE
GRIEVE
GRILLE
GRIPPE
GRISLY
GROCER
GROGGY
GROOVE
GROOVY
GROTTO
GROUCH
GROUND
GROUSE
GROVEL
GROWTH
GRUBBY
GRUDGE
GRUMPY
IRENIC
IRONIC
IRRUPT
ORACLE
ORANGE
ORATOR
ORCHID
ORDAIN
ORDEAL
ORDURE
ORGASM
ORIENT
ORIGIN
ORIOLE
ORISON
ORMOLU
ORNATE
ORNERY
ORNITH
ORPHAN
PRAISE
PRANCE
PRAYER
PREACH
PRECIS
PREFAB
PREFER
PREFIX
PRELIM
PREMED
PREMIX
PREPAY
PRESET
PRESTO

PRETTY
PREWAR
PRIEST
PRIMAL
PRIMER
PRINCE
PRINTF
PRIORY
PRISON
PRISSY
PRIVET
PROFIT
PROLIX
PROLOG
PROMPT
PRONTO
PROPEL
PROPER
PROTON
TRADER
TRAGIC
TRANCE
TRANSL
TRANSP
TRAUMA
TRAVEL
TREATY
TREBLE
TREMOR
TRENCH
TREPAN
TRIAGE
TRICKY
TRIFLE
TRIODE
TRIPLE
TRIPLY
TRIPOD
TRITON
TRIUNE
TRIVET
TRIVIA
TROCHE
TROIKA
TROJAN
TROPHY
TROPIC
TROUGH
TROUPE
TROWEL
TRUANT
TRUDGE
TRUISM
TRUSTY
TRYING
URACIL
URANIC

URANUS
URBANE
URCHIN
UREMIA
URETER
URGENT
URINAL
URSINE
WRAITH
WRASSE
WREATH
WRENCH
WRETCH
WRITER
WRITHE
ASCEND
ASCENT
ASHLAR
ASHORE
ASHRAM
ASLANT
ASLEEP
ASPECT
ASPIRE
ASSAIL
ASSENT
ASSERT
ASSESS
ASSIGN
ASSIST
ASSIZE
ASSORT
ASSUME
ASSURE
ASTERN
ASTHMA
ASTRAL
ASTRAY
ASTROL
ASTRON
ASTUTE
ASYLUM
ESCAPE
ESCHEW
ESCORT
ESCROW
ESCUDO
ESKIMO
ESPRIT
ESTATE
ESTEEM
ISLAND
ISOBAR
ISOMER
MSCDEX
OSMIUM
OSPREY

OSSIFY
OSTLER
PSEUDO
PSYCHE
PSYCHO
TSETSE
USABLE
USEFUL
USENET
USURER
ATOMIC
ATONAL
ATRIUM
ATTACH
ATTACK
ATTAIN
ATTEND
ATTEST
ATTIRE
ATTRIB
ATTUNE
ETHANE
ETHICS
ETHNIC
ETHNOL
ITALIC
ITSELF
OTIOSE
OTTAWA
STABLE
STAMEN
STANCE
STANCH
STANZA
STAPES
STAPLE
STARCH
STARVE
STATIC
STATUE
STATUS
STAVES
STEADY
STENCH
STEPPE
STEREO
STICKY
STIFLE
STIGMA
STINGY
STITCH
STOCKY
STODGY
STOLEN
STOLID
STOLON
STONED

STOOGE
STRAFE
STRAIN
STRAIT
STRAND
STREAK
STREAM
STREET
STRESS
STRICT
STRIDE
STRIFE
STRIKE
STRING
STRIPE
STRIVE
STROBE
STRODE
STROKE
STROLL
STRONG
STROVE
STRUCK
STRUNG
STUBBY
STUCCO
STUDIO
STUFFY
STUPID
STUPOR
STURDY
STYLUS
STYMIE
UTERUS
UTMOST
UTOPIA
AUBURN
AUGURY
AUGUST
AURORA
AUTHOR
AUTISM
AUTUMN
BUBBLE
BUCKET
BUCKLE
BUDGET
BUDGIE
BUFFER
BUFFET
BULBUL
BULLET
BUMMER
BUMPER
BUNDLE
BUNGLE
BUNION

BUNKER
BUNKUM
BUQSHA
BURDEN
BUREAU
BURGEE
BURGLE
BURIAL
BURLAP
BURNER
BURROW
BURSAR
BUSBOY
BUSHED
BUSHEL
BUSILY
BUSKIN
BUSTLE
BUTANE
BUTLER
BUTTER
BUTTON
BUZZER
CUBISM
CUCKOO
CUDDLE
CUDGEL
CUESTA
CUMBER
CUNNER
CUPOLA
CURATE
CURDLE
CURFEW
CURIUM
CURLEW
CURSOR
CURTSY
CURVET
CUSPID
CUSTOM
CUTLER
CUTLET
CUTOFF
CUTOUT
CUTTER
DUBBIN
DUENDE
DUENNA
DUFFER
DUGOUT
DULCET
DUMDUM
DUPLEX
DURESS
DURING
DUSTER

EUCHRE
EULOGY
EUNUCH
EUREKA
FUDDLE
FUHRER
FUMBLE
FUNGUS
FUNNEL
FURORE
FURROW
FUSION
FUTILE
FUTURE
GUFFAW
GUIDON
GUILTY
GUINEA
GUITAR
GULDEN
GULLET
GUNMAN
GUNNER
GURGLE
GURKHA
GUSHER
GUSSET
GUTTER
GUZZLE
HUBBUB
HUBCAP
HUBRIS
HUDDLE
HUMANE
HUMBLE
HUMBUG
HUMOUR
HUNGER
HUNKER
HURDLE
HURRAH
HURTLE
HUSSAR
HUSTLE
HUZZAH
JUDAIC
JUGGLE
JUICER
JUJUBE
JUMBLE
JUMPER
JUNGLE
JUNIOR
JUNKER
JUNKET
JUNKIE
JURIST

LUBBER
LUCENT
LUMBAR
LUMBER
LUMMOX
LUNACY
LUPINE
LUSTER
LUXURY
MUDDLE
MUFFIN
MUFFLE
MUKLUK
MULLET
MUMBLE
MUMMER
MURDER
MURMUR
MUSCLE
MUSEUM
MUSKEG
MUSKET
MUSLIM
MUSLIN
MUSSEL
MUSTER
MUTANT
MUTATE
MUTINY
MUTTER
MUTTON
MUTUAL
MUUMUU
MUZZLE
NUANCE
NUBBIN
NUBBLE
NUBILE
NUDISM
NUGGET
NUMBER
NUNCIO
NUTMEG
NUTRIA
NUZZLE
OUSTER
OUTBID
OUTCRY
OUTFIT
OUTFOX
OUTGUN
OUTING
OUTLAW
OUTLAY
OUTLET
OUTPUT
OUTRUN

OUTSET
OUTWIT
PUBLIC
PUCKER
PUDDLE
PUEBLO
PUFFIN
PULLET
PULLEY
PULPIT
PULSAR
PUMICE
PUMMEL
PUNDIT
PUNISH
PUNKIN
PUPPET
PURDAH
PURIFY
PURINE
PURISM
PURITY
PURPLE
PURSER
PURSUE
PURVEY
PUSHER
PUTOUT
PUTRID
PUTSCH
PUTTEE
PUTTER
PUZZLE
QUAHOG
QUAINT
QUAKER
QUARRY
QUARTO
QUARTZ
QUASAR
QUAVER
QUEASY
QUENCH
QUINCE
QUINSY
QUIVER
QUORUM
RUBBER
RUBBLE
RUBRIC
RUCKUS
RUDDER
RUFFLE
RUGGED
RUMBLE
RUMPLE
RUMPUS

RUNLET
RUNNEL
RUNNER
RUNOFF
RUNWAY
RUPIAH
RUSSET
RUSTIC
RUSTLE
SUBDUE
SUBLET
SUBMIT
SUBORN
SUBSET
SUBTLE
SUBURB
SUBWAY
SUCCOR
SUCKER
SUCKLE
SUDDEN
SUFFER
SUFFIX
SUITOR
SULFUR
SULLEN
SULTAN
SULTRY
SUMMER
SUMMIT
SUMMON
SUNDAE
SUNDAY
SUNDER
SUNDRY
SUNKEN
SUNLIT
SUNSET
SUNTAN
SUPERB
SUPINE
SUPPER
SUPPLE
SUPPLY
SURETY
SURREY
SURTAX
SURVEY
SUTURE
TUBING
TUBULE
TUCKER
TUGRIK
TUMBLE
TUMULT
TUNDRA
TUNNEL

TURBAN
TURBID
TURBOT
TUREEN
TURGID
TURING
TURKEY
TURNER
TURNIP
TURRET
TURTLE
TURVES
TUSKER
TUSSLE
TUXEDO
VULGAR
AVATAR
AVAUNT
AVENGE
AVENUE
AVERSE
AVIARY
AVOCET
AVOUCH
EVINCE
EVOLVE
OVERDO
OVERLY
SVELTE
AWAKEN
AWEARY
AWEIGH
AWHILE
AWHIRL
AWNING
KWACHA
SWATCH
SWATHE
SWERVE
SWITCH
SWIVEL
TWEEDY
TWELVE
TWENTY
TWINGE
TWITCH
EXCEED
EXCEPT
EXCESS
EXCISE
EXCITE
EXCUSE
EXEMPT
EXHALE
EXHORT
EXHUME
EXODUS
EXOTIC
EXPAND
EXPECT
EXPEND
EXPERT
EXPIRE
EXPORT
EXPOSE
EXTANT
EXTEND
EXTENT
EXTERN
EXTORT
OXFORD
OXYGEN
BYGONE
BYPASS
BYPATH
BYPLAY
BYWORD
CYGNET
CYMBAL
DYBBUK
DYNAMO
EYELET
EYELID
GYPSUM
GYRATE
HYAENA
HYBRID
HYPHEN
HYSSOP
LYCEUM
MYOPIA
MYRIAD
MYRTLE
MYSELF
MYSTIC
OYSTER
PYRITE
PYTHON
SYLVAN
SYMBOL
SYNTAX
SYPHON
SYSTEM
TYCOON
TYPHUS
TYPIFY
TYPIST
TYRANT
ZYGOTE
AZALEA

## 3RD LETTER

ABACUS
ABATIS
ACACIA
ADAGIO
AMAZON
ANADEM
ANALOG
APACHE
APATHY
ARABIC
ARABLE
AVATAR
AVAUNT
AWAKEN
AZALEA
BEACON
BEADLE
BEAGLE
BEAKER
BEANIE
BEAUTY
BEAVER
BLANCH
BLAZER
BLAZON
BOATER
BRAISE
BRANCH
BRANDY
BRAZEN
CHAFER
CHAISE
CHALET
CHANCE
CHANCY
CHANGE
CHAPEL
CHARGE
CHASER
CHASTE
CHATTY
CHAUNT
CLAMMY
CLAMOR
CLAQUE
CLARET
CLASSY
CLAUSE
COARSE
CRABBY
CRADLE
CRAFTY
CRANKY
CRANNY
CRATER
CRATON
CRAVAT
CRAVEN
CRAYON
DEACON
DEADEN
DEADLY
DEAFEN
DEARTH
DIADEM
DIAPER
DIATOM
DRAFTY
DRAGON
DRAPER
DRAWER
ELAPSE
ENABLE
ENAMEL
ENAMOR
FEALTY
FIANCE
FIASCO
FLABBY
FLACON
FLAGON
FLANGE
FLASHY
FLATUS
FLAUNT
FLAVOR
FLAXEN
FRACAS
FRAPPE
GLANCE
GOALIE
GOATEE
GRABEN
GRADER
GRAINY
GRANGE
GRATIS
GRAVEL
GRAVID
GRAYED
HEALTH
HEARSE
HEARTH
HEARTY
HEAVEN
HIATUS
HOAGIE
HOARSE
HYAENA
ITALIC
KLATCH
KWACHA
LEADEN
LEADER
LEAFED
LEAGUE
LEAVED
LEAVEN
LEAVES
LIABLE
LOADED
LOADER
LOATHE
MEADOW
MEAGER
MEASLY
MIASMA
NEARBY
NIACIN
NUANCE
OPAQUE
ORACLE
ORANGE
ORATOR
PEAHEN
PEAKED
PEANUT
PHAROS
PIAZZA
PLACER
PLACID
PLAGUE
PLAINT
PLANET
PLAQUE
PLASMA
PLATEN
PRAISE
PRANCE
PRAYER
QBASIC
QUAHOG
QUAINT
QUAKER
QUARRY
QUARTO
QUARTZ
QUASAR
QUAVER
REALLY
REALTY
REAMER
REASON
SCAMPI
SCANTY
SCARAB
SCARCE
SEABED
SEALER
SEAMAN
SEANCE
SEARCH
SEASON
SEAWAY
SHABBY
SHADOW
SHAGGY
SHAKER
SHAMAN
SHANTY
SHAVER
SHAVES
SLALOM
SLAVER
SLAVIC
SNATCH
SPADIX
SPARSE
SPATHE
SPAVIN
STABLE
STAMEN
STANCE
STANCH
STANZA
STAPES
STAPLE
STARCH
STARVE
STATIC
STATUE
STATUS
STAVES
SWATCH
SWATHE
TEACUP
TEAPOT
TEASEL
THANKS
THATCH
TRADER
TRAGIC
TRANCE
TRANSL
TRANSP
TRAUMA
TRAVEL
UNABLE
URACIL
URANIC
URANUS
USABLE
VIABLE
WEAKEN
WEAKLY
WEALTH
WEAPON
WEASEL
WHALER
WHAMMY
WRAITH
WRASSE
YEARLY
YEASTY
ZEALOT
ABBACY
ABBESS
ALBEIT
ALBINO
AMBUSH
AUBURN
BABBLE
BABOON
BOBBIN
BOBBLE
BOBCAT
BUBBLE
CABALA
CABANA
COBALT
COBBLE
COBWEB
CUBISM
DABBLE
DEBARK
DEBASE
DEBATE
DEBRIS
DEBTOR
DEBUNK
DIBBLE
DOBBIN
DUBBIN
DYBBUK
EMBALM
EMBANK
EMBARK
EMBLEM
EMBODY
EMBOSS
EMBRYO
ERBIUM
FABIAN
FABLED
FABRIC
FIBRIL
FIBRIN
FIBULA
GABBLE
GABBRO
GIBBER
GIBBET
GIBBON
GIBSON
GOBBET
GOBBLE
GOBLET
GOBLIN
HEBREW
HOBBLE
HOBNOB
HUBBUB
HUBCAP
HUBRIS
HYBRID
IMBIBE
IMBRUE
INBORN
INBRED
JABBER
JOBBER
KABUKI
KIBBLE
KIBOSH
KOBOLD
LABIAL
LABILE
LABIUM
LABOUR
LIBIDO
LIBYAN
LOBULE
LUBBER
MOBILE
NEBULA
NIBBLE
NOBODY
NUBBIN
NUBBLE
NUBILE
PEBBLE
PUBLIC
RABBET
RABBIT
RABBLE
RABIES
REBATE
REBORN
REBUFF
REBUKE
RIBALD
RIBAND
RIBBON
ROBBER
ROBUST
RUBBER
RUBBLE
RUBRIC
SUBDUE
SUBLET
SUBMIT
SUBORN
SUBSET
SUBTLE
SUBURB
SUBWAY
TABLET
TUBING
TUBULE
UNBEND
UNBIND
UNBOLT
UNBORN
UPBEAT
URBANE
WABBLE
WEBBED
WOBBLE
ACCEDE
ACCENT
ACCEPT
ACCESS
ACCORD
ACCOST
ACCRUE
ACCUSE
ALCOVE
ANCHOR
ARCADE
ARCANE
ARCCOS
ARCHON
ARCNET
ARCSIN
ARCTAN
ARCTIC
ASCEND
ASCENT
BACKER
BACKUP
BECALM
BECKON
BECOME
BICEPS
BICKER
BOCCIE
BUCKET
BUCKLE
CACHET
CACKLE
CACTUS
CICADA
COCCUS
COCCYX
COCKLE
COCOON
CUCKOO
DACTYL
DECADE
DECAMP
DECANT
DECEIT
DECENT
DECIDE
DECODE
DECREE
DICKER
DICKEY
DICTUM
DOCENT
DOCILE
DOCKET
DOCTOR
EBCDIC
ECCLES
ECCLUS
ENCAMP
ENCASE
ENCODE
ENCORE
ENCYST
ESCAPE
ESCHEW
ESCORT
ESCROW
ESCUDO
EUCHRE
EXCEED
EXCEPT
EXCESS
EXCISE
EXCITE
EXCUSE
FACADE
FACIAL
FACILE
FACING
FACTOR
FACULA
FECUND
FICKLE
HACKER
HACKIE
HACKLE
HECKLE
HECTIC
HECTOR
HICCUP
HOCKEY
INCASE
INCEST
INCISE
INCITE
INCOME

JACKAL
JACKET
JOCKEY
JOCOSE
JOCUND
LACKEY
LACTIC
LACUNA
LECTOR
LICHEE
LICHEN
LOCALE
LOCATE
LOCKER
LOCKET
LOCKUP
LOCUST
LUCENT
LYCEUM
MACAPP
MACRON
MICMAC
MICRON
MSCDEX
NECTAR
NICETY
NICKEL
NICKER
OCCULT
OCCUPY
ORCHID
PACIFY
PACKER
PACKET
PECTIN
PICKAX
PICKET
PICKLE
PICKUP
PICNIC
POCKET
PUCKER
RACEME
RACISM
RACKET
RECALL
RECANT
RECEDE
RECENT
RECESS
RECIPE
RECITE
RECKON
RECOIL
RECORD
RECOUP
RECTAL
RECTOR
RECTUM
RICHES
ROCKER
ROCKET
RUCKUS
SACHEM
SACHET
SACRED
SACRUM
SECEDE
SECOND
SECRET
SECTOR
SECURE
SICKEN
SICKLE
SOCCER
SOCIAL
SOCIOL
SOCKET
SUCCOR
SUCKER
SUCKLE
TACKLE
TACTIC
TICKER
TICKET
TICKLE
TOCSIN
TUCKER
TYCOON
UNCIAL
UNCLAD
UNCLOG
UNCOIL
UNCORK
UNCURL
URCHIN
VACANT
VACATE
VACUUM
VECTOR
VICTIM
VICTOR
VICUNA
WICKED
WICKER
WICKET
ABDUCT
ADDEND
ADDICT
ADDUCE
AIDMAN
ARDENT
BADGER
BEDAUB
BEDBUG
BEDECK
BEDLAM
BEDPAN
BODICE
BODILY
BODKIN
BUDGET
BUDGIE
CADDIE
CODDLE
CODGER
CODIFY
CUDDLE
CUDGEL
DEDUCE
DEDUCT
DODDER
ELDEST
ENDEAR
ENDING
ENDIVE
ENDRIN
ENDURE
ENDURO
FEDORA
FIDDLE
FIDGET
FODDER
FUDDLE
GADFLY
GADGET
GODSON
HUDDLE
INDEED
INDENT
INDIAN
INDICT
INDIGO
INDITE
INDIUM
INDOOR
INDUCE
INDUCT
IODIDE
IODINE
IODIZE
JUDAIC
KIDNAP
KIDNEY
LADDER
LADDIE
LADING
LEDGER
LODGER
MADAME
MADCAP
MADDEN
MADDER
MADMAN
MADRAS
MEDDLE
MEDIAL
MEDIAN
MEDICO
MEDIUM
MEDLEY
MIDAIR
MIDDAY
MIDDEN
MIDDLE
MIDGET
MIDWAY
MODERN
MODEST
MODIFY
MODISH
MODULE
MUDDLE
NODDLE
NODULE
NUDISM
ODDITY
OODLES
ORDAIN
ORDEAL
ORDURE
PADDLE
PEDANT
PEDDLE
PIDDLE
PIDGIN
PODIUM
PUDDLE
RADIAL
RADIAN
RADISH
RADIUM
RADIUS
REDACT
REDCAP
REDDEN
REDEEM
REDUCE
RIDDEN
RIDDLE
RODENT
RUDDER
SADDEN
SADDLE
SADISM
SEDATE
SEDUCE
SIDING
SODDEN
SODIUM
SODOMY
SUDDEN
TEDIUM
TIDBIT
TODDLE
UNDIES
UNDULY
UPDATE
WADDLE
ZODIAC
ACETIC
AGENCY
AGENDA
AMENDS
AMERCE
ANEMIA
APERCU
AVENGE
AVENUE
AVERSE
AWEARY
AWEIGH
BEETLE
BLEACH
BLEARY
BLENCH
BREACH
BREAST
BREATH
BREECH
BREEZE
BREVET
CAECUM
CAESAR
CHEEKY
CHEERY
CHEESE
CHEQUE
CHERRY
CHERUB
CLEAVE
CLENCH
CLERGY
CLERIC
CLEVER
CLEVIS
COERCE
COEVAL
CREASE
CREATE
CRECHE
CREDIT
CREEPY
CREOLE
CRETIN
CREWEL
CUESTA
DAEMON
DEEJAY
DEEPEN
DIESEL
DREARY
DREDGE
DRENCH
DRESSY
DUENDE
DUENNA
ELEVEN
EMERGE
EMETIC
ENERGY
EXEMPT
EYELET
EYELID
FAECAL
FAERIE
FEEBLE
FEELER
FIERCE
FIESTA
FLEECE
FLESHY
FOEMAN
FOETAL
FREEZE
FRENCH
FRENZY
FRESCO
GAELIC
GEEZER
GHETTO
GNEISS
GREASE
ICEBOX
ICEMAN
IPECAC
IRENIC
LEEWAY
MAENAD
NEEDLE
OCELOT
OMELET
ONEIDA
OVERDO
OVERLY
PEEWEE
PHENOL
PIERCE
PLEASE
PLEDGE
PLENTY
PLENUM
PLEXUS
POETRY
PREACH
PRECIS
PREFAB
PREFER
PREFIX
PRELIM
PREMED
PREMIX
PREPAY
PRESET
PRESTO
PRETTY
PREWAR
PSEUDO
PUEBLO
QUEASY
QUENCH
REEFER
SEEMLY
SEESAW
SEETHE
SHEATH
SHEAVE
SHEIKH
SHELVE
SHERRY
SIERRA
SIESTA
SKETCH
SKEWER
SLEAZY
SLEDGE
SLEEPY
SLEEVE
SLEIGH
SLEUTH
SNEEZE
SOEVER
SPECIE
SPECIF
SPEECH
STEADY
STENCH
STEPPE
STEREO
SVELTE
SWERVE
TEEPEE
TEETER
TEETHE
THEIRS
THEISM
THENCE
THEORY
THESIS
TREATY
TREBLE
TREMOR
TRENCH
TREPAN
TSETSE
TWEEDY
TWELVE
TWENTY
UNEASY
UNESCO
UNEVEN
UREMIA
URETER
USEFUL
USENET
UTERUS
WEEKLY
WEEVIL
WHEEZE
WHEEZY
WHENCE
WHERRY
WIENER
WOEFUL
WREATH
WRENCH
WRETCH
AFFAIR
AFFECT
AFFIRM
AFFORD
AFFRAY
BAFFLE
BEFALL
BEFORE
BEFOUL
BUFFER
BUFFET
CAFTAN
COFFEE
COFFER
COFFIN
DEFACE
DEFAME
DEFEAT
DEFECT
DEFEND
DEFILE
DEFINE
DEFORM
DEFRAY
DEFUSE
DIFFER
DUFFER
EFFACE
EFFECT
EFFETE
EFFIGY
EFFORT
ENFOLD
GAFFER
GIFTED
GUFFAW
INFAMY
INFANT
INFECT
INFEST
INFIRM
INFLOW
INFLUX
INFOLD
INFORM
INFUSE
MUFFIN
MUFFLE
OFFEND
OFFICE
OFFING
OFFISH
OFFSET
OXFORD
PIFFLE
PUFFIN
RAFFIA
RAFFLE
RAFTER
REFILL
REFINE
REFLEX
REFLUX
REFORM
REFRIG
REFUGE
REFUND
REFUSE
REFUTE
RUFFLE
SAFARI
SAFETY
SOFTEN
SUFFER
SUFFIX
TIFFIN
TOFFEE
UNFAIR
UNFOLD
UNFURL
WAFFLE
AFGHAN
ANGINA
ANGORA
ARGENT
ARGOSY
ARGYLE
AUGURY
AUGUST
BAGMAN
BAGNIO
BEGGAR
BEGONE
BIGAMY
BIGWIG
BOGGLE
BYGONE
COGENT
COGNAC
CYGNET
DAGGER
DEGREE
DIGEST
DOGGED
DOGLEG
DUGOUT
EAGLET
EDGING
EGGNOG
EIGHTY
ENGAGE
ENGINE
ENGRAM
ENGULF
FAGGOT
FIGURE
GAGGLE
GIGGLE
GIGOLO
GOGGLE
HAGGIS
HAGGLE
HEGIRA
INGEST
JAGGED
JAGUAR
JIGGER
JIGGLE
JIGSAW
JOGGLE
JUGGLE
KEGLER
LAGOON
LEGACY
LEGATE
LEGATO
LEGEND
LEGION
LEGMAN
LEGUME
LIGATE
LIGHTS
LOGGIA

LOGJAM
MAGGOT
MAGNET
MAGPIE
MAGYAR
MEGOHM
MIGHTY
NEGATE
NOGGIN
NUGGET
ORGASM
PAGODA
PIGEON
PIGLET
PIGNUT
PIGPEN
PIGSTY
POGROM
RAGGED
RAGLAN
RAGOUT
REGAIN
REGALE
REGARD
REGENT
REGIME
REGION
REGNAL
REGRET
RIGGER
RUGGED
SIGILL
SIGNAL
SIGNET
TIGHTS
TOGGLE
TUGRIK
UNGIRD
URGENT
VAGARY
VAGINA
VAGROM
WAGGLE
WIGGLE
WIGGLY
WIGLET
WIGWAG
WIGWAM
YOGURT
ZIGZAG
ZYGOTE
ADHERE
AGHAST
ASHLAR
ASHORE
ASHRAM
AWHILE
AWHIRL
BEHALF
BEHAVE
BEHEAD
BEHEST
BEHIND
BEHOLD
BEHOOF
CAHOOT
COHEIR
COHERE
COHORT
DAHLIA
DEHORN
ETHANE
ETHICS
ETHNIC
ETHNOL
EXHALE
EXHORT
EXHUME
FUHRER
INHALE
INHERE
INHUME
JOHNNY
MAHOUT
MOHAIR
MOHAWK
REHASH
SCHEME
SCHISM
SCHIST
SCHOOL
SCHUSS
SPHERE
SPHINX
UNHAND
UNHOLY
UNHOOK
UPHILL
UPHOLD
WAHINE
YAHWEH
AFIELD
AKIMBO
ALIGHT
ANIMAL
ANIMUS
APIARY
APICAL
APIECE
ARIGHT
AVIARY
BLIGHT
BLITHE
BOILER
BRIDAL
BRIDGE
BRIDLE
BRIGHT
BRITON
CAIMAN
CHICHI
CHICLE
CHILLY
CHINTZ
CHISEL
CHITIN
CLICHE
CLIENT
CLIMAX
CLINCH
CLINIC
CLIQUE
COITUS
CRINGE
CRISIS
CRITIC
DAINTY
DOINGS
DRIVEL
DRIVER
EDIBLE
ELICIT
ELIXIR
EMIGRE
ENIGMA
ENISLE
EVINCE
FAILLE
FAIRLY
FLIGHT
FLIMSY
FLINCH
FLITCH
FOIBLE
FRIARY
FRIDAY
FRIEND
FRIEZE
FRIGHT
FRIGID
FRINGE
FRISKY
GAIETY
GAITER
GEISHA
GLIDER
GLITCH
GOITER
GRIEVE
GRILLE
GRIPPE
GRISLY
GUIDON
GUILTY
GUINEA
GUITAR
HAIRDO
HEIFER
HEIGHT
IBIDEM
ICICLE
IDIOCY
JAILER
JOINER
JUICER
KAISER
KNIGHT
LOITER
MAIDEN
MAILED
MOIETY
ODIOUS
OJIBWA
OPIATE
ORIENT
ORIGIN
ORIOLE
ORISON
OTIOSE
PAIUTE
PHILOS
PLIANT
PLIERS
PLIGHT
PLINTH
POISON
PRIEST
PRIMAL
PRIMER
PRINCE
PRINTF
PRIORY
PRISON
PRISSY
PRIVET
QUINCE
QUINSY
QUIVER
RAISIN
SAILOR
SHIELD
SHIEST
SHIFTY
SHIMMY
SHINER
SHINNY
SHINTO
SHIVER
SKIMPY
SKINNY
SLIDER
SLIEST
SLIGHT
SLIPUP
SLIVER
SMILAX
SMIRCH
SMITHY
SNIPPY
SNITCH
SNIVEL
SOIGNE
SOIREE
SPIDER
SPIGOT
SPINAL
SPINEL
SPINET
SPIRAL
SPIREA
SPIRIT
STICKY
STIFLE
STIGMA
STINGY
STITCH
SUITOR
SWITCH
SWIVEL
TAILOR
THIEVE
THIRST
THIRTY
TOILET
TRIAGE
TRICKY
TRIFLE
TRIODE
TRIPLE
TRIPLY
TRIPOD
TRITON
TRIUNE
TRIVET
TRIVIA
TWINGE
TWITCH
UNICEF
UNIQUE
UNISEX
UNISON
UNITED
URINAL
VOICED
WAITER
WAIVER
WEIGHT
WHILOM
WHILST
WHIMSY
WHINNY
WHITEN
WRITER
WRITHE
ABJECT
ABJURE
ADJOIN
ADJURE
ADJUST
CAJOLE
ENJOIN
HIJACK
INJECT
INJURE
INJURY
JEJUNE
JUJUBE
OBJECT
REJECT
REJOIN
UNJUST
ALKALI
ANKLET
BAKERY
BIKINI
DAKOTA
ESKIMO
INKJET
LIKELY
LIKING
LIKUTA
MAKEUP
MAKUTA
MIKADO
MUKLUK
RAKISH
TAKING
UNKIND
UPKEEP
VIKING
ABLAZE
ABLOOM
AFLAME
AFLOAT
AGLEAM
ALLEGE
ALLIED
ALLUDE
ALLURE
APLOMB
ASLANT
ASLEEP
BALBOA
BALEEN
BALLAD
BALLET
BALLOT
BALSAM
BELDAM
BELFRY
BELIEF
BELIKE
BELLOW
BELONG
BELUGA
BILLET
BILLOW
BOLERO
BULBUL
BULLET
CALCIC
CALICO
CALIPH
CALLOW
CALLUS
CALVES
CELERY
CELLAR
CILIUM
COLLAR
COLLAT
COLLIE
COLLOQ
COLONY
COLUMN
DALASI
DELETE
DELUDE
DELUGE
DELUXE
DILATE
DILUTE
DOLLAR
DOLLOP
DOLMEN
DULCET
ECLAIR
ENLIST
EOLIAN
EULOGY
FALCON
FALLOW
FALTER
FELINE
FELLAH
FELLOW
FELONY
FILIAL
FILING
FILLER
FILLET
FILLIP
FILTER
FOLDER
FOLKSY
FOLLOW
GALAXY
GALENA
GALLEY
GALLIC
GALLON
GALLOP
GALORE
GALOSH
GOLDEN
GULDEN
GULLET
HALALA
HALITE
HALLOW
HALTER
HALVES
HELIUM
HELMET
HOLDUP
HOLLER
HOLLOW
ILLUME
ILLUST
INLAID
INLAND
ISLAND
JALOPY
KELVIN
KILTER
MALADY
MALIAN
MALICE
MALIGN
MALLET
MALLOW
MELLOW
MELODY
MILDEW
MILIEU
MILLER
MILLET
MOLDER
MOLEST
MOLTEN
MULLET
NELSON
OBLATE
OBLIGE
OBLONG
OOLITE
PALACE
PALATE
PALEON
PALING
PALLET
PALLID
PALLOR
PALMER
PALTER
PALTRY
PELAGE
PELLET
PELVIS
PHLEGM
PHLOEM
PILFER
PILING
PILLAR
PILLOW
POLDER
POLEAX
POLICE
POLICY
POLISH
POLITE
POLITY
POLLEN
PULLET
PULLEY
PULPIT
PULSAR
RELATE
RELENT
RELICT
RELIEF
RELISH
RELIVE
ROLLER
SALAAM
SALAMI
SALARY
SALINE
SALIVA
SALLOW
SALMON
SALOON
SALUTE
SALVER
SELDOM
SELECT
SELVES
SILAGE
SILENT
SILICA
SILVER
SOLACE
SOLDER
SOLEMN
SPLASH
SPLEEN
SPLICE
SPLINE
SPLINT
SULFUR
SULLEN
SULTAN
SULTRY
SYLVAN
TALENT
TALLOW
TALMUD
TELLER
TELNET
TILLER
ULLAGE
UNLACE
UNLADE
UNLESS
UNLIKE
UNLOAD
UNLOCK
UPLAND
UPLIFT
UPLOAD
VALISE
VALLEY
VALUED
VELLUM
VELOUR
VELVET
VILIFY
VILLUS
VOLLEY
VOLUME
VOLUTE
VULGAR
WALLET
WALLOP
WALLOW
WALNUT
WALRUS
WELKIN
WELTER
WILLOW
YELLOW
ADMIRE
ALMOND
ALMOST
ARMADA
ARMFUL
ARMLET
ARMORY
ARMPIT
BAMBOO

BEMIRE
BEMOAN
BEMUSE
BOMBER
BUMMER
BUMPER
CAMBER
CAMERA
CAMPER
CAMPUS
CEMENT
COMBAT
COMBER
COMDEX
COMEDY
COMELY
COMFIT
COMING
COMITY
COMMIT
COMMON
COMPAQ
COMPAR
COMPEL
COMPLY
CUMBER
CYMBAL
DAMAGE
DAMASK
DAMPEN
DAMPER
DAMSEL
DAMSON
DEMAND
DEMEAN
DEMISE
DEMODE
DEMOTE
DEMURE
DIMITY
DIMMER
DIMPLE
DOMAIN
DOMINO
DUMDUM
ENMESH
ENMITY
ERMINE
FAMILY
FAMINE
FAMISH
FAMOUS
FEMALE
FOMENT
FUMBLE
GAMBIT
GAMBLE
GAMBOL
GAMETE
GAMINE
GAMMER
GAMMON
GIMBAL
GIMLET
HAMLET
HAMMER
HAMPER
HOMAGE
HOMELY
HOMILY
HOMINY
HUMANE
HUMBLE
HUMBUG
HUMOUR
IMMUNE
IMMURE
INMATE
INMOST
JUMBLE
JUMPER
KIMONO
LAMENT
LAMINA
LIMBER
LIMPET
LIMPID
LUMBAR
LUMBER
LUMMOX
MAMMAL
MAMMON
MEMBER
MEMOIR
MEMORY
MIMOSA
MOMENT
MUMBLE
MUMMER
NAMELY
NIMBLE
NIMBUS
NIMROD
NUMBER
ORMOLU
OSMIUM
PAMPER
PCMCIA
PIMPLE
POMADE
POMMEL
POMPON
PUMICE
PUMMEL
RAMBLE
RAMIFY
RAMROD
REMAIN
REMAND
REMARK
REMEDY
REMIND
REMISS
REMORA
REMOTE
REMOVE
ROMANO
ROMPER
RUMBLE
RUMPLE
RUMPUS
SAMPAN
SAMPLE
SEMITE
SIMIAN
SIMILE
SIMMER
SIMONY
SIMPER
SIMPLE
SOMBER
SUMMER
SUMMIT
SUMMON
SYMBOL
TAMALE
TAMPER
TAMPON
TEMPER
TEMPLE
TIMBER
TIMBRE
TIMELY
TOMATO
TOMBOY
TOMCAT
TOMTIT
TUMBLE
TUMULT
UNMASK
UNMEET
UNMOOR
UPMOST
UTMOST
WAMBLE
WAMPUM
WIMBLE
WIMPLE
WOMBAT
YAMMER
ZOMBIE
ABNAKI
ANNALS
ANNEAL
ANNUAL
ARNICA
AWNING
BANANA
BANDED
BANDIT
BANGLE
BANISH
BANNER
BANTAM
BANTER
BANYAN
BANZAI
BENDER
BENIGN
BENUMB
BENZOL
BINARY
BINHEX
BONBON
BONITO
BONNET
BONSAI
BUNDLE
BUNGLE
BUNION
BUNKER
BUNKUM
CANAPE
CANARD
CANARY
CANCAN
CANCEL
CANCER
CANDID
CANDLE
CANDOR
CANINE
CANKER
CANNED
CANNON
CANNOT
CANOPY
CANTER
CANTLE
CANTON
CANTOR
CANVAS
CANYON
CENSER
CENSOR
CENSUS
CENTER
CENTRE
CINDER
CINEMA
CONCUR
CONDOM
CONDOR
CONFAB
CONFED
CONFER
CONSOL
CONSTR
CONSUL
CONVEX
CONVEY
CONVOY
CUNNER
DANDER
DANDLE
DANGER
DANGLE
DANISH
DENGUE
DENIAL
DENIER
DENOTE
DENTAL
DENTIN
DENUDE
DINGHY
DINGLE
DINGUS
DINNER
DONATE
DONKEY
DYNAMO
EUNUCH
FENDER
FENIAN
FENNEL
FINALE
FINDER
FINERY
FINGER
FINIAL
FINISH
FINITE
FONDLE
FONDUE
FUNGUS
FUNNEL
GANDER
GANNET
GANTRY
GENDER
GENERA
GENIAL
GENIUS
GENTLE
GENTRY
GINGER
GINKGO
GUNMAN
GUNNER
HANDLE
HANGAR
HANKER
HANSEL
HANSOM
HINDER
HONEST
HONOUR
HUNGER
HUNKER
IGNITE
IGNORE
INNATE
INNING
IONIZE
JANGLE
JENNET
JINGLE
JUNGLE
JUNIOR
JUNKER
JUNKET
JUNKIE
KENNEL
KINDLE
KINDLY
LANCER
LANCET
LANDAU
LANDED
LANDER
LENGTH
LENITY
LENTIL
LINAGE
LINDEN
LINEAL
LINEAR
LINEUP
LINGER
LINING
LINKED
LINKUP
LINNET
LINTEL
LONELY
LUNACY
MANAGE
MANANA
MANEGE
MANFUL
MANGER
MANGLE
MANIAC
MANIOC
MANNED
MANNER
MANQUE
MANTEL
MANTIS
MANTLE
MANTRA
MANUAL
MANURE
MENACE
MENAGE
MENIAL
MENINX
MENSES
MENTAL
MENTOR
MINDED
MINGLE
MINION
MINNOW
MINUET
MINUTE
MONDAY
MONGER
MONISM
MONKEY
MONODY
NINETY
NONAGE
NONCOM
NONFAT
NUNCIO
ORNATE
ORNERY
ORNITH
PANAMA
PANDER
PANTIE
PANTRY
PENCIL
PENMAN
PENNON
PENURY
PINCER
PINEAL
PINION
PINKIE
PONCHO
PONDER
PONGEE
PUNDIT
PUNISH
PUNKIN
QINTAR
RANCHO
RANCID
RANCOR
RANDOM
RANGER
RANKLE
RANSOM
RENDER
RENEGE
RENNET
RENNIN
RENOWN
RENTAL
RINGER
RUNLET
RUNNEL
RUNNER
RUNOFF
RUNWAY
SANDAL
SANITY
SENATE
SENECA
SENILE
SENIOR
SENITI
SENSOR
SENTRY
SINFUL
SINGLE
SINKER
SONATA
SONNET
SUNDAE
SUNDAY
SUNDER
SUNDRY
SUNKEN
SUNLIT
SUNSET
SUNTAN
SYNTAX
TANDEM
TANGLE
TANKER
TANNER
TANNIN
TENANT
TENDER
TENDON
TENNIS
TENPIN
TENURE
TINDER
TINGLE
TINKER
TINKLE
TINSEL
TONGUE
TONSIL
TUNDRA
TUNNEL
VANDAL
VANISH
VANITY
VENDEE
VENDER
VENDOR
VENEER
VENIAL
VENIRE
VENOUS
VINOUS
WANDER
WANGLE
WANTON
WINDER
WINDOW
WINDUP
WINGED
WINKER
WINKLE
WINNER
WINNOW
WINTER
WINTRY
WONDER
WONTED
YANKEE
YANQUI
YONDER
ZENANA
ZENITH
ZINNIA
ZONKED
ABOARD
ABOUND
AMOEBA
AMORAL
AMOUNT
ANOINT
APOGEE
AROUND
AROUSE
ATOMIC
ATONAL
AVOCET
AVOUCH
BAOBAB
BIOPSY
BIOTIC
BIOTIN
BLOTCH
BLOUSE
BLOWSY
BLOWUP
BOODLE
BOOKIE
BOOTEE
BROACH
BROGAN
BROGUE
BROKEN
BROKER
BRONCO
BRONZE
BROOCH
BROWSE
CHOICE
CHOKER
CHOLER
CHOOSE
CHOOSY
CHOPPY
CHORAL
CHOREA
CHORUS
CHOSEN
CLOCHE
CLOSET
CLOTHE
CLOVEN
CLOVER
COOKIE
COOLER
COOLIE
COOPER
COOTIE
CROCUS
CROTCH
CROUCH
DEODAR
DOODAD
DOODLE
DROGUE
DROPSY
DROVER
DROWSE
DROWSY
EGOISM
ENOUGH
EROTIC
EVOLVE
EXODUS
EXOTIC
FLOOZY
FLOPPY
FLORAL
FLORID
FLORIN
FLOSSY

| | | | | | | | | | |
|---|---|---|---|---|---|---|---|---|---|
| FLOWER | SHODDY | APPEAL | IMPEND | RUPIAH | BARFLY | CIRRUS | FORBID | IRRUPT | NORDIC |
| FOOTED | SHOULD | APPEAR | IMPERF | SEPSIS | BARIUM | CORBEL | FOREGO | JARGON | NORMAL |
| FROLIC | SHOVEL | APPEND | IMPISH | SEPTIC | BARKER | CORDON | FOREST | JERKIN | NORMAN |
| FROWSY | SHOWER | APPLET | IMPORT | SIPHON | BARLEY | CORNEA | FORGET | JERSEY | NORTON |
| FROZEN | SLOGAN | APPROX | IMPOSE | SUPERB | BARRED | CORNER | FORINT | JURIST | ONRUSH |
| GLOBAL | SLOPPY | ASPECT | IMPOST | SUPINE | BARREL | CORNET | FORKED | KARATE | PARADE |
| GLOSSY | SLOUCH | ASPIRE | IMPUGN | SUPPER | BARREN | CORONA | FORMAL | KERMIT | PARCEL |
| GLOWER | SLOUGH | BYPASS | IMPURE | SUPPLE | BARRIO | CORPSE | FORMAT | KERNEL | PARDON |
| GOOBER | SLOVEN | BYPATH | IMPUTE | SUPPLY | BARROW | CORPUS | FORMER | KIRTLE | PARENT |
| GOODLY | SMOOCH | BYPLAY | KIPPER | SYPHON | BARTER | CORRAL | FURORE | KOREAN | PARIAH |
| GROCER | SMOOTH | CAPFUL | KOPECK | TAPPET | BERATE | CORSET | FURROW | KORUNA | PARING |
| GROGGY | SNOBOL | CAPTOR | LAPDOG | TIPPET | BERBER | CORTEX | GARAGE | LARDER | PARISH |
| GROOVE | SNOOTY | CIPHER | LAPPET | TIPPLE | BEREFT | CORYZA | GARBLE | LARIAT | PARITY |
| GROOVY | SNOOZE | COPIER | LAPTOP | TIPTOE | BIRDIE | CURATE | GARCON | LARYNX | PARLAY |
| GROTTO | SOOTHE | COPING | LEPTON | TOPPLE | BORATE | CURDLE | GARDEN | LORDLY | PARLEY |
| GROUCH | SPOKEN | COPPER | LUPINE | TYPHUS | BORDER | CURFEW | GARGLE | MARACA | PARLOR |
| GROUND | SPONGE | COPTER | MOPPET | TYPIFY | BOREAL | CURIUM | GARISH | MARAUD | PARODY |
| GROUSE | SPOTTY | COPULA | NAPALM | TYPIST | BORROW | CURLEW | GARLIC | MARBLE | PAROLE |
| GROVEL | SPOUSE | CUPOLA | NAPERY | UMPIRE | BURDEN | CURSOR | GARNER | MARCEL | PARROT |
| GROWTH | STOCKY | DAPPER | NAPKIN | UNPACK | BUREAU | CURTSY | GARNET | MARGIN | PARSEC |
| HOODOO | STODGY | DAPPLE | NEPHEW | UNPILE | BURGEE | CURVET | GARRET | MARINA | PARSON |
| HOOKAH | STOLEN | DEPART | NIPPER | UNPLUG | BURGLE | DARING | GARTER | MARINE | PARTLY |
| HOOKER | STOLID | DEPEND | NIPPLE | UPPISH | BURIAL | DARKEN | GERBIL | MARKED | PERIOD |
| HOOKUP | STOLON | DEPICT | OPPOSE | UPPITY | BURLAP | DARNEL | GERMAN | MARKET | PERISH |
| HOOPLA | STONED | DEPLOY | ORPHAN | VAPORY | BURNER | DARTER | GERUND | MARKKA | PERMIT |
| IRONIC | STOOGE | DEPORT | OSPREY | WAPITI | BURROW | DERAIL | GIRDER | MARKUP | PERSON |
| ISOBAR | TAOISM | DEPOSE | PAPACY | ZEPHYR | BURSAR | DERIDE | GIRDLE | MARLIN | PERUKE |
| ISOMER | THORAX | DEPUTE | PAPAIN | ZIPPER | CARAFE | DERIVE | GURGLE | MARMOT | PERUSE |
| KAOLIN | THOUGH | DEPUTY | PAPAYA | ACQUIT | CARBON | DERMAL | GURKHA | MAROON | PHRASE |
| LOOPER | TOOTHY | DIPPER | PAPIST | BUQSHA | CARBOY | DERMIS | GYRATE | MARROW | PIRACY |
| LOOSEN | TROCHE | DOPANT | PAPULE | COQUET | CAREEN | DERRIS | HARASS | MARTEN | PIRATE |
| MAOISM | TROIKA | DUPLEX | PEPPER | LIQUID | CAREER | DIRECT | HARBOR | MARTIN | PORKER |
| MYOPIA | TROJAN | EEPROM | PEPSIN | LIQUOR | CARESS | DIRHAM | HARDEN | MARTYR | POROUS |
| NOODLE | TROPHY | EMPIRE | PEPTIC | PEQUOT | CARHOP | DIRNDL | HARDLY | MARVEL | PORTAL |
| PEOPLE | TROPIC | EMPLOY | PIPING | PIQUET | CARIES | DORMER | HARKEN | MERCER | PORTER |
| PHOBIA | TROUGH | ESPRIT | PIPKIN | SEQUEL | CARNAL | DORSAL | HARLOT | MERGER | PORTLY |
| PHOEBE | TROUPE | EXPAND | PIPPIN | SEQUIN | CARPAL | DURESS | HARROW | MERINO | PURDAH |
| PHONIC | TROWEL | EXPECT | POPGUN | ABRADE | CARPEL | DURING | HERALD | MERMAN | PURIFY |
| PHOTOG | UTOPIA | EXPEND | POPLAR | ABROAD | CARPET | EARTHY | HEREBY | MIRAGE | PURINE |
| PHOTON | VIOLET | EXPERT | POPLIN | ABRUPT | CARREL | EARWAX | HEREIN | MIRROR | PURISM |
| PLOVER | VIOLIN | EXPIRE | POPPER | ACROSS | CARROT | EARWIG | HEREOF | MORALE | PURITY |
| POODLE | VOODOO | EXPORT | PUPPET | ADRIFT | CARTEL | EGRESS | HEREON | MORBID | PURPLE |
| PROFIT | WHOLLY | EXPOSE | RAPIER | ADROIT | CARTON | ENRAGE | HERESY | MORGAN | PURSER |
| PROLIX | WOODED | GOPHER | RAPINE | AERATE | CARTOP | ENRICH | HERETO | MORGUE | PURSUE |
| PROLOG | WOODEN | GYPSUM | RAPPEN | AERIAL | CEREAL | ENROLL | HERMIT | MORMON | PURVEY |
| PROMPT | WOODSY | HAPPEN | REPAIR | AFRAID | CEREUS | ERRAND | HERNIA | MOROSE | PYRITE |
| PRONTO | WOOFER | HEPCAT | REPAST | AFRESH | CERISE | ERRANT | HEROIN | MORRIS | RAREFY |
| PROPEL | WOOLEN | HIPPED | REPEAL | AIRMAN | CERIUM | ERRATA | HERPES | MORROW | RARING |
| PROPER | WOOLLY | HIPPIE | REPEAT | AIRWAY | CERMET | EUREKA | HORNET | MORSEL | SARONG |
| PROTON | XMODEM | HOPPER | REPENT | ARRANT | CERVIX | FARINA | HORRID | MORTAL | SCRAPE |
| QUORUM | YEOMAN | HYPHEN | REPINE | ARREST | CHRISM | FARROW | HORROR | MORTAR | SCRAWL |
| RLOGIN | YMODEM | IMPACT | REPLAY | ARRIVE | CHRIST | FERRET | HORSEY | MURDER | SCREAM |
| ROOKIE | ZMODEM | IMPAIR | REPORT | ARROYO | CHROME | FERRIC | HURDLE | MURMUR | SCREEN |
| SCONCE | ALPACA | IMPALA | REPOSE | ATRIUM | CHROMO | FERULE | HURRAH | MYRIAD | SCREWY |
| SCORCH | ALPINE | IMPALE | REPUTE | AURORA | CIRCLE | FERVID | HURTLE | MYRTLE | SCRIBE |
| SCORIA | AMPERE | IMPART | RIPPLE | BARBER | CIRCUS | FERVOR | INROAD | NARROW | SCRIMP |
| SCOTCH | APPALL | IMPEDE | RIPSAW | BARELY | CIRQUE | FORAGE | INRUSH | NEREID | SCRIPT |

SCROLL
SCRUFF
SERAPE
SERAPH
SERENE
SERIAL
SERIES
SERMON
SERVER
SHREWD
SHRIEK
SHRIFT
SHRIKE
SHRILL
SHRIMP
SHRINE
SHRINK
SHRIVE
SHROUD
SORDID
SORREL
SORROW
SORTIE
SPRAIN
SPRAWL
SPREAD
SPRING
SPRINT
SPRITE
SPROUT
SPRUCE
SPRUNG
STRAFE
STRAIN
STRAIT
STRAND
STREAK
STREAM
STREET
STRESS
STRICT
STRIDE
STRIFE
STRIKE
STRING
STRIPE
STRIVE
STROBE
STRODE
STROKE
STROLL
STRONG
STROVE
STRUCK
STRUNG
SURETY
SURREY
SURTAX
SURVEY
TARGET
TARIFF
TARPON
TARSUS
TARTAN
TARTAR
TEREDO
TERROR
THRALL
THRASH
THREAD
THREAT
THRESH
THRICE
THRIFT
THRILL
THRIVE
THROAT
THRONE
THRONG
THROVE
THRUSH
THRUST
TIRADE
TORERO
TORPID
TORPOR
TORQUE
TORRID
TURBAN
TURBID
TURBOT
TUREEN
TURGID
TURING
TURKEY
TURNER
TURNIP
TURRET
TURTLE
TURVES
TYRANT
UNREAD
UNREAL
UNREEL
UNREST
UNRIPE
UNROBE
UNROLL
UNROOF
UNRULY
UPREAR
UPROAR
UPROOT
UPRUSH
VARIED
VARLET
VERBAL
VERGER
VERIFY
VERILY
VERITY
VERMIN
VERNAL
VERSED
VERSUS
VERTEX
VIRAGO
VIRGIN
VIRILE
VIRION
VIRTUE
VORTEX
WARBLE
WARDEN
WARDER
WARMTH
WARREN
WIRING
WORKER
WORSEN
WORTHY
YARROW
ZIRCON
ABSENT
ABSORB
ABSURD
ADSORB
ANSWER
ASSAIL
ASSENT
ASSERT
ASSESS
ASSIGN
ASSIST
ASSIZE
ASSORT
ASSUME
ASSURE
BASALT
BASKET
BASQUE
BESEEM
BESIDE
BESTIR
BESTOW
BISECT
BISHOP
BISQUE
BISTRO
BUSBOY
BUSHED
BUSHEL
BUSILY
BUSKIN
BUSTLE
CASABA
CASEIN
CASHEW
CASING
CASINO
CASKET
CASQUE
CASSIA
CASTER
CASTLE
CASUAL
CESIUM
COSINE
COSMIC
COSMOS
COSTLY
CUSPID
CUSTOM
DASHER
DESALT
DESCRY
DESERT
DESIGN
DESIRE
DESIST
DESKEW
DESPOT
DISARM
DISBAR
DISCUS
DISHED
DISMAL
DISMAY
DISOWN
DISPEL
DISTAL
DISUSE
DUSTER
EASTER
ENSIGN
ENSILE
ENSURE
ERSATZ
FASTEN
FESTAL
FESTER
FISCAL
FISHER
FOSSIL
FOSTER
FUSION
GASKET
GOSPEL
GOSSIP
GUSHER
GUSSET
HASSLE
HASTEN
HOSTEL
HUSSAR
HUSTLE
HYSSOP
INSANE
INSEAM
INSECT
INSERT
INSIDE
INSIST
INSOLE
INSTEP
INSULT
INSURE
ITSELF
JASPER
JESTER
JOSTLE
KISMET
KISSER
KOSHER
LASCAR
LASSIE
LESION
LESSEE
LESSEN
LESSER
LESSON
LESSOR
LISTEN
LUSTER
MASCON
MASCOT
MASQUE
MASSIF
MASTER
MASTIC
MESCAL
MESSRS
MISCUE
MISERY
MISFIT
MISHAP
MISLAY
MISSAL
MISTER
MISUSE
MOSAIC
MOSLEM
MOSQUE
MOSTLY
MUSCLE
MUSEUM
MUSKEG
MUSKET
MUSLIM
MUSLIN
MUSSEL
MUSTER
MYSELF
MYSTIC
NESTLE
OBSESS
OSSIFY
OUSTER
OYSTER
PASCAL
PASSEL
PASSIM
PASTEL
PASTOR
PASTRY
PESETA
PESEWA
PESTER
PESTLE
PISTIL
PISTOL
PISTON
POSEUR
POSSUM
POSTAL
POSTER
PUSHER
RASCAL
RASHER
RASTER
RESALE
RESCUE
RESENT
RESIDE
RESIGN
RESIST
RESORT
RESULT
RESUME
RISQUE
ROSARY
ROSTER
RUSSET
RUSTIC
RUSTLE
SASHAY
SESAME
SISTER
SYSTEM
TASSEL
TESTER
TESTIS
TISSUE
TUSKER
TUSSLE
ULSTER
UNSEAL
UNSEAT
UNSHIP
UNSHOD
UNSNAP
UNSTOP
UNSUNG
UPSHOT
UPSIDE
URSINE
VASSAL
VESPER
VESSEL
VESTAL
VESTEE
VESTRY
VISAGE
VISCID
VISCUS
VISION
VISUAL
WASHER
WESKIT
WISDOM
ACTING
ACTION
ACTIVE
ACTUAL
ALTAIR
ANTHEM
ANTHER
ANTLER
ANTRUM
ARTERY
ARTFUL
ARTIST
ASTERN
ASTHMA
ASTRAL
ASTRAY
ASTROL
ASTRON
ASTUTE
ATTACH
ATTACK
ATTAIN
ATTEND
ATTEST
ATTIRE
ATTRIB
ATTUNE
AUTHOR
AUTISM
AUTUMN
BATEAU
BATHOS
BATMAN
BATTEN
BATTER
BATTLE
BETAKE
BETHEL
BETIDE
BETRAY
BETTER
BETTOR
BITING
BITNET
BITTER
BOTANY
BOTHER
BOTTLE
BOTTOM
BUTANE
BUTLER
BUTTER
BUTTON
CATCHY
CATGUT
CATION
CATKIN
CATNAP
CATNIP
CATSUP
CATTLE
CITIFY
CITRON
CITRUS
COTTER
COTTON
CUTLER
CUTLET
CUTOFF
CUTOUT
CUTTER
DATIVE
DETACH
DETAIL
DETAIN
DETECT
DETEST
DETOUR
DITHER
DOTAGE
DOTARD
DOTTLE
EATERY
EITHER
ENTAIL
ENTICE
ENTIRE
ENTITY
ENTOMB
ENTRAP
ENTREE
ESTATE
ESTEEM
EXTANT
EXTEND
EXTENT
EXTERN
EXTORT
FATHER
FATHOM
FATTEN
FETISH
FETTER
FETTLE
FITFUL
FUTILE
FUTURE
GATHER
GOTHIC
GOTTEN
GUTTER
HATBOX
HATRED
HATTER
HITHER
HOTBED
HOTBOX
INTACT
INTAKE
INTEND
INTENT
INTERJ
INTERN
INTONE
INTROD
INTUIT
JETSAM
JITNEY
KETTLE
KITSCH
KITTEN
LATENT
LATHER
LATTER
LETHAL
LETTER
LITANY
LITCHI
LITMUS
LITTER
LITTLE
LOTION
MATINS
MATRIX
MATRON
MATTER
MATURE
METEOR
METHOD
METHYL
METIER
METRIC
METTLE
MITTEN
MOTHER
MOTILE
MOTION
MOTIVE
MOTLEY
MOTTLE
MUTANT
MUTATE
MUTINY
MUTTER
MUTTON
MUTUAL
NATION
NATIVE
NATURE
NETHER
NETTLE
NITRIC
NITWIT
NOTICE
NOTIFY
NOTION
NUTMEG
NUTRIA
OBTAIN
OBTUSE
OCTANE
OCTAVE
OCTAVO
OPTICS
OPTION
OSTLER
OTTAWA
OUTBID
OUTCRY
OUTFIT
OUTFOX
OUTGUN
OUTING
OUTLAW
OUTLAY
OUTLET
OUTPUT
OUTRUN
OUTSET
OUTWIT

PATACA
PATENT
PATHOS
PATINA
PATOIS
PATROL
PATRON
PATTER
PETARD
PETITE
PETREL
PETROL
POTAGE
POTASH
POTATO
POTBOY
POTEEN
POTENT
POTHER
POTION
POTPIE
POTTER
PUTOUT
PUTRID
PUTSCH
PUTTEE
PUTTER
PYTHON
RATHER
RATIFY
RATING
RATION
RATTAN
RATTER
RATTLE
RETAIL
RETAIN
RETAKE
RETARD
RETINA
RETIRE
RETORT
RETURN
RITUAL
ROTARY
ROTATE
ROTTEN
ROTUND
SATANG
SATEEN
SATIRE
SATRAP
SATURN
SETTEE
SETTER
SETTLE
SUTURE
TATTER
TATTLE
TATTOO
TETCHY
TETHER
TITBIT
TITLED
TITTER
TITTLE
TOTTER
ULTIMO
ULTRIX
UNTOLD
UNTRUE
UNTUNE
UPTAKE
UPTOWN
UPTURN
VITALS
VOTARY
VOTIVE
WATERY
WATTLE
WETHER
WITHAL
WITHER
WITHIN
WITTED
ZITHER
ACUITY
ACUMEN
ALUMNA
AMULET
BAUBLE
BLUING
BLUISH
BOUGHT
BOUNCE
BOUNTY
BOURSE
BRUISE
BRUNCH
BRUNET
BRUTAL
CAUCUS
CAUDAL
CAUGHT
CAUSAL
CHUBBY
CHUKKA
CHUMMY
CHUNKY
CHURCH
CLUMSY
CLUTCH
COUGAR
COULEE
COUNTY
COUPLE
COUPON
COURSE
COUSIN
CRUISE
CRUMMY
CRUNCH
CRUTCH
DOUBLE
DOUBLY
DOUCHE
DRUDGE
EQUATE
EQUINE
EQUITY
FAUCES
FAUCET
FEUDAL
FLUENT
FLUFFY
FLUNKY
FLURRY
FOUGHT
FOURTH
FRUGAL
FRUITY
FRUMPY
GAUCHE
GAUCHO
GLUTEN
GOURDE
GRUBBY
GRUDGE
GRUMPY
HAUNCH
IGUANA
JAUNTY
JOUNCE
LAUNCH
LAUREL
LOUNGE
LOUVER
MOUSER
MOUSSE
MOUTON
MUUMUU
NAUGHT
NAUSEA
NAUTCH
NEURAL
NEUROL
NEURON
NEUTER
NOUGAT
NOUGHT
OCULAR
OEUVRE
PAUNCH
PAUPER
PLUCKY
PLUNGE
PLURAL
PLUTON
POUNCE
ROUBLE
SAUCER
SCULPT
SCURRY
SCURVY
SCUZZY
SLUDGE
SLUICE
SLURRY
SMUDGE
SMUTCH
SOUGHT
SOURCE
SPURGE
SPUTUM
SQUALL
SQUARE
SQUASH
SQUAWK
SQUEAK
SQUEAL
SQUINT
SQUIRE
SQUIRM
SQUIRT
STUBBY
STUCCO
STUDIO
STUFFY
STUPID
STUPOR
STURDY
TAUGHT
TOUCAN
TOUCHE
TOUCHY
TOUPEE
TOUSLE
TRUANT
TRUDGE
TRUISM
TRUSTY
UNUSED
USURER
ZOUAVE
ZOUNDS
ADVENT
ADVERB
ADVERT
ADVICE
ADVISE
AMVETS
BOVINE
CAVEAT
CAVERN
CAVIAR
CAVITY
CAVORT
CIVICS
COVERT
DEVICE
DEVISE
DEVOID
DEVOIR
DEVOTE
DEVOUR
DEVOUT
DIVERS
DIVERT
DIVEST
DIVIDE
DIVINE
FAVOUR
GOVERN
INVADE
INVENT
INVERT
INVEST
INVITE
INVOKE
JOVIAL
LAVAGE
LAVISH
LEVITY
LIVELY
LIVERY
LIVING
LOVELY
LOVING
NAVAHO
NOVELL
NOVENA
NOVICE
PAVING
QIVIUT
RAVAGE
RAVINE
RAVISH
REVAMP
REVEAL
REVERB
REVERE
REVERS
REVERT
REVIEW
REVILE
REVISE
REVIVE
REVOKE
REVOLT
SAVAGE
SAVANT
SAVIOR
SEVERE
SOVIET
TAVERN
UNVEIL
VIVACE
VIVIFY
ALWAYS
BEWAIL
BEWARE
BOWLEG
BOWLER
BOWMAN
BYWORD
COWARD
COWBOY
COWMAN
COWPOX
DAWDLE
DEWLAP
DOWNER
GEWGAW
HAWKER
HAWSER
HOWDAH
HOWLER
INWARD
KOWTOW
LAWFUL
LAWMAN
LAWYER
LOWERY
NEWTON
NOWISE
ONWARD
PAWNEE
PAWPAW
PEWTER
POWDER
POWWOW
REWARD
SEWAGE
SEWING
TAWDRY
THWACK
THWART
TOWARD
TOWHEE
UNWELL
UNWEPT
UNWIND
UNWISE
UNWRAP
UPWARD
UPWELL
UPWIND
BOXCAR
BOXING
FIXITY
LUXURY
SEXISM
SEXPOT
SEXTET
SEXTON
SEXUAL
TUXEDO
ANYHOW
ANYONE
ANYWAY
ASYLUM
BEYOND
CAYMAN
CAYUGA
CAYUSE
COYOTE
DAYBED
FLYWAY
GAYETY
GEYSER
HAYMOW
HEYDAY
HOYDEN
JAYCEE
JAYGEE
JAYVEE
JOYFUL
JOYOUS
LAYMAN
LAYOFF
LAYOUT
MAYFLY
MAYHEM
OXYGEN
PAYOFF
PEYOTE
PHYLUM
PHYSIC
PSYCHE
PSYCHO
RHYTHM
SAYING
SCYTHE
SKYCAP
STYLUS
STYMIE
THYMUS
TRYING
UNYOKE
VOYAGE
VOYEUR
WAYLAY
ZOYSIA
BAZAAR
BUZZER
DAZZLE
ECZEMA
ENZYME
FIZZLE
GAZEBO
GUZZLE
HAZARD
HUZZAH
LIZARD
MIZZEN
MUZZLE
NOZZLE
NUZZLE
PUZZLE
SIZZLE
VIZARD
VIZIER
WIZARD

## 4TH LETTER

ABBACY
ABLAZE
ABNAKI
ABOARD
ABRADE
AERATE
AFFAIR
AFLAME
AFRAID
AGHAST
ALKALI
ALPACA
ALTAIR
ALWAYS
ANNALS
APIARY
APPALL
ARCADE
ARCANE
ARMADA
ARRANT
ASLANT
ASSAIL
ATTACH
ATTACK
ATTAIN
AVIARY
AWEARY
BANANA
BASALT
BAZAAR
BECALM
BEDAUB
BEFALL
BEHALF
BEHAVE
BERATE
BETAKE
BEWAIL
BEWARE
BIGAMY
BINARY
BLEACH
BLEARY
BORATE
BOTANY
BREACH
BREAST
BREATH
BROACH
BUTANE
BYPASS
BYPATH
CABALA
CABANA
CANAPE
CANARD
CANARY
CARAFE
CASABA
CICADA
CLEAVE
COBALT
COWARD
CREASE
CREATE
CURATE
DALASI
DAMAGE
DAMASK
DEBARK
DEBASE
DEBATE
DECADE
DECAMP
DECANT
DEFACE
DEFAME
DEMAND
DEPART
DERAIL
DESALT
DETACH
DETAIL
DETAIN
DILATE
DISARM
DOMAIN
DONATE
DOPANT
DOTAGE
DOTARD
DREARY
DYNAMO
ECLAIR
EFFACE
EMBALM
EMBANK
EMBARK
ENCAMP
ENCASE
ENGAGE
ENRAGE
ENTAIL
EQUATE
ERRAND
ERRANT
ERRATA
ERSATZ
ESCAPE
ESTATE
ETHANE
EXHALE
EXPAND
EXTANT
FACADE
FEMALE
FINALE
FORAGE
FRIARY
GALAXY
GARAGE
GREASE
GYRATE
HALALA
HARASS
HAZARD
HERALD
HIJACK
HOMAGE
HUMANE
IGUANA
IMPACT
IMPAIR
IMPALA
IMPALE
IMPART
INCASE
INFAMY
INFANT
INHALE
INLAID

INLAND
INMATE
INNATE
INSANE
INTACT
INTAKE
INVADE
INWARD
ISLAND
JUDAIC
KARATE
LAVAGE
LEGACY
LEGATE
LEGATO
LIGATE
LINAGE
LITANY
LIZARD
LOCALE
LOCATE
LUNACY
MACAPP
MADAME
MALADY
MANAGE
MANANA
MARACA
MARAUD
MENACE
MENAGE
MIDAIR
MIKADO
MIRAGE
MOHAIR
MOHAWK
MORALE
MOSAIC
MUTANT
MUTATE
NAPALM
NAVAHO
NEGATE
NONAGE
OBLATE
OBTAIN
OCTANE
OCTAVE
OCTAVO
ONWARD
OPIATE
ORDAIN
ORGASM
ORNATE
OTTAWA
PALACE
PALATE

PANAMA
PAPACY
PAPAIN
PAPAYA
PARADE
PATACA
PEDANT
PELAGE
PETARD
PHRASE
PIRACY
PIRATE
PLEASE
PLIANT
POMADE
POTAGE
POTASH
POTATO
PREACH
QUEASY
RAVAGE
REBATE
RECALL
RECANT
REDACT
REGAIN
REGALE
REGARD
REHASH
RELATE
REMAIN
REMAND
REMARK
REPAIR
REPAST
RESALE
RETAIL
RETAIN
RETAKE
RETARD
REVAMP
REWARD
RIBALD
RIBAND
ROMANO
ROSARY
ROTARY
ROTATE
SAFARI
SALAAM
SALAMI
SALARY
SATANG
SAVAGE
SAVANT
SCRAPE
SCRAWL

SEDATE
SENATE
SERAPE
SERAPH
SESAME
SEWAGE
SHEATH
SHEAVE
SILAGE
SLEAZY
SOLACE
SONATA
SPLASH
SPRAIN
SPRAWL
SQUALL
SQUARE
SQUASH
SQUAWK
STEADY
STRAFE
STRAIN
STRAIT
STRAND
TAMALE
TENANT
THRALL
THRASH
THWACK
THWART
TIRADE
TOMATO
TOWARD
TREATY
TRIAGE
TRUANT
TYRANT
ULLAGE
UNEASY
UNFAIR
UNHAND
UNLACE
UNLADE
UNMASK
UNPACK
UPDATE
UPLAND
UPTAKE
UPWARD
URBANE
VACANT
VACATE
VAGARY
VIRAGO
VISAGE
VITALS
VIVACE

VIZARD
VOTARY
VOYAGE
WIZARD
WREATH
ZENANA
ZOUAVE
ARABIC
ARABLE
BABBLE
BALBOA
BAMBOO
BAOBAB
BARBER
BAUBLE
BEDBUG
BERBER
BOBBIN
BOBBLE
BOMBER
BONBON
BUBBLE
BULBUL
BUSBOY
CAMBER
CARBON
CARBOY
CHUBBY
COBBLE
COMBAT
COMBER
CORBEL
COWBOY
CRABBY
CUMBER
CYMBAL
DABBLE
DAYBED
DIBBLE
DISBAR
DOBBIN
DOUBLE
DOUBLY
DUBBIN
DYBBUK
EDIBLE
ENABLE
FEEBLE
FLABBY
FOIBLE
FORBID
FUMBLE
GABBLE
GABBRO
GAMBIT
GAMBLE
GAMBOL

GARBLE
GERBIL
GIBBER
GIBBET
GIBBON
GIMBAL
GLOBAL
GOBBET
GOBBLE
GOOBER
GRABEN
GRUBBY
HARBOR
HATBOX
HOBBLE
HOTBED
HOTBOX
HUBBUB
HUMBLE
HUMBUG
ICEBOX
ISOBAR
JABBER
JOBBER
JUMBLE
KIBBLE
LIABLE
LIMBER
LUBBER
LUMBAR
LUMBER
MARBLE
MEMBER
MORBID
MUMBLE
NIBBLE
NIMBLE
NIMBUS
NUBBIN
NUBBLE
NUMBER
OJIBWA
OUTBID
PEBBLE
PHOBIA
POTBOY
PUEBLO
RABBET
RABBIT
RABBLE
RAMBLE
RIBBON
ROBBER
ROUBLE
RUBBER
RUBBLE
RUMBLE

SEABED
SHABBY
SNOBOL
SOMBER
STABLE
STUBBY
SYMBOL
TIDBIT
TIMBER
TIMBRE
TITBIT
TOMBOY
TREBLE
TUMBLE
TURBAN
TURBID
TURBOT
UNABLE
USABLE
VERBAL
VIABLE
WABBLE
WAMBLE
WARBLE
WEBBED
WIMBLE
WOBBLE
WOMBAT
ZOMBIE
ABACUS
ACACIA
APACHE
APICAL
ARCCOS
AVOCET
BEACON
BOBCAT
BOCCIE
BOXCAR
CAECUM
CALCIC
CANCAN
CANCEL
CANCER
CATCHY
CAUCUS
CHICHI
CHICLE
CIRCLE
CIRCUS
CLICHE
CLOCHE
COCCUS
COCCYX
CONCUR
CRECHE
CROCUS

DEACON
DESCRY
DISCUS
DOUCHE
DULCET
ELICIT
FAECAL
FALCON
FAUCES
FAUCET
FISCAL
FLACON
FRACAS
GARCON
GAUCHE
GAUCHO
GROCER
HEPCAT
HICCUP
HUBCAP
ICICLE
IPECAC
JAYCEE
JUICER
KWACHA
LANCER
LANCET
LASCAR
LITCHI
MADCAP
MARCEL
MASCON
MASCOT
MERCER
MESCAL
MISCUE
MUSCLE
NIACIN
NONCOM
NUNCIO
ORACLE
OUTCRY
PARCEL
PASCAL
PCMCIA
PENCIL
PINCER
PLACER
PLACID
PLUCKY
PONCHO
PRECIS
PSYCHE
PSYCHO
RANCHO
RANCID
RANCOR

RASCAL
REDCAP
RESCUE
SAUCER
SKYCAP
SOCCER
SPECIE
SPECIF
STICKY
STOCKY
STUCCO
SUCCOR
TEACUP
TETCHY
TOMCAT
TOUCAN
TOUCHE
TOUCHY
TRICKY
TROCHE
UNICEF
URACIL
VISCID
VISCUS
VOICED
ZIRCON
ANADEM
BANDED
BANDIT
BEADLE
BELDAM
BENDER
BIRDIE
BOODLE
BORDER
BRIDAL
BRIDGE
BRIDLE
BUNDLE
BURDEN
CADDIE
CANDID
CANDLE
CANDOR
CAUDAL
CINDER
CODDLE
COMDEX
CONDOM
CONDOR
CORDON
CRADLE
CREDIT
CUDDLE
CURDLE
DANDER
DANDLE

DAWDLE
DEADEN
DEADLY
DEODAR
DIADEM
DODDER
DOODAD
DOODLE
DREDGE
DRUDGE
DUMDUM
EBCDIC
EXODUS
FENDER
FEUDAL
FIDDLE
FINDER
FODDER
FOLDER
FONDLE
FONDUE
FRIDAY
FUDDLE
GANDER
GARDEN
GENDER
GIRDER
GIRDLE
GLIDER
GOLDEN
GOODLY
GRADER
GRUDGE
GUIDON
GULDEN
HANDLE
HARDEN
HARDLY
HEYDAY
HINDER
HOLDUP
HOODOO
HOWDAH
HOYDEN
HUDDLE
HURDLE
IBIDEM
KINDLE
KINDLY
LADDER
LADDIE
LANDAU
LANDED
LANDER
LAPDOG
LARDER
LEADEN

LEADER
LINDEN
LOADED
LOADER
LORDLY
MADDEN
MADDER
MAIDEN
MEADOW
MEDDLE
MIDDAY
MIDDEN
MIDDLE
MILDEW
MINDED
MOLDER
MONDAY
MSCDEX
MUDDLE
MURDER
NEEDLE
NODDLE
NOODLE
NORDIC
PADDLE
PANDER
PARDON
PEDDLE
PIDDLE
PLEDGE
POLDER
PONDER
POODLE
POWDER
PUDDLE
PUNDIT
PURDAH
RANDOM
REDDEN
RENDER
RIDDEN
RIDDLE
RUDDER
SADDEN
SADDLE
SANDAL
SELDOM
SHADOW
SHODDY
SLEDGE
SLIDER
SLUDGE
SMUDGE
SODDEN
SOLDER
SORDID
SPADIX

SPI**D**ER
STO**D**GY
STU**D**IO
SUB**D**UE
SUD**D**EN
SUN**D**AE
SUN**D**AY
SUN**D**ER
SUN**D**RY
TAN**D**EM
TAW**D**RY
TEN**D**ER
TEN**D**ON
TIN**D**ER
TOD**D**LE
TRA**D**ER
TRU**D**GE
TUN**D**RA
VAN**D**AL
VEN**D**EE
VEN**D**ER
VEN**D**OR
VOO**D**OO
WAD**D**LE
WAN**D**ER
WAR**D**EN
WAR**D**ER
WIN**D**ER
WIN**D**OW
WIN**D**UP
WIS**D**OM
WON**D**ER
WOO**D**ED
WOO**D**EN
WOO**D**SY
XMO**D**EM
YMO**D**EM
YON**D**ER
ZMO**D**EM
ABB**E**SS
ABJ**E**CT
ABS**E**NT
ACC**E**DE
ACC**E**NT
ACC**E**PT
ACC**E**SS
ADD**E**ND
ADH**E**RE
ADV**E**NT
ADV**E**RB
ADV**E**RT
AFF**E**CT
AFI**E**LD
AFR**E**SH
AGL**E**AM
ALB**E**IT
ALL**E**GE
AMO**E**BA
AMP**E**RE
AMV**E**TS
ANN**E**AL
API**E**CE
APP**E**AL
APP**E**AR
APP**E**ND
ARD**E**NT
ARG**E**NT
ARR**E**ST
ART**E**RY
ASC**E**ND
ASC**E**NT
ASL**E**EP
ASP**E**CT
ASS**E**NT
ASS**E**RT
ASS**E**SS
AST**E**RN
ATT**E**ND
ATT**E**ST
BAK**E**RY
BAL**E**EN
BAR**E**LY
BAT**E**AU
BED**E**CK
BEH**E**AD
BEH**E**ST
BER**E**FT
BES**E**EM
BIC**E**PS
BIS**E**CT
BOL**E**RO
BOR**E**AL
BRE**E**CH
BRE**E**ZE
BUR**E**AU
CAM**E**RA
CAR**E**EN
CAR**E**ER
CAR**E**SS
CAS**E**IN
CAV**E**AT
CAV**E**RN
CEL**E**RY
CEM**E**NT
CER**E**AL
CER**E**US
CHE**E**KY
CHE**E**RY
CHE**E**SE
CIN**E**MA
CLI**E**NT
COG**E**NT
COH**E**IR
COH**E**RE
COM**E**DY
COM**E**LY
COV**E**RT
CRE**E**PY
DEC**E**IT
DEC**E**NT
DEF**E**AT
DEF**E**CT
DEF**E**ND
DEL**E**TE
DEM**E**AN
DEP**E**ND
DES**E**RT
DET**E**CT
DET**E**ST
DIG**E**ST
DIR**E**CT
DIV**E**RS
DIV**E**RT
DIV**E**ST
DOC**E**NT
DUR**E**SS
EAT**E**RY
ECZ**E**MA
EFF**E**CT
EFF**E**TE
EGR**E**SS
ELD**E**ST
END**E**AR
ENM**E**SH
EST**E**EM
EUR**E**KA
EXC**E**ED
EXC**E**PT
EXC**E**SS
EXP**E**CT
EXP**E**ND
EXP**E**RT
EXT**E**ND
EXT**E**NT
EXT**E**RN
FIN**E**RY
FLE**E**CE
FLU**E**NT
FOM**E**NT
FOR**E**GO
FOR**E**ST
FRE**E**ZE
FRI**E**ND
FRI**E**ZE
GAI**E**TY
GAL**E**NA
GAM**E**TE
GAY**E**TY
GAZ**E**BO
GEN**E**RA
GOV**E**RN
GRI**E**VE
HER**E**BY
HER**E**IN
HER**E**OF
HER**E**ON
HER**E**SY
HER**E**TO
HOM**E**LY
HON**E**ST
HYA**E**NA
IMP**E**DE
IMP**E**ND
IMP**E**RF
INC**E**ST
IND**E**ED
IND**E**NT
INF**E**CT
INF**E**ST
ING**E**ST
INH**E**RE
INJ**E**CT
INS**E**AM
INS**E**CT
INS**E**RT
INT**E**ND
INT**E**NT
INT**E**RJ
INT**E**RN
INV**E**NT
INV**E**RT
INV**E**ST
ITS**E**LF
KOP**E**CK
KOR**E**AN
LAM**E**NT
LAT**E**NT
LEG**E**ND
LIK**E**LY
LIN**E**AL
LIN**E**AR
LIN**E**UP
LIV**E**LY
LIV**E**RY
LON**E**LY
LOV**E**LY
LOW**E**RY
LUC**E**NT
LYC**E**UM
MAK**E**UP
MAN**E**GE
MET**E**OR
MIS**E**RY
MOD**E**RN
MOD**E**ST
MOI**E**TY
MOL**E**ST
MOM**E**NT
MUS**E**UM
MYS**E**LF
NAM**E**LY
NAP**E**RY
NER**E**ID
NIC**E**TY
NIN**E**TY
NOV**E**LL
NOV**E**NA
OBJ**E**CT
OBS**E**SS
OFF**E**ND
ORD**E**AL
ORI**E**NT
ORN**E**RY
PAL**E**ON
PAR**E**NT
PAT**E**NT
PES**E**TA
PES**E**WA
PHL**E**GM
PHO**E**BE
PIG**E**ON
PIN**E**AL
PLI**E**RS
POL**E**AX
POS**E**UR
POT**E**EN
POT**E**NT
PRI**E**ST
RAC**E**ME
RAR**E**FY
REC**E**DE
REC**E**NT
REC**E**SS
RED**E**EM
REG**E**NT
REJ**E**CT
REL**E**NT
REM**E**DY
REN**E**GE
REP**E**AL
REP**E**AT
REP**E**NT
RES**E**NT
REV**E**AL
REV**E**RB
REV**E**RE
REV**E**RS
REV**E**RT
ROD**E**NT
SAF**E**TY
SAT**E**EN
SCH**E**ME
SCR**E**AM
SCR**E**EN
SCR**E**WY
SEC**E**DE
SEL**E**CT
SEN**E**CA
SER**E**NE
SEV**E**RE
SHI**E**LD
SHI**E**ST
SHR**E**WD
SIL**E**NT
SLE**E**PY
SLE**E**VE
SLI**E**ST
SNE**E**ZE
SOL**E**MN
SPE**E**CH
SPH**E**RE
SPL**E**EN
SPR**E**AD
SQU**E**AK
SQU**E**AL
STR**E**AK
STR**E**AM
STR**E**ET
STR**E**SS
SUP**E**RB
SUR**E**TY
TAL**E**NT
TAV**E**RN
TER**E**DO
THI**E**VE
THR**E**AD
THR**E**AT
THR**E**SH
TIM**E**LY
TOR**E**RO
TUR**E**EN
TUX**E**DO
TWE**E**DY
UNB**E**ND
UNL**E**SS
UNM**E**ET
UNR**E**AD
UNR**E**AL
UNR**E**EL
UNR**E**ST
UNS**E**AL
UNS**E**AT
UNV**E**IL
UNW**E**LL
UNW**E**PT
UPB**E**AT
UPK**E**EP
UPR**E**AR
UPW**E**LL
URG**E**NT
VEN**E**ER
VOY**E**UR
WAT**E**RY
WHE**E**ZE
WHE**E**ZY
ARM**F**UL
ART**F**UL
BAF**F**LE
BAR**F**LY
BEL**F**RY
BUF**F**ER
BUF**F**ET
CAP**F**UL
CHA**F**ER
COF**F**EE
COF**F**ER
COF**F**IN
COM**F**IT
CON**F**AB
CON**F**ED
CON**F**ER
CRA**F**TY
CUR**F**EW
DEA**F**EN
DIF**F**ER
DRA**F**TY
DUF**F**ER
FIT**F**UL
FLU**F**FY
GAD**F**LY
GAF**F**ER
GUF**F**AW
HEI**F**ER
JOY**F**UL
LAW**F**UL
LEA**F**ED
MAN**F**UL
MAY**F**LY
MIS**F**IT
MUF**F**IN
MUF**F**LE
NON**F**AT
OUT**F**IT
OUT**F**OX
PIF**F**LE
PIL**F**ER
PRE**F**AB
PRE**F**ER
PRE**F**IX
PRO**F**IT
PUF**F**IN
RAF**F**IA
RAF**F**LE
REE**F**ER
RUF**F**LE
SHI**F**TY
SIN**F**UL
STI**F**LE
STU**F**FY
SUF**F**ER
SUF**F**IX
SUL**F**UR
TIF**F**IN
TOF**F**EE
TRI**F**LE
USE**F**UL
WAF**F**LE
WOE**F**UL
WOO**F**ER
ADA**G**IO
ALI**G**HT
APO**G**EE
ARI**G**HT
BAD**G**ER
BAN**G**LE
BEA**G**LE
BEG**G**AR
BLI**G**HT
BOG**G**LE
BOU**G**HT
BRI**G**HT
BRO**G**AN
BRO**G**UE
BUD**G**ET
BUD**G**IE
BUN**G**LE
BUR**G**EE
BUR**G**LE
CAT**G**UT
CAU**G**HT
COD**G**ER
COU**G**AR
CUD**G**EL
DAG**G**ER
DAN**G**ER
DAN**G**LE
DEN**G**UE
DIN**G**HY
DIN**G**LE
DIN**G**US
DOG**G**ED
DRA**G**ON
DRO**G**UE
EMI**G**RE
ENI**G**MA
FAG**G**OT
FID**G**ET
FIN**G**ER
FLA**G**ON
FLI**G**HT
FOR**G**ET
FOU**G**HT
FRI**G**HT
FRI**G**ID
FRU**G**AL
FUN**G**US
GAD**G**ET
GAG**G**LE
GAR**G**LE
GEW**G**AW
GIG**G**LE
GIN**G**ER
GOG**G**LE
GRO**G**GY
GUR**G**LE
HAG**G**IS
HAG**G**LE
HAN**G**AR
HEI**G**HT
HOA**G**IE
HUN**G**ER
JAG**G**ED
JAN**G**LE
JAR**G**ON
JAY**G**EE
JIG**G**ER
JIG**G**LE
JIN**G**LE
JOG**G**LE
JUG**G**LE
JUN**G**LE
KNI**G**HT
LEA**G**UE
LED**G**ER
LEN**G**TH
LIN**G**ER
LOD**G**ER
LOG**G**IA
MAG**G**OT
MAN**G**ER
MAN**G**LE
MAR**G**IN
MEA**G**ER
MER**G**ER
MID**G**ET
MIN**G**LE
MON**G**ER
MOR**G**AN
MOR**G**UE
NAU**G**HT
NOG**G**IN
NOU**G**AT
NOU**G**HT
NUG**G**ET
ORI**G**IN
OUT**G**UN
OXY**G**EN
PID**G**IN
PLA**G**UE
PLI**G**HT
PON**G**EE
POP**G**UN
RAG**G**ED
RAN**G**ER
RIG**G**ER
RIN**G**ER
RLO**G**IN
RUG**G**ED
SHA**G**GY
SIN**G**LE
SLI**G**HT
SLO**G**AN
SOI**G**NE
SOU**G**HT
SPI**G**OT
STI**G**MA
TAN**G**LE
TAR**G**ET
TAU**G**HT
TIN**G**LE
TOG**G**LE
TON**G**UE
TRA**G**IC
TUR**G**ID
VER**G**ER
VIR**G**IN
VUL**G**AR
WAG**G**LE
WAN**G**LE
WEI**G**HT
WIG**G**LE
WIG**G**LY
WIN**G**ED
AFG**H**AN
ANC**H**OR
ANT**H**EM
ANT**H**ER
ANY**H**OW
ARC**H**ON
AST**H**MA
AUT**H**OR
BAT**H**OS
BET**H**EL
BIN**H**EX
BIS**H**OP
BOT**H**ER
BUS**H**ED
BUS**H**EL
CAC**H**ET
CAR**H**OP
CAS**H**EW
CIP**H**ER
DAS**H**ER
DIR**H**AM
DIS**H**ED
DIT**H**ER
EIG**H**TY
EIT**H**ER
ESC**H**EW
EUC**H**RE

FATHER
FATHOM
FISHER
GATHER
GOPHER
GOTHIC
GUSHER
HITHER
HYPHEN
KOSHER
LATHER
LETHAL
LICHEE
LICHEN
LIGHTS
MAYHEM
METHOD
METHYL
MIGHTY
MISHAP
MOTHER
NEPHEW
NETHER
ORCHID
ORPHAN
PATHOS
PEAHEN
POTHER
PUSHER
PYTHON
QUAHOG
RASHER
RATHER
RICHES
SACHEM
SACHET
SASHAY
SIPHON
SYPHON
TETHER
TIGHTS
TOWHEE
TYPHUS
UNSHIP
UNSHOD
UPSHOT
URCHIN
WASHER
WETHER
WITHAL
WITHER
WITHIN
ZEPHYR
ZITHER
ACTING
ACTION
ACTIVE
ACUITY
ADDICT
ADMIRE
ADRIFT
ADVICE
ADVISE
AERIAL
AFFIRM
ALBINO
ALLIED
ALPINE
ANGINA
ANOINT
ARNICA
ARRIVE
ARTIST
ASPIRE
ASSIGN
ASSIST
ASSIZE
ATRIUM
ATTIRE
AUTISM
AWEIGH
AWHILE
AWHIRL
AWNING
BANISH
BARIUM
BEHIND
BELIEF
BELIKE
BEMIRE
BENIGN
BESIDE
BETIDE
BIKINI
BITING
BLUING
BLUISH
BODICE
BODILY
BONITO
BOVINE
BOXING
BRAISE
BRUISE
BUNION
BURIAL
BUSILY
CALICO
CALIPH
CANINE
CARIES
CASING
CASINO
CATION
CAVIAR
CAVITY
CERISE
CERIUM
CESIUM
CHAISE
CHOICE
CHRISM
CHRIST
CILIUM
CITIFY
CIVICS
CODIFY
COMING
COMITY
COPIER
COPING
COSINE
CRUISE
CUBISM
CURIUM
DANISH
DARING
DATIVE
DECIDE
DEFILE
DEFINE
DEMISE
DENIAL
DENIER
DEPICT
DERIDE
DERIVE
DESIGN
DESIRE
DESIST
DEVICE
DEVISE
DIMITY
DIVIDE
DIVINE
DOCILE
DOMINO
DURING
EDGING
EFFIGY
EGOISM
EMPIRE
ENDING
ENDIVE
ENGINE
ENLIST
ENMITY
ENRICH
ENSIGN
ENSILE
ENTICE
ENTIRE
ENTITY
EOLIAN
EQUINE
EQUITY
ERBIUM
ERMINE
ESKIMO
ETHICS
EXCISE
EXCITE
EXPIRE
FABIAN
FACIAL
FACILE
FACING
FAMILY
FAMINE
FAMISH
FARINA
FELINE
FENIAN
FETISH
FILIAL
FILING
FINIAL
FINISH
FINITE
FIXITY
FORINT
FRUITY
FUSION
FUTILE
GAMINE
GARISH
GENIAL
GENIUS
GNEISS
GRAINY
HALITE
HEGIRA
HELIUM
HOMILY
HOMINY
IGNITE
IMBIBE
IMPISH
INCISE
INCITE
INDIAN
INDICT
INDIGO
INDITE
INDIUM
INFIRM
INNING
INSIDE
INSIST
INVITE
IODIDE
IODINE
IODIZE
IONIZE
JOVIAL
JUNIOR
JURIST
LABIAL
LABILE
LABIUM
LADING
LAMINA
LARIAT
LAVISH
LEGION
LENITY
LESION
LEVITY
LIBIDO
LIKING
LINING
LIVING
LOTION
LOVING
LUPINE
MALIAN
MALICE
MALIGN
MANIAC
MANIOC
MAOISM
MARINA
MARINE
MATINS
MEDIAL
MEDIAN
MEDICO
MEDIUM
MENIAL
MENINX
MERINO
METIER
MILIEU
MINION
MOBILE
MODIFY
MODISH
MONISM
MOTILE
MOTION
MOTIVE
MUTINY
MYRIAD
NATION
NATIVE
NOTICE
NOTIFY
NOTION
NOVICE
NOWISE
NUBILE
NUDISM
OBLIGE
ODDITY
OFFICE
OFFING
OFFISH
ONEIDA
OOLITE
OPTICS
OPTION
ORNITH
OSMIUM
OSSIFY
OUTING
PACIFY
PALING
PAPIST
PARIAH
PARING
PARISH
PARITY
PATINA
PAVING
PERIOD
PERISH
PETITE
PILING
PINION
PIPING
PLAINT
PODIUM
POLICE
POLICY
POLISH
POLITE
POLITY
POTION
PRAISE
PUMICE
PUNISH
PURIFY
PURINE
PURISM
PURITY
PYRITE
QIVIUT
QUAINT
RABIES
RACISM
RADIAL
RADIAN
RADISH
RADIUM
RADIUS
RAKISH
RAMIFY
RAPIER
RAPINE
RARING
RATIFY
RATING
RATION
RAVINE
RAVISH
RECIPE
RECITE
REFILL
REFINE
REGIME
REGION
RELICT
RELIEF
RELISH
RELIVE
REMIND
REMISS
REPINE
RESIDE
RESIGN
RESIST
RETINA
RETIRE
REVIEW
REVILE
REVISE
REVIVE
RUPIAH
SADISM
SALINE
SALIVA
SANITY
SATIRE
SAVIOR
SAYING
SCHISM
SCHIST
SCRIBE
SCRIMP
SCRIPT
SEMITE
SENILE
SENIOR
SENITI
SERIAL
SERIES
SEWING
SEXISM
SHEIKH
SHRIEK
SHRIFT
SHRIKE
SHRILL
SHRIMP
SHRINE
SHRINK
SHRIVE
SIDING
SIGILL
SILICA
SIMIAN
SIMILE
SLEIGH
SLUICE
SOCIAL
SOCIOL
SODIUM
SOVIET
SPHINX
SPLICE
SPLINE
SPLINT
SPRING
SPRINT
SPRITE
SQUINT
SQUIRE
SQUIRM
SQUIRT
STRICT
STRIDE
STRIFE
STRIKE
STRING
STRIPE
STRIVE
SUPINE
TAKING
TAOISM
TARIFF
TEDIUM
THEIRS
THEISM
THRICE
THRIFT
THRILL
THRIVE
TROIKA
TRUISM
TRYING
TUBING
TURING
TYPIFY
TYPIST
ULTIMO
UMPIRE
UNBIND
UNCIAL
UNDIES
UNGIRD
UNKIND
UNLIKE
UNPILE
UNRIPE
UNWIND
UNWISE
UPHILL
UPLIFT
UPPISH
UPPITY
UPSIDE
UPWIND
URSINE
VAGINA
VALISE
VANISH
VANITY
VARIED
VENIAL
VENIRE
VERIFY
VERILY
VERITY
VIKING
VILIFY
VIRILE
VIRION
VISION
VIVIFY
VIZIER
VOTIVE
WAHINE
WAPITI
WIRING
WRAITH
ZENITH
ZODIAC
DEEJAY
INKJET
LOGJAM
TROJAN
AWAKEN
BACKER
BACKUP
BARKER
BASKET
BEAKER
BECKON
BICKER
BODKIN
BOOKIE
BROKEN
BROKER
BUCKET
BUCKLE
BUNKER
BUNKUM
BUSKIN
CACKLE
CANKER
CASKET
CATKIN
CHOKER
CHUKKA
COCKLE
COOKIE
CUCKOO
DARKEN
DESKEW
DICKER
DICKEY
DOCKET
DONKEY
FICKLE
FOLKSY
FORKED
GASKET
GINKGO
GURKHA
HACKER
HACKIE
HACKLE
HANKER
HARKEN
HAWKER
HECKLE
HOCKEY
HOOKAH
HOOKER
HOOKUP
HUNKER
JACKAL
JACKET
JERKIN
JOCKEY
JUNKER
JUNKET
JUNKIE
LACKEY
LINKED
LINKUP
LOCKER
LOCKET
LOCKUP
MARKED
MARKET
MARKKA
MARKUP
MONKEY
MUSKEG

MUSKET
NAPKIN
NICKEL
NICKER
PACKER
PACKET
PEAKED
PICKAX
PICKET
PICKLE
PICKUP
PINKIE
PIPKIN
POCKET
PORKER
PUCKER
PUNKIN
QUAKER
RACKET
RANKLE
RECKON
ROCKER
ROCKET
ROOKIE
RUCKUS
SHAKER
SICKEN
SICKLE
SINKER
SOCKET
SPOKEN
SUCKER
SUCKLE
SUNKEN
TACKLE
TANKER
TICKER
TICKET
TICKLE
TINKER
TINKLE
TUCKER
TURKEY
TUSKER
WEAKEN
WEAKLY
WEEKLY
WELKIN
WESKIT
WICKED
WICKER
WICKET
WINKER
WINKLE
WORKER
YANKEE
ZONKED
AMULET
ANALOG
ANKLET
ANTLER
APPLET
ARMLET
ASHLAR
ASYLUM
AZALEA
BALLAD
BALLET
BALLOT
BARLEY
BEDLAM
BELLOW
BILLET
BILLOW
BOILER
BOWLEG
BOWLER
BULLET
BURLAP
BUTLER
BYPLAY
CALLOW
CALLUS
CELLAR
CHALET
CHILLY
CHOLER
COLLAR
COLLAT
COLLIE
COLLOQ
COOLER
COOLIE
COULEE
CURLEW
CUTLER
CUTLET
DAHLIA
DEPLOY
DEWLAP
DOGLEG
DOLLAR
DOLLOP
DUPLEX
EAGLET
ECCLES
ECCLUS
EMBLEM
EMPLOY
EVOLVE
EYELET
EYELID
FABLED
FAILLE
FALLOW
FEALTY
FEELER
FELLAH
FELLOW
FILLER
FILLET
FILLIP
FOLLOW
FROLIC
GAELIC
GALLEY
GALLIC
GALLON
GALLOP
GARLIC
GIMLET
GOALIE
GOBLET
GOBLIN
GRILLE
GUILTY
GULLET
HALLOW
HAMLET
HARLOT
HEALTH
HOLLER
HOLLOW
HOWLER
INFLOW
INFLUX
ITALIC
JAILER
KAOLIN
KEGLER
MAILED
MALLET
MALLOW
MARLIN
MEDLEY
MELLOW
MILLER
MILLET
MISLAY
MOSLEM
MOTLEY
MUKLUK
MULLET
MUSLIM
MUSLIN
OCELOT
OCULAR
OMELET
OODLES
OSTLER
OUTLAW
OUTLAY
OUTLET
PALLET
PALLID
PALLOR
PARLAY
PARLEY
PARLOR
PELLET
PHILOS
PHYLUM
PIGLET
PILLAR
PILLOW
POLLEN
POPLAR
POPLIN
PRELIM
PROLIX
PROLOG
PUBLIC
PULLET
PULLEY
RAGLAN
REALLY
REALTY
REFLEX
REFLUX
REPLAY
ROLLER
RUNLET
SAILOR
SALLOW
SCULPT
SEALER
SHELVE
SLALOM
SMILAX
STOLEN
STOLID
STOLON
STYLUS
SUBLET
SULLEN
SUNLIT
SVELTE
TABLET
TAILOR
TALLOW
TELLER
TILLER
TITLED
TOILET
TWELVE
UNCLAD
UNCLOG
UNPLUG
VALLEY
VARLET
VELLUM
VILLUS
VIOLET
VIOLIN
VOLLEY
WALLET
WALLOP
WALLOW
WAYLAY
WEALTH
WHALER
WHILOM
WHILST
WHOLLY
WIGLET
WILLOW
WOOLEN
WOOLLY
YELLOW
ZEALOT
ACUMEN
AIDMAN
AIRMAN
AKIMBO
ALUMNA
ANEMIA
ANIMAL
ANIMUS
ATOMIC
BAGMAN
BATMAN
BOWMAN
BUMMER
CAIMAN
CAYMAN
CERMET
CHUMMY
CLAMMY
CLAMOR
CLIMAX
CLUMSY
COMMIT
COMMON
COSMIC
COSMOS
COWMAN
CRUMMY
DAEMON
DERMAL
DERMIS
DIMMER
DISMAL
DISMAY
DOLMEN
DORMER
ENAMEL
ENAMOR
EXEMPT
FLIMSY
FOEMAN
FORMAL
FORMAT
FORMER
FRUMPY
GAMMER
GAMMON
GERMAN
GRUMPY
GUNMAN
HAMMER
HAYMOW
HELMET
HERMIT
ICEMAN
ISOMER
KERMIT
KISMET
LAWMAN
LAYMAN
LEGMAN
LITMUS
LUMMOX
MADMAN
MAMMAL
MAMMON
MARMOT
MERMAN
MICMAC
MORMON
MUMMER
MURMUR
MUUMUU
NORMAL
NORMAN
NUTMEG
PALMER
PENMAN
PERMIT
POMMEL
PREMED
PREMIX
PRIMAL
PRIMER
PROMPT
PUMMEL
REAMER
SALMON
SCAMPI
SEAMAN
SEEMLY
SERMON
SHAMAN
SHIMMY
SIMMER
SKIMPY
STAMEN
STYMIE
SUBMIT
SUMMER
SUMMIT
SUMMON
TALMUD
THYMUS
TREMOR
UREMIA
VERMIN
WARMTH
WHAMMY
WHIMSY
YAMMER
YEOMAN
AGENCY
AGENDA
AMENDS
ARCNET
ATONAL
AVENGE
AVENUE
BAGNIO
BANNER
BEANIE
BITNET
BLANCH
BLENCH
BONNET
BOUNCE
BOUNTY
BRANCH
BRANDY
BRONCO
BRONZE
BRUNCH
BRUNET
BURNER
CANNED
CANNON
CANNOT
CARNAL
CATNAP
CATNIP
CHANCE
CHANCY
CHANGE
CHINTZ
CHUNKY
CLENCH
CLINCH
CLINIC
COGNAC
CORNEA
CORNER
CORNET
COUNTY
CRANKY
CRANNY
CRINGE
CRUNCH
CUNNER
CYGNET
DAINTY
DARNEL
DINNER
DIRNDL
DOINGS
DOWNER
DRENCH
DUENDE
DUENNA
EGGNOG
ETHNIC
ETHNOL
EVINCE
FENNEL
FIANCE
FLANGE
FLINCH
FLUNKY
FRENCH
FRENZY
FRINGE
FUNNEL
GANNET
GARNER
GARNET
GLANCE
GRANGE
GUINEA
GUNNER
HAUNCH
HERNIA
HOBNOB
HORNET
IRENIC
IRONIC
JAUNTY
JENNET
JITNEY
JOHNNY
JOINER
JOUNCE
KENNEL
KERNEL
KIDNAP
KIDNEY
LAUNCH
LINNET
LOUNGE
MAENAD
MAGNET
MANNED
MANNER
MINNOW
NUANCE
ORANGE
PAUNCH
PAWNEE
PEANUT
PENNON
PHENOL
PHONIC
PICNIC
PIGNUT
PLANET
PLENTY
PLENUM
PLINTH
PLUNGE
POUNCE
PRANCE
PRINCE
PRINTF
PRONTO
QUENCH
QUINCE
QUINSY
REGNAL
RENNET
RENNIN
RUNNEL
RUNNER
SCANTY
SCONCE
SEANCE
SHANTY
SHINER
SHINNY
SHINTO
SIGNAL
SIGNET
SKINNY
SONNET
SPINAL
SPINEL
SPINET
SPONGE
STANCE
STANCH
STANZA
STENCH
STINGY
STONED
TANNER
TANNIN
TELNET
TENNIS
THANKS
THENCE
TRANCE
TRANSL
TRANSP
TRENCH
TUNNEL
TURNER
TURNIP
TWENTY
TWINGE
UNSNAP
URANIC
URANUS
URINAL
USENET
VERNAL
WALNUT
WHENCE
WHINNY
WIENER
WINNER
WINNOW
WRENCH
ZINNIA
ZOUNDS
ABLOOM
ABROAD
ABSORB
ACCORD
ACCOST
ACROSS
ADJOIN
ADROIT
ADSORB
AFFORD
AFLOAT
ALCOVE
ALMOND
ALMOST
ANGORA
ANYONE
APLOMB
ARGOSY
ARMORY
ARROYO
ASHORE
ASSORT
AURORA
BABOON
BECOME
BEFORE
BEFOUL
BEGONE
BEHOLD

BEHOOF
BELONG
BEMOAN
BEYOND
BROOCH
BYGONE
BYWORD
CAHOOT
CAJOLE
CANOPY
CAVORT
CHOOSE
CHOOSY
CHROME
CHROMO
COCOON
COHORT
COLONY
CORONA
COYOTE
CREOLE
CUPOLA
CUTOFF
CUTOUT
DAKOTA
DECODE
DEFORM
DEHORN
DEMODE
DEMOTE
DENOTE
DEPORT
DEPOSE
DETOUR
DEVOID
DEVOIR
DEVOTE
DEVOUR
DEVOUT
DISOWN
DUGOUT
EFFORT
EMBODY
EMBOSS
ENCODE
ENCORE
ENFOLD
ENJOIN
ENROLL
ENTOMB
ESCORT
EULOGY
EXHORT
EXPORT
EXPOSE
EXTORT
FAMOUS

FAVOUR
FEDORA
FELONY
FLOOZY
FURORE
GALORE
GALOSH
GIGOLO
GROOVE
GROOVY
HEROIN
HONOUR
HUMOUR
IDIOCY
IGNORE
IMPORT
IMPOSE
IMPOST
INBORN
INCOME
INDOOR
INFOLD
INFORM
INMOST
INROAD
INSOLE
INTONE
INVOKE
JALOPY
JOCOSE
JOYOUS
KIBOSH
KIMONO
KOBOLD
LABOUR
LAGOON
LAYOFF
LAYOUT
MAHOUT
MAROON
MEGOHM
MELODY
MEMOIR
MEMORY
MIMOSA
MONODY
MOROSE
NOBODY
OBLONG
ODIOUS
OPPOSE
ORIOLE
ORMOLU
OTIOSE
OXFORD
PAGODA
PARODY

PAROLE
PATOIS
PAYOFF
PEYOTE
PHLOEM
POROUS
PRIORY
PUTOUT
RAGOUT
REBORN
RECOIL
RECORD
RECOUP
REFORM
REJOIN
REMORA
REMOTE
REMOVE
RENOWN
REPORT
REPOSE
RESORT
RETORT
REVOKE
REVOLT
RUNOFF
SALOON
SARONG
SCHOOL
SCROLL
SECOND
SHROUD
SIMONY
SMOOCH
SMOOTH
SNOOTY
SNOOZE
SODOMY
SPROUT
STOOGE
STROBE
STRODE
STROKE
STROLL
STRONG
STROVE
SUBORN
THEORY
THROAT
THRONE
THRONG
THROVE
TRIODE
TYCOON
UNBOLT
UNBORN
UNCOIL

UNCORK
UNFOLD
UNHOLY
UNHOOK
UNLOAD
UNLOCK
UNMOOR
UNROBE
UNROLL
UNROOF
UNTOLD
UNYOKE
UPHOLD
UPLOAD
UPMOST
UPROAR
UPROOT
UPTOWN
UTMOST
VAPORY
VELOUR
VENOUS
VINOUS
ZYGOTE
ARMPIT
BEDPAN
BIOPSY
BUMPER
CAMPER
CAMPUS
CARPAL
CARPEL
CARPET
CHAPEL
CHOPPY
COMPAQ
COMPAR
COMPEL
COMPLY
COOPER
COPPER
CORPSE
CORPUS
COUPLE
COUPON
COWPOX
CUSPID
DAMPEN
DAMPER
DAPPER
DAPPLE
DEEPEN
DESPOT
DIAPER
DIMPLE
DIPPER
DISPEL

DRAPER
DROPSY
ELAPSE
FLOPPY
FRAPPE
GOSPEL
GRIPPE
HAMPER
HAPPEN
HERPES
HIPPED
HIPPIE
HOOPLA
HOPPER
JASPER
JUMPER
KIPPER
LAPPET
LIMPET
LIMPID
LOOPER
MAGPIE
MOPPET
MYOPIA
NIPPER
NIPPLE
OUTPUT
PAMPER
PAUPER
PAWPAW
PEOPLE
PEPPER
PIGPEN
PIMPLE
PIPPIN
POMPON
POPPER
POTPIE
PREPAY
PROPEL
PROPER
PULPIT
PUPPET
PURPLE
RAPPEN
RIPPLE
ROMPER
RUMPLE
RUMPUS
SAMPAN
SAMPLE
SEXPOT
SIMPER
SIMPLE
SLIPUP
SLOPPY
SNIPPY

STAPES
STAPLE
STEPPE
STUPID
STUPOR
SUPPER
SUPPLE
SUPPLY
TAMPER
TAMPON
TAPPET
TARPON
TEAPOT
TEEPEE
TEMPER
TEMPLE
TENPIN
TIPPET
TIPPLE
TOPPLE
TORPID
TORPOR
TOUPEE
TREPAN
TRIPLE
TRIPLY
TRIPOD
TROPHY
TROPIC
UTOPIA
VESPER
WAMPUM
WEAPON
WIMPLE
ZIPPER
BASQUE
BISQUE
CASQUE
CHEQUE
CIRQUE
CLAQUE
CLIQUE
MANQUE
MASQUE
MOSQUE
OPAQUE
PLAQUE
RISQUE
TORQUE
UNIQUE
YANQUI
ACCRUE
AFFRAY
AMERCE
AMORAL
ANTRUM
APERCU

APPROX
ASHRAM
ASTRAL
ASTRAY
ASTROL
ASTRON
ATTRIB
AVERSE
BARRED
BARREL
BARREN
BARRIO
BARROW
BETRAY
BORROW
BOURSE
BURROW
CARREL
CARROT
CHARGE
CHERRY
CHERUB
CHORAL
CHOREA
CHORUS
CHURCH
CIRRUS
CITRON
CITRUS
CLARET
CLERGY
CLERIC
COARSE
COERCE
CORRAL
COURSE
DEARTH
DEBRIS
DECREE
DEFRAY
DEGREE
DERRIS
EEPROM
EMBRYO
EMERGE
ENDRIN
ENERGY
ENGRAM
ENTRAP
ENTREE
ESCROW
ESPRIT
FABRIC
FAERIE
FAIRLY
FARROW
FERRET

FERRIC
FIBRIL
FIBRIN
FIERCE
FLORAL
FLORID
FLORIN
FLURRY
FOURTH
FUHRER
FURROW
GARRET
GOURDE
HAIRDO
HARROW
HATRED
HEARSE
HEARTH
HEARTY
HEBREW
HOARSE
HORRID
HORROR
HUBRIS
HURRAH
HYBRID
IMBRUE
INBRED
INTROD
LAUREL
MACRON
MADRAS
MARROW
MATRIX
MATRON
METRIC
MICRON
MIRROR
MORRIS
MORROW
NARROW
NEARBY
NEURAL
NEUROL
NEURON
NIMROD
NITRIC
NUTRIA
OSPREY
OUTRUN
OVERDO
OVERLY
PARROT
PATROL
PATRON
PETREL
PETROL

PHAROS
PIERCE
PLURAL
POGROM
PUTRID
QUARRY
QUARTO
QUARTZ
QUORUM
RAMROD
REFRIG
REGRET
RUBRIC
SACRED
SACRUM
SATRAP
SCARAB
SCARCE
SCORCH
SCORIA
SCURRY
SCURVY
SEARCH
SECRET
SHERRY
SIERRA
SLURRY
SMIRCH
SOIREE
SORREL
SORROW
SOURCE
SPARSE
SPIRAL
SPIREA
SPIRIT
SPURGE
STARCH
STARVE
STEREO
STURDY
SURREY
SWERVE
TERROR
THIRST
THIRTY
THORAX
TORRID
TUGRIK
TURRET
ULTRIX
UNTRUE
UNWRAP
USURER
UTERUS
VAGROM
WALRUS

WARREN
WHERRY
YARROW
YEARLY
ARCSIN
BALSAM
BONSAI
BUQSHA
BURSAR
CAESAR
CASSIA
CATSUP
CAUSAL
CENSER
CENSOR
CENSUS
CHASER
CHASTE
CHISEL
CHOSEN
CLASSY
CLOSET
CONSOL
CONSTR
CONSUL
CORSET
COUSIN
CRISIS
CUESTA
CURSOR
DAMSEL
DAMSON
DIESEL
DORSAL
DRESSY
ENISLE
FIASCO
FIESTA
FLASHY
FLESHY
FLOSSY
FOSSIL
FRESCO
FRISKY
GEISHA
GEYSER
GIBSON
GLOSSY
GODSON
GOSSIP
GRISLY
GUSSET
GYPSUM
HANSEL
HANSOM
HASSLE
HAWSER

HORSEY
HUSSAR
HYSSOP
JERSEY
JETSAM
JIGSAW
KAISER
KISSER
KITSCH
LASSIE
LESSEE
LESSEN
LESSER
LESSON
LESSOR
LOOSEN
MASSIF
MEASLY
MENSES
MESSRS
MIASMA
MISSAL
MORSEL
MOUSER
MOUSSE
MUSSEL
NAUSEA
NELSON
OFFSET
ORISON
OUTSET
PARSEC
PARSON
PASSEL
PASSIM
PEPSIN
PERSON
PHYSIC
PIGSTY
PLASMA
POISON
POSSUM
PRESET
PRESTO
PRISON
PRISSY
PULSAR
PURSER
PURSUE
PUTSCH
QBASIC
QUASAR
RAISIN
RANSOM
REASON
RIPSAW
RUSSET
SEASON
SEESAW
SENSOR
SEPSIS
SIESTA
SUBSET
SUNSET
TARSUS
TASSEL
TEASEL
THESIS
TINSEL
TISSUE
TOCSIN
TONSIL
TOUSLE
TRUSTY
TUSSLE
UNESCO
UNISEX
UNISON
UNUSED
VASSAL
VERSED
VERSUS
VESSEL
WEASEL
WORSEN
WRASSE
YEASTY
ZOYSIA
ABATIS
ACETIC
APATHY
ARCTAN
ARCTIC
AVATAR
BANTAM
BANTER
BARTER
BATTEN
BATTER
BATTLE
BEETLE
BESTIR
BESTOW
BETTER
BETTOR
BIOTIC
BIOTIN
BISTRO
BITTER
BLITHE
BLOTCH
BOATER
BOOTEE
BOTTLE
BOTTOM
BRITON
BRUTAL
BUSTLE
BUTTER
BUTTON
CACTUS
CAFTAN
CANTER
CANTLE
CANTON
CANTOR
CAPTOR
CARTEL
CARTON
CARTOP
CASTER
CASTLE
CATTLE
CENTER
CENTRE
CHATTY
CHITIN
CLOTHE
CLUTCH
COITUS
COOTIE
COPTER
CORTEX
COSTLY
COTTER
COTTON
CRATER
CRATON
CRETIN
CRITIC
CROTCH
CRUTCH
CURTSY
CUSTOM
CUTTER
DACTYL
DARTER
DEBTOR
DENTAL
DENTIN
DIATOM
DICTUM
DISTAL
DOCTOR
DOTTLE
DUSTER
EARTHY
EASTER
EMETIC
EROTIC
EXOTIC
FACTOR
FALTER
FASTEN
FATTEN
FESTAL
FESTER
FETTER
FETTLE
FILTER
FLATUS
FLITCH
FOETAL
FOOTED
FOSTER
GAITER
GANTRY
GARTER
GENTLE
GENTRY
GHETTO
GIFTED
GLITCH
GLUTEN
GOATEE
GOITER
GOTTEN
GRATIS
GROTTO
GUITAR
GUTTER
HALTER
HASTEN
HATTER
HECTIC
HECTOR
HIATUS
HOSTEL
HURTLE
HUSTLE
INSTEP
JESTER
JOSTLE
KETTLE
KILTER
KIRTLE
KITTEN
KLATCH
KOWTOW
LACTIC
LAPTOP
LATTER
LECTOR
LENTIL
LEPTON
LETTER
LINTEL
LISTEN
LITTER
LITTLE
LOATHE
LOITER
LUSTER
MANTEL
MANTIS
MANTLE
MANTRA
MARTEN
MARTIN
MARTYR
MASTER
MASTIC
MATTER
MENTAL
MENTOR
METTLE
MISTER
MITTEN
MOLTEN
MORTAL
MORTAR
MOSTLY
MOTTLE
MOUTON
MUSTER
MUTTER
MUTTON
MYRTLE
MYSTIC
NAUTCH
NECTAR
NESTLE
NETTLE
NEUTER
NEWTON
NORTON
ORATOR
OUSTER
OYSTER
PALTER
PALTRY
PANTIE
PANTRY
PARTLY
PASTEL
PASTOR
PASTRY
PATTER
PECTIN
PEPTIC
PESTER
PESTLE
PEWTER
PHOTOG
PHOTON
PISTIL
PISTOL
PISTON
PLATEN
PLUTON
POETRY
PORTAL
PORTER
PORTLY
POSTAL
POSTER
POTTER
PRETTY
PROTON
PUTTEE
PUTTER
QINTAR
RAFTER
RASTER
RATTAN
RATTER
RATTLE
RECTAL
RECTOR
RECTUM
RENTAL
RHYTHM
ROSTER
ROTTEN
RUSTIC
RUSTLE
SCOTCH
SCYTHE
SECTOR
SEETHE
SENTRY
SEPTIC
SETTEE
SETTER
SETTLE
SEXTET
SEXTON
SISTER
SKETCH
SMITHY
SMUTCH
SNATCH
SNITCH
SOFTEN
SOOTHE
SORTIE
SPATHE
SPOTTY
SPUTUM
STATIC
STATUE
STATUS
STITCH
SUBTLE
SUITOR
SULTAN
SULTRY
SUNTAN
SURTAX
SWATCH
SWATHE
SWITCH
SYNTAX
SYSTEM
TACTIC
TARTAN
TARTAR
TATTER
TATTLE
TATTOO
TEETER
TEETHE
TESTER
TESTIS
THATCH
TIPTOE
TITTER
TITTLE
TOMTIT
TOOTHY
TOTTER
TRITON
TSETSE
TURTLE
TWITCH
ULSTER
UNITED
UNSTOP
URETER
VECTOR
VERTEX
VESTAL
VESTEE
VESTRY
VICTIM
VICTOR
VIRTUE
VORTEX
WAITER
WANTON
WATTLE
WELTER
WHITEN
WINTER
WINTRY
WITTED
WONTED
WORTHY
WRETCH
WRITER
WRITHE
ABDUCT
ABJURE
ABOUND
ABRUPT
ABSURD
ACCUSE
ACQUIT
ACTUAL
ADDUCE
ADJURE
ADJUST
ALLUDE
ALLURE
AMBUSH
AMOUNT
ANNUAL
AROUND
AROUSE
ASSUME
ASSURE
ASTUTE
ATTUNE
AUBURN
AUGURY
AUGUST
AUTUMN
AVAUNT
AVOUCH
BEAUTY
BELUGA
BEMUSE
BENUMB
BLOUSE
CASUAL
CAYUGA
CAYUSE
CHAUNT
CLAUSE
COLUMN
COPULA
COQUET
CROUCH
DEBUNK
DEDUCE
DEDUCT
DEFUSE
DELUDE
DELUGE
DELUXE
DEMURE
DENUDE
DEPUTE
DEPUTY
DILUTE
DISUSE
ENDURE
ENDURO
ENGULF
ENOUGH
ENSURE
ESCUDO
EUNUCH
EXCUSE
EXHUME
FACULA
FECUND
FERULE
FIBULA
FIGURE
FLAUNT
FUTURE
GERUND
GROUCH
GROUND
GROUSE
ILLUME
ILLUST
IMMUNE
IMMURE
IMPUGN
IMPURE
IMPUTE
INDUCE
INDUCT
INFUSE
INHUME
INJURE
INJURY
INRUSH
INSULT
INSURE
INTUIT
IRRUPT
JAGUAR
JEJUNE
JOCUND
JUJUBE
KABUKI
KORUNA
LACUNA
LEGUME
LIKUTA
LIQUID
LIQUOR
LOBULE
LOCUST
LUXURY
MAKUTA
MANUAL
MANURE
MATURE
MINUET
MINUTE
MISUSE
MODULE
MUTUAL
NATURE
NEBULA
NODULE
OBTUSE
OCCULT
OCCUPY
ONRUSH
ORDURE
PAIUTE
PAPULE
PENURY
PEQUOT
PERUKE
PERUSE
PIQUET
PSEUDO
REBUFF
REBUKE
REDUCE
REFUGE
REFUND
REFUSE
REFUTE
REPUTE
RESULT
RESUME
RETURN
RITUAL
ROBUST
ROTUND
SALUTE
SATURN
SCHUSS
SCRUFF
SECURE
SEDUCE
SEQUEL
SEQUIN
SEXUAL
SHOULD
SLEUTH
SLOUCH
SLOUGH
SPOUSE
SPRUCE
SPRUNG
STRUCK
STRUNG
SUBURB
SUTURE
TENURE
THOUGH
THRUSH

THRUST
TRAUMA
TRIUNE
TROUGH
TROUPE
TUBULE
TUMULT
UNCURL
UNDULY
UNFURL
UNJUST
UNRULY
UNSUNG
UNTUNE
UPRUSH
UPTURN
VACUUM
VALUED
VICUNA
VISUAL
VOLUME
VOLUTE
YOGURT
BEAVER
BREVET
CALVES
CANVAS
CERVIX
CLEVER
CLEVIS
CLOVEN
CLOVER
COEVAL
CONVEX
CONVEY
CONVOY
CRAVAT
CRAVEN
CURVET
DRIVEL
DRIVER
DROVER
ELEVEN
FERVID
FERVOR
FLAVOR
GRAVEL
GRAVID
GROVEL
HALVES
HEAVEN
JAYVEE
KELVIN
LEAVED
LEAVEN
LEAVES
LOUVER
MARVEL
OEUVRE
PELVIS
PLOVER
PRIVET
PURVEY
QUAVER
QUIVER
SALVER
SELVES
SERVER
SHAVER
SHAVES
SHIVER
SHOVEL
SILVER
SLAVER
SLAVIC
SLIVER
SLOVEN
SNIVEL
SOEVER
SPAVIN
STAVES
SURVEY
SWIVEL
SYLVAN
TRAVEL
TRIVET
TRIVIA
TURVES
UNEVEN
VELVET
WAIVER
WEEVIL
AIRWAY
ANSWER
ANYWAY
BIGWIG
BLOWSY
BLOWUP
BROWSE
COBWEB
CREWEL
DRAWER
DROWSE
DROWSY
EARWAX
EARWIG
FLOWER
FLYWAY
FROWSY
GLOWER
GROWTH
LEEWAY
MIDWAY
NITWIT
OUTWIT
PEEWEE
POWWOW
PREWAR
RUNWAY
SEAWAY
SHOWER
SKEWER
SUBWAY
TROWEL
WIGWAG
WIGWAM
YAHWEH
ELIXIR
FLAXEN
PLEXUS
ARGYLE
BANYAN
CANYON
CORYZA
CRAYON
ENCYST
ENZYME
GRAYED
LARYNX
LAWYER
LIBYAN
MAGYAR
PRAYER
AMAZON
BANZAI
BENZOL
BLAZER
BLAZON
BRAZEN
BUZZER
DAZZLE
FIZZLE
FROZEN
GEEZER
GUZZLE
HUZZAH
MIZZEN
MUZZLE
NOZZLE
NUZZLE
PIAZZA
PUZZLE
SCUZZY
SIZZLE
ZIGZAG

## 5TH LETTER

ABROAD
ACTUAL
AERIAL
AFFRAY
AFGHAN
AFLOAT
AGLEAM
AIDMAN
AIRMAN
AIRWAY
AMORAL
ANIMAL
ANNEAL
ANNUAL
ANYWAY
APICAL
APPEAL
APPEAR
ARCTAN
ASHLAR
ASHRAM
ASTRAL
ASTRAY
ATONAL
AVATAR
BAGMAN
BALLAD
BALSAM
BANTAM
BANYAN
BANZAI
BAOBAB
BATEAU
BATMAN
BAZAAR
BEDLAM
BEDPAN
BEGGAR
BEHEAD
BELDAM
BEMOAN
BETRAY
BOBCAT
BONSAI
BOREAL
BOWMAN
BOXCAR
BRIDAL
BROGAN
BRUTAL
BUREAU
BURIAL
BURLAP
BURSAR
BYPLAY
CAESAR
CAFTAN
CAIMAN
CANCAN
CANVAS
CARNAL
CARPAL
CASUAL
CATNAP
CAUDAL
CAUSAL
CAVEAT
CAVIAR
CAYMAN
CELLAR
CEREAL
CHORAL
CLIMAX
COEVAL
COGNAC
COLLAR
COLLAT
COMBAT
COMPAQ
COMPAR
CONFAB
CORRAL
COUGAR
COWMAN
CRAVAT
CYMBAL
DEEJAY
DEFEAT
DEFRAY
DEMEAN
DENIAL
DENTAL
DEODAR
DERMAL
DEWLAP
DIRHAM
DISBAR
DISMAL
DISMAY
DISTAL
DOLLAR
DOODAD
DORSAL
EARWAX
ENDEAR
ENGRAM
ENTRAP
EOLIAN
FABIAN
FACIAL
FAECAL
FELLAH
FENIAN
FESTAL
FEUDAL
FILIAL
FINIAL
FISCAL
FLORAL
FLYWAY
FOEMAN
FOETAL
FORMAL
FORMAT
FRACAS
FRIDAY
FRUGAL
GENIAL
GERMAN
GEWGAW
GIMBAL
GLOBAL
GUFFAW
GUITAR
GUNMAN
HANGAR
HEPCAT
HEYDAY
HOOKAH
HOWDAH
HUBCAP
HURRAH
HUSSAR
HUZZAH
ICEMAN
INDIAN
INROAD
INSEAM
IPECAC
ISOBAR
JACKAL
JAGUAR
JETSAM
JIGSAW
JOVIAL
KIDNAP
KOREAN
LABIAL
LANDAU
LARIAT
LASCAR
LAWMAN
LAYMAN
LEEWAY
LEGMAN
LETHAL
LIBYAN
LINEAL
LINEAR
LOGJAM
LUMBAR
MADCAP
MADMAN
MADRAS
MAENAD
MAGYAR
MALIAN
MAMMAL
MANIAC
MANUAL
MEDIAL
MEDIAN
MENIAL
MENTAL
MERMAN
MESCAL
MICMAC
MIDDAY
MIDWAY
MISHAP
MISLAY
MISSAL
MONDAY
MORGAN
MORTAL
MORTAR
MUTUAL
MYRIAD
NECTAR
NEURAL
NONFAT
NORMAL
NORMAN
NOUGAT
OCULAR
ORDEAL
ORPHAN
OUTLAW
OUTLAY
PARIAH
PARLAY
PASCAL
PAWPAW
PENMAN
PICKAX
PILLAR
PINEAL
PLURAL
POLEAX
POPLAR
PORTAL
POSTAL
PREFAB
PREPAY
PREWAR
PRIMAL
PULSAR
PURDAH
QINTAR
QUASAR
RADIAL
RADIAN
RAGLAN
RASCAL
RATTAN
RECTAL
REDCAP
REGNAL
RENTAL
REPEAL
REPEAT
REPLAY
REVEAL
RIPSAW
RITUAL
RUNWAY
RUPIAH
SALAAM
SAMPAN
SANDAL
SASHAY
SATRAP
SCARAB
SCREAM
SEAMAN
SEAWAY
SEESAW
SERIAL
SEXUAL
SHAMAN
SIGNAL
SIMIAN
SKYCAP
SLOGAN
SMILAX
SOCIAL
SPINAL
SPIRAL
SPREAD
SQUEAK
SQUEAL
STREAK
STREAM
SUBWAY
SULTAN
SUNDAE
SUNDAY
SUNTAN
SURTAX
SYLVAN
SYNTAX
TARTAN
TARTAR
THORAX
THREAD
THREAT
THROAT
TOMCAT
TOUCAN
TREPAN
TROJAN
TURBAN
UNCIAL
UNCLAD
UNLOAD
UNREAD
UNREAL
UNSEAL
UNSEAT
UNSNAP
UNWRAP
UPBEAT
UPLOAD
UPREAR
UPROAR
URINAL
VANDAL
VASSAL
VENIAL
VERBAL
VERNAL
VESTAL
VISUAL
VULGAR
WAYLAY
WIGWAG
WIGWAM
WITHAL
WOMBAT
YEOMAN
ZIGZAG
ZODIAC
AKIMBO
AMOEBA
CASABA
CHUBBY
CRABBY
FLABBY
GAZEBO
GRUBBY
HEREBY
IMBIBE
JUJUBE
NEARBY
PHOEBE
SCRIBE
SHABBY
STROBE
STUBBY
UNROBE
ABBACY
ABDUCT
ABJECT
ADDICT
ADDUCE
ADVICE
AFFECT
AGENCY
ALPACA
AMERCE
APERCU
APIECE
ARNICA
ASPECT
ATTACH
ATTACK
AVOUCH
BEDECK
BISECT
BLANCH
BLEACH
BLENCH
BLOTCH
BODICE
BOUNCE
BRANCH
BREACH
BREECH
BROACH
BRONCO
BROOCH
BRUNCH
CALICO
CHANCE
CHANCY
CHOICE
CHURCH
CIVICS
CLENCH
CLINCH
CLUTCH
COERCE
CROTCH
CROUCH
CRUNCH
CRUTCH
DEDUCE
DEDUCT
DEFACE
DEFECT
DEPICT
DETACH
DETECT
DEVICE
DIRECT
DRENCH
EFFACE
EFFECT
ENRICH
ENTICE
ETHICS

EUNUCH
EVINCE
EXPECT
FIANCE
FIASCO
FIERCE
FLEECE
FLINCH
FLITCH
FRENCH
FRESCO
GLANCE
GLITCH
GROUCH
HAUNCH
HIJACK
IDIOCY
IMPACT
INDICT
INDUCE
INDUCT
INFECT
INJECT
INSECT
INTACT
JOUNCE
KITSCH
KLATCH
KOPECK
LAUNCH
LEGACY
LUNACY
MALICE
MARACA
MEDICO
MENACE
NAUTCH
NOTICE
NOVICE
NUANCE
OBJECT
OFFICE
OPTICS
PALACE
PAPACY
PATACA
PAUNCH
PIERCE
PIRACY
POLICE
POLICY
POUNCE
PRANCE
PREACH
PRINCE
PUMICE
PUTSCH
QUENCH
QUINCE
REDACT
REDUCE
REJECT
RELICT
SCARCE
SCONCE
SCORCH
SCOTCH
SEANCE
SEARCH
SEDUCE
SELECT
SENECA
SILICA
SKETCH
SLOUCH
SLUICE
SMIRCH
SMOOCH
SMUTCH
SNATCH
SNITCH
SOLACE
SOURCE
SPEECH
SPLICE
SPRUCE
STANCE
STANCH
STARCH
STENCH
STITCH
STRICT
STRUCK
STUCCO
SWATCH
SWITCH
THATCH
THENCE
THRICE
THWACK
TRANCE
TRENCH
TWITCH
UNESCO
UNLACE
UNLOCK
UNPACK
VIVACE
WHENCE
WRENCH
WRETCH
ABRADE
ACCEDE
AGENDA
ALLUDE
AMENDS
ARCADE
ARMADA
BESIDE
BETIDE
BRANDY
CICADA
COMEDY
DECADE
DECIDE
DECODE
DELUDE
DEMODE
DENUDE
DERIDE
DIRNDL
DIVIDE
DUENDE
EMBODY
ENCODE
ESCUDO
FACADE
GOURDE
HAIRDO
IMPEDE
INSIDE
INVADE
IODIDE
LIBIDO
MALADY
MELODY
MIKADO
MONODY
NOBODY
ONEIDA
OVERDO
PAGODA
PARADE
PARODY
POMADE
PSEUDO
RECEDE
REMEDY
RESIDE
SECEDE
SHODDY
STEADY
STRIDE
STRODE
STURDY
TEREDO
TIRADE
TRIODE
TUXEDO
TWEEDY
UNLADE
UPSIDE
ZOUNDS
ACUMEN
ALLIED
AMULET
ANADEM
ANKLET
ANSWER
ANTHEM
ANTHER
ANTLER
APOGEE
APPLET
ARCNET
ARMLET
ASLEEP
AVOCET
AWAKEN
AZALEA
BACKER
BADGER
BALEEN
BALLET
BANDED
BANNER
BANTER
BARBER
BARKER
BARLEY
BARRED
BARREL
BARREN
BARTER
BASKET
BATTEN
BATTER
BEAKER
BEAVER
BELIEF
BENDER
BERBER
BESEEM
BETHEL
BETTER
BICKER
BILLET
BINHEX
BITNET
BITTER
BLAZER
BOATER
BOILER
BOMBER
BONNET
BOOTEE
BORDER
BOTHER
BOWLEG
BOWLER
BRAZEN
BREVET
BROKEN
BROKER
BRUNET
BUCKET
BUDGET
BUFFER
BUFFET
BULLET
BUMMER
BUMPER
BUNKER
BURDEN
BURGEE
BURNER
BUSHED
BUSHEL
BUTLER
BUTTER
BUZZER
CACHET
CALVES
CAMBER
CAMPER
CANCEL
CANCER
CANKER
CANNED
CANTER
CAREEN
CAREER
CARIES
CARPEL
CARPET
CARREL
CARTEL
CASHEW
CASKET
CASTER
CENSER
CENTER
CERMET
CHAFER
CHALET
CHAPEL
CHASER
CHISEL
CHOKER
CHOLER
CHOREA
CHOSEN
CINDER
CIPHER
CLARET
CLEVER
CLOSET
CLOVEN
CLOVER
COBWEB
CODGER
COFFEE
COFFER
COMBER
COMDEX
COMPEL
CONFED
CONFER
CONVEX
CONVEY
COOLER
COOPER
COPIER
COPPER
COPTER
COQUET
CORBEL
CORNEA
CORNER
CORNET
CORSET
CORTEX
COTTER
COULEE
CRATER
CRAVEN
CREWEL
CUDGEL
CUMBER
CUNNER
CURFEW
CURLEW
CURVET
CUTLER
CUTLET
CUTTER
CYGNET
DAGGER
DAMPEN
DAMPER
DAMSEL
DANDER
DANGER
DAPPER
DARKEN
DARNEL
DARTER
DASHER
DAYBED
DEADEN
DEAFEN
DECREE
DEEPEN
DEGREE
DENIER
DESKEW
DIADEM
DIAPER
DICKER
DICKEY
DIESEL
DIFFER
DIMMER
DINNER
DIPPER
DISHED
DISPEL
DITHER
DOCKET
DODDER
DOGGED
DOGLEG
DOLMEN
DONKEY
DORMER
DOWNER
DRAPER
DRAWER
DRIVEL
DRIVER
DROVER
DUFFER
DULCET
DUPLEX
DUSTER
EAGLET
EASTER
ECCLES
EITHER
ELEVEN
EMBLEM
ENAMEL
ENTREE
ESCHEW
ESTEEM
EXCEED
EYELET
FABLED
FALTER
FASTEN
FATHER
FATTEN
FAUCES
FAUCET
FEELER
FENDER
FENNEL
FERRET
FESTER
FETTER
FIDGET
FILLER
FILLET
FILTER
FINDER
FINGER
FISHER
FLAXEN
FLOWER
FODDER
FOLDER
FOOTED
FORGET
FORKED
FORMER
FOSTER
FROZEN
FUHRER
FUNNEL
GADGET
GAFFER
GAITER
GALLEY
GAMMER
GANDER
GANNET
GARDEN
GARNER
GARNET
GARRET
GARTER
GASKET
GATHER
GEEZER
GENDER
GEYSER
GIBBER
GIBBET
GIFTED
GIMLET
GINGER
GIRDER
GLIDER
GLOWER
GLUTEN
GOATEE
GOBBET
GOBLET
GOITER
GOLDEN
GOOBER
GOPHER
GOSPEL
GOTTEN
GRABEN
GRADER
GRAVEL
GRAYED
GROCER
GROVEL
GUINEA
GULDEN
GULLET
GUNNER
GUSHER
GUSSET
GUTTER
HACKER
HALTER
HALVES
HAMLET
HAMMER
HAMPER
HANKER
HANSEL
HAPPEN
HARDEN
HARKEN
HASTEN
HATRED
HATTER
HAWKER
HAWSER
HEAVEN
HEBREW
HEIFER
HELMET
HERPES
HINDER
HIPPED
HITHER
HOCKEY
HOLLER
HOOKER
HOPPER
HORNET
HORSEY
HOSTEL
HOTBED
HOWLER
HOYDEN
HUNGER
HUNKER
HYPHEN
IBIDEM
INBRED
INDEED
INKJET
INSTEP
ISOMER
JABBER
JACKET
JAGGED
JAILER
JASPER
JAYCEE
JAYGEE
JAYVEE
JENNET
JERSEY
JESTER
JIGGER
JITNEY
JOBBER
JOCKEY
JOINER
JUICER
JUMPER
JUNKER
JUNKET
KAISER
KEGLER
KENNEL
KERNEL
KIDNEY
KILTER
KIPPER
KISMET
KISSER
KITTEN
KOSHER
LACKEY
LADDER
LANCER
LANCET
LANDED
LANDER
LAPPET
LARDER
LATHER
LATTER
LAUREL
LAWYER
LEADEN
LEADER
LEAFED
LEAVED
LEAVEN
LEAVES
LEDGER
LESSEE
LESSEN
LESSER
LETTER
LICHEE
LICHEN
LIMBER
LIMPET
LINDEN
LINGER

LINKED
LINNET
LINTEL
LISTEN
LITTER
LOADED
LOADER
LOCKER
LOCKET
LODGER
LOITER
LOOPER
LOOSEN
LOUVER
LUBBER
LUMBER
LUSTER
MADDEN
MADDER
MAGNET
MAIDEN
MAILED
MALLET
MANGER
MANNED
MANNER
MANTEL
MARCEL
MARKED
MARKET
MARTEN
MARVEL
MASTER
MATTER
MAYHEM
MEAGER
MEDLEY
MEMBER
MENSES
MERCER
MERGER
METIER
MIDDEN
MIDGET
MILDEW
MILIEU
MILLER
MILLET
MINDED
MINUET
MISTER
MITTEN
MIZZEN
MOLDER
MOLTEN
MONGER
MONKEY

MOPPET
MORSEL
MOSLEM
MOTHER
MOTLEY
MOUSER
MSCDEX
MULLET
MUMMER
MURDER
MUSKEG
MUSKET
MUSSEL
MUSTER
MUTTER
NAUSEA
NEPHEW
NETHER
NEUTER
NICKEL
NICKER
NIPPER
NUGGET
NUMBER
NUTMEG
OFFSET
OMELET
OODLES
OSPREY
OSTLER
OUSTER
OUTLET
OUTSET
OXYGEN
OYSTER
PACKER
PACKET
PALLET
PALMER
PALTER
PAMPER
PANDER
PARCEL
PARLEY
PARSEC
PASSEL
PASTEL
PATTER
PAUPER
PAWNEE
PEAHEN
PEAKED
PEEWEE
PELLET
PEPPER
PESTER
PETREL

PEWTER
PHLOEM
PICKET
PIGLET
PIGPEN
PILFER
PINCER
PIQUET
PLACER
PLANET
PLATEN
PLOVER
POCKET
POLDER
POLLEN
POMMEL
PONDER
PONGEE
POPPER
PORKER
PORTER
POSTER
POTEEN
POTHER
POTTER
POWDER
PRAYER
PREFER
PREMED
PRESET
PRIMER
PRIVET
PROPEL
PROPER
PUCKER
PULLET
PULLEY
PUMMEL
PUPPET
PURSER
PURVEY
PUSHER
PUTTEE
PUTTER
QUAKER
QUAVER
QUIVER
RABBET
RABIES
RACKET
RAFTER
RAGGED
RANGER
RAPIER
RAPPEN
RASHER
RASTER

RATHER
RATTER
REAMER
REDDEN
REDEEM
REEFER
REFLEX
REGRET
RELIEF
RENDER
RENNET
REVIEW
RICHES
RIDDEN
RIGGER
RINGER
ROBBER
ROCKER
ROCKET
ROLLER
ROMPER
ROSTER
ROTTEN
RUBBER
RUDDER
RUGGED
RUNLET
RUNNEL
RUNNER
RUSSET
SACHEM
SACHET
SACRED
SADDEN
SALVER
SATEEN
SAUCER
SCREEN
SEABED
SEALER
SECRET
SELVES
SEQUEL
SERIES
SERVER
SETTEE
SETTER
SEXTET
SHAKER
SHAVER
SHAVES
SHINER
SHIVER
SHOVEL
SHOWER
SHRIEK
SICKEN

SIGNET
SILVER
SIMMER
SIMPER
SINKER
SISTER
SKEWER
SLAVER
SLIDER
SLIVER
SLOVEN
SNIVEL
SOCCER
SOCKET
SODDEN
SOEVER
SOFTEN
SOIREE
SOLDER
SOMBER
SONNET
SORREL
SOVIET
SPIDER
SPINEL
SPINET
SPIREA
SPLEEN
SPOKEN
STAMEN
STAPES
STAVES
STEREO
STOLEN
STONED
STREET
SUBLET
SUBSET
SUCKER
SUDDEN
SUFFER
SULLEN
SUMMER
SUNDER
SUNKEN
SUNSET
SUPPER
SURREY
SURVEY
SWIVEL
SYSTEM
TABLET
TAMPER
TANDEM
TANKER
TANNER
TAPPET

TARGET
TASSEL
TATTER
TEASEL
TEEPEE
TEETER
TELLER
TELNET
TEMPER
TENDER
TESTER
TETHER
TICKER
TICKET
TILLER
TIMBER
TINDER
TINKER
TINSEL
TIPPET
TITLED
TITTER
TOFFEE
TOILET
TOTTER
TOUPEE
TOWHEE
TRADER
TRAVEL
TRIVET
TROWEL
TUCKER
TUNNEL
TUREEN
TURKEY
TURNER
TURRET
TURVES
TUSKER
ULSTER
UNDIES
UNEVEN
UNICEF
UNISEX
UNITED
UNMEET
UNREEL
UNUSED
UPKEEP
URETER
USENET
USURER
VALLEY
VALUED
VARIED
VARLET
VELVET

VENDEE
VENDER
VENEER
VERGER
VERSED
VERTEX
VESPER
VESSEL
VESTEE
VIOLET
VIZIER
VOICED
VOLLEY
VORTEX
WAITER
WAIVER
WALLET
WANDER
WARDEN
WARDER
WARREN
WASHER
WEAKEN
WEASEL
WEBBED
WELTER
WETHER
WHALER
WHITEN
WICKED
WICKER
WICKET
WIENER
WIGLET
WINDER
WINGED
WINKER
WINNER
WINTER
WITHER
WITTED
WONDER
WONTED
WOODED
WOODEN
WOOFER
WOOLEN
WORKER
WORSEN
WRITER
XMODEM
YAHWEH
YAMMER
YANKEE
YMODEM
YONDER
ZIPPER

ZITHER
ZMODEM
ZONKED
ADRIFT
BEREFT
CARAFE
CITIFY
CODIFY
CUTOFF
FLUFFY
LAYOFF
MODIFY
NOTIFY
OSSIFY
PACIFY
PAYOFF
PURIFY
RAMIFY
RAREFY
RATIFY
REBUFF
RUNOFF
SCRUFF
SHRIFT
STRAFE
STRIFE
STUFFY
TARIFF
THRIFT
TYPIFY
UPLIFT
VERIFY
VILIFY
VIVIFY
ALLEGE
ASSIGN
AVENGE
AWEIGH
BELUGA
BENIGN
BRIDGE
CAYUGA
CHANGE
CHARGE
CLERGY
CRINGE
DAMAGE
DELUGE
DESIGN
DOINGS
DOTAGE
DREDGE
DRUDGE
EFFIGY
EMERGE
ENERGY
ENGAGE

ENOUGH
ENRAGE
ENSIGN
EULOGY
FLANGE
FORAGE
FOREGO
FRINGE
GARAGE
GINKGO
GRANGE
GROGGY
GRUDGE
HOMAGE
IMPUGN
INDIGO
LAVAGE
LINAGE
LOUNGE
MALIGN
MANAGE
MANEGE
MENAGE
MIRAGE
NONAGE
OBLIGE
ORANGE
PELAGE
PHLEGM
PLEDGE
PLUNGE
POTAGE
RAVAGE
REFUGE
RENEGE
RESIGN
SAVAGE
SEWAGE
SHAGGY
SILAGE
SLEDGE
SLEIGH
SLOUGH
SLUDGE
SMUDGE
SPONGE
SPURGE
STINGY
STODGY
STOOGE
THOUGH
TRIAGE
TROUGH
TRUDGE
TWINGE
ULLAGE
VIRAGO

VISAGE
VOYAGE
ALIGHT
APACHE
APATHY
ARIGHT
BLIGHT
BLITHE
BOUGHT
BRIGHT
BUQSHA
CATCHY
CAUGHT
CHICHI
CLICHE
CLOCHE
CLOTHE
CRECHE
DINGHY
DOUCHE
EARTHY
FLASHY
FLESHY
FLIGHT
FOUGHT
FRIGHT
GAUCHE
GAUCHO
GEISHA
GURKHA
HEIGHT
KNIGHT
KWACHA
LITCHI
LOATHE
MEGOHM
NAUGHT
NAVAHO
NOUGHT
PLIGHT
PONCHO
PSYCHE
PSYCHO
RANCHO
RHYTHM
SCYTHE
SEETHE
SLIGHT
SMITHY
SOOTHE
SOUGHT
SPATHE
SWATHE
TAUGHT
TEETHE
TETCHY
TOOTHY

TOUCHE
TOUCHY
TROCHE
TROPHY
WEIGHT
WORTHY
WRITHE
ABATIS
ACACIA
ACETIC
ACQUIT
ADAGIO
ADJOIN
ADROIT
AFFAIR
AFRAID
ALBEIT
ALTAIR
ANEMIA
ARABIC
ARCSIN
ARCTIC
ARMPIT
ASSAIL
ATOMIC
ATTAIN
ATTRIB
BAGNIO
BANDIT
BARRIO
BEANIE
BESTIR
BEWAIL
BIGWIG
BIOTIC
BIOTIN
BIRDIE
BOBBIN
BOCCIE
BODKIN
BOOKIE
BUDGIE
BUSKIN
CADDIE
CALCIC
CANDID
CASEIN
CASSIA
CATKIN
CATNIP
CERVIX
CHITIN
CLERIC
CLEVIS
CLINIC
COFFIN
COHEIR

COLLIE
COMFIT
COMMIT
COOKIE
COOLIE
COOTIE
COSMIC
COUSIN
CREDIT
CRETIN
CRISIS
CRITIC
CUSPID
DAHLIA
DEBRIS
DECEIT
DENTIN
DERAIL
DERMIS
DERRIS
DETAIL
DETAIN
DEVOID
DEVOIR
DOBBIN
DOMAIN
DUBBIN
EARWIG
EBCDIC
ECLAIR
ELICIT
ELIXIR
EMETIC
ENDRIN
ENJOIN
ENTAIL
EROTIC
ESPRIT
ETHNIC
EXOTIC
EYELID
FABRIC
FAERIE
FERRIC
FERVID
FIBRIL
FIBRIN
FILLIP
FLORID
FLORIN
FORBID
FOSSIL
FRIGID
FROLIC
GAELIC
GALLIC
GAMBIT

GARLIC
GERBIL
GOALIE
GOBLIN
GOSSIP
GOTHIC
GRATIS
GRAVID
HACKIE
HAGGIS
HECTIC
HEREIN
HERMIT
HERNIA
HEROIN
HIPPIE
HOAGIE
HORRID
HUBRIS
HYBRID
IMPAIR
INLAID
INTUIT
IRENIC
IRONIC
ITALIC
JERKIN
JUDAIC
JUNKIE
KAOLIN
KELVIN
KERMIT
LACTIC
LADDIE
LASSIE
LENTIL
LIMPID
LIQUID
LOGGIA
MAGPIE
MANTIS
MARGIN
MARLIN
MARTIN
MASSIF
MASTIC
MATRIX
MEMOIR
METRIC
MIDAIR
MISFIT
MOHAIR
MORBID
MORRIS
MOSAIC
MUFFIN
MUSLIM

MUSLIN
MYOPIA
MYSTIC
NAPKIN
NEREID
NIACIN
NITRIC
NITWIT
NOGGIN
NORDIC
NUBBIN
NUNCIO
NUTRIA
OBTAIN
ORCHID
ORDAIN
ORIGIN
OUTBID
OUTFIT
OUTWIT
PALLID
PANTIE
PAPAIN
PASSIM
PATOIS
PCMCIA
PECTIN
PELVIS
PENCIL
PEPSIN
PEPTIC
PERMIT
PHOBIA
PHONIC
PHYSIC
PICNIC
PIDGIN
PINKIE
PIPKIN
PIPPIN
PISTIL
PLACID
POPLIN
POTPIE
PRECIS
PREFIX
PRELIM
PREMIX
PROFIT
PROLIX
PUBLIC
PUFFIN
PULPIT
PUNDIT
PUNKIN
PUTRID
QBASIC

RABBIT
RAFFIA
RAISIN
RANCID
RECOIL
REFRIG
REGAIN
REJOIN
REMAIN
RENNIN
REPAIR
RETAIL
RETAIN
RLOGIN
ROOKIE
RUBRIC
RUSTIC
SCORIA
SEPSIS
SEPTIC
SEQUIN
SLAVIC
SORDID
SORTIE
SPADIX
SPAVIN
SPECIE
SPECIF
SPIRIT
SPRAIN
STATIC
STOLID
STRAIN
STRAIT
STUDIO
STUPID
STYMIE
SUBMIT
SUFFIX
SUMMIT
SUNLIT
TACTIC
TANNIN
TENNIS
TENPIN
TESTIS
THESIS
TIDBIT
TIFFIN
TITBIT
TOCSIN
TOMTIT
TONSIL
TORPID
TORRID
TRAGIC
TRIVIA

TROPIC
TUGRIK
TURBID
TURGID
TURNIP
ULTRIX
UNCOIL
UNFAIR
UNSHIP
UNVEIL
URACIL
URANIC
URCHIN
UREMIA
UTOPIA
VERMIN
VICTIM
VIOLIN
VIRGIN
VISCID
WEEVIL
WELKIN
WESKIT
WITHIN
ZINNIA
ZOMBIE
ZOYSIA
ABNAKI
BELIKE
BETAKE
CHEEKY
CHUKKA
CHUNKY
CRANKY
EUREKA
FLUNKY
FRISKY
INTAKE
INVOKE
KABUKI
MARKKA
PERUKE
PLUCKY
REBUKE
RETAKE
REVOKE
SHEIKH
SHRIKE
STICKY
STOCKY
STRIKE
STROKE
THANKS
TRICKY
TROIKA
UNLIKE
UNYOKE

UPTAKE
AFIELD
ALKALI
ANNALS
APPALL
ARABLE
ARGYLE
AWHILE
BABBLE
BAFFLE
BANGLE
BARELY
BARFLY
BASALT
BATTLE
BAUBLE
BEADLE
BEAGLE
BECALM
BEETLE
BEFALL
BEHALF
BEHOLD
BOBBLE
BODILY
BOGGLE
BOODLE
BOTTLE
BRIDLE
BUBBLE
BUCKLE
BUNDLE
BUNGLE
BURGLE
BUSILY
BUSTLE
CABALA
CACKLE
CAJOLE
CANDLE
CANTLE
CASTLE
CATTLE
CHICLE
CHILLY
CIRCLE
COBALT
COBBLE
COCKLE
CODDLE
COMELY
COMPLY
COPULA
COSTLY
COUPLE
CRADLE
CREOLE

CUDDLE
CUPOLA
CURDLE
DABBLE
DANDLE
DANGLE
DAPPLE
DAWDLE
DAZZLE
DEADLY
DEFILE
DESALT
DIBBLE
DIMPLE
DINGLE
DOCILE
DOODLE
DOTTLE
DOUBLE
DOUBLY
EDIBLE
EMBALM
ENABLE
ENFOLD
ENGULF
ENISLE
ENROLL
ENSILE
EXHALE
FACILE
FACULA
FAILLE
FAIRLY
FAMILY
FEEBLE
FEMALE
FERULE
FETTLE
FIBULA
FICKLE
FIDDLE
FINALE
FIZZLE
FOIBLE
FONDLE
FUDDLE
FUMBLE
FUTILE
GABBLE
GADFLY
GAGGLE
GAMBLE
GARBLE
GARGLE
GENTLE
GIGGLE
GIGOLO

GIRDLE
GOBBLE
GOGGLE
GOODLY
GRILLE
GRISLY
GURGLE
GUZZLE
HACKLE
HAGGLE
HALALA
HANDLE
HARDLY
HASSLE
HECKLE
HERALD
HOBBLE
HOMELY
HOMILY
HOOPLA
HUDDLE
HUMBLE
HURDLE
HURTLE
HUSTLE
ICICLE
IMPALA
IMPALE
INFOLD
INHALE
INSOLE
INSULT
ITSELF
JANGLE
JIGGLE
JINGLE
JOGGLE
JOSTLE
JUGGLE
JUMBLE
JUNGLE
KETTLE
KIBBLE
KINDLE
KINDLY
KIRTLE
KOBOLD
LABILE
LIABLE
LIKELY
LITTLE
LIVELY
LOBULE
LOCALE
LONELY
LORDLY
LOVELY

MANGLE
MANTLE
MARBLE
MAYFLY
MEASLY
MEDDLE
METTLE
MIDDLE
MINGLE
MOBILE
MODULE
MORALE
MOSTLY
MOTILE
MOTTLE
MUDDLE
MUFFLE
MUMBLE
MUSCLE
MUZZLE
MYRTLE
MYSELF
NAMELY
NAPALM
NEBULA
NEEDLE
NESTLE
NETTLE
NIBBLE
NIMBLE
NIPPLE
NODDLE
NODULE
NOODLE
NOVELL
NOZZLE
NUBBLE
NUBILE
NUZZLE
OCCULT
ORACLE
ORIOLE
ORMOLU
OVERLY
PADDLE
PAPULE
PAROLE
PARTLY
PEBBLE
PEDDLE
PEOPLE
PESTLE
PICKLE
PIDDLE
PIFFLE
PIMPLE
POODLE

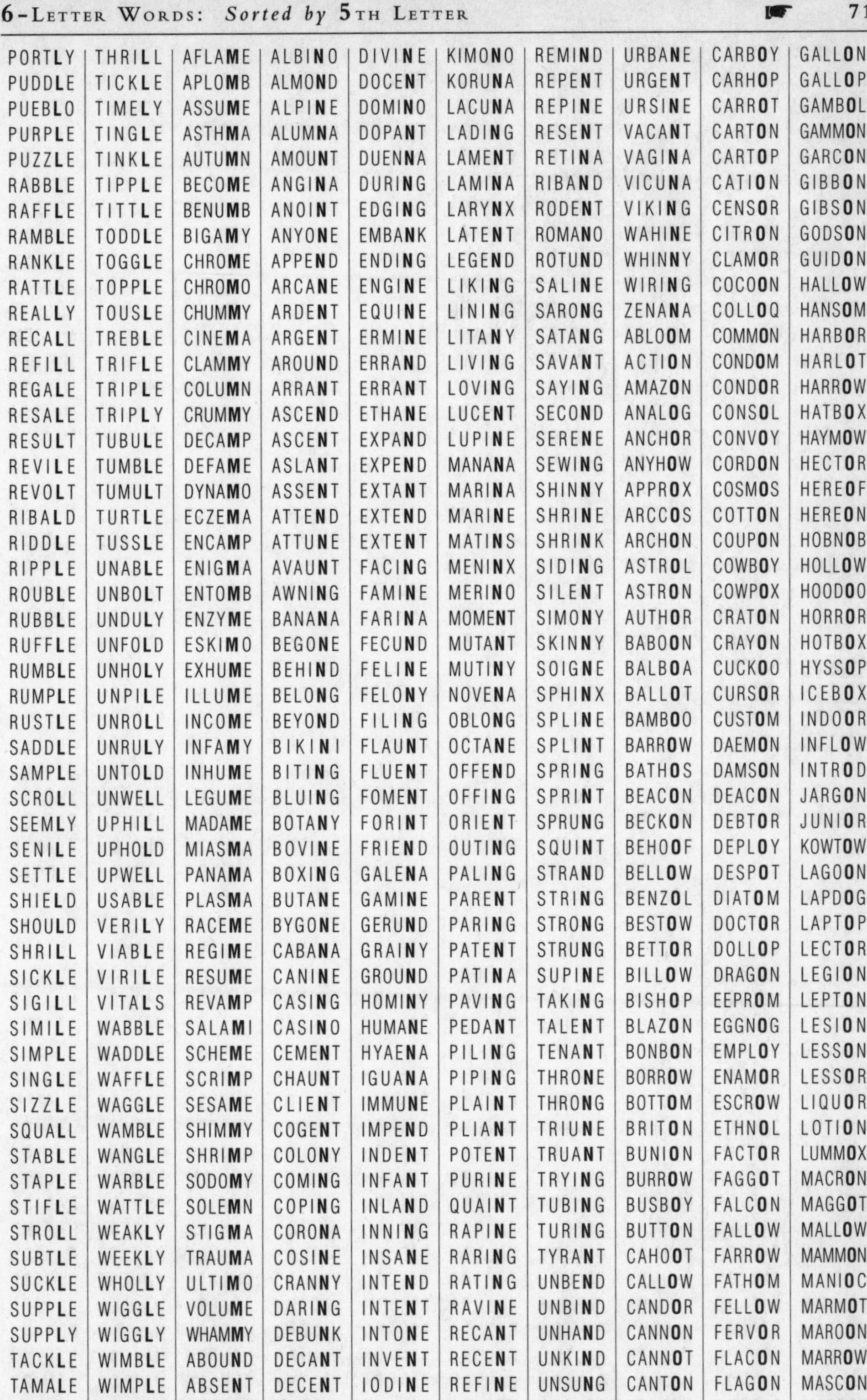

PORTLY
PUDDLE
PUEBLO
PURPLE
PUZZLE
RABBLE
RAFFLE
RAMBLE
RANKLE
RATTLE
REALLY
RECALL
REFILL
REGALE
RESALE
RESULT
REVILE
REVOLT
RIBALD
RIDDLE
RIPPLE
ROUBLE
RUBBLE
RUFFLE
RUMBLE
RUMPLE
RUSTLE
SADDLE
SAMPLE
SCROLL
SEEMLY
SENILE
SETTLE
SHIELD
SHOULD
SHRILL
SICKLE
SIGILL
SIMILE
SIMPLE
SINGLE
SIZZLE
SQUALL
STABLE
STAPLE
STIFLE
STROLL
SUBTLE
SUCKLE
SUPPLE
SUPPLY
TACKLE
TAMALE
TANGLE
TATTLE
TEMPLE
THRALL

THRILL
TICKLE
TIMELY
TINGLE
TINKLE
TIPPLE
TITTLE
TODDLE
TOGGLE
TOPPLE
TOUSLE
TREBLE
TRIFLE
TRIPLE
TRIPLY
TUBULE
TUMBLE
TUMULT
TURTLE
TUSSLE
UNABLE
UNBOLT
UNDULY
UNFOLD
UNHOLY
UNPILE
UNROLL
UNRULY
UNTOLD
UNWELL
UPHILL
UPHOLD
UPWELL
USABLE
VERILY
VIABLE
VIRILE
VITALS
WABBLE
WADDLE
WAFFLE
WAGGLE
WAMBLE
WANGLE
WARBLE
WATTLE
WEAKLY
WEEKLY
WHOLLY
WIGGLE
WIGGLY
WIMBLE
WIMPLE
WINKLE
WOBBLE
WOOLLY
YEARLY

AFLAME
APLOMB
ASSUME
ASTHMA
AUTUMN
BECOME
BENUMB
BIGAMY
CHROME
CHROMO
CHUMMY
CINEMA
CLAMMY
COLUMN
CRUMMY
DECAMP
DEFAME
DYNAMO
ECZEMA
ENCAMP
ENIGMA
ENTOMB
ENZYME
ESKIMO
EXHUME
ILLUME
INCOME
INFAMY
INHUME
LEGUME
MADAME
MIASMA
PANAMA
PLASMA
RACEME
REGIME
RESUME
REVAMP
SALAMI
SCHEME
SCRIMP
SESAME
SHIMMY
SHRIMP
SODOMY
SOLEMN
STIGMA
TRAUMA
ULTIMO
VOLUME
WHAMMY
ABOUND
ABSENT
ACCENT
ACTING
ADDEND
ADVENT

ALBINO
ALMOND
ALPINE
ALUMNA
AMOUNT
ANGINA
ANOINT
ANYONE
APPEND
ARCANE
ARDENT
ARGENT
AROUND
ARRANT
ASCEND
ASCENT
ASLANT
ASSENT
ATTEND
ATTUNE
AVAUNT
AWNING
BANANA
BEGONE
BEHIND
BELONG
BEYOND
BIKINI
BITING
BLUING
BOTANY
BOVINE
BOXING
BUTANE
BYGONE
CABANA
CANINE
CASING
CASINO
CEMENT
CHAUNT
CLIENT
COGENT
COLONY
COMING
COPING
CORONA
COSINE
CRANNY
DARING
DEBUNK
DECANT
DECENT
DEFEND
DEFINE
DEMAND
DEPEND

DIVINE
DOCENT
DOMINO
DOPANT
DUENNA
DURING
EDGING
EMBANK
ENDING
ENGINE
EQUINE
ERMINE
ERRAND
ERRANT
ETHANE
EXPAND
EXPEND
EXTANT
EXTEND
EXTENT
FACING
FAMINE
FARINA
FECUND
FELINE
FELONY
FILING
FLAUNT
FLUENT
FOMENT
FORINT
FRIEND
GALENA
GAMINE
GERUND
GRAINY
GROUND
HOMINY
HUMANE
HYAENA
IGUANA
IMMUNE
IMPEND
INDENT
INFANT
INLAND
INNING
INSANE
INTEND
INTENT
INTONE
INVENT
IODINE
ISLAND
JEJUNE
JOCUND
JOHNNY

KIMONO
KORUNA
LACUNA
LADING
LAMENT
LAMINA
LARYNX
LATENT
LEGEND
LIKING
LINING
LITANY
LIVING
LOVING
LUCENT
LUPINE
MANANA
MARINA
MARINE
MATINS
MENINX
MERINO
MOMENT
MUTANT
MUTINY
NOVENA
OBLONG
OCTANE
OFFEND
OFFING
ORIENT
OUTING
PALING
PARENT
PARING
PATENT
PATINA
PAVING
PEDANT
PILING
PIPING
PLAINT
PLIANT
POTENT
PURINE
QUAINT
RAPINE
RARING
RATING
RAVINE
RECANT
RECENT
REFINE
REFUND
REGENT
RELENT
REMAND

REMIND
REPENT
REPINE
RESENT
RETINA
RIBAND
RODENT
ROMANO
ROTUND
SALINE
SARONG
SATANG
SAVANT
SAYING
SECOND
SERENE
SEWING
SHINNY
SHRINE
SHRINK
SIDING
SILENT
SIMONY
SKINNY
SOIGNE
SPHINX
SPLINE
SPLINT
SPRING
SPRINT
SPRUNG
SQUINT
STRAND
STRING
STRONG
STRUNG
SUPINE
TAKING
TALENT
TENANT
THRONE
THRONG
TRIUNE
TRUANT
TRYING
TUBING
TURING
TYRANT
UNBEND
UNBIND
UNHAND
UNKIND
UNSUNG
UNTUNE
UNWIND
UPLAND
UPWIND

URBANE
URGENT
URSINE
VACANT
VAGINA
VICUNA
VIKING
WAHINE
WHINNY
WIRING
ZENANA
ABLOOM
ACTION
AMAZON
ANALOG
ANCHOR
ANYHOW
APPROX
ARCCOS
ARCHON
ASTROL
ASTRON
AUTHOR
BABOON
BALBOA
BALLOT
BAMBOO
BARROW
BATHOS
BEACON
BECKON
BEHOOF
BELLOW
BENZOL
BESTOW
BETTOR
BILLOW
BISHOP
BLAZON
BONBON
BORROW
BOTTOM
BRITON
BUNION
BURROW
BUSBOY
BUTTON
CAHOOT
CALLOW
CANDOR
CANNON
CANNOT
CANTON
CANTOR
CANYON
CAPTOR
CARBON

CARBOY
CARHOP
CARROT
CARTON
CARTOP
CATION
CENSOR
CITRON
CLAMOR
COCOON
COLLOQ
COMMON
CONDOM
CONDOR
CONSOL
CONVOY
CORDON
COSMOS
COTTON
COUPON
COWBOY
COWPOX
CRATON
CRAYON
CUCKOO
CURSOR
CUSTOM
DAEMON
DAMSON
DEACON
DEBTOR
DEPLOY
DESPOT
DIATOM
DOCTOR
DOLLOP
DRAGON
EEPROM
EGGNOG
EMPLOY
ENAMOR
ESCROW
ETHNOL
FACTOR
FAGGOT
FALCON
FALLOW
FARROW
FATHOM
FELLOW
FERVOR
FLACON
FLAGON
FLAVOR
FOLLOW
FURROW
FUSION

GALLON
GALLOP
GAMBOL
GAMMON
GARCON
GIBBON
GIBSON
GODSON
GUIDON
HALLOW
HANSOM
HARBOR
HARLOT
HARROW
HATBOX
HAYMOW
HECTOR
HEREOF
HEREON
HOBNOB
HOLLOW
HOODOO
HORROR
HOTBOX
HYSSOP
ICEBOX
INDOOR
INFLOW
INTROD
JARGON
JUNIOR
KOWTOW
LAGOON
LAPDOG
LAPTOP
LECTOR
LEGION
LEPTON
LESION
LESSON
LESSOR
LIQUOR
LOTION
LUMMOX
MACRON
MAGGOT
MALLOW
MAMMON
MANIOC
MARMOT
MAROON
MARROW
MASCON
MASCOT
MATRON
MEADOW
MELLOW

MENTOR
METEOR
METHOD
MICRON
MINION
MINNOW
MIRROR
MORMON
MORROW
MOTION
MOUTON
MUTTON
NARROW
NATION
NELSON
NEUROL
NEURON
NEWTON
NIMROD
NONCOM
NORTON
NOTION
OCELOT
OPTION
ORATOR
ORISON
OUTFOX
PALEON
PALLOR
PARDON
PARLOR
PARROT
PARSON
PASTOR
PATHOS
PATROL
PATRON
PENNON
PEQUOT
PERIOD
PERSON
PETROL
PHAROS
PHENOL
PHILOS
PHOTOG
PHOTON
PIGEON
PILLOW
PINION
PISTOL
PISTON
PLUTON
POGROM
POISON
POMPON
POTBOY

POTION
POWWOW
PRISON
PROLOG
PROTON
PYTHON
QUAHOG
RAMROD
RANCOR
RANDOM
RANSOM
RATION
REASON
RECKON
RECTOR
REGION
RIBBON
SAILOR
SALLOW
SALMON
SALOON
SAVIOR
SCHOOL
SEASON
SECTOR
SELDOM
SENIOR
SENSOR
SERMON
SEXPOT
SEXTON
SHADOW
SIPHON
SLALOM
SNOBOL
SOCIOL
SORROW
SPIGOT
STOLON
STUPOR
SUCCOR
SUITOR
SUMMON
SYMBOL
SYPHON
TAILOR
TALLOW
TAMPON
TARPON
TATTOO
TEAPOT
TENDON
TERROR
TIPTOE
TOMBOY
TORPOR
TREMOR

TRIPOD
TRITON
TURBOT
TYCOON
UNCLOG
UNHOOK
UNISON
UNMOOR
UNROOF
UNSHOD
UNSTOP
UPROOT
UPSHOT
VAGROM
VECTOR
VENDOR
VICTOR
VIRION
VISION
VOODOO
WALLOP
WALLOW
WANTON
WEAPON
WHILOM
WILLOW
WINDOW
WINNOW
WISDOM
YARROW
YELLOW
ZEALOT
ZIRCON
ABRUPT
ACCEPT
BICEPS
CALIPH
CANAPE
CANOPY
CHOPPY
CREEPY
ESCAPE
EXCEPT
EXEMPT
FLOPPY
FRAPPE
FRUMPY
GRIPPE
GRUMPY
IRRUPT
JALOPY
MACAPP
OCCUPY
PROMPT
RECIPE
SCAMPI
SCRAPE

SCRIPT
SCULPT
SERAPE
SERAPH
SKIMPY
SLEEPY
SLOPPY
SNIPPY
STEPPE
STRIPE
TROUPE
UNRIPE
UNWEPT
ABJURE
ABOARD
ABSORB
ABSURD
ACCORD
ADHERE
ADJURE
ADMIRE
ADSORB
ADVERB
ADVERT
AFFIRM
AFFORD
ALLURE
AMPERE
ANGORA
APIARY
ARMORY
ARTERY
ASHORE
ASPIRE
ASSERT
ASSORT
ASSURE
ASTERN
ATTIRE
AUBURN
AUGURY
AURORA
AVIARY
AWEARY
AWHIRL
BAKERY
BEFORE
BELFRY
BEMIRE
BEWARE
BINARY
BISTRO
BLEARY
BOLERO
BYWORD
CAMERA
CANARD

CANARY
CAVERN
CAVORT
CELERY
CENTRE
CHEERY
CHERRY
COHERE
COHORT
COVERT
COWARD
DEBARK
DEFORM
DEHORN
DEMURE
DEPART
DEPORT
DESCRY
DESERT
DESIRE
DISARM
DIVERS
DIVERT
DOTARD
DREARY
EATERY
EFFORT
EMBARK
EMIGRE
EMPIRE
ENCORE
ENDURE
ENDURO
ENSURE
ENTIRE
ESCORT
EUCHRE
EXHORT
EXPERT
EXPIRE
EXPORT
EXTERN
EXTORT
FEDORA
FIGURE
FINERY
FLURRY
FRIARY
FURORE
FUTURE
GABBRO
GALORE
GANTRY
GENERA
GENTRY
GOVERN
HAZARD

HEGIRA
IGNORE
IMMURE
IMPART
IMPERF
IMPORT
IMPURE
INBORN
INFIRM
INFORM
INHERE
INJURE
INJURY
INSERT
INSURE
INTERJ
INTERN
INVERT
INWARD
LIVERY
LIZARD
LOWERY
LUXURY
MANTRA
MANURE
MATURE
MEMORY
MESSRS
MISERY
MODERN
NAPERY
NATURE
OEUVRE
ONWARD
ORDURE
ORNERY
OUTCRY
OXFORD
PALTRY
PANTRY
PASTRY
PENURY
PETARD
PLIERS
POETRY
PRIORY
QUARRY
REBORN
RECORD
REFORM
REGARD
REMARK
REMORA
REPORT
RESORT
RETARD
RETIRE

RETORT
RETURN
REVERB
REVERE
REVERS
REVERT
REWARD
ROSARY
ROTARY
SAFARI
SALARY
SATIRE
SATURN
SCURRY
SECURE
SENTRY
SEVERE
SHERRY
SIERRA
SLURRY
SPHERE
SQUARE
SQUIRE
SQUIRM
SQUIRT
SUBORN
SUBURB
SULTRY
SUNDRY
SUPERB
SUTURE
TAVERN
TAWDRY
TENURE
THEIRS
THEORY
THWART
TIMBRE
TORERO
TOWARD
TUNDRA
UMPIRE
UNBORN
UNCORK
UNCURL
UNFURL
UNGIRD
UPTURN
UPWARD
VAGARY
VAPORY
VENIRE
VESTRY
VIZARD
VOTARY
WATERY
WHERRY

WINTRY
WIZARD
YOGURT
ABBESS
ACCESS
ACCOST
ACCUSE
ACROSS
ADJUST
ADVISE
AFRESH
AGHAST
ALMOST
AMBUSH
ARGOSY
AROUSE
ARREST
ARTIST
ASSESS
ASSIST
ATTEST
AUGUST
AUTISM
AVERSE
BANISH
BEHEST
BEMUSE
BIOPSY
BLOUSE
BLOWSY
BLUISH
BOURSE
BRAISE
BREAST
BROWSE
BRUISE
BYPASS
CARESS
CAYUSE
CERISE
CHAISE
CHEESE
CHOOSE
CHOOSY
CHRISM
CHRIST
CLASSY
CLAUSE
CLUMSY
COARSE
CORPSE
COURSE
CREASE
CRUISE
CUBISM
CURTSY
DALASI

DAMASK
DANISH
DEBASE
DEFUSE
DEMISE
DEPOSE
DESIST
DETEST
DEVISE
DIGEST
DISUSE
DIVEST
DRESSY
DROPSY
DROWSE
DROWSY
DURESS
EGOISM
EGRESS
ELAPSE
ELDEST
EMBOSS
ENCASE
ENCYST
ENLIST
ENMESH
EXCESS
EXCISE
EXCUSE
EXPOSE
FAMISH
FETISH
FINISH
FLIMSY
FLOSSY
FOLKSY
FOREST
FROWSY
GALOSH
GARISH
GLOSSY
GNEISS
GREASE
GROUSE
HARASS
HEARSE
HERESY
HOARSE
HONEST
ILLUST
IMPISH
IMPOSE
IMPOST
INCASE
INCEST
INCISE
INFEST

INFUSE
INGEST
INMOST
INRUSH
INSIST
INVEST
JOCOSE
JURIST
KIBOSH
LAVISH
LOCUST
MAOISM
MIMOSA
MISUSE
MODEST
MODISH
MOLEST
MONISM
MOROSE
MOUSSE
NOWISE
NUDISM
OBSESS
OBTUSE
OFFISH
ONRUSH
OPPOSE
ORGASM
OTIOSE
PAPIST
PARISH
PERISH
PERUSE
PHRASE
PLEASE
POLISH
POTASH
PRAISE
PRIEST
PRISSY
PUNISH
PURISM
QUEASY
QUINSY
RACISM
RADISH
RAKISH
RAVISH
RECESS
REFUSE
REHASH
RELISH
REMISS
REPAST
REPOSE
RESIST
REVISE

ROBUST
SADISM
SCHISM
SCHIST
SCHUSS
SEXISM
SHIEST
SLIEST
SPARSE
SPLASH
SPOUSE
SQUASH
STRESS
TAOISM
THEISM
THIRST
THRASH
THRESH
THRUSH
THRUST
TRANSL
TRANSP
TRUISM
TSETSE
TYPIST
UNEASY
UNJUST
UNLESS
UNMASK
UNREST
UNWISE
UPMOST
UPPISH
UPRUSH
UTMOST
VALISE
VANISH
WHILST
WHIMSY
WOODSY
WRASSE
ACUITY
AERATE
AMVETS
ASTUTE
BEAUTY
BERATE
BONITO
BORATE
BOUNTY
BREATH
BYPATH
CAVITY
CHASTE
CHATTY
CHINTZ
COMITY
CONSTR
COUNTY
COYOTE
CRAFTY
CREATE
CUESTA
CURATE
DAINTY
DAKOTA
DEARTH
DEBATE
DELETE
DEMOTE
DENOTE
DEPUTE
DEPUTY
DEVOTE
DILATE
DILUTE
DIMITY
DONATE
DRAFTY
EFFETE
EIGHTY
ENMITY
ENTITY
EQUATE
EQUITY
ERRATA
ERSATZ
ESTATE
EXCITE
FEALTY
FIESTA
FINITE
FIXITY
FOURTH
FRUITY
GAIETY
GAMETE
GAYETY
GHETTO
GROTTO
GROWTH
GUILTY
GYRATE
HALITE
HEALTH
HEARTH
HEARTY
HERETO
IGNITE
IMPUTE
INCITE
INDITE
INMATE
INNATE
INVITE
JAUNTY
KARATE
LEGATE
LEGATO
LENGTH
LENITY
LEVITY
LIGATE
LIGHTS
LIKUTA
LOCATE
MAKUTA
MIGHTY
MINUTE
MOIETY
MUTATE
NEGATE
NICETY
NINETY
OBLATE
ODDITY
OOLITE
OPIATE
ORNATE
ORNITH
PAIUTE
PALATE
PARITY
PESETA
PETITE
PEYOTE
PIGSTY
PIRATE
PLENTY
PLINTH
POLITE
POLITY
POTATO
PRESTO
PRETTY
PRINTF
PRONTO
PURITY
PYRITE
QUARTO
QUARTZ
REALTY
REBATE
RECITE
REFUTE
RELATE
REMOTE
REPUTE
ROTATE
SAFETY
SALUTE
SANITY
SCANTY
SEDATE
SEMITE
SENATE
SENITI
SHANTY
SHEATH
SHIFTY
SHINTO
SIESTA
SLEUTH
SMOOTH
SNOOTY
SONATA
SPOTTY
SPRITE
SURETY
SVELTE
THIRTY
TIGHTS
TOMATO
TREATY
TRUSTY
TWENTY
UPDATE
UPPITY
VACATE
VANITY
VERITY
VOLUTE
WAPITI
WARMTH
WEALTH
WRAITH
WREATH
YEASTY
ZENITH
ZYGOTE
ABACUS
ACCRUE
ANIMUS
ANTRUM
ARMFUL
ARTFUL
ASYLUM
ATRIUM
AVENUE
BACKUP
BARIUM
BASQUE
BEDAUB
BEDBUG
BEFOUL
BISQUE
BLOWUP
BROGUE
BULBUL
BUNKUM
CACTUS
CAECUM
CALLUS
CAMPUS
CAPFUL
CASQUE
CATGUT
CATSUP
CAUCUS
CENSUS
CEREUS
CERIUM
CESIUM
CHEQUE
CHERUB
CHORUS
CILIUM
CIRCUS
CIRQUE
CIRRUS
CITRUS
CLAQUE
CLIQUE
COCCUS
COITUS
CONCUR
CONSUL
CORPUS
CROCUS
CURIUM
CUTOUT
DENGUE
DETOUR
DEVOUR
DEVOUT
DICTUM
DINGUS
DISCUS
DROGUE
DUGOUT
DUMDUM
DYBBUK
ECCLUS
ERBIUM
EXODUS
FAMOUS
FAVOUR
FITFUL
FLATUS
FONDUE
FUNGUS
GENIUS
GYPSUM
HELIUM
HIATUS
HICCUP
HOLDUP
HONOUR
HOOKUP
HUBBUB
HUMBUG
HUMOUR
IMBRUE
INDIUM
INFLUX
JOYFUL
JOYOUS
LABIUM
LABOUR
LAWFUL
LAYOUT
LEAGUE
LINEUP
LINKUP
LITMUS
LOCKUP
LYCEUM
MAHOUT
MAKEUP
MANFUL
MANQUE
MARAUD
MARKUP
MASQUE
MEDIUM
MISCUE
MORGUE
MOSQUE
MUKLUK
MURMUR
MUSEUM
MUUMUU
NIMBUS
ODIOUS
OPAQUE
OSMIUM
OUTGUN
OUTPUT
OUTRUN
PEANUT
PHYLUM
PICKUP
PIGNUT
PLAGUE
PLAQUE
PLENUM
PLEXUS
PODIUM
POPGUN
POROUS
POSEUR
POSSUM
PURSUE
PUTOUT
QIVIUT
QUORUM
RADIUM
RADIUS
RAGOUT
RECOUP
RECTUM
REFLUX
RESCUE
RISQUE
RUCKUS
RUMPUS
SACRUM
SHROUD
SINFUL
SLIPUP
SODIUM
SPROUT
SPUTUM
STATUE
STATUS
STYLUS
SUBDUE
SULFUR
TALMUD
TARSUS
TEACUP
TEDIUM
THYMUS
TISSUE
TONGUE
TORQUE
TYPHUS
UNIQUE
UNPLUG
UNTRUE
URANUS
USEFUL
UTERUS
VACUUM
VELLUM
VELOUR
VENOUS
VERSUS
VILLUS
VINOUS
VIRTUE
VISCUS
VOYEUR
WALNUT
WALRUS
WAMPUM
WINDUP
WOEFUL
YANQUI
ACTIVE
ALCOVE
ARRIVE
BEHAVE
CLEAVE
DATIVE
DERIVE
ENDIVE
EVOLVE
GRIEVE
GROOVE
GROOVY
MOTIVE
NATIVE
OCTAVE
OCTAVO
RELIVE
REMOVE
REVIVE
SALIVA
SCURVY
SHEAVE
SHELVE
SHRIVE
SLEEVE
STARVE
STRIVE
STROVE
SWERVE
THIEVE
THRIVE
THROVE
TWELVE
VOTIVE
ZOUAVE
DISOWN
MOHAWK
OJIBWA
OTTAWA
PESEWA
RENOWN
SCRAWL
SCREWY
SHREWD
SPRAWL
SQUAWK
UPTOWN
DELUXE
GALAXY
ALWAYS
ARROYO
COCCYX
DACTYL
EMBRYO
MARTYR
METHYL
PAPAYA
ZEPHYR
ABLAZE
ASSIZE
BREEZE
BRONZE
CORYZA
FLOOZY
FREEZE
FRENZY
FRIEZE
IODIZE
IONIZE
PIAZZA
SCUZZY
SLEAZY
SNEEZE
SNOOZE
STANZA
WHEEZE
WHEEZY

### 6th Letter

ACACIA
AGENDA
ALPACA
ALUMNA
AMOEBA
ANEMIA
ANGINA
ANGORA
ARMADA
ARNICA
ASTHMA
AURORA
AZALEA
BALBOA
BANANA
BELUGA
BUQSHA
CABALA
CABANA
CAMERA
CASABA
CASSIA
CAYUGA
CHOREA
CHUKKA
CICADA
CINEMA
COPULA
CORNEA
CORONA
CORYZA
CUESTA
CUPOLA
DAHLIA
DAKOTA
DUENNA
ECZEMA
ENIGMA
ERRATA
EUREKA
FACULA
FARINA
FEDORA
FIBULA
FIESTA
GALENA
GEISHA
GENERA
GUINEA
GURKHA
HALALA
HEGIRA
HERNIA
HOOPLA
HYAENA
IGUANA
IMPALA
KORUNA
KWACHA
LACUNA
LAMINA
LIKUTA
LOGGIA
MAKUTA
MANANA
MANTRA
MARACA
MARINA
MARKKA
MIASMA
MIMOSA
MYOPIA
NAUSEA
NEBULA
NOVENA
NUTRIA
OJIBWA
ONEIDA
OTTAWA
PAGODA
PANAMA
PAPAYA
PATACA
PATINA
PCMCIA
PESETA
PESEWA
PHOBIA
PIAZZA

PLASMA
RAFFIA
REMORA
RETINA
SALIVA
SCORIA
SENECA
SIERRA
SIESTA
SILICA
SONATA
SPIREA
STANZA
STIGMA
TRAUMA
TRIVIA
TROIKA
TUNDRA
UREMIA
UTOPIA
VAGINA
VICUNA
ZENANA
ZINNIA
ZOYSIA
ABSORB
ADSORB
ADVERB
APLOMB
ATTRIB
BAOBAB
BEDAUB
BENUMB
CHERUB
COBWEB
CONFAB
ENTOMB
HOBNOB
HUBBUB
PREFAB
REVERB
SCARAB
SUBURB
SUPERB
ACETIC
ARABIC
ARCTIC
ATOMIC
BIOTIC
CALCIC
CLERIC
CLINIC
COGNAC
COSMIC
CRITIC
EBCDIC
EMETIC
EROTIC
ETHNIC
EXOTIC
FABRIC
FERRIC
FROLIC
GAELIC
GALLIC
GARLIC
GOTHIC
HECTIC
IPECAC
IRENIC
IRONIC
ITALIC
JUDAIC
LACTIC
MANIAC
MANIOC
MASTIC
METRIC
MICMAC
MOSAIC
MYSTIC
NITRIC
NORDIC
PARSEC
PEPTIC
PHONIC
PHYSIC
PICNIC
PUBLIC
QBASIC
RUBRIC
RUSTIC
SEPTIC
SLAVIC
STATIC
TACTIC
TRAGIC
TROPIC
URANIC
ZODIAC
ABOARD
ABOUND
ABROAD
ABSURD
ACCORD
ADDEND
AFFORD
AFIELD
AFRAID
ALLIED
ALMOND
APPEND
AROUND
ASCEND
ATTEND
BALLAD
BANDED
BARRED
BEHEAD
BEHIND
BEHOLD
BEYOND
BUSHED
BYWORD
CANARD
CANDID
CANNED
CONFED
COWARD
CUSPID
DAYBED
DEFEND
DEMAND
DEPEND
DEVOID
DISHED
DOGGED
DOODAD
DOTARD
ENFOLD
ERRAND
EXCEED
EXPAND
EXPEND
EXTEND
EYELID
FABLED
FECUND
FERVID
FLORID
FOOTED
FORBID
FORKED
FRIEND
FRIGID
GERUND
GIFTED
GRAVID
GRAYED
GROUND
HATRED
HAZARD
HERALD
HIPPED
HORRID
HOTBED
HYBRID
IMPEND
INBRED
INDEED
INFOLD
INLAID
INLAND
INROAD
INTEND
INTROD
INWARD
ISLAND
JAGGED
JOCUND
KOBOLD
LANDED
LEAFED
LEAVED
LEGEND
LIMPID
LINKED
LIQUID
LIZARD
LOADED
MAENAD
MAILED
MANNED
MARAUD
MARKED
METHOD
MINDED
MORBID
MYRIAD
NEREID
NIMROD
OFFEND
ONWARD
ORCHID
OUTBID
OXFORD
PALLID
PEAKED
PERIOD
PETARD
PLACID
PREMED
PUTRID
RAGGED
RAMROD
RANCID
RECORD
REFUND
REGARD
REMAND
REMIND
RETARD
REWARD
RIBALD
RIBAND
ROTUND
RUGGED
SACRED
SEABED
SECOND
SHIELD
SHOULD
SHREWD
SHROUD
SORDID
SPREAD
STOLID
STONED
STRAND
STUPID
TALMUD
THREAD
TITLED
TORPID
TORRID
TOWARD
TRIPOD
TURBID
TURGID
UNBEND
UNBIND
UNCLAD
UNFOLD
UNGIRD
UNHAND
UNITED
UNKIND
UNLOAD
UNREAD
UNSHOD
UNTOLD
UNUSED
UNWIND
UPHOLD
UPLAND
UPLOAD
UPWARD
UPWIND
VALUED
VARIED
VERSED
VISCID
VIZARD
VOICED
WEBBED
WICKED
WINGED
WITTED
WIZARD
WONTED
WOODED
ZONKED
ABJURE
ABLAZE
ABRADE
ACCEDE
ACCRUE
ACCUSE
ACTIVE
ADDUCE
ADHERE
ADJURE
ADMIRE
ADVICE
ADVISE
AERATE
AFLAME
ALCOVE
ALLEGE
ALLUDE
ALLURE
ALPINE
AMERCE
AMPERE
ANYONE
APACHE
APIECE
APOGEE
ARABLE
ARCADE
ARCANE
ARGYLE
AROUSE
ARRIVE
ASHORE
ASPIRE
ASSIZE
ASSUME
ASSURE
ASTUTE
ATTIRE
ATTUNE
AVENGE
AVENUE
AVERSE
AWHILE
BABBLE
BAFFLE
BANGLE
BASQUE
BATTLE
BAUBLE
BEADLE
BEAGLE
BEANIE
BECOME
BEETLE
BEFORE
BEGONE
BEHAVE
BELIKE
BEMIRE
BEMUSE
BERATE
BESIDE
BETAKE
BETIDE
BEWARE
BIRDIE
BISQUE
BLITHE
BLOUSE
BOBBLE
BOCCIE
BODICE
BOGGLE
BOODLE
BOOKIE
BOOTEE
BORATE
BOTTLE
BOUNCE
BOURSE
BOVINE
BRAISE
BREEZE
BRIDGE
BRIDLE
BROGUE
BRONZE
BROWSE
BRUISE
BUBBLE
BUCKLE
BUDGIE
BUNDLE
BUNGLE
BURGEE
BURGLE
BUSTLE
BUTANE
BYGONE
CACKLE
CADDIE
CAJOLE
CANAPE
CANDLE
CANINE
CANTLE
CARAFE
CASQUE
CASTLE
CATTLE
CAYUSE
CENTRE
CERISE
CHAISE
CHANCE
CHANGE
CHARGE
CHASTE
CHEESE
CHEQUE
CHICLE
CHOICE
CHOOSE
CHROME
CIRCLE
CIRQUE
CLAQUE
CLAUSE
CLEAVE
CLICHE
CLIQUE
CLOCHE
CLOTHE
COARSE
COBBLE
COCKLE
CODDLE
COERCE
COFFEE
COHERE
COLLIE
COOKIE
COOLIE
COOTIE
CORPSE
COSINE
COULEE
COUPLE
COURSE
COYOTE
CRADLE
CREASE
CREATE
CRECHE
CREOLE
CRINGE
CRUISE
CUDDLE
CURATE
CURDLE
DABBLE
DAMAGE
DANDLE
DANGLE
DAPPLE
DATIVE
DAWDLE
DAZZLE
DEBASE
DEBATE
DECADE
DECIDE
DECODE
DECREE
DEDUCE
DEFACE
DEFAME
DEFILE
DEFINE
DEFUSE
DEGREE
DELETE
DELUDE
DELUGE
DELUXE
DEMISE
DEMODE
DEMOTE
DEMURE
DENGUE
DENOTE
DENUDE
DEPOSE
DEPUTE
DERIDE
DERIVE
DESIRE
DEVICE
DEVISE
DEVOTE
DIBBLE
DILATE
DILUTE
DIMPLE
DINGLE
DISUSE
DIVIDE
DIVINE
DOCILE
DONATE
DOODLE
DOTAGE
DOTTLE
DOUBLE
DOUCHE
DREDGE
DROGUE
DROWSE
DRUDGE
DUENDE
EDIBLE
EFFACE
EFFETE
ELAPSE
EMERGE
EMIGRE
EMPIRE
ENABLE
ENCASE
ENCODE
ENCORE
ENDIVE
ENDURE
ENGAGE
ENGINE
ENISLE
ENRAGE
ENSILE
ENSURE
ENTICE
ENTIRE
ENTREE
ENZYME
EQUATE
EQUINE
ERMINE
ESCAPE
ESTATE
ETHANE
EUCHRE
EVINCE
EVOLVE
EXCISE
EXCITE
EXCUSE
EXHALE
EXHUME
EXPIRE
EXPOSE
FACADE
FACILE
FAERIE
FAILLE
FAMINE
FEEBLE
FELINE
FEMALE
FERULE
FETTLE
FIANCE
FICKLE
FIDDLE
FIERCE
FIGURE
FINALE
FINITE
FIZZLE
FLANGE
FLEECE
FOIBLE
FONDLE
FONDUE
FORAGE
FRAPPE
FREEZE
FRIEZE
FRINGE

FUDDLE
FUMBLE
FURORE
FUTILE
FUTURE
GABBLE
GAGGLE
GALORE
GAMBLE
GAMETE
GAMINE
GARAGE
GARBLE
GARGLE
GAUCHE
GENTLE
GIGGLE
GIRDLE
GLANCE
GOALIE
GOATEE
GOBBLE
GOGGLE
GOURDE
GRANGE
GREASE
GRIEVE
GRILLE
GRIPPE
GROOVE
GROUSE
GRUDGE
GURGLE
GUZZLE
GYRATE
HACKIE
HACKLE
HAGGLE
HALITE
HANDLE
HASSLE
HEARSE
HECKLE
HIPPIE
HOAGIE
HOARSE
HOBBLE
HOMAGE
HUDDLE
HUMANE
HUMBLE
HURDLE
HURTLE
HUSTLE
ICICLE
IGNITE
IGNORE
ILLUME
IMBIBE
IMBRUE
IMMUNE
IMMURE
IMPALE
IMPEDE
IMPOSE
IMPURE
IMPUTE
INCASE
INCISE
INCITE
INCOME
INDITE
INDUCE
INFUSE
INHALE
INHERE
INHUME
INJURE
INMATE
INNATE
INSANE
INSIDE
INSOLE
INSURE
INTAKE
INTONE
INVADE
INVITE
INVOKE
IODIDE
IODINE
IODIZE
IONIZE
JANGLE
JAYCEE
JAYGEE
JAYVEE
JEJUNE
JIGGLE
JINGLE
JOCOSE
JOGGLE
JOSTLE
JOUNCE
JUGGLE
JUJUBE
JUMBLE
JUNGLE
JUNKIE
KARATE
KETTLE
KIBBLE
KINDLE
KIRTLE
LABILE
LADDIE
LASSIE
LAVAGE
LEAGUE
LEGATE
LEGUME
LESSEE
LIABLE
LICHEE
LIGATE
LINAGE
LITTLE
LOATHE
LOBULE
LOCALE
LOCATE
LOUNGE
LUPINE
MADAME
MAGPIE
MALICE
MANAGE
MANEGE
MANGLE
MANQUE
MANTLE
MANURE
MARBLE
MARINE
MASQUE
MATURE
MEDDLE
MENACE
MENAGE
METTLE
MIDDLE
MINGLE
MINUTE
MIRAGE
MISCUE
MISUSE
MOBILE
MODULE
MORALE
MORGUE
MOROSE
MOSQUE
MOTILE
MOTIVE
MOTTLE
MOUSSE
MUDDLE
MUFFLE
MUMBLE
MUSCLE
MUTATE
MUZZLE
MYRTLE
NATIVE
NATURE
NEEDLE
NEGATE
NESTLE
NETTLE
NIBBLE
NIMBLE
NIPPLE
NODDLE
NODULE
NONAGE
NOODLE
NOTICE
NOVICE
NOWISE
NOZZLE
NUANCE
NUBBLE
NUBILE
NUZZLE
OBLATE
OBLIGE
OBTUSE
OCTANE
OCTAVE
OEUVRE
OFFICE
OOLITE
OPAQUE
OPIATE
OPPOSE
ORACLE
ORANGE
ORDURE
ORIOLE
ORNATE
OTIOSE
PADDLE
PAIUTE
PALACE
PALATE
PANTIE
PAPULE
PARADE
PAROLE
PAWNEE
PEBBLE
PEDDLE
PEEWEE
PELAGE
PEOPLE
PERUKE
PERUSE
PESTLE
PETITE
PEYOTE
PHOEBE
PHRASE
PICKLE
PIDDLE
PIERCE
PIFFLE
PIMPLE
PINKIE
PIRATE
PLAGUE
PLAQUE
PLEASE
PLEDGE
PLUNGE
POLICE
POLITE
POMADE
PONGEE
POODLE
POTAGE
POTPIE
POUNCE
PRAISE
PRANCE
PRINCE
PSYCHE
PUDDLE
PUMICE
PURINE
PURPLE
PURSUE
PUTTEE
PUZZLE
PYRITE
QUINCE
RABBLE
RACEME
RAFFLE
RAMBLE
RANKLE
RAPINE
RATTLE
RAVAGE
RAVINE
REBATE
REBUKE
RECEDE
RECIPE
RECITE
REDUCE
REFINE
REFUGE
REFUSE
REFUTE
REGALE
REGIME
RELATE
RELIVE
REMOTE
REMOVE
RENEGE
REPINE
REPOSE
REPUTE
RESALE
RESCUE
RESIDE
RESUME
RETAKE
RETIRE
REVERE
REVILE
REVISE
REVIVE
REVOKE
RIDDLE
RIPPLE
RISQUE
ROOKIE
ROTATE
ROUBLE
RUBBLE
RUFFLE
RUMBLE
RUMPLE
RUSTLE
SADDLE
SALINE
SALUTE
SAMPLE
SATIRE
SAVAGE
SCARCE
SCHEME
SCONCE
SCRAPE
SCRIBE
SCYTHE
SEANCE
SECEDE
SECURE
SEDATE
SEDUCE
SEETHE
SEMITE
SENATE
SENILE
SERAPE
SERENE
SESAME
SETTEE
SETTLE
SEVERE
SEWAGE
SHEAVE
SHELVE
SHRIKE
SHRINE
SHRIVE
SICKLE
SILAGE
SIMILE
SIMPLE
SINGLE
SIZZLE
SLEDGE
SLEEVE
SLUDGE
SLUICE
SMUDGE
SNEEZE
SNOOZE
SOIGNE
SOIREE
SOLACE
SOOTHE
SORTIE
SOURCE
SPARSE
SPATHE
SPECIE
SPHERE
SPLICE
SPLINE
SPONGE
SPOUSE
SPRITE
SPRUCE
SPURGE
SQUARE
SQUIRE
STABLE
STANCE
STAPLE
STARVE
STATUE
STEPPE
STIFLE
STOOGE
STRAFE
STRIDE
STRIFE
STRIKE
STRIPE
STRIVE
STROBE
STRODE
STROKE
STROVE
STYMIE
SUBDUE
SUBTLE
SUCKLE
SUNDAE
SUPINE
SUPPLE
SUTURE
SVELTE
SWATHE
SWERVE
TACKLE
TAMALE
TANGLE
TATTLE
TEEPEE
TEETHE
TEMPLE
TENURE
THENCE
THIEVE
THRICE
THRIVE
THRONE
THROVE
TICKLE
TIMBRE
TINGLE
TINKLE
TIPPLE
TIPTOE
TIRADE
TISSUE
TITTLE
TODDLE
TOFFEE
TOGGLE
TONGUE
TOPPLE
TORQUE
TOUCHE
TOUPEE
TOUSLE
TOWHEE
TRANCE
TREBLE
TRIAGE
TRIFLE
TRIODE
TRIPLE
TRIUNE
TROCHE
TROUPE
TRUDGE
TSETSE
TUBULE
TUMBLE
TURTLE
TUSSLE
TWELVE
TWINGE
ULLAGE
UMPIRE
UNABLE
UNIQUE
UNLACE
UNLADE
UNLIKE
UNPILE
UNRIPE
UNROBE
UNTRUE
UNTUNE
UNWISE
UNYOKE
UPDATE
UPSIDE
UPTAKE
URBANE
URSINE
USABLE
VACATE
VALISE
VENDEE
VENIRE
VESTEE
VIABLE
VIRILE
VIRTUE
VISAGE
VIVACE
VOLUME
VOLUTE
VOTIVE
VOYAGE
WABBLE
WADDLE
WAFFLE
WAGGLE
WAHINE
WAMBLE
WANGLE
WARBLE
WATTLE
WHEEZE
WHENCE
WIGGLE
WIMBLE
WIMPLE
WINKLE
WOBBLE
WRASSE
WRITHE
YANKEE
ZOMBIE
ZOUAVE
ZYGOTE
BEHALF
BEHOOF
BELIEF
CUTOFF
ENGULF
HEREOF
IMPERF
ITSELF
LAYOFF
MASSIF
MYSELF
PAYOFF
PRINTF
REBUFF
RELIEF
RUNOFF
SCRUFF
SPECIF
TARIFF
UNICEF
UNROOF
ACTING
ANALOG
AWNING
BEDBUG
BELONG
BIGWIG
BITING
BLUING
BOWLEG
BOXING
CASING
COMING
COPING
DARING
DOGLEG
DURING
EARWIG
EDGING
EGGNOG
ENDING
FACING
FILING
HUMBUG
INNING
LADING
LAPDOG
LIKING
LINING
LIVING
LOVING
MUSKEG
NUTMEG
OBLONG

OFFING
OUTING
PALING
PARING
PAVING
PHOTOG
PILING
PIPING
PROLOG
QUAHOG
RARING
RATING
REFRIG
SARONG
SATANG
SAYING
SEWING
SIDING
SPRING
SPRUNG
STRING
STRONG
STRUNG
TAKING
THRONG
TRYING
TUBING
TURING
UNCLOG
UNPLUG
UNSUNG
VIKING
WIGWAG
WIRING
ZIGZAG
AFRESH
AMBUSH
ATTACH
AVOUCH
AWEIGH
BANISH
BLANCH
BLEACH
BLENCH
BLOTCH
BLUISH
BRANCH
BREACH
BREATH
BREECH
BROACH
BROOCH
BRUNCH
BYPATH
CALIPH
CHURCH
CLENCH
CLINCH
CLUTCH
CROTCH
CROUCH
CRUNCH
CRUTCH
DANISH
DEARTH
DETACH
DRENCH
ENMESH
ENOUGH
ENRICH
EUNUCH
FAMISH
FELLAH
FETISH
FINISH
FLINCH
FLITCH
FOURTH
FRENCH
GALOSH
GARISH
GLITCH
GROUCH
GROWTH
HAUNCH
HEALTH
HEARTH
HOOKAH
HOWDAH
HURRAH
HUZZAH
IMPISH
INRUSH
KIBOSH
KITSCH
KLATCH
LAUNCH
LAVISH
LENGTH
MODISH
NAUTCH
OFFISH
ONRUSH
ORNITH
PARIAH
PARISH
PAUNCH
PERISH
PLINTH
POLISH
POTASH
PREACH
PUNISH
PURDAH
PUTSCH
QUENCH
RADISH
RAKISH
RAVISH
REHASH
RELISH
RUPIAH
SCORCH
SCOTCH
SEARCH
SERAPH
SHEATH
SHEIKH
SKETCH
SLEIGH
SLEUTH
SLOUCH
SLOUGH
SMIRCH
SMOOCH
SMOOTH
SMUTCH
SNATCH
SNITCH
SPEECH
SPLASH
SQUASH
STANCH
STARCH
STENCH
STITCH
SWATCH
SWITCH
THATCH
THOUGH
THRASH
THRESH
THRUSH
TRENCH
TROUGH
TWITCH
UPPISH
UPRUSH
VANISH
WARMTH
WEALTH
WRAITH
WREATH
WRENCH
WRETCH
YAHWEH
ZENITH
ABNAKI
ALKALI
BANZAI
BIKINI
BONSAI
CHICHI
DALASI
KABUKI
LITCHI
SAFARI
SALAMI
SCAMPI
SENITI
WAPITI
YANQUI
INTERJ
ATTACK
BEDECK
DAMASK
DEBARK
DEBUNK
DYBBUK
EMBANK
EMBARK
HIJACK
KOPECK
MOHAWK
MUKLUK
REMARK
SHRIEK
SHRINK
SQUAWK
SQUEAK
STREAK
STRUCK
THWACK
TUGRIK
UNCORK
UNHOOK
UNLOCK
UNMASK
UNPACK
ACTUAL
AERIAL
AMORAL
ANIMAL
ANNEAL
ANNUAL
APICAL
APPALL
APPEAL
ARMFUL
ARTFUL
ASSAIL
ASTRAL
ASTROL
ATONAL
AWHIRL
BARREL
BEFALL
BEFOUL
BENZOL
BETHEL
BEWAIL
BOREAL
BRIDAL
BRUTAL
BULBUL
BURIAL
BUSHEL
CANCEL
CAPFUL
CARNAL
CARPAL
CARPEL
CARREL
CARTEL
CASUAL
CAUDAL
CAUSAL
CEREAL
CHAPEL
CHISEL
CHORAL
COEVAL
COMPEL
CONSOL
CONSUL
CORBEL
CORRAL
CREWEL
CUDGEL
CYMBAL
DACTYL
DAMSEL
DARNEL
DENIAL
DENTAL
DERAIL
DERMAL
DETAIL
DIESEL
DIRNDL
DISMAL
DISPEL
DISTAL
DORSAL
DRIVEL
ENAMEL
ENROLL
ENTAIL
ETHNOL
FACIAL
FAECAL
FENNEL
FESTAL
FEUDAL
FIBRIL
FILIAL
FINIAL
FISCAL
FITFUL
FLORAL
FOETAL
FORMAL
FOSSIL
FRUGAL
FUNNEL
GAMBOL
GENIAL
GERBIL
GIMBAL
GLOBAL
GOSPEL
GRAVEL
GROVEL
HANSEL
HOSTEL
JACKAL
JOVIAL
JOYFUL
KENNEL
KERNEL
LABIAL
LAUREL
LAWFUL
LENTIL
LETHAL
LINEAL
LINTEL
MAMMAL
MANFUL
MANTEL
MANUAL
MARCEL
MARVEL
MEDIAL
MENIAL
MENTAL
MESCAL
METHYL
MISSAL
MORSEL
MORTAL
MUSSEL
MUTUAL
NEURAL
NEUROL
NICKEL
NORMAL
NOVELL
ORDEAL
PARCEL
PASCAL
PASSEL
PASTEL
PATROL
PENCIL
PETREL
PETROL
PHENOL
PINEAL
PISTIL
PISTOL
PLURAL
POMMEL
PORTAL
POSTAL
PRIMAL
PROPEL
PUMMEL
RADIAL
RASCAL
RECALL
RECOIL
RECTAL
REFILL
REGNAL
RENTAL
REPEAL
RETAIL
REVEAL
RITUAL
RUNNEL
SANDAL
SCHOOL
SCRAWL
SCROLL
SEQUEL
SERIAL
SEXUAL
SHOVEL
SHRILL
SIGILL
SIGNAL
SINFUL
SNIVEL
SNOBOL
SOCIAL
SOCIOL
SORREL
SPINAL
SPINEL
SPIRAL
SPRAWL
SQUALL
SQUEAL
STROLL
SWIVEL
SYMBOL
TASSEL
TEASEL
THRALL
THRILL
TINSEL
TONSIL
TRANSL
TRAVEL
TROWEL
TUNNEL
UNCIAL
UNCOIL
UNCURL
UNFURL
UNREAL
UNREEL
UNROLL
UNSEAL
UNVEIL
UNWELL
UPHILL
UPWELL
URACIL
URINAL
USEFUL
VANDAL
VASSAL
VENIAL
VERBAL
VERNAL
VESSEL
VESTAL
VISUAL
WEASEL
WEEVIL
WITHAL
WOEFUL
ABLOOM
AFFIRM
AGLEAM
ANADEM
ANTHEM
ANTRUM
ASHRAM
ASYLUM
ATRIUM
AUTISM
BALSAM
BANTAM
BARIUM
BECALM
BEDLAM
BELDAM
BESEEM
BOTTOM
BUNKUM
CAECUM
CERIUM
CESIUM
CHRISM
CILIUM
CONDOM
CUBISM
CURIUM
CUSTOM
DEFORM
DIADEM
DIATOM
DICTUM
DIRHAM
DISARM
DUMDUM
EEPROM
EGOISM
EMBALM
EMBLEM
ENGRAM
ERBIUM
ESTEEM
FATHOM
GYPSUM
HANSOM
HELIUM
IBIDEM
INDIUM
INFIRM
INFORM
INSEAM
JETSAM
LABIUM
LOGJAM
LYCEUM
MAOISM
MAYHEM
MEDIUM
MEGOHM
MONISM
MOSLEM
MUSEUM
MUSLIM
NAPALM
NONCOM
NUDISM
ORGASM
OSMIUM
PASSIM
PHLEGM
PHLOEM
PHYLUM
PLENUM
PODIUM
POGROM
POSSUM
PRELIM
PURISM
QUORUM
RACISM
RADIUM
RANDOM
RANSOM
RECTUM
REDEEM
REFORM
RHYTHM
SACHEM
SACRUM
SADISM
SALAAM
SCHISM
SCREAM
SELDOM
SEXISM
SLALOM
SODIUM
SPUTUM
SQUIRM
STREAM
SYSTEM
TANDEM
TAOISM
TEDIUM
THEISM
TRUISM
VACUUM
VAGROM
VELLUM
VICTIM
WAMPUM
WHILOM
WIGWAM
WISDOM
XMODEM
YMODEM
ZMODEM
ACTION
ACUMEN
ADJOIN
AFGHAN
AIDMAN
AIRMAN
AMAZON
ARCHON
ARCSIN
ARCTAN
ASSIGN
ASTERN
ASTRON
ATTAIN
AUBURN
AUTUMN
AWAKEN
BABOON
BAGMAN

BALEEN BANYAN BARREN BATMAN BATTEN BEACON BECKON BEDPAN BEMOAN BENIGN BIOTIN BLAZON BOBBIN BODKIN BONBON BOWMAN BRAZEN BRITON BROGAN BROKEN BUNION BURDEN BUSKIN BUTTON CAFTAN CAIMAN CANCAN CANNON CANTON CANYON CARBON CAREEN CARTON CASEIN CATION CATKIN CAVERN CAYMAN CHITIN CHOSEN CITRON CLOVEN COCOON COFFIN COLUMN COMMON CORDON COTTON COUPON COUSIN COWMAN CRATON CRAVEN CRAYON CRETIN DAEMON DAMPEN

DAMSON DARKEN DEACON DEADEN DEAFEN DEEPEN DEHORN DEMEAN DENTIN DESIGN DETAIN DISOWN DOBBIN DOLMEN DOMAIN DRAGON DUBBIN ELEVEN ENDRIN ENJOIN ENSIGN EOLIAN EXTERN FABIAN FALCON FASTEN FATTEN FENIAN FIBRIN FLACON FLAGON FLAXEN FLORIN FOEMAN FROZEN FUSION GALLON GAMMON GARCON GARDEN GERMAN GIBBON GIBSON GLUTEN GOBLIN GODSON GOLDEN GOTTEN GOVERN GRABEN GUIDON GULDEN GUNMAN HAPPEN HARDEN HARKEN HASTEN

HEAVEN HEREIN HEREON HEROIN HOYDEN HYPHEN ICEMAN IMPUGN INBORN INDIAN INTERN JARGON JERKIN KAOLIN KELVIN KITTEN KOREAN LAGOON LAWMAN LAYMAN LEADEN LEAVEN LEGION LEGMAN LEPTON LESION LESSEN LESSON LIBYAN LICHEN LINDEN LISTEN LOOSEN LOTION MACRON MADDEN MADMAN MAIDEN MALIAN MALIGN MAMMON MARGIN MARLIN MAROON MARTEN MARTIN MASCON MATRON MEDIAN MERMAN MICRON MIDDEN MINION MITTEN MIZZEN MODERN MOLTEN

MORGAN MORMON MOTION MOUTON MUFFIN MUSLIN MUTTON NAPKIN NATION NELSON NEURON NEWTON NIACIN NOGGIN NORMAN NORTON NOTION NUBBIN OBTAIN OPTION ORDAIN ORIGIN ORISON ORPHAN OUTGUN OUTRUN OXYGEN PALEON PAPAIN PARDON PARSON PATRON PEAHEN PECTIN PENMAN PENNON PEPSIN PERSON PHOTON PIDGIN PIGEON PIGPEN PINION PIPKIN PIPPIN PISTON PLATEN PLUTON POISON POLLEN POMPON POPGUN POPLIN POTEEN POTION PRISON PROTON

PUFFIN PUNKIN PYTHON RADIAN RAGLAN RAISIN RAPPEN RATION RATTAN REASON REBORN RECKON REDDEN REGAIN REGION REJOIN REMAIN RENNIN RENOWN RESIGN RETAIN RETURN RIBBON RIDDEN RLOGIN ROTTEN SADDEN SALMON SALOON SAMPAN SATEEN SATURN SCREEN SEAMAN SEASON SEQUIN SERMON SEXTON SHAMAN SICKEN SIMIAN SIPHON SLOGAN SLOVEN SODDEN SOFTEN SOLEMN SPAVIN SPLEEN SPOKEN SPRAIN STAMEN STOLEN STOLON STRAIN SUBORN SUDDEN

SULLEN SULTAN SUMMON SUNKEN SUNTAN SYLVAN SYPHON TAMPON TANNIN TARPON TARTAN TAVERN TENDON TENPIN TIFFIN TOCSIN TOUCAN TREPAN TRITON TROJAN TURBAN TUREEN TYCOON UNBORN UNEVEN UNISON UPTOWN UPTURN URCHIN VERMIN VIOLIN VIRGIN VIRION VISION WANTON WARDEN WARREN WEAKEN WEAPON WELKIN WHITEN WITHIN WOODEN WOOLEN WORSEN YEOMAN ZIRCON ADAGIO AKIMBO ALBINO ARROYO BAGNIO BAMBOO BARRIO BISTRO BOLERO BONITO

BRONCO CALICO CASINO CHROMO CUCKOO DOMINO DYNAMO EMBRYO ENDURO ESCUDO ESKIMO FIASCO FOREGO FRESCO GABBRO GAUCHO GAZEBO GHETTO GIGOLO GINKGO GROTTO HAIRDO HERETO HOODOO INDIGO KIMONO LEGATO LIBIDO MEDICO MERINO MIKADO NAVAHO NUNCIO OCTAVO OVERDO PONCHO POTATO PRESTO PRONTO PSEUDO PSYCHO PUEBLO QUARTO RANCHO ROMANO SHINTO STEREO STUCCO STUDIO TATTOO TEREDO TOMATO TORERO TUXEDO ULTIMO UNESCO VIRAGO

VOODOO ASLEEP BACKUP BISHOP BLOWUP BURLAP CARHOP CARTOP CATNAP CATNIP CATSUP DECAMP DEWLAP DOLLOP ENCAMP ENTRAP FILLIP GALLOP GOSSIP HICCUP HOLDUP HOOKUP HUBCAP HYSSOP INSTEP KIDNAP LAPTOP LINEUP LINKUP LOCKUP MACAPP MADCAP MAKEUP MARKUP MISHAP PICKUP RECOUP REDCAP REVAMP SATRAP SCRIMP SHRIMP SKYCAP SLIPUP TEACUP TRANSP TURNIP UNSHIP UNSNAP UNSTOP UNWRAP UPKEEP WALLOP WINDUP COLLOQ COMPAQ AFFAIR

ALTAIR ANCHOR ANSWER ANTHER ANTLER APPEAR ASHLAR AUTHOR AVATAR BACKER BADGER BANNER BANTER BARBER BARKER BARTER BATTER BAZAAR BEAKER BEAVER BEGGAR BENDER BERBER BESTIR BETTER BETTOR BICKER BITTER BLAZER BOATER BOILER BOMBER BORDER BOTHER BOWLER BOXCAR BROKER BUFFER BUMMER BUMPER BUNKER BURNER BURSAR BUTLER BUTTER BUZZER CAESAR CAMBER CAMPER CANCER CANDOR CANKER CANTER CANTOR CAPTOR CAREER CASTER

CAVIAR CELLAR CENSER CENSOR CENTER CHAFER CHASER CHOKER CHOLER CINDER CIPHER CLAMOR CLEVER CLOVER CODGER COFFER COHEIR COLLAR COMBER COMPAR CONCUR CONDOR CONFER CONSTR COOLER COOPER COPIER COPPER COPTER CORNER COTTER COUGAR CRATER CUMBER CUNNER CURSOR CUTLER CUTTER DAGGER DAMPER DANDER DANGER DAPPER DARTER DASHER DEBTOR DENIER DEODAR DETOUR DEVOIR DEVOUR DIAPER DICKER DIFFER DIMMER DINNER DIPPER

DISBAR
DITHER
DOCTOR
DODDER
DOLLAR
DORMER
DOWNER
DRAPER
DRAWER
DRIVER
DROVER
DUFFER
DUSTER
EASTER
ECLAIR
EITHER
ELIXIR
ENAMOR
ENDEAR
FACTOR
FALTER
FATHER
FAVOUR
FEELER
FENDER
FERVOR
FESTER
FETTER
FILLER
FILTER
FINDER
FINGER
FISHER
FLAVOR
FLOWER
FODDER
FOLDER
FORMER
FOSTER
FUHRER
GAFFER
GAITER
GAMMER
GANDER
GARNER
GARTER
GATHER
GEEZER
GENDER
GEYSER
GIBBER
GINGER
GIRDER
GLIDER
GLOWER
GOITER
GOOBER

GOPHER
GRADER
GROCER
GUITAR
GUNNER
GUSHER
GUTTER
HACKER
HALTER
HAMMER
HAMPER
HANGAR
HANKER
HARBOR
HATTER
HAWKER
HAWSER
HECTOR
HEIFER
HINDER
HITHER
HOLLER
HONOUR
HOOKER
HOPPER
HORROR
HOWLER
HUMOUR
HUNGER
HUNKER
HUSSAR
IMPAIR
INDOOR
ISOBAR
ISOMER
JABBER
JAGUAR
JAILER
JASPER
JESTER
JIGGER
JOBBER
JOINER
JUICER
JUMPER
JUNIOR
JUNKER
KAISER
KEGLER
KILTER
KIPPER
KISSER
KOSHER
LABOUR
LADDER
LANCER
LANDER

LARDER
LASCAR
LATHER
LATTER
LAWYER
LEADER
LECTOR
LEDGER
LESSER
LESSOR
LETTER
LIMBER
LINEAR
LINGER
LIQUOR
LITTER
LOADER
LOCKER
LODGER
LOITER
LOOPER
LOUVER
LUBBER
LUMBAR
LUMBER
LUSTER
MADDER
MAGYAR
MANGER
MANNER
MARTYR
MASTER
MATTER
MEAGER
MEMBER
MEMOIR
MENTOR
MERCER
MERGER
METEOR
METIER
MIDAIR
MILLER
MIRROR
MISTER
MOHAIR
MOLDER
MONGER
MORTAR
MOTHER
MOUSER
MUMMER
MURDER
MURMUR
MUSTER
MUTTER
NECTAR

NETHER
NEUTER
NICKER
NIPPER
NUMBER
OCULAR
ORATOR
OSTLER
OUSTER
OYSTER
PACKER
PALLOR
PALMER
PALTER
PAMPER
PANDER
PARLOR
PASTOR
PATTER
PAUPER
PEPPER
PESTER
PEWTER
PILFER
PILLAR
PINCER
PLACER
PLOVER
POLDER
PONDER
POPLAR
POPPER
PORKER
PORTER
POSEUR
POSTER
POTHER
POTTER
POWDER
PRAYER
PREFER
PREWAR
PRIMER
PROPER
PUCKER
PULSAR
PURSER
PUSHER
PUTTER
QINTAR
QUAKER
QUASAR
QUAVER
QUIVER
RAFTER
RANCOR
RANGER

RAPIER
RASHER
RASTER
RATHER
RATTER
REAMER
RECTOR
REEFER
RENDER
REPAIR
RIGGER
RINGER
ROBBER
ROCKER
ROLLER
ROMPER
ROSTER
RUBBER
RUDDER
RUNNER
SAILOR
SALVER
SAUCER
SAVIOR
SEALER
SECTOR
SENIOR
SENSOR
SERVER
SETTER
SHAKER
SHAVER
SHINER
SHIVER
SHOWER
SILVER
SIMMER
SIMPER
SINKER
SISTER
SKEWER
SLAVER
SLIDER
SLIVER
SOCCER
SOEVER
SOLDER
SOMBER
SPIDER
STUPOR
SUCCOR
SUCKER
SUFFER
SUITOR
SULFUR
SUMMER
SUNDER

SUPPER
TAILOR
TAMPER
TANKER
TANNER
TARTAR
TATTER
TEETER
TELLER
TEMPER
TENDER
TERROR
TESTER
TETHER
TICKER
TILLER
TIMBER
TINDER
TINKER
TITTER
TORPOR
TOTTER
TRADER
TREMOR
TUCKER
TURNER
TUSKER
ULSTER
UNFAIR
UNMOOR
UPREAR
UPROAR
URETER
USURER
VECTOR
VELOUR
VENDER
VENDOR
VENEER
VERGER
VESPER
VICTOR
VIZIER
VOYEUR
VULGAR
WAITER
WAIVER
WANDER
WARDER
WASHER
WELTER
WETHER
WHALER
WICKER
WIENER
WINDER
WINKER

WINNER
WINTER
WITHER
WONDER
WOOFER
WORKER
WRITER
YAMMER
YONDER
ZEPHYR
ZIPPER
ZITHER
ABACUS
ABATIS
ABBESS
ACCESS
ACROSS
ALWAYS
AMENDS
AMVETS
ANIMUS
ANNALS
ARCCOS
ASSESS
BATHOS
BICEPS
BYPASS
CACTUS
CALLUS
CALVES
CAMPUS
CANVAS
CARESS
CARIES
CAUCUS
CENSUS
CEREUS
CHORUS
CIRCUS
CIRRUS
CITRUS
CIVICS
CLEVIS
COCCUS
COITUS
CORPUS
COSMOS
CRISIS
CROCUS
DEBRIS
DERMIS
DERRIS
DINGUS
DISCUS
DIVERS
DOINGS
DURESS

ECCLES
ECCLUS
EGRESS
EMBOSS
ETHICS
EXCESS
EXODUS
FAMOUS
FAUCES
FLATUS
FRACAS
FUNGUS
GENIUS
GNEISS
GRATIS
HAGGIS
HALVES
HARASS
HERPES
HIATUS
HUBRIS
JOYOUS
LEAVES
LIGHTS
LITMUS
MADRAS
MANTIS
MATINS
MENSES
MESSRS
MORRIS
NIMBUS
OBSESS
ODIOUS
OODLES
OPTICS
PATHOS
PATOIS
PELVIS
PHAROS
PHILOS
PLEXUS
PLIERS
POROUS
PRECIS
RABIES
RADIUS
RECESS
REMISS
REVERS
RICHES
RUCKUS
RUMPUS
SCHUSS
SELVES
SEPSIS
SERIES

SHAVES
STAPES
STATUS
STAVES
STRESS
STYLUS
TARSUS
TENNIS
TESTIS
THANKS
THEIRS
THESIS
THYMUS
TIGHTS
TURVES
TYPHUS
UNDIES
UNLESS
URANUS
UTERUS
VENOUS
VERSUS
VILLUS
VINOUS
VISCUS
VITALS
WALRUS
ZOUNDS
ABDUCT
ABJECT
ABRUPT
ABSENT
ACCENT
ACCEPT
ACCOST
ACQUIT
ADDICT
ADJUST
ADRIFT
ADROIT
ADVENT
ADVERT
AFFECT
AFLOAT
AGHAST
ALBEIT
ALIGHT
ALMOST
AMOUNT
AMULET
ANKLET
ANOINT
APPLET
ARCNET
ARDENT
ARGENT
ARIGHT

ARMLET
ARMPIT
ARRANT
ARREST
ARTIST
ASCENT
ASLANT
ASPECT
ASSENT
ASSERT
ASSIST
ASSORT
ATTEST
AUGUST
AVAUNT
AVOCET
BALLET
BALLOT
BANDIT
BASALT
BASKET
BEHEST
BEREFT
BILLET
BISECT
BITNET
BLIGHT
BOBCAT
BONNET
BOUGHT
BREAST
BREVET
BRIGHT
BRUNET
BUCKET
BUDGET
BUFFET
BULLET
CACHET
CAHOOT
CANNOT
CARPET
CARROT
CASKET
CATGUT
CAUGHT
CAVEAT
CAVORT
CEMENT
CERMET
CHALET
CHAUNT
CHRIST
CLARET
CLIENT
CLOSET
COBALT

COGENT
COHORT
COLLAT
COMBAT
COMFIT
COMMIT
COQUET
CORNET
CORSET
COVERT
CRAVAT
CREDIT
CURVET
CUTLET
CUTOUT
CYGNET
DECANT
DECEIT
DECENT
DEDUCT
DEFEAT
DEFECT
DEPART
DEPICT
DEPORT
DESALT
DESERT
DESIST
DESPOT
DETECT
DETEST
DEVOUT
DIGEST
DIRECT
DIVERT
DIVEST
DOCENT
DOCKET
DOPANT
DUGOUT
DULCET
EAGLET
EFFECT
EFFORT
ELDEST
ELICIT
ENCYST
ENLIST
ERRANT
ESCORT
ESPRIT
EXCEPT
EXEMPT
EXHORT
EXPECT
EXPERT
EXPORT

EXTANT
EXTENT
EXTORT
EYELET
FAGGOT
FAUCET
FERRET
FIDGET
FILLET
FLAUNT
FLIGHT
FLUENT
FOMENT
FOREST
FORGET
FORINT
FORMAT
FOUGHT
FRIGHT
GADGET
GAMBIT
GANNET
GARNET
GARRET
GASKET
GIBBET
GIMLET
GOBBET
GOBLET
GULLET
GUSSET
HAMLET
HARLOT
HEIGHT
HELMET
HEPCAT
HERMIT
HONEST
HORNET
ILLUST
IMPACT
IMPART
IMPORT
IMPOST
INCEST
INDENT
INDICT
INDUCT
INFANT
INFECT
INFEST
INGEST
INJECT
INKJET
INMOST
INSECT
INSERT

INSIST
INSULT
INTACT
INTENT
INTUIT
INVENT
INVERT
INVEST
IRRUPT
JACKET
JENNET
JUNKET
JURIST
KERMIT
KISMET
KNIGHT
LAMENT
LANCET
LAPPET
LARIAT
LATENT
LAYOUT
LIMPET
LINNET
LOCKET
LOCUST
LUCENT
MAGGOT
MAGNET
MAHOUT
MALLET
MARKET
MARMOT
MASCOT
MIDGET
MILLET
MINUET
MISFIT
MODEST
MOLEST
MOMENT
MOPPET
MULLET
MUSKET
MUTANT
NAUGHT
NITWIT
NONFAT
NOUGAT
NOUGHT
NUGGET
OBJECT
OCCULT
OCELOT
OFFSET
OMELET
ORIENT

OUTFIT
OUTLET
OUTPUT
OUTSET
OUTWIT
PACKET
PALLET
PAPIST
PARENT
PARROT
PATENT
PEANUT
PEDANT
PELLET
PEQUOT
PERMIT
PICKET
PIGLET
PIGNUT
PIQUET
PLAINT
PLANET
PLIANT
PLIGHT
POCKET
POTENT
PRESET
PRIEST
PRIVET
PROFIT
PROMPT
PULLET
PULPIT
PUNDIT
PUPPET
PUTOUT
QIVIUT
QUAINT
RABBET
RABBIT
RACKET
RAGOUT
RECANT
RECENT
REDACT
REGENT
REGRET
REJECT
RELENT
RELICT
RENNET
REPAST
REPEAT
REPENT
REPORT
RESENT
RESIST

RESORT
RESULT
RETORT
REVERT
REVOLT
ROBUST
ROCKET
RODENT
RUNLET
RUSSET
SACHET
SAVANT
SCHIST
SCRIPT
SCULPT
SECRET
SELECT
SEXPOT
SEXTET
SHIEST
SHRIFT
SIGNET
SILENT
SLIEST
SLIGHT
SOCKET
SONNET
SOUGHT
SOVIET
SPIGOT
SPINET
SPIRIT
SPLINT
SPRINT
SPROUT
SQUINT
SQUIRT
STRAIT
STREET
STRICT
SUBLET
SUBMIT
SUBSET
SUMMIT
SUNLIT
SUNSET
TABLET
TALENT
TAPPET
TARGET
TAUGHT
TEAPOT
TELNET
TENANT
THIRST
THREAT
THRIFT

THROAT
THRUST
THWART
TICKET
TIDBIT
TIPPET
TITBIT
TOILET
TOMCAT
TOMTIT
TRIVET
TRUANT
TUMULT
TURBOT
TURRET
TYPIST
TYRANT
UNBOLT
UNJUST
UNMEET
UNREST
UNSEAT
UNWEPT
UPBEAT
UPLIFT
UPMOST
UPROOT
UPSHOT
URGENT
USENET
UTMOST
VACANT
VARLET
VELVET
VIOLET
WALLET
WALNUT
WEIGHT
WESKIT
WHILST
WICKET
WIGLET
WOMBAT
YOGURT
ZEALOT
APERCU
BATEAU
BUREAU
LANDAU
MILIEU
MUUMUU
ORMOLU
ANYHOW
BARROW
BELLOW
BESTOW
BILLOW

BORROW
BURROW
CALLOW
CASHEW
CURFEW
CURLEW
DESKEW
ESCHEW
ESCROW
FALLOW
FARROW
FELLOW
FOLLOW
FURROW
GEWGAW
GUFFAW
HALLOW
HARROW
HAYMOW
HEBREW
HOLLOW
INFLOW
JIGSAW
KOWTOW
MALLOW
MARROW
MEADOW
MELLOW
MILDEW
MINNOW
MORROW
NARROW
NEPHEW
OUTLAW
PAWPAW
PILLOW
POWWOW
REVIEW
RIPSAW
SALLOW
SEESAW
SHADOW
SORROW
TALLOW
WALLOW
WILLOW
WINDOW
WINNOW
YARROW
YELLOW
APPROX
BINHEX
CERVIX
CLIMAX
COCCYX
COMDEX
CONVEX

CORTEX
COWPOX
DUPLEX
EARWAX
HATBOX
HOTBOX
ICEBOX
INFLUX
LARYNX
LUMMOX
MATRIX
MENINX
MSCDEX
OUTFOX
PICKAX
POLEAX
PREFIX
PREMIX
PROLIX
REFLEX
REFLUX
SMILAX
SPADIX
SPHINX
SUFFIX
SURTAX
SYNTAX
THORAX
ULTRIX
UNISEX
VERTEX
VORTEX
ABBACY
ACUITY
AFFRAY
AGENCY
AIRWAY
ANYWAY
APATHY
APIARY
ARGOSY
ARMORY
ARTERY
ASTRAY
AUGURY
AVIARY
AWEARY
BAKERY
BARELY
BARFLY
BARLEY
BEAUTY
BELFRY
BETRAY
BIGAMY
BINARY
BIOPSY

BLEARY
BLOWSY
BODILY
BOTANY
BOUNTY
BRANDY
BUSBOY
BUSILY
BYPLAY
CANARY
CANOPY
CARBOY
CATCHY
CAVITY
CELERY
CHANCY
CHATTY
CHEEKY
CHEERY
CHERRY
CHILLY
CHOOSY
CHOPPY
CHUBBY
CHUMMY
CHUNKY
CITIFY
CLAMMY
CLASSY
CLERGY
CLUMSY
CODIFY
COLONY
COMEDY
COMELY
COMITY
COMPLY
CONVEY
CONVOY
COSTLY
COUNTY
COWBOY
CRABBY
CRAFTY
CRANKY
CRANNY
CREEPY
CRUMMY
CURTSY
DAINTY
DEADLY
DEEJAY
DEFRAY
DEPLOY
DEPUTY
DESCRY
DICKEY

DIMITY
DINGHY
DISMAY
DONKEY
DOUBLY
DRAFTY
DREARY
DRESSY
DROPSY
DROWSY
EARTHY
EATERY
EFFIGY
EIGHTY
EMBODY
EMPLOY
ENERGY
ENMITY
ENTITY
EQUITY
EULOGY
FAIRLY
FAMILY
FEALTY
FELONY
FINERY
FIXITY
FLABBY
FLASHY
FLESHY
FLIMSY
FLOOZY
FLOPPY
FLOSSY
FLUFFY
FLUNKY
FLURRY
FLYWAY
FOLKSY
FRENZY
FRIARY
FRIDAY
FRISKY
FROWSY
FRUITY
FRUMPY
GADFLY
GAIETY
GALAXY
GALLEY
GANTRY
GAYETY
GENTRY
GLOSSY
GOODLY
GRAINY
GRISLY

GROGG**Y**
GROOV**Y**
GRUBB**Y**
GRUMP**Y**
GUILT**Y**
HARDL**Y**
HEART**Y**
HEREB**Y**
HERES**Y**
HEYDA**Y**
HOCKE**Y**
HOMEL**Y**
HOMIL**Y**
HOMIN**Y**
HORSE**Y**
IDIOC**Y**
INFAM**Y**
INJUR**Y**
JALOP**Y**
JAUNT**Y**
JERSE**Y**
JITNE**Y**
JOCKE**Y**
JOHNN**Y**
KIDNE**Y**
KINDL**Y**
LACKE**Y**
LEEWA**Y**
LEGAC**Y**
LENIT**Y**
LEVIT**Y**
LIKEL**Y**
LITAN**Y**
LIVEL**Y**
LIVER**Y**
LONEL**Y**
LORDL**Y**
LOVEL**Y**
LOWER**Y**
LUNAC**Y**
LUXUR**Y**
MALAD**Y**
MAYFL**Y**
MEASL**Y**
MEDLE**Y**
MELOD**Y**
MEMOR**Y**
MIDDA**Y**
MIDWA**Y**
MIGHT**Y**
MISER**Y**
MISLA**Y**
MODIF**Y**
MOIET**Y**
MONDA**Y**
MONKE**Y**
MONOD**Y**
MOSTL**Y**
MOTLE**Y**
MUTIN**Y**
NAMEL**Y**
NAPER**Y**
NEARB**Y**
NICET**Y**
NINET**Y**
NOBOD**Y**
NOTIF**Y**
OCCUP**Y**
ODDIT**Y**
ORNER**Y**
OSPRE**Y**
OSSIF**Y**
OUTCR**Y**
OUTLA**Y**
OVERL**Y**
PACIF**Y**
PALTR**Y**
PANTR**Y**
PAPAC**Y**
PARIT**Y**
PARLA**Y**
PARLE**Y**
PAROD**Y**
PARTL**Y**
PASTR**Y**
PENUR**Y**
PIGST**Y**
PIRAC**Y**
PLENT**Y**
PLUCK**Y**
POETR**Y**
POLIC**Y**
POLIT**Y**
PORTL**Y**
POTBO**Y**
PREPA**Y**
PRETT**Y**
PRIOR**Y**
PRISS**Y**
PULLE**Y**
PURIF**Y**
PURIT**Y**
PURVE**Y**
QUARR**Y**
QUEAS**Y**
QUINS**Y**
RAMIF**Y**
RAREF**Y**
RATIF**Y**
REALL**Y**
REALT**Y**
REMED**Y**
REPLA**Y**
ROSAR**Y**
ROTAR**Y**
RUNWA**Y**
SAFET**Y**
SALAR**Y**
SANIT**Y**
SASHA**Y**
SCANT**Y**
SCREW**Y**
SCURR**Y**
SCURV**Y**
SCUZZ**Y**
SEAWA**Y**
SEEML**Y**
SENTR**Y**
SHABB**Y**
SHAGG**Y**
SHANT**Y**
SHERR**Y**
SHIFT**Y**
SHIMM**Y**
SHINN**Y**
SHODD**Y**
SIMON**Y**
SKIMP**Y**
SKINN**Y**
SLEAZ**Y**
SLEEP**Y**
SLOPP**Y**
SLURR**Y**
SMITH**Y**
SNIPP**Y**
SNOOT**Y**
SODOM**Y**
SPOTT**Y**
STEAD**Y**
STICK**Y**
STING**Y**
STOCK**Y**
STODG**Y**
STUBB**Y**
STUFF**Y**
STURD**Y**
SUBWA**Y**
SULTR**Y**
SUNDA**Y**
SUNDR**Y**
SUPPL**Y**
SURET**Y**
SURRE**Y**
SURVE**Y**
TAWDR**Y**
TETCH**Y**
THEOR**Y**
THIRT**Y**
TIMEL**Y**
TOMBO**Y**
TOOTH**Y**
TOUCH**Y**
TREAT**Y**
TRICK**Y**
TRIPL**Y**
TROPH**Y**
TRUST**Y**
TURKE**Y**
TWEED**Y**
TWENT**Y**
TYPIF**Y**
UNDUL**Y**
UNEAS**Y**
UNHOL**Y**
UNRUL**Y**
UPPIT**Y**
VAGAR**Y**
VALLE**Y**
VANIT**Y**
VAPOR**Y**
VERIF**Y**
VERIL**Y**
VERIT**Y**
VESTR**Y**
VILIF**Y**
VIVIF**Y**
VOLLE**Y**
VOTAR**Y**
WATER**Y**
WAYLA**Y**
WEAKL**Y**
WEEKL**Y**
WHAMM**Y**
WHEEZ**Y**
WHERR**Y**
WHIMS**Y**
WHINN**Y**
WHOLL**Y**
WIGGL**Y**
WINTR**Y**
WOODS**Y**
WOOLL**Y**
WORTH**Y**
YEARL**Y**
YEAST**Y**
CHINT**Z**
ERSAT**Z**
QUART**Z**

# 7 LETTER WORDS

1ST LETTER

ABALONE
ABANDON
ABDOMEN
ABILITY
ABOLISH
ABREAST
ABRIDGE
ABSCESS
ABSCOND
ABSENCE
ABSOLVE
ABSTAIN
ABYSMAL
ABYSSAL
ACADEME
ACADEMY
ACCLAIM
ACCOUNT
ACCUSAL
ACCUSED
ACETATE
ACETONE
ACHIEVE
ACIDIFY
ACOLYTE
ACONITE
ACQUIRE
ACREAGE
ACROBAT
ACRONYM
ACRYLIC
ACTUARY
ACTUATE
ADAMANT
ADAPTER
ADDRESS
ADENINE
ADENOID
ADIPOSE
ADJOURN
ADJUDGE
ADJUNCT
ADMIRAL
ADRENAL
ADULATE
ADVANCE
ADVERSE
ADVISED
AEROBIC
AEROSOL
AFFABLE
AFFLICT
AFFRONT
AFGHANI
AFRICAN
AGAINST
AGELESS
AGITATE
AGONIZE
AGROUND
AILERON
AILMENT
AIMLESS
AIRDROP
AIRFLOW
AIRFOIL
AIRLIFT
AIRLINE
AIRMAIL
AIRPORT
AIRPOST
AIRSHIP
AIRSICK
AIRWAVE
ALBUMEN
ALBUMIN
ALCALDE
ALCAZAR
ALCHEMY
ALCOHOL
ALEMBIC
ALEWIFE
ALFALFA
ALGEBRA
ALIMENT
ALIMONY
ALLEGRO
ALLERGY
ALMANAC
ALMONER
ALREADY
ALRIGHT
ALUMINA
ALUMNUS
AMALGAM
AMATEUR
AMATIVE
AMATORY
AMBIENT
AMENITY
AMERIND
AMIABLE
AMMETER
AMMONIA
AMNESIA
AMNESTY
AMOROUS
AMPHORA
AMPLIFY
AMPUTEE
AMYLASE
ANAEMIA
ANAGRAM
ANALOGY
ANALYZE
ANAPEST
ANARCHY
ANATOMY
ANCHOVY
ANCIENT
ANDANTE
ANDIRON
ANDROID
ANEMONE
ANGUISH
ANGULAR
ANILINE
ANIMATE
ANIMISM
ANNUITY
ANNULAR
ANODIZE
ANODYNE
ANOMALY
ANOTHER
ANTACID
ANTENNA
ANTHILL
ANTHRAX
ANTHROP
ANTIGEN
ANTIQUE
ANTONYM
ANXIETY
ANXIOUS
ANYBODY
ANYMORE
ANYTIME
ANYWISE
APANAGE
APATITE
APHASIA
APOLOGY
APOLUNE
APOSTLE
APPAREL
APPEASE
APPLAUD
APPLIED
APPOINT
APPRISE
APPROVE
APRICOT
APROPOS
AQUATIC
AQUAVIT
AQUEOUS
AQUIFER
ARAPAHO
ARBITER
ARBUTUS
ARCHAIC
ARCHERY
ARCHIVE
ARCHWAY
ARDUOUS
AREAWAY
ARMHOLE
ARMORER
ARMREST
ARPANET
ARRAIGN
ARRANGE
ARREARS
ARRIVAL
ARSENAL
ARSENIC
ARTICLE
ARTISAN
ARTISTE
ARTLESS
ASCETIC
ASCRIBE
ASEPTIC
ASEXUAL
ASHAMED
ASHTRAY
ASIATIC
ASININE
ASKANCE
ASPHALT
ASPIRIN
ASSAULT
ASSUAGE
ASSURED
ASTOUND
ASTRIDE
ASUNDER
ATAVISM
ATELIER
ATHEIST
ATHIRST
ATHLETE
ATHWART
ATOMIZE
ATROPHY
ATTACHE
ATTAINT
ATTEMPT
ATTRACT
AUCTION
AUDIBLE
AUDITOR
AUGMENT
AUREATE
AUREOLE
AURICLE
AUSPICE
AUSTERE
AUSTRAL
AUTOPSY
AVARICE
AVERAGE
AVOCADO
AWKWARD
AZIMUTH
BACKING
BACKLIT
BACKLOG
BADLAND
BAGASSE
BAGGAGE
BAGPIPE
BAILIFF
BALANCE
BALCONY
BALDING
BALDRIC
BALEFUL
BALLAST
BALLOON
BALONEY
BANDAGE
BANDBOX
BANNOCK
BANQUET
BANSHEE
BAPTISM
BAPTIST
BAPTIZE
BARBELL
BARGAIN
BARONET
BAROQUE
BARRAGE
BARRIER
BARRING
BARROOM
BASHFUL
BASSOON
BASTARD
BASTION
BATHTUB
BATISTE
BATSMAN
BATTERY
BATTING
BAUXITE
BAYONET
BAZOOKA
BEARING
BEASTLY
BEATIFY
BEATNIK
BECAUSE
BECLOUD
BEDDING
BEDEVIL
BEDFAST
BEDIZEN
BEDOUIN
BEDPOST
BEDROCK
BEDROLL
BEDROOM
BEDSIDE
BEDSORE
BEDTIME
BEEHIVE
BEELINE
BEESWAX
BEGGARY
BEGONIA
BEGRIME
BEGUILE
BEGUINE
BEHOOVE
BELABOR
BELATED
BELGIAN
BELIEVE
BELLBOY
BELLHOP
BELLOWS
BELOVED
BELTWAY
BENEATH
BENEFIT
BENISON
BENTHIC
BENTHOS
BENZENE
BENZINE
BENZOIN
BEQUEST
BERSERK
BESEECH
BESHREW
BESIDES
BESIEGE
BESMEAR
BESPEAK
BESTIAL
BETHINK
BETIMES
BETOKEN
BETROTH
BETWEEN
BETWIXT
BEWITCH
BIBELOT
BICYCLE
BIFOCAL
BIGHORN
BIKEWAY
BILIOUS
BILLION
BIMETAL
BINDING
BIOLOGY
BIOTITE
BIPLANE
BIPOLAR
BIRCHER
BIRETTA
BISCUIT
BISMUTH
BITTERN
BITTERS
BITUMEN
BIVALVE
BIVOUAC
BIZARRE
BLACKEN
BLADDER
BLANKET
BLARNEY
BLATANT
BLATHER
BLEEDER
BLEMISH
BLESSED
BLINDER
BLINKER
BLINTZE
BLISTER
BLOATER
BLOODED
BLOOPER
BLOSSOM
BLOTTER
BLOWGUN
BLOWOUT
BLUBBER
BLUCHER
BLUNDER
BLUSTER
BOATMAN
BOBSLED
BOLIVAR
BOLOGNA
BOLSTER
BOMBARD
BOMBAST
BONANZA
BONDAGE
BONDMAN
BONFIRE
BOOKEND
BOOKISH
BOOKLET
BOOTLEG
BOREDOM
BOROUGH
BORSCHT
BOUDOIR
BOULDER
BOUNCER
BOUNDEN
BOUQUET
BOURBON
BOWLDER
BOWLINE
BOWLING
BOYCOTT
BRACERO
BRACKEN
BRACKET
BRAHMAN
BRAHMIN
BRAILLE
BRAMBLE
BRAVADO
BRAVERY
BRAVURA
BRAZIER
BREADTH
BREAKER
BREAKUP
BREATHE
BRECCIA
BREVITY
BRIGADE
BRIGAND
BRIMFUL
BRIOCHE
BRISKET
BRISTLE
BRITISH
BRITTLE
BROADEN
BROCADE
BROIDER
BROILER
BROMIDE
BROMINE
BROODER
BROTHEL
BROTHER
BROUGHT
BROWNIE
BROWSER
BRUISER
BRUSQUE
BRUTISH
BUCKEYE
BUCKLER

BUCKRAM
BUCKSAW
BUCOLIC
BUFFALO
BUFFOON
BUGABOO
BUGBEAR
BULLDOG
BULLION
BULLOCK
BULRUSH
BULWARK
BUMPKIN
BUNTING
BURDOCK
BURETTE
BURGEON
BURGESS
BURGHER
BURMESE
BURNISH
BURNOUT
BUSHING
BUTCHER
BUTTOCK
BUZZARD
CABARET
CABBAGE
CABINET
CABOOSE
CADAVER
CADENCE
CADENZA
CADMIUM
CAESURA
CAISSON
CAITIFF
CALCIFY
CALCINE
CALCITE
CALCIUM
CALDERA
CALDRON
CALENDS
CALIBER
CALIPER
CALLING
CALLOUS
CALOMEL
CALORIC
CALORIE
CALUMET
CALUMNY
CALYPSO
CAMBIUM
CAMBRIC
CAMPHOR
CANASTA
CANDIED
CANNERY
CANNULA
CANTATA
CANTEEN
CANVASS
CAPABLE
CAPITAL
CAPITOL
CAPRICE
CAPSIZE
CAPSTAN
CAPSULE
CAPTAIN
CAPTION
CAPTIVE
CAPTURE
CARABAO
CARAMEL
CARAVAN
CARAVEL
CARAWAY
CARBIDE
CARBINE
CARCASS
CARDBUS
CARDIAC
CAREFUL
CARFARE
CARIBOU
CARIOUS
CARLOAD
CARMINE
CARNAGE
CAROTID
CAROUSE
CARPORT
CARRIER
CARRION
CARRYON
CARSICK
CARTAGE
CARTOON
CASCADE
CASCARA
CASHIER
CASSAVA
CASSOCK
CASTING
CASTLED
CATALOG
CATALPA
CATARRH
CATBIRD
CATBOAT
CATCALL
CATCHER
CATCHUP
CATFISH
CATHODE
CATLIKE
CATTAIL
CATWALK
CAUSTIC
CAUTION
CAVALRY
CAVEMAN
CEDILLA
CEILING
CELESTA
CELSIUS
CEMBALO
CENSURE
CENTARE
CENTAUR
CENTAVO
CENTIME
CENTIMO
CENTRAL
CENTURY
CERAMIC
CERTAIN
CERTIFY
CERUMEN
CESSION
CHABLIS
CHADIAN
CHAFFER
CHAGRIN
CHALICE
CHALLIS
CHAMBER
CHAMFER
CHAMOIS
CHANCEL
CHANCRE
CHANNEL
CHANSON
CHANTEY
CHANTRY
CHAPEAU
CHAPLET
CHAPMAN
CHAPTER
CHARGER
CHARIOT
CHARITY
CHARMER
CHARNEL
CHARTER
CHASSIS
CHASTEN
CHATEAU
CHATTEL
CHATTER
CHEAPEN
CHECKER
CHECKUP
CHEDDAR
CHEETAH
CHEMISE
CHEMIST
CHERISH
CHEROOT
CHEVIOT
CHEVRON
CHIANTI
CHICANE
CHICANO
CHICKEN
CHICORY
CHIFFON
CHIGGER
CHIGNON
CHIMERA
CHIMNEY
CHINESE
CHINOOK
CHINTZY
CHIPPER
CHOCTAW
CHOLERA
CHOPPER
CHORALE
CHORTLE
CHOWDER
CHROMIC
CHRONIC
CHUCKLE
CHUKKER
CHUTNEY
CILIATE
CIRCLET
CIRCUIT
CISTERN
CITADEL
CITIZEN
CIVILLY
CIVVIES
CLAMBER
CLANGOR
CLAPPER
CLARIFY
CLARION
CLARITY
CLASSIC
CLASTIC
CLATTER
CLAVIER
CLEANLY
CLEANSE
CLEANUP
CLEAVER
CLEMENT
CLIMATE
CLINKER
CLIPPER
CLOBBER
CLOSURE
CLOTHES
CLOTURE
CLUSTER
CLUTTER
COARSEN
COATING
COAXIAL
COBBLER
COCAINE
COCHLEA
COCKADE
COCKEYE
COCKNEY
COCKPIT
COCONUT
CODEINE
CODFISH
CODICIL
CODLING
COEQUAL
COEXIST
COGNATE
COHABIT
COINAGE
COLLAGE
COLLARD
COLLATE
COLLECT
COLLEEN
COLLEGE
COLLIDE
COLLIER
COLLOID
COLOGNE
COLONEL
COLORED
COMBINE
COMFORT
COMMAND
COMMEND
COMMENT
COMMODE
COMMUNE
COMMUTE
COMPACT
COMPANY
COMPARE
COMPASS
COMPEER
COMPETE
COMPILE
COMPLEX
COMPORT
COMPOSE
COMPOST
COMPOTE
COMPUTE
COMRADE
CONCAVE
CONCEAL
CONCEDE
CONCEIT
CONCEPT
CONCERN
CONCERT
CONCISE
CONCOCT
CONCORD
CONDEMN
CONDIGN
CONDOLE
CONDONE
CONDUCE
CONDUCT
CONDUIT
CONDYLE
CONFESS
CONFIDE
CONFINE
CONFIRM
CONFLUX
CONFORM
CONFUSE
CONFUTE
CONGEAL
CONGEST
CONICAL
CONIFER
CONJOIN
CONJURE
CONNECT
CONNIVE
CONNOTE
CONQUER
CONSENT
CONSIGN
CONSIST
CONSOLE
CONSORT
CONSULT
CONSUME
CONTACT
CONTAIN
CONTEMN
CONTEND
CONTENT
CONTEST
CONTEXT
CONTORT
CONTOUR
CONTRIB
CONTROL
CONVENE
CONVENT
CONVERT
CONVICT
CONVOKE
COOKERY
COOKOUT
COOLANT
COPILOT
COPIOUS
COPPICE
COPYBOY
COPYCAT
CORACLE
CORDAGE
CORDIAL
CORDITE
CORDOBA
CORINTH
CORNCOB
CORNICE
COROLLA
CORONAL
CORONER
CORONET
CORRECT
CORRODE
CORRUPT
CORSAGE
CORSAIR
CORTEGE
COSSACK
COSTIVE
COSTUME
COTERIE
COTTAGE
COULOMB
COUNCIL
COUNSEL
COUNTER
COUNTRY
COUPLET
COURAGE
COURIER
COURSER
COURTLY
COUTURE
COWBIRD
COWHAND
COWHIDE
COWLICK
COWLING
COWPOKE
COWSLIP
COXCOMB
CRABBED
CRACKER
CRACKLE
CRANIUM
CRAVING
CREATOR
CREMATE
CREVICE
CRICKET
CRIMSON
CRINKLE
CRIPPLE
CRITTER
CROCHET
CROOKED
CROPPER
CROQUET
CROSIER
CROUTON
CROWBAR
CRUCIAL
CRUCIFY
CRUISER
CRULLER
CRUMBLE
CRUMPET
CRUMPLE
CRUSADE
CRYBABY
CRYPTIC
CRYSTAL
CUBICLE
CUCKOLD
CUISINE
CULOTTE
CULPRIT
CULTURE
CULVERT
CUMULUS
CUNNING
CUPCAKE
CUPRITE
CURATOR
CURBING
CURIOUS
CURRANT
CURRENT
CURSIVE
CURSORY
CURTAIL
CURTAIN
CUSHION
CUSTARD
CUSTODY
CUTBACK
CUTICLE
CUTLASS
CUTLERY
CUTTING
CUTWORM
CYANIDE
CYCLIST
CYCLONE
CYPRESS
CZARINA
DANDIFY
DARLING
DASHIKI
DASHING
DASHPOT
DASTARD
DAUPHIN
DAYBOOK
DAYTIME
DEADPAN
DEALING
DEANERY
DEATHLY
DEBACLE
DEBAUCH
DEBOUCH
DEBRIEF
DECAGON
DECEASE
DECEIVE
DECENCY
DECIBEL
DECIDED
DECIMAL
DECLAIM
DECLARE
DECLINE
DECODER
DECORUM
DEERFLY
DEFAULT
DEFENSE
DEFIANT
DEFICIT
DEFLATE
DEFLECT
DEFRAUD
DEFROST
DEFUNCT
DEGAUSS
DEGRADE
DELIGHT
DELIMIT
DELIVER

DELOUSE
DEMERIT
DEMESNE
DEMIGOD
DEMONIC
DEMOTIC
DENIZEN
DENSITY
DENTATE
DENTIST
DENTURE
DEPLANE
DEPLETE
DEPLORE
DEPOSIT
DEPRAVE
DEPRESS
DEPRIVE
DERANGE
DERRICK
DERVISH
DESCANT
DESCEND
DESCENT
DESERVE
DESKTOP
DESPAIR
DESPISE
DESPITE
DESPOIL
DESPOND
DESSERT
DESTINE
DESTINY
DESTROY
DETENTE
DETRACT
DETRAIN
DEVALUE
DEVELOP
DEVIANT
DEVIATE
DEVILRY
DEVIOUS
DEVOLVE
DEVOTED
DEVOTEE
DEWCLAW
DEWDROP
DEXTRIN
DIAGRAM
DIALECT
DIAMOND
DIARIST
DICTATE
DICTION
DIEHARD
DIFFUSE
DIGITAL
DIGNIFY
DIGNITY
DIGRAPH
DIGRESS
DILEMMA
DILUENT
DINETTE
DIOCESE
DIPLOID
DIPLOMA
DIREFUL
DISABLE
DISAVOW
DISBAND
DISCARD
DISCERN
DISCORD
DISCUSS
DISDAIN
DISEASE
DISEUSE
DISGUST
DISHRAG
DISJOIN
DISLIKE
DISMISS
DISOBEY
DISPLAY
DISPORT
DISPOSE
DISPUTE
DISROBE
DISRUPT
DISSECT
DISSENT
DISTAFF
DISTANT
DISTEND
DISTICH
DISTILL
DISTORT
DISTURB
DIURNAL
DIVERGE
DIVERSE
DIVIDER
DIVISOR
DIVORCE
DIVULGE
DOCKAGE
DOGBANE
DOGCART
DOGFISH
DOGTROT
DOGWOOD
DOLEFUL
DOLPHIN
DOMINIE
DOORMAN
DOORMAT
DOORWAY
DORMANT
DOSSIER
DOUBLET
DOUGHTY
DOWAGER
DOYENNE
DRACHMA
DRAGNET
DRAGOON
DRAPERY
DRASTIC
DRAUGHT
DRAWING
DRESSER
DRIBBLE
DRIBLET
DRIFTER
DRIZZLE
DROPLET
DROPPER
DROUGHT
DRUMLIN
DRUMMER
DRUNKEN
DUBIETY
DUBIOUS
DUCHESS
DUCKPIN
DUCTILE
DUDGEON
DULLARD
DUMPING
DUNGEON
DURABLE
DURANCE
DUSTPAN
DUTEOUS
DUTIFUL
DWINDLE
DYNAMIC
DYNASTY
EARACHE
EARDRUM
EARLOBE
EARMARK
EARMUFF
EARNEST
EARPLUG
EARRING
EARSHOT
EARTHEN
EARTHLY
EASTERN
EBONITE
ECHELON
ECLIPSE
ECLOGUE
ECOLOGY
ECONOMY
ECSTASY
EDIFICE
EDITION
EDUCATE
EFFENDI
EGGHEAD
EGOTISM
EIDOLON
ELASTIC
ELDERLY
ELECTOR
ELEGIAC
ELEMENT
ELEVATE
ELISION
ELITISM
ELLIPSE
ELUSIVE
ELYSIUM
EMANATE
EMBARGO
EMBASSY
EMBOWER
EMBRACE
EMBROIL
EMBRYOL
EMERALD
EMERITA
EMINENT
EMITTER
EMOTION
EMPATHY
EMPEROR
EMPOWER
EMPRESS
EMULATE
ENAMOUR
ENCHAIN
ENCHANT
ENCLAVE
ENCLOSE
ENCRUST
ENDEMIC
ENDLESS
ENDMOST
ENDORSE
ENDWAYS
ENDWISE
ENFORCE
ENGLISH
ENGRAFT
ENGRAVE
ENGROSS
ENHANCE
ENLARGE
ENLIVEN
ENNOBLE
ENPLANE
ENQUIRE
ENSLAVE
ENSNARE
ENTENTE
ENTHUSE
ENTITLE
ENTRAIN
ENTRANT
ENTREAT
ENTROPY
ENTRUST
ENTWINE
ENVELOP
ENVENOM
ENVIOUS
EPAULET
EPERGNE
EPICURE
EPIGRAM
EPISODE
EPISTLE
EPITAPH
EPITHET
EPITOME
EQUABLE
EQUATOR
EQUERRY
EQUINOX
ERELONG
EREMITE
EROSION
EROSIVE
ERRATIC
ERRATUM
ESCAPEE
ESQUIRE
ESSENCE
ESTHETE
ESTUARY
ETCHING
ETERNAL
ETHANOL
ETHICAL
EUPHONY
EVACUEE
EVASION
EVENING
EVIDENT
EXAMINE
EXAMPLE
EXCERPT
EXCLAIM
EXCLUDE
EXCRETA
EXCRETE
EXECUTE
EXEGETE
EXHAUST
EXHIBIT
EXPANSE
EXPENSE
EXPIATE
EXPLAIN
EXPLODE
EXPLOIT
EXPLORE
EXPOUND
EXPRESS
EXPUNGE
EXTINCT
EXTRACT
EXTREME
EXTRUDE
EYEBALL
EYEBROW
EYELASH
EYESORE
EYEWASH
FACTION
FACTORY
FACTUAL
FACULTY
FAIENCE
FAILING
FAILURE
FAIRING
FAIRWAY
FALLACY
FALLOUT
FALSIFY
FANATIC
FANCIER
FANFARE
FANTAIL
FANTASY
FARAWAY
FARMING
FARRAGO
FARRIER
FARTHER
FASCISM
FASHION
FATBACK
FATEFUL
FATIGUE
FATUITY
FATUOUS
FAUVISM
FEARFUL
FEATHER
FEATURE
FEBRILE
FEDERAL
FEEDLOT
FEELING
FENCING
FERMENT
FERMIUM
FERNERY
FERROUS
FERRULE
FERTILE
FERVENT
FESTIVE
FESTOON
FETLOCK
FIANCEE
FIBROID
FICTION
FIFTEEN
FIGHTER
FIGMENT
FILBERT
FILLING
FILMDOM
FINAGLE
FINANCE
FINDING
FINESSE
FINFISH
FINICKY
FINNISH
FIREARM
FIREBOX
FIREBUG
FIREFLY
FIREMAN
FIRSTLY
FISHERY
FISHING
FISSILE
FISSION
FISSURE
FISTFUL
FISTULA
FITTING
FIXTURE
FLACCID
FLANKER
FLANNEL
FLAPPER
FLATBED
FLATCAR
FLATTEN
FLATTER
FLATTOP
FLAVOUR
FLEMING
FLEMISH
FLESHLY
FLEXURE
FLICKER
FLIGHTY
FLIPPER
FLIVVER
FLORIST
FLOTSAM
FLOUNCE
FLOWERY
FLUSTER
FLUTIST
FLUTTER
FLYABLE
FLYLEAF
FOGHORN
FOLDOUT
FOLIAGE
FOLKWAY
FONDANT
FOOLERY
FOOLISH
FOOTAGE
FOOTING
FOOTMAN
FOOTPAD
FORBEAR
FORBODE
FORCEPS
FOREARM
FOREIGN
FORELEG
FOREMAN
FORESEE
FORETOP
FOREVER
FORFEIT
FORFEND
FORGING
FORGIVE
FORLORN
FORMULA
FORSAKE
FORTIFY
FORTRAN
FORTUNE
FORWARD
FOULARD
FOULING
FOUNDER
FOUNDRY
FOXHOLE
FRACTAL
FRAGILE
FRAILTY
FRANTIC
FRAUGHT
FRAZZLE
FRECKLE
FREEBIE
FREEDOM
FREEMAN
FREEWAY
FREEZER
FREIGHT
FRESHEN
FRESHET
FRETFUL
FRETSAW
FRIABLE
FRIGATE
FRITTER
FRIZZLE
FROGMAN
FROWARD
FRUSTUM
FUCHSIA
FULCRUM
FULFILL
FULSOME
FUNERAL
FURBISH
FURIOUS
FURLONG
FURNACE
FURNISH
FURRIER
FURRING
FURTHER
FURTIVE
FUSTIAN
GABFEST
GAINFUL
GAINSAY
GALLANT
GALLEON
GALLERY
GALLIUM
GALLOWS
GAMBIAN
GANGWAY
GANTLET
GARBAGE
GARFISH
GARLAND
GARMENT
GARNISH

GARROTE
GASTRIC
GATEWAY
GAVOTTE
GAZELLE
GAZETTE
GEARBOX
GELATIN
GELDING
GENERAL
GENERIC
GENESIS
GENETIC
GENITAL
GENTEEL
GENTIAN
GENTILE
GENUINE
GEODESY
GEOLOGY
GERMANE
GESTAPO
GESTURE
GETAWAY
GHASTLY
GHERKIN
GIBBOUS
GIBLETS
GIMMICK
GINGHAM
GINSENG
GIRAFFE
GIZZARD
GLACIAL
GLACIER
GLADDEN
GLAMOUR
GLAZIER
GLEEMAN
GLIMMER
GLIMPSE
GLISTEN
GLISTER
GLITTER
GLOBULE
GLORIFY
GLOTTIS
GLUCOSE
GLUTTON
GOBBLER
GODDESS
GODHEAD
GODHOOD
GODLESS
GODLIKE
GODSEND
GOGGLES
GONDOLA
GOODMAN
GORILLA
GOSHAWK
GOSLING
GOULASH
GOURMET
GRACKLE
GRADUAL
GRAMMAR
GRANARY
GRANDAM
GRANDEE
GRANITE
GRANTEE
GRANULE
GRAPHIC
GRAPNEL
GRAPPLE
GRATIFY
GRATING
GRAUPEL
GRAVITY
GRAVURE
GRAZIER
GRECIAN
GREMLIN
GRENADE
GRIDDLE
GRIMACE
GRINDER
GRISTLE
GRIZZLY
GROMMET
GROUPER
GROUPIE
GRUMBLE
GRUNION
GUANINE
GUARANI
GUERDON
GUILDER
GUMBOIL
GUMDROP
GUMSHOE
GUNBOAT
GUNFIRE
GUNLOCK
GUNNERY
GUNSHOT
GUNWALE
HABITAT
HABITUE
HACKMAN
HACKNEY
HACKSAW
HADDOCK
HAFNIUM
HAGGARD
HAIRCUT
HAIRPIN
HALBERD
HALCYON
HALFWAY
HALIBUT
HALLWAY
HALTING
HALVERS
HALYARD
HAMMOCK
HAMSTER
HANDBAG
HANDCAR
HANDFUL
HANDGUN
HANDOUT
HANDSAW
HANDSEL
HANDSET
HANGDOG
HANGING
HANGMAN
HANGOUT
HAPLESS
HAPLOID
HAPPILY
HARBOUR
HARDPAN
HARDTOP
HARELIP
HARMONY
HARNESS
HARPOON
HARRIER
HARVARD
HARVEST
HASHING
HASHISH
HASSOCK
HATCHET
HAUBERK
HAUGHTY
HAULAGE
HAUTEUR
HAYCOCK
HAYFORK
HAYLOFT
HAYRICK
HAYSEED
HAYWIRE
HEADING
HEADMAN
HEADPIN
HEADSET
HEADWAY
HEALTHY
HEARING
HEARKEN
HEARSAY
HEARTEN
HEATHEN
HEATHER
HECTARE
HEINOUS
HEIRESS
HELICAL
HELLCAT
HELLENE
HELLION
HELPING
HEMLINE
HEMLOCK
HENPECK
HEPARIN
HEPATIC
HERBAGE
HEROICS
HEROINE
HEROISM
HERRING
HERSELF
HEXAGON
HEXAPOD
HIBACHI
HICKORY
HIDALGO
HIDEOUS
HIDEOUT
HIGHBOY
HIGHWAY
HILLOCK
HILLTOP
HIMSELF
HINTING
HIPBONE
HIPSTER
HIRSUTE
HISTORY
HOBNAIL
HOECAKE
HOEDOWN
HOGBACK
HOGWASH
HOLDING
HOLIDAY
HOLMIUM
HOLSTER
HOMBURG
HOMONYM
HOODLUM
HOOSIER
HOPHEAD
HORIZON
HORMONE
HORRIFY
HOSANNA
HOSIERY
HOSPICE
HOSTAGE
HOSTESS
HOSTILE
HOSTLER
HOTCAKE
HOTFOOT
HOTSHOT
HOUSING
HOWBEIT
HOWEVER
HOWLING
HULKING
HUMDRUM
HUMERUS
HUMIDOR
HUMMOCK
HUNDRED
HUNKERS
HUSBAND
HUSKING
HUTMENT
HYDRANT
HYDRATE
HYDROUS
HYGIENE
HYMNODY
ICEBERG
ICEBOAT
IDEALLY
IDOLIZE
IGNEOUS
IGNOBLE
ILEITIS
ILLEGAL
ILLICIT
ILLNESS
IMAGERY
IMAGINE
IMAGISM
IMITATE
IMMENSE
IMMERSE
IMMORAL
IMPANEL
IMPASSE
IMPASTO
IMPEACH
IMPEARL
IMPERIL
IMPETUS
IMPIETY
IMPINGE
IMPIOUS
IMPLODE
IMPLORE
IMPOUND
IMPRESS
IMPRINT
IMPROVE
IMPULSE
INBOARD
INBOUND
INCENSE
INCISOR
INCLINE
INCLOSE
INCLUDE
INCRUST
INCUBUS
INDEXED
INDICIA
INDOORS
INDORSE
INDULGE
INDWELL
INERTIA
INEXACT
INFANCY
INFARCT
INFERNO
INFIDEL
INFIELD
INFLAME
INFLATE
INFLECT
INFLICT
INGENUE
INGRAFT
INGRAIN
INGRATE
INGRESS
INGROWN
INHABIT
INHALER
INHERIT
INHIBIT
INHUMAN
INITIAL
INKHORN
INKLING
INKWELL
INNARDS
INNINGS
INQUEST
INQUIRE
INQUIRY
INSHORE
INSIDER
INSIGHT
INSIPID
INSPECT
INSPIRE
INSTALL
INSTANT
INSTATE
INSTEAD
INSTILL
INSULAR
INSULIN
INSURED
INSURER
INTEGER
INTENSE
INTERIM
INTRANS
INTROIT
INTRUDE
INTRUST
INVALID
INVEIGH
INVERSE
INVOICE
INVOLVE
IRANIAN
IRIDIUM
IRKSOME
IRONING
ISOLATE
ISOTOPE
ISRAELI
ISTHMUS
ITALIAN
ITEMIZE
ITERATE
JACINTH
JACKASS
JACKDAW
JACKLEG
JACKPOT
JANITOR
JANUARY
JASMINE
JAVELIN
JAYBIRD
JAYWALK
JEALOUS
JEHOVAH
JEJUNUM
JETPORT
JEWELER
JEWELRY
JITTERS
JOCULAR
JODHPUR
JOLLITY
JONQUIL
JOTTING
JOURNAL
JOURNEY
JOYANCE
JOYRIDE
JUBILEE
JUDAISM
JUGULAR
JUJITSU
JUKEBOX
JUNIPER
JUPITER
JUSTICE
JUSTIFY
KADDISH
KARAKUL
KATYDID
KEELSON
KEEPING
KERATIN
KERNING
KETCHUP
KEYHOLE
KEYNOTE
KHEDIVE
KIBBUTZ
KICKOFF
KIDSKIN
KILLING
KILLJOY
KILOTON
KINDRED
KINETIC
KINFOLK
KINGDOM
KINGPIN
KINSHIP
KINSMAN
KITCHEN
KNEECAP
KNOCKER
KNOWING
KNUCKLE
KREMLIN
KRYPTON
KUMQUAT
LABORED
LACONIC
LACQUER
LACTATE
LACTEAL
LACTOSE
LADYBUG
LAGGARD
LAMBENT
LAMINAR
LAMPOON
LAMPREY
LANDING
LANGUID
LANGUOR
LANOLIN
LANTANA
LANTERN
LANYARD
LAOTIAN
LAPWING
LARCENY
LARGESS
LASAGNA
LATAKIA
LATCHET
LATERAL
LATRINE
LATTICE
LATVIAN
LAUNDER
LAUNDRY
LAWLESS
LAWSUIT
LAYAWAY
LAYETTE
LEADING
LEAFAGE
LEAFLET
LEAGUER
LEAKAGE
LEARNED
LEATHER
LECHERY
LECTERN
LECTURE
LEEWARD
LEFTISM
LEGATEE
LEGGING
LEGHORN
LEGIBLE
LEISURE
LEMMING
LEMPIRA
LENIENT
LEONINE
LEOPARD
LEOTARD
LEPROSY
LESBIAN
LETDOWN
LETTUCE
LEXICON
LIAISON
LIBERAL

LIBERTY
LIBRARY
LICENSE
LIGHTEN
LIGHTER
LIGNIFY
LIGNITE
LIMBECK
LIMEADE
LIMITED
LINEAGE
LINEMAN
LINGUAL
LINKAGE
LINSEED
LIONIZE
LIQUEFY
LIQUEUR
LISSOME
LISTING
LITERAL
LITHIUM
LITURGY
LIVABLE
LOATHLY
LOBSTER
LOCATOR
LOCKJAW
LOCKNUT
LOCKOUT
LODGING
LONGBOW
LONGING
LOOKOUT
LOTTERY
LOWBROW
LOWDOWN
LOWLAND
LOZENGE
LUCERNE
LUCIFER
LUGGAGE
LULLABY
LUMBAGO
LUNATIC
LUNETTE
LUSTRAL
MACABRE
MACADAM
MACAQUE
MACDRAW
MACHETE
MACHINE
MACRAME
MADDING
MADEIRA
MAESTRO
MAFIOSO
MAGENTA
MAGNATE
MAGNETO
MAGNIFY
MAHATMA
MAHICAN
MAILBOX
MAILMAN
MAINTOP
MAJESTY
MAKINGS
MALAISE
MALARIA
MALEFIC
MALISON
MALLARD
MALLEUS
MALMSEY
MALTOSE
MAMMARY
MAMMOTH
MANACLE
MANAGER
MANDATE
MANDREL
MANDRIL
MANHOLE
MANHOOD
MANHUNT
MANIKIN
MANKIND
MANLIKE
MANNISH
MANSARD
MANSION
MANTEAU
MANUMIT
MARGENT
MARIMBA
MARINER
MARITAL
MARPLOT
MARQUEE
MARQUIS
MARSHAL
MARTIAL
MARTIAN
MARTINI
MARXISM
MASCARA
MASONIC
MASONRY
MASSAGE
MASSEUR
MASSIVE
MASTERY
MASTIFF
MASTOID
MATADOR
MATINEE
MATTINS
MATTOCK
MAUDLIN
MAUNDER
MAWKISH
MAXILLA
MAXIMAL
MAXIMUM
MAYPOLE
MAZURKA
MEANDER
MEANING
MEASLES
MEASURE
MEATMAN
MEDIATE
MEDICAL
MEDULLA
MEETING
MEGATON
MEIOSIS
MELANGE
MELANIC
MELANIN
MEMENTO
MENFOLK
MENTHOL
MENTION
MERCURY
MERMAID
MESSAGE
MESSIAH
MESTIZO
METHANE
MEXICAN
MICROBE
MIDLAND
MIDMOST
MIDRIFF
MIDTOWN
MIDWEEK
MIDWIFE
MIDYEAR
MIGRANT
MIGRATE
MILEAGE
MILITIA
MILKMAN
MILKSOP
MILLAGE
MILLDAM
MILLIME
MILLING
MILLION
MIMESIS
MIMETIC
MIMICRY
MINARET
MINDFUL
MINERAL
MINIBUS
MINIMAL
MINIMUM
MINSTER
MINUEND
MINUTIA
MIRACLE
MISCALL
MISDEED
MISFILE
MISFIRE
MISLEAD
MISLIKE
MISNAME
MISPLAY
MISREAD
MISRULE
MISSEND
MISSILE
MISSING
MISSION
MISSIVE
MISSTEP
MISTAKE
MISTRAL
MITOSIS
MIXTURE
MOBSTER
MODICUM
MODISTE
MODULAR
MOHEGAN
MOHICAN
MOISTEN
MOLDING
MOLLIFY
MOLLUSK
MONADIC
MONARCH
MONEYED
MONGREL
MONITOR
MONOCLE
MONOMER
MONSOON
MONSTER
MONTAGE
MOORING
MORAINE
MORDANT
MORNING
MOROCCO
MORPHIA
MORTIFY
MORTISE
MOUNTIE
MUDROOM
MUEZZIN
MUFFLER
MUGWUMP
MULATTO
MULLEIN
MULLION
MUNDANE
MURRAIN
MUSETTE
MUSICAL
MUSKRAT
MUSTANG
MUSTARD
MUTABLE
MYSTERY
MYSTIFY
NACELLE
NAIVETE
NAIVETY
NANKEEN
NAPHTHA
NARRATE
NARTHEX
NARWHAL
NASCENT
NATURAL
NAUGHTY
NECKTIE
NEEDFUL
NEGLECT
NEITHER
NEMESIS
NEOLOGY
NEPTUNE
NERVOUS
NETTING
NETWARE
NETWORK
NEUTRAL
NEUTRON
NEWBORN
NEWSBOY
NEWSMAN
NIAGARA
NIGGARD
NIGHTLY
NIOBIUM
NIRVANA
NITRATE
NITRIFY
NITRITE
NOCUOUS
NOISOME
NOMADIC
NOMINAL
NOMINEE
NONBOOK
NONHERO
NONPLUS
NONSKED
NONSTOP
NONUSER
NOONDAY
NORTHER
NOSEGAY
NOSTRIL
NOSTRUM
NOTABLE
NOTHING
NOURISH
NOVELLA
NOVELTY
NOWHERE
NOXIOUS
NUCLEAR
NUCLEON
NUCLEUS
NUCLIDE
NULLIFY
NUMERAL
NUMERIC
NUPTIAL
NURSERY
NURTURE
NUTPICK
OARLOCK
OARSMAN
OATCAKE
OATMEAL
OBELISK
OBLIQUE
OBLOQUY
OBSCENE
OBSCURE
OBSEQUY
OBSERVE
OBTRUDE
OBVERSE
OBVIATE
OBVIOUS
OCARINA
OCCLUDE
OCTAGON
OCTOBER
OCTOPUS
OCULIST
ODDBALL
ODDMENT
ODYSSEY
OEDIPAL
OFFBEAT
OFFENSE
OFFHAND
OFFICER
OFFSIDE
OILSKIN
OLDSTER
OLIVINE
OMINOUS
OMNIBUS
ONEROUS
ONESELF
ONETIME
ONGOING
ONSHORE
OPACITY
OPENING
OPERATE
OPINION
OPOSSUM
OPPRESS
OPTICAL
OPTIMAL
OPTIMUM
OPULENT
ORATION
ORATORY
ORBITER
ORCHARD
ORDERLY
ORDINAL
OREGANO
ORGANDY
ORGANIC
ORGANZA
ORIFICE
ORIGAMI
OROGENY
OROTUND
ORTOLAN
OSMOSIS
OSSUARY
OSTMARK
OSTRICH
OTTOMAN
OUTCAST
OUTCOME
OUTCROP
OUTDOOR
OUTDRAW
OUTFACE
OUTFLOW
OUTGROW
OUTLAST
OUTLINE
OUTLIVE
OUTLOOK
OUTPLAY
OUTPOST
OUTPULL
OUTRAGE
OUTRANK
OUTSELL
OUTSIDE
OUTSIZE
OUTSTAY
OUTVOTE
OUTWARD
OUTWEAR
OUTWORK
OUTWORN
OVATION
OVERACT
OVERAGE
OVERALL
OVERARM
OVERAWE
OVERFLY
OVERJOY
OVERLAP
OVERLAY
OVERRUN
OVERSEA
OVERSEE
OVERTOP
OVIDUCT
OVULATE
OXBLOOD
OXIDANT
OXIDIZE
PABULUM
PACIFIC
PACKAGE
PACKING
PADDING
PADDOCK
PADLOCK
PAGEANT
PAGEBOY
PAISLEY
PAJAMAS
PALADIN
PALAVER
PALETTE
PALFREY
PALMATE
PALPATE
PANACEA
PANACHE
PANCAKE
PANICLE
PANNIER
PANOPLY
PANTHER
PAPILLA
PAPOOSE
PAPRIKA
PAPYRUS
PARABLE
PARADOX
PARAGON
PARAPET
PARASOL
PARBOIL
PARESIS
PARFAIT
PARKWAY
PARLOUR
PARLOUS
PARQUET
PARSING
PARSLEY
PARSNIP
PARTAKE
PARTIAL
PARTING
PARTITE
PARTNER
PARTWAY
PARVENU
PASSAGE
PASSING
PASSION
PASSIVE
PASSKEY
PASTERN
PASTIME
PASTURE
PATELLA
PATHWAY
PATIENT
PATRIOT
PATROON
PATTERN
PAUCITY
PAYLOAD
PAYMENT
PAYROLL
PEACOCK
PEAFOWL
PEASANT
PECCARY
PECCAVI
PEDICAB
PEELING
PEEVISH
PELAGIC
PELICAN

PENALTY
PENANCE
PENATES
PENDANT
PENDENT
PENDING
PENGUIN
PENNANT
PENSION
PENSIVE
PENTIUM
PEPPERY
PERCALE
PERCENT
PERCEPT
PERFECT
PERFIDY
PERFORM
PERFUME
PERGOLA
PERHAPS
PERIGEE
PERIQUE
PERIWIG
PERJURY
PERLITE
PERPLEX
PERSIAN
PERSIST
PERTAIN
PERTURB
PERVADE
PERVERT
PETIOLE
PETRIFY
PETTISH
PETUNIA
PFENNIG
PHAETON
PHALANX
PHALLIC
PHALLUS
PHANTOM
PHARAOH
PHARYNX
PHILTER
PHOENIX
PHONEME
PHONICS
PHRENIC
PHYSICS
PHYSIOL
PIANIST
PIASTER
PIBROCH
PICCOLO
PICTURE
PIEBALD
PIGGISH
PIGMENT
PIGSKIN
PIGTAIL
PILGRIM
PILLAGE
PILLBOX
PILLION
PILLORY
PILSNER
PIMENTO
PINHOLE
PINKEYE
PINNACE
PINNATE
PINWORM
PIONEER
PIPETTE
PIQUANT
PIRANHA
PISMIRE
PITCHER
PITEOUS
PITFALL
PITIFUL
PIZZAZZ
PLACARD
PLACATE
PLACEBO
PLACKET
PLANTAR
PLANTER
PLASTER
PLASTIC
PLATEAU
PLATING
PLATOON
PLATTER
PLAUDIT
PLAYBOY
PLAYLET
PLAYPEN
PLENARY
PLIABLE
PLOTTER
PLOWBOY
PLOWMAN
PLUMAGE
PLUMBER
PLUMMET
PLUNDER
PLUNGER
PLUVIAL
PLYWOOD
POCOSIN
POINTED
POINTER
POLARIS
POLECAT
POLEMIC
POLITIC
POLLACK
POLLUTE
POLYGON
POLYMER
POMPANO
POMPOUS
PONIARD
PONTIFF
PONTOON
POPCORN
POPOVER
POPULAR
PORCINE
PORTAGE
PORTEND
PORTENT
PORTICO
PORTION
PORTRAY
POSSESS
POSTAGE
POSTBOY
POSTERN
POSTMAN
POSTURE
POSTWAR
POTABLE
POTHEAD
POTHERB
POTHOLE
POTHOOK
POTLUCK
POTSHOT
POTTAGE
POTTERY
POULTRY
POVERTY
PRAETOR
PRAIRIE
PRALINE
PRATTLE
PRAYING
PREBEND
PRECEDE
PRECEPT
PRECISE
PRECOOK
PREDATE
PREDICT
PREEMIE
PREEMPT
PREFACE
PREFECT
PREFORM
PREHEAT
PRELATE
PRELUDE
PREMIER
PREMISE
PREMIUM
PREPARE
PREPUCE
PRESAGE
PRESENT
PRESIDE
PRESOAK
PRESUME
PRETEEN
PRETEND
PRETEXT
PRETZEL
PREVAIL
PREVENT
PREVIEW
PRICKER
PRICKLE
PRIMACY
PRIMARY
PRIMATE
PRITHEE
PRIVACY
PRIVATE
PROBATE
PROBITY
PROBLEM
PROCEED
PROCESS
PROCTOR
PROCURE
PRODIGY
PRODUCE
PRODUCT
PROFANE
PROFESS
PROFFER
PROFILE
PROFUSE
PROGENY
PROGMAN
PROGRAM
PROJECT
PROLONG
PROMISE
PROMOTE
PRONOUN
PROPANE
PROPHET
PROPMAN
PROPOSE
PRORATE
PROSAIC
PROSODY
PROSPER
PROTEAN
PROTECT
PROTEGE
PROTEIN
PROTEST
PROVERB
PROVIDE
PROVISO
PROVOKE
PROVOST
PROWESS
PROXIMO
PRUDENT
PSALTER
PSYCHIC
PSYCHOL
PUBERTY
PUBLISH
PUDDING
PUERILE
PULLMAN
PULLOUT
PULSATE
PUMPKIN
PUNGENT
PUNSTER
PURITAN
PURLIEU
PURLOIN
PURPORT
PURPOSE
PURSUIT
PURVIEW
PUSTULE
PUTREFY
PYJAMAS
PYRAMID
PYRITES
QUALIFY
QUALITY
QUANTUM
QUARREL
QUARTER
QUARTET
QUETZAL
QUIBBLE
QUICKEN
QUICKIE
QUIETUS
QUININE
QUINTAL
QUINTET
QUONDAM
RACCOON
RACEWAY
RADIANT
RADIATE
RADICAL
RAFFISH
RAGTIME
RAGWEED
RAILING
RAILWAY
RAIMENT
RAINBOW
RAMBLER
RAMPAGE
RAMPANT
RAMPART
RANKING
RANSACK
RAPPORT
RAPTURE
RAREBIT
RATCHET
RATLINE
RATTLER
RATTRAP
RAUCOUS
RAUNCHY
RAVIOLI
RAWHIDE
REACTOR
READING
READOUT
REAGENT
REALISM
REALITY
REALIZE
REBIRTH
REBOUND
REBUILD
RECEIPT
RECEIVE
RECENCY
RECITAL
RECLAIM
RECLAME
RECLINE
RECLUSE
RECOUNT
RECOVER
RECRUIT
RECTIFY
RECTORY
RECYCLE
REDCOAT
REDDISH
REDHEAD
REDLINE
REDOUBT
REDOUND
REDRESS
REDSKIN
REDWOOD
REENTRY
REFEREE
REFINED
REFLECT
REFRACT
REFRAIN
REFRESH
REFUGEE
REGALIA
REGATTA
REGENCY
REGIMEN
REGNANT
REGRESS
REGROUP
REGULAR
REJOICE
RELAPSE
RELATED
RELATOR
RELEASE
RELIEVE
RELIQUE
REMAINS
REMNANT
REMODEL
REMORSE
REMOUNT
RENEWAL
REPLACE
REPLETE
REPLICA
REPRESS
REPRINT
REPRISE
REPROOF
REPROVE
REPTILE
REPULSE
REPUTED
REQUEST
REQUIEM
REQUIRE
REQUITE
REREDOS
RESCIND
RESEDIT
RESERVE
RESIDUE
RESOLVE
RESOUND
RESPECT
RESPITE
RESPOND
RESTIVE
RESTORE
RETINUE
RETIRED
RETIREE
RETOUCH
RETRACE
RETRACT
RETREAD
RETREAT
REUNION
REVENGE
REVENUE
REVERIE
REVERSE
REVIVAL
REVOLVE
RHENIUM
RHIZOME
RHODIUM
RHOMBUS
RHUBARB
RICKETS
RICKETY
RICKSHA
RIGGING
RIGHTLY
RINGLET
RIPOSTE
RISIBLE
RIVALRY
RIVULET
ROADBED
ROADWAY
ROASTER
ROBBERY
ROEBUCK
ROISTER
ROLLICK
ROMANCE
ROOFTOP
ROOKERY
ROOSTER
ROOTLET
ROSEATE
ROSEBUD
ROSETTE
ROSTRUM
ROTUNDA
ROUGHEN
ROUNDUP
ROUTINE
ROWBOAT
ROYALTY
RUBBISH
RUBELLA
RUFFIAN
RUINOUS
RUMMAGE
RUNAWAY
RUNDOWN
RUNNING
RUPTURE
RUSSIAN
SABBATH
SADIRON
SAFFRON
SAGUARO
SAILING
SAINTLY
SALIENT
SALTBOX
SALTINE
SALVAGE
SAMOVAR
SAMPLER
SAMURAI
SANCTUM
SANDBAG
SANDBAR
SANDHOG
SANDLOT
SANDMAN
SAPIENT
SAPLING
SAPWOOD
SARCASM
SARDINE
SATANIC
SATCHEL
SATIATE
SATIETY
SATISFY
SAUNTER
SAUSAGE
SAVANNA
SAWDUST
SAWMILL
SCALLOP
SCALPEL
SCAMPER
SCANDAL
SCANNER
SCAPULA
SCARIFY
SCARLET
SCATTER
SCENERY
SCEPTER
SCEPTIC
SCHOLAR
SCIENCE

SCOOTER
SCOURGE
SCRAPPY
SCRATCH
SCRAWNY
SCREECH
SCROTUM
SCRUFFY
SCRUPLE
SCUFFLE
SCUPPER
SCUTTLE
SEABIRD
SEAFOOD
SEALANT
SEAPORT
SEASICK
SEASIDE
SEATING
SEAWALL
SEAWARD
SEAWEED
SECLUDE
SECRECY
SECRETE
SECTARY
SECTION
SECULAR
SEEMING
SEGMENT
SEISMIC
SELFISH
SELTZER
SELVAGE
SEMINAL
SEMINAR
SENATOR
SENSORY
SENSUAL
SENTIMO
SEQUENT
SEQUOIA
SERIOUS
SERPENT
SERRATE
SERRIED
SERVANT
SERVICE
SERVILE
SERVING
SESSILE
SESSION
SETBACK
SETTING
SEVENTY
SEVERAL
SEXTANT
SHACKLE
SHADING
SHALLOP
SHALLOW
SHAMBLE
SHAMPOO
SHAPELY
SHARPEN
SHARPER
SHARPIE
SHATTER
SHAVING
SHAWNEE
SHEATHE
SHEBANG
SHELLAC
SHELTER
SHERBET
SHERIFF
SHIMMER
SHINGLE
SHOCKER
SHORING
SHORTEN
SHORTLY
SHOTGUN
SHOWMAN
SHRIVEL
SHUDDER
SHUFFLE
SHUTOUT
SHUTTER
SHUTTLE
SHYLOCK
SHYSTER
SIAMESE
SIBLING
SICKBED
SIDEARM
SIDECAR
SIDELIT
SIDEMAN
SIGHTED
SIGHTLY
SIGNIFY
SILENCE
SILICON
SIMILAR
SINCERE
SINUOUS
SIRLOIN
SIROCCO
SIXTEEN
SIZABLE
SKEPTIC
SKIFFLE
SKILLET
SKIPPER
SKITTER
SKIWEAR
SKYLARK
SKYLINE
SKYWARD
SLACKEN
SLACKER
SLANDER
SLATHER
SLAVERY
SLAVISH
SLEEPER
SLEIGHT
SLENDER
SLICKER
SLIPPER
SLITHER
SLOBBER
SLUMBER
SMELTER
SMIDGEN
SMOLDER
SMOTHER
SMUGGLE
SNAFFLE
SNEAKER
SNICKER
SNIFFLE
SNORKEL
SNUFFLE
SNUGGLE
SOCIETY
SOJOURN
SOLARIS
SOLDIER
SOLICIT
SOLUBLE
SOLVENT
SOMEDAY
SOMEHOW
SOMEONE
SOPHISM
SOPHIST
SOPRANO
SORCERY
SORGHUM
SOUFFLE
SOULFUL
SOUNDER
SOUPCON
SOYBEAN
SPANGLE
SPANIEL
SPANISH
SPARING
SPARKLE
SPARROW
SPASTIC
SPATIAL
SPATTER
SPATULA
SPEAKER
SPECIAL
SPECIES
SPECIFY
SPECKLE
SPECTER
SPEEDUP
SPELLER
SPICULE
SPINACH
SPINDLE
SPINDLY
SPIRANT
SPITTLE
SPLENIC
SPLOTCH
SPLURGE
SPOILER
SPONSOR
SPOTTER
SPOUSAL
SPUMONI
SPUTNIK
SPUTTER
SQUALID
SQUALOR
SQUEEZE
SQUELCH
STABILE
STADIUM
STAFFER
STAGGER
STAGING
STAMINA
STAMMER
STANDBY
STARTLE
STARTUP
STATELY
STATION
STATURE
STATUTE
STAUNCH
STEALTH
STEEPLE
STELLAR
STENCIL
STEPSON
STERILE
STERNUM
STEWARD
STICKER
STIFFEN
STILTED
STILTON
STIPEND
STIPPLE
STIRRUP
STOMACH
STOPGAP
STOPPER
STORAGE
STORIED
STRANGE
STRATUM
STRETCH
STRINGY
STROPHE
STRUDEL
STUBBLE
STUDENT
STUDIED
STUFFIT
STUMBLE
STUPEFY
STUTTER
STYLING
STYLISH
STYLIST
STYLIZE
STYPTIC
SUBJECT
SUBJOIN
SUBLIME
SUBSIDE
SUBSIDY
SUBSIST
SUBSOIL
SUBTILE
SUBVERT
SUCCEED
SUCCESS
SUCCUMB
SUCROSE
SUCTION
SUFFICE
SUFFUSE
SUGGEST
SUICIDE
SUITING
SULFATE
SULFIDE
SULTANA
SUMMARY
SUMMONS
SUNBATH
SUNBEAM
SUNBURN
SUNDIAL
SUNDOWN
SUNFISH
SUNLAMP
SUNRISE
SUNROOF
SUNSPOT
SUPPORT
SUPPOSE
SUPREME
SURFACE
SURFEIT
SURGEON
SURGERY
SURMISE
SURNAME
SURPASS
SURPLUS
SURTOUT
SURVIVE
SUSPECT
SUSPEND
SUSTAIN
SWADDLE
SWAGGER
SWAHILI
SWALLOW
SWARTHY
SWEATER
SWEDISH
SWEETEN
SWELTER
SWINDLE
SWOLLEN
SYMPTOM
SYNAPSE
SYNCOPE
SYNONYM
SYRINGE
SYSTOLE
TABLEAU
TABLOID
TABULAR
TACTICS
TACTILE
TADPOLE
TAFFETA
TAKEOFF
TALLYHO
TAMBALA
TANAGER
TANBARK
TANGENT
TANNERY
TANTRUM
TAPIOCA
TAPROOM
TAPROOT
TAPSTER
TARNISH
TATTING
TAXICAB
TECHNIC
TEDIOUS
TEENAGE
TEKTITE
TELLING
TEMPERA
TEMPEST
TENABLE
TENANCY
TENDRIL
TENFOLD
TENSILE
TENSION
TENUOUS
TENURED
TEQUILA
TERBIUM
TERMITE
TERNARY
TERRACE
TERRAIN
TERRIER
TERRIFY
TESTATE
TESTIFY
TETANUS
TEXTILE
TEXTURE
THEATER
THEOREM
THERAPY
THEREAT
THEREBY
THEREIN
THEREOF
THEREON
THERETO
THERMAL
THERMOS
THICKEN
THICKET
THIMBLE
THINNER
THISTLE
THITHER
THORIUM
THOUGHT
THREADY
THROATY
THROUGH
THRUWAY
THULIUM
THUNDER
THYMINE
THYROID
THYSELF
TIBETAN
TICKING
TIDINGS
TIEBACK
TIGHTEN
TILLAGE
TIMBREL
TIMOTHY
TIMPANI
TINFOIL
TINWARE
TIPSTER
TITANIC
TITULAR
TOASTER
TOBACCO
TOEHOLD
TOENAIL
TOGGERY
TOLUENE
TONIGHT
TONNAGE
TONNEAU
TONSURE
TOOLBOX
TOPCOAT
TOPICAL
TOPKNOT
TOPLESS
TOPMAST
TOPMOST
TOPPING
TOPSAIL
TOPSIDE
TOPSOIL
TORMENT
TORNADO
TORPEDO
TORRENT
TORSION
TORTONI
TORTURE
TOUGHEN
TOURIST
TOURNEY
TOWBOAT
TOWHEAD
TOWPATH
TOXEMIA
TRACERY
TRACHEA
TRACING
TRACTOR
TRADUCE
TRAFFIC
TRAGEDY
TRAILER
TRAINEE
TRAIPSE
TRAITOR
TRAMMEL
TRAMPLE
TRANSIT
TRANSOM
TRAPEZE
TRAVAIL
TREACLE
TREADLE
TREASON
TREFOIL
TRELLIS
TREMBLE
TREMOLO
TRESTLE
TRIBUNE
TRIBUTE
TRICEPS
TRICKLE
TRIDENT
TRIGGER
TRILOGY
TRINITY
TRINKET
TRIPLET
TRIPLEX
TRIREME
TRISECT
TRITIUM
TRIUMPH
TRIVIAL
TRIVIUM
TROCHEE
TRODDEN
TROLLEY
TROLLOP
TROOPER
TROPISM
TROUBLE
TROUNCE
TRUCKLE
TRUFFLE
TRUMPET
TRUNDLE
TRUSTEE
TSUNAMI
TUBULAR
TUESDAY
TUGBOAT
TUITION
TUMBLER
TUMBREL

TUNABLE
TUNEFUL
TURBINE
TURKISH
TURMOIL
TURNERY
TURNING
TURNKEY
TURNOFF
TURNOUT
TUSSOCK
TUTELAR
TWADDLE
TWEETER
TWIDDLE
TWILLED
TWINKLE
TWISTER
TWITTER
TWOSOME
TYPHOID
TYPHOON
TYPICAL
TYRANNY
UKULELE
ULULATE
UMBRAGE
UMPTEEN
UNARMED
UNAWARE
UNBLOCK
UNBOSOM
UNBOWED
UNCANNY
UNCHAIN
UNCIVIL
UNCLASP
UNCLEAN
UNCLOAK
UNCLOSE
UNCOUTH
UNCOVER
UNCROSS
UNCTION
UNDERGO
UNDOING
UNDRESS
UNDYING
UNEARTH
UNEQUAL
UNERASE
UNFROCK
UNGODLY
UNGROUP
UNGUENT
UNHANDY
UNHAPPY
UNHEARD
UNHINGE
UNHITCH
UNHORSE
UNICORN
UNIFORM
UNITARY
UNITIZE
UNKEMPT
UNKNOWN
UNLATCH
UNLEARN
UNLEASH
UNLOOSE
UNLUCKY
UNMANLY
UNMORAL
UNMOVED
UNNERVE
UNQUIET
UNQUOTE
UNRAVEL
UNSAVED
UNSCREW
UNSLING
UNSNARL
UNSOUND
UNSTRAP
UNTRIED
UNTRUTH
UNTWINE
UNTWIST
UNUSUAL
UNWEAVE
UPBRAID
UPCHUCK
UPDRAFT
UPGRADE
UPRAISE
UPRIGHT
UPRIVER
UPSHIFT
UPSTAGE
UPSTART
UPSTATE
UPSURGE
UPSWEPT
UPSWING
UPTIGHT
URANIUM
URANOUS
URETHRA
URINARY
URINATE
UROLOGY
USELESS
UTENSIL
UTILITY
UTILIZE
UTOPIAN
VACANCY
VACCINE
VACUITY
VACUOLE
VACUOUS
VAGRANT
VALANCE
VALENCE
VALIANT
VALUATE
VAMOOSE
VAMPIRE
VANDYKE
VANILLA
VANTAGE
VANWARD
VAQUERO
VARIANT
VARIETY
VARIOUS
VARMINT
VARNISH
VARSITY
VATICAN
VAULTED
VEDANTA
VEGETAL
VEHICLE
VEILING
VENISON
VENTRAL
VENTURE
VERANDA
VERBENA
VERBOSE
VERDANT
VERDICT
VERDURE
VERMEIL
VERNIER
VERSIFY
VERSION
VERTIGO
VERVAIN
VESICLE
VESPERS
VESTIGE
VESTING
VESTURE
VETERAN
VIADUCT
VIBRANT
VIBRATE
VIBRATO
VICEROY
VICINAL
VICIOUS
VICTORY
VICTUAL
VILLAGE
VILLAIN
VILLEIN
VILLOUS
VINEGAR
VINTAGE
VINTNER
VIOLATE
VIOLENT
VIRGULE
VIRTUAL
VISCERA
VISCOSE
VISCOUS
VISIBLE
VISITOR
VITAMIN
VITIATE
VITRIFY
VITRIOL
VITTLES
VOCABLE
VOCALIC
VOGUISH
VOLCANO
VOLTAGE
VOLTAIC
VOLUBLE
VOUCHER
VULGATE
VULPINE
VULTURE
WADABLE
WADDING
WAGGERY
WAGGISH
WAGONER
WAGTAIL
WAILFUL
WAKEFUL
WALKOUT
WALKWAY
WALLABY
WALLEYE
WALLOON
WANTING
WARBLER
WARFARE
WARHEAD
WARLESS
WARLIKE
WARLOCK
WARLORD
WARNING
WARPATH
WARRANT
WARRIOR
WARSHIP
WARTHOG
WARTIME
WASHING
WASHOUT
WASHTUB
WASPISH
WASSAIL
WASTAGE
WASTREL
WATTAGE
WAVELET
WAXWING
WAXWORK
WAYBILL
WAYSIDE
WAYWARD
WAYWORN
WEALTHY
WEASAND
WEATHER
WEBBING
WEDDING
WEDLOCK
WEEKDAY
WEEKEND
WEEPING
WEIGHTY
WELCOME
WELFARE
WESTERN
WETBACK
WETLAND
WHATNOT
WHEEDLE
WHEELER
WHEREAS
WHEREAT
WHEREBY
WHEREIN
WHEREOF
WHEREON
WHERETO
WHETHER
WHICKER
WHIMPER
WHIPPET
WHIPSAW
WHISKER
WHISKEY
WHISPER
WHISTLE
WHITHER
WHITING
WHITISH
WHITLOW
WHITTLE
WHOEVER
WHOOPLA
WHOPPER
WHORLED
WICKIUP
WIDGEON
WIDOWER
WIGGLER
WILDCAT
WILLFUL
WILLIES
WILLING
WILLOWY
WINDAGE
WINDBAG
WINDING
WINDOWS
WINDROW
WINNING
WINSOME
WIRETAP
WISHFUL
WISTFUL
WITHERS
WITHOUT
WITLESS
WITNESS
WITTING
WIZENED
WOLFRAM
WOMANLY
WOODCUT
WOODLOT
WOODMAN
WORDAGE
WORDING
WORKBAG
WORKBOX
WORKDAY
WORKING
WORKMAN
WORKOUT
WORLDLY
WORSHIP
WORSTED
WRANGLE
WRAPPER
WREATHE
WRECKER
WRESTLE
WRIGGLE
WRINGER
WRINKLE
WRITING
WRONGLY
WROUGHT
WRYNECK
WYSIWYG
YARDAGE
YARDARM
YARDMAN
YESHIVA
YIDDISH
YOUNKER
YTTRIUM
ZAMBIAN
ZEALOUS
ZEOLITE
ZILLION
ZIONISM
ZOOLOGY
ZYMURGY

## 2nd Letter

BACKING
BACKLIT
BACKLOG
BADLAND
BAGASSE
BAGGAGE
BAGPIPE
BAILIFF
BALANCE
BALCONY
BALDING
BALDRIC
BALEFUL
BALLAST
BALLOON
BALONEY
BANDAGE
BANDBOX
BANNOCK
BANQUET
BANSHEE
BAPTISM
BAPTIST
BAPTIZE
BARBELL
BARGAIN
BARONET
BAROQUE
BARRAGE
BARRIER
BARRING
BARROOM
BASHFUL
BASSOON
BASTARD
BASTION
BATHTUB
BATISTE
BATSMAN
BATTERY
BATTING
BAUXITE
BAYONET
BAZOOKA
CABARET
CABBAGE
CABINET
CABOOSE
CADAVER
CADENCE
CADENZA
CADMIUM
CAESURA
CAISSON
CAITIFF
CALCIFY
CALCINE
CALCITE
CALCIUM
CALDERA
CALDRON
CALENDS
CALIBER
CALIPER
CALLING
CALLOUS
CALOMEL
CALORIC
CALORIE
CALUMET
CALUMNY
CALYPSO
CAMBIUM
CAMBRIC
CAMPHOR
CANASTA
CANDIED
CANNERY
CANNULA
CANTATA
CANTEEN
CANVASS
CAPABLE
CAPITAL
CAPITOL
CAPRICE
CAPSIZE
CAPSTAN
CAPSULE
CAPTAIN
CAPTION
CAPTIVE
CAPTURE
CARABAO
CARAMEL
CARAVAN
CARAVEL
CARAWAY
CARBIDE
CARBINE
CARCASS
CARDBUS
CARDIAC
CAREFUL
CARFARE
CARIBOU
CARIOUS
CARLOAD
CARMINE
CARNAGE
CAROTID
CAROUSE
CARPORT
CARRIER
CARRION
CARRYON
CARSICK
CARTAGE
CARTOON
CASCADE
CASCARA
CASHIER
CASSAVA
CASSOCK
CASTING
CASTLED
CATALOG
CATALPA
CATARRH
CATBIRD
CATBOAT
CATCALL
CATCHER
CATCHUP
CATFISH
CATHODE
CATLIKE
CATTAIL
CATWALK
CAUSTIC
CAUTION
CAVALRY
CAVEMAN
DANDIFY
DARLING
DASHIKI

DASHING
DASHPOT
DASTARD
DAUPHIN
DAYBOOK
DAYTIME
EARACHE
EARDRUM
EARLOBE
EARMARK
EARMUFF
EARNEST
EARPLUG
EARRING
EARSHOT
EARTHEN
EARTHLY
EASTERN
FACTION
FACTORY
FACTUAL
FACULTY
FAIENCE
FAILING
FAILURE
FAIRING
FAIRWAY
FALLACY
FALLOUT
FALSIFY
FANATIC
FANCIER
FANFARE
FANTAIL
FANTASY
FARAWAY
FARMING
FARRAGO
FARRIER
FARTHER
FASCISM
FASHION
FATBACK
FATEFUL
FATIGUE
FATUITY
FATUOUS
FAUVISM
GABFEST
GAINFUL
GAINSAY
GALLANT
GALLEON
GALLERY
GALLIUM
GALLOWS
GAMBIAN
GANGWAY
GANTLET
GARBAGE
GARFISH
GARLAND
GARMENT
GARNISH
GARROTE
GASTRIC
GATEWAY
GAVOTTE
GAZELLE
GAZETTE
HABITAT
HABITUE
HACKMAN
HACKNEY
HACKSAW
HADDOCK
HAFNIUM
HAGGARD
HAIRCUT
HAIRPIN
HALBERD
HALCYON
HALFWAY
HALIBUT
HALLWAY
HALTING
HALVERS
HALYARD
HAMMOCK
HAMSTER
HANDBAG
HANDCAR
HANDFUL
HANDGUN
HANDOUT
HANDSAW
HANDSEL
HANDSET
HANGDOG
HANGING
HANGMAN
HANGOUT
HAPLESS
HAPLOID
HAPPILY
HARBOUR
HARDPAN
HARDTOP
HARELIP
HARMONY
HARNESS
HARPOON
HARRIER
HARVARD
HARVEST
HASHING
HASHISH
HASSOCK
HATCHET
HAUBERK
HAUGHTY
HAULAGE
HAUTEUR
HAYCOCK
HAYFORK
HAYLOFT
HAYRICK
HAYSEED
HAYWIRE
JACINTH
JACKASS
JACKDAW
JACKLEG
JACKPOT
JANITOR
JANUARY
JASMINE
JAVELIN
JAYBIRD
JAYWALK
KADDISH
KARAKUL
KATYDID
LABORED
LACONIC
LACQUER
LACTATE
LACTEAL
LACTOSE
LADYBUG
LAGGARD
LAMBENT
LAMINAR
LAMPOON
LAMPREY
LANDING
LANGUID
LANGUOR
LANOLIN
LANTANA
LANTERN
LANYARD
LAOTIAN
LAPWING
LARCENY
LARGESS
LASAGNA
LATAKIA
LATCHET
LATERAL
LATRINE
LATTICE
LATVIAN
LAUNDER
LAUNDRY
LAWLESS
LAWSUIT
LAYAWAY
LAYETTE
MACABRE
MACADAM
MACAQUE
MACDRAW
MACHETE
MACHINE
MACRAME
MADDING
MADEIRA
MAESTRO
MAFIOSO
MAGENTA
MAGNATE
MAGNETO
MAGNIFY
MAHATMA
MAHICAN
MAILBOX
MAILMAN
MAINTOP
MAJESTY
MAKINGS
MALAISE
MALARIA
MALEFIC
MALISON
MALLARD
MALLEUS
MALMSEY
MALTOSE
MAMMARY
MAMMOTH
MANACLE
MANAGER
MANDATE
MANDREL
MANDRIL
MANHOLE
MANHOOD
MANHUNT
MANIKIN
MANKIND
MANLIKE
MANNISH
MANSARD
MANSION
MANTEAU
MANUMIT
MARGENT
MARIMBA
MARINER
MARITAL
MARPLOT
MARQUEE
MARQUIS
MARSHAL
MARTIAL
MARTIAN
MARTINI
MARXISM
MASCARA
MASONIC
MASONRY
MASSAGE
MASSEUR
MASSIVE
MASTERY
MASTIFF
MASTOID
MATADOR
MATINEE
MATTINS
MATTOCK
MAUDLIN
MAUNDER
MAWKISH
MAXILLA
MAXIMAL
MAXIMUM
MAYPOLE
MAZURKA
NACELLE
NAIVETE
NAIVETY
NANKEEN
NAPHTHA
NARRATE
NARTHEX
NARWHAL
NASCENT
NATURAL
NAUGHTY
OARLOCK
OARSMAN
OATCAKE
OATMEAL
PABULUM
PACIFIC
PACKAGE
PACKING
PADDING
PADDOCK
PADLOCK
PAGEANT
PAGEBOY
PAISLEY
PAJAMAS
PALADIN
PALAVER
PALETTE
PALFREY
PALMATE
PALPATE
PANACEA
PANACHE
PANCAKE
PANICLE
PANNIER
PANOPLY
PANTHER
PAPILLA
PAPOOSE
PAPRIKA
PAPYRUS
PARABLE
PARADOX
PARAGON
PARAPET
PARASOL
PARBOIL
PARESIS
PARFAIT
PARKWAY
PARLOUR
PARLOUS
PARQUET
PARSING
PARSLEY
PARSNIP
PARTAKE
PARTIAL
PARTING
PARTITE
PARTNER
PARTWAY
PARVENU
PASSAGE
PASSING
PASSION
PASSIVE
PASSKEY
PASTERN
PASTIME
PASTURE
PATELLA
PATHWAY
PATIENT
PATRIOT
PATROON
PATTERN
PAUCITY
PAYLOAD
PAYMENT
PAYROLL
RACCOON
RACEWAY
RADIANT
RADIATE
RADICAL
RAFFISH
RAGTIME
RAGWEED
RAILING
RAILWAY
RAIMENT
RAINBOW
RAMBLER
RAMPAGE
RAMPANT
RAMPART
RANKING
RANSACK
RAPPORT
RAPTURE
RAREBIT
RATCHET
RATLINE
RATTLER
RATTRAP
RAUCOUS
RAUNCHY
RAVIOLI
RAWHIDE
SABBATH
SADIRON
SAFFRON
SAGUARO
SAILING
SAINTLY
SALIENT
SALTBOX
SALTINE
SALVAGE
SAMOVAR
SAMPLER
SAMURAI
SANCTUM
SANDBAG
SANDBAR
SANDHOG
SANDLOT
SANDMAN
SAPIENT
SAPLING
SAPWOOD
SARCASM
SARDINE
SATANIC
SATCHEL
SATIATE
SATIETY
SATISFY
SAUNTER
SAUSAGE
SAVANNA
SAWDUST
SAWMILL
TABLEAU
TABLOID
TABULAR
TACTICS
TACTILE
TADPOLE
TAFFETA
TAKEOFF
TALLYHO
TAMBALA
TANAGER
TANBARK
TANGENT
TANNERY
TANTRUM
TAPIOCA
TAPROOM
TAPROOT
TAPSTER
TARNISH
TATTING
TAXICAB
VACANCY
VACCINE
VACUITY
VACUOLE
VACUOUS
VAGRANT
VALANCE
VALENCE
VALIANT
VALUATE
VAMOOSE
VAMPIRE
VANDYKE
VANILLA
VANTAGE
VANWARD
VAQUERO
VARIANT
VARIETY
VARIOUS
VARMINT
VARNISH
VARSITY
VATICAN
VAULTED
WADABLE
WADDING
WAGGERY
WAGGISH
WAGONER
WAGTAIL
WAILFUL
WAKEFUL
WALKOUT
WALKWAY
WALLABY
WALLEYE
WALLOON
WANTING
WARBLER
WARFARE
WARHEAD
WARLESS
WARLIKE
WARLOCK
WARLORD
WARNING
WARPATH
WARRANT
WARRIOR
WARSHIP
WARTHOG
WARTIME
WASHING
WASHOUT
WASHTUB
WASPISH
WASSAIL
WASTAGE
WASTREL
WATTAGE
WAVELET
WAXWING
WAXWORK
WAYBILL
WAYSIDE
WAYWARD
WAYWORN
YARDAGE
YARDARM
YARDMAN
ZAMBIAN
ABALONE
ABANDON
ABDOMEN
ABILITY
ABOLISH
ABREAST
ABRIDGE
ABSCESS
ABSCOND
ABSENCE
ABSOLVE
ABSTAIN
ABYSMAL

ABYSSAL
EBONITE
OBELISK
OBLIQUE
OBLOQUY
OBSCENE
OBSCURE
OBSEQUY
OBSERVE
OBTRUDE
OBVERSE
OBVIATE
OBVIOUS
ACADEME
ACADEMY
ACCLAIM
ACCOUNT
ACCUSAL
ACCUSED
ACETATE
ACETONE
ACHIEVE
ACIDIFY
ACOLYTE
ACONITE
ACQUIRE
ACREAGE
ACROBAT
ACRONYM
ACRYLIC
ACTUARY
ACTUATE
ECHELON
ECLIPSE
ECLOGUE
ECOLOGY
ECONOMY
ECSTASY
ICEBERG
ICEBOAT
OCARINA
OCCLUDE
OCTAGON
OCTOBER
OCTOPUS
OCULIST
SCALLOP
SCALPEL
SCAMPER
SCANDAL
SCANNER
SCAPULA
SCARIFY
SCARLET
SCATTER
SCENERY
SCEPTER
SCEPTIC
SCHOLAR
SCIENCE
SCOOTER
SCOURGE
SCRAPPY
SCRATCH
SCRAWNY
SCREECH
SCROTUM
SCRUFFY
SCRUPLE
SCUFFLE
SCUPPER
SCUTTLE
ADAMANT
ADAPTER
ADDRESS
ADENINE
ADENOID
ADIPOSE
ADJOURN
ADJUDGE
ADJUNCT
ADMIRAL
ADRENAL
ADULATE
ADVANCE
ADVERSE
ADVISED
EDIFICE
EDITION
EDUCATE
IDEALLY
IDOLIZE
ODDBALL
ODDMENT
ODYSSEY
AEROBIC
AEROSOL
BEARING
BEASTLY
BEATIFY
BEATNIK
BECAUSE
BECLOUD
BEDDING
BEDEVIL
BEDFAST
BEDIZEN
BEDOUIN
BEDPOST
BEDROCK
BEDROLL
BEDROOM
BEDSIDE
BEDSORE
BEDTIME
BEEHIVE
BEELINE
BEESWAX
BEGGARY
BEGONIA
BEGRIME
BEGUILE
BEGUINE
BEHOOVE
BELABOR
BELATED
BELGIAN
BELIEVE
BELLBOY
BELLHOP
BELLOWS
BELOVED
BELTWAY
BENEATH
BENEFIT
BENISON
BENTHIC
BENTHOS
BENZENE
BENZINE
BENZOIN
BEQUEST
BERSERK
BESEECH
BESHREW
BESIDES
BESIEGE
BESMEAR
BESPEAK
BESTIAL
BETHINK
BETIMES
BETOKEN
BETROTH
BETWEEN
BETWIXT
BEWITCH
CEDILLA
CEILING
CELESTA
CELSIUS
CEMBALO
CENSURE
CENTARE
CENTAUR
CENTAVO
CENTIME
CENTIMO
CENTRAL
CENTURY
CERAMIC
CERTAIN
CERTIFY
CERUMEN
CESSION
DEADPAN
DEALING
DEANERY
DEATHLY
DEBACLE
DEBAUCH
DEBOUCH
DEBRIEF
DECAGON
DECEASE
DECEIVE
DECENCY
DECIBEL
DECIDED
DECIMAL
DECLAIM
DECLARE
DECLINE
DECODER
DECORUM
DEERFLY
DEFAULT
DEFENSE
DEFIANT
DEFICIT
DEFLATE
DEFLECT
DEFRAUD
DEFROST
DEFUNCT
DEGAUSS
DEGRADE
DELIGHT
DELIMIT
DELIVER
DELOUSE
DEMERIT
DEMESNE
DEMIGOD
DEMONIC
DEMOTIC
DENIZEN
DENSITY
DENTATE
DENTIST
DENTURE
DEPLANE
DEPLETE
DEPLORE
DEPOSIT
DEPRAVE
DEPRESS
DEPRIVE
DERANGE
DERRICK
DERVISH
DESCANT
DESCEND
DESCENT
DESERVE
DESKTOP
DESPAIR
DESPISE
DESPITE
DESPOIL
DESPOND
DESSERT
DESTINE
DESTINY
DESTROY
DETENTE
DETRACT
DETRAIN
DEVALUE
DEVELOP
DEVIANT
DEVIATE
DEVILRY
DEVIOUS
DEVOLVE
DEVOTED
DEVOTEE
DEWCLAW
DEWDROP
DEXTRIN
FEARFUL
FEATHER
FEATURE
FEBRILE
FEDERAL
FEEDLOT
FEELING
FENCING
FERMENT
FERMIUM
FERNERY
FERROUS
FERRULE
FERTILE
FERVENT
FESTIVE
FESTOON
FETLOCK
GEARBOX
GELATIN
GELDING
GENERAL
GENERIC
GENESIS
GENETIC
GENITAL
GENTEEL
GENTIAN
GENTILE
GENUINE
GEODESY
GEOLOGY
GERMANE
GESTAPO
GESTURE
GETAWAY
HEADING
HEADMAN
HEADPIN
HEADSET
HEADWAY
HEALTHY
HEARING
HEARKEN
HEARSAY
HEARTEN
HEATHEN
HEATHER
HECTARE
HEINOUS
HEIRESS
HELICAL
HELLCAT
HELLENE
HELLION
HELPING
HEMLINE
HEMLOCK
HENPECK
HEPARIN
HEPATIC
HERBAGE
HEROICS
HEROINE
HEROISM
HERRING
HERSELF
HEXAGON
HEXAPOD
JEALOUS
JEHOVAH
JEJUNUM
JETPORT
JEWELER
JEWELRY
KEELSON
KEEPING
KERATIN
KERNING
KETCHUP
KEYHOLE
KEYNOTE
LEADING
LEAFAGE
LEAFLET
LEAGUER
LEAKAGE
LEARNED
LEATHER
LECHERY
LECTERN
LECTURE
LEEWARD
LEFTISM
LEGATEE
LEGGING
LEGHORN
LEGIBLE
LEISURE
LEMMING
LEMPIRA
LENIENT
LEONINE
LEOPARD
LEOTARD
LEPROSY
LESBIAN
LETDOWN
LETTUCE
LEXICON
MEANDER
MEANING
MEASLES
MEASURE
MEATMAN
MEDIATE
MEDICAL
MEDULLA
MEETING
MEGATON
MEIOSIS
MELANGE
MELANIC
MELANIN
MEMENTO
MENFOLK
MENTHOL
MENTION
MERCURY
MERMAID
MESSAGE
MESSIAH
MESTIZO
METHANE
MEXICAN
NECKTIE
NEEDFUL
NEGLECT
NEITHER
NEMESIS
NEOLOGY
NEPTUNE
NERVOUS
NETTING
NETWARE
NETWORK
NEUTRAL
NEUTRON
NEWBORN
NEWSBOY
NEWSMAN
OEDIPAL
PEACOCK
PEAFOWL
PEASANT
PECCARY
PECCAVI
PEDICAB
PEELING
PEEVISH
PELAGIC
PELICAN
PENALTY
PENANCE
PENATES
PENDANT
PENDENT
PENDING
PENGUIN
PENNANT
PENSION
PENSIVE
PENTIUM
PEPPERY
PERCALE
PERCENT
PERCEPT
PERFECT
PERFIDY
PERFORM
PERFUME
PERGOLA
PERHAPS
PERIGEE
PERIQUE
PERIWIG
PERJURY
PERLITE
PERPLEX
PERSIAN
PERSIST
PERTAIN
PERTURB
PERVADE
PERVERT
PETIOLE
PETRIFY
PETTISH
PETUNIA
REACTOR
READING
READOUT
REAGENT
REALISM
REALITY
REALIZE
REBIRTH
REBOUND
REBUILD
RECEIPT
RECEIVE
RECENCY
RECITAL
RECLAIM
RECLAME
RECLINE
RECLUSE
RECOUNT
RECOVER
RECRUIT
RECTIFY
RECTORY
RECYCLE
REDCOAT
REDDISH
REDHEAD
REDLINE
REDOUBT
REDOUND
REDRESS
REDSKIN
REDWOOD
REENTRY
REFEREE
REFINED
REFLECT
REFRACT
REFRAIN
REFRESH
REFUGEE
REGALIA
REGATTA
REGENCY
REGIMEN
REGNANT
REGRESS
REGROUP
REGULAR
REJOICE
RELAPSE
RELATED
RELATOR
RELEASE

RELIEVE
RELIQUE
REMAINS
REMNANT
REMODEL
REMORSE
REMOUNT
RENEWAL
REPLACE
REPLETE
REPLICA
REPRESS
REPRINT
REPRISE
REPROOF
REPROVE
REPTILE
REPULSE
REPUTED
REQUEST
REQUIEM
REQUIRE
REQUITE
REREDOS
RESCIND
RESEDIT
RESERVE
RESIDUE
RESOLVE
RESOUND
RESPECT
RESPITE
RESPOND
RESTIVE
RESTORE
RETINUE
RETIRED
RETIREE
RETOUCH
RETRACE
RETRACT
RETREAD
RETREAT
REUNION
REVENGE
REVENUE
REVERIE
REVERSE
REVIVAL
REVOLVE
SEABIRD
SEAFOOD
SEALANT
SEAPORT
SEASICK
SEASIDE
SEATING
SEAWALL
SEAWARD
SEAWEED
SECLUDE
SECRECY
SECRETE
SECTARY
SECTION
SECULAR
SEEMING
SEGMENT
SEISMIC
SELFISH
SELTZER
SELVAGE
SEMINAL
SEMINAR
SENATOR
SENSORY
SENSUAL
SENTIMO
SEQUENT
SEQUOIA
SERIOUS
SERPENT
SERRATE
SERRIED
SERVANT
SERVICE
SERVILE
SERVING
SESSILE
SESSION
SETBACK
SETTING
SEVENTY
SEVERAL
SEXTANT
TECHNIC
TEDIOUS
TEENAGE
TEKTITE
TELLING
TEMPERA
TEMPEST
TENABLE
TENANCY
TENDRIL
TENFOLD
TENSILE
TENSION
TENUOUS
TENURED
TEQUILA
TERBIUM
TERMITE
TERNARY
TERRACE
TERRAIN
TERRIER
TERRIFY
TESTATE
TESTIFY
TETANUS
TEXTILE
TEXTURE
VEDANTA
VEGETAL
VEHICLE
VEILING
VENISON
VENTRAL
VENTURE
VERANDA
VERBENA
VERBOSE
VERDANT
VERDICT
VERDURE
VERMEIL
VERNIER
VERSIFY
VERSION
VERTIGO
VERVAIN
VESICLE
VESPERS
VESTIGE
VESTING
VESTURE
VETERAN
WEALTHY
WEASAND
WEATHER
WEBBING
WEDDING
WEDLOCK
WEEKDAY
WEEKEND
WEEPING
WEIGHTY
WELCOME
WELFARE
WESTERN
WETBACK
WETLAND
YESHIVA
ZEALOUS
ZEOLITE
AFFABLE
AFFLICT
AFFRONT
AFGHANI
AFRICAN
EFFENDI
OFFBEAT
OFFENSE
OFFHAND
OFFICER
OFFSIDE
PFENNIG
AGAINST
AGELESS
AGITATE
AGONIZE
AGROUND
EGGHEAD
EGOTISM
IGNEOUS
IGNOBLE
CHABLIS
CHADIAN
CHAFFER
CHAGRIN
CHALICE
CHALLIS
CHAMBER
CHAMFER
CHAMOIS
CHANCEL
CHANCRE
CHANNEL
CHANSON
CHANTEY
CHANTRY
CHAPEAU
CHAPLET
CHAPMAN
CHAPTER
CHARGER
CHARIOT
CHARITY
CHARMER
CHARNEL
CHARTER
CHASSIS
CHASTEN
CHATEAU
CHATTEL
CHATTER
CHEAPEN
CHECKER
CHECKUP
CHEDDAR
CHEETAH
CHEMISE
CHEMIST
CHERISH
CHEROOT
CHEVIOT
CHEVRON
CHIANTI
CHICANE
CHICANO
CHICKEN
CHICORY
CHIFFON
CHIGGER
CHIGNON
CHIMERA
CHIMNEY
CHINESE
CHINOOK
CHINTZY
CHIPPER
CHOCTAW
CHOLERA
CHOPPER
CHORALE
CHORTLE
CHOWDER
CHROMIC
CHRONIC
CHUCKLE
CHUKKER
CHUTNEY
GHASTLY
GHERKIN
KHEDIVE
PHAETON
PHALANX
PHALLIC
PHALLUS
PHANTOM
PHARAOH
PHARYNX
PHILTER
PHOENIX
PHONEME
PHONICS
PHRENIC
PHYSICS
PHYSIOL
RHENIUM
RHIZOME
RHODIUM
RHOMBUS
RHUBARB
SHACKLE
SHADING
SHALLOP
SHALLOW
SHAMBLE
SHAMPOO
SHAPELY
SHARPEN
SHARPER
SHARPIE
SHATTER
SHAVING
SHAWNEE
SHEATHE
SHEBANG
SHELLAC
SHELTER
SHERBET
SHERIFF
SHIMMER
SHINGLE
SHOCKER
SHORING
SHORTEN
SHORTLY
SHOTGUN
SHOWMAN
SHRIVEL
SHUDDER
SHUFFLE
SHUTOUT
SHUTTER
SHUTTLE
SHYLOCK
SHYSTER
THEATER
THEOREM
THERAPY
THEREAT
THEREBY
THEREIN
THEREOF
THEREON
THERETO
THERMAL
THERMOS
THICKEN
THICKET
THIMBLE
THINNER
THISTLE
THITHER
THORIUM
THOUGHT
THREADY
THROATY
THROUGH
THRUWAY
THULIUM
THUNDER
THYMINE
THYROID
THYSELF
WHATNOT
WHEEDLE
WHEELER
WHEREAS
WHEREAT
WHEREBY
WHEREIN
WHEREOF
WHEREON
WHERETO
WHETHER
WHICKER
WHIMPER
WHIPPET
WHIPSAW
WHISKER
WHISKEY
WHISPER
WHISTLE
WHITHER
WHITING
WHITISH
WHITLOW
WHITTLE
WHOEVER
WHOOPLA
WHOPPER
WHORLED
AILERON
AILMENT
AIMLESS
AIRDROP
AIRFLOW
AIRFOIL
AIRLIFT
AIRLINE
AIRMAIL
AIRPORT
AIRPOST
AIRSHIP
AIRSICK
AIRWAVE
BIBELOT
BICYCLE
BIFOCAL
BIGHORN
BIKEWAY
BILIOUS
BILLION
BIMETAL
BINDING
BIOLOGY
BIOTITE
BIPLANE
BIPOLAR
BIRCHER
BIRETTA
BISCUIT
BISMUTH
BITTERN
BITTERS
BITUMEN
BIVALVE
BIVOUAC
BIZARRE
CILIATE
CIRCLET
CIRCUIT
CISTERN
CITADEL
CITIZEN
CIVILLY
CIVVIES
DIAGRAM
DIALECT
DIAMOND
DIARIST
DICTATE
DICTION
DIEHARD
DIFFUSE
DIGITAL
DIGNIFY
DIGNITY
DIGRAPH
DIGRESS
DILEMMA
DILUENT
DINETTE
DIOCESE
DIPLOID
DIPLOMA
DIREFUL
DISABLE
DISAVOW
DISBAND
DISCARD
DISCERN
DISCORD
DISCUSS
DISDAIN
DISEASE
DISEUSE
DISGUST
DISHRAG
DISJOIN
DISLIKE
DISMISS
DISOBEY
DISPLAY
DISPORT
DISPOSE
DISPUTE
DISROBE
DISRUPT
DISSECT
DISSENT
DISTAFF
DISTANT
DISTEND
DISTICH
DISTILL
DISTORT
DISTURB
DIURNAL
DIVERGE
DIVERSE
DIVIDER
DIVISOR
DIVORCE
DIVULGE
EIDOLON
FIANCEE
FIBROID
FICTION
FIFTEEN
FIGHTER
FIGMENT
FILBERT
FILLING
FILMDOM
FINAGLE
FINANCE
FINDING
FINESSE
FINFISH
FINICKY
FINNISH
FIREARM
FIREBOX
FIREBUG
FIREFLY
FIREMAN
FIRSTLY
FISHERY
FISHING
FISSILE
FISSION
FISSURE
FISTFUL
FISTULA
FITTING
FIXTURE
GIBBOUS
GIBLETS
GIMMICK
GINGHAM
GINSENG
GIRAFFE
GIZZARD
HIBACHI
HICKORY
HIDALGO
HIDEOUS
HIDEOUT

HIGHBOY
HIGHWAY
HILLOCK
HILLTOP
HIMSELF
HINTING
HIPBONE
HIPSTER
HIRSUTE
HISTORY
JITTERS
KIBBUTZ
KICKOFF
KIDSKIN
KILLING
KILLJOY
KILOTON
KINDRED
KINETIC
KINFOLK
KINGDOM
KINGPIN
KINSHIP
KINSMAN
KITCHEN
LIAISON
LIBERAL
LIBERTY
LIBRARY
LICENSE
LIGHTEN
LIGHTER
LIGNIFY
LIGNITE
LIMBECK
LIMEADE
LIMITED
LINEAGE
LINEMAN
LINGUAL
LINKAGE
LINSEED
LIONIZE
LIQUEFY
LIQUEUR
LISSOME
LISTING
LITERAL
LITHIUM
LITURGY
LIVABLE
MICROBE
MIDLAND
MIDMOST
MIDRIFF
MIDTOWN
MIDWEEK
MIDWIFE
MIDYEAR
MIGRANT
MIGRATE
MILEAGE
MILITIA
MILKMAN
MILKSOP
MILLAGE
MILLDAM
MILLIME
MILLING
MILLION
MIMESIS
MIMETIC
MIMICRY
MINARET
MINDFUL
MINERAL
MINIBUS
MINIMAL
MINIMUM
MINSTER
MINUEND
MINUTIA
MIRACLE
MISCALL
MISDEED
MISFILE
MISFIRE
MISLEAD
MISLIKE
MISNAME
MISPLAY
MISREAD
MISRULE
MISSEND
MISSILE
MISSING
MISSION
MISSIVE
MISSTEP
MISTAKE
MISTRAL
MITOSIS
MIXTURE
NIAGARA
NIGGARD
NIGHTLY
NIOBIUM
NIRVANA
NITRATE
NITRIFY
NITRITE
OILSKIN
PIANIST
PIASTER
PIBROCH
PICCOLO
PICTURE
PIEBALD
PIGGISH
PIGMENT
PIGSKIN
PIGTAIL
PILGRIM
PILLAGE
PILLBOX
PILLION
PILLORY
PILSNER
PIMENTO
PINHOLE
PINKEYE
PINNACE
PINNATE
PINWORM
PIONEER
PIPETTE
PIQUANT
PIRANHA
PISMIRE
PITCHER
PITEOUS
PITFALL
PITIFUL
PIZZAZZ
RICKETS
RICKETY
RICKSHA
RIGGING
RIGHTLY
RINGLET
RIPOSTE
RISIBLE
RIVALRY
RIVULET
SIAMESE
SIBLING
SICKBED
SIDEARM
SIDECAR
SIDELIT
SIDEMAN
SIGHTED
SIGHTLY
SIGNIFY
SILENCE
SILICON
SIMILAR
SINCERE
SINUOUS
SIRLOIN
SIROCCO
SIXTEEN
SIZABLE
TIBETAN
TICKING
TIDINGS
TIEBACK
TIGHTEN
TILLAGE
TIMBREL
TIMOTHY
TIMPANI
TINFOIL
TINWARE
TIPSTER
TITANIC
TITULAR
VIADUCT
VIBRANT
VIBRATE
VIBRATO
VICEROY
VICINAL
VICIOUS
VICTORY
VICTUAL
VILLAGE
VILLAIN
VILLEIN
VILLOUS
VINEGAR
VINTAGE
VINTNER
VIOLATE
VIOLENT
VIRGULE
VIRTUAL
VISCERA
VISCOSE
VISCOUS
VISIBLE
VISITOR
VITAMIN
VITIATE
VITRIFY
VITRIOL
VITTLES
WICKIUP
WIDGEON
WIDOWER
WIGGLER
WILDCAT
WILLFUL
WILLIES
WILLING
WILLOWY
WINDAGE
WINDBAG
WINDING
WINDOWS
WINDROW
WINNING
WINSOME
WIRETAP
WISHFUL
WISTFUL
WITHERS
WITHOUT
WITLESS
WITNESS
WITTING
WIZENED
YIDDISH
ZILLION
ZIONISM
SKEPTIC
SKIFFLE
SKILLET
SKIPPER
SKITTER
SKIWEAR
SKYLARK
SKYLINE
SKYWARD
UKULELE
ALBUMEN
ALBUMIN
ALCALDE
ALCAZAR
ALCHEMY
ALCOHOL
ALEMBIC
ALEWIFE
ALFALFA
ALGEBRA
ALIMENT
ALIMONY
ALLEGRO
ALLERGY
ALMANAC
ALMONER
ALREADY
ALRIGHT
ALUMINA
ALUMNUS
BLACKEN
BLADDER
BLANKET
BLARNEY
BLATANT
BLATHER
BLEEDER
BLEMISH
BLESSED
BLINDER
BLINKER
BLINTZE
BLISTER
BLOATER
BLOODED
BLOOPER
BLOSSOM
BLOTTER
BLOWGUN
BLOWOUT
BLUBBER
BLUCHER
BLUNDER
BLUSTER
CLAMBER
CLANGOR
CLAPPER
CLARIFY
CLARION
CLARITY
CLASSIC
CLASTIC
CLATTER
CLAVIER
CLEANLY
CLEANSE
CLEANUP
CLEAVER
CLEMENT
CLIMATE
CLINKER
CLIPPER
CLOBBER
CLOSURE
CLOTHES
CLOTURE
CLUSTER
CLUTTER
ELASTIC
ELDERLY
ELECTOR
ELEGIAC
ELEMENT
ELEVATE
ELISION
ELITISM
ELLIPSE
ELUSIVE
ELYSIUM
FLACCID
FLANKER
FLANNEL
FLAPPER
FLATBED
FLATCAR
FLATTEN
FLATTER
FLATTOP
FLAVOUR
FLEMING
FLEMISH
FLESHLY
FLEXURE
FLICKER
FLIGHTY
FLIPPER
FLIVVER
FLORIST
FLOTSAM
FLOUNCE
FLOWERY
FLUSTER
FLUTIST
FLUTTER
FLYABLE
FLYLEAF
GLACIAL
GLACIER
GLADDEN
GLAMOUR
GLAZIER
GLEEMAN
GLIMMER
GLIMPSE
GLISTEN
GLISTER
GLITTER
GLOBULE
GLORIFY
GLOTTIS
GLUCOSE
GLUTTON
ILEITIS
ILLEGAL
ILLICIT
ILLNESS
OLDSTER
OLIVINE
PLACARD
PLACATE
PLACEBO
PLACKET
PLANTAR
PLANTER
PLASTER
PLASTIC
PLATEAU
PLATING
PLATOON
PLATTER
PLAUDIT
PLAYBOY
PLAYLET
PLAYPEN
PLENARY
PLIABLE
PLOTTER
PLOWBOY
PLOWMAN
PLUMAGE
PLUMBER
PLUMMET
PLUNDER
PLUNGER
PLUVIAL
PLYWOOD
SLACKEN
SLACKER
SLANDER
SLATHER
SLAVERY
SLAVISH
SLEEPER
SLEIGHT
SLENDER
SLICKER
SLIPPER
SLITHER
SLOBBER
SLUMBER
ULULATE
AMALGAM
AMATEUR
AMATIVE
AMATORY
AMBIENT
AMENITY
AMERIND
AMIABLE
AMMETER
AMMONIA
AMNESIA
AMNESTY
AMOROUS
AMPHORA
AMPLIFY
AMPUTEE
AMYLASE
EMANATE
EMBARGO
EMBASSY
EMBOWER
EMBRACE
EMBROIL
EMBRYOL
EMERALD
EMERITA
EMINENT
EMITTER
EMOTION
EMPATHY
EMPEROR
EMPOWER
EMPRESS
EMULATE
IMAGERY
IMAGINE
IMAGISM
IMITATE
IMMENSE
IMMERSE
IMMORAL
IMPANEL
IMPASSE
IMPASTO
IMPEACH
IMPEARL
IMPERIL
IMPETUS
IMPIETY
IMPINGE
IMPIOUS
IMPLODE
IMPLORE
IMPOUND
IMPRESS
IMPRINT
IMPROVE
IMPULSE
OMINOUS
OMNIBUS
SMELTER
SMIDGEN
SMOLDER
SMOTHER
SMUGGLE
UMBRAGE
UMPTEEN
ANAEMIA
ANAGRAM
ANALOGY
ANALYZE
ANAPEST
ANARCHY
ANATOMY
ANCHOVY
ANCIENT
ANDANTE
ANDIRON
ANDROID
ANEMONE
ANGUISH
ANGULAR
ANILINE
ANIMATE
ANIMISM
ANNUITY
ANNULAR

ANODIZE
ANODYNE
ANOMALY
ANOTHER
ANTACID
ANTENNA
ANTHILL
ANTHRAX
ANTHROP
ANTIGEN
ANTIQUE
ANTONYM
ANXIETY
ANXIOUS
ANYBODY
ANYMORE
ANYTIME
ANYWISE
ENAMOUR
ENCHAIN
ENCHANT
ENCLAVE
ENCLOSE
ENCRUST
ENDEMIC
ENDLESS
ENDMOST
ENDORSE
ENDWAYS
ENDWISE
ENFORCE
ENGLISH
ENGRAFT
ENGRAVE
ENGROSS
ENHANCE
ENLARGE
ENLIVEN
ENNOBLE
ENPLANE
ENQUIRE
ENSLAVE
ENSNARE
ENTENTE
ENTHUSE
ENTITLE
ENTRAIN
ENTRANT
ENTREAT
ENTROPY
ENTRUST
ENTWINE
ENVELOP
ENVENOM
ENVIOUS
INBOARD
INBOUND

INCENSE
INCISOR
INCLINE
INCLOSE
INCLUDE
INCRUST
INCUBUS
INDEXED
INDICIA
INDOORS
INDORSE
INDULGE
INDWELL
INERTIA
INEXACT
INFANCY
INFARCT
INFERNO
INFIDEL
INFIELD
INFLAME
INFLATE
INFLECT
INFLICT
INGENUE
INGRAFT
INGRAIN
INGRATE
INGRESS
INGROWN
INHABIT
INHALER
INHERIT
INHIBIT
INHUMAN
INITIAL
INKHORN
INKLING
INKWELL
INNARDS
INNINGS
INQUEST
INQUIRE
INQUIRY
INSHORE
INSIDER
INSIGHT
INSIPID
INSPECT
INSPIRE
INSTALL
INSTANT
INSTATE
INSTEAD
INSTILL
INSULAR
INSULIN

INSURED
INSURER
INTEGER
INTENSE
INTERIM
INTRANS
INTROIT
INTRUDE
INTRUST
INVALID
INVEIGH
INVERSE
INVOICE
INVOLVE
KNEECAP
KNOCKER
KNOWING
KNUCKLE
ONEROUS
ONESELF
ONETIME
ONGOING
ONSHORE
SNAFFLE
SNEAKER
SNICKER
SNIFFLE
SNORKEL
SNUFFLE
SNUGGLE
UNARMED
UNAWARE
UNBLOCK
UNBOSOM
UNBOWED
UNCANNY
UNCHAIN
UNCIVIL
UNCLASP
UNCLEAN
UNCLOAK
UNCLOSE
UNCOUTH
UNCOVER
UNCROSS
UNCTION
UNDERGO
UNDOING
UNDRESS
UNDYING
UNEARTH
UNEQUAL
UNERASE
UNFROCK
UNGODLY
UNGROUP
UNGUENT

UNHANDY
UNHAPPY
UNHEARD
UNHINGE
UNHITCH
UNHORSE
UNICORN
UNIFORM
UNITARY
UNITIZE
UNKEMPT
UNKNOWN
UNLATCH
UNLEARN
UNLEASH
UNLOOSE
UNLUCKY
UNMANLY
UNMORAL
UNMOVED
UNNERVE
UNQUIET
UNQUOTE
UNRAVEL
UNSAVED
UNSCREW
UNSLING
UNSNARL
UNSOUND
UNSTRAP
UNTRIED
UNTRUTH
UNTWINE
UNTWIST
UNUSUAL
UNWEAVE
BOATMAN
BOBSLED
BOLIVAR
BOLOGNA
BOLSTER
BOMBARD
BOMBAST
BONANZA
BONDAGE
BONDMAN
BONFIRE
BOOKEND
BOOKISH
BOOKLET
BOOTLEG
BOREDOM
BOROUGH
BORSCHT
BOUDOIR
BOULDER
BOUNCER

BOUNDEN
BOUQUET
BOURBON
BOWLDER
BOWLINE
BOWLING
BOYCOTT
COARSEN
COATING
COAXIAL
COBBLER
COCAINE
COCHLEA
COCKADE
COCKEYE
COCKNEY
COCKPIT
COCONUT
CODEINE
CODFISH
CODICIL
CODLING
COEQUAL
COEXIST
COGNATE
COHABIT
COINAGE
COLLAGE
COLLARD
COLLATE
COLLECT
COLLEEN
COLLEGE
COLLIDE
COLLIER
COLLOID
COLOGNE
COLONEL
COLORED
COMBINE
COMFORT
COMMAND
COMMEND
COMMENT
COMMODE
COMMUNE
COMMUTE
COMPACT
COMPANY
COMPARE
COMPASS
COMPEER
COMPETE
COMPILE
COMPLEX
COMPORT
COMPOSE

COMPOST
COMPOTE
COMPUTE
COMRADE
CONCAVE
CONCEAL
CONCEDE
CONCEIT
CONCEPT
CONCERN
CONCERT
CONCISE
CONCOCT
CONCORD
CONDEMN
CONDIGN
CONDOLE
CONDONE
CONDUCE
CONDUCT
CONDUIT
CONDYLE
CONFESS
CONFIDE
CONFINE
CONFIRM
CONFLUX
CONFORM
CONFUSE
CONFUTE
CONGEAL
CONGEST
CONICAL
CONIFER
CONJOIN
CONJURE
CONNECT
CONNIVE
CONNOTE
CONQUER
CONSENT
CONSIGN
CONSIST
CONSOLE
CONSORT
CONSULT
CONSUME
CONTACT
CONTAIN
CONTEMN
CONTEND
CONTENT
CONTEST
CONTEXT
CONTORT
CONTOUR
CONTRIB

CONTROL
CONVENE
CONVENT
CONVERT
CONVICT
CONVOKE
COOKERY
COOKOUT
COOLANT
COPILOT
COPIOUS
COPPICE
COPYBOY
COPYCAT
CORACLE
CORDAGE
CORDIAL
CORDITE
CORDOBA
CORINTH
CORNCOB
CORNICE
COROLLA
CORONAL
CORONER
CORONET
CORRECT
CORRODE
CORRUPT
CORSAGE
CORSAIR
CORTEGE
COSSACK
COSTIVE
COSTUME
COTERIE
COTTAGE
COULOMB
COUNCIL
COUNSEL
COUNTER
COUNTRY
COUPLET
COURAGE
COURIER
COURSER
COURTLY
COUTURE
COWBIRD
COWHAND
COWHIDE
COWLICK
COWLING
COWPOKE
COWSLIP
COXCOMB
DOCKAGE

DOGBANE
DOGCART
DOGFISH
DOGTROT
DOGWOOD
DOLEFUL
DOLPHIN
DOMINIE
DOORMAN
DOORMAT
DOORWAY
DORMANT
DOSSIER
DOUBLET
DOUGHTY
DOWAGER
DOYENNE
FOGHORN
FOLDOUT
FOLIAGE
FOLKWAY
FONDANT
FOOLERY
FOOLISH
FOOTAGE
FOOTING
FOOTMAN
FOOTPAD
FORBEAR
FORBODE
FORCEPS
FOREARM
FOREIGN
FORELEG
FOREMAN
FORESEE
FORETOP
FOREVER
FORFEIT
FORFEND
FORGING
FORGIVE
FORLORN
FORMULA
FORSAKE
FORTIFY
FORTRAN
FORTUNE
FORWARD
FOULARD
FOULING
FOUNDER
FOUNDRY
FOXHOLE
GOBBLER
GODDESS
GODHEAD

GODHOOD
GODLESS
GODLIKE
GODSEND
GOGGLES
GONDOLA
GOODMAN
GORILLA
GOSHAWK
GOSLING
GOULASH
GOURMET
HOBNAIL
HOECAKE
HOEDOWN
HOGBACK
HOGWASH
HOLDING
HOLIDAY
HOLMIUM
HOLSTER
HOMBURG
HOMONYM
HOODLUM
HOOSIER
HOPHEAD
HORIZON
HORMONE
HORRIFY
HOSANNA
HOSIERY
HOSPICE
HOSTAGE
HOSTESS
HOSTILE
HOSTLER
HOTCAKE
HOTFOOT
HOTSHOT
HOUSING
HOWBEIT
HOWEVER
HOWLING
JOCULAR
JODHPUR
JOLLITY
JONQUIL
JOTTING
JOURNAL
JOURNEY
JOYANCE
JOYRIDE
LOATHLY
LOBSTER
LOCATOR
LOCKJAW
LOCKNUT

LOCKOUT
LODGING
LONGBOW
LONGING
LOOKOUT
LOTTERY
LOWBROW
LOWDOWN
LOWLAND
LOZENGE
MOBSTER
MODICUM
MODISTE
MODULAR
MOHEGAN
MOHICAN
MOISTEN
MOLDING
MOLLIFY
MOLLUSK
MONADIC
MONARCH
MONEYED
MONGREL
MONITOR
MONOCLE
MONOMER
MONSOON
MONSTER
MONTAGE
MOORING
MORAINE
MORDANT
MORNING
MOROCCO
MORPHIA
MORTIFY
MORTISE
MOUNTIE
NOCUOUS
NOISOME
NOMADIC
NOMINAL
NOMINEE
NONBOOK
NONHERO
NONPLUS
NONSKED
NONSTOP
NONUSER
NOONDAY
NORTHER
NOSEGAY
NOSTRIL
NOSTRUM
NOTABLE
NOTHING
NOURISH
NOVELLA
NOVELTY
NOWHERE
NOXIOUS
POCOSIN
POINTED
POINTER
POLARIS
POLECAT
POLEMIC
POLITIC
POLLACK
POLLUTE
POLYGON
POLYMER
POMPANO
POMPOUS
PONIARD
PONTIFF
PONTOON
POPCORN
POPOVER
POPULAR
PORCINE
PORTAGE
PORTEND
PORTENT
PORTICO
PORTION
PORTRAY
POSSESS
POSTAGE
POSTBOY
POSTERN
POSTMAN
POSTURE
POSTWAR
POTABLE
POTHEAD
POTHERB
POTHOLE
POTHOOK
POTLUCK
POTSHOT
POTTAGE
POTTERY
POULTRY
POVERTY
ROADBED
ROADWAY
ROASTER
ROBBERY
ROEBUCK
ROISTER
ROLLICK
ROMANCE
ROOFTOP
ROOKERY
ROOSTER
ROOTLET
ROSEATE
ROSEBUD
ROSETTE
ROSTRUM
ROTUNDA
ROUGHEN
ROUNDUP
ROUTINE
ROWBOAT
ROYALTY
SOCIETY
SOJOURN
SOLARIS
SOLDIER
SOLICIT
SOLUBLE
SOLVENT
SOMEDAY
SOMEHOW
SOMEONE
SOPHISM
SOPHIST
SOPRANO
SORCERY
SORGHUM
SOUFFLE
SOULFUL
SOUNDER
SOUPCON
SOYBEAN
TOASTER
TOBACCO
TOEHOLD
TOENAIL
TOGGERY
TOLUENE
TONIGHT
TONNAGE
TONNEAU
TONSURE
TOOLBOX
TOPCOAT
TOPICAL
TOPKNOT
TOPLESS
TOPMAST
TOPMOST
TOPPING
TOPSAIL
TOPSIDE
TOPSOIL
TORMENT
TORNADO
TORPEDO
TORRENT
TORSION
TORTONI
TORTURE
TOUGHEN
TOURIST
TOURNEY
TOWBOAT
TOWHEAD
TOWPATH
TOXEMIA
VOCABLE
VOCALIC
VOGUISH
VOLCANO
VOLTAGE
VOLTAIC
VOLUBLE
VOUCHER
WOLFRAM
WOMANLY
WOODCUT
WOODLOT
WOODMAN
WORDAGE
WORDING
WORKBAG
WORKBOX
WORKDAY
WORKING
WORKMAN
WORKOUT
WORLDLY
WORSHIP
WORSTED
YOUNKER
ZOOLOGY
APANAGE
APATITE
APHASIA
APOLOGY
APOLUNE
APOSTLE
APPAREL
APPEASE
APPLAUD
APPLIED
APPOINT
APPRISE
APPROVE
APRICOT
APROPOS
EPAULET
EPERGNE
EPICURE
EPIGRAM
EPISODE
EPISTLE
EPITAPH
EPITHET
EPITOME
OPACITY
OPENING
OPERATE
OPINION
OPOSSUM
OPPRESS
OPTICAL
OPTIMAL
OPTIMUM
OPULENT
SPANGLE
SPANIEL
SPANISH
SPARING
SPARKLE
SPARROW
SPASTIC
SPATIAL
SPATTER
SPATULA
SPEAKER
SPECIAL
SPECIES
SPECIFY
SPECKLE
SPECTER
SPEEDUP
SPELLER
SPICULE
SPINACH
SPINDLE
SPINDLY
SPIRANT
SPITTLE
SPLENIC
SPLOTCH
SPLURGE
SPOILER
SPONSOR
SPOTTER
SPOUSAL
SPUMONI
SPUTNIK
SPUTTER
UPBRAID
UPCHUCK
UPDRAFT
UPGRADE
UPRAISE
UPRIGHT
UPRIVER
UPSHIFT
UPSTAGE
UPSTART
UPSTATE
UPSURGE
UPSWEPT
UPSWING
UPTIGHT
AQUATIC
AQUAVIT
AQUEOUS
AQUIFER
EQUABLE
EQUATOR
EQUERRY
EQUINOX
SQUALID
SQUALOR
SQUEEZE
SQUELCH
ARAPAHO
ARBITER
ARBUTUS
ARCHAIC
ARCHERY
ARCHIVE
ARCHWAY
ARDUOUS
AREAWAY
ARMHOLE
ARMORER
ARMREST
ARPANET
ARRAIGN
ARRANGE
ARREARS
ARRIVAL
ARSENAL
ARSENIC
ARTICLE
ARTISAN
ARTISTE
ARTLESS
BRACERO
BRACKEN
BRACKET
BRAHMAN
BRAHMIN
BRAILLE
BRAMBLE
BRAVADO
BRAVERY
BRAVURA
BRAZIER
BREADTH
BREAKER
BREAKUP
BREATHE
BRECCIA
BREVITY
BRIGADE
BRIGAND
BRIMFUL
BRIOCHE
BRISKET
BRISTLE
BRITISH
BRITTLE
BROADEN
BROCADE
BROIDER
BROILER
BROMIDE
BROMINE
BROODER
BROTHEL
BROTHER
BROUGHT
BROWNIE
BROWSER
BRUISER
BRUSQUE
BRUTISH
CRABBED
CRACKER
CRACKLE
CRANIUM
CRAVING
CREATOR
CREMATE
CREVICE
CRICKET
CRIMSON
CRINKLE
CRIPPLE
CRITTER
CROCHET
CROOKED
CROPPER
CROQUET
CROSIER
CROUTON
CROWBAR
CRUCIAL
CRUCIFY
CRUISER
CRULLER
CRUMBLE
CRUMPET
CRUMPLE
CRUSADE
CRYBABY
CRYPTIC
CRYSTAL
DRACHMA
DRAGNET
DRAGOON
DRAPERY
DRASTIC
DRAUGHT
DRAWING
DRESSER
DRIBBLE
DRIBLET
DRIFTER
DRIZZLE
DROPLET
DROPPER
DROUGHT
DRUMLIN
DRUMMER
DRUNKEN
ERELONG
EREMITE
EROSION
EROSIVE
ERRATIC
ERRATUM
FRACTAL
FRAGILE
FRAILTY
FRANTIC
FRAUGHT
FRAZZLE
FRECKLE
FREEBIE
FREEDOM
FREEMAN
FREEWAY
FREEZER
FREIGHT
FRESHEN
FRESHET
FRETFUL
FRETSAW
FRIABLE
FRIGATE
FRITTER
FRIZZLE
FROGMAN
FROWARD
FRUSTUM
GRACKLE
GRADUAL
GRAMMAR
GRANARY
GRANDAM
GRANDEE
GRANITE
GRANTEE
GRANULE
GRAPHIC
GRAPNEL
GRAPPLE
GRATIFY
GRATING
GRAUPEL
GRAVITY
GRAVURE
GRAZIER
GRECIAN
GREMLIN
GRENADE
GRIDDLE
GRIMACE
GRINDER
GRISTLE
GRIZZLY
GROMMET
GROUPER
GROUPIE
GRUMBLE
GRUNION
IRANIAN
IRIDIUM
IRKSOME
IRONING
KREMLIN
KRYPTON
ORATION
ORATORY
ORBITER
ORCHARD
ORDERLY
ORDINAL
OREGANO
ORGANDY
ORGANIC
ORGANZA
ORIFICE
ORIGAMI
OROGENY
OROTUND
ORTOLAN
PRAETOR
PRAIRIE
PRALINE
PRATTLE
PRAYING
PREBEND
PRECEDE
PRECEPT
PRECISE
PRECOOK
PREDATE
PREDICT
PREEMIE
PREEMPT
PREFACE

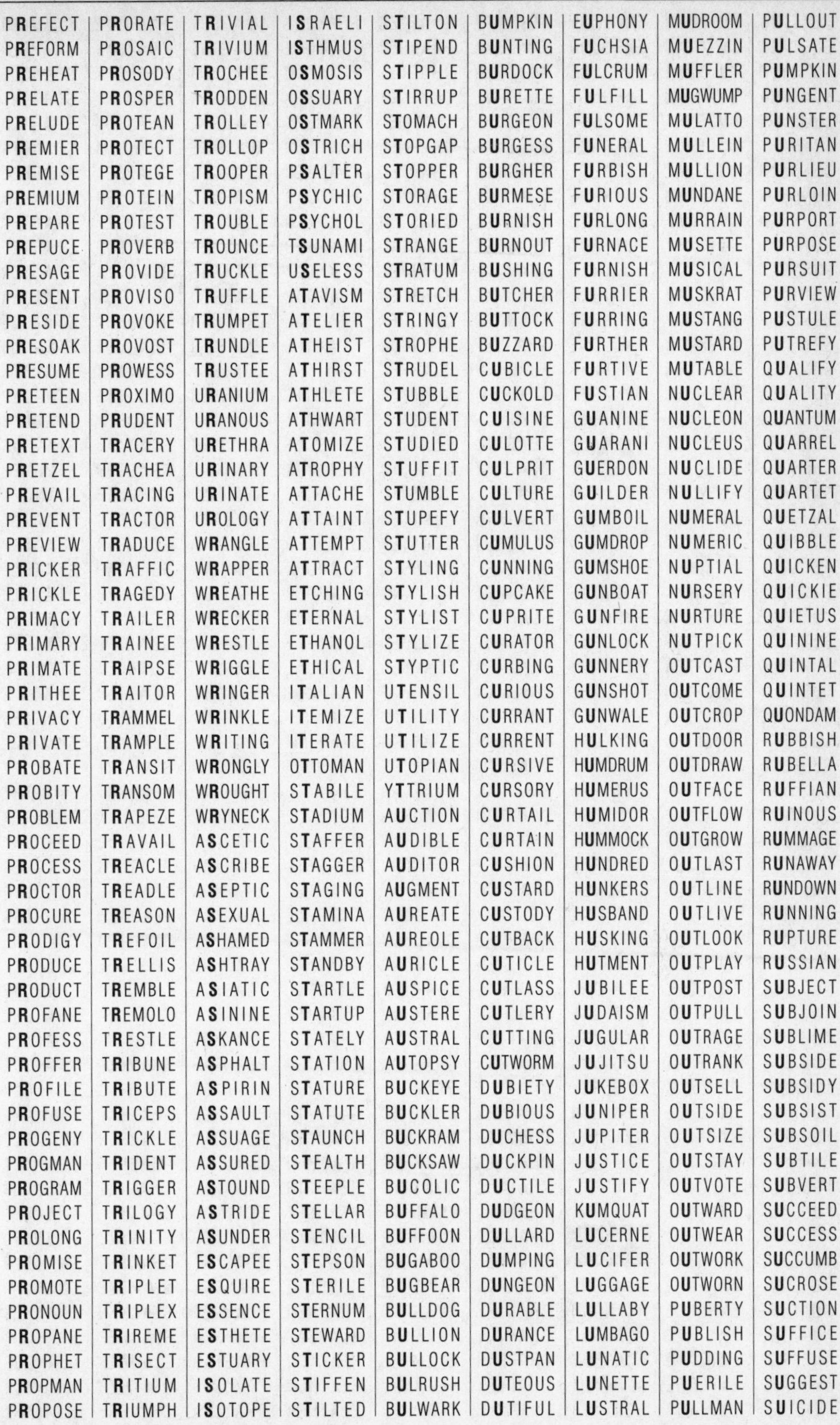

PREFECT
PREFORM
PREHEAT
PRELATE
PRELUDE
PREMIER
PREMISE
PREMIUM
PREPARE
PREPUCE
PRESAGE
PRESENT
PRESIDE
PRESOAK
PRESUME
PRETEEN
PRETEND
PRETEXT
PRETZEL
PREVAIL
PREVENT
PREVIEW
PRICKER
PRICKLE
PRIMACY
PRIMARY
PRIMATE
PRITHEE
PRIVACY
PRIVATE
PROBATE
PROBITY
PROBLEM
PROCEED
PROCESS
PROCTOR
PROCURE
PRODIGY
PRODUCE
PRODUCT
PROFANE
PROFESS
PROFFER
PROFILE
PROFUSE
PROGENY
PROGMAN
PROGRAM
PROJECT
PROLONG
PROMISE
PROMOTE
PRONOUN
PROPANE
PROPHET
PROPMAN
PROPOSE

PRORATE
PROSAIC
PROSODY
PROSPER
PROTEAN
PROTECT
PROTEGE
PROTEIN
PROTEST
PROVERB
PROVIDE
PROVISO
PROVOKE
PROVOST
PROWESS
PROXIMO
PRUDENT
TRACERY
TRACHEA
TRACING
TRACTOR
TRADUCE
TRAFFIC
TRAGEDY
TRAILER
TRAINEE
TRAIPSE
TRAITOR
TRAMMEL
TRAMPLE
TRANSIT
TRANSOM
TRAPEZE
TRAVAIL
TREACLE
TREADLE
TREASON
TREFOIL
TRELLIS
TREMBLE
TREMOLO
TRESTLE
TRIBUNE
TRIBUTE
TRICEPS
TRICKLE
TRIDENT
TRIGGER
TRILOGY
TRINITY
TRINKET
TRIPLET
TRIPLEX
TRIREME
TRISECT
TRITIUM
TRIUMPH

TRIVIAL
TRIVIUM
TROCHEE
TRODDEN
TROLLEY
TROLLOP
TROOPER
TROPISM
TROUBLE
TROUNCE
TRUCKLE
TRUFFLE
TRUMPET
TRUNDLE
TRUSTEE
URANIUM
URANOUS
URETHRA
URINARY
URINATE
UROLOGY
WRANGLE
WRAPPER
WREATHE
WRECKER
WRESTLE
WRIGGLE
WRINGER
WRINKLE
WRITING
WRONGLY
WROUGHT
WRYNECK
ASCETIC
ASCRIBE
ASEPTIC
ASEXUAL
ASHAMED
ASHTRAY
ASIATIC
ASININE
ASKANCE
ASPHALT
ASPIRIN
ASSAULT
ASSUAGE
ASSURED
ASTOUND
ASTRIDE
ASUNDER
ESCAPEE
ESQUIRE
ESSENCE
ESTHETE
ESTUARY
ISOLATE
ISOTOPE

ISRAELI
ISTHMUS
OSMOSIS
OSSUARY
OSTMARK
OSTRICH
PSALTER
PSYCHIC
PSYCHOL
TSUNAMI
USELESS
ATAVISM
ATELIER
ATHEIST
ATHIRST
ATHLETE
ATHWART
ATOMIZE
ATROPHY
ATTACHE
ATTAINT
ATTEMPT
ATTRACT
ETCHING
ETERNAL
ETHANOL
ETHICAL
ITALIAN
ITEMIZE
ITERATE
OTTOMAN
STABILE
STADIUM
STAFFER
STAGGER
STAGING
STAMINA
STAMMER
STANDBY
STARTLE
STARTUP
STATELY
STATION
STATURE
STATUTE
STAUNCH
STEALTH
STEEPLE
STELLAR
STENCIL
STEPSON
STERILE
STERNUM
STEWARD
STICKER
STIFFEN
STILTED

STILTON
STIPEND
STIPPLE
STIRRUP
STOMACH
STOPGAP
STOPPER
STORAGE
STORIED
STRANGE
STRATUM
STRETCH
STRINGY
STROPHE
STRUDEL
STUBBLE
STUDENT
STUDIED
STUFFIT
STUMBLE
STUPEFY
STUTTER
STYLING
STYLISH
STYLIST
STYLIZE
STYPTIC
UTENSIL
UTILITY
UTILIZE
UTOPIAN
YTTRIUM
AUCTION
AUDIBLE
AUDITOR
AUGMENT
AUREATE
AUREOLE
AURICLE
AUSPICE
AUSTERE
AUSTRAL
AUTOPSY
BUCKEYE
BUCKLER
BUCKRAM
BUCKSAW
BUCOLIC
BUFFALO
BUFFOON
BUGABOO
BUGBEAR
BULLDOG
BULLION
BULLOCK
BULRUSH
BULWARK

BUMPKIN
BUNTING
BURDOCK
BURETTE
BURGEON
BURGESS
BURGHER
BURMESE
BURNISH
BURNOUT
BUSHING
BUTCHER
BUTTOCK
BUZZARD
CUBICLE
CUCKOLD
CUISINE
CULOTTE
CULPRIT
CULTURE
CULVERT
CUMULUS
CUNNING
CUPCAKE
CUPRITE
CURATOR
CURBING
CURIOUS
CURRANT
CURRENT
CURSIVE
CURSORY
CURTAIL
CURTAIN
CUSHION
CUSTARD
CUSTODY
CUTBACK
CUTICLE
CUTLASS
CUTLERY
CUTTING
CUTWORM
DUBIETY
DUBIOUS
DUCHESS
DUCKPIN
DUCTILE
DUDGEON
DULLARD
DUMPING
DUNGEON
DURABLE
DURANCE
DUSTPAN
DUTEOUS
DUTIFUL

EUPHONY
FUCHSIA
FULCRUM
FULFILL
FULSOME
FUNERAL
FURBISH
FURIOUS
FURLONG
FURNACE
FURNISH
FURRIER
FURRING
FURTHER
FURTIVE
FUSTIAN
GUANINE
GUARANI
GUERDON
GUILDER
GUMBOIL
GUMDROP
GUMSHOE
GUNBOAT
GUNFIRE
GUNLOCK
GUNNERY
GUNSHOT
GUNWALE
HULKING
HUMDRUM
HUMERUS
HUMIDOR
HUMMOCK
HUNDRED
HUNKERS
HUSBAND
HUSKING
HUTMENT
JUBILEE
JUDAISM
JUGULAR
JUJITSU
JUKEBOX
JUNIPER
JUPITER
JUSTICE
JUSTIFY
KUMQUAT
LUCERNE
LUCIFER
LUGGAGE
LULLABY
LUMBAGO
LUNATIC
LUNETTE
LUSTRAL

MUDROOM
MUEZZIN
MUFFLER
MUGWUMP
MULATTO
MULLEIN
MULLION
MUNDANE
MURRAIN
MUSETTE
MUSICAL
MUSKRAT
MUSTANG
MUSTARD
MUTABLE
NUCLEAR
NUCLEON
NUCLEUS
NUCLIDE
NULLIFY
NUMERAL
NUMERIC
NUPTIAL
NURSERY
NURTURE
NUTPICK
OUTCAST
OUTCOME
OUTCROP
OUTDOOR
OUTDRAW
OUTFACE
OUTFLOW
OUTGROW
OUTLAST
OUTLINE
OUTLIVE
OUTLOOK
OUTPLAY
OUTPOST
OUTPULL
OUTRAGE
OUTRANK
OUTSELL
OUTSIDE
OUTSIZE
OUTSTAY
OUTVOTE
OUTWARD
OUTWEAR
OUTWORK
OUTWORN
PUBERTY
PUBLISH
PUDDING
PUERILE
PULLMAN

PULLOUT
PULSATE
PUMPKIN
PUNGENT
PUNSTER
PURITAN
PURLIEU
PURLOIN
PURPORT
PURPOSE
PURSUIT
PURVIEW
PUSTULE
PUTREFY
QUALIFY
QUALITY
QUANTUM
QUARREL
QUARTER
QUARTET
QUETZAL
QUIBBLE
QUICKEN
QUICKIE
QUIETUS
QUININE
QUINTAL
QUINTET
QUONDAM
RUBBISH
RUBELLA
RUFFIAN
RUINOUS
RUMMAGE
RUNAWAY
RUNDOWN
RUNNING
RUPTURE
RUSSIAN
SUBJECT
SUBJOIN
SUBLIME
SUBSIDE
SUBSIDY
SUBSIST
SUBSOIL
SUBTILE
SUBVERT
SUCCEED
SUCCESS
SUCCUMB
SUCROSE
SUCTION
SUFFICE
SUFFUSE
SUGGEST
SUICIDE

SUITING
SULFATE
SULFIDE
SULTANA
SUMMARY
SUMMONS
SUNBATH
SUNBEAM
SUNBURN
SUNDIAL
SUNDOWN
SUNFISH
SUNLAMP
SUNRISE
SUNROOF
SUNSPOT
SUPPORT
SUPPOSE
SUPREME
SURFACE
SURFEIT
SURGEON
SURGERY
SURMISE
SURNAME
SURPASS
SURPLUS
SURTOUT
SURVIVE
SUSPECT
SUSPEND
SUSTAIN
TUBULAR
TUESDAY
TUGBOAT
TUITION
TUMBLER
TUMBREL
TUNABLE
TUNEFUL
TURBINE
TURKISH
TURMOIL
TURNERY
TURNING
TURNKEY
TURNOFF
TURNOUT
TUSSOCK
TUTELAR
VULGATE
VULPINE
VULTURE
AVARICE
AVERAGE
AVOCADO
EVACUEE
EVASION
EVENING
EVIDENT
OVATION
OVERACT
OVERAGE
OVERALL
OVERARM
OVERAWE
OVERFLY
OVERJOY
OVERLAP
OVERLAY
OVERRUN
OVERSEA
OVERSEE
OVERTOP
OVIDUCT
OVULATE
AWKWARD
DWINDLE
SWADDLE
SWAGGER
SWAHILI
SWALLOW
SWARTHY
SWEATER
SWEDISH
SWEETEN
SWELTER
SWINDLE
SWOLLEN
TWADDLE
TWEETER
TWIDDLE
TWILLED
TWINKLE
TWISTER
TWITTER
TWOSOME
EXAMINE
EXAMPLE
EXCERPT
EXCLAIM
EXCLUDE
EXCRETA
EXCRETE
EXECUTE
EXEGETE
EXHAUST
EXHIBIT
EXPANSE
EXPENSE
EXPIATE
EXPLAIN
EXPLODE
EXPLOIT
EXPLORE
EXPOUND
EXPRESS
EXPUNGE
EXTINCT
EXTRACT
EXTREME
EXTRUDE
OXBLOOD
OXIDANT
OXIDIZE
CYANIDE
CYCLIST
CYCLONE
CYPRESS
DYNAMIC
DYNASTY
EYEBALL
EYEBROW
EYELASH
EYESORE
EYEWASH
HYDRANT
HYDRATE
HYDROUS
HYGIENE
HYMNODY
MYSTERY
MYSTIFY
PYJAMAS
PYRAMID
PYRITES
SYMPTOM
SYNAPSE
SYNCOPE
SYNONYM
SYRINGE
SYSTOLE
TYPHOID
TYPHOON
TYPICAL
TYRANNY
WYSIWYG
ZYMURGY
AZIMUTH
CZARINA

## 3RD LETTER

ABALONE
ABANDON
ACADEME
ACADEMY
ADAMANT
ADAPTER
AGAINST
AMALGAM
AMATEUR
AMATIVE
AMATORY
ANAEMIA
ANAGRAM
ANALOGY
ANALYZE
ANAPEST
ANARCHY
ANATOMY
APANAGE
APATITE
ARAPAHO
ATAVISM
AVARICE
BEARING
BEASTLY
BEATIFY
BEATNIK
BLACKEN
BLADDER
BLANKET
BLARNEY
BLATANT
BLATHER
BOATMAN
BRACERO
BRACKEN
BRACKET
BRAHMAN
BRAHMIN
BRAILLE
BRAMBLE
BRAVADO
BRAVERY
BRAVURA
BRAZIER
CHABLIS
CHADIAN
CHAFFER
CHAGRIN
CHALICE
CHALLIS
CHAMBER
CHAMFER
CHAMOIS
CHANCEL
CHANCRE
CHANNEL
CHANSON
CHANTEY
CHANTRY
CHAPEAU
CHAPLET
CHAPMAN
CHAPTER
CHARGER
CHARIOT
CHARITY
CHARMER
CHARNEL
CHARTER
CHASSIS
CHASTEN
CHATEAU
CHATTEL
CHATTER
CLAMBER
CLANGOR
CLAPPER
CLARIFY
CLARION
CLARITY
CLASSIC
CLASTIC
CLATTER
CLAVIER
COARSEN
COATING
COAXIAL
CRABBED
CRACKER
CRACKLE
CRANIUM
CRAVING
CYANIDE
CZARINA
DEADPAN
DEALING
DEANERY
DEATHLY
DIAGRAM
DIALECT
DIAMOND
DIARIST
DRACHMA
DRAGNET
DRAGOON
DRAPERY
DRASTIC
DRAUGHT
DRAWING
ELASTIC
EMANATE
ENAMOUR
EPAULET
EVACUEE
EVASION
EXAMINE
EXAMPLE
FEARFUL
FEATHER
FEATURE
FIANCEE
FLACCID
FLANKER
FLANNEL
FLAPPER
FLATBED
FLATCAR
FLATTEN
FLATTER
FLATTOP
FLAVOUR
FRACTAL
FRAGILE
FRAILTY
FRANTIC
FRAUGHT
FRAZZLE
GEARBOX
GHASTLY
GLACIAL
GLACIER
GLADDEN
GLAMOUR
GLAZIER
GRACKLE
GRADUAL
GRAMMAR
GRANARY
GRANDAM
GRANDEE
GRANITE
GRANTEE
GRANULE
GRAPHIC
GRAPNEL
GRAPPLE
GRATIFY
GRATING
GRAUPEL
GRAVITY
GRAVURE
GRAZIER
GUANINE
GUARANI
HEADING
HEADMAN
HEADPIN
HEADSET
HEADWAY
HEALTHY
HEARING
HEARKEN
HEARSAY
HEARTEN
HEATHEN
HEATHER
IMAGERY
IMAGINE
IMAGISM
IRANIAN
ITALIAN
JEALOUS
LEADING
LEAFAGE
LEAFLET
LEAGUER
LEAKAGE
LEARNED
LEATHER
LIAISON
LOATHLY
MEANDER
MEANING
MEASLES
MEASURE
MEATMAN
NIAGARA
OCARINA
OPACITY
ORATION
ORATORY
OVATION
PEACOCK
PEAFOWL
PEASANT
PHAETON
PHALANX
PHALLIC
PHALLUS
PHANTOM
PHARAOH
PHARYNX
PIANIST
PIASTER
PLACARD
PLACATE
PLACEBO
PLACKET
PLANTAR
PLANTER
PLASTER
PLASTIC
PLATEAU
PLATING
PLATOON
PLATTER
PLAUDIT
PLAYBOY
PLAYLET
PLAYPEN
PRAETOR
PRAIRIE
PRALINE
PRATTLE
PRAYING
PSALTER
QUALIFY
QUALITY
QUANTUM
QUARREL
QUARTER
QUARTET
REACTOR
READING
READOUT
REAGENT
REALISM
REALITY
REALIZE
ROADBED
ROADWAY
ROASTER
SCALLOP
SCALPEL
SCAMPER
SCANDAL
SCANNER
SCAPULA
SCARIFY
SCARLET
SCATTER
SEABIRD
SEAFOOD
SEALANT
SEAPORT
SEASICK
SEASIDE
SEATING
SEAWALL
SEAWARD
SEAWEED
SHACKLE
SHADING
SHALLOP
SHALLOW
SHAMBLE
SHAMPOO
SHAPELY
SHARPEN
SHARPER
SHARPIE
SHATTER
SHAVING
SHAWNEE
SIAMESE
SLACKEN
SLACKER
SLANDER
SLATHER
SLAVERY
SLAVISH
SNAFFLE
SPANGLE
SPANIEL
SPANISH
SPARING
SPARKLE
SPARROW
SPASTIC
SPATIAL
SPATTER
SPATULA
STABILE
STADIUM
STAFFER
STAGGER
STAGING
STAMINA
STAMMER
STANDBY
STARTLE
STARTUP
STATELY
STATION
STATURE
STATUTE
STAUNCH
SWADDLE
SWAGGER
SWAHILI
SWALLOW
SWARTHY
TOASTER
TRACERY
TRACHEA
TRACING
TRACTOR
TRADUCE
TRAFFIC
TRAGEDY
TRAILER
TRAINEE
TRAIPSE
TRAITOR
TRAMMEL
TRAMPLE
TRANSIT
TRANSOM
TRAPEZE
TRAVAIL
TWADDLE
UNARMED
UNAWARE
URANIUM
URANOUS
VIADUCT
WEALTHY

WE**A**SAND
WE**A**THER
WH**A**TNOT
WR**A**NGLE
WR**A**PPER
ZE**A**LOUS
AL**B**UMEN
AL**B**UMIN
AM**B**IENT
AR**B**ITER
AR**B**UTUS
BI**B**ELOT
BO**B**SLED
CA**B**ARET
CA**B**BAGE
CA**B**INET
CA**B**OOSE
CO**B**BLER
CU**B**ICLE
DE**B**ACLE
DE**B**AUCH
DE**B**OUCH
DE**B**RIEF
DU**B**IETY
DU**B**IOUS
EM**B**ARGO
EM**B**ASSY
EM**B**OWER
EM**B**RACE
EM**B**ROIL
EM**B**RYOL
FE**B**RILE
FI**B**ROID
GA**B**FEST
GI**B**BOUS
GI**B**LETS
GO**B**BLER
HA**B**ITAT
HA**B**ITUE
HI**B**ACHI
HO**B**NAIL
IN**B**OARD
IN**B**OUND
JU**B**ILEE
KI**B**BUTZ
LA**B**ORED
LI**B**ERAL
LI**B**ERTY
LI**B**RARY
LO**B**STER
MO**B**STER
OR**B**ITER
OX**B**LOOD
PA**B**ULUM
PI**B**ROCH
PU**B**ERTY
PU**B**LISH
RE**B**IRTH
RE**B**OUND
RE**B**UILD
RO**B**BERY
RU**B**BISH
RU**B**ELLA
SA**B**BATH
SI**B**LING
SU**B**JECT
SU**B**JOIN
SU**B**LIME
SU**B**SIDE
SU**B**SIDY
SU**B**SIST
SU**B**SOIL
SU**B**TILE
SU**B**VERT
TA**B**LEAU
TA**B**LOID
TA**B**ULAR
TI**B**ETAN
TO**B**ACCO
TU**B**ULAR
UM**B**RAGE
UN**B**LOCK
UN**B**OSOM
UN**B**OWED
UP**B**RAID
VI**B**RANT
VI**B**RATE
VI**B**RATO
WE**B**BING
AC**C**LAIM
AC**C**OUNT
AC**C**USAL
AC**C**USED
AL**C**ALDE
AL**C**AZAR
AL**C**HEMY
AL**C**OHOL
AN**C**HOVY
AN**C**IENT
AR**C**HAIC
AR**C**HERY
AR**C**HIVE
AR**C**HWAY
AS**C**ETIC
AS**C**RIBE
AU**C**TION
BA**C**KING
BA**C**KLIT
BA**C**KLOG
BE**C**AUSE
BE**C**LOUD
BI**C**YCLE
BU**C**KEYE
BU**C**KLER
BU**C**KRAM
BU**C**KSAW
BU**C**OLIC
CO**C**AINE
CO**C**HLEA
CO**C**KADE
CO**C**KEYE
CO**C**KNEY
CO**C**KPIT
CO**C**ONUT
CU**C**KOLD
CY**C**LIST
CY**C**LONE
DE**C**AGON
DE**C**EASE
DE**C**EIVE
DE**C**ENCY
DE**C**IBEL
DE**C**IDED
DE**C**IMAL
DE**C**LAIM
DE**C**LARE
DE**C**LINE
DE**C**ODER
DE**C**ORUM
DI**C**TATE
DI**C**TION
DO**C**KAGE
DU**C**HESS
DU**C**KPIN
DU**C**TILE
EN**C**HAIN
EN**C**HANT
EN**C**LAVE
EN**C**LOSE
EN**C**RUST
ES**C**APEE
ET**C**HING
EX**C**ERPT
EX**C**LAIM
EX**C**LUDE
EX**C**RETA
EX**C**RETE
FA**C**TION
FA**C**TORY
FA**C**TUAL
FA**C**ULTY
FI**C**TION
FU**C**HSIA
HA**C**KMAN
HA**C**KNEY
HA**C**KSAW
HE**C**TARE
HI**C**KORY
IN**C**ENSE
IN**C**ISOR
IN**C**LINE
IN**C**LOSE
IN**C**LUDE
IN**C**RUST
IN**C**UBUS
JA**C**INTH
JA**C**KASS
JA**C**KDAW
JA**C**KLEG
JA**C**KPOT
JO**C**ULAR
KI**C**KOFF
LA**C**ONIC
LA**C**QUER
LA**C**TATE
LA**C**TEAL
LA**C**TOSE
LE**C**HERY
LE**C**TERN
LE**C**TURE
LI**C**ENSE
LO**C**ATOR
LO**C**KJAW
LO**C**KNUT
LO**C**KOUT
LU**C**ERNE
LU**C**IFER
MA**C**ABRE
MA**C**ADAM
MA**C**AQUE
MA**C**DRAW
MA**C**HETE
MA**C**HINE
MA**C**RAME
MI**C**ROBE
NA**C**ELLE
NE**C**KTIE
NO**C**UOUS
NU**C**LEAR
NU**C**LEON
NU**C**LEUS
NU**C**LIDE
OC**C**LUDE
OR**C**HARD
PA**C**IFIC
PA**C**KAGE
PA**C**KING
PE**C**CARY
PE**C**CAVI
PI**C**COLO
PI**C**TURE
PO**C**OSIN
RA**C**COON
RA**C**EWAY
RE**C**EIPT
RE**C**EIVE
RE**C**ENCY
RE**C**ITAL
RE**C**LAIM
RE**C**LAME
RE**C**LINE
RE**C**LUSE
RE**C**OUNT
RE**C**OVER
RE**C**RUIT
RE**C**TIFY
RE**C**TORY
RE**C**YCLE
RI**C**KETS
RI**C**KETY
RI**C**KSHA
SE**C**LUDE
SE**C**RECY
SE**C**RETE
SE**C**TARY
SE**C**TION
SE**C**ULAR
SI**C**KBED
SO**C**IETY
SU**C**CEED
SU**C**CESS
SU**C**CUMB
SU**C**ROSE
SU**C**TION
TA**C**TICS
TA**C**TILE
TE**C**HNIC
TI**C**KING
UN**C**ANNY
UN**C**HAIN
UN**C**IVIL
UN**C**LASP
UN**C**LEAN
UN**C**LOAK
UN**C**LOSE
UN**C**OUTH
UN**C**OVER
UN**C**ROSS
UN**C**TION
UP**C**HUCK
VA**C**ANCY
VA**C**CINE
VA**C**UITY
VA**C**UOLE
VA**C**UOUS
VI**C**EROY
VI**C**INAL
VI**C**IOUS
VI**C**TORY
VI**C**TUAL
VO**C**ABLE
VO**C**ALIC
WI**C**KIUP
AB**D**OMEN
AD**D**RESS
AN**D**ANTE
AN**D**IRON
AN**D**ROID
AR**D**UOUS
AU**D**IBLE
AU**D**ITOR
BA**D**LAND
BE**D**DING
BE**D**EVIL
BE**D**FAST
BE**D**IZEN
BE**D**OUIN
BE**D**POST
BE**D**ROCK
BE**D**ROLL
BE**D**ROOM
BE**D**SIDE
BE**D**SORE
BE**D**TIME
CA**D**AVER
CA**D**ENCE
CA**D**ENZA
CA**D**MIUM
CE**D**ILLA
CO**D**EINE
CO**D**FISH
CO**D**ICIL
CO**D**LING
DU**D**GEON
EI**D**OLON
EL**D**ERLY
EN**D**EMIC
EN**D**LESS
EN**D**MOST
EN**D**ORSE
EN**D**WAYS
EN**D**WISE
FE**D**ERAL
GO**D**DESS
GO**D**HEAD
GO**D**HOOD
GO**D**LESS
GO**D**LIKE
GO**D**SEND
HA**D**DOCK
HI**D**ALGO
HI**D**EOUS
HI**D**EOUT
HY**D**RANT
HY**D**RATE
HY**D**ROUS
IN**D**EXED
IN**D**ICIA
IN**D**OORS
IN**D**ORSE
IN**D**ULGE
IN**D**WELL
JO**D**HPUR
JU**D**AISM
KA**D**DISH
KI**D**SKIN
LA**D**YBUG
LO**D**GING
MA**D**DING
MA**D**EIRA
ME**D**IATE
ME**D**ICAL
ME**D**ULLA
MI**D**LAND
MI**D**MOST
MI**D**RIFF
MI**D**TOWN
MI**D**WEEK
MI**D**WIFE
MI**D**YEAR
MO**D**ICUM
MO**D**ISTE
MO**D**ULAR
MU**D**ROOM
OD**D**BALL
OD**D**MENT
OE**D**IPAL
OL**D**STER
OR**D**ERLY
OR**D**INAL
PA**D**DING
PA**D**DOCK
PA**D**LOCK
PE**D**ICAB
PU**D**DING
RA**D**IANT
RA**D**IATE
RA**D**ICAL
RE**D**COAT
RE**D**DISH
RE**D**HEAD
RE**D**LINE
RE**D**OUBT
RE**D**OUND
RE**D**RESS
RE**D**SKIN
RE**D**WOOD
SA**D**IRON
SI**D**EARM
SI**D**ECAR
SI**D**ELIT
SI**D**EMAN
TA**D**POLE
TE**D**IOUS
TI**D**INGS
UN**D**ERGO
UN**D**OING
UN**D**RESS
UN**D**YING
UP**D**RAFT
VE**D**ANTA
WA**D**ABLE
WA**D**DING
WE**D**DING
WE**D**LOCK
WI**D**GEON
WI**D**OWER
YI**D**DISH
AC**E**TATE
AC**E**TONE
AD**E**NINE
AD**E**NOID
AG**E**LESS
AL**E**MBIC
AL**E**WIFE
AM**E**NITY
AM**E**RIND
AN**E**MONE
AR**E**AWAY
AS**E**PTIC
AS**E**XUAL
AT**E**LIER
AV**E**RAGE
BE**E**HIVE
BE**E**LINE
BE**E**SWAX
BL**E**EDER
BL**E**MISH
BL**E**SSED
BR**E**ADTH
BR**E**AKER
BR**E**AKUP
BR**E**ATHE
BR**E**CCIA
BR**E**VITY
CA**E**SURA
CH**E**APEN
CH**E**CKER
CH**E**CKUP
CH**E**DDAR
CH**E**ETAH
CH**E**MISE
CH**E**MIST
CH**E**RISH
CH**E**ROOT
CH**E**VIOT
CH**E**VRON
CL**E**ANLY
CL**E**ANSE
CL**E**ANUP
CL**E**AVER
CL**E**MENT
CO**E**QUAL
CO**E**XIST
CR**E**ATOR
CR**E**MATE
CR**E**VICE
DE**E**RFLY
DI**E**HARD
DR**E**SSER
EL**E**CTOR
EL**E**GIAC
EL**E**MENT
EL**E**VATE
EM**E**RALD
EM**E**RITA
EP**E**RGNE
ER**E**LONG
ER**E**MITE
ET**E**RNAL
EV**E**NING
EX**E**CUTE
EX**E**GETE
EY**E**BALL
EY**E**BROW
EY**E**LASH
EY**E**SORE
EY**E**WASH
FE**E**DLOT
FE**E**LING
FL**E**MING
FL**E**MISH
FL**E**SHLY
FL**E**XURE
FR**E**CKLE
FR**E**EBIE
FR**E**EDOM
FR**E**EMAN
FR**E**EWAY
FR**E**EZER
FR**E**IGHT
FR**E**SHEN
FR**E**SHET
FR**E**TFUL
FR**E**TSAW
GH**E**RKIN
GL**E**EMAN
GR**E**CIAN
GR**E**MLIN
GR**E**NADE
GU**E**RDON
HO**E**CAKE
HO**E**DOWN
IC**E**BERG
IC**E**BOAT
ID**E**ALLY
IL**E**ITIS
IN**E**RTIA
IN**E**XACT
IT**E**MIZE
IT**E**RATE
KE**E**LSON
KE**E**PING

KHEDIVE
KNEECAP
KREMLIN
LEEWARD
MAESTRO
MEETING
MUEZZIN
NEEDFUL
OBELISK
ONEROUS
ONESELF
ONETIME
OPENING
OPERATE
OREGANO
OVERACT
OVERAGE
OVERALL
OVERARM
OVERAWE
OVERFLY
OVERJOY
OVERLAP
OVERLAY
OVERRUN
OVERSEA
OVERSEE
OVERTOP
PEELING
PEEVISH
PFENNIG
PIEBALD
PLENARY
PREBEND
PRECEDE
PRECEPT
PRECISE
PRECOOK
PREDATE
PREDICT
PREEMIE
PREEMPT
PREFACE
PREFECT
PREFORM
PREHEAT
PRELATE
PRELUDE
PREMIER
PREMISE
PREMIUM
PREPARE
PREPUCE
PRESAGE
PRESENT
PRESIDE
PRESOAK
PRESUME
PRETEEN
PRETEND
PRETEXT
PRETZEL
PREVAIL
PREVENT
PREVIEW
PUERILE
QUETZAL
REENTRY
RHENIUM
ROEBUCK
SCENERY
SCEPTER
SCEPTIC
SEEMING
SHEATHE
SHEBANG
SHELLAC
SHELTER
SHERBET
SHERIFF
SKEPTIC
SLEEPER
SLEIGHT
SLENDER
SMELTER
SNEAKER
SPEAKER
SPECIAL
SPECIES
SPECIFY
SPECKLE
SPECTER
SPEEDUP
SPELLER
STEALTH
STEEPLE
STELLAR
STENCIL
STEPSON
STERILE
STERNUM
STEWARD
SWEATER
SWEDISH
SWEETEN
SWELTER
TEENAGE
THEATER
THEOREM
THERAPY
THEREAT
THEREBY
THEREIN
THEREOF
THEREON
THERETO
THERMAL
THERMOS
TIEBACK
TOEHOLD
TOENAIL
TREACLE
TREADLE
TREASON
TREFOIL
TRELLIS
TREMBLE
TREMOLO
TRESTLE
TUESDAY
TWEETER
UNEARTH
UNEQUAL
UNERASE
URETHRA
USELESS
UTENSIL
WEEKDAY
WEEKEND
WEEPING
WHEEDLE
WHEELER
WHEREAS
WHEREAT
WHEREBY
WHEREIN
WHEREOF
WHEREON
WHERETO
WHETHER
WREATHE
WRECKER
WRESTLE
AFFABLE
AFFLICT
AFFRONT
ALFALFA
BIFOCAL
BUFFALO
BUFFOON
DEFAULT
DEFENSE
DEFIANT
DEFICIT
DEFLATE
DEFLECT
DEFRAUD
DEFROST
DEFUNCT
DIFFUSE
EFFENDI
ENFORCE
FIFTEEN
HAFNIUM
INFANCY
INFARCT
INFERNO
INFIDEL
INFIELD
INFLAME
INFLATE
INFLECT
INFLICT
LEFTISM
MAFIOSO
MUFFLER
OFFBEAT
OFFENSE
OFFHAND
OFFICER
OFFSIDE
RAFFISH
REFEREE
REFINED
REFLECT
REFRACT
REFRAIN
REFRESH
REFUGEE
RUFFIAN
SAFFRON
SUFFICE
SUFFUSE
TAFFETA
UNFROCK
AFGHANI
ALGEBRA
ANGUISH
ANGULAR
AUGMENT
BAGASSE
BAGGAGE
BAGPIPE
BEGGARY
BEGONIA
BEGRIME
BEGUILE
BEGUINE
BIGHORN
BUGABOO
BUGBEAR
COGNATE
DEGAUSS
DEGRADE
DIGITAL
DIGNIFY
DIGNITY
DIGRAPH
DIGRESS
DOGBANE
DOGCART
DOGFISH
DOGTROT
DOGWOOD
EGGHEAD
ENGLISH
ENGRAFT
ENGRAVE
ENGROSS
FIGHTER
FIGMENT
FOGHORN
GOGGLES
HAGGARD
HIGHBOY
HIGHWAY
HOGBACK
HOGWASH
HYGIENE
INGENUE
INGRAFT
INGRAIN
INGRATE
INGRESS
INGROWN
JUGULAR
LAGGARD
LEGATEE
LEGGING
LEGHORN
LEGIBLE
LIGHTEN
LIGHTER
LIGNIFY
LIGNITE
LUGGAGE
MAGENTA
MAGNATE
MAGNETO
MAGNIFY
MEGATON
MIGRANT
MIGRATE
MUGWUMP
NEGLECT
NIGGARD
NIGHTLY
ONGOING
ORGANDY
ORGANIC
ORGANZA
PAGEANT
PAGEBOY
PIGGISH
PIGMENT
PIGSKIN
PIGTAIL
RAGTIME
RAGWEED
REGALIA
REGATTA
REGENCY
REGIMEN
REGNANT
REGRESS
REGROUP
REGULAR
RIGGING
RIGHTLY
SAGUARO
SEGMENT
SIGHTED
SIGHTLY
SIGNIFY
SUGGEST
TIGHTEN
TOGGERY
TUGBOAT
UNGODLY
UNGROUP
UNGUENT
UPGRADE
VAGRANT
VEGETAL
VOGUISH
WAGGERY
WAGGISH
WAGONER
WAGTAIL
WIGGLER
ACHIEVE
APHASIA
ASHAMED
ASHTRAY
ATHEIST
ATHIRST
ATHLETE
ATHWART
BEHOOVE
COHABIT
ECHELON
ENHANCE
ETHANOL
ETHICAL
EXHAUST
EXHIBIT
INHABIT
INHALER
INHERIT
INHIBIT
INHUMAN
JEHOVAH
MAHATMA
MAHICAN
MOHEGAN
MOHICAN
SCHOLAR
UNHANDY
UNHAPPY
UNHEARD
UNHINGE
UNHITCH
UNHORSE
VEHICLE
ABILITY
ACIDIFY
ADIPOSE
AGITATE
ALIMENT
ALIMONY
AMIABLE
ANILINE
ANIMATE
ANIMISM
ASIATIC
ASININE
AZIMUTH
BAILIFF
BLINDER
BLINKER
BLINTZE
BLISTER
BRIGADE
BRIGAND
BRIMFUL
BRIOCHE
BRISKET
BRISTLE
BRITISH
BRITTLE
CAISSON
CAITIFF
CEILING
CHIANTI
CHICANE
CHICANO
CHICKEN
CHICORY
CHIFFON
CHIGGER
CHIGNON
CHIMERA
CHIMNEY
CHINESE
CHINOOK
CHINTZY
CHIPPER
CLIMATE
CLINKER
CLIPPER
COINAGE
CRICKET
CRIMSON
CRINKLE
CRIPPLE
CRITTER
CUISINE
DRIBBLE
DRIBLET
DRIFTER
DRIZZLE
DWINDLE
EDIFICE
EDITION
ELISION
ELITISM
EMINENT
EMITTER
EPICURE
EPIGRAM
EPISODE
EPISTLE
EPITAPH
EPITHET
EPITOME
EVIDENT
FAIENCE
FAILING
FAILURE
FAIRING
FAIRWAY
FLICKER
FLIGHTY
FLIPPER
FLIVVER
FRIABLE
FRIGATE
FRITTER
FRIZZLE
GAINFUL
GAINSAY
GLIMMER
GLIMPSE
GLISTEN
GLISTER
GLITTER
GRIDDLE
GRIMACE
GRINDER
GRISTLE
GRIZZLY
GUILDER
HAIRCUT
HAIRPIN
HEINOUS
HEIRESS
IMITATE
INITIAL
IRIDIUM
LEISURE
MAILBOX
MAILMAN
MAINTOP
MEIOSIS
MOISTEN
NAIVETE
NAIVETY
NEITHER
NOISOME
OLIVINE
OMINOUS
OPINION
ORIFICE
ORIGAMI
OVIDUCT
OXIDANT
OXIDIZE
PAISLEY
PHILTER
PLIABLE
POINTED
POINTER
PRICKER
PRICKLE
PRIMACY
PRIMARY
PRIMATE
PRITHEE
PRIVACY
PRIVATE
QUIBBLE
QUICKEN
QUICKIE
QUIETUS
QUININE
QUINTAL
QUINTET
RAILING
RAILWAY
RAIMENT
RAINBOW
RHIZOME
ROISTER
RUINOUS
SAILING
SAINTLY
SCIENCE
SEISMIC
SHIMMER
SHINGLE
SKIFFLE
SKILLET
SKIPPER

SKITTER
SKIWEAR
SLICKER
SLIPPER
SLITHER
SMIDGEN
SNICKER
SNIFFLE
SPICULE
SPINACH
SPINDLE
SPINDLY
SPIRANT
SPITTLE
STICKER
STIFFEN
STILTED
STILTON
STIPEND
STIPPLE
STIRRUP
SUICIDE
SUITING
SWINDLE
THICKEN
THICKET
THIMBLE
THINNER
THISTLE
THITHER
TRIBUNE
TRIBUTE
TRICEPS
TRICKLE
TRIDENT
TRIGGER
TRILOGY
TRINITY
TRINKET
TRIPLET
TRIPLEX
TRIREME
TRISECT
TRITIUM
TRIUMPH
TRIVIAL
TRIVIUM
TUITION
TWIDDLE
TWILLED
TWINKLE
TWISTER
TWITTER
UNICORN
UNIFORM
UNITARY
UNITIZE

URINARY
URINATE
UTILITY
UTILIZE
VEILING
WAILFUL
WEIGHTY
WHICKER
WHIMPER
WHIPPET
WHIPSAW
WHISKER
WHISKEY
WHISPER
WHISTLE
WHITHER
WHITING
WHITISH
WHITLOW
WHITTLE
WRIGGLE
WRINGER
WRINKLE
WRITING
ADJOURN
ADJUDGE
ADJUNCT
JEJUNUM
JUJITSU
MAJESTY
PAJAMAS
PYJAMAS
REJOICE
SOJOURN
ASKANCE
AWKWARD
BIKEWAY
INKHORN
INKLING
INKWELL
IRKSOME
JUKEBOX
MAKINGS
TAKEOFF
TEKTITE
UNKEMPT
UNKNOWN
WAKEFUL
AILERON
AILMENT
ALLEGRO
ALLERGY
BALANCE
BALCONY
BALDING
BALDRIC
BALEFUL

BALLAST
BALLOON
BALONEY
BELABOR
BELATED
BELGIAN
BELIEVE
BELLBOY
BELLHOP
BELLOWS
BELOVED
BELTWAY
BILIOUS
BILLION
BOLIVAR
BOLOGNA
BOLSTER
BULLDOG
BULLION
BULLOCK
BULRUSH
BULWARK
CALCIFY
CALCINE
CALCITE
CALCIUM
CALDERA
CALDRON
CALENDS
CALIBER
CALIPER
CALLING
CALLOUS
CALOMEL
CALORIC
CALORIE
CALUMET
CALUMNY
CALYPSO
CELESTA
CELSIUS
CILIATE
COLLAGE
COLLARD
COLLATE
COLLECT
COLLEEN
COLLEGE
COLLIDE
COLLIER
COLLOID
COLOGNE
COLONEL
COLORED
CULOTTE
CULPRIT
CULTURE

CULVERT
DELIGHT
DELIMIT
DELIVER
DELOUSE
DILEMMA
DILUENT
DOLEFUL
DOLPHIN
DULLARD
ECLIPSE
ECLOGUE
ELLIPSE
ENLARGE
ENLIVEN
FALLACY
FALLOUT
FALSIFY
FILBERT
FILLING
FILMDOM
FOLDOUT
FOLIAGE
FOLKWAY
FULCRUM
FULFILL
FULSOME
GALLANT
GALLEON
GALLERY
GALLIUM
GALLOWS
GELATIN
GELDING
HALBERD
HALCYON
HALFWAY
HALIBUT
HALLWAY
HALTING
HALVERS
HALYARD
HELICAL
HELLCAT
HELLENE
HELLION
HELPING
HILLOCK
HILLTOP
HOLDING
HOLIDAY
HOLMIUM
HOLSTER
HULKING
ILLEGAL
ILLICIT
ILLNESS

JOLLITY
KILLING
KILLJOY
KILOTON
LULLABY
MALAISE
MALARIA
MALEFIC
MALISON
MALLARD
MALLEUS
MALMSEY
MALTOSE
MELANGE
MELANIC
MELANIN
MILEAGE
MILITIA
MILKMAN
MILKSOP
MILLAGE
MILLDAM
MILLIME
MILLING
MILLION
MOLDING
MOLLIFY
MOLLUSK
MULATTO
MULLEIN
MULLION
NULLIFY
OBLIQUE
OBLOQUY
OILSKIN
PALADIN
PALAVER
PALETTE
PALFREY
PALMATE
PALPATE
PELAGIC
PELICAN
PILGRIM
PILLAGE
PILLBOX
PILLION
PILLORY
PILSNER
POLARIS
POLECAT
POLEMIC
POLITIC
POLLACK
POLLUTE
POLYGON
POLYMER

PULLMAN
PULLOUT
PULSATE
RELAPSE
RELATED
RELATOR
RELEASE
RELIEVE
RELIQUE
ROLLICK
SALIENT
SALTBOX
SALTINE
SALVAGE
SELFISH
SELTZER
SELVAGE
SILENCE
SILICON
SOLARIS
SOLDIER
SOLICIT
SOLUBLE
SOLVENT
SPLENIC
SPLOTCH
SPLURGE
SULFATE
SULFIDE
SULTANA
TALLYHO
TELLING
TILLAGE
TOLUENE
UNLATCH
UNLEARN
UNLEASH
UNLOOSE
UNLUCKY
VALANCE
VALENCE
VALIANT
VALUATE
VILLAGE
VILLAIN
VILLEIN
VILLOUS
VOLCANO
VOLTAGE
VOLTAIC
VOLUBLE
VULGATE
VULPINE
VULTURE
WALKOUT
WALKWAY
WALLABY

WALLEYE
WALLOON
WELCOME
WELFARE
WILDCAT
WILLFUL
WILLIES
WILLING
WILLOWY
WOLFRAM
ZILLION
ADMIRAL
AIMLESS
ALMANAC
ALMONER
AMMETER
AMMONIA
ARMHOLE
ARMORER
ARMREST
BIMETAL
BOMBARD
BOMBAST
BUMPKIN
CAMBIUM
CAMBRIC
CAMPHOR
CEMBALO
COMBINE
COMFORT
COMMAND
COMMEND
COMMENT
COMMODE
COMMUNE
COMMUTE
COMPACT
COMPANY
COMPARE
COMPASS
COMPEER
COMPETE
COMPILE
COMPLEX
COMPORT
COMPOSE
COMPOST
COMPOTE
COMPUTE
COMRADE
CUMULUS
DEMERIT
DEMESNE
DEMIGOD
DEMONIC
DEMOTIC
DOMINIE

DUMPING
GAMBIAN
GIMMICK
GUMBOIL
GUMDROP
GUMSHOE
HAMMOCK
HAMSTER
HEMLINE
HEMLOCK
HIMSELF
HOMBURG
HOMONYM
HUMDRUM
HUMERUS
HUMIDOR
HUMMOCK
HYMNODY
IMMENSE
IMMERSE
IMMORAL
KUMQUAT
LAMBENT
LAMINAR
LAMPOON
LAMPREY
LEMMING
LEMPIRA
LIMBECK
LIMEADE
LIMITED
LUMBAGO
MAMMARY
MAMMOTH
MEMENTO
MIMESIS
MIMETIC
MIMICRY
NEMESIS
NOMADIC
NOMINAL
NOMINEE
NUMERAL
NUMERIC
OSMOSIS
PIMENTO
POMPANO
POMPOUS
PUMPKIN
RAMBLER
RAMPAGE
RAMPANT
RAMPART
REMAINS
REMNANT
REMODEL
REMORSE

REMOUNT
ROMANCE
RUMMAGE
SAMOVAR
SAMPLER
SAMURAI
SEMINAL
SEMINAR
SIMILAR
SOMEDAY
SOMEHOW
SOMEONE
SUMMARY
SUMMONS
SYMPTOM
TAMBALA
TEMPERA
TEMPEST
TIMBREL
TIMOTHY
TIMPANI
TUMBLER
TUMBREL
UNMANLY
UNMORAL
UNMOVED
VAMOOSE
VAMPIRE
WOMANLY
ZAMBIAN
ZYMURGY
AMNESIA
AMNESTY
ANNUITY
ANNULAR
BANDAGE
BANDBOX
BANNOCK
BANQUET
BANSHEE
BENEATH
BENEFIT
BENISON
BENTHIC
BENTHOS
BENZENE
BENZINE
BENZOIN
BINDING
BONANZA
BONDAGE
BONDMAN
BONFIRE
BUNTING
CANASTA
CANDIED
CANNERY

CANNULA
CANTATA
CANTEEN
CANVASS
CENSURE
CENTARE
CENTAUR
CENTAVO
CENTIME
CENTIMO
CENTRAL
CENTURY
CONCAVE
CONCEAL
CONCEDE
CONCEIT
CONCEPT
CONCERN
CONCERT
CONCISE
CONCOCT
CONCORD
CONDEMN
CONDIGN
CONDOLE
CONDONE
CONDUCE
CONDUCT
CONDUIT
CONDYLE
CONFESS
CONFIDE
CONFINE
CONFIRM
CONFLUX
CONFORM
CONFUSE
CONFUTE
CONGEAL
CONGEST
CONICAL
CONIFER
CONJOIN
CONJURE
CONNECT
CONNIVE
CONNOTE
CONQUER
CONSENT
CONSIGN
CONSIST
CONSOLE
CONSORT
CONSULT
CONSUME
CONTACT
CONTAIN
CONTEMN
CONTEND
CONTENT
CONTEST
CONTEXT
CONTORT
CONTOUR
CONTRIB
CONTROL
CONVENE
CONVENT
CONVERT
CONVICT
CONVOKE
CUNNING
DANDIFY
DENIZEN
DENSITY
DENTATE
DENTIST
DENTURE
DINETTE
DUNGEON
DYNAMIC
DYNASTY
ENNOBLE
FANATIC
FANCIER
FANFARE
FANTAIL
FANTASY
FENCING
FINAGLE
FINANCE
FINDING
FINESSE
FINFISH
FINICKY
FINNISH
FONDANT
FUNERAL
GANGWAY
GANTLET
GENERAL
GENERIC
GENESIS
GENETIC
GENITAL
GENTEEL
GENTIAN
GENTILE
GENUINE
GINGHAM
GINSENG
GONDOLA
GUNBOAT
GUNFIRE
GUNLOCK
GUNNERY
GUNSHOT
GUNWALE
HANDBAG
HANDCAR
HANDFUL
HANDGUN
HANDOUT
HANDSAW
HANDSEL
HANDSET
HANGDOG
HANGING
HANGMAN
HANGOUT
HENPECK
HINTING
HUNDRED
HUNKERS
IGNEOUS
IGNOBLE
INNARDS
INNINGS
JANITOR
JANUARY
JONQUIL
JUNIPER
KINDRED
KINETIC
KINFOLK
KINGDOM
KINGPIN
KINSHIP
KINSMAN
LANDING
LANGUID
LANGUOR
LANOLIN
LANTANA
LANTERN
LANYARD
LENIENT
LINEAGE
LINEMAN
LINGUAL
LINKAGE
LINSEED
LONGBOW
LONGING
LUNATIC
LUNETTE
MANACLE
MANAGER
MANDATE
MANDREL
MANDRIL
MANHOLE
MANHOOD
MANHUNT
MANIKIN
MANKIND
MANLIKE
MANNISH
MANSARD
MANSION
MANTEAU
MANUMIT
MENFOLK
MENTHOL
MENTION
MINARET
MINDFUL
MINERAL
MINIBUS
MINIMAL
MINIMUM
MINSTER
MINUEND
MINUTIA
MONADIC
MONARCH
MONEYED
MONGREL
MONITOR
MONOCLE
MONOMER
MONSOON
MONSTER
MONTAGE
MUNDANE
NANKEEN
NONBOOK
NONHERO
NONPLUS
NONSKED
NONSTOP
NONUSER
OMNIBUS
PANACEA
PANACHE
PANCAKE
PANICLE
PANNIER
PANOPLY
PANTHER
PENALTY
PENANCE
PENATES
PENDANT
PENDENT
PENDING
PENGUIN
PENNANT
PENSION
PENSIVE
PENTIUM
PINHOLE
PINKEYE
PINNACE
PINNATE
PINWORM
PONIARD
PONTIFF
PONTOON
PUNGENT
PUNSTER
RANKING
RANSACK
RENEWAL
RINGLET
RUNAWAY
RUNDOWN
RUNNING
SANCTUM
SANDBAG
SANDBAR
SANDHOG
SANDLOT
SANDMAN
SENATOR
SENSORY
SENSUAL
SENTIMO
SINCERE
SINUOUS
SUNBATH
SUNBEAM
SUNBURN
SUNDIAL
SUNDOWN
SUNFISH
SUNLAMP
SUNRISE
SUNROOF
SUNSPOT
SYNAPSE
SYNCOPE
SYNONYM
TANAGER
TANBARK
TANGENT
TANNERY
TANTRUM
TENABLE
TENANCY
TENDRIL
TENFOLD
TENSILE
TENSION
TENUOUS
TENURED
TINFOIL
TINWARE
TONIGHT
TONNAGE
TONNEAU
TONSURE
TUNABLE
TUNEFUL
UNNERVE
VANDYKE
VANILLA
VANTAGE
VANWARD
VENISON
VENTRAL
VENTURE
VINEGAR
VINTAGE
VINTNER
WANTING
WINDAGE
WINDBAG
WINDING
WINDOWS
WINDROW
WINNING
WINSOME
ABOLISH
ACOLYTE
ACONITE
AGONIZE
AMOROUS
ANODIZE
ANODYNE
ANOMALY
ANOTHER
APOLOGY
APOLUNE
APOSTLE
ATOMIZE
AVOCADO
BIOLOGY
BIOTITE
BLOATER
BLOODED
BLOOPER
BLOSSOM
BLOTTER
BLOWGUN
BLOWOUT
BOOKEND
BOOKISH
BOOKLET
BOOTLEG
BROADEN
BROCADE
BROIDER
BROILER
BROMIDE
BROMINE
BROODER
BROTHEL
BROTHER
BROUGHT
BROWNIE
BROWSER
CHOCTAW
CHOLERA
CHOPPER
CHORALE
CHORTLE
CHOWDER
CLOBBER
CLOSURE
CLOTHES
CLOTURE
COOKERY
COOKOUT
COOLANT
CROCHET
CROOKED
CROPPER
CROQUET
CROSIER
CROUTON
CROWBAR
DIOCESE
DOORMAN
DOORMAT
DOORWAY
DROPLET
DROPPER
DROUGHT
EBONITE
ECOLOGY
ECONOMY
EGOTISM
EMOTION
EROSION
EROSIVE
FLORIST
FLOTSAM
FLOUNCE
FLOWERY
FOOLERY
FOOLISH
FOOTAGE
FOOTING
FOOTMAN
FOOTPAD
FROGMAN
FROWARD
GEODESY
GEOLOGY
GLOBULE
GLORIFY
GLOTTIS
GOODMAN
GROMMET
GROUPER
GROUPIE
HOODLUM
HOOSIER
IDOLIZE
IRONING
ISOLATE
ISOTOPE
KNOCKER
KNOWING
LAOTIAN
LEONINE
LEOPARD
LEOTARD
LIONIZE
LOOKOUT
MOORING
NEOLOGY
NIOBIUM
NOONDAY
OPOSSUM
OROGENY
OROTUND
PHOENIX
PHONEME
PHONICS
PIONEER
PLOTTER
PLOWBOY
PLOWMAN
PROBATE
PROBITY
PROBLEM
PROCEED
PROCESS
PROCTOR
PROCURE
PRODIGY
PRODUCE
PRODUCT
PROFANE
PROFESS
PROFFER
PROFILE
PROFUSE
PROGENY
PROGMAN
PROGRAM
PROJECT
PROLONG
PROMISE
PROMOTE
PRONOUN
PROPANE
PROPHET
PROPMAN
PROPOSE
PRORATE
PROSAIC
PROSODY
PROSPER
PROTEAN
PROTECT
PROTEGE
PROTEIN
PROTEST
PROVERB
PROVIDE
PROVISO
PROVOKE
PROVOST
PROWESS
PROXIMO
QUONDAM
RHODIUM
RHOMBUS
ROOFTOP
ROOKERY
ROOSTER
ROOTLET
SCOOTER
SCOURGE
SHOCKER
SHORING
SHORTEN
SHORTLY
SHOTGUN
SHOWMAN
SLOBBER
SMOLDER
SMOTHER
SNORKEL
SPOILER
SPONSOR
SPOTTER
SPOUSAL
STOMACH
STOPGAP
STOPPER
STORAGE
STORIED
SWOLLEN
THORIUM
THOUGHT
TOOLBOX
TROCHEE
TRODDEN
TROLLEY

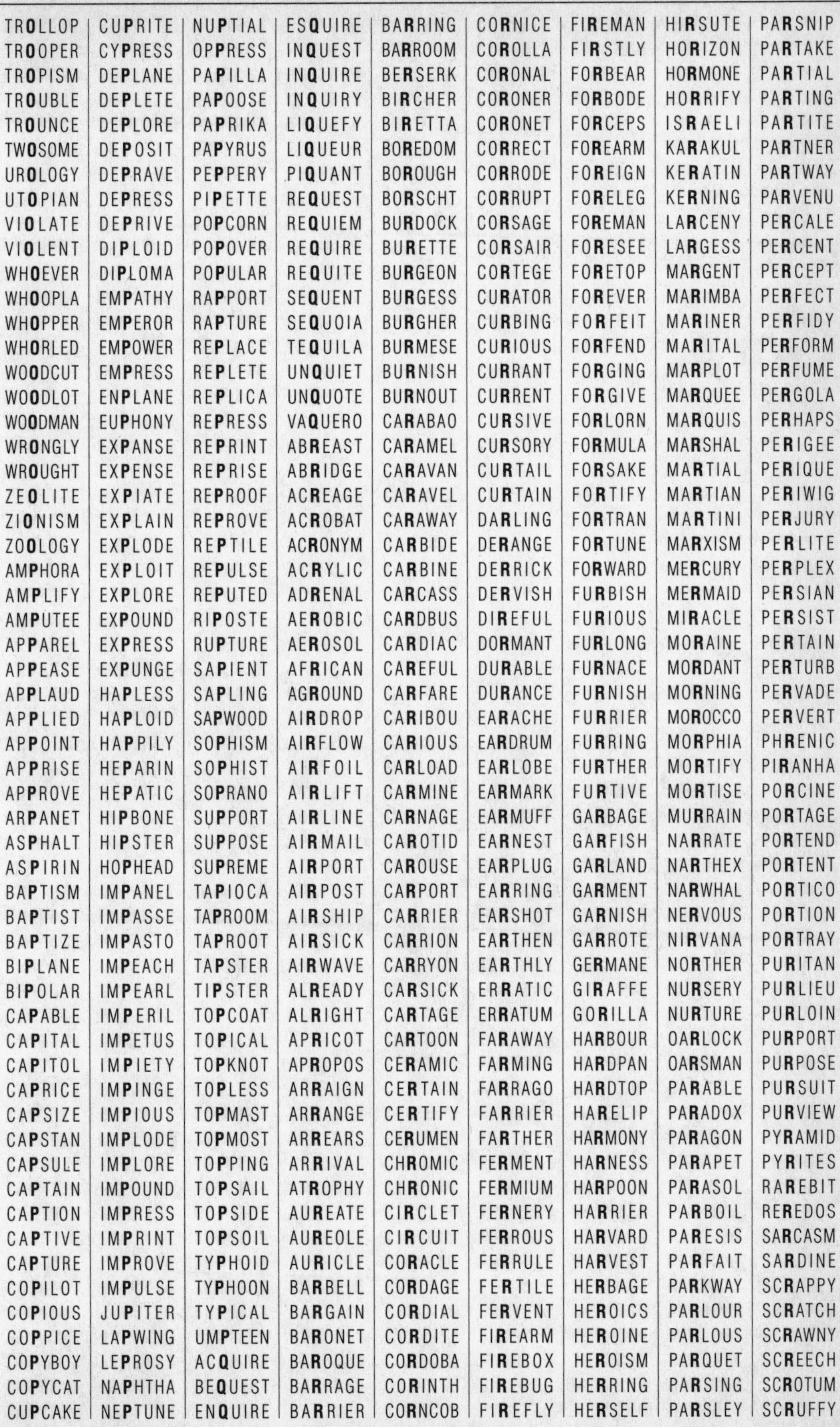

TROLLOP
TROOPER
TROPISM
TROUBLE
TROUNCE
TWOSOME
UROLOGY
UTOPIAN
VIOLATE
VIOLENT
WHOEVER
WHOOPLA
WHOPPER
WHORLED
WOODCUT
WOODLOT
WOODMAN
WRONGLY
WROUGHT
ZEOLITE
ZIONISM
ZOOLOGY
AMPHORA
AMPLIFY
AMPUTEE
APPAREL
APPEASE
APPLAUD
APPLIED
APPOINT
APPRISE
APPROVE
ARPANET
ASPHALT
ASPIRIN
BAPTISM
BAPTIST
BAPTIZE
BIPLANE
BIPOLAR
CAPABLE
CAPITAL
CAPITOL
CAPRICE
CAPSIZE
CAPSTAN
CAPSULE
CAPTAIN
CAPTION
CAPTIVE
CAPTURE
COPILOT
COPIOUS
COPPICE
COPYBOY
COPYCAT
CUPCAKE
CUPRITE
CYPRESS
DEPLANE
DEPLETE
DEPLORE
DEPOSIT
DEPRAVE
DEPRESS
DEPRIVE
DIPLOID
DIPLOMA
EMPATHY
EMPEROR
EMPOWER
EMPRESS
ENPLANE
EUPHONY
EXPANSE
EXPENSE
EXPIATE
EXPLAIN
EXPLODE
EXPLOIT
EXPLORE
EXPOUND
EXPRESS
EXPUNGE
HAPLESS
HAPLOID
HAPPILY
HEPARIN
HEPATIC
HIPBONE
HIPSTER
HOPHEAD
IMPANEL
IMPASSE
IMPASTO
IMPEACH
IMPEARL
IMPERIL
IMPETUS
IMPIETY
IMPINGE
IMPIOUS
IMPLODE
IMPLORE
IMPOUND
IMPRESS
IMPRINT
IMPROVE
IMPULSE
JUPITER
LAPWING
LEPROSY
NAPHTHA
NEPTUNE
NUPTIAL
OPPRESS
PAPILLA
PAPOOSE
PAPRIKA
PAPYRUS
PEPPERY
PIPETTE
POPCORN
POPOVER
POPULAR
RAPPORT
RAPTURE
REPLACE
REPLETE
REPLICA
REPRESS
REPRINT
REPRISE
REPROOF
REPROVE
REPTILE
REPULSE
REPUTED
RIPOSTE
RUPTURE
SAPIENT
SAPLING
SAPWOOD
SOPHISM
SOPHIST
SOPRANO
SUPPORT
SUPPOSE
SUPREME
TAPIOCA
TAPROOM
TAPROOT
TAPSTER
TIPSTER
TOPCOAT
TOPICAL
TOPKNOT
TOPLESS
TOPMAST
TOPMOST
TOPPING
TOPSAIL
TOPSIDE
TOPSOIL
TYPHOID
TYPHOON
TYPICAL
UMPTEEN
ACQUIRE
BEQUEST
ENQUIRE
ESQUIRE
INQUEST
INQUIRE
INQUIRY
LIQUEFY
LIQUEUR
PIQUANT
REQUEST
REQUIEM
REQUIRE
REQUITE
SEQUENT
SEQUOIA
TEQUILA
UNQUIET
UNQUOTE
VAQUERO
ABREAST
ABRIDGE
ACREAGE
ACROBAT
ACRONYM
ACRYLIC
ADRENAL
AEROBIC
AEROSOL
AFRICAN
AGROUND
AIRDROP
AIRFLOW
AIRFOIL
AIRLIFT
AIRLINE
AIRMAIL
AIRPORT
AIRPOST
AIRSHIP
AIRSICK
AIRWAVE
ALREADY
ALRIGHT
APRICOT
APROPOS
ARRAIGN
ARRANGE
ARREARS
ARRIVAL
ATROPHY
AUREATE
AUREOLE
AURICLE
BARBELL
BARGAIN
BARONET
BAROQUE
BARRAGE
BARRIER
BARRING
BARROOM
BERSERK
BIRCHER
BIRETTA
BOREDOM
BOROUGH
BORSCHT
BURDOCK
BURETTE
BURGEON
BURGESS
BURGHER
BURMESE
BURNISH
BURNOUT
CARABAO
CARAMEL
CARAVAN
CARAVEL
CARAWAY
CARBIDE
CARBINE
CARCASS
CARDBUS
CARDIAC
CAREFUL
CARFARE
CARIBOU
CARIOUS
CARLOAD
CARMINE
CARNAGE
CAROTID
CAROUSE
CARPORT
CARRIER
CARRION
CARRYON
CARSICK
CARTAGE
CARTOON
CERAMIC
CERTAIN
CERTIFY
CERUMEN
CHROMIC
CHRONIC
CIRCLET
CIRCUIT
CORACLE
CORDAGE
CORDIAL
CORDITE
CORDOBA
CORINTH
CORNCOB
CORNICE
COROLLA
CORONAL
CORONER
CORONET
CORRECT
CORRODE
CORRUPT
CORSAGE
CORSAIR
CORTEGE
CURATOR
CURBING
CURIOUS
CURRANT
CURRENT
CURSIVE
CURSORY
CURTAIL
CURTAIN
DARLING
DERANGE
DERRICK
DERVISH
DIREFUL
DORMANT
DURABLE
DURANCE
EARACHE
EARDRUM
EARLOBE
EARMARK
EARMUFF
EARNEST
EARPLUG
EARRING
EARSHOT
EARTHEN
EARTHLY
ERRATIC
ERRATUM
FARAWAY
FARMING
FARRAGO
FARRIER
FARTHER
FERMENT
FERMIUM
FERNERY
FERROUS
FERRULE
FERTILE
FERVENT
FIREARM
FIREBOX
FIREBUG
FIREFLY
FIREMAN
FIRSTLY
FORBEAR
FORBODE
FORCEPS
FOREARM
FOREIGN
FORELEG
FOREMAN
FORESEE
FORETOP
FOREVER
FORFEIT
FORFEND
FORGING
FORGIVE
FORLORN
FORMULA
FORSAKE
FORTIFY
FORTRAN
FORTUNE
FORWARD
FURBISH
FURIOUS
FURLONG
FURNACE
FURNISH
FURRIER
FURRING
FURTHER
FURTIVE
GARBAGE
GARFISH
GARLAND
GARMENT
GARNISH
GARROTE
GERMANE
GIRAFFE
GORILLA
HARBOUR
HARDPAN
HARDTOP
HARELIP
HARMONY
HARNESS
HARPOON
HARRIER
HARVARD
HARVEST
HERBAGE
HEROICS
HEROINE
HEROISM
HERRING
HERSELF
HIRSUTE
HORIZON
HORMONE
HORRIFY
ISRAELI
KARAKUL
KERATIN
KERNING
LARCENY
LARGESS
MARGENT
MARIMBA
MARINER
MARITAL
MARPLOT
MARQUEE
MARQUIS
MARSHAL
MARTIAL
MARTIAN
MARTINI
MARXISM
MERCURY
MERMAID
MIRACLE
MORAINE
MORDANT
MORNING
MOROCCO
MORPHIA
MORTIFY
MORTISE
MURRAIN
NARRATE
NARTHEX
NARWHAL
NERVOUS
NIRVANA
NORTHER
NURSERY
NURTURE
OARLOCK
OARSMAN
PARABLE
PARADOX
PARAGON
PARAPET
PARASOL
PARBOIL
PARESIS
PARFAIT
PARKWAY
PARLOUR
PARLOUS
PARQUET
PARSING
PARSLEY
PARSNIP
PARTAKE
PARTIAL
PARTING
PARTITE
PARTNER
PARTWAY
PARVENU
PERCALE
PERCENT
PERCEPT
PERFECT
PERFIDY
PERFORM
PERFUME
PERGOLA
PERHAPS
PERIGEE
PERIQUE
PERIWIG
PERJURY
PERLITE
PERPLEX
PERSIAN
PERSIST
PERTAIN
PERTURB
PERVADE
PERVERT
PHRENIC
PIRANHA
PORCINE
PORTAGE
PORTEND
PORTENT
PORTICO
PORTION
PORTRAY
PURITAN
PURLIEU
PURLOIN
PURPORT
PURPOSE
PURSUIT
PURVIEW
PYRAMID
PYRITES
RAREBIT
REREDOS
SARCASM
SARDINE
SCRAPPY
SCRATCH
SCRAWNY
SCREECH
SCROTUM
SCRUFFY

SCRUPLE
SERIOUS
SERPENT
SERRATE
SERRIED
SERVANT
SERVICE
SERVILE
SERVING
SHRIVEL
SIRLOIN
SIROCCO
SORCERY
SORGHUM
STRANGE
STRATUM
STRETCH
STRINGY
STROPHE
STRUDEL
SURFACE
SURFEIT
SURGEON
SURGERY
SURMISE
SURNAME
SURPASS
SURPLUS
SURTOUT
SURVIVE
SYRINGE
TARNISH
TERBIUM
TERMITE
TERNARY
TERRACE
TERRAIN
TERRIER
TERRIFY
THREADY
THROATY
THROUGH
THRUWAY
TORMENT
TORNADO
TORPEDO
TORRENT
TORSION
TORTONI
TORTURE
TURBINE
TURKISH
TURMOIL
TURNERY
TURNING
TURNKEY
TURNOFF
TURNOUT
TYRANNY
UNRAVEL
UPRAISE
UPRIGHT
UPRIVER
VARIANT
VARIETY
VARIOUS
VARMINT
VARNISH
VARSITY
VERANDA
VERBENA
VERBOSE
VERDANT
VERDICT
VERDURE
VERMEIL
VERNIER
VERSIFY
VERSION
VERTIGO
VERVAIN
VIRGULE
VIRTUAL
WARBLER
WARFARE
WARHEAD
WARLESS
WARLIKE
WARLOCK
WARLORD
WARNING
WARPATH
WARRANT
WARRIOR
WARSHIP
WARTHOG
WARTIME
WIRETAP
WORDAGE
WORDING
WORKBAG
WORKBOX
WORKDAY
WORKING
WORKMAN
WORKOUT
WORLDLY
WORSHIP
WORSTED
YARDAGE
YARDARM
YARDMAN
ABSCESS
ABSCOND
ABSENCE
ABSOLVE
ABSTAIN
ARSENAL
ARSENIC
ASSAULT
ASSUAGE
ASSURED
AUSPICE
AUSTERE
AUSTRAL
BASHFUL
BASSOON
BASTARD
BASTION
BESEECH
BESHREW
BESIDES
BESIEGE
BESMEAR
BESPEAK
BESTIAL
BISCUIT
BISMUTH
BUSHING
CASCADE
CASCARA
CASHIER
CASSAVA
CASSOCK
CASTING
CASTLED
CESSION
CISTERN
COSSACK
COSTIVE
COSTUME
CUSHION
CUSTARD
CUSTODY
DASHIKI
DASHING
DASHPOT
DASTARD
DESCANT
DESCEND
DESCENT
DESERVE
DESKTOP
DESPAIR
DESPISE
DESPITE
DESPOIL
DESPOND
DESSERT
DESTINE
DESTINY
DESTROY
DISABLE
DISAVOW
DISBAND
DISCARD
DISCERN
DISCORD
DISCUSS
DISDAIN
DISEASE
DISEUSE
DISGUST
DISHRAG
DISJOIN
DISLIKE
DISMISS
DISOBEY
DISPLAY
DISPORT
DISPOSE
DISPUTE
DISROBE
DISRUPT
DISSECT
DISSENT
DISTAFF
DISTANT
DISTEND
DISTICH
DISTILL
DISTORT
DISTURB
DOSSIER
DUSTPAN
EASTERN
ECSTASY
ENSLAVE
ENSNARE
ESSENCE
FASCISM
FASHION
FESTIVE
FESTOON
FISHERY
FISHING
FISSILE
FISSION
FISSURE
FISTFUL
FISTULA
FUSTIAN
GASTRIC
GESTAPO
GESTURE
GOSHAWK
GOSLING
HASHING
HASHISH
HASSOCK
HISTORY
HOSANNA
HOSIERY
HOSPICE
HOSTAGE
HOSTESS
HOSTILE
HOSTLER
HUSBAND
HUSKING
INSHORE
INSIDER
INSIGHT
INSIPID
INSPECT
INSPIRE
INSTALL
INSTANT
INSTATE
INSTEAD
INSTILL
INSULAR
INSULIN
INSURED
INSURER
JASMINE
JUSTICE
JUSTIFY
LASAGNA
LESBIAN
LISSOME
LISTING
LUSTRAL
MASCARA
MASONIC
MASONRY
MASSAGE
MASSEUR
MASSIVE
MASTERY
MASTIFF
MASTOID
MESSAGE
MESSIAH
MESTIZO
MISCALL
MISDEED
MISFILE
MISFIRE
MISLEAD
MISLIKE
MISNAME
MISPLAY
MISREAD
MISRULE
MISSEND
MISSILE
MISSING
MISSION
MISSIVE
MISSTEP
MISTAKE
MISTRAL
MUSETTE
MUSICAL
MUSKRAT
MUSTANG
MUSTARD
MYSTERY
MYSTIFY
NASCENT
NOSEGAY
NOSTRIL
NOSTRUM
OBSCENE
OBSCURE
OBSEQUY
OBSERVE
ONSHORE
OSSUARY
PASSAGE
PASSING
PASSION
PASSIVE
PASSKEY
PASTERN
PASTIME
PASTURE
PISMIRE
POSSESS
POSTAGE
POSTBOY
POSTERN
POSTMAN
POSTURE
POSTWAR
PUSTULE
RESCIND
RESEDIT
RESERVE
RESIDUE
RESOLVE
RESOUND
RESPECT
RESPITE
RESPOND
RESTIVE
RESTORE
RISIBLE
ROSEATE
ROSEBUD
ROSETTE
ROSTRUM
RUSSIAN
SESSILE
SESSION
SUSPECT
SUSPEND
SUSTAIN
SYSTOLE
TESTATE
TESTIFY
TUSSOCK
UNSAVED
UNSCREW
UNSLING
UNSNARL
UNSOUND
UNSTRAP
UPSHIFT
UPSTAGE
UPSTART
UPSTATE
UPSURGE
UPSWEPT
UPSWING
VESICLE
VESPERS
VESTIGE
VESTING
VESTURE
VISCERA
VISCOSE
VISCOUS
VISIBLE
VISITOR
WASHING
WASHOUT
WASHTUB
WASPISH
WASSAIL
WASTAGE
WASTREL
WESTERN
WISHFUL
WISTFUL
WYSIWYG
YESHIVA
ACTUARY
ACTUATE
ANTACID
ANTENNA
ANTHILL
ANTHRAX
ANTHROP
ANTIGEN
ANTIQUE
ANTONYM
ARTICLE
ARTISAN
ARTISTE
ARTLESS
ASTOUND
ASTRIDE
ATTACHE
ATTAINT
ATTEMPT
ATTRACT
AUTOPSY
BATHTUB
BATISTE
BATSMAN
BATTERY
BATTING
BETHINK
BETIMES
BETOKEN
BETROTH
BETWEEN
BETWIXT
BITTERN
BITTERS
BITUMEN
BUTCHER
BUTTOCK
CATALOG
CATALPA
CATARRH
CATBIRD
CATBOAT
CATCALL
CATCHER
CATCHUP
CATFISH
CATHODE
CATLIKE
CATTAIL
CATWALK
CITADEL
CITIZEN
COTERIE
COTTAGE
CUTBACK
CUTICLE
CUTLASS
CUTLERY
CUTTING
CUTWORM
DETENTE
DETRACT
DETRAIN
DUTEOUS
DUTIFUL
ENTENTE
ENTHUSE
ENTITLE
ENTRAIN
ENTRANT
ENTREAT
ENTROPY
ENTRUST
ENTWINE
ESTHETE
ESTUARY
EXTINCT
EXTRACT
EXTREME
EXTRUDE
FATBACK
FATEFUL
FATIGUE
FATUITY
FATUOUS
FETLOCK
FITTING
GATEWAY
GETAWAY
HATCHET
HOTCAKE
HOTFOOT
HOTSHOT
HUTMENT
INTEGER
INTENSE
INTERIM
INTRANS
INTROIT
INTRUDE
INTRUST
ISTHMUS
JETPORT
JITTERS
JOTTING
KATYDID
KETCHUP
KITCHEN
LATAKIA
LATCHET
LATERAL
LATRINE
LATTICE
LATVIAN
LETDOWN
LETTUCE
LITERAL
LITHIUM
LITURGY
LOTTERY
MATADOR
MATINEE
MATTINS
MATTOCK
METHANE

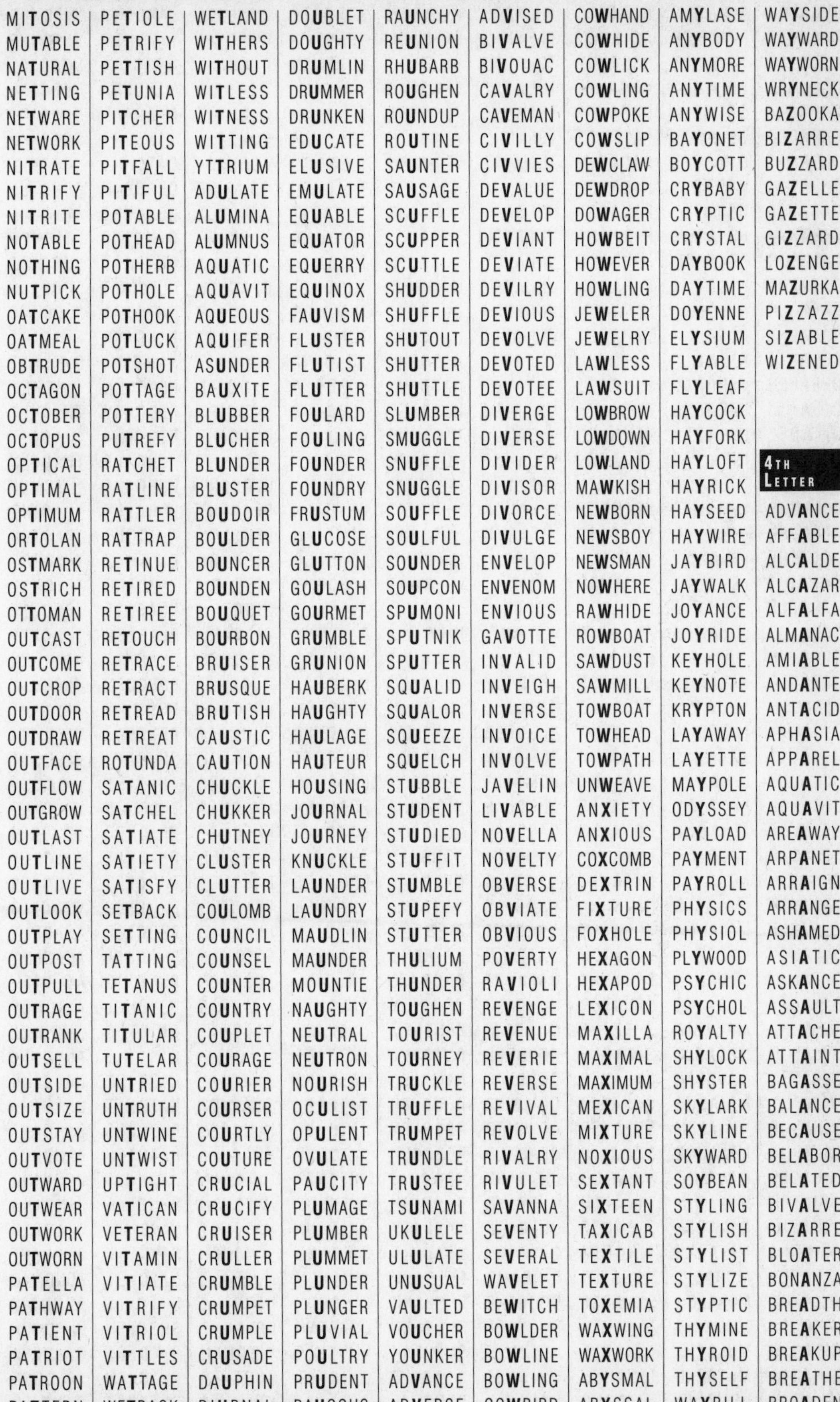

MITOSIS
MUTABLE
NATURAL
NETTING
NETWARE
NETWORK
NITRATE
NITRIFY
NITRITE
NOTABLE
NOTHING
NUTPICK
OATCAKE
OATMEAL
OBTRUDE
OCTAGON
OCTOBER
OCTOPUS
OPTICAL
OPTIMAL
OPTIMUM
ORTOLAN
OSTMARK
OSTRICH
OTTOMAN
OUTCAST
OUTCOME
OUTCROP
OUTDOOR
OUTDRAW
OUTFACE
OUTFLOW
OUTGROW
OUTLAST
OUTLINE
OUTLIVE
OUTLOOK
OUTPLAY
OUTPOST
OUTPULL
OUTRAGE
OUTRANK
OUTSELL
OUTSIDE
OUTSIZE
OUTSTAY
OUTVOTE
OUTWARD
OUTWEAR
OUTWORK
OUTWORN
PATELLA
PATHWAY
PATIENT
PATRIOT
PATROON
PATTERN
PETIOLE
PETRIFY
PETTISH
PETUNIA
PITCHER
PITEOUS
PITFALL
PITIFUL
POTABLE
POTHEAD
POTHERB
POTHOLE
POTHOOK
POTLUCK
POTSHOT
POTTAGE
POTTERY
PUTREFY
RATCHET
RATLINE
RATTLER
RATTRAP
RETINUE
RETIRED
RETIREE
RETOUCH
RETRACE
RETRACT
RETREAD
RETREAT
ROTUNDA
SATANIC
SATCHEL
SATIATE
SATIETY
SATISFY
SETBACK
SETTING
TATTING
TETANUS
TITANIC
TITULAR
TUTELAR
UNTRIED
UNTRUTH
UNTWINE
UNTWIST
UPTIGHT
VATICAN
VETERAN
VITAMIN
VITIATE
VITRIFY
VITRIOL
VITTLES
WATTAGE
WETBACK
WETLAND
WITHERS
WITHOUT
WITLESS
WITNESS
WITTING
YTTRIUM
ADULATE
ALUMINA
ALUMNUS
AQUATIC
AQUAVIT
AQUEOUS
AQUIFER
ASUNDER
BAUXITE
BLUBBER
BLUCHER
BLUNDER
BLUSTER
BOUDOIR
BOULDER
BOUNCER
BOUNDEN
BOUQUET
BOURBON
BRUISER
BRUSQUE
BRUTISH
CAUSTIC
CAUTION
CHUCKLE
CHUKKER
CHUTNEY
CLUSTER
CLUTTER
COULOMB
COUNCIL
COUNSEL
COUNTER
COUNTRY
COUPLET
COURAGE
COURIER
COURSER
COURTLY
COUTURE
CRUCIAL
CRUCIFY
CRUISER
CRULLER
CRUMBLE
CRUMPET
CRUMPLE
CRUSADE
DAUPHIN
DIURNAL
DOUBLET
DOUGHTY
DRUMLIN
DRUMMER
DRUNKEN
EDUCATE
ELUSIVE
EMULATE
EQUABLE
EQUATOR
EQUERRY
EQUINOX
FAUVISM
FLUSTER
FLUTIST
FLUTTER
FOULARD
FOULING
FOUNDER
FOUNDRY
FRUSTUM
GLUCOSE
GLUTTON
GOULASH
GOURMET
GRUMBLE
GRUNION
HAUBERK
HAUGHTY
HAULAGE
HAUTEUR
HOUSING
JOURNAL
JOURNEY
KNUCKLE
LAUNDER
LAUNDRY
MAUDLIN
MAUNDER
MOUNTIE
NAUGHTY
NEUTRAL
NEUTRON
NOURISH
OCULIST
OPULENT
OVULATE
PAUCITY
PLUMAGE
PLUMBER
PLUMMET
PLUNDER
PLUNGER
PLUVIAL
POULTRY
PRUDENT
RAUCOUS
RAUNCHY
REUNION
RHUBARB
ROUGHEN
ROUNDUP
ROUTINE
SAUNTER
SAUSAGE
SCUFFLE
SCUPPER
SCUTTLE
SHUDDER
SHUFFLE
SHUTOUT
SHUTTER
SHUTTLE
SLUMBER
SMUGGLE
SNUFFLE
SNUGGLE
SOUFFLE
SOULFUL
SOUNDER
SOUPCON
SPUMONI
SPUTNIK
SPUTTER
SQUALID
SQUALOR
SQUEEZE
SQUELCH
STUBBLE
STUDENT
STUDIED
STUFFIT
STUMBLE
STUPEFY
STUTTER
THULIUM
THUNDER
TOUGHEN
TOURIST
TOURNEY
TRUCKLE
TRUFFLE
TRUMPET
TRUNDLE
TRUSTEE
TSUNAMI
UKULELE
ULULATE
UNUSUAL
VAULTED
VOUCHER
YOUNKER
ADVANCE
ADVERSE
ADVISED
BIVALVE
BIVOUAC
CAVALRY
CAVEMAN
CIVILLY
CIVVIES
DEVALUE
DEVELOP
DEVIANT
DEVIATE
DEVILRY
DEVIOUS
DEVOLVE
DEVOTED
DEVOTEE
DIVERGE
DIVERSE
DIVIDER
DIVISOR
DIVORCE
DIVULGE
ENVELOP
ENVENOM
ENVIOUS
GAVOTTE
INVALID
INVEIGH
INVERSE
INVOICE
INVOLVE
JAVELIN
LIVABLE
NOVELLA
NOVELTY
OBVERSE
OBVIATE
OBVIOUS
POVERTY
RAVIOLI
REVENGE
REVENUE
REVERIE
REVERSE
REVIVAL
REVOLVE
RIVALRY
RIVULET
SAVANNA
SEVENTY
SEVERAL
WAVELET
BEWITCH
BOWLDER
BOWLINE
BOWLING
COWBIRD
COWHAND
COWHIDE
COWLICK
COWLING
COWPOKE
COWSLIP
DEWCLAW
DEWDROP
DOWAGER
HOWBEIT
HOWEVER
HOWLING
JEWELER
JEWELRY
LAWLESS
LAWSUIT
LOWBROW
LOWDOWN
LOWLAND
MAWKISH
NEWBORN
NEWSBOY
NEWSMAN
NOWHERE
RAWHIDE
ROWBOAT
SAWDUST
SAWMILL
TOWBOAT
TOWHEAD
TOWPATH
UNWEAVE
ANXIETY
ANXIOUS
COXCOMB
DEXTRIN
FIXTURE
FOXHOLE
HEXAGON
HEXAPOD
LEXICON
MAXILLA
MAXIMAL
MAXIMUM
MEXICAN
MIXTURE
NOXIOUS
SEXTANT
SIXTEEN
TAXICAB
TEXTILE
TEXTURE
TOXEMIA
WAXWING
WAXWORK
ABYSMAL
ABYSSAL
AMYLASE
ANYBODY
ANYMORE
ANYTIME
ANYWISE
BAYONET
BOYCOTT
CRYBABY
CRYPTIC
CRYSTAL
DAYBOOK
DAYTIME
DOYENNE
ELYSIUM
FLYABLE
FLYLEAF
HAYCOCK
HAYFORK
HAYLOFT
HAYRICK
HAYSEED
HAYWIRE
JAYBIRD
JAYWALK
JOYANCE
JOYRIDE
KEYHOLE
KEYNOTE
KRYPTON
LAYAWAY
LAYETTE
MAYPOLE
ODYSSEY
PAYLOAD
PAYMENT
PAYROLL
PHYSICS
PHYSIOL
PLYWOOD
PSYCHIC
PSYCHOL
ROYALTY
SHYLOCK
SHYSTER
SKYLARK
SKYLINE
SKYWARD
SOYBEAN
STYLING
STYLISH
STYLIST
STYLIZE
STYPTIC
THYMINE
THYROID
THYSELF
WAYBILL
WAYSIDE
WAYWARD
WAYWORN
WRYNECK
BAZOOKA
BIZARRE
BUZZARD
GAZELLE
GAZETTE
GIZZARD
LOZENGE
MAZURKA
PIZZAZZ
SIZABLE
WIZENED

## 4TH LETTER

ADVANCE
AFFABLE
ALCALDE
ALCAZAR
ALFALFA
ALMANAC
AMIABLE
ANDANTE
ANTACID
APHASIA
APPAREL
AQUATIC
AQUAVIT
AREAWAY
ARPANET
ARRAIGN
ARRANGE
ASHAMED
ASIATIC
ASKANCE
ASSAULT
ATTACHE
ATTAINT
BAGASSE
BALANCE
BECAUSE
BELABOR
BELATED
BIVALVE
BIZARRE
BLOATER
BONANZA
BREADTH
BREAKER
BREAKUP
BREATHE
BROADEN

BUGABOO
CABARET
CADAVER
CANASTA
CAPABLE
CARABAO
CARAMEL
CARAVAN
CARAVEL
CARAWAY
CATALOG
CATALPA
CATARRH
CAVALRY
CERAMIC
CHEAPEN
CHIANTI
CITADEL
CLEANLY
CLEANSE
CLEANUP
CLEAVER
COCAINE
COHABIT
CORACLE
CREATOR
CURATOR
DEBACLE
DEBAUCH
DECAGON
DEFAULT
DEGAUSS
DERANGE
DEVALUE
DISABLE
DISAVOW
DOWAGER
DURABLE
DURANCE
DYNAMIC
DYNASTY
EARACHE
EMBARGO
EMBASSY
EMPATHY
ENHANCE
ENLARGE
EQUABLE
EQUATOR
ERRATIC
ERRATUM
ESCAPEE
ETHANOL
EXHAUST
EXPANSE
FANATIC
FARAWAY

FINAGLE
FINANCE
FLYABLE
FRIABLE
GELATIN
GETAWAY
GIRAFFE
HEPARIN
HEPATIC
HEXAGON
HEXAPOD
HIBACHI
HIDALGO
HOSANNA
IDEALLY
IMPANEL
IMPASSE
IMPASTO
INFANCY
INFARCT
INHABIT
INHALER
INNARDS
INVALID
ISRAELI
JOYANCE
JUDAISM
KARAKUL
KERATIN
LASAGNA
LATAKIA
LAYAWAY
LEGATEE
LIVABLE
LOCATOR
LUNATIC
MACABRE
MACADAM
MACAQUE
MAHATMA
MALAISE
MALARIA
MANACLE
MANAGER
MATADOR
MEGATON
MELANGE
MELANIC
MELANIN
MINARET
MIRACLE
MONADIC
MONARCH
MORAINE
MULATTO
MUTABLE
NOMADIC

NOTABLE
OCTAGON
ORGANDY
ORGANIC
ORGANZA
PAJAMAS
PALADIN
PALAVER
PANACEA
PANACHE
PARABLE
PARADOX
PARAGON
PARAPET
PARASOL
PELAGIC
PENALTY
PENANCE
PENATES
PIRANHA
PLIABLE
POLARIS
POTABLE
PYJAMAS
PYRAMID
REGALIA
REGATTA
RELAPSE
RELATED
RELATOR
REMAINS
RIVALRY
ROMANCE
ROYALTY
RUNAWAY
SATANIC
SAVANNA
SCRAPPY
SCRATCH
SCRAWNY
SENATOR
SHEATHE
SIZABLE
SNEAKER
SOLARIS
SPEAKER
SQUALID
SQUALOR
STEALTH
STRANGE
STRATUM
SWEATER
SYNAPSE
TANAGER
TENABLE
TENANCY
TETANUS

THEATER
TITANIC
TOBACCO
TREACLE
TREADLE
TREASON
TUNABLE
TYRANNY
UNCANNY
UNEARTH
UNHANDY
UNHAPPY
UNLATCH
UNMANLY
UNRAVEL
UNSAVED
UPRAISE
VACANCY
VALANCE
VEDANTA
VERANDA
VITAMIN
VOCABLE
VOCALIC
WADABLE
WOMANLY
WREATHE
ANYBODY
BARBELL
BLUBBER
BOMBARD
BOMBAST
BUGBEAR
CABBAGE
CAMBIUM
CAMBRIC
CARBIDE
CARBINE
CATBIRD
CATBOAT
CEMBALO
CHABLIS
CLOBBER
COBBLER
COMBINE
COWBIRD
CRABBED
CRYBABY
CURBING
CUTBACK
DAYBOOK
DISBAND
DOGBANE
DOUBLET
DRIBBLE
DRIBLET
EYEBALL

EYEBROW
FATBACK
FILBERT
FORBEAR
FORBODE
FURBISH
GAMBIAN
GARBAGE
GIBBOUS
GLOBULE
GOBBLER
GUMBOIL
GUNBOAT
HALBERD
HARBOUR
HAUBERK
HERBAGE
HIPBONE
HOGBACK
HOMBURG
HOWBEIT
HUSBAND
ICEBERG
ICEBOAT
JAYBIRD
KIBBUTZ
LAMBENT
LESBIAN
LIMBECK
LOWBROW
LUMBAGO
NEWBORN
NIOBIUM
NONBOOK
ODDBALL
OFFBEAT
PARBOIL
PIEBALD
PREBEND
PROBATE
PROBITY
PROBLEM
QUIBBLE
RAMBLER
RHUBARB
ROBBERY
ROEBUCK
ROWBOAT
RUBBISH
SABBATH
SEABIRD
SETBACK
SHEBANG
SLOBBER
SOYBEAN
STABILE
STUBBLE

SUNBATH
SUNBEAM
SUNBURN
TAMBALA
TANBARK
TERBIUM
TIEBACK
TIMBREL
TOWBOAT
TRIBUNE
TRIBUTE
TUGBOAT
TUMBLER
TUMBREL
TURBINE
VERBENA
VERBOSE
WARBLER
WAYBILL
WEBBING
WETBACK
ZAMBIAN
ABSCESS
ABSCOND
AVOCADO
BALCONY
BIRCHER
BISCUIT
BLACKEN
BLUCHER
BOYCOTT
BRACERO
BRACKEN
BRACKET
BRECCIA
BROCADE
BUTCHER
CALCIFY
CALCINE
CALCITE
CALCIUM
CARCASS
CASCADE
CASCARA
CATCALL
CATCHER
CATCHUP
CHECKER
CHECKUP
CHICANE
CHICANO
CHICKEN
CHICORY
CHOCTAW
CHUCKLE
CIRCLET
CIRCUIT

CONCAVE
CONCEAL
CONCEDE
CONCEIT
CONCEPT
CONCERN
CONCERT
CONCISE
CONCOCT
CONCORD
COXCOMB
CRACKER
CRACKLE
CRICKET
CROCHET
CRUCIAL
CRUCIFY
CUPCAKE
DESCANT
DESCEND
DESCENT
DEWCLAW
DIOCESE
DISCARD
DISCERN
DISCORD
DISCUSS
DOGCART
DRACHMA
EDUCATE
ELECTOR
EPICURE
EVACUEE
EXECUTE
FANCIER
FASCISM
FENCING
FLACCID
FLICKER
FORCEPS
FRACTAL
FRECKLE
FULCRUM
GLACIAL
GLACIER
GLUCOSE
GRACKLE
GRECIAN
HALCYON
HATCHET
HAYCOCK
HOECAKE
HOTCAKE
KETCHUP
KITCHEN
KNOCKER
KNUCKLE

LARCENY
LATCHET
MASCARA
MERCURY
MISCALL
NASCENT
OATCAKE
OBSCENE
OBSCURE
OPACITY
OUTCAST
OUTCOME
OUTCROP
PANCAKE
PAUCITY
PEACOCK
PECCARY
PECCAVI
PERCALE
PERCENT
PERCEPT
PICCOLO
PITCHER
PLACARD
PLACATE
PLACEBO
PLACKET
POPCORN
PORCINE
PRECEDE
PRECEPT
PRECISE
PRECOOK
PRICKER
PRICKLE
PROCEED
PROCESS
PROCTOR
PROCURE
PSYCHIC
PSYCHOL
QUICKEN
QUICKIE
RACCOON
RATCHET
RAUCOUS
REACTOR
REDCOAT
RESCIND
SANCTUM
SARCASM
SATCHEL
SHACKLE
SHOCKER
SINCERE
SLACKEN
SLACKER

SLICKER
SNICKER
SORCERY
SPECIAL
SPECIES
SPECIFY
SPECKLE
SPECTER
SPICULE
STICKER
SUCCEED
SUCCESS
SUCCUMB
SUICIDE
SYNCOPE
THICKEN
THICKET
TOPCOAT
TRACERY
TRACHEA
TRACING
TRACTOR
TRICEPS
TRICKLE
TROCHEE
TRUCKLE
UNICORN
UNSCREW
VACCINE
VISCERA
VISCOSE
VISCOUS
VOLCANO
VOUCHER
WELCOME
WHICKER
WRECKER
ACADEME
ACADEMY
ACIDIFY
AIRDROP
ANODIZE
ANODYNE
BALDING
BALDRIC
BANDAGE
BANDBOX
BEDDING
BINDING
BLADDER
BONDAGE
BONDMAN
BOUDOIR
BURDOCK
CALDERA
CALDRON
CANDIED

CARDBUS
CARDIAC
CHADIAN
CHEDDAR
CONDEMN
CONDIGN
CONDOLE
CONDONE
CONDUCE
CONDUCT
CONDUIT
CONDYLE
CORDAGE
CORDIAL
CORDITE
CORDOBA
DANDIFY
DEADPAN
DEWDROP
DISDAIN
EARDRUM
EVIDENT
FEEDLOT
FINDING
FOLDOUT
FONDANT
GELDING
GEODESY
GLADDEN
GODDESS
GONDOLA
GOODMAN
GRADUAL
GRIDDLE
GUMDROP
HADDOCK
HANDBAG
HANDCAR
HANDFUL
HANDGUN
HANDOUT
HANDSAW
HANDSEL
HANDSET
HARDPAN
HARDTOP
HEADING
HEADMAN
HEADPIN
HEADSET
HEADWAY
HOEDOWN
HOLDING
HOODLUM
HUMDRUM
HUNDRED
IRIDIUM
KADDISH
KHEDIVE
KINDRED
LANDING
LEADING
LETDOWN
LOWDOWN
MACDRAW
MADDING
MANDATE
MANDREL
MANDRIL
MAUDLIN
MINDFUL
MISDEED
MOLDING
MORDANT
MUNDANE
NEEDFUL
OUTDOOR
OUTDRAW
OVIDUCT
OXIDANT
OXIDIZE
PADDING
PADDOCK
PENDANT
PENDENT
PENDING
PREDATE
PREDICT
PRODIGY
PRODUCE
PRODUCT
PRUDENT
PUDDING
READING
READOUT
REDDISH
RHODIUM
ROADBED
ROADWAY
RUNDOWN
SANDBAG
SANDBAR
SANDHOG
SANDLOT
SANDMAN
SARDINE
SAWDUST
SHADING
SHUDDER
SMIDGEN
SOLDIER
STADIUM
STUDENT
STUDIED
SUNDIAL
SUNDOWN
SWADDLE
SWEDISH
TENDRIL
TRADUCE
TRIDENT
TRODDEN
TWADDLE
TWIDDLE
VANDYKE
VERDANT
VERDICT
VERDURE
VIADUCT
WADDING
WEDDING
WILDCAT
WINDAGE
WINDBAG
WINDING
WINDOWS
WINDROW
WOODCUT
WOODLOT
WOODMAN
WORDAGE
WORDING
YARDAGE
YARDARM
YARDMAN
YIDDISH
ABREAST
ABSENCE
ACREAGE
ADRENAL
ADVERSE
AILERON
ALGEBRA
ALLEGRO
ALLERGY
ALREADY
AMMETER
AMNESIA
AMNESTY
ANAEMIA
ANTENNA
APPEASE
AQUEOUS
ARREARS
ARSENAL
ARSENIC
ASCETIC
ATHEIST
ATTEMPT
AUREATE
AUREOLE
BALEFUL
BEDEVIL
BENEATH
BENEFIT
BESEECH
BIBELOT
BIKEWAY
BIMETAL
BIRETTA
BLEEDER
BOREDOM
BURETTE
CADENCE
CADENZA
CALENDS
CAREFUL
CAVEMAN
CELESTA
CHEETAH
CODEINE
COTERIE
DECEASE
DECEIVE
DECENCY
DEFENSE
DEMERIT
DEMESNE
DESERVE
DETENTE
DEVELOP
DILEMMA
DINETTE
DIREFUL
DISEASE
DISEUSE
DIVERGE
DIVERSE
DOLEFUL
DOYENNE
DUTEOUS
ECHELON
EFFENDI
ELDERLY
EMPEROR
ENDEMIC
ENTENTE
ENVELOP
ENVENOM
EQUERRY
ESSENCE
EXCERPT
EXPENSE
FAIENCE
FATEFUL
FEDERAL
FINESSE
FIREARM
FIREBOX
FIREBUG
FIREFLY
FIREMAN
FOREARM
FOREIGN
FORELEG
FOREMAN
FORESEE
FORETOP
FOREVER
FREEBIE
FREEDOM
FREEMAN
FREEWAY
FREEZER
FUNERAL
GATEWAY
GAZELLE
GAZETTE
GENERAL
GENERIC
GENESIS
GENETIC
GLEEMAN
HARELIP
HIDEOUS
HIDEOUT
HOWEVER
HUMERUS
IGNEOUS
ILLEGAL
IMMENSE
IMMERSE
IMPEACH
IMPEARL
IMPERIL
IMPETUS
INCENSE
INDEXED
INFERNO
INGENUE
INHERIT
INTEGER
INTENSE
INTERIM
INVEIGH
INVERSE
JAVELIN
JEWELER
JEWELRY
JUKEBOX
KINETIC
KNEECAP
LATERAL
LAYETTE
LIBERAL
LIBERTY
LICENSE
LIMEADE
LINEAGE
LINEMAN
LITERAL
LOZENGE
LUCERNE
LUNETTE
MADEIRA
MAGENTA
MAJESTY
MALEFIC
MEMENTO
MILEAGE
MIMESIS
MIMETIC
MINERAL
MOHEGAN
MONEYED
MUSETTE
NACELLE
NEMESIS
NOSEGAY
NOVELLA
NOVELTY
NUMERAL
NUMERIC
OBSEQUY
OBSERVE
OBVERSE
OFFENSE
ORDERLY
PAGEANT
PAGEBOY
PALETTE
PARESIS
PATELLA
PHAETON
PHOENIX
PHRENIC
PIMENTO
PIPETTE
PITEOUS
POLECAT
POLEMIC
POVERTY
PRAETOR
PREEMIE
PREEMPT
PUBERTY
QUIETUS
RACEWAY
RAREBIT
RECEIPT
RECEIVE
RECENCY
REFEREE
REGENCY
RELEASE
RENEWAL
REREDOS
RESEDIT
RESERVE
REVENGE
REVENUE
REVERIE
REVERSE
ROSEATE
ROSEBUD
ROSETTE
RUBELLA
SCIENCE
SCREECH
SEVENTY
SEVERAL
SIDEARM
SIDECAR
SIDELIT
SIDEMAN
SILENCE
SLEEPER
SOMEDAY
SOMEHOW
SOMEONE
SPEEDUP
SPLENIC
SQUEEZE
SQUELCH
STEEPLE
STRETCH
SWEETEN
TAKEOFF
THREADY
TIBETAN
TOXEMIA
TUNEFUL
TUTELAR
TWEETER
UNDERGO
UNHEARD
UNKEMPT
UNLEARN
UNLEASH
UNNERVE
UNWEAVE
VALENCE
VEGETAL
VETERAN
VICEROY
VINEGAR
WAKEFUL
WAVELET
WHEEDLE
WHEELER
WHOEVER
WIRETAP
WIZENED
AIRFLOW
AIRFOIL
BEDFAST
BONFIRE
BUFFALO
BUFFOON
CARFARE
CATFISH
CHAFFER
CHIFFON
CODFISH
COMFORT
CONFESS
CONFIDE
CONFINE
CONFIRM
CONFLUX
CONFORM
CONFUSE
CONFUTE
DIFFUSE
DOGFISH
DRIFTER
EDIFICE
FANFARE
FINFISH
FORFEIT
FORFEND
FULFILL
GABFEST
GARFISH
GUNFIRE
HALFWAY
HAYFORK
HOTFOOT
KINFOLK
LEAFAGE
LEAFLET
MENFOLK
MISFILE
MISFIRE
MUFFLER
ORIFICE
OUTFACE
OUTFLOW
PALFREY
PARFAIT
PEAFOWL
PERFECT
PERFIDY
PERFORM
PERFUME
PITFALL
PREFACE
PREFECT
PREFORM
PROFANE
PROFESS
PROFFER
PROFILE
PROFUSE
RAFFISH
ROOFTOP
RUFFIAN
SAFFRON
SCUFFLE
SEAFOOD
SELFISH
SHUFFLE
SKIFFLE
SNAFFLE
SNIFFLE
SNUFFLE
SOUFFLE
STAFFER
STIFFEN
STUFFIT
SUFFICE
SUFFUSE
SULFATE
SULFIDE
SUNFISH
SURFACE
SURFEIT
TAFFETA
TENFOLD
TINFOIL
TRAFFIC
TREFOIL
TRUFFLE
UNIFORM
WARFARE
WELFARE
WOLFRAM
ANAGRAM
BAGGAGE
BARGAIN
BEGGARY
BELGIAN
BRIGADE
BRIGAND
BURGEON
BURGESS
BURGHER
CHAGRIN
CHIGGER
CHIGNON
CONGEAL
CONGEST
DIAGRAM

DISGUST
DOUGHTY
DRAGNET
DRAGOON
DUDGEON
DUNGEON
ELEGIAC
EPIGRAM
EXEGETE
FLIGHTY
FORGING
FORGIVE
FRAGILE
FRIGATE
FROGMAN
GANGWAY
GINGHAM
GOGGLES
HAGGARD
HANGDOG
HANGING
HANGMAN
HANGOUT
HAUGHTY
IMAGERY
IMAGINE
IMAGISM
KINGDOM
KINGPIN
LAGGARD
LANGUID
LANGUOR
LARGESS
LEAGUER
LEGGING
LINGUAL
LODGING
LONGBOW
LONGING
LUGGAGE
MARGENT
MONGREL
NAUGHTY
NIAGARA
NIGGARD
OREGANO
ORIGAMI
OROGENY
OUTGROW
PENGUIN
PERGOLA
PIGGISH
PILGRIM
PROGENY
PROGMAN
PROGRAM
PUNGENT
REAGENT
RIGGING
RINGLET
ROUGHEN
SMUGGLE
SNUGGLE
SORGHUM
STAGGER
STAGING
SUGGEST
SURGEON
SURGERY
SWAGGER
TANGENT
TOGGERY
TOUGHEN
TRAGEDY
TRIGGER
VIRGULE
VULGATE
WAGGERY
WAGGISH
WEIGHTY
WIDGEON
WIGGLER
WRIGGLE
AFGHANI
ALCHEMY
AMPHORA
ANCHOVY
ANTHILL
ANTHRAX
ANTHROP
ARCHAIC
ARCHERY
ARCHIVE
ARCHWAY
ARMHOLE
ASPHALT
BASHFUL
BATHTUB
BEEHIVE
BESHREW
BETHINK
BIGHORN
BRAHMAN
BRAHMIN
BUSHING
CASHIER
CATHODE
COCHLEA
COWHAND
COWHIDE
CUSHION
DASHIKI
DASHING
DASHPOT
DIEHARD
DISHRAG
DUCHESS
EGGHEAD
ENCHAIN
ENCHANT
ENTHUSE
ESTHETE
ETCHING
EUPHONY
FASHION
FIGHTER
FISHERY
FISHING
FOGHORN
FOXHOLE
FUCHSIA
GODHEAD
GODHOOD
GOSHAWK
HASHING
HASHISH
HIGHBOY
HIGHWAY
HOPHEAD
INKHORN
INSHORE
ISTHMUS
JODHPUR
KEYHOLE
LECHERY
LEGHORN
LIGHTEN
LIGHTER
LITHIUM
MACHETE
MACHINE
MANHOLE
MANHOOD
MANHUNT
METHANE
NAPHTHA
NIGHTLY
NONHERO
NOTHING
NOWHERE
OFFHAND
ONSHORE
ORCHARD
PATHWAY
PERHAPS
PINHOLE
POTHEAD
POTHERB
POTHOLE
POTHOOK
PREHEAT
RAWHIDE
REDHEAD
RIGHTLY
SIGHTED
SIGHTLY
SOPHISM
SOPHIST
SWAHILI
TECHNIC
TIGHTEN
TOEHOLD
TOWHEAD
TYPHOID
TYPHOON
UNCHAIN
UPCHUCK
UPSHIFT
WARHEAD
WASHING
WASHOUT
WASHTUB
WISHFUL
WITHERS
WITHOUT
YESHIVA
ABRIDGE
ACHIEVE
ADMIRAL
ADVISED
AFRICAN
AGAINST
ALRIGHT
AMBIENT
ANCIENT
ANDIRON
ANTIGEN
ANTIQUE
ANXIETY
ANXIOUS
APRICOT
AQUIFER
ARBITER
ARRIVAL
ARTICLE
ARTISAN
ARTISTE
ASPIRIN
ATHIRST
AUDIBLE
AUDITOR
AURICLE
BATISTE
BEDIZEN
BELIEVE
BENISON
BESIDES
BESIEGE
BETIMES
BEWITCH
BILIOUS
BOLIVAR
BRAILLE
BROIDER
BROILER
BRUISER
CABINET
CALIBER
CALIPER
CAPITAL
CAPITOL
CARIBOU
CARIOUS
CEDILLA
CILIATE
CITIZEN
CIVILLY
CODICIL
CONICAL
CONIFER
COPILOT
COPIOUS
CORINTH
CRUISER
CUBICLE
CURIOUS
CUTICLE
DECIBEL
DECIDED
DECIMAL
DEFIANT
DEFICIT
DELIGHT
DELIMIT
DELIVER
DEMIGOD
DENIZEN
DEVIANT
DEVIATE
DEVILRY
DEVIOUS
DIGITAL
DIVIDER
DIVISOR
DOMINIE
DUBIETY
DUBIOUS
DUTIFUL
ECLIPSE
ELLIPSE
ENLIVEN
ENTITLE
ENVIOUS
EQUINOX
ETHICAL
EXHIBIT
EXPIATE
EXTINCT
FATIGUE
FINICKY
FOLIAGE
FRAILTY
FREIGHT
FURIOUS
GENITAL
GORILLA
HABITAT
HABITUE
HALIBUT
HELICAL
HOLIDAY
HORIZON
HOSIERY
HUMIDOR
HYGIENE
ILEITIS
ILLICIT
IMPIETY
IMPINGE
IMPIOUS
INCISOR
INDICIA
INFIDEL
INFIELD
INHIBIT
INNINGS
INSIDER
INSIGHT
INSIPID
JACINTH
JANITOR
JUBILEE
JUJITSU
JUNIPER
JUPITER
LAMINAR
LEGIBLE
LENIENT
LEXICON
LIAISON
LIMITED
LUCIFER
MAFIOSO
MAHICAN
MAKINGS
MALISON
MANIKIN
MARIMBA
MARINER
MARITAL
MATINEE
MAXILLA
MAXIMAL
MAXIMUM
MEDIATE
MEDICAL
MEXICAN
MILITIA
MIMICRY
MINIBUS
MINIMAL
MINIMUM
MODICUM
MODISTE
MOHICAN
MONITOR
MUSICAL
NOMINAL
NOMINEE
NOXIOUS
OBLIQUE
OBVIATE
OBVIOUS
OEDIPAL
OFFICER
OMNIBUS
OPTICAL
OPTIMAL
OPTIMUM
ORBITER
ORDINAL
PACIFIC
PANICLE
PAPILLA
PATIENT
PEDICAB
PELICAN
PERIGEE
PERIQUE
PERIWIG
PETIOLE
PITIFUL
POLITIC
PONIARD
PRAIRIE
PURITAN
PYRITES
RADIANT
RADIATE
RADICAL
RAVIOLI
REBIRTH
RECITAL
REFINED
REGIMEN
RELIEVE
RELIQUE
RESIDUE
RETINUE
RETIRED
RETIREE
REVIVAL
RISIBLE
SADIRON
SALIENT
SAPIENT
SATIATE
SATIETY
SATISFY
SEMINAL
SEMINAR
SERIOUS
SHRIVEL
SILICON
SIMILAR
SLEIGHT
SOCIETY
SOLICIT
SPOILER
STRINGY
SYRINGE
TAPIOCA
TAXICAB
TEDIOUS
TIDINGS
TONIGHT
TOPICAL
TRAILER
TRAINEE
TRAIPSE
TRAITOR
TYPICAL
UNCIVIL
UNHINGE
UNHITCH
UPRIGHT
UPRIVER
UPTIGHT
VALIANT
VANILLA
VARIANT
VARIETY
VARIOUS
VATICAN
VEHICLE
VENISON
VESICLE
VICINAL
VICIOUS
VISIBLE
VISITOR
VITIATE
WYSIWYG
CONJOIN
CONJURE
DISJOIN
PERJURY
PROJECT
SUBJECT
SUBJOIN
BACKING
BACKLIT
BACKLOG
BOOKEND
BOOKISH
BOOKLET
BUCKEYE
BUCKLER
BUCKRAM
BUCKSAW
CHUKKER
COCKADE
COCKEYE
COCKNEY
COCKPIT
COOKERY
COOKOUT
CUCKOLD
DESKTOP
DOCKAGE
DUCKPIN
FOLKWAY
HACKMAN
HACKNEY
HACKSAW
HICKORY
HULKING
HUNKERS
HUSKING
JACKASS
JACKDAW
JACKLEG
JACKPOT
KICKOFF
LEAKAGE
LINKAGE
LOCKJAW
LOCKNUT
LOCKOUT
LOOKOUT
MANKIND
MAWKISH
MILKMAN
MILKSOP
MUSKRAT
NANKEEN
NECKTIE
PACKAGE
PACKING
PARKWAY
PINKEYE
RANKING
RICKETS

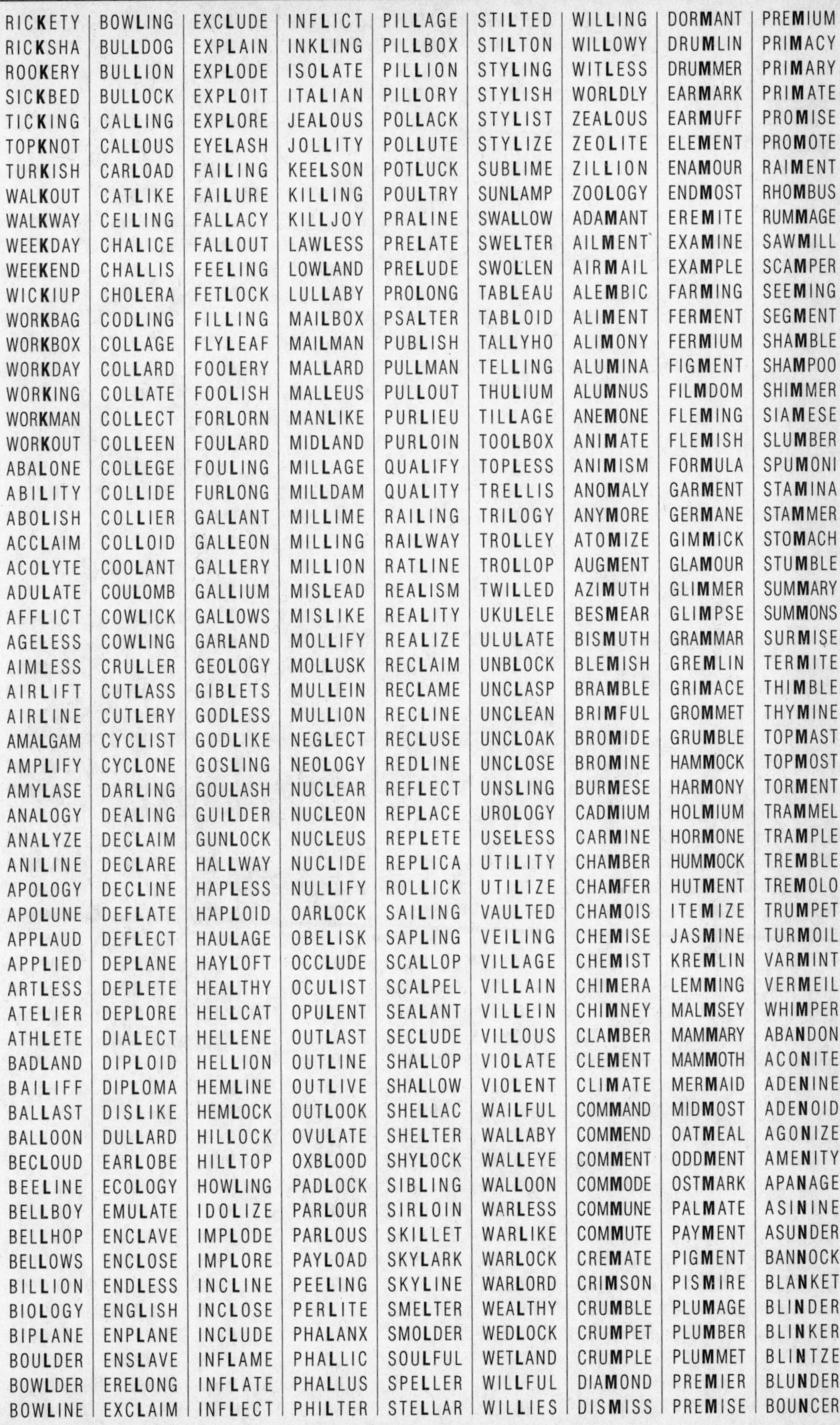

RICKETY
RICKSHA
ROOKERY
SICKBED
TICKING
TOPKNOT
TURKISH
WALKOUT
WALKWAY
WEEKDAY
WEEKEND
WICKIUP
WORKBAG
WORKBOX
WORKDAY
WORKING
WORKMAN
WORKOUT
ABALONE
ABILITY
ABOLISH
ACCLAIM
ACOLYTE
ADULATE
AFFLICT
AGELESS
AIMLESS
AIRLIFT
AIRLINE
AMALGAM
AMPLIFY
AMYLASE
ANALOGY
ANALYZE
ANILINE
APOLOGY
APOLUNE
APPLAUD
APPLIED
ARTLESS
ATELIER
ATHLETE
BADLAND
BAILIFF
BALLAST
BALLOON
BECLOUD
BEELINE
BELLBOY
BELLHOP
BELLOWS
BILLION
BIOLOGY
BIPLANE
BOULDER
BOWLDER
BOWLINE
BOWLING
BULLDOG
BULLION
BULLOCK
CALLING
CALLOUS
CARLOAD
CATLIKE
CEILING
CHALICE
CHALLIS
CHOLERA
CODLING
COLLAGE
COLLARD
COLLATE
COLLECT
COLLEEN
COLLEGE
COLLIDE
COLLIER
COLLOID
COOLANT
COULOMB
COWLICK
COWLING
CRULLER
CUTLASS
CUTLERY
CYCLIST
CYCLONE
DARLING
DEALING
DECLAIM
DECLARE
DECLINE
DEFLATE
DEFLECT
DEPLANE
DEPLETE
DEPLORE
DIALECT
DIPLOID
DIPLOMA
DISLIKE
DULLARD
EARLOBE
ECOLOGY
EMULATE
ENCLAVE
ENCLOSE
ENDLESS
ENGLISH
ENPLANE
ENSLAVE
ERELONG
EXCLAIM
EXCLUDE
EXPLAIN
EXPLODE
EXPLOIT
EXPLORE
EYELASH
FAILING
FAILURE
FALLACY
FALLOUT
FEELING
FETLOCK
FILLING
FLYLEAF
FOOLERY
FOOLISH
FORLORN
FOULARD
FOULING
FURLONG
GALLANT
GALLEON
GALLERY
GALLIUM
GALLOWS
GARLAND
GEOLOGY
GIBLETS
GODLESS
GODLIKE
GOSLING
GOULASH
GUILDER
GUNLOCK
HALLWAY
HAPLESS
HAPLOID
HAULAGE
HAYLOFT
HEALTHY
HELLCAT
HELLENE
HELLION
HEMLINE
HEMLOCK
HILLOCK
HILLTOP
HOWLING
IDOLIZE
IMPLODE
IMPLORE
INCLINE
INCLOSE
INCLUDE
INFLAME
INFLATE
INFLECT
INFLICT
INKLING
ISOLATE
ITALIAN
JEALOUS
JOLLITY
KEELSON
KILLING
KILLJOY
LAWLESS
LOWLAND
LULLABY
MAILBOX
MAILMAN
MALLARD
MALLEUS
MANLIKE
MIDLAND
MILLAGE
MILLDAM
MILLIME
MILLING
MILLION
MISLEAD
MISLIKE
MOLLIFY
MOLLUSK
MULLEIN
MULLION
NEGLECT
NEOLOGY
NUCLEAR
NUCLEON
NUCLEUS
NUCLIDE
NULLIFY
OARLOCK
OBELISK
OCCLUDE
OCULIST
OPULENT
OUTLAST
OUTLINE
OUTLIVE
OUTLOOK
OVULATE
OXBLOOD
PADLOCK
PARLOUR
PARLOUS
PAYLOAD
PEELING
PERLITE
PHALANX
PHALLIC
PHALLUS
PHILTER
PILLAGE
PILLBOX
PILLION
PILLORY
POLLACK
POLLUTE
POTLUCK
POULTRY
PRALINE
PRELATE
PRELUDE
PROLONG
PSALTER
PUBLISH
PULLMAN
PULLOUT
PURLIEU
PURLOIN
QUALIFY
QUALITY
RAILING
RAILWAY
RATLINE
REALISM
REALITY
REALIZE
RECLAIM
RECLAME
RECLINE
RECLUSE
REDLINE
REFLECT
REPLACE
REPLETE
REPLICA
ROLLICK
SAILING
SAPLING
SCALLOP
SCALPEL
SEALANT
SECLUDE
SHALLOP
SHALLOW
SHELLAC
SHELTER
SHYLOCK
SIBLING
SIRLOIN
SKILLET
SKYLARK
SKYLINE
SMELTER
SMOLDER
SOULFUL
SPELLER
STELLAR
STILTED
STILTON
STYLING
STYLISH
STYLIST
STYLIZE
SUBLIME
SUNLAMP
SWALLOW
SWELTER
SWOLLEN
TABLEAU
TABLOID
TALLYHO
TELLING
THULIUM
TILLAGE
TOOLBOX
TOPLESS
TRELLIS
TRILOGY
TROLLEY
TROLLOP
TWILLED
UKULELE
ULULATE
UNBLOCK
UNCLASP
UNCLEAN
UNCLOAK
UNCLOSE
UNSLING
UROLOGY
USELESS
UTILITY
UTILIZE
VAULTED
VEILING
VILLAGE
VILLAIN
VILLEIN
VILLOUS
VIOLATE
VIOLENT
WAILFUL
WALLABY
WALLEYE
WALLOON
WARLESS
WARLIKE
WARLOCK
WARLORD
WEALTHY
WEDLOCK
WETLAND
WILLFUL
WILLIES
WILLING
WILLOWY
WITLESS
WORLDLY
ZEALOUS
ZEOLITE
ZILLION
ZOOLOGY
ADAMANT
AILMENT
AIRMAIL
ALEMBIC
ALIMENT
ALIMONY
ALUMINA
ALUMNUS
ANEMONE
ANIMATE
ANIMISM
ANOMALY
ANYMORE
ATOMIZE
AUGMENT
AZIMUTH
BESMEAR
BISMUTH
BLEMISH
BRAMBLE
BRIMFUL
BROMIDE
BROMINE
BURMESE
CADMIUM
CARMINE
CHAMBER
CHAMFER
CHAMOIS
CHEMISE
CHEMIST
CHIMERA
CHIMNEY
CLAMBER
CLEMENT
CLIMATE
COMMAND
COMMEND
COMMENT
COMMODE
COMMUNE
COMMUTE
CREMATE
CRIMSON
CRUMBLE
CRUMPET
CRUMPLE
DIAMOND
DISMISS
DORMANT
DRUMLIN
DRUMMER
EARMARK
EARMUFF
ELEMENT
ENAMOUR
ENDMOST
EREMITE
EXAMINE
EXAMPLE
FARMING
FERMENT
FERMIUM
FIGMENT
FILMDOM
FLEMING
FLEMISH
FORMULA
GARMENT
GERMANE
GIMMICK
GLAMOUR
GLIMMER
GLIMPSE
GRAMMAR
GREMLIN
GRIMACE
GROMMET
GRUMBLE
HAMMOCK
HARMONY
HOLMIUM
HORMONE
HUMMOCK
HUTMENT
ITEMIZE
JASMINE
KREMLIN
LEMMING
MALMSEY
MAMMARY
MAMMOTH
MERMAID
MIDMOST
OATMEAL
ODDMENT
OSTMARK
PALMATE
PAYMENT
PIGMENT
PISMIRE
PLUMAGE
PLUMBER
PLUMMET
PREMIER
PREMISE
PREMIUM
PRIMACY
PRIMARY
PRIMATE
PROMISE
PROMOTE
RAIMENT
RHOMBUS
RUMMAGE
SAWMILL
SCAMPER
SEEMING
SEGMENT
SHAMBLE
SHAMPOO
SHIMMER
SIAMESE
SLUMBER
SPUMONI
STAMINA
STAMMER
STOMACH
STUMBLE
SUMMARY
SUMMONS
SURMISE
TERMITE
THIMBLE
THYMINE
TOPMAST
TOPMOST
TORMENT
TRAMMEL
TRAMPLE
TREMBLE
TREMOLO
TRUMPET
TURMOIL
VARMINT
VERMEIL
WHIMPER
ABANDON
ACONITE
ADENINE
ADENOID
AGONIZE
AMENITY
APANAGE
ASININE
ASUNDER
BANNOCK
BLANKET
BLINDER
BLINKER
BLINTZE
BLUNDER
BOUNCER

BOU**N**DEN
BUR**N**ISH
BUR**N**OUT
CAN**N**ERY
CAN**N**ULA
CAR**N**AGE
CHA**N**CEL
CHA**N**CRE
CHA**N**NEL
CHA**N**SON
CHA**N**TEY
CHA**N**TRY
CHI**N**ESE
CHI**N**OOK
CHI**N**TZY
CLA**N**GOR
CLI**N**KER
COG**N**ATE
COI**N**AGE
CON**N**ECT
CON**N**IVE
CON**N**OTE
COR**N**COB
COR**N**ICE
COU**N**CIL
COU**N**SEL
COU**N**TER
COU**N**TRY
CRA**N**IUM
CRI**N**KLE
CUN**N**ING
CYA**N**IDE
DEA**N**ERY
DIG**N**IFY
DIG**N**ITY
DRU**N**KEN
DWI**N**DLE
EAR**N**EST
EBO**N**ITE
ECO**N**OMY
EMA**N**ATE
EMI**N**ENT
ENS**N**ARE
EVE**N**ING
FER**N**ERY
FIA**N**CEE
FIN**N**ISH
FLA**N**KER
FLA**N**NEL
FOU**N**DER
FOU**N**DRY
FRA**N**TIC
FUR**N**ACE
FUR**N**ISH
GAI**N**FUL
GAI**N**SAY
GAR**N**ISH
GRA**N**ARY
GRA**N**DAM
GRA**N**DEE
GRA**N**ITE
GRA**N**TEE
GRA**N**ULE
GRE**N**ADE
GRI**N**DER
GRU**N**ION
GUA**N**INE
GUN**N**ERY
HAF**N**IUM
HAR**N**ESS
HEI**N**OUS
HOB**N**AIL
HYM**N**ODY
ILL**N**ESS
IRA**N**IAN
IRO**N**ING
KER**N**ING
KEY**N**OTE
LAU**N**DER
LAU**N**DRY
LEO**N**INE
LIG**N**IFY
LIG**N**ITE
LIO**N**IZE
MAG**N**ATE
MAG**N**ETO
MAG**N**IFY
MAI**N**TOP
MAN**N**ISH
MAU**N**DER
MEA**N**DER
MEA**N**ING
MIS**N**AME
MOR**N**ING
MOU**N**TIE
NOO**N**DAY
OMI**N**OUS
OPE**N**ING
OPI**N**ION
PAN**N**IER
PEN**N**ANT
PFE**N**NIG
PHA**N**TOM
PHO**N**EME
PHO**N**ICS
PIA**N**IST
PIN**N**ACE
PIN**N**ATE
PIO**N**EER
PLA**N**TAR
PLA**N**TER
PLE**N**ARY
PLU**N**DER
PLU**N**GER
POI**N**TED
POI**N**TER
PRO**N**OUN
QUA**N**TUM
QUI**N**INE
QUI**N**TAL
QUI**N**TET
QUO**N**DAM
RAI**N**BOW
RAU**N**CHY
REE**N**TRY
REG**N**ANT
REM**N**ANT
REU**N**ION
RHE**N**IUM
ROU**N**DUP
RUI**N**OUS
RUN**N**ING
SAI**N**TLY
SAU**N**TER
SCA**N**DAL
SCA**N**NER
SCE**N**ERY
SHI**N**GLE
SIG**N**IFY
SLA**N**DER
SLE**N**DER
SOU**N**DER
SPA**N**GLE
SPA**N**IEL
SPA**N**ISH
SPI**N**ACH
SPI**N**DLE
SPI**N**DLY
SPO**N**SOR
STA**N**DBY
STE**N**CIL
SUR**N**AME
SWI**N**DLE
TAN**N**ERY
TAR**N**ISH
TEE**N**AGE
TER**N**ARY
THI**N**NER
THU**N**DER
TOE**N**AIL
TON**N**AGE
TON**N**EAU
TOR**N**ADO
TRA**N**SIT
TRA**N**SOM
TRI**N**ITY
TRI**N**KET
TRU**N**DLE
TSU**N**AMI
TUR**N**ERY
TUR**N**ING
TUR**N**KEY
TUR**N**OFF
TUR**N**OUT
TWI**N**KLE
UNK**N**OWN
UNS**N**ARL
URA**N**IUM
URA**N**OUS
URI**N**ARY
URI**N**ATE
UTE**N**SIL
VAR**N**ISH
VER**N**IER
WAR**N**ING
WIN**N**ING
WIT**N**ESS
WRA**N**GLE
WRI**N**GER
WRI**N**KLE
WRO**N**GLY
WRY**N**ECK
YOU**N**KER
ZIO**N**ISM
ABD**O**MEN
ABS**O**LVE
ACC**O**UNT
ACR**O**BAT
ACR**O**NYM
ADJ**O**URN
AER**O**BIC
AER**O**SOL
AGR**O**UND
ALC**O**HOL
ALM**O**NER
AMM**O**NIA
ANT**O**NYM
APP**O**INT
APR**O**POS
ARM**O**RER
AST**O**UND
ATR**O**PHY
AUT**O**PSY
BAL**O**NEY
BAR**O**NET
BAR**O**QUE
BAY**O**NET
BAZ**O**OKA
BED**O**UIN
BEG**O**NIA
BEH**O**OVE
BEL**O**VED
BET**O**KEN
BIF**O**CAL
BIP**O**LAR
BIV**O**UAC
BLO**O**DED
BLO**O**PER
BOL**O**GNA
BOR**O**UGH
BRI**O**CHE
BRO**O**DER
BUC**O**LIC
CAB**O**OSE
CAL**O**MEL
CAL**O**RIC
CAL**O**RIE
CAR**O**TID
CAR**O**USE
CHR**O**MIC
CHR**O**NIC
COC**O**NUT
COL**O**GNE
COL**O**NEL
COL**O**RED
COR**O**LLA
COR**O**NAL
COR**O**NER
COR**O**NET
CRO**O**KED
CUL**O**TTE
DEB**O**UCH
DEC**O**DER
DEC**O**RUM
DEL**O**USE
DEM**O**NIC
DEM**O**TIC
DEP**O**SIT
DEV**O**LVE
DEV**O**TED
DEV**O**TEE
DIS**O**BEY
DIV**O**RCE
ECL**O**GUE
EID**O**LON
EMB**O**WER
EMP**O**WER
END**O**RSE
ENF**O**RCE
ENN**O**BLE
EXP**O**UND
GAV**O**TTE
HER**O**ICS
HER**O**INE
HER**O**ISM
HOM**O**NYM
IGN**O**BLE
IMM**O**RAL
IMP**O**UND
INB**O**ARD
INB**O**UND
IND**O**ORS
IND**O**RSE
INV**O**ICE
INV**O**LVE
JEH**O**VAH
KIL**O**TON
LAB**O**RED
LAC**O**NIC
LAN**O**LIN
MAS**O**NIC
MAS**O**NRY
MEI**O**SIS
MIT**O**SIS
MON**O**CLE
MON**O**MER
MOR**O**CCO
OBL**O**QUY
OCT**O**BER
OCT**O**PUS
ONG**O**ING
ORT**O**LAN
OSM**O**SIS
OTT**O**MAN
PAN**O**PLY
PAP**O**OSE
POC**O**SIN
POP**O**VER
REB**O**UND
REC**O**UNT
REC**O**VER
RED**O**UBT
RED**O**UND
REJ**O**ICE
REM**O**DEL
REM**O**RSE
REM**O**UNT
RES**O**LVE
RES**O**UND
RET**O**UCH
REV**O**LVE
RIP**O**STE
SAM**O**VAR
SCH**O**LAR
SCO**O**TER
SCR**O**TUM
SIR**O**CCO
SOJ**O**URN
SPL**O**TCH
STR**O**PHE
SYN**O**NYM
THE**O**REM
THR**O**ATY
THR**O**UGH
TIM**O**THY
TRO**O**PER
UNB**O**SOM
UNB**O**WED
UNC**O**UTH
UNC**O**VER
UND**O**ING
UNG**O**DLY
UNH**O**RSE
UNL**O**OSE
UNM**O**RAL
UNM**O**VED
UNS**O**UND
VAM**O**OSE
WAG**O**NER
WHO**O**PLA
WID**O**WER
ADA**P**TER
ADI**P**OSE
AIR**P**ORT
AIR**P**OST
ANA**P**EST
ARA**P**AHO
ASE**P**TIC
AUS**P**ICE
BAG**P**IPE
BED**P**OST
BES**P**EAK
BUM**P**KIN
CAM**P**HOR
CAR**P**ORT
CHA**P**EAU
CHA**P**LET
CHA**P**MAN
CHA**P**TER
CHI**P**PER
CHO**P**PER
CLA**P**PER
CLI**P**PER
COM**P**ACT
COM**P**ANY
COM**P**ARE
COM**P**ASS
COM**P**EER
COM**P**ETE
COM**P**ILE
COM**P**LEX
COM**P**ORT
COM**P**OSE
COM**P**OST
COM**P**OTE
COM**P**UTE
COP**P**ICE
COU**P**LET
COW**P**OKE
CRI**P**PLE
CRO**P**PER
CRY**P**TIC
CUL**P**RIT
DAU**P**HIN
DES**P**AIR
DES**P**ISE
DES**P**ITE
DES**P**OIL
DES**P**OND
DIS**P**LAY
DIS**P**ORT
DIS**P**OSE
DIS**P**UTE
DOL**P**HIN
DRA**P**ERY
DRO**P**LET
DRO**P**PER
DUM**P**ING
EAR**P**LUG
FLA**P**PER
FLI**P**PER
GRA**P**HIC
GRA**P**NEL
GRA**P**PLE
HAP**P**ILY
HAR**P**OON
HEL**P**ING
HEN**P**ECK
HOS**P**ICE
INS**P**ECT
INS**P**IRE
JET**P**ORT
KEE**P**ING
KRY**P**TON
LAM**P**OON
LAM**P**REY
LEM**P**IRA
LEO**P**ARD
MAR**P**LOT
MAY**P**OLE
MIS**P**LAY
MOR**P**HIA
NON**P**LUS
NUT**P**ICK
OUT**P**LAY
OUT**P**OST
OUT**P**ULL
PAL**P**ATE
PEP**P**ERY
PER**P**LEX
POM**P**ANO
POM**P**OUS
PRE**P**ARE
PRE**P**UCE
PRO**P**ANE
PRO**P**HET
PRO**P**MAN
PRO**P**OSE
PUM**P**KIN
PUR**P**ORT
PUR**P**OSE
RAM**P**AGE
RAM**P**ANT
RAM**P**ART
RAP**P**ORT
RES**P**ECT
RES**P**ITE
RES**P**OND
SAM**P**LER
SCA**P**ULA
SCE**P**TER
SCE**P**TIC
SCU**P**PER
SEA**P**ORT
SER**P**ENT
SHA**P**ELY
SKE**P**TIC
SKI**P**PER
SLI**P**PER
SOU**P**CON
STE**P**SON
STI**P**END
STI**P**PLE
STO**P**GAP
STO**P**PER
STU**P**EFY
STY**P**TIC
SUP**P**ORT
SUP**P**OSE
SUR**P**ASS
SUR**P**LUS
SUS**P**ECT
SUS**P**END
SYM**P**TOM
TAD**P**OLE
TEM**P**ERA
TEM**P**EST
TIM**P**ANI
TOP**P**ING
TOR**P**EDO
TOW**P**ATH
TRA**P**EZE
TRI**P**LET
TRI**P**LEX
TRO**P**ISM
UTO**P**IAN
VAM**P**IRE
VES**P**ERS
VUL**P**INE
WAR**P**ATH
WAS**P**ISH
WEE**P**ING
WHI**P**PET
WHI**P**SAW
WHO**P**PER
WRA**P**PER
BAN**Q**UET
BOU**Q**UET
COE**Q**UAL
CON**Q**UER
CRO**Q**UET
JON**Q**UIL
KUM**Q**UAT

LACQUER
MARQUEE
MARQUIS
PARQUET
UNEQUAL
ADDRESS
AFFRONT
AMERIND
AMOROUS
ANARCHY
ANDROID
APPRISE
APPROVE
ARMREST
ASCRIBE
ASTRIDE
ATTRACT
AVARICE
AVERAGE
BARRAGE
BARRIER
BARRING
BARROOM
BEARING
BEDROCK
BEDROLL
BEDROOM
BEGRIME
BETROTH
BLARNEY
BOURBON
BULRUSH
CAPRICE
CARRIER
CARRION
CARRYON
CHARGER
CHARIOT
CHARITY
CHARMER
CHARNEL
CHARTER
CHERISH
CHEROOT
CHORALE
CHORTLE
CLARIFY
CLARION
CLARITY
COARSEN
COMRADE
CORRECT
CORRODE
CORRUPT
COURAGE
COURIER
COURSER
COURTLY
CUPRITE
CURRANT
CURRENT
CYPRESS
CZARINA
DEBRIEF
DEERFLY
DEFRAUD
DEFROST
DEGRADE
DEPRAVE
DEPRESS
DEPRIVE
DERRICK
DETRACT
DETRAIN
DIARIST
DIGRAPH
DIGRESS
DISROBE
DISRUPT
DIURNAL
DOORMAN
DOORMAT
DOORWAY
EARRING
EMBRACE
EMBROIL
EMBRYOL
EMERALD
EMERITA
EMPRESS
ENCRUST
ENGRAFT
ENGRAVE
ENGROSS
ENTRAIN
ENTRANT
ENTREAT
ENTROPY
ENTRUST
EPERGNE
ETERNAL
EXCRETA
EXCRETE
EXPRESS
EXTRACT
EXTREME
EXTRUDE
FAIRING
FAIRWAY
FARRAGO
FARRIER
FEARFUL
FEBRILE
FERROUS
FERRULE
FIBROID
FLORIST
FURRIER
FURRING
GARROTE
GEARBOX
GHERKIN
GLORIFY
GOURMET
GUARANI
GUERDON
HAIRCUT
HAIRPIN
HARRIER
HAYRICK
HEARING
HEARKEN
HEARSAY
HEARTEN
HEIRESS
HERRING
HORRIFY
HYDRANT
HYDRATE
HYDROUS
IMPRESS
IMPRINT
IMPROVE
INCRUST
INERTIA
INGRAFT
INGRAIN
INGRATE
INGRESS
INGROWN
INTRANS
INTROIT
INTRUDE
INTRUST
ITERATE
JOURNAL
JOURNEY
JOYRIDE
LATRINE
LEARNED
LEPROSY
LIBRARY
MACRAME
MICROBE
MIDRIFF
MIGRANT
MIGRATE
MISREAD
MISRULE
MOORING
MUDROOM
MURRAIN
NARRATE
NITRATE
NITRIFY
NITRITE
NOURISH
OBTRUDE
OCARINA
ONEROUS
OPERATE
OPPRESS
OSTRICH
OUTRAGE
OUTRANK
OVERACT
OVERAGE
OVERALL
OVERARM
OVERAWE
OVERFLY
OVERJOY
OVERLAP
OVERLAY
OVERRUN
OVERSEA
OVERSEE
OVERTOP
PAPRIKA
PATRIOT
PATROON
PAYROLL
PETRIFY
PHARAOH
PHARYNX
PIBROCH
PRORATE
PUERILE
PUTREFY
QUARREL
QUARTER
QUARTET
RECRUIT
REDRESS
REFRACT
REFRAIN
REFRESH
REGRESS
REGROUP
REPRESS
REPRINT
REPRISE
REPROOF
REPROVE
RETRACE
RETRACT
RETREAD
RETREAT
SCARIFY
SCARLET
SECRECY
SECRETE
SERRATE
SERRIED
SHARPEN
SHARPER
SHARPIE
SHERBET
SHERIFF
SHORING
SHORTEN
SHORTLY
SNORKEL
SOPRANO
SPARING
SPARKLE
SPARROW
SPIRANT
STARTLE
STARTUP
STERILE
STERNUM
STIRRUP
STORAGE
STORIED
SUCROSE
SUNRISE
SUNROOF
SUPREME
SWARTHY
TAPROOM
TAPROOT
TERRACE
TERRAIN
TERRIER
TERRIFY
THERAPY
THEREAT
THEREBY
THEREIN
THEREOF
THEREON
THERETO
THERMAL
THERMOS
THORIUM
THYROID
TORRENT
TOURIST
TOURNEY
TRIREME
UMBRAGE
UNARMED
UNCROSS
UNDRESS
UNERASE
UNFROCK
UNGROUP
UNTRIED
UNTRUTH
UPBRAID
UPDRAFT
UPGRADE
VAGRANT
VIBRANT
VIBRATE
VIBRATO
VITRIFY
VITRIOL
WARRANT
WARRIOR
WHEREAS
WHEREAT
WHEREBY
WHEREIN
WHEREOF
WHEREON
WHERETO
WHORLED
YTTRIUM
ABYSMAL
ABYSSAL
AIRSHIP
AIRSICK
APOSTLE
BANSHEE
BASSOON
BATSMAN
BEASTLY
BEDSIDE
BEDSORE
BEESWAX
BERSERK
BLESSED
BLISTER
BLOSSOM
BLUSTER
BOBSLED
BOLSTER
BORSCHT
BRISKET
BRISTLE
BRUSQUE
CAESURA
CAISSON
CAPSIZE
CAPSTAN
CAPSULE
CARSICK
CASSAVA
CASSOCK
CAUSTIC
CELSIUS
CENSURE
CESSION
CHASSIS
CHASTEN
CLASSIC
CLASTIC
CLOSURE
CLUSTER
CONSENT
CONSIGN
CONSIST
CONSOLE
CONSORT
CONSULT
CONSUME
CORSAGE
CORSAIR
COSSACK
COWSLIP
CROSIER
CRUSADE
CRYSTAL
CUISINE
CURSIVE
CURSORY
DENSITY
DESSERT
DISSECT
DISSENT
DOSSIER
DRASTIC
DRESSER
EARSHOT
ELASTIC
ELISION
ELUSIVE
ELYSIUM
EPISODE
EPISTLE
EROSION
EROSIVE
EVASION
EYESORE
FALSIFY
FIRSTLY
FISSILE
FISSION
FISSURE
FLESHLY
FLUSTER
FORSAKE
FRESHEN
FRESHET
FRUSTUM
FULSOME
GHASTLY
GINSENG
GLISTEN
GLISTER
GODSEND
GRISTLE
GUMSHOE
GUNSHOT
HAMSTER
HASSOCK
HAYSEED
HERSELF
HIMSELF
HIPSTER
HIRSUTE
HOLSTER
HOOSIER
HOTSHOT
HOUSING
IRKSOME
KIDSKIN
KINSHIP
KINSMAN
LAWSUIT
LEISURE
LINSEED
LISSOME
LOBSTER
MAESTRO
MANSARD
MANSION
MARSHAL
MASSAGE
MASSEUR
MASSIVE
MEASLES
MEASURE
MESSAGE
MESSIAH
MINSTER
MISSEND
MISSILE
MISSING
MISSION
MISSIVE
MISSTEP
MOBSTER
MOISTEN
MONSOON
MONSTER
NEWSBOY
NEWSMAN
NOISOME
NONSKED
NONSTOP
NURSERY
OARSMAN
ODYSSEY
OFFSIDE
OILSKIN
OLDSTER
ONESELF
OPOSSUM
OUTSELL
OUTSIDE
OUTSIZE
OUTSTAY
PAISLEY
PARSING
PARSLEY
PARSNIP
PASSAGE
PASSING
PASSION
PASSIVE
PASSKEY
PEASANT
PENSION
PENSIVE
PERSIAN
PERSIST
PHYSICS
PHYSIOL
PIASTER
PIGSKIN
PILSNER
PLASTER
PLASTIC
POSSESS
POTSHOT
PRESAGE
PRESENT
PRESIDE
PRESOAK
PRESUME
PROSAIC
PROSODY
PROSPER
PULSATE
PUNSTER
PURSUIT
RANSACK
REDSKIN
ROASTER
ROISTER
ROOSTER
RUSSIAN
SAUSAGE
SEASICK
SEASIDE
SEISMIC
SENSORY
SENSUAL
SESSILE
SESSION

SHYSTER
SPASTIC
SUBSIDE
SUBSIDY
SUBSIST
SUBSOIL
SUNSPOT
TAPSTER
TENSILE
TENSION
THISTLE
THYSELF
TIPSTER
TOASTER
TONSURE
TOPSAIL
TOPSIDE
TOPSOIL
TORSION
TRESTLE
TRISECT
TRUSTEE
TUESDAY
TUSSOCK
TWISTER
TWOSOME
UNUSUAL
VARSITY
VERSIFY
VERSION
WARSHIP
WASSAIL
WAYSIDE
WEASAND
WHISKER
WHISKEY
WHISPER
WHISTLE
WINSOME
WORSHIP
WORSTED
WRESTLE
ABSTAIN
ACETATE
ACETONE
AGITATE
AMATEUR
AMATIVE
AMATORY
ANATOMY
ANOTHER
ANYTIME
APATITE
ASHTRAY
AUCTION
AUSTERE
AUSTRAL
BAPTISM
BAPTIST
BAPTIZE
BASTARD
BASTION
BATTERY
BATTING
BEATIFY
BEATNIK
BEDTIME
BELTWAY
BENTHIC
BENTHOS
BESTIAL
BIOTITE
BITTERN
BITTERS
BLATANT
BLATHER
BLOTTER
BOATMAN
BOOTLEG
BRITISH
BRITTLE
BROTHEL
BROTHER
BRUTISH
BUNTING
BUTTOCK
CAITIFF
CANTATA
CANTEEN
CAPTAIN
CAPTION
CAPTIVE
CAPTURE
CARTAGE
CARTOON
CASTING
CASTLED
CATTAIL
CAUTION
CENTARE
CENTAUR
CENTAVO
CENTIME
CENTIMO
CENTRAL
CENTURY
CERTAIN
CERTIFY
CHATEAU
CHATTEL
CHATTER
CHUTNEY
CISTERN
CLATTER
CLOTHES
CLOTURE
CLUTTER
COATING
CONTACT
CONTAIN
CONTEMN
CONTEND
CONTENT
CONTEST
CONTEXT
CONTORT
CONTOUR
CONTRIB
CONTROL
CORTEGE
COSTIVE
COSTUME
COTTAGE
COUTURE
CRITTER
CULTURE
CURTAIL
CURTAIN
CUSTARD
CUSTODY
CUTTING
DASTARD
DAYTIME
DEATHLY
DENTATE
DENTIST
DENTURE
DESTINE
DESTINY
DESTROY
DEXTRIN
DICTATE
DICTION
DISTAFF
DISTANT
DISTEND
DISTICH
DISTILL
DISTORT
DISTURB
DOGTROT
DUCTILE
DUSTPAN
EARTHEN
EARTHLY
EASTERN
ECSTASY
EDITION
EGOTISM
ELITISM
EMITTER
EMOTION
EPITAPH
EPITHET
EPITOME
FACTION
FACTORY
FACTUAL
FANTAIL
FANTASY
FARTHER
FEATHER
FEATURE
FERTILE
FESTIVE
FESTOON
FICTION
FIFTEEN
FISTFUL
FISTULA
FITTING
FIXTURE
FLATBED
FLATCAR
FLATTEN
FLATTER
FLATTOP
FLOTSAM
FLUTIST
FLUTTER
FOOTAGE
FOOTING
FOOTMAN
FOOTPAD
FORTIFY
FORTRAN
FORTUNE
FRETFUL
FRETSAW
FRITTER
FURTHER
FURTIVE
FUSTIAN
GANTLET
GASTRIC
GENTEEL
GENTIAN
GENTILE
GESTAPO
GESTURE
GLITTER
GLOTTIS
GLUTTON
GRATIFY
GRATING
HALTING
HAUTEUR
HEATHEN
HEATHER
HECTARE
HINTING
HISTORY
HOSTAGE
HOSTESS
HOSTILE
HOSTLER
IMITATE
INITIAL
INSTALL
INSTANT
INSTATE
INSTEAD
INSTILL
ISOTOPE
JITTERS
JOTTING
JUSTICE
JUSTIFY
LACTATE
LACTEAL
LACTOSE
LANTANA
LANTERN
LAOTIAN
LATTICE
LEATHER
LECTERN
LECTURE
LEFTISM
LEOTARD
LETTUCE
LISTING
LOATHLY
LOTTERY
LUSTRAL
MALTOSE
MANTEAU
MARTIAL
MARTIAN
MARTINI
MASTERY
MASTIFF
MASTOID
MATTINS
MATTOCK
MEATMAN
MEETING
MENTHOL
MENTION
MESTIZO
MIDTOWN
MISTAKE
MISTRAL
MIXTURE
MONTAGE
MORTIFY
MORTISE
MUSTANG
MUSTARD
MYSTERY
MYSTIFY
NARTHEX
NEITHER
NEPTUNE
NETTING
NEUTRAL
NEUTRON
NORTHER
NOSTRIL
NOSTRUM
NUPTIAL
NURTURE
ONETIME
ORATION
ORATORY
OROTUND
OVATION
PANTHER
PARTAKE
PARTIAL
PARTING
PARTITE
PARTNER
PARTWAY
PASTERN
PASTIME
PASTURE
PATTERN
PENTIUM
PERTAIN
PERTURB
PETTISH
PICTURE
PIGTAIL
PLATEAU
PLATING
PLATOON
PLATTER
PLOTTER
PONTIFF
PONTOON
PORTAGE
PORTEND
PORTENT
PORTICO
PORTION
PORTRAY
POSTAGE
POSTBOY
POSTERN
POSTMAN
POSTURE
POSTWAR
POTTAGE
POTTERY
PRATTLE
PRETEEN
PRETEND
PRETEXT
PRETZEL
PRITHEE
PROTEAN
PROTECT
PROTEGE
PROTEIN
PROTEST
PUSTULE
QUETZAL
RAGTIME
RAPTURE
RATTLER
RATTRAP
RECTIFY
RECTORY
REPTILE
RESTIVE
RESTORE
ROOTLET
ROSTRUM
ROUTINE
RUPTURE
SALTBOX
SALTINE
SCATTER
SCUTTLE
SEATING
SECTARY
SECTION
SELTZER
SENTIMO
SETTING
SEXTANT
SHATTER
SHOTGUN
SHUTOUT
SHUTTER
SHUTTLE
SIXTEEN
SKITTER
SLATHER
SLITHER
SMOTHER
SPATIAL
SPATTER
SPATULA
SPITTLE
SPOTTER
SPUTNIK
SPUTTER
STATELY
STATION
STATURE
STATUTE
STUTTER
SUBTILE
SUCTION
SUITING
SULTANA
SURTOUT
SUSTAIN
SYSTOLE
TACTICS
TACTILE
TANTRUM
TATTING
TEKTITE
TESTATE
TESTIFY
TEXTILE
TEXTURE
THITHER
TORTONI
TORTURE
TRITIUM
TUITION
TWITTER
UMPTEEN
UNCTION
UNITARY
UNITIZE
UNSTRAP
UPSTAGE
UPSTART
UPSTATE
URETHRA
VANTAGE
VENTRAL
VENTURE
VERTIGO
VESTIGE
VESTING
VESTURE
VICTORY
VICTUAL
VINTAGE
VINTNER
VIRTUAL
VITTLES
VOLTAGE
VOLTAIC
VULTURE
WAGTAIL
WANTING
WARTHOG
WARTIME
WASTAGE
WASTREL
WATTAGE
WEATHER
WESTERN
WHATNOT
WHETHER
WHITHER
WHITING
WHITISH
WHITLOW
WHITTLE
WISTFUL
WITTING
WRITING
ACCUSAL
ACCUSED
ACQUIRE
ACTUARY
ACTUATE
ADJUDGE
ADJUNCT
ALBUMEN
ALBUMIN
AMPUTEE
ANGUISH
ANGULAR
ANNUITY
ANNULAR
ARBUTUS
ARDUOUS
ASSUAGE
ASSURED
BEGUILE
BEGUINE
BEQUEST
BITUMEN
BROUGHT
CALUMET
CALUMNY
CERUMEN
CROUTON
CUMULUS
DEFUNCT
DILUENT
DIVULGE
DRAUGHT
DROUGHT
ENQUIRE
EPAULET
ESQUIRE
ESTUARY
EXPUNGE
FACULTY
FATUITY
FATUOUS
FLOUNCE
FRAUGHT

GENUINE
GRAUPEL
GROUPER
GROUPIE
IMPULSE
INCUBUS
INDULGE
INHUMAN
INQUEST
INQUIRE
INQUIRY
INSULAR
INSULIN
INSURED
INSURER
JANUARY
JEJUNUM
JOCULAR
JUGULAR
LIQUEFY
LIQUEUR
LITURGY
MANUMIT
MAZURKA
MEDULLA
MINUEND
MINUTIA
MODULAR
NATURAL
NOCUOUS
NONUSER
OSSUARY
PABULUM
PETUNIA
PIQUANT
PLAUDIT
POPULAR
REBUILD
REFUGEE
REGULAR
REPULSE
REPUTED
REQUEST
REQUIEM
REQUIRE
REQUITE
RIVULET
ROTUNDA
SAGUARO
SAMURAI
SCOURGE
SCRUFFY
SCRUPLE
SECULAR
SEQUENT
SEQUOIA
SINUOUS
SOLUBLE
SPLURGE
SPOUSAL
STAUNCH
STRUDEL
TABULAR
TENUOUS
TENURED
TEQUILA
THOUGHT
THRUWAY
TITULAR
TOLUENE
TRIUMPH
TROUBLE
TROUNCE
TUBULAR
UNGUENT
UNLUCKY
UNQUIET
UNQUOTE
UPSURGE
VACUITY
VACUOLE
VACUOUS
VALUATE
VAQUERO
VOGUISH
VOLUBLE
WROUGHT
ZYMURGY
ATAVISM
BRAVADO
BRAVERY
BRAVURA
BREVITY
CANVASS
CHEVIOT
CHEVRON
CIVVIES
CLAVIER
CONVENE
CONVENT
CONVERT
CONVICT
CONVOKE
CRAVING
CREVICE
CULVERT
DERVISH
ELEVATE
FAUVISM
FERVENT
FLAVOUR
FLIVVER
GRAVITY
GRAVURE
HALVERS
HARVARD
HARVEST
LATVIAN
NAIVETE
NAIVETY
NERVOUS
NIRVANA
OLIVINE
OUTVOTE
PARVENU
PEEVISH
PERVADE
PERVERT
PLUVIAL
PREVAIL
PREVENT
PREVIEW
PRIVACY
PRIVATE
PROVERB
PROVIDE
PROVISO
PROVOKE
PROVOST
PURVIEW
SALVAGE
SELVAGE
SERVANT
SERVICE
SERVILE
SERVING
SHAVING
SLAVERY
SLAVISH
SOLVENT
SUBVERT
SURVIVE
TRAVAIL
TRIVIAL
TRIVIUM
VERVAIN
AIRWAVE
ALEWIFE
ANYWISE
ATHWART
AWKWARD
BETWEEN
BETWIXT
BLOWGUN
BLOWOUT
BROWNIE
BROWSER
BULWARK
CATWALK
CHOWDER
CROWBAR
CUTWORM
DOGWOOD
DRAWING
ENDWAYS
ENDWISE
ENTWINE
EYEWASH
FLOWERY
FORWARD
FROWARD
GUNWALE
HAYWIRE
HOGWASH
INDWELL
INKWELL
JAYWALK
KNOWING
LAPWING
LEEWARD
MIDWEEK
MIDWIFE
MUGWUMP
NARWHAL
NETWARE
NETWORK
OUTWARD
OUTWEAR
OUTWORK
OUTWORN
PINWORM
PLOWBOY
PLOWMAN
PLYWOOD
PROWESS
RAGWEED
REDWOOD
SAPWOOD
SEAWALL
SEAWARD
SEAWEED
SHAWNEE
SHOWMAN
SKIWEAR
SKYWARD
STEWARD
TINWARE
UNAWARE
UNTWINE
UNTWIST
UPSWEPT
UPSWING
VANWARD
WAXWING
WAXWORK
WAYWARD
WAYWORN
ASEXUAL
BAUXITE
COAXIAL
COEXIST
FLEXURE
INEXACT
MARXISM
PROXIMO
ACRYLIC
BICYCLE
CALYPSO
COPYBOY
COPYCAT
HALYARD
KATYDID
LADYBUG
LANYARD
MIDYEAR
PAPYRUS
PLAYBOY
PLAYLET
PLAYPEN
POLYGON
POLYMER
PRAYING
RECYCLE
UNDYING
BENZENE
BENZINE
BENZOIN
BRAZIER
BUZZARD
DRIZZLE
FRAZZLE
FRIZZLE
GIZZARD
GLAZIER
GRAZIER
GRIZZLY
MUEZZIN
PIZZAZZ
RHIZOME

## 5th Letter

ABREAST
ABSTAIN
ACCLAIM
ACETATE
ACREAGE
ACTUARY
ACTUATE
ADAMANT
ADULATE
AFGHANI
AGITATE
AIRMAIL
AIRWAVE
ALREADY
AMYLASE
ANIMATE
ANOMALY
APANAGE
APPEASE
APPLAUD
ARAPAHO
ARCHAIC
ARREARS
ASPHALT
ASSUAGE
ATHWART
ATTRACT
AUREATE
AVERAGE
AVOCADO
AWKWARD
BADLAND
BAGGAGE
BALLAST
BANDAGE
BARGAIN
BARRAGE
BASTARD
BEDFAST
BEGGARY
BENEATH
BIPLANE
BLATANT
BOMBARD
BOMBAST
BONDAGE
BRAVADO
BRIGADE
BRIGAND
BROCADE
BUFFALO
BULWARK
BUZZARD
CABBAGE
CANTATA
CANVASS
CAPTAIN
CARCASS
CARFARE
CARNAGE
CARTAGE
CASCADE
CASCARA
CASSAVA
CATCALL
CATTAIL
CATWALK
CEMBALO
CENTARE
CENTAUR
CENTAVO
CERTAIN
CHICANE
CHICANO
CHORALE
CILIATE
CLIMATE
COCKADE
COGNATE
COINAGE
COLLAGE
COLLARD
COLLATE
COMMAND
COMPACT
COMPANY
COMPARE
COMPASS
COMRADE
CONCAVE
CONTACT
CONTAIN
COOLANT
CORDAGE
CORSAGE
CORSAIR
COSSACK
COTTAGE
COURAGE
COWHAND
CREMATE
CRUSADE
CRYBABY
CUPCAKE
CURRANT
CURTAIL
CURTAIN
CUSTARD
CUTBACK
CUTLASS
DASTARD
DECEASE
DECLAIM
DECLARE
DEFIANT
DEFLATE
DEFRAUD
DEGRADE
DENTATE
DEPLANE
DEPRAVE
DESCANT
DESPAIR
DETRACT
DETRAIN
DEVIANT
DEVIATE
DICTATE
DIEHARD
DIGRAPH
DISBAND
DISCARD
DISDAIN
DISEASE
DISTAFF
DISTANT
DOCKAGE
DOGBANE
DOGCART
DORMANT
DULLARD
EARMARK
ECSTASY
EDUCATE
ELEVATE
EMANATE
EMBRACE
EMERALD
EMULATE
ENCHAIN
ENCHANT
ENCLAVE
ENDWAYS
ENGRAFT
ENGRAVE
ENPLANE
ENSLAVE
ENSNARE
ENTRAIN
ENTRANT
EPITAPH
ESTUARY
EXCLAIM
EXPIATE
EXPLAIN
EXTRACT
EYEBALL
EYELASH
EYEWASH
FALLACY
FANFARE
FANTAIL
FANTASY
FARRAGO
FATBACK
FIREARM
FOLIAGE
FONDANT
FOOTAGE
FOREARM
FORSAKE
FORWARD
FOULARD
FRIGATE
FROWARD
FURNACE
GALLANT
GARBAGE
GARLAND
GERMANE
GESTAPO
GIZZARD
GOSHAWK
GOULASH
GRANARY
GRENADE
GRIMACE
GUARANI
GUNWALE
HAGGARD
HALYARD
HARVARD
HAULAGE
HECTARE
HERBAGE
HOBNAIL
HOECAKE
HOGBACK
HOGWASH
HOSTAGE
HOTCAKE
HUSBAND
HYDRANT
HYDRATE
IMITATE
IMPEACH
IMPEARL
INBOARD
INEXACT
INFLAME
INFLATE
INGRAFT
INGRAIN
INGRATE
INSTALL
INSTANT
INSTATE
INTRANS
ISOLATE
ITERATE
JACKASS
JANUARY
JAYWALK
LACTATE
LAGGARD
LANTANA
LANYARD
LEAFAGE
LEAKAGE

LEEWARD
LEOPARD
LEOTARD
LIBRARY
LIMEADE
LINEAGE
LINKAGE
LOWLAND
LUGGAGE
LULLABY
LUMBAGO
MACRAME
MAGNATE
MALLARD
MAMMARY
MANDATE
MANSARD
MASCARA
MASSAGE
MEDIATE
MERMAID
MESSAGE
METHANE
MIDLAND
MIGRANT
MIGRATE
MILEAGE
MILLAGE
MISCALL
MISNAME
MISTAKE
MONTAGE
MORDANT
MUNDANE
MURRAIN
MUSTANG
MUSTARD
NARRATE
NETWARE
NIAGARA
NIGGARD
NIRVANA
NITRATE
OATCAKE
OBVIATE
ODDBALL
OFFHAND
OPERATE
ORCHARD
OREGANO
ORIGAMI
OSSUARY
OSTMARK
OUTCAST
OUTFACE
OUTLAST
OUTRAGE
OUTRANK
OUTWARD
OVERACT
OVERAGE
OVERALL
OVERARM
OVERAWE
OVULATE
OXIDANT
PACKAGE
PAGEANT
PALMATE
PALPATE
PANCAKE
PARFAIT
PARTAKE
PASSAGE
PEASANT
PECCARY
PECCAVI
PENDANT
PENNANT
PERCALE
PERHAPS
PERTAIN
PERVADE
PHALANX
PHARAOH
PIEBALD
PIGTAIL
PILLAGE
PINNACE
PINNATE
PIQUANT
PITFALL
PIZZAZZ
PLACARD
PLACATE
PLENARY
PLUMAGE
POLLACK
POMPANO
PONIARD
PORTAGE
POSTAGE
POTTAGE
PREDATE
PREFACE
PRELATE
PREPARE
PRESAGE
PREVAIL
PRIMACY
PRIMARY
PRIMATE
PRIVACY
PRIVATE
PROBATE
PROFANE
PROPANE
PRORATE
PROSAIC
PULSATE
RADIANT
RADIATE
RAMPAGE
RAMPANT
RAMPART
RANSACK
RECLAIM
RECLAME
REFRACT
REFRAIN
REGNANT
RELEASE
REMNANT
REPLACE
RETRACE
RETRACT
RHUBARB
ROSEATE
RUMMAGE
SABBATH
SAGUARO
SALVAGE
SARCASM
SATIATE
SAUSAGE
SEALANT
SEAWALL
SEAWARD
SECTARY
SELVAGE
SERRATE
SERVANT
SETBACK
SEXTANT
SHEBANG
SIDEARM
SKYLARK
SKYWARD
SOPRANO
SPINACH
SPIRANT
STEWARD
STOMACH
STORAGE
SULFATE
SULTANA
SUMMARY
SUNBATH
SUNLAMP
SURFACE
SURNAME
SURPASS
SUSTAIN
TAMBALA
TANBARK
TEENAGE
TERNARY
TERRACE
TERRAIN
TESTATE
THERAPY
THREADY
THROATY
TIEBACK
TILLAGE
TIMPANI
TINWARE
TOENAIL
TONNAGE
TOPMAST
TOPSAIL
TORNADO
TOWPATH
TRAVAIL
TSUNAMI
ULULATE
UMBRAGE
UNAWARE
UNCHAIN
UNCLASP
UNERASE
UNHEARD
UNITARY
UNLEARN
UNLEASH
UNSNARL
UNWEAVE
UPBRAID
UPDRAFT
UPGRADE
UPSTAGE
UPSTART
UPSTATE
URINARY
URINATE
VAGRANT
VALIANT
VALUATE
VANTAGE
VANWARD
VARIANT
VERDANT
VERVAIN
VIBRANT
VIBRATE
VIBRATO
VILLAGE
VILLAIN
VINTAGE
VIOLATE
VITIATE
VOLCANO
VOLTAGE
VOLTAIC
VULGATE
WAGTAIL
WALLABY
WARFARE
WARPATH
WARRANT
WASSAIL
WASTAGE
WATTAGE
WAYWARD
WEASAND
WELFARE
WETBACK
WETLAND
WINDAGE
WORDAGE
YARDAGE
YARDARM
ACROBAT
AEROBIC
AFFABLE
ALEMBIC
ALGEBRA
AMIABLE
AUDIBLE
BANDBOX
BELABOR
BELLBOY
BLUBBER
BOURBON
BRAMBLE
BUGABOO
CALIBER
CAPABLE
CARABAO
CARDBUS
CARIBOU
CHAMBER
CLAMBER
CLOBBER
COHABIT
COPYBOY
CRABBED
CROWBAR
CRUMBLE
DECIBEL
DISABLE
DISOBEY
DRIBBLE
DURABLE
ENNOBLE
EQUABLE
EXHIBIT
FIREBOX
FIREBUG
FLATBED
FLYABLE
FREEBIE
FRIABLE
GEARBOX
GRUMBLE
HALIBUT
HANDBAG
HIGHBOY
IGNOBLE
INCUBUS
INHABIT
INHIBIT
JUKEBOX
LADYBUG
LEGIBLE
LIVABLE
LONGBOW
MACABRE
MAILBOX
MINIBUS
MUTABLE
NEWSBOY
NOTABLE
OCTOBER
OMNIBUS
PAGEBOY
PARABLE
PILLBOX
PLAYBOY
PLIABLE
PLOWBOY
PLUMBER
POSTBOY
POTABLE
QUIBBLE
RAINBOW
RAREBIT
RHOMBUS
RISIBLE
ROADBED
ROSEBUD
SALTBOX
SANDBAG
SANDBAR
SHAMBLE
SHERBET
SICKBED
SIZABLE
SLOBBER
SLUMBER
SOLUBLE
STUBBLE
STUMBLE
TENABLE
THIMBLE
TOOLBOX
TREMBLE
TROUBLE
TUNABLE
VISIBLE
VOCABLE
VOLUBLE
WADABLE
WINDBAG
WORKBAG
WORKBOX
AFRICAN
ANARCHY
ANTACID
APRICOT
ARTICLE
ATTACHE
AURICLE
BICYCLE
BIFOCAL
BORSCHT
BOUNCER
BRECCIA
BRIOCHE
CHANCEL
CHANCRE
CODICIL
CONICAL
COPYCAT
CORACLE
CORNCOB
COUNCIL
CUBICLE
CUTICLE
DEBACLE
DEFICIT
EARACHE
ETHICAL
FIANCEE
FINICKY
FLACCID
FLATCAR
HAIRCUT
HANDCAR
HELICAL
HELLCAT
HIBACHI
ILLICIT
INDICIA
KNEECAP
LEXICON
MAHICAN
MANACLE
MEDICAL
MEXICAN
MIMICRY
MIRACLE
MODICUM
MOHICAN
MONOCLE
MOROCCO
MUSICAL
OFFICER
OPTICAL
PANACEA
PANACHE
PANICLE
PEDICAB
PELICAN
POLECAT
RADICAL
RAUNCHY
RECYCLE
SIDECAR
SILICON
SIROCCO
SOLICIT
SOUPCON
STENCIL
TAXICAB
TOBACCO
TOPICAL
TREACLE
TYPICAL
UNLUCKY
VATICAN
VEHICLE
VESICLE
WILDCAT
WOODCUT
ABANDON
ABRIDGE
ADJUDGE
ASUNDER
BESIDES
BLADDER
BLEEDER
BLINDER
BLOODED
BLUNDER
BOREDOM
BOULDER
BOUNDEN
BOWLDER
BREADTH
BROADEN
BROIDER
BROODER
BULLDOG
CHEDDAR
CHOWDER
CITADEL
DECIDED
DECODER
DIVIDER
DWINDLE
FILMDOM
FOUNDER
FOUNDRY
FREEDOM
GLADDEN
GRANDAM
GRANDEE
GRIDDLE
GRINDER
GUERDON
GUILDER
HANGDOG
HOLIDAY
HUMIDOR
INFIDEL
INSIDER
JACKDAW
KATYDID
KINGDOM
LAUNDER
LAUNDRY
MACADAM
MATADOR
MAUNDER
MEANDER
MILLDAM
MONADIC
NOMADIC
NOONDAY
PALADIN
PARADOX
PLAUDIT
PLUNDER
QUONDAM
REMODEL
REREDOS
RESEDIT
RESIDUE
ROUNDUP
SCANDAL
SHUDDER
SLANDER
SLENDER
SMOLDER
SOMEDAY
SOUNDER
SPEEDUP
SPINDLE
SPINDLY
STANDBY
STRUDEL
SWADDLE

SWINDLE
THUNDER
TREADLE
TRODDEN
TRUNDLE
TUESDAY
TWADDLE
TWIDDLE
UNGODLY
WEEKDAY
WHEEDLE
WORKDAY
WORLDLY
ABSCESS
ACADEME
ACADEMY
ACHIEVE
ADDRESS
AGELESS
AILMENT
AIMLESS
ALCHEMY
ALIMENT
AMATEUR
AMBIENT
ANAPEST
ANCIENT
ANXIETY
ARCHERY
ARMREST
ARTLESS
ATHLETE
AUGMENT
AUSTERE
BARBELL
BATTERY
BELIEVE
BENZENE
BEQUEST
BERSERK
BESEECH
BESIEGE
BESMEAR
BESPEAK
BETWEEN
BITTERN
BITTERS
BOOKEND
BRACERO
BRAVERY
BUCKEYE
BUGBEAR
BURGEON
BURGESS
BURMESE
CALDERA
CANNERY
CANTEEN
CHAPEAU
CHATEAU
CHIMERA
CHINESE
CHOLERA
CISTERN
CLEMENT
COCKEYE
COLLECT
COLLEEN
COLLEGE
COMMEND
COMMENT
COMPEER
COMPETE
CONCEAL
CONCEDE
CONCEIT
CONCEPT
CONCERN
CONCERT
CONDEMN
CONFESS
CONGEAL
CONGEST
CONNECT
CONSENT
CONTEMN
CONTEND
CONTENT
CONTEST
CONTEXT
CONVENE
CONVENT
CONVERT
COOKERY
CORRECT
CORTEGE
CULVERT
CURRENT
CUTLERY
CYPRESS
DEANERY
DEFLECT
DEPLETE
DEPRESS
DESCEND
DESCENT
DESSERT
DIALECT
DIGRESS
DILUENT
DIOCESE
DISCERN
DISSECT
DISSENT
DISTEND
DRAPERY
DUBIETY
DUCHESS
DUDGEON
DUNGEON
EARNEST
EASTERN
EGGHEAD
ELEMENT
EMINENT
EMPRESS
ENDLESS
ENTREAT
ESTHETE
EVIDENT
EXCRETA
EXCRETE
EXEGETE
EXPRESS
EXTREME
FERMENT
FERNERY
FERVENT
FIFTEEN
FIGMENT
FILBERT
FISHERY
FLOWERY
FLYLEAF
FOOLERY
FORBEAR
FORCEPS
FORFEIT
FORFEND
GABFEST
GALLEON
GALLERY
GARMENT
GENTEEL
GEODESY
GIBLETS
GINSENG
GODDESS
GODHEAD
GODLESS
GODSEND
GUNNERY
HALBERD
HALVERS
HAPLESS
HARNESS
HARVEST
HAUBERK
HAUTEUR
HAYSEED
HEIRESS
HELLENE
HENPECK
HERSELF
HIMSELF
HOPHEAD
HOSIERY
HOSTESS
HOWBEIT
HUNKERS
HUTMENT
HYGIENE
ICEBERG
ILLNESS
IMAGERY
IMPIETY
IMPRESS
INDWELL
INFIELD
INFLECT
INGRESS
INKWELL
INQUEST
INSPECT
INSTEAD
ISRAELI
JITTERS
LACTEAL
LAMBENT
LANTERN
LARCENY
LARGESS
LAWLESS
LECHERY
LECTERN
LENIENT
LIMBECK
LINSEED
LIQUEFY
LIQUEUR
LOTTERY
MACHETE
MAGNETO
MALLEUS
MANTEAU
MARGENT
MASSEUR
MASTERY
MIDWEEK
MIDYEAR
MINUEND
MISDEED
MISLEAD
MISREAD
MISSEND
MULLEIN
MYSTERY
NAIVETE
NAIVETY
NANKEEN
NASCENT
NEGLECT
NONHERO
NOWHERE
NUCLEAR
NUCLEON
NUCLEUS
NURSERY
OATMEAL
OBSCENE
ODDMENT
OFFBEAT
ONESELF
OPPRESS
OPULENT
OROGENY
OUTSELL
OUTWEAR
PARVENU
PASTERN
PATIENT
PATTERN
PAYMENT
PENDENT
PEPPERY
PERCENT
PERCEPT
PERFECT
PERVERT
PHONEME
PIGMENT
PINKEYE
PIONEER
PLACEBO
PLATEAU
PORTEND
PORTENT
POSSESS
POSTERN
POTHEAD
POTHERB
POTTERY
PREBEND
PRECEDE
PRECEPT
PREFECT
PREHEAT
PRESENT
PRETEEN
PRETEND
PRETEXT
PREVENT
PROCEED
PROCESS
PROFESS
PROGENY
PROJECT
PROTEAN
PROTECT
PROTEGE
PROTEIN
PROTEST
PROVERB
PROWESS
PRUDENT
PUNGENT
PUTREFY
RAGWEED
RAIMENT
REAGENT
REDHEAD
REDRESS
REFLECT
REFRESH
REGRESS
RELIEVE
REPLETE
REPRESS
REQUEST
RESPECT
RETREAD
RETREAT
RICKETS
RICKETY
ROBBERY
ROOKERY
SALIENT
SAPIENT
SATIETY
SCENERY
SCREECH
SEAWEED
SECRECY
SECRETE
SEGMENT
SEQUENT
SERPENT
SHAPELY
SIAMESE
SINCERE
SIXTEEN
SKIWEAR
SLAVERY
SOCIETY
SOLVENT
SORCERY
SOYBEAN
SQUEEZE
STATELY
STIPEND
STUDENT
STUPEFY
SUBJECT
SUBVERT
SUCCEED
SUCCESS
SUGGEST
SUNBEAM
SUPREME
SURFEIT
SURGEON
SURGERY
SUSPECT
SUSPEND
TABLEAU
TAFFETA
TANGENT
TANNERY
TEMPERA
TEMPEST
THEREAT
THEREBY
THEREIN
THEREOF
THEREON
THERETO
THYSELF
TOGGERY
TOLUENE
TONNEAU
TOPLESS
TORMENT
TORPEDO
TORRENT
TOWHEAD
TRACERY
TRAGEDY
TRAPEZE
TRICEPS
TRIDENT
TRIREME
TRISECT
TURNERY
UKULELE
UMPTEEN
UNCLEAN
UNDRESS
UNGUENT
UPSWEPT
USELESS
VAQUERO
VARIETY
VERBENA
VERMEIL
VESPERS
VILLEIN
VIOLENT
VISCERA
WAGGERY
WALLEYE
WARHEAD
WARLESS
WEEKEND
WESTERN
WHEREAS
WHEREAT
WHEREBY
WHEREIN
WHEREOF
WHEREON
WHERETO
WIDGEON
WITHERS
WITLESS
WITNESS
WRYNECK
AQUIFER
BALEFUL
BASHFUL
BENEFIT
BRIMFUL
CAREFUL
CHAFFER
CHAMFER
CHIFFON
CONIFER
DEERFLY
DIREFUL
DOLEFUL
DUTIFUL
FATEFUL
FEARFUL
FIREFLY
FISTFUL
FRETFUL
GAINFUL
GIRAFFE
HANDFUL
LUCIFER
MALEFIC
MINDFUL
NEEDFUL
OVERFLY
PACIFIC
PITIFUL
PROFFER
SCRUFFY
SCUFFLE
SHUFFLE
SKIFFLE
SNAFFLE
SNIFFLE
SNUFFLE
SOUFFLE
SOULFUL
STAFFER
STIFFEN
STUFFIT
TRAFFIC
TRUFFLE
TUNEFUL
WAILFUL
WAKEFUL
WILLFUL
WISHFUL
WISTFUL
ALLEGRO
ALRIGHT
AMALGAM
ANTIGEN
BLOWGUN
BOLOGNA
BROUGHT
CHARGER
CHIGGER
CLANGOR
COLOGNE
DECAGON
DELIGHT
DEMIGOD
DOWAGER
DRAUGHT
DROUGHT
ECLOGUE
EPERGNE
FATIGUE
FINAGLE
FRAUGHT
FREIGHT
HANDGUN
HEXAGON
ILLEGAL
INSIGHT
INTEGER
LASAGNA
MANAGER
MOHEGAN
NOSEGAY
OCTAGON
PARAGON
PELAGIC
PERIGEE
PLUNGER
POLYGON
REFUGEE
SHINGLE
SHOTGUN
SLEIGHT
SMIDGEN
SMUGGLE
SNUGGLE
SPANGLE
STAGGER

STOP**G**AP
SWAG**G**ER
TANA**G**ER
THOU**G**HT
TONI**G**HT
TRIG**G**ER
UPRI**G**HT
UPTI**G**HT
VINE**G**AR
WRAN**G**LE
WRIG**G**LE
WRIN**G**ER
WRON**G**LY
WROU**G**HT
AIRS**H**IP
ALCO**H**OL
ANOT**H**ER
BANS**H**EE
BELL**H**OP
BENT**H**IC
BENT**H**OS
BIRC**H**ER
BLAT**H**ER
BLUC**H**ER
BROT**H**EL
BROT**H**ER
BURG**H**ER
BUTC**H**ER
CAMP**H**OR
CATC**H**ER
CATC**H**UP
CLOT**H**ES
CROC**H**ET
DAUP**H**IN
DEAT**H**LY
DOLP**H**IN
DOUG**H**TY
DRAC**H**MA
EARS**H**OT
EART**H**EN
EART**H**LY
EPIT**H**ET
FART**H**ER
FEAT**H**ER
FLES**H**LY
FLIG**H**TY
FRES**H**EN
FRES**H**ET
FURT**H**ER
GING**H**AM
GRAP**H**IC
GUMS**H**OE
GUNS**H**OT
HATC**H**ET
HAUG**H**TY
HEAT**H**EN
HEAT**H**ER

HOTS**H**OT
KETC**H**UP
KINS**H**IP
KITC**H**EN
LATC**H**ET
LEAT**H**ER
LOAT**H**LY
MARS**H**AL
MENT**H**OL
MORP**H**IA
NART**H**EX
NARW**H**AL
NAUG**H**TY
NEIT**H**ER
NORT**H**ER
PANT**H**ER
PITC**H**ER
POTS**H**OT
PRIT**H**EE
PROP**H**ET
PSYC**H**IC
PSYC**H**OL
RATC**H**ET
ROUG**H**EN
SAND**H**OG
SATC**H**EL
SLAT**H**ER
SLIT**H**ER
SMOT**H**ER
SOME**H**OW
SORG**H**UM
THIT**H**ER
TOUG**H**EN
TRAC**H**EA
TROC**H**EE
URET**H**RA
VOUC**H**ER
WARS**H**IP
WART**H**OG
WEAT**H**ER
WEIG**H**TY
WHET**H**ER
WHIT**H**ER
WORS**H**IP
ABIL**I**TY
ABOL**I**SH
ACID**I**FY
ACON**I**TE
ACQU**I**RE
ADEN**I**NE
AFFL**I**CT
AGON**I**ZE
AIRL**I**FT
AIRL**I**NE
AIRS**I**CK
ALEW**I**FE
ALUM**I**NA

AMAT**I**VE
AMEN**I**TY
AMER**I**ND
AMPL**I**FY
ANGU**I**SH
ANIL**I**NE
ANIM**I**SM
ANNU**I**TY
ANOD**I**ZE
ANTH**I**LL
ANYT**I**ME
ANYW**I**SE
APAT**I**TE
APPL**I**ED
APPO**I**NT
APPR**I**SE
ARCH**I**VE
ARRA**I**GN
ASCR**I**BE
ASIN**I**NE
ASTR**I**DE
ATAV**I**SM
ATEL**I**ER
ATHE**I**ST
ATOM**I**ZE
ATTA**I**NT
AUCT**I**ON
AUSP**I**CE
AVAR**I**CE
BACK**I**NG
BAGP**I**PE
BAIL**I**FF
BALD**I**NG
BAPT**I**SM
BAPT**I**ST
BAPT**I**ZE
BARR**I**ER
BARR**I**NG
BAST**I**ON
BATT**I**NG
BAUX**I**TE
BEAR**I**NG
BEAT**I**FY
BEDD**I**NG
BEDS**I**DE
BEDT**I**ME
BEEH**I**VE
BEEL**I**NE
BEGR**I**ME
BEGU**I**LE
BEGU**I**NE
BELG**I**AN
BENZ**I**NE
BEST**I**AL
BETH**I**NK
BETW**I**XT
BILL**I**ON

BIND**I**NG
BIOT**I**TE
BLEM**I**SH
BONF**I**RE
BOOK**I**SH
BOWL**I**NE
BOWL**I**NG
BRAZ**I**ER
BREV**I**TY
BRIT**I**SH
BROM**I**DE
BROM**I**NE
BRUT**I**SH
BULL**I**ON
BUNT**I**NG
BURN**I**SH
BUSH**I**NG
CADM**I**UM
CAIT**I**FF
CALC**I**FY
CALC**I**NE
CALC**I**TE
CALC**I**UM
CALL**I**NG
CAMB**I**UM
CAND**I**ED
CAPR**I**CE
CAPS**I**ZE
CAPT**I**ON
CAPT**I**VE
CARB**I**DE
CARB**I**NE
CARD**I**AC
CARM**I**NE
CARR**I**ER
CARR**I**ON
CARS**I**CK
CASH**I**ER
CAST**I**NG
CATB**I**RD
CATF**I**SH
CATL**I**KE
CAUT**I**ON
CEIL**I**NG
CELS**I**US
CENT**I**ME
CENT**I**MO
CERT**I**FY
CESS**I**ON
CHAD**I**AN
CHAL**I**CE
CHAR**I**OT
CHAR**I**TY
CHEM**I**SE
CHEM**I**ST
CHER**I**SH
CHEV**I**OT

CIVV**I**ES
CLAR**I**FY
CLAR**I**ON
CLAR**I**TY
CLAV**I**ER
COAT**I**NG
COAX**I**AL
COCA**I**NE
CODE**I**NE
CODF**I**SH
CODL**I**NG
COEX**I**ST
COLL**I**DE
COLL**I**ER
COMB**I**NE
COMP**I**LE
CONC**I**SE
COND**I**GN
CONF**I**DE
CONF**I**NE
CONF**I**RM
CONN**I**VE
CONS**I**GN
CONS**I**ST
CONV**I**CT
COPP**I**CE
CORD**I**AL
CORD**I**TE
CORN**I**CE
COST**I**VE
COUR**I**ER
COWB**I**RD
COWH**I**DE
COWL**I**CK
COWL**I**NG
CRAN**I**UM
CRAV**I**NG
CREV**I**CE
CROS**I**ER
CRUC**I**AL
CRUC**I**FY
CUIS**I**NE
CUNN**I**NG
CUPR**I**TE
CURB**I**NG
CURS**I**VE
CUSH**I**ON
CUTT**I**NG
CYAN**I**DE
CYCL**I**ST
CZAR**I**NA
DAND**I**FY
DARL**I**NG
DASH**I**KI
DASH**I**NG
DAYT**I**ME
DEAL**I**NG

DEBR**I**EF
DECE**I**VE
DECL**I**NE
DENS**I**TY
DENT**I**ST
DEPR**I**VE
DERR**I**CK
DERV**I**SH
DESP**I**SE
DESP**I**TE
DEST**I**NE
DEST**I**NY
DIAR**I**ST
DICT**I**ON
DIGN**I**FY
DIGN**I**TY
DISL**I**KE
DISM**I**SS
DIST**I**CH
DIST**I**LL
DOGF**I**SH
DOSS**I**ER
DRAW**I**NG
DUCT**I**LE
DUMP**I**NG
EARR**I**NG
EBON**I**TE
EDIF**I**CE
EDIT**I**ON
EGOT**I**SM
ELEG**I**AC
ELIS**I**ON
ELIT**I**SM
ELUS**I**VE
ELYS**I**UM
EMER**I**TA
EMOT**I**ON
ENDW**I**SE
ENGL**I**SH
ENQU**I**RE
ENTW**I**NE
EREM**I**TE
EROS**I**ON
EROS**I**VE
ESQU**I**RE
ETCH**I**NG
EVAS**I**ON
EVEN**I**NG
EXAM**I**NE
FACT**I**ON
FAIL**I**NG
FAIR**I**NG
FALS**I**FY
FANC**I**ER
FARM**I**NG
FARR**I**ER
FASC**I**SM

FASH**I**ON
FATU**I**TY
FAUV**I**SM
FEBR**I**LE
FEEL**I**NG
FENC**I**NG
FERM**I**UM
FERT**I**LE
FEST**I**VE
FICT**I**ON
FILL**I**NG
FIND**I**NG
FINF**I**SH
FINN**I**SH
FISH**I**NG
FISS**I**LE
FISS**I**ON
FITT**I**NG
FLEM**I**NG
FLEM**I**SH
FLOR**I**ST
FLUT**I**ST
FOOL**I**SH
FOOT**I**NG
FORE**I**GN
FORG**I**NG
FORG**I**VE
FORT**I**FY
FOUL**I**NG
FRAG**I**LE
FULF**I**LL
FURB**I**SH
FURN**I**SH
FURR**I**ER
FURR**I**NG
FURT**I**VE
FUST**I**AN
GALL**I**UM
GAMB**I**AN
GARF**I**SH
GARN**I**SH
GELD**I**NG
GENT**I**AN
GENT**I**LE
GENU**I**NE
GIMM**I**CK
GLAC**I**AL
GLAC**I**ER
GLAZ**I**ER
GLOR**I**FY
GODL**I**KE
GOSL**I**NG
GRAN**I**TE
GRAT**I**FY
GRAT**I**NG
GRAV**I**TY
GRAZ**I**ER

GREC**I**AN
GRUN**I**ON
GUAN**I**NE
GUNF**I**RE
HAFN**I**UM
HALT**I**NG
HANG**I**NG
HAPP**I**LY
HARR**I**ER
HASH**I**NG
HASH**I**SH
HAYR**I**CK
HAYW**I**RE
HEAD**I**NG
HEAR**I**NG
HELL**I**ON
HELP**I**NG
HEML**I**NE
HERO**I**CS
HERO**I**NE
HERO**I**SM
HERR**I**NG
HINT**I**NG
HOLD**I**NG
HOLM**I**UM
HOOS**I**ER
HORR**I**FY
HOSP**I**CE
HOST**I**LE
HOUS**I**NG
HOWL**I**NG
HULK**I**NG
HUSK**I**NG
IDOL**I**ZE
IMAG**I**NE
IMAG**I**SM
IMPR**I**NT
INCL**I**NE
INFL**I**CT
INIT**I**AL
INKL**I**NG
INQU**I**RE
INQU**I**RY
INSP**I**RE
INST**I**LL
INVE**I**GH
INVO**I**CE
IRAN**I**AN
IRID**I**UM
IRON**I**NG
ITAL**I**AN
ITEM**I**ZE
JASM**I**NE
JAYB**I**RD
JOLL**I**TY
JOTT**I**NG
JOYR**I**DE

JUDA**I**SM
JUST**I**CE
JUST**I**FY
KADD**I**SH
KEEP**I**NG
KERN**I**NG
KHED**I**VE
KILL**I**NG
KNOW**I**NG
LAND**I**NG
LAOT**I**AN
LAPW**I**NG
LATR**I**NE
LATT**I**CE
LATV**I**AN
LEAD**I**NG
LEFT**I**SM
LEGG**I**NG
LEMM**I**NG
LEMP**I**RA
LEON**I**NE
LESB**I**AN
LIGN**I**FY
LIGN**I**TE
LION**I**ZE
LIST**I**NG
LITH**I**UM
LODG**I**NG
LONG**I**NG
MACH**I**NE
MADD**I**NG
MADE**I**RA
MAGN**I**FY
MALA**I**SE
MANK**I**ND
MANL**I**KE
MANN**I**SH
MANS**I**ON
MART**I**AL
MART**I**AN
MART**I**NI
MARX**I**SM
MASS**I**VE
MAST**I**FF
MATT**I**NS
MAWK**I**SH
MEAN**I**NG
MEET**I**NG
MENT**I**ON
MESS**I**AH
MEST**I**ZO
MIDR**I**FF
MIDW**I**FE
MILL**I**ME
MILL**I**NG
MILL**I**ON
MISF**I**LE

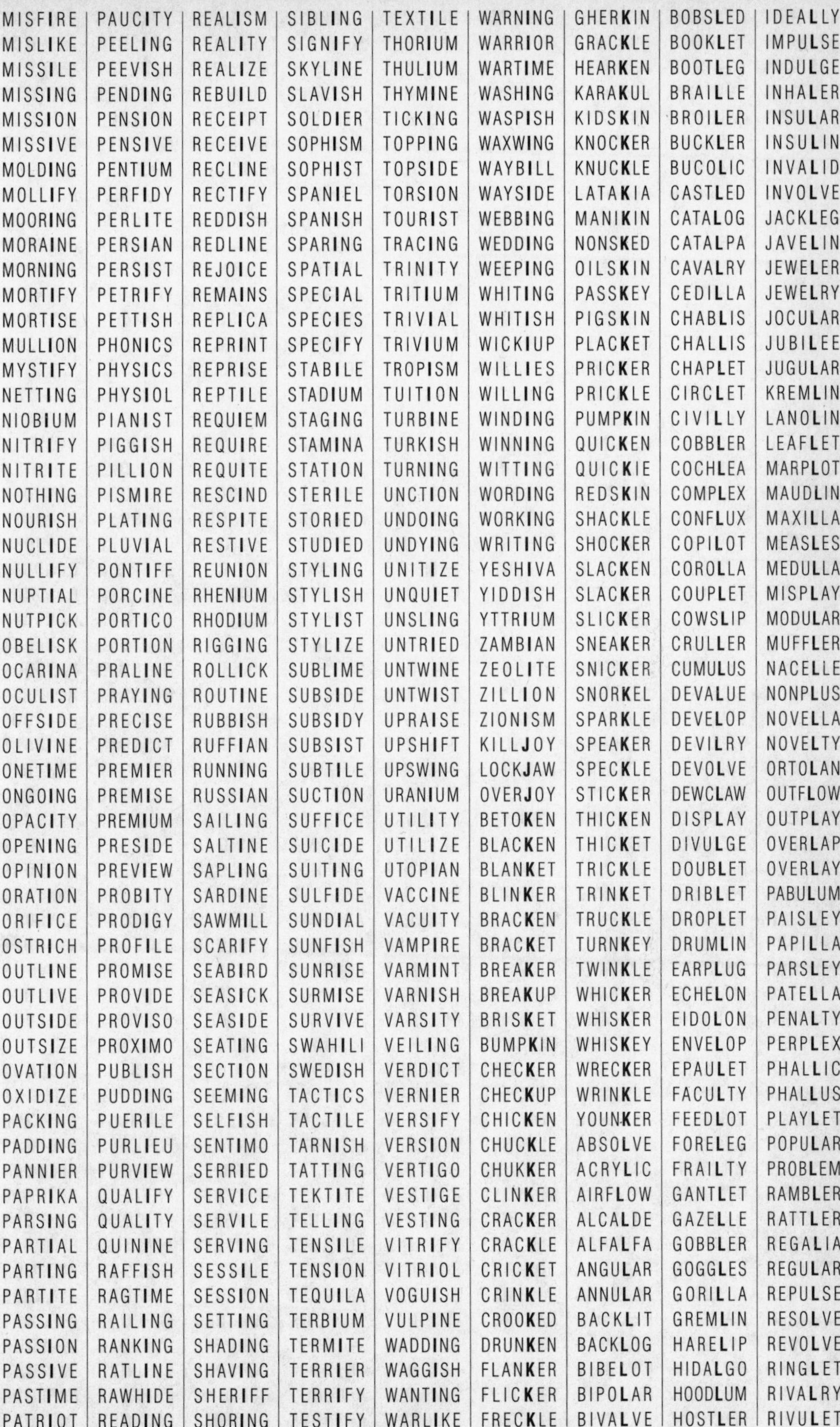

| | | | | | | | | |
|---|---|---|---|---|---|---|---|---|
| MISFIRE | PAUCITY | REALISM | SIBLING | TEXTILE | WARNING | GHERKIN | BOBSLED | IDEALLY |
| MISLIKE | PEELING | REALITY | SIGNIFY | THORIUM | WARRIOR | GRACKLE | BOOKLET | IMPULSE |
| MISSILE | PEEVISH | REALIZE | SKYLINE | THULIUM | WARTIME | HEARKEN | BOOTLEG | INDULGE |
| MISSING | PENDING | REBUILD | SLAVISH | THYMINE | WASHING | KARAKUL | BRAILLE | INHALER |
| MISSION | PENSION | RECEIPT | SOLDIER | TICKING | WASPISH | KIDSKIN | BROILER | INSULAR |
| MISSIVE | PENSIVE | RECEIVE | SOPHISM | TOPPING | WAXWING | KNOCKER | BUCKLER | INSULIN |
| MOLDING | PENTIUM | RECLINE | SOPHIST | TOPSIDE | WAYBILL | KNUCKLE | BUCOLIC | INVALID |
| MOLLIFY | PERFIDY | RECTIFY | SPANIEL | TORSION | WAYSIDE | LATAKIA | CASTLED | INVOLVE |
| MOORING | PERLITE | REDDISH | SPANISH | TOURIST | WEBBING | MANIKIN | CATALOG | JACKLEG |
| MORAINE | PERSIAN | REDLINE | SPARING | TRACING | WEDDING | NONSKED | CATALPA | JAVELIN |
| MORNING | PERSIST | REJOICE | SPATIAL | TRINITY | WEEPING | OILSKIN | CAVALRY | JEWELER |
| MORTIFY | PETRIFY | REMAINS | SPECIAL | TRITIUM | WHITING | PASSKEY | CEDILLA | JEWELRY |
| MORTISE | PETTISH | REPLICA | SPECIES | TRIVIAL | WHITISH | PIGSKIN | CHABLIS | JOCULAR |
| MULLION | PHONICS | REPRINT | SPECIFY | TRIVIUM | WICKIUP | PLACKET | CHALLIS | JUBILEE |
| MYSTIFY | PHYSICS | REPRISE | STABILE | TROPISM | WILLIES | PRICKER | CHAPLET | JUGULAR |
| NETTING | PHYSIOL | REPTILE | STADIUM | TUITION | WILLING | PRICKLE | CIRCLET | KREMLIN |
| NIOBIUM | PIANIST | REQUIEM | STAGING | TURBINE | WINDING | PUMPKIN | CIVILLY | LANOLIN |
| NITRIFY | PIGGISH | REQUIRE | STAMINA | TURKISH | WINNING | QUICKEN | COBBLER | LEAFLET |
| NITRITE | PILLION | REQUITE | STATION | TURNING | WITTING | QUICKIE | COCHLEA | MARPLOT |
| NOTHING | PISMIRE | RESCIND | STERILE | UNCTION | WORDING | REDSKIN | COMPLEX | MAUDLIN |
| NOURISH | PLATING | RESPITE | STORIED | UNDOING | WORKING | SHACKLE | CONFLUX | MAXILLA |
| NUCLIDE | PLUVIAL | RESTIVE | STUDIED | UNDYING | WRITING | SHOCKER | COPILOT | MEASLES |
| NULLIFY | PONTIFF | REUNION | STYLING | UNITIZE | YESHIVA | SLACKEN | COROLLA | MEDULLA |
| NUPTIAL | PORCINE | RHENIUM | STYLISH | UNQUIET | YIDDISH | SLACKER | COUPLET | MISPLAY |
| NUTPICK | PORTICO | RHODIUM | STYLIST | UNSLING | YTTRIUM | SLICKER | COWSLIP | MODULAR |
| OBELISK | PORTION | RIGGING | STYLIZE | UNTRIED | ZAMBIAN | SNEAKER | CRULLER | MUFFLER |
| OCARINA | PRALINE | ROLLICK | SUBLIME | UNTWINE | ZEOLITE | SNICKER | CUMULUS | NACELLE |
| OCULIST | PRAYING | ROUTINE | SUBSIDE | UNTWIST | ZILLION | SNORKEL | DEVALUE | NONPLUS |
| OFFSIDE | PRECISE | RUBBISH | SUBSIDY | UPRAISE | ZIONISM | SPARKLE | DEVELOP | NOVELLA |
| OLIVINE | PREDICT | RUFFIAN | SUBSIST | UPSHIFT | KILLJOY | SPEAKER | DEVILRY | NOVELTY |
| ONETIME | PREMIER | RUNNING | SUBTILE | UPSWING | LOCKJAW | SPECKLE | DEVOLVE | ORTOLAN |
| ONGOING | PREMISE | RUSSIAN | SUCTION | URANIUM | OVERJOY | STICKER | DEWCLAW | OUTFLOW |
| OPACITY | PREMIUM | SAILING | SUFFICE | UTILITY | BETOKEN | THICKEN | DISPLAY | OUTPLAY |
| OPENING | PRESIDE | SALTINE | SUICIDE | UTILIZE | BLACKEN | THICKET | DIVULGE | OVERLAP |
| OPINION | PREVIEW | SAPLING | SUITING | UTOPIAN | BLANKET | TRICKLE | DOUBLET | OVERLAY |
| ORATION | PROBITY | SARDINE | SULFIDE | VACCINE | BLINKER | TRINKET | DRIBLET | PABULUM |
| ORIFICE | PRODIGY | SAWMILL | SUNDIAL | VACUITY | BRACKEN | TRUCKLE | DROPLET | PAISLEY |
| OSTRICH | PROFILE | SCARIFY | SUNFISH | VAMPIRE | BRACKET | TURNKEY | DRUMLIN | PAPILLA |
| OUTLINE | PROMISE | SEABIRD | SUNRISE | VARMINT | BREAKER | TWINKLE | EARPLUG | PARSLEY |
| OUTLIVE | PROVIDE | SEASICK | SURMISE | VARNISH | BREAKUP | WHICKER | ECHELON | PATELLA |
| OUTSIDE | PROVISO | SEASIDE | SURVIVE | VARSITY | BRISKET | WHISKER | EIDOLON | PENALTY |
| OUTSIZE | PROXIMO | SEATING | SWAHILI | VEILING | BUMPKIN | WHISKEY | ENVELOP | PERPLEX |
| OVATION | PUBLISH | SECTION | SWEDISH | VERDICT | CHECKER | WRECKER | EPAULET | PHALLIC |
| OXIDIZE | PUDDING | SEEMING | TACTICS | VERNIER | CHECKUP | WRINKLE | FACULTY | PHALLUS |
| PACKING | PUERILE | SELFISH | TACTILE | VERSIFY | CHICKEN | YOUNKER | FEEDLOT | PLAYLET |
| PADDING | PURLIEU | SENTIMO | TARNISH | VERSION | CHUCKLE | ABSOLVE | FORELEG | POPULAR |
| PANNIER | PURVIEW | SERRIED | TATTING | VERTIGO | CHUKKER | ACRYLIC | FRAILTY | PROBLEM |
| PAPRIKA | QUALIFY | SERVICE | TEKTITE | VESTIGE | CLINKER | AIRFLOW | GANTLET | RAMBLER |
| PARSING | QUALITY | SERVILE | TELLING | VESTING | CRACKER | ALCALDE | GAZELLE | RATTLER |
| PARTIAL | QUININE | SERVING | TENSILE | VITRIFY | CRACKLE | ALFALFA | GOBBLER | REGALIA |
| PARTING | RAFFISH | SESSILE | TENSION | VITRIOL | CRICKET | ANGULAR | GOGGLES | REGULAR |
| PARTITE | RAGTIME | SESSION | TEQUILA | VOGUISH | CRINKLE | ANNULAR | GORILLA | REPULSE |
| PASSING | RAILING | SETTING | TERBIUM | VULPINE | CROOKED | BACKLIT | GREMLIN | RESOLVE |
| PASSION | RANKING | SHADING | TERMITE | WADDING | DRUNKEN | BACKLOG | HARELIP | REVOLVE |
| PASSIVE | RATLINE | SHAVING | TERRIER | WAGGISH | FLANKER | BIBELOT | HIDALGO | RINGLET |
| PASTIME | RAWHIDE | SHERIFF | TERRIFY | WANTING | FLICKER | BIPOLAR | HOODLUM | RIVALRY |
| PATRIOT | READING | SHORING | TESTIFY | WARLIKE | FRECKLE | BIVALVE | HOSTLER | RIVULET |

ROOTLET
ROYALTY
RUBELLA
SAMPLER
SANDLOT
SCALLOP
SCARLET
SCHOLAR
SECULAR
SHALLOP
SHALLOW
SHELLAC
SIDELIT
SIMILAR
SKILLET
SPELLER
SPOILER
SQUALID
SQUALOR
SQUELCH
STEALTH
STELLAR
SURPLUS
SWALLOW
SWOLLEN
TABULAR
TITULAR
TRAILER
TRELLIS
TRIPLET
TRIPLEX
TROLLEY
TROLLOP
TUBULAR
TUMBLER
TUTELAR
TWILLED
VANILLA
VITTLES
VOCALIC
WARBLER
WAVELET
WHEELER
WHITLOW
WHORLED
WIGGLER
WOODLOT
ABDOMEN
ABYSMAL
ALBUMEN
ALBUMIN
ANAEMIA
ASHAMED
ATTEMPT
BATSMAN
BETIMES
BITUMEN

BOATMAN
BONDMAN
BRAHMAN
BRAHMIN
CALOMEL
CALUMET
CALUMNY
CARAMEL
CAVEMAN
CERAMIC
CERUMEN
CHAPMAN
CHARMER
CHROMIC
DECIMAL
DELIMIT
DILEMMA
DOORMAN
DOORMAT
DRUMMER
DYNAMIC
ENDEMIC
FIREMAN
FOOTMAN
FOREMAN
FREEMAN
FROGMAN
GLEEMAN
GLIMMER
GOODMAN
GOURMET
GRAMMAR
GROMMET
HACKMAN
HANGMAN
HEADMAN
INHUMAN
ISTHMUS
KINSMAN
LINEMAN
MAILMAN
MANUMIT
MARIMBA
MAXIMAL
MAXIMUM
MEATMAN
MILKMAN
MINIMAL
MINIMUM
MONOMER
NEWSMAN
OARSMAN
OPTIMAL
OPTIMUM
OTTOMAN
PAJAMAS
PLOWMAN

PLUMMET
POLEMIC
POLYMER
POSTMAN
PREEMIE
PREEMPT
PROGMAN
PROPMAN
PULLMAN
PYJAMAS
PYRAMID
REGIMEN
SANDMAN
SEISMIC
SHIMMER
SHOWMAN
SIDEMAN
STAMMER
THERMAL
THERMOS
TOXEMIA
TRAMMEL
TRIUMPH
UNARMED
UNKEMPT
VITAMIN
WOODMAN
WORKMAN
YARDMAN
ABSENCE
ACRONYM
ADJUNCT
ADRENAL
ADVANCE
AGAINST
ALMANAC
ALMONER
ALUMNUS
AMMONIA
ANDANTE
ANTENNA
ANTONYM
ARPANET
ARRANGE
ARSENAL
ARSENIC
ASKANCE
BALANCE
BALONEY
BARONET
BAYONET
BEATNIK
BEGONIA
BLARNEY
BONANZA
BROWNIE
CABINET

CADENCE
CADENZA
CALENDS
CHANNEL
CHARNEL
CHIANTI
CHIGNON
CHIMNEY
CHRONIC
CHUTNEY
CLEANLY
CLEANSE
CLEANUP
COCKNEY
COCONUT
COLONEL
CORINTH
CORONAL
CORONER
CORONET
DECENCY
DEFENSE
DEFUNCT
DEMONIC
DERANGE
DETENTE
DIURNAL
DOMINIE
DOYENNE
DRAGNET
DURANCE
EFFENDI
ENHANCE
ENTENTE
ENVENOM
EQUINOX
ESSENCE
ETERNAL
ETHANOL
EXPANSE
EXPENSE
EXPUNGE
EXTINCT
FAIENCE
FINANCE
FLANNEL
FLOUNCE
GRAPNEL
HACKNEY
HOMONYM
HOSANNA
IMMENSE
IMPANEL
IMPINGE
INCENSE
INFANCY
INGENUE

INNINGS
INTENSE
JACINTH
JEJUNUM
JOURNAL
JOURNEY
JOYANCE
LACONIC
LAMINAR
LEARNED
LICENSE
LOCKNUT
LOZENGE
MAGENTA
MAKINGS
MARINER
MASONIC
MASONRY
MATINEE
MELANGE
MELANIC
MELANIN
MEMENTO
NOMINAL
NOMINEE
OFFENSE
ORDINAL
ORGANDY
ORGANIC
ORGANZA
PARSNIP
PARTNER
PENANCE
PETUNIA
PFENNIG
PHOENIX
PHRENIC
PILSNER
PIMENTO
PIRANHA
RECENCY
REFINED
REGENCY
RETINUE
REVENGE
REVENUE
ROMANCE
ROTUNDA
SATANIC
SAVANNA
SCANNER
SCIENCE
SEMINAL
SEMINAR
SEVENTY
SHAWNEE
SILENCE

SPLENIC
SPUTNIK
STAUNCH
STERNUM
STRANGE
STRINGY
SYNONYM
SYRINGE
TECHNIC
TENANCY
TETANUS
THINNER
TIDINGS
TITANIC
TOPKNOT
TOURNEY
TRAINEE
TROUNCE
TYRANNY
UNCANNY
UNHANDY
UNHINGE
UNMANLY
VACANCY
VALANCE
VALENCE
VEDANTA
VERANDA
VICINAL
VINTNER
WAGONER
WHATNOT
WIZENED
WOMANLY
ABALONE
ABSCOND
ACETONE
ADENOID
ADIPOSE
AFFRONT
AIRFOIL
AIRPORT
AIRPOST
ALIMONY
AMATORY
AMOROUS
AMPHORA
ANALOGY
ANATOMY
ANCHOVY
ANDROID
ANEMONE
ANXIOUS
ANYBODY
ANYMORE
APOLOGY
APPROVE

AQUEOUS
ARDUOUS
ARMHOLE
AUREOLE
BALCONY
BALLOON
BANNOCK
BARROOM
BASSOON
BAZOOKA
BECLOUD
BEDPOST
BEDROCK
BEDROLL
BEDROOM
BEDSORE
BEHOOVE
BELLOWS
BENZOIN
BETROTH
BIGHORN
BILIOUS
BIOLOGY
BLOWOUT
BOUDOIR
BOYCOTT
BUFFOON
BULLOCK
BURDOCK
BURNOUT
BUTTOCK
CABOOSE
CALLOUS
CARIOUS
CARLOAD
CARPORT
CARTOON
CASSOCK
CATBOAT
CATHODE
CHAMOIS
CHEROOT
CHICORY
CHINOOK
COLLOID
COMFORT
COMMODE
COMPORT
COMPOSE
COMPOST
COMPOTE
CONCOCT
CONCORD
CONDOLE
CONDONE
CONFORM
CONJOIN

CONNOTE
CONSOLE
CONSORT
CONTORT
CONTOUR
CONVOKE
COOKOUT
COPIOUS
CORDOBA
CORRODE
COULOMB
COWPOKE
COXCOMB
CUCKOLD
CURIOUS
CURSORY
CUSTODY
CUTWORM
CYCLONE
DAYBOOK
DEFROST
DEPLORE
DESPOIL
DESPOND
DEVIOUS
DIAMOND
DIPLOID
DIPLOMA
DISCORD
DISJOIN
DISPORT
DISPOSE
DISROBE
DISTORT
DOGWOOD
DRAGOON
DUBIOUS
DUTEOUS
EARLOBE
ECOLOGY
ECONOMY
EMBROIL
ENAMOUR
ENCLOSE
ENDMOST
ENGROSS
ENTROPY
ENVIOUS
EPISODE
EPITOME
ERELONG
EUPHONY
EXPLODE
EXPLOIT
EXPLORE
EYESORE
FACTORY

FALLOUT
FATUOUS
FERROUS
FESTOON
FETLOCK
FIBROID
FLAVOUR
FOGHORN
FOLDOUT
FORBODE
FORLORN
FOXHOLE
FULSOME
FURIOUS
FURLONG
GALLOWS
GARROTE
GEOLOGY
GIBBOUS
GLAMOUR
GLUCOSE
GODHOOD
GONDOLA
GUMBOIL
GUNBOAT
GUNLOCK
HADDOCK
HAMMOCK
HANDOUT
HANGOUT
HAPLOID
HARBOUR
HARMONY
HARPOON
HASSOCK
HAYCOCK
HAYFORK
HAYLOFT
HEINOUS
HEMLOCK
HICKORY
HIDEOUS
HIDEOUT
HILLOCK
HIPBONE
HISTORY
HOEDOWN
HORMONE
HOTFOOT
HUMMOCK
HYDROUS
HYMNODY
ICEBOAT
IGNEOUS
IMPIOUS
IMPLODE
IMPLORE

IMPROVE
INCLOSE
INDOORS
INGROWN
INKHORN
INSHORE
INTROIT
IRKSOME
ISOTOPE
JEALOUS
JETPORT
KEYHOLE
KEYNOTE
KICKOFF
KINFOLK
LACTOSE
LAMPOON
LEGHORN
LEPROSY
LETDOWN
LISSOME
LOCKOUT
LOOKOUT
LOWDOWN
MAFIOSO
MALTOSE
MAMMOTH
MANHOLE
MANHOOD
MASTOID
MATTOCK
MAYPOLE
MENFOLK
MICROBE
MIDMOST
MIDTOWN
MONSOON
MUDROOM
NEOLOGY
NERVOUS
NETWORK
NEWBORN
NOCUOUS
NOISOME
NONBOOK
NOXIOUS
OARLOCK
OBVIOUS
OMINOUS
ONEROUS
ONSHORE
ORATORY
OUTCOME
OUTDOOR
OUTLOOK
OUTPOST
OUTVOTE

OUTWORK
OUTWORN
OXBLOOD
PADDOCK
PADLOCK
PAPOOSE
PARBOIL
PARLOUR
PARLOUS
PATROON
PAYLOAD
PAYROLL
PEACOCK
PEAFOWL
PERFORM
PERGOLA
PETIOLE
PIBROCH
PICCOLO
PILLORY
PINHOLE
PINWORM
PITEOUS
PLATOON
PLYWOOD
POMPOUS
PONTOON
POPCORN
POTHOLE
POTHOOK
PRECOOK
PREFORM
PRESOAK
PROLONG
PROMOTE
PRONOUN
PROPOSE
PROSODY
PROVOKE
PROVOST
PULLOUT
PURLOIN
PURPORT
PURPOSE
RACCOON
RAPPORT
RAUCOUS
RAVIOLI
READOUT
RECTORY
REDCOAT
REDWOOD
REGROUP
REPROOF
REPROVE
RESPOND
RESTORE

RHIZOME
ROWBOAT
RUINOUS
RUNDOWN
SAPWOOD
SEAFOOD
SEAPORT
SENSORY
SEQUOIA
SERIOUS
SHUTOUT
SHYLOCK
SINUOUS
SIRLOIN
SOMEONE
SPUMONI
SUBJOIN
SUBSOIL
SUCROSE
SUMMONS
SUNDOWN
SUNROOF
SUPPORT
SUPPOSE
SURTOUT
SYNCOPE
SYSTOLE
TABLOID
TADPOLE
TAKEOFF
TAPIOCA
TAPROOM
TAPROOT
TEDIOUS
TENFOLD
TENUOUS
THYROID
TINFOIL
TOEHOLD
TOPCOAT
TOPMOST
TOPSOIL
TORTONI
TOWBOAT
TREFOIL
TREMOLO
TRILOGY
TUGBOAT
TURMOIL
TURNOFF
TURNOUT
TUSSOCK
TWOSOME
TYPHOID
TYPHOON
UNBLOCK
UNCLOAK

UNCLOSE
UNCROSS
UNFROCK
UNGROUP
UNICORN
UNIFORM
UNKNOWN
UNLOOSE
UNQUOTE
URANOUS
UROLOGY
VACUOLE
VACUOUS
VAMOOSE
VARIOUS
VERBOSE
VICIOUS
VICTORY
VILLOUS
VISCOSE
VISCOUS
WALKOUT
WALLOON
WARLOCK
WARLORD
WASHOUT
WAXWORK
WAYWORN
WEDLOCK
WELCOME
WILLOWY
WINDOWS
WINSOME
WITHOUT
WORKOUT
ZEALOUS
ZOOLOGY
APROPOS
ATROPHY
AUTOPSY
BLOOPER
CALIPER
CALYPSO
CHEAPEN
CHIPPER
CHOPPER
CLAPPER
CLIPPER
COCKPIT
CRIPPLE
CROPPER
CRUMPET
CRUMPLE
DASHPOT
DEADPAN
DROPPER
DUCKPIN

DUSTPAN
ECLIPSE
ELLIPSE
ESCAPEE
EXAMPLE
FLAPPER
FLIPPER
FOOTPAD
GLIMPSE
GRAPPLE
GRAUPEL
GROUPER
GROUPIE
HAIRPIN
HARDPAN
HEADPIN
HEXAPOD
INSIPID
JACKPOT
JODHPUR
JUNIPER
KINGPIN
OCTOPUS
OEDIPAL
PANOPLY
PARAPET
PLAYPEN
PROSPER
RELAPSE
SCALPEL
SCAMPER
SCRAPPY
SCRUPLE
SCUPPER
SHAMPOO
SHARPEN
SHARPER
SHARPIE
SKIPPER
SLEEPER
SLIPPER
STEEPLE
STIPPLE
STOPPER
STROPHE
SUNSPOT
SYNAPSE
TRAIPSE
TRAMPLE
TROOPER
TRUMPET
UNHAPPY
WHIMPER
WHIPPET
WHISPER
WHOOPLA
WHOPPER

WRAPPER
ANTIQUE
BAROQUE
BRUSQUE
MACAQUE
OBLIQUE
OBLOQUY
OBSEQUY
PERIQUE
RELIQUE
ADMIRAL
ADVERSE
AILERON
AIRDROP
ALLERGY
ANAGRAM
ANDIRON
ANTHRAX
ANTHROP
APPAREL
ARMORER
ASHTRAY
ASPIRIN
ASSURED
ATHIRST
AUSTRAL
BALDRIC
BESHREW
BIZARRE
BUCKRAM
CABARET
CALDRON
CALORIC
CALORIE
CAMBRIC
CATARRH
CENTRAL
CHAGRIN
CHEVRON
COLORED
CONTRIB
CONTROL
COTERIE
CULPRIT
DECORUM
DEMERIT
DESERVE
DESTROY
DEWDROP
DEXTRIN
DIAGRAM
DISHRAG
DIVERGE
DIVERSE
DIVORCE
DOGTROT
EARDRUM

ELDERLY
EMBARGO
EMPEROR
ENDORSE
ENFORCE
ENLARGE
EPIGRAM
EQUERRY
EXCERPT
EYEBROW
FEDERAL
FORTRAN
FULCRUM
FUNERAL
GASTRIC
GENERAL
GENERIC
GUMDROP
HEPARIN
HUMDRUM
HUMERUS
HUNDRED
IMMERSE
IMMORAL
IMPERIL
INDORSE
INFARCT
INFERNO
INHERIT
INNARDS
INSURED
INSURER
INTERIM
INVERSE
KINDRED
LABORED
LAMPREY
LATERAL
LIBERAL
LIBERTY
LITERAL
LITURGY
LOWBROW
LUCERNE
LUSTRAL
MACDRAW
MALARIA
MANDREL
MANDRIL
MAZURKA
MINARET
MINERAL
MISTRAL
MONARCH
MONGREL
MUSKRAT
NATURAL

NEUTRAL
NEUTRON
NOSTRIL
NOSTRUM
NUMERAL
NUMERIC
OBSERVE
OBVERSE
ORDERLY
OUTCROP
OUTDRAW
OUTGROW
OVERRUN
PALFREY
PAPYRUS
PILGRIM
POLARIS
PORTRAY
POVERTY
PRAIRIE
PROGRAM
PUBERTY
QUARREL
RATTRAP
REBIRTH
REFEREE
REMORSE
RESERVE
RETIRED
RETIREE
REVERIE
REVERSE
ROSTRUM
SADIRON
SAFFRON
SAMURAI
SCOURGE
SEVERAL
SOLARIS
SPARROW
SPLURGE
STIRRUP
TANTRUM
TENDRIL
TENURED
THEOREM
TIMBREL
TUMBREL
UNDERGO
UNEARTH
UNHORSE
UNMORAL
UNNERVE
UNSCREW
UNSTRAP
UPSURGE
VENTRAL

VETERAN
VICEROY
WASTREL
WINDROW
WOLFRAM
ZYMURGY
ABYSSAL
ACCUSAL
ACCUSED
ADVISED
AEROSOL
AMNESIA
AMNESTY
APHASIA
ARTISAN
ARTISTE
BAGASSE
BATISTE
BENISON
BLESSED
BLOSSOM
BROWSER
BRUISER
BUCKSAW
CAISSON
CANASTA
CELESTA
CHANSON
CHASSIS
CLASSIC
COARSEN
COUNSEL
COURSER
CRIMSON
CRUISER
DEMESNE
DEPOSIT
DIVISOR
DRESSER
DYNASTY
EMBASSY
FINESSE
FLOTSAM
FORESEE
FRETSAW
FUCHSIA
GAINSAY
GENESIS
HACKSAW
HANDSAW
HANDSEL
HANDSET
HEADSET
HEARSAY
IMPASSE
IMPASTO
INCISOR

KEELSON
LIAISON
MAJESTY
MALISON
MALMSEY
MEIOSIS
MILKSOP
MIMESIS
MITOSIS
MODISTE
NEMESIS
NONUSER
ODYSSEY
OPOSSUM
OSMOSIS
OVERSEA
OVERSEE
PARASOL
PARESIS
POCOSIN
RICKSHA
RIPOSTE
SATISFY
SPONSOR
SPOUSAL
STEPSON
TRANSIT
TRANSOM
TREASON
UNBOSOM
UTENSIL
VENISON
WHIPSAW
ADAPTER
AMMETER
AMPUTEE
APOSTLE
AQUATIC
ARBITER
ARBUTUS
ASCETIC
ASEPTIC
ASIATIC
AUDITOR
BATHTUB
BEASTLY
BELATED
BEWITCH
BIMETAL
BIRETTA
BLINTZE
BLISTER
BLOATER
BLOTTER
BLUSTER
BOLSTER
BREATHE
BRISTLE
BRITTLE
BURETTE
CAPITAL
CAPITOL
CAPSTAN
CAROTID
CAUSTIC
CHANTEY
CHANTRY
CHAPTER
CHARTER
CHASTEN
CHATTEL
CHATTER
CHEETAH
CHINTZY
CHOCTAW
CHORTLE
CLASTIC
CLATTER
CLUSTER
CLUTTER
COUNTER
COUNTRY
COURTLY
CREATOR
CRITTER
CROUTON
CRYPTIC
CRYSTAL
CULOTTE
CURATOR
DEMOTIC
DESKTOP
DEVOTED
DEVOTEE
DIGITAL
DINETTE
DRASTIC
DRIFTER
ELASTIC
ELECTOR
EMITTER
EMPATHY
ENTITLE
EPISTLE
EQUATOR
ERRATIC
ERRATUM
FANATIC
FIGHTER
FIRSTLY
FLATTEN
FLATTER
FLATTOP
FLUSTER
FLUTTER
FORETOP
FRACTAL
FRANTIC
FRITTER
FRUSTUM
GAVOTTE
GAZETTE
GELATIN
GENETIC
GENITAL
GHASTLY
GLISTEN
GLISTER
GLITTER
GLOTTIS
GLUTTON
GRANTEE
GRISTLE
HABITAT
HABITUE
HAMSTER
HARDTOP
HEALTHY
HEARTEN
HEPATIC
HILLTOP
HIPSTER
HOLSTER
ILEITIS
IMPETUS
INERTIA
JANITOR
JUJITSU
JUPITER
KERATIN
KILOTON
KINETIC
KRYPTON
LAYETTE
LEGATEE
LIGHTEN
LIGHTER
LIMITED
LOBSTER
LOCATOR
LUNATIC
LUNETTE
MAESTRO
MAHATMA
MAINTOP
MARITAL
MEGATON
MILITIA
MIMETIC
MINSTER
MINUTIA
MISSTEP
MOBSTER
MOISTEN
MONITOR
MONSTER
MOUNTIE
MULATTO
MUSETTE
NAPHTHA
NECKTIE
NIGHTLY
NONSTOP
OLDSTER
ORBITER
OUTSTAY
OVERTOP
PALETTE
PENATES
PHAETON
PHANTOM
PHILTER
PIASTER
PIPETTE
PLANTAR
PLANTER
PLASTER
PLASTIC
PLATTER
PLOTTER
POINTED
POINTER
POLITIC
POULTRY
PRAETOR
PRATTLE
PROCTOR
PSALTER
PUNSTER
PURITAN
PYRITES
QUANTUM
QUARTER
QUARTET
QUIETUS
QUINTAL
QUINTET
REACTOR
RECITAL
REENTRY
REGATTA
RELATED
RELATOR
REPUTED
RIGHTLY
ROASTER
ROISTER
ROOFTOP
ROOSTER
ROSETTE
SAINTLY
SANCTUM
SAUNTER
SCATTER
SCEPTER
SCEPTIC
SCOOTER
SCRATCH
SCROTUM
SCUTTLE
SENATOR
SHATTER
SHEATHE
SHELTER
SHORTEN
SHORTLY
SHUTTER
SHUTTLE
SHYSTER
SIGHTED
SIGHTLY
SKEPTIC
SKITTER
SMELTER
SPASTIC
SPATTER
SPECTER
SPITTLE
SPLOTCH
SPOTTER
SPUTTER
STARTLE
STARTUP
STILTED
STILTON
STRATUM
STRETCH
STUTTER
STYPTIC
SWARTHY
SWEATER
SWEETEN
SWELTER
SYMPTOM
TAPSTER
THEATER
THISTLE
TIBETAN
TIGHTEN
TIMOTHY
TIPSTER
TOASTER
TRACTOR
TRAITOR
TRESTLE
TRUSTEE
TWEETER
TWISTER
TWITTER
UNHITCH
UNLATCH
VAULTED
VEGETAL
VISITOR
WASHTUB
WEALTHY
WHISTLE
WHITTLE
WIRETAP
WORSTED
WREATHE
WRESTLE
ACCOUNT
ADJOURN
AGROUND
APOLUNE
ASEXUAL
ASSAULT
ASTOUND
AZIMUTH
BANQUET
BECAUSE
BEDOUIN
BISCUIT
BISMUTH
BIVOUAC
BOROUGH
BOUQUET
BRAVURA
BULRUSH
CAESURA
CANNULA
CAPSULE
CAPTURE
CAROUSE
CENSURE
CENTURY
CIRCUIT
CLOSURE
CLOTURE
COEQUAL
COMMUNE
COMMUTE
COMPUTE
CONDUCE
CONDUCT
CONDUIT
CONFUSE
CONFUTE
CONJURE
CONQUER
CONSULT
CONSUME
CORRUPT
COSTUME
COUTURE
CROQUET
CULTURE
DEBAUCH
DEBOUCH
DEFAULT
DEGAUSS
DELOUSE
DENTURE
DIFFUSE
DISCUSS
DISEUSE
DISGUST
DISPUTE
DISRUPT
DISTURB
EARMUFF
ENCRUST
ENTHUSE
ENTRUST
EPICURE
EVACUEE
EXCLUDE
EXECUTE
EXHAUST
EXPOUND
EXTRUDE
FACTUAL
FAILURE
FEATURE
FERRULE
FISSURE
FISTULA
FIXTURE
FLEXURE
FORMULA
FORTUNE
GESTURE
GLOBULE
GRADUAL
GRANULE
GRAVURE
HIRSUTE
HOMBURG
IMPOUND
INBOUND
INCLUDE
INCRUST
INTRUDE
INTRUST
JONQUIL
KIBBUTZ
KUMQUAT
LACQUER
LANGUID
LANGUOR
LAWSUIT
LEAGUER
LECTURE
LEISURE
LETTUCE
LINGUAL
MANHUNT
MARQUEE
MARQUIS
MEASURE
MERCURY
MISRULE
MIXTURE
MOLLUSK
MUGWUMP
NEPTUNE
NURTURE
OBSCURE
OBTRUDE
OCCLUDE
OROTUND
OUTPULL
OVIDUCT
PARQUET
PASTURE
PENGUIN
PERFUME
PERJURY
PERTURB
PICTURE
POLLUTE
POSTURE
POTLUCK
PRELUDE
PREPUCE
PRESUME
PROCURE
PRODUCE
PRODUCT
PROFUSE
PURSUIT
PUSTULE
RAPTURE
REBOUND
RECLUSE
RECOUNT
RECRUIT
REDOUBT
REDOUND
REMOUNT
RESOUND
RETOUCH
ROEBUCK
RUPTURE
SAWDUST
SCAPULA
SECLUDE
SENSUAL
SOJOURN
SPATULA
SPICULE
STATURE
STATUTE
SUCCUMB
SUFFUSE
SUNBURN
TEXTURE
THROUGH
TONSURE
TORTURE
TRADUCE
TRIBUNE
TRIBUTE
UNCOUTH
UNEQUAL
UNSOUND
UNTRUTH
UNUSUAL
UPCHUCK
VENTURE
VERDURE
VESTURE
VIADUCT
VICTUAL
VIRGULE
VIRTUAL
VULTURE
AQUAVIT
ARRIVAL
BEDEVIL
BELOVED
BOLIVAR
CADAVER
CARAVAN
CARAVEL
CLEAVER
DELIVER
DISAVOW
ENLIVEN
FLIVVER
FOREVER
HOWEVER
JEHOVAH
PALAVER
POPOVER
RECOVER
REVIVAL
SAMOVAR
SHRIVEL
UNCIVIL
UNCOVER
UNMOVED

UNRAVEL
UNSAVED
UPRIVER
WHOEVER
ARCHWAY
AREAWAY
BEESWAX
BELTWAY
BIKEWAY
CARAWAY
DOORWAY
EMBOWER
EMPOWER
FAIRWAY
FARAWAY
FOLKWAY
FREEWAY
GANGWAY
GATEWAY
GETAWAY
HALFWAY
HALLWAY
HEADWAY
HIGHWAY
LAYAWAY
PARKWAY
PARTWAY
PATHWAY
PERIWIG
POSTWAR
RACEWAY
RAILWAY
RENEWAL
ROADWAY
RUNAWAY
SCRAWNY
THRUWAY
UNBOWED
WALKWAY
WIDOWER
WYSIWYG
INDEXED
ACOLYTE
ANALYZE
ANODYNE
CARRYON
CONDYLE
EMBRYOL
HALCYON
MONEYED
PHARYNX
TALLYHO
VANDYKE
ALCAZAR
BEDIZEN
CITIZEN
DENIZEN

DRIZZLE
FRAZZLE
FREEZER
FRIZZLE
GRIZZLY
HORIZON
MUEZZIN
PRETZEL
QUETZAL
SELTZER

## 6th Letter

ABYSMAL
ABYSSAL
ACCUSAL
ACROBAT
ADMIRAL
ADRENAL
AFRICAN
ALCAZAR
ALMANAC
AMALGAM
ANAGRAM
ANGULAR
ANNULAR
ANTHRAX
ARCHWAY
AREAWAY
ARRIVAL
ARSENAL
ARTISAN
ASEXUAL
ASHTRAY
AUSTRAL
BATSMAN
BEESWAX
BELGIAN
BELTWAY
BESMEAR
BESPEAK
BESTIAL
BIFOCAL
BIKEWAY
BIMETAL
BIPOLAR
BIVOUAC
BOATMAN
BOLIVAR
BONDMAN
BRAHMAN
BUCKRAM
BUCKSAW
BUGBEAR
CAPITAL

CAPSTAN
CARABAO
CARAVAN
CARAWAY
CARDIAC
CARLOAD
CATBOAT
CAVEMAN
CENTRAL
CHADIAN
CHAPEAU
CHAPMAN
CHATEAU
CHEDDAR
CHEETAH
CHOCTAW
COAXIAL
COEQUAL
CONCEAL
CONGEAL
CONICAL
COPYCAT
CORDIAL
CORONAL
CROWBAR
CRUCIAL
CRYSTAL
DEADPAN
DECIMAL
DEWCLAW
DIAGRAM
DIGITAL
DISHRAG
DISPLAY
DIURNAL
DOORMAN
DOORMAT
DOORWAY
DUSTPAN
EGGHEAD
ELEGIAC
ENTREAT
EPIGRAM
ETERNAL
ETHICAL
FACTUAL
FAIRWAY
FARAWAY
FEDERAL
FIREMAN
FLATCAR
FLOTSAM
FLYLEAF
FOLKWAY
FOOTMAN
FOOTPAD
FORBEAR

FOREMAN
FORTRAN
FRACTAL
FREEMAN
FREEWAY
FRETSAW
FROGMAN
FUNERAL
FUSTIAN
GAINSAY
GAMBIAN
GANGWAY
GATEWAY
GENERAL
GENITAL
GENTIAN
GETAWAY
GINGHAM
GLACIAL
GLEEMAN
GODHEAD
GOODMAN
GRADUAL
GRAMMAR
GRANDAM
GRECIAN
GUNBOAT
HABITAT
HACKMAN
HACKSAW
HALFWAY
HALLWAY
HANDBAG
HANDCAR
HANDSAW
HANGMAN
HARDPAN
HEADMAN
HEADWAY
HEARSAY
HELICAL
HELLCAT
HIGHWAY
HOLIDAY
HOPHEAD
ICEBOAT
ILLEGAL
IMMORAL
INHUMAN
INITIAL
INSTEAD
INSULAR
IRANIAN
ITALIAN
JACKDAW
JEHOVAH
JOCULAR

JOURNAL
JUGULAR
KINSMAN
KNEECAP
KUMQUAT
LACTEAL
LAMINAR
LAOTIAN
LATERAL
LATVIAN
LAYAWAY
LESBIAN
LIBERAL
LINEMAN
LINGUAL
LITERAL
LOCKJAW
LUSTRAL
MACADAM
MACDRAW
MAHICAN
MAILMAN
MANTEAU
MARITAL
MARSHAL
MARTIAL
MARTIAN
MAXIMAL
MEATMAN
MEDICAL
MESSIAH
MEXICAN
MIDYEAR
MILKMAN
MILLDAM
MINERAL
MINIMAL
MISLEAD
MISPLAY
MISREAD
MISTRAL
MODULAR
MOHEGAN
MOHICAN
MUSICAL
MUSKRAT
NARWHAL
NATURAL
NEUTRAL
NEWSMAN
NOMINAL
NOONDAY
NOSEGAY
NUCLEAR
NUMERAL
NUPTIAL
OARSMAN

OATMEAL
OEDIPAL
OFFBEAT
OPTICAL
OPTIMAL
ORDINAL
ORTOLAN
OTTOMAN
OUTDRAW
OUTPLAY
OUTSTAY
OUTWEAR
OVERLAP
OVERLAY
PAJAMAS
PARKWAY
PARTIAL
PARTWAY
PATHWAY
PAYLOAD
PEDICAB
PELICAN
PERSIAN
PLANTAR
PLATEAU
PLOWMAN
PLUVIAL
POLECAT
POPULAR
PORTRAY
POSTMAN
POSTWAR
POTHEAD
PREHEAT
PRESOAK
PROGMAN
PROGRAM
PROPMAN
PROTEAN
PULLMAN
PURITAN
PYJAMAS
QUETZAL
QUINTAL
QUONDAM
RACEWAY
RADICAL
RAILWAY
RATTRAP
RECITAL
REDCOAT
REDHEAD
REGULAR
RENEWAL
RETREAD
RETREAT
REVIVAL

ROADWAY
ROWBOAT
RUFFIAN
RUNAWAY
RUSSIAN
SAMOVAR
SAMURAI
SANDBAG
SANDBAR
SANDMAN
SCANDAL
SCHOLAR
SECULAR
SEMINAL
SEMINAR
SENSUAL
SEVERAL
SHELLAC
SHOWMAN
SIDECAR
SIDEMAN
SIMILAR
SKIWEAR
SOMEDAY
SOYBEAN
SPATIAL
SPECIAL
SPOUSAL
STELLAR
STOPGAP
SUNBEAM
SUNDIAL
TABLEAU
TABULAR
TAXICAB
THEREAT
THERMAL
THRUWAY
TIBETAN
TITULAR
TONNEAU
TOPCOAT
TOPICAL
TOWBOAT
TOWHEAD
TRIVIAL
TUBULAR
TUESDAY
TUGBOAT
TUTELAR
TYPICAL
UNCLEAN
UNCLOAK
UNEQUAL
UNMORAL
UNSTRAP
UNUSUAL

UTOPIAN
VATICAN
VEGETAL
VENTRAL
VETERAN
VICINAL
VICTUAL
VINEGAR
VIRTUAL
WALKWAY
WARHEAD
WEEKDAY
WHEREAS
WHEREAT
WHIPSAW
WILDCAT
WINDBAG
WIRETAP
WOLFRAM
WOODMAN
WORKBAG
WORKDAY
WORKMAN
YARDMAN
ZAMBIAN
ASCRIBE
CORDOBA
CRYBABY
DISROBE
EARLOBE
LULLABY
MARIMBA
MICROBE
PLACEBO
REDOUBT
STANDBY
THEREBY
WALLABY
WHEREBY
ABSENCE
ADJUNCT
ADVANCE
AFFLICT
AIRSICK
ASKANCE
ATTRACT
AUSPICE
AVARICE
BALANCE
BANNOCK
BEDROCK
BESEECH
BEWITCH
BULLOCK
BURDOCK
BUTTOCK
CADENCE

CAPRICE
CARSICK
CASSOCK
CHALICE
COLLECT
COMPACT
CONCOCT
CONDUCE
CONDUCT
CONNECT
CONTACT
CONVICT
COPPICE
CORNICE
CORRECT
COSSACK
COWLICK
CREVICE
CUTBACK
DEBAUCH
DEBOUCH
DECENCY
DEFLECT
DEFUNCT
DERRICK
DETRACT
DIALECT
DISSECT
DISTICH
DIVORCE
DURANCE
EDIFICE
EMBRACE
ENFORCE
ENHANCE
ESSENCE
EXTINCT
EXTRACT
FAIENCE
FALLACY
FATBACK
FETLOCK
FINANCE
FLOUNCE
FURNACE
GIMMICK
GRIMACE
GUNLOCK
HADDOCK
HAMMOCK
HASSOCK
HAYCOCK
HAYRICK
HEMLOCK
HENPECK
HEROICS
HILLOCK

| HOGBACK | RESPECT | BRAVADO | TORNADO | BLUBBER | CHASTEN | CRULLER | FRITTER | KITCHEN |
|---|---|---|---|---|---|---|---|---|
| HOSPICE | RETOUCH | BRIGADE | TORPEDO | BLUCHER | CHATTEL | CRUMPET | FURRIER | KNOCKER |
| HUMMOCK | RETRACE | BROCADE | TRAGEDY | BLUNDER | CHATTER | DEBRIEF | FURTHER | LABORED |
| IMPEACH | RETRACT | BROMIDE | UNHANDY | BLUSTER | CHEAPEN | DECIBEL | GANTLET | LACQUER |
| INEXACT | ROEBUCK | CALENDS | UPGRADE | BOBSLED | CHECKER | DECIDED | GENTEEL | LAMPREY |
| INFANCY | ROLLICK | CARBIDE | VERANDA | BOLSTER | CHICKEN | DECODER | GLACIER | LATCHET |
| INFARCT | ROMANCE | CASCADE | WAYSIDE | BOOKLET | CHIGGER | DELIVER | GLADDEN | LAUNDER |
| INFLECT | SCIENCE | CATHODE | ABDOMEN | BOOTLEG | CHIMNEY | DENIZEN | GLAZIER | LEAFLET |
| INFLICT | SCRATCH | COCKADE | ACCUSED | BOULDER | CHIPPER | DEVOTED | GLIMMER | LEAGUER |
| INSPECT | SCREECH | COLLIDE | ADAPTER | BOUNCER | CHOPPER | DEVOTEE | GLISTEN | LEARNED |
| INVOICE | SEASICK | COMMODE | ADVISED | BOUNDEN | CHOWDER | DISOBEY | GLISTER | LEATHER |
| JOYANCE | SECRECY | COMRADE | ALBUMEN | BOUQUET | CHUKKER | DIVIDER | GLITTER | LEGATEE |
| JUSTICE | SERVICE | CONCEDE | ALMONER | BOWLDER | CHUTNEY | DOSSIER | GOBBLER | LIGHTEN |
| LATTICE | SETBACK | CONFIDE | AMMETER | BRACKEN | CIRCLET | DOUBLET | GOGGLES | LIGHTER |
| LETTUCE | SHYLOCK | CORRODE | AMPUTEE | BRACKET | CITADEL | DOWAGER | GOURMET | LIMITED |
| LIMBECK | SILENCE | COWHIDE | ANOTHER | BRAZIER | CITIZEN | DRAGNET | GRANDEE | LINSEED |
| MATTOCK | SIROCCO | CRUSADE | ANTIGEN | BREAKER | CIVVIES | DRESSER | GRANTEE | LOBSTER |
| MONARCH | SPINACH | CUSTODY | APPAREL | BRISKET | CLAMBER | DRIBLET | GRAPNEL | LUCIFER |
| MOROCCO | SPLOTCH | CYANIDE | APPLIED | BROADEN | CLAPPER | DRIFTER | GRAUPEL | MALMSEY |
| NEGLECT | SQUELCH | DEGRADE | AQUIFER | BROIDER | CLATTER | DROPLET | GRAZIER | MANAGER |
| NUTPICK | STAUNCH | EFFENDI | ARBITER | BROILER | CLAVIER | DROPPER | GRINDER | MANDREL |
| OARLOCK | STOMACH | EPISODE | ARMORER | BROODER | CLEAVER | DRUMMER | GROMMET | MARINER |
| ORIFICE | STRETCH | EXCLUDE | ARPANET | BROTHEL | CLINKER | DRUNKEN | GROUPER | MARQUEE |
| OSTRICH | SUBJECT | EXPLODE | ASHAMED | BROTHER | CLIPPER | EARTHEN | GUILDER | MATINEE |
| OUTFACE | SUFFICE | EXTRUDE | ASSURED | BROWSER | CLOBBER | EMBOWER | HACKNEY | MAUNDER |
| OVERACT | SURFACE | FORBODE | ASUNDER | BRUISER | CLOTHES | EMITTER | HAMSTER | MEANDER |
| OVIDUCT | SUSPECT | GRENADE | ATELIER | BUCKLER | CLUSTER | EMPOWER | HANDSEL | MEASLES |
| PADDOCK | TACTICS | HYMNODY | BALONEY | BURGHER | CLUTTER | ENLIVEN | HANDSET | MIDWEEK |
| PADLOCK | TAPIOCA | IMPLODE | BANQUET | BUTCHER | COARSEN | EPAULET | HARRIER | MINARET |
| PEACOCK | TENANCY | INCLUDE | BANSHEE | CABARET | COBBLER | EPITHET | HATCHET | MINSTER |
| PENANCE | TERRACE | INNARDS | BARONET | CABINET | COCHLEA | ESCAPEE | HAYSEED | MISDEED |
| PERFECT | TIEBACK | INTRUDE | BARRIER | CADAVER | COCKNEY | EVACUEE | HEADSET | MISSTEP |
| PHONICS | TOBACCO | JOYRIDE | BAYONET | CALIBER | COLLEEN | FANCIER | HEARKEN | MOBSTER |
| PHYSICS | TRADUCE | LIMEADE | BEDIZEN | CALIPER | COLLIER | FARRIER | HEARTEN | MOISTEN |
| PIBROCH | TRISECT | NUCLIDE | BELATED | CALOMEL | COLONEL | FARTHER | HEATHEN | MONEYED |
| PINNACE | TROUNCE | OBTRUDE | BELOVED | CALUMET | COLORED | FEATHER | HEATHER | MONGREL |
| POLLACK | TUSSOCK | OCCLUDE | BESHREW | CANDIED | COMPEER | FIANCEE | HIPSTER | MONOMER |
| PORTICO | UNBLOCK | OFFSIDE | BESIDES | CANTEEN | COMPLEX | FIFTEEN | HOLSTER | MONSTER |
| POTLUCK | UNFROCK | ORGANDY | BETIMES | CARAMEL | CONIFER | FIGHTER | HOOSIER | MUFFLER |
| PREDICT | UNHITCH | OUTSIDE | BETOKEN | CARAVEL | CONQUER | FLANKER | HOSTLER | NANKEEN |
| PREFACE | UNLATCH | PERFIDY | BETWEEN | CARRIER | CORONER | FLANNEL | HOWEVER | NARTHEX |
| PREFECT | UPCHUCK | PERVADE | BIRCHER | CASHIER | CORONET | FLAPPER | HUNDRED | NEITHER |
| PREPUCE | VACANCY | PRECEDE | BITUMEN | CASTLED | COUNSEL | FLATBED | IMPANEL | NOMINEE |
| PRIMACY | VALANCE | PRELUDE | BLACKEN | CATCHER | COUNTER | FLATTEN | INDEXED | NONSKED |
| PRIVACY | VALENCE | PRESIDE | BLADDER | CERUMEN | COUPLET | FLATTER | INFIDEL | NONUSER |
| PRODUCE | VERDICT | PROSODY | BLANKET | CHAFFER | COURIER | FLICKER | INHALER | NORTHER |
| PRODUCT | VIADUCT | PROVIDE | BLARNEY | CHAMBER | COURSER | FLIPPER | INSIDER | OCTOBER |
| PROJECT | WARLOCK | RAWHIDE | BLATHER | CHAMFER | CRABBED | FLIVVER | INSURED | ODYSSEY |
| PROTECT | WEDLOCK | ROTUNDA | BLEEDER | CHANCEL | CRACKER | FLUSTER | INSURER | OFFICER |
| RANSACK | WETBACK | SEASIDE | BLESSED | CHANNEL | CRICKET | FLUTTER | INTEGER | OLDSTER |
| RECENCY | WRYNECK | SECLUDE | BLINDER | CHANTEY | CRITTER | FORELEG | JACKLEG | ORBITER |
| REFLECT | ALCALDE | SUBSIDE | BLINKER | CHAPLET | CROCHET | FORESEE | JEWELER | OVERSEA |
| REFRACT | ALREADY | SUBSIDY | BLISTER | CHAPTER | CROOKED | FOREVER | JOURNEY | OVERSEE |
| REGENCY | ANYBODY | SUICIDE | BLOATER | CHARGER | CROPPER | FOUNDER | JUBILEE | PAISLEY |
| REJOICE | ASTRIDE | SULFIDE | BLOODED | CHARMER | CROQUET | FREEZER | JUNIPER | PALAVER |
| REPLACE | AVOCADO | THREADY | BLOOPER | CHARNEL | CROSIER | FRESHEN | JUPITER | PALFREY |
| REPLICA | BEDSIDE | TOPSIDE | BLOTTER | CHARTER | CRUISER | FRESHET | KINDRED | PANACEA |

PANNIER
PANTHER
PARAPET
PARQUET
PARSLEY
PARTNER
PASSKEY
PENATES
PERIGEE
PERPLEX
PHILTER
PIASTER
PILSNER
PIONEER
PITCHER
PLACKET
PLANTER
PLASTER
PLATTER
PLAYLET
PLAYPEN
PLOTTER
PLUMBER
PLUMMET
PLUNDER
PLUNGER
POINTED
POINTER
POLYMER
POPOVER
PREMIER
PRETEEN
PRETZEL
PREVIEW
PRICKER
PRITHEE
PROBLEM
PROCEED
PROFFER
PROPHET
PROSPER
PSALTER
PUNSTER
PURLIEU
PURVIEW
PYRITES
QUARREL
QUARTER
QUARTET
QUICKEN
QUINTET
RAGWEED
RAMBLER
RATCHET
RATTLER
RECOVER
REFEREE
REFINED
REFUGEE
REGIMEN
RELATED
REMODEL
REPUTED
REQUIEM
RETIRED
RETIREE
RINGLET
RIVULET
ROADBED
ROASTER
ROISTER
ROOSTER
ROOTLET
ROUGHEN
SAMPLER
SATCHEL
SAUNTER
SCALPEL
SCAMPER
SCANNER
SCARLET
SCATTER
SCEPTER
SCOOTER
SCUPPER
SEAWEED
SELTZER
SERRIED
SHARPEN
SHARPER
SHATTER
SHAWNEE
SHELTER
SHERBET
SHIMMER
SHOCKER
SHORTEN
SHRIVEL
SHUDDER
SHUTTER
SHYSTER
SICKBED
SIGHTED
SIXTEEN
SKILLET
SKIPPER
SKITTER
SLACKEN
SLACKER
SLANDER
SLATHER
SLEEPER
SLENDER
SLICKER
SLIPPER
SLITHER
SLOBBER
SLUMBER
SMELTER
SMIDGEN
SMOLDER
SMOTHER
SNEAKER
SNICKER
SNORKEL
SOLDIER
SOUNDER
SPANIEL
SPATTER
SPEAKER
SPECIES
SPECTER
SPELLER
SPOILER
SPOTTER
SPUTTER
STAFFER
STAGGER
STAMMER
STICKER
STIFFEN
STILTED
STOPPER
STORIED
STRUDEL
STUDIED
STUTTER
SUCCEED
SWAGGER
SWEATER
SWEETEN
SWELTER
SWOLLEN
TANAGER
TAPSTER
TENURED
TERRIER
THEATER
THEOREM
THICKEN
THICKET
THINNER
THITHER
THUNDER
TIGHTEN
TIMBREL
TIPSTER
TOASTER
TOUGHEN
TOURNEY
TRACHEA
TRAILER
TRAINEE
TRAMMEL
TRIGGER
TRINKET
TRIPLET
TRIPLEX
TROCHEE
TRODDEN
TROLLEY
TROOPER
TRUMPET
TRUSTEE
TUMBLER
TUMBREL
TURNKEY
TWEETER
TWILLED
TWISTER
TWITTER
UMPTEEN
UNARMED
UNBOWED
UNCOVER
UNMOVED
UNQUIET
UNRAVEL
UNSAVED
UNSCREW
UNTRIED
UPRIVER
VAULTED
VERNIER
VINTNER
VITTLES
VOUCHER
WAGONER
WARBLER
WASTREL
WAVELET
WEATHER
WHEELER
WHETHER
WHICKER
WHIMPER
WHIPPET
WHISKER
WHISKEY
WHISPER
WHITHER
WHOEVER
WHOPPER
WHORLED
WIDOWER
WIGGLER
WILLIES
WIZENED
WORSTED
WRAPPER
WRECKER
WRINGER
YOUNKER
ACIDIFY
AIRLIFT
ALEWIFE
ALFALFA
AMPLIFY
BAILIFF
BEATIFY
CAITIFF
CALCIFY
CERTIFY
CLARIFY
CRUCIFY
DANDIFY
DIGNIFY
DISTAFF
EARMUFF
ENGRAFT
FALSIFY
FORTIFY
GIRAFFE
GLORIFY
GRATIFY
HAYLOFT
HORRIFY
INGRAFT
JUSTIFY
KICKOFF
LIGNIFY
LIQUEFY
MAGNIFY
MASTIFF
MIDRIFF
MIDWIFE
MOLLIFY
MORTIFY
MYSTIFY
NITRIFY
NULLIFY
PETRIFY
PONTIFF
PUTREFY
QUALIFY
RECTIFY
SATISFY
SCARIFY
SCRUFFY
SHERIFF
SIGNIFY
SPECIFY
STUPEFY
TAKEOFF
TERRIFY
TESTIFY
TURNOFF
UPDRAFT
UPSHIFT
VERSIFY
VITRIFY
ABRIDGE
ACREAGE
ADJUDGE
ALLERGY
ANALOGY
APANAGE
APOLOGY
ARRAIGN
ARRANGE
ASSUAGE
AVERAGE
BAGGAGE
BANDAGE
BARRAGE
BESIEGE
BIOLOGY
BONDAGE
BOROUGH
CABBAGE
CARNAGE
CARTAGE
COINAGE
COLLAGE
COLLEGE
CONDIGN
CONSIGN
CORDAGE
CORSAGE
CORTEGE
COTTAGE
COURAGE
DERANGE
DIVERGE
DIVULGE
DOCKAGE
ECOLOGY
EMBARGO
ENLARGE
EXPUNGE
FARRAGO
FOLIAGE
FOOTAGE
FOREIGN
GARBAGE
GEOLOGY
HAULAGE
HERBAGE
HIDALGO
HOSTAGE
IMPINGE
INDULGE
INNINGS
INVEIGH
LEAFAGE
LEAKAGE
LINEAGE
LINKAGE
LITURGY
LOZENGE
LUGGAGE
LUMBAGO
MAKINGS
MASSAGE
MELANGE
MESSAGE
MILEAGE
MILLAGE
MONTAGE
NEOLOGY
OUTRAGE
OVERAGE
PACKAGE
PASSAGE
PILLAGE
PLUMAGE
PORTAGE
POSTAGE
POTTAGE
PRESAGE
PRODIGY
PROTEGE
RAMPAGE
REVENGE
RUMMAGE
SALVAGE
SAUSAGE
SCOURGE
SELVAGE
SPLURGE
STORAGE
STRANGE
STRINGY
SYRINGE
TEENAGE
THROUGH
TIDINGS
TILLAGE
TONNAGE
TRILOGY
UMBRAGE
UNDERGO
UNHINGE
UPSTAGE
UPSURGE
UROLOGY
VANTAGE
VERTIGO
VESTIGE
VILLAGE
VINTAGE
VOLTAGE
WASTAGE
WATTAGE
WINDAGE
WORDAGE
YARDAGE
ZOOLOGY
ZYMURGY
ALRIGHT
ANARCHY
ARAPAHO
ATROPHY
ATTACHE
BORSCHT
BREATHE
BRIOCHE
BROUGHT
DELIGHT
DRAUGHT
DROUGHT
EARACHE
EMPATHY
FRAUGHT
FREIGHT
HEALTHY
HIBACHI
INSIGHT
NAPHTHA
PANACHE
PIRANHA
RAUNCHY
RICKSHA
SHEATHE
SLEIGHT
STROPHE
SWARTHY
TALLYHO
THOUGHT
TIMOTHY
TONIGHT
UPRIGHT
UPTIGHT
WEALTHY
WREATHE
WROUGHT
ABSTAIN
ACCLAIM
ACRYLIC
ADENOID
AEROBIC
AIRFOIL
AIRMAIL
AIRSHIP
ALBUMIN
ALEMBIC
AMMONIA
AMNESIA
ANAEMIA
ANDROID
ANTACID
APHASIA
AQUATIC
AQUAVIT
ARCHAIC
ARSENIC
ASCETIC
ASEPTIC
ASIATIC
ASPIRIN
BACKLIT
BALDRIC
BARGAIN
BEATNIK
BEDEVIL
BEDOUIN
BEGONIA
BENEFIT
BENTHIC
BENZOIN
BISCUIT
BOUDOIR
BRAHMIN
BRECCIA
BROWNIE
BUCOLIC
BUMPKIN
CALORIC
CALORIE
CAMBRIC
CAPTAIN
CAROTID
CATTAIL
CAUSTIC
CERAMIC
CERTAIN
CHABLIS
CHAGRIN
CHALLIS
CHAMOIS
CHASSIS
CHROMIC
CHRONIC
CIRCUIT
CLASSIC
CLASTIC
COCKPIT
CODICIL
COHABIT
COLLOID
CONCEIT
CONDUIT
CONJOIN

CONTAIN
CONTRIB
CORSAIR
COTERIE
COUNCIL
COWSLIP
CRYPTIC
CULPRIT
CURTAIL
CURTAIN
DAUPHIN
DECLAIM
DEFICIT
DELIMIT
DEMERIT
DEMONIC
DEMOTIC
DEPOSIT
DESPAIR
DESPOIL
DETRAIN
DEXTRIN
DIPLOID
DISDAIN
DISJOIN
DOLPHIN
DOMINIE
DRASTIC
DRUMLIN
DUCKPIN
DYNAMIC
ELASTIC
EMBROIL
ENCHAIN
ENDEMIC
ENTRAIN
ERRATIC
EXCLAIM
EXHIBIT
EXPLAIN
EXPLOIT
FANATIC
FANTAIL
FIBROID
FLACCID
FORFEIT
FRANTIC
FREEBIE
FUCHSIA
GASTRIC
GELATIN
GENERIC
GENESIS
GENETIC
GHERKIN
GLOTTIS
GRAPHIC
GREMLIN
GROUPIE
GUMBOIL
HAIRPIN
HAPLOID
HARELIP
HEADPIN
HEPARIN
HEPATIC
HOBNAIL
HOWBEIT
ILEITIS
ILLICIT
IMPERIL
INDICIA
INERTIA
INGRAIN
INHABIT
INHERIT
INHIBIT
INSIPID
INSULIN
INTERIM
INTROIT
INVALID
JAVELIN
JONQUIL
KATYDID
KERATIN
KIDSKIN
KINETIC
KINGPIN
KINSHIP
KREMLIN
LACONIC
LANGUID
LANOLIN
LATAKIA
LAWSUIT
LUNATIC
MALARIA
MALEFIC
MANDRIL
MANIKIN
MANUMIT
MARQUIS
MASONIC
MASTOID
MAUDLIN
MEIOSIS
MELANIC
MELANIN
MERMAID
MILITIA
MIMESIS
MIMETIC
MINUTIA
MITOSIS
MONADIC
MORPHIA
MOUNTIE
MUEZZIN
MULLEIN
MURRAIN
NECKTIE
NEMESIS
NOMADIC
NOSTRIL
NUMERIC
OILSKIN
ORGANIC
OSMOSIS
PACIFIC
PALADIN
PARBOIL
PARESIS
PARFAIT
PARSNIP
PELAGIC
PENGUIN
PERIWIG
PERTAIN
PETUNIA
PFENNIG
PHALLIC
PHOENIX
PHRENIC
PIGSKIN
PIGTAIL
PILGRIM
PLASTIC
PLAUDIT
POCOSIN
POLARIS
POLEMIC
POLITIC
PRAIRIE
PREEMIE
PREVAIL
PROSAIC
PROTEIN
PSYCHIC
PUMPKIN
PURLOIN
PURSUIT
PYRAMID
QUICKIE
RAREBIT
RECLAIM
RECRUIT
REDSKIN
REFRAIN
REGALIA
RESEDIT
REVERIE
SATANIC
SCEPTIC
SEISMIC
SEQUOIA
SHARPIE
SIDELIT
SIRLOIN
SKEPTIC
SOLARIS
SOLICIT
SPASTIC
SPLENIC
SPUTNIK
SQUALID
STENCIL
STUFFIT
STYPTIC
SUBJOIN
SUBSOIL
SURFEIT
SUSTAIN
TABLOID
TECHNIC
TENDRIL
TERRAIN
THEREIN
THYROID
TINFOIL
TITANIC
TOENAIL
TOPSAIL
TOPSOIL
TOXEMIA
TRAFFIC
TRANSIT
TRAVAIL
TREFOIL
TRELLIS
TURMOIL
TYPHOID
UNCHAIN
UNCIVIL
UPBRAID
UTENSIL
VERMEIL
VERVAIN
VILLAIN
VILLEIN
VITAMIN
VOCALIC
VOLTAIC
WAGTAIL
WARSHIP
WASSAIL
WHEREIN
WORSHIP
BAZOOKA
CATLIKE
CONVOKE
COWPOKE
CUPCAKE
DASHIKI
DISLIKE
FINICKY
FORSAKE
GODLIKE
HOECAKE
HOTCAKE
MANLIKE
MAZURKA
MISLIKE
MISTAKE
OATCAKE
PANCAKE
PAPRIKA
PARTAKE
PROVOKE
UNLUCKY
VANDYKE
WARLIKE
AFFABLE
AMIABLE
ANOMALY
ANTHILL
APOSTLE
ARMHOLE
ARTICLE
ASPHALT
ASSAULT
AUDIBLE
AUREOLE
AURICLE
BARBELL
BEASTLY
BEDROLL
BEGUILE
BICYCLE
BRAILLE
BRAMBLE
BRISTLE
BRITTLE
BUFFALO
CANNULA
CAPABLE
CAPSULE
CATCALL
CATWALK
CEDILLA
CEMBALO
CHORALE
CHORTLE
CHUCKLE
CIVILLY
CLEANLY
COMPILE
CONDOLE
CONDYLE
CONSOLE
CONSULT
CORACLE
COROLLA
COURTLY
CRACKLE
CRINKLE
CRIPPLE
CRUMBLE
CRUMPLE
CUBICLE
CUCKOLD
CUTICLE
DEATHLY
DEBACLE
DEERFLY
DEFAULT
DISABLE
DISTILL
DRIBBLE
DRIZZLE
DUCTILE
DURABLE
DWINDLE
EARTHLY
ELDERLY
EMERALD
ENNOBLE
ENTITLE
EPISTLE
EQUABLE
EXAMPLE
EYEBALL
FEBRILE
FERRULE
FERTILE
FINAGLE
FIREFLY
FIRSTLY
FISSILE
FISTULA
FLESHLY
FLYABLE
FORMULA
FOXHOLE
FRAGILE
FRAZZLE
FRECKLE
FRIABLE
FRIZZLE
FULFILL
GAZELLE
GENTILE
GHASTLY
GLOBULE
GONDOLA
GORILLA
GRACKLE
GRANULE
GRAPPLE
GRIDDLE
GRISTLE
GRIZZLY
GRUMBLE
GUNWALE
HAPPILY
HERSELF
HIMSELF
HOSTILE
IDEALLY
IGNOBLE
INDWELL
INFIELD
INKWELL
INSTALL
INSTILL
ISRAELI
JAYWALK
KEYHOLE
KINFOLK
KNUCKLE
LEGIBLE
LIVABLE
LOATHLY
MANACLE
MANHOLE
MAXILLA
MAYPOLE
MEDULLA
MENFOLK
MIRACLE
MISCALL
MISFILE
MISRULE
MISSILE
MONOCLE
MUTABLE
NACELLE
NIGHTLY
NOTABLE
NOVELLA
ODDBALL
ONESELF
ORDERLY
OUTPULL
OUTSELL
OVERALL
OVERFLY
PANICLE
PANOPLY
PAPILLA
PARABLE
PATELLA
PAYROLL
PERCALE
PERGOLA
PETIOLE
PICCOLO
PIEBALD
PINHOLE
PITFALL
PLIABLE
POTABLE
POTHOLE
PRATTLE
PRICKLE
PROFILE
PUERILE
PUSTULE
QUIBBLE
RAVIOLI
REBUILD
RECYCLE
REPTILE
RIGHTLY
RISIBLE
RUBELLA
SAINTLY
SAWMILL
SCAPULA
SCRUPLE
SCUFFLE
SCUTTLE
SEAWALL
SERVILE
SESSILE
SHACKLE
SHAMBLE
SHAPELY
SHINGLE
SHORTLY
SHUFFLE
SHUTTLE
SIGHTLY
SIZABLE
SKIFFLE
SMUGGLE
SNAFFLE
SNIFFLE
SNUFFLE
SNUGGLE
SOLUBLE
SOUFFLE
SPANGLE
SPARKLE
SPATULA
SPECKLE
SPICULE
SPINDLE
SPINDLY
SPITTLE
STABILE
STARTLE
STATELY
STEEPLE
STERILE
STIPPLE
STUBBLE
STUMBLE
SUBTILE
SWADDLE
SWAHILI
SWINDLE
SYSTOLE
TACTILE
TADPOLE
TAMBALA
TENABLE
TENFOLD
TENSILE
TEQUILA
TEXTILE
THIMBLE
THISTLE
THYSELF
TOEHOLD
TRAMPLE
TREACLE
TREADLE
TREMBLE
TREMOLO
TRESTLE
TRICKLE
TROUBLE
TRUCKLE
TRUFFLE
TRUNDLE
TUNABLE
TWADDLE
TWIDDLE
TWINKLE
UKULELE
UNGODLY
UNMANLY
VACUOLE
VANILLA
VEHICLE
VESICLE
VIRGULE
VISIBLE
VOCABLE
VOLUBLE
WADABLE
WAYBILL

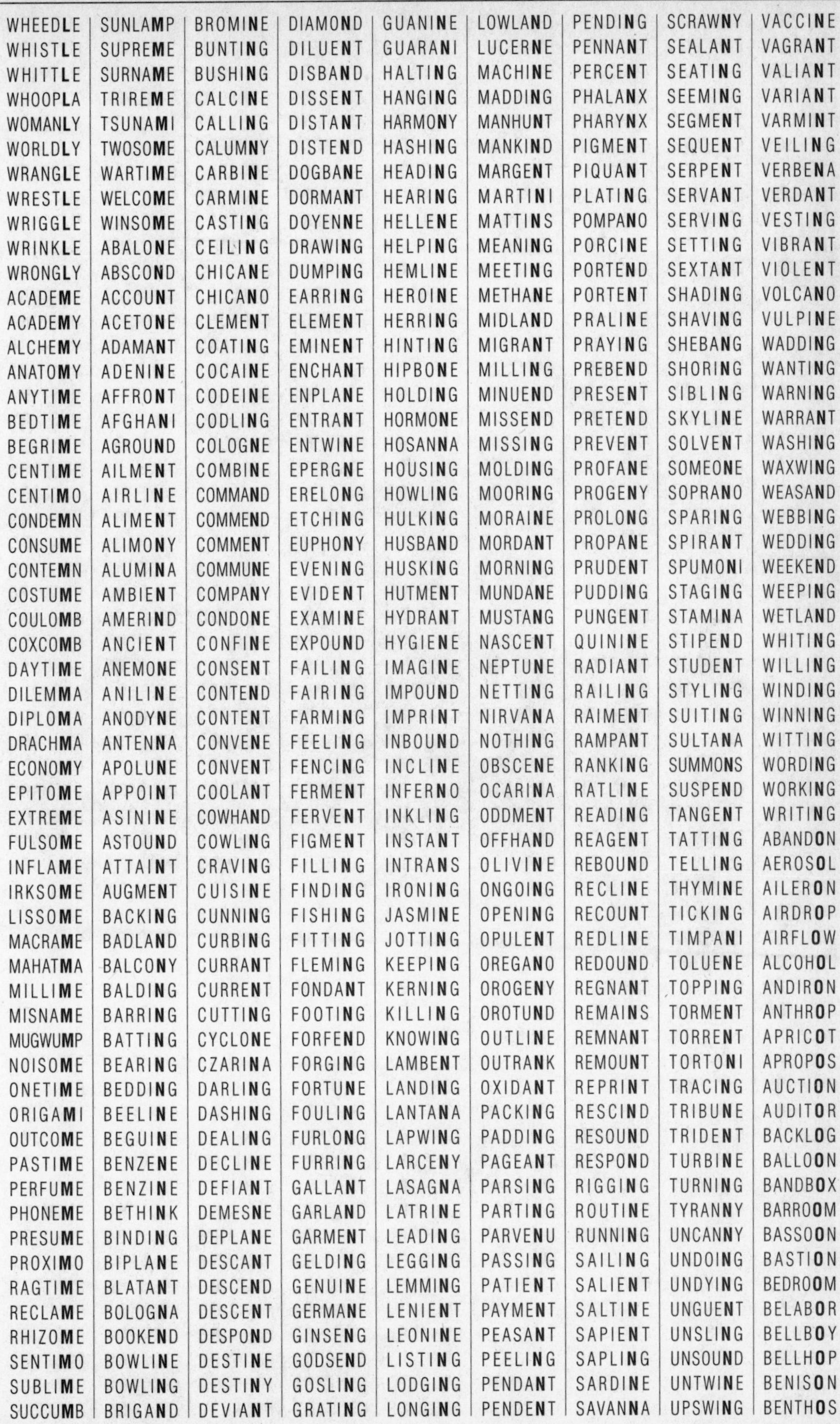

WHEEDLE
WHISTLE
WHITTLE
WHOOPLA
WOMANLY
WORLDLY
WRANGLE
WRESTLE
WRIGGLE
WRINKLE
WRONGLY
ACADEME
ACADEMY
ALCHEMY
ANATOMY
ANYTIME
BEDTIME
BEGRIME
CENTIME
CENTIMO
CONDEMN
CONSUME
CONTEMN
COSTUME
COULOMB
COXCOMB
DAYTIME
DILEMMA
DIPLOMA
DRACHMA
ECONOMY
EPITOME
EXTREME
FULSOME
INFLAME
IRKSOME
LISSOME
MACRAME
MAHATMA
MILLIME
MISNAME
MUGWUMP
NOISOME
ONETIME
ORIGAMI
OUTCOME
PASTIME
PERFUME
PHONEME
PRESUME
PROXIMO
RAGTIME
RECLAME
RHIZOME
SENTIMO
SUBLIME
SUCCUMB

SUNLAMP
SUPREME
SURNAME
TRIREME
TSUNAMI
TWOSOME
WARTIME
WELCOME
WINSOME
ABALONE
ABSCOND
ACCOUNT
ACETONE
ADAMANT
ADENINE
AFFRONT
AFGHANI
AGROUND
AILMENT
AIRLINE
ALIMENT
ALIMONY
ALUMINA
AMBIENT
AMERIND
ANCIENT
ANEMONE
ANILINE
ANODYNE
ANTENNA
APOLUNE
APPOINT
ASININE
ASTOUND
ATTAINT
AUGMENT
BACKING
BADLAND
BALCONY
BALDING
BARRING
BATTING
BEARING
BEDDING
BEELINE
BEGUINE
BENZENE
BENZINE
BETHINK
BINDING
BIPLANE
BLATANT
BOLOGNA
BOOKEND
BOWLINE
BOWLING
BRIGAND

BROMINE
BUNTING
BUSHING
CALCINE
CALLING
CALUMNY
CARBINE
CARMINE
CASTING
CEILING
CHICANE
CHICANO
CLEMENT
COATING
COCAINE
CODEINE
CODLING
COLOGNE
COMBINE
COMMAND
COMMEND
COMMENT
COMMUNE
COMPANY
CONDONE
CONFINE
CONSENT
CONTEND
CONTENT
CONVENE
CONVENT
COOLANT
COWHAND
COWLING
CRAVING
CUISINE
CUNNING
CURBING
CURRANT
CURRENT
CUTTING
CYCLONE
CZARINA
DARLING
DASHING
DEALING
DECLINE
DEFIANT
DEMESNE
DEPLANE
DESCANT
DESCEND
DESCENT
DESPOND
DESTINE
DESTINY
DEVIANT

DIAMOND
DILUENT
DISBAND
DISSENT
DISTANT
DISTEND
DOGBANE
DORMANT
DOYENNE
DRAWING
DUMPING
EARRING
ELEMENT
EMINENT
ENCHANT
ENPLANE
ENTRANT
ENTWINE
EPERGNE
ERELONG
ETCHING
EUPHONY
EVENING
EVIDENT
EXAMINE
EXPOUND
FAILING
FAIRING
FARMING
FEELING
FENCING
FERMENT
FERVENT
FIGMENT
FILLING
FINDING
FISHING
FITTING
FLEMING
FONDANT
FOOTING
FORFEND
FORGING
FORTUNE
FOULING
FURLONG
FURRING
GALLANT
GARLAND
GARMENT
GELDING
GENUINE
GERMANE
GINSENG
GODSEND
GOSLING
GRATING

GUANINE
GUARANI
HALTING
HANGING
HARMONY
HASHING
HEADING
HEARING
HELLENE
HELPING
HEMLINE
HEROINE
HERRING
HINTING
HIPBONE
HOLDING
HORMONE
HOSANNA
HOUSING
HOWLING
HULKING
HUSBAND
HUSKING
HUTMENT
HYDRANT
HYGIENE
IMAGINE
IMPOUND
IMPRINT
INBOUND
INCLINE
INFERNO
INKLING
INSTANT
INTRANS
IRONING
JASMINE
JOTTING
KEEPING
KERNING
KILLING
KNOWING
LAMBENT
LANDING
LANTANA
LAPWING
LARCENY
LASAGNA
LATRINE
LEADING
LEGGING
LEMMING
LENIENT
LEONINE
LISTING
LODGING
LONGING

LOWLAND
LUCERNE
MACHINE
MADDING
MANHUNT
MANKIND
MARGENT
MARTINI
MATTINS
MEANING
MEETING
METHANE
MIDLAND
MIGRANT
MILLING
MINUEND
MISSEND
MISSING
MOLDING
MOORING
MORAINE
MORDANT
MORNING
MUNDANE
MUSTANG
NASCENT
NEPTUNE
NETTING
NIRVANA
NOTHING
OBSCENE
OCARINA
ODDMENT
OFFHAND
OLIVINE
ONGOING
OPENING
OPULENT
OREGANO
OROGENY
OROTUND
OUTLINE
OUTRANK
OXIDANT
PACKING
PADDING
PAGEANT
PARSING
PARTING
PARVENU
PASSING
PATIENT
PAYMENT
PEASANT
PEELING
PENDANT
PENDENT

PENDING
PENNANT
PERCENT
PHALANX
PHARYNX
PIGMENT
PIQUANT
PLATING
POMPANO
PORCINE
PORTEND
PORTENT
PRALINE
PRAYING
PREBEND
PRESENT
PRETEND
PREVENT
PROFANE
PROGENY
PROLONG
PROPANE
PRUDENT
PUDDING
PUNGENT
QUININE
RADIANT
RAILING
RAIMENT
RAMPANT
RANKING
RATLINE
READING
REAGENT
REBOUND
RECLINE
RECOUNT
REDLINE
REDOUND
REGNANT
REMAINS
REMNANT
REMOUNT
REPRINT
RESCIND
RESOUND
RESPOND
RIGGING
ROUTINE
RUNNING
SAILING
SALIENT
SALTINE
SAPIENT
SAPLING
SARDINE
SAVANNA

SCRAWNY
SEALANT
SEATING
SEEMING
SEGMENT
SEQUENT
SERPENT
SERVANT
SERVING
SETTING
SEXTANT
SHADING
SHAVING
SHEBANG
SHORING
SIBLING
SKYLINE
SOLVENT
SOMEONE
SOPRANO
SPARING
SPIRANT
SPUMONI
STAGING
STAMINA
STIPEND
STUDENT
STYLING
SUITING
SULTANA
SUMMONS
SUSPEND
TANGENT
TATTING
TELLING
THYMINE
TICKING
TIMPANI
TOLUENE
TOPPING
TORMENT
TORRENT
TORTONI
TRACING
TRIBUNE
TRIDENT
TURBINE
TURNING
TYRANNY
UNCANNY
UNDOING
UNDYING
UNGUENT
UNSLING
UNSOUND
UNTWINE
UPSWING

VACCINE
VAGRANT
VALIANT
VARIANT
VARMINT
VEILING
VERBENA
VERDANT
VESTING
VIBRANT
VIOLENT
VOLCANO
VULPINE
WADDING
WANTING
WARNING
WARRANT
WASHING
WAXWING
WEASAND
WEBBING
WEDDING
WEEKEND
WEEPING
WETLAND
WHITING
WILLING
WINDING
WINNING
WITTING
WORDING
WORKING
WRITING
ABANDON
AEROSOL
AILERON
AIRDROP
AIRFLOW
ALCOHOL
ANDIRON
ANTHROP
APRICOT
APROPOS
AUCTION
AUDITOR
BACKLOG
BALLOON
BANDBOX
BARROOM
BASSOON
BASTION
BEDROOM
BELABOR
BELLBOY
BELLHOP
BENISON
BENTHOS

BIBELOT
BILLION
BLOSSOM
BOREDOM
BOURBON
BUFFOON
BUGABOO
BULLDOG
BULLION
BURGEON
CAISSON
CALDRON
CAMPHOR
CAPITOL
CAPTION
CARIBOU
CARRION
CARRYON
CARTOON
CATALOG
CAUTION
CESSION
CHANSON
CHARIOT
CHEROOT
CHEVIOT
CHEVRON
CHIFFON
CHIGNON
CHINOOK
CLANGOR
CLARION
CONTROL
COPILOT
COPYBOY
CORNCOB
CREATOR
CRIMSON
CROUTON
CURATOR
CUSHION
DASHPOT
DAYBOOK
DECAGON
DEMIGOD
DESKTOP
DESTROY
DEVELOP
DEWDROP
DICTION
DISAVOW
DIVISOR
DOGTROT
DOGWOOD
DRAGOON
DUDGEON
DUNGEON
EARSHOT
ECHELON
EDITION
EIDOLON
ELECTOR
ELISION
EMBRYOL
EMOTION
EMPEROR
ENVELOP
ENVENOM
EQUATOR
EQUINOX
EROSION
ETHANOL
EVASION
EYEBROW
FACTION
FASHION
FEEDLOT
FESTOON
FICTION
FILMDOM
FIREBOX
FISSION
FLATTOP
FORETOP
FREEDOM
GALLEON
GEARBOX
GLUTTON
GODHOOD
GRUNION
GUERDON
GUMDROP
GUMSHOE
GUNSHOT
HALCYON
HANGDOG
HARDTOP
HARPOON
HELLION
HEXAGON
HEXAPOD
HIGHBOY
HILLTOP
HORIZON
HOTFOOT
HOTSHOT
HUMIDOR
INCISOR
JACKPOT
JANITOR
JUKEBOX
KEELSON
KILLJOY
KILOTON
KINGDOM
KRYPTON
LAMPOON
LANGUOR
LEXICON
LIAISON
LOCATOR
LONGBOW
LOWBROW
MAILBOX
MAINTOP
MALISON
MANHOOD
MANSION
MARPLOT
MATADOR
MEGATON
MENTHOL
MENTION
MILKSOP
MILLION
MISSION
MONITOR
MONSOON
MUDROOM
MULLION
NEUTRON
NEWSBOY
NONBOOK
NONSTOP
NUCLEON
OCTAGON
OPINION
ORATION
OUTCROP
OUTDOOR
OUTFLOW
OUTGROW
OUTLOOK
OVATION
OVERJOY
OVERTOP
OXBLOOD
PAGEBOY
PARADOX
PARAGON
PARASOL
PASSION
PATRIOT
PATROON
PENSION
PHAETON
PHANTOM
PHARAOH
PHYSIOL
PILLBOX
PILLION
PLATOON
PLAYBOY
PLOWBOY
PLYWOOD
POLYGON
PONTOON
PORTION
POSTBOY
POTHOOK
POTSHOT
PRAETOR
PRECOOK
PROCTOR
PSYCHOL
RACCOON
RAINBOW
REACTOR
REDWOOD
RELATOR
REPROOF
REREDOS
REUNION
ROOFTOP
SADIRON
SAFFRON
SALTBOX
SANDHOG
SANDLOT
SAPWOOD
SCALLOP
SEAFOOD
SECTION
SENATOR
SESSION
SHALLOP
SHALLOW
SHAMPOO
SILICON
SOMEHOW
SOUPCON
SPARROW
SPONSOR
SQUALOR
STATION
STEPSON
STILTON
SUCTION
SUNROOF
SUNSPOT
SURGEON
SWALLOW
SYMPTOM
TAPROOM
TAPROOT
TENSION
THEREOF
THEREON
THERMOS
TOOLBOX
TOPKNOT
TORSION
TRACTOR
TRAITOR
TRANSOM
TREASON
TROLLOP
TUITION
TYPHOON
UNBOSOM
UNCTION
VENISON
VERSION
VICEROY
VISITOR
VITRIOL
WALLOON
WARRIOR
WARTHOG
WHATNOT
WHEREOF
WHEREON
WHITLOW
WIDGEON
WINDROW
WOODLOT
WORKBOX
ZILLION
ATTEMPT
BAGPIPE
CATALPA
CONCEPT
CORRUPT
DIGRAPH
DISRUPT
ENTROPY
EPITAPH
EXCERPT
FORCEPS
GESTAPO
ISOTOPE
PERCEPT
PERHAPS
PRECEPT
PREEMPT
RECEIPT
SCRAPPY
SYNCOPE
THERAPY
TRICEPS
TRIUMPH
UNHAPPY
UNKEMPT
UPSWEPT
ACQUIRE
ACTUARY
ADJOURN
AIRPORT
ALGEBRA
ALLEGRO
AMATORY
AMPHORA
ANYMORE
ARCHERY
ARREARS
ATHWART
AUSTERE
AWKWARD
BASTARD
BATTERY
BEDSORE
BEGGARY
BERSERK
BIGHORN
BITTERN
BITTERS
BIZARRE
BOMBARD
BONFIRE
BRACERO
BRAVERY
BRAVURA
BULWARK
BUZZARD
CAESURA
CALDERA
CANNERY
CAPTURE
CARFARE
CARPORT
CASCARA
CATARRH
CATBIRD
CAVALRY
CENSURE
CENTARE
CENTURY
CHANCRE
CHANTRY
CHICORY
CHIMERA
CHOLERA
CISTERN
CLOSURE
CLOTURE
COLLARD
COMFORT
COMPARE
COMPORT
CONCERN
CONCERT
CONCORD
CONFIRM
CONFORM
CONJURE
CONSORT
CONTORT
CONVERT
COOKERY
COUNTRY
COUTURE
COWBIRD
CULTURE
CULVERT
CURSORY
CUSTARD
CUTLERY
CUTWORM
DASTARD
DEANERY
DECLARE
DENTURE
DEPLORE
DESSERT
DEVILRY
DIEHARD
DISCARD
DISCERN
DISCORD
DISPORT
DISTORT
DISTURB
DOGCART
DRAPERY
DULLARD
EARMARK
EASTERN
ENQUIRE
ENSNARE
EPICURE
EQUERRY
ESQUIRE
ESTUARY
EXPLORE
EYESORE
FACTORY
FAILURE
FANFARE
FEATURE
FERNERY
FILBERT
FIREARM
FISHERY
FISSURE
FIXTURE
FLEXURE
FLOWERY
FOGHORN
FOOLERY
FOREARM
FORLORN
FORWARD
FOULARD
FOUNDRY
FROWARD
GALLERY
GESTURE
GIZZARD
GRANARY
GRAVURE
GUNFIRE
GUNNERY
HAGGARD
HALBERD
HALVERS
HALYARD
HARVARD
HAUBERK
HAYFORK
HAYWIRE
HECTARE
HICKORY
HISTORY
HOMBURG
HOSIERY
HUNKERS
ICEBERG
IMAGERY
IMPEARL
IMPLORE
INBOARD
INDOORS
INKHORN
INQUIRE
INQUIRY
INSHORE
INSPIRE
JANUARY
JAYBIRD
JETPORT
JEWELRY
JITTERS
LAGGARD
LANTERN
LANYARD
LAUNDRY
LECHERY
LECTERN
LECTURE
LEEWARD
LEGHORN
LEISURE
LEMPIRA
LEOPARD
LEOTARD
LIBRARY
LOTTERY
MACABRE
MADEIRA
MAESTRO
MALLARD
MAMMARY
MANSARD
MASCARA
MASONRY
MASTERY
MEASURE
MERCURY
MIMICRY
MISFIRE
MIXTURE
MUSTARD
MYSTERY
NETWARE
NETWORK
NEWBORN
NIAGARA
NIGGARD
NONHERO
NOWHERE
NURSERY
NURTURE
OBSCURE
ONSHORE
ORATORY
ORCHARD
OSSUARY
OSTMARK
OUTWARD
OUTWORK
OUTWORN
OVERARM
PASTERN
PASTURE
PATTERN
PECCARY
PEPPERY
PERFORM
PERJURY
PERTURB
PERVERT
PICTURE
PILLORY
PINWORM
PISMIRE
PLACARD
PLENARY
PONIARD
POPCORN
POSTERN
POSTURE
POTHERB
POTTERY

POULTRY
PREFORM
PREPARE
PRIMARY
PROCURE
PROVERB
PURPORT
RAMPART
RAPPORT
RAPTURE
RECTORY
REENTRY
REQUIRE
RESTORE
RHUBARB
RIVALRY
ROBBERY
ROOKERY
RUPTURE
SAGUARO
SCENERY
SEABIRD
SEAPORT
SEAWARD
SECTARY
SENSORY
SIDEARM
SINCERE
SKYLARK
SKYWARD
SLAVERY
SOJOURN
SORCERY
STATURE
STEWARD
SUBVERT
SUMMARY
SUNBURN
SUPPORT
SURGERY
TANBARK
TANNERY
TEMPERA
TERNARY
TEXTURE
TINWARE
TOGGERY
TONSURE
TORTURE
TRACERY
TURNERY
UNAWARE
UNHEARD
UNICORN
UNIFORM
UNITARY
UNLEARN
UNSNARL
UPSTART
URETHRA
URINARY
VAMPIRE
VANWARD
VAQUERO
VENTURE
VERDURE
VESPERS
VESTURE
VICTORY
VISCERA
VULTURE
WAGGERY
WARFARE
WARLORD
WAXWORK
WAYWARD
WAYWORN
WELFARE
WESTERN
WITHERS
YARDARM
ABOLISH
ABREAST
ABSCESS
ADDRESS
ADIPOSE
ADVERSE
AGAINST
AGELESS
AIMLESS
AIRPOST
AMYLASE
ANAPEST
ANGUISH
ANIMISM
ANYWISE
APPEASE
APPRISE
ARMREST
ARTLESS
ATAVISM
ATHEIST
ATHIRST
AUTOPSY
BAGASSE
BALLAST
BAPTISM
BAPTIST
BECAUSE
BEDFAST
BEDPOST
BEQUEST
BLEMISH
BOMBAST
BOOKISH
BRITISH
BRUTISH
BULRUSH
BURGESS
BURMESE
BURNISH
CABOOSE
CALYPSO
CANVASS
CARCASS
CAROUSE
CATFISH
CHEMISE
CHEMIST
CHERISH
CHINESE
CLEANSE
CODFISH
COEXIST
COMPASS
COMPOSE
COMPOST
CONCISE
CONFESS
CONFUSE
CONGEST
CONSIST
CONTEST
CUTLASS
CYCLIST
CYPRESS
DECEASE
DEFENSE
DEFROST
DEGAUSS
DELOUSE
DENTIST
DEPRESS
DERVISH
DESPISE
DIARIST
DIFFUSE
DIGRESS
DIOCESE
DISCUSS
DISEASE
DISEUSE
DISGUST
DISMISS
DISPOSE
DIVERSE
DOGFISH
DUCHESS
EARNEST
ECLIPSE
ECSTASY
EGOTISM
ELITISM
ELLIPSE
EMBASSY
EMPRESS
ENCLOSE
ENCRUST
ENDLESS
ENDMOST
ENDORSE
ENDWISE
ENGLISH
ENGROSS
ENTHUSE
ENTRUST
EXHAUST
EXPANSE
EXPENSE
EXPRESS
EYELASH
EYEWASH
FANTASY
FASCISM
FAUVISM
FINESSE
FINFISH
FINNISH
FLEMISH
FLORIST
FLUTIST
FOOLISH
FURBISH
FURNISH
GABFEST
GARFISH
GARNISH
GEODESY
GLIMPSE
GLUCOSE
GODDESS
GODLESS
GOULASH
HAPLESS
HARNESS
HARVEST
HASHISH
HEIRESS
HEROISM
HOGWASH
HOSTESS
ILLNESS
IMAGISM
IMMENSE
IMMERSE
IMPASSE
IMPRESS
IMPULSE
INCENSE
INCLOSE
INCRUST
INDORSE
INGRESS
INQUEST
INTENSE
INTRUST
INVERSE
JACKASS
JUDAISM
JUJITSU
KADDISH
LACTOSE
LARGESS
LAWLESS
LEFTISM
LEPROSY
LICENSE
MAFIOSO
MALAISE
MALTOSE
MANNISH
MARXISM
MAWKISH
MIDMOST
MOLLUSK
MORTISE
NOURISH
OBELISK
OBVERSE
OCULIST
OFFENSE
OPPRESS
OUTCAST
OUTLAST
OUTPOST
PAPOOSE
PEEVISH
PERSIST
PETTISH
PIANIST
PIGGISH
POSSESS
PRECISE
PREMISE
PROCESS
PROFESS
PROFUSE
PROMISE
PROPOSE
PROTEST
PROVISO
PROVOST
PROWESS
PUBLISH
PURPOSE
RAFFISH
REALISM
RECLUSE
REDDISH
REDRESS
REFRESH
REGRESS
RELAPSE
RELEASE
REMORSE
REPRESS
REPRISE
REPULSE
REQUEST
REVERSE
RUBBISH
SARCASM
SAWDUST
SELFISH
SIAMESE
SLAVISH
SOPHISM
SOPHIST
SPANISH
STYLISH
STYLIST
SUBSIST
SUCCESS
SUCROSE
SUFFUSE
SUGGEST
SUNFISH
SUNRISE
SUPPOSE
SURMISE
SURPASS
SWEDISH
SYNAPSE
TARNISH
TEMPEST
TOPLESS
TOPMAST
TOPMOST
TOURIST
TRAIPSE
TROPISM
TURKISH
UNCLASP
UNCLOSE
UNCROSS
UNDRESS
UNERASE
UNHORSE
UNLEASH
UNLOOSE
UNTWIST
UPRAISE
USELESS
VAMOOSE
VARNISH
VERBOSE
VISCOSE
VOGUISH
WAGGISH
WARLESS
WASPISH
WHITISH
WITLESS
WITNESS
YIDDISH
ZIONISM
ABILITY
ACETATE
ACOLYTE
ACONITE
ACTUATE
ADULATE
AGITATE
AMENITY
AMNESTY
ANDANTE
ANIMATE
ANNUITY
ANXIETY
APATITE
ARTISTE
ATHLETE
AUREATE
AZIMUTH
BATISTE
BAUXITE
BENEATH
BETROTH
BIOTITE
BIRETTA
BISMUTH
BOYCOTT
BREADTH
BREVITY
BURETTE
CALCITE
CANASTA
CANTATA
CELESTA
CHARITY
CHIANTI
CILIATE
CLARITY
CLIMATE
COGNATE
COLLATE
COMMUTE
COMPETE
COMPOTE
COMPUTE
CONFUTE
CONNOTE
CORDITE
CORINTH
CREMATE
CULOTTE
CUPRITE
DEFLATE
DENSITY
DENTATE
DEPLETE
DESPITE
DETENTE
DEVIATE
DICTATE
DIGNITY
DINETTE
DISPUTE
DOUGHTY
DUBIETY
DYNASTY
EBONITE
EDUCATE
ELEVATE
EMANATE
EMERITA
EMULATE
ENTENTE
EREMITE
ESTHETE
EXCRETA
EXCRETE
EXECUTE
EXEGETE
EXPIATE
FACULTY
FATUITY
FLIGHTY
FRAILTY
FRIGATE
GARROTE
GAVOTTE
GAZETTE
GIBLETS
GRANITE
GRAVITY
HAUGHTY
HIRSUTE
HYDRATE
IMITATE
IMPASTO
IMPIETY
INFLATE
INGRATE
INSTATE
ISOLATE
ITERATE
JACINTH
JOLLITY
KEYNOTE
KIBBUTZ
LACTATE
LAYETTE
LIBERTY
LIGNITE
LUNETTE
MACHETE
MAGENTA
MAGNATE
MAGNETO
MAJESTY
MAMMOTH
MANDATE
MEDIATE
MEMENTO
MIGRATE
MODISTE
MULATTO
MUSETTE
NAIVETE
NAIVETY
NARRATE
NAUGHTY
NITRATE
NITRITE
NOVELTY
OBVIATE
OPACITY
OPERATE
OUTVOTE
OVULATE
PALETTE
PALMATE
PALPATE
PARTITE
PAUCITY
PENALTY
PERLITE
PIMENTO
PINNATE
PIPETTE
PLACATE
POLLUTE
POVERTY
PREDATE
PRELATE
PRIMATE
PRIVATE
PROBATE
PROBITY
PROMOTE
PRORATE
PUBERTY

PULSATE
QUALITY
RADIATE
REALITY
REBIRTH
REGATTA
REPLETE
REQUITE
RESPITE
RICKETS
RICKETY
RIPOSTE
ROSEATE
ROSETTE
ROYALTY
SABBATH
SATIATE
SATIETY
SECRETE
SERRATE
SEVENTY
SOCIETY
STATUTE
STEALTH
SULFATE
SUNBATH
TAFFETA
TEKTITE
TERMITE
TESTATE
THERETO
THROATY
TOWPATH
TRIBUTE
TRINITY
ULULATE
UNCOUTH
UNEARTH
UNQUOTE
UNTRUTH
UPSTATE
URINATE
UTILITY
VACUITY
VALUATE
VARIETY
VARSITY
VEDANTA
VIBRATE
VIBRATO
VIOLATE
VITIATE
VULGATE
WARPATH
WEIGHTY
WHERETO
ZEOLITE

ALUMNUS
AMATEUR
AMOROUS
ANTIQUE
ANXIOUS
APPLAUD
AQUEOUS
ARBUTUS
ARDUOUS
BALEFUL
BAROQUE
BASHFUL
BATHTUB
BECLOUD
BILIOUS
BLOWGUN
BLOWOUT
BREAKUP
BRIMFUL
BRUSQUE
BURNOUT
CADMIUM
CALCIUM
CALLOUS
CAMBIUM
CARDBUS
CAREFUL
CARIOUS
CATCHUP
CELSIUS
CENTAUR
CHECKUP
CLEANUP
COCONUT
CONFLUX
CONTOUR
COOKOUT
COPIOUS
CRANIUM
CUMULUS
CURIOUS
DECORUM
DEFRAUD
DEVALUE
DEVIOUS
DIREFUL
DOLEFUL
DUBIOUS
DUTEOUS
DUTIFUL
EARDRUM
EARPLUG
ECLOGUE
ELYSIUM
ENAMOUR
ENVIOUS
ERRATUM

FALLOUT
FATEFUL
FATIGUE
FATUOUS
FEARFUL
FERMIUM
FERROUS
FIREBUG
FISTFUL
FLAVOUR
FOLDOUT
FRETFUL
FRUSTUM
FULCRUM
FURIOUS
GAINFUL
GALLIUM
GIBBOUS
GLAMOUR
HABITUE
HAFNIUM
HAIRCUT
HALIBUT
HANDFUL
HANDGUN
HANDOUT
HANGOUT
HARBOUR
HAUTEUR
HEINOUS
HIDEOUS
HIDEOUT
HOLMIUM
HOODLUM
HUMDRUM
HUMERUS
HYDROUS
IGNEOUS
IMPETUS
IMPIOUS
INCUBUS
INGENUE
IRIDIUM
ISTHMUS
JEALOUS
JEJUNUM
JODHPUR
KARAKUL
KETCHUP
LADYBUG
LIQUEUR
LITHIUM
LOCKNUT
LOCKOUT
LOOKOUT
MACAQUE
MALLEUS

MASSEUR
MAXIMUM
MINDFUL
MINIBUS
MINIMUM
MODICUM
NEEDFUL
NERVOUS
NIOBIUM
NOCUOUS
NONPLUS
NOSTRUM
NOXIOUS
NUCLEUS
OBLIQUE
OBLOQUY
OBSEQUY
OBVIOUS
OCTOPUS
OMINOUS
OMNIBUS
ONEROUS
OPOSSUM
OPTIMUM
OVERRUN
PABULUM
PAPYRUS
PARLOUR
PARLOUS
PENTIUM
PERIQUE
PHALLUS
PITEOUS
PITIFUL
POMPOUS
PREMIUM
PRONOUN
PULLOUT
QUANTUM
QUIETUS
RAUCOUS
READOUT
REGROUP
RELIQUE
RESIDUE
RETINUE
REVENUE
RHENIUM
RHODIUM
RHOMBUS
ROSEBUD
ROSTRUM
ROUNDUP
RUINOUS
SANCTUM
SCROTUM
SERIOUS

SHOTGUN
SHUTOUT
SINUOUS
SORGHUM
SOULFUL
SPEEDUP
STADIUM
STARTUP
STERNUM
STIRRUP
STRATUM
SURPLUS
SURTOUT
TANTRUM
TEDIOUS
TENUOUS
TERBIUM
TETANUS
THORIUM
THULIUM
TRITIUM
TRIVIUM
TUNEFUL
TURNOUT
UNGROUP
URANIUM
URANOUS
VACUOUS
VARIOUS
VICIOUS
VILLOUS
VISCOUS
WAILFUL
WAKEFUL
WALKOUT
WASHOUT
WASHTUB
WICKIUP
WILLFUL
WISHFUL
WISTFUL
WITHOUT
WOODCUT
WORKOUT
YTTRIUM
ZEALOUS
ABSOLVE
ACHIEVE
AIRWAVE
AMATIVE
ANCHOVY
APPROVE
ARCHIVE
BEEHIVE
BEHOOVE
BELIEVE
BIVALVE

CAPTIVE
CASSAVA
CENTAVO
CONCAVE
CONNIVE
COSTIVE
CURSIVE
DECEIVE
DEPRAVE
DEPRIVE
DESERVE
DEVOLVE
ELUSIVE
ENCLAVE
ENGRAVE
ENSLAVE
EROSIVE
FESTIVE
FORGIVE
FURTIVE
IMPROVE
INVOLVE
KHEDIVE
MASSIVE
MISSIVE
OBSERVE
OUTLIVE
PASSIVE
PECCAVI
PENSIVE
RECEIVE
RELIEVE
REPROVE
RESERVE
RESOLVE
RESTIVE
REVOLVE
SURVIVE
UNNERVE
UNWEAVE
YESHIVA
BELLOWS
GALLOWS
GOSHAWK
HOEDOWN
INGROWN
LETDOWN
LOWDOWN
MIDTOWN
OVERAWE
PEAFOWL
RUNDOWN
SUNDOWN
UNKNOWN
WILLOWY
WINDOWS
BETWIXT

CONTEXT
PRETEXT
ACRONYM
ANTONYM
BUCKEYE
COCKEYE
ENDWAYS
HOMONYM
PINKEYE
SYNONYM
WALLEYE
WYSIWYG
AGONIZE
ANALYZE
ANODIZE
ATOMIZE
BAPTIZE
BLINTZE
BONANZA
CADENZA
CAPSIZE
CHINTZY
IDOLIZE
ITEMIZE
LIONIZE
MESTIZO
ORGANZA
OUTSIZE
OXIDIZE
PIZZAZZ
REALIZE
SQUEEZE
STYLIZE
TRAPEZE
UNITIZE
UTILIZE

## 7TH LETTER

ALFALFA
ALGEBRA
ALUMINA
AMMONIA
AMNESIA
AMPHORA
ANAEMIA
ANTENNA
APHASIA
BAZOOKA
BEGONIA
BIRETTA
BOLOGNA
BONANZA
BRAVURA
BRECCIA

CADENZA
CAESURA
CALDERA
CANASTA
CANNULA
CANTATA
CASCARA
CASSAVA
CATALPA
CEDILLA
CELESTA
CHIMERA
CHOLERA
COCHLEA
CORDOBA
COROLLA
CZARINA
DILEMMA
DIPLOMA
DRACHMA
EMERITA
EXCRETA
FISTULA
FORMULA
FUCHSIA
GONDOLA
GORILLA
HOSANNA
INDICIA
INERTIA
LANTANA
LASAGNA
LATAKIA
LEMPIRA
MADEIRA
MAGENTA
MAHATMA
MALARIA
MARIMBA
MASCARA
MAXILLA
MAZURKA
MEDULLA
MILITIA
MINUTIA
MORPHIA
NAPHTHA
NIAGARA
NIRVANA
NOVELLA
OCARINA
ORGANZA
OVERSEA
PANACEA
PAPILLA
PAPRIKA
PATELLA

PERGOLA
PETUNIA
PIRANHA
REGALIA
REGATTA
REPLICA
RICKSHA
ROTUNDA
RUBELLA
SAVANNA
SCAPULA
SEQUOIA
SPATULA
STAMINA
SULTANA
TAFFETA
TAMBALA
TAPIOCA
TEMPERA
TEQUILA
TOXEMIA
TRACHEA
URETHRA
VANILLA
VEDANTA
VERANDA
VERBENA
VISCERA
WHOOPLA
YESHIVA
BATHTUB
CONTRIB
CORNCOB
COULOMB
COXCOMB
DISTURB
PEDICAB
PERTURB
POTHERB
PROVERB
RHUBARB
SUCCUMB
TAXICAB
WASHTUB
ACRYLIC
AEROBIC
ALEMBIC
ALMANAC
AQUATIC
ARCHAIC
ARSENIC
ASCETIC
ASEPTIC
ASIATIC
BALDRIC
BENTHIC
BIVOUAC

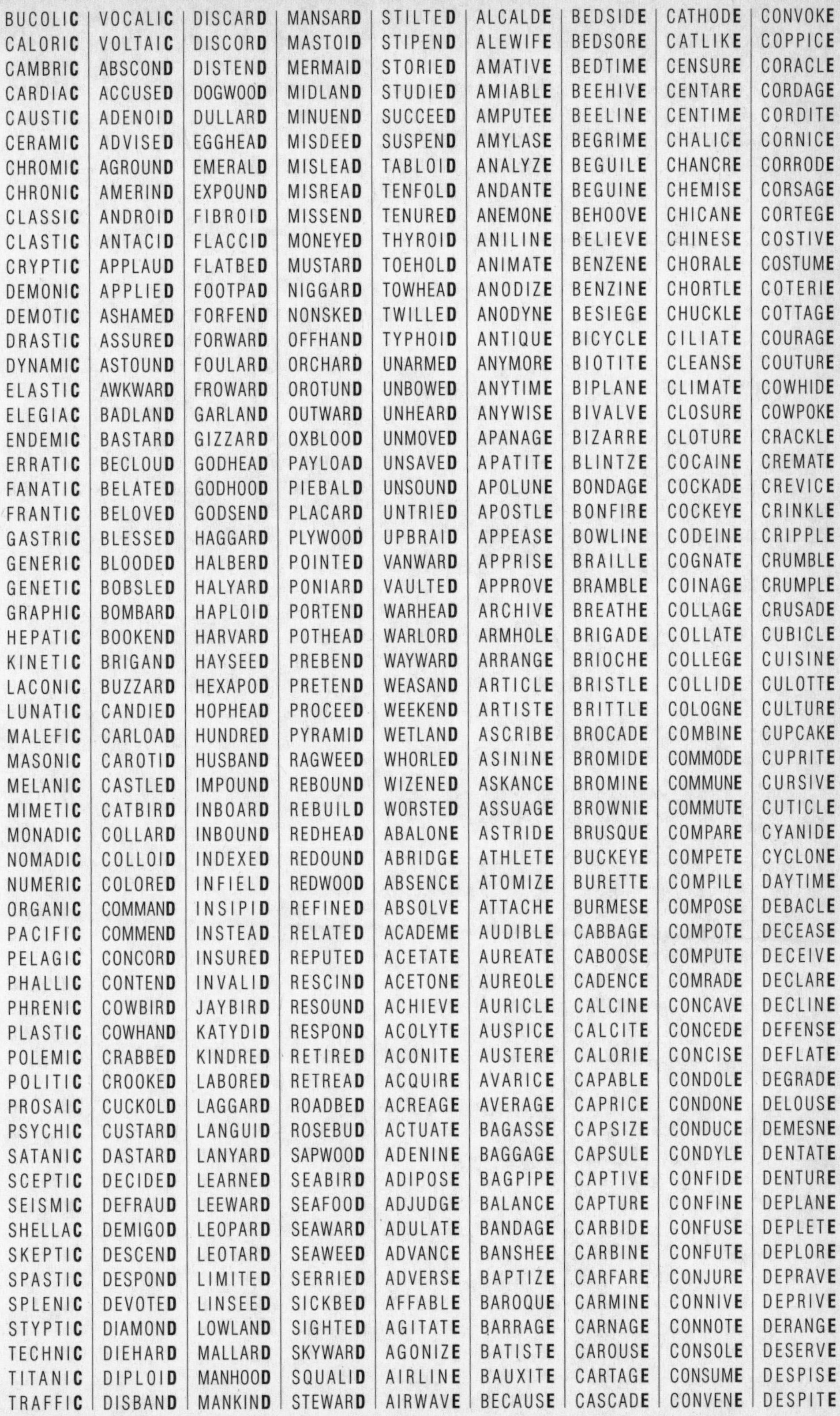

BUCOLIC
CALORIC
CAMBRIC
CARDIAC
CAUSTIC
CERAMIC
CHROMIC
CHRONIC
CLASSIC
CLASTIC
CRYPTIC
DEMONIC
DEMOTIC
DRASTIC
DYNAMIC
ELASTIC
ELEGIAC
ENDEMIC
ERRATIC
FANATIC
FRANTIC
GASTRIC
GENERIC
GENETIC
GRAPHIC
HEPATIC
KINETIC
LACONIC
LUNATIC
MALEFIC
MASONIC
MELANIC
MIMETIC
MONADIC
NOMADIC
NUMERIC
ORGANIC
PACIFIC
PELAGIC
PHALLIC
PHRENIC
PLASTIC
POLEMIC
POLITIC
PROSAIC
PSYCHIC
SATANIC
SCEPTIC
SEISMIC
SHELLAC
SKEPTIC
SPASTIC
SPLENIC
STYPTIC
TECHNIC
TITANIC
TRAFFIC

VOCALIC
VOLTAIC
ABSCOND
ACCUSED
ADENOID
ADVISED
AGROUND
AMERIND
ANDROID
ANTACID
APPLAUD
APPLIED
ASHAMED
ASSURED
ASTOUND
AWKWARD
BADLAND
BASTARD
BECLOUD
BELATED
BELOVED
BLESSED
BLOODED
BOBSLED
BOMBARD
BOOKEND
BRIGAND
BUZZARD
CANDIED
CARLOAD
CAROTID
CASTLED
CATBIRD
COLLARD
COLLOID
COLORED
COMMAND
COMMEND
CONCORD
CONTEND
COWBIRD
COWHAND
CRABBED
CROOKED
CUCKOLD
CUSTARD
DASTARD
DECIDED
DEFRAUD
DEMIGOD
DESCEND
DESPOND
DEVOTED
DIAMOND
DIEHARD
DIPLOID
DISBAND

DISCARD
DISCORD
DISTEND
DOGWOOD
DULLARD
EGGHEAD
EMERALD
EXPOUND
FIBROID
FLACCID
FLATBED
FOOTPAD
FORFEND
FORWARD
FOULARD
FROWARD
GARLAND
GIZZARD
GODHEAD
GODHOOD
GODSEND
HAGGARD
HALBERD
HALYARD
HAPLOID
HARVARD
HAYSEED
HEXAPOD
HOPHEAD
HUNDRED
HUSBAND
IMPOUND
INBOARD
INBOUND
INDEXED
INFIELD
INSIPID
INSTEAD
INSURED
INVALID
JAYBIRD
KATYDID
KINDRED
LABORED
LAGGARD
LANGUID
LANYARD
LEARNED
LEEWARD
LEOPARD
LEOTARD
LIMITED
LINSEED
LOWLAND
MALLARD
MANHOOD
MANKIND

MANSARD
MASTOID
MERMAID
MIDLAND
MINUEND
MISDEED
MISLEAD
MISREAD
MISSEND
MONEYED
MUSTARD
NIGGARD
NONSKED
OFFHAND
ORCHARD
OROTUND
OUTWARD
OXBLOOD
PAYLOAD
PIEBALD
PLACARD
PLYWOOD
POINTED
PONIARD
PORTEND
POTHEAD
PREBEND
PRETEND
PROCEED
PYRAMID
RAGWEED
REBOUND
REBUILD
REDHEAD
REDOUND
REDWOOD
REFINED
RELATED
REPUTED
RESCIND
RESOUND
RESPOND
RETIRED
RETREAD
ROADBED
ROSEBUD
SAPWOOD
SEABIRD
SEAFOOD
SEAWARD
SEAWEED
SERRIED
SICKBED
SIGHTED
SKYWARD
SQUALID
STEWARD

STILTED
STIPEND
STORIED
STUDIED
SUCCEED
SUSPEND
TABLOID
TENFOLD
TENURED
THYROID
TOEHOLD
TOWHEAD
TWILLED
TYPHOID
UNARMED
UNBOWED
UNHEARD
UNMOVED
UNSAVED
UNSOUND
UNTRIED
UPBRAID
VANWARD
VAULTED
WARHEAD
WARLORD
WAYWARD
WEASAND
WEEKEND
WETLAND
WHORLED
WIZENED
WORSTED
ABALONE
ABRIDGE
ABSENCE
ABSOLVE
ACADEME
ACETATE
ACETONE
ACHIEVE
ACOLYTE
ACONITE
ACQUIRE
ACREAGE
ACTUATE
ADENINE
ADIPOSE
ADJUDGE
ADULATE
ADVANCE
ADVERSE
AFFABLE
AGITATE
AGONIZE
AIRLINE
AIRWAVE

ALCALDE
ALEWIFE
AMATIVE
AMIABLE
AMPUTEE
AMYLASE
ANALYZE
ANDANTE
ANEMONE
ANILINE
ANIMATE
ANODIZE
ANODYNE
ANTIQUE
ANYMORE
ANYTIME
ANYWISE
APANAGE
APATITE
APOLUNE
APOSTLE
APPEASE
APPRISE
APPROVE
ARCHIVE
ARMHOLE
ARRANGE
ARTICLE
ARTISTE
ASCRIBE
ASININE
ASKANCE
ASSUAGE
ASTRIDE
ATHLETE
ATOMIZE
ATTACHE
AUDIBLE
AUREATE
AUREOLE
AURICLE
AUSPICE
AUSTERE
AVARICE
AVERAGE
BAGASSE
BAGGAGE
BAGPIPE
BALANCE
BANDAGE
BANSHEE
BAPTIZE
BAROQUE
BARRAGE
BATISTE
BAUXITE
BECAUSE

BEDSIDE
BEDSORE
BEDTIME
BEEHIVE
BEELINE
BEGRIME
BEGUILE
BEGUINE
BEHOOVE
BELIEVE
BENZENE
BENZINE
BESIEGE
BICYCLE
BIOTITE
BIPLANE
BIVALVE
BIZARRE
BLINTZE
BONDAGE
BONFIRE
BOWLINE
BRAILLE
BRAMBLE
BREATHE
BRIGADE
BRIOCHE
BRISTLE
BRITTLE
BROCADE
BROMIDE
BROMINE
BROWNIE
BRUSQUE
BUCKEYE
BURETTE
BURMESE
CABBAGE
CABOOSE
CADENCE
CALCINE
CALCITE
CALORIE
CAPABLE
CAPRICE
CAPSIZE
CAPSULE
CAPTIVE
CAPTURE
CARBIDE
CARBINE
CARFARE
CARMINE
CARNAGE
CAROUSE
CARTAGE
CASCADE

CATHODE
CATLIKE
CENSURE
CENTARE
CENTIME
CHALICE
CHANCRE
CHEMISE
CHICANE
CHINESE
CHORALE
CHORTLE
CHUCKLE
CILIATE
CLEANSE
CLIMATE
CLOSURE
CLOTURE
COCAINE
COCKADE
COCKEYE
CODEINE
COGNATE
COINAGE
COLLAGE
COLLATE
COLLEGE
COLLIDE
COLOGNE
COMBINE
COMMODE
COMMUNE
COMMUTE
COMPARE
COMPETE
COMPILE
COMPOSE
COMPOTE
COMPUTE
COMRADE
CONCAVE
CONCEDE
CONCISE
CONDOLE
CONDONE
CONDUCE
CONDYLE
CONFIDE
CONFINE
CONFUSE
CONFUTE
CONJURE
CONNIVE
CONNOTE
CONSOLE
CONSUME
CONVENE

CONVOKE
COPPICE
CORACLE
CORDAGE
CORDITE
CORNICE
CORRODE
CORSAGE
CORTEGE
COSTIVE
COSTUME
COTERIE
COTTAGE
COURAGE
COUTURE
COWHIDE
COWPOKE
CRACKLE
CREMATE
CREVICE
CRINKLE
CRIPPLE
CRUMBLE
CRUMPLE
CRUSADE
CUBICLE
CUISINE
CULOTTE
CULTURE
CUPCAKE
CUPRITE
CURSIVE
CUTICLE
CYANIDE
CYCLONE
DAYTIME
DEBACLE
DECEASE
DECEIVE
DECLARE
DECLINE
DEFENSE
DEFLATE
DEGRADE
DELOUSE
DEMESNE
DENTATE
DENTURE
DEPLANE
DEPLETE
DEPLORE
DEPRAVE
DEPRIVE
DERANGE
DESERVE
DESPISE
DESPITE

DESTINE
DETENTE
DEVALUE
DEVIATE
DEVOLVE
DEVOTEE
DICTATE
DIFFUSE
DINETTE
DIOCESE
DISABLE
DISEASE
DISEUSE
DISLIKE
DISPOSE
DISPUTE
DISROBE
DIVERGE
DIVERSE
DIVORCE
DIVULGE
DOCKAGE
DOGBANE
DOMINIE
DOYENNE
DRIBBLE
DRIZZLE
DUCTILE
DURABLE
DURANCE
DWINDLE
EARACHE
EARLOBE
EBONITE
ECLIPSE
ECLOGUE
EDIFICE
EDUCATE
ELEVATE
ELLIPSE
ELUSIVE
EMANATE
EMBRACE
EMULATE
ENCLAVE
ENCLOSE
ENDORSE
ENDWISE
ENFORCE
ENGRAVE
ENHANCE
ENLARGE
ENNOBLE
ENPLANE
ENQUIRE
ENSLAVE
ENSNARE
ENTENTE
ENTHUSE
ENTITLE
ENTWINE
EPERGNE
EPICURE
EPISODE
EPISTLE
EPITOME
EQUABLE
EREMITE
EROSIVE
ESCAPEE
ESQUIRE
ESSENCE
ESTHETE
EVACUEE
EXAMINE
EXAMPLE
EXCLUDE
EXCRETE
EXECUTE
EXEGETE
EXPANSE
EXPENSE
EXPIATE
EXPLODE
EXPLORE
EXPUNGE
EXTREME
EXTRUDE
EYESORE
FAIENCE
FAILURE
FANFARE
FATIGUE
FEATURE
FEBRILE
FERRULE
FERTILE
FESTIVE
FIANCEE
FINAGLE
FINANCE
FINESSE
FISSILE
FISSURE
FIXTURE
FLEXURE
FLOUNCE
FLYABLE
FOLIAGE
FOOTAGE
FORBODE
FORESEE
FORGIVE
FORSAKE
FORTUNE
FOXHOLE
FRAGILE
FRAZZLE
FRECKLE
FREEBIE
FRIABLE
FRIGATE
FRIZZLE
FULSOME
FURNACE
FURTIVE
GARBAGE
GARROTE
GAVOTTE
GAZELLE
GAZETTE
GENTILE
GENUINE
GERMANE
GESTURE
GIRAFFE
GLIMPSE
GLOBULE
GLUCOSE
GODLIKE
GRACKLE
GRANDEE
GRANITE
GRANTEE
GRANULE
GRAPPLE
GRAVURE
GRENADE
GRIDDLE
GRIMACE
GRISTLE
GROUPIE
GRUMBLE
GUANINE
GUMSHOE
GUNFIRE
GUNWALE
HABITUE
HAULAGE
HAYWIRE
HECTARE
HELLENE
HEMLINE
HERBAGE
HEROINE
HIPBONE
HIRSUTE
HOECAKE
HORMONE
HOSPICE
HOSTAGE
HOSTILE
HOTCAKE
HYDRATE
HYGIENE
IDOLIZE
IGNOBLE
IMAGINE
IMITATE
IMMENSE
IMMERSE
IMPASSE
IMPINGE
IMPLODE
IMPLORE
IMPROVE
IMPULSE
INCENSE
INCLINE
INCLOSE
INCLUDE
INDORSE
INDULGE
INFLAME
INFLATE
INGENUE
INGRATE
INQUIRE
INSHORE
INSPIRE
INSTATE
INTENSE
INTRUDE
INVERSE
INVOICE
INVOLVE
IRKSOME
ISOLATE
ISOTOPE
ITEMIZE
ITERATE
JASMINE
JOYANCE
JOYRIDE
JUBILEE
JUSTICE
KEYHOLE
KEYNOTE
KHEDIVE
KNUCKLE
LACTATE
LACTOSE
LATRINE
LATTICE
LAYETTE
LEAFAGE
LEAKAGE
LECTURE
LEGATEE
LEGIBLE
LEISURE
LEONINE
LETTUCE
LICENSE
LIGNITE
LIMEADE
LINEAGE
LINKAGE
LIONIZE
LISSOME
LIVABLE
LOZENGE
LUCERNE
LUGGAGE
LUNETTE
MACABRE
MACAQUE
MACHETE
MACHINE
MACRAME
MAGNATE
MALAISE
MALTOSE
MANACLE
MANDATE
MANHOLE
MANLIKE
MARQUEE
MASSAGE
MASSIVE
MATINEE
MAYPOLE
MEASURE
MEDIATE
MELANGE
MESSAGE
METHANE
MICROBE
MIDWIFE
MIGRATE
MILEAGE
MILLAGE
MILLIME
MIRACLE
MISFILE
MISFIRE
MISLIKE
MISNAME
MISRULE
MISSILE
MISSIVE
MISTAKE
MIXTURE
MODISTE
MONOCLE
MONTAGE
MORAINE
MORTISE
MOUNTIE
MUNDANE
MUSETTE
MUTABLE
NACELLE
NAIVETE
NARRATE
NECKTIE
NEPTUNE
NETWARE
NITRATE
NITRITE
NOISOME
NOMINEE
NOTABLE
NOWHERE
NUCLIDE
NURTURE
OATCAKE
OBLIQUE
OBSCENE
OBSCURE
OBSERVE
OBTRUDE
OBVERSE
OBVIATE
OCCLUDE
OFFENSE
OFFSIDE
OLIVINE
ONETIME
ONSHORE
OPERATE
ORIFICE
OUTCOME
OUTFACE
OUTLINE
OUTLIVE
OUTRAGE
OUTSIDE
OUTSIZE
OUTVOTE
OVERAGE
OVERAWE
OVERSEE
OVULATE
OXIDIZE
PACKAGE
PALETTE
PALMATE
PALPATE
PANACHE
PANCAKE
PANICLE
PAPOOSE
PARABLE
PARTAKE
PARTITE
PASSAGE
PASSIVE
PASTIME
PASTURE
PENANCE
PENSIVE
PERCALE
PERFUME
PERIGEE
PERIQUE
PERLITE
PERVADE
PETIOLE
PHONEME
PICTURE
PILLAGE
PINHOLE
PINKEYE
PINNACE
PINNATE
PIPETTE
PISMIRE
PLACATE
PLIABLE
PLUMAGE
POLLUTE
PORCINE
PORTAGE
POSTAGE
POSTURE
POTABLE
POTHOLE
POTTAGE
PRAIRIE
PRALINE
PRATTLE
PRECEDE
PRECISE
PREDATE
PREEMIE
PREFACE
PRELATE
PRELUDE
PREMISE
PREPARE
PREPUCE
PRESAGE
PRESIDE
PRESUME
PRICKLE
PRIMATE
PRITHEE
PRIVATE
PROBATE
PROCURE
PRODUCE
PROFANE
PROFILE
PROFUSE
PROMISE
PROMOTE
PROPANE
PROPOSE
PRORATE
PROTEGE
PROVIDE
PROVOKE
PUERILE
PULSATE
PURPOSE
PUSTULE
QUIBBLE
QUICKIE
QUININE
RADIATE
RAGTIME
RAMPAGE
RAPTURE
RATLINE
RAWHIDE
REALIZE
RECEIVE
RECLAME
RECLINE
RECLUSE
RECYCLE
REDLINE
REFEREE
REFUGEE
REJOICE
RELAPSE
RELEASE
RELIEVE
RELIQUE
REMORSE
REPLACE
REPLETE
REPRISE
REPROVE
REPTILE
REPULSE
REQUIRE
REQUITE
RESERVE
RESIDUE
RESOLVE
RESPITE
RESTIVE
RESTORE
RETINUE
RETIREE
RETRACE
REVENGE
REVENUE
REVERIE
REVERSE
REVOLVE
RHIZOME
RIPOSTE
RISIBLE
ROMANCE
ROSEATE
ROSETTE
ROUTINE
RUMMAGE
RUPTURE
SALTINE
SALVAGE
SARDINE
SATIATE
SAUSAGE
SCIENCE
SCOURGE
SCRUPLE
SCUFFLE
SCUTTLE
SEASIDE
SECLUDE
SECRETE
SELVAGE
SERRATE
SERVICE
SERVILE
SESSILE
SHACKLE
SHAMBLE
SHARPIE
SHAWNEE
SHEATHE
SHINGLE
SHUFFLE
SHUTTLE
SIAMESE
SILENCE
SINCERE
SIZABLE
SKIFFLE
SKYLINE
SMUGGLE
SNAFFLE
SNIFFLE
SNUFFLE
SNUGGLE
SOLUBLE
SOMEONE
SOUFFLE
SPANGLE

SPARKLE
SPECKLE
SPICULE
SPINDLE
SPITTLE
SPLURGE
SQUEEZE
STABILE
STARTLE
STATURE
STATUTE
STEEPLE
STERILE
STIPPLE
STORAGE
STRANGE
STROPHE
STUBBLE
STUMBLE
STYLIZE
SUBLIME
SUBSIDE
SUBTILE
SUCROSE
SUFFICE
SUFFUSE
SUICIDE
SULFATE
SULFIDE
SUNRISE
SUPPOSE
SUPREME
SURFACE
SURMISE
SURNAME
SURVIVE
SWADDLE
SWINDLE
SYNAPSE
SYNCOPE
SYRINGE
SYSTOLE
TACTILE
TADPOLE
TEENAGE
TEKTITE
TENABLE
TENSILE
TERMITE
TERRACE
TESTATE
TEXTILE
TEXTURE
THIMBLE
THISTLE
THYMINE
TILLAGE
TINWARE
TOLUENE
TONNAGE
TONSURE
TOPSIDE
TORTURE
TRADUCE
TRAINEE
TRAIPSE
TRAMPLE
TRAPEZE
TREACLE
TREADLE
TREMBLE
TRESTLE
TRIBUNE
TRIBUTE
TRICKLE
TRIREME
TROCHEE
TROUBLE
TROUNCE
TRUCKLE
TRUFFLE
TRUNDLE
TRUSTEE
TUNABLE
TURBINE
TWADDLE
TWIDDLE
TWINKLE
TWOSOME
UKULELE
ULULATE
UMBRAGE
UNAWARE
UNCLOSE
UNERASE
UNHINGE
UNHORSE
UNITIZE
UNLOOSE
UNNERVE
UNQUOTE
UNTWINE
UNWEAVE
UPGRADE
UPRAISE
UPSTAGE
UPSTATE
UPSURGE
URINATE
UTILIZE
VACCINE
VACUOLE
VALANCE
VALENCE
VALUATE
VAMOOSE
VAMPIRE
VANDYKE
VANTAGE
VEHICLE
VENTURE
VERBOSE
VERDURE
VESICLE
VESTIGE
VESTURE
VIBRATE
VILLAGE
VINTAGE
VIOLATE
VIRGULE
VISCOSE
VISIBLE
VITIATE
VOCABLE
VOLTAGE
VOLUBLE
VULGATE
VULPINE
VULTURE
WADABLE
WALLEYE
WARFARE
WARLIKE
WARTIME
WASTAGE
WATTAGE
WAYSIDE
WELCOME
WELFARE
WHEEDLE
WHISTLE
WHITTLE
WINDAGE
WINSOME
WORDAGE
WRANGLE
WREATHE
WRESTLE
WRIGGLE
WRINKLE
YARDAGE
ZEOLITE
BAILIFF
CAITIFF
DEBRIEF
DISTAFF
EARMUFF
FLYLEAF
HERSELF
HIMSELF
KICKOFF
MASTIFF
MIDRIFF
ONESELF
PONTIFF
REPROOF
SHERIFF
SUNROOF
TAKEOFF
THEREOF
THYSELF
TURNOFF
WHEREOF
BACKING
BACKLOG
BALDING
BARRING
BATTING
BEARING
BEDDING
BINDING
BOOTLEG
BOWLING
BULLDOG
BUNTING
BUSHING
CALLING
CASTING
CATALOG
CEILING
COATING
CODLING
COWLING
CRAVING
CUNNING
CURBING
CUTTING
DARLING
DASHING
DEALING
DISHRAG
DRAWING
DUMPING
EARPLUG
EARRING
ERELONG
ETCHING
EVENING
FAILING
FAIRING
FARMING
FEELING
FENCING
FILLING
FINDING
FIREBUG
FISHING
FITTING
FLEMING
FOOTING
FORELEG
FORGING
FOULING
FURLONG
FURRING
GELDING
GINSENG
GOSLING
GRATING
HALTING
HANDBAG
HANGDOG
HANGING
HASHING
HEADING
HEARING
HELPING
HERRING
HINTING
HOLDING
HOMBURG
HOUSING
HOWLING
HULKING
HUSKING
ICEBERG
INKLING
IRONING
JACKLEG
JOTTING
KEEPING
KERNING
KILLING
KNOWING
LADYBUG
LANDING
LAPWING
LEADING
LEGGING
LEMMING
LISTING
LODGING
LONGING
MADDING
MEANING
MEETING
MILLING
MISSING
MOLDING
MOORING
MORNING
MUSTANG
NETTING
NOTHING
ONGOING
OPENING
PACKING
PADDING
PARSING
PARTING
PASSING
PEELING
PENDING
PERIWIG
PFENNIG
PLATING
PRAYING
PROLONG
PUDDING
RAILING
RANKING
READING
RIGGING
RUNNING
SAILING
SANDBAG
SANDHOG
SAPLING
SEATING
SEEMING
SERVING
SETTING
SHADING
SHAVING
SHEBANG
SHORING
SIBLING
SPARING
STAGING
STYLING
SUITING
TATTING
TELLING
TICKING
TOPPING
TRACING
TURNING
UNDOING
UNDYING
UNSLING
UPSWING
VEILING
VESTING
WADDING
WANTING
WARNING
WARTHOG
WASHING
WAXWING
WEBBING
WEDDING
WEEPING
WHITING
WILLING
WINDBAG
WINDING
WINNING
WITTING
WORDING
WORKBAG
WORKING
WRITING
WYSIWYG
ABOLISH
ANGUISH
AZIMUTH
BENEATH
BESEECH
BETROTH
BEWITCH
BISMUTH
BLEMISH
BOOKISH
BOROUGH
BREADTH
BRITISH
BRUTISH
BULRUSH
BURNISH
CATARRH
CATFISH
CHEETAH
CHERISH
CODFISH
CORINTH
DEBAUCH
DEBOUCH
DERVISH
DIGRAPH
DISTICH
DOGFISH
ENGLISH
EPITAPH
EYELASH
EYEWASH
FINFISH
FINNISH
FLEMISH
FOOLISH
FURBISH
FURNISH
GARFISH
GARNISH
GOULASH
HASHISH
HOGWASH
IMPEACH
INVEIGH
JACINTH
JEHOVAH
KADDISH
MAMMOTH
MANNISH
MAWKISH
MESSIAH
MONARCH
NOURISH
OSTRICH
PEEVISH
PETTISH
PHARAOH
PIBROCH
PIGGISH
PUBLISH
RAFFISH
REBIRTH
REDDISH
REFRESH
RETOUCH
RUBBISH
SABBATH
SCRATCH
SCREECH
SELFISH
SLAVISH
SPANISH
SPINACH
SPLOTCH
SQUELCH
STAUNCH
STEALTH
STOMACH
STRETCH
STYLISH
SUNBATH
SUNFISH
SWEDISH
TARNISH
THROUGH
TOWPATH
TRIUMPH
TURKISH
UNCOUTH
UNEARTH
UNHITCH
UNLATCH
UNLEASH
UNTRUTH
VARNISH
VOGUISH
WAGGISH
WARPATH
WASPISH
WHITISH
YIDDISH
AFGHANI
CHIANTI
DASHIKI
EFFENDI
GUARANI
HIBACHI
ISRAELI
MARTINI
ORIGAMI
PECCAVI
RAVIOLI
SAMURAI
SPUMONI
SWAHILI
TIMPANI
TORTONI
TSUNAMI
AIRSICK
BANNOCK
BEATNIK
BEDROCK
BERSERK
BESPEAK
BETHINK
BULLOCK
BULWARK
BURDOCK
BUTTOCK
CARSICK
CASSOCK
CATWALK
CHINOOK
COSSACK
COWLICK
CUTBACK
DAYBOOK
DERRICK
EARMARK
FATBACK
FETLOCK
GIMMICK
GOSHAWK
GUNLOCK
HADDOCK
HAMMOCK
HASSOCK
HAUBERK
HAYCOCK
HAYFORK
HAYRICK
HEMLOCK
HENPECK
HILLOCK
HOGBACK
HUMMOCK
JAYWALK
KINFOLK

LIMBECK
MATTOCK
MENFOLK
MIDWEEK
MOLLUSK
NETWORK
NONBOOK
NUTPICK
OARLOCK
OBELISK
OSTMARK
OUTLOOK
OUTRANK
OUTWORK
PADDOCK
PADLOCK
PEACOCK
POLLACK
POTHOOK
POTLUCK
PRECOOK
PRESOAK
RANSACK
ROEBUCK
ROLLICK
SEASICK
SETBACK
SHYLOCK
SKYLARK
SPUTNIK
TANBARK
TIEBACK
TUSSOCK
UNBLOCK
UNCLOAK
UNFROCK
UPCHUCK
WARLOCK
WAXWORK
WEDLOCK
WETBACK
WRYNECK
ABYSMAL
ABYSSAL
ACCUSAL
ADMIRAL
ADRENAL
AEROSOL
AIRFOIL
AIRMAIL
ALCOHOL
ANTHILL
APPAREL
ARRIVAL
ARSENAL
ASEXUAL
AUSTRAL

BALEFUL
BARBELL
BASHFUL
BEDEVIL
BEDROLL
BESTIAL
BIFOCAL
BIMETAL
BRIMFUL
BROTHEL
CALOMEL
CAPITAL
CAPITOL
CARAMEL
CARAVEL
CAREFUL
CATCALL
CATTAIL
CENTRAL
CHANCEL
CHANNEL
CHARNEL
CHATTEL
CITADEL
COAXIAL
CODICIL
COEQUAL
COLONEL
CONCEAL
CONGEAL
CONICAL
CONTROL
CORDIAL
CORONAL
COUNCIL
COUNSEL
CRUCIAL
CRYSTAL
CURTAIL
DECIBEL
DECIMAL
DESPOIL
DIGITAL
DIREFUL
DISTILL
DIURNAL
DOLEFUL
DUTIFUL
EMBROIL
EMBRYOL
ETERNAL
ETHANOL
ETHICAL
EYEBALL
FACTUAL
FANTAIL
FATEFUL

FEARFUL
FEDERAL
FISTFUL
FLANNEL
FRACTAL
FRETFUL
FULFILL
FUNERAL
GAINFUL
GENERAL
GENITAL
GENTEEL
GLACIAL
GRADUAL
GRAPNEL
GRAUPEL
GUMBOIL
HANDFUL
HANDSEL
HELICAL
HOBNAIL
ILLEGAL
IMMORAL
IMPANEL
IMPEARL
IMPERIL
INDWELL
INFIDEL
INITIAL
INKWELL
INSTALL
INSTILL
JONQUIL
JOURNAL
KARAKUL
LACTEAL
LATERAL
LIBERAL
LINGUAL
LITERAL
LUSTRAL
MANDREL
MANDRIL
MARITAL
MARSHAL
MARTIAL
MAXIMAL
MEDICAL
MENTHOL
MINDFUL
MINERAL
MINIMAL
MISCALL
MISTRAL
MONGREL
MUSICAL
NARWHAL

NATURAL
NEEDFUL
NEUTRAL
NOMINAL
NOSTRIL
NUMERAL
NUPTIAL
OATMEAL
ODDBALL
OEDIPAL
OPTICAL
OPTIMAL
ORDINAL
OUTPULL
OUTSELL
OVERALL
PARASOL
PARBOIL
PARTIAL
PAYROLL
PEAFOWL
PHYSIOL
PIGTAIL
PITFALL
PITIFUL
PLUVIAL
PRETZEL
PREVAIL
PSYCHOL
QUARREL
QUETZAL
QUINTAL
RADICAL
RECITAL
REMODEL
RENEWAL
REVIVAL
SATCHEL
SAWMILL
SCALPEL
SCANDAL
SEAWALL
SEMINAL
SENSUAL
SEVERAL
SHRIVEL
SNORKEL
SOULFUL
SPANIEL
SPATIAL
SPECIAL
SPOUSAL
STENCIL
STRUDEL
SUBSOIL
SUNDIAL
TENDRIL

THERMAL
TIMBREL
TINFOIL
TOENAIL
TOPICAL
TOPSAIL
TOPSOIL
TRAMMEL
TRAVAIL
TREFOIL
TRIVIAL
TUMBREL
TUNEFUL
TURMOIL
TYPICAL
UNCIVIL
UNEQUAL
UNMORAL
UNRAVEL
UNSNARL
UNUSUAL
UTENSIL
VEGETAL
VENTRAL
VERMEIL
VICINAL
VICTUAL
VIRTUAL
VITRIOL
WAGTAIL
WAILFUL
WAKEFUL
WASSAIL
WASTREL
WAYBILL
WILLFUL
WISHFUL
WISTFUL
ACCLAIM
ACRONYM
AMALGAM
ANAGRAM
ANIMISM
ANTONYM
ATAVISM
BAPTISM
BARROOM
BEDROOM
BLOSSOM
BOREDOM
BUCKRAM
CADMIUM
CALCIUM
CAMBIUM
CONFIRM
CONFORM
CRANIUM

CUTWORM
DECLAIM
DECORUM
DIAGRAM
EARDRUM
EGOTISM
ELITISM
ELYSIUM
ENVENOM
EPIGRAM
ERRATUM
EXCLAIM
FASCISM
FAUVISM
FERMIUM
FILMDOM
FIREARM
FLOTSAM
FOREARM
FREEDOM
FRUSTUM
FULCRUM
GALLIUM
GINGHAM
GRANDAM
HAFNIUM
HEROISM
HOLMIUM
HOMONYM
HOODLUM
HUMDRUM
IMAGISM
INTERIM
IRIDIUM
JEJUNUM
JUDAISM
KINGDOM
LEFTISM
LITHIUM
MACADAM
MARXISM
MAXIMUM
MILLDAM
MINIMUM
MODICUM
MUDROOM
NIOBIUM
NOSTRUM
OPOSSUM
OPTIMUM
OVERARM
PABULUM
PENTIUM
PERFORM
PHANTOM
PILGRIM
PINWORM

PREFORM
PREMIUM
PROBLEM
PROGRAM
QUANTUM
QUONDAM
REALISM
RECLAIM
REQUIEM
RHENIUM
RHODIUM
ROSTRUM
SANCTUM
SARCASM
SCROTUM
SIDEARM
SOPHISM
SORGHUM
STADIUM
STERNUM
STRATUM
SUNBEAM
SYMPTOM
SYNONYM
TANTRUM
TAPROOM
TERBIUM
THEOREM
THORIUM
THULIUM
TRANSOM
TRITIUM
TRIVIUM
TROPISM
UNBOSOM
UNIFORM
URANIUM
WOLFRAM
YARDARM
YTTRIUM
ZIONISM
ABANDON
ABDOMEN
ABSTAIN
ADJOURN
AFRICAN
AILERON
ALBUMEN
ALBUMIN
ANDIRON
ANTIGEN
ARRAIGN
ARTISAN
ASPIRIN
AUCTION
BALLOON
BARGAIN

BASSOON
BASTION
BATSMAN
BEDIZEN
BEDOUIN
BELGIAN
BENISON
BENZOIN
BETOKEN
BETWEEN
BIGHORN
BILLION
BITTERN
BITUMEN
BLACKEN
BLOWGUN
BOATMAN
BONDMAN
BOUNDEN
BOURBON
BRACKEN
BRAHMAN
BRAHMIN
BROADEN
BUFFOON
BULLION
BUMPKIN
BURGEON
CAISSON
CALDRON
CANTEEN
CAPSTAN
CAPTAIN
CAPTION
CARAVAN
CARRION
CARRYON
CARTOON
CAUTION
CAVEMAN
CERTAIN
CERUMEN
CESSION
CHADIAN
CHAGRIN
CHANSON
CHAPMAN
CHASTEN
CHEAPEN
CHEVRON
CHICKEN
CHIFFON
CHIGNON
CISTERN
CITIZEN
CLARION
COARSEN

COLLEEN
CONCERN
CONDEMN
CONDIGN
CONJOIN
CONSIGN
CONTAIN
CONTEMN
CRIMSON
CROUTON
CURTAIN
CUSHION
DAUPHIN
DEADPAN
DECAGON
DENIZEN
DETRAIN
DEXTRIN
DICTION
DISCERN
DISDAIN
DISJOIN
DOLPHIN
DOORMAN
DRAGOON
DRUMLIN
DRUNKEN
DUCKPIN
DUDGEON
DUNGEON
DUSTPAN
EARTHEN
EASTERN
ECHELON
EDITION
EIDOLON
ELISION
EMOTION
ENCHAIN
ENLIVEN
ENTRAIN
EROSION
EVASION
EXPLAIN
FACTION
FASHION
FESTOON
FICTION
FIFTEEN
FIREMAN
FISSION
FLATTEN
FOGHORN
FOOTMAN
FOREIGN
FOREMAN
FORLORN

FORTRAN
FREEMAN
FRESHEN
FROGMAN
FUSTIAN
GALLEON
GAMBIAN
GELATIN
GENTIAN
GHERKIN
GLADDEN
GLEEMAN
GLISTEN
GLUTTON
GOODMAN
GRECIAN
GREMLIN
GRUNION
GUERDON
HACKMAN
HAIRPIN
HALCYON
HANDGUN
HANGMAN
HARDPAN
HARPOON
HEADMAN
HEADPIN
HEARKEN
HEARTEN
HEATHEN
HELLION
HEPARIN
HEXAGON
HOEDOWN
HORIZON
INGRAIN
INGROWN
INHUMAN
INKHORN
INSULIN
IRANIAN
ITALIAN
JAVELIN
KEELSON
KERATIN
KIDSKIN
KILOTON
KINGPIN
KINSMAN
KITCHEN
KREMLIN
KRYPTON
LAMPOON
LANOLIN
LANTERN
LAOTIAN
LATVIAN
LECTERN
LEGHORN
LESBIAN
LETDOWN
LEXICON
LIAISON
LIGHTEN
LINEMAN
LOWDOWN
MAHICAN
MAILMAN
MALISON
MANIKIN
MANSION
MARTIAN
MAUDLIN
MEATMAN
MEGATON
MELANIN
MENTION
MEXICAN
MIDTOWN
MILKMAN
MILLION
MISSION
MOHEGAN
MOHICAN
MOISTEN
MONSOON
MUEZZIN
MULLEIN
MULLION
MURRAIN
NANKEEN
NEUTRON
NEWBORN
NEWSMAN
NUCLEON
OARSMAN
OCTAGON
OILSKIN
OPINION
ORATION
ORTOLAN
OTTOMAN
OUTWORN
OVATION
OVERRUN
PALADIN
PARAGON
PASSION
PASTERN
PATROON
PATTERN
PELICAN
PENGUIN
PENSION
PERSIAN
PERTAIN
PHAETON
PIGSKIN
PILLION
PLATOON
PLAYPEN
PLOWMAN
POCOSIN
POLYGON
PONTOON
POPCORN
PORTION
POSTERN
POSTMAN
PRETEEN
PROGMAN
PRONOUN
PROPMAN
PROTEAN
PROTEIN
PULLMAN
PUMPKIN
PURITAN
PURLOIN
QUICKEN
RACCOON
REDSKIN
REFRAIN
REGIMEN
REUNION
ROUGHEN
RUFFIAN
RUNDOWN
RUSSIAN
SADIRON
SAFFRON
SANDMAN
SECTION
SESSION
SHARPEN
SHORTEN
SHOTGUN
SHOWMAN
SIDEMAN
SILICON
SIRLOIN
SIXTEEN
SLACKEN
SMIDGEN
SOJOURN
SOUPCON
SOYBEAN
STATION
STEPSON
STIFFEN
STILTON
SUBJOIN
SUCTION
SUNBURN
SUNDOWN
SURGEON
SUSTAIN
SWEETEN
SWOLLEN
TENSION
TERRAIN
THEREIN
THEREON
THICKEN
TIBETAN
TIGHTEN
TORSION
TOUGHEN
TREASON
TRODDEN
TUITION
TYPHOON
UMPTEEN
UNCHAIN
UNCLEAN
UNCTION
UNICORN
UNKNOWN
UNLEARN
UTOPIAN
VATICAN
VENISON
VERSION
VERVAIN
VETERAN
VILLAIN
VILLEIN
VITAMIN
WALLOON
WAYWORN
WESTERN
WHEREIN
WHEREON
WIDGEON
WOODMAN
WORKMAN
YARDMAN
ZAMBIAN
ZILLION
ALLEGRO
ARAPAHO
AVOCADO
BRACERO
BRAVADO
BUFFALO
BUGABOO
CALYPSO
CARABAO
CEMBALO
CENTAVO
CENTIMO
CHICANO
EMBARGO
FARRAGO
GESTAPO
HIDALGO
IMPASTO
INFERNO
LUMBAGO
MAESTRO
MAFIOSO
MAGNETO
MEMENTO
MESTIZO
MOROCCO
MULATTO
NONHERO
OREGANO
PICCOLO
PIMENTO
PLACEBO
POMPANO
PORTICO
PROVISO
PROXIMO
SAGUARO
SENTIMO
SHAMPOO
SIROCCO
SOPRANO
TALLYHO
THERETO
TOBACCO
TORNADO
TORPEDO
TREMOLO
UNDERGO
VAQUERO
VERTIGO
VIBRATO
VOLCANO
WHERETO
AIRDROP
AIRSHIP
ANTHROP
BELLHOP
BREAKUP
CATCHUP
CHECKUP
CLEANUP
COWSLIP
DESKTOP
DEVELOP
DEWDROP
ENVELOP
FLATTOP
FORETOP
GUMDROP
HARDTOP
HARELIP
HILLTOP
KETCHUP
KINSHIP
KNEECAP
MAINTOP
MILKSOP
MISSTEP
MUGWUMP
NONSTOP
OUTCROP
OVERLAP
OVERTOP
PARSNIP
RATTRAP
REGROUP
ROOFTOP
ROUNDUP
SCALLOP
SHALLOP
SPEEDUP
STARTUP
STIRRUP
STOPGAP
SUNLAMP
TROLLOP
UNCLASP
UNGROUP
UNSTRAP
WARSHIP
WICKIUP
WIRETAP
WORSHIP
ADAPTER
ALCAZAR
ALMONER
AMATEUR
AMMETER
ANGULAR
ANNULAR
ANOTHER
AQUIFER
ARBITER
ARMORER
ASUNDER
ATELIER
AUDITOR
BARRIER
BELABOR
BESMEAR
BIPOLAR
BIRCHER
BLADDER
BLATHER
BLEEDER
BLINDER
BLINKER
BLISTER
BLOATER
BLOOPER
BLOTTER
BLUBBER
BLUCHER
BLUNDER
BLUSTER
BOLIVAR
BOLSTER
BOUDOIR
BOULDER
BOUNCER
BOWLDER
BRAZIER
BREAKER
BROIDER
BROILER
BROODER
BROTHER
BROWSER
BRUISER
BUCKLER
BUGBEAR
BURGHER
BUTCHER
CADAVER
CALIBER
CALIPER
CAMPHOR
CARRIER
CASHIER
CATCHER
CENTAUR
CHAFFER
CHAMBER
CHAMFER
CHAPTER
CHARGER
CHARMER
CHARTER
CHATTER
CHECKER
CHEDDAR
CHIGGER
CHIPPER
CHOPPER
CHOWDER
CHUKKER
CLAMBER
CLANGOR
CLAPPER
CLATTER
CLAVIER
CLEAVER
CLINKER
CLIPPER
CLOBBER
CLUSTER
CLUTTER
COBBLER
COLLIER
COMPEER
CONIFER
CONQUER
CONTOUR
CORONER
CORSAIR
COUNTER
COURIER
COURSER
CRACKER
CREATOR
CRITTER
CROPPER
CROSIER
CROWBAR
CRUISER
CRULLER
CURATOR
DECODER
DELIVER
DESPAIR
DIVIDER
DIVISOR
DOSSIER
DOWAGER
DRESSER
DRIFTER
DROPPER
DRUMMER
ELECTOR
EMBOWER
EMITTER
EMPEROR
EMPOWER
ENAMOUR
EQUATOR
FANCIER
FARRIER
FARTHER
FEATHER
FIGHTER
FLANKER
FLAPPER
FLATCAR
FLATTER
FLAVOUR
FLICKER
FLIPPER
FLIVVER
FLUSTER
FLUTTER
FORBEAR
FOREVER
FOUNDER
FREEZER
FRITTER
FURRIER
FURTHER
GLACIER
GLAMOUR
GLAZIER
GLIMMER
GLISTER
GLITTER
GOBBLER
GRAMMAR
GRAZIER
GRINDER
GROUPER
GUILDER
HAMSTER
HANDCAR
HARBOUR
HARRIER
HAUTEUR
HEATHER
HIPSTER
HOLSTER
HOOSIER
HOSTLER
HOWEVER
HUMIDOR
INCISOR
INHALER
INSIDER
INSULAR
INSURER
INTEGER
JANITOR
JEWELER
JOCULAR
JODHPUR
JUGULAR
JUNIPER
JUPITER
KNOCKER
LACQUER
LAMINAR
LANGUOR
LAUNDER
LEAGUER
LEATHER
LIGHTER
LIQUEUR

LOBSTER
LOCATOR
LUCIFER
MANAGER
MARINER
MASSEUR
MATADOR
MAUNDER
MEANDER
MIDYEAR
MINSTER
MOBSTER
MODULAR
MONITOR
MONOMER
MONSTER
MUFFLER
NEITHER
NONUSER
NORTHER
NUCLEAR
OCTOBER
OFFICER
OLDSTER
ORBITER
OUTDOOR
OUTWEAR
PALAVER
PANNIER
PANTHER
PARLOUR
PARTNER
PHILTER
PIASTER
PILSNER
PIONEER
PITCHER
PLANTAR
PLANTER
PLASTER
PLATTER
PLOTTER
PLUMBER
PLUNDER
PLUNGER
POINTER
POLYMER
POPOVER
POPULAR
POSTWAR
PRAETOR
PREMIER
PRICKER
PROCTOR
PROFFER
PROSPER
PSALTER
PUNSTER
QUARTER
RAMBLER
RATTLER
REACTOR
RECOVER
REGULAR
RELATOR
ROASTER
ROISTER
ROOSTER
SAMOVAR
SAMPLER
SANDBAR
SAUNTER
SCAMPER
SCANNER
SCATTER
SCEPTER
SCHOLAR
SCOOTER
SCUPPER
SECULAR
SELTZER
SEMINAR
SENATOR
SHARPER
SHATTER
SHELTER
SHIMMER
SHOCKER
SHUDDER
SHUTTER
SHYSTER
SIDECAR
SIMILAR
SKIPPER
SKITTER
SKIWEAR
SLACKER
SLANDER
SLATHER
SLEEPER
SLENDER
SLICKER
SLIPPER
SLITHER
SLOBBER
SLUMBER
SMELTER
SMOLDER
SMOTHER
SNEAKER
SNICKER
SOLDIER
SOUNDER
SPATTER
SPEAKER
SPECTER
SPELLER
SPOILER
SPONSOR
SPOTTER
SPUTTER
SQUALOR
STAFFER
STAGGER
STAMMER
STELLAR
STICKER
STOPPER
STUTTER
SWAGGER
SWEATER
SWELTER
TABULAR
TANAGER
TAPSTER
TERRIER
THEATER
THINNER
THITHER
THUNDER
TIPSTER
TITULAR
TOASTER
TRACTOR
TRAILER
TRAITOR
TRIGGER
TROOPER
TUBULAR
TUMBLER
TUTELAR
TWEETER
TWISTER
TWITTER
UNCOVER
UPRIVER
VERNIER
VINEGAR
VINTNER
VISITOR
VOUCHER
WAGONER
WARBLER
WARRIOR
WEATHER
WHEELER
WHETHER
WHICKER
WHIMPER
WHISKER
WHISPER
WHITHER
WHOEVER
WHOPPER
WIDOWER
WIGGLER
WRAPPER
WRECKER
WRINGER
YOUNKER
ABSCESS
ADDRESS
AGELESS
AIMLESS
ALUMNUS
AMOROUS
ANXIOUS
APROPOS
AQUEOUS
ARBUTUS
ARDUOUS
ARREARS
ARTLESS
BELLOWS
BENTHOS
BESIDES
BETIMES
BILIOUS
BITTERS
BURGESS
CALENDS
CALLOUS
CANVASS
CARCASS
CARDBUS
CARIOUS
CELSIUS
CHABLIS
CHALLIS
CHAMOIS
CHASSIS
CIVVIES
CLOTHES
COMPASS
CONFESS
COPIOUS
CUMULUS
CURIOUS
CUTLASS
CYPRESS
DEGAUSS
DEPRESS
DEVIOUS
DIGRESS
DISCUSS
DISMISS
DUBIOUS
DUCHESS
DUTEOUS
EMPRESS
ENDLESS
ENDWAYS
ENGROSS
ENVIOUS
EXPRESS
FATUOUS
FERROUS
FORCEPS
FURIOUS
GALLOWS
GENESIS
GIBBOUS
GIBLETS
GLOTTIS
GODDESS
GODLESS
GOGGLES
HALVERS
HAPLESS
HARNESS
HEINOUS
HEIRESS
HEROICS
HIDEOUS
HOSTESS
HUMERUS
HUNKERS
HYDROUS
IGNEOUS
ILEITIS
ILLNESS
IMPETUS
IMPIOUS
IMPRESS
INCUBUS
INDOORS
INGRESS
INNARDS
INNINGS
INTRANS
ISTHMUS
JACKASS
JEALOUS
JITTERS
LARGESS
LAWLESS
MAKINGS
MALLEUS
MARQUIS
MATTINS
MEASLES
MEIOSIS
MIMESIS
MINIBUS
MITOSIS
NEMESIS
NERVOUS
NOCUOUS
NONPLUS
NOXIOUS
NUCLEUS
OBVIOUS
OCTOPUS
OMINOUS
OMNIBUS
ONEROUS
OPPRESS
OSMOSIS
PAJAMAS
PAPYRUS
PARESIS
PARLOUS
PENATES
PERHAPS
PHALLUS
PHONICS
PHYSICS
PITEOUS
POLARIS
POMPOUS
POSSESS
PROCESS
PROFESS
PROWESS
PYJAMAS
PYRITES
QUIETUS
RAUCOUS
REDRESS
REGRESS
REMAINS
REPRESS
REREDOS
RHOMBUS
RICKETS
RUINOUS
SERIOUS
SINUOUS
SOLARIS
SPECIES
SUCCESS
SUMMONS
SURPASS
SURPLUS
TACTICS
TEDIOUS
TENUOUS
TETANUS
THERMOS
TIDINGS
TOPLESS
TRELLIS
TRICEPS
UNCROSS
UNDRESS
URANOUS
USELESS
VACUOUS
VARIOUS
VESPERS
VICIOUS
VILLOUS
VISCOUS
VITTLES
WARLESS
WHEREAS
WILLIES
WINDOWS
WITHERS
WITLESS
WITNESS
ZEALOUS
ABREAST
ACCOUNT
ACROBAT
ADAMANT
ADJUNCT
AFFLICT
AFFRONT
AGAINST
AILMENT
AIRLIFT
AIRPORT
AIRPOST
ALIMENT
ALRIGHT
AMBIENT
ANAPEST
ANCIENT
APPOINT
APRICOT
AQUAVIT
ARMREST
ARPANET
ASPHALT
ASSAULT
ATHEIST
ATHIRST
ATHWART
ATTAINT
ATTEMPT
ATTRACT
AUGMENT
BACKLIT
BALLAST
BANQUET
BAPTIST
BARONET
BAYONET
BEDFAST
BEDPOST
BENEFIT
BEQUEST
BETWIXT
BIBELOT
BISCUIT
BLANKET
BLATANT
BLOWOUT
BOMBAST
BOOKLET
BORSCHT
BOUQUET
BOYCOTT
BRACKET
BRISKET
BROUGHT
BURNOUT
CABARET
CABINET
CALUMET
CARPORT
CATBOAT
CHAPLET
CHARIOT
CHEMIST
CHEROOT
CHEVIOT
CIRCLET
CIRCUIT
CLEMENT
COCKPIT
COCONUT
COEXIST
COHABIT
COLLECT
COMFORT
COMMENT
COMPACT
COMPORT
COMPOST
CONCEIT
CONCEPT
CONCERT
CONCOCT
CONDUCT
CONDUIT
CONGEST
CONNECT
CONSENT
CONSIST
CONSORT
CONSULT
CONTACT
CONTENT
CONTEST
CONTEXT
CONTORT
CONVENT
CONVERT
CONVICT
COOKOUT
COOLANT
COPILOT
COPYCAT
CORONET
CORRECT
CORRUPT
COUPLET
CRICKET
CROCHET
CROQUET
CRUMPET
CULPRIT
CULVERT
CURRANT
CURRENT
CYCLIST
DASHPOT
DEFAULT
DEFIANT
DEFICIT
DEFLECT
DEFROST
DEFUNCT
DELIGHT
DELIMIT
DEMERIT
DENTIST
DEPOSIT
DESCANT
DESCENT
DESSERT
DETRACT
DEVIANT
DIALECT
DIARIST
DILUENT
DISGUST
DISPORT
DISRUPT
DISSECT
DISSENT
DISTANT
DISTORT
DOGCART
DOGTROT
DOORMAT
DORMANT
DOUBLET
DRAGNET
DRAUGHT
DRIBLET

DROPLET
DROUGHT
EARNEST
EARSHOT
ELEMENT
EMINENT
ENCHANT
ENCRUST
ENDMOST
ENGRAFT
ENTRANT
ENTREAT
ENTRUST
EPAULET
EPITHET
EVIDENT
EXCERPT
EXHAUST
EXHIBIT
EXPLOIT
EXTINCT
EXTRACT
FALLOUT
FEEDLOT
FERMENT
FERVENT
FIGMENT
FILBERT
FLORIST
FLUTIST
FOLDOUT
FONDANT
FORFEIT
FRAUGHT
FREIGHT
FRESHET
GABFEST
GALLANT
GANTLET
GARMENT
GOURMET
GROMMET
GUNBOAT
GUNSHOT
HABITAT
HAIRCUT
HALIBUT
HANDOUT
HANDSET
HANGOUT
HARVEST
HATCHET
HAYLOFT
HEADSET
HELLCAT
HIDEOUT
HOTFOOT
HOTSHOT
HOWBEIT
HUTMENT
HYDRANT
ICEBOAT
ILLICIT
IMPRINT
INCRUST
INEXACT
INFARCT
INFLECT
INFLICT
INGRAFT
INHABIT
INHERIT
INHIBIT
INQUEST
INSIGHT
INSPECT
INSTANT
INTROIT
INTRUST
JACKPOT
JETPORT
KUMQUAT
LAMBENT
LATCHET
LAWSUIT
LEAFLET
LENIENT
LOCKNUT
LOCKOUT
LOOKOUT
MANHUNT
MANUMIT
MARGENT
MARPLOT
MIDMOST
MIGRANT
MINARET
MORDANT
MUSKRAT
NASCENT
NEGLECT
OCULIST
ODDMENT
OFFBEAT
OPULENT
OUTCAST
OUTLAST
OUTPOST
OVERACT
OVIDUCT
OXIDANT
PAGEANT
PARAPET
PARFAIT
PARQUET
PATIENT
PATRIOT
PAYMENT
PEASANT
PENDANT
PENDENT
PENNANT
PERCENT
PERCEPT
PERFECT
PERSIST
PERVERT
PIANIST
PIGMENT
PIQUANT
PLACKET
PLAUDIT
PLAYLET
PLUMMET
POLECAT
PORTENT
POTSHOT
PRECEPT
PREDICT
PREEMPT
PREFECT
PREHEAT
PRESENT
PRETEXT
PREVENT
PRODUCT
PROJECT
PROPHET
PROTECT
PROTEST
PROVOST
PRUDENT
PULLOUT
PUNGENT
PURPORT
PURSUIT
QUARTET
QUINTET
RADIANT
RAIMENT
RAMPANT
RAMPART
RAPPORT
RAREBIT
RATCHET
READOUT
REAGENT
RECEIPT
RECOUNT
RECRUIT
REDCOAT
REDOUBT
REFLECT
REFRACT
REGNANT
REMNANT
REMOUNT
REPRINT
REQUEST
RESEDIT
RESPECT
RETRACT
RETREAT
RINGLET
RIVULET
ROOTLET
ROWBOAT
SALIENT
SANDLOT
SAPIENT
SAWDUST
SCARLET
SEALANT
SEAPORT
SEGMENT
SEQUENT
SERPENT
SERVANT
SEXTANT
SHERBET
SHUTOUT
SIDELIT
SKILLET
SLEIGHT
SOLICIT
SOLVENT
SOPHIST
SPIRANT
STUDENT
STUFFIT
STYLIST
SUBJECT
SUBSIST
SUBVERT
SUGGEST
SUNSPOT
SUPPORT
SURFEIT
SURTOUT
SUSPECT
TANGENT
TAPROOT
TEMPEST
THEREAT
THICKET
THOUGHT
TONIGHT
TOPCOAT
TOPKNOT
TOPMAST
TOPMOST
TORMENT
TORRENT
TOURIST
TOWBOAT
TRANSIT
TRIDENT
TRINKET
TRIPLET
TRISECT
TRUMPET
TUGBOAT
TURNOUT
UNGUENT
UNKEMPT
UNQUIET
UNTWIST
UPDRAFT
UPRIGHT
UPSHIFT
UPSTART
UPSWEPT
UPTIGHT
VAGRANT
VALIANT
VARIANT
VARMINT
VERDANT
VERDICT
VIADUCT
VIBRANT
VIOLENT
WALKOUT
WARRANT
WASHOUT
WAVELET
WHATNOT
WHEREAT
WHIPPET
WILDCAT
WITHOUT
WOODCUT
WOODLOT
WORKOUT
WROUGHT
CARIBOU
CHAPEAU
CHATEAU
JUJITSU
MANTEAU
PARVENU
PLATEAU
PURLIEU
TABLEAU
TONNEAU
AIRFLOW
BESHREW
BUCKSAW
CHOCTAW
DEWCLAW
DISAVOW
EYEBROW
FRETSAW
HACKSAW
HANDSAW
JACKDAW
LOCKJAW
LONGBOW
LOWBROW
MACDRAW
OUTDRAW
OUTFLOW
OUTGROW
PREVIEW
PURVIEW
RAINBOW
SHALLOW
SOMEHOW
SPARROW
SWALLOW
UNSCREW
WHIPSAW
WHITLOW
WINDROW
ANTHRAX
BANDBOX
BEESWAX
COMPLEX
CONFLUX
EQUINOX
FIREBOX
GEARBOX
JUKEBOX
MAILBOX
NARTHEX
PARADOX
PERPLEX
PHALANX
PHARYNX
PHOENIX
PILLBOX
SALTBOX
TOOLBOX
TRIPLEX
WORKBOX
ABILITY
ACADEMY
ACIDIFY
ACTUARY
ALCHEMY
ALIMONY
ALLERGY
ALREADY
AMATORY
AMENITY
AMNESTY
AMPLIFY
ANALOGY
ANARCHY
ANATOMY
ANCHOVY
ANNUITY
ANOMALY
ANXIETY
ANYBODY
APOLOGY
ARCHERY
ARCHWAY
AREAWAY
ASHTRAY
ATROPHY
AUTOPSY
BALCONY
BALONEY
BATTERY
BEASTLY
BEATIFY
BEGGARY
BELLBOY
BELTWAY
BIKEWAY
BIOLOGY
BLARNEY
BRAVERY
BREVITY
CALCIFY
CALUMNY
CANNERY
CARAWAY
CAVALRY
CENTURY
CERTIFY
CHANTEY
CHANTRY
CHARITY
CHICORY
CHIMNEY
CHINTZY
CHUTNEY
CIVILLY
CLARIFY
CLARITY
CLEANLY
COCKNEY
COMPANY
COOKERY
COPYBOY
COUNTRY
COURTLY
CRUCIFY
CRYBABY
CURSORY
CUSTODY
CUTLERY
DANDIFY
DEANERY
DEATHLY
DECENCY
DEERFLY
DENSITY
DESTINY
DESTROY
DEVILRY
DIGNIFY
DIGNITY
DISOBEY
DISPLAY
DOORWAY
DOUGHTY
DRAPERY
DUBIETY
DYNASTY
EARTHLY
ECOLOGY
ECONOMY
ECSTASY
ELDERLY
EMBASSY
EMPATHY
ENTROPY
EQUERRY
ESTUARY
EUPHONY
FACTORY
FACULTY
FAIRWAY
FALLACY
FALSIFY
FANTASY
FARAWAY
FATUITY
FERNERY
FINICKY
FIREFLY
FIRSTLY
FISHERY
FLESHLY
FLIGHTY
FLOWERY
FOLKWAY
FOOLERY
FORTIFY
FOUNDRY
FRAILTY
FREEWAY
GAINSAY
GALLERY
GANGWAY
GATEWAY
GEODESY
GEOLOGY
GETAWAY
GHASTLY
GLORIFY
GRANARY
GRATIFY
GRAVITY
GRIZZLY
GUNNERY
HACKNEY
HALFWAY
HALLWAY
HAPPILY
HARMONY
HAUGHTY
HEADWAY
HEALTHY
HEARSAY
HICKORY
HIGHBOY
HIGHWAY
HISTORY
HOLIDAY
HORRIFY
HOSIERY
HYMNODY
IDEALLY
IMAGERY
IMPIETY
INFANCY
INQUIRY
JANUARY
JEWELRY
JOLLITY
JOURNEY
JUSTIFY
KILLJOY
LAMPREY
LARCENY
LAUNDRY
LAYAWAY
LECHERY
LEPROSY
LIBERTY
LIBRARY
LIGNIFY
LIQUEFY
LITURGY
LOATHLY
LOTTERY
LULLABY
MAGNIFY
MAJESTY

MALMSEY
MAMMARY
MASONRY
MASTERY
MERCURY
MIMICRY
MISPLAY
MOLLIFY
MORTIFY
MYSTERY
MYSTIFY
NAIVETY
NAUGHTY
NEOLOGY
NEWSBOY
NIGHTLY
NITRIFY
NOONDAY
NOSEGAY
NOVELTY
NULLIFY
NURSERY
OBLOQUY
OBSEQUY
ODYSSEY
OPACITY
ORATORY
ORDERLY
ORGANDY
OROGENY
OSSUARY
OUTPLAY
OUTSTAY
OVERFLY
OVERJOY
OVERLAY
PAGEBOY
PAISLEY
PALFREY
PANOPLY
PARKWAY
PARSLEY
PARTWAY
PASSKEY
PATHWAY
PAUCITY
PECCARY
PENALTY
PEPPERY
PERFIDY
PERJURY
PETRIFY
PILLORY
PLAYBOY
PLENARY
PLOWBOY
PORTRAY
POSTBOY
POTTERY
POULTRY
POVERTY
PRIMACY
PRIMARY
PRIVACY
PROBITY
PRODIGY
PROGENY
PROSODY
PUBERTY
PUTREFY
QUALIFY
QUALITY
RACEWAY
RAILWAY
RAUNCHY
REALITY
RECENCY
RECTIFY
RECTORY
REENTRY
REGENCY
RICKETY
RIGHTLY
RIVALRY
ROADWAY
ROBBERY
ROOKERY
ROYALTY
RUNAWAY
SAINTLY
SATIETY
SATISFY
SCARIFY
SCENERY
SCRAPPY
SCRAWNY
SCRUFFY
SECRECY
SECTARY
SENSORY
SEVENTY
SHAPELY
SHORTLY
SIGHTLY
SIGNIFY
SLAVERY
SOCIETY
SOMEDAY
SORCERY
SPECIFY
SPINDLY
STANDBY
STATELY
STRINGY
STUPEFY
SUBSIDY
SUMMARY
SURGERY
SWARTHY
TANNERY
TENANCY
TERNARY
TERRIFY
TESTIFY
THERAPY
THEREBY
THREADY
THROATY
THRUWAY
TIMOTHY
TOGGERY
TOURNEY
TRACERY
TRAGEDY
TRILOGY
TRINITY
TROLLEY
TUESDAY
TURNERY
TURNKEY
TYRANNY
UNCANNY
UNGODLY
UNHANDY
UNHAPPY
UNITARY
UNLUCKY
UNMANLY
URINARY
UROLOGY
UTILITY
VACANCY
VACUITY
VARIETY
VARSITY
VERSIFY
VICEROY
VICTORY
VITRIFY
WAGGERY
WALKWAY
WALLABY
WEALTHY
WEEKDAY
WEIGHTY
WHEREBY
WHISKEY
WILLOWY
WOMANLY
WORKDAY
WORLDLY
WRONGLY
ZOOLOGY
ZYMURGY
KIBBUTZ
PIZZAZZ

# 8 LETTER WORDS

1ST LETTER

AARDVARK
ABATTOIR
ABDICATE
ABEYANCE
ABLATION
ABLATIVE
ABLUTION
ABNEGATE
ABNORMAL
ABORNING
ABORTION
ABRASIVE
ABROGATE
ABSCISSA
ABSENTEE
ABSINTHE
ABSOLUTE
ABSTRACT
ABSTRUSE
ABUNDANT
ABUTMENT
ABUTTALS
ACADEMIC
ACANTHUS
ACCIDENT
ACCOLADE
ACCOUTRE
ACCREDIT
ACCURATE
ACCURSED
ACCUSTOM
ACERBATE
ACERBITY
ACIDHEAD
ACIDOSIS
ACOUSTIC
ACQUAINT
ACRIMONY
ACROSTIC
ACTINISM
ACTINIUM
ACTIVATE
ACTIVISM
ACTIVITY
ADDENDUM
ADDITION
ADDITIVE
ADEQUATE
ADHESION
ADHESIVE
ADJACENT
ADJUTANT
ADJUVANT
ADMONISH
ADOPTIVE
ADORABLE
ADULTERY
ADVISORY
ADVOCATE
AEROLOGY
AERONAUT
AESTHETE
AFFECTED
AFFERENT
AFFIANCE
AFFINITY
AFFLATUS
AFFRIGHT
AFLUTTER
AFTERTAX
AGERATUM
AGGRIEVE
AGITPROP
AGLITTER
AGNOSTIC
AGRARIAN
AGRONOMY
AIGRETTE
AIRBORNE
AIRBRUSH
AIRCRAFT
AIRDROME
AIRFIELD
AIRFRAME
AIRLINER
AIRPLANE
AIRSPACE
AIRSPEED
AIRSTRIP
AIRTIGHT
ALACRITY
ALARMIST
ALBACORE
ALBANIAN
ALDERMAN
ALEATORY
ALEHOUSE
ALFRESCO
ALGERIAN
ALIASING
ALIENATE
ALIENIST
ALIZARIN
ALKALOID
ALLEGORY
ALLELUIA
ALLERGEN
ALLEYWAY
ALLIANCE
ALLOCATE
ALLSPICE
ALLUVIUM
ALMIGHTY
ALOPECIA
ALPHABET
ALTHOUGH
ALTITUDE
ALTRUISM
ALUMINUM
AMARANTH
AMBIENCE
AMBITION
AMBROSIA
AMBULANT
AMENABLE
AMERICAN
AMETHYST
AMICABLE
AMMONIUM
AMOEBOID
AMORTIZE
AMPERAGE
AMPUTATE
ANACONDA
ANAEROBE
ANALOGUE
ANALYSIS
ANATHEMA
ANCESTOR
ANCESTRY
ANDROGEN
ANECDOTE
ANECHOIC
ANGELICA
ANGLICAN
ANGSTROM
ANISETTE
ANNOTATE
ANNOUNCE
ANTEATER
ANTEDATE
ANTELOPE
ANTERIOR
ANTEROOM
ANTHROPO
ANTIBODY
ANTIDOTE
ANTIMONY
ANTINOMY
ANTIPODE
ANTIPOPE
ANYPLACE
ANYTHING
ANYWHERE
APERITIF
APERTURE
APHANITE
APHELION
APHORISM
APOLOGIA
APOPLEXY
APOSTASY
APOTHEGM
APPANAGE
APPARENT
APPELLEE
APPENDIX
APPETITE
APPLAUSE
APPLIQUE
APPOSITE
APPRAISE
APPROACH
APPROVAL
APTITUDE
AQUACADE
AQUANAUT
AQUARIUM
AQUEDUCT
AQUILINE
ARACHNID
ARBALEST
ARBOREAL
ARCHDUKE
ARGUABLE
ARGUMENT
ARMAMENT
ARMATURE
ARMCHAIR
ARMORIAL
ARMYWORM
ARPEGGIO
ARROGANT
ARROGATE
ARTERIAL
ARTIFACT
ARTIFICE
ARTISTIC
ARTISTRY
ASBESTOS
ASPERITY
ASPHODEL
ASPHYXIA
ASPIRANT
ASPIRATE
ASSASSIN
ASSEMBLE
ASSEMBLY
ASSORTED
ASTATINE
ASTERISK
ASTEROID
ASTONISH
ATHLETIC
ATOMIZER
ATROCITY
ATROPINE
ATTITUDE
ATTORNEY
ATYPICAL
AUDIENCE
AUDITION
AUDITORY
AUSTRIAN
AUTOBAHN
AUTOGIRO
AUTOJOIN
AUTOMATE
AVERMENT
AVERSION
AVIATION
AVIATRIX
AVIONICS
AXLETREE
BABUSHKA
BACCARAT
BACHELOR
BACILLUS
BACKACHE
BACKBITE
BACKBONE
BACKDROP
BACKFIRE
BACKHAND
BACKLASH
BACKPACK
BACKREST
BACKSIDE
BACKSLAP
BACKSPIN
BACKSTOP
BACKWARD
BACKWASH
BADINAGE
BAEDEKER
BAGUETTE
BAILABLE
BAILSMAN
BAKESHOP
BALLROOM
BALLYHOO
BALUSTER
BANDANNA
BANISTER
BANKBOOK
BANKROLL
BANKRUPT
BANTLING
BARBARIC
BARBECUE
BARBERRY
BARBICAN
BARBITAL
BAREBACK
BAREFOOT
BARITONE
BARNACLE
BARNYARD
BARONAGE
BARONESS
BAROUCHE
BARRACKS
BARRATRY
BARRETTE
BASEBALL
BASEBORN
BASELESS
BASELINE
BASEMENT
BASILICA
BASILISK
BASSINET
BASSWOOD
BATHROBE
BATHROOM
BAYBERRY
BEANBALL
BEARSKIN
BEATIFIC
BEAUTIFY
BECHUANA
BECOMING
BEDAZZLE
BEDSTEAD
BEECHNUT
BEFRIEND
BEFUDDLE
BEGGARLY
BEGRUDGE
BEHAVIOR
BEHEMOTH
BEHOLDEN
BELITTLE
BENEDICT
BENEFICE
BENTWOOD
BENZOATE
BEQUEATH
BERCEUSE
BEREAVED
BERIBERI
BERMUDAS
BESMIRCH
BESTIARY
BESTRIDE
BETATRON
BEVERAGE
BEWILDER
BIANNUAL
BIATHLON
BIBULOUS
BICONVEX
BICUSPID
BIDDABLE
BIENNIAL
BIENNIUM
BIFOCALS
BILLFOLD
BILLHEAD
BINAURAL
BINNACLE
BIOCIDAL
BIRACIAL
BIRDBATH
BIRDLIME
BIRDSEED
BIRTHDAY
BISEXUAL
BITSTOCK
BIWEEKLY
BIYEARLY
BLACKING
BLACKOUT
BLACKTOP
BLESSING
BLISSFUL
BLIZZARD
BLOCKADE
BLOOMERS
BLOWPIPE
BLUDGEON
BLUEBELL
BLUEBIRD
BLUEFISH
BLUENOSE
BOASTFUL
BOBOLINK
BOBWHITE
BODILESS
BODYWORK
BOGEYMAN
BOHEMIAN
BOLDFACE
BOLLWORM
BONDSMAN
BONHOMIE
BOOKCASE
BOOKMARK
BOOKWORM
BOOTLESS
BORDELLO
BOTULISM
BOUFFANT
BOUILLON
BOUNDARY
BOUTIQUE
BOWSPRIT
BRACELET
BRACKISH
BRAGGART
BRAKEMAN
BRANDISH
BREAKAGE
BREAKOUT
BREEDING
BRETHREN

BREVIARY
BRICKBAT
BRIGHTEN
BRINDLED
BRISLING
BRITCHES
BROCCOLI
BROCHURE
BROMIDIC
BRONCHUS
BROOKLET
BROUGHAM
BROUHAHA
BROWBEAT
BROWNOUT
BUCKSHOT
BUCKSKIN
BUDDHISM
BUILDING
BULKHEAD
BULLDOZE
BULLETIN
BULLFROG
BULLHEAD
BUNDLING
BUNGALOW
BUNGHOLE
BUOYANCY
BURGLARY
BURGUNDY
BURNOOSE
BURSITIS
BUSINESS
BUSYBODY
BUSYWORK
BUTTRESS
CABOCHON
CABSTAND
CADUCEUS
CAFFEINE
CAGELING
CAKEWALK
CALABASH
CALADIUM
CALAMINE
CALAMITY
CALCULUS
CALENDAR
CALENDER
CALFSKIN
CALLBACK
CALLIOPE
CAMELLIA
CAMISOLE
CAMOMILE
CAMPAIGN
CAMPOREE
CAMSHAFT
CANADIAN
CANAILLE
CANALIZE
CANISTER
CANNABIS
CANNIBAL
CANONIZE
CANTICLE
CAPACITY
CAPESKIN
CAPRIOLE
CAPSICUM
CAPSULAR
CAPTIOUS
CAPUCHIN
CARACOLE
CARAPACE
CARDAMOM
CARDIGAN
CARDINAL
CAREFREE
CARELESS
CAREWORN
CARILLON
CARNAUBA
CARNIVAL
CAROTENE
CAROUSAL
CAROUSEL
CARRIAGE
CARRYALL
CARYATID
CASEMENT
CASEWORK
CASHMERE
CASSETTE
CASTAWAY
CASTRATE
CASUALTY
CATACOMB
CATALYZE
CATAPULT
CATARACT
CATCHALL
CATCHING
CATEGORY
CATHETER
CATHOLIC
CAUDILLO
CAULDRON
CAUSERIE
CAUSEWAY
CAUTIOUS
CAVALIER
CELERITY
CELIBACY
CELIBATE
CELLULAR
CEMENTUM
CEMETERY
CENOBITE
CENOTAPH
CENTERED
CENTRIST
CEPHALIC
CERAMIST
CEREBRUM
CEREMENT
CEREMONY
CERULEAN
CERVICAL
CESAREAN
CESSPOOL
CHAIRMAN
CHAMBRAY
CHAMPION
CHANCERY
CHANDLER
CHANUKAH
CHAPBOOK
CHAPERON
CHAPLAIN
CHARADES
CHARCOAL
CHARISMA
CHARMING
CHASTISE
CHASTITY
CHASUBLE
CHECKERS
CHECKOFF
CHECKOUT
CHECKSUM
CHEERFUL
CHEMICAL
CHEMURGY
CHENILLE
CHEROKEE
CHESTNUT
CHEYENNE
CHIPMUNK
CHIPPEWA
CHITCHAT
CHIVALRY
CHLORIDE
CHLORINE
CHLORITE
CHOIRBOY
CHOLERIC
CHOWCHOW
CHRISTEN
CHRISTIE
CHROMIUM
CHUTZPAH
CICATRIX
CICERONE
CINCHONA
CINCTURE
CINNABAR
CINNAMON
CIRCUITY
CIRCULAR
CISLUNAR
CITATION
CIVILIAN
CIVILITY
CIVILIZE
CLAIMANT
CLAMBAKE
CLAPTRAP
CLARINET
CLASSIFY
CLAVICLE
CLAYMORE
CLEARING
CLEAVAGE
CLEMATIS
CLEMENCY
CLERICAL
CLINCHER
CLINICAL
CLIPPING
CLITORIS
CLOISTER
CLOSEOUT
CLOTHIER
CLOTHING
CLOUDLET
CLUBFOOT
COACHMAN
COAGULUM
COALESCE
COAUTHOR
COCKATOO
COCKCROW
COCKEREL
COCKSURE
COCKTAIL
COGITATE
COGNOMEN
COGWHEEL
COHERENT
COHESION
COIFFEUR
COIFFURE
COINCIDE
COLANDER
COLESLAW
COLISEUM
COLLAPSE
COLLIERY
COLLOQUY
COLONIAL
COLONIST
COLONIZE
COLOPHON
COLOSSAL
COLOSSUS
COMANCHE
COMBINGS
COMEBACK
COMEDIAN
COMEDOWN
COMMANDO
COMMENCE
COMMERCE
COMMONER
COMMUNAL
COMPILER
COMPLAIN
COMPLEAT
COMPLETE
COMPOUND
COMPRESS
COMPRISE
COMPUTER
CONCEIVE
CONCERTO
CONCLAVE
CONCLUDE
CONCRETE
CONDENSE
CONFETTI
CONFINES
CONFLICT
CONFOCAL
CONFOUND
CONFRERE
CONFRONT
CONGENER
CONGRESS
CONJUGAL
CONJUNCT
CONQUEST
CONSERVE
CONSIDER
CONSOMME
CONSPIRE
CONSTANT
CONSTRUE
CONTEMPT
CONTINUE
CONTRACT
CONTRAIL
CONTRARY
CONTRAST
CONTRITE
CONTRIVE
CONVERGE
CONVERSE
CONVINCE
CONVULSE
COOKBOOK
COONSKIN
COPPERAS
COPULATE
COPYBOOK
COPYDESK
COQUETTE
CORDLESS
CORDOVAN
CORDUROY
CORNCRIB
CORNMEAL
CORONACH
CORONARY
CORPORAL
CORPSMAN
CORRIDOR
CORUNDUM
CORVETTE
COSIGNER
COSMETIC
COUCHANT
COUNTESS
COUPLING
COURTESY
COURTIER
COVENANT
COVERAGE
COVERALL
COVERLET
COXSWAIN
CRACKPOT
CRAWFISH
CRAYFISH
CREAMERY
CREATION
CREATURE
CREDENCE
CREDENZA
CREDIBLE
CREDITOR
CREEPING
CREMAINS
CREOSOTE
CRESCENT
CRETONNE
CREVASSE
CRIBBAGE
CRIMINAL
CRITICAL
CRITIQUE
CROCKERY
CROPLAND
CROSSBAR
CROSSBOW
CROSSCUT
CROSSING
CROTCHET
CROUPIER
CROWFOOT
CRUCIBLE
CRUCIFIX
CRUZEIRO
CRYOLITE
CUCUMBER
CULINARY
CULPABLE
CUPBOARD
CUPIDITY
CURATIVE
CURLICUE
CURRENCY
CUSPIDOR
CUSTOMER
CYCLAMEN
CYLINDER
CYNOSURE
CYTOLOGY
CYTOSINE
DAFFODIL
DAIQUIRI
DAIRYING
DAIRYMAN
DAMNABLE
DANDRUFF
DANSEUSE
DARKLING
DARKROOM
DARKSOME
DATABASE
DATELESS
DATELINE
DAUGHTER
DAYBREAK
DAYDREAM
DAYLIGHT
DEADBEAT
DEADLINE
DEADLOCK
DEADWOOD
DEATHBED
DEBILITY
DEBONAIR
DECANTER
DECEDENT
DECEMBER
DECIGRAM
DECIMATE
DECIPHER
DECISION
DECISIVE
DECKHAND
DECORATE
DECOROUS
DECREASE
DECREPIT
DEDICATE
DEERSKIN
DEFECATE
DEFIANCE
DEFINITE
DEFLOWER
DEFOREST
DEIONIZE
DEJECTED
DEKAGRAM
DELAWARE
DELEGATE
DELICACY
DELICATE
DELIRIUM
DELIVERY
DELUSION
DEMARCHE
DEMEANOR
DEMENTED
DEMENTIA
DEMIBOLD
DEMIJOHN
DEMOCRAT
DEMOLISH
DEMONIAC
DEMURRER
DENATURE
DENOUNCE
DEPONENT
DEPUTIZE
DERELICT
DEROGATE
DERRIERE
DESCRIBE
DESELECT
DESIROUS
DESOLATE
DESPATCH
DESTRUCT
DETACHED
DETHRONE
DETONATE
DETOXIFY
DETRITUS
DEVILISH
DEVOTION
DEWBERRY
DEXTROSE
DIABETES

DIABOLIC
DIAGONAL
DIALOGUE
DIALYSIS
DIAMETER
DIANTHUS
DIAPASON
DIARRHEA
DIASTOLE
DIATOMIC
DIATRIBE
DICTATOR
DIDACTIC
DIELDRIN
DILATORY
DILIGENT
DIMINISH
DINGBATS
DINOSAUR
DIPLOMAT
DIPSTICK
DIRECTOR
DISABUSE
DISAGREE
DISALLOW
DISARRAY
DISASTER
DISBURSE
DISCIPLE
DISCLAIM
DISCLOSE
DISCOLOR
DISCOUNT
DISCOVER
DISCREET
DISCRETE
DISFAVOR
DISGORGE
DISGRACE
DISGUISE
DISHEVEL
DISHONOR
DISINTER
DISJOINT
DISKETTE
DISLODGE
DISLOYAL
DISMOUNT
DISORDER
DISPATCH
DISPENSE
DISPERSE
DISPIRIT
DISPLACE
DISPOSAL
DISPROVE
DISQUIET

DISSEVER
DISSOLVE
DISSUADE
DISTANCE
DISTASTE
DISTINCT
DISTRACT
DISTRAIT
DISTRESS
DISTRICT
DISTRUST
DISUNITE
DISUNITY
DIURETIC
DIVAGATE
DIVIDEND
DIVINITY
DIVISION
DIVISIVE
DIVORCEE
DOCKHAND
DOCKYARD
DOCTRINE
DOCUMENT
DOGFIGHT
DOGGEREL
DOGHOUSE
DOLDRUMS
DOLOMITE
DOMESTIC
DOMICILE
DOMINATE
DOMINEER
DOMINION
DONATION
DOOMSDAY
DOORJAMB
DOORKNOB
DOORSTEP
DOORYARD
DORMOUSE
DOUBLOON
DOUBTFUL
DOUGHBOY
DOUGHNUT
DOVETAIL
DOWNBEAT
DOWNCAST
DOWNFALL
DOWNHILL
DOWNLOAD
DOWNPOUR
DOWNTOWN
DOWNTURN
DOWNWARD
DOWNWIND
DOXOLOGY

DRAGOMAN
DRAINAGE
DRAUGHTS
DRAWBACK
DREADFUL
DRESSAGE
DRESSING
DRIVEWAY
DROPKICK
DRUGGIST
DRUMBEAT
DRUNKARD
DUCKBILL
DUCKLING
DULCIMER
DUMBBELL
DUMPLING
DUNGAREE
DUNGHILL
DUODENUM
DURATION
DUTIABLE
DWELLING
DYESTUFF
DYNAMITE
DYSLEXIA
EARNINGS
EARPHONE
ECLIPTIC
ECONOMIC
EDGEWAYS
EDUCABLE
EFFERENT
EFFUSION
EGGPLANT
EGGSHELL
EGYPTIAN
EIGHTEEN
EKISTICS
ELECTION
ELECTIVE
ELECTRIC
ELECTRON
ELEGANCE
ELEPHANT
ELEVATOR
ELIGIBLE
ELLIPSIS
ELONGATE
ELOQUENT
EMACIATE
EMBATTLE
EMBEZZLE
EMBITTER
EMBLAZON
EMBOLDEN
EMBOLISM

EMERITUS
EMIGRATE
EMINENCE
EMISSARY
EMOTICON
EMPHASIS
EMPHATIC
EMPLOYEE
EMPORIUM
EMPYREAN
EMULSIFY
EMULSION
ENCEINTE
ENCIPHER
ENCIRCLE
ENCOMIUM
ENCROACH
ENCUMBER
ENDANGER
ENDEAVOR
ENERGIZE
ENERVATE
ENFEEBLE
ENFILADE
ENGAGING
ENGENDER
ENGINEER
ENORMITY
ENORMOUS
ENSCONCE
ENSEMBLE
ENSHRINE
ENSHROUD
ENSILAGE
ENTANGLE
ENTHRALL
ENTHRONE
ENTIRETY
ENTRAILS
ENTRANCE
ENTRENCH
ENURESIS
ENVELOPE
ENVIABLE
ENVIRONS
ENVISAGE
EPIDEMIC
EPILEPSY
EPILOGUE
EPIPHANY
EQUALIZE
EQUATION
EQUIPAGE
ERECTILE
ERECTION
ERYTHEMA
ESCALATE

ESCALLOP
ESCAPADE
ESCAPISM
ESCAROLE
ESOTERIC
ESPALIER
ESPECIAL
ESPOUSAL
ESPRESSO
ESTIMATE
ESTONIAN
ESTRANGE
ESTROGEN
ETERNITY
ETHEREAL
ETHERNET
ETHOLOGY
ETIOLOGY
ETRUSCAN
EUGENICS
EUPHORIA
EURASIAN
EUROBOND
EUROPEAN
EUROPIUM
EVACUATE
EVALUATE
EVENSONG
EVENTIDE
EVENTUAL
EVERMORE
EVERYDAY
EVERYONE
EVIDENCE
EXACTING
EXCAVATE
EXCHANGE
EXCURSUS
EXECRATE
EXECUTOR
EXEGESIS
EXEMPLAR
EXERCISE
EXIGENCY
EXIGUOUS
EXORCISE
EXORDIUM
EXPEDITE
EXPLICIT
EXPLODED
EXPONENT
EXPOSURE
EXTERIOR
EXTERNAL
EXTRADOS
EYEGLASS
EYELINER

EYEPIECE
EYESIGHT
EYETOOTH
FABULOUS
FACEDOWN
FACILITY
FACTIOUS
FACTOTUM
FADELESS
FAGOTING
FALCHION
FALLIBLE
FALSETTO
FALTBOAT
FAMILIAL
FAMILIAR
FANCIFUL
FANDANGO
FANLIGHT
FANTASIA
FAREWELL
FARMHAND
FARMLAND
FARMYARD
FAROUCHE
FARTHEST
FARTHING
FASCICLE
FASCISTA
FASTBACK
FASTNESS
FATALISM
FATALITY
FAUBOURG
FAVORITE
FEARLESS
FEARSOME
FEASIBLE
FEBRUARY
FECKLESS
FEDERATE
FEEDBACK
FELDSPAR
FELICITY
FELLATIO
FEMININE
FEMINISM
FEROCITY
FERVENCY
FESTIVAL
FETCHING
FIBROSIS
FIDELITY
FIGURINE
FILAMENT
FILIGREE
FILIPINO

FILTRATE
FINALIST
FINALIZE
FINESPUN
FIREBALL
FIREBOAT
FIREBOMB
FIRECLAY
FIREDAMP
FIREPLUG
FIRESIDE
FIRETRAP
FIREWOOD
FIREWORK
FIRMWARE
FISHBOWL
FISHHOOK
FISHWIFE
FIXATION
FIXATIVE
FLAGPOLE
FLAGRANT
FLAGSHIP
FLAMBEAU
FLAMENCO
FLAMEOUT
FLAMINGO
FLAPJACK
FLASHGUN
FLASHING
FLATBOAT
FLATFISH
FLATFOOT
FLATHEAD
FLATIRON
FLATLAND
FLATTERY
FLATWARE
FLAUTIST
FLEABANE
FLEABITE
FLEETING
FLESHPOT
FLEXIBLE
FLIMFLAM
FLIPPANT
FLOTILLA
FLOUNDER
FLOURISH
FLUIDRAM
FLUORIDE
FLUORINE
FLUORITE
FLYBLOWN
FLYPAPER
FLYSPECK
FLYWHEEL

FOLDAWAY
FOLDBOAT
FOLDEROL
FOLIATED
FOLKLORE
FOLLICLE
FOOLSCAP
FOOTBALL
FOOTFALL
FOOTHILL
FOOTHOLD
FOOTLESS
FOOTLING
FOOTNOTE
FOOTPATH
FOOTRACE
FOOTREST
FOOTSORE
FOOTSTEP
FOOTWEAR
FOOTWORK
FORCIBLE
FOREBEAR
FOREBODE
FORECAST
FOREDOOM
FOREFEND
FOREFOOT
FOREGONE
FOREHAND
FOREHEAD
FOREKNOW
FORELADY
FORELAND
FORELIMB
FORELOCK
FOREMAST
FOREMOST
FORENAME
FORENOON
FORENSIC
FOREPART
FORESAIL
FORESKIN
FORESTRY
FORETELL
FOREWARN
FOREWORD
FORKLIFT
FORMERLY
FORMLESS
FORSOOTH
FORSWEAR
FORTRESS
FORTUITY
FORWARDS
FOUNTAIN

FOURFOLD
FOURSOME
FOURTEEN
FOXGLOVE
FOXHOUND
FRACTION
FRACTURE
FRAGMENT
FRAGRANT
FRANCIUM
FREEBORN
FREEDMAN
FREEHAND
FREEHOLD
FREELOAD
FREEWILL
FRENETIC
FREQUENT
FRESHMAN
FRETWORK
FRICTION
FRIGHTEN
FRIPPERY
FRONTAGE
FRONTIER
FROSTING
FROUFROU
FRUCTIFY
FRUITION
FUGITIVE
FULLBACK
FUMAROLE
FUMIGANT
FUMIGATE
FUNCTION
FUNERARY
FUNEREAL
FURBELOW
FURLOUGH
FURTHEST
FUSELAGE
FUTILITY
FUTURISM
FUTURITY
GADABOUT
GALLUSES
GAMECOCK
GAMESOME
GAMESTER
GANGLAND
GANGLING
GANGLION
GANGPLOW
GANGRENE
GANGSTER
GARDENIA
GARGOYLE
GARRISON
GASLIGHT
GASOLINE
GASWORKS
GATEPOST
GAUNTLET
GEMINATE
GEMOLOGY
GEMSTONE
GENDARME
GENERATE
GENEROUS
GENETICS
GENITALS
GENITIVE
GENOCIDE
GEODESIC
GEOMETRY
GERANIUM
GERMINAL
GHANAIAN
GIGABYTE
GIGANTIC
GIMCRACK
GINGERLY
GIVEAWAY
GLABROUS
GLACIATE
GLADSOME
GLASSFUL
GLAUCOMA
GLOAMING
GLOBULIN
GLORIOUS
GLOSSARY
GLOWWORM
GLOXINIA
GLYCERIN
GLYCEROL
GLYCOGEN
GOALPOST
GOATHERD
GOATSKIN
GODCHILD
GOLDFISH
GONFALON
GOODNESS
GOODWIFE
GOODWILL
GOOFBALL
GORGEOUS
GOSSAMER
GOURMAND
GOVERNOR
GRACIOUS
GRADIENT
GRADUATE
GRAFFITO
GRANDEUR
GRANDSON
GRANULAR
GRAPHITE
GRASPING
GRATEFUL
GRATUITY
GRAVAMEN
GRAYLING
GREEKING
GREENERY
GREETING
GRIDIRON
GRIEVOUS
GRIZZLED
GROSBEAK
GROSCHEN
GROUNDER
GRUELING
GRUESOME
GUARANTY
GUARDIAN
GUERNSEY
GUIDANCE
GUMPTION
GUNFIGHT
GUNPOINT
GUNSMITH
GUTTURAL
GUYANESE
GYMKHANA
HABANERA
HABITANT
HABITUAL
HACIENDA
HACKWORD
HAIRLINE
HALFBACK
HALFTONE
HALLMARK
HANDBALL
HANDBILL
HANDBOOK
HANDCUFF
HANDICAP
HANDMADE
HANDPICK
HANDRAIL
HANDSOME
HANDYMAN
HANGNAIL
HANGOVER
HANUKKAH
HARANGUE
HARDBACK
HARDBALL
HARDHACK
HARDSHIP
HARDTACK
HARDWARE
HARDWOOD
HAREBELL
HARMONIC
HARRIDAN
HATCHING
HATCHWAY
HAUTBOIS
HAWAIIAN
HAWKWEED
HAWTHORN
HAYSTACK
HEADACHE
HEADBAND
HEADGEAR
HEADLAND
HEADLINE
HEADLOCK
HEADLONG
HEADREST
HEADROOM
HEADSHIP
HEADSMAN
HEADWORD
HEADWORK
HEAVYSET
HEBRAISM
HECATOMB
HEDGEHOG
HEDGEHOP
HEDGEROW
HEDONISM
HEGEMONY
HEIGHTEN
HEIRLOOM
HELICOID
HELIPORT
HELLHOLE
HELMSMAN
HELPMATE
HELPMEET
HEMATITE
HENCHMAN
HEPATICA
HERALDIC
HERALDRY
HERCULES
HERDSMAN
HEREDITY
HEREFORD
HEREUNTO
HEREUPON
HEREWITH
HERITAGE
HERMETIC
HESITANT
HESITATE
HIBISCUS
HIDEAWAY
HIGHBALL
HIGHBORN
HIGHBRED
HIGHBROW
HIGHLAND
HIGHNESS
HIGHROAD
HIGHTAIL
HILLSIDE
HINDMOST
HINDUISM
HIRELING
HISPANIC
HITHERTO
HOARDING
HOGSHEAD
HOLDOVER
HOLINESS
HOLOGRAM
HOLSTEIN
HOMEBODY
HOMEBRED
HOMELAND
HOMEMADE
HOMEROOM
HOMESICK
HOMESPUN
HOMEWARD
HOMEWORK
HOMICIDE
HONEYDEW
HONORARY
HOODWINK
HOOKWORM
HOOLIGAN
HOOSEGOW
HORMONAL
HORNBOOK
HORNPIPE
HOROLOGY
HORRIBLE
HORSEFLY
HORSEMAN
HOSPITAL
HOSTELRY
HOTHOUSE
HOUSEBOY
HOUSEFLY
HOUSETOP
HOWITZER
HUARACHE
HUCKSTER
HUGUENOT
HUMANISM
HUMANITY
HUMANIZE
HUMANOID
HUMIDIFY
HUMIDITY
HUMILITY
HUMPBACK
HUNTRESS
HUNTSMAN
HUSTINGS
HYACINTH
HYDROGEN
HYMENEAL
HYPNOSIS
HYPNOTIC
HYSTERIA
ICEBOUND
ICEHOUSE
IDEALISM
IDEALIZE
IDEATION
IDENTIFY
IDENTITY
IDEOGRAM
IDEOLOGY
IDOLATER
IDOLATRY
IGNITION
IGNORANT
ILLINOIS
ILLUMINE
ILLUSION
ILLUSIVE
ILLUSORY
IMBECILE
IMITABLE
IMMANENT
IMMATURE
IMMINENT
IMMOBILE
IMMODEST
IMMOLATE
IMMORTAL
IMMOTILE
IMMUNIZE
IMPACTED
IMPELLER
IMPERIAL
IMPETIGO
IMPLICIT
IMPOLITE
IMPOSING
IMPOSTOR
IMPOTENT
IMPRISON
IMPROPER
IMPUDENT
IMPUNITY
INCHOATE
INCHWORM
INCIDENT
INCISION
INCISIVE
INCOMING
INCREASE
INCUBATE
INCUMBER
INDEBTED
INDECENT
INDIAMAN
INDICATE
INDIGENT
INDIRECT
INDOLENT
INDUCTEE
INDURATE
INDUSTRY
INEDITED
INERRANT
INEXPERT
INFAMOUS
INFANTRY
INFERIOR
INFERNAL
INFINITE
INFINITY
INFOBAHN
INFORMAL
INFORMED
INFORMER
INFRADIG
INFRARED
INFRINGE
INGUINAL
INHALANT
INHERENT
INHUMANE
INIMICAL
INIQUITY
INITIATE
INKSTAND
INNOCENT
INNOVATE
INNUENDO
INSCRIBE
INSECURE
INSIGNIA
INSOLENT
INSOMNIA
INSOMUCH
INSPIRIT
INSTANCE
INSTINCT
INSTRUCT
INSULATE
INTAGLIO
INTEGRAL
INTENDED
INTERCOM
INTEREST
INTERIOR
INTERMIT
INTERMIX
INTERNAL
INTERNEE
INTERNET
INTERROG
INTERVAL
INTIMATE
INTRADOS
INTRENCH
INTREPID
INTRIGUE
INTROMIT
INUNDATE
INVASION
INVEIGLE
INVERTER
INVIABLE
INVITING
INVOLUTE
INVOLVED
INWARDLY
IRONCLAD
IRONWARE
IRONWEED
IRONWOOD
IRONWORK
IROQUOIS
IRRIGATE
IRRITATE
ISLANDER
ISOPRENE
ISOSTASY
ISOTHERM
ISOTONIC
ISSUANCE
ISTHMIAN
JACKBOOT
JACQUARD
JAILBIRD
JALOUSIE
JAMBOREE
JAPANESE
JAUNDICE
JEOPARDY
JEREMIAD
JETTISON
JINGOISM

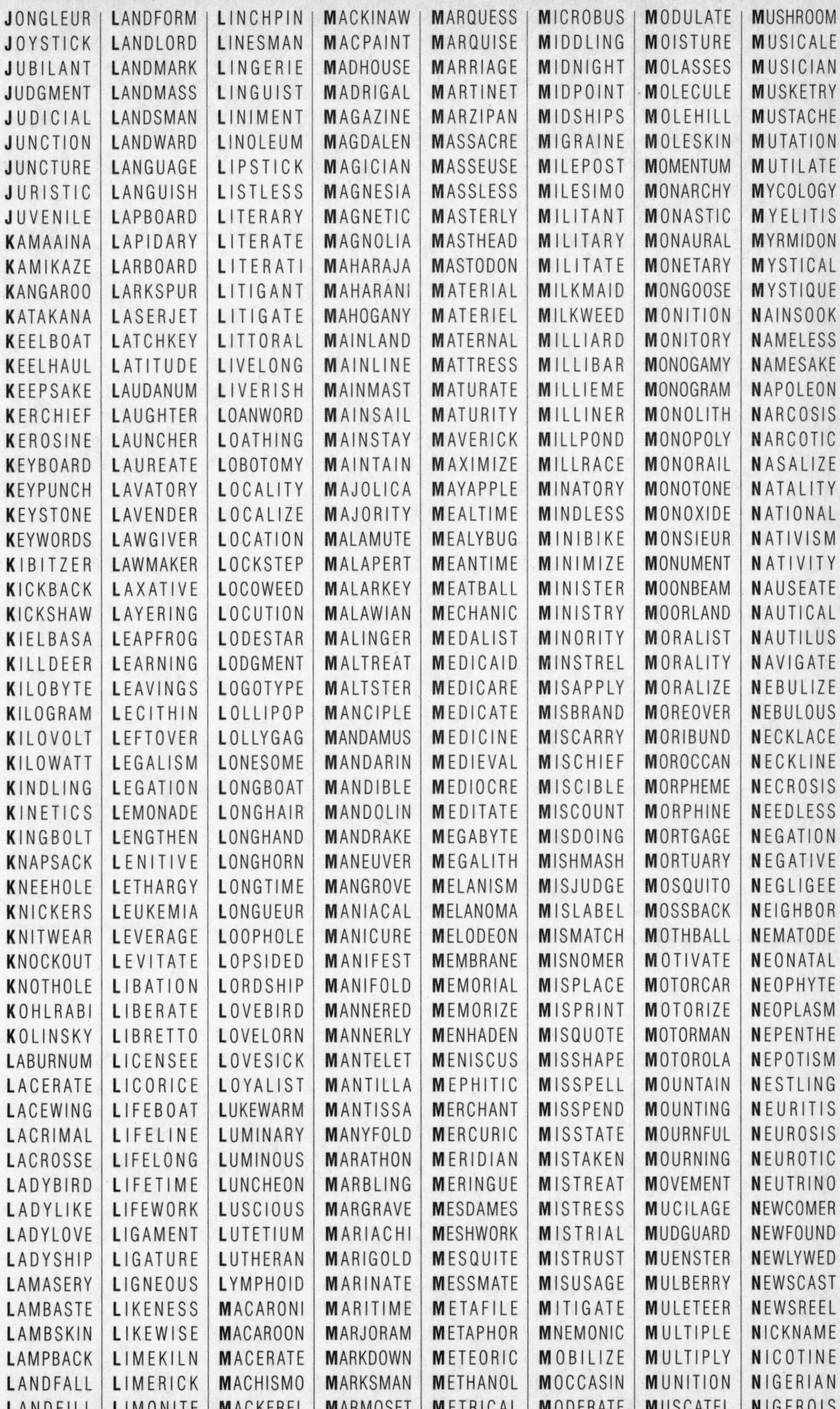

JONGLEUR
JOYSTICK
JUBILANT
JUDGMENT
JUDICIAL
JUNCTION
JUNCTURE
JURISTIC
JUVENILE
KAMAAINA
KAMIKAZE
KANGAROO
KATAKANA
KEELBOAT
KEELHAUL
KEEPSAKE
KERCHIEF
KEROSINE
KEYBOARD
KEYPUNCH
KEYSTONE
KEYWORDS
KIBITZER
KICKBACK
KICKSHAW
KIELBASA
KILLDEER
KILOBYTE
KILOGRAM
KILOVOLT
KILOWATT
KINDLING
KINETICS
KINGBOLT
KNAPSACK
KNEEHOLE
KNICKERS
KNITWEAR
KNOCKOUT
KNOTHOLE
KOHLRABI
KOLINSKY
LABURNUM
LACERATE
LACEWING
LACRIMAL
LACROSSE
LADYBIRD
LADYLIKE
LADYLOVE
LADYSHIP
LAMASERY
LAMBASTE
LAMBSKIN
LAMPBACK
LANDFALL
LANDFILL
LANDFORM
LANDLORD
LANDMARK
LANDMASS
LANDSMAN
LANDWARD
LANGUAGE
LANGUISH
LAPBOARD
LAPIDARY
LARBOARD
LARKSPUR
LASERJET
LATCHKEY
LATITUDE
LAUDANUM
LAUGHTER
LAUNCHER
LAUREATE
LAVATORY
LAVENDER
LAWGIVER
LAWMAKER
LAXATIVE
LAYERING
LEAPFROG
LEARNING
LEAVINGS
LECITHIN
LEFTOVER
LEGALISM
LEGATION
LEMONADE
LENGTHEN
LENITIVE
LETHARGY
LEUKEMIA
LEVERAGE
LEVITATE
LIBATION
LIBERATE
LIBRETTO
LICENSEE
LICORICE
LIFEBOAT
LIFELINE
LIFELONG
LIFETIME
LIFEWORK
LIGAMENT
LIGATURE
LIGNEOUS
LIKENESS
LIKEWISE
LIMEKILN
LIMERICK
LIMONITE
LINCHPIN
LINESMAN
LINGERIE
LINGUIST
LINIMENT
LINOLEUM
LIPSTICK
LISTLESS
LITERARY
LITERATE
LITERATI
LITIGANT
LITIGATE
LITTORAL
LIVELONG
LIVERISH
LOANWORD
LOATHING
LOBOTOMY
LOCALITY
LOCALIZE
LOCATION
LOCKSTEP
LOCOWEED
LOCUTION
LODESTAR
LODGMENT
LOGOTYPE
LOLLIPOP
LOLLYGAG
LONESOME
LONGBOAT
LONGHAIR
LONGHAND
LONGHORN
LONGTIME
LONGUEUR
LOOPHOLE
LOPSIDED
LORDSHIP
LOVEBIRD
LOVELORN
LOVESICK
LOYALIST
LUKEWARM
LUMINARY
LUMINOUS
LUNCHEON
LUSCIOUS
LUTETIUM
LUTHERAN
LYMPHOID
MACARONI
MACAROON
MACERATE
MACHISMO
MACKEREL
MACKINAW
MACPAINT
MADHOUSE
MADRIGAL
MAGAZINE
MAGDALEN
MAGICIAN
MAGNESIA
MAGNETIC
MAGNOLIA
MAHARAJA
MAHARANI
MAHOGANY
MAINLAND
MAINLINE
MAINMAST
MAINSAIL
MAINSTAY
MAINTAIN
MAJOLICA
MAJORITY
MALAMUTE
MALAPERT
MALARKEY
MALAWIAN
MALINGER
MALTREAT
MALTSTER
MANCIPLE
MANDAMUS
MANDARIN
MANDIBLE
MANDOLIN
MANDRAKE
MANEUVER
MANGROVE
MANIACAL
MANICURE
MANIFEST
MANIFOLD
MANNERED
MANNERLY
MANTELET
MANTILLA
MANTISSA
MANYFOLD
MARATHON
MARBLING
MARGRAVE
MARIACHI
MARIGOLD
MARINATE
MARITIME
MARJORAM
MARKDOWN
MARKSMAN
MARMOSET
MARQUESS
MARQUISE
MARRIAGE
MARTINET
MARZIPAN
MASSACRE
MASSEUSE
MASSLESS
MASTERLY
MASTHEAD
MASTODON
MATERIAL
MATERIEL
MATERNAL
MATTRESS
MATURATE
MATURITY
MAVERICK
MAXIMIZE
MAYAPPLE
MEALTIME
MEALYBUG
MEANTIME
MEATBALL
MECHANIC
MEDALIST
MEDICAID
MEDICARE
MEDICATE
MEDICINE
MEDIEVAL
MEDIOCRE
MEDITATE
MEGABYTE
MEGALITH
MELANISM
MELANOMA
MELODEON
MEMBRANE
MEMORIAL
MEMORIZE
MENHADEN
MENISCUS
MEPHITIC
MERCHANT
MERCURIC
MERIDIAN
MERINGUE
MESDAMES
MESHWORK
MESQUITE
MESSMATE
METAFILE
METAPHOR
METEORIC
METHANOL
METRICAL
MICROBUS
MIDDLING
MIDNIGHT
MIDPOINT
MIDSHIPS
MIGRAINE
MILEPOST
MILESIMO
MILITANT
MILITARY
MILITATE
MILKMAID
MILKWEED
MILLIARD
MILLIBAR
MILLIEME
MILLINER
MILLPOND
MILLRACE
MINATORY
MINDLESS
MINIBIKE
MINIMIZE
MINISTER
MINISTRY
MINORITY
MINSTREL
MISAPPLY
MISBRAND
MISCARRY
MISCHIEF
MISCIBLE
MISCOUNT
MISDOING
MISHMASH
MISJUDGE
MISLABEL
MISMATCH
MISNOMER
MISPLACE
MISPRINT
MISQUOTE
MISSHAPE
MISSPELL
MISSPEND
MISSTATE
MISTAKEN
MISTREAT
MISTRESS
MISTRIAL
MISTRUST
MISUSAGE
MITIGATE
MNEMONIC
MOBILIZE
MOCCASIN
MODERATE
MODULATE
MOISTURE
MOLASSES
MOLECULE
MOLEHILL
MOLESKIN
MOMENTUM
MONARCHY
MONASTIC
MONAURAL
MONETARY
MONGOOSE
MONITION
MONITORY
MONOGAMY
MONOGRAM
MONOLITH
MONOPOLY
MONORAIL
MONOTONE
MONOXIDE
MONSIEUR
MONUMENT
MOONBEAM
MOORLAND
MORALIST
MORALITY
MORALIZE
MOREOVER
MORIBUND
MOROCCAN
MORPHEME
MORPHINE
MORTGAGE
MORTUARY
MOSQUITO
MOSSBACK
MOTHBALL
MOTIVATE
MOTORCAR
MOTORIZE
MOTORMAN
MOTOROLA
MOUNTAIN
MOUNTING
MOURNFUL
MOURNING
MOVEMENT
MUCILAGE
MUDGUARD
MUENSTER
MULBERRY
MULETEER
MULTIPLE
MULTIPLY
MUNITION
MUSCATEL
MUSHROOM
MUSICALE
MUSICIAN
MUSKETRY
MUSTACHE
MUTATION
MUTILATE
MYCOLOGY
MYELITIS
MYRMIDON
MYSTICAL
MYSTIQUE
NAINSOOK
NAMELESS
NAMESAKE
NAPOLEON
NARCOSIS
NARCOTIC
NASALIZE
NATALITY
NATIONAL
NATIVISM
NATIVITY
NAUSEATE
NAUTICAL
NAUTILUS
NAVIGATE
NEBULIZE
NEBULOUS
NECKLACE
NECKLINE
NECROSIS
NEEDLESS
NEGATION
NEGATIVE
NEGLIGEE
NEIGHBOR
NEMATODE
NEONATAL
NEOPHYTE
NEOPLASM
NEPENTHE
NEPOTISM
NESTLING
NEURITIS
NEUROSIS
NEUROTIC
NEUTRINO
NEWCOMER
NEWFOUND
NEWLYWED
NEWSCAST
NEWSREEL
NICKNAME
NICOTINE
NIGERIAN
NIGEROIS

NIGGLING
NIHILISM
NINEPINS
NINETEEN
NITROGEN
NOBELIST
NOBELIUM
NOBILITY
NOBLEMAN
NOCTURNE
NOMINATE
NONDAIRY
NONESUCH
NONEVENT
NONMETAL
NONRIGID
NONSENSE
NONSTICK
NONUNION
NOONTIDE
NOONTIME
NORSEMAN
NOTARIAL
NOTARIZE
NOTATION
NOTEBOOK
NOTIONAL
NOVELIZE
NOVEMBER
NOWADAYS
NUCLEATE
NUGATORY
NUISANCE
NUMERATE
NUMEROUS
NUMSKULL
NURSLING
NUTHATCH
NUTRIENT
NUTSHELL
OBDURATE
OBEDIENT
OBITUARY
OBLATION
OBLIGATE
OBLIVION
OBSIDIAN
OBSOLETE
OBSTACLE
OBSTRUCT
OCCASION
OCCUPANT
ODOMETER
OFFICIAL
OFFPRINT
OFFSHOOT
OFFSHORE
OFFSTAGE
OHMMETER
OILCLOTH
OINTMENT
OLEANDER
ONCOMING
ONLOOKER
ONONDAGA
OPENWORK
OPERABLE
OPERANDS
OPERETTA
OPPONENT
OPPOSITE
OPTICIAN
OPTIMISM
OPUSCULE
ORANGERY
ORATORIO
ORDINARY
ORDINATE
ORDNANCE
ORGANISM
ORGANIST
ORGANIZE
ORGULOUS
ORIENTAL
ORIGINAL
ORNAMENT
ORTHODOX
ORTHOEPY
OSCULATE
OUTBOARD
OUTBOUND
OUTBREAK
OUTBURST
OUTCLASS
OUTDATED
OUTDOORS
OUTFIELD
OUTFIGHT
OUTFLANK
OUTGOING
OUTGUESS
OUTHOUSE
OUTLYING
OUTMODED
OUTPOINT
OUTREACH
OUTRIDER
OUTRIGHT
OUTSHINE
OUTSIDER
OUTSMART
OUTSPEND
OUTSTRIP
OUTWEIGH
OVENBIRD
OVERALLS
OVERCAST
OVERCOAT
OVERCOME
OVERDRAW
OVERFLOW
OVERGROW
OVERHAND
OVERHANG
OVERHAUL
OVERHEAD
OVERHEAR
OVERKILL
OVERLAID
OVERLAND
OVERLEAP
OVERLOOK
OVERLORD
OVERMUCH
OVERPASS
OVERPLAY
OVERRIDE
OVERRULE
OVERSEAS
OVERSHOE
OVERSIZE
OVERSTAY
OVERSTEP
OVERTAKE
OVERTIME
OVERTONE
OVERTURE
OVERTURN
OVERVIEW
PACIFIER
PACIFISM
PAGINATE
PAINTING
PALATINE
PALEFACE
PALINODE
PALISADE
PALLIATE
PALMETTO
PALOMINO
PALPABLE
PAMPHLET
PANATELA
PANCREAS
PANDEMIC
PANDOWDY
PANELING
PANELIST
PANORAMA
PANTHEON
PANTSUIT
PARABOLA
PARADIGM
PARADISE
PARAFFIN
PARAKEET
PARALLAX
PARALLEL
PARALYZE
PARAMOUR
PARANOIA
PARASITE
PARDONER
PARFOCAL
PARIETAL
PARLANCE
PARMESAN
PAROXYSM
PARTERRE
PARTIBLE
PARTICLE
PARTISAN
PASSABLE
PASSBOOK
PASSOVER
PASSPORT
PASSWORD
PASTICHE
PASTILLE
PASTORAL
PASTRAMI
PATERNAL
PATHETIC
PATHOGEN
PATIENCE
PAVEMENT
PAVILION
PAWNSHOP
PAYCHECK
PECTORAL
PECULATE
PECULIAR
PEDAGOGY
PEDERAST
PEDESTAL
PEDICURE
PEDIGREE
PEDIMENT
PEDUNCLE
PEEPHOLE
PEERLESS
PEIGNOIR
PELLAGRA
PELLUCID
PEMMICAN
PENALIZE
PENCHANT
PENDULUM
PENITENT
PENKNIFE
PENLIGHT
PENOLOGY
PENSTOCK
PENTAGON
PENUMBRA
PERCEIVE
PERFECTO
PERFORCE
PERILUNE
PERIODIC
PERMEATE
PEROXIDE
PERSONAL
PERSPIRE
PERSUADE
PERVERSE
PETITION
PETTIFOG
PETULANT
PHANTASM
PHANTASY
PHARISEE
PHARMACY
PHASEOUT
PHEASANT
PHENOLIC
PHOSPHOR
PHRASING
PHYSICAL
PHYSIQUE
PICAYUNE
PICKEREL
PICKINGS
PICKLOCK
PIDDLING
PIEPLANT
PILASTER
PILCHARD
PILOTAGE
PIMIENTO
PINAFORE
PINNACLE
PINOCHLE
PINPOINT
PINPRICK
PINWHEEL
PIPELINE
PITCHMAN
PITIABLE
PITILESS
PITTANCE
PIXELATE
PIZZERIA
PLACENTA
PLANGENT
PLANKING
PLANKTON
PLANTAIN
PLATFORM
PLATINUM
PLATYPUS
PLAYBACK
PLAYBILL
PLAYBOOK
PLAYGOER
PLAYMATE
PLAYSUIT
PLEASANT
PLEASING
PLEASURE
PLEBEIAN
PLECTRUM
PLETHORA
PLEURISY
PLUMBING
POCKMARK
PODIATRY
POIGNANT
POKEWEED
POLARITY
POLARIZE
POLESTAR
POLITICK
POLITICO
POLITICS
POLLIWOG
POLLSTER
POLONIUM
POLTROON
POLYGAMY
POLYGLOT
POLYMATH
PONYTAIL
POPINJAY
POPULACE
POPULATE
POPULIST
POPULOUS
PORPHYRY
PORPOISE
PORRIDGE
PORTABLE
PORTHOLE
PORTIERE
PORTRAIT
POSITION
POSITIVE
POSITRON
POSSIBLE
POSTCARD
POSTDATE
POSTHOLE
POSTLUDE
POSTMARK
POSTPAID
POSTPONE
POTATION
POTBELLY
POTSHERD
POULTICE
POUNDAGE
PRACTICE
PRATFALL
PRATIQUE
PREAMBLE
PRECINCT
PRECIOUS
PRECLUDE
PREEXIST
PREGNANT
PREJUDGE
PREMIERE
PREMOLAR
PRENATAL
PREPRESS
PRESENCE
PRESERVE
PRESIDIO
PRESSING
PRESSMAN
PRESSURE
PRESTIGE
PRETENSE
PRETERIT
PRETTIFY
PREVIOUS
PRIMEVAL
PRIMROSE
PRINCESS
PRINTING
PRINTOUT
PRISONER
PRISTINE
PROBABLE
PROCAINE
PROCEEDS
PROCLAIM
PRODIGAL
PROFOUND
PROGRESS
PROHIBIT
PROLIFIC
PROLOGUE
PROMOTER
PROPERTY
PROPHECY
PROPHESY
PROPOUND
PROROGUE
PROSPECT
PROSTATE
PROTOCOL
PROTRACT
PROTRUDE
PROVIDED
PROVINCE
PRURIENT
PSALMODY
PTOMAINE
PUBLICAN
PUDDLING
PUDENDUM
PUFFBALL
PUGILISM
PULLBACK
PULLOVER
PULMOTOR
PULPWOOD
PUNCHEON
PUNCTUAL
PUNCTURE
PUNITIVE
PURBLIND
PURCHASE
PUREBRED
PURSLANE
PURULENT
PUSHCART
PUSHDOWN
PUSHOVER
PUSSYCAT
PUTATIVE
PYORRHEA
QUADRANT
QUADROON
QUAGMIRE
QUALMISH
QUANDARY
QUANTITY
QUANTIZE
QUATRAIN
QUESTION
QUIETUDE
QUISLING
QUIXOTIC
QUOTABLE
QUOTIENT
RADIATOR
RADIOMAN
RAILLERY
RAILROAD
RAINCOAT
RAINDROP
RAINFALL
RATIONAL
RATTLING

RAVENING
RAVENOUS
RAWBONED
REACTANT
REACTION
REACTIVE
REARWARD
REASSURE
REBUTTAL
RECEIVER
RECEPTOR
RECKLESS
RECORDER
RECOURSE
RECREANT
RECREATE
REDOLENT
REFERENT
REFERRAL
REFINERY
REFOREST
REFORMER
REGICIDE
REGIMENT
REGIONAL
REGISTER
REGISTRY
REGOLITH
REGULATE
REHEARSE
REINDEER
RELATION
RELATIVE
RELAXANT
RELEGATE
RELEVANT
RELIABLE
RELIANCE
RELIGION
RELOCATE
REMEDIAL
REMEMBER
REMITTAL
RENEGADE
RENOUNCE
RENOVATE
REPARTEE
REPEATED
REPORTER
REPRIEVE
REPRISAL
REPROACH
REPUBLIC
RESCRIPT
RESEARCH
RESEMBLE
RESERVED
RESIDENT
RESIDUAL
RESIDUUM
RESIGNED
RESISTOR
RESOLUTE
RESONANT
RESONATE
RESORTER
RESOURCE
RESPONSE
RESTLESS
RESTRAIN
RESTRICT
RETAINER
RETARDED
RETICENT
RETIRING
RETRENCH
RETRIEVE
RETROFIT
RETURNEE
REVANCHE
REVEILLE
REVENUER
REVEREND
REVERENT
REVERSAL
REVIEWER
REVIVIFY
REVOLVER
RHAPSODY
RHEOLOGY
RHEOSTAT
RHETORIC
RHOMBOID
RHYOLITE
RIBOSOME
RICOCHET
RIDICULE
RIFFRAFF
RIGHTFUL
RINGWORM
RIPARIAN
RIVERBED
ROADSIDE
ROADSTER
ROADWORK
ROCKETRY
ROCKFALL
ROLLBACK
ROMANIAN
ROMANTIC
ROOFTREE
ROOMETTE
ROOMMATE
ROSEBUSH
ROSEMARY
ROSEWOOD
ROUGHAGE
ROULETTE
ROUTEMAN
ROYALIST
RUBICUND
RUBIDIUM
RUDIMENT
RUMANIAN
RUMBLING
RUMINANT
RUMINATE
RUNABOUT
RUNAGATE
RUTABAGA
RUTHLESS
SABOTAGE
SABOTEUR
SACRISTY
SADDUCEE
SAGAMORE
SAILBOAT
SAILFISH
SALESMAN
SALIVATE
SALUTARY
SAMARIUM
SANCTIFY
SANCTION
SANCTITY
SANDBANK
SANDWICH
SANGUINE
SANITARY
SANITIZE
SANSKRIT
SAPPHIRE
SARDONIC
SATURATE
SATURDAY
SAUCEPAN
SAUTERNE
SAWHORSE
SCABBARD
SCABROUS
SCAFFOLD
SCALABLE
SCALAWAG
SCALEPAN
SCALLION
SCANDIUM
SCAPULAR
SCARCELY
SCATHING
SCAVENGE
SCENARIO
SCHEDULE
SCHMALTZ
SCHOONER
SCIATICA
SCILICET
SCIMITAR
SCISSORS
SCOFFLAW
SCORPION
SCOTTISH
SCRABBLE
SCRAGGLY
SCRAMBLE
SCRIBBLE
SCROFULA
SCROUNGE
SCRUTINY
SCULLERY
SCULLION
SCULPTOR
SEABOARD
SEACOAST
SEAFARER
SEAGOING
SEALSKIN
SEAMOUNT
SEAPLANE
SEASCAPE
SEASHORE
SEAWATER
SECURITY
SEDATIVE
SEDIMENT
SEDITION
SEDULOUS
SEEDLING
SEEDTIME
SEIGNEUR
SELECTEE
SELENITE
SELENIUM
SELFLESS
SELFSAME
SEMANTIC
SEMESTER
SEMINARY
SEMINOLE
SEMISOFT
SENSIBLE
SENSUOUS
SENTENCE
SENTIENT
SENTINEL
SEPARATE
SEQUENCE
SERAGLIO
SERENADE
SERGEANT
SEROLOGY
SERVITOR
SETSCREW
SEWERAGE
SHAMBLES
SHAMROCK
SHANGHAI
SHANTUNG
SHEEPISH
SHEETING
SHELVING
SHEPHERD
SHILINGI
SHILLING
SHINBONE
SHINGLES
SHIPMATE
SHIPMENT
SHIPPING
SHIPWORM
SHIPYARD
SHIRRING
SHIRTING
SHOCKING
SHOELACE
SHOPLIFT
SHOPWORN
SHORTAGE
SHORTCUT
SHOSHONE
SHOULDER
SHOWCASE
SHOWDOWN
SHRAPNEL
SHREWISH
SHUTDOWN
SIBILANT
SICKNESS
SIDEKICK
SIDELONG
SIDEREAL
SIDERITE
SIDESHOW
SIDESTEP
SIDEWALK
SIDEWALL
SIDEWAYS
SIGNPOST
SILENCER
SILICATE
SILICIFY
SILICONE
SIMONIZE
SIMPLIFY
SIMULATE
SINECURE
SINGULAR
SINISTER
SINKHOLE
SITUATED
SIXPENCE
SKELETON
SKILLFUL
SKIMMING
SKIRMISH
SKITTISH
SKULLCAP
SKYLIGHT
SLATTERN
SLIPKNOT
SLIPPERY
SLIPSHOD
SLOVENLY
SLUGGARD
SLUGGISH
SLUMLORD
SMALLPOX
SNAPSHOT
SNOBBERY
SNOWBALL
SNOWBANK
SNOWDROP
SNOWFALL
SNOWPLOW
SNOWSHOE
SOBRIETY
SOCIABLE
SOFTBALL
SOFTWARE
SOFTWOOD
SOLARIUM
SOLDIERY
SOLECISM
SOLENOID
SOLIDIFY
SOLITARY
SOLITUDE
SOLSTICE
SOLUTION
SOLVENCY
SOMBRERO
SOMEBODY
SOMERSET
SOMETIME
SOMEWHAT
SONATINA
SONGBIRD
SONGSTER
SONOROUS
SORORITY
SORPTION
SOUTHPAW
SOUVENIR
SPACEMAN
SPACIOUS
SPANIARD
SPANKING
SPECIFIC
SPECIMEN
SPECIOUS
SPECTRAL
SPECTRUM
SPEEDWAY
SPHAGNUM
SPHEROID
SPILLWAY
SPINSTER
SPIRITED
SPITBALL
SPITTOON
SPLATTER
SPLENDID
SPLENDOR
SPLINTER
SPLUTTER
SPOOLING
SPORADIC
SPRINKLE
SPROCKET
SPURIOUS
SPYGLASS
SQUABBLE
SQUADRON
SQUANDER
SQUEEGEE
SQUIRREL
STACCATO
STAGNANT
STAGNATE
STAIRWAY
STAKEOUT
STALLION
STALWART
STAMPEDE
STANDARD
STANDING
STANDOFF
STANDOUT
STARFISH
STARLING
STATUARY
STEALTHY
STEERAGE
STERLING
STICKLER
STILETTO
STIMULUS
STINKBUG
STIRRING
STOCKADE
STOCKING
STOPPAGE
STOTINKA
STOWAWAY
STRADDLE
STRAGGLE
STRAIGHT
STRAITEN
STRANGER
STRANGLE
STRATEGY
STRATIFY
STREAMER
STRENGTH
STRICKEN
STRIDENT
STRIKING
STRINGED
STRINGER
STRUGGLE
STRUMPET
STUBBORN
STUDBOOK
STUDDING
STUDIOUS
STUFFING
STULTIFY
STUNNING
STURGEON
SUBMERGE
SUBMERSE
SUBPOENA
SUBSONIC
SUBTITLE
SUBTRACT
SUBURBIA
SUCCINCT
SUCHLIKE
SUCKLING
SUFFRAGE
SUITABLE
SUITCASE
SUKIYAKI
SULFURIC
SUNDRIES
SUNLIGHT
SUNSHADE
SUNSHINE
SUPEREGO
SUPERIOR
SUPERJET
SUPERNAL
SUPPLANT
SUPPOSED
SUPPRESS
SURCEASE
SUREFIRE

SURGICAL
SURMOUNT
SURPLICE
SURPRISE
SURROUND
SUSPENSE
SUZERAIN
SWASTIKA
SWAYBACK
SWEEPING
SWELLING
SWIMMING
SYBARITE
SYCAMORE
SYLLABLE
SYLLABUS
SYMBOLIC
SYMMETRY
SYMPATHY
SYMPHONY
SYNDROME
SYNOPSIS
SYNOPTIC
SYPHILIS
SYSADMIN
SYSTEMIC
TABULATE
TACITURN
TAFFRAIL
TAHITIAN
TAILCOAT
TAILGATE
TAILSPIN
TALESMAN
TALISMAN
TAMARACK
TAMARIND
TANGIBLE
TANTALUM
TAPESTRY
TAPEWORM
TARRAGON
TAXONOMY
TAXPAYER
TEACHING
TEAMSTER
TEAMWORK
TEASPOON
TEETHING
TEETOTAL
TELECAST
TELEFILM
TELEGRAM
TELEPLAY
TELETHON
TELEVIEW
TELEVISE
TELLTALE
TEMERITY
TEMPLATE
TEMPORAL
TENANTRY
TENDENCY
TENEMENT
TENPENNY
TENTACLE
TEOSINTE
TERMINAL
TERMINUS
TERRAPIN
TERRIBLE
TERRIFIC
TERTIARY
TESTATOR
TESTICLE
TEUTONIC
TEXTBOOK
THALAMUS
THALLIUM
THANKFUL
THEOLOGY
THEORIZE
THEREFOR
THESPIAN
THIAMINE
THICKSET
THIEVERY
THIRTEEN
THOROUGH
THOUSAND
THRASHER
THREATEN
THRENODY
THROMBUS
THROTTLE
THRUSTER
THURSDAY
TICKLISH
TIDELAND
TIGHTWAD
TIMBERED
TIMELESS
TIMEWORN
TIMOROUS
TINCTURE
TINPLATE
TINSMITH
TIRELESS
TIRESOME
TITANIUM
TITILATE
TITIVATE
TITMOUSE
TOBOGGAN
TOGETHER
TOILETRY
TOILETTE
TOILWORN
TOKENISM
TOLERATE
TOLLBOTH
TOLLGATE
TOMAHAWK
TOMORROW
TONALITY
TOPOLOGY
TOPSIDES
TOREADOR
TORTILLA
TORTOISE
TORTUOUS
TOTALITY
TOUCHING
TOWELING
TOWERING
TOWNSHIP
TOWNSMAN
TRACKAGE
TRACTATE
TRACTION
TRAINING
TRAINMAN
TRANQUIL
TRANSACT
TRANSEPT
TRANSFER
TRANSFIX
TRANSMIT
TRAPDOOR
TRAPPING
TRAPROCK
TRAVERSE
TRAVESTY
TREASURE
TREASURY
TREATISE
TRENCHER
TRESPASS
TRIANGLE
TRIBUNAL
TRICHINA
TRICKERY
TRICOLOR
TRICYCLE
TRIFLING
TRILLION
TRILLIUM
TRIMARAN
TRIMETER
TRIMMING
TRIPTYCH
TRIUMVIR
TROMBONE
TROUSERS
TRUCKAGE
TRUETYPE
TRUMPERY
TRUNCATE
TRUSTFUL
TRUTHFUL
TUBERCLE
TUBEROSE
TUBEROUS
TUNELESS
TUNGSTEN
TUNISIAN
TURBOFAN
TURBOJET
TURMERIC
TURNCOAT
TURNOVER
TURNPIKE
TURNSPIT
TUTELAGE
TUTELARY
TUTORIAL
TWEEZERS
TWILIGHT
TWOPENCE
TWOPENNY
TYMPANUM
TYPECAST
TYPEFACE
ULCERATE
ULTERIOR
ULTIMATE
UMBRELLA
UNAWARES
UNBEATEN
UNBELIEF
UNBIASED
UNBIDDEN
UNBODIED
UNBOLTED
UNBROKEN
UNBUCKLE
UNBURDEN
UNBUTTON
UNCHASTE
UNCHURCH
UNCLENCH
UNCLOTHE
UNCOMMON
UNCOUPLE
UNCTUOUS
UNDERACT
UNDERAGE
UNDERARM
UNDERBID
UNDERCUT
UNDERDOG
UNDERFUR
UNDERLIE
UNDERLIP
UNDERPAY
UNDERSEA
UNDERTOW
UNDULANT
UNDULATE
UNEARNED
UNENDING
UNERRING
UNFASTEN
UNFETTER
UNFILIAL
UNFORMED
UNFREEZE
UNGAINLY
UNGULATE
UNIAXIAL
UNICYCLE
UNIONISM
UNIONIZE
UNIVALVE
UNIVERSE
UNKINDLY
UNLAWFUL
UNLEADED
UNLIKELY
UNLIMBER
UNLOOSEN
UNLOVELY
UNMUZZLE
UNPERSON
UNRIDDLE
UNSADDLE
UNSAVORY
UNSEEMLY
UNSETTLE
UNSHAPED
UNSOUGHT
UNSPRUNG
UNSTABLE
UNSTEADY
UNSTRUNG
UNTANGLE
UNTAUGHT
UNTIMELY
UNTOWARD
UNVOICED
UNWIELDY
UNWONTED
UNWORTHY
UNZIPPED
UPCOMING
UPGROWTH
UPHEAVAL
UPPERCUT
UPRISING
UPSTAIRS
UPSTREAM
UPSTROKE
UPTHRUST
URBANITE
URBANIZE
USUFRUCT
USURIOUS
UUDECODE
UUENCODE
UXORIOUS
VACATION
VACCINIA
VAGABOND
VAGRANCY
VALIDATE
VALUABLE
VALVULAR
VANADIUM
VANGUARD
VANQUISH
VAPORING
VAPORISH
VAPORIZE
VAPOROUS
VARIABLE
VARIANCE
VARICOSE
VARIETAL
VARIORUM
VARISTOR
VASCULAR
VAULTING
VEGANISM
VEGETATE
VEHEMENT
VELLEITY
VELOCITY
VENATION
VENDETTA
VENERATE
VENEREAL
VENGEFUL
VENOMOUS
VENUSIAN
VERACITY
VERBATIM
VERBIAGE
VERBOTEN
VERMOUTH
VERONICA
VERSICLE
VERTEBRA
VERTICAL
VESICANT
VESTMENT
VEXATION
VIATICUM
VIBURNUM
VICARAGE
VICINAGE
VICINITY
VICTORIA
VIETCONG
VIGILANT
VIGNETTE
VIGOROUS
VILLAGER
VILLAINY
VINCIBLE
VINEGARY
VINEYARD
VIOLABLE
VIOLENCE
VIRGINAL
VIROLOGY
VIRTUOSO
VIRTUOUS
VIRULENT
VISCERAL
VISCOUNT
VISICALC
VISITANT
VITALITY
VITALIZE
VITREOUS
VIVACITY
VIVARIUM
VOCALIST
VOCALIZE
VOCATION
VOCATIVE
VOLATILE
VOLCANIC
VOLITION
VOLPLANE
VOYAGEUR
WAINSCOT
WAITRESS
WALKAWAY
WALKOVER
WARDROBE
WARDROOM
WARDSHIP
WAREROOM
WARFARIN
WARPLANE
WARRANTY
WASHABLE
WASHBOWL
WASHROOM
WATCHDOG
WATCHFUL
WATCHMAN
WATERLOO
WATERWAY
WAYFARER
WEAKFISH
WEAKLING
WEAKNESS
WEAPONRY
WELDMENT
WELLBORN
WELLHEAD
WEREWOLF
WHARFAGE
WHATEVER
WHENEVER
WHEREVER
WHIPCORD
WHIPLASH
WHITECAP
WHITEFLY
WHODUNIT
WHOMEVER
WHOPPING
WILDFIRE
WILDFOWL
WILDLIFE
WILDWOOD
WILLIWAW
WINDBURN
WINDFALL
WINDLASS
WINDMILL
WINDPIPE
WINDWARD
WINESHOP
WINGDING
WINGSPAN
WIREDRAW
WIREHAIR
WIRELESS
WIREWORM
WISEACRE
WISHBONE
WISTARIA
WISTERIA
WITCHERY
WITCHING
WITHDRAW
WITHHOLD
WIZARDRY
WOMANISH
WONDROUS
WOODBINE
WOODCOCK

WOODLAND
WOODNOTE
WOODPILE
WOODRUFF
WOODSHED
WOODSMAN
WOODWIND
WOODWORK
WOOLSACK
WORDBOOK
WORDPLAY
WORDSTAR
WORKABLE
WORKADAY
WORKBOOK
WORKROOM
WORKSHOP
WORMHOLE
WORMWOOD
WRAPPING
WRATHFUL
WRECKAGE
WRETCHED
WRIGGLER
WRISTLET
WRONGFUL
XENOLITH
YACHTING
YEARBOOK
YEARLING
YEARLONG
YEARNING
YEOMANRY
YIELDING
YOUNGISH
YOURSELF
YOUTHFUL
YUGOSLAV
YULETIDE
ZEPPELIN
ZOOPHYTE
ZOOSPORE
ZUCCHINI
ZWIEBACK

## 2nd Letter

AARDVARK
BABUSHKA
BACCARAT
BACHELOR
BACILLUS
BACKACHE
BACKBITE
BACKBONE
BACKDROP
BACKFIRE
BACKHAND
BACKLASH
BACKPACK
BACKREST
BACKSIDE
BACKSLAP
BACKSPIN
BACKSTOP
BACKWARD
BACKWASH
BADINAGE
BAEDEKER
BAGUETTE
BAILABLE
BAILSMAN
BAKESHOP
BALLROOM
BALLYHOO
BALUSTER
BANDANNA
BANISTER
BANKBOOK
BANKROLL
BANKRUPT
BANTLING
BARBARIC
BARBECUE
BARBERRY
BARBICAN
BARBITAL
BAREBACK
BAREFOOT
BARITONE
BARNACLE
BARNYARD
BARONAGE
BARONESS
BAROUCHE
BARRACKS
BARRATRY
BARRETTE
BASEBALL
BASEBORN
BASELESS
BASELINE
BASEMENT
BASILICA
BASILISK
BASSINET
BASSWOOD
BATHROBE
BATHROOM
BAYBERRY
CABOCHON
CABSTAND
CADUCEUS
CAFFEINE
CAGELING
CAKEWALK
CALABASH
CALADIUM
CALAMINE
CALAMITY
CALCULUS
CALENDAR
CALENDER
CALFSKIN
CALLBACK
CALLIOPE
CAMELLIA
CAMISOLE
CAMOMILE
CAMPAIGN
CAMPOREE
CAMSHAFT
CANADIAN
CANAILLE
CANALIZE
CANISTER
CANNABIS
CANNIBAL
CANONIZE
CANTICLE
CAPACITY
CAPESKIN
CAPRIOLE
CAPSICUM
CAPSULAR
CAPTIOUS
CAPUCHIN
CARACOLE
CARAPACE
CARDAMOM
CARDIGAN
CARDINAL
CAREFREE
CARELESS
CAREWORN
CARILLON
CARNAUBA
CARNIVAL
CAROTENE
CAROUSAL
CAROUSEL
CARRIAGE
CARRYALL
CARYATID
CASEMENT
CASEWORK
CASHMERE
CASSETTE
CASTAWAY
CASTRATE
CASUALTY
CATACOMB
CATALYZE
CATAPULT
CATARACT
CATCHALL
CATCHING
CATEGORY
CATHETER
CATHOLIC
CAUDILLO
CAULDRON
CAUSERIE
CAUSEWAY
CAUTIOUS
CAVALIER
DAFFODIL
DAIQUIRI
DAIRYING
DAIRYMAN
DAMNABLE
DANDRUFF
DANSEUSE
DARKLING
DARKROOM
DARKSOME
DATABASE
DATELESS
DATELINE
DAUGHTER
DAYBREAK
DAYDREAM
DAYLIGHT
EARNINGS
EARPHONE
FABULOUS
FACEDOWN
FACILITY
FACTIOUS
FACTOTUM
FADELESS
FAGOTING
FALCHION
FALLIBLE
FALSETTO
FALTBOAT
FAMILIAL
FAMILIAR
FANCIFUL
FANDANGO
FANLIGHT
FANTASIA
FAREWELL
FARMHAND
FARMLAND
FARMYARD
FAROUCHE
FARTHEST
FARTHING
FASCICLE
FASCISTA
FASTBACK
FASTNESS
FATALISM
FATALITY
FAUBOURG
FAVORITE
GADABOUT
GALLUSES
GAMECOCK
GAMESOME
GAMESTER
GANGLAND
GANGLING
GANGLION
GANGPLOW
GANGRENE
GANGSTER
GARDENIA
GARGOYLE
GARRISON
GASLIGHT
GASOLINE
GASWORKS
GATEPOST
GAUNTLET
HABANERA
HABITANT
HABITUAL
HACIENDA
HACKWORD
HAIRLINE
HALFBACK
HALFTONE
HALLMARK
HANDBALL
HANDBILL
HANDBOOK
HANDCUFF
HANDICAP
HANDMADE
HANDPICK
HANDRAIL
HANDSOME
HANDYMAN
HANGNAIL
HANGOVER
HANUKKAH
HARANGUE
HARDBACK
HARDBALL
HARDHACK
HARDSHIP
HARDTACK
HARDWARE
HARDWOOD
HAREBELL
HARMONIC
HARRIDAN
HATCHING
HATCHWAY
HAUTBOIS
HAWAIIAN
HAWKWEED
HAWTHORN
HAYSTACK
JACKBOOT
JACQUARD
JAILBIRD
JALOUSIE
JAMBOREE
JAPANESE
JAUNDICE
KAMAAINA
KAMIKAZE
KANGAROO
KATAKANA
LABURNUM
LACERATE
LACEWING
LACRIMAL
LACROSSE
LADYBIRD
LADYLIKE
LADYLOVE
LADYSHIP
LAMASERY
LAMBASTE
LAMBSKIN
LAMPBACK
LANDFALL
LANDFILL
LANDFORM
LANDLORD
LANDMARK
LANDMASS
LANDSMAN
LANDWARD
LANGUAGE
LANGUISH
LAPBOARD
LAPIDARY
LARBOARD
LARKSPUR
LASERJET
LATCHKEY
LATITUDE
LAUDANUM
LAUGHTER
LAUNCHER
LAUREATE
LAVATORY
LAVENDER
LAWGIVER
LAWMAKER
LAXATIVE
LAYERING
MACARONI
MACAROON
MACERATE
MACHISMO
MACKEREL
MACKINAW
MACPAINT
MADHOUSE
MADRIGAL
MAGAZINE
MAGDALEN
MAGICIAN
MAGNESIA
MAGNETIC
MAGNOLIA
MAHARAJA
MAHARANI
MAHOGANY
MAINLAND
MAINLINE
MAINMAST
MAINSAIL
MAINSTAY
MAINTAIN
MAJOLICA
MAJORITY
MALAMUTE
MALAPERT
MALARKEY
MALAWIAN
MALINGER
MALTREAT
MALTSTER
MANCIPLE
MANDAMUS
MANDARIN
MANDIBLE
MANDOLIN
MANDRAKE
MANEUVER
MANGROVE
MANIACAL
MANICURE
MANIFEST
MANIFOLD
MANNERED
MANNERLY
MANTELET
MANTILLA
MANTISSA
MANYFOLD
MARATHON
MARBLING
MARGRAVE
MARIACHI
MARIGOLD
MARINATE
MARITIME
MARJORAM
MARKDOWN
MARKSMAN
MARMOSET
MARQUESS
MARQUISE
MARRIAGE
MARTINET
MARZIPAN
MASSACRE
MASSEUSE
MASSLESS
MASTERLY
MASTHEAD
MASTODON
MATERIAL
MATERIEL
MATERNAL
MATTRESS
MATURATE
MATURITY
MAVERICK
MAXIMIZE
MAYAPPLE
NAINSOOK
NAMELESS
NAMESAKE
NAPOLEON
NARCOSIS
NARCOTIC
NASALIZE
NATALITY
NATIONAL
NATIVISM
NATIVITY
NAUSEATE
NAUTICAL
NAUTILUS
NAVIGATE
PACIFIER
PACIFISM
PAGINATE
PAINTING
PALATINE
PALEFACE
PALINODE
PALISADE
PALLIATE
PALMETTO

PALOMINO
PALPABLE
PAMPHLET
PANATELA
PANCREAS
PANDEMIC
PANDOWDY
PANELING
PANELIST
PANORAMA
PANTHEON
PANTSUIT
PARABOLA
PARADIGM
PARADISE
PARAFFIN
PARAKEET
PARALLAX
PARALLEL
PARALYZE
PARAMOUR
PARANOIA
PARASITE
PARDONER
PARFOCAL
PARIETAL
PARLANCE
PARMESAN
PAROXYSM
PARTERRE
PARTIBLE
PARTICLE
PARTISAN
PASSABLE
PASSBOOK
PASSOVER
PASSPORT
PASSWORD
PASTICHE
PASTILLE
PASTORAL
PASTRAMI
PATERNAL
PATHETIC
PATHOGEN
PATIENCE
PAVEMENT
PAVILION
PAWNSHOP
PAYCHECK
RADIATOR
RADIOMAN
RAILLERY
RAILROAD
RAINCOAT
RAINDROP
RAINFALL
RATIONAL
RATTLING
RAVENING
RAVENOUS
RAWBONED
SABOTAGE
SABOTEUR
SACRISTY
SADDUCEE
SAGAMORE
SAILBOAT
SAILFISH
SALESMAN
SALIVATE
SALUTARY
SAMARIUM
SANCTIFY
SANCTION
SANCTITY
SANDBANK
SANDWICH
SANGUINE
SANITARY
SANITIZE
SANSKRIT
SAPPHIRE
SARDONIC
SATURATE
SATURDAY
SAUCEPAN
SAUTERNE
SAWHORSE
TABULATE
TACITURN
TAFFRAIL
TAHITIAN
TAILCOAT
TAILGATE
TAILSPIN
TALESMAN
TALISMAN
TAMARACK
TAMARIND
TANGIBLE
TANTALUM
TAPESTRY
TAPEWORM
TARRAGON
TAXONOMY
TAXPAYER
VACATION
VACCINIA
VAGABOND
VAGRANCY
VALIDATE
VALUABLE
VALVULAR
VANADIUM
VANGUARD
VANQUISH
VAPORING
VAPORISH
VAPORIZE
VAPOROUS
VARIABLE
VARIANCE
VARICOSE
VARIETAL
VARIORUM
VARISTOR
VASCULAR
VAULTING
WAINSCOT
WAITRESS
WALKAWAY
WALKOVER
WARDROBE
WARDROOM
WARDSHIP
WAREROOM
WARFARIN
WARPLANE
WARRANTY
WASHABLE
WASHBOWL
WASHROOM
WATCHDOG
WATCHFUL
WATCHMAN
WATERLOO
WATERWAY
WAYFARER
YACHTING
ABATTOIR
ABDICATE
ABEYANCE
ABLATION
ABLATIVE
ABLUTION
ABNEGATE
ABNORMAL
ABORNING
ABORTION
ABRASIVE
ABROGATE
ABSCISSA
ABSENTEE
ABSINTHE
ABSOLUTE
ABSTRACT
ABSTRUSE
ABUNDANT
ABUTMENT
ABUTTALS
OBDURATE
OBEDIENT
OBITUARY
OBLATION
OBLIGATE
OBLIVION
OBSIDIAN
OBSOLETE
OBSTACLE
OBSTRUCT
ACADEMIC
ACANTHUS
ACCIDENT
ACCOLADE
ACCOUTRE
ACCREDIT
ACCURATE
ACCURSED
ACCUSTOM
ACERBATE
ACERBITY
ACIDHEAD
ACIDOSIS
ACOUSTIC
ACQUAINT
ACRIMONY
ACROSTIC
ACTINISM
ACTINIUM
ACTIVATE
ACTIVISM
ACTIVITY
ECLIPTIC
ECONOMIC
ICEBOUND
ICEHOUSE
OCCASION
OCCUPANT
SCABBARD
SCABROUS
SCAFFOLD
SCALABLE
SCALAWAG
SCALEPAN
SCALLION
SCANDIUM
SCAPULAR
SCARCELY
SCATHING
SCAVENGE
SCENARIO
SCHEDULE
SCHMALTZ
SCHOONER
SCIATICA
SCILICET
SCIMITAR
SCISSORS
SCOFFLAW
SCORPION
SCOTTISH
SCRABBLE
SCRAGGLY
SCRAMBLE
SCRIBBLE
SCROFULA
SCROUNGE
SCRUTINY
SCULLERY
SCULLION
SCULPTOR
ADDENDUM
ADDITION
ADDITIVE
ADEQUATE
ADHESION
ADHESIVE
ADJACENT
ADJUTANT
ADJUVANT
ADMONISH
ADOPTIVE
ADORABLE
ADULTERY
ADVISORY
ADVOCATE
EDGEWAYS
EDUCABLE
IDEALISM
IDEALIZE
IDEATION
IDENTIFY
IDENTITY
IDEOGRAM
IDEOLOGY
IDOLATER
IDOLATRY
ODOMETER
AEROLOGY
AERONAUT
AESTHETE
BEANBALL
BEARSKIN
BEATIFIC
BEAUTIFY
BECHUANA
BECOMING
BEDAZZLE
BEDSTEAD
BEECHNUT
BEFRIEND
BEFUDDLE
BEGGARLY
BEGRUDGE
BEHAVIOR
BEHEMOTH
BEHOLDEN
BELITTLE
BENEDICT
BENEFICE
BENTWOOD
BENZOATE
BEQUEATH
BERCEUSE
BEREAVED
BERIBERI
BERMUDAS
BESMIRCH
BESTIARY
BESTRIDE
BETATRON
BEVERAGE
BEWILDER
CELERITY
CELIBACY
CELIBATE
CELLULAR
CEMENTUM
CEMETERY
CENOBITE
CENOTAPH
CENTERED
CENTRIST
CEPHALIC
CERAMIST
CEREBRUM
CEREMENT
CEREMONY
CERULEAN
CERVICAL
CESAREAN
CESSPOOL
DEADBEAT
DEADLINE
DEADLOCK
DEADWOOD
DEATHBED
DEBILITY
DEBONAIR
DECANTER
DECEDENT
DECEMBER
DECIGRAM
DECIMATE
DECIPHER
DECISION
DECISIVE
DECKHAND
DECORATE
DECOROUS
DECREASE
DECREPIT
DEDICATE
DEERSKIN
DEFECATE
DEFIANCE
DEFINITE
DEFLOWER
DEFOREST
DEIONIZE
DEJECTED
DEKAGRAM
DELAWARE
DELEGATE
DELICACY
DELICATE
DELIRIUM
DELIVERY
DELUSION
DEMARCHE
DEMEANOR
DEMENTED
DEMENTIA
DEMIBOLD
DEMIJOHN
DEMOCRAT
DEMOLISH
DEMONIAC
DEMURRER
DENATURE
DENOUNCE
DEPONENT
DEPUTIZE
DERELICT
DEROGATE
DERRIERE
DESCRIBE
DESELECT
DESIROUS
DESOLATE
DESPATCH
DESTRUCT
DETACHED
DETHRONE
DETONATE
DETOXIFY
DETRITUS
DEVILISH
DEVOTION
DEWBERRY
DEXTROSE
FEARLESS
FEARSOME
FEASIBLE
FEBRUARY
FECKLESS
FEDERATE
FEEDBACK
FELDSPAR
FELICITY
FELLATIO
FEMININE
FEMINISM
FEROCITY
FERVENCY
FESTIVAL
FETCHING
GEMINATE
GEMOLOGY
GEMSTONE
GENDARME
GENERATE
GENEROUS
GENETICS
GENITALS
GENITIVE
GENOCIDE
GEODESIC
GEOMETRY
GERANIUM
GERMINAL
HEADACHE
HEADBAND
HEADGEAR
HEADLAND
HEADLINE
HEADLOCK
HEADLONG
HEADREST
HEADROOM
HEADSHIP
HEADSMAN
HEADWORD
HEADWORK
HEAVYSET
HEBRAISM
HECATOMB
HEDGEHOG
HEDGEHOP
HEDGEROW
HEDONISM
HEGEMONY
HEIGHTEN
HEIRLOOM
HELICOID
HELIPORT
HELLHOLE
HELMSMAN
HELPMATE
HELPMEET
HEMATITE
HENCHMAN
HEPATICA
HERALDIC
HERALDRY

HERCULES
HERDSMAN
HEREDITY
HEREFORD
HEREUNTO
HEREUPON
HEREWITH
HERITAGE
HERMETIC
HESITANT
HESITATE
JEOPARDY
JEREMIAD
JETTISON
KEELBOAT
KEELHAUL
KEEPSAKE
KERCHIEF
KEROSINE
KEYBOARD
KEYPUNCH
KEYSTONE
KEYWORDS
LEAPFROG
LEARNING
LEAVINGS
LECITHIN
LEFTOVER
LEGALISM
LEGATION
LEMONADE
LENGTHEN
LENITIVE
LETHARGY
LEUKEMIA
LEVERAGE
LEVITATE
MEALTIME
MEALYBUG
MEANTIME
MEATBALL
MECHANIC
MEDALIST
MEDICAID
MEDICARE
MEDICATE
MEDICINE
MEDIEVAL
MEDIOCRE
MEDITATE
MEGABYTE
MEGALITH
MELANISM
MELANOMA
MELODEON
MEMBRANE
MEMORIAL
MEMORIZE
MENHADEN
MENISCUS
MEPHITIC
MERCHANT
MERCURIC
MERIDIAN
MERINGUE
MESDAMES
MESHWORK
MESQUITE
MESSMATE
METAFILE
METAPHOR
METEORIC
METHANOL
METRICAL
NEBULIZE
NEBULOUS
NECKLACE
NECKLINE
NECROSIS
NEEDLESS
NEGATION
NEGATIVE
NEGLIGEE
NEIGHBOR
NEMATODE
NEONATAL
NEOPHYTE
NEOPLASM
NEPENTHE
NEPOTISM
NESTLING
NEURITIS
NEUROSIS
NEUROTIC
NEUTRINO
NEWCOMER
NEWFOUND
NEWLYWED
NEWSCAST
NEWSREEL
PECTORAL
PECULATE
PECULIAR
PEDAGOGY
PEDERAST
PEDESTAL
PEDICURE
PEDIGREE
PEDIMENT
PEDUNCLE
PEEPHOLE
PEERLESS
PEIGNOIR
PELLAGRA
PELLUCID
PEMMICAN
PENALIZE
PENCHANT
PENDULUM
PENITENT
PENKNIFE
PENLIGHT
PENOLOGY
PENSTOCK
PENTAGON
PENUMBRA
PERCEIVE
PERFECTO
PERFORCE
PERILUNE
PERIODIC
PERMEATE
PEROXIDE
PERSONAL
PERSPIRE
PERSUADE
PERVERSE
PETITION
PETTIFOG
PETULANT
REACTANT
REACTION
REACTIVE
REARWARD
REASSURE
REBUTTAL
RECEIVER
RECEPTOR
RECKLESS
RECORDER
RECOURSE
RECREANT
RECREATE
REDOLENT
REFERENT
REFERRAL
REFINERY
REFOREST
REFORMER
REGICIDE
REGIMENT
REGIONAL
REGISTER
REGISTRY
REGOLITH
REGULATE
REHEARSE
REINDEER
RELATION
RELATIVE
RELAXANT
RELEGATE
RELEVANT
RELIABLE
RELIANCE
RELIGION
RELOCATE
REMEDIAL
REMEMBER
REMITTAL
RENEGADE
RENOUNCE
RENOVATE
REPARTEE
REPEATED
REPORTER
REPRIEVE
REPRISAL
REPROACH
REPUBLIC
RESCRIPT
RESEARCH
RESEMBLE
RESERVED
RESIDENT
RESIDUAL
RESIDUUM
RESIGNED
RESISTOR
RESOLUTE
RESONANT
RESONATE
RESORTER
RESOURCE
RESPONSE
RESTLESS
RESTRAIN
RESTRICT
RETAINER
RETARDED
RETICENT
RETIRING
RETRENCH
RETRIEVE
RETROFIT
RETURNEE
REVANCHE
REVEILLE
REVENUER
REVEREND
REVERENT
REVERSAL
REVIEWER
REVIVIFY
REVOLVER
SEABOARD
SEACOAST
SEAFARER
SEAGOING
SEALSKIN
SEAMOUNT
SEAPLANE
SEASCAPE
SEASHORE
SEAWATER
SECURITY
SEDATIVE
SEDIMENT
SEDITION
SEDULOUS
SEEDLING
SEEDTIME
SEIGNEUR
SELECTEE
SELENITE
SELENIUM
SELFLESS
SELFSAME
SEMANTIC
SEMESTER
SEMINARY
SEMINOLE
SEMISOFT
SENSIBLE
SENSUOUS
SENTENCE
SENTIENT
SENTINEL
SEPARATE
SEQUENCE
SERAGLIO
SERENADE
SERGEANT
SEROLOGY
SERVITOR
SETSCREW
SEWERAGE
TEACHING
TEAMSTER
TEAMWORK
TEASPOON
TEETHING
TEETOTAL
TELECAST
TELEFILM
TELEGRAM
TELEPLAY
TELETHON
TELEVIEW
TELEVISE
TELLTALE
TEMERITY
TEMPLATE
TEMPORAL
TENANTRY
TENDENCY
TENEMENT
TENPENNY
TENTACLE
TEOSINTE
TERMINAL
TERMINUS
TERRAPIN
TERRIBLE
TERRIFIC
TERTIARY
TESTATOR
TESTICLE
TEUTONIC
TEXTBOOK
VEGANISM
VEGETATE
VEHEMENT
VELLEITY
VELOCITY
VENATION
VENDETTA
VENERATE
VENEREAL
VENGEFUL
VENOMOUS
VENUSIAN
VERACITY
VERBATIM
VERBIAGE
VERBOTEN
VERMOUTH
VERONICA
VERSICLE
VERTEBRA
VERTICAL
VESICANT
VESTMENT
VEXATION
WEAKFISH
WEAKLING
WEAKNESS
WEAPONRY
WELDMENT
WELLBORN
WELLHEAD
WEREWOLF
XENOLITH
YEARBOOK
YEARLING
YEARLONG
YEARNING
YEOMANRY
ZEPPELIN
AFFECTED
AFFERENT
AFFIANCE
AFFINITY
AFFLATUS
AFFRIGHT
AFLUTTER
AFTERTAX
EFFERENT
EFFUSION
OFFICIAL
OFFPRINT
OFFSHOOT
OFFSHORE
OFFSTAGE
AGERATUM
AGGRIEVE
AGITPROP
AGLITTER
AGNOSTIC
AGRARIAN
AGRONOMY
EGGPLANT
EGGSHELL
EGYPTIAN
IGNITION
IGNORANT
CHAIRMAN
CHAMBRAY
CHAMPION
CHANCERY
CHANDLER
CHANUKAH
CHAPBOOK
CHAPERON
CHAPLAIN
CHARADES
CHARCOAL
CHARISMA
CHARMING
CHASTISE
CHASTITY
CHASUBLE
CHECKERS
CHECKOFF
CHECKOUT
CHECKSUM
CHEERFUL
CHEMICAL
CHEMURGY
CHENILLE
CHEROKEE
CHESTNUT
CHEYENNE
CHIPMUNK
CHIPPEWA
CHITCHAT
CHIVALRY
CHLORIDE
CHLORINE
CHLORITE
CHOIRBOY
CHOLERIC
CHOWCHOW
CHRISTEN
CHRISTIE
CHROMIUM
CHUTZPAH
GHANAIAN
OHMMETER
PHANTASM
PHANTASY
PHARISEE
PHARMACY
PHASEOUT
PHEASANT
PHENOLIC
PHOSPHOR
PHRASING
PHYSICAL
PHYSIQUE
RHAPSODY
RHEOLOGY
RHEOSTAT
RHETORIC
RHOMBOID
RHYOLITE
SHAMBLES
SHAMROCK
SHANGHAI
SHANTUNG
SHEEPISH
SHEETING
SHELVING
SHEPHERD
SHILINGI
SHILLING
SHINBONE
SHINGLES
SHIPMATE
SHIPMENT
SHIPPING
SHIPWORM
SHIPYARD
SHIRRING
SHIRTING
SHOCKING
SHOELACE
SHOPLIFT
SHOPWORN
SHORTAGE
SHORTCUT
SHOSHONE
SHOULDER
SHOWCASE
SHOWDOWN
SHRAPNEL

SHREWISH
SHUTDOWN
THALAMUS
THALLIUM
THANKFUL
THEOLOGY
THEORIZE
THEREFOR
THESPIAN
THIAMINE
THICKSET
THIEVERY
THIRTEEN
THOROUGH
THOUSAND
THRASHER
THREATEN
THRENODY
THROMBUS
THROTTLE
THRUSTER
THURSDAY
WHARFAGE
WHATEVER
WHENEVER
WHEREVER
WHIPCORD
WHIPLASH
WHITECAP
WHITEFLY
WHODUNIT
WHOMEVER
WHOPPING
AIGRETTE
AIRBORNE
AIRBRUSH
AIRCRAFT
AIRDROME
AIRFIELD
AIRFRAME
AIRLINER
AIRPLANE
AIRSPACE
AIRSPEED
AIRSTRIP
AIRTIGHT
BIANNUAL
BIATHLON
BIBULOUS
BICONVEX
BICUSPID
BIDDABLE
BIENNIAL
BIENNIUM
BIFOCALS
BILLFOLD
BILLHEAD
BINAURAL
BINNACLE
BIOCIDAL
BIRACIAL
BIRDBATH
BIRDLIME
BIRDSEED
BIRTHDAY
BISEXUAL
BITSTOCK
BIWEEKLY
BIYEARLY
CICATRIX
CICERONE
CINCHONA
CINCTURE
CINNABAR
CINNAMON
CIRCUITY
CIRCULAR
CISLUNAR
CITATION
CIVILIAN
CIVILITY
CIVILIZE
DIABETES
DIABOLIC
DIAGONAL
DIALOGUE
DIALYSIS
DIAMETER
DIANTHUS
DIAPASON
DIARRHEA
DIASTOLE
DIATOMIC
DIATRIBE
DICTATOR
DIDACTIC
DIELDRIN
DILATORY
DILIGENT
DIMINISH
DINGBATS
DINOSAUR
DIPLOMAT
DIPSTICK
DIRECTOR
DISABUSE
DISAGREE
DISALLOW
DISARRAY
DISASTER
DISBURSE
DISCIPLE
DISCLAIM
DISCLOSE
DISCOLOR
DISCOUNT
DISCOVER
DISCREET
DISCRETE
DISFAVOR
DISGORGE
DISGRACE
DISGUISE
DISHEVEL
DISHONOR
DISINTER
DISJOINT
DISKETTE
DISLODGE
DISLOYAL
DISMOUNT
DISORDER
DISPATCH
DISPENSE
DISPERSE
DISPIRIT
DISPLACE
DISPOSAL
DISPROVE
DISQUIET
DISSEVER
DISSOLVE
DISSUADE
DISTANCE
DISTASTE
DISTINCT
DISTRACT
DISTRAIT
DISTRESS
DISTRICT
DISTRUST
DISUNITE
DISUNITY
DIURETIC
DIVAGATE
DIVIDEND
DIVINITY
DIVISION
DIVISIVE
DIVORCEE
EIGHTEEN
FIBROSIS
FIDELITY
FIGURINE
FILAMENT
FILIGREE
FILIPINO
FILTRATE
FINALIST
FINALIZE
FINESPUN
FIREBALL
FIREBOAT
FIREBOMB
FIRECLAY
FIREDAMP
FIREPLUG
FIRESIDE
FIRETRAP
FIREWOOD
FIREWORK
FIRMWARE
FISHBOWL
FISHHOOK
FISHWIFE
FIXATION
FIXATIVE
GIGABYTE
GIGANTIC
GIMCRACK
GINGERLY
GIVEAWAY
HIBISCUS
HIDEAWAY
HIGHBALL
HIGHBORN
HIGHBRED
HIGHBROW
HIGHLAND
HIGHNESS
HIGHROAD
HIGHTAIL
HILLSIDE
HINDMOST
HINDUISM
HIRELING
HISPANIC
HITHERTO
JINGOISM
KIBITZER
KICKBACK
KICKSHAW
KIELBASA
KILLDEER
KILOBYTE
KILOGRAM
KILOVOLT
KILOWATT
KINDLING
KINETICS
KINGBOLT
LIBATION
LIBERATE
LIBRETTO
LICENSEE
LICORICE
LIFEBOAT
LIFELINE
LIFELONG
LIFETIME
LIFEWORK
LIGAMENT
LIGATURE
LIGNEOUS
LIKENESS
LIKEWISE
LIMEKILN
LIMERICK
LIMONITE
LINCHPIN
LINESMAN
LINGERIE
LINGUIST
LINIMENT
LINOLEUM
LIPSTICK
LISTLESS
LITERARY
LITERATE
LITERATI
LITIGANT
LITIGATE
LITTORAL
LIVELONG
LIVERISH
MICROBUS
MIDDLING
MIDNIGHT
MIDPOINT
MIDSHIPS
MIGRAINE
MILEPOST
MILESIMO
MILITANT
MILITARY
MILITATE
MILKMAID
MILKWEED
MILLIARD
MILLIBAR
MILLIEME
MILLINER
MILLPOND
MILLRACE
MINATORY
MINDLESS
MINIBIKE
MINIMIZE
MINISTER
MINISTRY
MINORITY
MINSTREL
MISAPPLY
MISBRAND
MISCARRY
MISCHIEF
MISCIBLE
MISCOUNT
MISDOING
MISHMASH
MISJUDGE
MISLABEL
MISMATCH
MISNOMER
MISPLACE
MISPRINT
MISQUOTE
MISSHAPE
MISSPELL
MISSPEND
MISSTATE
MISTAKEN
MISTREAT
MISTRESS
MISTRIAL
MISTRUST
MISUSAGE
MITIGATE
NICKNAME
NICOTINE
NIGERIAN
NIGEROIS
NIGGLING
NIHILISM
NINEPINS
NINETEEN
NITROGEN
OILCLOTH
OINTMENT
PICAYUNE
PICKEREL
PICKINGS
PICKLOCK
PIDDLING
PIEPLANT
PILASTER
PILCHARD
PILOTAGE
PIMIENTO
PINAFORE
PINNACLE
PINOCHLE
PINPOINT
PINPRICK
PINWHEEL
PIPELINE
PITCHMAN
PITIABLE
PITILESS
PITTANCE
PIXELATE
PIZZERIA
RIBOSOME
RICOCHET
RIDICULE
RIFFRAFF
RIGHTFUL
RINGWORM
RIPARIAN
RIVERBED
SIBILANT
SICKNESS
SIDEKICK
SIDELONG
SIDEREAL
SIDERITE
SIDESHOW
SIDESTEP
SIDEWALK
SIDEWALL
SIDEWAYS
SIGNPOST
SILENCER
SILICATE
SILICIFY
SILICONE
SIMONIZE
SIMPLIFY
SIMULATE
SINECURE
SINGULAR
SINISTER
SINKHOLE
SITUATED
SIXPENCE
TICKLISH
TIDELAND
TIGHTWAD
TIMBERED
TIMELESS
TIMEWORN
TIMOROUS
TINCTURE
TINPLATE
TINSMITH
TIRELESS
TIRESOME
TITANIUM
TITILATE
TITIVATE
TITMOUSE
VIATICUM
VIBURNUM
VICARAGE
VICINAGE
VICINITY
VICTORIA
VIETCONG
VIGILANT
VIGNETTE
VIGOROUS
VILLAGER
VILLAINY
VINCIBLE
VINEGARY
VINEYARD
VIOLABLE
VIOLENCE
VIRGINAL
VIROLOGY
VIRTUOSO
VIRTUOUS
VIRULENT
VISCERAL
VISCOUNT
VISICALC
VISITANT
VITALITY
VITALIZE
VITREOUS
VIVACITY
VIVARIUM
WILDFIRE
WILDFOWL
WILDLIFE
WILDWOOD
WILLIWAW
WINDBURN
WINDFALL
WINDLASS
WINDMILL
WINDPIPE
WINDWARD
WINESHOP
WINGDING
WINGSPAN
WIREDRAW
WIREHAIR
WIRELESS
WIREWORM
WISEACRE
WISHBONE
WISTARIA
WISTERIA
WITCHERY
WITCHING
WITHDRAW
WITHHOLD
WIZARDRY
YIELDING
EKISTICS
SKELETON
SKILLFUL
SKIMMING
SKIRMISH
SKITTISH

SKULLCAP
SKYLIGHT
ALACRITY
ALARMIST
ALBACORE
ALBANIAN
ALDERMAN
ALEATORY
ALEHOUSE
ALFRESCO
ALGERIAN
ALIASING
ALIENATE
ALIENIST
ALIZARIN
ALKALOID
ALLEGORY
ALLELUIA
ALLERGEN
ALLEYWAY
ALLIANCE
ALLOCATE
ALLSPICE
ALLUVIUM
ALMIGHTY
ALOPECIA
ALPHABET
ALTHOUGH
ALTITUDE
ALTRUISM
ALUMINUM
BLACKING
BLACKOUT
BLACKTOP
BLESSING
BLISSFUL
BLIZZARD
BLOCKADE
BLOOMERS
BLOWPIPE
BLUDGEON
BLUEBELL
BLUEBIRD
BLUEFISH
BLUENOSE
CLAIMANT
CLAMBAKE
CLAPTRAP
CLARINET
CLASSIFY
CLAVICLE
CLAYMORE
CLEARING
CLEAVAGE
CLEMATIS
CLEMENCY
CLERICAL

CLINCHER
CLINICAL
CLIPPING
CLITORIS
CLOISTER
CLOSEOUT
CLOTHIER
CLOTHING
CLOUDLET
CLUBFOOT
ELECTION
ELECTIVE
ELECTRIC
ELECTRON
ELEGANCE
ELEPHANT
ELEVATOR
ELIGIBLE
ELLIPSIS
ELONGATE
ELOQUENT
FLAGPOLE
FLAGRANT
FLAGSHIP
FLAMBEAU
FLAMENCO
FLAMEOUT
FLAMINGO
FLAPJACK
FLASHGUN
FLASHING
FLATBOAT
FLATFISH
FLATFOOT
FLATHEAD
FLATIRON
FLATLAND
FLATTERY
FLATWARE
FLAUTIST
FLEABANE
FLEABITE
FLEETING
FLESHPOT
FLEXIBLE
FLIMFLAM
FLIPPANT
FLOTILLA
FLOUNDER
FLOURISH
FLUIDRAM
FLUORIDE
FLUORINE
FLUORITE
FLYBLOWN
FLYPAPER
FLYSPECK

FLYWHEEL
GLABROUS
GLACIATE
GLADSOME
GLASSFUL
GLAUCOMA
GLOAMING
GLOBULIN
GLORIOUS
GLOSSARY
GLOWWORM
GLOXINIA
GLYCERIN
GLYCEROL
GLYCOGEN
ILLINOIS
ILLUMINE
ILLUSION
ILLUSIVE
ILLUSORY
OLEANDER
PLACENTA
PLANGENT
PLANKING
PLANKTON
PLANTAIN
PLATFORM
PLATINUM
PLATYPUS
PLAYBACK
PLAYBILL
PLAYBOOK
PLAYGOER
PLAYMATE
PLAYSUIT
PLEASANT
PLEASING
PLEASURE
PLEBEIAN
PLECTRUM
PLETHORA
PLEURISY
PLUMBING
SLATTERN
SLIPKNOT
SLIPPERY
SLIPSHOD
SLOVENLY
SLUGGARD
SLUGGISH
SLUMLORD
ULCERATE
ULTERIOR
ULTIMATE
AMARANTH
AMBIENCE
AMBITION

AMBROSIA
AMBULANT
AMENABLE
AMERICAN
AMETHYST
AMICABLE
AMMONIUM
AMOEBOID
AMORTIZE
AMPERAGE
AMPUTATE
EMACIATE
EMBATTLE
EMBEZZLE
EMBITTER
EMBLAZON
EMBOLDEN
EMBOLISM
EMERITUS
EMIGRATE
EMINENCE
EMISSARY
EMOTICON
EMPHASIS
EMPHATIC
EMPLOYEE
EMPORIUM
EMPYREAN
EMULSIFY
EMULSION
IMBECILE
IMITABLE
IMMANENT
IMMATURE
IMMINENT
IMMOBILE
IMMODEST
IMMOLATE
IMMORTAL
IMMOTILE
IMMUNIZE
IMPACTED
IMPELLER
IMPERIAL
IMPETIGO
IMPLICIT
IMPOLITE
IMPOSING
IMPOSTOR
IMPOTENT
IMPRISON
IMPROPER
IMPUDENT
IMPUNITY
SMALLPOX
UMBRELLA
ANACONDA

ANAEROBE
ANALOGUE
ANALYSIS
ANATHEMA
ANCESTOR
ANCESTRY
ANDROGEN
ANECDOTE
ANECHOIC
ANGELICA
ANGLICAN
ANGSTROM
ANISETTE
ANNOTATE
ANNOUNCE
ANTEATER
ANTEDATE
ANTELOPE
ANTERIOR
ANTEROOM
ANTHROPO
ANTIBODY
ANTIDOTE
ANTIMONY
ANTINOMY
ANTIPODE
ANTIPOPE
ANYPLACE
ANYTHING
ANYWHERE
ENCEINTE
ENCIPHER
ENCIRCLE
ENCOMIUM
ENCROACH
ENCUMBER
ENDANGER
ENDEAVOR
ENERGIZE
ENERVATE
ENFEEBLE
ENFILADE
ENGAGING
ENGENDER
ENGINEER
ENORMITY
ENORMOUS
ENSCONCE
ENSEMBLE
ENSHRINE
ENSHROUD
ENSILAGE
ENTANGLE
ENTHRALL
ENTHRONE
ENTIRETY
ENTRAILS

ENTRANCE
ENTRENCH
ENURESIS
ENVELOPE
ENVIABLE
ENVIRONS
ENVISAGE
INCHOATE
INCHWORM
INCIDENT
INCISION
INCISIVE
INCOMING
INCREASE
INCUBATE
INCUMBER
INDEBTED
INDECENT
INDIAMAN
INDICATE
INDIGENT
INDIRECT
INDOLENT
INDUCTEE
INDURATE
INDUSTRY
INEDITED
INERRANT
INEXPERT
INFAMOUS
INFANTRY
INFERIOR
INFERNAL
INFINITE
INFINITY
INFOBAHN
INFORMAL
INFORMED
INFORMER
INFRADIG
INFRARED
INFRINGE
INGUINAL
INHALANT
INHERENT
INHUMANE
INIMICAL
INIQUITY
INITIATE
INKSTAND
INNOCENT
INNOVATE
INNUENDO
INSCRIBE
INSECURE
INSIGNIA
INSOLENT

INSOMNIA
INSOMUCH
INSPIRIT
INSTANCE
INSTINCT
INSTRUCT
INSULATE
INTAGLIO
INTEGRAL
INTENDED
INTERCOM
INTEREST
INTERIOR
INTERMIT
INTERMIX
INTERNAL
INTERNEE
INTERNET
INTERROG
INTERVAL
INTIMATE
INTRADOS
INTRENCH
INTREPID
INTRIGUE
INTROMIT
INUNDATE
INVASION
INVEIGLE
INVERTER
INVIABLE
INVITING
INVOLUTE
INVOLVED
INWARDLY
KNAPSACK
KNEEHOLE
KNICKERS
KNITWEAR
KNOCKOUT
KNOTHOLE
MNEMONIC
ONCOMING
ONLOOKER
ONONDAGA
SNAPSHOT
SNOBBERY
SNOWBALL
SNOWBANK
SNOWDROP
SNOWFALL
SNOWPLOW
SNOWSHOE
UNAWARES
UNBEATEN
UNBELIEF
UNBIASED

UNBIDDEN
UNBODIED
UNBOLTED
UNBROKEN
UNBUCKLE
UNBURDEN
UNBUTTON
UNCHASTE
UNCHURCH
UNCLENCH
UNCLOTHE
UNCOMMON
UNCOUPLE
UNCTUOUS
UNDERACT
UNDERAGE
UNDERARM
UNDERBID
UNDERCUT
UNDERDOG
UNDERFUR
UNDERLIE
UNDERLIP
UNDERPAY
UNDERSEA
UNDERTOW
UNDULANT
UNDULATE
UNEARNED
UNENDING
UNERRING
UNFASTEN
UNFETTER
UNFILIAL
UNFORMED
UNFREEZE
UNGAINLY
UNGULATE
UNIAXIAL
UNICYCLE
UNIONISM
UNIONIZE
UNIVALVE
UNIVERSE
UNKINDLY
UNLAWFUL
UNLEADED
UNLIKELY
UNLIMBER
UNLOOSEN
UNLOVELY
UNMUZZLE
UNPERSON
UNRIDDLE
UNSADDLE
UNSAVORY
UNSEEMLY

UNSETTLE
UNSHAPED
UNSOUGHT
UNSPRUNG
UNSTABLE
UNSTEADY
UNSTRUNG
UNTANGLE
UNTAUGHT
UNTIMELY
UNTOWARD
UNVOICED
UNWIELDY
UNWONTED
UNWORTHY
UNZIPPED
BOASTFUL
BOBOLINK
BOBWHITE
BODILESS
BODYWORK
BOGEYMAN
BOHEMIAN
BOLDFACE
BOLLWORM
BONDSMAN
BONHOMIE
BOOKCASE
BOOKMARK
BOOKWORM
BOOTLESS
BORDELLO
BOTULISM
BOUFFANT
BOUILLON
BOUNDARY
BOUTIQUE
BOWSPRIT
COACHMAN
COAGULUM
COALESCE
COAUTHOR
COCKATOO
COCKCROW
COCKEREL
COCKSURE
COCKTAIL
COGITATE
COGNOMEN
COGWHEEL
COHERENT
COHESION
COIFFEUR
COIFFURE
COINCIDE
COLANDER
COLESLAW
COLISEUM
COLLAPSE
COLLIERY
COLLOQUY
COLONIAL
COLONIST
COLONIZE
COLOPHON
COLOSSAL
COLOSSUS
COMANCHE
COMBINGS
COMEBACK
COMEDIAN
COMEDOWN
COMMANDO
COMMENCE
COMMERCE
COMMONER
COMMUNAL
COMPILER
COMPLAIN
COMPLEAT
COMPLETE
COMPOUND
COMPRESS
COMPRISE
COMPUTER
CONCEIVE
CONCERTO
CONCLAVE
CONCLUDE
CONCRETE
CONDENSE
CONFETTI
CONFINES
CONFLICT
CONFOCAL
CONFOUND
CONFRERE
CONFRONT
CONGENER
CONGRESS
CONJUGAL
CONJUNCT
CONQUEST
CONSERVE
CONSIDER
CONSOMME
CONSPIRE
CONSTANT
CONSTRUE
CONTEMPT
CONTINUE
CONTRACT
CONTRAIL
CONTRARY
CONTRAST
CONTRITE
CONTRIVE
CONVERGE
CONVERSE
CONVINCE
CONVULSE
COOKBOOK
COONSKIN
COPPERAS
COPULATE
COPYBOOK
COPYDESK
COQUETTE
CORDLESS
CORDOVAN
CORDUROY
CORNCRIB
CORNMEAL
CORONACH
CORONARY
CORPORAL
CORPSMAN
CORRIDOR
CORUNDUM
CORVETTE
COSIGNER
COSMETIC
COUCHANT
COUNTESS
COUPLING
COURTESY
COURTIER
COVENANT
COVERAGE
COVERALL
COVERLET
COXSWAIN
DOCKHAND
DOCKYARD
DOCTRINE
DOCUMENT
DOGFIGHT
DOGGEREL
DOGHOUSE
DOLDRUMS
DOLOMITE
DOMESTIC
DOMICILE
DOMINATE
DOMINEER
DOMINION
DONATION
DOOMSDAY
DOORJAMB
DOORKNOB
DOORSTEP
DOORYARD
DORMOUSE
DOUBLOON
DOUBTFUL
DOUGHBOY
DOUGHNUT
DOVETAIL
DOWNBEAT
DOWNCAST
DOWNFALL
DOWNHILL
DOWNLOAD
DOWNPOUR
DOWNTOWN
DOWNTURN
DOWNWARD
DOWNWIND
DOXOLOGY
FOLDAWAY
FOLDBOAT
FOLDEROL
FOLIATED
FOLKLORE
FOLLICLE
FOOLSCAP
FOOTBALL
FOOTFALL
FOOTHILL
FOOTHOLD
FOOTLESS
FOOTLING
FOOTNOTE
FOOTPATH
FOOTRACE
FOOTREST
FOOTSORE
FOOTSTEP
FOOTWEAR
FOOTWORK
FORCIBLE
FOREBEAR
FOREBODE
FORECAST
FOREDOOM
FOREFEND
FOREFOOT
FOREGONE
FOREHAND
FOREHEAD
FOREKNOW
FORELADY
FORELAND
FORELIMB
FORELOCK
FOREMAST
FOREMOST
FORENAME
FORENOON
FORENSIC
FOREPART
FORESAIL
FORESKIN
FORESTRY
FORETELL
FOREWARN
FOREWORD
FORKLIFT
FORMERLY
FORMLESS
FORSOOTH
FORSWEAR
FORTRESS
FORTUITY
FORWARDS
FOUNTAIN
FOURFOLD
FOURSOME
FOURTEEN
FOXGLOVE
FOXHOUND
GOALPOST
GOATHERD
GOATSKIN
GODCHILD
GOLDFISH
GONFALON
GOODNESS
GOODWIFE
GOODWILL
GOOFBALL
GORGEOUS
GOSSAMER
GOURMAND
GOVERNOR
HOARDING
HOGSHEAD
HOLDOVER
HOLINESS
HOLOGRAM
HOLSTEIN
HOMEBODY
HOMEBRED
HOMELAND
HOMEMADE
HOMEROOM
HOMESICK
HOMESPUN
HOMEWARD
HOMEWORK
HOMICIDE
HONEYDEW
HONORARY
HOODWINK
HOOKWORM
HOOLIGAN
HOOSEGOW
HORMONAL
HORNBOOK
HORNPIPE
HOROLOGY
HORRIBLE
HORSEFLY
HORSEMAN
HOSPITAL
HOSTELRY
HOTHOUSE
HOUSEBOY
HOUSEFLY
HOUSETOP
HOWITZER
JONGLEUR
JOYSTICK
KOHLRABI
KOLINSKY
LOANWORD
LOATHING
LOBOTOMY
LOCALITY
LOCALIZE
LOCATION
LOCKSTEP
LOCOWEED
LOCUTION
LODESTAR
LODGMENT
LOGOTYPE
LOLLIPOP
LOLLYGAG
LONESOME
LONGBOAT
LONGHAIR
LONGHAND
LONGHORN
LONGTIME
LONGUEUR
LOOPHOLE
LOPSIDED
LORDSHIP
LOVEBIRD
LOVELORN
LOVESICK
LOYALIST
MOBILIZE
MOCCASIN
MODERATE
MODULATE
MOISTURE
MOLASSES
MOLECULE
MOLEHILL
MOLESKIN
MOMENTUM
MONARCHY
MONASTIC
MONAURAL
MONETARY
MONGOOSE
MONITION
MONITORY
MONOGAMY
MONOGRAM
MONOLITH
MONOPOLY
MONORAIL
MONOTONE
MONOXIDE
MONSIEUR
MONUMENT
MOONBEAM
MOORLAND
MORALIST
MORALITY
MORALIZE
MOREOVER
MORIBUND
MOROCCAN
MORPHEME
MORPHINE
MORTGAGE
MORTUARY
MOSQUITO
MOSSBACK
MOTHBALL
MOTIVATE
MOTORCAR
MOTORIZE
MOTORMAN
MOTOROLA
MOUNTAIN
MOUNTING
MOURNFUL
MOURNING
MOVEMENT
NOBELIST
NOBELIUM
NOBILITY
NOBLEMAN
NOCTURNE
NOMINATE
NONDAIRY
NONESUCH
NONEVENT
NONMETAL
NONRIGID
NONSENSE
NONSTICK
NONUNION
NOONTIDE
NOONTIME
NORSEMAN
NOTARIAL
NOTARIZE
NOTATION
NOTEBOOK
NOTIONAL
NOVELIZE
NOVEMBER
NOWADAYS
POCKMARK
PODIATRY
POIGNANT
POKEWEED
POLARITY
POLARIZE
POLESTAR
POLITICK
POLITICO
POLITICS
POLLIWOG
POLLSTER
POLONIUM
POLTROON
POLYGAMY
POLYGLOT
POLYMATH
PONYTAIL
POPINJAY
POPULACE
POPULATE
POPULIST
POPULOUS
PORPHYRY
PORPOISE
PORRIDGE
PORTABLE
PORTHOLE
PORTIERE
PORTRAIT
POSITION
POSITIVE
POSITRON
POSSIBLE
POSTCARD
POSTDATE
POSTHOLE
POSTLUDE
POSTMARK
POSTPAID
POSTPONE
POTATION
POTBELLY
POTSHERD
POULTICE
POUNDAGE
ROADSIDE

ROADSTER
ROADWORK
ROCKETRY
ROCKFALL
ROLLBACK
ROMANIAN
ROMANTIC
ROOFTREE
ROOMETTE
ROOMMATE
ROSEBUSH
ROSEMARY
ROSEWOOD
ROUGHAGE
ROULETTE
ROUTEMAN
ROYALIST
SOBRIETY
SOCIABLE
SOFTBALL
SOFTWARE
SOFTWOOD
SOLARIUM
SOLDIERY
SOLECISM
SOLENOID
SOLIDIFY
SOLITARY
SOLITUDE
SOLSTICE
SOLUTION
SOLVENCY
SOMBRERO
SOMEBODY
SOMERSET
SOMETIME
SOMEWHAT
SONATINA
SONGBIRD
SONGSTER
SONOROUS
SORORITY
SORPTION
SOUTHPAW
SOUVENIR
TOBOGGAN
TOGETHER
TOILETRY
TOILETTE
TOILWORN
TOKENISM
TOLERATE
TOLLBOTH
TOLLGATE
TOMAHAWK
TOMORROW
TONALITY

TOPOLOGY
TOPSIDES
TOREADOR
TORTILLA
TORTOISE
TORTUOUS
TOTALITY
TOUCHING
TOWELING
TOWERING
TOWNSHIP
TOWNSMAN
VOCALIST
VOCALIZE
VOCATION
VOCATIVE
VOLATILE
VOLCANIC
VOLITION
VOLPLANE
VOYAGEUR
WOMANISH
WONDROUS
WOODBINE
WOODCOCK
WOODLAND
WOODNOTE
WOODPILE
WOODRUFF
WOODSHED
WOODSMAN
WOODWIND
WOODWORK
WOOLSACK
WORDBOOK
WORDPLAY
WORDSTAR
WORKABLE
WORKADAY
WORKBOOK
WORKROOM
WORKSHOP
WORMHOLE
WORMWOOD
YOUNGISH
YOURSELF
YOUTHFUL
ZOOPHYTE
ZOOSPORE
APERITIF
APERTURE
APHANITE
APHELION
APHORISM
APOLOGIA
APOPLEXY
APOSTASY

APOTHEGM
APPANAGE
APPARENT
APPELLEE
APPENDIX
APPETITE
APPLAUSE
APPLIQUE
APPOSITE
APPRAISE
APPROACH
APPROVAL
APTITUDE
EPIDEMIC
EPILEPSY
EPILOGUE
EPIPHANY
OPENWORK
OPERABLE
OPERANDS
OPERETTA
OPPONENT
OPPOSITE
OPTICIAN
OPTIMISM
OPUSCULE
SPACEMAN
SPACIOUS
SPANIARD
SPANKING
SPECIFIC
SPECIMEN
SPECIOUS
SPECTRAL
SPECTRUM
SPEEDWAY
SPHAGNUM
SPHEROID
SPILLWAY
SPINSTER
SPIRITED
SPITBALL
SPITTOON
SPLATTER
SPLENDID
SPLENDOR
SPLINTER
SPLUTTER
SPOOLING
SPORADIC
SPRINKLE
SPROCKET
SPURIOUS
SPYGLASS
UPCOMING
UPGROWTH
UPHEAVAL

UPPERCUT
UPRISING
UPSTAIRS
UPSTREAM
UPSTROKE
UPTHRUST
AQUACADE
AQUANAUT
AQUARIUM
AQUEDUCT
AQUILINE
EQUALIZE
EQUATION
EQUIPAGE
SQUABBLE
SQUADRON
SQUANDER
SQUEEGEE
SQUIRREL
ARACHNID
ARBALEST
ARBOREAL
ARCHDUKE
ARGUABLE
ARGUMENT
ARMAMENT
ARMATURE
ARMCHAIR
ARMORIAL
ARMYWORM
ARPEGGIO
ARROGANT
ARROGATE
ARTERIAL
ARTIFACT
ARTIFICE
ARTISTIC
ARTISTRY
BRACELET
BRACKISH
BRAGGART
BRAKEMAN
BRANDISH
BREAKAGE
BREAKOUT
BREEDING
BRETHREN
BREVIARY
BRICKBAT
BRIGHTEN
BRINDLED
BRISLING
BRITCHES
BROCCOLI
BROCHURE
BROMIDIC
BRONCHUS

BROOKLET
BROUGHAM
BROUHAHA
BROWBEAT
BROWNOUT
CRACKPOT
CRAWFISH
CRAYFISH
CREAMERY
CREATION
CREATURE
CREDENCE
CREDENZA
CREDIBLE
CREDITOR
CREEPING
CREMAINS
CREOSOTE
CRESCENT
CRETONNE
CREVASSE
CRIBBAGE
CRIMINAL
CRITICAL
CRITIQUE
CROCKERY
CROPLAND
CROSSBAR
CROSSBOW
CROSSCUT
CROSSING
CROTCHET
CROUPIER
CROWFOOT
CRUCIBLE
CRUCIFIX
CRUZEIRO
CRYOLITE
DRAGOMAN
DRAINAGE
DRAUGHTS
DRAWBACK
DREADFUL
DRESSAGE
DRESSING
DRIVEWAY
DROPKICK
DRUGGIST
DRUMBEAT
DRUNKARD
ERECTILE
ERECTION
ERYTHEMA
FRACTION
FRACTURE
FRAGMENT
FRAGRANT

FRANCIUM
FREEBORN
FREEDMAN
FREEHAND
FREEHOLD
FREELOAD
FREEWILL
FRENETIC
FREQUENT
FRESHMAN
FRETWORK
FRICTION
FRIGHTEN
FRIPPERY
FRONTAGE
FRONTIER
FROSTING
FROUFROU
FRUCTIFY
FRUITION
GRACIOUS
GRADIENT
GRADUATE
GRAFFITO
GRANDEUR
GRANDSON
GRANULAR
GRAPHITE
GRASPING
GRATEFUL
GRATUITY
GRAVAMEN
GRAYLING
GREEKING
GREENERY
GREETING
GRIDIRON
GRIEVOUS
GRIZZLED
GROSBEAK
GROSCHEN
GROUNDER
GRUELING
GRUESOME
IRONCLAD
IRONWARE
IRONWEED
IRONWOOD
IRONWORK
IROQUOIS
IRRIGATE
IRRITATE
ORANGERY
ORATORIO
ORDINARY
ORDINATE
ORDNANCE

ORGANISM
ORGANIST
ORGANIZE
ORGULOUS
ORIENTAL
ORIGINAL
ORNAMENT
ORTHODOX
ORTHOEPY
PRACTICE
PRATFALL
PRATIQUE
PREAMBLE
PRECINCT
PRECIOUS
PRECLUDE
PREEXIST
PREGNANT
PREJUDGE
PREMIERE
PREMOLAR
PRENATAL
PREPRESS
PRESENCE
PRESERVE
PRESIDIO
PRESSING
PRESSMAN
PRESSURE
PRESTIGE
PRETENSE
PRETERIT
PRETTIFY
PREVIOUS
PRIMEVAL
PRIMROSE
PRINCESS
PRINTING
PRINTOUT
PRISONER
PRISTINE
PROBABLE
PROCAINE
PROCEEDS
PROCLAIM
PRODIGAL
PROFOUND
PROGRESS
PROHIBIT
PROLIFIC
PROLOGUE
PROMOTER
PROPERTY
PROPHECY
PROPHESY
PROPOUND
PROROGUE

PROSPECT
PROSTATE
PROTOCOL
PROTRACT
PROTRUDE
PROVIDED
PROVINCE
PRURIENT
TRACKAGE
TRACTATE
TRACTION
TRAINING
TRAINMAN
TRANQUIL
TRANSACT
TRANSEPT
TRANSFER
TRANSFIX
TRANSMIT
TRAPDOOR
TRAPPING
TRAPROCK
TRAVERSE
TRAVESTY
TREASURE
TREASURY
TREATISE
TRENCHER
TRESPASS
TRIANGLE
TRIBUNAL
TRICHINA
TRICKERY
TRICOLOR
TRICYCLE
TRIFLING
TRILLION
TRILLIUM
TRIMARAN
TRIMETER
TRIMMING
TRIPTYCH
TRIUMVIR
TROMBONE
TROUSERS
TRUCKAGE
TRUETYPE
TRUMPERY
TRUNCATE
TRUSTFUL
TRUTHFUL
URBANITE
URBANIZE
WRAPPING
WRATHFUL
WRECKAGE
WRETCHED

WRIGGLER
WRISTLET
WRONGFUL
ASBESTOS
ASPERITY
ASPHODEL
ASPHYXIA
ASPIRANT
ASPIRATE
ASSASSIN
ASSEMBLE
ASSEMBLY
ASSORTED
ASTATINE
ASTERISK
ASTEROID
ASTONISH
ESCALATE
ESCALLOP
ESCAPADE
ESCAPISM
ESCAROLE
ESOTERIC
ESPALIER
ESPECIAL
ESPOUSAL
ESPRESSO
ESTIMATE
ESTONIAN
ESTRANGE
ESTROGEN
ISLANDER
ISOPRENE
ISOSTASY
ISOTHERM
ISOTONIC
ISSUANCE
ISTHMIAN
OSCULATE
PSALMODY
USUFRUCT
USURIOUS
ATHLETIC
ATOMIZER
ATROCITY
ATROPINE
ATTITUDE
ATTORNEY
ATYPICAL
ETERNITY
ETHEREAL
ETHERNET
ETHOLOGY
ETIOLOGY
ETRUSCAN
PTOMAINE
STACCATO
STAGNANT
STAGNATE
STAIRWAY
STAKEOUT
STALLION
STALWART
STAMPEDE
STANDARD
STANDING
STANDOFF
STANDOUT
STARFISH
STARLING
STATUARY
STEALTHY
STEERAGE
STERLING
STICKLER
STILETTO
STIMULUS
STINKBUG
STIRRING
STOCKADE
STOCKING
STOPPAGE
STOTINKA
STOWAWAY
STRADDLE
STRAGGLE
STRAIGHT
STRAITEN
STRANGER
STRANGLE
STRATEGY
STRATIFY
STREAMER
STRENGTH
STRICKEN
STRIDENT
STRIKING
STRINGED
STRINGER
STRUGGLE
STRUMPET
STUBBORN
STUDBOOK
STUDDING
STUDIOUS
STUFFING
STULTIFY
STUNNING
STURGEON
AUDIENCE
AUDITION
AUDITORY
AUSTRIAN
AUTOBAHN
AUTOGIRO
AUTOJOIN
AUTOMATE
BUCKSHOT
BUCKSKIN
BUDDHISM
BUILDING
BULKHEAD
BULLDOZE
BULLETIN
BULLFROG
BULLHEAD
BUNDLING
BUNGALOW
BUNGHOLE
BUOYANCY
BURGLARY
BURGUNDY
BURNOOSE
BURSITIS
BUSINESS
BUSYBODY
BUSYWORK
BUTTRESS
CUCUMBER
CULINARY
CULPABLE
CUPBOARD
CUPIDITY
CURATIVE
CURLICUE
CURRENCY
CUSPIDOR
CUSTOMER
DUCKBILL
DUCKLING
DULCIMER
DUMBBELL
DUMPLING
DUNGAREE
DUNGHILL
DUODENUM
DURATION
DUTIABLE
EUGENICS
EUPHORIA
EURASIAN
EUROBOND
EUROPEAN
EUROPIUM
FUGITIVE
FULLBACK
FUMAROLE
FUMIGANT
FUMIGATE
FUNCTION
FUNERARY
FUNEREAL
FURBELOW
FURLOUGH
FURTHEST
FUSELAGE
FUTILITY
FUTURISM
FUTURITY
GUARANTY
GUARDIAN
GUERNSEY
GUIDANCE
GUMPTION
GUNFIGHT
GUNPOINT
GUNSMITH
GUTTURAL
GUYANESE
HUARACHE
HUCKSTER
HUGUENOT
HUMANISM
HUMANITY
HUMANIZE
HUMANOID
HUMIDIFY
HUMIDITY
HUMILITY
HUMPBACK
HUNTRESS
HUNTSMAN
HUSTINGS
JUBILANT
JUDGMENT
JUDICIAL
JUNCTION
JUNCTURE
JURISTIC
JUVENILE
LUKEWARM
LUMINARY
LUMINOUS
LUNCHEON
LUSCIOUS
LUTETIUM
LUTHERAN
MUCILAGE
MUDGUARD
MUENSTER
MULBERRY
MULETEER
MULTIPLE
MULTIPLY
MUNITION
MUSCATEL
MUSHROOM
MUSICALE
MUSICIAN
MUSKETRY
MUSTACHE
MUTATION
MUTILATE
NUCLEATE
NUGATORY
NUISANCE
NUMERATE
NUMEROUS
NUMSKULL
NURSLING
NUTHATCH
NUTRIENT
NUTSHELL
OUTBOARD
OUTBOUND
OUTBREAK
OUTBURST
OUTCLASS
OUTDATED
OUTDOORS
OUTFIELD
OUTFIGHT
OUTFLANK
OUTGOING
OUTGUESS
OUTHOUSE
OUTLYING
OUTMODED
OUTPOINT
OUTREACH
OUTRIDER
OUTRIGHT
OUTSHINE
OUTSIDER
OUTSMART
OUTSPEND
OUTSTRIP
OUTWEIGH
PUBLICAN
PUDDLING
PUDENDUM
PUFFBALL
PUGILISM
PULLBACK
PULLOVER
PULMOTOR
PULPWOOD
PUNCHEON
PUNCTUAL
PUNCTURE
PUNITIVE
PURBLIND
PURCHASE
PUREBRED
PURSLANE
PURULENT
PUSHCART
PUSHDOWN
PUSHOVER
PUSSYCAT
PUTATIVE
QUADRANT
QUADROON
QUAGMIRE
QUALMISH
QUANDARY
QUANTITY
QUANTIZE
QUATRAIN
QUESTION
QUIETUDE
QUISLING
QUIXOTIC
QUOTABLE
QUOTIENT
RUBICUND
RUBIDIUM
RUDIMENT
RUMANIAN
RUMBLING
RUMINANT
RUMINATE
RUNABOUT
RUNAGATE
RUTABAGA
RUTHLESS
SUBMERGE
SUBMERSE
SUBPOENA
SUBSONIC
SUBTITLE
SUBTRACT
SUBURBIA
SUCCINCT
SUCHLIKE
SUCKLING
SUFFRAGE
SUITABLE
SUITCASE
SUKIYAKI
SULFURIC
SUNDRIES
SUNLIGHT
SUNSHADE
SUNSHINE
SUPEREGO
SUPERIOR
SUPERJET
SUPERNAL
SUPPLANT
SUPPOSED
SUPPRESS
SURCEASE
SUREFIRE
SURGICAL
SURMOUNT
SURPLICE
SURPRISE
SURROUND
SUSPENSE
SUZERAIN
TUBERCLE
TUBEROSE
TUBEROUS
TUNELESS
TUNGSTEN
TUNISIAN
TURBOFAN
TURBOJET
TURMERIC
TURNCOAT
TURNOVER
TURNPIKE
TURNSPIT
TUTELAGE
TUTELARY
TUTORIAL
UUDECODE
UUENCODE
YUGOSLAV
YULETIDE
ZUCCHINI
AVERMENT
AVERSION
AVIATION
AVIATRIX
AVIONICS
EVACUATE
EVALUATE
EVENSONG
EVENTIDE
EVENTUAL
EVERMORE
EVERYDAY
EVERYONE
EVIDENCE
OVENBIRD
OVERALLS
OVERCAST
OVERCOAT
OVERCOME
OVERDRAW
OVERFLOW
OVERGROW
OVERHAND
OVERHANG
OVERHAUL
OVERHEAD
OVERHEAR
OVERKILL
OVERLAID
OVERLAND
OVERLEAP
OVERLOOK
OVERLORD
OVERMUCH
OVERPASS
OVERPLAY
OVERRIDE
OVERRULE
OVERSEAS
OVERSHOE
OVERSIZE
OVERSTAY
OVERSTEP
OVERTAKE
OVERTIME
OVERTONE
OVERTURE
OVERTURN
OVERVIEW
DWELLING
SWASTIKA
SWAYBACK
SWEEPING
SWELLING
SWIMMING
TWEEZERS
TWILIGHT
TWOPENCE
TWOPENNY
ZWIEBACK
AXLETREE
EXACTING
EXCAVATE
EXCHANGE
EXCURSUS
EXECRATE
EXECUTOR
EXEGESIS
EXEMPLAR
EXERCISE
EXIGENCY
EXIGUOUS
EXORCISE
EXORDIUM
EXPEDITE
EXPLICIT
EXPLODED
EXPONENT
EXPOSURE
EXTERIOR
EXTERNAL
EXTRADOS
UXORIOUS
CYCLAMEN

CYLINDER
CYNOSURE
CYTOLOGY
CYTOSINE
DYESTUFF
DYNAMITE
DYSLEXIA
EYEGLASS
EYELINER
EYEPIECE
EYESIGHT
EYETOOTH
GYMKHANA
HYACINTH
HYDROGEN
HYMENEAL
HYPNOSIS
HYPNOTIC
HYSTERIA
LYMPHOID
MYCOLOGY
MYELITIS
MYRMIDON
MYSTICAL
MYSTIQUE
PYORRHEA
SYBARITE
SYCAMORE
SYLLABLE
SYLLABUS
SYMBOLIC
SYMMETRY
SYMPATHY
SYMPHONY
SYNDROME
SYNOPSIS
SYNOPTIC
SYPHILIS
SYSADMIN
SYSTEMIC
TYMPANUM
TYPECAST
TYPEFACE

## 3rd Letter

ABATTOIR
ACADEMIC
ACANTHUS
ALACRITY
ALARMIST
AMARANTH
ANACONDA
ANAEROBE
ANALOGUE
ANALYSIS
ANATHEMA
ARACHNID
BEANBALL
BEARSKIN
BEATIFIC
BEAUTIFY
BIANNUAL
BIATHLON
BLACKING
BLACKOUT
BLACKTOP
BOASTFUL
BRACELET
BRACKISH
BRAGGART
BRAKEMAN
BRANDISH
CHAIRMAN
CHAMBRAY
CHAMPION
CHANCERY
CHANDLER
CHANUKAH
CHAPBOOK
CHAPERON
CHAPLAIN
CHARADES
CHARCOAL
CHARISMA
CHARMING
CHASTISE
CHASTITY
CHASUBLE
CLAIMANT
CLAMBAKE
CLAPTRAP
CLARINET
CLASSIFY
CLAVICLE
CLAYMORE
COACHMAN
COAGULUM
COALESCE
COAUTHOR
CRACKPOT
CRAWFISH
CRAYFISH
DEADBEAT
DEADLINE
DEADLOCK
DEADWOOD
DEATHBED
DIABETES
DIABOLIC
DIAGONAL
DIALOGUE
DIALYSIS
DIAMETER
DIANTHUS
DIAPASON
DIARRHEA
DIASTOLE
DIATOMIC
DIATRIBE
DRAGOMAN
DRAINAGE
DRAUGHTS
DRAWBACK
EMACIATE
EVACUATE
EVALUATE
EXACTING
FEARLESS
FEARSOME
FEASIBLE
FLAGPOLE
FLAGRANT
FLAGSHIP
FLAMBEAU
FLAMENCO
FLAMEOUT
FLAMINGO
FLAPJACK
FLASHGUN
FLASHING
FLATBOAT
FLATFISH
FLATFOOT
FLATHEAD
FLATIRON
FLATLAND
FLATTERY
FLATWARE
FLAUTIST
FRACTION
FRACTURE
FRAGMENT
FRAGRANT
FRANCIUM
GHANAIAN
GLABROUS
GLACIATE
GLADSOME
GLASSFUL
GLAUCOMA
GOALPOST
GOATHERD
GOATSKIN
GRACIOUS
GRADIENT
GRADUATE
GRAFFITO
GRANDEUR
GRANDSON
GRANULAR
GRAPHITE
GRASPING
GRATEFUL
GRATUITY
GRAVAMEN
GRAYLING
GUARANTY
GUARDIAN
HEADACHE
HEADBAND
HEADGEAR
HEADLAND
HEADLINE
HEADLOCK
HEADLONG
HEADREST
HEADROOM
HEADSHIP
HEADSMAN
HEADWORD
HEADWORK
HEAVYSET
HOARDING
HUARACHE
HYACINTH
KNAPSACK
LEAPFROG
LEARNING
LEAVINGS
LOANWORD
LOATHING
MEALTIME
MEALYBUG
MEANTIME
MEATBALL
ORANGERY
ORATORIO
PHANTASM
PHANTASY
PHARISEE
PHARMACY
PHASEOUT
PLACENTA
PLANGENT
PLANKING
PLANKTON
PLANTAIN
PLATFORM
PLATINUM
PLATYPUS
PLAYBACK
PLAYBILL
PLAYBOOK
PLAYGOER
PLAYMATE
PLAYSUIT
PRACTICE
PRATFALL
PRATIQUE
PSALMODY
QUADRANT
QUADROON
QUAGMIRE
QUALMISH
QUANDARY
QUANTITY
QUANTIZE
QUATRAIN
REACTANT
REACTION
REACTIVE
REARWARD
REASSURE
RHAPSODY
ROADSIDE
ROADSTER
ROADWORK
SCABBARD
SCABROUS
SCAFFOLD
SCALABLE
SCALAWAG
SCALEPAN
SCALLION
SCANDIUM
SCAPULAR
SCARCELY
SCATHING
SCAVENGE
SEABOARD
SEACOAST
SEAFARER
SEAGOING
SEALSKIN
SEAMOUNT
SEAPLANE
SEASCAPE
SEASHORE
SEAWATER
SHAMBLES
SHAMROCK
SHANGHAI
SHANTUNG
SLATTERN
SMALLPOX
SNAPSHOT
SPACEMAN
SPACIOUS
SPANIARD
SPANKING
STACCATO
STAGNANT
STAGNATE
STAIRWAY
STAKEOUT
STALLION
STALWART
STAMPEDE
STANDARD
STANDING
STANDOFF
STANDOUT
STARFISH
STARLING
STATUARY
SWASTIKA
SWAYBACK
TEACHING
TEAMSTER
TEAMWORK
TEASPOON
THALAMUS
THALLIUM
THANKFUL
TRACKAGE
TRACTATE
TRACTION
TRAINING
TRAINMAN
TRANQUIL
TRANSACT
TRANSEPT
TRANSFER
TRANSFIX
TRANSMIT
TRAPDOOR
TRAPPING
TRAPROCK
TRAVERSE
TRAVESTY
UNAWARES
VIATICUM
WEAKFISH
WEAKLING
WEAKNESS
WEAPONRY
WHARFAGE
WHATEVER
WRAPPING
WRATHFUL
YEARBOOK
YEARLING
YEARLONG
YEARNING
ALBACORE
ALBANIAN
AMBIENCE
AMBITION
AMBROSIA
AMBULANT
ARBALEST
ARBOREAL
ASBESTOS
BABUSHKA
BIBULOUS
BOBOLINK
BOBWHITE
CABOCHON
CABSTAND
DEBILITY
DEBONAIR
EMBATTLE
EMBEZZLE
EMBITTER
EMBLAZON
EMBOLDEN
EMBOLISM
FABULOUS
FEBRUARY
FIBROSIS
HABANERA
HABITANT
HABITUAL
HEBRAISM
HIBISCUS
IMBECILE
JUBILANT
KIBITZER
LABURNUM
LIBATION
LIBERATE
LIBRETTO
LOBOTOMY
MOBILIZE
NEBULIZE
NEBULOUS
NOBELIST
NOBELIUM
NOBILITY
NOBLEMAN
PUBLICAN
REBUTTAL
RIBOSOME
RUBICUND
RUBIDIUM
SABOTAGE
SABOTEUR
SIBILANT
SOBRIETY
SUBMERGE
SUBMERSE
SUBPOENA
SUBSONIC
SUBTITLE
SUBTRACT
SUBURBIA
SYBARITE
TABULATE
TOBOGGAN
TUBERCLE
TUBEROSE
TUBEROUS
UMBRELLA
UNBEATEN
UNBELIEF
UNBIASED
UNBIDDEN
UNBODIED
UNBOLTED
UNBROKEN
UNBUCKLE
UNBURDEN
UNBUTTON
URBANITE
URBANIZE
VIBURNUM
ACCIDENT
ACCOLADE
ACCOUTRE
ACCREDIT
ACCURATE
ACCURSED
ACCUSTOM
ANCESTOR
ANCESTRY
ARCHDUKE
BACCARAT
BACHELOR
BACILLUS
BACKACHE
BACKBITE
BACKBONE
BACKDROP
BACKFIRE
BACKHAND
BACKLASH
BACKPACK
BACKREST
BACKSIDE
BACKSLAP
BACKSPIN
BACKSTOP
BACKWARD
BACKWASH
BECHUANA
BECOMING
BICONVEX
BICUSPID
BUCKSHOT
BUCKSKIN
CICATRIX
CICERONE
COCKATOO

CO**C**KCROW
CO**C**KEREL
CO**C**KSURE
CO**C**KTAIL
CU**C**UMBER
CY**C**LAMEN
DE**C**ANTER
DE**C**EDENT
DE**C**EMBER
DE**C**IGRAM
DE**C**IMATE
DE**C**IPHER
DE**C**ISION
DE**C**ISIVE
DE**C**KHAND
DE**C**ORATE
DE**C**OROUS
DE**C**REASE
DE**C**REPIT
DI**C**TATOR
DO**C**KHAND
DO**C**KYARD
DO**C**TRINE
DO**C**UMENT
DU**C**KBILL
DU**C**KLING
EN**C**EINTE
EN**C**IPHER
EN**C**IRCLE
EN**C**OMIUM
EN**C**ROACH
EN**C**UMBER
ES**C**ALATE
ES**C**ALLOP
ES**C**APADE
ES**C**APISM
ES**C**AROLE
EX**C**AVATE
EX**C**HANGE
EX**C**URSUS
FA**C**EDOWN
FA**C**ILITY
FA**C**TIOUS
FA**C**TOTUM
FE**C**KLESS
HA**C**IENDA
HA**C**KWORD
HE**C**ATOMB
HU**C**KSTER
IN**C**HOATE
IN**C**HWORM
IN**C**IDENT
IN**C**ISION
IN**C**ISIVE
IN**C**OMING
IN**C**REASE
IN**C**UBATE
IN**C**UMBER
JA**C**KBOOT
JA**C**QUARD
KI**C**KBACK
KI**C**KSHAW
LA**C**ERATE
LA**C**EWING
LA**C**RIMAL
LA**C**ROSSE
LE**C**ITHIN
LI**C**ENSEE
LI**C**ORICE
LO**C**ALITY
LO**C**ALIZE
LO**C**ATION
LO**C**KSTEP
LO**C**OWEED
LO**C**UTION
MA**C**ARONI
MA**C**AROON
MA**C**ERATE
MA**C**HISMO
MA**C**KEREL
MA**C**KINAW
MA**C**PAINT
ME**C**HANIC
MI**C**ROBUS
MO**C**CASIN
MU**C**ILAGE
MY**C**OLOGY
NE**C**KLACE
NE**C**KLINE
NE**C**ROSIS
NI**C**KNAME
NI**C**OTINE
NO**C**TURNE
NU**C**LEATE
OC**C**ASION
OC**C**UPANT
ON**C**OMING
OS**C**ULATE
PA**C**IFIER
PA**C**IFISM
PE**C**TORAL
PE**C**ULATE
PE**C**ULIAR
PI**C**AYUNE
PI**C**KEREL
PI**C**KINGS
PI**C**KLOCK
PO**C**KMARK
RE**C**EIVER
RE**C**EPTOR
RE**C**KLESS
RE**C**ORDER
RE**C**OURSE
RE**C**REANT
RE**C**REATE
RI**C**OCHET
RO**C**KETRY
RO**C**KFALL
SA**C**RISTY
SE**C**URITY
SI**C**KNESS
SO**C**IABLE
SU**C**CINCT
SU**C**HLIKE
SU**C**KLING
SY**C**AMORE
TA**C**ITURN
TI**C**KLISH
UL**C**ERATE
UN**C**HASTE
UN**C**HURCH
UN**C**LENCH
UN**C**LOTHE
UN**C**OMMON
UN**C**OUPLE
UN**C**TUOUS
UP**C**OMING
VA**C**ATION
VA**C**CINIA
VI**C**ARAGE
VI**C**INAGE
VI**C**INITY
VI**C**TORIA
VO**C**ALIST
VO**C**ALIZE
VO**C**ATION
VO**C**ATIVE
YA**C**HTING
ZU**C**CHINI
AB**D**ICATE
AD**D**ENDUM
AD**D**ITION
AD**D**ITIVE
AL**D**ERMAN
AN**D**ROGEN
AU**D**IENCE
AU**D**ITION
AU**D**ITORY
BA**D**INAGE
BE**D**AZZLE
BE**D**STEAD
BI**D**DABLE
BO**D**ILESS
BO**D**YWORK
BU**D**DHISM
CA**D**UCEUS
DE**D**ICATE
DI**D**ACTIC
EN**D**ANGER
EN**D**EAVOR
FA**D**ELESS
FE**D**ERATE
FI**D**ELITY
GA**D**ABOUT
GO**D**CHILD
HE**D**GEHOG
HE**D**GEHOP
HE**D**GEROW
HE**D**ONISM
HI**D**EAWAY
HY**D**ROGEN
IN**D**EBTED
IN**D**ECENT
IN**D**IAMAN
IN**D**ICATE
IN**D**IGENT
IN**D**IRECT
IN**D**OLENT
IN**D**UCTEE
IN**D**URATE
IN**D**USTRY
JU**D**GMENT
JU**D**ICIAL
LA**D**YBIRD
LA**D**YLIKE
LA**D**YLOVE
LA**D**YSHIP
LO**D**ESTAR
LO**D**GMENT
MA**D**HOUSE
MA**D**RIGAL
ME**D**ALIST
ME**D**ICAID
ME**D**ICARE
ME**D**ICATE
ME**D**ICINE
ME**D**IEVAL
ME**D**IOCRE
ME**D**ITATE
MI**D**DLING
MI**D**NIGHT
MI**D**POINT
MI**D**SHIPS
MO**D**ERATE
MO**D**ULATE
MU**D**GUARD
OB**D**URATE
OR**D**INARY
OR**D**INATE
OR**D**NANCE
PE**D**AGOGY
PE**D**ERAST
PE**D**ESTAL
PE**D**ICURE
PE**D**IGREE
PE**D**IMENT
PE**D**UNCLE
PI**D**DLING
PO**D**IATRY
PU**D**DLING
PU**D**ENDUM
RA**D**IATOR
RA**D**IOMAN
RE**D**OLENT
RI**D**ICULE
RU**D**IMENT
SA**D**DUCEE
SE**D**ATIVE
SE**D**IMENT
SE**D**ITION
SE**D**ULOUS
SI**D**EKICK
SI**D**ELONG
SI**D**EREAL
SI**D**ERITE
SI**D**ESHOW
SI**D**ESTEP
SI**D**EWALK
SI**D**EWALL
SI**D**EWAYS
TI**D**ELAND
UN**D**ERACT
UN**D**ERAGE
UN**D**ERARM
UN**D**ERBID
UN**D**ERCUT
UN**D**ERDOG
UN**D**ERFUR
UN**D**ERLIE
UN**D**ERLIP
UN**D**ERPAY
UN**D**ERSEA
UN**D**ERTOW
UN**D**ULANT
UN**D**ULATE
UU**D**ECODE
AB**E**YANCE
AC**E**RBATE
AC**E**RBITY
AD**E**QUATE
AG**E**RATUM
AL**E**ATORY
AL**E**HOUSE
AM**E**NABLE
AM**E**RICAN
AM**E**THYST
AN**E**CDOTE
AN**E**CHOIC
AP**E**RITIF
AP**E**RTURE
AV**E**RMENT
AV**E**RSION
BA**E**DEKER
BE**E**CHNUT
BI**E**NNIAL
BI**E**NNIUM
BL**E**SSING
BR**E**AKAGE
BR**E**AKOUT
BR**E**EDING
BR**E**THREN
BR**E**VIARY
CH**E**CKERS
CH**E**CKOFF
CH**E**CKOUT
CH**E**CKSUM
CH**E**ERFUL
CH**E**MICAL
CH**E**MURGY
CH**E**NILLE
CH**E**ROKEE
CH**E**STNUT
CH**E**YENNE
CL**E**ARING
CL**E**AVAGE
CL**E**MATIS
CL**E**MENCY
CL**E**RICAL
CR**E**AMERY
CR**E**ATION
CR**E**ATURE
CR**E**DENCE
CR**E**DENZA
CR**E**DIBLE
CR**E**DITOR
CR**E**EPING
CR**E**MAINS
CR**E**OSOTE
CR**E**SCENT
CR**E**TONNE
CR**E**VASSE
DE**E**RSKIN
DI**E**LDRIN
DR**E**ADFUL
DR**E**SSAGE
DR**E**SSING
DW**E**LLING
DY**E**STUFF
EL**E**CTION
EL**E**CTIVE
EL**E**CTRIC
EL**E**CTRON
EL**E**GANCE
EL**E**PHANT
EL**E**VATOR
EM**E**RITUS
EN**E**RGIZE
EN**E**RVATE
ER**E**CTILE
ER**E**CTION
ET**E**RNITY
EV**E**NSONG
EV**E**NTIDE
EV**E**NTUAL
EV**E**RMORE
EV**E**RYDAY
EV**E**RYONE
EX**E**CRATE
EX**E**CUTOR
EX**E**GESIS
EX**E**MPLAR
EX**E**RCISE
EY**E**GLASS
EY**E**LINER
EY**E**PIECE
EY**E**SIGHT
EY**E**TOOTH
FE**E**DBACK
FL**E**ABANE
FL**E**ABITE
FL**E**ETING
FL**E**SHPOT
FL**E**XIBLE
FR**E**EBORN
FR**E**EDMAN
FR**E**EHAND
FR**E**EHOLD
FR**E**ELOAD
FR**E**EWILL
FR**E**NETIC
FR**E**QUENT
FR**E**SHMAN
FR**E**TWORK
GR**E**EKING
GR**E**ENERY
GR**E**ETING
GU**E**RNSEY
IC**E**BOUND
IC**E**HOUSE
ID**E**ALISM
ID**E**ALIZE
ID**E**ATION
ID**E**NTIFY
ID**E**NTITY
ID**E**OGRAM
ID**E**OLOGY
IN**E**DITED
IN**E**RRANT
IN**E**XPERT
KE**E**LBOAT
KE**E**LHAUL
KE**E**PSAKE
KI**E**LBASA
KN**E**EHOLE
MN**E**MONIC
MU**E**NSTER
MY**E**LITIS
NE**E**DLESS
OB**E**DIENT
OL**E**ANDER
OP**E**NWORK
OP**E**RABLE
OP**E**RANDS
OP**E**RETTA
OV**E**NBIRD
OV**E**RALLS
OV**E**RCAST
OV**E**RCOAT
OV**E**RCOME
OV**E**RDRAW
OV**E**RFLOW
OV**E**RGROW
OV**E**RHAND
OV**E**RHANG
OV**E**RHAUL
OV**E**RHEAD
OV**E**RHEAR
OV**E**RKILL
OV**E**RLAID
OV**E**RLAND
OV**E**RLEAP
OV**E**RLOOK
OV**E**RLORD
OV**E**RMUCH
OV**E**RPASS
OV**E**RPLAY
OV**E**RRIDE
OV**E**RRULE
OV**E**RSEAS
OV**E**RSHOE
OV**E**RSIZE
OV**E**RSTAY
OV**E**RSTEP
OV**E**RTAKE
OV**E**RTIME
OV**E**RTONE
OV**E**RTURE
OV**E**RTURN
OV**E**RVIEW
PE**E**PHOLE
PE**E**RLESS
PH**E**ASANT
PH**E**NOLIC
PI**E**PLANT
PL**E**ASANT
PL**E**ASING
PL**E**ASURE
PL**E**BEIAN
PL**E**CTRUM
PL**E**THORA
PL**E**URISY
PR**E**AMBLE
PR**E**CINCT
PR**E**CIOUS
PR**E**CLUDE
PR**E**EXIST

PREGNANT
PREJUDGE
PREMIERE
PREMOLAR
PRENATAL
PREPRESS
PRESENCE
PRESERVE
PRESIDIO
PRESSING
PRESSMAN
PRESSURE
PRESTIGE
PRETENSE
PRETERIT
PRETTIFY
PREVIOUS
QUESTION
RHEOLOGY
RHEOSTAT
RHETORIC
SCENARIO
SEEDLING
SEEDTIME
SHEEPISH
SHEETING
SHELVING
SHEPHERD
SKELETON
SPECIFIC
SPECIMEN
SPECIOUS
SPECTRAL
SPECTRUM
SPEEDWAY
STEALTHY
STEERAGE
STERLING
SWEEPING
SWELLING
TEETHING
TEETOTAL
THEOLOGY
THEORIZE
THEREFOR
THESPIAN
TREASURE
TREASURY
TREATISE
TRENCHER
TRESPASS
TWEEZERS
UNEARNED
UNENDING
UNERRING
UUENCODE
VIETCONG

WHENEVER
WHEREVER
WRECKAGE
WRETCHED
YIELDING
AFFECTED
AFFERENT
AFFIANCE
AFFINITY
AFFLATUS
AFFRIGHT
ALFRESCO
BEFRIEND
BEFUDDLE
BIFOCALS
CAFFEINE
DAFFODIL
DEFECATE
DEFIANCE
DEFINITE
DEFLOWER
DEFOREST
EFFERENT
EFFUSION
ENFEEBLE
ENFILADE
INFAMOUS
INFANTRY
INFERIOR
INFERNAL
INFINITE
INFINITY
INFOBAHN
INFORMAL
INFORMED
INFORMER
INFRADIG
INFRARED
INFRINGE
LEFTOVER
LIFEBOAT
LIFELINE
LIFELONG
LIFETIME
LIFEWORK
OFFICIAL
OFFPRINT
OFFSHOOT
OFFSHORE
OFFSTAGE
PUFFBALL
REFERENT
REFERRAL
REFINERY
REFOREST
REFORMER
RIFFRAFF

SOFTBALL
SOFTWARE
SOFTWOOD
SUFFRAGE
TAFFRAIL
UNFASTEN
UNFETTER
UNFILIAL
UNFORMED
UNFREEZE
AGGRIEVE
AIGRETTE
ALGERIAN
ANGELICA
ANGLICAN
ANGSTROM
ARGUABLE
ARGUMENT
BAGUETTE
BEGGARLY
BEGRUDGE
BOGEYMAN
CAGELING
COGITATE
COGNOMEN
COGWHEEL
DOGFIGHT
DOGGEREL
DOGHOUSE
EDGEWAYS
EGGPLANT
EGGSHELL
EIGHTEEN
ENGAGING
ENGENDER
ENGINEER
EUGENICS
FAGOTING
FIGURINE
FUGITIVE
GIGABYTE
GIGANTIC
HEGEMONY
HIGHBALL
HIGHBORN
HIGHBRED
HIGHBROW
HIGHLAND
HIGHNESS
HIGHROAD
HIGHTAIL
HOGSHEAD
HUGUENOT
INGUINAL
LEGALISM
LEGATION
LIGAMENT

LIGATURE
LIGNEOUS
LOGOTYPE
MAGAZINE
MAGDALEN
MAGICIAN
MAGNESIA
MAGNETIC
MAGNOLIA
MEGABYTE
MEGALITH
MIGRAINE
NEGATION
NEGATIVE
NEGLIGEE
NIGERIAN
NIGEROIS
NIGGLING
NUGATORY
ORGANISM
ORGANIST
ORGANIZE
ORGULOUS
PAGINATE
PUGILISM
REGICIDE
REGIMENT
REGIONAL
REGISTER
REGISTRY
REGOLITH
REGULATE
RIGHTFUL
SAGAMORE
SIGNPOST
TIGHTWAD
TOGETHER
UNGAINLY
UNGULATE
UPGROWTH
VAGABOND
VAGRANCY
VEGANISM
VEGETATE
VIGILANT
VIGNETTE
VIGOROUS
YUGOSLAV
ADHESION
ADHESIVE
APHANITE
APHELION
APHORISM
ATHLETIC
BEHAVIOR
BEHEMOTH
BEHOLDEN

BOHEMIAN
COHERENT
COHESION
ETHEREAL
ETHERNET
ETHOLOGY
INHALANT
INHERENT
INHUMANE
KOHLRABI
MAHARAJA
MAHARANI
MAHOGANY
NIHILISM
REHEARSE
SCHEDULE
SCHMALTZ
SCHOONER
SPHAGNUM
SPHEROID
TAHITIAN
UPHEAVAL
VEHEMENT
ACIDHEAD
ACIDOSIS
AGITPROP
ALIASING
ALIENATE
ALIENIST
ALIZARIN
AMICABLE
ANISETTE
AVIATION
AVIATRIX
AVIONICS
BAILABLE
BAILSMAN
BLISSFUL
BLIZZARD
BRICKBAT
BRIGHTEN
BRINDLED
BRISLING
BRITCHES
BUILDING
CHIPMUNK
CHIPPEWA
CHITCHAT
CHIVALRY
CLINCHER
CLINICAL
CLIPPING
CLITORIS
COIFFEUR
COIFFURE
COINCIDE
CRIBBAGE

CRIMINAL
CRITICAL
CRITIQUE
DAIQUIRI
DAIRYING
DAIRYMAN
DEIONIZE
DRIVEWAY
EKISTICS
ELIGIBLE
EMIGRATE
EMINENCE
EMISSARY
EPIDEMIC
EPILEPSY
EPILOGUE
EPIPHANY
ETIOLOGY
EVIDENCE
EXIGENCY
EXIGUOUS
FLIMFLAM
FLIPPANT
FRICTION
FRIGHTEN
FRIPPERY
GRIDIRON
GRIEVOUS
GRIZZLED
GUIDANCE
HAIRLINE
HEIGHTEN
HEIRLOOM
IMITABLE
INIMICAL
INIQUITY
INITIATE
JAILBIRD
KNICKERS
KNITWEAR
MAINLAND
MAINLINE
MAINMAST
MAINSAIL
MAINSTAY
MAINTAIN
MOISTURE
NAINSOOK
NEIGHBOR
NUISANCE
OBITUARY
ORIENTAL
ORIGINAL
PAINTING
PEIGNOIR
POIGNANT
PRIMEVAL

PRIMROSE
PRINCESS
PRINTING
PRINTOUT
PRISONER
PRISTINE
QUIETUDE
QUISLING
QUIXOTIC
RAILLERY
RAILROAD
RAINCOAT
RAINDROP
RAINFALL
REINDEER
SAILBOAT
SAILFISH
SCIATICA
SCILICET
SCIMITAR
SCISSORS
SEIGNEUR
SHILINGI
SHILLING
SHINBONE
SHINGLES
SHIPMATE
SHIPMENT
SHIPPING
SHIPWORM
SHIPYARD
SHIRRING
SHIRTING
SKILLFUL
SKIMMING
SKIRMISH
SKITTISH
SLIPKNOT
SLIPPERY
SLIPSHOD
SPILLWAY
SPINSTER
SPIRITED
SPITBALL
SPITTOON
STICKLER
STILETTO
STIMULUS
STINKBUG
STIRRING
SUITABLE
SUITCASE
SWIMMING
TAILCOAT
TAILGATE
TAILSPIN
THIAMINE

THICKSET
THIEVERY
THIRTEEN
TOILETRY
TOILETTE
TOILWORN
TRIANGLE
TRIBUNAL
TRICHINA
TRICKERY
TRICOLOR
TRICYCLE
TRIFLING
TRILLION
TRILLIUM
TRIMARAN
TRIMETER
TRIMMING
TRIPTYCH
TRIUMVIR
TWILIGHT
UNIAXIAL
UNICYCLE
UNIONISM
UNIONIZE
UNIVALVE
UNIVERSE
WAINSCOT
WAITRESS
WHIPCORD
WHIPLASH
WHITECAP
WHITEFLY
WRIGGLER
WRISTLET
ZWIEBACK
ADJACENT
ADJUTANT
ADJUVANT
DEJECTED
MAJOLICA
MAJORITY
ALKALOID
BAKESHOP
CAKEWALK
DEKAGRAM
INKSTAND
LIKENESS
LIKEWISE
LUKEWARM
POKEWEED
SUKIYAKI
TOKENISM
UNKINDLY
ABLATION
ABLATIVE
ABLUTION

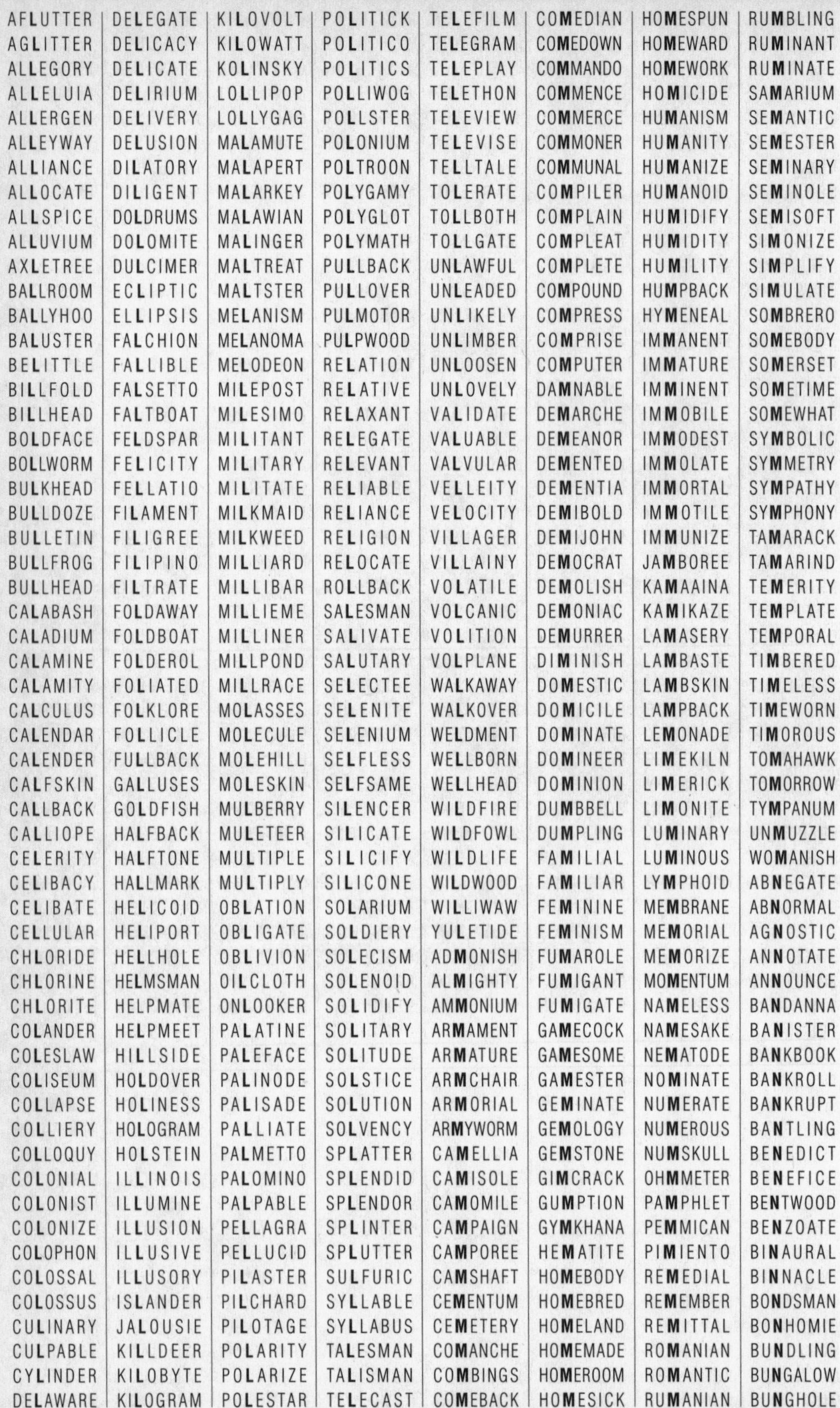

AFLUTTER
AGLITTER
ALLEGORY
ALLELUIA
ALLERGEN
ALLEYWAY
ALLIANCE
ALLOCATE
ALLSPICE
ALLUVIUM
AXLETREE
BALLROOM
BALLYHOO
BALUSTER
BELITTLE
BILLFOLD
BILLHEAD
BOLDFACE
BOLLWORM
BULKHEAD
BULLDOZE
BULLETIN
BULLFROG
BULLHEAD
CALABASH
CALADIUM
CALAMINE
CALAMITY
CALCULUS
CALENDAR
CALENDER
CALFSKIN
CALLBACK
CALLIOPE
CELERITY
CELIBACY
CELIBATE
CELLULAR
CHLORIDE
CHLORINE
CHLORITE
COLANDER
COLESLAW
COLISEUM
COLLAPSE
COLLIERY
COLLOQUY
COLONIAL
COLONIST
COLONIZE
COLOPHON
COLOSSAL
COLOSSUS
CULINARY
CULPABLE
CYLINDER
DELAWARE
DELEGATE
DELICACY
DELICATE
DELIRIUM
DELIVERY
DELUSION
DILATORY
DILIGENT
DOLDRUMS
DOLOMITE
DULCIMER
ECLIPTIC
ELLIPSIS
FALCHION
FALLIBLE
FALSETTO
FALTBOAT
FELDSPAR
FELICITY
FELLATIO
FILAMENT
FILIGREE
FILIPINO
FILTRATE
FOLDAWAY
FOLDBOAT
FOLDEROL
FOLIATED
FOLKLORE
FOLLICLE
FULLBACK
GALLUSES
GOLDFISH
HALFBACK
HALFTONE
HALLMARK
HELICOID
HELIPORT
HELLHOLE
HELMSMAN
HELPMATE
HELPMEET
HILLSIDE
HOLDOVER
HOLINESS
HOLOGRAM
HOLSTEIN
ILLINOIS
ILLUMINE
ILLUSION
ILLUSIVE
ILLUSORY
ISLANDER
JALOUSIE
KILLDEER
KILOBYTE
KILOGRAM
KILOVOLT
KILOWATT
KOLINSKY
LOLLIPOP
LOLLYGAG
MALAMUTE
MALAPERT
MALARKEY
MALAWIAN
MALINGER
MALTREAT
MALTSTER
MELANISM
MELANOMA
MELODEON
MILEPOST
MILESIMO
MILITANT
MILITARY
MILITATE
MILKMAID
MILKWEED
MILLIARD
MILLIBAR
MILLIEME
MILLINER
MILLPOND
MILLRACE
MOLASSES
MOLECULE
MOLEHILL
MOLESKIN
MULBERRY
MULETEER
MULTIPLE
MULTIPLY
OBLATION
OBLIGATE
OBLIVION
OILCLOTH
ONLOOKER
PALATINE
PALEFACE
PALINODE
PALISADE
PALLIATE
PALMETTO
PALOMINO
PALPABLE
PELLAGRA
PELLUCID
PILASTER
PILCHARD
PILOTAGE
POLARITY
POLARIZE
POLESTAR
POLITICK
POLITICO
POLITICS
POLLIWOG
POLLSTER
POLONIUM
POLTROON
POLYGAMY
POLYGLOT
POLYMATH
PULLBACK
PULLOVER
PULMOTOR
PULPWOOD
RELATION
RELATIVE
RELAXANT
RELEGATE
RELEVANT
RELIABLE
RELIANCE
RELIGION
RELOCATE
ROLLBACK
SALESMAN
SALIVATE
SALUTARY
SELECTEE
SELENITE
SELENIUM
SELFLESS
SELFSAME
SILENCER
SILICATE
SILICIFY
SILICONE
SOLARIUM
SOLDIERY
SOLECISM
SOLENOID
SOLIDIFY
SOLITARY
SOLITUDE
SOLSTICE
SOLUTION
SOLVENCY
SPLATTER
SPLENDID
SPLENDOR
SPLINTER
SPLUTTER
SULFURIC
SYLLABLE
SYLLABUS
TALESMAN
TALISMAN
TELECAST
TELEFILM
TELEGRAM
TELEPLAY
TELETHON
TELEVIEW
TELEVISE
TELLTALE
TOLERATE
TOLLBOTH
TOLLGATE
UNLAWFUL
UNLEADED
UNLIKELY
UNLIMBER
UNLOOSEN
UNLOVELY
VALIDATE
VALUABLE
VALVULAR
VELLEITY
VELOCITY
VILLAGER
VILLAINY
VOLATILE
VOLCANIC
VOLITION
VOLPLANE
WALKAWAY
WALKOVER
WELDMENT
WELLBORN
WELLHEAD
WILDFIRE
WILDFOWL
WILDLIFE
WILDWOOD
WILLIWAW
YULETIDE
ADMONISH
ALMIGHTY
AMMONIUM
ARMAMENT
ARMATURE
ARMCHAIR
ARMORIAL
ARMYWORM
CAMELLIA
CAMISOLE
CAMOMILE
CAMPAIGN
CAMPOREE
CAMSHAFT
CEMENTUM
CEMETERY
COMANCHE
COMBINGS
COMEBACK
COMEDIAN
COMEDOWN
COMMANDO
COMMENCE
COMMERCE
COMMONER
COMMUNAL
COMPILER
COMPLAIN
COMPLEAT
COMPLETE
COMPOUND
COMPRESS
COMPRISE
COMPUTER
DAMNABLE
DEMARCHE
DEMEANOR
DEMENTED
DEMENTIA
DEMIBOLD
DEMIJOHN
DEMOCRAT
DEMOLISH
DEMONIAC
DEMURRER
DIMINISH
DOMESTIC
DOMICILE
DOMINATE
DOMINEER
DOMINION
DUMBBELL
DUMPLING
FAMILIAL
FAMILIAR
FEMININE
FEMINISM
FUMAROLE
FUMIGANT
FUMIGATE
GAMECOCK
GAMESOME
GAMESTER
GEMINATE
GEMOLOGY
GEMSTONE
GIMCRACK
GUMPTION
GYMKHANA
HEMATITE
HOMEBODY
HOMEBRED
HOMELAND
HOMEMADE
HOMEROOM
HOMESICK
HOMESPUN
HOMEWARD
HOMEWORK
HOMICIDE
HUMANISM
HUMANITY
HUMANIZE
HUMANOID
HUMIDIFY
HUMIDITY
HUMILITY
HUMPBACK
HYMENEAL
IMMANENT
IMMATURE
IMMINENT
IMMOBILE
IMMODEST
IMMOLATE
IMMORTAL
IMMOTILE
IMMUNIZE
JAMBOREE
KAMAAINA
KAMIKAZE
LAMASERY
LAMBASTE
LAMBSKIN
LAMPBACK
LEMONADE
LIMEKILN
LIMERICK
LIMONITE
LUMINARY
LUMINOUS
LYMPHOID
MEMBRANE
MEMORIAL
MEMORIZE
MOMENTUM
NAMELESS
NAMESAKE
NEMATODE
NOMINATE
NUMERATE
NUMEROUS
NUMSKULL
OHMMETER
PAMPHLET
PEMMICAN
PIMIENTO
REMEDIAL
REMEMBER
REMITTAL
ROMANIAN
ROMANTIC
RUMANIAN
RUMBLING
RUMINANT
RUMINATE
SAMARIUM
SEMANTIC
SEMESTER
SEMINARY
SEMINOLE
SEMISOFT
SIMONIZE
SIMPLIFY
SIMULATE
SOMBRERO
SOMEBODY
SOMERSET
SOMETIME
SOMEWHAT
SYMBOLIC
SYMMETRY
SYMPATHY
SYMPHONY
TAMARACK
TAMARIND
TEMERITY
TEMPLATE
TEMPORAL
TIMBERED
TIMELESS
TIMEWORN
TIMOROUS
TOMAHAWK
TOMORROW
TYMPANUM
UNMUZZLE
WOMANISH
ABNEGATE
ABNORMAL
AGNOSTIC
ANNOTATE
ANNOUNCE
BANDANNA
BANISTER
BANKBOOK
BANKROLL
BANKRUPT
BANTLING
BENEDICT
BENEFICE
BENTWOOD
BENZOATE
BINAURAL
BINNACLE
BONDSMAN
BONHOMIE
BUNDLING
BUNGALOW
BUNGHOLE

CANADIAN
CANAILLE
CANALIZE
CANISTER
CANNABIS
CANNIBAL
CANONIZE
CANTICLE
CENOBITE
CENOTAPH
CENTERED
CENTRIST
CINCHONA
CINCTURE
CINNABAR
CINNAMON
CONCEIVE
CONCERTO
CONCLAVE
CONCLUDE
CONCRETE
CONDENSE
CONFETTI
CONFINES
CONFLICT
CONFOCAL
CONFOUND
CONFRERE
CONFRONT
CONGENER
CONGRESS
CONJUGAL
CONJUNCT
CONQUEST
CONSERVE
CONSIDER
CONSOMME
CONSPIRE
CONSTANT
CONSTRUE
CONTEMPT
CONTINUE
CONTRACT
CONTRAIL
CONTRARY
CONTRAST
CONTRITE
CONTRIVE
CONVERGE
CONVERSE
CONVINCE
CONVULSE
CYNOSURE
DANDRUFF
DANSEUSE
DENATURE
DENOUNCE
DINGBATS
DINOSAUR
DONATION
DUNGAREE
DUNGHILL
DYNAMITE
FANCIFUL
FANDANGO
FANLIGHT
FANTASIA
FINALIST
FINALIZE
FINESPUN
FUNCTION
FUNERARY
FUNEREAL
GANGLAND
GANGLING
GANGLION
GANGPLOW
GANGRENE
GANGSTER
GENDARME
GENERATE
GENEROUS
GENETICS
GENITALS
GENITIVE
GENOCIDE
GINGERLY
GONFALON
GUNFIGHT
GUNPOINT
GUNSMITH
HANDBALL
HANDBILL
HANDBOOK
HANDCUFF
HANDICAP
HANDMADE
HANDPICK
HANDRAIL
HANDSOME
HANDYMAN
HANGNAIL
HANGOVER
HANUKKAH
HENCHMAN
HINDMOST
HINDUISM
HONEYDEW
HONORARY
HUNTRESS
HUNTSMAN
IGNITION
IGNORANT
INNOCENT
INNOVATE
INNUENDO
JINGOISM
JONGLEUR
JUNCTION
JUNCTURE
KANGAROO
KINDLING
KINETICS
KINGBOLT
LANDFALL
LANDFILL
LANDFORM
LANDLORD
LANDMARK
LANDMASS
LANDSMAN
LANDWARD
LANGUAGE
LANGUISH
LENGTHEN
LENITIVE
LINCHPIN
LINESMAN
LINGERIE
LINGUIST
LINIMENT
LINOLEUM
LONESOME
LONGBOAT
LONGHAIR
LONGHAND
LONGHORN
LONGTIME
LONGUEUR
LUNCHEON
MANCIPLE
MANDAMUS
MANDARIN
MANDIBLE
MANDOLIN
MANDRAKE
MANEUVER
MANGROVE
MANIACAL
MANICURE
MANIFEST
MANIFOLD
MANNERED
MANNERLY
MANTELET
MANTILLA
MANTISSA
MANYFOLD
MENHADEN
MENISCUS
MINATORY
MINDLESS
MINIBIKE
MINIMIZE
MINISTER
MINISTRY
MINORITY
MINSTREL
MONARCHY
MONASTIC
MONAURAL
MONETARY
MONGOOSE
MONITION
MONITORY
MONOGAMY
MONOGRAM
MONOLITH
MONOPOLY
MONORAIL
MONOTONE
MONOXIDE
MONSIEUR
MONUMENT
MUNITION
NINEPINS
NINETEEN
NONDAIRY
NONESUCH
NONEVENT
NONMETAL
NONRIGID
NONSENSE
NONSTICK
NONUNION
OINTMENT
ORNAMENT
PANATELA
PANCREAS
PANDEMIC
PANDOWDY
PANELING
PANELIST
PANORAMA
PANTHEON
PANTSUIT
PENALIZE
PENCHANT
PENDULUM
PENITENT
PENKNIFE
PENLIGHT
PENOLOGY
PENSTOCK
PENTAGON
PENUMBRA
PINAFORE
PINNACLE
PINOCHLE
PINPOINT
PINPRICK
PINWHEEL
PONYTAIL
PUNCHEON
PUNCTUAL
PUNCTURE
PUNITIVE
RENEGADE
RENOUNCE
RENOVATE
RINGWORM
RUNABOUT
RUNAGATE
SANCTIFY
SANCTION
SANCTITY
SANDBANK
SANDWICH
SANGUINE
SANITARY
SANITIZE
SANSKRIT
SENSIBLE
SENSUOUS
SENTENCE
SENTIENT
SENTINEL
SINECURE
SINGULAR
SINISTER
SINKHOLE
SONATINA
SONGBIRD
SONGSTER
SONOROUS
SUNDRIES
SUNLIGHT
SUNSHADE
SUNSHINE
SYNDROME
SYNOPSIS
SYNOPTIC
TANGIBLE
TANTALUM
TENANTRY
TENDENCY
TENEMENT
TENPENNY
TENTACLE
TINCTURE
TINPLATE
TINSMITH
TONALITY
TUNELESS
TUNGSTEN
TUNISIAN
VANADIUM
VANGUARD
VANQUISH
VENATION
VENDETTA
VENERATE
VENEREAL
VENGEFUL
VENOMOUS
VENUSIAN
VINCIBLE
VINEGARY
VINEYARD
WINDBURN
WINDFALL
WINDLASS
WINDMILL
WINDPIPE
WINDWARD
WINESHOP
WINGDING
WINGSPAN
WONDROUS
XENOLITH
ABORNING
ABORTION
ACOUSTIC
ADOPTIVE
ADORABLE
ALOPECIA
AMOEBOID
AMORTIZE
APOLOGIA
APOPLEXY
APOSTASY
APOTHEGM
ATOMIZER
BIOCIDAL
BLOCKADE
BLOOMERS
BLOWPIPE
BOOKCASE
BOOKMARK
BOOKWORM
BOOTLESS
BROCCOLI
BROCHURE
BROMIDIC
BRONCHUS
BROOKLET
BROUGHAM
BROUHAHA
BROWBEAT
BROWNOUT
BUOYANCY
CHOIRBOY
CHOLERIC
CHOWCHOW
CLOISTER
CLOSEOUT
CLOTHIER
CLOTHING
CLOUDLET
COOKBOOK
COONSKIN
CROCKERY
CROPLAND
CROSSBAR
CROSSBOW
CROSSCUT
CROSSING
CROTCHET
CROUPIER
CROWFOOT
DOOMSDAY
DOORJAMB
DOORKNOB
DOORSTEP
DOORYARD
DROPKICK
DUODENUM
ECONOMIC
ELONGATE
ELOQUENT
EMOTICON
ENORMITY
ENORMOUS
ESOTERIC
EXORCISE
EXORDIUM
FLOTILLA
FLOUNDER
FLOURISH
FOOLSCAP
FOOTBALL
FOOTFALL
FOOTHILL
FOOTHOLD
FOOTLESS
FOOTLING
FOOTNOTE
FOOTPATH
FOOTRACE
FOOTREST
FOOTSORE
FOOTSTEP
FOOTWEAR
FOOTWORK
FRONTAGE
FRONTIER
FROSTING
FROUFROU
GEODESIC
GEOMETRY
GLOAMING
GLOBULIN
GLORIOUS
GLOSSARY
GLOWWORM
GLOXINIA
GOODNESS
GOODWIFE
GOODWILL
GOOFBALL
GROSBEAK
GROSCHEN
GROUNDER
HOODWINK
HOOKWORM
HOOLIGAN
HOOSEGOW
IDOLATER
IDOLATRY
IRONCLAD
IRONWARE
IRONWEED
IRONWOOD
IRONWORK
IROQUOIS
ISOPRENE
ISOSTASY
ISOTHERM
ISOTONIC
JEOPARDY
KNOCKOUT
KNOTHOLE
LOOPHOLE
MOONBEAM
MOORLAND
NEONATAL
NEOPHYTE
NEOPLASM
NOONTIDE
NOONTIME
ODOMETER
ONONDAGA
PHOSPHOR
PROBABLE
PROCAINE
PROCEEDS
PROCLAIM
PRODIGAL
PROFOUND
PROGRESS
PROHIBIT
PROLIFIC
PROLOGUE
PROMOTER
PROPERTY
PROPHECY

PR**O**PHESY
PR**O**POUND
PR**O**ROGUE
PR**O**SPECT
PR**O**STATE
PR**O**TOCOL
PR**O**TRACT
PR**O**TRUDE
PR**O**VIDED
PR**O**VINCE
PT**O**MAINE
PY**O**RRHEA
QU**O**TABLE
QU**O**TIENT
RH**O**MBOID
RO**O**FTREE
RO**O**METTE
RO**O**MMATE
SC**O**FFLAW
SC**O**RPION
SC**O**TTISH
SH**O**CKING
SH**O**ELACE
SH**O**PLIFT
SH**O**PWORN
SH**O**RTAGE
SH**O**RTCUT
SH**O**SHONE
SH**O**ULDER
SH**O**WCASE
SH**O**WDOWN
SL**O**VENLY
SN**O**BBERY
SN**O**WBALL
SN**O**WBANK
SN**O**WDROP
SN**O**WFALL
SN**O**WPLOW
SN**O**WSHOE
SP**O**OLING
SP**O**RADIC
ST**O**CKADE
ST**O**CKING
ST**O**PPAGE
ST**O**TINKA
ST**O**WAWAY
TE**O**SINTE
TH**O**ROUGH
TH**O**USAND
TR**O**MBONE
TR**O**USERS
TW**O**PENCE
TW**O**PENNY
UX**O**RIOUS
VI**O**LABLE
VI**O**LENCE
WH**O**DUNIT

WH**O**MEVER
WH**O**PPING
WO**O**DBINE
WO**O**DCOCK
WO**O**DLAND
WO**O**DNOTE
WO**O**DPILE
WO**O**DRUFF
WO**O**DSHED
WO**O**DSMAN
WO**O**DWIND
WO**O**DWORK
WO**O**LSACK
WR**O**NGFUL
YE**O**MANRY
ZO**O**PHYTE
ZO**O**SPORE
AL**P**HABET
AM**P**ERAGE
AM**P**UTATE
AP**P**ANAGE
AP**P**ARENT
AP**P**ELLEE
AP**P**ENDIX
AP**P**ETITE
AP**P**LAUSE
AP**P**LIQUE
AP**P**OSITE
AP**P**RAISE
AP**P**ROACH
AP**P**ROVAL
AR**P**EGGIO
AS**P**ERITY
AS**P**HODEL
AS**P**HYXIA
AS**P**IRANT
AS**P**IRATE
CA**P**ACITY
CA**P**ESKIN
CA**P**RIOLE
CA**P**SICUM
CA**P**SULAR
CA**P**TIOUS
CA**P**UCHIN
CE**P**HALIC
CO**P**PERAS
CO**P**ULATE
CO**P**YBOOK
CO**P**YDESK
CU**P**BOARD
CU**P**IDITY
DE**P**ONENT
DE**P**UTIZE
DI**P**LOMAT
DI**P**STICK
EM**P**HASIS
EM**P**HATIC

EM**P**LOYEE
EM**P**ORIUM
EM**P**YREAN
ES**P**ALIER
ES**P**ECIAL
ES**P**OUSAL
ES**P**RESSO
EU**P**HORIA
EX**P**EDITE
EX**P**LICIT
EX**P**LODED
EX**P**ONENT
EX**P**OSURE
HE**P**ATICA
HY**P**NOSIS
HY**P**NOTIC
IM**P**ACTED
IM**P**ELLER
IM**P**ERIAL
IM**P**ETIGO
IM**P**LICIT
IM**P**OLITE
IM**P**OSING
IM**P**OSTOR
IM**P**OTENT
IM**P**RISON
IM**P**ROPER
IM**P**UDENT
IM**P**UNITY
JA**P**ANESE
LA**P**BOARD
LA**P**IDARY
LI**P**STICK
LO**P**SIDED
ME**P**HITIC
NA**P**OLEON
NE**P**ENTHE
NE**P**OTISM
OP**P**ONENT
OP**P**OSITE
PI**P**ELINE
PO**P**INJAY
PO**P**ULACE
PO**P**ULATE
PO**P**ULIST
PO**P**ULOUS
RE**P**ARTEE
RE**P**EATED
RE**P**ORTER
RE**P**RIEVE
RE**P**RISAL
RE**P**ROACH
RE**P**UBLIC
RI**P**ARIAN
SA**P**PHIRE
SE**P**ARATE
SU**P**EREGO

SU**P**ERIOR
SU**P**ERJET
SU**P**ERNAL
SU**P**PLANT
SU**P**POSED
SU**P**PRESS
SY**P**HILIS
TA**P**ESTRY
TA**P**EWORM
TO**P**OLOGY
TO**P**SIDES
TY**P**ECAST
TY**P**EFACE
UN**P**ERSON
UP**P**ERCUT
VA**P**ORING
VA**P**ORISH
VA**P**ORIZE
VA**P**OROUS
ZE**P**PELIN
AC**Q**UAINT
BE**Q**UEATH
CO**Q**UETTE
SE**Q**UENCE
AA**R**DVARK
AB**R**ASIVE
AB**R**OGATE
AC**R**IMONY
AC**R**OSTIC
AE**R**OLOGY
AE**R**ONAUT
AG**R**ARIAN
AG**R**ONOMY
AI**R**BORNE
AI**R**BRUSH
AI**R**CRAFT
AI**R**DROME
AI**R**FIELD
AI**R**FRAME
AI**R**LINER
AI**R**PLANE
AI**R**SPACE
AI**R**SPEED
AI**R**STRIP
AI**R**TIGHT
AR**R**OGANT
AR**R**OGATE
AT**R**OCITY
AT**R**OPINE
BA**R**BARIC
BA**R**BECUE
BA**R**BERRY
BA**R**BICAN
BA**R**BITAL
BA**R**EBACK
BA**R**EFOOT
BA**R**ITONE

BA**R**NACLE
BA**R**NYARD
BA**R**ONAGE
BA**R**ONESS
BA**R**OUCHE
BA**R**RACKS
BA**R**RATRY
BA**R**RETTE
BE**R**CEUSE
BE**R**EAVED
BE**R**IBERI
BE**R**MUDAS
BI**R**ACIAL
BI**R**DBATH
BI**R**DLIME
BI**R**DSEED
BI**R**THDAY
BO**R**DELLO
BU**R**GLARY
BU**R**GUNDY
BU**R**NOOSE
BU**R**SITIS
CA**R**ACOLE
CA**R**APACE
CA**R**DAMOM
CA**R**DIGAN
CA**R**DINAL
CA**R**EFREE
CA**R**ELESS
CA**R**EWORN
CA**R**ILLON
CA**R**NAUBA
CA**R**NIVAL
CA**R**OTENE
CA**R**OUSAL
CA**R**OUSEL
CA**R**RIAGE
CA**R**RYALL
CA**R**YATID
CE**R**AMIST
CE**R**EBRUM
CE**R**EMENT
CE**R**EMONY
CE**R**ULEAN
CE**R**VICAL
CH**R**ISTEN
CH**R**ISTIE
CH**R**OMIUM
CI**R**CUITY
CI**R**CULAR
CO**R**DLESS
CO**R**DOVAN
CO**R**DUROY
CO**R**NCRIB
CO**R**NMEAL
CO**R**ONACH
CO**R**ONARY

CO**R**PORAL
CO**R**PSMAN
CO**R**RIDOR
CO**R**UNDUM
CO**R**VETTE
CU**R**ATIVE
CU**R**LICUE
CU**R**RENCY
DA**R**KLING
DA**R**KROOM
DA**R**KSOME
DE**R**ELICT
DE**R**OGATE
DE**R**RIERE
DI**R**ECTOR
DO**R**MOUSE
DU**R**ATION
EA**R**NINGS
EA**R**PHONE
ET**R**USCAN
EU**R**ASIAN
EU**R**OBOND
EU**R**OPEAN
EU**R**OPIUM
FA**R**EWELL
FA**R**MHAND
FA**R**MLAND
FA**R**MYARD
FA**R**OUCHE
FA**R**THEST
FA**R**THING
FE**R**OCITY
FE**R**VENCY
FI**R**EBALL
FI**R**EBOAT
FI**R**EBOMB
FI**R**ECLAY
FI**R**EDAMP
FI**R**EPLUG
FI**R**ESIDE
FI**R**ETRAP
FI**R**EWOOD
FI**R**EWORK
FI**R**MWARE
FO**R**CIBLE
FO**R**EBEAR
FO**R**EBODE
FO**R**ECAST
FO**R**EDOOM
FO**R**EFEND
FO**R**EFOOT
FO**R**EGONE
FO**R**EHAND
FO**R**EHEAD
FO**R**EKNOW
FO**R**ELADY
FO**R**ELAND

FO**R**ELIMB
FO**R**ELOCK
FO**R**EMAST
FO**R**EMOST
FO**R**ENAME
FO**R**ENOON
FO**R**ENSIC
FO**R**EPART
FO**R**ESAIL
FO**R**ESKIN
FO**R**ESTRY
FO**R**ETELL
FO**R**EWARN
FO**R**EWORD
FO**R**KLIFT
FO**R**MERLY
FO**R**MLESS
FO**R**SOOTH
FO**R**SWEAR
FO**R**TRESS
FO**R**TUITY
FO**R**WARDS
FU**R**BELOW
FU**R**LOUGH
FU**R**THEST
GA**R**DENIA
GA**R**GOYLE
GA**R**RISON
GE**R**ANIUM
GE**R**MINAL
GO**R**GEOUS
HA**R**ANGUE
HA**R**DBACK
HA**R**DBALL
HA**R**DHACK
HA**R**DSHIP
HA**R**DTACK
HA**R**DWARE
HA**R**DWOOD
HA**R**EBELL
HA**R**MONIC
HA**R**RIDAN
HE**R**ALDIC
HE**R**ALDRY
HE**R**CULES
HE**R**DSMAN
HE**R**EDITY
HE**R**EFORD
HE**R**EUNTO
HE**R**EUPON
HE**R**EWITH
HE**R**ITAGE
HE**R**METIC
HI**R**ELING
HO**R**MONAL
HO**R**NBOOK
HO**R**NPIPE

HO**R**OLOGY
HO**R**RIBLE
HO**R**SEFLY
HO**R**SEMAN
IR**R**IGATE
IR**R**ITATE
JE**R**EMIAD
JU**R**ISTIC
KE**R**CHIEF
KE**R**OSINE
LA**R**BOARD
LA**R**KSPUR
LO**R**DSHIP
MA**R**ATHON
MA**R**BLING
MA**R**GRAVE
MA**R**IACHI
MA**R**IGOLD
MA**R**INATE
MA**R**ITIME
MA**R**JORAM
MA**R**KDOWN
MA**R**KSMAN
MA**R**MOSET
MA**R**QUESS
MA**R**QUISE
MA**R**RIAGE
MA**R**TINET
MA**R**ZIPAN
ME**R**CHANT
ME**R**CURIC
ME**R**IDIAN
ME**R**INGUE
MO**R**ALIST
MO**R**ALITY
MO**R**ALIZE
MO**R**EOVER
MO**R**IBUND
MO**R**OCCAN
MO**R**PHEME
MO**R**PHINE
MO**R**TGAGE
MO**R**TUARY
MY**R**MIDON
NA**R**COSIS
NA**R**COTIC
NO**R**SEMAN
NU**R**SLING
PA**R**ABOLA
PA**R**ADIGM
PA**R**ADISE
PA**R**AFFIN
PA**R**AKEET
PA**R**ALLAX
PA**R**ALLEL
PA**R**ALYZE
PA**R**AMOUR

PARANOIA
PARASITE
PARDONER
PARFOCAL
PARIETAL
PARLANCE
PARMESAN
PAROXYSM
PARTERRE
PARTIBLE
PARTICLE
PARTISAN
PERCEIVE
PERFECTO
PERFORCE
PERILUNE
PERIODIC
PERMEATE
PEROXIDE
PERSONAL
PERSPIRE
PERSUADE
PERVERSE
PHRASING
PORPHYRY
PORPOISE
PORRIDGE
PORTABLE
PORTHOLE
PORTIERE
PORTRAIT
PURBLIND
PURCHASE
PUREBRED
PURSLANE
PURULENT
SARDONIC
SCRABBLE
SCRAGGLY
SCRAMBLE
SCRIBBLE
SCROFULA
SCROUNGE
SCRUTINY
SERAGLIO
SERENADE
SERGEANT
SEROLOGY
SERVITOR
SHRAPNEL
SHREWISH
SORORITY
SORPTION
SPRINKLE
SPROCKET
STRADDLE
STRAGGLE
STRAIGHT
STRAITEN
STRANGER
STRANGLE
STRATEGY
STRATIFY
STREAMER
STRENGTH
STRICKEN
STRIDENT
STRIKING
STRINGED
STRINGER
STRUGGLE
STRUMPET
SURCEASE
SUREFIRE
SURGICAL
SURMOUNT
SURPLICE
SURPRISE
SURROUND
TARRAGON
TERMINAL
TERMINUS
TERRAPIN
TERRIBLE
TERRIFIC
TERTIARY
THRASHER
THREATEN
THRENODY
THROMBUS
THROTTLE
THRUSTER
TIRELESS
TIRESOME
TOREADOR
TORTILLA
TORTOISE
TORTUOUS
TURBOFAN
TURBOJET
TURMERIC
TURNCOAT
TURNOVER
TURNPIKE
TURNSPIT
UNRIDDLE
UPRISING
VARIABLE
VARIANCE
VARICOSE
VARIETAL
VARIORUM
VARISTOR
VERACITY
VERBATIM
VERBIAGE
VERBOTEN
VERMOUTH
VERONICA
VERSICLE
VERTEBRA
VERTICAL
VIRGINAL
VIROLOGY
VIRTUOSO
VIRTUOUS
VIRULENT
WARDROBE
WARDROOM
WARDSHIP
WAREROOM
WARFARIN
WARPLANE
WARRANTY
WEREWOLF
WIREDRAW
WIREHAIR
WIRELESS
WIREWORM
WORDBOOK
WORDPLAY
WORDSTAR
WORKABLE
WORKADAY
WORKBOOK
WORKROOM
WORKSHOP
WORMHOLE
WORMWOOD
ABSCISSA
ABSENTEE
ABSINTHE
ABSOLUTE
ABSTRACT
ABSTRUSE
AESTHETE
ASSASSIN
ASSEMBLE
ASSEMBLY
ASSORTED
AUSTRIAN
BASEBALL
BASEBORN
BASELESS
BASELINE
BASEMENT
BASILICA
BASILISK
BASSINET
BASSWOOD
BESMIRCH
BESTIARY
BESTRIDE
BISEXUAL
BUSINESS
BUSYBODY
BUSYWORK
CASEMENT
CASEWORK
CASHMERE
CASSETTE
CASTAWAY
CASTRATE
CASUALTY
CESAREAN
CESSPOOL
CISLUNAR
COSIGNER
COSMETIC
CUSPIDOR
CUSTOMER
DESCRIBE
DESELECT
DESIROUS
DESOLATE
DESPATCH
DESTRUCT
DISABUSE
DISAGREE
DISALLOW
DISARRAY
DISASTER
DISBURSE
DISCIPLE
DISCLAIM
DISCLOSE
DISCOLOR
DISCOUNT
DISCOVER
DISCREET
DISCRETE
DISFAVOR
DISGORGE
DISGRACE
DISGUISE
DISHEVEL
DISHONOR
DISINTER
DISJOINT
DISKETTE
DISLODGE
DISLOYAL
DISMOUNT
DISORDER
DISPATCH
DISPENSE
DISPERSE
DISPIRIT
DISPLACE
DISPOSAL
DISPROVE
DISQUIET
DISSEVER
DISSOLVE
DISSUADE
DISTANCE
DISTASTE
DISTINCT
DISTRACT
DISTRAIT
DISTRESS
DISTRICT
DISTRUST
DISUNITE
DISUNITY
DYSLEXIA
ENSCONCE
ENSEMBLE
ENSHRINE
ENSHROUD
ENSILAGE
FASCICLE
FASCISTA
FASTBACK
FASTNESS
FESTIVAL
FISHBOWL
FISHHOOK
FISHWIFE
FUSELAGE
GASLIGHT
GASOLINE
GASWORKS
GOSSAMER
HESITANT
HESITATE
HISPANIC
HOSPITAL
HOSTELRY
HUSTINGS
HYSTERIA
INSCRIBE
INSECURE
INSIGNIA
INSOLENT
INSOMNIA
INSOMUCH
INSPIRIT
INSTANCE
INSTINCT
INSTRUCT
INSULATE
ISSUANCE
LASERJET
LISTLESS
LUSCIOUS
MASSACRE
MASSEUSE
MASSLESS
MASTERLY
MASTHEAD
MASTODON
MESDAMES
MESHWORK
MESQUITE
MESSMATE
MISAPPLY
MISBRAND
MISCARRY
MISCHIEF
MISCIBLE
MISCOUNT
MISDOING
MISHMASH
MISJUDGE
MISLABEL
MISMATCH
MISNOMER
MISPLACE
MISPRINT
MISQUOTE
MISSHAPE
MISSPELL
MISSPEND
MISSTATE
MISTAKEN
MISTREAT
MISTRESS
MISTRIAL
MISTRUST
MISUSAGE
MOSQUITO
MOSSBACK
MUSCATEL
MUSHROOM
MUSICALE
MUSICIAN
MUSKETRY
MUSTACHE
MYSTICAL
MYSTIQUE
NASALIZE
NESTLING
OBSIDIAN
OBSOLETE
OBSTACLE
OBSTRUCT
PASSABLE
PASSBOOK
PASSOVER
PASSPORT
PASSWORD
PASTICHE
PASTILLE
PASTORAL
PASTRAMI
POSITION
POSITIVE
POSITRON
POSSIBLE
POSTCARD
POSTDATE
POSTHOLE
POSTLUDE
POSTMARK
POSTPAID
POSTPONE
PUSHCART
PUSHDOWN
PUSHOVER
PUSSYCAT
RESCRIPT
RESEARCH
RESEMBLE
RESERVED
RESIDENT
RESIDUAL
RESIDUUM
RESIGNED
RESISTOR
RESOLUTE
RESONANT
RESONATE
RESORTER
RESOURCE
RESPONSE
RESTLESS
RESTRAIN
RESTRICT
ROSEBUSH
ROSEMARY
ROSEWOOD
SUSPENSE
SYSADMIN
SYSTEMIC
TESTATOR
TESTICLE
UNSADDLE
UNSAVORY
UNSEEMLY
UNSETTLE
UNSHAPED
UNSOUGHT
UNSPRUNG
UNSTABLE
UNSTEADY
UNSTRUNG
UPSTAIRS
UPSTREAM
UPSTROKE
VASCULAR
VESICANT
VESTMENT
VISCERAL
VISCOUNT
VISICALC
VISITANT
WASHABLE
WASHBOWL
WASHROOM
WISEACRE
WISHBONE
WISTARIA
WISTERIA
ACTINISM
ACTINIUM
ACTIVATE
ACTIVISM
ACTIVITY
AFTERTAX
ALTHOUGH
ALTITUDE
ALTRUISM
ANTEATER
ANTEDATE
ANTELOPE
ANTERIOR
ANTEROOM
ANTHROPO
ANTIBODY
ANTIDOTE
ANTIMONY
ANTINOMY
ANTIPODE
ANTIPOPE
APTITUDE
ARTERIAL
ARTIFACT
ARTIFICE
ARTISTIC
ARTISTRY
ASTATINE
ASTERISK
ASTEROID
ASTONISH
ATTITUDE
ATTORNEY
AUTOBAHN
AUTOGIRO
AUTOJOIN
AUTOMATE
BATHROBE
BATHROOM
BETATRON
BITSTOCK
BOTULISM

BUTTRESS
CATACOMB
CATALYZE
CATAPULT
CATARACT
CATCHALL
CATCHING
CATEGORY
CATHETER
CATHOLIC
CITATION
CYTOLOGY
CYTOSINE
DATABASE
DATELESS
DATELINE
DETACHED
DETHRONE
DETONATE
DETOXIFY
DETRITUS
DUTIABLE
ENTANGLE
ENTHRALL
ENTHRONE
ENTIRETY
ENTRAILS
ENTRANCE
ENTRENCH
ESTIMATE
ESTONIAN
ESTRANGE
ESTROGEN
EXTERIOR
EXTERNAL
EXTRADOS
FATALISM
FATALITY
FETCHING
FUTILITY
FUTURISM
FUTURITY
GATEPOST
GUTTURAL
HATCHING
HATCHWAY
HITHERTO
HOTHOUSE
INTAGLIO
INTEGRAL
INTENDED
INTERCOM
INTEREST
INTERIOR
INTERMIT
INTERMIX
INTERNAL
INTERNEE
INTERNET
INTERROG
INTERVAL
INTIMATE
INTRADOS
INTRENCH
INTREPID
INTRIGUE
INTROMIT
ISTHMIAN
JETTISON
KATAKANA
LATCHKEY
LATITUDE
LETHARGY
LITERARY
LITERATE
LITERATI
LITIGANT
LITIGATE
LITTORAL
LUTETIUM
LUTHERAN
MATERIAL
MATERIEL
MATERNAL
MATTRESS
MATURATE
MATURITY
METAFILE
METAPHOR
METEORIC
METHANOL
METRICAL
MITIGATE
MOTHBALL
MOTIVATE
MOTORCAR
MOTORIZE
MOTORMAN
MOTOROLA
MUTATION
MUTILATE
NATALITY
NATIONAL
NATIVISM
NATIVITY
NITROGEN
NOTARIAL
NOTARIZE
NOTATION
NOTEBOOK
NOTIONAL
NUTHATCH
NUTRIENT
NUTSHELL
OPTICIAN
OPTIMISM
ORTHODOX
ORTHOEPY
OUTBOARD
OUTBOUND
OUTBREAK
OUTBURST
OUTCLASS
OUTDATED
OUTDOORS
OUTFIELD
OUTFIGHT
OUTFLANK
OUTGOING
OUTGUESS
OUTHOUSE
OUTLYING
OUTMODED
OUTPOINT
OUTREACH
OUTRIDER
OUTRIGHT
OUTSHINE
OUTSIDER
OUTSMART
OUTSPEND
OUTSTRIP
OUTWEIGH
PATERNAL
PATHETIC
PATHOGEN
PATIENCE
PETITION
PETTIFOG
PETULANT
PITCHMAN
PITIABLE
PITILESS
PITTANCE
POTATION
POTBELLY
POTSHERD
PUTATIVE
RATIONAL
RATTLING
RETAINER
RETARDED
RETICENT
RETIRING
RETRENCH
RETRIEVE
RETROFIT
RETURNEE
RUTABAGA
RUTHLESS
SATURATE
SATURDAY
SETSCREW
SITUATED
TITANIUM
TITILATE
TITIVATE
TITMOUSE
TOTALITY
TUTELAGE
TUTELARY
TUTORIAL
ULTERIOR
ULTIMATE
UNTANGLE
UNTAUGHT
UNTIMELY
UNTOWARD
UPTHRUST
VITALITY
VITALIZE
VITREOUS
WATCHDOG
WATCHFUL
WATCHMAN
WATERLOO
WATERWAY
WITCHERY
WITCHING
WITHDRAW
WITHHOLD
ABUNDANT
ABUTMENT
ABUTTALS
ADULTERY
ALUMINUM
AQUACADE
AQUANAUT
AQUARIUM
AQUEDUCT
AQUILINE
BLUDGEON
BLUEBELL
BLUEBIRD
BLUEFISH
BLUENOSE
BOUFFANT
BOUILLON
BOUNDARY
BOUTIQUE
CAUDILLO
CAULDRON
CAUSERIE
CAUSEWAY
CAUTIOUS
CHUTZPAH
CLUBFOOT
COUCHANT
COUNTESS
COUPLING
COURTESY
COURTIER
CRUCIBLE
CRUCIFIX
CRUZEIRO
DAUGHTER
DIURETIC
DOUBLOON
DOUBTFUL
DOUGHBOY
DOUGHNUT
DRUGGIST
DRUMBEAT
DRUNKARD
EDUCABLE
EMULSIFY
EMULSION
ENURESIS
EQUALIZE
EQUATION
EQUIPAGE
FAUBOURG
FLUIDRAM
FLUORIDE
FLUORINE
FLUORITE
FOUNTAIN
FOURFOLD
FOURSOME
FOURTEEN
FRUCTIFY
FRUITION
GAUNTLET
GOURMAND
GRUELING
GRUESOME
HAUTBOIS
HOUSEBOY
HOUSEFLY
HOUSETOP
INUNDATE
JAUNDICE
LAUDANUM
LAUGHTER
LAUNCHER
LAUREATE
LEUKEMIA
MOUNTAIN
MOUNTING
MOURNFUL
MOURNING
NAUSEATE
NAUTICAL
NAUTILUS
NEURITIS
NEUROSIS
NEUROTIC
NEUTRINO
OPUSCULE
PLUMBING
POULTICE
POUNDAGE
PRURIENT
ROUGHAGE
ROULETTE
ROUTEMAN
SAUCEPAN
SAUTERNE
SCULLERY
SCULLION
SCULPTOR
SHUTDOWN
SKULLCAP
SLUGGARD
SLUGGISH
SLUMLORD
SOUTHPAW
SOUVENIR
SPURIOUS
SQUABBLE
SQUADRON
SQUANDER
SQUEEGEE
SQUIRREL
STUBBORN
STUDBOOK
STUDDING
STUDIOUS
STUFFING
STULTIFY
STUNNING
STURGEON
TEUTONIC
THURSDAY
TOUCHING
TRUCKAGE
TRUETYPE
TRUMPERY
TRUNCATE
TRUSTFUL
TRUTHFUL
USUFRUCT
USURIOUS
VAULTING
YOUNGISH
YOURSELF
YOUTHFUL
ADVISORY
ADVOCATE
BEVERAGE
CAVALIER
CIVILIAN
CIVILITY
CIVILIZE
COVENANT
COVERAGE
COVERALL
COVERLET
DEVILISH
DEVOTION
DIVAGATE
DIVIDEND
DIVINITY
DIVISION
DIVISIVE
DIVORCEE
DOVETAIL
ENVELOPE
ENVIABLE
ENVIRONS
ENVISAGE
FAVORITE
GIVEAWAY
GOVERNOR
INVASION
INVEIGLE
INVERTER
INVIABLE
INVITING
INVOLUTE
INVOLVED
JUVENILE
LAVATORY
LAVENDER
LEVERAGE
LEVITATE
LIVELONG
LIVERISH
LOVEBIRD
LOVELORN
LOVESICK
MAVERICK
MOVEMENT
NAVIGATE
NOVELIZE
NOVEMBER
PAVEMENT
PAVILION
RAVENING
RAVENOUS
REVANCHE
REVEILLE
REVENUER
REVEREND
REVERENT
REVERSAL
REVIEWER
REVIVIFY
REVOLVER
RIVERBED
UNVOICED
VIVACITY
VIVARIUM
BEWILDER
BIWEEKLY
BOWSPRIT
DEWBERRY
DOWNBEAT
DOWNCAST
DOWNFALL
DOWNHILL
DOWNLOAD
DOWNPOUR
DOWNTOWN
DOWNTURN
DOWNWARD
DOWNWIND
HAWAIIAN
HAWKWEED
HAWTHORN
HOWITZER
INWARDLY
LAWGIVER
LAWMAKER
NEWCOMER
NEWFOUND
NEWLYWED
NEWSCAST
NEWSREEL
NOWADAYS
PAWNSHOP
RAWBONED
SAWHORSE
SEWERAGE
TOWELING
TOWERING
TOWNSHIP
TOWNSMAN
UNWIELDY
UNWONTED
UNWORTHY
COXSWAIN
DEXTROSE
DOXOLOGY
FIXATION
FIXATIVE
FOXGLOVE
FOXHOUND
LAXATIVE
MAXIMIZE
PIXELATE
SIXPENCE
TAXONOMY
TAXPAYER
TEXTBOOK
VEXATION

AN**Y**PLACE
AN**Y**THING
AN**Y**WHERE
AT**Y**PICAL
BA**Y**BERRY
BI**Y**EARLY
CR**Y**OLITE
DA**Y**BREAK
DA**Y**DREAM
DA**Y**LIGHT
EG**Y**PTIAN
ER**Y**THEMA
FL**Y**BLOWN
FL**Y**PAPER
FL**Y**SPECK
FL**Y**WHEEL
GL**Y**CERIN
GL**Y**CEROL
GL**Y**COGEN
GU**Y**ANESE
HA**Y**STACK
JO**Y**STICK
KE**Y**BOARD
KE**Y**PUNCH
KE**Y**STONE
KE**Y**WORDS
LA**Y**ERING
LO**Y**ALIST
MA**Y**APPLE
PA**Y**CHECK
PH**Y**SICAL
PH**Y**SIQUE
RH**Y**OLITE
RO**Y**ALIST
SK**Y**LIGHT
SP**Y**GLASS
VO**Y**AGEUR
WA**Y**FARER
PI**Z**ZERIA
SU**Z**ERAIN
UN**Z**IPPED
WI**Z**ARDRY

### 4TH LETTER

ABL**A**TION
ABL**A**TIVE
ABR**A**SIVE
ADJ**A**CENT
AGR**A**RIAN
ALB**A**CORE
ALB**A**NIAN
ALE**A**TORY
ALI**A**SING
ALK**A**LOID
APH**A**NITE
APP**A**NAGE
APP**A**RENT
AQU**A**CADE
AQU**A**NAUT
AQU**A**RIUM
ARB**A**LEST
ARM**A**MENT
ARM**A**TURE
ASS**A**SSIN
AST**A**TINE
AVI**A**TION
AVI**A**TRIX
BED**A**ZZLE
BEH**A**VIOR
BET**A**TRON
BIN**A**URAL
BIR**A**CIAL
BRE**A**KAGE
BRE**A**KOUT
CAL**A**BASH
CAL**A**DIUM
CAL**A**MINE
CAL**A**MITY
CAN**A**DIAN
CAN**A**ILLE
CAN**A**LIZE
CAP**A**CITY
CAR**A**COLE
CAR**A**PACE
CAT**A**COMB
CAT**A**LYZE
CAT**A**PULT
CAT**A**RACT
CAV**A**LIER
CER**A**MIST
CES**A**REAN
CIC**A**TRIX
CIT**A**TION
CLE**A**RING
CLE**A**VAGE
COL**A**NDER
COM**A**NCHE
CRE**A**MERY
CRE**A**TION
CRE**A**TURE
CUR**A**TIVE
DAT**A**BASE
DEC**A**NTER
DEK**A**GRAM
DEL**A**WARE
DEM**A**RCHE
DEN**A**TURE
DET**A**CHED
DID**A**CTIC
DIL**A**TORY
DIS**A**BUSE
DIS**A**GREE
DIS**A**LLOW
DIS**A**RRAY
DIS**A**STER
DIV**A**GATE
DON**A**TION
DRE**A**DFUL
DUR**A**TION
DYN**A**MITE
EMB**A**TTLE
END**A**NGER
ENG**A**GING
ENT**A**NGLE
EQU**A**LIZE
EQU**A**TION
ESC**A**LATE
ESC**A**LLOP
ESC**A**PADE
ESC**A**PISM
ESC**A**ROLE
ESP**A**LIER
EUR**A**SIAN
EXC**A**VATE
FAT**A**LISM
FAT**A**LITY
FIL**A**MENT
FIN**A**LIST
FIN**A**LIZE
FIX**A**TION
FIX**A**TIVE
FLE**A**BANE
FLE**A**BITE
FUM**A**ROLE
GAD**A**BOUT
GER**A**NIUM
GIG**A**BYTE
GIG**A**NTIC
GLO**A**MING
GUY**A**NESE
HAB**A**NERA
HAR**A**NGUE
HAW**A**IIAN
HEC**A**TOMB
HEM**A**TITE
HEP**A**TICA
HER**A**LDIC
HER**A**LDRY
HUM**A**NISM
HUM**A**NITY
HUM**A**NIZE
HUM**A**NOID
IDE**A**LISM
IDE**A**LIZE
IDE**A**TION
IMM**A**NENT
IMM**A**TURE
IMP**A**CTED
INF**A**MOUS
INF**A**NTRY
INH**A**LANT
INT**A**GLIO
INV**A**SION
INW**A**RDLY
ISL**A**NDER
JAP**A**NESE
KAM**A**AINA
KAT**A**KANA
LAM**A**SERY
LAV**A**TORY
LAX**A**TIVE
LEG**A**LISM
LEG**A**TION
LIB**A**TION
LIG**A**MENT
LIG**A**TURE
LOC**A**LITY
LOC**A**LIZE
LOC**A**TION
LOY**A**LIST
MAC**A**RONI
MAC**A**ROON
MAG**A**ZINE
MAH**A**RAJA
MAH**A**RANI
MAL**A**MUTE
MAL**A**PERT
MAL**A**RKEY
MAL**A**WIAN
MAR**A**THON
MAY**A**PPLE
MED**A**LIST
MEG**A**BYTE
MEG**A**LITH
MEL**A**NISM
MEL**A**NOMA
MET**A**FILE
MET**A**PHOR
MIN**A**TORY
MIS**A**PPLY
MOL**A**SSES
MON**A**RCHY
MON**A**STIC
MON**A**URAL
MOR**A**LIST
MOR**A**LITY
MOR**A**LIZE
MUT**A**TION
NAS**A**LIZE
NAT**A**LITY
NEG**A**TION
NEG**A**TIVE
NEM**A**TODE
NOT**A**RIAL
NOT**A**RIZE
NOT**A**TION
NOW**A**DAYS
NUG**A**TORY
OBL**A**TION
OCC**A**SION
OLE**A**NDER
ORG**A**NISM
ORG**A**NIST
ORG**A**NIZE
ORN**A**MENT
PAL**A**TINE
PAN**A**TELA
PAR**A**BOLA
PAR**A**DIGM
PAR**A**DISE
PAR**A**FFIN
PAR**A**KEET
PAR**A**LLAX
PAR**A**LLEL
PAR**A**LYZE
PAR**A**MOUR
PAR**A**NOIA
PAR**A**SITE
PED**A**GOGY
PEN**A**LIZE
PHE**A**SANT
PHR**A**SING
PIC**A**YUNE
PIL**A**STER
PIN**A**FORE
PLE**A**SANT
PLE**A**SING
PLE**A**SURE
POL**A**RITY
POL**A**RIZE
POT**A**TION
PRE**A**MBLE
PUT**A**TIVE
REL**A**TION
REL**A**TIVE
REL**A**XANT
REP**A**RTEE
RET**A**INER
RET**A**RDED
REV**A**NCHE
RIP**A**RIAN
ROM**A**NIAN
ROM**A**NTIC
ROY**A**LIST
RUM**A**NIAN
RUN**A**BOUT
RUN**A**GATE
RUT**A**BAGA
SAG**A**MORE
SAM**A**RIUM
SCI**A**TICA
SCR**A**BBLE
SCR**A**GGLY
SCR**A**MBLE
SED**A**TIVE
SEM**A**NTIC
SEP**A**RATE
SER**A**GLIO
SHR**A**PNEL
SOL**A**RIUM
SON**A**TINA
SPH**A**GNUM
SPL**A**TTER
SQU**A**BBLE
SQU**A**DRON
SQU**A**NDER
STE**A**LTHY
STR**A**DDLE
STR**A**GGLE
STR**A**IGHT
STR**A**ITEN
STR**A**NGER
STR**A**NGLE
STR**A**TEGY
STR**A**TIFY
SYB**A**RITE
SYC**A**MORE
SYS**A**DMIN
TAM**A**RACK
TAM**A**RIND
TEN**A**NTRY
THI**A**MINE
THR**A**SHER
TIT**A**NIUM
TOM**A**HAWK
TON**A**LITY
TOT**A**LITY
TRE**A**SURE
TRE**A**SURY
TRE**A**TISE
TRI**A**NGLE
UNE**A**RNED
UNF**A**STEN
UNG**A**INLY
UNI**A**XIAL
UNL**A**WFUL
UNS**A**DDLE
UNS**A**VORY
UNT**A**NGLE
UNT**A**UGHT
URB**A**NITE
URB**A**NIZE
VAC**A**TION
VAG**A**BOND
VAN**A**DIUM
VEG**A**NISM
VEN**A**TION
VER**A**CITY
VEX**A**TION
VIC**A**RAGE
VIT**A**LITY
VIT**A**LIZE
VIV**A**CITY
VIV**A**RIUM
VOC**A**LIST
VOC**A**LIZE
VOC**A**TION
VOC**A**TIVE
VOL**A**TILE
VOY**A**GEUR
WIZ**A**RDRY
WOM**A**NISH
AIR**B**ORNE
AIR**B**RUSH
BAR**B**ARIC
BAR**B**ECUE
BAR**B**ERRY
BAR**B**ICAN
BAR**B**ITAL
BAY**B**ERRY
CLU**B**FOOT
COM**B**INGS
CRI**B**BAGE
CUP**B**OARD
DAY**B**REAK
DEW**B**ERRY
DIA**B**ETES
DIA**B**OLIC
DIS**B**URSE
DOU**B**LOON
DOU**B**TFUL
DUM**B**BELL
FAU**B**OURG
FLY**B**LOWN
FUR**B**ELOW
GLA**B**ROUS
GLO**B**ULIN
ICE**B**OUND
JAM**B**OREE
KEY**B**OARD
LAM**B**ASTE
LAM**B**SKIN
LAP**B**OARD
LAR**B**OARD
MAR**B**LING
MEM**B**RANE
MIS**B**RAND
MUL**B**ERRY
OUT**B**OARD
OUT**B**OUND
OUT**B**REAK
OUT**B**URST
PLE**B**EIAN
POT**B**ELLY
PRO**B**ABLE
PUR**B**LIND
RAW**B**ONED
RUM**B**LING
SCA**B**BARD
SCA**B**ROUS
SEA**B**OARD
SNO**B**BERY
SOM**B**RERO
STU**B**BORN
SYM**B**OLIC
TIM**B**ERED
TRI**B**UNAL
TUR**B**OFAN
TUR**B**OJET
VER**B**ATIM
VER**B**IAGE
VER**B**OTEN
ABS**C**ISSA
AIR**C**RAFT
ALA**C**RITY
AMI**C**ABLE
ANA**C**ONDA
ANE**C**DOTE
ANE**C**HOIC
ARA**C**HNID
ARM**C**HAIR
BAC**C**ARAT
BEE**C**HNUT
BER**C**EUSE
BIO**C**IDAL
BLA**C**KING
BLA**C**KOUT
BLA**C**KTOP
BLO**C**KADE
BRA**C**ELET
BRA**C**KISH
BRI**C**KBAT
BRO**C**COLI
BRO**C**HURE
CAL**C**ULUS
CAT**C**HALL
CAT**C**HING
CHE**C**KERS
CHE**C**KOFF
CHE**C**KOUT
CHE**C**KSUM
CIN**C**HONA
CIN**C**TURE
CIR**C**UITY
CIR**C**ULAR
COA**C**HMAN
CON**C**EIVE
CON**C**ERTO
CON**C**LAVE
CON**C**LUDE
CON**C**RETE
COU**C**HANT
CRA**C**KPOT

CRO**C**KERY
CRU**C**IBLE
CRU**C**IFIX
DES**C**RIBE
DIS**C**IPLE
DIS**C**LAIM
DIS**C**LOSE
DIS**C**OLOR
DIS**C**OUNT
DIS**C**OVER
DIS**C**REET
DIS**C**RETE
DUL**C**IMER
EDU**C**ABLE
ELE**C**TION
ELE**C**TIVE
ELE**C**TRIC
ELE**C**TRON
EMA**C**IATE
ENS**C**ONCE
ERE**C**TILE
ERE**C**TION
EVA**C**UATE
EXA**C**TING
EXE**C**RATE
EXE**C**UTOR
FAL**C**HION
FAN**C**IFUL
FAS**C**ICLE
FAS**C**ISTA
FET**C**HING
FOR**C**IBLE
FRA**C**TION
FRA**C**TURE
FRI**C**TION
FRU**C**TIFY
FUN**C**TION
GIM**C**RACK
GLA**C**IATE
GLY**C**ERIN
GLY**C**EROL
GLY**C**OGEN
GOD**C**HILD
GRA**C**IOUS
HAT**C**HING
HAT**C**HWAY
HEN**C**HMAN
HER**C**ULES
HYA**C**INTH
INS**C**RIBE
JUN**C**TION
JUN**C**TURE
KER**C**HIEF
KNI**C**KERS
KNO**C**KOUT
LAT**C**HKEY
LIN**C**HPIN

LUN**C**HEON
LUS**C**IOUS
MAN**C**IPLE
MER**C**HANT
MER**C**URIC
MIS**C**ARRY
MIS**C**HIEF
MIS**C**IBLE
MIS**C**OUNT
MOC**C**ASIN
MUS**C**ATEL
NAR**C**OSIS
NAR**C**OTIC
NEW**C**OMER
OIL**C**LOTH
OUT**C**LASS
PAN**C**REAS
PAY**C**HECK
PEN**C**HANT
PER**C**EIVE
PIL**C**HARD
PIT**C**HMAN
PLA**C**ENTA
PLE**C**TRUM
PRA**C**TICE
PRE**C**INCT
PRE**C**IOUS
PRE**C**LUDE
PRO**C**AINE
PRO**C**EEDS
PRO**C**LAIM
PUN**C**HEON
PUN**C**TUAL
PUN**C**TURE
PUR**C**HASE
REA**C**TANT
REA**C**TION
REA**C**TIVE
RES**C**RIPT
SAN**C**TIFY
SAN**C**TION
SAN**C**TITY
SAU**C**EPAN
SEA**C**OAST
SHO**C**KING
SPA**C**EMAN
SPA**C**IOUS
SPE**C**IFIC
SPE**C**IMEN
SPE**C**IOUS
SPE**C**TRAL
SPE**C**TRUM
STA**C**CATO
STI**C**KLER
STO**C**KADE
STO**C**KING
SUC**C**INCT

SUR**C**EASE
TEA**C**HING
THI**C**KSET
TIN**C**TURE
TOU**C**HING
TRA**C**KAGE
TRA**C**TATE
TRA**C**TION
TRI**C**HINA
TRI**C**KERY
TRI**C**OLOR
TRI**C**YCLE
TRU**C**KAGE
UNI**C**YCLE
VAC**C**INIA
VAS**C**ULAR
VIN**C**IBLE
VIS**C**ERAL
VIS**C**OUNT
VOL**C**ANIC
WAT**C**HDOG
WAT**C**HFUL
WAT**C**HMAN
WIT**C**HERY
WIT**C**HING
WRE**C**KAGE
ZUC**C**HINI
AAR**D**VARK
ACA**D**EMIC
ACI**D**HEAD
ACI**D**OSIS
AIR**D**ROME
BAE**D**EKER
BAN**D**ANNA
BID**D**ABLE
BIR**D**BATH
BIR**D**LIME
BIR**D**SEED
BLU**D**GEON
BOL**D**FACE
BON**D**SMAN
BOR**D**ELLO
BUD**D**HISM
BUN**D**LING
CAR**D**AMOM
CAR**D**IGAN
CAR**D**INAL
CAU**D**ILLO
CON**D**ENSE
COR**D**LESS
COR**D**OVAN
COR**D**UROY
CRE**D**ENCE
CRE**D**ENZA
CRE**D**IBLE
CRE**D**ITOR
DAN**D**RUFF

DAY**D**REAM
DEA**D**BEAT
DEA**D**LINE
DEA**D**LOCK
DEA**D**WOOD
DOL**D**RUMS
DUO**D**ENUM
EPI**D**EMIC
EVI**D**ENCE
FAN**D**ANGO
FEE**D**BACK
FEL**D**SPAR
FOL**D**AWAY
FOL**D**BOAT
FOL**D**EROL
GAR**D**ENIA
GEN**D**ARME
GEO**D**ESIC
GLA**D**SOME
GOL**D**FISH
GOO**D**NESS
GOO**D**WIFE
GOO**D**WILL
GRA**D**IENT
GRA**D**UATE
GRI**D**IRON
GUI**D**ANCE
HAN**D**BALL
HAN**D**BILL
HAN**D**BOOK
HAN**D**CUFF
HAN**D**ICAP
HAN**D**MADE
HAN**D**PICK
HAN**D**RAIL
HAN**D**SOME
HAN**D**YMAN
HAR**D**BACK
HAR**D**BALL
HAR**D**HACK
HAR**D**SHIP
HAR**D**TACK
HAR**D**WARE
HAR**D**WOOD
HEA**D**ACHE
HEA**D**BAND
HEA**D**GEAR
HEA**D**LAND
HEA**D**LINE
HEA**D**LOCK
HEA**D**LONG
HEA**D**REST
HEA**D**ROOM
HEA**D**SHIP
HEA**D**SMAN
HEA**D**WORD
HEA**D**WORK

HER**D**SMAN
HIN**D**MOST
HIN**D**UISM
HOL**D**OVER
HOO**D**WINK
INE**D**ITED
KIN**D**LING
LAN**D**FALL
LAN**D**FILL
LAN**D**FORM
LAN**D**LORD
LAN**D**MARK
LAN**D**MASS
LAN**D**SMAN
LAN**D**WARD
LAU**D**ANUM
LOR**D**SHIP
MAG**D**ALEN
MAN**D**AMUS
MAN**D**ARIN
MAN**D**IBLE
MAN**D**OLIN
MAN**D**RAKE
MES**D**AMES
MID**D**LING
MIN**D**LESS
MIS**D**OING
NEE**D**LESS
NON**D**AIRY
OBE**D**IENT
OUT**D**ATED
OUT**D**OORS
PAN**D**EMIC
PAN**D**OWDY
PAR**D**ONER
PEN**D**ULUM
PID**D**LING
PRO**D**IGAL
PUD**D**LING
QUA**D**RANT
QUA**D**ROON
ROA**D**SIDE
ROA**D**STER
ROA**D**WORK
SAD**D**UCEE
SAN**D**BANK
SAN**D**WICH
SAR**D**ONIC
SEE**D**LING
SEE**D**TIME
SOL**D**IERY
STU**D**BOOK
STU**D**DING
STU**D**IOUS
SUN**D**RIES
SYN**D**ROME
TEN**D**ENCY

VEN**D**ETTA
WAR**D**ROBE
WAR**D**ROOM
WAR**D**SHIP
WEL**D**MENT
WHO**D**UNIT
WIL**D**FIRE
WIL**D**FOWL
WIL**D**LIFE
WIL**D**WOOD
WIN**D**BURN
WIN**D**FALL
WIN**D**LASS
WIN**D**MILL
WIN**D**PIPE
WIN**D**WARD
WON**D**ROUS
WOO**D**BINE
WOO**D**COCK
WOO**D**LAND
WOO**D**NOTE
WOO**D**PILE
WOO**D**RUFF
WOO**D**SHED
WOO**D**SMAN
WOO**D**WIND
WOO**D**WORK
WOR**D**BOOK
WOR**D**PLAY
WOR**D**STAR
ABN**E**GATE
ABS**E**NTEE
ADD**E**NDUM
ADH**E**SION
ADH**E**SIVE
AFF**E**CTED
AFF**E**RENT
AFT**E**RTAX
ALD**E**RMAN
ALG**E**RIAN
ALI**E**NATE
ALI**E**NIST
ALL**E**GORY
ALL**E**LUIA
ALL**E**RGEN
ALL**E**YWAY
AMO**E**BOID
AMP**E**RAGE
ANA**E**ROBE
ANC**E**STOR
ANC**E**STRY
ANG**E**LICA
ANT**E**ATER
ANT**E**DATE
ANT**E**LOPE
ANT**E**RIOR
ANT**E**ROOM

APH**E**LION
APP**E**LLEE
APP**E**NDIX
APP**E**TITE
AQU**E**DUCT
ARP**E**GGIO
ART**E**RIAL
ASB**E**STOS
ASP**E**RITY
ASS**E**MBLE
ASS**E**MBLY
AST**E**RISK
AST**E**ROID
AXL**E**TREE
BAK**E**SHOP
BAR**E**BACK
BAR**E**FOOT
BAS**E**BALL
BAS**E**BORN
BAS**E**LESS
BAS**E**LINE
BAS**E**MENT
BEH**E**MOTH
BEN**E**DICT
BEN**E**FICE
BER**E**AVED
BEV**E**RAGE
BIS**E**XUAL
BIW**E**EKLY
BIY**E**ARLY
BLU**E**BELL
BLU**E**BIRD
BLU**E**FISH
BLU**E**NOSE
BOG**E**YMAN
BOH**E**MIAN
BRE**E**DING
CAG**E**LING
CAK**E**WALK
CAL**E**NDAR
CAL**E**NDER
CAM**E**LLIA
CAP**E**SKIN
CAR**E**FREE
CAR**E**LESS
CAR**E**WORN
CAS**E**MENT
CAS**E**WORK
CAT**E**GORY
CEL**E**RITY
CEM**E**NTUM
CEM**E**TERY
CER**E**BRUM
CER**E**MENT
CER**E**MONY
CHE**E**RFUL
CIC**E**RONE

COH**E**RENT
COH**E**SION
COL**E**SLAW
COM**E**BACK
COM**E**DIAN
COM**E**DOWN
COV**E**NANT
COV**E**RAGE
COV**E**RALL
COV**E**RLET
CRE**E**PING
DAT**E**LESS
DAT**E**LINE
DEC**E**DENT
DEC**E**MBER
DEF**E**CATE
DEJ**E**CTED
DEL**E**GATE
DEM**E**ANOR
DEM**E**NTED
DEM**E**NTIA
DER**E**LICT
DES**E**LECT
DIR**E**CTOR
DOM**E**STIC
DOV**E**TAIL
EDG**E**WAYS
EFF**E**RENT
EMB**E**ZZLE
ENC**E**INTE
END**E**AVOR
ENF**E**EBLE
ENG**E**NDER
ENS**E**MBLE
ENV**E**LOPE
ESP**E**CIAL
ETH**E**REAL
ETH**E**RNET
EUG**E**NICS
EXP**E**DITE
EXT**E**RIOR
EXT**E**RNAL
FAC**E**DOWN
FAD**E**LESS
FAR**E**WELL
FED**E**RATE
FID**E**LITY
FIN**E**SPUN
FIR**E**BALL
FIR**E**BOAT
FIR**E**BOMB
FIR**E**CLAY
FIR**E**DAMP
FIR**E**PLUG
FIR**E**SIDE
FIR**E**TRAP
FIR**E**WOOD

FIREWORK
FLEETING
FOREBEAR
FOREBODE
FORECAST
FOREDOOM
FOREFEND
FOREFOOT
FOREGONE
FOREHAND
FOREHEAD
FOREKNOW
FORELADY
FORELAND
FORELIMB
FORELOCK
FOREMAST
FOREMOST
FORENAME
FORENOON
FORENSIC
FOREPART
FORESAIL
FORESKIN
FORESTRY
FORETELL
FOREWARN
FOREWORD
FREEBORN
FREEDMAN
FREEHAND
FREEHOLD
FREELOAD
FREEWILL
FUNERARY
FUNEREAL
FUSELAGE
GAMECOCK
GAMESOME
GAMESTER
GATEPOST
GENERATE
GENEROUS
GENETICS
GIVEAWAY
GOVERNOR
GREEKING
GREENERY
GREETING
GRIEVOUS
GRUELING
GRUESOME
HAREBELL
HEGEMONY
HEREDITY
HEREFORD
HEREUNTO
HEREUPON
HEREWITH
HIDEAWAY
HIRELING
HOMEBODY
HOMEBRED
HOMELAND
HOMEMADE
HOMEROOM
HOMESICK
HOMESPUN
HOMEWARD
HOMEWORK
HONEYDEW
HYMENEAL
IMBECILE
IMPELLER
IMPERIAL
IMPETIGO
INDEBTED
INDECENT
INFERIOR
INFERNAL
INHERENT
INSECURE
INTEGRAL
INTENDED
INTERCOM
INTEREST
INTERIOR
INTERMIT
INTERMIX
INTERNAL
INTERNEE
INTERNET
INTERROG
INTERVAL
INVEIGLE
INVERTER
JEREMIAD
JUVENILE
KINETICS
KNEEHOLE
LACERATE
LACEWING
LASERJET
LAVENDER
LAYERING
LEVERAGE
LIBERATE
LICENSEE
LIFEBOAT
LIFELINE
LIFELONG
LIFETIME
LIFEWORK
LIKENESS
LIKEWISE
LIMEKILN
LIMERICK
LINESMAN
LITERARY
LITERATE
LITERATI
LIVELONG
LIVERISH
LODESTAR
LONESOME
LOVEBIRD
LOVELORN
LOVESICK
LUKEWARM
LUTETIUM
MACERATE
MANEUVER
MATERIAL
MATERIEL
MATERNAL
MAVERICK
METEORIC
MILEPOST
MILESIMO
MODERATE
MOLECULE
MOLEHILL
MOLESKIN
MOMENTUM
MONETARY
MOREOVER
MOVEMENT
MULETEER
NAMELESS
NAMESAKE
NEPENTHE
NIGERIAN
NIGEROIS
NINEPINS
NINETEEN
NOBELIST
NOBELIUM
NONESUCH
NONEVENT
NOTEBOOK
NOVELIZE
NOVEMBER
NUMERATE
NUMEROUS
ORIENTAL
PALEFACE
PANELING
PANELIST
PATERNAL
PAVEMENT
PEDERAST
PEDESTAL
PIPELINE
PIXELATE
POKEWEED
POLESTAR
PREEXIST
PUDENDUM
PUREBRED
QUIETUDE
RAVENING
RAVENOUS
RECEIVER
RECEPTOR
REFERENT
REFERRAL
REHEARSE
RELEGATE
RELEVANT
REMEDIAL
REMEMBER
RENEGADE
REPEATED
RESEARCH
RESEMBLE
RESERVED
REVEILLE
REVENUER
REVEREND
REVERENT
REVERSAL
RIVERBED
ROSEBUSH
ROSEMARY
ROSEWOOD
SALESMAN
SCHEDULE
SELECTEE
SELENITE
SELENIUM
SEMESTER
SERENADE
SEWERAGE
SHEEPISH
SHEETING
SHOELACE
SHREWISH
SIDEKICK
SIDELONG
SIDEREAL
SIDERITE
SIDESHOW
SIDESTEP
SIDEWALK
SIDEWALL
SIDEWAYS
SILENCER
SINECURE
SOLECISM
SOLENOID
SOMEBODY
SOMERSET
SOMETIME
SOMEWHAT
SPEEDWAY
SPHEROID
SPLENDID
SPLENDOR
SQUEEGEE
STEERAGE
STREAMER
STRENGTH
SUPEREGO
SUPERIOR
SUPERJET
SUPERNAL
SUREFIRE
SUZERAIN
SWEEPING
TALESMAN
TAPESTRY
TAPEWORM
TELECAST
TELEFILM
TELEGRAM
TELEPLAY
TELETHON
TELEVIEW
TELEVISE
TEMERITY
TENEMENT
THIEVERY
THREATEN
THRENODY
TIDELAND
TIMELESS
TIMEWORN
TIRELESS
TIRESOME
TOGETHER
TOKENISM
TOLERATE
TOREADOR
TOWELING
TOWERING
TRUETYPE
TUBERCLE
TUBEROSE
TUBEROUS
TUNELESS
TUTELAGE
TUTELARY
TWEEZERS
TYPECAST
TYPEFACE
ULCERATE
ULTERIOR
UNBEATEN
UNBELIEF
UNDERACT
UNDERAGE
UNDERARM
UNDERBID
UNDERCUT
UNDERDOG
UNDERFUR
UNDERLIE
UNDERLIP
UNDERPAY
UNDERSEA
UNDERTOW
UNFETTER
UNLEADED
UNPERSON
UNSEEMLY
UNSETTLE
UPHEAVAL
UPPERCUT
UUDECODE
VEGETATE
VEHEMENT
VENERATE
VENEREAL
VINEGARY
VINEYARD
WAREROOM
WATERLOO
WATERWAY
WEREWOLF
WINESHOP
WIREDRAW
WIREHAIR
WIRELESS
WIREWORM
WISEACRE
YULETIDE
ZWIEBACK
AIRFIELD
AIRFRAME
BOUFFANT
CAFFEINE
CALFSKIN
COIFFEUR
COIFFURE
CONFETTI
CONFINES
CONFLICT
CONFOCAL
CONFOUND
CONFRERE
CONFRONT
DAFFODIL
DISFAVOR
DOGFIGHT
GONFALON
GOOFBALL
GRAFFITO
GUNFIGHT
HALFBACK
HALFTONE
NEWFOUND
OUTFIELD
OUTFIGHT
OUTFLANK
PARFOCAL
PERFECTO
PERFORCE
PROFOUND
PUFFBALL
RIFFRAFF
ROOFTREE
SCAFFOLD
SCOFFLAW
SEAFARER
SELFLESS
SELFSAME
STUFFING
SUFFRAGE
SULFURIC
TAFFRAIL
TRIFLING
USUFRUCT
WARFARIN
WAYFARER
BEGGARLY
BRAGGART
BRIGHTEN
BUNGALOW
BUNGHOLE
BURGLARY
BURGUNDY
COAGULUM
CONGENER
CONGRESS
DAUGHTER
DIAGONAL
DINGBATS
DISGORGE
DISGRACE
DISGUISE
DOGGEREL
DOUGHBOY
DOUGHNUT
DRAGOMAN
DRUGGIST
DUNGAREE
DUNGHILL
ELEGANCE
ELIGIBLE
EMIGRATE
EXEGESIS
EXIGENCY
EXIGUOUS
EYEGLASS
FLAGPOLE
FLAGRANT
FLAGSHIP
FOXGLOVE
FRAGMENT
FRAGRANT
FRIGHTEN
GANGLAND
GANGLING
GANGLION
GANGPLOW
GANGRENE
GANGSTER
GARGOYLE
GINGERLY
GORGEOUS
HANGNAIL
HANGOVER
HEDGEHOG
HEDGEHOP
HEDGEROW
HEIGHTEN
JINGOISM
JONGLEUR
JUDGMENT
KANGAROO
KINGBOLT
LANGUAGE
LANGUISH
LAUGHTER
LAWGIVER
LENGTHEN
LINGERIE
LINGUIST
LODGMENT
LONGBOAT
LONGHAIR
LONGHAND
LONGHORN
LONGTIME
LONGUEUR
MANGROVE
MARGRAVE
MONGOOSE
MUDGUARD
NEIGHBOR
NIGGLING
ORIGINAL
OUTGOING
OUTGUESS
PEIGNOIR
POIGNANT

| PREGNANT | FISHWIFE | ACCIDENT | CIVILIAN | FAMILIAR | LECITHIN | OBSIDIAN | RUBICUND |
|---|---|---|---|---|---|---|---|
| PROGRESS | FOXHOUND | ACRIMONY | CIVILITY | FELICITY | LENITIVE | OFFICIAL | RUBIDIUM |
| QUAGMIRE | HIGHBALL | ACTINISM | CIVILIZE | FEMININE | LEVITATE | OPTICIAN | RUDIMENT |
| RINGWORM | HIGHBORN | ACTINIUM | CLAIMANT | FEMINISM | LINIMENT | OPTIMISM | RUMINANT |
| ROUGHAGE | HIGHBRED | ACTIVATE | CLOISTER | FILIGREE | LITIGANT | ORDINARY | RUMINATE |
| SANGUINE | HIGHBROW | ACTIVISM | COGITATE | FILIPINO | LITIGATE | ORDINATE | SALIVATE |
| SEAGOING | HIGHLAND | ACTIVITY | COLISEUM | FLUIDRAM | LUMINARY | PACIFIER | SANITARY |
| SEIGNEUR | HIGHNESS | ADDITION | COSIGNER | FOLIATED | LUMINOUS | PACIFISM | SANITIZE |
| SERGEANT | HIGHROAD | ADDITIVE | CULINARY | FRUITION | MAGICIAN | PAGINATE | SCRIBBLE |
| SINGULAR | HIGHTAIL | ADVISORY | CUPIDITY | FUGITIVE | MALINGER | PALINODE | SEDIMENT |
| SLUGGARD | HITHERTO | AFFIANCE | CYLINDER | FUMIGANT | MANIACAL | PALISADE | SEDITION |
| SLUGGISH | HOTHOUSE | AFFINITY | DEBILITY | FUMIGATE | MANICURE | PARIETAL | SEMINARY |
| SONGBIRD | ICEHOUSE | AGLITTER | DECIGRAM | FUTILITY | MANIFEST | PATIENCE | SEMINOLE |
| SONGSTER | INCHOATE | ALLIANCE | DECIMATE | GEMINATE | MANIFOLD | PAVILION | SEMISOFT |
| SPYGLASS | INCHWORM | ALMIGHTY | DECIPHER | GENITALS | MARIACHI | PEDICURE | SIBILANT |
| STAGNANT | ISTHMIAN | ALTITUDE | DECISION | GENITIVE | MARIGOLD | PEDIGREE | SILICATE |
| STAGNATE | LETHARGY | AMBIENCE | DECISIVE | HABITANT | MARINATE | PEDIMENT | SILICIFY |
| SURGICAL | LUTHERAN | AMBITION | DEDICATE | HABITUAL | MARITIME | PENITENT | SILICONE |
| TANGIBLE | MACHISMO | ANTIBODY | DEFIANCE | HACIENDA | MAXIMIZE | PERILUNE | SINISTER |
| TUNGSTEN | MADHOUSE | ANTIDOTE | DEFINITE | HELICOID | MEDICAID | PERIODIC | SOCIABLE |
| VANGUARD | MECHANIC | ANTIMONY | DELICACY | HELIPORT | MEDICARE | PETITION | SOLIDIFY |
| VENGEFUL | MENHADEN | ANTINOMY | DELICATE | HERITAGE | MEDICATE | PIMIENTO | SOLITARY |
| VIRGINAL | MEPHITIC | ANTIPODE | DELIRIUM | HESITANT | MEDICINE | PITIABLE | SOLITUDE |
| WINGDING | MESHWORK | ANTIPOPE | DELIVERY | HESITATE | MEDIEVAL | PITILESS | SPLINTER |
| WINGSPAN | METHANOL | APTITUDE | DEMIBOLD | HIBISCUS | MEDIOCRE | PODIATRY | SPRINKLE |
| WRIGGLER | MISHMASH | AQUILINE | DEMIJOHN | HOLINESS | MEDITATE | POLITICK | SQUIRREL |
| ALEHOUSE | MOTHBALL | ARTIFACT | DESIROUS | HOMICIDE | MENISCUS | POLITICO | STAIRWAY |
| ALPHABET | MUSHROOM | ARTIFICE | DEVILISH | HOWITZER | MERIDIAN | POLITICS | STRICKEN |
| ALTHOUGH | NUTHATCH | ARTISTIC | DILIGENT | HUMIDIFY | MERINGUE | POPINJAY | STRIDENT |
| ANTHROPO | ORTHODOX | ARTISTRY | DIMINISH | HUMIDITY | MILITANT | POSITION | STRIKING |
| ARCHDUKE | ORTHOEPY | ASPIRANT | DISINTER | HUMILITY | MILITARY | POSITIVE | STRINGED |
| ASPHODEL | OUTHOUSE | ASPIRATE | DIVIDEND | IGNITION | MILITATE | POSITRON | STRINGER |
| ASPHYXIA | PATHETIC | ATTITUDE | DIVINITY | ILLINOIS | MINIBIKE | PUGILISM | SUKIYAKI |
| BACHELOR | PATHOGEN | AUDIENCE | DIVISION | IMMINENT | MINIMIZE | PUNITIVE | TACITURN |
| BATHROBE | PROHIBIT | AUDITION | DIVISIVE | INCIDENT | MINISTER | RADIATOR | TAHITIAN |
| BATHROOM | PUSHCART | AUDITORY | DOMICILE | INCISION | MINISTRY | RADIOMAN | TALISMAN |
| BECHUANA | PUSHDOWN | BACILLUS | DOMINATE | INCISIVE | MITIGATE | RATIONAL | TITILATE |
| BONHOMIE | PUSHOVER | BADINAGE | DOMINEER | INDIAMAN | MOBILIZE | REFINERY | TITIVATE |
| CASHMERE | RIGHTFUL | BANISTER | DOMINION | INDICATE | MONITION | REGICIDE | TRAINING |
| CATHETER | RUTHLESS | BARITONE | DRAINAGE | INDIGENT | MONITORY | REGIMENT | TRAINMAN |
| CATHOLIC | SAWHORSE | BASILICA | DUTIABLE | INDIRECT | MORIBUND | REGIONAL | TUNISIAN |
| CEPHALIC | SUCHLIKE | BASILISK | ECLIPTIC | INFINITE | MOTIVATE | REGISTER | ULTIMATE |
| DETHRONE | SYPHILIS | BELITTLE | ELLIPSIS | INFINITY | MUCILAGE | REGISTRY | UNBIASED |
| DISHEVEL | TIGHTWAD | BERIBERI | EMBITTER | INSIGNIA | MUNITION | RELIABLE | UNBIDDEN |
| DISHONOR | UNCHASTE | BEWILDER | ENCIPHER | INTIMATE | MUSICALE | RELIANCE | UNFILIAL |
| DOGHOUSE | UNCHURCH | BODILESS | ENCIRCLE | INVIABLE | MUSICIAN | RELIGION | UNKINDLY |
| EIGHTEEN | UNSHAPED | BOUILLON | ENFILADE | INVITING | MUTILATE | REMITTAL | UNLIKELY |
| EMPHASIS | UPTHRUST | BUSINESS | ENGINEER | IRRIGATE | NATIONAL | RESIDENT | UNLIMBER |
| EMPHATIC | WASHABLE | CAMISOLE | ENSILAGE | IRRITATE | NATIVISM | RESIDUAL | UNRIDDLE |
| ENSHRINE | WASHBOWL | CANISTER | ENTIRETY | JUBILANT | NATIVITY | RESIDUUM | UNTIMELY |
| ENSHROUD | WASHROOM | CARILLON | ENVIABLE | JUDICIAL | NAVIGATE | RESIGNED | UNWIELDY |
| ENTHRALL | WISHBONE | CELIBACY | ENVIRONS | JURISTIC | NIHILISM | RESISTOR | UNZIPPED |
| ENTHRONE | WITHDRAW | CELIBATE | ENVISAGE | KAMIKAZE | NOBILITY | RETICENT | UPRISING |
| EUPHORIA | WITHHOLD | CHAIRMAN | EQUIPAGE | KIBITZER | NOMINATE | RETIRING | VALIDATE |
| EXCHANGE | YACHTING | CHOIRBOY | ESTIMATE | KOLINSKY | NOTIONAL | REVIEWER | VARIABLE |
| FISHBOWL | ABDICATE | CHRISTEN | FACILITY | LAPIDARY | OBLIGATE | REVIVIFY | VARIANCE |
| FISHHOOK | ABSINTHE | CHRISTIE | FAMILIAL | LATITUDE | OBLIVION | RIDICULE | VARICOSE |

VARIETAL
VARIORUM
VARISTOR
VESICANT
VICINAGE
VICINITY
VIGILANT
VISICALC
VISITANT
VOLITION
CONJUGAL
CONJUNCT
DISJOINT
MARJORAM
MISJUDGE
PREJUDGE
BACKACHE
BACKBITE
BACKBONE
BACKDROP
BACKFIRE
BACKHAND
BACKLASH
BACKPACK
BACKREST
BACKSIDE
BACKSLAP
BACKSPIN
BACKSTOP
BACKWARD
BACKWASH
BANKBOOK
BANKROLL
BANKRUPT
BOOKCASE
BOOKMARK
BOOKWORM
BRAKEMAN
BUCKSHOT
BUCKSKIN
BULKHEAD
COCKATOO
COCKCROW
COCKEREL
COCKSURE
COCKTAIL
COOKBOOK
DARKLING
DARKROOM
DARKSOME
DECKHAND
DISKETTE
DOCKHAND
DOCKYARD
DUCKBILL
DUCKLING
FECKLESS
FOLKLORE
FORKLIFT
GYMKHANA
HACKWORD
HAWKWEED
HOOKWORM
HUCKSTER
JACKBOOT
KICKBACK
KICKSHAW
LARKSPUR
LEUKEMIA
LOCKSTEP
MACKEREL
MACKINAW
MARKDOWN
MARKSMAN
MILKMAID
MILKWEED
MUSKETRY
NECKLACE
NECKLINE
NICKNAME
PENKNIFE
PICKEREL
PICKINGS
PICKLOCK
POCKMARK
RECKLESS
ROCKETRY
ROCKFALL
SICKNESS
SINKHOLE
STAKEOUT
SUCKLING
TICKLISH
WALKAWAY
WALKOVER
WEAKFISH
WEAKLING
WEAKNESS
WORKABLE
WORKADAY
WORKBOOK
WORKROOM
WORKSHOP
ADULTERY
AFFLATUS
AIRLINER
ANALOGUE
ANALYSIS
ANGLICAN
APOLOGIA
APPLAUSE
APPLIQUE
ATHLETIC
BAILABLE
BAILSMAN
BALLROOM
BALLYHOO
BILLFOLD
BILLHEAD
BOLLWORM
BUILDING
BULLDOZE
BULLETIN
BULLFROG
BULLHEAD
CALLBACK
CALLIOPE
CAULDRON
CELLULAR
CHOLERIC
CISLUNAR
COALESCE
COLLAPSE
COLLIERY
COLLOQUY
CURLICUE
CYCLAMEN
DAYLIGHT
DEFLOWER
DIALOGUE
DIALYSIS
DIELDRIN
DIPLOMAT
DISLODGE
DISLOYAL
DWELLING
DYSLEXIA
EMBLAZON
EMPLOYEE
EMULSIFY
EMULSION
EPILEPSY
EPILOGUE
EVALUATE
EXPLICIT
EXPLODED
EYELINER
FALLIBLE
FANLIGHT
FELLATIO
FOLLICLE
FOOLSCAP
FULLBACK
FURLOUGH
GALLUSES
GASLIGHT
GOALPOST
HALLMARK
HELLHOLE
HILLSIDE
HOOLIGAN
IDOLATER
IDOLATRY
IMPLICIT
JAILBIRD
KEELBOAT
KEELHAUL
KIELBASA
KILLDEER
KOHLRABI
LOLLIPOP
LOLLYGAG
MEALTIME
MEALYBUG
MILLIARD
MILLIBAR
MILLIEME
MILLINER
MILLPOND
MILLRACE
MISLABEL
MYELITIS
NEGLIGEE
NEWLYWED
NOBLEMAN
NUCLEATE
OUTLYING
PALLIATE
PARLANCE
PELLAGRA
PELLUCID
PENLIGHT
POLLIWOG
POLLSTER
POULTICE
PROLIFIC
PROLOGUE
PSALMODY
PUBLICAN
PULLBACK
PULLOVER
QUALMISH
RAILLERY
RAILROAD
ROLLBACK
ROULETTE
SAILBOAT
SAILFISH
SCALABLE
SCALAWAG
SCALEPAN
SCALLION
SCILICET
SCULLERY
SCULLION
SCULPTOR
SEALSKIN
SHELVING
SHILINGI
SHILLING
SKELETON
SKILLFUL
SKULLCAP
SKYLIGHT
SMALLPOX
SPILLWAY
STALLION
STALWART
STILETTO
STULTIFY
SUNLIGHT
SWELLING
SYLLABLE
SYLLABUS
TAILCOAT
TAILGATE
TAILSPIN
TELLTALE
THALAMUS
THALLIUM
TOILETRY
TOILETTE
TOILWORN
TOLLBOTH
TOLLGATE
TRILLION
TRILLIUM
TWILIGHT
UNCLENCH
UNCLOTHE
VAULTING
VELLEITY
VILLAGER
VILLAINY
VIOLABLE
VIOLENCE
WELLBORN
WELLHEAD
WILLIWAW
WOOLSACK
YIELDING
ALUMINUM
ATOMIZER
BERMUDAS
BESMIRCH
BROMIDIC
CHAMBRAY
CHAMPION
CHEMICAL
CHEMURGY
CLAMBAKE
CLEMATIS
CLEMENCY
COMMANDO
COMMENCE
COMMERCE
COMMONER
COMMUNAL
COSMETIC
CREMAINS
CRIMINAL
DIAMETER
DISMOUNT
DOOMSDAY
DORMOUSE
DRUMBEAT
EXEMPLAR
FARMHAND
FARMLAND
FARMYARD
FIRMWARE
FLAMBEAU
FLAMENCO
FLAMEOUT
FLAMINGO
FLIMFLAM
FORMERLY
FORMLESS
GEOMETRY
GERMINAL
HARMONIC
HELMSMAN
HERMETIC
HORMONAL
INIMICAL
LAWMAKER
MARMOSET
MISMATCH
MNEMONIC
MYRMIDON
NONMETAL
ODOMETER
OHMMETER
OUTMODED
PALMETTO
PARMESAN
PEMMICAN
PERMEATE
PLUMBING
PREMIERE
PREMOLAR
PRIMEVAL
PRIMROSE
PROMOTER
PTOMAINE
PULMOTOR
RHOMBOID
ROOMETTE
ROOMMATE
SCHMALTZ
SCIMITAR
SEAMOUNT
SHAMBLES
SHAMROCK
SKIMMING
SLUMLORD
STAMPEDE
STIMULUS
SUBMERGE
SUBMERSE
SURMOUNT
SWIMMING
SYMMETRY
TEAMSTER
TEAMWORK
TERMINAL
TERMINUS
TITMOUSE
TRIMARAN
TRIMETER
TRIMMING
TROMBONE
TRUMPERY
TURMERIC
VERMOUTH
WHOMEVER
WORMHOLE
WORMWOOD
YEOMANRY
ABUNDANT
ACANTHUS
AMENABLE
BARNACLE
BARNYARD
BEANBALL
BIANNUAL
BIENNIAL
BIENNIUM
BINNACLE
BOUNDARY
BRANDISH
BRINDLED
BRONCHUS
BURNOOSE
CANNABIS
CANNIBAL
CARNAUBA
CARNIVAL
CHANCERY
CHANDLER
CHANUKAH
CHENILLE
CINNABAR
CINNAMON
CLINCHER
CLINICAL
COGNOMEN
COINCIDE
COONSKIN
CORNCRIB
CORNMEAL
COUNTESS
DAMNABLE
DIANTHUS
DOWNBEAT
DOWNCAST
DOWNFALL
DOWNHILL
DOWNLOAD
DOWNPOUR
DOWNTOWN
DOWNTURN
DOWNWARD
DOWNWIND
DRUNKARD
EARNINGS
ECONOMIC
ELONGATE
EMINENCE
EVENSONG
EVENTIDE
EVENTUAL
FOUNTAIN
FRANCIUM
FRENETIC
FRONTAGE
FRONTIER
GAUNTLET
GHANAIAN
GRANDEUR
GRANDSON
GRANULAR
HORNBOOK
HORNPIPE
HYPNOSIS
HYPNOTIC
IDENTIFY
IDENTITY
INUNDATE
IRONCLAD
IRONWARE
IRONWEED
IRONWOOD
IRONWORK
JAUNDICE
LAUNCHER
LIGNEOUS
LOANWORD
MAGNESIA
MAGNETIC
MAGNOLIA
MAINLAND
MAINLINE
MAINMAST
MAINSAIL
MAINSTAY

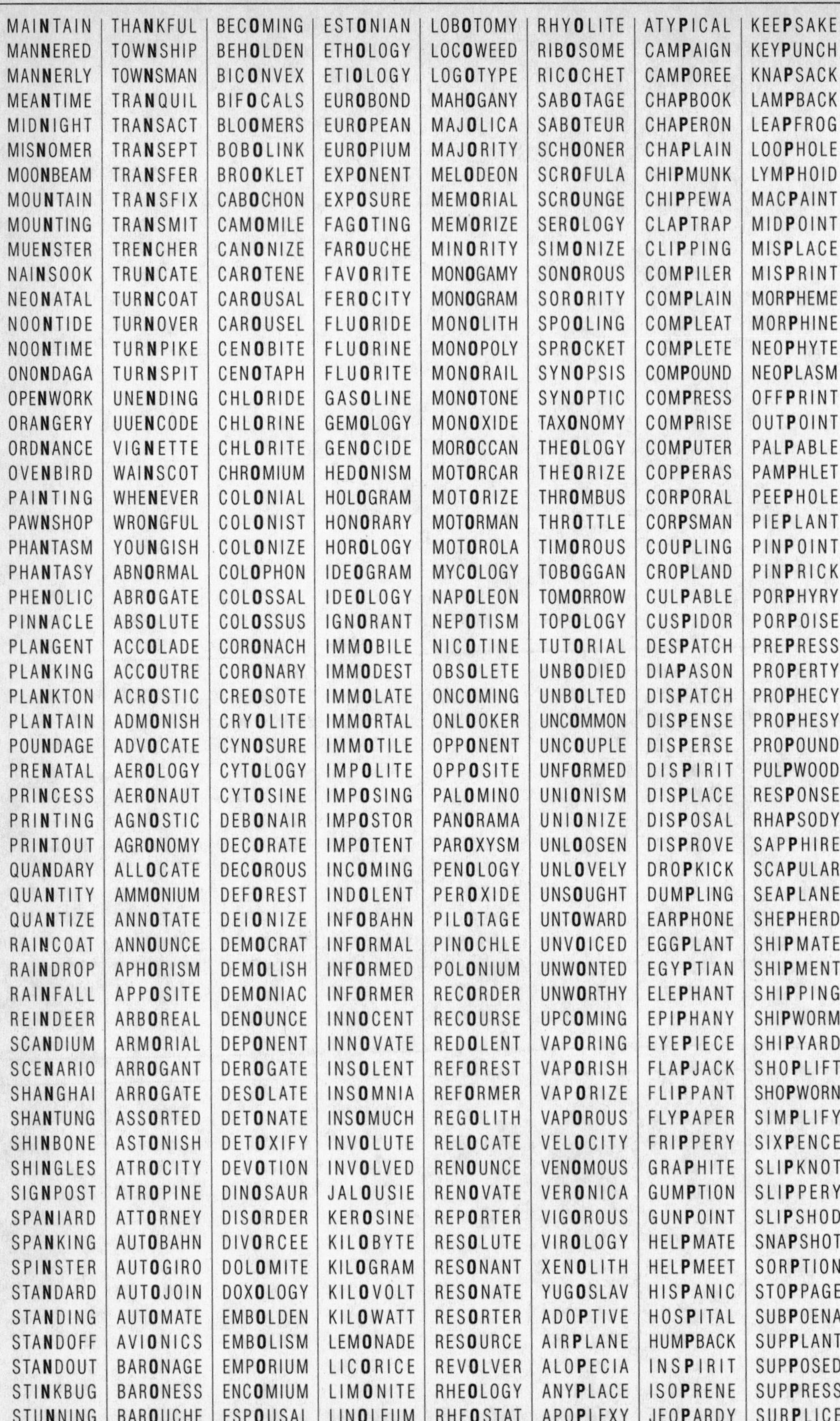

MAINTAIN
MANNERED
MANNERLY
MEANTIME
MIDNIGHT
MISNOMER
MOONBEAM
MOUNTAIN
MOUNTING
MUENSTER
NAINSOOK
NEONATAL
NOONTIDE
NOONTIME
ONONDAGA
OPENWORK
ORANGERY
ORDNANCE
OVENBIRD
PAINTING
PAWNSHOP
PHANTASM
PHANTASY
PHENOLIC
PINNACLE
PLANGENT
PLANKING
PLANKTON
PLANTAIN
POUNDAGE
PRENATAL
PRINCESS
PRINTING
PRINTOUT
QUANDARY
QUANTITY
QUANTIZE
RAINCOAT
RAINDROP
RAINFALL
REINDEER
SCANDIUM
SCENARIO
SHANGHAI
SHANTUNG
SHINBONE
SHINGLES
SIGNPOST
SPANIARD
SPANKING
SPINSTER
STANDARD
STANDING
STANDOFF
STANDOUT
STINKBUG
STUNNING
THANKFUL
TOWNSHIP
TOWNSMAN
TRANQUIL
TRANSACT
TRANSEPT
TRANSFER
TRANSFIX
TRANSMIT
TRENCHER
TRUNCATE
TURNCOAT
TURNOVER
TURNPIKE
TURNSPIT
UNENDING
UUENCODE
VIGNETTE
WAINSCOT
WHENEVER
WRONGFUL
YOUNGISH
ABNORMAL
ABROGATE
ABSOLUTE
ACCOLADE
ACCOUTRE
ACROSTIC
ADMONISH
ADVOCATE
AEROLOGY
AERONAUT
AGNOSTIC
AGRONOMY
ALLOCATE
AMMONIUM
ANNOTATE
ANNOUNCE
APHORISM
APPOSITE
ARBOREAL
ARMORIAL
ARROGANT
ARROGATE
ASSORTED
ASTONISH
ATROCITY
ATROPINE
ATTORNEY
AUTOBAHN
AUTOGIRO
AUTOJOIN
AUTOMATE
AVIONICS
BARONAGE
BARONESS
BAROUCHE
BECOMING
BEHOLDEN
BICONVEX
BIFOCALS
BLOOMERS
BOBOLINK
BROOKLET
CABOCHON
CAMOMILE
CANONIZE
CAROTENE
CAROUSAL
CAROUSEL
CENOBITE
CENOTAPH
CHLORIDE
CHLORINE
CHLORITE
CHROMIUM
COLONIAL
COLONIST
COLONIZE
COLOPHON
COLOSSAL
COLOSSUS
CORONACH
CORONARY
CREOSOTE
CRYOLITE
CYNOSURE
CYTOLOGY
CYTOSINE
DEBONAIR
DECORATE
DECOROUS
DEFOREST
DEIONIZE
DEMOCRAT
DEMOLISH
DEMONIAC
DENOUNCE
DEPONENT
DEROGATE
DESOLATE
DETONATE
DETOXIFY
DEVOTION
DINOSAUR
DISORDER
DIVORCEE
DOLOMITE
DOXOLOGY
EMBOLDEN
EMBOLISM
EMPORIUM
ENCOMIUM
ESPOUSAL
ESTONIAN
ETHOLOGY
ETIOLOGY
EUROBOND
EUROPEAN
EUROPIUM
EXPONENT
EXPOSURE
FAGOTING
FAROUCHE
FAVORITE
FEROCITY
FLUORIDE
FLUORINE
FLUORITE
GASOLINE
GEMOLOGY
GENOCIDE
HEDONISM
HOLOGRAM
HONORARY
HOROLOGY
IDEOGRAM
IDEOLOGY
IGNORANT
IMMOBILE
IMMODEST
IMMOLATE
IMMORTAL
IMMOTILE
IMPOLITE
IMPOSING
IMPOSTOR
IMPOTENT
INCOMING
INDOLENT
INFOBAHN
INFORMAL
INFORMED
INFORMER
INNOCENT
INNOVATE
INSOLENT
INSOMNIA
INSOMUCH
INVOLUTE
INVOLVED
JALOUSIE
KEROSINE
KILOBYTE
KILOGRAM
KILOVOLT
KILOWATT
LEMONADE
LICORICE
LIMONITE
LINOLEUM
LOBOTOMY
LOCOWEED
LOGOTYPE
MAHOGANY
MAJOLICA
MAJORITY
MELODEON
MEMORIAL
MEMORIZE
MINORITY
MONOGAMY
MONOGRAM
MONOLITH
MONOPOLY
MONORAIL
MONOTONE
MONOXIDE
MOROCCAN
MOTORCAR
MOTORIZE
MOTORMAN
MOTOROLA
MYCOLOGY
NAPOLEON
NEPOTISM
NICOTINE
OBSOLETE
ONCOMING
ONLOOKER
OPPONENT
OPPOSITE
PALOMINO
PANORAMA
PAROXYSM
PENOLOGY
PEROXIDE
PILOTAGE
PINOCHLE
POLONIUM
RECORDER
RECOURSE
REDOLENT
REFOREST
REFORMER
REGOLITH
RELOCATE
RENOUNCE
RENOVATE
REPORTER
RESOLUTE
RESONANT
RESONATE
RESORTER
RESOURCE
REVOLVER
RHEOLOGY
RHEOSTAT
RHYOLITE
RIBOSOME
RICOCHET
SABOTAGE
SABOTEUR
SCHOONER
SCROFULA
SCROUNGE
SEROLOGY
SIMONIZE
SONOROUS
SORORITY
SPOOLING
SPROCKET
SYNOPSIS
SYNOPTIC
TAXONOMY
THEOLOGY
THEORIZE
THROMBUS
THROTTLE
TIMOROUS
TOBOGGAN
TOMORROW
TOPOLOGY
TUTORIAL
UNBODIED
UNBOLTED
UNCOMMON
UNCOUPLE
UNFORMED
UNIONISM
UNIONIZE
UNLOOSEN
UNLOVELY
UNSOUGHT
UNTOWARD
UNVOICED
UNWONTED
UNWORTHY
UPCOMING
VAPORING
VAPORISH
VAPORIZE
VAPOROUS
VELOCITY
VENOMOUS
VERONICA
VIGOROUS
VIROLOGY
XENOLITH
YUGOSLAV
ADOPTIVE
AIRPLANE
ALOPECIA
ANYPLACE
APOPLEXY
ATYPICAL
CAMPAIGN
CAMPOREE
CHAPBOOK
CHAPERON
CHAPLAIN
CHIPMUNK
CHIPPEWA
CLAPTRAP
CLIPPING
COMPILER
COMPLAIN
COMPLEAT
COMPLETE
COMPOUND
COMPRESS
COMPRISE
COMPUTER
COPPERAS
CORPORAL
CORPSMAN
COUPLING
CROPLAND
CULPABLE
CUSPIDOR
DESPATCH
DIAPASON
DISPATCH
DISPENSE
DISPERSE
DISPIRIT
DISPLACE
DISPOSAL
DISPROVE
DROPKICK
DUMPLING
EARPHONE
EGGPLANT
EGYPTIAN
ELEPHANT
EPIPHANY
EYEPIECE
FLAPJACK
FLIPPANT
FLYPAPER
FRIPPERY
GRAPHITE
GUMPTION
GUNPOINT
HELPMATE
HELPMEET
HISPANIC
HOSPITAL
HUMPBACK
INSPIRIT
ISOPRENE
JEOPARDY
KEEPSAKE
KEYPUNCH
KNAPSACK
LAMPBACK
LEAPFROG
LOOPHOLE
LYMPHOID
MACPAINT
MIDPOINT
MISPLACE
MISPRINT
MORPHEME
MORPHINE
NEOPHYTE
NEOPLASM
OFFPRINT
OUTPOINT
PALPABLE
PAMPHLET
PEEPHOLE
PIEPLANT
PINPOINT
PINPRICK
PORPHYRY
PORPOISE
PREPRESS
PROPERTY
PROPHECY
PROPHESY
PROPOUND
PULPWOOD
RESPONSE
RHAPSODY
SAPPHIRE
SCAPULAR
SEAPLANE
SHEPHERD
SHIPMATE
SHIPMENT
SHIPPING
SHIPWORM
SHIPYARD
SHOPLIFT
SHOPWORN
SIMPLIFY
SIXPENCE
SLIPKNOT
SLIPPERY
SLIPSHOD
SNAPSHOT
SORPTION
STOPPAGE
SUBPOENA
SUPPLANT
SUPPOSED
SUPPRESS
SURPLICE

SUR**P**RISE
SUS**P**ENSE
SYM**P**ATHY
SYM**P**HONY
TAX**P**AYER
TEM**P**LATE
TEM**P**ORAL
TEN**P**ENNY
TIN**P**LATE
TRA**P**DOOR
TRA**P**PING
TRA**P**ROCK
TRI**P**TYCH
TWO**P**ENCE
TWO**P**ENNY
TYM**P**ANUM
UNS**P**RUNG
VOL**P**LANE
WAR**P**LANE
WEA**P**ONRY
WHI**P**CORD
WHI**P**LASH
WHO**P**PING
WRA**P**PING
ZEP**P**ELIN
ZOO**P**HYTE
ADE**Q**UATE
CON**Q**UEST
DAI**Q**UIRI
DIS**Q**UIET
ELO**Q**UENT
FRE**Q**UENT
INI**Q**UITY
IRO**Q**UOIS
JAC**Q**UARD
MAR**Q**UESS
MAR**Q**UISE
MES**Q**UITE
MIS**Q**UOTE
MOS**Q**UITO
VAN**Q**UISH
ABO**R**NING
ABO**R**TION
ACC**R**EDIT
ACE**R**BATE
ACE**R**BITY
ADO**R**ABLE
AFF**R**IGHT
AGE**R**ATUM
AGG**R**IEVE
AIG**R**ETTE
ALA**R**MIST
ALF**R**ESCO
ALT**R**UISM
AMA**R**ANTH
AMB**R**OSIA
AME**R**ICAN
AMO**R**TIZE
AND**R**OGEN
APE**R**ITIF
APE**R**TURE
APP**R**AISE
APP**R**OACH
APP**R**OVAL
AVE**R**MENT
AVE**R**SION
BAR**R**ACKS
BAR**R**ATRY
BAR**R**ETTE
BEA**R**SKIN
BEF**R**IEND
BEG**R**UDGE
CAP**R**IOLE
CAR**R**IAGE
CAR**R**YALL
CHA**R**ADES
CHA**R**COAL
CHA**R**ISMA
CHA**R**MING
CHE**R**OKEE
CLA**R**INET
CLE**R**ICAL
COR**R**IDOR
COU**R**TESY
COU**R**TIER
CUR**R**ENCY
DAI**R**YING
DAI**R**YMAN
DEC**R**EASE
DEC**R**EPIT
DEE**R**SKIN
DER**R**IERE
DET**R**ITUS
DIA**R**RHEA
DIU**R**ETIC
DOO**R**JAMB
DOO**R**KNOB
DOO**R**STEP
DOO**R**YARD
EME**R**ITUS
ENC**R**OACH
ENE**R**GIZE
ENE**R**VATE
ENO**R**MITY
ENO**R**MOUS
ENT**R**AILS
ENT**R**ANCE
ENT**R**ENCH
ENU**R**ESIS
ESP**R**ESSO
EST**R**ANGE
EST**R**OGEN
ETE**R**NITY
EVE**R**MORE
EVE**R**YDAY
EVE**R**YONE
EXE**R**CISE
EXO**R**CISE
EXO**R**DIUM
EXT**R**ADOS
FEA**R**LESS
FEA**R**SOME
FEB**R**UARY
FIB**R**OSIS
FOU**R**FOLD
FOU**R**SOME
FOU**R**TEEN
GAR**R**ISON
GLO**R**IOUS
GOU**R**MAND
GUA**R**ANTY
GUA**R**DIAN
GUE**R**NSEY
HAI**R**LINE
HAR**R**IDAN
HEB**R**AISM
HEI**R**LOOM
HOA**R**DING
HOR**R**IBLE
HUA**R**ACHE
HYD**R**OGEN
IMP**R**ISON
IMP**R**OPER
INC**R**EASE
INE**R**RANT
INF**R**ADIG
INF**R**ARED
INF**R**INGE
INT**R**ADOS
INT**R**ENCH
INT**R**EPID
INT**R**IGUE
INT**R**OMIT
LAC**R**IMAL
LAC**R**OSSE
LAU**R**EATE
LEA**R**NING
LIB**R**ETTO
MAD**R**IGAL
MAR**R**IAGE
MET**R**ICAL
MIC**R**OBUS
MIG**R**AINE
MOO**R**LAND
MOU**R**NFUL
MOU**R**NING
NEC**R**OSIS
NEU**R**ITIS
NEU**R**OSIS
NEU**R**OTIC
NIT**R**OGEN
NON**R**IGID
NUT**R**IENT
OPE**R**ABLE
OPE**R**ANDS
OPE**R**ETTA
OUT**R**EACH
OUT**R**IDER
OUT**R**IGHT
OVE**R**ALLS
OVE**R**CAST
OVE**R**COAT
OVE**R**COME
OVE**R**DRAW
OVE**R**FLOW
OVE**R**GROW
OVE**R**HAND
OVE**R**HANG
OVE**R**HAUL
OVE**R**HEAD
OVE**R**HEAR
OVE**R**KILL
OVE**R**LAID
OVE**R**LAND
OVE**R**LEAP
OVE**R**LOOK
OVE**R**LORD
OVE**R**MUCH
OVE**R**PASS
OVE**R**PLAY
OVE**R**RIDE
OVE**R**RULE
OVE**R**SEAS
OVE**R**SHOE
OVE**R**SIZE
OVE**R**STAY
OVE**R**STEP
OVE**R**TAKE
OVE**R**TIME
OVE**R**TONE
OVE**R**TURE
OVE**R**TURN
OVE**R**VIEW
PEE**R**LESS
PHA**R**ISEE
PHA**R**MACY
POR**R**IDGE
PRO**R**OGUE
PRU**R**IENT
PYO**R**RHEA
REA**R**WARD
REC**R**EANT
REC**R**EATE
REP**R**IEVE
REP**R**ISAL
REP**R**OACH
RET**R**ENCH
RET**R**IEVE
RET**R**OFIT
SAC**R**ISTY
SCA**R**CELY
SCO**R**PION
SHI**R**RING
SHI**R**TING
SHO**R**TAGE
SHO**R**TCUT
SKI**R**MISH
SOB**R**IETY
SPI**R**ITED
SPO**R**ADIC
SPU**R**IOUS
STA**R**FISH
STA**R**LING
STE**R**LING
STI**R**RING
STU**R**GEON
SUR**R**OUND
TAR**R**AGON
TER**R**APIN
TER**R**IBLE
TER**R**IFIC
THE**R**EFOR
THI**R**TEEN
THO**R**OUGH
THU**R**SDAY
UMB**R**ELLA
UNB**R**OKEN
UNE**R**RING
UNF**R**EEZE
UPG**R**OWTH
USU**R**IOUS
UXO**R**IOUS
VAG**R**ANCY
VIT**R**EOUS
WAR**R**ANTY
WHA**R**FAGE
WHE**R**EVER
YEA**R**BOOK
YEA**R**LING
YEA**R**LONG
YEA**R**NING
YOU**R**SELF
AIR**S**PACE
AIR**S**PEED
AIR**S**TRIP
ALL**S**PICE
ANG**S**TROM
ANI**S**ETTE
APO**S**TASY
BAS**S**INET
BAS**S**WOOD
BED**S**TEAD
BIT**S**TOCK
BLE**S**SING
BLI**S**SFUL
BOA**S**TFUL
BOW**S**PRIT
BRI**S**LING
BUR**S**ITIS
CAB**S**TAND
CAM**S**HAFT
CAP**S**ICUM
CAP**S**ULAR
CAS**S**ETTE
CAU**S**ERIE
CAU**S**EWAY
CES**S**POOL
CHA**S**TISE
CHA**S**TITY
CHA**S**UBLE
CHE**S**TNUT
CLA**S**SIFY
CLO**S**EOUT
CON**S**ERVE
CON**S**IDER
CON**S**OMME
CON**S**PIRE
CON**S**TANT
CON**S**TRUE
COX**S**WAIN
CRE**S**CENT
CRO**S**SBAR
CRO**S**SBOW
CRO**S**SCUT
CRO**S**SING
DAN**S**EUSE
DIA**S**TOLE
DIP**S**TICK
DIS**S**EVER
DIS**S**OLVE
DIS**S**UADE
DRE**S**SAGE
DRE**S**SING
DYE**S**TUFF
EGG**S**HELL
EKI**S**TICS
EMI**S**SARY
EYE**S**IGHT
FAL**S**ETTO
FEA**S**IBLE
FLA**S**HGUN
FLA**S**HING
FLE**S**HPOT
FLY**S**PECK
FOR**S**OOTH
FOR**S**WEAR
FRE**S**HMAN
FRO**S**TING
GEM**S**TONE
GLA**S**SFUL
GLO**S**SARY
GOS**S**AMER
GRA**S**PING
GRO**S**BEAK
GRO**S**CHEN
GUN**S**MITH
HAY**S**TACK
HOG**S**HEAD
HOL**S**TEIN
HOO**S**EGOW
HOR**S**EFLY
HOR**S**EMAN
HOU**S**EBOY
HOU**S**EFLY
HOU**S**ETOP
INK**S**TAND
ISO**S**TASY
JOY**S**TICK
KEY**S**TONE
LIP**S**TICK
LOP**S**IDED
MAS**S**ACRE
MAS**S**EUSE
MAS**S**LESS
MES**S**MATE
MID**S**HIPS
MIN**S**TREL
MIS**S**HAPE
MIS**S**PELL
MIS**S**PEND
MIS**S**TATE
MOI**S**TURE
MON**S**IEUR
MOS**S**BACK
NAU**S**EATE
NEW**S**CAST
NEW**S**REEL
NON**S**ENSE
NON**S**TICK
NOR**S**EMAN
NUI**S**ANCE
NUM**S**KULL
NUR**S**LING
NUT**S**HELL
OFF**S**HOOT
OFF**S**HORE
OFF**S**TAGE
OPU**S**CULE
OUT**S**HINE
OUT**S**IDER
OUT**S**MART
OUT**S**PEND
OUT**S**TRIP
PAS**S**ABLE
PAS**S**BOOK
PAS**S**OVER
PAS**S**PORT
PAS**S**WORD
PEN**S**TOCK
PER**S**ONAL
PER**S**PIRE
PER**S**UADE
PHA**S**EOUT
PHO**S**PHOR
PHY**S**ICAL
PHY**S**IQUE
POS**S**IBLE
POT**S**HERD
PRE**S**ENCE
PRE**S**ERVE
PRE**S**IDIO
PRE**S**SING
PRE**S**SMAN
PRE**S**SURE
PRE**S**TIGE
PRI**S**ONER
PRI**S**TINE
PRO**S**PECT
PRO**S**TATE
PUR**S**LANE
PUS**S**YCAT
QUE**S**TION
QUI**S**LING
REA**S**SURE
SAN**S**KRIT
SCI**S**SORS
SEA**S**CAPE
SEA**S**HORE
SEN**S**IBLE
SEN**S**UOUS
SET**S**CREW
SHO**S**HONE
SOL**S**TICE
SUB**S**ONIC
SUN**S**HADE
SUN**S**HINE
SWA**S**TIKA
TEA**S**POON
TEO**S**INTE
THE**S**PIAN
TIN**S**MITH
TOP**S**IDES
TRE**S**PASS
TRU**S**TFUL
VER**S**ICLE
WRI**S**TLET
ZOO**S**PORE
ABA**T**TOIR
ABS**T**RACT
ABS**T**RUSE
ABU**T**MENT
ABU**T**TALS
AES**T**HETE
AGI**T**PROP
AIR**T**IGHT
AME**T**HYST

ANATHEMA
ANYTHING
APOTHEGM
AUSTRIAN
BANTLING
BEATIFIC
BENTWOOD
BESTIARY
BESTRIDE
BIATHLON
BIRTHDAY
BOOTLESS
BOUTIQUE
BRETHREN
BRITCHES
BUTTRESS
CANTICLE
CAPTIOUS
CASTAWAY
CASTRATE
CAUTIOUS
CENTERED
CENTRIST
CHITCHAT
CHUTZPAH
CLITORIS
CLOTHIER
CLOTHING
CONTEMPT
CONTINUE
CONTRACT
CONTRAIL
CONTRARY
CONTRAST
CONTRITE
CONTRIVE
CRETONNE
CRITICAL
CRITIQUE
CROTCHET
CUSTOMER
DEATHBED
DESTRUCT
DEXTROSE
DIATOMIC
DIATRIBE
DICTATOR
DISTANCE
DISTASTE
DISTINCT
DISTRACT
DISTRAIT
DISTRESS
DISTRICT
DISTRUST
DOCTRINE
EMOTICON
ERYTHEMA
ESOTERIC
EYETOOTH
FACTIOUS
FACTOTUM
FALTBOAT
FANTASIA
FARTHEST
FARTHING
FASTBACK
FASTNESS
FESTIVAL
FILTRATE
FLATBOAT
FLATFISH
FLATFOOT
FLATHEAD
FLATIRON
FLATLAND
FLATTERY
FLATWARE
FLOTILLA
FOOTBALL
FOOTFALL
FOOTHILL
FOOTHOLD
FOOTLESS
FOOTLING
FOOTNOTE
FOOTPATH
FOOTRACE
FOOTREST
FOOTSORE
FOOTSTEP
FOOTWEAR
FOOTWORK
FORTRESS
FORTUITY
FRETWORK
FURTHEST
GOATHERD
GOATSKIN
GRATEFUL
GRATUITY
GUTTURAL
HAUTBOIS
HAWTHORN
HOSTELRY
HUNTRESS
HUNTSMAN
HUSTINGS
HYSTERIA
IMITABLE
INITIATE
INSTANCE
INSTINCT
INSTRUCT
ISOTHERM
ISOTONIC
JETTISON
KNITWEAR
KNOTHOLE
LEFTOVER
LISTLESS
LITTORAL
LOATHING
MALTREAT
MALTSTER
MANTELET
MANTILLA
MANTISSA
MARTINET
MASTERLY
MASTHEAD
MASTODON
MATTRESS
MEATBALL
MISTAKEN
MISTREAT
MISTRESS
MISTRIAL
MISTRUST
MORTGAGE
MORTUARY
MULTIPLE
MULTIPLY
MUSTACHE
MYSTICAL
MYSTIQUE
NAUTICAL
NAUTILUS
NESTLING
NEUTRINO
NOCTURNE
OBITUARY
OBSTACLE
OBSTRUCT
OINTMENT
ORATORIO
PANTHEON
PANTSUIT
PARTERRE
PARTIBLE
PARTICLE
PARTISAN
PASTICHE
PASTILLE
PASTORAL
PASTRAMI
PECTORAL
PENTAGON
PETTIFOG
PITTANCE
PLATFORM
PLATINUM
PLATYPUS
PLETHORA
POLTROON
PORTABLE
PORTHOLE
PORTIERE
PORTRAIT
POSTCARD
POSTDATE
POSTHOLE
POSTLUDE
POSTMARK
POSTPAID
POSTPONE
PRATFALL
PRATIQUE
PRETENSE
PRETERIT
PRETTIFY
PROTOCOL
PROTRACT
PROTRUDE
QUATRAIN
QUOTABLE
QUOTIENT
RATTLING
RESTLESS
RESTRAIN
RESTRICT
RHETORIC
ROUTEMAN
SAUTERNE
SCATHING
SCOTTISH
SENTENCE
SENTIENT
SENTINEL
SHUTDOWN
SKITTISH
SLATTERN
SOFTBALL
SOFTWARE
SOFTWOOD
SOUTHPAW
SPITBALL
SPITTOON
STATUARY
STOTINKA
SUBTITLE
SUBTRACT
SUITABLE
SUITCASE
SYSTEMIC
TANTALUM
TEETHING
TEETOTAL
TENTACLE
TERTIARY
TESTATOR
TESTICLE
TEUTONIC
TEXTBOOK
TORTILLA
TORTOISE
TORTUOUS
TRUTHFUL
UNCTUOUS
UNSTABLE
UNSTEADY
UNSTRUNG
UPSTAIRS
UPSTREAM
UPSTROKE
VERTEBRA
VERTICAL
VESTMENT
VIATICUM
VICTORIA
VIETCONG
VIRTUOSO
VIRTUOUS
WAITRESS
WHATEVER
WHITECAP
WHITEFLY
WISTARIA
WISTERIA
WRATHFUL
WRETCHED
YOUTHFUL
ABLUTION
ACCURATE
ACCURSED
ACCUSTOM
ACOUSTIC
ACQUAINT
ADJUTANT
ADJUVANT
AFLUTTER
ALLUVIUM
AMBULANT
AMPUTATE
ARGUABLE
ARGUMENT
BABUSHKA
BAGUETTE
BALUSTER
BEAUTIFY
BEFUDDLE
BEQUEATH
BIBULOUS
BICUSPID
BOTULISM
BROUGHAM
BROUHAHA
CADUCEUS
CAPUCHIN
CASUALTY
CERULEAN
CLOUDLET
COAUTHOR
COPULATE
COQUETTE
CORUNDUM
CROUPIER
CUCUMBER
DELUSION
DEMURRER
DEPUTIZE
DISUNITE
DISUNITY
DOCUMENT
DRAUGHTS
EFFUSION
ENCUMBER
ETRUSCAN
EXCURSUS
FABULOUS
FIGURINE
FLAUTIST
FLOUNDER
FLOURISH
FROUFROU
FUTURISM
FUTURITY
GLAUCOMA
GROUNDER
HANUKKAH
HUGUENOT
ILLUMINE
ILLUSION
ILLUSIVE
ILLUSORY
IMMUNIZE
IMPUDENT
IMPUNITY
INCUBATE
INCUMBER
INDUCTEE
INDURATE
INDUSTRY
INGUINAL
INHUMANE
INNUENDO
INSULATE
ISSUANCE
LABURNUM
LOCUTION
MATURATE
MATURITY
MISUSAGE
MODULATE
MONUMENT
NEBULIZE
NEBULOUS
NONUNION
OBDURATE
OCCUPANT
ORGULOUS
OSCULATE
PECULATE
PECULIAR
PEDUNCLE
PENUMBRA
PETULANT
PLEURISY
POPULACE
POPULATE
POPULIST
POPULOUS
PURULENT
REBUTTAL
REGULATE
REPUBLIC
RETURNEE
SALUTARY
SATURATE
SATURDAY
SCRUTINY
SECURITY
SEDULOUS
SEQUENCE
SHOULDER
SIMULATE
SITUATED
SOLUTION
SPLUTTER
STRUGGLE
STRUMPET
SUBURBIA
TABULATE
THOUSAND
THRUSTER
TRIUMVIR
TROUSERS
UNBUCKLE
UNBURDEN
UNBUTTON
UNDULANT
UNDULATE
UNGULATE
UNMUZZLE
VALUABLE
VENUSIAN
VIBURNUM
VIRULENT
BREVIARY
CERVICAL
CHIVALRY
CLAVICLE
CONVERGE
CONVERSE
CONVINCE
CONVULSE
CORVETTE
CREVASSE
DRIVEWAY
ELEVATOR
FERVENCY
GRAVAMEN
HEAVYSET
LEAVINGS
PERVERSE
PREVIOUS
PROVIDED
PROVINCE
SCAVENGE
SERVITOR
SLOVENLY
SOLVENCY
SOUVENIR
TRAVERSE
TRAVESTY
UNIVALVE
UNIVERSE
VALVULAR
ANYWHERE
BLOWPIPE
BOBWHITE
BROWBEAT
BROWNOUT
CHOWCHOW
COGWHEEL
CRAWFISH
CROWFOOT
DRAWBACK
FLYWHEEL
FORWARDS
GASWORKS
GLOWWORM
KEYWORDS
OUTWEIGH
PINWHEEL
SEAWATER
SHOWCASE
SHOWDOWN
SNOWBALL
SNOWBANK
SNOWDROP
SNOWFALL
SNOWPLOW
SNOWSHOE
STOWAWAY
UNAWARES

FLEXIBLE
GLOXINIA
INEXPERT
QUIXOTIC
ABEYANCE
ARMYWORM
BODYWORK
BUOYANCY
BUSYBODY
BUSYWORK
CARYATID
CHEYENNE
CLAYMORE
COPYBOOK
COPYDESK
CRAYFISH
EMPYREAN
GRAYLING
LADYBIRD
LADYLIKE
LADYLOVE
LADYSHIP
MANYFOLD
PLAYBACK
PLAYBILL
PLAYBOOK
PLAYGOER
PLAYMATE
PLAYSUIT
POLYGAMY
POLYGLOT
POLYMATH
PONYTAIL
SWAYBACK
ALIZARIN
BENZOATE
BLIZZARD
CRUZEIRO
GRIZZLED
MARZIPAN
PIZZERIA

## 5TH LETTER

ABEYANCE
ACQUAINT
ADORABLE
AFFIANCE
AFFLATUS
AGERATUM
ALIZARIN
ALLIANCE
ALPHABET
AMARANTH
AMENABLE
AMICABLE
ANTEATER
APPLAUSE
APPRAISE
ARGUABLE
BACCARAT
BACKACHE
BAILABLE
BANDANNA
BARBARIC
BARNACLE
BARRACKS
BARRATRY
BEGGARLY
BEREAVED
BIDDABLE
BINNACLE
BIYEARLY
BUNGALOW
BUOYANCY
CAMPAIGN
CANNABIS
CARDAMOM
CARNAUBA
CARYATID
CASTAWAY
CASUALTY
CEPHALIC
CHARADES
CHIVALRY
CINNABAR
CINNAMON
CLEMATIS
COCKATOO
COLLAPSE
COMMANDO
CREMAINS
CREVASSE
CULPABLE
CYCLAMEN
DAMNABLE
DEFIANCE
DEMEANOR
DESPATCH
DIAPASON
DICTATOR
DISFAVOR
DISPATCH
DISTANCE
DISTASTE
DUNGAREE
DUTIABLE
EDUCABLE
ELEGANCE
ELEVATOR
EMBLAZON
EMPHASIS
EMPHATIC
ENDEAVOR
ENTRAILS
ENTRANCE
ENVIABLE
ESTRANGE
EXCHANGE
EXTRADOS
FANDANGO
FANTASIA
FELLATIO
FLYPAPER
FOLDAWAY
FOLIATED
FORWARDS
GENDARME
GHANAIAN
GIVEAWAY
GONFALON
GOSSAMER
GRAVAMEN
GUARANTY
GUIDANCE
HEADACHE
HEBRAISM
HIDEAWAY
HISPANIC
HUARACHE
IDOLATER
IDOLATRY
IMITABLE
INDIAMAN
INFRADIG
INFRARED
INSTANCE
INTRADOS
INVIABLE
ISSUANCE
JEOPARDY
KAMAAINA
KANGAROO
LAMBASTE
LAUDANUM
LAWMAKER
LETHARGY
MACPAINT
MAGDALEN
MANDAMUS
MANDARIN
MANIACAL
MARIACHI
MASSACRE
MECHANIC
MENHADEN
MESDAMES
METHANOL
MIGRAINE
MISCARRY
MISLABEL
MISMATCH
MISTAKEN
MOCCASIN
MUSCATEL
MUSTACHE
NEONATAL
NONDAIRY
NUISANCE
NUTHATCH
OBSTACLE
OPERABLE
OPERANDS
ORDNANCE
OUTDATED
OVERALLS
PALPABLE
PARLANCE
PASSABLE
PELLAGRA
PENTAGON
PINNACLE
PITIABLE
PITTANCE
PODIATRY
PORTABLE
PRENATAL
PROBABLE
PROCAINE
PTOMAINE
QUOTABLE
RADIATOR
REHEARSE
RELIABLE
RELIANCE
REPEATED
RESEARCH
SCALABLE
SCALAWAG
SCENARIO
SCHMALTZ
SEAFARER
SEAWATER
SITUATED
SOCIABLE
SPORADIC
STOWAWAY
STREAMER
SUITABLE
SYLLABLE
SYLLABUS
SYMPATHY
TANTALUM
TARRAGON
TAXPAYER
TENTACLE
TERRAPIN
TESTATOR
THALAMUS
THREATEN
TOREADOR
TRIMARAN
TYMPANUM
UNAWARES
UNBEATEN
UNBIASED
UNCHASTE
UNIVALVE
UNLEADED
UNSHAPED
UNSTABLE
UPHEAVAL
UPSTAIRS
VAGRANCY
VALUABLE
VARIABLE
VARIANCE
VERBATIM
VILLAGER
VILLAINY
VIOLABLE
VOLCANIC
WALKAWAY
WARFARIN
WARRANTY
WASHABLE
WAYFARER
WISEACRE
WISTARIA
WORKABLE
WORKADAY
YEOMANRY
ACERBATE
ACERBITY
AMOEBOID
ANTIBODY
AUTOBAHN
BACKBITE
BACKBONE
BANKBOOK
BAREBACK
BASEBALL
BASEBORN
BEANBALL
BERIBERI
BIRDBATH
BLUEBELL
BLUEBIRD
BROWBEAT
BUSYBODY
CALABASH
CALLBACK
CELIBACY
CELIBATE
CENOBITE
CEREBRUM
CHAMBRAY
CHAPBOOK
CLAMBAKE
COMEBACK
COOKBOOK
COPYBOOK
CRIBBAGE
DATABASE
DEADBEAT
DEMIBOLD
DINGBATS
DISABUSE
DOWNBEAT
DRAWBACK
DRUMBEAT
DUCKBILL
DUMBBELL
EUROBOND
FALTBOAT
FASTBACK
FEEDBACK
FIREBALL
FIREBOAT
FIREBOMB
FISHBOWL
FLAMBEAU
FLATBOAT
FLEABANE
FLEABITE
FOLDBOAT
FOOTBALL
FOREBEAR
FOREBODE
FREEBORN
FULLBACK
GADABOUT
GIGABYTE
GOOFBALL
GROSBEAK
HALFBACK
HANDBALL
HANDBILL
HANDBOOK
HARDBACK
HARDBALL
HAREBELL
HAUTBOIS
HEADBAND
HIGHBALL
HIGHBORN
HIGHBRED
HIGHBROW
HOMEBODY
HOMEBRED
HORNBOOK
HUMPBACK
IMMOBILE
INCUBATE
INDEBTED
INFOBAHN
JACKBOOT
JAILBIRD
KEELBOAT
KICKBACK
KIELBASA
KILOBYTE
KINGBOLT
LADYBIRD
LAMPBACK
LIFEBOAT
LONGBOAT
LOVEBIRD
MEATBALL
MEGABYTE
MINIBIKE
MOONBEAM
MORIBUND
MOSSBACK
MOTHBALL
NOTEBOOK
OVENBIRD
PARABOLA
PASSBOOK
PLAYBACK
PLAYBILL
PLAYBOOK
PLUMBING
PUFFBALL
PULLBACK
PUREBRED
REPUBLIC
RHOMBOID
ROLLBACK
ROSEBUSH
RUNABOUT
RUTABAGA
SAILBOAT
SANDBANK
SCABBARD
SCRABBLE
SCRIBBLE
SHAMBLES
SHINBONE
SNOBBERY
SNOWBALL
SNOWBANK
SOFTBALL
SOMEBODY
SONGBIRD
SPITBALL
SQUABBLE
STUBBORN
STUDBOOK
SWAYBACK
TEXTBOOK
TOLLBOTH
TROMBONE
VAGABOND
WASHBOWL
WELLBORN
WINDBURN
WISHBONE
WOODBINE
WORDBOOK
WORKBOOK
YEARBOOK
ZWIEBACK
ABDICATE
ADJACENT
ADVOCATE
AFFECTED
ALBACORE
ALLOCATE
AQUACADE
ATROCITY
BIFOCALS
BIRACIAL
BOOKCASE
BRITCHES
BROCCOLI
BRONCHUS
CABOCHON
CADUCEUS
CAPACITY
CAPUCHIN
CARACOLE
CATACOMB
CHANCERY
CHARCOAL
CHITCHAT
CHOWCHOW
CLINCHER
COCKCROW
COINCIDE
CORNCRIB
CRESCENT
CROTCHET
DEDICATE
DEFECATE
DEJECTED
DELICACY
DELICATE
DEMOCRAT
DETACHED
DIDACTIC
DIRECTOR
DOMICILE
DOWNCAST

ESPECIAL
EXERCISE
EXORCISE
FELICITY
FEROCITY
FIRECLAY
FORECAST
FRANCIUM
GAMECOCK
GENOCIDE
GLAUCOMA
GROSCHEN
HANDCUFF
HELICOID
HOMICIDE
IMBECILE
IMPACTED
INDECENT
INDICATE
INDUCTEE
INNOCENT
INSECURE
IRONCLAD
JUDICIAL
LAUNCHER
MAGICIAN
MANICURE
MEDICAID
MEDICARE
MEDICATE
MEDICINE
MOLECULE
MOROCCAN
MUSICALE
MUSICIAN
NEWSCAST
OFFICIAL
OPTICIAN
OPUSCULE
OVERCAST
OVERCOAT
OVERCOME
PEDICURE
PINOCHLE
POSTCARD
PRINCESS
PUSHCART
RAINCOAT
REGICIDE
RELOCATE
RETICENT
RICOCHET
RIDICULE
RUBICUND
SCARCELY
SEASCAPE
SELECTEE
SETSCREW
SHOWCASE
SILICATE
SILICIFY
SILICONE
SINECURE
SOLECISM
SPROCKET
STACCATO
STRICKEN
SUITCASE
TAILCOAT
TELECAST
TRENCHER
TRUNCATE
TURNCOAT
TYPECAST
UNBUCKLE
UUDECODE
UUENCODE
VARICOSE
VELOCITY
VERACITY
VESICANT
VIETCONG
VISICALC
VIVACITY
WHIPCORD
WOODCOCK
WRETCHED
ABUNDANT
ACCIDENT
ANECDOTE
ANTEDATE
ANTIDOTE
AQUEDUCT
ARCHDUKE
BACKDROP
BEFUDDLE
BENEDICT
BOUNDARY
BRANDISH
BREEDING
BRINDLED
BUILDING
BULLDOZE
CALADIUM
CANADIAN
CAULDRON
CHANDLER
CLOUDLET
COMEDIAN
COMEDOWN
COPYDESK
CUPIDITY
DECEDENT
DIELDRIN
DIVIDEND
DREADFUL
EXORDIUM
EXPEDITE
FACEDOWN
FIREDAMP
FLUIDRAM
FOREDOOM
FREEDMAN
GRANDEUR
GRANDSON
GUARDIAN
HEREDITY
HOARDING
HUMIDIFY
HUMIDITY
IMMODEST
IMPUDENT
INCIDENT
INUNDATE
JAUNDICE
KILLDEER
LAPIDARY
MARKDOWN
MELODEON
MERIDIAN
NOWADAYS
OBSIDIAN
ONONDAGA
OVERDRAW
PARADIGM
PARADISE
POSTDATE
POUNDAGE
PUSHDOWN
QUANDARY
RAINDROP
REINDEER
REMEDIAL
RESIDENT
RESIDUAL
RESIDUUM
RUBIDIUM
SCANDIUM
SCHEDULE
SHOWDOWN
SHUTDOWN
SNOWDROP
SOLIDIFY
SPEEDWAY
SQUADRON
STANDARD
STANDING
STANDOFF
STANDOUT
STRADDLE
STRIDENT
STUDDING
SYSADMIN
TRAPDOOR
UNBIDDEN
UNBODIED
UNENDING
UNRIDDLE
UNSADDLE
VALIDATE
VANADIUM
WINGDING
WIREDRAW
WITHDRAW
YIELDING
ACADEMIC
ACCREDIT
AIGRETTE
ALFRESCO
ALOPECIA
AMBIENCE
ANISETTE
ATHLETIC
AUDIENCE
BACHELOR
BAEDEKER
BAGUETTE
BARBECUE
BARBERRY
BARRETTE
BAYBERRY
BEQUEATH
BERCEUSE
BIWEEKLY
BORDELLO
BRACELET
BRAKEMAN
BULLETIN
CAFFEINE
CASSETTE
CATHETER
CAUSERIE
CAUSEWAY
CENTERED
CHAPERON
CHEYENNE
CHOLERIC
CLEMENCY
CLOSEOUT
COALESCE
COCKEREL
COMMENCE
COMMERCE
CONCEIVE
CONCERTO
CONDENSE
CONFETTI
CONGENER
CONSERVE
CONTEMPT
CONVERGE
CONVERSE
COPPERAS
COQUETTE
CORVETTE
COSMETIC
CREDENCE
CREDENZA
CRUZEIRO
CURRENCY
DANSEUSE
DECREASE
DECREPIT
DEWBERRY
DIABETES
DIAMETER
DISHEVEL
DISKETTE
DISPENSE
DISPERSE
DISSEVER
DIURETIC
DOGGEREL
DRIVEWAY
DUODENUM
DYSLEXIA
EMINENCE
ENFEEBLE
ENTRENCH
ENURESIS
EPIDEMIC
EPILEPSY
ESOTERIC
ESPRESSO
EVIDENCE
EXEGESIS
EXIGENCY
FALSETTO
FERVENCY
FLAMENCO
FLAMEOUT
FOLDEROL
FORMERLY
FRENETIC
FURBELOW
GARDENIA
GEODESIC
GEOMETRY
GINGERLY
GLYCERIN
GLYCEROL
GORGEOUS
GRATEFUL
HACIENDA
HEDGEHOG
HEDGEHOP
HEDGEROW
HERMETIC
HITHERTO
HOOSEGOW
HORSEFLY
HORSEMAN
HOSTELRY
HOUSEBOY
HOUSEFLY
HOUSETOP
HUGUENOT
HYSTERIA
INCREASE
INNUENDO
INTRENCH
INTREPID
LAUREATE
LEUKEMIA
LIBRETTO
LIGNEOUS
LINGERIE
LUTHERAN
MACKEREL
MAGNESIA
MAGNETIC
MANNERED
MANNERLY
MANTELET
MASSEUSE
MASTERLY
MEDIEVAL
MULBERRY
MUSKETRY
NAUSEATE
NOBLEMAN
NONMETAL
NONSENSE
NORSEMAN
NUCLEATE
ODOMETER
OHMMETER
OPERETTA
OUTREACH
OUTWEIGH
PALMETTO
PANDEMIC
PARIETAL
PARMESAN
PARTERRE
PATHETIC
PATIENCE
PERCEIVE
PERFECTO
PERMEATE
PERVERSE
PHASEOUT
PICKEREL
PIMIENTO
PIZZERIA
PLACENTA
PLEBEIAN
POTBELLY
PRESENCE
PRESERVE
PRETENSE
PRETERIT
PRIMEVAL
PROCEEDS
PROPERTY
RECREANT
RECREATE
RETRENCH
REVIEWER
ROCKETRY
ROOMETTE
ROULETTE
ROUTEMAN
SAUCEPAN
SAUTERNE
SCALEPAN
SCAVENGE
SENTENCE
SEQUENCE
SERGEANT
SIXPENCE
SKELETON
SLOVENLY
SOLVENCY
SOUVENIR
SPACEMAN
SQUEEGEE
STAKEOUT
STILETTO
SUBMERGE
SUBMERSE
SURCEASE
SUSPENSE
SYMMETRY
SYSTEMIC
TENDENCY
TENPENNY
THEREFOR
TIMBERED
TOILETRY
TOILETTE
TRAVERSE
TRAVESTY
TRIMETER
TURMERIC
TWOPENCE
TWOPENNY
UMBRELLA
UNCLENCH
UNFREEZE
UNIVERSE
UNSEEMLY
UNSTEADY
UNWIELDY
VARIETAL
VELLEITY
VENDETTA
VENGEFUL
VERTEBRA
VIGNETTE
VIOLENCE
VISCERAL
VITREOUS
WHATEVER
WHENEVER
WHEREVER
WHITECAP
WHITEFLY
WHOMEVER
WISTERIA
ZEPPELIN
ARTIFACT
ARTIFICE
BACKFIRE
BAREFOOT
BENEFICE
BILLFOLD
BLUEFISH
BOLDFACE
BOUFFANT
BULLFROG
CAREFREE
CLUBFOOT
COIFFEUR
COIFFURE
CRAWFISH
CRAYFISH
CROWFOOT
DOWNFALL
FLATFISH
FLATFOOT
FLIMFLAM
FOOTFALL
FOREFEND
FOREFOOT
FOURFOLD
FROUFROU
GOLDFISH
GRAFFITO
HEREFORD
LANDFALL
LANDFILL
LANDFORM
LEAPFROG
MANIFEST
MANIFOLD

MANYFOLD
METAFILE
OVERFLOW
PACIFIER
PACIFISM
PALEFACE
PARAFFIN
PINAFORE
PLATFORM
PRATFALL
RAINFALL
ROCKFALL
SAILFISH
SCAFFOLD
SCOFFLAW
SCROFULA
SNOWFALL
STARFISH
STUFFING
SUREFIRE
TELEFILM
TYPEFACE
WEAKFISH
WHARFAGE
WILDFIRE
WILDFOWL
WINDFALL
ABNEGATE
ABROGATE
ALLEGORY
ALMIGHTY
ARPEGGIO
ARROGANT
ARROGATE
AUTOGIRO
BLUDGEON
BRAGGART
BROUGHAM
CATEGORY
COSIGNER
DECIGRAM
DEKAGRAM
DELEGATE
DEROGATE
DILIGENT
DISAGREE
DIVAGATE
DRAUGHTS
DRUGGIST
ELONGATE
ENERGIZE
ENGAGING
FILIGREE
FOREGONE
FUMIGANT
FUMIGATE
HEADGEAR

HOLOGRAM
IDEOGRAM
INDIGENT
INSIGNIA
INTAGLIO
INTEGRAL
IRRIGATE
KILOGRAM
LITIGANT
LITIGATE
MAHOGANY
MARIGOLD
MITIGATE
MONOGAMY
MONOGRAM
MORTGAGE
NAVIGATE
OBLIGATE
ORANGERY
OVERGROW
PEDAGOGY
PEDIGREE
PLANGENT
PLAYGOER
POLYGAMY
POLYGLOT
RELEGATE
RELIGION
RENEGADE
RESIGNED
RUNAGATE
SCRAGGLY
SERAGLIO
SHANGHAI
SHINGLES
SLUGGARD
SLUGGISH
SPHAGNUM
STRAGGLE
STRUGGLE
STURGEON
TAILGATE
TELEGRAM
TOBOGGAN
TOLLGATE
VINEGARY
VOYAGEUR
WRIGGLER
WRONGFUL
YOUNGISH
ACIDHEAD
AESTHETE
AMETHYST
ANATHEMA
ANECHOIC
ANYTHING
ANYWHERE

APOTHEGM
ARACHNID
ARMCHAIR
BACKHAND
BEECHNUT
BIATHLON
BILLHEAD
BIRTHDAY
BOBWHITE
BRETHREN
BRIGHTEN
BROCHURE
BROUHAHA
BUDDHISM
BULKHEAD
BULLHEAD
BUNGHOLE
CAMSHAFT
CATCHALL
CATCHING
CINCHONA
CLOTHIER
CLOTHING
COACHMAN
COGWHEEL
COUCHANT
DAUGHTER
DEATHBED
DECKHAND
DOCKHAND
DOUGHBOY
DOUGHNUT
DOWNHILL
DUNGHILL
EARPHONE
EGGSHELL
ELEPHANT
EPIPHANY
ERYTHEMA
FALCHION
FARMHAND
FARTHEST
FARTHING
FETCHING
FISHHOOK
FLASHGUN
FLASHING
FLATHEAD
FLESHPOT
FLYWHEEL
FOOTHILL
FOOTHOLD
FOREHAND
FOREHEAD
FREEHAND
FREEHOLD
FRESHMAN

FRIGHTEN
FURTHEST
GOATHERD
GODCHILD
GRAPHITE
GYMKHANA
HARDHACK
HATCHING
HATCHWAY
HAWTHORN
HEIGHTEN
HELLHOLE
HENCHMAN
HOGSHEAD
ISOTHERM
KEELHAUL
KERCHIEF
KNEEHOLE
KNOTHOLE
LATCHKEY
LAUGHTER
LINCHPIN
LOATHING
LONGHAIR
LONGHAND
LONGHORN
LOOPHOLE
LUNCHEON
LYMPHOID
MASTHEAD
MERCHANT
MIDSHIPS
MISCHIEF
MISSHAPE
MOLEHILL
MORPHEME
MORPHINE
NEIGHBOR
NEOPHYTE
NUTSHELL
OFFSHOOT
OFFSHORE
OUTSHINE
OVERHAND
OVERHANG
OVERHAUL
OVERHEAD
OVERHEAR
PAMPHLET
PANTHEON
PAYCHECK
PEEPHOLE
PENCHANT
PILCHARD
PINWHEEL
PITCHMAN
PLETHORA

PORPHYRY
PORTHOLE
POSTHOLE
POTSHERD
PROPHECY
PROPHESY
PUNCHEON
PURCHASE
ROUGHAGE
SAPPHIRE
SCATHING
SEASHORE
SHEPHERD
SHOSHONE
SINKHOLE
SOUTHPAW
SUNSHADE
SUNSHINE
SYMPHONY
TEACHING
TEETHING
TOMAHAWK
TOUCHING
TRICHINA
TRUTHFUL
WATCHDOG
WATCHFUL
WATCHMAN
WELLHEAD
WIREHAIR
WITCHERY
WITCHING
WITHHOLD
WORMHOLE
WRATHFUL
YOUTHFUL
ZOOPHYTE
ZUCCHINI
ABSCISSA
AFFRIGHT
AGGRIEVE
AIRFIELD
AIRLINER
AIRTIGHT
ALUMINUM
AMERICAN
ANGLICAN
APERITIF
APPLIQUE
ATOMIZER
ATYPICAL
BARBICAN
BARBITAL
BASSINET
BEATIFIC
BEFRIEND
BESMIRCH

BESTIARY
BIOCIDAL
BOUTIQUE
BREVIARY
BROMIDIC
BURSITIS
CALLIOPE
CANAILLE
CANNIBAL
CANTICLE
CAPRIOLE
CAPSICUM
CAPTIOUS
CARDIGAN
CARDINAL
CARNIVAL
CARRIAGE
CAUDILLO
CAUTIOUS
CERVICAL
CHARISMA
CHEMICAL
CHENILLE
CLARINET
CLAVICLE
CLERICAL
CLINICAL
COLLIERY
COMBINGS
COMPILER
CONFINES
CONSIDER
CONTINUE
CONVINCE
CORRIDOR
CREDIBLE
CREDITOR
CRIMINAL
CRITICAL
CRITIQUE
CRUCIBLE
CRUCIFIX
CURLICUE
CUSPIDOR
DAYLIGHT
DERRIERE
DETRITUS
DISCIPLE
DISPIRIT
DISTINCT
DOGFIGHT
DULCIMER
EARNINGS
ELIGIBLE
EMACIATE
EMERITUS
EMOTICON

ENCEINTE
EXPLICIT
EYELINER
EYEPIECE
EYESIGHT
FACTIOUS
FALLIBLE
FANCIFUL
FANLIGHT
FASCICLE
FASCISTA
FEASIBLE
FESTIVAL
FLAMINGO
FLATIRON
FLEXIBLE
FLOTILLA
FOLLICLE
FORCIBLE
GARRISON
GASLIGHT
GERMINAL
GLACIATE
GLORIOUS
GLOXINIA
GRACIOUS
GRADIENT
GRIDIRON
GUNFIGHT
HANDICAP
HARRIDAN
HAWAIIAN
HOOLIGAN
HORRIBLE
HOSPITAL
HUSTINGS
HYACINTH
IMPLICIT
IMPRISON
INEDITED
INFRINGE
INGUINAL
INIMICAL
INITIATE
INSPIRIT
INSTINCT
INTRIGUE
INVEIGLE
JETTISON
LACRIMAL
LAWGIVER
LEAVINGS
LOLLIPOP
LOPSIDED
LUSCIOUS
MACHISMO
MACKINAW

MADRIGAL
MANCIPLE
MANDIBLE
MANTILLA
MANTISSA
MARRIAGE
MARTINET
MARZIPAN
MEPHITIC
METRICAL
MIDNIGHT
MILLIARD
MILLIBAR
MILLIEME
MILLINER
MISCIBLE
MONSIEUR
MULTIPLE
MULTIPLY
MYELITIS
MYRMIDON
MYSTICAL
MYSTIQUE
NAUTICAL
NAUTILUS
NEGLIGEE
NEURITIS
NONRIGID
NUTRIENT
OBEDIENT
ORIGINAL
OUTFIELD
OUTFIGHT
OUTRIDER
OUTRIGHT
OUTSIDER
PALLIATE
PARTIBLE
PARTICLE
PARTISAN
PASTICHE
PASTILLE
PEMMICAN
PENLIGHT
PETTIFOG
PHARISEE
PHYSICAL
PHYSIQUE
PICKINGS
PLATINUM
POLLIWOG
PORRIDGE
PORTIERE
POSSIBLE
PRATIQUE
PRECINCT
PRECIOUS

PREMIERE
PRESIDIO
PREVIOUS
PRODIGAL
PROHIBIT
PROLIFIC
PROVIDED
PROVINCE
PRURIENT
PUBLICAN
QUOTIENT
RECEIVER
REPRIEVE
REPRISAL
RETAINER
RETRIEVE
REVEILLE
SACRISTY
SCILICET
SCIMITAR
SENSIBLE
SENTIENT
SENTINEL
SERVITOR
SHILINGI
SKYLIGHT
SOBRIETY
SOLDIERY
SPACIOUS
SPANIARD
SPECIFIC
SPECIMEN
SPECIOUS
SPIRITED
SPURIOUS
STOTINKA
STRAIGHT
STRAITEN
STUDIOUS
SUBTITLE
SUCCINCT
SUNLIGHT
SURGICAL
SYPHILIS
TANGIBLE
TEOSINTE
TERMINAL
TERMINUS
TERRIBLE
TERRIFIC
TERTIARY
TESTICLE
TOPSIDES
TORTILLA
TWILIGHT
UNGAINLY
UNVOICED

USURIOUS
UXORIOUS
VACCINIA
VERBIAGE
VERSICLE
VERTICAL
VIATICUM
VINCIBLE
VIRGINAL
WILLIWAW
AUTOJOIN
DEMIJOHN
DOORJAMB
FLAPJACK
BLACKING
BLACKOUT
BLACKTOP
BLOCKADE
BRACKISH
BREAKAGE
BREAKOUT
BRICKBAT
BROOKLET
CHECKERS
CHECKOFF
CHECKOUT
CHECKSUM
CRACKPOT
CROCKERY
DOORKNOB
DROPKICK
DRUNKARD
FOREKNOW
GREEKING
HANUKKAH
KAMIKAZE
KATAKANA
KNICKERS
KNOCKOUT
LIMEKILN
NUMSKULL
OVERKILL
PARAKEET
PLANKING
PLANKTON
SANSKRIT
SHOCKING
SIDEKICK
SLIPKNOT
SPANKING
STICKLER
STINKBUG
STOCKADE
STOCKING
STRIKING
THANKFUL
THICKSET

TRACKAGE
TRICKERY
TRUCKAGE
UNLIKELY
WRECKAGE
ABSOLUTE
ACCOLADE
AEROLOGY
AIRPLANE
ALKALOID
ALLELUIA
AMBULANT
ANGELICA
ANTELOPE
ANYPLACE
APHELION
APOPLEXY
APPELLEE
AQUILINE
ARBALEST
BACILLUS
BACKLASH
BANTLING
BASELESS
BASELINE
BASILICA
BASILISK
BEHOLDEN
BEWILDER
BIBULOUS
BIRDLIME
BOBOLINK
BODILESS
BOOTLESS
BOTULISM
BOUILLON
BRISLING
BUNDLING
BURGLARY
CAGELING
CAMELLIA
CANALIZE
CARELESS
CARILLON
CATALYZE
CAVALIER
CERULEAN
CHAPLAIN
CIVILIAN
CIVILITY
CIVILIZE
COMPLAIN
COMPLEAT
COMPLETE
CONCLAVE
CONCLUDE
CONFLICT

COPULATE
CORDLESS
COUPLING
CROPLAND
CRYOLITE
CYTOLOGY
DARKLING
DATELESS
DATELINE
DEADLINE
DEADLOCK
DEBILITY
DEMOLISH
DERELICT
DESELECT
DESOLATE
DEVILISH
DISALLOW
DISCLAIM
DISCLOSE
DISPLACE
DOUBLOON
DOWNLOAD
DOXOLOGY
DUCKLING
DUMPLING
DWELLING
EGGPLANT
EMBOLDEN
EMBOLISM
ENFILADE
ENSILAGE
ENVELOPE
EQUALIZE
ESCALATE
ESCALLOP
ESPALIER
ETHOLOGY
ETIOLOGY
EYEGLASS
FABULOUS
FACILITY
FADELESS
FAMILIAL
FAMILIAR
FARMLAND
FATALISM
FATALITY
FEARLESS
FECKLESS
FIDELITY
FINALIST
FINALIZE
FLATLAND
FLYBLOWN
FOLKLORE
FOOTLESS

FOOTLING
FORELADY
FORELAND
FORELIMB
FORELOCK
FORKLIFT
FORMLESS
FOXGLOVE
FREELOAD
FUSELAGE
FUTILITY
GANGLAND
GANGLING
GANGLION
GASOLINE
GEMOLOGY
GRAYLING
GRUELING
HAIRLINE
HEADLAND
HEADLINE
HEADLOCK
HEADLONG
HEIRLOOM
HERALDIC
HERALDRY
HIGHLAND
HIRELING
HOMELAND
HOROLOGY
HUMILITY
IDEALISM
IDEALIZE
IDEOLOGY
IMMOLATE
IMPELLER
IMPOLITE
INDOLENT
INHALANT
INSOLENT
INSULATE
INVOLUTE
INVOLVED
JONGLEUR
JUBILANT
KINDLING
LADYLIKE
LADYLOVE
LANDLORD
LEGALISM
LIFELINE
LIFELONG
LINOLEUM
LISTLESS
LIVELONG
LOCALITY
LOCALIZE

LOVELORN
LOYALIST
MAINLAND
MAINLINE
MAJOLICA
MARBLING
MASSLESS
MEDALIST
MEGALITH
MIDDLING
MINDLESS
MISPLACE
MOBILIZE
MODULATE
MONOLITH
MOORLAND
MORALIST
MORALITY
MORALIZE
MUCILAGE
MUTILATE
MYCOLOGY
NAMELESS
NAPOLEON
NASALIZE
NATALITY
NEBULIZE
NEBULOUS
NECKLACE
NECKLINE
NEEDLESS
NEOPLASM
NESTLING
NIGGLING
NIHILISM
NOBELIST
NOBELIUM
NOBILITY
NOVELIZE
NURSLING
OBSOLETE
OILCLOTH
ORGULOUS
OSCULATE
OUTCLASS
OUTFLANK
OVERLAID
OVERLAND
OVERLEAP
OVERLOOK
OVERLORD
PANELING
PANELIST
PARALLAX
PARALLEL
PARALYZE
PAVILION

PECULATE
PECULIAR
PEERLESS
PENALIZE
PENOLOGY
PERILUNE
PETULANT
PICKLOCK
PIDDLING
PIEPLANT
PIPELINE
PITILESS
PIXELATE
POPULACE
POPULATE
POPULIST
POPULOUS
POSTLUDE
PRECLUDE
PROCLAIM
PUDDLING
PUGILISM
PURBLIND
PURSLANE
PURULENT
QUISLING
RAILLERY
RATTLING
RECKLESS
REDOLENT
REGOLITH
REGULATE
RESOLUTE
RESTLESS
REVOLVER
RHEOLOGY
RHYOLITE
ROYALIST
RUMBLING
RUTHLESS
SCALLION
SCULLERY
SCULLION
SEAPLANE
SEDULOUS
SEEDLING
SELFLESS
SEROLOGY
SHILLING
SHOELACE
SHOPLIFT
SHOULDER
SIBILANT
SIDELONG
SIMPLIFY
SIMULATE
SKILLFUL

SKULLCAP
SLUMLORD
SMALLPOX
SPILLWAY
SPOOLING
SPYGLASS
STALLION
STARLING
STEALTHY
STERLING
SUCHLIKE
SUCKLING
SUPPLANT
SURPLICE
SWELLING
TABULATE
TEMPLATE
THALLIUM
THEOLOGY
TICKLISH
TIDELAND
TIMELESS
TINPLATE
TIRELESS
TITILATE
TONALITY
TOPOLOGY
TOTALITY
TOWELING
TRIFLING
TRILLION
TRILLIUM
TUNELESS
TUTELAGE
TUTELARY
UNBELIEF
UNBOLTED
UNDULANT
UNDULATE
UNFILIAL
UNGULATE
VIGILANT
VIROLOGY
VIRULENT
VITALITY
VITALIZE
VOCALIST
VOCALIZE
VOLPLANE
WARPLANE
WEAKLING
WHIPLASH
WILDLIFE
WINDLASS
WIRELESS
WOODLAND
XENOLITH

YEARLING
YEARLONG
ABUTMENT
ACRIMONY
ALARMIST
ANTIMONY
ARGUMENT
ARMAMENT
ASSEMBLE
ASSEMBLY
AUTOMATE
AVERMENT
BASEMENT
BECOMING
BEHEMOTH
BLOOMERS
BOHEMIAN
BOOKMARK
CALAMINE
CALAMITY
CAMOMILE
CASEMENT
CASHMERE
CERAMIST
CEREMENT
CEREMONY
CHARMING
CHIPMUNK
CHROMIUM
CLAIMANT
CLAYMORE
CORNMEAL
CREAMERY
CUCUMBER
DECEMBER
DECIMATE
DOCUMENT
DOLOMITE
DYNAMITE
ENCOMIUM
ENCUMBER
ENORMITY
ENORMOUS
ENSEMBLE
ESTIMATE
EVERMORE
FILAMENT
FOREMAST
FOREMOST
FRAGMENT
GLOAMING
GOURMAND
GUNSMITH
HALLMARK
HANDMADE
HEGEMONY
HELPMATE
HELPMEET
HINDMOST
HOMEMADE
ILLUMINE
INCOMING
INCUMBER
INFAMOUS
INHUMANE
INSOMNIA
INSOMUCH
INTIMATE
ISTHMIAN
JEREMIAD
JUDGMENT
LANDMARK
LANDMASS
LIGAMENT
LINIMENT
LODGMENT
MAINMAST
MALAMUTE
MAXIMIZE
MESSMATE
MILKMAID
MINIMIZE
MISHMASH
MONUMENT
MOVEMENT
NOVEMBER
OINTMENT
ONCOMING
OPTIMISM
ORNAMENT
OUTSMART
OVERMUCH
PALOMINO
PARAMOUR
PAVEMENT
PEDIMENT
PENUMBRA
PHARMACY
PLAYMATE
POCKMARK
POLYMATH
POSTMARK
PREAMBLE
PSALMODY
QUAGMIRE
QUALMISH
REGIMENT
REMEMBER
RESEMBLE
ROOMMATE
ROSEMARY
RUDIMENT
SAGAMORE
SCRAMBLE
SEDIMENT
SHIPMATE
SHIPMENT
SKIMMING
SKIRMISH
STRUMPET
SWIMMING
SYCAMORE
TENEMENT
THIAMINE
THROMBUS
TINSMITH
TRIMMING
TRIUMVIR
ULTIMATE
UNCOMMON
UNLIMBER
UNTIMELY
UPCOMING
VEHEMENT
VENOMOUS
VESTMENT
WELDMENT
WINDMILL
ABORNING
ABSENTEE
ABSINTHE
ACTINISM
ACTINIUM
ADDENDUM
ADMONISH
AERONAUT
AFFINITY
AGRONOMY
ALBANIAN
ALIENATE
ALIENIST
AMMONIUM
ANTINOMY
APHANITE
APPANAGE
APPENDIX
AQUANAUT
ASTONISH
AVIONICS
BADINAGE
BARONAGE
BARONESS
BIANNUAL
BICONVEX
BIENNIAL
BIENNIUM
BLUENOSE
BROWNOUT
BUSINESS
CALENDAR
CALENDER
CANONIZE
CEMENTUM
COLANDER
COLONIAL
COLONIST
COLONIZE
COMANCHE
CORONACH
CORONARY
CORUNDUM
COVENANT
CULINARY
CYLINDER
DEBONAIR
DECANTER
DEFINITE
DEIONIZE
DEMENTED
DEMENTIA
DEMONIAC
DEPONENT
DETONATE
DIMINISH
DISINTER
DISUNITE
DISUNITY
DIVINITY
DOMINATE
DOMINEER
DOMINION
DRAINAGE
ENDANGER
ENGENDER
ENGINEER
ENTANGLE
ESTONIAN
ETERNITY
EUGENICS
EXPONENT
FASTNESS
FEMININE
FEMINISM
FLOUNDER
FOOTNOTE
FORENAME
FORENOON
FORENSIC
GEMINATE
GERANIUM
GIGANTIC
GOODNESS
GREENERY
GROUNDER
GUERNSEY
GUYANESE
HABANERA
HANGNAIL
HARANGUE
HEDONISM
HIGHNESS
HOLINESS
HUMANISM
HUMANITY
HUMANIZE
HUMANOID
HYMENEAL
ILLINOIS
IMMANENT
IMMINENT
IMMUNIZE
IMPUNITY
INFANTRY
INFINITE
INFINITY
INTENDED
ISLANDER
JAPANESE
JUVENILE
KOLINSKY
LAVENDER
LEARNING
LEMONADE
LICENSEE
LIKENESS
LIMONITE
LUMINARY
LUMINOUS
MALINGER
MARINATE
MELANISM
MELANOMA
MERINGUE
MOMENTUM
MOURNFUL
MOURNING
NEPENTHE
NICKNAME
NOMINATE
NONUNION
OLEANDER
OPPONENT
ORDINARY
ORDINATE
ORGANISM
ORGANIST
ORGANIZE
ORIENTAL
PAGINATE
PALINODE
PARANOIA
PEDUNCLE
PEIGNOIR
PENKNIFE
POIGNANT
POLONIUM
POPINJAY
PREGNANT
PUDENDUM
RAVENING
RAVENOUS
REFINERY
RESONANT
RESONATE
REVANCHE
REVENUER
ROMANIAN
ROMANTIC
RUMANIAN
RUMINANT
RUMINATE
SEIGNEUR
SELENITE
SELENIUM
SEMANTIC
SEMINARY
SEMINOLE
SERENADE
SICKNESS
SILENCER
SIMONIZE
SOLENOID
SPLENDID
SPLENDOR
SPLINTER
SPRINKLE
SQUANDER
STAGNANT
STAGNATE
STRANGER
STRANGLE
STRENGTH
STRINGED
STRINGER
STUNNING
TAXONOMY
TENANTRY
THRENODY
TITANIUM
TOKENISM
TRAINING
TRAINMAN
TRIANGLE
UNIONISM
UNIONIZE
UNKINDLY
UNTANGLE
UNWONTED
URBANITE
URBANIZE
VEGANISM
VERONICA
VICINAGE
VICINITY
WEAKNESS
WOMANISH
WOODNOTE
YEARNING
ACIDOSIS
AIRBORNE
ALEHOUSE
ALTHOUGH
AMBROSIA
ANACONDA
ANALOGUE
ANDROGEN
APOLOGIA
APPROACH
APPROVAL
ASPHODEL
BENZOATE
BONHOMIE
BURNOOSE
CAMPOREE
CATHOLIC
CHEROKEE
CLITORIS
COGNOMEN
COLLOQUY
COMMONER
COMPOUND
CONFOCAL
CONFOUND
CONSOMME
CORDOVAN
CORPORAL
CRETONNE
CUPBOARD
CUSTOMER
DAFFODIL
DEFLOWER
DIABOLIC
DIAGONAL
DIALOGUE
DIATOMIC
DIPLOMAT
DISCOLOR
DISCOUNT
DISCOVER
DISGORGE
DISHONOR
DISJOINT
DISLODGE
DISLOYAL
DISMOUNT
DISPOSAL
DISSOLVE
DOGHOUSE
DORMOUSE
DRAGOMAN
ECONOMIC
EMPLOYEE
ENCROACH
ENSCONCE
EPILOGUE
ESTROGEN
EUPHORIA
EXPLODED
EYETOOTH
FACTOTUM
FAUBOURG
FIBROSIS
FORSOOTH
FOXHOUND
FURLOUGH
GARGOYLE
GASWORKS
GLYCOGEN
GUNPOINT
HANGOVER
HARMONIC
HOLDOVER
HORMONAL
HOTHOUSE
HYDROGEN
HYPNOSIS
HYPNOTIC
ICEBOUND
ICEHOUSE
IMPROPER
INCHOATE
INTROMIT
ISOTONIC
JAMBOREE
JINGOISM
KEYBOARD
KEYWORDS
LACROSSE
LAPBOARD
LARBOARD
LEFTOVER
LITTORAL
MADHOUSE
MAGNOLIA
MANDOLIN
MARJORAM
MARMOSET
MASTODON
MEDIOCRE
METEORIC
MICROBUS
MIDPOINT
MISCOUNT
MISDOING
MISNOMER
MNEMONIC

MONGOOSE
MOREOVER
NARCOSIS
NARCOTIC
NATIONAL
NECROSIS
NEUROSIS
NEUROTIC
NEWCOMER
NEWFOUND
NITROGEN
NOTIONAL
ONLOOKER
ORATORIO
ORTHODOX
ORTHOEPY
OUTBOARD
OUTBOUND
OUTDOORS
OUTGOING
OUTHOUSE
OUTMODED
OUTPOINT
PANDOWDY
PARDONER
PARFOCAL
PASSOVER
PASTORAL
PATHOGEN
PECTORAL
PERFORCE
PERIODIC
PERSONAL
PHENOLIC
PINPOINT
PORPOISE
PREMOLAR
PRISONER
PROFOUND
PROLOGUE
PROMOTER
PROPOUND
PROROGUE
PROTOCOL
PULLOVER
PULMOTOR
PUSHOVER
QUIXOTIC
RADIOMAN
RATIONAL
RAWBONED
REGIONAL
REPROACH
RESPONSE
RETROFIT
RHETORIC
SARDONIC
SAWHORSE
SCHOONER
SEABOARD
SEACOAST
SEAGOING
SEAMOUNT
SUBPOENA
SUBSONIC
SUPPOSED
SURMOUNT
SURROUND
SYMBOLIC
TEETOTAL
TEMPORAL
TEUTONIC
THOROUGH
TITMOUSE
TORTOISE
TRICOLOR
TURBOFAN
TURBOJET
TURNOVER
UNBROKEN
UNCLOTHE
UNLOOSEN
UPGROWTH
VARIORUM
VERBOTEN
VERMOUTH
VICTORIA
VISCOUNT
WALKOVER
WEAPONRY
AGITPROP
AIRSPACE
AIRSPEED
ALLSPICE
ANTIPODE
ANTIPOPE
ATROPINE
BACKPACK
BLOWPIPE
BOWSPRIT
CARAPACE
CATAPULT
CESSPOOL
CHAMPION
CHIPPEWA
CLIPPING
COLOPHON
CONSPIRE
CREEPING
CROUPIER
DECIPHER
DOWNPOUR
ECLIPTIC
ELLIPSIS
ENCIPHER
EQUIPAGE
ESCAPADE
ESCAPISM
EUROPEAN
EUROPIUM
EXEMPLAR
FILIPINO
FIREPLUG
FLAGPOLE
FLIPPANT
FLYSPECK
FOOTPATH
FOREPART
FRIPPERY
GANGPLOW
GATEPOST
GOALPOST
GRASPING
HANDPICK
HELIPORT
HORNPIPE
INEXPERT
MALAPERT
MAYAPPLE
METAPHOR
MILEPOST
MILLPOND
MISAPPLY
MISSPELL
MISSPEND
MONOPOLY
NINEPINS
OCCUPANT
OUTSPEND
OVERPASS
OVERPLAY
PASSPORT
PERSPIRE
PHOSPHOR
POSTPAID
POSTPONE
PROSPECT
RECEPTOR
SCORPION
SCULPTOR
SHEEPISH
SHIPPING
SHRAPNEL
SIGNPOST
SLIPPERY
SNOWPLOW
STAMPEDE
STOPPAGE
SWEEPING
SYNOPSIS
SYNOPTIC
TEASPOON
TELEPLAY
THESPIAN
TRAPPING
TRESPASS
TRUMPERY
TURNPIKE
UNZIPPED
WHOPPING
WINDPIPE
WOODPILE
WORDPLAY
WRAPPING
ZOOSPORE
TRANQUIL
ABNORMAL
ABSTRACT
ABSTRUSE
ACCURATE
ACCURSED
AFFERENT
AFTERTAX
AGRARIAN
AIRBRUSH
AIRCRAFT
AIRDROME
AIRFRAME
ALACRITY
ALDERMAN
ALGERIAN
ALLERGEN
AMPERAGE
ANAEROBE
ANTERIOR
ANTEROOM
ANTHROPO
APHORISM
APPARENT
AQUARIUM
ARBOREAL
ARMORIAL
ARTERIAL
ASPERITY
ASPIRANT
ASPIRATE
ASSORTED
ASTERISK
ASTEROID
ATTORNEY
AUSTRIAN
BACKREST
BALLROOM
BANKROLL
BANKRUPT
BATHROBE
BATHROOM
BESTRIDE
BEVERAGE
BUTTRESS
CASTRATE
CATARACT
CELERITY
CENTRIST
CESAREAN
CHAIRMAN
CHEERFUL
CHLORIDE
CHLORINE
CHLORITE
CHOIRBOY
CICERONE
CLEARING
COHERENT
COMPRESS
COMPRISE
CONCRETE
CONFRERE
CONFRONT
CONGRESS
CONTRACT
CONTRAIL
CONTRARY
CONTRAST
CONTRITE
CONTRIVE
COVERAGE
COVERALL
COVERLET
DANDRUFF
DARKROOM
DAYBREAK
DAYDREAM
DECORATE
DECOROUS
DEFOREST
DELIRIUM
DEMARCHE
DEMURRER
DESCRIBE
DESIROUS
DESTRUCT
DETHRONE
DEXTROSE
DIARRHEA
DIATRIBE
DISARRAY
DISCREET
DISCRETE
DISGRACE
DISORDER
DISPROVE
DISTRACT
DISTRAIT
DISTRESS
DISTRICT
DISTRUST
DIVORCEE
DOCTRINE
DOLDRUMS
EFFERENT
EMIGRATE
EMPORIUM
EMPYREAN
ENCIRCLE
ENSHRINE
ENSHROUD
ENTHRALL
ENTHRONE
ENTIRETY
ENVIRONS
ESCAROLE
ETHEREAL
ETHERNET
EXCURSUS
EXECRATE
EXTERIOR
EXTERNAL
FAVORITE
FEDERATE
FIGURINE
FILTRATE
FLAGRANT
FLOURISH
FLUORIDE
FLUORINE
FLUORITE
FOOTRACE
FOOTREST
FORTRESS
FRAGRANT
FUMAROLE
FUNERARY
FUNEREAL
FUTURISM
FUTURITY
GANGRENE
GENERATE
GENEROUS
GIMCRACK
GLABROUS
GOVERNOR
HANDRAIL
HEADREST
HEADROOM
HIGHROAD
HOMEROOM
HONORARY
HUNTRESS
IGNORANT
IMMORTAL
IMPERIAL
INDIRECT
INDURATE
INERRANT
INFERIOR
INFERNAL
INFORMAL
INFORMED
INFORMER
INHERENT
INSCRIBE
INSTRUCT
INTERCOM
INTEREST
INTERIOR
INTERMIT
INTERMIX
INTERNAL
INTERNEE
INTERNET
INTERROG
INTERVAL
INVERTER
INWARDLY
ISOPRENE
KOHLRABI
LABURNUM
LACERATE
LASERJET
LAYERING
LEVERAGE
LIBERATE
LICORICE
LIMERICK
LITERARY
LITERATE
LITERATI
LIVERISH
MACARONI
MACAROON
MACERATE
MAHARAJA
MAHARANI
MAJORITY
MALARKEY
MALTREAT
MANDRAKE
MANGROVE
MARGRAVE
MATERIAL
MATERIEL
MATERNAL
MATTRESS
MATURATE
MATURITY
MAVERICK
MEMBRANE
MEMORIAL
MEMORIZE
MILLRACE
MINORITY
MISBRAND
MISPRINT
MISTREAT
MISTRESS
MISTRIAL
MISTRUST
MODERATE
MONARCHY
MONORAIL
MOTORCAR
MOTORIZE
MOTORMAN
MOTOROLA
MUSHROOM
NEUTRINO
NEWSREEL
NIGERIAN
NIGEROIS
NOTARIAL
NOTARIZE
NUMERATE
NUMEROUS
OBDURATE
OBSTRUCT
OFFPRINT
OUTBREAK
OVERRIDE
OVERRULE
PANCREAS
PANORAMA
PASTRAMI
PATERNAL
PEDERAST
PINPRICK
PLEURISY
POLARITY
POLARIZE
POLTROON
PORTRAIT
PREPRESS
PRIMROSE
PROGRESS
PROTRACT
PROTRUDE
PYORRHEA
QUADRANT
QUADROON
QUATRAIN
RAILROAD
RECORDER
REFERENT
REFERRAL
REFOREST
REFORMER

REPARTEE
REPORTER
RESCRIPT
RESERVED
RESORTER
RESTRAIN
RESTRICT
RETARDED
RETIRING
RETURNEE
REVEREND
REVERENT
REVERSAL
RIFFRAFF
RIPARIAN
RIVERBED
SAMARIUM
SATURATE
SATURDAY
SCABROUS
SECURITY
SEPARATE
SEWERAGE
SHAMROCK
SHIRRING
SIDEREAL
SIDERITE
SOLARIUM
SOMBRERO
SOMERSET
SONOROUS
SORORITY
SPHEROID
SQUIRREL
STAIRWAY
STEERAGE
STIRRING
SUBTRACT
SUBURBIA
SUFFRAGE
SUNDRIES
SUPEREGO
SUPERIOR
SUPERJET
SUPERNAL
SUPPRESS
SURPRISE
SUZERAIN
SYBARITE
SYNDROME
TAFFRAIL
TAMARACK
TAMARIND
TEMERITY
THEORIZE
TIMOROUS
TOLERATE
TOMORROW
TOWERING
TRAPROCK
TUBERCLE
TUBEROSE
TUBEROUS
TUTORIAL
ULCERATE
ULTERIOR
UNBURDEN
UNDERACT
UNDERAGE
UNDERARM
UNDERBID
UNDERCUT
UNDERDOG
UNDERFUR
UNDERLIE
UNDERLIP
UNDERPAY
UNDERSEA
UNDERTOW
UNEARNED
UNERRING
UNFORMED
UNPERSON
UNSPRUNG
UNSTRUNG
UNWORTHY
UPPERCUT
UPSTREAM
UPSTROKE
UPTHRUST
USUFRUCT
VAPORING
VAPORISH
VAPORIZE
VAPOROUS
VENERATE
VENEREAL
VIBURNUM
VICARAGE
VIGOROUS
VIVARIUM
WAITRESS
WARDROBE
WARDROOM
WAREROOM
WASHROOM
WATERLOO
WATERWAY
WIZARDRY
WONDROUS
WOODRUFF
WORKROOM
ABRASIVE
ACCUSTOM
ACOUSTIC
ACROSTIC
ADHESION
ADHESIVE
ADVISORY
AGNOSTIC
ALIASING
ANCESTOR
ANCESTRY
APPOSITE
ARTISTIC
ARTISTRY
ASBESTOS
ASSASSIN
AVERSION
BABUSHKA
BACKSIDE
BACKSLAP
BACKSPIN
BACKSTOP
BAILSMAN
BAKESHOP
BALUSTER
BANISTER
BEARSKIN
BICUSPID
BIRDSEED
BLESSING
BLISSFUL
BONDSMAN
BUCKSHOT
BUCKSKIN
CALFSKIN
CAMISOLE
CANISTER
CAPESKIN
CHRISTEN
CHRISTIE
CLASSIFY
CLOISTER
COCKSURE
COHESION
COLESLAW
COLISEUM
COLOSSAL
COLOSSUS
COONSKIN
CORPSMAN
CREOSOTE
CROSSBAR
CROSSBOW
CROSSCUT
CROSSING
CYNOSURE
CYTOSINE
DARKSOME
DECISION
DECISIVE
DEERSKIN
DELUSION
DINOSAUR
DISASTER
DIVISION
DIVISIVE
DOMESTIC
DOOMSDAY
DOORSTEP
DRESSAGE
DRESSING
EFFUSION
EMISSARY
EMULSIFY
EMULSION
ENVISAGE
ETRUSCAN
EURASIAN
EVENSONG
EXPOSURE
FEARSOME
FELDSPAR
FINESPUN
FIRESIDE
FLAGSHIP
FOOLSCAP
FOOTSORE
FOOTSTEP
FORESAIL
FORESKIN
FORESTRY
FOURSOME
GAMESOME
GAMESTER
GANGSTER
GLADSOME
GLASSFUL
GLOSSARY
GOATSKIN
GRUESOME
HANDSOME
HARDSHIP
HEADSHIP
HEADSMAN
HELMSMAN
HERDSMAN
HIBISCUS
HILLSIDE
HOMESICK
HOMESPUN
HUCKSTER
HUNTSMAN
ILLUSION
ILLUSIVE
ILLUSORY
IMPOSING
IMPOSTOR
INCISION
INCISIVE
INDUSTRY
INVASION
JURISTIC
KEEPSAKE
KEROSINE
KICKSHAW
KNAPSACK
LADYSHIP
LAMASERY
LAMBSKIN
LANDSMAN
LARKSPUR
LINESMAN
LOCKSTEP
LODESTAR
LONESOME
LORDSHIP
LOVESICK
MAINSAIL
MAINSTAY
MALTSTER
MARKSMAN
MENISCUS
MILESIMO
MINISTER
MINISTRY
MISUSAGE
MOLASSES
MOLESKIN
MONASTIC
MUENSTER
NAINSOOK
NAMESAKE
NONESUCH
OCCASION
OPPOSITE
OVERSEAS
OVERSHOE
OVERSIZE
OVERSTAY
OVERSTEP
PALISADE
PANTSUIT
PARASITE
PAWNSHOP
PEDESTAL
PHEASANT
PHRASING
PILASTER
PLAYSUIT
PLEASANT
PLEASING
PLEASURE
POLESTAR
POLLSTER
PRESSING
PRESSMAN
PRESSURE
REASSURE
REGISTER
REGISTRY
RESISTOR
RHAPSODY
RHEOSTAT
RIBOSOME
ROADSIDE
ROADSTER
SALESMAN
SCISSORS
SEALSKIN
SELFSAME
SEMESTER
SEMISOFT
SIDESHOW
SIDESTEP
SINISTER
SLIPSHOD
SNAPSHOT
SNOWSHOE
SONGSTER
SPINSTER
TAILSPIN
TALESMAN
TALISMAN
TAPESTRY
TEAMSTER
THOUSAND
THRASHER
THRUSTER
THURSDAY
TIRESOME
TOWNSHIP
TOWNSMAN
TRANSACT
TRANSEPT
TRANSFER
TRANSFIX
TRANSMIT
TREASURE
TREASURY
TROUSERS
TUNGSTEN
TUNISIAN
TURNSPIT
UNFASTEN
UPRISING
VARISTOR
VENUSIAN
WAINSCOT
WARDSHIP
WINESHOP
WINGSPAN
WOODSHED
WOODSMAN
WOOLSACK
WORDSTAR
WORKSHOP
YOURSELF
YUGOSLAV
ABATTOIR
ABLATION
ABLATIVE
ABLUTION
ABORTION
ABUTTALS
ACANTHUS
ADDITION
ADDITIVE
ADJUTANT
ADOPTIVE
ADULTERY
AFLUTTER
AGLITTER
AIRSTRIP
ALEATORY
ALTITUDE
AMBITION
AMORTIZE
AMPUTATE
ANGSTROM
ANNOTATE
APERTURE
APOSTASY
APPETITE
APTITUDE
ARMATURE
ASTATINE
ATTITUDE
AUDITION
AUDITORY
AVIATION
AVIATRIX
AXLETREE
BARITONE
BEAUTIFY
BEDSTEAD
BELITTLE
BETATRON
BITSTOCK
BOASTFUL
CABSTAND
CAROTENE
CEMETERY
CENOTAPH
CHASTISE
CHASTITY
CHESTNUT
CICATRIX
CINCTURE
CITATION
CLAPTRAP
COAUTHOR
COCKTAIL
COGITATE
CONSTANT
CONSTRUE
COUNTESS
COURTESY
COURTIER
CREATION
CREATURE
CURATIVE
DENATURE
DEPUTIZE
DEVOTION
DIANTHUS
DIASTOLE
DILATORY
DIPSTICK
DONATION
DOUBTFUL
DOVETAIL
DOWNTOWN
DOWNTURN
DURATION
DYESTUFF
EGYPTIAN
EIGHTEEN
EKISTICS
ELECTION
ELECTIVE
ELECTRIC
ELECTRON
EMBATTLE
EMBITTER
EQUATION
ERECTILE
ERECTION
EVENTIDE
EVENTUAL
EXACTING
FAGOTING
FIRETRAP
FIXATION
FIXATIVE
FLATTERY
FLAUTIST
FLEETING
FORETELL
FOUNTAIN
FOURTEEN
FRACTION
FRACTURE
FRICTION
FRONTAGE

FRONTIER
FROSTING
FRUCTIFY
FRUITION
FUGITIVE
FUNCTION
GAUNTLET
GEMSTONE
GENETICS
GENITALS
GENITIVE
GREETING
GUMPTION
HABITANT
HABITUAL
HALFTONE
HARDTACK
HAYSTACK
HECATOMB
HEMATITE
HEPATICA
HERITAGE
HESITANT
HESITATE
HIGHTAIL
HOLSTEIN
HOWITZER
IDEATION
IDENTIFY
IDENTITY
IGNITION
IMMATURE
IMMOTILE
IMPETIGO
IMPOTENT
INKSTAND
INVITING
IRRITATE
ISOSTASY
JOYSTICK
JUNCTION
JUNCTURE
KEYSTONE
KIBITZER
KINETICS
LATITUDE
LAVATORY
LAXATIVE
LECITHIN
LEGATION
LENGTHEN
LENITIVE
LEVITATE
LIBATION
LIFETIME
LIGATURE
LIPSTICK
LOBOTOMY
LOCATION
LOCUTION
LOGOTYPE
LONGTIME
LUTETIUM
MAINTAIN
MARATHON
MARITIME
MEALTIME
MEANTIME
MEDITATE
MILITANT
MILITARY
MILITATE
MINATORY
MINSTREL
MISSTATE
MOISTURE
MONETARY
MONITION
MONITORY
MONOTONE
MOUNTAIN
MOUNTING
MULETEER
MUNITION
MUTATION
NEGATION
NEGATIVE
NEMATODE
NEPOTISM
NICOTINE
NINETEEN
NONSTICK
NOONTIDE
NOONTIME
NOTATION
NUGATORY
OBLATION
OFFSTAGE
OUTSTRIP
OVERTAKE
OVERTIME
OVERTONE
OVERTURE
OVERTURN
PAINTING
PALATINE
PANATELA
PENITENT
PENSTOCK
PETITION
PHANTASM
PHANTASY
PILOTAGE
PLANTAIN
PLECTRUM
POLITICK
POLITICO
POLITICS
PONYTAIL
POSITION
POSITIVE
POSITRON
POTATION
POULTICE
PRACTICE
PRESTIGE
PRETTIFY
PRINTING
PRINTOUT
PRISTINE
PROSTATE
PUNCTUAL
PUNCTURE
PUNITIVE
PUTATIVE
QUANTITY
QUANTIZE
QUESTION
QUIETUDE
REACTANT
REACTION
REACTIVE
REBUTTAL
RELATION
RELATIVE
REMITTAL
RIGHTFUL
ROOFTREE
SABOTAGE
SABOTEUR
SALUTARY
SANCTIFY
SANCTION
SANCTITY
SANITARY
SANITIZE
SCIATICA
SCOTTISH
SCRUTINY
SEDATIVE
SEDITION
SEEDTIME
SHANTUNG
SHEETING
SHIRTING
SHORTAGE
SHORTCUT
SKITTISH
SLATTERN
SOLITARY
SOLITUDE
SOLSTICE
SOLUTION
SOMETIME
SONATINA
SORPTION
SPECTRAL
SPECTRUM
SPITTOON
SPLATTER
SPLUTTER
STRATEGY
STRATIFY
STULTIFY
SWASTIKA
TACITURN
TAHITIAN
TELETHON
TELLTALE
THIRTEEN
THROTTLE
TIGHTWAD
TINCTURE
TOGETHER
TRACTATE
TRACTION
TREATISE
TRIPTYCH
TRUETYPE
TRUSTFUL
UNBUTTON
UNFETTER
UNSETTLE
VACATION
VAULTING
VEGETATE
VENATION
VEXATION
VISITANT
VOCATION
VOCATIVE
VOLATILE
VOLITION
WRISTLET
YACHTING
YULETIDE
ACCOUTRE
ADEQUATE
ALTRUISM
ANNOUNCE
BAROUCHE
BECHUANA
BEGRUDGE
BERMUDAS
BINAURAL
BURGUNDY
CALCULUS
CAPSULAR
CAROUSAL
CAROUSEL
CELLULAR
CHANUKAH
CHASUBLE
CHEMURGY
CIRCUITY
CIRCULAR
CISLUNAR
COAGULUM
COMMUNAL
COMPUTER
CONJUGAL
CONJUNCT
CONQUEST
CONVULSE
CORDUROY
DAIQUIRI
DENOUNCE
DISBURSE
DISGUISE
DISQUIET
DISSUADE
ELOQUENT
ESPOUSAL
EVACUATE
EVALUATE
EXECUTOR
EXIGUOUS
FAROUCHE
FEBRUARY
FORTUITY
FREQUENT
GALLUSES
GLOBULIN
GRADUATE
GRANULAR
GRATUITY
GUTTURAL
HERCULES
HEREUNTO
HEREUPON
HINDUISM
INIQUITY
IROQUOIS
JACQUARD
JALOUSIE
KEYPUNCH
LANGUAGE
LANGUISH
LINGUIST
LONGUEUR
MANEUVER
MARQUESS
MARQUISE
MERCURIC
MESQUITE
MISJUDGE
MISQUOTE
MONAURAL
MORTUARY
MOSQUITO
MUDGUARD
NOCTURNE
OBITUARY
OUTBURST
OUTGUESS
PELLUCID
PENDULUM
PERSUADE
PREJUDGE
RECOURSE
RENOUNCE
RESOURCE
SADDUCEE
SANGUINE
SCAPULAR
SCROUNGE
SENSUOUS
SINGULAR
STATUARY
STIMULUS
SULFURIC
TORTUOUS
TRIBUNAL
UNCHURCH
UNCOUPLE
UNCTUOUS
UNSOUGHT
UNTAUGHT
VALVULAR
VANGUARD
VANQUISH
VASCULAR
VIRTUOSO
VIRTUOUS
WHODUNIT
AARDVARK
ACTIVATE
ACTIVISM
ACTIVITY
ADJUVANT
ALLUVIUM
BEHAVIOR
CLEAVAGE
DELIVERY
ENERVATE
EXCAVATE
GRIEVOUS
INNOVATE
KILOVOLT
MOTIVATE
NATIVISM
NATIVITY
NONEVENT
OBLIVION
OVERVIEW
RELEVANT
RENOVATE
REVIVIFY
SALIVATE
SHELVING
TELEVIEW
TELEVISE
THIEVERY
TITIVATE
UNLOVELY
UNSAVORY
ARMYWORM
BACKWARD
BACKWASH
BASSWOOD
BENTWOOD
BODYWORK
BOLLWORM
BOOKWORM
BUSYWORK
CAKEWALK
CAREWORN
CASEWORK
COXSWAIN
DEADWOOD
DELAWARE
DOWNWARD
DOWNWIND
EDGEWAYS
FAREWELL
FIREWOOD
FIREWORK
FIRMWARE
FISHWIFE
FLATWARE
FOOTWEAR
FOOTWORK
FOREWARN
FOREWORD
FORSWEAR
FREEWILL
FRETWORK
GLOWWORM
GOODWIFE
GOODWILL
HACKWORD
HARDWARE
HARDWOOD
HAWKWEED
HEADWORD
HEADWORK
HEREWITH
HOMEWARD
HOMEWORK
HOODWINK
HOOKWORM
INCHWORM
IRONWARE
IRONWEED
IRONWOOD
IRONWORK
KILOWATT
KNITWEAR
LACEWING
LANDWARD
LIFEWORK
LIKEWISE
LOANWORD
LOCOWEED
LUKEWARM
MALAWIAN
MESHWORK
MILKWEED
OPENWORK
PASSWORD
POKEWEED
PULPWOOD
REARWARD
RINGWORM
ROADWORK
ROSEWOOD
SANDWICH
SHIPWORM
SHOPWORN
SHREWISH
SIDEWALK
SIDEWALL
SIDEWAYS
SOFTWARE
SOFTWOOD
SOMEWHAT
STALWART
TAPEWORM
TEAMWORK
TIMEWORN
TOILWORN
UNLAWFUL
UNTOWARD
WEREWOLF
WILDWOOD
WINDWARD
WIREWORM
WOODWIND
WOODWORK
WORMWOOD
BISEXUAL
DETOXIFY
MONOXIDE
PAROXYSM
PEROXIDE
PREEXIST

RELAXANT
UNIAXIAL
ALLEYWAY
ANALYSIS
ASPHYXIA
BALLYHOO
BARNYARD
BOGEYMAN
CARRYALL
DAIRYING
DAIRYMAN
DIALYSIS
DOCKYARD
DOORYARD
EVERYDAY
EVERYONE
FARMYARD
HANDYMAN
HEAVYSET
HONEYDEW
LOLLYGAG
MEALYBUG
NEWLYWED
OUTLYING
PICAYUNE
PLATYPUS
PUSSYCAT
SHIPYARD
SUKIYAKI
TRICYCLE
UNICYCLE
VINEYARD
BEDAZZLE
BLIZZARD
CHUTZPAH
EMBEZZLE
GRIZZLED
MAGAZINE
TWEEZERS
UNMUZZLE

## 6TH LETTER

AARDVARK
ABDICATE
ABNEGATE
ABROGATE
ABSTRACT
ABUNDANT
ABUTTALS
ACCOLADE
ACCURATE
ACERBATE
ACTIVATE
ADEQUATE
ADJUTANT
ADJUVANT
ADVOCATE
AERONAUT
AIRCRAFT
AIRFRAME
AIRPLANE
AIRSPACE
ALIENATE
ALLOCATE
AMBULANT
AMPERAGE
AMPUTATE
ANNOTATE
ANTEDATE
ANYPLACE
APOSTASY
APPANAGE
APPROACH
AQUACADE
AQUANAUT
ARMCHAIR
ARROGANT
ARROGATE
ARTIFACT
ASPIRANT
ASPIRATE
AUTOBAHN
AUTOMATE
BACKHAND
BACKLASH
BACKPACK
BACKWARD
BACKWASH
BADINAGE
BAREBACK
BARNYARD
BARONAGE
BASEBALL
BEANBALL
BECHUANA
BENZOATE
BEQUEATH
BESTIARY
BEVERAGE
BIFOCALS
BIRDBATH
BLIZZARD
BLOCKADE
BOLDFACE
BOOKCASE
BOOKMARK
BOUFFANT
BOUNDARY
BRAGGART
BREAKAGE
BREVIARY
BROUHAHA
BURGLARY
CABSTAND
CAKEWALK
CALABASH
CALLBACK
CAMSHAFT
CARAPACE
CARRIAGE
CARRYALL
CASTRATE
CATARACT
CATCHALL
CELIBACY
CELIBATE
CENOTAPH
CHAPLAIN
CLAIMANT
CLAMBAKE
CLEAVAGE
COCKTAIL
COGITATE
COMEBACK
COMPLAIN
CONCLAVE
CONSTANT
CONTRACT
CONTRAIL
CONTRARY
CONTRAST
COPULATE
CORONACH
CORONARY
COUCHANT
COVENANT
COVERAGE
COVERALL
COXSWAIN
CRIBBAGE
CROPLAND
CULINARY
CUPBOARD
DATABASE
DEBONAIR
DECIMATE
DECKHAND
DECORATE
DECREASE
DEDICATE
DEFECATE
DELAWARE
DELEGATE
DELICACY
DELICATE
DEROGATE
DESOLATE
DETONATE
DINGBATS
DINOSAUR
DISCLAIM
DISGRACE
DISPLACE
DISSUADE
DISTRACT
DISTRAIT
DIVAGATE
DOCKHAND
DOCKYARD
DOMINATE
DOORJAMB
DOORYARD
DOVETAIL
DOWNCAST
DOWNFALL
DOWNWARD
DRAINAGE
DRAWBACK
DRESSAGE
DRUNKARD
EDGEWAYS
EGGPLANT
ELEPHANT
ELONGATE
EMACIATE
EMIGRATE
EMISSARY
ENCROACH
ENERVATE
ENFILADE
ENSILAGE
ENTHRALL
ENVISAGE
EPIPHANY
EQUIPAGE
ESCALATE
ESCAPADE
ESTIMATE
EVACUATE
EVALUATE
EXCAVATE
EXECRATE
EYEGLASS
FARMHAND
FARMLAND
FARMYARD
FASTBACK
FEBRUARY
FEDERATE
FEEDBACK
FILTRATE
FIREBALL
FIREDAMP
FIRMWARE
FLAGRANT
FLAPJACK
FLATLAND
FLATWARE
FLEABANE
FLIPPANT
FOOTBALL
FOOTFALL
FOOTPATH
FOOTRACE
FORECAST
FOREHAND
FORELADY
FORELAND
FOREMAST
FORENAME
FOREPART
FORESAIL
FOREWARN
FOUNTAIN
FRAGRANT
FREEHAND
FRONTAGE
FULLBACK
FUMIGANT
FUMIGATE
FUNERARY
FUSELAGE
GANGLAND
GEMINATE
GENERATE
GENITALS
GIMCRACK
GLACIATE
GLOSSARY
GOOFBALL
GOURMAND
GRADUATE
GYMKHANA
HABITANT
HALFBACK
HALLMARK
HANDBALL
HANDMADE
HANDRAIL
HANGNAIL
HARDBACK
HARDBALL
HARDHACK
HARDTACK
HARDWARE
HAYSTACK
HEADBAND
HEADLAND
HELPMATE
HERITAGE
HESITANT
HESITATE
HIGHBALL
HIGHLAND
HIGHTAIL
HOMELAND
HOMEMADE
HOMEWARD
HONORARY
HUMPBACK
IGNORANT
IMMOLATE
INCHOATE
INCREASE
INCUBATE
INDICATE
INDURATE
INERRANT
INFOBAHN
INHALANT
INHUMANE
INITIATE
INKSTAND
INNOVATE
INSULATE
INTIMATE
INUNDATE
IRONWARE
IRRIGATE
IRRITATE
ISOSTASY
JACQUARD
JUBILANT
KAMIKAZE
KATAKANA
KEELHAUL
KEEPSAKE
KEYBOARD
KICKBACK
KIELBASA
KILOWATT
KNAPSACK
KOHLRABI
LACERATE
LAMPBACK
LANDFALL
LANDMARK
LANDMASS
LANDWARD
LANGUAGE
LAPBOARD
LAPIDARY
LARBOARD
LAUREATE
LEMONADE
LEVERAGE
LEVITATE
LIBERATE
LITERARY
LITERATE
LITERATI
LITIGANT
LITIGATE
LONGHAIR
LONGHAND
LUKEWARM
LUMINARY
MACERATE
MAHARAJA
MAHARANI
MAHOGANY
MAINLAND
MAINMAST
MAINSAIL
MAINTAIN
MANDRAKE
MARGRAVE
MARINATE
MARRIAGE
MATURATE
MEATBALL
MEDICAID
MEDICARE
MEDICATE
MEDITATE
MEMBRANE
MERCHANT
MESSMATE
MILITANT
MILITARY
MILITATE
MILKMAID
MILLIARD
MILLRACE
MISBRAND
MISHMASH
MISPLACE
MISSHAPE
MISSTATE
MISUSAGE
MITIGATE
MODERATE
MODULATE
MONETARY
MONOGAMY
MONORAIL
MOORLAND
MORTGAGE
MORTUARY
MOSSBACK
MOTHBALL
MOTIVATE
MOUNTAIN
MUCILAGE
MUDGUARD
MUSICALE
MUTILATE
NAMESAKE
NAUSEATE
NAVIGATE
NECKLACE
NEOPLASM
NEWSCAST
NICKNAME
NOMINATE
NOWADAYS
NUCLEATE
NUMERATE
OBDURATE
OBITUARY
OBLIGATE
OCCUPANT
OFFSTAGE
ONONDAGA
ORDINARY
ORDINATE
OSCULATE
OUTBOARD
OUTCLASS
OUTFLANK
OUTREACH
OUTSMART
OVERCAST
OVERHAND
OVERHANG
OVERHAUL
OVERLAID
OVERLAND
OVERPASS
OVERTAKE
PAGINATE
PALEFACE
PALISADE
PALLIATE
PANORAMA
PASTRAMI
PECULATE
PEDERAST
PENCHANT
PERMEATE
PERSUADE
PETULANT
PHANTASM
PHANTASY
PHARMACY
PHEASANT
PIEPLANT
PILCHARD
PILOTAGE
PIXELATE
PLANTAIN
PLAYBACK
PLAYMATE

| | | | | | | | |
|---|---|---|---|---|---|---|---|
| PLEASANT | SANITARY | TELLTALE | ALPHABET | PROBABLE | EMOTICON | VIATICUM | PORRIDGE |
| POCKMARK | SATURATE | TEMPLATE | AMENABLE | PROHIBIT | ENCIRCLE | WAINSCOT | PREJUDGE |
| POIGNANT | SCABBARD | TERTIARY | AMICABLE | QUOTABLE | ETRUSCAN | WHITECAP | PRESIDIO |
| POLYGAMY | SEABOARD | THOUSAND | ARGUABLE | RELIABLE | EXPLICIT | WISEACRE | PROVIDED |
| POLYMATH | SEACOAST | TIDELAND | ASSEMBLE | REMEMBER | FAROUCHE | ACCREDIT | PUDENDUM |
| PONYTAIL | SEAPLANE | TINPLATE | ASSEMBLY | RESEMBLE | FASCICLE | ADDENDUM | RECORDER |
| POPULACE | SEASCAPE | TITILATE | BAILABLE | RIVERBED | FOLLICLE | APPENDIX | RETARDED |
| POPULATE | SELFSAME | TITIVATE | BIDDABLE | SCALABLE | FOOLSCAP | ASPHODEL | SATURDAY |
| PORTRAIT | SEMINARY | TOLERATE | BRICKBAT | SCRABBLE | HANDICAP | BEFUDDLE | SHOULDER |
| POSTCARD | SEPARATE | TOLLGATE | CANNABIS | SCRAMBLE | HEADACHE | BEGRUDGE | SPLENDID |
| POSTDATE | SERENADE | TOMAHAWK | CANNIBAL | SCRIBBLE | HIBISCUS | BEHOLDEN | SPLENDOR |
| POSTMARK | SERGEANT | TRACKAGE | CHASUBLE | SENSIBLE | HUARACHE | BERMUDAS | SPORADIC |
| POSTPAID | SEWERAGE | TRACTATE | CHOIRBOY | SOCIABLE | IMPLICIT | BEWILDER | SQUANDER |
| POUNDAGE | SHIPMATE | TRANSACT | CINNABAR | SQUABBLE | INIMICAL | BIOCIDAL | STRADDLE |
| PRATFALL | SHIPYARD | TRESPASS | CREDIBLE | STINKBUG | INTERCOM | BIRTHDAY | THURSDAY |
| PREGNANT | SHOELACE | TRUCKAGE | CROSSBAR | SUBURBIA | MANIACAL | BROMIDIC | TOPSIDES |
| PROCLAIM | SHORTAGE | TRUNCATE | CROSSBOW | SUITABLE | MARIACHI | CALENDAR | TOREADOR |
| PROSTATE | SHOWCASE | TUTELAGE | CRUCIBLE | SYLLABLE | MASSACRE | CALENDER | UNBIDDEN |
| PROTRACT | SIBILANT | TUTELARY | CUCUMBER | SYLLABUS | MEDIOCRE | CHARADES | UNBURDEN |
| PUFFBALL | SIDEWALK | TYPECAST | CULPABLE | TANGIBLE | MENISCUS | COLANDER | UNDERDOG |
| PULLBACK | SIDEWALL | TYPEFACE | DAMNABLE | TERRIBLE | METRICAL | CONSIDER | UNKINDLY |
| PURCHASE | SIDEWAYS | ULCERATE | DEATHBED | THROMBUS | MONARCHY | CORRIDOR | UNLEADED |
| PURSLANE | SILICATE | ULTIMATE | DECEMBER | UNDERBID | MOROCCAN | CORUNDUM | UNRIDDLE |
| PUSHCART | SIMULATE | UNDERACT | DOUGHBOY | UNLIMBER | MOTORCAR | CUSPIDOR | UNSADDLE |
| QUADRANT | SLUGGARD | UNDERAGE | DUTIABLE | UNSTABLE | MUSTACHE | CYLINDER | WATCHDOG |
| QUANDARY | SNOWBALL | UNDERARM | EDUCABLE | VALUABLE | MYSTICAL | DAFFODIL | WIZARDRY |
| QUATRAIN | SNOWBANK | UNDULANT | ELIGIBLE | VARIABLE | NAUTICAL | DISLODGE | WORKADAY |
| RAINFALL | SNOWFALL | UNDULATE | ENCUMBER | VERTEBRA | OBSTACLE | DISORDER | ABUTMENT |
| REACTANT | SOFTBALL | UNGULATE | ENFEEBLE | VINCIBLE | PARFOCAL | DOOMSDAY | ACCIDENT |
| REARWARD | SOFTWARE | UNSTEADY | ENSEMBLE | VIOLABLE | PARTICLE | EMBOLDEN | ACIDHEAD |
| RECREANT | SOLITARY | UNTOWARD | ENVIABLE | WASHABLE | PASTICHE | ENGENDER | ADJACENT |
| RECREATE | SPANIARD | VALIDATE | FALLIBLE | WORKABLE | PEDUNCLE | EVERYDAY | ADULTERY |
| REGULATE | SPITBALL | VANGUARD | FEASIBLE | ALOPECIA | PELLUCID | EXPLODED | AESTHETE |
| RELAXANT | SPYGLASS | VEGETATE | FLEXIBLE | AMERICAN | PEMMICAN | EXTRADOS | AFFERENT |
| RELEGATE | STACCATO | VENERATE | FORCIBLE | ANGLICAN | PERFECTO | FLOUNDER | AGGRIEVE |
| RELEVANT | STAGNANT | VERBIAGE | HORRIBLE | ATYPICAL | PHYSICAL | GROUNDER | AIRFIELD |
| RELOCATE | STAGNATE | VESICANT | HOUSEBOY | BACKACHE | PINNACLE | HARRIDAN | AIRSPEED |
| RENEGADE | STALWART | VICARAGE | IMITABLE | BARBECUE | PROTOCOL | HERALDIC | ANATHEMA |
| RENOVATE | STANDARD | VICINAGE | INCUMBER | BARBICAN | PUBLICAN | HERALDRY | ANYWHERE |
| REPROACH | STATUARY | VIGILANT | INVIABLE | BARNACLE | PUSSYCAT | HONEYDEW | APOPLEXY |
| RESONANT | STEERAGE | VINEGARY | MANDIBLE | BAROUCHE | REVANCHE | INFRADIG | APOTHEGM |
| RESONATE | STOCKADE | VINEYARD | MEALYBUG | BARRACKS | SADDUCEE | INTENDED | APPARENT |
| RESTRAIN | STOPPAGE | VISICALC | MICROBUS | BINNACLE | SCILICET | INTRADOS | ARBALEST |
| RIFFRAFF | SUBTRACT | VISITANT | MILLIBAR | CANTICLE | SHORTCUT | INWARDLY | ARBOREAL |
| ROCKFALL | SUFFRAGE | VOLPLANE | MISCIBLE | CAPSICUM | SILENCER | ISLANDER | ARGUMENT |
| ROLLBACK | SUITCASE | WARPLANE | MISLABEL | CERVICAL | SKULLCAP | LAVENDER | ARMAMENT |
| ROOMMATE | SUKIYAKI | WHARFAGE | NEIGHBOR | CHEMICAL | SURGICAL | LOPSIDED | AVERMENT |
| ROSEMARY | SUNSHADE | WHIPLASH | NOVEMBER | CLAVICLE | TENTACLE | MASTODON | BACKREST |
| ROUGHAGE | SUPPLANT | WINDFALL | OPERABLE | CLERICAL | TESTICLE | MENHADEN | BARONESS |
| RUMINANT | SURCEASE | WINDLASS | PALPABLE | CLINICAL | TRICYCLE | MISJUDGE | BASELESS |
| RUMINATE | SUZERAIN | WINDWARD | PARTIBLE | COMANCHE | TUBERCLE | MYRMIDON | BASEMENT |
| RUNAGATE | SWAYBACK | WIREHAIR | PASSABLE | CONFOCAL | UNDERCUT | OLEANDER | BEDSTEAD |
| RUTABAGA | TABULATE | WOODLAND | PENUMBRA | CRITICAL | UNICYCLE | ORTHODOX | BEFRIEND |
| SABOTAGE | TAFFRAIL | WOOLSACK | PITIABLE | CROSSCUT | UNVOICED | OUTMODED | BERIBERI |
| SALIVATE | TAILGATE | WRECKAGE | PORTABLE | CURLICUE | UPPERCUT | OUTRIDER | BILLHEAD |
| SALUTARY | TAMARACK | ZWIEBACK | POSSIBLE | DEMARCHE | VERSICLE | OUTSIDER | BIRDSEED |
| SANDBANK | TELECAST | ADORABLE | PREAMBLE | DIVORCEE | VERTICAL | PERIODIC | BLOOMERS |

BLUDGEON
BLUEBELL
BODILESS
BOOTLESS
BROWBEAT
BULKHEAD
BULLHEAD
BUSINESS
BUTTRESS
CADUCEUS
CARELESS
CAROTENE
CASEMENT
CASHMERE
CEMETERY
CEREMENT
CERULEAN
CESAREAN
CHANCERY
CHECKERS
CHIPPEWA
COGWHEEL
COHERENT
COIFFEUR
COLISEUM
COLLIERY
COMPLEAT
COMPLETE
COMPRESS
CONCRETE
CONFRERE
CONGRESS
CONQUEST
COPYDESK
CORDLESS
CORNMEAL
COUNTESS
COURTESY
CREAMERY
CRESCENT
CROCKERY
DATELESS
DAYBREAK
DAYDREAM
DEADBEAT
DECEDENT
DEFOREST
DELIVERY
DEPONENT
DERRIERE
DESELECT
DILIGENT
DISCREET
DISCRETE
DISTRESS
DIVIDEND
DOCUMENT
DOMINEER
DOWNBEAT
DRUMBEAT
DUMBBELL
EFFERENT
EGGSHELL
EIGHTEEN
ELOQUENT
EMPYREAN
ENGINEER
ENTIRETY
ERYTHEMA
ETHEREAL
EUROPEAN
EXPONENT
EYEPIECE
FADELESS
FAREWELL
FARTHEST
FASTNESS
FEARLESS
FECKLESS
FILAMENT
FLAMBEAU
FLATHEAD
FLATTERY
FLYSPECK
FLYWHEEL
FOOTLESS
FOOTREST
FOOTWEAR
FOREBEAR
FOREFEND
FOREHEAD
FORETELL
FORMLESS
FORSWEAR
FORTRESS
FOURTEEN
FRAGMENT
FREQUENT
FRIPPERY
FUNEREAL
FURTHEST
GANGRENE
GOATHERD
GOODNESS
GRADIENT
GRANDEUR
GREENERY
GROSBEAK
GUYANESE
HABANERA
HAREBELL
HAWKWEED
HEADGEAR
HEADREST
HELPMEET
HIGHNESS
HOGSHEAD
HOLINESS
HOLSTEIN
HUNTRESS
HYMENEAL
IMMANENT
IMMINENT
IMMODEST
IMPOTENT
IMPUDENT
INCIDENT
INDECENT
INDIGENT
INDIRECT
INDOLENT
INEXPERT
INHERENT
INNOCENT
INSOLENT
INTEREST
IRONWEED
ISOPRENE
ISOTHERM
JAPANESE
JONGLEUR
JUDGMENT
KILLDEER
KNICKERS
KNITWEAR
LAMASERY
LIGAMENT
LIKENESS
LINIMENT
LINOLEUM
LISTLESS
LOCOWEED
LODGMENT
LONGUEUR
LUNCHEON
MALAPERT
MALTREAT
MANIFEST
MARQUESS
MASSLESS
MASTHEAD
MATTRESS
MELODEON
MILKWEED
MILLIEME
MINDLESS
MISSPELL
MISSPEND
MISTREAT
MISTRESS
MONSIEUR
MONUMENT
MOONBEAM
MORPHEME
MOVEMENT
MULETEER
NAMELESS
NAPOLEON
NEEDLESS
NEWSREEL
NINETEEN
NONEVENT
NUTRIENT
NUTSHELL
OBEDIENT
OBSOLETE
OINTMENT
OPPONENT
ORANGERY
ORNAMENT
ORTHOEPY
OUTBREAK
OUTFIELD
OUTGUESS
OUTSPEND
OVERHEAD
OVERHEAR
OVERLEAP
OVERSEAS
PANATELA
PANCREAS
PANTHEON
PARAKEET
PAVEMENT
PAYCHECK
PEDIMENT
PEERLESS
PENITENT
PINWHEEL
PITILESS
PLANGENT
POKEWEED
PORTIERE
POTSHERD
PREMIERE
PREPRESS
PRINCESS
PROCEEDS
PROGRESS
PROPHECY
PROPHESY
PROSPECT
PRURIENT
PUNCHEON
PURULENT
QUOTIENT
RAILLERY
RECKLESS
REDOLENT
REFERENT
REFINERY
REFOREST
REGIMENT
REINDEER
REPRIEVE
RESIDENT
RESTLESS
RETICENT
RETRIEVE
REVEREND
REVERENT
RUDIMENT
RUTHLESS
SABOTEUR
SCARCELY
SCULLERY
SEDIMENT
SEIGNEUR
SELFLESS
SENTIENT
SHEPHERD
SHIPMENT
SICKNESS
SIDEREAL
SLATTERN
SLIPPERY
SNOBBERY
SOBRIETY
SOLDIERY
SOMBRERO
STAMPEDE
STRATEGY
STRIDENT
STURGEON
SUBPOENA
SUPEREGO
SUPPRESS
TENEMENT
THIEVERY
THIRTEEN
TIMELESS
TIRELESS
TRANSEPT
TRICKERY
TROUSERS
TRUMPERY
TUNELESS
TWEEZERS
UNFREEZE
UNLIKELY
UNLOVELY
UNTIMELY
UPSTREAM
VEHEMENT
VENEREAL
VESTMENT
VIRULENT
VOYAGEUR
WAITRESS
WEAKNESS
WELDMENT
WELLHEAD
WIRELESS
WITCHERY
YOURSELF
BEATIFIC
BLISSFUL
BOASTFUL
CHEERFUL
CRUCIFIX
DOUBTFUL
DREADFUL
FANCIFUL
GLASSFUL
GRATEFUL
HORSEFLY
HOUSEFLY
MOURNFUL
PARAFFIN
PETTIFOG
PROLIFIC
RETROFIT
RIGHTFUL
SKILLFUL
SPECIFIC
TERRIFIC
THANKFUL
THEREFOR
TRANSFER
TRANSFIX
TRUSTFUL
TRUTHFUL
TURBOFAN
UNDERFUR
UNLAWFUL
VENGEFUL
WATCHFUL
WHITEFLY
WRATHFUL
WRONGFUL
YOUTHFUL
AFFRIGHT
AIRTIGHT
ALLERGEN
ANALOGUE
ANDROGEN
APOLOGIA
ARPEGGIO
CARDIGAN
CONJUGAL
DAYLIGHT
DIALOGUE
DOGFIGHT
ENDANGER
ENTANGLE
EPILOGUE
ESTROGEN
EYESIGHT
FANLIGHT
FLASHGUN
GASLIGHT
GLYCOGEN
GUNFIGHT
HARANGUE
HOOLIGAN
HOOSEGOW
HYDROGEN
INTRIGUE
INVEIGLE
LOLLYGAG
MADRIGAL
MALINGER
MERINGUE
MIDNIGHT
NEGLIGEE
NITROGEN
NONRIGID
OUTFIGHT
OUTRIGHT
PATHOGEN
PELLAGRA
PENLIGHT
PENTAGON
PRODIGAL
PROLOGUE
PROROGUE
SCRAGGLY
SKYLIGHT
SQUEEGEE
STRAGGLE
STRAIGHT
STRANGER
STRANGLE
STRENGTH
STRINGED
STRINGER
STRUGGLE
SUNLIGHT
TARRAGON
TOBOGGAN
TRIANGLE
TWILIGHT
UNSOUGHT
UNTANGLE
UNTAUGHT
VILLAGER
ACANTHUS
ALMIGHTY
BABUSHKA
BAKESHOP
BALLYHOO
BRITCHES
BRONCHUS
BROUGHAM
BUCKSHOT
CABOCHON
CAPUCHIN
CHITCHAT
CHOWCHOW
CLINCHER
COAUTHOR
COLOPHON
CROTCHET
DECIPHER
DETACHED
DIANTHUS
DIARRHEA
DRAUGHTS
ENCIPHER
FLAGSHIP
GROSCHEN
HARDSHIP
HEADSHIP
HEDGEHOG
HEDGEHOP
KICKSHAW
LADYSHIP
LAUNCHER
LECITHIN
LENGTHEN
LORDSHIP
MARATHON
METAPHOR
OVERSHOE
PAWNSHOP
PHOSPHOR
PINOCHLE
PYORRHEA
RICOCHET
SHANGHAI
SIDESHOW
SLIPSHOD
SNAPSHOT
SNOWSHOE
SOMEWHAT
TELETHON
THRASHER
TOGETHER
TOWNSHIP
TRENCHER
WARDSHIP
WINESHOP
WOODSHED
WORKSHOP
WRETCHED
ABLATION

ABLATIVE
ABLUTION
ABORNING
ABORTION
ABRASIVE
ACERBITY
ACQUAINT
ACTINISM
ACTINIUM
ACTIVISM
ACTIVITY
ADDITION
ADDITIVE
ADHESION
ADHESIVE
ADMONISH
ADOPTIVE
AFFINITY
AGRARIAN
ALACRITY
ALARMIST
ALBANIAN
ALGERIAN
ALIASING
ALIENIST
ALLSPICE
ALLUVIUM
ALTRUISM
AMBITION
AMMONIUM
AMORTIZE
ANGELICA
ANTERIOR
ANYTHING
APHANITE
APHELION
APHORISM
APPETITE
APPOSITE
APPRAISE
AQUARIUM
AQUILINE
ARMORIAL
ARTERIAL
ARTIFICE
ASPERITY
ASTATINE
ASTERISK
ASTONISH
ATROCITY
ATROPINE
AUDITION
AUSTRIAN
AUTOGIRO
AVERSION
AVIATION
AVIONICS
BACKBITE
BACKFIRE
BACKSIDE
BANTLING
BASELINE
BASILICA
BASILISK
BEAUTIFY
BECOMING
BEHAVIOR
BENEDICT
BENEFICE
BESTRIDE
BIENNIAL
BIENNIUM
BIRACIAL
BIRDLIME
BLACKING
BLESSING
BLOWPIPE
BLUEBIRD
BLUEFISH
BOBOLINK
BOBWHITE
BOHEMIAN
BOTULISM
BRACKISH
BRANDISH
BREEDING
BRISLING
BUDDHISM
BUILDING
BUNDLING
CAFFEINE
CAGELING
CALADIUM
CALAMINE
CALAMITY
CAMOMILE
CAMPAIGN
CANADIAN
CANALIZE
CANONIZE
CAPACITY
CATCHING
CAVALIER
CELERITY
CENOBITE
CENTRIST
CERAMIST
CHAMPION
CHARMING
CHASTISE
CHASTITY
CHLORIDE
CHLORINE
CHLORITE
CHROMIUM
CIRCUITY
CITATION
CIVILIAN
CIVILITY
CIVILIZE
CLASSIFY
CLEARING
CLIPPING
CLOTHIER
CLOTHING
COHESION
COINCIDE
COLONIAL
COLONIST
COLONIZE
COMEDIAN
COMPRISE
CONCEIVE
CONFLICT
CONSPIRE
CONTRITE
CONTRIVE
COUPLING
COURTIER
CRAWFISH
CRAYFISH
CREATION
CREEPING
CREMAINS
CROSSING
CROUPIER
CRUZEIRO
CRYOLITE
CUPIDITY
CURATIVE
CYTOSINE
DAIQUIRI
DAIRYING
DARKLING
DATELINE
DEADLINE
DEBILITY
DECISION
DECISIVE
DEFINITE
DEIONIZE
DELIRIUM
DELUSION
DEMOLISH
DEMONIAC
DEPUTIZE
DERELICT
DESCRIBE
DETOXIFY
DEVILISH
DEVOTION
DIATRIBE
DIMINISH
DIPSTICK
DISGUISE
DISJOINT
DISQUIET
DISTRICT
DISUNITE
DISUNITY
DIVINITY
DIVISION
DIVISIVE
DOCTRINE
DOLOMITE
DOMICILE
DOMINION
DONATION
DOWNHILL
DOWNWIND
DRESSING
DROPKICK
DRUGGIST
DUCKBILL
DUCKLING
DUMPLING
DUNGHILL
DURATION
DWELLING
DYNAMITE
EFFUSION
EGYPTIAN
EKISTICS
ELECTION
ELECTIVE
EMBOLISM
EMPORIUM
EMULSIFY
EMULSION
ENCOMIUM
ENERGIZE
ENGAGING
ENORMITY
ENSHRINE
ENTRAILS
EQUALIZE
EQUATION
ERECTILE
ERECTION
ESCAPISM
ESPALIER
ESPECIAL
ESTONIAN
ETERNITY
EUGENICS
EURASIAN
EUROPIUM
EVENTIDE
EXACTING
EXERCISE
EXORCISE
EXORDIUM
EXPEDITE
EXTERIOR
FACILITY
FAGOTING
FALCHION
FAMILIAL
FAMILIAR
FARTHING
FATALISM
FATALITY
FAVORITE
FELICITY
FEMININE
FEMINISM
FEROCITY
FETCHING
FIDELITY
FIGURINE
FILIPINO
FINALIST
FINALIZE
FIRESIDE
FISHWIFE
FIXATION
FIXATIVE
FLASHING
FLATFISH
FLAUTIST
FLEABITE
FLEETING
FLOURISH
FLUORIDE
FLUORINE
FLUORITE
FOOTHILL
FOOTLING
FORELIMB
FORKLIFT
FORTUITY
FRACTION
FRANCIUM
FREEWILL
FRICTION
FRONTIER
FROSTING
FRUCTIFY
FRUITION
FUGITIVE
FUNCTION
FUTILITY
FUTURISM
FUTURITY
GANGLING
GANGLION
GASOLINE
GENETICS
GENITIVE
GENOCIDE
GERANIUM
GHANAIAN
GLOAMING
GODCHILD
GOLDFISH
GOODWIFE
GOODWILL
GRAFFITO
GRAPHITE
GRASPING
GRATUITY
GRAYLING
GREEKING
GREETING
GRUELING
GUARDIAN
GUMPTION
GUNPOINT
GUNSMITH
HAIRLINE
HANDBILL
HANDPICK
HATCHING
HAWAIIAN
HEADLINE
HEBRAISM
HEDONISM
HEMATITE
HEPATICA
HEREDITY
HEREWITH
HILLSIDE
HINDUISM
HIRELING
HOARDING
HOMESICK
HOMICIDE
HOODWINK
HORNPIPE
HUMANISM
HUMANITY
HUMANIZE
HUMIDIFY
HUMIDITY
HUMILITY
IDEALISM
IDEALIZE
IDEATION
IDENTIFY
IDENTITY
IGNITION
ILLUMINE
ILLUSION
ILLUSIVE
IMBECILE
IMMOBILE
IMMOTILE
IMMUNIZE
IMPERIAL
IMPETIGO
IMPOLITE
IMPOSING
IMPUNITY
INCISION
INCISIVE
INCOMING
INFERIOR
INFINITE
INFINITY
INIQUITY
INSCRIBE
INTERIOR
INVASION
INVITING
ISTHMIAN
JAILBIRD
JAUNDICE
JEREMIAD
JINGOISM
JOYSTICK
JUDICIAL
JUNCTION
JUVENILE
KAMAAINA
KERCHIEF
KEROSINE
KINDLING
KINETICS
LACEWING
LADYBIRD
LADYLIKE
LANDFILL
LANGUISH
LAXATIVE
LAYERING
LEARNING
LEGALISM
LEGATION
LENITIVE
LIBATION
LICORICE
LIFELINE
LIFETIME
LIKEWISE
LIMEKILN
LIMERICK
LIMONITE
LINGUIST
LIPSTICK
LIVERISH
LOATHING
LOCALITY
LOCALIZE
LOCATION
LOCUTION
LONGTIME
LOVEBIRD
LOVESICK
LOYALIST
LUTETIUM
MACPAINT
MAGAZINE
MAGICIAN
MAINLINE
MAJOLICA
MAJORITY
MALAWIAN
MARBLING
MARITIME
MARQUISE
MATERIAL
MATERIEL
MATURITY
MAVERICK
MAXIMIZE
MEALTIME
MEANTIME
MEDALIST
MEDICINE
MEGALITH
MELANISM
MEMORIAL
MEMORIZE
MERIDIAN
MESQUITE
METAFILE
MIDDLING
MIDPOINT
MIDSHIPS
MIGRAINE
MILESIMO
MINIBIKE
MINIMIZE
MINORITY
MISCHIEF
MISDOING
MISPRINT
MISTRIAL
MOBILIZE
MOLEHILL
MONITION
MONOLITH
MONOXIDE
MORALIST
MORALITY
MORALIZE

MORPHINE
MOSQUITO
MOTORIZE
MOUNTING
MOURNING
MUNITION
MUSICIAN
MUTATION
NASALIZE
NATALITY
NATIVISM
NATIVITY
NEBULIZE
NECKLINE
NEGATION
NEGATIVE
NEPOTISM
NESTLING
NEUTRINO
NICOTINE
NIGERIAN
NIGGLING
NIHILISM
NINEPINS
NOBELIST
NOBELIUM
NOBILITY
NONDAIRY
NONSTICK
NONUNION
NOONTIDE
NOONTIME
NOTARIAL
NOTARIZE
NOTATION
NOVELIZE
NURSLING
OBLATION
OBLIVION
OBSIDIAN
OCCASION
OFFICIAL
OFFPRINT
ONCOMING
OPPOSITE
OPTICIAN
OPTIMISM
ORGANISM
ORGANIST
ORGANIZE
OUTGOING
OUTLYING
OUTPOINT
OUTSHINE
OUTWEIGH
OVENBIRD
OVERKILL

OVERRIDE
OVERSIZE
OVERTIME
OVERVIEW
PACIFIER
PACIFISM
PAINTING
PALATINE
PALOMINO
PANELING
PANELIST
PARADIGM
PARADISE
PARASITE
PAVILION
PECULIAR
PENALIZE
PENKNIFE
PERCEIVE
PEROXIDE
PERSPIRE
PETITION
PHRASING
PIDDLING
PINPOINT
PINPRICK
PIPELINE
PLANKING
PLAYBILL
PLEASING
PLEBEIAN
PLEURISY
PLUMBING
POLARITY
POLARIZE
POLITICK
POLITICO
POLITICS
POLONIUM
POPULIST
PORPOISE
POSITION
POSITIVE
POTATION
POULTICE
PRACTICE
PREEXIST
PRESSING
PRESTIGE
PRETTIFY
PRINTING
PRISTINE
PROCAINE
PTOMAINE
PUDDLING
PUGILISM
PUNITIVE

PURBLIND
PUTATIVE
QUAGMIRE
QUALMISH
QUANTITY
QUANTIZE
QUESTION
QUISLING
RATTLING
RAVENING
REACTION
REACTIVE
REGICIDE
REGOLITH
RELATION
RELATIVE
RELIGION
REMEDIAL
RESCRIPT
RESTRICT
RETIRING
REVIVIFY
RHYOLITE
RIPARIAN
ROADSIDE
ROMANIAN
ROYALIST
RUBIDIUM
RUMANIAN
RUMBLING
SAILFISH
SAMARIUM
SANCTIFY
SANCTION
SANCTITY
SANDWICH
SANGUINE
SANITIZE
SAPPHIRE
SCALLION
SCANDIUM
SCATHING
SCIATICA
SCORPION
SCOTTISH
SCRUTINY
SCULLION
SEAGOING
SECURITY
SEDATIVE
SEDITION
SEEDLING
SEEDTIME
SELENITE
SELENIUM
SHEEPISH
SHEETING

SHELVING
SHILLING
SHIPPING
SHIRRING
SHIRTING
SHOCKING
SHOPLIFT
SHREWISH
SIDEKICK
SIDERITE
SILICIFY
SIMONIZE
SIMPLIFY
SKIMMING
SKIRMISH
SKITTISH
SLUGGISH
SOLARIUM
SOLECISM
SOLIDIFY
SOLSTICE
SOLUTION
SOMETIME
SONATINA
SONGBIRD
SORORITY
SORPTION
SPANKING
SPOOLING
STALLION
STANDING
STARFISH
STARLING
STERLING
STIRRING
STOCKING
STRATIFY
STRIKING
STUDDING
STUFFING
STULTIFY
STUNNING
SUCHLIKE
SUCKLING
SUNDRIES
SUNSHINE
SUPERIOR
SUREFIRE
SURPLICE
SURPRISE
SWASTIKA
SWEEPING
SWELLING
SWIMMING
SYBARITE
TAHITIAN
TAMARIND

TEACHING
TEETHING
TELEFILM
TELEVIEW
TELEVISE
TEMERITY
THALLIUM
THEORIZE
THESPIAN
THIAMINE
TICKLISH
TINSMITH
TITANIUM
TOKENISM
TONALITY
TORTOISE
TOTALITY
TOUCHING
TOWELING
TOWERING
TRACTION
TRAINING
TRAPPING
TREATISE
TRICHINA
TRIFLING
TRILLION
TRILLIUM
TRIMMING
TUNISIAN
TURNPIKE
TUTORIAL
ULTERIOR
UNBELIEF
UNBODIED
UNENDING
UNERRING
UNFILIAL
UNIAXIAL
UNIONISM
UNIONIZE
UPCOMING
UPRISING
UPSTAIRS
URBANITE
URBANIZE
VACATION
VANADIUM
VANQUISH
VAPORING
VAPORISH
VAPORIZE
VAULTING
VEGANISM
VELLEITY
VELOCITY
VENATION

VENUSIAN
VERACITY
VERONICA
VEXATION
VICINITY
VILLAINY
VITALITY
VITALIZE
VIVACITY
VIVARIUM
VOCALIST
VOCALIZE
VOCATION
VOCATIVE
VOLATILE
VOLITION
WEAKFISH
WEAKLING
WHOPPING
WILDFIRE
WILDLIFE
WINDMILL
WINDPIPE
WINGDING
WITCHING
WOMANISH
WOODBINE
WOODPILE
WOODWIND
WRAPPING
XENOLITH
YACHTING
YEARLING
YEARNING
YIELDING
YOUNGISH
YULETIDE
ZUCCHINI
LASERJET
POPINJAY
SUPERJET
TURBOJET
BAEDEKER
BEARSKIN
BIWEEKLY
BUCKSKIN
CALFSKIN
CAPESKIN
CHANUKAH
CHEROKEE
COONSKIN
DEERSKIN
FORESKIN
GOATSKIN
HANUKKAH
LAMBSKIN
LATCHKEY

LAWMAKER
MALARKEY
MISTAKEN
MOLESKIN
ONLOOKER
SEALSKIN
SPRINKLE
SPROCKET
STRICKEN
UNBROKEN
UNBUCKLE
APPELLEE
BACHELOR
BACILLUS
BACKSLAP
BIATHLON
BORDELLO
BOUILLON
BRACELET
BRINDLED
BROOKLET
BUNGALOW
CALCULUS
CAMELLIA
CANAILLE
CAPSULAR
CARILLON
CASUALTY
CATHOLIC
CAUDILLO
CELLULAR
CEPHALIC
CHANDLER
CHENILLE
CHIVALRY
CIRCULAR
CLOUDLET
COAGULUM
COLESLAW
COMPILER
CONVULSE
COVERLET
DIABOLIC
DISALLOW
DISCOLOR
DISSOLVE
ESCALLOP
EXEMPLAR
FIRECLAY
FIREPLUG
FLIMFLAM
FLOTILLA
FURBELOW
GANGPLOW
GAUNTLET
GLOBULIN
GONFALON

GRANULAR
GRIZZLED
HERCULES
HOSTELRY
IMPELLER
INTAGLIO
IRONCLAD
MAGDALEN
MAGNOLIA
MANDOLIN
MANTELET
MANTILLA
NAUTILUS
OVERALLS
OVERFLOW
OVERPLAY
PAMPHLET
PARALLAX
PARALLEL
PASTILLE
PENDULUM
PHENOLIC
POLYGLOT
POTBELLY
PREMOLAR
REPUBLIC
REVEILLE
SCAPULAR
SCHMALTZ
SCOFFLAW
SERAGLIO
SHAMBLES
SHINGLES
SINGULAR
SNOWPLOW
STICKLER
STIMULUS
SYMBOLIC
SYPHILIS
TANTALUM
TELEPLAY
TORTILLA
TRICOLOR
UMBRELLA
UNDERLIE
UNDERLIP
UNIVALVE
UNWIELDY
VALVULAR
VASCULAR
WATERLOO
WORDPLAY
WRIGGLER
WRISTLET
YUGOSLAV
ZEPPELIN
ABNORMAL

ACADEMIC
ALDERMAN
BAILSMAN
BOGEYMAN
BONDSMAN
BONHOMIE
BRAKEMAN
CARDAMOM
CHAIRMAN
CINNAMON
COACHMAN
COGNOMEN
CONSOMME
CONTEMPT
CORPSMAN
CUSTOMER
CYCLAMEN
DAIRYMAN
DIATOMIC
DIPLOMAT
DRAGOMAN
DULCIMER
ECONOMIC
EPIDEMIC
FREEDMAN
FRESHMAN
GOSSAMER
GRAVAMEN
HANDYMAN
HEADSMAN
HELMSMAN
HENCHMAN
HERDSMAN
HORSEMAN
HUNTSMAN
INDIAMAN
INFORMAL
INFORMED
INFORMER
INTERMIT
INTERMIX
INTROMIT
LACRIMAL
LANDSMAN
LEUKEMIA
LINESMAN
MANDAMUS
MARKSMAN
MESDAMES
MISNOMER
MOTORMAN
NEWCOMER
NOBLEMAN
NORSEMAN
PANDEMIC
PITCHMAN
PRESSMAN
RADIOMAN
REFORMER
ROUTEMAN
SALESMAN
SPACEMAN
SPECIMEN
STREAMER
SYSADMIN
SYSTEMIC
TALESMAN
TALISMAN
THALAMUS
TOWNSMAN
TRAINMAN
TRANSMIT
UNCOMMON
UNFORMED
UNSEEMLY
WATCHMAN
WOODSMAN
ABEYANCE
AFFIANCE
AIRLINER
ALLIANCE
ALUMINUM
AMARANTH
AMBIENCE
ANACONDA
ANNOUNCE
ARACHNID
ATTORNEY
AUDIENCE
BANDANNA
BASSINET
BEECHNUT
BUOYANCY
BURGUNDY
CARDINAL
CHESTNUT
CHEYENNE
CISLUNAR
CLARINET
CLEMENCY
COMBINGS
COMMANDO
COMMENCE
COMMONER
COMMUNAL
CONDENSE
CONFINES
CONGENER
CONJUNCT
CONTINUE
CONVINCE
COSIGNER
CREDENCE
CREDENZA
CRETONNE
CRIMINAL
CURRENCY
DEFIANCE
DEMEANOR
DENOUNCE
DIAGONAL
DISHONOR
DISPENSE
DISTANCE
DISTINCT
DOORKNOB
DOUGHNUT
DUODENUM
EARNINGS
ELEGANCE
EMINENCE
ENCEINTE
ENSCONCE
ENTRANCE
ENTRENCH
ESTRANGE
ETHERNET
EVIDENCE
EXCHANGE
EXIGENCY
EXTERNAL
EYELINER
FANDANGO
FERVENCY
FLAMENCO
FLAMINGO
FOREKNOW
GARDENIA
GERMINAL
GLOXINIA
GOVERNOR
GUARANTY
GUIDANCE
HACIENDA
HARMONIC
HEREUNTO
HISPANIC
HORMONAL
HUGUENOT
HUSTINGS
HYACINTH
INFERNAL
INFRINGE
INGUINAL
INNUENDO
INSIGNIA
INSOMNIA
INSTANCE
INSTINCT
INTERNAL
INTERNEE
INTERNET
INTRENCH
ISOTONIC
ISSUANCE
KEYPUNCH
LABURNUM
LAUDANUM
LEAVINGS
MACKINAW
MARTINET
MATERNAL
MECHANIC
METHANOL
MILLINER
MNEMONIC
NATIONAL
NONSENSE
NOTIONAL
NUISANCE
OPERANDS
ORDNANCE
ORIGINAL
PARDONER
PARLANCE
PATERNAL
PATIENCE
PERSONAL
PICKINGS
PIMIENTO
PITTANCE
PLACENTA
PLATINUM
PRECINCT
PRESENCE
PRETENSE
PRISONER
PROVINCE
RATIONAL
RAWBONED
REGIONAL
RELIANCE
RENOUNCE
RESIGNED
RESPONSE
RETAINER
RETRENCH
RETURNEE
SARDONIC
SCAVENGE
SCHOONER
SCROUNGE
SENTENCE
SENTINEL
SEQUENCE
SHILINGI
SHRAPNEL
SIXPENCE
SLIPKNOT
SLOVENLY
SOLVENCY
SOUVENIR
SPHAGNUM
STOTINKA
SUBSONIC
SUCCINCT
SUPERNAL
SUSPENSE
TENDENCY
TENPENNY
TEOSINTE
TERMINAL
TERMINUS
TEUTONIC
TRIBUNAL
TWOPENCE
TWOPENNY
TYMPANUM
UNCLENCH
UNEARNED
UNGAINLY
VACCINIA
VAGRANCY
VARIANCE
VIBURNUM
VIOLENCE
VIRGINAL
VOLCANIC
WARRANTY
WEAPONRY
WHODUNIT
YEOMANRY
ABATTOIR
ACRIMONY
ADVISORY
AEROLOGY
AGRONOMY
AIRDROME
ALBACORE
ALEATORY
ALKALOID
ALLEGORY
AMOEBOID
ANAEROBE
ANECDOTE
ANECHOIC
ANTELOPE
ANTEROOM
ANTHROPO
ANTIBODY
ANTIDOTE
ANTIMONY
ANTINOMY
ANTIPODE
ANTIPOPE
ARMYWORM
ASTEROID
AUDITORY
AUTOJOIN
BACKBONE
BALLROOM
BANKBOOK
BANKROLL
BAREFOOT
BARITONE
BASEBORN
BASSWOOD
BATHROBE
BATHROOM
BEHEMOTH
BENTWOOD
BIBULOUS
BILLFOLD
BITSTOCK
BLACKOUT
BLUENOSE
BODYWORK
BOLLWORM
BOOKWORM
BREAKOUT
BROCCOLI
BROWNOUT
BULLDOZE
BUNGHOLE
BURNOOSE
BUSYBODY
BUSYWORK
CALLIOPE
CAMISOLE
CAPRIOLE
CAPTIOUS
CARACOLE
CAREWORN
CASEWORK
CATACOMB
CATEGORY
CAUTIOUS
CEREMONY
CESSPOOL
CHAPBOOK
CHARCOAL
CHECKOFF
CHECKOUT
CICERONE
CINCHONA
CLAYMORE
CLOSEOUT
CLUBFOOT
COMEDOWN
CONFRONT
COOKBOOK
COPYBOOK
CREOSOTE
CROWFOOT
CYTOLOGY
DARKROOM
DARKSOME
DEADLOCK
DEADWOOD
DECOROUS
DEMIBOLD
DEMIJOHN
DESIROUS
DETHRONE
DEXTROSE
DIASTOLE
DILATORY
DISCLOSE
DISPROVE
DOUBLOON
DOWNLOAD
DOWNPOUR
DOWNTOWN
DOXOLOGY
EARPHONE
ENORMOUS
ENSHROUD
ENTHRONE
ENVELOPE
ENVIRONS
ESCAROLE
ETHOLOGY
ETIOLOGY
EUROBOND
EVENSONG
EVERMORE
EVERYONE
EXIGUOUS
EYETOOTH
FABULOUS
FACEDOWN
FACTIOUS
FALTBOAT
FEARSOME
FIREBOAT
FIREBOMB
FIREWOOD
FIREWORK
FISHBOWL
FISHHOOK
FLAGPOLE
FLAMEOUT
FLATBOAT
FLATFOOT
FLYBLOWN
FOLDBOAT
FOLKLORE
FOOTHOLD
FOOTNOTE
FOOTSORE
FOOTWORK
FOREBODE
FOREDOOM
FOREFOOT
FOREGONE
FORELOCK
FOREMOST
FORENOON
FOREWORD
FORSOOTH
FOURFOLD
FOURSOME
FOXGLOVE
FREEBORN
FREEHOLD
FREELOAD
FRETWORK
FUMAROLE
GADABOUT
GAMECOCK
GAMESOME
GATEPOST
GEMOLOGY
GEMSTONE
GENEROUS
GLABROUS
GLADSOME
GLAUCOMA
GLORIOUS
GLOWWORM
GOALPOST
GORGEOUS
GRACIOUS
GRIEVOUS
GRUESOME
HACKWORD
HALFTONE
HANDBOOK
HANDSOME
HARDWOOD
HAUTBOIS
HAWTHORN
HEADLOCK
HEADLONG
HEADROOM
HEADWORD
HEADWORK
HECATOMB
HEGEMONY
HEIRLOOM
HELICOID
HELIPORT
HELLHOLE
HEREFORD
HIGHBORN
HIGHROAD

HINDMOST
HOMEBODY
HOMEROOM
HOMEWORK
HOOKWORM
HORNBOOK
HOROLOGY
HUMANOID
IDEOLOGY
ILLINOIS
ILLUSORY
INCHWORM
INFAMOUS
IRONWOOD
IRONWORK
IROQUOIS
JACKBOOT
KEELBOAT
KEYSTONE
KILOVOLT
KINGBOLT
KNEEHOLE
KNOCKOUT
KNOTHOLE
LADYLOVE
LANDFORM
LANDLORD
LAVATORY
LIFEBOAT
LIFELONG
LIFEWORK
LIGNEOUS
LIVELONG
LOANWORD
LOBOTOMY
LONESOME
LONGBOAT
LONGHORN
LOOPHOLE
LOVELORN
LUMINOUS
LUSCIOUS
LYMPHOID
MACARONI
MACAROON
MANGROVE
MANIFOLD
MANYFOLD
MARIGOLD
MARKDOWN
MELANOMA
MESHWORK
MILEPOST
MILLPOND
MINATORY
MISQUOTE
MONGOOSE
MONITORY
MONOPOLY
MONOTONE
MOTOROLA
MUSHROOM
MYCOLOGY
NAINSOOK
NEBULOUS
NEMATODE
NIGEROIS
NOTEBOOK
NUGATORY
NUMEROUS
OFFSHOOT
OFFSHORE
OILCLOTH
OPENWORK
ORGULOUS
OUTDOORS
OVERCOAT
OVERCOME
OVERLOOK
OVERLORD
OVERTONE
PALINODE
PARABOLA
PARAMOUR
PARANOIA
PASSBOOK
PASSPORT
PASSWORD
PEDAGOGY
PEEPHOLE
PEIGNOIR
PENOLOGY
PENSTOCK
PHASEOUT
PICKLOCK
PINAFORE
PLATFORM
PLAYBOOK
PLAYGOER
PLETHORA
POLTROON
POPULOUS
PORTHOLE
POSTHOLE
POSTPONE
PRECIOUS
PREVIOUS
PRIMROSE
PRINTOUT
PSALMODY
PULPWOOD
PUSHDOWN
QUADROON
RAILROAD
RAINCOAT
RAVENOUS
RHAPSODY
RHEOLOGY
RHOMBOID
RIBOSOME
RINGWORM
ROADWORK
ROSEWOOD
RUNABOUT
SAGAMORE
SAILBOAT
SCABROUS
SCAFFOLD
SCISSORS
SEASHORE
SEDULOUS
SEMINOLE
SEMISOFT
SENSUOUS
SEROLOGY
SHAMROCK
SHINBONE
SHIPWORM
SHOPWORN
SHOSHONE
SHOWDOWN
SHUTDOWN
SIDELONG
SIGNPOST
SILICONE
SINKHOLE
SLUMLORD
SOFTWOOD
SOLENOID
SOMEBODY
SONOROUS
SPACIOUS
SPECIOUS
SPHEROID
SPITTOON
SPURIOUS
STAKEOUT
STANDOFF
STANDOUT
STUBBORN
STUDBOOK
STUDIOUS
SYCAMORE
SYMPHONY
SYNDROME
TAILCOAT
TAPEWORM
TAXONOMY
TEAMWORK
TEASPOON
TEXTBOOK
THEOLOGY
THRENODY
TIMEWORN
TIMOROUS
TIRESOME
TOILWORN
TOLLBOTH
TOPOLOGY
TORTUOUS
TRAPDOOR
TRAPROCK
TROMBONE
TUBEROSE
TUBEROUS
TURNCOAT
UNCTUOUS
UNSAVORY
UPSTROKE
USURIOUS
UUDECODE
UUENCODE
UXORIOUS
VAGABOND
VAPOROUS
VARICOSE
VENOMOUS
VIETCONG
VIGOROUS
VIROLOGY
VIRTUOSO
VIRTUOUS
VITREOUS
WARDROBE
WARDROOM
WAREROOM
WASHBOWL
WASHROOM
WELLBORN
WEREWOLF
WHIPCORD
WILDFOWL
WILDWOOD
WIREWORM
WISHBONE
WITHHOLD
WONDROUS
WOODCOCK
WOODNOTE
WOODWORK
WORDBOOK
WORKBOOK
WORKROOM
WORMHOLE
WORMWOOD
YEARBOOK
YEARLONG
ZOOSPORE
BACKSPIN
BICUSPID
CHUTZPAH
COLLAPSE
CRACKPOT
DECREPIT
DISCIPLE
EPILEPSY
FELDSPAR
FINESPUN
FLESHPOT
FLYPAPER
HEREUPON
HOMESPUN
IMPROPER
INTREPID
LARKSPUR
LINCHPIN
LOLLIPOP
MANCIPLE
MARZIPAN
MAYAPPLE
MISAPPLY
MULTIPLE
MULTIPLY
PLATYPUS
SAUCEPAN
SCALEPAN
SMALLPOX
SOUTHPAW
STRUMPET
TAILSPIN
TERRAPIN
TURNSPIT
UNCOUPLE
UNDERPAY
UNSHAPED
UNZIPPED
WINGSPAN
APPLIQUE
BOUTIQUE
COLLOQUY
CRITIQUE
MYSTIQUE
PHYSIQUE
PRATIQUE
AGITPROP
AIRBORNE
AIRSTRIP
ALIZARIN
ANGSTROM
AVIATRIX
AXLETREE
BACCARAT
BACKDROP
BARBARIC
BARBERRY
BAYBERRY
BEGGARLY
BESMIRCH
BETATRON
BINAURAL
BIYEARLY
BOWSPRIT
BRETHREN
BULLFROG
CAMPOREE
CAREFREE
CAULDRON
CAUSERIE
CENTERED
CEREBRUM
CHAMBRAY
CHAPERON
CHEMURGY
CHOLERIC
CICATRIX
CLAPTRAP
CLITORIS
COCKCROW
COCKEREL
COMMERCE
CONCERTO
CONSERVE
CONSTRUE
CONVERGE
CONVERSE
COPPERAS
CORDUROY
CORNCRIB
CORPORAL
DECIGRAM
DEKAGRAM
DEMOCRAT
DEMURRER
DEWBERRY
DIELDRIN
DISAGREE
DISARRAY
DISBURSE
DISGORGE
DISPERSE
DISPIRIT
DOGGEREL
DUNGAREE
ELECTRIC
ELECTRON
ESOTERIC
EUPHORIA
FILIGREE
FIRETRAP
FLATIRON
FLUIDRAM
FOLDEROL
FORMERLY
FORWARDS
FROUFROU
GASWORKS
GENDARME
GINGERLY
GLYCERIN
GLYCEROL
GRIDIRON
GUTTURAL
HEDGEROW
HIGHBRED
HIGHBROW
HITHERTO
HOLOGRAM
HOMEBRED
HYSTERIA
IDEOGRAM
INFRARED
INSPIRIT
INTEGRAL
INTERROG
JAMBOREE
JEOPARDY
KANGAROO
KEYWORDS
KILOGRAM
LEAPFROG
LETHARGY
LINGERIE
LITTORAL
LUTHERAN
MACKEREL
MANDARIN
MANNERED
MANNERLY
MARJORAM
MASTERLY
MERCURIC
METEORIC
MINSTREL
MISCARRY
MONAURAL
MONOGRAM
MULBERRY
NOCTURNE
ORATORIO
OUTBURST
OUTSTRIP
OVERDRAW
OVERGROW
PARTERRE
PASTORAL
PECTORAL
PEDIGREE
PERFORCE
PERVERSE
PICKEREL
PIZZERIA
PLECTRUM
POSITRON
PRESERVE
PRETERIT
PROPERTY
PUREBRED
RAINDROP
RECOURSE
REFERRAL
REHEARSE
RESEARCH
RESOURCE
RHETORIC
ROOFTREE
SANSKRIT
SAUTERNE
SAWHORSE
SCENARIO
SEAFARER
SETSCREW
SNOWDROP
SPECTRAL
SPECTRUM
SQUADRON
SQUIRREL
SUBMERGE
SUBMERSE
SULFURIC
TELEGRAM
TEMPORAL
TIMBERED
TOMORROW
TRAVERSE
TRIMARAN
TURMERIC
UNAWARES
UNCHURCH
UNIVERSE
VARIORUM
VICTORIA
VISCERAL
WARFARIN
WAYFARER
WIREDRAW
WISTARIA
WISTERIA
WITHDRAW
ABSCISSA
ACCURSED
ACIDOSIS
ALFRESCO
AMBROSIA
ANALYSIS
ASSASSIN
CAROUSAL

CAROUSEL
CHARISMA
CHECKSUM
COALESCE
COLOSSAL
COLOSSUS
CREVASSE
DIALYSIS
DIAPASON
DISPOSAL
DISTASTE
ELLIPSIS
EMPHASIS
ENURESIS
ESPOUSAL
ESPRESSO
EXCURSUS
EXEGESIS
FANTASIA
FASCISTA
FIBROSIS
FORENSIC
GALLUSES
GARRISON
GEODESIC
GRANDSON
GUERNSEY
HEAVYSET
HYPNOSIS
IMPRISON
JALOUSIE
JETTISON
KOLINSKY
LACROSSE
LAMBASTE
LICENSEE
MACHISMO
MAGNESIA
MANTISSA
MARMOSET
MOCCASIN
MOLASSES
NARCOSIS
NECROSIS
NEUROSIS
PARMESAN
PARTISAN
PHARISEE
REPRISAL
REVERSAL
SACRISTY
SOMERSET
SUPPOSED
SYNOPSIS
THICKSET
TRAVESTY
UNBIASED
UNCHASTE
UNDERSEA
UNLOOSEN
UNPERSON
ABSENTEE
ABSINTHE
ACCOUTRE
ACCUSTOM
ACOUSTIC
ACROSTIC
AFFECTED
AFFLATUS
AFLUTTER
AFTERTAX
AGERATUM
AGLITTER
AGNOSTIC
AIGRETTE
ANCESTOR
ANCESTRY
ANISETTE
ANTEATER
APERITIF
ARTISTIC
ARTISTRY
ASBESTOS
ASSORTED
ATHLETIC
BACKSTOP
BAGUETTE
BALUSTER
BANISTER
BARBITAL
BARRATRY
BARRETTE
BELITTLE
BLACKTOP
BRIGHTEN
BULLETIN
BURSITIS
CANISTER
CARYATID
CASSETTE
CATHETER
CEMENTUM
CHRISTEN
CHRISTIE
CLEMATIS
CLOISTER
COCKATOO
COMPUTER
CONFETTI
COQUETTE
CORVETTE
COSMETIC
CREDITOR
DAUGHTER
DECANTER
DEJECTED
DEMENTED
DEMENTIA
DESPATCH
DETRITUS
DIABETES
DIAMETER
DICTATOR
DIDACTIC
DIRECTOR
DISASTER
DISINTER
DISKETTE
DISPATCH
DIURETIC
DOMESTIC
DOORSTEP
ECLIPTIC
ELEVATOR
EMBATTLE
EMBITTER
EMERITUS
EMPHATIC
EXECUTOR
FACTOTUM
FALSETTO
FELLATIO
FOLIATED
FOOTSTEP
FORESTRY
FRENETIC
FRIGHTEN
GAMESTER
GANGSTER
GEOMETRY
GIGANTIC
HEIGHTEN
HERMETIC
HOSPITAL
HOUSETOP
HUCKSTER
HYPNOTIC
IDOLATER
IDOLATRY
IMMORTAL
IMPACTED
IMPOSTOR
INDEBTED
INDUCTEE
INDUSTRY
INEDITED
INFANTRY
INVERTER
JURISTIC
LAUGHTER
LIBRETTO
LOCKSTEP
LODESTAR
MAGNETIC
MAINSTAY
MALTSTER
MEPHITIC
MINISTER
MINISTRY
MISMATCH
MOMENTUM
MONASTIC
MUENSTER
MUSCATEL
MUSKETRY
MYELITIS
NARCOTIC
NEONATAL
NEPENTHE
NEURITIS
NEUROTIC
NONMETAL
NUTHATCH
ODOMETER
OHMMETER
OPERETTA
ORIENTAL
OUTDATED
OVERSTAY
OVERSTEP
PALMETTO
PARIETAL
PATHETIC
PEDESTAL
PILASTER
PLANKTON
PODIATRY
POLESTAR
POLLSTER
PRENATAL
PROMOTER
PULMOTOR
QUIXOTIC
RADIATOR
REBUTTAL
RECEPTOR
REGISTER
REGISTRY
REMITTAL
REPARTEE
REPEATED
REPORTER
RESISTOR
RESORTER
RHEOSTAT
ROADSTER
ROCKETRY
ROMANTIC
ROOMETTE
ROULETTE
SCIMITAR
SCULPTOR
SEAWATER
SELECTEE
SEMANTIC
SEMESTER
SERVITOR
SIDESTEP
SINISTER
SITUATED
SKELETON
SONGSTER
SPINSTER
SPIRITED
SPLATTER
SPLINTER
SPLUTTER
STEALTHY
STILETTO
STRAITEN
SUBTITLE
SYMMETRY
SYMPATHY
SYNOPTIC
TAPESTRY
TEAMSTER
TEETOTAL
TENANTRY
TESTATOR
THREATEN
THROTTLE
THRUSTER
TOILETRY
TOILETTE
TRIMETER
TUNGSTEN
UNBEATEN
UNBOLTED
UNBUTTON
UNCLOTHE
UNDERTOW
UNFASTEN
UNFETTER
UNSETTLE
UNWONTED
UNWORTHY
VARIETAL
VARISTOR
VENDETTA
VERBATIM
VERBOTEN
VIGNETTE
WORDSTAR
ABSOLUTE
ABSTRUSE
AIRBRUSH
ALEHOUSE
ALLELUIA
ALTHOUGH
ALTITUDE
APERTURE
APPLAUSE
APTITUDE
AQUEDUCT
ARCHDUKE
ARMATURE
ATTITUDE
BANKRUPT
BERCEUSE
BIANNUAL
BISEXUAL
BROCHURE
CARNAUBA
CATAPULT
CHIPMUNK
CINCTURE
COCKSURE
COIFFURE
COMPOUND
CONCLUDE
CONFOUND
CREATURE
CYNOSURE
DANDRUFF
DANSEUSE
DENATURE
DESTRUCT
DISABUSE
DISCOUNT
DISMOUNT
DISTRUST
DOGHOUSE
DOLDRUMS
DORMOUSE
DOWNTURN
DYESTUFF
EVENTUAL
EXPOSURE
FAUBOURG
FOXHOUND
FRACTURE
FURLOUGH
HABITUAL
HANDCUFF
HOTHOUSE
ICEBOUND
ICEHOUSE
IMMATURE
INSECURE
INSOMUCH
INSTRUCT
INVOLUTE
JUNCTURE
LATITUDE
LIGATURE
MADHOUSE
MALAMUTE
MANICURE
MASSEUSE
MISCOUNT
MISTRUST
MOISTURE
MOLECULE
MORIBUND
NEWFOUND
NONESUCH
NUMSKULL
OBSTRUCT
OPUSCULE
OUTBOUND
OUTHOUSE
OVERMUCH
OVERRULE
OVERTURE
OVERTURN
PANTSUIT
PEDICURE
PERILUNE
PICAYUNE
PLAYSUIT
PLEASURE
POSTLUDE
PRECLUDE
PRESSURE
PROFOUND
PROPOUND
PROTRUDE
PUNCTUAL
PUNCTURE
QUIETUDE
REASSURE
RESIDUAL
RESIDUUM
RESOLUTE
REVENUER
RIDICULE
ROSEBUSH
RUBICUND
SCHEDULE
SCROFULA
SEAMOUNT
SHANTUNG
SINECURE
SOLITUDE
SURMOUNT
SURROUND
TACITURN
THOROUGH
TINCTURE
TITMOUSE
TRANQUIL
TREASURE
TREASURY
UNSPRUNG
UNSTRUNG
UPTHRUST
USUFRUCT
VERMOUTH
VISCOUNT
WINDBURN
WOODRUFF
APPROVAL
BEREAVED
BICONVEX
CARNIVAL
CORDOVAN
DISCOVER
DISFAVOR
DISHEVEL
DISSEVER
ENDEAVOR
FESTIVAL
HANGOVER
HOLDOVER
INTERVAL
INVOLVED
LAWGIVER
LEFTOVER
MANEUVER
MEDIEVAL
MOREOVER
PASSOVER
PRIMEVAL
PULLOVER
PUSHOVER
RECEIVER
RESERVED
REVOLVER
TRIUMVIR
TURNOVER
UPHEAVAL
WALKOVER
WHATEVER
WHENEVER
WHEREVER
WHOMEVER
ALLEYWAY
CASTAWAY
CAUSEWAY
DEFLOWER
DRIVEWAY
FOLDAWAY
GIVEAWAY
HATCHWAY
HIDEAWAY
NEWLYWED

PANDOWDY
POLLIWOG
REVIEWER
SCALAWAG
SPEEDWAY
SPILLWAY
STAIRWAY
STOWAWAY
TIGHTWAD
UPGROWTH
WALKAWAY
WATERWAY
WILLIWAW
ASPHYXIA
DYSLEXIA
AMETHYST
CATALYZE
DISLOYAL
EMPLOYEE
GARGOYLE
GIGABYTE
KILOBYTE
LOGOTYPE
MEGABYTE
NEOPHYTE
PARALYZE
PAROXYSM
PORPHYRY
TAXPAYER
TRIPTYCH
TRUETYPE
ZOOPHYTE
ATOMIZER
BEDAZZLE
EMBEZZLE
EMBLAZON
HOWITZER
KIBITZER
UNMUZZLE

## 7th Letter

ABNORMAL
ACIDHEAD
AFTERTAX
AGRARIAN
ALBANIAN
ALDERMAN
ALGERIAN
ALLEYWAY
AMERICAN
ANGLICAN
APPROVAL
ARBOREAL
ARMORIAL
ARTERIAL
ATYPICAL
AUSTRIAN
BACCARAT
BACKSLAP
BAILSMAN
BARBICAN
BARBITAL
BEDSTEAD
BERMUDAS
BIANNUAL
BIENNIAL
BILLHEAD
BINAURAL
BIOCIDAL
BIRACIAL
BIRTHDAY
BISEXUAL
BOGEYMAN
BOHEMIAN
BONDSMAN
BRAKEMAN
BRICKBAT
BROUGHAM
BROWBEAT
BULKHEAD
BULLHEAD
CALENDAR
CANADIAN
CANNIBAL
CAPSULAR
CARDIGAN
CARDINAL
CARNIVAL
CAROUSAL
CASTAWAY
CAUSEWAY
CELLULAR
CERULEAN
CERVICAL
CESAREAN
CHAIRMAN
CHAMBRAY
CHANUKAH
CHARCOAL
CHEMICAL
CHITCHAT
CHUTZPAH
CINNABAR
CIRCULAR
CISLUNAR
CIVILIAN
CLAPTRAP
CLERICAL
CLINICAL
COACHMAN
COLESLAW
COLONIAL
COLOSSAL
COMEDIAN
COMMUNAL
COMPLEAT
CONFOCAL
CONJUGAL
COPPERAS
CORDOVAN
CORNMEAL
CORPORAL
CORPSMAN
CRIMINAL
CRITICAL
CROSSBAR
DAIRYMAN
DAYBREAK
DAYDREAM
DEADBEAT
DECIGRAM
DEKAGRAM
DEMOCRAT
DEMONIAC
DIAGONAL
DIPLOMAT
DISARRAY
DISLOYAL
DISPOSAL
DOOMSDAY
DOWNBEAT
DOWNLOAD
DRAGOMAN
DRIVEWAY
DRUMBEAT
EGYPTIAN
EMPYREAN
ESPECIAL
ESPOUSAL
ESTONIAN
ETHEREAL
ETRUSCAN
EURASIAN
EUROPEAN
EVENTUAL
EVERYDAY
EXEMPLAR
EXTERNAL
FALTBOAT
FAMILIAL
FAMILIAR
FELDSPAR
FESTIVAL
FIREBOAT
FIRECLAY
FIRETRAP
FLAMBEAU
FLATBOAT
FLATHEAD
FLIMFLAM
FLUIDRAM
FOLDAWAY
FOLDBOAT
FOOLSCAP
FOOTWEAR
FOREBEAR
FOREHEAD
FORSWEAR
FREEDMAN
FREELOAD
FRESHMAN
FUNEREAL
GERMINAL
GHANAIAN
GIVEAWAY
GRANULAR
GROSBEAK
GUARDIAN
GUTTURAL
HABITUAL
HANDICAP
HANDYMAN
HANUKKAH
HARRIDAN
HATCHWAY
HAWAIIAN
HEADGEAR
HEADSMAN
HELMSMAN
HENCHMAN
HERDSMAN
HIDEAWAY
HIGHROAD
HOGSHEAD
HOLOGRAM
HOOLIGAN
HORMONAL
HORSEMAN
HOSPITAL
HUNTSMAN
HYMENEAL
IDEOGRAM
IMMORTAL
IMPERIAL
INDIAMAN
INFERNAL
INFORMAL
INGUINAL
INIMICAL
INTEGRAL
INTERNAL
INTERVAL
IRONCLAD
ISTHMIAN
JEREMIAD
JUDICIAL
KEELBOAT
KICKSHAW
KILOGRAM
KNITWEAR
LACRIMAL
LANDSMAN
LIFEBOAT
LINESMAN
LITTORAL
LODESTAR
LOLLYGAG
LONGBOAT
LUTHERAN
MACKINAW
MADRIGAL
MAGICIAN
MAINSTAY
MALAWIAN
MALTREAT
MANIACAL
MARJORAM
MARKSMAN
MARZIPAN
MASTHEAD
MATERIAL
MATERNAL
MEDIEVAL
MEMORIAL
MERIDIAN
METRICAL
MILLIBAR
MISTREAT
MISTRIAL
MONAURAL
MONOGRAM
MOONBEAM
MOROCCAN
MOTORCAR
MOTORMAN
MUSICIAN
MYSTICAL
NATIONAL
NAUTICAL
NEONATAL
NIGERIAN
NOBLEMAN
NONMETAL
NORSEMAN
NOTARIAL
NOTIONAL
OBSIDIAN
OFFICIAL
OPTICIAN
ORIENTAL
ORIGINAL
OUTBREAK
OVERCOAT
OVERDRAW
OVERHEAD
OVERHEAR
OVERLEAP
OVERPLAY
OVERSEAS
OVERSTAY
PANCREAS
PARALLAX
PARFOCAL
PARIETAL
PARMESAN
PARTISAN
PASTORAL
PATERNAL
PECTORAL
PECULIAR
PEDESTAL
PEMMICAN
PERSONAL
PHYSICAL
PITCHMAN
PLEBEIAN
POLESTAR
POPINJAY
PREMOLAR
PRENATAL
PRESSMAN
PRIMEVAL
PRODIGAL
PUBLICAN
PUNCTUAL
PUSSYCAT
RADIOMAN
RAILROAD
RAINCOAT
RATIONAL
REBUTTAL
REFERRAL
REGIONAL
REMEDIAL
REMITTAL
REPRISAL
RESIDUAL
REVERSAL
RHEOSTAT
RIPARIAN
ROMANIAN
ROUTEMAN
RUMANIAN
SAILBOAT
SALESMAN
SATURDAY
SAUCEPAN
SCALAWAG
SCALEPAN
SCAPULAR
SCIMITAR
SCOFFLAW
SHANGHAI
SIDEREAL
SINGULAR
SKULLCAP
SOMEWHAT
SOUTHPAW
SPACEMAN
SPECTRAL
SPEEDWAY
SPILLWAY
STAIRWAY
STOWAWAY
SUPERNAL
SURGICAL
TAHITIAN
TAILCOAT
TALESMAN
TALISMAN
TEETOTAL
TELEGRAM
TELEPLAY
TEMPORAL
TERMINAL
THESPIAN
THURSDAY
TIGHTWAD
TOBOGGAN
TOWNSMAN
TRAINMAN
TRIBUNAL
TRIMARAN
TUNISIAN
TURBOFAN
TURNCOAT
TUTORIAL
UNDERPAY
UNFILIAL
UNIAXIAL
UPHEAVAL
UPSTREAM
VALVULAR
VARIETAL
VASCULAR
VENEREAL
VENUSIAN
VERTICAL
VIRGINAL
VISCERAL
WALKAWAY
WATCHMAN
WATERWAY
WELLHEAD
WHITECAP
WILLIWAW
WINGSPAN
WIREDRAW
WITHDRAW
WOODSMAN
WORDPLAY
WORDSTAR
WORKADAY
YUGOSLAV
ANAEROBE
BATHROBE
CARNAUBA
DESCRIBE
DIATRIBE
INSCRIBE
KOHLRABI
WARDROBE
ABEYANCE
ABSTRACT
AFFIANCE
AIRSPACE
ALFRESCO
ALLIANCE
ALLSPICE
AMBIENCE
ANGELICA
ANNOUNCE
ANYPLACE
APPROACH
AQUEDUCT
ARTIFACT
ARTIFICE
AUDIENCE
AVIONICS
BACKPACK
BAREBACK
BASILICA
BENEDICT
BENEFICE
BESMIRCH
BITSTOCK
BOLDFACE
BUOYANCY
CALLBACK
CARAPACE
CATARACT
CELIBACY
CLEMENCY
COALESCE
COMEBACK
COMMENCE
COMMERCE
CONFLICT
CONJUNCT
CONTRACT
CONVINCE
CORONACH
CREDENCE

CURRENCY
DEADLOCK
DEFIANCE
DELICACY
DENOUNCE
DERELICT
DESELECT
DESPATCH
DESTRUCT
DIPSTICK
DISGRACE
DISPATCH
DISPLACE
DISTANCE
DISTINCT
DISTRACT
DISTRICT
DRAWBACK
DROPKICK
EKISTICS
ELEGANCE
EMINENCE
ENCROACH
ENSCONCE
ENTRANCE
ENTRENCH
EUGENICS
EVIDENCE
EXIGENCY
EYEPIECE
FASTBACK
FEEDBACK
FERVENCY
FLAMENCO
FLAPJACK
FLYSPECK
FOOTRACE
FORELOCK
FULLBACK
GAMECOCK
GENETICS
GIMCRACK
GUIDANCE
HALFBACK
HANDPICK
HARDBACK
HARDHACK
HARDTACK
HAYSTACK
HEADLOCK
HEPATICA
HOMESICK
HUMPBACK
INDIRECT
INSOMUCH
INSTANCE
INSTINCT
INSTRUCT
INTRENCH
ISSUANCE
JAUNDICE
JOYSTICK
KEYPUNCH
KICKBACK
KINETICS
KNAPSACK
LAMPBACK
LICORICE
LIMERICK
LIPSTICK
LOVESICK
MAJOLICA
MAVERICK
MILLRACE
MISMATCH
MISPLACE
MOSSBACK
NECKLACE
NONESUCH
NONSTICK
NUISANCE
NUTHATCH
OBSTRUCT
ORDNANCE
OUTREACH
OVERMUCH
PALEFACE
PARLANCE
PATIENCE
PAYCHECK
PENSTOCK
PERFORCE
PHARMACY
PICKLOCK
PINPRICK
PITTANCE
PLAYBACK
POLITICK
POLITICO
POLITICS
POPULACE
POULTICE
PRACTICE
PRECINCT
PRESENCE
PROPHECY
PROSPECT
PROTRACT
PROVINCE
PULLBACK
RELIANCE
RENOUNCE
REPROACH
RESEARCH
RESOURCE
RESTRICT
RETRENCH
ROLLBACK
SANDWICH
SCIATICA
SENTENCE
SEQUENCE
SHAMROCK
SHOELACE
SIDEKICK
SIXPENCE
SOLSTICE
SOLVENCY
SUBTRACT
SUCCINCT
SURPLICE
SWAYBACK
TAMARACK
TENDENCY
TRANSACT
TRAPROCK
TRIPTYCH
TWOPENCE
TYPEFACE
UNCHURCH
UNCLENCH
UNDERACT
USUFRUCT
VAGRANCY
VARIANCE
VERONICA
VIOLENCE
WOODCOCK
WOOLSACK
ZWIEBACK
ACCOLADE
ALTITUDE
ANACONDA
ANTIBODY
ANTIPODE
APTITUDE
AQUACADE
ATTITUDE
BACKSIDE
BESTRIDE
BLOCKADE
BURGUNDY
BUSYBODY
CHLORIDE
COINCIDE
COMMANDO
CONCLUDE
DISSUADE
ENFILADE
ESCAPADE
EVENTIDE
FIRESIDE
FLUORIDE
FOREBODE
FORELADY
FORWARDS
GENOCIDE
HACIENDA
HANDMADE
HILLSIDE
HOMEBODY
HOMEMADE
HOMICIDE
INNUENDO
JEOPARDY
KEYWORDS
LATITUDE
LEMONADE
MONOXIDE
NEMATODE
NOONTIDE
OPERANDS
OVERRIDE
PALINODE
PALISADE
PANDOWDY
PEROXIDE
PERSUADE
POSTLUDE
PRECLUDE
PROCEEDS
PROTRUDE
PSALMODY
QUIETUDE
REGICIDE
RENEGADE
RHAPSODY
ROADSIDE
SERENADE
SOLITUDE
SOMEBODY
STAMPEDE
STOCKADE
SUNSHADE
THRENODY
UNSTEADY
UNWIELDY
UUDECODE
UUENCODE
YULETIDE
ABSENTEE
ACCURSED
AFFECTED
AFLUTTER
AGLITTER
AIRLINER
AIRSPEED
ALLERGEN
ALPHABET
ANDROGEN
ANTEATER
APPELLEE
ASPHODEL
ASSORTED
ATOMIZER
ATTORNEY
AXLETREE
BAEDEKER
BALUSTER
BANISTER
BASSINET
BEHOLDEN
BEREAVED
BEWILDER
BICONVEX
BIRDSEED
BRACELET
BRETHREN
BRIGHTEN
BRINDLED
BRITCHES
BROOKLET
CALENDER
CAMPOREE
CANISTER
CAREFREE
CAROUSEL
CATHETER
CAVALIER
CENTERED
CHANDLER
CHARADES
CHEROKEE
CHRISTEN
CLARINET
CLINCHER
CLOISTER
CLOTHIER
CLOUDLET
COCKEREL
COGNOMEN
COGWHEEL
COLANDER
COMMONER
COMPILER
COMPUTER
CONFINES
CONGENER
CONSIDER
COSIGNER
COURTIER
COVERLET
CROTCHET
CROUPIER
CUCUMBER
CUSTOMER
CYCLAMEN
CYLINDER
DAUGHTER
DEATHBED
DECANTER
DECEMBER
DECIPHER
DEFLOWER
DEJECTED
DEMENTED
DEMURRER
DETACHED
DIABETES
DIAMETER
DIARRHEA
DISAGREE
DISASTER
DISCOVER
DISCREET
DISHEVEL
DISINTER
DISORDER
DISQUIET
DISSEVER
DIVORCEE
DOGGEREL
DOMINEER
DOORSTEP
DULCIMER
DUNGAREE
EIGHTEEN
EMBITTER
EMBOLDEN
EMPLOYEE
ENCIPHER
ENCUMBER
ENDANGER
ENGENDER
ENGINEER
ESPALIER
ESTROGEN
ETHERNET
EXPLODED
EYELINER
FILIGREE
FLOUNDER
FLYPAPER
FLYWHEEL
FOLIATED
FOOTSTEP
FOURTEEN
FRIGHTEN
FRONTIER
GALLUSES
GAMESTER
GANGSTER
GAUNTLET
GLYCOGEN
GOSSAMER
GRAVAMEN
GRIZZLED
GROSCHEN
GROUNDER
GUERNSEY
HANGOVER
HAWKWEED
HEAVYSET
HEIGHTEN
HELPMEET
HERCULES
HIGHBRED
HOLDOVER
HOMEBRED
HONEYDEW
HOWITZER
HUCKSTER
HYDROGEN
IDOLATER
IMPACTED
IMPELLER
IMPROPER
INCUMBER
INDEBTED
INDUCTEE
INEDITED
INFORMED
INFORMER
INFRARED
INTENDED
INTERNEE
INTERNET
INVERTER
INVOLVED
IRONWEED
ISLANDER
JAMBOREE
KERCHIEF
KIBITZER
KILLDEER
LASERJET
LATCHKEY
LAUGHTER
LAUNCHER
LAVENDER
LAWGIVER
LAWMAKER
LEFTOVER
LENGTHEN
LICENSEE
LOCKSTEP
LOCOWEED
LOPSIDED
MACKEREL
MAGDALEN
MALARKEY
MALINGER
MALTSTER
MANEUVER
MANNERED
MANTELET
MARMOSET
MARTINET
MATERIEL
MENHADEN
MESDAMES
MILKWEED
MILLINER
MINISTER
MINSTREL
MISCHIEF
MISLABEL
MISNOMER
MISTAKEN
MOLASSES
MOREOVER
MUENSTER
MULETEER
MUSCATEL
NEGLIGEE
NEWCOMER
NEWLYWED
NEWSREEL
NINETEEN
NITROGEN
NOVEMBER
ODOMETER
OHMMETER
OLEANDER
ONLOOKER
OUTDATED
OUTMODED
OUTRIDER
OUTSIDER
OVERSTEP
OVERVIEW
PACIFIER
PAMPHLET
PARAKEET
PARALLEL
PARDONER
PASSOVER
PATHOGEN
PEDIGREE
PHARISEE
PICKEREL
PILASTER
PINWHEEL
PLAYGOER
POKEWEED
POLLSTER

PRISONER
PROMOTER
PROVIDED
PULLOVER
PUREBRED
PUSHOVER
PYORRHEA
RAWBONED
RECEIVER
RECORDER
REFORMER
REGISTER
REINDEER
REMEMBER
REPARTEE
REPEATED
REPORTER
RESERVED
RESIGNED
RESORTER
RETAINER
RETARDED
RETURNEE
REVENUER
REVIEWER
REVOLVER
RICOCHET
RIVERBED
ROADSTER
ROOFTREE
SADDUCEE
SCHOONER
SCILICET
SEAFARER
SEAWATER
SELECTEE
SEMESTER
SENTINEL
SETSCREW
SHAMBLES
SHINGLES
SHOULDER
SHRAPNEL
SIDESTEP
SILENCER
SINISTER
SITUATED
SOMERSET
SONGSTER
SPECIMEN
SPINSTER
SPIRITED
SPLATTER
SPLINTER
SPLUTTER
SPROCKET
SQUANDER
SQUEEGEE
SQUIRREL
STICKLER
STRAITEN
STRANGER
STREAMER
STRICKEN
STRINGED
STRINGER
STRUMPET
SUNDRIES
SUPERJET
SUPPOSED
TAXPAYER
TEAMSTER
TELEVIEW
THICKSET
THIRTEEN
THRASHER
THREATEN
THRUSTER
TIMBERED
TOGETHER
TOPSIDES
TRANSFER
TRENCHER
TRIMETER
TUNGSTEN
TURBOJET
TURNOVER
UNAWARES
UNBEATEN
UNBELIEF
UNBIASED
UNBIDDEN
UNBODIED
UNBOLTED
UNBROKEN
UNBURDEN
UNDERSEA
UNEARNED
UNFASTEN
UNFETTER
UNFORMED
UNLEADED
UNLIMBER
UNLOOSEN
UNSHAPED
UNVOICED
UNWONTED
UNZIPPED
VERBOTEN
VILLAGER
WALKOVER
WAYFARER
WHATEVER
WHENEVER
WHEREVER
WHOMEVER
WOODSHED
WRETCHED
WRIGGLER
WRISTLET
AIRCRAFT
BEAUTIFY
CAMSHAFT
CHECKOFF
CLASSIFY
DANDRUFF
DETOXIFY
DYESTUFF
EMULSIFY
FISHWIFE
FORKLIFT
FRUCTIFY
GOODWIFE
HANDCUFF
HUMIDIFY
IDENTIFY
PENKNIFE
PRETTIFY
REVIVIFY
RIFFRAFF
SANCTIFY
SEMISOFT
SHOPLIFT
SILICIFY
SIMPLIFY
SOLIDIFY
STANDOFF
STRATIFY
STULTIFY
WILDLIFE
WOODRUFF
AEROLOGY
ALTHOUGH
AMPERAGE
APOTHEGM
APPANAGE
BADINAGE
BARONAGE
BEGRUDGE
BEVERAGE
BREAKAGE
CAMPAIGN
CARRIAGE
CHEMURGY
CLEAVAGE
COMBINGS
CONVERGE
COVERAGE
CRIBBAGE
CYTOLOGY
DISGORGE
DISLODGE
DOXOLOGY
DRAINAGE
DRESSAGE
EARNINGS
ENSILAGE
ENVISAGE
EQUIPAGE
ESTRANGE
ETHOLOGY
ETIOLOGY
EXCHANGE
FANDANGO
FLAMINGO
FRONTAGE
FURLOUGH
FUSELAGE
GEMOLOGY
HERITAGE
HOROLOGY
HUSTINGS
IDEOLOGY
IMPETIGO
INFRINGE
LANGUAGE
LEAVINGS
LETHARGY
LEVERAGE
MARRIAGE
MISJUDGE
MISUSAGE
MORTGAGE
MUCILAGE
MYCOLOGY
OFFSTAGE
ONONDAGA
OUTWEIGH
PARADIGM
PEDAGOGY
PENOLOGY
PICKINGS
PILOTAGE
PORRIDGE
POUNDAGE
PREJUDGE
PRESTIGE
RHEOLOGY
ROUGHAGE
RUTABAGA
SABOTAGE
SCAVENGE
SCROUNGE
SEROLOGY
SEWERAGE
SHILINGI
SHORTAGE
STEERAGE
STOPPAGE
STRATEGY
SUBMERGE
SUFFRAGE
SUPEREGO
THEOLOGY
THOROUGH
TOPOLOGY
TRACKAGE
TRUCKAGE
TUTELAGE
UNDERAGE
VERBIAGE
VICARAGE
VICINAGE
VIROLOGY
WHARFAGE
WRECKAGE
ABSINTHE
AFFRIGHT
AIRTIGHT
AUTOBAHN
BACKACHE
BAROUCHE
BROUHAHA
COMANCHE
DAYLIGHT
DEMARCHE
DEMIJOHN
DOGFIGHT
EYESIGHT
FANLIGHT
FAROUCHE
GASLIGHT
GUNFIGHT
HEADACHE
HUARACHE
INFOBAHN
MARIACHI
MIDNIGHT
MONARCHY
MUSTACHE
NEPENTHE
OUTFIGHT
OUTRIGHT
PASTICHE
PENLIGHT
REVANCHE
SKYLIGHT
STEALTHY
STRAIGHT
SUNLIGHT
SYMPATHY
TWILIGHT
UNCLOTHE
UNSOUGHT
UNTAUGHT
UNWORTHY
ABATTOIR
ACADEMIC
ACCREDIT
ACIDOSIS
ACOUSTIC
ACROSTIC
AGNOSTIC
AIRSTRIP
ALIZARIN
ALKALOID
ALLELUIA
ALOPECIA
AMBROSIA
AMOEBOID
ANALYSIS
ANECHOIC
APERITIF
APOLOGIA
APPENDIX
ARACHNID
ARMCHAIR
ARPEGGIO
ARTISTIC
ASPHYXIA
ASSASSIN
ASTEROID
ATHLETIC
AUTOJOIN
AVIATRIX
BACKSPIN
BARBARIC
BEARSKIN
BEATIFIC
BICUSPID
BONHOMIE
BOWSPRIT
BROMIDIC
BUCKSKIN
BULLETIN
BURSITIS
CALFSKIN
CAMELLIA
CANNABIS
CAPESKIN
CAPUCHIN
CARYATID
CATHOLIC
CAUSERIE
CEPHALIC
CHAPLAIN
CHOLERIC
CHRISTIE
CICATRIX
CLEMATIS
CLITORIS
COCKTAIL
COMPLAIN
CONTRAIL
COONSKIN
CORNCRIB
COSMETIC
COXSWAIN
CRUCIFIX
DAFFODIL
DEBONAIR
DECREPIT
DEERSKIN
DEMENTIA
DIABOLIC
DIALYSIS
DIATOMIC
DIDACTIC
DIELDRIN
DISCLAIM
DISPIRIT
DISTRAIT
DIURETIC
DOMESTIC
DOVETAIL
DYSLEXIA
ECLIPTIC
ECONOMIC
ELECTRIC
ELLIPSIS
EMPHASIS
EMPHATIC
ENURESIS
EPIDEMIC
ESOTERIC
EUPHORIA
EXEGESIS
EXPLICIT
FANTASIA
FELLATIO
FIBROSIS
FLAGSHIP
FORENSIC
FORESAIL
FORESKIN
FOUNTAIN
FRENETIC
GARDENIA
GEODESIC
GIGANTIC
GLOBULIN
GLOXINIA
GLYCERIN
GOATSKIN
HANDRAIL
HANGNAIL
HARDSHIP
HARMONIC
HAUTBOIS
HEADSHIP
HELICOID
HERALDIC
HERMETIC
HIGHTAIL
HISPANIC
HOLSTEIN
HUMANOID
HYPNOSIS
HYPNOTIC
HYSTERIA
ILLINOIS
IMPLICIT
INFRADIG
INSIGNIA
INSOMNIA
INSPIRIT
INTAGLIO
INTERMIT
INTERMIX
INTREPID
INTROMIT
IROQUOIS
ISOTONIC
JALOUSIE
JURISTIC
LADYSHIP
LAMBSKIN
LECITHIN
LEUKEMIA
LINCHPIN
LINGERIE
LONGHAIR
LORDSHIP
LYMPHOID
MAGNESIA
MAGNETIC
MAGNOLIA
MAINSAIL
MAINTAIN
MANDARIN
MANDOLIN
MECHANIC
MEDICAID
MEPHITIC
MERCURIC
METEORIC
MILKMAID
MNEMONIC
MOCCASIN
MOLESKIN
MONASTIC
MONORAIL
MOUNTAIN
MYELITIS
NARCOSIS
NARCOTIC

NECROSIS
NEURITIS
NEUROSIS
NEUROTIC
NIGEROIS
NONRIGID
ORATORIO
OUTSTRIP
OVERLAID
PANDEMIC
PANTSUIT
PARAFFIN
PARANOIA
PATHETIC
PEIGNOIR
PELLUCID
PERIODIC
PHENOLIC
PIZZERIA
PLANTAIN
PLAYSUIT
PONYTAIL
PORTRAIT
POSTPAID
PRESIDIO
PRETERIT
PROCLAIM
PROHIBIT
PROLIFIC
QUATRAIN
QUIXOTIC
REPUBLIC
RESTRAIN
RETROFIT
RHETORIC
RHOMBOID
ROMANTIC
SANSKRIT
SARDONIC
SCENARIO
SEALSKIN
SEMANTIC
SERAGLIO
SOLENOID
SOUVENIR
SPECIFIC
SPHEROID
SPLENDID
SPORADIC
SUBSONIC
SUBURBIA
SULFURIC
SUZERAIN
SYMBOLIC
SYNOPSIS
SYNOPTIC
SYPHILIS

SYSADMIN
SYSTEMIC
TAFFRAIL
TAILSPIN
TERRAPIN
TERRIFIC
TEUTONIC
TOWNSHIP
TRANQUIL
TRANSFIX
TRANSMIT
TRIUMVIR
TURMERIC
TURNSPIT
UNDERBID
UNDERLIE
UNDERLIP
VACCINIA
VERBATIM
VICTORIA
VOLCANIC
WARDSHIP
WARFARIN
WHODUNIT
WIREHAIR
WISTARIA
WISTERIA
ZEPPELIN
MAHARAJA
ARCHDUKE
BABUSHKA
BARRACKS
CLAMBAKE
GASWORKS
KEEPSAKE
KOLINSKY
LADYLIKE
MANDRAKE
MINIBIKE
NAMESAKE
OVERTAKE
STOTINKA
SUCHLIKE
SUKIYAKI
SWASTIKA
TURNPIKE
UPSTROKE
ABUTTALS
ADORABLE
AIRFIELD
AMENABLE
AMICABLE
ARGUABLE
ASSEMBLE
ASSEMBLY
BAILABLE
BANKROLL

BARNACLE
BASEBALL
BEANBALL
BEDAZZLE
BEFUDDLE
BEGGARLY
BELITTLE
BIDDABLE
BIFOCALS
BILLFOLD
BINNACLE
BIWEEKLY
BIYEARLY
BLUEBELL
BORDELLO
BROCCOLI
BUNGHOLE
CAKEWALK
CAMISOLE
CAMOMILE
CANAILLE
CANTICLE
CAPRIOLE
CARACOLE
CARRYALL
CATAPULT
CATCHALL
CAUDILLO
CHASUBLE
CHENILLE
CLAVICLE
COVERALL
CREDIBLE
CRUCIBLE
CULPABLE
DAMNABLE
DEMIBOLD
DIASTOLE
DISCIPLE
DOMICILE
DOWNFALL
DOWNHILL
DUCKBILL
DUMBBELL
DUNGHILL
DUTIABLE
EDUCABLE
EGGSHELL
ELIGIBLE
EMBATTLE
EMBEZZLE
ENCIRCLE
ENFEEBLE
ENSEMBLE
ENTANGLE
ENTHRALL
ENTRAILS

ENVIABLE
ERECTILE
ESCAROLE
FALLIBLE
FAREWELL
FASCICLE
FEASIBLE
FIREBALL
FLAGPOLE
FLEXIBLE
FLOTILLA
FOLLICLE
FOOTBALL
FOOTFALL
FOOTHILL
FOOTHOLD
FORCIBLE
FORETELL
FORMERLY
FOURFOLD
FREEHOLD
FREEWILL
FUMAROLE
GARGOYLE
GENITALS
GINGERLY
GODCHILD
GOODWILL
GOOFBALL
HANDBALL
HANDBILL
HARDBALL
HAREBELL
HELLHOLE
HIGHBALL
HORRIBLE
HORSEFLY
HOUSEFLY
IMBECILE
IMITABLE
IMMOBILE
IMMOTILE
INVEIGLE
INVIABLE
INWARDLY
JUVENILE
KILOVOLT
KINGBOLT
KNEEHOLE
KNOTHOLE
LANDFALL
LANDFILL
LIMEKILN
LOOPHOLE
MANCIPLE
MANDIBLE
MANIFOLD

MANNERLY
MANTILLA
MANYFOLD
MARIGOLD
MASTERLY
MAYAPPLE
MEATBALL
METAFILE
MISAPPLY
MISCIBLE
MISSPELL
MOLECULE
MOLEHILL
MONOPOLY
MOTHBALL
MOTOROLA
MULTIPLE
MULTIPLY
MUSICALE
NUMSKULL
NUTSHELL
OBSTACLE
OPERABLE
OPUSCULE
OUTFIELD
OVERALLS
OVERKILL
OVERRULE
PALPABLE
PANATELA
PARABOLA
PARTIBLE
PARTICLE
PASSABLE
PASTILLE
PEDUNCLE
PEEPHOLE
PINNACLE
PINOCHLE
PITIABLE
PLAYBILL
PORTABLE
PORTHOLE
POSSIBLE
POSTHOLE
POTBELLY
PRATFALL
PREAMBLE
PROBABLE
PUFFBALL
QUOTABLE
RAINFALL
RELIABLE
RESEMBLE
REVEILLE
RIDICULE
ROCKFALL

SCAFFOLD
SCALABLE
SCARCELY
SCHEDULE
SCRABBLE
SCRAGGLY
SCRAMBLE
SCRIBBLE
SCROFULA
SEMINOLE
SENSIBLE
SIDEWALK
SIDEWALL
SINKHOLE
SLOVENLY
SNOWBALL
SNOWFALL
SOCIABLE
SOFTBALL
SPITBALL
SPRINKLE
SQUABBLE
STRADDLE
STRAGGLE
STRANGLE
STRUGGLE
SUBTITLE
SUITABLE
SYLLABLE
TANGIBLE
TELEFILM
TELLTALE
TENTACLE
TERRIBLE
TESTICLE
THROTTLE
TORTILLA
TRIANGLE
TRICYCLE
TUBERCLE
UMBRELLA
UNBUCKLE
UNCOUPLE
UNGAINLY
UNICYCLE
UNKINDLY
UNLIKELY
UNLOVELY
UNMUZZLE
UNRIDDLE
UNSADDLE
UNSEEMLY
UNSETTLE
UNSTABLE
UNTANGLE
UNTIMELY
VALUABLE

VARIABLE
VERSICLE
VINCIBLE
VIOLABLE
VISICALC
VOLATILE
WASHABLE
WEREWOLF
WHITEFLY
WINDFALL
WINDMILL
WITHHOLD
WOODPILE
WORKABLE
WORMHOLE
YOURSELF
AGRONOMY
AIRDROME
AIRFRAME
ANATHEMA
ANTINOMY
BIRDLIME
CATACOMB
CHARISMA
CONSOMME
DARKSOME
DOLDRUMS
DOORJAMB
ERYTHEMA
FEARSOME
FIREBOMB
FIREDAMP
FORELIMB
FORENAME
FOURSOME
GAMESOME
GENDARME
GLADSOME
GLAUCOMA
GRUESOME
HANDSOME
HECATOMB
LIFETIME
LOBOTOMY
LONESOME
LONGTIME
MACHISMO
MARITIME
MEALTIME
MEANTIME
MELANOMA
MILESIMO
MILLIEME
MONOGAMY
MORPHEME
NICKNAME
NOONTIME

OVERCOME
OVERTIME
PANORAMA
PASTRAMI
POLYGAMY
RIBOSOME
SEEDTIME
SELFSAME
SOMETIME
SYNDROME
TAXONOMY
TIRESOME
ABORNING
ABUNDANT
ABUTMENT
ACCIDENT
ACQUAINT
ACRIMONY
ADJACENT
ADJUTANT
ADJUVANT
AFFERENT
AIRBORNE
AIRPLANE
ALIASING
AMBULANT
ANTIMONY
ANYTHING
APPARENT
AQUILINE
ARGUMENT
ARMAMENT
ARROGANT
ASPIRANT
ASTATINE
ATROPINE
AVERMENT
BACKBONE
BACKHAND
BANDANNA
BANTLING
BARITONE
BASELINE
BASEMENT
BECHUANA
BECOMING
BEFRIEND
BLACKING
BLESSING
BOBOLINK
BOUFFANT
BREEDING
BRISLING
BUILDING
BUNDLING
CABSTAND
CAFFEINE

CAGELING
CALAMINE
CAROTENE
CASEMENT
CATCHING
CEREMENT
CEREMONY
CHARMING
CHEYENNE
CHIPMUNK
CHLORINE
CICERONE
CINCHONA
CLAIMANT
CLEARING
CLIPPING
CLOTHING
COHERENT
COMPOUND
CONFOUND
CONFRONT
CONSTANT
COUCHANT
COUPLING
COVENANT
CREEPING
CREMAINS
CRESCENT
CRETONNE
CROPLAND
CROSSING
CYTOSINE
DAIRYING
DARKLING
DATELINE
DEADLINE
DECEDENT
DECKHAND
DEPONENT
DETHRONE
DILIGENT
DISCOUNT
DISJOINT
DISMOUNT
DIVIDEND
DOCKHAND
DOCTRINE
DOCUMENT
DOWNWIND
DRESSING
DUCKLING
DUMPLING
DWELLING
EARPHONE
EFFERENT
EGGPLANT
ELEPHANT
ELOQUENT
ENGAGING
ENSHRINE
ENTHRONE
ENVIRONS
EPIPHANY
EUROBOND
EVENSONG
EVERYONE
EXACTING
EXPONENT
FAGOTING
FARMHAND
FARMLAND
FARTHING
FEMININE
FETCHING
FIGURINE
FILAMENT
FILIPINO
FLAGRANT
FLASHING
FLATLAND
FLEABANE
FLEETING
FLIPPANT
FLUORINE
FOOTLING
FOREFEND
FOREGONE
FOREHAND
FORELAND
FOXHOUND
FRAGMENT
FRAGRANT
FRÉEHAND
FREQUENT
FROSTING
FUMIGANT
GANGLAND
GANGLING
GANGRENE
GASOLINE
GEMSTONE
GLOAMING
GOURMAND
GRADIENT
GRASPING
GRAYLING
GREEKING
GREETING
GRUELING
GUNPOINT
GYMKHANA
HABITANT
HAIRLINE
HALFTONE
HATCHING
HEADBAND
HEADLAND
HEADLINE
HEADLONG
HEGEMONY
HESITANT
HIGHLAND
HIRELING
HOARDING
HOMELAND
HOODWINK
ICEBOUND
IGNORANT
ILLUMINE
IMMANENT
IMMINENT
IMPOSING
IMPOTENT
IMPUDENT
INCIDENT
INCOMING
INDECENT
INDIGENT
INDOLENT
INERRANT
INHALANT
INHERENT
INHUMANE
INKSTAND
INNOCENT
INSOLENT
INVITING
ISOPRENE
JUBILANT
JUDGMENT
KAMAAINA
KATAKANA
KEROSINE
KEYSTONE
KINDLING
LACEWING
LAYERING
LEARNING
LIFELINE
LIFELONG
LIGAMENT
LINIMENT
LITIGANT
LIVELONG
LOATHING
LODGMENT
LONGHAND
MACARONI
MACPAINT
MAGAZINE
MAHARANI
MAHOGANY
MAINLAND
MAINLINE
MARBLING
MEDICINE
MEMBRANE
MERCHANT
MIDDLING
MIDPOINT
MIGRAINE
MILITANT
MILLPOND
MISBRAND
MISCOUNT
MISDOING
MISPRINT
MISSPEND
MONOTONE
MONUMENT
MOORLAND
MORIBUND
MORPHINE
MOUNTING
MOURNING
MOVEMENT
NECKLINE
NESTLING
NEUTRINO
NEWFOUND
NICOTINE
NIGGLING
NINEPINS
NOCTURNE
NONEVENT
NURSLING
NUTRIENT
OBEDIENT
OCCUPANT
OFFPRINT
OINTMENT
ONCOMING
OPPONENT
ORNAMENT
OUTBOUND
OUTFLANK
OUTGOING
OUTLYING
OUTPOINT
OUTSHINE
OUTSPEND
OVERHAND
OVERHANG
OVERLAND
OVERTONE
PAINTING
PALATINE
PALOMINO
PANELING
PAVEMENT
PEDIMENT
PENCHANT
PENITENT
PERILUNE
PETULANT
PHEASANT
PHRASING
PICAYUNE
PIDDLING
PIEPLANT
PINPOINT
PIPELINE
PLANGENT
PLANKING
PLEASANT
PLEASING
PLUMBING
POIGNANT
POSTPONE
PREGNANT
PRESSING
PRINTING
PRISTINE
PROCAINE
PROFOUND
PROPOUND
PRURIENT
PTOMAINE
PUDDLING
PURBLIND
PURSLANE
PURULENT
QUADRANT
QUISLING
QUOTIENT
RATTLING
RAVENING
REACTANT
RECREANT
REDOLENT
REFERENT
REGIMENT
RELAXANT
RELEVANT
RESIDENT
RESONANT
RETICENT
RETIRING
REVEREND
REVERENT
RUBICUND
RUDIMENT
RUMBLING
RUMINANT
SANDBANK
SANGUINE
SAUTERNE
SCATHING
SCRUTINY
SEAGOING
SEAMOUNT
SEAPLANE
SEDIMENT
SEEDLING
SENTIENT
SERGEANT
SHANTUNG
SHEETING
SHELVING
SHILLING
SHINBONE
SHIPMENT
SHIPPING
SHIRRING
SHIRTING
SHOCKING
SHOSHONE
SIBILANT
SIDELONG
SILICONE
SKIMMING
SNOWBANK
SONATINA
SPANKING
SPOOLING
STAGNANT
STANDING
STARLING
STERLING
STIRRING
STOCKING
STRIDENT
STRIKING
STUDDING
STUFFING
STUNNING
SUBPOENA
SUCKLING
SUNSHINE
SUPPLANT
SURMOUNT
SURROUND
SWEEPING
SWELLING
SWIMMING
SYMPHONY
TAMARIND
TEACHING
TEETHING
TENEMENT
TENPENNY
THIAMINE
THOUSAND
TIDELAND
TOUCHING
TOWELING
TOWERING
TRAINING
TRAPPING
TRICHINA
TRIFLING
TRIMMING
TROMBONE
TWOPENNY
UNDULANT
UNENDING
UNERRING
UNSPRUNG
UNSTRUNG
UPCOMING
UPRISING
VAGABOND
VAPORING
VAULTING
VEHEMENT
VESICANT
VESTMENT
VIETCONG
VIGILANT
VILLAINY
VIRULENT
VISCOUNT
VISITANT
VOLPLANE
WARPLANE
WEAKLING
WELDMENT
WHOPPING
WINGDING
WISHBONE
WITCHING
WOODBINE
WOODLAND
WOODWIND
WRAPPING
YACHTING
YEARLING
YEARLONG
YEARNING
YIELDING
ZUCCHINI
ABLATION
ABLUTION
ABORTION
ACCUSTOM
ADDITION
ADHESION
AGITPROP
AMBITION
ANCESTOR
ANGSTROM
ANTERIOR
ANTEROOM
APHELION
ASBESTOS
AUDITION
AVERSION
AVIATION
BACHELOR
BACKDROP
BACKSTOP
BAKESHOP
BALLROOM
BALLYHOO
BANKBOOK
BAREFOOT
BASSWOOD
BATHROOM
BEHAVIOR
BENTWOOD
BETATRON
BIATHLON
BLACKTOP
BLUDGEON
BOUILLON
BUCKSHOT
BULLFROG
BUNGALOW
CABOCHON
CARDAMOM
CARILLON
CAULDRON
CESSPOOL
CHAMPION
CHAPBOOK
CHAPERON
CHOIRBOY
CHOWCHOW
CINNAMON
CITATION
CLUBFOOT
COAUTHOR
COCKATOO
COCKCROW
COHESION
COLOPHON
COOKBOOK
COPYBOOK
CORDUROY
CORRIDOR
CRACKPOT
CREATION
CREDITOR
CROSSBOW
CROWFOOT
CUSPIDOR

DARKROOM
DEADWOOD
DECISION
DELUSION
DEMEANOR
DEVOTION
DIAPASON
DICTATOR
DIRECTOR
DISALLOW
DISCOLOR
DISFAVOR
DISHONOR
DIVISION
DOMINION
DONATION
DOORKNOB
DOUBLOON
DOUGHBOY
DURATION
EFFUSION
ELECTION
ELECTRON
ELEVATOR
EMBLAZON
EMOTICON
EMULSION
ENDEAVOR
EQUATION
ERECTION
ESCALLOP
EXECUTOR
EXTERIOR
EXTRADOS
FALCHION
FIREWOOD
FISHHOOK
FIXATION
FLATFOOT
FLATIRON
FLESHPOT
FOLDEROL
FOREDOOM
FOREFOOT
FOREKNOW
FORENOON
FRACTION
FRICTION
FROUFROU
FRUITION
FUNCTION
FURBELOW
GANGLION
GANGPLOW
GARRISON
GLYCEROL
GONFALON

GOVERNOR
GRANDSON
GRIDIRON
GUMPTION
HANDBOOK
HARDWOOD
HEADROOM
HEDGEHOG
HEDGEHOP
HEDGEROW
HEIRLOOM
HEREUPON
HIGHBROW
HOMEROOM
HOOSEGOW
HORNBOOK
HOUSEBOY
HOUSETOP
HUGUENOT
IDEATION
IGNITION
ILLUSION
IMPOSTOR
IMPRISON
INCISION
INFERIOR
INTERCOM
INTERIOR
INTERROG
INTRADOS
INVASION
IRONWOOD
JACKBOOT
JETTISON
JUNCTION
KANGAROO
LEAPFROG
LEGATION
LIBATION
LOCATION
LOCUTION
LOLLIPOP
LUNCHEON
MACAROON
MARATHON
MASTODON
MELODEON
METAPHOR
METHANOL
MONITION
MUNITION
MUSHROOM
MUTATION
MYRMIDON
NAINSOOK
NAPOLEON
NEGATION

NEIGHBOR
NONUNION
NOTATION
NOTEBOOK
OBLATION
OBLIVION
OCCASION
OFFSHOOT
ORTHODOX
OVERFLOW
OVERGROW
OVERLOOK
OVERSHOE
PANTHEON
PASSBOOK
PAVILION
PAWNSHOP
PENTAGON
PETITION
PETTIFOG
PHOSPHOR
PLANKTON
PLAYBOOK
POLLIWOG
POLTROON
POLYGLOT
POSITION
POSITRON
POTATION
PROTOCOL
PULMOTOR
PULPWOOD
PUNCHEON
QUADROON
QUESTION
RADIATOR
RAINDROP
REACTION
RECEPTOR
RELATION
RELIGION
RESISTOR
ROSEWOOD
SANCTION
SCALLION
SCORPION
SCULLION
SCULPTOR
SEDITION
SERVITOR
SIDESHOW
SKELETON
SLIPKNOT
SLIPSHOD
SMALLPOX
SNAPSHOT
SNOWDROP

SNOWPLOW
SNOWSHOE
SOFTWOOD
SOLUTION
SORPTION
SPITTOON
SPLENDOR
SQUADRON
STALLION
STUDBOOK
STURGEON
SUPERIOR
TARRAGON
TEASPOON
TELETHON
TESTATOR
TEXTBOOK
THEREFOR
TOMORROW
TOREADOR
TRACTION
TRAPDOOR
TRICOLOR
TRILLION
ULTERIOR
UNBUTTON
UNCOMMON
UNDERDOG
UNDERTOW
UNPERSON
VACATION
VARISTOR
VENATION
VEXATION
VOCATION
VOLITION
WAINSCOT
WARDROOM
WAREROOM
WASHROOM
WATCHDOG
WATERLOO
WILDWOOD
WINESHOP
WORDBOOK
WORKBOOK
WORKROOM
WORKSHOP
WORMWOOD
YEARBOOK
ANTELOPE
ANTHROPO
ANTIPOPE
BANKRUPT
BLOWPIPE
CALLIOPE
CENOTAPH

CONTEMPT
ENVELOPE
HORNPIPE
LOGOTYPE
MIDSHIPS
MISSHAPE
ORTHOEPY
RESCRIPT
SEASCAPE
TRANSEPT
TRUETYPE
WINDPIPE
AARDVARK
ACCOUTRE
ADULTERY
ADVISORY
ALBACORE
ALEATORY
ALLEGORY
ANCESTRY
ANYWHERE
APERTURE
ARMATURE
ARMYWORM
ARTISTRY
AUDITORY
AUTOGIRO
BACKFIRE
BACKWARD
BARBERRY
BARNYARD
BARRATRY
BASEBORN
BAYBERRY
BERIBERI
BESTIARY
BLIZZARD
BLOOMERS
BLUEBIRD
BODYWORK
BOLLWORM
BOOKMARK
BOOKWORM
BOUNDARY
BRAGGART
BREVIARY
BROCHURE
BURGLARY
BUSYWORK
CAREWORN
CASEWORK
CASHMERE
CATEGORY
CEMETERY
CHANCERY
CHECKERS
CHIVALRY

CINCTURE
CLAYMORE
COCKSURE
COIFFURE
COLLIERY
CONFRERE
CONSPIRE
CONTRARY
CORONARY
CREAMERY
CREATURE
CROCKERY
CRUZEIRO
CULINARY
CUPBOARD
CYNOSURE
DAIQUIRI
DELAWARE
DELIVERY
DENATURE
DERRIERE
DEWBERRY
DILATORY
DOCKYARD
DOORYARD
DOWNTURN
DOWNWARD
DRUNKARD
EMISSARY
EVERMORE
EXPOSURE
FARMYARD
FAUBOURG
FEBRUARY
FIREWORK
FIRMWARE
FLATTERY
FLATWARE
FOLKLORE
FOOTSORE
FOOTWORK
FOREPART
FORESTRY
FOREWARN
FOREWORD
FRACTURE
FREEBORN
FRETWORK
FRIPPERY
FUNERARY
GEOMETRY
GLOSSARY
GLOWWORM
GOATHERD
GREENERY
HABANERA
HACKWORD

HALLMARK
HARDWARE
HAWTHORN
HEADWORD
HEADWORK
HELIPORT
HERALDRY
HEREFORD
HIGHBORN
HOMEWARD
HOMEWORK
HONORARY
HOOKWORM
HOSTELRY
IDOLATRY
ILLUSORY
IMMATURE
INCHWORM
INDUSTRY
INEXPERT
INFANTRY
INSECURE
IRONWARE
IRONWORK
ISOTHERM
JACQUARD
JAILBIRD
JUNCTURE
KEYBOARD
KNICKERS
LADYBIRD
LAMASERY
LANDFORM
LANDLORD
LANDMARK
LANDWARD
LAPBOARD
LAPIDARY
LARBOARD
LAVATORY
LIFEWORK
LIGATURE
LITERARY
LOANWORD
LONGHORN
LOVEBIRD
LOVELORN
LUKEWARM
LUMINARY
MALAPERT
MANICURE
MASSACRE
MEDICARE
MEDIOCRE
MESHWORK
MILITARY
MILLIARD

MINATORY
MINISTRY
MISCARRY
MOISTURE
MONETARY
MONITORY
MORTUARY
MUDGUARD
MULBERRY
MUSKETRY
NONDAIRY
NUGATORY
OBITUARY
OFFSHORE
OPENWORK
ORANGERY
ORDINARY
OUTBOARD
OUTDOORS
OUTSMART
OVENBIRD
OVERLORD
OVERTURE
OVERTURN
PARTERRE
PASSPORT
PASSWORD
PEDICURE
PELLAGRA
PENUMBRA
PERSPIRE
PILCHARD
PINAFORE
PLATFORM
PLEASURE
PLETHORA
POCKMARK
PODIATRY
PORPHYRY
PORTIERE
POSTCARD
POSTMARK
POTSHERD
PREMIERE
PRESSURE
PUNCTURE
PUSHCART
QUAGMIRE
QUANDARY
RAILLERY
REARWARD
REASSURE
REFINERY
REGISTRY
RINGWORM
ROADWORK
ROCKETRY

ROSEMARY
SAGAMORE
SALUTARY
SANITARY
SAPPHIRE
SCABBARD
SCISSORS
SCULLERY
SEABOARD
SEASHORE
SEMINARY
SHEPHERD
SHIPWORM
SHIPYARD
SHOPWORN
SINECURE
SLATTERN
SLIPPERY
SLUGGARD
SLUMLORD
SNOBBERY
SOFTWARE
SOLDIERY
SOLITARY
SOMBRERO
SONGBIRD
SPANIARD
STALWART
STANDARD
STATUARY
STUBBORN
SUREFIRE
SYCAMORE
SYMMETRY
TACITURN
TAPESTRY
TAPEWORM
TEAMWORK
TENANTRY
TERTIARY
THIEVERY
TIMEWORN
TINCTURE
TOILETRY
TOILWORN
TREASURE
TREASURY
TRICKERY
TROUSERS
TRUMPERY
TUTELARY
TWEEZERS
UNDERARM
UNSAVORY
UNTOWARD
UPSTAIRS
VANGUARD
VERTEBRA
VINEGARY
VINEYARD
WEAPONRY
WELLBORN
WHIPCORD
WILDFIRE
WINDBURN
WINDWARD
WIREWORM
WISEACRE
WITCHERY
WIZARDRY
WOODWORK
YEOMANRY
ZOOSPORE
ABSCISSA
ABSTRUSE
ACTINISM
ACTIVISM
ADMONISH
AIRBRUSH
ALARMIST
ALEHOUSE
ALIENIST
ALTRUISM
AMETHYST
APHORISM
APOSTASY
APPLAUSE
APPRAISE
ARBALEST
ASTERISK
ASTONISH
BACKLASH
BACKREST
BACKWASH
BARONESS
BASELESS
BASILISK
BERCEUSE
BLUEFISH
BLUENOSE
BODILESS
BOOKCASE
BOOTLESS
BOTULISM
BRACKISH
BRANDISH
BUDDHISM
BURNOOSE
BUSINESS
BUTTRESS
CALABASH
CARELESS
CENTRIST
CERAMIST
CHASTISE
COLLAPSE
COLONIST
COMPRESS
COMPRISE
CONDENSE
CONGRESS
CONQUEST
CONTRAST
CONVERSE
CONVULSE
COPYDESK
CORDLESS
COUNTESS
COURTESY
CRAWFISH
CRAYFISH
CREVASSE
DANSEUSE
DATABASE
DATELESS
DECREASE
DEFOREST
DEMOLISH
DEVILISH
DEXTROSE
DIMINISH
DISABUSE
DISBURSE
DISCLOSE
DISGUISE
DISPENSE
DISPERSE
DISTRESS
DISTRUST
DOGHOUSE
DORMOUSE
DOWNCAST
DRUGGIST
EMBOLISM
EPILEPSY
ESCAPISM
ESPRESSO
EXERCISE
EXORCISE
EYEGLASS
FADELESS
FARTHEST
FASTNESS
FATALISM
FEARLESS
FECKLESS
FEMINISM
FINALIST
FLATFISH
FLAUTIST
FLOURISH
FOOTLESS
FOOTREST
FORECAST
FOREMAST
FOREMOST
FORMLESS
FORTRESS
FURTHEST
FUTURISM
GATEPOST
GOALPOST
GOLDFISH
GOODNESS
GUYANESE
HEADREST
HEBRAISM
HEDONISM
HIGHNESS
HINDMOST
HINDUISM
HOLINESS
HOTHOUSE
HUMANISM
HUNTRESS
ICEHOUSE
IDEALISM
IMMODEST
INCREASE
INTEREST
ISOSTASY
JAPANESE
JINGOISM
KIELBASA
LACROSSE
LANDMASS
LANGUISH
LEGALISM
LIKENESS
LIKEWISE
LINGUIST
LISTLESS
LIVERISH
LOYALIST
MADHOUSE
MAINMAST
MANIFEST
MANTISSA
MARQUESS
MARQUISE
MASSEUSE
MASSLESS
MATTRESS
MEDALIST
MELANISM
MILEPOST
MINDLESS
MISHMASH
MISTRESS
MISTRUST
MONGOOSE
MORALIST
NAMELESS
NATIVISM
NEEDLESS
NEOPLASM
NEPOTISM
NEWSCAST
NIHILISM
NOBELIST
NONSENSE
OPTIMISM
ORGANISM
ORGANIST
OUTBURST
OUTCLASS
OUTGUESS
OUTHOUSE
OVERCAST
OVERPASS
PACIFISM
PANELIST
PARADISE
PAROXYSM
PEDERAST
PEERLESS
PERVERSE
PHANTASM
PHANTASY
PITILESS
PLEURISY
POPULIST
PORPOISE
PREEXIST
PREPRESS
PRETENSE
PRIMROSE
PRINCESS
PROGRESS
PROPHESY
PUGILISM
PURCHASE
QUALMISH
RECKLESS
RECOURSE
REFOREST
REHEARSE
RESPONSE
RESTLESS
ROSEBUSH
ROYALIST
RUTHLESS
SAILFISH
SAWHORSE
SCOTTISH
SEACOAST
SELFLESS
SHEEPISH
SHOWCASE
SHREWISH
SICKNESS
SIGNPOST
SKIRMISH
SKITTISH
SLUGGISH
SOLECISM
SPYGLASS
STARFISH
SUBMERSE
SUITCASE
SUPPRESS
SURCEASE
SURPRISE
SUSPENSE
TELECAST
TELEVISE
TICKLISH
TIMELESS
TIRELESS
TITMOUSE
TOKENISM
TORTOISE
TRAVERSE
TREATISE
TRESPASS
TUBEROSE
TUNELESS
TYPECAST
UNIONISM
UNIVERSE
UPTHRUST
VANQUISH
VAPORISH
VARICOSE
VEGANISM
VIRTUOSO
VOCALIST
WAITRESS
WEAKFISH
WEAKNESS
WHIPLASH
WINDLASS
WIRELESS
WOMANISH
YOUNGISH
ABDICATE
ABNEGATE
ABROGATE
ABSOLUTE
ACCURATE
ACERBATE
ACERBITY
ACTIVATE
ACTIVITY
ADEQUATE
ADVOCATE
AESTHETE
AFFINITY
AIGRETTE
ALACRITY
ALIENATE
ALLOCATE
ALMIGHTY
AMARANTH
AMPUTATE
ANECDOTE
ANISETTE
ANNOTATE
ANTEDATE
ANTIDOTE
APHANITE
APPETITE
APPOSITE
ARROGATE
ASPERITY
ASPIRATE
ATROCITY
AUTOMATE
BACKBITE
BAGUETTE
BARRETTE
BEHEMOTH
BENZOATE
BEQUEATH
BIRDBATH
BOBWHITE
CALAMITY
CAPACITY
CASSETTE
CASTRATE
CASUALTY
CELERITY
CELIBATE
CENOBITE
CHASTITY
CHLORITE
CIRCUITY
CIVILITY
COGITATE
COMPLETE
CONCERTO
CONCRETE
CONFETTI
CONTRITE
COPULATE
COQUETTE
CORVETTE
CREOSOTE
CRYOLITE
CUPIDITY
DEBILITY
DECIMATE
DECORATE
DEDICATE
DEFECATE
DEFINITE
DELEGATE
DELICATE
DEROGATE
DESOLATE
DETONATE
DINGBATS
DISCRETE
DISKETTE
DISTASTE
DISUNITE
DISUNITY
DIVAGATE
DIVINITY
DOLOMITE
DOMINATE
DRAUGHTS
DYNAMITE
ELONGATE
EMACIATE
EMIGRATE
ENCEINTE
ENERVATE
ENORMITY
ENTIRETY
ESCALATE
ESTIMATE
ETERNITY
EVACUATE
EVALUATE
EXCAVATE
EXECRATE
EXPEDITE
EYETOOTH
FACILITY
FALSETTO
FASCISTA
FATALITY
FAVORITE
FEDERATE
FELICITY
FEROCITY
FIDELITY
FILTRATE
FLEABITE
FLUORITE
FOOTNOTE
FOOTPATH
FORSOOTH
FORTUITY
FUMIGATE

FUTILITY
FUTURITY
GEMINATE
GENERATE
GIGABYTE
GLACIATE
GRADUATE
GRAFFITO
GRAPHITE
GRATUITY
GUARANTY
GUNSMITH
HELPMATE
HEMATITE
HEREDITY
HEREUNTO
HEREWITH
HESITATE
HITHERTO
HUMANITY
HUMIDITY
HUMILITY
HYACINTH
IDENTITY
IMMOLATE
IMPOLITE
IMPUNITY
INCHOATE
INCUBATE
INDICATE
INDURATE
INFINITE
INFINITY
INIQUITY
INITIATE
INNOVATE
INSULATE
INTIMATE
INUNDATE
INVOLUTE
IRRIGATE
IRRITATE
KILOBYTE
KILOWATT
LACERATE
LAMBASTE
LAUREATE
LEVITATE
LIBERATE
LIBRETTO
LIMONITE
LITERATE
LITERATI
LITIGATE
LOCALITY
MACERATE
MAJORITY
MALAMUTE
MARINATE
MATURATE
MATURITY
MEDICATE
MEDITATE
MEGABYTE
MEGALITH
MESQUITE
MESSMATE
MILITATE
MINORITY
MISQUOTE
MISSTATE
MITIGATE
MODERATE
MODULATE
MONOLITH
MORALITY
MOSQUITO
MOTIVATE
MUTILATE
NATALITY
NATIVITY
NAUSEATE
NAVIGATE
NEOPHYTE
NOBILITY
NOMINATE
NUCLEATE
NUMERATE
OBDURATE
OBLIGATE
OBSOLETE
OILCLOTH
OPERETTA
OPPOSITE
ORDINATE
OSCULATE
PAGINATE
PALLIATE
PALMETTO
PARASITE
PECULATE
PERFECTO
PERMEATE
PIMIENTO
PIXELATE
PLACENTA
PLAYMATE
POLARITY
POLYMATH
POPULATE
POSTDATE
PROPERTY
PROSTATE
QUANTITY
RECREATE
REGOLITH
REGULATE
RELEGATE
RELOCATE
RENOVATE
RESOLUTE
RESONATE
RHYOLITE
ROOMETTE
ROOMMATE
ROULETTE
RUMINATE
RUNAGATE
SACRISTY
SALIVATE
SANCTITY
SATURATE
SCHMALTZ
SECURITY
SELENITE
SEPARATE
SHIPMATE
SIDERITE
SILICATE
SIMULATE
SOBRIETY
SORORITY
STACCATO
STAGNATE
STILETTO
STRENGTH
SYBARITE
TABULATE
TAILGATE
TEMERITY
TEMPLATE
TEOSINTE
TINPLATE
TINSMITH
TITILATE
TITIVATE
TOILETTE
TOLERATE
TOLLBOTH
TOLLGATE
TONALITY
TOTALITY
TRACTATE
TRAVESTY
TRUNCATE
ULCERATE
ULTIMATE
UNCHASTE
UNDULATE
UNGULATE
UPGROWTH
URBANITE
VALIDATE
VEGETATE
VELLEITY
VELOCITY
VENDETTA
VENERATE
VERACITY
VERMOUTH
VICINITY
VIGNETTE
VITALITY
VIVACITY
WARRANTY
WOODNOTE
XENOLITH
ZOOPHYTE
ACANTHUS
ACTINIUM
ADDENDUM
AERONAUT
AFFLATUS
AGERATUM
ALLUVIUM
ALUMINUM
AMMONIUM
ANALOGUE
APPLIQUE
AQUANAUT
AQUARIUM
BACILLUS
BARBECUE
BEECHNUT
BIBULOUS
BIENNIUM
BLACKOUT
BLISSFUL
BOASTFUL
BOUTIQUE
BREAKOUT
BRONCHUS
BROWNOUT
CADUCEUS
CALADIUM
CALCULUS
CAPSICUM
CAPTIOUS
CAUTIOUS
CEMENTUM
CEREBRUM
CHECKOUT
CHECKSUM
CHEERFUL
CHESTNUT
CHROMIUM
CLOSEOUT
COAGULUM
COIFFEUR
COLISEUM
COLLOQUY
COLOSSUS
CONSTRUE
CONTINUE
CORUNDUM
CRITIQUE
CROSSCUT
CURLICUE
DECOROUS
DELIRIUM
DESIROUS
DETRITUS
DIALOGUE
DIANTHUS
DINOSAUR
DOUBTFUL
DOUGHNUT
DOWNPOUR
DREADFUL
DUODENUM
EMERITUS
EMPORIUM
ENCOMIUM
ENORMOUS
ENSHROUD
EPILOGUE
EUROPIUM
EXCURSUS
EXIGUOUS
EXORDIUM
FABULOUS
FACTIOUS
FACTOTUM
FANCIFUL
FINESPUN
FIREPLUG
FLAMEOUT
FLASHGUN
FRANCIUM
GADABOUT
GENEROUS
GERANIUM
GLABROUS
GLASSFUL
GLORIOUS
GORGEOUS
GRACIOUS
GRANDEUR
GRATEFUL
GRIEVOUS
HARANGUE
HIBISCUS
HOMESPUN
INFAMOUS
INTRIGUE
JONGLEUR
KEELHAUL
KNOCKOUT
LABURNUM
LARKSPUR
LAUDANUM
LIGNEOUS
LINOLEUM
LONGUEUR
LUMINOUS
LUSCIOUS
LUTETIUM
MANDAMUS
MEALYBUG
MENISCUS
MERINGUE
MICROBUS
MOMENTUM
MONSIEUR
MOURNFUL
MYSTIQUE
NAUTILUS
NEBULOUS
NOBELIUM
NUMEROUS
ORGULOUS
OVERHAUL
PARAMOUR
PENDULUM
PHASEOUT
PHYSIQUE
PLATINUM
PLATYPUS
PLECTRUM
POLONIUM
POPULOUS
PRATIQUE
PRECIOUS
PREVIOUS
PRINTOUT
PROLOGUE
PROROGUE
PUDENDUM
RAVENOUS
RESIDUUM
RIGHTFUL
RUBIDIUM
RUNABOUT
SABOTEUR
SAMARIUM
SCABROUS
SCANDIUM
SEDULOUS
SEIGNEUR
SELENIUM
SENSUOUS
SHORTCUT
SKILLFUL
SOLARIUM
SONOROUS
SPACIOUS
SPECIOUS
SPECTRUM
SPHAGNUM
SPURIOUS
STAKEOUT
STANDOUT
STIMULUS
STINKBUG
STUDIOUS
SYLLABUS
TANTALUM
TERMINUS
THALAMUS
THALLIUM
THANKFUL
THROMBUS
TIMOROUS
TITANIUM
TORTUOUS
TRILLIUM
TRUSTFUL
TRUTHFUL
TUBEROUS
TYMPANUM
UNCTUOUS
UNDERCUT
UNDERFUR
UNLAWFUL
UPPERCUT
USURIOUS
UXORIOUS
VANADIUM
VAPOROUS
VARIORUM
VENGEFUL
VENOMOUS
VIATICUM
VIBURNUM
VIGOROUS
VIRTUOUS
VITREOUS
VIVARIUM
VOYAGEUR
WATCHFUL
WONDROUS
WRATHFUL
WRONGFUL
YOUTHFUL
ABLATIVE
ABRASIVE
ADDITIVE
ADHESIVE
ADOPTIVE
AGGRIEVE
CONCEIVE
CONCLAVE
CONSERVE
CONTRIVE
CURATIVE
DECISIVE
DISPROVE
DISSOLVE
DIVISIVE
ELECTIVE
FIXATIVE
FOXGLOVE
FUGITIVE
GENITIVE
ILLUSIVE
INCISIVE
LADYLOVE
LAXATIVE
LENITIVE
MANGROVE
MARGRAVE
NEGATIVE
PERCEIVE
POSITIVE
PRESERVE
PUNITIVE
PUTATIVE
REACTIVE
RELATIVE
REPRIEVE
RETRIEVE
SEDATIVE
UNIVALVE
VOCATIVE
CHIPPEWA
COMEDOWN
DOWNTOWN
FACEDOWN
FISHBOWL
FLYBLOWN
MARKDOWN
PUSHDOWN
SHOWDOWN
SHUTDOWN
TOMAHAWK
WASHBOWL
WILDFOWL
APOPLEXY
EDGEWAYS
NOWADAYS
SIDEWAYS
AMORTIZE
BULLDOZE
CANALIZE
CANONIZE
CATALYZE

CIVILIZE
COLONIZE
CREDENZA
DEIONIZE
DEPUTIZE
ENERGIZE
EQUALIZE
FINALIZE
HUMANIZE
IDEALIZE
IMMUNIZE
KAMIKAZE
LOCALIZE
MAXIMIZE
MEMORIZE
MINIMIZE
MOBILIZE
MORALIZE
MOTORIZE
NASALIZE
NEBULIZE
NOTARIZE
NOVELIZE
ORGANIZE
OVERSIZE
PARALYZE
PENALIZE
POLARIZE
QUANTIZE
SANITIZE
SIMONIZE
THEORIZE
UNFREEZE
UNIONIZE
URBANIZE
VAPORIZE
VITALIZE
VOCALIZE

## 8th Letter

ABSCISSA
ALLELUIA
ALOPECIA
AMBROSIA
ANACONDA
ANATHEMA
ANGELICA
APOLOGIA
ASPHYXIA
BABUSHKA
BANDANNA
BASILICA
BECHUANA
BROUHAHA
CAMELLIA
CARNAUBA
CHARISMA
CHIPPEWA
CINCHONA
CREDENZA
DEMENTIA
DIARRHEA
DYSLEXIA
ERYTHEMA
EUPHORIA
FANTASIA
FASCISTA
FLOTILLA
GARDENIA
GLAUCOMA
GLOXINIA
GYMKHANA
HABANERA
HACIENDA
HEPATICA
HYSTERIA
INSIGNIA
INSOMNIA
KAMAAINA
KATAKANA
KIELBASA
LEUKEMIA
MAGNESIA
MAGNOLIA
MAHARAJA
MAJOLICA
MANTILLA
MANTISSA
MELANOMA
MOTOROLA
ONONDAGA
OPERETTA
PANATELA
PANORAMA
PARABOLA
PARANOIA
PELLAGRA
PENUMBRA
PIZZERIA
PLACENTA
PLETHORA
PYORRHEA
RUTABAGA
SCIATICA
SCROFULA
SONATINA
STOTINKA
SUBPOENA
SUBURBIA
SWASTIKA
TORTILLA
TRICHINA
UMBRELLA
UNDERSEA
VACCINIA
VENDETTA
VERONICA
VERTEBRA
VICTORIA
WISTARIA
WISTERIA
CATACOMB
CORNCRIB
DOORJAMB
DOORKNOB
FIREBOMB
FORELIMB
HECATOMB
ACADEMIC
ACOUSTIC
ACROSTIC
AGNOSTIC
ANECHOIC
ARTISTIC
ATHLETIC
BARBARIC
BEATIFIC
BROMIDIC
CATHOLIC
CEPHALIC
CHOLERIC
COSMETIC
DEMONIAC
DIABOLIC
DIATOMIC
DIDACTIC
DIURETIC
DOMESTIC
ECLIPTIC
ECONOMIC
ELECTRIC
EMPHATIC
EPIDEMIC
ESOTERIC
FORENSIC
FRENETIC
GEODESIC
GIGANTIC
HARMONIC
HERALDIC
HERMETIC
HISPANIC
HYPNOTIC
ISOTONIC
JURISTIC
MAGNETIC
MECHANIC
MEPHITIC
MERCURIC
METEORIC
MNEMONIC
MONASTIC
NARCOTIC
NEUROTIC
PANDEMIC
PATHETIC
PERIODIC
PHENOLIC
PROLIFIC
QUIXOTIC
REPUBLIC
RHETORIC
ROMANTIC
SARDONIC
SEMANTIC
SPECIFIC
SPORADIC
SUBSONIC
SULFURIC
SYMBOLIC
SYNOPTIC
SYSTEMIC
TERRIFIC
TEUTONIC
TURMERIC
VISICALC
VOLCANIC
ACCURSED
ACIDHEAD
AFFECTED
AIRFIELD
AIRSPEED
ALKALOID
AMOEBOID
ARACHNID
ASSORTED
ASTEROID
BACKHAND
BACKWARD
BARNYARD
BASSWOOD
BEDSTEAD
BEFRIEND
BENTWOOD
BEREAVED
BICUSPID
BILLFOLD
BILLHEAD
BIRDSEED
BLIZZARD
BLUEBIRD
BRINDLED
BULKHEAD
BULLHEAD
CABSTAND
CARYATID
CENTERED
COMPOUND
CONFOUND
CROPLAND
CUPBOARD
DEADWOOD
DEATHBED
DECKHAND
DEJECTED
DEMENTED
DEMIBOLD
DETACHED
DIVIDEND
DOCKHAND
DOCKYARD
DOORYARD
DOWNLOAD
DOWNWARD
DOWNWIND
DRUNKARD
ENSHROUD
EUROBOND
EXPLODED
FARMHAND
FARMLAND
FARMYARD
FIREWOOD
FLATHEAD
FLATLAND
FOLIATED
FOOTHOLD
FOREFEND
FOREHAND
FOREHEAD
FORELAND
FOREWORD
FOURFOLD
FOXHOUND
FREEHAND
FREEHOLD
FREELOAD
GANGLAND
GOATHERD
GODCHILD
GOURMAND
GRIZZLED
HACKWORD
HARDWOOD
HAWKWEED
HEADBAND
HEADLAND
HEADWORD
HELICOID
HEREFORD
HIGHBRED
HIGHLAND
HIGHROAD
HOGSHEAD
HOMEBRED
HOMELAND
HOMEWARD
HUMANOID
ICEBOUND
IMPACTED
INDEBTED
INEDITED
INFORMED
INFRARED
INKSTAND
INTENDED
INTREPID
INVOLVED
IRONCLAD
IRONWEED
IRONWOOD
JACQUARD
JAILBIRD
JEREMIAD
KEYBOARD
LADYBIRD
LANDLORD
LANDWARD
LAPBOARD
LARBOARD
LOANWORD
LOCOWEED
LONGHAND
LOPSIDED
LOVEBIRD
LYMPHOID
MAINLAND
MANIFOLD
MANNERED
MANYFOLD
MARIGOLD
MASTHEAD
MEDICAID
MILKMAID
MILKWEED
MILLIARD
MILLPOND
MISBRAND
MISSPEND
MOORLAND
MORIBUND
MUDGUARD
NEWFOUND
NEWLYWED
NONRIGID
OUTBOARD
OUTBOUND
OUTDATED
OUTFIELD
OUTMODED
OUTSPEND
OVENBIRD
OVERHAND
OVERHEAD
OVERLAID
OVERLAND
OVERLORD
PASSWORD
PELLUCID
PILCHARD
POKEWEED
POSTCARD
POSTPAID
POTSHERD
PROFOUND
PROPOUND
PROVIDED
PULPWOOD
PURBLIND
PUREBRED
RAILROAD
RAWBONED
REARWARD
REPEATED
RESERVED
RESIGNED
RETARDED
REVEREND
RHOMBOID
RIVERBED
ROSEWOOD
RUBICUND
SCABBARD
SCAFFOLD
SEABOARD
SHEPHERD
SHIPYARD
SITUATED
SLIPSHOD
SLUGGARD
SLUMLORD
SOFTWOOD
SOLENOID
SONGBIRD
SPANIARD
SPHEROID
SPIRITED
SPLENDID
STANDARD
STRINGED
SUPPOSED
SURROUND
TAMARIND
THOUSAND
TIDELAND
TIGHTWAD
TIMBERED
UNBIASED
UNBODIED
UNBOLTED
UNDERBID
UNEARNED
UNFORMED
UNLEADED
UNSHAPED
UNTOWARD
UNVOICED
UNWONTED
UNZIPPED
VAGABOND
VANGUARD
VINEYARD
WELLHEAD
WHIPCORD
WILDWOOD
WINDWARD
WITHHOLD
WOODLAND
WOODSHED
WOODWIND
WORMWOOD
WRETCHED
ABDICATE
ABEYANCE
ABLATIVE
ABNEGATE
ABRASIVE
ABROGATE
ABSENTEE
ABSINTHE
ABSOLUTE
ABSTRUSE
ACCOLADE
ACCOUTRE
ACCURATE
ACERBATE
ACTIVATE
ADDITIVE
ADEQUATE
ADHESIVE
ADOPTIVE
ADORABLE
ADVOCATE
AESTHETE
AFFIANCE
AGGRIEVE
AIGRETTE
AIRBORNE
AIRDROME
AIRFRAME
AIRPLANE
AIRSPACE
ALBACORE

ALEHOUSE
ALIENATE
ALLIANCE
ALLOCATE
ALLSPICE
ALTITUDE
AMBIENCE
AMENABLE
AMICABLE
AMORTIZE
AMPERAGE
AMPUTATE
ANAEROBE
ANALOGUE
ANECDOTE
ANISETTE
ANNOTATE
ANNOUNCE
ANTEDATE
ANTELOPE
ANTIDOTE
ANTIPODE
ANTIPOPE
ANYPLACE
ANYWHERE
APERTURE
APHANITE
APPANAGE
APPELLEE
APPETITE
APPLAUSE
APPLIQUE
APPOSITE
APPRAISE
APTITUDE
AQUACADE
AQUILINE
ARCHDUKE
ARGUABLE
ARMATURE
ARROGATE
ARTIFICE
ASPIRATE
ASSEMBLE
ASTATINE
ATROPINE
ATTITUDE
AUDIENCE
AUTOMATE
AXLETREE
BACKACHE
BACKBITE
BACKBONE
BACKFIRE
BACKSIDE
BADINAGE
BAGUETTE
BAILABLE
BARBECUE
BARITONE
BARNACLE
BARONAGE
BAROUCHE
BARRETTE
BASELINE
BATHROBE
BEDAZZLE
BEFUDDLE
BEGRUDGE
BELITTLE
BENEFICE
BENZOATE
BERCEUSE
BESTRIDE
BEVERAGE
BIDDABLE
BINNACLE
BIRDLIME
BLOCKADE
BLOWPIPE
BLUENOSE
BOBWHITE
BOLDFACE
BONHOMIE
BOOKCASE
BOUTIQUE
BREAKAGE
BROCHURE
BULLDOZE
BUNGHOLE
BURNOOSE
CAFFEINE
CALAMINE
CALLIOPE
CAMISOLE
CAMOMILE
CAMPOREE
CANAILLE
CANALIZE
CANONIZE
CANTICLE
CAPRIOLE
CARACOLE
CARAPACE
CAREFREE
CAROTENE
CARRIAGE
CASHMERE
CASSETTE
CASTRATE
CATALYZE
CAUSERIE
CELIBATE
CENOBITE
CHASTISE
CHASUBLE
CHENILLE
CHEROKEE
CHEYENNE
CHLORIDE
CHLORINE
CHLORITE
CHRISTIE
CICERONE
CINCTURE
CIVILIZE
CLAMBAKE
CLAVICLE
CLAYMORE
CLEAVAGE
COALESCE
COCKSURE
COGITATE
COIFFURE
COINCIDE
COLLAPSE
COLONIZE
COMANCHE
COMMENCE
COMMERCE
COMPLETE
COMPRISE
CONCEIVE
CONCLAVE
CONCLUDE
CONCRETE
CONDENSE
CONFRERE
CONSERVE
CONSOMME
CONSPIRE
CONSTRUE
CONTINUE
CONTRITE
CONTRIVE
CONVERGE
CONVERSE
CONVINCE
CONVULSE
COPULATE
COQUETTE
CORVETTE
COVERAGE
CREATURE
CREDENCE
CREDIBLE
CREOSOTE
CRETONNE
CREVASSE
CRIBBAGE
CRITIQUE
CRUCIBLE
CRYOLITE
CULPABLE
CURATIVE
CURLICUE
CYNOSURE
CYTOSINE
DAMNABLE
DANSEUSE
DARKSOME
DATABASE
DATELINE
DEADLINE
DECIMATE
DECISIVE
DECORATE
DECREASE
DEDICATE
DEFECATE
DEFIANCE
DEFINITE
DEIONIZE
DELAWARE
DELEGATE
DELICATE
DEMARCHE
DENATURE
DENOUNCE
DEPUTIZE
DEROGATE
DERRIERE
DESCRIBE
DESOLATE
DETHRONE
DETONATE
DEXTROSE
DIALOGUE
DIASTOLE
DIATRIBE
DISABUSE
DISAGREE
DISBURSE
DISCIPLE
DISCLOSE
DISCRETE
DISGORGE
DISGRACE
DISGUISE
DISKETTE
DISLODGE
DISPENSE
DISPERSE
DISPLACE
DISPROVE
DISSOLVE
DISSUADE
DISTANCE
DISTASTE
DISUNITE
DIVAGATE
DIVISIVE
DIVORCEE
DOCTRINE
DOGHOUSE
DOLOMITE
DOMICILE
DOMINATE
DORMOUSE
DRAINAGE
DRESSAGE
DUNGAREE
DUTIABLE
DYNAMITE
EARPHONE
EDUCABLE
ELECTIVE
ELEGANCE
ELIGIBLE
ELONGATE
EMACIATE
EMBATTLE
EMBEZZLE
EMIGRATE
EMINENCE
EMPLOYEE
ENCEINTE
ENCIRCLE
ENERGIZE
ENERVATE
ENFEEBLE
ENFILADE
ENSCONCE
ENSEMBLE
ENSHRINE
ENSILAGE
ENTANGLE
ENTHRONE
ENTRANCE
ENVELOPE
ENVIABLE
ENVISAGE
EPILOGUE
EQUALIZE
EQUIPAGE
ERECTILE
ESCALATE
ESCAPADE
ESCAROLE
ESTIMATE
ESTRANGE
EVACUATE
EVALUATE
EVENTIDE
EVERMORE
EVERYONE
EVIDENCE
EXCAVATE
EXCHANGE
EXECRATE
EXERCISE
EXORCISE
EXPEDITE
EXPOSURE
EYEPIECE
FALLIBLE
FAROUCHE
FASCICLE
FAVORITE
FEARSOME
FEASIBLE
FEDERATE
FEMININE
FIGURINE
FILIGREE
FILTRATE
FINALIZE
FIRESIDE
FIRMWARE
FISHWIFE
FIXATIVE
FLAGPOLE
FLATWARE
FLEABANE
FLEABITE
FLEXIBLE
FLUORIDE
FLUORINE
FLUORITE
FOLKLORE
FOLLICLE
FOOTNOTE
FOOTRACE
FOOTSORE
FORCIBLE
FOREBODE
FOREGONE
FORENAME
FOURSOME
FOXGLOVE
FRACTURE
FRONTAGE
FUGITIVE
FUMAROLE
FUMIGATE
FUSELAGE
GAMESOME
GANGRENE
GARGOYLE
GASOLINE
GEMINATE
GEMSTONE
GENDARME
GENERATE
GENITIVE
GENOCIDE
GIGABYTE
GLACIATE
GLADSOME
GOODWIFE
GRADUATE
GRAPHITE
GRUESOME
GUIDANCE
GUYANESE
HAIRLINE
HALFTONE
HANDMADE
HANDSOME
HARANGUE
HARDWARE
HEADACHE
HEADLINE
HELLHOLE
HELPMATE
HEMATITE
HERITAGE
HESITATE
HILLSIDE
HOMEMADE
HOMICIDE
HORNPIPE
HORRIBLE
HOTHOUSE
HUARACHE
HUMANIZE
ICEHOUSE
IDEALIZE
ILLUMINE
ILLUSIVE
IMBECILE
IMITABLE
IMMATURE
IMMOBILE
IMMOLATE
IMMOTILE
IMMUNIZE
IMPOLITE
INCHOATE
INCISIVE
INCREASE
INCUBATE
INDICATE
INDUCTEE
INDURATE
INFINITE
INFRINGE
INHUMANE
INITIATE
INNOVATE
INSCRIBE
INSECURE
INSTANCE
INSULATE
INTERNEE
INTIMATE
INTRIGUE
INUNDATE
INVEIGLE
INVIABLE
INVOLUTE
IRONWARE
IRRIGATE
IRRITATE
ISOPRENE
ISSUANCE
JALOUSIE
JAMBOREE
JAPANESE
JAUNDICE
JUNCTURE
JUVENILE
KAMIKAZE
KEEPSAKE
KEROSINE
KEYSTONE
KILOBYTE
KNEEHOLE
KNOTHOLE
LACERATE
LACROSSE
LADYLIKE
LADYLOVE
LAMBASTE
LANGUAGE
LATITUDE
LAUREATE
LAXATIVE
LEMONADE
LENITIVE
LEVERAGE
LEVITATE
LIBERATE
LICENSEE
LICORICE
LIFELINE
LIFETIME
LIGATURE
LIKEWISE
LIMONITE
LINGERIE
LITERATE
LITIGATE
LOCALIZE
LOGOTYPE
LONESOME

LONGTIME
LOOPHOLE
MACERATE
MADHOUSE
MAGAZINE
MAINLINE
MALAMUTE
MANCIPLE
MANDIBLE
MANDRAKE
MANGROVE
MANICURE
MARGRAVE
MARINATE
MARITIME
MARQUISE
MARRIAGE
MASSACRE
MASSEUSE
MATURATE
MAXIMIZE
MAYAPPLE
MEALTIME
MEANTIME
MEDICARE
MEDICATE
MEDICINE
MEDIOCRE
MEDITATE
MEGABYTE
MEMBRANE
MEMORIZE
MERINGUE
MESQUITE
MESSMATE
METAFILE
MIGRAINE
MILITATE
MILLIEME
MILLRACE
MINIBIKE
MINIMIZE
MISCIBLE
MISJUDGE
MISPLACE
MISQUOTE
MISSHAPE
MISSTATE
MISUSAGE
MITIGATE
MOBILIZE
MODERATE
MODULATE
MOISTURE
MOLECULE
MONGOOSE
MONOTONE
MONOXIDE
MORALIZE
MORPHEME
MORPHINE
MORTGAGE
MOTIVATE
MOTORIZE
MUCILAGE
MULTIPLE
MUSICALE
MUSTACHE
MUTILATE
MYSTIQUE
NAMESAKE
NASALIZE
NAUSEATE
NAVIGATE
NEBULIZE
NECKLACE
NECKLINE
NEGATIVE
NEGLIGEE
NEMATODE
NEOPHYTE
NEPENTHE
NICKNAME
NICOTINE
NOCTURNE
NOMINATE
NONSENSE
NOONTIDE
NOONTIME
NOTARIZE
NOVELIZE
NUCLEATE
NUISANCE
NUMERATE
OBDURATE
OBLIGATE
OBSOLETE
OBSTACLE
OFFSHORE
OFFSTAGE
OPERABLE
OPPOSITE
OPUSCULE
ORDINATE
ORDNANCE
ORGANIZE
OSCULATE
OUTHOUSE
OUTSHINE
OVERCOME
OVERRIDE
OVERRULE
OVERSHOE
OVERSIZE
OVERTAKE
OVERTIME
OVERTONE
OVERTURE
PAGINATE
PALATINE
PALEFACE
PALINODE
PALISADE
PALLIATE
PALPABLE
PARADISE
PARALYZE
PARASITE
PARLANCE
PARTERRE
PARTIBLE
PARTICLE
PASSABLE
PASTICHE
PASTILLE
PATIENCE
PECULATE
PEDICURE
PEDIGREE
PEDUNCLE
PEEPHOLE
PENALIZE
PENKNIFE
PERCEIVE
PERFORCE
PERILUNE
PERMEATE
PEROXIDE
PERSPIRE
PERSUADE
PERVERSE
PHARISEE
PHYSIQUE
PICAYUNE
PILOTAGE
PINAFORE
PINNACLE
PINOCHLE
PIPELINE
PITIABLE
PITTANCE
PIXELATE
PLAYMATE
PLEASURE
POLARIZE
POPULACE
POPULATE
PORPOISE
PORRIDGE
PORTABLE
PORTHOLE
PORTIERE
POSITIVE
POSSIBLE
POSTDATE
POSTHOLE
POSTLUDE
POSTPONE
POULTICE
POUNDAGE
PRACTICE
PRATIQUE
PREAMBLE
PRECLUDE
PREJUDGE
PREMIERE
PRESENCE
PRESERVE
PRESSURE
PRESTIGE
PRETENSE
PRIMROSE
PRISTINE
PROBABLE
PROCAINE
PROLOGUE
PROROGUE
PROSTATE
PROTRUDE
PROVINCE
PTOMAINE
PUNCTURE
PUNITIVE
PURCHASE
PURSLANE
PUTATIVE
QUAGMIRE
QUANTIZE
QUIETUDE
QUOTABLE
REACTIVE
REASSURE
RECOURSE
RECREATE
REGICIDE
REGULATE
REHEARSE
RELATIVE
RELEGATE
RELIABLE
RELIANCE
RELOCATE
RENEGADE
RENOUNCE
RENOVATE
REPARTEE
REPRIEVE
RESEMBLE
RESOLUTE
RESONATE
RESOURCE
RESPONSE
RETRIEVE
RETURNEE
REVANCHE
REVEILLE
RHYOLITE
RIBOSOME
RIDICULE
ROADSIDE
ROOFTREE
ROOMETTE
ROOMMATE
ROUGHAGE
ROULETTE
RUMINATE
RUNAGATE
SABOTAGE
SADDUCEE
SAGAMORE
SALIVATE
SANGUINE
SANITIZE
SAPPHIRE
SATURATE
SAUTERNE
SAWHORSE
SCALABLE
SCAVENGE
SCHEDULE
SCRABBLE
SCRAMBLE
SCRIBBLE
SCROUNGE
SEAPLANE
SEASCAPE
SEASHORE
SEDATIVE
SEEDTIME
SELECTEE
SELENITE
SELFSAME
SEMINOLE
SENSIBLE
SENTENCE
SEPARATE
SEQUENCE
SERENADE
SEWERAGE
SHINBONE
SHIPMATE
SHOELACE
SHORTAGE
SHOSHONE
SHOWCASE
SIDERITE
SILICATE
SILICONE
SIMONIZE
SIMULATE
SINECURE
SINKHOLE
SIXPENCE
SNOWSHOE
SOCIABLE
SOFTWARE
SOLITUDE
SOLSTICE
SOMETIME
SPRINKLE
SQUABBLE
SQUEEGEE
STAGNATE
STAMPEDE
STEERAGE
STOCKADE
STOPPAGE
STRADDLE
STRAGGLE
STRANGLE
STRUGGLE
SUBMERGE
SUBMERSE
SUBTITLE
SUCHLIKE
SUFFRAGE
SUITABLE
SUITCASE
SUNSHADE
SUNSHINE
SURCEASE
SUREFIRE
SURPLICE
SURPRISE
SUSPENSE
SYBARITE
SYCAMORE
SYLLABLE
SYNDROME
TABULATE
TAILGATE
TANGIBLE
TELEVISE
TELLTALE
TEMPLATE
TENTACLE
TEOSINTE
TERRIBLE
TESTICLE
THEORIZE
THIAMINE
THROTTLE
TINCTURE
TINPLATE
TIRESOME
TITILATE
TITIVATE
TITMOUSE
TOILETTE
TOLERATE
TOLLGATE
TORTOISE
TRACKAGE
TRACTATE
TRAVERSE
TREASURE
TREATISE
TRIANGLE
TRICYCLE
TROMBONE
TRUCKAGE
TRUETYPE
TRUNCATE
TUBERCLE
TUBEROSE
TURNPIKE
TUTELAGE
TWOPENCE
TYPEFACE
ULCERATE
ULTIMATE
UNBUCKLE
UNCHASTE
UNCLOTHE
UNCOUPLE
UNDERAGE
UNDERLIE
UNDULATE
UNFREEZE
UNGULATE
UNICYCLE
UNIONIZE
UNIVALVE
UNIVERSE
UNMUZZLE
UNRIDDLE
UNSADDLE
UNSETTLE
UNSTABLE
UNTANGLE
UPSTROKE
URBANITE
URBANIZE
UUDECODE
UUENCODE
VALIDATE
VALUABLE
VAPORIZE
VARIABLE
VARIANCE
VARICOSE
VEGETATE
VENERATE
VERBIAGE
VERSICLE
VICARAGE
VICINAGE
VIGNETTE
VINCIBLE
VIOLABLE
VIOLENCE
VITALIZE
VOCALIZE
VOCATIVE
VOLATILE
VOLPLANE
WARDROBE
WARPLANE
WASHABLE
WHARFAGE
WILDFIRE
WILDLIFE
WINDPIPE
WISEACRE
WISHBONE
WOODBINE
WOODNOTE
WOODPILE
WORKABLE
WORMHOLE
WRECKAGE
YULETIDE
ZOOPHYTE
ZOOSPORE
APERITIF
CHECKOFF
DANDRUFF
DYESTUFF
HANDCUFF
KERCHIEF
MISCHIEF
RIFFRAFF
STANDOFF
UNBELIEF
WEREWOLF
WOODRUFF
YOURSELF
ABORNING
ALIASING
ANYTHING
BANTLING
BECOMING
BLACKING
BLESSING
BREEDING
BRISLING

BUILDING
BULLFROG
BUNDLING
CAGELING
CATCHING
CHARMING
CLEARING
CLIPPING
CLOTHING
COUPLING
CREEPING
CROSSING
DAIRYING
DARKLING
DRESSING
DUCKLING
DUMPLING
DWELLING
ENGAGING
EVENSONG
EXACTING
FAGOTING
FARTHING
FAUBOURG
FETCHING
FIREPLUG
FLASHING
FLEETING
FOOTLING
FROSTING
GANGLING
GLOAMING
GRASPING
GRAYLING
GREEKING
GREETING
GRUELING
HATCHING
HEADLONG
HEDGEHOG
HIRELING
HOARDING
IMPOSING
INCOMING
INFRADIG
INTERROG
INVITING
KINDLING
LACEWING
LAYERING
LEAPFROG
LEARNING
LIFELONG
LIVELONG
LOATHING
LOLLYGAG
MARBLING
MEALYBUG
MIDDLING
MISDOING
MOUNTING
MOURNING
NESTLING
NIGGLING
NURSLING
ONCOMING
OUTGOING
OUTLYING
OVERHANG
PAINTING
PANELING
PETTIFOG
PHRASING
PIDDLING
PLANKING
PLEASING
PLUMBING
POLLIWOG
PRESSING
PRINTING
PUDDLING
QUISLING
RATTLING
RAVENING
RETIRING
RUMBLING
SCALAWAG
SCATHING
SEAGOING
SEEDLING
SHANTUNG
SHEETING
SHELVING
SHILLING
SHIPPING
SHIRRING
SHIRTING
SHOCKING
SIDELONG
SKIMMING
SPANKING
SPOOLING
STANDING
STARLING
STERLING
STINKBUG
STIRRING
STOCKING
STRIKING
STUDDING
STUFFING
STUNNING
SUCKLING
SWEEPING
SWELLING
SWIMMING
TEACHING
TEETHING
TOUCHING
TOWELING
TOWERING
TRAINING
TRAPPING
TRIFLING
TRIMMING
UNDERDOG
UNENDING
UNERRING
UNSPRUNG
UNSTRUNG
UPCOMING
UPRISING
VAPORING
VAULTING
VIETCONG
WATCHDOG
WEAKLING
WHOPPING
WINGDING
WITCHING
WRAPPING
YACHTING
YEARLING
YEARLONG
YEARNING
YIELDING
ADMONISH
AIRBRUSH
ALTHOUGH
AMARANTH
APPROACH
ASTONISH
BACKLASH
BACKWASH
BEHEMOTH
BEQUEATH
BESMIRCH
BIRDBATH
BLUEFISH
BRACKISH
BRANDISH
CALABASH
CENOTAPH
CHANUKAH
CHUTZPAH
CORONACH
CRAWFISH
CRAYFISH
DEMOLISH
DESPATCH
DEVILISH
DIMINISH
DISPATCH
ENCROACH
ENTRENCH
EYETOOTH
FLATFISH
FLOURISH
FOOTPATH
FORSOOTH
FURLOUGH
GOLDFISH
GUNSMITH
HANUKKAH
HEREWITH
HYACINTH
INSOMUCH
INTRENCH
KEYPUNCH
LANGUISH
LIVERISH
MEGALITH
MISHMASH
MISMATCH
MONOLITH
NONESUCH
NUTHATCH
OILCLOTH
OUTREACH
OUTWEIGH
OVERMUCH
POLYMATH
QUALMISH
REGOLITH
REPROACH
RESEARCH
RETRENCH
ROSEBUSH
SAILFISH
SANDWICH
SCOTTISH
SHEEPISH
SHREWISH
SKIRMISH
SKITTISH
SLUGGISH
STARFISH
STRENGTH
THOROUGH
TICKLISH
TINSMITH
TOLLBOTH
TRIPTYCH
UNCHURCH
UNCLENCH
UPGROWTH
VANQUISH
VAPORISH
VERMOUTH
WEAKFISH
WHIPLASH
WOMANISH
XENOLITH
YOUNGISH
BERIBERI
BROCCOLI
CONFETTI
DAIQUIRI
KOHLRABI
LITERATI
MACARONI
MAHARANI
MARIACHI
PASTRAMI
SHANGHAI
SHILINGI
SUKIYAKI
ZUCCHINI
AARDVARK
ASTERISK
BACKPACK
BANKBOOK
BAREBACK
BASILISK
BITSTOCK
BOBOLINK
BODYWORK
BOOKMARK
BUSYWORK
CAKEWALK
CALLBACK
CASEWORK
CHAPBOOK
CHIPMUNK
COMEBACK
COOKBOOK
COPYBOOK
COPYDESK
DAYBREAK
DEADLOCK
DIPSTICK
DRAWBACK
DROPKICK
FASTBACK
FEEDBACK
FIREWORK
FISHHOOK
FLAPJACK
FLYSPECK
FOOTWORK
FORELOCK
FRETWORK
FULLBACK
GAMECOCK
GIMCRACK
GROSBEAK
HALFBACK
HALLMARK
HANDBOOK
HANDPICK
HARDBACK
HARDHACK
HARDTACK
HAYSTACK
HEADLOCK
HEADWORK
HOMESICK
HOMEWORK
HOODWINK
HORNBOOK
HUMPBACK
IRONWORK
JOYSTICK
KICKBACK
KNAPSACK
LAMPBACK
LANDMARK
LIFEWORK
LIMERICK
LIPSTICK
LOVESICK
MAVERICK
MESHWORK
MOSSBACK
NAINSOOK
NONSTICK
NOTEBOOK
OPENWORK
OUTBREAK
OUTFLANK
OVERLOOK
PASSBOOK
PAYCHECK
PENSTOCK
PICKLOCK
PINPRICK
PLAYBACK
PLAYBOOK
POCKMARK
POLITICK
POSTMARK
PULLBACK
ROADWORK
ROLLBACK
SANDBANK
SHAMROCK
SIDEKICK
SIDEWALK
SNOWBANK
STUDBOOK
SWAYBACK
TAMARACK
TEAMWORK
TEXTBOOK
TOMAHAWK
TRAPROCK
WOODCOCK
WOODWORK
WOOLSACK
WORDBOOK
WORKBOOK
YEARBOOK
ZWIEBACK
ABNORMAL
APPROVAL
ARBOREAL
ARMORIAL
ARTERIAL
ASPHODEL
ATYPICAL
BANKROLL
BARBITAL
BASEBALL
BEANBALL
BIANNUAL
BIENNIAL
BINAURAL
BIOCIDAL
BIRACIAL
BISEXUAL
BLISSFUL
BLUEBELL
BOASTFUL
CANNIBAL
CARDINAL
CARNIVAL
CAROUSAL
CAROUSEL
CARRYALL
CATCHALL
CERVICAL
CESSPOOL
CHARCOAL
CHEERFUL
CHEMICAL
CLERICAL
CLINICAL
COCKEREL
COCKTAIL
COGWHEEL
COLONIAL
COLOSSAL
COMMUNAL
CONFOCAL
CONJUGAL
CONTRAIL
CORNMEAL
CORPORAL
COVERALL
CRIMINAL
CRITICAL
DAFFODIL
DIAGONAL
DISHEVEL
DISLOYAL
DISPOSAL
DOGGEREL
DOUBTFUL
DOVETAIL
DOWNFALL
DOWNHILL
DREADFUL
DUCKBILL
DUMBBELL
DUNGHILL
EGGSHELL
ENTHRALL
ESPECIAL
ESPOUSAL
ETHEREAL
EVENTUAL
EXTERNAL
FAMILIAL
FANCIFUL
FAREWELL
FESTIVAL
FIREBALL
FISHBOWL
FLYWHEEL
FOLDEROL
FOOTBALL
FOOTFALL
FOOTHILL
FORESAIL
FORETELL
FREEWILL
FUNEREAL
GERMINAL
GLASSFUL
GLYCEROL
GOODWILL
GOOFBALL
GRATEFUL
GUTTURAL
HABITUAL
HANDBALL
HANDBILL
HANDRAIL
HANGNAIL
HARDBALL
HAREBELL
HIGHBALL
HIGHTAIL
HORMONAL
HOSPITAL
HYMENEAL

IMMORTAL
IMPERIAL
INFERNAL
INFORMAL
INGUINAL
INIMICAL
INTEGRAL
INTERNAL
INTERVAL
JUDICIAL
KEELHAUL
LACRIMAL
LANDFALL
LANDFILL
LITTORAL
MACKEREL
MADRIGAL
MAINSAIL
MANIACAL
MATERIAL
MATERIEL
MATERNAL
MEATBALL
MEDIEVAL
MEMORIAL
METHANOL
METRICAL
MINSTREL
MISLABEL
MISSPELL
MISTRIAL
MOLEHILL
MONAURAL
MONORAIL
MOTHBALL
MOURNFUL
MUSCATEL
MYSTICAL
NATIONAL
NAUTICAL
NEONATAL
NEWSREEL
NONMETAL
NOTARIAL
NOTIONAL
NUMSKULL
NUTSHELL
OFFICIAL
ORIENTAL
ORIGINAL
OVERHAUL
OVERKILL
PARALLEL
PARFOCAL
PARIETAL
PASTORAL
PATERNAL
PECTORAL
PEDESTAL
PERSONAL
PHYSICAL
PICKEREL
PINWHEEL
PLAYBILL
PONYTAIL
PRATFALL
PRENATAL
PRIMEVAL
PRODIGAL
PROTOCOL
PUFFBALL
PUNCTUAL
RAINFALL
RATIONAL
REBUTTAL
REFERRAL
REGIONAL
REMEDIAL
REMITTAL
REPRISAL
RESIDUAL
REVERSAL
RIGHTFUL
ROCKFALL
SENTINEL
SHRAPNEL
SIDEREAL
SIDEWALL
SKILLFUL
SNOWBALL
SNOWFALL
SOFTBALL
SPECTRAL
SPITBALL
SQUIRREL
SUPERNAL
SURGICAL
TAFFRAIL
TEETOTAL
TEMPORAL
TERMINAL
THANKFUL
TRANQUIL
TRIBUNAL
TRUSTFUL
TRUTHFUL
TUTORIAL
UNFILIAL
UNIAXIAL
UNLAWFUL
UPHEAVAL
VARIETAL
VENEREAL
VENGEFUL
VERTICAL
VIRGINAL
VISCERAL
WASHBOWL
WATCHFUL
WILDFOWL
WINDFALL
WINDMILL
WRATHFUL
WRONGFUL
YOUTHFUL
ACCUSTOM
ACTINISM
ACTINIUM
ACTIVISM
ADDENDUM
AGERATUM
ALLUVIUM
ALTRUISM
ALUMINUM
AMMONIUM
ANGSTROM
ANTEROOM
APHORISM
APOTHEGM
AQUARIUM
ARMYWORM
BALLROOM
BATHROOM
BIENNIUM
BOLLWORM
BOOKWORM
BOTULISM
BROUGHAM
BUDDHISM
CALADIUM
CAPSICUM
CARDAMOM
CEMENTUM
CEREBRUM
CHECKSUM
CHROMIUM
COAGULUM
COLISEUM
CORUNDUM
DARKROOM
DAYDREAM
DECIGRAM
DEKAGRAM
DELIRIUM
DISCLAIM
DUODENUM
EMBOLISM
EMPORIUM
ENCOMIUM
ESCAPISM
EUROPIUM
EXORDIUM
FACTOTUM
FATALISM
FEMINISM
FLIMFLAM
FLUIDRAM
FOREDOOM
FRANCIUM
FUTURISM
GERANIUM
GLOWWORM
HEADROOM
HEBRAISM
HEDONISM
HEIRLOOM
HINDUISM
HOLOGRAM
HOMEROOM
HOOKWORM
HUMANISM
IDEALISM
IDEOGRAM
INCHWORM
INTERCOM
ISOTHERM
JINGOISM
KILOGRAM
LABURNUM
LANDFORM
LAUDANUM
LEGALISM
LINOLEUM
LUKEWARM
LUTETIUM
MARJORAM
MELANISM
MOMENTUM
MONOGRAM
MOONBEAM
MUSHROOM
NATIVISM
NEOPLASM
NEPOTISM
NIHILISM
NOBELIUM
OPTIMISM
ORGANISM
PACIFISM
PARADIGM
PAROXYSM
PENDULUM
PHANTASM
PLATFORM
PLATINUM
PLECTRUM
POLONIUM
PROCLAIM
PUDENDUM
PUGILISM
RESIDUUM
RINGWORM
RUBIDIUM
SAMARIUM
SCANDIUM
SELENIUM
SHIPWORM
SOLARIUM
SOLECISM
SPECTRUM
SPHAGNUM
TANTALUM
TAPEWORM
TELEFILM
TELEGRAM
THALLIUM
TITANIUM
TOKENISM
TRILLIUM
TYMPANUM
UNDERARM
UNIONISM
UPSTREAM
VANADIUM
VARIORUM
VEGANISM
VERBATIM
VIATICUM
VIBURNUM
VIVARIUM
WARDROOM
WAREROOM
WASHROOM
WIREWORM
WORKROOM
ABLATION
ABLUTION
ABORTION
ADDITION
ADHESION
AGRARIAN
ALBANIAN
ALDERMAN
ALGERIAN
ALIZARIN
ALLERGEN
AMBITION
AMERICAN
ANDROGEN
ANGLICAN
APHELION
ASSASSIN
AUDITION
AUSTRIAN
AUTOBAHN
AUTOJOIN
AVERSION
AVIATION
BACKSPIN
BAILSMAN
BARBICAN
BASEBORN
BEARSKIN
BEHOLDEN
BETATRON
BIATHLON
BLUDGEON
BOGEYMAN
BOHEMIAN
BONDSMAN
BOUILLON
BRAKEMAN
BRETHREN
BRIGHTEN
BUCKSKIN
BULLETIN
CABOCHON
CALFSKIN
CAMPAIGN
CANADIAN
CAPESKIN
CAPUCHIN
CARDIGAN
CAREWORN
CARILLON
CAULDRON
CERULEAN
CESAREAN
CHAIRMAN
CHAMPION
CHAPERON
CHAPLAIN
CHRISTEN
CINNAMON
CITATION
CIVILIAN
COACHMAN
COGNOMEN
COHESION
COLOPHON
COMEDIAN
COMEDOWN
COMPLAIN
COONSKIN
CORDOVAN
CORPSMAN
COXSWAIN
CREATION
CYCLAMEN
DAIRYMAN
DECISION
DEERSKIN
DELUSION
DEMIJOHN
DEVOTION
DIAPASON
DIELDRIN
DIVISION
DOMINION
DONATION
DOUBLOON
DOWNTOWN
DOWNTURN
DRAGOMAN
DURATION
EFFUSION
EGYPTIAN
EIGHTEEN
ELECTION
ELECTRON
EMBLAZON
EMBOLDEN
EMOTICON
EMPYREAN
EMULSION
EQUATION
ERECTION
ESTONIAN
ESTROGEN
ETRUSCAN
EURASIAN
EUROPEAN
FACEDOWN
FALCHION
FINESPUN
FIXATION
FLASHGUN
FLATIRON
FLYBLOWN
FORENOON
FORESKIN
FOREWARN
FOUNTAIN
FOURTEEN
FRACTION
FREEBORN
FREEDMAN
FRESHMAN
FRICTION
FRIGHTEN
FRUITION
FUNCTION
GANGLION
GARRISON
GHANAIAN
GLOBULIN
GLYCERIN
GLYCOGEN
GOATSKIN
GONFALON
GRANDSON
GRAVAMEN
GRIDIRON
GROSCHEN
GUARDIAN
GUMPTION
HANDYMAN
HARRIDAN
HAWAIIAN
HAWTHORN
HEADSMAN
HEIGHTEN
HELMSMAN
HENCHMAN
HERDSMAN
HEREUPON
HIGHBORN
HOLSTEIN
HOMESPUN
HOOLIGAN
HORSEMAN
HUNTSMAN
HYDROGEN
IDEATION
IGNITION
ILLUSION
IMPRISON
INCISION
INDIAMAN
INFOBAHN
INVASION
ISTHMIAN
JETTISON
JUNCTION
LAMBSKIN
LANDSMAN
LECITHIN
LEGATION
LENGTHEN
LIBATION
LIMEKILN
LINCHPIN
LINESMAN
LOCATION
LOCUTION
LONGHORN
LOVELORN
LUNCHEON
LUTHERAN
MACAROON
MAGDALEN
MAGICIAN
MAINTAIN
MALAWIAN
MANDARIN
MANDOLIN

MARATHON
MARKDOWN
MARKSMAN
MARZIPAN
MASTODON
MELODEON
MENHADEN
MERIDIAN
MISTAKEN
MOCCASIN
MOLESKIN
MONITION
MOROCCAN
MOTORMAN
MOUNTAIN
MUNITION
MUSICIAN
MUTATION
MYRMIDON
NAPOLEON
NEGATION
NIGERIAN
NINETEEN
NITROGEN
NOBLEMAN
NONUNION
NORSEMAN
NOTATION
OBLATION
OBLIVION
OBSIDIAN
OCCASION
OPTICIAN
OVERTURN
PANTHEON
PARAFFIN
PARMESAN
PARTISAN
PATHOGEN
PAVILION
PEMMICAN
PENTAGON
PETITION
PITCHMAN
PLANKTON
PLANTAIN
PLEBEIAN
POLTROON
POSITION
POSITRON
POTATION
PRESSMAN
PUBLICAN
PUNCHEON
PUSHDOWN
QUADROON
QUATRAIN
QUESTION
RADIOMAN
REACTION
RELATION
RELIGION
RESTRAIN
RIPARIAN
ROMANIAN
ROUTEMAN
RUMANIAN
SALESMAN
SANCTION
SAUCEPAN
SCALEPAN
SCALLION
SCORPION
SCULLION
SEALSKIN
SEDITION
SHOPWORN
SHOWDOWN
SHUTDOWN
SKELETON
SLATTERN
SOLUTION
SORPTION
SPACEMAN
SPECIMEN
SPITTOON
SQUADRON
STALLION
STRAITEN
STRICKEN
STUBBORN
STURGEON
SUZERAIN
SYSADMIN
TACITURN
TAHITIAN
TAILSPIN
TALESMAN
TALISMAN
TARRAGON
TEASPOON
TELETHON
TERRAPIN
THESPIAN
THIRTEEN
THREATEN
TIMEWORN
TOBOGGAN
TOILWORN
TOWNSMAN
TRACTION
TRAINMAN
TRILLION
TRIMARAN
TUNGSTEN
TUNISIAN
TURBOFAN
UNBEATEN
UNBIDDEN
UNBROKEN
UNBURDEN
UNBUTTON
UNCOMMON
UNFASTEN
UNLOOSEN
UNPERSON
VACATION
VENATION
VENUSIAN
VERBOTEN
VEXATION
VOCATION
VOLITION
WARFARIN
WATCHMAN
WELLBORN
WINDBURN
WINGSPAN
WOODSMAN
ZEPPELIN
ALFRESCO
ANTHROPO
ARPEGGIO
AUTOGIRO
BALLYHOO
BORDELLO
CAUDILLO
COCKATOO
COMMANDO
CONCERTO
CRUZEIRO
ESPRESSO
FALSETTO
FANDANGO
FELLATIO
FILIPINO
FLAMENCO
FLAMINGO
GRAFFITO
HEREUNTO
HITHERTO
IMPETIGO
INNUENDO
INTAGLIO
KANGAROO
LIBRETTO
MACHISMO
MILESIMO
MOSQUITO
NEUTRINO
ORATORIO
PALMETTO
PALOMINO
PERFECTO
PIMIENTO
POLITICO
PRESIDIO
SCENARIO
SERAGLIO
SOMBRERO
STACCATO
STILETTO
SUPEREGO
VIRTUOSO
WATERLOO
AGITPROP
AIRSTRIP
BACKDROP
BACKSLAP
BACKSTOP
BAKESHOP
BLACKTOP
CLAPTRAP
DOORSTEP
ESCALLOP
FIREDAMP
FIRETRAP
FLAGSHIP
FOOLSCAP
FOOTSTEP
HANDICAP
HARDSHIP
HEADSHIP
HEDGEHOP
HOUSETOP
LADYSHIP
LOCKSTEP
LOLLIPOP
LORDSHIP
OUTSTRIP
OVERLEAP
OVERSTEP
PAWNSHOP
RAINDROP
SIDESTEP
SKULLCAP
SNOWDROP
TOWNSHIP
UNDERLIP
WARDSHIP
WHITECAP
WINESHOP
WORKSHOP
ABATTOIR
AFLUTTER
AGLITTER
AIRLINER
ANCESTOR
ANTEATER
ANTERIOR
ARMCHAIR
ATOMIZER
BACHELOR
BAEDEKER
BALUSTER
BANISTER
BEHAVIOR
BEWILDER
CALENDAR
CALENDER
CANISTER
CAPSULAR
CATHETER
CAVALIER
CELLULAR
CHANDLER
CINNABAR
CIRCULAR
CISLUNAR
CLINCHER
CLOISTER
CLOTHIER
COAUTHOR
COIFFEUR
COLANDER
COMMONER
COMPILER
COMPUTER
CONGENER
CONSIDER
CORRIDOR
COSIGNER
COURTIER
CREDITOR
CROSSBAR
CROUPIER
CUCUMBER
CUSPIDOR
CUSTOMER
CYLINDER
DAUGHTER
DEBONAIR
DECANTER
DECEMBER
DECIPHER
DEFLOWER
DEMEANOR
DEMURRER
DIAMETER
DICTATOR
DINOSAUR
DIRECTOR
DISASTER
DISCOLOR
DISCOVER
DISFAVOR
DISHONOR
DISINTER
DISORDER
DISSEVER
DOMINEER
DOWNPOUR
DULCIMER
ELEVATOR
EMBITTER
ENCIPHER
ENCUMBER
ENDANGER
ENDEAVOR
ENGENDER
ENGINEER
ESPALIER
EXECUTOR
EXEMPLAR
EXTERIOR
EYELINER
FAMILIAR
FELDSPAR
FLOUNDER
FLYPAPER
FOOTWEAR
FOREBEAR
FORSWEAR
FRONTIER
GAMESTER
GANGSTER
GOSSAMER
GOVERNOR
GRANDEUR
GRANULAR
GROUNDER
HANGOVER
HEADGEAR
HOLDOVER
HOWITZER
HUCKSTER
IDOLATER
IMPELLER
IMPOSTOR
IMPROPER
INCUMBER
INFERIOR
INFORMER
INTERIOR
INVERTER
ISLANDER
JONGLEUR
KIBITZER
KILLDEER
KNITWEAR
LARKSPUR
LAUGHTER
LAUNCHER
LAVENDER
LAWGIVER
LAWMAKER
LEFTOVER
LODESTAR
LONGHAIR
LONGUEUR
MALINGER
MALTSTER
MANEUVER
METAPHOR
MILLIBAR
MILLINER
MINISTER
MISNOMER
MONSIEUR
MOREOVER
MOTORCAR
MUENSTER
MULETEER
NEIGHBOR
NEWCOMER
NOVEMBER
ODOMETER
OHMMETER
OLEANDER
ONLOOKER
OUTRIDER
OUTSIDER
OVERHEAR
PACIFIER
PARAMOUR
PARDONER
PASSOVER
PECULIAR
PEIGNOIR
PHOSPHOR
PILASTER
PLAYGOER
POLESTAR
POLLSTER
PREMOLAR
PRISONER
PROMOTER
PULLOVER
PULMOTOR
PUSHOVER
RADIATOR
RECEIVER
RECEPTOR
RECORDER
REFORMER
REGISTER
REINDEER
REMEMBER
REPORTER
RESISTOR
RESORTER
RETAINER
REVENUER
REVIEWER
REVOLVER
ROADSTER
SABOTEUR
SCAPULAR
SCHOONER
SCIMITAR
SCULPTOR
SEAFARER
SEAWATER
SEIGNEUR
SEMESTER
SERVITOR
SHOULDER
SILENCER
SINGULAR
SINISTER
SONGSTER
SOUVENIR
SPINSTER
SPLATTER
SPLENDOR
SPLINTER
SPLUTTER
SQUANDER
STICKLER
STRANGER
STREAMER
STRINGER
SUPERIOR
TAXPAYER
TEAMSTER
TESTATOR
THEREFOR
THRASHER
THRUSTER
TOGETHER
TOREADOR
TRANSFER
TRAPDOOR
TRENCHER
TRICOLOR
TRIMETER
TRIUMVIR
TURNOVER
ULTERIOR
UNDERFUR
UNFETTER
UNLIMBER
VALVULAR
VARISTOR
VASCULAR
VILLAGER

VOYAGEUR
WALKOVER
WAYFARER
WHATEVER
WHENEVER
WHEREVER
WHOMEVER
WIREHAIR
WORDSTAR
WRIGGLER
ABUTTALS
ACANTHUS
ACIDOSIS
AFFLATUS
ANALYSIS
ASBESTOS
AVIONICS
BACILLUS
BARONESS
BARRACKS
BASELESS
BERMUDAS
BIBULOUS
BIFOCALS
BLOOMERS
BODILESS
BOOTLESS
BRITCHES
BRONCHUS
BURSITIS
BUSINESS
BUTTRESS
CADUCEUS
CALCULUS
CANNABIS
CAPTIOUS
CARELESS
CAUTIOUS
CHARADES
CHECKERS
CLEMATIS
CLITORIS
COLOSSUS
COMBINGS
COMPRESS
CONFINES
CONGRESS
COPPERAS
CORDLESS
COUNTESS
CREMAINS
DATELESS
DECOROUS
DESIROUS
DETRITUS
DIABETES
DIALYSIS
DIANTHUS
DINGBATS
DISTRESS
DOLDRUMS
DRAUGHTS
EARNINGS
EDGEWAYS
EKISTICS
ELLIPSIS
EMERITUS
EMPHASIS
ENORMOUS
ENTRAILS
ENURESIS
ENVIRONS
EUGENICS
EXCURSUS
EXEGESIS
EXIGUOUS
EXTRADOS
EYEGLASS
FABULOUS
FACTIOUS
FADELESS
FASTNESS
FEARLESS
FECKLESS
FIBROSIS
FOOTLESS
FORMLESS
FORTRESS
FORWARDS
GALLUSES
GASWORKS
GENEROUS
GENETICS
GENITALS
GLABROUS
GLORIOUS
GOODNESS
GORGEOUS
GRACIOUS
GRIEVOUS
HAUTBOIS
HERCULES
HIBISCUS
HIGHNESS
HOLINESS
HUNTRESS
HUSTINGS
HYPNOSIS
ILLINOIS
INFAMOUS
INTRADOS
IROQUOIS
KEYWORDS
KINETICS
KNICKERS
LANDMASS
LEAVINGS
LIGNEOUS
LIKENESS
LISTLESS
LUMINOUS
LUSCIOUS
MANDAMUS
MARQUESS
MASSLESS
MATTRESS
MENISCUS
MESDAMES
MICROBUS
MIDSHIPS
MINDLESS
MISTRESS
MOLASSES
MYELITIS
NAMELESS
NARCOSIS
NAUTILUS
NEBULOUS
NECROSIS
NEEDLESS
NEURITIS
NEUROSIS
NIGEROIS
NINEPINS
NOWADAYS
NUMEROUS
OPERANDS
ORGULOUS
OUTCLASS
OUTDOORS
OUTGUESS
OVERALLS
OVERPASS
OVERSEAS
PANCREAS
PEERLESS
PICKINGS
PITILESS
PLATYPUS
POLITICS
POPULOUS
PRECIOUS
PREPRESS
PREVIOUS
PRINCESS
PROCEEDS
PROGRESS
RAVENOUS
RECKLESS
RESTLESS
RUTHLESS
SCABROUS
SCISSORS
SEDULOUS
SELFLESS
SENSUOUS
SHAMBLES
SHINGLES
SICKNESS
SIDEWAYS
SONOROUS
SPACIOUS
SPECIOUS
SPURIOUS
SPYGLASS
STIMULUS
STUDIOUS
SUNDRIES
SUPPRESS
SYLLABUS
SYNOPSIS
SYPHILIS
TERMINUS
THALAMUS
THROMBUS
TIMELESS
TIMOROUS
TIRELESS
TOPSIDES
TORTUOUS
TRESPASS
TROUSERS
TUBEROUS
TUNELESS
TWEEZERS
UNAWARES
UNCTUOUS
UPSTAIRS
USURIOUS
UXORIOUS
VAPOROUS
VENOMOUS
VIGOROUS
VIRTUOUS
VITREOUS
WAITRESS
WEAKNESS
WINDLASS
WIRELESS
WONDROUS
ABSTRACT
ABUNDANT
ABUTMENT
ACCIDENT
ACCREDIT
ACQUAINT
ADJACENT
ADJUTANT
ADJUVANT
AERONAUT
AFFERENT
AFFRIGHT
AIRCRAFT
AIRTIGHT
ALARMIST
ALIENIST
ALPHABET
AMBULANT
AMETHYST
APPARENT
AQUANAUT
AQUEDUCT
ARBALEST
ARGUMENT
ARMAMENT
ARROGANT
ARTIFACT
ASPIRANT
AVERMENT
BACCARAT
BACKREST
BANKRUPT
BAREFOOT
BASEMENT
BASSINET
BEECHNUT
BENEDICT
BLACKOUT
BOUFFANT
BOWSPRIT
BRACELET
BRAGGART
BREAKOUT
BRICKBAT
BROOKLET
BROWBEAT
BROWNOUT
BUCKSHOT
CAMSHAFT
CASEMENT
CATAPULT
CATARACT
CENTRIST
CERAMIST
CEREMENT
CHECKOUT
CHESTNUT
CHITCHAT
CLAIMANT
CLARINET
CLOSEOUT
CLOUDLET
CLUBFOOT
COHERENT
COLONIST
COMPLEAT
CONFLICT
CONFRONT
CONJUNCT
CONQUEST
CONSTANT
CONTEMPT
CONTRACT
CONTRAST
COUCHANT
COVENANT
COVERLET
CRACKPOT
CRESCENT
CROSSCUT
CROTCHET
CROWFOOT
DAYLIGHT
DEADBEAT
DECEDENT
DECREPIT
DEFOREST
DEMOCRAT
DEPONENT
DERELICT
DESELECT
DESTRUCT
DILIGENT
DIPLOMAT
DISCOUNT
DISCREET
DISJOINT
DISMOUNT
DISPIRIT
DISQUIET
DISTINCT
DISTRACT
DISTRAIT
DISTRICT
DISTRUST
DOCUMENT
DOGFIGHT
DOUGHNUT
DOWNBEAT
DOWNCAST
DRUGGIST
DRUMBEAT
EFFERENT
EGGPLANT
ELEPHANT
ELOQUENT
ETHERNET
EXPLICIT
EXPONENT
EYESIGHT
FALTBOAT
FANLIGHT
FARTHEST
FILAMENT
FINALIST
FIREBOAT
FLAGRANT
FLAMEOUT
FLATBOAT
FLATFOOT
FLAUTIST
FLESHPOT
FLIPPANT
FOLDBOAT
FOOTREST
FORECAST
FOREFOOT
FOREMAST
FOREMOST
FOREPART
FORKLIFT
FRAGMENT
FRAGRANT
FREQUENT
FUMIGANT
FURTHEST
GADABOUT
GASLIGHT
GATEPOST
GAUNTLET
GOALPOST
GRADIENT
GUNFIGHT
GUNPOINT
HABITANT
HEADREST
HEAVYSET
HELIPORT
HELPMEET
HESITANT
HINDMOST
HUGUENOT
IGNORANT
IMMANENT
IMMINENT
IMMODEST
IMPLICIT
IMPOTENT
IMPUDENT
INCIDENT
INDECENT
INDIGENT
INDIRECT
INDOLENT
INERRANT
INEXPERT
INHALANT
INHERENT
INNOCENT
INSOLENT
INSPIRIT
INSTINCT
INSTRUCT
INTEREST
INTERMIT
INTERNET
INTROMIT
JACKBOOT
JUBILANT
JUDGMENT
KEELBOAT
KILOVOLT
KILOWATT
KINGBOLT
KNOCKOUT
LASERJET
LIFEBOAT
LIGAMENT
LINGUIST
LINIMENT
LITIGANT
LODGMENT
LONGBOAT
LOYALIST
MACPAINT
MAINMAST
MALAPERT
MALTREAT
MANIFEST
MANTELET
MARMOSET
MARTINET
MEDALIST
MERCHANT
MIDNIGHT
MIDPOINT
MILEPOST
MILITANT
MISCOUNT
MISPRINT
MISTREAT
MISTRUST
MONUMENT
MORALIST
MOVEMENT
NEWSCAST
NOBELIST
NONEVENT
NUTRIENT
OBEDIENT
OBSTRUCT
OCCUPANT
OFFPRINT
OFFSHOOT
OINTMENT
OPPONENT

ORGANIST
ORNAMENT
OUTBURST
OUTFIGHT
OUTPOINT
OUTRIGHT
OUTSMART
OVERCAST
OVERCOAT
PAMPHLET
PANELIST
PANTSUIT
PARAKEET
PASSPORT
PAVEMENT
PEDERAST
PEDIMENT
PENCHANT
PENITENT
PENLIGHT
PETULANT
PHASEOUT
PHEASANT
PIEPLANT
PINPOINT
PLANGENT
PLAYSUIT
PLEASANT
POIGNANT
POLYGLOT
POPULIST
PORTRAIT
PRECINCT
PREEXIST
PREGNANT
PRETERIT
PRINTOUT
PROHIBIT
PROSPECT
PROTRACT
PRURIENT
PURULENT
PUSHCART
PUSSYCAT
QUADRANT
QUOTIENT
RAINCOAT
REACTANT
RECREANT
REDOLENT
REFERENT
REFOREST
REGIMENT
RELAXANT
RELEVANT
RESCRIPT
RESIDENT
RESONANT
RESTRICT
RETICENT
RETROFIT
REVERENT
RHEOSTAT
RICOCHET
ROYALIST
RUDIMENT
RUMINANT
RUNABOUT
SAILBOAT
SANSKRIT
SCILICET
SEACOAST
SEAMOUNT
SEDIMENT
SEMISOFT
SENTIENT
SERGEANT
SHIPMENT
SHOPLIFT
SHORTCUT
SIBILANT
SIGNPOST
SKYLIGHT
SLIPKNOT
SNAPSHOT
SOMERSET
SOMEWHAT
SPROCKET
STAGNANT
STAKEOUT
STALWART
STANDOUT
STRAIGHT
STRIDENT
STRUMPET
SUBTRACT
SUCCINCT
SUNLIGHT
SUPERJET
SUPPLANT
SURMOUNT
TAILCOAT
TELECAST
TENEMENT
THICKSET
TRANSACT
TRANSEPT
TRANSMIT
TURBOJET
TURNCOAT
TURNSPIT
TWILIGHT
TYPECAST
UNDERACT
UNDERCUT
UNDULANT
UNSOUGHT
UNTAUGHT
UPPERCUT
UPTHRUST
USUFRUCT
VEHEMENT
VESICANT
VESTMENT
VIGILANT
VIRULENT
VISCOUNT
VISITANT
VOCALIST
WAINSCOT
WELDMENT
WHODUNIT
WRISTLET
FLAMBEAU
FROUFROU
YUGOSLAV
BUNGALOW
CHOWCHOW
COCKCROW
COLESLAW
CROSSBOW
DISALLOW
FOREKNOW
FURBELOW
GANGPLOW
HEDGEROW
HIGHBROW
HONEYDEW
HOOSEGOW
KICKSHAW
MACKINAW
OVERDRAW
OVERFLOW
OVERGROW
OVERVIEW
SCOFFLAW
SETSCREW
SIDESHOW
SNOWPLOW
SOUTHPAW
TELEVIEW
TOMORROW
UNDERTOW
WILLIWAW
WIREDRAW
WITHDRAW
AFTERTAX
APPENDIX
AVIATRIX
BICONVEX
CICATRIX
CRUCIFIX
INTERMIX
ORTHODOX
PARALLAX
SMALLPOX
TRANSFIX
ACERBITY
ACRIMONY
ACTIVITY
ADULTERY
ADVISORY
AEROLOGY
AFFINITY
AGRONOMY
ALACRITY
ALEATORY
ALLEGORY
ALLEYWAY
ALMIGHTY
ANCESTRY
ANTIBODY
ANTIMONY
ANTINOMY
APOPLEXY
APOSTASY
ARTISTRY
ASPERITY
ASSEMBLY
ATROCITY
ATTORNEY
AUDITORY
BARBERRY
BARRATRY
BAYBERRY
BEAUTIFY
BEGGARLY
BESTIARY
BIRTHDAY
BIWEEKLY
BIYEARLY
BOUNDARY
BREVIARY
BUOYANCY
BURGLARY
BURGUNDY
BUSYBODY
CALAMITY
CAPACITY
CASTAWAY
CASUALTY
CATEGORY
CAUSEWAY
CELERITY
CELIBACY
CEMETERY
CEREMONY
CHAMBRAY
CHANCERY
CHASTITY
CHEMURGY
CHIVALRY
CHOIRBOY
CIRCUITY
CIVILITY
CLASSIFY
CLEMENCY
COLLIERY
COLLOQUY
CONTRARY
CORDUROY
CORONARY
COURTESY
CREAMERY
CROCKERY
CULINARY
CUPIDITY
CURRENCY
CYTOLOGY
DEBILITY
DELICACY
DELIVERY
DETOXIFY
DEWBERRY
DILATORY
DISARRAY
DISUNITY
DIVINITY
DOOMSDAY
DOUGHBOY
DOXOLOGY
DRIVEWAY
EMISSARY
EMULSIFY
ENORMITY
ENTIRETY
EPILEPSY
EPIPHANY
ETERNITY
ETHOLOGY
ETIOLOGY
EVERYDAY
EXIGENCY
FACILITY
FATALITY
FEBRUARY
FELICITY
FEROCITY
FERVENCY
FIDELITY
FIRECLAY
FLATTERY
FOLDAWAY
FORELADY
FORESTRY
FORMERLY
FORTUITY
FRIPPERY
FRUCTIFY
FUNERARY
FUTILITY
FUTURITY
GEMOLOGY
GEOMETRY
GINGERLY
GIVEAWAY
GLOSSARY
GRATUITY
GREENERY
GUARANTY
GUERNSEY
HATCHWAY
HEGEMONY
HERALDRY
HEREDITY
HIDEAWAY
HOMEBODY
HONORARY
HOROLOGY
HORSEFLY
HOSTELRY
HOUSEBOY
HOUSEFLY
HUMANITY
HUMIDIFY
HUMIDITY
HUMILITY
IDENTIFY
IDENTITY
IDEOLOGY
IDOLATRY
ILLUSORY
IMPUNITY
INDUSTRY
INFANTRY
INFINITY
INIQUITY
INWARDLY
ISOSTASY
JEOPARDY
KOLINSKY
LAMASERY
LAPIDARY
LATCHKEY
LAVATORY
LETHARGY
LITERARY
LOBOTOMY
LOCALITY
LUMINARY
MAHOGANY
MAINSTAY
MAJORITY
MALARKEY
MANNERLY
MASTERLY
MATURITY
MILITARY
MINATORY
MINISTRY
MINORITY
MISAPPLY
MISCARRY
MONARCHY
MONETARY
MONITORY
MONOGAMY
MONOPOLY
MORALITY
MORTUARY
MULBERRY
MULTIPLY
MUSKETRY
MYCOLOGY
NATALITY
NATIVITY
NOBILITY
NONDAIRY
NUGATORY
OBITUARY
ORANGERY
ORDINARY
ORTHOEPY
OVERPLAY
OVERSTAY
PANDOWDY
PEDAGOGY
PENOLOGY
PHANTASY
PHARMACY
PLEURISY
PODIATRY
POLARITY
POLYGAMY
POPINJAY
PORPHYRY
POTBELLY
PRETTIFY
PROPERTY
PROPHECY
PROPHESY
PSALMODY
QUANDARY
QUANTITY
RAILLERY
REFINERY
REGISTRY
REVIVIFY
RHAPSODY
RHEOLOGY
ROCKETRY
ROSEMARY
SACRISTY
SALUTARY
SANCTIFY
SANCTITY
SANITARY
SATURDAY
SCARCELY
SCRAGGLY
SCRUTINY
SCULLERY
SECURITY
SEMINARY
SEROLOGY
SILICIFY
SIMPLIFY
SLIPPERY
SLOVENLY
SNOBBERY
SOBRIETY
SOLDIERY
SOLIDIFY
SOLITARY
SOLVENCY
SOMEBODY
SORORITY
SPEEDWAY
SPILLWAY
STAIRWAY
STATUARY
STEALTHY
STOWAWAY
STRATEGY
STRATIFY
STULTIFY
SYMMETRY
SYMPATHY
SYMPHONY
TAPESTRY
TAXONOMY
TELEPLAY
TEMERITY
TENANTRY
TENDENCY
TENPENNY
TERTIARY
THEOLOGY
THIEVERY
THRENODY
THURSDAY
TOILETRY
TONALITY
TOPOLOGY
TOTALITY
TRAVESTY

TREASURY
TRICKERY
TRUMPERY
TUTELARY
TWOPENNY
UNDERPAY
UNGAINLY
UNKINDLY
UNLIKELY
UNLOVELY
UNSAVORY
UNSEEMLY
UNSTEADY
UNTIMELY
UNWIELDY
UNWORTHY
VAGRANCY
VELLEITY
VELOCITY
VERACITY
VICINITY
VILLAINY
VINEGARY
VIROLOGY
VITALITY
VIVACITY
WALKAWAY
WARRANTY
WATERWAY
WEAPONRY
WHITEFLY
WITCHERY
WIZARDRY
WORDPLAY
WORKADAY
YEOMANRY
SCHMALTZ

# 9 LETTER WORDS

**1ST LETTER**

ABANDONED
ABATEMENT
ABHORRENT
ABOMINATE
ABORIGINE
ABSORBENT
ACCESSION
ACCESSORY
ACCIDENCE
ACCLIMATE
ACCLIVITY
ACCOMPANY
ACCORDION
ACCRETION
ACETYLENE
ACIDULATE
ACIDULOUS
ACOUSTICS
ACQUIESCE
ACROPOLIS
ADDICTION
ADDRESSEE
ADIABATIC
ADJECTIVE
ADJOINING
ADMIRABLE
ADMIRALTY
ADMISSION
ADMIXTURE
ADSORBATE
ADSORBENT
ADUMBRATE
ADVANTAGE
ADVENTURE
ADVERSARY
ADVERSITY
ADVERTISE
ADVISABLE
AERIALIST
AERODROME
AEROPAUSE
AEROPLANE
AEROSPACE
AESTHETIC
AESTIVATE
AFFECTING
AFFECTION
AFFIDAVIT
AFFILIATE
AFFLUENCE
AFORESAID
AFRIKAANS
AFTERCARE
AFTERDECK
AFTERGLOW
AFTERLIFE
AFTERMATH
AFTERNOON
AFTERWARD
AGGRAVATE
AGGREGATE
AGREEABLE
AGREEMENT
AILANTHUS
AIRMOBILE
AIRWORTHY
ALABASTER
ALBATROSS
ALCOHOLIC
ALEATORIC
ALGONQUIN
ALGORITHM
ALIENABLE
ALLERGIST
ALLEVIATE
ALLIGATOR
ALLOWANCE
ALMANDITE
ALMSHOUSE
ALONGSIDE
ALTERNATE
ALTIMETER
ALUMINIUM
ALUMINIZE
AMARYLLIS
AMBERGRIS
AMBIGUOUS
AMBITIOUS
AMBULANCE
AMBUSCADE
AMENDMENT
AMERICANA
AMERICIUM
AMIDSHIPS
AMORPHOUS
AMPERSAND
AMPHIBIAN
AMPHIBOLE
AMPLITUDE
ANAEROBIC
ANALGESIA
ANALGESIC
ANALOGOUS
ANARCHISM
ANATOMIZE
ANCHORAGE
ANCHORITE
ANCHORMAN
ANCILLARY
ANGELFISH
ANGLEWORM
ANGLICIZE
ANGUISHED
ANHYDROUS
ANIMALISM
ANIMATION
ANIMOSITY
ANKLEBONE
ANNOUNCER
ANNOYANCE
ANNUITANT
ANOMALOUS
ANONYMOUS
ANOPHELES
ANTARCTIC
ANTECHOIR
ANTHOLOGY
ANTICLINE
ANTIKNOCK
ANTINOVEL
ANTIPASTO
ANTIPATHY
ANTIQUARY
ANTIQUITY
ANTISERUM
ANTITOXIN
ANTITUMOR
ANTIVENIN
APARTHEID
APARTMENT
APOCRYPHA
APOLOGIZE
APOSTOLIC
APPALOOSA
APPARATUS
APPELLANT
APPELLATE
APPENDAGE
APPERTAIN
APPETIZER
APPLEJACK
APPLETALK
APPLIANCE
APPLICANT
APPOINTEE
APPORTION
APPREHEND
AQUAPLANE
ARABESQUE
ARBITRARY
ARBITRATE
ARBORETUM
ARCHANGEL
ARCHENEMY
ARCHETYPE
ARCHFIEND
ARCHITECT
ARCHIVIST
ARGENTINE
ARGENTITE
ARMADILLO
ARMISTICE
ARROWHEAD
ARROWROOT
ARTERIOLE
ARTHRITIS
ARTHROPOD
ARTICHOKE
ARTICULAR
ARTIFICER
ARTILLERY
ASAFETIDA
ASCENDANT
ASCENDERS
ASCENSION
ASCERTAIN
ASPARAGUS
ASPERSION
ASSEMBLER
ASSERTION
ASSIDUOUS
ASSISTANT
ASSOCIATE
ASSONANCE
ASSURANCE
ASTRADDLE
ASTRAKHAN
ASTROLABE
ASTROLOGY
ASTRONAUT
ASTRONOMY
ASYMPTOTE
ATHENAEUM
ATHLETICS
ATONEMENT
ATROCIOUS
ATTAINDER
ATTENDANT
ATTENTION
ATTENUATE
ATTRIBUTE
ATTRITION
AUCTORIAL
AUDACIOUS
AUDIOLOGY
AURICULAR
AUTHENTIC
AUTHORITY
AUTHORIZE
AUTOCRACY
AUTOGRAPH
AUTOMATIC
AUTOMATON
AUTOTRACE
AUXILIARY
AVAILABLE
AVALANCHE
AVOCATION
AVUNCULAR
AWESTRUCK
BACCHANAL
BACKBOARD
BACKFIELD
BACKPEDAL
BACKSLASH
BACKSLIDE
BACKSTAGE
BACKSWEPT
BACKTRACK
BACKWATER
BACKWOODS
BACTERIUM
BADMINTON
BAGATELLE
BAILIWICK
BAKSHEESH
BALALAIKA
BALDACHIN
BALLADEER
BALLERINA
BAMBOOZLE
BANDEROLE
BANDOLIER
BANDSTAND
BANDWAGON
BANDWIDTH
BANQUETTE
BANTUSTAN
BARBARIAN
BARBARISM
BARBAROUS
BARCAROLE
BAREFACED
BARKEEPER
BARNSTORM
BAROGRAPH
BAROMETER
BARRACUDA
BARRICADE
BARRISTER
BARTENDER
BASEBOARD
BASTINADO
BATHHOUSE
BATHOLITH
BATTALION
BEACHHEAD
BEATITUDE
BEAUTEOUS
BEAUTIFUL
BEDFELLOW
BEDRIDDEN
BEDSPREAD
BEEFEATER
BEEFSTEAK
BEEKEEPER
BELEAGUER
BELLICOSE
BELLYACHE
BELVEDERE
BENIGHTED
BENIGNANT
BENTONITE
BERKELIUM
BERYLLIUM
BESETTING
BESPANGLE
BESPATTER
BETROTHED
BICAMERAL
BICONCAVE
BIFURCATE
BILATERAL
BILINGUAL
BILLBOARD
BILLIARDS
BIMONTHLY
BINOCULAR
BINOMINAL
BIOGRAPHY
BIOSPHERE
BIPARTITE
BIRDHOUSE
BIRTHMARK
BIRTHRATE
BISHOPRIC
BLACKBALL
BLACKBIRD
BLACKBODY
BLACKFOOT
BLACKHEAD
BLACKJACK
BLACKLIST
BLACKMAIL
BLASPHEME
BLASPHEMY
BLEACHERS
BLINDFOLD
BLOCKHEAD
BLOODBATH
BLOODLINE
BLOODROOT
BLOODSHED
BLOODSHOT
BLOWTORCH
BLUEBERRY
BLUEBLACK
BLUEGRASS
BLUEPOINT
BLUEPRINT
BOARDWALK
BOATSWAIN
BODYGUARD
BOLSHEVIK
BOMBAZINE
BOMBPROOF
BOMBSHELL
BOMBSIGHT
BONDWOMAN
BOOKMAKER
BOOKPLATE
BOOKSHELF
BOOMERANG
BOONDOCKS
BOOTBLACK
BOULEVARD
BOUNTEOUS
BOUNTIFUL
BOURGEOIS
BOWSTRING
BRASSERIE
BRASSIERE
BRAZILIAN
BREAKDOWN
BREAKFAST
BREEZEWAY
BRIEFCASE
BRILLIANT
BRIMSTONE
BRIQUETTE
BRITANNIC
BROADBAND
BROADCAST
BROADLOOM
BROADSIDE
BROADTAIL
BROCHETTE
BROKERAGE
BRONCHIAL
BRUSHWOOD
BRUTALIZE
BUCCANEER
BUCKBOARD
BUCKTOOTH
BUCKWHEAT
BULGARIAN
BULLFIGHT
BULLFINCH
BUMBLEBEE
BUMPTIOUS
BURLESQUE
BURUNDIAN
BUSHWHACK
BUTTERCUP
BUTTERFAT
BUTTERFLY
BUTTERNUT
BYSTANDER
CABLEGRAM
CABRIOLET
CACOPHONY
CAFETERIA
CALABOOSE
CALCIMINE
CALCULATE
CALENDULA

CALIBRATE
CALLOSITY
CALORIFIC
CALVINISM
CAMELBACK
CAMEMBERT
CAMPANILE
CAMPSTOOL
CANALBOAT
CANDIDACY
CANDIDATE
CANDLEMAS
CANDLEPIN
CANEBRAKE
CANNONADE
CANNONEER
CANONICAL
CANTABILE
CANTHARIS
CAPACIOUS
CAPACITOR
CAPARISON
CAPILLARY
CAPITALLY
CAPRICCIO
CAPSULATE
CAPTIVATE
CARBONATE
CARBUNCLE
CARBURIZE
CARCINOMA
CARDBOARD
CARETAKER
CARIBBEAN
CARNATION
CARNELIAN
CARNIVORA
CARNIVORE
CARPENTER
CARPETBAG
CARPETING
CARROUSEL
CARTILAGE
CARTRIDGE
CARTWHEEL
CASSEROLE
CASSOWARY
CASTANETS
CASTIGATE
CASUISTRY
CATACLYSM
CATALEPSY
CATALYSIS
CATAMARAN
CATAMOUNT
CATATONIC
CATCHMENT

CATCHWORD
CATECHISM
CATERWAUL
CATHARSIS
CATHARTIC
CATHEDRAL
CAUCASIAN
CAUSATION
CAUTERIZE
CAVALCADE
CEASELESS
CELANDINE
CELEBRATE
CELEBRITY
CELESTIAL
CELLARAGE
CELLULOSE
CENTENARY
CENTESIMO
CENTIGRAM
CENTIPEDE
CENTURION
CEREBRATE
CERECLOTH
CERTAINTY
CERTITUDE
CESSATION
CHAFFINCH
CHALKBORD
CHALLENGE
CHAMELEON
CHAMOMILE
CHAMPAGNE
CHAMPAIGN
CHANCROID
CHANTEUSE
CHAPARRAL
CHARABANC
CHARACTER
CHARLATAN
CHARWOMAN
CHAUFFEUR
CHECKBOOK
CHECKLIST
CHECKMATE
CHECKROOM
CHEEKBONE
CHEERLESS
CHEMISTRY
CHEVALIER
CHICANERY
CHICKADEE
CHICKASAW
CHICKWEED
CHIEFTAIN
CHILBLAIN
CHILDHOOD

CHIROPODY
CHIVALRIC
CHLORDANE
CHOCOLATE
CHONDRITE
CHONDRULE
CHOPHOUSE
CHOPSTICK
CHORISTER
CHRISTIAN
CHRISTMAS
CHROMATIC
CHRONICLE
CHRYSALIS
CHUCKHOLE
CHURCHMAN
CIGARETTE
CIGARILLO
CIRCADIAN
CIRCUITRY
CIRCULATE
CIRRHOSIS
CITIZENRY
CLAMSHELL
CLAPBOARD
CLASSICAL
CLASSMATE
CLASSROOM
CLEARANCE
CLERGYMAN
CLIENTELE
CLINICIAN
CLIPBOARD
CLIPSHEET
CLOCKWISE
CLOCKWORK
CLOISONNE
CLUBHOUSE
COADJUTOR
COAGULANT
COAGULATE
COALFIELD
COALITION
COASTLINE
COCHINEAL
COCKATIEL
COCKFIGHT
COCKROACH
COFEATURE
COFFEEPOT
COFFERDAM
COGNITION
COIFFEUSE
COLLATION
COLLEAGUE
COLLECTED
COLLEGIAN

COLLEGIUM
COLLIMATE
COLLODION
COLLUSION
COLLUVIUM
COLONNADE
COLORCAST
COLORFAST
COLUMBINE
COLUMNIST
COMFORTER
COMMANDER
COMMINGLE
COMMISSAR
COMMITTEE
COMMODITY
COMMODORE
COMMOTION
COMMUNION
COMMUNISM
COMMUNITY
COMPANION
COMPETENT
COMPLAINT
COMPONENT
COMPOSITE
COMPOSURE
CONCERNED
CONCERTED
CONCIERGE
CONCORDAT
CONCOURSE
CONCUBINE
CONDENSER
CONDIMENT
CONDITION
CONDUCTOR
CONESTOGA
CONFESSOR
CONFIDANT
CONFUSION
CONGENIAL
CONGERIES
CONGRUITY
CONJUGATE
CONNUBIAL
CONSCIOUS
CONSCRIPT
CONSENSUS
CONSONANT
CONSTABLE
CONSTANCY
CONSTRAIN
CONSTRICT
CONSTRUCT
CONTAGION
CONTAINER

CONTENTED
CONTINENT
CONTINUAL
CONTINUUM
CONTRALTO
CONTUMELY
CONTUSION
CONUNDRUM
CONVIVIAL
COONHOUND
COOPERATE
COPARTNER
COPYRIGHT
CORELDRAW
CORIANDER
CORKSCREW
CORMORANT
CORNSTALK
COROLLARY
CORPORATE
CORPOREAL
CORPUSCLE
CORRELATE
CORRUGATE
CORTISONE
CORUSCATE
COSMOGONY
COSMOLOGY
COSMONAUT
COSPONSOR
COTILLION
COTYLEDON
COUNSELOR
COUNTDOWN
COUNTLESS
COURTEOUS
COURTESAN
COURTROOM
COURTSHIP
COURTYARD
COUTURIER
COVALENCE
CRABGRASS
CRACKDOWN
CRAFTSMAN
CRANBERRY
CRANKCASE
CREDULOUS
CREMATORY
CRESCENDO
CRETINISM
CRINOLINE
CRITERION
CRITICISM
CRITICIZE
CROCODILE
CROISSANT

CROQUETTE
CROSSOVER
CROSSROAD
CROSSWALK
CROSSWAYS
CROSSWISE
CRUCIFORM
CRYOGENIC
CUBBYHOLE
CULLENDER
CULMINATE
CULTIVATE
CUNEIFORM
CUPBEARER
CURETTAGE
CURRYCOMB
CURVATURE
CUSTODIAL
CUSTODIAN
CUSTOMARY
CUSTOMIZE
CUTANEOUS
CUTTHROAT
CYCLAMATE
CYCLOTRON
CYTOPLASM
DACHSHUND
DAIRYMAID
DALMATION
DAMASCENE
DAMNATION
DAMSELFLY
DANDELION
DANGEROUS
DAREDEVIL
DARWINISM
DASHBOARD
DAUNTLESS
DAVENPORT
DEATHBLOW
DEATHLESS
DEBENTURE
DEBUTANTE
DECADENCE
DECALOGUE
DECATHLON
DECEITFUL
DECENNIAL
DECEPTION
DECIDUOUS
DECILITER
DECIMETER
DECISTERE
DECLIVITY
DECOLLETE
DECOMPOSE
DECONTROL

DECORATOR
DECOUPAGE
DECREMENT
DEDUCTION
DEFEATISM
DEFECTIVE
DEFENDANT
DEFENSIVE
DEFERENCE
DEFERMENT
DEFICIENT
DEFLATION
DEFOLIANT
DEFOLIATE
DEFORMITY
DEHYDRATE
DEJECTION
DEKALITER
DEKAMETER
DEKASTERE
DELFTWARE
DELICIOUS
DELIGHTED
DELIMITER
DELINEATE
DEMAGOGUE
DEMARCATE
DEMIMONDE
DEMITASSE
DEMOCRACY
DEMULCENT
DEMURRAGE
DENIGRATE
DENTITION
DEODORANT
DEODORIZE
DEOXIDIZE
DEPARTURE
DEPENDENT
DEPRECATE
DEPRESSED
DERRINGER
DESCENDER
DESECRATE
DESICCANT
DESICCATE
DESIGNATE
DESIGNING
DESIRABLE
DESPERADO
DESPERATE
DESTITUTE
DESTROYER
DESUETUDE
DESULTORY
DETECTIVE
DETENTION

DETERGENT
DETERMINE
DETERRENT
DETONATOR
DETRIMENT
DEUTERIUM
DEVASTATE
DEVILMENT
DEXTERITY
DEXTEROUS
DHRYSTONE
DIACRITIC
DIAERESIS
DIAGNOSIS
DIALECTIC
DIAMETRIC
DIAPHRAGM
DIATHERMY
DIATOMITE
DICHOTOMY
DIETETICS
DIFFERENT
DIFFICULT
DIFFIDENT
DIGITALIS
DIGITIZED
DIGNIFIED
DIGNITARY
DIMENSION
DIMORPHIC
DIPHTHONG
DIPLOMACY
DIPTEROUS
DIRECTION
DIRECTIVE
DIRECTORY
DIRIGIBLE
DISAFFECT
DISAPPEAR
DISBURDEN
DISCHARGE
DISCOMFIT
DISCOURSE
DISCREDIT
DISEMBARK
DISEMBODY
DISENGAGE
DISESTEEM
DISFIGURE
DISHCLOTH
DISHONEST
DISHWATER
DISINFECT
DISLOCATE
DISMANTLE
DISMEMBER
DISOBLIGE

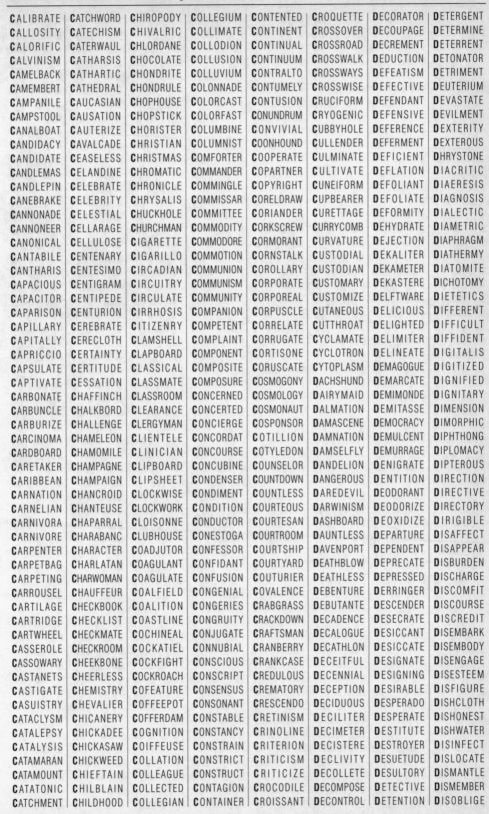

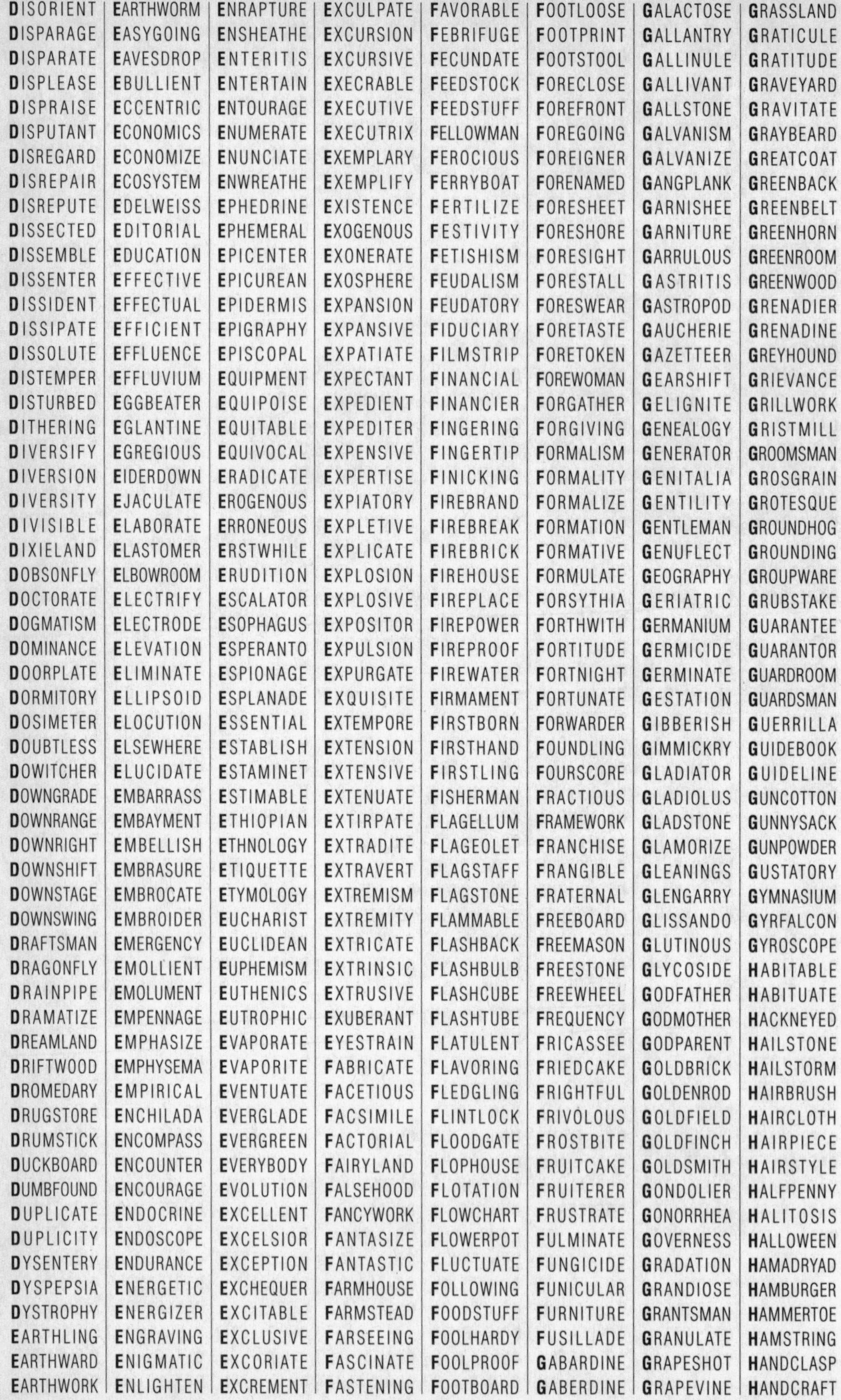

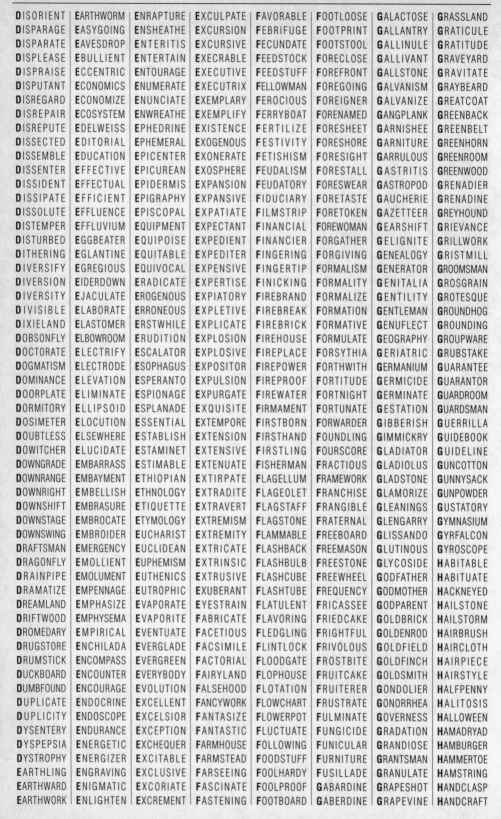

DISORIENT
DISPARAGE
DISPARATE
DISPLEASE
DISPRAISE
DISPUTANT
DISREGARD
DISREPAIR
DISREPUTE
DISSECTED
DISSEMBLE
DISSENTER
DISSIDENT
DISSIPATE
DISSOLUTE
DISTEMPER
DISTURBED
DITHERING
DIVERSIFY
DIVERSION
DIVERSITY
DIVISIBLE
DIXIELAND
DOBSONFLY
DOCTORATE
DOGMATISM
DOMINANCE
DOORPLATE
DORMITORY
DOSIMETER
DOUBTLESS
DOWITCHER
DOWNGRADE
DOWNRANGE
DOWNRIGHT
DOWNSHIFT
DOWNSTAGE
DOWNSWING
DRAFTSMAN
DRAGONFLY
DRAINPIPE
DRAMATIZE
DREAMLAND
DRIFTWOOD
DROMEDARY
DRUGSTORE
DRUMSTICK
DUCKBOARD
DUMBFOUND
DUPLICATE
DUPLICITY
DYSENTERY
DYSPEPSIA
DYSTROPHY
EARTHLING
EARTHWARD
EARTHWORK
EARTHWORM
EASYGOING
EAVESDROP
EBULLIENT
ECCENTRIC
ECONOMICS
ECONOMIZE
ECOSYSTEM
EDELWEISS
EDITORIAL
EDUCATION
EFFECTIVE
EFFECTUAL
EFFICIENT
EFFLUENCE
EFFLUVIUM
EGGBEATER
EGLANTINE
EGREGIOUS
EIDERDOWN
EJACULATE
ELABORATE
ELASTOMER
ELBOWROOM
ELECTRIFY
ELECTRODE
ELEVATION
ELIMINATE
ELLIPSOID
ELOCUTION
ELSEWHERE
ELUCIDATE
EMBARRASS
EMBAYMENT
EMBELLISH
EMBRASURE
EMBROCATE
EMBROIDER
EMERGENCY
EMOLLIENT
EMOLUMENT
EMPENNAGE
EMPHASIZE
EMPHYSEMA
EMPIRICAL
ENCHILADA
ENCOMPASS
ENCOUNTER
ENCOURAGE
ENDOCRINE
ENDOSCOPE
ENDURANCE
ENERGETIC
ENERGIZER
ENGRAVING
ENIGMATIC
ENLIGHTEN
ENRAPTURE
ENSHEATHE
ENTERITIS
ENTERTAIN
ENTOURAGE
ENUMERATE
ENUNCIATE
ENWREATHE
EPHEDRINE
EPHEMERAL
EPICENTER
EPICUREAN
EPIDERMIS
EPIGRAPHY
EPISCOPAL
EQUIPMENT
EQUIPOISE
EQUITABLE
EQUIVOCAL
ERADICATE
EROGENOUS
ERRONEOUS
ERSTWHILE
ERUDITION
ESCALATOR
ESOPHAGUS
ESPERANTO
ESPIONAGE
ESPLANADE
ESSENTIAL
ESTABLISH
ESTAMINET
ESTIMABLE
ETHIOPIAN
ETHNOLOGY
ETIQUETTE
ETYMOLOGY
EUCHARIST
EUCLIDEAN
EUPHEMISM
EUTHENICS
EUTROPHIC
EVAPORATE
EVAPORITE
EVENTUATE
EVERGLADE
EVERGREEN
EVERYBODY
EVOLUTION
EXCELLENT
EXCELSIOR
EXCEPTION
EXCHEQUER
EXCITABLE
EXCLUSIVE
EXCORIATE
EXCREMENT
EXCULPATE
EXCURSION
EXCURSIVE
EXECRABLE
EXECUTIVE
EXECUTRIX
EXEMPLARY
EXEMPLIFY
EXISTENCE
EXOGENOUS
EXONERATE
EXOSPHERE
EXPANSION
EXPANSIVE
EXPATIATE
EXPECTANT
EXPEDIENT
EXPEDITER
EXPENSIVE
EXPERTISE
EXPIATORY
EXPLETIVE
EXPLICATE
EXPLOSION
EXPLOSIVE
EXPOSITOR
EXPULSION
EXPURGATE
EXQUISITE
EXTEMPORE
EXTENSION
EXTENSIVE
EXTENUATE
EXTIRPATE
EXTRADITE
EXTRAVERT
EXTREMISM
EXTREMITY
EXTRICATE
EXTRINSIC
EXTRUSIVE
EXUBERANT
EYESTRAIN
FABRICATE
FACETIOUS
FACSIMILE
FACTORIAL
FAIRYLAND
FALSEHOOD
FANCYWORK
FANTASIZE
FANTASTIC
FARMHOUSE
FARMSTEAD
FARSEEING
FASCINATE
FASTENING
FAVORABLE
FEBRIFUGE
FECUNDATE
FEEDSTOCK
FEEDSTUFF
FELLOWMAN
FEROCIOUS
FERRYBOAT
FERTILIZE
FESTIVITY
FETISHISM
FEUDALISM
FEUDATORY
FIDUCIARY
FILMSTRIP
FINANCIAL
FINANCIER
FINGERING
FINGERTIP
FINICKING
FIREBRAND
FIREBREAK
FIREBRICK
FIREHOUSE
FIREPLACE
FIREPOWER
FIREPROOF
FIREWATER
FIRMAMENT
FIRSTBORN
FIRSTHAND
FIRSTLING
FISHERMAN
FLAGELLUM
FLAGEOLET
FLAGSTAFF
FLAGSTONE
FLAMMABLE
FLASHBACK
FLASHBULB
FLASHCUBE
FLASHTUBE
FLATULENT
FLAVORING
FLEDGLING
FLINTLOCK
FLOODGATE
FLOPHOUSE
FLOTATION
FLOWCHART
FLOWERPOT
FLUCTUATE
FOLLOWING
FOODSTUFF
FOOLHARDY
FOOLPROOF
FOOTBOARD
FOOTLOOSE
FOOTPRINT
FOOTSTOOL
FORECLOSE
FOREFRONT
FOREGOING
FOREIGNER
FORENAMED
FORESHEET
FORESHORE
FORESIGHT
FORESTALL
FORESWEAR
FORETASTE
FORETOKEN
FOREWOMAN
FORGATHER
FORGIVING
FORMALISM
FORMALITY
FORMALIZE
FORMATION
FORMATIVE
FORMULATE
FORSYTHIA
FORTHWITH
FORTITUDE
FORTNIGHT
FORTUNATE
FORWARDER
FOUNDLING
FOURSCORE
FRACTIOUS
FRAMEWORK
FRANCHISE
FRANGIBLE
FRATERNAL
FREEBOARD
FREEMASON
FREESTONE
FREEWHEEL
FREQUENCY
FRICASSEE
FRIEDCAKE
FRIGHTFUL
FRIVOLOUS
FROSTBITE
FRUITCAKE
FRUITERER
FRUSTRATE
FULMINATE
FUNGICIDE
FUNICULAR
FURNITURE
FUSILLADE
GABARDINE
GABERDINE
GALACTOSE
GALLANTRY
GALLINULE
GALLIVANT
GALLSTONE
GALVANISM
GALVANIZE
GANGPLANK
GARNISHEE
GARNITURE
GARRULOUS
GASTRITIS
GASTROPOD
GAUCHERIE
GAZETTEER
GEARSHIFT
GELIGNITE
GENEALOGY
GENERATOR
GENITALIA
GENTILITY
GENTLEMAN
GENUFLECT
GEOGRAPHY
GERIATRIC
GERMANIUM
GERMICIDE
GERMINATE
GESTATION
GIBBERISH
GIMMICKRY
GLADIATOR
GLADIOLUS
GLADSTONE
GLAMORIZE
GLEANINGS
GLENGARRY
GLISSANDO
GLUTINOUS
GLYCOSIDE
GODFATHER
GODMOTHER
GODPARENT
GOLDBRICK
GOLDENROD
GOLDFIELD
GOLDFINCH
GOLDSMITH
GONDOLIER
GONORRHEA
GOVERNESS
GRADATION
GRANDIOSE
GRANTSMAN
GRANULATE
GRAPESHOT
GRAPEVINE
GRASSLAND
GRATICULE
GRATITUDE
GRAVEYARD
GRAVITATE
GRAYBEARD
GREATCOAT
GREENBACK
GREENBELT
GREENHORN
GREENROOM
GREENWOOD
GRENADIER
GRENADINE
GREYHOUND
GRIEVANCE
GRILLWORK
GRISTMILL
GROOMSMAN
GROSGRAIN
GROTESQUE
GROUNDHOG
GROUNDING
GROUPWARE
GRUBSTAKE
GUARANTEE
GUARANTOR
GUARDROOM
GUARDSMAN
GUERRILLA
GUIDEBOOK
GUIDELINE
GUNCOTTON
GUNNYSACK
GUNPOWDER
GUSTATORY
GYMNASIUM
GYRFALCON
GYROSCOPE
HABITABLE
HABITUATE
HACKNEYED
HAILSTONE
HAILSTORM
HAIRBRUSH
HAIRCLOTH
HAIRPIECE
HAIRSTYLE
HALFPENNY
HALITOSIS
HALLOWEEN
HAMADRYAD
HAMBURGER
HAMMERTOE
HAMSTRING
HANDCLASP
HANDCRAFT

HANDIWORK
HANDSHAKE
HANDSPIKE
HANDSTAND
HANDWOVEN
HAPHAZARD
HAPPENING
HAPPINESS
HARBINGER
HARBORAGE
HARDBOARD
HARDBOUND
HARDCOVER
HARDIHOOD
HARDSTAND
HARLEQUIN
HARMONICA
HARMONICS
HARMONIUM
HARMONIZE
HARTSHORN
HATCHMENT
HAVERSACK
HEADBOARD
HEADDRESS
HEADFIRST
HEADLIGHT
HEADPHONE
HEADPIECE
HEADSTALL
HEADSTONE
HEADWATER
HEALTHFUL
HEARTACHE
HEARTBEAT
HEARTBURN
HEARTFELT
HEARTLESS
HEARTSICK
HEARTWOOD
HECTOGRAM
HELLEBORE
HELLENISM
HELVETIAN
HELVETICA
HEMISTICH
HEMSTITCH
HEPATITIS
HERBALIST
HERBARIUM
HERBICIDE
HERCULEAN
HEREAFTER
HEREUNDER
HERITABLE
HERMITAGE
HETERODOX
HEURISTIC
HEXAMETER
HIBERNATE
HIDEBOUND
HIERARCHY
HIGHLIGHT
HILARIOUS
HILLBILLY
HINDRANCE
HINDSIGHT
HISTAMINE
HISTOGRAM
HISTORIAN
HITCHHIKE
HOARFROST
HOBGOBLIN
HOLLYHOCK
HOLOCAUST
HOLOGRAPH
HOLYSTONE
HOMEGROWN
HOMEMAKER
HOMESTEAD
HOMOGRAPH
HOMOPHONE
HONEYCOMB
HONEYMOON
HONORABLE
HONORIFIC
HOPSCOTCH
HOREHOUND
HOROSCOPE
HORSEBACK
HORSEHAIR
HORSEHIDE
HORSEPLAY
HORSESHOE
HORSETAIL
HORSEWHIP
HORTATIVE
HORTATORY
HOTHEADED
HOURGLASS
HOUSEBOAT
HOUSECOAT
HOUSEHOLD
HOUSEMAID
HOUSEWIFE
HOUSEWORK
HOWSOEVER
HUMANKIND
HUMDINGER
HUMILIATE
HUNCHBACK
HUNGARIAN
HURRICANE
HUSBANDRY
HYDRANGEA
HYDRAULIC
HYDROFOIL
HYDROLOGY
HYDROXIDE
HYPERBOLA
HYPERBOLE
HYPERCARD
HYPERTEXT
HYPHENATE
HYPOCRISY
HYSTERICS
ICELANDER
ICELANDIC
IDENTICAL
IGNORANCE
ILLEGIBLE
ILLIBERAL
ILLOGICAL
IMAGINARY
IMBALANCE
IMBROGLIO
IMITATION
IMITATIVE
IMMEDIACY
IMMEDIATE
IMMIGRANT
IMMIGRATE
IMMOVABLE
IMMUTABLE
IMPARTIAL
IMPASSIVE
IMPATIENS
IMPATIENT
IMPEDANCE
IMPERFECT
IMPERIOUS
IMPETUOUS
IMPLEMENT
IMPLICATE
IMPOLITIC
IMPORTANT
IMPORTUNE
IMPOSTURE
IMPRECATE
IMPRECISE
IMPROMPTU
IMPROVISE
IMPRUDENT
IMPULSION
IMPULSIVE
INABILITY
INAMORATA
INANIMATE
INANITION
INAUGURAL
INCAPABLE
INCARNATE
INCENTIVE
INCEPTION
INCESSANT
INCIDENCE
INCIPIENT
INCLEMENT
INCOGNITO
INCOMMODE
INCORRECT
INCREMENT
INCUBATOR
INCULCATE
INCULPATE
INCUMBENT
INCURABLE
INCURIOUS
INCURSION
INDELIBLE
INDEMNIFY
INDEMNITY
INDENTION
INDENTURE
INDIGNANT
INDIGNITY
INDUCTION
INDUCTIVE
INEBRIATE
INEFFABLE
INELEGANT
INFANTILE
INFATUATE
INFECTION
INFERENCE
INFERTILE
INFIRMARY
INFIRMITY
INFLATION
INFLEXION
INFLUENCE
INFLUENZA
INFORMANT
INFURIATE
INFUSIBLE
INGENIOUS
INGENUITY
INGENUOUS
INGLENOOK
INGROWING
INHALATOR
INJECTION
INJUSTICE
INNERMOST
INNERSOLE
INNKEEPER
INNOCENCE
INNOCUOUS
INOCULATE
INORGANIC
INPATIENT
INSATIATE
INSENSATE
INSERTION
INSIDIOUS
INSINCERE
INSINUATE
INSISTENT
INSOLUBLE
INSOLVENT
INSTANTER
INSTANTLY
INSTIGATE
INSTITUTE
INSURABLE
INSURANCE
INSURGENT
INTEGRATE
INTEGRITY
INTELLECT
INTENDANT
INTENSIFY
INTENSITY
INTENSIVE
INTENTION
INTERCEDE
INTERCEPT
INTERDICT
INTERFACE
INTERFERE
INTERFUSE
INTERJECT
INTERLACE
INTERLARD
INTERLEAF
INTERLINE
INTERLINK
INTERLOCK
INTERLOPE
INTERLUDE
INTERMENT
INTERNIST
INTERNODE
INTERPLAY
INTERPOSE
INTERPRET
INTERRUPT
INTERSECT
INTERVENE
INTERVIEW
INTESTATE
INTESTINE
INTRICATE
INTRINSIC
INTRODUCE
INTROVERT
INTUITION
INTUMESCE
INVECTIVE
INVENTION
INVENTIVE
INVENTORY
INVERNESS
INVERSION
INVIDIOUS
INVIOLATE
INVISIBLE
INVOLUCRE
IRASCIBLE
IRONBOUND
IRONSTONE
IRRADIATE
IRREGULAR
IRRITABLE
ISINGLASS
ISOSCELES
ISRAELITE
ITALICIZE
ITERATION
ITINERANT
ITINERARY
JACARANDA
JACKKNIFE
JACKSCREW
JACKSTRAW
JAILBREAK
JAUNDICED
JELLYFISH
JERKWATER
JESSAMINE
JEWELWEED
JINRIKSHA
JITTERBUG
JOBHOLDER
JUDICIARY
JUDICIOUS
JURIDICAL
JUXTAPOSE
KICKSTAND
KILOCYCLE
KILOHERTZ
KILOLITER
KILOMETER
KINESCOPE
KINSWOMAN
KNOCKDOWN
KNOWLEDGE
LABORIOUS
LABYRINTH
LACCOLITH
LAGNIAPPE
LAMEBRAIN
LAMINATED
LANDOWNER
LANDSCAPE
LANDSLIDE
LANTHANUM
LASSITUDE
LATECOMER
LAUDATORY
LAUNCHPAD
LAVALIERE
LAZYBONES
LEAFSTALK
LEASEHOLD
LEASTWISE
LEAVENING
LEGENDARY
LEGISLATE
LEITMOTIV
LEUKOCYTE
LEVIATHAN
LIABILITY
LIBERTINE
LIBRARIAN
LIFEBLOOD
LIFEGUARD
LIGHTFACE
LIGHTNING
LIGHTSHIP
LIGHTSOME
LIMBURGER
LIMELIGHT
LIMESTONE
LIMOUSINE
LINEAMENT
LIQUIDATE
LITERATIM
LITHESOME
LITHOLOGY
LITIGIOUS
LITTERBUG
LIVERWORT
LIVERYMAN
LIVESTOCK
LOADSTONE
LOATHSOME
LOCKSMITH
LOCOMOTOR
LODESTONE
LOGARITHM
LOGISTICS
LOINCLOTH
LONGEVITY
LONGITUDE
LORGNETTE
LOWERCASE
LUBRICANT
LUBRICATE
LUCRATIVE
LUDICROUS
LUNCHROOM
LUXURIANT
LUXURIATE
MACHINERY
MACHINIST
MACINTOSH
MACROCOSM
MAELSTROM
MAGISTRAL
MAGNESIUM
MAGNETISM
MAGNETITE
MAGNETIZE
MAGNIFICO
MAGNITUDE
MAHARISHI
MAINFRAME
MAJORDOMO
MAJORETTE
MAJUSCULE
MAKESHIFT
MALACHITE
MALADROIT
MALATHION
MALAYSIAN
MALIGNANT
MALLEABLE
MANDATORY
MANGANESE
MANHANDLE
MANHATTAN
MANIFESTO
MANNEQUIN
MANNERISM
MANOEUVRE
MANOMETER
MANSLAYER
MARGARINE
MARIJUANA
MARMALADE
MARMOREAL
MARQUETRY
MARSUPIAL
MARTYRDOM
MARVELOUS
MASCULINE
MASOCHISM
MASTERFUL
MASTICATE
MATCHBOOK
MATCHLOCK
MATCHWOOD
MATERNITY
MATRIARCH
MATRICIDE

MATRIMONY
MATUTINAL
MAUSOLEUM
MAYFLOWER
MEANWHILE
MECHANICS
MECHANISM
MECHANIZE
MEDALLION
MEDICABLE
MEDICINAL
MEGACYCLE
MEGADEATH
MEGAHERTZ
MEGAPHONE
MEGAPIXEL
MELIORATE
MELODIOUS
MELODRAMA
MELTWATER
MEMORABLE
MENAGERIE
MENDICANT
MENOPAUSE
MENTALITY
MERCENARY
MERCERIZE
MERCURIAL
MERCUROUS
MERGANSER
MERRIMENT
MESCALINE
MESMERIZE
MESSENGER
MESSIEURS
METALWARE
METALWORK
METEORITE
METEOROID
METHADONE
METHODIST
METHODIZE
METRICIZE
METROLOGY
METRONOME
MEZZANINE
MICROCOPY
MICROCOSM
MICROFILM
MICROGRAM
MICROSOFT
MICROWAVE
MIDDLEMAN
MIDSTREAM
MIDSUMMER
MIDWINTER
MILESTONE
MILLIGRAM
MILLINERY
MILLIPEDE
MILLIVOLT
MILLSTONE
MINCEMEAT
MINELAYER
MINIATURE
MINISCULE
MINISKIRT
MINISTATE
MINUSCULE
MINUTEMAN
MISBEHAVE
MISCHANCE
MISCREANT
MISDIRECT
MISERABLE
MISGIVING
MISGOVERN
MISHANDLE
MISINFORM
MISMANAGE
MISORIENT
MISSILERY
MISSIONER
MISTLETOE
MODERATOR
MODERNISM
MODERNIZE
MOLDBOARD
MOMENTARY
MOMENTOUS
MONASTERY
MONGOLIAN
MONGOLISM
MONGOLOID
MONKSHOOD
MONOGRAPH
MONOLOGUE
MONOMANIA
MONOPLANE
MONOSPACE
MONSIGNOR
MOONLIGHT
MOONSCAPE
MOONSHINE
MOONSTONE
MORTICIAN
MOTORBIKE
MOTORBOAT
MOTORCADE
MOUSETRAP
MOUSTACHE
MOUTHPART
MOUTHWASH
MUCKRAKER
MULTIFORM
MULTISCAN
MULTISPIN
MULTISYNC
MULTITUDE
MUNICIPAL
MURDEROUS
MUSKMELON
MUSSULMAN
MYSTICISM
MYTHOLOGY
NAMEPLATE
NANOMETER
NARCISSUS
NARCOTIZE
NARRATIVE
NATURALLY
NAVIGABLE
NECESSARY
NECESSITY
NECROLOGY
NECTARINE
NEFARIOUS
NEGLIGENT
NEGOTIANT
NEGOTIATE
NEGRITUDE
NEODYMIUM
NEOLOGISM
NEPHRITIC
NEPHRITIS
NEPTUNIUM
NEURALGIA
NEUROLOGY
NEVERMORE
NEWSPAPER
NEWSPRINT
NEWSSTAND
NICOTINIC
NIGHTCLUB
NIGHTFALL
NIGHTGOWN
NIGHTHAWK
NIGHTLIFE
NIGHTMARE
NIGHTTIME
NIGRITUDE
NOCTURNAL
NONCREDIT
NONENTITY
NONPAREIL
NONPERSON
NONPROFIT
NONREADER
NORMALIZE
NORMATIVE
NORTHEAST
NORTHWEST
NORWEGIAN
NOSEBLEED
NOSEPIECE
NOSTALGIA
NOTCHBACK
NOTORIOUS
NOVELETTE
NOVITIATE
NUMERATOR
NUMERICAL
NURSEMAID
NUTRIMENT
NUTRITION
OBBLIGATO
OBEISANCE
OBFUSCATE
OBJECTIFY
OBJECTIVE
OBJURGATE
OBLIVIOUS
OBNOXIOUS
OBSERVANT
OBSESSION
OBSTINATE
OCCULTISM
OCCUPANCY
OFFENSIVE
OFFERTORY
OFFICIANT
OFFICIATE
OFFICIOUS
OFFSPRING
OLFACTORY
OLIGARCHY
OMBUDSMAN
ONIONSKIN
ONSLAUGHT
OPERATION
OPERATIVE
OPPORTUNE
OPTOMETRY
ORANGEADE
ORCHESTRA
ORDINANCE
ORGIASTIC
ORIENTATE
ORIFLAMME
ORIGINATE
ORPHANAGE
OSCILLATE
OSTRACIZE
OTHERWISE
OUBLIETTE
OURSELVES
OUTERMOST
OUTGROWTH
OUTNUMBER
OUTRIGGER
OUTSKIRTS
OUTSPOKEN
OUTSPREAD
OUTWARDLY
OVERBLOWN
OVERBOARD
OVERCLOUD
OVERDRAFT
OVERDRIVE
OVERMATCH
OVERNIGHT
OVERPOWER
OVERPRINT
OVERREACH
OVERSEXED
OVERSHOOT
OVERSIGHT
OVERSLEEP
OVERSTATE
OVERTHROW
OVERTRICK
OVERWEIGH
OVERWHELM
OVERWRITE
OVIPAROUS
OXIDATION
OXYGENATE
PACEMAKER
PACHYDERM
PACKHORSE
PAGEMAKER
PAKISTANI
PALAESTRA
PALANQUIN
PALATABLE
PALLADIUM
PALMISTRY
PALPITATE
PANEGYRIC
PANHANDLE
PANTHEISM
PANTOMIME
PAPERBACK
PAPILLOTE
PARACHUTE
PARAGRAPH
PARALYSIS
PARAMETER
PARAMOUNT
PARATHION
PARCHMENT
PAREGORIC
PAROCHIAL
PARQUETRY
PARRICIDE
PARSIMONY
PARSONAGE
PARTITION
PARTITIVE
PARTRIDGE
PASSENGER
PASSERINE
PASTORALE
PASTURAGE
PATCHWORK
PATERNITY
PATHOLOGY
PATRIARCH
PATRICIAN
PATRICIDE
PATRIMONY
PATRISTIC
PATROLMAN
PATRONAGE
PATRONIZE
PAYMASTER
PEACETIME
PECUNIARY
PEDAGOGUE
PEDOMETER
PEGMATITE
PEKINGESE
PENDULOUS
PENEPLAIN
PENETRATE
PENHOLDER
PENINSULA
PENTECOST
PENTHOUSE
PENURIOUS
PERCHANCE
PERCOLATE
PERDITION
PERENNIAL
PERFORATE
PERFUMERY
PERIMETER
PERIPHERY
PERISCOPE
PERISTYLE
PERMANENT
PERMEABLE
PERPETUAL
PERPLEXED
PERSECUTE
PERSEVERE
PERSIMMON
PERSONAGE
PERSONATE
PERSONIFY
PERSONNEL
PERTINENT
PESSIMISM
PESTHOUSE
PESTICIDE
PESTILENT
PETROLEUM
PETROLOGY
PETTICOAT
PHALAROPE
PHEROMONE
PHILANDER
PHILATELY
PHILIPPIC
PHILOLOGY
PHLEBITIS
PHONETICS
PHONOLOGY
PHOSPHATE
PHOTOCELL
PHOTOCOPY
PHOTOPLAY
PHRENETIC
PHYSICIAN
PHYSICIST
PICKABACK
PICTORIAL
PIECEMEAL
PIECEWORK
PIGGYBACK
PIGHEADED
PIKESTAFF
PIMPERNEL
PINEAPPLE
PINSTRIPE
PIROUETTE
PISTACHIO
PITCHFORK
PITUITARY
PIZZICATO
PLACEKICK
PLACEMENT
PLAINTIFF
PLAINTIVE
PLANELOAD
PLANETOID
PLATITUDE
PLAUSIBLE
PLAYHOUSE
PLAYTHING
PLENITUDE
PLENTEOUS
PLENTIFUL
PLOWSHARE
PLURALITY
PLURALIZE
PLUTONIUM
PNEUMATIC
PNEUMONIA
POETASTER
POINCIANA
POLICEMAN
POLITBURO
POLITESSE
POLITICAL
POLYESTER
POLYGRAPH
POLYPHONY
POMPADOUR
PONDEROUS
POORHOUSE
POPPYCOCK
PORCELAIN
PORCUPINE
PORRINGER
PORTFOLIO
PORTULACA
POSTERIOR
POSTERITY
POSTHASTE
POSTILION
POSTNATAL
POSTULANT
POSTULATE
POTASSIUM
POTBOILER
POTENTATE
POTENTIAL
POTPOURRI
POULTERER
POURBOIRE
POWERBOAT
PRACTICAL
PRAGMATIC
PRAYERFUL
PRECANCEL
PRECEDENT
PRECEDING
PRECENTOR
PRECEPTOR
PRECIPICE
PRECISION
PRECURSOR
PREDATION
PREDATORY
PREDICATE
PREFIGURE
PREFLIGHT
PREGNABLE
PREJUDICE
PRELAUNCH
PREMATURE
PREOCCUPY
PREORDAIN
PRERECORD
PRESBYTER

PRESCHOOL
PRESCRIBE
PRESENTLY
PRESHRUNK
PRESIDENT
PRESIDIUM
PRESSROOM
PRESTRESS
PREVALENT
PREVERBAL
PREVISION
PRICELESS
PRIMARILY
PRIMITIVE
PRINCIPAL
PRINCIPLE
PRINTABLE
PRIVATEER
PRIVATION
PRIVILEGE
PROBATION
PROBATIVE
PROBOSCIS
PROCEDURE
PROCESSOR
PROCONSUL
PROCREATE
PROFANITY
PROFESSOR
PROFITEER
PROGNOSIS
PROJECTOR
PROMENADE
PROMINENT
PROMISING
PRONGHORN
PRONOUNCE
PROOFREAD
PROPAGATE
PROPELLER
PROPHETIC
PROPONENT
PROPRIETY
PROSCRIBE
PROSECUTE
PROSELYTE
PROSTRATE
PROTECTOR
PROTOTYPE
PROTOZOAN
PROVENCAL
PROVENDER
PROVIDENT
PROVISION
PROVOLONE
PROXIMATE
PROXIMITY
PSEUDONYM
PSORIASIS
PSYCHOSIS
PTARMIGAN
PUBESCENT
PUBLICIST
PUBLICITY
PUBLICIZE
PUERPERAL
PUISSANCE
PULMONARY
PULVERIZE
PUNCTILIO
PUNCTUATE
PUPPETEER
PUREBLOOD
PURGATION
PURGATIVE
PURGATORY
PURSUANCE
PUSSYFOOT
PYRETHRUM
PYROLYSIS
PYROMANIA
PYROMETER
QUADRATIC
QUADRILLE
QUADRUPED
QUADRUPLE
QUARTERLY
QUARTZITE
QUERULOUS
QUICKDRAW
QUICKLIME
QUICKSAND
QUICKSORT
QUICKSTEP
QUICKTIME
QUIESCENT
QUINTUPLE
QUITTANCE
QUIZZICAL
QUOTIDIAN
RABBINATE
RACEHORSE
RACETRACK
RACIALISM
RACKETEER
RACONTEUR
RADIOGRAM
RADIOLOGY
RAGPICKER
RAINSPOUT
RAINSTORM
RAINWATER
RANCHLAND
RANDOMIZE
RANGELAND
RAPACIOUS
RASPBERRY
RASTERIZE
RATIONALE
RAUWOLFIA
REACTANCE
REBELLION
RECEPTION
RECEPTIVE
RECESSION
RECESSIVE
RECHERCHE
RECIPIENT
RECKONING
RECOGNIZE
RECOLLECT
RECOMMEND
RECONCILE
RECONDITE
RECORDING
RECORDIST
RECTANGLE
RECTIFIER
RECTITUDE
RECUMBENT
RECURSION
REDACTION
REDBREAST
REDUCTION
REDUNDANT
REENFORCE
REENTRANT
REFECTION
REFECTORY
REFERENCE
REFLECTOR
REFLEXIVE
REFRACTOR
REFURBISH
REGARDING
REGISTRAR
REHEARING
REHEARSAL
REIMBURSE
REINFORCE
REINSTATE
REITERATE
REJOINDER
RELEVANCE
RELEVANCY
RELIGIOUS
RELIQUARY
RELUCTANT
REMAINDER
REMINISCE
REMISSION
RENCONTRE
RENDITION
REPAIRMAN
REPELLENT
REPERTORY
REPLENISH
REPLETION
REPLICATE
REPORTAGE
REPOSSESS
REPREHEND
REPRESENT
REPRIMAND
REPROBATE
REPRODUCE
REPUDIATE
REPUGNANT
REPULSION
REPULSIVE
REPUTABLE
REQUISITE
RESECTION
RESERPINE
RESERVIST
RESERVOIR
RESHUFFLE
RESIDENCE
RESIDENCY
RESIDUARY
RESISTANT
RESONANCE
RESONATOR
RESTRAINT
RESURRECT
RETALIATE
RETARDATE
RETENTION
RETENTIVE
RETRIEVER
RETROFIRE
REVERENCE
REVERSION
REVOCABLE
REVOLTING
REVULSION
RHEOMETER
RIDGEPOLE
RIGHTEOUS
RIGMAROLE
RIVERBANK
RIVERBOAT
RIVERSIDE
ROADBLOCK
ROADSTEAD
ROCKBOUND
ROOTSTOCK
ROSEWATER
ROUGHNECK
ROUMANIAN
ROUNDELAY
ROUNDWORM
RUINATION
RUMRUNNER
RUNAROUND
RUSTICATE
RUTHENIUM
SACCHARIN
SACKCLOTH
SACRAMENT
SACRIFICE
SACRILEGE
SACRISTAN
SADDLEBOW
SAFEGUARD
SAFFLOWER
SAGACIOUS
SAGEBRUSH
SAILCLOTH
SAILPLANE
SALACIOUS
SALESGIRL
SALTPETER
SALTWATER
SALVATION
SANCTUARY
SANDBLAST
SANDPAPER
SANDPIPER
SANDSTONE
SANDSTORM
SANGFROID
SAPSUCKER
SARTORIAL
SASSAFRAS
SATELLITE
SATINWOOD
SATURNINE
SAXIFRAGE
SAXOPHONE
SCANTLING
SCAPEGOAT
SCARECROW
SCAVENGER
SCHEELITE
SCHEMATIC
SCHILLING
SCHLEMIEL
SCHNAUZER
SCHOOLBOY
SCINTILLA
SCLEROSIS
SCOUNDREL
SCRAPBOOK
SCREENING
SCREWBALL
SCRIMMAGE
SCRIMSHAW
SCRIPTURE
SCRIVENER
SCULPTURE
SCUTCHEON
SEAFARING
SEASONING
SEAWORTHY
SEBACEOUS
SECESSION
SECLUSION
SECONDARY
SECRETARY
SECRETION
SECRETIVE
SECTARIAN
SECTIONAL
SEDENTARY
SEGREGATE
SELECTION
SELECTMAN
SEMANTICS
SEMAPHORE
SEMBLANCE
SEMICOLON
SEMIFINAL
SEMIFLUID
SEMILUNAR
SEMIWORKS
SENIORITY
SENSATION
SENSITIVE
SENSITIZE
SENTIMENT
SEPARABLE
SEPARATOR
SEPTEMBER
SEPULCHER
SEPULTURE
SEQUESTER
SERIGRAPH
SERVITUDE
SEVENTEEN
SHADOWBOX
SHAKEDOWN
SHAPELESS
SHAREWARE
SHARKSKIN
SHEATHING
SHEEPFOLD
SHEEPSKIN
SHELLFIRE
SHELLFISH
SHIFTLESS
SHIPBOARD
SHIPSHAPE
SHIPWRECK
SHOEMAKER
SHOREBIRD
SHORTCAKE
SHORTHAND
SHORTHORN
SHORTSTOP
SHORTWAVE
SHOWPIECE
SHOWPLACE
SHRINKAGE
SHRUBBERY
SIDEBOARD
SIDEBURNS
SIDEPIECE
SIDESWIPE
SIDETRACK
SIGNALIZE
SIGNALMAN
SIGNATORY
SIGNATURE
SIGNBOARD
SILICEOUS
SILICOSIS
SILTSTONE
SIMPATICO
SIMPLETON
SINGLETON
SINUSITIS
SITUATION
SKIMOBILE
SKINFLINT
SKINTIGHT
SKYDIVING
SKYJACKER
SKYLOUNGE
SKYROCKET
SLAUGHTER
SLINGSHOT
SLUICEWAY
SMALLTALK
SNAKEBIRD
SNAKEBITE
SNOWDRIFT
SNOWFIELD
SNOWFLAKE
SNOWSTORM
SOAPSTONE
SOBRIQUET
SOCIALISM
SOCIALITE
SOCIALIZE
SOCIOLOGY
SOFTBOUND
SOLEMNIZE
SOLICITOR
SOLILOQUY
SOLITAIRE
SOMETHING
SOMETIMES
SOMEWHERE
SOMNOLENT
SOPHISTIC
SOPHISTRY
SOPHOMORE
SOPORIFIC
SOUBRETTE
SOUTHEAST
SOUTHWEST
SOVEREIGN
SPACESHIP
SPAGHETTI
SPEAKEASY
SPEARHEAD
SPEARMINT
SPECIALTY
SPECTACLE
SPECTATOR
SPECULATE
SPEEDBOAT
SPEEDWELL
SPELUNKER
SPHINCTER
SPICEBUSH
SPINDLING
SPINDRIFT
SPINNAKER
SPIRITUAL
SPLENETIC
SPLITTING
SPOKESMAN
SPOONBILL
SPORTSMAN
SPOTLIGHT
SPRIGHTLY
SQUEAMISH
STABILIZE
STAIRCASE
STAIRWELL
STALEMATE
STAMINATE
STANCHION
STANDPIPE
STARBOARD
STARLIGHT
STARTLING
STATEMENT
STATEROOM
STATESIDE
STATESMAN
STATIONER
STATISTIC
STATUETTE

STATUTORY
STEADFAST
STEAMBOAT
STEAMSHIP
STEELYARD
STEPCHILD
STERILIZE
STEVEDORE
STILLBORN
STIMULANT
STIMULATE
STIPULATE
STOCKPILE
STOCKYARD
STOMACHER
STOMACHIC
STOPLIGHT
STOPWATCH
STOREROOM
STRAPLESS
STRAPPING
STRATAGEM
STREAMBED
STREAMLET
STREETCAR
STRENUOUS
STRETCHER
STRICTURE
STRIKEOUT
STRIPLING
STRONTIUM
STRUCTURE
SUBALPINE
SUBALTERN
SUBATOMIC
SUBDIVIDE
SUBJUGATE
SUBLIMATE
SUBLUNARY
SUBMARINE
SUBNORMAL
SUBSCRIBE
SUBSCRIPT
SUBSIDIZE
SUBSTANCE
SUCCESSOR
SUCCOTASH
SUCCULENT
SUFFERING
SUFFOCATE
SUFFRAGAN
SUGARCANE
SUGARPLUM
SULFUROUS
SUMMARIZE
SUMMATION
SUMPTUOUS
SUNBONNET
SUNFLOWER
SUNSEEKER
SUNSTROKE
SUPERNOVA
SUPERPOSE
SUPERSEDE
SUPERVENE
SUPERVISE
SUPPLIANT
SUPPOSING
SUPPURATE
SUPREMACY
SURCHARGE
SURCINGLE
SURFBOARD
SURRENDER
SURROGATE
SURVEYING
SUSPENDER
SUSPICION
SWAMPLAND
SWANSDOWN
SWEATSHOP
SWEETMEAT
SWELLHEAD
SWITCHMAN
SWORDFISH
SWORDPLAY
SWORDSMAN
SWORDTAIL
SYCOPHANT
SYLLABIFY
SYLLOGISM
SYMBIOSIS
SYMBOLISM
SYMBOLIZE
SYMPOSIUM
SYNAGOGUE
SYNDICATE
SYNERGISM
SYNTHESIS
SYNTHETIC
SYSTEMIZE
TABLELAND
TABLEWARE
TAILLIGHT
TALKATIVE
TANGERINE
TANTALIZE
TANZANIAN
TARANTULA
TARPAULIN
TAUTOLOGY
TAXIDERMY
TEAKETTLE
TECHNICAL
TECHNIQUE
TECTONICS
TECTONISM
TELEGENIC
TELEGRAPH
TELEMETER
TELEPATHY
TELEPHONE
TELEPHONY
TELEPHOTO
TELESCOPE
TELLURIUM
TEMPERATE
TEMPORARY
TEMPORIZE
TENACIOUS
TENDERIZE
TENEBROUS
TENTATIVE
TERMAGANT
TERMINATE
TERRARIUM
TERRITORY
TERRORISM
TERRORIZE
TESTAMENT
TESTIMONY
THANKLESS
THEATRICS
THEOCRACY
THEOSOPHY
THEREFORE
THEREFROM
THEREUNTO
THEREUPON
THEREWITH
THESAURUS
THICKNESS
THIGHBONE
THRALLDOM
THREEFOLD
THREESOME
THRESHOLD
THROWAWAY
THROWBACK
THUMBNAIL
THUMBTACK
THYROXINE
TIDEWATER
TIGHTROPE
TIMBERING
TIMEPIECE
TIMETABLE
TINDERBOX
TOADSTOOL
TOLERABLE
TOLERANCE
TOLLHOUSE
TOMBSTONE
TONSORIAL
TOOTHACHE
TOOTHPICK
TOOTHSOME
TOUCHDOWN
TOWNSFOLK
TRACKBALL
TRACTABLE
TRADEMARK
TRADESMAN
TRADITION
TRAGEDIAN
TRAINLOAD
TRANSCEND
TRANSDUCE
TRANSFORM
TRANSFUSE
TRANSIENT
TRANSLATE
TRANSMUTE
TRANSONIC
TRANSPIRE
TRANSPORT
TRANSPOSE
TRANSSHIP
TRAPEZOID
TRAPPINGS
TREACHERY
TREADMILL
TREASURER
TREATMENT
TREMATODE
TREMULOUS
TRENCHANT
TRIBESMAN
TRIBUTARY
TRICKSTER
TRIENNIAL
TRIFOCALS
TRIMESTER
TRITURATE
TRIWEEKLY
TROOPSHIP
TROUSSEAU
TRUCKLOAD
TRUCULENT
TRUNCHEON
TULAREMIA
TURBOPROP
TURBULENT
TURNABOUT
TURNSTILE
TURNTABLE
TURPITUDE
TURQUOISE
TUSCARORA
TWINKLING
TYPEWRITE
TYRANNIZE
TYRANNOUS
UKRAINIAN
ULTIMATUM
ULTRAHIGH
ULTRAPURE
UMBILICUS
UNADVISED
UNALIGNED
UNALLOYED
UNANIMOUS
UNBEKNOWN
UNBENDING
UNBLESSED
UNBOUNDED
UNBRIDLED
UNCEASING
UNCERTAIN
UNCHARTED
UNCLEANLY
UNCONCERN
UNCOUNTED
UNDAUNTED
UNDECEIVE
UNDECIDED
UNDERBODY
UNDERBRED
UNDERCOAT
UNDERDONE
UNDERFEED
UNDERFOOT
UNDERGIRD
UNDERHAND
UNDERLINE
UNDERLING
UNDERMINE
UNDERMOST
UNDERPART
UNDERPASS
UNDERPLAY
UNDERRATE
UNDERSELL
UNDERSHOT
UNDERSIDE
UNDERTAKE
UNDERTONE
UNDERWEAR
UNDERWOOD
UNDOUBTED
UNEARTHLY
UNEQUALED
UNFAILING
UNFEELING
UNFEIGNED
UNFLEDGED
UNFOUNDED
UNGUARDED
UNHARNESS
UNHEALTHY
UNISEXUAL
UNITARIAN
UNIVALENT
UNIVERSAL
UNKNOWING
UNLEARNED
UNMEANING
UNMINDFUL
UNNATURAL
UNPLUMBED
UNPOPULAR
UNRIVALED
UNRUFFLED
UNSCATHED
UNSELFISH
UNSETTLED
UNSHACKLE
UNSHEATHE
UNSIGHTLY
UNSKILLED
UNSPARING
UNSPOTTED
UNSTUDIED
UNTUTORED
UNWILLING
UNWITTING
UNWORLDLY
UNWRITTEN
UPANISHAD
UPHOLSTER
UPPERCASE
UPPERMOST
URTICARIA
UTTERANCE
UTTERMOST
VACCINATE
VACILLATE
VAGARIOUS
VAGINITIS
VAINGLORY
VALENTINE
VALUATION
VANDALISM
VANDALIZE
VAPORIZER
VAPORWARE
VARIATION
VARIEGATE
VASECTOMY
VASSALAGE
VEGETABLE
VEHEMENCE
VELVETEEN
VENERABLE
VENGEANCE
VENIREMAN
VENTILATE
VENTRICLE
VENTUROUS
VERACIOUS
VERBALIZE
VERDIGRIS
VERIDICAL
VERITABLE
VERMIFORM
VERMIFUGE
VERMILION
VERNALIZE
VERSATILE
VERTEBRAL
VESTIBULE
VESTRYMAN
VEXATIOUS
VIBRATION
VIBRATORY
VICARIOUS
VICENNIAL
VICEREGAL
VICTIMIZE
VICTORIAN
VICTUALER
VIDELICET
VIDEOTAPE
VIEWPOINT
VIGESIMAL
VIGILANCE
VIGILANTE
VILLENAGE
VINDICATE
VIOLATION
VIRGINITY
VISCOSITY
VISIONARY
VISUALIZE
VIVACIOUS
VOICELESS
VOLCANISM
VOLTMETER
VOLUNTARY
VOLUNTEER
VOODOOISM
VORACIOUS
VOUCHSAFE
VULCANISM
VULCANIZE
VULGARIAN
VULGARISM
VULGARITY
VULGARIZE
WAGONETTE
WAISTBAND
WAISTCOAT
WAISTLINE
WALLBOARD
WALLOPING
WALLPAPER
WARBONNET
WAREHOUSE
WARMONGER
WASHBASIN
WASHBOARD
WASHCLOTH
WASHHOUSE
WASHSTAND
WASHWOMAN
WASTELAND
WATCHBAND
WATCHCASE
WATCHWORD
WATERFALL
WATERFOWL
WATERLINE
WATERMARK
WATERSHED
WATERSIDE
WAVETABLE
WEARISOME
WEDNESDAY
WHALEBOAT
WHALEBONE
WHEELBASE
WHEREFORE
WHEREUPON
WHEREWITH
WHETSTONE
WHICHEVER
WHIMSICAL
WHIRLIGIG
WHIRLPOOL
WHIRLWIND
WHITEBAIT
WHITEFISH
WHITEHALL
WHITEHEAD
WHITENESS
WHITETAIL
WHITEWALL
WHITEWASH
WHITEWOOD
WHOLESALE
WHOLESOME
WHOSOEVER
WILLPOWER
WINDBLOWN
WINDBREAK
WINDCHILL

WINDPROOF
WINDSTORM
WINDSWEPT
WINEPRESS
WINTERIZE
WIREFRAME
WISECRACK
WITHDRAWN
WITHSTAND
WITTICISM
WOEBEGONE
WOLFHOUND
WOLFSBANE
WOLVERINE
WOMANHOOD
WOMANKIND
WOMANLIKE
WOMENFOLK
WONDERFUL
WOODBLOCK
WOODCHUCK
WOODCRAFT
WORKBENCH
WORKGROUP
WORKHORSE
WORKHOUSE
WORKPLACE
WORKTABLE
WORLDLING
WORLDWIDE
WORRISOME
WORRYWART
WORTHLESS
WRESTLING
WRISTBAND
WRONGDOER
XANTHIPPE
XEROPHYTE
XYLOPHONE
YACHTSMAN
YARDSTICK
YESTERDAY
YOUNGLING
YOUNGSTER
YTTERBIUM
ZEITGEIST
ZIRCONIUM
ZUCCHETTO
ZWINGLIAN

## 2ND LETTER

BACCHANAL
BACKBOARD
BACKFIELD
BACKPEDAL
BACKSLASH
BACKSLIDE
BACKSTAGE
BACKSWEPT
BACKTRACK
BACKWATER
BACKWOODS
BACTERIUM
BADMINTON
BAGATELLE
BAILIWICK
BAKSHEESH
BALALAIKA
BALDACHIN
BALLADEER
BALLERINA
BAMBOOZLE
BANDEROLE
BANDOLIER
BANDSTAND
BANDWAGON
BANDWIDTH
BANQUETTE
BANTUSTAN
BARBARIAN
BARBARISM
BARBAROUS
BARCAROLE
BAREFACED
BARKEEPER
BARNSTORM
BAROGRAPH
BAROMETER
BARRACUDA
BARRICADE
BARRISTER
BARTENDER
BASEBOARD
BASTINADO
BATHHOUSE
BATHOLITH
BATTALION
CABLEGRAM
CABRIOLET
CACOPHONY
CAFETERIA
CALABOOSE
CALCIMINE
CALCULATE
CALENDULA
CALIBRATE
CALLOSITY
CALORIFIC
CALVINISM
CAMELBACK
CAMEMBERT
CAMPANILE
CAMPSTOOL
CANALBOAT
CANDIDACY
CANDIDATE
CANDLEMAS
CANDLEPIN
CANEBRAKE
CANNONADE
CANNONEER
CANONICAL
CANTABILE
CANTHARIS
CAPACIOUS
CAPACITOR
CAPARISON
CAPILLARY
CAPITALLY
CAPRICCIO
CAPSULATE
CAPTIVATE
CARBONATE
CARBUNCLE
CARBURIZE
CARCINOMA
CARDBOARD
CARETAKER
CARIBBEAN
CARNATION
CARNELIAN
CARNIVORA
CARNIVORE
CARPENTER
CARPETBAG
CARPETING
CARROUSEL
CARTILAGE
CARTRIDGE
CARTWHEEL
CASSEROLE
CASSOWARY
CASTANETS
CASTIGATE
CASUISTRY
CATACLYSM
CATALEPSY
CATALYSIS
CATAMARAN
CATAMOUNT
CATATONIC
CATCHMENT
CATCHWORD
CATECHISM
CATERWAUL
CATHARSIS
CATHARTIC
CATHEDRAL
CAUCASIAN
CAUSATION
CAUTERIZE
CAVALCADE
DACHSHUND
DAIRYMAID
DALMATION
DAMASCENE
DAMNATION
DAMSELFLY
DANDELION
DANGEROUS
DAREDEVIL
DARWINISM
DASHBOARD
DAUNTLESS
DAVENPORT
EARTHLING
EARTHWARD
EARTHWORK
EARTHWORM
EASYGOING
EAVESDROP
FABRICATE
FACETIOUS
FACSIMILE
FACTORIAL
FAIRYLAND
FALSEHOOD
FANCYWORK
FANTASIZE
FANTASTIC
FARMHOUSE
FARMSTEAD
FARSEEING
FASCINATE
FASTENING
FAVORABLE
GABARDINE
GABERDINE
GALACTOSE
GALLANTRY
GALLINULE
GALLIVANT
GALLSTONE
GALVANISM
GALVANIZE
GANGPLANK
GARNISHEE
GARNITURE
GARRULOUS
GASTRITIS
GASTROPOD
GAUCHERIE
GAZETTEER
HABITABLE
HABITUATE
HACKNEYED
HAILSTONE
HAILSTORM
HAIRBRUSH
HAIRCLOTH
HAIRPIECE
HAIRSTYLE
HALFPENNY
HALITOSIS
HALLOWEEN
HAMADRYAD
HAMBURGER
HAMMERTOE
HAMSTRING
HANDCLASP
HANDCRAFT
HANDIWORK
HANDSHAKE
HANDSPIKE
HANDSTAND
HANDWOVEN
HAPHAZARD
HAPPENING
HAPPINESS
HARBINGER
HARBORAGE
HARDBOARD
HARDBOUND
HARDCOVER
HARDIHOOD
HARDSTAND
HARLEQUIN
HARMONICA
HARMONICS
HARMONIUM
HARMONIZE
HARTSHORN
HATCHMENT
HAVERSACK
JACARANDA
JACKKNIFE
JACKSCREW
JACKSTRAW
JAILBREAK
JAUNDICED
LABORIOUS
LABYRINTH
LACCOLITH
LAGNIAPPE
LAMEBRAIN
LAMINATED
LANDOWNER
LANDSCAPE
LANDSLIDE
LANTHANUM
LASSITUDE
LATECOMER
LAUDATORY
LAUNCHPAD
LAVALIERE
LAZYBONES
MACHINERY
MACHINIST
MACINTOSH
MACROCOSM
MAELSTROM
MAGISTRAL
MAGNESIUM
MAGNETISM
MAGNETITE
MAGNETIZE
MAGNIFICO
MAGNITUDE
MAHARISHI
MAINFRAME
MAJORDOMO
MAJORETTE
MAJUSCULE
MAKESHIFT
MALACHITE
MALADROIT
MALATHION
MALAYSIAN
MALIGNANT
MALLEABLE
MANDATORY
MANGANESE
MANHANDLE
MANHATTAN
MANIFESTO
MANNEQUIN
MANNERISM
MANOEUVRE
MANOMETER
MANSLAYER
MARGARINE
MARIJUANA
MARMALADE
MARMOREAL
MARQUETRY
MARSUPIAL
MARTYRDOM
MARVELOUS
MASCULINE
MASOCHISM
MASTERFUL
MASTICATE
MATCHBOOK
MATCHLOCK
MATCHWOOD
MATERNITY
MATRIARCH
MATRICIDE
MATRIMONY
MATUTINAL
MAUSOLEUM
MAYFLOWER
NAMEPLATE
NANOMETER
NARCISSUS
NARCOTIZE
NARRATIVE
NATURALLY
NAVIGABLE
PACEMAKER
PACHYDERM
PACKHORSE
PAGEMAKER
PAKISTANI
PALAESTRA
PALANQUIN
PALATABLE
PALLADIUM
PALMISTRY
PALPITATE
PANEGYRIC
PANHANDLE
PANTHEISM
PANTOMIME
PAPERBACK
PAPILLOTE
PARACHUTE
PARAGRAPH
PARALYSIS
PARAMETER
PARAMOUNT
PARATHION
PARCHMENT
PAREGORIC
PAROCHIAL
PARQUETRY
PARRICIDE
PARSIMONY
PARSONAGE
PARTITION
PARTITIVE
PARTRIDGE
PASSENGER
PASSERINE
PASTORALE
PASTURAGE
PATCHWORK
PATERNITY
PATHOLOGY
PATRIARCH
PATRICIAN
PATRICIDE
PATRIMONY
PATRISTIC
PATROLMAN
PATRONAGE
PATRONIZE
PAYMASTER
RABBINATE
RACEHORSE
RACETRACK
RACIALISM
RACKETEER
RACONTEUR
RADIOGRAM
RADIOLOGY
RAGPICKER
RAINSPOUT
RAINSTORM
RAINWATER
RANCHLAND
RANDOMIZE
RANGELAND
RAPACIOUS
RASPBERRY
RASTERIZE
RATIONALE
RAUWOLFIA
SACCHARIN
SACKCLOTH
SACRAMENT
SACRIFICE
SACRILEGE
SACRISTAN
SADDLEBOW
SAFEGUARD
SAFFLOWER
SAGACIOUS
SAGEBRUSH
SAILCLOTH
SAILPLANE
SALACIOUS
SALESGIRL
SALTPETER
SALTWATER
SALVATION
SANCTUARY
SANDBLAST
SANDPAPER
SANDPIPER
SANDSTONE
SANDSTORM
SANGFROID
SAPSUCKER
SARTORIAL
SASSAFRAS
SATELLITE
SATINWOOD
SATURNINE
SAXIFRAGE
SAXOPHONE
TABLELAND
TABLEWARE

TAILLIGHT
TALKATIVE
TANGERINE
TANTALIZE
TANZANIAN
TARANTULA
TARPAULIN
TAUTOLOGY
TAXIDERMY
VACCINATE
VACILLATE
VAGARIOUS
VAGINITIS
VAINGLORY
VALENTINE
VALUATION
VANDALISM
VANDALIZE
VAPORIZER
VAPORWARE
VARIATION
VARIEGATE
VASECTOMY
VASSALAGE
WAGONETTE
WAISTBAND
WAISTCOAT
WAISTLINE
WALLBOARD
WALLOPING
WALLPAPER
WARBONNET
WAREHOUSE
WARMONGER
WASHBASIN
WASHBOARD
WASHCLOTH
WASHHOUSE
WASHSTAND
WASHWOMAN
WASTELAND
WATCHBAND
WATCHCASE
WATCHWORD
WATERFALL
WATERFOWL
WATERLINE
WATERMARK
WATERSHED
WATERSIDE
WAVETABLE
XANTHIPPE
YACHTSMAN
YARDSTICK
ABANDONED
ABATEMENT
ABHORRENT
ABOMINATE
ABORIGINE
ABSORBENT
EBULLIENT
OBBLIGATO
OBEISANCE
OBFUSCATE
OBJECTIFY
OBJECTIVE
OBJURGATE
OBLIVIOUS
OBNOXIOUS
OBSERVANT
OBSESSION
OBSTINATE
ACCESSION
ACCESSORY
ACCIDENCE
ACCLIMATE
ACCLIVITY
ACCOMPANY
ACCORDION
ACCRETION
ACETYLENE
ACIDULATE
ACIDULOUS
ACOUSTICS
ACQUIESCE
ACROPOLIS
ECCENTRIC
ECONOMICS
ECONOMIZE
ECOSYSTEM
ICELANDER
ICELANDIC
OCCULTISM
OCCUPANCY
SCANTLING
SCAPEGOAT
SCARECROW
SCAVENGER
SCHEELITE
SCHEMATIC
SCHILLING
SCHLEMIEL
SCHNAUZER
SCHOOLBOY
SCINTILLA
SCLEROSIS
SCOUNDREL
SCRAPBOOK
SCREENING
SCREWBALL
SCRIMMAGE
SCRIMSHAW
SCRIPTURE
SCRIVENER
SCULPTURE
SCUTCHEON
ADDICTION
ADDRESSEE
ADIABATIC
ADJECTIVE
ADJOINING
ADMIRABLE
ADMIRALTY
ADMISSION
ADMIXTURE
ADSORBATE
ADSORBENT
ADUMBRATE
ADVANTAGE
ADVENTURE
ADVERSARY
ADVERSITY
ADVERTISE
ADVISABLE
EDELWEISS
EDITORIAL
EDUCATION
IDENTICAL
AERIALIST
AERODROME
AEROPAUSE
AEROPLANE
AEROSPACE
AESTHETIC
AESTIVATE
BEACHHEAD
BEATITUDE
BEAUTEOUS
BEAUTIFUL
BEDFELLOW
BEDRIDDEN
BEDSPREAD
BEEFEATER
BEEFSTEAK
BEEKEEPER
BELEAGUER
BELLICOSE
BELLYACHE
BELVEDERE
BENIGHTED
BENIGNANT
BENTONITE
BERKELIUM
BERYLLIUM
BESETTING
BESPANGLE
BESPATTER
BETROTHED
CEASELESS
CELANDINE
CELEBRATE
CELEBRITY
CELESTIAL
CELLARAGE
CELLULOSE
CENTENARY
CENTESIMO
CENTIGRAM
CENTIPEDE
CENTURION
CEREBRATE
CERECLOTH
CERTAINTY
CERTITUDE
CESSATION
DEATHBLOW
DEATHLESS
DEBENTURE
DEBUTANTE
DECADENCE
DECALOGUE
DECATHLON
DECEITFUL
DECENNIAL
DECEPTION
DECIDUOUS
DECILITER
DECIMETER
DECISTERE
DECLIVITY
DECOLLETE
DECOMPOSE
DECONTROL
DECORATOR
DECOUPAGE
DECREMENT
DEDUCTION
DEFEATISM
DEFECTIVE
DEFENDANT
DEFENSIVE
DEFERENCE
DEFERMENT
DEFICIENT
DEFLATION
DEFOLIANT
DEFOLIATE
DEFORMITY
DEHYDRATE
DEJECTION
DEKALITER
DEKAMETER
DEKASTERE
DELFTWARE
DELICIOUS
DELIGHTED
DELIMETER
DELINEATE
DEMAGOGUE
DEMARCATE
DEMIMONDE
DEMITASSE
DEMOCRACY
DEMULCENT
DEMURRAGE
DENIGRATE
DENTITION
DEODORANT
DEODORIZE
DEOXIDIZE
DEPARTURE
DEPENDENT
DEPRECATE
DEPRESSED
DERRINGER
DESCENDER
DESECRATE
DESICCANT
DESICCATE
DESIGNATE
DESIGNING
DESIRABLE
DESPERADO
DESPERATE
DESTITUTE
DESTROYER
DESUETUDE
DESULTORY
DETECTIVE
DETENTION
DETERGENT
DETERMINE
DETERRENT
DETONATOR
DETRIMENT
DEUTERIUM
DEVASTATE
DEVILMENT
DEXTERITY
DEXTEROUS
FEBRIFUGE
FECUNDATE
FEEDSTOCK
FEEDSTUFF
FELLOWMAN
FEROCIOUS
FERRYBOAT
FERTILIZE
FESTIVITY
FETISHISM
FEUDALISM
FEUDATORY
GEARSHIFT
GELIGNITE
GENEALOGY
GENERATOR
GENITALIA
GENTILITY
GENTLEMAN
GENUFLECT
GEOGRAPHY
GERIATRIC
GERMANIUM
GERMICIDE
GERMINATE
GESTATION
HEADBOARD
HEADDRESS
HEADFIRST
HEADLIGHT
HEADPHONE
HEADPIECE
HEADSTALL
HEADSTONE
HEADWATER
HEALTHFUL
HEARTACHE
HEARTBEAT
HEARTBURN
HEARTFELT
HEARTLESS
HEARTSICK
HEARTWOOD
HECTOGRAM
HELLEBORE
HELLENISM
HELVETIAN
HELVETICA
HEMISTICH
HEMSTITCH
HEPATITIS
HERBALIST
HERBARIUM
HERBICIDE
HERCULEAN
HEREAFTER
HEREUNDER
HERITABLE
HERMITAGE
HETERODOX
HEURISTIC
HEXAMETER
JELLYFISH
JERKWATER
JESSAMINE
JEWELWEED
LEAFSTALK
LEASEHOLD
LEASTWISE
LEAVENING
LEGENDARY
LEGISLATE
LEITMOTIV
LEUKOCYTE
LEVIATHAN
MEANWHILE
MECHANICS
MECHANISM
MECHANIZE
MEDALLION
MEDICABLE
MEDICINAL
MEGACYCLE
MEGADEATH
MEGAHERTZ
MEGAPHONE
MEGAPIXEL
MELIORATE
MELODIOUS
MELODRAMA
MELTWATER
MEMORABLE
MENAGERIE
MENDICANT
MENOPAUSE
MENTALITY
MERCENARY
MERCERIZE
MERCURIAL
MERCUROUS
MERGANSER
MERRIMENT
MESCALINE
MESMERIZE
MESSENGER
MESSIEURS
METALWARE
METALWORK
METEORITE
METEOROID
METHADONE
METHODIST
METHODIZE
METRICIZE
METROLOGY
METRONOME
MEZZANINE
NECESSARY
NECESSITY
NECROLOGY
NECTARINE
NEFARIOUS
NEGLIGENT
NEGOTIANT
NEGOTIATE
NEGRITUDE
NEODYMIUM
NEOLOGISM
NEPHRITIC
NEPHRITIS
NEPTUNIUM
NEURALGIA
NEUROLOGY
NEVERMORE
NEWSPAPER
NEWSPRINT
NEWSSTAND
PEACETIME
PECUNIARY
PEDAGOGUE
PEDOMETER
PEGMATITE
PEKINGESE
PENDULOUS
PENEPLAIN
PENETRATE
PENHOLDER
PENINSULA
PENTECOST
PENTHOUSE
PENURIOUS
PERCHANCE
PERCOLATE
PERDITION
PERENNIAL
PERFORATE
PERFUMERY
PERIMETER
PERIPHERY
PERISCOPE
PERISTYLE
PERMANENT
PERMEABLE
PERPETUAL
PERPLEXED
PERSECUTE
PERSEVERE
PERSIMMON
PERSONAGE
PERSONATE
PERSONIFY
PERSONNEL
PERTINENT
PESSIMISM
PESTHOUSE
PESTICIDE
PESTILENT
PETROLEUM
PETROLOGY
PETTICOAT
REACTANCE
REBELLION
RECEPTION
RECEPTIVE
RECESSION
RECESSIVE

RECHERCHE
RECIPIENT
RECKONING
RECOGNIZE
RECOLLECT
RECOMMEND
RECONCILE
RECONDITE
RECORDING
RECORDIST
RECTANGLE
RECTIFIER
RECTITUDE
RECUMBENT
RECURSION
REDACTION
REDBREAST
REDUCTION
REDUNDANT
REENFORCE
REENTRANT
REFECTION
REFECTORY
REFERENCE
REFLECTOR
REFLEXIVE
REFRACTOR
REFURBISH
REGARDING
REGISTRAR
REHEARING
REHEARSAL
REIMBURSE
REINFORCE
REINSTATE
REITERATE
REJOINDER
RELEVANCE
RELEVANCY
RELIGIOUS
RELIQUARY
RELUCTANT
REMAINDER
REMINISCE
REMISSION
RENCONTRE
RENDITION
REPAIRMAN
REPELLENT
REPERTORY
REPLENISH
REPLETION
REPLICATE
REPORTAGE
REPOSSESS
REPREHEND
REPRESENT
REPRIMAND
REPROBATE
REPRODUCE
REPUDIATE
REPUGNANT
REPULSION
REPULSIVE
REPUTABLE
REQUISITE
RESECTION
RESERPINE
RESERVIST
RESERVOIR
RESHUFFLE
RESIDENCE
RESIDENCY
RESIDUARY
RESISTANT
RESONANCE
RESONATOR
RESTRAINT
RESURRECT
RETALIATE
RETARDATE
RETENTION
RETENTIVE
RETRIEVER
RETROFIRE
REVERENCE
REVERSION
REVOCABLE
REVOLTING
REVULSION
SEAFARING
SEASONING
SEAWORTHY
SEBACEOUS
SECESSION
SECLUSION
SECONDARY
SECRETARY
SECRETION
SECRETIVE
SECTARIAN
SECTIONAL
SEDENTARY
SEGREGATE
SELECTION
SELECTMAN
SEMANTICS
SEMAPHORE
SEMBLANCE
SEMICOLON
SEMIFINAL
SEMIFLUID
SEMILUNAR
SEMIWORKS
SENIORITY
SENSATION
SENSITIVE
SENSITIZE
SENTIMENT
SEPARABLE
SEPARATOR
SEPTEMBER
SEPULCHER
SEPULTURE
SEQUESTER
SERIGRAPH
SERVITUDE
SEVENTEEN
TEAKETTLE
TECHNICAL
TECHNIQUE
TECTONICS
TECTONISM
TELEGENIC
TELEGRAPH
TELEMETER
TELEPATHY
TELEPHONE
TELEPHONY
TELEPHOTO
TELESCOPE
TELLURIUM
TEMPERATE
TEMPORARY
TEMPORIZE
TENACIOUS
TENDERIZE
TENEBROUS
TENTATIVE
TERMAGANT
TERMINATE
TERRARIUM
TERRITORY
TERRORISM
TERRORIZE
TESTAMENT
TESTIMONY
VEGETABLE
VEHEMENCE
VELVETEEN
VENERABLE
VENGEANCE
VENIREMAN
VENTILATE
VENTRICLE
VENTUROUS
VERACIOUS
VERBALIZE
VERDIGRIS
VERIDICAL
VERITABLE
VERMIFORM
VERMIFUGE
VERMILION
VERNALIZE
VERSATILE
VERTEBRAL
VESTIBULE
VESTRYMAN
VEXATIOUS
WEARISOME
WEDNESDAY
XEROPHYTE
YESTERDAY
ZEITGEIST
AFFECTING
AFFECTION
AFFIDAVIT
AFFILIATE
AFFLUENCE
AFORESAID
AFRIKAANS
AFTERCARE
AFTERDECK
AFTERGLOW
AFTERLIFE
AFTERMATH
AFTERNOON
AFTERWARD
EFFECTIVE
EFFECTUAL
EFFICIENT
EFFLUENCE
EFFLUVIUM
OFFENSIVE
OFFERTORY
OFFICIANT
OFFICIATE
OFFICIOUS
OFFSPRING
AGGRAVATE
AGGREGATE
AGREEABLE
AGREEMENT
EGGBEATER
EGLANTINE
EGREGIOUS
IGNORANCE
CHAFFINCH
CHALKBORD
CHALLENGE
CHAMELEON
CHAMOMILE
CHAMPAGNE
CHAMPAIGN
CHANCROID
CHANTEUSE
CHAPARRAL
CHARABANC
CHARACTER
CHARLATAN
CHARWOMAN
CHAUFFEUR
CHECKBOOK
CHECKLIST
CHECKMATE
CHECKROOM
CHEEKBONE
CHEERLESS
CHEMISTRY
CHEVALIER
CHICANERY
CHICKADEE
CHICKASAW
CHICKWEED
CHIEFTAIN
CHILBLAIN
CHILDHOOD
CHIROPODY
CHIVALRIC
CHLORDANE
CHOCOLATE
CHONDRITE
CHONDRULE
CHOPHOUSE
CHOPSTICK
CHORISTER
CHRISTIAN
CHRISTMAS
CHROMATIC
CHRONICLE
CHRYSALIS
CHUCKHOLE
CHURCHMAN
DHRYSTONE
PHALAROPE
PHEROMONE
PHILANDER
PHILATELY
PHILIPPIC
PHILOLOGY
PHLEBITIS
PHONETICS
PHONOLOGY
PHOSPHATE
PHOTOCELL
PHOTOCOPY
PHOTOPLAY
PHRENETIC
PHYSICIAN
PHYSICIST
RHEOMETER
SHADOWBOX
SHAKEDOWN
SHAPELESS
SHAREWARE
SHARKSKIN
SHEATHING
SHEEPFOLD
SHEEPSKIN
SHELLFIRE
SHELLFISH
SHIFTLESS
SHIPBOARD
SHIPSHAPE
SHIPWRECK
SHOEMAKER
SHOREBIRD
SHORTCAKE
SHORTHAND
SHORTHORN
SHORTSTOP
SHORTWAVE
SHOWPIECE
SHOWPLACE
SHRINKAGE
SHRUBBERY
THANKLESS
THEATRICS
THEOCRACY
THEOSOPHY
THEREFORE
THEREFROM
THEREUNTO
THEREUPON
THEREWITH
THESAURUS
THICKNESS
THIGHBONE
THRALLDOM
THREEFOLD
THREESOME
THRESHOLD
THROWAWAY
THROWBACK
THUMBNAIL
THUMBTACK
THYROXINE
WHALEBOAT
WHALEBONE
WHEELBASE
WHEREFORE
WHEREUPON
WHEREWITH
WHETSTONE
WHICHEVER
WHIMSICAL
WHIRLIGIG
WHIRLPOOL
WHIRLWIND
WHITEBAIT
WHITEFISH
WHITEHALL
WHITEHEAD
WHITENESS
WHITETAIL
WHITEWALL
WHITEWASH
WHITEWOOD
WHOLESALE
WHOLESOME
WHOSOEVER
AILANTHUS
AIRMOBILE
AIRWORTHY
BICAMERAL
BICONCAVE
BIFURCATE
BILATERAL
BILINGUAL
BILLBOARD
BILLIARDS
BIMONTHLY
BINOCULAR
BINOMINAL
BIOGRAPHY
BIOSPHERE
BIPARTITE
BIRDHOUSE
BIRTHMARK
BIRTHRATE
BISHOPRIC
CIGARETTE
CIGARILLO
CIRCADIAN
CIRCUITRY
CIRCULATE
CIRRHOSIS
CITIZENRY
DIACRITIC
DIAERESIS
DIAGNOSIS
DIALECTIC
DIAMETRIC
DIAPHRAGM
DIATHERMY
DIATOMITE
DICHOTOMY
DIETETICS
DIFFERENT
DIFFICULT
DIFFIDENT
DIGITALIS
DIGITIZED
DIGNIFIED
DIGNITARY
DIMENSION
DIMORPHIC
DIPHTHONG
DIPLOMACY
DIPTEROUS
DIRECTION
DIRECTIVE
DIRECTORY
DIRIGIBLE
DISAFFECT
DISAPPEAR
DISBURDEN
DISCHARGE
DISCOMFIT
DISCOURSE
DISCREDIT
DISEMBARK
DISEMBODY
DISENGAGE
DISESTEEM
DISFIGURE
DISHCLOTH
DISHONEST
DISHWATER
DISINFECT
DISLOCATE
DISMANTLE
DISMEMBER
DISOBLIGE
DISORIENT
DISPARAGE
DISPARATE
DISPLEASE
DISPRAISE
DISPUTANT
DISREGARD
DISREPAIR
DISREPUTE
DISSECTED
DISSEMBLE
DISSENTER
DISSIDENT
DISSIPATE
DISSOLUTE
DISTEMPER
DISTURBED
DITHERING
DIVERSIFY
DIVERSION
DIVERSITY
DIVISIBLE
DIXIELAND
EIDERDOWN
FIDUCIARY
FILMSTRIP
FINANCIAL
FINANCIER
FINGERING
FINGERTIP
FINICKING

FIREBRAND
FIREBREAK
FIREBRICK
FIREHOUSE
FIREPLACE
FIREPOWER
FIREPROOF
FIREWATER
FIRMAMENT
FIRSTBORN
FIRSTHAND
FIRSTLING
FISHERMAN
GIBBERISH
GIMMICKRY
HIBERNATE
HIDEBOUND
HIERARCHY
HIGHLIGHT
HILARIOUS
HILLBILLY
HINDRANCE
HINDSIGHT
HISTAMINE
HISTOGRAM
HISTORIAN
HITCHHIKE
JINRIKSHA
JITTERBUG
KICKSTAND
KILOCYCLE
KILOHERTZ
KILOLITER
KILOMETER
KINESCOPE
KINSWOMAN
LIABILITY
LIBERTINE
LIBRARIAN
LIFEBLOOD
LIFEGUARD
LIGHTFACE
LIGHTNING
LIGHTSHIP
LIGHTSOME
LIMBURGER
LIMELIGHT
LIMESTONE
LIMOUSINE
LINEAMENT
LIQUIDATE
LITERATIM
LITHESOME
LITHOLOGY
LITIGIOUS
LITTERBUG
LIVERWORT
LIVERYMAN
LIVESTOCK
MICROCOPY
MICROCOSM
MICROFILM
MICROGRAM
MICROSOFT
MICROWAVE
MIDDLEMAN
MIDSTREAM
MIDSUMMER
MIDWINTER
MILESTONE
MILLIGRAM
MILLINERY
MILLIPEDE
MILLIVOLT
MILLSTONE
MINCEMEAT
MINELAYER
MINIATURE
MINISCULE
MINISKIRT
MINISTATE
MINUSCULE
MINUTEMAN
MISBEHAVE
MISCHANCE
MISCREANT
MISDIRECT
MISERABLE
MISGIVING
MISGOVERN
MISHANDLE
MISINFORM
MISMANAGE
MISORIENT
MISSILERY
MISSIONER
MISTLETOE
NICOTINIC
NIGHTCLUB
NIGHTFALL
NIGHTGOWN
NIGHTHAWK
NIGHTLIFE
NIGHTMARE
NIGHTTIME
NIGRITUDE
PICKABACK
PICTORIAL
PIECEMEAL
PIECEWORK
PIGGYBACK
PIGHEADED
PIKESTAFF
PIMPERNEL
PINEAPPLE
PINSTRIPE
PIROUETTE
PISTACHIO
PITCHFORK
PITUITARY
PIZZICATO
RIDGEPOLE
RIGHTEOUS
RIGMAROLE
RIVERBANK
RIVERBOAT
RIVERSIDE
SIDEBOARD
SIDEBURNS
SIDEPIECE
SIDESWIPE
SIDETRACK
SIGNALIZE
SIGNALMAN
SIGNATORY
SIGNATURE
SIGNBOARD
SILICEOUS
SILICOSIS
SILTSTONE
SIMPATICO
SIMPLETON
SINGLETON
SINUSITIS
SITUATION
TIDEWATER
TIGHTROPE
TIMBERING
TIMEPIECE
TIMETABLE
TINDERBOX
VIBRATION
VIBRATORY
VICARIOUS
VICENNIAL
VICEREGAL
VICTIMIZE
VICTORIAN
VICTUALER
VIDELICET
VIDEOTAPE
VIEWPOINT
VIGESIMAL
VIGILANCE
VIGILANTE
VILLENAGE
VINDICATE
VIOLATION
VIRGINITY
VISCOSITY
VISIONARY
VISUALIZE
VIVACIOUS
WILLPOWER
WINDBLOWN
WINDBREAK
WINDCHILL
WINDPROOF
WINDSTORM
WINDSWEPT
WINEPRESS
WINTERIZE
WIREFRAME
WISECRACK
WITHDRAWN
WITHSTAND
WITTICISM
ZIRCONIUM
EJACULATE
SKIMOBILE
SKINFLINT
SKINTIGHT
SKYDIVING
SKYJACKER
SKYLOUNGE
SKYROCKET
UKRAINIAN
ALABASTER
ALBATROSS
ALCOHOLIC
ALEATORIC
ALGONQUIN
ALGORITHM
ALIENABLE
ALLERGIST
ALLEVIATE
ALLIGATOR
ALLOWANCE
ALMANDITE
ALMSHOUSE
ALONGSIDE
ALTERNATE
ALTIMETER
ALUMINIUM
ALUMINIZE
BLACKBALL
BLACKBIRD
BLACKBODY
BLACKFOOT
BLACKHEAD
BLACKJACK
BLACKLIST
BLACKMAIL
BLASPHEME
BLASPHEMY
BLEACHERS
BLINDFOLD
BLOCKHEAD
BLOODBATH
BLOODLINE
BLOODROOT
BLOODSHED
BLOODSHOT
BLOWTORCH
BLUEBERRY
BLUEBLACK
BLUEGRASS
BLUEPOINT
BLUEPRINT
CLAMSHELL
CLAPBOARD
CLASSICAL
CLASSMATE
CLASSROOM
CLEARANCE
CLERGYMAN
CLIENTELE
CLINICIAN
CLIPBOARD
CLIPSHEET
CLOCKWISE
CLOCKWORK
CLOISONNE
CLUBHOUSE
ELABORATE
ELASTOMER
ELBOWROOM
ELECTRIFY
ELECTRODE
ELEVATION
ELIMINATE
ELLIPSOID
ELOCUTION
ELSEWHERE
ELUCIDATE
FLAGELLUM
FLAGEOLET
FLAGSTAFF
FLAGSTONE
FLAMMABLE
FLASHBACK
FLASHBULB
FLASHCUBE
FLASHTUBE
FLATULENT
FLAVORING
FLEDGLING
FLINTLOCK
FLOODGATE
FLOPHOUSE
FLOTATION
FLOWCHART
FLOWERPOT
FLUCTUATE
GLADIATOR
GLADIOLUS
GLADSTONE
GLAMORIZE
GLEANINGS
GLENGARRY
GLISSANDO
GLUTINOUS
GLYCOSIDE
ILLEGIBLE
ILLIBERAL
ILLOGICAL
OLFACTORY
OLIGARCHY
PLACEKICK
PLACEMENT
PLAINTIFF
PLAINTIVE
PLANELOAD
PLANETOID
PLATITUDE
PLAUSIBLE
PLAYHOUSE
PLAYTHING
PLENITUDE
PLENTEOUS
PLENTIFUL
PLOWSHARE
PLURALITY
PLURALIZE
PLUTONIUM
SLAUGHTER
SLINGSHOT
SLUICEWAY
ULTIMATUM
ULTRAHIGH
ULTRAPURE
AMARYLLIS
AMBERGRIS
AMBIGUOUS
AMBITIOUS
AMBULANCE
AMBUSCADE
AMENDMENT
AMERICANA
AMERICIUM
AMIDSHIPS
AMORPHOUS
AMPERSAND
AMPHIBIAN
AMPHIBOLE
AMPLITUDE
EMBARRASS
EMBAYMENT
EMBELLISH
EMBRASURE
EMBROCATE
EMBROIDER
EMERGENCY
EMOLLIENT
EMOLUMENT
EMPENNAGE
EMPHASIZE
EMPHYSEMA
EMPIRICAL
IMAGINARY
IMBALANCE
IMBROGLIO
IMITATION
IMITATIVE
IMMEDIACY
IMMEDIATE
IMMIGRANT
IMMIGRATE
IMMOVABLE
IMMUTABLE
IMPARTIAL
IMPASSIVE
IMPATIENS
IMPATIENT
IMPEDANCE
IMPERFECT
IMPERIOUS
IMPETUOUS
IMPLEMENT
IMPLICATE
IMPOLITIC
IMPORTANT
IMPORTUNE
IMPOSTURE
IMPRECATE
IMPRECISE
IMPROMPTU
IMPROVISE
IMPRUDENT
IMPULSION
IMPULSIVE
OMBUDSMAN
SMALLTALK
UMBILICUS
ANAEROBIC
ANALGESIA
ANALGESIC
ANALOGOUS
ANARCHISM
ANATOMIZE
ANCHORAGE
ANCHORITE
ANCHORMAN
ANCILLARY
ANGELFISH
ANGLEWORM
ANGLICIZE
ANGUISHED
ANHYDROUS
ANIMALISM
ANIMATION
ANIMOSITY
ANKLEBONE
ANNOUNCER
ANNOYANCE
ANNUITANT
ANOMALOUS
ANONYMOUS
ANOPHELES
ANTARCTIC
ANTECHOIR
ANTHOLOGY
ANTICLINE
ANTIKNOCK
ANTINOVEL
ANTIPASTO
ANTIPATHY
ANTIQUARY
ANTIQUITY
ANTISERUM
ANTITOXIN
ANTITUMOR
ANTIVENIN
ENCHILADA
ENCOMPASS
ENCOUNTER
ENCOURAGE
ENDOCRINE
ENDOSCOPE
ENDURANCE
ENERGETIC
ENERGIZER
ENGRAVING
ENIGMATIC
ENLIGHTEN
ENRAPTURE
ENSHEATHE
ENTERITIS
ENTERTAIN
ENTOURAGE
ENUMERATE
ENUNCIATE
ENWREATHE
INABILITY
INAMORATA
INANIMATE
INANITION
INAUGURAL
INCAPABLE
INCARNATE
INCENTIVE
INCEPTION
INCESSANT
INCIDENCE
INCIPIENT
INCLEMENT

INCOGNITO
INCOMMODE
INCORRECT
INCREMENT
INCUBATOR
INCULCATE
INCULPATE
INCUMBENT
INCURABLE
INCURIOUS
INCURSION
INDELIBLE
INDEMNIFY
INDEMNITY
INDENTION
INDENTURE
INDIGNANT
INDIGNITY
INDUCTION
INDUCTIVE
INEBRIATE
INEFFABLE
INELEGANT
INFANTILE
INFATUATE
INFECTION
INFERENCE
INFERTILE
INFIRMARY
INFIRMITY
INFLATION
INFLEXION
INFLUENCE
INFLUENZA
INFORMANT
INFURIATE
INFUSIBLE
INGENIOUS
INGENUITY
INGENUOUS
INGLENOOK
INGROWING
INHALATOR
INJECTION
INJUSTICE
INNERMOST
INNERSOLE
INNKEEPER
INNOCENCE
INNOCUOUS
INOCULATE
INORGANIC
INPATIENT
INSATIATE
INSENSATE
INSERTION
INSIDIOUS

INSINCERE
INSINUATE
INSISTENT
INSOLUBLE
INSOLVENT
INSTANTER
INSTANTLY
INSTIGATE
INSTITUTE
INSURABLE
INSURANCE
INSURGENT
INTEGRATE
INTEGRITY
INTELLECT
INTENDANT
INTENSIFY
INTENSITY
INTENSIVE
INTENTION
INTERCEDE
INTERCEPT
INTERDICT
INTERFACE
INTERFERE
INTERFUSE
INTERJECT
INTERLACE
INTERLARD
INTERLEAF
INTERLINE
INTERLINK
INTERLOCK
INTERLOPE
INTERLUDE
INTERMENT
INTERNIST
INTERNODE
INTERPLAY
INTERPOSE
INTERPRET
INTERRUPT
INTERSECT
INTERVENE
INTERVIEW
INTESTATE
INTESTINE
INTRICATE
INTRINSIC
INTRODUCE
INTROVERT
INTUITION
INTUMESCE
INVECTIVE
INVENTION
INVENTIVE
INVENTORY

INVERNESS
INVERSION
INVIDIOUS
INVIOLATE
INVISIBLE
INVOLUCRE
KNOCKDOWN
KNOWLEDGE
ONIONSKIN
ONSLAUGHT
PNEUMATIC
PNEUMONIA
SNAKEBIRD
SNAKEBITE
SNOWDRIFT
SNOWFIELD
SNOWFLAKE
SNOWSTORM
UNADVISED
UNALIGNED
UNALLOYED
UNANIMOUS
UNBEKNOWN
UNBENDING
UNBLESSED
UNBOUNDED
UNBRIDLED
UNCEASING
UNCERTAIN
UNCHARTED
UNCLEANLY
UNCONCERN
UNCOUNTED
UNDAUNTED
UNDECEIVE
UNDECIDED
UNDERBODY
UNDERBRED
UNDERCOAT
UNDERDONE
UNDERFEED
UNDERFOOT
UNDERGIRD
UNDERHAND
UNDERLINE
UNDERLING
UNDERMINE
UNDERMOST
UNDERPART
UNDERPASS
UNDERPLAY
UNDERRATE
UNDERSELL
UNDERSHOT
UNDERSIDE
UNDERTAKE
UNDERTONE

UNDERWEAR
UNDERWOOD
UNDOUBTED
UNEARTHLY
UNEQUALED
UNFAILING
UNFEELING
UNFEIGNED
UNFLEDGED
UNFOUNDED
UNGUARDED
UNHARNESS
UNHEALTHY
UNISEXUAL
UNITARIAN
UNIVALENT
UNIVERSAL
UNKNOWING
UNLEARNED
UNMEANING
UNMINDFUL
UNNATURAL
UNPLUMBED
UNPOPULAR
UNRIVALED
UNRUFFLED
UNSCATHED
UNSELFISH
UNSETTLED
UNSHACKLE
UNSHEATHE
UNSIGHTLY
UNSKILLED
UNSPARING
UNSPOTTED
UNSTUDIED
UNTUTORED
UNWILLING
UNWITTING
UNWORLDLY
UNWRITTEN
BOARDWALK
BOATSWAIN
BODYGUARD
BOLSHEVIK
BOMBAZINE
BOMBPROOF
BOMBSHELL
BOMBSIGHT
BONDWOMAN
BOOKMAKER
BOOKPLATE
BOOKSHELF
BOOMERANG
BOONDOCKS
BOOTBLACK
BOULEVARD

BOUNTEOUS
BOUNTIFUL
BOURGEOIS
BOWSTRING
COADJUTOR
COAGULANT
COAGULATE
COALFIELD
COALITION
COASTLINE
COCHINEAL
COCKATIEL
COCKFIGHT
COCKROACH
COFEATURE
COFFEEPOT
COFFERDAM
COGNITION
COIFFEUSE
COLLATION
COLLEAGUE
COLLECTED
COLLEGIAN
COLLEGIUM
COLLIMATE
COLLODION
COLLUSION
COLLUVIUM
COLONNADE
COLORCAST
COLORFAST
COLUMBINE
COLUMNIST
COMFORTER
COMMANDER
COMMINGLE
COMMISSAR
COMMITTEE
COMMODITY
COMMODORE
COMMOTION
COMMUNION
COMMUNISM
COMMUNITY
COMPANION
COMPETENT
COMPLAINT
COMPONENT
COMPOSITE
COMPOSURE
CONCERNED
CONCERTED
CONCIERGE
CONCORDAT
CONCOURSE
CONCUBINE
CONDENSER

CONDIMENT
CONDITION
CONDUCTOR
CONESTOGA
CONFESSOR
CONFIDANT
CONFUSION
CONGENIAL
CONGERIES
CONGRUITY
CONJUGATE
CONNUBIAL
CONSCIOUS
CONSCRIPT
CONSENSUS
CONSONANT
CONSTABLE
CONSTANCY
CONSTRAIN
CONSTRICT
CONSTRUCT
CONTAGION
CONTAINER
CONTENTED
CONTINENT
CONTINUAL
CONTINUUM
CONTRALTO
CONTUMELY
CONTUSION
CONUNDRUM
CONVIVIAL
COONHOUND
COOPERATE
COPARTNER
COPYRIGHT
CORELDRAW
CORIANDER
CORKSCREW
CORMORANT
CORNSTALK
COROLLARY
CORPORATE
CORPOREAL
CORPUSCLE
CORRELATE
CORRUGATE
CORTISONE
CORUSCATE
COSMOGONY
COSMOLOGY
COSMONAUT
COSPONSOR
COTILLION
COTYLEDON
COUNSELOR
COUNTDOWN

COUNTLESS
COURTEOUS
COURTESAN
COURTROOM
COURTSHIP
COURTYARD
COUTURIER
COVALENCE
DOBSONFLY
DOCTORATE
DOGMATISM
DOMINANCE
DOORPLATE
DORMITORY
DOSIMETER
DOUBTLESS
DOWITCHER
DOWNGRADE
DOWNRANGE
DOWNRIGHT
DOWNSHIFT
DOWNSTAGE
DOWNSWING
FOLLOWING
FOODSTUFF
FOOLHARDY
FOOLPROOF
FOOTBOARD
FOOTLOOSE
FOOTPRINT
FOOTSTOOL
FORECLOSE
FOREFRONT
FOREGOING
FOREIGNER
FORENAMED
FORESHEET
FORESHORE
FORESIGHT
FORESTALL
FORESWEAR
FORETASTE
FORETOKEN
FOREWOMAN
FORGATHER
FORGIVING
FORMALISM
FORMALITY
FORMALIZE
FORMATION
FORMATIVE
FORMULATE
FORSYTHIA
FORTHWITH
FORTITUDE
FORTNIGHT
FORTUNATE

FORWARDER
FOUNDLING
FOURSCORE
GODFATHER
GODMOTHER
GODPARENT
GOLDBRICK
GOLDENROD
GOLDFIELD
GOLDFINCH
GOLDSMITH
GONDOLIER
GONORRHEA
GOVERNESS
HOARFROST
HOBGOBLIN
HOLLYHOCK
HOLOCAUST
HOLOGRAPH
HOLYSTONE
HOMEGROWN
HOMEMAKER
HOMESTEAD
HOMOGRAPH
HOMOPHONE
HONEYCOMB
HONEYMOON
HONORABLE
HONORIFIC
HOPSCOTCH
HOREHOUND
HOROSCOPE
HORSEBACK
HORSEHAIR
HORSEHIDE
HORSEPLAY
HORSESHOE
HORSETAIL
HORSEWHIP
HORTATIVE
HORTATORY
HOTHEADED
HOURGLASS
HOUSEBOAT
HOUSECOAT
HOUSEHOLD
HOUSEMAID
HOUSEWIFE
HOUSEWORK
HOWSOEVER
JOBHOLDER
LOADSTONE
LOATHSOME
LOCKSMITH
LOCOMOTOR
LODESTONE
LOGARITHM

LOGISTICS
LOINCLOTH
LONGEVITY
LONGITUDE
LORGNETTE
LOWERCASE
MODERATOR
MODERNISM
MODERNIZE
MOLDBOARD
MOMENTARY
MOMENTOUS
MONASTERY
MONGOLIAN
MONGOLISM
MONGOLOID
MONKSHOOD
MONOGRAPH
MONOLOGUE
MONOMANIA
MONOPLANE
MONOSPACE
MONSIGNOR
MOONLIGHT
MOONSCAPE
MOONSHINE
MOONSTONE
MORTICIAN
MOTORBIKE
MOTORBOAT
MOTORCADE
MOUSETRAP
MOUSTACHE
MOUTHPART
MOUTHWASH
NOCTURNAL
NONCREDIT
NONENTITY
NONPAREIL
NONPERSON
NONPROFIT
NONREADER
NORMALIZE
NORMATIVE
NORTHEAST
NORTHWEST
NORWEGIAN
NOSEBLEED
NOSEPIECE
NOSTALGIA
NOTCHBACK
NOTORIOUS
NOVELETTE
NOVITIATE
POETASTER
POINCIANA
POLICEMAN
POLITBURO
POLITESSE
POLITICAL
POLYESTER
POLYGRAPH
POLYPHONY
POMPADOUR
PONDEROUS
POORHOUSE
POPPYCOCK
PORCELAIN
PORCUPINE
PORRINGER
PORTFOLIO
PORTULACA
POSTERIOR
POSTERITY
POSTHASTE
POSTILION
POSTNATAL
POSTULANT
POSTULATE
POTASSIUM
POTBOILER
POTENTATE
POTENTIAL
POTPOURRI
POULTERER
POURBOIRE
POWERBOAT
ROADBLOCK
ROADSTEAD
ROCKBOUND
ROOTSTOCK
ROSEWATER
ROUGHNECK
ROUMANIAN
ROUNDELAY
ROUNDWORM
SOAPSTONE
SOBRIQUET
SOCIALISM
SOCIALITE
SOCIALIZE
SOCIOLOGY
SOFTBOUND
SOLEMNIZE
SOLICITOR
SOLILOQUY
SOLITAIRE
SOMETHING
SOMETIMES
SOMEWHERE
SOMNOLENT
SOPHISTIC
SOPHISTRY
SOPHOMORE
SOPORIFIC
SOUBRETTE
SOUTHEAST
SOUTHWEST
SOVEREIGN
TOADSTOOL
TOLERABLE
TOLERANCE
TOLLHOUSE
TOMBSTONE
TONSORIAL
TOOTHACHE
TOOTHPICK
TOOTHSOME
TOUCHDOWN
TOWNSFOLK
VOICELESS
VOLCANISM
VOLTMETER
VOLUNTARY
VOLUNTEER
VOODOOISM
VORACIOUS
VOUCHSAFE
WOEBEGONE
WOLFHOUND
WOLFSBANE
WOLVERINE
WOMANHOOD
WOMANKIND
WOMANLIKE
WOMENFOLK
WONDERFUL
WOODBLOCK
WOODCHUCK
WOODCRAFT
WORKBENCH
WORKGROUP
WORKHORSE
WORKHOUSE
WORKPLACE
WORKTABLE
WORLDLING
WORLDWIDE
WORRISOME
WORRYWART
WORTHLESS
YOUNGLING
YOUNGSTER
APARTHEID
APARTMENT
APOCRYPHA
APOLOGIZE
APOSTOLIC
APPALOOSA
APPARATUS
APPELLANT
APPELLATE
APPENDAGE
APPERTAIN
APPETIZER
APPLEJACK
APPLETALK
APPLIANCE
APPLICANT
APPOINTEE
APPORTION
APPREHEND
EPHEDRINE
EPHEMERAL
EPICENTER
EPICUREAN
EPIDERMIS
EPIGRAPHY
EPISCOPAL
OPERATION
OPERATIVE
OPPORTUNE
OPTOMETRY
SPACESHIP
SPAGHETTI
SPEAKEASY
SPEARHEAD
SPEARMINT
SPECIALTY
SPECTACLE
SPECTATOR
SPECULATE
SPEEDBOAT
SPEEDWELL
SPELUNKER
SPHINCTER
SPICEBUSH
SPINDLING
SPINDRIFT
SPINNAKER
SPIRITUAL
SPLENETIC
SPLITTING
SPOKESMAN
SPOONBILL
SPORTSMAN
SPOTLIGHT
SPRIGHTLY
UPANISHAD
UPHOLSTER
UPPERCASE
UPPERMOST
AQUAPLANE
EQUIPMENT
EQUIPOISE
EQUITABLE
EQUIVOCAL
SQUEAMISH
ARABESQUE
ARBITRARY
ARBITRATE
ARBORETUM
ARCHANGEL
ARCHENEMY
ARCHETYPE
ARCHFIEND
ARCHITECT
ARCHIVIST
ARGENTINE
ARGENTITE
ARMADILLO
ARMISTICE
ARROWHEAD
ARROWROOT
ARTERIOLE
ARTHRITIS
ARTHROPOD
ARTICHOKE
ARTICULAR
ARTIFICER
ARTILLERY
BRASSERIE
BRASSIERE
BRAZILIAN
BREAKDOWN
BREAKFAST
BREEZEWAY
BRIEFCASE
BRILLIANT
BRIMSTONE
BRIQUETTE
BRITANNIC
BROADBAND
BROADCAST
BROADLOOM
BROADSIDE
BROADTAIL
BROCHETTE
BROKERAGE
BRONCHIAL
BRUSHWOOD
BRUTALIZE
CRABGRASS
CRACKDOWN
CRAFTSMAN
CRANBERRY
CRANKCASE
CREDULOUS
CREMATORY
CRESCENDO
CRETINISM
CRINOLINE
CRITERION
CRITICISM
CRITICIZE
CROCODILE
CROISSANT
CROQUETTE
CROSSOVER
CROSSROAD
CROSSWALK
CROSSWAYS
CROSSWISE
CRUCIFORM
CRYOGENIC
DRAFTSMAN
DRAGONFLY
DRAINPIPE
DRAMATIZE
DREAMLAND
DRIFTWOOD
DROMEDARY
DRUGSTORE
DRUMSTICK
ERADICATE
EROGENOUS
ERRONEOUS
ERSTWHILE
ERUDITION
FRACTIOUS
FRAMEWORK
FRANCHISE
FRANGIBLE
FRATERNAL
FREEBOARD
FREEMASON
FREESTONE
FREEWHEEL
FREQUENCY
FRICASSEE
FRIEDCAKE
FRIGHTFUL
FRIVOLOUS
FROSTBITE
FRUITCAKE
FRUITERER
FRUSTRATE
GRADATION
GRANDIOSE
GRANTSMAN
GRANULATE
GRAPESHOT
GRAPEVINE
GRASSLAND
GRATICULE
GRATITUDE
GRAVEYARD
GRAVITATE
GRAYBEARD
GREATCOAT
GREENBACK
GREENBELT
GREENHORN
GREENROOM
GREENWOOD
GRENADIER
GRENADINE
GREYHOUND
GRIEVANCE
GRILLWORK
GRISTMILL
GROOMSMAN
GROSGRAIN
GROTESQUE
GROUNDHOG
GROUNDING
GROUPWARE
GRUBSTAKE
IRASCIBLE
IRONBOUND
IRONSTONE
IRRADIATE
IRREGULAR
IRRITABLE
ORANGEADE
ORCHESTRA
ORDINANCE
ORGIASTIC
ORIENTATE
ORIFLAMME
ORIGINATE
ORPHANAGE
PRACTICAL
PRAGMATIC
PRAYERFUL
PRECANCEL
PRECEDENT
PRECEDING
PRECENTOR
PRECEPTOR
PRECIPICE
PRECISION
PRECURSOR
PREDATION
PREDATORY
PREDICATE
PREFIGURE
PREFLIGHT
PREGNABLE
PREJUDICE
PRELAUNCH
PREMATURE
PREOCCUPY
PREORDAIN
PRERECORD
PRESBYTER
PRESCHOOL
PRESCRIBE
PRESENTLY
PRESHRUNK
PRESIDENT
PRESIDIUM
PRESSROOM
PRESTRESS
PREVALENT
PREVERBAL
PREVISION
PRICELESS
PRIMARILY
PRIMITIVE
PRINCIPAL
PRINCIPLE
PRINTABLE
PRIVATEER
PRIVATION
PRIVILEGE
PROBATION
PROBATIVE
PROBOSCIS
PROCEDURE
PROCESSOR
PROCONSUL
PROCREATE
PROFANITY
PROFESSOR
PROFITEER
PROGNOSIS
PROJECTOR
PROMENADE
PROMINENT
PROMISING
PRONGHORN
PRONOUNCE
PROOFREAD
PROPAGATE
PROPELLER
PROPHETIC
PROPONENT
PROPRIETY
PROSCRIBE
PROSECUTE
PROSELYTE
PROSTRATE
PROTECTOR
PROTOTYPE
PROTOZOAN
PROVENCAL
PROVENDER
PROVIDENT
PROVISION
PROVOLONE
PROXIMATE
PROXIMITY
TRACKBALL
TRACTABLE
TRADEMARK

TRADESMAN
TRADITION
TRAGEDIAN
TRAINLOAD
TRANSCEND
TRANSDUCE
TRANSFORM
TRANSFUSE
TRANSIENT
TRANSLATE
TRANSMUTE
TRANSONIC
TRANSPIRE
TRANSPORT
TRANSPOSE
TRANSSHIP
TRAPEZOID
TRAPPINGS
TREACHERY
TREADMILL
TREASURER
TREATMENT
TREMATODE
TREMULOUS
TRENCHANT
TRIBESMAN
TRIBUTARY
TRICKSTER
TRIENNIAL
TRIFOCALS
TRIMESTER
TRITURATE
TRIWEEKLY
TROOPSHIP
TROUSSEAU
TRUCKLOAD
TRUCULENT
TRUNCHEON
URTICARIA
WRESTLING
WRISTBAND
WRONGDOER
ASAFETIDA
ASCENDANT
ASCENDERS
ASCENSION
ASCERTAIN
ASPARAGUS
ASPERSION
ASSEMBLER
ASSERTION
ASSIDUOUS
ASSISTANT
ASSOCIATE
ASSONANCE
ASSURANCE
ASTRADDLE

ASTRAKHAN
ASTROLABE
ASTROLOGY
ASTRONAUT
ASTRONOMY
ASYMPTOTE
ESCALATOR
ESOPHAGUS
ESPERANTO
ESPIONAGE
ESPLANADE
ESSENTIAL
ESTABLISH
ESTAMINET
ESTIMABLE
ISINGLASS
ISOSCELES
ISRAELITE
OSCILLATE
OSTRACIZE
PSEUDONYM
PSORIASIS
PSYCHOSIS
ATHENAEUM
ATHLETICS
ATONEMENT
ATROCIOUS
ATTAINDER
ATTENDANT
ATTENTION
ATTENUATE
ATTRIBUTE
ATTRITION
ETHIOPIAN
ETHNOLOGY
ETIQUETTE
ETYMOLOGY
ITALICIZE
ITERATION
ITINERANT
ITINERARY
OTHERWISE
PTARMIGAN
STABILIZE
STAIRCASE
STAIRWELL
STALEMATE
STAMINATE
STANCHION
STANDPIPE
STARBOARD
STARLIGHT
STARTLING
STATEMENT
STATEROOM
STATESIDE
STATESMAN

STATIONER
STATISTIC
STATUETTE
STATUTORY
STEADFAST
STEAMBOAT
STEAMSHIP
STEELYARD
STEPCHILD
STERILIZE
STEVEDORE
STILLBORN
STIMULANT
STIMULATE
STIPULATE
STOCKPILE
STOCKYARD
STOMACHER
STOMACHIC
STOPLIGHT
STOPWATCH
STOREROOM
STRAPLESS
STRAPPING
STRATAGEM
STREAMBED
STREAMLET
STREETCAR
STRENUOUS
STRETCHER
STRICTURE
STRIKEOUT
STRIPLING
STRONTIUM
STRUCTURE
UTTERANCE
UTTERMOST
YTTERBIUM
AUCTORIAL
AUDACIOUS
AUDIOLOGY
AURICULAR
AUTHENTIC
AUTHORITY
AUTHORIZE
AUTOCRACY
AUTOGRAPH
AUTOMATIC
AUTOMATON
AUTOTRACE
AUXILIARY
BUCCANEER
BUCKBOARD
BUCKTOOTH
BUCKWHEAT
BULGARIAN
BULLFIGHT

BULLFINCH
BUMBLEBEE
BUMPTIOUS
BURLESQUE
BURUNDIAN
BUSHWHACK
BUTTERCUP
BUTTERFAT
BUTTERFLY
BUTTERNUT
CUBBYHOLE
CULLENDER
CULMINATE
CULTIVATE
CUNEIFORM
CUPBEARER
CURETTAGE
CURRYCOMB
CURVATURE
CUSTODIAL
CUSTODIAN
CUSTOMARY
CUSTOMIZE
CUTANEOUS
CUTTHROAT
DUCKBOARD
DUMBFOUND
DUPLICATE
DUPLICITY
EUCHARIST
EUCLIDEAN
EUPHEMISM
EUTHENICS
EUTROPHIC
FULMINATE
FUNGICIDE
FUNICULAR
FURNITURE
FUSILLADE
GUARANTEE
GUARANTOR
GUARDROOM
GUARDSMAN
GUERRILLA
GUIDEBOOK
GUIDELINE
GUNCOTTON
GUNNYSACK
GUNPOWDER
GUSTATORY
HUMANKIND
HUMDINGER
HUMILIATE
HUNCHBACK
HUNGARIAN
HURRICANE
HUSBANDRY

JUDICIARY
JUDICIOUS
JURIDICAL
JUXTAPOSE
LUBRICANT
LUBRICATE
LUCRATIVE
LUDICROUS
LUNCHROOM
LUXURIANT
LUXURIATE
MUCKRAKER
MULTIFORM
MULTISCAN
MULTISPIN
MULTISYNC
MULTITUDE
MUNICIPAL
MURDEROUS
MUSKMELON
MUSSULMAN
NUMERATOR
NUMERICAL
NURSEMAID
NUTRIMENT
NUTRITION
OUBLIETTE
OURSELVES
OUTERMOST
OUTGROWTH
OUTNUMBER
OUTRIGGER
OUTSKIRTS
OUTSPOKEN
OUTSPREAD
OUTWARDLY
PUBESCENT
PUBLICIST
PUBLICITY
PUBLICIZE
PUERPERAL
PUISSANCE
PULMONARY
PULVERIZE
PUNCTILIO
PUNCTUATE
PUPPETEER
PUREBLOOD
PURGATION
PURGATIVE
PURGATORY
PURSUANCE
PUSSYFOOT
QUADRATIC
QUADRILLE
QUADRUPED
QUADRUPLE

QUARTERLY
QUARTZITE
QUERULOUS
QUICKDRAW
QUICKLIME
QUICKSAND
QUICKSORT
QUICKSTEP
QUICKTIME
QUIESCENT
QUINTUPLE
QUITTANCE
QUIZZICAL
QUOTIDIAN
RUINATION
RUMRUNNER
RUNAROUND
RUSTICATE
RUTHENIUM
SUBALPINE
SUBALTERN
SUBATOMIC
SUBDIVIDE
SUBJUGATE
SUBLIMATE
SUBLUNARY
SUBMARINE
SUBNORMAL
SUBSCRIBE
SUBSCRIPT
SUBSIDIZE
SUBSTANCE
SUCCESSOR
SUCCOTASH
SUCCULENT
SUFFERING
SUFFOCATE
SUFFRAGAN
SUGARCANE
SUGARPLUM
SULFUROUS
SUMMARIZE
SUMMATION
SUMPTUOUS
SUNBONNET
SUNFLOWER
SUNSEEKER
SUNSTROKE
SUPERNOVA
SUPERPOSE
SUPERSEDE
SUPERVENE
SUPERVISE
SUPPLIANT
SUPPOSING
SUPPURATE
SUPREMACY

SURCHARGE
SURCINGLE
SURFBOARD
SURRENDER
SURROGATE
SURVEYING
SUSPENDER
SUSPICION
TULAREMIA
TURBOPROP
TURBULENT
TURNABOUT
TURNSTILE
TURNTABLE
TURPITUDE
TURQUOISE
TUSCARORA
VULCANISM
VULCANIZE
VULGARIAN
VULGARISM
VULGARITY
VULGARIZE
ZUCCHETTO
AVAILABLE
AVALANCHE
AVOCATION
AVUNCULAR
EVAPORATE
EVAPORITE
EVENTUATE
EVERGLADE
EVERGREEN
EVERYBODY
EVOLUTION
OVERBLOWN
OVERBOARD
OVERCLOUD
OVERDRAFT
OVERDRIVE
OVERMATCH
OVERNIGHT
OVERPOWER
OVERPRINT
OVERREACH
OVERSEXED
OVERSHOOT
OVERSIGHT
OVERSLEEP
OVERSTATE
OVERTHROW
OVERTRICK
OVERWEIGH
OVERWHELM
OVERWRITE
OVIPAROUS
AWESTRUCK

SWAMPLAND
SWANSDOWN
SWEATSHOP
SWEETMEAT
SWELLHEAD
SWITCHMAN
SWORDFISH
SWORDPLAY
SWORDSMAN
SWORDTAIL
TWINKLING
ZWINGLIAN
EXCELLENT
EXCELSIOR
EXCEPTION
EXCHEQUER
EXCITABLE
EXCLUSIVE
EXCORIATE
EXCREMENT
EXCULPATE
EXCURSION
EXCURSIVE
EXECRABLE
EXECUTIVE
EXECUTRIX
EXEMPLARY
EXEMPLIFY
EXISTENCE
EXOGENOUS
EXONERATE
EXOSPHERE
EXPANSION
EXPANSIVE
EXPATIATE
EXPECTANT
EXPEDIENT
EXPEDITER
EXPENSIVE
EXPERTISE
EXPIATORY
EXPLETIVE
EXPLICATE
EXPLOSION
EXPLOSIVE
EXPOSITOR
EXPULSION
EXPURGATE
EXQUISITE
EXTEMPORE
EXTENSION
EXTENSIVE
EXTENUATE
EXTIRPATE
EXTRADITE
EXTRAVERT
EXTREMISM

EXTREMITY
EXTRICATE
EXTRINSIC
EXTRUSIVE
EXUBERANT
OXIDATION
OXYGENATE
BYSTANDER
CYCLAMATE
CYCLOTRON
CYTOPLASM
DYSENTERY
DYSPEPSIA
DYSTROPHY
EYESTRAIN
GYMNASIUM
GYRFALCON
GYROSCOPE
HYDRANGEA
HYDRAULIC
HYDROFOIL
HYDROLOGY
HYDROXIDE
HYPERBOLA
HYPERBOLE
HYPERCARD
HYPERTEXT
HYPHENATE
HYPOCRISY
HYSTERICS
MYSTICISM
MYTHOLOGY
PYRETHRUM
PYROLYSIS
PYROMANIA
PYROMETER
SYCOPHANT
SYLLABIFY
SYLLOGISM
SYMBIOSIS
SYMBOLISM
SYMBOLIZE
SYMPOSIUM
SYNAGOGUE
SYNDICATE
SYNERGISM
SYNTHESIS
SYNTHETIC
SYSTEMIZE
TYPEWRITE
TYRANNIZE
TYRANNOUS
XYLOPHONE

**3RD LETTER**

ABANDONED
ABATEMENT
ALABASTER
AMARYLLIS
ANAEROBIC
ANALGESIA
ANALGESIC
ANALOGOUS
ANARCHISM
ANATOMIZE
APARTHEID
APARTMENT
ARABESQUE
ASAFETIDA
AVAILABLE
AVALANCHE
BEACHHEAD
BEATITUDE
BEAUTEOUS
BEAUTIFUL
BLACKBALL
BLACKBIRD
BLACKBODY
BLACKFOOT
BLACKHEAD
BLACKJACK
BLACKLIST
BLACKMAIL
BLASPHEME
BLASPHEMY
BOARDWALK
BOATSWAIN
BRASSERIE
BRASSIERE
BRAZILIAN
CEASELESS
CHAFFINCH
CHALKBORD
CHALLENGE
CHAMELEON
CHAMOMILE
CHAMPAGNE
CHAMPAIGN
CHANCROID
CHANTEUSE
CHAPARRAL
CHARABANC
CHARACTER
CHARLATAN
CHARWOMAN
CHAUFFEUR
CLAMSHELL
CLAPBOARD
CLASSICAL
CLASSMATE
CLASSROOM
COADJUTOR
COAGULANT
COAGULATE
COALFIELD
COALITION
COASTLINE
CRABGRASS
CRACKDOWN
CRAFTSMAN
CRANBERRY
CRANKCASE
DEATHBLOW
DEATHLESS
DIACRITIC
DIAERESIS
DIAGNOSIS
DIALECTIC
DIAMETRIC
DIAPHRAGM
DIATHERMY
DIATOMITE
DRAFTSMAN
DRAGONFLY
DRAINPIPE
DRAMATIZE
EJACULATE
ELABORATE
ELASTOMER
ERADICATE
EVAPORATE
EVAPORITE
FLAGELLUM
FLAGEOLET
FLAGSTAFF
FLAGSTONE
FLAMMABLE
FLASHBACK
FLASHBULB
FLASHCUBE
FLASHTUBE
FLATULENT
FLAVORING
FRACTIOUS
FRAMEWORK
FRANCHISE
FRANGIBLE
FRATERNAL
GEARSHIFT
GLADIATOR
GLADIOLUS
GLADSTONE
GLAMORIZE
GRADATION
GRANDIOSE
GRANTSMAN
GRANULATE
GRAPESHOT
GRAPEVINE
GRASSLAND
GRATICULE
GRATITUDE
GRAVEYARD
GRAVITATE
GRAYBEARD
GUARANTEE
GUARANTOR
GUARDROOM
GUARDSMAN
HEADBOARD
HEADDRESS
HEADFIRST
HEADLIGHT
HEADPHONE
HEADPIECE
HEADSTALL
HEADSTONE
HEADWATER
HEALTHFUL
HEARTACHE
HEARTBEAT
HEARTBURN
HEARTFELT
HEARTLESS
HEARTSICK
HEARTWOOD
HOARFROST
IMAGINARY
INABILITY
INAMORATA
INANIMATE
INANITION
INAUGURAL
IRASCIBLE
ITALICIZE
LEAFSTALK
LEASEHOLD
LEASTWISE
LEAVENING
LIABILITY
LOADSTONE
LOATHSOME
MEANWHILE
ORANGEADE
PEACETIME
PHALAROPE
PLACEKICK
PLACEMENT
PLAINTIFF
PLAINTIVE
PLANELOAD
PLANETOID
PLATITUDE
PLAUSIBLE
PLAYHOUSE
PLAYTHING
PRACTICAL
PRAGMATIC
PRAYERFUL
PTARMIGAN
QUADRATIC
QUADRILLE
QUADRUPED
QUADRUPLE
QUARTERLY
QUARTZITE
REACTANCE
ROADBLOCK
ROADSTEAD
SCANTLING
SCAPEGOAT
SCARECROW
SCAVENGER
SEAFARING
SEASONING
SEAWORTHY
SHADOWBOX
SHAKEDOWN
SHAPELESS
SHAREWARE
SHARKSKIN
SLAUGHTER
SMALLTALK
SNAKEBIRD
SNAKEBITE
SOAPSTONE
SPACESHIP
SPAGHETTI
STABILIZE
STAIRCASE
STAIRWELL
STALEMATE
STAMINATE
STANCHION
STANDPIPE
STARBOARD
STARLIGHT
STARTLING
STATEMENT
STATEROOM
STATESIDE
STATESMAN
STATIONER
STATISTIC
STATUETTE
STATUTORY
SWAMPLAND
SWANSDOWN
TEAKETTLE
THANKLESS
TOADSTOOL
TRACKBALL
TRACTABLE
TRADEMARK
TRADESMAN
TRADITION
TRAGEDIAN
TRAINLOAD
TRANSCEND
TRANSDUCE
TRANSFORM
TRANSFUSE
TRANSIENT
TRANSLATE
TRANSMUTE
TRANSONIC
TRANSPIRE
TRANSPORT
TRANSPOSE
TRANSSHIP
TRAPEZOID
TRAPPINGS
UNADVISED
UNALIGNED
UNALLOYED
UNANIMOUS
UPANISHAD
WEARISOME
WHALEBOAT
WHALEBONE
ALBATROSS
AMBERGRIS
AMBIGUOUS
AMBITIOUS
AMBULANCE
AMBUSCADE
ARBITRARY
ARBITRATE
ARBORETUM
CABLEGRAM
CABRIOLET
CUBBYHOLE
DEBENTURE
DEBUTANTE
DOBSONFLY
ELBOWROOM
EMBARRASS
EMBAYMENT
EMBELLISH
EMBRASURE
EMBROCATE
EMBROIDER
FABRICATE
FEBRIFUGE
GABARDINE
GABERDINE
GIBBERISH
HABITABLE
HABITUATE
HIBERNATE
HOBGOBLIN
IMBALANCE
IMBROGLIO
JOBHOLDER
LABORIOUS
LABYRINTH
LIBERTINE
LIBRARIAN
LUBRICANT
LUBRICATE
OBBLIGATO
OMBUDSMAN
OUBLIETTE
PUBESCENT
PUBLICIST
PUBLICITY
PUBLICIZE
RABBINATE
REBELLION
SEBACEOUS
SOBRIQUET
SUBALPINE
SUBALTERN
SUBATOMIC
SUBDIVIDE
SUBJUGATE
SUBLIMATE
SUBLUNARY
SUBMARINE
SUBNORMAL
SUBSCRIBE
SUBSCRIPT
SUBSIDIZE
SUBSTANCE
TABLELAND
TABLEWARE
UMBILICUS
UNBEKNOWN
UNBENDING
UNBLESSED
UNBOUNDED
UNBRIDLED
VIBRATION
VIBRATORY
ACCESSION
ACCESSORY
ACCIDENCE
ACCLIMATE
ACCLIVITY
ACCOMPANY
ACCORDION
ACCRETION
ALCOHOLIC
ANCHORAGE
ANCHORITE
ANCHORMAN
ANCILLARY
ARCHANGEL
ARCHENEMY
ARCHETYPE
ARCHFIEND
ARCHITECT
ARCHIVIST
ASCENDANT
ASCENDERS
ASCENSION
ASCERTAIN
AUCTORIAL
BACCHANAL
BACKBOARD
BACKFIELD
BACKPEDAL
BACKSLASH
BACKSLIDE
BACKSTAGE
BACKSWEPT
BACKTRACK
BACKWATER
BACKWOODS
BACTERIUM
BICAMERAL
BICONCAVE
BUCCANEER
BUCKBOARD
BUCKTOOTH
BUCKWHEAT
CACOPHONY
COCHINEAL
COCKATIEL
COCKFIGHT
COCKROACH
CYCLAMATE
CYCLOTRON
DACHSHUND
DECADENCE
DECALOGUE
DECATHLON
DECEITFUL
DECENNIAL
DECEPTION
DECIDUOUS
DECILITER
DECIMETER
DECISTERE
DECLIVITY
DECOLLETE
DECOMPOSE
DECONTROL
DECORATOR
DECOUPAGE
DECREMENT
DICHOTOMY

DOCTORATE
DUCKBOARD
ECCENTRIC
ENCHILADA
ENCOMPASS
ENCOUNTER
ENCOURAGE
ESCALATOR
EUCHARIST
EUCLIDEAN
EXCELLENT
EXCELSIOR
EXCEPTION
EXCHEQUER
EXCITABLE
EXCLUSIVE
EXCORIATE
EXCREMENT
EXCULPATE
EXCURSION
EXCURSIVE
FACETIOUS
FACSIMILE
FACTORIAL
FECUNDATE
HACKNEYED
HECTOGRAM
INCAPABLE
INCARNATE
INCENTIVE
INCEPTION
INCESSANT
INCIDENCE
INCIPIENT
INCLEMENT
INCOGNITO
INCOMMODE
INCORRECT
INCREMENT
INCUBATOR
INCULCATE
INCULPATE
INCUMBENT
INCURABLE
INCURIOUS
INCURSION
JACARANDA
JACKKNIFE
JACKSCREW
JACKSTRAW
KICKSTAND
LACCOLITH
LOCKSMITH
LOCOMOTOR
LUCRATIVE
MACHINERY
MACHINIST
MACINTOSH
MACROCOSM
MECHANICS
MECHANISM
MECHANIZE
MICROCOPY
MICROCOSM
MICROFILM
MICROGRAM
MICROSOFT
MICROWAVE
MUCKRAKER
NECESSARY
NECESSITY
NECROLOGY
NECTARINE
NICOTINIC
NOCTURNAL
OCCULTISM
OCCUPANCY
ORCHESTRA
OSCILLATE
PACEMAKER
PACHYDERM
PACKHORSE
PECUNIARY
PICKABACK
PICTORIAL
RACEHORSE
RACETRACK
RACIALISM
RACKETEER
RACONTEUR
RECEPTION
RECEPTIVE
RECESSION
RECESSIVE
RECHERCHE
RECIPIENT
RECKONING
RECOGNIZE
RECOLLECT
RECOMMEND
RECONCILE
RECONDITE
RECORDING
RECORDIST
RECTANGLE
RECTIFIER
RECTITUDE
RECUMBENT
RECURSION
ROCKBOUND
SACCHARIN
SACKCLOTH
SACRAMENT
SACRIFICE
SACRILEGE
SACRISTAN
SECESSION
SECLUSION
SECONDARY
SECRETARY
SECRETION
SECRETIVE
SECTARIAN
SECTIONAL
SOCIALISM
SOCIALITE
SOCIALIZE
SOCIOLOGY
SUCCESSOR
SUCCOTASH
SUCCULENT
SYCOPHANT
TECHNICAL
TECHNIQUE
TECTONICS
TECTONISM
UNCEASING
UNCERTAIN
UNCHARTED
UNCLEANLY
UNCONCERN
UNCOUNTED
VACCINATE
VACILLATE
VICARIOUS
VICENNIAL
VICEREGAL
VICTIMIZE
VICTORIAN
VICTUALER
YACHTSMAN
ZUCCHETTO
ADDICTION
ADDRESSEE
AUDACIOUS
AUDIOLOGY
BADMINTON
BEDFELLOW
BEDRIDDEN
BEDSPREAD
BODYGUARD
DEDUCTION
EIDERDOWN
ENDOCRINE
ENDOSCOPE
ENDURANCE
FIDUCIARY
GODFATHER
GODMOTHER
GODPARENT
HIDEBOUND
HYDRANGEA
HYDRAULIC
HYDROFOIL
HYDROLOGY
HYDROXIDE
INDELIBLE
INDEMNIFY
INDEMNITY
INDENTION
INDENTURE
INDIGNANT
INDIGNITY
INDUCTION
INDUCTIVE
JUDICIARY
JUDICIOUS
LODESTONE
LUDICROUS
MEDALLION
MEDICABLE
MEDICINAL
MIDDLEMAN
MIDSTREAM
MIDSUMMER
MIDWINTER
MODERATOR
MODERNISM
MODERNIZE
ORDINANCE
PEDAGOGUE
PEDOMETER
RADIOGRAM
RADIOLOGY
REDACTION
REDBREAST
REDUCTION
REDUNDANT
RIDGEPOLE
SADDLEBOW
SEDENTARY
SIDEBOARD
SIDEBURNS
SIDEPIECE
SIDESWIPE
SIDETRACK
TIDEWATER
UNDAUNTED
UNDECEIVE
UNDECIDED
UNDERBODY
UNDERBRED
UNDERCOAT
UNDERDONE
UNDERFEED
UNDERFOOT
UNDERGIRD
UNDERHAND
UNDERLINE
UNDERLING
UNDERMINE
UNDERMOST
UNDERPART
UNDERPASS
UNDERPLAY
UNDERRATE
UNDERSELL
UNDERSHOT
UNDERSIDE
UNDERTAKE
UNDERTONE
UNDERWEAR
UNDERWOOD
UNDOUBTED
VIDELICET
VIDEOTAPE
WEDNESDAY
ACETYLENE
ALEATORIC
AMENDMENT
AMERICANA
AMERICIUM
AWESTRUCK
BEEFEATER
BEEFSTEAK
BEEKEEPER
BLEACHERS
BREAKDOWN
BREAKFAST
BREEZEWAY
CHECKBOOK
CHECKLIST
CHECKMATE
CHECKROOM
CHEEKBONE
CHEERLESS
CHEMISTRY
CHEVALIER
CLEARANCE
CLERGYMAN
CREDULOUS
CREMATORY
CRESCENDO
CRETINISM
DIETETICS
DREAMLAND
EDELWEISS
ELECTRIFY
ELECTRODE
ELEVATION
EMERGENCY
ENERGETIC
ENERGIZER
EVENTUATE
EVERGLADE
EVERGREEN
EVERYBODY
EXECRABLE
EXECUTIVE
EXECUTRIX
EXEMPLARY
EXEMPLIFY
EYESTRAIN
FEEDSTOCK
FEEDSTUFF
FLEDGLING
FREEBOARD
FREEMASON
FREESTONE
FREEWHEEL
FREQUENCY
GLEANINGS
GLENGARRY
GREATCOAT
GREENBACK
GREENBELT
GREENHORN
GREENROOM
GREENWOOD
GRENADIER
GRENADINE
GREYHOUND
GUERRILLA
HIERARCHY
ICELANDER
ICELANDIC
IDENTICAL
INEBRIATE
INEFFABLE
INELEGANT
ITERATION
MAELSTROM
OBEISANCE
OPERATION
OPERATIVE
OVERBLOWN
OVERBOARD
OVERCLOUD
OVERDRAFT
OVERDRIVE
OVERMATCH
OVERNIGHT
OVERPOWER
OVERPRINT
OVERREACH
OVERSEXED
OVERSHOOT
OVERSIGHT
OVERSLEEP
OVERSTATE
OVERTHROW
OVERTRICK
OVERWEIGH
OVERWHELM
OVERWRITE
PHEROMONE
PIECEMEAL
PIECEWORK
PLENITUDE
PLENTEOUS
PLENTIFUL
PNEUMATIC
PNEUMONIA
POETASTER
PRECANCEL
PRECEDENT
PRECEDING
PRECENTOR
PRECEPTOR
PRECIPICE
PRECISION
PRECURSOR
PREDATION
PREDATORY
PREDICATE
PREFIGURE
PREFLIGHT
PREGNABLE
PREJUDICE
PRELAUNCH
PREMATURE
PREOCCUPY
PREORDAIN
PRERECORD
PRESBYTER
PRESCHOOL
PRESCRIBE
PRESENTLY
PRESHRUNK
PRESIDENT
PRESIDIUM
PRESSROOM
PRESTRESS
PREVALENT
PREVERBAL
PREVISION
PSEUDONYM
PUERPERAL
QUERULOUS
REENFORCE
REENTRANT
RHEOMETER
SHEATHING
SHEEPFOLD
SHEEPSKIN
SHELLFIRE
SHELLFISH
SPEAKEASY
SPEARHEAD
SPEARMINT
SPECIALTY
SPECTACLE
SPECTATOR
SPECULATE
SPEEDBOAT
SPEEDWELL
SPELUNKER
STEADFAST
STEAMBOAT
STEAMSHIP
STEELYARD
STEPCHILD
STERILIZE
STEVEDORE
SWEATSHOP
SWEETMEAT
SWELLHEAD
THEATRICS
THEOCRACY
THEOSOPHY
THEREFORE
THEREFROM
THEREUNTO
THEREUPON
THEREWITH
THESAURUS
TREACHERY
TREADMILL
TREASURER
TREATMENT
TREMATODE
TREMULOUS
TRENCHANT
UNEARTHLY
UNEQUALED
VIEWPOINT
WHEELBASE
WHEREFORE
WHEREUPON
WHEREWITH
WHETSTONE
WOEBEGONE
WRESTLING
AFFECTING
AFFECTION
AFFIDAVIT
AFFILIATE
AFFLUENCE
BIFURCATE
CAFETERIA
COFEATURE
COFFEEPOT
COFFERDAM
DEFEATISM
DEFECTIVE
DEFENDANT

DEFENSIVE
DEFERENCE
DEFERMENT
DEFICIENT
DEFLATION
DEFOLIANT
DEFOLIATE
DEFORMITY
DIFFERENT
DIFFICULT
DIFFIDENT
EFFECTIVE
EFFECTUAL
EFFICIENT
EFFLUENCE
EFFLUVIUM
INFANTILE
INFATUATE
INFECTION
INFERENCE
INFERTILE
INFIRMARY
INFIRMITY
INFLATION
INFLEXION
INFLUENCE
INFLUENZA
INFORMANT
INFURIATE
INFUSIBLE
LIFEBLOOD
LIFEGUARD
NEFARIOUS
OBFUSCATE
OFFENSIVE
OFFERTORY
OFFICIANT
OFFICIATE
OFFICIOUS
OFFSPRING
OLFACTORY
REFECTION
REFECTORY
REFERENCE
REFLECTOR
REFLEXIVE
REFRACTOR
REFURBISH
SAFEGUARD
SAFFLOWER
SOFTBOUND
SUFFERING
SUFFOCATE
SUFFRAGAN
UNFAILING
UNFEELING
UNFEIGNED
UNFLEDGED
UNFOUNDED
AGGRAVATE
AGGREGATE
ALGONQUIN
ALGORITHM
ANGELFISH
ANGLEWORM
ANGLICIZE
ANGUISHED
ARGENTINE
ARGENTITE
BAGATELLE
CIGARETTE
CIGARILLO
COGNITION
DIGITALIS
DIGITIZED
DIGNIFIED
DIGNITARY
DOGMATISM
EGGBEATER
ENGRAVING
HIGHLIGHT
INGENIOUS
INGENUITY
INGENUOUS
INGLENOOK
INGROWING
LAGNIAPPE
LEGENDARY
LEGISLATE
LIGHTFACE
LIGHTNING
LIGHTSHIP
LIGHTSOME
LOGARITHM
LOGISTICS
MAGISTRAL
MAGNESIUM
MAGNETISM
MAGNETITE
MAGNETIZE
MAGNIFICO
MAGNITUDE
MEGACYCLE
MEGADEATH
MEGAHERTZ
MEGAPHONE
MEGAPIXEL
NEGLIGENT
NEGOTIANT
NEGOTIATE
NEGRITUDE
NIGHTCLUB
NIGHTFALL
NIGHTGOWN
NIGHTHAWK
NIGHTLIFE
NIGHTMARE
NIGHTTIME
NIGRITUDE
ORGIASTIC
PAGEMAKER
PEGMATITE
PIGGYBACK
PIGHEADED
RAGPICKER
REGARDING
REGISTRAR
RIGHTEOUS
RIGMAROLE
SAGACIOUS
SAGEBRUSH
SEGREGATE
SIGNALIZE
SIGNALMAN
SIGNATORY
SIGNATURE
SIGNBOARD
SUGARCANE
SUGARPLUM
TIGHTROPE
UNGUARDED
VAGARIOUS
VAGINITIS
VEGETABLE
VIGESIMAL
VIGILANCE
VIGILANTE
WAGONETTE
ABHORRENT
ANHYDROUS
ATHENAEUM
ATHLETICS
DEHYDRATE
EPHEDRINE
EPHEMERAL
ETHIOPIAN
ETHNOLOGY
INHALATOR
MAHARISHI
OTHERWISE
REHEARING
REHEARSAL
SCHEELITE
SCHEMATIC
SCHILLING
SCHLEMIEL
SCHNAUZER
SCHOOLBOY
SPHINCTER
UNHARNESS
UNHEALTHY
UPHOLSTER
VEHEMENCE
ACIDULATE
ACIDULOUS
ADIABATIC
ALIENABLE
AMIDSHIPS
ANIMALISM
ANIMATION
ANIMOSITY
BAILIWICK
BLINDFOLD
BRIEFCASE
BRILLIANT
BRIMSTONE
BRIQUETTE
BRITANNIC
CHICANERY
CHICKADEE
CHICKASAW
CHICKWEED
CHIEFTAIN
CHILBLAIN
CHILDHOOD
CHIROPODY
CHIVALRIC
CLIENTELE
CLINICIAN
CLIPBOARD
CLIPSHEET
COIFFEUSE
CRINOLINE
CRITERION
CRITICISM
CRITICIZE
DAIRYMAID
DRIFTWOOD
EDITORIAL
ELIMINATE
ENIGMATIC
EPICENTER
EPICUREAN
EPIDERMIS
EPIGRAPHY
EPISCOPAL
ETIQUETTE
EXISTENCE
FAIRYLAND
FLINTLOCK
FRICASSEE
FRIEDCAKE
FRIGHTFUL
FRIVOLOUS
GLISSANDO
GRIEVANCE
GRILLWORK
GRISTMILL
GUIDEBOOK
GUIDELINE
HAILSTONE
HAILSTORM
HAIRBRUSH
HAIRCLOTH
HAIRPIECE
HAIRSTYLE
IMITATION
IMITATIVE
ISINGLASS
ITINERANT
ITINERARY
JAILBREAK
LEITMOTIV
LOINCLOTH
MAINFRAME
OLIGARCHY
ONIONSKIN
ORIENTATE
ORIFLAMME
ORIGINATE
OVIPAROUS
OXIDATION
PHILANDER
PHILATELY
PHILIPPIC
PHILOLOGY
POINCIANA
PRICELESS
PRIMARILY
PRIMITIVE
PRINCIPAL
PRINCIPLE
PRINTABLE
PRIVATEER
PRIVATION
PRIVILEGE
PUISSANCE
QUICKDRAW
QUICKLIME
QUICKSAND
QUICKSORT
QUICKSTEP
QUICKTIME
QUIESCENT
QUINTUPLE
QUITTANCE
QUIZZICAL
RAINSPOUT
RAINSTORM
RAINWATER
REIMBURSE
REINFORCE
REINSTATE
REITERATE
RUINATION
SAILCLOTH
SAILPLANE
SCINTILLA
SHIFTLESS
SHIPBOARD
SHIPSHAPE
SHIPWRECK
SKIMOBILE
SKINFLINT
SKINTIGHT
SLINGSHOT
SPICEBUSH
SPINDLING
SPINDRIFT
SPINNAKER
SPIRITUAL
STILLBORN
STIMULANT
STIMULATE
STIPULATE
SWITCHMAN
TAILLIGHT
THICKNESS
THIGHBONE
TRIBESMAN
TRIBUTARY
TRICKSTER
TRIENNIAL
TRIFOCALS
TRIMESTER
TRITURATE
TRIWEEKLY
TWINKLING
UNISEXUAL
UNITARIAN
UNIVALENT
UNIVERSAL
VAINGLORY
VOICELESS
WAISTBAND
WAISTCOAT
WAISTLINE
WHICHEVER
WHIMSICAL
WHIRLIGIG
WHIRLPOOL
WHIRLWIND
WHITEBAIT
WHITEFISH
WHITEHALL
WHITEHEAD
WHITENESS
WHITETAIL
WHITEWALL
WHITEWASH
WHITEWOOD
WRISTBAND
ZEITGEIST
ZWINGLIAN
ADJECTIVE
ADJOINING
DEJECTION
INJECTION
INJUSTICE
MAJORDOMO
MAJORETTE
MAJUSCULE
OBJECTIFY
OBJECTIVE
OBJURGATE
REJOINDER
ANKLEBONE
BAKSHEESH
DEKALITER
DEKAMETER
DEKASTERE
MAKESHIFT
PAKISTANI
PEKINGESE
PIKESTAFF
UNKNOWING
AILANTHUS
ALLERGIST
ALLEVIATE
ALLIGATOR
ALLOWANCE
BALALAIKA
BALDACHIN
BALLADEER
BALLERINA
BELEAGUER
BELLICOSE
BELLYACHE
BELVEDERE
BILATERAL
BILINGUAL
BILLBOARD
BILLIARDS
BOLSHEVIK
BULGARIAN
BULLFIGHT
BULLFINCH
CALABOOSE
CALCIMINE
CALCULATE
CALENDULA
CALIBRATE
CALLOSITY
CALORIFIC
CALVINISM
CELANDINE
CELEBRATE
CELEBRITY
CELESTIAL
CELLARAGE
CELLULOSE
CHLORDANE
COLLATION
COLLEAGUE
COLLECTED
COLLEGIAN
COLLEGIUM
COLLIMATE
COLLODION
COLLUSION
COLLUVIUM
COLONNADE
COLORCAST
COLORFAST
COLUMBINE
COLUMNIST
CULLENDER
CULMINATE
CULTIVATE
DALMATION
DELFTWARE
DELICIOUS
DELIGHTED
DELIMITER
DELINEATE
EGLANTINE
ELLIPSOID
ENLIGHTEN
FALSEHOOD
FELLOWMAN
FILMSTRIP
FOLLOWING
FULMINATE
GALACTOSE
GALLANTRY
GALLINULE
GALLIVANT
GALLSTONE
GALVANISM
GALVANIZE
GELIGNITE
GOLDBRICK
GOLDENROD
GOLDFIELD
GOLDFINCH
GOLDSMITH
HALFPENNY
HALITOSIS
HALLOWEEN
HELLEBORE
HELLENISM
HELVETIAN
HELVETICA
HILARIOUS
HILLBILLY
HOLLYHOCK

HOLOCAUST
HOLOGRAPH
HOLYSTONE
ILLEGIBLE
ILLIBERAL
ILLOGICAL
JELLYFISH
KILOCYCLE
KILOHERTZ
KILOLITER
KILOMETER
MALACHITE
MALADROIT
MALATHION
MALAYSIAN
MALIGNANT
MALLEABLE
MELIORATE
MELODIOUS
MELODRAMA
MELTWATER
MILESTONE
MILLIGRAM
MILLINERY
MILLIPEDE
MILLIVOLT
MILLSTONE
MOLDBOARD
MULTIFORM
MULTISCAN
MULTISPIN
MULTISYNC
MULTITUDE
OBLIVIOUS
PALAESTRA
PALANQUIN
PALATABLE
PALLADIUM
PALMISTRY
PALPITATE
PHLEBITIS
POLICEMAN
POLITBURO
POLITESSE
POLITICAL
POLYESTER
POLYGRAPH
POLYPHONY
PULMONARY
PULVERIZE
RELEVANCE
RELEVANCY
RELIGIOUS
RELIQUARY
RELUCTANT
SALACIOUS
SALESGIRL
SALTPETER
SALTWATER
SALVATION
SCLEROSIS
SELECTION
SELECTMAN
SILICEOUS
SILICOSIS
SILTSTONE
SOLEMNIZE
SOLICITOR
SOLILOQUY
SOLITAIRE
SPLENETIC
SPLITTING
SULFUROUS
SYLLABIFY
SYLLOGISM
TALKATIVE
TELEGENIC
TELEGRAPH
TELEMETER
TELEPATHY
TELEPHONE
TELEPHONY
TELEPHOTO
TELESCOPE
TELLURIUM
TOLERABLE
TOLERANCE
TOLLHOUSE
TULAREMIA
UNLEARNED
VALENTINE
VALUATION
VELVETEEN
VILLENAGE
VOLCANISM
VOLTMETER
VOLUNTARY
VOLUNTEER
VULCANISM
VULCANIZE
VULGARIAN
VULGARISM
VULGARITY
VULGARIZE
WALLBOARD
WALLOPING
WALLPAPER
WILLPOWER
WOLFHOUND
WOLFSBANE
WOLVERINE
XYLOPHONE
ADMIRABLE
ADMIRALTY
ADMISSION
ADMIXTURE
ALMANDITE
ALMSHOUSE
ARMADILLO
ARMISTICE
BAMBOOZLE
BIMONTHLY
BOMBAZINE
BOMBPROOF
BOMBSHELL
BOMBSIGHT
BUMBLEBEE
BUMPTIOUS
CAMELBACK
CAMEMBERT
CAMPANILE
CAMPSTOOL
COMFORTER
COMMANDER
COMMINGLE
COMMISSAR
COMMITTEE
COMMODITY
COMMODORE
COMMOTION
COMMUNION
COMMUNISM
COMMUNITY
COMPANION
COMPETENT
COMPLAINT
COMPONENT
COMPOSITE
COMPOSURE
DAMASCENE
DAMNATION
DAMSELFLY
DEMAGOGUE
DEMARCATE
DEMIMONDE
DEMITASSE
DEMOCRACY
DEMULCENT
DEMURRAGE
DIMENSION
DIMORPHIC
DOMINANCE
DUMBFOUND
GIMMICKRY
GYMNASIUM
HAMADRYAD
HAMBURGER
HAMMERTOE
HAMSTRING
HEMISTICH
HEMSTITCH
HOMEGROWN
HOMEMAKER
HOMESTEAD
HOMOGRAPH
HOMOPHONE
HUMANKIND
HUMDINGER
HUMILIATE
IMMEDIACY
IMMEDIATE
IMMIGRANT
IMMIGRATE
IMMOVABLE
IMMUTABLE
LAMEBRAIN
LAMINATED
LIMBURGER
LIMELIGHT
LIMESTONE
LIMOUSINE
MEMORABLE
MOMENTARY
MOMENTOUS
NAMEPLATE
NUMERATOR
NUMERICAL
PIMPERNEL
POMPADOUR
REMAINDER
REMINISCE
REMISSION
RUMRUNNER
SEMANTICS
SEMAPHORE
SEMBLANCE
SEMICOLON
SEMIFINAL
SEMIFLUID
SEMILUNAR
SEMIWORKS
SIMPATICO
SIMPLETON
SOMETHING
SOMETIMES
SOMEWHERE
SOMNOLENT
SUMMARIZE
SUMMATION
SUMPTUOUS
SYMBIOSIS
SYMBOLISM
SYMBOLIZE
SYMPOSIUM
TEMPERATE
TEMPORARY
TEMPORIZE
TIMBERING
TIMEPIECE
TIMETABLE
TOMBSTONE
UNMEANING
UNMINDFUL
WOMANHOOD
WOMANKIND
WOMANLIKE
WOMENFOLK
ANNOUNCER
ANNOYANCE
ANNUITANT
BANDEROLE
BANDOLIER
BANDSTAND
BANDWAGON
BANDWIDTH
BANQUETTE
BANTUSTAN
BENIGHTED
BENIGNANT
BENTONITE
BINOCULAR
BINOMINAL
BONDWOMAN
CANALBOAT
CANDIDACY
CANDIDATE
CANDLEMAS
CANDLEPIN
CANEBRAKE
CANNONADE
CANNONEER
CANONICAL
CANTABILE
CANTHARIS
CENTENARY
CENTESIMO
CENTIGRAM
CENTIPEDE
CENTURION
CONCERNED
CONCERTED
CONCIERGE
CONCORDAT
CONCOURSE
CONCUBINE
CONDENSER
CONDIMENT
CONDITION
CONDUCTOR
CONESTOGA
CONFESSOR
CONFIDANT
CONFUSION
CONGENIAL
CONGERIES
CONGRUITY
CONJUGATE
CONNUBIAL
CONSCIOUS
CONSCRIPT
CONSENSUS
CONSONANT
CONSTABLE
CONSTANCY
CONSTRAIN
CONSTRICT
CONSTRUCT
CONTAGION
CONTAINER
CONTENTED
CONTINENT
CONTINUAL
CONTINUUM
CONTRALTO
CONTUMELY
CONTUSION
CONUNDRUM
CONVIVIAL
CUNEIFORM
DANDELION
DANGEROUS
DENIGRATE
DENTITION
FANCYWORK
FANTASIZE
FANTASTIC
FINANCIAL
FINANCIER
FINGERING
FINGERTIP
FINICKING
FUNGICIDE
FUNICULAR
GANGPLANK
GENEALOGY
GENERATOR
GENITALIA
GENTILITY
GENTLEMAN
GENUFLECT
GONDOLIER
GONORRHEA
GUNCOTTON
GUNNYSACK
GUNPOWDER
HANDCLASP
HANDCRAFT
HANDIWORK
HANDSHAKE
HANDSPIKE
HANDSTAND
HANDWOVEN
HINDRANCE
HINDSIGHT
HONEYCOMB
HONEYMOON
HONORABLE
HONORIFIC
HUNCHBACK
HUNGARIAN
IGNORANCE
INNERMOST
INNERSOLE
INNKEEPER
INNOCENCE
INNOCUOUS
JINRIKSHA
KINESCOPE
KINSWOMAN
LANDOWNER
LANDSCAPE
LANDSLIDE
LANTHANUM
LINEAMENT
LONGEVITY
LONGITUDE
LUNCHROOM
MANDATORY
MANGANESE
MANHANDLE
MANHATTAN
MANIFESTO
MANNEQUIN
MANNERISM
MANOEUVRE
MANOMETER
MANSLAYER
MENAGERIE
MENDICANT
MENOPAUSE
MENTALITY
MINCEMEAT
MINELAYER
MINIATURE
MINISCULE
MINISKIRT
MINISTATE
MINUSCULE
MINUTEMAN
MONASTERY
MONGOLIAN
MONGOLISM
MONGOLOID
MONKSHOOD
MONOGRAPH
MONOLOGUE
MONOMANIA
MONOPLANE
MONOSPACE
MONSIGNOR
MUNICIPAL
NANOMETER
NONCREDIT
NONENTITY
NONPAREIL
NONPERSON
NONPROFIT
NONREADER
OBNOXIOUS
PANEGYRIC
PANHANDLE
PANTHEISM
PANTOMIME
PENDULOUS
PENEPLAIN
PENETRATE
PENHOLDER
PENINSULA
PENTECOST
PENTHOUSE
PENURIOUS
PINEAPPLE
PINSTRIPE
PONDEROUS
PUNCTILIO
PUNCTUATE
RANCHLAND
RANDOMIZE
RANGELAND
RENCONTRE
RENDITION
RUNAROUND
SANCTUARY
SANDBLAST
SANDPAPER
SANDPIPER
SANDSTONE
SANDSTORM
SANGFROID
SENIORITY
SENSATION
SENSITIVE
SENSITIZE
SENTIMENT
SINGLETON
SINUSITIS
SUNBONNET
SUNFLOWER
SUNSEEKER
SUNSTROKE
SYNAGOGUE
SYNDICATE
SYNERGISM
SYNTHESIS
SYNTHETIC
TANGERINE

TANTALIZE
TANZANIAN
TENACIOUS
TENDERIZE
TENEBROUS
TENTATIVE
TINDERBOX
TONSORIAL
UNNATURAL
VANDALISM
VANDALIZE
VENERABLE
VENGEANCE
VENIREMAN
VENTILATE
VENTRICLE
VENTUROUS
VINDICATE
WINDBLOWN
WINDBREAK
WINDCHILL
WINDPROOF
WINDSTORM
WINDSWEPT
WINEPRESS
WINTERIZE
WONDERFUL
XANTHIPPE
ABOMINATE
ABORIGINE
ACOUSTICS
AFORESAID
ALONGSIDE
AMORPHOUS
ANOMALOUS
ANONYMOUS
ANOPHELES
APOCRYPHA
APOLOGIZE
APOSTOLIC
ATONEMENT
AVOCATION
BIOGRAPHY
BIOSPHERE
BLOCKHEAD
BLOODBATH
BLOODLINE
BLOODROOT
BLOODSHED
BLOODSHOT
BLOWTORCH
BOOKMAKER
BOOKPLATE
BOOKSHELF
BOOMERANG
BOONDOCKS
BOOTBLACK

BROADBAND
BROADCAST
BROADLOOM
BROADSIDE
BROADTAIL
BROCHETTE
BROKERAGE
BRONCHIAL
CHOCOLATE
CHONDRITE
CHONDRULE
CHOPHOUSE
CHOPSTICK
CHORISTER
CLOCKWISE
CLOCKWORK
CLOISONNE
COONHOUND
COOPERATE
CROCODILE
CROISSANT
CROQUETTE
CROSSOVER
CROSSROAD
CROSSWALK
CROSSWAYS
CROSSWISE
DEODORANT
DEODORIZE
DEOXIDIZE
DOORPLATE
DROMEDARY
ECONOMICS
ECONOMIZE
ECOSYSTEM
ELOCUTION
EMOLLIENT
EMOLUMENT
EROGENOUS
ESOPHAGUS
EVOLUTION
EXOGENOUS
EXONERATE
EXOSPHERE
FLOODGATE
FLOPHOUSE
FLOTATION
FLOWCHART
FLOWERPOT
FOODSTUFF
FOOLHARDY
FOOLPROOF
FOOTBOARD
FOOTLOOSE
FOOTPRINT
FOOTSTOOL
FROSTBITE

GEOGRAPHY
GROOMSMAN
GROSGRAIN
GROTESQUE
GROUNDHOG
GROUNDING
GROUPWARE
INOCULATE
INORGANIC
IRONBOUND
IRONSTONE
ISOSCELES
KNOCKDOWN
KNOWLEDGE
MOONLIGHT
MOONSCAPE
MOONSHINE
MOONSTONE
NEODYMIUM
NEOLOGISM
PHONETICS
PHONOLOGY
PHOSPHATE
PHOTOCELL
PHOTOCOPY
PHOTOPLAY
PLOWSHARE
POORHOUSE
PROBATION
PROBATIVE
PROBOSCIS
PROCEDURE
PROCESSOR
PROCONSUL
PROCREATE
PROFANITY
PROFESSOR
PROFITEER
PROGNOSIS
PROJECTOR
PROMENADE
PROMINENT
PROMISING
PRONGHORN
PRONOUNCE
PROOFREAD
PROPAGATE
PROPELLER
PROPHETIC
PROPONENT
PROPRIETY
PROSCRIBE
PROSECUTE
PROSELYTE
PROSTRATE
PROTECTOR
PROTOTYPE

PROTOZOAN
PROVENCAL
PROVENDER
PROVIDENT
PROVISION
PROVOLONE
PROXIMATE
PROXIMITY
PSORIASIS
QUOTIDIAN
ROOTSTOCK
SCOUNDREL
SHOEMAKER
SHOREBIRD
SHORTCAKE
SHORTHAND
SHORTHORN
SHORTSTOP
SHORTWAVE
SHOWPIECE
SHOWPLACE
SNOWDRIFT
SNOWFIELD
SNOWFLAKE
SNOWSTORM
SPOKESMAN
SPOONBILL
SPORTSMAN
SPOTLIGHT
STOCKPILE
STOCKYARD
STOMACHER
STOMACHIC
STOPLIGHT
STOPWATCH
STOREROOM
SWORDFISH
SWORDPLAY
SWORDSMAN
SWORDTAIL
TOOTHACHE
TOOTHPICK
TOOTHSOME
TROOPSHIP
TROUSSEAU
VIOLATION
VOODOOISM
WHOLESALE
WHOLESOME
WHOSOEVER
WOODBLOCK
WOODCHUCK
WOODCRAFT
WRONGDOER
AMPERSAND
AMPHIBIAN
AMPHIBOLE

AMPLITUDE
APPALOOSA
APPARATUS
APPELLANT
APPELLATE
APPENDAGE
APPERTAIN
APPETIZER
APPLEJACK
APPLETALK
APPLIANCE
APPLICANT
APPOINTEE
APPORTION
APPREHEND
ASPARAGUS
ASPERSION
BIPARTITE
CAPACIOUS
CAPACITOR
CAPARISON
CAPILLARY
CAPITALLY
CAPRICCIO
CAPSULATE
CAPTIVATE
COPARTNER
COPYRIGHT
CUPBEARER
DEPARTURE
DEPENDENT
DEPRECATE
DEPRESSED
DIPHTHONG
DIPLOMACY
DIPTEROUS
DUPLICATE
DUPLICITY
EMPENNAGE
EMPHASIZE
EMPHYSEMA
EMPIRICAL
ESPERANTO
ESPIONAGE
ESPLANADE
EUPHEMISM
EXPANSION
EXPANSIVE
EXPATIATE
EXPECTANT
EXPEDIENT
EXPEDITER
EXPENSIVE
EXPERTISE
EXPIATORY
EXPLETIVE
EXPLICATE

EXPLOSION
EXPLOSIVE
EXPOSITOR
EXPULSION
EXPURGATE
HAPHAZARD
HAPPENING
HAPPINESS
HEPATITIS
HOPSCOTCH
HYPERBOLA
HYPERBOLE
HYPERCARD
HYPERTEXT
HYPHENATE
HYPOCRISY
IMPARTIAL
IMPASSIVE
IMPATIENS
IMPATIENT
IMPEDANCE
IMPERFECT
IMPERIOUS
IMPETUOUS
IMPLEMENT
IMPLICATE
IMPOLITIC
IMPORTANT
IMPORTUNE
IMPOSTURE
IMPRECATE
IMPRECISE
IMPROMPTU
IMPROVISE
IMPRUDENT
IMPULSION
IMPULSIVE
INPATIENT
NEPHRITIC
NEPHRITIS
NEPTUNIUM
OPPORTUNE
ORPHANAGE
PAPERBACK
PAPILLOTE
POPPYCOCK
PUPPETEER
RAPACIOUS
REPAIRMAN
REPELLENT
REPERTORY
REPLENISH
REPLETION
REPLICATE
REPORTAGE
REPOSSESS
REPREHEND

REPRESENT
REPRIMAND
REPROBATE
REPRODUCE
REPUDIATE
REPUGNANT
REPULSION
REPULSIVE
REPUTABLE
SAPSUCKER
SEPARABLE
SEPARATOR
SEPTEMBER
SEPULCHER
SEPULTURE
SOPHISTIC
SOPHISTRY
SOPHOMORE
SOPORIFIC
SUPERNOVA
SUPERPOSE
SUPERSEDE
SUPERVENE
SUPERVISE
SUPPLIANT
SUPPOSING
SUPPURATE
SUPREMACY
TYPEWRITE
UNPLUMBED
UNPOPULAR
UPPERCASE
UPPERMOST
VAPORIZER
VAPORWARE
ACQUIESCE
EXQUISITE
LIQUIDATE
REQUISITE
SEQUESTER
ACROPOLIS
AERIALIST
AERODROME
AEROPAUSE
AEROPLANE
AEROSPACE
AFRIKAANS
AGREEABLE
AGREEMENT
AIRMOBILE
AIRWORTHY
ARROWHEAD
ARROWROOT
ATROCIOUS
AURICULAR
BARBARIAN
BARBARISM

BARBAROUS
BARCAROLE
BAREFACED
BARKEEPER
BARNSTORM
BAROGRAPH
BAROMETER
BARRACUDA
BARRICADE
BARRISTER
BARTENDER
BERKELIUM
BERYLLIUM
BIRDHOUSE
BIRTHMARK
BIRTHRATE
BURLESQUE
BURUNDIAN
CARBONATE
CARBUNCLE
CARBURIZE
CARCINOMA
CARDBOARD
CARETAKER
CARIBBEAN
CARNATION
CARNELIAN
CARNIVORA
CARNIVORE
CARPENTER
CARPETBAG
CARPETING
CARROUSEL
CARTILAGE
CARTRIDGE
CARTWHEEL
CEREBRATE
CERECLOTH
CERTAINTY
CERTITUDE
CHRISTIAN
CHRISTMAS
CHROMATIC
CHRONICLE
CHRYSALIS
CIRCADIAN
CIRCUITRY
CIRCULATE
CIRRHOSIS
CORELDRAW
CORIANDER
CORKSCREW
CORMORANT
CORNSTALK
COROLLARY
CORPORATE
CORPOREAL

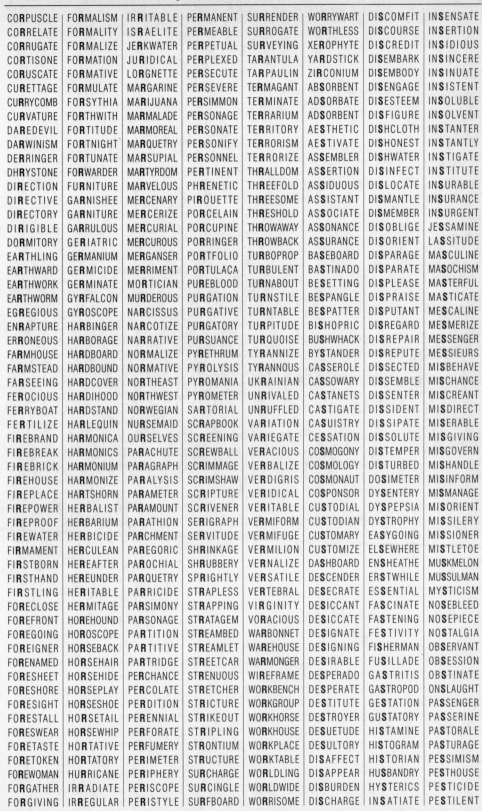

CORPUSCLE
CORRELATE
CORRUGATE
CORTISONE
CORUSCATE
CURETTAGE
CURRYCOMB
CURVATURE
DAREDEVIL
DARWINISM
DERRINGER
DHRYSTONE
DIRECTION
DIRECTIVE
DIRECTORY
DIRIGIBLE
DORMITORY
EARTHLING
EARTHWARD
EARTHWORK
EARTHWORM
EGREGIOUS
ENRAPTURE
ERRONEOUS
FARMHOUSE
FARMSTEAD
FARSEEING
FEROCIOUS
FERRYBOAT
FERTILIZE
FIREBRAND
FIREBREAK
FIREBRICK
FIREHOUSE
FIREPLACE
FIREPOWER
FIREPROOF
FIREWATER
FIRMAMENT
FIRSTBORN
FIRSTHAND
FIRSTLING
FORECLOSE
FOREFRONT
FOREGOING
FOREIGNER
FORENAMED
FORESHEET
FORESHORE
FORESIGHT
FORESTALL
FORESWEAR
FORETASTE
FORETOKEN
FOREWOMAN
FORGATHER
FORGIVING
FORMALISM
FORMALITY
FORMALIZE
FORMATION
FORMATIVE
FORMULATE
FORSYTHIA
FORTHWITH
FORTITUDE
FORTNIGHT
FORTUNATE
FORWARDER
FURNITURE
GARNISHEE
GARNITURE
GARRULOUS
GERIATRIC
GERMANIUM
GERMICIDE
GERMINATE
GYRFALCON
GYROSCOPE
HARBINGER
HARBORAGE
HARDBOARD
HARDBOUND
HARDCOVER
HARDIHOOD
HARDSTAND
HARLEQUIN
HARMONICA
HARMONICS
HARMONIUM
HARMONIZE
HARTSHORN
HERBALIST
HERBARIUM
HERBICIDE
HERCULEAN
HEREAFTER
HEREUNDER
HERITABLE
HERMITAGE
HOREHOUND
HOROSCOPE
HORSEBACK
HORSEHAIR
HORSEHIDE
HORSEPLAY
HORSESHOE
HORSETAIL
HORSEWHIP
HORTATIVE
HORTATORY
HURRICANE
IRRADIATE
IRREGULAR
IRRITABLE
ISRAELITE
JERKWATER
JURIDICAL
LORGNETTE
MARGARINE
MARIJUANA
MARMALADE
MARMOREAL
MARQUETRY
MARSUPIAL
MARTYRDOM
MARVELOUS
MERCENARY
MERCERIZE
MERCURIAL
MERCUROUS
MERGANSER
MERRIMENT
MORTICIAN
MURDEROUS
NARCISSUS
NARCOTIZE
NARRATIVE
NORMALIZE
NORMATIVE
NORTHEAST
NORTHWEST
NORWEGIAN
NURSEMAID
OURSELVES
PARACHUTE
PARAGRAPH
PARALYSIS
PARAMETER
PARAMOUNT
PARATHION
PARCHMENT
PAREGORIC
PAROCHIAL
PARQUETRY
PARRICIDE
PARSIMONY
PARSONAGE
PARTITION
PARTITIVE
PARTRIDGE
PERCHANCE
PERCOLATE
PERDITION
PERENNIAL
PERFORATE
PERFUMERY
PERIMETER
PERIPHERY
PERISCOPE
PERISTYLE
PERMANENT
PERMEABLE
PERPETUAL
PERPLEXED
PERSECUTE
PERSEVERE
PERSIMMON
PERSONAGE
PERSONATE
PERSONIFY
PERSONNEL
PERTINENT
PHRENETIC
PIROUETTE
PORCELAIN
PORCUPINE
PORRINGER
PORTFOLIO
PORTULACA
PUREBLOOD
PURGATION
PURGATIVE
PURGATORY
PURSUANCE
PYRETHRUM
PYROLYSIS
PYROMANIA
PYROMETER
SARTORIAL
SCRAPBOOK
SCREENING
SCREWBALL
SCRIMMAGE
SCRIMSHAW
SCRIPTURE
SCRIVENER
SERIGRAPH
SERVITUDE
SHRINKAGE
SHRUBBERY
SPRIGHTLY
STRAPLESS
STRAPPING
STRATAGEM
STREAMBED
STREAMLET
STREETCAR
STRENUOUS
STRETCHER
STRICTURE
STRIKEOUT
STRIPLING
STRONTIUM
STRUCTURE
SURCHARGE
SURCINGLE
SURFBOARD
SURRENDER
SURROGATE
SURVEYING
TARANTULA
TARPAULIN
TERMAGANT
TERMINATE
TERRARIUM
TERRITORY
TERRORISM
TERRORIZE
THRALLDOM
THREEFOLD
THREESOME
THRESHOLD
THROWAWAY
THROWBACK
TURBOPROP
TURBULENT
TURNABOUT
TURNSTILE
TURNTABLE
TURPITUDE
TURQUOISE
TYRANNIZE
TYRANNOUS
UKRAINIAN
UNRIVALED
UNRUFFLED
VARIATION
VARIEGATE
VERACIOUS
VERBALIZE
VERDIGRIS
VERIDICAL
VERITABLE
VERMIFORM
VERMIFUGE
VERMILION
VERNALIZE
VERSATILE
VERTEBRAL
VIRGINITY
VORACIOUS
WARBONNET
WAREHOUSE
WARMONGER
WIREFRAME
WORKBENCH
WORKGROUP
WORKHORSE
WORKHOUSE
WORKPLACE
WORKTABLE
WORLDLING
WORLDWIDE
WORRISOME
WORRYWART
WORTHLESS
XEROPHYTE
YARDSTICK
ZIRCONIUM
ABSORBENT
ADSORBATE
ADSORBENT
AESTHETIC
AESTIVATE
ASSEMBLER
ASSERTION
ASSIDUOUS
ASSISTANT
ASSOCIATE
ASSONANCE
ASSURANCE
BASEBOARD
BASTINADO
BESETTING
BESPANGLE
BESPATTER
BISHOPRIC
BUSHWHACK
BYSTANDER
CASSEROLE
CASSOWARY
CASTANETS
CASTIGATE
CASUISTRY
CESSATION
COSMOGONY
COSMOLOGY
COSMONAUT
COSPONSOR
CUSTODIAL
CUSTODIAN
CUSTOMARY
CUSTOMIZE
DASHBOARD
DESCENDER
DESECRATE
DESICCANT
DESICCATE
DESIGNATE
DESIGNING
DESIRABLE
DESPERADO
DESPERATE
DESTITUTE
DESTROYER
DESUETUDE
DESULTORY
DISAFFECT
DISAPPEAR
DISBURDEN
DISCHARGE
DISCOMFIT
DISCOURSE
DISCREDIT
DISEMBARK
DISEMBODY
DISENGAGE
DISESTEEM
DISFIGURE
DISHCLOTH
DISHONEST
DISHWATER
DISINFECT
DISLOCATE
DISMANTLE
DISMEMBER
DISOBLIGE
DISORIENT
DISPARAGE
DISPARATE
DISPLEASE
DISPRAISE
DISPUTANT
DISREGARD
DISREPAIR
DISREPUTE
DISSECTED
DISSEMBLE
DISSENTER
DISSIDENT
DISSIPATE
DISSOLUTE
DISTEMPER
DISTURBED
DOSIMETER
DYSENTERY
DYSPEPSIA
DYSTROPHY
EASYGOING
ELSEWHERE
ENSHEATHE
ERSTWHILE
ESSENTIAL
FASCINATE
FASTENING
FESTIVITY
FISHERMAN
FUSILLADE
GASTRITIS
GASTROPOD
GESTATION
GUSTATORY
HISTAMINE
HISTOGRAM
HISTORIAN
HUSBANDRY
HYSTERICS
INSATIATE
INSENSATE
INSERTION
INSIDIOUS
INSINCERE
INSINUATE
INSISTENT
INSOLUBLE
INSOLVENT
INSTANTER
INSTANTLY
INSTIGATE
INSTITUTE
INSURABLE
INSURANCE
INSURGENT
JESSAMINE
LASSITUDE
MASCULINE
MASOCHISM
MASTERFUL
MASTICATE
MESCALINE
MESMERIZE
MESSENGER
MESSIEURS
MISBEHAVE
MISCHANCE
MISCREANT
MISDIRECT
MISERABLE
MISGIVING
MISGOVERN
MISHANDLE
MISINFORM
MISMANAGE
MISORIENT
MISSILERY
MISSIONER
MISTLETOE
MUSKMELON
MUSSULMAN
MYSTICISM
NOSEBLEED
NOSEPIECE
NOSTALGIA
OBSERVANT
OBSESSION
OBSTINATE
ONSLAUGHT
PASSENGER
PASSERINE
PASTORALE
PASTURAGE
PESSIMISM
PESTHOUSE
PESTICIDE
PESTILENT

PI**S**TACHIO
PO**S**TERIOR
PO**S**TERITY
PO**S**THASTE
PO**S**TILION
PO**S**TNATAL
PO**S**TULANT
PO**S**TULATE
PU**S**SYFOOT
RA**S**PBERRY
RA**S**TERIZE
RE**S**ECTION
RE**S**ERPINE
RE**S**ERVIST
RE**S**ERVOIR
RE**S**HUFFLE
RE**S**IDENCE
RE**S**IDENCY
RE**S**IDUARY
RE**S**ISTANT
RE**S**ONANCE
RE**S**ONATOR
RE**S**TRAINT
RE**S**URRECT
RO**S**EWATER
RU**S**TICATE
SA**S**SAFRAS
SU**S**PENDER
SU**S**PICION
SY**S**TEMIZE
TE**S**TAMENT
TE**S**TIMONY
TU**S**CARORA
UN**S**CATHED
UN**S**ELFISH
UN**S**ETTLED
UN**S**HACKLE
UN**S**HEATHE
UN**S**IGHTLY
UN**S**KILLED
UN**S**PARING
UN**S**POTTED
UN**S**TUDIED
VA**S**ECTOMY
VA**S**SALAGE
VE**S**TIBULE
VE**S**TRYMAN
VI**S**COSITY
VI**S**IONARY
VI**S**UALIZE
WA**S**HBASIN
WA**S**HBOARD
WA**S**HCLOTH
WA**S**HHOUSE
WA**S**HSTAND
WA**S**HWOMAN
WA**S**TELAND
WI**S**ECRACK
YE**S**TERDAY
AF**T**ERCARE
AF**T**ERDECK
AF**T**ERGLOW
AF**T**ERLIFE
AF**T**ERMATH
AF**T**ERNOON
AF**T**ERWARD
AL**T**ERNATE
AL**T**IMETER
AN**T**ARCTIC
AN**T**ECHOIR
AN**T**HOLOGY
AN**T**ICLINE
AN**T**IKNOCK
AN**T**INOVEL
AN**T**IPASTO
AN**T**IPATHY
AN**T**IQUARY
AN**T**IQUITY
AN**T**ISERUM
AN**T**ITOXIN
AN**T**ITUMOR
AN**T**IVENIN
AR**T**ERIOLE
AR**T**HRITIS
AR**T**HROPOD
AR**T**ICHOKE
AR**T**ICULAR
AR**T**IFICER
AR**T**ILLERY
AS**T**RADDLE
AS**T**RAKHAN
AS**T**ROLABE
AS**T**ROLOGY
AS**T**RONAUT
AS**T**RONOMY
AT**T**AINDER
AT**T**ENDANT
AT**T**ENTION
AT**T**ENUATE
AT**T**RIBUTE
AT**T**RITION
AU**T**HENTIC
AU**T**HORITY
AU**T**HORIZE
AU**T**OCRACY
AU**T**OGRAPH
AU**T**OMATIC
AU**T**OMATON
AU**T**OTRACE
BA**T**HHOUSE
BA**T**HOLITH
BA**T**TALION
BE**T**ROTHED
BU**T**TERCUP
BU**T**TERFAT
BU**T**TERFLY
BU**T**TERNUT
CA**T**ACLYSM
CA**T**ALEPSY
CA**T**ALYSIS
CA**T**AMARAN
CA**T**AMOUNT
CA**T**ATONIC
CA**T**CHMENT
CA**T**CHWORD
CA**T**ECHISM
CA**T**ERWAUL
CA**T**HARSIS
CA**T**HARTIC
CA**T**HEDRAL
CI**T**IZENRY
CO**T**ILLION
CO**T**YLEDON
CU**T**ANEOUS
CU**T**THROAT
CY**T**OPLASM
DE**T**ECTIVE
DE**T**ENTION
DE**T**ERGENT
DE**T**ERMINE
DE**T**ERRENT
DE**T**ONATOR
DE**T**RIMENT
DI**T**HERING
EN**T**ERITIS
EN**T**ERTAIN
EN**T**OURAGE
ES**T**ABLISH
ES**T**AMINET
ES**T**IMABLE
EU**T**HENICS
EU**T**ROPHIC
EX**T**EMPORE
EX**T**ENSION
EX**T**ENSIVE
EX**T**ENUATE
EX**T**IRPATE
EX**T**RADITE
EX**T**RAVERT
EX**T**REMISM
EX**T**REMITY
EX**T**RICATE
EX**T**RINSIC
EX**T**RUSIVE
FE**T**ISHISM
HA**T**CHMENT
HE**T**ERODOX
HI**T**CHHIKE
HO**T**HEADED
IN**T**EGRATE
IN**T**EGRITY
IN**T**ELLECT
IN**T**ENDANT
IN**T**ENSIFY
IN**T**ENSITY
IN**T**ENSIVE
IN**T**ENTION
IN**T**ERCEDE
IN**T**ERCEPT
IN**T**ERDICT
IN**T**ERFACE
IN**T**ERFERE
IN**T**ERFUSE
IN**T**ERJECT
IN**T**ERLACE
IN**T**ERLARD
IN**T**ERLEAF
IN**T**ERLINE
IN**T**ERLINK
IN**T**ERLOCK
IN**T**ERLOPE
IN**T**ERLUDE
IN**T**ERMENT
IN**T**ERNIST
IN**T**ERNODE
IN**T**ERPLAY
IN**T**ERPOSE
IN**T**ERPRET
IN**T**ERRUPT
IN**T**ERSECT
IN**T**ERVENE
IN**T**ERVIEW
IN**T**ESTATE
IN**T**ESTINE
IN**T**RICATE
IN**T**RINSIC
IN**T**RODUCE
IN**T**ROVERT
IN**T**UITION
IN**T**UMESCE
JI**T**TERBUG
LA**T**ECOMER
LI**T**ERATIM
LI**T**HESOME
LI**T**HOLOGY
LI**T**IGIOUS
LI**T**TERBUG
MA**T**CHBOOK
MA**T**CHLOCK
MA**T**CHWOOD
MA**T**ERNITY
MA**T**RIARCH
MA**T**RICIDE
MA**T**RIMONY
MA**T**UTINAL
ME**T**ALWARE
ME**T**ALWORK
ME**T**EORITE
ME**T**EOROID
ME**T**HADONE
ME**T**HODIST
ME**T**HODIZE
ME**T**RICIZE
ME**T**ROLOGY
ME**T**RONOME
MO**T**ORBIKE
MO**T**ORBOAT
MO**T**ORCADE
MY**T**HOLOGY
NA**T**URALLY
NO**T**CHBACK
NO**T**ORIOUS
NU**T**RIMENT
NU**T**RITION
OP**T**OMETRY
OS**T**RACIZE
OU**T**ERMOST
OU**T**GROWTH
OU**T**NUMBER
OU**T**RIGGER
OU**T**SKIRTS
OU**T**SPOKEN
OU**T**SPREAD
OU**T**WARDLY
PA**T**CHWORK
PA**T**ERNITY
PA**T**HOLOGY
PA**T**RIARCH
PA**T**RICIAN
PA**T**RICIDE
PA**T**RIMONY
PA**T**RISTIC
PA**T**ROLMAN
PA**T**RONAGE
PA**T**RONIZE
PE**T**ROLEUM
PE**T**ROLOGY
PE**T**TICOAT
PI**T**CHFORK
PI**T**UITARY
PO**T**ASSIUM
PO**T**BOILER
PO**T**ENTATE
PO**T**ENTIAL
PO**T**POURRI
RA**T**IONALE
RE**T**ALIATE
RE**T**ARDATE
RE**T**ENTION
RE**T**ENTIVE
RE**T**RIEVER
RE**T**ROFIRE
RU**T**HENIUM
SA**T**ELLITE
SA**T**INWOOD
SA**T**URNINE
SI**T**UATION
UL**T**IMATUM
UL**T**RAHIGH
UL**T**RAPURE
UN**T**UTORED
UR**T**ICARIA
UT**T**ERANCE
UT**T**ERMOST
WA**T**CHBAND
WA**T**CHCASE
WA**T**CHWORD
WA**T**ERFALL
WA**T**ERFOWL
WA**T**ERLINE
WA**T**ERMARK
WA**T**ERSHED
WA**T**ERSIDE
WI**T**HDRAWN
WI**T**HSTAND
WI**T**TICISM
YT**T**ERBIUM
AD**U**MBRATE
AL**U**MINIUM
AL**U**MINIZE
AQ**U**APLANE
AV**U**NCULAR
BL**U**EBERRY
BL**U**EBLACK
BL**U**EGRASS
BL**U**EPOINT
BL**U**EPRINT
BO**U**LEVARD
BO**U**NTEOUS
BO**U**NTIFUL
BO**U**RGEOIS
BR**U**SHWOOD
BR**U**TALIZE
CA**U**CASIAN
CA**U**SATION
CA**U**TERIZE
CH**U**CKHOLE
CH**U**RCHMAN
CL**U**BHOUSE
CO**U**NSELOR
CO**U**NTDOWN
CO**U**NTLESS
CO**U**RTEOUS
CO**U**RTESAN
CO**U**RTROOM
CO**U**RTSHIP
CO**U**RTYARD
CO**U**TURIER
CR**U**CIFORM
DA**U**NTLESS
DE**U**TERIUM
DO**U**BTLESS
DR**U**GSTORE
DR**U**MSTICK
EB**U**LLIENT
ED**U**CATION
EL**U**CIDATE
EN**U**MERATE
EN**U**NCIATE
EQ**U**IPMENT
EQ**U**IPOISE
EQ**U**ITABLE
EQ**U**IVOCAL
ER**U**DITION
EX**U**BERANT
FE**U**DALISM
FE**U**DATORY
FL**U**CTUATE
FO**U**NDLING
FO**U**RSCORE
FR**U**ITCAKE
FR**U**ITERER
FR**U**STRATE
GA**U**CHERIE
GL**U**TINOUS
GR**U**BSTAKE
HE**U**RISTIC
HO**U**RGLASS
HO**U**SEBOAT
HO**U**SECOAT
HO**U**SEHOLD
HO**U**SEMAID
HO**U**SEWIFE
HO**U**SEWORK
JA**U**NDICED
LA**U**DATORY
LA**U**NCHPAD
LE**U**KOCYTE
MA**U**SOLEUM
MO**U**SETRAP
MO**U**STACHE
MO**U**THPART
MO**U**THWASH
NE**U**RALGIA
NE**U**ROLOGY
PL**U**RALITY
PL**U**RALIZE
PL**U**TONIUM
PO**U**LTERER
PO**U**RBOIRE
RA**U**WOLFIA
RO**U**GHNECK
RO**U**MANIAN
RO**U**NDELAY
RO**U**NDWORM
SC**U**LPTURE
SC**U**TCHEON
SL**U**ICEWAY
SO**U**BRETTE
SO**U**THEAST
SO**U**THWEST
SQ**U**EAMISH
TA**U**TOLOGY
TH**U**MBNAIL
TH**U**MBTACK
TO**U**CHDOWN
TR**U**CKLOAD
TR**U**CULENT
TR**U**NCHEON
VO**U**CHSAFE
YO**U**NGLING
YO**U**NGSTER
AD**V**ANTAGE
AD**V**ENTURE
AD**V**ERSARY
AD**V**ERSITY
AD**V**ERTISE
AD**V**ISABLE
CA**V**ALCADE
CO**V**ALENCE
DA**V**ENPORT
DE**V**ASTATE
DE**V**ILMENT
DI**V**ERSIFY
DI**V**ERSION
DI**V**ERSITY
DI**V**ISIBLE
EA**V**ESDROP
FA**V**ORABLE
GO**V**ERNESS
HA**V**ERSACK
IN**V**ECTIVE
IN**V**ENTION
IN**V**ENTIVE
IN**V**ENTORY
IN**V**ERNESS
IN**V**ERSION
IN**V**IDIOUS
IN**V**IOLATE
IN**V**ISIBLE
IN**V**OLUCRE
LA**V**ALIERE
LE**V**IATHAN
LI**V**ERWORT
LI**V**ERYMAN
LI**V**ESTOCK
NA**V**IGABLE
NE**V**ERMORE

NOVELETTE
NOVITIATE
REVERENCE
REVERSION
REVOCABLE
REVOLTING
REVULSION
RIVERBANK
RIVERBOAT
RIVERSIDE
SEVENTEEN
SOVEREIGN
VIVACIOUS
WAVETABLE
BOWSTRING
DOWITCHER
DOWNGRADE
DOWNRANGE
DOWNRIGHT
DOWNSHIFT
DOWNSTAGE
DOWNSWING
ENWREATHE
HOWSOEVER
JEWELWEED
LOWERCASE
NEWSPAPER
NEWSPRINT
NEWSSTAND
POWERBOAT
TOWNSFOLK
UNWILLING
UNWITTING
UNWORLDLY
UNWRITTEN
AUXILIARY
DEXTERITY
DEXTEROUS
DIXIELAND
HEXAMETER
JUXTAPOSE
LUXURIANT
LUXURIATE
SAXIFRAGE
SAXOPHONE
TAXIDERMY
VEXATIOUS
ASYMPTOTE
CRYOGENIC
ETYMOLOGY
GLYCOSIDE
MAYFLOWER
OXYGENATE
PAYMASTER
PHYSICIAN
PHYSICIST
PSYCHOSIS
SKYDIVING
SKYJACKER
SKYLOUNGE
SKYROCKET
THYROXINE
GAZETTEER
LAZYBONES
MEZZANINE
PIZZICATO

### 4TH LETTER

ADIABATIC
ADVANTAGE
AILANTHUS
ALBATROSS
ALEATORIC
ALMANDITE
ANTARCTIC
APPALOOSA
APPARATUS
AQUAPLANE
ARMADILLO
ASPARAGUS
ATTAINDER
AUDACIOUS
BAGATELLE
BALALAIKA
BICAMERAL
BILATERAL
BIPARTITE
BLEACHERS
BREAKDOWN
BREAKFAST
BROADBAND
BROADCAST
BROADLOOM
BROADSIDE
BROADTAIL
CALABOOSE
CANALBOAT
CAPACIOUS
CAPACITOR
CAPARISON
CATACLYSM
CATALEPSY
CATALYSIS
CATAMARAN
CATAMOUNT
CATATONIC
CAVALCADE
CELANDINE
CIGARETTE
CIGARILLO
CLEARANCE
COPARTNER
COVALENCE
CUTANEOUS
DAMASCENE
DECADENCE
DECALOGUE
DECATHLON
DEKALITER
DEKAMETER
DEKASTERE
DEMAGOGUE
DEMARCATE
DEPARTURE
DEVASTATE
DISAFFECT
DISAPPEAR
DREAMLAND
EGLANTINE
EMBARRASS
EMBAYMENT
ENRAPTURE
ESCALATOR
ESTABLISH
ESTAMINET
EXPANSION
EXPANSIVE
EXPATIATE
FINANCIAL
FINANCIER
GABARDINE
GALACTOSE
GLEANINGS
GREATCOAT
HAMADRYAD
HEPATITIS
HEXAMETER
HILARIOUS
HUMANKIND
IMBALANCE
IMPARTIAL
IMPASSIVE
IMPATIENS
IMPATIENT
INCAPABLE
INCARNATE
INFANTILE
INFATUATE
INHALATOR
INPATIENT
INSATIATE
IRRADIATE
ISRAELITE
JACARANDA
LAVALIERE
LOGARITHM
MAHARISHI
MALACHITE
MALADROIT
MALATHION
MALAYSIAN
MEDALLION
MEGACYCLE
MEGADEATH
MEGAHERTZ
MEGAPHONE
MEGAPIXEL
MENAGERIE
METALWARE
METALWORK
MONASTERY
NEFARIOUS
OLFACTORY
PALAESTRA
PALANQUIN
PALATABLE
PARACHUTE
PARAGRAPH
PARALYSIS
PARAMETER
PARAMOUNT
PARATHION
PEDAGOGUE
POTASSIUM
RAPACIOUS
REDACTION
REGARDING
REMAINDER
REPAIRMAN
RETALIATE
RETARDATE
RUNAROUND
SAGACIOUS
SALACIOUS
SCRAPBOOK
SEBACEOUS
SEMANTICS
SEMAPHORE
SEPARABLE
SEPARATOR
SHEATHING
SPEAKEASY
SPEARHEAD
SPEARMINT
STEADFAST
STEAMBOAT
STEAMSHIP
STRAPLESS
STRAPPING
STRATAGEM
SUBALPINE
SUBALTERN
SUBATOMIC
SUGARCANE
SUGARPLUM
SWEATSHOP
SYNAGOGUE
TARANTULA
TENACIOUS
THEATRICS
THRALLDOM
TREACHERY
TREADMILL
TREASURER
TREATMENT
TULAREMIA
TYRANNIZE
TYRANNOUS
UKRAINIAN
UNDAUNTED
UNEARTHLY
UNFAILING
UNHARNESS
UNNATURAL
VAGARIOUS
VERACIOUS
VEXATIOUS
VICARIOUS
VIVACIOUS
VORACIOUS
WOMANHOOD
WOMANKIND
WOMANLIKE
ALABASTER
ARABESQUE
BAMBOOZLE
BARBARIAN
BARBARISM
BARBAROUS
BOMBAZINE
BOMBPROOF
BOMBSHELL
BOMBSIGHT
BUMBLEBEE
CARBONATE
CARBUNCLE
CARBURIZE
CLUBHOUSE
CRABGRASS
CUBBYHOLE
CUPBEARER
DISBURDEN
DOUBTLESS
DUMBFOUND
EGGBEATER
ELABORATE
EXUBERANT
GIBBERISH
GRUBSTAKE
HAMBURGER
HARBINGER
HARBORAGE
HERBALIST
HERBARIUM
HERBICIDE
HUSBANDRY
INABILITY
INEBRIATE
LIABILITY
LIMBURGER
MISBEHAVE
POTBOILER
PROBATION
PROBATIVE
PROBOSCIS
RABBINATE
REDBREAST
SEMBLANCE
SOUBRETTE
STABILIZE
SUNBONNET
SYMBIOSIS
SYMBOLISM
SYMBOLIZE
TIMBERING
TOMBSTONE
TRIBESMAN
TRIBUTARY
TURBOPROP
TURBULENT
VERBALIZE
WARBONNET
WOEBEGONE
APOCRYPHA
AVOCATION
BACCHANAL
BARCAROLE
BEACHHEAD
BLACKBALL
BLACKBIRD
BLACKBODY
BLACKFOOT
BLACKHEAD
BLACKJACK
BLACKLIST
BLACKMAIL
BLOCKHEAD
BROCHETTE
BUCCANEER
CALCIMINE
CALCULATE
CARCINOMA
CATCHMENT
CATCHWORD
CAUCASIAN
CHECKBOOK
CHECKLIST
CHECKMATE
CHECKROOM
CHICANERY
CHICKADEE
CHICKASAW
CHICKWEED
CHOCOLATE
CHUCKHOLE
CIRCADIAN
CIRCUITRY
CIRCULATE
CLOCKWISE
CLOCKWORK
CONCERNED
CONCERTED
CONCIERGE
CONCORDAT
CONCOURSE
CONCUBINE
CRACKDOWN
CROCODILE
CRUCIFORM
DESCENDER
DIACRITIC
DISCHARGE
DISCOMFIT
DISCOURSE
DISCREDIT
EDUCATION
EJACULATE
ELECTRIFY
ELECTRODE
ELOCUTION
ELUCIDATE
EPICENTER
EPICUREAN
EXECRABLE
EXECUTIVE
EXECUTRIX
FANCYWORK
FASCINATE
FLUCTUATE
FRACTIOUS
FRICASSEE
GAUCHERIE
GLYCOSIDE
GUNCOTTON
HATCHMENT
HERCULEAN
HITCHHIKE
HUNCHBACK
INOCULATE
KNOCKDOWN
LACCOLITH
LUNCHROOM
MASCULINE
MATCHBOOK
MATCHLOCK
MATCHWOOD
MERCENARY
MERCERIZE
MERCURIAL
MERCUROUS
MESCALINE
MINCEMEAT
MISCHANCE
MISCREANT
NARCISSUS
NARCOTIZE
NONCREDIT
NOTCHBACK
PARCHMENT
PATCHWORK
PEACETIME
PERCHANCE
PERCOLATE
PIECEMEAL
PIECEWORK
PITCHFORK
PLACEKICK
PLACEMENT
PORCELAIN
PORCUPINE
PRACTICAL
PRECANCEL
PRECEDENT
PRECEDING
PRECENTOR
PRECEPTOR
PRECIPICE
PRECISION
PRECURSOR
PRICELESS
PROCEDURE
PROCESSOR
PROCONSUL
PROCREATE
PSYCHOSIS
PUNCTILIO
PUNCTUATE
QUICKDRAW
QUICKLIME
QUICKSAND
QUICKSORT
QUICKSTEP
QUICKTIME
RANCHLAND
REACTANCE

RENCONTRE
SACCHARIN
SANCTUARY
SPACESHIP
SPECIALTY
SPECTACLE
SPECTATOR
SPECULATE
SPICEBUSH
STOCKPILE
STOCKYARD
SUCCESSOR
SUCCOTASH
SUCCULENT
SURCHARGE
SURCINGLE
THICKNESS
TOUCHDOWN
TRACKBALL
TRACTABLE
TRICKSTER
TRUCKLOAD
TRUCULENT
TUSCARORA
UNSCATHED
VACCINATE
VISCOSITY
VOICELESS
VOLCANISM
VOUCHSAFE
VULCANISM
VULCANIZE
WATCHBAND
WATCHCASE
WATCHWORD
WHICHEVER
ZIRCONIUM
ZUCCHETTO
ACIDULATE
ACIDULOUS
AMIDSHIPS
BALDACHIN
BANDEROLE
BANDOLIER
BANDSTAND
BANDWAGON
BANDWIDTH
BIRDHOUSE
BONDWOMAN
CANDIDACY
CANDIDATE
CANDLEMAS
CANDLEPIN
CARDBOARD
COADJUTOR
CONDENSER
CONDIMENT
CONDITION
CONDUCTOR
CREDULOUS
DANDELION
DEODORANT
DEODORIZE
EPIDERMIS
ERADICATE
ERUDITION
FEEDSTOCK
FEEDSTUFF
FEUDALISM
FEUDATORY
FLEDGLING
FOODSTUFF
GLADIATOR
GLADIOLUS
GLADSTONE
GOLDBRICK
GOLDENROD
GOLDFIELD
GOLDFINCH
GOLDSMITH
GONDOLIER
GRADATION
GUIDEBOOK
GUIDELINE
HANDCLASP
HANDCRAFT
HANDIWORK
HANDSHAKE
HANDSPIKE
HANDSTAND
HANDWOVEN
HARDBOARD
HARDBOUND
HARDCOVER
HARDIHOOD
HARDSTAND
HEADBOARD
HEADDRESS
HEADFIRST
HEADLIGHT
HEADPHONE
HEADPIECE
HEADSTALL
HEADSTONE
HEADWATER
HINDRANCE
HINDSIGHT
HUMDINGER
LANDOWNER
LANDSCAPE
LANDSLIDE
LAUDATORY
LOADSTONE
MANDATORY
MENDICANT
MIDDLEMAN
MISDIRECT
MOLDBOARD
MURDEROUS
NEODYMIUM
OXIDATION
PENDULOUS
PERDITION
PONDEROUS
PREDATION
PREDATORY
PREDICATE
QUADRATIC
QUADRILLE
QUADRUPED
QUADRUPLE
RANDOMIZE
RENDITION
ROADBLOCK
ROADSTEAD
SADDLEBOW
SANDBLAST
SANDPAPER
SANDPIPER
SANDSTONE
SANDSTORM
SHADOWBOX
SKYDIVING
SUBDIVIDE
SYNDICATE
TENDERIZE
TINDERBOX
TOADSTOOL
TRADEMARK
TRADESMAN
TRADITION
UNADVISED
VANDALISM
VANDALIZE
VERDIGRIS
VINDICATE
VOODOOISM
WINDBLOWN
WINDBREAK
WINDCHILL
WINDPROOF
WINDSTORM
WINDSWEPT
WONDERFUL
WOODBLOCK
WOODCHUCK
WOODCRAFT
YARDSTICK
ACCESSION
ACCESSORY
ADJECTIVE
ADVENTURE
ADVERSARY
ADVERSITY
ADVERTISE
AFFECTING
AFFECTION
AFTERCARE
AFTERDECK
AFTERGLOW
AFTERLIFE
AFTERMATH
AFTERNOON
AFTERWARD
AGREEABLE
AGREEMENT
ALIENABLE
ALLERGIST
ALLEVIATE
ALTERNATE
AMBERGRIS
AMPERSAND
ANAEROBIC
ANGELFISH
ANTECHOIR
APPELLANT
APPELLATE
APPENDAGE
APPERTAIN
APPETIZER
ARGENTINE
ARGENTITE
ARTERIOLE
ASCENDANT
ASCENDERS
ASCENSION
ASCERTAIN
ASPERSION
ASSEMBLER
ASSERTION
ATHENAEUM
ATTENDANT
ATTENTION
ATTENUATE
BAREFACED
BASEBOARD
BELEAGUER
BESETTING
BLUEBERRY
BLUEBLACK
BLUEGRASS
BLUEPOINT
BLUEPRINT
BREEZEWAY
BRIEFCASE
CAFETERIA
CALENDULA
CAMELBACK
CAMEMBERT
CANEBRAKE
CARETAKER
CATECHISM
CATERWAUL
CELEBRATE
CELEBRITY
CELESTIAL
CEREBRATE
CERECLOTH
CHEEKBONE
CHEERLESS
CHIEFTAIN
CLIENTELE
COFEATURE
CONESTOGA
CORELDRAW
CUNEIFORM
CURETTAGE
DAREDEVIL
DAVENPORT
DEBENTURE
DECEITFUL
DECENNIAL
DECEPTION
DEFEATISM
DEFECTIVE
DEFENDANT
DEFENSIVE
DEFERENCE
DEFERMENT
DEJECTION
DEPENDENT
DESECRATE
DETECTIVE
DETENTION
DETERGENT
DETERMINE
DETERRENT
DIAERESIS
DIMENSION
DIRECTION
DIRECTIVE
DIRECTORY
DISEMBARK
DISEMBODY
DISENGAGE
DISESTEEM
DIVERSIFY
DIVERSION
DIVERSITY
DYSENTERY
EAVESDROP
ECCENTRIC
EFFECTIVE
EFFECTUAL
EGREGIOUS
EIDERDOWN
ELSEWHERE
EMBELLISH
EMPENNAGE
ENTERITIS
ENTERTAIN
EPHEDRINE
EPHEMERAL
ESPERANTO
ESSENTIAL
EXCELLENT
EXCELSIOR
EXCEPTION
EXPECTANT
EXPEDIENT
EXPEDITER
EXPENSIVE
EXPERTISE
EXTEMPORE
EXTENSION
EXTENSIVE
EXTENUATE
FACETIOUS
FIREBRAND
FIREBREAK
FIREBRICK
FIREHOUSE
FIREPLACE
FIREPOWER
FIREPROOF
FIREWATER
FORECLOSE
FOREFRONT
FOREGOING
FOREIGNER
FORENAMED
FORESHEET
FORESHORE
FORESIGHT
FORESTALL
FORESWEAR
FORETASTE
FORETOKEN
FOREWOMAN
FREEBOARD
FREEMASON
FREESTONE
FREEWHEEL
FRIEDCAKE
GABERDINE
GAZETTEER
GENEALOGY
GENERATOR
GOVERNESS
GREENBACK
GREENBELT
GREENHORN
GREENROOM
GREENWOOD
GRIEVANCE
HAVERSACK
HEREAFTER
HEREUNDER
HETERODOX
HIBERNATE
HIDEBOUND
HOMEGROWN
HOMEMAKER
HOMESTEAD
HONEYCOMB
HONEYMOON
HOREHOUND
HYPERBOLA
HYPERBOLE
HYPERCARD
HYPERTEXT
ILLEGIBLE
IMMEDIACY
IMMEDIATE
IMPEDANCE
IMPERFECT
IMPERIOUS
IMPETUOUS
INCENTIVE
INCEPTION
INCESSANT
INDELIBLE
INDEMNIFY
INDEMNITY
INDENTION
INDENTURE
INFECTION
INFERENCE
INFERTILE
INGENIOUS
INGENUITY
INGENUOUS
INJECTION
INNERMOST
INNERSOLE
INSENSATE
INSERTION
INTEGRATE
INTEGRITY
INTELLECT
INTENDANT
INTENSIFY
INTENSITY
INTENSIVE
INTENTION
INTERCEDE
INTERCEPT
INTERDICT
INTERFACE
INTERFERE
INTERFUSE
INTERJECT
INTERLACE
INTERLARD
INTERLEAF
INTERLINE
INTERLINK
INTERLOCK
INTERLOPE
INTERLUDE
INTERMENT
INTERNIST
INTERNODE
INTERPLAY
INTERPOSE
INTERPRET
INTERRUPT
INTERSECT
INTERVENE
INTERVIEW
INTESTATE
INTESTINE
INVECTIVE
INVENTION
INVENTIVE
INVENTORY
INVERNESS
INVERSION
IRREGULAR
JEWELWEED
KINESCOPE
LAMEBRAIN
LATECOMER
LEGENDARY
LIBERTINE
LIFEBLOOD
LIFEGUARD
LIMELIGHT
LIMESTONE
LINEAMENT
LITERATIM
LIVERWORT
LIVERYMAN
LIVESTOCK
LODESTONE
LOWERCASE
MAKESHIFT
MATERNITY
METEORITE
METEOROID
MILESTONE
MINELAYER
MISERABLE
MODERATOR
MODERNISM
MODERNIZE

MOM**E**NTARY
MOM**E**NTOUS
NAM**E**PLATE
NEC**E**SSARY
NEC**E**SSITY
NEV**E**RMORE
NON**E**NTITY
NOS**E**BLEED
NOS**E**PIECE
NOV**E**LETTE
NUM**E**RATOR
NUM**E**RICAL
OBJ**E**CTIFY
OBJ**E**CTIVE
OBS**E**RVANT
OBS**E**SSION
OFF**E**NSIVE
OFF**E**RTORY
ORI**E**NTATE
OTH**E**RWISE
OUT**E**RMOST
PAC**E**MAKER
PAG**E**MAKER
PAN**E**GYRIC
PAP**E**RBACK
PAR**E**GORIC
PAT**E**RNITY
PEN**E**PLAIN
PEN**E**TRATE
PER**E**NNIAL
PHL**E**BITIS
PHR**E**NETIC
PIK**E**STAFF
PIN**E**APPLE
POT**E**NTATE
POT**E**NTIAL
POW**E**RBOAT
PUB**E**SCENT
PUR**E**BLOOD
PYR**E**THRUM
QUI**E**SCENT
RAC**E**HORSE
RAC**E**TRACK
REB**E**LLION
REC**E**PTION
REC**E**PTIVE
REC**E**SSION
REC**E**SSIVE
REF**E**CTION
REF**E**CTORY
REF**E**RENCE
REH**E**ARING
REH**E**ARSAL
REL**E**VANCE
REL**E**VANCY
REP**E**LLENT
REP**E**RTORY
RES**E**CTION
RES**E**RPINE
RES**E**RVIST
RES**E**RVOIR
RET**E**NTION
RET**E**NTIVE
REV**E**RENCE
REV**E**RSION
RIV**E**RBANK
RIV**E**RBOAT
RIV**E**RSIDE
ROS**E**WATER
SAF**E**GUARD
SAG**E**BRUSH
SAL**E**SGIRL
SAT**E**LLITE
SCH**E**ELITE
SCH**E**MATIC
SCL**E**ROSIS
SCR**E**ENING
SCR**E**WBALL
SEC**E**SSION
SED**E**NTARY
SEL**E**CTION
SEL**E**CTMAN
SEV**E**NTEEN
SHE**E**PFOLD
SHE**E**PSKIN
SHO**E**MAKER
SID**E**BOARD
SID**E**BURNS
SID**E**PIECE
SID**E**SWIPE
SID**E**TRACK
SOL**E**MNIZE
SOM**E**THING
SOM**E**TIMES
SOM**E**WHERE
SOV**E**REIGN
SPE**E**DBOAT
SPE**E**DWELL
SPL**E**NETIC
SQU**E**AMISH
STE**E**LYARD
STR**E**AMBED
STR**E**AMLET
STR**E**ETCAR
STR**E**NUOUS
STR**E**TCHER
SUP**E**RNOVA
SUP**E**RPOSE
SUP**E**RSEDE
SUP**E**RVENE
SUP**E**RVISE
SWE**E**TMEAT
SYN**E**RGISM
TEL**E**GENIC
TEL**E**GRAPH
TEL**E**METER
TEL**E**PATHY
TEL**E**PHONE
TEL**E**PHONY
TEL**E**PHOTO
TEL**E**SCOPE
TEN**E**BROUS
THR**E**EFOLD
THR**E**ESOME
THR**E**SHOLD
TID**E**WATER
TIM**E**PIECE
TIM**E**TABLE
TOL**E**RABLE
TOL**E**RANCE
TRI**E**NNIAL
TYP**E**WRITE
UNB**E**KNOWN
UNB**E**NDING
UNC**E**ASING
UNC**E**RTAIN
UND**E**CEIVE
UND**E**CIDED
UND**E**RBODY
UND**E**RBRED
UND**E**RCOAT
UND**E**RDONE
UND**E**RFEED
UND**E**RFOOT
UND**E**RGIRD
UND**E**RHAND
UND**E**RLINE
UND**E**RLING
UND**E**RMINE
UND**E**RMOST
UND**E**RPART
UND**E**RPASS
UND**E**RPLAY
UND**E**RRATE
UND**E**RSELL
UND**E**RSHOT
UND**E**RSIDE
UND**E**RTAKE
UND**E**RTONE
UND**E**RWEAR
UND**E**RWOOD
UNF**E**ELING
UNF**E**IGNED
UNH**E**ALTHY
UNL**E**ARNED
UNM**E**ANING
UNS**E**LFISH
UNS**E**TTLED
UPP**E**RCASE
UPP**E**RMOST
UTT**E**RANCE
UTT**E**RMOST
VAL**E**NTINE
VAS**E**CTOMY
VEG**E**TABLE
VEH**E**MENCE
VEN**E**RABLE
VIC**E**NNIAL
VIC**E**REGAL
VID**E**LICET
VID**E**OTAPE
VIG**E**SIMAL
WAR**E**HOUSE
WAT**E**RFALL
WAT**E**RFOWL
WAT**E**RLINE
WAT**E**RMARK
WAT**E**RSHED
WAT**E**RSIDE
WAV**E**TABLE
WHE**E**LBASE
WIN**E**PRESS
WIR**E**FRAME
WIS**E**CRACK
WOM**E**NFOLK
YTT**E**RBIUM
ASA**F**ETIDA
BED**F**ELLOW
BEE**F**EATER
BEE**F**STEAK
CHA**F**FINCH
COF**F**EEPOT
COF**F**ERDAM
COI**F**FEUSE
COM**F**ORTER
CON**F**ESSOR
CON**F**IDANT
CON**F**USION
CRA**F**TSMAN
DEL**F**TWARE
DIF**F**ERENT
DIF**F**ICULT
DIF**F**IDENT
DIS**F**IGURE
DRA**F**TSMAN
DRI**F**TWOOD
GOD**F**ATHER
GYR**F**ALCON
HAL**F**PENNY
INE**F**FABLE
LEA**F**STALK
MAY**F**LOWER
ORI**F**LAMME
PER**F**ORATE
PER**F**UMERY
PRE**F**IGURE
PRE**F**LIGHT
PRO**F**ANITY
PRO**F**ESSOR
PRO**F**ITEER
SAF**F**LOWER
SEA**F**ARING
SHI**F**TLESS
SUF**F**ERING
SUF**F**OCATE
SUF**F**RAGAN
SUL**F**UROUS
SUN**F**LOWER
SUR**F**BOARD
TRI**F**OCALS
WOL**F**HOUND
WOL**F**SBANE
BIO**G**RAPHY
BUL**G**ARIAN
COA**G**ULANT
COA**G**ULATE
CON**G**ENIAL
CON**G**ERIES
CON**G**RUITY
DAN**G**EROUS
DIA**G**NOSIS
DRA**G**ONFLY
DRU**G**STORE
ENI**G**MATIC
EPI**G**RAPHY
ERO**G**ENOUS
EXO**G**ENOUS
FIN**G**ERING
FIN**G**ERTIP
FLA**G**ELLUM
FLA**G**EOLET
FLA**G**STAFF
FLA**G**STONE
FOR**G**ATHER
FOR**G**IVING
FRI**G**HTFUL
FUN**G**ICIDE
GAN**G**PLANK
GEO**G**RAPHY
HOB**G**OBLIN
HUN**G**ARIAN
IMA**G**INARY
LON**G**EVITY
LON**G**ITUDE
LOR**G**NETTE
MAN**G**ANESE
MAR**G**ARINE
MER**G**ANSER
MIS**G**IVING
MIS**G**OVERN
MON**G**OLIAN
MON**G**OLISM
MON**G**OLOID
OLI**G**ARCHY
ORI**G**INATE
OUT**G**ROWTH
OXY**G**ENATE
PIG**G**YBACK
PRA**G**MATIC
PRE**G**NABLE
PRO**G**NOSIS
PUR**G**ATION
PUR**G**ATIVE
PUR**G**ATORY
RAN**G**ELAND
RID**G**EPOLE
ROU**G**HNECK
SAN**G**FROID
SIN**G**LETON
SPA**G**HETTI
TAN**G**ERINE
THI**G**HBONE
TRA**G**EDIAN
VEN**G**EANCE
VIR**G**INITY
VUL**G**ARIAN
VUL**G**ARISM
VUL**G**ARITY
VUL**G**ARIZE
AMP**H**IBIAN
AMP**H**IBOLE
ANC**H**ORAGE
ANC**H**ORITE
ANC**H**ORMAN
ANT**H**OLOGY
ARC**H**ANGEL
ARC**H**ENEMY
ARC**H**ETYPE
ARC**H**FIEND
ARC**H**ITECT
ARC**H**IVIST
ART**H**RITIS
ART**H**ROPOD
AUT**H**ENTIC
AUT**H**ORITY
AUT**H**ORIZE
BAT**H**HOUSE
BAT**H**OLITH
BIS**H**OPRIC
BUS**H**WHACK
CAT**H**ARSIS
CAT**H**ARTIC
CAT**H**EDRAL
COC**H**INEAL
DAC**H**SHUND
DAS**H**BOARD
DIC**H**OTOMY
DIP**H**THONG
DIS**H**CLOTH
DIS**H**ONEST
DIS**H**WATER
DIT**H**ERING
EMP**H**ASIZE
EMP**H**YSEMA
ENC**H**ILADA
ENS**H**EATHE
EUC**H**ARIST
EUP**H**EMISM
EUT**H**ENICS
EXC**H**EQUER
FIS**H**ERMAN
HAP**H**AZARD
HIG**H**LIGHT
HOT**H**EADED
HYP**H**ENATE
JOB**H**OLDER
LIG**H**TFACE
LIG**H**TNING
LIG**H**TSHIP
LIG**H**TSOME
LIT**H**ESOME
LIT**H**OLOGY
MAC**H**INERY
MAC**H**INIST
MAN**H**ANDLE
MAN**H**ATTAN
MEC**H**ANICS
MEC**H**ANISM
MEC**H**ANIZE
MET**H**ADONE
MET**H**ODIST
MET**H**ODIZE
MIS**H**ANDLE
MYT**H**OLOGY
NEP**H**RITIC
NEP**H**RITIS
NIG**H**TCLUB
NIG**H**TFALL
NIG**H**TGOWN
NIG**H**THAWK
NIG**H**TLIFE
NIG**H**TMARE
NIG**H**TTIME
ORC**H**ESTRA
ORP**H**ANAGE
PAC**H**YDERM
PAN**H**ANDLE
PAT**H**OLOGY
PEN**H**OLDER
PIG**H**EADED
REC**H**ERCHE
RES**H**UFFLE
RIG**H**TEOUS
RUT**H**ENIUM
SOP**H**ISTIC
SOP**H**ISTRY
SOP**H**OMORE
TEC**H**NICAL
TEC**H**NIQUE
TIG**H**TROPE
UNC**H**ARTED
UNS**H**ACKLE
UNS**H**EATHE
WAS**H**BASIN
WAS**H**BOARD
WAS**H**CLOTH
WAS**H**HOUSE
WAS**H**STAND
WAS**H**WOMAN
WIT**H**DRAWN
WIT**H**STAND
YAC**H**TSMAN
ACC**I**DENCE
ADD**I**CTION
ADM**I**RABLE
ADM**I**RALTY
ADM**I**SSION
ADM**I**XTURE
ADV**I**SABLE
AER**I**ALIST
AFF**I**DAVIT
AFF**I**LIATE
AFR**I**KAANS
ALL**I**GATOR
ALT**I**METER
AMB**I**GUOUS
AMB**I**TIOUS
ANC**I**LLARY
ANT**I**CLINE
ANT**I**KNOCK
ANT**I**NOVEL
ANT**I**PASTO
ANT**I**PATHY
ANT**I**QUARY
ANT**I**QUITY
ANT**I**SERUM
ANT**I**TOXIN
ANT**I**TUMOR
ANT**I**VENIN
ARB**I**TRARY
ARB**I**TRATE
ARM**I**STICE
ART**I**CHOKE
ART**I**CULAR
ART**I**FICER
ART**I**LLERY
ASS**I**DUOUS
ASS**I**STANT
AUD**I**OLOGY
AUR**I**CULAR
AUX**I**LIARY
AVA**I**LABLE
BEN**I**GHTED
BEN**I**GNANT
BIL**I**NGUAL
CAL**I**BRATE

CAPILLARY
CAPITALLY
CARIBBEAN
CHRISTIAN
CHRISTMAS
CITIZENRY
CLOISONNE
CORIANDER
COTILLION
CROISSANT
DECIDUOUS
DECILITER
DECIMETER
DECISTERE
DEFICIENT
DELICIOUS
DELIGHTED
DELIMITER
DELINEATE
DEMIMONDE
DEMITASSE
DENIGRATE
DESICCANT
DESICCATE
DESIGNATE
DESIGNING
DESIRABLE
DEVILMENT
DIGITALIS
DIGITIZED
DIRIGIBLE
DISINFECT
DIVISIBLE
DIXIELAND
DOMINANCE
DOSIMETER
DOWITCHER
DRAINPIPE
EFFICIENT
ELLIPSOID
EMPIRICAL
ENLIGHTEN
EQUIPMENT
EQUIPOISE
EQUITABLE
EQUIVOCAL
ESPIONAGE
ESTIMABLE
ETHIOPIAN
EXCITABLE
EXPIATORY
EXTIRPATE
FETISHISM
FINICKING
FRUITCAKE
FRUITERER
FUNICULAR

FUSILLADE
GELIGNITE
GENITALIA
GERIATRIC
HABITABLE
HABITUATE
HALITOSIS
HEMISTICH
HERITABLE
HUMILIATE
ILLIBERAL
IMMIGRANT
IMMIGRATE
INCIDENCE
INCIPIENT
INDIGNANT
INDIGNITY
INFIRMARY
INFIRMITY
INSIDIOUS
INSINCERE
INSINUATE
INSISTENT
INVIDIOUS
INVIOLATE
INVISIBLE
IRRITABLE
JUDICIARY
JUDICIOUS
JURIDICAL
LAMINATED
LEGISLATE
LEVIATHAN
LITIGIOUS
LOGISTICS
LUDICROUS
MACINTOSH
MAGISTRAL
MALIGNANT
MANIFESTO
MARIJUANA
MEDICABLE
MEDICINAL
MELIORATE
MINIATURE
MINISCULE
MINISKIRT
MINISTATE
MISINFORM
MUNICIPAL
NAVIGABLE
NOVITIATE
OBEISANCE
OBLIVIOUS
OFFICIANT
OFFICIATE
OFFICIOUS

ORDINANCE
ORGIASTIC
OSCILLATE
PAKISTANI
PAPILLOTE
PEKINGESE
PENINSULA
PERIMETER
PERIPHERY
PERISCOPE
PERISTYLE
PLAINTIFF
PLAINTIVE
POLICEMAN
POLITBURO
POLITESSE
POLITICAL
RACIALISM
RADIOGRAM
RADIOLOGY
RATIONALE
RECIPIENT
REGISTRAR
RELIGIOUS
RELIQUARY
REMINISCE
REMISSION
RESIDENCE
RESIDENCY
RESIDUARY
RESISTANT
SATINWOOD
SAXIFRAGE
SCHILLING
SCRIMMAGE
SCRIMSHAW
SCRIPTURE
SCRIVENER
SEMICOLON
SEMIFINAL
SEMIFLUID
SEMILUNAR
SEMIWORKS
SENIORITY
SERIGRAPH
SHRINKAGE
SILICEOUS
SILICOSIS
SLUICEWAY
SOCIALISM
SOCIALITE
SOCIALIZE
SOCIOLOGY
SOLICITOR
SOLILOQUY
SOLITAIRE
SPHINCTER

SPLITTING
SPRIGHTLY
STAIRCASE
STAIRWELL
STRICTURE
STRIKEOUT
STRIPLING
TAXIDERMY
TRAINLOAD
ULTIMATUM
UMBILICUS
UNMINDFUL
UNRIVALED
UNSIGHTLY
UNWILLING
UNWITTING
URTICARIA
VACILLATE
VAGINITIS
VARIATION
VARIEGATE
VENIREMAN
VERIDICAL
VERITABLE
VIGILANCE
VIGILANTE
VISIONARY
CONJUGATE
PREJUDICE
PROJECTOR
SKYJACKER
SUBJUGATE
BACKBOARD
BACKFIELD
BACKPEDAL
BACKSLASH
BACKSLIDE
BACKSTAGE
BACKSWEPT
BACKTRACK
BACKWATER
BACKWOODS
BARKEEPER
BEEKEEPER
BERKELIUM
BOOKMAKER
BOOKPLATE
BOOKSHELF
BROKERAGE
BUCKBOARD
BUCKTOOTH
BUCKWHEAT
COCKATIEL
COCKFIGHT
COCKROACH
CORKSCREW
DUCKBOARD

HACKNEYED
INNKEEPER
JACKKNIFE
JACKSCREW
JACKSTRAW
JERKWATER
KICKSTAND
LEUKOCYTE
LOCKSMITH
MONKSHOOD
MUCKRAKER
MUSKMELON
PACKHORSE
PICKABACK
RACKETEER
RECKONING
ROCKBOUND
SACKCLOTH
SHAKEDOWN
SNAKEBIRD
SNAKEBITE
SPOKESMAN
TALKATIVE
TEAKETTLE
UNSKILLED
WORKBENCH
WORKGROUP
WORKHORSE
WORKHOUSE
WORKPLACE
WORKTABLE
ACCLIMATE
ACCLIVITY
AFFLUENCE
AMPLITUDE
ANALGESIA
ANALGESIC
ANALOGOUS
ANGLEWORM
ANGLICIZE
ANKLEBONE
APOLOGIZE
APPLEJACK
APPLETALK
APPLIANCE
APPLICANT
ATHLETICS
AVALANCHE
BAILIWICK
BALLADEER
BALLERINA
BELLICOSE
BELLYACHE
BILLBOARD
BILLIARDS
BOULEVARD
BRILLIANT

BULLFIGHT
BULLFINCH
BURLESQUE
CABLEGRAM
CALLOSITY
CELLARAGE
CELLULOSE
CHALKBORD
CHALLENGE
CHILBLAIN
CHILDHOOD
COALFIELD
COALITION
COLLATION
COLLEAGUE
COLLECTED
COLLEGIAN
COLLEGIUM
COLLIMATE
COLLODION
COLLUSION
COLLUVIUM
CULLENDER
CYCLAMATE
CYCLOTRON
DECLIVITY
DEFLATION
DIALECTIC
DIPLOMACY
DISLOCATE
DUPLICATE
DUPLICITY
EBULLIENT
EDELWEISS
EFFLUENCE
EFFLUVIUM
EMOLLIENT
EMOLUMENT
ESPLANADE
EUCLIDEAN
EVOLUTION
EXCLUSIVE
EXPLETIVE
EXPLICATE
EXPLOSION
EXPLOSIVE
FELLOWMAN
FOLLOWING
FOOLHARDY
FOOLPROOF
GALLANTRY
GALLINULE
GALLIVANT
GALLSTONE
GRILLWORK
HAILSTONE
HAILSTORM

HALLOWEEN
HARLEQUIN
HEALTHFUL
HELLEBORE
HELLENISM
HILLBILLY
HOLLYHOCK
ICELANDER
ICELANDIC
IMPLEMENT
IMPLICATE
INCLEMENT
INELEGANT
INFLATION
INFLEXION
INFLUENCE
INFLUENZA
INGLENOOK
ITALICIZE
JAILBREAK
JELLYFISH
MAELSTROM
MALLEABLE
MILLIGRAM
MILLINERY
MILLIPEDE
MILLIVOLT
MILLSTONE
NEGLIGENT
NEOLOGISM
OBBLIGATO
ONSLAUGHT
OUBLIETTE
PALLADIUM
PHALAROPE
PHILANDER
PHILATELY
PHILIPPIC
PHILOLOGY
POULTERER
PRELAUNCH
PUBLICIST
PUBLICITY
PUBLICIZE
REFLECTOR
REFLEXIVE
REPLENISH
REPLETION
REPLICATE
SAILCLOTH
SAILPLANE
SCHLEMIEL
SCULPTURE
SECLUSION
SHELLFIRE
SHELLFISH
SKYLOUNGE

SMALLTALK
SPELUNKER
STALEMATE
STILLBORN
SUBLIMATE
SUBLUNARY
SWELLHEAD
SYLLABIFY
SYLLOGISM
TABLELAND
TABLEWARE
TAILLIGHT
TELLURIUM
TOLLHOUSE
UNALIGNED
UNALLOYED
UNBLESSED
UNCLEANLY
UNFLEDGED
UNPLUMBED
VILLENAGE
VIOLATION
WALLBOARD
WALLOPING
WALLPAPER
WHALEBOAT
WHALEBONE
WHOLESALE
WHOLESOME
WILLPOWER
WORLDLING
WORLDWIDE
ABOMINATE
ADUMBRATE
AIRMOBILE
ALUMINIUM
ALUMINIZE
ANIMALISM
ANIMATION
ANIMOSITY
ANOMALOUS
ASYMPTOTE
BADMINTON
BOOMERANG
BRIMSTONE
CHAMELEON
CHAMOMILE
CHAMPAGNE
CHAMPAIGN
CHEMISTRY
CLAMSHELL
COMMANDER
COMMINGLE
COMMISSAR
COMMITTEE
COMMODITY
COMMODORE

COMMOTION
COMMUNION
COMMUNISM
COMMUNITY
CORMORANT
COSMOGONY
COSMOLOGY
COSMONAUT
CREMATORY
CULMINATE
DALMATION
DIAMETRIC
DISMANTLE
DISMEMBER
DOGMATISM
DORMITORY
DRAMATIZE
DROMEDARY
DRUMSTICK
ELIMINATE
ENUMERATE
ETYMOLOGY
EXEMPLARY
EXEMPLIFY
FARMHOUSE
FARMSTEAD
FILMSTRIP
FIRMAMENT
FLAMMABLE
FORMALISM
FORMALITY
FORMALIZE
FORMATION
FORMATIVE
FORMULATE
FRAMEWORK
FULMINATE
GERMANIUM
GERMICIDE
GERMINATE
GIMMICKRY
GLAMORIZE
GODMOTHER
HAMMERTOE
HARMONICA
HARMONICS
HARMONIUM
HARMONIZE
HERMITAGE
INAMORATA
MARMALADE
MARMOREAL
MESMERIZE
MISMANAGE
NORMALIZE
NORMATIVE
PALMISTRY

PAYMASTER
PEGMATITE
PERMANENT
PERMEABLE
PREMATURE
PRIMARILY
PRIMITIVE
PROMENADE
PROMINENT
PROMISING
PULMONARY
REIMBURSE
RIGMAROLE
ROUMANIAN
SKIMOBILE
STAMINATE
STIMULANT
STIMULATE
STOMACHER
STOMACHIC
SUBMARINE
SUMMARIZE
SUMMATION
SWAMPLAND
TERMAGANT
TERMINATE
THUMBNAIL
THUMBTACK
TREMATODE
TREMULOUS
TRIMESTER
VERMIFORM
VERMIFUGE
VERMILION
WARMONGER
WHIMSICAL
ABANDONED
ALONGSIDE
AMENDMENT
ANONYMOUS
ATONEMENT
AVUNCULAR
BARNSTORM
BLINDFOLD
BOONDOCKS
BOUNTEOUS
BOUNTIFUL
BRONCHIAL
CANNONADE
CANNONEER
CARNATION
CARNELIAN
CARNIVORA
CARNIVORE
CHANCROID
CHANTEUSE
CHONDRITE

CHONDRULE
CLINICIAN
COGNITION
CONNUBIAL
COONHOUND
CORNSTALK
COUNSELOR
COUNTDOWN
COUNTLESS
CRANBERRY
CRANKCASE
CRINOLINE
DAMNATION
DAUNTLESS
DIGNIFIED
DIGNITARY
DOWNGRADE
DOWNRANGE
DOWNRIGHT
DOWNSHIFT
DOWNSTAGE
DOWNSWING
ECONOMICS
ECONOMIZE
ENUNCIATE
ETHNOLOGY
EVENTUATE
EXONERATE
FLINTLOCK
FOUNDLING
FRANCHISE
FRANGIBLE
FURNITURE
GARNISHEE
GARNITURE
GLENGARRY
GRANDIOSE
GRANTSMAN
GRANULATE
GRENADIER
GRENADINE
GUNNYSACK
GYMNASIUM
IDENTICAL
INANIMATE
INANITION
IRONBOUND
IRONSTONE
ISINGLASS
ITINERANT
ITINERARY
JAUNDICED
LAGNIAPPE
LAUNCHPAD
LOINCLOTH
MAGNESIUM
MAGNETISM

MAGNETITE
MAGNETIZE
MAGNIFICO
MAGNITUDE
MAINFRAME
MANNEQUIN
MANNERISM
MEANWHILE
MOONLIGHT
MOONSCAPE
MOONSHINE
MOONSTONE
ORANGEADE
OUTNUMBER
PHONETICS
PHONOLOGY
PLANELOAD
PLANETOID
PLENITUDE
PLENTEOUS
PLENTIFUL
POINCIANA
PRINCIPAL
PRINCIPLE
PRINTABLE
PRONGHORN
PRONOUNCE
QUINTUPLE
RAINSPOUT
RAINSTORM
RAINWATER
REENFORCE
REENTRANT
REINFORCE
REINSTATE
ROUNDELAY
ROUNDWORM
RUINATION
SCANTLING
SCHNAUZER
SCINTILLA
SIGNALIZE
SIGNALMAN
SIGNATORY
SIGNATURE
SIGNBOARD
SKINFLINT
SKINTIGHT
SLINGSHOT
SOMNOLENT
SPINDLING
SPINDRIFT
SPINNAKER
STANCHION
STANDPIPE
SUBNORMAL
SWANSDOWN

THANKLESS
TOWNSFOLK
TRANSCEND
TRANSDUCE
TRANSFORM
TRANSFUSE
TRANSIENT
TRANSLATE
TRANSMUTE
TRANSONIC
TRANSPIRE
TRANSPORT
TRANSPOSE
TRANSSHIP
TRENCHANT
TRUNCHEON
TURNABOUT
TURNSTILE
TURNTABLE
TWINKLING
UNANIMOUS
UNKNOWING
UPANISHAD
VAINGLORY
VERNALIZE
WEDNESDAY
WRONGDOER
YOUNGLING
YOUNGSTER
ZWINGLIAN
ABHORRENT
ABSORBENT
ACCOMPANY
ACCORDION
ACROPOLIS
ADJOINING
ADSORBATE
ADSORBENT
AERODROME
AEROPAUSE
AEROPLANE
AEROSPACE
ALCOHOLIC
ALGONQUIN
ALGORITHM
ALLOWANCE
ANNOUNCER
ANNOYANCE
APPOINTEE
APPORTION
ARBORETUM
ARROWHEAD
ARROWROOT
ASSOCIATE
ASSONANCE
ATROCIOUS
AUTOCRACY

AUTOGRAPH
AUTOMATIC
AUTOMATON
AUTOTRACE
BAROGRAPH
BAROMETER
BICONCAVE
BIMONTHLY
BINOCULAR
BINOMINAL
BLOODBATH
BLOODLINE
BLOODROOT
BLOODSHED
BLOODSHOT
CACOPHONY
CALORIFIC
CANONICAL
CHLORDANE
CHROMATIC
CHRONICLE
COLONNADE
COLORCAST
COLORFAST
COROLLARY
CRYOGENIC
CYTOPLASM
DECOLLETE
DECOMPOSE
DECONTROL
DECORATOR
DECOUPAGE
DEFOLIANT
DEFOLIATE
DEFORMITY
DEMOCRACY
DETONATOR
DIMORPHIC
DISOBLIGE
DISORIENT
ELBOWROOM
ENCOMPASS
ENCOUNTER
ENCOURAGE
ENDOCRINE
ENDOSCOPE
ENTOURAGE
ERRONEOUS
EXCORIATE
EXPOSITOR
FAVORABLE
FEROCIOUS
FLOODGATE
GONORRHEA
GROOMSMAN
GYROSCOPE
HOLOCAUST

HOLOGRAPH
HOMOGRAPH
HOMOPHONE
HONORABLE
HONORIFIC
HOROSCOPE
HYPOCRISY
IGNORANCE
ILLOGICAL
IMMOVABLE
IMPOLITIC
IMPORTANT
IMPORTUNE
IMPOSTURE
INCOGNITO
INCOMMODE
INCORRECT
INFORMANT
INNOCENCE
INNOCUOUS
INSOLUBLE
INSOLVENT
INVOLUCRE
KILOCYCLE
KILOHERTZ
KILOLITER
KILOMETER
LABORIOUS
LIMOUSINE
LOCOMOTOR
MAJORDOMO
MAJORETTE
MANOEUVRE
MANOMETER
MASOCHISM
MELODIOUS
MELODRAMA
MEMORABLE
MENOPAUSE
MISORIENT
MONOGRAPH
MONOLOGUE
MONOMANIA
MONOPLANE
MONOSPACE
MOTORBIKE
MOTORBOAT
MOTORCADE
NANOMETER
NEGOTIANT
NEGOTIATE
NICOTINIC
NOTORIOUS
OBNOXIOUS
ONIONSKIN
OPPORTUNE
OPTOMETRY

PAROCHIAL
PEDOMETER
PIROUETTE
PREOCCUPY
PREORDAIN
PROOFREAD
PYROLYSIS
PYROMANIA
PYROMETER
RACONTEUR
RECOGNIZE
RECOLLECT
RECOMMEND
RECONCILE
RECONDITE
RECORDING
RECORDIST
REJOINDER
REPORTAGE
REPOSSESS
RESONANCE
RESONATOR
REVOCABLE
REVOLTING
RHEOMETER
SAXOPHONE
SCHOOLBOY
SECONDARY
SOPORIFIC
SPOONBILL
STRONTIUM
SYCOPHANT
THEOCRACY
THEOSOPHY
THROWAWAY
THROWBACK
TROOPSHIP
UNBOUNDED
UNCONCERN
UNCOUNTED
UNDOUBTED
UNFOUNDED
UNPOPULAR
UNWORLDLY
UPHOLSTER
VAPORIZER
VAPORWARE
WAGONETTE
XEROPHYTE
XYLOPHONE
ANOPHELES
BESPANGLE
BESPATTER
BUMPTIOUS
CAMPANILE
CAMPSTOOL
CARPENTER

CARPETBAG
CARPETING
CHAPARRAL
CHOPHOUSE
CHOPSTICK
CLAPBOARD
CLIPBOARD
CLIPSHEET
COMPANION
COMPETENT
COMPLAINT
COMPONENT
COMPOSITE
COMPOSURE
COOPERATE
CORPORATE
CORPOREAL
CORPUSCLE
COSPONSOR
DESPERADO
DESPERATE
DIAPHRAGM
DISPARAGE
DISPARATE
DISPLEASE
DISPRAISE
DISPUTANT
DYSPEPSIA
ESOPHAGUS
EVAPORATE
EVAPORITE
FLOPHOUSE
GODPARENT
GRAPESHOT
GRAPEVINE
GUNPOWDER
HAPPENING
HAPPINESS
NONPAREIL
NONPERSON
NONPROFIT
OVIPAROUS
PALPITATE
PERPETUAL
PERPLEXED
PIMPERNEL
POMPADOUR
POPPYCOCK
POTPOURRI
PROPAGATE
PROPELLER
PROPHETIC
PROPONENT
PROPRIETY
PUPPETEER
RAGPICKER
RASPBERRY
SCAPEGOAT
SHAPELESS
SHIPBOARD
SHIPSHAPE
SHIPWRECK
SIMPATICO
SIMPLETON
SOAPSTONE
STEPCHILD
STIPULATE
STOPLIGHT
STOPWATCH
SUMPTUOUS
SUPPLIANT
SUPPOSING
SUPPURATE
SUSPENDER
SUSPICION
SYMPOSIUM
TARPAULIN
TEMPERATE
TEMPORARY
TEMPORIZE
TRAPEZOID
TRAPPINGS
TURPITUDE
UNSPARING
UNSPOTTED
BANQUETTE
BRIQUETTE
CROQUETTE
ETIQUETTE
FREQUENCY
MARQUETRY
PARQUETRY
TURQUOISE
UNEQUALED
ABORIGINE
ACCRETION
ADDRESSEE
AFORESAID
AGGRAVATE
AGGREGATE
AMARYLLIS
AMERICANA
AMERICIUM
AMORPHOUS
ANARCHISM
APARTHEID
APARTMENT
APPREHEND
ASTRADDLE
ASTRAKHAN
ASTROLABE
ASTROLOGY
ASTRONAUT
ASTRONOMY
ATTRIBUTE
ATTRITION
BARRACUDA
BARRICADE
BARRISTER
BEDRIDDEN
BETROTHED
BOARDWALK
BOURGEOIS
CABRIOLET
CAPRICCIO
CARROUSEL
CHARABANC
CHARACTER
CHARLATAN
CHARWOMAN
CHIROPODY
CHORISTER
CHURCHMAN
CIRRHOSIS
CLERGYMAN
CORRELATE
CORRUGATE
COURTEOUS
COURTESAN
COURTROOM
COURTSHIP
COURTYARD
CURRYCOMB
DAIRYMAID
DECREMENT
DEPRECATE
DEPRESSED
DERRINGER
DETRIMENT
DISREGARD
DISREPAIR
DISREPUTE
DOORPLATE
EMBRASURE
EMBROCATE
EMBROIDER
EMERGENCY
ENERGETIC
ENERGIZER
ENGRAVING
ENWREATHE
EUTROPHIC
EVERGLADE
EVERGREEN
EVERYBODY
EXCREMENT
EXTRADITE
EXTRAVERT
EXTREMISM
EXTREMITY
EXTRICATE
EXTRINSIC
EXTRUSIVE
FABRICATE
FAIRYLAND
FEBRIFUGE
FERRYBOAT
FOURSCORE
GARRULOUS
GEARSHIFT
GUARANTEE
GUARANTOR
GUARDROOM
GUARDSMAN
GUERRILLA
HAIRBRUSH
HAIRCLOTH
HAIRPIECE
HAIRSTYLE
HEARTACHE
HEARTBEAT
HEARTBURN
HEARTFELT
HEARTLESS
HEARTSICK
HEARTWOOD
HEURISTIC
HIERARCHY
HOARFROST
HOURGLASS
HURRICANE
HYDRANGEA
HYDRAULIC
HYDROFOIL
HYDROLOGY
HYDROXIDE
IMBROGLIO
IMPRECATE
IMPRECISE
IMPROMPTU
IMPROVISE
IMPRUDENT
INCREMENT
INGROWING
INORGANIC
INTRICATE
INTRINSIC
INTRODUCE
INTROVERT
ITERATION
JINRIKSHA
LIBRARIAN
LUBRICANT
LUBRICATE
LUCRATIVE
MACROCOSM
MATRIARCH
MATRICIDE
MATRIMONY
MERRIMENT
METRICIZE
METROLOGY
METRONOME
MICROCOPY
MICROCOSM
MICROFILM
MICROGRAM
MICROSOFT
MICROWAVE
NARRATIVE
NECROLOGY
NEGRITUDE
NEURALGIA
NEUROLOGY
NIGRITUDE
NONREADER
NUTRIMENT
NUTRITION
OPERATION
OPERATIVE
OSTRACIZE
OUTRIGGER
OVERBLOWN
OVERBOARD
OVERCLOUD
OVERDRAFT
OVERDRIVE
OVERMATCH
OVERNIGHT
OVERPOWER
OVERPRINT
OVERREACH
OVERSEXED
OVERSHOOT
OVERSIGHT
OVERSLEEP
OVERSTATE
OVERTHROW
OVERTRICK
OVERWEIGH
OVERWHELM
OVERWRITE
PARRICIDE
PATRIARCH
PATRICIAN
PATRICIDE
PATRIMONY
PATRISTIC
PATROLMAN
PATRONAGE
PATRONIZE
PETROLEUM
PETROLOGY
PHEROMONE
PLURALITY
PLURALIZE
POORHOUSE
PORRINGER
POURBOIRE
PRERECORD
PSORIASIS
PTARMIGAN
PUERPERAL
QUARTERLY
QUARTZITE
QUERULOUS
REFRACTOR
REPREHEND
REPRESENT
REPRIMAND
REPROBATE
REPRODUCE
RETRIEVER
RETROFIRE
RUMRUNNER
SACRAMENT
SACRIFICE
SACRILEGE
SACRISTAN
SCARECROW
SECRETARY
SECRETION
SECRETIVE
SEGREGATE
SHAREWARE
SHARKSKIN
SHOREBIRD
SHORTCAKE
SHORTHAND
SHORTHORN
SHORTSTOP
SHORTWAVE
SKYROCKET
SOBRIQUET
SPIRITUAL
SPORTSMAN
STARBOARD
STARLIGHT
STARTLING
STERILIZE
STOREROOM
SUPREMACY
SURRENDER
SURROGATE
SWORDFISH
SWORDPLAY
SWORDSMAN
SWORDTAIL
TERRARIUM
TERRITORY
TERRORISM
TERRORIZE
THEREFORE
THEREFROM
THEREUNTO
THEREUPON
THEREWITH
THYROXINE
ULTRAHIGH
ULTRAPURE
UNBRIDLED
UNWRITTEN
VIBRATION
VIBRATORY
WEARISOME
WHEREFORE
WHEREUPON
WHEREWITH
WHIRLIGIG
WHIRLPOOL
WHIRLWIND
WORRISOME
WORRYWART
ALMSHOUSE
APOSTOLIC
AWESTRUCK
BAKSHEESH
BEDSPREAD
BIOSPHERE
BLASPHEME
BLASPHEMY
BOLSHEVIK
BOWSTRING
BRASSERIE
BRASSIERE
BRUSHWOOD
CAPSULATE
CASSEROLE
CASSOWARY
CAUSATION
CEASELESS
CESSATION
CLASSICAL
CLASSMATE
CLASSROOM
COASTLINE
CONSCIOUS
CONSCRIPT
CONSENSUS
CONSONANT
CONSTABLE
CONSTANCY
CONSTRAIN
CONSTRICT
CONSTRUCT
CRESCENDO
CROSSOVER
CROSSROAD
CROSSWALK
CROSSWAYS
CROSSWISE
DAMSELFLY
DISSECTED
DISSEMBLE
DISSENTER
DISSIDENT
DISSIPATE
DISSOLUTE
DOBSONFLY
ECOSYSTEM
ELASTOMER
EPISCOPAL
EXISTENCE
EXOSPHERE
EYESTRAIN
FACSIMILE
FALSEHOOD
FARSEEING
FIRSTBORN
FIRSTHAND
FIRSTLING
FLASHBACK
FLASHBULB
FLASHCUBE
FLASHTUBE
FORSYTHIA
FROSTBITE
FRUSTRATE
GLISSANDO
GRASSLAND
GRISTMILL
GROSGRAIN
HAMSTRING
HEMSTITCH
HOPSCOTCH
HORSEBACK
HORSEHAIR
HORSEHIDE
HORSEPLAY
HORSESHOE
HORSETAIL
HORSEWHIP
HOUSEBOAT
HOUSECOAT
HOUSEHOLD
HOUSEMAID
HOUSEWIFE
HOUSEWORK
HOWSOEVER
IRASCIBLE
ISOSCELES
JESSAMINE
KINSWOMAN
LASSITUDE
LEASEHOLD
LEASTWISE

MANSLAYER
MARSUPIAL
MAUSOLEUM
MESSENGER
MESSIEURS
MIDSTREAM
MIDSUMMER
MISSILERY
MISSIONER
MONSIGNOR
MOUSETRAP
MOUSTACHE
MUSSULMAN
NEWSPAPER
NEWSPRINT
NEWSSTAND
NURSEMAID
OFFSPRING
OURSELVES
OUTSKIRTS
OUTSPOKEN
OUTSPREAD
PARSIMONY
PARSONAGE
PASSENGER
PASSERINE
PERSECUTE
PERSEVERE
PERSIMMON
PERSONAGE
PERSONATE
PERSONIFY
PERSONNEL
PESSIMISM
PHOSPHATE
PHYSICIAN
PHYSICIST
PINSTRIPE
PRESBYTER
PRESCHOOL
PRESCRIBE
PRESENTLY
PRESHRUNK
PRESIDENT
PRESIDIUM
PRESSROOM
PRESTRESS
PROSCRIBE
PROSECUTE
PROSELYTE
PROSTRATE
PUISSANCE
PURSUANCE
PUSSYFOOT
SAPSUCKER
SASSAFRAS
SEASONING

SENSATION
SENSITIVE
SENSITIZE
SUBSCRIBE
SUBSCRIPT
SUBSIDIZE
SUBSTANCE
SUNSEEKER
SUNSTROKE
THESAURUS
TONSORIAL
UNISEXUAL
VASSALAGE
VERSATILE
WAISTBAND
WAISTCOAT
WAISTLINE
WHOSOEVER
WRESTLING
WRISTBAND
ABATEMENT
ACETYLENE
AESTHETIC
AESTIVATE
ANATOMIZE
AUCTORIAL
BACTERIUM
BANTUSTAN
BARTENDER
BASTINADO
BATTALION
BEATITUDE
BENTONITE
BIRTHMARK
BIRTHRATE
BOATSWAIN
BOOTBLACK
BRITANNIC
BRUTALIZE
BUTTERCUP
BUTTERFAT
BUTTERFLY
BUTTERNUT
BYSTANDER
CANTABILE
CANTHARIS
CAPTIVATE
CARTILAGE
CARTRIDGE
CARTWHEEL
CASTANETS
CASTIGATE
CAUTERIZE
CENTENARY
CENTESIMO
CENTIGRAM
CENTIPEDE

CENTURION
CERTAINTY
CERTITUDE
CONTAGION
CONTAINER
CONTENTED
CONTINENT
CONTINUAL
CONTINUUM
CONTRALTO
CONTUMELY
CONTUSION
CORTISONE
COUTURIER
CRETINISM
CRITERION
CRITICISM
CRITICIZE
CULTIVATE
CUSTODIAL
CUSTODIAN
CUSTOMARY
CUSTOMIZE
CUTTHROAT
DEATHBLOW
DEATHLESS
DENTITION
DESTITUTE
DESTROYER
DEUTERIUM
DEXTERITY
DEXTEROUS
DIATHERMY
DIATOMITE
DIETETICS
DIPTEROUS
DISTEMPER
DISTURBED
DOCTORATE
DYSTROPHY
EARTHLING
EARTHWARD
EARTHWORK
EARTHWORM
EDITORIAL
ERSTWHILE
FACTORIAL
FANTASIZE
FANTASTIC
FASTENING
FERTILIZE
FESTIVITY
FLATULENT
FLOTATION
FOOTBOARD
FOOTLOOSE
FOOTPRINT

FOOTSTOOL
FORTHWITH
FORTITUDE
FORTNIGHT
FORTUNATE
FRATERNAL
GASTRITIS
GASTROPOD
GENTILITY
GENTLEMAN
GESTATION
GLUTINOUS
GRATICULE
GRATITUDE
GROTESQUE
GUSTATORY
HARTSHORN
HECTOGRAM
HISTAMINE
HISTOGRAM
HISTORIAN
HORTATIVE
HORTATORY
HYSTERICS
IMITATION
IMITATIVE
INSTANTER
INSTANTLY
INSTIGATE
INSTITUTE
JITTERBUG
JUXTAPOSE
LANTHANUM
LEITMOTIV
LITTERBUG
LOATHSOME
MARTYRDOM
MASTERFUL
MASTICATE
MELTWATER
MENTALITY
MISTLETOE
MORTICIAN
MOUTHPART
MOUTHWASH
MULTIFORM
MULTISCAN
MULTISPIN
MULTISYNC
MULTITUDE
MYSTICISM
NECTARINE
NEPTUNIUM
NOCTURNAL
NORTHEAST
NORTHWEST
NOSTALGIA

OBSTINATE
PANTHEISM
PANTOMIME
PARTITION
PARTITIVE
PARTRIDGE
PASTORALE
PASTURAGE
PENTECOST
PENTHOUSE
PERTINENT
PESTHOUSE
PESTICIDE
PESTILENT
PETTICOAT
PHOTOCELL
PHOTOCOPY
PHOTOPLAY
PICTORIAL
PISTACHIO
PLATITUDE
PLUTONIUM
POETASTER
PORTFOLIO
PORTULACA
POSTERIOR
POSTERITY
POSTHASTE
POSTILION
POSTNATAL
POSTULANT
POSTULATE
PROTECTOR
PROTOTYPE
PROTOZOAN
QUITTANCE
QUOTIDIAN
RASTERIZE
RECTANGLE
RECTIFIER
RECTITUDE
REITERATE
RESTRAINT
ROOTSTOCK
RUSTICATE
SALTPETER
SALTWATER
SARTORIAL
SCUTCHEON
SECTARIAN
SECTIONAL
SENTIMENT
SEPTEMBER
SILTSTONE
SOFTBOUND
SOUTHEAST
SOUTHWEST

SPOTLIGHT
STATEMENT
STATEROOM
STATESIDE
STATESMAN
STATIONER
STATISTIC
STATUETTE
STATUTORY
SWITCHMAN
SYNTHESIS
SYNTHETIC
SYSTEMIZE
TANTALIZE
TAUTOLOGY
TECTONICS
TECTONISM
TENTATIVE
TESTAMENT
TESTIMONY
TOOTHACHE
TOOTHPICK
TOOTHSOME
TRITURATE
UNITARIAN
UNSTUDIED
VENTILATE
VENTRICLE
VENTUROUS
VERTEBRAL
VESTIBULE
VESTRYMAN
VICTIMIZE
VICTORIAN
VICTUALER
VOLTMETER
WASTELAND
WHETSTONE
WHITEBAIT
WHITEFISH
WHITEHALL
WHITEHEAD
WHITENESS
WHITETAIL
WHITEWALL
WHITEWASH
WHITEWOOD
WINTERIZE
WITTICISM
WORTHLESS
XANTHIPPE
YESTERDAY
ZEITGEIST
ACOUSTICS
ACQUIESCE
AMBULANCE
AMBUSCADE

ANGUISHED
ANNUITANT
ASSURANCE
BEAUTEOUS
BEAUTIFUL
BIFURCATE
BURUNDIAN
CASUISTRY
CHAUFFEUR
COLUMBINE
COLUMNIST
CONUNDRUM
CORUSCATE
DEBUTANTE
DEDUCTION
DEMULCENT
DEMURRAGE
DESUETUDE
DESULTORY
ENDURANCE
EXCULPATE
EXCURSION
EXCURSIVE
EXPULSION
EXPURGATE
EXQUISITE
FECUNDATE
FIDUCIARY
GENUFLECT
GROUNDHOG
GROUNDING
GROUPWARE
IMMUTABLE
IMPULSION
IMPULSIVE
INAUGURAL
INCUBATOR
INCULCATE
INCULPATE
INCUMBENT
INCURABLE
INCURIOUS
INCURSION
INDUCTION
INDUCTIVE
INFURIATE
INFUSIBLE
INJUSTICE
INSURABLE
INSURANCE
INSURGENT
INTUITION
INTUMESCE
LIQUIDATE
LUXURIANT
LUXURIATE
MAJUSCULE

MATUTINAL
MINUSCULE
MINUTEMAN
NATURALLY
OBFUSCATE
OBJURGATE
OCCULTISM
OCCUPANCY
OMBUDSMAN
PECUNIARY
PENURIOUS
PITUITARY
PLAUSIBLE
PNEUMATIC
PNEUMONIA
PSEUDONYM
RECUMBENT
RECURSION
REDUCTION
REDUNDANT
REFURBISH
RELUCTANT
REPUDIATE
REPUGNANT
REPULSION
REPULSIVE
REPUTABLE
REQUISITE
RESURRECT
REVULSION
SATURNINE
SCOUNDREL
SEPULCHER
SEPULTURE
SEQUESTER
SHRUBBERY
SINUSITIS
SITUATION
SLAUGHTER
STRUCTURE
TROUSSEAU
UNGUARDED
UNRUFFLED
UNTUTORED
VALUATION
VISUALIZE
VOLUNTARY
VOLUNTEER
BELVEDERE
CALVINISM
CHEVALIER
CHIVALRIC
CONVIVIAL
CURVATURE
ELEVATION
FLAVORING
FRIVOLOUS

GALVANISM
GALVANIZE
GRAVEYARD
GRAVITATE
HELVETIAN
HELVETICA
LEAVENING
MARVELOUS
PREVALENT
PREVERBAL
PREVISION
PRIVATEER
PRIVATION
PRIVILEGE
PROVENCAL
PROVENDER
PROVIDENT
PROVISION
PROVOLONE
PULVERIZE
SALVATION
SCAVENGER
SERVITUDE
STEVEDORE
SURVEYING
UNIVALENT
UNIVERSAL
VELVETEEN
WOLVERINE
AIRWORTHY
BLOWTORCH
DARWINISM
FLOWCHART
FLOWERPOT
FORWARDER
KNOWLEDGE
MIDWINTER
NORWEGIAN
OUTWARDLY
PLOWSHARE
RAUWOLFIA
SEAWORTHY
SHOWPIECE
SHOWPLACE
SNOWDRIFT
SNOWFIELD
SNOWFLAKE
SNOWSTORM
TRIWEEKLY
VIEWPOINT
DEOXIDIZE
PROXIMATE
PROXIMITY
ANHYDROUS
BERYLLIUM
BODYGUARD
CHRYSALIS
COPYRIGHT
COTYLEDON
DEHYDRATE
DHRYSTONE
EASYGOING
GRAYBEARD
GREYHOUND
HOLYSTONE
LABYRINTH
LAZYBONES
PLAYHOUSE
PLAYTHING
POLYESTER
POLYGRAPH
POLYPHONY
PRAYERFUL
BRAZILIAN
MEZZANINE
PIZZICATO
QUIZZICAL
TANZANIAN

### 5TH LETTER

AERIALIST
AGGRAVATE
ALABASTER
ANIMALISM
ANIMATION
ANOMALOUS
ARCHANGEL
ASTRADDLE
ASTRAKHAN
AVALANCHE
AVOCATION
BALDACHIN
BALLADEER
BARBARIAN
BARBARISM
BARBAROUS
BARCAROLE
BARRACUDA
BATTALION
BELEAGUER
BESPANGLE
BESPATTER
BOMBAZINE
BRITANNIC
BRUTALIZE
BUCCANEER
BULGARIAN
BYSTANDER
CAMPANILE
CANTABILE
CARNATION
CASTANETS
CATHARSIS
CATHARTIC
CAUCASIAN
CAUSATION
CELLARAGE
CERTAINTY
CESSATION
CHAPARRAL
CHARABANC
CHARACTER
CHEVALIER
CHICANERY
CHIVALRIC
CIRCADIAN
COCKATIEL
COFEATURE
COLLATION
COMMANDER
COMPANION
CONTAGION
CONTAINER
CORIANDER
CREMATORY
CURVATURE
CYCLAMATE
DALMATION
DAMNATION
DEFEATISM
DEFLATION
DISMANTLE
DISPARAGE
DISPARATE
DOGMATISM
DRAMATIZE
EDUCATION
ELEVATION
EMBRASURE
EMPHASIZE
ENGRAVING
ESPLANADE
EUCHARIST
EXPIATORY
EXTRADITE
EXTRAVERT
FANTASIZE
FANTASTIC
FEUDALISM
FEUDATORY
FIRMAMENT
FLOTATION
FORGATHER
FORMALISM
FORMALITY
FORMALIZE
FORMATION
FORMATIVE
FORWARDER
FRICASSEE
GALLANTRY
GALVANISM
GALVANIZE
GENEALOGY
GERIATRIC
GERMANIUM
GESTATION
GODFATHER
GODPARENT
GRADATION
GRENADIER
GRENADINE
GUARANTEE
GUARANTOR
GUSTATORY
GYMNASIUM
GYRFALCON
HAPHAZARD
HERBALIST
HERBARIUM
HEREAFTER
HIERARCHY
HISTAMINE
HORTATIVE
HORTATORY
HUNGARIAN
HUSBANDRY
HYDRANGEA
HYDRAULIC
ICELANDER
ICELANDIC
IMITATION
IMITATIVE
INFLATION
INSTANTER
INSTANTLY
ITERATION
JESSAMINE
JUXTAPOSE
LAUDATORY
LEVIATHAN
LIBRARIAN
LINEAMENT
LUCRATIVE
MANDATORY
MANGANESE
MANHANDLE
MANHATTAN
MARGARINE
MARMALADE
MECHANICS
MECHANISM
MECHANIZE
MENTALITY
MERGANSER
MESCALINE
METHADONE
MEZZANINE
MINIATURE
MISHANDLE
MISMANAGE
NARRATIVE
NECTARINE
NEURALGIA
NONPAREIL
NORMALIZE
NORMATIVE
NOSTALGIA
OLIGARCHY
ONSLAUGHT
OPERATION
OPERATIVE
ORGIASTIC
ORPHANAGE
OSTRACIZE
OUTWARDLY
OVIPAROUS
OXIDATION
PALLADIUM
PANHANDLE
PAYMASTER
PEGMATITE
PERMANENT
PHALAROPE
PHILANDER
PHILATELY
PICKABACK
PINEAPPLE
PISTACHIO
PLURALITY
PLURALIZE
POETASTER
POMPADOUR
PRECANCEL
PREDATION
PREDATORY
PRELAUNCH
PREMATURE
PREVALENT
PRIMARILY
PRIVATEER
PRIVATION
PROBATION
PROBATIVE
PROFANITY
PROPAGATE
PURGATION
PURGATIVE
PURGATORY
RACIALISM
RECTANGLE
REFRACTOR
REHEARING
REHEARSAL
RIGMAROLE
ROUMANIAN
RUINATION
SACRAMENT
SALVATION
SASSAFRAS
SCHNAUZER
SEAFARING
SECTARIAN
SENSATION
SIGNALIZE
SIGNALMAN
SIGNATORY
SIGNATURE
SIMPATICO
SITUATION
SKYJACKER
SOCIALISM
SOCIALITE
SOCIALIZE
SQUEAMISH
STOMACHER
STOMACHIC
STREAMBED
STREAMLET
SUBMARINE
SUMMARIZE
SUMMATION
SYLLABIFY
TALKATIVE
TANTALIZE
TANZANIAN
TARPAULIN
TENTATIVE
TERMAGANT
TERRARIUM
TESTAMENT
THESAURUS
TREMATODE
TURNABOUT
TUSCARORA
ULTRAHIGH
ULTRAPURE
UNCEASING
UNCHARTED
UNGUARDED
UNHEALTHY
UNITARIAN
UNIVALENT
UNLEARNED
UNMEANING
UNSCATHED
UNSHACKLE
UNSPARING
VALUATION
VANDALISM
VANDALIZE
VARIATION
VASSALAGE
VERBALIZE
VERNALIZE
VERSATILE
VIBRATION
VIBRATORY
VIOLATION
VISUALIZE
VOLCANISM
VULCANISM
VULCANIZE
VULGARIAN
VULGARISM
VULGARITY
VULGARIZE
ADIABATIC
ADUMBRATE
BACKBOARD
BASEBOARD
BILLBOARD
BLUEBERRY
BLUEBLACK
BOOTBLACK
BUCKBOARD
CALABOOSE
CALIBRATE
CANEBRAKE
CARDBOARD
CARIBBEAN
CELEBRATE
CELEBRITY
CEREBRATE
CHILBLAIN
CLAPBOARD
CLIPBOARD
CRANBERRY
DASHBOARD
DISOBLIGE
DUCKBOARD
ESTABLISH
FIREBRAND
FIREBREAK
FIREBRICK
FOOTBOARD
FREEBOARD
GOLDBRICK
GRAYBEARD
HAIRBRUSH
HARDBOARD
HARDBOUND
HEADBOARD
HIDEBOUND
HILLBILLY
ILLIBERAL
INCUBATOR
IRONBOUND
JAILBREAK
LAMEBRAIN
LAZYBONES
LIFEBLOOD
MOLDBOARD
NOSEBLEED
OVERBLOWN
OVERBOARD
PHLEBITIS
POURBOIRE
PRESBYTER
PUREBLOOD
RASPBERRY
REIMBURSE
ROADBLOCK
ROCKBOUND
SAGEBRUSH
SANDBLAST
SHIPBOARD
SHRUBBERY
SIDEBOARD
SIDEBURNS
SIGNBOARD
SOFTBOUND
STARBOARD
SURFBOARD
TENEBROUS
THUMBNAIL
THUMBTACK
WALLBOARD
WASHBASIN
WASHBOARD
WINDBLOWN
WINDBREAK
WOODBLOCK
WORKBENCH
ADDICTION
ADJECTIVE
AFFECTING
AFFECTION
ANARCHISM
ANTECHOIR
ANTICLINE
ARTICHOKE
ARTICULAR
ASSOCIATE
ATROCIOUS
AUDACIOUS
AURICULAR
AUTOCRACY
AVUNCULAR
BINOCULAR
BLEACHERS
BRONCHIAL
CAPACIOUS

CAPACITOR
CATACLYSM
CATECHISM
CERECLOTH
CHANCROID
CHURCHMAN
CONSCIOUS
CONSCRIPT
CRESCENDO
DEDUCTION
DEFECTIVE
DEFICIENT
DEJECTION
DELICIOUS
DEMOCRACY
DESECRATE
DESICCANT
DESICCATE
DETECTIVE
DIRECTION
DIRECTIVE
DIRECTORY
DISHCLOTH
EFFECTIVE
EFFECTUAL
EFFICIENT
ENDOCRINE
ENUNCIATE
EPISCOPAL
EXPECTANT
FEROCIOUS
FIDUCIARY
FINICKING
FLOWCHART
FORECLOSE
FRANCHISE
FUNICULAR
GALACTOSE
HAIRCLOTH
HANDCLASP
HANDCRAFT
HARDCOVER
HOLOCAUST
HOPSCOTCH
HYPOCRISY
INDUCTION
INDUCTIVE
INFECTION
INJECTION
INNOCENCE
INNOCUOUS
INVECTIVE
IRASCIBLE
ISOSCELES
JUDICIARY
JUDICIOUS
KILOCYCLE
LATECOMER
LAUNCHPAD
LOINCLOTH
LUDICROUS
MALACHITE
MASOCHISM
MEDICABLE
MEDICINAL
MEGACYCLE
MUNICIPAL
OBJECTIFY
OBJECTIVE
OFFICIANT
OFFICIATE
OFFICIOUS
OLFACTORY
OVERCLOUD
PARACHUTE
PAROCHIAL
POINCIANA
POLICEMAN
PREOCCUPY
PRESCHOOL
PRESCRIBE
PRINCIPAL
PRINCIPLE
PROSCRIBE
RAPACIOUS
REDACTION
REDUCTION
REFECTION
REFECTORY
RELUCTANT
RESECTION
REVOCABLE
SACKCLOTH
SAGACIOUS
SAILCLOTH
SALACIOUS
SCUTCHEON
SEBACEOUS
SELECTION
SELECTMAN
SEMICOLON
SILICEOUS
SILICOSIS
SLUICEWAY
SOLICITOR
STANCHION
STEPCHILD
STRICTURE
STRUCTURE
SUBSCRIBE
SUBSCRIPT
SWITCHMAN
TENACIOUS
THEOCRACY
TREACHERY
TRENCHANT
TRUNCHEON
UNDECEIVE
UNDECIDED
URTICARIA
VASECTOMY
VERACIOUS
VIVACIOUS
VORACIOUS
WASHCLOTH
WINDCHILL
WISECRACK
WOODCHUCK
WOODCRAFT
ABANDONED
ACCIDENCE
AERODROME
AFFIDAVIT
AMENDMENT
ANHYDROUS
ARMADILLO
ASSIDUOUS
BLINDFOLD
BLOODBATH
BLOODLINE
BLOODROOT
BLOODSHED
BLOODSHOT
BOARDWALK
BOONDOCKS
BROADBAND
BROADCAST
BROADLOOM
BROADSIDE
BROADTAIL
CHILDHOOD
CHONDRITE
CHONDRULE
DAREDEVIL
DECADENCE
DECIDUOUS
DEHYDRATE
EPHEDRINE
EXPEDIENT
EXPEDITER
FLOODGATE
FOUNDLING
FRIEDCAKE
GRANDIOSE
GUARDROOM
GUARDSMAN
HAMADRYAD
HEADDRESS
IMMEDIACY
IMMEDIATE
IMPEDANCE
INCIDENCE
INSIDIOUS
INVIDIOUS
IRRADIATE
JAUNDICED
JURIDICAL
MALADROIT
MEGADEATH
MELODIOUS
MELODRAMA
OMBUDSMAN
OVERDRAFT
OVERDRIVE
PSEUDONYM
REPUDIATE
RESIDENCE
RESIDENCY
RESIDUARY
ROUNDELAY
ROUNDWORM
SNOWDRIFT
SPEEDBOAT
SPEEDWELL
SPINDLING
SPINDRIFT
STANDPIPE
STEADFAST
SWORDFISH
SWORDPLAY
SWORDSMAN
SWORDTAIL
TAXIDERMY
TREADMILL
VERIDICAL
WITHDRAWN
WORLDLING
WORLDWIDE
ABATEMENT
ACCRETION
ADDRESSEE
AFORESAID
AGGREGATE
AGREEABLE
AGREEMENT
ANGLEWORM
ANKLEBONE
APPLEJACK
APPLETALK
APPREHEND
ARABESQUE
ARCHENEMY
ARCHETYPE
ASAFETIDA
ATHLETICS
ATONEMENT
AUTHENTIC
BACTERIUM
BALLERINA
BANDEROLE
BARKEEPER
BARTENDER
BEDFELLOW
BEEFEATER
BEEKEEPER
BELVEDERE
BERKELIUM
BOOMERANG
BOULEVARD
BROKERAGE
BURLESQUE
BUTTERCUP
BUTTERFAT
BUTTERFLY
BUTTERNUT
CABLEGRAM
CARNELIAN
CARPENTER
CARPETBAG
CARPETING
CASSEROLE
CATHEDRAL
CAUTERIZE
CEASELESS
CENTENARY
CENTESIMO
CHAMELEON
COFFEEPOT
COFFERDAM
COLLEAGUE
COLLECTED
COLLEGIAN
COLLEGIUM
COMPETENT
CONCERNED
CONCERTED
CONDENSER
CONFESSOR
CONGENIAL
CONGERIES
CONSENSUS
CONTENTED
COOPERATE
CORRELATE
CRITERION
CULLENDER
CUPBEARER
DAMSELFLY
DANDELION
DANGEROUS
DECREMENT
DEPRECATE
DEPRESSED
DESCENDER
DESPERADO
DESPERATE
DESUETUDE
DEUTERIUM
DEXTERITY
DEXTEROUS
DIALECTIC
DIAMETRIC
DIETETICS
DIFFERENT
DIPTEROUS
DISMEMBER
DISREGARD
DISREPAIR
DISREPUTE
DISSECTED
DISSEMBLE
DISSENTER
DISTEMPER
DITHERING
DIXIELAND
DROMEDARY
DYSPEPSIA
EGGBEATER
ENSHEATHE
ENUMERATE
ENWREATHE
EPICENTER
EPIDERMIS
EROGENOUS
EUPHEMISM
EUTHENICS
EXCHEQUER
EXCREMENT
EXOGENOUS
EXONERATE
EXPLETIVE
EXTREMISM
EXTREMITY
EXUBERANT
FALSEHOOD
FARSEEING
FASTENING
FINGERING
FINGERTIP
FISHERMAN
FLAGELLUM
FLAGEOLET
FLOWERPOT
FRAMEWORK
FRATERNAL
GIBBERISH
GOLDENROD
GRAPESHOT
GRAPEVINE
GRAVEYARD
GROTESQUE
GUIDEBOOK
GUIDELINE
HAMMERTOE
HAPPENING
HARLEQUIN
HELLEBORE
HELLENISM
HELVETIAN
HELVETICA
HORSEBACK
HORSEHAIR
HORSEHIDE
HORSEPLAY
HORSESHOE
HORSETAIL
HORSEWHIP
HOTHEADED
HOUSEBOAT
HOUSECOAT
HOUSEHOLD
HOUSEMAID
HOUSEWIFE
HOUSEWORK
HYPHENATE
HYSTERICS
IMPLEMENT
IMPRECATE
IMPRECISE
INCLEMENT
INCREMENT
INELEGANT
INFLEXION
INGLENOOK
INNKEEPER
ISRAELITE
ITINERANT
ITINERARY
JITTERBUG
LEASEHOLD
LEAVENING
LITHESOME
LITTERBUG
LONGEVITY
MAGNESIUM
MAGNETISM
MAGNETITE
MAGNETIZE
MALLEABLE
MANNEQUIN
MANNERISM
MANOEUVRE
MARVELOUS
MASTERFUL
MERCENARY
MERCERIZE
MESMERIZE
MESSENGER
MINCEMEAT
MISBEHAVE
MOUSETRAP
MURDEROUS
NONPERSON
NONREADER
NORWEGIAN
NURSEMAID
ORCHESTRA
OURSELVES
OXYGENATE
PALAESTRA
PASSENGER
PASSERINE
PEACETIME
PENTECOST
PERMEABLE
PERPETUAL
PERSECUTE
PERSEVERE
PHONETICS
PIECEMEAL
PIECEWORK
PIGHEADED
PIMPERNEL
PLACEKICK
PLACEMENT
PLANELOAD
PLANETOID
POLYESTER
PONDEROUS
PORCELAIN
POSTERIOR
POSTERITY
PRAYERFUL
PRECEDENT
PRECEDING
PRECENTOR
PRECEPTOR
PRERECORD
PRESENTLY
PREVERBAL
PRICELESS
PROCEDURE
PROCESSOR
PROFESSOR
PROJECTOR
PROMENADE
PROPELLER
PROSECUTE
PROSELYTE
PROTECTOR
PROVENCAL
PROVENDER
PULVERIZE
PUPPETEER
RACKETEER
RANGELAND

RASTERIZE
RECHERCHE
REFLECTOR
REFLEXIVE
REITERATE
REPLENISH
REPLETION
REPREHEND
REPRESENT
RIDGEPOLE
RUTHENIUM
SCAPEGOAT
SCARECROW
SCAVENGER
SCHEELITE
SCHLEMIEL
SCREENING
SECRETARY
SECRETION
SECRETIVE
SEGREGATE
SEPTEMBER
SEQUESTER
SHAKEDOWN
SHAPELESS
SHAREWARE
SHOREBIRD
SNAKEBIRD
SNAKEBITE
SPACESHIP
SPICEBUSH
SPOKESMAN
STALEMATE
STATEMENT
STATEROOM
STATESIDE
STATESMAN
STEVEDORE
STOREROOM
STREETCAR
SUCCESSOR
SUFFERING
SUNSEEKER
SUPREMACY
SURRENDER
SURVEYING
SUSPENDER
SYSTEMIZE
TABLELAND
TABLEWARE
TANGERINE
TEAKETTLE
TEMPERATE
TENDERIZE
THEREFORE
THEREFROM
THEREUNTO
THEREUPON
THEREWITH
THREEFOLD
THREESOME
TIMBERING
TINDERBOX
TRADEMARK
TRADESMAN
TRAGEDIAN
TRAPEZOID
TRIBESMAN
TRIMESTER
TRIWEEKLY
UNBLESSED
UNCLEANLY
UNFEELING
UNFLEDGED
UNISEXUAL
UNIVERSAL
UNSHEATHE
VARIEGATE
VELVETEEN
VENGEANCE
VERTEBRAL
VILLENAGE
VOICELESS
WASTELAND
WEDNESDAY
WHALEBOAT
WHALEBONE
WHEREFORE
WHEREUPON
WHEREWITH
WHITEBAIT
WHITEFISH
WHITEHALL
WHITEHEAD
WHITENESS
WHITETAIL
WHITEWALL
WHITEWASH
WHITEWOOD
WHOLESALE
WHOLESOME
WINTERIZE
WOEBEGONE
WOLVERINE
WONDERFUL
YESTERDAY
ARCHFIEND
ARTIFICER
BACKFIELD
BAREFACED
BRIEFCASE
BULLFIGHT
BULLFINCH
CHAFFINCH
CHAUFFEUR
CHIEFTAIN
COALFIELD
COCKFIGHT
COIFFEUSE
DISAFFECT
DUMBFOUND
FOREFRONT
GENUFLECT
GOLDFIELD
GOLDFINCH
HEADFIRST
HOARFROST
INEFFABLE
MAINFRAME
MANIFESTO
PORTFOLIO
PROOFREAD
REENFORCE
REINFORCE
SANGFROID
SAXIFRAGE
SEMIFINAL
SEMIFLUID
SKINFLINT
SNOWFIELD
SNOWFLAKE
UNRUFFLED
WIREFRAME
ALLIGATOR
ALONGSIDE
AMBIGUOUS
ANALGESIA
ANALGESIC
AUTOGRAPH
BAROGRAPH
BENIGHTED
BENIGNANT
BLUEGRASS
BODYGUARD
BOURGEOIS
CLERGYMAN
CRABGRASS
CRYOGENIC
DELIGHTED
DEMAGOGUE
DENIGRATE
DESIGNATE
DESIGNING
DIRIGIBLE
DOWNGRADE
EASYGOING
EGREGIOUS
EMERGENCY
ENERGETIC
ENERGIZER
ENLIGHTEN
EVERGLADE
EVERGREEN
FLEDGLING
FOREGOING
FRANGIBLE
GELIGNITE
GLENGARRY
GROSGRAIN
HOLOGRAPH
HOMEGROWN
HOMOGRAPH
HOURGLASS
ILLEGIBLE
ILLOGICAL
IMMIGRANT
IMMIGRATE
INAUGURAL
INCOGNITO
INDIGNANT
INDIGNITY
INORGANIC
INTEGRATE
INTEGRITY
IRREGULAR
ISINGLASS
LIFEGUARD
LITIGIOUS
MALIGNANT
MENAGERIE
MONOGRAPH
NAVIGABLE
ORANGEADE
PANEGYRIC
PARAGRAPH
PAREGORIC
PEDAGOGUE
POLYGRAPH
PRONGHORN
RECOGNIZE
RELIGIOUS
REPUGNANT
SAFEGUARD
SERIGRAPH
SLAUGHTER
SLINGSHOT
SPRIGHTLY
SYNAGOGUE
TELEGENIC
TELEGRAPH
UNSIGHTLY
VAINGLORY
WORKGROUP
WRONGDOER
YOUNGLING
YOUNGSTER
ZEITGEIST
ZWINGLIAN
AESTHETIC
ALCOHOLIC
ALMSHOUSE
ANOPHELES
BACCHANAL
BAKSHEESH
BATHHOUSE
BEACHHEAD
BIRDHOUSE
BIRTHMARK
BIRTHRATE
BOLSHEVIK
BROCHETTE
BRUSHWOOD
CANTHARIS
CATCHMENT
CATCHWORD
CHOPHOUSE
CIRRHOSIS
CLUBHOUSE
COONHOUND
CUTTHROAT
DEATHBLOW
DEATHLESS
DIAPHRAGM
DIATHERMY
DISCHARGE
EARTHLING
EARTHWARD
EARTHWORK
EARTHWORM
ESOPHAGUS
FARMHOUSE
FIREHOUSE
FLASHBACK
FLASHBULB
FLASHCUBE
FLASHTUBE
FLOPHOUSE
FOOLHARDY
FORTHWITH
FRIGHTFUL
GAUCHERIE
GREYHOUND
HATCHMENT
HITCHHIKE
HOREHOUND
HUNCHBACK
KILOHERTZ
LANTHANUM
LOATHSOME
LUNCHROOM
MATCHBOOK
MATCHLOCK
MATCHWOOD
MEGAHERTZ
MISCHANCE
MOUTHPART
MOUTHWASH
NORTHEAST
NORTHWEST
NOTCHBACK
PACKHORSE
PANTHEISM
PARCHMENT
PATCHWORK
PENTHOUSE
PERCHANCE
PESTHOUSE
PITCHFORK
PLAYHOUSE
POORHOUSE
POSTHASTE
PRESHRUNK
PROPHETIC
PSYCHOSIS
RACEHORSE
RANCHLAND
ROUGHNECK
SACCHARIN
SOUTHEAST
SOUTHWEST
SPAGHETTI
SURCHARGE
SYNTHESIS
SYNTHETIC
THIGHBONE
TOLLHOUSE
TOOTHACHE
TOOTHPICK
TOOTHSOME
TOUCHDOWN
VOUCHSAFE
WAREHOUSE
WASHHOUSE
WATCHBAND
WATCHCASE
WATCHWORD
WHICHEVER
WOLFHOUND
WORKHORSE
WORKHOUSE
WORTHLESS
XANTHIPPE
ZUCCHETTO
ABOMINATE
ABORIGINE
ACCLIMATE
ACCLIVITY
ACQUIESCE
ADJOINING
AESTIVATE
ALUMINIUM
ALUMINIZE
AMERICANA
AMERICIUM
AMPHIBIAN
AMPHIBOLE
AMPLITUDE
ANGLICIZE
ANGUISHED
ANNUITANT
APPLIANCE
APPLICANT
APPOINTEE
ARCHITECT
ARCHIVIST
ATTAINDER
ATTRIBUTE
ATTRITION
BADMINTON
BAILIWICK
BARRICADE
BARRISTER
BASTINADO
BEATITUDE
BEDRIDDEN
BELLICOSE
BILLIARDS
BRAZILIAN
CABRIOLET
CALCIMINE
CALVINISM
CANDIDACY
CANDIDATE
CAPRICCIO
CAPTIVATE
CARCINOMA
CARNIVORA
CARNIVORE
CARTILAGE
CASTIGATE
CASUISTRY
CENTIGRAM
CENTIPEDE
CERTITUDE
CHEMISTRY
CHORISTER
CLINICIAN
COALITION
COCHINEAL
COGNITION
COLLIMATE
COMMINGLE
COMMISSAR
COMMITTEE
CONCIERGE
CONDIMENT
CONDITION
CONFIDANT
CONTINENT
CONTINUAL
CONTINUUM
CONVIVIAL
CORTISONE
CRETINISM
CRITICISM
CRITICIZE
CRUCIFORM
CULMINATE
CULTIVATE
CUNEIFORM
DARWINISM
DECEITFUL
DECLIVITY
DENTITION
DEOXIDIZE
DERRINGER
DESTITUTE
DETRIMENT
DIFFICULT
DIFFIDENT
DIGNIFIED
DIGNITARY
DISFIGURE
DISSIDENT
DISSIPATE
DORMITORY
DUPLICATE
DUPLICITY
ELIMINATE
ELUCIDATE
ENCHILADA
ERADICATE
ERUDITION
EUCLIDEAN
EXPLICATE
EXQUISITE
EXTRICATE
EXTRINSIC
FABRICATE
FACSIMILE
FASCINATE
FEBRIFUGE
FERTILIZE
FESTIVITY
FOREIGNER
FORGIVING
FORTITUDE
FULMINATE
FUNGICIDE
FURNITURE
GALLINULE
GALLIVANT
GARNISHEE
GARNITURE
GENTILITY
GERMICIDE

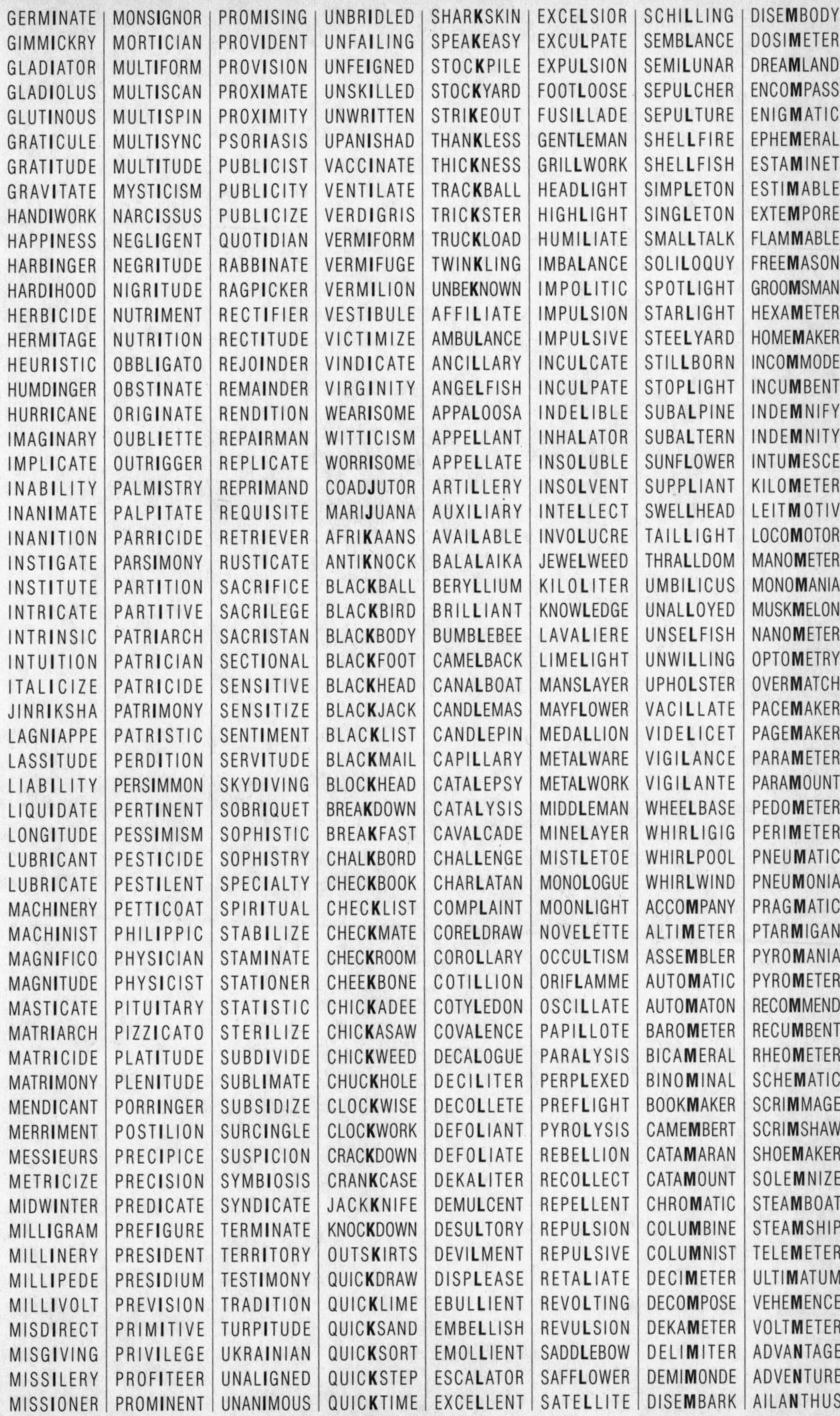

GERMINATE
GIMMICKRY
GLADIATOR
GLADIOLUS
GLUTINOUS
GRATICULE
GRATITUDE
GRAVITATE
HANDIWORK
HAPPINESS
HARBINGER
HARDIHOOD
HERBICIDE
HERMITAGE
HEURISTIC
HUMDINGER
HURRICANE
IMAGINARY
IMPLICATE
INABILITY
INANIMATE
INANITION
INSTIGATE
INSTITUTE
INTRICATE
INTRINSIC
INTUITION
ITALICIZE
JINRIKSHA
LAGNIAPPE
LASSITUDE
LIABILITY
LIQUIDATE
LONGITUDE
LUBRICANT
LUBRICATE
MACHINERY
MACHINIST
MAGNIFICO
MAGNITUDE
MASTICATE
MATRIARCH
MATRICIDE
MATRIMONY
MENDICANT
MERRIMENT
MESSIEURS
METRICIZE
MIDWINTER
MILLIGRAM
MILLINERY
MILLIPEDE
MILLIVOLT
MISDIRECT
MISGIVING
MISSILERY
MISSIONER
MONSIGNOR
MORTICIAN
MULTIFORM
MULTISCAN
MULTISPIN
MULTISYNC
MULTITUDE
MYSTICISM
NARCISSUS
NEGLIGENT
NEGRITUDE
NIGRITUDE
NUTRIMENT
NUTRITION
OBBLIGATO
OBSTINATE
ORIGINATE
OUBLIETTE
OUTRIGGER
PALMISTRY
PALPITATE
PARRICIDE
PARSIMONY
PARTITION
PARTITIVE
PATRIARCH
PATRICIAN
PATRICIDE
PATRIMONY
PATRISTIC
PERDITION
PERSIMMON
PERTINENT
PESSIMISM
PESTICIDE
PESTILENT
PETTICOAT
PHILIPPIC
PHYSICIAN
PHYSICIST
PITUITARY
PIZZICATO
PLATITUDE
PLENITUDE
PORRINGER
POSTILION
PRECIPICE
PRECISION
PREDICATE
PREFIGURE
PRESIDENT
PRESIDIUM
PREVISION
PRIMITIVE
PRIVILEGE
PROFITEER
PROMINENT
PROMISING
PROVIDENT
PROVISION
PROXIMATE
PROXIMITY
PSORIASIS
PUBLICIST
PUBLICITY
PUBLICIZE
QUOTIDIAN
RABBINATE
RAGPICKER
RECTIFIER
RECTITUDE
REJOINDER
REMAINDER
RENDITION
REPAIRMAN
REPLICATE
REPRIMAND
REQUISITE
RETRIEVER
RUSTICATE
SACRIFICE
SACRILEGE
SACRISTAN
SECTIONAL
SENSITIVE
SENSITIZE
SENTIMENT
SERVITUDE
SKYDIVING
SOBRIQUET
SOPHISTIC
SOPHISTRY
SPECIALTY
SPIRITUAL
STABILIZE
STAMINATE
STATIONER
STATISTIC
STERILIZE
SUBDIVIDE
SUBLIMATE
SUBSIDIZE
SURCINGLE
SUSPICION
SYMBIOSIS
SYNDICATE
TERMINATE
TERRITORY
TESTIMONY
TRADITION
TURPITUDE
UKRAINIAN
UNALIGNED
UNANIMOUS
UNBRIDLED
UNFAILING
UNFEIGNED
UNSKILLED
UNWRITTEN
UPANISHAD
VACCINATE
VENTILATE
VERDIGRIS
VERMIFORM
VERMIFUGE
VERMILION
VESTIBULE
VICTIMIZE
VINDICATE
VIRGINITY
WEARISOME
WITTICISM
WORRISOME
COADJUTOR
MARIJUANA
AFRIKAANS
ANTIKNOCK
BLACKBALL
BLACKBIRD
BLACKBODY
BLACKFOOT
BLACKHEAD
BLACKJACK
BLACKLIST
BLACKMAIL
BLOCKHEAD
BREAKDOWN
BREAKFAST
CHALKBORD
CHECKBOOK
CHECKLIST
CHECKMATE
CHECKROOM
CHEEKBONE
CHICKADEE
CHICKASAW
CHICKWEED
CHUCKHOLE
CLOCKWISE
CLOCKWORK
CRACKDOWN
CRANKCASE
JACKKNIFE
KNOCKDOWN
OUTSKIRTS
QUICKDRAW
QUICKLIME
QUICKSAND
QUICKSORT
QUICKSTEP
QUICKTIME
SHARKSKIN
SPEAKEASY
STOCKPILE
STOCKYARD
STRIKEOUT
THANKLESS
THICKNESS
TRACKBALL
TRICKSTER
TRUCKLOAD
TWINKLING
UNBEKNOWN
AFFILIATE
AMBULANCE
ANCILLARY
ANGELFISH
APPALOOSA
APPELLANT
APPELLATE
ARTILLERY
AUXILIARY
AVAILABLE
BALALAIKA
BERYLLIUM
BRILLIANT
BUMBLEBEE
CAMELBACK
CANALBOAT
CANDLEMAS
CANDLEPIN
CAPILLARY
CATALEPSY
CATALYSIS
CAVALCADE
CHALLENGE
CHARLATAN
COMPLAINT
CORELDRAW
COROLLARY
COTILLION
COTYLEDON
COVALENCE
DECALOGUE
DECILITER
DECOLLETE
DEFOLIANT
DEFOLIATE
DEKALITER
DEMULCENT
DESULTORY
DEVILMENT
DISPLEASE
EBULLIENT
EMBELLISH
EMOLLIENT
ESCALATOR
EXCELLENT
EXCELSIOR
EXCULPATE
EXPULSION
FOOTLOOSE
FUSILLADE
GENTLEMAN
GRILLWORK
HEADLIGHT
HIGHLIGHT
HUMILIATE
IMBALANCE
IMPOLITIC
IMPULSION
IMPULSIVE
INCULCATE
INCULPATE
INDELIBLE
INHALATOR
INSOLUBLE
INSOLVENT
INTELLECT
INVOLUCRE
JEWELWEED
KILOLITER
KNOWLEDGE
LAVALIERE
LIMELIGHT
MANSLAYER
MAYFLOWER
MEDALLION
METALWARE
METALWORK
MIDDLEMAN
MINELAYER
MISTLETOE
MONOLOGUE
MOONLIGHT
NOVELETTE
OCCULTISM
ORIFLAMME
OSCILLATE
PAPILLOTE
PARALYSIS
PERPLEXED
PREFLIGHT
PYROLYSIS
REBELLION
RECOLLECT
REPELLENT
REPULSION
REPULSIVE
RETALIATE
REVOLTING
REVULSION
SADDLEBOW
SAFFLOWER
SATELLITE
SCHILLING
SEMBLANCE
SEMILUNAR
SEPULCHER
SEPULTURE
SHELLFIRE
SHELLFISH
SIMPLETON
SINGLETON
SMALLTALK
SOLILOQUY
SPOTLIGHT
STARLIGHT
STEELYARD
STILLBORN
STOPLIGHT
SUBALPINE
SUBALTERN
SUNFLOWER
SUPPLIANT
SWELLHEAD
TAILLIGHT
THRALLDOM
UMBILICUS
UNALLOYED
UNSELFISH
UNWILLING
UPHOLSTER
VACILLATE
VIDELICET
VIGILANCE
VIGILANTE
WHEELBASE
WHIRLIGIG
WHIRLPOOL
WHIRLWIND
ACCOMPANY
ALTIMETER
ASSEMBLER
AUTOMATIC
AUTOMATON
BAROMETER
BICAMERAL
BINOMINAL
BOOKMAKER
CAMEMBERT
CATAMARAN
CATAMOUNT
CHROMATIC
COLUMBINE
COLUMNIST
DECIMETER
DECOMPOSE
DEKAMETER
DELIMITER
DEMIMONDE
DISEMBARK
DISEMBODY
DOSIMETER
DREAMLAND
ENCOMPASS
ENIGMATIC
EPHEMERAL
ESTAMINET
ESTIMABLE
EXTEMPORE
FLAMMABLE
FREEMASON
GROOMSMAN
HEXAMETER
HOMEMAKER
INCOMMODE
INCUMBENT
INDEMNIFY
INDEMNITY
INTUMESCE
KILOMETER
LEITMOTIV
LOCOMOTOR
MANOMETER
MONOMANIA
MUSKMELON
NANOMETER
OPTOMETRY
OVERMATCH
PACEMAKER
PAGEMAKER
PARAMETER
PARAMOUNT
PEDOMETER
PERIMETER
PNEUMATIC
PNEUMONIA
PRAGMATIC
PTARMIGAN
PYROMANIA
PYROMETER
RECOMMEND
RECUMBENT
RHEOMETER
SCHEMATIC
SCRIMMAGE
SCRIMSHAW
SHOEMAKER
SOLEMNIZE
STEAMBOAT
STEAMSHIP
TELEMETER
ULTIMATUM
VEHEMENCE
VOLTMETER
ADVANTAGE
ADVENTURE
AILANTHUS

ALGONQUIN
ALIENABLE
ALMANDITE
ANTINOVEL
APPENDAGE
ARGENTINE
ARGENTITE
ASCENDANT
ASCENDERS
ASCENSION
ASSONANCE
ATHENAEUM
ATTENDANT
ATTENTION
ATTENUATE
BICONCAVE
BILINGUAL
BIMONTHLY
BURUNDIAN
CALENDULA
CANONICAL
CELANDINE
CHRONICLE
CLIENTELE
COLONNADE
CONUNDRUM
CUTANEOUS
DAVENPORT
DEBENTURE
DECENNIAL
DECONTROL
DEFENDANT
DEFENSIVE
DELINEATE
DEPENDENT
DETENTION
DETONATOR
DIAGNOSIS
DIMENSION
DISENGAGE
DISINFECT
DOMINANCE
DRAINPIPE
DYSENTERY
ECCENTRIC
EGLANTINE
EMPENNAGE
ERRONEOUS
ESSENTIAL
EXPANSION
EXPANSIVE
EXPENSIVE
EXTENSION
EXTENSIVE
EXTENUATE
FECUNDATE
FINANCIAL
FINANCIER
FORENAMED
FORTNIGHT
GLEANINGS
GREENBACK
GREENBELT
GREENHORN
GREENROOM
GREENWOOD
GROUNDHOG
GROUNDING
HACKNEYED
HUMANKIND
INCENTIVE
INDENTION
INDENTURE
INFANTILE
INGENIOUS
INGENUITY
INGENUOUS
INSENSATE
INSINCERE
INSINUATE
INTENDANT
INTENSIFY
INTENSITY
INTENSIVE
INTENTION
INVENTION
INVENTIVE
INVENTORY
LAMINATED
LEGENDARY
LORGNETTE
MACINTOSH
MISINFORM
MOMENTARY
MOMENTOUS
NONENTITY
OFFENSIVE
ONIONSKIN
ORDINANCE
ORIENTATE
OVERNIGHT
PALANQUIN
PECUNIARY
PEKINGESE
PENINSULA
PERENNIAL
PHRENETIC
PLAINTIFF
PLAINTIVE
POSTNATAL
POTENTATE
POTENTIAL
PREGNABLE
PROGNOSIS
RACONTEUR
RECONCILE
RECONDITE
REDUNDANT
REMINISCE
RESONANCE
RESONATOR
RETENTION
RETENTIVE
SATINWOOD
SCOUNDREL
SECONDARY
SEDENTARY
SEMANTICS
SEVENTEEN
SHRINKAGE
SPHINCTER
SPINNAKER
SPLENETIC
SPOONBILL
STRENUOUS
STRONTIUM
TARANTULA
TECHNICAL
TECHNIQUE
TRAINLOAD
TRIENNIAL
TYRANNIZE
TYRANNOUS
UNBENDING
UNCONCERN
UNMINDFUL
VAGINITIS
VALENTINE
VICENNIAL
VOLUNTARY
VOLUNTEER
WAGONETTE
WOMANHOOD
WOMANKIND
WOMANLIKE
WOMENFOLK
AIRMOBILE
AIRWORTHY
ANALOGOUS
ANATOMIZE
ANCHORAGE
ANCHORITE
ANCHORMAN
ANIMOSITY
ANTHOLOGY
APOLOGIZE
ASTROLABE
ASTROLOGY
ASTRONAUT
ASTRONOMY
AUCTORIAL
AUDIOLOGY
AUTHORITY
AUTHORIZE
BAMBOOZLE
BANDOLIER
BATHOLITH
BENTONITE
BETROTHED
BISHOPRIC
CALLOSITY
CANNONADE
CANNONEER
CARBONATE
CARROUSEL
CASSOWARY
CHAMOMILE
CHIROPODY
CHOCOLATE
COLLODION
COMFORTER
COMMODITY
COMMODORE
COMMOTION
COMPONENT
COMPOSITE
COMPOSURE
CONCORDAT
CONCOURSE
CONSONANT
CORMORANT
CORPORATE
CORPOREAL
COSMOGONY
COSMOLOGY
COSMONAUT
COSPONSOR
CRINOLINE
CROCODILE
CUSTODIAL
CUSTODIAN
CUSTOMARY
CUSTOMIZE
CYCLOTRON
DEODORANT
DEODORIZE
DIATOMITE
DICHOTOMY
DIPLOMACY
DISCOMFIT
DISCOURSE
DISHONEST
DISLOCATE
DISSOLUTE
DOBSONFLY
DOCTORATE
DRAGONFLY
ECONOMICS
ECONOMIZE
EDITORIAL
ELABORATE
EMBROCATE
EMBROIDER
ESPIONAGE
ETHIOPIAN
ETHNOLOGY
ETYMOLOGY
EUTROPHIC
EVAPORATE
EVAPORITE
EXPLOSION
EXPLOSIVE
FACTORIAL
FELLOWMAN
FLAVORING
FOLLOWING
FRIVOLOUS
GLAMORIZE
GLYCOSIDE
GODMOTHER
GONDOLIER
GUNCOTTON
GUNPOWDER
HALLOWEEN
HARBORAGE
HARMONICA
HARMONICS
HARMONIUM
HARMONIZE
HECTOGRAM
HISTOGRAM
HISTORIAN
HOBGOBLIN
HOWSOEVER
HYDROFOIL
HYDROLOGY
HYDROXIDE
IMBROGLIO
IMPROMPTU
IMPROVISE
INAMORATA
INGROWING
INTRODUCE
INTROVERT
INVIOLATE
JOBHOLDER
LACCOLITH
LANDOWNER
LEUKOCYTE
LITHOLOGY
MACROCOSM
MARMOREAL
MAUSOLEUM
MELIORATE
METEORITE
METEOROID
METHODIST
METHODIZE
METROLOGY
METRONOME
MICROCOPY
MICROCOSM
MICROFILM
MICROGRAM
MICROSOFT
MICROWAVE
MISGOVERN
MONGOLIAN
MONGOLISM
MONGOLOID
MYTHOLOGY
NARCOTIZE
NECROLOGY
NEOLOGISM
NEUROLOGY
PANTOMIME
PARSONAGE
PASTORALE
PATHOLOGY
PATROLMAN
PATRONAGE
PATRONIZE
PENHOLDER
PERCOLATE
PERFORATE
PERSONAGE
PERSONATE
PERSONIFY
PERSONNEL
PETROLEUM
PETROLOGY
PHEROMONE
PHILOLOGY
PHONOLOGY
PHOTOCELL
PHOTOCOPY
PHOTOPLAY
PICTORIAL
PLUTONIUM
POTBOILER
POTPOURRI
PROBOSCIS
PROCONSUL
PRONOUNCE
PROPONENT
PROTOTYPE
PROTOZOAN
PROVOLONE
PULMONARY
RADIOGRAM
RADIOLOGY
RANDOMIZE
RATIONALE
RAUWOLFIA
RECKONING
RENCONTRE
REPROBATE
REPRODUCE
RETROFIRE
SARTORIAL
SCHOOLBOY
SEASONING
SEAWORTHY
SENIORITY
SHADOWBOX
SKIMOBILE
SKYLOUNGE
SKYROCKET
SOCIOLOGY
SOMNOLENT
SOPHOMORE
SUBNORMAL
SUCCOTASH
SUFFOCATE
SUNBONNET
SUPPOSING
SURROGATE
SYLLOGISM
SYMBOLISM
SYMBOLIZE
SYMPOSIUM
TAUTOLOGY
TECTONICS
TECTONISM
TEMPORARY
TEMPORIZE
TERRORISM
TERRORIZE
THYROXINE
TONSORIAL
TRIFOCALS
TURBOPROP
UNKNOWING
UNSPOTTED
VICTORIAN
VIDEOTAPE
VISCOSITY
VISIONARY
VOODOOISM
WALLOPING
WARBONNET
WARMONGER
WHOSOEVER
ZIRCONIUM
ACROPOLIS
AEROPAUSE
AEROPLANE
AMORPHOUS
ANTIPASTO
ANTIPATHY
AQUAPLANE
ASYMPTOTE
BACKPEDAL
BEDSPREAD
BIOSPHERE
BLASPHEME
BLASPHEMY
BLUEPOINT
BLUEPRINT
BOMBPROOF
BOOKPLATE
CACOPHONY
CHAMPAGNE
CHAMPAIGN
CYTOPLASM
DECEPTION
DISAPPEAR
DOORPLATE
ELLIPSOID
ENRAPTURE
EQUIPMENT
EQUIPOISE
EXCEPTION
EXEMPLARY
EXEMPLIFY
EXOSPHERE
FIREPLACE
FIREPOWER
FIREPROOF
FOOLPROOF
FOOTPRINT
GANGPLANK
GROUPWARE
HAIRPIECE
HALFPENNY
HEADPHONE
HEADPIECE
HOMOPHONE
INCAPABLE
INCEPTION
INCIPIENT
MEGAPHONE
MEGAPIXEL
MENOPAUSE
MONOPLANE
NAMEPLATE
NEWSPAPER
NEWSPRINT
NOSEPIECE
OCCUPANCY
OFFSPRING
OUTSPOKEN
OUTSPREAD
OVERPOWER
OVERPRINT
PENEPLAIN

PERIPHERY
PHOSPHATE
POLYPHONY
PUERPERAL
RECEPTION
RECEPTIVE
RECIPIENT
SAILPLANE
SALTPETER
SANDPAPER
SANDPIPER
SAXOPHONE
SCRAPBOOK
SCRIPTURE
SCULPTURE
SEMAPHORE
SHEEPFOLD
SHEEPSKIN
SHOWPIECE
SHOWPLACE
SIDEPIECE
STRAPLESS
STRAPPING
STRIPLING
SWAMPLAND
SYCOPHANT
TELEPATHY
TELEPHONE
TELEPHONY
TELEPHOTO
TIMEPIECE
TRAPPINGS
TROOPSHIP
UNPOPULAR
VIEWPOINT
WALLPAPER
WILLPOWER
WINDPROOF
WINEPRESS
WORKPLACE
XEROPHYTE
XYLOPHONE
ANTIQUARY
ANTIQUITY
RELIQUARY
ABHORRENT
ABSORBENT
ACCORDION
ADMIRABLE
ADMIRALTY
ADSORBATE
ADSORBENT
ADVERSARY
ADVERSITY
ADVERTISE
AFTERCARE
AFTERDECK
AFTERGLOW
AFTERLIFE
AFTERMATH
AFTERNOON
AFTERWARD
ALGORITHM
ALLERGIST
ALTERNATE
AMBERGRIS
AMPERSAND
ANAEROBIC
ANTARCTIC
APOCRYPHA
APPARATUS
APPERTAIN
APPORTION
ARBORETUM
ARTERIOLE
ARTHRITIS
ARTHROPOD
ASCERTAIN
ASPARAGUS
ASPERSION
ASSERTION
ASSURANCE
BIFURCATE
BIOGRAPHY
BIPARTITE
CALORIFIC
CAPARISON
CARTRIDGE
CATERWAUL
CHEERLESS
CHLORDANE
CIGARETTE
CIGARILLO
CLEARANCE
COCKROACH
COLORCAST
COLORFAST
CONGRUITY
CONTRALTO
COPARTNER
COPYRIGHT
DECORATOR
DEFERENCE
DEFERMENT
DEFORMITY
DEMARCATE
DEMURRAGE
DEPARTURE
DESIRABLE
DESTROYER
DETERGENT
DETERMINE
DETERRENT
DIACRITIC
DIAERESIS
DIMORPHIC
DISCREDIT
DISORIENT
DISPRAISE
DIVERSIFY
DIVERSION
DIVERSITY
DOWNRANGE
DOWNRIGHT
DYSTROPHY
EIDERDOWN
EMBARRASS
EMPIRICAL
ENDURANCE
ENTERITIS
ENTERTAIN
EPIGRAPHY
ESPERANTO
EXCORIATE
EXCURSION
EXCURSIVE
EXECRABLE
EXPERTISE
EXPURGATE
EXTIRPATE
FAVORABLE
GABARDINE
GABERDINE
GASTRITIS
GASTROPOD
GENERATOR
GEOGRAPHY
GONORRHEA
GOVERNESS
GUERRILLA
HAVERSACK
HETERODOX
HIBERNATE
HILARIOUS
HINDRANCE
HONORABLE
HONORIFIC
HYPERBOLA
HYPERBOLE
HYPERCARD
HYPERTEXT
IGNORANCE
IMPARTIAL
IMPERFECT
IMPERIOUS
IMPORTANT
IMPORTUNE
INCARNATE
INCORRECT
INCURABLE
INCURIOUS
INCURSION
INEBRIATE
INFERENCE
INFERTILE
INFIRMARY
INFIRMITY
INFORMANT
INFURIATE
INNERMOST
INNERSOLE
INSERTION
INSURABLE
INSURANCE
INSURGENT
INTERCEDE
INTERCEPT
INTERDICT
INTERFACE
INTERFERE
INTERFUSE
INTERJECT
INTERLACE
INTERLARD
INTERLEAF
INTERLINE
INTERLINK
INTERLOCK
INTERLOPE
INTERLUDE
INTERMENT
INTERNIST
INTERNODE
INTERPLAY
INTERPOSE
INTERPRET
INTERRUPT
INTERSECT
INTERVENE
INTERVIEW
INVERNESS
INVERSION
JACARANDA
LABORIOUS
LABYRINTH
LIBERTINE
LITERATIM
LIVERWORT
LIVERYMAN
LOGARITHM
LOWERCASE
LUXURIANT
LUXURIATE
MAHARISHI
MAJORDOMO
MAJORETTE
MATERNITY
MEMORABLE
MISCREANT
MISERABLE
MISORIENT
MODERATOR
MODERNISM
MODERNIZE
MOTORBIKE
MOTORBOAT
MOTORCADE
MUCKRAKER
NATURALLY
NEFARIOUS
NEPHRITIC
NEPHRITIS
NEVERMORE
NONCREDIT
NONPROFIT
NOTORIOUS
NUMERATOR
NUMERICAL
OBJURGATE
OBSERVANT
OFFERTORY
OPPORTUNE
OTHERWISE
OUTERMOST
OUTGROWTH
OVERREACH
PAPERBACK
PARTRIDGE
PATERNITY
PENURIOUS
POWERBOAT
PREORDAIN
PROCREATE
PROPRIETY
QUADRATIC
QUADRILLE
QUADRUPED
QUADRUPLE
RECORDING
RECORDIST
RECURSION
REDBREAST
REFERENCE
REFURBISH
REGARDING
REPERTORY
REPORTAGE
RESERPINE
RESERVIST
RESERVOIR
RESTRAINT
RESURRECT
RETARDATE
REVERENCE
REVERSION
RIVERBANK
RIVERBOAT
RIVERSIDE
RUNAROUND
SATURNINE
SCLEROSIS
SEPARABLE
SEPARATOR
SOPORIFIC
SOUBRETTE
SOVEREIGN
SPEARHEAD
SPEARMINT
STAIRCASE
STAIRWELL
SUFFRAGAN
SUGARCANE
SUGARPLUM
SUPERNOVA
SUPERPOSE
SUPERSEDE
SUPERVENE
SUPERVISE
SYNERGISM
TOLERABLE
TOLERANCE
TULAREMIA
UNCERTAIN
UNDERBODY
UNDERBRED
UNDERCOAT
UNDERDONE
UNDERFEED
UNDERFOOT
UNDERGIRD
UNDERHAND
UNDERLINE
UNDERLING
UNDERMINE
UNDERMOST
UNDERPART
UNDERPASS
UNDERPLAY
UNDERRATE
UNDERSELL
UNDERSHOT
UNDERSIDE
UNDERTAKE
UNDERTONE
UNDERWEAR
UNDERWOOD
UNEARTHLY
UNHARNESS
UNWORLDLY
UPPERCASE
UPPERMOST
UTTERANCE
UTTERMOST
VAGARIOUS
VAPORIZER
VAPORWARE
VENERABLE
VENIREMAN
VENTRICLE
VESTRYMAN
VICARIOUS
VICEREGAL
WATERFALL
WATERFOWL
WATERLINE
WATERMARK
WATERSHED
WATERSIDE
YTTERBIUM
ACCESSION
ACCESSORY
ACOUSTICS
ADMISSION
ADVISABLE
AEROSPACE
AMBUSCADE
AMIDSHIPS
ANTISERUM
ARMISTICE
ASSISTANT
BACKSLASH
BACKSLIDE
BACKSTAGE
BACKSWEPT
BANDSTAND
BARNSTORM
BEEFSTEAK
BOATSWAIN
BOMBSHELL
BOMBSIGHT
BOOKSHELF
BRASSERIE
BRASSIERE
BRIMSTONE
CAMPSTOOL
CELESTIAL
CHOPSTICK
CHRISTIAN
CHRISTMAS
CHRYSALIS
CLAMSHELL
CLASSICAL
CLASSMATE
CLASSROOM
CLIPSHEET
CLOISONNE
CONESTOGA
CORKSCREW
CORNSTALK
CORUSCATE
COUNSELOR
CROISSANT
CROSSOVER
CROSSROAD
CROSSWALK
CROSSWAYS
CROSSWISE
DACHSHUND
DAMASCENE
DECISTERE
DEKASTERE
DEVASTATE
DHRYSTONE
DISESTEEM
DIVISIBLE
DOWNSHIFT
DOWNSTAGE
DOWNSWING
DRUGSTORE
DRUMSTICK
EAVESDROP
ENDOSCOPE
EXPOSITOR
FARMSTEAD
FEEDSTOCK
FEEDSTUFF
FETISHISM
FILMSTRIP
FLAGSTAFF
FLAGSTONE
FOODSTUFF
FOOTSTOOL
FORESHEET
FORESHORE
FORESIGHT
FORESTALL
FORESWEAR
FOURSCORE
FREESTONE
GALLSTONE
GEARSHIFT
GLADSTONE
GLISSANDO
GOLDSMITH
GRASSLAND
GRUBSTAKE
GYROSCOPE
HAILSTONE
HAILSTORM
HAIRSTYLE
HANDSHAKE
HANDSPIKE
HANDSTAND
HARDSTAND
HARTSHORN
HEADSTALL

HEADSTONE
HEMISTICH
HINDSIGHT
HOLYSTONE
HOMESTEAD
HOROSCOPE
IMPASSIVE
IMPOSTURE
INCESSANT
INFUSIBLE
INJUSTICE
INSISTENT
INTESTATE
INTESTINE
INVISIBLE
IRONSTONE
JACKSCREW
JACKSTRAW
KICKSTAND
KINESCOPE
LANDSCAPE
LANDSLIDE
LEAFSTALK
LEGISLATE
LIMESTONE
LIVESTOCK
LOADSTONE
LOCKSMITH
LODESTONE
LOGISTICS
MAELSTROM
MAGISTRAL
MAJUSCULE
MAKESHIFT
MILESTONE
MILLSTONE
MINISCULE
MINISKIRT
MINISTATE
MINUSCULE
MONASTERY
MONKSHOOD
MONOSPACE
MOONSCAPE
MOONSHINE
MOONSTONE
NECESSARY
NECESSITY
NEWSSTAND
OBEISANCE
OBFUSCATE
OBSESSION
OVERSEXED
OVERSHOOT
OVERSIGHT
OVERSLEEP
OVERSTATE
PAKISTANI
PERISCOPE
PERISTYLE
PIKESTAFF
PLAUSIBLE
PLOWSHARE
POTASSIUM
PRESSROOM
PUBESCENT
PUISSANCE
QUIESCENT
RAINSPOUT
RAINSTORM
RECESSION
RECESSIVE
REGISTRAR
REINSTATE
REMISSION
REPOSSESS
RESISTANT
ROADSTEAD
ROOTSTOCK
SALESGIRL
SANDSTONE
SANDSTORM
SECESSION
SHIPSHAPE
SIDESWIPE
SILTSTONE
SINUSITIS
SNOWSTORM
SOAPSTONE
SWANSDOWN
TELESCOPE
THEOSOPHY
THRESHOLD
TOADSTOOL
TOMBSTONE
TOWNSFOLK
TRANSCEND
TRANSDUCE
TRANSFORM
TRANSFUSE
TRANSIENT
TRANSLATE
TRANSMUTE
TRANSONIC
TRANSPIRE
TRANSPORT
TRANSPOSE
TRANSSHIP
TREASURER
TROUSSEAU
TURNSTILE
VIGESIMAL
WASHSTAND
WHETSTONE
WHIMSICAL
WINDSTORM
WINDSWEPT
WITHSTAND
WOLFSBANE
YARDSTICK
ALBATROSS
ALEATORIC
AMBITIOUS
ANTITOXIN
ANTITUMOR
APARTHEID
APARTMENT
APOSTOLIC
APPETIZER
ARBITRARY
ARBITRATE
AUTOTRACE
AWESTRUCK
BACKTRACK
BAGATELLE
BEAUTEOUS
BEAUTIFUL
BESETTING
BILATERAL
BLOWTORCH
BOUNTEOUS
BOUNTIFUL
BOWSTRING
BUCKTOOTH
BUMPTIOUS
CAFETERIA
CAPITALLY
CARETAKER
CATATONIC
CHANTEUSE
COASTLINE
CONSTABLE
CONSTANCY
CONSTRAIN
CONSTRICT
CONSTRUCT
COUNTDOWN
COUNTLESS
COURTEOUS
COURTESAN
COURTROOM
COURTSHIP
COURTYARD
CRAFTSMAN
CURETTAGE
DAUNTLESS
DEBUTANTE
DECATHLON
DELFTWARE
DEMITASSE
DIGITALIS
DIGITIZED
DIPHTHONG
DOUBTLESS
DOWITCHER
DRAFTSMAN
DRIFTWOOD
ELASTOMER
ELECTRIFY
ELECTRODE
EQUITABLE
EVENTUATE
EXCITABLE
EXISTENCE
EXPATIATE
EYESTRAIN
FACETIOUS
FIRSTBORN
FIRSTHAND
FIRSTLING
FLINTLOCK
FLUCTUATE
FORETASTE
FORETOKEN
FRACTIOUS
FROSTBITE
FRUITCAKE
FRUITERER
FRUSTRATE
GAZETTEER
GENITALIA
GRANTSMAN
GREATCOAT
GRISTMILL
HABITABLE
HABITUATE
HALITOSIS
HAMSTRING
HEALTHFUL
HEARTACHE
HEARTBEAT
HEARTBURN
HEARTFELT
HEARTLESS
HEARTSICK
HEARTWOOD
HEMSTITCH
HEPATITIS
HERITABLE
IDENTICAL
IMMUTABLE
IMPATIENS
IMPATIENT
IMPETUOUS
INFATUATE
INPATIENT
INSATIATE
IRRITABLE
LEASTWISE
LIGHTFACE
LIGHTNING
LIGHTSHIP
LIGHTSOME
MALATHION
MATUTINAL
MIDSTREAM
MINUTEMAN
MOUSTACHE
NEGOTIANT
NEGOTIATE
NICOTINIC
NIGHTCLUB
NIGHTFALL
NIGHTGOWN
NIGHTHAWK
NIGHTLIFE
NIGHTMARE
NIGHTTIME
NOVITIATE
OVERTHROW
OVERTRICK
PALATABLE
PARATHION
PENETRATE
PINSTRIPE
PLAYTHING
PLENTEOUS
PLENTIFUL
POLITBURO
POLITESSE
POLITICAL
POULTERER
PRACTICAL
PRESTRESS
PRINTABLE
PROSTRATE
PUNCTILIO
PUNCTUATE
PYRETHRUM
QUARTERLY
QUARTZITE
QUINTUPLE
QUITTANCE
RACETRACK
REACTANCE
REENTRANT
REPUTABLE
RIGHTEOUS
SANCTUARY
SCANTLING
SCINTILLA
SHEATHING
SHIFTLESS
SHORTCAKE
SHORTHAND
SHORTHORN
SHORTSTOP
SHORTWAVE
SIDETRACK
SKINTIGHT
SOLITAIRE
SOMETHING
SOMETIMES
SPECTACLE
SPECTATOR
SPLITTING
SPORTSMAN
STARTLING
STRATAGEM
STRETCHER
SUBATOMIC
SUBSTANCE
SUMPTUOUS
SUNSTROKE
SWEATSHOP
SWEETMEAT
THEATRICS
TIGHTROPE
TIMETABLE
TRACTABLE
TREATMENT
TURNTABLE
UNNATURAL
UNSETTLED
UNTUTORED
UNWITTING
VEGETABLE
VERITABLE
VEXATIOUS
WAISTBAND
WAISTCOAT
WAISTLINE
WAVETABLE
WORKTABLE
WRESTLING
WRISTBAND
YACHTSMAN
ACIDULATE
ACIDULOUS
AFFLUENCE
ANNOUNCER
BANQUETTE
BANTUSTAN
BRIQUETTE
CALCULATE
CAPSULATE
CARBUNCLE
CARBURIZE
CELLULOSE
CENTURION
CIRCUITRY
CIRCULATE
COAGULANT
COAGULATE
COLLUSION
COLLUVIUM
COMMUNION
COMMUNISM
COMMUNITY
CONCUBINE
CONDUCTOR
CONFUSION
CONJUGATE
CONNUBIAL
CONTUMELY
CONTUSION
CORPUSCLE
CORRUGATE
COUTURIER
CREDULOUS
CROQUETTE
DECOUPAGE
DISBURDEN
DISPUTANT
DISTURBED
EFFLUENCE
EFFLUVIUM
EJACULATE
ELOCUTION
EMOLUMENT
ENCOUNTER
ENCOURAGE
ENTOURAGE
EPICUREAN
ETIQUETTE
EVOLUTION
EXCLUSIVE
EXECUTIVE
EXECUTRIX
EXTRUSIVE
FLATULENT
FORMULATE
FORTUNATE
FREQUENCY
GARRULOUS
GRANULATE
HAMBURGER
HERCULEAN
HEREUNDER
IMPRUDENT
INFLUENCE
INFLUENZA
INOCULATE
LIMBURGER
LIMOUSINE
MARQUETRY
MARSUPIAL
MASCULINE
MERCURIAL
MERCUROUS
MIDSUMMER
MUSSULMAN
NEPTUNIUM
NOCTURNAL
OUTNUMBER
PARQUETRY
PASTURAGE
PENDULOUS
PERFUMERY
PIROUETTE
PORCUPINE
PORTULACA
POSTULANT
POSTULATE
PRECURSOR
PREJUDICE
PURSUANCE
QUERULOUS
RESHUFFLE
RUMRUNNER
SAPSUCKER
SECLUSION
SPECULATE
SPELUNKER
STATUETTE
STATUTORY
STIMULANT
STIMULATE
STIPULATE
SUBJUGATE
SUBLUNARY
SUCCULENT
SULFUROUS
SUPPURATE
TELLURIUM
TREMULOUS
TRIBUTARY
TRITURATE
TRUCULENT
TURBULENT
TURQUOISE
UNBOUNDED
UNCOUNTED
UNDAUNTED
UNDOUBTED
UNEQUALED
UNFOUNDED
UNPLUMBED
UNSTUDIED
VENTUROUS
VICTUALER
ALLEVIATE
ANTIVENIN
EQUIVOCAL
GRIEVANCE
IMMOVABLE

OBLIVIOUS
RELEVANCE
RELEVANCY
SCRIVENER
UNADVISED
UNRIVALED
ALLOWANCE
ARROWHEAD
ARROWROOT
BACKWATER
BACKWOODS
BANDWAGON
BANDWIDTH
BONDWOMAN
BUCKWHEAT
BUSHWHACK
CARTWHEEL
CHARWOMAN
DISHWATER
EDELWEISS
ELBOWROOM
ELSEWHERE
ERSTWHILE
FIREWATER
FOREWOMAN
FREEWHEEL
HANDWOVEN
HEADWATER
JERKWATER
KINSWOMAN
MEANWHILE
MELTWATER
OVERWEIGH
OVERWHELM
OVERWRITE
RAINWATER
ROSEWATER
SALTWATER
SCREWBALL
SEMIWORKS
SHIPWRECK
SOMEWHERE
STOPWATCH
THROWAWAY
THROWBACK
TIDEWATER
TYPEWRITE
WASHWOMAN
ADMIXTURE
OBNOXIOUS
ACETYLENE
AMARYLLIS
ANNOYANCE
ANONYMOUS
BELLYACHE
CUBBYHOLE
CURRYCOMB

DAIRYMAID
ECOSYSTEM
EMBAYMENT
EMPHYSEMA
EVERYBODY
FAIRYLAND
FANCYWORK
FERRYBOAT
FORSYTHIA
GUNNYSACK
HOLLYHOCK
HONEYCOMB
HONEYMOON
JELLYFISH
MALAYSIAN
MARTYRDOM
NEODYMIUM
PACHYDERM
PIGGYBACK
POPPYCOCK
PUSSYFOOT
WORRYWART
BREEZEWAY
CITIZENRY
QUIZZICAL

## 6th Letter

ADIABATIC
ADMIRABLE
ADMIRALTY
ADVISABLE
AEROPAUSE
AFFIDAVIT
AFRIKAANS
AGREEABLE
ALIENABLE
ALLIGATOR
ALLOWANCE
AMBULANCE
ANNOYANCE
ANTIPASTO
ANTIPATHY
APPARATUS
APPLIANCE
ASPARAGUS
ASSONANCE
ASSURANCE
ATHENAEUM
AUTOMATIC
AUTOMATON
AVAILABLE
BACCHANAL
BACKWATER
BALALAIKA

BANDWAGON
BAREFACED
BEEFEATER
BELLYACHE
BILLIARDS
BIOGRAPHY
BOOKMAKER
CANTHARIS
CAPITALLY
CARETAKER
CATAMARAN
CHAMPAGNE
CHAMPAIGN
CHARLATAN
CHICKADEE
CHICKASAW
CHROMATIC
CHRYSALIS
CLEARANCE
COLLEAGUE
COMPLAINT
CONSTABLE
CONSTANCY
CONTRALTO
CUPBEARER
DEBUTANTE
DECORATOR
DEMITASSE
DESIRABLE
DETONATOR
DIGITALIS
DISCHARGE
DISHWATER
DISPRAISE
DOMINANCE
DOWNRANGE
EGGBEATER
ENDURANCE
ENIGMATIC
ENSHEATHE
ENWREATHE
EPIGRAPHY
EQUITABLE
ESCALATOR
ESOPHAGUS
ESPERANTO
ESTIMABLE
EXCITABLE
EXECRABLE
FAVORABLE
FIREWATER
FLAMMABLE
FOOLHARDY
FORENAMED
FORETASTE
FREEMASON
GENERATOR

GENITALIA
GEOGRAPHY
GLADIATOR
GLENGARRY
GLISSANDO
GRIEVANCE
HABITABLE
HEADWATER
HEARTACHE
HERITABLE
HINDRANCE
HOLOCAUST
HOMEMAKER
HONORABLE
HOTHEADED
IGNORANCE
IMBALANCE
IMMOVABLE
IMMUTABLE
IMPEDANCE
INCAPABLE
INCUBATOR
INCURABLE
INEFFABLE
INHALATOR
INORGANIC
INSURABLE
INSURANCE
IRRITABLE
JACARANDA
JERKWATER
LAGNIAPPE
LAMINATED
LANTHANUM
LITERATIM
MALLEABLE
MANSLAYER
MATRIARCH
MEDICABLE
MELTWATER
MEMORABLE
MENOPAUSE
MINELAYER
MISCHANCE
MISERABLE
MODERATOR
MONOMANIA
MOUSTACHE
MUCKRAKER
NATURALLY
NAVIGABLE
NEWSPAPER
NONREADER
NUMERATOR
OBEISANCE
OCCUPANCY
ORDINANCE

ORIFLAMME
OVERMATCH
PACEMAKER
PAGEMAKER
PALATABLE
PATRIARCH
PERCHANCE
PERMEABLE
PIGHEADED
PNEUMATIC
POSTHASTE
POSTNATAL
PRAGMATIC
PREGNABLE
PRINTABLE
PSORIASIS
PUISSANCE
PURSUANCE
PYROMANIA
QUADRATIC
QUITTANCE
RAINWATER
REACTANCE
RELEVANCE
RELEVANCY
REPUTABLE
RESONANCE
RESONATOR
RESTRAINT
REVOCABLE
ROSEWATER
SACCHARIN
SALTWATER
SANDPAPER
SCHEMATIC
SEMBLANCE
SEPARABLE
SEPARATOR
SHOEMAKER
SOLITAIRE
SPECIALTY
SPECTACLE
SPECTATOR
SPINNAKER
STOPWATCH
STRATAGEM
SUBSTANCE
SUFFRAGAN
SURCHARGE
TELEPATHY
THROWAWAY
TIDEWATER
TIMETABLE
TOLERABLE
TOLERANCE
TOOTHACHE
TRACTABLE

TURNTABLE
ULTIMATUM
UNCLEANLY
UNEQUALED
UNRIVALED
UNSHEATHE
URTICARIA
UTTERANCE
VEGETABLE
VENERABLE
VENGEANCE
VERITABLE
VICTUALER
VIGILANCE
VIGILANTE
WALLPAPER
WASHBASIN
WAVETABLE
WORKTABLE
ABSORBENT
ADSORBATE
ADSORBENT
AIRMOBILE
AMPHIBIAN
AMPHIBOLE
ANKLEBONE
ASSEMBLER
ATTRIBUTE
BLACKBALL
BLACKBIRD
BLACKBODY
BLOODBATH
BROADBAND
CAMELBACK
CAMEMBERT
CANALBOAT
CANTABILE
CARIBBEAN
CHALKBORD
CHARABANC
CHECKBOOK
CHEEKBONE
COLUMBINE
CONCUBINE
CONNUBIAL
DEATHBLOW
DISEMBARK
DISEMBODY
EVERYBODY
FERRYBOAT
FIRSTBORN
FLASHBACK
FLASHBULB
FROSTBITE
GREENBACK
GREENBELT
GUIDEBOOK

HEARTBEAT
HEARTBURN
HELLEBORE
HOBGOBLIN
HORSEBACK
HOUSEBOAT
HUNCHBACK
HYPERBOLA
HYPERBOLE
INCUMBENT
MATCHBOOK
MOTORBIKE
MOTORBOAT
NOTCHBACK
PAPERBACK
PICKABACK
PIGGYBACK
POLITBURO
POWERBOAT
RECUMBENT
REFURBISH
REPROBATE
RIVERBANK
RIVERBOAT
SCRAPBOOK
SCREWBALL
SHOREBIRD
SHRUBBERY
SKIMOBILE
SNAKEBIRD
SNAKEBITE
SPEEDBOAT
SPICEBUSH
SPOONBILL
STEAMBOAT
STILLBORN
SYLLABIFY
THIGHBONE
THROWBACK
TRACKBALL
TURNABOUT
UNDERBODY
UNDERBRED
UNDOUBTED
VERTEBRAL
VESTIBULE
WAISTBAND
WATCHBAND
WHALEBOAT
WHALEBONE
WHEELBASE
WHITEBAIT
WOLFSBANE
WRISTBAND
YTTERBIUM
AFTERCARE
AMBUSCADE

AMERICANA
AMERICIUM
ANGLICIZE
ANTARCTIC
APPLICANT
BALDACHIN
BARRACUDA
BARRICADE
BELLICOSE
BICONCAVE
BIFURCATE
BRIEFCASE
BROADCAST
CAPRICCIO
CAVALCADE
CHARACTER
CLINICIAN
COLLECTED
COLORCAST
CONDUCTOR
CORKSCREW
CORUSCATE
CRANKCASE
CRITICISM
CRITICIZE
CURRYCOMB
DAMASCENE
DEMARCATE
DEMULCENT
DEPRECATE
DESICCANT
DESICCATE
DIALECTIC
DIFFICULT
DISLOCATE
DISSECTED
DOWITCHER
DUPLICATE
DUPLICITY
EMBROCATE
ENDOSCOPE
ERADICATE
EXPLICATE
EXTRICATE
FABRICATE
FINANCIAL
FINANCIER
FLASHCUBE
FOURSCORE
FRIEDCAKE
FRUITCAKE
FUNGICIDE
GERMICIDE
GIMMICKRY
GRATICULE
GREATCOAT
GYROSCOPE

HERBICIDE
HONEYCOMB
HOROSCOPE
HOUSECOAT
HURRICANE
HYPERCARD
IMPLICATE
IMPRECATE
IMPRECISE
INCULCATE
INSINCERE
INTERCEDE
INTERCEPT
INTRICATE
ITALICIZE
JACKSCREW
KINESCOPE
LANDSCAPE
LEUKOCYTE
LOWERCASE
LUBRICANT
LUBRICATE
MACROCOSM
MAJUSCULE
MASTICATE
MATRICIDE
MENDICANT
METRICIZE
MICROCOPY
MICROCOSM
MINISCULE
MINUSCULE
MOONSCAPE
MORTICIAN
MOTORCADE
MYSTICISM
NIGHTCLUB
OBFUSCATE
OSTRACIZE
PARRICIDE
PATRICIAN
PATRICIDE
PENTECOST
PERISCOPE
PERSECUTE
PESTICIDE
PETTICOAT
PHOTOCELL
PHOTOCOPY
PHYSICIAN
PHYSICIST
PISTACHIO
PIZZICATO
POPPYCOCK
PREDICATE
PREOCCUPY
PRERECORD
PROJECTOR
PROSECUTE
PROTECTOR
PUBESCENT
PUBLICIST
PUBLICITY
PUBLICIZE
QUIESCENT
RAGPICKER
RECONCILE
REFLECTOR
REFRACTOR
REPLICATE
RUSTICATE
SAPSUCKER
SCARECROW
SEPULCHER
SHORTCAKE
SKYJACKER
SKYROCKET
SPHINCTER
STAIRCASE
STOMACHER
STOMACHIC
STRETCHER
SUFFOCATE
SUGARCANE
SUSPICION
SYNDICATE
TELESCOPE
TRANSCEND
TRIFOCALS
UNCONCERN
UNDERCOAT
UNSHACKLE
UPPERCASE
VINDICATE
WAISTCOAT
WATCHCASE
WITTICISM
ACCORDION
AFTERDECK
ALMANDITE
APPENDAGE
ASCENDANT
ASCENDERS
ASTRADDLE
ATTENDANT
BALLADEER
BEDRIDDEN
BELVEDERE
BREAKDOWN
BURUNDIAN
CALENDULA
CANDIDACY
CANDIDATE
CATHEDRAL
CELANDINE
CHLORDANE
CIRCADIAN
COLLODION
COMMODITY
COMMODORE
CONFIDANT
CONUNDRUM
CORELDRAW
COUNTDOWN
CRACKDOWN
CROCODILE
CUSTODIAL
CUSTODIAN
DEFENDANT
DEOXIDIZE
DEPENDENT
DIFFIDENT
DISSIDENT
DROMEDARY
EAVESDROP
EIDERDOWN
ELUCIDATE
EUCLIDEAN
EXTRADITE
FECUNDATE
GABARDINE
GABERDINE
GRENADIER
GRENADINE
GROUNDHOG
GROUNDING
IMPRUDENT
INTENDANT
INTERDICT
INTRODUCE
KNOCKDOWN
LEGENDARY
LIQUIDATE
MAJORDOMO
METHADONE
METHODIST
METHODIZE
PACHYDERM
PALLADIUM
POMPADOUR
PRECEDENT
PRECEDING
PREJUDICE
PREORDAIN
PRESIDENT
PRESIDIUM
PROCEDURE
PROVIDENT
QUICKDRAW
QUOTIDIAN
RECONDITE
RECORDING
RECORDIST
REDUNDANT
REGARDING
REPRODUCE
RETARDATE
SCOUNDREL
SECONDARY
SHAKEDOWN
STEVEDORE
SUBSIDIZE
SWANSDOWN
TOUCHDOWN
TRAGEDIAN
TRANSDUCE
UNBENDING
UNBRIDLED
UNDERDONE
UNFLEDGED
UNMINDFUL
UNSTUDIED
WRONGDOER
ACCIDENCE
ACQUIESCE
AESTHETIC
AFFLUENCE
ALTIMETER
ANALGESIA
ANALGESIC
ANOPHELES
ANTISERUM
ANTIVENIN
ARBORETUM
BACKPEDAL
BAGATELLE
BAKSHEESH
BANQUETTE
BARKEEPER
BAROMETER
BEAUTEOUS
BEEKEEPER
BICAMERAL
BILATERAL
BLUEBERRY
BOLSHEVIK
BOUNTEOUS
BOURGEOIS
BRASSERIE
BREEZEWAY
BRIQUETTE
BROCHETTE
BUMBLEBEE
CAFETERIA
CANDLEMAS
CANDLEPIN
CATALEPSY
CHALLENGE
CHANTEUSE
CIGARETTE
CITIZENRY
COFFEEPOT
COIFFEUSE
CONCIERGE
COTYLEDON
COUNSELOR
COURTEOUS
COURTESAN
COVALENCE
CRANBERRY
CRESCENDO
CROQUETTE
CRYOGENIC
CUTANEOUS
DAREDEVIL
DECADENCE
DECIMETER
DEFERENCE
DEKAMETER
DELINEATE
DIAERESIS
DIATHERMY
DISCREDIT
DISPLEASE
DOSIMETER
EDELWEISS
EFFLUENCE
EMERGENCY
ENERGETIC
EPHEMERAL
ERRONEOUS
ETIQUETTE
EXISTENCE
FARSEEING
FREQUENCY
FRUITERER
GAUCHERIE
GENTLEMAN
GRAYBEARD
HACKNEYED
HALFPENNY
HEXAMETER
HOWSOEVER
ILLIBERAL
INCIDENCE
INFERENCE
INFLUENCE
INFLUENZA
INNKEEPER
INNOCENCE
INTUMESCE
ISOSCELES
KILOHERTZ
KILOMETER
KNOWLEDGE
LORGNETTE
MAJORETTE
MANIFESTO
MANOMETER
MARQUETRY
MEGADEATH
MEGAHERTZ
MENAGERIE
MESSIEURS
MIDDLEMAN
MINUTEMAN
MISCREANT
MISTLETOE
MUSKMELON
NANOMETER
NONCREDIT
NORTHEAST
NOVELETTE
OPTOMETRY
ORANGEADE
OUBLIETTE
OVERREACH
OVERSEXED
OVERWEIGH
PANTHEISM
PARAMETER
PARQUETRY
PEDOMETER
PERIMETER
PERPLEXED
PHRENETIC
PIROUETTE
PLENTEOUS
POLICEMAN
POLITESSE
POULTERER
PROCREATE
PROPHETIC
PUERPERAL
PYROMETER
QUARTERLY
RASPBERRY
REDBREAST
REFERENCE
RESIDENCE
RESIDENCY
RETRIEVER
REVERENCE
RHEOMETER
RIGHTEOUS
ROUNDELAY
SADDLEBOW
SALTPETER
SCRIVENER
SEBACEOUS
SILICEOUS
SIMPLETON
SINGLETON
SLUICEWAY
SOUBRETTE
SOUTHEAST
SOVEREIGN
SPAGHETTI
SPEAKEASY
SPLENETIC
STATUETTE
STRIKEOUT
SUNSEEKER
SYNTHESIS
SYNTHETIC
TAXIDERMY
TELEGENIC
TELEMETER
TRIWEEKLY
TULAREMIA
UNDECEIVE
VEHEMENCE
VENIREMAN
VICEREGAL
VOLTMETER
WAGONETTE
WHICHEVER
WHOSOEVER
WORKBENCH
ZEITGEIST
ZUCCHETTO
ANGELFISH
BLACKFOOT
BLINDFOLD
BREAKFAST
CHAUFFEUR
COLORFAST
CRUCIFORM
CUNEIFORM
DIGNIFIED
DISAFFECT
DISINFECT
FEBRIFUGE
HEARTFELT
HEREAFTER
HYDROFOIL
IMPERFECT
INTERFACE
INTERFERE
INTERFUSE
JELLYFISH
LIGHTFACE
MAGNIFICO
MICROFILM
MISINFORM
MULTIFORM
NIGHTFALL
PITCHFORK
PUSSYFOOT
RECTIFIER
RESHUFFLE
RETROFIRE
SACRIFICE
SASSAFRAS
SHEEPFOLD
SHELLFIRE
SHELLFISH
STEADFAST
SWORDFISH
THEREFORE
THEREFROM
THREEFOLD
TOWNSFOLK
TRANSFORM
TRANSFUSE
UNDERFEED
UNDERFOOT
UNRUFFLED
UNSELFISH
VERMIFORM
VERMIFUGE
WATERFALL
WATERFOWL
WHEREFORE
WHITEFISH
WOMENFOLK
ABORIGINE
AFTERGLOW
AGGREGATE
ALLERGIST
AMBERGRIS
ANALOGOUS
APOLOGIZE
BELEAGUER
BILINGUAL
CABLEGRAM
CASTIGATE
CENTIGRAM
COLLEGIAN
COLLEGIUM
CONJUGATE
CONTAGION
CORRUGATE
COSMOGONY
DETERGENT
DISENGAGE
DISFIGURE
DISREGARD
EXPURGATE
FLOODGATE
FOREIGNER
HECTOGRAM
HISTOGRAM
IMBROGLIO
INELEGANT
INSTIGATE

INSURGENT
MICROGRAM
MILLIGRAM
MONSIGNOR
NEGLIGENT
NEOLOGISM
NIGHTGOWN
NORWEGIAN
OBBLIGATO
OBJURGATE
OUTRIGGER
PEKINGESE
PREFIGURE
PROPAGATE
RADIOGRAM
SALESGIRL
SCAPEGOAT
SEGREGATE
SUBJUGATE
SURROGATE
SYLLOGISM
SYNERGISM
TERMAGANT
UNALIGNED
UNDERGIRD
UNFEIGNED
VARIEGATE
VERDIGRIS
WOEBEGONE
AMIDSHIPS
AMORPHOUS
ANARCHISM
ANTECHOIR
APARTHEID
APPREHEND
ARROWHEAD
ARTICHOKE
BEACHHEAD
BENIGHTED
BIOSPHERE
BLACKHEAD
BLASPHEME
BLASPHEMY
BLEACHERS
BLOCKHEAD
BOMBSHELL
BOOKSHELF
BRONCHIAL
BUCKWHEAT
BUSHWHACK
CACOPHONY
CARTWHEEL
CATECHISM
CHILDHOOD
CHUCKHOLE
CHURCHMAN
CLAMSHELL
CLIPSHEET
CUBBYHOLE
DACHSHUND
DECATHLON
DELIGHTED
DIPHTHONG
DOWNSHIFT
ELSEWHERE
ENLIGHTEN
ERSTWHILE
EXOSPHERE
FALSEHOOD
FETISHISM
FIRSTHAND
FLOWCHART
FORESHEET
FORESHORE
FRANCHISE
FREEWHEEL
GEARSHIFT
GREENHORN
HANDSHAKE
HARDIHOOD
HARTSHORN
HEADPHONE
HEALTHFUL
HITCHHIKE
HOLLYHOCK
HOMOPHONE
HORSEHAIR
HORSEHIDE
HOUSEHOLD
LAUNCHPAD
LEASEHOLD
MAKESHIFT
MALACHITE
MALATHION
MASOCHISM
MEANWHILE
MEGAPHONE
MISBEHAVE
MONKSHOOD
MOONSHINE
NIGHTHAWK
OVERSHOOT
OVERTHROW
OVERWHELM
PARACHUTE
PARATHION
PAROCHIAL
PERIPHERY
PHOSPHATE
PLAYTHING
PLOWSHARE
POLYPHONY
PRESCHOOL
PRONGHORN
PYRETHRUM
REPREHEND
SAXOPHONE
SCUTCHEON
SEMAPHORE
SHEATHING
SHIPSHAPE
SHORTHAND
SHORTHORN
SLAUGHTER
SOMETHING
SOMEWHERE
SPEARHEAD
SPRIGHTLY
STANCHION
STEPCHILD
SWELLHEAD
SWITCHMAN
SYCOPHANT
TELEPHONE
TELEPHONY
TELEPHOTO
THRESHOLD
TREACHERY
TRENCHANT
TRUNCHEON
ULTRAHIGH
UNDERHAND
UNSIGHTLY
WHITEHALL
WHITEHEAD
WINDCHILL
WOMANHOOD
WOODCHUCK
XEROPHYTE
XYLOPHONE
AFFILIATE
ALGORITHM
ALLEVIATE
AMBITIOUS
APPETIZER
ARCHFIEND
ARMADILLO
ARTERIOLE
ARTHRITIS
ARTIFICER
ASSOCIATE
ATROCIOUS
AUDACIOUS
AUXILIARY
BACKFIELD
BANDWIDTH
BEAUTIFUL
BINOMINAL
BOMBSIGHT
BOUNTIFUL
BRASSIERE
BRILLIANT
BULLFIGHT
BULLFINCH
BUMPTIOUS
CALORIFIC
CANONICAL
CAPACIOUS
CAPACITOR
CAPARISON
CARTRIDGE
CERTAINTY
CHAFFINCH
CHRONICLE
CIGARILLO
CIRCUITRY
CLASSICAL
COALFIELD
COCKFIGHT
CONSCIOUS
CONTAINER
COPYRIGHT
DECILITER
DEFICIENT
DEFOLIANT
DEFOLIATE
DEKALITER
DELICIOUS
DELIMITER
DIACRITIC
DIGITIZED
DIRIGIBLE
DISORIENT
DIVISIBLE
DOWNRIGHT
EBULLIENT
EFFICIENT
EGREGIOUS
EMBROIDER
EMOLLIENT
EMPIRICAL
ENERGIZER
ENTERITIS
ENUNCIATE
ESTAMINET
EXCORIATE
EXPATIATE
EXPEDIENT
EXPEDITER
EXPOSITOR
FACETIOUS
FEROCIOUS
FIDUCIARY
FORESIGHT
FORTNIGHT
FRACTIOUS
FRANGIBLE
GASTRITIS
GLEANINGS
GOLDFIELD
GOLDFINCH
GRANDIOSE
GUERRILLA
HAIRPIECE
HEADFIRST
HEADLIGHT
HEADPIECE
HEMSTITCH
HEPATITIS
HIGHLIGHT
HILARIOUS
HILLBILLY
HINDSIGHT
HONORIFIC
HUMILIATE
IDENTICAL
ILLEGIBLE
ILLOGICAL
IMMEDIACY
IMMEDIATE
IMPATIENS
IMPATIENT
IMPERIOUS
IMPOLITIC
INCIPIENT
INCURIOUS
INDELIBLE
INEBRIATE
INFURIATE
INFUSIBLE
INGENIOUS
INPATIENT
INSATIATE
INSIDIOUS
INVIDIOUS
INVISIBLE
IRASCIBLE
IRRADIATE
JAUNDICED
JUDICIARY
JUDICIOUS
JURIDICAL
KILOLITER
LABORIOUS
LABYRINTH
LAVALIERE
LIMELIGHT
LITIGIOUS
LOGARITHM
LUXURIANT
LUXURIATE
MAHARISHI
MATUTINAL
MEDICINAL
MEGAPIXEL
MELODIOUS
MISORIENT
MOONLIGHT
MUNICIPAL
NEFARIOUS
NEGOTIANT
NEGOTIATE
NEPHRITIC
NEPHRITIS
NICOTINIC
NOSEPIECE
NOTORIOUS
NOVITIATE
NUMERICAL
OBLIVIOUS
OBNOXIOUS
OFFICIANT
OFFICIATE
OFFICIOUS
OUTSKIRTS
OVERNIGHT
OVERSIGHT
PARTRIDGE
PECUNIARY
PENURIOUS
PHLEBITIS
PLAUSIBLE
PLENTIFUL
POINCIANA
POLITICAL
POTBOILER
PRACTICAL
PREFLIGHT
PRINCIPAL
PRINCIPLE
PROPRIETY
PTARMIGAN
PUNCTILIO
QUADRILLE
QUIZZICAL
RAPACIOUS
RECIPIENT
RELIGIOUS
REMINISCE
REPUDIATE
RETALIATE
SAGACIOUS
SALACIOUS
SANDPIPER
SCINTILLA
SEMIFINAL
SHOWPIECE
SIDEPIECE
SINUSITIS
SKINTIGHT
SNOWFIELD
SOLICITOR
SOMETIMES
SOPORIFIC
SPOTLIGHT
STARLIGHT
STOPLIGHT
SUPPLIANT
TAILLIGHT
TECHNICAL
TECHNIQUE
TENACIOUS
TIMEPIECE
TRANSIENT
TRAPPINGS
UMBILICUS
UNADVISED
UNDECIDED
VAGARIOUS
VAGINITIS
VAPORIZER
VENTRICLE
VERACIOUS
VERIDICAL
VEXATIOUS
VICARIOUS
VIDELICET
VIGESIMAL
VIVACIOUS
VORACIOUS
WHIMSICAL
WHIRLIGIG
XANTHIPPE
APPLEJACK
BLACKJACK
INTERJECT
ASTRAKHAN
FINICKING
HUMANKIND
JINRIKSHA
MINISKIRT
PLACEKICK
SHRINKAGE
WOMANKIND
ACETYLENE
ACIDULATE
ACIDULOUS
AERIALIST
AEROPLANE
AFTERLIFE
AMARYLLIS
ANCILLARY
ANIMALISM
ANOMALOUS
ANTHOLOGY
ANTICLINE
APPELLANT
APPELLATE
AQUAPLANE
ARTILLERY
ASTROLABE
ASTROLOGY
AUDIOLOGY
BACKSLASH
BACKSLIDE
BANDOLIER
BATHOLITH
BATTALION
BEDFELLOW
BERKELIUM
BERYLLIUM
BLACKLIST
BLOODLINE
BLUEBLACK
BOOKPLATE
BOOTBLACK
BRAZILIAN
BROADLOOM
BRUTALIZE
CALCULATE
CAPILLARY
CAPSULATE
CARNELIAN
CARTILAGE
CATACLYSM
CEASELESS
CELLULOSE
CERECLOTH
CHAMELEON
CHECKLIST
CHEERLESS
CHEVALIER
CHILBLAIN
CHIVALRIC
CHOCOLATE
CIRCULATE
COAGULANT
COAGULATE
COASTLINE
COROLLARY
CORRELATE
COSMOLOGY
COTILLION
COUNTLESS
CREDULOUS
CRINOLINE
CYTOPLASM
DAMSELFLY
DANDELION
DAUNTLESS
DEATHLESS
DECOLLETE
DISHCLOTH
DISOBLIGE
DISSOLUTE
DIXIELAND

DOORPLATE
DOUBTLESS
DREAMLAND
EARTHLING
EJACULATE
EMBELLISH
ENCHILADA
ESTABLISH
ETHNOLOGY
ETYMOLOGY
EVERGLADE
EXCELLENT
EXEMPLARY
EXEMPLIFY
FAIRYLAND
FERTILIZE
FEUDALISM
FIREPLACE
FIRSTLING
FLAGELLUM
FLATULENT
FLEDGLING
FLINTLOCK
FORECLOSE
FORMALISM
FORMALITY
FORMALIZE
FORMULATE
FOUNDLING
FRIVOLOUS
FUSILLADE
GANGPLANK
GARRULOUS
GENEALOGY
GENTILITY
GENUFLECT
GONDOLIER
GRANULATE
GRASSLAND
GUIDELINE
GYRFALCON
HAIRCLOTH
HANDCLASP
HEARTLESS
HERBALIST
HERCULEAN
HOURGLASS
HYDROLOGY
INABILITY
INOCULATE
INTELLECT
INTERLACE
INTERLARD
INTERLEAF
INTERLINE
INTERLINK
INTERLOCK
INTERLOPE
INTERLUDE
INVIOLATE
ISINGLASS
ISRAELITE
JOBHOLDER
LACCOLITH
LANDSLIDE
LEGISLATE
LIABILITY
LIFEBLOOD
LITHOLOGY
LOINCLOTH
MARMALADE
MARVELOUS
MASCULINE
MATCHLOCK
MAUSOLEUM
MEDALLION
MENTALITY
MESCALINE
METROLOGY
MISSILERY
MONGOLIAN
MONGOLISM
MONGOLOID
MONOPLANE
MUSSULMAN
MYTHOLOGY
NAMEPLATE
NECROLOGY
NEURALGIA
NEUROLOGY
NIGHTLIFE
NORMALIZE
NOSEBLEED
NOSTALGIA
OSCILLATE
OURSELVES
OVERBLOWN
OVERCLOUD
OVERSLEEP
PAPILLOTE
PATHOLOGY
PATROLMAN
PENDULOUS
PENEPLAIN
PENHOLDER
PERCOLATE
PESTILENT
PETROLEUM
PETROLOGY
PHILOLOGY
PHONOLOGY
PLANELOAD
PLURALITY
PLURALIZE
PORCELAIN
PORTULACA
POSTILION
POSTULANT
POSTULATE
PREVALENT
PRICELESS
PRIVILEGE
PROPELLER
PROSELYTE
PROVOLONE
PUREBLOOD
QUERULOUS
QUICKLIME
RACIALISM
RADIOLOGY
RANCHLAND
RANGELAND
RAUWOLFIA
REBELLION
RECOLLECT
REPELLENT
ROADBLOCK
SACKCLOTH
SACRILEGE
SAILCLOTH
SAILPLANE
SANDBLAST
SATELLITE
SCANTLING
SCHEELITE
SCHILLING
SCHOOLBOY
SEMIFLUID
SHAPELESS
SHIFTLESS
SHOWPLACE
SIGNALIZE
SIGNALMAN
SKINFLINT
SNOWFLAKE
SOCIALISM
SOCIALITE
SOCIALIZE
SOCIOLOGY
SOMNOLENT
SPECULATE
SPINDLING
STABILIZE
STARTLING
STERILIZE
STIMULANT
STIMULATE
STIPULATE
STRAPLESS
STRIPLING
SUCCULENT
SWAMPLAND
SYMBOLISM
SYMBOLIZE
TABLELAND
TANTALIZE
TAUTOLOGY
THANKLESS
THRALLDOM
TRAINLOAD
TRANSLATE
TREMULOUS
TRUCKLOAD
TRUCULENT
TURBULENT
TWINKLING
UNDERLINE
UNDERLING
UNFAILING
UNFEELING
UNHEALTHY
UNIVALENT
UNSKILLED
UNWILLING
UNWORLDLY
VACILLATE
VAINGLORY
VANDALISM
VANDALIZE
VASSALAGE
VENTILATE
VERBALIZE
VERMILION
VERNALIZE
VISUALIZE
VOICELESS
WAISTLINE
WASHCLOTH
WASTELAND
WATERLINE
WINDBLOWN
WOMANLIKE
WOODBLOCK
WORKPLACE
WORLDLING
WORTHLESS
WRESTLING
YOUNGLING
ZWINGLIAN
ABATEMENT
ACCLIMATE
AFTERMATH
AGREEMENT
AMENDMENT
ANATOMIZE
ANONYMOUS
APARTMENT
ATONEMENT
BIRTHMARK
BLACKMAIL
CALCIMINE
CATCHMENT
CHAMOMILE
CHECKMATE
CLASSMATE
COLLIMATE
CONDIMENT
CONTUMELY
CUSTOMARY
CUSTOMIZE
CYCLAMATE
DAIRYMAID
DECREMENT
DEFERMENT
DEFORMITY
DETERMINE
DETRIMENT
DEVILMENT
DIATOMITE
DIPLOMACY
DISCOMFIT
DISMEMBER
DISSEMBLE
DISTEMPER
ECONOMICS
ECONOMIZE
EMBAYMENT
EMOLUMENT
EQUIPMENT
EUPHEMISM
EXCREMENT
EXTREMISM
EXTREMITY
FACSIMILE
FIRMAMENT
GOLDSMITH
GRISTMILL
HATCHMENT
HISTAMINE
HONEYMOON
HOUSEMAID
IMPLEMENT
IMPROMPTU
INANIMATE
INCLEMENT
INCOMMODE
INCREMENT
INFIRMARY
INFIRMITY
INFORMANT
INNERMOST
INTERMENT
JESSAMINE
LINEAMENT
LOCKSMITH
MATRIMONY
MERRIMENT
MIDSUMMER
MINCEMEAT
NEODYMIUM
NEVERMORE
NIGHTMARE
NURSEMAID
NUTRIMENT
OUTERMOST
OUTNUMBER
PANTOMIME
PARCHMENT
PARSIMONY
PATRIMONY
PERFUMERY
PERSIMMON
PESSIMISM
PHEROMONE
PIECEMEAL
PLACEMENT
PROXIMATE
PROXIMITY
RANDOMIZE
RECOMMEND
REPRIMAND
SACRAMENT
SCHLEMIEL
SCRIMMAGE
SENTIMENT
SEPTEMBER
SOPHOMORE
SPEARMINT
SQUEAMISH
STALEMATE
STATEMENT
STREAMBED
STREAMLET
SUBLIMATE
SUPREMACY
SWEETMEAT
SYSTEMIZE
TESTAMENT
TESTIMONY
TRADEMARK
TRANSMUTE
TREADMILL
TREATMENT
UNANIMOUS
UNDERMINE
UNDERMOST
UNPLUMBED
UPPERMOST
UTTERMOST
VICTIMIZE
WATERMARK
ABOMINATE
ADJOINING
AFTERNOON
ALTERNATE
ALUMINIUM
ALUMINIZE
ANNOUNCER
ANTIKNOCK
APPOINTEE
ARCHANGEL
ARCHENEMY
ASTRONAUT
ASTRONOMY
ATTAINDER
AUTHENTIC
AVALANCHE
BADMINTON
BARTENDER
BASTINADO
BENIGNANT
BENTONITE
BESPANGLE
BRITANNIC
BUCCANEER
BYSTANDER
CALVINISM
CAMPANILE
CANNONADE
CANNONEER
CARBONATE
CARBUNCLE
CARCINOMA
CARPENTER
CASTANETS
CENTENARY
CHICANERY
COCHINEAL
COLONNADE
COLUMNIST
COMMANDER
COMMINGLE
COMMUNION
COMMUNISM
COMMUNITY
COMPANION
COMPONENT
CONDENSER
CONGENIAL
CONSENSUS
CONSONANT
CONTENTED
CONTINENT
CONTINUAL
CONTINUUM
CORIANDER
COSMONAUT
COSPONSOR
CRETINISM
CULLENDER
CULMINATE
DARWINISM
DECENNIAL
DERRINGER
DESCENDER
DESIGNATE
DESIGNING
DISHONEST
DISMANTLE
DISSENTER
DOBSONFLY
DRAGONFLY
ELIMINATE
EMPENNAGE
ENCOUNTER
EPICENTER
EROGENOUS
ESPIONAGE
ESPLANADE
EUTHENICS
EXOGENOUS
EXTRINSIC
FASCINATE
FASTENING
FORTUNATE
FULMINATE
GALLANTRY
GALLINULE
GALVANISM
GALVANIZE
GELIGNITE
GERMANIUM
GERMINATE
GLUTINOUS
GOLDENROD
GOVERNESS
GUARANTEE
GUARANTOR
HAPPENING
HAPPINESS
HARBINGER
HARMONICA
HARMONICS
HARMONIUM
HARMONIZE
HELLENISM
HEREUNDER
HIBERNATE
HUMDINGER
HUSBANDRY
HYDRANGEA
HYPHENATE
ICELANDER
ICELANDIC
IMAGINARY
INCARNATE

INCOGNITO
INDEMNIFY
INDEMNITY
INDIGNANT
INDIGNITY
INGLENOOK
INSTANTER
INSTANTLY
INTERNIST
INTERNODE
INTRINSIC
INVERNESS
JACKKNIFE
LEAVENING
LIGHTNING
MACHINERY
MACHINIST
MALIGNANT
MANGANESE
MANHANDLE
MATERNITY
MECHANICS
MECHANISM
MECHANIZE
MERCENARY
MERGANSER
MESSENGER
METRONOME
MEZZANINE
MIDWINTER
MILLINERY
MISHANDLE
MISMANAGE
MODERNISM
MODERNIZE
NEPTUNIUM
OBSTINATE
ORIGINATE
ORPHANAGE
OXYGENATE
PANHANDLE
PARSONAGE
PASSENGER
PATERNITY
PATRONAGE
PATRONIZE
PERENNIAL
PERMANENT
PERSONAGE
PERSONATE
PERSONIFY
PERSONNEL
PERTINENT
PHILANDER
PLUTONIUM
PORRINGER
PRECANCEL
PRECENTOR
PRESENTLY
PROCONSUL
PROFANITY
PROMENADE
PROMINENT
PROPONENT
PROVENCAL
PROVENDER
PULMONARY
RABBINATE
RATIONALE
RECKONING
RECOGNIZE
RECTANGLE
REJOINDER
REMAINDER
RENCONTRE
REPLENISH
REPUGNANT
ROUGHNECK
ROUMANIAN
RUMRUNNER
RUTHENIUM
SATURNINE
SCAVENGER
SCREENING
SEASONING
SOLEMNIZE
SPELUNKER
STAMINATE
SUBLUNARY
SUNBONNET
SUPERNOVA
SURCINGLE
SURRENDER
SUSPENDER
TANZANIAN
TECTONICS
TECTONISM
TERMINATE
THICKNESS
THUMBNAIL
TRIENNIAL
TYRANNIZE
TYRANNOUS
UKRAINIAN
UNBEKNOWN
UNBOUNDED
UNCOUNTED
UNDAUNTED
UNFOUNDED
UNHARNESS
UNMEANING
VACCINATE
VICENNIAL
VILLENAGE
VIRGINITY
VISIONARY
VOLCANISM
VULCANISM
VULCANIZE
WARBONNET
WARMONGER
WHITENESS
ZIRCONIUM
ABANDONED
ACROPOLIS
ALCOHOLIC
ALEATORIC
ALMSHOUSE
ANAEROBIC
ANTINOVEL
ANTITOXIN
APOSTOLIC
APPALOOSA
ARTHROPOD
BACKBOARD
BACKWOODS
BAMBOOZLE
BASEBOARD
BATHHOUSE
BILLBOARD
BIRDHOUSE
BLOWTORCH
BLUEPOINT
BONDWOMAN
BOONDOCKS
BUCKBOARD
BUCKTOOTH
CABRIOLET
CALABOOSE
CARDBOARD
CATAMOUNT
CATATONIC
CHARWOMAN
CHOPHOUSE
CIRRHOSIS
CLAPBOARD
CLIPBOARD
CLOISONNE
CLUBHOUSE
COCKROACH
COONHOUND
CROSSOVER
DASHBOARD
DECALOGUE
DEMAGOGUE
DEMIMONDE
DESTROYER
DIAGNOSIS
DUCKBOARD
DUMBFOUND
DYSTROPHY
EASYGOING
ELASTOMER
EPISCOPAL
EQUIPOISE
EQUIVOCAL
FARMHOUSE
FIREHOUSE
FIREPOWER
FLAGEOLET
FLOPHOUSE
FOOTBOARD
FOOTLOOSE
FOREGOING
FORETOKEN
FOREWOMAN
FREEBOARD
GASTROPOD
GLADIOLUS
GREYHOUND
HALITOSIS
HANDWOVEN
HARDBOARD
HARDBOUND
HARDCOVER
HEADBOARD
HETERODOX
HIDEBOUND
HOPSCOTCH
HOREHOUND
IRONBOUND
KINSWOMAN
LATECOMER
LAZYBONES
LEITMOTIV
LOCOMOTOR
MAYFLOWER
MISSIONER
MOLDBOARD
MONOLOGUE
NONPROFIT
OUTGROWTH
OUTSPOKEN
OVERBOARD
OVERPOWER
PACKHORSE
PARAMOUNT
PAREGORIC
PEDAGOGUE
PENTHOUSE
PESTHOUSE
PLAYHOUSE
PNEUMONIA
POORHOUSE
PORTFOLIO
POURBOIRE
PROGNOSIS
PSEUDONYM
PSYCHOSIS
RACEHORSE
REENFORCE
REINFORCE
ROCKBOUND
RUNAROUND
SAFFLOWER
SCLEROSIS
SECTIONAL
SEMICOLON
SEMIWORKS
SHIPBOARD
SIDEBOARD
SIGNBOARD
SILICOSIS
SOFTBOUND
SOLILOQUY
STARBOARD
STATIONER
SUBATOMIC
SUNFLOWER
SURFBOARD
SYMBIOSIS
SYNAGOGUE
THEOSOPHY
TOLLHOUSE
TRANSONIC
TURQUOISE
UNALLOYED
UNTUTORED
VIEWPOINT
VOODOOISM
WALLBOARD
WAREHOUSE
WASHBOARD
WASHHOUSE
WASHWOMAN
WILLPOWER
WOLFHOUND
WORKHORSE
WORKHOUSE
ACCOMPANY
AEROSPACE
BISHOPRIC
CENTIPEDE
CHIROPODY
DAVENPORT
DECOMPOSE
DECOUPAGE
DIMORPHIC
DISAPPEAR
DISREPAIR
DISREPUTE
DISSIPATE
DRAINPIPE
DYSPEPSIA
ENCOMPASS
ETHIOPIAN
EUTROPHIC
EXCULPATE
EXTEMPORE
EXTIRPATE
HANDSPIKE
HORSEPLAY
INCULPATE
INTERPLAY
INTERPOSE
INTERPRET
JUXTAPOSE
MARSUPIAL
MILLIPEDE
MONOSPACE
MOUTHPART
PHILIPPIC
PHOTOPLAY
PINEAPPLE
PORCUPINE
PRECEPTOR
PRECIPICE
RAINSPOUT
RESERPINE
RIDGEPOLE
STANDPIPE
STOCKPILE
STRAPPING
SUBALPINE
SUGARPLUM
SUPERPOSE
SWORDPLAY
TOOTHPICK
TRANSPIRE
TRANSPORT
TRANSPOSE
TURBOPROP
ULTRAPURE
UNDERPART
UNDERPASS
UNDERPLAY
WALLOPING
WHIRLPOOL
ALGONQUIN
EXCHEQUER
HARLEQUIN
MANNEQUIN
PALANQUIN
SOBRIQUET
ABHORRENT
ADUMBRATE
AERODROME
AIRWORTHY
ALBATROSS
ANCHORAGE
ANCHORITE
ANCHORMAN
ANHYDROUS
ARBITRARY
ARBITRATE
ARROWROOT
AUCTORIAL
AUTHORITY
AUTHORIZE
AUTOCRACY
AUTOGRAPH
AUTOTRACE
AWESTRUCK
BACKTRACK
BACTERIUM
BALLERINA
BANDEROLE
BARBARIAN
BARBARISM
BARBAROUS
BARCAROLE
BAROGRAPH
BEDSPREAD
BIRTHRATE
BLOODROOT
BLUEGRASS
BLUEPRINT
BOMBPROOF
BOOMERANG
BOWSTRING
BROKERAGE
BULGARIAN
BUTTERCUP
BUTTERFAT
BUTTERFLY
BUTTERNUT
CALIBRATE
CANEBRAKE
CARBURIZE
CASSEROLE
CATHARSIS
CATHARTIC
CAUTERIZE
CELEBRATE
CELEBRITY
CELLARAGE
CENTURION
CEREBRATE
CHANCROID
CHAPARRAL
CHECKROOM
CHONDRITE
CHONDRULE
CLASSROOM
COFFERDAM
COMFORTER
CONCERNED
CONCERTED
CONCORDAT
CONGERIES
CONSCRIPT
CONSTRAIN
CONSTRICT
CONSTRUCT
COOPERATE
CORMORANT
CORPORATE
CORPOREAL
COURTROOM
COUTURIER
CRABGRASS
CRITERION
CROSSROAD
CUTTHROAT
DANGEROUS
DEHYDRATE
DEMOCRACY
DEMURRAGE
DENIGRATE
DEODORANT
DEODORIZE
DESECRATE
DESPERADO
DESPERATE
DETERRENT
DEUTERIUM
DEXTERITY
DEXTEROUS
DIAPHRAGM
DIFFERENT
DIPTEROUS
DISBURDEN
DISPARAGE
DISPARATE
DISTURBED
DITHERING
DOCTORATE
DOWNGRADE
EDITORIAL
ELABORATE
ELBOWROOM
ELECTRIFY
ELECTRODE
EMBARRASS
ENCOURAGE
ENDOCRINE
ENTOURAGE
ENUMERATE
EPHEDRINE
EPICUREAN
EPIDERMIS
EUCHARIST
EVAPORATE
EVAPORITE
EVERGREEN
EXONERATE

EXUBERANT
EYESTRAIN
FACTORIAL
FINGERING
FINGERTIP
FIREBRAND
FIREBREAK
FIREBRICK
FIREPROOF
FISHERMAN
FLAVORING
FLOWERPOT
FOOLPROOF
FOOTPRINT
FOREFRONT
FORWARDER
FRATERNAL
FRUSTRATE
GIBBERISH
GLAMORIZE
GODPARENT
GOLDBRICK
GONORRHEA
GREENROOM
GROSGRAIN
GUARDROOM
HAIRBRUSH
HAMADRYAD
HAMBURGER
HAMMERTOE
HAMSTRING
HANDCRAFT
HARBORAGE
HEADDRESS
HERBARIUM
HIERARCHY
HISTORIAN
HOARFROST
HOLOGRAPH
HOMEGROWN
HOMOGRAPH
HUNGARIAN
HYPOCRISY
HYSTERICS
IMMIGRANT
IMMIGRATE
INAMORATA
INCORRECT
INTEGRATE
INTEGRITY
INTERRUPT
ITINERANT
ITINERARY
JAILBREAK
JITTERBUG
LAMEBRAIN
LIBRARIAN
LIMBURGER
LITTERBUG
LUDICROUS
LUNCHROOM
MAINFRAME
MALADROIT
MANNERISM
MARGARINE
MARMOREAL
MARTYRDOM
MASTERFUL
MELIORATE
MELODRAMA
MERCERIZE
MERCURIAL
MERCUROUS
MESMERIZE
METEORITE
METEOROID
MIDSTREAM
MISDIRECT
MONOGRAPH
MURDEROUS
NECTARINE
NEWSPRINT
NOCTURNAL
NONPAREIL
NONPERSON
OFFSPRING
OLIGARCHY
OUTSPREAD
OUTWARDLY
OVERDRAFT
OVERDRIVE
OVERPRINT
OVERTRICK
OVERWRITE
OVIPAROUS
PARAGRAPH
PASSERINE
PASTORALE
PASTURAGE
PENETRATE
PERFORATE
PHALAROPE
PICTORIAL
PIMPERNEL
PINSTRIPE
POLYGRAPH
PONDEROUS
POSTERIOR
POSTERITY
PRAYERFUL
PRECURSOR
PRESCRIBE
PRESHRUNK
PRESSROOM
PRESTRESS
PREVERBAL
PRIMARILY
PROOFREAD
PROSCRIBE
PROSTRATE
PULVERIZE
RACETRACK
RASTERIZE
RECHERCHE
REENTRANT
REHEARING
REHEARSAL
REITERATE
REPAIRMAN
RESURRECT
RIGMAROLE
SAGEBRUSH
SANGFROID
SARTORIAL
SAXIFRAGE
SEAFARING
SEAWORTHY
SECTARIAN
SENIORITY
SERIGRAPH
SHIPWRECK
SIDETRACK
SNOWDRIFT
SPINDRIFT
STATEROOM
STOREROOM
SUBMARINE
SUBNORMAL
SUBSCRIBE
SUBSCRIPT
SUFFERING
SULFUROUS
SUMMARIZE
SUNSTROKE
SUPPURATE
TANGERINE
TELEGRAPH
TELLURIUM
TEMPERATE
TEMPORARY
TEMPORIZE
TENDERIZE
TENEBROUS
TERRARIUM
TERRORISM
TERRORIZE
THEATRICS
THEOCRACY
TIGHTROPE
TIMBERING
TINDERBOX
TONSORIAL
TRITURATE
TUSCARORA
TYPEWRITE
UNCHARTED
UNDERRATE
UNGUARDED
UNITARIAN
UNIVERSAL
UNLEARNED
UNSPARING
VENTUROUS
VICTORIAN
VULGARIAN
VULGARISM
VULGARITY
VULGARIZE
WINDBREAK
WINDPROOF
WINEPRESS
WINTERIZE
WIREFRAME
WISECRACK
WITHDRAWN
WOLVERINE
WONDERFUL
WOODCRAFT
WORKGROUP
YESTERDAY
ACCESSION
ACCESSORY
ADDRESSEE
ADMISSION
ADVERSARY
ADVERSITY
AFORESAID
ALABASTER
ALONGSIDE
AMPERSAND
ANGUISHED
ANIMOSITY
ARABESQUE
ASCENSION
ASPERSION
BANTUSTAN
BARRISTER
BLOODSHED
BLOODSHOT
BROADSIDE
BURLESQUE
CALLOSITY
CASUISTRY
CAUCASIAN
CENTESIMO
CHEMISTRY
CHORISTER
COLLUSION
COMMISSAR
COMPOSITE
COMPOSURE
CONFESSOR
CONFUSION
CONTUSION
CORPUSCLE
CORTISONE
COURTSHIP
CRAFTSMAN
CROISSANT
DEFENSIVE
DEPRESSED
DIMENSION
DIVERSIFY
DIVERSION
DIVERSITY
DRAFTSMAN
ECOSYSTEM
ELLIPSOID
EMBRASURE
EMPHASIZE
EMPHYSEMA
EXCELSIOR
EXCLUSIVE
EXCURSION
EXCURSIVE
EXPANSION
EXPANSIVE
EXPENSIVE
EXPLOSION
EXPLOSIVE
EXPULSION
EXQUISITE
EXTENSION
EXTENSIVE
EXTRUSIVE
FANTASIZE
FANTASTIC
FRICASSEE
GARNISHEE
GLYCOSIDE
GRANTSMAN
GRAPESHOT
GROOMSMAN
GROTESQUE
GUARDSMAN
GUNNYSACK
GYMNASIUM
HAVERSACK
HEARTSICK
HEURISTIC
HORSESHOE
IMPASSIVE
IMPULSION
IMPULSIVE
INCESSANT
INCURSION
INNERSOLE
INSENSATE
INTENSIFY
INTENSITY
INTENSIVE
INTERSECT
INVERSION
LIGHTSHIP
LIGHTSOME
LIMOUSINE
LITHESOME
LOATHSOME
MAGNESIUM
MALAYSIAN
MICROSOFT
MULTISCAN
MULTISPIN
MULTISYNC
NARCISSUS
NECESSARY
NECESSITY
OBSESSION
OFFENSIVE
OMBUDSMAN
ONIONSKIN
ORCHESTRA
ORGIASTIC
PALAESTRA
PALMISTRY
PATRISTIC
PAYMASTER
PENINSULA
POETASTER
POLYESTER
POTASSIUM
PRECISION
PREVISION
PROBOSCIS
PROCESSOR
PROFESSOR
PROMISING
PROVISION
QUICKSAND
QUICKSORT
QUICKSTEP
RECESSION
RECESSIVE
RECURSION
REMISSION
REPOSSESS
REPRESENT
REPULSION
REPULSIVE
REQUISITE
REVERSION
REVULSION
RIVERSIDE
SACRISTAN
SCRIMSHAW
SECESSION
SECLUSION
SEQUESTER
SHARKSKIN
SHEEPSKIN
SHORTSTOP
SLINGSHOT
SOPHISTIC
SOPHISTRY
SPACESHIP
SPOKESMAN
SPORTSMAN
STATESIDE
STATESMAN
STATISTIC
STEAMSHIP
SUCCESSOR
SUPERSEDE
SUPPOSING
SWEATSHOP
SWORDSMAN
SYMPOSIUM
THREESOME
TOOTHSOME
TRADESMAN
TRANSSHIP
TRIBESMAN
TRICKSTER
TRIMESTER
TROOPSHIP
TROUSSEAU
UNBLESSED
UNCEASING
UNDERSELL
UNDERSHOT
UNDERSIDE
UPANISHAD
UPHOLSTER
VISCOSITY
VOUCHSAFE
WATERSHED
WATERSIDE
WEARISOME
WEDNESDAY
WHOLESALE
WHOLESOME
WORRISOME
YACHTSMAN
YOUNGSTER
ACCRETION
ACOUSTICS
ADDICTION
ADJECTIVE
ADMIXTURE
ADVANTAGE
ADVENTURE
ADVERTISE
AFFECTING
AFFECTION
AILANTHUS
AMPLITUDE
ANIMATION
ANNUITANT
APPERTAIN
APPLETALK
APPORTION
ARCHETYPE
ARCHITECT
ARGENTINE
ARGENTITE
ARMISTICE
ASAFETIDA
ASCERTAIN
ASSERTION
ASSISTANT
ASYMPTOTE
ATHLETICS
ATTENTION
ATTRITION
AVOCATION
BACKSTAGE
BANDSTAND
BARNSTORM
BEATITUDE
BEEFSTEAK
BESETTING
BESPATTER
BETROTHED
BIMONTHLY
BIPARTITE
BRIMSTONE
BROADTAIL
CAMPSTOOL
CARNATION
CARPETBAG
CARPETING
CAUSATION
CELESTIAL
CERTITUDE
CESSATION
CHIEFTAIN
CHOPSTICK
CHRISTIAN
CHRISTMAS
CLIENTELE
COALITION
COCKATIEL
COFEATURE
COGNITION
COLLATION
COMMITTEE

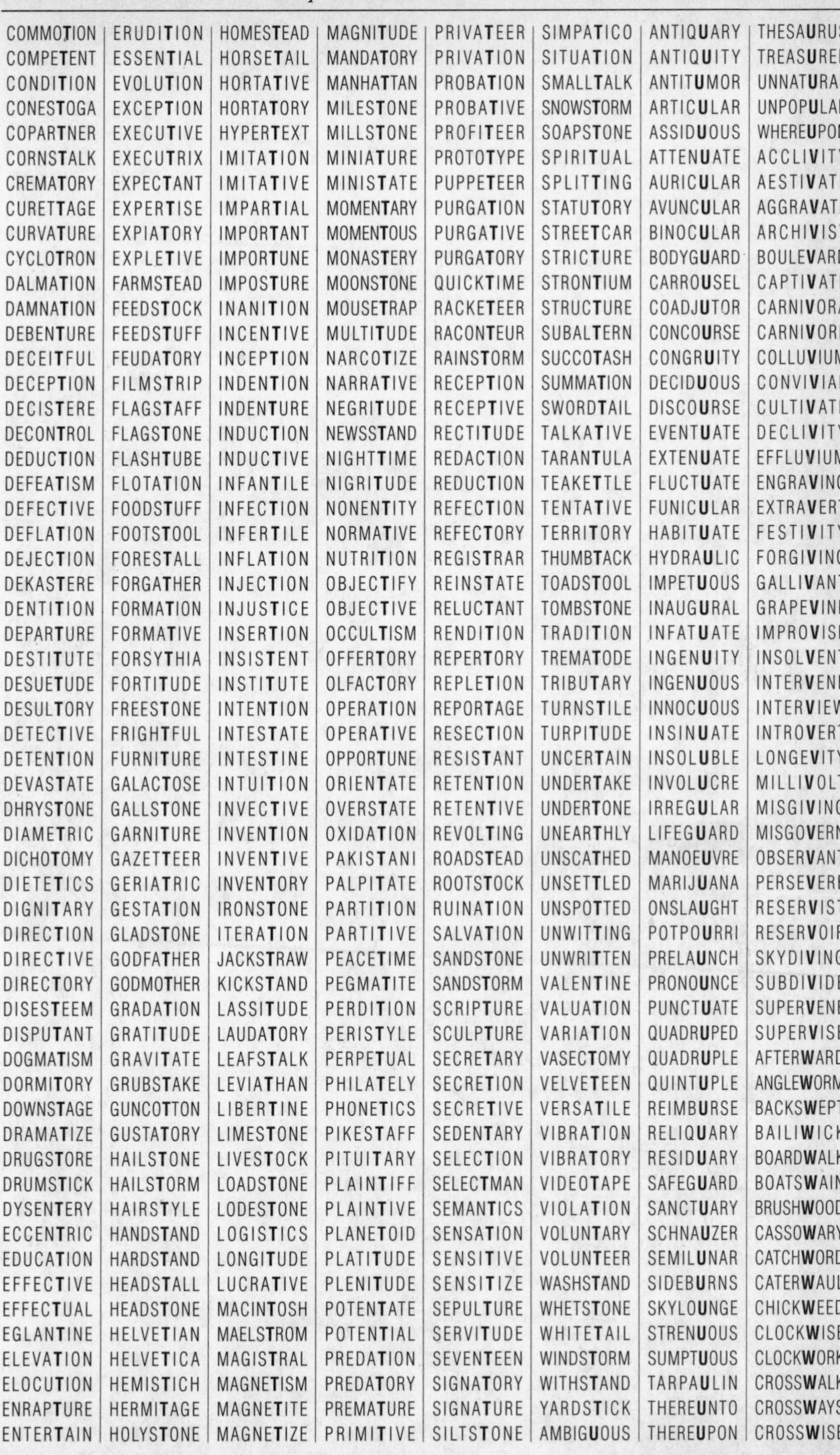

COMMOTION
COMPETENT
CONDITION
CONESTOGA
COPARTNER
CORNSTALK
CREMATORY
CURETTAGE
CURVATURE
CYCLOTRON
DALMATION
DAMNATION
DEBENTURE
DECEITFUL
DECEPTION
DECISTERE
DECONTROL
DEDUCTION
DEFEATISM
DEFECTIVE
DEFLATION
DEJECTION
DEKASTERE
DENTITION
DEPARTURE
DESTITUTE
DESUETUDE
DESULTORY
DETECTIVE
DETENTION
DEVASTATE
DHRYSTONE
DIAMETRIC
DICHOTOMY
DIETETICS
DIGNITARY
DIRECTION
DIRECTIVE
DIRECTORY
DISESTEEM
DISPUTANT
DOGMATISM
DORMITORY
DOWNSTAGE
DRAMATIZE
DRUGSTORE
DRUMSTICK
DYSENTERY
ECCENTRIC
EDUCATION
EFFECTIVE
EFFECTUAL
EGLANTINE
ELEVATION
ELOCUTION
ENRAPTURE
ENTERTAIN
ERUDITION
ESSENTIAL
EVOLUTION
EXCEPTION
EXECUTIVE
EXECUTRIX
EXPECTANT
EXPERTISE
EXPIATORY
EXPLETIVE
FARMSTEAD
FEEDSTOCK
FEEDSTUFF
FEUDATORY
FILMSTRIP
FLAGSTAFF
FLAGSTONE
FLASHTUBE
FLOTATION
FOODSTUFF
FOOTSTOOL
FORESTALL
FORGATHER
FORMATION
FORMATIVE
FORSYTHIA
FORTITUDE
FREESTONE
FRIGHTFUL
FURNITURE
GALACTOSE
GALLSTONE
GARNITURE
GAZETTEER
GERIATRIC
GESTATION
GLADSTONE
GODFATHER
GODMOTHER
GRADATION
GRATITUDE
GRAVITATE
GRUBSTAKE
GUNCOTTON
GUSTATORY
HAILSTONE
HAILSTORM
HAIRSTYLE
HANDSTAND
HARDSTAND
HEADSTALL
HEADSTONE
HELVETIAN
HELVETICA
HEMISTICH
HERMITAGE
HOLYSTONE
HOMESTEAD
HORSETAIL
HORTATIVE
HORTATORY
HYPERTEXT
IMITATION
IMITATIVE
IMPARTIAL
IMPORTANT
IMPORTUNE
IMPOSTURE
INANITION
INCENTIVE
INCEPTION
INDENTION
INDENTURE
INDUCTION
INDUCTIVE
INFANTILE
INFECTION
INFERTILE
INFLATION
INJECTION
INJUSTICE
INSERTION
INSISTENT
INSTITUTE
INTENTION
INTESTATE
INTESTINE
INTUITION
INVECTIVE
INVENTION
INVENTIVE
INVENTORY
IRONSTONE
ITERATION
JACKSTRAW
KICKSTAND
LASSITUDE
LAUDATORY
LEAFSTALK
LEVIATHAN
LIBERTINE
LIMESTONE
LIVESTOCK
LOADSTONE
LODESTONE
LOGISTICS
LONGITUDE
LUCRATIVE
MACINTOSH
MAELSTROM
MAGISTRAL
MAGNETISM
MAGNETITE
MAGNETIZE
MAGNITUDE
MANDATORY
MANHATTAN
MILESTONE
MILLSTONE
MINIATURE
MINISTATE
MOMENTARY
MOMENTOUS
MONASTERY
MOONSTONE
MOUSETRAP
MULTITUDE
NARCOTIZE
NARRATIVE
NEGRITUDE
NEWSSTAND
NIGHTTIME
NIGRITUDE
NONENTITY
NORMATIVE
NUTRITION
OBJECTIFY
OBJECTIVE
OCCULTISM
OFFERTORY
OLFACTORY
OPERATION
OPERATIVE
OPPORTUNE
ORIENTATE
OVERSTATE
OXIDATION
PAKISTANI
PALPITATE
PARTITION
PARTITIVE
PEACETIME
PEGMATITE
PERDITION
PERISTYLE
PERPETUAL
PHILATELY
PHONETICS
PIKESTAFF
PITUITARY
PLAINTIFF
PLAINTIVE
PLANETOID
PLATITUDE
PLENITUDE
POTENTATE
POTENTIAL
PREDATION
PREDATORY
PREMATURE
PRIMITIVE
PRIVATEER
PRIVATION
PROBATION
PROBATIVE
PROFITEER
PROTOTYPE
PUPPETEER
PURGATION
PURGATIVE
PURGATORY
QUICKTIME
RACKETEER
RACONTEUR
RAINSTORM
RECEPTION
RECEPTIVE
RECTITUDE
REDACTION
REDUCTION
REFECTION
REFECTORY
REGISTRAR
REINSTATE
RELUCTANT
RENDITION
REPERTORY
REPLETION
REPORTAGE
RESECTION
RESISTANT
RETENTION
RETENTIVE
REVOLTING
ROADSTEAD
ROOTSTOCK
RUINATION
SALVATION
SANDSTONE
SANDSTORM
SCRIPTURE
SCULPTURE
SECRETARY
SECRETION
SECRETIVE
SEDENTARY
SELECTION
SELECTMAN
SEMANTICS
SENSATION
SENSITIVE
SENSITIZE
SEPULTURE
SERVITUDE
SEVENTEEN
SIGNATORY
SIGNATURE
SILTSTONE
SIMPATICO
SITUATION
SMALLTALK
SNOWSTORM
SOAPSTONE
SPIRITUAL
SPLITTING
STATUTORY
STREETCAR
STRICTURE
STRONTIUM
STRUCTURE
SUBALTERN
SUCCOTASH
SUMMATION
SWORDTAIL
TALKATIVE
TARANTULA
TEAKETTLE
TENTATIVE
TERRITORY
THUMBTACK
TOADSTOOL
TOMBSTONE
TRADITION
TREMATODE
TRIBUTARY
TURNSTILE
TURPITUDE
UNCERTAIN
UNDERTAKE
UNDERTONE
UNEARTHLY
UNSCATHED
UNSETTLED
UNSPOTTED
UNWITTING
UNWRITTEN
VALENTINE
VALUATION
VARIATION
VASECTOMY
VELVETEEN
VERSATILE
VIBRATION
VIBRATORY
VIDEOTAPE
VIOLATION
VOLUNTARY
VOLUNTEER
WASHSTAND
WHETSTONE
WHITETAIL
WINDSTORM
WITHSTAND
YARDSTICK
AMBIGUOUS
ANTIQUARY
ANTIQUITY
ANTITUMOR
ARTICULAR
ASSIDUOUS
ATTENUATE
AURICULAR
AVUNCULAR
BINOCULAR
BODYGUARD
CARROUSEL
COADJUTOR
CONCOURSE
CONGRUITY
DECIDUOUS
DISCOURSE
EVENTUATE
EXTENUATE
FLUCTUATE
FUNICULAR
HABITUATE
HYDRAULIC
IMPETUOUS
INAUGURAL
INFATUATE
INGENUITY
INGENUOUS
INNOCUOUS
INSINUATE
INSOLUBLE
INVOLUCRE
IRREGULAR
LIFEGUARD
MANOEUVRE
MARIJUANA
ONSLAUGHT
POTPOURRI
PRELAUNCH
PRONOUNCE
PUNCTUATE
QUADRUPED
QUADRUPLE
QUINTUPLE
REIMBURSE
RELIQUARY
RESIDUARY
SAFEGUARD
SANCTUARY
SCHNAUZER
SEMILUNAR
SIDEBURNS
SKYLOUNGE
STRENUOUS
SUMPTUOUS
TARPAULIN
THEREUNTO
THEREUPON
THESAURUS
TREASURER
UNNATURAL
UNPOPULAR
WHEREUPON
ACCLIVITY
AESTIVATE
AGGRAVATE
ARCHIVIST
BOULEVARD
CAPTIVATE
CARNIVORA
CARNIVORE
COLLUVIUM
CONVIVIAL
CULTIVATE
DECLIVITY
EFFLUVIUM
ENGRAVING
EXTRAVERT
FESTIVITY
FORGIVING
GALLIVANT
GRAPEVINE
IMPROVISE
INSOLVENT
INTERVENE
INTERVIEW
INTROVERT
LONGEVITY
MILLIVOLT
MISGIVING
MISGOVERN
OBSERVANT
PERSEVERE
RESERVIST
RESERVOIR
SKYDIVING
SUBDIVIDE
SUPERVENE
SUPERVISE
AFTERWARD
ANGLEWORM
BACKSWEPT
BAILIWICK
BOARDWALK
BOATSWAIN
BRUSHWOOD
CASSOWARY
CATCHWORD
CATERWAUL
CHICKWEED
CLOCKWISE
CLOCKWORK
CROSSWALK
CROSSWAYS
CROSSWISE

DELFTWARE
DOWNSWING
DRIFTWOOD
EARTHWARD
EARTHWORK
EARTHWORM
FANCYWORK
FELLOWMAN
FOLLOWING
FORESWEAR
FORTHWITH
FRAMEWORK
GREENWOOD
GRILLWORK
GROUPWARE
GUNPOWDER
HALLOWEEN
HANDIWORK
HEARTWOOD
HORSEWHIP
HOUSEWIFE
HOUSEWORK
INGROWING
JEWELWEED
LANDOWNER
LEASTWISE
LIVERWORT
MATCHWOOD
METALWARE
METALWORK
MICROWAVE
MOUTHWASH
NORTHWEST
OTHERWISE
PATCHWORK
PIECEWORK
ROUNDWORM
SATINWOOD
SHADOWBOX
SHAREWARE
SHORTWAVE
SIDESWIPE
SOUTHWEST
SPEEDWELL
STAIRWELL
TABLEWARE
THEREWITH
UNDERWEAR
UNDERWOOD
UNKNOWING
VAPORWARE
WATCHWORD
WHEREWITH
WHIRLWIND
WHITEWALL
WHITEWASH
WHITEWOOD
WINDSWEPT
WORLDWIDE
WORRYWART
HYDROXIDE
INFLEXION
REFLEXIVE
THYROXINE
UNISEXUAL
APOCRYPHA
CATALYSIS
CLERGYMAN
COURTYARD
GRAVEYARD
KILOCYCLE
LIVERYMAN
MEGACYCLE
PANEGYRIC
PARALYSIS
PRESBYTER
PYROLYSIS
STEELYARD
STOCKYARD
SURVEYING
VESTRYMAN
BOMBAZINE
HAPHAZARD
PROTOZOAN
QUARTZITE
TRAPEZOID

## 7th Letter

ABOMINATE
ACCLIMATE
ACCOMPANY
ACIDULATE
ADSORBATE
ADUMBRATE
ADVANTAGE
ADVERSARY
AEROPLANE
AEROSPACE
AESTIVATE
AFFILIATE
AFORESAID
AFRIKAANS
AFTERCARE
AFTERMATH
AFTERWARD
AGGRAVATE
AGGREGATE
ALLEVIATE
ALTERNATE
AMBUSCADE
AMERICANA
AMPERSAND
ANCHORAGE
ANCILLARY
ANNUITANT
ANTIQUARY
APPELLANT
APPELLATE
APPENDAGE
APPERTAIN
APPLEJACK
APPLETALK
APPLICANT
AQUAPLANE
ARBITRARY
ARBITRATE
ASCENDANT
ASCERTAIN
ASSISTANT
ASSOCIATE
ASTROLABE
ASTRONAUT
ATTENDANT
ATTENUATE
AUTOCRACY
AUTOGRAPH
AUTOTRACE
AUXILIARY
BACKBOARD
BACKSLASH
BACKSTAGE
BACKTRACK
BANDSTAND
BAROGRAPH
BARRICADE
BASEBOARD
BASTINADO
BENIGNANT
BICONCAVE
BIFURCATE
BILLBOARD
BIRTHMARK
BIRTHRATE
BLACKBALL
BLACKJACK
BLACKMAIL
BLOODBATH
BLUEBLACK
BLUEGRASS
BOARDWALK
BOATSWAIN
BODYGUARD
BOOKPLATE
BOOMERANG
BOOTBLACK
BOULEVARD
BREAKFAST
BRIEFCASE
BRILLIANT
BROADBAND
BROADCAST
BROADTAIL
BROKERAGE
BUCKBOARD
BUSHWHACK
CALCULATE
CALIBRATE
CAMELBACK
CANDIDACY
CANDIDATE
CANEBRAKE
CANNONADE
CAPILLARY
CAPSULATE
CAPTIVATE
CARBONATE
CARDBOARD
CARTILAGE
CASSOWARY
CASTIGATE
CATERWAUL
CAVALCADE
CELEBRATE
CELLARAGE
CENTENARY
CEREBRATE
CHARABANC
CHECKMATE
CHIEFTAIN
CHILBLAIN
CHLORDANE
CHOCOLATE
CIRCULATE
CLAPBOARD
CLASSMATE
CLIPBOARD
COAGULANT
COAGULATE
COCKROACH
COLLIMATE
COLONNADE
COLORCAST
COLORFAST
CONFIDANT
CONJUGATE
CONSONANT
CONSTRAIN
COOPERATE
CORMORANT
CORNSTALK
COROLLARY
CORPORATE
CORRELATE
CORRUGATE
CORUSCATE
COSMONAUT
COURTYARD
CRABGRASS
CRANKCASE
CROISSANT
CROSSWALK
CROSSWAYS
CULMINATE
CULTIVATE
CURETTAGE
CUSTOMARY
CYCLAMATE
CYTOPLASM
DAIRYMAID
DASHBOARD
DECOUPAGE
DEFENDANT
DEFOLIANT
DEFOLIATE
DEHYDRATE
DELFTWARE
DELINEATE
DEMARCATE
DEMOCRACY
DEMURRAGE
DENIGRATE
DEODORANT
DEPRECATE
DESECRATE
DESICCANT
DESICCATE
DESIGNATE
DESPERADO
DESPERATE
DEVASTATE
DIAPHRAGM
DIGNITARY
DIPLOMACY
DISEMBARK
DISENGAGE
DISLOCATE
DISPARAGE
DISPARATE
DISPLEASE
DISPUTANT
DISREGARD
DISREPAIR
DISSIPATE
DIXIELAND
DOCTORATE
DOORPLATE
DOWNGRADE
DOWNSTAGE
DREAMLAND
DROMEDARY
DUCKBOARD
DUPLICATE
EARTHWARD
EJACULATE
ELABORATE
ELIMINATE
ELUCIDATE
EMBARRASS
EMBROCATE
EMPENNAGE
ENCHILADA
ENCOMPASS
ENCOURAGE
ENTERTAIN
ENTOURAGE
ENUMERATE
ENUNCIATE
ERADICATE
ESPIONAGE
ESPLANADE
EVAPORATE
EVENTUATE
EVERGLADE
EXCORIATE
EXCULPATE
EXEMPLARY
EXONERATE
EXPATIATE
EXPECTANT
EXPLICATE
EXPURGATE
EXTENUATE
EXTIRPATE
EXTRICATE
EXUBERANT
EYESTRAIN
FABRICATE
FAIRYLAND
FASCINATE
FECUNDATE
FIDUCIARY
FIREBRAND
FIREPLACE
FIRSTHAND
FLAGSTAFF
FLASHBACK
FLOODGATE
FLOWCHART
FLUCTUATE
FOOTBOARD
FORESTALL
FORMULATE
FORTUNATE
FREEBOARD
FRIEDCAKE
FRUITCAKE
FRUSTRATE
FULMINATE
FUSILLADE
GALLIVANT
GANGPLANK
GERMINATE
GRANULATE
GRASSLAND
GRAVEYARD
GRAVITATE
GRAYBEARD
GREENBACK
GROSGRAIN
GROUPWARE
GRUBSTAKE
GUNNYSACK
HABITUATE
HANDCLASP
HANDCRAFT
HANDSHAKE
HANDSTAND
HAPHAZARD
HARBORAGE
HARDBOARD
HARDSTAND
HAVERSACK
HEADBOARD
HEADSTALL
HERMITAGE
HIBERNATE
HOLOGRAPH
HOMOGRAPH
HORSEBACK
HORSEHAIR
HORSETAIL
HOURGLASS
HOUSEMAID
HUMILIATE
HUNCHBACK
HURRICANE
HYPERCARD
HYPHENATE
IMAGINARY
IMMEDIACY
IMMEDIATE
IMMIGRANT
IMMIGRATE
IMPLICATE
IMPORTANT
IMPRECATE
INAMORATA
INANIMATE
INCARNATE
INCESSANT
INCULCATE
INCULPATE
INDIGNANT
INEBRIATE
INELEGANT
INFATUATE
INFIRMARY
INFORMANT
INFURIATE
INOCULATE
INSATIATE
INSENSATE
INSINUATE
INSTIGATE
INTEGRATE
INTENDANT
INTERFACE
INTERLACE
INTERLARD
INTESTATE
INTRICATE
INVIOLATE
IRRADIATE
ISINGLASS
ITINERANT
ITINERARY
JUDICIARY
KICKSTAND
LAMEBRAIN
LANDSCAPE
LEAFSTALK
LEGENDARY
LEGISLATE
LIFEGUARD
LIGHTFACE
LIQUIDATE
LOWERCASE
LUBRICANT
LUBRICATE
LUXURIANT
LUXURIATE
MAINFRAME
MALIGNANT
MARIJUANA
MARMALADE
MASTICATE
MEGADEATH
MELIORATE
MELODRAMA
MENDICANT
MERCENARY
METALWARE
MICROWAVE
MINISTATE
MISBEHAVE
MISCREANT
MISMANAGE
MOLDBOARD
MOMENTARY
MONOGRAPH
MONOPLANE
MONOSPACE
MOONSCAPE

MOTORCADE
MOUTHPART
MOUTHWASH
NAMEPLATE
NECESSARY
NEGOTIANT
NEGOTIATE
NEWSSTAND
NIGHTFALL
NIGHTHAWK
NIGHTMARE
NORTHEAST
NOTCHBACK
NOVITIATE
NURSEMAID
OBBLIGATO
OBFUSCATE
OBJURGATE
OBSERVANT
OBSTINATE
OFFICIANT
OFFICIATE
ORANGEADE
ORIENTATE
ORIGINATE
ORPHANAGE
OSCILLATE
OVERBOARD
OVERDRAFT
OVERREACH
OVERSTATE
OXYGENATE
PAKISTANI
PALPITATE
PAPERBACK
PARAGRAPH
PARSONAGE
PASTORALE
PASTURAGE
PATRONAGE
PECUNIARY
PENEPLAIN
PENETRATE
PERCOLATE
PERFORATE
PERSONAGE
PERSONATE
PHOSPHATE
PICKABACK
PIGGYBACK
PIKESTAFF
PITUITARY
PIZZICATO
PLOWSHARE
POINCIANA
POLYGRAPH
PORCELAIN
PORTULACA
POSTULANT
POSTULATE
POTENTATE
PREDICATE
PREORDAIN
PROCREATE
PROMENADE
PROPAGATE
PROSTRATE
PROXIMATE
PULMONARY
PUNCTUATE
QUICKSAND
RABBINATE
RACETRACK
RANCHLAND
RANGELAND
RATIONALE
REDBREAST
REDUNDANT
REENTRANT
REINSTATE
REITERATE
RELIQUARY
RELUCTANT
REPLICATE
REPORTAGE
REPRIMAND
REPROBATE
REPUDIATE
REPUGNANT
RESIDUARY
RESISTANT
RETALIATE
RETARDATE
RIVERBANK
RUSTICATE
SAFEGUARD
SAILPLANE
SANCTUARY
SANDBLAST
SAXIFRAGE
SCREWBALL
SCRIMMAGE
SECONDARY
SECRETARY
SEDENTARY
SEGREGATE
SERIGRAPH
SHAREWARE
SHIPBOARD
SHIPSHAPE
SHORTCAKE
SHORTHAND
SHORTWAVE
SHOWPLACE
SHRINKAGE
SIDEBOARD
SIDETRACK
SIGNBOARD
SMALLTALK
SNOWFLAKE
SOUTHEAST
SPEAKEASY
SPECULATE
STAIRCASE
STALEMATE
STAMINATE
STARBOARD
STEADFAST
STEELYARD
STIMULANT
STIMULATE
STIPULATE
STOCKYARD
SUBJUGATE
SUBLIMATE
SUBLUNARY
SUCCOTASH
SUFFOCATE
SUGARCANE
SUPPLIANT
SUPPURATE
SUPREMACY
SURFBOARD
SURROGATE
SWAMPLAND
SWORDTAIL
SYCOPHANT
SYNDICATE
TABLELAND
TABLEWARE
TELEGRAPH
TEMPERATE
TEMPORARY
TERMAGANT
TERMINATE
THEOCRACY
THROWBACK
THUMBNAIL
THUMBTACK
TRACKBALL
TRADEMARK
TRANSLATE
TRENCHANT
TRIBUTARY
TRIFOCALS
TRITURATE
UNCERTAIN
UNDERHAND
UNDERPART
UNDERPASS
UNDERRATE
UNDERTAKE
UPPERCASE
VACCINATE
VACILLATE
VAPORWARE
VARIEGATE
VASSALAGE
VENTILATE
VIDEOTAPE
VILLENAGE
VINDICATE
VISIONARY
VOLUNTARY
VOUCHSAFE
WAISTBAND
WALLBOARD
WASHBOARD
WASHSTAND
WASTELAND
WATCHBAND
WATCHCASE
WATERFALL
WATERMARK
WHEELBASE
WHITEBAIT
WHITEHALL
WHITETAIL
WHITEWALL
WHITEWASH
WHOLESALE
WIREFRAME
WISECRACK
WITHDRAWN
WITHSTAND
WOLFSBANE
WOODCRAFT
WORKPLACE
WORRYWART
WRISTBAND
ADMIRABLE
ADVISABLE
AGREEABLE
ALIENABLE
ANAEROBIC
AVAILABLE
BUMBLEBEE
CARPETBAG
CONSTABLE
DESIRABLE
DIRIGIBLE
DISMEMBER
DISSEMBLE
DISTURBED
DIVISIBLE
EQUITABLE
ESTIMABLE
EXCITABLE
EXECRABLE
FAVORABLE
FLAMMABLE
FRANGIBLE
HABITABLE
HERITABLE
HONORABLE
ILLEGIBLE
IMMOVABLE
IMMUTABLE
INCAPABLE
INCURABLE
INDELIBLE
INEFFABLE
INFUSIBLE
INSOLUBLE
INSURABLE
INVISIBLE
IRASCIBLE
IRRITABLE
JITTERBUG
LITTERBUG
MALLEABLE
MEDICABLE
MEMORABLE
MISERABLE
NAVIGABLE
OUTNUMBER
PALATABLE
PERMEABLE
PLAUSIBLE
PREGNABLE
PREVERBAL
PRINTABLE
REPUTABLE
REVOCABLE
SADDLEBOW
SCHOOLBOY
SEPARABLE
SEPTEMBER
SHADOWBOX
STREAMBED
TIMETABLE
TINDERBOX
TOLERABLE
TRACTABLE
TURNTABLE
UNPLUMBED
VEGETABLE
VENERABLE
VERITABLE
WAVETABLE
WORKTABLE
ANNOUNCER
ARTIFICER
AVALANCHE
BAREFACED
BELLYACHE
BOONDOCKS
BUTTERCUP
CANONICAL
CAPRICCIO
CARBUNCLE
CHRONICLE
CLASSICAL
CORPUSCLE
EMPIRICAL
EQUIVOCAL
GYRFALCON
HEARTACHE
HIERARCHY
IDENTICAL
ILLOGICAL
INVOLUCRE
JAUNDICED
JURIDICAL
KILOCYCLE
MEGACYCLE
MOUSTACHE
MULTISCAN
NUMERICAL
OLIGARCHY
POLITICAL
PRACTICAL
PRECANCEL
PROBOSCIS
PROVENCAL
QUIZZICAL
RECHERCHE
SPECTACLE
STREETCAR
TECHNICAL
TOOTHACHE
UMBILICUS
VENTRICLE
VERIDICAL
VIDELICET
WHIMSICAL
ASTRADDLE
ATTAINDER
BACKPEDAL
BANDWIDTH
BARTENDER
BEDRIDDEN
BYSTANDER
CARTRIDGE
CHICKADEE
COFFERDAM
COMMANDER
CONCORDAT
CORIANDER
COTYLEDON
CULLENDER
DESCENDER
DISBURDEN
DISCREDIT
EMBROIDER
FORWARDER
GUNPOWDER
HEREUNDER
HETERODOX
HOTHEADED
HUSBANDRY
ICELANDER
ICELANDIC
JOBHOLDER
KNOWLEDGE
MANHANDLE
MARTYRDOM
MISHANDLE
NONCREDIT
NONREADER
OUTWARDLY
PANHANDLE
PARTRIDGE
PENHOLDER
PHILANDER
PIGHEADED
PROVENDER
REJOINDER
REMAINDER
SURRENDER
SUSPENDER
THRALLDOM
UNBOUNDED
UNDECIDED
UNFOUNDED
UNGUARDED
UNWORLDLY
WEDNESDAY
YESTERDAY
ABATEMENT
ABHORRENT
ABSORBENT
ACETYLENE
ADSORBENT
AFTERDECK
AGREEMENT
AMENDMENT
APARTHEID
APARTMENT
APPREHEND
ARCHENEMY
ARCHFIEND
ARCHITECT
ARROWHEAD
ARTILLERY
ASCENDERS
ATHENAEUM
ATONEMENT
BACKFIELD
BACKSWEPT
BAKSHEESH
BALLADEER
BEACHHEAD
BEDSPREAD
BEEFSTEAK
BELVEDERE
BIOSPHERE
BLACKHEAD
BLASPHEME
BLASPHEMY
BLEACHERS
BLOCKHEAD
BOMBSHELL
BOOKSHELF
BRASSIERE
BUCCANEER
BUCKWHEAT
CAMEMBERT
CANNONEER
CARIBBEAN
CARTWHEEL
CASTANETS
CATCHMENT
CEASELESS
CENTIPEDE
CHAMELEON
CHAUFFEUR
CHEERLESS
CHICANERY
CHICKWEED
CLAMSHELL
CLIENTELE
CLIPSHEET
COALFIELD
COCHINEAL
COMPETENT
COMPONENT
CONDIMENT
CONTINENT
CONTUMELY
CORPOREAL
COUNTLESS
DAMASCENE
DAUNTLESS
DEATHLESS
DECISTERE
DECOLLETE
DECREMENT
DEFERMENT
DEFICIENT
DEKASTERE
DEMULCENT
DEPENDENT
DETERGENT
DETERRENT
DETRIMENT

DEVILMENT
DIFFERENT
DIFFIDENT
DISAFFECT
DISAPPEAR
DISESTEEM
DISHONEST
DISINFECT
DISORIENT
DISSIDENT
DOUBTLESS
DYSENTERY
EBULLIENT
EFFICIENT
ELSEWHERE
EMBAYMENT
EMOLLIENT
EMOLUMENT
EMPHYSEMA
EPICUREAN
EQUIPMENT
EUCLIDEAN
EVERGREEN
EXCELLENT
EXCREMENT
EXOSPHERE
EXPEDIENT
EXTRAVERT
FARMSTEAD
FIREBREAK
FIRMAMENT
FLATULENT
FORESHEET
FORESWEAR
FREEWHEEL
GAZETTEER
GENUFLECT
GODPARENT
GOLDFIELD
GOVERNESS
GREENBELT
HAIRPIECE
HALLOWEEN
HAPPINESS
HATCHMENT
HEADDRESS
HEADPIECE
HEARTBEAT
HEARTFELT
HEARTLESS
HERCULEAN
HOMESTEAD
HYPERTEXT
IMPATIENS
IMPATIENT
IMPERFECT
IMPLEMENT
IMPRUDENT
INCIPIENT
INCLEMENT
INCORRECT
INCREMENT
INCUMBENT
INPATIENT
INSINCERE
INSISTENT
INSOLVENT
INSURGENT
INTELLECT
INTERCEDE
INTERCEPT
INTERFERE
INTERJECT
INTERLEAF
INTERMENT
INTERSECT
INTERVENE
INTROVERT
INVERNESS
JAILBREAK
JEWELWEED
LAVALIERE
LINEAMENT
MACHINERY
MANGANESE
MARMOREAL
MAUSOLEUM
MERRIMENT
MIDSTREAM
MILLINERY
MILLIPEDE
MINCEMEAT
MISDIRECT
MISGOVERN
MISORIENT
MISSILERY
MONASTERY
NEGLIGENT
NONPAREIL
NORTHWEST
NOSEBLEED
NOSEPIECE
NUTRIMENT
OUTSPREAD
OVERSLEEP
OVERWHELM
PACHYDERM
PARCHMENT
PEKINGESE
PERFUMERY
PERIPHERY
PERMANENT
PERSEVERE
PERTINENT
PESTILENT
PETROLEUM
PHILATELY
PHOTOCELL
PIECEMEAL
PLACEMENT
PRECEDENT
PRESIDENT
PRESTRESS
PREVALENT
PRICELESS
PRIVATEER
PRIVILEGE
PROFITEER
PROMINENT
PROOFREAD
PROPONENT
PROPRIETY
PROVIDENT
PUBESCENT
PUPPETEER
QUIESCENT
RACKETEER
RACONTEUR
RECIPIENT
RECOLLECT
RECOMMEND
RECUMBENT
REPELLENT
REPOSSESS
REPREHEND
REPRESENT
RESURRECT
ROADSTEAD
ROUGHNECK
SACRAMENT
SACRILEGE
SCUTCHEON
SENTIMENT
SEVENTEEN
SHAPELESS
SHIFTLESS
SHIPWRECK
SHOWPIECE
SHRUBBERY
SIDEPIECE
SNOWFIELD
SOMEWHERE
SOMNOLENT
SOUTHWEST
SPEARHEAD
SPEEDWELL
STAIRWELL
STATEMENT
STRAPLESS
SUBALTERN
SUCCULENT
SUPERSEDE
SUPERVENE
SWEETMEAT
SWELLHEAD
TESTAMENT
THANKLESS
THICKNESS
TIMEPIECE
TRANSCEND
TRANSIENT
TREACHERY
TREATMENT
TROUSSEAU
TRUCULENT
TRUNCHEON
TURBULENT
UNCONCERN
UNDERFEED
UNDERSELL
UNDERWEAR
UNHARNESS
UNIVALENT
VELVETEEN
VOICELESS
VOLUNTEER
WHITEHEAD
WHITENESS
WINDBREAK
WINDSWEPT
WINEPRESS
WORTHLESS
BEAUTIFUL
BOUNTIFUL
BUTTERFAT
BUTTERFLY
CALORIFIC
DAMSELFLY
DECEITFUL
DISCOMFIT
DOBSONFLY
DRAGONFLY
FRIGHTFUL
HEALTHFUL
HONORIFIC
MASTERFUL
NONPROFIT
PLENTIFUL
PRAYERFUL
RAUWOLFIA
RESHUFFLE
SOPORIFIC
UNMINDFUL
WONDERFUL
ARCHANGEL
ASPARAGUS
BANDWAGON
BESPANGLE
BOMBSIGHT
BULLFIGHT
CHAMPAGNE
COCKFIGHT
COLLEAGUE
COMMINGLE
COPYRIGHT
DECALOGUE
DEMAGOGUE
DERRINGER
DOWNRIGHT
ESOPHAGUS
FORESIGHT
FORTNIGHT
HAMBURGER
HARBINGER
HEADLIGHT
HIGHLIGHT
HINDSIGHT
HUMDINGER
HYDRANGEA
LIMBURGER
LIMELIGHT
MESSENGER
MONOLOGUE
MOONLIGHT
NEURALGIA
NOSTALGIA
ONSLAUGHT
OUTRIGGER
OVERNIGHT
OVERSIGHT
PASSENGER
PEDAGOGUE
PORRINGER
PREFLIGHT
PTARMIGAN
RECTANGLE
SCAVENGER
SKINTIGHT
SPOTLIGHT
STARLIGHT
STOPLIGHT
STRATAGEM
SUFFRAGAN
SURCINGLE
SYNAGOGUE
TAILLIGHT
UNFLEDGED
VICEREGAL
WARMONGER
WHIRLIGIG
AILANTHUS
ANGUISHED
ASTRAKHAN
BALDACHIN
BETROTHED
BIMONTHLY
BLOODSHED
BLOODSHOT
COURTSHIP
DIMORPHIC
DOWITCHER
EUTROPHIC
FORGATHER
FORSYTHIA
GARNISHEE
GODFATHER
GODMOTHER
GONORRHEA
GRAPESHOT
GROUNDHOG
HORSESHOE
HORSEWHIP
LEVIATHAN
LIGHTSHIP
PISTACHIO
SCRIMSHAW
SEPULCHER
SLINGSHOT
SPACESHIP
STEAMSHIP
STOMACHER
STOMACHIC
STRETCHER
SWEATSHOP
TRANSSHIP
TROOPSHIP
UNDERSHOT
UNEARTHLY
UNSCATHED
UPANISHAD
WATERSHED
ABORIGINE
ACCESSION
ACCLIVITY
ACCORDION
ACCRETION
ACOUSTICS
ADDICTION
ADJECTIVE
ADJOINING
ADMISSION
ADVERSITY
ADVERTISE
AERIALIST
AFFECTING
AFFECTION
AFTERLIFE
AIRMOBILE
ALLERGIST
ALMANDITE
ALONGSIDE
ALUMINIUM
ALUMINIZE
AMERICIUM
AMIDSHIPS
AMPHIBIAN
ANARCHISM
ANATOMIZE
ANCHORITE
ANGELFISH
ANGLICIZE
ANIMALISM
ANIMATION
ANIMOSITY
ANTICLINE
ANTIQUITY
APOLOGIZE
APPORTION
ARCHIVIST
ARGENTINE
ARGENTITE
ARMISTICE
ASAFETIDA
ASCENSION
ASPERSION
ASSERTION
ATHLETICS
ATTENTION
ATTRITION
AUCTORIAL
AUTHORITY
AUTHORIZE
AVOCATION
BACKSLIDE
BACTERIUM
BAILIWICK
BALALAIKA
BALLERINA
BANDOLIER
BARBARIAN
BARBARISM
BATHOLITH
BATTALION
BENTONITE
BERKELIUM
BERYLLIUM
BESETTING
BIPARTITE
BLACKBIRD
BLACKLIST
BLOODLINE
BLUEPOINT
BLUEPRINT
BOMBAZINE
BOWSTRING
BRAZILIAN
BROADSIDE
BRONCHIAL
BRUTALIZE
BULGARIAN
BURUNDIAN
CALCIMINE
CALLOSITY
CALVINISM
CAMPANILE
CANTABILE
CARBURIZE
CARNATION
CARNELIAN
CARPETING
CATECHISM
CAUCASIAN
CAUSATION
CAUTERIZE
CELANDINE
CELEBRITY
CELESTIAL
CENTESIMO
CENTURION
CESSATION
CHAMOMILE
CHAMPAIGN
CHECKLIST
CHEVALIER
CHONDRITE
CHOPSTICK
CHRISTIAN
CIRCADIAN
CLINICIAN
CLOCKWISE
COALITION
COASTLINE
COCKATIEL
COGNITION
COLLATION
COLLEGIAN
COLLEGIUM
COLLODION
COLLUSION
COLLUVIUM
COLUMBINE
COLUMNIST
COMMODITY
COMMOTION
COMMUNION
COMMUNISM
COMMUNITY
COMPANION
COMPLAINT
COMPOSITE
CONCUBINE
CONDITION
CONFUSION
CONGENIAL
CONGERIES
CONGRUITY

CONNUBIAL
CONSCRIPT
CONSTRICT
CONTAGION
CONTUSION
CONVIVIAL
COTILLION
COUTURIER
CRETINISM
CRINOLINE
CRITERION
CRITICISM
CRITICIZE
CROCODILE
CROSSWISE
CUSTODIAL
CUSTODIAN
CUSTOMIZE
DALMATION
DAMNATION
DANDELION
DARWINISM
DECENNIAL
DECEPTION
DECLIVITY
DEDUCTION
DEFEATISM
DEFECTIVE
DEFENSIVE
DEFLATION
DEFORMITY
DEJECTION
DENTITION
DEODORIZE
DEOXIDIZE
DESIGNING
DETECTIVE
DETENTION
DETERMINE
DEUTERIUM
DEXTERITY
DIATOMITE
DIETETICS
DIGNIFIED
DIMENSION
DIRECTION
DIRECTIVE
DISOBLIGE
DISPRAISE
DITHERING
DIVERSIFY
DIVERSION
DIVERSITY
DOGMATISM
DOWNSHIFT
DOWNSWING
DRAINPIPE

DRAMATIZE
DRUMSTICK
DUPLICITY
EARTHLING
EASYGOING
ECONOMICS
ECONOMIZE
EDELWEISS
EDITORIAL
EDUCATION
EFFECTIVE
EFFLUVIUM
EGLANTINE
ELECTRIFY
ELEVATION
ELOCUTION
EMBELLISH
EMPHASIZE
ENDOCRINE
ENGRAVING
EPHEDRINE
EQUIPOISE
ERSTWHILE
ERUDITION
ESSENTIAL
ESTABLISH
ETHIOPIAN
EUCHARIST
EUPHEMISM
EUTHENICS
EVAPORITE
EVOLUTION
EXCELSIOR
EXCEPTION
EXCLUSIVE
EXCURSION
EXCURSIVE
EXECUTIVE
EXEMPLIFY
EXPANSION
EXPANSIVE
EXPENSIVE
EXPERTISE
EXPLETIVE
EXPLOSION
EXPLOSIVE
EXPULSION
EXQUISITE
EXTENSION
EXTENSIVE
EXTRADITE
EXTREMISM
EXTREMITY
EXTRUSIVE
FACSIMILE
FACTORIAL
FANTASIZE

FARSEEING
FASTENING
FERTILIZE
FESTIVITY
FETISHISM
FEUDALISM
FINANCIAL
FINANCIER
FINGERING
FINICKING
FIREBRICK
FIRSTLING
FLAVORING
FLEDGLING
FLOTATION
FOLLOWING
FOOTPRINT
FOREGOING
FORGIVING
FORMALISM
FORMALITY
FORMALIZE
FORMATION
FORMATIVE
FORTHWITH
FOUNDLING
FRANCHISE
FROSTBITE
FUNGICIDE
GABARDINE
GABERDINE
GALVANISM
GALVANIZE
GEARSHIFT
GELIGNITE
GENTILITY
GERMANIUM
GERMICIDE
GESTATION
GIBBERISH
GLAMORIZE
GLYCOSIDE
GOLDBRICK
GOLDSMITH
GONDOLIER
GRADATION
GRAPEVINE
GRENADIER
GRENADINE
GRISTMILL
GROUNDING
GUIDELINE
GYMNASIUM
HAMSTRING
HANDSPIKE
HAPPENING
HARMONICA

HARMONICS
HARMONIUM
HARMONIZE
HEARTSICK
HELLENISM
HELVETIAN
HELVETICA
HEMISTICH
HERBALIST
HERBARIUM
HERBICIDE
HISTAMINE
HISTORIAN
HITCHHIKE
HORSEHIDE
HORTATIVE
HOUSEWIFE
HUMANKIND
HUNGARIAN
HYDROXIDE
HYPOCRISY
HYSTERICS
IMITATION
IMITATIVE
IMPARTIAL
IMPASSIVE
IMPRECISE
IMPROVISE
IMPULSION
IMPULSIVE
INABILITY
INANITION
INCENTIVE
INCEPTION
INCOGNITO
INCURSION
INDEMNIFY
INDEMNITY
INDENTION
INDIGNITY
INDUCTION
INDUCTIVE
INFANTILE
INFECTION
INFERTILE
INFIRMITY
INFLATION
INFLEXION
INGENUITY
INGROWING
INJECTION
INJUSTICE
INSERTION
INTEGRITY
INTENSIFY
INTENSITY
INTENSIVE

INTENTION
INTERDICT
INTERLINE
INTERLINK
INTERNIST
INTERVIEW
INTESTINE
INTUITION
INVECTIVE
INVENTION
INVENTIVE
INVERSION
ISRAELITE
ITALICIZE
ITERATION
JACKKNIFE
JELLYFISH
JESSAMINE
LACCOLITH
LANDSLIDE
LEASTWISE
LEAVENING
LIABILITY
LIBERTINE
LIBRARIAN
LIGHTNING
LIMOUSINE
LOCKSMITH
LOGISTICS
LONGEVITY
LUCRATIVE
MACHINIST
MAGNESIUM
MAGNETISM
MAGNETITE
MAGNETIZE
MAGNIFICO
MAKESHIFT
MALACHITE
MALATHION
MALAYSIAN
MANNERISM
MARGARINE
MARSUPIAL
MASCULINE
MASOCHISM
MATERNITY
MATRICIDE
MEANWHILE
MECHANICS
MECHANISM
MECHANIZE
MEDALLION
MENTALITY
MERCERIZE
MERCURIAL
MESCALINE

MESMERIZE
METEORITE
METHODIST
METHODIZE
METRICIZE
MEZZANINE
MICROFILM
MINISKIRT
MISGIVING
MODERNISM
MODERNIZE
MONGOLIAN
MONGOLISM
MOONSHINE
MORTICIAN
MOTORBIKE
MYSTICISM
NARCOTIZE
NARRATIVE
NECESSITY
NECTARINE
NEODYMIUM
NEOLOGISM
NEPTUNIUM
NEWSPRINT
NIGHTLIFE
NIGHTTIME
NONENTITY
NORMALIZE
NORMATIVE
NORWEGIAN
NUTRITION
OBJECTIFY
OBJECTIVE
OBSESSION
OCCULTISM
OFFENSIVE
OFFSPRING
OPERATION
OPERATIVE
OSTRACIZE
OTHERWISE
OVERDRIVE
OVERPRINT
OVERTRICK
OVERWEIGH
OVERWRITE
OXIDATION
PALLADIUM
PANTHEISM
PANTOMIME
PARATHION
PAROCHIAL
PARRICIDE
PARTITION
PARTITIVE
PASSERINE

PATERNITY
PATRICIAN
PATRICIDE
PATRONIZE
PEACETIME
PEGMATITE
PERDITION
PERENNIAL
PERSONIFY
PESSIMISM
PESTICIDE
PHONETICS
PHYSICIAN
PHYSICIST
PICTORIAL
PINSTRIPE
PLACEKICK
PLAINTIFF
PLAINTIVE
PLAYTHING
PLURALITY
PLURALIZE
PLUTONIUM
PORCUPINE
POSTERIOR
POSTERITY
POSTILION
POTASSIUM
POTENTIAL
POURBOIRE
PRECEDING
PRECIPICE
PRECISION
PREDATION
PREJUDICE
PRESCRIBE
PRESIDIUM
PREVISION
PRIMARILY
PRIMITIVE
PRIVATION
PROBATION
PROBATIVE
PROFANITY
PROMISING
PROSCRIBE
PROVISION
PROXIMITY
PUBLICIST
PUBLICITY
PUBLICIZE
PULVERIZE
PURGATION
PURGATIVE
QUARTZITE
QUICKLIME
QUICKTIME

QUOTIDIAN
RACIALISM
RANDOMIZE
RASTERIZE
REBELLION
RECEPTION
RECEPTIVE
RECESSION
RECESSIVE
RECKONING
RECOGNIZE
RECONCILE
RECONDITE
RECORDING
RECORDIST
RECTIFIER
RECURSION
REDACTION
REDUCTION
REFECTION
REFLEXIVE
REFURBISH
REGARDING
REHEARING
REMISSION
RENDITION
REPLENISH
REPLETION
REPULSION
REPULSIVE
REQUISITE
RESECTION
RESERPINE
RESERVIST
RESTRAINT
RETENTION
RETENTIVE
RETROFIRE
REVERSION
REVOLTING
REVULSION
RIVERSIDE
ROUMANIAN
RUINATION
RUTHENIUM
SACRIFICE
SALESGIRL
SALVATION
SARTORIAL
SATELLITE
SATURNINE
SCANTLING
SCHEELITE
SCHILLING
SCHLEMIEL
SCREENING
SEAFARING

SEASONING
SECESSION
SECLUSION
SECRETION
SECRETIVE
SECTARIAN
SELECTION
SEMANTICS
SENIORITY
SENSATION
SENSITIVE
SENSITIZE
SHEATHING
SHELLFIRE
SHELLFISH
SHOREBIRD
SIDESWIPE
SIGNALIZE
SIMPATICO
SITUATION
SKIMOBILE
SKINFLINT
SKYDIVING
SNAKEBIRD
SNAKEBITE
SNOWDRIFT
SOCIALISM
SOCIALITE
SOCIALIZE
SOLEMNIZE
SOLITAIRE
SOMETHING
SOVEREIGN
SPEARMINT
SPINDLING
SPINDRIFT
SPLITTING
SPOONBILL
SQUEAMISH
STABILIZE
STANCHION
STANDPIPE
STARTLING
STATESIDE
STEPCHILD
STERILIZE
STOCKPILE
STRAPPING
STRIPLING
STRONTIUM
SUBALPINE
SUBDIVIDE
SUBMARINE
SUBSCRIBE
SUBSCRIPT
SUBSIDIZE
SUFFERING
SUMMARIZE
SUMMATION
SUPERVISE
SUPPOSING
SURVEYING
SUSPICION
SWORDFISH
SYLLABIFY
SYLLOGISM
SYMBOLISM
SYMBOLIZE
SYMPOSIUM
SYNERGISM
SYSTEMIZE
TALKATIVE
TANGERINE
TANTALIZE
TANZANIAN
TECTONICS
TECTONISM
TELLURIUM
TEMPORIZE
TENDERIZE
TENTATIVE
TERRARIUM
TERRORISM
TERRORIZE
THEATRICS
THEREWITH
THYROXINE
TIMBERING
TONSORIAL
TOOTHPICK
TRADITION
TRAGEDIAN
TRANSPIRE
TREADMILL
TRIENNIAL
TURNSTILE
TURQUOISE
TWINKLING
TYPEWRITE
TYRANNIZE
UKRAINIAN
ULTRAHIGH
UNBENDING
UNCEASING
UNDECEIVE
UNDERGIRD
UNDERLINE
UNDERLING
UNDERMINE
UNDERSIDE
UNFAILING
UNFEELING
UNITARIAN
UNKNOWING
UNMEANING
UNSELFISH
UNSPARING
UNSTUDIED
UNWILLING
UNWITTING
VALENTINE
VALUATION
VANDALISM
VANDALIZE
VARIATION
VERBALIZE
VERMILION
VERNALIZE
VERSATILE
VIBRATION
VICENNIAL
VICTIMIZE
VICTORIAN
VIEWPOINT
VIOLATION
VIRGINITY
VISCOSITY
VISUALIZE
VOLCANISM
VOODOOISM
VULCANISM
VULCANIZE
VULGARIAN
VULGARISM
VULGARITY
VULGARIZE
WAISTLINE
WALLOPING
WATERLINE
WATERSIDE
WHEREWITH
WHIRLWIND
WHITEFISH
WINDCHILL
WINTERIZE
WITTICISM
WOLVERINE
WOMANKIND
WOMANLIKE
WORLDLING
WORLDWIDE
WRESTLING
YARDSTICK
YOUNGLING
YTTERBIUM
ZEITGEIST
ZIRCONIUM
ZWINGLIAN
BOOKMAKER
CARETAKER
FORETOKEN
GIMMICKRY
HOMEMAKER
MUCKRAKER
ONIONSKIN
OUTSPOKEN
PACEMAKER
PAGEMAKER
RAGPICKER
SAPSUCKER
SHARKSKIN
SHEEPSKIN
SHOEMAKER
SKYJACKER
SKYROCKET
SPELUNKER
SPINNAKER
SUNSEEKER
TRIWEEKLY
UNSHACKLE
ACROPOLIS
ADMIRALTY
AFTERGLOW
ALCOHOLIC
AMARYLLIS
ANOPHELES
APOSTOLIC
ARMADILLO
ARTICULAR
ASSEMBLER
AURICULAR
AVUNCULAR
BAGATELLE
BEDFELLOW
BINOCULAR
CABRIOLET
CAPITALLY
CHRYSALIS
CIGARILLO
CONTRALTO
COUNSELOR
DEATHBLOW
DECATHLON
DIGITALIS
FLAGELLUM
FLAGEOLET
FUNICULAR
GENITALIA
GLADIOLUS
GUERRILLA
HILLBILLY
HOBGOBLIN
HORSEPLAY
HYDRAULIC
IMBROGLIO
INTERPLAY
IRREGULAR
ISOSCELES
MUSKMELON
NATURALLY
NIGHTCLUB
PHOTOPLAY
PORTFOLIO
POTBOILER
PROPELLER
PUNCTILIO
QUADRILLE
ROUNDELAY
SCINTILLA
SEMICOLON
SPECIALTY
STREAMLET
SUGARPLUM
SWORDPLAY
TARPAULIN
UNBRIDLED
UNDERPLAY
UNEQUALED
UNPOPULAR
UNRIVALED
UNRUFFLED
UNSETTLED
UNSKILLED
VICTUALER
ANCHORMAN
ANTITUMOR
BONDWOMAN
CANDLEMAS
CHARWOMAN
CHRISTMAS
CHURCHMAN
CLERGYMAN
CRAFTSMAN
DRAFTSMAN
ELASTOMER
EPIDERMIS
FELLOWMAN
FISHERMAN
FORENAMED
FOREWOMAN
GENTLEMAN
GRANTSMAN
GROOMSMAN
GUARDSMAN
KINSWOMAN
LATECOMER
LIVERYMAN
MIDDLEMAN
MIDSUMMER
MINUTEMAN
MUSSULMAN
OMBUDSMAN
ORIFLAMME
PATROLMAN
PERSIMMON
POLICEMAN
REPAIRMAN
SELECTMAN
SIGNALMAN
SOMETIMES
SPOKESMAN
SPORTSMAN
STATESMAN
SUBATOMIC
SUBNORMAL
SWITCHMAN
SWORDSMAN
TRADESMAN
TRIBESMAN
TULAREMIA
VENIREMAN
VESTRYMAN
VIGESIMAL
WASHWOMAN
YACHTSMAN
ABANDONED
ACCIDENCE
AFFLUENCE
ALLOWANCE
AMBULANCE
ANNOYANCE
ANTIVENIN
APPLIANCE
ASSONANCE
ASSURANCE
BACCHANAL
BINOMINAL
BRITANNIC
BULLFINCH
BUTTERNUT
CATATONIC
CERTAINTY
CHAFFINCH
CHALLENGE
CITIZENRY
CLEARANCE
CLOISONNE
CONCERNED
CONSTANCY
CONTAINER
COPARTNER
COVALENCE
CRESCENDO
CRYOGENIC
DEBUTANTE
DECADENCE
DEFERENCE
DEMIMONDE
DOMINANCE
DOWNRANGE
EFFLUENCE
EMERGENCY
ENDURANCE
ESPERANTO
ESTAMINET
EXISTENCE
FOREIGNER
FRATERNAL
FREQUENCY
GLEANINGS
GLISSANDO
GOLDFINCH
GRIEVANCE
HALFPENNY
HINDRANCE
IGNORANCE
IMBALANCE
IMPEDANCE
INCIDENCE
INFERENCE
INFLUENCE
INFLUENZA
INNOCENCE
INORGANIC
INSURANCE
JACARANDA
LABYRINTH
LANDOWNER
LANTHANUM
LAZYBONES
MATUTINAL
MEDICINAL
MISCHANCE
MISSIONER
MONOMANIA
MONSIGNOR
NICOTINIC
NOCTURNAL
OBEISANCE
OCCUPANCY
ORDINANCE
PERCHANCE
PERSONNEL
PIMPERNEL
PNEUMONIA
PRELAUNCH
PRONOUNCE
PSEUDONYM
PUISSANCE
PURSUANCE
PYROMANIA
QUITTANCE
REACTANCE
REFERENCE
RELEVANCE
RELEVANCY
RESIDENCE
RESIDENCY
RESONANCE
REVERENCE
RUMRUNNER
SCRIVENER
SECTIONAL
SEMBLANCE
SEMIFINAL
SEMILUNAR
SKYLOUNGE
STATIONER
SUBSTANCE
SUNBONNET
TELEGENIC
THEREUNTO
TOLERANCE
TRANSONIC
TRAPPINGS
UNALIGNED
UNCLEANLY
UNFEIGNED
UNLEARNED
UTTERANCE
VEHEMENCE
VENGEANCE
VIGILANCE
VIGILANTE
WARBONNET
WORKBENCH
ACCESSORY
ACIDULOUS
AERODROME
AFTERNOON
ALBATROSS
AMBIGUOUS
AMBITIOUS
AMORPHOUS
AMPHIBOLE
ANALOGOUS
ANGLEWORM
ANHYDROUS
ANKLEBONE
ANOMALOUS
ANONYMOUS
ANTECHOIR
ANTHOLOGY
ANTIKNOCK
APPALOOSA
ARROWROOT
ARTERIOLE
ARTICHOKE
ASSIDUOUS
ASTROLOGY
ASTRONOMY
ASYMPTOTE
ATROCIOUS
AUDACIOUS
AUDIOLOGY
BACKWOODS

BANDEROLE
BARBAROUS
BARCAROLE
BARNSTORM
BEAUTEOUS
BELLICOSE
BLACKBODY
BLACKFOOT
BLINDFOLD
BLOODROOT
BOMBPROOF
BOUNTEOUS
BOURGEOIS
BREAKDOWN
BRIMSTONE
BROADLOOM
BRUSHWOOD
BUCKTOOTH
BUMPTIOUS
CACOPHONY
CALABOOSE
CAMPSTOOL
CANALBOAT
CAPACIOUS
CARCINOMA
CARNIVORA
CARNIVORE
CASSEROLE
CATCHWORD
CELLULOSE
CERECLOTH
CHALKBORD
CHANCROID
CHECKBOOK
CHECKROOM
CHEEKBONE
CHILDHOOD
CHIROPODY
CHUCKHOLE
CLASSROOM
CLOCKWORK
COMMODORE
CONESTOGA
CONSCIOUS
CORTISONE
COSMOGONY
COSMOLOGY
COUNTDOWN
COURTEOUS
COURTROOM
CRACKDOWN
CREDULOUS
CREMATORY
CROSSROAD
CRUCIFORM
CUBBYHOLE
CUNEIFORM
CURRYCOMB
CUTANEOUS
CUTTHROAT
DANGEROUS
DAVENPORT
DECIDUOUS
DECOMPOSE
DELICIOUS
DESULTORY
DEXTEROUS
DHRYSTONE
DICHOTOMY
DIPHTHONG
DIPTEROUS
DIRECTORY
DISEMBODY
DISHCLOTH
DORMITORY
DRIFTWOOD
DRUGSTORE
EARTHWORK
EARTHWORM
EGREGIOUS
EIDERDOWN
ELBOWROOM
ELECTRODE
ELLIPSOID
ENDOSCOPE
EROGENOUS
ERRONEOUS
ETHNOLOGY
ETYMOLOGY
EVERYBODY
EXOGENOUS
EXPIATORY
EXTEMPORE
FACETIOUS
FALSEHOOD
FANCYWORK
FEEDSTOCK
FEROCIOUS
FERRYBOAT
FEUDATORY
FIREPROOF
FIRSTBORN
FLAGSTONE
FLINTLOCK
FOOLPROOF
FOOTLOOSE
FOOTSTOOL
FORECLOSE
FOREFRONT
FORESHORE
FOURSCORE
FRACTIOUS
FRAMEWORK
FREESTONE
FRIVOLOUS
GALACTOSE
GALLSTONE
GARRULOUS
GENEALOGY
GLADSTONE
GLUTINOUS
GRANDIOSE
GREATCOAT
GREENHORN
GREENROOM
GREENWOOD
GRILLWORK
GUARDROOM
GUIDEBOOK
GUSTATORY
GYROSCOPE
HAILSTONE
HAILSTORM
HAIRCLOTH
HANDIWORK
HARDIHOOD
HARTSHORN
HEADPHONE
HEADSTONE
HEARTWOOD
HELLEBORE
HILARIOUS
HOARFROST
HOLLYHOCK
HOLYSTONE
HOMEGROWN
HOMOPHONE
HONEYCOMB
HONEYMOON
HOROSCOPE
HORTATORY
HOUSEBOAT
HOUSECOAT
HOUSEHOLD
HOUSEWORK
HYDROFOIL
HYDROLOGY
HYPERBOLA
HYPERBOLE
IMPERIOUS
IMPETUOUS
INCOMMODE
INCURIOUS
INGENIOUS
INGENUOUS
INGLENOOK
INNERMOST
INNERSOLE
INNOCUOUS
INSIDIOUS
INTERLOCK
INTERLOPE
INTERNODE
INTERPOSE
INVENTORY
INVIDIOUS
IRONSTONE
JUDICIOUS
JUXTAPOSE
KINESCOPE
KNOCKDOWN
LABORIOUS
LAUDATORY
LEASEHOLD
LIFEBLOOD
LIGHTSOME
LIMESTONE
LITHESOME
LITHOLOGY
LITIGIOUS
LIVERWORT
LIVESTOCK
LOADSTONE
LOATHSOME
LODESTONE
LOINCLOTH
LUDICROUS
LUNCHROOM
MACINTOSH
MACROCOSM
MAJORDOMO
MALADROIT
MANDATORY
MARVELOUS
MATCHBOOK
MATCHLOCK
MATCHWOOD
MATRIMONY
MEGAPHONE
MELODIOUS
MERCUROUS
METALWORK
METEOROID
METHADONE
METROLOGY
METRONOME
MICROCOPY
MICROCOSM
MICROSOFT
MILESTONE
MILLIVOLT
MILLSTONE
MISINFORM
MOMENTOUS
MONGOLOID
MONKSHOOD
MOONSTONE
MOTORBOAT
MULTIFORM
MURDEROUS
MYTHOLOGY
NECROLOGY
NEFARIOUS
NEUROLOGY
NEVERMORE
NIGHTGOWN
NOTORIOUS
OBLIVIOUS
OBNOXIOUS
OFFERTORY
OFFICIOUS
OLFACTORY
OUTERMOST
OVERBLOWN
OVERCLOUD
OVERSHOOT
OVIPAROUS
PAPILLOTE
PARSIMONY
PATCHWORK
PATHOLOGY
PATRIMONY
PENDULOUS
PENTECOST
PENURIOUS
PERISCOPE
PETROLOGY
PETTICOAT
PHALAROPE
PHEROMONE
PHILOLOGY
PHONOLOGY
PHOTOCOPY
PIECEWORK
PITCHFORK
PLANELOAD
PLANETOID
PLENTEOUS
POLYPHONY
POMPADOUR
PONDEROUS
POPPYCOCK
POWERBOAT
PREDATORY
PRERECORD
PRESCHOOL
PRESSROOM
PRONGHORN
PROTOZOAN
PROVOLONE
PUREBLOOD
PURGATORY
PUSSYFOOT
QUERULOUS
QUICKSORT
RADIOLOGY
RAINSPOUT
RAINSTORM
RAPACIOUS
REFECTORY
RELIGIOUS
REPERTORY
RESERVOIR
RIDGEPOLE
RIGHTEOUS
RIGMAROLE
RIVERBOAT
ROADBLOCK
ROOTSTOCK
ROUNDWORM
SACKCLOTH
SAGACIOUS
SAILCLOTH
SALACIOUS
SANDSTONE
SANDSTORM
SANGFROID
SATINWOOD
SAXOPHONE
SCAPEGOAT
SCRAPBOOK
SEBACEOUS
SEMAPHORE
SHAKEDOWN
SHEEPFOLD
SHORTHORN
SIGNATORY
SILICEOUS
SILTSTONE
SNOWSTORM
SOAPSTONE
SOCIOLOGY
SOPHOMORE
SPEEDBOAT
STATEROOM
STATUTORY
STEAMBOAT
STEVEDORE
STILLBORN
STOREROOM
STRENUOUS
STRIKEOUT
SULFUROUS
SUMPTUOUS
SUNSTROKE
SUPERNOVA
SUPERPOSE
SWANSDOWN
TAUTOLOGY
TELEPHONE
TELEPHONY
TELEPHOTO
TELESCOPE
TENACIOUS
TENEBROUS
TERRITORY
TESTIMONY
THEREFORE
THIGHBONE
THREEFOLD
THREESOME
THRESHOLD
TIGHTROPE
TOADSTOOL
TOMBSTONE
TOOTHSOME
TOUCHDOWN
TOWNSFOLK
TRAINLOAD
TRANSFORM
TRANSPORT
TRANSPOSE
TRAPEZOID
TREMATODE
TREMULOUS
TRUCKLOAD
TURNABOUT
TUSCARORA
TYRANNOUS
UNANIMOUS
UNBEKNOWN
UNDERBODY
UNDERCOAT
UNDERDONE
UNDERFOOT
UNDERMOST
UNDERTONE
UNDERWOOD
UPPERMOST
UTTERMOST
VAGARIOUS
VAINGLORY
VASECTOMY
VENTUROUS
VERACIOUS
VERMIFORM
VEXATIOUS
VIBRATORY
VICARIOUS
VIVACIOUS
VORACIOUS
WAISTCOAT
WASHCLOTH
WATCHWORD
WATERFOWL
WEARISOME
WHALEBOAT
WHALEBONE
WHEREFORE
WHETSTONE
WHIRLPOOL
WHITEWOOD
WHOLESOME
WINDBLOWN
WINDPROOF
WINDSTORM
WOEBEGONE
WOMANHOOD
WOMENFOLK
WOODBLOCK
WORKGROUP
WORRISOME
WRONGDOER
XYLOPHONE
APOCRYPHA
ARTHROPOD
BARKEEPER
BEEKEEPER
BIOGRAPHY
CANDLEPIN
CATALEPSY
COFFEEPOT
DISTEMPER
DYSTROPHY
EPIGRAPHY
EPISCOPAL
FLOWERPOT
GASTROPOD
GEOGRAPHY
IMPROMPTU
INNKEEPER
LAGNIAPPE
LAUNCHPAD
MULTISPIN
MUNICIPAL
NEWSPAPER
PHILIPPIC
PINEAPPLE
PRINCIPAL
PRINCIPLE
QUADRUPED
QUADRUPLE
QUINTUPLE
SANDPAPER
SANDPIPER
THEOSOPHY
THEREUPON
WALLPAPER
WHEREUPON
XANTHIPPE
ARABESQUE
BURLESQUE
GROTESQUE
SOLILOQUY
TECHNIQUE
ALEATORIC

AMBERG**R**IS
ANTISE**R**UM
BICAME**R**AL
BILATE**R**AL
BILLIA**R**DS
BISHOP**R**IC
BLOWTO**R**CH
BLUEBE**R**RY
BRASSE**R**IE
CABLEG**R**AM
CAFETE**R**IA
CANTHA**R**IS
CATAMA**R**AN
CATHED**R**AL
CENTIG**R**AM
CHAPAR**R**AL
CHIVAL**R**IC
CONCIE**R**GE
CONCOU**R**SE
CONUND**R**UM
CORELD**R**AW
CORKSC**R**EW
CRANBE**R**RY
CUPBEA**R**ER
CYCLOT**R**ON
DECONT**R**OL
DIAMET**R**IC
DIATHE**R**MY
DISCHA**R**GE
DISCOU**R**SE
EAVESD**R**OP
ECCENT**R**IC
EPHEME**R**AL
EXECUT**R**IX
FILMST**R**IP
FOOLHA**R**DY
FRUITE**R**ER
GAUCHE**R**IE
GERIAT**R**IC
GLENGA**R**RY
GOLDEN**R**OD
HEADFI**R**ST
HECTOG**R**AM
HISTOG**R**AM
ILLIBE**R**AL
INAUGU**R**AL
INTERP**R**ET
JACKSC**R**EW
JACKST**R**AW
KILOHE**R**TZ
MAELST**R**OM
MAGIST**R**AL
MATRIA**R**CH
MEGAHE**R**TZ
MENAGE**R**IE
MICROG**R**AM
MILLIG**R**AM
MOUSET**R**AP
OUTSKI**R**TS
OVERTH**R**OW
PACKHO**R**SE
PANEGY**R**IC
PAREGO**R**IC
PATRIA**R**CH
POTPOU**R**RI
POULTE**R**ER
PUERPE**R**AL
PYRETH**R**UM
QUARTE**R**LY
QUICKD**R**AW
RACEHO**R**SE
RADIOG**R**AM
RASPBE**R**RY
REENFO**R**CE
REGIST**R**AR
REIMBU**R**SE
REINFO**R**CE
SACCHA**R**IN
SASSAF**R**AS
SCAREC**R**OW
SCOUND**R**EL
SEMIWO**R**KS
SIDEBU**R**NS
SURCHA**R**GE
TAXIDE**R**MY
THEREF**R**OM
THESAU**R**US
TREASU**R**ER
TURBOP**R**OP
UNDERB**R**ED
UNNATU**R**AL
UNTUTO**R**ED
URTICA**R**IA
VERDIG**R**IS
VERTEB**R**AL
WORKHO**R**SE
ACQUIE**S**CE
ADDRES**S**EE
ANALGE**S**IA
ANALGE**S**IC
ANTIPA**S**TO
CAPARI**S**ON
CARROU**S**EL
CATALY**S**IS
CATHAR**S**IS
CHICKA**S**AW
CIRRHO**S**IS
COMMIS**S**AR
CONDEN**S**ER
CONFES**S**OR
CONSEN**S**US
COSPON**S**OR
COURTE**S**AN
DEMITA**S**SE
DEPRES**S**ED
DIAERE**S**IS
DIAGNO**S**IS
DYSPEP**S**IA
EXTRIN**S**IC
FORETA**S**TE
FREEMA**S**ON
FRICAS**S**EE
HALITO**S**IS
INTRIN**S**IC
INTUME**S**CE
JINRIK**S**HA
MAHARI**S**HI
MANIFE**S**TO
MERGAN**S**ER
NARCIS**S**US
NONPER**S**ON
PARALY**S**IS
POLITE**S**SE
POSTHA**S**TE
PRECUR**S**OR
PROCES**S**OR
PROCON**S**UL
PROFES**S**OR
PROGNO**S**IS
PSORIA**S**IS
PSYCHO**S**IS
PYROLY**S**IS
REHEAR**S**AL
REMINI**S**CE
SCLERO**S**IS
SILICO**S**IS
SUCCES**S**OR
SYMBIO**S**IS
SYNTHE**S**IS
UNADVI**S**ED
UNBLES**S**ED
UNIVER**S**AL
WASHBA**S**IN
ADIABA**T**IC
AESTHE**T**IC
AIRWOR**T**HY
ALABAS**T**ER
ALGORI**T**HM
ALLIGA**T**OR
ALTIME**T**ER
ANTARC**T**IC
ANTIPA**T**HY
APPARA**T**US
APPOIN**T**EE
ARBORE**T**UM
ARTHRI**T**IS
AUTHEN**T**IC
AUTOMA**T**IC
AUTOMA**T**ON
BACKWA**T**ER
BADMIN**T**ON
BANQUE**T**TE
BANTUS**T**AN
BAROME**T**ER
BARRIS**T**ER
BEEFEA**T**ER
BENIGH**T**ED
BESPAT**T**ER
BRIQUE**T**TE
BROCHE**T**TE
CAPACI**T**OR
CARPEN**T**ER
CASUIS**T**RY
CATHAR**T**IC
CHARAC**T**ER
CHARLA**T**AN
CHEMIS**T**RY
CHORIS**T**ER
CHROMA**T**IC
CIGARE**T**TE
CIRCUI**T**RY
COADJU**T**OR
COLLEC**T**ED
COMFOR**T**ER
COMMIT**T**EE
CONCER**T**ED
CONDUC**T**OR
CONTEN**T**ED
CROQUE**T**TE
DECILI**T**ER
DECIME**T**ER
DECORA**T**OR
DEKALI**T**ER
DEKAME**T**ER
DELIGH**T**ED
DELIME**T**ER
DETONA**T**OR
DIACRI**T**IC
DIALEC**T**IC
DISHWA**T**ER
DISMAN**T**LE
DISSEC**T**ED
DISSEN**T**ER
DOSIME**T**ER
ECOSYS**T**EM
EGGBEA**T**ER
ENCOUN**T**ER
ENERGE**T**IC
ENIGMA**T**IC
ENLIGH**T**EN
ENSHEA**T**HE
ENTERI**T**IS
ENWREA**T**HE
EPICEN**T**ER
ESCALA**T**OR
ETIQUE**T**TE
EXPEDI**T**ER
EXPOSI**T**OR
FANTAS**T**IC
FINGER**T**IP
FIREWA**T**ER
GALLAN**T**RY
GASTRI**T**IS
GENERA**T**OR
GLADIA**T**OR
GUARAN**T**EE
GUARAN**T**OR
GUNCOT**T**ON
HAMMER**T**OE
HEADWA**T**ER
HEMSTI**T**CH
HEPATI**T**IS
HEREAF**T**ER
HEURIS**T**IC
HEXAME**T**ER
HOPSCO**T**CH
IMPOLI**T**IC
INCUBA**T**OR
INHALA**T**OR
INSTAN**T**ER
INSTAN**T**LY
JERKWA**T**ER
KILOLI**T**ER
KILOME**T**ER
LAMINA**T**ED
LEITMO**T**IV
LITERA**T**IM
LOCOMO**T**OR
LOGARI**T**HM
LORGNE**T**TE
MAJORE**T**TE
MANHAT**T**AN
MANOME**T**ER
MARQUE**T**RY
MELTWA**T**ER
MIDWIN**T**ER
MISTLE**T**OE
MODERA**T**OR
NANOME**T**ER
NEPHRI**T**IC
NEPHRI**T**IS
NOVELE**T**TE
NUMERA**T**OR
OPTOME**T**RY
ORCHES**T**RA
ORGIAS**T**IC
OUBLIE**T**TE
OVERMA**T**CH
PALAES**T**RA
PALMIS**T**RY
PARAME**T**ER
PARQUE**T**RY
PATRIS**T**IC
PAYMAS**T**ER
PEDOME**T**ER
PERIME**T**ER
PHLEBI**T**IS
PHRENE**T**IC
PIROUE**T**TE
PNEUMA**T**IC
POETAS**T**ER
POLYES**T**ER
POSTNA**T**AL
PRAGMA**T**IC
PRECEN**T**OR
PRECEP**T**OR
PRESBY**T**ER
PRESEN**T**LY
PROJEC**T**OR
PROPHE**T**IC
PROTEC**T**OR
PYROME**T**ER
QUADRA**T**IC
QUICKS**T**EP
RAINWA**T**ER
REFLEC**T**OR
REFRAC**T**OR
RENCON**T**RE
RESONA**T**OR
RHEOME**T**ER
ROSEWA**T**ER
SACRIS**T**AN
SALTPE**T**ER
SALTWA**T**ER
SCHEMA**T**IC
SEAWOR**T**HY
SEPARA**T**OR
SEQUES**T**ER
SHORTS**T**OP
SIMPLE**T**ON
SINGLE**T**ON
SINUSI**T**IS
SLAUGH**T**ER
SOLICI**T**OR
SOPHIS**T**IC
SOPHIS**T**RY
SOUBRE**T**TE
SPAGHE**T**TI
SPECTA**T**OR
SPHINC**T**ER
SPLENE**T**IC
SPRIGH**T**LY
STATIS**T**IC
STATUE**T**TE
STOPWA**T**CH
SYNTHE**T**IC
TEAKET**T**LE
TELEME**T**ER
TELEPA**T**HY
TIDEWA**T**ER
TRICKS**T**ER
TRIMES**T**ER
ULTIMA**T**UM
UNCHAR**T**ED
UNCOUN**T**ED
UNDAUN**T**ED
UNDOUB**T**ED
UNHEAL**T**HY
UNSHEA**T**HE
UNSIGH**T**LY
UNSPOT**T**ED
UNWRIT**T**EN
UPHOLS**T**ER
VAGINI**T**IS
VOLTME**T**ER
WAGONE**T**TE
YOUNGS**T**ER
ZUCCHE**T**TO
ADMIXT**U**RE
ADVENT**U**RE
AEROPA**U**SE
ALGONQ**U**IN
ALMSHO**U**SE
AMPLIT**U**DE
ATTRIB**U**TE
AWESTR**U**CK
BARRAC**U**DA
BATHHO**U**SE
BEATIT**U**DE
BELEAG**U**ER
BILING**U**AL
BIRDHO**U**SE
CALEND**U**LA
CATAMO**U**NT
CERTIT**U**DE
CHANTE**U**SE
CHONDR**U**LE
CHOPHO**U**SE
CLUBHO**U**SE
COFEAT**U**RE
COIFFE**U**SE
COMPOS**U**RE
CONSTR**U**CT
CONTIN**U**AL
CONTIN**U**UM
COONHO**U**ND
CURVAT**U**RE
DACHSH**U**ND
DEBENT**U**RE
DEPART**U**RE
DESTIT**U**TE
DESUET**U**DE
DIFFIC**U**LT
DISFIG**U**RE
DISREP**U**TE
DISSOL**U**TE
DUMBFO**U**ND
EFFECT**U**AL
EMBRAS**U**RE
ENRAPT**U**RE
EXCHEQ**U**ER
FARMHO**U**SE
FEBRIF**U**GE
FEEDST**U**FF
FIREHO**U**SE
FLASHB**U**LB
FLASHC**U**BE
FLASHT**U**BE
FLOPHO**U**SE
FOODST**U**FF
FORTIT**U**DE
FURNIT**U**RE
GALLIN**U**LE
GARNIT**U**RE
GRATIC**U**LE
GRATIT**U**DE
GREYHO**U**ND
HAIRBR**U**SH
HARDBO**U**ND
HARLEQ**U**IN
HEARTB**U**RN
HIDEBO**U**ND
HOLOCA**U**ST
HOREHO**U**ND
IMPORT**U**NE
IMPOST**U**RE
INDENT**U**RE
INSTIT**U**TE
INTERF**U**SE
INTERL**U**DE
INTERR**U**PT
INTROD**U**CE
IRONBO**U**ND
LASSIT**U**DE
LONGIT**U**DE
MAGNIT**U**DE
MAJUSC**U**LE
MANNEQ**U**IN
MENOPA**U**SE
MESSIE**U**RS
MINIAT**U**RE
MINISC**U**LE
MINUSC**U**LE
MULTIT**U**DE
NEGRIT**U**DE
NIGRIT**U**DE
OPPORT**U**NE
PALANQ**U**IN
PARACH**U**TE
PARAMO**U**NT
PENINS**U**LA
PENTHO**U**SE
PERPET**U**AL
PERSEC**U**TE
PESTHO**U**SE
PLATIT**U**DE

PLAYHOUSE
PLENITUDE
POLITBURO
POORHOUSE
PREFIGURE
PREMATURE
PREOCCUPY
PRESHRUNK
PROCEDURE
PROSECUTE
RECTITUDE
REPRODUCE
ROCKBOUND
RUNAROUND
SAGEBRUSH
SCRIPTURE
SCULPTURE
SEMIFLUID
SEPULTURE
SERVITUDE
SIGNATURE
SOBRIQUET
SOFTBOUND
SPICEBUSH
SPIRITUAL
STRICTURE
STRUCTURE
TARANTULA
TOLLHOUSE
TRANSDUCE
TRANSFUSE
TRANSMUTE
TURPITUDE
ULTRAPURE
UNISEXUAL
VERMIFUGE
VESTIBULE
WAREHOUSE
WASHHOUSE
WOLFHOUND
WOODCHUCK
WORKHOUSE
AFFIDAVIT
ANTINOVEL
BOLSHEVIK
CROSSOVER
DAREDEVIL
HANDWOVEN
HARDCOVER
HOWSOEVER
MANOEUVRE
OURSELVES
RETRIEVER
WHICHEVER
WHOSOEVER
BREEZEWAY
FIREPOWER
MAYFLOWER
OUTGROWTH
OVERPOWER
SAFFLOWER
SLUICEWAY
SUNFLOWER
THROWAWAY
WILLPOWER
ANTITOXIN
MEGAPIXEL
OVERSEXED
PERPLEXED
ARCHETYPE
CATACLYSM
DESTROYER
HACKNEYED
HAIRSTYLE
HAMADRYAD
LEUKOCYTE
MANSLAYER
MINELAYER
MULTISYNC
PERISTYLE
PROSELYTE
PROTOTYPE
UNALLOYED
XEROPHYTE
APPETIZER
BAMBOOZLE
DIGITIZED
ENERGIZER
SCHNAUZER
VAPORIZER

## 8th Letter

AMPHIBIAN
ANCHORMAN
ARROWHEAD
ARTICULAR
ASTRAKHAN
AUCTORIAL
AURICULAR
AVUNCULAR
BACCHANAL
BACKPEDAL
BANTUSTAN
BARBARIAN
BEACHHEAD
BEDSPREAD
BEEFSTEAK
BICAMERAL
BILATERAL
BILINGUAL
BINOCULAR
BINOMINAL
BLACKHEAD
BLOCKHEAD
BONDWOMAN
BRAZILIAN
BREEZEWAY
BRONCHIAL
BUCKWHEAT
BULGARIAN
BURUNDIAN
BUTTERFAT
CABLEGRAM
CANALBOAT
CANDLEMAS
CANONICAL
CARIBBEAN
CARNELIAN
CARPETBAG
CATAMARAN
CATHEDRAL
CAUCASIAN
CELESTIAL
CENTIGRAM
CHAPARRAL
CHARLATAN
CHARWOMAN
CHICKASAW
CHRISTIAN
CHRISTMAS
CHURCHMAN
CIRCADIAN
CLASSICAL
CLERGYMAN
CLINICIAN
COCHINEAL
COFFERDAM
COLLEGIAN
COMMISSAR
CONCORDAT
CONGENIAL
CONNUBIAL
CONTINUAL
CONVIVIAL
CORELDRAW
CORPOREAL
COURTESAN
CRAFTSMAN
CROSSROAD
CUSTODIAL
CUSTODIAN
CUTTHROAT
DECENNIAL
DISAPPEAR
DRAFTSMAN
EDITORIAL
EFFECTUAL
EMPIRICAL
EPHEMERAL
EPICUREAN
EPISCOPAL
EQUIVOCAL
ESSENTIAL
ETHIOPIAN
EUCLIDEAN
FACTORIAL
FARMSTEAD
FELLOWMAN
FERRYBOAT
FINANCIAL
FIREBREAK
FISHERMAN
FORESWEAR
FOREWOMAN
FRATERNAL
FUNICULAR
GENTLEMAN
GRANTSMAN
GREATCOAT
GROOMSMAN
GUARDSMAN
HAMADRYAD
HEARTBEAT
HECTOGRAM
HELVETIAN
HERCULEAN
HISTOGRAM
HISTORIAN
HOMESTEAD
HORSEPLAY
HOUSEBOAT
HOUSECOAT
HUNGARIAN
IDENTICAL
ILLIBERAL
ILLOGICAL
IMPARTIAL
INAUGURAL
INTERLEAF
INTERPLAY
IRREGULAR
JACKSTRAW
JAILBREAK
JURIDICAL
KINSWOMAN
LAUNCHPAD
LEVIATHAN
LIBRARIAN
LIVERYMAN
MAGISTRAL
MALAYSIAN
MANHATTAN
MARMOREAL
MARSUPIAL
MATUTINAL
MEDICINAL
MERCURIAL
MICROGRAM
MIDDLEMAN
MIDSTREAM
MILLIGRAM
MINCEMEAT
MINUTEMAN
MONGOLIAN
MORTICIAN
MOTORBOAT
MOUSETRAP
MULTISCAN
MUNICIPAL
MUSSULMAN
NOCTURNAL
NORWEGIAN
NUMERICAL
OMBUDSMAN
OUTSPREAD
PAROCHIAL
PATRICIAN
PATROLMAN
PERENNIAL
PERPETUAL
PETTICOAT
PHOTOPLAY
PHYSICIAN
PICTORIAL
PIECEMEAL
PLANELOAD
POLICEMAN
POLITICAL
POSTNATAL
POTENTIAL
POWERBOAT
PRACTICAL
PREVERBAL
PRINCIPAL
PROOFREAD
PROTOZOAN
PROVENCAL
PTARMIGAN
PUERPERAL
QUICKDRAW
QUIZZICAL
QUOTIDIAN
RADIOGRAM
REGISTRAR
REHEARSAL
REPAIRMAN
RIVERBOAT
ROADSTEAD
ROUMANIAN
ROUNDELAY
SACRISTAN
SARTORIAL
SASSAFRAS
SCAPEGOAT
SCRIMSHAW
SECTARIAN
SECTIONAL
SELECTMAN
SEMIFINAL
SEMILUNAR
SIGNALMAN
SLUICEWAY
SPEARHEAD
SPEEDBOAT
SPIRITUAL
SPOKESMAN
SPORTSMAN
STATESMAN
STEAMBOAT
STREETCAR
SUBNORMAL
SUFFRAGAN
SWEETMEAT
SWELLHEAD
SWITCHMAN
SWORDPLAY
SWORDSMAN
TANZANIAN
TECHNICAL
THROWAWAY
TONSORIAL
TRADESMAN
TRAGEDIAN
TRAINLOAD
TRIBESMAN
TRIENNIAL
TROUSSEAU
TRUCKLOAD
UKRAINIAN
UNDERCOAT
UNDERPLAY
UNDERWEAR
UNISEXUAL
UNITARIAN
UNIVERSAL
UNNATURAL
UNPOPULAR
UPANISHAD
VENIREMAN
VERIDICAL
VERTEBRAL
VESTRYMAN
VICENNIAL
VICEREGAL
VICTORIAN
VIGESIMAL
VULGARIAN
WASHWOMAN
WAISTCOAT
WEDNESDAY
WHALEBOAT
WHIMSICAL
WHITEHEAD
WINDBREAK
YACHTSMAN
YESTERDAY
ZWINGLIAN
ASTROLABE
FLASHCUBE
FLASHTUBE
PRESCRIBE
PROSCRIBE
SUBSCRIBE
ACCIDENCE
ACOUSTICS
ACQUIESCE
AEROSPACE
AFFLUENCE
AFTERDECK
ALLOWANCE
AMBULANCE
ANNOYANCE
ANTIKNOCK
APPLEJACK
APPLIANCE
ARCHITECT
ARMISTICE
ASSONANCE
ASSURANCE
ATHLETICS
AUTOCRACY
AUTOTRACE
AWESTRUCK
BACKTRACK
BAILIWICK
BLACKJACK
BLOWTORCH
BLUEBLACK
BOOTBLACK
BULLFINCH
BUSHWHACK
CAMELBACK
CANDIDACY
CHAFFINCH
CHOPSTICK
CLEARANCE
COCKROACH
CONSTANCY
CONSTRICT
CONSTRUCT
COVALENCE
DECADENCE
DEFERENCE
DEMOCRACY
DIETETICS
DIPLOMACY
DISAFFECT
DISINFECT
DOMINANCE
DRUMSTICK
ECONOMICS
EFFLUENCE
EMERGENCY
ENDURANCE
EUTHENICS
EXISTENCE
FEEDSTOCK
FIREBRICK
FIREPLACE
FLASHBACK
FLINTLOCK
FREQUENCY
GENUFLECT
GOLDBRICK
GOLDFINCH
GREENBACK
GRIEVANCE
GUNNYSACK
HAIRPIECE
HARMONICA
HARMONICS
HAVERSACK
HEADPIECE
HEARTSICK
HELVETICA
HEMISTICH
HEMSTITCH
HINDRANCE
HOLLYHOCK
HOPSCOTCH
HORSEBACK
HUNCHBACK
HYSTERICS
IGNORANCE
IMBALANCE
IMMEDIACY
IMPEDANCE
IMPERFECT
INCIDENCE
INCORRECT
INFERENCE
INFLUENCE
INJUSTICE
INNOCENCE
INSURANCE
INTELLECT
INTERDICT
INTERFACE
INTERJECT
INTERLACE
INTERLOCK
INTERSECT
INTRODUCE

INTUMESCE
LIGHTFACE
LIVESTOCK
LOGISTICS
MAGNIFICO
MATCHLOCK
MATRIARCH
MECHANICS
MISCHANCE
MISDIRECT
MONOSPACE
NOSEPIECE
NOTCHBACK
OBEISANCE
OCCUPANCY
ORDINANCE
OVERMATCH
OVERREACH
OVERTRICK
PAPERBACK
PATRIARCH
PERCHANCE
PHONETICS
PICKABACK
PIGGYBACK
PLACEKICK
POPPYCOCK
PORTULACA
PRECIPICE
PREJUDICE
PRELAUNCH
PRONOUNCE
PUISSANCE
PURSUANCE
QUITTANCE
RACETRACK
REACTANCE
RECOLLECT
REENFORCE
REFERENCE
REINFORCE
RELEVANCE
RELEVANCY
REMINISCE
REPRODUCE
RESIDENCE
RESIDENCY
RESONANCE
RESURRECT
REVERENCE
ROADBLOCK
ROOTSTOCK
ROUGHNECK
SACRIFICE
SEMANTICS
SEMBLANCE
SHIPWRECK
SHOWPIECE
SHOWPLACE
SIDEPIECE
SIDETRACK
SIMPATICO
STOPWATCH
SUBSTANCE
SUPREMACY
TECTONICS
THEATRICS
THEOCRACY
THROWBACK
THUMBTACK
TIMEPIECE
TOLERANCE
TOOTHPICK
TRANSDUCE
UTTERANCE
VEHEMENCE
VENGEANCE
VIGILANCE
WISECRACK
WOODBLOCK
WOODCHUCK
WORKBENCH
WORKPLACE
YARDSTICK
ALONGSIDE
AMBUSCADE
AMPLITUDE
ASAFETIDA
BACKSLIDE
BACKWOODS
BARRACUDA
BARRICADE
BASTINADO
BEATITUDE
BILLIARDS
BLACKBODY
BROADSIDE
CANNONADE
CAVALCADE
CENTIPEDE
CERTITUDE
CHIROPODY
COLONNADE
CRESCENDO
DEMIMONDE
DESPERADO
DESUETUDE
DISEMBODY
DOWNGRADE
ELECTRODE
ENCHILADA
ESPLANADE
EVERGLADE
EVERYBODY
FOOLHARDY
FORTITUDE
FUNGICIDE
FUSILLADE
GERMICIDE
GLISSANDO
GLYCOSIDE
GRATITUDE
HERBICIDE
HORSEHIDE
HYDROXIDE
INCOMMODE
INTERCEDE
INTERLUDE
INTERNODE
JACARANDA
LANDSLIDE
LASSITUDE
LONGITUDE
MAGNITUDE
MARMALADE
MATRICIDE
MILLIPEDE
MOTORCADE
MULTITUDE
NEGRITUDE
NIGRITUDE
ORANGEADE
PARRICIDE
PATRICIDE
PESTICIDE
PLATITUDE
PLENITUDE
PROMENADE
RECTITUDE
RIVERSIDE
SERVITUDE
STATESIDE
SUBDIVIDE
SUPERSEDE
TREMATODE
TURPITUDE
UNDERBODY
UNDERSIDE
WATERSIDE
WORLDWIDE
ABANDONED
ADDRESSEE
ALABASTER
ALTIMETER
ANGUISHED
ANNOUNCER
ANOPHELES
ANTINOVEL
APPETIZER
APPOINTEE
ARCHANGEL
ARTIFICER
ASSEMBLER
ATTAINDER
BACKWATER
BALLADEER
BANDOLIER
BAREFACED
BARKEEPER
BAROMETER
BARRISTER
BARTENDER
BEDRIDDEN
BEEFEATER
BEEKEEPER
BELEAGUER
BENIGHTED
BESPATTER
BETROTHED
BLOODSHED
BOOKMAKER
BUCCANEER
BUMBLEBEE
BYSTANDER
CABRIOLET
CANNONEER
CARETAKER
CARPENTER
CARROUSEL
CARTWHEEL
CHARACTER
CHEVALIER
CHICKADEE
CHICKWEED
CHORISTER
CLIPSHEET
COCKATIEL
COLLECTED
COMFORTER
COMMANDER
COMMITTEE
CONCERNED
CONCERTED
CONDENSER
CONGERIES
CONTAINER
CONTENTED
COPARTNER
CORIANDER
CORKSCREW
COUTURIER
CROSSOVER
CULLENDER
CUPBEARER
DECILITER
DECIMETER
DEKALITER
DEKAMETER
DELIGHTED
DELIMITER
DEPRESSED
DERRINGER
DESCENDER
DESTROYER
DIGITIZED
DIGNIFIED
DISBURDEN
DISESTEEM
DISHWATER
DISMEMBER
DISSECTED
DISSENTER
DISTEMPER
DISTURBED
DOSIMETER
DOWITCHER
ECOSYSTEM
EGGBEATER
ELASTOMER
EMBROIDER
ENCOUNTER
ENERGIZER
ENLIGHTEN
EPICENTER
ESTAMINET
EVERGREEN
EXCHEQUER
EXPEDITER
FINANCIER
FIREPOWER
FIREWATER
FLAGEOLET
FOREIGNER
FORENAMED
FORESHEET
FORETOKEN
FORGATHER
FORWARDER
FREEWHEEL
FRICASSEE
FRUITERER
GARNISHEE
GAZETTEER
GODFATHER
GODMOTHER
GONDOLIER
GONORRHEA
GRENADIER
GUARANTEE
GUNPOWDER
HACKNEYED
HALLOWEEN
HAMBURGER
HANDWOVEN
HARBINGER
HARDCOVER
HEADWATER
HEREAFTER
HEREUNDER
HEXAMETER
HOMEMAKER
HOTHEADED
HOWSOEVER
HUMDINGER
HYDRANGEA
ICELANDER
INNKEEPER
INSTANTER
INTERPRET
INTERVIEW
ISOSCELES
JACKSCREW
JAUNDICED
JERKWATER
JEWELWEED
JOBHOLDER
KILOLITER
KILOMETER
LAMINATED
LANDOWNER
LATECOMER
LAZYBONES
LIMBURGER
MANOMETER
MANSLAYER
MAYFLOWER
MEGAPIXEL
MELTWATER
MERGANSER
MESSENGER
MIDSUMMER
MIDWINTER
MINELAYER
MISSIONER
MUCKRAKER
NANOMETER
NEWSPAPER
NONREADER
NOSEBLEED
OURSELVES
OUTNUMBER
OUTRIGGER
OUTSPOKEN
OVERPOWER
OVERSEXED
OVERSLEEP
PACEMAKER
PAGEMAKER
PARAMETER
PASSENGER
PAYMASTER
PEDOMETER
PENHOLDER
PERIMETER
PERPLEXED
PERSONNEL
PHILANDER
PIGHEADED
PIMPERNEL
POETASTER
POLYESTER
PORRINGER
POTBOILER
POULTERER
PRECANCEL
PRESBYTER
PRIVATEER
PROFITEER
PROPELLER
PROVENDER
PUPPETEER
PYROMETER
QUADRUPED
QUICKSTEP
RACKETEER
RAGPICKER
RAINWATER
RECTIFIER
REJOINDER
REMAINDER
RETRIEVER
RHEOMETER
ROSEWATER
RUMRUNNER
SAFFLOWER
SALTPETER
SALTWATER
SANDPAPER
SANDPIPER
SAPSUCKER
SCAVENGER
SCHLEMIEL
SCHNAUZER
SCOUNDREL
SCRIVENER
SEPTEMBER
SEPULCHER
SEQUESTER
SEVENTEEN
SHOEMAKER
SKYJACKER
SKYROCKET
SLAUGHTER
SOBRIQUET
SOMETIMES
SPELUNKER
SPHINCTER
SPINNAKER
STATIONER
STOMACHER
STRATAGEM
STREAMBED
STREAMLET
STRETCHER
SUNBONNET
SUNFLOWER
SUNSEEKER
SURRENDER
SUSPENDER
TELEMETER
TIDEWATER
TREASURER
TRICKSTER
TRIMESTER
UNADVISED
UNALIGNED
UNALLOYED
UNBLESSED
UNBOUNDED
UNBRIDLED
UNCHARTED
UNCOUNTED
UNDAUNTED
UNDECIDED
UNDERBRED
UNDERFEED
UNDOUBTED
UNEQUALED
UNFEIGNED
UNFLEDGED
UNFOUNDED
UNGUARDED
UNLEARNED
UNPLUMBED
UNRIVALED
UNRUFFLED
UNSCATHED
UNSETTLED
UNSKILLED
UNSPOTTED
UNSTUDIED
UNTUTORED
UNWRITTEN
UPHOLSTER
VAPORIZER
VELVETEEN
VICTUALER
VIDELICET
VOLTMETER
VOLUNTEER
WALLPAPER
WARBONNET
WARMONGER
WATERSHED
WHICHEVER
WHOSOEVER

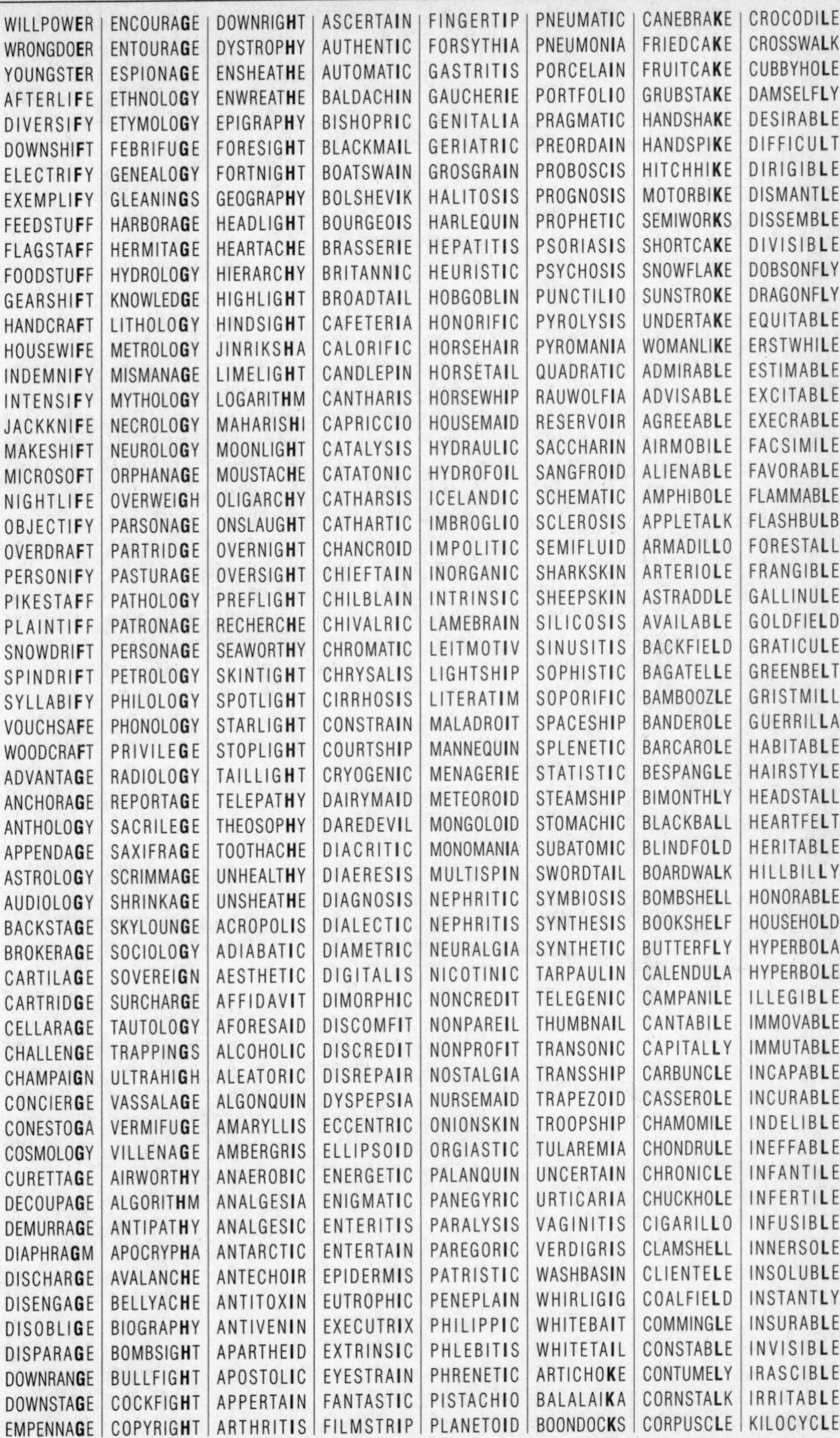

WILLPOWER
WRONGDOER
YOUNGSTER
AFTERLIFE
DIVERSIFY
DOWNSHIFT
ELECTRIFY
EXEMPLIFY
FEEDSTUFF
FLAGSTAFF
FOODSTUFF
GEARSHIFT
HANDCRAFT
HOUSEWIFE
INDEMNIFY
INTENSIFY
JACKKNIFE
MAKESHIFT
MICROSOFT
NIGHTLIFE
OBJECTIFY
OVERDRAFT
PERSONIFY
PIKESTAFF
PLAINTIFF
SNOWDRIFT
SPINDRIFT
SYLLABIFY
VOUCHSAFE
WOODCRAFT
ADVANTAGE
ANCHORAGE
ANTHOLOGY
APPENDAGE
ASTROLOGY
AUDIOLOGY
BACKSTAGE
BROKERAGE
CARTILAGE
CARTRIDGE
CELLARAGE
CHALLENGE
CHAMPAIGN
CONCIERGE
CONESTOGA
COSMOLOGY
CURETTAGE
DECOUPAGE
DEMURRAGE
DIAPHRAGM
DISCHARGE
DISENGAGE
DISOBLIGE
DISPARAGE
DOWNRANGE
DOWNSTAGE
EMPENNAGE

ENCOURAGE
ENTOURAGE
ESPIONAGE
ETHNOLOGY
ETYMOLOGY
FEBRIFUGE
GENEALOGY
GLEANINGS
HARBORAGE
HERMITAGE
HYDROLOGY
KNOWLEDGE
LITHOLOGY
METROLOGY
MISMANAGE
MYTHOLOGY
NECROLOGY
NEUROLOGY
ORPHANAGE
OVERWEIGH
PARSONAGE
PARTRIDGE
PASTURAGE
PATHOLOGY
PATRONAGE
PERSONAGE
PETROLOGY
PHILOLOGY
PHONOLOGY
PRIVILEGE
RADIOLOGY
REPORTAGE
SACRILEGE
SAXIFRAGE
SCRIMMAGE
SHRINKAGE
SKYLOUNGE
SOCIOLOGY
SOVEREIGN
SURCHARGE
TAUTOLOGY
TRAPPINGS
ULTRAHIGH
VASSALAGE
VERMIFUGE
VILLENAGE
AIRWORTHY
ALGORITHM
ANTIPATHY
APOCRYPHA
AVALANCHE
BELLYACHE
BIOGRAPHY
BOMBSIGHT
BULLFIGHT
COCKFIGHT
COPYRIGHT

DOWNRIGHT
DYSTROPHY
ENSHEATHE
ENWREATHE
EPIGRAPHY
FORESIGHT
FORTNIGHT
GEOGRAPHY
HEADLIGHT
HEARTACHE
HIERARCHY
HIGHLIGHT
HINDSIGHT
JINRIKSHA
LIMELIGHT
LOGARITHM
MAHARISHI
MOONLIGHT
MOUSTACHE
OLIGARCHY
ONSLAUGHT
OVERNIGHT
OVERSIGHT
PREFLIGHT
RECHERCHE
SEAWORTHY
SKINTIGHT
SPOTLIGHT
STARLIGHT
STOPLIGHT
TAILLIGHT
TELEPATHY
THEOSOPHY
TOOTHACHE
UNHEALTHY
UNSHEATHE
ACROPOLIS
ADIABATIC
AESTHETIC
AFFIDAVIT
AFORESAID
ALCOHOLIC
ALEATORIC
ALGONQUIN
AMARYLLIS
AMBERGRIS
ANAEROBIC
ANALGESIA
ANALGESIC
ANTARCTIC
ANTECHOIR
ANTITOXIN
ANTIVENIN
APARTHEID
APOSTOLIC
APPERTAIN
ARTHRITIS

ASCERTAIN
AUTHENTIC
AUTOMATIC
BALDACHIN
BISHOPRIC
BLACKMAIL
BOATSWAIN
BOLSHEVIK
BOURGEOIS
BRASSERIE
BRITANNIC
BROADTAIL
CAFETERIA
CALORIFIC
CANDLEPIN
CANTHARIS
CAPRICCIO
CATALYSIS
CATATONIC
CATHARSIS
CATHARTIC
CHANCROID
CHIEFTAIN
CHILBLAIN
CHIVALRIC
CHROMATIC
CHRYSALIS
CIRRHOSIS
CONSTRAIN
COURTSHIP
CRYOGENIC
DAIRYMAID
DAREDEVIL
DIACRITIC
DIAERESIS
DIAGNOSIS
DIALECTIC
DIAMETRIC
DIGITALIS
DIMORPHIC
DISCOMFIT
DISCREDIT
DISREPAIR
DYSPEPSIA
ECCENTRIC
ELLIPSOID
ENERGETIC
ENIGMATIC
ENTERITIS
ENTERTAIN
EPIDERMIS
EUTROPHIC
EXECUTRIX
EXTRINSIC
EYESTRAIN
FANTASTIC
FILMSTRIP

FINGERTIP
FORSYTHIA
GASTRITIS
GAUCHERIE
GENITALIA
GERIATRIC
GROSGRAIN
HALITOSIS
HARLEQUIN
HEPATITIS
HEURISTIC
HOBGOBLIN
HONORIFIC
HORSEHAIR
HORSETAIL
HORSEWHIP
HOUSEMAID
HYDRAULIC
HYDROFOIL
ICELANDIC
IMBROGLIO
IMPOLITIC
INORGANIC
INTRINSIC
LAMEBRAIN
LEITMOTIV
LIGHTSHIP
LITERATIM
MALADROIT
MANNEQUIN
MENAGERIE
METEOROID
MONGOLOID
MONOMANIA
MULTISPIN
NEPHRITIC
NEPHRITIS
NEURALGIA
NICOTINIC
NONCREDIT
NONPAREIL
NONPROFIT
NOSTALGIA
NURSEMAID
ONIONSKIN
ORGIASTIC
PALANQUIN
PANEGYRIC
PARALYSIS
PAREGORIC
PATRISTIC
PENEPLAIN
PHILIPPIC
PHLEBITIS
PHRENETIC
PISTACHIO
PLANETOID

PNEUMATIC
PNEUMONIA
PORCELAIN
PORTFOLIO
PRAGMATIC
PREORDAIN
PROBOSCIS
PROGNOSIS
PROPHETIC
PSORIASIS
PSYCHOSIS
PUNCTILIO
PYROLYSIS
PYROMANIA
QUADRATIC
RAUWOLFIA
RESERVOIR
SACCHARIN
SANGFROID
SCHEMATIC
SCLEROSIS
SEMIFLUID
SHARKSKIN
SHEEPSKIN
SILICOSIS
SINUSITIS
SOPHISTIC
SOPORIFIC
SPACESHIP
SPLENETIC
STATISTIC
STEAMSHIP
STOMACHIC
SUBATOMIC
SWORDTAIL
SYMBIOSIS
SYNTHESIS
SYNTHETIC
TARPAULIN
TELEGENIC
THUMBNAIL
TRANSONIC
TRANSSHIP
TRAPEZOID
TROOPSHIP
TULAREMIA
UNCERTAIN
URTICARIA
VAGINITIS
VERDIGRIS
WASHBASIN
WHIRLIGIG
WHITEBAIT
WHITETAIL
ARTICHOKE
BALALAIKA
BOONDOCKS

CANEBRAKE
FRIEDCAKE
FRUITCAKE
GRUBSTAKE
HANDSHAKE
HANDSPIKE
HITCHHIKE
MOTORBIKE
SEMIWORKS
SHORTCAKE
SNOWFLAKE
SUNSTROKE
UNDERTAKE
WOMANLIKE
ADMIRABLE
ADVISABLE
AGREEABLE
AIRMOBILE
ALIENABLE
AMPHIBOLE
APPLETALK
ARMADILLO
ARTERIOLE
ASTRADDLE
AVAILABLE
BACKFIELD
BAGATELLE
BAMBOOZLE
BANDEROLE
BARCAROLE
BESPANGLE
BIMONTHLY
BLACKBALL
BLINDFOLD
BOARDWALK
BOMBSHELL
BOOKSHELF
BUTTERFLY
CALENDULA
CAMPANILE
CANTABILE
CAPITALLY
CARBUNCLE
CASSEROLE
CHAMOMILE
CHONDRULE
CHRONICLE
CHUCKHOLE
CIGARILLO
CLAMSHELL
CLIENTELE
COALFIELD
COMMINGLE
CONSTABLE
CONTUMELY
CORNSTALK
CORPUSCLE

CROCODILE
CROSSWALK
CUBBYHOLE
DAMSELFLY
DESIRABLE
DIFFICULT
DIRIGIBLE
DISMANTLE
DISSEMBLE
DIVISIBLE
DOBSONFLY
DRAGONFLY
EQUITABLE
ERSTWHILE
ESTIMABLE
EXCITABLE
EXECRABLE
FACSIMILE
FAVORABLE
FLAMMABLE
FLASHBULB
FORESTALL
FRANGIBLE
GALLINULE
GOLDFIELD
GRATICULE
GREENBELT
GRISTMILL
GUERRILLA
HABITABLE
HAIRSTYLE
HEADSTALL
HEARTFELT
HERITABLE
HILLBILLY
HONORABLE
HOUSEHOLD
HYPERBOLA
HYPERBOLE
ILLEGIBLE
IMMOVABLE
IMMUTABLE
INCAPABLE
INCURABLE
INDELIBLE
INEFFABLE
INFANTILE
INFERTILE
INFUSIBLE
INNERSOLE
INSOLUBLE
INSTANTLY
INSURABLE
INVISIBLE
IRASCIBLE
IRRITABLE
KILOCYCLE

LEAFSTALK
LEASEHOLD
MAJUSCULE
MALLEABLE
MANHANDLE
MEANWHILE
MEDICABLE
MEGACYCLE
MEMORABLE
MICROFILM
MILLIVOLT
MINISCULE
MINUSCULE
MISERABLE
MISHANDLE
NATURALLY
NAVIGABLE
NIGHTFALL
OUTWARDLY
OVERWHELM
PALATABLE
PANHANDLE
PASTORALE
PENINSULA
PERISTYLE
PERMEABLE
PHILATELY
PHOTOCELL
PINEAPPLE
PLAUSIBLE
PREGNABLE
PRESENTLY
PRIMARILY
PRINCIPLE
PRINTABLE
QUADRILLE
QUADRUPLE
QUARTERLY
QUINTUPLE
RATIONALE
RECONCILE
RECTANGLE
REPUTABLE
RESHUFFLE
REVOCABLE
RIDGEPOLE
RIGMAROLE
SCINTILLA
SCREWBALL
SEPARABLE
SHEEPFOLD
SKIMOBILE
SMALLTALK
SNOWFIELD
SPECTACLE
SPEEDWELL
SPOONBILL
SPRIGHTLY
STAIRWELL
STEPCHILD
STOCKPILE
SURCINGLE
TARANTULA
TEAKETTLE
THREEFOLD
THRESHOLD
TIMETABLE
TOLERABLE
TOWNSFOLK
TRACKBALL
TRACTABLE
TREADMILL
TRIFOCALS
TRIWEEKLY
TURNSTILE
TURNTABLE
UNCLEANLY
UNDERSELL
UNEARTHLY
UNSHACKLE
UNSIGHTLY
UNWORLDLY
VEGETABLE
VENERABLE
VENTRICLE
VERITABLE
VERSATILE
VESTIBULE
WATERFALL
WAVETABLE
WHITEHALL
WHITEWALL
WHOLESALE
WINDCHILL
WOMENFOLK
WORKTABLE
AERODROME
ARCHENEMY
ASTRONOMY
BLASPHEME
BLASPHEMY
CARCINOMA
CENTESIMO
CURRYCOMB
DIATHERMY
DICHOTOMY
EMPHYSEMA
HONEYCOMB
LIGHTSOME
LITHESOME
LOATHSOME
MAINFRAME
MAJORDOMO
MELODRAMA
METRONOME
NIGHTTIME
ORIFLAMME
PANTOMIME
PEACETIME
QUICKLIME
QUICKTIME
TAXIDERMY
THREESOME
TOOTHSOME
VASECTOMY
WEARISOME
WHOLESOME
WIREFRAME
WORRISOME
ABATEMENT
ABHORRENT
ABORIGINE
ABSORBENT
ACCOMPANY
ACETYLENE
ADJOINING
ADSORBENT
AEROPLANE
AFFECTING
AFRIKAANS
AGREEMENT
AMENDMENT
AMERICANA
AMPERSAND
ANKLEBONE
ANNUITANT
ANTICLINE
APARTMENT
APPELLANT
APPLICANT
APPREHEND
AQUAPLANE
ARCHFIEND
ARGENTINE
ASCENDANT
ASSISTANT
ATONEMENT
ATTENDANT
BALLERINA
BANDSTAND
BENIGNANT
BESETTING
BLOODLINE
BLUEPOINT
BLUEPRINT
BOMBAZINE
BOOMERANG
BOWSTRING
BRILLIANT
BRIMSTONE
BROADBAND
CACOPHONY
CALCIMINE
CARPETING
CATAMOUNT
CATCHMENT
CELANDINE
CHAMPAGNE
CHARABANC
CHEEKBONE
CHLORDANE
CLOISONNE
COAGULANT
COASTLINE
COLUMBINE
COMPETENT
COMPLAINT
COMPONENT
CONCUBINE
CONDIMENT
CONFIDANT
CONSONANT
CONTINENT
COONHOUND
CORMORANT
CORTISONE
COSMOGONY
CRINOLINE
CROISSANT
DACHSHUND
DAMASCENE
DECREMENT
DEFENDANT
DEFERMENT
DEFICIENT
DEFOLIANT
DEMULCENT
DEODORANT
DEPENDENT
DESICCANT
DESIGNING
DETERGENT
DETERMINE
DETERRENT
DETRIMENT
DEVILMENT
DHRYSTONE
DIFFERENT
DIFFIDENT
DIPHTHONG
DISORIENT
DISPUTANT
DISSIDENT
DITHERING
DIXIELAND
DOWNSWING
DREAMLAND
DUMBFOUND
EARTHLING
EASYGOING
EBULLIENT
EFFICIENT
EGLANTINE
EMBAYMENT
EMOLLIENT
EMOLUMENT
ENDOCRINE
ENGRAVING
EPHEDRINE
EQUIPMENT
EXCELLENT
EXCREMENT
EXPECTANT
EXPEDIENT
EXUBERANT
FAIRYLAND
FARSEEING
FASTENING
FINGERING
FINICKING
FIREBRAND
FIRMAMENT
FIRSTHAND
FIRSTLING
FLAGSTONE
FLATULENT
FLAVORING
FLEDGLING
FOLLOWING
FOOTPRINT
FOREFRONT
FOREGOING
FORGIVING
FOUNDLING
FREESTONE
GABARDINE
GABERDINE
GALLIVANT
GALLSTONE
GANGPLANK
GLADSTONE
GODPARENT
GRAPEVINE
GRASSLAND
GRENADINE
GREYHOUND
GROUNDING
GUIDELINE
HAILSTONE
HALFPENNY
HAMSTRING
HANDSTAND
HAPPENING
HARDBOUND
HARDSTAND
HATCHMENT
HEADPHONE
HEADSTONE
HIDEBOUND
HISTAMINE
HOLYSTONE
HOMOPHONE
HOREHOUND
HUMANKIND
HURRICANE
IMMIGRANT
IMPATIENS
IMPATIENT
IMPLEMENT
IMPORTANT
IMPORTUNE
IMPRUDENT
INCESSANT
INCIPIENT
INCLEMENT
INCREMENT
INCUMBENT
INDIGNANT
INELEGANT
INFORMANT
INGROWING
INPATIENT
INSISTENT
INSOLVENT
INSURGENT
INTENDANT
INTERLINE
INTERLINK
INTERMENT
INTERVENE
INTESTINE
IRONBOUND
IRONSTONE
ITINERANT
JESSAMINE
KICKSTAND
LEAVENING
LIBERTINE
LIGHTNING
LIMESTONE
LIMOUSINE
LINEAMENT
LOADSTONE
LODESTONE
LUBRICANT
LUXURIANT
MALIGNANT
MARGARINE
MARIJUANA
MASCULINE
MATRIMONY
MEGAPHONE
MENDICANT
MERRIMENT
MESCALINE
METHADONE
MEZZANINE
MILESTONE
MILLSTONE
MISCREANT
MISGIVING
MISORIENT
MONOPLANE
MOONSHINE
MOONSTONE
MULTISYNC
NECTARINE
NEGLIGENT
NEGOTIANT
NEWSPRINT
NEWSSTAND
NUTRIMENT
OBSERVANT
OFFICIANT
OFFSPRING
OPPORTUNE
OVERPRINT
PAKISTANI
PARAMOUNT
PARCHMENT
PARSIMONY
PASSERINE
PATRIMONY
PERMANENT
PERTINENT
PESTILENT
PHEROMONE
PLACEMENT
PLAYTHING
POINCIANA
POLYPHONY
PORCUPINE
POSTULANT
PRECEDENT
PRECEDING
PRESHRUNK
PRESIDENT
PREVALENT
PROMINENT
PROMISING
PROPONENT
PROVIDENT
PROVOLONE
PUBESCENT
QUICKSAND
QUIESCENT
RANCHLAND
RANGELAND
RECIPIENT
RECKONING
RECOMMEND
RECORDING
RECUMBENT
REDUNDANT
REENTRANT
REGARDING
REHEARING
RELUCTANT
REPELLENT
REPREHEND
REPRESENT
REPRIMAND
REPUGNANT
RESERPINE
RESISTANT
RESTRAINT
REVOLTING
RIVERBANK
ROCKBOUND
RUNAROUND
SACRAMENT
SAILPLANE
SANDSTONE
SATURNINE
SAXOPHONE
SCANTLING
SCHILLING
SCREENING
SEAFARING
SEASONING
SENTIMENT
SHEATHING
SHORTHAND
SIDEBURNS
SILTSTONE
SKINFLINT
SKYDIVING
SOAPSTONE
SOFTBOUND
SOMETHING
SOMNOLENT
SPEARMINT
SPINDLING
SPLITTING
STARTLING
STATEMENT
STIMULANT
STRAPPING
STRIPLING
SUBALPINE
SUBMARINE
SUCCULENT
SUFFERING
SUGARCANE
SUPERVENE
SUPPLIANT

SUPPOSING
SURVEYING
SWAMPLAND
SYCOPHANT
TABLELAND
TANGERINE
TELEPHONE
TELEPHONY
TERMAGANT
TESTAMENT
TESTIMONY
THIGHBONE
THYROXINE
TIMBERING
TOMBSTONE
TRANSCEND
TRANSIENT
TREATMENT
TRENCHANT
TRUCULENT
TURBULENT
TWINKLING
UNBENDING
UNCEASING
UNDERDONE
UNDERHAND
UNDERLINE
UNDERLING
UNDERMINE
UNDERTONE
UNFAILING
UNFEELING
UNIVALENT
UNKNOWING
UNMEANING
UNSPARING
UNWILLING
UNWITTING
VALENTINE
VIEWPOINT
WAISTBAND
WAISTLINE
WALLOPING
WASHSTAND
WASTELAND
WATCHBAND
WATERLINE
WHALEBONE
WHETSTONE
WHIRLWIND
WITHSTAND
WOEBEGONE
WOLFHOUND
WOLFSBANE
WOLVERINE
WOMANKIND
WORLDLING

WRESTLING
WRISTBAND
XYLOPHONE
YOUNGLING
ACCESSION
ACCORDION
ACCRETION
ADDICTION
ADMISSION
AFFECTION
AFTERGLOW
AFTERNOON
ALLIGATOR
ANIMATION
ANTITUMOR
APPORTION
ARROWROOT
ARTHROPOD
ASCENSION
ASPERSION
ASSERTION
ATTENTION
ATTRITION
AUTOMATON
AVOCATION
BADMINTON
BANDWAGON
BATTALION
BEDFELLOW
BLACKFOOT
BLOODROOT
BLOODSHOT
BOMBPROOF
BROADLOOM
BRUSHWOOD
CAMPSTOOL
CAPACITOR
CAPARISON
CARNATION
CAUSATION
CENTURION
CESSATION
CHAMELEON
CHECKBOOK
CHECKROOM
CHILDHOOD
CLASSROOM
COADJUTOR
COALITION
COFFEEPOT
COGNITION
COLLATION
COLLODION
COLLUSION
COMMOTION
COMMUNION
COMPANION

CONDITION
CONDUCTOR
CONFESSOR
CONFUSION
CONTAGION
CONTUSION
COSPONSOR
COTILLION
COTYLEDON
COUNSELOR
COURTROOM
CRITERION
CYCLOTRON
DALMATION
DAMNATION
DANDELION
DEATHBLOW
DECATHLON
DECEPTION
DECONTROL
DECORATOR
DEDUCTION
DEFLATION
DEJECTION
DENTITION
DETENTION
DETONATOR
DIMENSION
DIRECTION
DIVERSION
DRIFTWOOD
EAVESDROP
EDUCATION
ELBOWROOM
ELEVATION
ELOCUTION
ERUDITION
ESCALATOR
EVOLUTION
EXCELSIOR
EXCEPTION
EXCURSION
EXPANSION
EXPLOSION
EXPOSITOR
EXPULSION
EXTENSION
FALSEHOOD
FIREPROOF
FLOTATION
FLOWERPOT
FOOLPROOF
FOOTSTOOL
FORMATION
FREEMASON
GASTROPOD
GENERATOR

GESTATION
GLADIATOR
GOLDENROD
GRADATION
GRAPESHOT
GREENROOM
GREENWOOD
GROUNDHOG
GUARANTOR
GUARDROOM
GUIDEBOOK
GUNCOTTON
GYRFALCON
HAMMERTOE
HARDIHOOD
HEARTWOOD
HETERODOX
HONEYMOON
HORSESHOE
IMITATION
IMPULSION
INANITION
INCEPTION
INCUBATOR
INCURSION
INDENTION
INDUCTION
INFECTION
INFLATION
INFLEXION
INGLENOOK
INHALATOR
INJECTION
INSERTION
INTENTION
INTUITION
INVENTION
INVERSION
ITERATION
LIFEBLOOD
LOCOMOTOR
LUNCHROOM
MAELSTROM
MALATHION
MARTYRDOM
MATCHBOOK
MATCHWOOD
MEDALLION
MISTLETOE
MODERATOR
MONKSHOOD
MONSIGNOR
MUSKMELON
NONPERSON
NUMERATOR
NUTRITION
OBSESSION

OPERATION
OVERSHOOT
OVERTHROW
OXIDATION
PARATHION
PARTITION
PERDITION
PERSIMMON
POSTERIOR
POSTILION
PRECENTOR
PRECEPTOR
PRECISION
PRECURSOR
PREDATION
PRESCHOOL
PRESSROOM
PREVISION
PRIVATION
PROBATION
PROCESSOR
PROFESSOR
PROJECTOR
PROTECTOR
PROVISION
PUREBLOOD
PURGATION
PUSSYFOOT
REBELLION
RECEPTION
RECESSION
RECURSION
REDACTION
REDUCTION
REFECTION
REFLECTOR
REFRACTOR
REMISSION
RENDITION
REPLETION
REPULSION
RESECTION
RESONATOR
RETENTION
REVERSION
REVULSION
RUINATION
SADDLEBOW
SALVATION
SATINWOOD
SCARECROW
SCHOOLBOY
SCRAPBOOK
SCUTCHEON
SECESSION
SECLUSION
SECRETION

SELECTION
SEMICOLON
SENSATION
SEPARATOR
SHADOWBOX
SHORTSTOP
SIMPLETON
SINGLETON
SITUATION
SLINGSHOT
SOLICITOR
SPECTATOR
STANCHION
STATEROOM
STOREROOM
SUCCESSOR
SUMMATION
SUSPICION
SWEATSHOP
THEREFROM
THEREUPON
THRALLDOM
TINDERBOX
TOADSTOOL
TRADITION
TRUNCHEON
TURBOPROP
UNDERFOOT
UNDERSHOT
UNDERWOOD
VALUATION
VARIATION
VERMILION
VIBRATION
VIOLATION
WHEREUPON
WHIRLPOOL
WHITEWOOD
WINDPROOF
WOMANHOOD
AMIDSHIPS
ARCHETYPE
AUTOGRAPH
BACKSWEPT
BAROGRAPH
CONSCRIPT
DRAINPIPE
ENDOSCOPE
GYROSCOPE
HOLOGRAPH
HOMOGRAPH
HOROSCOPE
INTERCEPT
INTERLOPE
INTERRUPT
KINESCOPE
LAGNIAPPE

LANDSCAPE
MICROCOPY
MONOGRAPH
MOONSCAPE
PARAGRAPH
PERISCOPE
PHALAROPE
PHOTOCOPY
PINSTRIPE
POLYGRAPH
PREOCCUPY
PROTOTYPE
SERIGRAPH
SHIPSHAPE
SIDESWIPE
STANDPIPE
SUBSCRIPT
TELEGRAPH
TELESCOPE
TIGHTROPE
VIDEOTAPE
WINDSWEPT
XANTHIPPE
ACCESSORY
ADMIXTURE
ADVENTURE
ADVERSARY
AFTERCARE
AFTERWARD
ANCILLARY
ANGLEWORM
ANTIQUARY
ARBITRARY
ARTILLERY
ASCENDERS
AUXILIARY
BACKBOARD
BARNSTORM
BASEBOARD
BELVEDERE
BILLBOARD
BIOSPHERE
BIRTHMARK
BLACKBIRD
BLEACHERS
BLUEBERRY
BODYGUARD
BOULEVARD
BRASSIERE
BUCKBOARD
CAMEMBERT
CAPILLARY
CARDBOARD
CARNIVORA
CARNIVORE
CASSOWARY
CASUISTRY

CATCHWORD
CENTENARY
CHALKBORD
CHEMISTRY
CHICANERY
CIRCUITRY
CITIZENRY
CLAPBOARD
CLIPBOARD
CLOCKWORK
COFEATURE
COMMODORE
COMPOSURE
COROLLARY
COURTYARD
CRANBERRY
CREMATORY
CRUCIFORM
CUNEIFORM
CURVATURE
CUSTOMARY
DASHBOARD
DAVENPORT
DEBENTURE
DECISTERE
DEKASTERE
DELFTWARE
DEPARTURE
DESULTORY
DIGNITARY
DIRECTORY
DISEMBARK
DISFIGURE
DISREGARD
DORMITORY
DROMEDARY
DRUGSTORE
DUCKBOARD
DYSENTERY
EARTHWARD
EARTHWORK
EARTHWORM
ELSEWHERE
EMBRASURE
ENRAPTURE
EXEMPLARY
EXOSPHERE
EXPIATORY
EXTEMPORE
EXTRAVERT
FANCYWORK
FEUDATORY
FIDUCIARY
FIRSTBORN
FLOWCHART
FOOTBOARD
FORESHORE

FOURSCO**R**E
FRAMEWO**R**K
FREEBOA**R**D
FURNITU**R**E
GALLANT**R**Y
GARNITU**R**E
GIMMICK**R**Y
GLENGAR**R**Y
GRAVEYA**R**D
GRAYBEA**R**D
GREENHO**R**N
GRILLWO**R**K
GROUPWA**R**E
GUSTATO**R**Y
HAILSTO**R**M
HANDIWO**R**K
HAPHAZA**R**D
HARDBOA**R**D
HARTSHO**R**N
HEADBOA**R**D
HEARTBU**R**N
HELLEBO**R**E
HORTATO**R**Y
HOUSEWO**R**K
HUSBAND**R**Y
HYPERCA**R**D
IMAGINA**R**Y
IMPOSTU**R**E
INDENTU**R**E
INFIRMA**R**Y
INSINCE**R**E
INTERFE**R**E
INTERLA**R**D
INTROVE**R**T
INVENTO**R**Y
INVOLUC**R**E
ITINERA**R**Y
JUDICIA**R**Y
LAUDATO**R**Y
LAVALIE**R**E
LEGENDA**R**Y
LIFEGUA**R**D
LIVERWO**R**T
MACHINE**R**Y
MANDATO**R**Y
MANOEUV**R**E
MARQUET**R**Y
MERCENA**R**Y
MESSIEU**R**S
METALWA**R**E
METALWO**R**K
MILLINE**R**Y
MINIATU**R**E
MINISKI**R**T
MISGOVE**R**N
MISINFO**R**M
MISSILE**R**Y
MOLDBOA**R**D
MOMENTA**R**Y
MONASTE**R**Y
MOUTHPA**R**T
MULTIFO**R**M
NECESSA**R**Y
NEVERMO**R**E
NIGHTMA**R**E
OFFERTO**R**Y
OLFACTO**R**Y
OPTOMET**R**Y
ORCHEST**R**A
OVERBOA**R**D
PACHYDE**R**M
PALAEST**R**A
PALMIST**R**Y
PARQUET**R**Y
PATCHWO**R**K
PECUNIA**R**Y
PERFUME**R**Y
PERIPHE**R**Y
PERSEVE**R**E
PIECEWO**R**K
PITCHFO**R**K
PITUITA**R**Y
PLOWSHA**R**E
POLITBU**R**O
POTPOUR**R**I
POURBOI**R**E
PREDATO**R**Y
PREFIGU**R**E
PREMATU**R**E
PRERECO**R**D
PROCEDU**R**E
PRONGHO**R**N
PULMONA**R**Y
PURGATO**R**Y
QUICKSO**R**T
RAINSTO**R**M
RASPBER**R**Y
REFECTO**R**Y
RELIQUA**R**Y
RENCONT**R**E
REPERTO**R**Y
RESIDUA**R**Y
RETROFI**R**E
ROUNDWO**R**M
SAFEGUA**R**D
SALESGI**R**L
SANCTUA**R**Y
SANDSTO**R**M
SCRIPTU**R**E
SCULPTU**R**E
SECONDA**R**Y
SECRETA**R**Y
SEDENTA**R**Y
SEMAPHO**R**E
SEPULTU**R**E
SHAREWA**R**E
SHELLFI**R**E
SHIPBOA**R**D
SHOREBI**R**D
SHORTHO**R**N
SHRUBBE**R**Y
SIDEBOA**R**D
SIGNATO**R**Y
SIGNATU**R**E
SIGNBOA**R**D
SNAKEBI**R**D
SNOWSTO**R**M
SOLITAI**R**E
SOMEWHE**R**E
SOPHIST**R**Y
SOPHOMO**R**E
STARBOA**R**D
STATUTO**R**Y
STEELYA**R**D
STEVEDO**R**E
STILLBO**R**N
STOCKYA**R**D
STRICTU**R**E
STRUCTU**R**E
SUBALTE**R**N
SUBLUNA**R**Y
SURFBOA**R**D
TABLEWA**R**E
TEMPORA**R**Y
TERRITO**R**Y
THEREFO**R**E
TRADEMA**R**K
TRANSFO**R**M
TRANSPI**R**E
TRANSPO**R**T
TREACHE**R**Y
TRIBUTA**R**Y
TUSCARO**R**A
ULTRAPU**R**E
UNCONCE**R**N
UNDERGI**R**D
UNDERPA**R**T
VAINGLO**R**Y
VAPORWA**R**E
VERMIFO**R**M
VIBRATO**R**Y
VISIONA**R**Y
VOLUNTA**R**Y
WALLBOA**R**D
WASHBOA**R**D
WATCHWO**R**D
WATERMA**R**K
WHEREFO**R**E
WINDSTO**R**M
WORRYWA**R**T
ADVERTI**S**E
AERIALI**S**T
AEROPAU**S**E
ALBATRO**S**S
ALLERGI**S**T
ALMSHOU**S**E
ANARCHI**S**M
ANGELFI**S**H
ANIMALI**S**M
APPALOO**S**A
ARCHIVI**S**T
BACKSLA**S**H
BAKSHEE**S**H
BARBARI**S**M
BATHHOU**S**E
BELLICO**S**E
BIRDHOU**S**E
BLACKLI**S**T
BLUEGRA**S**S
BREAKFA**S**T
BRIEFCA**S**E
BROADCA**S**T
CALABOO**S**E
CALVINI**S**M
CATACLY**S**M
CATALEP**S**Y
CATECHI**S**M
CEASELE**S**S
CELLULO**S**E
CHANTEU**S**E
CHECKLI**S**T
CHEERLE**S**S
CHOPHOU**S**E
CLOCKWI**S**E
CLUBHOU**S**E
COIFFEU**S**E
COLORCA**S**T
COLORFA**S**T
COLUMNI**S**T
COMMUNI**S**M
CONCOUR**S**E
COUNTLE**S**S
CRABGRA**S**S
CRANKCA**S**E
CRETINI**S**M
CRITICI**S**M
CROSSWI**S**E
CYTOPLA**S**M
DARWINI**S**M
DAUNTLE**S**S
DEATHLE**S**S
DECOMPO**S**E
DEFEATI**S**M
DEMITAS**S**E
DISCOUR**S**E
DISHONE**S**T
DISPLEA**S**E
DISPRAI**S**E
DOGMATI**S**M
DOUBTLE**S**S
EDELWEI**S**S
EMBARRA**S**S
EMBELLI**S**H
ENCOMPA**S**S
EQUIPOI**S**E
ESTABLI**S**H
EUCHARI**S**T
EUPHEMI**S**M
EXPERTI**S**E
EXTREMI**S**M
FARMHOU**S**E
FETISHI**S**M
FEUDALI**S**M
FIREHOU**S**E
FLOPHOU**S**E
FOOTLOO**S**E
FORECLO**S**E
FORMALI**S**M
FRANCHI**S**E
GALACTO**S**E
GALVANI**S**M
GIBBERI**S**H
GOVERNE**S**S
GRANDIO**S**E
HAIRBRU**S**H
HANDCLA**S**P
HAPPINE**S**S
HEADDRE**S**S
HEADFIR**S**T
HEARTLE**S**S
HELLENI**S**M
HERBALI**S**T
HOARFRO**S**T
HOLOCAU**S**T
HOURGLA**S**S
HYPOCRI**S**Y
IMPRECI**S**E
IMPROVI**S**E
INNERMO**S**T
INTERFU**S**E
INTERNI**S**T
INTERPO**S**E
INVERNE**S**S
ISINGLA**S**S
JELLYFI**S**H
JUXTAPO**S**E
LEASTWI**S**E
LOWERCA**S**E
MACHINI**S**T
MACINTO**S**H
MACROCO**S**M
MAGNETI**S**M
MANGANE**S**E
MANNERI**S**M
MASOCHI**S**M
MECHANI**S**M
MENOPAU**S**E
METHODI**S**T
MICROCO**S**M
MODERNI**S**M
MONGOLI**S**M
MOUTHWA**S**H
MYSTICI**S**M
NEOLOGI**S**M
NORTHEA**S**T
NORTHWE**S**T
OCCULTI**S**M
OTHERWI**S**E
OUTERMO**S**T
PACKHOR**S**E
PANTHEI**S**M
PEKINGE**S**E
PENTECO**S**T
PENTHOU**S**E
PESSIMI**S**M
PESTHOU**S**E
PHYSICI**S**T
PLAYHOU**S**E
POLITES**S**E
POORHOU**S**E
PRESTRE**S**S
PRICELE**S**S
PUBLICI**S**T
RACEHOR**S**E
RACIALI**S**M
RECORDI**S**T
REDBREA**S**T
REFURBI**S**H
REIMBUR**S**E
REPLENI**S**H
REPOSSE**S**S
RESERVI**S**T
SAGEBRU**S**H
SANDBLA**S**T
SHAPELE**S**S
SHELLFI**S**H
SHIFTLE**S**S
SOCIALI**S**M
SOUTHEA**S**T
SOUTHWE**S**T
SPEAKEA**S**Y
SPICEBU**S**H
SQUEAMI**S**H
STAIRCA**S**E
STEADFA**S**T
STRAPLE**S**S
SUCCOTA**S**H
SUPERPO**S**E
SUPERVI**S**E
SWORDFI**S**H
SYLLOGI**S**M
SYMBOLI**S**M
SYNERGI**S**M
TECTONI**S**M
TERRORI**S**M
THANKLE**S**S
THICKNE**S**S
TOLLHOU**S**E
TRANSFU**S**E
TRANSPO**S**E
TURQUOI**S**E
UNDERMO**S**T
UNDERPA**S**S
UNHARNE**S**S
UNSELFI**S**H
UPPERCA**S**E
UPPERMO**S**T
UTTERMO**S**T
VANDALI**S**M
VOICELE**S**S
VOLCANI**S**M
VOODOOI**S**M
VULCANI**S**M
VULGARI**S**M
WAREHOU**S**E
WASHHOU**S**E
WATCHCA**S**E
WHEELBA**S**E
WHITEFI**S**H
WHITENE**S**S
WHITEWA**S**H
WINEPRE**S**S
WITTICI**S**M
WORKHOR**S**E
WORKHOU**S**E
WORTHLE**S**S
ZEITGEI**S**T
ABOMINA**T**E
ACCLIMA**T**E
ACCLIVI**T**Y
ACIDULA**T**E
ADMIRAL**T**Y
ADSORBA**T**E
ADUMBRA**T**E
ADVERSI**T**Y
AESTIVA**T**E
AFFILIA**T**E
AFTERMA**T**H
AGGRAVA**T**E
AGGREGA**T**E
ALLEVIA**T**E
ALMANDI**T**E
ALTERNA**T**E
ANCHORI**T**E
ANIMOSI**T**Y
ANTIPAS**T**O
ANTIQUI**T**Y
APPELLA**T**E
ARBITRA**T**E
ARGENTI**T**E
ASSOCIA**T**E
ASYMPTO**T**E
ATTENUA**T**E
ATTRIBU**T**E
AUTHORI**T**Y
BANDWID**T**H
BANQUET**T**E
BATHOLI**T**H
BENTONI**T**E
BIFURCA**T**E
BIPARTI**T**E
BIRTHRA**T**E
BLOODBA**T**H
BOOKPLA**T**E
BRIQUET**T**E
BROCHET**T**E
BUCKTOO**T**H
CALCULA**T**E
CALIBRA**T**E
CALLOSI**T**Y
CANDIDA**T**E
CAPSULA**T**E
CAPTIVA**T**E
CARBONA**T**E
CASTANE**T**S
CASTIGA**T**E
CELEBRA**T**E
CELEBRI**T**Y
CEREBRA**T**E
CERECLO**T**H
CERTAIN**T**Y
CHECKMA**T**E
CHOCOLA**T**E
CHONDRI**T**E
CIGARET**T**E
CIRCULA**T**E
CLASSMA**T**E
COAGULA**T**E
COLLIMA**T**E
COMMODI**T**Y
COMMUNI**T**Y
COMPOSI**T**E
CONGRUI**T**Y
CONJUGA**T**E
CONTRAL**T**O
COOPERA**T**E
CORPORA**T**E
CORRELA**T**E
CORRUGA**T**E
CORUSCA**T**E
CROQUET**T**E
CULMINA**T**E
CULTIVA**T**E
CYCLAMA**T**E
DEBUTAN**T**E
DECLIVI**T**Y

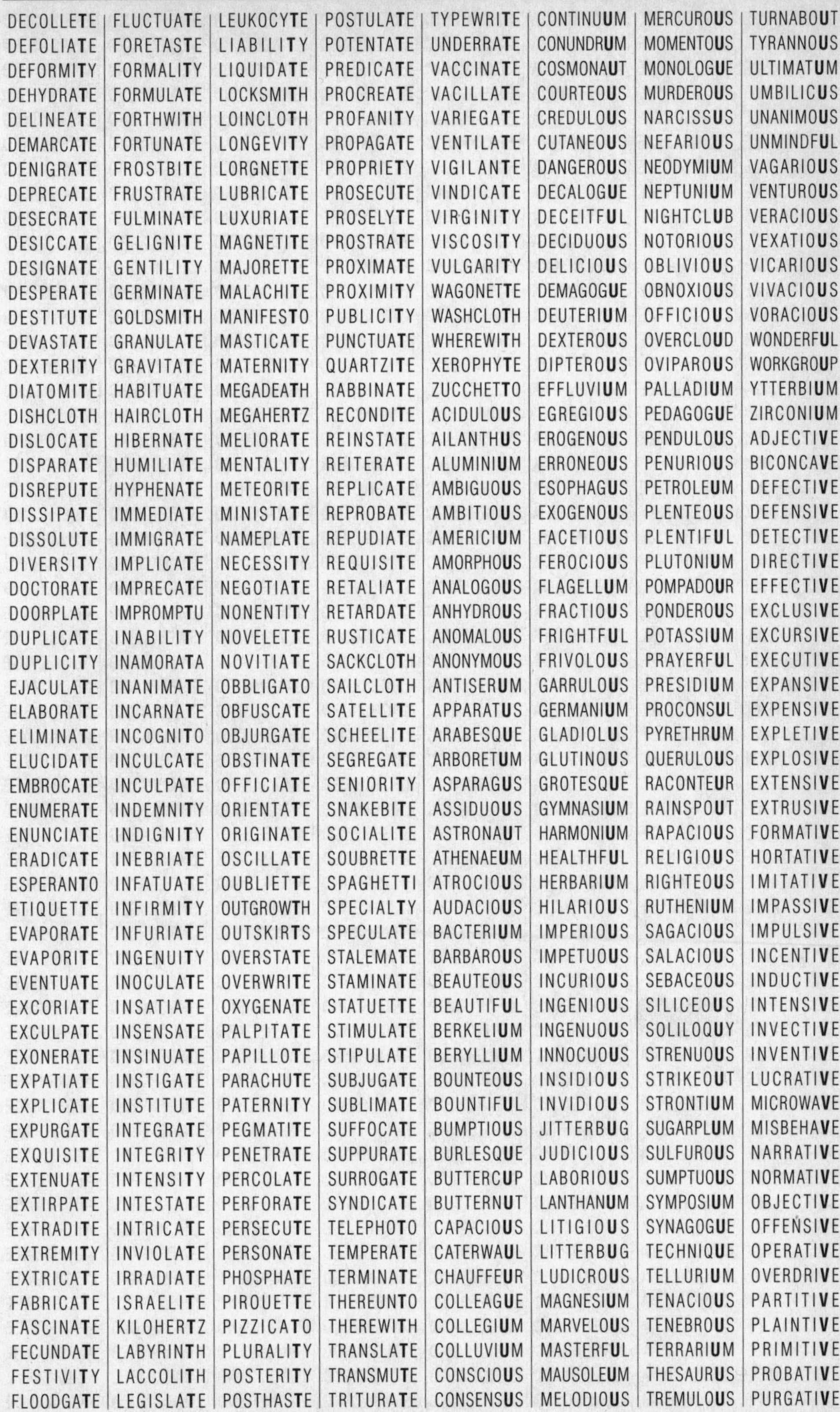

DECOLLETE
DEFOLIATE
DEFORMITY
DEHYDRATE
DELINEATE
DEMARCATE
DENIGRATE
DEPRECATE
DESECRATE
DESICCATE
DESIGNATE
DESPERATE
DESTITUTE
DEVASTATE
DEXTERITY
DIATOMITE
DISHCLOTH
DISLOCATE
DISPARATE
DISREPUTE
DISSIPATE
DISSOLUTE
DIVERSITY
DOCTORATE
DOORPLATE
DUPLICATE
DUPLICITY
EJACULATE
ELABORATE
ELIMINATE
ELUCIDATE
EMBROCATE
ENUMERATE
ENUNCIATE
ERADICATE
ESPERANTO
ETIQUETTE
EVAPORATE
EVAPORITE
EVENTUATE
EXCORIATE
EXCULPATE
EXONERATE
EXPATIATE
EXPLICATE
EXPURGATE
EXQUISITE
EXTENUATE
EXTIRPATE
EXTRADITE
EXTREMITY
EXTRICATE
FABRICATE
FASCINATE
FECUNDATE
FESTIVITY
FLOODGATE
FLUCTUATE
FORETASTE
FORMALITY
FORMULATE
FORTHWITH
FORTUNATE
FROSTBITE
FRUSTRATE
FULMINATE
GELIGNITE
GENTILITY
GERMINATE
GOLDSMITH
GRANULATE
GRAVITATE
HABITUATE
HAIRCLOTH
HIBERNATE
HUMILIATE
HYPHENATE
IMMEDIATE
IMMIGRATE
IMPLICATE
IMPRECATE
IMPROMPTU
INABILITY
INAMORATA
INANIMATE
INCARNATE
INCOGNITO
INCULCATE
INCULPATE
INDEMNITY
INDIGNITY
INEBRIATE
INFATUATE
INFIRMITY
INFURIATE
INGENUITY
INOCULATE
INSATIATE
INSENSATE
INSINUATE
INSTIGATE
INSTITUTE
INTEGRATE
INTEGRITY
INTENSITY
INTESTATE
INTRICATE
INVIOLATE
IRRADIATE
ISRAELITE
KILOHERTZ
LABYRINTH
LACCOLITH
LEGISLATE
LEUKOCYTE
LIABILITY
LIQUIDATE
LOCKSMITH
LOINCLOTH
LONGEVITY
LORGNETTE
LUBRICATE
LUXURIATE
MAGNETITE
MAJORETTE
MALACHITE
MANIFESTO
MASTICATE
MATERNITY
MEGADEATH
MEGAHERTZ
MELIORATE
MENTALITY
METEORITE
MINISTATE
NAMEPLATE
NECESSITY
NEGOTIATE
NONENTITY
NOVELETTE
NOVITIATE
OBBLIGATO
OBFUSCATE
OBJURGATE
OBSTINATE
OFFICIATE
ORIENTATE
ORIGINATE
OSCILLATE
OUBLIETTE
OUTGROWTH
OUTSKIRTS
OVERSTATE
OVERWRITE
OXYGENATE
PALPITATE
PAPILLOTE
PARACHUTE
PATERNITY
PEGMATITE
PENETRATE
PERCOLATE
PERFORATE
PERSECUTE
PERSONATE
PHOSPHATE
PIROUETTE
PIZZICATO
PLURALITY
POSTERITY
POSTHASTE
POSTULATE
POTENTATE
PREDICATE
PROCREATE
PROFANITY
PROPAGATE
PROPRIETY
PROSECUTE
PROSELYTE
PROSTRATE
PROXIMATE
PROXIMITY
PUBLICITY
PUNCTUATE
QUARTZITE
RABBINATE
RECONDITE
REINSTATE
REITERATE
REPLICATE
REPROBATE
REPUDIATE
REQUISITE
RETALIATE
RETARDATE
RUSTICATE
SACKCLOTH
SAILCLOTH
SATELLITE
SCHEELITE
SEGREGATE
SENIORITY
SNAKEBITE
SOCIALITE
SOUBRETTE
SPAGHETTI
SPECIALTY
SPECULATE
STALEMATE
STAMINATE
STATUETTE
STIMULATE
STIPULATE
SUBJUGATE
SUBLIMATE
SUFFOCATE
SUPPURATE
SURROGATE
SYNDICATE
TELEPHOTO
TEMPERATE
TERMINATE
THEREUNTO
THEREWITH
TRANSLATE
TRANSMUTE
TRITURATE
TYPEWRITE
UNDERRATE
VACCINATE
VACILLATE
VARIEGATE
VENTILATE
VIGILANTE
VINDICATE
VIRGINITY
VISCOSITY
VULGARITY
WAGONETTE
WASHCLOTH
WHEREWITH
XEROPHYTE
ZUCCHETTO
ACIDULOUS
AILANTHUS
ALUMINIUM
AMBIGUOUS
AMBITIOUS
AMERICIUM
AMORPHOUS
ANALOGOUS
ANHYDROUS
ANOMALOUS
ANONYMOUS
ANTISERUM
APPARATUS
ARABESQUE
ARBORETUM
ASPARAGUS
ASSIDUOUS
ASTRONAUT
ATHENAEUM
ATROCIOUS
AUDACIOUS
BACTERIUM
BARBAROUS
BEAUTEOUS
BEAUTIFUL
BERKELIUM
BERYLLIUM
BOUNTEOUS
BOUNTIFUL
BUMPTIOUS
BURLESQUE
BUTTERCUP
BUTTERNUT
CAPACIOUS
CATERWAUL
CHAUFFEUR
COLLEAGUE
COLLEGIUM
COLLUVIUM
CONSCIOUS
CONSENSUS
CONTINUUM
CONUNDRUM
COSMONAUT
COURTEOUS
CREDULOUS
CUTANEOUS
DANGEROUS
DECALOGUE
DECEITFUL
DECIDUOUS
DELICIOUS
DEMAGOGUE
DEUTERIUM
DEXTEROUS
DIPTEROUS
EFFLUVIUM
EGREGIOUS
EROGENOUS
ERRONEOUS
ESOPHAGUS
EXOGENOUS
FACETIOUS
FEROCIOUS
FLAGELLUM
FRACTIOUS
FRIGHTFUL
FRIVOLOUS
GARRULOUS
GERMANIUM
GLADIOLUS
GLUTINOUS
GROTESQUE
GYMNASIUM
HARMONIUM
HEALTHFUL
HERBARIUM
HILARIOUS
IMPERIOUS
IMPETUOUS
INCURIOUS
INGENIOUS
INGENUOUS
INNOCUOUS
INSIDIOUS
INVIDIOUS
JITTERBUG
JUDICIOUS
LABORIOUS
LANTHANUM
LITIGIOUS
LITTERBUG
LUDICROUS
MAGNESIUM
MARVELOUS
MASTERFUL
MAUSOLEUM
MELODIOUS
MERCUROUS
MOMENTOUS
MONOLOGUE
MURDEROUS
NARCISSUS
NEFARIOUS
NEODYMIUM
NEPTUNIUM
NIGHTCLUB
NOTORIOUS
OBLIVIOUS
OBNOXIOUS
OFFICIOUS
OVERCLOUD
OVIPAROUS
PALLADIUM
PEDAGOGUE
PENDULOUS
PENURIOUS
PETROLEUM
PLENTEOUS
PLENTIFUL
PLUTONIUM
POMPADOUR
PONDEROUS
POTASSIUM
PRAYERFUL
PRESIDIUM
PROCONSUL
PYRETHRUM
QUERULOUS
RACONTEUR
RAINSPOUT
RAPACIOUS
RELIGIOUS
RIGHTEOUS
RUTHENIUM
SAGACIOUS
SALACIOUS
SEBACEOUS
SILICEOUS
SOLILOQUY
STRENUOUS
STRIKEOUT
STRONTIUM
SUGARPLUM
SULFUROUS
SUMPTUOUS
SYMPOSIUM
SYNAGOGUE
TECHNIQUE
TELLURIUM
TENACIOUS
TENEBROUS
TERRARIUM
THESAURUS
TREMULOUS
TURNABOUT
TYRANNOUS
ULTIMATUM
UMBILICUS
UNANIMOUS
UNMINDFUL
VAGARIOUS
VENTUROUS
VERACIOUS
VEXATIOUS
VICARIOUS
VIVACIOUS
VORACIOUS
WONDERFUL
WORKGROUP
YTTERBIUM
ZIRCONIUM
ADJECTIVE
BICONCAVE
DEFECTIVE
DEFENSIVE
DETECTIVE
DIRECTIVE
EFFECTIVE
EXCLUSIVE
EXCURSIVE
EXECUTIVE
EXPANSIVE
EXPENSIVE
EXPLETIVE
EXPLOSIVE
EXTENSIVE
EXTRUSIVE
FORMATIVE
HORTATIVE
IMITATIVE
IMPASSIVE
IMPULSIVE
INCENTIVE
INDUCTIVE
INTENSIVE
INVECTIVE
INVENTIVE
LUCRATIVE
MICROWAVE
MISBEHAVE
NARRATIVE
NORMATIVE
OBJECTIVE
OFFENSIVE
OPERATIVE
OVERDRIVE
PARTITIVE
PLAINTIVE
PRIMITIVE
PROBATIVE
PURGATIVE

RECEPTIVE
RECESSIVE
REFLEXIVE
REPULSIVE
RETENTIVE
SECRETIVE
SENSITIVE
SHORTWAVE
SUPERNOVA
TALKATIVE
TENTATIVE
UNDECEIVE
BREAKDOWN
COUNTDOWN
CRACKDOWN
EIDERDOWN
HOMEGROWN
KNOCKDOWN
NIGHTGOWN
NIGHTHAWK
OVERBLOWN
SHAKEDOWN
SWANSDOWN
TOUCHDOWN
UNBEKNOWN
WATERFOWL
WINDBLOWN
WITHDRAWN
HYPERTEXT
CROSSWAYS
PSEUDONYM
ALUMINIZE
ANATOMIZE
ANGLICIZE
APOLOGIZE
AUTHORIZE
BRUTALIZE
CARBURIZE
CAUTERIZE
CRITICIZE
CUSTOMIZE
DEODORIZE
DEOXIDIZE
DRAMATIZE
ECONOMIZE
EMPHASIZE
FANTASIZE
FERTILIZE
FORMALIZE
GALVANIZE
GLAMORIZE
HARMONIZE
INFLUENZA
ITALICIZE
MAGNETIZE
MECHANIZE
MERCERIZE
MESMERIZE
METHODIZE
METRICIZE
MODERNIZE
NARCOTIZE
NORMALIZE
OSTRACIZE
PATRONIZE
PLURALIZE
PUBLICIZE
PULVERIZE
RANDOMIZE
RASTERIZE
RECOGNIZE
SENSITIZE
SIGNALIZE
SOCIALIZE
SOLEMNIZE
STABILIZE
STERILIZE
SUBSIDIZE
SUMMARIZE
SYMBOLIZE
SYSTEMIZE
TANTALIZE
TEMPORIZE
TENDERIZE
TERRORIZE
TYRANNIZE
VANDALIZE
VERBALIZE
VERNALIZE
VICTIMIZE
VISUALIZE
VULCANIZE
VULGARIZE
WINTERIZE

## 9TH LETTER

AMERICANA
ANALGESIA
APOCRYPHA
APPALOOSA
ASAFETIDA
BALALAIKA
BALLERINA
BARRACUDA
CAFETERIA
CALENDULA
CARCINOMA
CARNIVORA
CONESTOGA
DYSPEPSIA
EMPHYSEMA
ENCHILADA
FORSYTHIA
GENITALIA
GONORRHEA
GUERRILLA
HARMONICA
HELVETICA
HYDRANGEA
HYPERBOLA
INAMORATA
INFLUENZA
JACARANDA
JINRIKSHA
MARIJUANA
MELODRAMA
MONOMANIA
NEURALGIA
NOSTALGIA
ORCHESTRA
PALAESTRA
PENINSULA
PNEUMONIA
POINCIANA
PORTULACA
PYROMANIA
RAUWOLFIA
SCINTILLA
SUPERNOVA
TARANTULA
TULAREMIA
TUSCARORA
URTICARIA
CURRYCOMB
FLASHBULB
HONEYCOMB
NIGHTCLUB
ADIABATIC
AESTHETIC
ALCOHOLIC
ALEATORIC
ANAEROBIC
ANALGESIC
ANTARCTIC
APOSTOLIC
AUTHENTIC
AUTOMATIC
BISHOPRIC
BRITANNIC
CALORIFIC
CATATONIC
CATHARTIC
CHARABANC
CHIVALRIC
CHROMATIC
CRYOGENIC
DIACRITIC
DIALECTIC
DIAMETRIC
DIMORPHIC
ECCENTRIC
ENERGETIC
ENIGMATIC
EUTROPHIC
EXTRINSIC
FANTASTIC
GERIATRIC
HEURISTIC
HONORIFIC
HYDRAULIC
ICELANDIC
IMPOLITIC
INORGANIC
INTRINSIC
MULTISYNC
NEPHRITIC
NICOTINIC
ORGIASTIC
PANEGYRIC
PAREGORIC
PATRISTIC
PHILIPPIC
PHRENETIC
PNEUMATIC
PRAGMATIC
PROPHETIC
QUADRATIC
SCHEMATIC
SOPHISTIC
SOPORIFIC
SPLENETIC
STATISTIC
STOMACHIC
SUBATOMIC
SYNTHETIC
TELEGENIC
TRANSONIC
ABANDONED
AFORESAID
AFTERWARD
AMPERSAND
ANGUISHED
APARTHEID
APPREHEND
ARCHFIEND
ARROWHEAD
ARTHROPOD
BACKBOARD
BACKFIELD
BANDSTAND
BAREFACED
BASEBOARD
BEACHHEAD
BEDSPREAD
BENIGHTED
BETROTHED
BILLBOARD
BLACKBIRD
BLACKHEAD
BLINDFOLD
BLOCKHEAD
BLOODSHED
BODYGUARD
BOULEVARD
BROADBAND
BRUSHWOOD
BUCKBOARD
CARDBOARD
CATCHWORD
CHALKBORD
CHANCROID
CHICKWEED
CHILDHOOD
CLAPBOARD
CLIPBOARD
COALFIELD
COLLECTED
CONCERNED
CONCERTED
CONTENTED
COONHOUND
COURTYARD
CROSSROAD
DACHSHUND
DAIRYMAID
DASHBOARD
DELIGHTED
DEPRESSED
DIGITIZED
DIGNIFIED
DISREGARD
DISSECTED
DISTURBED
DIXIELAND
DREAMLAND
DRIFTWOOD
DUCKBOARD
DUMBFOUND
EARTHWARD
ELLIPSOID
FAIRYLAND
FALSEHOOD
FARMSTEAD
FIREBRAND
FIRSTHAND
FOOTBOARD
FORENAMED
FREEBOARD
GASTROPOD
GOLDENROD
GOLDFIELD
GRASSLAND
GRAVEYARD
GRAYBEARD
GREENWOOD
GREYHOUND
HACKNEYED
HAMADRYAD
HANDSTAND
HAPHAZARD
HARDBOARD
HARDBOUND
HARDIHOOD
HARDSTAND
HEADBOARD
HEARTWOOD
HIDEBOUND
HOMESTEAD
HOREHOUND
HOTHEADED
HOUSEHOLD
HOUSEMAID
HUMANKIND
HYPERCARD
INTERLARD
IRONBOUND
JAUNDICED
JEWELWEED
KICKSTAND
LAMINATED
LAUNCHPAD
LEASEHOLD
LIFEBLOOD
LIFEGUARD
MATCHWOOD
METEOROID
MOLDBOARD
MONGOLOID
MONKSHOOD
NEWSSTAND
NOSEBLEED
NURSEMAID
OUTSPREAD
OVERBOARD
OVERCLOUD
OVERSEXED
PERPLEXED
PIGHEADED
PLANELOAD
PLANETOID
PRERECORD
PROOFREAD
PUREBLOOD
QUADRUPED
QUICKSAND
RANCHLAND
RANGELAND
RECOMMEND
REPREHEND
REPRIMAND
ROADSTEAD
ROCKBOUND
RUNAROUND
SAFEGUARD
SANGFROID
SATINWOOD
SEMIFLUID
SHEEPFOLD
SHIPBOARD
SHOREBIRD
SHORTHAND
SIDEBOARD
SIGNBOARD
SNAKEBIRD
SNOWFIELD
SOFTBOUND
SPEARHEAD
STARBOARD
STEELYARD
STEPCHILD
STOCKYARD
STREAMBED
SURFBOARD
SWAMPLAND
SWELLHEAD
TABLELAND
THREEFOLD
THRESHOLD
TRAINLOAD
TRANSCEND
TRAPEZOID
TRUCKLOAD
UNADVISED
UNALIGNED
UNALLOYED
UNBLESSED
UNBOUNDED
UNBRIDLED
UNCHARTED
UNCOUNTED
UNDAUNTED
UNDECIDED
UNDERBRED
UNDERFEED
UNDERGIRD
UNDERHAND
UNDERWOOD
UNDOUBTED
UNEQUALED
UNFEIGNED
UNFLEDGED
UNFOUNDED
UNGUARDED
UNLEARNED
UNPLUMBED
UNRIVALED
UNRUFFLED
UNSCATHED
UNSETTLED
UNSKILLED
UNSPOTTED
UNSTUDIED
UNTUTORED
UPANISHAD
WAISTBAND
WALLBOARD
WASHBOARD
WASHSTAND
WASTELAND
WATCHBAND
WATCHWORD
WATERSHED
WHIRLWIND
WHITEHEAD
WHITEWOOD
WITHSTAND
WOLFHOUND
WOMANHOOD
WOMANKIND
WRISTBAND
ABOMINATE
ABORIGINE
ACCIDENCE
ACCLIMATE
ACETYLENE
ACIDULATE
ACQUIESCE
ADDRESSEE
ADJECTIVE
ADMIRABLE
ADMIXTURE
ADSORBATE
ADUMBRATE
ADVANTAGE
ADVENTURE
ADVERTISE
ADVISABLE
AERODROME
AEROPAUSE
AEROPLANE
AEROSPACE
AESTIVATE
AFFILIATE
AFFLUENCE
AFTERCARE
AFTERLIFE
AGGRAVATE
AGGREGATE
AGREEABLE
AIRMOBILE
ALIENABLE
ALLEVIATE
ALLOWANCE

ALMANDITE
ALMSHOUSE
ALONGSIDE
ALTERNATE
ALUMINIZE
AMBULANCE
AMBUSCADE
AMPHIBOLE
AMPLITUDE
ANATOMIZE
ANCHORAGE
ANCHORITE
ANGLICIZE
ANKLEBONE
ANNOYANCE
ANTICLINE
APOLOGIZE
APPELLATE
APPENDAGE
APPLIANCE
APPOINTEE
AQUAPLANE
ARABESQUE
ARBITRATE
ARCHETYPE
ARGENTINE
ARGENTITE
ARMISTICE
ARTERIOLE
ARTICHOKE
ASSOCIATE
ASSONANCE
ASSURANCE
ASTRADDLE
ASTROLABE
ASYMPTOTE
ATTENUATE
ATTRIBUTE
AUTHORIZE
AUTOTRACE
AVAILABLE
AVALANCHE
BACKSLIDE
BACKSTAGE
BAGATELLE
BAMBOOZLE
BANDEROLE
BANQUETTE
BARCAROLE
BARRICADE
BATHHOUSE
BEATITUDE
BELLICOSE
BELLYACHE
BELVEDERE
BENTONITE
BESPANGLE
BICONCAVE
BIFURCATE
BIOSPHERE
BIPARTITE
BIRDHOUSE
BIRTHRATE
BLASPHEME
BLOODLINE
BOMBAZINE
BOOKPLATE
BRASSERIE
BRASSIERE
BRIEFCASE
BRIMSTONE
BRIQUETTE
BROADSIDE
BROCHETTE
BROKERAGE
BRUTALIZE
BUMBLEBEE
BURLESQUE
CALABOOSE
CALCIMINE
CALCULATE
CALIBRATE
CAMPANILE
CANDIDATE
CANEBRAKE
CANNONADE
CANTABILE
CAPSULATE
CAPTIVATE
CARBONATE
CARBUNCLE
CARBURIZE
CARNIVORE
CARTILAGE
CARTRIDGE
CASSEROLE
CASTIGATE
CAUTERIZE
CAVALCADE
CELANDINE
CELEBRATE
CELLARAGE
CELLULOSE
CENTIPEDE
CEREBRATE
CERTITUDE
CHALLENGE
CHAMOMILE
CHAMPAGNE
CHANTEUSE
CHECKMATE
CHEEKBONE
CHICKADEE
CHLORDANE
CHOCOLATE
CHONDRITE
CHONDRULE
CHOPHOUSE
CHRONICLE
CHUCKHOLE
CIGARETTE
CIRCULATE
CLASSMATE
CLEARANCE
CLIENTELE
CLOCKWISE
CLOISONNE
CLUBHOUSE
COAGULATE
COASTLINE
COFEATURE
COIFFEUSE
COLLEAGUE
COLLIMATE
COLONNADE
COLUMBINE
COMMINGLE
COMMITTEE
COMMODORE
COMPOSITE
COMPOSURE
CONCIERGE
CONCOURSE
CONCUBINE
CONJUGATE
CONSTABLE
COOPERATE
CORPORATE
CORPUSCLE
CORRELATE
CORRUGATE
CORTISONE
CORUSCATE
COVALENCE
CRANKCASE
CRINOLINE
CRITICIZE
CROCODILE
CROQUETTE
CROSSWISE
CUBBYHOLE
CULMINATE
CULTIVATE
CURETTAGE
CURVATURE
CUSTOMIZE
CYCLAMATE
DAMASCENE
DEBENTURE
DEBUTANTE
DECADENCE
DECALOGUE
DECISTERE
DECOLLETE
DECOMPOSE
DECOUPAGE
DEFECTIVE
DEFENSIVE
DEFERENCE
DEFOLIATE
DEHYDRATE
DEKASTERE
DELFTWARE
DELINEATE
DEMAGOGUE
DEMARCATE
DEMIMONDE
DEMITASSE
DEMURRAGE
DENIGRATE
DEODORIZE
DEOXIDIZE
DEPARTURE
DEPRECATE
DESECRATE
DESICCATE
DESIGNATE
DESIRABLE
DESPERATE
DESTITUTE
DESUETUDE
DETECTIVE
DETERMINE
DEVASTATE
DHRYSTONE
DIATOMITE
DIRECTIVE
DIRIGIBLE
DISCHARGE
DISCOURSE
DISENGAGE
DISFIGURE
DISLOCATE
DISMANTLE
DISOBLIGE
DISPARAGE
DISPARATE
DISPLEASE
DISPRAISE
DISREPUTE
DISSEMBLE
DISSIPATE
DISSOLUTE
DIVISIBLE
DOCTORATE
DOMINANCE
DOORPLATE
DOWNGRADE
DOWNRANGE
DOWNSTAGE
DRAINPIPE
DRAMATIZE
DRUGSTORE
DUPLICATE
ECONOMIZE
EFFECTIVE
EFFLUENCE
EGLANTINE
EJACULATE
ELABORATE
ELECTRODE
ELIMINATE
ELSEWHERE
ELUCIDATE
EMBRASURE
EMBROCATE
EMPENNAGE
EMPHASIZE
ENCOURAGE
ENDOCRINE
ENDOSCOPE
ENDURANCE
ENRAPTURE
ENSHEATHE
ENTOURAGE
ENUMERATE
ENUNCIATE
ENWREATHE
EPHEDRINE
EQUIPOISE
EQUITABLE
ERADICATE
ERSTWHILE
ESPIONAGE
ESPLANADE
ESTIMABLE
ETIQUETTE
EVAPORATE
EVAPORITE
EVENTUATE
EVERGLADE
EXCITABLE
EXCLUSIVE
EXCORIATE
EXCULPATE
EXCURSIVE
EXECRABLE
EXECUTIVE
EXISTENCE
EXONERATE
EXOSPHERE
EXPANSIVE
EXPATIATE
EXPENSIVE
EXPERTISE
EXPLETIVE
EXPLICATE
EXPLOSIVE
EXPURGATE
EXQUISITE
EXTEMPORE
EXTENSIVE
EXTENUATE
EXTIRPATE
EXTRADITE
EXTRICATE
EXTRUSIVE
FABRICATE
FACSIMILE
FANTASIZE
FARMHOUSE
FASCINATE
FAVORABLE
FEBRIFUGE
FECUNDATE
FERTILIZE
FIREHOUSE
FIREPLACE
FLAGSTONE
FLAMMABLE
FLASHCUBE
FLASHTUBE
FLOODGATE
FLOPHOUSE
FLUCTUATE
FOOTLOOSE
FORECLOSE
FORESHORE
FORETASTE
FORMALIZE
FORMATIVE
FORMULATE
FORTITUDE
FORTUNATE
FOURSCORE
FRANCHISE
FRANGIBLE
FREESTONE
FRICASSEE
FRIEDCAKE
FROSTBITE
FRUITCAKE
FRUSTRATE
FULMINATE
FUNGICIDE
FURNITURE
FUSILLADE
GABARDINE
GABERDINE
GALACTOSE
GALLINULE
GALLSTONE
GALVANIZE
GARNISHEE
GARNITURE
GAUCHERIE
GELIGNITE
GERMICIDE
GERMINATE
GLADSTONE
GLAMORIZE
GLYCOSIDE
GRANDIOSE
GRANULATE
GRAPEVINE
GRATICULE
GRATITUDE
GRAVITATE
GRENADINE
GRIEVANCE
GROTESQUE
GROUPWARE
GRUBSTAKE
GUARANTEE
GUIDELINE
GYROSCOPE
HABITABLE
HABITUATE
HAILSTONE
HAIRPIECE
HAIRSTYLE
HAMMERTOE
HANDSHAKE
HANDSPIKE
HARBORAGE
HARMONIZE
HEADPHONE
HEADPIECE
HEADSTONE
HEARTACHE
HELLEBORE
HERBICIDE
HERITABLE
HERMITAGE
HIBERNATE
HINDRANCE
HISTAMINE
HITCHHIKE
HOLYSTONE
HOMOPHONE
HONORABLE
HOROSCOPE
HORSEHIDE
HORSESHOE
HORTATIVE
HOUSEWIFE
HUMILIATE
HURRICANE
HYDROXIDE
HYPERBOLE
HYPHENATE
IGNORANCE
ILLEGIBLE
IMBALANCE
IMITATIVE
IMMEDIATE
IMMIGRATE
IMMOVABLE
IMMUTABLE
IMPASSIVE
IMPEDANCE
IMPLICATE
IMPORTUNE
IMPOSTURE
IMPRECATE
IMPRECISE
IMPROVISE
IMPULSIVE
INANIMATE
INCAPABLE
INCARNATE
INCENTIVE
INCIDENCE
INCOMMODE
INCULCATE
INCULPATE
INCURABLE
INDELIBLE
INDENTURE
INDUCTIVE
INEBRIATE
INEFFABLE
INFANTILE
INFATUATE
INFERENCE
INFERTILE
INFLUENCE
INFURIATE
INFUSIBLE
INJUSTICE
INNERSOLE
INNOCENCE
INOCULATE
INSATIATE
INSENSATE
INSINCERE
INSINUATE
INSOLUBLE
INSTIGATE
INSTITUTE
INSURABLE
INSURANCE
INTEGRATE
INTENSIVE
INTERCEDE
INTERFACE

INTERFERE
INTERFUSE
INTERLACE
INTERLINE
INTERLOPE
INTERLUDE
INTERNODE
INTERPOSE
INTERVENE
INTESTATE
INTESTINE
INTRICATE
INTRODUCE
INTUMESCE
INVECTIVE
INVENTIVE
INVIOLATE
INVISIBLE
INVOLUCRE
IRASCIBLE
IRONSTONE
IRRADIATE
IRRITABLE
ISRAELITE
ITALICIZE
JACKKNIFE
JESSAMINE
JUXTAPOSE
KILOCYCLE
KINESCOPE
KNOWLEDGE
LAGNIAPPE
LANDSCAPE
LANDSLIDE
LASSITUDE
LAVALIERE
LEASTWISE
LEGISLATE
LEUKOCYTE
LIBERTINE
LIGHTFACE
LIGHTSOME
LIMESTONE
LIMOUSINE
LIQUIDATE
LITHESOME
LOADSTONE
LOATHSOME
LODESTONE
LONGITUDE
LORGNETTE
LOWERCASE
LUBRICATE
LUCRATIVE
LUXURIATE
MAGNETITE
MAGNETIZE

MAGNITUDE
MAINFRAME
MAJORETTE
MAJUSCULE
MALACHITE
MALLEABLE
MANGANESE
MANHANDLE
MANOEUVRE
MARGARINE
MARMALADE
MASCULINE
MASTICATE
MATRICIDE
MEANWHILE
MECHANIZE
MEDICABLE
MEGACYCLE
MEGAPHONE
MELIORATE
MEMORABLE
MENAGERIE
MENOPAUSE
MERCERIZE
MESCALINE
MESMERIZE
METALWARE
METEORITE
METHADONE
METHODIZE
METRICIZE
METRONOME
MEZZANINE
MICROWAVE
MILESTONE
MILLIPEDE
MILLSTONE
MINIATURE
MINISCULE
MINISTATE
MINUSCULE
MISBEHAVE
MISCHANCE
MISERABLE
MISHANDLE
MISMANAGE
MISTLETOE
MODERNIZE
MONOLOGUE
MONOPLANE
MONOSPACE
MOONSCAPE
MOONSHINE
MOONSTONE
MOTORBIKE
MOTORCADE
MOUSTACHE

MULTITUDE
NAMEPLATE
NARCOTIZE
NARRATIVE
NAVIGABLE
NECTARINE
NEGOTIATE
NEGRITUDE
NEVERMORE
NIGHTLIFE
NIGHTMARE
NIGHTTIME
NIGRITUDE
NORMALIZE
NORMATIVE
NOSEPIECE
NOVELETTE
NOVITIATE
OBEISANCE
OBFUSCATE
OBJECTIVE
OBJURGATE
OBSTINATE
OFFENSIVE
OFFICIATE
OPERATIVE
OPPORTUNE
ORANGEADE
ORDINANCE
ORIENTATE
ORIFLAMME
ORIGINATE
ORPHANAGE
OSCILLATE
OSTRACIZE
OTHERWISE
OUBLIETTE
OVERDRIVE
OVERSTATE
OVERWRITE
OXYGENATE
PACKHORSE
PALATABLE
PALPITATE
PANHANDLE
PANTOMIME
PAPILLOTE
PARACHUTE
PARRICIDE
PARSONAGE
PARTITIVE
PARTRIDGE
PASSERINE
PASTORALE
PASTURAGE
PATRICIDE
PATRONAGE

PATRONIZE
PEACETIME
PEDAGOGUE
PEGMATITE
PEKINGESE
PENETRATE
PENTHOUSE
PERCHANCE
PERCOLATE
PERFORATE
PERISCOPE
PERISTYLE
PERMEABLE
PERSECUTE
PERSEVERE
PERSONAGE
PERSONATE
PESTHOUSE
PESTICIDE
PHALAROPE
PHEROMONE
PHOSPHATE
PINEAPPLE
PINSTRIPE
PIROUETTE
PLAINTIVE
PLATITUDE
PLAUSIBLE
PLAYHOUSE
PLENITUDE
PLOWSHARE
PLURALIZE
POLITESSE
POORHOUSE
PORCUPINE
POSTHASTE
POSTULATE
POTENTATE
POURBOIRE
PRECIPICE
PREDICATE
PREFIGURE
PREGNABLE
PREJUDICE
PREMATURE
PRESCRIBE
PRIMITIVE
PRINCIPLE
PRINTABLE
PRIVILEGE
PROBATIVE
PROCEDURE
PROCREATE
PROMENADE
PRONOUNCE
PROPAGATE
PROSCRIBE

PROSECUTE
PROSELYTE
PROSTRATE
PROTOTYPE
PROVOLONE
PROXIMATE
PUBLICIZE
PUISSANCE
PULVERIZE
PUNCTUATE
PURGATIVE
PURSUANCE
QUADRILLE
QUADRUPLE
QUARTZITE
QUICKLIME
QUICKTIME
QUINTUPLE
QUITTANCE
RABBINATE
RACEHORSE
RANDOMIZE
RASTERIZE
RATIONALE
REACTANCE
RECEPTIVE
RECESSIVE
RECHERCHE
RECOGNIZE
RECONCILE
RECONDITE
RECTANGLE
RECTITUDE
REENFORCE
REFERENCE
REFLEXIVE
REIMBURSE
REINFORCE
REINSTATE
REITERATE
RELEVANCE
REMINISCE
RENCONTRE
REPLICATE
REPORTAGE
REPROBATE
REPRODUCE
REPUDIATE
REPULSIVE
REPUTABLE
REQUISITE
RESERPINE
RESHUFFLE
RESIDENCE
RESONANCE
RETALIATE
RETARDATE

RETENTIVE
RETROFIRE
REVERENCE
REVOCABLE
RIDGEPOLE
RIGMAROLE
RIVERSIDE
RUSTICATE
SACRIFICE
SACRILEGE
SAILPLANE
SANDSTONE
SATELLITE
SATURNINE
SAXIFRAGE
SAXOPHONE
SCHEELITE
SCRIMMAGE
SCRIPTURE
SCULPTURE
SECRETIVE
SEGREGATE
SEMAPHORE
SEMBLANCE
SENSITIVE
SENSITIZE
SEPARABLE
SEPULTURE
SERVITUDE
SHAREWARE
SHELLFIRE
SHIPSHAPE
SHORTCAKE
SHORTWAVE
SHOWPIECE
SHOWPLACE
SHRINKAGE
SIDEPIECE
SIDESWIPE
SIGNALIZE
SIGNATURE
SILTSTONE
SKIMOBILE
SKYLOUNGE
SNAKEBITE
SNOWFLAKE
SOAPSTONE
SOCIALITE
SOCIALIZE
SOLEMNIZE
SOLITAIRE
SOMEWHERE
SOPHOMORE
SOUBRETTE
SPECTACLE
SPECULATE
STABILIZE

STAIRCASE
STALEMATE
STAMINATE
STANDPIPE
STATESIDE
STATUETTE
STERILIZE
STEVEDORE
STIMULATE
STIPULATE
STOCKPILE
STRICTURE
STRUCTURE
SUBALPINE
SUBDIVIDE
SUBJUGATE
SUBLIMATE
SUBMARINE
SUBSCRIBE
SUBSIDIZE
SUBSTANCE
SUFFOCATE
SUGARCANE
SUMMARIZE
SUNSTROKE
SUPERPOSE
SUPERSEDE
SUPERVENE
SUPERVISE
SUPPURATE
SURCHARGE
SURCINGLE
SURROGATE
SYMBOLIZE
SYNAGOGUE
SYNDICATE
SYSTEMIZE
TABLEWARE
TALKATIVE
TANGERINE
TANTALIZE
TEAKETTLE
TECHNIQUE
TELEPHONE
TELESCOPE
TEMPERATE
TEMPORIZE
TENDERIZE
TENTATIVE
TERMINATE
TERRORIZE
THEREFORE
THIGHBONE
THREESOME
THYROXINE
TIGHTROPE
TIMEPIECE

TIMETABLE
TOLERABLE
TOLERANCE
TOLLHOUSE
TOMBSTONE
TOOTHACHE
TOOTHSOME
TRACTABLE
TRANSDUCE
TRANSFUSE
TRANSLATE
TRANSMUTE
TRANSPIRE
TRANSPOSE
TREMATODE
TRITURATE
TURNSTILE
TURNTABLE
TURPITUDE
TURQUOISE
TYPEWRITE
TYRANNIZE
ULTRAPURE
UNDECEIVE
UNDERDONE
UNDERLINE
UNDERMINE
UNDERRATE
UNDERSIDE
UNDERTAKE
UNDERTONE
UNSHACKLE
UNSHEATHE
UPPERCASE
UTTERANCE
VACCINATE
VACILLATE
VALENTINE
VANDALIZE
VAPORWARE
VARIEGATE
VASSALAGE
VEGETABLE
VEHEMENCE
VENERABLE
VENGEANCE
VENTILATE
VENTRICLE
VERBALIZE
VERITABLE
VERMIFUGE
VERNALIZE
VERSATILE
VESTIBULE
VICTIMIZE
VIDEOTAPE
VIGILANCE

VIGILANTE
VILLENAGE
VINDICATE
VISUALIZE
VOUCHSAFE
VULCANIZE
VULGARIZE
WAGONETTE
WAISTLINE
WAREHOUSE
WASHHOUSE
WATCHCASE
WATERLINE
WATERSIDE
WAVETABLE
WEARISOME
WHALEBONE
WHEELBASE
WHEREFORE
WHETSTONE
WHOLESALE
WHOLESOME
WINTERIZE
WIREFRAME
WOEBEGONE
WOLFSBANE
WOLVERINE
WOMANLIKE
WORKHORSE
WORKHOUSE
WORKPLACE
WORKTABLE
WORLDWIDE
WORRISOME
XANTHIPPE
XEROPHYTE
XYLOPHONE
BOMBPROOF
BOOKSHELF
FEEDSTUFF
FIREPROOF
FLAGSTAFF
FOODSTUFF
FOOLPROOF
INTERLEAF
PIKESTAFF
PLAINTIFF
WINDPROOF
ADJOINING
AFFECTING
BESETTING
BOOMERANG
BOWSTRING
CARPETBAG
CARPETING
DESIGNING
DIPHTHONG
DITHERING
DOWNSWING
EARTHLING
EASYGOING
ENGRAVING
FARSEEING
FASTENING
FINGERING
FINICKING
FIRSTLING
FLAVORING
FLEDGLING
FOLLOWING
FOREGOING
FORGIVING
FOUNDLING
GROUNDHOG
GROUNDING
HAMSTRING
HAPPENING
INGROWING
JITTERBUG
LEAVENING
LIGHTNING
LITTERBUG
MISGIVING
OFFSPRING
PLAYTHING
PRECEDING
PROMISING
RECKONING
RECORDING
REGARDING
REHEARING
REVOLTING
SCANTLING
SCHILLING
SCREENING
SEAFARING
SEASONING
SHEATHING
SKYDIVING
SOMETHING
SPINDLING
SPLITTING
STARTLING
STRAPPING
STRIPLING
SUFFERING
SUPPOSING
SURVEYING
TIMBERING
TWINKLING
UNBENDING
UNCEASING
UNDERLING
UNFAILING
UNFEELING
UNKNOWING
UNMEANING
UNSPARING
UNWILLING
UNWITTING
WALLOPING
WHIRLIGIG
WORLDLING
WRESTLING
YOUNGLING
AFTERMATH
ANGELFISH
AUTOGRAPH
BACKSLASH
BAKSHEESH
BANDWIDTH
BAROGRAPH
BATHOLITH
BLOODBATH
BLOWTORCH
BUCKTOOTH
BULLFINCH
CERECLOTH
CHAFFINCH
COCKROACH
DISHCLOTH
EMBELLISH
ESTABLISH
FORTHWITH
GIBBERISH
GOLDFINCH
GOLDSMITH
HAIRBRUSH
HAIRCLOTH
HEMISTICH
HEMSTITCH
HOLOGRAPH
HOMOGRAPH
HOPSCOTCH
JELLYFISH
LABYRINTH
LACCOLITH
LOCKSMITH
LOINCLOTH
MACINTOSH
MATRIARCH
MEGADEATH
MONOGRAPH
MOUTHWASH
OUTGROWTH
OVERMATCH
OVERREACH
OVERWEIGH
PARAGRAPH
PATRIARCH
POLYGRAPH
PRELAUNCH
REFURBISH
REPLENISH
SACKCLOTH
SAGEBRUSH
SAILCLOTH
SERIGRAPH
SHELLFISH
SPICEBUSH
SQUEAMISH
STOPWATCH
SUCCOTASH
SWORDFISH
TELEGRAPH
THEREWITH
ULTRAHIGH
UNSELFISH
WASHCLOTH
WHEREWITH
WHITEFISH
WHITEWASH
WORKBENCH
MAHARISHI
PAKISTANI
POTPOURRI
SPAGHETTI
AFTERDECK
ANTIKNOCK
APPLEJACK
APPLETALK
AWESTRUCK
BACKTRACK
BAILIWICK
BEEFSTEAK
BIRTHMARK
BLACKJACK
BLUEBLACK
BOARDWALK
BOLSHEVIK
BOOTBLACK
BUSHWHACK
CAMELBACK
CHECKBOOK
CHOPSTICK
CLOCKWORK
CORNSTALK
CROSSWALK
DISEMBARK
DRUMSTICK
EARTHWORK
FANCYWORK
FEEDSTOCK
FIREBREAK
FIREBRICK
FLASHBACK
FLINTLOCK
FRAMEWORK
GANGPLANK
GOLDBRICK
GREENBACK
GRILLWORK
GUIDEBOOK
GUNNYSACK
HANDIWORK
HAVERSACK
HEARTSICK
HOLLYHOCK
HORSEBACK
HOUSEWORK
HUNCHBACK
INGLENOOK
INTERLINK
INTERLOCK
JAILBREAK
LEAFSTALK
LIVESTOCK
MATCHBOOK
MATCHLOCK
METALWORK
NIGHTHAWK
NOTCHBACK
OVERTRICK
PAPERBACK
PATCHWORK
PICKABACK
PIECEWORK
PIGGYBACK
PITCHFORK
PLACEKICK
POPPYCOCK
PRESHRUNK
RACETRACK
RIVERBANK
ROADBLOCK
ROOTSTOCK
ROUGHNECK
SCRAPBOOK
SHIPWRECK
SIDETRACK
SMALLTALK
THROWBACK
THUMBTACK
TOOTHPICK
TOWNSFOLK
TRADEMARK
WATERMARK
WINDBREAK
WISECRACK
WOMENFOLK
WOODBLOCK
WOODCHUCK
YARDSTICK
ANTINOVEL
ARCHANGEL
AUCTORIAL
BACCHANAL
BACKPEDAL
BEAUTIFUL
BICAMERAL
BILATERAL
BILINGUAL
BINOMINAL
BLACKBALL
BLACKMAIL
BOMBSHELL
BOUNTIFUL
BROADTAIL
BRONCHIAL
CAMPSTOOL
CANONICAL
CARROUSEL
CARTWHEEL
CATERWAUL
CATHEDRAL
CELESTIAL
CHAPARRAL
CLAMSHELL
CLASSICAL
COCHINEAL
COCKATIEL
CONGENIAL
CONNUBIAL
CONTINUAL
CONVIVIAL
CORPOREAL
CUSTODIAL
DAREDEVIL
DECEITFUL
DECENNIAL
DECONTROL
EDITORIAL
EFFECTUAL
EMPIRICAL
EPHEMERAL
EPISCOPAL
EQUIVOCAL
ESSENTIAL
FACTORIAL
FINANCIAL
FOOTSTOOL
FORESTALL
FRATERNAL
FREEWHEEL
FRIGHTFUL
GRISTMILL
HEADSTALL
HEALTHFUL
HORSETAIL
HYDROFOIL
IDENTICAL
ILLIBERAL
ILLOGICAL
IMPARTIAL
INAUGURAL
JURIDICAL
MAGISTRAL
MARMOREAL
MARSUPIAL
MASTERFUL
MATUTINAL
MEDICINAL
MEGAPIXEL
MERCURIAL
MUNICIPAL
NIGHTFALL
NOCTURNAL
NONPAREIL
NUMERICAL
PAROCHIAL
PERENNIAL
PERPETUAL
PERSONNEL
PHOTOCELL
PICTORIAL
PIECEMEAL
PIMPERNEL
PLENTIFUL
POLITICAL
POSTNATAL
POTENTIAL
PRACTICAL
PRAYERFUL
PRECANCEL
PRESCHOOL
PREVERBAL
PRINCIPAL
PROCONSUL
PROVENCAL
PUERPERAL
QUIZZICAL
REHEARSAL
SALESGIRL
SARTORIAL
SCHLEMIEL
SCOUNDREL
SCREWBALL
SECTIONAL
SEMIFINAL
SPEEDWELL
SPIRITUAL
SPOONBILL
STAIRWELL
SUBNORMAL
SWORDTAIL
TECHNICAL
THUMBNAIL
TOADSTOOL
TONSORIAL
TRACKBALL
TREADMILL
TRIENNIAL
UNDERSELL
UNISEXUAL
UNIVERSAL
UNMINDFUL
UNNATURAL
VERIDICAL
VERTEBRAL
VICENNIAL
VICEREGAL
VIGESIMAL
WATERFALL
WATERFOWL
WHIMSICAL
WHIRLPOOL
WHITEHALL
WHITETAIL
WHITEWALL
WINDCHILL
WONDERFUL
ALGORITHM
ALUMINIUM
AMERICIUM
ANARCHISM
ANGLEWORM
ANIMALISM
ANTISERUM
ARBORETUM
ATHENAEUM
BACTERIUM
BARBARISM
BARNSTORM
BERKELIUM
BERYLLIUM
BROADLOOM
CABLEGRAM
CALVINISM
CATACLYSM
CATECHISM
CENTIGRAM
CHECKROOM
CLASSROOM
COFFERDAM
COLLEGIUM
COLLUVIUM
COMMUNISM
CONTINUUM
CONUNDRUM
COURTROOM
CRETINISM
CRITICISM
CRUCIFORM
CUNEIFORM
CYTOPLASM
DARWINISM

DEFEATISM
DEUTERIUM
DIAPHRAGM
DISESTEEM
DOGMATISM
EARTHWORM
ECOSYSTEM
EFFLUVIUM
ELBOWROOM
EUPHEMISM
EXTREMISM
FETISHISM
FEUDALISM
FLAGELLUM
FORMALISM
GALVANISM
GERMANIUM
GREENROOM
GUARDROOM
GYMNASIUM
HAILSTORM
HARMONIUM
HECTOGRAM
HELLENISM
HERBARIUM
HISTOGRAM
LANTHANUM
LITERATIM
LOGARITHM
LUNCHROOM
MACROCOSM
MAELSTROM
MAGNESIUM
MAGNETISM
MANNERISM
MARTYRDOM
MASOCHISM
MAUSOLEUM
MECHANISM
MICROCOSM
MICROFILM
MICROGRAM
MIDSTREAM
MILLIGRAM
MISINFORM
MODERNISM
MONGOLISM
MULTIFORM
MYSTICISM
NEODYMIUM
NEOLOGISM
NEPTUNIUM
OCCULTISM
OVERWHELM
PACHYDERM
PALLADIUM
PANTHEISM
PESSIMISM
PETROLEUM
PLUTONIUM
POTASSIUM
PRESIDIUM
PRESSROOM
PSEUDONYM
PYRETHRUM
RACIALISM
RADIOGRAM
RAINSTORM
ROUNDWORM
RUTHENIUM
SANDSTORM
SNOWSTORM
SOCIALISM
STATEROOM
STOREROOM
STRATAGEM
STRONTIUM
SUGARPLUM
SYLLOGISM
SYMBOLISM
SYMPOSIUM
SYNERGISM
TECTONISM
TELLURIUM
TERRARIUM
TERRORISM
THEREFROM
THRALLDOM
TRANSFORM
ULTIMATUM
VANDALISM
VERMIFORM
VOLCANISM
VOODOOISM
VULCANISM
VULGARISM
WINDSTORM
WITTICISM
YTTERBIUM
ZIRCONIUM
ACCESSION
ACCORDION
ACCRETION
ADDICTION
ADMISSION
AFFECTION
AFTERNOON
ALGONQUIN
AMPHIBIAN
ANCHORMAN
ANIMATION
ANTITOXIN
ANTIVENIN
APPERTAIN
APPORTION
ASCENSION
ASCERTAIN
ASPERSION
ASSERTION
ASTRAKHAN
ATTENTION
ATTRITION
AUTOMATON
AVOCATION
BADMINTON
BALDACHIN
BANDWAGON
BANTUSTAN
BARBARIAN
BATTALION
BEDRIDDEN
BOATSWAIN
BONDWOMAN
BRAZILIAN
BREAKDOWN
BULGARIAN
BURUNDIAN
CANDLEPIN
CAPARISON
CARIBBEAN
CARNATION
CARNELIAN
CATAMARAN
CAUCASIAN
CAUSATION
CENTURION
CESSATION
CHAMELEON
CHAMPAIGN
CHARLATAN
CHARWOMAN
CHIEFTAIN
CHILBLAIN
CHRISTIAN
CHURCHMAN
CIRCADIAN
CLERGYMAN
CLINICIAN
COALITION
COGNITION
COLLATION
COLLEGIAN
COLLODION
COLLUSION
COMMOTION
COMMUNION
COMPANION
CONDITION
CONFUSION
CONSTRAIN
CONTAGION
CONTUSION
COTILLION
COTYLEDON
COUNTDOWN
COURTESAN
CRACKDOWN
CRAFTSMAN
CRITERION
CUSTODIAN
CYCLOTRON
DALMATION
DAMNATION
DANDELION
DECATHLON
DECEPTION
DEDUCTION
DEFLATION
DEJECTION
DENTITION
DETENTION
DIMENSION
DIRECTION
DISBURDEN
DIVERSION
DRAFTSMAN
EDUCATION
EIDERDOWN
ELEVATION
ELOCUTION
ENLIGHTEN
ENTERTAIN
EPICUREAN
ERUDITION
ETHIOPIAN
EUCLIDEAN
EVERGREEN
EVOLUTION
EXCEPTION
EXCURSION
EXPANSION
EXPLOSION
EXPULSION
EXTENSION
EYESTRAIN
FELLOWMAN
FIRSTBORN
FISHERMAN
FLOTATION
FORETOKEN
FOREWOMAN
FORMATION
FREEMASON
GENTLEMAN
GESTATION
GRADATION
GRANTSMAN
GREENHORN
GROOMSMAN
GROSGRAIN
GUARDSMAN
GUNCOTTON
GYRFALCON
HALLOWEEN
HANDWOVEN
HARLEQUIN
HARTSHORN
HEARTBURN
HELVETIAN
HERCULEAN
HISTORIAN
HOBGOBLIN
HOMEGROWN
HONEYMOON
HUNGARIAN
IMITATION
IMPULSION
INANITION
INCEPTION
INCURSION
INDENTION
INDUCTION
INFECTION
INFLATION
INFLEXION
INJECTION
INSERTION
INTENTION
INTUITION
INVENTION
INVERSION
ITERATION
KINSWOMAN
KNOCKDOWN
LAMEBRAIN
LEVIATHAN
LIBRARIAN
LIVERYMAN
MALATHION
MALAYSIAN
MANHATTAN
MANNEQUIN
MEDALLION
MIDDLEMAN
MINUTEMAN
MISGOVERN
MONGOLIAN
MORTICIAN
MULTISCAN
MULTISPIN
MUSKMELON
MUSSULMAN
NIGHTGOWN
NONPERSON
NORWEGIAN
NUTRITION
OBSESSION
OMBUDSMAN
ONIONSKIN
OPERATION
OUTSPOKEN
OVERBLOWN
OXIDATION
PALANQUIN
PARATHION
PARTITION
PATRICIAN
PATROLMAN
PENEPLAIN
PERDITION
PERSIMMON
PHYSICIAN
POLICEMAN
PORCELAIN
POSTILION
PRECISION
PREDATION
PREORDAIN
PREVISION
PRIVATION
PROBATION
PRONGHORN
PROTOZOAN
PROVISION
PTARMIGAN
PURGATION
QUOTIDIAN
REBELLION
RECEPTION
RECESSION
RECURSION
REDACTION
REDUCTION
REFECTION
REMISSION
RENDITION
REPAIRMAN
REPLETION
REPULSION
RESECTION
RETENTION
REVERSION
REVULSION
ROUMANIAN
RUINATION
SACCHARIN
SACRISTAN
SALVATION
SCUTCHEON
SECESSION
SECLUSION
SECRETION
SECTARIAN
SELECTION
SELECTMAN
SEMICOLON
SENSATION
SEVENTEEN
SHAKEDOWN
SHARKSKIN
SHEEPSKIN
SHORTHORN
SIGNALMAN
SIMPLETON
SINGLETON
SITUATION
SOVEREIGN
SPOKESMAN
SPORTSMAN
STANCHION
STATESMAN
STILLBORN
SUBALTERN
SUFFRAGAN
SUMMATION
SUSPICION
SWANSDOWN
SWITCHMAN
SWORDSMAN
TANZANIAN
TARPAULIN
THEREUPON
TOUCHDOWN
TRADESMAN
TRADITION
TRAGEDIAN
TRIBESMAN
TRUNCHEON
UKRAINIAN
UNBEKNOWN
UNCERTAIN
UNCONCERN
UNITARIAN
UNWRITTEN
VALUATION
VARIATION
VELVETEEN
VENIREMAN
VERMILION
VESTRYMAN
VIBRATION
VICTORIAN
VIOLATION
VULGARIAN
WASHBASIN
WASHWOMAN
WHEREUPON
WINDBLOWN
WITHDRAWN
YACHTSMAN
ZWINGLIAN
ANTIPASTO
ARMADILLO
BASTINADO
CAPRICCIO
CENTESIMO
CIGARILLO
CONTRALTO
CRESCENDO
DESPERADO
ESPERANTO
GLISSANDO
IMBROGLIO
INCOGNITO
MAGNIFICO
MAJORDOMO
MANIFESTO
OBBLIGATO
PISTACHIO
PIZZICATO
POLITBURO
PORTFOLIO
PUNCTILIO
SIMPATICO
TELEPHOTO
THEREUNTO
ZUCCHETTO
BUTTERCUP
COURTSHIP
EAVESDROP
FILMSTRIP
FINGERTIP
HANDCLASP
HORSEWHIP
LIGHTSHIP
MOUSETRAP
OVERSLEEP
QUICKSTEP
SHORTSTOP
SPACESHIP
STEAMSHIP
SWEATSHOP
TRANSSHIP
TROOPSHIP
TURBOPROP
WORKGROUP
ALABASTER
ALLIGATOR
ALTIMETER
ANNOUNCER
ANTECHOIR
ANTITUMOR
APPETIZER
ARTICULAR
ARTIFICER
ASSEMBLER

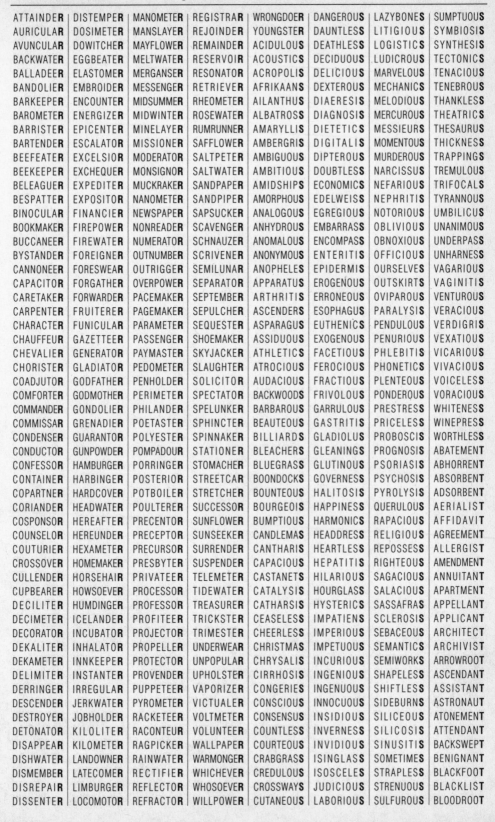

ATTAINDER
AURICULAR
AVUNCULAR
BACKWATER
BALLADEER
BANDOLIER
BARKEEPER
BAROMETER
BARRISTER
BARTENDER
BEEFEATER
BEEKEEPER
BELEAGUER
BESPATTER
BINOCULAR
BOOKMAKER
BUCCANEER
BYSTANDER
CANNONEER
CAPACITOR
CARETAKER
CARPENTER
CHARACTER
CHAUFFEUR
CHEVALIER
CHORISTER
COADJUTOR
COMFORTER
COMMANDER
COMMISSAR
CONDENSER
CONDUCTOR
CONFESSOR
CONTAINER
COPARTNER
CORIANDER
COSPONSOR
COUNSELOR
COUTURIER
CROSSOVER
CULLENDER
CUPBEARER
DECILITER
DECIMETER
DECORATOR
DEKALITER
DEKAMETER
DELIMITER
DERRINGER
DESCENDER
DESTROYER
DETONATOR
DISAPPEAR
DISHWATER
DISMEMBER
DISREPAIR
DISSENTER
DISTEMPER
DOSIMETER
DOWITCHER
EGGBEATER
ELASTOMER
EMBROIDER
ENCOUNTER
ENERGIZER
EPICENTER
ESCALATOR
EXCELSIOR
EXCHEQUER
EXPEDITER
EXPOSITOR
FINANCIER
FIREPOWER
FIREWATER
FOREIGNER
FORESWEAR
FORGATHER
FORWARDER
FRUITERER
FUNICULAR
GAZETTEER
GENERATOR
GLADIATOR
GODFATHER
GODMOTHER
GONDOLIER
GRENADIER
GUARANTOR
GUNPOWDER
HAMBURGER
HARBINGER
HARDCOVER
HEADWATER
HEREAFTER
HEREUNDER
HEXAMETER
HOMEMAKER
HORSEHAIR
HOWSOEVER
HUMDINGER
ICELANDER
INCUBATOR
INHALATOR
INNKEEPER
INSTANTER
IRREGULAR
JERKWATER
JOBHOLDER
KILOLITER
KILOMETER
LANDOWNER
LATECOMER
LIMBURGER
LOCOMOTOR
MANOMETER
MANSLAYER
MAYFLOWER
MELTWATER
MERGANSER
MESSENGER
MIDSUMMER
MIDWINTER
MINELAYER
MISSIONER
MODERATOR
MONSIGNOR
MUCKRAKER
NANOMETER
NEWSPAPER
NONREADER
NUMERATOR
OUTNUMBER
OUTRIGGER
OVERPOWER
PACEMAKER
PAGEMAKER
PARAMETER
PASSENGER
PAYMASTER
PEDOMETER
PENHOLDER
PERIMETER
PHILANDER
POETASTER
POLYESTER
POMPADOUR
PORRINGER
POSTERIOR
POTBOILER
POULTERER
PRECENTOR
PRECEPTOR
PRECURSOR
PRESBYTER
PRIVATEER
PROCESSOR
PROFESSOR
PROFITEER
PROJECTOR
PROPELLER
PROTECTOR
PROVENDER
PUPPETEER
PYROMETER
RACKETEER
RACONTEUR
RAGPICKER
RAINWATER
RECTIFIER
REFLECTOR
REFRACTOR
REGISTRAR
REJOINDER
REMAINDER
RESERVOIR
RESONATOR
RETRIEVER
RHEOMETER
ROSEWATER
RUMRUNNER
SAFFLOWER
SALTPETER
SALTWATER
SANDPAPER
SANDPIPER
SAPSUCKER
SCAVENGER
SCHNAUZER
SCRIVENER
SEMILUNAR
SEPARATOR
SEPTEMBER
SEPULCHER
SEQUESTER
SHOEMAKER
SKYJACKER
SLAUGHTER
SOLICITOR
SPECTATOR
SPELUNKER
SPHINCTER
SPINNAKER
STATIONER
STOMACHER
STREETCAR
STRETCHER
SUCCESSOR
SUNFLOWER
SUNSEEKER
SURRENDER
SUSPENDER
TELEMETER
TIDEWATER
TREASURER
TRICKSTER
TRIMESTER
UNDERWEAR
UNPOPULAR
UPHOLSTER
VAPORIZER
VICTUALER
VOLTMETER
VOLUNTEER
WALLPAPER
WARMONGER
WHICHEVER
WHOSOEVER
WILLPOWER
WRONGDOER
YOUNGSTER
ACIDULOUS
ACOUSTICS
ACROPOLIS
AFRIKAANS
AILANTHUS
ALBATROSS
AMARYLLIS
AMBERGRIS
AMBIGUOUS
AMBITIOUS
AMIDSHIPS
AMORPHOUS
ANALOGOUS
ANHYDROUS
ANOMALOUS
ANONYMOUS
ANOPHELES
APPARATUS
ARTHRITIS
ASCENDERS
ASPARAGUS
ASSIDUOUS
ATHLETICS
ATROCIOUS
AUDACIOUS
BACKWOODS
BARBAROUS
BEAUTEOUS
BILLIARDS
BLEACHERS
BLUEGRASS
BOONDOCKS
BOUNTEOUS
BOURGEOIS
BUMPTIOUS
CANDLEMAS
CANTHARIS
CAPACIOUS
CASTANETS
CATALYSIS
CATHARSIS
CEASELESS
CHEERLESS
CHRISTMAS
CHRYSALIS
CIRRHOSIS
CONGERIES
CONSCIOUS
CONSENSUS
COUNTLESS
COURTEOUS
CRABGRASS
CREDULOUS
CROSSWAYS
CUTANEOUS
DANGEROUS
DAUNTLESS
DEATHLESS
DECIDUOUS
DELICIOUS
DEXTEROUS
DIAERESIS
DIAGNOSIS
DIETETICS
DIGITALIS
DIPTEROUS
DOUBTLESS
ECONOMICS
EDELWEISS
EGREGIOUS
EMBARRASS
ENCOMPASS
ENTERITIS
EPIDERMIS
EROGENOUS
ERRONEOUS
ESOPHAGUS
EUTHENICS
EXOGENOUS
FACETIOUS
FEROCIOUS
FRACTIOUS
FRIVOLOUS
GARRULOUS
GASTRITIS
GLADIOLUS
GLEANINGS
GLUTINOUS
GOVERNESS
HALITOSIS
HAPPINESS
HARMONICS
HEADDRESS
HEARTLESS
HEPATITIS
HILARIOUS
HOURGLASS
HYSTERICS
IMPATIENS
IMPERIOUS
IMPETUOUS
INCURIOUS
INGENIOUS
INGENUOUS
INNOCUOUS
INSIDIOUS
INVERNESS
INVIDIOUS
ISINGLASS
ISOSCELES
JUDICIOUS
LABORIOUS
LAZYBONES
LITIGIOUS
LOGISTICS
LUDICROUS
MARVELOUS
MECHANICS
MELODIOUS
MERCUROUS
MESSIEURS
MOMENTOUS
MURDEROUS
NARCISSUS
NEFARIOUS
NEPHRITIS
NOTORIOUS
OBLIVIOUS
OBNOXIOUS
OFFICIOUS
OURSELVES
OUTSKIRTS
OVIPAROUS
PARALYSIS
PENDULOUS
PENURIOUS
PHLEBITIS
PHONETICS
PLENTEOUS
PONDEROUS
PRESTRESS
PRICELESS
PROBOSCIS
PROGNOSIS
PSORIASIS
PSYCHOSIS
PYROLYSIS
QUERULOUS
RAPACIOUS
RELIGIOUS
REPOSSESS
RIGHTEOUS
SAGACIOUS
SALACIOUS
SASSAFRAS
SCLEROSIS
SEBACEOUS
SEMANTICS
SEMIWORKS
SHAPELESS
SHIFTLESS
SIDEBURNS
SILICEOUS
SILICOSIS
SINUSITIS
SOMETIMES
STRAPLESS
STRENUOUS
SULFUROUS
SUMPTUOUS
SYMBIOSIS
SYNTHESIS
TECTONICS
TENACIOUS
TENEBROUS
THANKLESS
THEATRICS
THESAURUS
THICKNESS
TRAPPINGS
TREMULOUS
TRIFOCALS
TYRANNOUS
UMBILICUS
UNANIMOUS
UNDERPASS
UNHARNESS
VAGARIOUS
VAGINITIS
VENTUROUS
VERACIOUS
VERDIGRIS
VEXATIOUS
VICARIOUS
VIVACIOUS
VOICELESS
VORACIOUS
WHITENESS
WINEPRESS
WORTHLESS
ABATEMENT
ABHORRENT
ABSORBENT
ADSORBENT
AERIALIST
AFFIDAVIT
AGREEMENT
ALLERGIST
AMENDMENT
ANNUITANT
APARTMENT
APPELLANT
APPLICANT
ARCHITECT
ARCHIVIST
ARROWROOT
ASCENDANT
ASSISTANT
ASTRONAUT
ATONEMENT
ATTENDANT
BACKSWEPT
BENIGNANT
BLACKFOOT
BLACKLIST
BLOODROOT

BLOODSHOT
BLUEPOINT
BLUEPRINT
BOMBSIGHT
BREAKFAST
BRILLIANT
BROADCAST
BUCKWHEAT
BULLFIGHT
BUTTERFAT
BUTTERNUT
CABRIOLET
CAMEMBERT
CANALBOAT
CATAMOUNT
CATCHMENT
CHECKLIST
CLIPSHEET
COAGULANT
COCKFIGHT
COFFEEPOT
COLORCAST
COLORFAST
COLUMNIST
COMPETENT
COMPLAINT
COMPONENT
CONCORDAT
CONDIMENT
CONFIDANT
CONSCRIPT
CONSONANT
CONSTRICT
CONSTRUCT
CONTINENT
COPYRIGHT
CORMORANT
COSMONAUT
CROISSANT
CUTTHROAT
DAVENPORT
DECREMENT
DEFENDANT
DEFERMENT
DEFICIENT
DEFOLIANT
DEMULCENT
DEODORANT
DEPENDENT
DESICCANT
DETERGENT
DETERRENT
DETRIMENT
DEVILMENT
DIFFERENT
DIFFICULT
DIFFIDENT
DISAFFECT
DISCOMFIT
DISCREDIT
DISHONEST
DISINFECT
DISORIENT
DISPUTANT
DISSIDENT
DOWNRIGHT
DOWNSHIFT
EBULLIENT
EFFICIENT
EMBAYMENT
EMOLLIENT
EMOLUMENT
EQUIPMENT
ESTAMINET
EUCHARIST
EXCELLENT
EXCREMENT
EXPECTANT
EXPEDIENT
EXTRAVERT
EXUBERANT
FERRYBOAT
FIRMAMENT
FLAGEOLET
FLATULENT
FLOWCHART
FLOWERPOT
FOOTPRINT
FOREFRONT
FORESHEET
FORESIGHT
FORTNIGHT
GALLIVANT
GEARSHIFT
GENUFLECT
GODPARENT
GRAPESHOT
GREATCOAT
GREENBELT
HANDCRAFT
HATCHMENT
HEADFIRST
HEADLIGHT
HEARTBEAT
HEARTFELT
HERBALIST
HIGHLIGHT
HINDSIGHT
HOARFROST
HOLOCAUST
HOUSEBOAT
HOUSECOAT
HYPERTEXT
IMMIGRANT
IMPATIENT
IMPERFECT
IMPLEMENT
IMPORTANT
IMPRUDENT
INCESSANT
INCIPIENT
INCLEMENT
INCORRECT
INCREMENT
INCUMBENT
INDIGNANT
INELEGANT
INFORMANT
INNERMOST
INPATIENT
INSISTENT
INSOLVENT
INSURGENT
INTELLECT
INTENDANT
INTERCEPT
INTERDICT
INTERJECT
INTERMENT
INTERNIST
INTERPRET
INTERRUPT
INTERSECT
INTROVERT
ITINERANT
LIMELIGHT
LINEAMENT
LIVERWORT
LUBRICANT
LUXURIANT
MACHINIST
MAKESHIFT
MALADROIT
MALIGNANT
MENDICANT
MERRIMENT
METHODIST
MICROSOFT
MILLIVOLT
MINCEMEAT
MINISKIRT
MISCREANT
MISDIRECT
MISORIENT
MOONLIGHT
MOTORBOAT
MOUTHPART
NEGLIGENT
NEGOTIANT
NEWSPRINT
NONCREDIT
NONPROFIT
NORTHEAST
NORTHWEST
NUTRIMENT
OBSERVANT
OFFICIANT
ONSLAUGHT
OUTERMOST
OVERDRAFT
OVERNIGHT
OVERPRINT
OVERSHOOT
OVERSIGHT
PARAMOUNT
PARCHMENT
PENTECOST
PERMANENT
PERTINENT
PESTILENT
PETTICOAT
PHYSICIST
PLACEMENT
POSTULANT
POWERBOAT
PRECEDENT
PREFLIGHT
PRESIDENT
PREVALENT
PROMINENT
PROPONENT
PROVIDENT
PUBESCENT
PUBLICIST
PUSSYFOOT
QUICKSORT
QUIESCENT
RAINSPOUT
RECIPIENT
RECOLLECT
RECORDIST
RECUMBENT
REDBREAST
REDUNDANT
REENTRANT
RELUCTANT
REPELLENT
REPRESENT
REPUGNANT
RESERVIST
RESISTANT
RESTRAINT
RESURRECT
RIVERBOAT
SACRAMENT
SANDBLAST
SCAPEGOAT
SENTIMENT
SKINFLINT
SKINTIGHT
SKYROCKET
SLINGSHOT
SNOWDRIFT
SOBRIQUET
SOMNOLENT
SOUTHEAST
SOUTHWEST
SPEARMINT
SPEEDBOAT
SPINDRIFT
SPOTLIGHT
STARLIGHT
STATEMENT
STEADFAST
STEAMBOAT
STIMULANT
STOPLIGHT
STREAMLET
STRIKEOUT
SUBSCRIPT
SUCCULENT
SUNBONNET
SUPPLIANT
SWEETMEAT
SYCOPHANT
TAILLIGHT
TERMAGANT
TESTAMENT
TRANSIENT
TRANSPORT
TREATMENT
TRENCHANT
TRUCULENT
TURBULENT
TURNABOUT
UNDERCOAT
UNDERFOOT
UNDERMOST
UNDERPART
UNDERSHOT
UNIVALENT
UPPERMOST
UTTERMOST
VIDELICET
VIEWPOINT
WAISTCOAT
WARBONNET
WHALEBOAT
WHITEBAIT
WINDSWEPT
WOODCRAFT
WORRYWART
ZEITGEIST
IMPROMPTU
TROUSSEAU
LEITMOTIV
AFTERGLOW
BEDFELLOW
CHICKASAW
CORELDRAW
CORKSCREW
DEATHBLOW
INTERVIEW
JACKSCREW
JACKSTRAW
OVERTHROW
QUICKDRAW
SADDLEBOW
SCARECROW
SCRIMSHAW
EXECUTRIX
HETERODOX
SHADOWBOX
TINDERBOX
ACCESSORY
ACCLIVITY
ACCOMPANY
ADMIRALTY
ADVERSARY
ADVERSITY
AIRWORTHY
ANCILLARY
ANIMOSITY
ANTHOLOGY
ANTIPATHY
ANTIQUARY
ANTIQUITY
ARBITRARY
ARCHENEMY
ARTILLERY
ASTROLOGY
ASTRONOMY
AUDIOLOGY
AUTHORITY
AUTOCRACY
AUXILIARY
BIMONTHLY
BIOGRAPHY
BLACKBODY
BLASPHEMY
BLUEBERRY
BREEZEWAY
BUTTERFLY
CACOPHONY
CALLOSITY
CANDIDACY
CAPILLARY
CAPITALLY
CASSOWARY
CASUISTRY
CATALEPSY
CELEBRITY
CENTENARY
CERTAINTY
CHEMISTRY
CHICANERY
CHIROPODY
CIRCUITRY
CITIZENRY
COMMODITY
COMMUNITY
CONGRUITY
CONSTANCY
CONTUMELY
COROLLARY
COSMOGONY
COSMOLOGY
CRANBERRY
CREMATORY
CUSTOMARY
DAMSELFLY
DECLIVITY
DEFORMITY
DEMOCRACY
DESULTORY
DEXTERITY
DIATHERMY
DICHOTOMY
DIGNITARY
DIPLOMACY
DIRECTORY
DISEMBODY
DIVERSIFY
DIVERSITY
DOBSONFLY
DORMITORY
DRAGONFLY
DROMEDARY
DUPLICITY
DYSENTERY
DYSTROPHY
ELECTRIFY
EMERGENCY
EPIGRAPHY
ETHNOLOGY
ETYMOLOGY
EVERYBODY
EXEMPLARY
EXEMPLIFY
EXPIATORY
EXTREMITY
FESTIVITY
FEUDATORY
FIDUCIARY
FOOLHARDY
FORMALITY
FREQUENCY
GALLANTRY
GENEALOGY
GENTILITY
GEOGRAPHY
GIMMICKRY
GLENGARRY
GUSTATORY
HALFPENNY
HIERARCHY
HILLBILLY
HORSEPLAY
HORTATORY
HUSBANDRY
HYDROLOGY
HYPOCRISY
IMAGINARY
IMMEDIACY
INABILITY
INDEMNIFY
INDEMNITY
INDIGNITY
INFIRMARY
INFIRMITY
INGENUITY
INSTANTLY
INTEGRITY
INTENSIFY
INTENSITY
INTERPLAY
INVENTORY
ITINERARY
JUDICIARY
LAUDATORY
LEGENDARY
LIABILITY
LITHOLOGY
LONGEVITY
MACHINERY
MANDATORY
MARQUETRY
MATERNITY
MATRIMONY
MENTALITY
MERCENARY
METROLOGY
MICROCOPY
MILLINERY
MISSILERY
MOMENTARY
MONASTERY
MYTHOLOGY
NATURALLY
NECESSARY
NECESSITY
NECROLOGY
NEUROLOGY
NONENTITY
OBJECTIFY
OCCUPANCY

OFFERTORY
OLFACTORY
OLIGARCHY
OPTOMETRY
OUTWARDLY
PALMISTRY
PARQUETRY
PARSIMONY
PATERNITY
PATHOLOGY
PATRIMONY
PECUNIARY
PERFUMERY
PERIPHERY
PERSONIFY
PETROLOGY
PHILATELY
PHILOLOGY
PHONOLOGY
PHOTOCOPY
PHOTOPLAY
PITUITARY
PLURALITY
POLYPHONY
POSTERITY
PREDATORY
PREOCCUPY
PRESENTLY
PRIMARILY
PROFANITY
PROPRIETY
PROXIMITY
PUBLICITY
PULMONARY
PURGATORY
QUARTERLY
RADIOLOGY
RASPBERRY
REFECTORY
RELEVANCY
RELIQUARY
REPERTORY
RESIDENCY
RESIDUARY
ROUNDELAY
SANCTUARY
SCHOOLBOY
SEAWORTHY
SECONDARY
SECRETARY
SEDENTARY
SENIORITY
SHRUBBERY
SIGNATORY
SLUICEWAY
SOCIOLOGY
SOLILOQUY
SOPHISTRY
SPEAKEASY
SPECIALTY
SPRIGHTLY
STATUTORY
SUBLUNARY
SUPREMACY
SWORDPLAY
SYLLABIFY
TAUTOLOGY
TAXIDERMY
TELEPATHY
TELEPHONY
TEMPORARY
TERRITORY
TESTIMONY
THEOCRACY
THEOSOPHY
THROWAWAY
TREACHERY
TRIBUTARY
TRIWEEKLY
UNCLEANLY
UNDERBODY
UNDERPLAY
UNEARTHLY
UNHEALTHY
UNSIGHTLY
UNWORLDLY
VAINGLORY
VASECTOMY
VIBRATORY
VIRGINITY
VISCOSITY
VISIONARY
VOLUNTARY
VULGARITY
WEDNESDAY
YESTERDAY
KILOHERTZ
MEGAHERTZ

# 10 LETTER WORDS

**1st Letter**

ABBREVIATE
ABERRATION
ABOMINABLE
ABORIGINAL
ABOVEBOARD
ABSCISSION
ABSOLUTION
ABSOLUTISM
ABSORPTION
ABSTEMIOUS
ABSTINENCE
ACCELERATE
ACCENTUATE
ACCEPTABLE
ACCEPTANCE
ACCESSIBLE
ACCIDENTAL
ACCOMPLICE
ACCOMPLISH
ACCORDANCE
ACCOUNTANT
ACCOUNTING
ACCUMULATE
ACCUSATIVE
ACCUSTOMED
ACHROMATIC
ACROBATICS
ACROPHOBIA
ACTIONABLE
ADDITIONAL
ADJUDICATE
ADMINISTER
ADMISSIBLE
ADMITTANCE
ADRENALINE
ADULTERANT
ADULTERATE
ADVENTURER
ADVISEMENT
AEROBATICS
AESTHETICS
AFFLICTIVE
AFICIONADO
AFTERBIRTH
AFTERIMAGE
AFTERTASTE
AGGRANDIZE
AGGRESSION
AGGRESSIVE
AIRFREIGHT
ALBUMINOUS
ALCOHOLISM
ALIMENTARY
ALKALINIZE
ALLEGIANCE
ALLHALLOWS
ALLITERATE
ALONGSHORE
ALPHABETIC
ALTARPIECE
ALTERNATOR
ALTOGETHER
AMALGAMATE
AMANUENSIS
AMBASSADOR
AMBULATORY
AMELIORATE
AMERINDIAN
AMMUNITION
AMPHIBIOUS
ANEMOMETER
ANESTHESIA
ANESTHETIC
ANGIOSPERM
ANGLOPHILE
ANGLOPHOBE
ANIMADVERT
ANIMALCULE
ANNIHILATE
ANNUNCIATE
ANSWERABLE
ANTAGONISM
ANTAGONIST
ANTAGONIZE
ANTEBELLUM
ANTECEDENT
ANTEPENULT
ANTHRACITE
ANTHROPOID
ANTIBIOTIC
ANTICANCER
ANTICHRIST
ANTICIPATE
ANTICLIMAX
ANTIFREEZE
ANTIMATTER
ANTINOMIAN
ANTIPHONAL
ANTIPROTON
ANTIQUATED
ANTISEPTIC
ANTISOCIAL
ANTITHESIS
APOCALYPSE
APOCRYPHAL
APOLITICAL
APOLOGETIC
APOSTROPHE
APOTHECARY
APOTHEOSIS
APPARITION
APPEARANCE
APPETIZING
APPLICABLE
APPLICATOR
APPOINTIVE
APPOSITION
APPOSITIVE
APPRECIATE
APPRENTICE
AQUALUNGER
AQUAMARINE
ARBITRATOR
ARBORVITAE
ARCHBISHOP
ARCHDEACON
ARCHITRAVE
ARITHMETIC
ARMAGEDDON
ARTICULATE
ARTIFICIAL
ASCENDANCY
ASPHYXIATE
ASPIRATION
ASSEMBLAGE
ASSEVERATE
ASSIGNMENT
ASSIMILATE
ASSORTMENT
ASSUMPTION
ASTRINGENT
ASYMMETRIC
ATMOSPHERE
ATTACHMENT
ATTAINMENT
ATTENDANCE
ATTRACTANT
ATTRACTION
AUCTIONEER
AUDIOPHILE
AUDITORIUM
AURIFEROUS
AUSPICIOUS
AUSTRALIAN
AUTHORSHIP
AUTOMATION
AUTOMATIZE
AUTOMOBILE
AUTOMOTIVE
AUTONOMOUS
AUTOSTRADA
BACKGAMMON
BACKGROUND
BACKHANDED
BACKSTAIRS
BACKSTROKE
BALBRIGGAN
BALDERDASH
BALLISTICS
BALUSTRADE
BAPTISTERY
BAREHEADED
BASKETBALL
BASTARDIZE
BATHYSCAPH
BATRACHIAN
BATTLEMENT
BATTLESHIP
BEAUJOLAIS
BEAUTICIAN
BEDCLOTHES
BEDRAGGLED
BEFOREHAND
BEHINDHAND
BELLADONNA
BELLETRIST
BELLWETHER
BELONGINGS
BENCHMARKS
BENEFACTOR
BENEFICENT
BENEFICIAL
BESPRINKLE
BESTIALITY
BETTERMENT
BICHLORIDE
BIMETALLIC
BIOMEDICAL
BIOPHYSICS
BIPARENTAL
BIPARIETAL
BIPARTISAN
BIRTHPLACE
BIRTHRIGHT
BIRTHSTONE
BITUMINOUS
BLACKAMOOR
BLACKBERRY
BLACKBOARD
BLACKGUARD
BLACKSMITH
BLACKTHORN
BLANCMANGE
BLITZKRIEG
BLOCKHOUSE
BLOODHOUND
BLOODSTAIN
BLOODSTONE
BLUEBONNET
BLUEBOTTLE
BLUECOLLAR
BLUEJACKET
BOISTEROUS
BOLSHEVISM
BOMBARDIER
BONDHOLDER
BOOKKEEPER
BOOKMOBILE
BOOKSELLER
BOONDOGGLE
BORDERLAND
BOTTLENECK
BOTTOMLAND
BOWDLERIZE
BRAHMANISM
BRAINCHILD
BRAINSTORM
BREADBOARD
BREADFRUIT
BREADSTUFF
BREAKFRONT
BREAKWATER
BREASTBONE
BREASTWORK
BRICKLAYER
BRIDEGROOM
BRIDESMAID
BRIDGEHEAD
BRIDGEWORK
BRIGANTINE
BROADCLOTH
BROADSWORD
BRONCHITIS
BRONTOSAUR
BROWNSTONE
BUDGERIGAR
BULLHEADED
BUSHMASTER
BUTTERMILK
BUTTONHOLE
BUTTONHOOK
CACCIATORE
CADAVEROUS
CALCAREOUS
CALCULATED
CALUMNIATE
CAMELOPARD
CAMOUFLAGE
CAMPHORATE
CANDELABRA
CANDESCENT
CANDLEWICK
CANKERWORM
CANNONBALL
CANONICALS
CANTALOUPE
CANTILEVER
CANTONMENT
CANVASBACK
CAOUTCHOUC
CAPACITATE
CAPITALISM
CAPITALIST
CAPITALIZE
CAPITATION
CAPITULATE
CAPOREGIME
CARABINEER
CARBOLATED
CARBURETOR
CARCINOGEN
CARDIOGRAM
CARDIOLOGY
CARICATURE
CATABOLISM
CATAFALQUE
CATCHPENNY
CATECHUMEN
CATEGORIZE
CAVITATION
CELEBRATED
CELLARETTE
CELLOPHANE
CENSORIOUS
CENSORSHIP
CENTENNIAL
CENTESIMAL
CENTIGRADE
CENTILITER
CENTIMETER
CENTRALIZE
CENTRIFUGE
CEREBELLUM
CEREMONIAL
CHALCEDONY
CHANCELLOR
CHANDELIER
CHANGELING
CHANGEOVER
CHANNELIZE
CHAPFALLEN
CHARACTERY
CHARITABLE
CHARLESTON
CHARTREUSE
CHATELAINE
CHATTERBOX
CHAUVINISM
CHEAPSKATE
CHECKPOINT
CHEESECAKE
CHIFFONIER
CHILDBIRTH
CHIMERICAL
CHIMPANZEE
CHINCHILLA
CHIROMANCY
CHIVALROUS
CHLORINATE
CHLOROFORM
CHROMOSOME
CHRONOLOGY
CHRYSOLITE
CHURCHGOER
CHURCHLESS
CHURCHYARD
CINERARIUM
CINQUEFOIL
CIRCUITOUS
CIRCUMCISE
CIRCUMFLEX
CIRCUMVENT
CITRONELLA
CLASSICISM
CLASSIFIED

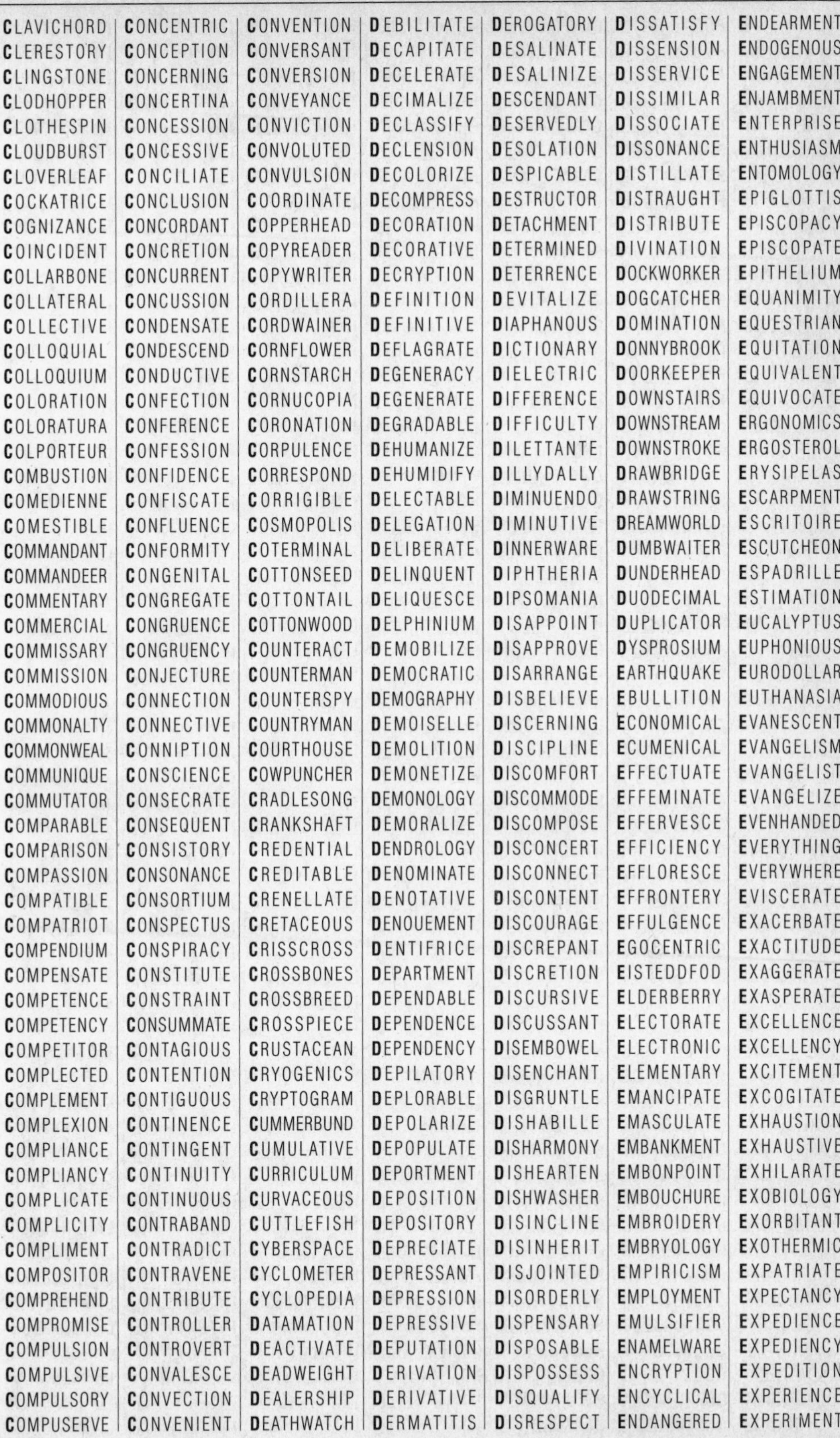

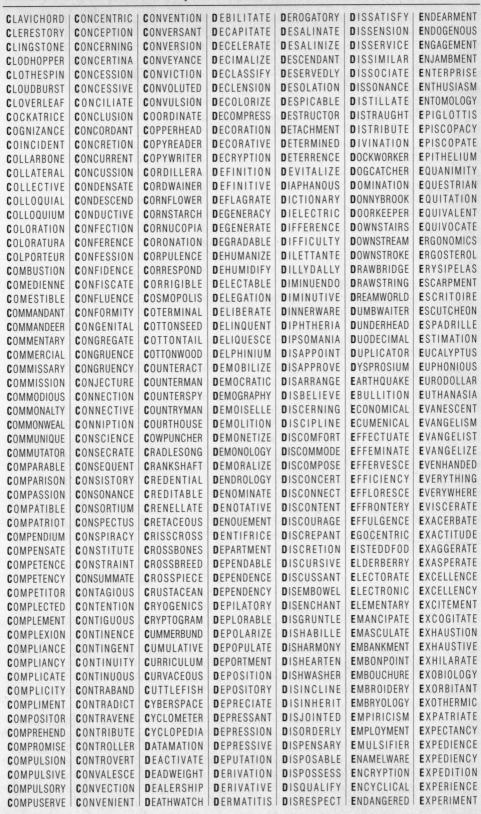

CLAVICHORD
CLERESTORY
CLINGSTONE
CLODHOPPER
CLOTHESPIN
CLOUDBURST
CLOVERLEAF
COCKATRICE
COGNIZANCE
COINCIDENT
COLLARBONE
COLLATERAL
COLLECTIVE
COLLOQUIAL
COLLOQUIUM
COLORATION
COLORATURA
COLPORTEUR
COMBUSTION
COMEDIENNE
COMESTIBLE
COMMANDANT
COMMANDEER
COMMENTARY
COMMERCIAL
COMMISSARY
COMMISSION
COMMODIOUS
COMMONALTY
COMMONWEAL
COMMUNIQUE
COMMUTATOR
COMPARABLE
COMPARISON
COMPASSION
COMPATIBLE
COMPATRIOT
COMPENDIUM
COMPENSATE
COMPETENCE
COMPETENCY
COMPETITOR
COMPLECTED
COMPLEMENT
COMPLEXION
COMPLIANCE
COMPLIANCY
COMPLICATE
COMPLICITY
COMPLIMENT
COMPOSITOR
COMPREHEND
COMPROMISE
COMPULSION
COMPULSIVE
COMPULSORY
COMPUSERVE
CONCENTRIC
CONCEPTION
CONCERNING
CONCERTINA
CONCESSION
CONCESSIVE
CONCILIATE
CONCLUSION
CONCORDANT
CONCRETION
CONCURRENT
CONCUSSION
CONDENSATE
CONDESCEND
CONDUCTIVE
CONFECTION
CONFERENCE
CONFESSION
CONFIDENCE
CONFISCATE
CONFLUENCE
CONFORMITY
CONGENITAL
CONGREGATE
CONGRUENCE
CONGRUENCY
CONJECTURE
CONNECTION
CONNECTIVE
CONNIPTION
CONSCIENCE
CONSECRATE
CONSEQUENT
CONSISTORY
CONSONANCE
CONSORTIUM
CONSPECTUS
CONSPIRACY
CONSTITUTE
CONSTRAINT
CONSUMMATE
CONTAGIOUS
CONTENTION
CONTIGUOUS
CONTINENCE
CONTINGENT
CONTINUITY
CONTINUOUS
CONTRABAND
CONTRADICT
CONTRAVENE
CONTRIBUTE
CONTROLLER
CONTROVERT
CONVALESCE
CONVECTION
CONVENIENT
CONVENTION
CONVERSANT
CONVERSION
CONVEYANCE
CONVICTION
CONVOLUTED
CONVULSION
COORDINATE
COPPERHEAD
COPYREADER
COPYWRITER
CORDILLERA
CORDWAINER
CORNFLOWER
CORNSTARCH
CORNUCOPIA
CORONATION
CORPULENCE
CORRESPOND
CORRIGIBLE
COSMOPOLIS
COTERMINAL
COTTONSEED
COTTONTAIL
COTTONWOOD
COUNTERACT
COUNTERMAN
COUNTERSPY
COUNTRYMAN
COURTHOUSE
COWPUNCHER
CRADLESONG
CRANKSHAFT
CREDENTIAL
CREDITABLE
CRENELLATE
CRETACEOUS
CRISSCROSS
CROSSBONES
CROSSBREED
CROSSPIECE
CRUSTACEAN
CRYOGENICS
CRYPTOGRAM
CUMMERBUND
CUMULATIVE
CURRICULUM
CURVACEOUS
CUTTLEFISH
CYBERSPACE
CYCLOMETER
CYCLOPEDIA
DATAMATION
DEACTIVATE
DEADWEIGHT
DEALERSHIP
DEATHWATCH
DEBILITATE
DECAPITATE
DECELERATE
DECIMALIZE
DECLASSIFY
DECLENSION
DECOLORIZE
DECOMPRESS
DECORATION
DECORATIVE
DECRYPTION
DEFINITION
DEFINITIVE
DEFLAGRATE
DEGENERACY
DEGENERATE
DEGRADABLE
DEHUMANIZE
DEHUMIDIFY
DELECTABLE
DELEGATION
DELIBERATE
DELINQUENT
DELIQUESCE
DELPHINIUM
DEMOBILIZE
DEMOCRATIC
DEMOGRAPHY
DEMOISELLE
DEMOLITION
DEMONETIZE
DEMONOLOGY
DEMORALIZE
DENDROLOGY
DENOMINATE
DENOTATIVE
DENOUEMENT
DENTIFRICE
DEPARTMENT
DEPENDABLE
DEPENDENCE
DEPENDENCY
DEPILATORY
DEPLORABLE
DEPOLARIZE
DEPOPULATE
DEPORTMENT
DEPOSITION
DEPOSITORY
DEPRECIATE
DEPRESSANT
DEPRESSION
DEPRESSIVE
DEPUTATION
DERIVATION
DERIVATIVE
DERMATITIS
DEROGATORY
DESALINATE
DESALINIZE
DESCENDANT
DESERVEDLY
DESOLATION
DESPICABLE
DESTRUCTOR
DETACHMENT
DETERMINED
DETERRENCE
DEVITALIZE
DIAPHANOUS
DICTIONARY
DIELECTRIC
DIFFERENCE
DIFFICULTY
DILETTANTE
DILLYDALLY
DIMINUENDO
DIMINUTIVE
DINNERWARE
DIPHTHERIA
DIPSOMANIA
DISAPPOINT
DISAPPROVE
DISARRANGE
DISBELIEVE
DISCERNING
DISCIPLINE
DISCOMFORT
DISCOMMODE
DISCOMPOSE
DISCONCERT
DISCONNECT
DISCONTENT
DISCOURAGE
DISCREPANT
DISCRETION
DISCURSIVE
DISCUSSANT
DISEMBOWEL
DISENCHANT
DISGRUNTLE
DISHABILLE
DISHARMONY
DISHEARTEN
DISHWASHER
DISINCLINE
DISINHERIT
DISJOINTED
DISORDERLY
DISPENSARY
DISPOSABLE
DISPOSSESS
DISQUALIFY
DISRESPECT
DISSATISFY
DISSENSION
DISSERVICE
DISSIMILAR
DISSOCIATE
DISSONANCE
DISTILLATE
DISTRAUGHT
DISTRIBUTE
DIVINATION
DOCKWORKER
DOGCATCHER
DOMINATION
DONNYBROOK
DOORKEEPER
DOWNSTAIRS
DOWNSTREAM
DOWNSTROKE
DRAWBRIDGE
DRAWSTRING
DREAMWORLD
DUMBWAITER
DUNDERHEAD
DUODECIMAL
DUPLICATOR
DYSPROSIUM
EARTHQUAKE
EBULLITION
ECONOMICAL
ECUMENICAL
EFFECTUATE
EFFEMINATE
EFFERVESCE
EFFICIENCY
EFFLORESCE
EFFRONTERY
EFFULGENCE
EGOCENTRIC
EISTEDDFOD
ELDERBERRY
ELECTORATE
ELECTRONIC
ELEMENTARY
EMANCIPATE
EMASCULATE
EMBANKMENT
EMBONPOINT
EMBOUCHURE
EMBROIDERY
EMBRYOLOGY
EMPIRICISM
EMPLOYMENT
EMULSIFIER
ENAMELWARE
ENCRYPTION
ENCYCLICAL
ENDANGERED
ENDEARMENT
ENDOGENOUS
ENGAGEMENT
ENJAMBMENT
ENTERPRISE
ENTHUSIASM
ENTOMOLOGY
EPIGLOTTIS
EPISCOPACY
EPISCOPATE
EPITHELIUM
EQUANIMITY
EQUESTRIAN
EQUITATION
EQUIVALENT
EQUIVOCATE
ERGONOMICS
ERGOSTEROL
ERYSIPELAS
ESCARPMENT
ESCRITOIRE
ESCUTCHEON
ESPADRILLE
ESTIMATION
EUCALYPTUS
EUPHONIOUS
EURODOLLAR
EUTHANASIA
EVANESCENT
EVANGELISM
EVANGELIST
EVANGELIZE
EVENHANDED
EVERYTHING
EVERYWHERE
EVISCERATE
EXACERBATE
EXACTITUDE
EXAGGERATE
EXASPERATE
EXCELLENCE
EXCELLENCY
EXCITEMENT
EXCOGITATE
EXHAUSTION
EXHAUSTIVE
EXHILARATE
EXOBIOLOGY
EXORBITANT
EXOTHERMIC
EXPATRIATE
EXPECTANCY
EXPEDIENCE
EXPEDIENCY
EXPEDITION
EXPERIENCE
EXPERIMENT

EXPLICABLE
EXPOSITION
EXPRESSION
EXPRESSMAN
EXPRESSWAY
EXTINGUISH
EXTRAMURAL
EXTRANEOUS
EXURBANITE
EYEDROPPER
EYEWITNESS
FACILITATE
FACTITIOUS
FAHRENHEIT
FAIRGROUND
FALLACIOUS
FAMILARIZE
FARFETCHED
FARSIGHTED
FASTIDIOUS
FATHERLAND
FATHOMLESS
FAVORITISM
FEDERALISM
FEDERALIST
FEDERALIZE
FEDERATION
FELICITATE
FELICITOUS
FELLOWSHIP
FERTILIZER
FIBERBOARD
FIBERGLASS
FIBRINOGEN
FICTITIOUS
FIELDPIECE
FIGURATION
FIGURATIVE
FIGUREHEAD
FILIBUSTER
FINGERLING
FINGERNAIL
FISTICUFFS
FLAGELLATE
FLAGITIOUS
FLAMBOYANT
FLASHLIGHT
FLOODLIGHT
FLOODPLAIN
FLOODWATER
FLOORBOARD
FLUIDOUNCE
FLUORIDATE
FLUORINATE
FLYCATCHER
FOLKSINGER
FOOTBRIDGE
FOOTLIGHTS
FOOTLOCKER
FORBIDDING
FORECASTLE
FOREFATHER
FOREFINGER
FOREGATHER
FOREGROUND
FOREHANDED
FOREORDAIN
FORERUNNER
FORESHADOW
FORFEITURE
FORMIDABLE
FORTHRIGHT
FORTISSIMO
FORTUITOUS
FOSTERLING
FOUNDATION
FOURSQUARE
FRANCHISEE
FRANCHISER
FRANCHISOR
FRATERNITY
FRATERNIZE
FRATRICIDE
FRAUDULENT
FREEBOOTER
FRESHWATER
FUSSBUDGET
FUTURISTIC
GADOLINIUM
GAMEKEEPER
GARGANTUAN
GASTRONOMY
GATEKEEPER
GENERALITY
GENERALIZE
GENERATION
GENTLEFOLK
GEOCENTRIC
GEOPHYSICS
GEOSCIENCE
GEOTHERMAL
GERIATRICS
GESUNDHEIT
GHOSTWRITE
GINGERSNAP
GINGIVITIS
GLACIOLOGY
GOALKEEPER
GOLDBEATER
GONOCOCCUS
GOOSEBERRY
GOOSEFLESH
GORGONZOLA
GORMANDIZE
GOVERNMENT
GRADUALISM
GRADUATION
GRAINFIELD
GRAMOPHONE
GRANDCHILD
GRANDSTAND
GRAPEFRUIT
GRATUITOUS
GRAVESTONE
GRAVIMETER
GREENHOUSE
GREENSWARD
GREGARIOUS
GRINDSTONE
GROUNDLING
GROUNDMASS
GROUNDWORK
GUARDHOUSE
GUILLOTINE
GUNSLINGER
GYMNASTICS
GYMNOSPERM
GYNECOLOGY
HABILIMENT
HABITATION
HALLELUJAH
HAMMERHEAD
HAMMERLOCK
HANDBARROW
HANDICRAFT
HANDLEBARS
HANDMAIDEN
HANDSPRING
HARDHEADED
HARMONIOUS
HEADMASTER
HEADSTRONG
HEADWAITER
HEARTBREAK
HEARTHSIDE
HEARTTHROB
HEATSTROKE
HECTOLITER
HECTOMETER
HELICOPTER
HELIOGRAPH
HELIOTROPE
HEMATOLOGY
HEMISPHERE
HEMOGLOBIN
HEMOPHILIA
HEMORRHAGE
HEMORRHOID
HENCEFORTH
HEPTAMETER
HEREABOUTS
HEREDITARY
HERETOFORE
HIEROPHANT
HIGHLANDER
HIGHWAYMAN
HINTERLAND
HIPPODROME
HISTRIONIC
HOBBYHORSE
HODGEPODGE
HOLLOWWARE
HOLOGRAPHY
HOMECOMING
HOMEOPATHY
HOMOGENIZE
HOMOLOGOUS
HOMOSEXUAL
HONORARIUM
HOOTENANNY
HORIZONTAL
HORRENDOUS
HORSEFLESH
HORSELAUGH
HORSEPOWER
HORSEWOMAN
HOSPITABLE
HOUSECLEAN
HOUSEWARES
HULLABALOO
HUSBANDMAN
HYDRAULICS
HYDROLYSIS
HYDROMETER
HYDROPHONE
HYDROPLANE
HYGROMETER
HYPERBARIC
HYPOCENTER
HYPODERMIC
HYPOTENUSE
HYPOTHESIS
ICEBREAKER
ICONOCLASM
ICONOCLAST
IDIOPATHIC
IGNORAMOUS
ILLITERATE
ILLUMINATE
ILLUSTRATE
IMAGINABLE
IMBIBITION
IMMACULATE
IMMATERIAL
IMMEMORIAL
IMMISCIBLE
IMMOBILIZE
IMMODERATE
IMMORALITY
IMMUNOLOGY
IMPALPABLE
IMPASSABLE
IMPASSIBLE
IMPATIENCE
IMPECCABLE
IMPEDIMENT
IMPENITENT
IMPERATIVE
IMPERSONAL
IMPERVIOUS
IMPLACABLE
IMPORTANCE
IMPOSSIBLE
IMPOVERISH
IMPREGNATE
IMPRESARIO
IMPRESSION
IMPRESSIVE
IMPRIMATUR
IMPROBABLE
INACTIVATE
INADEQUATE
INAPTITUDE
INAUGURATE
INBREEDING
INCAPACITY
INCENDIARY
INCIDENTAL
INCINERATE
INCIVILITY
INCLINABLE
INCOHERENT
INCOMPLETE
INCONSTANT
INCREDIBLE
INCULPABLE
INCUMBENCY
INDECISION
INDECISIVE
INDECOROUS
INDEFINITE
INDELICATE
INDICATIVE
INDIGENOUS
INDISCREET
INDISPOSED
INDISTINCT
INDIVIDUAL
INDONESIAN
INDUCEMENT
INDUCTANCE
INDULGENCE
INDUSTRIAL
INELIGIBLE
INEQUALITY
INEVITABLE
INEXORABLE
INEXPIABLE
INFALLIBLE
INFIDELITY
INFIGHTING
INFILTRATE
INFINITIVE
INFINITUDE
INFLECTION
INFLEXIBLE
INFRACTION
INFRASONIC
INFREQUENT
INGLORIOUS
INGRATIATE
INGREDIENT
INHABITANT
INHIBITION
INHUMANITY
INIMITABLE
INITIATIVE
INITIATORY
INJUNCTION
INNOMINATE
INNOVATION
INOPERABLE
INORDINATE
INQUIETUDE
INSATIABLE
INSEMINATE
INSENSIBLE
INSENTIENT
INSISTENCE
INSOLATION
INSOLVABLE
INSTRUCTOR
INSTRUMENT
INTANGIBLE
INTEGUMENT
INTERBLOCK
INTERBREED
INTERFAITH
INTERFERON
INTERLEAVE
INTERLUNAR
INTERMARRY
INTERMEZZO
INTERNMENT
INTERSTATE
INTERSTICE
INTERTIDAL
INTERTWINE
INTERTWIST
INTERURBAN
INTERWEAVE
INTIMIDATE
INTINCTION
INTOLERANT
INTONATION
INTOXICANT
INTOXICATE
INTRAMURAL
INTRASTATE
INVALIDATE
INVALUABLE
INVARIABLE
INVESTMENT
INVETERATE
INVIGORATE
INVINCIBLE
INVIOLABLE
INVOCATION
INVOLUTION
IONOSPHERE
IRRATIONAL
IRRELEVANT
IRRESOLUTE
ISOMETRICS
ISOTHERMAL
JACKANAPES
JACKHAMMER
JACKRABBIT
JARDINIERE
JAWBREAKER
JIMSONWEED
JINRIKISHA
JOURNALESE
JOURNALISM
JOURNEYMAN
JUBILATION
JUDICATURE
JUGGERNAUT
KETTLEDRUM
KIESELGUHR
KINEMATICS
KINGFISHER
KNICKKNACK
KNIGHTHOOD
KNOCKWURST
KRUGERRAND
LABORATORY
LACHRYMOSE
LACKLUSTER
LADYFINGER
LANDHOLDER
LANDLOCKED
LANDLUBBER
LARYNGITIS
LASCIVIOUS
LAWBREAKER
LAWRENCIUM
LEAFHOPPER
LEDERHOSEN

LEGITIMATE
LENGTHWISE
LEPRECHAUN
LETTERHEAD
LIBERALISM
LIBIDINOUS
LICENTIATE
LICENTIOUS
LIEUTENANT
LIFESAVING
LIGHTHOUSE
LIGHTPROOF
LIKELIHOOD
LINEBACKER
LIPREADING
LITERALISM
LITERATURE
LITHUANIAN
LIVELIHOOD
LIVERWURST
LOCOMOTION
LOCOMOTIVE
LOGANBERRY
LOGGERHEAD
LOGROLLING
LOQUACIOUS
LOVEMAKING
LUBRICIOUS
LUGUBRIOUS
LUMBERJACK
LUMBERYARD
MACKINTOSH
MAGISTRATE
MAIDENHAIR
MAIDENHEAD
MAIDENHOOD
MAINSPRING
MAINSTREAM
MAISONETTE
MALADAPTED
MALAPROPOS
MALCONTENT
MALEFACTOR
MALEFICENT
MALEVOLENT
MALODOROUS
MALTHUSIAN
MANAGEMENT
MANDELBROT
MANDRAGORA
MANICURIST
MANIPULATE
MANSERVANT
MANSUETUDE
MANTLEROCK
MANUSCRIPT
MARASCHINO
MARGINALIA
MARGUERITE
MARIONETTE
MARROWBONE
MARTINGALE
MASQUERADE
MASTERMIND
MASTERSHIP
MASTERWORK
MATCHMAKER
MATURATION
MAYONNAISE
MEADOWLARK
MECHANICAL
MEDDLESOME
MEDICAMENT
MEERSCHAUM
MELANCHOLY
MELANESIAN
MEMBERSHIP
MEMORANDUM
MENDACIOUS
MENINGITIS
MENSURABLE
MERCANTILE
MESOSPHERE
METABOLISM
METABOLITE
METACARPUS
METAGALAXY
METALLURGY
METASTASIS
METATARSAL
METATARSUS
METICULOUS
METROPOLIS
METTLESOME
MICROFICHE
MICROGRAPH
MICROMETER
MICROPHONE
MICROPROBE
MICROSCOPE
MICROSTATE
MIDDLEBROW
MIDSHIPMAN
MIGNONETTE
MILITARISM
MILITARIZE
MILLENNIUM
MILLILITER
MILLIMETER
MILLSTREAM
MILLWRIGHT
MIMEOGRAPH
MINERALIZE
MINERALOGY
MINESTRONE
MINISCROLL
MINISTRANT
MISALIGNED
MISCELLANY
MISCONDUCT
MISFORTUNE
MISOGAMIST
MISOGYNIST
MISSILEMAN
MISSIONARY
MISTAKABLE
MIZZENMAST
MOHAMMEDAN
MOLYBDENUM
MONARCHIST
MONOCHROME
MONOPHONIC
MONOTHEISM
MONOTONOUS
MONSTRANCE
MONUMENTAL
MOONSTRUCK
MORATORIUM
MORPHOLOGY
MOTHERHOOD
MOTHERLAND
MOTORCYCLE
MOTORTRUCK
MOUNTEBANK
MOUTHPIECE
MOZZARELLA
MUDSLINGER
MUHAMMADAN
MULTILEVEL
MULTIMEDIA
MULTIPLIER
MULTISENSE
MULTISTAGE
MULTISTORY
MUNIFICENT
MUSICOLOGY
MYRIAMETER
NANOSECOND
NAPOLEONIC
NASTURTIUM
NATATORIUM
NATIONWIDE
NATURALISM
NATURALIST
NATURALIZE
NEBULOSITY
NECROMANCY
NECROPOLIS
NEEDLEWORK
NEGATIVISM
NEGLIGIBLE
NEIGHBORLY
NEOCLASSIC
NETHERMOST
NETTLESOME
NEUTRALISM
NEUTRALITY
NEUTRALIZE
NEWFANGLED
NEWSGROUPS
NEWSLETTER
NEWSWORTHY
NIGHTDRESS
NIGHTSHADE
NIGHTSHIRT
NIGHTSTICK
NINCOMPOOP
NOISEMAKER
NOMINATIVE
NONCHALANT
NONDRINKER
NONSTARTER
NONSUPPORT
NOTABILITY
NOTEWORTHY
NOTICEABLE
NOURISHING
NUCLEONICS
NUMBERLESS
NUMEROLOGY
NURSERYMAN
NUTCRACKER
OBLIGATION
OBLITERATE
OBSEQUIOUS
OBSERVABLE
OBSERVANCE
OBSTETRICS
OCCASIONAL
OCCIDENTAL
OCCUPATION
OCCURRENCE
OCEANARIUM
OCEANFRONT
OCEANGOING
OCEANOLOGY
OCTOTHORPE
OESOPHAGUS
OFTENTIMES
OLEAGINOUS
OMNIPOTENT
OMNISCIENT
OMNIVOROUS
OPALESCENT
OPHTHALMIC
OPPRESSION
OPPROBRIUM
ORATORICAL
ORDINATION
ORGANGUTAN
OSTENSIBLE
OSTEOPATHY
OTHERWORLD
OUTBALANCE
OUTGENERAL
OUTLANDISH
OUTPATIENT
OUTPERFORM
OUTPOURING
OUTRAGEOUS
OVERCHARGE
OVERMASTER
OVERSHADOW
OVERSPREAD
OVERWINTER
PACKSADDLE
PACKTHREAD
PAGINATION
PAINKILLER
PAINTBRUSH
PALATALIZE
PALATINATE
PALIMPSEST
PALINDROME
PALLBEARER
PANJANDRUM
PANTALOONS
PANTYWAIST
PAPERBOARD
PARAMECIUM
PARAPHRASE
PARAPLEGIA
PARATROOPS
PARLIAMENT
PARMIGIANA
PARTICIPLE
PARTICULAR
PASSAGEWAY
PASTEBOARD
PASTEURIZE
PATHFINDER
PATRONYMIC
PAWNBROKER
PEACEMAKER
PEASHOOTER
PECCADILLO
PEDESTRIAN
PEDIATRICS
PEJORATIVE
PENICILLIN
PENMANSHIP
PENNYROYAL
PENTAMETER
PEPPERCORN
PEPPERMINT
PERCENTAGE
PERCENTILE
PERCEPTION
PERCEPTIVE
PERCEPTUAL
PERCIPIENT
PERCUSSION
PERDURABLE
PEREMPTORY
PERFECTION
PERIHELION
PERIODICAL
PERIPHERAL
PERISHABLE
PERITONEUM
PERIWINKLE
PERMAFROST
PERMISSION
PERMISSIVE
PERNICIOUS
PERORATION
PERPETRATE
PERPETUATE
PERPETUITY
PERQUISITE
PERSIFLAGE
PERSONABLE
PERSONALTY
PERSUASION
PERVERSION
PESTILENCE
PETNAPPING
PETROLATUM
PHENOMENON
PHILISTINE
PHILOSOPHY
PHLEBOTOMY
PHLEGMATIC
PHONOGRAPH
PHOSPHORUS
PHOTOFLASH
PHOTOGENIC
PHOTOGRAPH
PHOTOMETER
PHOTOMURAL
PHOTOPAINT
PHRENOLOGY
PHYLACTERY
PHYSIOLOGY
PIANISSIMO
PIANOFORTE
PICARESQUE
PICCALILLI
PICKANINNY
PICKPOCKET
PICOSECOND
PIGEONHOLE
PILGRIMAGE
PILLOWCASE
PILOTHOUSE
PINCUSHION
PINFEATHER
PLAGIARIZE
PLANTATION
PLAYACTING
PLAYGROUND
PLAYWRIGHT
PLEASANTRY
PLEBISCITE
PLUPERFECT
PLUTOCRACY
POCKETBOOK
POINSETTIA
POLITICIAN
POLYCLINIC
POLYHEDRON
POLYNESIAN
POLYTHEISM
POPULATION
PORTCULLIS
PORTENTOUS
PORTUGUESE
POSSESSION
POSSESSIVE
POSTHUMOUS
POSTMASTER
POSTMORTEM
POSTPARTUM
POSTSCRIPT
POTENTIATE
POULTRYMAN
POURPARLER
POWERHOUSE
POWERLINES
PRAGMATISM
PREARRANGE
PREBENDARY
PRECARIOUS
PRECAUTION
PRECEDENCE
PRECESSION
PRECIOSITY
PRECOCIOUS
PREDACEOUS
PREDECEASE
PREDESTINE
PREDICABLE
PREDISPOSE
PREEMINENT
PREEMPTIVE
PREFERENCE
PREFERMENT
PREHENSILE
PREMARITAL

PREMEDICAL
PREPACKAGE
PREPOSSESS
PRESBYOPIA
PRESBYTERY
PRESCIENCE
PRESSURIZE
PRESUPPOSE
PRIMORDIAL
PRINCELING
PRINCIPLED
PRIVILEGED
PRIZEFIGHT
PROCEEDING
PROCESSION
PROCLIVITY
PROCURATOR
PRODIGIOUS
PRODUCTION
PROFESSION
PROFICIENT
PROFLIGATE
PROGENITOR
PROGNOSTIC
PROGRAMMED
PROGRAMMER
PROJECTILE
PROMETHIUM
PROMINENCE
PROMISSORY
PROMONTORY
PROMPTBOOK
PROMULGATE
PRONOUNCED
PROPAGANDA
PROPELLANT
PROPENSITY
PROPERTIED
PROPITIATE
PROPITIOUS
PROPORTION
PROPRIETOR
PROPRINTER
PROPULSION
PROSCENIUM
PROSPECTUS
PROSPERITY
PROSPEROUS
PROSTHESIS
PROSTITUTE
PROTECTION
PROTESTANT
PROTOPLASM
PROTRACTOR
PROVENANCE
PROVIDENCE

PROVINCIAL
PSEUDOCODE
PSYCHIATRY
PSYCHOLOGY
PSYCHOPATH
PUBESCENCE
PUGNACIOUS
PUNISHMENT
PUTRESCENT
PYRIMIDINE
QUADRANGLE
QUADRATICS
QUADRIVIUM
QUADRUPLET
QUARANTINE
QUATREFOIL
QUICKBASIC
QUINTUPLET
RACECOURSE
RADARSCOPE
RADICALIZE
RADIOGENIC
RADIOGRAPH
RADIOMETER
RADIOPHONE
RADIOSONDE
RAGAMUFFIN
RAINMAKING
RAMSHACKLE
RATTLETRAP
REACTIVATE
READERSHIP
REASONABLE
REBELLIOUS
RECEIVABLE
RECEPTACLE
RECIDIVISM
RECIPROCAL
RECITATION
RECOILLESS
RECOMPENSE
RECONSIDER
RECREATION
RECUPERATE
REDEMPTION
REDISTRICT
REDUNDANCY
REFERENDUM
REFINEMENT
REFRACTION
REFRACTORY
REFRINGENT
REFULGENCE
REGENERACY
REGENERATE
REGISTRANT

REGRESSION
REGULATION
REJUVENATE
RELATIONAL
RELATIVITY
RELAXATION
RELENTLESS
RELINQUISH
RELUCTANCE
REMARKABLE
REMEDIABLE
REMITTANCE
REMUNERATE
RENASCENCE
RENDEZVOUS
REPAGINATE
REPARATION
REPARATIVE
REPATRIATE
REPERTOIRE
REPETITION
REPETITIVE
REPORTEDLY
REPOSITORY
REPUBLICAN
REPUGNANCE
REPUTATION
RESILIENCE
RESILIENCY
RESISTANCE
RESOLUTION
RESORPTION
RESOUNDING
RESPECTING
RESPECTIVE
RESPIRATOR
RESPONDENT
RESPONSIVE
RESTAURANT
RESTORABLE
RESTRAINED
RESURGENCE
RETRACTILE
RETROGRADE
RETROGRESS
RETROSPECT
REVELATION
REVITALIZE
REVOCATION
REVOLUTION
RHEUMATISM
RHINESTONE
RHINOCEROS
RIBOFLAVIN
RICKETTSIA
RIDICULOUS

RINGLEADER
RINGMASTER
RISIBILITY
ROADRUNNER
ROLLERBALL
ROLLICKING
ROTISSERIE
ROUGHHOUSE
ROUNDABOUT
ROUNDHOUSE
ROUSTABOUT
RUBBERNECK
SACCHARINE
SACERDOTAL
SACROILIAC
SACROSANCT
SALAMANDER
SALESWOMAN
SALTCELLAR
SALUBRIOUS
SALUTATION
SANATORIUM
SANDALWOOD
SANGUINARY
SANITARIAN
SANITARIUM
SANITATION
SAPROPHYTE
SAUERKRAUT
SCAPEGRACE
SCARLATINA
SCHISMATIC
SCHOLASTIC
SCHOOLGIRL
SCHOOLMARM
SCHOOLMATE
SCHOOLROOM
SCRUTINIZE
SCURRILOUS
SEAMANSHIP
SEAMSTRESS
SEARCHWARE
SEASONABLE
SECONDHAND
SECULARISM
SECULARIZE
SEERSUCKER
SEISMOGRAM
SEISMOLOGY
SELENOLOGY
SEMIDRYING
SEMPSTRESS
SENEGALESE
SENESCENCE
SEPARATION
SEPARATIST

SEPARATIVE
SEPTICEMIA
SEPTUAGINT
SEPULCHRAL
SERPENTINE
SERVICEMAN
SERVOMOTOR
SETTLEMENT
SHAMEFACED
SHENANIGAN
SHIBBOLETH
SHILLELAGH
SHIPFITTER
SHIPWRIGHT
SHOESTRING
SHOPKEEPER
SHORTENING
SHUNPIKING
SHUTTERBUG
SIDESTROKE
SIDEWINDER
SILHOUETTE
SILVERFISH
SILVERWARE
SIMILITUDE
SIMPLICITY
SIMPLISTIC
SINGLETREE
SISTERHOOD
SKATEBOARD
SKEPTICISM
SKYSCRAPER
SKYWRITING
SLENDERIZE
SLIPSTREAM
SLUMBEROUS
SMATTERING
SMOKESTACK
SNAPDRAGON
SNOWMOBILE
SOLICITOUS
SOLICITUDE
SOLIDARITY
SOMERSAULT
SOOTHSAYER
SOPHOMORIC
SPACECRAFT
SPECIALIST
SPECIALIZE
SPELLBOUND
SPIRITUOUS
SPIROCHETE
SPITTLEBUG
SPLASHDOWN
SPOILSPORT
SPOLIATION

SPORTSCAST
SPRINGTIME
SPRINKLING
STAGECOACH
STALACTITE
STALAGMITE
STANDPOINT
STANDSTILL
STARVELING
STATECRAFT
STATEHOUSE
STATIONARY
STATIONERY
STATISTICS
STATUESQUE
STENTORIAN
STEPFATHER
STEPLADDER
STEPMOTHER
STEPPARENT
STEPSISTER
STEREOTYPE
STIGMATIZE
STILLBIRTH
STOCHASTIC
STOREHOUSE
STRAIGHTEN
STRAWBERRY
STRENGTHEN
STRINGENCY
STRIPTEASE
STRONGHOLD
STRYCHNINE
STUPENDOUS
SUBCOMPACT
SUBJECTIVE
SUBLIMINAL
SUBORBITAL
SUBROUTINE
SUBSEQUENT
SUBSIDIARY
SUBSTATION
SUBSTITUTE
SUBSTRATUM
SUBSURFACE
SUBTERFUGE
SUBTRAHEND
SUBVENTION
SUCCESSION
SUCCESSIVE
SUFFERANCE
SUFFICIENT
SUFFRAGIST
SUGGESTION
SUGGESTIVE
SUNGLASSES

SUPERCARGO
SUPERSONIC
SUPERTWIST
SUPPLEMENT
SUPPLICANT
SUPPLICATE
SURREALISM
SUSPENSION
SUSPENSORY
SUSPICIOUS
SUSTENANCE
SWEETBREAD
SWEETBRIER
SWEETHEART
SWITCHBACK
SYMPATHIZE
TABERNACLE
TABLECLOTH
TABLESPOON
TACHOMETER
TAMBOURINE
TANTAMOUNT
TARANTELLA
TASKMASTER
TATTERSALL
TATTLETALE
TEARJERKER
TECHNETIUM
TECHNICIAN
TECHNOLOGY
TEETHRIDGE
TELEGRAPHY
TELESCOPIC
TELEVISION
TEMPERANCE
TEMPTATION
TENDERFOOT
TENDERLOIN
TENEBRIOUS
TERMINATOR
TESSELLATE
TETRAMETER
THEATRICAL
THEMSELVES
THEREAFTER
THERMISTOR
THERMOSTAT
THOUGHTFUL
THREADBARE
THREEPENCE
THREESCORE
THROMBOSIS
THROUGHOUT
THROUGHPUT
THROUGHWAY
THUMBSCREW

THUNDEROUS
TIMBERLINE
TIMEKEEPER
TOMFOOLERY
TOOTHBRUSH
TOOTHPASTE
TOPOGRAPHY
TORRENTIAL
TOUCHSTONE
TOURMALINE
TOURNAMENT
TOURNIQUET
TOXICOLOGY
TRAJECTORY
TRAMPOLINE
TRANSCRIBE
TRANSCRIPT
TRANSDUCER
TRANSGRESS
TRANSISTOR
TRANSITION
TRANSITIVE
TRANSITORY
TRANSPLANT
TRANSPOLAR
TRANSVERSE
TRAVELOGUE
TRAVERTINE
TREMENDOUS
TRIFOLIATE
TRIMONTHLY
TRIPARTITE
TRIPLICATE
TROLLEYBUS
TROUBADOUR
TRUNCATION
TUBERCULAR
TUBERCULIN
TUMBLEDOWN
TUMBLEWEED
TUMULTUOUS
TURBULENCE
TURNBUCKLE
TURPENTINE
TURTLEDOVE
TURTLENECK
TYPESCRIPT
TYPESETTER
TYPEWRITER
TYPOGRAPHY
TYRANNICAL
UBIQUITOUS
ULTRASHORT
ULTRASONIC
ULTRASOUND
UNABRIDGED
UNAFFECTED
UNASSUMING
UNATTACHED
UNAVAILING
UNBALANCED
UNBEARABLE
UNBEATABLE
UNBECOMING
UNBELIEVER
UNBLUSHING
UNCRITICAL
UNDENIABLE
UNDERBELLY
UNDERBRUSH
UNDERCOVER
UNDERCROFT
UNDERLYING
UNDERNEATH
UNDERPANTS
UNDERSCORE
UNDERSEXED
UNDERSHIRT
UNDERSHOOT
UNDERSIZED
UNDERSKIRT
UNDERSLUNG
UNDERSTAND
UNDERSTATE
UNDERSTOOD
UNDERSTORY
UNDERSTUDY
UNDERTAKER
UNDERTRICK
UNDERVALUE
UNDERWAIST
UNDERWATER
UNDERWORLD
UNDERWRITE
UNDULATION
UNEMPLOYED
UNEVENTFUL
UNEXAMPLED
UNEXPECTED
UNFAITHFUL
UNFAMILIAR
UNFRIENDLY
UNFRUITFUL
UNGENEROUS
UNGRACEFUL
UNGRACIOUS
UNGRATEFUL
UNGROUNDED
UNHALLOWED
UNHANDSOME
UNICAMERAL
UNIFORMITY
UNILATERAL
UNIVERSITY
UNLETTERED
UNMANNERLY
UNMERCIFUL
UNNUMBERED
UNOCCUPIED
UNPLEASANT
UNREASONED
UNRESERVED
UNSCHOOLED
UNSCRAMBLE
UNSKILLFUL
UNSUITABLE
UNTHINKING
UNYIELDING
UPBRINGING
UPHOLSTERY
UPROARIOUS
UPSTANDING
URETHRITIS
URINALYSIS
UROGENITAL
VARICOSITY
VAUDEVILLE
VEGETARIAN
VEGETATION
VEGETATIVE
VELOCIPEDE
VERMICELLI
VERNACULAR
VERTEBRATE
VESPERTINE
VETERINARY
VIBRAPHONE
VICEGERENT
VICTORIOUS
VICTUALLER
VIDEOPHONE
VIETNAMESE
VILLAINOUS
VINDICTIVE
VIRTUOSITY
VISIBILITY
VISITATION
VITUPERATE
VIVIPAROUS
VOCABULARY
VOCIFERATE
VOCIFEROUS
VOICEPRINT
VOLLEYBALL
VOLUMETRIC
VOLUMINOUS
VOLUPTUARY
VOLUPTUOUS
VULNERABLE
WAINWRIGHT
WALLFLOWER
WANDERLUST
WASTEPAPER
WATCHMAKER
WATCHTOWER
WATERBORNE
WATERCOLOR
WATERCRAFT
WATERCRESS
WATERFRONT
WATERMELON
WATERPOWER
WATERPROOF
WATERSPOUT
WATERTIGHT
WATERWHEEL
WATERWORKS
WAVELENGTH
WEAPONLESS
WEATHERING
WEATHERMAN
WEIGHTLESS
WELLSPRING
WESTERNIZE
WHARFINGER
WHATSOEVER
WHEELCHAIR
WHEELHORSE
WHEELHOUSE
WHENSOEVER
WHIRLYBIRD
WHITSUNDAY
WHOMSOEVER
WICKERWORK
WIDESPREAD
WILDEBEEST
WILDERNESS
WILLOWWARE
WINCHESTER
WINDFLOWER
WINDJAMMER
WINDOWPANE
WINDOWSILL
WINDSHIELD
WINEGROWER
WINGSPREAD
WINTERTIDE
WINTERTIME
WIREHAIRED
WITCHCRAFT
WITCHGRASS
WITHDRAWAL
WONDERLAND
WONDERMENT
WOODCUTTER
WOODENWARE
WOODPECKER
WORKBASKET
WORKINGMAN
WORSHIPFUL
WORTHWHILE
WRAPAROUND
WRISTWATCH
XENOPHOBIA
XEROGRAPHY
YARDMASTER
YESTERYEAR

## 2nd Letter

BACKGAMMON
BACKGROUND
BACKHANDED
BACKSTAIRS
BACKSTROKE
BALBRIGGAN
BALDERDASH
BALLISTICS
BALUSTRADE
BAPTISTERY
BAREHEADED
BASKETBALL
BASTARDIZE
BATHYSCAPH
BATRACHIAN
BATTLEMENT
BATTLESHIP
CACCIATORE
CADAVEROUS
CALCAREOUS
CALCULATED
CALUMNIATE
CAMELOPARD
CAMOUFLAGE
CAMPHORATE
CANDELABRA
CANDESCENT
CANDLEWICK
CANKERWORM
CANNONBALL
CANONICALS
CANTALOUPE
CANTILEVER
CANTONMENT
CANVASBACK
CAOUTCHOUC
CAPACITATE
CAPITALISM
CAPITALIST
CAPITALIZE
CAPITATION
CAPITULATE
CAPOREGIME
CARABINEER
CARBOLATED
CARBURETOR
CARCINOGEN
CARDIOGRAM
CARDIOLOGY
CARICATURE
CATABOLISM
CATAFALQUE
CATCHPENNY
CATECHUMEN
CATEGORIZE
CAVITATION
DATAMATION
EARTHQUAKE
FACILITATE
FACTITIOUS
FAHRENHEIT
FAIRGROUND
FALLACIOUS
FAMILARIZE
FARFETCHED
FARSIGHTED
FASTIDIOUS
FATHERLAND
FATHOMLESS
FAVORITISM
GADOLINIUM
GAMEKEEPER
GARGANTUAN
GASTRONOMY
GATEKEEPER
HABILIMENT
HABITATION
HALLELUJAH
HAMMERHEAD
HAMMERLOCK
HANDBARROW
HANDICRAFT
HANDLEBARS
HANDMAIDEN
HANDSPRING
HARDHEADED
HARMONIOUS
JACKANAPES
JACKHAMMER
JACKRABBIT
JARDINIERE
JAWBREAKER
LABORATORY
LACHRYMOSE
LACKLUSTER
LADYFINGER
LANDHOLDER
LANDLOCKED
LANDLUBBER
LARYNGITIS
LASCIVIOUS
LAWBREAKER
LAWRENCIUM
MACKINTOSH
MAGISTRATE
MAIDENHAIR
MAIDENHEAD
MAIDENHOOD
MAINSPRING
MAINSTREAM
MAISONETTE
MALADAPTED
MALAPROPOS
MALCONTENT
MALEFACTOR
MALEFICENT
MALEVOLENT
MALODOROUS
MALTHUSIAN
MANAGEMENT
MANDELBROT
MANDRAGORA
MANICURIST
MANIPULATE
MANSERVANT
MANSUETUDE
MANTLEROCK
MANUSCRIPT
MARASCHINO
MARGINALIA
MARGUERITE
MARIONETTE
MARROWBONE
MARTINGALE
MASQUERADE
MASTERMIND
MASTERSHIP
MASTERWORK
MATCHMAKER
MATURATION
MAYONNAISE
NANOSECOND
NAPOLEONIC
NARCISSISM
NASTURTIUM
NATATORIUM
NATIONWIDE
NATURALISM
NATURALIST
NATURALIZE

PACKSADDLE
PACKTHREAD
PAGINATION
PAINKILLER
PAINTBRUSH
PALATALIZE
PALATINATE
PALIMPSEST
PALINDROME
PALLBEARER
PANJANDRUM
PANTALOONS
PANTYWAIST
PAPERBOARD
PARAMECIUM
PARAPHRASE
PARAPLEGIA
PARATROOPS
PARLIAMENT
PARMIGIANA
PARTICIPLE
PARTICULAR
PASSAGEWAY
PASTEBOARD
PASTEURIZE
PATHFINDER
PATRONYMIC
PAWNBROKER
RACECOURSE
RADARSCOPE
RADICALIZE
RADIOGENIC
RADIOGRAPH
RADIOMETER
RADIOPHONE
RADIOSONDE
RAGAMUFFIN
RAINMAKING
RAMSHACKLE
RATTLETRAP
SACCHARINE
SACERDOTAL
SACROILIAC
SACROSANCT
SALAMANDER
SALESWOMAN
SALTCELLAR
SALUBRIOUS
SALUTATION
SANATORIUM
SANDALWOOD
SANGUINARY
SANITARIAN
SANITARIUM
SANITATION
SAPROPHYTE
SAUERKRAUT
TABERNACLE
TABLECLOTH
TABLESPOON
TACHOMETER
TAMBOURINE
TANTAMOUNT
TARANTELLA
TASKMASTER
TATTERSALL
TATTLETALE
VARICOSITY
VAUDEVILLE
WAINWRIGHT
WALLFLOWER
WANDERLUST
WASTEPAPER
WATCHMAKER
WATCHTOWER
WATERBORNE
WATERCOLOR
WATERCRAFT
WATERCRESS
WATERFRONT
WATERMELON
WATERPOWER
WATERPROOF
WATERSPOUT
WATERTIGHT
WATERWHEEL
WATERWORKS
WAVELENGTH
YARDMASTER
ABBREVIATE
ABERRATION
ABOMINABLE
ABORIGINAL
ABOVEBOARD
ABSCISSION
ABSOLUTION
ABSOLUTISM
ABSORPTION
ABSTEMIOUS
ABSTINENCE
EBULLITION
OBLIGATION
OBLITERATE
OBSEQUIOUS
OBSERVABLE
OBSERVANCE
OBSTETRICS
UBIQUITOUS
ACCELERATE
ACCENTUATE
ACCEPTABLE
ACCEPTANCE
ACCESSIBLE
ACCIDENTAL
ACCOMPLICE
ACCOMPLISH
ACCORDANCE
ACCOUNTANT
ACCOUNTING
ACCUMULATE
ACCUSATIVE
ACCUSTOMED
ACHROMATIC
ACROBATICS
ACROPHOBIA
ACTIONABLE
ECONOMICAL
ECUMENICAL
ICEBREAKER
ICONOCLASM
ICONOCLAST
OCCASIONAL
OCCIDENTAL
OCCUPATION
OCCURRENCE
OCEANARIUM
OCEANFRONT
OCEANGOING
OCEANOLOGY
OCTOTHORPE
SCAPEGRACE
SCARLATINA
SCHISMATIC
SCHOLASTIC
SCHOOLGIRL
SCHOOLMARM
SCHOOLMATE
SCHOOLROOM
SCRUTINIZE
SCURRILOUS
ADDITIONAL
ADJUDICATE
ADMINISTER
ADMISSIBLE
ADMITTANCE
ADRENALINE
ADULTERANT
ADULTERATE
ADVENTURER
ADVISEMENT
IDIOPATHIC
AEROBATICS
AESTHETICS
BEAUJOLAIS
BEAUTICIAN
BEDCLOTHES
BEDRAGGLED
BEFOREHAND
BEHINDHAND
BELLADONNA
BELLETRIST
BELLWETHER
BELONGINGS
BENCHMARKS
BENEFACTOR
BENEFICENT
BENEFICIAL
BESPRINKLE
BESTIALITY
BETTERMENT
CELEBRATED
CELLARETTE
CELLOPHANE
CENSORIOUS
CENSORSHIP
CENTENNIAL
CENTESIMAL
CENTIGRADE
CENTILITER
CENTIMETER
CENTRALIZE
CENTRIFUGE
CEREBELLUM
CEREMONIAL
DEACTIVATE
DEADWEIGHT
DEALERSHIP
DEATHWATCH
DEBILITATE
DECAPITATE
DECELERATE
DECIMALIZE
DECLASSIFY
DECLENSION
DECOLORIZE
DECOMPRESS
DECORATION
DECORATIVE
DECRYPTION
DEFINITION
DEFINITIVE
DEFLAGRATE
DEGENERACY
DEGENERATE
DEGRADABLE
DEHUMANIZE
DEHUMIDIFY
DELECTABLE
DELEGATION
DELIBERATE
DELINQUENT
DELIQUESCE
DELPHINIUM
DEMOBILIZE
DEMOCRATIC
DEMOGRAPHY
DEMOISELLE
DEMOLITION
DEMONETIZE
DEMONOLOGY
DEMORALIZE
DENDROLOGY
DENOMINATE
DENOTATIVE
DENOUEMENT
DENTIFRICE
DEPARTMENT
DEPENDABLE
DEPENDENCE
DEPENDENCY
DEPILATORY
DEPLORABLE
DEPOLARIZE
DEPOPULATE
DEPORTMENT
DEPOSITION
DEPOSITORY
DEPRECIATE
DEPRESSANT
DEPRESSION
DEPRESSIVE
DEPUTATION
DERIVATION
DERIVATIVE
DERMATITIS
DEROGATORY
DESALINATE
DESALINIZE
DESCENDANT
DESERVEDLY
DESOLATION
DESPICABLE
DESTRUCTOR
DETACHMENT
DETERMINED
DETERRENCE
DEVITALIZE
FEDERALISM
FEDERALIST
FEDERALIZE
FEDERATION
FELICITATE
FELICITOUS
FELLOWSHIP
FERTILIZER
GENERALITY
GENERALIZE
GENERATION
GENTLEFOLK
GEOCENTRIC
GEOPHYSICS
GEOSCIENCE
GEOTHERMAL
GERIATRICS
GESUNDHEIT
HEADMASTER
HEADSTRONG
HEADWAITER
HEARTBREAK
HEARTHSIDE
HEARTTHROB
HEATSTROKE
HECTOLITER
HECTOMETER
HELICOPTER
HELIOGRAPH
HELIOTROPE
HEMATOLOGY
HEMISPHERE
HEMOGLOBIN
HEMOPHILIA
HEMORRHAGE
HEMORRHOID
HENCEFORTH
HEPTAMETER
HEREABOUTS
HEREDITARY
HERETOFORE
KETTLEDRUM
LEAFHOPPER
LEDERHOSEN
LEGITIMATE
LENGTHWISE
LEPRECHAUN
LETTERHEAD
MEADOWLARK
MECHANICAL
MEDDLESOME
MEDICAMENT
MEERSCHAUM
MELANCHOLY
MELANESIAN
MEMBERSHIP
MEMORANDUM
MENDACIOUS
MENINGITIS
MENSURABLE
MERCANTILE
MESOSPHERE
METABOLISM
METABOLITE
METACARPUS
METAGALAXY
METALLURGY
METASTASIS
METATARSAL
METATARSUS
METICULOUS
METROPOLIS
METTLESOME
NEBULOSITY
NECROMANCY
NECROPOLIS
NEEDLEWORK
NEGATIVISM
NEGLIGIBLE
NEIGHBORLY
NEOCLASSIC
NETHERMOST
NETTLESOME
NEUTRALISM
NEUTRALITY
NEUTRALIZE
NEWFANGLED
NEWSGROUPS
NEWSLETTER
NEWSWORTHY
OESOPHAGUS
PEACEMAKER
PEASHOOTER
PECCADILLO
PEDESTRIAN
PEDIATRICS
PEJORATIVE
PENICILLIN
PENMANSHIP
PENNYROYAL
PENTAMETER
PEPPERCORN
PEPPERMINT
PERCENTAGE
PERCENTILE
PERCEPTION
PERCEPTIVE
PERCEPTUAL
PERCIPIENT
PERCUSSION
PERDURABLE
PEREMPTORY
PERFECTION
PERIHELION
PERIODICAL
PERIPHERAL
PERISHABLE
PERITONEUM
PERIWINKLE
PERMAFROST
PERMISSION
PERMISSIVE
PERNICIOUS
PERORATION
PERPETRATE
PERPETUATE
PERPETUITY
PERQUISITE
PERSIFLAGE
PERSONABLE
PERSONALTY
PERSUASION

PERVERSION
PESTILENCE
PETNAPPING
PETROLATUM
REACTIVATE
READERSHIP
REASONABLE
REBELLIOUS
RECEIVABLE
RECEPTACLE
RECIDIVISM
RECIPROCAL
RECITATION
RECOILLESS
RECOMPENSE
RECONSIDER
RECREATION
RECUPERATE
REDEMPTION
REDISTRICT
REDUNDANCY
REFERENDUM
REFINEMENT
REFRACTION
REFRACTORY
REFRINGENT
REFULGENCE
REGENERACY
REGENERATE
REGISTRANT
REGRESSION
REGULATION
REJUVENATE
RELATIONAL
RELATIVITY
RELAXATION
RELENTLESS
RELINQUISH
RELUCTANCE
REMARKABLE
REMEDIABLE
REMITTANCE
REMUNERATE
RENASCENCE
RENDEZVOUS
REPAGINATE
REPARATION
REPARATIVE
REPATRIATE
REPERTOIRE
REPETITION
REPETITIVE
REPORTEDLY
REPOSITORY
REPUBLICAN
REPUGNANCE
REPUTATION

RESILIENCE
RESILIENCY
RESISTANCE
RESOLUTION
RESORPTION
RESOUNDING
RESPECTING
RESPECTIVE
RESPIRATOR
RESPONDENT
RESPONSIVE
RESTAURANT
RESTORABLE
RESTRAINED
RESURGENCE
RETRACTILE
RETROGRADE
RETROGRESS
RETROSPECT
REVELATION
REVITALIZE
REVOCATION
REVOLUTION
SEAMANSHIP
SEAMSTRESS
SEARCHWARE
SEASONABLE
SECONDHAND
SECULARISM
SECULARIZE
SEERSUCKER
SEISMOGRAM
SEISMOLOGY
SELENOLOGY
SEMIDRYING
SEMPSTRESS
SENEGALESE
SENESCENCE
SEPARATION
SEPARATIST
SEPARATIVE
SEPTICEMIA
SEPTUAGINT
SEPULCHRAL
SERPENTINE
SERVICEMAN
SERVOMOTOR
SETTLEMENT
TEARJERKER
TECHNETIUM
TECHNICIAN
TECHNOLOGY
TEETHRIDGE
TELEGRAPHY
TELESCOPIC
TELEVISION
TEMPERANCE

TEMPTATION
TENDERFOOT
TENDERLOIN
TENEBRIOUS
TERMINATOR
TESSELLATE
TETRAMETER
VEGETARIAN
VEGETATION
VEGETATIVE
VELOCIPEDE
VERMICELLI
VERNACULAR
VERTEBRATE
VESPERTINE
VETERINARY
WEAPONLESS
WEATHERING
WEATHERMAN
WEIGHTLESS
WELLSPRING
WESTERNIZE
XENOPHOBIA
XEROGRAPHY
YESTERYEAR
AFFLICTIVE
AFICIONADO
AFTERBIRTH
AFTERIMAGE
AFTERTASTE
EFFECTUATE
EFFEMINATE
EFFERVESCE
EFFICIENCY
EFFLORESCE
EFFRONTERY
EFFULGENCE
OFTENTIMES
AGGRANDIZE
AGGRESSION
AGGRESSIVE
EGOCENTRIC
IGNORAMOUS
CHALCEDONY
CHANCELLOR
CHANDELIER
CHANGELING
CHANGEOVER
CHANNELIZE
CHAPFALLEN
CHARACTERY
CHARITABLE
CHARLESTON
CHARTREUSE
CHATELAINE
CHATTERBOX
CHAUVINISM

CHEAPSKATE
CHECKPOINT
CHEESECAKE
CHIFFONIER
CHILDBIRTH
CHIMERICAL
CHIMPANZEE
CHINCHILLA
CHIROMANCY
CHIVALROUS
CHLORINATE
CHLOROFORM
CHROMOSOME
CHRONOLOGY
CHRYSOLITE
CHURCHGOER
CHURCHLESS
CHURCHYARD
GHOSTWRITE
PHENOMENON
PHILISTINE
PHILOSOPHY
PHLEBOTOMY
PHLEGMATIC
PHONOGRAPH
PHOSPHORUS
PHOTOFLASH
PHOTOGENIC
PHOTOGRAPH
PHOTOMETER
PHOTOMURAL
PHOTOPAINT
PHRENOLOGY
PHYLACTERY
PHYSIOLOGY
RHEUMATISM
RHINESTONE
RHINOCEROS
SHAMEFACED
SHENANIGAN
SHIBBOLETH
SHILLELAGH
SHIPFITTER
SHIPWRIGHT
SHOESTRING
SHOPKEEPER
SHORTENING
SHUNPIKING
SHUTTERBUG
THEATRICAL
THEMSELVES
THEREAFTER
THERMISTOR
THERMOSTAT
THOUGHTFUL
THREADBARE
THREEPENCE

THREESCORE
THROMBOSIS
THROUGHOUT
THROUGHPUT
THROUGHWAY
THUMBSCREW
THUNDEROUS
WHARFINGER
WHATSOEVER
WHEELCHAIR
WHEELHORSE
WHEELHOUSE
WHENSOEVER
WHIRLYBIRD
WHITSUNDAY
WHOMSOEVER
AIRFREIGHT
BICHLORIDE
BIMETALLIC
BIOMEDICAL
BIOPHYSICS
BIPARENTAL
BIPARIETAL
BIPARTISAN
BIRTHPLACE
BIRTHRIGHT
BIRTHSTONE
BITUMINOUS
CINERARIUM
CINQUEFOIL
CIRCUITOUS
CIRCUMCISE
CIRCUMFLEX
CIRCUMVENT
CITRONELLA
DIAPHANOUS
DICTIONARY
DIELECTRIC
DIFFERENCE
DIFFICULTY
DILETTANTE
DILLYDALLY
DIMINUENDO
DIMINUTIVE
DINNERWARE
DIPHTHERIA
DIPSOMANIA
DISAPPOINT
DISAPPROVE
DISARRANGE
DISBELIEVE
DISCERNING
DISCIPLINE
DISCOMFORT
DISCOMMODE
DISCOMPOSE
DISCONCERT

DISCONNECT
DISCONTENT
DISCOURAGE
DISCREPANT
DISCRETION
DISCURSIVE
DISCUSSANT
DISEMBOWEL
DISENCHANT
DISGRUNTLE
DISHABILLE
DISHARMONY
DISHEARTEN
DISHWASHER
DISINCLINE
DISINHERIT
DISJOINTED
DISORDERLY
DISPENSARY
DISPOSABLE
DISPOSSESS
DISQUALIFY
DISRESPECT
DISSATISFY
DISSENSION
DISSERVICE
DISSIMILAR
DISSOCIATE
DISSONANCE
DISTILLATE
DISTRAUGHT
DISTRIBUTE
DIVINATION
EISTEDDFOD
FIBERBOARD
FIBERGLASS
FIBRINOGEN
FICTITIOUS
FIELDPIECE
FIGURATION
FIGURATIVE
FIGUREHEAD
FILIBUSTER
FINGERLING
FINGERNAIL
FISTICUFFS
GINGERSNAP
GINGIVITIS
HIEROPHANT
HIGHLANDER
HIGHWAYMAN
HINTERLAND
HIPPODROME
HISTRIONIC
JIMSONWEED
JINRIKISHA
KIESELGUHR

KINEMATICS
KINGFISHER
LIBERALISM
LIBIDINOUS
LICENTIATE
LICENTIOUS
LIEUTENANT
LIFESAVING
LIGHTHOUSE
LIGHTPROOF
LIKELIHOOD
LINEBACKER
LIPREADING
LITERALISM
LITERATURE
LITHUANIAN
LIVELIHOOD
LIVERWURST
MICROFICHE
MICROGRAPH
MICROMETER
MICROPHONE
MICROPROBE
MICROSCOPE
MICROSTATE
MIDDLEBROW
MIDSHIPMAN
MIGNONETTE
MILITARISM
MILITARIZE
MILLENNIUM
MILLILITER
MILLIMETER
MILLSTREAM
MILLWRIGHT
MIMEOGRAPH
MINERALIZE
MINERALOGY
MINESTRONE
MINISCROLL
MINISTRANT
MISALIGNED
MISCELLANY
MISCONDUCT
MISFORTUNE
MISOGAMIST
MISOGYNIST
MISSILEMAN
MISSIONARY
MISTAKABLE
MIZZENMAST
NIGHTDRESS
NIGHTSHADE
NIGHTSHIRT
NIGHTSTICK
NINCOMPOOP
PIANISSIMO

PIANOFORTE
PICARESQUE
PICCALILLI
PICKANINNY
PICKPOCKET
PICOSECOND
PIGEONHOLE
PILGRIMAGE
PILLOWCASE
PILOTHOUSE
PINCUSHION
PINFEATHER
RIBOFLAVIN
RICKETTSIA
RIDICULOUS
RINGLEADER
RINGMASTER
RISIBILITY
SIDESTROKE
SIDEWINDER
SILHOUETTE
SILVERFISH
SILVERWARE
SIMILITUDE
SIMPLICITY
SIMPLISTIC
SINGLETREE
SISTERHOOD
TIMBERLINE
TIMEKEEPER
VIBRAPHONE
VICEGERENT
VICTORIOUS
VICTUALLER
VIDEOPHONE
VIETNAMESE
VILLAINOUS
VINDICTIVE
VIRTUOSITY
VISIBILITY
VISITATION
VITUPERATE
VIVIPAROUS
WICKERWORK
WIDESPREAD
WILDEBEEST
WILDERNESS
WILLOWWARE
WINCHESTER
WINDFLOWER
WINDJAMMER
WINDOWPANE
WINDOWSILL
WINDSHIELD
WINEGROWER
WINGSPREAD
WINTERTIDE

WINTERTIME
WIREHAIRED
WITCHCRAFT
WITCHGRASS
WITHDRAWAL
SKATEBOARD
SKEPTICISM
SKYSCRAPER
SKYWRITING
ALBUMINOUS
ALCOHOLISM
ALIMENTARY
ALKALINIZE
ALLEGIANCE
ALLHALLOWS
ALLITERATE
ALONGSHORE
ALPHABETIC
ALTARPIECE
ALTERNATOR
ALTOGETHER
BLACKAMOOR
BLACKBERRY
BLACKBOARD
BLACKGUARD
BLACKSMITH
BLACKTHORN
BLANCMANGE
BLITZKRIEG
BLOCKHOUSE
BLOODHOUND
BLOODSTAIN
BLOODSTONE
BLUEBONNET
BLUEBOTTLE
BLUECOLLAR
BLUEJACKET
CLASSICISM
CLASSIFIED
CLAVICHORD
CLERESTORY
CLINGSTONE
CLODHOPPER
CLOTHESPIN
CLOUDBURST
CLOVERLEAF
ELDERBERRY
ELECTORATE
ELECTRONIC
ELEMENTARY
FLAGELLATE
FLAGITIOUS
FLAMBOYANT
FLASHLIGHT
FLOODLIGHT
FLOODPLAIN
FLOODWATER

FLOORBOARD
FLUIDOUNCE
FLUORIDATE
FLUORINATE
FLYCATCHER
GLACIOLOGY
ILLITERATE
ILLUMINATE
ILLUSTRATE
OLEAGINOUS
PLAGIARIZE
PLANTATION
PLAYACTING
PLAYGROUND
PLAYWRIGHT
PLEASANTRY
PLEBISCITE
PLUPERFECT
PLUTOCRACY
SLENDERIZE
SLIPSTREAM
SLUMBEROUS
ULTRASHORT
ULTRASONIC
ULTRASOUND
AMALGAMATE
AMANUENSIS
AMBASSADOR
AMBULATORY
AMELIORATE
AMERINDIAN
AMMUNITION
AMPHIBIOUS
EMANCIPATE
EMASCULATE
EMBANKMENT
EMBONPOINT
EMBOUCHURE
EMBROIDERY
EMBRYOLOGY
EMPIRICISM
EMPLOYMENT
EMULSIFIER
IMAGINABLE
IMBIBITION
IMMACULATE
IMMATERIAL
IMMEMORIAL
IMMISCIBLE
IMMOBILIZE
IMMODERATE
IMMORALITY
IMMUNOLOGY
IMPALPABLE
IMPASSABLE
IMPASSIBLE
IMPATIENCE

IMPECCABLE
IMPEDIMENT
IMPENITENT
IMPERATIVE
IMPERSONAL
IMPERVIOUS
IMPLACABLE
IMPORTANCE
IMPOSSIBLE
IMPOVERISH
IMPREGNATE
IMPRESARIO
IMPRESSION
IMPRESSIVE
IMPRIMATUR
IMPROBABLE
OMNIPOTENT
OMNISCIENT
OMNIVOROUS
SMATTERING
SMOKESTACK
ANEMOMETER
ANESTHESIA
ANESTHETIC
ANGIOSPERM
ANGLOPHILE
ANGLOPHOBE
ANIMADVERT
ANIMALCULE
ANNIHILATE
ANNUNCIATE
ANSWERABLE
ANTAGONISM
ANTAGONIST
ANTAGONIZE
ANTEBELLUM
ANTECEDENT
ANTEPENULT
ANTHRACITE
ANTHROPOID
ANTIBIOTIC
ANTICANCER
ANTICHRIST
ANTICIPATE
ANTICLIMAX
ANTIFREEZE
ANTIMATTER
ANTINOMIAN
ANTIPHONAL
ANTIPROTON
ANTIQUATED
ANTISEPTIC
ANTISOCIAL
ANTITHESIS
ENAMELWARE
ENCRYPTION
ENCYCLICAL

ENDANGERED
ENDEARMENT
ENDOGENOUS
ENGAGEMENT
ENJAMBMENT
ENTERPRISE
ENTHUSIASM
ENTOMOLOGY
INACTIVATE
INADEQUATE
INAPTITUDE
INAUGURATE
INBREEDING
INCAPACITY
INCENDIARY
INCIDENTAL
INCINERATE
INCIVILITY
INCLINABLE
INCOHERENT
INCOMPLETE
INCONSTANT
INCREDIBLE
INCULPABLE
INCUMBENCY
INDECISION
INDECISIVE
INDECOROUS
INDEFINITE
INDELICATE
INDICATIVE
INDIGENOUS
INDISCREET
INDISPOSED
INDISTINCT
INDIVIDUAL
INDONESIAN
INDUCEMENT
INDUCTANCE
INDULGENCE
INDUSTRIAL
INELIGIBLE
INEQUALITY
INEVITABLE
INEXORABLE
INEXPIABLE
INFALLIBLE
INFIDELITY
INFIGHTING
INFILTRATE
INFINITIVE
INFINITUDE
INFLECTION
INFLEXIBLE
INFRACTION
INFRASONIC
INFREQUENT

INGLORIOUS
INGRATIATE
INGREDIENT
INHABITANT
INHIBITION
INHUMANITY
INIMITABLE
INITIATIVE
INITIATORY
INJUNCTION
INNOMINATE
INNOVATION
INOPERABLE
INORDINATE
INQUIETUDE
INSATIABLE
INSEMINATE
INSENSIBLE
INSENTIENT
INSISTENCE
INSOLATION
INSOLVABLE
INSTRUCTOR
INSTRUMENT
INTANGIBLE
INTEGUMENT
INTERBLOCK
INTERBREED
INTERFAITH
INTERFERON
INTERLEAVE
INTERLUNAR
INTERMARRY
INTERMEZZO
INTERNMENT
INTERSTATE
INTERSTICE
INTERTIDAL
INTERTWINE
INTERTWIST
INTERURBAN
INTERWEAVE
INTIMIDATE
INTINCTION
INTOLERANT
INTONATION
INTOXICANT
INTOXICATE
INTRAMURAL
INTRASTATE
INVALIDATE
INVALUABLE
INVARIABLE
INVESTMENT
INVETERATE
INVIGORATE
INVINCIBLE

INVIOLABLE
INVOCATION
INVOLUTION
KNICKKNACK
KNIGHTHOOD
KNOCKWURST
SNAPDRAGON
SNOWMOBILE
UNABRIDGED
UNAFFECTED
UNASSUMING
UNATTACHED
UNAVAILING
UNBALANCED
UNBEARABLE
UNBEATABLE
UNBECOMING
UNBELIEVER
UNBLUSHING
UNCRITICAL
UNDENIABLE
UNDERBELLY
UNDERBRUSH
UNDERCOVER
UNDERCROFT
UNDERLYING
UNDERNEATH
UNDERPANTS
UNDERSCORE
UNDERSEXED
UNDERSHIRT
UNDERSHOOT
UNDERSIZED
UNDERSKIRT
UNDERSLUNG
UNDERSTAND
UNDERSTATE
UNDERSTOOD
UNDERSTORY
UNDERSTUDY
UNDERTAKER
UNDERTRICK
UNDERVALUE
UNDERWAIST
UNDERWATER
UNDERWORLD
UNDERWRITE
UNDULATION
UNEMPLOYED
UNEVENTFUL
UNEXAMPLED
UNEXPECTED
UNFAITHFUL
UNFAMILIAR
UNFRIENDLY
UNFRUITFUL
UNGENEROUS

UNGRACEFUL
UNGRACIOUS
UNGRATEFUL
UNGROUNDED
UNHALLOWED
UNHANDSOME
UNICAMERAL
UNIFORMITY
UNILATERAL
UNIVERSITY
UNLETTERED
UNMANNERLY
UNMERCIFUL
UNNUMBERED
UNOCCUPIED
UNPLEASANT
UNREASONED
UNRESERVED
UNSCHOOLED
UNSCRAMBLE
UNSKILLFUL
UNSUITABLE
UNTHINKING
UNYIELDING
BOISTEROUS
BOLSHEVISM
BOMBARDIER
BONDHOLDER
BOOKKEEPER
BOOKMOBILE
BOOKSELLER
BOONDOGGLE
BORDERLAND
BOTTLENECK
BOTTOMLAND
BOWDLERIZE
COCKATRICE
COGNIZANCE
COINCIDENT
COLLARBONE
COLLATERAL
COLLECTIVE
COLLOQUIAL
COLLOQUIUM
COLORATION
COLORATURA
COLPORTEUR
COMBUSTION
COMEDIENNE
COMESTIBLE
COMMANDANT
COMMANDEER
COMMENTARY
COMMERCIAL
COMMISSARY
COMMISSION
COMMODIOUS
COMMONALTY
COMMONWEAL
COMMUNIQUE
COMMUTATOR
COMPARABLE
COMPARISON
COMPASSION
COMPATIBLE
COMPATRIOT
COMPENDIUM
COMPENSATE
COMPETENCE
COMPETENCY
COMPETITOR
COMPLECTED
COMPLEMENT
COMPLEXION
COMPLIANCE
COMPLIANCY
COMPLICATE
COMPLICITY
COMPLIMENT
COMPOSITOR
COMPREHEND
COMPROMISE
COMPULSION
COMPULSIVE
COMPULSORY
COMPUSERVE
CONCENTRIC
CONCEPTION
CONCERNING
CONCERTINA
CONCESSION
CONCESSIVE
CONCILIATE
CONCLUSION
CONCORDANT
CONCRETION
CONCURRENT
CONCUSSION
CONDENSATE
CONDESCEND
CONDUCTIVE
CONFECTION
CONFERENCE
CONFESSION
CONFIDENCE
CONFISCATE
CONFLUENCE
CONFORMITY
CONGENITAL
CONGREGATE
CONGRUENCE
CONGRUENCY
CONJECTURE
CONNECTION
CONNECTIVE
CONNIPTION
CONSCIENCE
CONSECRATE
CONSEQUENT
CONSISTORY
CONSONANCE
CONSORTIUM
CONSPECTUS
CONSPIRACY
CONSTITUTE
CONSTRAINT
CONSUMMATE
CONTAGIOUS
CONTENTION
CONTIGUOUS
CONTINENCE
CONTINGENT
CONTINUITY
CONTINUOUS
CONTRABAND
CONTRADICT
CONTRAVENE
CONTRIBUTE
CONTROLLER
CONTROVERT
CONVALESCE
CONVECTION
CONVENIENT
CONVENTION
CONVERSANT
CONVERSION
CONVEYANCE
CONVICTION
CONVOLUTED
CONVULSION
COORDINATE
COPPERHEAD
COPYREADER
COPYWRITER
CORDILLERA
CORDWAINER
CORNFLOWER
CORNSTARCH
CORNUCOPIA
CORONATION
CORPULENCE
CORRESPOND
CORRIGIBLE
COSMOPOLIS
COTERMINAL
COTTONSEED
COTTONTAIL
COTTONWOOD
COUNTERACT
COUNTERMAN
COUNTERSPY
COUNTRYMAN
COURTHOUSE
COWPUNCHER
DOCKWORKER
DOGCATCHER
DOMINATION
DONNYBROOK
DOORKEEPER
DOWNSTAIRS
DOWNSTREAM
DOWNSTROKE
FOLKSINGER
FOOTBRIDGE
FOOTLIGHTS
FOOTLOCKER
FORBIDDING
FORECASTLE
FOREFATHER
FOREFINGER
FOREGATHER
FOREGROUND
FOREHANDED
FOREORDAIN
FORERUNNER
FORESHADOW
FORFEITURE
FORMIDABLE
FORTHRIGHT
FORTISSIMO
FORTUITOUS
FOSTERLING
FOUNDATION
FOURSQUARE
GOALKEEPER
GOLDBEATER
GONOCOCCUS
GOOSEBERRY
GOOSEFLESH
GORGONZOLA
GORMANDIZE
GOVERNMENT
HOBBYHORSE
HODGEPODGE
HOLLOWWARE
HOLOGRAPHY
HOMECOMING
HOMEOPATHY
HOMOGENIZE
HOMOLOGOUS
HOMOSEXUAL
HONORARIUM
HOOTENANNY
HORIZONTAL
HORRENDOUS
HORSEFLESH
HORSELAUGH
HORSEPOWER
HORSEWOMAN
HOSPITABLE
HOUSECLEAN
HOUSEWARES
IONOSPHERE
JOURNALESE
JOURNALISM
JOURNEYMAN
LOCOMOTION
LOCOMOTIVE
LOGANBERRY
LOGGERHEAD
LOGROLLING
LOQUACIOUS
LOVEMAKING
MOHAMMEDAN
MOLYBDENUM
MONARCHIST
MONOCHROME
MONOPHONIC
MONOTHEISM
MONOTONOUS
MONSTRANCE
MONUMENTAL
MOONSTRUCK
MORATORIUM
MORPHOLOGY
MOTHERHOOD
MOTHERLAND
MOTORCYCLE
MOTORTRUCK
MOUNTEBANK
MOUTHPIECE
MOZZARELLA
NOISEMAKER
NOMINATIVE
NONCHALANT
NONDRINKER
NONSTARTER
NONSUPPORT
NOTABILITY
NOTEWORTHY
NOTICEABLE
NOURISHING
POCKETBOOK
POINSETTIA
POLITICIAN
POLYCLINIC
POLYHEDRON
POLYNESIAN
POLYTHEISM
POPULATION
PORTCULLIS
PORTENTOUS
PORTUGUESE
POSSESSION
POSSESSIVE
POSTHUMOUS
POSTMASTER
POSTMORTEM
POSTPARTUM
POSTSCRIPT
POTENTIATE
POULTRYMAN
POURPARLER
POWERHOUSE
POWERLINES
ROADRUNNER
ROLLERBALL
ROLLICKING
ROTISSERIE
ROUGHHOUSE
ROUNDABOUT
ROUNDHOUSE
ROUSTABOUT
SOLICITOUS
SOLICITUDE
SOLIDARITY
SOMERSAULT
SOOTHSAYER
SOPHOMORIC
TOMFOOLERY
TOOTHBRUSH
TOOTHPASTE
TOPOGRAPHY
TORRENTIAL
TOUCHSTONE
TOURMALINE
TOURNAMENT
TOURNIQUET
TOXICOLOGY
VOCABULARY
VOCIFERATE
VOCIFEROUS
VOICEPRINT
VOLLEYBALL
VOLUMETRIC
VOLUMINOUS
VOLUPTUARY
VOLUPTUOUS
WONDERLAND
WONDERMENT
WOODCUTTER
WOODENWARE
WOODPECKER
WORKBASKET
WORKINGMAN
WORSHIPFUL
WORTHWHILE
APOCALYPSE
APOCRYPHAL
APOLITICAL
APOLOGETIC
APOSTROPHE
APOTHECARY
APOTHEOSIS
APPARITION
APPEARANCE
APPETIZING
APPLICABLE
APPLICATOR
APPOINTIVE
APPOSITION
APPOSITIVE
APPRECIATE
APPRENTICE
EPIGLOTTIS
EPISCOPACY
EPISCOPATE
EPITHELIUM
OPALESCENT
OPHTHALMIC
OPPRESSION
OPPROBRIUM
SPACECRAFT
SPECIALIST
SPECIALIZE
SPELLBOUND
SPIRITUOUS
SPIROCHETE
SPITTLEBUG
SPLASHDOWN
SPOILSPORT
SPOLIATION
SPORTSCAST
SPRINGTIME
SPRINKLING
UPBRINGING
UPHOLSTERY
UPROARIOUS
UPSTANDING
AQUALUNGER
AQUAMARINE
EQUANIMITY
EQUESTRIAN
EQUITATION
EQUIVALENT
EQUIVOCATE
ARBITRATOR
ARBORVITAE
ARCHBISHOP
ARCHDEACON
ARCHITRAVE
ARITHMETIC
ARMAGEDDON
ARTICULATE
ARTIFICIAL
BRAHMANISM
BRAINCHILD
BRAINSTORM
BREADBOARD

BREADFRUIT
BREADSTUFF
BREAKFRONT
BREAKWATER
BREASTBONE
BREASTWORK
BRICKLAYER
BRIDEGROOM
BRIDESMAID
BRIDGEHEAD
BRIDGEWORK
BRIGANTINE
BROADCLOTH
BROADSWORD
BRONCHITIS
BRONTOSAUR
BROWNSTONE
CRADLESONG
CRANKSHAFT
CREDENTIAL
CREDITABLE
CRENELLATE
CRETACEOUS
CRISSCROSS
CROSSBONES
CROSSBREED
CROSSPIECE
CRUSTACEAN
CRYOGENICS
CRYPTOGRAM
DRAWBRIDGE
DRAWSTRING
DREAMWORLD
ERGONOMICS
ERGOSTEROL
ERYSIPELAS
FRANCHISEE
FRANCHISER
FRANCHISOR
FRATERNITY
FRATERNIZE
FRATRICIDE
FRAUDULENT
FREEBOOTER
FRESHWATER
GRADUALISM
GRADUATION
GRAINFIELD
GRAMOPHONE
GRANDCHILD
GRANDSTAND
GRAPEFRUIT
GRATUITOUS
GRAVESTONE
GRAVIMETER
GREENHOUSE
GREENSWARD
GREGARIOUS
GRINDSTONE
GROUNDLING
GROUNDMASS
GROUNDWORK
IRRATIONAL
IRRELEVANT
IRRESOLUTE
KRUGERRAND
ORATORICAL
ORDINATION
ORGANGUTAN
PRAGMATISM
PREARRANGE
PREBENDARY
PRECARIOUS
PRECAUTION
PRECEDENCE
PRECESSION
PRECIOSITY
PRECOCIOUS
PREDACEOUS
PREDECEASE
PREDESTINE
PREDICABLE
PREDISPOSE
PREEMINENT
PREEMPTIVE
PREFERENCE
PREFERMENT
PREHENSILE
PREMARITAL
PREMEDICAL
PREPACKAGE
PREPOSSESS
PRESBYOPIA
PRESBYTERY
PRESCIENCE
PRESSURIZE
PRESUPPOSE
PRIMORDIAL
PRINCELING
PRINCIPLED
PRIVILEGED
PRIZEFIGHT
PROCEEDING
PROCESSION
PROCLIVITY
PROCURATOR
PRODIGIOUS
PRODUCTION
PROFESSION
PROFICIENT
PROFLIGATE
PROGENITOR
PROGNOSTIC
PROGRAMMED
PROGRAMMER
PROJECTILE
PROMETHIUM
PROMINENCE
PROMISSORY
PROMONTORY
PROMPTBOOK
PROMULGATE
PRONOUNCED
PROPAGANDA
PROPELLANT
PROPENSITY
PROPERTIED
PROPITIATE
PROPITIOUS
PROPORTION
PROPRIETOR
PROPRINTER
PROPULSION
PROSCENIUM
PROSPECTUS
PROSPERITY
PROSPEROUS
PROSTHESIS
PROSTITUTE
PROTECTION
PROTESTANT
PROTOPLASM
PROTRACTOR
PROVENANCE
PROVIDENCE
PROVINCIAL
TRAJECTORY
TRAMPOLINE
TRANSCRIBE
TRANSCRIPT
TRANSDUCER
TRANSGRESS
TRANSISTOR
TRANSITION
TRANSITIVE
TRANSITORY
TRANSPLANT
TRANSPOLAR
TRANSVERSE
TRAVELOGUE
TRAVERTINE
TREMENDOUS
TRIFOLIATE
TRIMONTHLY
TRIPARTITE
TRIPLICATE
TROLLEYBUS
TROUBADOUR
TRUNCATION
URETHRITIS
URINALYSIS
UROGENITAL
WRAPAROUND
WRISTWATCH
ASCENDANCY
ASPHYXIATE
ASPIRATION
ASSEMBLAGE
ASSEVERATE
ASSIGNMENT
ASSIMILATE
ASSORTMENT
ASSUMPTION
ASTRINGENT
ASYMMETRIC
ESCARPMENT
ESCRITOIRE
ESCUTCHEON
ESPADRILLE
ESTIMATION
ISOMETRICS
ISOTHERMAL
OSTENSIBLE
OSTEOPATHY
PSEUDOCODE
PSYCHIATRY
PSYCHOLOGY
PSYCHOPATH
ATMOSPHERE
ATTACHMENT
ATTAINMENT
ATTENDANCE
ATTRACTANT
ATTRACTION
OTHERWORLD
STAGECOACH
STALACTITE
STALAGMITE
STANDPOINT
STANDSTILL
STARVELING
STATECRAFT
STATEHOUSE
STATIONARY
STATIONERY
STATISTICS
STATUESQUE
STENTORIAN
STEPFATHER
STEPLADDER
STEPMOTHER
STEPPARENT
STEPSISTER
STEREOTYPE
STIGMATIZE
STILLBIRTH
STOCHASTIC
STOREHOUSE
STRAIGHTEN
STRAWBERRY
STRENGTHEN
STRINGENCY
STRIPTEASE
STRONGHOLD
STRYCHNINE
STUPENDOUS
AUCTIONEER
AUDIOPHILE
AUDITORIUM
AURIFEROUS
AUSPICIOUS
AUSTRALIAN
AUTHORSHIP
AUTOMATION
AUTOMATIZE
AUTOMOBILE
AUTOMOTIVE
AUTONOMOUS
AUTOSTRADA
BUDGERIGAR
BULLHEADED
BUSHMASTER
BUTTERMILK
BUTTONHOLE
BUTTONHOOK
CUMMERBUND
CUMULATIVE
CURRICULUM
CURVACEOUS
CUTTLEFISH
DUMBWAITER
DUNDERHEAD
DUODECIMAL
DUPLICATOR
EUCALYPTUS
EUPHONIOUS
EURODOLLAR
EUTHANASIA
FUSSBUDGET
FUTURISTIC
GUARDHOUSE
GUILLOTINE
GUNSLINGER
HULLABALOO
HUSBANDMAN
JUBILATION
JUDICATURE
JUGGERNAUT
LUBRICIOUS
LUGUBRIOUS
LUMBERJACK
LUMBERYARD
MUDSLINGER
MUHAMMADAN
MULTILEVEL
MULTIMEDIA
MULTIPLIER
MULTISENSE
MULTISTAGE
MULTISTORY
MUNIFICENT
MUSICOLOGY
NUCLEONICS
NUMBERLESS
NUMEROLOGY
NURSERYMAN
NUTCRACKER
OUTBALANCE
OUTGENERAL
OUTLANDISH
OUTPATIENT
OUTPERFORM
OUTPOURING
OUTRAGEOUS
PUBESCENCE
PUGNACIOUS
PUNISHMENT
PUTRESCENT
QUADRANGLE
QUADRATICS
QUADRIVIUM
QUADRUPLET
QUARANTINE
QUATREFOIL
QUICKBASIC
QUINTUPLET
RUBBERNECK
SUBCOMPACT
SUBJECTIVE
SUBLIMINAL
SUBORBITAL
SUBROUTINE
SUBSEQUENT
SUBSIDIARY
SUBSTATION
SUBSTITUTE
SUBSTRATUM
SUBSURFACE
SUBTERFUGE
SUBTRAHEND
SUBVENTION
SUCCESSION
SUCCESSIVE
SUFFERANCE
SUFFICIENT
SUFFRAGIST
SUGGESTION
SUGGESTIVE
SUNGLASSES
SUPERCARGO
SUPERSONIC
SUPERTWIST
SUPPLEMENT
SUPPLICANT
SUPPLICATE
SURREALISM
SUSPENSION
SUSPENSORY
SUSPICIOUS
SUSTENANCE
TUBERCULAR
TUBERCULIN
TUMBLEDOWN
TUMBLEWEED
TUMULTUOUS
TURBULENCE
TURNBUCKLE
TURPENTINE
TURTLEDOVE
TURTLENECK
VULNERABLE
EVANESCENT
EVANGELISM
EVANGELIST
EVANGELIZE
EVENHANDED
EVERYTHING
EVERYWHERE
EVISCERATE
OVERCHARGE
OVERMASTER
OVERSHADOW
OVERSPREAD
OVERWINTER
SWEETBREAD
SWEETBRIER
SWEETHEART
SWITCHBACK
EXACERBATE
EXACTITUDE
EXAGGERATE
EXASPERATE
EXCELLENCE
EXCELLENCY
EXCITEMENT
EXCOGITATE
EXHAUSTION
EXHAUSTIVE
EXHILARATE
EXOBIOLOGY
EXORBITANT
EXOTHERMIC
EXPATRIATE
EXPECTANCY
EXPEDIENCE
EXPEDIENCY
EXPEDITION
EXPERIENCE
EXPERIMENT

EXPLICABLE
EXPOSITION
EXPRESSION
EXPRESSMAN
EXPRESSWAY
EXTINGUISH
EXTRAMURAL
EXTRANEOUS
EXURBANITE
CYBERSPACE
CYCLOMETER
CYCLOPEDIA
DYSPROSIUM
EYEDROPPER
EYEWITNESS
GYMNASTICS
GYMNOSPERM
GYNECOLOGY
HYDRAULICS
HYDROLYSIS
HYDROMETER
HYDROPHONE
HYDROPLANE
HYGROMETER
HYPERBARIC
HYPOCENTER
HYPODERMIC
HYPOTENUSE
HYPOTHESIS
MYRIAMETER
PYRIMIDINE
SYMPATHIZE
TYPESCRIPT
TYPESETTER
TYPEWRITER
TYPOGRAPHY
TYRANNICAL

### 3rd Letter

AMALGAMATE
AMANUENSIS
BEAUJOLAIS
BEAUTICIAN
BLACKAMOOR
BLACKBERRY
BLACKBOARD
BLACKGUARD
BLACKSMITH
BLACKTHORN
BLANCMANGE
BRAHMANISM
BRAINCHILD
BRAINSTORM
CHALCEDONY
CHANCELLOR
CHANDELIER
CHANGELING
CHANGEOVER
CHANNELIZE
CHAPFALLEN
CHARACTERY
CHARITABLE
CHARLESTON
CHARTREUSE
CHATELAINE
CHATTERBOX
CHAUVINISM
CLASSICISM
CLASSIFIED
CLAVICHORD
CRADLESONG
CRANKSHAFT
DEACTIVATE
DEADWEIGHT
DEALERSHIP
DEATHWATCH
DIAPHANOUS
DRAWBRIDGE
DRAWSTRING
EMANCIPATE
EMASCULATE
ENAMELWARE
EVANESCENT
EVANGELISM
EVANGELIST
EVANGELIZE
EXACERBATE
EXACTITUDE
EXAGGERATE
EXASPERATE
FLAGELLATE
FLAGITIOUS
FLAMBOYANT
FLASHLIGHT
FRANCHISEE
FRANCHISER
FRANCHISOR
FRATERNITY
FRATERNIZE
FRATRICIDE
FRAUDULENT
GLACIOLOGY
GOALKEEPER
GRADUALISM
GRADUATION
GRAINFIELD
GRAMOPHONE
GRANDCHILD
GRANDSTAND
GRAPEFRUIT
GRATUITOUS
GRAVESTONE
GRAVIMETER
GUARDHOUSE
HEADMASTER
HEADSTRONG
HEADWAITER
HEARTBREAK
HEARTHSIDE
HEARTTHROB
HEATSTROKE
IMAGINABLE
INACTIVATE
INADEQUATE
INAPTITUDE
INAUGURATE
LEAFHOPPER
MEADOWLARK
OPALESCENT
ORATORICAL
PEACEMAKER
PEASHOOTER
PIANISSIMO
PIANOFORTE
PLAGIARIZE
PLANTATION
PLAYACTING
PLAYGROUND
PLAYWRIGHT
PRAGMATISM
QUADRANGLE
QUADRATICS
QUADRIVIUM
QUADRUPLET
QUARANTINE
QUATREFOIL
REACTIVATE
READERSHIP
REASONABLE
ROADRUNNER
SCAPEGRACE
SCARLATINA
SEAMANSHIP
SEAMSTRESS
SEARCHWARE
SEASONABLE
SHAMEFACED
SKATEBOARD
SMATTERING
SNAPDRAGON
SPACECRAFT
STAGECOACH
STALACTITE
STALAGMITE
STANDPOINT
STANDSTILL
STARVELING
STATECRAFT
STATEHOUSE
STATIONARY
STATIONERY
STATISTICS
STATUESQUE
TEARJERKER
TRAJECTORY
TRAMPOLINE
TRANSCRIBE
TRANSCRIPT
TRANSDUCER
TRANSGRESS
TRANSISTOR
TRANSITION
TRANSITIVE
TRANSITORY
TRANSPLANT
TRANSPOLAR
TRANSVERSE
TRAVELOGUE
TRAVERTINE
UNABRIDGED
UNAFFECTED
UNASSUMING
UNATTACHED
UNAVAILING
WEAPONLESS
WEATHERING
WEATHERMAN
WHARFINGER
WHATSOEVER
WRAPAROUND
ABBREVIATE
ALBUMINOUS
AMBASSADOR
AMBULATORY
ARBITRATOR
ARBORVITAE
CYBERSPACE
DEBILITATE
EMBANKMENT
EMBONPOINT
EMBOUCHURE
EMBROIDERY
EMBRYOLOGY
FIBERBOARD
FIBERGLASS
FIBRINOGEN
HABILIMENT
HABITATION
HOBBYHORSE
IMBIBITION
INBREEDING
JUBILATION
LABORATORY
LIBERALISM
LIBIDINOUS
LUBRICIOUS
NEBULOSITY
PUBESCENCE
REBELLIOUS
RIBOFLAVIN
RUBBERNECK
SUBCOMPACT
SUBJECTIVE
SUBLIMINAL
SUBORBITAL
SUBROUTINE
SUBSEQUENT
SUBSIDIARY
SUBSTATION
SUBSTITUTE
SUBSTRATUM
SUBSURFACE
SUBTERFUGE
SUBTRAHEND
SUBVENTION
TABERNACLE
TABLECLOTH
TABLESPOON
TUBERCULAR
TUBERCULIN
UNBALANCED
UNBEARABLE
UNBEATABLE
UNBECOMING
UNBELIEVER
UNBLUSHING
UPBRINGING
VIBRAPHONE
ACCELERATE
ACCENTUATE
ACCEPTABLE
ACCEPTANCE
ACCESSIBLE
ACCIDENTAL
ACCOMPLICE
ACCOMPLISH
ACCORDANCE
ACCOUNTANT
ACCOUNTING
ACCUMULATE
ACCUSATIVE
ACCUSTOMED
ALCOHOLISM
ARCHBISHOP
ARCHDEACON
ARCHITRAVE
ASCENDANCY
AUCTIONEER
BACKGAMMON
BACKGROUND
BACKHANDED
BACKSTAIRS
BACKSTROKE
BICHLORIDE
CACCIATORE
COCKATRICE
CYCLOMETER
CYCLOPEDIA
DECAPITATE
DECELERATE
DECIMALIZE
DECLASSIFY
DECLENSION
DECOLORIZE
DECOMPRESS
DECORATION
DECORATIVE
DECRYPTION
DICTIONARY
DOCKWORKER
ENCRYPTION
ENCYCLICAL
ESCARPMENT
ESCRITOIRE
ESCUTCHEON
EUCALYPTUS
EXCELLENCE
EXCELLENCY
EXCITEMENT
EXCOGITATE
FACILITATE
FACTITIOUS
FICTITIOUS
HECTOLITER
HECTOMETER
INCAPACITY
INCENDIARY
INCIDENTAL
INCINERATE
INCIVILITY
INCLINABLE
INCOHERENT
INCOMPLETE
INCONSTANT
INCREDIBLE
INCULPABLE
INCUMBENCY
JACKANAPES
JACKHAMMER
JACKRABBIT
LACHRYMOSE
LACKLUSTER
LICENTIATE
LICENTIOUS
LOCOMOTION
LOCOMOTIVE
MACKINTOSH
MECHANICAL
MICROFICHE
MICROGRAPH
MICROMETER
MICROPHONE
MICROPROBE
MICROSCOPE
MICROSTATE
NECROMANCY
NECROPOLIS
NUCLEONICS
OCCASIONAL
OCCIDENTAL
OCCUPATION
OCCURRENCE
PACKSADDLE
PACKTHREAD
PECCADILLO
PICARESQUE
PICCALILLI
PICKANINNY
PICKPOCKET
PICOSECOND
POCKETBOOK
RACECOURSE
RECEIVABLE
RECEPTACLE
RECIDIVISM
RECIPROCAL
RECITATION
RECOILLESS
RECOMPENSE
RECONSIDER
RECREATION
RECUPERATE
RICKETTSIA
SACCHARINE
SACERDOTAL
SACROILIAC
SACROSANCT
SECONDHAND
SECULARISM
SECULARIZE
SUCCESSION
SUCCESSIVE
TACHOMETER
TECHNETIUM
TECHNICIAN
TECHNOLOGY
UNCRITICAL
VICEGERENT
VICTORIOUS
VICTUALLER
VOCABULARY
VOCIFERATE
VOCIFEROUS
WICKERWORK
ADDITIONAL
AUDIOPHILE

AU**D**ITORIUM
BE**D**CLOTHES
BE**D**RAGGLED
BU**D**GERIGAR
CA**D**AVEROUS
EL**D**ERBERRY
EN**D**ANGERED
EN**D**EARMENT
EN**D**OGENOUS
FE**D**ERALISM
FE**D**ERALIST
FE**D**ERALIZE
FE**D**ERATION
GA**D**OLINIUM
HO**D**GEPODGE
HY**D**RAULICS
HY**D**ROLYSIS
HY**D**ROMETER
HY**D**ROPHONE
HY**D**ROPLANE
IN**D**ECISION
IN**D**ECISIVE
IN**D**ECOROUS
IN**D**EFINITE
IN**D**ELICATE
IN**D**ICATIVE
IN**D**IGENOUS
IN**D**ISCREET
IN**D**ISPOSED
IN**D**ISTINCT
IN**D**IVIDUAL
IN**D**ONESIAN
IN**D**UCEMENT
IN**D**UCTANCE
IN**D**ULGENCE
IN**D**USTRIAL
JU**D**ICATURE
LA**D**YFINGER
LE**D**ERHOSEN
ME**D**DLESOME
ME**D**ICAMENT
MI**D**DLEBROW
MI**D**SHIPMAN
MU**D**SLINGER
OR**D**INATION
PE**D**ESTRIAN
PE**D**IATRICS
RA**D**ARSCOPE
RA**D**ICALIZE
RA**D**IOGENIC
RA**D**IOGRAPH
RA**D**IOMETER
RA**D**IOPHONE
RA**D**IOSONDE
RE**D**EMPTION
RE**D**ISTRICT
RE**D**UNDANCY
RI**D**ICULOUS
SI**D**ESTROKE
SI**D**EWINDER
UN**D**ENIABLE
UN**D**ERBELLY
UN**D**ERBRUSH
UN**D**ERCOVER
UN**D**ERCROFT
UN**D**ERLYING
UN**D**ERNEATH
UN**D**ERPANTS
UN**D**ERSCORE
UN**D**ERSEXED
UN**D**ERSHIRT
UN**D**ERSHOOT
UN**D**ERSIZED
UN**D**ERSKIRT
UN**D**ERSLUNG
UN**D**ERSTAND
UN**D**ERSTATE
UN**D**ERSTOOD
UN**D**ERSTORY
UN**D**ERSTUDY
UN**D**ERTAKER
UN**D**ERTRICK
UN**D**ERVALUE
UN**D**ERWAIST
UN**D**ERWATER
UN**D**ERWORLD
UN**D**ERWRITE
UN**D**ULATION
VI**D**EOPHONE
WI**D**ESPREAD
AB**E**RRATION
AM**E**LIORATE
AM**E**RINDIAN
AN**E**MOMETER
AN**E**STHESIA
AN**E**STHETIC
BR**E**ADBOARD
BR**E**ADFRUIT
BR**E**ADSTUFF
BR**E**AKFRONT
BR**E**AKWATER
BR**E**ASTBONE
BR**E**ASTWORK
CH**E**APSKATE
CH**E**CKPOINT
CH**E**ESECAKE
CL**E**RESTORY
CR**E**DENTIAL
CR**E**DITABLE
CR**E**NELLATE
CR**E**TACEOUS
DI**E**LECTRIC
DR**E**AMWORLD
EL**E**CTORATE
EL**E**CTRONIC
EL**E**MENTARY
EV**E**NHANDED
EV**E**RYTHING
EV**E**RYWHERE
EY**E**DROPPER
EY**E**WITNESS
FI**E**LDPIECE
FR**E**EBOOTER
FR**E**SHWATER
GR**E**ENHOUSE
GR**E**ENSWARD
GR**E**GARIOUS
HI**E**ROPHANT
IC**E**BREAKER
IN**E**LIGIBLE
IN**E**QUALITY
IN**E**VITABLE
IN**E**XORABLE
IN**E**XPIABLE
KI**E**SELGUHR
LI**E**UTENANT
ME**E**RSCHAUM
NE**E**DLEWORK
OC**E**ANARIUM
OC**E**ANFRONT
OC**E**ANGOING
OC**E**ANOLOGY
OL**E**AGINOUS
OV**E**RCHARGE
OV**E**RMASTER
OV**E**RSHADOW
OV**E**RSPREAD
OV**E**RWINTER
PH**E**NOMENON
PL**E**ASANTRY
PL**E**BISCITE
PR**E**ARRANGE
PR**E**BENDARY
PR**E**CARIOUS
PR**E**CAUTION
PR**E**CEDENCE
PR**E**CESSION
PR**E**CIOSITY
PR**E**COCIOUS
PR**E**DACEOUS
PR**E**DECEASE
PR**E**DESTINE
PR**E**DICABLE
PR**E**DISPOSE
PR**E**EMINENT
PR**E**EMPTIVE
PR**E**FERENCE
PR**E**FERMENT
PR**E**HENSILE
PR**E**MARITAL
PR**E**MEDICAL
PR**E**PACKAGE
PR**E**POSSESS
PR**E**SBYOPIA
PR**E**SBYTERY
PR**E**SCIENCE
PR**E**SSURIZE
PR**E**SUPPOSE
PS**E**UDOCODE
RH**E**UMATISM
SE**E**RSUCKER
SH**E**NANIGAN
SK**E**PTICISM
SL**E**NDERIZE
SP**E**CIALIST
SP**E**CIALIZE
SP**E**LLBOUND
ST**E**NTORIAN
ST**E**PFATHER
ST**E**PLADDER
ST**E**PMOTHER
ST**E**PPARENT
ST**E**PSISTER
ST**E**REOTYPE
SW**E**ETBREAD
SW**E**ETBRIER
SW**E**ETHEART
TE**E**THRIDGE
TH**E**ATRICAL
TH**E**MSELVES
TH**E**REAFTER
TH**E**RMISTOR
TH**E**RMOSTAT
TR**E**MENDOUS
UN**E**MPLOYED
UN**E**VENTFUL
UN**E**XAMPLED
UN**E**XPECTED
UR**E**THRITIS
VI**E**TNAMESE
WH**E**ELCHAIR
WH**E**ELHORSE
WH**E**ELHOUSE
WH**E**NSOEVER
AF**F**LICTIVE
BE**F**OREHAND
DE**F**INITION
DE**F**INITIVE
DE**F**LAGRATE
DI**F**FERENCE
DI**F**FICULTY
EF**F**ECTUATE
EF**F**EMINATE
EF**F**ERVESCE
EF**F**ICIENCY
EF**F**LORESCE
EF**F**RONTERY
EF**F**ULGENCE
IN**F**ALLIBLE
IN**F**IDELITY
IN**F**IGHTING
IN**F**ILTRATE
IN**F**INITIVE
IN**F**INITUDE
IN**F**LECTION
IN**F**LEXIBLE
IN**F**RACTION
IN**F**RASONIC
IN**F**REQUENT
LI**F**ESAVING
RE**F**ERENDUM
RE**F**INEMENT
RE**F**RACTION
RE**F**RACTORY
RE**F**RINGENT
RE**F**ULGENCE
SU**F**FERANCE
SU**F**FICIENT
SU**F**FRAGIST
UN**F**AITHFUL
UN**F**AMILIAR
UN**F**RIENDLY
UN**F**RUITFUL
AG**G**RANDIZE
AG**G**RESSION
AG**G**RESSIVE
AN**G**IOSPERM
AN**G**LOPHILE
AN**G**LOPHOBE
CO**G**NIZANCE
DE**G**ENERACY
DE**G**ENERATE
DE**G**RADABLE
DO**G**CATCHER
EN**G**AGEMENT
ER**G**ONOMICS
ER**G**OSTEROL
FI**G**URATION
FI**G**URATIVE
FI**G**UREHEAD
HI**G**HLANDER
HI**G**HWAYMAN
HY**G**ROMETER
IN**G**LORIOUS
IN**G**RATIATE
IN**G**REDIENT
JU**G**GERNAUT
LE**G**ITIMATE
LI**G**HTHOUSE
LI**G**HTPROOF
LO**G**ANBERRY
LO**G**GERHEAD
LO**G**ROLLING
LU**G**UBRIOUS
MA**G**ISTRATE
MI**G**NONETTE
NE**G**ATIVISM
NE**G**LIGIBLE
NI**G**HTDRESS
NI**G**HTSHADE
NI**G**HTSHIRT
NI**G**HTSTICK
OR**G**ANGUTAN
PA**G**INATION
PI**G**EONHOLE
PU**G**NACIOUS
RA**G**AMUFFIN
RE**G**ENERACY
RE**G**ENERATE
RE**G**ISTRANT
RE**G**RESSION
RE**G**ULATION
SU**G**GESTION
SU**G**GESTIVE
UN**G**ENEROUS
UN**G**RACEFUL
UN**G**RACIOUS
UN**G**RATEFUL
UN**G**ROUNDED
VE**G**ETARIAN
VE**G**ETATION
VE**G**ETATIVE
AC**H**ROMATIC
BE**H**INDHAND
DE**H**UMANIZE
DE**H**UMIDIFY
EX**H**AUSTION
EX**H**AUSTIVE
EX**H**ILARATE
FA**H**RENHEIT
IN**H**ABITANT
IN**H**IBITION
IN**H**UMANITY
MO**H**AMMEDAN
MU**H**AMMADAN
OP**H**THALMIC
OT**H**ERWORLD
SC**H**ISMATIC
SC**H**OLASTIC
SC**H**OOLGIRL
SC**H**OOLMARM
SC**H**OOLMATE
SC**H**OOLROOM
UN**H**ALLOWED
UN**H**ANDSOME
UP**H**OLSTERY
AF**I**CIONADO
AL**I**MENTARY
AN**I**MADVERT
AN**I**MALCULE
AR**I**THMETIC
BL**I**TZKRIEG
BO**I**STEROUS
BR**I**CKLAYER
BR**I**DEGROOM
BR**I**DESMAID
BR**I**DGEHEAD
BR**I**DGEWORK
BR**I**GANTINE
CH**I**FFONIER
CH**I**LDBIRTH
CH**I**MERICAL
CH**I**MPANZEE
CH**I**NCHILLA
CH**I**ROMANCY
CH**I**VALROUS
CL**I**NGSTONE
CO**I**NCIDENT
CR**I**SSCROSS
EP**I**GLOTTIS
EP**I**SCOPACY
EP**I**SCOPATE
EP**I**THELIUM
EV**I**SCERATE
FA**I**RGROUND
GR**I**NDSTONE
GU**I**LLOTINE
ID**I**OPATHIC
IN**I**MITABLE
IN**I**TIATIVE
IN**I**TIATORY
KN**I**CKKNACK
KN**I**GHTHOOD
MA**I**DENHAIR
MA**I**DENHEAD
MA**I**DENHOOD
MA**I**NSPRING
MA**I**NSTREAM
MA**I**SONETTE
NE**I**GHBORLY
NO**I**SEMAKER
PA**I**NKILLER
PA**I**NTBRUSH
PH**I**LISTINE
PH**I**LOSOPHY
PO**I**NSETTIA
PR**I**MORDIAL
PR**I**NCELING
PR**I**NCIPLED
PR**I**VILEGED
PR**I**ZEFIGHT
QU**I**CKBASIC
QU**I**NTUPLET
RA**I**NMAKING
RH**I**NESTONE
RH**I**NOCEROS
SE**I**SMOGRAM
SE**I**SMOLOGY
SH**I**BBOLETH

SH**I**LLELAGH
SH**I**PFITTER
SH**I**PWRIGHT
SL**I**PSTREAM
SP**I**RITUOUS
SP**I**ROCHETE
SP**I**TTLEBUG
ST**I**GMATIZE
ST**I**LLBIRTH
SW**I**TCHBACK
TR**I**FOLIATE
TR**I**MONTHLY
TR**I**PARTITE
TR**I**PLICATE
UB**I**QUITOUS
UN**I**CAMERAL
UN**I**FORMITY
UN**I**LATERAL
UN**I**VERSITY
UR**I**NALYSIS
VO**I**CEPRINT
WA**I**NWRIGHT
WE**I**GHTLESS
WH**I**RLYBIRD
WH**I**TSUNDAY
WR**I**STWATCH
AD**J**UDICATE
EN**J**AMBMENT
IN**J**UNCTION
PE**J**ORATIVE
RE**J**UVENATE
AL**K**ALINIZE
LI**K**ELIHOOD
AL**L**EGIANCE
AL**L**HALLOWS
AL**L**ITERATE
BA**L**BRIGGAN
BA**L**DERDASH
BA**L**LISTICS
BA**L**USTRADE
BE**L**LADONNA
BE**L**LETRIST
BE**L**LWETHER
BE**L**ONGINGS
BO**L**SHEVISM
BU**L**LHEADED
CA**L**CAREOUS
CA**L**CULATED
CA**L**UMNIATE
CE**L**EBRATED
CE**L**LARETTE
CE**L**LOPHANE
CH**L**ORINATE
CH**L**OROFORM
CO**L**LARBONE
CO**L**LATERAL
CO**L**LECTIVE
CO**L**LOQUIAL
CO**L**LOQUIUM
CO**L**ORATION
CO**L**ORATURA
CO**L**PORTEUR
DE**L**ECTABLE
DE**L**EGATION
DE**L**IBERATE
DE**L**INQUENT
DE**L**IQUESCE
DE**L**PHINIUM
DI**L**ETTANTE
DI**L**LYDALLY
FA**L**LACIOUS
FE**L**ICITATE
FE**L**ICITOUS
FE**L**LOWSHIP
FI**L**IBUSTER
FO**L**KSINGER
GO**L**DBEATER
HA**L**LELUJAH
HE**L**ICOPTER
HE**L**IOGRAPH
HE**L**IOTROPE
HO**L**LOWWARE
HO**L**OGRAPHY
HU**L**LABALOO
IL**L**ITERATE
IL**L**UMINATE
IL**L**USTRATE
MA**L**ADAPTED
MA**L**APROPOS
MA**L**CONTENT
MA**L**EFACTOR
MA**L**EFICENT
MA**L**EVOLENT
MA**L**ODOROUS
MA**L**THUSIAN
ME**L**ANCHOLY
ME**L**ANESIAN
MI**L**ITARISM
MI**L**ITARIZE
MI**L**LENNIUM
MI**L**LILITER
MI**L**LIMETER
MI**L**LSTREAM
MI**L**LWRIGHT
MO**L**YBDENUM
MU**L**TILEVEL
MU**L**TIMEDIA
MU**L**TIPLIER
MU**L**TISENSE
MU**L**TISTAGE
MU**L**TISTORY
OB**L**IGATION
OB**L**ITERATE
PA**L**ATALIZE
PA**L**ATINATE
PA**L**IMPSEST
PA**L**INDROME
PA**L**LBEARER
PH**L**EBOTOMY
PH**L**EGMATIC
PI**L**GRIMAGE
PI**L**LOWCASE
PI**L**OTHOUSE
PO**L**ITICIAN
PO**L**YCLINIC
PO**L**YHEDRON
PO**L**YNESIAN
PO**L**YTHEISM
RE**L**ATIONAL
RE**L**ATIVITY
RE**L**AXATION
RE**L**ENTLESS
RE**L**INQUISH
RE**L**UCTANCE
RO**L**LERBALL
RO**L**LICKING
SA**L**AMANDER
SA**L**ESWOMAN
SA**L**TCELLAR
SA**L**UBRIOUS
SA**L**UTATION
SE**L**ENOLOGY
SI**L**HOUETTE
SI**L**VERFISH
SI**L**VERWARE
SO**L**ICITOUS
SO**L**ICITUDE
SO**L**IDARITY
SP**L**ASHDOWN
TE**L**EGRAPHY
TE**L**ESCOPIC
TE**L**EVISION
UN**L**ETTERED
VE**L**OCIPEDE
VI**L**LAINOUS
VO**L**LEYBALL
VO**L**UMETRIC
VO**L**UMINOUS
VO**L**UPTUARY
VO**L**UPTUOUS
VU**L**NERABLE
WA**L**LFLOWER
WE**L**LSPRING
WI**L**DEBEEST
WI**L**DERNESS
WI**L**LOWWARE
AD**M**INISTER
AD**M**ISSIBLE
AD**M**ITTANCE
AM**M**UNITION
AR**M**AGEDDON
AT**M**OSPHERE
BI**M**ETALLIC
BO**M**BARDIER
CA**M**ELOPARD
CA**M**OUFLAGE
CA**M**PHORATE
CO**M**BUSTION
CO**M**EDIENNE
CO**M**ESTIBLE
CO**M**MANDANT
CO**M**MANDEER
CO**M**MENTARY
CO**M**MERCIAL
CO**M**MISSARY
CO**M**MISSION
CO**M**MODIOUS
CO**M**MONALTY
CO**M**MONWEAL
CO**M**MUNIQUE
CO**M**MUTATOR
CO**M**PARABLE
CO**M**PARISON
CO**M**PASSION
CO**M**PATIBLE
CO**M**PATRIOT
CO**M**PENDIUM
CO**M**PENSATE
CO**M**PETENCE
CO**M**PETENCY
CO**M**PETITOR
CO**M**PLECTED
CO**M**PLEMENT
CO**M**PLEXION
CO**M**PLIANCE
CO**M**PLIANCY
CO**M**PLICATE
CO**M**PLICITY
CO**M**PLIMENT
CO**M**POSITOR
CO**M**PREHEND
CO**M**PROMISE
CO**M**PULSION
CO**M**PULSIVE
CO**M**PULSORY
CO**M**PUSERVE
CU**M**MERBUND
CU**M**ULATIVE
DE**M**OBILIZE
DE**M**OCRATIC
DE**M**OGRAPHY
DE**M**OISELLE
DE**M**OLITION
DE**M**ONETIZE
DE**M**ONOLOGY
DE**M**ORALIZE
DI**M**INUENDO
DI**M**INUTIVE
DO**M**INATION
DU**M**BWAITER
FA**M**ILARIZE
GA**M**EKEEPER
GY**M**NASTICS
GY**M**NOSPERM
HA**M**MERHEAD
HA**M**MERLOCK
HE**M**ATOLOGY
HE**M**ISPHERE
HE**M**OGLOBIN
HE**M**OPHILIA
HE**M**ORRHAGE
HE**M**ORRHOID
HO**M**ECOMING
HO**M**EOPATHY
HO**M**OGENIZE
HO**M**OLOGOUS
HO**M**OSEXUAL
IM**M**ACULATE
IM**M**ATERIAL
IM**M**EMORIAL
IM**M**ISCIBLE
IM**M**OBILIZE
IM**M**ODERATE
IM**M**ORALITY
IM**M**UNOLOGY
JI**M**SONWEED
LU**M**BERJACK
LU**M**BERYARD
ME**M**BERSHIP
ME**M**ORANDUM
MI**M**EOGRAPH
NO**M**INATIVE
NU**M**BERLESS
NU**M**EROLOGY
RA**M**SHACKLE
RE**M**ARKABLE
RE**M**EDIABLE
RE**M**ITTANCE
RE**M**UNERATE
SE**M**IDRYING
SE**M**PSTRESS
SI**M**ILITUDE
SI**M**PLICITY
SI**M**PLISTIC
SO**M**ERSAULT
SY**M**PATHIZE
TA**M**BOURINE
TE**M**PERANCE
TE**M**PTATION
TI**M**BERLINE
TI**M**EKEEPER
TO**M**FOOLERY
TU**M**BLEDOWN
TU**M**BLEWEED
TU**M**ULTUOUS
UN**M**ANNERLY
UN**M**ERCIFUL
AN**N**IHILATE
AN**N**UNCIATE
BE**N**CHMARKS
BE**N**EFACTOR
BE**N**EFICENT
BE**N**EFICIAL
BO**N**DHOLDER
CA**N**DELABRA
CA**N**DESCENT
CA**N**DLEWICK
CA**N**KERWORM
CA**N**NONBALL
CA**N**ONICALS
CA**N**TALOUPE
CA**N**TILEVER
CA**N**TONMENT
CA**N**VASBACK
CE**N**SORIOUS
CE**N**SORSHIP
CE**N**TENNIAL
CE**N**TESIMAL
CE**N**TIGRADE
CE**N**TILITER
CE**N**TIMETER
CE**N**TRALIZE
CE**N**TRIFUGE
CI**N**ERARIUM
CI**N**QUEFOIL
CO**N**CENTRIC
CO**N**CEPTION
CO**N**CERNING
CO**N**CERTINA
CO**N**CESSION
CO**N**CESSIVE
CO**N**CILIATE
CO**N**CLUSION
CO**N**CORDANT
CO**N**CRETION
CO**N**CURRENT
CO**N**CUSSION
CO**N**DENSATE
CO**N**DESCEND
CO**N**DUCTIVE
CO**N**FECTION
CO**N**FERENCE
CO**N**FESSION
CO**N**FIDENCE
CO**N**FISCATE
CO**N**FLUENCE
CO**N**FORMITY
CO**N**GENITAL
CO**N**GREGATE
CO**N**GRUENCE
CO**N**GRUENCY
CO**N**JECTURE
CO**N**NECTION
CO**N**NECTIVE
CO**N**NIPTION
CO**N**SCIENCE
CO**N**SECRATE
CO**N**SEQUENT
CO**N**SISTORY
CO**N**SONANCE
CO**N**SORTIUM
CO**N**SPECTUS
CO**N**SPIRACY
CO**N**STITUTE
CO**N**STRAINT
CO**N**SUMMATE
CO**N**TAGIOUS
CO**N**TENTION
CO**N**TIGUOUS
CO**N**TINENCE
CO**N**TINGENT
CO**N**TINUITY
CO**N**TINUOUS
CO**N**TRABAND
CO**N**TRADICT
CO**N**TRAVENE
CO**N**TRIBUTE
CO**N**TROLLER
CO**N**TROVERT
CO**N**VALESCE
CO**N**VECTION
CO**N**VENIENT
CO**N**VENTION
CO**N**VERSANT
CO**N**VERSION
CO**N**VEYANCE
CO**N**VICTION
CO**N**VOLUTED
CO**N**VULSION
DE**N**DROLOGY
DE**N**OMINATE
DE**N**OTATIVE
DE**N**OUEMENT
DE**N**TIFRICE
DI**N**NERWARE
DO**N**NYBROOK
DU**N**DERHEAD
FI**N**GERLING
FI**N**GERNAIL
GE**N**ERALITY
GE**N**ERALIZE
GE**N**ERATION
GE**N**TLEFOLK
GI**N**GERSNAP
GI**N**GIVITIS
GO**N**OCOCCUS
GU**N**SLINGER
GY**N**ECOLOGY
HA**N**DBARROW

HANDICRAFT
HANDLEBARS
HANDMAIDEN
HANDSPRING
HENCEFORTH
HINTERLAND
HONORARIUM
IGNORAMOUS
INNOMINATE
INNOVATION
IONOSPHERE
JINRIKISHA
KINEMATICS
KINGFISHER
LANDHOLDER
LANDLOCKED
LANDLUBBER
LENGTHWISE
LINEBACKER
MANAGEMENT
MANDELBROT
MANDRAGORA
MANICURIST
MANIPULATE
MANSERVANT
MANSUETUDE
MANTLEROCK
MANUSCRIPT
MENDACIOUS
MENINGITIS
MENSURABLE
MINERALIZE
MINERALOGY
MINESTRONE
MINISCROLL
MINISTRANT
MONARCHIST
MONOCHROME
MONOPHONIC
MONOTHEISM
MONOTONOUS
MONSTRANCE
MONUMENTAL
MUNIFICENT
NANOSECOND
NINCOMPOOP
NONCHALANT
NONDRINKER
NONSTARTER
NONSUPPORT
OMNIPOTENT
OMNISCIENT
OMNIVOROUS
PANJANDRUM
PANTALOONS
PANTYWAIST
PENICILLIN
PENMANSHIP
PENNYROYAL
PENTAMETER
PINCUSHION
PINFEATHER
PUNISHMENT
RENASCENCE
RENDEZVOUS
RINGLEADER
RINGMASTER
SANATORIUM
SANDALWOOD
SANGUINARY
SANITARIAN
SANITARIUM
SANITATION
SENEGALESE
SENESCENCE
SINGLETREE
SUNGLASSES
TANTAMOUNT
TENDERFOOT
TENDERLOIN
TENEBRIOUS
UNNUMBERED
VINDICTIVE
WANDERLUST
WINCHESTER
WINDFLOWER
WINDJAMMER
WINDOWPANE
WINDOWSILL
WINDSHIELD
WINEGROWER
WINGSPREAD
WINTERTIDE
WINTERTIME
WONDERLAND
WONDERMENT
XENOPHOBIA
ABOMINABLE
ABORIGINAL
ABOVEBOARD
ALONGSHORE
APOCALYPSE
APOCRYPHAL
APOLITICAL
APOLOGETIC
APOSTROPHE
APOTHECARY
APOTHEOSIS
BIOMEDICAL
BIOPHYSICS
BLOCKHOUSE
BLOODHOUND
BLOODSTAIN
BLOODSTONE
BOOKKEEPER
BOOKMOBILE
BOOKSELLER
BOONDOGGLE
BROADCLOTH
BROADSWORD
BRONCHITIS
BRONTOSAUR
BROWNSTONE
CAOUTCHOUC
CLODHOPPER
CLOTHESPIN
CLOUDBURST
CLOVERLEAF
COORDINATE
CROSSBONES
CROSSBREED
CROSSPIECE
DOORKEEPER
DUODECIMAL
ECONOMICAL
EGOCENTRIC
EXOBIOLOGY
EXORBITANT
EXOTHERMIC
FLOODLIGHT
FLOODPLAIN
FLOODWATER
FLOORBOARD
FOOTBRIDGE
FOOTLIGHTS
FOOTLOCKER
GEOCENTRIC
GEOPHYSICS
GEOSCIENCE
GEOTHERMAL
GHOSTWRITE
GOOSEBERRY
GOOSEFLESH
GROUNDLING
GROUNDMASS
GROUNDWORK
HOOTENANNY
ICONOCLASM
ICONOCLAST
INOPERABLE
INORDINATE
ISOMETRICS
ISOTHERMAL
KNOCKWURST
MOONSTRUCK
NEOCLASSIC
PHONOGRAPH
PHOSPHORUS
PHOTOFLASH
PHOTOGENIC
PHOTOGRAPH
PHOTOMETER
PHOTOMURAL
PHOTOPAINT
PROCEEDING
PROCESSION
PROCLIVITY
PROCURATOR
PRODIGIOUS
PRODUCTION
PROFESSION
PROFICIENT
PROFLIGATE
PROGENITOR
PROGNOSTIC
PROGRAMMED
PROGRAMMER
PROJECTILE
PROMETHIUM
PROMINENCE
PROMISSORY
PROMONTORY
PROMPTBOOK
PROMULGATE
PRONOUNCED
PROPAGANDA
PROPELLANT
PROPENSITY
PROPERTIED
PROPITIATE
PROPITIOUS
PROPORTION
PROPRIETOR
PROPRINTER
PROPULSION
PROSCENIUM
PROSPECTUS
PROSPERITY
PROSPEROUS
PROSTHESIS
PROSTITUTE
PROTECTION
PROTESTANT
PROTOPLASM
PROTRACTOR
PROVENANCE
PROVIDENCE
PROVINCIAL
SHOESTRING
SHOPKEEPER
SHORTENING
SMOKESTACK
SNOWMOBILE
SOOTHSAYER
SPOILSPORT
SPOLIATION
SPORTSCAST
STOCHASTIC
STOREHOUSE
THOUGHTFUL
TOOTHBRUSH
TOOTHPASTE
TROLLEYBUS
TROUBADOUR
UNOCCUPIED
UROGENITAL
WHOMSOEVER
WOODCUTTER
WOODENWARE
WOODPECKER
ALPHABETIC
AMPHIBIOUS
APPARITION
APPEARANCE
APPETIZING
APPLICABLE
APPLICATOR
APPOINTIVE
APPOSITION
APPOSITIVE
APPRECIATE
APPRENTICE
ASPHYXIATE
ASPIRATION
BAPTISTERY
BIPARENTAL
BIPARIETAL
BIPARTISAN
CAPACITATE
CAPITALISM
CAPITALIST
CAPITALIZE
CAPITATION
CAPITULATE
CAPOREGIME
COPPERHEAD
COPYREADER
COPYWRITER
DEPARTMENT
DEPENDABLE
DEPENDENCE
DEPENDENCY
DEPILATORY
DEPLORABLE
DEPOLARIZE
DEPOPULATE
DEPORTMENT
DEPOSITION
DEPOSITORY
DEPRECIATE
DEPRESSANT
DEPRESSION
DEPRESSIVE
DEPUTATION
DIPHTHERIA
DIPSOMANIA
DUPLICATOR
EMPIRICISM
EMPLOYMENT
ESPADRILLE
EUPHONIOUS
EXPATRIATE
EXPECTANCY
EXPEDIENCE
EXPEDIENCY
EXPEDITION
EXPERIENCE
EXPERIMENT
EXPLICABLE
EXPOSITION
EXPRESSION
EXPRESSMAN
EXPRESSWAY
HEPTAMETER
HIPPODROME
HYPERBARIC
HYPOCENTER
HYPODERMIC
HYPOTENUSE
HYPOTHESIS
IMPALPABLE
IMPASSABLE
IMPASSIBLE
IMPATIENCE
IMPECCABLE
IMPEDIMENT
IMPENITENT
IMPERATIVE
IMPERSONAL
IMPERVIOUS
IMPLACABLE
IMPORTANCE
IMPOSSIBLE
IMPOVERISH
IMPREGNATE
IMPRESARIO
IMPRESSION
IMPRESSIVE
IMPRIMATUR
IMPROBABLE
LEPRECHAUN
LIPREADING
NAPOLEONIC
OPPRESSION
OPPROBRIUM
PAPERBOARD
PEPPERCORN
PEPPERMINT
POPULATION
REPAGINATE
REPARATION
REPARATIVE
REPATRIATE
REPERTOIRE
REPETITION
REPETITIVE
REPORTEDLY
REPOSITORY
REPUBLICAN
REPUGNANCE
REPUTATION
SAPROPHYTE
SEPARATION
SEPARATIST
SEPARATIVE
SEPTICEMIA
SEPTUAGINT
SEPULCHRAL
SOPHOMORIC
SUPERCARGO
SUPERSONIC
SUPERTWIST
SUPPLEMENT
SUPPLICANT
SUPPLICATE
TOPOGRAPHY
TYPESCRIPT
TYPESETTER
TYPEWRITER
TYPOGRAPHY
UNPLEASANT
INQUIETUDE
LOQUACIOUS
ACROBATICS
ACROPHOBIA
ADRENALINE
AEROBATICS
AIRFREIGHT
AURIFEROUS
BAREHEADED
BIRTHPLACE
BIRTHRIGHT
BIRTHSTONE
BORDERLAND
CARABINEER
CARBOLATED
CARBURETOR
CARCINOGEN
CARDIOGRAM
CARDIOLOGY
CARICATURE
CEREBELLUM
CEREMONIAL
CHROMOSOME
CHRONOLOGY
CHRYSOLITE
CIRCUITOUS
CIRCUMCISE
CIRCUMFLEX

CIRCUMVENT
CORDILLERA
CORDWAINER
CORNFLOWER
CORNSTARCH
CORNUCOPIA
CORONATION
CORPULENCE
CORRESPOND
CORRIGIBLE
CURRICULUM
CURVACEOUS
DERIVATION
DERIVATIVE
DERMATITIS
DEROGATORY
EARTHQUAKE
EURODOLLAR
FARFETCHED
FARSIGHTED
FERTILIZER
FORBIDDING
FORECASTLE
FOREFATHER
FOREFINGER
FOREGATHER
FOREGROUND
FOREHANDED
FOREORDAIN
FORERUNNER
FORESHADOW
FORFEITURE
FORMIDABLE
FORTHRIGHT
FORTISSIMO
FORTUITOUS
GARGANTUAN
GERIATRICS
GORGONZOLA
GORMANDIZE
HARDHEADED
HARMONIOUS
HEREABOUTS
HEREDITARY
HERETOFORE
HORIZONTAL
HORRENDOUS
HORSEFLESH
HORSELAUGH
HORSEPOWER
HORSEWOMAN
IRRATIONAL
IRRELEVANT
IRRESOLUTE
JARDINIERE
LARYNGITIS
MARASCHINO
MARGINALIA
MARGUERITE
MARIONETTE
MARROWBONE
MARTINGALE
MERCANTILE
MORATORIUM
MORPHOLOGY
MYRIAMETER
NARCISSISM
NURSERYMAN
PARAMECIUM
PARAPHRASE
PARAPLEGIA
PARATROOPS
PARLIAMENT
PARMIGIANA
PARTICIPLE
PARTICULAR
PERCENTAGE
PERCENTILE
PERCEPTION
PERCEPTIVE
PERCEPTUAL
PERCIPIENT
PERCUSSION
PERDURABLE
PEREMPTORY
PERFECTION
PERIHELION
PERIODICAL
PERIPHERAL
PERISHABLE
PERITONEUM
PERIWINKLE
PERMAFROST
PERMISSION
PERMISSIVE
PERNICIOUS
PERORATION
PERPETRATE
PERPETUATE
PERPETUITY
PERQUISITE
PERSIFLAGE
PERSONABLE
PERSONALTY
PERSUASION
PERVERSION
PHRENOLOGY
PORTCULLIS
PORTENTOUS
PORTUGUESE
PYRIMIDINE
SCRUTINIZE
SERPENTINE
SERVICEMAN
SERVOMOTOR
SPRINGTIME
SPRINKLING
STRAIGHTEN
STRAWBERRY
STRENGTHEN
STRINGENCY
STRIPTEASE
STRONGHOLD
STRYCHNINE
SURREALISM
TARANTELLA
TERMINATOR
THREADBARE
THREEPENCE
THREESCORE
THROMBOSIS
THROUGHOUT
THROUGHPUT
THROUGHWAY
TORRENTIAL
TURBULENCE
TURNBUCKLE
TURPENTINE
TURTLEDOVE
TURTLENECK
TYRANNICAL
UNREASONED
UNRESERVED
UPROARIOUS
VARICOSITY
VERMICELLI
VERNACULAR
VERTEBRATE
VIRTUOSITY
WIREHAIRED
WORKBASKET
WORKINGMAN
WORSHIPFUL
WORTHWHILE
XEROGRAPHY
YARDMASTER
ABSCISSION
ABSOLUTION
ABSOLUTISM
ABSORPTION
ABSTEMIOUS
ABSTINENCE
AESTHETICS
ANSWERABLE
ASSEMBLAGE
ASSEVERATE
ASSIGNMENT
ASSIMILATE
ASSORTMENT
ASSUMPTION
AUSPICIOUS
AUSTRALIAN
BASKETBALL
BASTARDIZE
BESPRINKLE
BESTIALITY
BUSHMASTER
COSMOPOLIS
DESALINATE
DESALINIZE
DESCENDANT
DESERVEDLY
DESOLATION
DESPICABLE
DESTRUCTOR
DISAPPOINT
DISAPPROVE
DISARRANGE
DISBELIEVE
DISCERNING
DISCIPLINE
DISCOMFORT
DISCOMMODE
DISCOMPOSE
DISCONCERT
DISCONNECT
DISCONTENT
DISCOURAGE
DISCREPANT
DISCRETION
DISCURSIVE
DISCUSSANT
DISEMBOWEL
DISENCHANT
DISGRUNTLE
DISHABILLE
DISHARMONY
DISHEARTEN
DISHWASHER
DISINCLINE
DISINHERIT
DISJOINTED
DISORDERLY
DISPENSARY
DISPOSABLE
DISPOSSESS
DISQUALIFY
DISRESPECT
DISSATISFY
DISSENSION
DISSERVICE
DISSIMILAR
DISSOCIATE
DISSONANCE
DISTILLATE
DISTRAUGHT
DISTRIBUTE
DYSPROSIUM
EISTEDDFOD
FASTIDIOUS
FISTICUFFS
FOSTERLING
FUSSBUDGET
GASTRONOMY
GESUNDHEIT
HISTRIONIC
HOSPITABLE
HUSBANDMAN
INSATIABLE
INSEMINATE
INSENSIBLE
INSENTIENT
INSISTENCE
INSOLATION
INSOLVABLE
INSTRUCTOR
INSTRUMENT
LASCIVIOUS
MASQUERADE
MASTERMIND
MASTERSHIP
MASTERWORK
MESOSPHERE
MISALIGNED
MISCELLANY
MISCONDUCT
MISFORTUNE
MISOGAMIST
MISOGYNIST
MISSILEMAN
MISSIONARY
MISTAKABLE
MUSICOLOGY
NASTURTIUM
OBSEQUIOUS
OBSERVABLE
OBSERVANCE
OBSTETRICS
OESOPHAGUS
PASSAGEWAY
PASTEBOARD
PASTEURIZE
PESTILENCE
POSSESSION
POSSESSIVE
POSTHUMOUS
POSTMASTER
POSTMORTEM
POSTPARTUM
POSTSCRIPT
RESILIENCE
RESILIENCY
RESISTANCE
RESOLUTION
RESORPTION
RESOUNDING
RESPECTING
RESPECTIVE
RESPIRATOR
RESPONDENT
RESPONSIVE
RESTAURANT
RESTORABLE
RESTRAINED
RESURGENCE
RISIBILITY
SISTERHOOD
SUSPENSION
SUSPENSORY
SUSPICIOUS
SUSTENANCE
TASKMASTER
TESSELLATE
UNSCHOOLED
UNSCRAMBLE
UNSKILLFUL
UNSUITABLE
UPSTANDING
VESPERTINE
VISIBILITY
VISITATION
WASTEPAPER
WESTERNIZE
YESTERYEAR
ACTIONABLE
AFTERBIRTH
AFTERIMAGE
AFTERTASTE
ALTARPIECE
ALTERNATOR
ALTOGETHER
ANTAGONISM
ANTAGONIST
ANTAGONIZE
ANTEBELLUM
ANTECEDENT
ANTEPENULT
ANTHRACITE
ANTHROPOID
ANTIBIOTIC
ANTICANCER
ANTICHRIST
ANTICIPATE
ANTICLIMAX
ANTIFREEZE
ANTIMATTER
ANTINOMIAN
ANTIPHONAL
ANTIPROTON
ANTIQUATED
ANTISEPTIC
ANTISOCIAL
ANTITHESIS
ARTICULATE
ARTIFICIAL
ASTRINGENT
ATTACHMENT
ATTAINMENT
ATTENDANCE
ATTRACTANT
ATTRACTION
AUTHORSHIP
AUTOMATION
AUTOMATIZE
AUTOMOBILE
AUTOMOTIVE
AUTONOMOUS
AUTOSTRADA
BATHYSCAPH
BATRACHIAN
BATTLEMENT
BATTLESHIP
BETTERMENT
BITUMINOUS
BOTTLENECK
BOTTOMLAND
BUTTERMILK
BUTTONHOLE
BUTTONHOOK
CATABOLISM
CATAFALQUE
CATCHPENNY
CATECHUMEN
CATEGORIZE
CITRONELLA
COTERMINAL
COTTONSEED
COTTONTAIL
COTTONWOOD
CUTTLEFISH
DATAMATION
DETACHMENT
DETERMINED
DETERRENCE
ENTERPRISE
ENTHUSIASM
ENTOMOLOGY
ESTIMATION
EUTHANASIA
EXTINGUISH
EXTRAMURAL
EXTRANEOUS
FATHERLAND
FATHOMLESS
FUTURISTIC
GATEKEEPER
INTANGIBLE
INTEGUMENT
INTERBLOCK

INTERBREED
INTERFAITH
INTERFERON
INTERLEAVE
INTERLUNAR
INTERMARRY
INTERMEZZO
INTERNMENT
INTERSTATE
INTERSTICE
INTERTIDAL
INTERTWINE
INTERTWIST
INTERURBAN
INTERWEAVE
INTIMIDATE
INTINCTION
INTOLERANT
INTONATION
INTOXICANT
INTOXICATE
INTRAMURAL
INTRASTATE
KETTLEDRUM
LETTERHEAD
LITERALISM
LITERATURE
LITHUANIAN
MATCHMAKER
MATURATION
METABOLISM
METABOLITE
METACARPUS
METAGALAXY
METALLURGY
METASTASIS
METATARSAL
METATARSUS
METICULOUS
METROPOLIS
METTLESOME
MOTHERHOOD
MOTHERLAND
MOTORCYCLE
MOTORTRUCK
NATATORIUM
NATIONWIDE
NATURALISM
NATURALIST
NATURALIZE
NETHERMOST
NETTLESOME
NOTABILITY
NOTEWORTHY
NOTICEABLE
NUTCRACKER

OCTOTHORPE
OFTENTIMES
OSTENSIBLE
OSTEOPATHY
OUTBALANCE
OUTGENERAL
OUTLANDISH
OUTPATIENT
OUTPERFORM
OUTPOURING
OUTRAGEOUS
PATHFINDER
PATRONYMIC
PETNAPPING
PETROLATUM
POTENTIATE
PUTRESCENT
RATTLETRAP
RETRACTILE
RETROGRADE
RETROGRESS
RETROSPECT
ROTISSERIE
SETTLEMENT
TATTERSALL
TATTLETALE
TETRAMETER
ULTRASHORT
ULTRASONIC
ULTRASOUND
UNTHINKING
VETERINARY
VITUPERATE
WATCHMAKER
WATCHTOWER
WATERBORNE
WATERCOLOR
WATERCRAFT
WATERCRESS
WATERFRONT
WATERMELON
WATERPOWER
WATERPROOF
WATERSPOUT
WATERTIGHT
WATERWHEEL
WATERWORKS
WITCHCRAFT
WITCHGRASS
WITHDRAWAL
ADULTERANT
ADULTERATE
AQUALUNGER
AQUAMARINE
BLUEBONNET
BLUEBOTTLE

BLUECOLLAR
BLUEJACKET
CHURCHGOER
CHURCHLESS
CHURCHYARD
COUNTERACT
COUNTERMAN
COUNTERSPY
COUNTRYMAN
COURTHOUSE
CRUSTACEAN
EBULLITION
ECUMENICAL
EMULSIFIER
EQUANIMITY
EQUESTRIAN
EQUITATION
EQUIVALENT
EQUIVOCATE
EXURBANITE
FLUIDOUNCE
FLUORIDATE
FLUORINATE
FOUNDATION
FOURSQUARE
HOUSECLEAN
HOUSEWARES
JOURNALESE
JOURNALISM
JOURNEYMAN
KRUGERRAND
MOUNTEBANK
MOUTHPIECE
NEUTRALISM
NEUTRALITY
NEUTRALIZE
NOURISHING
PLUPERFECT
PLUTOCRACY
POULTRYMAN
POURPARLER
ROUGHHOUSE
ROUNDABOUT
ROUNDHOUSE
ROUSTABOUT
SAUERKRAUT
SCURRILOUS
SHUNPIKING
SHUTTERBUG
SLUMBEROUS
STUPENDOUS
THUMBSCREW
THUNDEROUS
TOUCHSTONE
TOURMALINE
TOURNAMENT

TOURNIQUET
TRUNCATION
VAUDEVILLE
ADVENTURER
ADVISEMENT
CAVITATION
DEVITALIZE
DIVINATION
FAVORITISM
GOVERNMENT
INVALIDATE
INVALUABLE
INVARIABLE
INVESTMENT
INVETERATE
INVIGORATE
INVINCIBLE
INVIOLABLE
INVOCATION
INVOLUTION
LIVELIHOOD
LIVERWURST
LOVEMAKING
REVELATION
REVITALIZE
REVOCATION
REVOLUTION
VIVIPAROUS
WAVELENGTH
BOWDLERIZE
COWPUNCHER
DOWNSTAIRS
DOWNSTREAM
DOWNSTROKE
JAWBREAKER
LAWBREAKER
LAWRENCIUM
NEWFANGLED
NEWSGROUPS
NEWSLETTER
NEWSWORTHY
PAWNBROKER
POWERHOUSE
POWERLINES
TOXICOLOGY
ASYMMETRIC
CRYOGENICS
CRYPTOGRAM
ERYSIPELAS
FLYCATCHER
MAYONNAISE
PHYLACTERY
PHYSIOLOGY
PSYCHIATRY
PSYCHOLOGY
PSYCHOPATH

SKYSCRAPER
SKYWRITING
UNYIELDING
MIZZENMAST
MOZZARELLA

**4TH LETTER**

ALKALINIZE
ALTARPIECE
AMBASSADOR
ANTAGONISM
ANTAGONIST
ANTAGONIZE
APPARITION
AQUALUNGER
AQUAMARINE
ARMAGEDDON
ATTACHMENT
ATTAINMENT
BIPARENTAL
BIPARIETAL
BIPARTISAN
BREADBOARD
BREADFRUIT
BREADSTUFF
BREAKFRONT
BREAKWATER
BREASTBONE
BREASTWORK
BROADCLOTH
BROADSWORD
CADAVEROUS
CAPACITATE
CARABINEER
CATABOLISM
CATAFALQUE
CHEAPSKATE
DATAMATION
DECAPITATE
DEPARTMENT
DESALINATE
DESALINIZE
DETACHMENT
DISAPPOINT
DISAPPROVE
DISARRANGE
DREAMWORLD
EMBANKMENT
ENDANGERED
ENGAGEMENT
ENJAMBMENT
EQUANIMITY
ESCARPMENT

ESPADRILLE
EUCALYPTUS
EXHAUSTION
EXHAUSTIVE
EXPATRIATE
HEMATOLOGY
IMMACULATE
IMMATERIAL
IMPALPABLE
IMPASSABLE
IMPASSIBLE
IMPATIENCE
INCAPACITY
INFALLIBLE
INHABITANT
INSATIABLE
INTANGIBLE
INVALIDATE
INVALUABLE
INVARIABLE
IRRATIONAL
LOGANBERRY
MALADAPTED
MALAPROPOS
MANAGEMENT
MARASCHINO
MELANCHOLY
MELANESIAN
METABOLISM
METABOLITE
METACARPUS
METAGALAXY
METALLURGY
METASTASIS
METATARSAL
METATARSUS
MISALIGNED
MOHAMMEDAN
MONARCHIST
MORATORIUM
MUHAMMADAN
NATATORIUM
NEGATIVISM
NOTABILITY
OCCASIONAL
OCEANARIUM
OCEANFRONT
OCEANGOING
OCEANOLOGY
OLEAGINOUS
ORGANGUTAN
PALATALIZE
PALATINATE
PARAMECIUM
PARAPHRASE
PARAPLEGIA

PARATROOPS
PICARESQUE
PLEASANTRY
PREARRANGE
RADARSCOPE
RAGAMUFFIN
RELATIONAL
RELATIVITY
RELAXATION
REMARKABLE
RENASCENCE
REPAGINATE
REPARATION
REPARATIVE
REPATRIATE
SALAMANDER
SANATORIUM
SEPARATION
SEPARATIST
SEPARATIVE
SPLASHDOWN
STRAIGHTEN
STRAWBERRY
TARANTELLA
THEATRICAL
TYRANNICAL
UNBALANCED
UNFAITHFUL
UNFAMILIAR
UNHALLOWED
UNHANDSOME
UNMANNERLY
VOCABULARY
BALBRIGGAN
BOMBARDIER
CARBOLATED
CARBURETOR
COMBUSTION
DISBELIEVE
DUMBWAITER
EXOBIOLOGY
FORBIDDING
HOBBYHORSE
HUSBANDMAN
ICEBREAKER
JAWBREAKER
LAWBREAKER
LUMBERJACK
LUMBERYARD
MEMBERSHIP
NUMBERLESS
OUTBALANCE
PLEBISCITE
PREBENDARY
RUBBERNECK
SHIBBOLETH

TAM**B**OURINE
TIM**B**ERLINE
TUM**B**LEDOWN
TUM**B**LEWEED
TUR**B**ULENCE
UNA**B**RIDGED
ABS**C**ISSION
AFI**C**IONADO
APO**C**ALYPSE
APO**C**RYPHAL
BED**C**LOTHES
BEN**C**HMARKS
BLA**C**KAMOOR
BLA**C**KBERRY
BLA**C**KBOARD
BLA**C**KGUARD
BLA**C**KSMITH
BLA**C**KTHORN
BLO**C**KHOUSE
BRI**C**KLAYER
CAC**C**IATORE
CAL**C**AREOUS
CAL**C**ULATED
CAR**C**INOGEN
CAT**C**HPENNY
CHE**C**KPOINT
CIR**C**UITOUS
CIR**C**UMCISE
CIR**C**UMFLEX
CIR**C**UMVENT
CON**C**ENTRIC
CON**C**EPTION
CON**C**ERNING
CON**C**ERTINA
CON**C**ESSION
CON**C**ESSIVE
CON**C**ILIATE
CON**C**LUSION
CON**C**ORDANT
CON**C**RETION
CON**C**URRENT
CON**C**USSION
DEA**C**TIVATE
DES**C**ENDANT
DIS**C**ERNING
DIS**C**IPLINE
DIS**C**OMFORT
DIS**C**OMMODE
DIS**C**OMPOSE
DIS**C**ONCERT
DIS**C**ONNECT
DIS**C**ONTENT
DIS**C**OURAGE
DIS**C**REPANT
DIS**C**RETION
DIS**C**URSIVE
DIS**C**USSANT
DOG**C**ATCHER
EGO**C**ENTRIC
ELE**C**TORATE
ELE**C**TRONIC
EXA**C**ERBATE
EXA**C**TITUDE
FLY**C**ATCHER
GEO**C**ENTRIC
GLA**C**IOLOGY
HEN**C**EFORTH
INA**C**TIVATE
KNI**C**KKNACK
KNO**C**KWURST
LAS**C**IVIOUS
MAL**C**ONTENT
MAT**C**HMAKER
MER**C**ANTILE
MIS**C**ELLANY
MIS**C**ONDUCT
NAR**C**ISSISM
NEO**C**LASSIC
NIN**C**OMPOOP
NON**C**HALANT
NUT**C**RACKER
PEA**C**EMAKER
PEC**C**ADILLO
PER**C**ENTAGE
PER**C**ENTILE
PER**C**EPTION
PER**C**EPTIVE
PER**C**EPTUAL
PER**C**IPIENT
PER**C**USSION
PIC**C**ALILLI
PIN**C**USHION
PRE**C**ARIOUS
PRE**C**AUTION
PRE**C**EDENCE
PRE**C**ESSION
PRE**C**IOSITY
PRE**C**OCIOUS
PRO**C**EEDING
PRO**C**ESSION
PRO**C**LIVITY
PRO**C**URATOR
PSY**C**HIATRY
PSY**C**HOLOGY
PSY**C**HOPATH
QUI**C**KBASIC
REA**C**TIVATE
SAC**C**HARINE
SPA**C**ECRAFT
SPE**C**IALIST
SPE**C**IALIZE
STO**C**HASTIC
SUB**C**OMPACT
SUC**C**ESSION
SUC**C**ESSIVE
TOU**C**HSTONE
UNI**C**AMERAL
UNO**C**CUPIED
UNS**C**HOOLED
UNS**C**RAMBLE
VOI**C**EPRINT
WAT**C**HMAKER
WAT**C**HTOWER
WIN**C**HESTER
WIT**C**HCRAFT
WIT**C**HGRASS
BAL**D**ERDASH
BON**D**HOLDER
BOR**D**ERLAND
BOW**D**LERIZE
BRI**D**EGROOM
BRI**D**ESMAID
BRI**D**GEHEAD
BRI**D**GEWORK
CAN**D**ELABRA
CAN**D**ESCENT
CAN**D**LEWICK
CAR**D**IOGRAM
CAR**D**IOLOGY
CLO**D**HOPPER
CON**D**ENSATE
CON**D**ESCEND
CON**D**UCTIVE
COR**D**ILLERA
COR**D**WAINER
CRA**D**LESONG
CRE**D**ENTIAL
CRE**D**ITABLE
DEA**D**WEIGHT
DEN**D**ROLOGY
DUN**D**ERHEAD
DUO**D**ECIMAL
EYE**D**ROPPER
GOL**D**BEATER
GRA**D**UALISM
GRA**D**UATION
HAN**D**BARROW
HAN**D**ICRAFT
HAN**D**LEBARS
HAN**D**MAIDEN
HAN**D**SPRING
HAR**D**HEADED
HEA**D**MASTER
HEA**D**STRONG
HEA**D**WAITER
INA**D**EQUATE
JAR**D**INIERE
LAN**D**HOLDER
LAN**D**LOCKED
LAN**D**LUBBER
MAI**D**ENHAIR
MAI**D**ENHEAD
MAI**D**ENHOOD
MAN**D**ELBROT
MAN**D**RAGORA
MEA**D**OWLARK
MED**D**LESOME
MEN**D**ACIOUS
MID**D**LEBROW
NEE**D**LEWORK
NON**D**RINKER
PER**D**URABLE
PRE**D**ACEOUS
PRE**D**ECEASE
PRE**D**ESTINE
PRE**D**ICABLE
PRE**D**ISPOSE
PRO**D**IGIOUS
PRO**D**UCTION
QUA**D**RANGLE
QUA**D**RATICS
QUA**D**RIVIUM
QUA**D**RUPLET
REA**D**ERSHIP
REN**D**EZVOUS
ROA**D**RUNNER
SAN**D**ALWOOD
TEN**D**ERFOOT
TEN**D**ERLOIN
VAU**D**EVILLE
VIN**D**ICTIVE
WAN**D**ERLUST
WIL**D**EBEEST
WIL**D**ERNESS
WIN**D**FLOWER
WIN**D**JAMMER
WIN**D**OWPANE
WIN**D**OWSILL
WIN**D**SHIELD
WON**D**ERLAND
WON**D**ERMENT
WOO**D**CUTTER
WOO**D**ENWARE
WOO**D**PECKER
YAR**D**MASTER
ACC**E**LERATE
ACC**E**NTUATE
ACC**E**PTABLE
ACC**E**PTANCE
ACC**E**SSIBLE
ADR**E**NALINE
ADV**E**NTURER
AFT**E**RBIRTH
AFT**E**RIMAGE
AFT**E**RTASTE
ALL**E**GIANCE
ALT**E**RNATOR
ANT**E**BELLUM
ANT**E**CEDENT
ANT**E**PENULT
APP**E**ARANCE
APP**E**TIZING
ASC**E**NDANCY
ASS**E**MBLAGE
ASS**E**VERATE
ATT**E**NDANCE
BAR**E**HEADED
BEN**E**FACTOR
BEN**E**FICENT
BEN**E**FICIAL
BIM**E**TALLIC
BLU**E**BONNET
BLU**E**BOTTLE
BLU**E**COLLAR
BLU**E**JACKET
CAM**E**LOPARD
CAT**E**CHUMEN
CAT**E**GORIZE
CEL**E**BRATED
CER**E**BELLUM
CER**E**MONIAL
CHE**E**SECAKE
CIN**E**RARIUM
COM**E**DIENNE
COM**E**STIBLE
COT**E**RMINAL
CYB**E**RSPACE
DEC**E**LERATE
DEG**E**NERACY
DEG**E**NERATE
DEL**E**CTABLE
DEL**E**GATION
DEP**E**NDABLE
DEP**E**NDENCE
DEP**E**NDENCY
DES**E**RVEDLY
DET**E**RMINED
DET**E**RRENCE
DIL**E**TTANTE
DIS**E**MBOWEL
DIS**E**NCHANT
EFF**E**CTUATE
EFF**E**MINATE
EFF**E**RVESCE
ELD**E**RBERRY
END**E**ARMENT
ENT**E**RPRISE
EQU**E**STRIAN
EXC**E**LLENCE
EXC**E**LLENCY
EXP**E**CTANCY
EXP**E**DIENCE
EXP**E**DIENCY
EXP**E**DITION
EXP**E**RIENCE
EXP**E**RIMENT
FED**E**RALISM
FED**E**RALIST
FED**E**RALIZE
FED**E**RATION
FIB**E**RBOARD
FIB**E**RGLASS
FOR**E**CASTLE
FOR**E**FATHER
FOR**E**FINGER
FOR**E**GATHER
FOR**E**GROUND
FOR**E**HANDED
FOR**E**ORDAIN
FOR**E**RUNNER
FOR**E**SHADOW
FRE**E**BOOTER
GAM**E**KEEPER
GAT**E**KEEPER
GEN**E**RALITY
GEN**E**RALIZE
GEN**E**RATION
GOV**E**RNMENT
GRE**E**NHOUSE
GRE**E**NSWARD
GYN**E**COLOGY
HER**E**ABOUTS
HER**E**DITARY
HER**E**TOFORE
HOM**E**COMING
HOM**E**OPATHY
HYP**E**RBARIC
IMM**E**MORIAL
IMP**E**CCABLE
IMP**E**DIMENT
IMP**E**NITENT
IMP**E**RATIVE
IMP**E**RSONAL
IMP**E**RVIOUS
INC**E**NDIARY
IND**E**CISION
IND**E**CISIVE
IND**E**COROUS
IND**E**FINITE
IND**E**LICATE
INS**E**MINATE
INS**E**NSIBLE
INS**E**NTIENT
INT**E**GUMENT
INT**E**RBLOCK
INT**E**RBREED
INT**E**RFAITH
INT**E**RFERON
INT**E**RLEAVE
INT**E**RLUNAR
INT**E**RMARRY
INT**E**RMEZZO
INT**E**RNMENT
INT**E**RSTATE
INT**E**RSTICE
INT**E**RTIDAL
INT**E**RTWINE
INT**E**RTWIST
INT**E**RURBAN
INT**E**RWEAVE
INV**E**STMENT
INV**E**TERATE
IRR**E**LEVANT
IRR**E**SOLUTE
KIN**E**MATICS
LED**E**RHOSEN
LIB**E**RALISM
LIC**E**NTIATE
LIC**E**NTIOUS
LIF**E**SAVING
LIK**E**LIHOOD
LIN**E**BACKER
LIT**E**RALISM
LIT**E**RATURE
LIV**E**LIHOOD
LIV**E**RWURST
LOV**E**MAKING
MAL**E**FACTOR
MAL**E**FICENT
MAL**E**VOLENT
MIM**E**OGRAPH
MIN**E**RALIZE
MIN**E**RALOGY
MIN**E**STRONE
NOT**E**WORTHY
NUM**E**ROLOGY
OBS**E**QUIOUS
OBS**E**RVABLE
OBS**E**RVANCE
OFT**E**NTIMES
OST**E**NSIBLE
OST**E**OPATHY
OTH**E**RWORLD
PAP**E**RBOARD
PED**E**STRIAN
PER**E**MPTORY
PHL**E**BOTOMY
PHL**E**GMATIC
PHR**E**NOLOGY
PIG**E**ONHOLE
POT**E**NTIATE
POW**E**RHOUSE

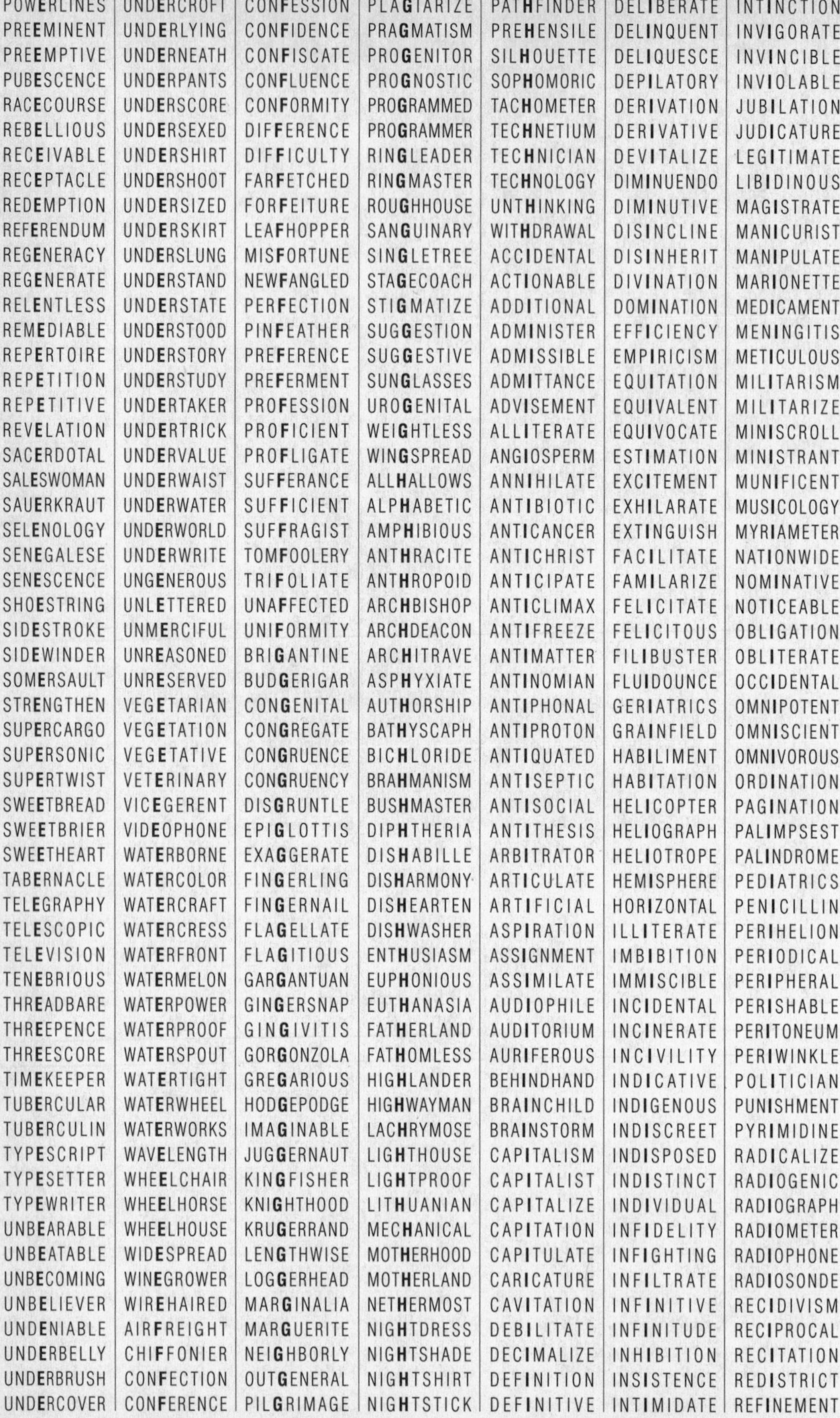

POWERLINES
PREEMINENT
PREEMPTIVE
PUBESCENCE
RACECOURSE
REBELLIOUS
RECEIVABLE
RECEPTACLE
REDEMPTION
REFERENDUM
REGENERACY
REGENERATE
RELENTLESS
REMEDIABLE
REPERTOIRE
REPETITION
REPETITIVE
REVELATION
SACERDOTAL
SALESWOMAN
SAUERKRAUT
SELENOLOGY
SENEGALESE
SENESCENCE
SHOESTRING
SIDESTROKE
SIDEWINDER
SOMERSAULT
STRENGTHEN
SUPERCARGO
SUPERSONIC
SUPERTWIST
SWEETBREAD
SWEETBRIER
SWEETHEART
TABERNACLE
TELEGRAPHY
TELESCOPIC
TELEVISION
TENEBRIOUS
THREADBARE
THREEPENCE
THREESCORE
TIMEKEEPER
TUBERCULAR
TUBERCULIN
TYPESCRIPT
TYPESETTER
TYPEWRITER
UNBEARABLE
UNBEATABLE
UNBECOMING
UNBELIEVER
UNDENIABLE
UNDERBELLY
UNDERBRUSH
UNDERCOVER

UNDERCROFT
UNDERLYING
UNDERNEATH
UNDERPANTS
UNDERSCORE
UNDERSEXED
UNDERSHIRT
UNDERSHOOT
UNDERSIZED
UNDERSKIRT
UNDERSLUNG
UNDERSTAND
UNDERSTATE
UNDERSTOOD
UNDERSTORY
UNDERSTUDY
UNDERTAKER
UNDERTRICK
UNDERVALUE
UNDERWAIST
UNDERWATER
UNDERWORLD
UNDERWRITE
UNGENEROUS
UNLETTERED
UNMERCIFUL
UNREASONED
UNRESERVED
VEGETARIAN
VEGETATION
VEGETATIVE
VETERINARY
VICEGERENT
VIDEOPHONE
WATERBORNE
WATERCOLOR
WATERCRAFT
WATERCRESS
WATERFRONT
WATERMELON
WATERPOWER
WATERPROOF
WATERSPOUT
WATERTIGHT
WATERWHEEL
WATERWORKS
WAVELENGTH
WHEELCHAIR
WHEELHORSE
WHEELHOUSE
WIDESPREAD
WINEGROWER
WIREHAIRED
AIRFREIGHT
CHIFFONIER
CONFECTION
CONFERENCE

CONFESSION
CONFIDENCE
CONFISCATE
CONFLUENCE
CONFORMITY
DIFFERENCE
DIFFICULTY
FARFETCHED
FORFEITURE
LEAFHOPPER
MISFORTUNE
NEWFANGLED
PERFECTION
PINFEATHER
PREFERENCE
PREFERMENT
PROFESSION
PROFICIENT
PROFLIGATE
SUFFERANCE
SUFFICIENT
SUFFRAGIST
TOMFOOLERY
TRIFOLIATE
UNAFFECTED
UNIFORMITY
BRIGANTINE
BUDGERIGAR
CONGENITAL
CONGREGATE
CONGRUENCE
CONGRUENCY
DISGRUNTLE
EPIGLOTTIS
EXAGGERATE
FINGERLING
FINGERNAIL
FLAGELLATE
FLAGITIOUS
GARGANTUAN
GINGERSNAP
GINGIVITIS
GORGONZOLA
GREGARIOUS
HODGEPODGE
IMAGINABLE
JUGGERNAUT
KINGFISHER
KNIGHTHOOD
KRUGERRAND
LENGTHWISE
LOGGERHEAD
MARGINALIA
MARGUERITE
NEIGHBORLY
OUTGENERAL
PILGRIMAGE

PLAGIARIZE
PRAGMATISM
PROGENITOR
PROGNOSTIC
PROGRAMMED
PROGRAMMER
RINGLEADER
RINGMASTER
ROUGHHOUSE
SANGUINARY
SINGLETREE
STAGECOACH
STIGMATIZE
SUGGESTION
SUGGESTIVE
SUNGLASSES
UROGENITAL
WEIGHTLESS
WINGSPREAD
ALLHALLOWS
ALPHABETIC
AMPHIBIOUS
ANTHRACITE
ANTHROPOID
ARCHBISHOP
ARCHDEACON
ARCHITRAVE
ASPHYXIATE
AUTHORSHIP
BATHYSCAPH
BICHLORIDE
BRAHMANISM
BUSHMASTER
DIPHTHERIA
DISHABILLE
DISHARMONY
DISHEARTEN
DISHWASHER
ENTHUSIASM
EUPHONIOUS
EUTHANASIA
FATHERLAND
FATHOMLESS
HIGHLANDER
HIGHWAYMAN
LACHRYMOSE
LIGHTHOUSE
LIGHTPROOF
LITHUANIAN
MECHANICAL
MOTHERHOOD
MOTHERLAND
NETHERMOST
NIGHTDRESS
NIGHTSHADE
NIGHTSHIRT
NIGHTSTICK

PATHFINDER
PREHENSILE
SILHOUETTE
SOPHOMORIC
TACHOMETER
TECHNETIUM
TECHNICIAN
TECHNOLOGY
UNTHINKING
WITHDRAWAL
ACCIDENTAL
ACTIONABLE
ADDITIONAL
ADMINISTER
ADMISSIBLE
ADMITTANCE
ADVISEMENT
ALLITERATE
ANGIOSPERM
ANNIHILATE
ANTIBIOTIC
ANTICANCER
ANTICHRIST
ANTICIPATE
ANTICLIMAX
ANTIFREEZE
ANTIMATTER
ANTINOMIAN
ANTIPHONAL
ANTIPROTON
ANTIQUATED
ANTISEPTIC
ANTISOCIAL
ANTITHESIS
ARBITRATOR
ARTICULATE
ARTIFICIAL
ASPIRATION
ASSIGNMENT
ASSIMILATE
AUDIOPHILE
AUDITORIUM
AURIFEROUS
BEHINDHAND
BRAINCHILD
BRAINSTORM
CAPITALISM
CAPITALIST
CAPITALIZE
CAPITATION
CAPITULATE
CARICATURE
CAVITATION
DEBILITATE
DECIMALIZE
DEFINITION
DEFINITIVE

DELIBERATE
DELINQUENT
DELIQUESCE
DEPILATORY
DERIVATION
DERIVATIVE
DEVITALIZE
DIMINUENDO
DIMINUTIVE
DISINCLINE
DISINHERIT
DIVINATION
DOMINATION
EFFICIENCY
EMPIRICISM
EQUITATION
EQUIVALENT
EQUIVOCATE
ESTIMATION
EXCITEMENT
EXHILARATE
EXTINGUISH
FACILITATE
FAMILARIZE
FELICITATE
FELICITOUS
FILIBUSTER
FLUIDOUNCE
GERIATRICS
GRAINFIELD
HABILIMENT
HABITATION
HELICOPTER
HELIOGRAPH
HELIOTROPE
HEMISPHERE
HORIZONTAL
ILLITERATE
IMBIBITION
IMMISCIBLE
INCIDENTAL
INCINERATE
INCIVILITY
INDICATIVE
INDIGENOUS
INDISCREET
INDISPOSED
INDISTINCT
INDIVIDUAL
INFIDELITY
INFIGHTING
INFILTRATE
INFINITIVE
INFINITUDE
INHIBITION
INSISTENCE
INTIMIDATE

INTINCTION
INVIGORATE
INVINCIBLE
INVIOLABLE
JUBILATION
JUDICATURE
LEGITIMATE
LIBIDINOUS
MAGISTRATE
MANICURIST
MANIPULATE
MARIONETTE
MEDICAMENT
MENINGITIS
METICULOUS
MILITARISM
MILITARIZE
MINISCROLL
MINISTRANT
MUNIFICENT
MUSICOLOGY
MYRIAMETER
NATIONWIDE
NOMINATIVE
NOTICEABLE
OBLIGATION
OBLITERATE
OCCIDENTAL
OMNIPOTENT
OMNISCIENT
OMNIVOROUS
ORDINATION
PAGINATION
PALIMPSEST
PALINDROME
PEDIATRICS
PENICILLIN
PERIHELION
PERIODICAL
PERIPHERAL
PERISHABLE
PERITONEUM
PERIWINKLE
POLITICIAN
PUNISHMENT
PYRIMIDINE
RADICALIZE
RADIOGENIC
RADIOGRAPH
RADIOMETER
RADIOPHONE
RADIOSONDE
RECIDIVISM
RECIPROCAL
RECITATION
REDISTRICT
REFINEMENT

REG**I**STRANT
REL**I**NQUISH
REM**I**TTANCE
RES**I**LIENCE
RES**I**LIENCY
RES**I**STANCE
REV**I**TALIZE
RID**I**CULOUS
RIS**I**BILITY
ROT**I**SSERIE
SAN**I**TARIAN
SAN**I**TARIUM
SAN**I**TATION
SCH**I**SMATIC
SEM**I**DRYING
SIM**I**LITUDE
SOL**I**CITOUS
SOL**I**CITUDE
SOL**I**DARITY
SPO**I**LSPORT
SPR**I**NGTIME
SPR**I**NKLING
STR**I**NGENCY
STR**I**PTEASE
TOX**I**COLOGY
UNY**I**ELDING
VAR**I**COSITY
VIS**I**BILITY
VIS**I**TATION
VIV**I**PAROUS
VOC**I**FERATE
VOC**I**FEROUS
CON**J**ECTURE
DIS**J**OINTED
PAN**J**ANDRUM
PRO**J**ECTILE
SUB**J**ECTIVE
TRA**J**ECTORY
BAC**K**GAMMON
BAC**K**GROUND
BAC**K**HANDED
BAC**K**STAIRS
BAC**K**STROKE
BAS**K**ETBALL
BOO**K**KEEPER
BOO**K**MOBILE
BOO**K**SELLER
CAN**K**ERWORM
COC**K**ATRICE
DOC**K**WORKER
FOL**K**SINGER
JAC**K**ANAPES
JAC**K**HAMMER
JAC**K**RABBIT
LAC**K**LUSTER
MAC**K**INTOSH
PAC**K**SADDLE
PAC**K**THREAD
PIC**K**ANINNY
PIC**K**POCKET
POC**K**ETBOOK
RIC**K**ETTSIA
SMO**K**ESTACK
TAS**K**MASTER
UNS**K**ILLFUL
WIC**K**ERWORK
WOR**K**BASKET
WOR**K**INGMAN
ADU**L**TERANT
ADU**L**TERATE
AFF**L**ICTIVE
AMA**L**GAMATE
AME**L**IORATE
ANG**L**OPHILE
ANG**L**OPHOBE
APO**L**ITICAL
APO**L**OGETIC
APP**L**ICABLE
APP**L**ICATOR
BAL**L**ISTICS
BEL**L**ADONNA
BEL**L**ETRIST
BEL**L**WETHER
BUL**L**HEADED
CEL**L**ARETTE
CEL**L**OPHANE
CHA**L**CEDONY
CHI**L**DBIRTH
COL**L**ARBONE
COL**L**ATERAL
COL**L**ECTIVE
COL**L**OQUIAL
COL**L**OQUIUM
CYC**L**OMETER
CYC**L**OPEDIA
DEA**L**ERSHIP
DEC**L**ASSIFY
DEC**L**ENSION
DEF**L**AGRATE
DEP**L**ORABLE
DIE**L**ECTRIC
DIL**L**YDALLY
DUP**L**ICATOR
EBU**L**LITION
EFF**L**ORESCE
EMP**L**OYMENT
EMU**L**SIFIER
EXP**L**ICABLE
FAL**L**ACIOUS
FEL**L**OWSHIP
FIE**L**DPIECE
GOA**L**KEEPER
GUI**L**LOTINE
HAL**L**ELUJAH
HOL**L**OWWARE
HUL**L**ABALOO
IMP**L**ACABLE
INC**L**INABLE
INE**L**IGIBLE
INF**L**ECTION
INF**L**EXIBLE
ING**L**ORIOUS
MIL**L**ENNIUM
MIL**L**ILITER
MIL**L**IMETER
MIL**L**STREAM
MIL**L**WRIGHT
NEG**L**IGIBLE
NUC**L**EONICS
OPA**L**ESCENT
OUT**L**ANDISH
PAL**L**BEARER
PAR**L**IAMENT
PHI**L**ISTINE
PHI**L**OSOPHY
PHY**L**ACTERY
PIL**L**OWCASE
POU**L**TRYMAN
ROL**L**ERBALL
ROL**L**ICKING
SHI**L**LELAGH
SPE**L**LBOUND
SPO**L**IATION
STA**L**ACTITE
STA**L**AGMITE
STI**L**LBIRTH
SUB**L**IMINAL
TAB**L**ECLOTH
TAB**L**ESPOON
TRO**L**LEYBUS
UNB**L**USHING
UNI**L**ATERAL
UNP**L**EASANT
VIL**L**AINOUS
VOL**L**EYBALL
WAL**L**FLOWER
WEL**L**SPRING
WIL**L**OWWARE
ABO**M**INABLE
ALI**M**ENTARY
ANE**M**OMETER
ANI**M**ADVERT
ANI**M**ALCULE
ASY**M**METRIC
BIO**M**EDICAL
CHI**M**ERICAL
CHI**M**PANZEE
COM**M**ANDANT
COM**M**ANDEER
COM**M**ENTARY
COM**M**ERCIAL
COM**M**ISSARY
COM**M**ISSION
COM**M**ODIOUS
COM**M**ONALTY
COM**M**ONWEAL
COM**M**UNIQUE
COM**M**UTATOR
COS**M**OPOLIS
CUM**M**ERBUND
DER**M**ATITIS
ECU**M**ENICAL
ELE**M**ENTARY
ENA**M**ELWARE
FLA**M**BOYANT
FOR**M**IDABLE
GOR**M**ANDIZE
GRA**M**OPHONE
HAM**M**ERHEAD
HAM**M**ERLOCK
HAR**M**ONIOUS
INI**M**ITABLE
ISO**M**ETRICS
PAR**M**IGIANA
PEN**M**ANSHIP
PER**M**AFROST
PER**M**ISSION
PER**M**ISSIVE
PRE**M**ARITAL
PRE**M**EDICAL
PRI**M**ORDIAL
PRO**M**ETHIUM
PRO**M**INENCE
PRO**M**ISSORY
PRO**M**ONTORY
PRO**M**PTBOOK
PRO**M**ULGATE
SEA**M**ANSHIP
SEA**M**STRESS
SHA**M**EFACED
SLU**M**BEROUS
TER**M**INATOR
THE**M**SELVES
THU**M**BSCREW
TRA**M**POLINE
TRE**M**ENDOUS
TRI**M**ONTHLY
UNE**M**PLOYED
VER**M**ICELLI
WHO**M**SOEVER
ALO**N**GSHORE
AMA**N**UENSIS
BLA**N**CMANGE
BOO**N**DOGGLE
BRO**N**CHITIS
BRO**N**TOSAUR
CAN**N**ONBALL
CHA**N**CELLOR
CHA**N**DELIER
CHA**N**GELING
CHA**N**GEOVER
CHA**N**NELIZE
CHI**N**CHILLA
CLI**N**GSTONE
COG**N**IZANCE
COI**N**CIDENT
CON**N**ECTION
CON**N**ECTIVE
CON**N**IPTION
COR**N**FLOWER
COR**N**STARCH
COR**N**UCOPIA
COU**N**TERACT
COU**N**TERMAN
COU**N**TERSPY
COU**N**TRYMAN
CRA**N**KSHAFT
CRE**N**ELLATE
DIN**N**ERWARE
DON**N**YBROOK
DOW**N**STAIRS
DOW**N**STREAM
DOW**N**STROKE
ECO**N**OMICAL
EMA**N**CIPATE
EVA**N**ESCENT
EVA**N**GELISM
EVA**N**GELIST
EVA**N**GELIZE
EVE**N**HANDED
FOU**N**DATION
FRA**N**CHISEE
FRA**N**CHISER
FRA**N**CHISOR
GRA**N**DCHILD
GRA**N**DSTAND
GRI**N**DSTONE
GYM**N**ASTICS
GYM**N**OSPERM
ICO**N**OCLASM
ICO**N**OCLAST
MAI**N**SPRING
MAI**N**STREAM
MIG**N**ONETTE
MOO**N**STRUCK
MOU**N**TEBANK
PAI**N**KILLER
PAI**N**TBRUSH
PAW**N**BROKER
PEN**N**YROYAL
PER**N**ICIOUS
PET**N**APPING
PHE**N**OMENON
PHO**N**OGRAPH
PIA**N**ISSIMO
PIA**N**OFORTE
PLA**N**TATION
POI**N**SETTIA
PRI**N**CELING
PRI**N**CIPLED
PRO**N**OUNCED
PUG**N**ACIOUS
QUI**N**TUPLET
RAI**N**MAKING
RHI**N**ESTONE
RHI**N**OCEROS
ROU**N**DABOUT
ROU**N**DHOUSE
SHE**N**ANIGAN
SHU**N**PIKING
SLE**N**DERIZE
STA**N**DPOINT
STA**N**DSTILL
STE**N**TORIAN
THU**N**DEROUS
TRA**N**SCRIBE
TRA**N**SCRIPT
TRA**N**SDUCER
TRA**N**SGRESS
TRA**N**SISTOR
TRA**N**SITION
TRA**N**SITIVE
TRA**N**SITORY
TRA**N**SPLANT
TRA**N**SPOLAR
TRA**N**SVERSE
TRU**N**CATION
TUR**N**BUCKLE
URI**N**ALYSIS
VER**N**ACULAR
VUL**N**ERABLE
WAI**N**WRIGHT
WHE**N**SOEVER
ABS**O**LUTION
ABS**O**LUTISM
ABS**O**RPTION
ACC**O**MPLICE
ACC**O**MPLISH
ACC**O**RDANCE
ACC**O**UNTANT
ACC**O**UNTING
ACR**O**BATICS
ACR**O**PHOBIA
AER**O**BATICS
ALC**O**HOLISM
ALT**O**GETHER
APP**O**INTIVE
APP**O**SITION
APP**O**SITIVE
ARB**O**RVITAE
ASS**O**RTMENT
ATM**O**SPHERE
AUT**O**MATION
AUT**O**MATIZE
AUT**O**MOBILE
AUT**O**MOTIVE
AUT**O**NOMOUS
AUT**O**STRADA
BEF**O**REHAND
BEL**O**NGINGS
BLO**O**DHOUND
BLO**O**DSTAIN
BLO**O**DSTONE
CAM**O**UFLAGE
CAN**O**NICALS
CAP**O**REGIME
CHL**O**RINATE
CHL**O**ROFORM
CHR**O**MOSOME
CHR**O**NOLOGY
COL**O**RATION
COL**O**RATURA
COR**O**NATION
CRY**O**GENICS
DEC**O**LORIZE
DEC**O**MPRESS
DEC**O**RATION
DEC**O**RATIVE
DEM**O**BILIZE
DEM**O**CRATIC
DEM**O**GRAPHY
DEM**O**ISELLE
DEM**O**LITION
DEM**O**NETIZE
DEM**O**NOLOGY
DEM**O**RALIZE
DEN**O**MINATE
DEN**O**TATIVE
DEN**O**UEMENT
DEP**O**LARIZE
DEP**O**PULATE
DEP**O**RTMENT
DEP**O**SITION
DEP**O**SITORY
DER**O**GATORY
DES**O**LATION
DIS**O**RDERLY
EMB**O**NPOINT
EMB**O**UCHURE
END**O**GENOUS
ENT**O**MOLOGY
ERG**O**NOMICS
ERG**O**STEROL
EUR**O**DOLLAR
EXC**O**GITATE
EXP**O**SITION
FAV**O**RITISM
FLO**O**DLIGHT
FLO**O**DPLAIN

FLOODWATER
FLOORBOARD
FLUORIDATE
FLUORINATE
GADOLINIUM
GONOCOCCUS
HEMOGLOBIN
HEMOPHILIA
HEMORRHAGE
HEMORRHOID
HOLOGRAPHY
HOMOGENIZE
HOMOLOGOUS
HOMOSEXUAL
HONORARIUM
HYPOCENTER
HYPODERMIC
HYPOTENUSE
HYPOTHESIS
IDIOPATHIC
IGNORAMOUS
IMMOBILIZE
IMMODERATE
IMMORALITY
IMPORTANCE
IMPOSSIBLE
IMPOVERISH
INCOHERENT
INCOMPLETE
INCONSTANT
INDONESIAN
INNOMINATE
INNOVATION
INSOLATION
INSOLVABLE
INTOLERANT
INTONATION
INTOXICANT
INTOXICATE
INVOCATION
INVOLUTION
IONOSPHERE
LABORATORY
LOCOMOTION
LOCOMOTIVE
MALODOROUS
MAYONNAISE
MEMORANDUM
MESOSPHERE
MISOGAMIST
MISOGYNIST
MONOCHROME
MONOPHONIC
MONOTHEISM
MONOTONOUS
MOTORCYCLE
MOTORTRUCK
NANOSECOND
NAPOLEONIC
OCTOTHORPE
OESOPHAGUS
PEJORATIVE
PERORATION
PICOSECOND
PILOTHOUSE
RECOILLESS
RECOMPENSE
RECONSIDER
REPORTEDLY
REPOSITORY
RESOLUTION
RESORPTION
RESOUNDING
REVOCATION
REVOLUTION
RIBOFLAVIN
SCHOLASTIC
SCHOOLGIRL
SCHOOLMARM
SCHOOLMATE
SCHOOLROOM
SECONDHAND
STRONGHOLD
SUBORBITAL
THROMBOSIS
THROUGHOUT
THROUGHPUT
THROUGHWAY
TOPOGRAPHY
TYPOGRAPHY
UPHOLSTERY
UPROARIOUS
VELOCIPEDE
XENOPHOBIA
XEROGRAPHY
AUSPICIOUS
BESPRINKLE
BIOPHYSICS
CAMPHORATE
CHAPFALLEN
COLPORTEUR
COMPARABLE
COMPARISON
COMPASSION
COMPATIBLE
COMPATRIOT
COMPENDIUM
COMPENSATE
COMPETENCE
COMPETENCY
COMPETITOR
COMPLECTED
COMPLEMENT
COMPLEXION
COMPLIANCE
COMPLIANCY
COMPLICATE
COMPLICITY
COMPLIMENT
COMPOSITOR
COMPREHEND
COMPROMISE
COMPULSION
COMPULSIVE
COMPULSORY
COMPUSERVE
COPPERHEAD
CORPULENCE
COWPUNCHER
CRYPTOGRAM
DELPHINIUM
DESPICABLE
DIAPHANOUS
DISPENSARY
DISPOSABLE
DISPOSSESS
DYSPROSIUM
GEOPHYSICS
GRAPEFRUIT
HIPPODROME
HOSPITABLE
INAPTITUDE
INOPERABLE
MORPHOLOGY
OUTPATIENT
OUTPERFORM
OUTPOURING
PEPPERCORN
PEPPERMINT
PERPETRATE
PERPETUATE
PERPETUITY
PLUPERFECT
PREPACKAGE
PREPOSSESS
PROPAGANDA
PROPELLANT
PROPENSITY
PROPERTIED
PROPITIATE
PROPITIOUS
PROPORTION
PROPRIETOR
PROPRINTER
PROPULSION
RESPECTING
RESPECTIVE
RESPIRATOR
RESPONDENT
RESPONSIVE
SCAPEGRACE
SEMPSTRESS
SERPENTINE
SHIPFITTER
SHIPWRIGHT
SHOPKEEPER
SIMPLICITY
SIMPLISTIC
SKEPTICISM
SLIPSTREAM
SNAPDRAGON
STEPFATHER
STEPLADDER
STEPMOTHER
STEPPARENT
STEPSISTER
STUPENDOUS
SUPPLEMENT
SUPPLICANT
SUPPLICATE
SUSPENSION
SUSPENSORY
SUSPICIOUS
SYMPATHIZE
TEMPERANCE
TEMPTATION
TRIPARTITE
TRIPLICATE
TURPENTINE
VESPERTINE
WEAPONLESS
WRAPAROUND
CINQUEFOIL
DISQUALIFY
INEQUALITY
MASQUERADE
PERQUISITE
UBIQUITOUS
ABBREVIATE
ABERRATION
ABORIGINAL
ACHROMATIC
AGGRANDIZE
AGGRESSION
AGGRESSIVE
AMERINDIAN
APPRECIATE
APPRENTICE
ASTRINGENT
ATTRACTANT
ATTRACTION
BATRACHIAN
BEDRAGGLED
CHARACTERY
CHARITABLE
CHARLESTON
CHARTREUSE
CHIROMANCY
CHURCHGOER
CHURCHLESS
CHURCHYARD
CITRONELLA
CLERESTORY
COORDINATE
CORRESPOND
CORRIGIBLE
COURTHOUSE
CURRICULUM
DECRYPTION
DEGRADABLE
DEPRECIATE
DEPRESSANT
DEPRESSION
DEPRESSIVE
DISRESPECT
DOORKEEPER
EFFRONTERY
EMBROIDERY
EMBRYOLOGY
ENCRYPTION
ESCRITOIRE
EVERYTHING
EVERYWHERE
EXORBITANT
EXPRESSION
EXPRESSMAN
EXPRESSWAY
EXTRAMURAL
EXTRANEOUS
EXURBANITE
FAHRENHEIT
FAIRGROUND
FIBRINOGEN
FOURSQUARE
GUARDHOUSE
HEARTBREAK
HEARTHSIDE
HEARTTHROB
HIEROPHANT
HORRENDOUS
HYDRAULICS
HYDROLYSIS
HYDROMETER
HYDROPHONE
HYDROPLANE
HYGROMETER
IMPREGNATE
IMPRESARIO
IMPRESSION
IMPRESSIVE
IMPRIMATUR
IMPROBABLE
INBREEDING
INCREDIBLE
INFRACTION
INFRASONIC
INFREQUENT
INGRATIATE
INGREDIENT
INORDINATE
INTRAMURAL
INTRASTATE
JINRIKISHA
JOURNALESE
JOURNALISM
JOURNEYMAN
LAWRENCIUM
LEPRECHAUN
LIPREADING
LOGROLLING
LUBRICIOUS
MARROWBONE
MEERSCHAUM
METROPOLIS
MICROFICHE
MICROGRAPH
MICROMETER
MICROPHONE
MICROPROBE
MICROSCOPE
MICROSTATE
NECROMANCY
NECROPOLIS
NOURISHING
OPPRESSION
OPPROBRIUM
OUTRAGEOUS
OVERCHARGE
OVERMASTER
OVERSHADOW
OVERSPREAD
OVERWINTER
PATRONYMIC
PETROLATUM
POURPARLER
PUTRESCENT
QUARANTINE
RECREATION
REFRACTION
REFRACTORY
REFRINGENT
REGRESSION
RETRACTILE
RETROGRADE
RETROGRESS
RETROSPECT
SACROILIAC
SACROSANCT
SAPROPHYTE
SCARLATINA
SCURRILOUS
SEARCHWARE
SEERSUCKER
SHORTENING
SPIRITUOUS
SPIROCHETE
SPORTSCAST
STARVELING
STEREOTYPE
STOREHOUSE
SUBROUTINE
SURREALISM
TEARJERKER
TETRAMETER
THEREAFTER
THERMISTOR
THERMOSTAT
TORRENTIAL
TOURMALINE
TOURNAMENT
TOURNIQUET
ULTRASHORT
ULTRASONIC
ULTRASOUND
UNCRITICAL
UNFRIENDLY
UNFRUITFUL
UNGRACEFUL
UNGRACIOUS
UNGRATEFUL
UNGROUNDED
UPBRINGING
VIBRAPHONE
WHARFINGER
WHIRLYBIRD
ANESTHESIA
ANESTHETIC
APOSTROPHE
BOISTEROUS
BOLSHEVISM
CENSORIOUS
CENSORSHIP
CLASSICISM
CLASSIFIED
CONSCIENCE
CONSECRATE
CONSEQUENT
CONSISTORY
CONSONANCE
CONSORTIUM
CONSPECTUS
CONSPIRACY
CONSTITUTE
CONSTRAINT
CONSUMMATE
CRISSCROSS
CROSSBONES
CROSSBREED
CROSSPIECE

CRUSTACEAN
DIPSOMANIA
DISSATISFY
DISSENSION
DISSERVICE
DISSIMILAR
DISSOCIATE
DISSONANCE
EMASCULATE
EPISCOPACY
EPISCOPATE
ERYSIPELAS
EVISCERATE
EXASPERATE
FARSIGHTED
FLASHLIGHT
FRESHWATER
FUSSBUDGET
GEOSCIENCE
GHOSTWRITE
GOOSEBERRY
GOOSEFLESH
GUNSLINGER
HORSEFLESH
HORSELAUGH
HORSEPOWER
HORSEWOMAN
HOUSECLEAN
HOUSEWARES
JIMSONWEED
KIESELGUHR
MAISONETTE
MANSERVANT
MANSUETUDE
MENSURABLE
MIDSHIPMAN
MISSILEMAN
MISSIONARY
MONSTRANCE
MUDSLINGER
NEWSGROUPS
NEWSLETTER
NEWSWORTHY
NOISEMAKER
NONSTARTER
NONSUPPORT
NURSERYMAN
PASSAGEWAY
PEASHOOTER
PERSIFLAGE
PERSONABLE
PERSONALTY
PERSUASION
PHOSPHORUS
PHYSIOLOGY
POSSESSION
POSSESSIVE

PRESBYOPIA
PRESBYTERY
PRESCIENCE
PRESSURIZE
PRESUPPOSE
PROSCENIUM
PROSPECTUS
PROSPERITY
PROSPEROUS
PROSTHESIS
PROSTITUTE
RAMSHACKLE
REASONABLE
ROUSTABOUT
SEASONABLE
SEISMOGRAM
SEISMOLOGY
SKYSCRAPER
SUBSEQUENT
SUBSIDIARY
SUBSTATION
SUBSTITUTE
SUBSTRATUM
SUBSURFACE
TESSELLATE
UNASSUMING
WORSHIPFUL
WRISTWATCH
ABSTEMIOUS
ABSTINENCE
AESTHETICS
APOTHECARY
APOTHEOSIS
ARITHMETIC
AUCTIONEER
AUSTRALIAN
BAPTISTERY
BASTARDIZE
BATTLEMENT
BATTLESHIP
BESTIALITY
BETTERMENT
BIRTHPLACE
BIRTHRIGHT
BIRTHSTONE
BLITZKRIEG
BOTTLENECK
BOTTOMLAND
BUTTERMILK
BUTTONHOLE
BUTTONHOOK
CANTALOUPE
CANTILEVER
CANTONMENT
CENTENNIAL
CENTESIMAL
CENTIGRADE

CENTILITER
CENTIMETER
CENTRALIZE
CENTRIFUGE
CHATELAINE
CHATTERBOX
CLOTHESPIN
CONTAGIOUS
CONTENTION
CONTIGUOUS
CONTINENCE
CONTINGENT
CONTINUITY
CONTINUOUS
CONTRABAND
CONTRADICT
CONTRAVENE
CONTRIBUTE
CONTROLLER
CONTROVERT
COTTONSEED
COTTONTAIL
COTTONWOOD
CRETACEOUS
CUTTLEFISH
DEATHWATCH
DENTIFRICE
DESTRUCTOR
DICTIONARY
DISTILLATE
DISTRAUGHT
DISTRIBUTE
EARTHQUAKE
EISTEDDFOD
EPITHELIUM
EXOTHERMIC
FACTITIOUS
FASTIDIOUS
FERTILIZER
FICTITIOUS
FISTICUFFS
FOOTBRIDGE
FOOTLIGHTS
FOOTLOCKER
FORTHRIGHT
FORTISSIMO
FORTUITOUS
FOSTERLING
FRATERNITY
FRATERNIZE
FRATRICIDE
GASTRONOMY
GENTLEFOLK
GEOTHERMAL
GRATUITOUS
HEATSTROKE
HECTOLITER

HECTOMETER
HEPTAMETER
HINTERLAND
HISTRIONIC
HOOTENANNY
INITIATIVE
INITIATORY
INSTRUCTOR
INSTRUMENT
ISOTHERMAL
KETTLEDRUM
LETTERHEAD
MALTHUSIAN
MANTLEROCK
MARTINGALE
MASTERMIND
MASTERSHIP
MASTERWORK
METTLESOME
MISTAKABLE
MOUTHPIECE
MULTILEVEL
MULTIMEDIA
MULTIPLIER
MULTISENSE
MULTISTAGE
MULTISTORY
NASTURTIUM
NETTLESOME
NEUTRALISM
NEUTRALITY
NEUTRALIZE
OBSTETRICS
OPHTHALMIC
ORATORICAL
PANTALOONS
PANTYWAIST
PARTICIPLE
PARTICULAR
PASTEBOARD
PASTEURIZE
PENTAMETER
PESTILENCE
PHOTOFLASH
PHOTOGENIC
PHOTOGRAPH
PHOTOMETER
PHOTOMURAL
PHOTOPAINT
PLUTOCRACY
PORTCULLIS
PORTENTOUS
PORTUGUESE
POSTHUMOUS
POSTMASTER
POSTMORTEM
POSTPARTUM

POSTSCRIPT
PROTECTION
PROTESTANT
PROTOPLASM
PROTRACTOR
QUATREFOIL
RATTLETRAP
RESTAURANT
RESTORABLE
RESTRAINED
SALTCELLAR
SEPTICEMIA
SEPTUAGINT
SETTLEMENT
SHUTTERBUG
SISTERHOOD
SKATEBOARD
SMATTERING
SOOTHSAYER
SPITTLEBUG
STATECRAFT
STATEHOUSE
STATIONARY
STATIONERY
STATISTICS
STATUESQUE
SUBTERFUGE
SUBTRAHEND
SUSTENANCE
SWITCHBACK
TANTAMOUNT
TATTERSALL
TATTLETALE
TEETHRIDGE
TOOTHBRUSH
TOOTHPASTE
TURTLEDOVE
TURTLENECK
UNATTACHED
UPSTANDING
URETHRITIS
VERTEBRATE
VICTORIOUS
VICTUALLER
VIETNAMESE
VIRTUOSITY
WASTEPAPER
WEATHERING
WEATHERMAN
WESTERNIZE
WHATSOEVER
WHITSUNDAY
WINTERTIDE
WINTERTIME
WORTHWHILE
YESTERYEAR
ACCUMULATE

ACCUSATIVE
ACCUSTOMED
ADJUDICATE
ALBUMINOUS
AMBULATORY
AMMUNITION
ANNUNCIATE
ASSUMPTION
BALUSTRADE
BEAUJOLAIS
BEAUTICIAN
BITUMINOUS
CALUMNIATE
CAOUTCHOUC
CHAUVINISM
CLOUDBURST
CUMULATIVE
DEHUMANIZE
DEHUMIDIFY
DEPUTATION
EFFULGENCE
ESCUTCHEON
FIGURATION
FIGURATIVE
FIGUREHEAD
FRAUDULENT
FUTURISTIC
GESUNDHEIT
GROUNDLING
GROUNDMASS
GROUNDWORK
ILLUMINATE
ILLUSTRATE
IMMUNOLOGY
INAUGURATE
INCULPABLE
INCUMBENCY
INDUCEMENT
INDUCTANCE
INDULGENCE
INDUSTRIAL
INHUMANITY
INJUNCTION
INQUIETUDE
LIEUTENANT
LOQUACIOUS
LUGUBRIOUS
MANUSCRIPT
MATURATION
MONUMENTAL
NATURALISM
NATURALIST
NATURALIZE
NEBULOSITY
OCCUPATION
OCCURRENCE
POPULATION

PSEUDOCODE
RECUPERATE
REDUNDANCY
REFULGENCE
REGULATION
REJUVENATE
RELUCTANCE
REMUNERATE
REPUBLICAN
REPUGNANCE
REPUTATION
RESURGENCE
RHEUMATISM
SALUBRIOUS
SALUTATION
SCRUTINIZE
SECULARISM
SECULARIZE
SEPULCHRAL
THOUGHTFUL
TROUBADOUR
TUMULTUOUS
UNDULATION
UNNUMBERED
UNSUITABLE
VITUPERATE
VOLUMETRIC
VOLUMINOUS
VOLUPTUARY
VOLUPTUOUS
ABOVEBOARD
CANVASBACK
CHIVALROUS
CLAVICHORD
CLOVERLEAF
CONVALESCE
CONVECTION
CONVENIENT
CONVENTION
CONVERSANT
CONVERSION
CONVEYANCE
CONVICTION
CONVOLUTED
CONVULSION
CURVACEOUS
GRAVESTONE
GRAVIMETER
INEVITABLE
PERVERSION
PRIVILEGED
PROVENANCE
PROVIDENCE
PROVINCIAL
SERVICEMAN
SERVOMOTOR
SILVERFISH

SILVERWARE
SUBVENTION
TRAVELOGUE
TRAVERTINE
UNAVAILING
UNEVENTFUL
UNIVERSITY
ANSWERABLE
BROWNSTONE
DRAWBRIDGE
DRAWSTRING
EYEWITNESS
SKYWRITING
SNOWMOBILE
INEXORABLE
INEXPIABLE
UNEXAMPLED
UNEXPECTED
CHRYSOLITE
COPYREADER
COPYWRITER
ENCYCLICAL
LADYFINGER
LARYNGITIS
MOLYBDENUM
PLAYACTING
PLAYGROUND
PLAYWRIGHT
POLYCLINIC
POLYHEDRON
POLYNESIAN
POLYTHEISM
STRYCHNINE
MIZZENMAST
MOZZARELLA
PRIZEFIGHT

## 5TH LETTER

AGGRANDIZE
ALLHALLOWS
ALPHABETIC
ANIMADVERT
ANIMALCULE
APOCALYPSE
APPEARANCE
ATTRACTANT
ATTRACTION
BASTARDIZE
BATRACHIAN
BEDRAGGLED
BELLADONNA
BOMBARDIER
BRIGANTINE
CALCAREOUS
CANTALOUPE
CANVASBACK
CELLARETTE
CHARACTERY
CHIVALROUS
COCKATRICE
COLLARBONE
COLLATERAL
COMMANDANT
COMMANDEER
COMPARABLE
COMPARISON
COMPASSION
COMPATIBLE
COMPATRIOT
CONTAGIOUS
CONVALESCE
CRETACEOUS
CURVACEOUS
DECLASSIFY
DEFLAGRATE
DEGRADABLE
DERMATITIS
DISHABILLE
DISHARMONY
DISSATISFY
DOGCATCHER
ENDEARMENT
EUTHANASIA
EXTRAMURAL
EXTRANEOUS
FALLACIOUS
FLYCATCHER
GARGANTUAN
GERIATRICS
GORMANDIZE
GREGARIOUS
GYMNASTICS
HEPTAMETER
HEREABOUTS
HULLABALOO
HUSBANDMAN
HYDRAULICS
IMPLACABLE
INFRACTION
INFRASONIC
INGRATIATE
INTRAMURAL
INTRASTATE
JACKANAPES
LOQUACIOUS
MECHANICAL
MENDACIOUS
MERCANTILE
MISTAKABLE
MOZZARELLA
MYRIAMETER
NEWFANGLED
OUTBALANCE
OUTLANDISH
OUTPATIENT
OUTRAGEOUS
PANJANDRUM
PANTALOONS
PASSAGEWAY
PECCADILLO
PEDIATRICS
PENMANSHIP
PENTAMETER
PERMAFROST
PETNAPPING
PHYLACTERY
PICCALILLI
PICKANINNY
PLAYACTING
PRECARIOUS
PRECAUTION
PREDACEOUS
PREMARITAL
PREPACKAGE
PROPAGANDA
PUGNACIOUS
QUARANTINE
REFRACTION
REFRACTORY
RESTAURANT
RETRACTILE
SANDALWOOD
SEAMANSHIP
SHENANIGAN
STALACTITE
STALAGMITE
SYMPATHIZE
TANTAMOUNT
TETRAMETER
THREADBARE
TRIPARTITE
ULTRASHORT
ULTRASONIC
ULTRASOUND
UNAVAILING
UNBEARABLE
UNBEATABLE
UNEXAMPLED
UNGRACEFUL
UNGRACIOUS
UNGRATEFUL
UNICAMERAL
UNILATERAL
UNREASONED
UPROARIOUS
UPSTANDING
URINALYSIS
VERNACULAR
VIBRAPHONE
VILLAINOUS
WRAPAROUND
ACROBATICS
AEROBATICS
ANTEBELLUM
ANTIBIOTIC
ARCHBISHOP
BLUEBONNET
BLUEBOTTLE
CARABINEER
CATABOLISM
CELEBRATED
CEREBELLUM
DELIBERATE
DEMOBILIZE
DRAWBRIDGE
EXORBITANT
EXURBANITE
FILIBUSTER
FLAMBOYANT
FOOTBRIDGE
FREEBOOTER
FUSSBUDGET
GOLDBEATER
HANDBARROW
IMBIBITION
IMMOBILIZE
INHABITANT
INHIBITION
LINEBACKER
LUGUBRIOUS
METABOLISM
METABOLITE
MOLYBDENUM
NOTABILITY
PALLBEARER
PAWNBROKER
PHLEBOTOMY
PRESBYOPIA
PRESBYTERY
REPUBLICAN
RISIBILITY
SALUBRIOUS
SHIBBOLETH
SLUMBEROUS
TENEBRIOUS
THUMBSCREW
TROUBADOUR
TURNBUCKLE
VISIBILITY
VOCABULARY
WORKBASKET
ANTECEDENT
ANTICANCER
ANTICHRIST
ANTICIPATE
ANTICLIMAX
ARTICULATE
ATTACHMENT
BLANCMANGE
BLUECOLLAR
BRONCHITIS
CAPACITATE
CARICATURE
CATECHUMEN
CHALCEDONY
CHANCELLOR
CHINCHILLA
CHURCHGOER
CHURCHLESS
CHURCHYARD
COINCIDENT
CONSCIENCE
DELECTABLE
DEMOCRATIC
DETACHMENT
EFFECTUATE
EFFICIENCY
EMANCIPATE
EMASCULATE
ENCYCLICAL
EPISCOPACY
EPISCOPATE
EVISCERATE
EXPECTANCY
FELICITATE
FELICITOUS
FORECASTLE
FRANCHISEE
FRANCHISER
FRANCHISOR
GEOSCIENCE
GONOCOCCUS
GYNECOLOGY
HELICOPTER
HOMECOMING
HYPOCENTER
IMMACULATE
IMPECCABLE
INDECISION
INDECISIVE
INDECOROUS
INDICATIVE
INDUCEMENT
INDUCTANCE
INVOCATION
JUDICATURE
MANICURIST
MEDICAMENT
METACARPUS
METICULOUS
MONOCHROME
MUSICOLOGY
NOTICEABLE
OVERCHARGE
PENICILLIN
POLYCLINIC
PORTCULLIS
PRESCIENCE
PRINCELING
PRINCIPLED
PROSCENIUM
RACECOURSE
RADICALIZE
RELUCTANCE
REVOCATION
RIDICULOUS
SALTCELLAR
SEARCHWARE
SKYSCRAPER
SOLICITOUS
SOLICITUDE
STRYCHNINE
SWITCHBACK
TOXICOLOGY
TRUNCATION
UNBECOMING
UNOCCUPIED
VARICOSITY
VELOCIPEDE
WOODCUTTER
ACCIDENTAL
ADJUDICATE
ARCHDEACON
BLOODHOUND
BLOODSTAIN
BLOODSTONE
BOONDOGGLE
BREADBOARD
BREADFRUIT
BREADSTUFF
BROADCLOTH
BROADSWORD
CHANDELIER
CHILDBIRTH
CLOUDBURST
COMEDIENNE
COORDINATE
ESPADRILLE
EURODOLLAR
EXPEDIENCE
EXPEDIENCY
EXPEDITION
FIELDPIECE
FLOODLIGHT
FLOODPLAIN
FLOODWATER
FLUIDOUNCE
FOUNDATION
FRAUDULENT
GRANDCHILD
GRANDSTAND
GRINDSTONE
GUARDHOUSE
HEREDITARY
HYPODERMIC
IMMODERATE
IMPEDIMENT
INCIDENTAL
INFIDELITY
INORDINATE
LIBIDINOUS
MALADAPTED
MALODOROUS
OCCIDENTAL
PSEUDOCODE
RECIDIVISM
REMEDIABLE
ROUNDABOUT
ROUNDHOUSE
SEMIDRYING
SLENDERIZE
SNAPDRAGON
SOLIDARITY
STANDPOINT
STANDSTILL
THUNDEROUS
WITHDRAWAL
ABBREVIATE
ABOVEBOARD
ABSTEMIOUS
AGGRESSION
AGGRESSIVE
ALIMENTARY
ANSWERABLE
APPRECIATE
APPRENTICE
BALDERDASH
BASKETBALL
BELLETRIST
BETTERMENT
BIOMEDICAL
BORDERLAND
BRIDEGROOM
BRIDESMAID
BUDGERIGAR
BUTTERMILK
CANDELABRA
CANDESCENT
CANKERWORM
CENTENNIAL
CENTESIMAL
CHATELAINE
CHIMERICAL
CLERESTORY
CLOVERLEAF
COLLECTIVE

COMMENTARY
COMMERCIAL
COMPENDIUM
COMPENSATE
COMPETENCE
COMPETENCY
COMPETITOR
CONCENTRIC
CONCEPTION
CONCERNING
CONCERTINA
CONCESSION
CONCESSIVE
CONDENSATE
CONDESCEND
CONFECTION
CONFERENCE
CONFESSION
CONGENITAL
CONJECTURE
CONNECTION
CONNECTIVE
CONSECRATE
CONSEQUENT
CONTENTION
CONVECTION
CONVENIENT
CONVENTION
CONVERSANT
CONVERSION
CONVEYANCE
COPPERHEAD
CORRESPOND
CREDENTIAL
CRENELLATE
CUMMERBUND
DEALERSHIP
DECLENSION
DEPRECIATE
DEPRESSANT
DEPRESSION
DEPRESSIVE
DESCENDANT
DIELECTRIC
DIFFERENCE
DINNERWARE
DISBELIEVE
DISCERNING
DISHEARTEN
DISPENSARY
DISRESPECT
DISSENSION
DISSERVICE
DUNDERHEAD
DUODECIMAL
ECUMENICAL
EGOCENTRIC
EISTEDDFOD
ELEMENTARY
ENAMELWARE
EVANESCENT
EXACERBATE
EXPRESSION
EXPRESSMAN
EXPRESSWAY
FAHRENHEIT
FARFETCHED
FATHERLAND
FINGERLING
FINGERNAIL
FLAGELLATE
FORFEITURE
FOSTERLING
FRATERNITY
FRATERNIZE
GEOCENTRIC
GINGERSNAP
GOOSEBERRY
GOOSEFLESH
GRAPEFRUIT
GRAVESTONE
HALLELUJAH
HAMMERHEAD
HAMMERLOCK
HENCEFORTH
HINTERLAND
HODGEPODGE
HOOTENANNY
HORRENDOUS
HORSEFLESH
HORSELAUGH
HORSEPOWER
HORSEWOMAN
HOUSECLEAN
HOUSEWARES
IMPREGNATE
IMPRESARIO
IMPRESSION
IMPRESSIVE
INADEQUATE
INBREEDING
INCREDIBLE
INFLECTION
INFLEXIBLE
INFREQUENT
INGREDIENT
INOPERABLE
ISOMETRICS
JUGGERNAUT
KIESELGUHR
KRUGERRAND
LAWRENCIUM
LEPRECHAUN
LETTERHEAD
LIPREADING
LOGGERHEAD
LUMBERJACK
LUMBERYARD
MAIDENHAIR
MAIDENHEAD
MAIDENHOOD
MANDELBROT
MANSERVANT
MASTERMIND
MASTERSHIP
MASTERWORK
MEMBERSHIP
MILLENNIUM
MISCELLANY
MIZZENMAST
MOTHERHOOD
MOTHERLAND
NETHERMOST
NOISEMAKER
NUCLEONICS
NUMBERLESS
NURSERYMAN
OBSTETRICS
OPALESCENT
OPPRESSION
OUTGENERAL
OUTPERFORM
PASTEBOARD
PASTEURIZE
PEACEMAKER
PEPPERCORN
PEPPERMINT
PERCENTAGE
PERCENTILE
PERCEPTION
PERCEPTIVE
PERCEPTUAL
PERFECTION
PERPETRATE
PERPETUATE
PERPETUITY
PERVERSION
PINFEATHER
PLUPERFECT
POCKETBOOK
PORTENTOUS
POSSESSION
POSSESSIVE
PREBENDARY
PRECEDENCE
PRECESSION
PREDECEASE
PREDESTINE
PREFERENCE
PREFERMENT
PREHENSILE
PREMEDICAL
PRIZEFIGHT
PROCEEDING
PROCESSION
PROFESSION
PROGENITOR
PROJECTILE
PROMETHIUM
PROPELLANT
PROPENSITY
PROPERTIED
PROTECTION
PROTESTANT
PROVENANCE
PUTRESCENT
READERSHIP
RECREATION
REGRESSION
RENDEZVOUS
RESPECTING
RESPECTIVE
RHINESTONE
RICKETTSIA
ROLLERBALL
RUBBERNECK
SCAPEGRACE
SERPENTINE
SHAMEFACED
SILVERFISH
SILVERWARE
SISTERHOOD
SKATEBOARD
SMOKESTACK
SPACECRAFT
STAGECOACH
STATECRAFT
STATEHOUSE
STEREOTYPE
STOREHOUSE
STUPENDOUS
SUBJECTIVE
SUBSEQUENT
SUBTERFUGE
SUBVENTION
SUCCESSION
SUCCESSIVE
SUFFERANCE
SUGGESTION
SUGGESTIVE
SURREALISM
SUSPENSION
SUSPENSORY
SUSTENANCE
TABLECLOTH
TABLESPOON
TATTERSALL
TEMPERANCE
TENDERFOOT
TENDERLOIN
TESSELLATE
THEREAFTER
THREEPENCE
THREESCORE
TIMBERLINE
TORRENTIAL
TRAJECTORY
TRAVELOGUE
TRAVERTINE
TREMENDOUS
TURPENTINE
UNEVENTFUL
UNIVERSITY
UNPLEASANT
UNYIELDING
UROGENITAL
VAUDEVILLE
VERTEBRATE
VESPERTINE
VOICEPRINT
VOLLEYBALL
VULNERABLE
WANDERLUST
WASTEPAPER
WESTERNIZE
WICKERWORK
WILDEBEEST
WILDERNESS
WINTERTIDE
WINTERTIME
WONDERLAND
WONDERMENT
WOODENWARE
YESTERYEAR
ANTIFREEZE
ARTIFICIAL
AURIFEROUS
BENEFACTOR
BENEFICENT
BENEFICIAL
CATAFALQUE
CHAPFALLEN
CHIFFONIER
CORNFLOWER
FOREFATHER
FOREFINGER
INDEFINITE
KINGFISHER
LADYFINGER
MALEFACTOR
MALEFICENT
MUNIFICENT
PATHFINDER
RIBOFLAVIN
SHIPFITTER
STEPFATHER
UNAFFECTED
VOCIFERATE
VOCIFEROUS
WALLFLOWER
WHARFINGER
WINDFLOWER
ALLEGIANCE
ALONGSHORE
ALTOGETHER
AMALGAMATE
ANTAGONISM
ANTAGONIST
ANTAGONIZE
ARMAGEDDON
ASSIGNMENT
BACKGAMMON
BACKGROUND
BRIDGEHEAD
BRIDGEWORK
CATEGORIZE
CHANGELING
CHANGEOVER
CLINGSTONE
CRYOGENICS
DELEGATION
DEMOGRAPHY
DEROGATORY
ENDOGENOUS
ENGAGEMENT
EVANGELISM
EVANGELIST
EVANGELIZE
EXAGGERATE
EXCOGITATE
FAIRGROUND
FOREGATHER
FOREGROUND
HEMOGLOBIN
HOLOGRAPHY
HOMOGENIZE
INAUGURATE
INDIGENOUS
INFIGHTING
INTEGUMENT
INVIGORATE
MANAGEMENT
METAGALAXY
MISOGAMIST
MISOGYNIST
NEWSGROUPS
OBLIGATION
OLEAGINOUS
PHLEGMATIC
PLAYGROUND
REPAGINATE
REPUGNANCE
SENEGALESE
TELEGRAPHY
THOUGHTFUL
TOPOGRAPHY
TYPOGRAPHY
VICEGERENT
WINEGROWER
XEROGRAPHY
AESTHETICS
ALCOHOLISM
ANNIHILATE
APOTHECARY
APOTHEOSIS
ARITHMETIC
BACKHANDED
BAREHEADED
BENCHMARKS
BIOPHYSICS
BIRTHPLACE
BIRTHRIGHT
BIRTHSTONE
BOLSHEVISM
BONDHOLDER
BULLHEADED
CAMPHORATE
CATCHPENNY
CLODHOPPER
CLOTHESPIN
DEATHWATCH
DELPHINIUM
DIAPHANOUS
EARTHQUAKE
EPITHELIUM
EVENHANDED
EXOTHERMIC
FLASHLIGHT
FOREHANDED
FORTHRIGHT
FRESHWATER
GEOPHYSICS
GEOTHERMAL
HARDHEADED
INCOHERENT
ISOTHERMAL
JACKHAMMER
KNIGHTHOOD
LANDHOLDER
LEAFHOPPER
MALTHUSIAN
MATCHMAKER
MIDSHIPMAN
MORPHOLOGY
MOUTHPIECE
NEIGHBORLY
NONCHALANT
OPHTHALMIC
PEASHOOTER

PERIHELION
POLYHEDRON
POSTHUMOUS
PSYCHIATRY
PSYCHOLOGY
PSYCHOPATH
RAMSHACKLE
ROUGHHOUSE
SACCHARINE
SOOTHSAYER
STOCHASTIC
TEETHRIDGE
TOOTHBRUSH
TOOTHPASTE
TOUCHSTONE
UNSCHOOLED
URETHRITIS
WATCHMAKER
WATCHTOWER
WEATHERING
WEATHERMAN
WEIGHTLESS
WINCHESTER
WIREHAIRED
WITCHCRAFT
WITCHGRASS
WORSHIPFUL
WORTHWHILE
ABOMINABLE
ABORIGINAL
ABSCISSION
ABSTINENCE
AFFLICTIVE
AFICIONADO
AMELIORATE
AMERINDIAN
AMPHIBIOUS
APOLITICAL
APPLICABLE
APPLICATOR
APPOINTIVE
ARCHITRAVE
ASTRINGENT
ATTAINMENT
AUCTIONEER
AUSPICIOUS
BALLISTICS
BAPTISTERY
BESTIALITY
CACCIATORE
CANTILEVER
CARCINOGEN
CARDIOGRAM
CARDIOLOGY
CENTIGRADE
CENTILITER
CENTIMETER
CHARITABLE
CLAVICHORD
COGNIZANCE
COMMISSARY
COMMISSION
CONCILIATE
CONFIDENCE
CONFISCATE
CONNIPTION
CONSISTORY
CONTIGUOUS
CONTINENCE
CONTINGENT
CONTINUITY
CONTINUOUS
CONVICTION
CORDILLERA
CORRIGIBLE
CREDITABLE
CURRICULUM
DEMOISELLE
DENTIFRICE
DESPICABLE
DICTIONARY
DIFFICULTY
DISCIPLINE
DISSIMILAR
DISTILLATE
DUPLICATOR
ERYSIPELAS
ESCRITOIRE
EXOBIOLOGY
EXPLICABLE
EYEWITNESS
FACTITIOUS
FARSIGHTED
FASTIDIOUS
FERTILIZER
FIBRINOGEN
FICTITIOUS
FISTICUFFS
FLAGITIOUS
FORBIDDING
FORMIDABLE
FORTISSIMO
GINGIVITIS
GLACIOLOGY
GRAVIMETER
HANDICRAFT
HOSPITABLE
IMAGINABLE
IMPRIMATUR
INCLINABLE
INELIGIBLE
INEVITABLE
INIMITABLE
INITIATIVE
INITIATORY
INQUIETUDE
JARDINIERE
JINRIKISHA
LASCIVIOUS
LUBRICIOUS
MACKINTOSH
MARGINALIA
MARTINGALE
MILLILITER
MILLIMETER
MISSILEMAN
MISSIONARY
MULTILEVEL
MULTIMEDIA
MULTIPLIER
MULTISENSE
MULTISTAGE
MULTISTORY
NARCISSISM
NEGLIGIBLE
NOURISHING
PARLIAMENT
PARMIGIANA
PARTICIPLE
PARTICULAR
PERCIPIENT
PERMISSION
PERMISSIVE
PERNICIOUS
PERSIFLAGE
PESTILENCE
PHILISTINE
PHYSIOLOGY
PIANISSIMO
PLAGIARIZE
PLEBISCITE
PRECIOSITY
PREDICABLE
PREDISPOSE
PRIVILEGED
PRODIGIOUS
PROFICIENT
PROMINENCE
PROMISSORY
PROPITIATE
PROPITIOUS
PROVIDENCE
PROVINCIAL
RECEIVABLE
RECOILLESS
REFRINGENT
RESPIRATOR
ROLLICKING
SEPTICEMIA
SERVICEMAN
SPECIALIST
SPECIALIZE
SPIRITUOUS
SPOLIATION
STATIONARY
STATIONERY
STATISTICS
STRAIGHTEN
SUBLIMINAL
SUBSIDIARY
SUFFICIENT
SUSPICIOUS
TERMINATOR
UNCRITICAL
UNFAITHFUL
UNFRIENDLY
UNSKILLFUL
UNSUITABLE
UNTHINKING
UPBRINGING
VERMICELLI
VINDICTIVE
WORKINGMAN
BEAUJOLAIS
BLUEJACKET
TEARJERKER
WINDJAMMER
BLACKAMOOR
BLACKBERRY
BLACKBOARD
BLACKGUARD
BLACKSMITH
BLACKTHORN
BLOCKHOUSE
BOOKKEEPER
BREAKFRONT
BREAKWATER
BRICKLAYER
CHECKPOINT
CRANKSHAFT
DOORKEEPER
GAMEKEEPER
GATEKEEPER
GOALKEEPER
KNICKKNACK
KNOCKWURST
PAINKILLER
QUICKBASIC
SHOPKEEPER
TIMEKEEPER
ABSOLUTION
ABSOLUTISM
ACCELERATE
ALKALINIZE
AMBULATORY
AQUALUNGER
BATTLEMENT
BATTLESHIP
BEDCLOTHES
BICHLORIDE
BOTTLENECK
BOWDLERIZE
CAMELOPARD
CANDLEWICK
CHARLESTON
COMPLECTED
COMPLEMENT
COMPLEXION
COMPLIANCE
COMPLIANCY
COMPLICATE
COMPLICITY
COMPLIMENT
CONCLUSION
CONFLUENCE
CRADLESONG
CUMULATIVE
CUTTLEFISH
DEBILITATE
DECELERATE
DECOLORIZE
DEMOLITION
DEPILATORY
DEPOLARIZE
DESALINATE
DESALINIZE
DESOLATION
EBULLITION
EFFULGENCE
EPIGLOTTIS
EUCALYPTUS
EXCELLENCE
EXCELLENCY
EXHILARATE
FACILITATE
FAMILARIZE
FOOTLIGHTS
FOOTLOCKER
GADOLINIUM
GENTLEFOLK
GUILLOTINE
GUNSLINGER
HABILIMENT
HANDLEBARS
HIGHLANDER
HOMOLOGOUS
IMPALPABLE
INCULPABLE
INDELICATE
INDULGENCE
INFALLIBLE
INFILTRATE
INSOLATION
INSOLVABLE
INTOLERANT
INVALIDATE
INVALUABLE
INVOLUTION
IRRELEVANT
JUBILATION
KETTLEDRUM
LACKLUSTER
LANDLOCKED
LANDLUBBER
LIKELIHOOD
LIVELIHOOD
MANTLEROCK
MEDDLESOME
METALLURGY
METTLESOME
MIDDLEBROW
MISALIGNED
MUDSLINGER
NAPOLEONIC
NEBULOSITY
NEEDLEWORK
NEOCLASSIC
NETTLESOME
NEWSLETTER
POPULATION
PROCLIVITY
PROFLIGATE
RATTLETRAP
REBELLIOUS
REFULGENCE
REGULATION
RESILIENCE
RESILIENCY
RESOLUTION
REVELATION
REVOLUTION
RINGLEADER
SCARLATINA
SCHOLASTIC
SECULARISM
SECULARIZE
SEPULCHRAL
SETTLEMENT
SHILLELAGH
SIMILITUDE
SIMPLICITY
SIMPLISTIC
SINGLETREE
SPELLBOUND
SPOILSPORT
STEPLADDER
STILLBIRTH
SUNGLASSES
SUPPLEMENT
SUPPLICANT
SUPPLICATE
TATTLETALE
TRIPLICATE
TROLLEYBUS
TUMBLEDOWN
TUMBLEWEED
TUMULTUOUS
TURTLEDOVE
TURTLENECK
UNBALANCED
UNBELIEVER
UNDULATION
UNHALLOWED
UPHOLSTERY
WAVELENGTH
WHEELCHAIR
WHEELHORSE
WHEELHOUSE
WHIRLYBIRD
ACCOMPLICE
ACCOMPLISH
ACCUMULATE
ALBUMINOUS
ANTIMATTER
AQUAMARINE
ASSEMBLAGE
ASSIMILATE
ASSUMPTION
ASYMMETRIC
AUTOMATION
AUTOMATIZE
AUTOMOBILE
AUTOMOTIVE
BITUMINOUS
BOOKMOBILE
BRAHMANISM
BUSHMASTER
CALUMNIATE
CEREMONIAL
CHROMOSOME
DATAMATION
DECIMALIZE
DECOMPRESS
DEHUMANIZE
DEHUMIDIFY
DENOMINATE
DISEMBOWEL
DREAMWORLD
EFFEMINATE
ENJAMBMENT
ENTOMOLOGY
ESTIMATION
HANDMAIDEN
HEADMASTER
ILLUMINATE
IMMEMORIAL
INCOMPLETE
INCUMBENCY
INHUMANITY

INNOMINATE
INSEMINATE
INTIMIDATE
KINEMATICS
LOCOMOTION
LOCOMOTIVE
LOVEMAKING
MOHAMMEDAN
MONUMENTAL
MUHAMMADAN
OVERMASTER
PALIMPSEST
PARAMECIUM
PEREMPTORY
POSTMASTER
POSTMORTEM
PRAGMATISM
PREEMINENT
PREEMPTIVE
PYRIMIDINE
RAGAMUFFIN
RAINMAKING
RECOMPENSE
REDEMPTION
RHEUMATISM
RINGMASTER
SALAMANDER
SEISMOGRAM
SEISMOLOGY
SNOWMOBILE
STEPMOTHER
STIGMATIZE
TASKMASTER
THERMISTOR
THERMOSTAT
THROMBOSIS
TOURMALINE
UNFAMILIAR
UNNUMBERED
VOLUMETRIC
VOLUMINOUS
YARDMASTER
ACCENTUATE
ADMINISTER
ADRENALINE
ADVENTURER
AMMUNITION
ANNUNCIATE
ANTINOMIAN
ASCENDANCY
ATTENDANCE
AUTONOMOUS
BEHINDHAND
BELONGINGS
BRAINCHILD
BRAINSTORM
BROWNSTONE

CANONICALS
CHANNELIZE
CHRONOLOGY
CORONATION
DEFINITION
DEFINITIVE
DEGENERACY
DEGENERATE
DELINQUENT
DEMONETIZE
DEMONOLOGY
DEPENDABLE
DEPENDENCE
DEPENDENCY
DIMINUENDO
DIMINUTIVE
DISENCHANT
DISINCLINE
DISINHERIT
DIVINATION
DOMINATION
EMBANKMENT
EMBONPOINT
ENDANGERED
EQUANIMITY
ERGONOMICS
EXTINGUISH
GESUNDHEIT
GRAINFIELD
GREENHOUSE
GREENSWARD
GROUNDLING
GROUNDMASS
GROUNDWORK
IMMUNOLOGY
IMPENITENT
INCENDIARY
INCINERATE
INCONSTANT
INDONESIAN
INFINITIVE
INFINITUDE
INJUNCTION
INSENSIBLE
INSENTIENT
INTANGIBLE
INTINCTION
INTONATION
INVINCIBLE
JOURNALESE
JOURNALISM
JOURNEYMAN
LARYNGITIS
LICENTIATE
LICENTIOUS
LOGANBERRY
MAYONNAISE

MELANCHOLY
MELANESIAN
MENINGITIS
NOMINATIVE
OCEANARIUM
OCEANFRONT
OCEANGOING
OCEANOLOGY
OFTENTIMES
ORDINATION
ORGANGUTAN
OSTENSIBLE
PAGINATION
PALINDROME
PHRENOLOGY
POLYNESIAN
POTENTIATE
PROGNOSTIC
RECONSIDER
REDUNDANCY
REFINEMENT
REGENERACY
REGENERATE
RELENTLESS
RELINQUISH
REMUNERATE
SECONDHAND
SELENOLOGY
SPRINGTIME
SPRINKLING
STRENGTHEN
STRINGENCY
STRONGHOLD
TARANTELLA
TECHNETIUM
TECHNICIAN
TECHNOLOGY
TOURNAMENT
TOURNIQUET
TYRANNICAL
UNDENIABLE
UNGENEROUS
UNHANDSOME
UNMANNERLY
VIETNAMESE
ACHROMATIC
ACTIONABLE
ANEMOMETER
ANGIOSPERM
ANGLOPHILE
ANGLOPHOBE
APOLOGETIC
AUDIOPHILE
AUTHORSHIP
BOTTOMLAND
BUTTONHOLE
BUTTONHOOK

CANNONBALL
CANTONMENT
CARBOLATED
CELLOPHANE
CENSORIOUS
CENSORSHIP
CHIROMANCY
CITRONELLA
COLLOQUIAL
COLLOQUIUM
COLPORTEUR
COMMODIOUS
COMMONALTY
COMMONWEAL
COMPOSITOR
CONCORDANT
CONFORMITY
CONSONANCE
CONSORTIUM
CONVOLUTED
COSMOPOLIS
COTTONSEED
COTTONTAIL
COTTONWOOD
CYCLOMETER
CYCLOPEDIA
DEPLORABLE
DIPSOMANIA
DISCOMFORT
DISCOMMODE
DISCOMPOSE
DISCONCERT
DISCONNECT
DISCONTENT
DISCOURAGE
DISJOINTED
DISPOSABLE
DISPOSSESS
DISSOCIATE
DISSONANCE
ECONOMICAL
EFFLORESCE
EFFRONTERY
EMBROIDERY
EMPLOYMENT
EUPHONIOUS
FATHOMLESS
FELLOWSHIP
FOREORDAIN
GORGONZOLA
GRAMOPHONE
GYMNOSPERM
HARMONIOUS
HECTOLITER
HECTOMETER
HELIOGRAPH
HELIOTROPE

HIEROPHANT
HIPPODROME
HOLLOWWARE
HOMEOPATHY
HYDROLYSIS
HYDROMETER
HYDROPHONE
HYDROPLANE
HYGROMETER
ICONOCLASM
ICONOCLAST
IMPROBABLE
INEXORABLE
INGLORIOUS
INVIOLABLE
JIMSONWEED
LOGROLLING
MAISONETTE
MALCONTENT
MARIONETTE
MARROWBONE
MEADOWLARK
METROPOLIS
MICROFICHE
MICROGRAPH
MICROMETER
MICROPHONE
MICROPROBE
MICROSCOPE
MICROSTATE
MIGNONETTE
MIMEOGRAPH
MISCONDUCT
MISFORTUNE
NATIONWIDE
NECROMANCY
NECROPOLIS
NINCOMPOOP
OPPROBRIUM
ORATORICAL
OSTEOPATHY
OUTPOURING
PATRONYMIC
PERIODICAL
PERSONABLE
PERSONALTY
PETROLATUM
PHENOMENON
PHILOSOPHY
PHONOGRAPH
PHOTOFLASH
PHOTOGENIC
PHOTOGRAPH
PHOTOMETER
PHOTOMURAL
PHOTOPAINT
PIANOFORTE

PIGEONHOLE
PILLOWCASE
PLUTOCRACY
PRECOCIOUS
PREPOSSESS
PRIMORDIAL
PROMONTORY
PRONOUNCED
PROPORTION
PROTOPLASM
RADIOGENIC
RADIOGRAPH
RADIOMETER
RADIOPHONE
RADIOSONDE
REASONABLE
RESPONDENT
RESPONSIVE
RESTORABLE
RETROGRADE
RETROGRESS
RETROSPECT
RHINOCEROS
SACROILIAC
SACROSANCT
SAPROPHYTE
SCHOOLGIRL
SCHOOLMARM
SCHOOLMATE
SCHOOLROOM
SEASONABLE
SERVOMOTOR
SILHOUETTE
SOPHOMORIC
SPIROCHETE
SUBCOMPACT
SUBROUTINE
TACHOMETER
TAMBOURINE
TOMFOOLERY
TRIFOLIATE
TRIMONTHLY
UNGROUNDED
UNIFORMITY
VICTORIOUS
VIDEOPHONE
WEAPONLESS
WILLOWWARE
WINDOWPANE
WINDOWSILL
ACCEPTABLE
ACCEPTANCE
ACROPHOBIA
ANTEPENULT
ANTIPHONAL
ANTIPROTON
CHEAPSKATE

CHIMPANZEE
CONSPECTUS
CONSPIRACY
DECAPITATE
DEPOPULATE
DISAPPOINT
DISAPPROVE
EXASPERATE
HEMOPHILIA
IDIOPATHIC
INCAPACITY
INEXPIABLE
MALAPROPOS
MANIPULATE
MONOPHONIC
OCCUPATION
OESOPHAGUS
OMNIPOTENT
PARAPHRASE
PARAPLEGIA
PERIPHERAL
PHOSPHORUS
PICKPOCKET
POSTPARTUM
POURPARLER
PROMPTBOOK
PROSPECTUS
PROSPERITY
PROSPEROUS
RECEPTACLE
RECIPROCAL
RECUPERATE
SHUNPIKING
STEPPARENT
STRIPTEASE
TRAMPOLINE
UNEMPLOYED
UNEXPECTED
VITUPERATE
VIVIPAROUS
VOLUPTUARY
VOLUPTUOUS
WOODPECKER
XENOPHOBIA
ANTIQUATED
DELIQUESCE
OBSEQUIOUS
ABERRATION
ABSORPTION
ACCORDANCE
AFTERBIRTH
AFTERIMAGE
AFTERTASTE
AIRFREIGHT
ALTARPIECE
ALTERNATOR
ANTHRACITE

ANTH**R**OPOID
APOC**R**YPHAL
APPA**R**ITION
ARBO**R**VITAE
ASPI**R**ATION
ASSO**R**TMENT
AUST**R**ALIAN
BALB**R**IGGAN
BEFO**R**EHAND
BESP**R**INKLE
BIPA**R**ENTAL
BIPA**R**IETAL
BIPA**R**TISAN
CAPO**R**EGIME
CENT**R**ALIZE
CENT**R**IFUGE
CHLO**R**INATE
CHLO**R**OFORM
CINE**R**ARIUM
COLO**R**ATION
COLO**R**ATURA
COMP**R**EHEND
COMP**R**OMISE
CONC**R**ETION
CONG**R**EGATE
CONG**R**UENCE
CONG**R**UENCY
CONT**R**ABAND
CONT**R**ADICT
CONT**R**AVENE
CONT**R**IBUTE
CONT**R**OLLER
CONT**R**OVERT
COPY**R**EADER
COTE**R**MINAL
CYBE**R**SPACE
DECO**R**ATION
DECO**R**ATIVE
DEMO**R**ALIZE
DEND**R**OLOGY
DEPA**R**TMENT
DEPO**R**TMENT
DESE**R**VEDLY
DEST**R**UCTOR
DETE**R**MINED
DETE**R**RENCE
DISA**R**RANGE
DISC**R**EPANT
DISC**R**ETION
DISG**R**UNTLE
DISO**R**DERLY
DIST**R**AUGHT
DIST**R**IBUTE
DYSP**R**OSIUM
EFFE**R**VESCE
ELDE**R**BERRY
EMPI**R**ICISM
ENTE**R**PRISE
ESCA**R**PMENT
EXPE**R**IENCE
EXPE**R**IMENT
EYED**R**OPPER
FAVO**R**ITISM
FEDE**R**ALISM
FEDE**R**ALIST
FEDE**R**ALIZE
FEDE**R**ATION
FIBE**R**BOARD
FIBE**R**GLASS
FIGU**R**ATION
FIGU**R**ATIVE
FIGU**R**EHEAD
FLOO**R**BOARD
FLUO**R**IDATE
FLUO**R**INATE
FORE**R**UNNER
FRAT**R**ICIDE
FUTU**R**ISTIC
GAST**R**ONOMY
GENE**R**ALITY
GENE**R**ALIZE
GENE**R**ATION
GOVE**R**NMENT
HEMO**R**RHAGE
HEMO**R**RHOID
HIST**R**IONIC
HONO**R**ARIUM
HYPE**R**BARIC
ICEB**R**EAKER
IGNO**R**AMOUS
IMMO**R**ALITY
IMPE**R**ATIVE
IMPE**R**SONAL
IMPE**R**VIOUS
IMPO**R**TANCE
INST**R**UCTOR
INST**R**UMENT
INTE**R**BLOCK
INTE**R**BREED
INTE**R**FAITH
INTE**R**FERON
INTE**R**LEAVE
INTE**R**LUNAR
INTE**R**MARRY
INTE**R**MEZZO
INTE**R**NMENT
INTE**R**STATE
INTE**R**STICE
INTE**R**TIDAL
INTE**R**TWINE
INTE**R**TWIST
INTE**R**URBAN
INTE**R**WEAVE
INVA**R**IABLE
JACK**R**ABBIT
JAWB**R**EAKER
LABO**R**ATORY
LACH**R**YMOSE
LAWB**R**EAKER
LEDE**R**HOSEN
LIBE**R**ALISM
LITE**R**ALISM
LITE**R**ATURE
LIVE**R**WURST
MAND**R**AGORA
MATU**R**ATION
MEMO**R**ANDUM
MINE**R**ALIZE
MINE**R**ALOGY
MONA**R**CHIST
MOTO**R**CYCLE
MOTO**R**TRUCK
NATU**R**ALISM
NATU**R**ALIST
NATU**R**ALIZE
NEUT**R**ALISM
NEUT**R**ALITY
NEUT**R**ALIZE
NOND**R**INKER
NUME**R**OLOGY
NUTC**R**ACKER
OBSE**R**VABLE
OBSE**R**VANCE
OCCU**R**RENCE
OTHE**R**WORLD
PAPE**R**BOARD
PEJO**R**ATIVE
PERO**R**ATION
PICA**R**ESQUE
PILG**R**IMAGE
POWE**R**HOUSE
POWE**R**LINES
PREA**R**RANGE
PROG**R**AMMED
PROG**R**AMMER
PROP**R**IETOR
PROP**R**INTER
PROT**R**ACTOR
QUAD**R**ANGLE
QUAD**R**ATICS
QUAD**R**IVIUM
QUAD**R**UPLET
QUAT**R**EFOIL
RADA**R**SCOPE
REFE**R**ENDUM
REMA**R**KABLE
REPA**R**ATION
REPA**R**ATIVE
REPE**R**TOIRE
REPO**R**TEDLY
RESO**R**PTION
REST**R**AINED
RESU**R**GENCE
ROAD**R**UNNER
SACE**R**DOTAL
SAUE**R**KRAUT
SCUR**R**ILOUS
SEPA**R**ATION
SEPA**R**ATIST
SEPA**R**ATIVE
SKYW**R**ITING
SOME**R**SAULT
SUBO**R**BITAL
SUBT**R**AHEND
SUFF**R**AGIST
SUPE**R**CARGO
SUPE**R**SONIC
SUPE**R**TWIST
TABE**R**NACLE
TUBE**R**CULAR
TUBE**R**CULIN
UNAB**R**IDGED
UNDE**R**BELLY
UNDE**R**BRUSH
UNDE**R**COVER
UNDE**R**CROFT
UNDE**R**LYING
UNDE**R**NEATH
UNDE**R**PANTS
UNDE**R**SCORE
UNDE**R**SEXED
UNDE**R**SHIRT
UNDE**R**SHOOT
UNDE**R**SIZED
UNDE**R**SKIRT
UNDE**R**SLUNG
UNDE**R**STAND
UNDE**R**STATE
UNDE**R**STOOD
UNDE**R**STORY
UNDE**R**STUDY
UNDE**R**TAKER
UNDE**R**TRICK
UNDE**R**VALUE
UNDE**R**WAIST
UNDE**R**WATER
UNDE**R**WORLD
UNDE**R**WRITE
UNME**R**CIFUL
UNSC**R**AMBLE
VETE**R**INARY
WATE**R**BORNE
WATE**R**COLOR
WATE**R**CRAFT
WATE**R**CRESS
WATE**R**FRONT
WATE**R**MELON
WATE**R**POWER
WATE**R**PROOF
WATE**R**SPOUT
WATE**R**TIGHT
WATE**R**WHEEL
WATE**R**WORKS
ACCE**S**SIBLE
ACCU**S**ATIVE
ACCU**S**TOMED
ADMI**S**SIBLE
ADVI**S**EMENT
AMBA**S**SADOR
ANTI**S**EPTIC
ANTI**S**OCIAL
APPO**S**ITION
APPO**S**ITIVE
ATMO**S**PHERE
AUTO**S**TRADA
BACK**S**TAIRS
BACK**S**TROKE
BALU**S**TRADE
BOOK**S**ELLER
BREA**S**TBONE
BREA**S**TWORK
CHEE**S**ECAKE
CHRY**S**OLITE
CLAS**S**ICISM
CLAS**S**IFIED
COME**S**TIBLE
CORN**S**TARCH
CRIS**S**CROSS
CROS**S**BONES
CROS**S**BREED
CROS**S**PIECE
DEPO**S**ITION
DEPO**S**ITORY
DOWN**S**TAIRS
DOWN**S**TREAM
DOWN**S**TROKE
DRAW**S**TRING
EMUL**S**IFIER
EQUE**S**TRIAN
ERGO**S**TEROL
EXPO**S**ITION
FOLK**S**INGER
FORE**S**HADOW
FOUR**S**QUARE
HAND**S**PRING
HEAD**S**TRONG
HEAT**S**TROKE
HEMI**S**PHERE
HOMO**S**EXUAL
ILLU**S**TRATE
IMMI**S**CIBLE
IMPA**S**SABLE
IMPA**S**SIBLE
IMPO**S**SIBLE
INDI**S**CREET
INDI**S**POSED
INDI**S**TINCT
INDU**S**TRIAL
INSI**S**TENCE
INVE**S**TMENT
IONO**S**PHERE
IRRE**S**OLUTE
LIFE**S**AVING
MAGI**S**TRATE
MAIN**S**PRING
MAIN**S**TREAM
MANU**S**CRIPT
MARA**S**CHINO
MEER**S**CHAUM
MESO**S**PHERE
META**S**TASIS
MILL**S**TREAM
MINE**S**TRONE
MINI**S**CROLL
MINI**S**TRANT
MOON**S**TRUCK
NANO**S**ECOND
OCCA**S**IONAL
OMNI**S**CIENT
OVER**S**HADOW
OVER**S**PREAD
PACK**S**ADDLE
PEDE**S**TRIAN
PERI**S**HABLE
PICO**S**ECOND
PLEA**S**ANTRY
POIN**S**ETTIA
POST**S**CRIPT
PRES**S**URIZE
PUBE**S**CENCE
PUNI**S**HMENT
REDI**S**TRICT
REGI**S**TRANT
RENA**S**CENCE
REPO**S**ITORY
RESI**S**TANCE
ROTI**S**SERIE
SALE**S**WOMAN
SCHI**S**MATIC
SEAM**S**TRESS
SEER**S**UCKER
SEMP**S**TRESS
SENE**S**CENCE
SHOE**S**TRING
SIDE**S**TROKE
SLIP**S**TREAM
SPLA**S**HDOWN
STEP**S**ISTER
TELE**S**COPIC
THEM**S**ELVES
TRAN**S**CRIBE
TRAN**S**CRIPT
TRAN**S**DUCER
TRAN**S**GRESS
TRAN**S**ISTOR
TRAN**S**ITION
TRAN**S**ITIVE
TRAN**S**ITORY
TRAN**S**PLANT
TRAN**S**POLAR
TRAN**S**VERSE
TYPE**S**CRIPT
TYPE**S**ETTER
UNAS**S**UMING
UNRE**S**ERVED
WELL**S**PRING
WHAT**S**OEVER
WHEN**S**OEVER
WHIT**S**UNDAY
WHOM**S**OEVER
WIDE**S**PREAD
WIND**S**HIELD
WING**S**PREAD
ADDI**T**IONAL
ADMI**T**TANCE
ADUL**T**ERANT
ADUL**T**ERATE
ALLI**T**ERATE
ANES**T**HESIA
ANES**T**HETIC
ANTI**T**HESIS
APOS**T**ROPHE
APPE**T**IZING
ARBI**T**RATOR
AUDI**T**ORIUM
BEAU**T**ICIAN
BIME**T**ALLIC
BOIS**T**EROUS
BRON**T**OSAUR
CAOU**T**CHOUC
CAPI**T**ALISM
CAPI**T**ALIST
CAPI**T**ALIZE
CAPI**T**ATION
CAPI**T**ULATE
CAVI**T**ATION
CHAR**T**REUSE
CHAT**T**ERBOX
CONS**T**ITUTE
CONS**T**RAINT
COUN**T**ERACT
COUN**T**ERMAN
COUN**T**ERSPY
COUN**T**RYMAN
COUR**T**HOUSE
CRUS**T**ACEAN
CRYP**T**OGRAM
DEAC**T**IVATE
DENO**T**ATIVE

DEPUTATION
DEVITALIZE
DILETTANTE
DIPHTHERIA
ELECTORATE
ELECTRONIC
EQUITATION
ESCUTCHEON
EXACTITUDE
EXCITEMENT
EXPATRIATE
GHOSTWRITE
HABITATION
HEARTBREAK
HEARTHSIDE
HEARTTHROB
HEMATOLOGY
HERETOFORE
HYPOTENUSE
HYPOTHESIS
ILLITERATE
IMMATERIAL
IMPATIENCE
INACTIVATE
INAPTITUDE
INSATIABLE
INVETERATE
IRRATIONAL
LEGITIMATE
LENGTHWISE
LIEUTENANT
LIGHTHOUSE
LIGHTPROOF
METATARSAL
METATARSUS
MILITARISM
MILITARIZE
MONOTHEISM
MONOTONOUS
MONSTRANCE
MORATORIUM
MOUNTEBANK
NATATORIUM
NEGATIVISM
NIGHTDRESS
NIGHTSHADE
NIGHTSHIRT
NIGHTSTICK
NONSTARTER
OBLITERATE
OCTOTHORPE
PACKTHREAD
PAINTBRUSH
PALATALIZE
PALATINATE
PARATROOPS
PERITONEUM

PILOTHOUSE
PLANTATION
POLITICIAN
POLYTHEISM
POULTRYMAN
PROSTHESIS
PROSTITUTE
QUINTUPLET
REACTIVATE
RECITATION
RELATIONAL
RELATIVITY
REMITTANCE
REPATRIATE
REPETITION
REPETITIVE
REPUTATION
REVITALIZE
ROUSTABOUT
SALUTATION
SANATORIUM
SANITARIAN
SANITARIUM
SANITATION
SCRUTINIZE
SHORTENING
SHUTTERBUG
SKEPTICISM
SMATTERING
SPITTLEBUG
SPORTSCAST
STENTORIAN
SUBSTATION
SUBSTITUTE
SUBSTRATUM
SWEETBREAD
SWEETBRIER
SWEETHEART
TEMPTATION
THEATRICAL
UNATTACHED
UNLETTERED
VEGETARIAN
VEGETATION
VEGETATIVE
VISITATION
WRISTWATCH
ACCOUNTANT
ACCOUNTING
AMANUENSIS
CALCULATED
CAMOUFLAGE
CARBURETOR
CINQUEFOIL
CIRCUITOUS
CIRCUMCISE
CIRCUMFLEX

CIRCUMVENT
COMBUSTION
COMMUNIQUE
COMMUTATOR
COMPULSION
COMPULSIVE
COMPULSORY
COMPUSERVE
CONCURRENT
CONCUSSION
CONDUCTIVE
CONSUMMATE
CONVULSION
CORNUCOPIA
CORPULENCE
COWPUNCHER
DENOUEMENT
DISCURSIVE
DISCUSSANT
DISQUALIFY
EMBOUCHURE
ENTHUSIASM
EXHAUSTION
EXHAUSTIVE
FORTUITOUS
GRADUALISM
GRADUATION
GRATUITOUS
INEQUALITY
LITHUANIAN
MANSUETUDE
MARGUERITE
MASQUERADE
MENSURABLE
NASTURTIUM
NONSUPPORT
PERCUSSION
PERDURABLE
PERQUISITE
PERSUASION
PINCUSHION
PORTUGUESE
PRESUPPOSE
PROCURATOR
PRODUCTION
PROMULGATE
PROPULSION
RESOUNDING
SANGUINARY
SEPTUAGINT
STATUESQUE
SUBSURFACE
THROUGHOUT
THROUGHPUT
THROUGHWAY
TURBULENCE
UBIQUITOUS

UNBLUSHING
UNFRUITFUL
VICTUALLER
VIRTUOSITY
ASSEVERATE
CADAVEROUS
CHAUVINISM
DERIVATION
DERIVATIVE
EQUIVALENT
EQUIVOCATE
IMPOVERISH
INCIVILITY
INDIVIDUAL
INNOVATION
MALEVOLENT
OMNIVOROUS
REJUVENATE
STARVELING
TELEVISION
BELLWETHER
COPYWRITER
CORDWAINER
DEADWEIGHT
DISHWASHER
DOCKWORKER
DUMBWAITER
HEADWAITER
HIGHWAYMAN
MILLWRIGHT
NEWSWORTHY
NOTEWORTHY
OVERWINTER
PERIWINKLE
PLAYWRIGHT
SHIPWRIGHT
SIDEWINDER
STRAWBERRY
TYPEWRITER
WAINWRIGHT
INTOXICANT
INTOXICATE
RELAXATION
ASPHYXIATE
BATHYSCAPH
DECRYPTION
DILLYDALLY
DONNYBROOK
EMBRYOLOGY
ENCRYPTION
EVERYTHING
EVERYWHERE
HOBBYHORSE
PANTYWAIST
PENNYROYAL
BLITZKRIEG
HORIZONTAL

## 6th Letter

ABERRATION
ACCUSATIVE
ACROBATICS
ADRENALINE
AEROBATICS
AMALGAMATE
AMBULATORY
ANTHRACITE
ANTICANCER
ANTIMATTER
AQUAMARINE
ASPIRATION
AUSTRALIAN
AUTOMATION
AUTOMATIZE
BACKGAMMON
BACKHANDED
BENEFACTOR
BESTIALITY
BIMETALLIC
BLACKAMOOR
BLUEJACKET
BRAHMANISM
BUSHMASTER
CACCIATORE
CAPITALISM
CAPITALIST
CAPITALIZE
CAPITATION
CARICATURE
CATAFALQUE
CAVITATION
CENTRALIZE
CHAPFALLEN
CHIMPANZEE
CINERARIUM
COLORATION
COLORATURA
CONTRABAND
CONTRADICT
CONTRAVENE
CORDWAINER
CORONATION
CRUSTACEAN
CUMULATIVE
DATAMATION
DECIMALIZE
DECORATION
DECORATIVE
DEHUMANIZE
DELEGATION
DEMORALIZE
DENOTATIVE
DEPILATORY
DEPOLARIZE

DEPUTATION
DERIVATION
DERIVATIVE
DEROGATORY
DESOLATION
DEVITALIZE
DIAPHANOUS
DISHEARTEN
DISHWASHER
DISQUALIFY
DISTRAUGHT
DIVINATION
DOMINATION
DUMBWAITER
EQUITATION
EQUIVALENT
ESTIMATION
EVENHANDED
EXHILARATE
EXURBANITE
FAMILARIZE
FEDERALISM
FEDERALIST
FEDERALIZE
FEDERATION
FIGURATION
FIGURATIVE
FORECASTLE
FOREFATHER
FOREGATHER
FOREHANDED
FOUNDATION
GENERALITY
GENERALIZE
GENERATION
GRADUALISM
GRADUATION
HABITATION
HANDBARROW
HANDMAIDEN
HEADMASTER
HEADWAITER
HIGHLANDER
HIGHWAYMAN
HONORARIUM
IDIOPATHIC
IGNORAMOUS
IMMORALITY
IMPERATIVE
INCAPACITY
INDICATIVE
INEQUALITY
INHUMANITY
INITIATIVE
INITIATORY
INNOVATION
INSOLATION

INTONATION
INVOCATION
JACKHAMMER
JACKRABBIT
JOURNALESE
JOURNALISM
JUBILATION
JUDICATURE
KINEMATICS
LABORATORY
LIBERALISM
LIFESAVING
LINEBACKER
LIPREADING
LITERALISM
LITERATURE
LITHUANIAN
LOVEMAKING
MALADAPTED
MALEFACTOR
MANDRAGORA
MATURATION
MEDICAMENT
MEMORANDUM
METACARPUS
METAGALAXY
METATARSAL
METATARSUS
MILITARISM
MILITARIZE
MINERALIZE
MINERALOGY
MISOGAMIST
NATURALISM
NATURALIST
NATURALIZE
NEOCLASSIC
NEUTRALISM
NEUTRALITY
NEUTRALIZE
NOMINATIVE
NONCHALANT
NONSTARTER
NUTCRACKER
OBLIGATION
OCCUPATION
OCEANARIUM
OPHTHALMIC
ORDINATION
OVERMASTER
PACKSADDLE
PAGINATION
PALATALIZE
PARLIAMENT
PEJORATIVE
PERORATION
PERSUASION

PINFEATHER
PLAGIARIZE
PLANTATION
PLEASANTRY
POPULATION
POSTMASTER
POSTPARTUM
POURPARLER
PRAGMATISM
PROGRAMMED
PROGRAMMER
PROTRACTOR
QUADRANGLE
QUADRATICS
RADICALIZE
RAINMAKING
RAMSHACKLE
RECITATION
RECREATION
REGULATION
RELAXATION
REPARATION
REPARATIVE
REPUTATION
RESTRAINED
REVELATION
REVITALIZE
REVOCATION
RHEUMATISM
RINGMASTER
ROUNDABOUT
ROUSTABOUT
SACCHARINE
SALAMANDER
SALUTATION
SANITARIAN
SANITARIUM
SANITATION
SCARLATINA
SCHOLASTIC
SECULARISM
SECULARIZE
SENEGALESE
SEPARATION
SEPARATIST
SEPARATIVE
SEPTUAGINT
SOLIDARITY
SPECIALIST
SPECIALIZE
SPOLIATION
STEPFATHER
STEPLADDER
STEPPARENT
STIGMATIZE
STOCHASTIC
SUBSTATION
SUBTRAHEND
SUFFRAGIST
SUNGLASSES
SURREALISM
TASKMASTER
TEMPTATION
THEREAFTER
TOURMALINE
TOURNAMENT
TROUBADOUR
TRUNCATION
UNATTACHED
UNBALANCED
UNDULATION
UNPLEASANT
UNSCRAMBLE
VEGETARIAN
VEGETATION
VEGETATIVE
VICTUALLER
VIETNAMESE
VISITATION
VIVIPAROUS
WINDJAMMER
WIREHAIRED
WORKBASKET
YARDMASTER
ABOVEBOARD
AFTERBIRTH
ALPHABETIC
AMPHIBIOUS
ASSEMBLAGE
BLACKBERRY
BLACKBOARD
BREADBOARD
CHILDBIRTH
CLOUDBURST
CROSSBONES
CROSSBREED
DISEMBOWEL
DISHABILLE
DONNYBROOK
ELDERBERRY
ENJAMBMENT
FIBERBOARD
FLOORBOARD
GOOSEBERRY
HEARTBREAK
HEREABOUTS
HULLABALOO
HYPERBARIC
IMPROBABLE
INCUMBENCY
INTERBLOCK
INTERBREED
LOGANBERRY
NEIGHBORLY
OPPROBRIUM
PAINTBRUSH
PAPERBOARD
PASTEBOARD
QUICKBASIC
SKATEBOARD
SPELLBOUND
STILLBIRTH
STRAWBERRY
SUBORBITAL
SWEETBREAD
SWEETBRIER
THROMBOSIS
TOOTHBRUSH
UNDERBELLY
UNDERBRUSH
UNNUMBERED
VERTEBRATE
WATERBORNE
WILDEBEEST
AFFLICTIVE
ANNUNCIATE
APPLICABLE
APPLICATOR
APPRECIATE
ATTRACTANT
ATTRACTION
AUSPICIOUS
BATRACHIAN
BRAINCHILD
BROADCLOTH
CAOUTCHOUC
CHARACTERY
CLAVICHORD
COLLECTIVE
CONDUCTIVE
CONFECTION
CONJECTURE
CONNECTION
CONNECTIVE
CONSECRATE
CONVECTION
CONVICTION
CORNUCOPIA
CRETACEOUS
CRISSCROSS
CURRICULUM
CURVACEOUS
DEPRECIATE
DESPICABLE
DIELECTRIC
DIFFICULTY
DISENCHANT
DISINCLINE
DISSOCIATE
DUODECIMAL
DUPLICATOR
EMBOUCHURE
ESCUTCHEON
EXPLICABLE
FALLACIOUS
FISTICUFFS
GRANDCHILD
HANDICRAFT
HOUSECLEAN
ICONOCLASM
ICONOCLAST
IMMISCIBLE
IMPECCABLE
IMPLACABLE
INDISCREET
INFLECTION
INFRACTION
INJUNCTION
INTINCTION
INVINCIBLE
LEPRECHAUN
LOQUACIOUS
LUBRICIOUS
MANUSCRIPT
MARASCHINO
MEERSCHAUM
MELANCHOLY
MENDACIOUS
MINISCROLL
MONARCHIST
MOTORCYCLE
OMNISCIENT
PARTICIPLE
PARTICULAR
PERFECTION
PERNICIOUS
PHYLACTERY
PLAYACTING
PLUTOCRACY
POSTSCRIPT
PRECOCIOUS
PREDACEOUS
PREDECEASE
PREDICABLE
PREPACKAGE
PRODUCTION
PROFICIENT
PROJECTILE
PROTECTION
PUBESCENCE
PUGNACIOUS
REFRACTION
REFRACTORY
RENASCENCE
RESPECTING
RESPECTIVE
RETRACTILE
RHINOCEROS
ROLLICKING
SENESCENCE
SEPTICEMIA
SEPULCHRAL
SERVICEMAN
SPACECRAFT
SPIROCHETE
STAGECOACH
STALACTITE
STATECRAFT
SUBJECTIVE
SUFFICIENT
SUPERCARGO
SUSPICIOUS
TABLECLOTH
TELESCOPIC
TRAJECTORY
TRANSCRIBE
TRANSCRIPT
TUBERCULAR
TUBERCULIN
TYPESCRIPT
UNDERCOVER
UNDERCROFT
UNGRACEFUL
UNGRACIOUS
UNMERCIFUL
VERMICELLI
VERNACULAR
VINDICTIVE
WATERCOLOR
WATERCRAFT
WATERCRESS
WHEELCHAIR
WITCHCRAFT
ACCORDANCE
ANIMADVERT
ASCENDANCY
ATTENDANCE
BEHINDHAND
BELLADONNA
BIOMEDICAL
COMMODIOUS
CONFIDENCE
DEGRADABLE
DEPENDABLE
DEPENDENCE
DEPENDENCY
DILLYDALLY
DISORDERLY
EISTEDDFOD
FASTIDIOUS
FORBIDDING
FORMIDABLE
GESUNDHEIT
GROUNDLING
GROUNDMASS
GROUNDWORK
HIPPODROME
INCENDIARY
INCREDIBLE
INGREDIENT
MOLYBDENUM
NIGHTDRESS
PALINDROME
PECCADILLO
PERIODICAL
PRECEDENCE
PREMEDICAL
PROVIDENCE
REDUNDANCY
SACERDOTAL
SECONDHAND
SUBSIDIARY
THREADBARE
TRANSDUCER
UNHANDSOME
ACCELERATE
ACCIDENTAL
ADULTERANT
ADULTERATE
ADVISEMENT
AESTHETICS
AIRFREIGHT
ALLITERATE
ALTOGETHER
AMANUENSIS
ANTEBELLUM
ANTECEDENT
ANTEPENULT
ANTISEPTIC
APOTHECARY
APOTHEOSIS
ARCHDEACON
ARMAGEDDON
ASSEVERATE
ASYMMETRIC
AURIFEROUS
BAREHEADED
BATTLEMENT
BATTLESHIP
BEFOREHAND
BELLWETHER
BIPARENTAL
BOISTEROUS
BOLSHEVISM
BOOKKEEPER
BOOKSELLER
BOTTLENECK
BOWDLERIZE
BRIDGEHEAD
BRIDGEWORK
BULLHEADED
CADAVEROUS
CANDLEWICK
CAPOREGIME
CEREBELLUM
CHALCEDONY
CHANCELLOR
CHANDELIER
CHANGELING
CHANGEOVER
CHANNELIZE
CHARLESTON
CHATTERBOX
CHEESECAKE
CINQUEFOIL
CLOTHESPIN
COMPLECTED
COMPLEMENT
COMPLEXION
COMPREHEND
CONCRETION
CONGREGATE
CONSPECTUS
COPYREADER
COUNTERACT
COUNTERMAN
COUNTERSPY
CRADLESONG
CRYOGENICS
CUTTLEFISH
DEADWEIGHT
DECELERATE
DEGENERACY
DEGENERATE
DELIBERATE
DEMONETIZE
DENOUEMENT
DISCREPANT
DISCRETION
DOORKEEPER
ENDOGENOUS
ENGAGEMENT
EPITHELIUM
EVANGELISM
EVANGELIST
EVANGELIZE
EVISCERATE
EXAGGERATE
EXASPERATE
EXCITEMENT
EXOTHERMIC
FIGUREHEAD
GAMEKEEPER
GATEKEEPER
GENTLEFOLK
GEOTHERMAL
GOALKEEPER
GOLDBEATER
HANDLEBARS

HARDHEADED
HOMOGENIZE
HOMOSEXUAL
HYPOCENTER
HYPODERMIC
HYPOTENUSE
ICEBREAKER
ILLITERATE
IMMATERIAL
IMMODERATE
IMPOVERISH
INBREEDING
INCIDENTAL
INCINERATE
INCOHERENT
INDIGENOUS
INDONESIAN
INDUCEMENT
INFIDELITY
INQUIETUDE
INTOLERANT
INVETERATE
IRRELEVANT
ISOTHERMAL
JAWBREAKER
JOURNEYMAN
KETTLEDRUM
LAWBREAKER
LIEUTENANT
MANAGEMENT
MANSUETUDE
MANTLEROCK
MARGUERITE
MASQUERADE
MEDDLESOME
MELANESIAN
METTLESOME
MIDDLEBROW
MONUMENTAL
MOUNTEBANK
NANOSECOND
NAPOLEONIC
NEEDLEWORK
NETTLESOME
NEWSLETTER
NOTICEABLE
OBLITERATE
OCCIDENTAL
PALLBEARER
PARAMECIUM
PERIHELION
PICARESQUE
PICOSECOND
POINSETTIA
POLYHEDRON
POLYNESIAN
PRINCELING

PROCEEDING
PROSCENIUM
PROSPECTUS
PROSPERITY
PROSPEROUS
QUATREFOIL
RATTLETRAP
RECUPERATE
REFERENDUM
REFINEMENT
REGENERACY
REGENERATE
REJUVENATE
REMUNERATE
RINGLEADER
SALTCELLAR
SETTLEMENT
SHILLELAGH
SHOPKEEPER
SHORTENING
SHUTTERBUG
SINGLETREE
SLENDERIZE
SLUMBEROUS
SMATTERING
STARVELING
STATUESQUE
SUPPLEMENT
TATTLETALE
TEARJERKER
TECHNETIUM
THEMSELVES
THUNDEROUS
TIMEKEEPER
TROLLEYBUS
TUMBLEDOWN
TUMBLEWEED
TURTLEDOVE
TURTLENECK
TYPESETTER
UNAFFECTED
UNEXPECTED
UNFRIENDLY
UNGENEROUS
UNRESERVED
VICEGERENT
VITUPERATE
VOCIFERATE
VOCIFEROUS
VOLUMETRIC
WAVELENGTH
WEATHERING
WEATHERMAN
WINCHESTER
WOODPECKER
BREADFRUIT
BREAKFRONT

CAMOUFLAGE
DENTIFRICE
GOOSEFLESH
GRAINFIELD
GRAPEFRUIT
HENCEFORTH
HORSEFLESH
INTERFAITH
INTERFERON
MICROFICHE
OCEANFRONT
PERMAFROST
PERSIFLAGE
PHOTOFLASH
PIANOFORTE
PRIZEFIGHT
SHAMEFACED
WATERFRONT
ABORIGINAL
APOLOGETIC
BEDRAGGLED
BELONGINGS
BLACKGUARD
BRIDEGROOM
CENTIGRADE
CONTAGIOUS
CONTIGUOUS
CORRIGIBLE
DEFLAGRATE
EFFULGENCE
ENDANGERED
EXTINGUISH
FARSIGHTED
FIBERGLASS
HELIOGRAPH
IMPREGNATE
INDULGENCE
INELIGIBLE
INTANGIBLE
LARYNGITIS
MENINGITIS
MICROGRAPH
MIMEOGRAPH
NEGLIGIBLE
OCEANGOING
ORGANGUTAN
OUTRAGEOUS
PARMIGIANA
PASSAGEWAY
PHONOGRAPH
PHOTOGENIC
PHOTOGRAPH
PORTUGUESE
PRODIGIOUS
PROPAGANDA
RADIOGENIC
RADIOGRAPH

REFULGENCE
RESURGENCE
RETROGRADE
RETROGRESS
SCAPEGRACE
SPRINGTIME
STALAGMITE
STRAIGHTEN
STRENGTHEN
STRINGENCY
STRONGHOLD
THROUGHOUT
THROUGHPUT
THROUGHWAY
TRANSGRESS
WITCHGRASS
ACROPHOBIA
ANESTHESIA
ANESTHETIC
ANTICHRIST
ANTIPHONAL
ANTITHESIS
ATTACHMENT
BLOCKHOUSE
BLOODHOUND
BRONCHITIS
CATECHUMEN
CHINCHILLA
CHURCHGOER
CHURCHLESS
CHURCHYARD
COURTHOUSE
DETACHMENT
DIPHTHERIA
DISINHERIT
FORESHADOW
FRANCHISEE
FRANCHISER
FRANCHISOR
GREENHOUSE
GUARDHOUSE
HEARTHSIDE
HEMOPHILIA
HOBBYHORSE
HYPOTHESIS
INFIGHTING
LEDERHOSEN
LENGTHWISE
LIGHTHOUSE
MONOCHROME
MONOPHONIC
MONOTHEISM
OCTOTHORPE
OESOPHAGUS
OVERCHARGE
OVERSHADOW
PACKTHREAD

PARAPHRASE
PERIPHERAL
PERISHABLE
PHOSPHORUS
PILOTHOUSE
POLYTHEISM
POWERHOUSE
PROSTHESIS
PUNISHMENT
ROUGHHOUSE
ROUNDHOUSE
SEARCHWARE
SPLASHDOWN
STATEHOUSE
STOREHOUSE
STRYCHNINE
SWEETHEART
SWITCHBACK
THOUGHTFUL
WHEELHORSE
WHEELHOUSE
WINDSHIELD
XENOPHOBIA
ADDITIONAL
ADJUDICATE
ADMINISTER
AFTERIMAGE
ALBUMINOUS
ALKALINIZE
ALLEGIANCE
AMMUNITION
ANNIHILATE
ANTIBIOTIC
ANTICIPATE
APPARITION
APPETIZING
APPOSITION
APPOSITIVE
ARCHBISHOP
ARTIFICIAL
ASSIMILATE
BALBRIGGAN
BEAUTICIAN
BENEFICENT
BENEFICIAL
BESPRINKLE
BIPARIETAL
BITUMINOUS
CANONICALS
CAPACITATE
CARABINEER
CENTRIFUGE
CHAUVINISM
CHLORINATE
CIRCUITOUS
CLASSICISM
CLASSIFIED

COINCIDENT
COMEDIENNE
COMPLIANCE
COMPLIANCY
COMPLICATE
COMPLICITY
COMPLIMENT
CONSCIENCE
CONSPIRACY
CONSTITUTE
CONTRIBUTE
COORDINATE
DEACTIVATE
DEBILITATE
DECAPITATE
DEFINITION
DEFINITIVE
DEHUMIDIFY
DELPHINIUM
DEMOBILIZE
DEMOLITION
DENOMINATE
DEPOSITION
DEPOSITORY
DESALINATE
DESALINIZE
DISJOINTED
DISTRIBUTE
EBULLITION
EFFEMINATE
EFFICIENCY
EMANCIPATE
EMBROIDERY
EMPIRICISM
EMULSIFIER
EQUANIMITY
EXACTITUDE
EXCOGITATE
EXORBITANT
EXPEDIENCE
EXPEDIENCY
EXPEDITION
EXPERIENCE
EXPERIMENT
EXPOSITION
FACILITATE
FAVORITISM
FELICITATE
FELICITOUS
FLUORIDATE
FLUORINATE
FOLKSINGER
FOOTLIGHTS
FOREFINGER
FORFEITURE
FORTUITOUS
FRATRICIDE

FUTURISTIC
GADOLINIUM
GEOSCIENCE
GRATUITOUS
GUNSLINGER
HABILIMENT
HEREDITARY
HISTRIONIC
ILLUMINATE
IMBIBITION
IMMOBILIZE
IMPATIENCE
IMPEDIMENT
IMPENITENT
INACTIVATE
INAPTITUDE
INCIVILITY
INDECISION
INDECISIVE
INDEFINITE
INDELICATE
INDIVIDUAL
INEXPIABLE
INFINITIVE
INFINITUDE
INHABITANT
INHIBITION
INNOMINATE
INORDINATE
INSATIABLE
INSEMINATE
INTIMIDATE
INTOXICANT
INTOXICATE
INVALIDATE
INVARIABLE
IRRATIONAL
KINGFISHER
LADYFINGER
LEGITIMATE
LIBIDINOUS
LIKELIHOOD
LIVELIHOOD
MALEFICENT
MIDSHIPMAN
MISALIGNED
MUDSLINGER
MUNIFICENT
NEGATIVISM
NONDRINKER
NOTABILITY
OCCASIONAL
OLEAGINOUS
OVERWINTER
PAINKILLER
PALATINATE
PATHFINDER

PENICILLIN
PERIWINKLE
PERQUISITE
PILGRIMAGE
POLITICIAN
PREEMINENT
PRESCIENCE
PRINCIPLED
PROCLIVITY
PROFLIGATE
PROPRIETOR
PROPRINTER
PROSTITUTE
PSYCHIATRY
PYRIMIDINE
QUADRIVIUM
REACTIVATE
RECIDIVISM
RELATIONAL
RELATIVITY
REMEDIABLE
REPAGINATE
REPETITION
REPETITIVE
REPOSITORY
RESILIENCE
RESILIENCY
RISIBILITY
SACROILIAC
SANGUINARY
SCRUTINIZE
SCURRILOUS
SHIPFITTER
SHUNPIKING
SIDEWINDER
SIMILITUDE
SIMPLICITY
SIMPLISTIC
SKEPTICISM
SKYWRITING
SOLICITOUS
SOLICITUDE
STEPSISTER
SUBSTITUTE
SUPPLICANT
SUPPLICATE
TECHNICIAN
TELEVISION
THERMISTOR
TOURNIQUET
TRANSISTOR
TRANSITION
TRANSITIVE
TRANSITORY
TRIPLICATE
UBIQUITOUS
UNABRIDGED
UNAVAILING
UNBELIEVER
UNDENIABLE
UNFAMILIAR
UNFRUITFUL
VELOCIPEDE
VETERINARY
VILLAINOUS
VISIBILITY
VOLUMINOUS
WHARFINGER
WORSHIPFUL
BLITZKRIEG
EMBANKMENT
JINRIKISHA
KNICKKNACK
MISTAKABLE
REMARKABLE
SAUERKRAUT
SPRINKLING
ALLHALLOWS
ANIMALCULE
ANTICLIMAX
APOCALYPSE
BRICKLAYER
CALCULATED
CANDELABRA
CANTALOUPE
CANTILEVER
CARBOLATED
CENTILITER
CHATELAINE
CHIVALROUS
COMPULSION
COMPULSIVE
COMPULSORY
CONCILIATE
CONVALESCE
CONVOLUTED
CONVULSION
CORDILLERA
CORNFLOWER
CORPULENCE
CRENELLATE
DISBELIEVE
DISTILLATE
ENAMELWARE
ENCYCLICAL
EXCELLENCE
EXCELLENCY
FERTILIZER
FLAGELLATE
FLASHLIGHT
FLOODLIGHT
HALLELUJAH
HECTOLITER
HEMOGLOBIN
HORSELAUGH
HYDROLYSIS
INFALLIBLE
INTERLEAVE
INTERLUNAR
INVIOLABLE
KIESELGUHR
LOGROLLING
MANDELBROT
METALLURGY
MILLILITER
MISCELLANY
MISSILEMAN
MULTILEVEL
OUTBALANCE
PANTALOONS
PARAPLEGIA
PESTILENCE
PETROLATUM
PICCALILLI
POLYCLINIC
POWERLINES
PRIVILEGED
PROMULGATE
PROPELLANT
PROPULSION
REBELLIOUS
RECOILLESS
REPUBLICAN
RIBOFLAVIN
SANDALWOOD
SCHOOLGIRL
SCHOOLMARM
SCHOOLMATE
SCHOOLROOM
SPITTLEBUG
TESSELLATE
TRAVELOGUE
TRIFOLIATE
TURBULENCE
UNDERLYING
UNEMPLOYED
UNHALLOWED
UNSKILLFUL
UNYIELDING
URINALYSIS
WALLFLOWER
WINDFLOWER
ABSTEMIOUS
ACHROMATIC
ANEMOMETER
ARITHMETIC
BENCHMARKS
BLANCMANGE
BOTTOMLAND
CENTIMETER
CHIROMANCY
CIRCUMCISE
CIRCUMFLEX
CIRCUMVENT
CONSUMMATE
COTERMINAL
CYCLOMETER
DETERMINED
DIPSOMANIA
DISCOMFORT
DISCOMMODE
DISCOMPOSE
DISSIMILAR
ECONOMICAL
EXTRAMURAL
FATHOMLESS
GRAVIMETER
HECTOMETER
HEPTAMETER
HYDROMETER
HYGROMETER
IMPRIMATUR
INTERMARRY
INTERMEZZO
INTRAMURAL
MATCHMAKER
MICROMETER
MILLIMETER
MOHAMMEDAN
MUHAMMADAN
MULTIMEDIA
MYRIAMETER
NECROMANCY
NINCOMPOOP
NOISEMAKER
PEACEMAKER
PENTAMETER
PHENOMENON
PHLEGMATIC
PHOTOMETER
PHOTOMURAL
RADIOMETER
SCHISMATIC
SERVOMOTOR
SOPHOMORIC
SUBCOMPACT
SUBLIMINAL
TACHOMETER
TANTAMOUNT
TETRAMETER
UNEXAMPLED
UNICAMERAL
WATCHMAKER
WATERMELON
ABOMINABLE
ABSTINENCE
ACCOUNTANT
ACCOUNTING
ACTIONABLE
AGGRANDIZE
ALIMENTARY
ALTERNATOR
AMERINDIAN
APPOINTIVE
APPRENTICE
ASSIGNMENT
ASTRINGENT
ATTAINMENT
BRIGANTINE
BUTTONHOLE
BUTTONHOOK
CALUMNIATE
CANNONBALL
CANTONMENT
CARCINOGEN
CENTENNIAL
CITRONELLA
COMMANDANT
COMMANDEER
COMMENTARY
COMMONALTY
COMMONWEAL
COMMUNIQUE
COMPENDIUM
COMPENSATE
CONCENTRIC
CONDENSATE
CONGENITAL
CONSONANCE
CONTENTION
CONTINENCE
CONTINGENT
CONTINUITY
CONTINUOUS
CONVENIENT
CONVENTION
COTTONSEED
COTTONTAIL
COTTONWOOD
COWPUNCHER
CREDENTIAL
DECLENSION
DESCENDANT
DISCONCERT
DISCONNECT
DISCONTENT
DISPENSARY
DISSENSION
DISSONANCE
ECUMENICAL
EFFRONTERY
EGOCENTRIC
ELEMENTARY
EUPHONIOUS
EUTHANASIA
EXTRANEOUS
FAHRENHEIT
FIBRINOGEN
GARGANTUAN
GEOCENTRIC
GORGONZOLA
GORMANDIZE
GOVERNMENT
HARMONIOUS
HOOTENANNY
HORRENDOUS
HUSBANDMAN
IMAGINABLE
INCLINABLE
INTERNMENT
JACKANAPES
JARDINIERE
JIMSONWEED
LAWRENCIUM
MACKINTOSH
MAIDENHAIR
MAIDENHEAD
MAIDENHOOD
MAISONETTE
MALCONTENT
MARGINALIA
MARIONETTE
MARTINGALE
MAYONNAISE
MECHANICAL
MERCANTILE
MIGNONETTE
MILLENNIUM
MISCONDUCT
MIZZENMAST
NATIONWIDE
NEWFANGLED
OUTGENERAL
OUTLANDISH
PANJANDRUM
PATRONYMIC
PENMANSHIP
PERCENTAGE
PERCENTILE
PERSONABLE
PERSONALTY
PICKANINNY
PIGEONHOLE
PORTENTOUS
PREBENDARY
PREHENSILE
PROGENITOR
PROMINENCE
PROMONTORY
PROPENSITY
PROVENANCE
PROVINCIAL
QUARANTINE
REASONABLE
REFRINGENT
REPUGNANCE
RESOUNDING
RESPONDENT
RESPONSIVE
SEAMANSHIP
SEASONABLE
SERPENTINE
SHENANIGAN
STUPENDOUS
SUBVENTION
SUSPENSION
SUSPENSORY
SUSTENANCE
TABERNACLE
TERMINATOR
TORRENTIAL
TREMENDOUS
TRIMONTHLY
TURPENTINE
TYRANNICAL
UNDERNEATH
UNEVENTFUL
UNMANNERLY
UNTHINKING
UPBRINGING
UPSTANDING
UROGENITAL
WEAPONLESS
WOODENWARE
WORKINGMAN
AFICIONADO
ALCOHOLISM
AMELIORATE
ANTAGONISM
ANTAGONIST
ANTAGONIZE
ANTHROPOID
ANTINOMIAN
ANTISOCIAL
AUCTIONEER
AUDITORIUM
AUTOMOBILE
AUTOMOTIVE
AUTONOMOUS
BEAUJOLAIS
BEDCLOTHES
BICHLORIDE
BLUEBONNET
BLUEBOTTLE
BLUECOLLAR
BONDHOLDER
BOOKMOBILE
BOONDOGGLE
BRONTOSAUR

CAMELOPARD
CAMPHORATE
CARDIOGRAM
CARDIOLOGY
CATABOLISM
CATEGORIZE
CEREMONIAL
CHIFFONIER
CHLOROFORM
CHROMOSOME
CHRONOLOGY
CHRYSOLITE
CLODHOPPER
COMPROMISE
CONTROLLER
CONTROVERT
CRYPTOGRAM
DECOLORIZE
DEMONOLOGY
DENDROLOGY
DICTIONARY
DOCKWORKER
DYSPROSIUM
ELECTORATE
EMBRYOLOGY
ENTOMOLOGY
EPIGLOTTIS
EPISCOPACY
EPISCOPATE
EQUIVOCATE
ERGONOMICS
EURODOLLAR
EXOBIOLOGY
EYEDROPPER
FLAMBOYANT
FLUIDOUNCE
FOOTLOCKER
FREEBOOTER
GASTRONOMY
GLACIOLOGY
GONOCOCCUS
GUILLOTINE
GYNECOLOGY
HELICOPTER
HEMATOLOGY
HERETOFORE
HOMECOMING
HOMOLOGOUS
HORIZONTAL
IMMEMORIAL
IMMUNOLOGY
INDECOROUS
INVIGORATE
IRRESOLUTE
LANDHOLDER
LANDLOCKED
LEAFHOPPER
LOCOMOTION
LOCOMOTIVE
MALEVOLENT
MALODOROUS
METABOLISM
METABOLITE
MISSIONARY
MONOTONOUS
MORATORIUM
MORPHOLOGY
MUSICOLOGY
NATATORIUM
NEBULOSITY
NEWSWORTHY
NOTEWORTHY
NUCLEONICS
NUMEROLOGY
OCEANOLOGY
OMNIPOTENT
OMNIVOROUS
PEASHOOTER
PERITONEUM
PHLEBOTOMY
PHRENOLOGY
PHYSIOLOGY
PICKPOCKET
POSTMORTEM
PRECIOSITY
PROGNOSTIC
PSEUDOCODE
PSYCHOLOGY
PSYCHOPATH
RACECOURSE
SANATORIUM
SEISMOGRAM
SEISMOLOGY
SELENOLOGY
SHIBBOLETH
SNOWMOBILE
STATIONARY
STATIONERY
STENTORIAN
STEPMOTHER
STEREOTYPE
TECHNOLOGY
THERMOSTAT
TOMFOOLERY
TOXICOLOGY
TRAMPOLINE
UNBECOMING
UNSCHOOLED
VARICOSITY
VIRTUOSITY
WHATSOEVER
WHENSOEVER
WHOMSOEVER
ABSORPTION
ACCOMPLICE
ACCOMPLISH
ALTARPIECE
ANGLOPHILE
ANGLOPHOBE
ASSUMPTION
ATMOSPHERE
AUDIOPHILE
BIRTHPLACE
CATCHPENNY
CELLOPHANE
CHECKPOINT
CONCEPTION
CONNIPTION
COSMOPOLIS
CROSSPIECE
CYCLOPEDIA
DECOMPRESS
DECRYPTION
DISAPPOINT
DISAPPROVE
DISCIPLINE
EMBONPOINT
ENCRYPTION
ENTERPRISE
ERYSIPELAS
ESCARPMENT
FIELDPIECE
FLOODPLAIN
GRAMOPHONE
HANDSPRING
HEMISPHERE
HIEROPHANT
HODGEPODGE
HOMEOPATHY
HORSEPOWER
HYDROPHONE
HYDROPLANE
IMPALPABLE
INCOMPLETE
INCULPABLE
INDISPOSED
IONOSPHERE
LIGHTPROOF
MAINSPRING
MESOSPHERE
METROPOLIS
MICROPHONE
MICROPROBE
MOUTHPIECE
MULTIPLIER
NECROPOLIS
NONSUPPORT
OSTEOPATHY
OVERSPREAD
PALIMPSEST
PERCEPTION
PERCEPTIVE
PERCEPTUAL
PERCIPIENT
PEREMPTORY
PETNAPPING
PHOTOPAINT
PREEMPTIVE
PRESUPPOSE
PROTOPLASM
RADIOPHONE
RECOMPENSE
REDEMPTION
RESORPTION
SAPROPHYTE
STANDPOINT
THREEPENCE
TOOTHPASTE
TRANSPLANT
TRANSPOLAR
UNDERPANTS
VIBRAPHONE
VIDEOPHONE
VOICEPRINT
WASTEPAPER
WATERPOWER
WATERPROOF
WELLSPRING
WIDESPREAD
WINGSPREAD
COLLOQUIAL
COLLOQUIUM
CONSEQUENT
DELINQUENT
EARTHQUAKE
FOURSQUARE
INADEQUATE
INFREQUENT
RELINQUISH
SUBSEQUENT
ANSWERABLE
ANTIFREEZE
ANTIPROTON
APOSTROPHE
APPEARANCE
ARBITRATOR
AUTHORSHIP
BACKGROUND
BALDERDASH
BASTARDIZE
BETTERMENT
BIRTHRIGHT
BOMBARDIER
BORDERLAND
BUDGERIGAR
BUTTERMILK
CALCAREOUS
CANKERWORM
CARBURETOR
CELEBRATED
CELLARETTE
CENSORIOUS
CENSORSHIP
CHARTREUSE
CHIMERICAL
CLOVERLEAF
COLLARBONE
COLPORTEUR
COMMERCIAL
COMPARABLE
COMPARISON
CONCERNING
CONCERTINA
CONCORDANT
CONCURRENT
CONFERENCE
CONFORMITY
CONSORTIUM
CONSTRAINT
CONVERSANT
CONVERSION
COPPERHEAD
COPYWRITER
COUNTRYMAN
CUMMERBUND
DEALERSHIP
DEMOCRATIC
DEMOGRAPHY
DEPLORABLE
DETERRENCE
DIFFERENCE
DINNERWARE
DISARRANGE
DISCERNING
DISCURSIVE
DISHARMONY
DISSERVICE
DRAWBRIDGE
DUNDERHEAD
EFFLORESCE
ELECTRONIC
ENDEARMENT
ESPADRILLE
EXACERBATE
EXPATRIATE
FAIRGROUND
FATHERLAND
FINGERLING
FINGERNAIL
FOOTBRIDGE
FOREGROUND
FOREORDAIN
FORTHRIGHT
FOSTERLING
FRATERNITY
FRATERNIZE
GINGERSNAP
GREGARIOUS
HAMMERHEAD
HAMMERLOCK
HEMORRHAGE
HEMORRHOID
HINTERLAND
HOLOGRAPHY
INEXORABLE
INGLORIOUS
INOPERABLE
JUGGERNAUT
KRUGERRAND
LETTERHEAD
LOGGERHEAD
LUGUBRIOUS
LUMBERJACK
LUMBERYARD
MALAPROPOS
MANSERVANT
MASTERMIND
MASTERSHIP
MASTERWORK
MEMBERSHIP
MENSURABLE
MILLWRIGHT
MISFORTUNE
MONSTRANCE
MOTHERHOOD
MOTHERLAND
MOZZARELLA
NASTURTIUM
NETHERMOST
NEWSGROUPS
NUMBERLESS
NURSERYMAN
OCCURRENCE
ORATORICAL
OUTPERFORM
PARATROOPS
PAWNBROKER
PENNYROYAL
PEPPERCORN
PEPPERMINT
PERDURABLE
PERVERSION
PLAYGROUND
PLAYWRIGHT
PLUPERFECT
POULTRYMAN
PREARRANGE
PRECARIOUS
PREFERENCE
PREFERMENT
PREMARITAL
PRIMORDIAL
PROCURATOR
PROPERTIED
PROPORTION
READERSHIP
RECIPROCAL
REPATRIATE
RESPIRATOR
RESTORABLE
ROLLERBALL
RUBBERNECK
SALUBRIOUS
SEMIDRYING
SHIPWRIGHT
SILVERFISH
SILVERWARE
SISTERHOOD
SKYSCRAPER
SNAPDRAGON
SUBSTRATUM
SUBSURFACE
SUBTERFUGE
SUFFERANCE
TATTERSALL
TEETHRIDGE
TELEGRAPHY
TEMPERANCE
TENDERFOOT
TENDERLOIN
TENEBRIOUS
THEATRICAL
TIMBERLINE
TOPOGRAPHY
TRAVERTINE
TRIPARTITE
TYPEWRITER
TYPOGRAPHY
UNBEARABLE
UNIFORMITY
UNIVERSITY
UPROARIOUS
URETHRITIS
VESPERTINE
VICTORIOUS
VULNERABLE
WAINWRIGHT
WANDERLUST
WESTERNIZE
WICKERWORK
WILDERNESS
WINEGROWER
WINTERTIDE
WINTERTIME
WITHDRAWAL
WONDERLAND
WONDERMENT
WRAPAROUND
XEROGRAPHY

YESTE**R**YEAR
ABSCI**S**SION
ACCES**S**IBLE
ADMIS**S**IBLE
AGGRE**S**SION
AGGRE**S**SIVE
ALONG**S**HORE
AMBAS**S**ADOR
ANGIO**S**PERM
BALLI**S**TICS
BAPTI**S**TERY
BATHY**S**CAPH
BIRTH**S**TONE
BLACK**S**MITH
BLOOD**S**TAIN
BLOOD**S**TONE
BRAIN**S**TORM
BREAD**S**TUFF
BRIDE**S**MAID
BROAD**S**WORD
BROWN**S**TONE
CANDE**S**CENT
CANVA**S**BACK
CENTE**S**IMAL
CHEAP**S**KATE
CLERE**S**TORY
CLING**S**TONE
COMBU**S**TION
COMMI**S**SARY
COMMI**S**SION
COMPA**S**SION
COMPO**S**ITOR
COMPU**S**ERVE
CONCE**S**SION
CONCE**S**SIVE
CONCU**S**SION
CONDE**S**CEND
CONFE**S**SION
CONFI**S**CATE
CONSI**S**TORY
CORRE**S**POND
CRANK**S**HAFT
CYBER**S**PACE
DECLA**S**SIFY
DEMOI**S**ELLE
DEPRE**S**SANT
DEPRE**S**SION
DEPRE**S**SIVE
DISCU**S**SANT
DISPO**S**ABLE
DISPO**S**SESS
DISRE**S**PECT
ENTHU**S**IASM
EVANE**S**CENT
EXHAU**S**TION
EXHAU**S**TIVE
EXPRE**S**SION

EXPRE**S**SMAN
EXPRE**S**SWAY
FORTI**S**SIMO
GRAND**S**TAND
GRAVE**S**TONE
GREEN**S**WARD
GRIND**S**TONE
GYMNA**S**TICS
GYMNO**S**PERM
IMPAS**S**ABLE
IMPAS**S**IBLE
IMPER**S**ONAL
IMPOS**S**IBLE
IMPRE**S**ARIO
IMPRE**S**SION
IMPRE**S**SIVE
INCON**S**TANT
INFRA**S**ONIC
INSEN**S**IBLE
INTER**S**TATE
INTER**S**TICE
INTRA**S**TATE
MICRO**S**COPE
MICRO**S**TATE
MULTI**S**ENSE
MULTI**S**TAGE
MULTI**S**TORY
NARCI**S**SISM
NIGHT**S**HADE
NIGHT**S**HIRT
NIGHT**S**TICK
NOURI**S**HING
OPALE**S**CENT
OPPRE**S**SION
OSTEN**S**IBLE
PERCU**S**SION
PERMI**S**SION
PERMI**S**SIVE
PHILI**S**TINE
PHILO**S**OPHY
PIANI**S**SIMO
PINCU**S**HION
PLEBI**S**CITE
POSSE**S**SION
POSSE**S**SIVE
PRECE**S**SION
PREDE**S**TINE
PREDI**S**POSE
PREPO**S**SESS
PROCE**S**SION
PROFE**S**SION
PROMI**S**SORY
PROTE**S**TANT
PUTRE**S**CENT
RADAR**S**COPE
RADIO**S**ONDE
RECON**S**IDER

REGRE**S**SION
RETRO**S**PECT
RHINE**S**TONE
ROTIS**S**ERIE
SACRO**S**ANCT
SMOKE**S**TACK
SOMER**S**AULT
SOOTH**S**AYER
SPOIL**S**PORT
SPORT**S**CAST
STAND**S**TILL
STATI**S**TICS
SUCCE**S**SION
SUCCE**S**SIVE
SUGGE**S**TION
SUGGE**S**TIVE
SUPER**S**ONIC
TABLE**S**POON
THREE**S**CORE
THUMB**S**CREW
TOUCH**S**TONE
ULTRA**S**HORT
ULTRA**S**ONIC
ULTRA**S**OUND
UNBLU**S**HING
UNDER**S**CORE
UNDER**S**EXED
UNDER**S**HIRT
UNDER**S**HOOT
UNDER**S**IZED
UNDER**S**KIRT
UNDER**S**LUNG
UNDER**S**TAND
UNDER**S**TATE
UNDER**S**TOOD
UNDER**S**TORY
UNDER**S**TUDY
UNREA**S**ONED
UPHOL**S**TERY
WATER**S**POUT
ACCEN**T**UATE
ACCEP**T**ABLE
ACCEP**T**ANCE
ACCUS**T**OMED
ADMIT**T**ANCE
ADVEN**T**URER
AFTER**T**ASTE
APOLI**T**ICAL
ARCHI**T**RAVE
ASSOR**T**MENT
AUTOS**T**RADA
BACKS**T**AIRS
BACKS**T**ROKE
BALUS**T**RADE
BASKE**T**BALL
BELLE**T**RIST
BIPAR**T**ISAN

BLACK**T**HORN
BREAS**T**BONE
BREAS**T**WORK
CHARI**T**ABLE
COCKA**T**RICE
COLLA**T**ERAL
COMES**T**IBLE
COMMU**T**ATOR
COMPA**T**IBLE
COMPA**T**RIOT
COMPE**T**ENCE
COMPE**T**ENCY
COMPE**T**ITOR
CORNS**T**ARCH
CREDI**T**ABLE
DELEC**T**ABLE
DEPAR**T**MENT
DEPOR**T**MENT
DERMA**T**ITIS
DILET**T**ANTE
DISSA**T**ISFY
DOGCA**T**CHER
DOWNS**T**AIRS
DOWNS**T**REAM
DOWNS**T**ROKE
DRAWS**T**RING
EFFEC**T**UATE
EQUES**T**RIAN
ERGOS**T**EROL
ESCRI**T**OIRE
EVERY**T**HING
EXPEC**T**ANCY
EYEWI**T**NESS
FACTI**T**IOUS
FARFE**T**CHED
FICTI**T**IOUS
FLAGI**T**IOUS
FLYCA**T**CHER
GERIA**T**RICS
HEADS**T**RONG
HEART**T**HROB
HEATS**T**ROKE
HELIO**T**ROPE
HOSPI**T**ABLE
ILLUS**T**RATE
IMPOR**T**ANCE
INDIS**T**INCT
INDUC**T**ANCE
INDUS**T**RIAL
INEVI**T**ABLE
INFIL**T**RATE
INGRA**T**IATE
INIMI**T**ABLE
INSEN**T**IENT
INSIS**T**ENCE
INTER**T**IDAL
INTER**T**WINE

INTER**T**WIST
INVES**T**MENT
ISOME**T**RICS
KNIGH**T**HOOD
LICEN**T**IATE
LICEN**T**IOUS
MAGIS**T**RATE
MAINS**T**REAM
METAS**T**ASIS
MILLS**T**REAM
MINES**T**RONE
MINIS**T**RANT
MOONS**T**RUCK
MOTOR**T**RUCK
OBSTE**T**RICS
OFTEN**T**IMES
OUTPA**T**IENT
PEDES**T**RIAN
PEDIA**T**RICS
PERPE**T**RATE
PERPE**T**UATE
PERPE**T**UITY
POCKE**T**BOOK
POTEN**T**IATE
PROME**T**HIUM
PROMP**T**BOOK
PROPI**T**IATE
PROPI**T**IOUS
RECEP**T**ACLE
REDIS**T**RICT
REGIS**T**RANT
RELEN**T**LESS
RELUC**T**ANCE
REMIT**T**ANCE
REPER**T**OIRE
REPOR**T**EDLY
RESIS**T**ANCE
RICKE**T**TSIA
SEAMS**T**RESS
SEMPS**T**RESS
SHOES**T**RING
SIDES**T**ROKE
SLIPS**T**REAM
SPIRI**T**UOUS
STRIP**T**EASE
SUPER**T**WIST
SYMPA**T**HIZE
TARAN**T**ELLA
TUMUL**T**UOUS
UNBEA**T**ABLE
UNCRI**T**ICAL
UNDER**T**AKER
UNDER**T**RICK
UNFAI**T**HFUL
UNGRA**T**EFUL
UNILA**T**ERAL
UNLET**T**ERED

UNSUI**T**ABLE
VOLUP**T**UARY
VOLUP**T**UOUS
WATCH**T**OWER
WATER**T**IGHT
WEIGH**T**LESS
ABSOL**U**TION
ABSOL**U**TISM
ACCUM**U**LATE
ANTIQ**U**ATED
AQUAL**U**NGER
ARTIC**U**LATE
CAPIT**U**LATE
CONCL**U**SION
CONFL**U**ENCE
CONGR**U**ENCE
CONGR**U**ENCY
DELIQ**U**ESCE
DEPOP**U**LATE
DESTR**U**CTOR
DIMIN**U**ENDO
DIMIN**U**TIVE
DISCO**U**RAGE
DISGR**U**NTLE
EMASC**U**LATE
FILIB**U**STER
FORER**U**NNER
FRAUD**U**LENT
FUSSB**U**DGET
HYDRA**U**LICS
IMMAC**U**LATE
INAUG**U**RATE
INSTR**U**CTOR
INSTR**U**MENT
INTEG**U**MENT
INTER**U**RBAN
INVAL**U**ABLE
INVOL**U**TION
LACKL**U**STER
LANDL**U**BBER
MALTH**U**SIAN
MANIC**U**RIST
MANIP**U**LATE
METIC**U**LOUS
OBSEQ**U**IOUS
OUTPO**U**RING
PASTE**U**RIZE
PORTC**U**LLIS
POSTH**U**MOUS
PRECA**U**TION
PRESS**U**RIZE
PRONO**U**NCED
QUADR**U**PLET
QUINT**U**PLET
RAGAM**U**FFIN
RESOL**U**TION
RESTA**U**RANT

REVOL**U**TION
RIDIC**U**LOUS
ROADR**U**NNER
SEERS**U**CKER
SILHO**U**ETTE
SUBRO**U**TINE
TAMBO**U**RINE
TURNB**U**CKLE
UNASS**U**MING
UNGRO**U**NDED
UNOCC**U**PIED
VOCAB**U**LARY
WHITS**U**NDAY
WOODC**U**TTER
ABBRE**V**IATE
ARBOR**V**ITAE
DESER**V**EDLY
EFFER**V**ESCE
GINGI**V**ITIS
IMPER**V**IOUS
INSOL**V**ABLE
LASCI**V**IOUS
OBSER**V**ABLE
OBSER**V**ANCE
RECEI**V**ABLE
TRANS**V**ERSE
UNDER**V**ALUE
VAUDE**V**ILLE
BREAK**W**ATER
DEATH**W**ATCH
DREAM**W**ORLD
EVERY**W**HERE
FELLO**W**SHIP
FLOOD**W**ATER
FRESH**W**ATER
GHOST**W**RITE
HOLLO**W**WARE
HORSE**W**OMAN
HOUSE**W**ARES
INTER**W**EAVE
KNOCK**W**URST
LIVER**W**URST
MARRO**W**BONE
MEADO**W**LARK
OTHER**W**ORLD
PANTY**W**AIST
PILLO**W**CASE
SALES**W**OMAN
UNDER**W**AIST
UNDER**W**ATER
UNDER**W**ORLD
UNDER**W**RITE
WATER**W**HEEL
WATER**W**ORKS
WILLO**W**WARE
WINDO**W**PANE
WINDO**W**SILL

WORTHWHILE
WRISTWATCH
ASPHYXIATE
INFLEXIBLE
APOCRYPHAL
BIOPHYSICS
CONVEYANCE
EMPLOYMENT
EUCALYPTUS
GEOPHYSICS
LACHRYMOSE
MISOGYNIST
PRESBYOPIA
PRESBYTERY
VOLLEYBALL
WHIRLYBIRD
COGNIZANCE
RENDEZVOUS

## 7th Letter

ABOMINABLE
ACCEPTABLE
ACCEPTANCE
ACCORDANCE
ACHROMATIC
ACTIONABLE
ADMITTANCE
AFTERTASTE
ALLEGIANCE
ALTERNATOR
AMBASSADOR
ANSWERABLE
ANTIQUATED
APPEARANCE
APPLICABLE
APPLICATOR
ARBITRATOR
ARCHDEACON
ASCENDANCY
ATTENDANCE
BACKSTAIRS
BAREHEADED
BENCHMARKS
BLANCMANGE
BREAKWATER
BRICKLAYER
BULLHEADED
CALCULATED
CANDELABRA
CARBOLATED
CELEBRATED
CHARITABLE
CHATELAINE
CHIROMANCY
COGNIZANCE
COMMONALTY
COMMUTATOR
COMPARABLE
COMPLIANCE
COMPLIANCY
CONSONANCE
CONSTRAINT
CONVEYANCE
COPYREADER
CORNSTARCH
CREDITABLE
DEATHWATCH
DEGRADABLE
DELECTABLE
DEMOCRATIC
DEMOGRAPHY
DEPENDABLE
DEPLORABLE
DESPICABLE
DILETTANTE
DILLYDALLY
DIPSOMANIA
DISARRANGE
DISPOSABLE
DISSONANCE
DOWNSTAIRS
DUPLICATOR
EUTHANASIA
EXPECTANCY
EXPLICALBE
FLOODWATER
FORESHADOW
FORMIDABLE
FRESHWATER
GOLDBEATER
HARDHEADED
HOLOGRAPHY
HOMEOPATHY
HOOTENANNY
HORSELAUGH
HOSPITABLE
HOUSEWARES
HULLABALOO
HYPERBARIC
ICEBREAKER
IMAGINABLE
IMPALPABLE
IMPASSABLE
IMPECCABLE
IMPLACABLE
IMPORTANCE
IMPRESARIO
IMPRIMATUR
IMPROBABLE
INCLINABLE
INCULPABLE
INDUCTANCE
INEVITABLE
INEXORABLE
INEXPIABLE
INIMITABLE
INOPERABLE
INSATIABLE
INSOLVABLE
INTERFAITH
INTERMARRY
INVALUABLE
INVARIABLE
INVIOLABLE
JACKANAPES
JAWBREAKER
LAWBREAKER
MARGINALIA
MATCHMAKER
MAYONNAISE
MENSURABLE
METASTASIS
MISTAKABLE
MONSTRANCE
MUHAMMADAN
NECROMANCY
NOISEMAKER
NOTICEABLE
OBSERVABLE
OBSERVANCE
OESOPHAGUS
OSTEOPATHY
OUTBALANCE
OVERCHARGE
OVERSHADOW
PALLBEARER
PANTYWAIST
PEACEMAKER
PERDURABLE
PERISHABLE
PERSONABLE
PERSONALTY
PETROLATUM
PHLEGMATIC
PHOTOPAINT
PREARRANGE
PREDICABLE
PROCURATOR
PROPAGANDA
PROVENANCE
PSYCHIATRY
QUICKBASIC
REASONABLE
RECEIVABLE
RECEPTACLE
REDUNDANCY
RELUCTANCE
REMARKABLE
REMEDIABLE
REMITTANCE
REPUGNANCE
RESISTANCE
RESPIRATOR
RESTORABLE
RIBOFLAVIN
RINGLEADER
SACROSANCT
SCHISMATIC
SEASONABLE
SHAMEFACED
SKYSCRAPER
SNAPDRAGON
SOMERSAULT
SOOTHSAYER
SUBSTRATUM
SUFFERANCE
SUPERCARGO
SUSTENANCE
TABERNACLE
TELEGRAPHY
TEMPERANCE
TERMINATOR
TOOTHPASTE
TOPOGRAPHY
TYPOGRAPHY
UNBEARABLE
UNBEATABLE
UNDENIABLE
UNDERPANTS
UNDERTAKER
UNDERVALUE
UNDERWAIST
UNDERWATER
UNSUITABLE
VULNERABLE
WASTEPAPER
WATCHMAKER
WITHDRAWAL
WRISTWATCH
XEROGRAPHY
AUTOMOBILE
BASKETBALL
BOOKMOBILE
BREASTBONE
CANNONBALL
CANVASBACK
COLLARBONE
CONTRABAND
CONTRIBUTE
CUMMERBUND
DISTRIBUTE
EXACERBATE
HANDLEBARS
JACKRABBIT
LANDLUBBER
MANDELBROT
MARROWBONE
MIDDLEBROW
MOUNTEBANK
POCKETBOOK
PROMPTBOOK
ROLLERBALL
ROUNDABOUT
ROUSTABOUT
SNOWMOBILE
SWITCHBACK
THREADBARE
VOLLEYBALL
WHIRLYBIRD
ADJUDICATE
ANIMALCULE
ANTHRACITE
ANTISOCIAL
APOTHECARY
ARTIFICIAL
BATHYSCAPH
BEAUTICIAN
BENEFACTOR
BENEFICENT
BENEFICIAL
BLUEJACKET
CANDESCENT
CANONICALS
CHEESECAKE
CIRCUMCISE
CLASSICISM
COMMERCIAL
COMPLECTED
COMPLICATE
COMPLICITY
CONDESCEND
CONFISCATE
CONSPECTUS
COWPUNCHER
CRUSTACEAN
DESTRUCTOR
DISCONCERT
DOGCATCHER
EMPIRICISM
EQUIVOCATE
EVANESCENT
FARFETCHED
FLYCATCHER
FOOTLOCKER
FRATRICIDE
GONOCOCCUS
INCAPACITY
INDELICATE
INSTRUCTOR
INTOXICANT
INTOXICATE
LANDLOCKED
LAWRENCIUM
LINEBACKER
MALEFACTOR
MALEFICENT
MICROSCOPE
MUNIFICENT
NANOSECOND
NUTCRACKER
OPALESCENT
PARAMECIUM
PEPPERCORN
PICKPOCKET
PICOSECOND
PILLOWCASE
PLEBISCITE
POLITICIAN
PROSPECTUS
PROTRACTOR
PROVINCIAL
PSEUDOCODE
PUTRESCENT
RADARSCOPE
RAMSHACKLE
SEERSUCKER
SIMPLICITY
SKEPTICISM
SPORTSCAST
SUPPLICANT
SUPPLICATE
TECHNICIAN
THREESCORE
THUMBSCREW
TRIPLICATE
TURNBUCKLE
UNAFFECTED
UNATTACHED
UNDERSCORE
UNEXPECTED
WOODPECKER
AGGRANDIZE
AMERINDIAN
ANTECEDENT
ARMAGEDDON
BALDERDASH
BASTARDIZE
BOMBARDIER
CHALCEDONY
COINCIDENT
COMMANDANT
COMMANDEER
COMPENDIUM
CONCORDANT
CONTRADICT
DEHUMIDIFY
DESCENDANT
EISTEDDFOD
EMBROIDERY
FLUORIDATE
FORBIDDING
FOREORDAIN
FUSSBUDGET
GORMANDIZE
HORRENDOUS
HUSBANDMAN
INBREEDING
INDIVIDUAL
INTIMIDATE
INVALIDATE
KETTLEDRUM
LIPREADING
MISCONDUCT
OUTLANDISH
PACKSADDLE
PANJANDRUM
POLYHEDRON
PREBENDARY
PRIMORDIAL
PROCEEDING
PYRIMIDINE
RESOUNDING
RESPONDENT
SPLASHDOWN
STEPLADDER
STUPENDOUS
TREMENDOUS
TROUBADOUR
TUMBLEDOWN
TURTLEDOVE
UNABRIDGED
UNYIELDING
UPSTANDING
ABSTINENCE
ALPHABETIC
ANEMOMETER
ANESTHESIA
ANESTHETIC
ANTIFREEZE
ANTITHESIS
APOLOGETIC
ARITHMETIC
BIPARIETAL
BLACKBERRY
BOOKKEEPER
CALCAREOUS
CANTILEVER
CARBURETOR
CATCHPENNY
CELLARETTE
CENTIMETER
CHARTREUSE
CITRONELLA
COLLATERAL
COMEDIENNE
COMPETENCE

COMPETENCY
COMPUSERVE
CONFERENCE
CONFIDENCE
CONFLUENCE
CONGRUENCE
CONGRUENCY
CONSCIENCE
CONTINENCE
CONVALESCE
CORPULENCE
CRETACEOUS
CURVACEOUS
CYCLOMETER
CYCLOPEDIA
DELIQUESCE
DEMOISELLE
DEPENDENCE
DEPENDENCY
DESERVEDLY
DETERRENCE
DIFFERENCE
DIMINUENDO
DIPHTHERIA
DISINHERIT
DISORDERLY
DOORKEEPER
EFFERVESCE
EFFICIENCY
EFFLORESCE
EFFULGENCE
ELDERBERRY
ENDANGERED
ERGOSTEROL
ERYSIPELAS
EXCELLENCE
EXCELLENCY
EXPEDIENCE
EXPEDIENCY
EXPERIENCE
EXTRANEOUS
GAMEKEEPER
GATEKEEPER
GEOSCIENCE
GOALKEEPER
GOOSEBERRY
GRAVIMETER
HECTOMETER
HEPTAMETER
HYDROMETER
HYGROMETER
HYPOTHESIS
IMPATIENCE
INCUMBENCY
INDULGENCE
INSISTENCE
INTERFERON
INTERLEAVE
INTERMEZZO
INTERWEAVE
LOGANBERRY
MAISONETTE
MARIONETTE
MICROMETER
MIGNONETTE
MILLIMETER
MISSILEMAN
MOHAMMEDAN
MOLYBDENUM
MONOTHEISM
MOZZARELLA
MULTILEVEL
MULTIMEDIA
MULTISENSE
MYRIAMETER
OCCURRENCE
OUTGENERAL
OUTRAGEOUS
PARAPLEGIA
PASSAGEWAY
PENTAMETER
PERIPHERAL
PESTILENCE
PHENOMENON
PHOTOGENIC
PHOTOMETER
POLYTHEISM
PRECEDENCE
PREDACEOUS
PREDECEASE
PREFERENCE
PRESCIENCE
PRIVILEGED
PROMINENCE
PROPRIETOR
PROSTHESIS
PROVIDENCE
PUBESCENCE
RADIOGENIC
RADIOMETER
RECOMPENSE
REFULGENCE
RENASCENCE
REPORTEDLY
RESILIENCE
RESILIENCY
RESURGENCE
RHINOCEROS
ROTISSERIE
SENESCENCE
SEPTICEMIA
SERVICEMAN
SHOPKEEPER
SILHOUETTE
SPITTLEBUG
STRAWBERRY
STRINGENCY
STRIPTEASE
SWEETHEART
TACHOMETER
TARANTELLA
TETRAMETER
THREEPENCE
TIMEKEEPER
TRANSVERSE
TURBULENCE
UNBELIEVER
UNDERBELLY
UNDERNEATH
UNDERSEXED
UNGRACEFUL
UNGRATEFUL
UNICAMERAL
UNILATERAL
UNLETTERED
UNMANNERLY
UNNUMBERED
VERMICELLI
WATERMELON
WHATSOEVER
WHENSOEVER
WHOMSOEVER
WILDEBEEST
CENTRIFUGE
CHLOROFORM
CINQUEFOIL
CIRCUMFLEX
CLASSIFIED
CUTTLEFISH
DISCOMFORT
EMULSIFIER
GENTLEFOLK
HERETOFORE
OUTPERFORM
PLUPERFECT
QUATREFOIL
RAGAMUFFIN
SILVERFISH
SUBSURFACE
SUBTERFUGE
TENDERFOOT
THEREAFTER
ASTRINGENT
BALBRIGGAN
BEDRAGGLED
BOONDOGGLE
CAPOREGIME
CARDIOGRAM
CHURCHGOER
CONGREGATE
CONTINGENT
CRYPTOGRAM
FOOTLIGHTS
HOMOLOGOUS
KIESELGUHR
MANDRAGORA
MARTINGALE
MISALIGNED
NEWFANGLED
PROFLIGATE
PROMULGATE
REFRINGENT
SCHOOLGIRL
SEISMOGRAM
SEPTUAGINT
SUFFRAGIST
UPBRINGING
WORKINGMAN
ALONGSHORE
ANGLOPHILE
ANGLOPHOBE
ATMOSPHERE
AUDIOPHILE
BATRACHIAN
BEFOREHAND
BEHINDHAND
BLACKTHORN
BRAINCHILD
BRIDGEHEAD
BUTTONHOLE
BUTTONHOOK
CAOUTCHOUC
CELLOPHANE
CLAVICHORD
COMPREHEND
COPPERHEAD
CRANKSHAFT
DISENCHANT
DUNDERHEAD
EMBOUCHURE
ESCUTCHEON
EVERYTHING
EVERYWHERE
FAHRENHEIT
FARSIGHTED
FIGUREHEAD
GESUNDHEIT
GRAMOPHONE
GRANDCHILD
HAMMERHEAD
HEARTTHROB
HEMISPHERE
HEMORRHAGE
HEMORRHOID
HIEROPHANT
HYDROPHONE
IONOSPHERE
KNIGHTHOOD
LEPRECHAUN
LETTERHEAD
LIKELIHOOD
LIVELIHOOD
LOGGERHEAD
MAIDENHAIR
MAIDENHEAD
MAIDENHOOD
MARASCHINO
MEERSCHAUM
MELANCHOLY
MESOSPHERE
MICROPHONE
MONARCHIST
MOTHERHOOD
NIGHTSHADE
NIGHTSHIRT
NOURISHING
PIGEONHOLE
PINCUSHION
PROMETHIUM
RADIOPHONE
SAPROPHYTE
SECONDHAND
SEPULCHRAL
SISTERHOOD
SPIROCHETE
STRAIGHTEN
STRONGHOLD
SUBTRAHEND
SYMPATHIZE
THROUGHOUT
THROUGHPUT
THROUGHWAY
ULTRASHORT
UNBLUSHING
UNDERSHIRT
UNDERSHOOT
UNFAITHFUL
VIBRAPHONE
VIDEOPHONE
WATERWHEEL
WHEELCHAIR
WORTHWHILE
ABBREVIATE
ABORIGINAL
ABSTEMIOUS
ACCESSIBLE
ADMISSIBLE
AFTERBIRTH
AIRFREIGHT
ALTARPIECE
AMPHIBIOUS
ANNUNCIATE
ANTICLIMAX
APOLITICAL
APPRECIATE
ARBORVITAE
ASPHYXIATE
AUSPICIOUS
BELONGINGS
BIOMEDICAL
BIPARTISAN
BIRTHRIGHT
BRONCHITIS
BUDGERIGAR
CALUMNIATE
CENSORIOUS
CENTESIMAL
CENTILITER
CHILDBIRTH
CHIMERICAL
CHINCHILLA
COMESTIBLE
COMMODIOUS
COMMUNIQUE
COMPARISON
COMPATIBLE
COMPETITOR
COMPOSITOR
CONCILIATE
CONGENITAL
CONTAGIOUS
CONVENIENT
COPYWRITER
CORDWAINER
CORRIGIBLE
COTERMINAL
CROSSPIECE
DEADWEIGHT
DEPRECIATE
DERMATITIS
DETERMINED
DISBELIEVE
DISHABILLE
DISSATISFY
DISSIMILAR
DISSOCIATE
DRAWBRIDGE
DUMBWAITER
DUODECIMAL
ECONOMICAL
ECUMENICAL
ENCYCLICAL
ENTHUSIASM
ESPADRILLE
EUPHONIOUS
EXPATRIATE
FACTITIOUS
FALLACIOUS
FASTIDIOUS
FERTILIZER
FICTITIOUS
FIELDPIECE
FLAGITIOUS
FLASHLIGHT
FLOODLIGHT
FOOTBRIDGE
FORTHRIGHT
FRANCHISEE
FRANCHISER
FRANCHISOR
GINGIVITIS
GRAINFIELD
GREGARIOUS
HANDMAIDEN
HARMONIOUS
HEADWAITER
HECTOLITER
HEMOPHILIA
IMMISCIBLE
IMPASSIBLE
IMPERVIOUS
IMPOSSIBLE
INCENDIARY
INCREDIBLE
INDISTINCT
INELIGIBLE
INFALLIBLE
INFLEXIBLE
INGLORIOUS
INGRATIATE
INGREDIENT
INSENSIBLE
INSENTIENT
INTANGIBLE
INTERTIDAL
INVINCIBLE
JARDINIERE
JINRIKISHA
LARYNGITIS
LASCIVIOUS
LICENTIATE
LICENTIOUS
LOQUACIOUS
LUBRICIOUS
LUGUBRIOUS
MECHANICAL
MENDACIOUS
MENINGITIS
MICROFICHE
MILLILITER
MILLWRIGHT
MOUTHPIECE
NEGLIGIBLE
OBSEQUIOUS
OFTENTIMES
OMNISCIENT
ORATORICAL
OSTENSIBLE
OUTPATIENT

PARMIGIANA
PARTICIPLE
PECCADILLO
PERCIPIENT
PERIODICAL
PERNICIOUS
PICCALILLI
PICKANINNY
PLAYWRIGHT
POLYCLINIC
POTENTIATE
POWERLINES
PRECARIOUS
PRECOCIOUS
PREMARITAL
PREMEDICAL
PRIZEFIGHT
PRODIGIOUS
PROFICIENT
PROGENITOR
PROPITIATE
PROPITIOUS
PUGNACIOUS
REBELLIOUS
RECONSIDER
REPATRIATE
REPUBLICAN
RESTRAINED
SALUBRIOUS
SHENANIGAN
SHIPWRIGHT
STILLBIRTH
SUBLIMINAL
SUBORBITAL
SUBSIDIARY
SUFFICIENT
SUSPICIOUS
TEETHRIDGE
TENEBRIOUS
THEATRICAL
TRIFOLIATE
TYPEWRITER
TYRANNICAL
UNCRITICAL
UNDERSIZED
UNGRACIOUS
UNMERCIFUL
UPROARIOUS
URETHRITIS
UROGENITAL
VAUDEVILLE
VICTORIOUS
WAINWRIGHT
WATERTIGHT
WINDSHIELD
WIREHAIRED
LUMBERJACK

CHEAPSKATE
LOVEMAKING
PREPACKAGE
RAINMAKING
ROLLICKING
SHUNPIKING
UNDERSKIRT
UNTHINKING
ACCOMPLICE
ACCOMPLISH
ACCUMULATE
ADRENALINE
ALCOHOLISM
ALLHALLOWS
ANNIHILATE
ANTEBELLUM
ARTICULATE
ASSEMBLAGE
ASSIMILATE
AUSTRALIAN
BEAUJOLAIS
BESTIALITY
BIMETALLIC
BIRTHPLACE
BLUECOLLAR
BONDHOLDER
BOOKSELLER
BORDERLAND
BOTTOMLAND
BROADCLOTH
CAMOUFLAGE
CAPITALISM
CAPITALIST
CAPITALIZE
CAPITULATE
CARDIOLOGY
CATABOLISM
CATAFALQUE
CENTRALIZE
CEREBELLUM
CHANCELLOR
CHANDELIER
CHANGELING
CHANNELIZE
CHAPFALLEN
CHRONOLOGY
CHRYSOLITE
CHURCHLESS
CLOVERLEAF
CONTROLLER
CORDILLERA
CRENELLATE
DECIMALIZE
DEMOBILIZE
DEMONOLOGY
DEMORALIZE
DENDROLOGY

DEPOPULATE
DEVITALIZE
DISCIPLINE
DISINCLINE
DISQUALIFY
DISTILLATE
EMASCULATE
EMBRYOLOGY
ENTOMOLOGY
EPITHELIUM
EQUIVALENT
EURODOLLAR
EVANGELISM
EVANGELIST
EVANGELIZE
EXOBIOLOGY
FATHERLAND
FATHOMLESS
FEDERALISM
FEDERALIST
FEDERALIZE
FIBERGLASS
FINGERLING
FLAGELLATE
FLOODPLAIN
FOSTERLING
FRAUDULENT
GENERALITY
GENERALIZE
GLACIOLOGY
GOOSEFLESH
GRADUALISM
GROUNDLING
GYNECOLOGY
HAMMERLOCK
HEMATOLOGY
HINTERLAND
HORSEFLESH
HOUSECLEAN
HYDRAULICS
HYDROPLANE
ICONOCLASM
ICONOCLAST
IMMACULATE
IMMOBILIZE
IMMORALITY
IMMUNOLOGY
INCIVILITY
INCOMPLETE
INEQUALITY
INFIDELITY
INTERBLOCK
IRRESOLUTE
JOURNALESE
JOURNALISM
LANDHOLDER
LIBERALISM

LITERALISM
LOGROLLING
MALEVOLENT
MANIPULATE
MEADOWLARK
METABOLISM
METABOLITE
METAGALAXY
METICULOUS
MINERALIZE
MINERALOGY
MISCELLANY
MORPHOLOGY
MOTHERLAND
MULTIPLIER
MUSICOLOGY
NATURALISM
NATURALIST
NATURALIZE
NEUTRALISM
NEUTRALITY
NEUTRALIZE
NONCHALANT
NOTABILITY
NUMBERLESS
NUMEROLOGY
OCEANOLOGY
OPHTHALMIC
PAINKILLER
PALATALIZE
PENICILLIN
PERIHELION
PERSIFLAGE
PHOTOFLASH
PHRENOLOGY
PHYSIOLOGY
PORTCULLIS
PRINCELING
PROPELLANT
PROTOPLASM
PSYCHOLOGY
RADICALIZE
RECOILLESS
RELENTLESS
REVITALIZE
RIDICULOUS
RISIBILITY
SACROILIAC
SALTCELLAR
SCURRILOUS
SEISMOLOGY
SELENOLOGY
SENEGALESE
SHIBBOLETH
SHILLELAGH
SPECIALIST
SPECIALIZE

SPRINKLING
STARVELING
SURREALISM
TABLECLOTH
TECHNOLOGY
TENDERLOIN
TESSELLATE
THEMSELVES
TIMBERLINE
TOMFOOLERY
TOURMALINE
TOXICOLOGY
TRAMPOLINE
TRANSPLANT
UNAVAILING
UNDERSLUNG
UNFAMILIAR
UNSKILLFUL
VICTUALLER
VISIBILITY
VOCABULARY
WANDERLUST
WEAPONLESS
WEIGHTLESS
WONDERLAND
ADVISEMENT
AFTERIMAGE
AMALGAMATE
ANTINOMIAN
ASSIGNMENT
ASSORTMENT
ATTACHMENT
ATTAINMENT
AUTONOMOUS
BACKGAMMON
BATTLEMENT
BETTERMENT
BLACKAMOOR
BLACKSMITH
BRIDESMAID
BUTTERMILK
CANTONMENT
COMPLEMENT
COMPLIMENT
COMPROMISE
CONFORMITY
CONSUMMATE
DENOUEMENT
DEPARTMENT
DEPORTMENT
DETACHMENT
DISCOMMODE
DISHARMONY
EMBANKMENT
EMPLOYMENT
ENDEARMENT
ENGAGEMENT

ENJAMBMENT
EQUANIMITY
ERGONOMICS
ESCARPMENT
EXCITEMENT
EXPERIMENT
GOVERNMENT
GROUNDMASS
HABILIMENT
HOMECOMING
IGNORAMOUS
IMPEDIMENT
INDUCEMENT
INSTRUMENT
INTEGUMENT
INTERNMENT
INVESTMENT
JACKHAMMER
LACHRYMOSE
LEGITIMATE
MANAGEMENT
MASTERMIND
MEDICAMENT
MISOGAMIST
MIZZENMAST
NETHERMOST
PARLIAMENT
PEPPERMINT
PILGRIMAGE
POSTHUMOUS
PREFERMENT
PROGRAMMED
PROGRAMMER
PUNISHMENT
REFINEMENT
SCHOOLMARM
SCHOOLMATE
SETTLEMENT
STALAGMITE
SUPPLEMENT
TOURNAMENT
UNASSUMING
UNBECOMING
UNIFORMITY
UNSCRAMBLE
VIETNAMESE
WINDJAMMER
WONDERMENT
ACCIDENTAL
AFICIONADO
ALBUMINOUS
ALKALINIZE
AMANUENSIS
ANTAGONISM
ANTAGONIST
ANTAGONIZE
ANTEPENULT

ANTICANCER
AQUALUNGER
AUCTIONEER
BACKHANDED
BESPRINKLE
BIPARENTAL
BITUMINOUS
BLUEBONNET
BOTTLENECK
BRAHMANISM
CARABINEER
CENTENNIAL
CEREMONIAL
CHAUVINISM
CHIFFONIER
CHIMPANZEE
CHLORINATE
CONCERNING
COORDINATE
CRYOGENICS
DEHUMANIZE
DELPHINIUM
DENOMINATE
DESALINATE
DESALINIZE
DIAPHANOUS
DICTIONARY
DISCERNING
DISCONNECT
DISGRUNTLE
DISJOINTED
EFFEMINATE
ENDOGENOUS
EVENHANDED
EXURBANITE
EYEWITNESS
FINGERNAIL
FLUORINATE
FOLKSINGER
FOREFINGER
FOREHANDED
FORERUNNER
FRATERNITY
FRATERNIZE
GADOLINIUM
GASTRONOMY
GUNSLINGER
HIGHLANDER
HOMOGENIZE
HORIZONTAL
HYPOCENTER
HYPOTENUSE
ILLUMINATE
IMPREGNATE
INCIDENTAL
INDEFINITE
INDIGENOUS

INHUMANITY
INNOMINATE
INORDINATE
INSEMINATE
JUGGERNAUT
KNICKKNACK
LADYFINGER
LIBIDINOUS
LIEUTENANT
LITHUANIAN
MEMORANDUM
MILLENNIUM
MISOGYNIST
MISSIONARY
MONOTONOUS
MONUMENTAL
MUDSLINGER
NONDRINKER
NUCLEONICS
OCCIDENTAL
OLEAGINOUS
OVERWINTER
PALATINATE
PATHFINDER
PERITONEUM
PERIWINKLE
PLEASANTRY
PREEMINENT
PRONOUNCED
PROPRINTER
PROSCENIUM
QUADRANGLE
REFERENDUM
REJUVENATE
REPAGINATE
ROADRUNNER
RUBBERNECK
SALAMANDER
SANGUINARY
SCRUTINIZE
SHORTENING
SIDEWINDER
STATIONARY
STATIONERY
STRYCHNINE
TURTLENECK
UNBALANCED
UNFRIENDLY
UNGROUNDED
VETERINARY
VILLAINOUS
VOLUMINOUS
WAVELENGTH
WESTERNIZE
WHARFINGER
WHITSUNDAY
WILDERNESS
ABOVEBOARD
ACCUSTOMED
ACROPHOBIA
ADDITIONAL
ANTIBIOTIC
ANTIPHONAL
ANTIPROTON
APOSTROPHE
APOTHEOSIS
BACKGROUND
BELLADONNA
BLACKBOARD
BLOCKHOUSE
BLOODHOUND
BREADBOARD
CANTALOUPE
CARCINOGEN
CHANGEOVER
CHECKPOINT
CORNFLOWER
CORNUCOPIA
COSMOPOLIS
COURTHOUSE
CROSSBONES
DISAPPOINT
DISEMBOWEL
DREAMWORLD
ELECTRONIC
EMBONPOINT
ESCRITOIRE
FAIRGROUND
FIBERBOARD
FIBRINOGEN
FLOORBOARD
FOREGROUND
FREEBOOTER
GREENHOUSE
GUARDHOUSE
HEMOGLOBIN
HENCEFORTH
HEREABOUTS
HISTRIONIC
HOBBYHORSE
HODGEPODGE
HORSEPOWER
HORSEWOMAN
IMPERSONAL
INDISPOSED
INFRASONIC
IRRATIONAL
LEDERHOSEN
LIGHTHOUSE
MALAPROPOS
METROPOLIS
MONOPHONIC
NAPOLEONIC
NECROPOLIS
NEIGHBORLY
NEWSGROUPS
OCCASIONAL
OCEANGOING
OCTOTHORPE
OTHERWORLD
PANTALOONS
PAPERBOARD
PARATROOPS
PASTEBOARD
PAWNBROKER
PEASHOOTER
PENNYROYAL
PHILOSOPHY
PHOSPHORUS
PIANOFORTE
PILOTHOUSE
PLAYGROUND
POWERHOUSE
PRESBYOPIA
RADIOSONDE
RECIPROCAL
RELATIONAL
REPERTOIRE
ROUGHHOUSE
ROUNDHOUSE
SACERDOTAL
SALESWOMAN
SERVOMOTOR
SKATEBOARD
SOPHOMORIC
SPELLBOUND
STAGECOACH
STANDPOINT
STATEHOUSE
STOREHOUSE
SUPERSONIC
TANTAMOUNT
TELESCOPIC
THROMBOSIS
TRANSPOLAR
TRAVELOGUE
ULTRASONIC
ULTRASOUND
UNDERCOVER
UNDERWORLD
UNEMPLOYED
UNHALLOWED
UNREASONED
UNSCHOOLED
WALLFLOWER
WATCHTOWER
WATERBORNE
WATERCOLOR
WATERPOWER
WATERWORKS
WHEELHORSE
WHEELHOUSE
WINDFLOWER
WINEGROWER
WRAPAROUND
XENOPHOBIA
ANGIOSPERM
ANTHROPOID
ANTICIPATE
ANTISEPTIC
APOCRYPHAL
CAMELOPARD
CLODHOPPER
CORRESPOND
CYBERSPACE
DISCOMPOSE
DISCREPANT
DISRESPECT
EMANCIPATE
EPISCOPACY
EPISCOPATE
EUCALYPTUS
EYEDROPPER
GYMNOSPERM
HELICOPTER
LEAFHOPPER
MALADAPTED
MIDSHIPMAN
NINCOMPOOP
NONSUPPORT
PETNAPPING
PREDISPOSE
PRESUPPOSE
PRINCIPLED
PSYCHOPATH
QUADRUPLET
QUINTUPLET
RETROSPECT
SPOILSPORT
SUBCOMPACT
TABLESPOON
UNEXAMPLED
UNOCCUPIED
VELOCIPEDE
WATERSPOUT
WINDOWPANE
WORSHIPFUL
TOURNIQUET
ACCELERATE
ADULTERANT
ADULTERATE
ALLITERATE
AMELIORATE
ANTICHRIST
AQUAMARINE
ARCHITRAVE
ASSEVERATE
AUDITORIUM
AURIFEROUS
AUTOSTRADA
BACKSTROKE
BALUSTRADE
BELLETRIST
BICHLORIDE
BLITZKRIEG
BOISTEROUS
BOWDLERIZE
BREADFRUIT
BREAKFRONT
BRIDEGROOM
CADAVEROUS
CAMPHORATE
CATEGORIZE
CENTIGRADE
CHATTERBOX
CHIVALROUS
CINERARIUM
COCKATRICE
COMPATRIOT
CONCURRENT
CONSECRATE
CONSPIRACY
COUNTERACT
COUNTERMAN
COUNTERSPY
CRISSCROSS
CROSSBREED
DECELERATE
DECOLORIZE
DECOMPRESS
DEFLAGRATE
DEGENERACY
DEGENERATE
DELIBERATE
DENTIFRICE
DEPOLARIZE
DISAPPROVE
DISCOURAGE
DISHEARTEN
DOCKWORKER
DONNYBROOK
DOWNSTREAM
DOWNSTROKE
DRAWSTRING
ELECTORATE
ENTERPRISE
EQUESTRIAN
EVISCERATE
EXAGGERATE
EXASPERATE
EXHILARATE
EXOTHERMIC
FAMILARIZE
GEOTHERMAL
GERIATRICS
GHOSTWRITE
GRAPEFRUIT
HANDBARROW
HANDICRAFT
HANDSPRING
HEADSTRONG
HEARTBREAK
HEATSTROKE
HELIOGRAPH
HELIOTROPE
HIPPODROME
HONORARIUM
HYPODERMIC
ILLITERATE
ILLUSTRATE
IMMATERIAL
IMMEMORIAL
IMMODERATE
IMPOVERISH
INAUGURATE
INCINERATE
INCOHERENT
INDECOROUS
INDISCREET
INDUSTRIAL
INFILTRATE
INTERBREED
INTERURBAN
INTOLERANT
INVETERATE
INVIGORATE
ISOMETRICS
ISOTHERMAL
KRUGERRAND
LIGHTPROOF
MAGISTRATE
MAINSPRING
MAINSTREAM
MALODOROUS
MANICURIST
MANTLEROCK
MANUSCRIPT
MARGUERITE
MASQUERADE
METACARPUS
METATARSAL
METATARSUS
MICROGRAPH
MICROPROBE
MILITARISM
MILITARIZE
MILLSTREAM
MIMEOGRAPH
MINESTRONE
MINISCROLL
MINISTRANT
MONOCHROME
MOONSTRUCK
MORATORIUM
MOTORTRUCK
NATATORIUM
NEWSWORTHY
NIGHTDRESS
NONSTARTER
NOTEWORTHY
OBLITERATE
OBSTETRICS
OCEANARIUM
OCEANFRONT
OMNIVOROUS
OPPROBRIUM
OUTPOURING
OVERSPREAD
PACKTHREAD
PAINTBRUSH
PALINDROME
PARAPHRASE
PASTEURIZE
PEDESTRIAN
PEDIATRICS
PERMAFROST
PERPETRATE
PHONOGRAPH
PHOTOGRAPH
PLAGIARIZE
PLUTOCRACY
POSTMORTEM
POSTPARTUM
POSTSCRIPT
POURPARLER
PRESSURIZE
PROSPERITY
PROSPEROUS
RADIOGRAPH
RECUPERATE
REDISTRICT
REGENERACY
REGENERATE
REGISTRANT
REMUNERATE
RESTAURANT
RETROGRADE
RETROGRESS
SACCHARINE
SANATORIUM
SANITARIAN
SANITARIUM
SAUERKRAUT
SCAPEGRACE
SCHOOLROOM
SEAMSTRESS
SECULARISM
SECULARIZE
SEMPSTRESS

SHOESTRING
SHUTTERBUG
SIDESTROKE
SLENDERIZE
SLIPSTREAM
SLUMBEROUS
SMATTERING
SOLIDARITY
SPACECRAFT
STATECRAFT
STENTORIAN
STEPPARENT
SWEETBREAD
SWEETBRIER
TAMBOURINE
TEARJERKER
THUNDEROUS
TOOTHBRUSH
TRANSCRIBE
TRANSCRIPT
TRANSGRESS
TYPESCRIPT
UNDERBRUSH
UNDERCROFT
UNDERTRICK
UNDERWRITE
UNGENEROUS
UNRESERVED
VEGETARIAN
VERTEBRATE
VICEGERENT
VITUPERATE
VIVIPAROUS
VOCIFERATE
VOCIFEROUS
VOICEPRINT
WATERCRAFT
WATERCRESS
WATERFRONT
WATERPROOF
WEATHERING
WEATHERMAN
WELLSPRING
WIDESPREAD
WINGSPREAD
WITCHCRAFT
WITCHGRASS
ABSCISSION
ADMINISTER
AGGRESSION
AGGRESSIVE
ARCHBISHOP
AUTHORSHIP
BATTLESHIP
BIOPHYSICS
BRONTOSAUR
BUSHMASTER
CENSORSHIP
CHARLESTON
CHROMOSOME
CLOTHESPIN
COMMISSARY
COMMISSION
COMPASSION
COMPENSATE
COMPULSION
COMPULSIVE
COMPULSORY
CONCESSION
CONCESSIVE
CONCLUSION
CONCUSSION
CONDENSATE
CONFESSION
CONVERSANT
CONVERSION
CONVULSION
COTTONSEED
CRADLESONG
DEALERSHIP
DECLASSIFY
DECLENSION
DEPRESSANT
DEPRESSION
DEPRESSIVE
DISCURSIVE
DISCUSSANT
DISHWASHER
DISPENSARY
DISPOSSESS
DISSENSION
DYSPROSIUM
EXPRESSION
EXPRESSMAN
EXPRESSWAY
FELLOWSHIP
FILIBUSTER
FORECASTLE
FORTISSIMO
FUTURISTIC
GEOPHYSICS
GINGERSNAP
HEADMASTER
HEARTHSIDE
IMPRESSION
IMPRESSIVE
INDECISION
INDECISIVE
INDONESIAN
KINGFISHER
LACKLUSTER
MALTHUSIAN
MASTERSHIP
MEDDLESOME
MELANESIAN
MEMBERSHIP
METTLESOME
NARCISSISM
NEBULOSITY
NEOCLASSIC
NETTLESOME
OPPRESSION
OVERMASTER
PALIMPSEST
PENMANSHIP
PERCUSSION
PERMISSION
PERMISSIVE
PERQUISITE
PERSUASION
PERVERSION
PIANISSIMO
PICARESQUE
POLYNESIAN
POSSESSION
POSSESSIVE
POSTMASTER
PRECESSION
PRECIOSITY
PREHENSILE
PREPOSSESS
PROCESSION
PROFESSION
PROGNOSTIC
PROMISSORY
PROPENSITY
PROPULSION
READERSHIP
REGRESSION
RESPONSIVE
RINGMASTER
SCHOLASTIC
SEAMANSHIP
SIMPLISTIC
STATUESQUE
STEPSISTER
STOCHASTIC
SUCCESSION
SUCCESSIVE
SUNGLASSES
SUSPENSION
SUSPENSORY
TATTERSALL
TASKMASTER
TELEVISION
THERMISTOR
THERMOSTAT
TRANSISTOR
UNHANDSOME
UNIVERSITY
UNPLEASANT
VARICOSITY
VIRTUOSITY
WINCHESTER
WINDOWSILL
WORKBASKET
YARDMASTER
ABERRATION
ABSOLUTION
ABSOLUTISM
ABSORPTION
ACCOUNTANT
ACCOUNTING
ACCUSATIVE
ACROBATICS
AEROBATICS
AESTHETICS
AFFLICTIVE
ALIMENTARY
ALTOGETHER
AMBULATORY
AMMUNITION
ANTIMATTER
APPARITION
APPOINTIVE
APPOSITION
APPOSITIVE
APPRENTICE
ASPIRATION
ASSUMPTION
ASYMMETRIC
ATTRACTANT
ATTRACTION
AUTOMATION
AUTOMATIZE
AUTOMOTIVE
BALLISTICS
BAPTISTERY
BEDCLOTHES
BELLWETHER
BIRTHSTONE
BLOODSTAIN
BLOODSTONE
BLUEBOTTLE
BRAINSTORM
BREADSTUFF
BRIGANTINE
BROWNSTONE
CACCIATORE
CAPACITATE
CAPITATION
CARICATURE
CAVITATION
CHARACTERY
CIRCUITOUS
CLERESTORY
CLINGSTONE
COLLECTIVE
COLORATION
COLORATURA
COLPORTEUR
COMBUSTION
COMMENTARY
CONCENTRIC
CONCEPTION
CONCERTINA
CONCRETION
CONDUCTIVE
CONFECTION
CONJECTURE
CONNECTION
CONNECTIVE
CONNIPTION
CONSISTORY
CONSORTIUM
CONSTITUTE
CONTENTION
CONVECTION
CONVENTION
CONVICTION
CORONATION
COTTONTAIL
CREDENTIAL
CUMULATIVE
DATAMATION
DEBILITATE
DECAPITATE
DECORATION
DECORATIVE
DECRYPTION
DEFINITION
DEFINITIVE
DELEGATION
DEMOLITION
DEMONETIZE
DENOTATIVE
DEPILATORY
DEPOSITION
DEPOSITORY
DEPUTATION
DERIVATION
DERIVATIVE
DEROGATORY
DESOLATION
DIELECTRIC
DIMINUTIVE
DISCONTENT
DISCRETION
DIVINATION
DOMINATION
EBULLITION
EFFRONTERY
EGOCENTRIC
ELEMENTARY
ENCRYPTION
EPIGLOTTIS
EQUITATION
ESTIMATION
EXACTITUDE
EXCOGITATE
EXHAUSTION
EXHAUSTIVE
EXORBITANT
EXPEDITION
EXPOSITION
FACILITATE
FAVORITISM
FEDERATION
FELICITATE
FELICITOUS
FIGURATION
FIGURATIVE
FOREFATHER
FOREGATHER
FORFEITURE
FORTUITOUS
FOUNDATION
GARGANTUAN
GENERATION
GEOCENTRIC
GRADUATION
GRANDSTAND
GRATUITOUS
GRAVESTONE
GRINDSTONE
GUILLOTINE
GYMNASTICS
HABITATION
HEREDITARY
IDIOPATHIC
IMBIBITION
IMPENITENT
IMPERATIVE
INAPTITUDE
INCONSTANT
INDICATIVE
INFIGHTING
INFINITIVE
INFINITUDE
INFLECTION
INFRACTION
INHABITANT
INHIBITION
INITIATIVE
INITIATORY
INJUNCTION
INNOVATION
INQUIETUDE
INSOLATION
INTERSTATE
INTERSTICE
INTINCTION
INTONATION
INTRASTATE
INVOCATION
INVOLUTION
JUBILATION
JUDICATURE
KINEMATICS
LABORATORY
LITERATURE
LOCOMOTION
LOCOMOTIVE
MACKINTOSH
MALCONTENT
MANSUETUDE
MATURATION
MERCANTILE
MICROSTATE
MISFORTUNE
MULTISTAGE
MULTISTORY
NASTURTIUM
NEWSLETTER
NIGHTSTICK
NOMINATIVE
OBLIGATION
OCCUPATION
OMNIPOTENT
ORDINATION
PAGINATION
PEJORATIVE
PERCENTAGE
PERCENTILE
PERCEPTION
PERCEPTIVE
PERCEPTUAL
PEREMPTORY
PERFECTION
PERORATION
PHILISTINE
PHLEBOTOMY
PHYLACTERY
PINFEATHER
PLANTATION
PLAYACTING
POINSETTIA
POPULATION
PORTENTOUS
PRAGMATISM
PRECAUTION
PREDESTINE
PREEMPTIVE
PRESBYTERY
PRODUCTION
PROJECTILE
PROMONTORY
PROPERTIED
PROPORTION

PROSTITUTE
PROTECTION
PROTESTANT
QUADRATICS
QUARANTINE
RATTLETRAP
RECITATION
RECREATION
REDEMPTION
REFRACTION
REFRACTORY
REGULATION
RELAXATION
REPARATION
REPARATIVE
REPETITION
REPETITIVE
REPOSITORY
REPUTATION
RESOLUTION
RESORPTION
RESPECTING
RESPECTIVE
RETRACTILE
REVELATION
REVOCATION
REVOLUTION
RHEUMATISM
RHINESTONE
RICKETTSIA
SALUTATION
SANITATION
SCARLATINA
SEPARATION
SEPARATIST
SEPARATIVE
SERPENTINE
SHIPFITTER
SIMILITUDE
SINGLETREE
SKYWRITING
SMOKESTACK
SOLICITOUS
SOLICITUDE
SPOLIATION
SPRINGTIME
STALACTITE
STANDSTILL
STATISTICS
STEPFATHER
STEPMOTHER
STEREOTYPE
STIGMATIZE
STRENGTHEN
SUBJECTIVE
SUBROUTINE
SUBSTATION
SUBSTITUTE
SUBVENTION
SUGGESTION
SUGGESTIVE
TATTLETALE
TECHNETIUM
TEMPTATION
THOUGHTFUL
TORRENTIAL
TOUCHSTONE
TRAJECTORY
TRANSITION
TRANSITIVE
TRANSITORY
TRAVERTINE
TRIMONTHLY
TRIPARTITE
TRUNCATION
TURPENTINE
TYPESETTER
UBIQUITOUS
UNDERSTAND
UNDERSTATE
UNDERSTOOD
UNDERSTORY
UNDERSTUDY
UNDULATION
UNEVENTFUL
UNFRUITFUL
UPHOLSTERY
VEGETATION
VEGETATIVE
VESPERTINE
VINDICTIVE
VISITATION
VOLUMETRIC
WINTERTIDE
WINTERTIME
WOODCUTTER
ACCENTUATE
ADVENTURER
BLACKGUARD
CATECHUMEN
CLOUDBURST
COLLOQUIAL
COLLOQUIUM
CONSEQUENT
CONTIGUOUS
CONTINUITY
CONTINUOUS
CONVOLUTED
CURRICULUM
DELINQUENT
DIFFICULTY
DISTRAUGHT
EARTHQUAKE
EFFECTUATE
EXTINGUISH
EXTRAMURAL
FISTICUFFS
FLUIDOUNCE
FOURSQUARE
HALLELUJAH
INADEQUATE
INFREQUENT
INTERLUNAR
INTRAMURAL
KNOCKWURST
LIVERWURST
METALLURGY
ORGANGUTAN
PARTICULAR
PERPETUATE
PERPETUITY
PHOTOMURAL
PORTUGUESE
RACECOURSE
RELINQUISH
SPIRITUOUS
SUBSEQUENT
TRANSDUCER
TUBERCULAR
TUBERCULIN
TUMULTUOUS
VERNACULAR
VOLUPTUARY
VOLUPTUOUS
ANIMADVERT
BOLSHEVISM
CIRCUMVENT
CONTRAVENE
CONTROVERT
DEACTIVATE
DISSERVICE
INACTIVATE
IRRELEVANT
LIFESAVING
MANSERVANT
NEGATIVISM
PROCLIVITY
QUADRIVIUM
REACTIVATE
RECIDIVISM
RELATIVITY
RENDEZVOUS
BREASTWORK
BRIDGEWORK
BROADSWORD
CANDLEWICK
CANKERWORM
COMMONWEAL
COTTONWOOD
DINNERWARE
ENAMELWARE
GREENSWARD
GROUNDWORK
HOLLOWWARE
INTERTWINE
INTERTWIST
JIMSONWEED
LENGTHWISE
MASTERWORK
NATIONWIDE
NEEDLEWORK
SANDALWOOD
SEARCHWARE
SILVERWARE
SUPERTWIST
TUMBLEWEED
WICKERWORK
WILLOWWARE
WOODENWARE
COMPLEXION
HOMOSEXUAL
APOCALYPSE
CHURCHYARD
COUNTRYMAN
FLAMBOYANT
HIGHWAYMAN
HYDROLYSIS
JOURNEYMAN
LUMBERYARD
MOTORCYCLE
NURSERYMAN
PATRONYMIC
POULTRYMAN
SEMIDRYING
TROLLEYBUS
UNDERLYING
URINALYSIS
YESTERYEAR
APPETIZING
GORGONZOLA

## 8TH LETTER

ABBREVIATE
ABOVEBOARD
ACCELERATE
ACCENTUATE
ACCOUNTANT
ACCUMULATE
ADJUDICATE
ADULTERANT
ADULTERATE
AFICIONADO
AFTERIMAGE
ALIMENTARY
ALLITERATE
AMALGAMATE
AMELIORATE
ANNIHILATE
ANNUNCIATE
ANTICIPATE
APOTHECARY
APPRECIATE
ARCHITRAVE
ARTICULATE
ASPHYXIATE
ASSEMBLAGE
ASSEVERATE
ASSIMILATE
ATTRACTANT
AUTOSTRADA
BALDERDASH
BALUSTRADE
BASKETBALL
BATHYSCAPH
BEAUJOLAIS
BEFOREHAND
BEHINDHAND
BIRTHPLACE
BLACKBOARD
BLACKGUARD
BLOODSTAIN
BORDERLAND
BOTTOMLAND
BREADBOARD
BRIDESMAID
BRONTOSAUR
CALUMNIATE
CAMELOPARD
CAMOUFLAGE
CAMPHORATE
CANNONBALL
CANONICALS
CANVASBACK
CAPACITATE
CAPITULATE
CELLOPHANE
CENTIGRADE
CHEAPSKATE
CHEESECAKE
CHLORINATE
CHURCHYARD
COMMANDANT
COMMENTARY
COMMISSARY
COMPENSATE
COMPLICATE
CONCILIATE
CONCORDANT
CONDENSATE
CONFISCATE
CONGREGATE
CONSECRATE
CONSPIRACY
CONSUMMATE
CONTRABAND
CONVERSANT
COORDINATE
COTTONTAIL
COUNTERACT
CRANKSHAFT
CRENELLATE
CYBERSPACE
DEACTIVATE
DEBILITATE
DECAPITATE
DECELERATE
DEFLAGRATE
DEGENERACY
DEGENERATE
DELIBERATE
DENOMINATE
DEPOPULATE
DEPRECIATE
DEPRESSANT
DESALINATE
DESCENDANT
DICTIONARY
DINNERWARE
DISCOURAGE
DISCREPANT
DISCUSSANT
DISENCHANT
DISPENSARY
DISSOCIATE
DISTILLATE
EARTHQUAKE
EFFECTUATE
EFFEMINATE
ELECTORATE
ELEMENTARY
EMANCIPATE
EMASCULATE
ENAMELWARE
ENTHUSIASM
EPISCOPACY
EPISCOPATE
EQUIVOCATE
EVISCERATE
EXACERBATE
EXAGGERATE
EXASPERATE
EXCOGITATE
EXHILARATE
EXORBITANT
EXPATRIATE
FACILITATE
FATHERLAND
FELICITATE
FIBERBOARD
FIBERGLASS
FINGERNAIL
FLAGELLATE
FLAMBOYANT
FLOODPLAIN
FLOORBOARD
FLUORIDATE
FLUORINATE
FOREORDAIN
FOURSQUARE
GRANDSTAND
GREENSWARD
GROUNDMASS
HANDICRAFT
HANDLEBARS
HELIOGRAPH
HEMORRHAGE
HEREDITARY
HIEROPHANT
HINTERLAND
HOLLOWWARE
HYDROPLANE
ICONOCLASM
ICONOCLAST
ILLITERATE
ILLUMINATE
ILLUSTRATE
IMMACULATE
IMMODERATE
IMPREGNATE
INACTIVATE
INADEQUATE
INAUGURATE
INCENDIARY
INCINERATE
INCONSTANT
INDELICATE
INFILTRATE
INGRATIATE
INHABITANT
INNOMINATE
INORDINATE
INSEMINATE
INTERLEAVE
INTERSTATE
INTERWEAVE
INTIMIDATE
INTOLERANT
INTOXICANT
INTOXICATE
INTRASTATE
INVALIDATE
INVETERATE
INVIGORATE
IRRELEVANT
JUGGERNAUT
KNICKKNACK

KRUGERRAND
LEGITIMATE
LEPRECHAUN
LICENTIATE
LIEUTENANT
LUMBERJACK
LUMBERYARD
MAGISTRATE
MAIDENHAIR
MANIPULATE
MANSERVANT
MARTINGALE
MASQUERADE
MEADOWLARK
MEERSCHAUM
METAGALAXY
MICROGRAPH
MICROSTATE
MIMEOGRAPH
MINISTRANT
MISCELLANY
MISSIONARY
MIZZENMAST
MOTHERLAND
MOUNTEBANK
MULTISTAGE
NIGHTSHADE
NONCHALANT
OBLITERATE
PALATINATE
PAPERBOARD
PARAPHRASE
PARMIGIANA
PASTEBOARD
PERCENTAGE
PERPETRATE
PERPETUATE
PERSIFLAGE
PHONOGRAPH
PHOTOFLASH
PHOTOGRAPH
PILGRIMAGE
PILLOWCASE
PLUTOCRACY
POTENTIATE
PREBENDARY
PREDECEASE
PREPACKAGE
PROFLIGATE
PROMULGATE
PROPELLANT
PROPITIATE
PROTESTANT
PROTOPLASM
PSYCHOPATH
RADIOGRAPH
REACTIVATE

RECUPERATE
REGENERACY
REGENERATE
REGISTRANT
REJUVENATE
REMUNERATE
REPAGINATE
REPATRIATE
RESTAURANT
RETROGRADE
ROLLERBALL
SANGUINARY
SAUERKRAUT
SCAPEGRACE
SCHOOLMARM
SCHOOLMATE
SEARCHWARE
SECONDHAND
SHILLELAGH
SILVERWARE
SKATEBOARD
SMOKESTACK
SPACECRAFT
SPORTSCAST
STAGECOACH
STATECRAFT
STATIONARY
STRIPTEASE
SUBCOMPACT
SUBSIDIARY
SUBSURFACE
SUPPLICANT
SUPPLICATE
SWEETHEART
SWITCHBACK
TATTERSALL
TATTLETALE
TESSELLATE
THREADBARE
TRANSPLANT
TRIFOLIATE
TRIPLICATE
UNDERNEATH
UNDERSTAND
UNDERSTATE
UNPLEASANT
VERTEBRATE
VETERINARY
VITUPERATE
VOCABULARY
VOCIFERATE
VOLLEYBALL
VOLUPTUARY
WATERCRAFT
WHEELCHAIR
WILLOWWARE
WINDOWPANE

WITCHCRAFT
WITCHGRASS
WONDERLAND
WOODENWARE
ABOMINABLE
ACCEPTABLE
ACCESSIBLE
ACROPHOBIA
ACTIONABLE
ADMISSIBLE
ANSWERABLE
APPLICABLE
CANDELABRA
CHARITABLE
CHATTERBOX
COMESTIBLE
COMPARABLE
COMPATIBLE
CORRIGIBLE
CREDITABLE
DEGRADABLE
DELECTABLE
DEPENDABLE
DEPLORABLE
DESPICABLE
DISPOSABLE
EXPLICABLE
FORMIDABLE
HEMOGLOBIN
HOSPITABLE
IMAGINABLE
IMMISCIBLE
IMPALPABLE
IMPASSABLE
IMPASSIBLE
IMPECCABLE
IMPLACABLE
IMPOSSIBLE
IMPROBABLE
INCLINABLE
INCREDIBLE
INCULPABLE
INELIGIBLE
INEVITABLE
INEXORABLE
INEXPIABLE
INFALLIBLE
INFLEXIBLE
INIMITABLE
INOPERABLE
INSATIABLE
INSENSIBLE
INSOLVABLE
INTANGIBLE
INTERURBAN
INVALUABLE
INVARIABLE

INVINCIBLE
INVIOLABLE
JACKRABBIT
LANDLUBBER
MENSURABLE
MISTAKABLE
NEGLIGIBLE
NOTICEABLE
OBSERVABLE
OSTENSIBLE
PERDURABLE
PERISHABLE
PERSONABLE
PREDICABLE
REASONABLE
RECEIVABLE
REMARKABLE
REMEDIABLE
RESTORABLE
SEASONABLE
SHUTTERBUG
SPITTLEBUG
TROLLEYBUS
UNBEARABLE
UNBEATABLE
UNDENIABLE
UNSCRAMBLE
UNSUITABLE
VULNERABLE
XENOPHOBIA
ANTICANCER
APOLITICAL
ARCHDEACON
BIOMEDICAL
CHIMERICAL
ECONOMICAL
ECUMENICAL
ENCYCLICAL
GONOCOCCUS
MECHANICAL
MICROFICHE
MOTORCYCLE
ORATORICAL
PERIODICAL
PREMEDICAL
PRONOUNCED
RECEPTACLE
RECIPROCAL
REPUBLICAN
SHAMEFACED
TABERNACLE
THEATRICAL
TRANSDUCER
TYRANNICAL
UNBALANCED
UNCRITICAL
AMBASSADOR

ARMAGEDDON
BACKHANDED
BAREHEADED
BONDHOLDER
BULLHEADED
COPYREADER
CYCLOPEDIA
DESERVEDLY
DRAWBRIDGE
EVENHANDED
FOOTBRIDGE
FOREHANDED
FORESHADOW
HANDMAIDEN
HARDHEADED
HIGHLANDER
HODGEPODGE
INTERTIDAL
LANDHOLDER
MEMORANDUM
MOHAMMEDAN
MUHAMMADAN
MULTIMEDIA
OVERSHADOW
PACKSADDLE
PATHFINDER
RECONSIDER
REFERENDUM
REPORTEDLY
RINGLEADER
SALAMANDER
SIDEWINDER
STEPLADDER
TEETHRIDGE
UNFRIENDLY
UNGROUNDED
WHITSUNDAY
ADVISEMENT
ALTARPIECE
ANGIOSPERM
ANIMADVERT
ANTECEDENT
ANTIFREEZE
ASSIGNMENT
ASSORTMENT
ASTRINGENT
ATMOSPHERE
ATTACHMENT
ATTAINMENT
AUCTIONEER
BAPTISTERY
BATTLEMENT
BENEFICENT
BETTERMENT
BOTTLENECK
BRIDGEHEAD
CANDESCENT

CANTONMENT
CARABINEER
CHARACTERY
CHURCHLESS
CIRCUMVENT
CLOVERLEAF
COINCIDENT
COLPORTEUR
COMMANDEER
COMMONWEAL
COMPLEMENT
COMPLIMENT
COMPREHEND
CONCURRENT
CONDESCEND
CONSEQUENT
CONTINGENT
CONTRAVENE
CONTROVERT
CONVENIENT
COPPERHEAD
CORDILLERA
COTTONSEED
CROSSBREED
CROSSPIECE
CRUSTACEAN
DECOMPRESS
DELINQUENT
DENOUEMENT
DEPARTMENT
DEPORTMENT
DETACHMENT
DISBELIEVE
DISCONCERT
DISCONNECT
DISCONTENT
DISPOSSESS
DISRESPECT
DOWNSTREAM
DUNDERHEAD
EFFRONTERY
EMBANKMENT
EMBROIDERY
EMPLOYMENT
ENDEARMENT
ENGAGEMENT
ENJAMBMENT
EQUIVALENT
ESCARPMENT
ESCUTCHEON
EVANESCENT
EVERYWHERE
EXCITEMENT
EXPERIMENT
EYEWITNESS
FAHRENHEIT
FATHOMLESS

FIELDPIECE
FIGUREHEAD
FRAUDULENT
GESUNDHEIT
GOOSEFLESH
GOVERNMENT
GRAINFIELD
GYMNOSPERM
HABILIMENT
HAMMERHEAD
HEARTBREAK
HEMISPHERE
HORSEFLESH
HOUSECLEAN
IMPEDIMENT
IMPENITENT
INCOHERENT
INCOMPLETE
INDISCREET
INDUCEMENT
INFREQUENT
INGREDIENT
INSENTIENT
INSTRUMENT
INTEGUMENT
INTERBREED
INTERNMENT
INVESTMENT
IONOSPHERE
JARDINIERE
JIMSONWEED
JOURNALESE
LETTERHEAD
LOGGERHEAD
MAIDENHEAD
MAINSTREAM
MALCONTENT
MALEFICENT
MALEVOLENT
MANAGEMENT
MEDICAMENT
MESOSPHERE
MILLSTREAM
MOUTHPIECE
MUNIFICENT
NIGHTDRESS
NUMBERLESS
OMNIPOTENT
OMNISCIENT
OPALESCENT
OUTPATIENT
OVERSPREAD
PACKTHREAD
PALIMPSEST
PARLIAMENT
PERCIPIENT
PERITONEUM

PHYLACTERY
PLUPERFECT
PORTUGUESE
PREEMINENT
PREFERMENT
PREPOSSESS
PRESBYTERY
PROFICIENT
PUNISHMENT
PUTRESCENT
RECOILLESS
REFINEMENT
REFRINGENT
RELENTLESS
RESPONDENT
RETROGRESS
RETROSPECT
RUBBERNECK
SEAMSTRESS
SEMPSTRESS
SENEGALESE
SETTLEMENT
SHIBBOLETH
SLIPSTREAM
SPIROCHETE
STATIONERY
STEPPARENT
SUBSEQUENT
SUBTRAHEND
SUFFICIENT
SUPPLEMENT
SWEETBREAD
TOMFOOLERY
TOURNAMENT
TRANSGRESS
TUMBLEWEED
TURTLENECK
UPHOLSTERY
VELOCIPEDE
VICEGERENT
VIETNAMESE
WATERCRESS
WATERWHEEL
WEAPONLESS
WEIGHTLESS
WIDESPREAD
WILDEBEEST
WILDERNESS
WINDSHIELD
WINGSPREAD
WONDERMENT
YESTERYEAR
EISTEDDFOD
FISTICUFFS
RAGAMUFFIN
THOUGHTFUL
UNEVENTFUL
UNFAITHFUL
UNFRUITFUL
UNGRACEFUL
UNGRATEFUL
UNMERCIFUL
UNSKILLFUL
WORSHIPFUL
AIRFREIGHT
AQUALUNGER
BALBRIGGAN
BIRTHRIGHT
BOONDOGGLE
BUDGERIGAR
CARCINOGEN
DEADWEIGHT
DISTRAUGHT
FIBRINOGEN
FLASHLIGHT
FLOODLIGHT
FOLKSINGER
FOREFINGER
FORTHRIGHT
FUSSBUDGET
GUNSLINGER
LADYFINGER
MILLWRIGHT
MUDSLINGER
OESOPHAGUS
PARAPLEGIA
PLAYWRIGHT
PRIVILEGED
PRIZEFIGHT
QUADRANGLE
SHENANIGAN
SHIPWRIGHT
SNAPDRAGON
TRAVELOGUE
UNABRIDGED
WAINWRIGHT
WATERTIGHT
WAVELENGTH
WHARFINGER
ALTOGETHER
APOCRYPHAL
ARCHBISHOP
AUTHORSHIP
BATTLESHIP
BEDCLOTHES
BELLWETHER
CENSORSHIP
COWPUNCHER
DEALERSHIP
DISHWASHER
DOGCATCHER
FARFETCHED
FELLOWSHIP
FLYCATCHER
FOOTLIGHTS
FOREFATHER
FOREGATHER
IDIOPATHIC
KINGFISHER
MASTERSHIP
MEMBERSHIP
PENMANSHIP
PINFEATHER
READERSHIP
SEAMANSHIP
STEPFATHER
STEPMOTHER
STRENGTHEN
TRIMONTHLY
UNATTACHED
ABERRATION
ABSCISSION
ABSOLUTION
ABSOLUTISM
ABSORPTION
ACCOMPLICE
ACCOMPLISH
ACCOUNTING
ACCUSATIVE
ACROBATICS
ADRENALINE
AEROBATICS
AESTHETICS
AFFLICTIVE
AGGRANDIZE
AGGRESSION
AGGRESSIVE
ALCOHOLISM
ALKALINIZE
AMERINDIAN
AMMUNITION
ANGLOPHILE
ANTAGONISM
ANTAGONIST
ANTAGONIZE
ANTHRACITE
ANTICHRIST
ANTINOMIAN
ANTISOCIAL
APPARITION
APPETIZING
APPOINTIVE
APPOSITION
APPOSITIVE
APPRENTICE
AQUAMARINE
ARTIFICIAL
ASPIRATION
ASSUMPTION
ATTRACTION
AUDIOPHILE
AUDITORIUM
AUSTRALIAN
AUTOMATION
AUTOMATIZE
AUTOMOBILE
AUTOMOTIVE
BACKSTAIRS
BALLISTICS
BASTARDIZE
BATRACHIAN
BEAUTICIAN
BELLETRIST
BENEFICIAL
BESTIALITY
BICHLORIDE
BIOPHYSICS
BLACKSMITH
BLITZKRIEG
BOLSHEVISM
BOMBARDIER
BOOKMOBILE
BOWDLERIZE
BRAHMANISM
BRAINCHILD
BRIGANTINE
BUTTERMILK
CANDLEWICK
CAPITALISM
CAPITALIST
CAPITALIZE
CAPITATION
CAPOREGIME
CATABOLISM
CATEGORIZE
CAVITATION
CENTENNIAL
CENTRALIZE
CEREMONIAL
CHANDELIER
CHANGELING
CHANNELIZE
CHATELAINE
CHAUVINISM
CHECKPOINT
CHIFFONIER
CHRYSOLITE
CINERARIUM
CIRCUMCISE
CLASSICISM
CLASSIFIED
COCKATRICE
COLLECTIVE
COLLOQUIAL
COLLOQUIUM
COLORATION
COMBUSTION
COMMERCIAL
COMMISSION
COMPASSION
COMPATRIOT
COMPENDIUM
COMPLEXION
COMPLICITY
COMPROMISE
COMPULSION
COMPULSIVE
CONCEPTION
CONCERNING
CONCERTINA
CONCESSION
CONCESSIVE
CONCLUSION
CONCRETION
CONCUSSION
CONDUCTIVE
CONFECTION
CONFESSION
CONFORMITY
CONNECTION
CONNECTIVE
CONNIPTION
CONSORTIUM
CONSTRAINT
CONTENTION
CONTINUITY
CONTRADICT
CONVECTION
CONVENTION
CONVERSION
CONVICTION
CONVULSION
CORONATION
CREDENTIAL
CRYOGENICS
CUMULATIVE
CUTTLEFISH
DATAMATION
DECIMALIZE
DECLASSIFY
DECLENSION
DECOLORIZE
DECORATION
DECORATIVE
DECRYPTION
DEFINITION
DEFINITIVE
DEHUMANIZE
DEHUMIDIFY
DELEGATION
DELPHINIUM
DEMOBILIZE
DEMOLITION
DEMONETIZE
DEMORALIZE
DENOTATIVE
DENTIFRICE
DEPOLARIZE
DEPOSITION
DEPRESSION
DEPRESSIVE
DEPUTATION
DERIVATION
DERIVATIVE
DESALINIZE
DESOLATION
DEVITALIZE
DIMINUTIVE
DISAPPOINT
DISCERNING
DISCIPLINE
DISCRETION
DISCURSIVE
DISINCLINE
DISQUALIFY
DISSENSION
DISSERVICE
DIVINATION
DOMINATION
DOWNSTAIRS
DRAWSTRING
DYSPROSIUM
EBULLITION
EMBONPOINT
EMPIRICISM
EMULSIFIER
ENCRYPTION
ENTERPRISE
EPITHELIUM
EQUANIMITY
EQUESTRIAN
EQUITATION
ERGONOMICS
ESCRITOIRE
ESTIMATION
EVANGELISM
EVANGELIST
EVANGELIZE
EVERYTHING
EXHAUSTION
EXHAUSTIVE
EXPEDITION
EXPOSITION
EXPRESSION
EXTINGUISH
EXURBANITE
FAMILARIZE
FAVORITISM
FEDERALISM
FEDERALIST
FEDERALIZE
FEDERATION
FIGURATION
FIGURATIVE
FINGERLING
FORBIDDING
FORTISSIMO
FOSTERLING
FOUNDATION
FRATERNITY
FRATERNIZE
FRATRICIDE
GADOLINIUM
GENERALITY
GENERALIZE
GENERATION
GEOPHYSICS
GERIATRICS
GHOSTWRITE
GORMANDIZE
GRADUALISM
GRADUATION
GRANDCHILD
GROUNDLING
GUILLOTINE
GYMNASTICS
HABITATION
HANDSPRING
HEARTHSIDE
HOMECOMING
HOMOGENIZE
HONORARIUM
HYDRAULICS
IMBIBITION
IMMATERIAL
IMMEMORIAL
IMMOBILIZE
IMMORALITY
IMPERATIVE
IMPOVERISH
IMPRESSION
IMPRESSIVE
INBREEDING
INCAPACITY
INCIVILITY
INDECISION
INDECISIVE
INDEFINITE
INDICATIVE
INDONESIAN
INDUSTRIAL
INEQUALITY
INFIDELITY
INFIGHTING
INFINITIVE
INFLECTION
INFRACTION
INHIBITION
INHUMANITY

INITIATIVE
INJUNCTION
INNOVATION
INSOLATION
INTERFAITH
INTERSTICE
INTERTWINE
INTERTWIST
INTINCTION
INTONATION
INVOCATION
INVOLUTION
ISOMETRICS
JOURNALISM
JUBILATION
KINEMATICS
LAWRENCIUM
LENGTHWISE
LIBERALISM
LIFESAVING
LIPREADING
LITERALISM
LITHUANIAN
LOCOMOTION
LOCOMOTIVE
LOGROLLING
LOVEMAKING
MAINSPRING
MALTHUSIAN
MANICURIST
MANUSCRIPT
MARASCHINO
MARGUERITE
MASTERMIND
MATURATION
MAYONNAISE
MELANESIAN
MERCANTILE
METABOLISM
METABOLITE
MILITARISM
MILITARIZE
MILLENNIUM
MINERALIZE
MISOGAMIST
MISOGYNIST
MONARCHIST
MONOTHEISM
MORATORIUM
MULTIPLIER
NARCISSISM
NASTURTIUM
NATATORIUM
NATIONWIDE
NATURALISM
NATURALIST
NATURALIZE
NEBULOSITY
NEGATIVISM
NEUTRALISM
NEUTRALITY
NEUTRALIZE
NIGHTSHIRT
NIGHTSTICK
NOMINATIVE
NOTABILITY
NOURISHING
NUCLEONICS
OBLIGATION
OBSTETRICS
OCCUPATION
OCEANARIUM
OCEANGOING
OPPRESSION
OPPROBRIUM
ORDINATION
OUTLANDISH
OUTPOURING
PAGINATION
PALATALIZE
PANTYWAIST
PARAMECIUM
PASTEURIZE
PEDESTRIAN
PEDIATRICS
PEJORATIVE
PEPPERMINT
PERCENTILE
PERCEPTION
PERCEPTIVE
PERCUSSION
PERFECTION
PERIHELION
PERMISSION
PERMISSIVE
PERORATION
PERPETUITY
PERQUISITE
PERSUASION
PERVERSION
PETNAPPING
PHILISTINE
PHOTOPAINT
PIANISSIMO
PINCUSHION
PLAGIARIZE
PLANTATION
PLAYACTING
PLEBISCITE
POLITICIAN
POLYNESIAN
POLYTHEISM
POPULATION
POSSESSION
POSSESSIVE
POSTSCRIPT
PRAGMATISM
PRECAUTION
PRECESSION
PRECIOSITY
PREDESTINE
PREEMPTIVE
PREHENSILE
PRESSURIZE
PRIMORDIAL
PRINCELING
PROCEEDING
PROCESSION
PROCLIVITY
PRODUCTION
PROFESSION
PROJECTILE
PROMETHIUM
PROPENSITY
PROPERTIED
PROPORTION
PROPULSION
PROSCENIUM
PROSPERITY
PROTECTION
PROVINCIAL
PYRIMIDINE
QUADRATICS
QUADRIVIUM
QUARANTINE
RADICALIZE
RAINMAKING
RECIDIVISM
RECITATION
RECREATION
REDEMPTION
REDISTRICT
REFRACTION
REGRESSION
REGULATION
RELATIVITY
RELAXATION
RELINQUISH
REPARATION
REPARATIVE
REPERTOIRE
REPETITION
REPETITIVE
REPUTATION
RESOLUTION
RESORPTION
RESOUNDING
RESPECTING
RESPECTIVE
RESPONSIVE
RETRACTILE
REVELATION
REVITALIZE
REVOCATION
REVOLUTION
RHEUMATISM
RISIBILITY
ROLLICKING
SACCHARINE
SACROILIAC
SALUTATION
SANATORIUM
SANITARIAN
SANITARIUM
SANITATION
SCARLATINA
SCHOOLGIRL
SCRUTINIZE
SECULARISM
SECULARIZE
SEMIDRYING
SEPARATION
SEPARATIST
SEPARATIVE
SEPTUAGINT
SERPENTINE
SHOESTRING
SHORTENING
SHUNPIKING
SILVERFISH
SIMPLICITY
SKEPTICISM
SKYWRITING
SLENDERIZE
SMATTERING
SNOWMOBILE
SOLIDARITY
SPECIALIST
SPECIALIZE
SPOLIATION
SPRINGTIME
SPRINKLING
STALACTITE
STALAGMITE
STANDPOINT
STANDSTILL
STARVELING
STATISTICS
STENTORIAN
STIGMATIZE
STRYCHNINE
SUBJECTIVE
SUBROUTINE
SUBSTATION
SUBVENTION
SUCCESSION
SUCCESSIVE
SUFFRAGIST
SUGGESTION
SUGGESTIVE
SUPERTWIST
SURREALISM
SUSPENSION
SWEETBRIER
SYMPATHIZE
TAMBOURINE
TECHNETIUM
TECHNICIAN
TELEVISION
TEMPTATION
TIMBERLINE
TORRENTIAL
TOURMALINE
TRAMPOLINE
TRANSCRIBE
TRANSCRIPT
TRANSITION
TRANSITIVE
TRAVERTINE
TRIPARTITE
TRUNCATION
TURPENTINE
TYPESCRIPT
UNASSUMING
UNAVAILING
UNBECOMING
UNBLUSHING
UNDERLYING
UNDERSHIRT
UNDERSKIRT
UNDERTRICK
UNDERWAIST
UNDERWRITE
UNDULATION
UNFAMILIAR
UNIFORMITY
UNIVERSITY
UNOCCUPIED
UNTHINKING
UNYIELDING
UPBRINGING
UPSTANDING
VARICOSITY
VEGETARIAN
VEGETATION
VEGETATIVE
VESPERTINE
VINDICTIVE
VIRTUOSITY
VISIBILITY
VISITATION
VOICEPRINT
WEATHERING
WELLSPRING
WESTERNIZE
WHIRLYBIRD
WINDOWSILL
WINTERTIDE
WINTERTIME
WORTHWHILE
HALLELUJAH
BESPRINKLE
BLUEJACKET
DOCKWORKER
FOOTLOCKER
ICEBREAKER
JAWBREAKER
LANDLOCKED
LAWBREAKER
LINEBACKER
MATCHMAKER
NOISEMAKER
NONDRINKER
NUTCRACKER
PAWNBROKER
PEACEMAKER
PERIWINKLE
PICKPOCKET
RAMSHACKLE
SEERSUCKER
TEARJERKER
TURNBUCKLE
UNDERTAKER
WATCHMAKER
WOODPECKER
WORKBASKET
ANTEBELLUM
BEDRAGGLED
BIMETALLIC
BLUECOLLAR
BOOKSELLER
CEREBELLUM
CHANCELLOR
CHAPFALLEN
CHINCHILLA
CIRCUMFLEX
CITRONELLA
COMMONALTY
CONTROLLER
COSMOPOLIS
CURRICULUM
DEMOISELLE
DIFFICULTY
DILLYDALLY
DISHABILLE
DISSIMILAR
ERYSIPELAS
ESPADRILLE
EURODOLLAR
HEMOPHILIA
HULLABALOO
MARGINALIA
METROPOLIS
MOZZARELLA
NECROPOLIS
NEWFANGLED
PAINKILLER
PARTICULAR
PECCADILLO
PENICILLIN
PERSONALTY
PICCALILLI
PORTCULLIS
POURPARLER
PRINCIPLED
QUADRUPLET
QUINTUPLET
SALTCELLAR
TARANTELLA
TRANSPOLAR
TUBERCULAR
TUBERCULIN
UNDERBELLY
UNDERVALUE
UNEXAMPLED
UNSCHOOLED
VAUDEVILLE
VERMICELLI
VERNACULAR
VICTUALLER
WATERCOLOR
WATERMELON
ACCUSTOMED
ANTICLIMAX
BACKGAMMON
CATECHUMEN
CENTESIMAL
COUNTERMAN
COUNTRYMAN
DUODECIMAL
EXOTHERMIC
EXPRESSMAN
GEOTHERMAL
HIGHWAYMAN
HORSEWOMAN
HUSBANDMAN
HYPODERMIC
ISOTHERMAL
JACKHAMMER
JOURNEYMAN
MIDSHIPMAN
MISSILEMAN
NURSERYMAN
OFTENTIMES
OPHTHALMIC
PATRONYMIC
POULTRYMAN
PROGRAMMED
PROGRAMMER

SALESWOMAN
SEPTICEMIA
SERVICEMAN
WEATHERMAN
WINDJAMMER
WORKINGMAN
ABORIGINAL
ABSTINENCE
ACCEPTANCE
ACCORDANCE
ADDITIONAL
ADMITTANCE
ALLEGIANCE
ANTIPHONAL
APPEARANCE
ASCENDANCY
ATTENDANCE
BELLADONNA
BELONGINGS
BLANCMANGE
BLUEBONNET
CATCHPENNY
CHIROMANCY
COGNIZANCE
COMEDIENNE
COMPETENCE
COMPETENCY
COMPLIANCE
COMPLIANCY
CONFERENCE
CONFIDENCE
CONFLUENCE
CONGRUENCE
CONGRUENCY
CONSCIENCE
CONSONANCE
CONTINENCE
CONVEYANCE
CORDWAINER
CORPULENCE
COTERMINAL
CROSSBONES
DEPENDENCE
DEPENDENCY
DETERMINED
DETERRENCE
DIFFERENCE
DILETTANTE
DIMINUENDO
DIPSOMANIA
DISARRANGE
DISSONANCE
EFFICIENCY
EFFULGENCE
ELECTRONIC
EXCELLENCE
EXCELLENCY
EXPECTANCY
EXPEDIENCE
EXPEDIENCY
EXPERIENCE
FLUIDOUNCE
FORERUNNER
GEOSCIENCE
GINGERSNAP
HISTRIONIC
HOOTENANNY
IMPATIENCE
IMPERSONAL
IMPORTANCE
INCUMBENCY
INDISTINCT
INDUCTANCE
INDULGENCE
INFRASONIC
INSISTENCE
INTERLUNAR
IRRATIONAL
MISALIGNED
MOLYBDENUM
MONOPHONIC
MONSTRANCE
MULTISENSE
NAPOLEONIC
NECROMANCY
OBSERVANCE
OCCASIONAL
OCCURRENCE
OUTBALANCE
PESTILENCE
PHENOMENON
PHOTOGENIC
PICKANINNY
POLYCLINIC
POWERLINES
PREARRANGE
PRECEDENCE
PREFERENCE
PRESCIENCE
PROMINENCE
PROPAGANDA
PROVENANCE
PROVIDENCE
PUBESCENCE
RADIOGENIC
RADIOSONDE
RECOMPENSE
REDUNDANCY
REFULGENCE
RELATIONAL
RELUCTANCE
REMITTANCE
RENASCENCE
REPUGNANCE
RESILIENCE
RESILIENCY
RESISTANCE
RESTRAINED
RESURGENCE
ROADRUNNER
SACROSANCT
SENESCENCE
STRINGENCY
SUBLIMINAL
SUFFERANCE
SUPERSONIC
SUSTENANCE
TEMPERANCE
THREEPENCE
TURBULENCE
ULTRASONIC
UNDERPANTS
UNREASONED
ABSTEMIOUS
ALBUMINOUS
ALLHALLOWS
ALONGSHORE
AMBULATORY
AMPHIBIOUS
ANGLOPHOBE
ANTHROPOID
AURIFEROUS
AUSPICIOUS
AUTONOMOUS
BACKSTROKE
BIRTHSTONE
BITUMINOUS
BLACKAMOOR
BLACKTHORN
BLOODSTONE
BOISTEROUS
BRAINSTORM
BREAKFRONT
BREASTBONE
BREASTWORK
BRIDEGROOM
BRIDGEWORK
BROADCLOTH
BROADSWORD
BROWNSTONE
BUTTONHOLE
BUTTONHOOK
CACCIATORE
CADAVEROUS
CALCAREOUS
CANKERWORM
CAOUTCHOUC
CARDIOLOGY
CENSORIOUS
CHALCEDONY
CHIVALROUS
CHLOROFORM
CHROMOSOME
CHRONOLOGY
CHURCHGOER
CINQUEFOIL
CIRCUITOUS
CLAVICHORD
CLERESTORY
CLINGSTONE
COLLARBONE
COMMODIOUS
COMPULSORY
CONSISTORY
CONTAGIOUS
CONTIGUOUS
CONTINUOUS
CORRESPOND
COTTONWOOD
CRADLESONG
CRETACEOUS
CRISSCROSS
CURVACEOUS
DEMONOLOGY
DENDROLOGY
DEPILATORY
DEPOSITORY
DEROGATORY
DIAPHANOUS
DISAPPROVE
DISCOMFORT
DISCOMMODE
DISCOMPOSE
DISHARMONY
DONNYBROOK
DOWNSTROKE
EMBRYOLOGY
ENDOGENOUS
ENTOMOLOGY
EUPHONIOUS
EXOBIOLOGY
EXTRANEOUS
FACTITIOUS
FALLACIOUS
FASTIDIOUS
FELICITOUS
FICTITIOUS
FLAGITIOUS
FORTUITOUS
GASTRONOMY
GENTLEFOLK
GLACIOLOGY
GORGONZOLA
GRAMOPHONE
GRATUITOUS
GRAVESTONE
GREGARIOUS
GRINDSTONE
GROUNDWORK
GYNECOLOGY
HAMMERLOCK
HARMONIOUS
HEADSTRONG
HEATSTROKE
HELIOTROPE
HEMATOLOGY
HEMORRHOID
HERETOFORE
HIPPODROME
HOMOLOGOUS
HORRENDOUS
HYDROPHONE
IGNORAMOUS
IMMUNOLOGY
IMPERVIOUS
INDECOROUS
INDIGENOUS
INGLORIOUS
INITIATORY
INTERBLOCK
KNIGHTHOOD
LABORATORY
LACHRYMOSE
LASCIVIOUS
LIBIDINOUS
LICENTIOUS
LIGHTPROOF
LIKELIHOOD
LIVELIHOOD
LOQUACIOUS
LUBRICIOUS
LUGUBRIOUS
MACKINTOSH
MAIDENHOOD
MALODOROUS
MANDRAGORA
MANTLEROCK
MARROWBONE
MASTERWORK
MEDDLESOME
MELANCHOLY
MENDACIOUS
METICULOUS
METTLESOME
MICROPHONE
MICROPROBE
MICROSCOPE
MINERALOGY
MINESTRONE
MINISCROLL
MONOCHROME
MONOTONOUS
MORPHOLOGY
MOTHERHOOD
MULTISTORY
MUSICOLOGY
NANOSECOND
NEEDLEWORK
NETHERMOST
NETTLESOME
NINCOMPOOP
NONSUPPORT
NUMEROLOGY
OBSEQUIOUS
OCEANFRONT
OCEANOLOGY
OLEAGINOUS
OMNIVOROUS
OUTPERFORM
OUTRAGEOUS
PALINDROME
PANTALOONS
PARATROOPS
PEPPERCORN
PEREMPTORY
PERMAFROST
PERNICIOUS
PHLEBOTOMY
PHRENOLOGY
PHYSIOLOGY
PICOSECOND
PIGEONHOLE
POCKETBOOK
PORTENTOUS
POSTHUMOUS
PRECARIOUS
PRECOCIOUS
PREDACEOUS
PREDISPOSE
PRESUPPOSE
PRODIGIOUS
PROMISSORY
PROMONTORY
PROMPTBOOK
PROPITIOUS
PROSPEROUS
PSEUDOCODE
PSYCHOLOGY
PUGNACIOUS
QUATREFOIL
RADARSCOPE
RADIOPHONE
REBELLIOUS
REFRACTORY
RENDEZVOUS
REPOSITORY
RHINESTONE
RIDICULOUS
ROUNDABOUT
ROUSTABOUT
SALUBRIOUS
SANDALWOOD
SCHOOLROOM
SCURRILOUS
SEISMOLOGY
SELENOLOGY
SIDESTROKE
SISTERHOOD
SLUMBEROUS
SOLICITOUS
SPIRITUOUS
SPLASHDOWN
SPOILSPORT
STRONGHOLD
STUPENDOUS
SUSPENSORY
SUSPICIOUS
TABLECLOTH
TABLESPOON
TECHNOLOGY
TENDERFOOT
TENDERLOIN
TENEBRIOUS
THREESCORE
THROUGHOUT
THUNDEROUS
TOUCHSTONE
TOXICOLOGY
TRAJECTORY
TRANSITORY
TREMENDOUS
TROUBADOUR
TUMBLEDOWN
TUMULTUOUS
TURTLEDOVE
UBIQUITOUS
ULTRASHORT
UNDERCROFT
UNDERSCORE
UNDERSHOOT
UNDERSTOOD
UNDERSTORY
UNGENEROUS
UNGRACIOUS
UNHANDSOME
UPROARIOUS
VIBRAPHONE
VICTORIOUS
VIDEOPHONE
VILLAINOUS
VIVIPAROUS
VOCIFEROUS
VOLUMINOUS
VOLUPTUOUS
WATERFRONT
WATERPROOF
WATERSPOUT
WICKERWORK
APOCALYPSE

APOSTROPHE
BOOKKEEPER
CLODHOPPER
CLOTHESPIN
CORNUCOPIA
DEMOGRAPHY
DOORKEEPER
EYEDROPPER
GAMEKEEPER
GATEKEEPER
GOALKEEPER
HOLOGRAPHY
JACKANAPES
LEAFHOPPER
MALAPROPOS
METACARPUS
PARTICIPLE
PHILOSOPHY
PRESBYOPIA
SHOPKEEPER
SKYSCRAPER
TELEGRAPHY
TELESCOPIC
THROUGHPUT
TIMEKEEPER
TOPOGRAPHY
TYPOGRAPHY
WASTEPAPER
XEROGRAPHY
CATAFALQUE
COMMUNIQUE
PICARESQUE
STATUESQUE
ADVENTURER
AFTERBIRTH
ASYMMETRIC
BENCHMARKS
BLACKBERRY
CARDIOGRAM
CHILDBIRTH
CLOUDBURST
COLLATERAL
COMPUSERVE
CONCENTRIC
CORNSTARCH
CRYPTOGRAM
DIELECTRIC
DIPHTHERIA
DISINHERIT
DISORDERLY
DREAMWORLD
EGOCENTRIC
ELDERBERRY
ENDANGERED
ERGOSTEROL
EXTRAMURAL
GEOCENTRIC

GOOSEBERRY
HANDBARROW
HEARTTHROB
HENCEFORTH
HOBBYHORSE
HOUSEWARES
HYPERBARIC
IMPRESARIO
INTERFERON
INTERMARRY
INTRAMURAL
KETTLEDRUM
KNOCKWURST
LIVERWURST
LOGANBERRY
MANDELBROT
METALLURGY
MIDDLEBROW
NEIGHBORLY
OCTOTHORPE
OTHERWORLD
OUTGENERAL
OVERCHARGE
PALLBEARER
PANJANDRUM
PERIPHERAL
PHOSPHORUS
PHOTOMURAL
PIANOFORTE
POLYHEDRON
RACECOURSE
RATTLETRAP
RHINOCEROS
ROTISSERIE
SEISMOGRAM
SEPULCHRAL
SINGLETREE
SOPHOMORIC
STILLBIRTH
STRAWBERRY
SUPERCARGO
THUMBSCREW
TRANSVERSE
UNDERWORLD
UNICAMERAL
UNILATERAL
UNLETTERED
UNMANNERLY
UNNUMBERED
VOLUMETRIC
WATERBORNE
WATERWORKS
WHEELHORSE
WIREHAIRED
AFTERTASTE
AMANUENSIS
ANESTHESIA

ANTITHESIS
APOTHEOSIS
BIPARTISAN
COMPARISON
CONVALESCE
COUNTERSPY
DELIQUESCE
DISSATISFY
EFFERVESCE
EFFLORESCE
EUTHANASIA
FRANCHISEE
FRANCHISER
FRANCHISOR
HYDROLYSIS
HYPOTHESIS
INDISPOSED
JINRIKISHA
LEDERHOSEN
METASTASIS
METATARSAL
METATARSUS
NEOCLASSIC
PROSTHESIS
QUICKBASIC
RICKETTSIA
SUNGLASSES
THROMBOSIS
TOOTHPASTE
URINALYSIS
ACCIDENTAL
ACHROMATIC
ADMINISTER
ALPHABETIC
ALTERNATOR
ANEMOMETER
ANESTHETIC
ANTIBIOTIC
ANTIMATTER
ANTIPROTON
ANTIQUATED
ANTISEPTIC
APOLOGETIC
APPLICATOR
ARBITRATOR
ARBORVITAE
ARITHMETIC
BENEFACTOR
BIPARENTAL
BIPARIETAL
BLUEBOTTLE
BREAKWATER
BRONCHITIS
BUSHMASTER
CALCULATED
CARBOLATED
CARBURETOR

CELEBRATED
CELLARETTE
CENTILITER
CENTIMETER
CHARLESTON
COMMUTATOR
COMPETITOR
COMPLECTED
COMPOSITOR
CONGENITAL
CONSPECTUS
CONVOLUTED
COPYWRITER
CYCLOMETER
DEATHWATCH
DEMOCRATIC
DERMATITIS
DESTRUCTOR
DISGRUNTLE
DISHEARTEN
DISJOINTED
DUMBWAITER
DUPLICATOR
EPIGLOTTIS
EUCALYPTUS
FARSIGHTED
FILIBUSTER
FLOODWATER
FORECASTLE
FREEBOOTER
FRESHWATER
FUTURISTIC
GINGIVITIS
GOLDBEATER
GRAVIMETER
HEADMASTER
HEADWAITER
HECTOLITER
HECTOMETER
HELICOPTER
HEPTAMETER
HOMEOPATHY
HORIZONTAL
HYDROMETER
HYGROMETER
HYPOCENTER
IMPRIMATUR
INCIDENTAL
INSTRUCTOR
LACKLUSTER
LARYNGITIS
MAISONETTE
MALADAPTED
MALEFACTOR
MARIONETTE
MENINGITIS
MICROMETER

MIGNONETTE
MILLILITER
MILLIMETER
MONUMENTAL
MYRIAMETER
NEWSLETTER
NEWSWORTHY
NONSTARTER
NOTEWORTHY
OCCIDENTAL
ORGANGUTAN
OSTEOPATHY
OVERMASTER
OVERWINTER
PEASHOOTER
PENTAMETER
PETROLATUM
PHLEGMATIC
PHOTOMETER
PLEASANTRY
POINSETTIA
POSTMASTER
POSTMORTEM
POSTPARTUM
PREMARITAL
PROCURATOR
PROGENITOR
PROGNOSTIC
PROPRIETOR
PROPRINTER
PROSPECTUS
PROTRACTOR
PSYCHIATRY
RADIOMETER
RESPIRATOR
RINGMASTER
SACERDOTAL
SCHISMATIC
SCHOLASTIC
SERVOMOTOR
SHIPFITTER
SILHOUETTE
SIMPLISTIC
STEPSISTER
STOCHASTIC
STRAIGHTEN
SUBORBITAL
SUBSTRATUM
TACHOMETER
TASKMASTER
TERMINATOR
TETRAMETER
THEREAFTER
THERMISTOR
THERMOSTAT
TRANSISTOR
TYPESETTER

TYPEWRITER
UNAFFECTED
UNDERWATER
UNEXPECTED
URETHRITIS
UROGENITAL
WINCHESTER
WOODCUTTER
WRISTWATCH
YARDMASTER
ANIMALCULE
ANTEPENULT
BACKGROUND
BLOCKHOUSE
BLOODHOUND
BREADFRUIT
BREADSTUFF
CANTALOUPE
CARICATURE
CENTRIFUGE
CHARTREUSE
COLORATURA
CONJECTURE
CONSTITUTE
CONTRIBUTE
COURTHOUSE
CUMMERBUND
DISTRIBUTE
EMBOUCHURE
EXACTITUDE
FAIRGROUND
FOREGROUND
FORFEITURE
GARGANTUAN
GRAPEFRUIT
GREENHOUSE
GUARDHOUSE
HEREABOUTS
HOMOSEXUAL
HORSELAUGH
HYPOTENUSE
INAPTITUDE
INDIVIDUAL
INFINITUDE
INQUIETUDE
IRRESOLUTE
JUDICATURE
KIESELGUHR
LIGHTHOUSE
LITERATURE
MANSUETUDE
MISCONDUCT
MISFORTUNE
MOONSTRUCK
MOTORTRUCK
NEWSGROUPS
PAINTBRUSH

PERCEPTUAL
PILOTHOUSE
PLAYGROUND
POWERHOUSE
PROSTITUTE
ROUGHHOUSE
ROUNDHOUSE
SIMILITUDE
SOLICITUDE
SOMERSAULT
SPELLBOUND
STATEHOUSE
STOREHOUSE
SUBSTITUTE
SUBTERFUGE
TANTAMOUNT
TOOTHBRUSH
TOURNIQUET
ULTRASOUND
UNDERBRUSH
UNDERSLUNG
UNDERSTUDY
WANDERLUST
WHEELHOUSE
WRAPAROUND
CANTILEVER
CHANGEOVER
MULTILEVEL
RIBOFLAVIN
THEMSELVES
UNBELIEVER
UNDERCOVER
UNRESERVED
WHATSOEVER
WHENSOEVER
WHOMSOEVER
CORNFLOWER
DISEMBOWEL
EXPRESSWAY
HORSEPOWER
PASSAGEWAY
THROUGHWAY
UNHALLOWED
WALLFLOWER
WATCHTOWER
WATERPOWER
WINDFLOWER
WINEGROWER
WITHDRAWAL
UNDERSEXED
BRICKLAYER
PENNYROYAL
SAPROPHYTE
SOOTHSAYER
STEREOTYPE
UNEMPLOYED
CHIMPANZEE

FERTILIZER
INTERMEZZO
UNDERSIZED

## 9TH LETTER

ABORIGINAL
ACCIDENTAL
ADDITIONAL
AMERINDIAN
ANTICLIMAX
ANTINOMIAN
ANTIPHONAL
ANTISOCIAL
APOCRYPHAL
APOLITICAL
ARBORVITAE
ARTIFICIAL
AUSTRALIAN
BALBRIGGAN
BATRACHIAN
BEAUTICIAN
BENEFICIAL
BIOMEDICAL
BIPARENTAL
BIPARIETAL
BIPARTISAN
BLUECOLLAR
BRIDGEHEAD
BUDGERIGAR
CARDIOGRAM
CENTENNIAL
CENTESIMAL
CEREMONIAL
CHIMERICAL
CLOVERLEAF
COLLATERAL
COLLOQUIAL
COMMERCIAL
COMMONWEAL
CONGENITAL
COPPERHEAD
COTERMINAL
COUNTERMAN
COUNTRYMAN
CREDENTIAL
CRUSTACEAN
CRYPTOGRAM
DISSIMILAR
DOWNSTREAM
DUNDERHEAD
DUODECIMAL
ECONOMICAL
ECUMENICAL
ENCYCLICAL
EQUESTRIAN
ERYSIPELAS
EURODOLLAR
EXPRESSMAN
EXPRESSWAY
EXTRAMURAL
FIGUREHEAD
GARGANTUAN
GEOTHERMAL
GINGERSNAP
HALLELUJAH
HAMMERHEAD
HEARTBREAK
HIGHWAYMAN
HOMOSEXUAL
HORIZONTAL
HORSEWOMAN
HOUSECLEAN
HUSBANDMAN
IMMATERIAL
IMMEMORIAL
IMPERSONAL
INCIDENTAL
INDIVIDUAL
INDONESIAN
INDUSTRIAL
INTERLUNAR
INTERTIDAL
INTERURBAN
INTRAMURAL
IRRATIONAL
ISOTHERMAL
JOURNEYMAN
LETTERHEAD
LITHUANIAN
LOGGERHEAD
MAIDENHEAD
MAINSTREAM
MALTHUSIAN
MECHANICAL
MELANESIAN
METATARSAL
MIDSHIPMAN
MILLSTREAM
MISSILEMAN
MOHAMMEDAN
MONUMENTAL
MUHAMMADAN
NURSERYMAN
OCCASIONAL
OCCIDENTAL
ORATORICAL
ORGANGUTAN
OUTGENERAL
OVERSPREAD
PACKTHREAD
PARTICULAR
PASSAGEWAY
PEDESTRIAN
PENNYROYAL
PERCEPTUAL
PERIODICAL
PERIPHERAL
PHOTOMURAL
POLITICIAN
POLYNESIAN
POULTRYMAN
PREMARITAL
PREMEDICAL
PRIMORDIAL
PROVINCIAL
RATTLETRAP
RECIPROCAL
RELATIONAL
REPUBLICAN
SACERDOTAL
SACROILIAC
SALESWOMAN
SALTCELLAR
SANITARIAN
SEISMOGRAM
SEPULCHRAL
SERVICEMAN
SHENANIGAN
SLIPSTREAM
STENTORIAN
SUBLIMINAL
SUBORBITAL
SWEETBREAD
TECHNICIAN
THEATRICAL
THERMOSTAT
THROUGHWAY
TORRENTIAL
TRANSPOLAR
TUBERCULAR
TYRANNICAL
UNCRITICAL
UNFAMILIAR
UNICAMERAL
UNILATERAL
UROGENITAL
VEGETARIAN
VERNACULAR
WEATHERMAN
WHITSUNDAY
WIDESPREAD
WINGSPREAD
WITHDRAWAL
WORKINGMAN
YESTERYEAR
ANGLOPHOBE
MICROPROBE
TRANSCRIBE
ABSTINENCE
ACCEPTANCE
ACCOMPLICE
ACCORDANCE
ACROBATICS
ADMITTANCE
AEROBATICS
AESTHETICS
ALLEGIANCE
ALTARPIECE
APPEARANCE
APPRENTICE
ASCENDANCY
ATTENDANCE
BALLISTICS
BIOPHYSICS
BIRTHPLACE
BOTTLENECK
CANDLEWICK
CANVASBACK
CHIROMANCY
COCKATRICE
COGNIZANCE
COMPETENCE
COMPETENCY
COMPLIANCE
COMPLIANCY
CONFERENCE
CONFIDENCE
CONFLUENCE
CONGRUENCE
CONGRUENCY
CONSCIENCE
CONSONANCE
CONSPIRACY
CONTINENCE
CONTRADICT
CONVALESCE
CONVEYANCE
CORNSTARCH
CORPULENCE
COUNTERACT
CROSSPIECE
CRYOGENICS
CYBERSPACE
DEATHWATCH
DEGENERACY
DELIQUESCE
DENTIFRICE
DEPENDENCE
DEPENDENCY
DETERRENCE
DIFFERENCE
DISCONNECT
DISRESPECT
DISSERVICE
DISSONANCE
EFFERVESCE
EFFICIENCY
EFFLORESCE
EFFULGENCE
EPISCOPACY
ERGONOMICS
EXCELLENCE
EXCELLENCY
EXPECTANCY
EXPEDIENCE
EXPEDIENCY
EXPERIENCE
FIELDPIECE
FLUIDOUNCE
GEOPHYSICS
GEOSCIENCE
GERIATRICS
GYMNASTICS
HAMMERLOCK
HYDRAULICS
IMPATIENCE
IMPORTANCE
INCUMBENCY
INDISTINCT
INDUCTANCE
INDULGENCE
INSISTENCE
INTERBLOCK
INTERSTICE
ISOMETRICS
KINEMATICS
KNICKKNACK
LUMBERJACK
MANTLEROCK
MISCONDUCT
MONSTRANCE
MOONSTRUCK
MOTORTRUCK
MOUTHPIECE
NECROMANCY
NIGHTSTICK
NUCLEONICS
OBSERVANCE
OBSTETRICS
OCCURRENCE
OUTBALANCE
PEDIATRICS
PESTILENCE
PLUPERFECT
PLUTOCRACY
PRECEDENCE
PREFERENCE
PRESCIENCE
PROMINENCE
PROVENANCE
PROVIDENCE
PUBESCENCE
QUADRATICS
REDISTRICT
REDUNDANCY
REFULGENCE
REGENERACY
RELUCTANCE
REMITTANCE
RENASCENCE
REPUGNANCE
RESILIENCE
RESILIENCY
RESISTANCE
RESURGENCE
RETROSPECT
RUBBERNECK
SACROSANCT
SCAPEGRACE
SENESCENCE
SMOKESTACK
STAGECOACH
STATISTICS
STRINGENCY
SUBCOMPACT
SUBSURFACE
SUFFERANCE
SUSTENANCE
SWITCHBACK
TEMPERANCE
THREEPENCE
TURBULENCE
TURTLENECK
UNDERTRICK
WRISTWATCH
AFICIONADO
AUTOSTRADA
BALUSTRADE
BICHLORIDE
CENTIGRADE
DIMINUENDO
DISCOMMODE
EXACTITUDE
FRATRICIDE
HEARTHSIDE
INAPTITUDE
INFINITUDE
INQUIETUDE
MANSUETUDE
MASQUERADE
NATIONWIDE
NIGHTSHADE
PROPAGANDA
PSEUDOCODE
RADIOSONDE
RETROGRADE
SIMILITUDE
SOLICITUDE
UNDERSTUDY
VELOCIPEDE
WINTERTIDE
ACCUSTOMED
ADMINISTER
ADVENTURER
ALTOGETHER
ANEMOMETER
ANTICANCER
ANTIMATTER
ANTIQUATED
AQUALUNGER
AUCTIONEER
BACKHANDED
BAREHEADED
BEDCLOTHES
BEDRAGGLED
BELLWETHER
BLITZKRIEG
BLUEBONNET
BLUEJACKET
BOMBARDIER
BONDHOLDER
BOOKKEEPER
BOOKSELLER
BREAKWATER
BRICKLAYER
BULLHEADED
BUSHMASTER
CALCULATED
CANTILEVER
CARABINEER
CARBOLATED
CARCINOGEN
CATECHUMEN
CELEBRATED
CENTILITER
CENTIMETER
CHANDELIER
CHANGEOVER
CHAPFALLEN
CHIFFONIER
CHIMPANZEE
CHURCHGOER
CIRCUMFLEX
CLASSIFIED
CLODHOPPER
COMMANDEER
COMPLECTED
CONTROLLER
CONVOLUTED
COPYREADER
COPYWRITER
CORDWAINER
CORNFLOWER
COTTONSEED
COWPUNCHER
CROSSBONES

CROSSBREED
CYCLOMETER
DETERMINED
DISEMBOWEL
DISHEARTEN
DISHWASHER
DISJOINTED
DOCKWORKER
DOGCATCHER
DOORKEEPER
DUMBWAITER
EMULSIFIER
ENDANGERED
EVENHANDED
EYEDROPPER
FARFETCHED
FARSIGHTED
FERTILIZER
FIBRINOGEN
FILIBUSTER
FLOODWATER
FLYCATCHER
FOLKSINGER
FOOTLOCKER
FOREFATHER
FOREFINGER
FOREGATHER
FOREHANDED
FORERUNNER
FRANCHISEE
FRANCHISER
FREEBOOTER
FRESHWATER
FUSSBUDGET
GAMEKEEPER
GATEKEEPER
GOALKEEPER
GOLDBEATER
GRAVIMETER
GUNSLINGER
HANDMAIDEN
HARDHEADED
HEADMASTER
HEADWAITER
HECTOLITER
HECTOMETER
HELICOPTER
HEPTAMETER
HIGHLANDER
HORSEPOWER
HOUSEWARES
HYDROMETER
HYGROMETER
HYPOCENTER
ICEBREAKER
INDISCREET
INDISPOSED
INTERBREED
JACKANAPES
JACKHAMMER
JAWBREAKER
JIMSONWEED
KINGFISHER
LACKLUSTER
LADYFINGER
LANDHOLDER
LANDLOCKED
LANDLUBBER
LAWBREAKER
LEAFHOPPER
LEDERHOSEN
LINEBACKER
MALADAPTED
MATCHMAKER
MICROMETER
MILLILITER
MILLIMETER
MISALIGNED
MUDSLINGER
MULTILEVEL
MULTIPLIER
MYRIAMETER
NEWFANGLED
NEWSLETTER
NOISEMAKER
NONDRINKER
NONSTARTER
NUTCRACKER
OFTENTIMES
OVERMASTER
OVERWINTER
PAINKILLER
PALLBEARER
PATHFINDER
PAWNBROKER
PEACEMAKER
PEASHOOTER
PENTAMETER
PHOTOMETER
PICKPOCKET
PINFEATHER
POSTMASTER
POSTMORTEM
POURPARLER
POWERLINES
PRINCIPLED
PRIVILEGED
PROGRAMMED
PROGRAMMER
PRONOUNCED
PROPERTIED
PROPRINTER
QUADRUPLET
QUINTUPLET
RADIOMETER
RECONSIDER
RESTRAINED
RINGLEADER
RINGMASTER
ROADRUNNER
SALAMANDER
SEERSUCKER
SHAMEFACED
SHIPFITTER
SHOPKEEPER
SIDEWINDER
SINGLETREE
SKYSCRAPER
SOOTHSAYER
STEPFATHER
STEPLADDER
STEPMOTHER
STEPSISTER
STRAIGHTEN
STRENGTHEN
SUNGLASSES
SWEETBRIER
TACHOMETER
TASKMASTER
TEARJERKER
TETRAMETER
THEMSELVES
THEREAFTER
THUMBSCREW
TIMEKEEPER
TOURNIQUET
TRANSDUCER
TUMBLEWEED
TYPESETTER
TYPEWRITER
UNABRIDGED
UNAFFECTED
UNATTACHED
UNBALANCED
UNBELIEVER
UNDERCOVER
UNDERSEXED
UNDERSIZED
UNDERTAKER
UNDERWATER
UNEMPLOYED
UNEXAMPLED
UNEXPECTED
UNGROUNDED
UNHALLOWED
UNLETTERED
UNNUMBERED
UNOCCUPIED
UNREASONED
UNRESERVED
UNSCHOOLED
VICTUALLER
WALLFLOWER
WASTEPAPER
WATCHMAKER
WATCHTOWER
WATERPOWER
WATERWHEEL
WHARFINGER
WHATSOEVER
WHENSOEVER
WHOMSOEVER
WINCHESTER
WINDFLOWER
WINDJAMMER
WINEGROWER
WIREHAIRED
WOODCUTTER
WOODPECKER
WORKBASKET
YARDMASTER
BREADSTUFF
CRANKSHAFT
DECLASSIFY
DEHUMIDIFY
DISQUALIFY
DISSATISFY
FISTICUFFS
HANDICRAFT
SPACECRAFT
STATECRAFT
UNDERCROFT
WATERCRAFT
WITCHCRAFT
AFTERIMAGE
ASSEMBLAGE
BELONGINGS
BLANCMANGE
CAMOUFLAGE
CARDIOLOGY
CENTRIFUGE
CHRONOLOGY
DEMONOLOGY
DENDROLOGY
DISARRANGE
DISCOURAGE
DRAWBRIDGE
EMBRYOLOGY
ENTOMOLOGY
EXOBIOLOGY
FOOTBRIDGE
GLACIOLOGY
GYNECOLOGY
HEMATOLOGY
HEMORRHAGE
HODGEPODGE
HORSELAUGH
IMMUNOLOGY
METALLURGY
MINERALOGY
MORPHOLOGY
MULTISTAGE
MUSICOLOGY
NUMEROLOGY
OCEANOLOGY
OVERCHARGE
PERCENTAGE
PERSIFLAGE
PHRENOLOGY
PHYSIOLOGY
PILGRIMAGE
PREARRANGE
PREPACKAGE
PSYCHOLOGY
SEISMOLOGY
SELENOLOGY
SHILLELAGH
SUBTERFUGE
SUPERCARGO
TECHNOLOGY
TEETHRIDGE
TOXICOLOGY
AIRFREIGHT
APOSTROPHE
BIRTHRIGHT
DEADWEIGHT
DEMOGRAPHY
DISTRAUGHT
FLASHLIGHT
FLOODLIGHT
FORTHRIGHT
HOLOGRAPHY
HOMEOPATHY
JINRIKISHA
KIESELGUHR
MICROFICHE
MILLWRIGHT
NEWSWORTHY
NOTEWORTHY
OSTEOPATHY
PHILOSOPHY
PLAYWRIGHT
PRIZEFIGHT
SHIPWRIGHT
TELEGRAPHY
TOPOGRAPHY
TYPOGRAPHY
WAINWRIGHT
WATERTIGHT
XEROGRAPHY
ACHROMATIC
ACROPHOBIA
ALPHABETIC
AMANUENSIS
ANESTHESIA
ANESTHETIC
ANTHROPOID
ANTIBIOTIC
ANTISEPTIC
ANTITHESIS
APOLOGETIC
APOTHEOSIS
ARITHMETIC
ASYMMETRIC
AUTHORSHIP
BATTLESHIP
BEAUJOLAIS
BIMETALLIC
BLOODSTAIN
BREADFRUIT
BRIDESMAID
BRONCHITIS
CENSORSHIP
CINQUEFOIL
CLOTHESPIN
CONCENTRIC
CORNUCOPIA
COSMOPOLIS
COTTONTAIL
CYCLOPEDIA
DEALERSHIP
DEMOCRATIC
DERMATITIS
DIELECTRIC
DIPHTHERIA
DIPSOMANIA
DISINHERIT
EGOCENTRIC
ELECTRONIC
EPIGLOTTIS
EUTHANASIA
EXOTHERMIC
FAHRENHEIT
FELLOWSHIP
FINGERNAIL
FLOODPLAIN
FOREORDAIN
FUTURISTIC
GEOCENTRIC
GESUNDHEIT
GINGIVITIS
GRAPEFRUIT
HEMOGLOBIN
HEMOPHILIA
HEMORRHOID
HISTRIONIC
HYDROLYSIS
HYPERBARIC
HYPODERMIC
HYPOTHESIS
IDIOPATHIC
IMPRESARIO
INFRASONIC
JACKRABBIT
LARYNGITIS
MAIDENHAIR
MARGINALIA
MASTERSHIP
MEMBERSHIP
MENINGITIS
METASTASIS
METROPOLIS
MONOPHONIC
MULTIMEDIA
NAPOLEONIC
NECROPOLIS
NEOCLASSIC
OPHTHALMIC
PARAPLEGIA
PATRONYMIC
PENICILLIN
PENMANSHIP
PHLEGMATIC
PHOTOGENIC
POINSETTIA
POLYCLINIC
PORTCULLIS
PRESBYOPIA
PROGNOSTIC
PROSTHESIS
QUATREFOIL
QUICKBASIC
RADIOGENIC
RAGAMUFFIN
READERSHIP
RIBOFLAVIN
RICKETTSIA
ROTISSERIE
SCHISMATIC
SCHOLASTIC
SEAMANSHIP
SEPTICEMIA
SIMPLISTIC
SOPHOMORIC
STOCHASTIC
SUPERSONIC
TELESCOPIC
TENDERLOIN
THROMBOSIS
TUBERCULIN
ULTRASONIC
URETHRITIS
URINALYSIS
VOLUMETRIC
WHEELCHAIR
XENOPHOBIA
BACKSTROKE
BENCHMARKS
CHEESECAKE

DOWNSTROKE
EARTHQUAKE
HEATSTROKE
SIDESTROKE
WATERWORKS
ABOMINABLE
ACCEPTABLE
ACCESSIBLE
ACTIONABLE
ADMISSIBLE
ANGLOPHILE
ANIMALCULE
ANSWERABLE
ANTEPENULT
APPLICABLE
AUDIOPHILE
AUTOMOBILE
BASKETBALL
BESPRINKLE
BLUEBOTTLE
BOOKMOBILE
BOONDOGGLE
BRAINCHILD
BUTTERMILK
BUTTONHOLE
CANNONBALL
CANONICALS
CHARITABLE
CHINCHILLA
CITRONELLA
COMESTIBLE
COMPARABLE
COMPATIBLE
CORRIGIBLE
CREDITABLE
DEGRADABLE
DELECTABLE
DEMOISELLE
DEPENDABLE
DEPLORABLE
DESERVEDLY
DESPICABLE
DILLYDALLY
DISGRUNTLE
DISHABILLE
DISORDERLY
DISPOSABLE
DREAMWORLD
ESPADRILLE
EXPLICABLE
FORECASTLE
FORMIDABLE
GENTLEFOLK
GORGONZOLA
GRAINFIELD
GRANDCHILD
HOSPITABLE

IMAGINABLE
IMMISCIBLE
IMPALPABLE
IMPASSABLE
IMPASSIBLE
IMPECCABLE
IMPLACABLE
IMPOSSIBLE
IMPROBABLE
INCLINABLE
INCREDIBLE
INCULPABLE
INELIGIBLE
INEVITABLE
INEXORABLE
INEXPIABLE
INFALLIBLE
INFLEXIBLE
INIMITABLE
INOPERABLE
INSATIABLE
INSENSIBLE
INSOLVABLE
INTANGIBLE
INVALUABLE
INVARIABLE
INVINCIBLE
INVIOLABLE
MARTINGALE
MELANCHOLY
MENSURABLE
MERCANTILE
MINISCROLL
MISTAKABLE
MOTORCYCLE
MOZZARELLA
NEGLIGIBLE
NEIGHBORLY
NOTICEABLE
OBSERVABLE
OSTENSIBLE
OTHERWORLD
PACKSADDLE
PARTICIPLE
PECCADILLO
PERCENTILE
PERDURABLE
PERISHABLE
PERIWINKLE
PERSONABLE
PICCALILLI
PIGEONHOLE
PREDICABLE
PREHENSILE
PROJECTILE
QUADRANGLE
RAMSHACKLE

REASONABLE
RECEIVABLE
RECEPTACLE
REMARKABLE
REMEDIABLE
REPORTEDLY
RESTORABLE
RETRACTILE
ROLLERBALL
SEASONABLE
SNOWMOBILE
SOMERSAULT
STANDSTILL
STRONGHOLD
TABERNACLE
TARANTELLA
TATTERSALL
TATTLETALE
TRIMONTHLY
TURNBUCKLE
UNBEARABLE
UNBEATABLE
UNDENIABLE
UNDERBELLY
UNDERWORLD
UNFRIENDLY
UNMANNERLY
UNSCRAMBLE
UNSUITABLE
VAUDEVILLE
VERMICELLI
VOLLEYBALL
VULNERABLE
WINDOWSILL
WINDSHIELD
WORTHWHILE
CAPOREGIME
CHROMOSOME
FORTISSIMO
GASTRONOMY
HIPPODROME
MEDDLESOME
METTLESOME
MONOCHROME
NETTLESOME
PALINDROME
PHLEBOTOMY
PIANISSIMO
SPRINGTIME
UNHANDSOME
WINTERTIME
ACCOUNTANT
ACCOUNTING
ADRENALINE
ADULTERANT
ADVISEMENT
ANTECEDENT

APPETIZING
AQUAMARINE
ASSIGNMENT
ASSORTMENT
ASTRINGENT
ATTACHMENT
ATTAINMENT
ATTRACTANT
BACKGROUND
BATTLEMENT
BEFOREHAND
BEHINDHAND
BELLADONNA
BENEFICENT
BETTERMENT
BIRTHSTONE
BLOODHOUND
BLOODSTONE
BORDERLAND
BOTTOMLAND
BREAKFRONT
BREASTBONE
BRIGANTINE
BROWNSTONE
CANDESCENT
CANTONMENT
CATCHPENNY
CELLOPHANE
CHALCEDONY
CHANGELING
CHATELAINE
CHECKPOINT
CIRCUMVENT
CLINGSTONE
COINCIDENT
COLLARBONE
COMEDIENNE
COMMANDANT
COMPLEMENT
COMPLIMENT
COMPREHEND
CONCERNING
CONCERTINA
CONCORDANT
CONCURRENT
CONDESCEND
CONSEQUENT
CONSTRAINT
CONTINGENT
CONTRABAND
CONTRAVENE
CONVENIENT
CONVERSANT
CORRESPOND
CRADLESONG
CUMMERBUND
DELINQUENT

DENOUEMENT
DEPARTMENT
DEPORTMENT
DEPRESSANT
DESCENDANT
DETACHMENT
DISAPPOINT
DISÇERNING
DISCIPLINE
DISCONTENT
DISCREPANT
DISCUSSANT
DISENCHANT
DISHARMONY
DISINCLINE
DRAWSTRING
EMBANKMENT
EMBONPOINT
EMPLOYMENT
ENDEARMENT
ENGAGEMENT
ENJAMBMENT
EQUIVALENT
ESCARPMENT
EVANESCENT
EVERYTHING
EXCITEMENT
EXORBITANT
EXPERIMENT
FAIRGROUND
FATHERLAND
FINGERLING
FLAMBOYANT
FORBIDDING
FOREGROUND
FOSTERLING
FRAUDULENT
GOVERNMENT
GRAMOPHONE
GRANDSTAND
GRAVESTONE
GRINDSTONE
GROUNDLING
GUILLOTINE
HABILIMENT
HANDSPRING
HEADSTRONG
HIEROPHANT
HINTERLAND
HOMECOMING
HOOTENANNY
HYDROPHONE
HYDROPLANE
IMPEDIMENT
IMPENITENT
INBREEDING
INCOHERENT

INCONSTANT
INDUCEMENT
INFIGHTING
INFREQUENT
INGREDIENT
INHABITANT
INSENTIENT
INSTRUMENT
INTEGUMENT
INTERNMENT
INTERTWINE
INTOLERANT
INTOXICANT
INVESTMENT
IRRELEVANT
KRUGERRAND
LIEUTENANT
LIFESAVING
LIPREADING
LOGROLLING
LOVEMAKING
MAINSPRING
MALCONTENT
MALEFICENT
MALEVOLENT
MANAGEMENT
MANSERVANT
MARASCHINO
MARROWBONE
MASTERMIND
MEDICAMENT
MICROPHONE
MINESTRONE
MINISTRANT
MISCELLANY
MISFORTUNE
MOTHERLAND
MOUNTEBANK
NANOSECOND
NONCHALANT
NOURISHING
OCEANFRONT
OCEANGOING
OMNIPOTENT
OMNISCIENT
OPALESCENT
OUTPATIENT
OUTPOURING
PANTALOONS
PARLIAMENT
PARMIGIANA
PEPPERMINT
PERCIPIENT
PETNAPPING
PHILISTINE
PHOTOPAINT
PICKANINNY

PICOSECOND
PLAYACTING
PLAYGROUND
PREDESTINE
PREEMINENT
PREFERMENT
PRINCELING
PROCEEDING
PROFICIENT
PROPELLANT
PROTESTANT
PUNISHMENT
PUTRESCENT
PYRIMIDINE
QUARANTINE
RADIOPHONE
RAINMAKING
REFINEMENT
REFRINGENT
REGISTRANT
RESOUNDING
RESPECTING
RESPONDENT
RESTAURANT
RHINESTONE
ROLLICKING
SACCHARINE
SCARLATINA
SECONDHAND
SEMIDRYING
SEPTUAGINT
SERPENTINE
SETTLEMENT
SHOESTRING
SHORTENING
SHUNPIKING
SKYWRITING
SMATTERING
SPELLBOUND
SPRINKLING
STANDPOINT
STARVELING
STEPPARENT
STRYCHNINE
SUBROUTINE
SUBSEQUENT
SUBTRAHEND
SUFFICIENT
SUPPLEMENT
SUPPLICANT
TAMBOURINE
TANTAMOUNT
TIMBERLINE
TOUCHSTONE
TOURMALINE
TOURNAMENT
TRAMPOLINE

TRANSPLANT
TRAVERTINE
TURPENTINE
ULTRASOUND
UNASSUMING
UNAVAILING
UNBECOMING
UNBLUSHING
UNDERLYING
UNDERSLUNG
UNDERSTAND
UNPLEASANT
UNTHINKING
UNYIELDING
UPBRINGING
UPSTANDING
VESPERTINE
VIBRAPHONE
VICEGERENT
VIDEOPHONE
VOICEPRINT
WATERBORNE
WATERFRONT
WEATHERING
WELLSPRING
WINDOWPANE
WONDERLAND
WONDERMENT
WRAPAROUND
ABERRATION
ABSCISSION
ABSOLUTION
ABSORPTION
AGGRESSION
ALTERNATOR
AMBASSADOR
AMMUNITION
ANTIPROTON
APPARITION
APPLICATOR
APPOSITION
ARBITRATOR
ARCHBISHOP
ARCHDEACON
ARMAGEDDON
ASPIRATION
ASSUMPTION
ATTRACTION
AUTOMATION
BACKGAMMON
BENEFACTOR
BLACKAMOOR
BRIDEGROOM
BUTTONHOOK
CAPITATION
CARBURETOR
CAVITATION
CHANCELLOR
CHARLESTON
CHATTERBOX
COLORATION
COMBUSTION
COMMISSION
COMMUTATOR
COMPARISON
COMPASSION
COMPATRIOT
COMPETITOR
COMPLEXION
COMPOSITOR
COMPULSION
CONCEPTION
CONCESSION
CONCLUSION
CONCRETION
CONCUSSION
CONFECTION
CONFESSION
CONNECTION
CONNIPTION
CONTENTION
CONVECTION
CONVENTION
CONVERSION
CONVICTION
CONVULSION
CORONATION
COTTONWOOD
DATAMATION
DECLENSION
DECORATION
DECRYPTION
DEFINITION
DELEGATION
DEMOLITION
DEPOSITION
DEPRESSION
DEPUTATION
DERIVATION
DESOLATION
DESTRUCTOR
DISCRETION
DISSENSION
DIVINATION
DOMINATION
DONNYBROOK
DUPLICATOR
EBULLITION
EISTEDDFOD
ENCRYPTION
EQUITATION
ERGOSTEROL
ESCUTCHEON
ESTIMATION
EXHAUSTION
EXPEDITION
EXPOSITION
EXPRESSION
FEDERATION
FIGURATION
FORESHADOW
FOUNDATION
FRANCHISOR
GENERATION
GRADUATION
HABITATION
HANDBARROW
HEARTTHROB
HULLABALOO
IMBIBITION
IMPRESSION
INDECISION
INFLECTION
INFRACTION
INHIBITION
INJUNCTION
INNOVATION
INSOLATION
INSTRUCTOR
INTERFERON
INTINCTION
INTONATION
INVOCATION
INVOLUTION
JUBILATION
KNIGHTHOOD
LIGHTPROOF
LIKELIHOOD
LIVELIHOOD
LOCOMOTION
MAIDENHOOD
MALAPROPOS
MALEFACTOR
MANDLEBROT
MATURATION
MIDDLEBROW
MOTHERHOOD
NINCOMPOOP
OBLIGATION
OCCUPATION
OPPRESSION
ORDINATION
OVERSHADOW
PAGINATION
PERCEPTION
PERCUSSION
PERFECTION
PERIHELION
PERMISSION
PERORATION
PERSUASION
PERVERSION
PHENOMENON
PINCUSHION
PLANTATION
POCKETBOOK
POLYHEDRON
POPULATION
POSSESSION
PRECAUTION
PRECESSION
PROCESSION
PROCURATOR
PRODUCTION
PROFESSION
PROGENITOR
PROMPTBOOK
PROPORTION
PROPRIETOR
PROPULSION
PROTECTION
PROTRACTOR
RECITATION
RECREATION
REDEMPTION
REFRACTION
REGRESSION
REGULATION
RELAXATION
REPARATION
REPETITION
REPUTATION
RESOLUTION
RESORPTION
RESPIRATOR
REVELATION
REVOCATION
REVOLUTION
RHINOCEROS
SALUTATION
SANDALWOOD
SANITATION
SCHOOLROOM
SEPARATION
SERVOMOTOR
SISTERHOOD
SNAPDRAGON
SPOLIATION
SUBSTATION
SUBVENTION
SUCCESSION
SUGGESTION
SUSPENSION
TABLESPOON
TELEVISION
TEMPTATION
TENDERFOOT
TERMINATOR
THERMISTOR
TRANSISTOR
TRANSITION
TRUNCATION
UNDERSHOOT
UNDERSTOOD
UNDULATION
VEGETATION
VISITATION
WATERCOLOR
WATERMELON
WATERPROOF
BATHYSCAPH
CANTALOUPE
COUNTERSPY
HELIOGRAPH
HELIOTROPE
MANUSCRIPT
MICROGRAPH
MICROSCOPE
MIMEOGRAPH
NEWSGROUPS
OCTOTHORPE
PARATROOPS
PHONOGRAPH
PHOTOGRAPH
POSTSCRIPT
RADARSCOPE
RADIOGRAPH
STEREOTYPE
TRANSCRIPT
TYPESCRIPT
ABOVEBOARD
ALIMENTARY
ALONGSHORE
AMBULATORY
ANGIOSPERM
ANIMADVERT
APOTHECARY
ATMOSPHERE
BACKSTAIRS
BAPTISTERY
BLACKBERRY
BLACKBOARD
BLACKGUARD
BLACKTHORN
BRAINSTORM
BREADBOARD
BREASTWORK
BRIDGEWORK
BROADSWORD
CACCIATORE
CAMELOPARD
CANDELABRA
CANKERWORM
CARICATURE
CHARACTERY
CHLOROFORM
CHURCHYARD
CLAVICHORD
CLERESTORY
COLORATURA
COMMENTARY
COMMISSARY
COMPULSORY
CONJECTURE
CONSISTORY
CONTROVERT
CORDILLERA
DEPILATORY
DEPOSITORY
DEROGATORY
DICTIONARY
DINNERWARE
DISCOMFORT
DISCONCERT
DISPENSARY
DOWNSTAIRS
EFFRONTERY
ELDERBERRY
ELEMENTARY
EMBOUCHURE
EMBROIDERY
ENAMELWARE
ESCRITOIRE
EVERYWHERE
FIBERBOARD
FLOORBOARD
FORFEITURE
FOURSQUARE
GOOSEBERRY
GREENSWARD
GROUNDWORK
GYMNOSPERM
HANDLEBARS
HEMISPHERE
HEREDITARY
HERETOFORE
HOLLOWWARE
INCENDIARY
INITIATORY
INTERMARRY
IONOSPHERE
JARDINIERE
JUDICATURE
LABORATORY
LITERATURE
LOGANBERRY
LUMBERYARD
MANDRAGORA
MASTERWORK
MEADOWLARK
MESOSPHERE
MISSIONARY
MULTISTORY
NEEDLEWORK
NIGHTSHIRT
NONSUPPORT
OUTPERFORM
PAPERBOARD
PASTEBOARD
PEPPERCORN
PEREMPTORY
PHYLACTERY
PLEASANTRY
PREBENDARY
PRESBYTERY
PROMISSORY
PROMONTORY
PSYCHIATRY
REFRACTORY
REPERTOIRE
REPOSITORY
SANGUINARY
SCHOOLGIRL
SCHOOLMARM
SEARCHWARE
SILVERWARE
SKATEBOARD
SPOILSPORT
STATIONARY
STATIONERY
STRAWBERRY
SUBSIDIARY
SUSPENSORY
SWEETHEART
THREADBARE
THREESCORE
TOMFOOLERY
TRAJECTORY
TRANSITORY
ULTRASHORT
UNDERSCORE
UNDERSHIRT
UNDERSKIRT
UNDERSTORY
UPHOLSTERY
VETERINARY
VOCABULARY
VOLUPTUARY
WHIRLYBIRD
WICKERWORK
WILLOWWARE
WOODENWARE
ABSOLUTISM
ACCOMPLISH
ALCOHOLISM
ANTAGONISM
ANTAGONIST
ANTICHRIST
APOCALYPSE

BALDERDASH
BELLETRIST
BLOCKHOUSE
BOLSHEVISM
BRAHMANISM
CAPITALISM
CAPITALIST
CATABOLISM
CHARTREUSE
CHAUVINISM
CHURCHLESS
CIRCUMCISE
CLASSICISM
CLOUDBURST
COMPROMISE
COURTHOUSE
CRISSCROSS
CUTTLEFISH
DECOMPRESS
DISCOMPOSE
DISPOSSESS
EMPIRICISM
ENTERPRISE
ENTHUSIASM
EVANGELISM
EVANGELIST
EXTINGUISH
EYEWITNESS
FATHOMLESS
FAVORITISM
FEDERALISM
FEDERALIST
FIBERGLASS
GOOSEFLESH
GRADUALISM
GREENHOUSE
GROUNDMASS
GUARDHOUSE
HOBBYHORSE
HORSEFLESH
HYPOTENUSE
ICONOCLASM
ICONOCLAST
IMPOVERISH
INTERTWIST
JOURNALESE
JOURNALISM
KNOCKWURST
LACHRYMOSE
LENGTHWISE
LIBERALISM
LIGHTHOUSE
LITERALISM
LIVERWURST
MACKINTOSH
MANICURIST
MAYONNAISE
METABOLISM
MILITARISM
MISOGAMIST
MISOGYNIST
MIZZENMAST
MONARCHIST
MONOTHEISM
MULTISENSE
NARCISSISM
NATURALISM
NATURALIST
NEGATIVISM
NETHERMOST
NEUTRALISM
NIGHTDRESS
NUMBERLESS
OUTLANDISH
PAINTBRUSH
PALIMPSEST
PANTYWAIST
PARAPHRASE
PERMAFROST
PHOTOFLASH
PILLOWCASE
PILOTHOUSE
POLYTHEISM
PORTUGUESE
POWERHOUSE
PRAGMATISM
PREDECEASE
PREDISPOSE
PREPOSSESS
PRESUPPOSE
PROTOPLASM
RACECOURSE
RECIDIVISM
RECOILLESS
RECOMPENSE
RELENTLESS
RELINQUISH
RETROGRESS
RHEUMATISM
ROUGHHOUSE
ROUNDHOUSE
SEAMSTRESS
SECULARISM
SEMPSTRESS
SENEGALESE
SEPARATIST
SILVERFISH
SKEPTICISM
SPECIALIST
SPORTSCAST
STATEHOUSE
STOREHOUSE
STRIPTEASE
SUFFRAGIST
SUPERTWIST
SURREALISM
TOOTHBRUSH
TRANSGRESS
TRANSVERSE
UNDERBRUSH
UNDERWAIST
VIETNAMESE
WANDERLUST
WATERCRESS
WEAPONLESS
WEIGHTLESS
WHEELHORSE
WHEELHOUSE
WILDEBEEST
WILDERNESS
WITCHGRASS
ABBREVIATE
ACCELERATE
ACCENTUATE
ACCUMULATE
ADJUDICATE
ADULTERATE
AFTERBIRTH
AFTERTASTE
ALLITERATE
AMALGAMATE
AMELIORATE
ANNIHILATE
ANNUNCIATE
ANTHRACITE
ANTICIPATE
APPRECIATE
ARTICULATE
ASPHYXIATE
ASSEVERATE
ASSIMILATE
BESTIALITY
BLACKSMITH
BROADCLOTH
CALUMNIATE
CAMPHORATE
CAPACITATE
CAPITULATE
CELLARETTE
CHEAPSKATE
CHILDBIRTH
CHLORINATE
CHRYSOLITE
COMMONALTY
COMPENSATE
COMPLICATE
COMPLICITY
CONCILIATE
CONDENSATE
CONFISCATE
CONFORMITY
CONGREGATE
CONSECRATE
CONSTITUTE
CONSUMMATE
CONTINUITY
CONTRIBUTE
COORDINATE
CRENELLATE
DEACTIVATE
DEBILITATE
DECAPITATE
DECELERATE
DEFLAGRATE
DEGENERATE
DELIBERATE
DENOMINATE
DEPOPULATE
DEPRECIATE
DESALINATE
DIFFICULTY
DILETTANTE
DISSOCIATE
DISTILLATE
DISTRIBUTE
EFFECTUATE
EFFEMINATE
ELECTORATE
EMANCIPATE
EMASCULATE
EPISCOPATE
EQUANIMITY
EQUIVOCATE
EVISCERATE
EXACERBATE
EXAGGERATE
EXASPERATE
EXCOGITATE
EXHILARATE
EXPATRIATE
EXURBANITE
FACILITATE
FELICITATE
FLAGELLATE
FLUORIDATE
FLUORINATE
FOOTLIGHTS
FRATERNITY
GENERALITY
GHOSTWRITE
HENCEFORTH
HEREABOUTS
ILLITERATE
ILLUMINATE
ILLUSTRATE
IMMACULATE
IMMODERATE
IMMORALITY
IMPREGNATE
INACTIVATE
INADEQUATE
INAUGURATE
INCAPACITY
INCINERATE
INCIVILITY
INCOMPLETE
INDEFINITE
INDELICATE
INEQUALITY
INFIDELITY
INFILTRATE
INGRATIATE
INHUMANITY
INNOMINATE
INORDINATE
INSEMINATE
INTERFAITH
INTERSTATE
INTIMIDATE
INTOXICATE
INTRASTATE
INVALIDATE
INVETERATE
INVIGORATE
IRRESOLUTE
LEGITIMATE
LICENTIATE
MAGISTRATE
MAISONETTE
MANIPULATE
MARGUERITE
MARIONETTE
METABOLITE
MICROSTATE
MIGNONETTE
NEBULOSITY
NEUTRALITY
NOTABILITY
OBLITERATE
PALATINATE
PERPETRATE
PERPETUATE
PERPETUITY
PERQUISITE
PERSONALTY
PIANOFORTE
PLEBISCITE
POTENTIATE
PRECIOSITY
PROCLIVITY
PROFLIGATE
PROMULGATE
PROPENSITY
PROPITIATE
PROSPERITY
PROSTITUTE
PSYCHOPATH
REACTIVATE
RECUPERATE
REGENERATE
REJUVENATE
RELATIVITY
REMUNERATE
REPAGINATE
REPATRIATE
RISIBILITY
SAPROPHYTE
SCHOOLMATE
SHIBBOLETH
SILHOUETTE
SIMPLICITY
SOLIDARITY
SPIROCHETE
STALACTITE
STALAGMITE
STILLBIRTH
SUBSTITUTE
SUPPLICATE
TABLECLOTH
TESSELLATE
TOOTHPASTE
TRIFOLIATE
TRIPARTITE
TRIPLICATE
UNDERNEATH
UNDERPANTS
UNDERSTATE
UNDERWRITE
UNIFORMITY
UNIVERSITY
VARICOSITY
VERTEBRATE
VIRTUOSITY
VISIBILITY
VITUPERATE
VOCIFERATE
WAVELENGTH
ABSTEMIOUS
ALBUMINOUS
AMPHIBIOUS
ANTEBELLUM
AUDITORIUM
AURIFEROUS
AUSPICIOUS
AUTONOMOUS
BITUMINOUS
BOISTEROUS
BRONTOSAUR
CADAVEROUS
CALCAREOUS
CAOUTCHOUC
CATAFALQUE
CENSORIOUS
CEREBELLUM
CHIVALROUS
CINERARIUM
CIRCUITOUS
COLLOQUIUM
COLPORTEUR
COMMODIOUS
COMMUNIQUE
COMPENDIUM
CONSORTIUM
CONSPECTUS
CONTAGIOUS
CONTIGUOUS
CONTINUOUS
CRETACEOUS
CURRICULUM
CURVACEOUS
DELPHINIUM
DIAPHANOUS
DYSPROSIUM
ENDOGENOUS
EPITHELIUM
EUCALYPTUS
EUPHONIOUS
EXTRANEOUS
FACTITIOUS
FALLACIOUS
FASTIDIOUS
FELICITOUS
FICTITIOUS
FLAGITIOUS
FORTUITOUS
GADOLINIUM
GONOCOCCUS
GRATUITOUS
GREGARIOUS
HARMONIOUS
HOMOLOGOUS
HONORARIUM
HORRENDOUS
IGNORAMOUS
IMPERVIOUS
IMPRIMATUR
INDECOROUS
INDIGENOUS
INGLORIOUS
JUGGERNAUT
KETTLEDRUM
LASCIVIOUS
LAWRENCIUM
LEPRECHAUN
LIBIDINOUS
LICENTIOUS
LOQUACIOUS
LUBRICIOUS
LUGUBRIOUS

MALODOROUS
MEERSCHAUM
MEMORANDUM
MENDACIOUS
METACARPUS
METATARSUS
METICULOUS
MILLENNIUM
MOLYBDENUM
MONOTONOUS
MORATORIUM
NASTURTIUM
NATATORIUM
OBSEQUIOUS
OCEANARIUM
OESOPHAGUS
OLEAGINOUS
OMNIVOROUS
OPPROBRIUM
OUTRAGEOUS
PANJANDRUM
PARAMECIUM
PERITONEUM
PERNICIOUS
PETROLATUM
PHOSPHORUS
PICARESQUE
PORTENTOUS
POSTHUMOUS
POSTPARTUM
PRECARIOUS
PRECOCIOUS
PREDACEOUS
PRODIGIOUS
PROMETHIUM
PROPITIOUS
PROSCENIUM
PROSPECTUS
PROSPEROUS
PUGNACIOUS
QUADRIVIUM
REBELLIOUS
REFERENDUM
RENDEZVOUS
RIDICULOUS
ROUNDABOUT
ROUSTABOUT
SALUBRIOUS
SANATORIUM
SANITARIUM
SAUERKRAUT
SCURRILOUS
SHUTTERBUG
SLUMBEROUS
SOLICITOUS
SPIRITUOUS
SPITTLEBUG

STATUESQUE
STUPENDOUS
SUBSTRATUM
SUSPICIOUS
TECHNETIUM
TENEBRIOUS
THOUGHTFUL
THROUGHOUT
THROUGHPUT
THUNDEROUS
TRAVELOGUE
TREMENDOUS
TROLLEYBUS
TROUBADOUR
TUMULTUOUS
UBIQUITOUS
UNDERVALUE
UNEVENTFUL
UNFAITHFUL
UNFRUITFUL
UNGENEROUS
UNGRACEFUL
UNGRACIOUS
UNGRATEFUL
UNMERCIFUL
UNSKILLFUL
UPROARIOUS
VICTORIOUS
VILLAINOUS
VIVIPAROUS
VOCIFEROUS
VOLUMINOUS
VOLUPTUOUS
WATERSPOUT
WORSHIPFUL
ACCUSATIVE
AFFLICTIVE
AGGRESSIVE
APPOINTIVE
APPOSITIVE
ARCHITRAVE
AUTOMOTIVE
COLLECTIVE
COMPULSIVE
COMPUSERVE
CONCESSIVE
CONDUCTIVE
CONNECTIVE
CUMULATIVE
DECORATIVE
DEFINITIVE
DENOTATIVE
DEPRESSIVE
DERIVATIVE
DIMINUTIVE
DISAPPROVE
DISBELIEVE

DISCURSIVE
EXHAUSTIVE
FIGURATIVE
IMPERATIVE
IMPRESSIVE
INDECISIVE
INDICATIVE
INFINITIVE
INITIATIVE
INTERLEAVE
INTERWEAVE
LOCOMOTIVE
NOMINATIVE
PEJORATIVE
PERCEPTIVE
PERMISSIVE
POSSESSIVE
PREEMPTIVE
REPARATIVE
REPETITIVE
RESPECTIVE
RESPONSIVE
SEPARATIVE
SUBJECTIVE
SUCCESSIVE
SUGGESTIVE
TRANSITIVE
TURTLEDOVE
VEGETATIVE
VINDICTIVE
ALLHALLOWS
SPLASHDOWN
TUMBLEDOWN
METAGALAXY
AGGRANDIZE
ALKALINIZE
ANTAGONIZE
ANTIFREEZE
AUTOMATIZE
BASTARDIZE
BOWDLERIZE
CAPITALIZE
CATEGORIZE
CENTRALIZE
CHANNELIZE
DECIMALIZE
DECOLORIZE
DEHUMANIZE
DEMOBILIZE
DEMONETIZE
DEMORALIZE
DEPOLARIZE
DESALINIZE
DEVITALIZE
EVANGELIZE
FAMILARIZE
FEDERALIZE

FRATERNIZE
GENERALIZE
GORMANDIZE
HOMOGENIZE
IMMOBILIZE
INTERMEZZO
MILITARIZE
MINERALIZE
NATURALIZE
NEUTRALIZE
PALATALIZE
PASTEURIZE
PLAGIARIZE
PRESSURIZE
RADICALIZE
REVITALIZE
SCRUTINIZE
SECULARIZE
SLENDERIZE
SPECIALIZE
STIGMATIZE
SYMPATHIZE
WESTERNIZE

### 10th Letter

ACROPHOBIA
ANESTHESIA
AUTOSTRADA
BELLADONNA
CANDELABRA
CHINCHILLA
CITRONELLA
COLORATURA
CONCERTINA
CORDILLERA
CORNUCOPIA
CYCLOPEDIA
DIPHTHERIA
DIPSOMANIA
EUTHANASIA
GORGONZOLA
HEMOPHILIA
JINRIKISHA
MANDRAGORA
MARGINALIA
MOZZARELLA
MULTIMEDIA
PARAPLEGIA
PARMIGIANA
POINSETTIA
PRESBYOPIA
PROPAGANDA
RICKETTSIA
SCARLATINA

SEPTICEMIA
TARANTELLA
XENOPHOBIA
HEARTTHROB
ACHROMATIC
ALPHABETIC
ANESTHETIC
ANTIBIOTIC
ANTISEPTIC
APOLOGETIC
ARITHMETIC
ASYMMETRIC
BIMETALLIC
CAOUTCHOUC
CONCENTRIC
DEMOCRATIC
DIELECTRIC
EGOCENTRIC
ELECTRONIC
EXOTHERMIC
FUTURISTIC
GEOCENTRIC
HISTRIONIC
HYPERBARIC
HYPODERMIC
IDIOPATHIC
INFRASONIC
MONOPHONIC
NAPOLEONIC
NEOCLASSIC
OPHTHALMIC
PATRONYMIC
PHLEGMATIC
PHOTOGENIC
POLYCLINIC
PROGNOSTIC
QUICKBASIC
RADIOGENIC
SACROILIAC
SCHISMATIC
SCHOLASTIC
SIMPLISTIC
SOPHOMORIC
STOCHASTIC
SUPERSONIC
TELESCOPIC
ULTRASONIC
VOLUMETRIC
ABOVEBOARD
ACCUSTOMED
ANTHROPOID
ANTIQUATED
BACKGROUND
BACKHANDED
BAREHEADED
BEDRAGGLED
BEFOREHAND

BEHINDHAND
BLACKBOARD
BLACKGUARD
BLOODHOUND
BORDERLAND
BOTTOMLAND
BRAINCHILD
BREADBOARD
BRIDESMAID
BRIDGEHEAD
BROADSWORD
BULLHEADED
CALCULATED
CAMELOPARD
CARBOLATED
CELEBRATED
CHURCHYARD
CLASSIFIED
CLAVICHORD
COMPLECTED
COMPREHEND
CONDESCEND
CONTRABAND
CONVOLUTED
COPPERHEAD
CORRESPOND
COTTONSEED
COTTONWOOD
CROSSBREED
CUMMERBUND
DETERMINED
DISJOINTED
DREAMWORLD
DUNDERHEAD
EISTEDDFOD
ENDANGERED
EVENHANDED
FAIRGROUND
FARFETCHED
FARSIGHTED
FATHERLAND
FIBERBOARD
FIGUREHEAD
FLOORBOARD
FOREGROUND
FOREHANDED
GRAINFIELD
GRANDCHILD
GRANDSTAND
GREENSWARD
HAMMERHEAD
HARDHEADED
HEMORRHOID
HINTERLAND
INDISPOSED
INTERBREED
JIMSONWEED

KNIGHTHOOD
KRUGERRAND
LANDLOCKED
LETTERHEAD
LIKELIHOOD
LIVELIHOOD
LOGGERHEAD
LUMBERYARD
MAIDENHEAD
MAIDENHOOD
MALADAPTED
MASTERMIND
MISALIGNED
MOTHERHOOD
MOTHERLAND
NANOSECOND
NEWFANGLED
OTHERWORLD
OVERSPREAD
PACKTHREAD
PAPERBOARD
PASTEBOARD
PICOSECOND
PLAYGROUND
PRINCIPLED
PRIVILEGED
PROGRAMMED
PRONOUNCED
PROPERTIED
RESTRAINED
SANDALWOOD
SECONDHAND
SHAMEFACED
SISTERHOOD
SKATEBOARD
SPELLBOUND
STRONGHOLD
SUBTRAHEND
SWEETBREAD
TUMBLEWEED
ULTRASOUND
UNABRIDGED
UNAFFECTED
UNATTACHED
UNBALANCED
UNDERSEXED
UNDERSIZED
UNDERSTAND
UNDERSTOOD
UNDERWORLD
UNEMPLOYED
UNEXAMPLED
UNEXPECTED
UNGROUNDED
UNHALLOWED
UNLETTERED
UNNUMBERED

UNOCCUPIED
UNREASONED
UNRESERVED
UNSCHOOLED
WHIRLYBIRD
WIDESPREAD
WINDSHIELD
WINGSPREAD
WIREHAIRED
WONDERLAND
WRAPAROUND
ABBREVIATE
ABOMINABLE
ABSTINENCE
ACCELERATE
ACCENTUATE
ACCEPTABLE
ACCEPTANCE
ACCESSIBLE
ACCOMPLICE
ACCORDANCE
ACCUMULATE
ACCUSATIVE
ACTIONABLE
ADJUDICATE
ADMISSIBLE
ADMITTANCE
ADRENALINE
ADULTERATE
AFFLICTIVE
AFTERIMAGE
AFTERTASTE
AGGRANDIZE
AGGRESSIVE
ALKALINIZE
ALLEGIANCE
ALLITERATE
ALONGSHORE
ALTARPIECE
AMALGAMATE
AMELIORATE
ANGLOPHILE
ANGLOPHOBE
ANIMALCULE
ANNIHILATE
ANNUNCIATE
ANSWERABLE
ANTAGONIZE
ANTHRACITE
ANTICIPATE
ANTIFREEZE
APOCALYPSE
APOSTROPHE
APPEARANCE
APPLICABLE
APPOINTIVE
APPOSITIVE

APPRECIATE
APPRENTICE
AQUAMARINE
ARBORVITAE
ARCHITRAVE
ARTICULATE
ASPHYXIATE
ASSEMBLAGE
ASSEVERATE
ASSIMILATE
ATMOSPHERE
ATTENDANCE
AUDIOPHILE
AUTOMATIZE
AUTOMOBILE
AUTOMOTIVE
BACKSTROKE
BALUSTRADE
BASTARDIZE
BESPRINKLE
BICHLORIDE
BIRTHPLACE
BIRTHSTONE
BLANCMANGE
BLOCKHOUSE
BLOODSTONE
BLUEBOTTLE
BOOKMOBILE
BOONDOGGLE
BOWDLERIZE
BREASTBONE
BRIGANTINE
BROWNSTONE
BUTTONHOLE
CACCIATORE
CALUMNIATE
CAMOUFLAGE
CAMPHORATE
CANTALOUPE
CAPACITATE
CAPITALIZE
CAPITULATE
CAPOREGIME
CARICATURE
CATAFALQUE
CATEGORIZE
CELLARETTE
CELLOPHANE
CENTIGRADE
CENTRALIZE
CENTRIFUGE
CHANNELIZE
CHARITABLE
CHARTREUSE
CHATELAINE
CHEAPSKATE
CHEESECAKE

CHIMPANZEE
CHLORINATE
CHROMOSOME
CHRYSOLITE
CIRCUMCISE
CLINGSTONE
COCKATRICE
COGNIZANCE
COLLARBONE
COLLECTIVE
COMEDIENNE
COMESTIBLE
COMMUNIQUE
COMPARABLE
COMPATIBLE
COMPENSATE
COMPETENCE
COMPLIANCE
COMPLICATE
COMPROMISE
COMPULSIVE
COMPUSERVE
CONCESSIVE
CONCILIATE
CONDENSATE
CONDUCTIVE
CONFERENCE
CONFIDENCE
CONFISCATE
CONFLUENCE
CONGREGATE
CONGRUENCE
CONJECTURE
CONNECTIVE
CONSCIENCE
CONSECRATE
CONSONANCE
CONSTITUTE
CONSUMMATE
CONTINENCE
CONTRAVENE
CONTRIBUTE
CONVALESCE
CONVEYANCE
COORDINATE
CORPULENCE
CORRIGIBLE
COURTHOUSE
CREDITABLE
CRENELLATE
CROSSPIECE
CUMULATIVE
CYBERSPACE
DEACTIVATE
DEBILITATE
DECAPITATE
DECELERATE

DECIMALIZE
DECOLORIZE
DECORATIVE
DEFINITIVE
DEFLAGRATE
DEGENERATE
DEGRADABLE
DEHUMANIZE
DELECTABLE
DELIBERATE
DELIQUESCE
DEMOBILIZE
DEMOISELLE
DEMONETIZE
DEMORALIZE
DENOMINATE
DENOTATIVE
DENTIFRICE
DEPENDABLE
DEPENDENCE
DEPLORABLE
DEPOLARIZE
DEPOPULATE
DEPRECIATE
DEPRESSIVE
DERIVATIVE
DESALINATE
DESALINIZE
DESPICABLE
DETERRENCE
DEVITALIZE
DIFFERENCE
DILETTANTE
DIMINUTIVE
DINNERWARE
DISAPPROVE
DISARRANGE
DISBELIEVE
DISCIPLINE
DISCOMMODE
DISCOMPOSE
DISCOURAGE
DISCURSIVE
DISGRUNTLE
DISHABILLE
DISINCLINE
DISPOSABLE
DISSERVICE
DISSOCIATE
DISSONANCE
DISTILLATE
DISTRIBUTE
DOWNSTROKE
DRAWBRIDGE
EARTHQUAKE
EFFECTUATE
EFFEMINATE

EFFERVESCE
EFFLORESCE
EFFULGENCE
ELECTORATE
EMANCIPATE
EMASCULATE
EMBOUCHURE
ENAMELWARE
ENTERPRISE
EPISCOPATE
EQUIVOCATE
ESCRITOIRE
ESPADRILLE
EVANGELIZE
EVERYWHERE
EVISCERATE
EXACERBATE
EXACTITUDE
EXAGGERATE
EXASPERATE
EXCELLENCE
EXCOGITATE
EXHAUSTIVE
EXHILARATE
EXPATRIATE
EXPEDIENCE
EXPERIENCE
EXPLICABLE
EXURBANITE
FACILITATE
FAMILARIZE
FEDERALIZE
FELICITATE
FIELDPIECE
FIGURATIVE
FLAGELLATE
FLUIDOUNCE
FLUORIDATE
FLUORINATE
FOOTBRIDGE
FORECASTLE
FORFEITURE
FORMIDABLE
FOURSQUARE
FRANCHISEE
FRATERNIZE
FRATRICIDE
GENERALIZE
GEOSCIENCE
GHOSTWRITE
GORMANDIZE
GRAMOPHONE
GRAVESTONE
GREENHOUSE
GRINDSTONE
GUARDHOUSE
GUILLOTINE

HEARTHSIDE
HEATSTROKE
HELIOTROPE
HEMISPHERE
HEMORRHAGE
HERETOFORE
HIPPODROME
HOBBYHORSE
HODGEPODGE
HOLLOWWARE
HOMOGENIZE
HOSPITABLE
HYDROPHONE
HYDROPLANE
HYPOTENUSE
ILLITERATE
ILLUMINATE
ILLUSTRATE
IMAGINABLE
IMMACULATE
IMMISCIBLE
IMMOBILIZE
IMMODERATE
IMPALPABLE
IMPASSABLE
IMPASSIBLE
IMPATIENCE
IMPECCABLE
IMPERATIVE
IMPLACABLE
IMPORTANCE
IMPOSSIBLE
IMPREGNATE
IMPRESSIVE
IMPROBABLE
INACTIVATE
INADEQUATE
INAPTITUDE
INAUGURATE
INCINERATE
INCLINABLE
INCOMPLETE
INCREDIBLE
INCULPABLE
INDECISIVE
INDEFINITE
INDELICATE
INDICATIVE
INDUCTANCE
INDULGENCE
INELIGIBLE
INEVITABLE
INEXORABLE
INEXPIABLE
INFALLIBLE
INFILTRATE
INFINITIVE

INFINITUDE
INFLEXIBLE
INGRATIATE
INIMITABLE
INITIATIVE
INNOMINATE
INOPERABLE
INORDINATE
INQUIETUDE
INSATIABLE
INSEMINATE
INSENSIBLE
INSISTENCE
INSOLVABLE
INTANGIBLE
INTERLEAVE
INTERSTATE
INTERSTICE
INTERTWINE
INTERWEAVE
INTIMIDATE
INTOXICATE
INTRASTATE
INVALIDATE
INVALUABLE
INVARIABLE
INVETERATE
INVIGORATE
INVINCIBLE
INVIOLABLE
IONOSPHERE
IRRESOLUTE
JARDINIERE
JOURNALESE
JUDICATURE
LACHRYMOSE
LEGITIMATE
LENGTHWISE
LICENTIATE
LIGHTHOUSE
LITERATURE
LOCOMOTIVE
MAGISTRATE
MAISONETTE
MANIPULATE
MANSUETUDE
MARGUERITE
MARIONETTE
MARROWBONE
MARTINGALE
MASQUERADE
MAYONNAISE
MEDDLESOME
MENSURABLE
MERCANTILE
MESOSPHERE
METABOLITE

METTLESOME
MICROFICHE
MICROPHONE
MICROPROBE
MICROSCOPE
MICROSTATE
MIGNONETTE
MILITARIZE
MINERALIZE
MINESTRONE
MISFORTUNE
MISTAKABLE
MONOCHROME
MONSTRANCE
MOTORCYCLE
MOUTHPIECE
MULTISENSE
MULTISTAGE
NATIONWIDE
NATURALIZE
NEGLIGIBLE
NETTLESOME
NEUTRALIZE
NIGHTSHADE
NOMINATIVE
NOTICEABLE
OBLITERATE
OBSERVABLE
OBSERVANCE
OCCURRENCE
OCTOTHORPE
OSTENSIBLE
OUTBALANCE
OVERCHARGE
PACKSADDLE
PALATALIZE
PALATINATE
PALINDROME
PARAPHRASE
PARTICIPLE
PASTEURIZE
PEJORATIVE
PERCENTAGE
PERCENTILE
PERCEPTIVE
PERDURABLE
PERISHABLE
PERIWINKLE
PERMISSIVE
PERPETRATE
PERPETUATE
PERQUISITE
PERSIFLAGE
PERSONABLE
PESTILENCE
PHILISTINE
PIANOFORTE
PICARESQUE
PIGEONHOLE
PILGRIMAGE
PILLOWCASE
PILOTHOUSE
PLAGIARIZE
PLEBISCITE
PORTUGUESE
POSSESSIVE
POTENTIATE
POWERHOUSE
PREARRANGE
PRECEDENCE
PREDECEASE
PREDESTINE
PREDICABLE
PREDISPOSE
PREEMPTIVE
PREFERENCE
PREHENSILE
PREPACKAGE
PRESCIENCE
PRESSURIZE
PRESUPPOSE
PROFLIGATE
PROJECTILE
PROMINENCE
PROMULGATE
PROPITIATE
PROSTITUTE
PROVENANCE
PROVIDENCE
PSEUDOCODE
PUBESCENCE
PYRIMIDINE
QUADRANGLE
QUARANTINE
RACECOURSE
RADARSCOPE
RADICALIZE
RADIOPHONE
RADIOSONDE
RAMSHACKLE
REACTIVATE
REASONABLE
RECEIVABLE
RECEPTACLE
RECOMPENSE
RECUPERATE
REFULGENCE
REGENERATE
REJUVENATE
RELUCTANCE
REMARKABLE
REMEDIABLE
REMITTANCE
REMUNERATE
RENASCENCE
REPAGINATE
REPARATIVE
REPATRIATE
REPERTOIRE
REPETITIVE
REPUGNANCE
RESILIENCE
RESISTANCE
RESPECTIVE
RESPONSIVE
RESTORABLE
RESURGENCE
RETRACTILE
RETROGRADE
REVITALIZE
RHINESTONE
ROTISSERIE
ROUGHHOUSE
ROUNDHOUSE
SACCHARINE
SAPROPHYTE
SCAPEGRACE
SCHOOLMATE
SCRUTINIZE
SEARCHWARE
SEASONABLE
SECULARIZE
SENEGALESE
SENESCENCE
SEPARATIVE
SERPENTINE
SIDESTROKE
SILHOUETTE
SILVERWARE
SIMILITUDE
SINGLETREE
SLENDERIZE
SNOWMOBILE
SOLICITUDE
SPECIALIZE
SPIROCHETE
SPRINGTIME
STALACTITE
STALAGMITE
STATEHOUSE
STATUESQUE
STEREOTYPE
STIGMATIZE
STOREHOUSE
STRIPTEASE
STRYCHNINE
SUBJECTIVE
SUBROUTINE
SUBSTITUTE
SUBSURFACE
SUBTERFUGE
SUCCESSIVE
SUFFERANCE
SUGGESTIVE
SUPPLICATE
SUSTENANCE
SYMPATHIZE
TABERNACLE
TAMBOURINE
TATTLETALE
TEETHRIDGE
TEMPERANCE
TESSELLATE
THREADBARE
THREEPENCE
THREESCORE
TIMBERLINE
TOOTHPASTE
TOUCHSTONE
TOURMALINE
TRAMPOLINE
TRANSCRIBE
TRANSITIVE
TRANSVERSE
TRAVELOGUE
TRAVERTINE
TRIFOLIATE
TRIPARTITE
TRIPLICATE
TURBULENCE
TURNBUCKLE
TURPENTINE
TURTLEDOVE
UNBEARABLE
UNBEATABLE
UNDENIABLE
UNDERSCORE
UNDERSTATE
UNDERVALUE
UNDERWRITE
UNHANDSOME
UNSCRAMBLE
UNSUITABLE
VAUDEVILLE
VEGETATIVE
VELOCIPEDE
VERTEBRATE
VESPERTINE
VIBRAPHONE
VIDEOPHONE
VIETNAMESE
VINDICTIVE
VITUPERATE
VOCIFERATE
VULNERABLE
WATERBORNE
WESTERNIZE
WHEELHORSE
WHEELHOUSE
WILLOWWARE
WINDOWPANE
WINTERTIDE
WINTERTIME
WOODENWARE
WORTHWHILE
BREADSTUFF
CLOVERLEAF
LIGHTPROOF
WATERPROOF
ACCOUNTING
APPETIZING
BLITZKRIEG
CHANGELING
CONCERNING
CRADLESONG
DISCERNING
DRAWSTRING
EVERYTHING
FINGERLING
FORBIDDING
FOSTERLING
GROUNDLING
HANDSPRING
HEADSTRONG
HOMECOMING
INBREEDING
INFIGHTING
LIFESAVING
LIPREADING
LOGROLLING
LOVEMAKING
MAINSPRING
NOURISHING
OCEANGOING
OUTPOURING
PETNAPPING
PLAYACTING
PRINCELING
PROCEEDING
RAINMAKING
RESOUNDING
RESPECTING
ROLLICKING
SEMIDRYING
SHOESTRING
SHORTENING
SHUNPIKING
SHUTTERBUG
SKYWRITING
SMATTERING
SPITTLEBUG
SPRINKLING
STARVELING
UNASSUMING
UNAVAILING
UNBECOMING
UNBLUSHING
UNDERLYING
UNDERSLUNG
UNTHINKING
UNYIELDING
UPBRINGING
UPSTANDING
WEATHERING
WELLSPRING
ACCOMPLISH
AFTERBIRTH
BALDERDASH
BATHYSCAPH
BLACKSMITH
BROADCLOTH
CHILDBIRTH
CORNSTARCH
CUTTLEFISH
DEATHWATCH
EXTINGUISH
GOOSEFLESH
HALLELUJAH
HELIOGRAPH
HENCEFORTH
HORSEFLESH
HORSELAUGH
IMPOVERISH
INTERFAITH
MACKINTOSH
MICROGRAPH
MIMEOGRAPH
OUTLANDISH
PAINTBRUSH
PHONOGRAPH
PHOTOFLASH
PHOTOGRAPH
PSYCHOPATH
RADIOGRAPH
RELINQUISH
SHIBBOLETH
SHILLELAGH
SILVERFISH
STAGECOACH
STILLBIRTH
TABLECLOTH
TOOTHBRUSH
UNDERBRUSH
UNDERNEATH
WAVELENGTH
WRISTWATCH
PICCALILLI
VERMICELLI
BOTTLENECK
BREASTWORK
BRIDGEWORK
BUTTERMILK
BUTTONHOOK
CANDLEWICK
CANVASBACK
DONNYBROOK
GENTLEFOLK
GROUNDWORK
HAMMERLOCK
HEARTBREAK
INTERBLOCK
KNICKKNACK
LUMBERJACK
MANTLEROCK
MASTERWORK
MEADOWLARK
MOONSTRUCK
MOTORTRUCK
MOUNTEBANK
NEEDLEWORK
NIGHTSTICK
POCKETBOOK
PROMPTBOOK
RUBBERNECK
SMOKESTACK
SWITCHBACK
TURTLENECK
UNDERTRICK
WICKERWORK
ABORIGINAL
ACCIDENTAL
ADDITIONAL
ANTIPHONAL
ANTISOCIAL
APOCRYPHAL
APOLITICAL
ARTIFICIAL
BASKETBALL
BENEFICIAL
BIOMEDICAL
BIPARENTAL
BIPARIETAL
CANNONBALL
CENTENNIAL
CENTESIMAL
CEREMONIAL
CHIMERICAL
CINQUEFOIL
COLLATERAL
COLLOQUIAL
COMMERCIAL
COMMONWEAL
CONGENITAL
COTERMINAL
COTTONTAIL
CREDENTIAL
DISEMBOWEL
DUODECIMAL
ECONOMICAL

ECUMENICAL
ENCYCLICAL
ERGOSTEROL
EXTRAMURAL
FINGERNAIL
GEOTHERMAL
HOMOSEXUAL
HORIZONTAL
IMMATERIAL
IMMEMORIAL
IMPERSONAL
INCIDENTAL
INDIVIDUAL
INDUSTRIAL
INTERTIDAL
INTRAMURAL
IRRATIONAL
ISOTHERMAL
MECHANICAL
METATARSAL
MINISCROLL
MONUMENTAL
MULTILEVEL
OCCASIONAL
OCCIDENTAL
ORATORICAL
OUTGENERAL
PENNYROYAL
PERCEPTUAL
PERIODICAL
PERIPHERAL
PHOTOMURAL
PREMARITAL
PREMEDICAL
PRIMORDIAL
PROVINCIAL
QUATREFOIL
RECIPROCAL
RELATIONAL
ROLLERBALL
SACERDOTAL
SCHOOLGIRL
SEPULCHRAL
STANDSTILL
SUBLIMINAL
SUBORBITAL
TATTERSALL
THEATRICAL
THOUGHTFUL
TORRENTIAL
TYRANNICAL
UNCRITICAL
UNEVENTFUL
UNFAITHFUL
UNFRUITFUL
UNGRACEFUL
UNGRATEFUL
UNICAMERAL
UNILATERAL
UNMERCIFUL
UNSKILLFUL
UROGENITAL
VOLLEYBALL
WATERWHEEL
WINDOWSILL
WITHDRAWAL
WORSHIPFUL
ABSOLUTISM
ALCOHOLISM
ANGIOSPERM
ANTAGONISM
ANTEBELLUM
AUDITORIUM
BOLSHEVISM
BRAHMANISM
BRAINSTORM
BRIDEGROOM
CANKERWORM
CAPITALISM
CARDIOGRAM
CATABOLISM
CEREBELLUM
CHAUVINISM
CHLOROFORM
CINERARIUM
CLASSICISM
COLLOQUIUM
COMPENDIUM
CONSORTIUM
CRYPTOGRAM
CURRICULUM
DELPHINIUM
DOWNSTREAM
DYSPROSIUM
EMPIRICISM
ENTHUSIASM
EPITHELIUM
EVANGELISM
FAVORITISM
FEDERALISM
GADOLINIUM
GRADUALISM
GYMNOSPERM
HONORARIUM
ICONOCLASM
JOURNALISM
KETTLEDRUM
LAWRENCIUM
LIBERALISM
LITERALISM
MAINSTREAM
MEERSCHAUM
MEMORANDUM
METABOLISM
MILITARISM
MILLENNIUM
MILLSTREAM
MOLYBDENUM
MONOTHEISM
MORATORIUM
NARCISSISM
NASTURTIUM
NATATORIUM
NATURALISM
NEGATIVISM
NEUTRALISM
OCEANARIUM
OPPROBRIUM
OUTPERFORM
PANJANDRUM
PARAMECIUM
PERITONEUM
PETROLATUM
POLYTHEISM
POSTMORTEM
POSTPARTUM
PRAGMATISM
PROMETHIUM
PROSCENIUM
PROTOPLASM
QUADRIVIUM
RECIDIVISM
REFERENDUM
RHEUMATISM
SANATORIUM
SANITARIUM
SCHOOLMARM
SCHOOLROOM
SECULARISM
SEISMOGRAM
SKEPTICISM
SLIPSTREAM
SUBSTRATUM
SURREALISM
TECHNETIUM
ABERRATION
ABSCISSION
ABSOLUTION
ABSORPTION
AGGRESSION
AMERINDIAN
AMMUNITION
ANTINOMIAN
ANTIPROTON
APPARITION
APPOSITION
ARCHDEACON
ARMAGEDDON
ASPIRATION
ASSUMPTION
ATTRACTION
AUSTRALIAN
AUTOMATION
BACKGAMMON
BALBRIGGAN
BATRACHIAN
BEAUTICIAN
BIPARTISAN
BLACKTHORN
BLOODSTAIN
CAPITATION
CARCINOGEN
CATECHUMEN
CAVITATION
CHAPFALLEN
CHARLESTON
CLOTHESPIN
COLORATION
COMBUSTION
COMMISSION
COMPARISON
COMPASSION
COMPLEXION
COMPULSION
CONCEPTION
CONCESSION
CONCLUSION
CONCRETION
CONCUSSION
CONFECTION
CONFESSION
CONNECTION
CONNIPTION
CONTENTION
CONVECTION
CONVENTION
CONVERSION
CONVICTION
CONVULSION
CORONATION
COUNTERMAN
COUNTRYMAN
CRUSTACEAN
DATAMATION
DECLENSION
DECORATION
DECRYPTION
DEFINITION
DELEGATION
DEMOLITION
DEPOSITION
DEPRESSION
DEPUTATION
DERIVATION
DESOLATION
DISCRETION
DISHEARTEN
DISSENSION
DIVINATION
DOMINATION
EBULLITION
ENCRYPTION
EQUESTRIAN
EQUITATION
ESCUTCHEON
ESTIMATION
EXHAUSTION
EXPEDITION
EXPOSITION
EXPRESSION
EXPRESSMAN
FEDERATION
FIBRINOGEN
FIGURATION
FLOODPLAIN
FOREORDAIN
FOUNDATION
GARGANTUAN
GENERATION
GRADUATION
HABITATION
HANDMAIDEN
HEMOGLOBIN
HIGHWAYMAN
HORSEWOMAN
HOUSECLEAN
HUSBANDMAN
IMBIBITION
IMPRESSION
INDECISION
INDONESIAN
INFLECTION
INFRACTION
INHIBITION
INJUNCTION
INNOVATION
INSOLATION
INTERFERON
INTERURBAN
INTINCTION
INTONATION
INVOCATION
INVOLUTION
JOURNEYMAN
JUBILATION
LEDERHOSEN
LEPRECHAUN
LITHUANIAN
LOCOMOTION
MALTHUSIAN
MATURATION
MELANESIAN
MIDSHIPMAN
MISSILEMAN
MOHAMMEDAN
MUHAMMADAN
NURSERYMAN
OBLIGATION
OCCUPATION
OPPRESSION
ORDINATION
ORGANGUTAN
PAGINATION
PEDESTRIAN
PENICILLIN
PEPPERCORN
PERCEPTION
PERCUSSION
PERFECTION
PERIHELION
PERMISSION
PERORATION
PERSUASION
PERVERSION
PHENOMENON
PINCUSHION
PLANTATION
POLITICIAN
POLYHEDRON
POLYNESIAN
POPULATION
POSSESSION
POULTRYMAN
PRECAUTION
PRECESSION
PROCESSION
PRODUCTION
PROFESSION
PROPORTION
PROPULSION
PROTECTION
RAGAMUFFIN
RECITATION
RECREATION
REDEMPTION
REFRACTION
REGRESSION
REGULATION
RELAXATION
REPARATION
REPETITION
REPUBLICAN
REPUTATION
RESOLUTION
RESORPTION
REVELATION
REVOCATION
REVOLUTION
RIBOFLAVIN
SALESWOMAN
SALUTATION
SANITARIAN
SANITATION
SEPARATION
SERVICEMAN
SHENANIGAN
SNAPDRAGON
SPLASHDOWN
SPOLIATION
STENTORIAN
STRAIGHTEN
STRENGTHEN
SUBSTATION
SUBVENTION
SUCCESSION
SUGGESTION
SUSPENSION
TABLESPOON
TECHNICIAN
TELEVISION
TEMPTATION
TENDERLOIN
TRANSITION
TRUNCATION
TUBERCULIN
TUMBLEDOWN
UNDULATION
VEGETARIAN
VEGETATION
VISITATION
WATERMELON
WEATHERMAN
WORKINGMAN
AFICIONADO
DIMINUENDO
FORTISSIMO
HULLABALOO
IMPRESARIO
INTERMEZZO
MARASCHINO
PECCADILLO
PIANISSIMO
SUPERCARGO
ARCHBISHOP
AUTHORSHIP
BATTLESHIP
CENSORSHIP
DEALERSHIP
FELLOWSHIP
GINGERSNAP
MASTERSHIP
MEMBERSHIP
NINCOMPOOP
PENMANSHIP
RATTLETRAP
READERSHIP
SEAMANSHIP
ADMINISTER
ADVENTURER

ALTERNATOR
ALTOGETHER
AMBASSADOR
ANEMOMETER
ANTICANCER
ANTIMATTER
APPLICATOR
AQUALUNGER
ARBITRATOR
AUCTIONEER
BELLWETHER
BENEFACTOR
BLACKAMOOR
BLUECOLLAR
BOMBARDIER
BONDHOLDER
BOOKKEEPER
BOOKSELLER
BREAKWATER
BRICKLAYER
BRONTOSAUR
BUDGERIGAR
BUSHMASTER
CANTILEVER
CARABINEER
CARBURETOR
CENTILITER
CENTIMETER
CHANCELLOR
CHANDELIER
CHANGEOVER
CHIFFONIER
CHURCHGOER
CLODHOPPER
COLPORTEUR
COMMANDEER
COMMUTATOR
COMPETITOR
COMPOSITOR
CONTROLLER
COPYREADER
COPYWRITER
CORDWAINER
CORNFLOWER
COWPUNCHER
CYCLOMETER
DESTRUCTOR
DISHWASHER
DISSIMILAR
DOCKWORKER
DOGCATCHER
DOORKEEPER
DUMBWAITER
DUPLICATOR
EMULSIFIER
EURODOLLAR
EYEDROPPER
FERTILIZER
FILIBUSTER
FLOODWATER
FLYCATCHER
FOLKSINGER
FOOTLOCKER
FOREFATHER
FOREFINGER
FOREGATHER
FORERUNNER
FRANCHISER
FRANCHISOR
FREEBOOTER
FRESHWATER
GAMEKEEPER
GATEKEEPER
GOALKEEPER
GOLDBEATER
GRAVIMETER
GUNSLINGER
HEADMASTER
HEADWAITER
HECTOLITER
HECTOMETER
HELICOPTER
HEPTAMETER
HIGHLANDER
HORSEPOWER
HYDROMETER
HYGROMETER
HYPOCENTER
ICEBREAKER
IMPRIMATUR
INSTRUCTOR
INTERLUNAR
JACKHAMMER
JAWBREAKER
KIESELGUHR
KINGFISHER
LACKLUSTER
LADYFINGER
LANDHOLDER
LANDLUBBER
LAWBREAKER
LEAFHOPPER
LINEBACKER
MAIDENHAIR
MALEFACTOR
MATCHMAKER
MICROMETER
MILLILITER
MILLIMETER
MUDSLINGER
MULTIPLIER
MYRIAMETER
NEWSLETTER
NOISEMAKER
NONDRINKER
NONSTARTER
NUTCRACKER
OVERMASTER
OVERWINTER
PAINKILLER
PALLBEARER
PARTICULAR
PATHFINDER
PAWNBROKER
PEACEMAKER
PEASHOOTER
PENTAMETER
PHOTOMETER
PINFEATHER
POSTMASTER
POURPARLER
PROCURATOR
PROGENITOR
PROGRAMMER
PROPRIETOR
PROPRINTER
PROTRACTOR
RADIOMETER
RECONSIDER
RESPIRATOR
RINGLEADER
RINGMASTER
ROADRUNNER
SALAMANDER
SALTCELLAR
SEERSUCKER
SERVOMOTOR
SHIPFITTER
SHOPKEEPER
SIDEWINDER
SKYSCRAPER
SOOTHSAYER
STEPFATHER
STEPLADDER
STEPMOTHER
STEPSISTER
SWEETBRIER
TACHOMETER
TASKMASTER
TEARJERKER
TERMINATOR
TETRAMETER
THEREAFTER
THERMISTOR
TIMEKEEPER
TRANSDUCER
TRANSISTOR
TRANSPOLAR
TROUBADOUR
TUBERCULAR
TYPESETTER
TYPEWRITER
UNBELIEVER
UNDERCOVER
UNDERTAKER
UNDERWATER
UNFAMILIAR
VERNACULAR
VICTUALLER
WALLFLOWER
WASTEPAPER
WATCHMAKER
WATCHTOWER
WATERCOLOR
WATERPOWER
WHARFINGER
WHATSOEVER
WHEELCHAIR
WHENSOEVER
WHOMSOEVER
WINCHESTER
WINDFLOWER
WINDJAMMER
WINEGROWER
WOODCUTTER
WOODPECKER
YARDMASTER
YESTERYEAR
ABSTEMIOUS
ACROBATICS
AEROBATICS
AESTHETICS
ALBUMINOUS
ALLHALLOWS
AMANUENSIS
AMPHIBIOUS
ANTITHESIS
APOTHEOSIS
AURIFEROUS
AUSPICIOUS
AUTONOMOUS
BACKSTAIRS
BALLISTICS
BEAUJOLAIS
BEDCLOTHES
BELONGINGS
BENCHMARKS
BIOPHYSICS
BITUMINOUS
BOISTEROUS
BRONCHITIS
CADAVEROUS
CALCAREOUS
CANONICALS
CENSORIOUS
CHIVALROUS
CHURCHLESS
CIRCUITOUS
COMMODIOUS
CONSPECTUS
CONTAGIOUS
CONTIGUOUS
CONTINUOUS
COSMOPOLIS
CRETACEOUS
CRISSCROSS
CROSSBONES
CRYOGENICS
CURVACEOUS
DECOMPRESS
DERMATITIS
DIAPHANOUS
DISPOSSESS
DOWNSTAIRS
ENDOGENOUS
EPIGLOTTIS
ERGONOMICS
ERYSIPELAS
EUCALYPTUS
EUPHONIOUS
EXTRANEOUS
EYEWITNESS
FACTITIOUS
FALLACIOUS
FASTIDIOUS
FATHOMLESS
FELICITOUS
FIBERGLASS
FICTITIOUS
FISTICUFFS
FLAGITIOUS
FOOTLIGHTS
FORTUITOUS
GEOPHYSICS
GERIATRICS
GINGIVITIS
GONOCOCCUS
GRATUITOUS
GREGARIOUS
GROUNDMASS
GYMNASTICS
HANDLEBARS
HARMONIOUS
HEREABOUTS
HOMOLOGOUS
HORRENDOUS
HOUSEWARES
HYDRAULICS
HYDROLYSIS
HYPOTHESIS
IGNORAMOUS
IMPERVIOUS
INDECOROUS
INDIGENOUS
INGLORIOUS
ISOMETRICS
JACKANAPES
KINEMATICS
LARYNGITIS
LASCIVIOUS
LIBIDINOUS
LICENTIOUS
LOQUACIOUS
LUBRICIOUS
LUGUBRIOUS
MALAPROPOS
MALODOROUS
MENDACIOUS
MENINGITIS
METACARPUS
METASTASIS
METATARSUS
METICULOUS
METROPOLIS
MONOTONOUS
NECROPOLIS
NEWSGROUPS
NIGHTDRESS
NUCLEONICS
NUMBERLESS
OBSEQUIOUS
OBSTETRICS
OESOPHAGUS
OFTENTIMES
OLEAGINOUS
OMNIVOROUS
OUTRAGEOUS
PANTALOONS
PARATROOPS
PEDIATRICS
PERNICIOUS
PHOSPHORUS
PORTCULLIS
PORTENTOUS
POSTHUMOUS
POWERLINES
PRECARIOUS
PRECOCIOUS
PREDACEOUS
PREPOSSESS
PRODIGIOUS
PROPITIOUS
PROSPECTUS
PROSPEROUS
PROSTHESIS
PUGNACIOUS
QUADRATICS
REBELLIOUS
RECOILLESS
RELENTLESS
RENDEZVOUS
RETROGRESS
RHINOCEROS
RIDICULOUS
SALUBRIOUS
SCURRILOUS
SEAMSTRESS
SEMPSTRESS
SLUMBEROUS
SOLICITOUS
SPIRITUOUS
STATISTICS
STUPENDOUS
SUNGLASSES
SUSPICIOUS
TENEBRIOUS
THEMSELVES
THROMBOSIS
THUNDEROUS
TRANSGRESS
TREMENDOUS
TROLLEYBUS
TUMULTUOUS
UBIQUITOUS
UNDERPANTS
UNGENEROUS
UNGRACIOUS
UPROARIOUS
URETHRITIS
URINALYSIS
VICTORIOUS
VILLAINOUS
VIVIPAROUS
VOCIFEROUS
VOLUMINOUS
VOLUPTUOUS
WATERCRESS
WATERWORKS
WEAPONLESS
WEIGHTLESS
WILDERNESS
WITCHGRASS
ACCOUNTANT
ADULTERANT
ADVISEMENT
AIRFREIGHT
ANIMADVERT
ANTAGONIST
ANTECEDENT
ANTEPENULT
ANTICHRIST
ASSIGNMENT
ASSORTMENT
ASTRINGENT
ATTACHMENT
ATTAINMENT
ATTRACTANT
BATTLEMENT
BELLETRIST

BENEFICENT
BETTERMENT
BIRTHRIGHT
BLUEBONNET
BLUEJACKET
BREADFRUIT
BREAKFRONT
CANDESCENT
CANTONMENT
CAPITALIST
CHECKPOINT
CIRCUMVENT
CLOUDBURST
COINCIDENT
COMMANDANT
COMPATRIOT
COMPLEMENT
COMPLIMENT
CONCORDANT
CONCURRENT
CONSEQUENT
CONSTRAINT
CONTINGENT
CONTRADICT
CONTROVERT
CONVENIENT
CONVERSANT
COUNTERACT
CRANKSHAFT
DEADWEIGHT
DELINQUENT
DENOUEMENT
DEPARTMENT
DEPORTMENT
DEPRESSANT
DESCENDANT
DETACHMENT
DISAPPOINT
DISCOMFORT
DISCONCERT
DISCONNECT
DISCONTENT
DISCREPANT
DISCUSSANT
DISENCHANT
DISINHERIT
DISRESPECT
DISTRAUGHT
EMBANKMENT
EMBONPOINT
EMPLOYMENT
ENDEARMENT
ENGAGEMENT
ENJAMBMENT
EQUIVALENT
ESCARPMENT
EVANESCENT
EVANGELIST
EXCITEMENT
EXORBITANT
EXPERIMENT
FAHRENHEIT
FEDERALIST
FLAMBOYANT
FLASHLIGHT
FLOODLIGHT
FORTHRIGHT
FRAUDULENT
FUSSBUDGET
GESUNDHEIT
GOVERNMENT
GRAPEFRUIT
HABILIMENT
HANDICRAFT
HIEROPHANT
ICONOCLAST
IMPEDIMENT
IMPENITENT
INCOHERENT
INCONSTANT
INDISCREET
INDISTINCT
INDUCEMENT
INFREQUENT
INGREDIENT
INHABITANT
INSENTIENT
INSTRUMENT
INTEGUMENT
INTERNMENT
INTERTWIST
INTOLERANT
INTOXICANT
INVESTMENT
IRRELEVANT
JACKRABBIT
JUGGERNAUT
KNOCKWURST
LIEUTENANT
LIVERWURST
MALCONTENT
MALEFICENT
MALEVOLENT
MANAGEMENT
MANDELBROT
MANICURIST
MANSERVANT
MANUSCRIPT
MEDICAMENT
MILLWRIGHT
MINISTRANT
MISCONDUCT
MISOGAMIST
MISOGYNIST
MIZZENMAST
MONARCHIST
MUNIFICENT
NATURALIST
NETHERMOST
NIGHTSHIRT
NONCHALANT
NONSUPPORT
OCEANFRONT
OMNIPOTENT
OMNISCIENT
OPALESCENT
OUTPATIENT
PALIMPSEST
PANTYWAIST
PARLIAMENT
PEPPERMINT
PERCIPIENT
PERMAFROST
PHOTOPAINT
PICKPOCKET
PLAYWRIGHT
PLUPERFECT
POSTSCRIPT
PREEMINENT
PREFERMENT
PRIZEFIGHT
PROFICIENT
PROPELLANT
PROTESTANT
PUNISHMENT
PUTRESCENT
QUADRUPLET
QUINTUPLET
REDISTRICT
REFINEMENT
REFRINGENT
REGISTRANT
RESPONDENT
RESTAURANT
RETROSPECT
ROUNDABOUT
ROUSTABOUT
SACROSANCT
SAUERKRAUT
SEPARATIST
SEPTUAGINT
SETTLEMENT
SHIPWRIGHT
SOMERSAULT
SPACECRAFT
SPECIALIST
SPOILSPORT
SPORTSCAST
STANDPOINT
STATECRAFT
STEPPARENT
SUBCOMPACT
SUBSEQUENT
SUFFICIENT
SUFFRAGIST
SUPERTWIST
SUPPLEMENT
SUPPLICANT
SWEETHEART
TANTAMOUNT
TENDERFOOT
THERMOSTAT
THROUGHOUT
THROUGHPUT
TOURNAMENT
TOURNIQUET
TRANSCRIPT
TRANSPLANT
TYPESCRIPT
ULTRASHORT
UNDERCROFT
UNDERSHIRT
UNDERSHOOT
UNDERSKIRT
UNDERWAIST
UNPLEASANT
VICEGERENT
VOICEPRINT
WAINWRIGHT
WANDERLUST
WATERCRAFT
WATERFRONT
WATERSPOUT
WATERTIGHT
WILDEBEEST
WITCHCRAFT
WONDERMENT
WORKBASKET
FORESHADOW
HANDBARROW
MIDDLEBROW
OVERSHADOW
THUMBSCREW
ANTICLIMAX
CHATTERBOX
CIRCUMFLEX
ALIMENTARY
AMBULATORY
APOTHECARY
ASCENDANCY
BAPTISTERY
BESTIALITY
BLACKBERRY
CARDIOLOGY
CATCHPENNY
CHALCEDONY
CHARACTERY
CHIROMANCY
CHRONOLOGY
CLERESTORY
COMMENTARY
COMMISSARY
COMMONALTY
COMPETENCY
COMPLIANCY
COMPLICITY
COMPULSORY
CONFORMITY
CONGRUENCY
CONSISTORY
CONSPIRACY
CONTINUITY
COUNTERSPY
DECLASSIFY
DEGENERACY
DEHUMIDIFY
DEMOGRAPHY
DEMONOLOGY
DENDROLOGY
DEPENDENCY
DEPILATORY
DEPOSITORY
DEROGATORY
DESERVEDLY
DICTIONARY
DIFFICULTY
DILLYDALLY
DISHARMONY
DISORDERLY
DISPENSARY
DISQUALIFY
DISSATISFY
EFFICIENCY
EFFRONTERY
ELDERBERRY
ELEMENTARY
EMBROIDERY
EMBRYOLOGY
ENTOMOLOGY
EPISCOPACY
EQUANIMITY
EXCELLENCY
EXOBIOLOGY
EXPECTANCY
EXPEDIENCY
EXPRESSWAY
FRATERNITY
GASTRONOMY
GENERALITY
GLACIOLOGY
GOOSEBERRY
GYNECOLOGY
HEMATOLOGY
HEREDITARY
HOLOGRAPHY
HOMEOPATHY
HOOTENANNY
IMMORALITY
IMMUNOLOGY
INCAPACITY
INCENDIARY
INCIVILITY
INCUMBENCY
INEQUALITY
INFIDELITY
INHUMANITY
INITIATORY
INTERMARRY
LABORATORY
LOGANBERRY
MELANCHOLY
METAGALAXY
METALLURGY
MINERALOGY
MISCELLANY
MISSIONARY
MORPHOLOGY
MULTISTORY
MUSICOLOGY
NEBULOSITY
NECROMANCY
NEIGHBORLY
NEUTRALITY
NEWSWORTHY
NOTABILITY
NOTEWORTHY
NUMEROLOGY
OCEANOLOGY
OSTEOPATHY
PASSAGEWAY
PEREMPTORY
PERPETUITY
PERSONALTY
PHILOSOPHY
PHLEBOTOMY
PHRENOLOGY
PHYLACTERY
PHYSIOLOGY
PICKANINNY
PLEASANTRY
PLUTOCRACY
PREBENDARY
PRECIOSITY
PRESBYTERY
PROCLIVITY
PROMISSORY
PROMONTORY
PROPENSITY
PROSPERITY
PSYCHIATRY
PSYCHOLOGY
REDUNDANCY
REFRACTORY
REGENERACY
RELATIVITY
REPORTEDLY
REPOSITORY
RESILIENCY
RISIBILITY
SANGUINARY
SEISMOLOGY
SELENOLOGY
SIMPLICITY
SOLIDARITY
STATIONARY
STATIONERY
STRAWBERRY
STRINGENCY
SUBSIDIARY
SUSPENSORY
TECHNOLOGY
TELEGRAPHY
THROUGHWAY
TOMFOOLERY
TOPOGRAPHY
TOXICOLOGY
TRAJECTORY
TRANSITORY
TRIMONTHLY
TYPOGRAPHY
UNDERBELLY
UNDERSTORY
UNDERSTUDY
UNFRIENDLY
UNIFORMITY
UNIVERSITY
UNMANNERLY
UPHOLSTERY
VARICOSITY
VETERINARY
VIRTUOSITY
VISIBILITY
VOCABULARY
VOLUPTUARY
WHITSUNDAY
XEROGRAPHY

# 11 LETTER WORDS

**1st Letter**

ABECEDARIAN
ABOMINATION
ABORTIONIST
ABRACADABRA
ABSENTEEISM
ABSTRACTION
ACADEMICIAN
ACADEMICISM
ACCELERANDO
ACCELERATOR
ACCEPTATION
ACCLAMATION
ACCLIMATIZE
ACCOMMODATE
ACCORDINGLY
ACCOUNTABLE
ACCUMULATOR
ACKNOWLEDGE
ACQUIREMENT
ACQUISITION
ACQUISITIVE
ACUPUNCTURE
ADOLESCENCE
ADVERSATIVE
ADVERTISING
AERONAUTICS
AFFECTATION
AFFIRMATIVE
AFTERBURNER
AFTEREFFECT
AGGLOMERATE
AGGLUTINATE
AGGREGATION
AGORAPHOBIA
AGRICULTURE
ALEXANDRIAN
ALEXANDRINE
ALPHABETIZE
ALTERCATION
ALTERNATIVE
AMBIVALENCE
AMONTILLADO
AMPHETAMINE
ANACHRONISM
ANAESTHESIA
ANASTOMOSIS
ANNIVERSARY
ANNUNCIATOR
ANTECHAMBER
ANTICYCLONE
ANTIGRAVITY
ANTINEUTRON
ANTIOXIDANT
ANTIPOVERTY
ANTIQUARIAN
APHRODISIAC
APOCYNTHION
APPELLATION
APPLICATION
APPOINTMENT
APPRECIABLE
APPROBATION
APPROPRIATE
APPROXIMATE
AQUICULTURE
ARBITRAMENT
ARCHAEOLOGY
ARCHDIOCESE
ARCHIPELAGO
ARISTOCRACY
ASSASSINATE
ASSEMBLYMAN
ASSIGNATION
ASSOCIATION
ASSOCIATIVE
ASTIGMATISM
ATTRIBUTIVE
AUDIOVISUAL
AVOIRDUPOIS
BACCHANALIA
BACKSTRETCH
BALLCARRIER
BALLETOMANE
BARBITURATE
BATHYSCAPHE
BATHYSPHERE
BATTLEFIELD
BATTLEWAGON
BEACHCOMBER
BEHAVIORISM
BELLIGERENT
BENEDICTION
BENEFACTION
BENEFICENCE
BENEFICIARY
BENEVOLENCE
BIBLIOPHILE
BICARBONATE
BICENTENARY
BIMETALLISM
BIOFEEDBACK
BITTERSWEET
BLAMEWORTHY
BLOCKBUSTER
BLOODMOBILE
BLOODSTREAM
BLOODSUCKER
BLUNDERBUSS
BOILERMAKER
BOURGEOISIE
BOUTONNIERE
BOYSENBERRY
BRAGGADOCIO
BREADBASKET
BREADWINNER
BREAKPOINTS
BREASTPLATE
BROTHERHOOD
BUREAUCRACY
BURGOMASTER
BUSINESSMAN
CABINETWORK
CALCIFEROUS
CALCULATING
CALCULATION
CALIFORNIUM
CALLIGRAPHY
CALORIMETER
CAMARADERIE
CAMEROONIAN
CAMPANOLOGY
CANDELABRUM
CANDIDATURE
CANDLELIGHT
CANDLESTICK
CANNIBALIZE
CAPACITANCE
CAPILLARITY
CARAVANSARY
CARDINALATE
CARDINALITY
CARDIOGRAPH
CARDSHARPER
CARMINATIVE
CARNIVOROUS
CARRAGEENAN
CARTOGRAPHY
CASSITERITE
CASTELLATED
CATASTROPHE
CATEGORICAL
CATERCORNER
CATERPILLAR
CATHOLICITY
CAULIFLOWER
CEMENTATION
CENTENARIAN
CENTERBOARD
CENTERPIECE
CENTRIFUGAL
CENTRIPETAL
CEREMONIOUS
CERTIFICATE
CHAMBERLAIN
CHAMBERMAID
CHANCELLERY
CHANTICLEER
CHEERLEADER
CHEESECLOTH
CHIAROSCURO
CHIROGRAPHY
CHLOROPHYLL
CHOCKABLOCK
CHOIRMASTER
CHOLESTEROL
CHRISTENDOM
CHRISTIANIA
CHRONOGRAPH
CHRONOMETER
CIRCULARITY
CIRCULARIZE
CIRCUMLUNAR
CIRCUMPOLAR
CIRCUMSPECT
CLAIRVOYANT
CLANDESTINE
CLEARHEADED
CLERICALISM
CLIMACTERIC
CLIMATOLOGY
CLOSEFISTED
COBBLESTONE
COCKLESHELL
COEDUCATION
COEFFICIENT
COEXTENSIVE
COFFEEHOUSE
COGNOSCENTE
COINCIDENCE
COLLABORATE
COLLOCATION
COLONIALISM
COLORCASTER
COMBINATION
COMBUSTIBLE
COMEUPPANCE
COMFORTABLE
COMMANDMENT
COMMEMORATE
COMMENTATOR
COMMINATION
COMMISERATE
COMMONPLACE
COMMUNICANT
COMMUNICATE
COMMUTATION
COMMUTATIVE
COMPARATIVE
COMPARTMENT
COMPETITION
COMPLACENCE
COMPLACENCY
COMPLICATED
COMPORTMENT
COMPOSITION
COMPTROLLER
COMPUNCTION
COMPUTERIZE
CONCENTRATE
CONCERNMENT
CONCOMITANT
CONCORDANCE
CONCURRENCE
CONDITIONAL
CONDITIONED
CONDOMINIUM
CONDUCTANCE
CONFEDERACY
CONFEDERATE
CONFESSEDLY
CONFORMANCE
CONGRESSMAN
CONJUGATION
CONJUNCTION
CONJUNCTIVA
CONJUNCTIVE
CONJUNCTURE
CONNOISSEUR
CONNOTATION
CONNOTATIVE
CONSECUTIVE
CONSEQUENCE
CONSERVANCY
CONSERVATOR
CONSIDERATE
CONSIDERING
CONSIGNMENT
CONSISTENCE
CONSISTENCY
CONSOLIDATE
CONSPICUOUS
CONSTITUENT
CONSUMERISM
CONSUMPTION
CONSUMPTIVE
CONTAMINANT
CONTAMINATE
CONTEMPLATE
CONTENTMENT
CONTINENTAL
CONTINGENCY
CONTINUANCE
CONTRACTILE
CONTRAPTION
CONTRARIETY
CONTRETEMPS
CONTRIVANCE
CONTROVERSY
CONURBATION
CONVENIENCE
CONVENTICLE
CONVERTIBLE
CONVOCATION
CONVOLUTION
COOPERATIVE
COPROCESSOR
CORNERSTONE
CORPORATION
CORRELATIVE
CORRIGENDUM
CORROBORATE
COSIGNATORY
COTERMINOUS
COTTONMOUTH
COUNTENANCE
COUNTERFEIT
COUNTERMAND
COUNTERPANE
COUNTERPART
COUNTERSIGN
COUNTERSINK
COUNTERVAIL
COUNTRIFIED
COUNTRYSIDE
CRACKERJACK
CRAPSHOOTER
CREPUSCULAR
CRESTFALLEN
CRIMINOLOGY
CRUCIFIXION
CRYSTALLIZE
CUSTOMHOUSE
CYBERNATION
CYBERNETICS
DECLARATIVE
DECRESCENDO
DEFALCATION
DEFLORATION
DELECTATION
DELETERIOUS
DELINQUENCY
DEMAGNETIZE
DEMOCRATIZE
DEMONSTRATE
DENOMINATOR
DEPRECATORY
DEPREDATION
DEPRIVATION
DERELICTION
DERMATOLOGY
DESCRIPTION
DESEGREGATE
DESENSITIZE
DESIDERATUM
DESPERATION
DESPONDENCY
DESTINATION
DESTRUCTION
DETERIORATE
DETERMINANT
DETERMINATE
DETERMINISM
DIAMAGNETIC
DIAMONDBACK
DIAPHORETIC
DICOTYLEDON
DICTATORIAL
DIFFRACTION
DILAPIDATED
DIPLOMATIST
DIRECTORATE
DISAPPROVAL
DISASSEMBLE
DISCONTINUE
DISCOTHEQUE

DISCOURTESY
DISCREPANCY
DISENCUMBER
DISENTANGLE
DISILLUSION
DISORGANIZE
DISPENSABLE
DISPLEASURE
DISPOSITION
DISPUTATION
DISQUIETUDE
DISSEMINATE
DISSIMULATE
DISSOLUTION
DISTINCTION
DISTINCTIVE
DISTINGUISH
DISTRIBUTOR
DOCTRINAIRE
DOCUMENTARY
DOMESTICATE
DOMESTICITY
DOWNHEARTED
DOWNTRODDEN
DREADNOUGHT
DRILLMASTER
DYNAMOMETER
EARTHENWARE
EDIFICATION
EFFICACIOUS
EINSTEINIUM
ELECTIONEER
ELECTRICIAN
ELECTRICITY
ELECTROCUTE
ELECTROFORM
ELECTROLYTE
ELECTRONICS
ELECTROTYPE
ELEPHANTINE
ELIZABETHAN
EMPLACEMENT
ENCAPSULATE
ENDOTHERMIC
ENFRANCHISE
ENGINEERING
ENVIRONMENT
EPINEPHRINE
EQUIDISTANT
EQUILATERAL
EQUILIBRIUM
EVANGELICAL
EVENTUALITY
EVERLASTING
EXCEEDINGLY
EXCEPTIONAL
EXCRESCENCE
EXHAUSTLESS
EXPECTATION
EXPECTORANT
EXPECTORATE
EXPEDITIOUS
EXPENDITURE
EXPERIENCED
EXPOSTULATE
EXPROPRIATE
EXTEMPORARY
EXTEMPORIZE
EXTERMINATE
EXTRADITION
EXTRAPOLATE
EXTRAVAGANT
FAMILIARITY
FARINACEOUS
FARTHERMOST
FARTHINGALE
FASHIONABLE
FAULTFINDER
FEATHEREDGE
FIDDLESTICK
FILMOGRAPHY
FINGERBOARD
FINGERPRINT
FIRECRACKER
FLABBERGAST
FLANNELETTE
FLOORWALKER
FLORESCENCE
FLUOROSCOPE
FORECLOSURE
FOREQUARTER
FORESHORTEN
FORETHOUGHT
FOREVERMORE
FORMFITTING
FORNICATION
FORTHCOMING
FORTNIGHTLY
FOULMOUTHED
FRAGMENTARY
FRANKFURTER
FREETHINKER
FUNCTIONARY
FUNDAMENTAL
FURNISHINGS
FURTHERMORE
FURTHERMOST
GALLBLADDER
GALLIMAUFRY
GARNISHMENT
GEANTICLINE
GENDARMERIE
GENERALSHIP
GENTLEWOMAN
GEOMAGNETIC
GEOPOLITICS
GEOSYNCLINE
GERONTOLOGY
GERRYMANDER
GESTICULATE
GINGERBREAD
GLOSSOLALIA
GODDAUGHTER
GRANDFATHER
GRANDMOTHER
GRANDPARENT
GRANITEWARE
GRASSHOPPER
GRAVITATION
GREASEPAINT
GREENGROCER
GROUNDSHEET
GROUNDWATER
GUTTERSNIPE
GYROCOMPASS
HABERDASHER
HABITUATION
HAEMORRHAGE
HAGIOGRAPHY
HAIRBREADTH
HAIRDRESSER
HAIRSTYLIST
HALFHEARTED
HALLUCINATE
HANDICAPPER
HANDSHAKING
HANDWRITING
HARDHEARTED
HARDWORKING
HAREBRAINED
HARPSICHORD
HEARTBROKEN
HEARTHSTONE
HEAVYWEIGHT
HELLENISTIC
HERBIVOROUS
HERPETOLOGY
HERRINGBONE
HEXADECIMAL
HIGHFALUTIN
HINDQUARTER
HISTORICITY
HISTRIONICS
HOMEOSTASIS
HOMESTEADER
HOMESTRETCH
HOMOGENEOUS
HONEYSUCKLE
HORSEPLAYER
HORSERADISH
HOSPITALITY
HOSPITALIZE
HOUSEBROKEN
HOUSEKEEPER
HOUSELIGHTS
HOUSEMOTHER
HUCKLEBERRY
HUMMINGBIRD
HYDROCARBON
HYDROGENATE
HYDROGRAPHY
HYDROPHOBIA
HYDROPONICS
HYDROSPHERE
HYDROSTATIC
HYGROSCOPIC
HYPERACTIVE
HYPERBOREAN
HYPERTROPHY
HYPHENATION
HYPOTHECATE
HYPOTHESIZE
ICHTHYOLOGY
IDENTIFIERS
IGNOMINIOUS
ILLIMITABLE
ILLUSIONISM
ILLUSTRIOUS
IMAGESETTER
IMAGINATION
IMBRICATION
IMMITIGABLE
IMMORTALITY
IMMORTALIZE
IMPASSIONED
IMPECUNIOUS
IMPEDIMENTA
IMPERFORATE
IMPERIALISM
IMPERMANENT
IMPERMEABLE
IMPERSONATE
IMPERTINENT
IMPLAUSIBLE
IMPORTATION
IMPORTUNATE
IMPRACTICAL
IMPREGNABLE
IMPROPRIETY
IMPROVEMENT
IMPROVIDENT
IMPUISSANCE
INADVERTENT
INALIENABLE
INATTENTION
INCANTATION
INCARCERATE
INCARNADINE
INCARNATION
INCERTITUDE
INCINERATOR
INCLINATION
INCOMPETENT
INCONGRUENT
INCONGRUOUS
INCONTINENT
INCORPORATE
INCORPOREAL
INCREDULOUS
INCREMENTAL
INCRIMINATE
INCUNABULUM
INDEFINABLE
INDENTATION
INDEPENDENT
INDIFFERENT
INDIGESTION
INDIGNATION
INDIVIDUATE
INDIVISIBLE
INDOMITABLE
INDUBITABLE
INDUSTRIOUS
INEFFECTIVE
INEFFECTUAL
INEFFICIENT
INELUCTABLE
INESCAPABLE
INESTIMABLE
INEXCUSABLE
INFANTICIDE
INFLAMMABLE
INFORMATION
INFORMATIVE
INGATHERING
INGRATITUDE
INNERSPRING
INNUMERABLE
INOPERATIVE
INOPPORTUNE
INQUISITION
INQUISITIVE
INSCRUTABLE
INSECTICIDE
INSEPARABLE
INSINUATING
INSOUCIANCE
INSPIRATION
INSTABILITY
INSTALLMENT
INSTANTIATE
INSTITUTION
INSTRUCTION
INSTRUCTIVE
INSUPERABLE
INTELLIGENT
INTENTIONAL
INTERACTION
INTERACTIVE
INTERATOMIC
INTERCALARY
INTERCALATE
INTERCEPTOR
INTERCHANGE
INTERCOURSE
INTERESTING
INTERLACING
INTERLINEAR
INTERLINING
INTERMEDDLE
INTERMINGLE
INTERNECINE
INTERNUNCIO
INTEROFFICE
INTERPOLATE
INTERPRETER
INTERRACIAL
INTERREGNUM
INTERRELATE
INTERROGATE
INTERSPERSE
INTOLERABLE
INTRACTABLE
INTRAVENOUS
INVESTIGATE
INVESTITURE
INVOLUNTARY
IRIDESCENCE
IRREDENTISM
IRREDUCIBLE
IRREFUTABLE
IRRELIGIOUS
IRREMOVABLE
IRREPARABLE
IRREVERENCE
IRREVOCABLE
JABBERWOCKY
JUVENOCRACY
KINDHEARTED
KINESTHESIA
KITCHENETTE
KITCHENWARE
KLEPTOMANIA
KNUCKLEBONE
KWASHIORKOR
LABORSAVING
LABRADORITE
LACRIMATION
LAMPLIGHTER
LASERWRITER
LATCHSTRING
LATTICEWORK
LEATHERNECK
LEGERDEMAIN
LEGISLATION
LEGISLATIVE
LEGISLATURE
LETTERPRESS
LEVELHEADED
LIBERTARIAN
LICKSPITTLE
LIGHTWEIGHT
LILLIPUTIAN
LINGUISTICS
LIONHEARTED
LITHOGRAPHY
LITHOSPHERE
LITTERATEUR
LOUDMOUTHED
LOUDSPEAKER
LUCUBRATION
MACHINATION
MACROBIOTIC
MACROSCOPIC
MAGISTERIAL
MAGNANIMOUS
MAGNIFICENT
MAIDSERVANT
MALADJUSTED
MALAPROPISM
MALEDICTION
MALFEASANCE
MALFUNCTION
MALPRACTICE
MANTELPIECE
MANUFACTORY
MANUFACTURE
MARCHIONESS
MARKETPLACE
MARQUISETTE
MARSHMALLOW
MASSACHUSET
MASTERPIECE
MATERIALISM
MATERIALIZE
MATHEMATICS
MATRICULATE
MEADOWSWEET
MEASUREMENT
MECHANISTIC
MEDIUMISTIC
MEGALOMANIA
MEGALOPOLIS
MELANCHOLIA
MELANCHOLIC
MELLIFLUOUS
MEMORABILIA
MENDELEVIUM
MENSURATION

MERCHANDISE
MERCHANTMAN
MERITOCRACY
MERITORIOUS
MERRYMAKING
MESALLIANCE
METAPHYSICS
METEOROLOGY
METHODOLOGY
METRICATION
MICROCAPSUL
MICROSCOPIC
MICROSECOND
MILLIAMPERE
MILLIONAIRE
MILLISECOND
MINESWEEPER
MINIATURIZE
MINNESINGER
MISALLIANCE
MISANTHROPE
MISBEGOTTEN
MISBELIEVER
MISCHIEVOUS
MISCONCEIVE
MISCONSTRUE
MISDEMEANOR
MISFEASANCE
MISGUIDANCE
MOCKINGBIRD
MODULARIZED
MOLLYCODDLE
MOMENTARILY
MONASTICISM
MONEYLENDER
MONKEYSHINE
MONOLINGUAL
MONSEIGNEUR
MORTARBOARD
MOTHERBOARD
MOUNTAINEER
MOUNTAINTOP
MULTIFAMILY
MULTIRACIAL
MUSCULATURE
MUSKELLUNGE
MUTTONCHOPS
NAPHTHALENE
NARRAGANSET
NATIONALISM
NATIONALIST
NATIONALITY
NATIONALIZE
NEANDERTHAL
NEARSIGHTED
NECESSITATE
NECESSITOUS

NECKERCHIEF
NEEDLEPOINT
NEEDLEWOMAN
NETHERWORLD
NICKELODEON
NIGHTINGALE
NIGHTWALKER
NINNYHAMMER
NONDESCRIPT
NONDOCUMENT
NONETHELESS
NONNEGATIVE
NONPARTISAN
NONRESIDENT
NONVIOLENCE
NORTHEASTER
NOTHINGNESS
NOURISHMENT
NUMISMATICS
NURSERYMAID
NYMPHOMANIA
OBSERVATION
OBSERVATORY
OBSTRUCTION
OBSOLESCENT
OFFICIALDOM
OFFICIALISM
OMNIPRESENT
OPINIONATED
OPPORTUNISM
OPPORTUNITY
OPPROBRIOUS
ORCHESTRATE
ORNITHOLOGY
ORTHODONTIA
ORTHOGRAPHY
ORTHOPEDICS
OSTENTATION
OUTBUILDING
OUTDISTANCE
OUTMANEUVER
OUTSTANDING
OVERBALANCE
OVERBEARING
OVERSTUFFED
OVERWEENING
OVERWROUGHT
OZONOSPHERE
PACHYSANDRA
PAINSTAKING
PALEOGRAPHY
PANDEMONIUM
PAPERHANGER
PAPERWEIGHT
PARAMEDICAL
PARATHYROID
PARATROOPER

PARATYPHOID
PARENTHESIS
PARISHIONER
PARTICIPATE
PARTICULATE
PARTURITION
PATERNALISM
PENETRATING
PENNYWEIGHT
PENTECOSTAL
PENULTIMATE
PERAMBULATE
PERCEPTIBLE
PERFECTIBLE
PERFORMANCE
PERFUNCTORY
PERIODONTAL
PERIPATETIC
PERIPHRASIS
PERISTALSIS
PERITONITIS
PERMISSIBLE
PERMUTATION
PERSNICKETY
PERSONALITY
PERSONALIZE
PERSPECTIVE
PERSPICUOUS
PESTIFEROUS
PETROGRAPHY
PHARISAICAL
PHILOSOPHER
PHOTOGRAPHY
PHOTOSPHERE
PHRASEOLOGY
PHYSIOGNOMY
PICTURESQUE
PISCATORIAL
PITCHBLENDE
PLACEHOLDER
PLAINSPOKEN
PLANETARIUM
PLANETOLOGY
PLEASURABLE
POCKETKNIFE
POINTILLISM
POLLINATION
POLTERGEIST
POLYNOMINAL
POLYSTYRENE
POLYTECHNIC
POMEGRANATE
PONTIFICALS
PONTIFICATE
PORNOGRAPHY
PORTERHOUSE
PORTIONLESS

PORTMANTEAU
PORTRAITIST
PORTRAITURE
PRACTICABLE
PREASSIGNED
PRECIPITATE
PRECIPITOUS
PRECONCEIVE
PREDECESSOR
PREDICAMENT
PREDOMINATE
PREHISTORIC
PREIGNITION
PRELIMINARY
PREMEDITATE
PREMONITION
PREOCCUPIED
PREPOSITION
PREROGATIVE
PRESUMPTION
PRETENTIOUS
PRETERMINAL
PREVARICATE
PRIMITIVISM
PRIZEWINNER
PROBATIONER
PROBLEMATIC
PROCRUSTEAN
PROFANATORY
PROGNATHOUS
PROGRAMMING
PROGRESSION
PROGRESSIVE
PROHIBITION
PROLETARIAN
PROLETARIAT
PROLIFERATE
PROMISCUOUS
PROMPTITUDE
PROPHYLAXIS
PROPINQUITY
PROPOSITION
PROPRIETARY
PROSELYTIZE
PROSTATITIS
PROSTHETICS
PROTAGONIST
PROTOMARTYR
PROTUBERANT
PROVENIENCE
PROVISIONAL
PSYCHEDELIA
PSYCHEDELIC
PSYCHODRAMA
PSYCHOGENIC
PUBLICATION
PULCHRITUDE

PUNCTILIOUS
PUNCTUATION
QUACKSALVER
QUADRENNIAL
QUADRENNIUM
QUALITATIVE
QUARTERBACK
QUARTERDECK
QUICKSILVER
RADIOCARBON
RADIOMETRIC
RAPSCALLION
RATHSKELLER
RATIONALISM
RATIONALITY
RATIONALIZE
RATTLESNAKE
REACTIONARY
REALPOLITIK
RECESSIONAL
RECIPROCATE
RECIPROCITY
RECOGNITION
RECONNOITER
RECONSTRUCT
RECRIMINATE
RECTILINEAR
REDOUBTABLE
REFORMATION
REFORMATORY
REFRESHMENT
REFRIGERATE
REGIMENTALS
REGURGITATE
REINFECTION
RELOCATABLE
REMEMBRANCE
REMINISCENT
REMONSTRANT
REMONSTRATE
RENAISSANCE
REPETITIOUS
REPLACEMENT
REPLICATION
REPROBATION
REQUIREMENT
REQUISITION
RESEMBLANCE
RESERVATION
RESIDENTIAL
RESIGNATION
RESISTIVITY
RESPECTABLE
RESPIRATION
RESPLENDENT
RESPONSIBLE
RESTITUTION

RESTORATION
RESTORATIVE
RESTRICTION
RESUSCITATE
RETRIBUTION
RETROACTIVE
REVERBERATE
REVERENTIAL
ROADABILITY
ROMANTICISM
ROTOGRAVURE
ROTTENSTONE
SAFEKEEPING
SARCOPHAGUS
SCAFFOLDING
SCHOLARSHIP
SCHOOLHOUSE
SCINTILLATE
SCREWDRIVER
SCRUMPTIOUS
SCUTTLEBUTT
SEARCHLIGHT
SEISMOGRAPH
SEISMOMETER
SEMITRAILER
SENSATIONAL
SENSIBILITY
SENTENTIOUS
SENTIMENTAL
SEQUESTRATE
SERENDIPITY
SERVICEABLE
SHAREHOLDER
SHELLACKING
SHIPBUILDER
SHORTCHANGE
SHORTCOMING
SHORTHANDED
SHUTTLECOCK
SIGNIFICANT
SLEEPWALKER
SMITHEREENS
SMORGASBORD
SOLILOQUIZE
SOVEREIGNTY
SPACEFLIGHT
SPECTACULAR
SPECTROGRAM
SPEEDOMETER
SPELLBINDER
SPENDTHRIFT
SPONTANEOUS
SPREADSHEET
SPRINGBOARD
STANDARDIZE
STEAMROLLER
STENOGRAPHY

STEPBROTHER
STEREOSCOPE
STEREOSCOPY
STEREOTYPED
STETHOSCOPE
STOCKBROKER
STOCKHOLDER
STOCKINETTE
STOMACHACHE
STOREKEEPER
STORYTELLER
STRAIGHTWAY
STRAITLACED
STRANGULATE
STRAWFLOWER
STREAMLINED
STREAMLINER
STROBOSCOPE
SUBASSEMBLY
SUBJUNCTIVE
SUBMERSIBLE
SUBORDINATE
SUBSISTENCE
SUBSTANDARD
SUBSTANTIAL
SUBSTANTIVE
SUBTROPICAL
SUBURBANITE
SUFFICIENCY
SUFFRAGETTE
SUMMERHOUSE
SUPERFICIAL
SUPERFLUOUS
SUPERIMPOSE
SUPERINTEND
SUPERLATIVE
SUPERMARKET
SUPERSCRIBE
SUPERSCRIPT
SUPERSONICS
SUPPOSITION
SUPPOSITORY
SUPPRESSANT
SUPREMACIST
SUSCEPTIBLE
SWALLOWTAIL
SWEEPSTAKES
SWITCHBLADE
SWITCHBOARD
SYNCHROMESH
SYNCHRONIZE
SYNCHRONOUS
SYNCOPATION
SYNTHESIZER
SYSTEMATIZE
TACHYCARDIA
TEASPOONFUL

TECHNOCRACY
TELEPRINTER
TEMPERAMENT
TEMPERATURE
TEMPESTUOUS
TENDENTIOUS
TERMINOLOGY
TERRESTRIAL
TERRITORIAL
TESTIMONIAL
THALIDOMIDE
THEATRICALS
THENCEFORTH
THEORETICAL
THERAPEUTIC
THEREABOUTS
THEREWITHAL
THERMOCLINE
THERMOMETER
THISTLEDOWN
THITHERWARD
THOUGHTLESS
THUNDERBOLT
THUNDERCLAP
THUNDERHEAD
TIGHTFISTED
TIMESHARING
TOASTMASTER
TOBACCONIST
TONSILLITIS
TOPDRESSING
TOTALIZATOR
TOWNSPEOPLE
TRAGEDIENNE
TRAILBLAZER
TRANQUILIZE
TRANSACTION
TRANSCEIVER
TRANSFIGURE
TRANSLUCENT
TRANSMITTER
TRANSPARENT
TREACHEROUS
TRENCHERMAN
TREPIDATION
TRIANGULATE
TRIBULATION
TRICHINOSIS
TRINIDADIAN
TRINITARIAN
TRIUMVIRATE
TROPOSPHERE
TRUEHEARTED
TRUSTEESHIP
TRUSTWORTHY
TUBERCULATE
TWELVEMONTH
TYPEFOUNDER
TYPESETTING
TYPEWRITING
TYPOGRAPHER
ULTRAMARINE
ULTRAMODERN
ULTRASONICS
ULTRAVIOLET
UNACCOUNTED
UNALIENABLE
UNAVOIDABLE
UNCERTAINTY
UNCHRISTIAN
UNCIVILIZED
UNCOMMITTED
UNCONCERNED
UNCONSCIOUS
UNDERCHARGE
UNDEREXPOSE
UNDERGROUND
UNDERGROWTH
UNDERHANDED
UNDERSHORTS
UNDERSIGNED
UNDERTAKING
UNDERWEIGHT
UNDESIGNING
UNDESIRABLE
UNDEVIATING
UNEQUIVOCAL
UNFAVORABLE
UNFLAPPABLE
UNFLINCHING
UNFORTUNATE
UNICELLULAR
UNIFICATION
UNINHIBITED
UNMITIGATED
UNOBTRUSIVE
UNORGANIZED
UNPRINTABLE
UNQUALIFIED
UNREASONING
UNRELENTING
UNREMITTING
UNRIGHTEOUS
UNSATURATED
UNSPEAKABLE
UNTHINKABLE
UNTOUCHABLE
UNUTTERABLE
UNVARNISHED
UNWHOLESOME
UTILITARIAN
VACATIONIST
VACCINATION
VALEDICTION
VALEDICTORY
VARICOLORED
VENTILATION
VENTRILOQUY
VENTURESOME
VERMICULITE
VERTIGINOUS
VICHYSSOISE
VICISSITUDE
VINAIGRETTE
VINDICATION
VIOLONCELLO
VIRIDESCENT
VITICULTURE
VIVISECTION
VOLCANOLOGY
WAINSCOTING
WARMHEARTED
WASHERWOMAN
WASTEBASKET
WATERCOURSE
WATERLOGGED
WEATHERCOCK
WEATHERWORN
WHEELBARROW
WHEELWRIGHT
WHEREABOUTS
WHERESOEVER
WHEREWITHAL
WHICHSOEVER
WHIFFLETREE
WHIPPLETREE
WIDEMOUTHED
WINTERGREEN
WITENAGEMOT
WOODCHOPPER
WORDPERFECT
WORKMANLIKE
WORKMANSHIP
WORKSTATION
WRONGHEADED
ZOOMORPHISM
ZOOPLANKTON

## 2ND LETTER

BACCHANALIA
BACKSTRETCH
BALLCARRIER
BALLETOMANE
BARBITURATE
BATHYSCAPHE
BATHYSPHERE
BATTLEFIELD
BATTLEWAGON
CABINETWORK
CALCIFEROUS
CALCULATING
CALCULATION
CALIFORNIUM
CALLIGRAPHY
CALORIMETER
CAMARADERIE
CAMEROONIAN
CAMPANOLOGY
CANDELABRUM
CANDIDATURE
CANDLELIGHT
CANDLESTICK
CANNIBALIZE
CAPACITANCE
CAPILLARITY
CARAVANSARY
CARDINALATE
CARDINALITY
CARDIOGRAPH
CARDSHARPER
CARMINATIVE
CARNIVOROUS
CARRAGEENAN
CARTOGRAPHY
CASSITERITE
CASTELLATED
CATASTROPHE
CATEGORICAL
CATERCORNER
CATERPILLAR
CATHOLICITY
CAULIFLOWER
EARTHENWARE
FAMILIARITY
FARINACEOUS
FARTHERMOST
FARTHINGALE
FASHIONABLE
FAULTFINDER
GALLBLADDER
GALLIMAUFRY
GARNISHMENT
HABERDASHER
HABITUATION
HAEMORRHAGE
HAGIOGRAPHY
HAGIOGRAPHY
HAIRBREADTH
HAIRDRESSER
HAIRSTYLIST
HALFHEARTED
HALLUCINATE
HANDICAPPER
HANDSHAKING
HANDWRITING
HARDHEARTED
HARDWORKING
HAREBRAINED
HARPSICHORD
JABBERWOCKY
LABORSAVING
LABRADORITE
LACRIMATION
LAMPLIGHTER
LASERWRITER
LATCHSTRING
LATTICEWORK
MACHINATION
MACROBIOTIC
MACROSCOPIC
MAGISTERIAL
MAGNANIMOUS
MAGNIFICENT
MAIDSERVANT
MALADJUSTED
MALAPROPISM
MALEDICTION
MALFEASANCE
MALFUNCTION
MALPRACTICE
MANTELPIECE
MANUFACTORY
MANUFACTURE
MARCHIONESS
MARKETPLACE
MARQUISETTE
MARSHMALLOW
MASSACHUSET
MASTERPIECE
MATERIALISM
MATERIALIZE
MATHEMATICS
MATRICULATE
NAPHTHALENE
NARRAGANSET
NATIONALISM
NATIONALIST
NATIONALITY
NATIONALIZE
PACHYSANDRA
PAINSTAKING
PALEOGRAPHY
PANDEMONIUM
PAPERHANGER
PAPERWEIGHT
PARAMEDICAL
PARATHYROID
PARATROOPER
PARATYPHOID
PARENTHESIS
PARISHIONER
PARTICIPATE
PARTICULATE
PARTURITION
PATERNALISM
RADIOCARBON
RADIOMETRIC
RAPSCALLION
RATHSKELLER
RATIONALISM
RATIONALITY
RATIONALIZE
RATTLESNAKE
SAFEKEEPING
SARCOPHAGUS
TACHYCARDIA
VACATIONIST
VACCINATION
VALEDICTION
VALEDICTORY
VARICOLORED
WAINSCOTING
WARMHEARTED
WASHERWOMAN
WASTEBASKET
WATERCOURSE
WATERLOGGED
ABECEDARIAN
ABOMINATION
ABORTIONIST
ABRACADABRA
ABSENTEEISM
ABSTRACTION
OBSERVATION
OBSERVATORY
OBSOLESCENT
OBSTRUCTION
ACADEMICIAN
ACADEMICISM
ACCELERANDO
ACCELERATOR
ACCEPTATION
ACCLAMATION
ACCLIMATIZE
ACCOMMODATE
ACCORDINGLY
ACCOUNTABLE
ACCUMULATOR
ACKNOWLEDGE
ACQUIREMENT
ACQUISITION
ACQUISITIVE
ACUPUNCTURE
ICHTHYOLOGY
SCAFFOLDING
SCHOLARSHIP
SCHOOLHOUSE
SCINTILLATE
SCREWDRIVER
SCRUMPTIOUS
SCUTTLEBUTT
ADOLESCENCE
ADVERSATIVE
ADVERTISING
EDIFICATION
IDENTIFIERS
AERONAUTICS
BEACHCOMBER
BEHAVIORISM
BELLIGERENT
BENEDICTION
BENEFACTION
BENEFICENCE
BENEFICIARY
BENEVOLENCE
CEMENTATION
CENTENARIAN
CENTERBOARD
CENTERPIECE
CENTRIFUGAL
CENTRIPETAL
CEREMONIOUS
CERTIFICATE
DECLARATIVE
DECRESCENDO
DEFALCATION
DEFLORATION
DELECTATION
DELETERIOUS
DELINQUENCY
DEMAGNETIZE
DEMOCRATIZE
DEMONSTRATE
DENOMINATOR
DEPRECATORY
DEPREDATION
DEPRIVATION
DERELICTION
DERMATOLOGY
DESCRIPTION
DESEGREGATE
DESENSITIZE
DESIDERATUM
DESPERATION
DESPONDENCY
DESTINATION
DESTRUCTION
DETERIORATE
DETERMINANT
DETERMINATE
DETERMINISM
FEATHEREDGE
GEANTICLINE
GENDARMERIE
GENERALSHIP
GENTLEWOMAN

GEOMAGNETIC
GEOPOLITICS
GEOSYNCLINE
GERONTOLOGY
GERRYMANDER
GESTICULATE
HEARTBROKEN
HEARTHSTONE
HEAVYWEIGHT
HELLENISTIC
HERBIVOROUS
HERPETOLOGY
HERRINGBONE
HEXADECIMAL
LEATHERNECK
LEGERDEMAIN
LEGISLATION
LEGISLATIVE
LEGISLATURE
LETTERPRESS
LEVELHEADED
MEADOWSWEET
MEASUREMENT
MECHANISTIC
MEDIUMISTIC
MEGALOMANIA
MEGALOPOLIS
MELANCHOLIA
MELANCHOLIC
MELLIFLUOUS
MEMORABILIA
MENDELEVIUM
MENSURATION
MERCHANDISE
MERCHANTMAN
MERITOCRACY
MERITORIOUS
MERRYMAKING
MESALLIANCE
METAPHYSICS
METEOROLOGY
METHODOLOGY
METRICATION
NEANDERTHAL
NEARSIGHTED
NECESSITATE
NECESSITOUS
NECKERCHIEF
NEEDLEPOINT
NEEDLEWOMAN
NETHERWORLD
PENETRATING
PENNYWEIGHT
PENTECOSTAL
PENULTIMATE
PERAMBULATE
PERCEPTIBLE
PERFECTIBLE
PERFORMANCE
PERFUNCTORY
PERIODONTAL
PERIPATETIC
PERIPHRASIS
PERISTALSIS
PERITONITIS
PERMISSIBLE
PERMUTATION
PERSNICKETY
PERSONALITY
PERSONALIZE
PERSPECTIVE
PERSPICUOUS
PESTIFEROUS
PETROGRAPHY
REACTIONARY
REALPOLITIK
RECESSIONAL
RECIPROCATE
RECIPROCITY
RECOGNITION
RECONNOITER
RECONSTRUCT
RECRIMINATE
RECTILINEAR
REDOUBTABLE
REFORMATION
REFORMATORY
REFRESHMENT
REFRIGERATE
REGIMENTALS
REGURGITATE
REINFECTION
RELOCATABLE
REMEMBRANCE
REMINISCENT
REMONSTRANT
REMONSTRATE
RENAISSANCE
REPETITIOUS
REPLACEMENT
REPLICATION
REPROBATION
REQUIREMENT
REQUISITION
RESEMBLANCE
RESERVATION
RESIDENTIAL
RESIGNATION
RESISTIVITY
RESPECTABLE
RESPIRATION
RESPLENDENT
RESPONSIBLE
RESTITUTION
RESTORATION
RESTORATIVE
RESTRICTION
RESUSCITATE
RETRIBUTION
RETROACTIVE
REVERBERATE
REVERENTIAL
SEARCHLIGHT
SEISMOGRAPH
SEISMOMETER
SEMITRAILER
SENSATIONAL
SENSIBILITY
SENTENTIOUS
SENTIMENTAL
SEQUESTRATE
SERENDIPITY
SERVICEABLE
TEASPOONFUL
TECHNOCRACY
TELEPRINTER
TEMPERAMENT
TEMPERATURE
TEMPESTUOUS
TENDENTIOUS
TERMINOLOGY
TERRESTRIAL
TERRITORIAL
TESTIMONIAL
VENTILATION
VENTRILOQUY
VENTURESOME
VERMICULITE
VERTIGINOUS
WEATHERCOCK
WEATHERWORN
AFFECTATION
AFFIRMATIVE
AFTERBURNER
AFTEREFFECT
EFFICACIOUS
OFFICIALDOM
OFFICIALISM
AGGLOMERATE
AGGLUTINATE
AGGREGATION
AGORAPHOBIA
AGRICULTURE
IGNOMINIOUS
CHAMBERLAIN
CHAMBERMAID
CHANCELLERY
CHANTICLEER
CHEERLEADER
CHEESECLOTH
CHIAROSCURO
CHIROGRAPHY
CHLOROPHYLL
CHOCKABLOCK
CHOIRMASTER
CHOLESTEROL
CHRISTENDOM
CHRISTIANIA
CHRONOGRAPH
CHRONOMETER
PHARISAICAL
PHILOSOPHER
PHOTOGRAPHY
PHOTOSPHERE
PHRASEOLOGY
PHYSIOGNOMY
SHAREHOLDER
SHELLACKING
SHIPBUILDER
SHORTCHANGE
SHORTCOMING
SHORTHANDED
SHUTTLECOCK
THALIDOMIDE
THEATRICALS
THENCEFORTH
THEORETICAL
THERAPEUTIC
THEREABOUTS
THEREWITHAL
THERMOCLINE
THERMOMETER
THISTLEDOWN
THITHERWARD
THOUGHTLESS
THUNDERBOLT
THUNDERCLAP
THUNDERHEAD
WHEELBARROW
WHEELWRIGHT
WHEREABOUTS
WHERESOEVER
WHEREWITHAL
WHICHSOEVER
WHIFFLETREE
WHIPPLETREE
BIBLIOPHILE
BICARBONATE
BICENTENARY
BIMETALLISM
BIOFEEDBACK
BITTERSWEET
CIRCULARITY
CIRCULARIZE
CIRCUMLUNAR
CIRCUMPOLAR
CIRCUMSPECT
DIAMAGNETIC
DIAMONDBACK
DIAPHORETIC
DICOTYLEDON
DICTATORIAL
DIFFRACTION
DILAPIDATED
DIPLOMATIST
DIRECTORATE
DISAPPROVAL
DISASSEMBLE
DISCONTINUE
DISCOTHEQUE
DISCOURTESY
DISCREPANCY
DISENCUMBER
DISENTANGLE
DISILLUSION
DISORGANIZE
DISPENSABLE
DISPLEASURE
DISPOSITION
DISPUTATION
DISQUIETUDE
DISSEMINATE
DISSIMULATE
DISSOLUTION
DISTINCTION
DISTINCTIVE
DISTINGUISH
DISTRIBUTOR
EINSTEINIUM
FIDDLESTICK
FILMOGRAPHY
FINGERBOARD
FINGERPRINT
FIRECRACKER
GINGERBREAD
HIGHFALUTIN
HINDQUARTER
HISTORICITY
HISTRIONICS
KINDHEARTED
KINESTHESIA
KITCHENETTE
KITCHENWARE
LIBERTARIAN
LICKSPITTLE
LIGHTWEIGHT
LILLIPUTIAN
LINGUISTICS
LIONHEARTED
LITHOGRAPHY
LITHOSPHERE
LITTERATEUR
MICROCAPSUL
MICROSCOPIC
MICROSECOND
MILLIAMPERE
MILLIONAIRE
MILLISECOND
MINESWEEPER
MINIATURIZE
MINNESINGER
MISALLIANCE
MISANTHROPE
MISBEGOTTEN
MISBELIEVER
MISCHIEVOUS
MISCONCEIVE
MISCONSTRUE
MISDEMEANOR
MISFEASANCE
MISGUIDANCE
NICKELODEON
NIGHTINGALE
NIGHTWALKER
NINNYHAMMER
PICTURESQUE
PISCATORIAL
PITCHBLENDE
SIGNIFICANT
TIGHTFISTED
TIMESHARING
VICHYSSOISE
VICISSITUDE
VINAIGRETTE
VINDICATION
VIOLONCELLO
VIRIDESCENT
VITICULTURE
VIVISECTION
WIDEMOUTHED
WINTERGREEN
WITENAGEMOT
ALEXANDRIAN
ALEXANDRINE
ALPHABETIZE
ALTERCATION
ALTERNATIVE
BLAMEWORTHY
BLOCKBUSTER
BLOODMOBILE
BLOODSTREAM
BLOODSUCKER
BLUNDERBUSS
CLAIRVOYANT
CLANDESTINE
CLEARHEADED
CLERICALISM
CLIMACTERIC
CLIMATOLOGY
CLOSEFISTED
ELECTIONEER
ELECTRICIAN
ELECTRICITY
ELECTROCUTE
ELECTROFORM
ELECTROLYTE
ELECTRONICS
ELECTROTYPE
ELEPHANTINE
ELIZABETHAN
FLABBERGAST
FLANNELETTE
FLOORWALKER
FLORESCENCE
FLUOROSCOPE
GLOSSOLALIA
ILLIMITABLE
ILLUSIONISM
ILLUSTRIOUS
KLEPTOMANIA
PLACEHOLDER
PLAINSPOKEN
PLANETARIUM
PLANETOLOGY
PLEASURABLE
SLEEPWALKER
ULTRAMARINE
ULTRAMODERN
ULTRASONICS
ULTRAVIOLET
AMBIVALENCE
AMONTILLADO
AMPHETAMINE
EMPLACEMENT
IMAGESETTER
IMAGINATION
IMBRICATION
IMMITIGABLE
IMMORTALITY
IMMORTALIZE
IMPASSIONED
IMPECUNIOUS
IMPEDIMENTA
IMPERFORATE
IMPERIALISM
IMPERMANENT
IMPERMEABLE
IMPERSONATE
IMPERTINENT
IMPLAUSIBLE
IMPORTATION
IMPORTUNATE
IMPRACTICAL
IMPREGNABLE
IMPROPRIETY
IMPROVEMENT
IMPROVIDENT
IMPUISSANCE
OMNIPRESENT

SMITHEREENS
SMORGASBORD
ANACHRONISM
ANAESTHESIA
ANASTOMOSIS
ANNIVERSARY
ANNUNCIATOR
ANTECHAMBER
ANTICYCLONE
ANTIGRAVITY
ANTINEUTRON
ANTIOXIDANT
ANTIPOVERTY
ANTIQUARIAN
ENCAPSULATE
ENDOTHERMIC
ENFRANCHISE
ENGINEERING
ENVIRONMENT
INADVERTENT
INALIENABLE
INATTENTION
INCANTATION
INCARCERATE
INCARNADINE
INCARNATION
INCERTITUDE
INCINERATOR
INCLINATION
INCOMPETENT
INCONGRUENT
INCONGRUOUS
INCONTINENT
INCORPORATE
INCORPOREAL
INCREDULOUS
INCREMENTAL
INCRIMINATE
INCUNABULUM
INDEFINABLE
INDENTATION
INDEPENDENT
INDIFFERENT
INDIGESTION
INDIGNATION
INDIVIDUATE
INDIVISIBLE
INDOMITABLE
INDUBITABLE
INDUSTRIOUS
INEFFECTIVE
INEFFECTUAL
INEFFICIENT
INELUCTABLE
INESCAPABLE
INESTIMABLE
INEXCUSABLE
INFANTICIDE
INFLAMMABLE
INFORMATION
INFORMATIVE
INGATHERING
INGRATITUDE
INNERSPRING
INNUMERABLE
INOPERATIVE
INOPPORTUNE
INQUISITION
INQUISITIVE
INSCRUTABLE
INSECTICIDE
INSEPARABLE
INSINUATING
INSOUCIANCE
INSPIRATION
INSTABILITY
INSTALLMENT
INSTANTIATE
INSTITUTION
INSTRUCTION
INSTRUCTIVE
INSUPERABLE
INTELLIGENT
INTENTIONAL
INTERACTION
INTERACTIVE
INTERATOMIC
INTERCALARY
INTERCALATE
INTERCEPTOR
INTERCHANGE
INTERCOURSE
INTERESTING
INTERLACING
INTERLINEAR
INTERLINING
INTERMEDDLE
INTERMINGLE
INTERNECINE
INTERNUNCIO
INTEROFFICE
INTERPOLATE
INTERPRETER
INTERRACIAL
INTERREGNUM
INTERRELATE
INTERROGATE
INTERSPERSE
INTOLERABLE
INTRACTABLE
INTRAVENOUS
INVESTIGATE
INVESTITURE
INVOLUNTARY
KNUCKLEBONE
UNACCOUNTED
UNALIENABLE
UNAVOIDABLE
UNCERTAINTY
UNCHRISTIAN
UNCIVILIZED
UNCOMMITTED
UNCONCERNED
UNCONSCIOUS
UNDERCHARGE
UNDEREXPOSE
UNDERGROUND
UNDERGROWTH
UNDERHANDED
UNDERSHORTS
UNDERSIGNED
UNDERTAKING
UNDERWEIGHT
UNDESIGNING
UNDESIRABLE
UNDEVIATING
UNEQUIVOCAL
UNFAVORABLE
UNFLAPPABLE
UNFLINCHING
UNFORTUNATE
UNICELLULAR
UNIFICATION
UNINHIBITED
UNMITIGATED
UNOBTRUSIVE
UNORGANIZED
UNPRINTABLE
UNQUALIFIED
UNREASONING
UNRELENTING
UNREMITTING
UNRIGHTEOUS
UNSATURATED
UNSPEAKABLE
UNTHINKABLE
UNTOUCHABLE
UNUTTERABLE
UNVARNISHED
UNWHOLESOME
BOILERMAKER
BOURGEOISIE
BOUTONNIERE
BOYSENBERRY
COBBLESTONE
COCKLESHELL
COEDUCATION
COEFFICIENT
COEXTENSIVE
COFFEEHOUSE
COGNOSCENTE
COINCIDENCE
COLLABORATE
COLLOCATION
COLONIALISM
COLORCASTER
COMBINATION
COMBUSTIBLE
COMEUPPANCE
COMFORTABLE
COMMANDMENT
COMMEMORATE
COMMENTATOR
COMMINATION
COMMISERATE
COMMONPLACE
COMMUNICANT
COMMUNICATE
COMMUTATION
COMMUTATIVE
COMPARATIVE
COMPARTMENT
COMPETITION
COMPLACENCE
COMPLACENCY
COMPLICATED
COMPORTMENT
COMPOSITION
COMPTROLLER
COMPUNCTION
COMPUTERIZE
CONCENTRATE
CONCERNMENT
CONCOMITANT
CONCORDANCE
CONCURRENCE
CONDITIONAL
CONDITIONED
CONDOMINIUM
CONDUCTANCE
CONFEDERACY
CONFEDERATE
CONFESSEDLY
CONFORMANCE
CONGRESSMAN
CONJUGATION
CONJUNCTION
CONJUNCTIVA
CONJUNCTIVE
CONJUNCTURE
CONNOISSEUR
CONNOTATION
CONNOTATIVE
CONSECUTIVE
CONSEQUENCE
CONSERVANCY
CONSERVATOR
CONSIDERATE
CONSIDERING
CONSIGNMENT
CONSISTENCE
CONSISTENCY
CONSOLIDATE
CONSPICUOUS
CONSTITUENT
CONSUMERISM
CONSUMPTION
CONSUMPTIVE
CONTAMINANT
CONTAMINATE
CONTEMPLATE
CONTENTMENT
CONTINENTAL
CONTINGENCY
CONTINUANCE
CONTRACTILE
CONTRAPTION
CONTRARIETY
CONTRETEMPS
CONTRIVANCE
CONTROVERSY
CONURBATION
CONVENIENCE
CONVENTICLE
CONVERTIBLE
CONVOCATION
CONVOLUTION
COOPERATIVE
COPROCESSOR
CORNERSTONE
CORPORATION
CORRELATIVE
CORRIGENDUM
CORROBORATE
COSIGNATORY
COTERMINOUS
COTTONMOUTH
COUNTENANCE
COUNTERFEIT
COUNTERMAND
COUNTERPANE
COUNTERPART
COUNTERSIGN
COUNTERSINK
COUNTERVAIL
COUNTRIFIED
COUNTRYSIDE
DOCTRINAIRE
DOCUMENTARY
DOMESTICATE
DOMESTICITY
DOWNHEARTED
DOWNTRODDEN
FORECLOSURE
FOREQUARTER
FORESHORTEN
FORETHOUGHT
FOREVERMORE
FORMFITTING
FORNICATION
FORTHCOMING
FORTNIGHTLY
FOULMOUTHED
GODDAUGHTER
HOMEOSTASIS
HOMESTEADER
HOMESTRETCH
HOMOGENEOUS
HONEYSUCKLE
HORSEPLAYER
HORSERADISH
HOSPITALITY
HOSPITALIZE
HOUSEBROKEN
HOUSEKEEPER
HOUSELIGHTS
HOUSEMOTHER
LOUDMOUTHED
LOUDSPEAKER
MOCKINGBIRD
MODULARIZED
MOLLYCODDLE
MOMENTARILY
MONASTICISM
MONEYLENDER
MONKEYSHINE
MONOLINGUAL
MONSEIGNEUR
MORTARBOARD
MOTHERBOARD
MOUNTAINEER
MOUNTAINTOP
NONDESCRIPT
NONDOCUMENT
NONETHELESS
NONNEGATIVE
NONPARTISAN
NONRESIDENT
NONVIOLENCE
NORTHEASTER
NOTHINGNESS
NOURISHMENT
POCKETKNIFE
POINTILLISM
POLLINATION
POLTERGEIST
POLYNOMINAL
POLYSTYRENE
POLYTECHNIC
POMEGRANATE
PONTIFICALS
PONTIFICATE
PORNOGRAPHY
PORTERHOUSE
PORTIONLESS
PORTMANTEAU
PORTRAITIST
PORTRAITURE
ROADABILITY
ROMANTICISM
ROTOGRAVURE
ROTTENSTONE
SOLILOQUIZE
SOVEREIGNTY
TOASTMASTER
TOBACCONIST
TONSILLITIS
TOPDRESSING
TOTALIZATOR
TOWNSPEOPLE
VOLCANOLOGY
WOODCHOPPER
WORDPERFECT
WORKMANLIKE
WORKMANSHIP
WORKSTATION
ZOOMORPHISM
ZOOPLANKTON
APHRODISIAC
APOCYNTHION
APPELLATION
APPLICATION
APPOINTMENT
APPRECIABLE
APPROBATION
APPROPRIATE
APPROXIMATE
EPINEPHRINE
OPINIONATED
OPPORTUNISM
OPPORTUNITY
OPPROBRIOUS
SPACEFLIGHT
SPECTACULAR
SPECTROGRAM
SPEEDOMETER
SPELLBINDER
SPENDTHRIFT
SPONTANEOUS
SPREADSHEET
SPRINGBOARD
AQUICULTURE
EQUIDISTANT
EQUILATERAL
EQUILIBRIUM
ARBITRAMENT
ARCHAEOLOGY
ARCHDIOCESE
ARCHIPELAGO

ARISTOCRACY
BRAGGADOCIO
BREADBASKET
BREADWINNER
BREAKPOINTS
BREASTPLATE
BROTHERHOOD
CRACKERJACK
CRAPSHOOTER
CREPUSCULAR
CRESTFALLEN
CRIMINOLOGY
CRUCIFIXION
CRYSTALLIZE
DREADNOUGHT
DRILLMASTER
FRAGMENTARY
FRANKFURTER
FREETHINKER
GRANDFATHER
GRANDMOTHER
GRANDPARENT
GRANITEWARE
GRASSHOPPER
GRAVITATION
GREASEPAINT
GREENGROCER
GROUNDSHEET
GROUNDWATER
IRIDESCENCE
IRREDENTISM
IRREDUCIBLE
IRREFUTABLE
IRRELIGIOUS
IRREMOVABLE
IRREPARABLE
IRREVERENCE
IRREVOCABLE
ORCHESTRATE
ORNITHOLOGY
ORTHODONTIA
ORTHOGRAPHY
ORTHOPEDICS
PRACTICABLE
PREASSIGNED
PRECIPITATE
PRECIPITOUS
PRECONCEIVE
PREDECESSOR
PREDICAMENT
PREDOMINATE
PREHISTORIC
PREIGNITION
PRELIMINARY
PREMEDITATE
PREMONITION
PREOCCUPIED
PREPOSITION
PREROGATIVE
PRESUMPTION
PRETENTIOUS
PRETERMINAL
PREVARICATE
PRIMITIVISM
PRIZEWINNER
PROBATIONER
PROBLEMATIC
PROCRUSTEAN
PROFANATORY
PROGNATHOUS
PROGRAMMING
PROGRESSION
PROGRESSIVE
PROHIBITION
PROLETARIAN
PROLETARIAT
PROLIFERATE
PROMISCUOUS
PROMPTITUDE
PROPHYLAXIS
PROPINQUITY
PROPOSITION
PROPRIETARY
PROSELYTIZE
PROSTATITIS
PROSTHETICS
PROTAGONIST
PROTOMARTYR
PROTUBERANT
PROVENIENCE
PROVISIONAL
TRAGEDIENNE
TRAILBLAZER
TRANQUILIZE
TRANSACTION
TRANSCEIVER
TRANSFIGURE
TRANSLUCENT
TRANSMITTER
TRANSPARENT
TREACHEROUS
TRENCHERMAN
TREPIDATION
TRIANGULATE
TRIBULATION
TRICHINOSIS
TRINIDADIAN
TRINITARIAN
TRIUMVIRATE
TROPOSPHERE
TRUEHEARTED
TRUSTEESHIP
TRUSTWORTHY
WRONGHEADED
ASSASSINATE
ASSEMBLYMAN
ASSIGNATION
ASSOCIATION
ASSOCIATIVE
ASTIGMATISM
OSTENTATION
PSYCHEDELIA
PSYCHEDELIC
PSYCHODRAMA
PSYCHOGENIC
ATTRIBUTIVE
STANDARDIZE
STEAMROLLER
STENOGRAPHY
STEPBROTHER
STEREOSCOPE
STEREOSCOPY
STEREOTYPED
STETHOSCOPE
STOCKBROKER
STOCKHOLDER
STOCKINETTE
STOMACHACHE
STOREKEEPER
STORYTELLER
STRAIGHTWAY
STRAITLACED
STRANGULATE
STRAWFLOWER
STREAMLINED
STREAMLINER
STROBOSCOPE
UTILITARIAN
AUDIOVISUAL
BUREAUCRACY
BURGOMASTER
BUSINESSMAN
CUSTOMHOUSE
FUNCTIONARY
FUNDAMENTAL
FURNISHINGS
FURTHERMORE
FURTHERMOST
GUTTERSNIPE
HUCKLEBERRY
HUMMINGBIRD
JUVENOCRACY
LUCUBRATION
MULTIFAMILY
MULTIRACIAL
MUSCULATURE
MUSKELLUNGE
MUTTONCHOPS
NUMISMATICS
NURSERYMAID
OUTBUILDING
OUTDISTANCE
OUTMANEUVER
OUTSTANDING
PUBLICATION
PULCHRITUDE
PUNCTILIOUS
PUNCTUATION
QUACKSALVER
QUADRENNIAL
QUADRENNIUM
QUALITATIVE
QUARTERBACK
QUARTERDECK
QUICKSILVER
SUBASSEMBLY
SUBJUNCTIVE
SUBMERSIBLE
SUBORDINATE
SUBSISTENCE
SUBSTANDARD
SUBSTANTIAL
SUBSTANTIVE
SUBTROPICAL
SUBURBANITE
SUFFICIENCY
SUFFRAGETTE
SUMMERHOUSE
SUPERFICIAL
SUPERFLUOUS
SUPERIMPOSE
SUPERINTEND
SUPERLATIVE
SUPERMARKET
SUPERSCRIBE
SUPERSCRIPT
SUPERSONICS
SUPPOSITION
SUPPOSITORY
SUPPRESSANT
SUPREMACIST
SUSCEPTIBLE
TUBERCULATE
AVOIRDUPOIS
EVANGELICAL
EVENTUALITY
EVERLASTING
OVERBALANCE
OVERBEARING
OVERSTUFFED
OVERWEENING
OVERWROUGHT
KWASHIORKOR
SWALLOWTAIL
SWEEPSTAKES
SWITCHBLADE
SWITCHBOARD
TWELVEMONTH
EXCEEDINGLY
EXCEPTIONAL
EXCRESCENCE
EXHAUSTLESS
EXPECTATION
EXPECTORANT
EXPECTORATE
EXPEDITIOUS
EXPENDITURE
EXPERIENCED
EXPOSTULATE
EXPROPRIATE
EXTEMPORARY
EXTEMPORIZE
EXTERMINATE
EXTRADITION
EXTRAPOLATE
EXTRAVAGANT
CYBERNATION
CYBERNETICS
DYNAMOMETER
GYROCOMPASS
HYDROCARBON
HYDROGENATE
HYDROGRAPHY
HYDROPHOBIA
HYDROPONICS
HYDROSPHERE
HYDROSTATIC
HYGROSCOPIC
HYPERACTIVE
HYPERBOREAN
HYPERTROPHY
HYPHENATION
HYPOTHECATE
HYPOTHESIZE
NYMPHOMANIA
SYNCHROMESH
SYNCHRONIZE
SYNCHRONOUS
SYNCOPATION
SYNTHESIZER
SYSTEMATIZE
TYPEFOUNDER
TYPESETTING
TYPEWRITING
TYPOGRAPHER
OZONOSPHERE

## 3rd Letter

ACADEMICIAN
ACADEMICISM
ANACHRONISM
ANAESTHESIA
ANASTOMOSIS
BEACHCOMBER
BLAMEWORTHY
BRAGGADOCIO
CHAMBERLAIN
CHAMBERMAID
CHANCELLERY
CHANTICLEER
CLAIRVOYANT
CLANDESTINE
CRACKERJACK
CRAPSHOOTER
DIAMAGNETIC
DIAMONDBACK
DIAPHORETIC
EVANGELICAL
FEATHEREDGE
FLABBERGAST
FLANNELETTE
FRAGMENTARY
FRANKFURTER
GEANTICLINE
GRANDFATHER
GRANDMOTHER
GRANDPARENT
GRANITEWARE
GRASSHOPPER
GRAVITATION
HEARTBROKEN
HEARTHSTONE
HEAVYWEIGHT
IMAGESETTER
IMAGINATION
INADVERTENT
INALIENABLE
INATTENTION
KWASHIORKOR
LEATHERNECK
MEADOWSWEET
MEASUREMENT
NEANDERTHAL
NEARSIGHTED
PHARISAICAL
PLACEHOLDER
PLAINSPOKEN
PLANETARIUM
PLANETOLOGY
PRACTICABLE
QUACKSALVER
QUADRENNIAL
QUADRENNIUM
QUALITATIVE
QUARTERBACK
QUARTERDECK
REACTIONARY
REALPOLITIK
ROADABILITY
SCAFFOLDING
SEARCHLIGHT
SHAREHOLDER
SPACEFLIGHT
STANDARDIZE
SWALLOWTAIL
TEASPOONFUL
THALIDOMIDE
TOASTMASTER
TRAGEDIENNE
TRAILBLAZER
TRANQUILIZE
TRANSACTION
TRANSCEIVER
TRANSFIGURE
TRANSLUCENT
TRANSMITTER
TRANSPARENT
UNACCOUNTED
UNALIENABLE
UNAVOIDABLE
WEATHERCOCK
WEATHERWORN
AMBIVALENCE
ARBITRAMENT
BIBLIOPHILE
CABINETWORK
COBBLESTONE
CYBERNATION
CYBERNETICS
HABERDASHER
HABITUATION
IMBRICATION
JABBERWOCKY
LABORSAVING
LABRADORITE
LIBERTARIAN
PUBLICATION
SUBASSEMBLY
SUBJUNCTIVE
SUBMERSIBLE
SUBORDINATE
SUBSISTENCE
SUBSTANDARD
SUBSTANTIAL
SUBSTANTIVE
SUBTROPICAL
SUBURBANITE
TOBACCONIST
TUBERCULATE
ACCELERANDO
ACCELERATOR
ACCEPTATION
ACCLAMATION
ACCLIMATIZE
ACCOMMODATE
ACCORDINGLY

ACCOUNTABLE
ACCUMULATOR
ARCHAEOLOGY
ARCHDIOCESE
ARCHIPELAGO
BACCHANALIA
BACKSTRETCH
BICARBONATE
BICENTENARY
COCKLESHELL
DECLARATIVE
DECRESCENDO
DICOTYLEDON
DICTATORIAL
DOCTRINAIRE
DOCUMENTARY
ENCAPSULATE
EXCEEDINGLY
EXCEPTIONAL
EXCRESCENCE
HUCKLEBERRY
INCANTATION
INCARCERATE
INCARNADINE
INCARNATION
INCERTITUDE
INCINERATOR
INCLINATION
INCOMPETENT
INCONGRUENT
INCONGRUOUS
INCONTINENT
INCORPORATE
INCORPOREAL
INCREDULOUS
INCREMENTAL
INCRIMINATE
INCUNABULUM
LACRIMATION
LICKSPITTLE
LUCUBRATION
MACHINATION
MACROBIOTIC
MACROSCOPIC
MECHANISTIC
MICROCAPSUL
MICROSCOPIC
MICROSECOND
MOCKINGBIRD
NECESSITATE
NECESSITOUS
NECKERCHIEF
NICKELODEON
ORCHESTRATE
PACHYSANDRA
PICTURESQUE
POCKETKNIFE
RECESSIONAL
RECIPROCATE
RECIPROCITY
RECOGNITION
RECONNOITER
RECONSTRUCT
RECRIMINATE
RECTILINEAR
TACHYCARDIA
TECHNOCRACY
UNCERTAINTY
UNCHRISTIAN
UNCIVILIZED
UNCOMMITTED
UNCONCERNED
UNCONSCIOUS
VACATIONIST
VACCINATION
VICHYSSOISE
VICISSITUDE
AUDIOVISUAL
ENDOTHERMIC
FIDDLESTICK
GODDAUGHTER
HYDROCARBON
HYDROGENATE
HYDROGRAPHY
HYDROPHOBIA
HYDROPONICS
HYDROSPHERE
HYDROSTATIC
INDEFINABLE
INDENTATION
INDEPENDENT
INDIFFERENT
INDIGESTION
INDIGNATION
INDIVIDUATE
INDIVISIBLE
INDOMITABLE
INDUBITABLE
INDUSTRIOUS
MEDIUMISTIC
MODULARIZED
RADIOCARBON
RADIOMETRIC
REDOUBTABLE
UNDERCHARGE
UNDEREXPOSE
UNDERGROUND
UNDERGROWTH
UNDERHANDED
UNDERSHORTS
UNDERSIGNED
UNDERTAKING
UNDERWEIGHT
UNDESIGNING
UNDESIRABLE
UNDEVIATING
WIDEMOUTHED
ABECEDARIAN
ALEXANDRIAN
ALEXANDRINE
BREADBASKET
BREADWINNER
BREAKPOINTS
BREASTPLATE
CHEERLEADER
CHEESECLOTH
CLEARHEADED
CLERICALISM
COEDUCATION
COEFFICIENT
COEXTENSIVE
CREPUSCULAR
CRESTFALLEN
DREADNOUGHT
ELECTIONEER
ELECTRICIAN
ELECTRICITY
ELECTROCUTE
ELECTROFORM
ELECTROLYTE
ELECTRONICS
ELECTROTYPE
ELEPHANTINE
EVENTUALITY
EVERLASTING
FREETHINKER
GREASEPAINT
GREENGROCER
HAEMORRHAGE
IDENTIFIERS
INEFFECTIVE
INEFFECTUAL
INEFFICIENT
INELUCTABLE
INESCAPABLE
INESTIMABLE
INEXCUSABLE
KLEPTOMANIA
NEEDLEPOINT
NEEDLEWOMAN
OVERBALANCE
OVERBEARING
OVERSTUFFED
OVERWEENING
OVERWROUGHT
PLEASURABLE
PREASSIGNED
PRECIPITATE
PRECIPITOUS
PRECONCEIVE
PREDECESSOR
PREDICAMENT
PREDOMINATE
PREHISTORIC
PREIGNITION
PRELIMINARY
PREMEDITATE
PREMONITION
PREOCCUPIED
PREPOSITION
PREROGATIVE
PRESUMPTION
PRETENTIOUS
PRETERMINAL
PREVARICATE
SHELLACKING
SLEEPWALKER
SPECTACULAR
SPECTROGRAM
SPEEDOMETER
SPELLBINDER
SPENDTHRIFT
STEAMROLLER
STENOGRAPHY
STEPBROTHER
STEREOSCOPE
STEREOSCOPY
STEREOTYPED
STETHOSCOPE
SWEEPSTAKES
THEATRICALS
THENCEFORTH
THEORETICAL
THERAPEUTIC
THEREABOUTS
THEREWITHAL
THERMOCLINE
THERMOMETER
TREACHEROUS
TRENCHERMAN
TREPIDATION
TWELVEMONTH
UNEQUIVOCAL
WHEELBARROW
WHEELWRIGHT
WHEREABOUTS
WHERESOEVER
WHEREWITHAL
AFFECTATION
AFFIRMATIVE
COFFEEHOUSE
DEFALCATION
DEFLORATION
DIFFRACTION
EFFICACIOUS
ENFRANCHISE
INFANTICIDE
INFLAMMABLE
INFORMATION
INFORMATIVE
OFFICIALDOM
OFFICIALISM
REFORMATION
REFORMATORY
REFRESHMENT
REFRIGERATE
SAFEKEEPING
SUFFICIENCY
SUFFRAGETTE
UNFAVORABLE
UNFLAPPABLE
UNFLINCHING
UNFORTUNATE
AGGLOMERATE
AGGLUTINATE
AGGREGATION
COGNOSCENTE
ENGINEERING
HAGIOGRAPHY
HIGHFALUTIN
HYGROSCOPIC
INGATHERING
INGRATITUDE
LEGERDEMAIN
LEGISLATION
LEGISLATIVE
LEGISLATURE
LIGHTWEIGHT
MAGISTERIAL
MAGNANIMOUS
MAGNIFICENT
MEGALOMANIA
MEGALOPOLIS
NIGHTINGALE
NIGHTWALKER
REGIMENTALS
REGURGITATE
SIGNIFICANT
TIGHTFISTED
APHRODISIAC
BEHAVIORISM
EXHAUSTLESS
ICHTHYOLOGY
SCHOLARSHIP
SCHOOLHOUSE
ARISTOCRACY
BOILERMAKER
CHIAROSCURO
CHIROGRAPHY
CLIMACTERIC
CLIMATOLOGY
COINCIDENCE
CRIMINOLOGY
DRILLMASTER
EDIFICATION
ELIZABETHAN
EPINEPHRINE
HAIRBREADTH
HAIRDRESSER
HAIRSTYLIST
IRIDESCENCE
MAIDSERVANT
OPINIONATED
PAINSTAKING
PHILOSOPHER
POINTILLISM
PRIMITIVISM
PRIZEWINNER
QUICKSILVER
REINFECTION
SCINTILLATE
SEISMOGRAPH
SEISMOMETER
SHIPBUILDER
SMITHEREENS
SWITCHBLADE
SWITCHBOARD
THISTLEDOWN
THITHERWARD
TRIANGULATE
TRIBULATION
TRICHINOSIS
TRINIDADIAN
TRINITARIAN
TRIUMVIRATE
UNICELLULAR
UNIFICATION
UNINHIBITED
UTILITARIAN
WAINSCOTING
WHICHSOEVER
WHIFFLETREE
WHIPPLETREE
ACKNOWLEDGE
BALLCARRIER
BALLETOMANE
BELLIGERENT
CALCIFEROUS
CALCULATING
CALCULATION
CALIFORNIUM
CALLIGRAPHY
CALORIMETER
CHLOROPHYLL
COLLABORATE
COLLOCATION
COLONIALISM
COLORCASTER
DELECTATION
DELETERIOUS
DELINQUENCY
DILAPIDATED
FILMOGRAPHY
GALLBLADDER
GALLIMAUFRY
HALFHEARTED
HALLUCINATE
HELLENISTIC
ILLIMITABLE
ILLUSIONISM
ILLUSTRIOUS
LILLIPUTIAN
MALADJUSTED
MALAPROPISM
MALEDICTION
MALFEASANCE
MALFUNCTION
MALPRACTICE
MELANCHOLIA
MELANCHOLIC
MELLIFLUOUS
MILLIAMPERE
MILLIONAIRE
MILLISECOND
MOLLYCODDLE
MULTIFAMILY
MULTIRACIAL
PALEOGRAPHY
POLLINATION
POLTERGEIST
POLYNOMINAL
POLYSTYRENE
POLYTECHNIC
PULCHRITUDE
RELOCATABLE
SOLILOQUIZE
TELEPRINTER
VALEDICTION
VALEDICTORY
VOLCANOLOGY
BIMETALLISM
CAMARADERIE
CAMEROONIAN
CAMPANOLOGY
CEMENTATION
COMBINATION
COMBUSTIBLE
COMEUPPANCE
COMFORTABLE
COMMANDMENT
COMMEMORATE
COMMENTATOR
COMMINATION
COMMISERATE
COMMONPLACE
COMMUNICANT
COMMUNICATE
COMMUTATION
COMMUTATIVE

CO**M**PARATIVE
CO**M**PARTMENT
CO**M**PETITION
CO**M**PLACENCE
CO**M**PLACENCY
CO**M**PLICATED
CO**M**PORTMENT
CO**M**POSITION
CO**M**PTROLLER
CO**M**PUNCTION
CO**M**PUTERIZE
DE**M**AGNETIZE
DE**M**OCRATIZE
DE**M**ONSTRATE
DO**M**ESTICATE
DO**M**ESTICITY
FA**M**ILIARITY
HO**M**EOSTASIS
HO**M**ESTEADER
HO**M**ESTRETCH
HO**M**OGENEOUS
HU**M**MINGBIRD
IM**M**ITIGABLE
IM**M**ORTALITY
IM**M**ORTALIZE
LA**M**PLIGHTER
ME**M**ORABILIA
MO**M**ENTARILY
NU**M**ISMATICS
NY**M**PHOMANIA
PO**M**EGRANATE
RE**M**EMBRANCE
RE**M**INISCENT
RE**M**ONSTRANT
RE**M**ONSTRATE
RO**M**ANTICISM
SE**M**ITRAILER
SU**M**MERHOUSE
TE**M**PERAMENT
TE**M**PERATURE
TE**M**PESTUOUS
TI**M**ESHARING
UN**M**ITIGATED
AN**N**IVERSARY
AN**N**UNCIATOR
BE**N**EDICTION
BE**N**EFACTION
BE**N**EFICENCE
BE**N**EFICIARY
BE**N**EVOLENCE
CA**N**DELABRUM
CA**N**DIDATURE
CA**N**DLELIGHT
CA**N**DLESTICK
CA**N**NIBALIZE
CE**N**TENARIAN
CE**N**TERBOARD
CE**N**TERPIECE
CE**N**TRIFUGAL
CE**N**TRIPETAL
CO**N**CENTRATE
CO**N**CERNMENT
CO**N**COMITANT
CO**N**CORDANCE
CO**N**CURRENCE
CO**N**DITIONAL
CO**N**DITIONED
CO**N**DOMINIUM
CO**N**DUCTANCE
CO**N**FEDERACY
CO**N**FEDERATE
CO**N**FESSEDLY
CO**N**FORMANCE
CO**N**GRESSMAN
CO**N**JUGATION
CO**N**JUNCTION
CO**N**JUNCTIVA
CO**N**JUNCTIVE
CO**N**JUNCTURE
CO**N**NOISSEUR
CO**N**NOTATION
CO**N**NOTATIVE
CO**N**SECUTIVE
CO**N**SEQUENCE
CO**N**SERVANCY
CO**N**SERVATOR
CO**N**SIDERATE
CO**N**SIDERING
CO**N**SIGNMENT
CO**N**SISTENCE
CO**N**SISTENCY
CO**N**SOLIDATE
CO**N**SPICUOUS
CO**N**STITUENT
CO**N**SUMERISM
CO**N**SUMPTION
CO**N**SUMPTIVE
CO**N**TAMINANT
CO**N**TAMINATE
CO**N**TEMPLATE
CO**N**TENTMENT
CO**N**TINENTAL
CO**N**TINGENCY
CO**N**TINUANCE
CO**N**TRACTILE
CO**N**TRAPTION
CO**N**TRARIETY
CO**N**TRETEMPS
CO**N**TRIVANCE
CO**N**TROVERSY
CO**N**URBATION
CO**N**VENIENCE
CO**N**VENTICLE
CO**N**VERTIBLE
CO**N**VOCATION
CO**N**VOLUTION
DE**N**OMINATOR
DY**N**AMOMETER
EI**N**STEINIUM
FI**N**GERBOARD
FI**N**GERPRINT
FU**N**CTIONARY
FU**N**DAMENTAL
GE**N**DARMERIE
GE**N**ERALSHIP
GE**N**TLEWOMAN
GI**N**GERBREAD
HA**N**DICAPPER
HA**N**DSHAKING
HA**N**DWRITING
HI**N**DQUARTER
HO**N**EYSUCKLE
IG**N**OMINIOUS
IN**N**ERSPRING
IN**N**UMERABLE
KI**N**DHEARTED
KI**N**ESTHESIA
LI**N**GUISTICS
MA**N**TELPIECE
MA**N**UFACTORY
MA**N**UFACTURE
ME**N**DELEVIUM
ME**N**SURATION
MI**N**ESWEEPER
MI**N**IATURIZE
MI**N**NESINGER
MO**N**ASTICISM
MO**N**EYLENDER
MO**N**KEYSHINE
MO**N**OLINGUAL
MO**N**SEIGNEUR
NI**N**NYHAMMER
NO**N**DESCRIPT
NO**N**DOCUMENT
NO**N**ETHELESS
NO**N**NEGATIVE
NO**N**PARTISAN
NO**N**RESIDENT
NO**N**VIOLENCE
OM**N**IPRESENT
OR**N**ITHOLOGY
PA**N**DEMONIUM
PE**N**ETRATING
PE**N**NYWEIGHT
PE**N**TECOSTAL
PE**N**ULTIMATE
PO**N**TIFICALS
PO**N**TIFICATE
PU**N**CTILIOUS
PU**N**CTUATION
RE**N**AISSANCE
SE**N**SATIONAL
SE**N**SIBILITY
SE**N**TENTIOUS
SE**N**TIMENTAL
SY**N**CHROMESH
SY**N**CHRONIZE
SY**N**CHRONOUS
SY**N**COPATION
SY**N**THESIZER
TE**N**DENTIOUS
TO**N**SILLITIS
VE**N**TILATION
VE**N**TRILOQUY
VE**N**TURESOME
VI**N**AIGRETTE
VI**N**DICATION
WI**N**TERGREEN
AB**O**MINATION
AB**O**RTIONIST
AD**O**LESCENCE
AG**O**RAPHOBIA
AM**O**NTILLADO
AP**O**CYNTHION
AV**O**IRDUPOIS
BI**O**FEEDBACK
BL**O**CKBUSTER
BL**O**ODMOBILE
BL**O**ODSTREAM
BL**O**ODSUCKER
BR**O**THERHOOD
CH**O**CKABLOCK
CH**O**IRMASTER
CH**O**LESTEROL
CL**O**SEFISTED
CO**O**PERATIVE
FL**O**ORWALKER
FL**O**RESCENCE
GE**O**MAGNETIC
GE**O**POLITICS
GE**O**SYNCLINE
GL**O**SSOLALIA
GR**O**UNDSHEET
GR**O**UNDWATER
IN**O**PERATIVE
IN**O**PPORTUNE
LI**O**NHEARTED
OZ**O**NOSPHERE
PH**O**TOGRAPHY
PH**O**TOSPHERE
PR**O**BATIONER
PR**O**BLEMATIC
PR**O**CRUSTEAN
PR**O**FANATORY
PR**O**GNATHOUS
PR**O**GRAMMING
PR**O**GRESSION
PR**O**GRESSIVE
PR**O**HIBITION
PR**O**LETARIAN
PR**O**LETARIAT
PR**O**LIFERATE
PR**O**MISCUOUS
PR**O**MPTITUDE
PR**O**PHYLAXIS
PR**O**PINQUITY
PR**O**POSITION
PR**O**PRIETARY
PR**O**SELYTIZE
PR**O**STATITIS
PR**O**STHETICS
PR**O**TAGONIST
PR**O**TOMARTYR
PR**O**TUBERANT
PR**O**VENIENCE
PR**O**VISIONAL
SH**O**RTCHANGE
SH**O**RTCOMING
SH**O**RTHANDED
SM**O**RGASBORD
SP**O**NTANEOUS
ST**O**CKBROKER
ST**O**CKHOLDER
ST**O**CKINETTE
ST**O**MACHACHE
ST**O**REKEEPER
ST**O**RYTELLER
TH**O**UGHTLESS
TR**O**POSPHERE
UN**O**BTRUSIVE
UN**O**RGANIZED
VI**O**LONCELLO
WO**O**DCHOPPER
WR**O**NGHEADED
ZO**O**MORPHISM
ZO**O**PLANKTON
AL**P**HABETIZE
AM**P**HETAMINE
AP**P**ELLATION
AP**P**LICATION
AP**P**OINTMENT
AP**P**RECIABLE
AP**P**ROBATION
AP**P**ROPRIATE
AP**P**ROXIMATE
CA**P**ACITANCE
CA**P**ILLARITY
CO**P**ROCESSOR
DE**P**RECATORY
DE**P**REDATION
DE**P**RIVATION
DI**P**LOMATIST
EM**P**LACEMENT
EX**P**ECTATION
EX**P**ECTORANT
EX**P**ECTORATE
EX**P**EDITIOUS
EX**P**ENDITURE
EX**P**ERIENCED
EX**P**OSTULATE
EX**P**ROPRIATE
HY**P**ERACTIVE
HY**P**ERBOREAN
HY**P**ERTROPHY
HY**P**HENATION
HY**P**OTHECATE
HY**P**OTHESIZE
IM**P**ASSIONED
IM**P**ECUNIOUS
IM**P**EDIMENTA
IM**P**ERFORATE
IM**P**ERIALISM
IM**P**ERMANENT
IM**P**ERMEABLE
IM**P**ERSONATE
IM**P**ERTINENT
IM**P**LAUSIBLE
IM**P**ORTATION
IM**P**ORTUNATE
IM**P**RACTICAL
IM**P**REGNABLE
IM**P**ROPRIETY
IM**P**ROVEMENT
IM**P**ROVIDENT
IM**P**UISSANCE
NA**P**HTHALENE
OP**P**ORTUNISM
OP**P**ORTUNITY
OP**P**ROBRIOUS
PA**P**ERHANGER
PA**P**ERWEIGHT
RA**P**SCALLION
RE**P**ETITIOUS
RE**P**LACEMENT
RE**P**LICATION
RE**P**ROBATION
SU**P**ERFICIAL
SU**P**ERFLUOUS
SU**P**ERIMPOSE
SU**P**ERINTEND
SU**P**ERLATIVE
SU**P**ERMARKET
SU**P**ERSCRIBE
SU**P**ERSCRIPT
SU**P**ERSONICS
SU**P**POSITION
SU**P**POSITORY
SU**P**PRESSANT
SU**P**REMACIST
TO**P**DRESSING
TY**P**EFOUNDER
TY**P**ESETTING
TY**P**EWRITING
TY**P**OGRAPHER
UN**P**RINTABLE
AC**Q**UIREMENT
AC**Q**UISITION
AC**Q**UISITIVE
IN**Q**UISITION
IN**Q**UISITIVE
RE**Q**UIREMENT
RE**Q**UISITION
SE**Q**UESTRATE
UN**Q**UALIFIED
AB**R**ACADABRA
AE**R**ONAUTICS
AG**R**ICULTURE
BA**R**BITURATE
BU**R**EAUCRACY
BU**R**GOMASTER
CA**R**AVANSARY
CA**R**DINALATE
CA**R**DINALITY
CA**R**DIOGRAPH
CA**R**DSHARPER
CA**R**MINATIVE
CA**R**NIVOROUS
CA**R**RAGEENAN
CA**R**TOGRAPHY
CE**R**EMONIOUS
CE**R**TIFICATE
CH**R**ISTENDOM
CH**R**ISTIANIA
CH**R**ONOGRAPH
CH**R**ONOMETER
CI**R**CULARITY
CI**R**CULARIZE
CI**R**CUMLUNAR
CI**R**CUMPOLAR
CI**R**CUMSPECT
CO**R**NERSTONE
CO**R**PORATION
CO**R**RELATIVE
CO**R**RIGENDUM
CO**R**ROBORATE
DE**R**ELICTION
DE**R**MATOLOGY
DI**R**ECTORATE
EA**R**THENWARE
FA**R**INACEOUS
FA**R**THERMOST
FA**R**THINGALE
FI**R**ECRACKER
FO**R**ECLOSURE
FO**R**EQUARTER
FO**R**ESHORTEN
FO**R**ETHOUGHT
FO**R**EVERMORE
FO**R**MFITTING

FO**R**NICATION
FO**R**THCOMING
FO**R**TNIGHTLY
FU**R**NISHINGS
FU**R**THERMORE
FU**R**THERMOST
GA**R**NISHMENT
GE**R**ONTOLOGY
GE**R**RYMANDER
GY**R**OCOMPASS
HA**R**DHEARTED
HA**R**DWORKING
HA**R**EBRAINED
HA**R**PSICHORD
HE**R**BIVOROUS
HE**R**PETOLOGY
HE**R**RINGBONE
HO**R**SEPLAYER
HO**R**SERADISH
IR**R**EDENTISM
IR**R**EDUCIBLE
IR**R**EFUTABLE
IR**R**ELIGIOUS
IR**R**EMOVABLE
IR**R**EPARABLE
IR**R**EVERENCE
IR**R**EVOCABLE
MA**R**CHIONESS
MA**R**KETPLACE
MA**R**QUISETTE
MA**R**SHMALLOW
ME**R**CHANDISE
ME**R**CHANTMAN
ME**R**ITOCRACY
ME**R**ITORIOUS
ME**R**RYMAKING
MO**R**TARBOARD
NA**R**RAGANSET
NO**R**THEASTER
NU**R**SERYMAID
PA**R**AMEDICAL
PA**R**ATHYROID
PA**R**ATROOPER
PA**R**ATYPHOID
PA**R**ENTHESIS
PA**R**ISHIONER
PA**R**TICIPATE
PA**R**TICULATE
PA**R**TURITION
PE**R**AMBULATE
PE**R**CEPTIBLE
PE**R**FECTIBLE
PE**R**FORMANCE
PE**R**FUNCTORY
PE**R**IODONTAL
PE**R**IPATETIC
PE**R**IPHRASIS
PE**R**ISTALSIS
PE**R**ITONITIS
PE**R**MISSIBLE
PE**R**MUTATION
PE**R**SNICKETY
PE**R**SONALITY
PE**R**SONALIZE
PE**R**SPECTIVE
PE**R**SPICUOUS
PH**R**ASEOLOGY
PO**R**NOGRAPHY
PO**R**TERHOUSE
PO**R**TIONLESS
PO**R**TMANTEAU
PO**R**TRAITIST
PO**R**TRAITURE
SA**R**COPHAGUS
SC**R**EWDRIVER
SC**R**UMPTIOUS
SE**R**ENDIPITY
SE**R**VICEABLE
SP**R**EADSHEET
SP**R**INGBOARD
ST**R**AIGHTWAY
ST**R**AITLACED
ST**R**ANGULATE
ST**R**AWFLOWER
ST**R**EAMLINED
ST**R**EAMLINER
ST**R**OBOSCOPE
TE**R**MINOLOGY
TE**R**RESTRIAL
TE**R**RITORIAL
UN**R**EASONING
UN**R**ELENTING
UN**R**EMITTING
UN**R**IGHTEOUS
VA**R**ICOLORED
VE**R**MICULITE
VE**R**TIGINOUS
VI**R**IDESCENT
WA**R**MHEARTED
WO**R**DPERFECT
WO**R**KMANLIKE
WO**R**KMANSHIP
WO**R**KSTATION
AB**S**ENTEEISM
AB**S**TRACTION
AS**S**ASSINATE
AS**S**EMBLYMAN
AS**S**IGNATION
AS**S**OCIATION
AS**S**OCIATIVE
BU**S**INESSMAN
CA**S**SITERITE
CA**S**TELLATED
CO**S**IGNATORY
CU**S**TOMHOUSE
DE**S**CRIPTION
DE**S**EGREGATE
DE**S**ENSITIZE
DE**S**IDERATUM
DE**S**PERATION
DE**S**PONDENCY
DE**S**TINATION
DE**S**TRUCTION
DI**S**APPROVAL
DI**S**ASSEMBLE
DI**S**CONTINUE
DI**S**COTHEQUE
DI**S**COURTESY
DI**S**CREPANCY
DI**S**ENCUMBER
DI**S**ENTANGLE
DI**S**ILLUSION
DI**S**ORGANIZE
DI**S**PENSABLE
DI**S**PLEASURE
DI**S**POSITION
DI**S**PUTATION
DI**S**QUIETUDE
DI**S**SEMINATE
DI**S**SIMULATE
DI**S**SOLUTION
DI**S**TINCTION
DI**S**TINCTIVE
DI**S**TINGUISH
DI**S**TRIBUTOR
FA**S**HIONABLE
GE**S**TICULATE
HI**S**TORICITY
HI**S**TRIONICS
HO**S**PITALITY
HO**S**PITALIZE
IN**S**CRUTABLE
IN**S**ECTICIDE
IN**S**EPARABLE
IN**S**INUATING
IN**S**OUCIANCE
IN**S**PIRATION
IN**S**TABILITY
IN**S**TALLMENT
IN**S**TANTIATE
IN**S**TITUTION
IN**S**TRUCTION
IN**S**TRUCTIVE
IN**S**UPERABLE
LA**S**ERWRITER
MA**S**SACHUSET
MA**S**TERPIECE
ME**S**ALLIANCE
MI**S**ALLIANCE
MI**S**ANTHROPE
MI**S**BEGOTTEN
MI**S**BELIEVER
MI**S**CHIEVOUS
MI**S**CONCEIVE
MI**S**CONSTRUE
MI**S**DEMEANOR
MI**S**FEASANCE
MI**S**GUIDANCE
MU**S**CULATURE
MU**S**KELLUNGE
OB**S**ERVATION
OB**S**ERVATORY
OB**S**OLESCENT
OB**S**TRUCTION
PE**S**TIFEROUS
PI**S**CATORIAL
RE**S**EMBLANCE
RE**S**ERVATION
RE**S**IDENTIAL
RE**S**IGNATION
RE**S**ISTIVITY
RE**S**PECTABLE
RE**S**PIRATION
RE**S**PLENDENT
RE**S**PONSIBLE
RE**S**TITUTION
RE**S**TORATION
RE**S**TORATIVE
RE**S**TRICTION
RE**S**USCITATE
SU**S**CEPTIBLE
SY**S**TEMATIZE
TE**S**TIMONIAL
UN**S**ATURATED
UN**S**PEAKABLE
WA**S**HERWOMAN
WA**S**TEBASKET
AF**T**ERBURNER
AF**T**EREFFECT
AL**T**ERCATION
AL**T**ERNATIVE
AN**T**ECHAMBER
AN**T**ICYCLONE
AN**T**IGRAVITY
AN**T**INEUTRON
AN**T**IOXIDANT
AN**T**IPOVERTY
AN**T**IQUARIAN
AS**T**IGMATISM
AT**T**RIBUTIVE
BA**T**HYSCAPHE
BA**T**HYSPHERE
BA**T**TLEFIELD
BA**T**TLEWAGON
BI**T**TERSWEET
CA**T**ASTROPHE
CA**T**EGORICAL
CA**T**ERCORNER
CA**T**ERPILLAR
CA**T**HOLICITY
CO**T**ERMINOUS
CO**T**TONMOUTH
DE**T**ERIORATE
DE**T**ERMINANT
DE**T**ERMINATE
DE**T**ERMINISM
EX**T**EMPORARY
EX**T**EMPORIZE
EX**T**ERMINATE
EX**T**RADITION
EX**T**RAPOLATE
EX**T**RAVAGANT
GU**T**TERSNIPE
IN**T**ELLIGENT
IN**T**ENTIONAL
IN**T**ERACTION
IN**T**ERACTIVE
IN**T**ERATOMIC
IN**T**ERCALARY
IN**T**ERCALATE
IN**T**ERCEPTOR
IN**T**ERCHANGE
IN**T**ERCOURSE
IN**T**ERESTING
IN**T**ERLACING
IN**T**ERLINEAR
IN**T**ERLINING
IN**T**ERMEDDLE
IN**T**ERMINGLE
IN**T**ERNECINE
IN**T**ERNUNCIO
IN**T**EROFFICE
IN**T**ERPOLATE
IN**T**ERPRETER
IN**T**ERRACIAL
IN**T**ERREGNUM
IN**T**ERRELATE
IN**T**ERROGATE
IN**T**ERSPERSE
IN**T**OLERABLE
IN**T**RACTABLE
IN**T**RAVENOUS
KI**T**CHENETTE
KI**T**CHENWARE
LA**T**CHSTRING
LA**T**TICEWORK
LE**T**TERPRESS
LI**T**HOGRAPHY
LI**T**HOSPHERE
LI**T**TERATEUR
MA**T**ERIALISM
MA**T**ERIALIZE
MA**T**HEMATICS
MA**T**RICULATE
ME**T**APHYSICS
ME**T**EOROLOGY
ME**T**HODOLOGY
ME**T**RICATION
MO**T**HERBOARD
MU**T**TONCHOPS
NA**T**IONALISM
NA**T**IONALIST
NA**T**IONALITY
NA**T**IONALIZE
NE**T**HERWORLD
NO**T**HINGNESS
OR**T**HODONTIA
OR**T**HOGRAPHY
OR**T**HOPEDICS
OS**T**ENTATION
OU**T**BUILDING
OU**T**DISTANCE
OU**T**MANEUVER
OU**T**STANDING
PA**T**ERNALISM
PE**T**ROGRAPHY
PI**T**CHBLENDE
RA**T**HSKELLER
RA**T**IONALISM
RA**T**IONALITY
RA**T**IONALIZE
RA**T**TLESNAKE
RE**T**RIBUTION
RE**T**ROACTIVE
RO**T**OGRAVURE
RO**T**TENSTONE
TO**T**ALIZATOR
UL**T**RAMARINE
UL**T**RAMODERN
UL**T**RASONICS
UL**T**RAVIOLET
UN**T**HINKABLE
UN**T**OUCHABLE
VI**T**ICULTURE
WA**T**ERCOURSE
WA**T**ERLOGGED
WI**T**ENAGEMOT
AC**U**PUNCTURE
AQ**U**ICULTURE
BL**U**NDERBUSS
BO**U**RGEOISIE
BO**U**TONNIERE
CA**U**LIFLOWER
CO**U**NTENANCE
CO**U**NTERFEIT
CO**U**NTERMAND
CO**U**NTERPANE
CO**U**NTERPART
CO**U**NTERSIGN
CO**U**NTERSINK
CO**U**NTERVAIL
CO**U**NTRIFIED
CO**U**NTRYSIDE
CR**U**CIFIXION
EQ**U**IDISTANT
EQ**U**ILATERAL
EQ**U**ILIBRIUM
FA**U**LTFINDER
FL**U**OROSCOPE
FO**U**LMOUTHED
HO**U**SEBROKEN
HO**U**SEKEEPER
HO**U**SELIGHTS
HO**U**SEMOTHER
KN**U**CKLEBONE
LO**U**DMOUTHED
LO**U**DSPEAKER
MO**U**NTAINEER
MO**U**NTAINTOP
NO**U**RISHMENT
SC**U**TTLEBUTT
SH**U**TTLECOCK
TH**U**NDERBOLT
TH**U**NDERCLAP
TH**U**NDERHEAD
TR**U**EHEARTED
TR**U**STEESHIP
TR**U**STWORTHY
UN**U**TTERABLE
AD**V**ERSATIVE
AD**V**ERTISING
EN**V**IRONMENT
IN**V**ESTIGATE
IN**V**ESTITURE
IN**V**OLUNTARY
JU**V**ENOCRACY
LE**V**ELHEADED
RE**V**ERBERATE
RE**V**ERENTIAL
SO**V**EREIGNTY
UN**V**ARNISHED
VI**V**ISECTION
DO**W**NHEARTED
DO**W**NTRODDEN
TO**W**NSPEOPLE
UN**W**HOLESOME
HE**X**ADECIMAL
BO**Y**SENBERRY
CR**Y**STALLIZE
PH**Y**SIOGNOMY
PS**Y**CHEDELIA
PS**Y**CHEDELIC
PS**Y**CHODRAMA
PS**Y**CHOGENIC

**4th Letter**

ABRACADABRA
ASSASSINATE
BEHAVIORISM
BICARBONATE
BREADBASKET
BREADWINNER
BREAKPOINTS
BREASTPLATE
CAMARADERIE
CAPACITANCE
CARAVANSARY
CATASTROPHE
CHIAROSCURO
CLEARHEADED
DEFALCATION
DEMAGNETIZE
DILAPIDATED
DISAPPROVAL
DISASSEMBLE
DREADNOUGHT
DYNAMOMETER
ENCAPSULATE
EXHAUSTLESS
GREASEPAINT
HEXADECIMAL
IMPASSIONED
INCANTATION
INCARCERATE
INCARNADINE
INCARNATION
INFANTICIDE
INGATHERING
MALADJUSTED
MALAPROPISM
MEGALOMANIA
MEGALOPOLIS
MELANCHOLIA
MELANCHOLIC
MESALLIANCE
METAPHYSICS
MISALLIANCE
MISANTHROPE
MONASTICISM
PARAMEDICAL
PARATHYROID
PARATROOPER
PARATYPHOID
PERAMBULATE
PHRASEOLOGY
PLEASURABLE
PREASSIGNED
RENAISSANCE
ROMANTICISM
STEAMROLLER
STRAIGHTWAY
STRAITLACED
STRANGULATE
STRAWFLOWER
SUBASSEMBLY
THEATRICALS
TOBACCONIST
TOTALIZATOR
TREACHEROUS
TRIANGULATE
UNFAVORABLE
UNSATURATED
UNVARNISHED
VACATIONIST
VINAIGRETTE
BARBITURATE
COBBLESTONE
COMBINATION
COMBUSTIBLE
FLABBERGAST
HERBIVOROUS
JABBERWOCKY
MISBEGOTTEN
MISBELIEVER
OUTBUILDING
PROBATIONER
PROBLEMATIC
TRIBULATION
UNOBTRUSIVE
ABECEDARIAN
ANACHRONISM
APOCYNTHION
BACCHANALIA
BEACHCOMBER
BLOCKBUSTER
CALCIFEROUS
CALCULATING
CALCULATION
CHOCKABLOCK
CIRCULARITY
CIRCULARIZE
CIRCUMLUNAR
CIRCUMPOLAR
CIRCUMSPECT
CONCENTRATE
CONCERNMENT
CONCOMITANT
CONCORDANCE
CONCURRENCE
CRACKERJACK
CRUCIFIXION
DESCRIPTION
DISCONTINUE
DISCOTHEQUE
DISCOURTESY
DISCREPANCY
ELECTIONEER
ELECTRICIAN
ELECTRICITY
ELECTROCUTE
ELECTROFORM
ELECTROLYTE
ELECTRONICS
ELECTROTYPE
FUNCTIONARY
INSCRUTABLE
KITCHENETTE
KITCHENWARE
KNUCKLEBONE
LATCHSTRING
MARCHIONESS
MERCHANDISE
MERCHANTMAN
MISCHIEVOUS
MISCONCEIVE
MISCONSTRUE
MUSCULATURE
PERCEPTIBLE
PISCATORIAL
PITCHBLENDE
PLACEHOLDER
PRACTICABLE
PRECIPITATE
PRECIPITOUS
PRECONCEIVE
PROCRUSTEAN
PSYCHEDELIA
PSYCHEDELIC
PSYCHODRAMA
PSYCHOGENIC
PULCHRITUDE
PUNCTILIOUS
PUNCTUATION
QUACKSALVER
QUICKSILVER
REACTIONARY
SARCOPHAGUS
SPACEFLIGHT
SPECTACULAR
SPECTROGRAM
STOCKBROKER
STOCKHOLDER
STOCKINETTE
SUSCEPTIBLE
SYNCHROMESH
SYNCHRONIZE
SYNCHRONOUS
SYNCOPATION
TRICHINOSIS
UNACCOUNTED
UNICELLULAR
VACCINATION
VOLCANOLOGY
WHICHSOEVER
ACADEMICIAN
ACADEMICISM
CANDELABRUM
CANDIDATURE
CANDLELIGHT
CANDLESTICK
CARDINALATE
CARDINALITY
CARDIOGRAPH
CARDSHARPER
COEDUCATION
CONDITIONAL
CONDITIONED
CONDOMINIUM
CONDUCTANCE
FIDDLESTICK
FUNDAMENTAL
GENDARMERIE
GODDAUGHTER
HANDICAPPER
HANDSHAKING
HANDWRITING
HARDHEARTED
HARDWORKING
HINDQUARTER
INADVERTENT
IRIDESCENCE
KINDHEARTED
LOUDMOUTHED
LOUDSPEAKER
MAIDSERVANT
MEADOWSWEET
MENDELEVIUM
MISDEMEANOR
NEEDLEPOINT
NEEDLEWOMAN
NONDESCRIPT
NONDOCUMENT
OUTDISTANCE
PANDEMONIUM
PREDECESSOR
PREDICAMENT
PREDOMINATE
QUADRENNIAL
QUADRENNIUM
ROADABILITY
TENDENTIOUS
TOPDRESSING
VINDICATION
WOODCHOPPER
WORDPERFECT
ABSENTEEISM
ACCELERANDO
ACCELERATOR
ACCEPTATION
ADVERSATIVE
ADVERTISING
AFFECTATION
AFTERBURNER
AFTEREFFECT
ALTERCATION
ALTERNATIVE
ANAESTHESIA
ANTECHAMBER
APPELLATION
ASSEMBLYMAN
BENEDICTION
BENEFACTION
BENEFICENCE
BENEFICIARY
BENEVOLENCE
BICENTENARY
BIMETALLISM
BUREAUCRACY
CAMEROONIAN
CATEGORICAL
CATERCORNER
CATERPILLAR
CEMENTATION
CEREMONIOUS
CHEERLEADER
CHEESECLOTH
COMEUPPANCE
COTERMINOUS
CYBERNATION
CYBERNETICS
DELECTATION
DELETERIOUS
DERELICTION
DESEGREGATE
DESENSITIZE
DETERIORATE
DETERMINANT
DETERMINATE
DETERMINISM
DIRECTORATE
DISENCUMBER
DISENTANGLE
DOMESTICATE
DOMESTICITY
EXCEEDINGLY
EXCEPTIONAL
EXPECTATION
EXPECTORANT
EXPECTORATE
EXPEDITIOUS
EXPENDITURE
EXPERIENCED
EXTEMPORARY
EXTEMPORIZE
EXTERMINATE
FIRECRACKER
FORECLOSURE
FOREQUARTER
FORESHORTEN
FORETHOUGHT
FOREVERMORE
FREETHINKER
GENERALSHIP
GREENGROCER
HABERDASHER
HAREBRAINED
HOMEOSTASIS
HOMESTEADER
HOMESTRETCH
HONEYSUCKLE
HYPERACTIVE
HYPERBOREAN
HYPERTROPHY
IMPECUNIOUS
IMPEDIMENTA
IMPERFORATE
IMPERIALISM
IMPERMANENT
IMPERMEABLE
IMPERSONATE
IMPERTINENT
INCERTITUDE
INDEFINABLE
INDENTATION
INDEPENDENT
INNERSPRING
INSECTICIDE
INSEPARABLE
INTELLIGENT
INTENTIONAL
INTERACTION
INTERACTIVE
INTERATOMIC
INTERCALARY
INTERCALATE
INTERCEPTOR
INTERCHANGE
INTERCOURSE
INTERESTING
INTERLACING
INTERLINEAR
INTERLINING
INTERMEDDLE
INTERMINGLE
INTERNECINE
INTERNUNCIO
INTEROFFICE
INTERPOLATE
INTERPRETER
INTERRACIAL
INTERREGNUM
INTERRELATE
INTERROGATE
INTERSPERSE
INVESTIGATE
INVESTITURE
IRREDENTISM
IRREDUCIBLE
IRREFUTABLE
IRRELIGIOUS
IRREMOVABLE
IRREPARABLE
IRREVERENCE
IRREVOCABLE
JUVENOCRACY
KINESTHESIA
LASERWRITER
LEGERDEMAIN
LEVELHEADED
LIBERTARIAN
MALEDICTION
MATERIALISM
MATERIALIZE
METEOROLOGY
MINESWEEPER
MOMENTARILY
MONEYLENDER
NECESSITATE
NECESSITOUS
NONETHELESS
OBSERVATION
OBSERVATORY
OSTENTATION
PALEOGRAPHY
PAPERHANGER
PAPERWEIGHT
PARENTHESIS
PATERNALISM
PENETRATING
POMEGRANATE
RECESSIONAL
REMEMBRANCE
REPETITIOUS
RESEMBLANCE
RESERVATION
REVERBERATE
REVERENTIAL
SAFEKEEPING
SCREWDRIVER
SERENDIPITY
SLEEPWALKER
SOVEREIGNTY
SPEEDOMETER
SPREADSHEET
STREAMLINED
STREAMLINER
SUPERFICIAL
SUPERFLUOUS
SUPERIMPOSE
SUPERINTEND
SUPERLATIVE
SUPERMARKET
SUPERSCRIBE

SUP**E**RSCRIPT
SUP**E**RSONICS
SWE**E**PSTAKES
TEL**E**PRINTER
TIM**E**SHARING
TRU**E**HEARTED
TUB**E**RCULATE
TYP**E**FOUNDER
TYP**E**SETTING
TYP**E**WRITING
UNC**E**RTAINTY
UND**E**RCHARGE
UND**E**REXPOSE
UND**E**RGROUND
UND**E**RGROWTH
UND**E**RHANDED
UND**E**RSHORTS
UND**E**RSIGNED
UND**E**RTAKING
UND**E**RWEIGHT
UND**E**SIGNING
UND**E**SIRABLE
UND**E**VIATING
UNR**E**ASONING
UNR**E**LENTING
UNR**E**MITTING
VAL**E**DICTION
VAL**E**DICTORY
WAT**E**RCOURSE
WAT**E**RLOGGED
WHE**E**LBARROW
WHE**E**LWRIGHT
WID**E**MOUTHED
WIT**E**NAGEMOT
BIO**F**EEDBACK
COE**F**FICIENT
COF**F**EEHOUSE
COM**F**ORTABLE
CON**F**EDERACY
CON**F**EDERATE
CON**F**ESSEDLY
CON**F**ORMANCE
DIF**F**RACTION
EDI**F**ICATION
HAL**F**HEARTED
INE**F**FECTIVE
INE**F**FECTUAL
INE**F**FICIENT
MAL**F**EASANCE
MAL**F**UNCTION
MIS**F**EASANCE
PER**F**ECTIBLE
PER**F**ORMANCE
PER**F**UNCTORY
PRO**F**ANATORY
SCA**F**FOLDING
SUF**F**ICIENCY
SUF**F**RAGETTE
UNI**F**ICATION
WHI**F**FLETREE
BRA**G**GADOCIO
BUR**G**OMASTER
CON**G**RESSMAN
FIN**G**ERBOARD
FIN**G**ERPRINT
FRA**G**MENTARY
GIN**G**ERBREAD
IMA**G**ESETTER
IMA**G**INATION
LIN**G**UISTICS
MIS**G**UIDANCE
PRO**G**NATHOUS
PRO**G**RAMMING
PRO**G**RESSION
PRO**G**RESSIVE
TRA**G**EDIENNE
ALP**H**ABETIZE
AMP**H**ETAMINE
ARC**H**AEOLOGY
ARC**H**DIOCESE
ARC**H**IPELAGO
BAT**H**YSCAPHE
BAT**H**YSPHERE
CAT**H**OLICITY
FAS**H**IONABLE
HIG**H**FALUTIN
HYP**H**ENATION
LIG**H**TWEIGHT
LIT**H**OGRAPHY
LIT**H**OSPHERE
MAC**H**INATION
MAT**H**EMATICS
MEC**H**ANISTIC
MET**H**ODOLOGY
MOT**H**ERBOARD
NAP**H**THALENE
NET**H**ERWORLD
NIG**H**TINGALE
NIG**H**TWALKER
NOT**H**INGNESS
ORC**H**ESTRATE
ORT**H**ODONTIA
ORT**H**OGRAPHY
ORT**H**OPEDICS
PAC**H**YSANDRA
PRE**H**ISTORIC
PRO**H**IBITION
RAT**H**SKELLER
TAC**H**YCARDIA
TEC**H**NOCRACY
TIG**H**TFISTED
UNC**H**RISTIAN
UNT**H**INKABLE
UNW**H**OLESOME
VIC**H**YSSOISE
WAS**H**ERWOMAN
AFF**I**RMATIVE
AGR**I**CULTURE
AMB**I**VALENCE
ANN**I**VERSARY
ANT**I**CYCLONE
ANT**I**GRAVITY
ANT**I**NEUTRON
ANT**I**OXIDANT
ANT**I**POVERTY
ANT**I**QUARIAN
AQU**I**CULTURE
ARB**I**TRAMENT
ASS**I**GNATION
AST**I**GMATISM
AUD**I**OVISUAL
AVO**I**RDUPOIS
BUS**I**NESSMAN
CAB**I**NETWORK
CAL**I**FORNIUM
CAP**I**LLARITY
CHO**I**RMASTER
CHR**I**STENDOM
CHR**I**STIANIA
CLA**I**RVOYANT
COS**I**GNATORY
DEL**I**NQUENCY
DES**I**DERATUM
DIS**I**LLUSION
EFF**I**CACIOUS
ENG**I**NEERING
ENV**I**RONMENT
EQU**I**DISTANT
EQU**I**LATERAL
EQU**I**LIBRIUM
FAM**I**LIARITY
FAR**I**NACEOUS
HAB**I**TUATION
HAG**I**OGRAPHY
ILL**I**MITABLE
IMM**I**TIGABLE
INC**I**NERATOR
IND**I**FFERENT
IND**I**GESTION
IND**I**GNATION
IND**I**VIDUATE
IND**I**VISIBLE
INS**I**NUATING
LEG**I**SLATION
LEG**I**SLATIVE
LEG**I**SLATURE
MAG**I**STERIAL
MED**I**UMISTIC
MER**I**TOCRACY
MER**I**TORIOUS
MIN**I**ATURIZE
NAT**I**ONALISM
NAT**I**ONALIST
NAT**I**ONALITY
NAT**I**ONALIZE
NUM**I**SMATICS
OFF**I**CIALDOM
OFF**I**CIALISM
OMN**I**PRESENT
ORN**I**THOLOGY
PAR**I**SHIONER
PER**I**ODONTAL
PER**I**PATETIC
PER**I**PHRASIS
PER**I**STALSIS
PER**I**TONITIS
PLA**I**NSPOKEN
PRE**I**GNITION
RAD**I**OCARBON
RAD**I**OMETRIC
RAT**I**ONALISM
RAT**I**ONALITY
RAT**I**ONALIZE
REC**I**PROCATE
REC**I**PROCITY
REG**I**MENTALS
REM**I**NISCENT
RES**I**DENTIAL
RES**I**GNATION
RES**I**STIVITY
SEM**I**TRAILER
SOL**I**LOQUIZE
SPR**I**NGBOARD
TRA**I**LBLAZER
UNC**I**VILIZED
UNM**I**TIGATED
UNR**I**GHTEOUS
VAR**I**COLORED
VIC**I**SSITUDE
VIR**I**DESCENT
VIT**I**CULTURE
VIV**I**SECTION
CON**J**UGATION
CON**J**UNCTION
CON**J**UNCTIVA
CON**J**UNCTIVE
CON**J**UNCTURE
SUB**J**UNCTIVE
BAC**K**STRETCH
COC**K**LESHELL
HUC**K**LEBERRY
LIC**K**SPITTLE
MAR**K**ETPLACE
MOC**K**INGBIRD
MON**K**EYSHINE
MUS**K**ELLUNGE
NEC**K**ERCHIEF
NIC**K**ELODEON
POC**K**ETKNIFE
WOR**K**MANLIKE
WOR**K**MANSHIP
WOR**K**STATION
ACC**L**AMATION
ACC**L**IMATIZE
ADO**L**ESCENCE
AGG**L**OMERATE
AGG**L**UTINATE
APP**L**ICATION
BAL**L**CARRIER
BAL**L**ETOMANE
BEL**L**IGERENT
BIB**L**IOPHILE
BOI**L**ERMAKER
CAL**L**IGRAPHY
CAU**L**IFLOWER
CHO**L**ESTEROL
COL**L**ABORATE
COL**L**OCATION
DEC**L**ARATIVE
DEF**L**ORATION
DIP**L**OMATIST
DRI**L**LMASTER
EMP**L**ACEMENT
FAU**L**TFINDER
FOU**L**MOUTHED
GAL**L**BLADDER
GAL**L**IMAUFRY
HAL**L**UCINATE
HEL**L**ENISTIC
IMP**L**AUSIBLE
INA**L**IENABLE
INC**L**INATION
INE**L**UCTABLE
INF**L**AMMABLE
LIL**L**IPUTIAN
MEL**L**IFLUOUS
MIL**L**IAMPERE
MIL**L**IONAIRE
MIL**L**ISECOND
MOL**L**YCODDLE
PHI**L**OSOPHER
POL**L**INATION
PRE**L**IMINARY
PRO**L**ETARIAN
PRO**L**ETARIAT
PRO**L**IFERATE
PUB**L**ICATION
QUA**L**ITATIVE
REA**L**POLITIK
REP**L**ACEMENT
REP**L**ICATION
SHE**L**LACKING
SPE**L**LBINDER
SWA**L**LOWTAIL
THA**L**IDOMIDE
TWE**L**VEMONTH
UNA**L**IENABLE
UNF**L**APPABLE
UNF**L**INCHING
UTI**L**ITARIAN
VIO**L**ONCELLO
ABO**M**INATION
BLA**M**EWORTHY
CAR**M**INATIVE
CHA**M**BERLAIN
CHA**M**BERMAID
CLI**M**ACTERIC
CLI**M**ATOLOGY
COM**M**ANDMENT
COM**M**EMORATE
COM**M**ENTATOR
COM**M**INATION
COM**M**ISERATE
COM**M**ONPLACE
COM**M**UNICANT
COM**M**UNICATE
COM**M**UTATION
COM**M**UTATIVE
CRI**M**INOLOGY
DER**M**ATOLOGY
DIA**M**AGNETIC
DIA**M**ONDBACK
FIL**M**OGRAPHY
FOR**M**FITTING
GEO**M**AGNETIC
HAE**M**ORRHAGE
HUM**M**INGBIRD
OUT**M**ANEUVER
PER**M**ISSIBLE
PER**M**UTATION
PRE**M**EDITATE
PRE**M**ONITION
PRI**M**ITIVISM
PRO**M**ISCUOUS
PRO**M**PTITUDE
STO**M**ACHACHE
SUB**M**ERSIBLE
SUM**M**ERHOUSE
TER**M**INOLOGY
VER**M**ICULITE
WAR**M**HEARTED
ZOO**M**ORPHISM
ACK**N**OWLEDGE
AMO**N**TILLADO
BLU**N**DERBUSS
CAN**N**IBALIZE
CAR**N**IVOROUS
CHA**N**CELLERY
CHA**N**TICLEER
CLA**N**DESTINE
COG**N**OSCENTE
COI**N**CIDENCE
CON**N**OISSEUR
CON**N**OTATION
CON**N**OTATIVE
COR**N**ERSTONE
COU**N**TENANCE
COU**N**TERFEIT
COU**N**TERMAND
COU**N**TERPANE
COU**N**TERPART
COU**N**TERSIGN
COU**N**TERSINK
COU**N**TERVAIL
COU**N**TRIFIED
COU**N**TRYSIDE
DOW**N**HEARTED
DOW**N**TRODDEN
EPI**N**EPHRINE
EVA**N**GELICAL
EVE**N**TUALITY
FLA**N**NELETTE
FOR**N**ICATION
FRA**N**KFURTER
FUR**N**ISHINGS
GAR**N**ISHMENT
GEA**N**TICLINE
GRA**N**DFATHER
GRA**N**DMOTHER
GRA**N**DPARENT
GRA**N**ITEWARE
IDE**N**TIFIERS
LIO**N**HEARTED
MAG**N**ANIMOUS
MAG**N**IFICENT
MIN**N**ESINGER
MOU**N**TAINEER
MOU**N**TAINTOP
NEA**N**DERTHAL
NIN**N**YHAMMER
NON**N**EGATIVE
OPI**N**IONATED
OZO**N**OSPHERE
PAI**N**STAKING
PEN**N**YWEIGHT
PLA**N**ETARIUM
PLA**N**ETOLOGY
POI**N**TILLISM
POR**N**OGRAPHY
REI**N**FECTION
SCI**N**TILLATE
SIG**N**IFICANT
SPE**N**DTHRIFT
SPO**N**TANEOUS
STA**N**DARDIZE
STE**N**OGRAPHY
THE**N**CEFORTH
THU**N**DERBOLT
THU**N**DERCLAP

THUNDERHEAD
TOWNSPEOPLE
TRANQUILIZE
TRANSACTION
TRANSCEIVER
TRANSFIGURE
TRANSLUCENT
TRANSMITTER
TRANSPARENT
TRENCHERMAN
TRINIDADIAN
TRINITARIAN
UNINHIBITED
WAINSCOTING
WRONGHEADED
ACCOMMODATE
ACCORDINGLY
ACCOUNTABLE
AERONAUTICS
APPOINTMENT
ASSOCIATION
ASSOCIATIVE
BLOODMOBILE
BLOODSTREAM
BLOODSUCKER
CALORIMETER
CHLOROPHYLL
CHRONOGRAPH
CHRONOMETER
COLONIALISM
COLORCASTER
DEMOCRATIZE
DEMONSTRATE
DENOMINATOR
DICOTYLEDON
DISORGANIZE
ENDOTHERMIC
EXPOSTULATE
FLOORWALKER
FLUOROSCOPE
GERONTOLOGY
GYROCOMPASS
HOMOGENEOUS
HYPOTHECATE
HYPOTHESIZE
IGNOMINIOUS
IMMORTALITY
IMMORTALIZE
IMPORTATION
IMPORTUNATE
INCOMPETENT
INCONGRUENT
INCONGRUOUS
INCONTINENT
INCORPORATE
INCORPOREAL
INDOMITABLE

INFORMATION
INFORMATIVE
INSOUCIANCE
INTOLERABLE
INVOLUNTARY
LABORSAVING
MEMORABILIA
MONOLINGUAL
OBSOLESCENT
OPPORTUNISM
OPPORTUNITY
PREOCCUPIED
RECOGNITION
RECONNOITER
RECONSTRUCT
REDOUBTABLE
REFORMATION
REFORMATORY
RELOCATABLE
REMONSTRANT
REMONSTRATE
ROTOGRAVURE
SCHOLARSHIP
SCHOOLHOUSE
STROBOSCOPE
SUBORDINATE
THEORETICAL
TYPOGRAPHER
UNCOMMITTED
UNCONCERNED
UNCONSCIOUS
UNFORTUNATE
UNTOUCHABLE
ACUPUNCTURE
CAMPANOLOGY
COMPARATIVE
COMPARTMENT
COMPETITION
COMPLACENCE
COMPLACENCY
COMPLICATED
COMPORTMENT
COMPOSITION
COMPTROLLER
COMPUNCTION
COMPUTERIZE
COOPERATIVE
CORPORATION
CRAPSHOOTER
CREPUSCULAR
DESPERATION
DESPONDENCY
DIAPHORETIC
DISPENSABLE
DISPLEASURE
DISPOSITION
DISPUTATION

ELEPHANTINE
GEOPOLITICS
HARPSICHORD
HERPETOLOGY
HOSPITALITY
HOSPITALIZE
INOPERATIVE
INOPPORTUNE
INSPIRATION
KLEPTOMANIA
LAMPLIGHTER
MALPRACTICE
NONPARTISAN
NYMPHOMANIA
PREPOSITION
PROPHYLAXIS
PROPINQUITY
PROPOSITION
PROPRIETARY
RESPECTABLE
RESPIRATION
RESPLENDENT
RESPONSIBLE
SHIPBUILDER
STEPBROTHER
SUPPOSITION
SUPPOSITORY
SUPPRESSANT
TEMPERAMENT
TEMPERATURE
TEMPESTUOUS
TREPIDATION
TROPOSPHERE
UNSPEAKABLE
WHIPPLETREE
ZOOPLANKTON
DISQUIETUDE
MARQUISETTE
UNEQUIVOCAL
ABORTIONIST
AGGREGATION
AGORAPHOBIA
APHRODISIAC
APPRECIABLE
APPROBATION
APPROPRIATE
APPROXIMATE
ATTRIBUTIVE
BOURGEOISIE
CARRAGEENAN
CHIROGRAPHY
CLERICALISM
COPROCESSOR
CORRELATIVE
CORRIGENDUM
CORROBORATE
DECRESCENDO

DEPRECATORY
DEPREDATION
DEPRIVATION
ENFRANCHISE
EVERLASTING
EXCRESCENCE
EXPROPRIATE
EXTRADITION
EXTRAPOLATE
EXTRAVAGANT
FLORESCENCE
GERRYMANDER
HAIRBREADTH
HAIRDRESSER
HAIRSTYLIST
HEARTBROKEN
HEARTHSTONE
HERRINGBONE
HYDROCARBON
HYDROGENATE
HYDROGRAPHY
HYDROPHOBIA
HYDROPONICS
HYDROSPHERE
HYDROSTATIC
HYGROSCOPIC
IMBRICATION
IMPRACTICAL
IMPREGNABLE
IMPROPRIETY
IMPROVEMENT
IMPROVIDENT
INCREDULOUS
INCREMENTAL
INCRIMINATE
INGRATITUDE
INTRACTABLE
INTRAVENOUS
LABRADORITE
LACRIMATION
MACROBIOTIC
MACROSCOPIC
MATRICULATE
MERRYMAKING
METRICATION
MICROCAPSUL
MICROSCOPIC
MICROSECOND
NARRAGANSET
NEARSIGHTED
NONRESIDENT
NOURISHMENT
OPPROBRIOUS
OVERBALANCE
OVERBEARING
OVERSTUFFED
OVERWEENING

OVERWROUGHT
PETROGRAPHY
PHARISAICAL
PREROGATIVE
QUARTERBACK
QUARTERDECK
RECRIMINATE
REFRESHMENT
REFRIGERATE
REPROBATION
RETRIBUTION
RETROACTIVE
SEARCHLIGHT
SHAREHOLDER
SHORTCHANGE
SHORTCOMING
SHORTHANDED
SMORGASBORD
STEREOSCOPE
STEREOSCOPY
STEREOTYPED
STOREKEEPER
STORYTELLER
SUPREMACIST
TERRESTRIAL
TERRITORIAL
THERAPEUTIC
THEREABOUTS
THEREWITHAL
THERMOCLINE
THERMOMETER
ULTRAMARINE
ULTRAMODERN
ULTRASONICS
ULTRAVIOLET
UNORGANIZED
UNPRINTABLE
WHEREABOUTS
WHERESOEVER
WHEREWITHAL
ANASTOMOSIS
ARISTOCRACY
BOYSENBERRY
CASSITERITE
CLOSEFISTED
CONSECUTIVE
CONSEQUENCE
CONSERVANCY
CONSERVATOR
CONSIDERATE
CONSIDERING
CONSIGNMENT
CONSISTENCE
CONSISTENCY
CONSOLIDATE
CONSPICUOUS
CONSTITUENT

CONSUMERISM
CONSUMPTION
CONSUMPTIVE
CRESTFALLEN
CRYSTALLIZE
DISSEMINATE
DISSIMULATE
DISSOLUTION
EINSTEINIUM
GEOSYNCLINE
GLOSSOLALIA
GRASSHOPPER
HORSEPLAYER
HORSERADISH
HOUSEBROKEN
HOUSEKEEPER
HOUSELIGHTS
HOUSEMOTHER
INESCAPABLE
INESTIMABLE
KWASHIORKOR
MARSHMALLOW
MASSACHUSET
MEASUREMENT
MENSURATION
MONSEIGNEUR
NURSERYMAID
OUTSTANDING
PERSNICKETY
PERSONALITY
PERSONALIZE
PERSPECTIVE
PERSPICUOUS
PHYSIOGNOMY
PRESUMPTION
PROSELYTIZE
PROSTATITIS
PROSTHETICS
RAPSCALLION
SEISMOGRAPH
SEISMOMETER
SENSATIONAL
SENSIBILITY
SUBSISTENCE
SUBSTANDARD
SUBSTANTIAL
SUBSTANTIVE
TEASPOONFUL
THISTLEDOWN
TOASTMASTER
TONSILLITIS
TRUSTEESHIP
TRUSTWORTHY
ABSTRACTION
BATTLEFIELD
BATTLEWAGON
BITTERSWEET

BOUTONNIERE
BROTHERHOOD
CARTOGRAPHY
CASTELLATED
CENTENARIAN
CENTERBOARD
CENTERPIECE
CENTRIFUGAL
CENTRIPETAL
CERTIFICATE
CONTAMINANT
CONTAMINATE
CONTEMPLATE
CONTENTMENT
CONTINENTAL
CONTINGENCY
CONTINUANCE
CONTRACTILE
CONTRAPTION
CONTRARIETY
CONTRETEMPS
CONTRIVANCE
CONTROVERSY
COTTONMOUTH
CUSTOMHOUSE
DESTINATION
DESTRUCTION
DICTATORIAL
DISTINCTION
DISTINCTIVE
DISTINGUISH
DISTRIBUTOR
DOCTRINAIRE
EARTHENWARE
FARTHERMOST
FARTHINGALE
FEATHEREDGE
FORTHCOMING
FORTNIGHTLY
FURTHERMORE
FURTHERMOST
GENTLEWOMAN
GESTICULATE
GUTTERSNIPE
HISTORICITY
HISTRIONICS
ICHTHYOLOGY
INATTENTION
INSTABILITY
INSTALLMENT
INSTANTIATE
INSTITUTION
INSTRUCTION
INSTRUCTIVE
LATTICEWORK
LEATHERNECK
LETTERPRESS

LITTERATEUR
MANTELPIECE
MASTERPIECE
MORTARBOARD
MULTIFAMILY
MULTIRACIAL
MUTTONCHOPS
NORTHEASTER
OBSTRUCTION
PARTICIPATE
PARTICULATE
PARTURITION
PENTECOSTAL
PESTIFEROUS
PHOTOGRAPHY
PHOTOSPHERE
PICTURESQUE
POLTERGEIST
PONTIFICALS
PONTIFICATE
PORTERHOUSE
PORTIONLESS
PORTMANTEAU
PORTRAITIST
PORTRAITURE
PRETENTIOUS
PRETERMINAL
PROTAGONIST
PROTOMARTYR
PROTUBERANT
RATTLESNAKE
RECTILINEAR
RESTITUTION
RESTORATION
RESTORATIVE
RESTRICTION
ROTTENSTONE
SCUTTLEBUTT
SENTENTIOUS
SENTIMENTAL
SHUTTLECOCK
SMITHEREENS
STETHOSCOPE
SUBTROPICAL
SWITCHBLADE
SWITCHBOARD
SYNTHESIZER
SYSTEMATIZE
TESTIMONIAL
THITHERWARD
UNUTTERABLE
VENTILATION
VENTRILOQUY
VENTURESOME
VERTIGINOUS
WASTEBASKET
WEATHERCOCK
WEATHERWORN
WINTERGREEN
ACCUMULATOR
ACQUIREMENT
ACQUISITION
ACQUISITIVE
ANNUNCIATOR
CONURBATION
DOCUMENTARY
GROUNDSHEET
GROUNDWATER
ILLUSIONISM
ILLUSTRIOUS
IMPUISSANCE
INCUNABULUM
INDUBITABLE
INDUSTRIOUS
INNUMERABLE
INQUISITION
INQUISITIVE
INSUPERABLE
LUCUBRATION
MANUFACTORY
MANUFACTURE
MODULARIZED
PENULTIMATE
REGURGITATE
REQUIREMENT
REQUISITION
RESUSCITATE
SCRUMPTIOUS
SEQUESTRATE
SUBURBANITE
THOUGHTLESS
TRIUMVIRATE
UNQUALIFIED
CONVENIENCE
CONVENTICLE
CONVERTIBLE
CONVOCATION
CONVOLUTION
GRAVITATION
HEAVYWEIGHT
NONVIOLENCE
PREVARICATE
PROVENIENCE
PROVISIONAL
SERVICEABLE
UNAVOIDABLE
ALEXANDRIAN
ALEXANDRINE
COEXTENSIVE
INEXCUSABLE
POLYNOMINAL
POLYSTYRENE
POLYTECHNIC
ELIZABETHAN
PRIZEWINNER

## 5TH LETTER

ACCLAMATION
AGORAPHOBIA
ALEXANDRIAN
ALEXANDRINE
ALPHABETIZE
ARCHAEOLOGY
BUREAUCRACY
CAMPANOLOGY
CARRAGEENAN
CLIMACTERIC
CLIMATOLOGY
COLLABORATE
COMMANDMENT
COMPARATIVE
COMPARTMENT
CONTAMINANT
CONTAMINATE
DECLARATIVE
DERMATOLOGY
DIAMAGNETIC
DICTATORIAL
ELIZABETHAN
EMPLACEMENT
ENFRANCHISE
EXTRADITION
EXTRAPOLATE
EXTRAVAGANT
FUNDAMENTAL
GENDARMERIE
GEOMAGNETIC
GODDAUGHTER
IMPLAUSIBLE
IMPRACTICAL
INFLAMMABLE
INGRATITUDE
INSTABILITY
INSTALLMENT
INSTANTIATE
INTRACTABLE
INTRAVENOUS
LABRADORITE
MAGNANIMOUS
MASSACHUSET
MECHANISTIC
MINIATURIZE
MORTARBOARD
NARRAGANSET
NONPARTISAN
OUTMANEUVER
PISCATORIAL
PREVARICATE
PROBATIONER
PROFANATORY
PROTAGONIST
REPLACEMENT
ROADABILITY
SENSATIONAL
SPREADSHEET
STOMACHACHE
STREAMLINED
STREAMLINER
THERAPEUTIC
ULTRAMARINE
ULTRAMODERN
ULTRASONICS
ULTRAVIOLET
UNFLAPPABLE
UNQUALIFIED
UNREASONING
VOLCANOLOGY
CHAMBERLAIN
CHAMBERMAID
FLABBERGAST
GALLBLADDER
HAIRBREADTH
HAREBRAINED
INDUBITABLE
LUCUBRATION
OVERBALANCE
OVERBEARING
SHIPBUILDER
STEPBROTHER
STROBOSCOPE
ABRACADABRA
AFFECTATION
AGRICULTURE
ANTECHAMBER
ANTICYCLONE
AQUICULTURE
ASSOCIATION
ASSOCIATIVE
BALLCARRIER
CAPACITANCE
CHANCELLERY
COINCIDENCE
DELECTATION
DEMOCRATIZE
DIRECTORATE
EFFICACIOUS
EXPECTATION
EXPECTORANT
EXPECTORATE
FIRECRACKER
FORECLOSURE
GYROCOMPASS
IMPECUNIOUS
INESCAPABLE
INEXCUSABLE
INSECTICIDE
OFFICIALDOM
OFFICIALISM
PREOCCUPIED
RAPSCALLION
RELOCATABLE
SEARCHLIGHT
SWITCHBLADE
SWITCHBOARD
THENCEFORTH
TOBACCONIST
TREACHEROUS
TRENCHERMAN
UNACCOUNTED
VARICOLORED
VITICULTURE
WOODCHOPPER
ARCHDIOCESE
BENEDICTION
BLOODMOBILE
BLOODSTREAM
BLOODSUCKER
BLUNDERBUSS
BREADBASKET
BREADWINNER
CLANDESTINE
DESIDERATUM
DREADNOUGHT
EQUIDISTANT
EXPEDITIOUS
GRANDFATHER
GRANDMOTHER
GRANDPARENT
HAIRDRESSER
HEXADECIMAL
IMPEDIMENTA
IRREDENTISM
IRREDUCIBLE
MALADJUSTED
MALEDICTION
NEANDERTHAL
RESIDENTIAL
SPEEDOMETER
SPENDTHRIFT
STANDARDIZE
THUNDERBOLT
THUNDERCLAP
THUNDERHEAD
VALEDICTION
VALEDICTORY
VIRIDESCENT
ABECEDARIAN
ACADEMICIAN
ACADEMICISM
ADOLESCENCE
AGGREGATION
AMPHETAMINE
APPRECIABLE
BALLETOMANE
BIOFEEDBACK
BITTERSWEET
BLAMEWORTHY
BOILERMAKER
BOYSENBERRY
CANDELABRUM
CASTELLATED
CENTENARIAN
CENTERBOARD
CENTERPIECE
CHOLESTEROL
CLOSEFISTED
COFFEEHOUSE
COMMEMORATE
COMMENTATOR
COMPETITION
CONCENTRATE
CONCERNMENT
CONFEDERACY
CONFEDERATE
CONFESSEDLY
CONSECUTIVE
CONSEQUENCE
CONSERVANCY
CONSERVATOR
CONTEMPLATE
CONTENTMENT
CONVENIENCE
CONVENTICLE
CONVERTIBLE
COOPERATIVE
CORNERSTONE
CORRELATIVE
DECRESCENDO
DEPRECATORY
DEPREDATION
DESPERATION
DISPENSABLE
DISSEMINATE
EPINEPHRINE
EXCEEDINGLY
EXCRESCENCE
FINGERBOARD
FINGERPRINT
FLORESCENCE
GINGERBREAD
GUTTERSNIPE
HELLENISTIC
HERPETOLOGY
HORSEPLAYER
HORSERADISH
HOUSEBROKEN
HOUSEKEEPER
HOUSELIGHTS
HOUSEMOTHER
HYPHENATION
IMAGESETTER
IMPREGNABLE
INCREDULOUS
INCREMENTAL
INOPERATIVE
IRIDESCENCE
JABBERWOCKY
LETTERPRESS
LITTERATEUR
MALFEASANCE
MANTELPIECE
MARKETPLACE
MASTERPIECE
MATHEMATICS
MENDELEVIUM
MINNESINGER
MISBEGOTTEN
MISBELIEVER
MISDEMEANOR
MISFEASANCE
MONKEYSHINE
MONSEIGNEUR
MOTHERBOARD
MUSKELLUNGE
NECKERCHIEF
NETHERWORLD
NICKELODEON
NONDESCRIPT
NONNEGATIVE
NONRESIDENT
NURSERYMAID
ORCHESTRATE
PANDEMONIUM
PENTECOSTAL
PERCEPTIBLE
PERFECTIBLE
PLACEHOLDER
PLANETARIUM
PLANETOLOGY
POCKETKNIFE
POLTERGEIST
PORTERHOUSE
PREDECESSOR
PREMEDITATE
PRETENTIOUS
PRETERMINAL
PRIZEWINNER
PROLETARIAN
PROLETARIAT

PROSELYTIZE
PROVENIENCE
REFRESHMENT
RESPECTABLE
ROTTENSTONE
SENTENTIOUS
SEQUESTRATE
SHAREHOLDER
SPACEFLIGHT
STEREOSCOPE
STEREOSCOPY
STEREOTYPED
STOREKEEPER
SUBMERSIBLE
SUMMERHOUSE
SUPREMACIST
SUSCEPTIBLE
SYSTEMATIZE
TEMPERAMENT
TEMPERATURE
TEMPESTUOUS
TENDENTIOUS
TERRESTRIAL
THEREABOUTS
THEREWITHAL
TRAGEDIENNE
UNICELLULAR
UNSPEAKABLE
WASHERWOMAN
WASTEBASKET
WHEREABOUTS
WHERESOEVER
WHEREWITHAL
WINTERGREEN
BENEFACTION
BENEFICENCE
BENEFICIARY
CALIFORNIUM
COEFFICIENT
FORMFITTING
HIGHFALUTIN
INDEFINABLE
INDIFFERENT
INEFFECTIVE
INEFFECTUAL
INEFFICIENT
IRREFUTABLE
MANUFACTORY
MANUFACTURE
REINFECTION
SCAFFOLDING
TYPEFOUNDER
WHIFFLETREE
ANTIGRAVITY
ASSIGNATION
ASTIGMATISM
BOURGEOISIE
BRAGGADOCIO
CATEGORICAL
COSIGNATORY
DEMAGNETIZE
DESEGREGATE
EVANGELICAL
HOMOGENEOUS
INDIGESTION
INDIGNATION
POMEGRANATE
PREIGNITION
RECOGNITION
RESIGNATION
ROTOGRAVURE
SMORGASBORD
THOUGHTLESS
TYPOGRAPHER
UNORGANIZED
UNRIGHTEOUS
WRONGHEADED
ANACHRONISM
BACCHANALIA
BEACHCOMBER
BROTHERHOOD
DIAPHORETIC
DOWNHEARTED
EARTHENWARE
ELEPHANTINE
FARTHERMOST
FARTHINGALE
FEATHEREDGE
FORTHCOMING
FURTHERMORE
FURTHERMOST
HALFHEARTED
HARDHEARTED
ICHTHYOLOGY
KINDHEARTED
KITCHENETTE
KITCHENWARE
KWASHIORKOR
LATCHSTRING
LEATHERNECK
LIONHEARTED
MARCHIONESS
MARSHMALLOW
MERCHANDISE
MERCHANTMAN
MISCHIEVOUS
NORTHEASTER
NYMPHOMANIA
PITCHBLENDE
PROPHYLAXIS
PSYCHEDELIA
PSYCHEDELIC
PSYCHODRAMA
PSYCHOGENIC
PULCHRITUDE
SMITHEREENS
STETHOSCOPE
SYNCHROMESH
SYNCHRONIZE
SYNCHRONOUS
SYNTHESIZER
THITHERWARD
TRICHINOSIS
TRUEHEARTED
UNINHIBITED
WARMHEARTED
WEATHERCOCK
WEATHERWORN
WHICHSOEVER
ABOMINATION
ACCLIMATIZE
ACQUIREMENT
ACQUISITION
ACQUISITIVE
APPLICATION
APPOINTMENT
ARCHIPELAGO
ATTRIBUTIVE
BARBITURATE
BELLIGERENT
BIBLIOPHILE
CALCIFEROUS
CALLIGRAPHY
CANDIDATURE
CANNIBALIZE
CARDINALATE
CARDINALITY
CARDIOGRAPH
CARMINATIVE
CARNIVOROUS
CASSITERITE
CAULIFLOWER
CERTIFICATE
CLERICALISM
COMBINATION
COMMINATION
COMMISERATE
CONDITIONAL
CONDITIONED
CONSIDERATE
CONSIDERING
CONSIGNMENT
CONSISTENCE
CONSISTENCY
CONTINENTAL
CONTINGENCY
CONTINUANCE
CORRIGENDUM
CRIMINOLOGY
CRUCIFIXION
DEPRIVATION
DESTINATION
DISSIMULATE
DISTINCTION
DISTINCTIVE
DISTINGUISH
EDIFICATION
FASHIONABLE
FORNICATION
FURNISHINGS
GALLIMAUFRY
GARNISHMENT
GESTICULATE
GRANITEWARE
GRAVITATION
HANDICAPPER
HERBIVOROUS
HERRINGBONE
HOSPITALITY
HOSPITALIZE
HUMMINGBIRD
IMAGINATION
IMBRICATION
IMPUISSANCE
INALIENABLE
INCLINATION
INCRIMINATE
INQUISITION
INQUISITIVE
INSPIRATION
INSTITUTION
LACRIMATION
LATTICEWORK
LILLIPUTIAN
MACHINATION
MAGNIFICENT
MATRICULATE
MELLIFLUOUS
METRICATION
MILLIAMPERE
MILLIONAIRE
MILLISECOND
MOCKINGBIRD
MULTIFAMILY
MULTIRACIAL
NONVIOLENCE
NOTHINGNESS
NOURISHMENT
OPINIONATED
OUTDISTANCE
PARTICIPATE
PARTICULATE
PERMISSIBLE
PESTIFEROUS
PHARISAICAL
PHYSIOGNOMY
POLLINATION
PONTIFICALS
PONTIFICATE
PORTIONLESS
PRECIPITATE
PRECIPITOUS
PREDICAMENT
PREHISTORIC
PRELIMINARY
PRIMITIVISM
PROHIBITION
PROLIFERATE
PROMISCUOUS
PROPINQUITY
PROVISIONAL
PUBLICATION
QUALITATIVE
RECRIMINATE
RECTILINEAR
REFRIGERATE
RENAISSANCE
REPLICATION
REQUIREMENT
REQUISITION
RESPIRATION
RESTITUTION
RETRIBUTION
SENSIBILITY
SENTIMENTAL
SERVICEABLE
SIGNIFICANT
STRAIGHTWAY
STRAITLACED
SUBSISTENCE
SUFFICIENCY
TERMINOLOGY
TERRITORIAL
TESTIMONIAL
THALIDOMIDE
TONSILLITIS
TREPIDATION
TRINIDADIAN
TRINITARIAN
UNALIENABLE
UNFLINCHING
UNIFICATION
UNPRINTABLE
UNTHINKABLE
UTILITARIAN
VACCINATION
VENTILATION
VERMICULITE
VERTIGINOUS
VINAIGRETTE
VINDICATION
BLOCKBUSTER
BREAKPOINTS
CHOCKABLOCK
CRACKERJACK
FRANKFURTER
KNUCKLEBONE
QUACKSALVER
QUICKSILVER
SAFEKEEPING
STOCKBROKER
STOCKHOLDER
STOCKINETTE
ACCELERANDO
ACCELERATOR
APPELLATION
BATTLEFIELD
BATTLEWAGON
CANDLELIGHT
CANDLESTICK
CAPILLARITY
COBBLESTONE
COCKLESHELL
COMPLACENCE
COMPLACENCY
COMPLICATED
DEFALCATION
DERELICTION
DISILLUSION
DISPLEASURE
DRILLMASTER
EQUILATERAL
EQUILIBRIUM
EVERLASTING
FAMILIARITY
FIDDLESTICK
GENTLEWOMAN
HUCKLEBERRY
INTELLIGENT
INTOLERABLE
INVOLUNTARY
IRRELIGIOUS
LAMPLIGHTER
LEVELHEADED
MEGALOMANIA
MEGALOPOLIS
MESALLIANCE
MISALLIANCE
MODULARIZED
MONOLINGUAL
NEEDLEPOINT
NEEDLEWOMAN
OBSOLESCENT
PENULTIMATE
PROBLEMATIC
RATTLESNAKE
RESPLENDENT
SCHOLARSHIP
SHELLACKING
SOLILOQUIZE
SPELLBINDER
SWALLOWTAIL
TOTALIZATOR
TRAILBLAZER
UNRELENTING
WHEELBARROW
WHEELWRIGHT
ZOOPLANKTON
ACCOMMODATE
ACCUMULATOR
ASSEMBLYMAN
CEREMONIOUS
DENOMINATOR
DOCUMENTARY
DYNAMOMETER
EXTEMPORARY
EXTEMPORIZE
FOULMOUTHED
FRAGMENTARY
IGNOMINIOUS
ILLIMITABLE
INCOMPETENT
INDOMITABLE
INNUMERABLE
IRREMOVABLE
LOUDMOUTHED
PARAMEDICAL
PERAMBULATE
PORTMANTEAU
REGIMENTALS
REMEMBRANCE
RESEMBLANCE
SCRUMPTIOUS
SEISMOGRAPH
SEISMOMETER
STEAMROLLER
THERMOCLINE
THERMOMETER
TRIUMVIRATE
UNCOMMITTED
UNREMITTING
WIDEMOUTHED
WORKMANLIKE
WORKMANSHIP
ABSENTEEISM
AERONAUTICS
ANNUNCIATOR
ANTINEUTRON
BICENTENARY
BUSINESSMAN
CABINETWORK
CEMENTATION

CHRONOGRAPH
CHRONOMETER
COLONIALISM
DELINQUENCY
DEMONSTRATE
DESENSITIZE
DISENCUMBER
DISENTANGLE
ENGINEERING
EXPENDITURE
FARINACEOUS
FLANNELETTE
FORTNIGHTLY
GERONTOLOGY
GREENGROCER
GROUNDSHEET
GROUNDWATER
INCANTATION
INCINERATOR
INCONGRUENT
INCONGRUOUS
INCONTINENT
INCUNABULUM
INDENTATION
INFANTICIDE
INSINUATING
INTENTIONAL
JUVENOCRACY
MELANCHOLIA
MELANCHOLIC
MISANTHROPE
MOMENTARILY
OSTENTATION
PARENTHESIS
PERSNICKETY
PLAINSPOKEN
POLYNOMINAL
PROGNATHOUS
RECONNOITER
RECONSTRUCT
REMINISCENT
REMONSTRANT
REMONSTRATE
ROMANTICISM
SERENDIPITY
SPRINGBOARD
STRANGULATE
TECHNOCRACY
TRIANGULATE
UNCONCERNED
UNCONSCIOUS
WITENAGEMOT
ACKNOWLEDGE
AGGLOMERATE
ANTIOXIDANT
APHRODISIAC
APPROBATION
APPROPRIATE
APPROXIMATE
AUDIOVISUAL
BOUTONNIERE
BURGOMASTER
CARTOGRAPHY
CATHOLICITY
CHIROGRAPHY
COGNOSCENTE
COLLOCATION
COMFORTABLE
COMMONPLACE
COMPORTMENT
COMPOSITION
CONCOMITANT
CONCORDANCE
CONDOMINIUM
CONFORMANCE
CONNOISSEUR
CONNOTATION
CONNOTATIVE
CONSOLIDATE
CONVOCATION
CONVOLUTION
COPROCESSOR
CORPORATION
CORROBORATE
COTTONMOUTH
CUSTOMHOUSE
DEFLORATION
DESPONDENCY
DIAMONDBACK
DIPLOMATIST
DISCONTINUE
DISCOTHEQUE
DISCOURTESY
DISPOSITION
DISSOLUTION
EXPROPRIATE
FILMOGRAPHY
GEOPOLITICS
HAEMORRHAGE
HAGIOGRAPHY
HISTORICITY
HOMEOSTASIS
HYDROCARBON
HYDROGENATE
HYDROGRAPHY
HYDROPHOBIA
HYDROPONICS
HYDROSPHERE
HYDROSTATIC
HYGROSCOPIC
IMPROPRIETY
IMPROVEMENT
IMPROVIDENT
LITHOGRAPHY
LITHOSPHERE
MACROBIOTIC
MACROSCOPIC
MEADOWSWEET
METEOROLOGY
METHODOLOGY
MICROCAPSUL
MICROSCOPIC
MICROSECOND
MISCONCEIVE
MISCONSTRUE
MUTTONCHOPS
NATIONALISM
NATIONALIST
NATIONALITY
NATIONALIZE
NONDOCUMENT
OPPROBRIOUS
ORTHODONTIA
ORTHOGRAPHY
ORTHOPEDICS
OZONOSPHERE
PALEOGRAPHY
PERFORMANCE
PERIODONTAL
PERSONALITY
PERSONALIZE
PETROGRAPHY
PHILOSOPHER
PHOTOGRAPHY
PHOTOSPHERE
PORNOGRAPHY
PRECONCEIVE
PREDOMINATE
PREMONITION
PREPOSITION
PREROGATIVE
PROPOSITION
PROTOMARTYR
RADIOCARBON
RADIOMETRIC
RATIONALISM
RATIONALITY
RATIONALIZE
REPROBATION
RESPONSIBLE
RESTORATION
RESTORATIVE
RETROACTIVE
SARCOPHAGUS
SCHOOLHOUSE
STENOGRAPHY
SUPPOSITION
SUPPOSITORY
SYNCOPATION
TROPOSPHERE
UNAVOIDABLE
UNWHOLESOME
VIOLONCELLO
ZOOMORPHISM
ACCEPTATION
ANTIPOVERTY
CONSPICUOUS
DILAPIDATED
DISAPPROVAL
ENCAPSULATE
EXCEPTIONAL
INDEPENDENT
INOPPORTUNE
INSEPARABLE
INSUPERABLE
IRREPARABLE
MALAPROPISM
METAPHYSICS
OMNIPRESENT
PERIPATETIC
PERIPHRASIS
PERSPECTIVE
PERSPICUOUS
PROMPTITUDE
REALPOLITIK
RECIPROCATE
RECIPROCITY
SLEEPWALKER
SWEEPSTAKES
TEASPOONFUL
TELEPRINTER
WHIPPLETREE
WORDPERFECT
ANTIQUARIAN
FOREQUARTER
HINDQUARTER
TRANQUILIZE
ABSTRACTION
ACCORDINGLY
ADVERSATIVE
ADVERTISING
AFFIRMATIVE
AFTERBURNER
AFTEREFFECT
ALTERCATION
ALTERNATIVE
AVOIRDUPOIS
BICARBONATE
CALORIMETER
CAMARADERIE
CAMEROONIAN
CATERCORNER
CATERPILLAR
CENTRIFUGAL
CENTRIPETAL
CHEERLEADER
CHIAROSCURO
CHLOROPHYLL
CHOIRMASTER
CLAIRVOYANT
CLEARHEADED
COLORCASTER
CONGRESSMAN
CONTRACTILE
CONTRAPTION
CONTRARIETY
CONTRETEMPS
CONTRIVANCE
CONTROVERSY
CONURBATION
COTERMINOUS
CYBERNATION
CYBERNETICS
DESCRIPTION
DESTRUCTION
DETERIORATE
DETERMINANT
DETERMINATE
DETERMINISM
DIFFRACTION
DISCREPANCY
DISORGANIZE
DISTRIBUTOR
DOCTRINAIRE
ENVIRONMENT
EXPERIENCED
EXTERMINATE
FLOORWALKER
FLUOROSCOPE
GENERALSHIP
HABERDASHER
HISTRIONICS
HYPERACTIVE
HYPERBOREAN
HYPERTROPHY
IMMORTALITY
IMMORTALIZE
IMPERFORATE
IMPERIALISM
IMPERMANENT
IMPERMEABLE
IMPERSONATE
IMPERTINENT
IMPORTATION
IMPORTUNATE
INCARCERATE
INCARNADINE
INCARNATION
INCERTITUDE
INCORPORATE
INCORPOREAL
INFORMATION
INFORMATIVE
INNERSPRING
INSCRUTABLE
INSTRUCTION
INSTRUCTIVE
INTERACTION
INTERACTIVE
INTERATOMIC
INTERCALARY
INTERCALATE
INTERCEPTOR
INTERCHANGE
INTERCOURSE
INTERESTING
INTERLACING
INTERLINEAR
INTERLINING
INTERMEDDLE
INTERMINGLE
INTERNECINE
INTERNUNCIO
INTEROFFICE
INTERPOLATE
INTERPRETER
INTERRACIAL
INTERREGNUM
INTERRELATE
INTERROGATE
INTERSPERSE
LABORSAVING
LASERWRITER
LEGERDEMAIN
LIBERTARIAN
MALPRACTICE
MATERIALISM
MATERIALIZE
MEMORABILIA
OBSERVATION
OBSERVATORY
OBSTRUCTION
OPPORTUNISM
OPPORTUNITY
PAPERHANGER
PAPERWEIGHT
PATERNALISM
PORTRAITIST
PORTRAITURE
PROCRUSTEAN
PROGRAMMING
PROGRESSION
PROGRESSIVE
PROPRIETARY
QUADRENNIAL
QUADRENNIUM
REFORMATION
REFORMATORY
REGURGITATE
RESERVATION
RESTRICTION
REVERBERATE
REVERENTIAL
SOVEREIGNTY
SUBORDINATE
SUBTROPICAL
SUBURBANITE
SUFFRAGETTE
SUPERFICIAL
SUPERFLUOUS
SUPERIMPOSE
SUPERINTEND
SUPERLATIVE
SUPERMARKET
SUPERSCRIBE
SUPERSCRIPT
SUPERSONICS
SUPPRESSANT
THEORETICAL
TOPDRESSING
TUBERCULATE
UNCERTAINTY
UNCHRISTIAN
UNDERCHARGE
UNDEREXPOSE
UNDERGROUND
UNDERGROWTH
UNDERHANDED
UNDERSHORTS
UNDERSIGNED
UNDERTAKING
UNDERWEIGHT
UNFORTUNATE
UNVARNISHED
VENTRILOQUY
WATERCOURSE
WATERLOGGED
ANAESTHESIA
ASSASSINATE
BACKSTRETCH
BREASTPLATE
CARDSHARPER
CATASTROPHE
CHEESECLOTH
CHRISTENDOM
CHRISTIANIA
CRAPSHOOTER
DISASSEMBLE
DOMESTICATE
DOMESTICITY
EXPOSTULATE
FORESHORTEN
GLOSSOLALIA
GRASSHOPPER
GREASEPAINT
HAIRSTYLIST
HANDSHAKING
HARPSICHORD
HOMESTEADER

HOME**S**TRETCH
ILLU**S**IONISM
ILLU**S**TRIOUS
IMPA**S**SIONED
INDU**S**TRIOUS
INVE**S**TIGATE
INVE**S**TITURE
KINE**S**THESIA
LEGI**S**LATION
LEGI**S**LATIVE
LEGI**S**LATURE
LICK**S**PITTLE
LOUD**S**PEAKER
MAGI**S**TERIAL
MAID**S**ERVANT
MINE**S**WEEPER
MONA**S**TICISM
NEAR**S**IGHTED
NECE**S**SITATE
NECE**S**SITOUS
NUMI**S**MATICS
OVER**S**TUFFED
PAIN**S**TAKING
PARI**S**HIONER
PERI**S**TALSIS
PHRA**S**EOLOGY
PLEA**S**URABLE
POLY**S**TYRENE
PREA**S**SIGNED
RATH**S**KELLER
RECE**S**SIONAL
RESI**S**TIVITY
RESU**S**CITATE
SUBA**S**SEMBLY
TIME**S**HARING
TOWN**S**PEOPLE
TRAN**S**ACTION
TRAN**S**CEIVER
TRAN**S**FIGURE
TRAN**S**LUCENT
TRAN**S**MITTER
TRAN**S**PARENT
TYPE**S**ETTING
UNDE**S**IGNING
UNDE**S**IRABLE
VICI**S**SITUDE
VIVI**S**ECTION
WAIN**S**COTING
WORK**S**TATION
ABOR**T**IONIST
AMON**T**ILLADO
ANAS**T**OMOSIS
ARBI**T**RAMENT
ARIS**T**OCRACY
BIME**T**ALLISM
CHAN**T**ICLEER
COEX**T**ENSIVE

COMP**T**ROLLER
CONS**T**ITUENT
COUN**T**ENANCE
COUN**T**ERFEIT
COUN**T**ERMAND
COUN**T**ERPANE
COUN**T**ERPART
COUN**T**ERSIGN
COUN**T**ERSINK
COUN**T**ERVAIL
COUN**T**RIFIED
COUN**T**RYSIDE
CRES**T**FALLEN
CRYS**T**ALLIZE
DELE**T**ERIOUS
DICO**T**YLEDON
DOWN**T**RODDEN
EINS**T**EINIUM
ELEC**T**IONEER
ELEC**T**RICIAN
ELEC**T**RICITY
ELEC**T**ROCUTE
ELEC**T**ROFORM
ELEC**T**ROLYTE
ELEC**T**RONICS
ELEC**T**ROTYPE
ENDO**T**HERMIC
EVEN**T**UALITY
FAUL**T**FINDER
FORE**T**HOUGHT
FREE**T**HINKER
FUNC**T**IONARY
GEAN**T**ICLINE
HABI**T**UATION
HEAR**T**BROKEN
HEAR**T**HSTONE
HYPO**T**HECATE
HYPO**T**HESIZE
IDEN**T**IFIERS
IMMI**T**IGABLE
INAT**T**ENTION
INES**T**IMABLE
INGA**T**HERING
KLEP**T**OMANIA
LIGH**T**WEIGHT
MERI**T**OCRACY
MERI**T**ORIOUS
MOUN**T**AINEER
MOUN**T**AINTOP
NAPH**T**HALENE
NIGH**T**INGALE
NIGH**T**WALKER
NONE**T**HELESS
ORNI**T**HOLOGY
OUTS**T**ANDING
PARA**T**HYROID
PARA**T**ROOPER

PARA**T**YPHOID
PENE**T**RATING
PERI**T**ONITIS
POIN**T**ILLISM
POLY**T**ECHNIC
PRAC**T**ICABLE
PROS**T**ATITIS
PROS**T**HETICS
PUNC**T**ILIOUS
PUNC**T**UATION
QUAR**T**ERBACK
QUAR**T**ERDECK
REAC**T**IONARY
REPE**T**ITIOUS
SCIN**T**ILLATE
SCUT**T**LEBUTT
SEMI**T**RAILER
SHOR**T**CHANGE
SHOR**T**COMING
SHOR**T**HANDED
SHUT**T**LECOCK
SPEC**T**ACULAR
SPEC**T**ROGRAM
SPON**T**ANEOUS
SUBS**T**ANDARD
SUBS**T**ANTIAL
SUBS**T**ANTIVE
THEA**T**RICALS
THIS**T**LEDOWN
TIGH**T**FISTED
TOAS**T**MASTER
TRUS**T**EESHIP
TRUS**T**WORTHY
UNMI**T**IGATED
UNOB**T**RUSIVE
UNSA**T**URATED
UNUT**T**ERABLE
VACA**T**IONIST
ACCO**U**NTABLE
ACUP**U**NCTURE
AGGL**U**TINATE
CALC**U**LATING
CALC**U**LATION
CIRC**U**LARITY
CIRC**U**LARIZE
CIRC**U**MLUNAR
CIRC**U**MPOLAR
CIRC**U**MSPECT
COED**U**CATION
COMB**U**STIBLE
COME**U**PPANCE
COMM**U**NICANT
COMM**U**NICATE
COMM**U**TATION
COMM**U**TATIVE
COMP**U**NCTION
COMP**U**TERIZE

CONC**U**RRENCE
COND**U**CTANCE
CONJ**U**GATION
CONJ**U**NCTION
CONJ**U**NCTIVA
CONJ**U**NCTIVE
CONJ**U**NCTURE
CONS**U**MERISM
CONS**U**MPTION
CONS**U**MPTIVE
CREP**U**SCULAR
DISP**U**TATION
DISQ**U**IETUDE
EXHA**U**STLESS
HALL**U**CINATE
INEL**U**CTABLE
INSO**U**CIANCE
LING**U**ISTICS
MALF**U**NCTION
MARQ**U**ISETTE
MEAS**U**REMENT
MEDI**U**MISTIC
MENS**U**RATION
MISG**U**IDANCE
MUSC**U**LATURE
OUTB**U**ILDING
PART**U**RITION
PERF**U**NCTORY
PERM**U**TATION
PICT**U**RESQUE
PRES**U**MPTION
PROT**U**BERANT
REDO**U**BTABLE
SUBJ**U**NCTIVE
TRIB**U**LATION
UNEQ**U**IVOCAL
UNTO**U**CHABLE
VENT**U**RESOME
AMBI**V**ALENCE
ANNI**V**ERSARY
BEHA**V**IORISM
BENE**V**OLENCE
CARA**V**ANSARY
FORE**V**ERMORE
INAD**V**ERTENT
INDI**V**IDUATE
INDI**V**ISIBLE
IRRE**V**ERENCE
IRRE**V**OCABLE
TWEL**V**EMONTH
UNCI**V**ILIZED
UNDE**V**IATING
UNFA**V**ORABLE
HAND**W**RITING
HARD**W**ORKING
OVER**W**EENING
OVER**W**ROUGHT

SCRE**W**DRIVER
STRA**W**FLOWER
TYPE**W**RITING
APOC**Y**NTHION
BATH**Y**SCAPHE
BATH**Y**SPHERE
GEOS**Y**NCLINE
GERR**Y**MANDER
HEAV**Y**WEIGHT
HONE**Y**SUCKLE
MERR**Y**MAKING
MOLL**Y**CODDLE
MONE**Y**LENDER
NINN**Y**HAMMER
PACH**Y**SANDRA
PENN**Y**WEIGHT
STOR**Y**TELLER
TACH**Y**CARDIA
VICH**Y**SSOISE

## 6th Letter

ABRAC**A**DABRA
ABSTR**A**CTION
AERON**A**UTICS
AMBIV**A**LENCE
BACCH**A**NALIA
BALLC**A**RRIER
BENEF**A**CTION
BIMET**A**LLISM
BRAGG**A**DOCIO
CAMAR**A**DERIE
CARAV**A**NSARY
CHOCK**A**BLOCK
COMPL**A**CENCE
COMPL**A**CENCY
CONTR**A**CTILE
CONTR**A**PTION
CONTR**A**RIETY
CRYST**A**LLIZE
DIFFR**A**CTION
EFFIC**A**CIOUS
ELEPH**A**NTINE
EQUIL**A**TERAL
EVERL**A**STING
FARIN**A**CEOUS
GENER**A**LSHIP
HIGHF**A**LUTIN
HYPER**A**CTIVE
INCUN**A**BULUM
INESC**A**PABLE
INSEP**A**RABLE
INTER**A**CTION
INTER**A**CTIVE
INTER**A**TOMIC

IRREP**A**RABLE
MALFE**A**SANCE
MALPR**A**CTICE
MANUF**A**CTORY
MANUF**A**CTURE
MEMOR**A**BILIA
MERCH**A**NDISE
MERCH**A**NTMAN
MILLI**A**MPERE
MISFE**A**SANCE
MODUL**A**RIZED
MOUNT**A**INEER
MOUNT**A**INTOP
OUTST**A**NDING
OVERB**A**LANCE
PERIP**A**TETIC
PORTM**A**NTEAU
PORTR**A**ITIST
PORTR**A**ITURE
PROGN**A**THOUS
PROGR**A**MMING
PROST**A**TITIS
RAPSC**A**LLION
RELOC**A**TABLE
RETRO**A**CTIVE
SCHOL**A**RSHIP
SHELL**A**CKING
SMORG**A**SBORD
SPECT**A**CULAR
SPONT**A**NEOUS
STAND**A**RDIZE
SUBST**A**NDARD
SUBST**A**NTIAL
SUBST**A**NTIVE
SUFFR**A**GETTE
THERE**A**BOUTS
TRANS**A**CTION
UNORG**A**NIZED
UNSPE**A**KABLE
WHERE**A**BOUTS
WITEN**A**GEMOT
WORKM**A**NLIKE
WORKM**A**NSHIP
ZOOPL**A**NKTON
AFTER**B**URNER
ALPHA**B**ETIZE
APPRO**B**ATION
ASSEM**B**LYMAN
ATTRI**B**UTIVE
BICAR**B**ONATE
BLOCK**B**USTER
BREAD**B**ASKET
CANNI**B**ALIZE
COLLA**B**ORATE
CONUR**B**ATION
CORRO**B**ORATE
ELIZA**B**ETHAN

HEART**B**ROKEN
HOUSE**B**ROKEN
HYPER**B**OREAN
INSTA**B**ILITY
MACRO**B**IOTIC
OPPRO**B**RIOUS
PERAM**B**ULATE
PITCH**B**LENDE
PROHI**B**ITION
PROTU**B**ERANT
REDOU**B**TABLE
REMEM**B**RANCE
REPRO**B**ATION
RESEM**B**LANCE
RETRI**B**UTION
REVER**B**ERATE
ROADA**B**ILITY
SENSI**B**ILITY
SPELL**B**INDER
STOCK**B**ROKER
SUBUR**B**ANITE
TRAIL**B**LAZER
WASTE**B**ASKET
WHEEL**B**ARROW
ALTER**C**ATION
ANNUN**C**IATOR
APPLI**C**ATION
APPRE**C**IABLE
BEACH**C**OMBER
CATER**C**ORNER
CLERI**C**ALISM
CLIMA**C**TERIC
COEDU**C**ATION
COLLO**C**ATION
COLOR**C**ASTER
CONDU**C**TANCE
CONSE**C**UTIVE
CONVO**C**ATION
COPRO**C**ESSOR
DEFAL**C**ATION
DEPRE**C**ATORY
DISEN**C**UMBER
EDIFI**C**ATION
EMPLA**C**EMENT
FORNI**C**ATION
FORTH**C**OMING
GESTI**C**ULATE
HALLU**C**INATE
HANDI**C**APPER
HYDRO**C**ARBON
IMBRI**C**ATION
IMPRA**C**TICAL
INCAR**C**ERATE
INELU**C**TABLE
INSOU**C**IANCE
INTER**C**ALARY
INTER**C**ALATE

INTERCEPTOR
INTERCHANGE
INTERCOURSE
INTRACTABLE
LATTICEWORK
MASSACHUSET
MATRICULATE
MELANCHOLIA
MELANCHOLIC
METRICATION
MICROCAPSUL
MOLLYCODDLE
NONDOCUMENT
PARTICIPATE
PARTICULATE
PENTECOSTAL
PERFECTIBLE
PREDECESSOR
PREDICAMENT
PREOCCUPIED
PUBLICATION
RADIOCARBON
REPLACEMENT
REPLICATION
RESPECTABLE
RESUSCITATE
SERVICEABLE
SHORTCHANGE
SHORTCOMING
STOMACHACHE
SUFFICIENCY
TACHYCARDIA
TOBACCONIST
TRANSCEIVER
TUBERCULATE
UNCONCERNED
UNDERCHARGE
UNIFICATION
UNTOUCHABLE
VERMICULITE
VINDICATION
WAINSCOTING
WATERCOURSE
ABECEDARIAN
ACCORDINGLY
APHRODISIAC
AVOIRDUPOIS
CANDIDATURE
CONFEDERACY
CONFEDERATE
CONSIDERATE
CONSIDERING
DEPREDATION
EXCEEDINGLY
EXPENDITURE
EXTRADITION
GROUNDSHEET

GROUNDWATER
HABERDASHER
INCREDULOUS
LABRADORITE
LEGERDEMAIN
METHODOLOGY
ORTHODONTIA
PERIODONTAL
PREMEDITATE
SCREWDRIVER
SERENDIPITY
SPREADSHEET
SUBORDINATE
THALIDOMIDE
TRAGEDIENNE
TREPIDATION
TRINIDADIAN
ACCELERANDO
ACCELERATOR
AFTEREFFECT
ANNIVERSARY
ANTINEUTRON
ARCHAEOLOGY
BATTLEFIELD
BATTLEWAGON
BIOFEEDBACK
BLUNDERBUSS
BOURGEOISIE
BROTHERHOOD
BUSINESSMAN
CABINETWORK
CANDLELIGHT
CANDLESTICK
CHAMBERLAIN
CHAMBERMAID
CHANCELLERY
CHEESECLOTH
CLANDESTINE
COBBLESTONE
COCKLESHELL
COEXTENSIVE
COFFEEHOUSE
CONGRESSMAN
CONTRETEMPS
COUNTENANCE
COUNTERFEIT
COUNTERMAND
COUNTERPANE
COUNTERPART
COUNTERSIGN
COUNTERSINK
COUNTERVAIL
CRACKERJACK
DELETERIOUS
DESIDERATUM
DISCREPANCY
DISPLEASURE

DOCUMENTARY
DOWNHEARTED
EARTHENWARE
EINSTEINIUM
ENGINEERING
EVANGELICAL
FARTHERMOST
FEATHEREDGE
FIDDLESTICK
FLABBERGAST
FLANNELETTE
FOREVERMORE
FRAGMENTARY
FURTHERMORE
FURTHERMOST
GENTLEWOMAN
GREASEPAINT
HALFHEARTED
HARDHEARTED
HEXADECIMAL
HOMOGENEOUS
HUCKLEBERRY
INADVERTENT
INALIENABLE
INATTENTION
INCINERATOR
INDEPENDENT
INDIGESTION
INEFFECTIVE
INEFFECTUAL
INNUMERABLE
INSUPERABLE
INTERESTING
INTOLERABLE
IRREDENTISM
IRREVERENCE
KINDHEARTED
KITCHENETTE
KITCHENWARE
LEATHERNECK
LIONHEARTED
MAIDSERVANT
NEANDERTHAL
NEEDLEPOINT
NEEDLEWOMAN
NORTHEASTER
OBSOLESCENT
OVERBEARING
OVERWEENING
PARAMEDICAL
PERSPECTIVE
PHRASEOLOGY
POLYTECHNIC
PROBLEMATIC
PROGRESSION
PROGRESSIVE
PSYCHEDELIA

PSYCHEDELIC
QUADRENNIAL
QUADRENNIUM
QUARTERBACK
QUARTERDECK
RATTLESNAKE
REGIMENTALS
REINFECTION
RESIDENTIAL
RESPLENDENT
REVERENTIAL
SAFEKEEPING
SMITHEREENS
SOVEREIGNTY
SUPPRESSANT
SYNTHESIZER
THENCEFORTH
THEORETICAL
THITHERWARD
THUNDERBOLT
THUNDERCLAP
THUNDERHEAD
TOPDRESSING
TRUEHEARTED
TRUSTEESHIP
TWELVEMONTH
TYPESETTING
UNALIENABLE
UNDEREXPOSE
UNRELENTING
UNUTTERABLE
VIRIDESCENT
VIVISECTION
WARMHEARTED
WEATHERCOCK
WEATHERWORN
WORDPERFECT
CALCIFEROUS
CAULIFLOWER
CERTIFICATE
CLOSEFISTED
CRESTFALLEN
CRUCIFIXION
FAULTFINDER
FRANKFURTER
GRANDFATHER
IMPERFORATE
INDIFFERENT
MAGNIFICENT
MELLIFLUOUS
MULTIFAMILY
PESTIFEROUS
PONTIFICALS
PONTIFICATE
PROLIFERATE
SIGNIFICANT
SPACEFLIGHT

STRAWFLOWER
SUPERFICIAL
SUPERFLUOUS
TIGHTFISTED
TRANSFIGURE
AGGREGATION
BELLIGERENT
CALLIGRAPHY
CARRAGEENAN
CARTOGRAPHY
CHIROGRAPHY
CONJUGATION
CONSIGNMENT
CORRIGENDUM
DIAMAGNETIC
DISORGANIZE
FILMOGRAPHY
GEOMAGNETIC
GREENGROCER
HAGIOGRAPHY
HYDROGENATE
HYDROGRAPHY
IMPREGNABLE
INCONGRUENT
INCONGRUOUS
LITHOGRAPHY
MISBEGOTTEN
NARRAGANSET
NONNEGATIVE
ORTHOGRAPHY
PALEOGRAPHY
PETROGRAPHY
PHOTOGRAPHY
PORNOGRAPHY
PREROGATIVE
PROTAGONIST
REFRIGERATE
REGURGITATE
SPRINGBOARD
STENOGRAPHY
STRAIGHTWAY
STRANGULATE
TRIANGULATE
UNDERGROUND
UNDERGROWTH
VERTIGINOUS
VINAIGRETTE
ANTECHAMBER
CARDSHARPER
CLEARHEADED
CRAPSHOOTER
ENDOTHERMIC
FORESHORTEN
FORETHOUGHT
FREETHINKER
GRASSHOPPER
HANDSHAKING

HEARTHSTONE
HYPOTHECATE
HYPOTHESIZE
INGATHERING
LEVELHEADED
METAPHYSICS
NAPHTHALENE
NINNYHAMMER
NONETHELESS
ORNITHOLOGY
PAPERHANGER
PARATHYROID
PARISHIONER
PERIPHRASIS
PLACEHOLDER
PROSTHETICS
SEARCHLIGHT
SHAREHOLDER
SHORTHANDED
STOCKHOLDER
SWITCHBLADE
SWITCHBOARD
THOUGHTLESS
TIMESHARING
TREACHEROUS
TRENCHERMAN
UNDERHANDED
UNRIGHTEOUS
WOODCHOPPER
WRONGHEADED
ABORTIONIST
AMONTILLADO
ARCHDIOCESE
ASSOCIATION
ASSOCIATIVE
BEHAVIORISM
BENEDICTION
BENEFICENCE
BENEFICIARY
CALORIMETER
CAPACITANCE
CENTRIFUGAL
CENTRIPETAL
CHANTICLEER
COEFFICIENT
COINCIDENCE
COLONIALISM
COMPLICATED
CONNOISSEUR
CONSPICUOUS
CONSTITUENT
CONTRIVANCE
DENOMINATOR
DERELICTION
DESCRIPTION
DETERIORATE
DILAPIDATED

DISQUIETUDE
DISTRIBUTOR
DOCTRINAIRE
ELECTIONEER
EQUIDISTANT
EQUILIBRIUM
EXPEDITIOUS
EXPERIENCED
FAMILIARITY
FARTHINGALE
FORMFITTING
FORTNIGHTLY
FUNCTIONARY
GEANTICLINE
HARPSICHORD
HISTRIONICS
IDENTIFIERS
IGNOMINIOUS
ILLIMITABLE
ILLUSIONISM
IMMITIGABLE
IMPEDIMENTA
IMPERIALISM
INDEFINABLE
INDIVIDUATE
INDIVISIBLE
INDOMITABLE
INDUBITABLE
INEFFICIENT
INESTIMABLE
IRRELIGIOUS
KWASHIORKOR
LAMPLIGHTER
LINGUISTICS
MALEDICTION
MARCHIONESS
MARQUISETTE
MATERIALISM
MATERIALIZE
MISCHIEVOUS
MISGUIDANCE
MONOLINGUAL
MONSEIGNEUR
NEARSIGHTED
NIGHTINGALE
OFFICIALDOM
OFFICIALISM
OUTBUILDING
PERSNICKETY
PERSPICUOUS
POINTILLISM
PRACTICABLE
PROPRIETARY
PUNCTILIOUS
REACTIONARY
REMINISCENT
REPETITIOUS

RESTR**I**CTION
SCINT**I**LLATE
STOCK**I**NETTE
SUPER**I**MPOSE
SUPER**I**NTEND
TOTAL**I**ZATOR
TRICH**I**NOSIS
UNAVO**I**DABLE
UNCHR**I**STIAN
UNCIV**I**LIZED
UNDES**I**GNING
UNDES**I**RABLE
UNDEV**I**ATING
UNEQU**I**VOCAL
UNINH**I**BITED
UNMIT**I**GATED
UNREM**I**TTING
VACAT**I**ONIST
VALED**I**CTION
VALED**I**CTORY
VENTR**I**LOQUY
MALAD**J**USTED
HOUSE**K**EEPER
RATHS**K**ELLER
STORE**K**EEPER
APPEL**L**ATION
CALCU**L**ATING
CALCU**L**ATION
CANDE**L**ABRUM
CAPIL**L**ARITY
CASTE**L**LATED
CATHO**L**ICITY
CHEER**L**EADER
CIRCU**L**ARITY
CIRCU**L**ARIZE
CONSO**L**IDATE
CONVO**L**UTION
CORRE**L**ATIVE
DISIL**L**USION
DISSO**L**UTION
FOREC**L**OSURE
GALLB**L**ADDER
GEOPO**L**ITICS
HOUSE**L**IGHTS
INSTA**L**LMENT
INTEL**L**IGENT
INTER**L**ACING
INTER**L**INEAR
INTER**L**INING
KNUCK**L**EBONE
LEGIS**L**ATION
LEGIS**L**ATIVE
LEGIS**L**ATURE
MANTE**L**PIECE
MENDE**L**EVIUM
MESAL**L**IANCE
MISAL**L**IANCE

MISBE**L**IEVER
MONEY**L**ENDER
MUSCU**L**ATURE
MUSKE**L**LUNGE
NICKE**L**ODEON
PROSE**L**YTIZE
RECTI**L**INEAR
SCHOO**L**HOUSE
SCUTT**L**EBUTT
SHUTT**L**ECOCK
SUPER**L**ATIVE
THIST**L**EDOWN
TONSI**L**LITIS
TRANS**L**UCENT
TRIBU**L**ATION
UNICE**L**LULAR
UNQUA**L**IFIED
UNWHO**L**ESOME
VENTI**L**ATION
WATER**L**OGGED
WHIFF**L**ETREE
WHIPP**L**ETREE
ACADE**M**ICIAN
ACADE**M**ICISM
ACCLA**M**ATION
ACCLI**M**ATIZE
ACCOM**M**ODATE
AFFIR**M**ATIVE
AGGLO**M**ERATE
ASTIG**M**ATISM
BLOOD**M**OBILE
BURGO**M**ASTER
CHOIR**M**ASTER
CIRCU**M**LUNAR
CIRCU**M**POLAR
CIRCU**M**SPECT
COMME**M**ORATE
CONCO**M**ITANT
CONDO**M**INIUM
CONSU**M**ERISM
CONSU**M**PTION
CONSU**M**PTIVE
CONTA**M**INANT
CONTA**M**INATE
CONTE**M**PLATE
COTER**M**INOUS
CUSTO**M**HOUSE
DETER**M**INANT
DETER**M**INATE
DETER**M**INISM
DIPLO**M**ATIST
DISSE**M**INATE
DISSI**M**ULATE
DRILL**M**ASTER
EXTER**M**INATE
FUNDA**M**ENTAL
GALLI**M**AUFRY

GERRY**M**ANDER
GRAND**M**OTHER
HOUSE**M**OTHER
IMPER**M**ANENT
IMPER**M**EABLE
INCRE**M**ENTAL
INCRI**M**INATE
INFLA**M**MABLE
INFOR**M**ATION
INFOR**M**ATIVE
INTER**M**EDDLE
INTER**M**INGLE
LACRI**M**ATION
MARSH**M**ALLOW
MATHE**M**ATICS
MEDIU**M**ISTIC
MERRY**M**AKING
MISDE**M**EANOR
NUMIS**M**ATICS
PANDE**M**ONIUM
PREDO**M**INATE
PRELI**M**INARY
PRESU**M**PTION
PROTO**M**ARTYR
RADIO**M**ETRIC
RECRI**M**INATE
REFOR**M**ATION
REFOR**M**ATORY
SENTI**M**ENTAL
STREA**M**LINED
STREA**M**LINER
SUPER**M**ARKET
SUPRE**M**ACIST
SYSTE**M**ATIZE
TESTI**M**ONIAL
TOAST**M**ASTER
TRANS**M**ITTER
ULTRA**M**ARINE
ULTRA**M**ODERN
UNCOM**M**ITTED
ABOMI**N**ATION
ACCOU**N**TABLE
ACUPU**N**CTURE
ALEXA**N**DRIAN
ALEXA**N**DRINE
ALTER**N**ATIVE
APOCY**N**THION
APPOI**N**TMENT
ASSIG**N**ATION
BOUTO**N**NIERE
BOYSE**N**BERRY
CAMPA**N**OLOGY
CARDI**N**ALATE
CARDI**N**ALITY
CARMI**N**ATIVE
CENTE**N**ARIAN
COMBI**N**ATION

COMMA**N**DMENT
COMME**N**TATOR
COMMI**N**ATION
COMMO**N**PLACE
COMMU**N**ICANT
COMMU**N**ICATE
COMPU**N**CTION
CONCE**N**TRATE
CONJU**N**CTION
CONJU**N**CTIVA
CONJU**N**CTIVE
CONJU**N**CTURE
CONTE**N**TMENT
CONTI**N**ENTAL
CONTI**N**GENCY
CONTI**N**UANCE
CONVE**N**IENCE
CONVE**N**TICLE
COSIG**N**ATORY
COTTO**N**MOUTH
CRIMI**N**OLOGY
CYBER**N**ATION
CYBER**N**ETICS
DEMAG**N**ETIZE
DESPO**N**DENCY
DESTI**N**ATION
DIAMO**N**DBACK
DISCO**N**TINUE
DISPE**N**SABLE
DISTI**N**CTION
DISTI**N**CTIVE
DISTI**N**GUISH
DREAD**N**OUGHT
ENFRA**N**CHISE
GEOSY**N**CLINE
HELLE**N**ISTIC
HERRI**N**GBONE
HUMMI**N**GBIRD
HYPHE**N**ATION
IMAGI**N**ATION
INCAR**N**ADINE
INCAR**N**ATION
INCLI**N**ATION
INDIG**N**ATION
INSTA**N**TIATE
INTER**N**ECINE
INTER**N**UNCIO
MACHI**N**ATION
MAGNA**N**IMOUS
MALFU**N**CTION
MECHA**N**ISTIC
MISCO**N**CEIVE
MISCO**N**STRUE
MOCKI**N**GBIRD
MUTTO**N**CHOPS
NATIO**N**ALISM
NATIO**N**ALIST

NATIO**N**ALITY
NATIO**N**ALIZE
NOTHI**N**GNESS
OUTMA**N**EUVER
PATER**N**ALISM
PERFU**N**CTORY
PERSO**N**ALITY
PERSO**N**ALIZE
POLLI**N**ATION
PRECO**N**CEIVE
PREIG**N**ITION
PREMO**N**ITION
PRETE**N**TIOUS
PROFA**N**ATORY
PROPI**N**QUITY
PROVE**N**IENCE
RATIO**N**ALISM
RATIO**N**ALITY
RATIO**N**ALIZE
RECOG**N**ITION
RECON**N**OITER
RESIG**N**ATION
RESPO**N**SIBLE
ROTTE**N**STONE
SENTE**N**TIOUS
SUBJU**N**CTIVE
TENDE**N**TIOUS
TERMI**N**OLOGY
UNFLI**N**CHING
UNPRI**N**TABLE
UNTHI**N**KABLE
UNVAR**N**ISHED
VACCI**N**ATION
VIOLO**N**CELLO
VOLCA**N**OLOGY
ANAST**O**MOSIS
ANTIP**O**VERTY
ARIST**O**CRACY
BENEV**O**LENCE
BIBLI**O**PHILE
CALIF**O**RNIUM
CAMER**O**ONIAN
CARDI**O**GRAPH
CATEG**O**RICAL
CEREM**O**NIOUS
CHIAR**O**SCURO
CHLOR**O**PHYLL
CHRON**O**GRAPH
CHRON**O**METER
CONTR**O**VERSY
DIAPH**O**RETIC
DYNAM**O**METER
ENVIR**O**NMENT
FASHI**O**NABLE
FLUOR**O**SCOPE
FOULM**O**UTHED
GLOSS**O**LALIA

GYROC**O**MPASS
HARDW**O**RKING
INOPP**O**RTUNE
INTER**O**FFICE
IRREM**O**VABLE
IRREV**O**CABLE
JUVEN**O**CRACY
KLEPT**O**MANIA
LOUDM**O**UTHED
MEGAL**O**MANIA
MEGAL**O**POLIS
MERIT**O**CRACY
MERIT**O**RIOUS
MILLI**O**NAIRE
NONVI**O**LENCE
NYMPH**O**MANIA
OPINI**O**NATED
PERIT**O**NITIS
PHYSI**O**GNOMY
POLYN**O**MINAL
PORTI**O**NLESS
PSYCH**O**DRAMA
PSYCH**O**GENIC
REALP**O**LITIK
SCAFF**O**LDING
SEISM**O**GRAPH
SEISM**O**METER
SOLIL**O**QUIZE
SPEED**O**METER
STERE**O**SCOPE
STERE**O**SCOPY
STERE**O**TYPED
STETH**O**SCOPE
STROB**O**SCOPE
SUBTR**O**PICAL
SWALL**O**WTAIL
TEASP**O**ONFUL
TECHN**O**CRACY
THERM**O**CLINE
THERM**O**METER
TYPEF**O**UNDER
UNACC**O**UNTED
UNFAV**O**RABLE
VARIC**O**LORED
WIDEM**O**UTHED
AGORA**P**HOBIA
APPRO**P**RIATE
ARCHI**P**ELAGO
BREAK**P**OINTS
CATER**P**ILLAR
COMEU**P**PANCE
DISAP**P**ROVAL
EPINE**P**HRINE
EXPRO**P**RIATE
EXTEM**P**ORARY
EXTEM**P**ORIZE
EXTRA**P**OLATE

GRAND**P**ARENT
HORSE**P**LAYER
HYDRO**P**HOBIA
HYDRO**P**ONICS
IMPRO**P**RIETY
INCOM**P**ETENT
INCOR**P**ORATE
INCOR**P**OREAL
INTER**P**OLATE
INTER**P**RETER
LICKS**P**ITTLE
LILLI**P**UTIAN
LOUDS**P**EAKER
ORTHO**P**EDICS
PERCE**P**TIBLE
PRECI**P**ITATE
PRECI**P**ITOUS
SARCO**P**HAGUS
SCRUM**P**TIOUS
SUSCE**P**TIBLE
SYNCO**P**ATION
THERA**P**EUTIC
TOWNS**P**EOPLE
TRANS**P**ARENT
UNFLA**P**PABLE
CONSE**Q**UENCE
DELIN**Q**UENCY
ACQUI**R**EMENT
ANACH**R**ONISM
ANTIG**R**AVITY
ARBIT**R**AMENT
BITTE**R**SWEET
BOILE**R**MAKER
CENTE**R**BOARD
CENTE**R**PIECE
COMFO**R**TABLE
COMPA**R**ATIVE
COMPA**R**TMENT
COMPO**R**TMENT
COMPT**R**OLLER
CONCE**R**NMENT
CONCO**R**DANCE
CONCU**R**RENCE
CONFO**R**MANCE
CONSE**R**VANCY
CONSE**R**VATOR
CONVE**R**TIBLE
COOPE**R**ATIVE
CORNE**R**STONE
CORPO**R**ATION
COUNT**R**IFIED
COUNT**R**YSIDE
DECLA**R**ATIVE
DEFLO**R**ATION
DEMOC**R**ATIZE
DESEG**R**EGATE
DESPE**R**ATION

DOWNTRODDEN
ELECTRICIAN
ELECTRICITY
ELECTROCUTE
ELECTROFORM
ELECTROLYTE
ELECTRONICS
ELECTROTYPE
FINGERBOARD
FINGERPRINT
FIRECRACKER
GENDARMERIE
GINGERBREAD
GUTTERSNIPE
HAEMORRHAGE
HAIRBREADTH
HAIRDRESSER
HANDWRITING
HAREBRAINED
HISTORICITY
HORSERADISH
INOPERATIVE
INSPIRATION
INTERRACIAL
INTERREGNUM
INTERRELATE
INTERROGATE
JABBERWOCKY
LETTERPRESS
LITTERATEUR
LUCUBRATION
MALAPROPISM
MASTERPIECE
MEASUREMENT
MENSURATION
METEOROLOGY
MORTARBOARD
MOTHERBOARD
MULTIRACIAL
NECKERCHIEF
NETHERWORLD
NONPARTISAN
NURSERYMAID
OMNIPRESENT
OVERWROUGHT
PARATROOPER
PARTURITION
PENETRATING
PERFORMANCE
PICTURESQUE
POLTERGEIST
POMEGRANATE
PORTERHOUSE
PRETERMINAL
PREVARICATE
PULCHRITUDE
RECIPROCATE
RECIPROCITY
REQUIREMENT
RESPIRATION
RESTORATION
RESTORATIVE
ROTOGRAVURE
SEMITRAILER
SPECTROGRAM
STEAMROLLER
STEPBROTHER
SUBMERSIBLE
SUMMERHOUSE
SYNCHROMESH
SYNCHRONIZE
SYNCHRONOUS
TELEPRINTER
TEMPERAMENT
TEMPERATURE
THEATRICALS
TYPEWRITING
TYPOGRAPHER
UNOBTRUSIVE
VENTURESOME
WASHERWOMAN
WINTERGREEN
ZOOMORPHISM
ACQUISITION
ACQUISITIVE
ADOLESCENCE
ADVERSATIVE
ASSASSINATE
BATHYSPHERE
BATHYSCAPHE
BLOODSTREAM
BLOODSUCKER
CHOLESTEROL
COGNOSCENTE
COMBUSTIBLE
COMMISERATE
COMPOSITION
CONFESSEDLY
CONSISTENCE
CONSISTENCY
CREPUSCULAR
DECRESCENDO
DEMONSTRATE
DESENSITIZE
DISASSEMBLE
DISPOSITION
ENCAPSULATE
EXCRESCENCE
EXHAUSTLESS
FLORESCENCE
FURNISHINGS
GARNISHMENT
HOMEOSTASIS
HONEYSUCKLE
HYDROSPHERE
HYDROSTATIC
HYGROSCOPIC
IMAGESETTER
IMPASSIONED
IMPERSONATE
IMPUISSANCE
INNERSPRING
INQUISITION
INQUISITIVE
INTERSPERSE
IRIDESCENCE
LABORSAVING
LATCHSTRING
LITHOSPHERE
MACROSCOPIC
MICROSCOPIC
MICROSECOND
MILLISECOND
MINNESINGER
NECESSITATE
NECESSITOUS
NONDESCRIPT
NONRESIDENT
NOURISHMENT
ORCHESTRATE
OUTDISTANCE
OZONOSPHERE
PACHYSANDRA
PERMISSIBLE
PHARISAICAL
PHILOSOPHER
PHOTOSPHERE
PLAINSPOKEN
PREASSIGNED
PREHISTORIC
PREPOSITION
PROMISCUOUS
PROPOSITION
PROVISIONAL
QUACKSALVER
QUICKSILVER
RECESSIONAL
RECONSTRUCT
REFRESHMENT
REMONSTRANT
REMONSTRATE
RENAISSANCE
REQUISITION
SEQUESTRATE
SUBASSEMBLY
SUBSISTENCE
SUPERSCRIBE
SUPERSCRIPT
SUPERSONICS
SUPPOSITION
SUPPOSITORY
SWEEPSTAKES
TEMPESTUOUS
TERRESTRIAL
TROPOSPHERE
ULTRASONICS
UNCONSCIOUS
UNDERSHORTS
UNDERSIGNED
UNREASONING
VICHYSSOISE
VICISSITUDE
WHERESOEVER
WHICHSOEVER
ABSENTEEISM
ACCEPTATION
ADVERTISING
AFFECTATION
AGGLUTINATE
AMPHETAMINE
ANAESTHESIA
BACKSTRETCH
BALLETOMANE
BARBITURATE
BICENTENARY
BREASTPLATE
CASSITERITE
CATASTROPHE
CEMENTATION
CHRISTENDOM
CHRISTIANIA
CLIMATOLOGY
COMMUTATION
COMMUTATIVE
COMPETITION
COMPUTERIZE
CONDITIONAL
CONDITIONED
CONNOTATION
CONNOTATIVE
DELECTATION
DERMATOLOGY
DICTATORIAL
DIRECTORATE
DISCOTHEQUE
DISENTANGLE
DISPUTATION
DOMESTICATE
DOMESTICITY
EXCEPTIONAL
EXPECTATION
EXPECTORANT
EXPECTORATE
EXPOSTULATE
GERONTOLOGY
GRANITEWARE
GRAVITATION
HAIRSTYLIST
HERPETOLOGY
HOMESTEADER
HOMESTRETCH
HOSPITALITY
HOSPITALIZE
HYPERTROPHY
ILLUSTRIOUS
IMMORTALITY
IMMORTALIZE
IMPERTINENT
IMPORTATION
IMPORTUNATE
INCANTATION
INCERTITUDE
INCONTINENT
INDENTATION
INDUSTRIOUS
INFANTICIDE
INGRATITUDE
INSECTICIDE
INSTITUTION
INTENTIONAL
INVESTIGATE
INVESTITURE
KINESTHESIA
LIBERTARIAN
MAGISTERIAL
MARKETPLACE
MINIATURIZE
MISANTHROPE
MOMENTARILY
MONASTICISM
OPPORTUNISM
OPPORTUNITY
OSTENTATION
OVERSTUFFED
PAINSTAKING
PARENTHESIS
PENULTIMATE
PERISTALSIS
PERMUTATION
PISCATORIAL
PLANETARIUM
PLANETOLOGY
POCKETKNIFE
POLYSTYRENE
PRIMITIVISM
PROBATIONER
PROLETARIAN
PROLETARIAT
PROMPTITUDE
QUALITATIVE
RESISTIVITY
RESTITUTION
ROMANTICISM
SENSATIONAL
SPENDTHRIFT
STORYTELLER
STRAITLACED
TERRITORIAL
TRINITARIAN
UNCERTAINTY
UNDERTAKING
UNFORTUNATE
UTILITARIAN
WORKSTATION
ACCUMULATOR
AGRICULTURE
ANTIQUARIAN
AQUICULTURE
BUREAUCRACY
DESTRUCTION
DISCOURTESY
EVENTUALITY
FOREQUARTER
GODDAUGHTER
HABITUATION
HINDQUARTER
IMPECUNIOUS
IMPLAUSIBLE
INEXCUSABLE
INSCRUTABLE
INSINUATING
INSTRUCTION
INSTRUCTIVE
INVOLUNTARY
IRREDUCIBLE
IRREFUTABLE
OBSTRUCTION
PLEASURABLE
PROCRUSTEAN
PUNCTUATION
SHIPBUILDER
TRANQUILIZE
UNSATURATED
VITICULTURE
AUDIOVISUAL
CARNIVOROUS
CLAIRVOYANT
DEPRIVATION
EXTRAVAGANT
HERBIVOROUS
IMPROVEMENT
IMPROVIDENT
INTRAVENOUS
OBSERVATION
OBSERVATORY
RESERVATION
TRIUMVIRATE
ULTRAVIOLET
ACKNOWLEDGE
BLAMEWORTHY
BREADWINNER
FLOORWALKER
HEAVYWEIGHT
LASERWRITER
LIGHTWEIGHT
MEADOWSWEET
MINESWEEPER
NIGHTWALKER
PAPERWEIGHT
PENNYWEIGHT
PRIZEWINNER
SLEEPWALKER
THEREWITHAL
TRUSTWORTHY
UNDERWEIGHT
WHEELWRIGHT
WHEREWITHAL
ANTIOXIDANT
APPROXIMATE
ANTICYCLONE
DICOTYLEDON
ICHTHYOLOGY
MONKEYSHINE
PARATYPHOID
PROPHYLAXIS

## 7TH LETTER

ABECEDARIAN
ABOMINATION
ACCEPTATION
ACCLAMATION
ACCLIMATIZE
ADVERSATIVE
AFFECTATION
AFFIRMATIVE
AGGREGATION
ALTERCATION
ALTERNATIVE
AMPHETAMINE
ANTECHAMBER
ANTIGRAVITY
ANTIQUARIAN
APPELLATION
APPLICATION
APPROBATION
ARBITRAMENT
ASSIGNATION
ASSOCIATION
ASSOCIATIVE
ASTIGMATISM
BREADBASKET
BURGOMASTER
CALCULATING
CALCULATION
CANDELABRUM
CANDIDATURE

CANNIBALIZE
CAPILLARITY
CARDINALATE
CARDINALITY
CARDSHARPER
CARMINATIVE
CEMENTATION
CENTENARIAN
CHOIRMASTER
CIRCULARITY
CIRCULARIZE
CLERICALISM
COEDUCATION
COLLOCATION
COLONIALISM
COLORCASTER
COMBINATION
COMMINATION
COMMUTATION
COMMUTATIVE
COMPARATIVE
CONJUGATION
CONNOTATION
CONNOTATIVE
CONURBATION
CONVOCATION
COOPERATIVE
CORPORATION
CORRELATIVE
COSIGNATORY
CRESTFALLEN
CYBERNATION
DECLARATIVE
DEFALCATION
DEFLORATION
DELECTATION
DEMOCRATIZE
DEPRECATORY
DEPREDATION
DEPRIVATION
DESPERATION
DESTINATION
DIPLOMATIST
DISENTANGLE
DISORGANIZE
DISPLEASURE
DISPUTATION
DOWNHEARTED
DRILLMASTER
EDIFICATION
EVENTUALITY
EXPECTATION
EXTRAVAGANT
FAMILIARITY
FIRECRACKER
FLOORWALKER
FOREQUARTER
FORNICATION
GALLBLADDER
GALLIMAUFRY
GERRYMANDER
GRANDFATHER
GRANDPARENT
GRAVITATION
HABERDASHER
HABITUATION
HALFHEARTED
HANDICAPPER
HANDSHAKING
HARDHEARTED
HAREBRAINED
HINDQUARTER
HORSERADISH
HOSPITALITY
HOSPITALIZE
HYDROCARBON
HYPHENATION
IMAGINATION
IMBRICATION
IMMORTALITY
IMMORTALIZE
IMPERIALISM
IMPERMANENT
IMPORTATION
INCANTATION
INCARNADINE
INCARNATION
INCLINATION
INDENTATION
INDIGNATION
INFORMATION
INFORMATIVE
INOPERATIVE
INSINUATING
INSPIRATION
INTERCALARY
INTERCALATE
INTERLACING
INTERRACIAL
KINDHEARTED
LABORSAVING
LACRIMATION
LEGISLATION
LEGISLATIVE
LEGISLATURE
LIBERTARIAN
LIONHEARTED
LITTERATEUR
LUCUBRATION
MACHINATION
MARSHMALLOW
MATERIALISM
MATERIALIZE
MATHEMATICS
MENSURATION
MERRYMAKING
METRICATION
MICROCAPSUL
MOMENTARILY
MULTIFAMILY
MULTIRACIAL
MUSCULATURE
NAPHTHALENE
NARRAGANSET
NATIONALISM
NATIONALIST
NATIONALITY
NATIONALIZE
NIGHTWALKER
NINNYHAMMER
NONNEGATIVE
NORTHEASTER
NUMISMATICS
OBSERVATION
OBSERVATORY
OFFICIALDOM
OFFICIALISM
OSTENTATION
OVERBEARING
PACHYSANDRA
PAINSTAKING
PAPERHANGER
PATERNALISM
PENETRATING
PERISTALSIS
PERMUTATION
PERSONALITY
PERSONALIZE
PHARISAICAL
PLANETARIUM
POLLINATION
POMEGRANATE
PREDICAMENT
PREROGATIVE
PROFANATORY
PROLETARIAN
PROLETARIAT
PROTOMARTYR
PUBLICATION
PUNCTUATION
QUACKSALVER
QUALITATIVE
RADIOCARBON
RATIONALISM
RATIONALITY
RATIONALIZE
REFORMATION
REFORMATORY
REPLICATION
REPROBATION
RESERVATION
RESIGNATION
RESPIRATION
RESTORATION
RESTORATIVE
ROTOGRAVURE
SEMITRAILER
SHORTHANDED
SLEEPWALKER
SUBURBANITE
SUPERLATIVE
SUPERMARKET
SUPREMACIST
SYNCOPATION
SYSTEMATIZE
TACHYCARDIA
TEMPERAMENT
TEMPERATURE
TIMESHARING
TOASTMASTER
TRANSPARENT
TREPIDATION
TRIBULATION
TRINIDADIAN
TRINITARIAN
TRUEHEARTED
TYPOGRAPHER
ULTRAMARINE
UNCERTAINTY
UNDERHANDED
UNDERTAKING
UNDEVIATING
UNIFICATION
UTILITARIAN
VACCINATION
VENTILATION
VINDICATION
WARMHEARTED
WASTEBASKET
WHEELBARROW
WORKSTATION
BOYSENBERRY
CENTERBOARD
CHOCKABLOCK
DISTRIBUTOR
EQUILIBRIUM
FINGERBOARD
GINGERBREAD
HUCKLEBERRY
INCUNABULUM
MEMORABILIA
MORTARBOARD
MOTHERBOARD
SPRINGBOARD
SWITCHBLADE
SWITCHBOARD
THEREABOUTS
UNINHIBITED
WHEREABOUTS
ABSTRACTION
ACUPUNCTURE
ADOLESCENCE
ANTICYCLONE
ARISTOCRACY
BATHYSCAPHE
BENEDICTION
BENEFACTION
BENEFICENCE
BENEFICIARY
BUREAUCRACY
CHANTICLEER
CHEESECLOTH
COEFFICIENT
COGNOSCENTE
COMPLACENCE
COMPLACENCY
COMPLICATED
COMPUNCTION
CONJUNCTION
CONJUNCTIVA
CONJUNCTIVE
CONJUNCTURE
CONSPICUOUS
CONTRACTILE
CREPUSCULAR
DECRESCENDO
DERELICTION
DESTRUCTION
DIFFRACTION
DISTINCTION
DISTINCTIVE
EFFICACIOUS
ENFRANCHISE
EXCRESCENCE
FARINACEOUS
FLORESCENCE
GEANTICLINE
GEOSYNCLINE
HARPSICHORD
HEXADECIMAL
HYGROSCOPIC
HYPERACTIVE
INEFFECTIVE
INEFFECTUAL
INEFFICIENT
INSTRUCTION
INSTRUCTIVE
INTERACTION
INTERACTIVE
IRIDESCENCE
IRREDUCIBLE
IRREVOCABLE
JUVENOCRACY
MACROSCOPIC
MALEDICTION
MALFUNCTION
MALPRACTICE
MANUFACTORY
MANUFACTURE
MERITOCRACY
MICROSCOPIC
MISCONCEIVE
MUTTONCHOPS
NECKERCHIEF
NONDESCRIPT
OBSTRUCTION
PERFUNCTORY
PERSNICKETY
PERSPECTIVE
PERSPICUOUS
POLYTECHNIC
PRACTICABLE
PRECONCEIVE
PROMISCUOUS
REINFECTION
RESTRICTION
RETROACTIVE
SHELLACKING
SPECTACULAR
SUBJUNCTIVE
SUPERSCRIBE
SUPERSCRIPT
TECHNOCRACY
THERMOCLINE
TRANSACTION
UNCONSCIOUS
UNFLINCHING
VALEDICTION
VALEDICTORY
VIOLONCELLO
VIVISECTION
ABRACADABRA
ALEXANDRIAN
ALEXANDRINE
BIOFEEDBACK
BRAGGADOCIO
CAMARADERIE
COINCIDENCE
COMMANDMENT
CONCORDANCE
DESPONDENCY
DIAMONDBACK
DILAPIDATED
INDIVIDUATE
MISGUIDANCE
PARAMEDICAL
PSYCHEDELIA
PSYCHEDELIC
PSYCHODRAMA
UNAVOIDABLE
ABSENTEEISM
ACQUIREMENT
AGGLOMERATE
ALPHABETIZE
ARCHIPELAGO
BELLIGERENT
BICENTENARY
CALCIFEROUS
CARRAGEENAN
CASSITERITE
CHEERLEADER
CHRISTENDOM
CLEARHEADED
COMMISERATE
COMPUTERIZE
CONFEDERACY
CONFEDERATE
CONSIDERATE
CONSIDERING
CONSUMERISM
CONTINENTAL
COPROCESSOR
CORRIGENDUM
CYBERNETICS
DEMAGNETIZE
DESEGREGATE
DISASSEMBLE
DISQUIETUDE
ELIZABETHAN
EMPLACEMENT
ENDOTHERMIC
ENGINEERING
EXPERIENCED
FUNDAMENTAL
GRANITEWARE
HAIRBREADTH
HAIRDRESSER
HEAVYWEIGHT
HOMESTEADER
HOUSEKEEPER
HYDROGENATE
HYPOTHECATE
HYPOTHESIZE
IMAGESETTER
IMPERMEABLE
IMPROVEMENT
INCARCERATE
INCOMPETENT
INCREMENTAL
INDIFFERENT
INGATHERING
INTERCEPTOR
INTERMEDDLE
INTERNECINE
INTERREGNUM
INTERRELATE
INTRAVENOUS
KNUCKLEBONE
LATTICEWORK

LEGERD**E**MAIN
LEVELH**E**ADED
LIGHTW**E**IGHT
LOUDSP**E**AKER
MAGIST**E**RIAL
MEASUR**E**MENT
MENDEL**E**VIUM
MICROS**E**COND
MILLIS**E**COND
MINESW**E**EPER
MISCHI**E**VOUS
MISDEM**E**ANOR
MONEYL**E**NDER
NONETH**E**LESS
OMNIPR**E**SENT
ORTHOP**E**DICS
OUTMAN**E**UVER
OVERWE**E**NING
PAPERW**E**IGHT
PENNYW**E**IGHT
PESTIF**E**ROUS
PICTUR**E**SQUE
PREDEC**E**SSOR
PROLIF**E**RATE
PROPRI**E**TARY
PROSTH**E**TICS
PROTUB**E**RANT
RADIOM**E**TRIC
RATHSK**E**LLER
REFRIG**E**RATE
REPLAC**E**MENT
REQUIR**E**MENT
REVERB**E**RATE
SAFEKE**E**PING
SCUTTL**E**BUTT
SENTIM**E**NTAL
SERVIC**E**ABLE
SHUTTL**E**COCK
STOREK**E**EPER
STORYT**E**LLER
SUBASS**E**MBLY
THERAP**E**UTIC
THISTL**E**DOWN
TOWNSP**E**OPLE
TRANSC**E**IVER
TREACH**E**ROUS
TRENCH**E**RMAN
TRUSTE**E**SHIP
UNCONC**E**RNED
UNDERW**E**IGHT
UNWHOL**E**SOME
VENTUR**E**SOME
WHIFFL**E**TREE
WHIPPL**E**TREE
WRONGH**E**ADED
AFTERE**F**FECT
BATTLE**F**IELD
CENTRI**F**UGAL
IDENTI**F**IERS
INTERO**F**FICE
THENCE**F**ORTH
CARDIO**G**RAPH
CHRONO**G**RAPH
CONTIN**G**ENCY
DISTIN**G**UISH
FORTNI**G**HTLY
GODDAU**G**HTER
HERRIN**G**BONE
HUMMIN**G**BIRD
IMMITI**G**ABLE
IRRELI**G**IOUS
LAMPLI**G**HTER
MOCKIN**G**BIRD
MONSEI**G**NEUR
NEARSI**G**HTED
NOTHIN**G**NESS
PHYSIO**G**NOMY
POLTER**G**EIST
PSYCHO**G**ENIC
SEISMO**G**RAPH
SUFFRA**G**ETTE
UNDESI**G**NING
UNMITI**G**ATED
WINTER**G**REEN
WITENA**G**EMOT
AGORAP**H**OBIA
ANAEST**H**ESIA
COFFEE**H**OUSE
CUSTOM**H**OUSE
DISCOT**H**EQUE
EPINEP**H**RINE
FURNIS**H**INGS
GARNIS**H**MENT
HYDROP**H**OBIA
INTERC**H**ANGE
KINEST**H**ESIA
MASSAC**H**USET
MELANC**H**OLIA
MELANC**H**OLIC
MISANT**H**ROPE
NOURIS**H**MENT
PARENT**H**ESIS
PORTER**H**OUSE
REFRES**H**MENT
SARCOP**H**AGUS
SCHOOL**H**OUSE
SHORTC**H**ANGE
SPENDT**H**RIFT
STOMAC**H**ACHE
STRAIG**H**TWAY
SUMMER**H**OUSE
UNDERC**H**ARGE
UNDERS**H**ORTS
UNTOUC**H**ABLE
ACADEM**I**CIAN
ACADEM**I**CISM
ACCORD**I**NGLY
ACQUIS**I**TION
ACQUIS**I**TIVE
ADVERT**I**SING
AGGLUT**I**NATE
ANNUNC**I**ATOR
ANTIOX**I**DANT
APHROD**I**SIAC
APPREC**I**ABLE
APPROX**I**MATE
ASSASS**I**NATE
AUDIOV**I**SUAL
BREADW**I**NNER
CATERP**I**LLAR
CATHOL**I**CITY
CERTIF**I**CATE
CHRIST**I**ANIA
CLOSEF**I**STED
COMMUN**I**CANT
COMMUN**I**CATE
COMPET**I**TION
COMPOS**I**TION
CONCOM**I**TANT
CONDIT**I**ONAL
CONDIT**I**ONED
CONDOM**I**NIUM
CONSOL**I**DATE
CONTAM**I**NANT
CONTAM**I**NATE
CONVEN**I**ENCE
COTERM**I**NOUS
COUNTR**I**FIED
CRUCIF**I**XION
DESENS**I**TIZE
DETERM**I**NANT
DETERM**I**NATE
DETERM**I**NISM
DISPOS**I**TION
DISSEM**I**NATE
DOMEST**I**CATE
DOMEST**I**CITY
EINSTE**I**NIUM
ELECTR**I**CIAN
ELECTR**I**CITY
EXCEED**I**NGLY
EXCEPT**I**ONAL
EXPEND**I**TURE
EXTERM**I**NATE
EXTRAD**I**TION
FAULTF**I**NDER
FREETH**I**NKER
GEOPOL**I**TICS
HALLUC**I**NATE
HANDWR**I**TING
HELLEN**I**STIC
HISTOR**I**CITY
HOUSEL**I**GHTS
IMPASS**I**ONED
IMPERT**I**NENT
IMPROV**I**DENT
INCERT**I**TUDE
INCONT**I**NENT
INCRIM**I**NATE
INFANT**I**CIDE
INGRAT**I**TUDE
INQUIS**I**TION
INQUIS**I**TIVE
INSECT**I**CIDE
INSOUC**I**ANCE
INSTAB**I**LITY
INTELL**I**GENT
INTENT**I**ONAL
INTERL**I**NEAR
INTERL**I**NING
INTERM**I**NGLE
INVEST**I**GATE
INVEST**I**TURE
LICKSP**I**TTLE
MACROB**I**OTIC
MAGNAN**I**MOUS
MAGNIF**I**CENT
MECHAN**I**STIC
MEDIUM**I**STIC
MESALL**I**ANCE
MINNES**I**NGER
MISALL**I**ANCE
MISBEL**I**EVER
MONAST**I**CISM
MOUNTA**I**NEER
MOUNTA**I**NTOP
NECESS**I**TATE
NECESS**I**TOUS
NONRES**I**DENT
PARISH**I**ONER
PARTIC**I**PATE
PARTUR**I**TION
PENULT**I**MATE
PONTIF**I**CALS
PONTIF**I**CATE
PORTRA**I**TIST
PORTRA**I**TURE
PREASS**I**GNED
PRECIP**I**TATE
PRECIP**I**TOUS
PREDOM**I**NATE
PREIGN**I**TION
PRELIM**I**NARY
PREMED**I**TATE
PREMON**I**TION
PREPOS**I**TION
PREVAR**I**CATE
PRIMIT**I**VISM
PRIZEW**I**NNER
PROBAT**I**ONER
PROHIB**I**TION
PROMPT**I**TUDE
PROPOS**I**TION
PROVEN**I**ENCE
PROVIS**I**ONAL
PULCHR**I**TUDE
QUICKS**I**LVER
RECESS**I**ONAL
RECOGN**I**TION
RECRIM**I**NATE
RECTIL**I**NEAR
REGURG**I**TATE
REQUIS**I**TION
RESIST**I**VITY
RESUSC**I**TATE
ROADAB**I**LITY
ROMANT**I**CISM
SENSAT**I**ONAL
SENSIB**I**LITY
SEREND**I**PITY
SHIPBU**I**LDER
SIGNIF**I**CANT
SOVERE**I**GNTY
SPELLB**I**NDER
SUBORD**I**NATE
SUFFIC**I**ENCY
SUPERF**I**CIAL
SUPPOS**I**TION
SUPPOS**I**TORY
TELEPR**I**NTER
THEATR**I**CALS
THEREW**I**THAL
TIGHTF**I**STED
TRAGED**I**ENNE
TRANQU**I**LIZE
TRANSF**I**GURE
TRANSM**I**TTER
TRIUMV**I**RATE
TYPEWR**I**TING
ULTRAV**I**OLET
UNCOMM**I**TTED
UNDERS**I**GNED
UNQUAL**I**FIED
UNVARN**I**SHED
VERTIG**I**NOUS
VICISS**I**TUDE
WHEREW**I**THAL
POCKET**K**NIFE
UNSPEA**K**ABLE
UNTHIN**K**ABLE
ACCUMU**L**ATOR
ACKNOW**L**EDGE
AGRICU**L**TURE
AMBIVA**L**ENCE
AMONTI**L**LADO
AQUICU**L**TURE
ASSEMB**L**YMAN
BENEVO**L**ENCE
BIMETA**L**LISM
CANDLE**L**IGHT
CASTEL**L**ATED
CAULIF**L**OWER
CHANCE**L**LERY
CIRCUM**L**UNAR
CRYSTA**L**LIZE
DICOTY**L**EDON
EVANGE**L**ICAL
FLANNE**L**ETTE
GENERA**L**SHIP
GLOSSO**L**ALIA
HIGHFA**L**UTIN
HORSEP**L**AYER
INSTAL**L**MENT
MELLIF**L**UOUS
MUSKEL**L**UNGE
NONVIO**L**ENCE
OUTBUI**L**DING
OVERBA**L**ANCE
PITCHB**L**ENDE
POINTI**L**LISM
PROPHY**L**AXIS
PUNCTI**L**IOUS
RAPSCA**L**LION
REALPO**L**ITIK
RESEMB**L**ANCE
SCAFFO**L**DING
SCINTI**L**LATE
SEARCH**L**IGHT
SPACEF**L**IGHT
STRAIT**L**ACED
STRAWF**L**OWER
STREAM**L**INED
STREAM**L**INER
SUPERF**L**UOUS
TONSIL**L**ITIS
TRAILB**L**AZER
UNCIVI**L**IZED
UNICEL**L**ULAR
VARICO**L**ORED
VENTRI**L**OQUY
VITICU**L**TURE
ANASTO**M**OSIS
BOILER**M**AKER
CALORI**M**ETER
CHRONO**M**ETER
CONFOR**M**ANCE
COTTON**M**OUTH
DYNAMO**M**ETER
GENDAR**M**ERIE
GYROCO**M**PASS
IMPEDI**M**ENTA
INESTI**M**ABLE
INFLAM**M**ABLE
KLEPTO**M**ANIA
MEGALO**M**ANIA
MILLIA**M**PERE
NYMPHO**M**ANIA
PERFOR**M**ANCE
POLYNO**M**INAL
PRETER**M**INAL
PROBLE**M**ATIC
PROGRA**M**MING
SEISMO**M**ETER
SPEEDO**M**ETER
SUPERI**M**POSE
THERMO**M**ETER
TWELVE**M**ONTH
BACCHA**N**ALIA
BOUTON**N**IERE
CARAVA**N**SARY
CEREMO**N**IOUS
COEXTE**N**SIVE
CONCER**N**MENT
CONSIG**N**MENT
COUNTE**N**ANCE
DENOMI**N**ATOR
DIAMAG**N**ETIC
DOCTRI**N**AIRE
DOCUME**N**TARY
EARTHE**N**WARE
ELEPHA**N**TINE
ENVIRO**N**MENT
FARTHI**N**GALE
FASHIO**N**ABLE
FRAGME**N**TARY
GEOMAG**N**ETIC
HOMOGE**N**EOUS
IGNOMI**N**IOUS
IMPECU**N**IOUS
IMPREG**N**ABLE
INALIE**N**ABLE
INATTE**N**TION
INDEFI**N**ABLE
INDEPE**N**DENT
INVOLU**N**TARY
IRREDE**N**TISM
KITCHE**N**ETTE
KITCHE**N**WARE
MERCHA**N**DISE
MERCHA**N**TMAN
MILLIO**N**AIRE
MONOLI**N**GUAL
NIGHTI**N**GALE
OPINIO**N**ATED
OUTSTA**N**DING
PERITO**N**ITIS
PORTIO**N**LESS
PORTMA**N**TEAU
QUADRE**N**NIAL

QUADRENNIUM
REGIMENTALS
RESIDENTIAL
RESPLENDENT
REVERENTIAL
SPONTANEOUS
STOCKINETTE
SUBSTANDARD
SUBSTANTIAL
SUBSTANTIVE
SUPERINTEND
TRICHINOSIS
UNALIENABLE
UNORGANIZED
UNRELENTING
WORKMANLIKE
WORKMANSHIP
ZOOPLANKTON
ABORTIONIST
ACCOMMODATE
ANACHRONISM
ARCHAEOLOGY
ARCHDIOCESE
BALLETOMANE
BEACHCOMBER
BEHAVIORISM
BICARBONATE
BLAMEWORTHY
BLOODMOBILE
BOURGEOISIE
BREAKPOINTS
CAMEROONIAN
CAMPANOLOGY
CARNIVOROUS
CATERCORNER
CLAIRVOYANT
CLIMATOLOGY
COLLABORATE
COMMEMORATE
COMPTROLLER
CORROBORATE
CRAPSHOOTER
CRIMINOLOGY
DERMATOLOGY
DETERIORATE
DICTATORIAL
DIRECTORATE
DOWNTRODDEN
DREADNOUGHT
ELECTIONEER
ELECTROCUTE
ELECTROFORM
ELECTROLYTE
ELECTRONICS
ELECTROTYPE
EXPECTORANT
EXPECTORATE

EXTEMPORARY
EXTEMPORIZE
EXTRAPOLATE
FORECLOSURE
FORESHORTEN
FORETHOUGHT
FORTHCOMING
FUNCTIONARY
GERONTOLOGY
GRANDMOTHER
GRASSHOPPER
HERBIVOROUS
HERPETOLOGY
HISTRIONICS
HOUSEMOTHER
HYDROPONICS
HYPERBOREAN
ICHTHYOLOGY
ILLUSIONISM
IMPERFORATE
IMPERSONATE
INCORPORATE
INCORPOREAL
INTERCOURSE
INTERPOLATE
INTERROGATE
KWASHIORKOR
LABRADORITE
MALAPROPISM
MARCHIONESS
METEOROLOGY
METHODOLOGY
MISBEGOTTEN
MOLLYCODDLE
NICKELODEON
ORNITHOLOGY
ORTHODONTIA
OVERWROUGHT
PANDEMONIUM
PARATROOPER
PENTECOSTAL
PERIODONTAL
PHILOSOPHER
PHRASEOLOGY
PISCATORIAL
PLACEHOLDER
PLANETOLOGY
PROTAGONIST
REACTIONARY
RECIPROCATE
RECIPROCITY
RECONNOITER
SHAREHOLDER
SHORTCOMING
SPECTROGRAM
STEAMROLLER
STEPBROTHER

STOCKHOLDER
SUPERSONICS
SYNCHROMESH
SYNCHRONIZE
SYNCHRONOUS
TEASPOONFUL
TERMINOLOGY
TERRITORIAL
TESTIMONIAL
THALIDOMIDE
TOBACCONIST
TRUSTWORTHY
ULTRAMODERN
ULTRASONICS
UNREASONING
VACATIONIST
VOLCANOLOGY
WAINSCOTING
WATERCOURSE
WATERLOGGED
WHERESOEVER
WHICHSOEVER
WOODCHOPPER
BATHYSPHERE
BIBLIOPHILE
BREASTPLATE
CENTERPIECE
CENTRIPETAL
CHLOROPHYLL
CIRCUMPOLAR
COMEUPPANCE
COMMONPLACE
CONSUMPTION
CONSUMPTIVE
CONTEMPLATE
CONTRAPTION
DESCRIPTION
DISCREPANCY
FINGERPRINT
GREASEPAINT
HYDROSPHERE
INESCAPABLE
INNERSPRING
INTERSPERSE
LETTERPRESS
LITHOSPHERE
MANTELPIECE
MARKETPLACE
MASTERPIECE
MEGALOPOLIS
NEEDLEPOINT
OZONOSPHERE
PARATYPHOID
PHOTOSPHERE
PLAINSPOKEN
PRESUMPTION
SUBTROPICAL

TROPOSPHERE
UNFLAPPABLE
ZOOMORPHISM
PROPINQUITY
SOLILOQUIZE
ACCELERANDO
ACCELERATOR
ANNIVERSARY
APPROPRIATE
BACKSTRETCH
BALLCARRIER
BLUNDERBUSS
BROTHERHOOD
CALIFORNIUM
CALLIGRAPHY
CARTOGRAPHY
CATASTROPHE
CATEGORICAL
CHAMBERLAIN
CHAMBERMAID
CHIROGRAPHY
CONCURRENCE
CONTRARIETY
COUNTERFEIT
COUNTERMAND
COUNTERPANE
COUNTERPART
COUNTERSIGN
COUNTERSINK
COUNTERVAIL
CRACKERJACK
DELETERIOUS
DESIDERATUM
DIAPHORETIC
DISAPPROVAL
DISCOURTESY
EXPROPRIATE
FARTHERMOST
FEATHEREDGE
FILMOGRAPHY
FLABBERGAST
FOREVERMORE
FURTHERMORE
FURTHERMOST
GREENGROCER
HAEMORRHAGE
HAGIOGRAPHY
HARDWORKING
HEARTBROKEN
HOMESTRETCH
HOUSEBROKEN
HYDROGRAPHY
HYPERTROPHY
ILLUSTRIOUS
IMPROPRIETY
INADVERTENT
INCINERATOR

INCONGRUENT
INCONGRUOUS
INDUSTRIOUS
INNUMERABLE
INOPPORTUNE
INSEPARABLE
INSUPERABLE
INTERPRETER
INTOLERABLE
IRREPARABLE
IRREVERENCE
LASERWRITER
LEATHERNECK
LITHOGRAPHY
MAIDSERVANT
MERITORIOUS
MODULARIZED
NEANDERTHAL
OPPROBRIOUS
ORTHOGRAPHY
PALEOGRAPHY
PERIPHRASIS
PETROGRAPHY
PHOTOGRAPHY
PLEASURABLE
PORNOGRAPHY
QUARTERBACK
QUARTERDECK
REMEMBRANCE
SCHOLARSHIP
SCREWDRIVER
SMITHEREENS
STANDARDIZE
STENOGRAPHY
STOCKBROKER
THITHERWARD
THUNDERBOLT
THUNDERCLAP
THUNDERHEAD
UNDERGROUND
UNDERGROWTH
UNDESIRABLE
UNFAVORABLE
UNSATURATED
UNUTTERABLE
VINAIGRETTE
WEATHERCOCK
WEATHERWORN
WHEELWRIGHT
WORDPERFECT
BITTERSWEET
BUSINESSMAN
CANDLESTICK
CHIAROSCURO
CIRCUMSPECT
CLANDESTINE
COBBLESTONE

COCKLESHELL
CONFESSEDLY
CONGRESSMAN
CONNOISSEUR
CORNERSTONE
DISPENSABLE
EQUIDISTANT
EVERLASTING
FIDDLESTICK
FLUOROSCOPE
GROUNDSHEET
GUTTERSNIPE
HEARTHSTONE
IMPLAUSIBLE
IMPUISSANCE
INDIGESTION
INDIVISIBLE
INEXCUSABLE
INTERESTING
LINGUISTICS
MALFEASANCE
MARQUISETTE
MEADOWSWEET
MISCONSTRUE
MISFEASANCE
MONKEYSHINE
OBSOLESCENT
PERMISSIBLE
PROCRUSTEAN
PROGRESSION
PROGRESSIVE
RATTLESNAKE
REMINISCENT
RENAISSANCE
RESPONSIBLE
ROTTENSTONE
SMORGASBORD
SPREADSHEET
STEREOSCOPE
STEREOSCOPY
STETHOSCOPE
STROBOSCOPE
SUBMERSIBLE
SUPPRESSANT
SYNTHESIZER
TOPDRESSING
UNCHRISTIAN
VICHYSSOISE
VIRIDESCENT
ACCOUNTABLE
APOCYNTHION
APPOINTMENT
BLOODSTREAM
CABINETWORK
CAPACITANCE
CHOLESTEROL
CLIMACTERIC

COMBUSTIBLE
COMFORTABLE
COMMENTATOR
COMPARTMENT
COMPORTMENT
CONCENTRATE
CONDUCTANCE
CONSISTENCE
CONSISTENCY
CONSTITUENT
CONTENTMENT
CONTRETEMPS
CONVENTICLE
CONVERTIBLE
DEMONSTRATE
DISCONTINUE
EQUILATERAL
EXHAUSTLESS
EXPEDITIOUS
FORMFITTING
HOMEOSTASIS
HYDROSTATIC
ILLIMITABLE
IMPRACTICAL
INDOMITABLE
INDUBITABLE
INELUCTABLE
INSCRUTABLE
INSTANTIATE
INTERATOMIC
INTRACTABLE
IRREFUTABLE
LATCHSTRING
NONPARTISAN
ORCHESTRATE
OUTDISTANCE
PERCEPTIBLE
PERFECTIBLE
PERIPATETIC
PREHISTORIC
PRETENTIOUS
PROGNATHOUS
PROSTATITIS
RECONSTRUCT
REDOUBTABLE
RELOCATABLE
REMONSTRANT
REMONSTRATE
REPETITIOUS
RESPECTABLE
SCRUMPTIOUS
SENTENTIOUS
SEQUESTRATE
STEREOTYPED
SUBSISTENCE
SUSCEPTIBLE
SWEEPSTAKES

TEMPES**T**UOUS
TENDEN**T**IOUS
TERRES**T**RIAL
THEORE**T**ICAL
THOUGH**T**LESS
TYPESE**T**TING
UNPRIN**T**ABLE
UNREMI**T**TING
UNRIGH**T**EOUS
AERONA**U**TICS
AFTERB**U**RNER
ANTINE**U**TRON
ATTRIB**U**TIVE
AVOIRD**U**POIS
BARBIT**U**RATE
BLOCKB**U**STER
BLOODS**U**CKER
CONSEC**U**TIVE
CONSEQ**U**ENCE
CONTIN**U**ANCE
CONVOL**U**TION
DELINQ**U**ENCY
DISENC**U**MBER
DISILL**U**SION
DISSIM**U**LATE
DISSOL**U**TION
ENCAPS**U**LATE
EXPOST**U**LATE
FOULMO**U**THED
FRANKF**U**RTER
GESTIC**U**LATE
HONEYS**U**CKLE
IMPORT**U**NATE
INCRED**U**LOUS
INSTIT**U**TION
INTERN**U**NCIO
LILLIP**U**TIAN
LOUDMO**U**THED
MALADJ**U**STED
MATRIC**U**LATE
MINIAT**U**RIZE
NONDOC**U**MENT
OPPORT**U**NISM
OPPORT**U**NITY
OVERST**U**FFED
PARTIC**U**LATE
PERAMB**U**LATE
PREOCC**U**PIED
RESTIT**U**TION
RETRIB**U**TION
STRANG**U**LATE
TRANSL**U**CENT
TRIANG**U**LATE
TUBERC**U**LATE
TYPEFO**U**NDER
UNACCO**U**NTED
UNFORT**U**NATE
UNOBTR**U**SIVE
VERMIC**U**LITE
WIDEMO**U**THED
ANTIPO**V**ERTY
CONSER**V**ANCY
CONSER**V**ATOR
CONTRI**V**ANCE
CONTRO**V**ERSY
IRREMO**V**ABLE
UNEQUI**V**OCAL
BATTLE**W**AGON
GENTLE**W**OMAN
GROUND**W**ATER
JABBER**W**OCKY
NEEDLE**W**OMAN
NETHER**W**ORLD
SWALLO**W**TAIL
WASHER**W**OMAN
UNDERE**X**POSE
COUNTR**Y**SIDE
HAIRST**Y**LIST
METAPH**Y**SICS
NURSER**Y**MAID
PARATH**Y**ROID
POLYST**Y**RENE
PROSEL**Y**TIZE
TOTALI**Z**ATOR

## 8TH LETTER

ABRACAD**A**BRA
ACCELER**A**NDO
ACCELER**A**TOR
ACCOUNT**A**BLE
ACCUMUL**A**TOR
ANNUNCI**A**TOR
APPRECI**A**BLE
BACCHAN**A**LIA
BATHYSC**A**PHE
BATTLEW**A**GON
BOILERM**A**KER
CALLIGR**A**PHY
CAPACIT**A**NCE
CARTOGR**A**PHY
CASTELL**A**TED
CHEERLE**A**DER
CHIROGR**A**PHY
CHRISTI**A**NIA
CLEARHE**A**DED
COMEUPP**A**NCE
COMFORT**A**BLE
COMMENT**A**TOR
COMPLIC**A**TED
CONCORD**A**NCE
CONDUCT**A**NCE
CONFORM**A**NCE
CONSERV**A**NCY
CONSERV**A**TOR
CONTINU**A**NCE
CONTRIV**A**NCE
COUNTEN**A**NCE
DENOMIN**A**TOR
DESIDER**A**TUM
DILAPID**A**TED
DISCREP**A**NCY
DISPENS**A**BLE
DOCTRIN**A**IRE
FASHION**A**BLE
FILMOGR**A**PHY
GLOSSOL**A**LIA
GREASEP**A**INT
GROUNDW**A**TER
HAGIOGR**A**PHY
HAIRBRE**A**DTH
HOMEOST**A**SIS
HOMESTE**A**DER
HORSEPL**A**YER
HYDROGR**A**PHY
HYDROST**A**TIC
ILLIMIT**A**BLE
IMMITIG**A**BLE
IMPERME**A**BLE
IMPREGN**A**BLE
IMPUISS**A**NCE
INALIEN**A**BLE
INCINER**A**TOR
INDEFIN**A**BLE
INDOMIT**A**BLE
INDUBIT**A**BLE
INELUCT**A**BLE
INESCAP**A**BLE
INESTIM**A**BLE
INEXCUS**A**BLE
INFLAMM**A**BLE
INNUMER**A**BLE
INSCRUT**A**BLE
INSEPAR**A**BLE
INSOUCI**A**NCE
INSUPER**A**BLE
INTERCH**A**NGE
INTOLER**A**BLE
INTRACT**A**BLE
IRREFUT**A**BLE
IRREMOV**A**BLE
IRREPAR**A**BLE
IRREVOC**A**BLE
KLEPTOM**A**NIA
LEVELHE**A**DED
LITHOGR**A**PHY
LOUDSPE**A**KER
MALFEAS**A**NCE
MEGALOM**A**NIA
MESALLI**A**NCE
MILLION**A**IRE
MISALLI**A**NCE
MISDEME**A**NOR
MISFEAS**A**NCE
MISGUID**A**NCE
NYMPHOM**A**NIA
OPINION**A**TED
ORTHOGR**A**PHY
OUTDIST**A**NCE
OVERBAL**A**NCE
PALEOGR**A**PHY
PERFORM**A**NCE
PERIPHR**A**SIS
PETROGR**A**PHY
PHOTOGR**A**PHY
PLEASUR**A**BLE
PORNOGR**A**PHY
PRACTIC**A**BLE
PROBLEM**A**TIC
PROPHYL**A**XIS
REDOUBT**A**BLE
RELOCAT**A**BLE
REMEMBR**A**NCE
RENAISS**A**NCE
RESEMBL**A**NCE
RESPECT**A**BLE
SARCOPH**A**GUS
SERVICE**A**BLE
SHORTCH**A**NGE
STENOGR**A**PHY
STOMACH**A**CHE
STRAITL**A**CED
SWEEPST**A**KES
TOTALIZ**A**TOR
TRAILBL**A**ZER
UNALIEN**A**BLE
UNAVOID**A**BLE
UNDERCH**A**RGE
UNDESIR**A**BLE
UNFAVOR**A**BLE
UNFLAPP**A**BLE
UNMITIG**A**TED
UNPRINT**A**BLE
UNSATUR**A**TED
UNSPEAK**A**BLE
UNTHINK**A**BLE
UNTOUCH**A**BLE
UNUTTER**A**BLE
WRONGHE**A**DED
BIOFEED**B**ACK
BLOODMO**B**ILE
BLUNDER**B**USS
CANDELA**B**RUM
DIAMOND**B**ACK
HERRING**B**ONE
HUMMING**B**IRD
KNUCKLE**B**ONE
MOCKING**B**IRD
QUARTER**B**ACK
SCUTTLE**B**UTT
SMORGAS**B**ORD
THUNDER**B**OLT
ACADEMI**C**IAN
ACADEMI**C**ISM
ARCHDIO**C**ESE
BLOODSU**C**KER
CATHOLI**C**ITY
CERTIFI**C**ATE
CHIAROS**C**URO
COMMUNI**C**ANT
COMMUNI**C**ATE
DOMESTI**C**ATE
DOMESTI**C**ITY
ELECTRI**C**IAN
ELECTRI**C**ITY
ELECTRO**C**UTE
FIRECRA**C**KER
FLUOROS**C**OPE
HISTORI**C**ITY
HONEYSU**C**KLE
HYPOTHE**C**ATE
INFANTI**C**IDE
INSECTI**C**IDE
INTERLA**C**ING
INTERNE**C**INE
INTERRA**C**IAL
MAGNIFI**C**ENT
MICROSE**C**OND
MILLISE**C**OND
MONASTI**C**ISM
MULTIRA**C**IAL
OBSOLES**C**ENT
PONTIFI**C**ALS
PONTIFI**C**ATE
PREVARI**C**ATE
RECIPRO**C**ATE
RECIPRO**C**ITY
REMINIS**C**ENT
ROMANTI**C**ISM
SHUTTLE**C**OCK
SIGNIFI**C**ANT
STEREOS**C**OPE
STEREOS**C**OPY
STETHOS**C**OPE
STROBOS**C**OPE
SUPERFI**C**IAL
SUPREMA**C**IST
THEATRI**C**ALS
THUNDER**C**LAP
TRANSLU**C**ENT
VIRIDES**C**ENT
WEATHER**C**OCK
ACCOMMO**D**ATE
ANTIOXI**D**ANT
CONSOLI**D**ATE
DOWNTRO**D**DEN
GALLBLA**D**DER
HORSERA**D**ISH
IMPROVI**D**ENT
INCARNA**D**INE
INDEPEN**D**ENT
INTERME**D**DLE
MERCHAN**D**ISE
MOLLYCO**D**DLE
NICKELO**D**EON
NONRESI**D**ENT
ORTHOPE**D**ICS
OUTBUIL**D**ING
OUTSTAN**D**ING
QUARTER**D**ECK
RESPLEN**D**ENT
SCAFFOL**D**ING
STANDAR**D**IZE
SUBSTAN**D**ARD
THISTLE**D**OWN
TRINIDA**D**IAN
ULTRAMO**D**ERN
ABSENTE**E**ISM
ACKNOWL**E**DGE
ADOLESC**E**NCE
AMBIVAL**E**NCE
ANAESTH**E**SIA
ANTIPOV**E**RTY
BACKSTR**E**TCH
BENEFIC**E**NCE
BENEVOL**E**NCE
BOYSENB**E**RRY
CALORIM**E**TER
CAMARAD**E**RIE
CARRAGE**E**NAN
CENTRIP**E**TAL
CHOLEST**E**ROL
CHRONOM**E**TER
CLIMACT**E**RIC
COGNOSC**E**NTE
COINCID**E**NCE
COMPLAC**E**NCE
COMPLAC**E**NCY
CONCURR**E**NCE
CONFESS**E**DLY
CONSEQU**E**NCE
CONSIST**E**NCE
CONSIST**E**NCY
CONTING**E**NCY
CONTRET**E**MPS
CONTROV**E**RSY
CONVENI**E**NCE
DECRESC**E**NDO
DELINQU**E**NCY
DESPOND**E**NCY
DIAMAGN**E**TIC
DIAPHOR**E**TIC
DICOTYL**E**DON
DISCOTH**E**QUE
DYNAMOM**E**TER
EQUILAT**E**RAL
EXCRESC**E**NCE
FARINAC**E**OUS
FEATHER**E**DGE
FLANNEL**E**TTE
FLORESC**E**NCE
GENDARM**E**RIE
GEOMAGN**E**TIC
HOMESTR**E**TCH
HOMOGEN**E**OUS
HOUSEKE**E**PER
HUCKLEB**E**RRY
IMPEDIM**E**NTA
INTERPR**E**TER
INTERSP**E**RSE
IRIDESC**E**NCE
IRREVER**E**NCE
KINESTH**E**SIA
KITCHEN**E**TTE
MARQUIS**E**TTE
MINESWE**E**PER
MISBELI**E**VER
MISCONC**E**IVE
NONVIOL**E**NCE
PARENTH**E**SIS
PERIPAT**E**TIC
PITCHBL**E**NDE
POLTERG**E**IST
PRECONC**E**IVE
PROVENI**E**NCE
PSYCHED**E**LIA
PSYCHED**E**LIC
PSYCHOG**E**NIC
SEISMOM**E**TER
SMITHER**E**ENS
SPEEDOM**E**TER
SPONTAN**E**OUS
STOCKIN**E**TTE
STOREKE**E**PER
SUBSIST**E**NCE
SUFFICI**E**NCY
SUFFRAG**E**TTE
THERMOM**E**TER
TRAGEDI**E**NNE
UNRIGHT**E**OUS
VINAIGR**E**TTE
VIOLONC**E**LLO
WHERESO**E**VER
WHICHSO**E**VER
WITENAG**E**MOT
AFTEREF**F**ECT
COUNTER**F**EIT

COUNTRIFIED
ELECTROFORM
INTEROFFICE
OVERSTUFFED
UNQUALIFIED
WORDPERFECT
DESEGREGATE
EXTRAVAGANT
FARTHINGALE
FLABBERGAST
HOUSELIGHTS
INTELLIGENT
INTERREGNUM
INTERROGATE
INVESTIGATE
MONOLINGUAL
NIGHTINGALE
PREASSIGNED
SOVEREIGNTY
SPECTROGRAM
TRANSFIGURE
UNDERSIGNED
WATERLOGGED
APOCYNTHION
BATHYSPHERE
BIBLIOPHILE
BROTHERHOOD
CHLOROPHYLL
COCKLESHELL
ENFRANCHISE
FORTNIGHTLY
GODDAUGHTER
GROUNDSHEET
HAEMORRHAGE
HARPSICHORD
HYDROSPHERE
LAMPLIGHTER
LITHOSPHERE
MONKEYSHINE
MUTTONCHOPS
NEARSIGHTED
NECKERCHIEF
OZONOSPHERE
PARATYPHOID
PHOTOSPHERE
POLYTECHNIC
PROGNATHOUS
SPREADSHEET
THUNDERHEAD
TROPOSPHERE
UNFLINCHING
ZOOMORPHISM
APPROPRIATE
BATTLEFIELD
BENEFICIARY
BOURGEOISIE
BOUTONNIERE
BREAKPOINTS
CANDLELIGHT
CATEGORICAL
CENTERPIECE
CEREMONIOUS
COEFFICIENT
COMBUSTIBLE
CONTRARIETY
CONVENTICLE
CONVERTIBLE
DELETERIOUS
DISCONTINUE
EFFICACIOUS
EVANGELICAL
EXPEDITIOUS
EXPROPRIATE
FURNISHINGS
HAREBRAINED
HEAVYWEIGHT
HEXADECIMAL
IDENTIFIERS
IGNOMINIOUS
ILLUSTRIOUS
IMPECUNIOUS
IMPLAUSIBLE
IMPRACTICAL
IMPROPRIETY
INDIVISIBLE
INDUSTRIOUS
INEFFICIENT
INSTANTIATE
IRREDUCIBLE
IRRELIGIOUS
LASERWRITER
LIGHTWEIGHT
MANTELPIECE
MASTERPIECE
MEMORABILIA
MERITORIOUS
MODULARIZED
NONPARTISAN
OPPROBRIOUS
PAPERWEIGHT
PARAMEDICAL
PENNYWEIGHT
PERCEPTIBLE
PERFECTIBLE
PERITONITIS
PERMISSIBLE
PHARISAICAL
POLYNOMINAL
PRETENTIOUS
PRETERMINAL
PROSTATITIS
PUNCTILIOUS
REALPOLITIK
RECONNOITER
REPETITIOUS
RESPONSIBLE
SCREWDRIVER
SCRUMPTIOUS
SEARCHLIGHT
SEMITRAILER
SENTENTIOUS
SPACEFLIGHT
STREAMLINED
STREAMLINER
SUBMERSIBLE
SUBTROPICAL
SUSCEPTIBLE
SYNTHESIZER
TENDENTIOUS
THEORETICAL
TONSILLITIS
TRANSCEIVER
UNCERTAINTY
UNCIVILIZED
UNCONSCIOUS
UNDERWEIGHT
UNINHIBITED
UNORGANIZED
WHEELWRIGHT
CRACKERJACK
HANDSHAKING
HARDWORKING
MERRYMAKING
PAINSTAKING
PERSNICKETY
SHELLACKING
UNDERTAKING
ZOOPLANKTON
AMONTILLADO
ANTICYCLONE
ARCHAEOLOGY
ARCHIPELAGO
BIMETALLISM
BREASTPLATE
CAMPANOLOGY
CANNIBALIZE
CARDINALATE
CARDINALITY
CATERPILLAR
CHAMBERLAIN
CHANCELLERY
CHANTICLEER
CHEESECLOTH
CHOCKABLOCK
CLERICALISM
CLIMATOLOGY
COLONIALISM
COMMONPLACE
COMPTROLLER
CONTEMPLATE
CRESTFALLEN
CRIMINOLOGY
CRYSTALLIZE
DERMATOLOGY
DISSIMULATE
ELECTROLYTE
ENCAPSULATE
EVENTUALITY
EXHAUSTLESS
EXPOSTULATE
EXTRAPOLATE
FLOORWALKER
GEANTICLINE
GEOSYNCLINE
GERONTOLOGY
GESTICULATE
HAIRSTYLIST
HERPETOLOGY
HOSPITALITY
HOSPITALIZE
ICHTHYOLOGY
IMMORTALITY
IMMORTALIZE
IMPERIALISM
INCREDULOUS
INSTABILITY
INTERCALARY
INTERCALATE
INTERPOLATE
INTERRELATE
MARKETPLACE
MARSHMALLOW
MATERIALISM
MATERIALIZE
MATRICULATE
METEOROLOGY
METHODOLOGY
NAPHTHALENE
NATIONALISM
NATIONALIST
NATIONALITY
NATIONALIZE
NIGHTWALKER
NONETHELESS
OFFICIALDOM
OFFICIALISM
ORNITHOLOGY
PARTICULATE
PATERNALISM
PERAMBULATE
PERISTALSIS
PERSONALITY
PERSONALIZE
PHRASEOLOGY
PLACEHOLDER
PLANETOLOGY
POINTILLISM
PORTIONLESS
QUACKSALVER
QUICKSILVER
RAPSCALLION
RATHSKELLER
RATIONALISM
RATIONALITY
RATIONALIZE
ROADABILITY
SCINTILLATE
SENSIBILITY
SHAREHOLDER
SHIPBUILDER
SLEEPWALKER
STEAMROLLER
STOCKHOLDER
STORYTELLER
STRANGULATE
SWITCHBLADE
TERMINOLOGY
THERMOCLINE
THOUGHTLESS
TRANQUILIZE
TRIANGULATE
TUBERCULATE
VERMICULITE
VOLCANOLOGY
WORKMANLIKE
ACQUIREMENT
AMPHETAMINE
ANTECHAMBER
APPOINTMENT
APPROXIMATE
ARBITRAMENT
BALLETOMANE
BEACHCOMBER
CHAMBERMAID
COMMANDMENT
COMPARTMENT
COMPORTMENT
CONCERNMENT
CONSIGNMENT
CONTENTMENT
COUNTERMAND
DISASSEMBLE
DISENCUMBER
EMPLACEMENT
ENVIRONMENT
FARTHERMOST
FOREVERMORE
FORTHCOMING
FURTHERMORE
FURTHERMOST
GARNISHMENT
IMPROVEMENT
INSTALLMENT
LEGERDEMAIN
MAGNANIMOUS
MEASUREMENT
MULTIFAMILY
NINNYHAMMER
NONDOCUMENT
NOURISHMENT
NURSERYMAID
PENULTIMATE
PREDICAMENT
PROGRAMMING
REFRESHMENT
REPLACEMENT
REQUIREMENT
SHORTCOMING
SUBASSEMBLY
SYNCHROMESH
TEMPERAMENT
THALIDOMIDE
ABORTIONIST
ACCORDINGLY
AGGLUTINATE
ANACHRONISM
ASSASSINATE
BICARBONATE
BICENTENARY
BREADWINNER
CALIFORNIUM
CAMEROONIAN
CHRISTENDOM
CONDOMINIUM
CONTAMINANT
CONTAMINATE
CONTINENTAL
CORRIGENDUM
COTERMINOUS
DETERMINANT
DETERMINATE
DETERMINISM
DISENTANGLE
DISORGANIZE
DISSEMINATE
EINSTEINIUM
ELECTIONEER
ELECTRONICS
EXCEEDINGLY
EXPERIENCED
EXTERMINATE
FAULTFINDER
FREETHINKER
FUNCTIONARY
FUNDAMENTAL
GERRYMANDER
GUTTERSNIPE
HALLUCINATE
HISTRIONICS
HYDROGENATE
HYDROPONICS
ILLUSIONISM
IMPERMANENT
IMPERSONATE
IMPERTINENT
IMPORTUNATE
INCONTINENT
INCREMENTAL
INCRIMINATE
INTERLINEAR
INTERLINING
INTERMINGLE
INTERNUNCIO
INTRAVENOUS
LEATHERNECK
MARCHIONESS
MINNESINGER
MONEYLENDER
MONSEIGNEUR
MOUNTAINEER
MOUNTAINTOP
NARRAGANSET
NOTHINGNESS
OPPORTUNISM
OPPORTUNITY
ORTHODONTIA
OVERWEENING
PACHYSANDRA
PANDEMONIUM
PAPERHANGER
PERIODONTAL
PHYSIOGNOMY
POCKETKNIFE
POMEGRANATE
PREDOMINATE
PRELIMINARY
PRIZEWINNER
PROTAGONIST
QUADRENNIAL
QUADRENNIUM
RATTLESNAKE
REACTIONARY
RECRIMINATE
RECTILINEAR
SENTIMENTAL
SHORTHANDED
SPELLBINDER
SUBORDINATE
SUBURBANITE
SUPERSONICS
SYNCHRONIZE
SYNCHRONOUS
TEASPOONFUL
TELEPRINTER
TESTIMONIAL
TOBACCONIST
TYPEFOUNDER
ULTRASONICS
UNACCOUNTED

UNDERHANDED
UNDESIGNING
UNFORTUNATE
UNREASONING
VACATIONIST
VERTIGINOUS
AGORAPHOBIA
ANASTOMOSIS
BRAGGADOCIO
CATASTROPHE
CAULIFLOWER
CENTERBOARD
CIRCUMPOLAR
COFFEEHOUSE
CONDITIONAL
CONDITIONED
COTTONMOUTH
CRAPSHOOTER
CUSTOMHOUSE
DISAPPROVAL
EXCEPTIONAL
FINGERBOARD
GENTLEWOMAN
GREENGROCER
HEARTBROKEN
HOUSEBROKEN
HYDROPHOBIA
HYGROSCOPIC
HYPERTROPHY
IMPASSIONED
INTENTIONAL
INTERATOMIC
JABBERWOCKY
MACROBIOTIC
MACROSCOPIC
MEGALOPOLIS
MELANCHOLIA
MELANCHOLIC
MICROSCOPIC
MORTARBOARD
MOTHERBOARD
NEEDLEPOINT
NEEDLEWOMAN
NETHERWORLD
PARATROOPER
PARISHIONER
PLAINSPOKEN
PORTERHOUSE
PREHISTORIC
PROBATIONER
PROVISIONAL
RECESSIONAL
SCHOOLHOUSE
SENSATIONAL
SPRINGBOARD
STOCKBROKER
STRAWFLOWER

SUMMERHOUSE
SWITCHBOARD
THENCEFORTH
THEREABOUTS
TOWNSPEOPLE
TRICHINOSIS
TWELVEMONTH
ULTRAVIOLET
UNDERGROUND
UNDERGROWTH
UNDERSHORTS
UNEQUIVOCAL
VARICOLORED
VENTRILOQUY
VICHYSSOISE
WASHERWOMAN
WHEREABOUTS
AVOIRDUPOIS
CIRCUMSPECT
COUNTERPANE
COUNTERPART
GRASSHOPPER
GYROCOMPASS
HANDICAPPER
INTERCEPTOR
MALAPROPISM
MICROCAPSUL
MILLIAMPERE
PARTICIPATE
PHILOSOPHER
PREOCCUPIED
SAFEKEEPING
SERENDIPITY
SUPERIMPOSE
TYPOGRAPHER
UNDEREXPOSE
WOODCHOPPER
ABECEDARIAN
AFTERBURNER
AGGLOMERATE
ALEXANDRIAN
ALEXANDRINE
ANTIQUARIAN
ARISTOCRACY
BALLCARRIER
BARBITURATE
BEHAVIORISM
BELLIGERENT
BLAMEWORTHY
BLOODSTREAM
BUREAUCRACY
CALCIFEROUS
CAPILLARITY
CARDIOGRAPH
CARDSHARPER
CARNIVOROUS
CASSITERITE

CATERCORNER
CENTENARIAN
CHRONOGRAPH
CIRCULARITY
CIRCULARIZE
COLLABORATE
COMMEMORATE
COMMISERATE
COMPUTERIZE
CONCENTRATE
CONFEDERACY
CONFEDERATE
CONSIDERATE
CONSIDERING
CONSUMERISM
CORROBORATE
DEMONSTRATE
DETERIORATE
DICTATORIAL
DIRECTORATE
DOWNHEARTED
ENDOTHERMIC
ENGINEERING
EPINEPHRINE
EQUILIBRIUM
EXPECTORANT
EXPECTORATE
EXTEMPORARY
EXTEMPORIZE
FAMILIARITY
FINGERPRINT
FOREQUARTER
FORESHORTEN
FRANKFURTER
GINGERBREAD
GRANDPARENT
HALFHEARTED
HARDHEARTED
HERBIVOROUS
HINDQUARTER
HYDROCARBON
HYPERBOREAN
IMPERFORATE
INCARCERATE
INCORPORATE
INCORPOREAL
INDIFFERENT
INGATHERING
INNERSPRING
JUVENOCRACY
KINDHEARTED
KWASHIORKOR
LABRADORITE
LATCHSTRING
LETTERPRESS
LIBERTARIAN
LIONHEARTED

MAGISTERIAL
MERITOCRACY
MINIATURIZE
MISANTHROPE
MOMENTARILY
NONDESCRIPT
ORCHESTRATE
OVERBEARING
PARATHYROID
PESTIFEROUS
PISCATORIAL
PLANETARIUM
POLYSTYRENE
PROLETARIAN
PROLETARIAT
PROLIFERATE
PROTOMARTYR
PROTUBERANT
PSYCHODRAMA
RADIOCARBON
RECONSTRUCT
REFRIGERATE
REMONSTRANT
REMONSTRATE
REVERBERATE
SEISMOGRAPH
SEQUESTRATE
SPENDTHRIFT
SUPERMARKET
SUPERSCRIBE
SUPERSCRIPT
TACHYCARDIA
TECHNOCRACY
TERRESTRIAL
TERRITORIAL
TIMESHARING
TRANSPARENT
TREACHEROUS
TRENCHERMAN
TRINITARIAN
TRIUMVIRATE
TRUEHEARTED
TRUSTWORTHY
ULTRAMARINE
UNCONCERNED
UTILITARIAN
WARMHEARTED
WHEELBARROW
WINTERGREEN
ADVERTISING
ANNIVERSARY
APHRODISIAC
AUDIOVISUAL
BLOCKBUSTER
BREADBASKET
BURGOMASTER
BUSINESSMAN

CARAVANSARY
CHOIRMASTER
CLOSEFISTED
COEXTENSIVE
COLORCASTER
CONGRESSMAN
CONNOISSEUR
COPROCESSOR
COUNTERSIGN
COUNTERSINK
COUNTRYSIDE
DISILLUSION
DISPLEASURE
DRILLMASTER
FORECLOSURE
GENERALSHIP
HABERDASHER
HAIRDRESSER
HELLENISTIC
HYPOTHESIZE
MALADJUSTED
MECHANISTIC
MEDIUMISTIC
METAPHYSICS
NORTHEASTER
OMNIPRESENT
PENTECOSTAL
PICTURESQUE
PREDECESSOR
PROGRESSION
PROGRESSIVE
SCHOLARSHIP
SUPPRESSANT
TIGHTFISTED
TOASTMASTER
TOPDRESSING
TRUSTEESHIP
UNOBTRUSIVE
UNVARNISHED
UNWHOLESOME
VENTURESOME
WASTEBASKET
WORKMANSHIP
ABOMINATION
ABSTRACTION
ACCEPTATION
ACCLAMATION
ACCLIMATIZE
ACQUISITION
ACQUISITIVE
ACUPUNCTURE
ADVERSATIVE
AERONAUTICS
AFFECTATION
AFFIRMATIVE
AGGREGATION
AGRICULTURE

ALPHABETIZE
ALTERCATION
ALTERNATIVE
ANTINEUTRON
APPELLATION
APPLICATION
APPROBATION
AQUICULTURE
ASSIGNATION
ASSOCIATION
ASSOCIATIVE
ASTIGMATISM
ATTRIBUTIVE
BENEDICTION
BENEFACTION
CALCULATING
CALCULATION
CANDIDATURE
CANDLESTICK
CARMINATIVE
CEMENTATION
CLANDESTINE
COBBLESTONE
COEDUCATION
COLLOCATION
COMBINATION
COMMINATION
COMMUTATION
COMMUTATIVE
COMPARATIVE
COMPETITION
COMPOSITION
COMPUNCTION
CONCOMITANT
CONJUGATION
CONJUNCTION
CONJUNCTIVA
CONJUNCTIVE
CONJUNCTURE
CONNOTATION
CONNOTATIVE
CONSECUTIVE
CONSUMPTION
CONSUMPTIVE
CONTRACTILE
CONTRAPTION
CONURBATION
CONVOCATION
CONVOLUTION
COOPERATIVE
CORNERSTONE
CORPORATION
CORRELATIVE
COSIGNATORY
CYBERNATION
CYBERNETICS
DECLARATIVE

DEFALCATION
DEFLORATION
DELECTATION
DEMAGNETIZE
DEMOCRATIZE
DEPRECATORY
DEPREDATION
DEPRIVATION
DERELICTION
DESCRIPTION
DESENSITIZE
DESPERATION
DESTINATION
DESTRUCTION
DIFFRACTION
DIPLOMATIST
DISCOURTESY
DISPOSITION
DISPUTATION
DISQUIETUDE
DISSOLUTION
DISTINCTION
DISTINCTIVE
DOCUMENTARY
EDIFICATION
ELECTROTYPE
ELEPHANTINE
ELIZABETHAN
EQUIDISTANT
EVERLASTING
EXPECTATION
EXPENDITURE
EXTRADITION
FIDDLESTICK
FORMFITTING
FORNICATION
FOULMOUTHED
FRAGMENTARY
GEOPOLITICS
GRANDFATHER
GRANDMOTHER
GRAVITATION
HABITUATION
HANDWRITING
HEARTHSTONE
HOUSEMOTHER
HYPERACTIVE
HYPHENATION
IMAGESETTER
IMAGINATION
IMBRICATION
IMPORTATION
INADVERTENT
INATTENTION
INCANTATION
INCARNATION
INCERTITUDE

INCLINATION
INCOMPETENT
INDENTATION
INDIGESTION
INDIGNATION
INEFFECTIVE
INEFFECTUAL
INFORMATION
INFORMATIVE
INGRATITUDE
INOPERATIVE
INOPPORTUNE
INQUISITION
INQUISITIVE
INSINUATING
INSPIRATION
INSTITUTION
INSTRUCTION
INSTRUCTIVE
INTERACTION
INTERACTIVE
INTERESTING
INVESTITURE
INVOLUNTARY
IRREDENTISM
LACRIMATION
LEGISLATION
LEGISLATIVE
LEGISLATURE
LICKSPITTLE
LILLIPUTIAN
LINGUISTICS
LITTERATEUR
LOUDMOUTHED
LUCUBRATION
MACHINATION
MALEDICTION
MALFUNCTION
MALPRACTICE
MANUFACTORY
MANUFACTURE
MATHEMATICS
MENSURATION
MERCHANTMAN
METRICATION
MISBEGOTTEN
MISCONSTRUE
MUSCULATURE
NEANDERTHAL
NECESSITATE
NECESSITOUS
NONNEGATIVE
NUMISMATICS
OBSERVATION
OBSERVATORY
OBSTRUCTION
OSTENTATION
PARTURITION
PENETRATING
PERFUNCTORY
PERMUTATION
PERSPECTIVE
POLLINATION
PORTMANTEAU
PORTRAITIST
PORTRAITURE
PRECIPITATE
PRECIPITOUS
PREIGNITION
PREMEDITATE
PREMONITION
PREPOSITION
PREROGATIVE
PRESUMPTION
PROCRUSTEAN
PROFANATORY
PROHIBITION
PROMPTITUDE
PROPOSITION
PROPRIETARY
PROSELYTIZE
PROSTHETICS
PUBLICATION
PULCHRITUDE
PUNCTUATION
QUALITATIVE
RADIOMETRIC
RECOGNITION
REFORMATION
REFORMATORY
REGIMENTALS
REGURGITATE
REINFECTION
REPLICATION
REPROBATION
REQUISITION
RESERVATION
RESIDENTIAL
RESIGNATION
RESPIRATION
RESTITUTION
RESTORATION
RESTORATIVE
RESTRICTION
RESUSCITATE
RETRIBUTION
RETROACTIVE
REVERENTIAL
ROTTENSTONE
STEPBROTHER
STRAIGHTWAY
SUBJUNCTIVE
SUBSTANTIAL
SUBSTANTIVE
SUPERINTEND
SUPERLATIVE
SUPPOSITION
SUPPOSITORY
SWALLOWTAIL
SYNCOPATION
SYSTEMATIZE
TEMPERATURE
THEREWITHAL
TRANSACTION
TRANSMITTER
TREPIDATION
TRIBULATION
TYPESETTING
TYPEWRITING
UNCHRISTIAN
UNCOMMITTED
UNDEVIATING
UNIFICATION
UNRELENTING
UNREMITTING
VACCINATION
VALEDICTION
VALEDICTORY
VENTILATION
VICISSITUDE
VINDICATION
VITICULTURE
VIVISECTION
WAINSCOTING
WHEREWITHAL
WHIFFLETREE
WHIPPLETREE
WIDEMOUTHED
WORKSTATION
CENTRIFUGAL
CIRCUMLUNAR
CONSPICUOUS
CONSTITUENT
CREPUSCULAR
DISTINGUISH
DISTRIBUTOR
DREADNOUGHT
FORETHOUGHT
GALLIMAUFRY
HIGHFALUTIN
INCONGRUENT
INCONGRUOUS
INCUNABULUM
INDIVIDUATE
INTERCOURSE
MASSACHUSET
MELLIFLUOUS
MUSKELLUNGE
OUTMANEUVER
OVERWROUGHT
PERSPICUOUS
PROMISCUOUS
PROPINQUITY
SOLILOQUIZE
SPECTACULAR
SUPERFLUOUS
TEMPESTUOUS
THERAPEUTIC
UNICELLULAR
WATERCOURSE
ANTIGRAVITY
COUNTERVAIL
LABORSAVING
MAIDSERVANT
MENDELEVIUM
MISCHIEVOUS
PRIMITIVISM
RESISTIVITY
ROTOGRAVURE
BITTERSWEET
CABINETWORK
EARTHENWARE
GRANITEWARE
KITCHENWARE
LATTICEWORK
MEADOWSWEET
THITHERWARD
WEATHERWORN
CRUCIFIXION
ASSEMBLYMAN
CLAIRVOYANT
STEREOTYPED

### 9th Letter

ACCOMMODATE
AGGLOMERATE
AGGLUTINATE
AMONTILLADO
ANNIVERSARY
ANTIOXIDANT
APPROPRIATE
APPROXIMATE
ARCHIPELAGO
ARISTOCRACY
ASSASSINATE
BALLETOMANE
BARBITURATE
BENEFICIARY
BICARBONATE
BICENTENARY
BIOFEEDBACK
BREASTPLATE
BUREAUCRACY
CARAVANSARY
CARDINALATE
CARDIOGRAPH
CENTERBOARD
CERTIFICATE
CHAMBERLAIN
CHAMBERMAID
CHRONOGRAPH
CLAIRVOYANT
COLLABORATE
COMMEMORATE
COMMISERATE
COMMONPLACE
COMMUNICANT
COMMUNICATE
CONCENTRATE
CONCOMITANT
CONFEDERACY
CONFEDERATE
CONSIDERATE
CONSOLIDATE
CONTAMINANT
CONTAMINATE
CONTEMPLATE
CORROBORATE
COUNTERMAND
COUNTERPANE
COUNTERPART
COUNTERVAIL
CRACKERJACK
DEMONSTRATE
DESEGREGATE
DETERIORATE
DETERMINANT
DETERMINATE
DIAMONDBACK
DIRECTORATE
DISSEMINATE
DISSIMULATE
DOCUMENTARY
DOMESTICATE
EARTHENWARE
ENCAPSULATE
EQUIDISTANT
EXPECTORANT
EXPECTORATE
EXPOSTULATE
EXPROPRIATE
EXTEMPORARY
EXTERMINATE
EXTRAPOLATE
EXTRAVAGANT
FARTHINGALE
FINGERBOARD
FLABBERGAST
FRAGMENTARY
FUNCTIONARY
GESTICULATE
GRANITEWARE
GYROCOMPASS
HAEMORRHAGE
HALLUCINATE
HYDROGENATE
HYPOTHECATE
IMPERFORATE
IMPERSONATE
IMPORTUNATE
INCARCERATE
INCORPORATE
INCRIMINATE
INDIVIDUATE
INSTANTIATE
INTERCALARY
INTERCALATE
INTERPOLATE
INTERRELATE
INTERROGATE
INVESTIGATE
INVOLUNTARY
JUVENOCRACY
KITCHENWARE
LEGERDEMAIN
MAIDSERVANT
MARKETPLACE
MATRICULATE
MERITOCRACY
MORTARBOARD
MOTHERBOARD
NECESSITATE
NIGHTINGALE
NURSERYMAID
ORCHESTRATE
PARTICIPATE
PARTICULATE
PENULTIMATE
PERAMBULATE
POMEGRANATE
PONTIFICALS
PONTIFICATE
PRECIPITATE
PREDOMINATE
PRELIMINARY
PREMEDITATE
PREVARICATE
PROLIFERATE
PROPRIETARY
PROTUBERANT
PSYCHODRAMA
QUARTERBACK
RATTLESNAKE
REACTIONARY
RECIPROCATE
RECRIMINATE
REFRIGERATE
REGIMENTALS
REGURGITATE
REMONSTRANT
REMONSTRATE
RESUSCITATE
REVERBERATE
SCINTILLATE
SEISMOGRAPH
SEQUESTRATE
SIGNIFICANT
SPRINGBOARD
STRANGULATE
SUBORDINATE
SUBSTANDARD
SUPPRESSANT
SWALLOWTAIL
SWITCHBLADE
SWITCHBOARD
TECHNOCRACY
THEATRICALS
THITHERWARD
TRIANGULATE
TRIUMVIRATE
TUBERCULATE
UNFORTUNATE
ABRACADABRA
ACCOUNTABLE
AGORAPHOBIA
ANTECHAMBER
APPRECIABLE
BEACHCOMBER
COMBUSTIBLE
COMFORTABLE
CONVERTIBLE
DISASSEMBLE
DISENCUMBER
DISPENSABLE
FASHIONABLE
HYDROCARBON
HYDROPHOBIA
ILLIMITABLE
IMMITIGABLE
IMPERMEABLE
IMPLAUSIBLE
IMPREGNABLE
INALIENABLE
INDEFINABLE
INDIVISIBLE
INDOMITABLE
INDUBITABLE
INELUCTABLE
INESCAPABLE
INESTIMABLE
INEXCUSABLE
INFLAMMABLE
INNUMERABLE
INSCRUTABLE
INSEPARABLE
INSUPERABLE

INTOLERABLE
INTRACTABLE
IRREDUCIBLE
IRREFUTABLE
IRREMOVABLE
IRREPARABLE
IRREVOCABLE
PERCEPTIBLE
PERFECTIBLE
PERMISSIBLE
PLEASURABLE
PRACTICABLE
RADIOCARBON
REDOUBTABLE
RELOCATABLE
RESPECTABLE
RESPONSIBLE
SERVICEABLE
SUBASSEMBLY
SUBMERSIBLE
SUSCEPTIBLE
UNALIENABLE
UNAVOIDABLE
UNDESIRABLE
UNFAVORABLE
UNFLAPPABLE
UNPRINTABLE
UNSPEAKABLE
UNTHINKABLE
UNTOUCHABLE
UNUTTERABLE
BRAGGADOCIO
CATEGORICAL
CONVENTICLE
EVANGELICAL
EXPERIENCED
GREENGROCER
IMPRACTICAL
INTERNUNCIO
JABBERWOCKY
PARAMEDICAL
PHARISAICAL
STOMACHACHE
STRAITLACED
SUBTROPICAL
THEORETICAL
UNEQUIVOCAL
ACKNOWLEDGE
CHEERLEADER
CHRISTENDOM
CLEARHEADED
CONFESSEDLY
CORRIGENDUM
DICOTYLEDON
DOWNTRODDEN
FAULTFINDER
FEATHEREDGE
GALLBLADDER
GERRYMANDER
HAIRBREADTH
HOMESTEADER
INTERMEDDLE
LEVELHEADED
MOLLYCODDLE
MONEYLENDER
OFFICIALDOM
PACHYSANDRA
PLACEHOLDER
SHAREHOLDER
SHIPBUILDER
SHORTHANDED
SPELLBINDER
STOCKHOLDER
TACHYCARDIA
TYPEFOUNDER
UNDERHANDED
WRONGHEADED
ACQUIREMENT
AFTEREFFECT
APPOINTMENT
ARBITRAMENT
ARCHDIOCESE
BATHYSPHERE
BATTLEFIELD
BELLIGERENT
BITTERSWEET
BLOODSTREAM
BOUTONNIERE
CENTERPIECE
CHANCELLERY
CHANTICLEER
CIRCUMSPECT
COCKLESHELL
COEFFICIENT
COMMANDMENT
COMPARTMENT
COMPORTMENT
CONCERNMENT
CONNOISSEUR
CONSIGNMENT
CONSTITUENT
CONTENTMENT
CONTRARIETY
COUNTERFEIT
DISCOURTESY
ELECTIONEER
EMPLACEMENT
ENVIRONMENT
EXHAUSTLESS
GARNISHMENT
GINGERBREAD
GRANDPARENT
GROUNDSHEET
HYDROSPHERE
HYPERBOREAN
IDENTIFIERS
IMPERMANENT
IMPERTINENT
IMPROPRIETY
IMPROVEMENT
IMPROVIDENT
INADVERTENT
INCOMPETENT
INCONGRUENT
INCONTINENT
INCORPOREAL
INDEPENDENT
INDIFFERENT
INEFFICIENT
INSTALLMENT
INTELLIGENT
INTERLINEAR
LEATHERNECK
LETTERPRESS
LITHOSPHERE
LITTERATEUR
MAGNIFICENT
MANTELPIECE
MARCHIONESS
MASTERPIECE
MEADOWSWEET
MEASUREMENT
MILLIAMPERE
MONSEIGNEUR
MOUNTAINEER
NAPHTHALENE
NICKELODEON
NONDOCUMENT
NONETHELESS
NONRESIDENT
NOTHINGNESS
NOURISHMENT
OBSOLESCENT
OMNIPRESENT
OZONOSPHERE
PERSNICKETY
PHOTOSPHERE
POLYSTYRENE
PORTIONLESS
PORTMANTEAU
PREDICAMENT
PROCRUSTEAN
QUARTERDECK
RECTILINEAR
REFRESHMENT
REMINISCENT
REPLACEMENT
REQUIREMENT
RESPLENDENT
SMITHEREENS
SPREADSHEET
SUPERINTEND
SYNCHROMESH
TEMPERAMENT
THOUGHTLESS
THUNDERHEAD
TRANSLUCENT
TRANSPARENT
TROPOSPHERE
ULTRAMODERN
VIRIDESCENT
WINTERGREEN
WORDPERFECT
GALLIMAUFRY
OVERSTUFFED
TEASPOONFUL
ACCORDINGLY
BATTLEWAGON
CANDLELIGHT
CENTRIFUGAL
DISENTANGLE
DREADNOUGHT
EXCEEDINGLY
FORETHOUGHT
HEAVYWEIGHT
INTERMINGLE
LIGHTWEIGHT
MINNESINGER
OVERWROUGHT
PAPERHANGER
PAPERWEIGHT
PENNYWEIGHT
SARCOPHAGUS
SEARCHLIGHT
SPACEFLIGHT
UNDERWEIGHT
WATERLOGGED
WHEELWRIGHT
ELIZABETHAN
FOULMOUTHED
GENERALSHIP
GRANDFATHER
GRANDMOTHER
HABERDASHER
HOUSELIGHTS
HOUSEMOTHER
LOUDMOUTHED
NEANDERTHAL
PHILOSOPHER
SCHOLARSHIP
STEPBROTHER
THEREWITHAL
TRUSTEESHIP
TYPOGRAPHER
UNVARNISHED
WHEREWITHAL
WIDEMOUTHED
WORKMANSHIP
ABECEDARIAN
ABOMINATION
ABORTIONIST
ABSENTEEISM
ABSTRACTION
ACADEMICIAN
ACADEMICISM
ACCEPTATION
ACCLAMATION
ACCLIMATIZE
ACQUISITION
ACQUISITIVE
ADVERSATIVE
ADVERTISING
AERONAUTICS
AFFECTATION
AFFIRMATIVE
AGGREGATION
ALEXANDRIAN
ALEXANDRINE
ALPHABETIZE
ALTERCATION
ALTERNATIVE
AMPHETAMINE
ANACHRONISM
ANTIGRAVITY
ANTIQUARIAN
APHRODISIAC
APOCYNTHION
APPELLATION
APPLICATION
APPROBATION
ASSIGNATION
ASSOCIATION
ASSOCIATIVE
ASTIGMATISM
ATTRIBUTIVE
BALLCARRIER
BEHAVIORISM
BENEDICTION
BENEFACTION
BIBLIOPHILE
BIMETALLISM
BLOODMOBILE
CALCULATING
CALCULATION
CALIFORNIUM
CAMEROONIAN
CANDLESTICK
CANNIBALIZE
CAPILLARITY
CARDINALITY
CARMINATIVE
CASSITERITE
CATHOLICITY
CEMENTATION
CENTENARIAN
CIRCULARITY
CIRCULARIZE
CLANDESTINE
CLERICALISM
COEDUCATION
COEXTENSIVE
COLLOCATION
COLONIALISM
COMBINATION
COMMINATION
COMMUTATION
COMMUTATIVE
COMPARATIVE
COMPETITION
COMPOSITION
COMPUNCTION
COMPUTERIZE
CONDOMINIUM
CONJUGATION
CONJUNCTION
CONJUNCTIVA
CONJUNCTIVE
CONNOTATION
CONNOTATIVE
CONSECUTIVE
CONSIDERING
CONSUMERISM
CONSUMPTION
CONSUMPTIVE
CONTRACTILE
CONTRAPTION
CONURBATION
CONVOCATION
CONVOLUTION
COOPERATIVE
CORPORATION
CORRELATIVE
COUNTERSIGN
COUNTERSINK
COUNTRIFIED
COUNTRYSIDE
CRUCIFIXION
CRYSTALLIZE
CYBERNATION
CYBERNETICS
DECLARATIVE
DEFALCATION
DEFLORATION
DELECTATION
DEMAGNETIZE
DEMOCRATIZE
DEPREDATION
DEPRIVATION
DERELICTION
DESCRIPTION
DESENSITIZE
DESPERATION
DESTINATION
DESTRUCTION
DETERMINISM
DICTATORIAL
DIFFRACTION
DIPLOMATIST
DISILLUSION
DISORGANIZE
DISPOSITION
DISPUTATION
DISSOLUTION
DISTINCTION
DISTINCTIVE
DISTINGUISH
DOCTRINAIRE
DOMESTICITY
EDIFICATION
EINSTEINIUM
ELECTRICIAN
ELECTRICITY
ELECTRONICS
ELEPHANTINE
ENFRANCHISE
ENGINEERING
EPINEPHRINE
EQUILIBRIUM
EVENTUALITY
EVERLASTING
EXPECTATION
EXTEMPORIZE
EXTRADITION
FAMILIARITY
FIDDLESTICK
FINGERPRINT
FORMFITTING
FORNICATION
FORTHCOMING
GEANTICLINE
GEOPOLITICS
GEOSYNCLINE
GRAVITATION
GREASEPAINT
GUTTERSNIPE
HABITUATION
HAIRSTYLIST
HANDSHAKING
HANDWRITING
HARDWORKING
HISTORICITY
HISTRIONICS
HORSERADISH
HOSPITALITY
HOSPITALIZE
HUMMINGBIRD
HYDROPONICS
HYPERACTIVE
HYPHENATION

HYPOTHESIZE
ILLUSIONISM
IMAGINATION
IMBRICATION
IMMORTALITY
IMMORTALIZE
IMPERIALISM
IMPORTATION
INATTENTION
INCANTATION
INCARNADINE
INCARNATION
INCLINATION
INDENTATION
INDIGESTION
INDIGNATION
INEFFECTIVE
INFANTICIDE
INFORMATION
INFORMATIVE
INGATHERING
INNERSPRING
INOPERATIVE
INQUISITION
INQUISITIVE
INSECTICIDE
INSINUATING
INSPIRATION
INSTABILITY
INSTITUTION
INSTRUCTION
INSTRUCTIVE
INTERACTION
INTERACTIVE
INTERESTING
INTERLACING
INTERLINING
INTERNECINE
INTEROFFICE
INTERRACIAL
IRREDENTISM
LABORSAVING
LABRADORITE
LACRIMATION
LATCHSTRING
LEGISLATION
LEGISLATIVE
LIBERTARIAN
LILLIPUTIAN
LINGUISTICS
LUCUBRATION
MACHINATION
MAGISTERIAL
MALAPROPISM
MALEDICTION
MALFUNCTION
MALPRACTICE

MATERIALISM
MATERIALIZE
MATHEMATICS
MENDELEVIUM
MENSURATION
MERCHANDISE
MERRYMAKING
METAPHYSICS
METRICATION
MILLIONAIRE
MINIATURIZE
MISCONCEIVE
MOCKINGBIRD
MOMENTARILY
MONASTICISM
MONKEYSHINE
MULTIFAMILY
MULTIRACIAL
NATIONALISM
NATIONALIST
NATIONALITY
NATIONALIZE
NECKERCHIEF
NEEDLEPOINT
NONDESCRIPT
NONNEGATIVE
NUMISMATICS
OBSERVATION
OBSTRUCTION
OFFICIALISM
OPPORTUNISM
OPPORTUNITY
ORTHOPEDICS
OSTENTATION
OUTBUILDING
OUTSTANDING
OVERBEARING
OVERWEENING
PAINSTAKING
PANDEMONIUM
PARTURITION
PATERNALISM
PENETRATING
PERMUTATION
PERSONALITY
PERSONALIZE
PERSPECTIVE
PISCATORIAL
PLANETARIUM
POCKETKNIFE
POINTILLISM
POLLINATION
POLTERGEIST
PORTRAITIST
PRECONCEIVE
PREIGNITION
PREMONITION

PREOCCUPIED
PREPOSITION
PREROGATIVE
PRESUMPTION
PRIMITIVISM
PROGRAMMING
PROGRESSION
PROGRESSIVE
PROHIBITION
PROLETARIAN
PROLETARIAT
PROPINQUITY
PROPOSITION
PROSELYTIZE
PROSTHETICS
PROTAGONIST
PUBLICATION
PUNCTUATION
QUADRENNIAL
QUADRENNIUM
QUALITATIVE
RAPSCALLION
RATIONALISM
RATIONALITY
RATIONALIZE
RECIPROCITY
RECOGNITION
REFORMATION
REINFECTION
REPLICATION
REPROBATION
REQUISITION
RESERVATION
RESIDENTIAL
RESIGNATION
RESISTIVITY
RESPIRATION
RESTITUTION
RESTORATION
RESTORATIVE
RESTRICTION
RETRIBUTION
RETROACTIVE
REVERENTIAL
ROADABILITY
ROMANTICISM
SAFEKEEPING
SCAFFOLDING
SENSIBILITY
SERENDIPITY
SHELLACKING
SHORTCOMING
SOLILOQUIZE
SPENDTHRIFT
STANDARDIZE
SUBJUNCTIVE
SUBSTANTIAL

SUBSTANTIVE
SUBURBANITE
SUPERFICIAL
SUPERLATIVE
SUPERSCRIBE
SUPERSCRIPT
SUPERSONICS
SUPPOSITION
SUPREMACIST
SYNCHRONIZE
SYNCOPATION
SYSTEMATIZE
TERRESTRIAL
TERRITORIAL
TESTIMONIAL
THALIDOMIDE
THERMOCLINE
TIMESHARING
TOBACCONIST
TOPDRESSING
TRANQUILIZE
TRANSACTION
TREPIDATION
TRIBULATION
TRINIDADIAN
TRINITARIAN
TYPESETTING
TYPEWRITING
ULTRAMARINE
ULTRASONICS
UNCHRISTIAN
UNDERTAKING
UNDESIGNING
UNDEVIATING
UNFLINCHING
UNIFICATION
UNOBTRUSIVE
UNQUALIFIED
UNREASONING
UNRELENTING
UNREMITTING
UTILITARIAN
VACATIONIST
VACCINATION
VALEDICTION
VENTILATION
VERMICULITE
VICHYSSOISE
VINDICATION
VIVISECTION
WAINSCOTING
WORKMANLIKE
WORKSTATION
ZOOMORPHISM
BLOODSUCKER
BOILERMAKER
BREADBASKET

FIRECRACKER
FLOORWALKER
FREETHINKER
HEARTBROKEN
HONEYSUCKLE
HOUSEBROKEN
KWASHIORKOR
LOUDSPEAKER
NIGHTWALKER
PLAINSPOKEN
SLEEPWALKER
STOCKBROKER
SUPERMARKET
SWEEPSTAKES
WASTEBASKET
BACCHANALIA
CATERPILLAR
CIRCUMPOLAR
COMPTROLLER
CREPUSCULAR
CRESTFALLEN
GLOSSOLALIA
INCUNABULUM
MARSHMALLOW
MEGALOPOLIS
MELANCHOLIA
MELANCHOLIC
MEMORABILIA
PSYCHEDELIA
PSYCHEDELIC
RATHSKELLER
SEMITRAILER
SPECTACULAR
STEAMROLLER
STORYTELLER
THUNDERCLAP
ULTRAVIOLET
UNICELLULAR
VIOLONCELLO
ASSEMBLYMAN
BUSINESSMAN
CONGRESSMAN
CONTRETEMPS
ENDOTHERMIC
GENTLEWOMAN
HEXADECIMAL
INTERATOMIC
MERCHANTMAN
NEEDLEWOMAN
NINNYHAMMER
TRENCHERMAN
WASHERWOMAN
WITENAGEMOT
ACCELERANDO
ADOLESCENCE
AFTERBURNER
AMBIVALENCE

BENEFICENCE
BENEVOLENCE
BREADWINNER
BREAKPOINTS
CAPACITANCE
CARRAGEENAN
CATERCORNER
CHRISTIANIA
CIRCUMLUNAR
COGNOSCENTE
COINCIDENCE
COMEUPPANCE
COMPLACENCE
COMPLACENCY
CONCORDANCE
CONCURRENCE
CONDITIONAL
CONDITIONED
CONDUCTANCE
CONFORMANCE
CONSEQUENCE
CONSERVANCY
CONSISTENCE
CONSISTENCY
CONTINGENCY
CONTINUANCE
CONTRIVANCE
CONVENIENCE
COUNTENANCE
DECRESCENDO
DELINQUENCY
DESPONDENCY
DISCONTINUE
DISCREPANCY
EXCEPTIONAL
EXCRESCENCE
FLORESCENCE
FURNISHINGS
HAREBRAINED
IMPASSIONED
IMPEDIMENTA
IMPUISSANCE
INSOUCIANCE
INTENTIONAL
INTERCHANGE
INTERREGNUM
IRIDESCENCE
IRREVERENCE
KLEPTOMANIA
MALFEASANCE
MEGALOMANIA
MESALLIANCE
MISALLIANCE
MISDEMEANOR
MISFEASANCE
MISGUIDANCE
MUSKELLUNGE

NONVIOLENCE
NYMPHOMANIA
OUTDISTANCE
OVERBALANCE
PARISHIONER
PERFORMANCE
PITCHBLENDE
POLYNOMINAL
POLYTECHNIC
PREASSIGNED
PRETERMINAL
PRIZEWINNER
PROBATIONER
PROVENIENCE
PROVISIONAL
PSYCHOGENIC
RECESSIONAL
REMEMBRANCE
RENAISSANCE
RESEMBLANCE
SENSATIONAL
SHORTCHANGE
SOVEREIGNTY
STREAMLINED
STREAMLINER
SUBSISTENCE
SUFFICIENCY
TRAGEDIENNE
TWELVEMONTH
UNCERTAINTY
UNCONCERNED
UNDERSIGNED
ANTICYCLONE
ARCHAEOLOGY
AVOIRDUPOIS
BROTHERHOOD
CABINETWORK
CALCIFEROUS
CAMPANOLOGY
CARNIVOROUS
CEREMONIOUS
CHEESECLOTH
CHOCKABLOCK
CLIMATOLOGY
COBBLESTONE
CONSPICUOUS
CORNERSTONE
COSIGNATORY
COTERMINOUS
CRIMINOLOGY
DELETERIOUS
DEPRECATORY
DERMATOLOGY
EFFICACIOUS
ELECTROFORM
EXPEDITIOUS
FARINACEOUS

FARTHERMOST
FLUOROSCOPE
FOREVERMORE
FURTHERMORE
FURTHERMOST
GERONTOLOGY
HARPSICHORD
HEARTHSTONE
HERBIVOROUS
HERPETOLOGY
HERRINGBONE
HOMOGENEOUS
ICHTHYOLOGY
IGNOMINIOUS
ILLUSTRIOUS
IMPECUNIOUS
INCONGRUOUS
INCREDULOUS
INDUSTRIOUS
INTRAVENOUS
IRRELIGIOUS
KNUCKLEBONE
LATTICEWORK
MAGNANIMOUS
MANUFACTORY
MELLIFLUOUS
MERITORIOUS
METEOROLOGY
METHODOLOGY
MICROSECOND
MILLISECOND
MISANTHROPE
MISCHIEVOUS
MUTTONCHOPS
NECESSITOUS
OBSERVATORY
OPPROBRIOUS
ORNITHOLOGY
PARATHYROID
PARATYPHOID
PERFUNCTORY
PERSPICUOUS
PESTIFEROUS
PHRASEOLOGY
PHYSIOGNOMY
PLANETOLOGY
PRECIPITOUS
PRETENTIOUS
PROFANATORY
PROGNATHOUS
PROMISCUOUS
PUNCTILIOUS
REFORMATORY
REPETITIOUS
ROTTENSTONE
SCRUMPTIOUS
SENTENTIOUS
SHUTTLECOCK
SMORGASBORD
SPONTANEOUS
STEREOSCOPE
STEREOSCOPY
STETHOSCOPE
STROBOSCOPE
SUPERFLUOUS
SUPERIMPOSE
SUPPOSITORY
SYNCHRONOUS
TEMPESTUOUS
TENDENTIOUS
TERMINOLOGY
THISTLEDOWN
THUNDERBOLT
TREACHEROUS
UNCONSCIOUS
UNDEREXPOSE
UNRIGHTEOUS
UNWHOLESOME
VALEDICTORY
VENTURESOME
VERTIGINOUS
VOLCANOLOGY
WEATHERCOCK
WEATHERWORN
BATHYSCAPHE
CALLIGRAPHY
CARDSHARPER
CARTOGRAPHY
CATASTROPHE
CHIROGRAPHY
FILMOGRAPHY
GRASSHOPPER
HAGIOGRAPHY
HANDICAPPER
HOUSEKEEPER
HYDROGRAPHY
HYGROSCOPIC
HYPERTROPHY
LITHOGRAPHY
MACROSCOPIC
MICROSCOPIC
MINESWEEPER
ORTHOGRAPHY
PALEOGRAPHY
PARATROOPER
PETROGRAPHY
PHOTOGRAPHY
PORNOGRAPHY
STENOGRAPHY
STEREOTYPED
STOREKEEPER
TOWNSPEOPLE
WOODCHOPPER
DISCOTHEQUE
PICTURESQUE
VENTRILOQUY
ANTINEUTRON
ANTIPOVERTY
BOYSENBERRY
CAMARADERIE
CANDELABRUM
CHOLESTEROL
CLIMACTERIC
CONTROVERSY
EQUILATERAL
GENDARMERIE
HUCKLEBERRY
INTERCOURSE
INTERSPERSE
MISCONSTRUE
NETHERWORLD
PREHISTORIC
RADIOMETRIC
SPECTROGRAM
THENCEFORTH
UNDERCHARGE
UNDERSHORTS
VARICOLORED
WATERCOURSE
WHEELBARROW
WHIFFLETREE
WHIPPLETREE
ANAESTHESIA
ANASTOMOSIS
BOURGEOISIE
COPROCESSOR
HAIRDRESSER
HOMEOSTASIS
KINESTHESIA
MASSACHUSET
MICROCAPSUL
NARRAGANSET
NONPARTISAN
PARENTHESIS
PERIPHRASIS
PERISTALSIS
PREDECESSOR
TRICHINOSIS
ACCELERATOR
ACCUMULATOR
ANNUNCIATOR
BACKSTRETCH
BLAMEWORTHY
BLOCKBUSTER
BURGOMASTER
CALORIMETER
CASTELLATED
CENTRIPETAL
CHOIRMASTER
CHRONOMETER
CLOSEFISTED
COLORCASTER
COMMENTATOR
COMPLICATED
CONSERVATOR
CONTINENTAL
CRAPSHOOTER
DENOMINATOR
DESIDERATUM
DIAMAGNETIC
DIAPHORETIC
DILAPIDATED
DISTRIBUTOR
DOWNHEARTED
DRILLMASTER
DYNAMOMETER
FLANNELETTE
FOREQUARTER
FORESHORTEN
FORTNIGHTLY
FRANKFURTER
FUNDAMENTAL
GEOMAGNETIC
GODDAUGHTER
GROUNDWATER
HALFHEARTED
HARDHEARTED
HELLENISTIC
HIGHFALUTIN
HINDQUARTER
HOMESTRETCH
HYDROSTATIC
IMAGESETTER
INCINERATOR
INCREMENTAL
INTERCEPTOR
INTERPRETER
KINDHEARTED
KITCHENETTE
LAMPLIGHTER
LASERWRITER
LICKSPITTLE
LIONHEARTED
MACROBIOTIC
MALADJUSTED
MARQUISETTE
MECHANISTIC
MEDIUMISTIC
MISBEGOTTEN
MOUNTAINTOP
NEARSIGHTED
NORTHEASTER
OPINIONATED
ORTHODONTIA
PENTECOSTAL
PERIODONTAL
PERIPATETIC
PERITONITIS
PROBLEMATIC
PROSTATITIS
PROTOMARTYR
REALPOLITIK
RECONNOITER
SEISMOMETER
SENTIMENTAL
SPEEDOMETER
STOCKINETTE
SUFFRAGETTE
TELEPRINTER
THERAPEUTIC
THERMOMETER
TIGHTFISTED
TOASTMASTER
TONSILLITIS
TOTALIZATOR
TRANSMITTER
TRUEHEARTED
TRUSTWORTHY
UNACCOUNTED
UNCOMMITTED
UNINHIBITED
UNMITIGATED
UNSATURATED
VINAIGRETTE
WARMHEARTED
ZOOPLANKTON
ACUPUNCTURE
AGRICULTURE
AQUICULTURE
AUDIOVISUAL
BLUNDERBUSS
CANDIDATURE
CHIAROSCURO
COFFEEHOUSE
CONJUNCTURE
COTTONMOUTH
CUSTOMHOUSE
DISPLEASURE
DISQUIETUDE
ELECTROCUTE
EXPENDITURE
FORECLOSURE
INCERTITUDE
INEFFECTUAL
INGRATITUDE
INOPPORTUNE
INVESTITURE
LEGISLATURE
MANUFACTURE
MONOLINGUAL
MUSCULATURE
PORTERHOUSE
PORTRAITURE
PROMPTITUDE
PULCHRITUDE
RECONSTRUCT
ROTOGRAVURE
SCHOOLHOUSE
SCUTTLEBUTT
SUMMERHOUSE
TEMPERATURE
THEREABOUTS
TRANSFIGURE
UNDERGROUND
VICISSITUDE
VITICULTURE
WHEREABOUTS
DISAPPROVAL
MISBELIEVER
OUTMANEUVER
QUACKSALVER
QUICKSILVER
SCREWDRIVER
TRANSCEIVER
WHERESOEVER
WHICHSOEVER
CAULIFLOWER
STRAIGHTWAY
STRAWFLOWER
UNDERGROWTH
PROPHYLAXIS
CHLOROPHYLL
ELECTROLYTE
ELECTROTYPE
HORSEPLAYER
MODULARIZED
SYNTHESIZER
TRAILBLAZER
UNCIVILIZED
UNORGANIZED

## 10th Letter

ABECEDARIAN
ACADEMICIAN
ALEXANDRIAN
ANTIQUARIAN
APHRODISIAC
ASSEMBLYMAN
AUDIOVISUAL
BLOODSTREAM
BUSINESSMAN
CAMEROONIAN
CARRAGEENAN
CATEGORICAL
CATERPILLAR
CENTENARIAN
CENTRIFUGAL
CENTRIPETAL
CIRCUMLUNAR
CIRCUMPOLAR
CONDITIONAL
CONGRESSMAN
CONTINENTAL
CREPUSCULAR
DICTATORIAL
DISAPPROVAL
ELECTRICIAN
ELIZABETHAN
EQUILATERAL
EVANGELICAL
EXCEPTIONAL
FUNDAMENTAL
GENTLEWOMAN
GINGERBREAD
HEXADECIMAL
HYPERBOREAN
IMPRACTICAL
INCORPOREAL
INCREMENTAL
INEFFECTUAL
INTENTIONAL
INTERLINEAR
INTERRACIAL
LIBERTARIAN
LILLIPUTIAN
MAGISTERIAL
MERCHANTMAN
MONOLINGUAL
MULTIRACIAL
NEANDERTHAL
NEEDLEWOMAN
NONPARTISAN
PARAMEDICAL
PENTECOSTAL
PERIODONTAL
PHARISAICAL
PISCATORIAL
POLYNOMINAL
PORTMANTEAU
PRETERMINAL
PROCRUSTEAN
PROLETARIAN
PROLETARIAT
PROVISIONAL
QUADRENNIAL
RECESSIONAL
RECTILINEAR
RESIDENTIAL
REVERENTIAL
SENSATIONAL
SENTIMENTAL
SPECTACULAR
SPECTROGRAM
STRAIGHTWAY
SUBSTANTIAL
SUBTROPICAL

SUPERFICIAL
TERRESTRIAL
TERRITORIAL
TESTIMONIAL
THEORETICAL
THEREWITHAL
THUNDERCLAP
THUNDERHEAD
TRENCHERMAN
TRINIDADIAN
TRINITARIAN
UNCHRISTIAN
UNEQUIVOCAL
UNICELLULAR
UTILITARIAN
WASHERWOMAN
WHEREWITHAL
SUPERSCRIBE
ADOLESCENCE
AERONAUTICS
AFTEREFFECT
AMBIVALENCE
ARISTOCRACY
BACKSTRETCH
BENEFICENCE
BENEVOLENCE
BIOFEEDBACK
BUREAUCRACY
CANDLESTICK
CAPACITANCE
CENTERPIECE
CHOCKABLOCK
CIRCUMSPECT
COINCIDENCE
COMEUPPANCE
COMMONPLACE
COMPLACENCE
COMPLACENCY
CONCORDANCE
CONCURRENCE
CONDUCTANCE
CONFEDERACY
CONFORMANCE
CONSEQUENCE
CONSERVANCY
CONSISTENCE
CONSISTENCY
CONTINGENCY
CONTINUANCE
CONTRIVANCE
CONVENIENCE
COUNTENANCE
CRACKERJACK
CYBERNETICS
DELINQUENCY
DESPONDENCY
DIAMONDBACK
DISCREPANCY
ELECTRONICS
EXCRESCENCE
FIDDLESTICK
FLORESCENCE
GEOPOLITICS
HISTRIONICS
HOMESTRETCH
HYDROPONICS
IMPUISSANCE
INSOUCIANCE
INTEROFFICE
IRIDESCENCE
IRREVERENCE
JUVENOCRACY
LEATHERNECK
LINGUISTICS
MALFEASANCE
MALPRACTICE
MANTELPIECE
MARKETPLACE
MASTERPIECE
MATHEMATICS
MERITOCRACY
MESALLIANCE
METAPHYSICS
MISALLIANCE
MISFEASANCE
MISGUIDANCE
NONVIOLENCE
NUMISMATICS
ORTHOPEDICS
OUTDISTANCE
OVERBALANCE
PERFORMANCE
PROSTHETICS
PROVENIENCE
QUARTERBACK
QUARTERDECK
RECONSTRUCT
REMEMBRANCE
RENAISSANCE
RESEMBLANCE
SHUTTLECOCK
SUBSISTENCE
SUFFICIENCY
SUPERSONICS
TECHNOCRACY
ULTRASONICS
WEATHERCOCK
WORDPERFECT
ACCELERANDO
AMONTILLADO
COUNTRYSIDE
DECRESCENDO
DISQUIETUDE
INCERTITUDE
INFANTICIDE
INGRATITUDE
INSECTICIDE
PITCHBLENDE
PROMPTITUDE
PULCHRITUDE
SWITCHBLADE
THALIDOMIDE
VICISSITUDE
AFTERBURNER
ANTECHAMBER
BALLCARRIER
BEACHCOMBER
BITTERSWEET
BLOCKBUSTER
BLOODSUCKER
BOILERMAKER
BREADBASKET
BREADWINNER
BURGOMASTER
CALORIMETER
CARDSHARPER
CASTELLATED
CATERCORNER
CAULIFLOWER
CHANTICLEER
CHEERLEADER
CHOIRMASTER
CHRONOMETER
CLEARHEADED
CLOSEFISTED
COLORCASTER
COMPLICATED
COMPTROLLER
CONDITIONED
COUNTRIFIED
CRAPSHOOTER
CRESTFALLEN
DILAPIDATED
DISENCUMBER
DOWNHEARTED
DOWNTRODDEN
DRILLMASTER
DYNAMOMETER
ELECTIONEER
EXPERIENCED
FAULTFINDER
FIRECRACKER
FLOORWALKER
FOREQUARTER
FORESHORTEN
FOULMOUTHED
FRANKFURTER
FREETHINKER
GALLBLADDER
GERRYMANDER
GODDAUGHTER
GRANDFATHER
GRANDMOTHER
GRASSHOPPER
GREENGROCER
GROUNDSHEET
GROUNDWATER
HABERDASHER
HAIRDRESSER
HALFHEARTED
HANDICAPPER
HARDHEARTED
HAREBRAINED
HEARTBROKEN
HINDQUARTER
HOMESTEADER
HORSEPLAYER
HOUSEBROKEN
HOUSEKEEPER
HOUSEMOTHER
IMAGESETTER
IMPASSIONED
INTERPRETER
KINDHEARTED
LAMPLIGHTER
LASERWRITER
LEVELHEADED
LIONHEARTED
LOUDMOUTHED
LOUDSPEAKER
MALADJUSTED
MASSACHUSET
MEADOWSWEET
MINESWEEPER
MINNESINGER
MISBEGOTTEN
MISBELIEVER
MODULARIZED
MONEYLENDER
MOUNTAINEER
NARRAGANSET
NEARSIGHTED
NECKERCHIEF
NIGHTWALKER
NINNYHAMMER
NORTHEASTER
OPINIONATED
OUTMANEUVER
OVERSTUFFED
PAPERHANGER
PARATROOPER
PARISHIONER
PHILOSOPHER
PLACEHOLDER
PLAINSPOKEN
PREASSIGNED
PREOCCUPIED
PRIZEWINNER
PROBATIONER
QUACKSALVER
QUICKSILVER
RATHSKELLER
RECONNOITER
SCREWDRIVER
SEISMOMETER
SEMITRAILER
SHAREHOLDER
SHIPBUILDER
SHORTHANDED
SLEEPWALKER
SPEEDOMETER
SPELLBINDER
SPREADSHEET
STEAMROLLER
STEPBROTHER
STEREOTYPED
STOCKBROKER
STOCKHOLDER
STOREKEEPER
STORYTELLER
STRAITLACED
STRAWFLOWER
STREAMLINED
STREAMLINER
SUPERMARKET
SWEEPSTAKES
SYNTHESIZER
TELEPRINTER
THERMOMETER
TIGHTFISTED
TOASTMASTER
TRAILBLAZER
TRANSCEIVER
TRANSMITTER
TRUEHEARTED
TYPEFOUNDER
TYPOGRAPHER
ULTRAVIOLET
UNACCOUNTED
UNCIVILIZED
UNCOMMITTED
UNCONCERNED
UNDERHANDED
UNDERSIGNED
UNINHIBITED
UNMITIGATED
UNORGANIZED
UNQUALIFIED
UNSATURATED
UNVARNISHED
VARICOLORED
WARMHEARTED
WASTEBASKET
WATERLOGGED
WHERESOEVER
WHICHSOEVER
WHIFFLETREE
WHIPPLETREE
WIDEMOUTHED
WINTERGREEN
WOODCHOPPER
WRONGHEADED
POCKETKNIFE
SPENDTHRIFT
ACKNOWLEDGE
ARCHAEOLOGY
ARCHIPELAGO
CAMPANOLOGY
CLIMATOLOGY
COUNTERSIGN
CRIMINOLOGY
DERMATOLOGY
FEATHEREDGE
FURNISHINGS
GERONTOLOGY
HAEMORRHAGE
HERPETOLOGY
ICHTHYOLOGY
INTERCHANGE
METEOROLOGY
METHODOLOGY
MUSKELLUNGE
ORNITHOLOGY
PHRASEOLOGY
PLANETOLOGY
SHORTCHANGE
TERMINOLOGY
UNDERCHARGE
VOLCANOLOGY
BATHYSCAPHE
BLAMEWORTHY
CALLIGRAPHY
CANDLELIGHT
CARTOGRAPHY
CATASTROPHE
CHIROGRAPHY
DREADNOUGHT
FILMOGRAPHY
FORETHOUGHT
HAGIOGRAPHY
HEAVYWEIGHT
HYDROGRAPHY
HYPERTROPHY
LIGHTWEIGHT
LITHOGRAPHY
ORTHOGRAPHY
OVERWROUGHT
PALEOGRAPHY
PAPERWEIGHT
PENNYWEIGHT
PETROGRAPHY
PHOTOGRAPHY
PORNOGRAPHY
SEARCHLIGHT
SPACEFLIGHT
STENOGRAPHY
STOMACHACHE
TRUSTWORTHY
UNDERWEIGHT
WHEELWRIGHT
AGORAPHOBIA
ANAESTHESIA
ANASTOMOSIS
AVOIRDUPOIS
BACCHANALIA
BOURGEOISIE
BRAGGADOCIO
CAMARADERIE
CHAMBERLAIN
CHAMBERMAID
CHRISTIANIA
CLIMACTERIC
COUNTERFEIT
COUNTERVAIL
DIAMAGNETIC
DIAPHORETIC
ENDOTHERMIC
GENDARMERIE
GENERALSHIP
GEOMAGNETIC
GLOSSOLALIA
HELLENISTIC
HIGHFALUTIN
HOMEOSTASIS
HYDROPHOBIA
HYDROSTATIC
HYGROSCOPIC
INTERATOMIC
INTERNUNCIO
KINESTHESIA
KLEPTOMANIA
LEGERDEMAIN
MACROBIOTIC
MACROSCOPIC
MECHANISTIC
MEDIUMISTIC
MEGALOMANIA
MEGALOPOLIS
MELANCHOLIA
MELANCHOLIC
MEMORABILIA
MICROSCOPIC
NURSERYMAID
NYMPHOMANIA
ORTHODONTIA
PARATHYROID
PARATYPHOID
PARENTHESIS
PERIPATETIC

PERIPHRASIS
PERISTALSIS
PERITONITIS
POLYTECHNIC
PREHISTORIC
PROBLEMATIC
PROPHYLAXIS
PROSTATITIS
PSYCHEDELIA
PSYCHEDELIC
PSYCHOGENIC
RADIOMETRIC
REALPOLITIK
SCHOLARSHIP
SWALLOWTAIL
TACHYCARDIA
THERAPEUTIC
TONSILLITIS
TRICHINOSIS
TRUSTEESHIP
WORKMANSHIP
JABBERWOCKY
RATTLESNAKE
WORKMANLIKE
ACCORDINGLY
ACCOUNTABLE
APPRECIABLE
BATTLEFIELD
BIBLIOPHILE
BLOODMOBILE
CHLOROPHYLL
COCKLESHELL
COMBUSTIBLE
COMFORTABLE
CONFESSEDLY
CONTRACTILE
CONVENTICLE
CONVERTIBLE
DISASSEMBLE
DISENTANGLE
DISPENSABLE
EXCEEDINGLY
FARTHINGALE
FASHIONABLE
FORTNIGHTLY
HONEYSUCKLE
ILLIMITABLE
IMMITIGABLE
IMPERMEABLE
IMPLAUSIBLE
IMPREGNABLE
INALIENABLE
INDEFINABLE
INDIVISIBLE
INDOMITABLE
INDUBITABLE
INELUCTABLE
INESCAPABLE
INESTIMABLE
INEXCUSABLE
INFLAMMABLE
INNUMERABLE
INSCRUTABLE
INSEPARABLE
INSUPERABLE
INTERMEDDLE
INTERMINGLE
INTOLERABLE
INTRACTABLE
IRREDUCIBLE
IRREFUTABLE
IRREMOVABLE
IRREPARABLE
IRREVOCABLE
LICKSPITTLE
MOLLYCODDLE
MOMENTARILY
MULTIFAMILY
NETHERWORLD
NIGHTINGALE
PERCEPTIBLE
PERFECTIBLE
PERMISSIBLE
PLEASURABLE
PONTIFICALS
PRACTICABLE
REDOUBTABLE
REGIMENTALS
RELOCATABLE
RESPECTABLE
RESPONSIBLE
SERVICEABLE
SUBASSEMBLY
SUBMERSIBLE
SUSCEPTIBLE
THEATRICALS
THUNDERBOLT
TOWNSPEOPLE
UNALIENABLE
UNAVOIDABLE
UNDESIRABLE
UNFAVORABLE
UNFLAPPABLE
UNPRINTABLE
UNSPEAKABLE
UNTHINKABLE
UNTOUCHABLE
UNUTTERABLE
VIOLONCELLO
PHYSIOGNOMY
PSYCHODRAMA
UNWHOLESOME
VENTURESOME
ACQUIREMENT
ADVERTISING
ALEXANDRINE
AMPHETAMINE
ANTICYCLONE
ANTIOXIDANT
APPOINTMENT
ARBITRAMENT
BALLETOMANE
BELLIGERENT
CALCULATING
CLAIRVOYANT
CLANDESTINE
COBBLESTONE
COEFFICIENT
COMMANDMENT
COMMUNICANT
COMPARTMENT
COMPORTMENT
CONCERNMENT
CONCOMITANT
CONSIDERING
CONSIGNMENT
CONSTITUENT
CONTAMINANT
CONTENTMENT
CORNERSTONE
COUNTERMAND
COUNTERPANE
COUNTERSINK
DETERMINANT
ELEPHANTINE
EMPLACEMENT
ENGINEERING
ENVIRONMENT
EPINEPHRINE
EQUIDISTANT
EVERLASTING
EXPECTORANT
EXTRAVAGANT
FINGERPRINT
FORMFITTING
FORTHCOMING
GARNISHMENT
GEANTICLINE
GEOSYNCLINE
GRANDPARENT
GREASEPAINT
HANDSHAKING
HANDWRITING
HARDWORKING
HEARTHSTONE
HERRINGBONE
IMPERMANENT
IMPERTINENT
IMPROVEMENT
IMPROVIDENT
INADVERTENT
INCARNADINE
INCOMPETENT
INCONGRUENT
INCONTINENT
INDEPENDENT
INDIFFERENT
INEFFICIENT
INGATHERING
INNERSPRING
INOPPORTUNE
INSINUATING
INSTALLMENT
INTELLIGENT
INTERESTING
INTERLACING
INTERLINING
INTERNECINE
KNUCKLEBONE
LABORSAVING
LATCHSTRING
MAGNIFICENT
MAIDSERVANT
MEASUREMENT
MERRYMAKING
MICROSECOND
MILLISECOND
MONKEYSHINE
NAPHTHALENE
NEEDLEPOINT
NONDOCUMENT
NONRESIDENT
NOURISHMENT
OBSOLESCENT
OMNIPRESENT
OUTBUILDING
OUTSTANDING
OVERBEARING
OVERWEENING
PAINSTAKING
PENETRATING
POLYSTYRENE
PREDICAMENT
PROGRAMMING
PROTUBERANT
REFRESHMENT
REMINISCENT
REMONSTRANT
REPLACEMENT
REQUIREMENT
RESPLENDENT
ROTTENSTONE
SAFEKEEPING
SCAFFOLDING
SHELLACKING
SHORTCOMING
SIGNIFICANT
SMITHEREENS
SUPERINTEND
SUPPRESSANT
TEMPERAMENT
THERMOCLINE
TIMESHARING
TOPDRESSING
TRAGEDIENNE
TRANSLUCENT
TRANSPARENT
TYPESETTING
TYPEWRITING
ULTRAMARINE
UNDERGROUND
UNDERTAKING
UNDESIGNING
UNDEVIATING
UNFLINCHING
UNREASONING
UNRELENTING
UNREMITTING
VIRIDESCENT
WAINSCOTING
ABOMINATION
ABSTRACTION
ACCELERATOR
ACCEPTATION
ACCLAMATION
ACCUMULATOR
ACQUISITION
AFFECTATION
AGGREGATION
ALTERCATION
ANNUNCIATOR
ANTINEUTRON
APOCYNTHION
APPELLATION
APPLICATION
APPROBATION
ASSIGNATION
ASSOCIATION
BATTLEWAGON
BENEDICTION
BENEFACTION
BROTHERHOOD
CALCULATION
CEMENTATION
CHOLESTEROL
CHRISTENDOM
COEDUCATION
COLLOCATION
COMBINATION
COMMENTATOR
COMMINATION
COMMUTATION
COMPETITION
COMPOSITION
COMPUNCTION
CONJUGATION
CONJUNCTION
CONNOTATION
CONSERVATOR
CONSUMPTION
CONTRAPTION
CONURBATION
CONVOCATION
CONVOLUTION
COPROCESSOR
CORPORATION
CRUCIFIXION
CYBERNATION
DEFALCATION
DEFLORATION
DELECTATION
DENOMINATOR
DEPREDATION
DEPRIVATION
DERELICTION
DESCRIPTION
DESPERATION
DESTINATION
DESTRUCTION
DICOTYLEDON
DIFFRACTION
DISILLUSION
DISPOSITION
DISPUTATION
DISSOLUTION
DISTINCTION
DISTRIBUTOR
EDIFICATION
EXPECTATION
EXTRADITION
FORNICATION
GRAVITATION
HABITUATION
HYDROCARBON
HYPHENATION
IMAGINATION
IMBRICATION
IMPORTATION
INATTENTION
INCANTATION
INCARNATION
INCINERATOR
INCLINATION
INDENTATION
INDIGESTION
INDIGNATION
INFORMATION
INQUISITION
INSPIRATION
INSTITUTION
INSTRUCTION
INTERACTION
INTERCEPTOR
KWASHIORKOR
LACRIMATION
LEGISLATION
LUCUBRATION
MACHINATION
MALEDICTION
MALFUNCTION
MARSHMALLOW
MENSURATION
METRICATION
MISDEMEANOR
MOUNTAINTOP
NICKELODEON
OBSERVATION
OBSTRUCTION
OFFICIALDOM
OSTENTATION
PARTURITION
PERMUTATION
POLLINATION
PREDECESSOR
PREIGNITION
PREMONITION
PREPOSITION
PRESUMPTION
PROGRESSION
PROHIBITION
PROPOSITION
PUBLICATION
PUNCTUATION
RADIOCARBON
RAPSCALLION
RECOGNITION
REFORMATION
REINFECTION
REPLICATION
REPROBATION
REQUISITION
RESERVATION
RESIGNATION
RESPIRATION
RESTITUTION
RESTORATION
RESTRICTION
RETRIBUTION
SUPPOSITION
SYNCOPATION
TOTALIZATOR
TRANSACTION
TREPIDATION
TRIBULATION
UNIFICATION
VACCINATION
VALEDICTION
VENTILATION
VINDICATION

VIVISECTION
WHEELBARROW
WITENAGEMOT
WORKSTATION
ZOOPLANKTON
CARDIOGRAPH
CHRONOGRAPH
CONTRETEMPS
ELECTROTYPE
FLUOROSCOPE
GUTTERSNIPE
MISANTHROPE
MUTTONCHOPS
NONDESCRIPT
SEISMOGRAPH
STEREOSCOPE
STEREOSCOPY
STETHOSCOPE
STROBOSCOPE
SUPERSCRIPT
ABRACADABRA
ACUPUNCTURE
AGRICULTURE
ANNIVERSARY
AQUICULTURE
BATHYSPHERE
BENEFICIARY
BICENTENARY
BOUTONNIERE
BOYSENBERRY
CABINETWORK
CANDIDATURE
CARAVANSARY
CENTERBOARD
CHANCELLERY
CHIAROSCURO
CONJUNCTURE
COSIGNATORY
COUNTERPART
DEPRECATORY
DISPLEASURE
DOCTRINAIRE
DOCUMENTARY
EARTHENWARE
ELECTROFORM
EXPENDITURE
EXTEMPORARY
FINGERBOARD
FORECLOSURE
FOREVERMORE
FRAGMENTARY
FUNCTIONARY
FURTHERMORE
GALLIMAUFRY
GRANITEWARE
HARPSICHORD
HUCKLEBERRY

HUMMINGBIRD
HYDROSPHERE
IDENTIFIERS
INTERCALARY
INVESTITURE
INVOLUNTARY
KITCHENWARE
LATTICEWORK
LEGISLATURE
LITHOSPHERE
MANUFACTORY
MANUFACTURE
MILLIAMPERE
MILLIONAIRE
MOCKINGBIRD
MORTARBOARD
MOTHERBOARD
MUSCULATURE
OBSERVATORY
OZONOSPHERE
PACHYSANDRA
PERFUNCTORY
PHOTOSPHERE
PORTRAITURE
PRELIMINARY
PROFANATORY
PROPRIETARY
REACTIONARY
REFORMATORY
ROTOGRAVURE
SMORGASBORD
SPRINGBOARD
SUBSTANDARD
SUPPOSITORY
SWITCHBOARD
TEMPERATURE
THITHERWARD
TRANSFIGURE
TROPOSPHERE
ULTRAMODERN
VALEDICTORY
VITICULTURE
WEATHERWORN
ABORTIONIST
ABSENTEEISM
ACADEMICISM
ANACHRONISM
ARCHDIOCESE
ASTIGMATISM
BEHAVIORISM
BIMETALLISM
BLUNDERBUSS
CLERICALISM
COFFEEHOUSE
COLONIALISM
CONSUMERISM
CONTROVERSY

CUSTOMHOUSE
DETERMINISM
DIPLOMATIST
DISCOURTESY
DISTINGUISH
ENFRANCHISE
EXHAUSTLESS
FARTHERMOST
FLABBERGAST
FURTHERMOST
GYROCOMPASS
HAIRSTYLIST
HORSERADISH
ILLUSIONISM
IMPERIALISM
INTERCOURSE
INTERSPERSE
IRREDENTISM
LETTERPRESS
MALAPROPISM
MARCHIONESS
MATERIALISM
MERCHANDISE
MONASTICISM
NATIONALISM
NATIONALIST
NONETHELESS
NOTHINGNESS
OFFICIALISM
OPPORTUNISM
PATERNALISM
POINTILLISM
POLTERGEIST
PORTERHOUSE
PORTIONLESS
PORTRAITIST
PRIMITIVISM
PROTAGONIST
RATIONALISM
ROMANTICISM
SCHOOLHOUSE
SUMMERHOUSE
SUPERIMPOSE
SUPREMACIST
SYNCHROMESH
THOUGHTLESS
TOBACCONIST
UNDEREXPOSE
VACATIONIST
VICHYSSOISE
WATERCOURSE
ZOOMORPHISM
ACCOMMODATE
AGGLOMERATE
AGGLUTINATE
ANTIGRAVITY
ANTIPOVERTY

APPROPRIATE
APPROXIMATE
ASSASSINATE
BARBITURATE
BICARBONATE
BREAKPOINTS
BREASTPLATE
CAPILLARITY
CARDINALATE
CARDINALITY
CASSITERITE
CATHOLICITY
CERTIFICATE
CHEESECLOTH
CIRCULARITY
COGNOSCENTE
COLLABORATE
COMMEMORATE
COMMISERATE
COMMUNICATE
CONCENTRATE
CONFEDERATE
CONSIDERATE
CONSOLIDATE
CONTAMINATE
CONTEMPLATE
CONTRARIETY
CORROBORATE
COTTONMOUTH
DEMONSTRATE
DESEGREGATE
DETERIORATE
DETERMINATE
DIRECTORATE
DISSEMINATE
DISSIMULATE
DOMESTICATE
DOMESTICITY
ELECTRICITY
ELECTROCUTE
ELECTROLYTE
ENCAPSULATE
EVENTUALITY
EXPECTORATE
EXPOSTULATE
EXPROPRIATE
EXTERMINATE
EXTRAPOLATE
FAMILIARITY
FLANNELETTE
GESTICULATE
HAIRBREADTH
HALLUCINATE
HISTORICITY
HOSPITALITY
HOUSELIGHTS
HYDROGENATE

HYPOTHECATE
IMMORTALITY
IMPEDIMENTA
IMPERFORATE
IMPERSONATE
IMPORTUNATE
IMPROPRIETY
INCARCERATE
INCORPORATE
INCRIMINATE
INDIVIDUATE
INSTABILITY
INSTANTIATE
INTERCALATE
INTERPOLATE
INTERRELATE
INTERROGATE
INVESTIGATE
KITCHENETTE
LABRADORITE
MARQUISETTE
MATRICULATE
NATIONALITY
NECESSITATE
OPPORTUNITY
ORCHESTRATE
PARTICIPATE
PARTICULATE
PENULTIMATE
PERAMBULATE
PERSNICKETY
PERSONALITY
POMEGRANATE
PONTIFICATE
PRECIPITATE
PREDOMINATE
PREMEDITATE
PREVARICATE
PROLIFERATE
PROPINQUITY
RATIONALITY
RECIPROCATE
RECIPROCITY
RECRIMINATE
REFRIGERATE
REGURGITATE
REMONSTRATE
RESISTIVITY
RESUSCITATE
REVERBERATE
ROADABILITY
SCINTILLATE
SCUTTLEBUTT
SENSIBILITY
SEQUESTRATE
SERENDIPITY
SOVEREIGNTY

STOCKINETTE
STRANGULATE
SUBORDINATE
SUBURBANITE
SUFFRAGETTE
THENCEFORTH
THEREABOUTS
TRIANGULATE
TRIUMVIRATE
TUBERCULATE
TWELVEMONTH
UNCERTAINTY
UNDERGROWTH
UNDERSHORTS
UNFORTUNATE
VERMICULITE
VINAIGRETTE
WHEREABOUTS
CALCIFEROUS
CALIFORNIUM
CANDELABRUM
CARNIVOROUS
CEREMONIOUS
CONDOMINIUM
CONNOISSEUR
CONSPICUOUS
CORRIGENDUM
COTERMINOUS
DELETERIOUS
DESIDERATUM
DISCONTINUE
DISCOTHEQUE
EFFICACIOUS
EINSTEINIUM
EQUILIBRIUM
EXPEDITIOUS
FARINACEOUS
HERBIVOROUS
HOMOGENEOUS
IGNOMINIOUS
ILLUSTRIOUS
IMPECUNIOUS
INCONGRUOUS
INCREDULOUS
INCUNABULUM
INDUSTRIOUS
INTERREGNUM
INTRAVENOUS
IRRELIGIOUS
LITTERATEUR
MAGNANIMOUS
MELLIFLUOUS
MENDELEVIUM
MERITORIOUS
MICROCAPSUL
MISCHIEVOUS
MISCONSTRUE

MONSEIGNEUR
NECESSITOUS
OPPROBRIOUS
PANDEMONIUM
PERSPICUOUS
PESTIFEROUS
PICTURESQUE
PLANETARIUM
PRECIPITOUS
PRETENTIOUS
PROGNATHOUS
PROMISCUOUS
PUNCTILIOUS
QUADRENNIUM
REPETITIOUS
SARCOPHAGUS
SCRUMPTIOUS
SENTENTIOUS
SPONTANEOUS
SUPERFLUOUS
SYNCHRONOUS
TEASPOONFUL
TEMPESTUOUS
TENDENTIOUS
TREACHEROUS
UNCONSCIOUS
UNRIGHTEOUS
VENTRILOQUY
VERTIGINOUS
ACQUISITIVE
ADVERSATIVE
AFFIRMATIVE
ALTERNATIVE
ASSOCIATIVE
ATTRIBUTIVE
CARMINATIVE
COEXTENSIVE
COMMUTATIVE
COMPARATIVE
CONJUNCTIVA
CONJUNCTIVE
CONNOTATIVE
CONSECUTIVE
CONSUMPTIVE
COOPERATIVE
CORRELATIVE
DECLARATIVE
DISTINCTIVE
HYPERACTIVE
INEFFECTIVE
INFORMATIVE
INOPERATIVE
INQUISITIVE
INSTRUCTIVE
INTERACTIVE
LEGISLATIVE
MISCONCEIVE

NONNEGATIVE
PERSPECTIVE
PRECONCEIVE
PREROGATIVE
PROGRESSIVE
QUALITATIVE
RESTORATIVE
RETROACTIVE
SUBJUNCTIVE
SUBSTANTIVE
SUPERLATIVE
UNOBTRUSIVE
THISTLEDOWN
PROTOMARTYR
ACCLIMATIZE
ALPHABETIZE
CANNIBALIZE
CIRCULARIZE
COMPUTERIZE
CRYSTALLIZE
DEMAGNETIZE
DEMOCRATIZE
DESENSITIZE
DISORGANIZE
EXTEMPORIZE
HOSPITALIZE
HYPOTHESIZE
IMMORTALIZE
MATERIALIZE
MINIATURIZE
NATIONALIZE
PERSONALIZE
PROSELYTIZE
RATIONALIZE
SOLILOQUIZE
STANDARDIZE
SYNCHRONIZE
SYSTEMATIZE
TRANQUILIZE

## 11TH LETTER

ABRACADABRA
AGORAPHOBIA
ANAESTHESIA
BACCHANALIA
CHRISTIANIA
CONJUNCTIVA
GLOSSOLALIA
HYDROPHOBIA
IMPEDIMENTA
KINESTHESIA
KLEPTOMANIA
MEGALOMANIA
MELANCHOLIA
MEMORABILIA
NYMPHOMANIA
ORTHODONTIA
PACHYSANDRA
PSYCHEDELIA
PSYCHODRAMA
TACHYCARDIA
APHRODISIAC
CLIMACTERIC
DIAMAGNETIC
DIAPHORETIC
ENDOTHERMIC
GEOMAGNETIC
HELLENISTIC
HYDROSTATIC
HYGROSCOPIC
INTERATOMIC
MACROBIOTIC
MACROSCOPIC
MECHANISTIC
MEDIUMISTIC
MELANCHOLIC
MICROSCOPIC
PERIPATETIC
POLYTECHNIC
PREHISTORIC
PROBLEMATIC
PSYCHEDELIC
PSYCHOGENIC
RADIOMETRIC
THERAPEUTIC
BATTLEFIELD
BROTHERHOOD
CASTELLATED
CENTERBOARD
CHAMBERMAID
CLEARHEADED
CLOSEFISTED
COMPLICATED
CONDITIONED
COUNTERMAND
COUNTRIFIED
DILAPIDATED
DOWNHEARTED
EXPERIENCED
FINGERBOARD
FOULMOUTHED
GINGERBREAD
HALFHEARTED
HARDHEARTED
HAREBRAINED
HARPSICHORD
HUMMINGBIRD
IMPASSIONED
KINDHEARTED
LEVELHEADED
LIONHEARTED
LOUDMOUTHED
MALADJUSTED
MICROSECOND
MILLISECOND
MOCKINGBIRD
MODULARIZED
MORTARBOARD
MOTHERBOARD
NEARSIGHTED
NETHERWORLD
NURSERYMAID
OPINIONATED
OVERSTUFFED
PARATHYROID
PARATYPHOID
PREASSIGNED
PREOCCUPIED
SHORTHANDED
SMORGASBORD
SPRINGBOARD
STEREOTYPED
STRAITLACED
STREAMLINED
SUBSTANDARD
SWITCHBOARD
THITHERWARD
THUNDERHEAD
TIGHTFISTED
TRUEHEARTED
UNACCOUNTED
UNCIVILIZED
UNCOMMITTED
UNCONCERNED
UNDERGROUND
UNDERHANDED
UNDERSIGNED
UNINHIBITED
UNMITIGATED
UNORGANIZED
UNQUALIFIED
UNSATURATED
UNVARNISHED
VARICOLORED
WARMHEARTED
WATERLOGGED
WIDEMOUTHED
WRONGHEADED
ACCLIMATIZE
ACCOMMODATE
ACCOUNTABLE
ACKNOWLEDGE
ACQUISITIVE
ACUPUNCTURE
ADOLESCENCE
ADVERSATIVE
AFFIRMATIVE
AGGLOMERATE
AGGLUTINATE
AGRICULTURE
ALEXANDRINE
ALPHABETIZE
ALTERNATIVE
AMBIVALENCE
AMPHETAMINE
ANTICYCLONE
APPRECIABLE
APPROPRIATE
APPROXIMATE
AQUICULTURE
ARCHDIOCESE
ASSASSINATE
ASSOCIATIVE
ATTRIBUTIVE
BALLETOMANE
BARBITURATE
BATHYSCAPHE
BATHYSPHERE
BENEFICENCE
BENEVOLENCE
BIBLIOPHILE
BICARBONATE
BLOODMOBILE
BOURGEOISIE
BOUTONNIERE
BREASTPLATE
CAMARADERIE
CANDIDATURE
CANNIBALIZE
CAPACITANCE
CARDINALATE
CARMINATIVE
CASSITERITE
CATASTROPHE
CENTERPIECE
CERTIFICATE
CIRCULARIZE
CLANDESTINE
COBBLESTONE
COEXTENSIVE
COFFEEHOUSE
COGNOSCENTE
COINCIDENCE
COLLABORATE
COMBUSTIBLE
COMEUPPANCE
COMFORTABLE
COMMEMORATE
COMMISERATE
COMMONPLACE
COMMUNICATE
COMMUTATIVE
COMPARATIVE
COMPLACENCE
COMPUTERIZE
CONCENTRATE
CONCORDANCE
CONCURRENCE
CONDUCTANCE
CONFEDERATE
CONFORMANCE
CONJUNCTIVE
CONJUNCTURE
CONNOTATIVE
CONSECUTIVE
CONSEQUENCE
CONSIDERATE
CONSISTENCE
CONSOLIDATE
CONSUMPTIVE
CONTAMINATE
CONTEMPLATE
CONTINUANCE
CONTRACTILE
CONTRIVANCE
CONVENIENCE
CONVENTICLE
CONVERTIBLE
COOPERATIVE
CORNERSTONE
CORRELATIVE
CORROBORATE
COUNTENANCE
COUNTERPANE
COUNTRYSIDE
CRYSTALLIZE
CUSTOMHOUSE
DECLARATIVE
DEMAGNETIZE
DEMOCRATIZE
DEMONSTRATE
DESEGREGATE
DESENSITIZE
DETERIORATE
DETERMINATE
DIRECTORATE
DISASSEMBLE
DISCONTINUE
DISCOTHEQUE
DISENTANGLE
DISORGANIZE
DISPENSABLE
DISPLEASURE
DISQUIETUDE
DISSEMINATE
DISSIMULATE
DISTINCTIVE
DOCTRINAIRE
DOMESTICATE
EARTHENWARE
ELECTROCUTE
ELECTROLYTE
ELECTROTYPE
ELEPHANTINE
ENCAPSULATE
ENFRANCHISE
EPINEPHRINE
EXCRESCENCE
EXPECTORATE
EXPENDITURE
EXPOSTULATE
EXPROPRIATE
EXTEMPORIZE
EXTERMINATE
EXTRAPOLATE
FARTHINGALE
FASHIONABLE
FEATHEREDGE
FLANNELETTE
FLORESCENCE
FLUOROSCOPE
FORECLOSURE
FOREVERMORE
FURTHERMORE
GEANTICLINE
GENDARMERIE
GEOSYNCLINE
GESTICULATE
GRANITEWARE
GUTTERSNIPE
HAEMORRHAGE
HALLUCINATE
HEARTHSTONE
HERRINGBONE
HONEYSUCKLE
HOSPITALIZE
HYDROGENATE
HYDROSPHERE
HYPERACTIVE
HYPOTHECATE
HYPOTHESIZE
ILLIMITABLE
IMMITIGABLE
IMMORTALIZE
IMPERFORATE
IMPERMEABLE
IMPERSONATE
IMPLAUSIBLE
IMPORTUNATE
IMPREGNABLE
IMPUISSANCE
INALIENABLE
INCARCERATE
INCARNADINE
INCERTITUDE
INCORPORATE
INCRIMINATE
INDEFINABLE
INDIVIDUATE
INDIVISIBLE
INDOMITABLE
INDUBITABLE
INEFFECTIVE
INELUCTABLE
INESCAPABLE
INESTIMABLE
INEXCUSABLE
INFANTICIDE
INFLAMMABLE
INFORMATIVE
INGRATITUDE
INNUMERABLE
INOPERATIVE
INOPPORTUNE
INQUISITIVE
INSCRUTABLE
INSECTICIDE
INSEPARABLE
INSOUCIANCE
INSTANTIATE
INSTRUCTIVE
INSUPERABLE
INTERACTIVE
INTERCALATE
INTERCHANGE
INTERCOURSE
INTERMEDDLE
INTERMINGLE
INTERNECINE
INTEROFFICE
INTERPOLATE
INTERRELATE
INTERROGATE
INTERSPERSE
INTOLERABLE
INTRACTABLE
INVESTIGATE
INVESTITURE
IRIDESCENCE
IRREDUCIBLE
IRREFUTABLE
IRREMOVABLE
IRREPARABLE
IRREVERENCE
IRREVOCABLE
KITCHENETTE
KITCHENWARE
KNUCKLEBONE
LABRADORITE
LEGISLATIVE
LEGISLATURE
LICKSPITTLE
LITHOSPHERE
MALFEASANCE
MALPRACTICE
MANTELPIECE

MANUFACTURE
MARKETPLACE
MARQUISETTE
MASTERPIECE
MATERIALIZE
MATRICULATE
MERCHANDISE
MESALLIANCE
MILLIAMPERE
MILLIONAIRE
MINIATURIZE
MISALLIANCE
MISANTHROPE
MISCONCEIVE
MISCONSTRUE
MISFEASANCE
MISGUIDANCE
MOLLYCODDLE
MONKEYSHINE
MUSCULATURE
MUSKELLUNGE
NAPHTHALENE
NATIONALIZE
NECESSITATE
NIGHTINGALE
NONNEGATIVE
NONVIOLENCE
ORCHESTRATE
OUTDISTANCE
OVERBALANCE
OZONOSPHERE
PARTICIPATE
PARTICULATE
PENULTIMATE
PERAMBULATE
PERCEPTIBLE
PERFECTIBLE
PERFORMANCE
PERMISSIBLE
PERSONALIZE
PERSPECTIVE
PHOTOSPHERE
PICTURESQUE
PITCHBLENDE
PLEASURABLE
POCKETKNIFE
POLYSTYRENE
POMEGRANATE
PONTIFICATE
PORTERHOUSE
PORTRAITURE
PRACTICABLE
PRECIPITATE
PRECONCEIVE
PREDOMINATE
PREMEDITATE
PREROGATIVE

PREVARICATE
PROGRESSIVE
PROLIFERATE
PROMPTITUDE
PROSELYTIZE
PROVENIENCE
PULCHRITUDE
QUALITATIVE
RATIONALIZE
RATTLESNAKE
RECIPROCATE
RECRIMINATE
REDOUBTABLE
REFRIGERATE
REGURGITATE
RELOCATABLE
REMEMBRANCE
REMONSTRATE
RENAISSANCE
RESEMBLANCE
RESPECTABLE
RESPONSIBLE
RESTORATIVE
RESUSCITATE
RETROACTIVE
REVERBERATE
ROTOGRAVURE
ROTTENSTONE
SCHOOLHOUSE
SCINTILLATE
SEQUESTRATE
SERVICEABLE
SHORTCHANGE
SOLILOQUIZE
STANDARDIZE
STEREOSCOPE
STETHOSCOPE
STOCKINETTE
STOMACHACHE
STRANGULATE
STROBOSCOPE
SUBJUNCTIVE
SUBMERSIBLE
SUBORDINATE
SUBSISTENCE
SUBSTANTIVE
SUBURBANITE
SUFFRAGETTE
SUMMERHOUSE
SUPERIMPOSE
SUPERLATIVE
SUPERSCRIBE
SUSCEPTIBLE
SWITCHBLADE
SYNCHRONIZE
SYSTEMATIZE
TEMPERATURE

THALIDOMIDE
THERMOCLINE
TOWNSPEOPLE
TRAGEDIENNE
TRANQUILIZE
TRANSFIGURE
TRIANGULATE
TRIUMVIRATE
TROPOSPHERE
TUBERCULATE
ULTRAMARINE
UNALIENABLE
UNAVOIDABLE
UNDERCHARGE
UNDEREXPOSE
UNDESIRABLE
UNFAVORABLE
UNFLAPPABLE
UNFORTUNATE
UNOBTRUSIVE
UNPRINTABLE
UNSPEAKABLE
UNTHINKABLE
UNTOUCHABLE
UNUTTERABLE
UNWHOLESOME
VENTURESOME
VERMICULITE
VICHYSSOISE
VICISSITUDE
VINAIGRETTE
VITICULTURE
WATERCOURSE
WHIFFLETREE
WHIPPLETREE
WORKMANLIKE
NECKERCHIEF
ADVERTISING
CALCULATING
CONSIDERING
ENGINEERING
EVERLASTING
FORMFITTING
FORTHCOMING
HANDSHAKING
HANDWRITING
HARDWORKING
INGATHERING
INNERSPRING
INSINUATING
INTERESTING
INTERLACING
INTERLINING
LABORSAVING
LATCHSTRING
MERRYMAKING
OUTBUILDING

OUTSTANDING
OVERBEARING
OVERWEENING
PAINSTAKING
PENETRATING
PROGRAMMING
SAFEKEEPING
SCAFFOLDING
SHELLACKING
SHORTCOMING
TIMESHARING
TOPDRESSING
TYPESETTING
TYPEWRITING
UNDERTAKING
UNDESIGNING
UNDEVIATING
UNFLINCHING
UNREASONING
UNRELENTING
UNREMITTING
WAINSCOTING
BACKSTRETCH
CARDIOGRAPH
CHEESECLOTH
CHRONOGRAPH
COTTONMOUTH
DISTINGUISH
HAIRBREADTH
HOMESTRETCH
HORSERADISH
SEISMOGRAPH
SYNCHROMESH
THENCEFORTH
TWELVEMONTH
UNDERGROWTH
BIOFEEDBACK
CABINETWORK
CANDLESTICK
CHOCKABLOCK
COUNTERSINK
CRACKERJACK
DIAMONDBACK
FIDDLESTICK
LATTICEWORK
LEATHERNECK
QUARTERBACK
QUARTERDECK
REALPOLITIK
SHUTTLECOCK
WEATHERCOCK
AUDIOVISUAL
CATEGORICAL
CENTRIFUGAL
CENTRIPETAL
CHLOROPHYLL
CHOLESTEROL

COCKLESHELL
CONDITIONAL
CONTINENTAL
COUNTERVAIL
DICTATORIAL
DISAPPROVAL
EQUILATERAL
EVANGELICAL
EXCEPTIONAL
FUNDAMENTAL
HEXADECIMAL
IMPRACTICAL
INCORPOREAL
INCREMENTAL
INEFFECTUAL
INTENTIONAL
INTERRACIAL
MAGISTERIAL
MICROCAPSUL
MONOLINGUAL
MULTIRACIAL
NEANDERTHAL
PARAMEDICAL
PENTECOSTAL
PERIODONTAL
PHARISAICAL
PISCATORIAL
POLYNOMINAL
PRETERMINAL
PROVISIONAL
QUADRENNIAL
RECESSIONAL
RESIDENTIAL
REVERENTIAL
SENSATIONAL
SENTIMENTAL
SUBSTANTIAL
SUBTROPICAL
SUPERFICIAL
SWALLOWTAIL
TEASPOONFUL
TERRESTRIAL
TERRITORIAL
TESTIMONIAL
THEORETICAL
THEREWITHAL
UNEQUIVOCAL
WHEREWITHAL
ABSENTEEISM
ACADEMICISM
ANACHRONISM
ASTIGMATISM
BEHAVIORISM
BIMETALLISM
BLOODSTREAM
CALIFORNIUM
CANDELABRUM

CHRISTENDOM
CLERICALISM
COLONIALISM
CONDOMINIUM
CONSUMERISM
CORRIGENDUM
DESIDERATUM
DETERMINISM
EINSTEINIUM
ELECTROFORM
EQUILIBRIUM
ILLUSIONISM
IMPERIALISM
INCUNABULUM
INTERREGNUM
IRREDENTISM
MALAPROPISM
MATERIALISM
MENDELEVIUM
MONASTICISM
NATIONALISM
OFFICIALDOM
OFFICIALISM
OPPORTUNISM
PANDEMONIUM
PATERNALISM
PLANETARIUM
POINTILLISM
PRIMITIVISM
QUADRENNIUM
RATIONALISM
ROMANTICISM
SPECTROGRAM
ZOOMORPHISM
ABECEDARIAN
ABOMINATION
ABSTRACTION
ACADEMICIAN
ACCEPTATION
ACCLAMATION
ACQUISITION
AFFECTATION
AGGREGATION
ALEXANDRIAN
ALTERCATION
ANTINEUTRON
ANTIQUARIAN
APOCYNTHION
APPELLATION
APPLICATION
APPROBATION
ASSEMBLYMAN
ASSIGNATION
ASSOCIATION
BATTLEWAGON
BENEDICTION
BENEFACTION

BUSINESSMAN
CALCULATION
CAMEROONIAN
CARRAGEENAN
CEMENTATION
CENTENARIAN
CHAMBERLAIN
COEDUCATION
COLLOCATION
COMBINATION
COMMINATION
COMMUTATION
COMPETITION
COMPOSITION
COMPUNCTION
CONGRESSMAN
CONJUGATION
CONJUNCTION
CONNOTATION
CONSUMPTION
CONTRAPTION
CONURBATION
CONVOCATION
CONVOLUTION
CORPORATION
COUNTERSIGN
CRESTFALLEN
CRUCIFIXION
CYBERNATION
DEFALCATION
DEFLORATION
DELECTATION
DEPREDATION
DEPRIVATION
DERELICTION
DESCRIPTION
DESPERATION
DESTINATION
DESTRUCTION
DICOTYLEDON
DIFFRACTION
DISILLUSION
DISPOSITION
DISPUTATION
DISSOLUTION
DISTINCTION
DOWNTRODDEN
EDIFICATION
ELECTRICIAN
ELIZABETHAN
EXPECTATION
EXTRADITION
FORESHORTEN
FORNICATION
GENTLEWOMAN
GRAVITATION
HABITUATION

HEARTBROKEN
HIGHFALUTIN
HOUSEBROKEN
HYDROCARBON
HYPERBOREAN
HYPHENATION
IMAGINATION
IMBRICATION
IMPORTATION
INATTENTION
INCANTATION
INCARNATION
INCLINATION
INDENTATION
INDIGESTION
INDIGNATION
INFORMATION
INQUISITION
INSPIRATION
INSTITUTION
INSTRUCTION
INTERACTION
LACRIMATION
LEGERDEMAIN
LEGISLATION
LIBERTARIAN
LILLIPUTIAN
LUCUBRATION
MACHINATION
MALEDICTION
MALFUNCTION
MENSURATION
MERCHANTMAN
METRICATION
MISBEGOTTEN
NEEDLEWOMAN
NICKELODEON
NONPARTISAN
OBSERVATION
OBSTRUCTION
OSTENTATION
PARTURITION
PERMUTATION
PLAINSPOKEN
POLLINATION
PREIGNITION
PREMONITION
PREPOSITION
PRESUMPTION
PROCRUSTEAN
PROGRESSION
PROHIBITION
PROLETARIAN
PROPOSITION
PUBLICATION
PUNCTUATION
RADIOCARBON
RAPSCALLION
RECOGNITION
REFORMATION
REINFECTION
REPLICATION
REPROBATION
REQUISITION
RESERVATION
RESIGNATION
RESPIRATION
RESTITUTION
RESTORATION
RESTRICTION
RETRIBUTION
SUPPOSITION
SYNCOPATION
THISTLEDOWN
TRANSACTION
TRENCHERMAN
TREPIDATION
TRIBULATION
TRINIDADIAN
TRINITARIAN
ULTRAMODERN
UNCHRISTIAN
UNIFICATION
UTILITARIAN
VACCINATION
VALEDICTION
VENTILATION
VINDICATION
VIVISECTION
WASHERWOMAN
WEATHERWORN
WINTERGREEN
WORKSTATION
ZOOPLANKTON
ACCELERANDO
AMONTILLADO
ARCHIPELAGO
BRAGGADOCIO
CHIAROSCURO
DECRESCENDO
INTERNUNCIO
VIOLONCELLO
GENERALSHIP
MOUNTAINTOP
SCHOLARSHIP
THUNDERCLAP
TRUSTEESHIP
WORKMANSHIP
ACCELERATOR
ACCUMULATOR
AFTERBURNER
ANNUNCIATOR
ANTECHAMBER
BALLCARRIER
BEACHCOMBER
BLOCKBUSTER
BLOODSUCKER
BOILERMAKER
BREADWINNER
BURGOMASTER
CALORIMETER
CARDSHARPER
CATERCORNER
CATERPILLAR
CAULIFLOWER
CHANTICLEER
CHEERLEADER
CHOIRMASTER
CHRONOMETER
CIRCUMLUNAR
CIRCUMPOLAR
COLORCASTER
COMMENTATOR
COMPTROLLER
CONNOISSEUR
CONSERVATOR
COPROCESSOR
CRAPSHOOTER
CREPUSCULAR
DENOMINATOR
DISENCUMBER
DISTRIBUTOR
DRILLMASTER
DYNAMOMETER
ELECTIONEER
FAULTFINDER
FIRECRACKER
FLOORWALKER
FOREQUARTER
FRANKFURTER
FREETHINKER
GALLBLADDER
GERRYMANDER
GODDAUGHTER
GRANDFATHER
GRANDMOTHER
GRASSHOPPER
GREENGROCER
GROUNDWATER
HABERDASHER
HAIRDRESSER
HANDICAPPER
HINDQUARTER
HOMESTEADER
HORSEPLAYER
HOUSEKEEPER
HOUSEMOTHER
IMAGESETTER
INCINERATOR
INTERCEPTOR
INTERLINEAR
INTERPRETER
KWASHIORKOR
LAMPLIGHTER
LASERWRITER
LITTERATEUR
LOUDSPEAKER
MINESWEEPER
MINNESINGER
MISBELIEVER
MISDEMEANOR
MONEYLENDER
MONSEIGNEUR
MOUNTAINEER
NIGHTWALKER
NINNYHAMMER
NORTHEASTER
OUTMANEUVER
PAPERHANGER
PARATROOPER
PARISHIONER
PHILOSOPHER
PLACEHOLDER
PREDECESSOR
PRIZEWINNER
PROBATIONER
PROTOMARTYR
QUACKSALVER
QUICKSILVER
RATHSKELLER
RECONNOITER
RECTILINEAR
SCREWDRIVER
SEISMOMETER
SEMITRAILER
SHAREHOLDER
SHIPBUILDER
SLEEPWALKER
SPECTACULAR
SPEEDOMETER
SPELLBINDER
STEAMROLLER
STEPBROTHER
STOCKBROKER
STOCKHOLDER
STOREKEEPER
STORYTELLER
STRAWFLOWER
STREAMLINER
SYNTHESIZER
TELEPRINTER
THERMOMETER
TOASTMASTER
TOTALIZATOR
TRAILBLAZER
TRANSCEIVER
TRANSMITTER
TYPEFOUNDER
TYPOGRAPHER
UNICELLULAR
WHERESOEVER
WHICHSOEVER
WOODCHOPPER
AERONAUTICS
ANASTOMOSIS
AVOIRDUPOIS
BLUNDERBUSS
BREAKPOINTS
CALCIFEROUS
CARNIVOROUS
CEREMONIOUS
CONSPICUOUS
CONTRETEMPS
COTERMINOUS
CYBERNETICS
DELETERIOUS
EFFICACIOUS
ELECTRONICS
EXHAUSTLESS
EXPEDITIOUS
FARINACEOUS
FURNISHINGS
GEOPOLITICS
GYROCOMPASS
HERBIVOROUS
HISTRIONICS
HOMEOSTASIS
HOMOGENEOUS
HOUSELIGHTS
HYDROPONICS
IDENTIFIERS
IGNOMINIOUS
ILLUSTRIOUS
IMPECUNIOUS
INCONGRUOUS
INCREDULOUS
INDUSTRIOUS
INTRAVENOUS
IRRELIGIOUS
LETTERPRESS
LINGUISTICS
MAGNANIMOUS
MARCHIONESS
MATHEMATICS
MEGALOPOLIS
MELLIFLUOUS
MERITORIOUS
METAPHYSICS
MISCHIEVOUS
MUTTONCHOPS
NECESSITOUS
NONETHELESS
NOTHINGNESS
NUMISMATICS
OPPROBRIOUS
ORTHOPEDICS
PARENTHESIS
PERIPHRASIS
PERISTALSIS
PERITONITIS
PERSPICUOUS
PESTIFEROUS
PONTIFICALS
PORTIONLESS
PRECIPITOUS
PRETENTIOUS
PROGNATHOUS
PROMISCUOUS
PROPHYLAXIS
PROSTATITIS
PROSTHETICS
PUNCTILIOUS
REGIMENTALS
REPETITIOUS
SARCOPHAGUS
SCRUMPTIOUS
SENTENTIOUS
SMITHEREENS
SPONTANEOUS
SUPERFLUOUS
SUPERSONICS
SWEEPSTAKES
SYNCHRONOUS
TEMPESTUOUS
TENDENTIOUS
THEATRICALS
THEREABOUTS
THOUGHTLESS
TONSILLITIS
TREACHEROUS
TRICHINOSIS
ULTRASONICS
UNCONSCIOUS
UNDERSHORTS
UNRIGHTEOUS
VERTIGINOUS
WHEREABOUTS
ABORTIONIST
ACQUIREMENT
AFTEREFFECT
ANTIOXIDANT
APPOINTMENT
ARBITRAMENT
BELLIGERENT
BITTERSWEET
BREADBASKET
CANDLELIGHT
CIRCUMSPECT
CLAIRVOYANT
COEFFICIENT
COMMANDMENT
COMMUNICANT
COMPARTMENT
COMPORTMENT
CONCERNMENT
CONCOMITANT
CONSIGNMENT
CONSTITUENT
CONTAMINANT
CONTENTMENT
COUNTERFEIT
COUNTERPART
DETERMINANT
DIPLOMATIST
DREADNOUGHT
EMPLACEMENT
ENVIRONMENT
EQUIDISTANT
EXPECTORANT
EXTRAVAGANT
FARTHERMOST
FINGERPRINT
FLABBERGAST
FORETHOUGHT
FURTHERMOST
GARNISHMENT
GRANDPARENT
GREASEPAINT
GROUNDSHEET
HAIRSTYLIST
HEAVYWEIGHT
IMPERMANENT
IMPERTINENT
IMPROVEMENT
IMPROVIDENT
INADVERTENT
INCOMPETENT
INCONGRUENT
INCONTINENT
INDEPENDENT
INDIFFERENT
INEFFICIENT
INSTALLMENT
INTELLIGENT
LIGHTWEIGHT
MAGNIFICENT
MAIDSERVANT
MASSACHUSET
MEADOWSWEET
MEASUREMENT
NARRAGANSET
NATIONALIST
NEEDLEPOINT
NONDESCRIPT
NONDOCUMENT
NONRESIDENT
NOURISHMENT
OBSOLESCENT
OMNIPRESENT

OVERWROUGHT
PAPERWEIGHT
PENNYWEIGHT
POLTERGEIST
PORTRAITIST
PREDICAMENT
PROLETARIAT
PROTAGONIST
PROTUBERANT
RECONSTRUCT
REFRESHMENT
REMINISCENT
REMONSTRANT
REPLACEMENT
REQUIREMENT
RESPLENDENT
SCUTTLEBUTT
SEARCHLIGHT
SIGNIFICANT
SPACEFLIGHT
SPENDTHRIFT
SPREADSHEET
SUPERMARKET
SUPERSCRIPT
SUPPRESSANT
SUPREMACIST
TEMPERAMENT
THUNDERBOLT
TOBACCONIST
TRANSLUCENT
TRANSPARENT
ULTRAVIOLET
UNDERWEIGHT
VACATIONIST
VIRIDESCENT
WASTEBASKET
WHEELWRIGHT
WITENAGEMOT
WORDPERFECT
PORTMANTEAU
MARSHMALLOW
WHEELBARROW
ACCORDINGLY
ANNIVERSARY
ANTIGRAVITY
ANTIPOVERTY
ARCHAEOLOGY
ARISTOCRACY
BENEFICIARY
BICENTENARY
BLAMEWORTHY
BOYSENBERRY
BUREAUCRACY
CALLIGRAPHY
CAMPANOLOGY
CAPILLARITY
CARAVANSARY
CARDINALITY
CARTOGRAPHY
CATHOLICITY
CHANCELLERY
CHIROGRAPHY
CIRCULARITY
CLIMATOLOGY
COMPLACENCY
CONFEDERACY
CONFESSEDLY
CONSERVANCY
CONSISTENCY
CONTINGENCY
CONTRARIETY
CONTROVERSY
COSIGNATORY
CRIMINOLOGY
DELINQUENCY
DEPRECATORY
DERMATOLOGY
DESPONDENCY
DISCOURTESY
DISCREPANCY
DOCUMENTARY
DOMESTICITY
ELECTRICITY
EVENTUALITY
EXCEEDINGLY
EXTEMPORARY
FAMILIARITY
FILMOGRAPHY
FORTNIGHTLY
FRAGMENTARY
FUNCTIONARY
GALLIMAUFRY
GERONTOLOGY
HAGIOGRAPHY
HERPETOLOGY
HISTORICITY
HOSPITALITY
HUCKLEBERRY
HYDROGRAPHY
HYPERTROPHY
ICHTHYOLOGY
IMMORTALITY
IMPROPRIETY
INSTABILITY
INTERCALARY
INVOLUNTARY
JABBERWOCKY
JUVENOCRACY
LITHOGRAPHY
MANUFACTORY
MERITOCRACY
METEOROLOGY
METHODOLOGY
MOMENTARILY
MULTIFAMILY
NATIONALITY
OBSERVATORY
OPPORTUNITY
ORNITHOLOGY
ORTHOGRAPHY
PALEOGRAPHY
PERFUNCTORY
PERSNICKETY
PERSONALITY
PETROGRAPHY
PHOTOGRAPHY
PHRASEOLOGY
PHYSIOGNOMY
PLANETOLOGY
PORNOGRAPHY
PRELIMINARY
PROFANATORY
PROPINQUITY
PROPRIETARY
RATIONALITY
REACTIONARY
RECIPROCITY
REFORMATORY
RESISTIVITY
ROADABILITY
SENSIBILITY
SERENDIPITY
SOVEREIGNTY
STENOGRAPHY
STEREOSCOPY
STRAIGHTWAY
SUBASSEMBLY
SUFFICIENCY
SUPPOSITORY
TECHNOCRACY
TERMINOLOGY
TRUSTWORTHY
UNCERTAINTY
VALEDICTORY
VENTRILOQUY
VOLCANOLOGY

# 12 LETTER WORDS

1st Letter

ABBREVIATION
ABOLITIONISM
ABSENTMINDED
ACCOMPLISHED
ACQUAINTANCE
ADVENTITIOUS
AERODYNAMICS
AFORETHOUGHT
AFTERTHOUGHT
ALLITERATION
ALPHANUMERIC
AMBIDEXTROUS
AMPHITHEATER
ANATHEMATIZE
ANNUNCIATION
ANTEDILUVIAN
ANTHROPOLOGY
ANTIALIASING
ANTIELECTRON
ANTIMACASSAR
ANTIMAGNETIC
ANTIPARTICLE
ANTITHETICAL
APOSTROPHIZE
APPENDECTOMY
APPENDICITIS
APPRECIATIVE
APPREHENSIVE
APPURTENANCE
ARCHITECTURE
ARGILLACEOUS
ASTRONAUTICS
ASTRONOMICAL
ASTROPHYSICS
ASYNCHRONOUS
ATMOSPHERICS
ATTITUDINIZE
AUDIOVISUALS
AUSTRONESIAN
AUTHENTICATE
AVITAMINOSIS
BACKTRACKING
BACTERICIDAL
BACTERIOLOGY
BELLIGERENCY
BIBLIOGRAPHY
BICENTENNIAL
BILLINGSGATE
BIOCHEMISTRY
BIOGEOGRAPHY
BIOSATELLITE
BIOTELEMETRY
BLANDISHMENT
BLATHERSKITE
BLOCKBUSTING
BLOODLETTING
BLOODTHIRSTY
BLUESTOCKING
BRAINWASHING
BREAKTHROUGH
BREASTSTROKE
BREATHTAKING
BRILLIANTINE
BUTTERSCOTCH
CABINETMAKER
CALISTHENICS
CANTANKEROUS
CARBOHYDRATE
CARBONACEOUS
CARILLONNEUR
CARPETBAGGER
CHALCOPYRITE
CHAMPIONSHIP
CHARACTERIZE
CHECKERBERRY
CHECKERBOARD
CHEESEBURGER
CHEESEPARING
CHEMOTHERAPY
CHESTERFIELD
CHILDBEARING
CHIROPRACTIC
CHITTERLINGS
CHOREOGRAPHY
CHRISTIANITY
CHRISTIANIZE
CHROMATICITY
CHROMOSPHERE
CHURCHWARDEN
CINEMATHEQUE
CIRCUMSCRIBE
CIRCUMSTANCE
CIVILIZATION
CLOSEMOUTHED
CLOTHESHORSE
CLOTHESPRESS
COELENTERATE
COLLECTIVISM
COLLECTIVIZE
COLLEGIALITY
COMMENCEMENT
COMMENSURATE
COMMISSARIAT
COMMISSIONER
COMMONWEALTH
COMMUNICABLE
COMPANIONWAY
COMPLAISANCE
CONCELEBRANT
CONCRESCENCE
CONFECTIONER
CONFESSIONAL
CONFIDENTIAL
CONFIRMATION
CONFORMATION
CONFUCIANISM
CONGLOMERATE
CONGRATULATE
CONGREGATION
CONQUISTADOR
CONSERVATION
CONSERVATISM
CONSERVATIVE
CONSERVATORY
CONSIDERABLE
CONSTABULARY
CONSTIPATION
CONSTITUENCY
CONSTITUTION
CONSTITUTIVE
CONSTRUCTION
CONTAINERIZE
CONTEMPORARY
CONTEMPTIBLE
CONTEMPTUOUS
CONTERMINOUS
CONTINUATION
CONTRAPUNTAL
CONTRARIWISE
CONTUMACIOUS
CONTUMELIOUS
CONVENTIONAL
CONVERSATION
CORESPONDENT
COSMOPOLITAN
COUNTERCLAIM
COUNTERPOINT
COUNTERPOISE
COUNTERTENOR
CROSSCURRENT
CRYPTOGRAPHY
CUMULONIMBUS
DECALCOMANIA
DECASYLLABIC
DECOMMISSION
DECONGESTANT
DELIBERATIVE
DELICATESSEN
DEMILITARIZE
DEMIMONDAINE
DEMINERALIZE
DEMONSTRABLE
DENOMINATION
DENSITOMETER
DENUNCIATION
DESPOLIATION
DESTRUCTIBLE
DETERMINABLE
DIASTROPHISM
DICTATORSHIP
DIFFERENTIAL
DISACCHARIDE
DISADVANTAGE
DISAGREEABLE
DISASSOCIATE
DISCIPLINARY
DISCONNECTED
DISCONSOLATE
DISCOURTEOUS
DISCRIMINATE
DISESTABLISH
DISFRANCHISE
DISINGENUOUS
DISINTEGRATE
DISOBEDIENCE
DISPENSATION
DISPLACEMENT
DISPUTATIOUS
DISQUISITION
DISREPUTABLE
DISSERTATION
DISTILLATION
DISTRIBUTIVE
EARSPLITTING
EARTHSHAKING
ECCLESIASTIC
ECHOLOCATION
EDITORIALIZE
ELECTROLYSIS
ELECTROPLATE
ELEEMOSYNARY
ENCEPHALITIS
ENCYCLOPEDIA
ENTERPRISING
ENTREPRENEUR
EPISCOPALIAN
EPITHALAMIUM
EQUESTRIENNE
EVERBLOOMING
EXCRUCIATING
EXTORTIONATE
EXTRAMARITAL
EXTRASENSORY
EXTRAVAGANZA
FAINTHEARTED
FEEBLEMINDED
FENESTRATION
FERMENTATION
FIBRILLATION
FLAMETHROWER
FLUORESCENCE
FLUOROCARBON
FORMALDEHYDE
FOUNTAINHEAD
FRANKENSTEIN
FRANKINCENSE
FREESTANDING
FRONTISPIECE
GALVANOMETER
GEOCHEMISTRY
GLASSBLOWING
GLOCKENSPIEL
GOBBLEDYGOOK
GREATHEARTED
HABERDASHERY
HAIRSPLITTER
HALLUCINOGEN
HANDKERCHIEF
HEADMISTRESS
HEADQUARTERS
HEARTRENDING
HEARTSTRINGS
HEARTWARMING
HEAVYHEARTED
HELIOCENTRIC
HELLGRAMMITE
HENCEFORWARD
HETEROSEXUAL
HIERARCHICAL
HIEROGLYPHIC
HIPPOPOTAMUS
HORTICULTURE
HOUSEWARMING
HUMANITARIAN
HYDROTHERAPY
HYDROTHERMAL
HYPERACIDITY
HYPERTENSION
HYPOCHONDRIA
HYPOGLYCEMIA
HYSTERECTOMY
IDIOSYNCRASY
ILLEGITIMATE
ILLUSTRATION
ILLUSTRATIVE
IMMEASURABLE
IMPENETRABLE
IMPERCEPTIVE
IMPERCIPIENT
IMPERFECTION
IMPERISHABLE
IMPONDERABLE
INARTICULATE
INCALCULABLE
INCANDESCENT
INCAPACITATE
INCOMPARABLE
INCOMPATIBLE
INCONSOLABLE
INCONVENIENT
INCORRIGIBLE
INCRUSTATION
INDECLINABLE
INDEFEASIBLE
INDEPENDENCE
INDIGESTIBLE
INDISPUTABLE
INDISSOLUBLE
INDOCTRINATE
INEFFACEABLE
INEXPERIENCE
INEXPLICABLE
INEXTRICABLE
INFELICITOUS
INFLAMMATION
INFLAMMATORY
INFLATIONARY
INFLATIONISM
INGRATIATING
INSALUBRIOUS
INSTRUMENTAL
INSUFFERABLE
INSUFFICIENT
INSURRECTION

INTELLECTUAL
INTELLIGENCE
INTELLIGIBLE
INTEMPERANCE
INTERCESSION
INTERFERENCE
INTERGLACIAL
INTERJECTION
INTERLOCUTOR
INTERMEDIARY
INTERMEDIATE
INTERMINABLE
INTERMISSION
INTERMITTENT
INTERSECTION
INTERSTELLAR
INTERVOCALIC
INTRANSIGENT
INTRANSITIVE
INVERTEBRATE
INVITATIONAL
INVULNERABLE
IRREDEEMABLE
IRREFRAGABLE
IRREMEDIABLE
IRRESISTIBLE
IRRESPECTIVE
IRREVERSIBLE
ISOLATIONISM
JURISDICTION
KALEIDOSCOPE
KINDERGARTEN
LEXICOGRAPHY
LIGHTHEARTED
LONGITUDINAL
LONGSHOREMAN
LUMINESCENCE
LUNCHEONETTE
MADEMOISELLE
MAGNETOMETER
MAGNILOQUENT
MALFORMATION
MALNOURISHED
MALNUTRITION
MALOCCLUSION
MANSLAUGHTER
MARLINESPIKE
MASTERSTROKE
MASTURBATION
MEALYMOUTHED
MEETINGHOUSE
MENSTRUATION
MERCHANTABLE
MERETRICIOUS
MESSEIGNEURS
METALANGUAGE
METAMORPHISM
MICROBIOLOGY
MICROCIRCUIT
MICROCLIMATE
MICROSPACING
MICROSURGERY
MIDDLEWEIGHT
MINICOMPUTER
MISADVENTURE
MISAPPREHEND
MISCALCULATE
MISINTERPRET
MISPRONOUNCE
MISREPRESENT
MONOFILAMENT
MONOSYLLABLE
MOUNTAINSIDE
MUDDLEHEADED
MULLIGATAWNY
MULTICOLORED
MULTIFACETED
MULTIFARIOUS
MULTILATERAL
MULTILINGUAL
MULTIPLICAND
MULTIPLICITY
MULTIPURPOSE
MULTISESSION
MULTITASKING
MULTIVERSITY
MULTIVITAMIN
MUNICIPALITY
NEIGHBORHOOD
NEURASTHENIA
NEUROSCIENCE
NEVERTHELESS
NEWSMAGAZINE
NEWSPAPERMAN
NIGHTCLOTHES
NOMENCLATURE
NONAGENARIAN
NONCOMBATANT
NONCOMMITTAL
NONCONDUCTOR
NONOBJECTIVE
NONSCHEDULED
OBSCURANTISM
OBSTREPEROUS
OCEANOGRAPHY
OCTOGENARIAN
OCTOSYLLABIC
OFFICEHOLDER
ONOMATOPOEIA
ORGANIZATION
OSCILLOSCOPE
OTHERWORLDLY
OUTSTRETCHED
OVEREXPOSURE
OXYACETYLENE
PACKINGHOUSE
PALEONTOLOGY
PANCHROMATIC
PARADISIACAL
PARAMILITARY
PARASITOLOGY
PARENTHESIZE
PEACEKEEPING
PENITENTIARY
PERADVENTURE
PERAMBULATOR
PERICYNTHION
PERSPICACITY
PERTINACIOUS
PESTILENTIAL
PHARMACOLOGY
PHILANTHROPY
PHILHARMONIC
PHILODENDRON
PHILOSOPHIZE
PHOTOCOMPOSE
PHOTOENGRAVE
PHOTOGRAVURE
PHYSIOGRAPHY
PICKERELWEED
PIGMENTATION
PLANETESIMAL
PLASTERBOARD
POLARIZATION
POLICYHOLDER
POLYETHYLENE
POLYMORPHISM
POLYSYLLABIC
POLYSYLLABLE
PORCELAINIZE
POSTDOCTORAL
POSTGRADUATE
POSTHYPNOTIC
POSTMISTRESS
PRACTITIONER
PRASEODYMIUM
PREAMPLIFIER
PRECANCEROUS
PRECIPITANCY
PRECONCERTED
PRECONDITION
PREDESIGNATE
PREDETERMINE
PREDIGESTION
PREDILECTION
PREFABRICATE
PREINDUCTION
PREMENSTRUAL
PREOPERATIVE
PREPAREDNESS
PREPONDERATE
PREPOSTEROUS
PREREQUISITE
PRESBYTERIAN
PRESCRIPTION
PRESENTIMENT
PRESUMPTUOUS
PRIMOGENITOR
PRINCIPALITY
PROCATHEDRAL
PROCESSIONAL
PROFESSIONAL
PROGRAMMABLE
PROLEGOMENON
PROPAGANDIZE
PROPHYLACTIC
PROPORTIONAL
PROTACTINIUM
PROTECTORATE
PROTHALAMION
PROTUBERANCE
PROVIDENTIAL
PSYCHOACTIVE
PSYCHOSEXUAL
PSYCHOTROPIC
PUMPERNICKEL
PYROTECHNICS
QUANTITATIVE
QUARTERSTAFF
QUESTIONABLE
QUINTESSENCE
RADIOISOTOPE
RADIOTHERAPY
RAMBUNCTIOUS
RECALCITRANT
RECAPITULATE
RECEIVERSHIP
RECEPTIONIST
RECOGNIZANCE
RECOLLECTION
RECONSTITUTE
REGISTRATION
REHABILITATE
RELATIONSHIP
RELATIVISTIC
REMINISCENCE
REMONSTRANCE
REMUNERATION
REMUNERATIVE
RENUNCIATION
REPERCUSSION
RESPECTIVELY
RESTAURATEUR
RESURRECTION
RHODODENDRON
SARSAPARILLA
SATISFACTION
SATISFACTORY
SCANDINAVIAN
SCATOLOGICAL
SCHOOLFELLOW
SCHOOLMASTER
SECRETARIATE
SELENOGRAPHY
SENSITOMETER
SEXAGENARIAN
SHARECROPPER
SHARPSHOOTER
SHORTSIGHTED
SHUFFLEBOARD
SIGNIFICANCE
SIMULTANEOUS
SLEDGEHAMMER
SOMNAMBULISM
SPECTROGRAPH
SPECTROMETER
SPECTROSCOPE
SPERMATOZOON
SPIRITUALISM
SPORTSWRITER
STEEPLECHASE
STEPDAUGHTER
STEREOPHONIC
STEREOSCOPIC
STRAIGHTAWAY
STRAIGHTEDGE
STRAITJACKET
STRATIGRAPHY
STRATOSPHERE
STREETWALKER
STREPTOMYCIN
SUBCOMMITTEE
SUBCONSCIOUS
SUBCONTINENT
SUBCUTANEOUS
SUBDIRECTORY
SUBMINIATURE
SUBSCRIPTION
SUBSERVIENCE
SUBSTANTIATE
SUBSTRUCTURE
SUBTERRANEAN
SUPERANNUATE
SUPERCHARGER
SUPERCILIOUS
SUPERHIGHWAY
SUPERNATURAL
SUPERSTITION
SURROUNDINGS
SURVEILLANCE
SWASHBUCKLER
TECHNICALITY
TENDEROMETER
TERCENTENARY
TESTOSTERONE
THANKSGIVING
THERAPEUTICS
THERMOSPHERE
THOROUGHBRED
THOROUGHFARE
THUNDERCLOUD
THUNDERSTORM
TOTALITARIAN
TRADESPEOPLE
TRANQUILIZER
TRANSCENDENT
TRANSFERENCE
TRANSMIGRATE
TRANSMISSION
TRANSMOGRIFY
TRANSOCEANIC
TRANSPACIFIC
TRANSVESTISM
TRAPSHOOTING
TRIGNOMETRIC
TRIGONOMETRY
TROUBLEMAKER
TUBERCULOSIS
ULTRAMONTANE
UNACCUSTOMED
UNASSAILABLE
UNBELIEVABLE
UNCHARITABLE
UNDERCLOTHES
UNDERCOATING
UNDERCURRENT
UNDERDRAWERS
UNDERGARMENT
UNDERPINNING
UNDERSURFACE
UNDOCUMENTED
UNEMPLOYMENT
UNFREQUENTED
UNGOVERNABLE
UNINTERESTED
UNIVERSALIST
UNIVERSALITY
UNIVERSALIZE
UNLIKELIHOOD
UNMISTAKABLE
UNPARALLELED
UNPRINCIPLED
UNPROFITABLE
UNREASONABLE
UNREGENERATE
UNRESTRAINED
UNSCIENTIFIC
UNSCRUPULOUS
UNSEARCHABLE
UNSEASONABLE
UNSEGREGATED
VACATIONLAND

**V**AINGLORIOUS
**V**ALENCIENNES
**V**ALORIZATION
**V**ENIPUNCTURE
**V**ERTICILLATE
**V**ETERINARIAN
**W**EATHERBOARD
**W**EATHERGLASS
**W**EATHERPROOF
**W**ELTERWEIGHT
**W**HIPPOORWILL
**W**HOLEHEARTED
**Z**OOGEOGRAPHY

## 2ND LETTER

B**A**CKTRACKING
B**A**CTERICIDAL
B**A**CTERIOLOGY
C**A**BINETMAKER
C**A**LISTHENICS
C**A**NTANKEROUS
C**A**RBOHYDRATE
C**A**RBONACEOUS
C**A**RILLONNEUR
C**A**RPETBAGGER
E**A**RSPLITTING
E**A**RTHSHAKING
F**A**INTHEARTED
G**A**LVANOMETER
H**A**BERDASHERY
H**A**IRSPLITTER
H**A**LLUCINOGEN
H**A**NDKERCHIEF
K**A**LEIDOSCOPE
M**A**DEMOISELLE
M**A**GNETOMETER
M**A**GNILOQUENT
M**A**LFORMATION
M**A**LNOURISHED
M**A**LNUTRITION
M**A**LOCCLUSION
M**A**NSLAUGHTER
M**A**RLINESPIKE
M**A**STERSTROKE
M**A**STURBATION
P**A**CKINGHOUSE
P**A**LEONTOLOGY
P**A**NCHROMATIC
P**A**RADISIACAL
P**A**RAMILITARY
P**A**RASITOLOGY
P**A**RENTHESIZE
R**A**DIOISOTOPE
R**A**DIOTHERAPY
R**A**MBUNCTIOUS
S**A**RSAPARILLA
S**A**TISFACTION
S**A**TISFACTORY
V**A**CATIONLAND
V**A**INGLORIOUS
V**A**LENCIENNES
V**A**LORIZATION
A**B**BREVIATION
A**B**OLITIONISM
A**B**SENTMINDED
O**B**SCURANTISM
O**B**STREPEROUS
A**C**COMPLISHED
A**C**QUAINTANCE
E**C**CLESIASTIC
E**C**HOLOCATION
O**C**EANOGRAPHY
O**C**TOGENARIAN
O**C**TOSYLLABIC
S**C**ANDINAVIAN
S**C**ATOLOGICAL
S**C**HOOLFELLOW
S**C**HOOLMASTER
A**D**VENTITIOUS
E**D**ITORIALIZE
I**D**IOSYNCRASY
A**E**RODYNAMICS
B**E**LLIGERENCY
D**E**CALCOMANIA
D**E**CASYLLABIC
D**E**COMMISSION
D**E**CONGESTANT
D**E**LIBERATIVE
D**E**LICATESSEN
D**E**MILITARIZE
D**E**MIMONDAINE
D**E**MINERALIZE
D**E**MONSTRABLE
D**E**NOMINATION
D**E**NSITOMETER
D**E**NUNCIATION
D**E**SPOLIATION
D**E**STRUCTIBLE
D**E**TERMINABLE
F**E**EBLEMINDED
F**E**NESTRATION
F**E**RMENTATION
G**E**OCHEMISTRY
H**E**ADMISTRESS
H**E**ADQUARTERS
H**E**ARTRENDING
H**E**ARTSTRINGS
H**E**ARTWARMING
H**E**AVYHEARTED
H**E**LIOCENTRIC
H**E**LLGRAMMITE
H**E**NCEFORWARD
H**E**TEROSEXUAL
L**E**XICOGRAPHY
M**E**ALYMOUTHED
M**E**ETINGHOUSE
M**E**NSTRUATION
M**E**RCHANTABLE
M**E**RETRICIOUS
M**E**SSEIGNEURS
M**E**TALANGUAGE
M**E**TAMORPHISM
N**E**IGHBORHOOD
N**E**URASTHENIA
N**E**UROSCIENCE
N**E**VERTHELESS
N**E**WSMAGAZINE
N**E**WSPAPERMAN
P**E**ACEKEEPING
P**E**NITENTIARY
P**E**RADVENTURE
P**E**RAMBULATOR
P**E**RICYNTHION
P**E**RSPICACITY
P**E**RTINACIOUS
P**E**STILENTIAL
R**E**CALCITRANT
R**E**CAPITULATE
R**E**CEIVERSHIP
R**E**CEPTIONIST
R**E**COGNIZANCE
R**E**COLLECTION
R**E**CONSTITUTE
R**E**GISTRATION
R**E**HABILITATE
R**E**LATIONSHIP
R**E**LATIVISTIC
R**E**MINISCENCE
R**E**MONSTRANCE
R**E**MUNERATION
R**E**MUNERATIVE
R**E**NUNCIATION
R**E**PERCUSSION
R**E**SPECTIVELY
R**E**STAURATEUR
R**E**SURRECTION
S**E**CRETARIATE
S**E**LENOGRAPHY
S**E**NSITOMETER
S**E**XAGENARIAN
T**E**CHNICALITY
T**E**NDEROMETER
T**E**RCENTENARY
T**E**STOSTERONE
V**E**NIPUNCTURE
V**E**RTICILLATE
V**E**TERINARIAN
W**E**ATHERBOARD
W**E**ATHERGLASS
W**E**ATHERPROOF
W**E**LTERWEIGHT
A**F**ORETHOUGHT
A**F**TERTHOUGHT
O**F**FICEHOLDER
C**H**ALCOPYRITE
C**H**AMPIONSHIP
C**H**ARACTERIZE
C**H**ECKERBERRY
C**H**ECKERBOARD
C**H**EESEBURGER
C**H**EESEPARING
C**H**EMOTHERAPY
C**H**ESTERFIELD
C**H**ILDBEARING
C**H**IROPRACTIC
C**H**ITTERLINGS
C**H**OREOGRAPHY
C**H**RISTIANITY
C**H**RISTIANIZE
C**H**ROMATICITY
C**H**ROMOSPHERE
C**H**URCHWARDEN
P**H**ARMACOLOGY
P**H**ILANTHROPY
P**H**ILHARMONIC
P**H**ILODENDRON
P**H**ILOSOPHIZE
P**H**OTOCOMPOSE
P**H**OTOENGRAVE
P**H**OTOGRAVURE
P**H**YSIOGRAPHY
R**H**ODODENDRON
S**H**ARECROPPER
S**H**ARPSHOOTER
S**H**ORTSIGHTED
S**H**UFFLEBOARD
T**H**ANKSGIVING
T**H**ERAPEUTICS
T**H**ERMOSPHERE
T**H**OROUGHBRED
T**H**OROUGHFARE
T**H**UNDERCLOUD
T**H**UNDERSTORM
W**H**IPPOORWILL
W**H**OLEHEARTED
B**I**BLIOGRAPHY
B**I**CENTENNIAL
B**I**LLINGSGATE
B**I**OCHEMISTRY
B**I**OGEOGRAPHY
B**I**OSATELLITE
B**I**OTELEMETRY
C**I**NEMATHEQUE
C**I**RCUMSCRIBE
C**I**RCUMSTANCE
C**I**VILIZATION
D**I**ASTROPHISM
D**I**CTATORSHIP
D**I**FFERENTIAL
D**I**SACCHARIDE
D**I**SADVANTAGE
D**I**SAGREEABLE
D**I**SASSOCIATE
D**I**SCIPLINARY
D**I**SCONNECTED
D**I**SCONSOLATE
D**I**SCOURTEOUS
D**I**SCRIMINATE
D**I**SESTABLISH
D**I**SFRANCHISE
D**I**SINGENUOUS
D**I**SINTEGRATE
D**I**SOBEDIENCE
D**I**SPENSATION
D**I**SPLACEMENT
D**I**SPUTATIOUS
D**I**SQUISITION
D**I**SREPUTABLE
D**I**SSERTATION
D**I**STILLATION
D**I**STRIBUTIVE
F**I**BRILLATION
H**I**ERARCHICAL
H**I**EROGLYPHIC
H**I**PPOPOTAMUS
K**I**NDERGARTEN
L**I**GHTHEARTED
M**I**CROBIOLOGY
M**I**CROCIRCUIT
M**I**CROCLIMATE
M**I**CROSPACING
M**I**CROSURGERY
M**I**DDLEWEIGHT
M**I**NICOMPUTER
M**I**SADVENTURE
M**I**SAPPREHEND
M**I**SCALCULATE
M**I**SINTERPRET
M**I**SPRONOUNCE
M**I**SREPRESENT
N**I**GHTCLOTHES
P**I**CKERELWEED
P**I**GMENTATION
S**I**GNIFICANCE
S**I**MULTANEOUS
A**L**LITERATION
A**L**PHANUMERIC
B**L**ANDISHMENT
B**L**ATHERSKITE
B**L**OCKBUSTING
B**L**OODLETTING
B**L**OODTHIRSTY
B**L**UESTOCKING
C**L**OSEMOUTHED
C**L**OTHESHORSE
C**L**OTHESPRESS
E**L**ECTROLYSIS
E**L**ECTROPLATE
E**L**EEMOSYNARY
F**L**AMETHROWER
F**L**UORESCENCE
F**L**UOROCARBON
G**L**ASSBLOWING
G**L**OCKENSPIEL
I**L**LEGITIMATE
I**L**LUSTRATION
I**L**LUSTRATIVE
P**L**ANETESIMAL
P**L**ASTERBOARD
S**L**EDGEHAMMER
U**L**TRAMONTANE
A**M**BIDEXTROUS
A**M**PHITHEATER
I**M**MEASURABLE
I**M**PENETRABLE
I**M**PERCEPTIVE
I**M**PERCIPIENT
I**M**PERFECTION
I**M**PERISHABLE
I**M**PONDERABLE
A**N**ATHEMATIZE
A**N**NUNCIATION
A**N**TEDILUVIAN
A**N**THROPOLOGY
A**N**TIALIASING
A**N**TIELECTRON
A**N**TIMACASSAR
A**N**TIMAGNETIC
A**N**TIPARTICLE
A**N**TITHETICAL
E**N**CEPHALITIS
E**N**CYCLOPEDIA
E**N**TERPRISING
E**N**TREPRENEUR
I**N**ARTICULATE
I**N**CALCULABLE
I**N**CANDESCENT
I**N**CAPACITATE
I**N**COMPARABLE
I**N**COMPATIBLE
I**N**CONSOLABLE
I**N**CONVENIENT
I**N**CORRIGIBLE
I**N**CRUSTATION
I**N**DECLINABLE
I**N**DEFEASIBLE
I**N**DEPENDENCE
I**N**DIGESTIBLE
I**N**DISPUTABLE

INDISSOLUBLE
INDOCTRINATE
INEFFACEABLE
INEXPERIENCE
INEXPLICABLE
INEXTRICABLE
INFELICITOUS
INFLAMMATION
INFLAMMATORY
INFLATIONARY
INFLATIONISM
INGRATIATING
INSALUBRIOUS
INSTRUMENTAL
INSUFFERABLE
INSUFFICIENT
INSURRECTION
INTELLECTUAL
INTELLIGENCE
INTELLIGIBLE
INTEMPERANCE
INTERCESSION
INTERFERENCE
INTERGLACIAL
INTERJECTION
INTERLOCUTOR
INTERMEDIARY
INTERMEDIATE
INTERMINABLE
INTERMISSION
INTERMITTENT
INTERSECTION
INTERSTELLAR
INTERVOCALIC
INTRANSIGENT
INTRANSITIVE
INVERTEBRATE
INVITATIONAL
INVULNERABLE
ONOMATOPOEIA
UNACCUSTOMED
UNASSAILABLE
UNBELIEVABLE
UNCHARITABLE
UNDERCLOTHES
UNDERCOATING
UNDERCURRENT
UNDERDRAWERS
UNDERGARMENT
UNDERPINNING
UNDERSURFACE
UNDOCUMENTED
UNEMPLOYMENT
UNFREQUENTED
UNGOVERNABLE
UNINTERESTED
UNIVERSALIST
UNIVERSALITY
UNIVERSALIZE
UNLIKELIHOOD
UNMISTAKABLE
UNPARALLELED
UNPRINCIPLED
UNPROFITABLE
UNREASONABLE
UNREGENERATE
UNRESTRAINED
UNSCIENTIFIC
UNSCRUPULOUS
UNSEARCHABLE
UNSEASONABLE
UNSEGREGATED
COELENTERATE
COLLECTIVISM
COLLECTIVIZE
COLLEGIALITY
COMMENCEMENT
COMMENSURATE
COMMISSARIAT
COMMISSIONER
COMMONWEALTH
COMMUNICABLE
COMPANIONWAY
COMPLAISANCE
CONCELEBRANT
CONCRESCENCE
CONFECTIONER
CONFESSIONAL
CONFIDENTIAL
CONFIRMATION
CONFORMATION
CONFUCIANISM
CONGLOMERATE
CONGRATULATE
CONGREGATION
CONQUISTADOR
CONSERVATION
CONSERVATISM
CONSERVATIVE
CONSERVATORY
CONSIDERABLE
CONSTABULARY
CONSTIPATION
CONSTITUENCY
CONSTITUTION
CONSTITUTIVE
CONSTRUCTION
CONTAINERIZE
CONTEMPORARY
CONTEMPTIBLE
CONTEMPTUOUS
CONTERMINOUS
CONTINUATION
CONTRAPUNTAL
CONTRARIWISE
CONTUMACIOUS
CONTUMELIOUS
CONVENTIONAL
CONVERSATION
CORESPONDENT
COSMOPOLITAN
COUNTERCLAIM
COUNTERPOINT
COUNTERPOISE
COUNTERTENOR
FORMALDEHYDE
FOUNTAINHEAD
GOBBLEDYGOOK
HORTICULTURE
HOUSEWARMING
LONGITUDINAL
LONGSHOREMAN
MONOFILAMENT
MONOSYLLABLE
MOUNTAINSIDE
NOMENCLATURE
NONAGENARIAN
NONCOMBATANT
NONCOMMITTAL
NONCONDUCTOR
NONOBJECTIVE
NONSCHEDULED
POLARIZATION
POLICYHOLDER
POLYETHYLENE
POLYMORPHISM
POLYSYLLABIC
POLYSYLLABLE
PORCELAINIZE
POSTDOCTORAL
POSTGRADUATE
POSTHYPNOTIC
POSTMISTRESS
SOMNAMBULISM
TOTALITARIAN
ZOOGEOGRAPHY
APOSTROPHIZE
APPENDECTOMY
APPENDICITIS
APPRECIATIVE
APPREHENSIVE
APPURTENANCE
EPISCOPALIAN
EPITHALAMIUM
SPECTROGRAPH
SPECTROMETER
SPECTROSCOPE
SPERMATOZOON
SPIRITUALISM
SPORTSWRITER
EQUESTRIENNE
ARCHITECTURE
ARGILLACEOUS
BRAINWASHING
BREAKTHROUGH
BREASTSTROKE
BREATHTAKING
BRILLIANTINE
CROSSCURRENT
CRYPTOGRAPHY
FRANKENSTEIN
FRANKINCENSE
FREESTANDING
FRONTISPIECE
GREATHEARTED
IRREDEEMABLE
IRREFRAGABLE
IRREMEDIABLE
IRRESISTIBLE
IRRESPECTIVE
IRREVERSIBLE
ORGANIZATION
PRACTITIONER
PRASEODYMIUM
PREAMPLIFIER
PRECANCEROUS
PRECIPITANCY
PRECONCERTED
PRECONDITION
PREDESIGNATE
PREDETERMINE
PREDIGESTION
PREDILECTION
PREFABRICATE
PREINDUCTION
PREMENSTRUAL
PREOPERATIVE
PREPAREDNESS
PREPONDERATE
PREPOSTEROUS
PREREQUISITE
PRESBYTERIAN
PRESCRIPTION
PRESENTIMENT
PRESUMPTUOUS
PRIMOGENITOR
PRINCIPALITY
PROCATHEDRAL
PROCESSIONAL
PROFESSIONAL
PROGRAMMABLE
PROLEGOMENON
PROPAGANDIZE
PROPHYLACTIC
PROPORTIONAL
PROTACTINIUM
PROTECTORATE
PROTHALAMION
PROTUBERANCE
PROVIDENTIAL
TRADESPEOPLE
TRANQUILIZER
TRANSCENDENT
TRANSFERENCE
TRANSMIGRATE
TRANSMISSION
TRANSMOGRIFY
TRANSOCEANIC
TRANSPACIFIC
TRANSVESTISM
TRAPSHOOTING
TRIGNOMETRIC
TRIGONOMETRY
TROUBLEMAKER
ASTRONAUTICS
ASTRONOMICAL
ASTROPHYSICS
ASYNCHRONOUS
ISOLATIONISM
OSCILLOSCOPE
PSYCHOACTIVE
PSYCHOSEXUAL
PSYCHOTROPIC
ATMOSPHERICS
ATTITUDINIZE
OTHERWORLDLY
STEEPLECHASE
STEPDAUGHTER
STEREOPHONIC
STEREOSCOPIC
STRAIGHTAWAY
STRAIGHTEDGE
STRAITJACKET
STRATIGRAPHY
STRATOSPHERE
STREETWALKER
STREPTOMYCIN
AUDIOVISUALS
AUSTRONESIAN
AUTHENTICATE
BUTTERSCOTCH
CUMULONIMBUS
HUMANITARIAN
JURISDICTION
LUMINESCENCE
LUNCHEONETTE
MUDDLEHEADED
MULLIGATAWNY
MULTICOLORED
MULTIFACETED
MULTIFARIOUS
MULTILATERAL
MULTILINGUAL
MULTIPLICAND
MULTIPLICITY
MULTIPURPOSE
MULTISESSION
MULTITASKING
MULTIVERSITY
MULTIVITAMIN
MUNICIPALITY
OUTSTRETCHED
PUMPERNICKEL
QUANTITATIVE
QUARTERSTAFF
QUESTIONABLE
QUINTESSENCE
SUBCOMMITTEE
SUBCONSCIOUS
SUBCONTINENT
SUBCUTANEOUS
SUBDIRECTORY
SUBMINIATURE
SUBSCRIPTION
SUBSERVIENCE
SUBSTANTIATE
SUBSTRUCTURE
SUBTERRANEAN
SUPERANNUATE
SUPERCHARGER
SUPERCILIOUS
SUPERHIGHWAY
SUPERNATURAL
SUPERSTITION
SURROUNDINGS
SURVEILLANCE
TUBERCULOSIS
AVITAMINOSIS
EVERBLOOMING
OVEREXPOSURE
SWASHBUCKLER
EXCRUCIATING
EXTORTIONATE
EXTRAMARITAL
EXTRASENSORY
EXTRAVAGANZA
OXYACETYLENE
HYDROTHERAPY
HYDROTHERMAL
HYPERACIDITY
HYPERTENSION
HYPOCHONDRIA
HYPOGLYCEMIA
HYSTERECTOMY
PYROTECHNICS

## 3RD LETTER

ANATHEMATIZE
BLANDISHMENT

BLATHERSKITE
BRAINWASHING
CHALCOPYRITE
CHAMPIONSHIP
CHARACTERIZE
DIASTROPHISM
FLAMETHROWER
FRANKENSTEIN
FRANKINCENSE
GLASSBLOWING
HEADMISTRESS
HEADQUARTERS
HEARTRENDING
HEARTSTRINGS
HEARTWARMING
HEAVYHEARTED
INARTICULATE
MEALYMOUTHED
PEACEKEEPING
PHARMACOLOGY
PLANETESIMAL
PLASTERBOARD
PRACTITIONER
PRASEODYMIUM
QUANTITATIVE
QUARTERSTAFF
SCANDINAVIAN
SCATOLOGICAL
SHARECROPPER
SHARPSHOOTER
SWASHBUCKLER
THANKSGIVING
TRADESPEOPLE
TRANQUILIZER
TRANSCENDENT
TRANSFERENCE
TRANSMIGRATE
TRANSMISSION
TRANSMOGRIFY
TRANSOCEANIC
TRANSPACIFIC
TRANSVESTISM
TRAPSHOOTING
UNACCUSTOMED
UNASSAILABLE
WEATHERBOARD
WEATHERGLASS
WEATHERPROOF
ABBREVIATION
AMBIDEXTROUS
BIBLIOGRAPHY
CABINETMAKER
FIBRILLATION
GOBBLEDYGOOK
HABERDASHERY
SUBCOMMITTEE
SUBCONSCIOUS
SUBCONTINENT
SUBCUTANEOUS
SUBDIRECTORY
SUBMINIATURE
SUBSCRIPTION
SUBSERVIENCE
SUBSTANTIATE
SUBSTRUCTURE
SUBTERRANEAN
TUBERCULOSIS
UNBELIEVABLE
ACCOMPLISHED
ARCHITECTURE
BACKTRACKING
BACTERICIDAL
BACTERIOLOGY
BICENTENNIAL
DECALCOMANIA
DECASYLLABIC
DECOMMISSION
DECONGESTANT
DICTATORSHIP
ECCLESIASTIC
ENCEPHALITIS
ENCYCLOPEDIA
EXCRUCIATING
INCALCULABLE
INCANDESCENT
INCAPACITATE
INCOMPARABLE
INCOMPATIBLE
INCONSOLABLE
INCONVENIENT
INCORRIGIBLE
INCRUSTATION
MICROBIOLOGY
MICROCIRCUIT
MICROCLIMATE
MICROSPACING
MICROSURGERY
OSCILLOSCOPE
PACKINGHOUSE
PICKERELWEED
RECALCITRANT
RECAPITULATE
RECEIVERSHIP
RECEPTIONIST
RECOGNIZANCE
RECOLLECTION
RECONSTITUTE
SECRETARIATE
TECHNICALITY
UNCHARITABLE
VACATIONLAND
AUDIOVISUALS
HYDROTHERAPY
HYDROTHERMAL
INDECLINABLE
INDEFEASIBLE
INDEPENDENCE
INDIGESTIBLE
INDISPUTABLE
INDISSOLUBLE
INDOCTRINATE
MADEMOISELLE
MIDDLEWEIGHT
MUDDLEHEADED
RADIOISOTOPE
RADIOTHERAPY
UNDERCLOTHES
UNDERCOATING
UNDERCURRENT
UNDERDRAWERS
UNDERGARMENT
UNDERPINNING
UNDERSURFACE
UNDOCUMENTED
BREAKTHROUGH
BREASTSTROKE
BREATHTAKING
CHECKERBERRY
CHECKERBOARD
CHEESEBURGER
CHEESEPARING
CHEMOTHERAPY
CHESTERFIELD
COELENTERATE
ELECTROLYSIS
ELECTROPLATE
ELEEMOSYNARY
EVERBLOOMING
FEEBLEMINDED
FREESTANDING
GREATHEARTED
HIERARCHICAL
HIEROGLYPHIC
INEFFACEABLE
INEXPERIENCE
INEXPLICABLE
INEXTRICABLE
MEETINGHOUSE
OCEANOGRAPHY
OVEREXPOSURE
PREAMPLIFIER
PRECANCEROUS
PRECIPITANCY
PRECONCERTED
PRECONDITION
PREDESIGNATE
PREDETERMINE
PREDIGESTION
PREDILECTION
PREFABRICATE
PREINDUCTION
PREMENSTRUAL
PREOPERATIVE
PREPAREDNESS
PREPONDERATE
PREPOSTEROUS
PREREQUISITE
PRESBYTERIAN
PRESCRIPTION
PRESENTIMENT
PRESUMPTUOUS
QUESTIONABLE
SLEDGEHAMMER
SPECTROGRAPH
SPECTROMETER
SPECTROSCOPE
SPERMATOZOON
STEEPLECHASE
STEPDAUGHTER
STEREOPHONIC
STEREOSCOPIC
THERAPEUTICS
THERMOSPHERE
UNEMPLOYMENT
DIFFERENTIAL
INFELICITOUS
INFLAMMATION
INFLAMMATORY
INFLATIONARY
INFLATIONISM
OFFICEHOLDER
UNFREQUENTED
ARGILLACEOUS
INGRATIATING
LIGHTHEARTED
MAGNETOMETER
MAGNILOQUENT
NIGHTCLOTHES
ORGANIZATION
PIGMENTATION
REGISTRATION
SIGNIFICANCE
UNGOVERNABLE
ECHOLOCATION
OTHERWORLDLY
REHABILITATE
SCHOOLFELLOW
SCHOOLMASTER
AVITAMINOSIS
BRILLIANTINE
CHILDBEARING
CHIROPRACTIC
CHITTERLINGS
EDITORIALIZE
EPISCOPALIAN
EPITHALAMIUM
FAINTHEARTED
HAIRSPLITTER
IDIOSYNCRASY
NEIGHBORHOOD
PHILANTHROPY
PHILHARMONIC
PHILODENDRON
PHILOSOPHIZE
PRIMOGENITOR
PRINCIPALITY
QUINTESSENCE
SPIRITUALISM
TRIGNOMETRIC
TRIGONOMETRY
UNINTERESTED
UNIVERSALIST
UNIVERSALITY
UNIVERSALIZE
VAINGLORIOUS
WHIPPOORWILL
ALLITERATION
BELLIGERENCY
BILLINGSGATE
CALISTHENICS
COLLECTIVISM
COLLECTIVIZE
COLLEGIALITY
DELIBERATIVE
DELICATESSEN
GALVANOMETER
HALLUCINOGEN
HELIOCENTRIC
HELLGRAMMITE
ILLEGITIMATE
ILLUSTRATION
ILLUSTRATIVE
KALEIDOSCOPE
MALFORMATION
MALNOURISHED
MALNUTRITION
MALOCCLUSION
MULLIGATAWNY
MULTICOLORED
MULTIFACETED
MULTIFARIOUS
MULTILATERAL
MULTILINGUAL
MULTIPLICAND
MULTIPLICITY
MULTIPURPOSE
MULTISESSION
MULTITASKING
MULTIVERSITY
MULTIVITAMIN
PALEONTOLOGY
POLARIZATION
POLICYHOLDER
POLYETHYLENE
POLYMORPHISM
POLYSYLLABIC
POLYSYLLABLE
RELATIONSHIP
RELATIVISTIC
SELENOGRAPHY
UNLIKELIHOOD
VALENCIENNES
VALORIZATION
WELTERWEIGHT
ATMOSPHERICS
COMMENCEMENT
COMMENSURATE
COMMISSARIAT
COMMISSIONER
COMMONWEALTH
COMMUNICABLE
COMPANIONWAY
COMPLAISANCE
CUMULONIMBUS
DEMILITARIZE
DEMIMONDAINE
DEMINERALIZE
DEMONSTRABLE
HUMANITARIAN
IMMEASURABLE
LUMINESCENCE
NOMENCLATURE
PUMPERNICKEL
RAMBUNCTIOUS
REMINISCENCE
REMONSTRANCE
REMUNERATION
REMUNERATIVE
SIMULTANEOUS
SOMNAMBULISM
UNMISTAKABLE
ANNUNCIATION
CANTANKEROUS
CINEMATHEQUE
CONCELEBRANT
CONCRESCENCE
CONFECTIONER
CONFESSIONAL
CONFIDENTIAL
CONFIRMATION
CONFORMATION
CONFUCIANISM
CONGLOMERATE
CONGRATULATE
CONGREGATION
CONQUISTADOR
CONSERVATION
CONSERVATISM
CONSERVATIVE
CONSERVATORY
CONSIDERABLE
CONSTABULARY

CONSTIPATION
CONSTITUENCY
CONSTITUTION
CONSTITUTIVE
CONSTRUCTION
CONTAINERIZE
CONTEMPORARY
CONTEMPTIBLE
CONTEMPTUOUS
CONTERMINOUS
CONTINUATION
CONTRAPUNTAL
CONTRARIWISE
CONTUMACIOUS
CONTUMELIOUS
CONVENTIONAL
CONVERSATION
DENOMINATION
DENSITOMETER
DENUNCIATION
FENESTRATION
HANDKERCHIEF
HENCEFORWARD
KINDERGARTEN
LONGITUDINAL
LONGSHOREMAN
LUNCHEONETTE
MANSLAUGHTER
MENSTRUATION
MINICOMPUTER
MONOFILAMENT
MONOSYLLABLE
MUNICIPALITY
NONAGENARIAN
NONCOMBATANT
NONCOMMITTAL
NONCONDUCTOR
NONOBJECTIVE
NONSCHEDULED
PANCHROMATIC
PENITENTIARY
RENUNCIATION
SENSITOMETER
TENDEROMETER
VENIPUNCTURE
ABOLITIONISM
AFORETHOUGHT
APOSTROPHIZE
BIOCHEMISTRY
BIOGEOGRAPHY
BIOSATELLITE
BIOTELEMETRY
BLOCKBUSTING
BLOODLETTING
BLOODTHIRSTY
CHOREOGRAPHY
CLOSEMOUTHED
CLOTHESHORSE
CLOTHESPRESS
CROSSCURRENT
FRONTISPIECE
GEOCHEMISTRY
GLOCKENSPIEL
ISOLATIONISM
ONOMATOPOEIA
PHOTOCOMPOSE
PHOTOENGRAVE
PHOTOGRAVURE
PROCATHEDRAL
PROCESSIONAL
PROFESSIONAL
PROGRAMMABLE
PROLEGOMENON
PROPAGANDIZE
PROPHYLACTIC
PROPORTIONAL
PROTACTINIUM
PROTECTORATE
PROTHALAMION
PROTUBERANCE
PROVIDENTIAL
RHODODENDRON
SHORTSIGHTED
SPORTSWRITER
THOROUGHBRED
THOROUGHFARE
TROUBLEMAKER
WHOLEHEARTED
ZOOGEOGRAPHY
ALPHANUMERIC
AMPHITHEATER
APPENDECTOMY
APPENDICITIS
APPRECIATIVE
APPREHENSIVE
APPURTENANCE
HIPPOPOTAMUS
HYPERACIDITY
HYPERTENSION
HYPOCHONDRIA
HYPOGLYCEMIA
IMPENETRABLE
IMPERCEPTIVE
IMPERCIPIENT
IMPERFECTION
IMPERISHABLE
IMPONDERABLE
REPERCUSSION
SUPERANNUATE
SUPERCHARGER
SUPERCILIOUS
SUPERHIGHWAY
SUPERNATURAL
SUPERSTITION
UNPARALLELED
UNPRINCIPLED
UNPROFITABLE
ACQUAINTANCE
AERODYNAMICS
CARBOHYDRATE
CARBONACEOUS
CARILLONNEUR
CARPETBAGGER
CHRISTIANITY
CHRISTIANIZE
CHROMATICITY
CHROMOSPHERE
CIRCUMSCRIBE
CIRCUMSTANCE
CORESPONDENT
EARSPLITTING
EARTHSHAKING
FERMENTATION
FORMALDEHYDE
HORTICULTURE
IRREDEEMABLE
IRREFRAGABLE
IRREMEDIABLE
IRRESISTIBLE
IRRESPECTIVE
IRREVERSIBLE
JURISDICTION
MARLINESPIKE
MERCHANTABLE
MERETRICIOUS
PARADISIACAL
PARAMILITARY
PARASITOLOGY
PARENTHESIZE
PERADVENTURE
PERAMBULATOR
PERICYNTHION
PERSPICACITY
PERTINACIOUS
PORCELAINIZE
PYROTECHNICS
SARSAPARILLA
STRAIGHTAWAY
STRAIGHTEDGE
STRAITJACKET
STRATIGRAPHY
STRATOSPHERE
STREETWALKER
STREPTOMYCIN
SURROUNDINGS
SURVEILLANCE
TERCENTENARY
UNREASONABLE
UNREGENERATE
UNRESTRAINED
VERTICILLATE
ABSENTMINDED
AUSTRONESIAN
COSMOPOLITAN
DESPOLIATION
DESTRUCTIBLE
DISACCHARIDE
DISADVANTAGE
DISAGREEABLE
DISASSOCIATE
DISCIPLINARY
DISCONNECTED
DISCONSOLATE
DISCOURTEOUS
DISCRIMINATE
DISESTABLISH
DISFRANCHISE
DISINGENUOUS
DISINTEGRATE
DISOBEDIENCE
DISPENSATION
DISPLACEMENT
DISPUTATIOUS
DISQUISITION
DISREPUTABLE
DISSERTATION
DISTILLATION
DISTRIBUTIVE
HYSTERECTOMY
INSALUBRIOUS
INSTRUMENTAL
INSUFFERABLE
INSUFFICIENT
INSURRECTION
MASTERSTROKE
MASTURBATION
MESSEIGNEURS
MISADVENTURE
MISAPPREHEND
MISCALCULATE
MISINTERPRET
MISPRONOUNCE
MISREPRESENT
OBSCURANTISM
OBSTREPEROUS
PESTILENTIAL
POSTDOCTORAL
POSTGRADUATE
POSTHYPNOTIC
POSTMISTRESS
RESPECTIVELY
RESTAURATEUR
RESURRECTION
TESTOSTERONE
UNSCIENTIFIC
UNSCRUPULOUS
UNSEARCHABLE
UNSEASONABLE
UNSEGREGATED
AFTERTHOUGHT
ANTEDILUVIAN
ANTHROPOLOGY
ANTIALIASING
ANTIELECTRON
ANTIMACASSAR
ANTIMAGNETIC
ANTIPARTICLE
ANTITHETICAL
ASTRONAUTICS
ASTRONOMICAL
ASTROPHYSICS
ATTITUDINIZE
AUTHENTICATE
BUTTERSCOTCH
DETERMINABLE
ENTERPRISING
ENTREPRENEUR
EXTORTIONATE
EXTRAMARITAL
EXTRASENSORY
EXTRAVAGANZA
HETEROSEXUAL
INTELLECTUAL
INTELLIGENCE
INTELLIGIBLE
INTEMPERANCE
INTERCESSION
INTERFERENCE
INTERGLACIAL
INTERJECTION
INTERLOCUTOR
INTERMEDIARY
INTERMEDIATE
INTERMINABLE
INTERMISSION
INTERMITTENT
INTERSECTION
INTERSTELLAR
INTERVOCALIC
INTRANSIGENT
INTRANSITIVE
METALANGUAGE
METAMORPHISM
OCTOGENARIAN
OCTOSYLLABIC
OUTSTRETCHED
SATISFACTION
SATISFACTORY
TOTALITARIAN
ULTRAMONTANE
VETERINARIAN
BLUESTOCKING
CHURCHWARDEN
COUNTERCLAIM
COUNTERPOINT
COUNTERPOISE
COUNTERTENOR
EQUESTRIENNE
FLUORESCENCE
FLUOROCARBON
FOUNTAINHEAD
HOUSEWARMING
MOUNTAINSIDE
NEURASTHENIA
NEUROSCIENCE
SHUFFLEBOARD
THUNDERCLOUD
THUNDERSTORM
ADVENTITIOUS
CIVILIZATION
INVERTEBRATE
INVITATIONAL
INVULNERABLE
NEVERTHELESS
NEWSMAGAZINE
NEWSPAPERMAN
LEXICOGRAPHY
SEXAGENARIAN
ASYNCHRONOUS
CRYPTOGRAPHY
OXYACETYLENE
PHYSIOGRAPHY
PSYCHOACTIVE
PSYCHOSEXUAL
PSYCHOTROPIC

## 4th Letter

BREAKTHROUGH
BREASTSTROKE
BREATHTAKING
DECALCOMANIA
DECASYLLABIC
DISACCHARIDE
DISADVANTAGE
DISAGREEABLE
DISASSOCIATE
GREATHEARTED
HUMANITARIAN
INCALCULABLE
INCANDESCENT
INCAPACITATE
INSALUBRIOUS
METALANGUAGE
METAMORPHISM
MISADVENTURE
MISAPPREHEND
NONAGENARIAN
OCEANOGRAPHY
ORGANIZATION

OXY**A**CETYLENE
PAR**A**DISIACAL
PAR**A**MILITARY
PAR**A**SITOLOGY
PER**A**DVENTURE
PER**A**MBULATOR
POL**A**RIZATION
PRE**A**MPLIFIER
REC**A**LCITRANT
REC**A**PITULATE
REH**A**BILITATE
REL**A**TIONSHIP
REL**A**TIVISTIC
SEX**A**GENARIAN
STR**A**IGHTAWAY
STR**A**IGHTEDGE
STR**A**ITJACKET
STR**A**TIGRAPHY
STR**A**TOSPHERE
TOT**A**LITARIAN
UNP**A**RALLELED
VAC**A**TIONLAND
CAR**B**OHYDRATE
CAR**B**ONACEOUS
FEE**B**LEMINDED
GOB**B**LEDYGOOK
RAM**B**UNCTIOUS
BIO**C**HEMISTRY
BLO**C**KBUSTING
CHE**C**KERBERRY
CHE**C**KERBOARD
CIR**C**UMSCRIBE
CIR**C**UMSTANCE
CON**C**ELEBRANT
CON**C**RESCENCE
DIS**C**IPLINARY
DIS**C**ONNECTED
DIS**C**ONSOLATE
DIS**C**OURTEOUS
DIS**C**RIMINATE
ELE**C**TROLYSIS
ELE**C**TROPLATE
GEO**C**HEMISTRY
GLO**C**KENSPIEL
HEN**C**EFORWARD
LUN**C**HEONETTE
MER**C**HANTABLE
MIS**C**ALCULATE
NON**C**OMBATANT
NON**C**OMMITTAL
NON**C**ONDUCTOR
OBS**C**URANTISM
PAN**C**HROMATIC
PEA**C**EKEEPING
POR**C**ELAINIZE
PRA**C**TITIONER
PRE**C**ANCEROUS

PRE**C**IPITANCY
PRE**C**ONCERTED
PRE**C**ONDITION
PRO**C**ATHEDRAL
PRO**C**ESSIONAL
PSY**C**HOACTIVE
PSY**C**HOSEXUAL
PSY**C**HOTROPIC
SPE**C**TROGRAPH
SPE**C**TROMETER
SPE**C**TROSCOPE
SUB**C**OMMITTEE
SUB**C**ONSCIOUS
SUB**C**ONTINENT
SUB**C**UTANEOUS
TER**C**ENTENARY
UNA**C**CUSTOMED
UNS**C**IENTIFIC
UNS**C**RUPULOUS
HAN**D**KERCHIEF
HEA**D**MISTRESS
HEA**D**QUARTERS
KIN**D**ERGARTEN
MID**D**LEWEIGHT
MUD**D**LEHEADED
PRE**D**ESIGNATE
PRE**D**ETERMINE
PRE**D**IGESTION
PRE**D**ILECTION
RHO**D**ODENDRON
SLE**D**GEHAMMER
SUB**D**IRECTORY
TEN**D**EROMETER
TRA**D**ESPEOPLE
ABS**E**NTMINDED
ADV**E**NTITIOUS
AFT**E**RTHOUGHT
ANT**E**DILUVIAN
APP**E**NDECTOMY
APP**E**NDICITIS
BIC**E**NTENNIAL
BLU**E**STOCKING
CHE**E**SEBURGER
CHE**E**SEPARING
CIN**E**MATHEQUE
COR**E**SPONDENT
DET**E**RMINABLE
DIS**E**STABLISH
ELE**E**MOSYNARY
ENC**E**PHALITIS
ENT**E**RPRISING
EQU**E**STRIENNE
FEN**E**STRATION
FRE**E**STANDING
HAB**E**RDASHERY
HET**E**ROSEXUAL
HYP**E**RACIDITY

HYP**E**RTENSION
ILL**E**GITIMATE
IMM**E**ASURABLE
IMP**E**NETRABLE
IMP**E**RCEPTIVE
IMP**E**RCIPIENT
IMP**E**RFECTION
IMP**E**RISHABLE
IND**E**CLINABLE
IND**E**FEASIBLE
IND**E**PENDENCE
INF**E**LICITOUS
INT**E**LLECTUAL
INT**E**LLIGENCE
INT**E**LLIGIBLE
INT**E**MPERANCE
INT**E**RCESSION
INT**E**RFERENCE
INT**E**RGLACIAL
INT**E**RJECTION
INT**E**RLOCUTOR
INT**E**RMEDIARY
INT**E**RMEDIATE
INT**E**RMINABLE
INT**E**RMISSION
INT**E**RMITTENT
INT**E**RSECTION
INT**E**RSTELLAR
INT**E**RVOCALIC
INV**E**RTEBRATE
IRR**E**DEEMABLE
IRR**E**FRAGABLE
IRR**E**MEDIABLE
IRR**E**SISTIBLE
IRR**E**SPECTIVE
IRR**E**VERSIBLE
KAL**E**IDOSCOPE
MAD**E**MOISELLE
MER**E**TRICIOUS
NEV**E**RTHELESS
NOM**E**NCLATURE
OTH**E**RWORLDLY
PAL**E**ONTOLOGY
PAR**E**NTHESIZE
REC**E**IVERSHIP
REC**E**PTIONIST
REP**E**RCUSSION
SEL**E**NOGRAPHY
STE**E**PLECHASE
STR**E**ETWALKER
STR**E**PTOMYCIN
SUP**E**RANNUATE
SUP**E**RCHARGER
SUP**E**RCILIOUS
SUP**E**RHIGHWAY
SUP**E**RNATURAL
SUP**E**RSTITION

TUB**E**RCULOSIS
UNB**E**LIEVABLE
UND**E**RCLOTHES
UND**E**RCOATING
UND**E**RCURRENT
UND**E**RDRAWERS
UND**E**RGARMENT
UND**E**RPINNING
UND**E**RSURFACE
UNR**E**ASONABLE
UNR**E**GENERATE
UNR**E**STRAINED
UNS**E**ARCHABLE
UNS**E**ASONABLE
UNS**E**GREGATED
VAL**E**NCIENNES
VET**E**RINARIAN
CON**F**ECTIONER
CON**F**ESSIONAL
CON**F**IDENTIAL
CON**F**IRMATION
CON**F**ORMATION
CON**F**UCIANISM
DIF**F**ERENTIAL
DIS**F**RANCHISE
INE**F**FACEABLE
MAL**F**ORMATION
PRE**F**ABRICATE
PRO**F**ESSIONAL
SHU**F**FLEBOARD
BIO**G**EOGRAPHY
CON**G**LOMERATE
CON**G**RATULATE
CON**G**REGATION
LON**G**ITUDINAL
LON**G**SHOREMAN
NEI**G**HBORHOOD
PRO**G**RAMMABLE
TRI**G**NOMETRIC
TRI**G**ONOMETRY
ZOO**G**EOGRAPHY
ALP**H**ANUMERIC
AMP**H**ITHEATER
ANT**H**ROPOLOGY
ARC**H**ITECTURE
AUT**H**ENTICATE
LIG**H**THEARTED
NIG**H**TCLOTHES
TEC**H**NICALITY
UNC**H**ARITABLE
ALL**I**TERATION
AMB**I**DEXTROUS
ANT**I**ALIASING
ANT**I**ELECTRON
ANT**I**MACASSAR
ANT**I**MAGNETIC
ANT**I**PARTICLE

ANT**I**THETICAL
ARG**I**LLACEOUS
ATT**I**TUDINIZE
AUD**I**OVISUALS
BRA**I**NWASHING
CAB**I**NETMAKER
CAL**I**STHENICS
CAR**I**LLONNEUR
CHR**I**STIANITY
CHR**I**STIANIZE
CIV**I**LIZATION
DEL**I**BERATIVE
DEL**I**CATESSEN
DEM**I**LITARIZE
DEM**I**MONDAINE
DEM**I**NERALIZE
DIS**I**NGENUOUS
DIS**I**NTEGRATE
HEL**I**OCENTRIC
IND**I**GESTIBLE
IND**I**SPUTABLE
IND**I**SSOLUBLE
INV**I**TATIONAL
JUR**I**SDICTION
LEX**I**COGRAPHY
LUM**I**NESCENCE
MIN**I**COMPUTER
MIS**I**NTERPRET
MUN**I**CIPALITY
OFF**I**CEHOLDER
OSC**I**LLOSCOPE
PEN**I**TENTIARY
PER**I**CYNTHION
POL**I**CYHOLDER
PRE**I**NDUCTION
RAD**I**OISOTOPE
RAD**I**OTHERAPY
REG**I**STRATION
REM**I**NISCENCE
SAT**I**SFACTION
SAT**I**SFACTORY
UNL**I**KELIHOOD
UNM**I**STAKABLE
VEN**I**PUNCTURE
BAC**K**TRACKING
PAC**K**INGHOUSE
PIC**K**ERELWEED
ABO**L**ITIONISM
BEL**L**IGERENCY
BIB**L**IOGRAPHY
BIL**L**INGSGATE
BRI**L**LIANTINE
CHA**L**COPYRITE
CHI**L**DBEARING
COE**L**ENTERATE
COL**L**ECTIVISM
COL**L**ECTIVIZE

COL**L**EGIALITY
ECC**L**ESIASTIC
HAL**L**UCINOGEN
HEL**L**GRAMMITE
INF**L**AMMATION
INF**L**AMMATORY
INF**L**ATIONARY
INF**L**ATIONISM
ISO**L**ATIONISM
MAR**L**INESPIKE
MEA**L**YMOUTHED
MUL**L**IGATAWNY
PHI**L**ANTHROPY
PHI**L**HARMONIC
PHI**L**ODENDRON
PHI**L**OSOPHIZE
PRO**L**EGOMENON
WHO**L**EHEARTED
CHA**M**PIONSHIP
CHE**M**OTHERAPY
COM**M**ENCEMENT
COM**M**ENSURATE
COM**M**ISSARIAT
COM**M**ISSIONER
COM**M**ONWEALTH
COM**M**UNICABLE
COS**M**OPOLITAN
FER**M**ENTATION
FLA**M**ETHROWER
FOR**M**ALDEHYDE
ONO**M**ATOPOEIA
PIG**M**ENTATION
PRE**M**ENSTRUAL
PRI**M**OGENITOR
SUB**M**INIATURE
UNE**M**PLOYMENT
ASY**N**CHRONOUS
BLA**N**DISHMENT
COU**N**TERCLAIM
COU**N**TERPOINT
COU**N**TERPOISE
COU**N**TERTENOR
FAI**N**THEARTED
FOU**N**TAINHEAD
FRA**N**KENSTEIN
FRA**N**KINCENSE
FRO**N**TISPIECE
MAG**N**ETOMETER
MAG**N**ILOQUENT
MAL**N**OURISHED
MAL**N**UTRITION
MOU**N**TAINSIDE
PLA**N**ETESIMAL
PRI**N**CIPALITY
QUA**N**TITATIVE
QUI**N**TESSENCE
SCA**N**DINAVIAN

SIG**N**IFICANCE
SOM**N**AMBULISM
THA**N**KSGIVING
THU**N**DERCLOUD
THU**N**DERSTORM
TRA**N**QUILIZER
TRA**N**SCENDENT
TRA**N**SFERENCE
TRA**N**SMIGRATE
TRA**N**SMISSION
TRA**N**SMOGRIFY
TRA**N**SOCEANIC
TRA**N**SPACIFIC
TRA**N**SVESTISM
UNI**N**TERESTED
VAI**N**GLORIOUS
ACC**O**MPLISHED
AER**O**DYNAMICS
ATM**O**SPHERICS
BLO**O**DLETTING
BLO**O**DTHIRSTY
CHR**O**MATICITY
CHR**O**MOSPHERE
DEC**O**MMISSION
DEC**O**NGESTANT
DEM**O**NSTRABLE
DEN**O**MINATION
DIS**O**BEDIENCE
ECH**O**LOCATION
EXT**O**RTIONATE
FLU**O**RESCENCE
FLU**O**ROCARBON
HYP**O**CHONDRIA
HYP**O**GLYCEMIA
IDI**O**SYNCRASY
IMP**O**NDERABLE
INC**O**MPARABLE
INC**O**MPATIBLE
INC**O**NSOLABLE
INC**O**NVENIENT
INC**O**RRIGIBLE
IND**O**CTRINATE
MAL**O**CCLUSION
MON**O**FILAMENT
MON**O**SYLLABLE
NON**O**BJECTIVE
OCT**O**GENARIAN
OCT**O**SYLLABIC
PRE**O**PERATIVE
PYR**O**TECHNICS
REC**O**GNIZANCE
REC**O**LLECTION
REC**O**NSTITUTE
REM**O**NSTRANCE
SCH**O**OLFELLOW
SCH**O**OLMASTER
UND**O**CUMENTED

UNG**O**VERNABLE
VAL**O**RIZATION
CAR**P**ETBAGGER
COM**P**ANIONWAY
COM**P**LAISANCE
CRY**P**TOGRAPHY
DES**P**OLIATION
DIS**P**ENSATION
DIS**P**LACEMENT
DIS**P**UTATIOUS
HIP**P**OPOTAMUS
MIS**P**RONOUNCE
PRE**P**AREDNESS
PRE**P**ONDERATE
PRE**P**OSTEROUS
PRO**P**AGANDIZE
PRO**P**HYLACTIC
PRO**P**ORTIONAL
PUM**P**ERNICKEL
RES**P**ECTIVELY
STE**P**DAUGHTER
TRA**P**SHOOTING
WHI**P**POORWILL
CON**Q**UISTADOR
DIS**Q**UISITION
ABB**R**EVIATION
AFO**R**ETHOUGHT
APP**R**ECIATIVE
APP**R**EHENSIVE
AST**R**ONAUTICS
AST**R**ONOMICAL
AST**R**OPHYSICS
CHA**R**ACTERIZE
CHI**R**OPRACTIC
CHO**R**EOGRAPHY
CHU**R**CHWARDEN
DIS**R**EPUTABLE
ENT**R**EPRENEUR
EVE**R**BLOOMING
EXC**R**UCIATING
EXT**R**AMARITAL
EXT**R**ASENSORY
EXT**R**AVAGANZA
FIB**R**ILLATION
HAI**R**SPLITTER
HEA**R**TRENDING
HEA**R**TSTRINGS
HEA**R**TWARMING
HIE**R**ARCHICAL
HIE**R**OGLYPHIC
HYD**R**OTHERAPY
HYD**R**OTHERMAL
INA**R**TICULATE
INC**R**USTATION
ING**R**ATIATING
INT**R**ANSIGENT
INT**R**ANSITIVE

MIC**R**OBIOLOGY
MIC**R**OCIRCUIT
MIC**R**OCLIMATE
MIC**R**OSPACING
MIC**R**OSURGERY
MIS**R**EPRESENT
NEU**R**ASTHENIA
NEU**R**OSCIENCE
OVE**R**EXPOSURE
PHA**R**MACOLOGY
PRE**R**EQUISITE
QUA**R**TERSTAFF
SEC**R**ETARIATE
SHA**R**ECROPPER
SHA**R**PSHOOTER
SHO**R**TSIGHTED
SPE**R**MATOZOON
SPI**R**ITUALISM
SPO**R**TSWRITER
STE**R**EOPHONIC
STE**R**EOSCOPIC
SUR**R**OUNDINGS
THE**R**APEUTICS
THE**R**MOSPHERE
THO**R**OUGHBRED
THO**R**OUGHFARE
ULT**R**AMONTANE
UNF**R**EQUENTED
UNP**R**INCIPLED
UNP**R**OFITABLE
APO**S**TROPHIZE
BIO**S**ATELLITE
CHE**S**TERFIELD
CLO**S**EMOUTHED
CON**S**ERVATION
CON**S**ERVATISM
CON**S**ERVATIVE
CON**S**ERVATORY
CON**S**IDERABLE
CON**S**TABULARY
CON**S**TIPATION
CON**S**TITUENCY
CON**S**TITUTION
CON**S**TITUTIVE
CON**S**TRUCTION
CRO**S**SCURRENT
DEN**S**ITOMETER
DIA**S**TROPHISM
DIS**S**ERTATION
EAR**S**PLITTING
EPI**S**COPALIAN
GLA**S**SBLOWING
HOU**S**EWARMING
MAN**S**LAUGHTER
MEN**S**TRUATION
MES**S**EIGNEURS
NEW**S**MAGAZINE

NEW**S**PAPERMAN
NON**S**CHEDULED
OUT**S**TRETCHED
PER**S**PICACITY
PHY**S**IOGRAPHY
PLA**S**TERBOARD
PRA**S**EODYMIUM
PRE**S**BYTERIAN
PRE**S**CRIPTION
PRE**S**ENTIMENT
PRE**S**UMPTUOUS
QUE**S**TIONABLE
SAR**S**APARILLA
SEN**S**ITOMETER
SUB**S**CRIPTION
SUB**S**ERVIENCE
SUB**S**TANTIATE
SUB**S**TRUCTURE
SWA**S**HBUCKLER
UNA**S**SAILABLE
ANA**T**HEMATIZE
AUS**T**RONESIAN
AVI**T**AMINOSIS
BAC**T**ERICIDAL
BAC**T**ERIOLOGY
BIO**T**ELEMETRY
BLA**T**HERSKITE
BUT**T**ERSCOTCH
CAN**T**ANKEROUS
CHI**T**TERLINGS
CLO**T**HESHORSE
CLO**T**HESPRESS
CON**T**AINERIZE
CON**T**EMPORARY
CON**T**EMPTIBLE
CON**T**EMPTUOUS
CON**T**ERMINOUS
CON**T**INUATION
CON**T**RAPUNTAL
CON**T**RARIWISE
CON**T**UMACIOUS
CON**T**UMELIOUS
DES**T**RUCTIBLE
DIC**T**ATORSHIP
DIS**T**ILLATION
DIS**T**RIBUTIVE
EAR**T**HSHAKING
EDI**T**ORIALIZE
EPI**T**HALAMIUM
HOR**T**ICULTURE
HYS**T**ERECTOMY
INS**T**RUMENTAL
MAS**T**ERSTROKE
MAS**T**URBATION
MEE**T**INGHOUSE
MUL**T**ICOLORED
MUL**T**IFACETED

MUL**T**IFARIOUS
MUL**T**ILATERAL
MUL**T**ILINGUAL
MUL**T**IPLICAND
MUL**T**IPLICITY
MUL**T**IPURPOSE
MUL**T**ISESSION
MUL**T**ITASKING
MUL**T**IVERSITY
MUL**T**IVITAMIN
OBS**T**REPEROUS
PER**T**INACIOUS
PES**T**ILENTIAL
PHO**T**OCOMPOSE
PHO**T**OENGRAVE
PHO**T**OGRAVURE
POS**T**DOCTORAL
POS**T**GRADUATE
POS**T**HYPNOTIC
POS**T**MISTRESS
PRO**T**ACTINIUM
PRO**T**ECTORATE
PRO**T**HALAMION
PRO**T**UBERANCE
RES**T**AURATEUR
SCA**T**OLOGICAL
SUB**T**ERRANEAN
TES**T**OSTERONE
VER**T**ICILLATE
WEA**T**HERBOARD
WEA**T**HERGLASS
WEA**T**HERPROOF
WEL**T**ERWEIGHT
ACQ**U**AINTANCE
ANN**U**NCIATION
APP**U**RTENANCE
CUM**U**LONIMBUS
DEN**U**NCIATION
ILL**U**STRATION
ILL**U**STRATIVE
INS**U**FFERABLE
INS**U**FFICIENT
INS**U**RRECTION
INV**U**LNERABLE
REM**U**NERATION
REM**U**NERATIVE
REN**U**NCIATION
RES**U**RRECTION
SIM**U**LTANEOUS
TRO**U**BLEMAKER
CON**V**ENTIONAL
CON**V**ERSATION
GAL**V**ANOMETER
HEA**V**YHEARTED
PRO**V**IDENTIAL
SUR**V**EILLANCE
UNI**V**ERSALIST

UNI**V**ERSALITY
UNI**V**ERSALIZE
INE**X**PERIENCE
INE**X**PLICABLE
INE**X**TRICABLE
ENC**Y**CLOPEDIA
POL**Y**ETHYLENE
POL**Y**MORPHISM
POL**Y**SYLLABIC
POL**Y**SYLLABLE

## 5TH LETTER

ACQU**A**INTANCE
ALPH**A**NUMERIC
ANTI**A**LIASING
AVIT**A**MINOSIS
BIOS**A**TELLITE
CANT**A**NKEROUS
CHAR**A**CTERIZE
COMP**A**NIONWAY
CONT**A**INERIZE
DICT**A**TORSHIP
EXTR**A**MARITAL
EXTR**A**SENSORY
EXTR**A**VAGANZA
FORM**A**LDEHYDE
GALV**A**NOMETER
HIER**A**RCHICAL
IMME**A**SURABLE
INFL**A**MMATION
INFL**A**MMATORY
INFL**A**TIONARY
INFL**A**TIONISM
INGR**A**TIATING
INTR**A**NSIGENT
INTR**A**NSITIVE
ISOL**A**TIONISM
MISC**A**LCULATE
NEUR**A**STHENIA
ONOM**A**TOPOEIA
PHIL**A**NTHROPY
PREC**A**NCEROUS
PREF**A**BRICATE
PREP**A**REDNESS
PROC**A**THEDRAL
PROP**A**GANDIZE
PROT**A**CTINIUM
REST**A**URATEUR
SARS**A**PARILLA
SOMN**A**MBULISM
THER**A**PEUTICS
ULTR**A**MONTANE
UNCH**A**RITABLE
UNRE**A**SONABLE

UNSEARCHABLE
UNSEASONABLE
DELIBERATIVE
DISOBEDIENCE
EVERBLOOMING
NONOBJECTIVE
PRESBYTERIAN
REHABILITATE
TROUBLEMAKER
ASYNCHRONOUS
CHALCOPYRITE
CHURCHWARDEN
DELICATESSEN
DISACCHARIDE
ENCYCLOPEDIA
EPISCOPALIAN
HYPOCHONDRIA
INDECLINABLE
INDOCTRINATE
LEXICOGRAPHY
MALOCCLUSION
MINICOMPUTER
MUNICIPALITY
NONSCHEDULED
OFFICEHOLDER
OXYACETYLENE
PERICYNTHION
POLICYHOLDER
PRESCRIPTION
PRINCIPALITY
SUBSCRIPTION
UNACCUSTOMED
UNDOCUMENTED
AERODYNAMICS
AMBIDEXTROUS
ANTEDILUVIAN
BLANDISHMENT
BLOODLETTING
BLOODTHIRSTY
CHILDBEARING
DISADVANTAGE
IRREDEEMABLE
MISADVENTURE
PARADISIACAL
PERADVENTURE
POSTDOCTORAL
SCANDINAVIAN
STEPDAUGHTER
THUNDERCLOUD
THUNDERSTORM
ABBREVIATION
AFORETHOUGHT
ANTIELECTRON
APPRECIATIVE
APPREHENSIVE
AUTHENTICATE
BACTERICIDAL
BACTERIOLOGY
BIOGEOGRAPHY
BIOTELEMETRY
BUTTERSCOTCH
CARPETBAGGER
CHOREOGRAPHY
CLOSEMOUTHED
COELENTERATE
COLLECTIVISM
COLLECTIVIZE
COLLEGIALITY
COMMENCEMENT
COMMENSURATE
CONCELEBRANT
CONFECTIONER
CONFESSIONAL
CONSERVATION
CONSERVATISM
CONSERVATIVE
CONSERVATORY
CONTEMPORARY
CONTEMPTIBLE
CONTEMPTUOUS
CONTERMINOUS
CONVENTIONAL
CONVERSATION
DIFFERENTIAL
DISPENSATION
DISREPUTABLE
DISSERTATION
ECCLESIASTIC
ENTREPRENEUR
FERMENTATION
FLAMETHROWER
HENCEFORWARD
HOUSEWARMING
HYSTERECTOMY
KINDERGARTEN
MAGNETOMETER
MASTERSTROKE
MESSEIGNEURS
MISREPRESENT
OVEREXPOSURE
PEACEKEEPING
PICKERELWEED
PIGMENTATION
PLANETESIMAL
POLYETHYLENE
PORCELAINIZE
PRASEODYMIUM
PREDESIGNATE
PREDETERMINE
PREMENSTRUAL
PREREQUISITE
PRESENTIMENT
PROCESSIONAL
PROFESSIONAL
PROLEGOMENON
PROTECTORATE
PUMPERNICKEL
RESPECTIVELY
SECRETARIATE
SHARECROPPER
STEREOPHONIC
STEREOSCOPIC
STREETWALKER
SUBSERVIENCE
SUBTERRANEAN
SURVEILLANCE
TENDEROMETER
TERCENTENARY
TRADESPEOPLE
UNFREQUENTED
UNIVERSALIST
UNIVERSALITY
UNIVERSALIZE
WELTERWEIGHT
WHOLEHEARTED
ZOOGEOGRAPHY
INDEFEASIBLE
INEFFACEABLE
INSUFFERABLE
INSUFFICIENT
IRREFRAGABLE
MONOFILAMENT
SHUFFLEBOARD
DISAGREEABLE
HELLGRAMMITE
HYPOGLYCEMIA
ILLEGITIMATE
INDIGESTIBLE
NONAGENARIAN
OCTOGENARIAN
POSTGRADUATE
RECOGNIZANCE
SEXAGENARIAN
SLEDGEHAMMER
UNREGENERATE
UNSEGREGATED
VAINGLORIOUS
ANATHEMATIZE
BIOCHEMISTRY
BLATHERSKITE
CLOTHESHORSE
CLOTHESPRESS
EARTHSHAKING
EPITHALAMIUM
GEOCHEMISTRY
LUNCHEONETTE
MERCHANTABLE
NEIGHBORHOOD
PANCHROMATIC
PHILHARMONIC
POSTHYPNOTIC
PROPHYLACTIC
PROTHALAMION
PSYCHOACTIVE
PSYCHOSEXUAL
PSYCHOTROPIC
SWASHBUCKLER
WEATHERBOARD
WEATHERGLASS
WEATHERPROOF
ABOLITIONISM
AMPHITHEATER
ARCHITECTURE
BELLIGERENCY
BIBLIOGRAPHY
BILLINGSGATE
COMMISSARIAT
COMMISSIONER
CONFIDENTIAL
CONFIRMATION
CONSIDERABLE
CONTINUATION
DENSITOMETER
DISCIPLINARY
DISTILLATION
FIBRILLATION
HORTICULTURE
KALEIDOSCOPE
LONGITUDINAL
MAGNILOQUENT
MARLINESPIKE
MEETINGHOUSE
MULLIGATAWNY
MULTICOLORED
MULTIFACETED
MULTIFARIOUS
MULTILATERAL
MULTILINGUAL
MULTIPLICAND
MULTIPLICITY
MULTIPURPOSE
MULTISESSION
MULTITASKING
MULTIVERSITY
MULTIVITAMIN
PACKINGHOUSE
PERTINACIOUS
PESTILENTIAL
PHYSIOGRAPHY
PRECIPITANCY
PREDIGESTION
PREDILECTION
PROVIDENTIAL
RECEIVERSHIP
SENSITOMETER
SIGNIFICANCE
SPIRITUALISM
STRAIGHTAWAY
STRAIGHTEDGE
STRAITJACKET
SUBDIRECTORY
SUBMINIATURE
UNPRINCIPLED
UNSCIENTIFIC
VERTICILLATE
BLOCKBUSTING
BREAKTHROUGH
CHECKERBERRY
CHECKERBOARD
FRANKENSTEIN
FRANKINCENSE
GLOCKENSPIEL
HANDKERCHIEF
THANKSGIVING
UNLIKELIHOOD
ARGILLACEOUS
BRILLIANTINE
CARILLONNEUR
CIVILIZATION
COMPLAISANCE
CONGLOMERATE
CUMULONIMBUS
DECALCOMANIA
DEMILITARIZE
DISPLACEMENT
ECHOLOCATION
FEEBLEMINDED
GOBBLEDYGOOK
INCALCULABLE
INFELICITOUS
INSALUBRIOUS
INTELLECTUAL
INTELLIGENCE
INTELLIGIBLE
INVULNERABLE
MANSLAUGHTER
METALANGUAGE
MIDDLEWEIGHT
MUDDLEHEADED
OSCILLOSCOPE
RECALCITRANT
RECOLLECTION
SIMULTANEOUS
TOTALITARIAN
UNBELIEVABLE
ACCOMPLISHED
ANTIMACASSAR
ANTIMAGNETIC
CHROMATICITY
CHROMOSPHERE
CINEMATHEQUE
DECOMMISSION
DEMIMONDAINE
DENOMINATION
ELEEMOSYNARY
HEADMISTRESS
INCOMPARABLE
INCOMPATIBLE
INTEMPERANCE
IRREMEDIABLE
MADEMOISELLE
METAMORPHISM
NEWSMAGAZINE
PARAMILITARY
PERAMBULATOR
PHARMACOLOGY
POLYMORPHISM
POSTMISTRESS
PREAMPLIFIER
SPERMATOZOON
THERMOSPHERE
ABSENTMINDED
ADVENTITIOUS
ANNUNCIATION
APPENDECTOMY
APPENDICITIS
BICENTENNIAL
BRAINWASHING
CABINETMAKER
DECONGESTANT
DEMINERALIZE
DEMONSTRABLE
DENUNCIATION
DISINGENUOUS
DISINTEGRATE
HUMANITARIAN
IMPENETRABLE
IMPONDERABLE
INCANDESCENT
INCONSOLABLE
INCONVENIENT
LUMINESCENCE
MISINTERPRET
NOMENCLATURE
OCEANOGRAPHY
ORGANIZATION
PARENTHESIZE
PREINDUCTION
RECONSTITUTE
REMINISCENCE
REMONSTRANCE
REMUNERATION
REMUNERATIVE
RENUNCIATION
SELENOGRAPHY
TECHNICALITY
TRIGNOMETRIC
VALENCIENNES
ASTRONAUTICS
ASTRONOMICAL
ASTROPHYSICS
AUDIOVISUALS

CARB**O**HYDRATE
CARB**O**NACEOUS
CHEM**O**THERAPY
CHIR**O**PRACTIC
COMM**O**NWEALTH
CONF**O**RMATION
COSM**O**POLITAN
DESP**O**LIATION
DISC**O**NNECTED
DISC**O**NSOLATE
DISC**O**URTEOUS
EDIT**O**RIALIZE
HELI**O**CENTRIC
HIER**O**GLYPHIC
HIPP**O**POTAMUS
HYDR**O**THERAPY
HYDR**O**THERMAL
MALF**O**RMATION
MALN**O**URISHED
MICR**O**BIOLOGY
MICR**O**CIRCUIT
MICR**O**CLIMATE
MICR**O**SPACING
MICR**O**SURGERY
NEUR**O**SCIENCE
NONC**O**MBATANT
NONC**O**MMITTAL
NONC**O**NDUCTOR
PALE**O**NTOLOGY
PHIL**O**DENDRON
PHIL**O**SOPHIZE
PHOT**O**COMPOSE
PHOT**O**ENGRAVE
PHOT**O**GRAVURE
PREC**O**NCERTED
PREC**O**NDITION
PREP**O**NDERATE
PREP**O**STEROUS
PRIM**O**GENITOR
PROP**O**RTIONAL
RADI**O**ISOTOPE
RADI**O**THERAPY
RHOD**O**DENDRON
SCAT**O**LOGICAL
SCHO**O**LFELLOW
SCHO**O**LMASTER
SUBC**O**MMITTEE
SUBC**O**NSCIOUS
SUBC**O**NTINENT
SURR**O**UNDINGS
TEST**O**STERONE
THOR**O**UGHBRED
THOR**O**UGHFARE
TRIG**O**NOMETRY
UNPR**O**FITABLE
ANTI**P**ARTICLE
CHAM**P**IONSHIP
EARS**P**LITTING
ENCE**P**HALITIS
INCA**P**ACITATE
INDE**P**ENDENCE
INEX**P**ERIENCE
INEX**P**LICABLE
MISA**P**PREHEND
NEWS**P**APERMAN
PERS**P**ICACITY
PREO**P**ERATIVE
RECA**P**ITULATE
RECE**P**TIONIST
SHAR**P**SHOOTER
STEE**P**LECHASE
STRE**P**TOMYCIN
UNEM**P**LOYMENT
VENI**P**UNCTURE
WHIP**P**OORWILL
HEAD**Q**UARTERS
TRAN**Q**UILIZER
AFTE**R**THOUGHT
ANTH**R**OPOLOGY
APPU**R**TENANCE
AUST**R**ONESIAN
CONC**R**ESCENCE
CONG**R**ATULATE
CONG**R**EGATION
CONT**R**APUNTAL
CONT**R**ARIWISE
DEST**R**UCTIBLE
DETE**R**MINABLE
DISC**R**IMINATE
DISF**R**ANCHISE
DIST**R**IBUTIVE
ENTE**R**PRISING
EXTO**R**TIONATE
FLUO**R**ESCENCE
FLUO**R**OCARBON
HABE**R**DASHERY
HETE**R**OSEXUAL
HYPE**R**ACIDITY
HYPE**R**TENSION
IMPE**R**CEPTIVE
IMPE**R**CIPIENT
IMPE**R**FECTION
IMPE**R**ISHABLE
INCO**R**RIGIBLE
INST**R**UMENTAL
INSU**R**RECTION
INTE**R**CESSION
INTE**R**FERENCE
INTE**R**GLACIAL
INTE**R**JECTION
INTE**R**LOCUTOR
INTE**R**MEDIARY
INTE**R**MEDIATE
INTE**R**MINABLE
INTE**R**MISSION
INTE**R**MITTENT
INTE**R**SECTION
INTE**R**STELLAR
INTE**R**VOCALIC
INVE**R**TEBRATE
MISP**R**ONOUNCE
NEVE**R**THELESS
OBST**R**EPEROUS
OTHE**R**WORLDLY
POLA**R**IZATION
PROG**R**AMMABLE
REPE**R**CUSSION
RESU**R**RECTION
SUPE**R**ANNUATE
SUPE**R**CHARGER
SUPE**R**CILIOUS
SUPE**R**HIGHWAY
SUPE**R**NATURAL
SUPE**R**STITION
TUBE**R**CULOSIS
UNDE**R**CLOTHES
UNDE**R**COATING
UNDE**R**CURRENT
UNDE**R**DRAWERS
UNDE**R**GARMENT
UNDE**R**PINNING
UNDE**R**SURFACE
UNPA**R**ALLELED
UNSC**R**UPULOUS
VALO**R**IZATION
VETE**R**INARIAN
ATMO**S**PHERICS
BLUE**S**TOCKING
BREA**S**TSTROKE
CALI**S**THENICS
CHEE**S**EBURGER
CHEE**S**EPARING
CHRI**S**TIANITY
CHRI**S**TIANIZE
CORE**S**PONDENT
CROS**S**CURRENT
DECA**S**YLLABIC
DISA**S**SOCIATE
DISE**S**TABLISH
EQUE**S**TRIENNE
FENE**S**TRATION
FREE**S**TANDING
GLAS**S**BLOWING
HAIR**S**PLITTER
IDIO**S**YNCRASY
ILLU**S**TRATION
ILLU**S**TRATIVE
INDI**S**PUTABLE
INDI**S**SOLUBLE
IRRE**S**ISTIBLE
IRRE**S**PECTIVE
JURI**S**DICTION
LONG**S**HOREMAN
MONO**S**YLLABLE
OCTO**S**YLLABIC
PARA**S**ITOLOGY
POLY**S**YLLABIC
POLY**S**YLLABLE
REGI**S**TRATION
SATI**S**FACTION
SATI**S**FACTORY
TRAN**S**CENDENT
TRAN**S**FERENCE
TRAN**S**MIGRATE
TRAN**S**MISSION
TRAN**S**MOGRIFY
TRAN**S**OCEANIC
TRAN**S**PACIFIC
TRAN**S**VESTISM
TRAP**S**HOOTING
UNAS**S**AILABLE
UNMI**S**TAKABLE
UNRE**S**TRAINED
ALLI**T**ERATION
ANTI**T**HETICAL
APOS**T**ROPHIZE
ATTI**T**UDINIZE
BACK**T**RACKING
BREA**T**HTAKING
CHES**T**ERFIELD
CHIT**T**ERLINGS
CONS**T**ABULARY
CONS**T**IPATION
CONS**T**ITUENCY
CONS**T**ITUTION
CONS**T**ITUTIVE
CONS**T**RUCTION
COUN**T**ERCLAIM
COUN**T**ERPOINT
COUN**T**ERPOISE
COUN**T**ERTENOR
CRYP**T**OGRAPHY
DIAS**T**ROPHISM
ELEC**T**ROLYSIS
ELEC**T**ROPLATE
FAIN**T**HEARTED
FOUN**T**AINHEAD
FRON**T**ISPIECE
GREA**T**HEARTED
HEAR**T**RENDING
HEAR**T**STRINGS
HEAR**T**WARMING
INAR**T**ICULATE
INEX**T**RICABLE
INVI**T**ATIONAL
LIGH**T**HEARTED
MENS**T**RUATION
MERE**T**RICIOUS
MOUN**T**AINSIDE
NIGH**T**CLOTHES
OUTS**T**RETCHED
PENI**T**ENTIARY
PLAS**T**ERBOARD
PRAC**T**ITIONER
PYRO**T**ECHNICS
QUAN**T**ITATIVE
QUAR**T**ERSTAFF
QUES**T**IONABLE
QUIN**T**ESSENCE
RELA**T**IONSHIP
RELA**T**IVISTIC
SHOR**T**SIGHTED
SPEC**T**ROGRAPH
SPEC**T**ROMETER
SPEC**T**ROSCOPE
SPOR**T**SWRITER
STRA**T**IGRAPHY
STRA**T**OSPHERE
SUBS**T**ANTIATE
SUBS**T**RUCTURE
UNIN**T**ERESTED
VACA**T**IONLAND
CIRC**U**MSCRIBE
CIRC**U**MSTANCE
COMM**U**NICABLE
CONF**U**CIANISM
CONQ**U**ISTADOR
CONT**U**MACIOUS
CONT**U**MELIOUS
DISP**U**TATIOUS
DISQ**U**ISITION
EXCR**U**CIATING
HALL**U**CINOGEN
INCR**U**STATION
MALN**U**TRITION
MAST**U**RBATION
OBSC**U**RANTISM
PRES**U**MPTUOUS
PROT**U**BERANCE
RAMB**U**NCTIOUS
SUBC**U**TANEOUS
IRRE**V**ERSIBLE
UNGO**V**ERNABLE
HEAV**Y**HEARTED
MEAL**Y**MOUTHED

## 6th Letter

ANTIM**A**CASSAR
ANTIM**A**GNETIC
ANTIP**A**RTICLE
CHROM**A**TICITY
CINEM**A**THEQUE
COMPL**A**ISANCE
CONGR**A**TULATE
CONST**A**BULARY
CONTR**A**PUNTAL
CONTR**A**RIWISE
DELIC**A**TESSEN
DISFR**A**NCHISE
DISPL**A**CEMENT
EPITH**A**LAMIUM
FOUNT**A**INHEAD
HYPER**A**CIDITY
INCAP**A**CITATE
INEFF**A**CEABLE
INVIT**A**TIONAL
MANSL**A**UGHTER
MERCH**A**NTABLE
METAL**A**NGUAGE
MOUNT**A**INSIDE
NEWSM**A**GAZINE
NEWSP**A**PERMAN
PHARM**A**COLOGY
PHILH**A**RMONIC
PROGR**A**MMABLE
PROTH**A**LAMION
SPERM**A**TOZOON
STEPD**A**UGHTER
SUBST**A**NTIATE
SUPER**A**NNUATE
UNASS**A**ILABLE
UNPAR**A**LLELED
BLOCK**B**USTING
CHILD**B**EARING
GLASS**B**LOWING
MICRO**B**IOLOGY
NEIGH**B**ORHOOD
PERAM**B**ULATOR
PREFA**B**RICATE
PROTU**B**ERANCE
SWASH**B**UCKLER
ANNUN**C**IATION
APPRE**C**IATIVE
CHARA**C**TERIZE
COLLE**C**TIVISM
COLLE**C**TIVIZE
CONFE**C**TIONER
CONFU**C**IANISM
CROSS**C**URRENT
DECAL**C**OMANIA
DENUN**C**IATION
DISAC**C**HARIDE
EXCRU**C**IATING
HALLU**C**INOGEN
HELIO**C**ENTRIC
HORTI**C**ULTURE
IMPER**C**EPTIVE
IMPER**C**IPIENT
INCAL**C**ULABLE

INTERCESSION
MALOCCLUSION
MICROCIRCUIT
MICROCLIMATE
MULTICOLORED
NIGHTCLOTHES
NOMENCLATURE
PHOTOCOMPOSE
PROTACTINIUM
PROTECTORATE
RECALCITRANT
RENUNCIATION
REPERCUSSION
RESPECTIVELY
SHARECROPPER
SUPERCHARGER
SUPERCILIOUS
TRANSCENDENT
TUBERCULOSIS
UNDERCLOTHES
UNDERCOATING
UNDERCURRENT
VALENCIENNES
VERTICILLATE
APPENDECTOMY
APPENDICITIS
CONFIDENTIAL
CONSIDERABLE
HABERDASHERY
IMPONDERABLE
INCANDESCENT
JURISDICTION
KALEIDOSCOPE
PHILODENDRON
PREINDUCTION
PROVIDENTIAL
RHODODENDRON
UNDERDRAWERS
ALLITERATION
AMBIDEXTROUS
ANATHEMATIZE
BIOCHEMISTRY
BLATHERSKITE
CABINETMAKER
CHECKERBERRY
CHECKERBOARD
CHEESEBURGER
CHEESEPARING
CHESTERFIELD
CHITTERLINGS
CLOTHESHORSE
CLOTHESPRESS
CONCRESCENCE
CONGREGATION
COUNTERCLAIM
COUNTERPOINT
COUNTERPOISE

COUNTERTENOR
DELIBERATIVE
DEMINERALIZE
DISOBEDIENCE
FEEBLEMINDED
FLUORESCENCE
FRANKENSTEIN
GEOCHEMISTRY
GLOCKENSPIEL
GOBBLEDYGOOK
HANDKERCHIEF
IMPENETRABLE
INDEFEASIBLE
INDEPENDENCE
INDIGESTIBLE
INEXPERIENCE
IRREDEEMABLE
IRREMEDIABLE
IRREVERSIBLE
LUMINESCENCE
LUNCHEONETTE
MIDDLEWEIGHT
MUDDLEHEADED
NONAGENARIAN
OBSTREPEROUS
OCTOGENARIAN
OFFICEHOLDER
OXYACETYLENE
PENITENTIARY
PHOTOENGRAVE
PLASTERBOARD
PREOPERATIVE
PYROTECHNICS
QUARTERSTAFF
QUINTESSENCE
REMUNERATION
REMUNERATIVE
SEXAGENARIAN
SLEDGEHAMMER
THUNDERCLOUD
THUNDERSTORM
UNGOVERNABLE
UNINTERESTED
UNLIKELIHOOD
UNREGENERATE
UNSCIENTIFIC
WEATHERBOARD
WEATHERGLASS
WEATHERPROOF
HENCEFORWARD
IMPERFECTION
INSUFFERABLE
INSUFFICIENT
INTERFERENCE
MULTIFACETED
MULTIFARIOUS
SATISFACTION

SATISFACTORY
SIGNIFICANCE
TRANSFERENCE
UNPROFITABLE
BELLIGERENCY
COLLEGIALITY
DECONGESTANT
DISINGENUOUS
HIEROGLYPHIC
INTERGLACIAL
MULLIGATAWNY
PHOTOGRAVURE
PREDIGESTION
PRIMOGENITOR
PROLEGOMENON
PROPAGANDIZE
STRAIGHTAWAY
STRAIGHTEDGE
UNDERGARMENT
ANTITHETICAL
APPREHENSIVE
ASYNCHRONOUS
BREATHTAKING
CARBOHYDRATE
CHURCHWARDEN
ENCEPHALITIS
FAINTHEARTED
GREATHEARTED
HEAVYHEARTED
HYPOCHONDRIA
LIGHTHEARTED
LONGSHOREMAN
NONSCHEDULED
SUPERHIGHWAY
TRAPSHOOTING
WHOLEHEARTED
ACQUAINTANCE
ANTEDILUVIAN
BLANDISHMENT
BRILLIANTINE
CHAMPIONSHIP
CIVILIZATION
CONQUISTADOR
CONSTIPATION
CONSTITUENCY
CONSTITUTION
CONSTITUTIVE
CONTAINERIZE
DEMILITARIZE
DENOMINATION
DISCRIMINATE
DISQUISITION
DISTRIBUTIVE
FRANKINCENSE
FRONTISPIECE
HEADMISTRESS
HUMANITARIAN

ILLEGITIMATE
IMPERISHABLE
INARTICULATE
INFELICITOUS
IRRESISTIBLE
MESSEIGNEURS
MONOFILAMENT
MUNICIPALITY
ORGANIZATION
PARADISIACAL
PARAMILITARY
PARASITOLOGY
PERSPICACITY
POLARIZATION
POSTMISTRESS
PRACTITIONER
PRINCIPALITY
QUANTITATIVE
QUESTIONABLE
RADIOISOTOPE
RECAPITULATE
REHABILITATE
RELATIONSHIP
RELATIVISTIC
REMINISCENCE
SCANDINAVIAN
STRATIGRAPHY
SURVEILLANCE
TECHNICALITY
TOTALITARIAN
UNBELIEVABLE
VACATIONLAND
VALORIZATION
VETERINARIAN
INTERJECTION
NONOBJECTIVE
PEACEKEEPING
ANTIALIASING
ANTIELECTRON
ARGILLACEOUS
BIOTELEMETRY
BLOODLETTING
CARILLONNEUR
CONCELEBRANT
DESPOLIATION
DISTILLATION
EARSPLITTING
ENCYCLOPEDIA
EVERBLOOMING
FIBRILLATION
FORMALDEHYDE
HYPOGLYCEMIA
INDECLINABLE
INEXPLICABLE
INTELLECTUAL
INTELLIGENCE
INTELLIGIBLE

INTERLOCUTOR
MAGNILOQUENT
MISCALCULATE
MULTILATERAL
MULTILINGUAL
OSCILLOSCOPE
PESTILENTIAL
PORCELAINIZE
PREDILECTION
RECOLLECTION
SCATOLOGICAL
SCHOOLFELLOW
SCHOOLMASTER
SHUFFLEBOARD
STEEPLECHASE
TROUBLEMAKER
UNEMPLOYMENT
VAINGLORIOUS
AVITAMINOSIS
CIRCUMSCRIBE
CIRCUMSTANCE
CLOSEMOUTHED
CONTEMPORARY
CONTEMPTIBLE
CONTEMPTUOUS
CONTUMACIOUS
CONTUMELIOUS
DECOMMISSION
DETERMINABLE
EXTRAMARITAL
INFLAMMATION
INFLAMMATORY
INTERMEDIARY
INTERMEDIATE
INTERMINABLE
INTERMISSION
INTERMITTENT
MEALYMOUTHED
NONCOMBATANT
NONCOMMITTAL
PRESUMPTUOUS
SOMNAMBULISM
SUBCOMMITTEE
TRANSMIGRATE
TRANSMISSION
TRANSMOGRIFY
ULTRAMONTANE
ALPHANUMERIC
ASTRONAUTICS
ASTRONOMICAL
AUTHENTICATE
BILLINGSGATE
CANTANKEROUS
CARBONACEOUS
COELENTERATE
COMMENCEMENT
COMMENSURATE

COMMONWEALTH
COMMUNICABLE
COMPANIONWAY
CONTINUATION
CONVENTIONAL
DISCONNECTED
DISCONSOLATE
DISPENSATION
FERMENTATION
GALVANOMETER
INTRANSIGENT
INTRANSITIVE
INVULNERABLE
MARLINESPIKE
MEETINGHOUSE
NONCONDUCTOR
PACKINGHOUSE
PALEONTOLOGY
PERTINACIOUS
PHILANTHROPY
PIGMENTATION
PRECANCEROUS
PRECONCERTED
PRECONDITION
PREMENSTRUAL
PREPONDERATE
PRESENTIMENT
RAMBUNCTIOUS
RECOGNIZANCE
SUBCONSCIOUS
SUBCONTINENT
SUBMINIATURE
SUPERNATURAL
TERCENTENARY
TRIGONOMETRY
UNPRINCIPLED
ANTHROPOLOGY
AUSTRONESIAN
BIBLIOGRAPHY
BIOGEOGRAPHY
CHALCOPYRITE
CHOREOGRAPHY
CHROMOSPHERE
CONGLOMERATE
CRYPTOGRAPHY
CUMULONIMBUS
DEMIMONDAINE
ECHOLOCATION
ELEEMOSYNARY
EPISCOPALIAN
FLUOROCARBON
HETEROSEXUAL
LEXICOGRAPHY
MADEMOISELLE
METAMORPHISM
MINICOMPUTER
MISPRONOUNCE

OCEAN**O**GRAPHY
PHYSI**O**GRAPHY
POLYM**O**RPHISM
POSTD**O**CTORAL
PRASE**O**DYMIUM
PSYCH**O**ACTIVE
PSYCH**O**SEXUAL
PSYCH**O**TROPIC
SELEN**O**GRAPHY
STERE**O**PHONIC
STERE**O**SCOPIC
STRAT**O**SPHERE
THERM**O**SPHERE
TRANS**O**CEANIC
TRIGN**O**METRIC
WHIPP**O**ORWILL
ZOOGE**O**GRAPHY
ACCOM**P**LISHED
ASTRO**P**HYSICS
ATMOS**P**HERICS
CHIRO**P**RACTIC
CORES**P**ONDENT
COSMO**P**OLITAN
DISCI**P**LINARY
DISRE**P**UTABLE
ENTER**P**RISING
ENTRE**P**RENEUR
HAIRS**P**LITTER
HIPPO**P**OTAMUS
INCOM**P**ARABLE
INCOM**P**ATIBLE
INDIS**P**UTABLE
INTEM**P**ERANCE
IRRES**P**ECTIVE
MISAP**P**REHEND
MISRE**P**RESENT
MULTI**P**LICAND
MULTI**P**LICITY
MULTI**P**URPOSE
PREAM**P**LIFIER
PRECI**P**ITANCY
SARSA**P**ARILLA
THERA**P**EUTICS
TRANS**P**ACIFIC
UNDER**P**INNING
PRERE**Q**UISITE
UNFRE**Q**UENTED
APOST**R**OPHIZE
BACKT**R**ACKING
BACTE**R**ICIDAL
BACTE**R**IOLOGY
BUTTE**R**SCOTCH
CONFI**R**MATION
CONFO**R**MATION
CONSE**R**VATION
CONSE**R**VATISM
CONSE**R**VATIVE
CONSE**R**VATORY
CONST**R**UCTION
CONTE**R**MINOUS
CONVE**R**SATION
DIAST**R**OPHISM
DIFFE**R**ENTIAL
DISAG**R**EEABLE
DISSE**R**TATION
EDITO**R**IALIZE
ELECT**R**OLYSIS
ELECT**R**OPLATE
HEART**R**ENDING
HELLG**R**AMMITE
HIERA**R**CHICAL
HYSTE**R**ECTOMY
INCOR**R**IGIBLE
INEXT**R**ICABLE
INSUR**R**ECTION
IRREF**R**AGABLE
KINDE**R**GARTEN
MALFO**R**MATION
MASTE**R**STROKE
MASTU**R**BATION
MENST**R**UATION
MERET**R**ICIOUS
OBSCU**R**ANTISM
OUTST**R**ETCHED
PANCH**R**OMATIC
PICKE**R**ELWEED
POSTG**R**ADUATE
PREPA**R**EDNESS
PRESC**R**IPTION
PROPO**R**TIONAL
PUMPE**R**NICKEL
RESUR**R**ECTION
SPECT**R**OGRAPH
SPECT**R**OMETER
SPECT**R**OSCOPE
SUBDI**R**ECTORY
SUBSC**R**IPTION
SUBSE**R**VIENCE
SUBST**R**UCTURE
SUBTE**R**RANEAN
TENDE**R**OMETER
UNCHA**R**ITABLE
UNIVE**R**SALIST
UNIVE**R**SALITY
UNIVE**R**SALIZE
UNSEA**R**CHABLE
UNSEG**R**EGATED
WELTE**R**WEIGHT
COMMI**S**SARIAT
COMMI**S**SIONER
CONFE**S**SIONAL
DEMON**S**TRABLE
DISAS**S**OCIATE
EARTH**S**HAKING
ECCLE**S**IASTIC
EXTRA**S**ENSORY
HEART**S**TRINGS
IMMEA**S**URABLE
INCON**S**OLABLE
INCRU**S**TATION
INDIS**S**OLUBLE
INTER**S**ECTION
INTER**S**TELLAR
MICRO**S**PACING
MICRO**S**URGERY
MULTI**S**ESSION
NEURA**S**THENIA
NEURO**S**CIENCE
PHILO**S**OPHIZE
PREDE**S**IGNATE
PREPO**S**TEROUS
PROCE**S**SIONAL
PROFE**S**SIONAL
RECON**S**TITUTE
REMON**S**TRANCE
SHARP**S**HOOTER
SHORT**S**IGHTED
SPORT**S**WRITER
SUPER**S**TITION
TESTO**S**TERONE
THANK**S**GIVING
TRADE**S**PEOPLE
UNDER**S**URFACE
UNREA**S**ONABLE
UNSEA**S**ONABLE
ABOLI**T**IONISM
ABSEN**T**MINDED
ADVEN**T**ITIOUS
AFORE**T**HOUGHT
AFTER**T**HOUGHT
AMPHI**T**HEATER
APPUR**T**ENANCE
ARCHI**T**ECTURE
BICEN**T**ENNIAL
BIOSA**T**ELLITE
BLOOD**T**HIRSTY
BLUES**T**OCKING
BREAK**T**HROUGH
BREAS**T**STROKE
CALIS**T**HENICS
CARPE**T**BAGGER
CHEMO**T**HERAPY
CHRIS**T**IANITY
CHRIS**T**IANIZE
DENSI**T**OMETER
DICTA**T**ORSHIP
DISES**T**ABLISH
DISIN**T**EGRATE
DISPU**T**ATIOUS
EQUES**T**RIENNE
EXTOR**T**IONATE
FENES**T**RATION
FLAME**T**HROWER
FREES**T**ANDING
HYDRO**T**HERAPY
HYDRO**T**HERMAL
HYPER**T**ENSION
ILLUS**T**RATION
ILLUS**T**RATIVE
INDOC**T**RINATE
INFLA**T**IONARY
INFLA**T**IONISM
INGRA**T**IATING
INVER**T**EBRATE
ISOLA**T**IONISM
LONGI**T**UDINAL
MAGNE**T**OMETER
MALNU**T**RITION
MISIN**T**ERPRET
MULTI**T**ASKING
NEVER**T**HELESS
ONOMA**T**OPOEIA
PAREN**T**HESIZE
PLANE**T**ESIMAL
POLYE**T**HYLENE
PREDE**T**ERMINE
PROCA**T**HEDRAL
RADIO**T**HERAPY
RECEP**T**IONIST
REGIS**T**RATION
SECRE**T**ARIATE
SENSI**T**OMETER
SIMUL**T**ANEOUS
SPIRI**T**UALISM
STRAI**T**JACKET
STREE**T**WALKER
STREP**T**OMYCIN
SUBCU**T**ANEOUS
UNMIS**T**AKABLE
UNRES**T**RAINED
ATTIT**U**DINIZE
DESTR**U**CTIBLE
DISCO**U**RTEOUS
HEADQ**U**ARTERS
INSAL**U**BRIOUS
INSTR**U**MENTAL
MALNO**U**RISHED
RESTA**U**RATEUR
SURRO**U**NDINGS
THORO**U**GHBRED
THORO**U**GHFARE
TRANQ**U**ILIZER
UNACC**U**STOMED
UNDOC**U**MENTED
UNSCR**U**PULOUS
VENIP**U**NCTURE
ABBRE**V**IATION
AUDIO**V**ISUALS
DISAD**V**ANTAGE
EXTRA**V**AGANZA
INCON**V**ENIENT
INTER**V**OCALIC
MISAD**V**ENTURE
MULTI**V**ERSITY
MULTI**V**ITAMIN
PERAD**V**ENTURE
RECEI**V**ERSHIP
TRANS**V**ESTISM
BRAIN**W**ASHING
HEART**W**ARMING
HOUSE**W**ARMING
OTHER**W**ORLDLY
OVERE**X**POSURE
AEROD**Y**NAMICS
DECAS**Y**LLABIC
IDIOS**Y**NCRASY
MONOS**Y**LLABLE
OCTOS**Y**LLABIC
PERIC**Y**NTHION
POLIC**Y**HOLDER
POLYS**Y**LLABIC
POLYS**Y**LLABLE
POSTH**Y**PNOTIC
PRESB**Y**TERIAN
PROPH**Y**LACTIC

## 7th Letter

ARGILL**A**CEOUS
ASTRON**A**UTICS
BACKTR**A**CKING
BRAINW**A**SHING
BRILLI**A**NTINE
CARBON**A**CEOUS
CONTUM**A**CIOUS
DISADV**A**NTAGE
DISEST**A**BLISH
DISPUT**A**TIOUS
ENCEPH**A**LITIS
EXTRAM**A**RITAL
EXTRAV**A**GANZA
FREEST**A**NDING
HABERD**A**SHERY
HEADQU**A**RTERS
HEARTW**A**RMING
HELLGR**A**MMITE
HOUSEW**A**RMING
INCOMP**A**RABLE
INCOMP**A**TIBLE
INDEFE**A**SIBLE
IRREFR**A**GABLE
MULLIG**A**TAWNY
MULTIF**A**CETED
MULTIF**A**RIOUS
MULTIL**A**TERAL
MULTIT**A**SKING
OBSCUR**A**NTISM
PERTIN**A**CIOUS
PORCEL**A**INIZE
POSTGR**A**DUATE
PROPAG**A**NDIZE
PSYCHO**A**CTIVE
SARSAP**A**RILLA
SATISF**A**CTION
SATISF**A**CTORY
SECRET**A**RIATE
SIMULT**A**NEOUS
SUBCUT**A**NEOUS
SUPERN**A**TURAL
TRANSP**A**CIFIC
UNDERG**A**RMENT
UNMIST**A**KABLE
CARPET**B**AGGER
CHEESE**B**URGER
CONSTA**B**ULARY
DISTRI**B**UTIVE
INSALU**B**RIOUS
MASTUR**B**ATION
NONCOM**B**ATANT
SOMNAM**B**ULISM
ANTIMA**C**ASSAR
COMMEN**C**EMENT
DESTRU**C**TIBLE
DISPLA**C**EMENT
ECHOLO**C**ATION
FLUORO**C**ARBON
HIERAR**C**HICAL
HYPERA**C**IDITY
INARTI**C**ULATE
INCAPA**C**ITATE
INEFFA**C**EABLE
INFELI**C**ITOUS
MISCAL**C**ULATE
NEUROS**C**IENCE
PERSPI**C**ACITY
PHARMA**C**OLOGY
POSTDO**C**TORAL
PRECAN**C**EROUS
PRECON**C**ERTED
PYROTE**C**HNICS
RAMBUN**C**TIOUS
TECHNI**C**ALITY
TRANSO**C**EANIC
UNPRIN**C**IPLED
UNSEAR**C**HABLE
ATTITU**D**INIZE
DISOBE**D**IENCE
FORMAL**D**EHYDE
GOBBLE**D**YGOOK
IRREME**D**IABLE

NONCONDUCTOR
PRASEODYMIUM
PRECONDITION
PREPONDERATE
ANTIELECTRON
ANTITHETICAL
APPENDECTOMY
APPREHENSIVE
APPURTENANCE
ARCHITECTURE
BELLIGERENCY
BICENTENNIAL
BIOSATELLITE
BIOTELEMETRY
BLOODLETTING
CHILDBEARING
CONCELEBRANT
CONFIDENTIAL
CONSIDERABLE
CONTUMELIOUS
DECONGESTANT
DIFFERENTIAL
DISAGREEABLE
DISINGENUOUS
DISINTEGRATE
EXTRASENSORY
FAINTHEARTED
GREATHEARTED
HEARTRENDING
HEAVYHEARTED
HELIOCENTRIC
HYPERTENSION
HYSTERECTOMY
IMPERCEPTIVE
IMPERFECTION
IMPONDERABLE
INCANDESCENT
INCONVENIENT
INSUFFERABLE
INSURRECTION
INTELLECTUAL
INTEMPERANCE
INTERCESSION
INTERFERENCE
INTERJECTION
INTERMEDIARY
INTERMEDIATE
INTERSECTION
INVERTEBRATE
INVULNERABLE
IRREDEEMABLE
IRRESPECTIVE
LIGHTHEARTED
MARLINESPIKE
MISADVENTURE
MISINTERPRET
MULTISESSION

MULTIVERSITY
NONOBJECTIVE
NONSCHEDULED
OUTSTRETCHED
PEACEKEEPING
PERADVENTURE
PESTILENTIAL
PHILODENDRON
PICKERELWEED
PLANETESIMAL
PREDETERMINE
PREDIGESTION
PREDILECTION
PREPAREDNESS
PRIMOGENITOR
PROTUBERANCE
PROVIDENTIAL
RECEIVERSHIP
RECOLLECTION
RESURRECTION
RHODODENDRON
SHUFFLEBOARD
STEEPLECHASE
SUBDIRECTORY
THERAPEUTICS
TRANSCENDENT
TRANSFERENCE
TRANSVESTISM
TROUBLEMAKER
UNBELIEVABLE
UNSEGREGATED
WHOLEHEARTED
SCHOOLFELLOW
ANTIMAGNETIC
BIBLIOGRAPHY
BILLINGSGATE
BIOGEOGRAPHY
CHOREOGRAPHY
CONGREGATION
CRYPTOGRAPHY
KINDERGARTEN
LEXICOGRAPHY
MEETINGHOUSE
MESSEIGNEURS
NEWSMAGAZINE
OCEANOGRAPHY
PACKINGHOUSE
PHYSIOGRAPHY
SELENOGRAPHY
STRATIGRAPHY
THANKSGIVING
THOROUGHBRED
THOROUGHFARE
ZOOGEOGRAPHY
AFORETHOUGHT
AFTERTHOUGHT
AMPHITHEATER

ASTROPHYSICS
ATMOSPHERICS
BLOODTHIRSTY
BREAKTHROUGH
CALISTHENICS
CHEMOTHERAPY
DISACCHARIDE
EARTHSHAKING
FLAMETHROWER
HYDROTHERAPY
HYDROTHERMAL
MUDDLEHEADED
NEVERTHELESS
OFFICEHOLDER
PARENTHESIZE
POLICYHOLDER
POLYETHYLENE
PROCATHEDRAL
RADIOTHERAPY
SHARPSHOOTER
SLEDGEHAMMER
STRAIGHTAWAY
STRAIGHTEDGE
SUPERCHARGER
ABBREVIATION
ABOLITIONISM
ADVENTITIOUS
ANNUNCIATION
ANTIALIASING
APPENDICITIS
APPRECIATIVE
AUDIOVISUALS
AVITAMINOSIS
BACTERICIDAL
BACTERIOLOGY
CHRISTIANITY
CHRISTIANIZE
COLLEGIALITY
COMMUNICABLE
COMPANIONWAY
COMPLAISANCE
CONFUCIANISM
DECOMMISSION
DENUNCIATION
DESPOLIATION
DETERMINABLE
EARSPLITTING
ECCLESIASTIC
EDITORIALIZE
EXCRUCIATING
EXTORTIONATE
FOUNTAINHEAD
HALLUCINOGEN
IMPERCIPIENT
INCORRIGIBLE
INDECLINABLE
INEXPLICABLE

INEXTRICABLE
INFLATIONARY
INFLATIONISM
INGRATIATING
INSUFFICIENT
INTELLIGENCE
INTELLIGIBLE
INTERMINABLE
INTERMISSION
INTERMITTENT
ISOLATIONISM
JURISDICTION
MADEMOISELLE
MERETRICIOUS
MICROBIOLOGY
MICROCIRCUIT
MOUNTAINSIDE
MULTILINGUAL
MULTIVITAMIN
PRECIPITANCY
PREDESIGNATE
PRESCRIPTION
RECALCITRANT
RECEPTIONIST
RECOGNIZANCE
RENUNCIATION
SHORTSIGHTED
SIGNIFICANCE
SUBMINIATURE
SUBSCRIPTION
SUPERCILIOUS
SUPERHIGHWAY
TRANQUILIZER
TRANSMIGRATE
TRANSMISSION
UNASSAILABLE
UNCHARITABLE
UNDERPINNING
UNPROFITABLE
VALENCIENNES
VERTICILLATE
STRAITJACKET
CANTANKEROUS
ACCOMPLISHED
ANTEDILUVIAN
DECASYLLABIC
DISCIPLINARY
DISTILLATION
EPITHALAMIUM
FIBRILLATION
GLASSBLOWING
HAIRSPLITTER
HIEROGLYPHIC
INTERGLACIAL
MALOCCLUSION
MICROCLIMATE
MONOFILAMENT

MONOSYLLABLE
MULTIPLICAND
MULTIPLICITY
NIGHTCLOTHES
NOMENCLATURE
OCTOSYLLABIC
PARAMILITARY
POLYSYLLABIC
POLYSYLLABLE
PREAMPLIFIER
PROPHYLACTIC
PROTHALAMION
REHABILITATE
SURVEILLANCE
UNDERCLOTHES
UNLIKELIHOOD
UNPARALLELED
ABSENTMINDED
ANATHEMATIZE
BIOCHEMISTRY
CONFIRMATION
CONFORMATION
CONGLOMERATE
CONTERMINOUS
DISCRIMINATE
FEEBLEMINDED
GEOCHEMISTRY
INFLAMMATION
INFLAMMATORY
INSTRUMENTAL
MALFORMATION
MINICOMPUTER
NONCOMMITTAL
PROGRAMMABLE
SCHOOLMASTER
SUBCOMMITTEE
TRIGNOMETRIC
UNDOCUMENTED
ACQUAINTANCE
AERODYNAMICS
AUSTRONESIAN
CONTAINERIZE
CUMULONIMBUS
DEMIMONDAINE
DENOMINATION
DISCONNECTED
DISFRANCHISE
FRANKENSTEIN
FRANKINCENSE
GLOCKENSPIEL
IDIOSYNCRASY
INDEPENDENCE
MERCHANTABLE
METALANGUAGE
MISPRONOUNCE
NONAGENARIAN
OCTOGENARIAN

PENITENTIARY
PERICYNTHION
PHOTOENGRAVE
PUMPERNICKEL
SCANDINAVIAN
SEXAGENARIAN
SUBSTANTIATE
SUPERANNUATE
SURROUNDINGS
UNREGENERATE
UNSCIENTIFIC
VENIPUNCTURE
VETERINARIAN
APOSTROPHIZE
ASTRONOMICAL
BLUESTOCKING
CARILLONNEUR
CHAMPIONSHIP
CLOSEMOUTHED
CORESPONDENT
COSMOPOLITAN
DECALCOMANIA
DENSITOMETER
DIASTROPHISM
DICTATORSHIP
DISASSOCIATE
ELECTROLYSIS
ELECTROPLATE
ENCYCLOPEDIA
EVERBLOOMING
GALVANOMETER
HENCEFORWARD
HIPPOPOTAMUS
HYPOCHONDRIA
INCONSOLABLE
INDISSOLUBLE
INTERLOCUTOR
INTERVOCALIC
KALEIDOSCOPE
LONGSHOREMAN
LUNCHEONETTE
MAGNETOMETER
MAGNILOQUENT
MEALYMOUTHED
MULTICOLORED
NEIGHBORHOOD
ONOMATOPOEIA
OSCILLOSCOPE
OTHERWORLDLY
PANCHROMATIC
PHILOSOPHIZE
PHOTOCOMPOSE
PROLEGOMENON
QUESTIONABLE
RELATIONSHIP
SCATOLOGICAL
SENSITOMETER

SPECTR**O**GRAPH
SPECTR**O**METER
SPECTR**O**SCOPE
STREPT**O**MYCIN
TENDER**O**METER
TRANSM**O**GRIFY
TRAPSH**O**OTING
TRIGON**O**METRY
ULTRAM**O**NTANE
UNDERC**O**ATING
UNEMPL**O**YMENT
UNREAS**O**NABLE
UNSEAS**O**NABLE
VACATI**O**NLAND
VAINGL**O**RIOUS
WHIPPO**O**RWILL
ANTHRO**P**OLOGY
CHALCO**P**YRITE
CHEESE**P**ARING
CONSTI**P**ATION
CONTEM**P**ORARY
CONTEM**P**TIBLE
CONTEM**P**TUOUS
CONTRA**P**UNTAL
EPISCO**P**ALIAN
MICROS**P**ACING
MUNICI**P**ALITY
NEWSPA**P**ERMAN
OBSTRE**P**EROUS
OVEREX**P**OSURE
POSTHY**P**NOTIC
PRESUM**P**TUOUS
PRINCI**P**ALITY
STEREO**P**HONIC
TRADES**P**EOPLE
UNSCRU**P**ULOUS
ALLITE**R**ATION
ANTIPA**R**TICLE
ASYNCH**R**ONOUS
BLATHE**R**SKITE
CHECKE**R**BERRY
CHECKE**R**BOARD
CHESTE**R**FIELD
CHIROP**R**ACTIC
CHITTE**R**LINGS
CONTRA**R**IWISE
COUNTE**R**CLAIM
COUNTE**R**POINT
COUNTE**R**POISE
COUNTE**R**TENOR
DELIBE**R**ATIVE
DEMINE**R**ALIZE
DISCOU**R**TEOUS
ENTERP**R**ISING
ENTREP**R**ENEUR
EQUEST**R**IENNE
FENEST**R**ATION
HANDKE**R**CHIEF
ILLUST**R**ATION
ILLUST**R**ATIVE
INDOCT**R**INATE
INEXPE**R**IENCE
IRREVE**R**SIBLE
MALNOU**R**ISHED
MALNUT**R**ITION
METAMO**R**PHISM
MISAPP**R**EHEND
MISREP**R**ESENT
PHILHA**R**MONIC
PHOTOG**R**AVURE
PLASTE**R**BOARD
POLYMO**R**PHISM
PREFAB**R**ICATE
PREOPE**R**ATIVE
QUARTE**R**STAFF
REGIST**R**ATION
REMUNE**R**ATION
REMUNE**R**ATIVE
RESTAU**R**ATEUR
SHAREC**R**OPPER
SUBTER**R**ANEAN
THUNDE**R**CLOUD
THUNDE**R**STORM
UNDERD**R**AWERS
UNGOVE**R**NABLE
UNINTE**R**ESTED
UNREST**R**AINED
WEATHE**R**BOARD
WEATHE**R**GLASS
WEATHE**R**PROOF
BLANDI**S**HMENT
BREAST**S**TROKE
BUTTER**S**COTCH
CHROMO**S**PHERE
CIRCUM**S**CRIBE
CIRCUM**S**TANCE
CLOTHE**S**HORSE
CLOTHE**S**PRESS
COMMEN**S**URATE
COMMIS**S**ARIAT
COMMIS**S**IONER
CONCRE**S**CENCE
CONFES**S**IONAL
CONQUI**S**TADOR
CONVER**S**ATION
DISCON**S**OLATE
DISPEN**S**ATION
DISQUI**S**ITION
ELEEMO**S**YNARY
FLUORE**S**CENCE
FRONTI**S**PIECE
HEADMI**S**TRESS
HETERO**S**EXUAL
IMPERI**S**HABLE
INDIGE**S**TIBLE
INTRAN**S**IGENT
INTRAN**S**ITIVE
IRRESI**S**TIBLE
LUMINE**S**CENCE
MASTER**S**TROKE
PARADI**S**IACAL
POSTMI**S**TRESS
PREMEN**S**TRUAL
PROCES**S**IONAL
PROFES**S**IONAL
PSYCHO**S**EXUAL
QUINTE**S**SENCE
RADIOI**S**OTOPE
REMINI**S**CENCE
STEREO**S**COPIC
STRATO**S**PHERE
SUBCON**S**CIOUS
THERMO**S**PHERE
UNACCU**S**TOMED
UNIVER**S**ALIST
UNIVER**S**ALITY
UNIVER**S**ALIZE
AUTHEN**T**ICATE
BREATH**T**AKING
CABINE**T**MAKER
CHARAC**T**ERIZE
CHROMA**T**ICITY
CINEMA**T**HEQUE
COELEN**T**ERATE
COLLEC**T**IVISM
COLLEC**T**IVIZE
CONFEC**T**IONER
CONGRA**T**ULATE
CONSTI**T**UENCY
CONSTI**T**UTION
CONSTI**T**UTIVE
CONVEN**T**IONAL
DELICA**T**ESSEN
DEMILI**T**ARIZE
DEMONS**T**RABLE
DISSER**T**ATION
FERMEN**T**ATION
HEARTS**T**RINGS
HUMANI**T**ARIAN
ILLEGI**T**IMATE
IMPENE**T**RABLE
INCRUS**T**ATION
INTERS**T**ELLAR
INVITA**T**IONAL
NEURAS**T**HENIA
OXYACE**T**YLENE
PALEON**T**OLOGY
PARASI**T**OLOGY
PHILAN**T**HROPY
PIGMEN**T**ATION
PRACTI**T**IONER
PREPOS**T**EROUS
PRESBY**T**ERIAN
PRESEN**T**IMENT
PROPOR**T**IONAL
PROTAC**T**INIUM
PROTEC**T**ORATE
PSYCHO**T**ROPIC
QUANTI**T**ATIVE
RECAPI**T**ULATE
RECONS**T**ITUTE
REMONS**T**RANCE
RESPEC**T**IVELY
SPERMA**T**OZOON
SUBCON**T**INENT
SUPERS**T**ITION
TERCEN**T**ENARY
TESTOS**T**ERONE
TOTALI**T**ARIAN
ALPHAN**U**MERIC
BLOCKB**U**STING
CONSTR**U**CTION
CONTIN**U**ATION
CROSSC**U**RRENT
DISREP**U**TABLE
HORTIC**U**LTURE
IMMEAS**U**RABLE
INCALC**U**LABLE
INDISP**U**TABLE
LONGIT**U**DINAL
MANSLA**U**GHTER
MENSTR**U**ATION
MICROS**U**RGERY
MULTIP**U**RPOSE
PERAMB**U**LATOR
PREIND**U**CTION
PREREQ**U**ISITE
REPERC**U**SSION
SPIRIT**U**ALISM
STEPDA**U**GHTER
SUBSTR**U**CTURE
SWASHB**U**CKLER
TUBERC**U**LOSIS
UNDERC**U**RRENT
UNDERS**U**RFACE
UNFREQ**U**ENTED
CONSER**V**ATION
CONSER**V**ATISM
CONSER**V**ATIVE
CONSER**V**ATORY
RELATI**V**ISTIC
SUBSER**V**IENCE
CHURCH**W**ARDEN
COMMON**W**EALTH
MIDDLE**W**EIGHT
SPORTS**W**RITER
STREET**W**ALKER
WELTER**W**EIGHT
AMBIDE**X**TROUS
CARBOH**Y**DRATE
HYPOGL**Y**CEMIA
CIVILI**Z**ATION
ORGANI**Z**ATION
POLARI**Z**ATION
VALORI**Z**ATION

## 8TH LETTER

ABBREVI**A**TION
AERODYN**A**MICS
ALLITER**A**TION
ANATHEM**A**TIZE
ANNUNCI**A**TION
ANTIALI**A**SING
ANTIMAC**A**SSAR
APPRECI**A**TIVE
BREATHT**A**KING
CARPETB**A**GGER
CHEESEP**A**RING
CHILDBE**A**RING
CHIROPR**A**CTIC
CHRISTI**A**NITY
CHRISTI**A**NIZE
CHURCHW**A**RDEN
CIVILIZ**A**TION
COLLEGI**A**LITY
COMMISS**A**RIAT
CONFIRM**A**TION
CONFORM**A**TION
CONFUCI**A**NISM
CONGREG**A**TION
CONSERV**A**TION
CONSERV**A**TISM
CONSERV**A**TIVE
CONSERV**A**TORY
CONSTIP**A**TION
CONTINU**A**TION
CONVERS**A**TION
DELIBER**A**TIVE
DEMILIT**A**RIZE
DEMINER**A**LIZE
DENOMIN**A**TION
DENUNCI**A**TION
DESPOLI**A**TION
DISACCH**A**RIDE
DISPENS**A**TION
DISSERT**A**TION
DISTILL**A**TION
EARTHSH**A**KING
ECCLESI**A**STIC
ECHOLOC**A**TION
EDITORI**A**LIZE
EPISCOP**A**LIAN
EPITHAL**A**MIUM
EXCRUCI**A**TING
FAINTHE**A**RTED
FENESTR**A**TION
FERMENT**A**TION
FIBRILL**A**TION
FLUOROC**A**RBON
GREATHE**A**RTED
HEAVYHE**A**RTED
HUMANIT**A**RIAN
ILLUSTR**A**TION
ILLUSTR**A**TIVE
INCRUST**A**TION
INFLAMM**A**TION
INFLAMM**A**TORY
INGRATI**A**TING
INTERGL**A**CIAL
KINDERG**A**RTEN
LIGHTHE**A**RTED
MALFORM**A**TION
MASTURB**A**TION
MENSTRU**A**TION
MICROSP**A**CING
MONOFIL**A**MENT
MUNICIP**A**LITY
NEWSMAG**A**ZINE
NOMENCL**A**TURE
NONAGEN**A**RIAN
NONCOMB**A**TANT
OCTOGEN**A**RIAN
ORGANIZ**A**TION
PERSPIC**A**CITY
PHOTOGR**A**VURE
PIGMENT**A**TION
POLARIZ**A**TION
PREOPER**A**TIVE
PRINCIP**A**LITY
PROPHYL**A**CTIC
PROTHAL**A**MION
QUANTIT**A**TIVE
REGISTR**A**TION
REMUNER**A**TION
REMUNER**A**TIVE
RENUNCI**A**TION
RESTAUR**A**TEUR
SCANDIN**A**VIAN
SCHOOLM**A**STER
SEXAGEN**A**RIAN
SLEDGEH**A**MMER
SPIRITU**A**LISM
STRAITJ**A**CKET
STREETW**A**LKER
SUBMINI**A**TURE
SUBTERR**A**NEAN
SUPERCH**A**RGER
TECHNIC**A**LITY
TOTALIT**A**RIAN

UNDERCOATING
UNDERDRAWERS
UNIVERSALIST
UNIVERSALITY
UNIVERSALIZE
UNRESTRAINED
VALORIZATION
VETERINARIAN
WHOLEHEARTED
CHECKERBERRY
CHECKERBOARD
CONCELEBRANT
DISESTABLISH
INVERTEBRATE
PLASTERBOARD
SHUFFLEBOARD
WEATHERBOARD
ANTIELECTRON
APPENDECTOMY
APPENDICITIS
ARCHITECTURE
ARGILLACEOUS
BACKTRACKING
BACTERICIDAL
BLUESTOCKING
BUTTERSCOTCH
CARBONACEOUS
CIRCUMSCRIBE
COMMUNICABLE
CONCRESCENCE
CONSTRUCTION
CONTUMACIOUS
COUNTERCLAIM
DISASSOCIATE
DISFRANCHISE
FLUORESCENCE
FRANKINCENSE
HANDKERCHIEF
HYPOGLYCEMIA
HYSTERECTOMY
IDIOSYNCRASY
IMPERFECTION
INEXPLICABLE
INEXTRICABLE
INSUFFICIENT
INSURRECTION
INTELLECTUAL
INTERJECTION
INTERLOCUTOR
INTERSECTION
INTERVOCALIC
IRRESPECTIVE
JURISDICTION
LUMINESCENCE
MERETRICIOUS
MULTIFACETED
NONOBJECTIVE

PERTINACIOUS
PREDILECTION
PREINDUCTION
PSYCHOACTIVE
RECOLLECTION
REMINISCENCE
RESURRECTION
SATISFACTION
SATISFACTORY
SIGNIFICANCE
STEEPLECHASE
STEREOSCOPIC
SUBCONSCIOUS
SUBDIRECTORY
SUBSTRUCTURE
SWASHBUCKLER
THUNDERCLOUD
TRANSPACIFIC
VENIPUNCTURE
CARBOHYDRATE
DEMIMONDAINE
INDEPENDENCE
INTERMEDIARY
INTERMEDIATE
LONGITUDINAL
NONSCHEDULED
POSTGRADUATE
PREPAREDNESS
SURROUNDINGS
AMPHITHEATER
ATMOSPHERICS
AUSTRONESIAN
CALISTHENICS
CANTANKEROUS
CHARACTERIZE
CHEMOTHERAPY
COELENTERATE
COMMENCEMENT
COMMONWEALTH
CONGLOMERATE
CONTAINERIZE
DELICATESSEN
DISAGREEABLE
DISCONNECTED
DISPLACEMENT
ENTREPRENEUR
FORMALDEHYDE
HETEROSEXUAL
HYDROTHERAPY
HYDROTHERMAL
INEFFACEABLE
INSTRUMENTAL
INTERSTELLAR
MIDDLEWEIGHT
MISAPPREHEND
MISREPRESENT
MUDDLEHEADED

NEVERTHELESS
NEWSPAPERMAN
OBSTREPEROUS
PARENTHESIZE
PEACEKEEPING
PRECANCEROUS
PRECONCERTED
PREPONDERATE
PREPOSTEROUS
PRESBYTERIAN
PROCATHEDRAL
PSYCHOSEXUAL
RADIOTHERAPY
SCHOOLFELLOW
TERCENTENARY
TESTOSTERONE
TRADESPEOPLE
TRANSOCEANIC
TRIGNOMETRIC
UNDOCUMENTED
UNFREQUENTED
UNINTERESTED
UNREGENERATE
VALENCIENNES
WELTERWEIGHT
CHESTERFIELD
DISINTEGRATE
EXTRAVAGANZA
INCORRIGIBLE
INTELLIGENCE
INTELLIGIBLE
IRREFRAGABLE
MANSLAUGHTER
METALANGUAGE
PHOTOENGRAVE
PREDESIGNATE
SCATOLOGICAL
SHORTSIGHTED
SPECTROGRAPH
STEPDAUGHTER
SUPERHIGHWAY
TRANSMIGRATE
TRANSMOGRIFY
UNSEGREGATED
WEATHERGLASS
BLANDISHMENT
CINEMATHEQUE
CLOTHESHORSE
HIERARCHICAL
IMPERISHABLE
MEETINGHOUSE
NEURASTHENIA
PACKINGHOUSE
PHILANTHROPY
PYROTECHNICS
STEREOPHONIC
THOROUGHBRED

THOROUGHFARE
UNSEARCHABLE
ABSENTMINDED
ACCOMPLISHED
ATTITUDINIZE
AUTHENTICATE
BIOCHEMISTRY
BLOODTHIRSTY
CHROMATICITY
COLLECTIVISM
COLLECTIVIZE
COMMISSIONER
CONFECTIONER
CONFESSIONAL
CONTERMINOUS
CONTRARIWISE
CONVENTIONAL
CUMULONIMBUS
DISCIPLINARY
DISCRIMINATE
DISOBEDIENCE
DISQUISITION
ENTERPRISING
EQUESTRIENNE
FEEBLEMINDED
GEOCHEMISTRY
HAIRSPLITTER
HYPERACIDITY
ILLEGITIMATE
INCAPACITATE
INDOCTRINATE
INEXPERIENCE
INFELICITOUS
INTRANSIGENT
INTRANSITIVE
INVITATIONAL
IRREMEDIABLE
MALNOURISHED
MALNUTRITION
MICROCLIMATE
MULTIPLICAND
MULTIPLICITY
NEUROSCIENCE
NONCOMMITTAL
PARADISIACAL
PARAMILITARY
PORCELAINIZE
PRACTITIONER
PREAMPLIFIER
PRECONDITION
PREFABRICATE
PREREQUISITE
PRESENTIMENT
PROCESSIONAL
PROFESSIONAL
PROPORTIONAL
PROTACTINIUM

PUMPERNICKEL
RECONSTITUTE
REHABILITATE
RELATIVISTIC
RESPECTIVELY
SUBCOMMITTEE
SUBCONTINENT
SUBSERVIENCE
SUPERSTITION
THANKSGIVING
UNLIKELIHOOD
UNPRINCIPLED
UNMISTAKABLE
BIOSATELLITE
CHITTERLINGS
CONTUMELIOUS
COSMOPOLITAN
DECASYLLABIC
ELECTROLYSIS
ENCEPHALITIS
HORTICULTURE
INCALCULABLE
INCONSOLABLE
INDISSOLUBLE
MONOSYLLABLE
MULTICOLORED
OCTOSYLLABIC
PERAMBULATOR
PICKERELWEED
POLYSYLLABIC
POLYSYLLABLE
SUPERCILIOUS
SURVEILLANCE
TRANQUILIZER
TUBERCULOSIS
UNASSAILABLE
UNPARALLELED
VERTICILLATE
ALPHANUMERIC
ASTRONOMICAL
BIOTELEMETRY
CABINETMAKER
DECALCOMANIA
DENSITOMETER
GALVANOMETER
HELLGRAMMITE
IRREDEEMABLE
MAGNETOMETER
PANCHROMATIC
PHILHARMONIC
PHOTOCOMPOSE
PROGRAMMABLE
PROLEGOMENON
SENSITOMETER
SPECTROMETER
STREPTOMYCIN
TENDEROMETER

TRIGONOMETRY
TROUBLEMAKER
ANTIMAGNETIC
APPREHENSIVE
APPURTENANCE
AVITAMINOSIS
BICENTENNIAL
BRILLIANTINE
CARILLONNEUR
CHAMPIONSHIP
CONFIDENTIAL
CORESPONDENT
DETERMINABLE
DIFFERENTIAL
DISADVANTAGE
DISINGENUOUS
EXTRASENSORY
FOUNTAINHEAD
FREESTANDING
HALLUCINOGEN
HEARTRENDING
HELIOCENTRIC
HYPERTENSION
HYPOCHONDRIA
INCONVENIENT
INDECLINABLE
INTERMINABLE
LUNCHEONETTE
MESSEIGNEURS
MISADVENTURE
MOUNTAINSIDE
MULTILINGUAL
OBSCURANTISM
PERADVENTURE
PESTILENTIAL
PHILODENDRON
POSTHYPNOTIC
PRIMOGENITOR
PROPAGANDIZE
PROVIDENTIAL
QUESTIONABLE
RELATIONSHIP
RHODODENDRON
SIMULTANEOUS
SUBCUTANEOUS
SUPERANNUATE
TRANSCENDENT
ULTRAMONTANE
UNDERPINNING
UNGOVERNABLE
UNREASONABLE
UNSEASONABLE
VACATIONLAND
ABOLITIONISM
AFORETHOUGHT
AFTERTHOUGHT
ANTHROPOLOGY

ASYNCHR**O**NOUS
BACTERI**O**LOGY
COMPANI**O**NWAY
CONTEMP**O**RARY
DISCONS**O**LATE
EVERBLO**O**MING
EXTORTI**O**NATE
GLASSBL**O**WING
INFLATI**O**NARY
INFLATI**O**NISM
ISOLATI**O**NISM
MICROBI**O**LOGY
MISPRON**O**UNCE
NIGHTCL**O**THES
OFFICEH**O**LDER
OVEREXP**O**SURE
PALEONT**O**LOGY
PARASIT**O**LOGY
PHARMAC**O**LOGY
POLICYH**O**LDER
PROTECT**O**RATE
RADIOIS**O**TOPE
RECEPTI**O**NIST
SHARECR**O**PPER
SHARPSH**O**OTER
SPERMAT**O**ZOON
TRAPSHO**O**TING
UNDERCL**O**THES
APOSTRO**P**HIZE
CHROMOS**P**HERE
CLOTHES**P**RESS
COUNTER**P**OINT
COUNTER**P**OISE
DIASTRO**P**HISM
ELECTRO**P**LATE
ENCYCLO**P**EDIA
FRONTIS**P**IECE
IMPERCE**P**TIVE
IMPERCI**P**IENT
METAMOR**P**HISM
MINICOM**P**UTER
ONOMATO**P**OEIA
PHILOSO**P**HIZE
POLYMOR**P**HISM
PRESCRI**P**TION
STRATOS**P**HERE
SUBSCRI**P**TION
THERMOS**P**HERE
WEATHER**P**ROOF
MAGNILO**Q**UENT
BELLIGE**R**ENCY
BIBLIOG**R**APHY
BIOGEOG**R**APHY
BREAKTH**R**OUGH
CHOREOG**R**APHY
CONSIDE**R**ABLE
CROSSCU**R**RENT
CRYPTOG**R**APHY
DEMONST**R**ABLE
DICTATO**R**SHIP
EXTRAMA**R**ITAL
FLAMETH**R**OWER
HEADQUA**R**TERS
HEARTST**R**INGS
HEARTWA**R**MING
HENCEFO**R**WARD
HOUSEWA**R**MING
IMMEASU**R**ABLE
IMPENET**R**ABLE
IMPONDE**R**ABLE
INCOMPA**R**ABLE
INSALUB**R**IOUS
INSUFFE**R**ABLE
INTEMPE**R**ANCE
INTERFE**R**ENCE
INVULNE**R**ABLE
LEXICOG**R**APHY
LONGSHO**R**EMAN
MICROCI**R**CUIT
MICROSU**R**GERY
MISINTE**R**PRET
MULTIFA**R**IOUS
MULTIPU**R**POSE
MULTIVE**R**SITY
NEIGHBO**R**HOOD
OCEANOG**R**APHY
OTHERWO**R**LDLY
PHYSIOG**R**APHY
PREDETE**R**MINE
PROTUBE**R**ANCE
PSYCHOT**R**OPIC
RECEIVE**R**SHIP
REMONST**R**ANCE
SARSAPA**R**ILLA
SECRETA**R**IATE
SELENOG**R**APHY
SPORTSW**R**ITER
STRATIG**R**APHY
TRANSFE**R**ENCE
UNDERCU**R**RENT
UNDERGA**R**MENT
UNDERSU**R**FACE
VAINGLO**R**IOUS
WHIPPOO**R**WILL
ZOOGEOG**R**APHY
AUDIOVI**S**UALS
BILLING**S**GATE
BLATHER**S**KITE
BLOCKBU**S**TING
BRAINWA**S**HING
COMPLAI**S**ANCE
DECOMMI**S**SION
DECONGE**S**TANT
FRANKEN**S**TEIN
GLOCKEN**S**PIEL
HABERDA**S**HERY
INCANDE**S**CENT
INDEFEA**S**IBLE
INTERCE**S**SION
INTERMI**S**SION
IRREVER**S**IBLE
KALEIDO**S**COPE
MADEMOI**S**ELLE
MARLINE**S**PIKE
MULTISE**S**SION
MULTITA**S**KING
OSCILLO**S**COPE
PLANETE**S**IMAL
PREDIGE**S**TION
QUARTER**S**TAFF
QUINTES**S**ENCE
REPERCU**S**SION
SPECTRO**S**COPE
THUNDER**S**TORM
TRANSMI**S**SION
TRANSVE**S**TISM
ACQUAIN**T**ANCE
ADVENTI**T**IOUS
AMBIDEX**T**ROUS
ANTIPAR**T**ICLE
ANTITHE**T**ICAL
BLOODLE**T**TING
BREASTS**T**ROKE
CIRCUMS**T**ANCE
CONQUIS**T**ADOR
CONTEMP**T**IBLE
CONTEMP**T**UOUS
COUNTER**T**ENOR
DESTRUC**T**IBLE
DISCOUR**T**EOUS
DISPUTA**T**IOUS
DISREPU**T**ABLE
EARSPLI**T**TING
HEADMIS**T**RESS
HIPPOPO**T**AMUS
INCOMPA**T**IBLE
INDIGES**T**IBLE
INDISPU**T**ABLE
INTERMI**T**TENT
IRRESIS**T**IBLE
MASTERS**T**ROKE
MERCHAN**T**ABLE
MULLIGA**T**AWNY
MULTILA**T**ERAL
MULTIVI**T**AMIN
OUTSTRE**T**CHED
PENITEN**T**IARY
PERICYN**T**HION
POSTDOC**T**ORAL
POSTMIS**T**RESS
PRECIPI**T**ANCY
PREMENS**T**RUAL
PRESUMP**T**UOUS
RAMBUNC**T**IOUS
RECALCI**T**RANT
STRAIGH**T**AWAY
STRAIGH**T**EDGE
SUBSTAN**T**IATE
SUPERNA**T**URAL
UNACCUS**T**OMED
UNCHARI**T**ABLE
UNPROFI**T**ABLE
UNSCIEN**T**IFIC
ANTEDIL**U**VIAN
ASTRONA**U**TICS
CHEESEB**U**RGER
CLOSEMO**U**THED
COMMENS**U**RATE
CONGRAT**U**LATE
CONSTAB**U**LARY
CONSTIT**U**ENCY
CONSTIT**U**TION
CONSTIT**U**TIVE
CONTRAP**U**NTAL
DISTRIB**U**TIVE
INARTIC**U**LATE
MALOCCL**U**SION
MEALYMO**U**THED
MISCALC**U**LATE
NONCOND**U**CTOR
RECAPIT**U**LATE
SOMNAMB**U**LISM
THERAPE**U**TICS
UNSCRUP**U**LOUS
UNBELIE**V**ABLE
ASTROPH**Y**SICS
CHALCOP**Y**RITE
ELEEMOS**Y**NARY
GOBBLED**Y**GOOK
HIEROGL**Y**PHIC
OXYACET**Y**LENE
POLYETH**Y**LENE
PRASEOD**Y**MIUM
UNEMPLO**Y**MENT
RECOGNI**Z**ANCE

## 9th Letter

ACQUAINT**A**NCE
AMPHITHE**A**TER
APPURTEN**A**NCE
BIBLIOGR**A**PHY
BIOGEOGR**A**PHY
CABINETM**A**KER
CHOREOGR**A**PHY
CIRCUMST**A**NCE
COMMONWE**A**LTH
COMMUNIC**A**BLE
COMPLAIS**A**NCE
CONQUIST**A**DOR
CONSIDER**A**BLE
CRYPTOGR**A**PHY
DECALCOM**A**NIA
DECASYLL**A**BIC
DEMIMOND**A**INE
DEMONSTR**A**BLE
DETERMIN**A**BLE
DISAGREE**A**BLE
DISREPUT**A**BLE
EXTRAVAG**A**NZA
HIPPOPOT**A**MUS
IMMEASUR**A**BLE
IMPENETR**A**BLE
IMPERISH**A**BLE
IMPONDER**A**BLE
INCALCUL**A**BLE
INCOMPAR**A**BLE
INCONSOL**A**BLE
INDECLIN**A**BLE
INDISPUT**A**BLE
INEFFACE**A**BLE
INEXPLIC**A**BLE
INEXTRIC**A**BLE
INSUFFER**A**BLE
INTEMPER**A**NCE
INTERMIN**A**BLE
INTERVOC**A**LIC
INVULNER**A**BLE
IRREDEEM**A**BLE
IRREFRAG**A**BLE
IRREMEDI**A**BLE
LEXICOGR**A**PHY
MERCHANT**A**BLE
MONOSYLL**A**BLE
MUDDLEHE**A**DED
MULLIGAT**A**WNY
MULTIVIT**A**MIN
OCEANOGR**A**PHY
OCTOSYLL**A**BIC
PANCHROM**A**TIC
PARADISI**A**CAL
PERAMBUL**A**TOR
PHYSIOGR**A**PHY
POLYSYLL**A**BIC
POLYSYLL**A**BLE
PRECIPIT**A**NCY
PROGRAMM**A**BLE
PROTUBER**A**NCE
QUESTION**A**BLE
RECOGNIZ**A**NCE
REMONSTR**A**NCE
SELENOGR**A**PHY
SIGNIFIC**A**NCE
STRAIGHT**A**WAY
STRATIGR**A**PHY
SURVEILL**A**NCE
TRANSOCE**A**NIC
TROUBLEM**A**KER
UNASSAIL**A**BLE
UNBELIEV**A**BLE
UNCHARIT**A**BLE
UNGOVERN**A**BLE
UNMISTAK**A**BLE
UNPROFIT**A**BLE
UNREASON**A**BLE
UNSEARCH**A**BLE
UNSEASON**A**BLE
UNSEGREG**A**TED
ZOOGEOGR**A**PHY
THOROUGH**B**RED
AUTHENTI**C**ATE
CHIROPRA**C**TIC
CHROMATI**C**ITY
DISCONNE**C**TED
INCANDES**C**ENT
INTERGLA**C**IAL
KALEIDOS**C**OPE
MICROCIR**C**UIT
MICROSPA**C**ING
MULTIPLI**C**AND
MULTIPLI**C**ITY
NONCONDU**C**TOR
OSCILLOS**C**OPE
OUTSTRET**C**HED
PERSPICA**C**ITY
PREFABRI**C**ATE
PROPHYLA**C**TIC
PUMPERNI**C**KEL
SPECTROS**C**OPE
STRAITJA**C**KET
CORESPON**D**ENT
FREESTAN**D**ING
HEARTREN**D**ING
HYPERACI**D**ITY
HYPOCHON**D**RIA
PHILODEN**D**RON
PROCATHE**D**RAL
PROPAGAN**D**IZE
RHODODEN**D**RON
TRANSCEN**D**ENT
ALPHANUM**E**RIC
ANTIMAGN**E**TIC
ARGILLAC**E**OUS
BELLIGER**E**NCY
BIOTELEM**E**TRY
CARBONAC**E**OUS
CHECKERB**E**RRY
CINEMATH**E**QUE
CONCRESC**E**NCE
CONSTITU**E**NCY

COUNTERTENOR
DENSITOMETER
DISCOURTEOUS
DISOBEDIENCE
ENCYCLOPEDIA
EQUESTRIENNE
FLUORESCENCE
FRANKINCENSE
GALVANOMETER
HYPOGLYCEMIA
INDEPENDENCE
INEXPERIENCE
INTELLIGENCE
INTERFERENCE
LONGSHOREMAN
LUMINESCENCE
LUNCHEONETTE
MADEMOISELLE
MAGNETOMETER
MESSEIGNEURS
MULTIFACETED
MULTILATERAL
NEURASTHENIA
NEUROSCIENCE
PROLEGOMENON
QUINTESSENCE
REMINISCENCE
SENSITOMETER
SIMULTANEOUS
SPECTROMETER
STRAIGHTEDGE
SUBCUTANEOUS
SUBSERVIENCE
TENDEROMETER
TRANSFERENCE
TRIGONOMETRY
UNPARALLELED
PREAMPLIFIER
THOROUGHFARE
UNDERSURFACE
BILLINGSGATE
CARPETBAGGER
GOBBLEDYGOOK
INTRANSIGENT
MICROSURGERY
MULTILINGUAL
APOSTROPHIZE
BRAINWASHING
CHROMOSPHERE
DIASTROPHISM
DISFRANCHISE
FORMALDEHYDE
FOUNTAINHEAD
HABERDASHERY
HANDKERCHIEF
MANSLAUGHTER
METAMORPHISM
MISAPPREHEND
NEIGHBORHOOD
PERICYNTHION
PHILOSOPHIZE
POLYMORPHISM
SHORTSIGHTED
STEEPLECHASE
STEPDAUGHTER
STRATOSPHERE
SUPERHIGHWAY
THERMOSPHERE
UNLIKELIHOOD
ADVENTITIOUS
ANTIPARTICLE
ANTITHETICAL
APPENDICITIS
ASTRONOMICAL
BACTERICIDAL
CHESTERFIELD
CHITTERLINGS
CONTEMPTIBLE
CONTUMACIOUS
CONTUMELIOUS
COSMOPOLITAN
DESTRUCTIBLE
DISASSOCIATE
DISPUTATIOUS
ENCEPHALITIS
EXTRAMARITAL
FRONTISPIECE
HEARTSTRINGS
HIERARCHICAL
IMPERCIPIENT
INCOMPATIBLE
INCONVENIENT
INCORRIGIBLE
INDEFEASIBLE
INDIGESTIBLE
INSALUBRIOUS
INSUFFICIENT
INTELLIGIBLE
INTERMEDIARY
INTERMEDIATE
IRRESISTIBLE
IRREVERSIBLE
LONGITUDINAL
MERETRICIOUS
MIDDLEWEIGHT
MULTIFARIOUS
PENITENTIARY
PERTINACIOUS
PLANETESIMAL
PRIMOGENITOR
RAMBUNCTIOUS
SARSAPARILLA
SCATOLOGICAL
SECRETARIATE
SPORTSWRITER
SUBCONSCIOUS
SUBSTANTIATE
SUPERCILIOUS
SURROUNDINGS
TRANQUILIZER
TRANSPACIFIC
UNRESTRAINED
UNSCIENTIFIC
VAINGLORIOUS
WELTERWEIGHT
BACKTRACKING
BLATHERSKITE
BLUESTOCKING
BREATHTAKING
EARTHSHAKING
MULTITASKING
SWASHBUCKLER
ANTHROPOLOGY
BACTERIOLOGY
BIOSATELLITE
COLLEGIALITY
CONGRATULATE
CONSTABULARY
COUNTERCLAIM
DEMINERALIZE
DISCONSOLATE
DISESTABLISH
EDITORIALIZE
ELECTROPLATE
EPISCOPALIAN
INARTICULATE
INTERSTELLAR
MICROBIOLOGY
MISCALCULATE
MUNICIPALITY
NEVERTHELESS
OFFICEHOLDER
OTHERWORLDLY
OXYACETYLENE
PALEONTOLOGY
PARASITOLOGY
PHARMACOLOGY
POLICYHOLDER
POLYETHYLENE
PRINCIPALITY
RECAPITULATE
SCHOOLFELLOW
SOMNAMBULISM
SPIRITUALISM
STREETWALKER
TECHNICALITY
THUNDERCLOUD
UNIVERSALIST
UNIVERSALITY
UNIVERSALIZE
UNSCRUPULOUS
VACATIONLAND
VERTICILLATE
WEATHERGLASS
AERODYNAMICS
BLANDISHMENT
COMMENCEMENT
CUMULONIMBUS
DISPLACEMENT
EPITHALAMIUM
EVERBLOOMING
HEARTWARMING
HELLGRAMMITE
HOUSEWARMING
ILLEGITIMATE
MICROCLIMATE
MONOFILAMENT
PRASEODYMIUM
PREDETERMINE
PRESENTIMENT
PROTHALAMION
SLEDGEHAMMER
UNDERGARMENT
UNEMPLOYMENT
ABOLITIONISM
ABSENTMINDED
ASYNCHRONOUS
ATTITUDINIZE
BICENTENNIAL
CALISTHENICS
CARILLONNEUR
CHRISTIANITY
CHRISTIANIZE
COMPANIONWAY
CONFUCIANISM
CONTERMINOUS
CONTRAPUNTAL
DISCIPLINARY
DISCRIMINATE
ELEEMOSYNARY
ENTREPRENEUR
EXTORTIONATE
FEEBLEMINDED
INDOCTRINATE
INFLATIONARY
INFLATIONISM
INSTRUMENTAL
ISOLATIONISM
PORCELAINIZE
PREDESIGNATE
PREPAREDNESS
PROTACTINIUM
PYROTECHNICS
RECEPTIONIST
SUBCONTINENT
SUBTERRANEAN
TERCENTENARY
UNDERPINNING
UNDOCUMENTED
UNFREQUENTED
VALENCIENNES
AVITAMINOSIS
BREAKTHROUGH
BUTTERSCOTCH
CHECKERBOARD
CLOTHESHORSE
COMMISSIONER
CONFECTIONER
CONFESSIONAL
CONVENTIONAL
COUNTERPOINT
COUNTERPOISE
FLAMETHROWER
HALLUCINOGEN
INVITATIONAL
MEETINGHOUSE
MULTICOLORED
ONOMATOPOEIA
PACKINGHOUSE
PHILHARMONIC
PLASTERBOARD
POSTDOCTORAL
POSTHYPNOTIC
PRACTITIONER
PROCESSIONAL
PROFESSIONAL
PROPORTIONAL
PSYCHOTROPIC
SHARPSHOOTER
SHUFFLEBOARD
STEREOPHONIC
STEREOSCOPIC
TRADESPEOPLE
TUBERCULOSIS
UNACCUSTOMED
WEATHERBOARD
GLOCKENSPIEL
HIEROGLYPHIC
MARLINESPIKE
MISINTERPRET
MULTIPURPOSE
PEACEKEEPING
PHOTOCOMPOSE
SHARECROPPER
UNPRINCIPLED
AMBIDEXTROUS
ATMOSPHERICS
BLOODTHIRSTY
BREASTSTROKE
CANTANKEROUS
CARBOHYDRATE
CHALCOPYRITE
CHARACTERIZE
CHEESEBURGER
CHEESEPARING
CHEMOTHERAPY
CHILDBEARING
CHURCHWARDEN
CIRCUMSCRIBE
CLOTHESPRESS
COELENTERATE
COMMENSURATE
COMMISSARIAT
CONCELEBRANT
CONGLOMERATE
CONTAINERIZE
CONTEMPORARY
CROSSCURRENT
DEMILITARIZE
DISACCHARIDE
DISINTEGRATE
FAINTHEARTED
FLUOROCARBON
GREATHEARTED
HEADMISTRESS
HEAVYHEARTED
HUMANITARIAN
HYDROTHERAPY
HYDROTHERMAL
IDIOSYNCRASY
INVERTEBRATE
KINDERGARTEN
LIGHTHEARTED
MASTERSTROKE
NEWSPAPERMAN
NONAGENARIAN
OBSTREPEROUS
OCTOGENARIAN
PHILANTHROPY
PHOTOENGRAVE
POSTMISTRESS
PRECANCEROUS
PRECONCERTED
PREMENSTRUAL
PREPONDERATE
PREPOSTEROUS
PRESBYTERIAN
PROTECTORATE
RADIOTHERAPY
RECALCITRANT
SEXAGENARIAN
SPECTROGRAPH
SUPERCHARGER
TESTOSTERONE
TOTALITARIAN
TRANSMIGRATE
TRANSMOGRIFY
UNDERCURRENT
UNREGENERATE
VETERINARIAN
WEATHERPROOF
WHOLEHEARTED

ACCOMPLI**S**HED
ANTIALIA**S**ING
ANTIMACA**S**SAR
APPREHEN**S**IVE
ASTROPHY**S**ICS
AUSTRONE**S**IAN
BIOCHEMI**S**TRY
CHAMPION**S**HIP
DECOMMIS**S**ION
DELICATE**S**SEN
DICTATOR**S**HIP
ECCLESIA**S**TIC
ENTERPRI**S**ING
EXTRASEN**S**ORY
GEOCHEMI**S**TRY
HYPERTEN**S**ION
INTERCES**S**ION
INTERMIS**S**ION
MALNOURI**S**HED
MALOCCLU**S**ION
MISREPRE**S**ENT
MOUNTAIN**S**IDE
MULTISES**S**ION
MULTIVER**S**ITY
OVEREXPO**S**URE
PARENTHE**S**IZE
PREREQUI**S**ITE
RECEIVER**S**HIP
RELATION**S**HIP
RELATIVI**S**TIC
REPERCUS**S**ION
SCHOOLMA**S**TER
TRANSMIS**S**ION
UNINTERE**S**TED
ABBREVIA**T**ION
ALLITERA**T**ION
ANATHEMA**T**IZE
ANNUNCIA**T**ION
ANTIELEC**T**RON
APPENDEC**T**OMY
APPRECIA**T**IVE
ARCHITEC**T**URE
ASTRONAU**T**ICS
BLOCKBUS**T**ING
BLOODLET**T**ING
BRILLIAN**T**INE
CIVILIZA**T**ION
CLOSEMOU**T**HED
CONFIDEN**T**IAL
CONFIRMA**T**ION
CONFORMA**T**ION
CONGREGA**T**ION
CONSERVA**T**ION
CONSERVA**T**ISM
CONSERVA**T**IVE
CONSERVA**T**ORY
CONSTIPA**T**ION
CONSTITU**T**ION
CONSTITU**T**IVE
CONSTRUC**T**ION
CONTINUA**T**ION
CONVERSA**T**ION
DECONGES**T**ANT
DELIBERA**T**IVE
DENOMINA**T**ION
DENUNCIA**T**ION
DESPOLIA**T**ION
DIFFEREN**T**IAL
DISADVAN**T**AGE
DISPENSA**T**ION
DISQUISI**T**ION
DISSERTA**T**ION
DISTILLA**T**ION
DISTRIBU**T**IVE
EARSPLIT**T**ING
ECHOLOCA**T**ION
EXCRUCIA**T**ING
FENESTRA**T**ION
FERMENTA**T**ION
FIBRILLA**T**ION
FRANKENS**T**EIN
HAIRSPLI**T**TER
HEADQUAR**T**ERS
HELIOCEN**T**RIC
HORTICUL**T**URE
HYSTEREC**T**OMY
ILLUSTRA**T**ION
ILLUSTRA**T**IVE
IMPERCEP**T**IVE
IMPERFEC**T**ION
INCAPACI**T**ATE
INCRUSTA**T**ION
INFELICI**T**OUS
INFLAMMA**T**ION
INFLAMMA**T**ORY
INGRATIA**T**ING
INSURREC**T**ION
INTELLEC**T**UAL
INTERJEC**T**ION
INTERMIT**T**ENT
INTERSEC**T**ION
INTRANSI**T**IVE
IRRESPEC**T**IVE
JURISDIC**T**ION
MALFORMA**T**ION
MALNUTRI**T**ION
MASTURBA**T**ION
MEALYMOU**T**HED
MENSTRUA**T**ION
MISADVEN**T**URE
NIGHTCLO**T**HES
NOMENCLA**T**URE
NONCOMBA**T**ANT
NONCOMMI**T**TAL
NONOBJEC**T**IVE
OBSCURAN**T**ISM
ORGANIZA**T**ION
PARAMILI**T**ARY
PERADVEN**T**URE
PESTILEN**T**IAL
PIGMENTA**T**ION
POLARIZA**T**ION
PRECONDI**T**ION
PREDIGES**T**ION
PREDILEC**T**ION
PREINDUC**T**ION
PREOPERA**T**IVE
PRESCRIP**T**ION
PROVIDEN**T**IAL
PSYCHOAC**T**IVE
QUANTITA**T**IVE
QUARTERS**T**AFF
RADIOISO**T**OPE
RECOLLEC**T**ION
RECONSTI**T**UTE
REGISTRA**T**ION
REHABILI**T**ATE
REMUNERA**T**ION
REMUNERA**T**IVE
RENUNCIA**T**ION
RESTAURA**T**EUR
RESURREC**T**ION
SATISFAC**T**ION
SATISFAC**T**ORY
SUBCOMMI**T**TEE
SUBDIREC**T**ORY
SUBMINIA**T**URE
SUBSCRIP**T**ION
SUBSTRUC**T**URE
SUPERSTI**T**ION
THERAPEU**T**ICS
THUNDERS**T**ORM
TRANSVES**T**ISM
TRAPSHOO**T**ING
TRIGNOME**T**RIC
ULTRAMON**T**ANE
UNDERCLO**T**HES
UNDERCOA**T**ING
VALORIZA**T**ION
VENIPUNC**T**URE
AFORETHO**U**GHT
AFTERTHO**U**GHT
AUDIOVIS**U**ALS
CONTEMPT**U**OUS
DISINGEN**U**OUS
INDISSOL**U**BLE
INTERLOC**U**TOR
MAGNILOQ**U**ENT
METALANG**U**AGE
MINICOMP**U**TER
MISPRONO**U**NCE
NONSCHED**U**LED
POSTGRAD**U**ATE
PRESUMPT**U**OUS
SUPERANN**U**ATE
SUPERNAT**U**RAL
ANTEDILU**V**IAN
COLLECTI**V**ISM
COLLECTI**V**IZE
PHOTOGRA**V**URE
RESPECTI**V**ELY
SCANDINA**V**IAN
THANKSGI**V**ING
CONTRARI**W**ISE
GLASSBLO**W**ING
HENCEFOR**W**ARD
PICKEREL**W**EED
UNDERDRA**W**ERS
WHIPPOOR**W**ILL
HETEROSE**X**UAL
PSYCHOSE**X**UAL
ELECTROL**Y**SIS
STREPTOM**Y**CIN
NEWSMAGA**Z**INE
SPERMATO**Z**OON

## 10TH LETTER

AUDIOVISU**A**LS
AUTHENTIC**A**TE
BILLINGSG**A**TE
CARBOHYDR**A**TE
CHECKERBO**A**RD
CHEMOTHER**A**PY
COELENTER**A**TE
COMMENSUR**A**TE
CONCELEBR**A**NT
CONGLOMER**A**TE
CONGRATUL**A**TE
CONSTABUL**A**RY
CONTEMPOR**A**RY
COUNTERCL**A**IM
DECONGEST**A**NT
DISADVANT**A**GE
DISASSOCI**A**TE
DISCIPLIN**A**RY
DISCONSOL**A**TE
DISCRIMIN**A**TE
DISINTEGR**A**TE
ELECTROPL**A**TE
ELEEMOSYN**A**RY
EXTORTION**A**TE
HENCEFORW**A**RD
HYDROTHER**A**PY
IDIOSYNCR**A**SY
ILLEGITIM**A**TE
INARTICUL**A**TE
INCAPACIT**A**TE
INDOCTRIN**A**TE
INFLATION**A**RY
INTERMEDI**A**RY
INTERMEDI**A**TE
INVERTEBR**A**TE
METALANGU**A**GE
MICROCLIM**A**TE
MISCALCUL**A**TE
MULTIPLIC**A**ND
NONCOMBAT**A**NT
PARAMILIT**A**RY
PENITENTI**A**RY
PHOTOENGR**A**VE
PLASTERBO**A**RD
POSTGRADU**A**TE
PREDESIGN**A**TE
PREFABRIC**A**TE
PREPONDER**A**TE
PROTECTOR**A**TE
QUARTERST**A**FF
RADIOTHER**A**PY
RECALCITR**A**NT
RECAPITUL**A**TE
REHABILIT**A**TE
SECRETARI**A**TE
SHUFFLEBO**A**RD
SPECTROGR**A**PH
STEEPLECH**A**SE
SUBSTANTI**A**TE
SUPERANNU**A**TE
TERCENTEN**A**RY
THOROUGHF**A**RE
TRANSMIGR**A**TE
ULTRAMONT**A**NE
UNDERSURF**A**CE
UNREGENER**A**TE
VACATIONL**A**ND
VERTICILL**A**TE
WEATHERBO**A**RD
WEATHERGL**A**SS
COMMUNICA**B**LE
CONSIDERA**B**LE
CONTEMPTI**B**LE
CUMULONIM**B**US
DECASYLLA**B**IC
DEMONSTRA**B**LE
DESTRUCTI**B**LE
DETERMINA**B**LE
DISAGREEA**B**LE
DISREPUTA**B**LE
FLUOROCAR**B**ON
IMMEASURA**B**LE
IMPENETRA**B**LE
IMPERISHA**B**LE
IMPONDERA**B**LE
INCALCULA**B**LE
INCOMPARA**B**LE
INCOMPATI**B**LE
INCONSOLA**B**LE
INCORRIGI**B**LE
INDECLINA**B**LE
INDEFEASI**B**LE
INDIGESTI**B**LE
INDISPUTA**B**LE
INDISSOLU**B**LE
INEFFACEA**B**LE
INEXPLICA**B**LE
INEXTRICA**B**LE
INSUFFERA**B**LE
INTELLIGI**B**LE
INTERMINA**B**LE
INVULNERA**B**LE
IRREDEEMA**B**LE
IRREFRAGA**B**LE
IRREMEDIA**B**LE
IRRESISTI**B**LE
IRREVERSI**B**LE
MERCHANTA**B**LE
MONOSYLLA**B**LE
OCTOSYLLA**B**IC
POLYSYLLA**B**IC
POLYSYLLA**B**LE
PROGRAMMA**B**LE
QUESTIONA**B**LE
UNASSAILA**B**LE
UNBELIEVA**B**LE
UNCHARITA**B**LE
UNGOVERNA**B**LE
UNMISTAKA**B**LE
UNPROFITA**B**LE
UNREASONA**B**LE
UNSEARCHA**B**LE
UNSEASONA**B**LE
ANTIPARTI**C**LE
ANTITHETI**C**AL
ASTRONOMI**C**AL
HIERARCHI**C**AL
PARADISIA**C**AL
SCATOLOGI**C**AL
STREPTOMY**C**IN
ABSENTMIN**D**ED
BACTERICI**D**AL
CHURCHWAR**D**EN
CONQUISTA**D**OR
ENCYCLOPE**D**IA
FEEBLEMIN**D**ED
MUDDLEHEA**D**ED
OFFICEHOL**D**ER
OTHERWORL**D**LY
POLICYHOL**D**ER
STRAIGHTE**D**GE
BLANDISHM**E**NT

CARILLONNEUR
CHESTERFIELD
CHROMOSPHERE
CLOTHESPRESS
COMMENCEMENT
CORESPONDENT
CROSSCURRENT
DISPLACEMENT
ENTREPRENEUR
FOUNTAINHEAD
FRANKENSTEIN
FRONTISPIECE
HABERDASHERY
HEADMISTRESS
HEADQUARTERS
IMPERCIPIENT
INCANDESCENT
INCONVENIENT
INSUFFICIENT
INTERMITTENT
INTRANSIGENT
MAGNILOQUENT
MICROSURGERY
MISAPPREHEND
MISREPRESENT
MONOFILAMENT
NEVERTHELESS
ONOMATOPOEIA
OXYACETYLENE
PICKERELWEED
POLYETHYLENE
POSTMISTRESS
PREPAREDNESS
PRESENTIMENT
RESPECTIVELY
RESTAURATEUR
STRATOSPHERE
SUBCONTINENT
SUBTERRANEAN
THERMOSPHERE
TRANSCENDENT
UNDERCURRENT
UNDERDRAWERS
UNDERGARMENT
UNEMPLOYMENT
TRANSPACIFIC
UNSCIENTIFIC
AFORETHOUGHT
AFTERTHOUGHT
CARPETBAGGER
CHEESEBURGER
HALLUCINOGEN
MIDDLEWEIGHT
SUPERCHARGER
WELTERWEIGHT
ACCOMPLISHED
CHAMPIONSHIP

CLOSEMOUTHED
DICTATORSHIP
HIEROGLYPHIC
MALNOURISHED
MEALYMOUTHED
NIGHTCLOTHES
OUTSTRETCHED
RECEIVERSHIP
RELATIONSHIP
UNDERCLOTHES
ABBREVIATION
ABOLITIONISM
AERODYNAMICS
ALLITERATION
ANATHEMATIZE
ANNUNCIATION
ANTEDILUVIAN
ANTIALIASING
APOSTROPHIZE
APPRECIATIVE
APPREHENSIVE
ASTRONAUTICS
ASTROPHYSICS
ATMOSPHERICS
ATTITUDINIZE
AUSTRONESIAN
BACKTRACKING
BICENTENNIAL
BIOSATELLITE
BLATHERSKITE
BLOCKBUSTING
BLOODLETTING
BLUESTOCKING
BRAINWASHING
BREATHTAKING
BRILLIANTINE
CALISTHENICS
CHALCOPYRITE
CHARACTERIZE
CHEESEPARING
CHILDBEARING
CHRISTIANITY
CHRISTIANIZE
CHROMATICITY
CIRCUMSCRIBE
CIVILIZATION
COLLECTIVISM
COLLECTIVIZE
COLLEGIALITY
COMMISSARIAT
CONFIDENTIAL
CONFIRMATION
CONFORMATION
CONFUCIANISM
CONGREGATION
CONSERVATION
CONSERVATISM

CONSERVATIVE
CONSTIPATION
CONSTITUTION
CONSTITUTIVE
CONSTRUCTION
CONTAINERIZE
CONTINUATION
CONTRARIWISE
CONVERSATION
COUNTERPOINT
COUNTERPOISE
DECOMMISSION
DELIBERATIVE
DEMILITARIZE
DEMIMONDAINE
DEMINERALIZE
DENOMINATION
DENUNCIATION
DESPOLIATION
DIASTROPHISM
DIFFERENTIAL
DISACCHARIDE
DISESTABLISH
DISFRANCHISE
DISPENSATION
DISQUISITION
DISSERTATION
DISTILLATION
DISTRIBUTIVE
EARSPLITTING
EARTHSHAKING
ECHOLOCATION
EDITORIALIZE
ENTERPRISING
EPISCOPALIAN
EPITHALAMIUM
EVERBLOOMING
EXCRUCIATING
FENESTRATION
FERMENTATION
FIBRILLATION
FREESTANDING
GLASSBLOWING
GLOCKENSPIEL
HANDKERCHIEF
HEARTRENDING
HEARTWARMING
HELLGRAMMITE
HOUSEWARMING
HUMANITARIAN
HYPERACIDITY
HYPERTENSION
ILLUSTRATION
ILLUSTRATIVE
IMPERCEPTIVE
IMPERFECTION
INCRUSTATION

INFLAMMATION
INFLATIONISM
INGRATIATING
INSURRECTION
INTERCESSION
INTERGLACIAL
INTERJECTION
INTERMISSION
INTERSECTION
INTRANSITIVE
IRRESPECTIVE
ISOLATIONISM
JURISDICTION
MALFORMATION
MALNUTRITION
MALOCCLUSION
MARLINESPIKE
MASTURBATION
MENSTRUATION
METAMORPHISM
MICROSPACING
MOUNTAINSIDE
MULTIPLICITY
MULTISESSION
MULTITASKING
MULTIVERSITY
MUNICIPALITY
NEWSMAGAZINE
NONAGENARIAN
NONOBJECTIVE
OBSCURANTISM
OCTOGENARIAN
ORGANIZATION
PARENTHESIZE
PEACEKEEPING
PERICYNTHION
PERSPICACITY
PESTILENTIAL
PHILOSOPHIZE
PIGMENTATION
POLARIZATION
POLYMORPHISM
PORCELAINIZE
PRASEODYMIUM
PREAMPLIFIER
PRECONDITION
PREDETERMINE
PREDIGESTION
PREDILECTION
PREINDUCTION
PREOPERATIVE
PREREQUISITE
PRESBYTERIAN
PRESCRIPTION
PRINCIPALITY
PROPAGANDIZE
PROTACTINIUM

PROTHALAMION
PROVIDENTIAL
PSYCHOACTIVE
PYROTECHNICS
QUANTITATIVE
RECEPTIONIST
RECOLLECTION
REGISTRATION
REMUNERATION
REMUNERATIVE
RENUNCIATION
REPERCUSSION
RESURRECTION
SATISFACTION
SCANDINAVIAN
SEXAGENARIAN
SOMNAMBULISM
SPIRITUALISM
SUBSCRIPTION
SUPERSTITION
TECHNICALITY
THANKSGIVING
THERAPEUTICS
TOTALITARIAN
TRANSMISSION
TRANSMOGRIFY
TRANSVESTISM
TRAPSHOOTING
UNDERCOATING
UNDERPINNING
UNIVERSALIST
UNIVERSALITY
UNIVERSALIZE
VALORIZATION
VETERINARIAN
WHIPPOORWILL
CABINETMAKER
PUMPERNICKEL
STRAITJACKET
STREETWALKER
TROUBLEMAKER
COMMONWEALTH
INTERSTELLAR
INTERVOCALIC
MADEMOISELLE
NONSCHEDULED
SARSAPARILLA
SCHOOLFELLOW
SWASHBUCKLER
UNPARALLELED
UNPRINCIPLED
HIPPOPOTAMUS
HYDROTHERMAL
HYPOGLYCEMIA
LONGSHOREMAN
MULTIVITAMIN
NEWSPAPERMAN

PLANETESIMAL
SLEDGEHAMMER
UNACCUSTOMED
ACQUAINTANCE
APPURTENANCE
BELLIGERENCY
CHITTERLINGS
CIRCUMSTANCE
COMMISSIONER
COMPLAISANCE
CONCRESCENCE
CONFECTIONER
CONFESSIONAL
CONSTITUENCY
CONVENTIONAL
COUNTERTENOR
DECALCOMANIA
DISOBEDIENCE
EQUESTRIENNE
EXTRAVAGANZA
FLUORESCENCE
FRANKINCENSE
HEARTSTRINGS
INDEPENDENCE
INEXPERIENCE
INTELLIGENCE
INTEMPERANCE
INTERFERENCE
INVITATIONAL
LONGITUDINAL
LUMINESCENCE
MISPRONOUNCE
NEURASTHENIA
NEUROSCIENCE
PHILHARMONIC
PRACTITIONER
PRECIPITANCY
PROCESSIONAL
PROFESSIONAL
PROLEGOMENON
PROPORTIONAL
PROTUBERANCE
QUINTESSENCE
RECOGNIZANCE
REMINISCENCE
REMONSTRANCE
SIGNIFICANCE
STEREOPHONIC
SUBSERVIENCE
SURROUNDINGS
SURVEILLANCE
TRANSFERENCE
TRANSOCEANIC
UNRESTRAINED
VALENCIENNES
ADVENTITIOUS
AMBIDEXTROUS

ANTHROPOLOGY
APPENDECTOMY
ARGILLACEOUS
ASYNCHRONOUS
BACTERIOLOGY
BREASTSTROKE
CANTANKEROUS
CARBONACEOUS
CONSERVATORY
CONTEMPTUOUS
CONTERMINOUS
CONTUMACIOUS
CONTUMELIOUS
DISCOURTEOUS
DISINGENUOUS
DISPUTATIOUS
EXTRASENSORY
GOBBLEDYGOOK
HYSTERECTOMY
INFELICITOUS
INFLAMMATORY
INSALUBRIOUS
KALEIDOSCOPE
MASTERSTROKE
MERETRICIOUS
MICROBIOLOGY
MULTIFARIOUS
MULTIPURPOSE
NEIGHBORHOOD
OBSTREPEROUS
OSCILLOSCOPE
PALEONTOLOGY
PARASITOLOGY
PERTINACIOUS
PHARMACOLOGY
PHILANTHROPY
PHOTOCOMPOSE
PRECANCEROUS
PREPOSTEROUS
PRESUMPTUOUS
RADIOISOTOPE
RAMBUNCTIOUS
SATISFACTORY
SIMULTANEOUS
SPECTROSCOPE
SPERMATOZOON
SUBCONSCIOUS
SUBCUTANEOUS
SUBDIRECTORY
SUPERCILIOUS
TESTOSTERONE
THUNDERCLOUD
THUNDERSTORM
UNLIKELIHOOD
UNSCRUPULOUS
VAINGLORIOUS
WEATHERPROOF

BIBLIOGRAPHY
BIOGEOGRAPHY
CHOREOGRAPHY
CRYPTOGRAPHY
LEXICOGRAPHY
OCEANOGRAPHY
PHYSIOGRAPHY
PSYCHOTROPIC
SELENOGRAPHY
SHARECROPPER
STEREOSCOPIC
STRATIGRAPHY
TRADESPEOPLE
ZOOGEOGRAPHY
CINEMATHEQUE
ALPHANUMERIC
ANTIELECTRON
CHECKERBERRY
CLOTHESHORSE
HELIOCENTRIC
HYPOCHONDRIA
MISINTERPRET
MULTICOLORED
MULTILATERAL
PHILODENDRON
POSTDOCTORAL
PROCATHEDRAL
RHODODENDRON
SUPERNATURAL
THOROUGHBRED
TRIGNOMETRIC
ANTIMACASSAR
AVITAMINOSIS
BLOODTHIRSTY
DELICATESSEN
ELECTROLYSIS
TUBERCULOSIS
AMPHITHEATER
ANTIMAGNETIC
APPENDICITIS
BIOCHEMISTRY
BIOTELEMETRY
BUTTERSCOTCH
CHIROPRACTIC
CONTRAPUNTAL
COSMOPOLITAN
DENSITOMETER
DISCONNECTED
ECCLESIASTIC
ENCEPHALITIS
EXTRAMARITAL
FAINTHEARTED
GALVANOMETER
GEOCHEMISTRY
GREATHEARTED
HAIRSPLITTER
HEAVYHEARTED

INSTRUMENTAL
INTERLOCUTOR
KINDERGARTEN
LIGHTHEARTED
LUNCHEONETTE
MAGNETOMETER
MANSLAUGHTER
MINICOMPUTER
MULTIFACETED
NONCOMMITTAL
NONCONDUCTOR
PANCHROMATIC
PERAMBULATOR
POSTHYPNOTIC
PRECONCERTED
PRIMOGENITOR
PROPHYLACTIC
RELATIVISTIC
SCHOOLMASTER
SENSITOMETER
SHARPSHOOTER
SHORTSIGHTED
SPECTROMETER
SPORTSWRITER
STEPDAUGHTER
SUBCOMMITTEE
TENDEROMETER
TRIGONOMETRY
UNDOCUMENTED
UNFREQUENTED
UNINTERESTED
UNSEGREGATED
WHOLEHEARTED
ARCHITECTURE
BREAKTHROUGH
HETEROSEXUAL
HORTICULTURE
INTELLECTUAL
MEETINGHOUSE
MESSEIGNEURS
MICROCIRCUIT
MISADVENTURE
MULTILINGUAL
NOMENCLATURE
OVEREXPOSURE
PACKINGHOUSE
PERADVENTURE
PHOTOGRAVURE
PREMENSTRUAL
PSYCHOSEXUAL
RECONSTITUTE
SUBMINIATURE
SUBSTRUCTURE
VENIPUNCTURE
COMPANIONWAY
FLAMETHROWER
MULLIGATAWNY

STRAIGHTAWAY
SUPERHIGHWAY
FORMALDEHYDE
TRANQUILIZER

## 11th Letter

ANTEDILUVIAN
ANTIMACASSAR
ANTITHETICAL
ASTRONOMICAL
AUSTRONESIAN
BACTERICIDAL
BICENTENNIAL
COMMISSARIAT
COMPANIONWAY
CONFESSIONAL
CONFIDENTIAL
CONTRAPUNTAL
CONVENTIONAL
COSMOPOLITAN
DIFFERENTIAL
EPISCOPALIAN
EXTRAMARITAL
FOUNTAINHEAD
HETEROSEXUAL
HIERARCHICAL
HUMANITARIAN
HYDROTHERMAL
INSTRUMENTAL
INTELLECTUAL
INTERGLACIAL
INTERSTELLAR
INVITATIONAL
LONGITUDINAL
LONGSHOREMAN
MULTILATERAL
MULTILINGUAL
NEWSPAPERMAN
NONAGENARIAN
NONCOMMITTAL
OCTOGENARIAN
PARADISIACAL
PESTILENTIAL
PLANETESIMAL
POSTDOCTORAL
PREMENSTRUAL
PRESBYTERIAN
PROCATHEDRAL
PROCESSIONAL
PROFESSIONAL
PROPORTIONAL
PROVIDENTIAL
PSYCHOSEXUAL
SCANDINAVIAN

SCATOLOGICAL
SEXAGENARIAN
STRAIGHTAWAY
SUBTERRANEAN
SUPERHIGHWAY
SUPERNATURAL
TOTALITARIAN
VETERINARIAN
CIRCUMSCRIBE
ACQUAINTANCE
AERODYNAMICS
APPURTENANCE
ASTRONAUTICS
ASTROPHYSICS
ATMOSPHERICS
BELLIGERENCY
BUTTERSCOTCH
CALISTHENICS
CIRCUMSTANCE
COMPLAISANCE
CONCRESCENCE
CONSTITUENCY
DISOBEDIENCE
FLUORESCENCE
FRONTISPIECE
INDEPENDENCE
INEXPERIENCE
INTELLIGENCE
INTEMPERANCE
INTERFERENCE
LUMINESCENCE
MISPRONOUNCE
NEUROSCIENCE
PRECIPITANCY
PROTUBERANCE
PYROTECHNICS
QUINTESSENCE
RECOGNIZANCE
REMINISCENCE
REMONSTRANCE
SIGNIFICANCE
SUBSERVIENCE
SURVEILLANCE
THERAPEUTICS
TRANSFERENCE
UNDERSURFACE
DISACCHARIDE
FORMALDEHYDE
MOUNTAINSIDE
ABSENTMINDED
ACCOMPLISHED
AMPHITHEATER
CABINETMAKER
CARPETBAGGER
CHEESEBURGER
CHURCHWARDEN
CLOSEMOUTHED

COMMISSIONER
CONFECTIONER
DELICATESSEN
DENSITOMETER
DISCONNECTED
FAINTHEARTED
FEEBLEMINDED
FLAMETHROWER
GALVANOMETER
GLOCKENSPIEL
GREATHEARTED
HAIRSPLITTER
HALLUCINOGEN
HANDKERCHIEF
HEAVYHEARTED
KINDERGARTEN
LIGHTHEARTED
MAGNETOMETER
MALNOURISHED
MANSLAUGHTER
MEALYMOUTHED
MINICOMPUTER
MISINTERPRET
MUDDLEHEADED
MULTICOLORED
MULTIFACETED
NIGHTCLOTHES
NONSCHEDULED
OFFICEHOLDER
OUTSTRETCHED
PICKERELWEED
POLICYHOLDER
PRACTITIONER
PREAMPLIFIER
PRECONCERTED
PUMPERNICKEL
SCHOOLMASTER
SENSITOMETER
SHARECROPPER
SHARPSHOOTER
SHORTSIGHTED
SLEDGEHAMMER
SPECTROMETER
SPORTSWRITER
STEPDAUGHTER
STRAITJACKET
STREETWALKER
SUBCOMMITTEE
SUPERCHARGER
SWASHBUCKLER
TENDEROMETER
THOROUGHBRED
TRANQUILIZER
TROUBLEMAKER
UNACCUSTOMED
UNDERCLOTHES
UNDOCUMENTED

UNFREQUENTED
UNINTERESTED
UNPARALLELED
UNPRINCIPLED
UNRESTRAINED
UNSEGREGATED
VALENCIENNES
WHOLEHEARTED
QUARTERSTAFF
TRANSMOGRIFY
ANTHROPOLOGY
BACTERIOLOGY
BREAKTHROUGH
CHITTERLINGS
DISADVANTAGE
HEARTSTRINGS
METALANGUAGE
MICROBIOLOGY
PALEONTOLOGY
PARASITOLOGY
PHARMACOLOGY
STRAIGHTEDGE
SURROUNDINGS
AFORETHOUGHT
AFTERTHOUGHT
BIBLIOGRAPHY
BIOGEOGRAPHY
CHOREOGRAPHY
CRYPTOGRAPHY
LEXICOGRAPHY
MIDDLEWEIGHT
OCEANOGRAPHY
PHYSIOGRAPHY
SELENOGRAPHY
STRATIGRAPHY
WELTERWEIGHT
ZOOGEOGRAPHY
ALPHANUMERIC
ANTIMAGNETIC
APPENDICITIS
AVITAMINOSIS
CHAMPIONSHIP
CHIROPRACTIC
COUNTERCLAIM
DECALCOMANIA
DECASYLLABIC
DICTATORSHIP
ECCLESIASTIC
ELECTROLYSIS
ENCEPHALITIS
ENCYCLOPEDIA
FRANKENSTEIN
HELIOCENTRIC
HIEROGLYPHIC
HYPOCHONDRIA
HYPOGLYCEMIA
INTERVOCALIC
MICROCIRCUIT
MULTIVITAMIN
NEURASTHENIA
OCTOSYLLABIC
ONOMATOPEIA
PANCHROMATIC
PHILHARMONIC
POLYSYLLABIC
POSTHYPNOTIC
PROPHYLACTIC
PSYCHOTROPIC
RECEIVERSHIP
RELATIONSHIP
RELATIVISTIC
STEREOPHONIC
STEREOSCOPIC
STREPTOMYCIN
TRANSOCEANIC
TRANSPACIFIC
TRIGNOMETRIC
TUBERCULOSIS
UNSCIENTIFIC
BREASTSTROKE
MARLINESPIKE
MASTERSTROKE
ANTIPARTICLE
AUDIOVISUALS
CHESTERFIELD
COMMUNICABLE
CONSIDERABLE
CONTEMPTIBLE
DEMONSTRABLE
DESTRUCTIBLE
DETERMINABLE
DISAGREEABLE
DISREPUTABLE
IMMEASURABLE
IMPENETRABLE
IMPERISHABLE
IMPONDERABLE
INCALCULABLE
INCOMPARABLE
INCOMPATIBLE
INCONSOLABLE
INCORRIGIBLE
INDECLINABLE
INDEFEASIBLE
INDIGESTIBLE
INDISPUTABLE
INDISSOLUBLE
INEFFACEABLE
INEXPLICABLE
INEXTRICABLE
INSUFFERABLE
INTELLIGIBLE
INTERMINABLE
INVULNERABLE
IRREDEEMABLE
IRREFRAGABLE
IRREMEDIABLE
IRRESISTIBLE
IRREVERSIBLE
MADEMOISELLE
MERCHANTABLE
MONOSYLLABLE
OTHERWORLDLY
POLYSYLLABLE
PROGRAMMABLE
QUESTIONABLE
RESPECTIVELY
SARSAPARILLA
TRADESPEOPLE
UNASSAILABLE
UNBELIEVABLE
UNCHARITABLE
UNGOVERNABLE
UNMISTAKABLE
UNPROFITABLE
UNREASONABLE
UNSEARCHABLE
UNSEASONABLE
WHIPPOORWILL
APPENDECTOMY
HYSTERECTOMY
ANTIALIASING
BACKTRACKING
BLANDISHMENT
BLOCKBUSTING
BLOODLETTING
BLUESTOCKING
BRAINWASHING
BREATHTAKING
BRILLIANTINE
CHEESEPARING
CHILDBEARING
COMMENCEMENT
CONCELEBRANT
CORESPONDENT
COUNTERPOINT
CROSSCURRENT
DECONGESTANT
DEMIMONDAINE
DISPLACEMENT
EARSPLITTING
EARTHSHAKING
ENTERPRISING
EQUESTRIENNE
EVERBLOOMING
EXCRUCIATING
FREESTANDING
GLASSBLOWING
HEARTRENDING
HEARTWARMING
HOUSEWARMING
IMPERCIPIENT
INCANDESCENT
INCONVENIENT
INGRATIATING
INSUFFICIENT
INTERMITTENT
INTRANSIGENT
MAGNILOQUENT
MICROSPACING
MISAPPREHEND
MISREPRESENT
MONOFILAMENT
MULLIGATAWNY
MULTIPLICAND
MULTITASKING
NEWSMAGAZINE
NONCOMBATANT
OXYACETYLENE
PEACEKEEPING
POLYETHYLENE
PREDETERMINE
PRESENTIMENT
RECALCITRANT
SUBCONTINENT
TESTOSTERONE
THANKSGIVING
TRANSCENDENT
TRAPSHOOTING
ULTRAMONTANE
UNDERCOATING
UNDERCURRENT
UNDERGARMENT
UNDERPINNING
UNEMPLOYMENT
VACATIONLAND
ABBREVIATION
ALLITERATION
ANNUNCIATION
ANTIELECTRON
CIVILIZATION
CONFIRMATION
CONFORMATION
CONGREGATION
CONQUISTADOR
CONSERVATION
CONSTIPATION
CONSTITUTION
CONSTRUCTION
CONTINUATION
CONVERSATION
COUNTERTENOR
DECOMMISSION
DENOMINATION
DENUNCIATION
DESPOLIATION
DISPENSATION
DISQUISITION
DISSERTATION
DISTILLATION
ECHOLOCATION
FENESTRATION
FERMENTATION
FIBRILLATION
FLUOROCARBON
GOBBLEDYGOOK
HYPERTENSION
ILLUSTRATION
IMPERFECTION
INCRUSTATION
INFLAMMATION
INSURRECTION
INTERCESSION
INTERJECTION
INTERLOCUTOR
INTERMISSION
INTERSECTION
JURISDICTION
MALFORMATION
MALNUTRITION
MALOCCLUSION
MASTURBATION
MENSTRUATION
MULTISESSION
NEIGHBORHOOD
NONCONDUCTOR
ORGANIZATION
PERAMBULATOR
PERICYNTHION
PHILODENDRON
PIGMENTATION
POLARIZATION
PRECONDITION
PREDIGESTION
PREDILECTION
PREINDUCTION
PRESCRIPTION
PRIMOGENITOR
PROLEGOMENON
PROTHALAMION
RECOLLECTION
REGISTRATION
REMUNERATION
RENUNCIATION
REPERCUSSION
RESURRECTION
RHODODENDRON
SATISFACTION
SCHOOLFELLOW
SPERMATOZOON
SUBSCRIPTION
SUPERSTITION
TRANSMISSION
UNLIKELIHOOD
VALORIZATION
WEATHERPROOF
CHEMOTHERAPY
HYDROTHERAPY
KALEIDOSCOPE
OSCILLOSCOPE
PHILANTHROPY
RADIOISOTOPE
RADIOTHERAPY
SPECTROGRAPH
SPECTROSCOPE
ARCHITECTURE
BIOCHEMISTRY
BIOTELEMETRY
CHECKERBERRY
CHECKERBOARD
CHROMOSPHERE
CONSERVATORY
CONSTABULARY
CONTEMPORARY
DISCIPLINARY
ELEEMOSYNARY
EXTRASENSORY
GEOCHEMISTRY
HABERDASHERY
HEADQUARTERS
HENCEFORWARD
HORTICULTURE
INFLAMMATORY
INFLATIONARY
INTERMEDIARY
MESSEIGNEURS
MICROSURGERY
MISADVENTURE
NOMENCLATURE
OVEREXPOSURE
PARAMILITARY
PENITENTIARY
PERADVENTURE
PHOTOGRAVURE
PLASTERBOARD
SATISFACTORY
SHUFFLEBOARD
STRATOSPHERE
SUBDIRECTORY
SUBMINIATURE
SUBSTRUCTURE
TERCENTENARY
THERMOSPHERE
THOROUGHFARE
THUNDERSTORM
TRIGONOMETRY
UNDERDRAWERS
VENIPUNCTURE
WEATHERBOARD
ABOLITIONISM
CLOTHESHORSE
CLOTHESPRESS

COLLECTIVISM
CONFUCIANISM
CONSERVATISM
CONTRARIWISE
COUNTERPOISE
DIASTROPHISM
DISESTABLISH
DISFRANCHISE
FRANKINCENSE
HEADMISTRESS
IDIOSYNCRASY
INFLATIONISM
ISOLATIONISM
MEETINGHOUSE
METAMORPHISM
MULTIPURPOSE
NEVERTHELESS
OBSCURANTISM
PACKINGHOUSE
PHOTOCOMPOSE
POLYMORPHISM
POSTMISTRESS
PREPAREDNESS
RECEPTIONIST
SOMNAMBULISM
SPIRITUALISM
STEEPLECHASE
TRANSVESTISM
UNIVERSALIST
WEATHERGLASS
AUTHENTICATE
BILLINGSGATE
BIOSATELLITE
BLATHERSKITE
BLOODTHIRSTY
CARBOHYDRATE
CHALCOPYRITE
CHRISTIANITY
CHROMATICITY
COELENTERATE
COLLEGIALITY
COMMENSURATE
COMMONWEALTH
CONGLOMERATE
CONGRATULATE
DISASSOCIATE
DISCONSOLATE
DISCRIMINATE
DISINTEGRATE
ELECTROPLATE
EXTORTIONATE
HELLGRAMMITE
HYPERACIDITY
ILLEGITIMATE
INARTICULATE
INCAPACITATE
INDOCTRINATE

INTERMEDIATE
INVERTEBRATE
LUNCHEONETTE
MICROCLIMATE
MISCALCULATE
MULTIPLICITY
MULTIVERSITY
MUNICIPALITY
PERSPICACITY
POSTGRADUATE
PREDESIGNATE
PREFABRICATE
PREPONDERATE
PREREQUISITE
PRINCIPALITY
PROTECTORATE
RECAPITULATE
RECONSTITUTE
REHABILITATE
SECRETARIATE
SUBSTANTIATE
SUPERANNUATE
TECHNICALITY
TRANSMIGRATE
UNIVERSALITY
UNREGENERATE
VERTICILLATE
ADVENTITIOUS
AMBIDEXTROUS
ARGILLACEOUS
ASYNCHRONOUS
CANTANKEROUS
CARBONACEOUS
CARILLONNEUR
CINEMATHEQUE
CONTEMPTUOUS
CONTERMINOUS
CONTUMACIOUS
CONTUMELIOUS
CUMULONIMBUS
DISCOURTEOUS
DISINGENUOUS
DISPUTATIOUS
ENTREPRENEUR
EPITHALAMIUM
HIPPOPOTAMUS
INFELICITOUS
INSALUBRIOUS
MERETRICIOUS
MULTIFARIOUS
OBSTREPEROUS
PERTINACIOUS
PRASEODYMIUM
PRECANCEROUS
PREPOSTEROUS
PRESUMPTUOUS
PROTACTINIUM

RAMBUNCTIOUS
RESTAURATEUR
SIMULTANEOUS
SUBCONSCIOUS
SUBCUTANEOUS
SUPERCILIOUS
THUNDERCLOUD
UNSCRUPULOUS
VAINGLORIOUS
APPRECIATIVE
APPREHENSIVE
CONSERVATIVE
CONSTITUTIVE
DELIBERATIVE
DISTRIBUTIVE
ILLUSTRATIVE
IMPERCEPTIVE
INTRANSITIVE
IRRESPECTIVE
NONOBJECTIVE
PHOTOENGRAVE
PREOPERATIVE
PSYCHOACTIVE
QUANTITATIVE
REMUNERATIVE
ANATHEMATIZE
APOSTROPHIZE
ATTITUDINIZE
CHARACTERIZE
CHRISTIANIZE
COLLECTIVIZE
CONTAINERIZE
DEMILITARIZE
DEMINERALIZE
EDITORIALIZE
EXTRAVAGANZA
PARENTHESIZE
PHILOSOPHIZE
PORCELAINIZE
PROPAGANDIZE
UNIVERSALIZE

## 12TH LETTER

DECALCOMANIA
ENCYCLOPEDIA
EXTRAVAGANZA
HYPOCHONDRIA
HYPOGLYCEMIA
NEURASTHENIA
ONOMATOPOEIA
SARSAPARILLA
ALPHANUMERIC
ANTIMAGNETIC
CHIROPRACTIC

DECASYLLABIC
ECCLESIASTIC
HELIOCENTRIC
HIEROGLYPHIC
INTERVOCALIC
OCTOSYLLABIC
PANCHROMATIC
PHILHARMONIC
POLYSYLLABIC
POSTHYPNOTIC
PROPHYLACTIC
PSYCHOTROPIC
RELATIVISTIC
STEREOPHONIC
STEREOSCOPIC
TRANSOCEANIC
TRANSPACIFIC
TRIGNOMETRIC
UNSCIENTIFIC
ABSENTMINDED
ACCOMPLISHED
CHECKERBOARD
CHESTERFIELD
CLOSEMOUTHED
DISCONNECTED
FAINTHEARTED
FEEBLEMINDED
FOUNTAINHEAD
GREATHEARTED
HEAVYHEARTED
HENCEFORWARD
LIGHTHEARTED
MALNOURISHED
MEALYMOUTHED
MISAPPREHEND
MUDDLEHEADED
MULTICOLORED
MULTIFACETED
MULTIPLICAND
NEIGHBORHOOD
NONSCHEDULED
OUTSTRETCHED
PICKERELWEED
PLASTERBOARD
PRECONCERTED
SHORTSIGHTED
SHUFFLEBOARD
THOROUGHBRED
THUNDERCLOUD
UNACCUSTOMED
UNDOCUMENTED
UNFREQUENTED
UNINTERESTED
UNLIKELIHOOD
UNPARALLELED
UNPRINCIPLED
UNRESTRAINED

UNSEGREGATED
VACATIONLAND
WEATHERBOARD
WHOLEHEARTED
ACQUAINTANCE
ANATHEMATIZE
ANTIPARTICLE
APOSTROPHIZE
APPRECIATIVE
APPREHENSIVE
APPURTENANCE
ARCHITECTURE
ATTITUDINIZE
AUTHENTICATE
BILLINGSGATE
BIOSATELLITE
BLATHERSKITE
BREASTSTROKE
BRILLIANTINE
CARBOHYDRATE
CHALCOPYRITE
CHARACTERIZE
CHRISTIANIZE
CHROMOSPHERE
CINEMATHEQUE
CIRCUMSCRIBE
CIRCUMSTANCE
CLOTHESHORSE
COELENTERATE
COLLECTIVIZE
COMMENSURATE
COMMUNICABLE
COMPLAISANCE
CONCRESCENCE
CONGLOMERATE
CONGRATULATE
CONSERVATIVE
CONSIDERABLE
CONSTITUTIVE
CONTAINERIZE
CONTEMPTIBLE
CONTRARIWISE
COUNTERPOISE
DELIBERATIVE
DEMILITARIZE
DEMIMONDAINE
DEMINERALIZE
DEMONSTRABLE
DESTRUCTIBLE
DETERMINABLE
DISACCHARIDE
DISADVANTAGE
DISAGREEABLE
DISASSOCIATE
DISCONSOLATE
DISCRIMINATE
DISFRANCHISE

DISINTEGRATE
DISOBEDIENCE
DISREPUTABLE
DISTRIBUTIVE
EDITORIALIZE
ELECTROPLATE
EQUESTRIENNE
EXTORTIONATE
FLUORESCENCE
FORMALDEHYDE
FRANKINCENSE
FRONTISPIECE
HELLGRAMMITE
HORTICULTURE
ILLEGITIMATE
ILLUSTRATIVE
IMMEASURABLE
IMPENETRABLE
IMPERCEPTIVE
IMPERISHABLE
IMPONDERABLE
INARTICULATE
INCALCULABLE
INCAPACITATE
INCOMPARABLE
INCOMPATIBLE
INCONSOLABLE
INCORRIGIBLE
INDECLINABLE
INDEFEASIBLE
INDEPENDENCE
INDIGESTIBLE
INDISPUTABLE
INDISSOLUBLE
INDOCTRINATE
INEFFACEABLE
INEXPERIENCE
INEXPLICABLE
INEXTRICABLE
INSUFFERABLE
INTELLIGENCE
INTELLIGIBLE
INTEMPERANCE
INTERFERENCE
INTERMEDIATE
INTERMINABLE
INTRANSITIVE
INVERTEBRATE
INVULNERABLE
IRREDEEMABLE
IRREFRAGABLE
IRREMEDIABLE
IRRESISTIBLE
IRRESPECTIVE
IRREVERSIBLE
KALEIDOSCOPE
LUMINESCENCE

LUNCHEONETTE
MADEMOISELLE
MARLINESPIKE
MASTERSTROKE
MEETINGHOUSE
MERCHANTABLE
METALANGUAGE
MICROCLIMATE
MISADVENTURE
MISCALCULATE
MISPRONOUNCE
MONOSYLLABLE
MOUNTAINSIDE
MULTIPURPOSE
NEUROSCIENCE
NEWSMAGAZINE
NOMENCLATURE
NONOBJECTIVE
OSCILLOSCOPE
OVEREXPOSURE
OXYACETYLENE
PACKINGHOUSE
PARENTHESIZE
PERADVENTURE
PHILOSOPHIZE
PHOTOCOMPOSE
PHOTOENGRAVE
PHOTOGRAVURE
POLYETHYLENE
POLYSYLLABLE
PORCELAINIZE
POSTGRADUATE
PREDESIGNATE
PREDETERMINE
PREFABRICATE
PREOPERATIVE
PREPONDERATE
PREREQUISITE
PROGRAMMABLE
PROPAGANDIZE
PROTECTORATE
PROTUBERANCE
PSYCHOACTIVE
QUANTITATIVE
QUESTIONABLE
QUINTESSENCE
RADIOISOTOPE
RECAPITULATE
RECOGNIZANCE
RECONSTITUTE
REHABILITATE
REMINISCENCE
REMONSTRANCE
REMUNERATIVE
SECRETARIATE
SIGNIFICANCE
SPECTROSCOPE
STEEPLECHASE
STRAIGHTEDGE
STRATOSPHERE
SUBCOMMITTEE
SUBMINIATURE
SUBSERVIENCE
SUBSTANTIATE
SUBSTRUCTURE
SUPERANNUATE
SURVEILLANCE
TESTOSTERONE
THERMOSPHERE
THOROUGHFARE
TRADESPEOPLE
TRANSFERENCE
TRANSMIGRATE
ULTRAMONTANE
UNASSAILABLE
UNBELIEVABLE
UNCHARITABLE
UNDERSURFACE
UNGOVERNABLE
UNIVERSALIZE
UNMISTAKABLE
UNPROFITABLE
UNREASONABLE
UNREGENERATE
UNSEARCHABLE
UNSEASONABLE
VENIPUNCTURE
VERTICILLATE
HANDKERCHIEF
QUARTERSTAFF
WEATHERPROOF
ANTIALIASING
BACKTRACKING
BLOCKBUSTING
BLOODLETTING
BLUESTOCKING
BRAINWASHING
BREATHTAKING
CHEESEPARING
CHILDBEARING
EARSPLITTING
EARTHSHAKING
ENTERPRISING
EVERBLOOMING
EXCRUCIATING
FREESTANDING
GLASSBLOWING
HEARTRENDING
HEARTWARMING
HOUSEWARMING
INGRATIATING
MICROSPACING
MULTITASKING
PEACEKEEPING
THANKSGIVING
TRAPSHOOTING
UNDERCOATING
UNDERPINNING
BREAKTHROUGH
BUTTERSCOTCH
COMMONWEALTH
DISESTABLISH
SPECTROGRAPH
GOBBLEDYGOOK
ANTITHETICAL
ASTRONOMICAL
BACTERICIDAL
BICENTENNIAL
CONFESSIONAL
CONFIDENTIAL
CONTRAPUNTAL
CONVENTIONAL
DIFFERENTIAL
EXTRAMARITAL
GLOCKENSPIEL
HETEROSEXUAL
HIERARCHICAL
HYDROTHERMAL
INSTRUMENTAL
INTELLECTUAL
INTERGLACIAL
INVITATIONAL
LONGITUDINAL
MULTILATERAL
MULTILINGUAL
NONCOMMITTAL
PARADISIACAL
PESTILENTIAL
PLANETESIMAL
POSTDOCTORAL
PREMENSTRUAL
PROCATHEDRAL
PROCESSIONAL
PROFESSIONAL
PROPORTIONAL
PROVIDENTIAL
PSYCHOSEXUAL
PUMPERNICKEL
SCATOLOGICAL
SUPERNATURAL
WHIPPOORWILL
ABOLITIONISM
COLLECTIVISM
CONFUCIANISM
CONSERVATISM
COUNTERCLAIM
DIASTROPHISM
EPITHALAMIUM
INFLATIONISM
ISOLATIONISM
METAMORPHISM
OBSCURANTISM
POLYMORPHISM
PRASEODYMIUM
PROTACTINIUM
SOMNAMBULISM
SPIRITUALISM
THUNDERSTORM
TRANSVESTISM
ABBREVIATION
ALLITERATION
ANNUNCIATION
ANTEDILUVIAN
ANTIELECTRON
AUSTRONESIAN
CHURCHWARDEN
CIVILIZATION
CONFIRMATION
CONFORMATION
CONGREGATION
CONSERVATION
CONSTIPATION
CONSTITUTION
CONSTRUCTION
CONTINUATION
CONVERSATION
COSMOPOLITAN
DECOMMISSION
DELICATESSEN
DENOMINATION
DENUNCIATION
DESPOLIATION
DISPENSATION
DISQUISITION
DISSERTATION
DISTILLATION
ECHOLOCATION
EPISCOPALIAN
FENESTRATION
FERMENTATION
FIBRILLATION
FLUOROCARBON
FRANKENSTEIN
HALLUCINOGEN
HUMANITARIAN
HYPERTENSION
ILLUSTRATION
IMPERFECTION
INCRUSTATION
INFLAMMATION
INSURRECTION
INTERCESSION
INTERJECTION
INTERMISSION
INTERSECTION
JURISDICTION
KINDERGARTEN
LONGSHOREMAN
MALFORMATION
MALNUTRITION
MALOCCLUSION
MASTURBATION
MENSTRUATION
MULTISESSION
MULTIVITAMIN
NEWSPAPERMAN
NONAGENARIAN
OCTOGENARIAN
ORGANIZATION
PERICYNTHION
PHILODENDRON
PIGMENTATION
POLARIZATION
PRECONDITION
PREDIGESTION
PREDILECTION
PREINDUCTION
PRESBYTERIAN
PRESCRIPTION
PROLEGOMENON
PROTHALAMION
RECOLLECTION
REGISTRATION
REMUNERATION
RENUNCIATION
REPERCUSSION
RESURRECTION
RHODODENDRON
SATISFACTION
SCANDINAVIAN
SEXAGENARIAN
SPERMATOZOON
STREPTOMYCIN
SUBSCRIPTION
SUBTERRANEAN
SUPERSTITION
TOTALITARIAN
TRANSMISSION
VALORIZATION
VETERINARIAN
CHAMPIONSHIP
DICTATORSHIP
RECEIVERSHIP
RELATIONSHIP
AMPHITHEATER
ANTIMACASSAR
CABINETMAKER
CARILLONNEUR
CARPETBAGGER
CHEESEBURGER
COMMISSIONER
CONFECTIONER
CONQUISTADOR
COUNTERTENOR
DENSITOMETER
ENTREPRENEUR
FLAMETHROWER
GALVANOMETER
HAIRSPLITTER
INTERLOCUTOR
INTERSTELLAR
MAGNETOMETER
MANSLAUGHTER
MINICOMPUTER
NONCONDUCTOR
OFFICEHOLDER
PERAMBULATOR
POLICYHOLDER
PRACTITIONER
PREAMPLIFIER
PRIMOGENITOR
RESTAURATEUR
SCHOOLMASTER
SENSITOMETER
SHARECROPPER
SHARPSHOOTER
SLEDGEHAMMER
SPECTROMETER
SPORTSWRITER
STEPDAUGHTER
STREETWALKER
SUPERCHARGER
SWASHBUCKLER
TENDEROMETER
TRANQUILIZER
TROUBLEMAKER
ADVENTITIOUS
AERODYNAMICS
AMBIDEXTROUS
APPENDICITIS
ARGILLACEOUS
ASTRONAUTICS
ASTROPHYSICS
ASYNCHRONOUS
ATMOSPHERICS
AUDIOVISUALS
AVITAMINOSIS
CALISTHENICS
CANTANKEROUS
CARBONACEOUS
CHITTERLINGS
CLOTHESPRESS
CONTEMPTUOUS
CONTERMINOUS
CONTUMACIOUS
CONTUMELIOUS
CUMULONIMBUS
DISCOURTEOUS
DISINGENUOUS
DISPUTATIOUS
ELECTROLYSIS
ENCEPHALITIS

HEADMISTRESS
HEADQUARTERS
HEARTSTRINGS
HIPPOPOTAMUS
INFELICITOUS
INSALUBRIOUS
MERETRICIOUS
MESSEIGNEURS
MULTIFARIOUS
NEVERTHELESS
NIGHTCLOTHES
OBSTREPEROUS
PERTINACIOUS
POSTMISTRESS
PRECANCEROUS
PREPAREDNESS
PREPOSTEROUS
PRESUMPTUOUS
PYROTECHNICS
RAMBUNCTIOUS
SIMULTANEOUS
SUBCONSCIOUS
SUBCUTANEOUS
SUPERCILIOUS
SURROUNDINGS
THERAPEUTICS
TUBERCULOSIS
UNDERCLOTHES
UNDERDRAWERS
UNSCRUPULOUS
VAINGLORIOUS
VALENCIENNES
WEATHERGLASS
AFORETHOUGHT
AFTERTHOUGHT
BLANDISHMENT
COMMENCEMENT
COMMISSARIAT
CONCELEBRANT
CORESPONDENT
COUNTERPOINT
CROSSCURRENT
DECONGESTANT
DISPLACEMENT
IMPERCIPIENT
INCANDESCENT
INCONVENIENT
INSUFFICIENT
INTERMITTENT
INTRANSIGENT
MAGNILOQUENT
MICROCIRCUIT
MIDDLEWEIGHT
MISINTERPRET
MISREPRESENT
MONOFILAMENT
NONCOMBATANT
PRESENTIMENT
RECALCITRANT
RECEPTIONIST
STRAITJACKET
SUBCONTINENT
TRANSCENDENT
UNDERCURRENT
UNDERGARMENT
UNEMPLOYMENT
UNIVERSALIST
WELTERWEIGHT
SCHOOLFELLOW
ANTHROPOLOGY
APPENDECTOMY
BACTERIOLOGY
BELLIGERENCY
BIBLIOGRAPHY
BIOCHEMISTRY
BIOGEOGRAPHY
BIOTELEMETRY
BLOODTHIRSTY
CHECKERBERRY
CHEMOTHERAPY
CHOREOGRAPHY
CHRISTIANITY
CHROMATICITY
COLLEGIALITY
COMPANIONWAY
CONSERVATORY
CONSTABULARY
CONSTITUENCY
CONTEMPORARY
CRYPTOGRAPHY
DISCIPLINARY
ELEEMOSYNARY
EXTRASENSORY
GEOCHEMISTRY
HABERDASHERY
HYDROTHERAPY
HYPERACIDITY
HYSTERECTOMY
IDIOSYNCRASY
INFLAMMATORY
INFLATIONARY
INTERMEDIARY
LEXICOGRAPHY
MICROBIOLOGY
MICROSURGERY
MULLIGATAWNY
MULTIPLICITY
MULTIVERSITY
MUNICIPALITY
OCEANOGRAPHY
OTHERWORLDLY
PALEONTOLOGY
PARAMILITARY
PARASITOLOGY
PENITENTIARY
PERSPICACITY
PHARMACOLOGY
PHILANTHROPY
PHYSIOGRAPHY
PRECIPITANCY
PRINCIPALITY
RADIOTHERAPY
RESPECTIVELY
SATISFACTORY
SELENOGRAPHY
STRAIGHTAWAY
STRATIGRAPHY
SUBDIRECTORY
SUPERHIGHWAY
TECHNICALITY
TERCENTENARY
TRANSMOGRIFY
TRIGONOMETRY
UNIVERSALITY
ZOOGEOGRAPHY

# 13 LETTER WORDS

**1st Letter**

ACCELEROMETER
ACCOMMODATING
ACCOMMODATION
ACCOMPANIMENT
ACCULTURATION
ACETYLCHOLINE
ADMINISTRATOR
ADVENTURESOME
ADVERTISEMENT
AFFORESTATION
AGGIORNAMENTO
AMNIOCENTESIS
ANTICOAGULANT
ANTIFERTILITY
ANTIHISTAMINE
ANTILOGARITHM
ANTIPERSONNEL
ANTIPOLLUTION
APPROPRIATION
ARCHIMANDRITE
ARCHITECTONIC
ARGUMENTATION
ARGUMENTATIVE
AUTHORITARIAN
AUTHORITATIVE
AUTOBIOGRAPHY
AUTOCHTHONOUS
BACCALAUREATE
BACTERIOPHAGE
BIODEGRADABLE
BLOODCURDLING
BOARDINGHOUSE
BOUILLABAISSE
BROKENHEARTED
CARBONIFEROUS
CERTIFICATION
CHRISTMASTIDE
CHRYSANTHEMUM
CINEMATOGRAPH
CIRCUMABULATE
CIRCUMFERENCE
CLEARINGHOUSE
COLLOQUIALISM
COMMEMORATIVE
COMMENSURABLE
COMMERCIALISM
COMMERCIALIZE
COMMUNICATION
COMPLIMENTARY
CONCATENATION
CONCENTRATION
CONCEPTUALIZE
CONCERTMASTER
CONCUPISCENCE
CONFABULATION
CONFECTIONERY
CONFEDERATION
CONFIGURATION
CONFLAGRATION
CONFRATERNITY
CONSANGUINITY
CONSCIENTIOUS
CONSEQUENTIAL
CONSIDERATION
CONSTELLATION
CONSTERNATION
CONTAINERSHIP
CONTORTIONIST
CONTRACEPTION
CORRESPONDENT
COSMETOLOGIST
COUNTERATTACK
COUNTERWEIGHT
COUNTINGHOUSE
DAGUERREOTYPE
DECONTAMINATE
DEHYDROGENATE
DEMONSTRATIVE
DETERMINATION
DIFFERENTIATE
DISINTERESTED
DISPASSIONATE
DISPROPORTION
DISTINGUISHED
EFFLORESCENCE
ELECTROLOGIST
ELECTROMAGNET
ELEPHANTIASIS
ESTABLISHMENT
EUROPOCENTRIC
EXCEPTIONABLE
EXCOMMUNICATE
EXHIBITIONISM
EXPEDITIONARY
EXPRESSIONISM
EXTRAGALACTIC
EXTRAORDINARY
FEATHERWEIGHT
FERROMAGNETIC
FRAGMENTATION
GENERALISSIMO
GENITOURINARY
GEOCHRONOLOGY
GEOMORPHOLOGY
GEOSTATIONARY
GONADOTROPHIC
GONADOTROPHIN
GRANDDAUGHTER
GRANTSMANSHIP
GUBERNATORIAL
HALLUCINATION
HEARTBREAKING
HERMAPHRODITE
HETEROGENEOUS
HOUSEBREAKING
HUNDREDWEIGHT
HYDROCEPHALUS
HYDRODYNAMICS
HYDROELECTRIC
HYPERCRITICAL
HYPERDOCUMENT
IMPERCEPTIBLE
IMPERMISSIBLE
IMPERTURBABLE
IMPRACTICABLE
IMPRESSIONISM
IMPRESSIONIST
INAPPRECIABLE
INCOMBUSTIBLE
INCOMMUNICADO
INCONSIDERATE
INCONSPICUOUS
INCONTESTABLE
INCONVENIENCE
INCORRUPTIBLE
INDEFATIGABLE
INDESCRIBABLE
INDETERMINATE
INDISPENSABLE
INDIVIDUALISM
INDIVIDUALIST
INDIVIDUALITY
INDIVIDUALIZE
INDUSTRIALIST
INDUSTRIALIZE
INEXHAUSTIBLE
INEXPRESSIBLE
INFINITESIMAL
INFLORESCENCE
INSECTIVOROUS
INSTANTANEOUS
INSUBORDINATE
INSUBSTANTIAL
INSUPPORTABLE
INTERCULTURAL
INTERGALACTIC
INTERLOCUTORY
INTERMARRIAGE
INTERNATIONAL
INTERPERSONAL
INTERROGATIVE
INTERROGATORY
INTRAMUSCULAR
INTRANSIGENCE
INTROSPECTION
IRRECLAIMABLE
IRRECOVERABLE
IRREPLACEABLE
IRREPRESSIBLE
IRRESPONSIBLE
IRRETRIEVABLE
JOLLIFICATION
JURISPRUDENCE
JUSTIFICATION
KAFFEEKLATSCH
KNOWLEDGEABLE
LACKADAISICAL
LAUGHINGSTOCK
MACHICOLATION
MAGNETOSPHERE
MALADMINISTER
MANIFESTATION
METAMORPHOSIS
MICROCOMPUTER
MICROORGANISM
MISALLOCATION
MISCEGENATION
MISCELLANEOUS
MISUNDERSTAND
MONOCHROMATIC
MONOCOTYLEDON
MONONUCLEOSIS
MULTINATIONAL
NITRIFICATION
NITROGLYCERIN
NONCONFORMIST
NONINTERLACED
NONRESISTANCE
OLEOMARGARINE
OPHTHALMOLOGY
ORTHONDONTICS
OVERQUALIFIED
OVERSUBSCRIBE
PARALLELOGRAM
PARAPHERNALIA
PARTICULARIZE
PATERFAMILIAS
PEREGRINATION
PERFECTIONIST
PERPENDICULAR
PETROCHEMICAL
PHARMACOPOEIA
PHENOBARBITAL
PHOTOCHEMICAL
PHOTOELECTRIC
PHOTOELECTRON
PHOTOEMISSION
PHYSIOTHERAPY
POLIOMYELITIS
POSTOPERATIVE
PRECIPITATION
PREOCCUPATION
PREPOSSESSING
PREPOSSESSION
PRETERNATURAL
PRIMOGENITURE
PROCRASTINATE
PROFESSORIATE
PROGNOSTICATE
PROJECTIONIST
PRONOUNCEMENT
PRONUNCIATION
PROTECTIONIST
PSYCHOSOMATIC
PSYCHOTHERAPY
PUSILLANIMOUS
QUADRILATERAL
QUADRIPARTITE
QUADRUPLICATE
QUALIFICATION
QUARTERMASTER
QUESTIONNAIRE
QUINTUPLICATE
RADIOACTIVITY
RAPPROCHEMENT
RATIOCINATION
RECRUDESCENCE
REINCARNATION
REPREHENSIBLE
REVOLUTIONARY
REVOLUTIONIST
REVOLUTIONIZE
ROENTGENOLOGY
SANCTIMONIOUS
SCANDALMONGER
SCHIZOPHRENIA
SCHOOLTEACHER
SEMIAUTOMATIC
SEMICONDUCTOR
SEMIPERMEABLE
SOPHISTICATED
SPECIFICATION
STRANGULATION
STREPTOCOCCUS
STRIKEBREAKER
SUBDISCIPLINE
SULFANILAMIDE
SUPERABUNDANT
SUPERCOMPUTER
SUPERNUMERARY
SUPRANATIONAL
SURREPTITIOUS
SYLLABICATION
TABLESPOONFUL
TENDERHEARTED
TERCENTENNIAL
THENCEFORWARD
THERMONUCLEAR
THERMOPLASTIC
THOROUGHGOING
THUNDERSHOWER
THUNDERSTRUCK
TONSILLECTOMY
TORTOISESHELL
TRANSATLANTIC
TRANSCRIPTION
TRANSISTORIZE
TRANSNATIONAL
TURBOELECTRIC
UNACCOMPANIED
UNACCOUNTABLE
UNADULTERATED
UNCEREMONIOUS
UNCIRCUMCISED
UNCOMFORTABLE
UNCONDITIONAL
UNCONDITIONED
UNCONQUERABLE
UNDERACHIEVER
UNDERCARRIAGE
UNDERCLASSMAN
UNDERCLOTHING
UNDEREMPLOYED
UNDERESTIMATE

UNDERGRADUATE
UNDERSTANDING
UNFORGETTABLE
UNIMPEACHABLE
UNINTELLIGENT
UNINTENTIONAL
UNINTERRUPTED
UNMENTIONABLE
UNNECESSARILY
UNPRECEDENTED
UNPREDICTABLE
UNPRETENTIOUS
UNQUESTIONING
UNSUBSTANTIAL
UNWARRANTABLE
UPPERCLASSMAN
VALEDICTORIAN
VENTRILOQUISM
VERSIFICATION
VOCATIONALISM
WHITHERSOEVER
WOOLGATHERING

## 2nd Letter

BACCALAUREATE
BACTERIOPHAGE
CARBONIFEROUS
DAGUERREOTYPE
HALLUCINATION
KAFFEEKLATSCH
LACKADAISICAL
LAUGHINGSTOCK
MACHICOLATION
MAGNETOSPHERE
MALADMINISTER
MANIFESTATION
PARALLELOGRAM
PARAPHERNALIA
PARTICULARIZE
PATERFAMILIAS
RADIOACTIVITY
RAPPROCHEMENT
RATIOCINATION
SANCTIMONIOUS
TABLESPOONFUL
VALEDICTORIAN
ACCELEROMETER
ACCOMMODATING
ACCOMMODATION
ACCOMPANIMENT
ACCULTURATION
ACETYLCHOLINE
SCANDALMONGER
SCHIZOPHRENIA
SCHOOLTEACHER
ADMINISTRATOR
ADVENTURESOME
ADVERTISEMENT
CERTIFICATION
DECONTAMINATE
DEHYDROGENATE
DEMONSTRATIVE
DETERMINATION
FEATHERWEIGHT
FERROMAGNETIC
GENERALISSIMO
GENITOURINARY
GEOCHRONOLOGY
GEOMORPHOLOGY
GEOSTATIONARY
HEARTBREAKING
HERMAPHRODITE
HETEROGENEOUS
METAMORPHOSIS
PEREGRINATION
PERFECTIONIST
PERPENDICULAR
PETROCHEMICAL
RECRUDESCENCE
REINCARNATION
REPREHENSIBLE
REVOLUTIONARY
REVOLUTIONIST
REVOLUTIONIZE
SEMIAUTOMATIC
SEMICONDUCTOR
SEMIPERMEABLE
TENDERHEARTED
TERCENTENNIAL
VENTRILOQUISM
VERSIFICATION
AFFORESTATION
EFFLORESCENCE
AGGIORNAMENTO
CHRISTMASTIDE
CHRYSANTHEMUM
PHARMACOPOEIA
PHENOBARBITAL
PHOTOCHEMICAL
PHOTOELECTRIC
PHOTOELECTRON
PHOTOEMISSION
PHYSIOTHERAPY
THENCEFORWARD
THERMONUCLEAR
THERMOPLASTIC
THOROUGHGOING
THUNDERSHOWER
THUNDERSTRUCK
WHITHERSOEVER
BIODEGRADABLE
CINEMATOGRAPH
CIRCUMAMBULATE
CIRCUMFERENCE
DIFFERENTIATE
DISINTERESTED
DISPASSIONATE
DISPROPORTION
DISTINGUISHED
MICROCOMPUTER
MICROORGANISM
MISALLOCATION
MISCEGENATION
MISCELLANEOUS
MISUNDERSTAND
NITRIFICATION
NITROGLYCERIN
BLOODCURDLING
CLEARINGHOUSE
ELECTROLOGIST
ELECTROMAGNET
ELEPHANTIASIS
OLEOMARGARINE
AMNIOCENTESIS
IMPERCEPTIBLE
IMPERMISSIBLE
IMPERTURBABLE
IMPRACTICABLE
IMPRESSIONISM
IMPRESSIONIST
ANTICOAGULANT
ANTIFERTILITY
ANTIHISTAMINE
ANTILOGARITHM
ANTIPERSONNEL
ANTIPOLLUTION
INAPPRECIABLE
INCOMBUSTIBLE
INCOMMUNICADO
INCONSIDERATE
INCONSPICUOUS
INCONTESTABLE
INCONVENIENCE
INCORRUPTIBLE
INDEFATIGABLE
INDESCRIBABLE
INDETERMINATE
INDISPENSABLE
INDIVIDUALISM
INDIVIDUALIST
INDIVIDUALITY
INDIVIDUALIZE
INDUSTRIALIST
INDUSTRIALIZE
INEXHAUSTIBLE
INEXPRESSIBLE
INFINITESIMAL
INFLORESCENCE
INSECTIVOROUS
INSTANTANEOUS
INSUBORDINATE
INSUBSTANTIAL
INSUPPORTABLE
INTERCULTURAL
INTERGALACTIC
INTERLOCUTORY
INTERMARRIAGE
INTERNATIONAL
INTERPERSONAL
INTERROGATIVE
INTERROGATORY
INTRAMUSCULAR
INTRANSIGENCE
INTROSPECTION
KNOWLEDGEABLE
UNACCOMPANIED
UNACCOUNTABLE
UNADULTERATED
UNCEREMONIOUS
UNCIRCUMCISED
UNCOMFORTABLE
UNCONDITIONAL
UNCONDITIONED
UNCONQUERABLE
UNDERACHIEVER
UNDERCARRIAGE
UNDERCLASSMAN
UNDERCLOTHING
UNDEREMPLOYED
UNDERESTIMATE
UNDERGRADUATE
UNDERSTANDING
UNFORGETTABLE
UNIMPEACHABLE
UNINTELLIGENT
UNINTENTIONAL
UNINTERRUPTED
UNMENTIONABLE
UNNECESSARILY
UNPRECEDENTED
UNPREDICTABLE
UNPRETENTIOUS
UNQUESTIONING
UNSUBSTANTIAL
UNWARRANTABLE
BOARDINGHOUSE
BOUILLABAISSE
COLLOQUIALISM
COMMEMORATIVE
COMMENSURABLE
COMMERCIALISM
COMMERCIALIZE
COMMUNICATION
COMPLIMENTARY
CONCATENATION
CONCENTRATION
CONCEPTUALIZE
CONCERTMASTER
CONCUPISCENCE
CONFABULATION
CONFECTIONERY
CONFEDERATION
CONFIGURATION
CONFLAGRATION
CONFRATERNITY
CONSANGUINITY
CONSCIENTIOUS
CONSEQUENTIAL
CONSIDERATION
CONSTELLATION
CONSTERNATION
CONTAINERSHIP
CONTORTIONIST
CONTRACEPTION
CORRESPONDENT
COSMETOLOGIST
COUNTERATTACK
COUNTERWEIGHT
COUNTINGHOUSE
GONADOTROPHIC
GONADOTROPHIN
HOUSEBREAKING
JOLLIFICATION
MONOCHROMATIC
MONOCOTYLEDON
MONONUCLEOSIS
NONCONFORMIST
NONINTERLACED
NONRESISTANCE
POLIOMYELITIS
POSTOPERATIVE
ROENTGENOLOGY
SOPHISTICATED
TONSILLECTOMY
TORTOISESHELL
VOCATIONALISM
WOOLGATHERING
APPROPRIATION
OPHTHALMOLOGY
SPECIFICATION
UPPERCLASSMAN
ARCHIMANDRITE
ARCHITECTONIC
ARGUMENTATION
ARGUMENTATIVE
BROKENHEARTED
FRAGMENTATION
GRANDDAUGHTER
GRANTSMANSHIP
IRRECLAIMABLE
IRRECOVERABLE
IRREPLACEABLE
IRREPRESSIBLE
IRRESPONSIBLE
IRRETRIEVABLE
ORTHONDONTICS
PRECIPITATION
PREOCCUPATION
PREPOSSESSING
PREPOSSESSION
PRETERNATURAL
PRIMOGENITURE
PROCRASTINATE
PROFESSORIATE
PROGNOSTICATE
PROJECTIONIST
PRONOUNCEMENT
PRONUNCIATION
PROTECTIONIST
TRANSATLANTIC
TRANSCRIPTION
TRANSISTORIZE
TRANSNATIONAL
ESTABLISHMENT
PSYCHOSOMATIC
PSYCHOTHERAPY
STRANGULATION
STREPTOCOCCUS
STRIKEBREAKER
AUTHORITARIAN
AUTHORITATIVE
AUTOBIOGRAPHY
AUTOCHTHONOUS
EUROPOCENTRIC
GUBERNATORIAL
HUNDREDWEIGHT
JURISPRUDENCE
JUSTIFICATION
MULTINATIONAL
PUSILLANIMOUS
QUADRILATERAL
QUADRIPARTITE
QUADRUPLICATE
QUALIFICATION
QUARTERMASTER
QUESTIONNAIRE
QUINTUPLICATE
SUBDISCIPLINE
SULFANILAMIDE
SUPERABUNDANT
SUPERCOMPUTER
SUPERNUMERARY
SUPRANATIONAL
SURREPTITIOUS
TURBOELECTRIC
OVERQUALIFIED
OVERSUBSCRIBE
EXCEPTIONABLE
EXCOMMUNICATE

EXHIBITIONISM
EXPEDITIONARY
EXPRESSIONISM
EXTRAGALACTIC
EXTRAORDINARY
HYDROCEPHALUS
HYDRODYNAMICS
HYDROELECTRIC
HYPERCRITICAL
HYPERDOCUMENT
SYLLABICATION

## 3rd Letter

BOARDINGHOUSE
FEATHERWEIGHT
FRAGMENTATION
GRANDDAUGHTER
GRANTSMANSHIP
HEARTBREAKING
INAPPRECIABLE
PHARMACOPOEIA
QUADRILATERAL
QUADRIPARTITE
QUADRUPLICATE
QUALIFICATION
QUARTERMASTER
SCANDALMONGER
TRANSATLANTIC
TRANSCRIPTION
TRANSISTORIZE
TRANSNATIONAL
UNACCOMPANIED
UNACCOUNTABLE
UNADULTERATED
GUBERNATORIAL
SUBDISCIPLINE
TABLESPOONFUL
ACCELEROMETER
ACCOMMODATING
ACCOMMODATION
ACCOMPANIMENT
ACCULTURATION
ARCHIMANDRITE
ARCHITECTONIC
BACCALAUREATE
BACTERIOPHAGE
DECONTAMINATE
EXCEPTIONABLE
EXCOMMUNICATE
INCOMBUSTIBLE
INCOMMUNICADO
INCONSIDERATE
INCONSPICUOUS
INCONTESTABLE
INCONVENIENCE
INCORRUPTIBLE
LACKADAISICAL
MACHICOLATION
MICROCOMPUTER
MICROORGANISM
RECRUDESCENCE
UNCEREMONIOUS
UNCIRCUMCISED
UNCOMFORTABLE
UNCONDITIONAL
UNCONDITIONED
UNCONQUERABLE
VOCATIONALISM
HYDROCEPHALUS
HYDRODYNAMICS
HYDROELECTRIC
INDEFATIGABLE
INDESCRIBABLE
INDETERMINATE
INDISPENSABLE
INDIVIDUALISM
INDIVIDUALIST
INDIVIDUALITY
INDIVIDUALIZE
INDUSTRIALIST
INDUSTRIALIZE
RADIOACTIVITY
UNDERACHIEVER
UNDERCARRIAGE
UNDERCLASSMAN
UNDERCLOTHING
UNDEREMPLOYED
UNDERESTIMATE
UNDERGRADUATE
UNDERSTANDING
ACETYLCHOLINE
CLEARINGHOUSE
ELECTROLOGIST
ELECTROMAGNET
ELEPHANTIASIS
INEXHAUSTIBLE
INEXPRESSIBLE
OLEOMARGARINE
OVERQUALIFIED
OVERSUBSCRIBE
PHENOBARBITAL
PRECIPITATION
PREOCCUPATION
PREPOSSESSING
PREPOSSESSION
PRETERNATURAL
QUESTIONNAIRE
ROENTGENOLOGY
SPECIFICATION
THENCEFORWARD
THERMONUCLEAR
THERMOPLASTIC
AFFORESTATION
DIFFERENTIATE
EFFLORESCENCE
INFINITESIMAL
INFLORESCENCE
KAFFEEKLATSCH
UNFORGETTABLE
AGGIORNAMENTO
ARGUMENTATION
ARGUMENTATIVE
DAGUERREOTYPE
MAGNETOSPHERE
DEHYDROGENATE
EXHIBITIONISM
OPHTHALMOLOGY
SCHIZOPHRENIA
SCHOOLTEACHER
PRIMOGENITURE
QUINTUPLICATE
REINCARNATION
UNIMPEACHABLE
UNINTELLIGENT
UNINTENTIONAL
UNINTERRUPTED
WHITHERSOEVER
COLLOQUIALISM
HALLUCINATION
JOLLIFICATION
MALADMINISTER
MULTINATIONAL
POLIOMYELITIS
SULFANILAMIDE
SYLLABICATION
VALEDICTORIAN
ADMINISTRATOR
COMMEMORATIVE
COMMENSURABLE
COMMERCIALISM
COMMERCIALIZE
COMMUNICATION
COMPLIMENTARY
DEMONSTRATIVE
SEMIAUTOMATIC
SEMICONDUCTOR
SEMIPERMEABLE
UNMENTIONABLE
AMNIOCENTESIS
CINEMATOGRAPH
CONCATENATION
CONCENTRATION
CONCEPTUALIZE
CONCERTMASTER
CONCUPISCENCE
CONFABULATION
CONFECTIONERY
CONFEDERATION
CONFIGURATION
CONFLAGRATION
CONFRATERNITY
CONSANGUINITY
CONSCIENTIOUS
CONSEQUENTIAL
CONSIDERATION
CONSTELLATION
CONSTERNATION
CONTAINERSHIP
CONTORTIONIST
CONTRACEPTION
GENERALISSIMO
GENITOURINARY
GONADOTROPHIC
GONADOTROPHIN
HUNDREDWEIGHT
MANIFESTATION
MONOCHROMATIC
MONOCOTYLEDON
MONONUCLEOSIS
NONCONFORMIST
NONINTERLACED
NONRESISTANCE
SANCTIMONIOUS
TENDERHEARTED
TONSILLECTOMY
UNNECESSARILY
VENTRILOQUISM
BIODEGRADABLE
BLOODCURDLING
BROKENHEARTED
GEOCHRONOLOGY
GEOMORPHOLOGY
GEOSTATIONARY
KNOWLEDGEABLE
PHOTOCHEMICAL
PHOTOELECTRIC
PHOTOELECTRON
PHOTOEMISSION
PROCRASTINATE
PROFESSORIATE
PROGNOSTICATE
PROJECTIONIST
PRONOUNCEMENT
PRONUNCIATION
PROTECTIONIST
THOROUGHGOING
WOOLGATHERING
APPROPRIATION
EXPEDITIONARY
EXPRESSIONISM
HYPERCRITICAL
HYPERDOCUMENT
IMPERCEPTIBLE
IMPERMISSIBLE
IMPERTURBABLE
IMPRACTICABLE
IMPRESSIONISM
IMPRESSIONIST
RAPPROCHEMENT
REPREHENSIBLE
SOPHISTICATED
SUPERABUNDANT
SUPERCOMPUTER
SUPERNUMERARY
SUPRANATIONAL
UNPRECEDENTED
UNPREDICTABLE
UNPRETENTIOUS
UPPERCLASSMAN
UNQUESTIONING
CARBONIFEROUS
CERTIFICATION
CHRISTMASTIDE
CHRYSANTHEMUM
CIRCUMABULATE
CIRCUMFERENCE
CORRESPONDENT
EUROPOCENTRIC
FERROMAGNETIC
HERMAPHRODITE
IRRECLAIMABLE
IRRECOVERABLE
IRREPLACEABLE
IRREPRESSIBLE
IRRESPONSIBLE
IRRETRIEVABLE
JURISPRUDENCE
PARALLELOGRAM
PARAPHERNALIA
PARTICULARIZE
PEREGRINATION
PERFECTIONIST
PERPENDICULAR
STRANGULATION
STREPTOCOCCUS
STRIKEBREAKER
SURREPTITIOUS
TERCENTENNIAL
TORTOISESHELL
TURBOELECTRIC
VERSIFICATION
COSMETOLOGIST
DISINTERESTED
DISPASSIONATE
DISPROPORTION
DISTINGUISHED
INSECTIVOROUS
INSTANTANEOUS
INSUBORDINATE
INSUBSTANTIAL
INSUPPORTABLE
JUSTIFICATION
MISALLOCATION
MISCEGENATION
MISCELLANEOUS
MISUNDERSTAND
POSTOPERATIVE
PUSILLANIMOUS
UNSUBSTANTIAL
ANTICOAGULANT
ANTIFERTILITY
ANTIHISTAMINE
ANTILOGARITHM
ANTIPERSONNEL
ANTIPOLLUTION
AUTHORITARIAN
AUTHORITATIVE
AUTOBIOGRAPHY
AUTOCHTHONOUS
DETERMINATION
ESTABLISHMENT
EXTRAGALACTIC
EXTRAORDINARY
HETEROGENEOUS
INTERCULTURAL
INTERGALACTIC
INTERLOCUTORY
INTERMARRIAGE
INTERNATIONAL
INTERPERSONAL
INTERROGATIVE
INTERROGATORY
INTRAMUSCULAR
INTRANSIGENCE
INTROSPECTION
METAMORPHOSIS
NITRIFICATION
NITROGLYCERIN
ORTHONDONTICS
PATERFAMILIAS
PETROCHEMICAL
RATIOCINATION
BOUILLABAISSE
COUNTERATTACK
COUNTERWEIGHT
COUNTINGHOUSE
HOUSEBREAKING
LAUGHINGSTOCK
THUNDERSHOWER
THUNDERSTRUCK
ADVENTURESOME
ADVERTISEMENT
REVOLUTIONARY
REVOLUTIONIST
REVOLUTIONIZE
UNWARRANTABLE
PHYSIOTHERAPY
PSYCHOSOMATIC
PSYCHOTHERAPY

**4th Letter**

CLEARINGHOUSE
ESTABLISHMENT
GONADOTROPHIC
GONADOTROPHIN
MALADMINISTER
METAMORPHOSIS
MISALLOCATION
PARALLELOGRAM
PARAPHERNALIA
STRANGULATION
UNWARRANTABLE
VOCATIONALISM
CARBONIFEROUS
TURBOELECTRIC
BACCALAUREATE
CIRCUMABULATE
CIRCUMFERENCE
CONCATENATION
CONCENTRATION
CONCEPTUALIZE
CONCERTMASTER
CONCUPISCENCE
ELECTROLOGIST
ELECTROMAGNET
GEOCHRONOLOGY
MISCEGENATION
MISCELLANEOUS
NONCONFORMIST
PRECIPITATION
PROCRASTINATE
PSYCHOSOMATIC
PSYCHOTHERAPY
SANCTIMONIOUS
SPECIFICATION
TERCENTENNIAL
UNACCOMPANIED
UNACCOUNTABLE
BIODEGRADABLE
HUNDREDWEIGHT
QUADRILATERAL
QUADRIPARTITE
QUADRUPLICATE
SUBDISCIPLINE
TENDERHEARTED
UNADULTERATED
ACCELEROMETER
ADVENTURESOME
ADVERTISEMENT
CINEMATOGRAPH
DETERMINATION
EXCEPTIONABLE
EXPEDITIONARY
GENERALISSIMO
GUBERNATORIAL
HETEROGENEOUS
HYPERCRITICAL
HYPERDOCUMENT
IMPERCEPTIBLE
IMPERMISSIBLE
IMPERTURBABLE
INDEFATIGABLE
INDESCRIBABLE
INDETERMINATE
INSECTIVOROUS
INTERCULTURAL
INTERGALACTIC
INTERLOCUTORY
INTERMARRIAGE
INTERNATIONAL
INTERPERSONAL
INTERROGATIVE
INTERROGATORY
IRRECLAIMABLE
IRRECOVERABLE
IRREPLACEABLE
IRREPRESSIBLE
IRRESPONSIBLE
IRRETRIEVABLE
PATERFAMILIAS
PEREGRINATION
STREPTOCOCCUS
SUPERABUNDANT
SUPERCOMPUTER
SUPERNUMERARY
UNCEREMONIOUS
UNDERACHIEVER
UNDERCARRIAGE
UNDERCLASSMAN
UNDERCLOTHING
UNDEREMPLOYED
UNDERESTIMATE
UNDERGRADUATE
UNDERSTANDING
UNMENTIONABLE
UNNECESSARILY
UPPERCLASSMAN
VALEDICTORIAN
CONFABULATION
CONFECTIONERY
CONFEDERATION
CONFIGURATION
CONFLAGRATION
CONFRATERNITY
DIFFERENTIATE
KAFFEEKLATSCH
PERFECTIONIST
PROFESSORIATE
SULFANILAMIDE
FRAGMENTATION
LAUGHINGSTOCK
PROGNOSTICATE
ARCHIMANDRITE
ARCHITECTONIC
AUTHORITARIAN
AUTHORITATIVE
MACHICOLATION
ORTHONDONTICS
SOPHISTICATED
ADMINISTRATOR
AGGIORNAMENTO
AMNIOCENTESIS
ANTICOAGULANT
ANTIFERTILITY
ANTIHISTAMINE
ANTILOGARITHM
ANTIPERSONNEL
ANTIPOLLUTION
BOUILLABAISSE
CHRISTMASTIDE
DISINTERESTED
EXHIBITIONISM
GENITOURINARY
INDISPENSABLE
INDIVIDUALISM
INDIVIDUALIST
INDIVIDUALITY
INDIVIDUALIZE
INFINITESIMAL
JURISPRUDENCE
MANIFESTATION
NONINTERLACED
POLIOMYELITIS
PUSILLANIMOUS
RADIOACTIVITY
RATIOCINATION
SCHIZOPHRENIA
SEMIAUTOMATIC
SEMICONDUCTOR
SEMIPERMEABLE
STRIKEBREAKER
UNCIRCUMCISED
PROJECTIONIST
BROKENHEARTED
LACKADAISICAL
COLLOQUIALISM
EFFLORESCENCE
HALLUCINATION
INFLORESCENCE
JOLLIFICATION
QUALIFICATION
SYLLABICATION
TABLESPOONFUL
WOOLGATHERING
COMMEMORATIVE
COMMENSURABLE
COMMERCIALISM
COMMERCIALIZE
COMMUNICATION
COSMETOLOGIST
GEOMORPHOLOGY
HERMAPHRODITE
PRIMOGENITURE
UNIMPEACHABLE
COUNTERATTACK
COUNTERWEIGHT
COUNTINGHOUSE
GRANDDAUGHTER
GRANTSMANSHIP
MAGNETOSPHERE
PHENOBARBITAL
PRONOUNCEMENT
PRONUNCIATION
QUINTUPLICATE
REINCARNATION
ROENTGENOLOGY
SCANDALMONGER
THENCEFORWARD
THUNDERSHOWER
THUNDERSTRUCK
TRANSATLANTIC
TRANSCRIPTION
TRANSISTORIZE
TRANSNATIONAL
UNINTELLIGENT
UNINTENTIONAL
UNINTERRUPTED
ACCOMMODATING
ACCOMMODATION
ACCOMPANIMENT
AFFORESTATION
AUTOBIOGRAPHY
AUTOCHTHONOUS
BLOODCURDLING
DECONTAMINATE
DEMONSTRATIVE
EUROPOCENTRIC
EXCOMMUNICATE
INCOMBUSTIBLE
INCOMMUNICADO
INCONSIDERATE
INCONSPICUOUS
INCONTESTABLE
INCONVENIENCE
INCORRUPTIBLE
MONOCHROMATIC
MONOCOTYLEDON
MONONUCLEOSIS
OLEOMARGARINE
PREOCCUPATION
REVOLUTIONARY
REVOLUTIONIST
REVOLUTIONIZE
SCHOOLTEACHER
UNCOMFORTABLE
UNCONDITIONAL
UNCONDITIONED
UNCONQUERABLE
UNFORGETTABLE
COMPLIMENTARY
DISPASSIONATE
DISPROPORTION
ELEPHANTIASIS
INAPPRECIABLE
PERPENDICULAR
PREPOSSESSING
PREPOSSESSION
RAPPROCHEMENT
APPROPRIATION
BOARDINGHOUSE
CORRESPONDENT
EXPRESSIONISM
EXTRAGALACTIC
EXTRAORDINARY
FERROMAGNETIC
HEARTBREAKING
HYDROCEPHALUS
HYDRODYNAMICS
HYDROELECTRIC
IMPRACTICABLE
IMPRESSIONISM
IMPRESSIONIST
INTRAMUSCULAR
INTRANSIGENCE
INTROSPECTION
MICROCOMPUTER
MICROORGANISM
NITRIFICATION
NITROGLYCERIN
NONRESISTANCE
OVERQUALIFIED
OVERSUBSCRIBE
PETROCHEMICAL
PHARMACOPOEIA
QUARTERMASTER
RECRUDESCENCE
REPREHENSIBLE
SUPRANATIONAL
SURREPTITIOUS
THERMONUCLEAR
THERMOPLASTIC
THOROUGHGOING
UNPRECEDENTED
UNPREDICTABLE
UNPRETENTIOUS
CONSANGUINITY
CONSCIENTIOUS
CONSEQUENTIAL
CONSIDERATION
CONSTELLATION
CONSTERNATION
GEOSTATIONARY
HOUSEBREAKING
PHYSIOTHERAPY
QUESTIONNAIRE
TONSILLECTOMY
VERSIFICATION
ACETYLCHOLINE
BACTERIOPHAGE
CERTIFICATION
CONTAINERSHIP
CONTORTIONIST
CONTRACEPTION
DISTINGUISHED
FEATHERWEIGHT
INSTANTANEOUS
JUSTIFICATION
MULTINATIONAL
OPHTHALMOLOGY
PARTICULARIZE
PHOTOCHEMICAL
PHOTOELECTRIC
PHOTOELECTRON
PHOTOEMISSION
POSTOPERATIVE
PRETERNATURAL
PROTECTIONIST
TORTOISESHELL
VENTRILOQUISM
WHITHERSOEVER
ACCULTURATION
ARGUMENTATION
ARGUMENTATIVE
DAGUERREOTYPE
INDUSTRIALIST
INDUSTRIALIZE
INSUBORDINATE
INSUBSTANTIAL
INSUPPORTABLE
MISUNDERSTAND
UNQUESTIONING
UNSUBSTANTIAL
KNOWLEDGEABLE
INEXHAUSTIBLE
INEXPRESSIBLE
CHRYSANTHEMUM
DEHYDROGENATE

**5th Letter**

BACCALAUREATE
CONCATENATION
CONFABULATION
CONSANGUINITY
CONTAINERSHIP
DISPASSIONATE
EXTRAGALACTIC
EXTRAORDINARY
HERMAPHRODITE

IMPR**A**CTICABLE
INST**A**NTANEOUS
INTR**A**MUSCULAR
INTR**A**NSIGENCE
LACK**A**DAISICAL
SEMI**A**UTOMATIC
SULF**A**NILAMIDE
SUPR**A**NATIONAL
SYLL**A**BICATION
AUTO**B**IOGRAPHY
ESTA**B**LISHMENT
EXHI**B**ITIONISM
INSU**B**ORDINATE
INSU**B**STANTIAL
UNSU**B**STANTIAL
ANTI**C**OAGULANT
AUTO**C**HTHONOUS
CONS**C**IENTIOUS
INSE**C**TIVOROUS
IRRE**C**LAIMABLE
IRRE**C**OVERABLE
MONO**C**HROMATIC
MONO**C**OTYLEDON
PREO**C**CUPATION
REIN**C**ARNATION
SEMI**C**ONDUCTOR
THEN**C**EFORWARD
UNAC**C**OMPANIED
UNAC**C**OUNTABLE
UNNE**C**ESSARILY
BLOO**D**CURDLING
BOAR**D**INGHOUSE
DEHY**D**ROGENATE
EXPE**D**ITIONARY
GONA**D**OTROPHIC
GONA**D**OTROPHIN
GRAN**D**DAUGHTER
MALA**D**MINISTER
SCAN**D**ALMONGER
THUN**D**ERSHOWER
THUN**D**ERSTRUCK
VALE**D**ICTORIAN
BACT**E**RIOPHAGE
BIOD**E**GRADABLE
BROK**E**NHEARTED
COMM**E**MORATIVE
COMM**E**NSURABLE
COMM**E**RCIALISM
COMM**E**RCIALIZE
CONC**E**NTRATION
CONC**E**PTUALIZE
CONC**E**RTMASTER
CONF**E**CTIONERY
CONF**E**DERATION
CONS**E**QUENTIAL
CORR**E**SPONDENT
COSM**E**TOLOGIST
DAGU**E**RREOTYPE
DIFF**E**RENTIATE
EXPR**E**SSIONISM
HOUS**E**BREAKING
IMPR**E**SSIONISM
IMPR**E**SSIONIST
KAFF**E**EKLATSCH
MAGN**E**TOSPHERE
MISC**E**GENATION
MISC**E**LLANEOUS
NONR**E**SISTANCE
PERF**E**CTIONIST
PERP**E**NDICULAR
PRET**E**RNATURAL
PROF**E**SSORIATE
PROJ**E**CTIONIST
PROT**E**CTIONIST
REPR**E**HENSIBLE
SURR**E**PTITIOUS
TABL**E**SPOONFUL
TEND**E**RHEARTED
TERC**E**NTENNIAL
UNPR**E**CEDENTED
UNPR**E**DICTABLE
UNPR**E**TENTIOUS
UNQU**E**STIONING
ANTI**F**ERTILITY
INDE**F**ATIGABLE
MANI**F**ESTATION
PERE**G**RINATION
WOOL**G**ATHERING
ANTI**H**ISTAMINE
ELEP**H**ANTIASIS
FEAT**H**ERWEIGHT
GEOC**H**RONOLOGY
INEX**H**AUSTIBLE
LAUG**H**INGSTOCK
OPHT**H**ALMOLOGY
PSYC**H**OSOMATIC
PSYC**H**OTHERAPY
WHIT**H**ERSOEVER
ARCH**I**MANDRITE
ARCH**I**TECTONIC
CERT**I**FICATION
CONF**I**GURATION
CONS**I**DERATION
DIST**I**NGUISHED
JOLL**I**FICATION
JUST**I**FICATION
MACH**I**COLATION
MULT**I**NATIONAL
NITR**I**FICATION
PART**I**CULARIZE
PHYS**I**OTHERAPY
PREC**I**PITATION
QUAL**I**FICATION
SOPH**I**STICATED
SPEC**I**FICATION
SUBD**I**SCIPLINE
TONS**I**LLECTOMY
VERS**I**FICATION
STRI**K**EBREAKER
ACCE**L**EROMETER
ACCU**L**TURATION
ANTI**L**OGARITHM
BOUI**L**LABAISSE
COMP**L**IMENTARY
CONF**L**AGRATION
KNOW**L**EDGEABLE
MISA**L**LOCATION
PARA**L**LELOGRAM
PUSI**L**LANIMOUS
REVO**L**UTIONARY
REVO**L**UTIONIST
REVO**L**UTIONIZE
ACCO**M**MODATING
ACCO**M**MODATION
ACCO**M**PANIMENT
ARGU**M**ENTATION
ARGU**M**ENTATIVE
CINE**M**ATOGRAPH
EXCO**M**MUNICATE
FRAG**M**ENTATION
INCO**M**BUSTIBLE
INCO**M**MUNICADO
META**M**ORPHOSIS
OLEO**M**ARGARINE
PHAR**M**ACOPOEIA
THER**M**ONUCLEAR
THER**M**OPLASTIC
UNCO**M**FORTABLE
ADMI**N**ISTRATOR
ADVE**N**TURESOME
DECO**N**TAMINATE
DEMO**N**STRATIVE
DISI**N**TERESTED
INCO**N**SIDERATE
INCO**N**SPICUOUS
INCO**N**TESTABLE
INCO**N**VENIENCE
INFI**N**ITESIMAL
MISU**N**DERSTAND
MONO**N**UCLEOSIS
NONI**N**TERLACED
PROG**N**OSTICATE
STRA**N**GULATION
UNCO**N**DITIONAL
UNCO**N**DITIONED
UNCO**N**QUERABLE
UNME**N**TIONABLE
AGGI**O**RNAMENTO
AMNI**O**CENTESIS
APPR**O**PRIATION
AUTH**O**RITARIAN
AUTH**O**RITATIVE
CARB**O**NIFEROUS
COLL**O**QUIALISM
CONT**O**RTIONIST
EFFL**O**RESCENCE
FERR**O**MAGNETIC
GEOM**O**RPHOLOGY
HYDR**O**CEPHALUS
HYDR**O**DYNAMICS
HYDR**O**ELECTRIC
INFL**O**RESCENCE
INTR**O**SPECTION
MICR**O**COMPUTER
MICR**O**ORGANISM
NITR**O**GLYCERIN
NONC**O**NFORMIST
ORTH**O**NDONTICS
PETR**O**CHEMICAL
PHEN**O**BARBITAL
PHOT**O**CHEMICAL
PHOT**O**ELECTRIC
PHOT**O**ELECTRON
PHOT**O**EMISSION
POLI**O**MYELITIS
POST**O**PERATIVE
PREP**O**SSESSING
PREP**O**SSESSION
PRIM**O**GENITURE
PRON**O**UNCEMENT
RADI**O**ACTIVITY
RATI**O**CINATION
SCHO**O**LTEACHER
THOR**O**UGHGOING
TORT**O**ISESHELL
TURB**O**ELECTRIC
ANTI**P**ERSONNEL
ANTI**P**OLLUTION
EURO**P**OCENTRIC
EXCE**P**TIONABLE
INAP**P**RECIABLE
INEX**P**RESSIBLE
INSU**P**PORTABLE
IRRE**P**LACEABLE
IRRE**P**RESSIBLE
PARA**P**HERNALIA
SEMI**P**ERMEABLE
STRE**P**TOCOCCUS
UNIM**P**EACHABLE
OVER**Q**UALIFIED
ADVE**R**TISEMENT
AFFO**R**ESTATION
CLEA**R**INGHOUSE
CONF**R**ATERNITY
CONT**R**ACEPTION
DETE**R**MINATION
DISP**R**OPORTION
GENE**R**ALISSIMO
GUBE**R**NATORIAL
HETE**R**OGENEOUS
HUND**R**EDWEIGHT
HYPE**R**CRITICAL
HYPE**R**DOCUMENT
IMPE**R**CEPTIBLE
IMPE**R**MISSIBLE
IMPE**R**TURBABLE
INCO**R**RUPTIBLE
INTE**R**CULTURAL
INTE**R**GALACTIC
INTE**R**LOCUTORY
INTE**R**MARRIAGE
INTE**R**NATIONAL
INTE**R**PERSONAL
INTE**R**ROGATIVE
INTE**R**ROGATORY
PATE**R**FAMILIAS
PROC**R**ASTINATE
QUAD**R**ILATERAL
QUAD**R**IPARTITE
QUAD**R**UPLICATE
RAPP**R**OCHEMENT
SUPE**R**ABUNDANT
SUPE**R**COMPUTER
SUPE**R**NUMERARY
UNCE**R**EMONIOUS
UNCI**R**CUMCISED
UNDE**R**ACHIEVER
UNDE**R**CARRIAGE
UNDE**R**CLASSMAN
UNDE**R**CLOTHING
UNDE**R**EMPLOYED
UNDE**R**ESTIMATE
UNDE**R**GRADUATE
UNDE**R**STANDING
UNFO**R**GETTABLE
UNWA**R**RANTABLE
UPPE**R**CLASSMAN
VENT**R**ILOQUISM
CHRI**S**TMASTIDE
CHRY**S**ANTHEMUM
INDE**S**CRIBABLE
INDI**S**PENSABLE
INDU**S**TRIALIST
INDU**S**TRIALIZE
IRRE**S**PONSIBLE
JURI**S**PRUDENCE
OVER**S**UBSCRIBE
TRAN**S**ATLANTIC
TRAN**S**CRIPTION
TRAN**S**ISTORIZE
TRAN**S**NATIONAL
CONS**T**ELLATION
CONS**T**ERNATION
COUN**T**ERATTACK
COUN**T**ERWEIGHT
COUN**T**INGHOUSE
ELEC**T**ROLOGIST
ELEC**T**ROMAGNET
GENI**T**OURINARY
GEOS**T**ATIONARY
GRAN**T**SMANSHIP
HEAR**T**BREAKING
INDE**T**ERMINATE
IRRE**T**RIEVABLE
QUAR**T**ERMASTER
QUES**T**IONNAIRE
QUIN**T**UPLICATE
ROEN**T**GENOLOGY
SANC**T**IMONIOUS
UNIN**T**ELLIGENT
UNIN**T**ENTIONAL
UNIN**T**ERRUPTED
VOCA**T**IONALISM
CIRC**U**MABULATE
CIRC**U**MFERENCE
COMM**U**NICATION
CONC**U**PISCENCE
HALL**U**CINATION
PRON**U**NCIATION
RECR**U**DESCENCE
UNAD**U**LTERATED
INDI**V**IDUALISM
INDI**V**IDUALIST
INDI**V**IDUALITY
INDI**V**IDUALIZE
ACET**Y**LCHOLINE
SCHI**Z**OPHRENIA

## 6TH LETTER

CHRYS**A**NTHEMUM
CINEM**A**TOGRAPH
CONFL**A**GRATION
CONFR**A**TERNITY
CONTR**A**CEPTION
ELEPH**A**NTIASIS
GENER**A**LISSIMO
GEOST**A**TIONARY
INDEF**A**TIGABLE
INEXH**A**USTIBLE
OLEOM**A**RGARINE
OPHTH**A**MOLOGY
PHARM**A**COPOEIA
PROCR**A**STINATE
RADIO**A**CTIVITY
REINC**A**RNATION
SCAND**A**LMONGER
SUPER**A**BUNDANT
TRANS**A**TLANTIC
UNDER**A**CHIEVER

WOOLG**A**THERING
CONFA**B**ULATION
HEART**B**REAKING
HOUSE**B**REAKING
INCOM**B**USTIBLE
PHENO**B**ARBITAL
SYLLA**B**ICATION
AMNIO**C**ENTESIS
BLOOD**C**URDLING
CONFE**C**TIONERY
HALLU**C**INATION
HYDRO**C**EPHALUS
HYPER**C**RITICAL
IMPER**C**EPTIBLE
IMPRA**C**TICABLE
INDES**C**RIBABLE
INTER**C**ULTURAL
MACHI**C**OLATION
MICRO**C**OMPUTER
PARTI**C**ULARIZE
PERFE**C**TIONIST
PETRO**C**HEMICAL
PHOTO**C**HEMICAL
PREOC**C**UPATION
PROJE**C**TIONIST
PROTE**C**TIONIST
RATIO**C**INATION
SUPER**C**OMPUTER
TRANS**C**RIPTION
UNCIR**C**UMCISED
UNDER**C**ARRIAGE
UNDER**C**LASSMAN
UNDER**C**LOTHING
UNPRE**C**EDENTED
UPPER**C**LASSMAN
CONFE**D**ERATION
CONSI**D**ERATION
GRAND**D**AUGHTER
HYDRO**D**YNAMICS
HYPER**D**OCUMENT
LACKA**D**AISICAL
MISUN**D**ERSTAND
RECRU**D**ESCENCE
UNCON**D**ITIONAL
UNCON**D**ITIONED
UNPRE**D**ICTABLE
ACCEL**E**ROMETER
AFFOR**E**STATION
ANTIF**E**RTILITY
ANTIP**E**RSONNEL
ARGUM**E**NTATION
ARGUM**E**NTATIVE
CONST**E**LLATION
CONST**E**RNATION
COUNT**E**RATTACK
COUNT**E**RWEIGHT
FEATH**E**RWEIGHT
FRAGM**E**NTATION
HUNDR**E**DWEIGHT
HYDRO**E**LECTRIC
INDET**E**RMINATE
KAFFE**E**KLATSCH
KNOWL**E**DGEABLE
MANIF**E**STATION
PHOTO**E**LECTRIC
PHOTO**E**LECTRON
PHOTO**E**MISSION
QUART**E**RMASTER
SEMIP**E**RMEABLE
STRIK**E**BREAKER
THENC**E**FORWARD
THUND**E**RSHOWER
THUND**E**RSTRUCK
TURBO**E**LECTRIC
UNCER**E**MONIOUS
UNDER**E**MPLOYED
UNDER**E**STIMATE
UNIMP**E**ACHABLE
UNINT**E**LLIGENT
UNINT**E**NTIONAL
UNINT**E**RRUPTED
UNNEC**E**SSARILY
WHITH**E**RSOEVER
CERTI**F**ICATION
JOLLI**F**ICATION
JUSTI**F**ICATION
NITRI**F**ICATION
PATER**F**AMILIAS
QUALI**F**ICATION
SPECI**F**ICATION
UNCOM**F**ORTABLE
VERSI**F**ICATION
BIODE**G**RADABLE
CONFI**G**URATION
EXTRA**G**ALACTIC
INTER**G**ALACTIC
MISCE**G**ENATION
NITRO**G**LYCERIN
PRIMO**G**ENITURE
ROENT**G**ENOLOGY
STRAN**G**ULATION
UNDER**G**RADUATE
UNFOR**G**ETTABLE
AUTOC**H**THONOUS
MONOC**H**ROMATIC
PARAP**H**ERNALIA
REPRE**H**ENSIBLE
ADMIN**I**STRATOR
ANTIH**I**STAMINE
AUTOB**I**OGRAPHY
BOARD**I**NGHOUSE
CLEAR**I**NGHOUSE
COMPL**I**MENTARY
CONSC**I**ENTIOUS
CONTA**I**NERSHIP
COUNT**I**NGHOUSE
EXHIB**I**TIONISM
EXPED**I**TIONARY
INDIV**I**DUALISM
INDIV**I**DUALIST
INDIV**I**DUALITY
INDIV**I**DUALIZE
INFIN**I**TESIMAL
LAUGH**I**NGSTOCK
QUADR**I**LATERAL
QUADR**I**PARTITE
QUEST**I**ONNAIRE
SANCT**I**MONIOUS
TORTO**I**SESHELL
TRANS**I**STORIZE
VALED**I**CTORIAN
VENTR**I**LOQUISM
VOCAT**I**ONALISM
ACETY**L**CHOLINE
BACCA**L**AUREATE
BOUIL**L**ABAISSE
ESTAB**L**ISHMENT
INTER**L**OCUTORY
IRREC**L**AIMABLE
IRREP**L**ACEABLE
MISAL**L**OCATION
MISCE**L**LANEOUS
PARAL**L**ELOGRAM
PUSIL**L**ANIMOUS
SCHOO**L**TEACHER
TONSI**L**LECTOMY
UNADU**L**TERATED
ACCOM**M**ODATING
ACCOM**M**ODATION
ARCHI**M**ANDRITE
CIRCU**M**ABULATE
CIRCU**M**FERENCE
COMME**M**ORATIVE
DETER**M**INATION
EXCOM**M**UNICATE
FERRO**M**AGNETIC
IMPER**M**ISSIBLE
INCOM**M**UNICADO
INTER**M**ARRIAGE
INTRA**M**USCULAR
MALAD**M**INISTER
POLIO**M**YELITIS
BROKE**N**HEARTED
CARBO**N**IFEROUS
COMME**N**SURABLE
COMMU**N**ICATION
CONCE**N**TRATION
CONSA**N**GUINITY
DISTI**N**GUISHED
GUBER**N**ATORIAL
INSTA**N**TANEOUS
INTER**N**ATIONAL
INTRA**N**SIGENCE
MULTI**N**ATIONAL
NONCO**N**FORMIST
ORTHO**N**DONTICS
PERPE**N**DICULAR
PRONU**N**CIATION
SULFA**N**ILAMIDE
SUPER**N**UMERARY
SUPRA**N**ATIONAL
TERCE**N**TENNIAL
TRANS**N**ATIONAL
ANTIC**O**AGULANT
ANTIL**O**GARITHM
ANTIP**O**LLUTION
DISPR**O**PORTION
EUROP**O**CENTRIC
EXTRA**O**RDINARY
GENIT**O**URINARY
GONAD**O**TROPHIC
GONAD**O**TROPHIN
HETER**O**GENEOUS
INSUB**O**RDINATE
IRREC**O**VERABLE
METAM**O**RPHOSIS
MICRO**O**RGANISM
MONOC**O**TYLEDON
PHYSI**O**THERAPY
PROGN**O**STICATE
PSYCH**O**SOMATIC
PSYCH**O**THERAPY
RAPPR**O**CHEMENT
SCHIZ**O**PHRENIA
SEMIC**O**NDUCTOR
THERM**O**NUCLEAR
THERM**O**PLASTIC
UNACC**O**MPANIED
UNACC**O**UNTABLE
ACCOM**P**ANIMENT
APPRO**P**RIATION
CONCE**P**TUALIZE
CONCU**P**ISCENCE
HERMA**P**HRODITE
INDIS**P**ENSABLE
INSUP**P**ORTABLE
INTER**P**ERSONAL
IRRES**P**ONSIBLE
JURIS**P**RUDENCE
POSTO**P**ERATIVE
PRECI**P**ITATION
SURRE**P**TITIOUS
COLLO**Q**UIALISM
CONSE**Q**UENTIAL
UNCON**Q**UERABLE
AGGIO**R**NAMENTO
AUTHO**R**ITARIAN
AUTHO**R**ITATIVE
BACTE**R**IOPHAGE
COMME**R**CIALISM
COMME**R**CIALIZE
CONCE**R**TMASTER
CONTO**R**TIONIST
DAGUE**R**REOTYPE
DEHYD**R**OGENATE
DIFFE**R**ENTIATE
EFFLO**R**ESCENCE
ELECT**R**OLOGIST
ELECT**R**OMAGNET
GEOCH**R**ONOLOGY
GEOMO**R**PHOLOGY
INAPP**R**ECIABLE
INCOR**R**UPTIBLE
INEXP**R**ESSIBLE
INFLO**R**ESCENCE
INTER**R**OGATIVE
INTER**R**OGATORY
IRREP**R**ESSIBLE
IRRET**R**IEVABLE
PEREG**R**INATION
PRETE**R**NATURAL
TENDE**R**HEARTED
UNWAR**R**ANTABLE
CORRE**S**PONDENT
DEMON**S**TRATIVE
DISPA**S**SIONATE
EXPRE**S**SIONISM
GRANT**S**MANSHIP
IMPRE**S**SIONISM
IMPRE**S**SIONIST
INCON**S**IDERATE
INCON**S**PICUOUS
INSUB**S**TANTIAL
INTRO**S**PECTION
NONRE**S**ISTANCE
PREPO**S**SESSING
PREPO**S**SESSION
PROFE**S**SORIATE
SOPHI**S**TICATED
SUBDI**S**CIPLINE
TABLE**S**POONFUL
UNDER**S**TANDING
UNQUE**S**TIONING
UNSUB**S**TANTIAL
ACCUL**T**URATION
ADVEN**T**URESOME
ADVER**T**ISEMENT
ARCHI**T**ECTONIC
CHRIS**T**MASTIDE
CONCA**T**ENATION
COSME**T**OLOGIST
DECON**T**AMINATE
DISIN**T**ERESTED
EXCEP**T**IONABLE
IMPER**T**URBABLE
INCON**T**ESTABLE
INDUS**T**RIALIST
INDUS**T**RIALIZE
INSEC**T**IVOROUS
MAGNE**T**OSPHERE
NONIN**T**ERLACED
STREP**T**OCOCCUS
UNMEN**T**IONABLE
UNPRE**T**ENTIOUS
MONON**U**CLEOSIS
OVERQ**U**ALIFIED
OVERS**U**BSCRIBE
PRONO**U**NCEMENT
QUADR**U**PLICATE
QUINT**U**PLICATE
REVOL**U**TIONARY
REVOL**U**TIONIST
REVOL**U**TIONIZE
SEMIA**U**TOMATIC
THORO**U**GHGOING
INCON**V**ENIENCE

### 7th Letter

ACCOMP**A**NIMENT
ANTICO**A**GULANT
ARCHIM**A**NDRITE
BACCAL**A**UREATE
BOUILL**A**BAISSE
CIRCUM**A**BULATE
DECONT**A**MINATE
EXTRAG**A**LACTIC
FERROM**A**GNETIC
GRANDD**A**UGHTER
GUBERN**A**TORIAL
INTERG**A**LACTIC
INTERM**A**RRIAGE
INTERN**A**TIONAL
IRRECL**A**IMABLE
IRREPL**A**CEABLE
LACKAD**A**ISICAL
MULTIN**A**TIONAL
OVERQU**A**LIFIED
PATERF**A**MILIAS
PHENOB**A**RBITAL
PUSILL**A**NIMOUS
SUPRAN**A**TIONAL
TRANSN**A**TIONAL
UNDERC**A**RRIAGE
UNIMPE**A**CHABLE
UNWARR**A**NTABLE
OVERSU**B**SCRIBE
STRIKE**B**REAKER
SUPERA**B**UNDANT
ACETYL**C**HOLINE

COMMER**C**IALISM
COMMER**C**IALIZE
CONTRA**C**EPTION
EUROPO**C**ENTRIC
MONONU**C**LEOSIS
PHARMA**C**OPOEIA
PRONUN**C**IATION
RADIOA**C**TIVITY
RAPPRO**C**HEMENT
SUBDIS**C**IPLINE
UNDERA**C**HIEVER
VALEDI**C**TORIAN
HUNDRE**D**WEIGHT
INDIVI**D**UALISM
INDIVI**D**UALIST
INDIVI**D**UALITY
INDIVI**D**UALIZE
KNOWLE**D**GEABLE
ORTHON**D**ONTICS
PERPEN**D**ICULAR
AMNIOC**E**NTESIS
ARCHIT**E**CTONIC
CONCAT**E**NATION
CONFED**E**RATION
CONSCI**E**NTIOUS
CONSID**E**RATION
DIFFER**E**NTIATE
DISINT**E**RESTED
EFFLOR**E**SCENCE
HYDROC**E**PHALUS
IMPERC**E**PTIBLE
INAPPR**E**CIABLE
INCONT**E**STABLE
INCONV**E**NIENCE
INDISP**E**NSABLE
INEXPR**E**SSIBLE
INFLOR**E**SCENCE
INTERP**E**RSONAL
IRREPR**E**SSIBLE
MISCEG**E**NATION
MISUND**E**RSTAND
NONINT**E**RLACED
PARALL**E**LOGRAM
PARAPH**E**RNALIA
POSTOP**E**RATIVE
PRIMOG**E**NITURE
RECRUD**E**SCENCE
REPREH**E**NSIBLE
ROENTG**E**NOLOGY
UNFORG**E**TTABLE
UNPREC**E**DENTED
UNPRET**E**NTIOUS
CIRCUM**F**ERENCE
NONCON**F**ORMIST
THENCE**F**ORWARD
ANTILO**G**ARITHM
CONFLA**G**RATION
CONSAN**G**UINITY
DISTIN**G**UISHED
HETERO**G**ENEOUS
THOROU**G**HGOING
BROKEN**H**EARTED
HERMAP**H**RODITE
PETROC**H**EMICAL
PHOTOC**H**EMICAL
TENDER**H**EARTED
ADVERT**I**SEMENT
AUTHOR**I**TARIAN
AUTHOR**I**TATIVE
BACTER**I**OPHAGE
CARBON**I**FEROUS
CERTIF**I**CATION
COMMUN**I**CATION
CONCUP**I**SCENCE
DETERM**I**NATION
ESTABL**I**SHMENT
EXCEPT**I**ONABLE
HALLUC**I**NATION
IMPERM**I**SSIBLE
INCONS**I**DERATE
INSECT**I**VOROUS
IRRETR**I**EVABLE
JOLLIF**I**CATION
JUSTIF**I**CATION
MALADM**I**NISTER
NITRIF**I**CATION
NONRES**I**STANCE
PEREGR**I**NATION
PRECIP**I**TATION
QUALIF**I**CATION
RATIOC**I**NATION
SPECIF**I**CATION
SULFAN**I**LAMIDE
SYLLAB**I**CATION
UNCOND**I**TIONAL
UNCOND**I**TIONED
UNMENT**I**ONABLE
UNPRED**I**CTABLE
VERSIF**I**CATION
KAFFEE**K**LATSCH
ANTIPO**L**LUTION
CONSTE**L**LATION
GENERA**L**ISSIMO
HYDROE**L**ECTRIC
MISCEL**L**ANEOUS
NITROG**L**YCERIN
OPHTHA**L**MOLOGY
PHOTOE**L**ECTRIC
PHOTOE**L**ECTRON
QUADRI**L**ATERAL
SCANDA**L**MONGER
TONSIL**L**ECTOMY
TURBOE**L**ECTRIC
UNDERC**L**ASSMAN
UNDERC**L**OTHING
UNINTE**L**LIGENT
UPPERC**L**ASSMAN
VENTRI**L**OQUISM
CHRIST**M**ASTIDE
COMPLI**M**ENTARY
GRANTS**M**ANSHIP
PHOTOE**M**ISSION
SANCTI**M**ONIOUS
UNACCO**M**PANIED
UNCERE**M**ONIOUS
UNDERE**M**PLOYED
AGGIOR**N**AMENTO
ARGUME**N**TATION
ARGUME**N**TATIVE
BOARDI**N**GHOUSE
CHRYSA**N**THEMUM
CLEARI**N**GHOUSE
CONTAI**N**ERSHIP
COUNTI**N**GHOUSE
ELEPHA**N**TIASIS
FRAGME**N**TATION
LAUGHI**N**GSTOCK
PRETER**N**ATURAL
PRONOU**N**CEMENT
SEMICO**N**DUCTOR
THERMO**N**UCLEAR
UNINTE**N**TIONAL
ACCOMM**O**DATING
ACCOMM**O**DATION
AUTOBI**O**GRAPHY
COMMEM**O**RATIVE
COSMET**O**LOGIST
DEHYDR**O**GENATE
ELECTR**O**LOGIST
ELECTR**O**MAGNET
GEOCHR**O**NOLOGY
HYPERD**O**CUMENT
INSUPP**O**RTABLE
INTERL**O**CUTORY
INTERR**O**GATIVE
INTERR**O**GATORY
IRRESP**O**NSIBLE
MACHIC**O**LATION
MAGNET**O**SPHERE
MICROC**O**MPUTER
MISALL**O**CATION
QUESTI**O**NNAIRE
STREPT**O**COCCUS
SUPERC**O**MPUTER
UNCOMF**O**RTABLE
VOCATI**O**NALISM
CORRES**P**ONDENT
DISPRO**P**ORTION
GEOMOR**P**HOLOGY
INCONS**P**ICUOUS
INTROS**P**ECTION
QUADRI**P**ARTITE
QUADRU**P**LICATE
QUINTU**P**LICATE
SCHIZO**P**HRENIA
TABLES**P**OONFUL
THERMO**P**LASTIC
ACCELE**R**OMETER
ANTIFE**R**TILITY
ANTIPE**R**SONNEL
APPROP**R**IATION
BIODEG**R**ADABLE
CONSTE**R**NATION
COUNTE**R**ATTACK
COUNTE**R**WEIGHT
DAGUER**R**EOTYPE
EXTRAO**R**DINARY
FEATHE**R**WEIGHT
HEARTB**R**EAKING
HOUSEB**R**EAKING
HYPERC**R**ITICAL
INDESC**R**IBABLE
INDETE**R**MINATE
INDUST**R**IALIST
INDUST**R**IALIZE
INSUBO**R**DINATE
JURISP**R**UDENCE
METAMO**R**PHOSIS
MICROO**R**GANISM
MONOCH**R**OMATIC
OLEOMA**R**GARINE
QUARTE**R**MASTER
REINCA**R**NATION
SEMIPE**R**MEABLE
THUNDE**R**SHOWER
THUNDE**R**STRUCK
TRANSC**R**IPTION
UNDERG**R**ADUATE
UNINTE**R**RUPTED
WHITHE**R**SOEVER
ADMINI**S**TRATOR
AFFORE**S**TATION
ANTIHI**S**TAMINE
COMMEN**S**URABLE
DISPAS**S**IONATE
EXPRES**S**IONISM
IMPRES**S**IONISM
IMPRES**S**IONIST
INTRAN**S**IGENCE
MANIFE**S**TATION
PREPOS**S**ESSING
PREPOS**S**ESSION
PROCRA**S**TINATE
PROFES**S**ORIATE
PROGNO**S**TICATE
PSYCHO**S**OMATIC
TORTOI**S**ESHELL
TRANSI**S**TORIZE
UNDERE**S**TIMATE
UNNECE**S**SARILY
AUTOCH**T**HONOUS
CINEMA**T**OGRAPH
CONCEN**T**RATION
CONCEP**T**UALIZE
CONCER**T**MASTER
CONFEC**T**IONERY
CONFRA**T**ERNITY
CONTOR**T**IONIST
DEMONS**T**RATIVE
EXHIBI**T**IONISM
EXPEDI**T**IONARY
GEOSTA**T**IONARY
GONADO**T**ROPHIC
GONADO**T**ROPHIN
IMPRAC**T**ICABLE
INDEFA**T**IGABLE
INFINI**T**ESIMAL
INSTAN**T**ANEOUS
INSUBS**T**ANTIAL
MONOCO**T**YLEDON
PERFEC**T**IONIST
PHYSIO**T**HERAPY
PSYCHO**T**HERAPY
PROJEC**T**IONIST
PROTEC**T**IONIST
REVOLU**T**IONARY
REVOLU**T**IONIST
REVOLU**T**IONIZE
SCHOOL**T**EACHER
SEMIAU**T**OMATIC
SOPHIS**T**ICATED
SURREP**T**ITIOUS
TERCEN**T**ENNIAL
TRANSA**T**LANTIC
UNADUL**T**ERATED
UNDERS**T**ANDING
UNQUES**T**IONING
UNSUBS**T**ANTIAL
WOOLGA**T**HERING
ACCULT**U**RATION
ADVENT**U**RESOME
BLOODC**U**RDLING
COLLOQ**U**IALISM
CONFAB**U**LATION
CONFIG**U**RATION
CONSEQ**U**ENTIAL
EXCOMM**U**NICATE
GENITO**U**RINARY
IMPERT**U**RBABLE
INCOMB**U**STIBLE
INCOMM**U**NICADO
INCORR**U**PTIBLE
INEXHA**U**STIBLE
INTERC**U**LTURAL
INTRAM**U**SCULAR
PARTIC**U**LARIZE
PREOCC**U**PATION
STRANG**U**LATION
SUPERN**U**MERARY
UNACCO**U**NTABLE
UNCIRC**U**MCISED
UNCONQ**U**ERABLE
IRRECO**V**ERABLE
HYDROD**Y**NAMICS
POLIOM**Y**ELITIS

## 8th Letter

AGGIORN**A**MENTO
ANTILOG**A**RITHM
BIODEGR**A**DABLE
CHRISTM**A**STIDE
COUNTER**A**TTACK
GRANTSM**A**NSHIP
INSTANT**A**NEOUS
INSUBST**A**NTIAL
MISCELL**A**NEOUS
PRETERN**A**TURAL
QUADRIL**A**TERAL
QUADRIP**A**RTITE
UNDERCL**A**SSMAN
UNDERGR**A**DUATE
UNDERST**A**NDING
UNSUBST**A**NTIAL
UPPERCL**A**SSMAN
BOUILLA**B**AISSE
CIRCUMA**B**ULATE
ARCHITE**C**TONIC
CERTIFI**C**ATION
COMMUNI**C**ATION
HYPERDO**C**UMENT
INAPPRE**C**IABLE
INTERLO**C**UTORY
IRREPLA**C**EABLE
JOLLIFI**C**ATION
JUSTIFI**C**ATION
MISALLO**C**ATION
NITRIFI**C**ATION
PRONOUN**C**EMENT
QUALIFI**C**ATION
SPECIFI**C**ATION
STREPTO**C**OCCUS
SYLLABI**C**ATION
UNIMPEA**C**HABLE
UNPREDI**C**TABLE
VERSIFI**C**ATION
ACCOMMO**D**ATING
ACCOMMO**D**ATION
EXTRAOR**D**INARY
INCONSI**D**ERATE

INSUBOR**D**INATE
SEMICON**D**UCTOR
UNPRECE**D**ENTED
BROKENH**E**ARTED
CIRCUMF**E**RENCE
COMPLIM**E**NTARY
CONFRAT**E**RNITY
CONSEQU**E**NTIAL
CONTAIN**E**RSHIP
CONTRAC**E**PTION
DAGUERR**E**OTYPE
EUROPOC**E**NTRIC
HEARTBR**E**AKING
HETEROG**E**NEOUS
HOUSEBR**E**AKING
HYDROEL**E**CTRIC
INFINIT**E**SIMAL
INTROSP**E**CTION
IRRECOV**E**RABLE
IRRETRI**E**VABLE
PETROCH**E**MICAL
PHOTOCH**E**MICAL
PHOTOEL**E**CTRIC
PHOTOEL**E**CTRON
POLIOMY**E**LITIS
PREPOSS**E**SSING
PREPOSS**E**SSION
SCHOOLT**E**ACHER
TENDERH**E**ARTED
TERCENT**E**NNIAL
TONSILL**E**CTOMY
TORTOIS**E**SHELL
TURBOEL**E**CTRIC
UNADULT**E**RATED
UNCONQU**E**RABLE
CARBONI**F**EROUS
ANTICOA**G**ULANT
AUTOBIO**G**RAPHY
BOARDIN**G**HOUSE
CLEARIN**G**HOUSE
COUNTIN**G**HOUSE
DEHYDRO**G**ENATE
FERROMA**G**NETIC
INTERRO**G**ATIVE
INTERRO**G**ATORY
KNOWLED**G**EABLE
LAUGHIN**G**STOCK
MICROOR**G**ANISM
OLEOMAR**G**ARINE
ACETYLC**H**OLINE
AUTOCHT**H**ONOUS
GEOMORP**H**OLOGY
PHYSIOT**H**ERAPY
PSYCHOT**H**ERAPY
RAPPROC**H**EMENT
SCHIZOP**H**RENIA
THOROUG**H**GOING
UNDERAC**H**IEVER
WOOLGAT**H**ERING
APPROPR**I**ATION
COLLOQU**I**ALISM
COMMERC**I**ALISM
COMMERC**I**ALIZE
CONFECT**I**ONERY
CONTORT**I**ONIST
DISPASS**I**ONATE
EXHIBIT**I**ONISM
EXPEDIT**I**ONARY
EXPRESS**I**ONISM
GENERAL**I**SSIMO
GEOSTAT**I**ONARY
HYPERCR**I**TICAL
IMPRACT**I**CABLE
IMPRESS**I**ONISM
IMPRESS**I**ONIST
INCONSP**I**CUOUS
INDEFAT**I**GABLE
INDESCR**I**BABLE
INDUSTR**I**ALIST
INDUSTR**I**ALIZE
INTRANS**I**GENCE
IRRECLA**I**MABLE
LACKADA**I**SICAL
PERFECT**I**ONIST
PERPEND**I**CULAR
PHOTOEM**I**SSION
PROJECT**I**ONIST
PRONUNC**I**ATION
PROTECT**I**ONIST
REVOLUT**I**ONARY
REVOLUT**I**ONIST
REVOLUT**I**ONIZE
SOPHIST**I**CATED
SUBDISC**I**PLINE
SURREPT**I**TIOUS
TRANSCR**I**PTION
UNQUEST**I**ONING
ANTIPOL**L**UTION
CONFABU**L**ATION
CONSTEL**L**ATION
COSMETO**L**OGIST
ELECTRO**L**OGIST
EXTRAGA**L**ACTIC
INTERCU**L**TURAL
INTERGA**L**ACTIC
KAFFEEK**L**ATSCH
MACHICO**L**ATION
MONONUC**L**EOSIS
OVERQUA**L**IFIED
PARALLE**L**OGRAM
PARTICU**L**ARIZE
QUADRUP**L**ICATE
QUINTUP**L**ICATE
STRANGU**L**ATION
SULFANI**L**AMIDE
THERMOP**L**ASTIC
TRANSAT**L**ANTIC
UNINTEL**L**IGENT
CONCERT**M**ASTER
DECONTA**M**INATE
ELECTRO**M**AGNET
INDETER**M**INATE
MICROCO**M**PUTER
OPHTHAL**M**OLOGY
PATERFA**M**ILIAS
QUARTER**M**ASTER
SCANDAL**M**ONGER
SEMIPER**M**EABLE
SUPERCO**M**PUTER
SUPERNU**M**ERARY
UNCIRCU**M**CISED
ACCOMPA**N**IMENT
AMNIOCE**N**TESIS
ARCHIMA**N**DRITE
CONCATE**N**ATION
CONSCIE**N**TIOUS
CONSTER**N**ATION
DETERMI**N**ATION
DIFFERE**N**TIATE
EXCOMMU**N**ICATE
GEOCHRO**N**OLOGY
HALLUCI**N**ATION
HYDRODY**N**AMICS
INCOMMU**N**ICADO
INCONVE**N**IENCE
INDISPE**N**SABLE
IRRESPO**N**SIBLE
MALADMI**N**ISTER
MISCEGE**N**ATION
PEREGRI**N**ATION
PRIMOGE**N**ITURE
PUSILLA**N**IMOUS
QUESTIO**N**NAIRE
RATIOCI**N**ATION
REINCAR**N**ATION
REPREHE**N**SIBLE
ROENTGE**N**OLOGY
UNACCOU**N**TABLE
UNPRETE**N**TIOUS
UNWARRA**N**TABLE
VOCATIO**N**ALISM
ACCELER**O**METER
BACTERI**O**PHAGE
CINEMAT**O**GRAPH
CORRESP**O**NDENT
DISPROP**O**RTION
EXCEPTI**O**NABLE
MONOCHR**O**MATIC
NONCONF**O**RMIST
ORTHOND**O**NTICS
PHARMAC**O**POEIA
PROFESS**O**RIATE
PSYCHOS**O**MATIC
SANCTIM**O**NIOUS
SEMIAUT**O**MATIC
TABLESP**O**ONFUL
THENCEF**O**RWARD
UNCEREM**O**NIOUS
UNDERCL**O**THING
UNMENTI**O**NABLE
VENTRIL**O**QUISM
HYDROCE**P**HALUS
IMPERCE**P**TIBLE
INCORRU**P**TIBLE
METAMOR**P**HOSIS
PREOCCU**P**ATION
UNACCOM**P**ANIED
UNDEREM**P**LOYED
ACCULTU**R**ATION
ADVENTU**R**ESOME
BLOODCU**R**DLING
COMMEMO**R**ATIVE
CONCENT**R**ATION
CONFEDE**R**ATION
CONFIGU**R**ATION
CONFLAG**R**ATION
CONSIDE**R**ATION
DEMONST**R**ATIVE
DISINTE**R**ESTED
GENITOU**R**INARY
GONADOT**R**OPHIC
GONADOT**R**OPHIN
HERMAPH**R**ODITE
IMPERTU**R**BABLE
INSUPPO**R**TABLE
INTERMA**R**RIAGE
INTERPE**R**SONAL
MISUNDE**R**STAND
NONINTE**R**LACED
PARAPHE**R**NALIA
PHENOBA**R**BITAL
POSTOPE**R**ATIVE
STRIKEB**R**EAKER
UNCOMFO**R**TABLE
UNDERCA**R**RIAGE
UNINTER**R**UPTED
ADVERTI**S**EMENT
ANTIPER**S**ONNEL
CONCUPI**S**CENCE
EFFLORE**S**CENCE
ESTABLI**S**HMENT
IMPERMI**S**SIBLE
INCOMBU**S**TIBLE
INCONTE**S**TABLE
INEXHAU**S**TIBLE
INEXPRE**S**SIBLE
INFLORE**S**CENCE
INTRAMU**S**CULAR
IRREPRE**S**SIBLE
MAGNETO**S**PHERE
NONRESI**S**TANCE
OVERSUB**S**CRIBE
RECRUDE**S**CENCE
THUNDER**S**HOWER
THUNDER**S**TRUCK
UNNECES**S**ARILY
WHITHER**S**OEVER
ADMINIS**T**RATOR
AFFORES**T**ATION
ANTIFER**T**ILITY
ANTIHIS**T**AMINE
ARGUMEN**T**ATION
ARGUMEN**T**ATIVE
AUTHORI**T**ARIAN
AUTHORI**T**ATIVE
CHRYSAN**T**HEMUM
ELEPHAN**T**IASIS
FRAGMEN**T**ATION
GUBERNA**T**ORIAL
INTERNA**T**IONAL
MANIFES**T**ATION
MULTINA**T**IONAL
PRECIPI**T**ATION
PROCRAS**T**INATE
PROGNOS**T**ICATE
RADIOAC**T**IVITY
SUPRANA**T**IONAL
TRANSIS**T**ORIZE
TRANSNA**T**IONAL
UNCONDI**T**IONAL
UNCONDI**T**IONED
UNDERES**T**IMATE
UNFORGE**T**TABLE
UNINTEN**T**IONAL
VALEDIC**T**ORIAN
BACCALA**U**REATE
COMMENS**U**RABLE
CONCEPT**U**ALIZE
CONSANG**U**INITY
DISTING**U**ISHED
GRANDDA**U**GHTER
INDIVID**U**ALISM
INDIVID**U**ALIST
INDIVID**U**ALITY
INDIVID**U**ALIZE
JURISPR**U**DENCE
SUPERAB**U**NDANT
THERMON**U**CLEAR
INSECTI**V**OROUS
COUNTER**W**EIGHT
FEATHER**W**EIGHT
HUNDRED**W**EIGHT
MONOCOT**Y**LEDON
NITROGL**Y**CERIN

## 9th Letter

ACCOMMOD**A**TING
ACCOMMOD**A**TION
ACCULTUR**A**TION
AFFOREST**A**TION
ANTIHIST**A**MINE
APPROPRI**A**TION
ARGUMENT**A**TION
ARGUMENT**A**TIVE
AUTHORIT**A**RIAN
AUTHORIT**A**TIVE
BOUILLAB**A**ISSE
BROKENHE**A**RTED
CERTIFIC**A**TION
COLLOQUI**A**LISM
COMMEMOR**A**TIVE
COMMERCI**A**LISM
COMMERCI**A**LIZE
COMMUNIC**A**TION
CONCATEN**A**TION
CONCENTR**A**TION
CONCEPTU**A**LIZE
CONCERTM**A**STER
CONFABUL**A**TION
CONFEDER**A**TION
CONFIGUR**A**TION
CONFLAGR**A**TION
CONSIDER**A**TION
CONSTELL**A**TION
CONSTERN**A**TION
DEMONSTR**A**TIVE
DETERMIN**A**TION
ELECTROM**A**GNET
EXTRAGAL**A**CTIC
FRAGMENT**A**TION
HALLUCIN**A**TION
HEARTBRE**A**KING
HOUSEBRE**A**KING
HYDRODYN**A**MICS
INDIVIDU**A**LISM
INDIVIDU**A**LIST
INDIVIDU**A**LITY
INDIVIDU**A**LIZE
INDUSTRI**A**LIST
INDUSTRI**A**LIZE
INTERGAL**A**CTIC
INTERROG**A**TIVE
INTERROG**A**TORY
JOLLIFIC**A**TION
JUSTIFIC**A**TION
KAFFEEKL**A**TSCH
MACHICOL**A**TION
MANIFEST**A**TION
MICROORG**A**NISM
MISALLOC**A**TION
MISCEGEN**A**TION

NITRIFICATION
OLEOMARGARINE
PARTICULARIZE
PEREGRINATION
POSTOPERATIVE
PRECIPITATION
PREOCCUPATION
PRONUNCIATION
QUALIFICATION
QUARTERMASTER
RATIOCINATION
REINCARNATION
SCHOOLTEACHER
SPECIFICATION
STRANGULATION
SULFANILAMIDE
SYLLABICATION
TENDERHEARTED
THERMOPLASTIC
TRANSATLANTIC
UNACCOMPANIED
UNNECESSARILY
VERSIFICATION
VOCATIONALISM
IMPERTURBABLE
INDESCRIBABLE
PHENOBARBITAL
CONCUPISCENCE
EFFLORESCENCE
HYDROELECTRIC
IMPRACTICABLE
INCONSPICUOUS
INFLORESCENCE
INTRAMUSCULAR
INTROSPECTION
NITROGLYCERIN
OVERSUBSCRIBE
PERPENDICULAR
PHOTOELECTRIC
PHOTOELECTRON
RECRUDESCENCE
SOPHISTICATED
THERMONUCLEAR
TONSILLECTOMY
TURBOELECTRIC
UNCIRCUMCISED
ARCHIMANDRITE
BIODEGRADABLE
BLOODCURDLING
JURISPRUDENCE
UNDERGRADUATE
ADVENTURESOME
ADVERTISEMENT
CARBONIFEROUS
COUNTERWEIGHT
DEHYDROGENATE
DISINTERESTED

FEATHERWEIGHT
HUNDREDWEIGHT
INCONSIDERATE
IRREPLACEABLE
KNOWLEDGEABLE
MONONUCLEOSIS
PHYSIOTHERAPY
PSYCHOTHERAPY
PRONOUNCEMENT
RAPPROCHEMENT
SEMIPERMEABLE
STRIKEBREAKER
SUPERNUMERARY
UNPRECEDENTED
WOOLGATHERING
CINEMATOGRAPH
GRANDDAUGHTER
INDEFATIGABLE
INTRANSIGENCE
THOROUGHGOING
BOARDINGHOUSE
CHRYSANTHEMUM
CLEARINGHOUSE
COUNTINGHOUSE
ESTABLISHMENT
HYDROCEPHALUS
METAMORPHOSIS
THUNDERSHOWER
UNIMPEACHABLE
ACCOMPANIMENT
ANTIFERTILITY
CONSANGUINITY
DECONTAMINATE
DISTINGUISHED
ELEPHANTIASIS
EXCOMMUNICATE
EXTRAORDINARY
GENITOURINARY
INAPPRECIABLE
INCOMMUNICADO
INCONVENIENCE
INDETERMINATE
INSUBORDINATE
INTERNATIONAL
MALADMINISTER
MULTINATIONAL
OVERQUALIFIED
PATERFAMILIAS
PRIMOGENITURE
PROCRASTINATE
PROGNOSTICATE
PUSILLANIMOUS
QUADRUPLICATE
QUINTUPLICATE
RADIOACTIVITY
SUPRANATIONAL
TRANSNATIONAL

UNCONDITIONAL
UNCONDITIONED
UNDERACHIEVER
UNDERESTIMATE
UNINTELLIGENT
UNINTENTIONAL
MONOCOTYLEDON
NONINTERLACED
POLIOMYELITIS
UNDEREMPLOYED
ACCELEROMETER
AGGIORNAMENTO
IRRECLAIMABLE
MONOCHROMATIC
PETROCHEMICAL
PHOTOCHEMICAL
PSYCHOSOMATIC
SEMIAUTOMATIC
COMPLIMENTARY
CONSEQUENTIAL
CORRESPONDENT
EUROPOCENTRIC
EXCEPTIONABLE
FERROMAGNETIC
GRANTSMANSHIP
HETEROGENEOUS
INSTANTANEOUS
INSUBSTANTIAL
MISCELLANEOUS
ORTHONDONTICS
PARAPHERNALIA
QUESTIONNAIRE
SANCTIMONIOUS
SUPERABUNDANT
TERCENTENNIAL
UNCEREMONIOUS
UNDERSTANDING
UNMENTIONABLE
UNSUBSTANTIAL
ACETYLCHOLINE
ANTIPERSONNEL
AUTOCHTHONOUS
CONFECTIONERY
CONTORTIONIST
COSMETOLOGIST
DAGUERREOTYPE
DISPASSIONATE
ELECTROLOGIST
EXHIBITIONISM
EXPEDITIONARY
EXPRESSIONISM
GEOCHRONOLOGY
GEOMORPHOLOGY
GEOSTATIONARY
GONADOTROPHIC
GONADOTROPHIN
GUBERNATORIAL

HERMAPHRODITE
IMPRESSIONISM
IMPRESSIONIST
INSECTIVOROUS
OPHTHALMOLOGY
PARALLELOGRAM
PERFECTIONIST
PROJECTIONIST
PROTECTIONIST
REVOLUTIONARY
REVOLUTIONIST
REVOLUTIONIZE
ROENTGENOLOGY
SCANDALMONGER
STREPTOCOCCUS
TABLESPOONFUL
TRANSISTORIZE
UNQUESTIONING
VALEDICTORIAN
WHITHERSOEVER
BACTERIOPHAGE
CONTRACEPTION
MAGNETOSPHERE
MICROCOMPUTER
PHARMACOPOEIA
SUBDISCIPLINE
SUPERCOMPUTER
TRANSCRIPTION
VENTRILOQUISM
ADMINISTRATOR
ANTILOGARITHM
AUTOBIOGRAPHY
BACCALAUREATE
CIRCUMFERENCE
COMMENSURABLE
CONFRATERNITY
CONTAINERSHIP
DISPROPORTION
INTERMARRIAGE
IRRECOVERABLE
NONCONFORMIST
PROFESSORIATE
QUADRIPARTITE
SCHIZOPHRENIA
THENCEFORWARD
UNADULTERATED
UNCONQUERABLE
UNDERCARRIAGE
CHRISTMASTIDE
GENERALISSIMO
IMPERMISSIBLE
INDISPENSABLE
INEXPRESSIBLE
INFINITESIMAL
INTERPERSONAL
IRREPRESSIBLE
IRRESPONSIBLE

LACKADAISICAL
LAUGHINGSTOCK
MISUNDERSTAND
PHOTOEMISSION
PREPOSSESSING
PREPOSSESSION
REPREHENSIBLE
TORTOISESHELL
UNDERCLASSMAN
UPPERCLASSMAN
AMNIOCENTESIS
ARCHITECTONIC
CONSCIENTIOUS
COUNTERATTACK
DIFFERENTIATE
HYPERCRITICAL
IMPERCEPTIBLE
INCOMBUSTIBLE
INCONTESTABLE
INCORRUPTIBLE
INEXHAUSTIBLE
INSUPPORTABLE
INTERCULTURAL
NONRESISTANCE
PRETERNATURAL
QUADRILATERAL
SURREPTITIOUS
THUNDERSTRUCK
UNACCOUNTABLE
UNCOMFORTABLE
UNDERCLOTHING
UNFORGETTABLE
UNPREDICTABLE
UNPRETENTIOUS
UNWARRANTABLE
ANTICOAGULANT
ANTIPOLLUTION
CIRCUMABULATE
HYPERDOCUMENT
INTERLOCUTORY
SEMICONDUCTOR
UNINTERRUPTED
IRRETRIEVABLE

## 10TH LETTER

ADMINISTRATOR
AUTOBIOGRAPHY
BIODEGRADABLE
COMMENSURABLE
ELEPHANTIASIS
EXCEPTIONABLE
HYDROCEPHALUS
IMPERTURBABLE
IMPRACTICABLE

INAPPRECIABLE
INCONTESTABLE
INDEFATIGABLE
INDESCRIBABLE
INDISPENSABLE
INSUPPORTABLE
IRRECLAIMABLE
IRRECOVERABLE
IRREPLACEABLE
IRRETRIEVABLE
KNOWLEDGEABLE
MONOCHROMATIC
NONINTERLACED
NONRESISTANCE
PARAPHERNALIA
PSYCHOSOMATIC
QUESTIONNAIRE
SEMIAUTOMATIC
SEMIPERMEABLE
SOPHISTICATED
STRIKEBREAKER
UNACCOUNTABLE
UNADULTERATED
UNCOMFORTABLE
UNCONQUERABLE
UNFORGETTABLE
UNIMPEACHABLE
UNMENTIONABLE
UNPREDICTABLE
UNWARRANTABLE
EXCOMMUNICATE
EXTRAGALACTIC
INCOMMUNICADO
INTERGALACTIC
PROGNOSTICATE
QUADRUPLICATE
QUINTUPLICATE
SCHOOLTEACHER
SEMICONDUCTOR
STREPTOCOCCUS
CORRESPONDENT
HERMAPHRODITE
SUPERABUNDANT
UNDERSTANDING
ACCELEROMETER
AGGIORNAMENTO
AMNIOCENTESIS
BACCALAUREATE
CHRYSANTHEMUM
CIRCUMFERENCE
CONCUPISCENCE
EFFLORESCENCE
FERROMAGNETIC
HETEROGENEOUS
INCONVENIENCE
INFLORESCENCE
INSTANTANEOUS

INTRANSIGENCE
JURISPRUDENCE
MISCELLANEOUS
MONOCOTYLEDON
NITROGLYCERIN
QUADRILATERAL
RECRUDESCENCE
SCHIZOPHRENIA
UNDERACHIEVER
WHITHERSOEVER
OVERQUALIFIED
COSMETOLOGIST
ELECTROLOGIST
ELECTROMAGNET
PARALLELOGRAM
UNINTELLIGENT
BACTERIOPHAGE
GRANDDAUGHTER
MAGNETOSPHERE
TORTOISESHELL
UNDERCLOTHING
ANTILOGARITHM
BOUILLABAISSE
CONSCIENTIOUS
COUNTERWEIGHT
DIFFERENTIATE
FEATHERWEIGHT
HUNDREDWEIGHT
HYPERCRITICAL
IMPERCEPTIBLE
IMPERMISSIBLE
INCOMBUSTIBLE
INCORRUPTIBLE
INEXHAUSTIBLE
INEXPRESSIBLE
INFINITESIMAL
INTERMARRIAGE
IRREPRESSIBLE
IRRESPONSIBLE
LACKADAISICAL
PETROCHEMICAL
PHENOBARBITAL
PHOTOCHEMICAL
POLIOMYELITIS
PROFESSORIATE
REPREHENSIBLE
SANCTIMONIOUS
SURREPTITIOUS
UNCEREMONIOUS
UNCIRCUMCISED
UNDERCARRIAGE
UNPRETENTIOUS
HEARTBREAKING
HOUSEBREAKING
ACETYLCHOLINE
ANTICOAGULANT
ANTIFERTILITY

BLOODCURDLING
CIRCUMABULATE
COLLOQUIALISM
COMMERCIALISM
COMMERCIALIZE
CONCEPTUALIZE
GEOCHRONOLOGY
GEOMORPHOLOGY
INDIVIDUALISM
INDIVIDUALIST
INDIVIDUALITY
INDIVIDUALIZE
OPHTHALMOLOGY
INDUSTRIALIST
INDUSTRIALIZE
PATERFAMILIAS
ROENTGENOLOGY
SUBDISCIPLINE
THERMONUCLEAR
VOCATIONALISM
ACCOMPANIMENT
ADVERTISEMENT
ANTIHISTAMINE
ESTABLISHMENT
HYDRODYNAMICS
HYPERDOCUMENT
NONCONFORMIST
PRONOUNCEMENT
PUSILLANIMOUS
RAPPROCHEMENT
SULFANILAMIDE
UNDERESTIMATE
ANTIPERSONNEL
AUTOCHTHONOUS
CONFECTIONERY
CONFRATERNITY
CONSANGUINITY
CONTORTIONIST
DECONTAMINATE
DEHYDROGENATE
DISPASSIONATE
EXHIBITIONISM
EXPEDITIONARY
EXPRESSIONISM
EXTRAORDINARY
GENITOURINARY
GEOSTATIONARY
IMPRESSIONISM
IMPRESSIONIST
INDETERMINATE
INSUBORDINATE
MICROORGANISM
PERFECTIONIST
PROCRASTINATE
PROJECTIONIST
PROTECTIONIST
REVOLUTIONARY

REVOLUTIONIST
REVOLUTIONIZE
SCANDALMONGER
TABLESPOONFUL
TERCENTENNIAL
TRANSATLANTIC
UNACCOMPANIED
UNPRECEDENTED
UNQUESTIONING
ARCHITECTONIC
BOARDINGHOUSE
CLEARINGHOUSE
COUNTINGHOUSE
INTERNATIONAL
INTERPERSONAL
METAMORPHOSIS
MONONUCLEOSIS
MULTINATIONAL
PHARMACOPOEIA
SUPRANATIONAL
THOROUGHGOING
THUNDERSHOWER
TRANSNATIONAL
UNCONDITIONAL
UNCONDITIONED
UNDEREMPLOYED
UNINTENTIONAL
GONADOTROPHIC
GONADOTROPHIN
UNINTERRUPTED
ARCHIMANDRITE
AUTHORITARIAN
BROKENHEARTED
CARBONIFEROUS
CINEMATOGRAPH
GUBERNATORIAL
INCONSIDERATE
INSECTIVOROUS
OLEOMARGARINE
OVERSUBSCRIBE
PARTICULARIZE
PHYSIOTHERAPY
PSYCHOTHERAPY
SUPERNUMERARY
TENDERHEARTED
THUNDERSTRUCK
TRANSISTORIZE
UNNECESSARILY
VALEDICTORIAN
WOOLGATHERING
ADVENTURESOME
CONCERTMASTER
CONTAINERSHIP
DISINTERESTED
DISTINGUISHED
GENERALISSIMO
GRANTSMANSHIP

MALADMINISTER
PHOTOEMISSION
PREPOSSESSING
PREPOSSESSION
QUARTERMASTER
THERMOPLASTIC
UNDERCLASSMAN
UPPERCLASSMAN
ACCOMMODATING
ACCOMMODATION
ACCULTURATION
AFFORESTATION
ANTIPOLLUTION
APPROPRIATION
ARGUMENTATION
ARGUMENTATIVE
AUTHORITATIVE
CERTIFICATION
CHRISTMASTIDE
COMMEMORATIVE
COMMUNICATION
COMPLIMENTARY
CONCATENATION
CONCENTRATION
CONFABULATION
CONFEDERATION
CONFIGURATION
CONFLAGRATION
CONSEQUENTIAL
CONSIDERATION
CONSTELLATION
CONSTERNATION
CONTRACEPTION
COUNTERATTACK
DAGUERREOTYPE
DEMONSTRATIVE
DETERMINATION
DISPROPORTION
EUROPOCENTRIC
FRAGMENTATION
HALLUCINATION
HYDROELECTRIC
INSUBSTANTIAL
INTERLOCUTORY
INTERROGATIVE
INTERROGATORY
INTROSPECTION
JOLLIFICATION
JUSTIFICATION
KAFFEEKLATSCH
LAUGHINGSTOCK
MACHICOLATION
MANIFESTATION
MISALLOCATION
MISCEGENATION
MISUNDERSTAND
NITRIFICATION

ORTHONDONTICS
PEREGRINATION
PHOTOELECTRIC
PHOTOELECTRON
POSTOPERATIVE
PRECIPITATION
PREOCCUPATION
PRIMOGENITURE
PRONUNCIATION
QUADRIPARTITE
QUALIFICATION
RATIOCINATION
REINCARNATION
SPECIFICATION
STRANGULATION
SYLLABICATION
TONSILLECTOMY
TRANSCRIPTION
TURBOELECTRIC
UNSUBSTANTIAL
VERSIFICATION
INCONSPICUOUS
INTERCULTURAL
INTRAMUSCULAR
MICROCOMPUTER
PERPENDICULAR
PRETERNATURAL
SUPERCOMPUTER
UNDERGRADUATE
VENTRILOQUISM
RADIOACTIVITY
THENCEFORWARD

## 11th Letter

ANTICOAGULANT
BACCALAUREATE
BACTERIOPHAGE
CINEMATOGRAPH
CIRCUMABULATE
COMPLIMENTARY
COUNTERATTACK
DECONTAMINATE
DEHYDROGENATE
DIFFERENTIATE
DISPASSIONATE
EXCOMMUNICATE
EXPEDITIONARY
EXTRAORDINARY
GENITOURINARY
GEOSTATIONARY
INCOMMUNICADO
INCONSIDERATE
INDETERMINATE
INSUBORDINATE

INTERMARRIAGE
MISUNDERSTAND
PHYSIOTHERAPY
PSYCHOTHERAPY
PROCRASTINATE
PROFESSORIATE
PROGNOSTICATE
QUADRUPLICATE
QUINTUPLICATE
REVOLUTIONARY
SUPERABUNDANT
SUPERNUMERARY
THENCEFORWARD
UNDERCARRIAGE
UNDERESTIMATE
UNDERGRADUATE
BIODEGRADABLE
COMMENSURABLE
EXCEPTIONABLE
IMPERCEPTIBLE
IMPERMISSIBLE
IMPERTURBABLE
IMPRACTICABLE
INAPPRECIABLE
INCOMBUSTIBLE
INCONTESTABLE
INCORRUPTIBLE
INDEFATIGABLE
INDESCRIBABLE
INDISPENSABLE
INEXHAUSTIBLE
INEXPRESSIBLE
INSUPPORTABLE
IRRECLAIMABLE
IRRECOVERABLE
IRREPLACEABLE
IRREPRESSIBLE
IRRESPONSIBLE
IRRETRIEVABLE
KNOWLEDGEABLE
REPREHENSIBLE
SEMIPERMEABLE
UNACCOUNTABLE
UNCOMFORTABLE
UNCONQUERABLE
UNFORGETTABLE
UNIMPEACHABLE
UNMENTIONABLE
UNPREDICTABLE
UNWARRANTABLE
HYPERCRITICAL
LACKADAISICAL
NONINTERLACED
PETROCHEMICAL
PHOTOCHEMICAL
STREPTOCOCCUS
MONOCOTYLEDON

ACCOMPANIMENT
ADVERTISEMENT
CONFECTIONERY
CORRESPONDENT
ESTABLISHMENT
HYPERDOCUMENT
MAGNETOSPHERE
PHARMACOPOEIA
PRONOUNCEMENT
RAPPROCHEMENT
THERMONUCLEAR
TORTOISESHELL
UNINTELLIGENT
TABLESPOONFUL
COUNTERWEIGHT
FEATHERWEIGHT
HUNDREDWEIGHT
SCANDALMONGER
CONTAINERSHIP
DISTINGUISHED
GONADOTROPHIC
GONADOTROPHIN
GRANTSMANSHIP
SCHOOLTEACHER
ACCOMMODATING
ACCOMMODATION
ACCULTURATION
ACETYLCHOLINE
AFFORESTATION
ANTIFERTILITY
ANTIHISTAMINE
ANTIPOLLUTION
APPROPRIATION
ARCHIMANDRITE
ARGUMENTATION
ARGUMENTATIVE
AUTHORITARIAN
AUTHORITATIVE
BLOODCURDLING
CERTIFICATION
CHRISTMASTIDE
COLLOQUIALISM
COMMEMORATIVE
COMMERCIALISM
COMMERCIALIZE
COMMUNICATION
CONCATENATION
CONCENTRATION
CONCEPTUALIZE
CONFABULATION
CONFEDERATION
CONFIGURATION
CONFLAGRATION
CONFRATERNITY
CONSANGUINITY
CONSEQUENTIAL
CONSIDERATION
CONSTELLATION
CONSTERNATION
CONTORTIONIST
CONTRACEPTION
COSMETOLOGIST
DEMONSTRATIVE
DETERMINATION
DISPROPORTION
ELECTROLOGIST
EXHIBITIONISM
EXPRESSIONISM
FRAGMENTATION
GENERALISSIMO
GUBERNATORIAL
HALLUCINATION
HEARTBREAKING
HERMAPHRODITE
HOUSEBREAKING
HYDRODYNAMICS
IMPRESSIONISM
IMPRESSIONIST
INDIVIDUALISM
INDIVIDUALIST
INDIVIDUALITY
INDIVIDUALIZE
INDUSTRIALIST
INDUSTRIALIZE
INSUBSTANTIAL
INTERROGATIVE
INTROSPECTION
JOLLIFICATION
JUSTIFICATION
MACHICOLATION
MANIFESTATION
MICROORGANISM
MISALLOCATION
MISCEGENATION
NITRIFICATION
NONCONFORMIST
OLEOMARGARINE
ORTHONDONTICS
OVERQUALIFIED
OVERSUBSCRIBE
PARTICULARIZE
PATERFAMILIAS
PEREGRINATION
PERFECTIONIST
PHOTOEMISSION
POSTOPERATIVE
PRECIPITATION
PREOCCUPATION
PREPOSSESSING
PREPOSSESSION
PROJECTIONIST
PRONUNCIATION
PROTECTIONIST
QUADRIPARTITE
QUALIFICATION
QUESTIONNAIRE
RADIOACTIVITY
RATIOCINATION
REINCARNATION
REVOLUTIONIST
REVOLUTIONIZE
SPECIFICATION
STRANGULATION
SUBDISCIPLINE
SULFANILAMIDE
SYLLABICATION
TERCENTENNIAL
THOROUGHGOING
TRANSCRIPTION
TRANSISTORIZE
UNACCOMPANIED
UNDERCLOTHING
UNDERSTANDING
UNNECESSARILY
UNQUESTIONING
UNSUBSTANTIAL
VALEDICTORIAN
VENTRILOQUISM
VERSIFICATION
VOCATIONALISM
WOOLGATHERING
STRIKEBREAKER
HYDROCEPHALUS
INTRAMUSCULAR
PARAPHERNALIA
PERPENDICULAR
CHRYSANTHEMUM
INFINITESIMAL
UNDERCLASSMAN
UPPERCLASSMAN
AGGIORNAMENTO
ANTIPERSONNEL
ARCHITECTONIC
CIRCUMFERENCE
CONCUPISCENCE
EFFLORESCENCE
ELECTROMAGNET
INCONVENIENCE
INFLORESCENCE
INTERNATIONAL
INTERPERSONAL
INTRANSIGENCE
JURISPRUDENCE
MULTINATIONAL
NONRESISTANCE
RECRUDESCENCE
SCHIZOPHRENIA
SUPRANATIONAL
TRANSNATIONAL
UNCONDITIONAL
UNCONDITIONED
UNINTENTIONAL
ADVENTURESOME
AUTOCHTHONOUS
CARBONIFEROUS
CONSCIENTIOUS
GEOCHRONOLOGY
GEOMORPHOLOGY
HETEROGENEOUS
INCONSPICUOUS
INSECTIVOROUS
INSTANTANEOUS
INTERLOCUTORY
INTERROGATORY
LAUGHINGSTOCK
MISCELLANEOUS
OPHTHALMOLOGY
PUSILLANIMOUS
ROENTGENOLOGY
SANCTIMONIOUS
SURREPTITIOUS
TONSILLECTOMY
UNCEREMONIOUS
UNPRETENTIOUS
AUTOBIOGRAPHY
EUROPOCENTRIC
HYDROELECTRIC
INTERCULTURAL
NITROGLYCERIN
PARALLELOGRAM
PHOTOELECTRIC
PHOTOELECTRON
PRETERNATURAL
QUADRILATERAL
TURBOELECTRIC
AMNIOCENTESIS
BOUILLABAISSE
ELEPHANTIASIS
KAFFEEKLATSCH
METAMORPHOSIS
MONONUCLEOSIS
UNCIRCUMCISED
ACCELEROMETER
ADMINISTRATOR
ANTILOGARITHM
BROKENHEARTED
CONCERTMASTER
DISINTERESTED
EXTRAGALACTIC
FERROMAGNETIC
GRANDDAUGHTER
INTERGALACTIC
MALADMINISTER
MICROCOMPUTER
MONOCHROMATIC
PHENOBARBITAL
POLIOMYELITIS
PSYCHOSOMATIC
QUARTERMASTER
SEMIAUTOMATIC
SEMICONDUCTOR
SOPHISTICATED
SUPERCOMPUTER
TENDERHEARTED
THERMOPLASTIC
TRANSATLANTIC
UNADULTERATED
UNINTERRUPTED
UNPRECEDENTED
BOARDINGHOUSE
CLEARINGHOUSE
COUNTINGHOUSE
PRIMOGENITURE
THUNDERSTRUCK
UNDERACHIEVER
WHITHERSOEVER
THUNDERSHOWER
DAGUERREOTYPE
UNDEREMPLOYED

## 12th Letter

AUTHORITARIAN
CONSEQUENTIAL
GUBERNATORIAL
HYPERCRITICAL
INFINITESIMAL
INSUBSTANTIAL
INTERCULTURAL
INTERNATIONAL
INTERPERSONAL
INTRAMUSCULAR
LACKADAISICAL
MULTINATIONAL
PARALLELOGRAM
PATERFAMILIAS
PERPENDICULAR
PETROCHEMICAL
PHENOBARBITAL
PHOTOCHEMICAL
PRETERNATURAL
QUADRILATERAL
SUPRANATIONAL
TERCENTENNIAL
THERMONUCLEAR
TRANSNATIONAL
UNCONDITIONAL
UNDERCLASSMAN
UNINTENTIONAL
UNSUBSTANTIAL
UPPERCLASSMAN
VALEDICTORIAN
OVERSUBSCRIBE
CIRCUMFERENCE
CONCUPISCENCE
COUNTERATTACK
EFFLORESCENCE
HYDRODYNAMICS
INCONVENIENCE
INFLORESCENCE
INTRANSIGENCE
JURISPRUDENCE
KAFFEEKLATSCH
LAUGHINGSTOCK
NONRESISTANCE
ORTHONDONTICS
RECRUDESCENCE
THUNDERSTRUCK
CHRISTMASTIDE
INCOMMUNICADO
SULFANILAMIDE
ACCELEROMETER
ANTIPERSONNEL
BROKENHEARTED
CONCERTMASTER
DISINTERESTED
DISTINGUISHED
ELECTROMAGNET
GRANDDAUGHTER
MALADMINISTER
MICROCOMPUTER
NONINTERLACED
OVERQUALIFIED
QUARTERMASTER
SCANDALMONGER
SCHOOLTEACHER
SOPHISTICATED
STRIKEBREAKER
SUPERCOMPUTER
TENDERHEARTED
THUNDERSHOWER
UNACCOMPANIED
UNADULTERATED
UNCIRCUMCISED
UNCONDITIONED
UNDERACHIEVER
UNDEREMPLOYED
UNINTERRUPTED
UNPRECEDENTED
WHITHERSOEVER
BACTERIOPHAGE
GEOCHRONOLOGY
GEOMORPHOLOGY
INTERMARRIAGE
OPHTHALMOLOGY
ROENTGENOLOGY
UNDERCARRIAGE
ANTILOGARITHM
AUTOBIOGRAPHY
COUNTERWEIGHT

FEATHERWEIGHT
HUNDREDWEIGHT
AMNIOCENTESIS
ARCHITECTONIC
CONTAINERSHIP
ELEPHANTIASIS
EUROPOCENTRIC
EXTRAGALACTIC
FERROMAGNETIC
GONADOTROPHIC
GONADOTROPHIN
GRANTSMANSHIP
HYDROELECTRIC
INTERGALACTIC
METAMORPHOSIS
MONOCHROMATIC
MONONUCLEOSIS
NITROGLYCERIN
PARAPHERNALIA
PHARMACOPOEIA
PHOTOELECTRIC
POLIOMYELITIS
PSYCHOSOMATIC
SCHIZOPHRENIA
SEMIAUTOMATIC
THERMOPLASTIC
TRANSATLANTIC
TURBOELECTRIC
BIODEGRADABLE
COMMENSURABLE
EXCEPTIONABLE
IMPERCEPTIBLE
IMPERMISSIBLE
IMPERTURBABLE
IMPRACTICABLE
INAPPRECIABLE
INCOMBUSTIBLE
INCONTESTABLE
INCORRUPTIBLE
INDEFATIGABLE
INDESCRIBABLE
INDISPENSABLE
INEXHAUSTIBLE
INEXPRESSIBLE
INSUPPORTABLE
IRRECLAIMABLE
IRRECOVERABLE
IRREPLACEABLE
IRREPRESSIBLE
IRRESPONSIBLE
IRRETRIEVABLE
KNOWLEDGEABLE
REPREHENSIBLE
SEMIPERMEABLE
TORTOISESHELL
UNACCOUNTABLE
UNCOMFORTABLE
UNCONQUERABLE
UNFORGETTABLE
UNIMPEACHABLE
UNMENTIONABLE
UNNECESSARILY
UNPREDICTABLE
UNWARRANTABLE
ADVENTURESOME
GENERALISSIMO
TONSILLECTOMY
ACCOMMODATING
ACCOMPANIMENT
ACETYLCHOLINE
ADVERTISEMENT
ANTICOAGULANT
ANTIHISTAMINE
BLOODCURDLING
CORRESPONDENT
ESTABLISHMENT
HEARTBREAKING
HOUSEBREAKING
HYPERDOCUMENT
MISUNDERSTAND
OLEOMARGARINE
PREPOSSESSING
PRONOUNCEMENT
RAPPROCHEMENT
SUBDISCIPLINE
SUPERABUNDANT
THOROUGHGOING
UNDERCLOTHING
UNDERSTANDING
UNINTELLIGENT
UNQUESTIONING
WOOLGATHERING
ACCOMMODATION
ACCULTURATION
ADMINISTRATOR
AFFORESTATION
ANTIPOLLUTION
APPROPRIATION
ARGUMENTATION
CERTIFICATION
COMMUNICATION
CONCATENATION
CONCENTRATION
CONFABULATION
CONFEDERATION
CONFIGURATION
CONFLAGRATION
CONSIDERATION
CONSTELLATION
CONSTERNATION
CONTRACEPTION
DETERMINATION
DISPROPORTION
FRAGMENTATION
HALLUCINATION
INTROSPECTION
JOLLIFICATION
JUSTIFICATION
MACHICOLATION
MANIFESTATION
MISALLOCATION
MISCEGENATION
MONOCOTYLEDON
NITRIFICATION
PEREGRINATION
PHOTOELECTRON
PHOTOEMISSION
PRECIPITATION
PREOCCUPATION
PREPOSSESSION
PRONUNCIATION
QUALIFICATION
RATIOCINATION
REINCARNATION
SEMICONDUCTOR
SPECIFICATION
STRANGULATION
SYLLABICATION
TRANSCRIPTION
VERSIFICATION
CINEMATOGRAPH
DAGUERREOTYPE
PHYSIOTHERAPY
PSCHOTHERAPY
COMPLIMENTARY
CONFECTIONERY
EXPEDITIONARY
EXTRAORDINARY
GENITOURINARY
GEOSTATIONARY
INTERLOCUTORY
INTERROGATORY
MAGNETOSPHERE
PRIMOGENITURE
QUESTIONNAIRE
REVOLUTIONARY
SUPERNUMERARY
THENCEFORWARD
BOARDINGHOUSE
BOUILLABAISSE
CLEARINGHOUSE
COLLOQUIALISM
COMMERCIALISM
CONTORTIONIST
COSMETOLOGIST
COUNTINGHOUSE
ELECTROLOGIST
EXHIBITIONISM
EXPRESSIONISM
IMPRESSIONISM
IMPRESSIONIST
INDIVIDUALISM
INDIVIDUALIST
INDUSTRIALIST
MICROORGANISM
NONCONFORMIST
PERFECTIONIST
PROJECTIONIST
PROTECTIONIST
REVOLUTIONIST
VENTRILOQUISM
VOCATIONALISM
AGGIORNAMENTO
ANTIFERTILITY
ARCHIMANDRITE
BACCALAUREATE
CIRCUMABULATE
CONFRATERNITY
CONSANGUINITY
DECONTAMINATE
DEHYDROGENATE
DIFFERENTIATE
DISPASSIONATE
EXCOMMUNICATE
HERMAPHRODITE
INCONSIDERATE
INDETERMINATE
INDIVIDUALITY
INSUBORDINATE
PROCRASTINATE
PROFESSORIATE
PROGNOSTICATE
QUADRIPARTITE
QUADRUPLICATE
QUINTUPLICATE
RADIOACTIVITY
UNDERESTIMATE
UNDERGRADUATE
AUTOCHTHONOUS
CARBONIFEROUS
CHRYSANTHEMUM
CONSCIENTIOUS
HETEROGENEOUS
HYDROCEPHALUS
INCONSPICUOUS
INSECTIVOROUS
INSTANTANEOUS
MISCELLANEOUS
PUSILLANIMOUS
SANCTIMONIOUS
STREPTOCOCCUS
SURREPTITIOUS
TABLESPOONFUL
UNCEREMONIOUS
UNPRETENTIOUS
ARGUMENTATIVE
AUTHORITATIVE
COMMEMORATIVE
DEMONSTRATIVE
INTERROGATIVE
POSTOPERATIVE
COMMERCIALIZE
CONCEPTUALIZE
INDIVIDUALIZE
INDUSTRIALIZE
PARTICULARIZE
REVOLUTIONIZE
TRANSISTORIZE

## 13th Letter

PARAPHERNALIA
PHARMACOPOEIA
SCHIZOPHRENIA
ARCHITECTONIC
EUROPOCENTRIC
EXTRAGALACTIC
FERROMAGNETIC
GONADOTROPHIC
HYDROELECTRIC
INTERGALACTIC
MONOCHROMATIC
PHOTOELECTRIC
PSYCHOSOMATIC
SEMIAUTOMATIC
THERMOPLASTIC
TRANSATLANTIC
TURBOELECTRIC
BROKENHEARTED
DISINTERESTED
DISTINGUISHED
MISUNDERSTAND
NONINTERLACED
OVERQUALIFIED
SOPHISTICATED
TENDERHEARTED
THENCEFORWARD
UNACCOMPANIED
UNADULTERATED
UNCIRCUMCISED
UNCONDITIONED
UNDEREMPLOYED
UNINTERRUPTED
UNPRECEDENTED
ACETYLCHOLINE
ADVENTURESOME
ANTIHISTAMINE
ARCHIMANDRITE
ARGUMENTATIVE
AUTHORITATIVE
BACCALAUREATE
BACTERIOPHAGE
BIODEGRADABLE
BOARDINGHOUSE
BOUILLABAISSE
CHRISTMASTIDE
CIRCUMABULATE
CIRCUMFERENCE
CLEARINGHOUSE
COMMEMORATIVE
COMMENSURABLE
COMMERCIALIZE
CONCEPTUALIZE
CONCUPISCENCE
COUNTINGHOUSE
DAGUERREOTYPE
DECONTAMINATE
DEHYDROGENATE
DEMONSTRATIVE
DIFFERENTIATE
DISPASSIONATE
EFFLORESCENCE
EXCEPTIONABLE
EXCOMMUNICATE
HERMAPHRODITE
IMPERCEPTIBLE
IMPERMISSIBLE
IMPERTURBABLE
IMPRACTICABLE
INAPPRECIABLE
INCOMBUSTIBLE
INCONSIDERATE
INCONTESTABLE
INCONVENIENCE
INCORRUPTIBLE
INDEFATIGABLE
INDESCRIBABLE
INDETERMINATE
INDISPENSABLE
INDIVIDUALIZE
INDUSTRIALIZE
INEXHAUSTIBLE
INEXPRESSIBLE
INFLORESCENCE
INSUBORDINATE
INSUPPORTABLE
INTERMARRIAGE
INTERROGATIVE
INTRANSIGENCE
IRRECLAIMABLE
IRRECOVERABLE
IRREPLACEABLE
IRREPRESSIBLE
IRRESPONSIBLE
IRRETRIEVABLE
JURISPRUDENCE
KNOWLEDGEABLE
MAGNETOSPHERE
NONRESISTANCE
OLEOMARGARINE

OVERSUBSCRIBE
PARTICULARIZE
POSTOPERATIVE
PRIMOGENITURE
PROCRASTINATE
PROFESSORIATE
PROGNOSTICATE
QUADRIPARTITE
QUADRUPLICATE
QUESTIONNAIRE
QUINTUPLICATE
RECRUDESCENCE
REPREHENSIBLE
REVOLUTIONIZE
SEMIPERMEABLE
SUBDISCIPLINE
SULFANILAMIDE
TRANSISTORIZE
UNACCOUNTABLE
UNCOMFORTABLE
UNCONQUERABLE
UNDERCARRIAGE
UNDERESTIMATE
UNDERGRADUATE
UNFORGETTABLE
UNIMPEACHABLE
UNMENTIONABLE
UNPREDICTABLE
UNWARRANTABLE
ACCOMMODATING
BLOODCURDLING
HEARTBREAKING
HOUSEBREAKING
PREPOSSESSING
THOROUGHGOING
UNDERCLOTHING
UNDERSTANDING
UNQUESTIONING
WOOLGATHERING
CINEMATOGRAPH
KAFFEEKLATSCH
COUNTERATTACK
LAUGHINGSTOCK
THUNDERSTRUCK
ANTIPERSONNEL
CONSEQUENTIAL
GUBERNATORIAL
HYPERCRITICAL
INFINITESIMAL
INSUBSTANTIAL
INTERCULTURAL
INTERNATIONAL
INTERPERSONAL
LACKADAISICAL
MULTINATIONAL
PETROCHEMICAL
PHENOBARBITAL
PHOTOCHEMICAL
PRETERNATURAL
QUADRILATERAL
SUPRANATIONAL
TABLESPOONFUL
TERCENTENNIAL
TORTOISESHELL
TRANSNATIONAL
UNCONDITIONAL
UNINTENTIONAL
UNSUBSTANTIAL
ANTILOGARITHM
CHRYSANTHEMUM
COLLOQUIALISM
COMMERCIALISM
EXHIBITIONISM
EXPRESSIONISM
IMPRESSIONISM
INDIVIDUALISM
MICROORGANISM
PARALLELOGRAM
VENTRILOQUISM
VOCATIONALISM
ACCOMMODATION
ACCULTURATION
AFFORESTATION
ANTIPOLLUTION
APPROPRIATION
ARGUMENTATION
AUTHORITARIAN
CERTIFICATION
COMMUNICATION
CONCATENATION
CONCENTRATION
CONFABULATION
CONFEDERATION
CONFIGURATION
CONFLAGRATION
CONSIDERATION
CONSTELLATION
CONSTERNATION
CONTRACEPTION
DETERMINATION
DISPROPORTION
FRAGMENTATION
GONADOTROPHIN
HALLUCINATION
INTROSPECTION
JOLLIFICATION
JUSTIFICATION
MACHICOLATION
MANIFESTATION
MISALLOCATION
MISCEGENATION
MONOCOTYLEDON
NITRIFICATION
NITROGLYCERIN
PEREGRINATION
PHOTOELECTRON
PHOTOEMISSION
PRECIPITATION
PREOCCUPATION
PREPOSSESSION
PRONUNCIATION
QUALIFICATION
RATIOCINATION
REINCARNATION
SPECIFICATION
STRANGULATION
SYLLABICATION
TRANSCRIPTION
UNDERCLASSMAN
UPPERCLASSMAN
VALEDICTORIAN
VERSIFICATION
AGGIORNAMENTO
GENERALISSIMO
INCOMMUNICADO
CONTAINERSHIP
GRANTSMANSHIP
ACCELEROMETER
ADMINISTRATOR
CONCERTMASTER
GRANDDAUGHTER
INTRAMUSCULAR
MALADMINISTER
MICROCOMPUTER
PERPENDICULAR
QUARTERMASTER
SCANDALMONGER
SCHOOLTEACHER
SEMICONDUCTOR
STRIKEBREAKER
SUPERCOMPUTER
THERMONUCLEAR
THUNDERSHOWER
UNDERACHIEVER
WHITHERSOEVER
AMNIOCENTESIS
AUTOCHTHONOUS
CARBONIFEROUS
CONSCIENTIOUS
ELEPHANTIASIS
HETEROGENEOUS
HYDROCEPHALUS
HYDRODYNAMICS
INCONSPICUOUS
INSECTIVOROUS
INSTANTANEOUS
METAMORPHOSIS
MISCELLANEOUS
MONONUCLEOSIS
ORTHONDONTICS
PATERFAMILIAS
POLIOMYELITIS
PUSILLANIMOUS
SANCTIMONIOUS
STREPTOCOCCUS
SURREPTITIOUS
UNCEREMONIOUS
UNPRETENTIOUS
ACCOMPANIMENT
ADVERTISEMENT
ANTICOAGULANT
CONTORTIONIST
CORRESPONDENT
COSMETOLOGIST
COUNTERWEIGHT
ELECTROLOGIST
ELECTROMAGNET
ESTABLISHMENT
FEATHERWEIGHT
HUNDREDWEIGHT
HYPERDOCUMENT
IMPRESSIONIST
INDIVIDUALIST
INDUSTRIALIST
NONCONFORMIST
PERFECTIONIST
PROJECTIONIST
PRONOUNCEMENT
PROTECTIONIST
RAPPROCHEMENT
REVOLUTIONIST
SUPERABUNDANT
UNINTELLIGENT
ANTIFERTILITY
AUTOBIOGRAPHY
COMPLIMENTARY
CONFECTIONERY
CONFRATERNITY
CONSANGUINITY
EXPEDITIONARY
EXTRAORDINARY
GENITOURINARY
GEOCHRONOLOGY
GEOMORPHOLOGY
GEOSTATIONARY
INDIVIDUALITY
INTERLOCUTORY
INTERROGATORY
OPHTHALMOLOGY
PHYSIOTHERAPY
RADIOACTIVITY
PSYCHOTHERAPY
REVOLUTIONARY
ROENTGENOLOGY
SUPERNUMERARY
TONSILLECTOMY
UNNECESSARILY

# 14 LETTER WORDS

**1st Letter**

ACCOMPLISHMENT
ADMINISTRATION
AFOREMENTIONED
ANESTHESIOLOGY
ANTIDEPRESSANT
ANTINEOPLASTIC
ANTIPERSPIRANT
ARCHIEPISCOPAL
ARCHITECTONICS
BUTTERFINGERED
CAPITALIZATION
CARDIOVASCULAR
CHARACTERISTIC
CHEMOSTERILANT
CHICKENHEARTED
CHROMATOGRAPHY
CINEMATOGRAPHY
CIRCUMLOCUTION
CIRCUMNAVIGATE
CIRCUMSTANTIAL
CLAUSTROPHOBIA
CONGREGATIONAL
CONJUNCTIVITIS
CONSTITUTIONAL
CORRESPONDENCE
COSMOCHEMISTRY
COUNTERBALANCE
COUNTERCULTURE
COUNTERMEASURE
DECOMPENSATION
DINOFLAGELLATE
DISAPPROBATION
DISCIPLINARIAN
DISCOMBOBULATE
DISCOUNTENANCE
DISCRIMINATING
DISCRIMINATORY
DISENFRANCHISE
DISEQUILIBRIUM
DISINCLINATION
ECCLESIASTICAL
EGALITARIANISM
ELECTRODEPOSIT
ELECTROSTATICS
EXISTENTIALISM
EXTEMPORANEOUS
EXTRAVEHICULAR
FEATHERBEDDING
FUNDAMENTALISM
GENERALIZATION
GRANDILOQUENCE
HYPERSENSITIVE
HYPOTHYROIDISM
IDENTIFICATION
IMPRESSIONABLE
INCOMMENSURATE
INCOMMUNICABLE
INCOMPRESSIBLE
INCONSIDERABLE
INDISCRIMINATE
INSURMOUNTABLE
INTELLIGENTSIA
INTERDEPENDENT
INTERFEROMETER
INTERMOLECULAR
INTERPLANETARY
INTERPRETATION
INTRAMOLECULAR
INTRANSIGEANCE
IRRECONCILABLE
IRREPROACHABLE
KINDERGARTENER
KREMLINOLOGIST
LATITUDINARIAN
MESDEMOISELLES
METEMPSYCHOSIS
MICROMETEORITE
MICROMETEOROID
MICROMINIATURE
MICROPROCESSOR
MISAPPROPRIATE
MULTIPLICATION
NEOCOLONIALISM
NITROCELLULOSE
NONCOOPERATION
NONRESTRICTIVE
OBSTRUCTIONIST
OPHTHALMOSCOPE
ORGANOCHLORINE
OTOLARYNGOLOGY
PALEOMAGNETISM
PARAPSYCHOLOGY
PHANTASMAGORIA
PHARMACEUTICAL
PHOTOENGRAVING
PHOTOSENSITIVE
PHOTOSYNTHESIS
PNEUMOCONIOSIS
PREADOLESCENCE
PREDESTINATION
PRONUNCIAMENTO
PSYCHOANALYSIS
PSYCHOCHEMICAL
RADIOTELEGRAPH
RADIOTELEMETRY
RADIOTELEPHONE
RECOMMENDATION
RECONNAISSANCE
RECONSTRUCTION
REPRESENTATION
REPRESENTATIVE
RESPONSIBILITY
SCHOOLMISTRESS
SEGREGATIONIST
SENSATIONALISM
SENTIMENTALIZE
SEPTUAGENARIAN
SERVOMECHANISM
SESQUIPEDALIAN
SLAUGHTERHOUSE
SOCIORELIGIOUS
STAPHYLOCOCCUS
SUBMICROSCOPIC
SUPERSTRUCTURE
TATTERDEMALION
TELETYPEWRITER
THERMODYNAMICS
TRANSCENDENTAL
TROUBLESHOOTER
ULTRAMINIATURE
UNCOMPROMISING
UNCONSCIONABLE
UNCONTROLLABLE
UNCONVENTIONAL
UNDERDEVELOPED
UNDEREMPHASIZE
UNDERNOURISHED
UNDERSECRETARY
UNIDIRECTIONAL
UNINTELLIGIBLE
UNPROFESSIONAL
UNQUESTIONABLE
UTILITARIANISM
VALETUDINARIAN
VERISIMILITUDE
VIETNAMIZATION
WEATHERABILITY
WHIPPERSNAPPER
ZOROASTRIANISM

**2nd Letter**

CAPITALIZATION
CARDIOVASCULAR
LATITUDINARIAN
PALEOMAGNETISM
PARAPSYCHOLOGY
RADIOTELEGRAPH
RADIOTELEMETRY
RADIOTELEPHONE
TATTERDEMALION
VALETUDINARIAN
OBSTRUCTIONIST
ACCOMPLISHMENT
ECCLESIASTICAL
SCHOOLMISTRESS
ADMINISTRATION
IDENTIFICATION
DECOMPENSATION
FEATHERBEDDING
GENERALIZATION
MESDEMOISELLES
METEMPSYCHOSIS
NEOCOLONIALISM
RECOMMENDATION
RECONNAISSANCE
RECONSTRUCTION
REPRESENTATION
REPRESENTATIVE
RESPONSIBILITY
SEGREGATIONIST
SENSATIONALISM
SENTIMENTALIZE
SEPTUAGENARIAN
SERVOMECHANISM
SESQUIPEDALIAN
TELETYPEWRITER
VERISIMILITUDE
WEATHERABILITY
AFOREMENTIONED
EGALITARIANISM
CHARACTERISTIC
CHEMOSTERILANT
CHICKENHEARTED
CHROMATOGRAPHY
PHANTASMAGORIA
PHARMACEUTICAL
PHOTOENGRAVING
PHOTOSENSITIVE
PHOTOSYNTHESIS
THERMODYNAMICS
WHIPPERSNAPPER
CINEMATOGRAPHY
CIRCUMLOCUTION
CIRCUMNAVIGATE
CIRCUMSTANTIAL
DINOFLAGELLATE
DISAPPROBATION
DISCIPLINARIAN
DISCOMBOBULATE
DISCOUNTENANCE
DISCRIMINATING
DISCRIMINATORY
DISENFRANCHISE
DISEQUILIBRIUM
DISINCLINATION
KINDERGARTENER
MICROMETEORITE
MICROMETEOROID
MICROMINIATURE
MICROPROCESSOR
MISAPPROPRIATE
NITROCELLULOSE
VIETNAMIZATION
CLAUSTROPHOBIA
ELECTRODEPOSIT
ELECTROSTATICS
SLAUGHTERHOUSE
ULTRAMINIATURE
IMPRESSIONABLE
ANESTHESIOLOGY
ANTIDEPRESSANT
ANTINEOPLASTIC
ANTIPERSPIRANT
INCOMMENSURATE
INCOMMUNICABLE
INCOMPRESSIBLE
INCONSIDERABLE
INDISCRIMINATE
INSURMOUNTABLE
INTELLIGENTSIA
INTERDEPENDENT
INTERFEROMETER
INTERMOLECULAR
INTERPLANETARY
INTERPRETATION
INTRAMOLECULAR
INTRANSIGEANCE
PNEUMOCONIOSIS
UNCOMPROMISING
UNCONSCIONABLE
UNCONTROLLABLE

U**N**CONVENTIONAL
U**N**DERDEVELOPED
U**N**DEREMPHASIZE
U**N**DERNOURISHED
U**N**DERSECRETARY
U**N**IDIRECTIONAL
U**N**INTELLIGIBLE
U**N**PROFESSIONAL
U**N**QUESTIONABLE
C**O**NGREGATIONAL
C**O**NJUNCTIVITIS
C**O**NSTITUTIONAL
C**O**RRESPONDENCE
C**O**SMOCHEMISTRY
C**O**UNTERBALANCE
C**O**UNTERCULTURE
C**O**UNTERMEASURE
N**O**NCOOPERATION
N**O**NRESTRICTIVE
S**O**CIORELIGIOUS
Z**O**ROASTRIANISM
O**P**HTHALMOSCOPE
A**R**CHIEPISCOPAL
A**R**CHITECTONICS
G**R**ANDILOQUENCE
I**R**RECONCILABLE
I**R**REPROACHABLE
K**R**EMLINOLOGIST
O**R**GANOCHLORINE
P**R**EADOLESCENCE
P**R**EDESTINATION
P**R**ONUNCIAMENTO
T**R**ANSCENDENTAL
T**R**OUBLESHOOTER
P**S**YCHOANALYSIS
P**S**YCHOCHEMICAL
O**T**OLARYNGOLOGY
S**T**APHYLOCOCCUS
U**T**ILITARIANISM
B**U**TTERFINGERED
F**U**NDAMENTALISM
M**U**LTIPLICATION
S**U**BMICROSCOPIC
S**U**PERSTRUCTURE
E**X**ISTENTIALISM
E**X**TEMPORANEOUS
E**X**TRAVEHICULAR
H**Y**PERSENSITIVE
H**Y**POTHYROIDISM

## 3RD LETTER

CH**A**RACTERISTIC
CL**A**USTROPHOBIA
EG**A**LITARIANISM
FE**A**THERBEDDING
GR**A**NDILOQUENCE
PH**A**NTASMAGORIA
PH**A**RMACEUTICAL
SL**A**UGHTERHOUSE
ST**A**PHYLOCOCCUS
TR**A**NSCENDENTAL
WE**A**THERABILITY
SU**B**MICROSCOPIC
AC**C**OMPLISHMENT
AR**C**HIEPISCOPAL
AR**C**HITECTONICS
DE**C**OMPENSATION
EC**C**LESIASTICAL
IN**C**OMMENSURATE
IN**C**OMMUNICABLE
IN**C**OMPRESSIBLE
IN**C**ONSIDERABLE
MI**C**ROMETEORITE
MI**C**ROMETEOROID
MI**C**ROMINIATURE
MI**C**ROPROCESSOR
RE**C**OMMENDATION
RE**C**ONNAISSANCE
RE**C**ONSTRUCTION
SO**C**IORELIGIOUS
UN**C**OMPROMISING
UN**C**ONSCIONABLE
UN**C**ONTROLLABLE
UN**C**ONVENTIONAL
IN**D**ISCRIMINATE
RA**D**IOTELEGRAPH
RA**D**IOTELEMETRY
RA**D**IOTELEPHONE
UN**D**ERDEVELOPED
UN**D**EREMPHASIZE
UN**D**ERNOURISHED
UN**D**ERSECRETARY
AN**E**STHESIOLOGY
CH**E**MOSTERILANT
EL**E**CTRODEPOSIT
EL**E**CTROSTATICS
ID**E**NTIFICATION
KR**E**MLINOLOGIST
PN**E**UMOCONIOSIS
PR**E**ADOLESCENCE
PR**E**DESTINATION
TH**E**RMODYNAMICS
VI**E**TNAMIZATION
OR**G**ANOCHLORINE
SE**G**REGATIONIST
OP**H**THALMOSCOPE
SC**H**OOLMISTRESS
CH**I**CKENHEARTED
EX**I**STENTIALISM
UN**I**DIRECTIONAL
UN**I**NTELLIGIBLE
UT**I**LITARIANISM
WH**I**PPERSNAPPER
MU**L**TIPLICATION
PA**L**EOMAGNETISM
TE**L**ETYPEWRITER
VA**L**ETUDINARIAN
AD**M**INISTRATION
CI**N**EMATOGRAPHY
CO**N**GREGATIONAL
CO**N**JUNCTIVITIS
CO**N**STITUTIONAL
DI**N**OFLAGELLATE
FU**N**DAMENTALISM
GE**N**ERALIZATION
KI**N**DERGARTENER
NO**N**COOPERATION
NO**N**RESTRICTIVE
SE**N**SATIONALISM
SE**N**TIMENTALIZE
AF**O**REMENTIONED
NE**O**COLONIALISM
OT**O**LARYNGOLOGY
PH**O**TOENGRAVING
PH**O**TOSENSITIVE
PH**O**TOSYNTHESIS
PR**O**NUNCIAMENTO
TR**O**UBLESHOOTER
CA**P**ITALIZATION
HY**P**ERSENSITIVE
HY**P**OTHYROIDISM
IM**P**RESSIONABLE
RE**P**RESENTATION
RE**P**RESENTATIVE
SE**P**TUAGENARIAN
SU**P**ERSTRUCTURE
UN**P**ROFESSIONAL
UN**Q**UESTIONABLE
CA**R**DIOVASCULAR
CH**R**OMATOGRAPHY
CI**R**CUMLOCUTION
CI**R**CUMNAVIGATE
CI**R**CUMSTANTIAL
CO**R**RESPONDENCE
IR**R**ECONCILABLE
IR**R**EPROACHABLE
PA**R**APSYCHOLOGY
SE**R**VOMECHANISM
VE**R**ISIMILITUDE
ZO**R**OASTRIANISM
CO**S**MOCHEMISTRY
DI**S**APPROBATION
DI**S**CIPLINARIAN
DI**S**COMBOBULATE
DI**S**COUNTENANCE
DI**S**CRIMINATING
DI**S**CRIMINATORY
DI**S**ENFRANCHISE
DI**S**EQUILIBRIUM
DI**S**INCLINATION
IN**S**URMOUNTABLE
ME**S**DEMOISELLES
MI**S**APPROPRIATE
OB**S**TRUCTIONIST
RE**S**PONSIBILITY
SE**S**QUIPEDALIAN
AN**T**IDEPRESSANT
AN**T**INEOPLASTIC
AN**T**IPERSPIRANT
BU**T**TERFINGERED
EX**T**EMPORANEOUS
EX**T**RAVEHICULAR
IN**T**ELLIGENTSIA
IN**T**ERDEPENDENT
IN**T**ERFEROMETER
IN**T**ERMOLECULAR
IN**T**ERPLANETARY
IN**T**ERPRETATION
IN**T**RAMOLECULAR
IN**T**RANSIGEANCE
LA**T**ITUDINARIAN
ME**T**EMPSYCHOSIS
NI**T**ROCELLULOSE
TA**T**TERDEMALION
UL**T**RAMINIATURE
CO**U**NTERBALANCE
CO**U**NTERCULTURE
CO**U**NTERMEASURE
PS**Y**CHOANALYSIS
PS**Y**CHOCHEMICAL

## 4TH LETTER

DIS**A**PPROBATION
MIS**A**PPROPRIATE
ORG**A**NOCHLORINE
PAR**A**PSYCHOLOGY
PRE**A**DOLESCENCE
CHI**C**KENHEARTED
CIR**C**UMLOCUTION
CIR**C**UMNAVIGATE
CIR**C**UMSTANTIAL
DIS**C**IPLINARIAN
DIS**C**OMBOBULATE
DIS**C**OUNTENANCE
DIS**C**RIMINATING
DIS**C**RIMINATORY
ELE**C**TRODEPOSIT
ELE**C**TROSTATICS
NEO**C**OLONIALISM
NON**C**OOPERATION
PSY**C**HOANALYSIS
PSY**C**HOCHEMICAL
CAR**D**IOVASCULAR
FUN**D**AMENTALISM
KIN**D**ERGARTENER
MES**D**EMOISELLES
PRE**D**ESTINATION
UNI**D**IRECTIONAL
CIN**E**MATOGRAPHY
DIS**E**NFRANCHISE
DIS**E**QUILIBRIUM
EXT**E**MPORANEOUS
GEN**E**RALIZATION
HYP**E**RSENSITIVE
INT**E**LLIGENTSIA
INT**E**RDEPENDENT
INT**E**RFEROMETER
INT**E**RMOLECULAR
INT**E**RPLANETARY
INT**E**RPRETATION
IRR**E**CONCILABLE
IRR**E**PROACHABLE
MET**E**MPSYCHOSIS
PAL**E**OMAGNETISM
SUP**E**RSTRUCTURE
TEL**E**TYPEWRITER
UND**E**RDEVELOPED
UND**E**REMPHASIZE
UND**E**RNOURISHED
UND**E**RSECRETARY
VAL**E**TUDINARIAN
CON**G**REGATIONAL
ARC**H**IEPISCOPAL
ARC**H**ITECTONICS
ADM**I**NISTRATION
ANT**I**DEPRESSANT
ANT**I**NEOPLASTIC
ANT**I**PERSPIRANT
CAP**I**TALIZATION
DIS**I**NCLINATION
IND**I**SCRIMINATE
LAT**I**TUDINARIAN
RAD**I**OTELEGRAPH
RAD**I**OTELEMETRY
RAD**I**OTELEPHONE
SOC**I**ORELIGIOUS
VER**I**SIMILITUDE
CON**J**UNCTIVITIS
ECC**L**ESIASTICAL
EGA**L**ITARIANISM
OTO**L**ARYNGOLOGY
UTI**L**ITARIANISM
CHE**M**OSTERILANT
COS**M**OCHEMISTRY
KRE**M**LINOLOGIST
SUB**M**ICROSCOPIC
COU**N**TERBALANCE
COU**N**TERCULTURE
COU**N**TERMEASURE

GRA**N**DILOQUENCE
IDE**N**TIFICATION
PHA**N**TASMAGORIA
PRO**N**UNCIAMENTO
TRA**N**SCENDENTAL
UNI**N**TELLIGIBLE
ACC**O**MPLISHMENT
CHR**O**MATOGRAPHY
DEC**O**MPENSATION
DIN**O**FLAGELLATE
HYP**O**THYROIDISM
INC**O**MMENSURATE
INC**O**MMUNICABLE
INC**O**MPRESSIBLE
INC**O**NSIDERABLE
REC**O**MMENDATION
REC**O**NNAISSANCE
REC**O**NSTRUCTION
SCH**O**OLMISTRESS
UNC**O**MPROMISING
UNC**O**NSCIONABLE
UNC**O**NTROLLABLE
UNC**O**NVENTIONAL
ZOR**O**ASTRIANISM
RES**P**ONSIBILITY
STA**P**HYLOCOCCUS
WHI**P**PERSNAPPER
SES**Q**UIPEDALIAN
AFO**R**EMENTIONED
CHA**R**ACTERISTIC
COR**R**ESPONDENCE
EXT**R**AVEHICULAR
IMP**R**ESSIONABLE
INT**R**AMOLECULAR
INT**R**ANSIGEANCE
MIC**R**OMETEORITE
MIC**R**OMETEOROID
MIC**R**OMINIATURE
MIC**R**OPROCESSOR
NIT**R**OCELLULOSE
NON**R**ESTRICTIVE
PHA**R**MACEUTICAL
REP**R**ESENTATION
REP**R**ESENTATIVE
SEG**R**EGATIONIST
THE**R**MODYNAMICS
ULT**R**AMINIATURE
UNP**R**OFESSIONAL
ANE**S**THESIOLOGY
CON**S**TITUTIONAL
EXI**S**TENTIALISM
SEN**S**ATIONALISM
BUT**T**ERFINGERED
FEA**T**HERBEDDING
MUL**T**IPLICATION
OBS**T**RUCTIONIST
OPH**T**HALMOSCOPE
PHO**T**OENGRAVING
PHO**T**OSENSITIVE
PHO**T**OSYNTHESIS
SEN**T**IMENTALIZE
SEP**T**UAGENARIAN
TAT**T**ERDEMALION
VIE**T**NAMIZATION
WEA**T**HERABILITY
CLA**U**STROPHOBIA
INS**U**RMOUNTABLE
PNE**U**MOCONIOSIS
SLA**U**GHTERHOUSE
TRO**U**BLESHOOTER
UNQ**U**ESTIONABLE
SER**V**OMECHANISM

## 5th Letter

CHAR**A**CTERISTIC
EXTR**A**VEHICULAR
FUND**A**MENTALISM
INTR**A**MOLECULAR
INTR**A**NSIGEANCE
OTOL**A**RYNGOLOGY
SENS**A**TIONALISM
ULTR**A**MINIATURE
ZORO**A**STRIANISM
TROU**B**LESHOOTER
IRRE**C**ONCILABLE
ANTI**D**EPRESSANT
GRAN**D**ILOQUENCE
PREA**D**OLESCENCE
AFOR**E**MENTIONED
BUTT**E**RFINGERED
CORR**E**SPONDENCE
ECCL**E**SIASTICAL
IMPR**E**SSIONABLE
KIND**E**RGARTENER
MESD**E**MOISELLES
NONR**E**STRICTIVE
PRED**E**STINATION
REPR**E**SENTATION
REPR**E**SENTATIVE
SEGR**E**GATIONIST
TATT**E**RDEMALION
UNQU**E**STIONABLE
DINO**F**LAGELLATE
SLAU**G**HTERHOUSE
FEAT**H**ERBEDDING
OPHT**H**ALMOSCOPE
PSYC**H**OANALYSIS
PSYC**H**OCHEMICAL
STAP**H**YLOCOCCUS
WEAT**H**ERABILITY
ARCH**I**EPISCOPAL
ARCH**I**TECTONICS
CARD**I**OVASCULAR
DISC**I**PLINARIAN
EGAL**I**TARIANISM
MULT**I**PLICATION
SENT**I**MENTALIZE
SUBM**I**CROSCOPIC
UNID**I**RECTIONAL
UTIL**I**TARIANISM
CHIC**K**ENHEARTED
INTE**L**LIGENTSIA
KREM**L**INOLOGIST
ACCO**M**PLISHMENT
CHRO**M**ATOGRAPHY
CINE**M**ATOGRAPHY
DECO**M**PENSATION
EXTE**M**PORANEOUS
INCO**M**MENSURATE
INCO**M**MUNICABLE
INCO**M**PRESSIBLE
METE**M**PSYCHOSIS
PHAR**M**ACEUTICAL
PNEU**M**OCONIOSIS
RECO**M**MENDATION
THER**M**ODYNAMICS
UNCO**M**PROMISING
ADMI**N**ISTRATION
ANTI**N**EOPLASTIC
DISE**N**FRANCHISE
DISI**N**CLINATION
INCO**N**SIDERABLE
ORGA**N**OCHLORINE
RECO**N**NAISSANCE
RECO**N**STRUCTION
UNCO**N**SCIONABLE
UNCO**N**TROLLABLE
UNCO**N**VENTIONAL
VIET**N**AMIZATION
CHEM**O**STERILANT
COSM**O**CHEMISTRY
DISC**O**MBOBULATE
DISC**O**UNTENANCE
MICR**O**METEORITE
MICR**O**METEOROID
MICR**O**MINIATURE
MICR**O**PROCESSOR
NEOC**O**LONIALISM
NITR**O**CELLULOSE
NONC**O**OPERATION
PALE**O**MAGNETISM
PHOT**O**ENGRAVING
PHOT**O**SENSITIVE
PHOT**O**SYNTHESIS
RADI**O**TELEGRAPH
RADI**O**TELEMETRY
RADI**O**TELEPHONE
RESP**O**NSIBILITY
SCHO**O**LMISTRESS
SERV**O**MECHANISM
SOCI**O**RELIGIOUS
UNPR**O**FESSIONAL
ANTI**P**ERSPIRANT
DISA**P**PROBATION
IRRE**P**ROACHABLE
MISA**P**PROPRIATE
PARA**P**SYCHOLOGY
WHIP**P**ERSNAPPER
DISE**Q**UILIBRIUM
CONG**R**EGATIONAL
DISC**R**IMINATING
DISC**R**IMINATORY
GENE**R**ALIZATION
HYPE**R**SENSITIVE
INSU**R**MOUNTABLE
INTE**R**DEPENDENT
INTE**R**FEROMETER
INTE**R**MOLECULAR
INTE**R**PLANETARY
INTE**R**PRETATION
OBST**R**UCTIONIST
SUPE**R**STRUCTURE
UNDE**R**DEVELOPED
UNDE**R**EMPHASIZE
UNDE**R**NOURISHED
UNDE**R**SECRETARY
CLAU**S**TROPHOBIA
INDI**S**CRIMINATE
TRAN**S**CENDENTAL
VERI**S**IMILITUDE
ANES**T**HESIOLOGY
CAPI**T**ALIZATION
CONS**T**ITUTIONAL
COUN**T**ERBALANCE
COUN**T**ERCULTURE
COUN**T**ERMEASURE
ELEC**T**RODEPOSIT
ELEC**T**ROSTATICS
EXIS**T**ENTIALISM
HYPO**T**HYROIDISM
IDEN**T**IFICATION
LATI**T**UDINARIAN
PHAN**T**ASMAGORIA
TELE**T**YPEWRITER
UNIN**T**ELLIGIBLE
VALE**T**UDINARIAN
CIRC**U**MLOCUTION
CIRC**U**MNAVIGATE
CIRC**U**MSTANTIAL
CONJ**U**NCTIVITIS
PRON**U**NCIAMENTO
SEPT**U**AGENARIAN
SESQ**U**IPEDALIAN

## 6th Letter

CAPIT**A**LIZATION
CHROM**A**TOGRAPHY
CINEM**A**TOGRAPHY
GENER**A**LIZATION
OPHTH**A**LMOSCOPE
PHANT**A**SMAGORIA
PHARM**A**CEUTICAL
SEPTU**A**GENARIAN
VIETN**A**MIZATION
CHARA**C**TERISTIC
COSMO**C**HEMISTRY
DISIN**C**LINATION
INDIS**C**RIMINATE
NITRO**C**ELLULOSE
SUBMI**C**ROSCOPIC
TRANS**C**ENDENTAL
INTER**D**EPENDENT
UNDER**D**EVELOPED
ANTID**E**PRESSANT
ANTIN**E**OPLASTIC
ANTIP**E**RSPIRANT
ARCHI**E**PISCOPAL
CHICK**E**NHEARTED
CONGR**E**GATIONAL
COUNT**E**RBALANCE
COUNT**E**RCULTURE
COUNT**E**RMEASURE
EXIST**E**NTIALISM
FEATH**E**RBEDDING
PHOTO**E**NGRAVING
UNDER**E**MPHASIZE
UNINT**E**LLIGIBLE
WEATH**E**RABILITY
WHIPP**E**RSNAPPER
DISEN**F**RANCHISE
INTER**F**EROMETER
UNPRO**F**ESSIONAL
SEGRE**G**ATIONIST
ANEST**H**ESIOLOGY
HYPOT**H**YROIDISM
SLAUG**H**TERHOUSE
ADMIN**I**STRATION
CONST**I**TUTIONAL
DISCR**I**MINATING
DISCR**I**MINATORY
GRAND**I**LOQUENCE
IDENT**I**FICATION
KREML**I**NOLOGIST
SESQU**I**PEDALIAN
VERIS**I**MILITUDE
DINOF**L**AGELLATE
INTEL**L**IGENTSIA
NEOCO**L**ONIALISM
SCHOO**L**MISTRESS
TROUB**L**ESHOOTER

AFORE**M**ENTIONED
CIRCU**M**LOCUTION
CIRCU**M**NAVIGATE
CIRCU**M**STANTIAL
DISCO**M**BOBULATE
FUNDA**M**ENTALISM
INCOM**M**ENSURATE
INCOM**M**UNICABLE
INSUR**M**OUNTABLE
INTER**M**OLECULAR
INTRA**M**OLECULAR
MESDE**M**OISELLES
MICRO**M**ETEORITE
MICRO**M**ETEOROID
MICRO**M**INIATURE
PALEO**M**AGNETISM
RECOM**M**ENDATION
SENTI**M**ENTALIZE
SERVO**M**ECHANISM
ULTRA**M**INIATURE
CONJU**N**CTIVITIS
INTRA**N**SIGEANCE
PRONU**N**CIAMENTO
RECON**N**AISSANCE
RESPO**N**SIBILITY
UNDER**N**OURISHED
CARDI**O**VASCULAR
IRREC**O**NCILABLE
NONCO**O**PERATION
ORGAN**O**CHLORINE
PNEUM**O**CONIOSIS
PREAD**O**LESCENCE
PSYCH**O**ANALYSIS
PSYCH**O**CHEMICAL
THERM**O**DYNAMICS
ACCOM**P**LISHMENT
DECOM**P**ENSATION
DISAP**P**ROBATION
DISCI**P**LINARIAN
EXTEM**P**ORANEOUS
INCOM**P**RESSIBLE
INTER**P**LANETARY
INTER**P**RETATION
METEM**P**SYCHOSIS
MICRO**P**ROCESSOR
MISAP**P**ROPRIATE
MULTI**P**LICATION
UNCOM**P**ROMISING
BUTTE**R**FINGERED
ELECT**R**ODEPOSIT
ELECT**R**OSTATICS
IRREP**R**OACHABLE
KINDE**R**GARTENER
OTOLA**R**YNGOLOGY
SOCIO**R**ELIGIOUS
TATTE**R**DEMALION
UNIDI**R**ECTIONAL
CHEMO**S**TERILANT
CORRE**S**PONDENCE
ECCLE**S**IASTICAL
HYPER**S**ENSITIVE
IMPRE**S**SIONABLE
INCON**S**IDERABLE
NONRE**S**TRICTIVE
PARAP**S**YCHOLOGY
PHOTO**S**ENSITIVE
PHOTO**S**YNTHESIS
PREDE**S**TINATION
RECON**S**TRUCTION
REPRE**S**ENTATION
REPRE**S**ENTATIVE
SUPER**S**TRUCTURE
UNCON**S**CIONABLE
UNDER**S**ECRETARY
UNQUE**S**TIONABLE
ZOROA**S**TRIANISM
ARCHI**T**ECTONICS
CLAUS**T**ROPHOBIA
EGALI**T**ARIANISM
RADIO**T**ELEGRAPH
RADIO**T**ELEMETRY
RADIO**T**ELEPHONE
SENSA**T**IONALISM
UNCON**T**ROLLABLE
UTILI**T**ARIANISM
DISCO**U**NTENANCE
DISEQ**U**ILIBRIUM
LATIT**U**DINARIAN
OBSTR**U**CTIONIST
VALET**U**DINARIAN
EXTRA**V**EHICULAR
UNCON**V**ENTIONAL
STAPH**Y**LOCOCCUS
TELET**Y**PEWRITER

## 7TH LETTER

DINOFL**A**GELLATE
EGALIT**A**RIANISM
PALEOM**A**GNETISM
PSYCHO**A**NALYSIS
RECONN**A**ISSANCE
SEGREG**A**TIONIST
UTILIT**A**RIANISM
DISCOM**B**OBULATE
CONJUN**C**TIVITIS
OBSTRU**C**TIONIST
ORGANO**C**HLORINE
PHARMA**C**EUTICAL
PNEUMO**C**ONIOSIS
PRONUN**C**IAMENTO
PSYCHO**C**HEMICAL
UNCONS**C**IONABLE
LATITU**D**INARIAN
TATTER**D**EMALION
THERMO**D**YNAMICS
VALETU**D**INARIAN
AFOREM**E**NTIONED
ANESTH**E**SIOLOGY
ARCHIT**E**CTONICS
DECOMP**E**NSATION
EXTRAV**E**HICULAR
FUNDAM**E**NTALISM
HYPERS**E**NSITIVE
INCOMM**E**NSURATE
INTERD**E**PENDENT
INTERF**E**ROMETER
MICROM**E**TEORITE
MICROM**E**TEOROID
NITROC**E**LLULOSE
PHOTOS**E**NSITIVE
RADIOT**E**LEGRAPH
RADIOT**E**LEMETRY
RADIOT**E**LEPHONE
RECOMM**E**NDATION
REPRES**E**NTATION
REPRES**E**NTATIVE
SENTIM**E**NTALIZE
SERVOM**E**CHANISM
SOCIOR**E**LIGIOUS
TRANSC**E**NDENTAL
TROUBL**E**SHOOTER
UNCONV**E**NTIONAL
UNDERD**E**VELOPED
UNDERS**E**CRETARY
UNIDIR**E**CTIONAL
UNPROF**E**SSIONAL
BUTTER**F**INGERED
IDENTI**F**ICATION
CONGRE**G**ATIONAL
KINDER**G**ARTENER
SEPTUA**G**ENARIAN
COSMOC**H**EMISTRY
DISEQU**I**LIBRIUM
ECCLES**I**ASTICAL
INCONS**I**DERABLE
INTELL**I**GENTSIA
MICROM**I**NIATURE
SENSAT**I**ONALISM
ULTRAM**I**NIATURE
ACCOMP**L**ISHMENT
CAPITA**L**IZATION
CIRCUM**L**OCUTION
DISCIP**L**INARIAN
DISINC**L**INATION
GENERA**L**IZATION
GRANDI**L**OQUENCE
INTERP**L**ANETARY
MULTIP**L**ICATION
OPHTHA**L**MOSCOPE
PREADO**L**ESCENCE
STAPHY**L**OCOCCUS
UNINTE**L**LIGIBLE
DISCRI**M**INATING
DISCRI**M**INATORY
SCHOOL**M**ISTRESS
UNDERE**M**PHASIZE
VERISI**M**ILITUDE
VIETNA**M**IZATION
CHICKE**N**HEARTED
CIRCUM**N**AVIGATE
DISCOU**N**TENANCE
EXISTE**N**TIALISM
IRRECO**N**CILABLE
KREMLI**N**OLOGIST
PHOTOE**N**GRAVING
ANTINE**O**PLASTIC
ELECTR**O**DEPOSIT
ELECTR**O**STATICS
EXTEMP**O**RANEOUS
INSURM**O**UNTABLE
INTERM**O**LECULAR
INTRAM**O**LECULAR
IRREPR**O**ACHABLE
MESDEM**O**ISELLES
NEOCOL**O**NIALISM
UNDERN**O**URISHED
ANTIDE**P**RESSANT
ARCHIE**P**ISCOPAL
CORRES**P**ONDENCE
NONCOO**P**ERATION
SESQUI**P**EDALIAN
TELETY**P**EWRITER
ANTIPE**R**SPIRANT
CLAUST**R**OPHOBIA
COUNTE**R**BALANCE
COUNTE**R**CULTURE
COUNTE**R**MEASURE
DISAPP**R**OBATION
DISENF**R**ANCHISE
FEATHE**R**BEDDING
INCOMP**R**ESSIBLE
INDISC**R**IMINATE
INTERP**R**ETATION
MICROP**R**OCESSOR
MISAPP**R**OPRIATE
SUBMIC**R**OSCOPIC
UNCOMP**R**OMISING
UNCONT**R**OLLABLE
WEATHE**R**ABILITY
WHIPPE**R**SNAPPER
ADMINI**S**TRATION
CIRCUM**S**TANTIAL
IMPRES**S**IONABLE
INTRAN**S**IGEANCE
METEMP**S**YCHOSIS
PHANTA**S**MAGORIA
RESPON**S**IBILITY
CHARAC**T**ERISTIC
CHEMOS**T**ERILANT
CHROMA**T**OGRAPHY
CINEMA**T**OGRAPHY
CONSTI**T**UTIONAL
NONRES**T**RICTIVE
PREDES**T**INATION
RECONS**T**RUCTION
SLAUGH**T**ERHOUSE
SUPERS**T**RUCTURE
UNQUES**T**IONABLE
ZOROAS**T**RIANISM
INCOMM**U**NICABLE
CARDIO**V**ASCULAR
HYPOTH**Y**ROIDISM
OTOLAR**Y**NGOLOGY
PARAPS**Y**CHOLOGY
PHOTOS**Y**NTHESIS

## 8TH LETTER

CARDIOV**A**SCULAR
CIRCUMN**A**VIGATE
CONGREG**A**TIONAL
DISENFR**A**NCHISE
ECCLESI**A**STICAL
INTERPL**A**NETARY
IRREPRO**A**CHABLE
KINDERG**A**RTENER
WEATHER**A**BILITY
COUNTER**B**ALANCE
FEATHER**B**EDDING
ARCHITE**C**TONICS
COUNTER**C**ULTURE
IRRECON**C**ILABLE
PARAPSY**C**HOLOGY
SERVOME**C**HANISM
UNDERSE**C**RETARY
UNIDIRE**C**TIONAL
ELECTRO**D**EPOSIT
INCONSI**D**ERABLE
CHARACT**E**RISTIC
CHEMOST**E**RILANT
COSMOCH**E**MISTRY
INCOMPR**E**SSIBLE
INTERPR**E**TATION
NONCOOP**E**RATION
PHARMAC**E**UTICAL
PREADOL**E**SCENCE
SEPTUAG**E**NARIAN
SESQUIP**E**DALIAN
SLAUGHT**E**RHOUSE
TATTERD**E**MALION

TELETYP**E**WRITER
DINOFLA**G**ELLATE
INTELLI**G**ENTSIA
PALEOMA**G**NETISM
PHOTOEN**G**RAVING
CHICKEN**H**EARTED
EXTRAVE**H**ICULAR
ORGANOC**H**LORINE
PSYCHOC**H**EMICAL
ACCOMPL**I**SHMENT
ARCHIEP**I**SCOPAL
BUTTERF**I**NGERED
CAPITAL**I**ZATION
DISCIPL**I**NARIAN
DISCRIM**I**NATING
DISCRIM**I**NATORY
DISINCL**I**NATION
GENERAL**I**ZATION
IDENTIF**I**CATION
IMPRESS**I**ONABLE
INDISCR**I**MINATE
INTRANS**I**GEANCE
LATITUD**I**NARIAN
MESDEMO**I**SELLES
MULTIPL**I**CATION
PREDEST**I**NATION
PRONUNC**I**AMENTO
RECONNA**I**SSANCE
RESPONS**I**BILITY
SCHOOLM**I**STRESS
UNCONSC**I**ONABLE
UNQUEST**I**ONABLE
VALETUD**I**NARIAN
VERISIM**I**LITUDE
VIETNAM**I**ZATION
DISEQUI**L**IBRIUM
INTERMO**L**ECULAR
INTRAMO**L**ECULAR
NITROCE**L**LULOSE
RADIOTE**L**EGRAPH
RADIOTE**L**EMETRY
RADIOTE**L**EPHONE
SOCIORE**L**IGIOUS
UNINTEL**L**IGIBLE
COUNTER**M**EASURE
OPHTHAL**M**OSCOPE
PHANTAS**M**AGORIA
AFOREME**N**TIONED
DECOMPE**N**SATION
FUNDAME**N**TALISM
HYPERSE**N**SITIVE
INCOMME**N**SURATE
INCOMMU**N**ICABLE
MICROMI**N**IATURE
NEOCOLO**N**IALISM
OTOLARY**N**GOLOGY
PHOTOSE**N**SITIVE
PHOTOSY**N**THESIS
PSYCHOA**N**ALYSIS
RECOMME**N**DATION
REPRESE**N**TATION
REPRESE**N**TATIVE
SENTIME**N**TALIZE
TRANSCE**N**DENTAL
ULTRAMI**N**IATURE
UNCONVE**N**TIONAL
CHROMAT**O**GRAPHY
CINEMAT**O**GRAPHY
CIRCUML**O**CUTION
CLAUSTR**O**PHOBIA
CORRESP**O**NDENCE
DISAPPR**O**BATION
DISCOMB**O**BULATE
GRANDIL**O**QUENCE
KREMLIN**O**LOGIST
MICROPR**O**CESSOR
MISAPPR**O**PRIATE
PNEUMOC**O**NIOSIS
SENSATI**O**NALISM
STAPHYL**O**COCCUS
SUBMICR**O**SCOPIC
UNCOMPR**O**MISING
UNCONTR**O**LLABLE
ANTINEO**P**LASTIC
INTERDE**P**ENDENT
UNDEREM**P**HASIZE
ANTIDEP**R**ESSANT
EGALITA**R**IANISM
EXTEMPO**R**ANEOUS
HYPOTHY**R**OIDISM
INTERFE**R**OMETER
NONREST**R**ICTIVE
RECONST**R**UCTION
SUPERST**R**UCTURE
UTILITA**R**IANISM
ZOROAST**R**IANISM
ANESTHE**S**IOLOGY
ANTIPER**S**PIRANT
ELECTRO**S**TATICS
TROUBLE**S**HOOTER
UNPROFE**S**SIONAL
WHIPPER**S**NAPPER
ADMINIS**T**RATION
CIRCUMS**T**ANTIAL
CONJUNC**T**IVITIS
DISCOUN**T**ENANCE
EXISTEN**T**IALISM
MICROME**T**EORITE
MICROME**T**EOROID
OBSTRUC**T**IONIST
SEGREGA**T**IONIST
CONSTIT**U**TIONAL
INSURMO**U**NTABLE
UNDERNO**U**RISHED
UNDERDE**V**ELOPED
METEMPS**Y**CHOSIS
THERMOD**Y**NAMICS

## 9th Letter

CIRCUMST**A**NTIAL
COUNTERB**A**LANCE
EXTEMPOR**A**NEOUS
PHANTASM**A**GORIA
PRONUNCI**A**MENTO
PSYCHOAN**A**LYSIS
DISAPPRO**B**ATION
DISCOMBO**B**ULATE
RESPONSI**B**ILITY
WEATHERA**B**ILITY
CIRCUMLO**C**UTION
IDENTIFI**C**ATION
IRREPROA**C**HABLE
METEMPSY**C**HOSIS
MICROPRO**C**ESSOR
MULTIPLI**C**ATION
STAPHYLO**C**OCCUS
RECOMMEN**D**ATION
SESQUIPE**D**ALIAN
TRANSCEN**D**ENTAL
ANTIDEPR**E**SSANT
CHICKENH**E**ARTED
COUNTERM**E**ASURE
DINOFLAG**E**LLATE
DISCOUNT**E**NANCE
ELECTROD**E**POSIT
FEATHERB**E**DDING
INCONSID**E**RABLE
INTELLIG**E**NTSIA
INTERDEP**E**NDENT
INTERMOL**E**CULAR
INTRAMOL**E**CULAR
MICROMET**E**ORITE
MICROMET**E**OROID
PSYCHOCH**E**MICAL
RADIOTEL**E**GRAPH
RADIOTEL**E**METRY
RADIOTEL**E**PHONE
UNDERDEV**E**LOPED
CHROMATO**G**RAPHY
CINEMATO**G**RAPHY
INTRANSI**G**EANCE
OTOLARYN**G**OLOGY
PARAPSYC**H**OLOGY
SERVOMEC**H**ANISM
TROUBLES**H**OOTER
UNDEREMP**H**ASIZE
ANESTHES**I**OLOGY
CONJUNCT**I**VITIS
DISEQUIL**I**BRIUM
EGALITAR**I**ANISM
EXISTENT**I**ALISM
EXTRAVEH**I**CULAR
INCOMMUN**I**CABLE
IRRECONC**I**LABLE
MICROMIN**I**ATURE
NEOCOLON**I**ALISM
NONRESTR**I**CTIVE
OBSTRUCT**I**ONIST
SEGREGAT**I**ONIST
SOCIOREL**I**GIOUS
ULTRAMIN**I**ATURE
UNINTELL**I**GIBLE
UTILITAR**I**ANISM
ZOROASTR**I**ANISM
ANTINEOP**L**ASTIC
KREMLINO**L**OGIST
NITROCEL**L**ULOSE
ORGANOCH**L**ORINE
UNCONTRO**L**LABLE
VERISIMI**L**ITUDE
COSMOCHE**M**ISTRY
INDISCRI**M**INATE
TATTERDE**M**ALION
UNCOMPRO**M**ISING
BUTTERFI**N**GERED
CORRESPO**N**DENCE
DISCIPLI**N**ARIAN
DISCRIMI**N**ATING
DISCRIMI**N**ATORY
DISENFRA**N**CHISE
DISINCLI**N**ATION
INSURMOU**N**TABLE
INTERPLA**N**ETARY
LATITUDI**N**ARIAN
PALEOMAG**N**ETISM
PNEUMOCO**N**IOSIS
PREDESTI**N**ATION
SENSATIO**N**ALISM
SEPTUAGE**N**ARIAN
THERMODY**N**AMICS
VALETUDI**N**ARIAN
WHIPPERS**N**APPER
HYPOTHYR**O**IDISM
IMPRESSI**O**NABLE
INTERFER**O**METER
OPHTHALM**O**SCOPE
UNCONSCI**O**NABLE
UNQUESTI**O**NABLE
ANTIPERS**P**IRANT
CLAUSTRO**P**HOBIA
MISAPPRO**P**RIATE
GRANDILO**Q**UENCE
ADMINIST**R**ATION
CHARACTE**R**ISTIC
CHEMOSTE**R**ILANT
KINDERGA**R**TENER
NONCOOPE**R**ATION
PHOTOENG**R**AVING
SLAUGHTE**R**HOUSE
UNDERNOU**R**ISHED
UNDERSEC**R**ETARY
ACCOMPLI**S**HMENT
ARCHIEPI**S**COPAL
CARDIOVA**S**CULAR
DECOMPEN**S**ATION
ECCLESIA**S**TICAL
HYPERSEN**S**ITIVE
INCOMMEN**S**URATE
INCOMPRE**S**SIBLE
MESDEMOI**S**ELLES
PHOTOSEN**S**ITIVE
PREADOLE**S**CENCE
RECONNAI**S**SANCE
SCHOOLMI**S**TRESS
SUBMICRO**S**COPIC
UNPROFES**S**IONAL
AFOREMEN**T**IONED
ARCHITEC**T**ONICS
CONGREGA**T**IONAL
CONSTITU**T**IONAL
ELECTROS**T**ATICS
FUNDAMEN**T**ALISM
INTERPRE**T**ATION
PHOTOSYN**T**HESIS
REPRESEN**T**ATION
REPRESEN**T**ATIVE
SENTIMEN**T**ALIZE
UNCONVEN**T**IONAL
UNIDIREC**T**IONAL
COUNTERC**U**LTURE
PHARMACE**U**TICAL
RECONSTR**U**CTION
SUPERSTR**U**CTURE
CIRCUMNA**V**IGATE
TELETYPE**W**RITER
CAPITALI**Z**ATION
GENERALI**Z**ATION
VIETNAMI**Z**ATION

## 10th Letter

ADMINISTR**A**TION
ANTINEOPL**A**STIC
CAPITALIZ**A**TION
CHICKENHE**A**RTED
COUNTERME**A**SURE
DECOMPENS**A**TION
DISAPPROB**A**TION
DISCIPLIN**A**RIAN
DISCRIMIN**A**TING

DISCRIMINATORY
DISINCLINATION
EGALITARIANISM
ELECTROSTATICS
EXISTENTIALISM
FUNDAMENTALISM
GENERALIZATION
IDENTIFICATION
INTERPRETATION
LATITUDINARIAN
MICROMINIATURE
MULTIPLICATION
NEOCOLONIALISM
NONCOOPERATION
PHOTOENGRAVING
PREDESTINATION
RECOMMENDATION
REPRESENTATION
REPRESENTATIVE
SENSATIONALISM
SENTIMENTALIZE
SEPTUAGENARIAN
SERVOMECHANISM
SESQUIPEDALIAN
TATTERDEMALION
THERMODYNAMICS
ULTRAMINIATURE
UNDEREMPHASIZE
UTILITARIANISM
VALETUDINARIAN
VIETNAMIZATION
WHIPPERSNAPPER
ZOROASTRIANISM
DISEQUILIBRIUM
ARCHIEPISCOPAL
CARDIOVASCULAR
DISENFRANCHISE
EXTRAVEHICULAR
INCOMMUNICABLE
INTERMOLECULAR
INTRAMOLECULAR
NONRESTRICTIVE
PREADOLESCENCE
RECONSTRUCTION
SUBMICROSCOPIC
SUPERSTRUCTURE
CORRESPONDENCE
FEATHERBEDDING
INTERPLANETARY
INTRANSIGEANCE
MESDEMOISELLES
MICROPROCESSOR
PALEOMAGNETISM
TRANSCENDENTAL
UNDERSECRETARY
BUTTERFINGERED
PHANTASMAGORIA
RADIOTELEGRAPH
SOCIORELIGIOUS
UNINTELLIGIBLE
ACCOMPLISHMENT
CLAUSTROPHOBIA
IRREPROACHABLE
METEMPSYCHOSIS
PHOTOSYNTHESIS
SLAUGHTERHOUSE
AFOREMENTIONED
ANTIPERSPIRANT
CHARACTERISTIC
CHEMOSTERILANT
CIRCUMNAVIGATE
CONGREGATIONAL
CONSTITUTIONAL
COSMOCHEMISTRY
HYPERSENSITIVE
HYPOTHYROIDISM
INDISCRIMINATE
PHOTOSENSITIVE
PNEUMOCONIOSIS
RESPONSIBILITY
UNCOMPROMISING
UNCONVENTIONAL
UNDERNOURISHED
UNIDIRECTIONAL
UNPROFESSIONAL
VERISIMILITUDE
WEATHERABILITY
COUNTERBALANCE
COUNTERCULTURE
DINOFLAGELLATE
IRRECONCILABLE
PSYCHOANALYSIS
UNCONTROLLABLE
UNDERDEVELOPED
INTERFEROMETER
PRONUNCIAMENTO
PSYCHOCHEMICAL
RADIOTELEMETRY
CIRCUMSTANTIAL
DISCOUNTENANCE
EXTEMPORANEOUS
IMPRESSIONABLE
INTELLIGENTSIA
INTERDEPENDENT
UNCONSCIONABLE
UNQUESTIONABLE
ANESTHESIOLOGY
ARCHITECTONICS
KREMLINOLOGIST
MICROMETEORITE
MICROMETEOROID
OBSTRUCTIONIST
ORGANOCHLORINE
OTOLARYNGOLOGY
PARAPSYCHOLOGY
SEGREGATIONIST
STAPHYLOCOCCUS
TROUBLESHOOTER
ELECTRODEPOSIT
RADIOTELEPHONE
CHROMATOGRAPHY
CINEMATOGRAPHY
INCONSIDERABLE
MISAPPROPRIATE
TELETYPEWRITER
ANTIDEPRESSANT
INCOMPRESSIBLE
OPHTHALMOSCOPE
RECONNAISSANCE
ECCLESIASTICAL
INSURMOUNTABLE
KINDERGARTENER
PHARMACEUTICAL
SCHOOLMISTRESS
CIRCUMLOCUTION
DISCOMBOBULATE
GRANDILOQUENCE
INCOMMENSURATE
NITROCELLULOSE
CONJUNCTIVITIS

## 11th Letter

CHROMATOGRAPHY
CINEMATOGRAPHY
COUNTERBALANCE
DISCOUNTENANCE
IMPRESSIONABLE
INCOMMUNICABLE
INCONSIDERABLE
INSURMOUNTABLE
INTRANSIGEANCE
IRRECONCILABLE
IRREPROACHABLE
RECONNAISSANCE
UNCONSCIONABLE
UNCONTROLLABLE
UNQUESTIONABLE
OPHTHALMOSCOPE
STAPHYLOCOCCUS
FEATHERBEDDING
HYPOTHYROIDISM
INTERDEPENDENT
BUTTERFINGERED
CORRESPONDENCE
EXTEMPORANEOUS
GRANDILOQUENCE
INTERFEROMETER
KINDERGARTENER
PHOTOSYNTHESIS
PREADOLESCENCE
PRONUNCIAMENTO
RADIOTELEMETRY
CIRCUMNAVIGATE
KREMLINOLOGIST
DISENFRANCHISE
RADIOTELEPHONE
CONJUNCTIVITIS
ECCLESIASTICAL
INCOMPRESSIBLE
MISAPPROPRIATE
PHARMACEUTICAL
PSYCHOCHEMICAL
SOCIORELIGIOUS
TELETYPEWRITER
UNINTELLIGIBLE
ANESTHESIOLOGY
CHEMOSTERILANT
DINOFLAGELLATE
DISCOMBOBULATE
EXISTENTIALISM
FUNDAMENTALISM
MESDEMOISELLES
NEOCOLONIALISM
NITROCELLULOSE
OTOLARYNGOLOGY
PARAPSYCHOLOGY
RESPONSIBILITY
SENSATIONALISM
SENTIMENTALIZE
SESQUIPEDALIAN
TATTERDEMALION
WEATHERABILITY
ACCOMPLISHMENT
THERMODYNAMICS
ARCHITECTONICS
EGALITARIANISM
INDISCRIMINATE
OBSTRUCTIONIST
SEGREGATIONIST
SERVOMECHANISM
TRANSCENDENTAL
UTILITARIANISM
ZOROASTRIANISM
AFOREMENTIONED
ARCHIEPISCOPAL
CLAUSTROPHOBIA
CONGREGATIONAL
CONSTITUTIONAL
ELECTRODEPOSIT
METEMPSYCHOSIS
PHANTASMAGORIA
PNEUMOCONIOSIS
SLAUGHTERHOUSE
SUBMICROSCOPIC
TROUBLESHOOTER
UNCONVENTIONAL
UNDERDEVELOPED
UNIDIRECTIONAL
UNPROFESSIONAL
WHIPPERSNAPPER
ANTIPERSPIRANT
CHICKENHEARTED
DISCIPLINARIAN
DISEQUILIBRIUM
INCOMMENSURATE
LATITUDINARIAN
MICROMETEORITE
MICROMETEOROID
ORGANOCHLORINE
RADIOTELEGRAPH
SCHOOLMISTRESS
SEPTUAGENARIAN
VALETUDINARIAN
ANTIDEPRESSANT
ANTINEOPLASTIC
CHARACTERISTIC
COSMOCHEMISTRY
COUNTERMEASURE
MICROPROCESSOR
UNCOMPROMISING
UNDEREMPHASIZE
UNDERNOURISHED
ADMINISTRATION
CAPITALIZATION
CIRCUMLOCUTION
CIRCUMSTANTIAL
COUNTERCULTURE
DECOMPENSATION
DISAPPROBATION
DISCRIMINATING
DISCRIMINATORY
DISINCLINATION
ELECTROSTATICS
GENERALIZATION
HYPERSENSITIVE
IDENTIFICATION
INTELLIGENTSIA
INTERPLANETARY
INTERPRETATION
MICROMINIATURE
MULTIPLICATION
NONCOOPERATION
NONRESTRICTIVE
PALEOMAGNETISM
PHOTOSENSITIVE
PREDESTINATION
RECOMMENDATION
RECONSTRUCTION
REPRESENTATION
REPRESENTATIVE
SUPERSTRUCTURE
ULTRAMINIATURE

UNDERSECRETARY
VERISIMILITUDE
VIETNAMIZATION
CARDIOVASCULAR
EXTRAVEHICULAR
INTERMOLECULAR
INTRAMOLECULAR
PHOTOENGRAVING
PSYCHOANALYSIS

## 12th Letter

ANTIDEPRESSANT
ANTIPERSPIRANT
CHEMOSTERILANT
CIRCUMNAVIGATE
DINOFLAGELLATE
DISCOMBOBULATE
INCOMMENSURATE
INDISCRIMINATE
INTERPLANETARY
MISAPPROPRIATE
RADIOTELEGRAPH
UNDERSECRETARY
CLAUSTROPHOBIA
IMPRESSIONABLE
INCOMMUNICABLE
INCOMPRESSIBLE
INCONSIDERABLE
INSURMOUNTABLE
IRRECONCILABLE
IRREPROACHABLE
UNCONSCIONABLE
UNCONTROLLABLE
UNINTELLIGIBLE
UNQUESTIONABLE
ECCLESIASTICAL
PHARMACEUTICAL
PSYCHOCHEMICAL
STAPHYLOCOCCUS
ACCOMPLISHMENT
INTERDEPENDENT
SCHOOLMISTRESS
UNDERNOURISHED
ADMINISTRATION
ARCHITECTONICS
CAPITALIZATION
CIRCUMLOCUTION
CIRCUMSTANTIAL
DECOMPENSATION
DISAPPROBATION
DISCIPLINARIAN
DISCRIMINATING
DISENFRANCHISE
DISEQUILIBRIUM
DISINCLINATION
EGALITARIANISM
ELECTROSTATICS
EXISTENTIALISM
FEATHERBEDDING
FUNDAMENTALISM
GENERALIZATION
HYPERSENSITIVE
HYPOTHYROIDISM
IDENTIFICATION
INTERPRETATION
KREMLINOLOGIST
LATITUDINARIAN
MICROMETEORITE
MULTIPLICATION
NEOCOLONIALISM
NONCOOPERATION
NONRESTRICTIVE
OBSTRUCTIONIST
ORGANOCHLORINE
PALEOMAGNETISM
PHOTOENGRAVING
PHOTOSENSITIVE
PREDESTINATION
RECOMMENDATION
RECONSTRUCTION
REPRESENTATION
REPRESENTATIVE
RESPONSIBILITY
SEGREGATIONIST
SENSATIONALISM
SENTIMENTALIZE
SEPTUAGENARIAN
SERVOMECHANISM
SESQUIPEDALIAN
TATTERDEMALION
THERMODYNAMICS
UNCOMPROMISING
UNDEREMPHASIZE
UTILITARIANISM
VALETUDINARIAN
VIETNAMIZATION
WEATHERABILITY
ZOROASTRIANISM
CARDIOVASCULAR
EXTRAVEHICULAR
INTERMOLECULAR
INTRAMOLECULAR
MESDEMOISELLES
AFOREMENTIONED
CONGREGATIONAL
CONSTITUTIONAL
CORRESPONDENCE
COUNTERBALANCE
DISCOUNTENANCE
GRANDILOQUENCE
INTRANSIGEANCE
KINDERGARTENER
PREADOLESCENCE
PRONUNCIAMENTO
RECONNAISSANCE
UNCONVENTIONAL
UNIDIRECTIONAL
UNPROFESSIONAL
ANESTHESIOLOGY
DISCRIMINATORY
EXTEMPORANEOUS
MICROMETEOROID
NITROCELLULOSE
OPHTHALMOSCOPE
OTOLARYNGOLOGY
PARAPSYCHOLOGY
RADIOTELEPHONE
SOCIORELIGIOUS
ARCHIEPISCOPAL
CHROMATOGRAPHY
CINEMATOGRAPHY
SUBMICROSCOPIC
UNDERDEVELOPED
WHIPPERSNAPPER
BUTTERFINGERED
PHANTASMAGORIA
ELECTRODEPOSIT
INTELLIGENTSIA
METEMPSYCHOSIS
MICROPROCESSOR
PHOTOSYNTHESIS
PNEUMOCONIOSIS
PSYCHOANALYSIS
ANTINEOPLASTIC
CHARACTERISTIC
CHICKENHEARTED
CONJUNCTIVITIS
COSMOCHEMISTRY
INTERFEROMETER
RADIOTELEMETRY
TELETYPEWRITER
TRANSCENDENTAL
TROUBLESHOOTER
COUNTERCULTURE
COUNTERMEASURE
MICROMINIATURE
SLAUGHTERHOUSE
SUPERSTRUCTURE
ULTRAMINIATURE
VERISIMILITUDE

## 13th Letter

ARCHIEPISCOPAL
CARDIOVASCULAR
CIRCUMSTANTIAL
CONGREGATIONAL
CONSTITUTIONAL
DISCIPLINARIAN
ECCLESIASTICAL
EXTRAVEHICULAR
INTERMOLECULAR
INTRAMOLECULAR
LATITUDINARIAN
PHARMACEUTICAL
PSYCHOCHEMICAL
SEPTUAGENARIAN
SESQUIPEDALIAN
TRANSCENDENTAL
UNCONVENTIONAL
UNIDIRECTIONAL
UNPROFESSIONAL
VALETUDINARIAN
ARCHITECTONICS
CORRESPONDENCE
COUNTERBALANCE
DISCOUNTENANCE
ELECTROSTATICS
GRANDILOQUENCE
INTRANSIGEANCE
PREADOLESCENCE
RECONNAISSANCE
THERMODYNAMICS
VERISIMILITUDE
AFOREMENTIONED
BUTTERFINGERED
CHICKENHEARTED
INTERFEROMETER
KINDERGARTENER
MESDEMOISELLES
TELETYPEWRITER
TROUBLESHOOTER
UNDERDEVELOPED
UNDERNOURISHED
WHIPPERSNAPPER
ANESTHESIOLOGY
OTOLARYNGOLOGY
PARAPSYCHOLOGY
CHROMATOGRAPHY
CINEMATOGRAPHY
ANTINEOPLASTIC
CHARACTERISTIC
CLAUSTROPHOBIA
CONJUNCTIVITIS
ELECTRODEPOSIT
INTELLIGENTSIA
METEMPSYCHOSIS
MICROMETEOROID
PHANTASMAGORIA
PHOTOSYNTHESIS
PNEUMOCONIOSIS
PSYCHOANALYSIS
SUBMICROSCOPIC
IMPRESSIONABLE
INCOMMUNICABLE
INCOMPRESSIBLE
INCONSIDERABLE
INSURMOUNTABLE
IRRECONCILABLE
IRREPROACHABLE
UNCONSCIONABLE
UNCONTROLLABLE
UNINTELLIGIBLE
UNQUESTIONABLE
ACCOMPLISHMENT
ANTIDEPRESSANT
ANTIPERSPIRANT
CHEMOSTERILANT
DISCRIMINATING
FEATHERBEDDING
INTERDEPENDENT
ORGANOCHLORINE
PHOTOENGRAVING
RADIOTELEPHONE
UNCOMPROMISING
ADMINISTRATION
CAPITALIZATION
CIRCUMLOCUTION
DECOMPENSATION
DISAPPROBATION
DISINCLINATION
GENERALIZATION
IDENTIFICATION
INTERPRETATION
MICROPROCESSOR
MULTIPLICATION
NONCOOPERATION
PREDESTINATION
RECOMMENDATION
RECONSTRUCTION
REPRESENTATION
TATTERDEMALION
VIETNAMIZATION
OPHTHALMOSCOPE
RADIOTELEGRAPH
COSMOCHEMISTRY
COUNTERCULTURE
COUNTERMEASURE
DISCRIMINATORY
INTERPLANETARY
MICROMINIATURE
RADIOTELEMETRY
SUPERSTRUCTURE
ULTRAMINIATURE
UNDERSECRETARY
DISENFRANCHISE
EGALITARIANISM
EXISTENTIALISM
FUNDAMENTALISM
HYPOTHYROIDISM

KREMLINOLOGI**S**T
NEOCOLONIALI**S**M
NITROCELLULO**S**E
OBSTRUCTIONI**S**T
PALEOMAGNETI**S**M
SCHOOLMISTRE**S**S
SEGREGATIONI**S**T
SENSATIONALI**S**M
SERVOMECHANI**S**M
SLAUGHTERHOU**S**E
UTILITARIANI**S**M
ZOROASTRIANI**S**M
CIRCUMNAVIGA**T**E
DINOFLAGELLA**T**E
DISCOMBOBULA**T**E
INCOMMENSURA**T**E
INDISCRIMINA**T**E
MICROMETEORI**T**E
MISAPPROPRIA**T**E
PRONUNCIAMEN**T**O
RESPONSIBILI**T**Y
WEATHERABILI**T**Y
DISEQUILIBRI**U**M
EXTEMPORANEO**U**S
SOCIORELIGIO**U**S
STAPHYLOCOCC**U**S
HYPERSENSITI**V**E
NONRESTRICTI**V**E
PHOTOSENSITI**V**E
REPRESENTATI**V**E
SENTIMENTALI**Z**E
UNDEREMPHASI**Z**E

## 14TH LETTER

CLAUSTROPHOBI**A**
INTELLIGENTSI**A**
PHANTASMAGORI**A**
ANTINEOPLASTI**C**
CHARACTERISTI**C**
SUBMICROSCOPI**C**
AFOREMENTIONE**D**
BUTTERFINGERE**D**
CHICKENHEARTE**D**
MICROMETEOROI**D**
UNDERDEVELOPE**D**
UNDERNOURISHE**D**
CIRCUMNAVIGAT**E**
CORRESPONDENC**E**
COUNTERBALANC**E**
COUNTERCULTUR**E**
COUNTERMEASUR**E**
DINOFLAGELLAT**E**
DISCOMBOBULAT**E**
DISCOUNTENANC**E**
DISENFRANCHIS**E**
GRANDILOQUENC**E**
HYPERSENSITIV**E**
IMPRESSIONABL**E**
INCOMMENSURAT**E**
INCOMMUNICABL**E**
INCOMPRESSIBL**E**
INCONSIDERABL**E**
INDISCRIMINAT**E**
INSURMOUNTABL**E**
INTRANSIGEANC**E**
IRRECONCILABL**E**
IRREPROACHABL**E**
MICROMETEORIT**E**
MICROMINIATUR**E**
MISAPPROPRIAT**E**
NITROCELLULOS**E**
NONRESTRICTIV**E**
OPHTHALMOSCOP**E**
ORGANOCHLORIN**E**
PHOTOSENSITIV**E**
PREADOLESCENC**E**
RADIOTELEPHON**E**
RECONNAISSANC**E**
REPRESENTATIV**E**
SENTIMENTALIZ**E**
SLAUGHTERHOUS**E**
SUPERSTRUCTUR**E**
ULTRAMINIATUR**E**
UNCONSCIONABL**E**
UNCONTROLLABL**E**
UNDEREMPHASIZ**E**
UNINTELLIGIBL**E**
UNQUESTIONABL**E**
VERISIMILITUD**E**
DISCRIMINATIN**G**
FEATHERBEDDIN**G**
PHOTOENGRAVIN**G**
UNCOMPROMISIN**G**
RADIOTELEGRAP**H**
ARCHIEPISCOPA**L**
CIRCUMSTANTIA**L**
CONGREGATIONA**L**
CONSTITUTIONA**L**
ECCLESIASTICA**L**
PHARMACEUTICA**L**
PSYCHOCHEMICA**L**
TRANSCENDENTA**L**
UNCONVENTIONA**L**
UNIDIRECTIONA**L**
UNPROFESSIONA**L**
DISEQUILIBRIU**M**
EGALITARIANIS**M**
EXISTENTIALIS**M**
FUNDAMENTALIS**M**
HYPOTHYROIDIS**M**
NEOCOLONIALIS**M**
PALEOMAGNETIS**M**
SENSATIONALIS**M**
SERVOMECHANIS**M**
UTILITARIANIS**M**
ZOROASTRIANIS**M**
ADMINISTRATIO**N**
CAPITALIZATIO**N**
CIRCUMLOCUTIO**N**
DECOMPENSATIO**N**
DISAPPROBATIO**N**
DISCIPLINARIA**N**
DISINCLINATIO**N**
GENERALIZATIO**N**
IDENTIFICATIO**N**
INTERPRETATIO**N**
LATITUDINARIA**N**
MULTIPLICATIO**N**
NONCOOPERATIO**N**
PREDESTINATIO**N**
RECOMMENDATIO**N**
RECONSTRUCTIO**N**
REPRESENTATIO**N**
SEPTUAGENARIA**N**
SESQUIPEDALIA**N**
TATTERDEMALIO**N**
VALETUDINARIA**N**
VIETNAMIZATIO**N**
PRONUNCIAMENT**O**
CARDIOVASCULA**R**
EXTRAVEHICULA**R**
INTERFEROMETE**R**
INTERMOLECULA**R**
INTRAMOLECULA**R**
KINDERGARTENE**R**
MICROPROCESSO**R**
TELETYPEWRITE**R**
TROUBLESHOOTE**R**
WHIPPERSNAPPE**R**
ARCHITECTONIC**S**
CONJUNCTIVITI**S**
ELECTROSTATIC**S**
EXTEMPORANEOU**S**
MESDEMOISELLE**S**
METEMPSYCHOSI**S**
PHOTOSYNTHESI**S**
PNEUMOCONIOSI**S**
PSYCHOANALYSI**S**
SCHOOLMISTRES**S**
SOCIORELIGIOU**S**
STAPHYLOCOCCU**S**
THERMODYNAMIC**S**
ACCOMPLISHMEN**T**
ANTIDEPRESSAN**T**
ANTIPERSPIRAN**T**
CHEMOSTERILAN**T**
ELECTRODEPOSI**T**
INTERDEPENDEN**T**
KREMLINOLOGIS**T**
OBSTRUCTIONIS**T**
SEGREGATIONIS**T**
ANESTHESIOLOG**Y**
CHROMATOGRAPH**Y**
CINEMATOGRAPH**Y**
COSMOCHEMISTR**Y**
DISCRIMINATOR**Y**
INTERPLANETAR**Y**
OTOLARYNGOLOG**Y**
PARAPSYCHOLOG**Y**
RADIOTELEMETR**Y**
RESPONSIBILIT**Y**
UNDERSECRETAR**Y**
WEATHERABILIT**Y**

# 15 LETTER WORDS

## 1st Letter

**A**NTHROPOCENTRIC
**A**THEROSCLEROSIS
**C**ONSERVATIONIST
**C**ONSTRUCTIONIST
**C**ONTEMPORANEOUS
**C**ONVENTIONALIZE
**C**RYSTALLOGRAPHY
**D**ISINTOXICATION
**D**ISSATISFACTION
**E**LECTRODYNAMICS
**E**LECTROMAGNETIC
**E**LECTROPHORESIS
**E**XTRACURRICULAR
**F**LIBBERTIGIBBET
**H**ISTORIOGRAPHER
**H**YPERTHYROIDISM
**I**NCONSEQUENTIAL
**I**NSTRUMENTALIST
**I**NSTRUMENTALITY
**I**NSTRUMENTATION
**I**NTELLECTUALISM
**I**NTERCOLLEGIATE
**I**NTERSCHOLASTIC
**I**NTERVENTIONISM
**M**ETHAMPHETAMINE
**M**ICROCONTROLLER
**M**ICROPHOTOGRAPH
**M**ULTIPROCESSING
**N**ONINTERVENTION
**N**ONPRESCRIPTION
**N**OTWITHSTANDING
**O**RGANOPHOSPHATE
**P**ARLIAMENTARIAN
**P**ARTHENOGENESIS
**P**HOSPHORESCENCE
**P**HOTOMICROGRAPH
**P**ITHECANTHROPUS
**P**LAINCLOTHESMAN
**P**LENIPOTENTIARY
**P**OLYCRYSTALLINE
**P**OLYUNSATURATED
**P**OSTCONSONANTAL
**P**ROFESSIONALISM
**P**ROFESSIONALIZE
**S**TRAIGHTFORWARD
**T**HERMOREGULATOR
**U**LTRACENTRIFUGE
**U**LTRAMICROSCOPE
**U**NCOMMUNICATIVE
**U**NDEMONSTRATIVE
**U**NDERPRIVILEGED
**U**NDERPRODUCTION
**U**NEXCEPTIONABLE
**U**NINTERRUPTIBLE
**U**NPARLIAMENTARY
**U**NRECONSTRUCTED
**U**NSOPHISTICATED
**V**ASOCONSTRICTOR
**W**EATHERBOARDING

## 2nd Letter

P**A**RLIAMENTARIAN
P**A**RTHENOGENESIS
V**A**SOCONSTRICTOR
M**E**THAMPHETAMINE
W**E**ATHERBOARDING
P**H**OSPHORESCENCE
P**H**OTOMICROGRAPH
T**H**ERMOREGULATOR
D**I**SINTOXICATION
D**I**SSATISFACTION
H**I**STORIOGRAPHER
M**I**CROCONTROLLER
M**I**CROPHOTOGRAPH
P**I**THECANTHROPUS
E**L**ECTRODYNAMICS
E**L**ECTROMAGNETIC
E**L**ECTROPHORESIS
F**L**IBBERTIGIBBET
P**L**AINCLOTHESMAN
P**L**ENIPOTENTIARY
U**L**TRACENTRIFUGE
U**L**TRAMICROSCOPE
A**N**THROPOCENTRIC
I**N**CONSEQUENTIAL
I**N**STRUMENTALIST
I**N**STRUMENTALITY
I**N**STRUMENTATION
I**N**TELLECTUALISM
I**N**TERCOLLEGIATE
I**N**TERSCHOLASTIC
I**N**TERVENTIONISM
U**N**COMMUNICATIVE
U**N**DEMONSTRATIVE
U**N**DERPRIVILEGED
U**N**DERPRODUCTION
U**N**EXCEPTIONABLE
U**N**INTERRUPTIBLE
U**N**PARLIAMENTARY
U**N**RECONSTRUCTED
U**N**SOPHISTICATED
C**O**NSERVATIONIST
C**O**NSTRUCTIONIST
C**O**NTEMPORANEOUS
C**O**NVENTIONALIZE
N**O**NINTERVENTION
N**O**NPRESCRIPTION
N**O**TWITHSTANDING
P**O**LYCRYSTALLINE
P**O**LYUNSATURATED
P**O**STCONSONANTAL
C**R**YSTALLOGRAPHY
O**R**GANOPHOSPHATE
P**R**OFESSIONALISM
P**R**OFESSIONALIZE
A**T**HEROSCLEROSIS
S**T**RAIGHTFORWARD
M**U**LTIPROCESSING
E**X**TRACURRICULAR
H**Y**PERTHYROIDISM

## 3rd Letter

PL**A**INCLOTHESMAN
WE**A**THERBOARDING
IN**C**ONSEQUENTIAL
MI**C**ROCONTROLLER
MI**C**ROPHOTOGRAPH
UN**C**OMMUNICATIVE
UN**D**EMONSTRATIVE
UN**D**ERPRIVILEGED
UN**D**ERPRODUCTION
EL**E**CTRODYNAMICS
EL**E**CTROMAGNETIC
EL**E**CTROPHORESIS
PL**E**NIPOTENTIARY
TH**E**RMOREGULATOR
UN**E**XCEPTIONABLE
OR**G**ANOPHOSPHATE
AT**H**EROSCLEROSIS
FL**I**BBERTIGIBBET
UN**I**NTERRUPTIBLE
MU**L**TIPROCESSING
PO**L**YCRYSTALLINE
PO**L**YUNSATURATED
CO**N**SERVATIONIST
CO**N**STRUCTIONIST
CO**N**TEMPORANEOUS
CO**N**VENTIONALIZE
NO**N**INTERVENTION
NO**N**PRESCRIPTION
PH**O**SPHORESCENCE
PH**O**TOMICROGRAPH
PR**O**FESSIONALISM
PR**O**FESSIONALIZE
HY**P**ERTHYROIDISM
UN**P**ARLIAMENTARY
PA**R**LIAMENTARIAN
PA**R**THENOGENESIS
ST**R**AIGHTFORWARD
UN**R**ECONSTRUCTED
DI**S**INTOXICATION
DI**S**SATISFACTION
HI**S**TORIOGRAPHER
IN**S**TRUMENTALIST
IN**S**TRUMENTALITY
IN**S**TRUMENTATION
PO**S**TCONSONANTAL
UN**S**OPHISTICATED
VA**S**OCONSTRICTOR
AN**T**HROPOCENTRIC
EX**T**RACURRICULAR
IN**T**ELLECTUALISM
IN**T**ERCOLLEGIATE
IN**T**ERSCHOLASTIC
IN**T**ERVENTIONISM
ME**T**HAMPHETAMINE
NO**T**WITHSTANDING
PI**T**HECANTHROPUS
UL**T**RACENTRIFUGE
UL**T**RAMICROSCOPE
CR**Y**STALLOGRAPHY

## 4th Letter

ORG**A**NOPHOSPHATE
STR**A**IGHTFORWARD
UNP**A**RLIAMENTARY
FLI**B**BERTIGIBBET
ELE**C**TRODYNAMICS
ELE**C**TROMAGNETIC
ELE**C**TROPHORESIS
ATH**E**ROSCLEROSIS
HYP**E**RTHYROIDISM
INT**E**LLECTUALISM
INT**E**RCOLLEGIATE
INT**E**RSCHOLASTIC
INT**E**RVENTIONISM
UND**E**MONSTRATIVE
UND**E**RPRIVILEGED
UND**E**RPRODUCTION
UNR**E**CONSTRUCTED
PRO**F**ESSIONALISM
PRO**F**ESSIONALIZE
ANT**H**ROPOCENTRIC
MET**H**AMPHETAMINE
PIT**H**ECANTHROPUS
DIS**I**NTOXICATION
NON**I**NTERVENTION
PLA**I**NCLOTHESMAN
PAR**L**IAMENTARIAN
PLE**N**IPOTENTIARY
UNI**N**TERRUPTIBLE
INC**O**NSEQUENTIAL
UNC**O**MMUNICATIVE
UNS**O**PHISTICATED
VAS**O**CONSTRICTOR
NON**P**RESCRIPTION
EXT**R**ACURRICULAR
MIC**R**OCONTROLLER
MIC**R**OPHOTOGRAPH
THE**R**MOREGULATOR
ULT**R**ACENTRIFUGE
ULT**R**AMICROSCOPE
CON**S**ERVATIONIST
CON**S**TRUCTIONIST
CRY**S**TALLOGRAPHY
DIS**S**ATISFACTION
PHO**S**PHORESCENCE
CON**T**EMPORANEOUS
HIS**T**ORIOGRAPHER
INS**T**RUMENTALIST
INS**T**RUMENTALITY
INS**T**RUMENTATION
MUL**T**IPROCESSING
PAR**T**HENOGENESIS
PHO**T**OMICROGRAPH
POS**T**CONSONANTAL
WEA**T**HERBOARDING
CON**V**ENTIONALIZE
NOT**W**ITHSTANDING
UNE**X**CEPTIONABLE
POL**Y**CRYSTALLINE
POL**Y**UNSATURATED

## 5th Letter

DISSATISFACTION
EXTRACURRICULAR
METHAMPHETAMINE
ULTRACENTRIFUGE
ULTRAMICROSCOPE
FLIBBERTIGIBBET
POLYCRYSTALLINE
POSTCONSONANTAL
UNEXCEPTIONABLE
UNRECONSTRUCTED
VASOCONSTRICTOR
CONSERVATIONIST
CONTEMPORANEOUS
CONVENTIONALIZE
PITHECANTHROPUS
PROFESSIONALISM
PROFESSIONALIZE
PARTHENOGENESIS
WEATHERBOARDING
MULTIPROCESSING
NOTWITHSTANDING
PARLIAMENTARIAN
PLENIPOTENTIARY
STRAIGHTFORWARD
INTELLECTUALISM
THERMOREGULATOR
UNCOMMUNICATIVE
UNDEMONSTRATIVE
DISINTOXICATION
INCONSEQUENTIAL
NONINTERVENTION
ORGANOPHOSPHATE
PLAINCLOTHESMAN
HISTORIOGRAPHER
MICROCONTROLLER
MICROPHOTOGRAPH
PHOTOMICROGRAPH
PHOSPHORESCENCE
UNSOPHISTICATED
ANTHROPOCENTRIC
ATHEROSCLEROSIS
HYPERTHYROIDISM
INSTRUMENTALIST
INSTRUMENTALITY
INSTRUMENTATION
INTERCOLLEGIATE
INTERSCHOLASTIC
INTERVENTIONISM
NONPRESCRIPTION
UNDERPRIVILEGED
UNDERPRODUCTION
UNPARLIAMENTARY
CONSTRUCTIONIST
CRYSTALLOGRAPHY
ELECTRODYNAMICS
ELECTROMAGNETIC
ELECTROPHORESIS
UNINTERRUPTIBLE
POLYUNSATURATED

## 6th Letter

CRYSTALLOGRAPHY
PARLIAMENTARIAN
EXTRACURRICULAR
INTERCOLLEGIATE
MICROCONTROLLER
PITHECANTHROPUS
PLAINCLOTHESMAN
ULTRACENTRIFUGE
FLIBBERTIGIBBET
NONPRESCRIPTION
PARTHENOGENESIS
UNEXCEPTIONABLE
UNINTERRUPTIBLE
WEATHERBOARDING
STRAIGHTFORWARD
PHOSPHORESCENCE
UNSOPHISTICATED
INTELLECTUALISM
UNPARLIAMENTARY
CONTEMPORANEOUS
METHAMPHETAMINE
PHOTOMICROGRAPH
ULTRAMICROSCOPE
UNCOMMUNICATIVE
CONVENTIONALIZE
POLYUNSATURATED
ANTHROPOCENTRIC
ATHEROSCLEROSIS
ORGANOPHOSPHATE
POSTCONSONANTAL
THERMOREGULATOR
UNDEMONSTRATIVE
UNRECONSTRUCTED
VASOCONSTRICTOR
MICROPHOTOGRAPH
MULTIPROCESSING
PLENIPOTENTIARY
UNDERPRIVILEGED
UNDERPRODUCTION
CONSERVATIONIST
CONSTRUCTIONIST
ELECTRODYNAMICS
ELECTROMAGNETIC
ELECTROPHORESIS
HISTORIOGRAPHER
POLYCRYSTALLINE
INCONSEQUENTIAL
INTERSCHOLASTIC
PROFESSIONALISM
PROFESSIONALIZE
DISINTOXICATION
DISSATISFACTION
HYPERTHYROIDISM
NONINTERVENTION
NOTWITHSTANDING
INSTRUMENTALIST
INSTRUMENTALITY
INSTRUMENTATION
INTERVENTIONISM

## 7th Letter

PITHECANTHROPUS
INTERSCHOLASTIC
INCONSEQUENTIAL
INTELLECTUALISM
INTERVENTIONISM
NONINTERVENTION
ULTRACENTRIFUGE
HYPERTHYROIDISM
MICROPHOTOGRAPH
NOTWITHSTANDING
STRAIGHTFORWARD
DISSATISFACTION
HISTORIOGRAPHER
PHOTOMICROGRAPH
ULTRAMICROSCOPE
UNPARLIAMENTARY
UNSOPHISTICATED
CRYSTALLOGRAPHY
PLAINCLOTHESMAN
INSTRUMENTALIST
INSTRUMENTALITY
INSTRUMENTATION
PARLIAMENTARIAN
PARTHENOGENESIS
POSTCONSONANTAL
UNDEMONSTRATIVE
UNRECONSTRUCTED
VASOCONSTRICTOR
DISINTOXICATION
ELECTRODYNAMICS
ELECTROMAGNETIC
ELECTROPHORESIS
INTERCOLLEGIATE
MICROCONTROLLER
PHOSPHORESCENCE
PLENIPOTENTIARY
ANTHROPOCENTRIC
CONTEMPORANEOUS
METHAMPHETAMINE
ORGANOPHOSPHATE
UNEXCEPTIONABLE
FLIBBERTIGIBBET
MULTIPROCESSING
THERMOREGULATOR
UNDERPRIVILEGED
UNDERPRODUCTION
UNINTERRUPTIBLE
WEATHERBOARDING
ATHEROSCLEROSIS
NONPRESCRIPTION
POLYUNSATURATED
PROFESSIONALISM
PROFESSIONALIZE
CONVENTIONALIZE
CONSTRUCTIONIST
EXTRACURRICULAR
UNCOMMUNICATIVE
CONSERVATIONIST
POLYCRYSTALLINE

## 8th Letter

CONSERVATIONIST
POLYUNSATURATED
UNPARLIAMENTARY
WEATHERBOARDING
ATHEROSCLEROSIS
CONSTRUCTIONIST
INTELLECTUALISM
NONPRESCRIPTION
PHOTOMICROGRAPH
ULTRAMICROSCOPE
ELECTRODYNAMICS
INSTRUMENTALIST
INSTRUMENTALITY
INSTRUMENTATION
PARLIAMENTARIAN
THERMOREGULATOR
INTERSCHOLASTIC
METHAMPHETAMINE
ORGANOPHOSPHATE
CONVENTIONALIZE
PROFESSIONALISM
PROFESSIONALIZE
UNDERPRIVILEGED
CRYSTALLOGRAPHY
INTERCOLLEGIATE
ELECTROMAGNETIC
INTERVENTIONISM
MICROCONTROLLER
PITHECANTHROPUS
ULTRACENTRIFUGE
UNCOMMUNICATIVE
ANTHROPOCENTRIC
CONTEMPORANEOUS
HISTORIOGRAPHER
MICROPHOTOGRAPH
MULTIPROCESSING
PARTHENOGENESIS
PLAINCLOTHESMAN
UNDERPRODUCTION
ELECTROPHORESIS
INCONSEQUENTIAL
EXTRACURRICULAR
NONINTERVENTION
PHOSPHORESCENCE
UNINTERRUPTIBLE
DISSATISFACTION
NOTWITHSTANDING
POLYCRYSTALLINE
POSTCONSONANTAL
UNDEMONSTRATIVE
UNRECONSTRUCTED
UNSOPHISTICATED
VASOCONSTRICTOR
FLIBBERTIGIBBET
PLENIPOTENTIARY
STRAIGHTFORWARD
UNEXCEPTIONABLE
DISINTOXICATION
HYPERTHYROIDISM

## 9th Letter

ELECTROMAGNETIC
ANTHROPOCENTRIC
MULTIPROCESSING
UNDERPRODUCTION
METHAMPHETAMINE
PHOSPHORESCENCE
PLENIPOTENTIARY
DISSATISFACTION
STRAIGHTFORWARD
HISTORIOGRAPHER
PARTHENOGENESIS
THERMOREGULATOR
ELECTROPHORESIS
DISINTOXICATION
FLIBBERTIGIBBET
UNCOMMUNICATIVE
UNEXCEPTIONABLE
ATHEROSCLEROSIS
INTERCOLLEGIATE
UNPARLIAMENTARY
INSTRUMENTALIST
INSTRUMENTALITY
INSTRUMENTATION
PARLIAMENTARIAN
CONVENTIONALIZE
CRYSTALLOGRAPHY
INTERSCHOLASTIC

ORGANOPHOSPHATE
POSTCONSONANTAL
PROFESSIONALISM
PROFESSIONALIZE
WEATHERBOARDING
CONTEMPORANEOUS
EXTRACURRICULAR
HYPERTHYROIDISM
NONPRESCRIPTION
PHOTOMICROGRAPH
ULTRAMICROSCOPE
CONSERVATIONIST
CONSTRUCTIONIST
INTELLECTUALISM
INTERVENTIONISM
MICROCONTROLLER
MICROPHOTOGRAPH
NOTWITHSTANDING
PITHECANTHROPUS
PLAINCLOTHESMAN
POLYCRYSTALLINE
POLYUNSATURATED
ULTRACENTRIFUGE
UNDEMONSTRATIVE
UNRECONSTRUCTED
UNSOPHISTICATED
VASOCONSTRICTOR
INCONSEQUENTIAL
UNINTERRUPTIBLE
NONINTERVENTION
UNDERPRIVILEGED
ELECTRODYNAMICS

## 10th Letter

CONTEMPORANEOUS
DISSATISFACTION
NOTWITHSTANDING
POLYCRYSTALLINE
WEATHERBOARDING
DISINTOXICATION
UNCOMMUNICATIVE
ANTHROPOCENTRIC
ATHEROSCLEROSIS
INCONSEQUENTIAL
INTERCOLLEGIATE
MULTIPROCESSING
NONINTERVENTION
PARTHENOGENESIS
UNPARLIAMENTARY
CRYSTALLOGRAPHY
ELECTROMAGNETIC
FLIBBERTIGIBBET
PITHECANTHROPUS
PLAINCLOTHESMAN
CONSERVATIONIST
CONSTRUCTIONIST
EXTRACURRICULAR
INTERVENTIONISM
NONPRESCRIPTION
UNDERPRIVILEGED
UNSOPHISTICATED
INTERSCHOLASTIC
CONVENTIONALIZE
ELECTRODYNAMICS
PLENIPOTENTIARY
POSTCONSONANTAL
PROFESSIONALISM
PROFESSIONALIZE
ELECTROPHORESIS
HYPERTHYROIDISM
MICROPHOTOGRAPH
PHOTOMICROGRAPH
STRAIGHTFORWARD
ULTRAMICROSCOPE
UNEXCEPTIONABLE
UNINTERRUPTIBLE
HISTORIOGRAPHER
MICROCONTROLLER
ULTRACENTRIFUGE
UNDEMONSTRATIVE
UNRECONSTRUCTED
VASOCONSTRICTOR
ORGANOPHOSPHATE
PHOSPHORESCENCE
INSTRUMENTALIST
INSTRUMENTALITY
INSTRUMENTATION
METHAMPHETAMINE
PARLIAMENTARIAN
INTELLECTUALISM
POLYUNSATURATED
THERMOREGULATOR
UNDERPRODUCTION

## 11th Letter

CONVENTIONALIZE
DISINTOXICATION
ELECTRODYNAMICS
HISTORIOGRAPHER
INSTRUMENTALIST
INSTRUMENTALITY
INSTRUMENTATION
INTELLECTUALISM
INTERSCHOLASTIC
METHAMPHETAMINE
PARLIAMENTARIAN
POSTCONSONANTAL
PROFESSIONALISM
PROFESSIONALIZE
UNCOMMUNICATIVE
UNDEMONSTRATIVE
DISSATISFACTION
EXTRACURRICULAR
PHOSPHORESCENCE
UNDERPRODUCTION
UNSOPHISTICATED
PLAINCLOTHESMAN
INTERCOLLEGIATE
MICROPHOTOGRAPH
PHOTOMICROGRAPH
FLIBBERTIGIBBET
HYPERTHYROIDISM
ULTRACENTRIFUGE
VASOCONSTRICTOR
POLYCRYSTALLINE
THERMOREGULATOR
UNDERPRIVILEGED
ANTHROPOCENTRIC
CONTEMPORANEOUS
ELECTROMAGNETIC
INCONSEQUENTIAL
NONINTERVENTION
NOTWITHSTANDING
PARTHENOGENESIS
UNEXCEPTIONABLE
UNPARLIAMENTARY
CONSERVATIONIST
CONSTRUCTIONIST
INTERVENTIONISM
MICROCONTROLLER
NONPRESCRIPTION
ORGANOPHOSPHATE
ATHEROSCLEROSIS
CRYSTALLOGRAPHY
ELECTROPHORESIS
PITHECANTHROPUS
POLYUNSATURATED
STRAIGHTFORWARD
WEATHERBOARDING
MULTIPROCESSING
ULTRAMICROSCOPE
PLENIPOTENTIARY
UNINTERRUPTIBLE
UNRECONSTRUCTED

## 12th Letter

CRYSTALLOGRAPHY
POLYUNSATURATED
THERMOREGULATOR
UNEXCEPTIONABLE
UNSOPHISTICATED
FLIBBERTIGIBBET
ULTRAMICROSCOPE
UNRECONSTRUCTED
VASOCONSTRICTOR
HYPERTHYROIDISM
NOTWITHSTANDING
WEATHERBOARDING
CONTEMPORANEOUS
ELECTROMAGNETIC
ELECTROPHORESIS
PARTHENOGENESIS
PHOSPHORESCENCE
UNDERPRIVILEGED
ULTRACENTRIFUGE
ORGANOPHOSPHATE
INTERCOLLEGIATE
PLENIPOTENTIARY
UNINTERRUPTIBLE
CONVENTIONALIZE
INSTRUMENTALIST
INSTRUMENTALITY
INTELLECTUALISM
MICROCONTROLLER
POLYCRYSTALLINE
PROFESSIONALISM
PROFESSIONALIZE
ELECTRODYNAMICS
METHAMPHETAMINE
CONSERVATIONIST
CONSTRUCTIONIST
INTERVENTIONISM
POSTCONSONANTAL
ATHEROSCLEROSIS
PITHECANTHROPUS
HISTORIOGRAPHER
MICROPHOTOGRAPH
PARLIAMENTARIAN
PHOTOMICROGRAPH
INTERSCHOLASTIC
MULTIPROCESSING
PLAINCLOTHESMAN
ANTHROPOCENTRIC
DISINTOXICATION
DISSATISFACTION
INCONSEQUENTIAL
INSTRUMENTATION
NONINTERVENTION
NONPRESCRIPTION
UNCOMMUNICATIVE
UNDEMONSTRATIVE
UNDERPRODUCTION
UNPARLIAMENTARY
EXTRACURRICULAR
STRAIGHTFORWARD

## 13th Letter

INTERCOLLEGIATE
MICROPHOTOGRAPH
ORGANOPHOSPHATE
PHOTOMICROGRAPH
PLENIPOTENTIARY
STRAIGHTFORWARD
UNPARLIAMENTARY
FLIBBERTIGIBBET
UNEXCEPTIONABLE
UNINTERRUPTIBLE
UNDERPRIVILEGED
HISTORIOGRAPHER
CONSERVATIONIST
CONSTRUCTIONIST
CONVENTIONALIZE
DISINTOXICATION
DISSATISFACTION
ELECTRODYNAMICS
HYPERTHYROIDISM
INCONSEQUENTIAL
INSTRUMENTALIST
INSTRUMENTALITY
INSTRUMENTATION
INTELLECTUALISM
INTERVENTIONISM
METHAMPHETAMINE
MULTIPROCESSING
NONINTERVENTION
NONPRESCRIPTION
NOTWITHSTANDING
PARLIAMENTARIAN
POLYCRYSTALLINE
PROFESSIONALISM
PROFESSIONALIZE
UNCOMMUNICATIVE
UNDEMONSTRATIVE
UNDERPRODUCTION
WEATHERBOARDING
EXTRACURRICULAR
MICROCONTROLLER
PLAINCLOTHESMAN
PHOSPHORESCENCE
CONTEMPORANEOUS
ULTRAMICROSCOPE
CRYSTALLOGRAPHY
PITHECANTHROPUS
ANTHROPOCENTRIC
ATHEROSCLEROSIS
ELECTROPHORESIS
PARTHENOGENESIS
ELECTROMAGNETIC
INTERSCHOLASTIC
POLYUNSATURATED
POSTCONSONANTAL
THERMOREGULATOR

UNRECONSTRUC**T**ED
UNSOPHISTICA**T**ED
VASOCONSTRIC**T**OR
ULTRACENTRIF**U**GE

## 14th Letter

EXTRACURRICUL**A**R
INCONSEQUENTI**A**L
PARLIAMENTARI**A**N
PLAINCLOTHESM**A**N
POSTCONSONANT**A**L
ELECTRODYNAMI**C**S
PHOSPHORESCEN**C**E
FLIBBERTIGIBB**E**T
HISTORIOGRAPH**E**R
MICROCONTROLL**E**R
POLYUNSATURAT**E**D
UNDERPRIVILEG**E**D
UNRECONSTRUCT**E**D
UNSOPHISTICAT**E**D
ULTRACENTRIFU**G**E
CRYSTALLOGRAP**H**Y
ANTHROPOCENTR**I**C
ATHEROSCLEROS**I**S
ELECTROMAGNET**I**C
ELECTROPHORES**I**S
INTERSCHOLAST**I**C
PARTHENOGENES**I**S
UNEXCEPTIONAB**L**E
UNINTERRUPTIB**L**E
METHAMPHETAMI**N**E
MULTIPROCESSI**N**G
NOTWITHSTANDI**N**G
POLYCRYSTALLI**N**E
WEATHERBOARDI**N**G
DISINTOXICATI**O**N
DISSATISFACTI**O**N
INSTRUMENTATI**O**N
NONINTERVENTI**O**N
NONPRESCRIPTI**O**N
THERMOREGULAT**O**R
UNDERPRODUCTI**O**N
VASOCONSTRICT**O**R
MICROPHOTOGRA**P**H
PHOTOMICROGRA**P**H
ULTRAMICROSCO**P**E
PLENIPOTENTIA**R**Y
STRAIGHTFORWA**R**D
UNPARLIAMENTA**R**Y
CONSERVATIONI**S**T
CONSTRUCTIONI**S**T
HYPERTHYROIDI**S**M
INSTRUMENTALI**S**T
INTELLECTUALI**S**M
INTERVENTIONI**S**M
PROFESSIONALI**S**M
INSTRUMENTALI**T**Y
INTERCOLLEGIA**T**E
ORGANOPHOSPHA**T**E
CONTEMPORANEO**U**S
PITHECANTHROP**U**S
UNCOMMUNICATI**V**E
UNDEMONSTRATI**V**E
CONVENTIONALI**Z**E
PROFESSIONALI**Z**E

## 15th Letter

ANTHROPOCENTRI**C**
ELECTROMAGNETI**C**
INTERSCHOLASTI**C**
POLYUNSATURATE**D**
STRAIGHTFORWAR**D**
UNDERPRIVILEGE**D**
UNRECONSTRUCTE**D**
UNSOPHISTICATE**D**
CONVENTIONALIZ**E**
INTERCOLLEGIAT**E**
METHAMPHETAMIN**E**
ORGANOPHOSPHAT**E**
PHOSPHORESCENC**E**
POLYCRYSTALLIN**E**
PROFESSIONALIZ**E**
ULTRACENTRIFUG**E**
ULTRAMICROSCOP**E**
UNCOMMUNICATIV**E**
UNDEMONSTRATIV**E**
UNEXCEPTIONABL**E**
UNINTERRUPTIBL**E**
MULTIPROCESSIN**G**
NOTWITHSTANDIN**G**
WEATHERBOARDIN**G**
MICROPHOTOGRAP**H**
PHOTOMICROGRAP**H**
INCONSEQUENTIA**L**
POSTCONSONANTA**L**
HYPERTHYROIDIS**M**
INTELLECTUALIS**M**
INTERVENTIONIS**M**
PROFESSIONALIS**M**
DISINTOXICATIO**N**
DISSATISFACTIO**N**
INSTRUMENTATIO**N**
NONINTERVENTIO**N**
NONPRESCRIPTIO**N**
PARLIAMENTARIA**N**
PLAINCLOTHESMA**N**
UNDERPRODUCTIO**N**
EXTRACURRICULA**R**
HISTORIOGRAPHE**R**
MICROCONTROLLE**R**
THERMOREGULATO**R**
VASOCONSTRICTO**R**
ATHEROSCLEROSI**S**
CONTEMPORANEOU**S**
ELECTRODYNAMIC**S**
ELECTROPHORESI**S**
PARTHENOGENESI**S**
PITHECANTHROPU**S**
CONSERVATIONIS**T**
CONSTRUCTIONIS**T**
FLIBBERTIGIBBE**T**
INSTRUMENTALIS**T**
CRYSTALLOGRAPH**Y**
INSTRUMENTALIT**Y**
PLENIPOTENTIAR**Y**
UNPARLIAMENTAR**Y**

# 16 LETTER WORDS

### 1st Letter

**A**NTHROPOMORPHISM
**A**NTIHYPERTENSIVE
**A**RTERIOSCLEROSIS
**A**UTOINTOXICATION
**C**OMPARTMENTALIZE
**C**ONTAINERIZATION
**C**OUNTERCLOCKWISE
**C**OUNTERESPIONAGE
**C**OUNTEROFFENSIVE
**D**ECENTRALIZATION
**E**LECTROCHEMISTRY
**E**LECTROHYDRAULIC
**E**LECTROMAGNETISM
**E**NVIRONMENTALIST
**E**XTRATERRESTRIAL
**E**XTRATERRITORIAL
**G**ASTROENTEROLOGY
**G**ASTROINTESTINAL
**I**NCOMPREHENSIBLE
**I**NCONTROVERTIBLE
**I**NTERCONTINENTAL
**I**NTERNATIONALISM
**I**NTERNATIONALIZE
**M**ICROELECTRONICS
**M**ICROENCAPSULATE
**M**ISCOMMUNICATION
**M**ISUNDERSTANDING
**M**ULTIDIMENSIONAL
**M**ULTIMILLIONAIRE
**M**ULTIPROGRAMMING
**N**ONPROLIFERATION
**O**RGANOPHOSPHORUS
**P**ARAPROFESSIONAL
**P**IEZOELECTRICITY
**P**RESTIDIGITATION
**S**ESQUICENTENNIAL
**T**INTINNABULATION
**T**RANSCONTINENTAL
**U**LTRAFASHIONABLE
**U**LTRAMICROSCOPIC
**U**NCONSTITUTIONAL
**U**NDERREPRESENTED
**V**ASOCONSTRICTION

### 2nd Letter

G**A**STROENTEROLOGY
G**A**STROINTESTINAL
P**A**RAPROFESSIONAL
V**A**SOCONSTRICTION
D**E**CENTRALIZATION
S**E**SQUICENTENNIAL
M**I**CROELECTRONICS
M**I**CROENCAPSULATE
M**I**SCOMMUNICATION
M**I**SUNDERSTANDING
P**I**EZOELECTRICITY
T**I**NTINNABULATION
E**L**ECTROCHEMISTRY
E**L**ECTROHYDRAULIC
E**L**ECTROMAGNETISM
U**L**TRAFASHIONABLE
U**L**TRAMICROSCOPIC
A**N**THROPOMORPHISM
A**N**TIHYPERTENSIVE
E**N**VIRONMENTALIST
I**N**COMPREHENSIBLE
I**N**CONTROVERTIBLE
I**N**TERCONTINENTAL
I**N**TERNATIONALISM
I**N**TERNATIONALIZE
U**N**CONSTITUTIONAL
U**N**DERREPRESENTED
C**O**MPARTMENTALIZE
C**O**NTAINERIZATION
C**O**UNTERCLOCKWISE
C**O**UNTERESPIONAGE
C**O**UNTEROFFENSIVE
N**O**NPROLIFERATION
A**R**TERIOSCLEROSIS
O**R**GANOPHOSPHORUS
P**R**ESTIDIGITATION
T**R**ANSCONTINENTAL
A**U**TOINTOXICATION
M**U**LTIDIMENSIONAL
M**U**LTIMILLIONAIRE
M**U**LTIPROGRAMMING
E**X**TRATERRESTRIAL
E**X**TRATERRITORIAL

### 3rd Letter

TR**A**NSCONTINENTAL
DE**C**ENTRALIZATION
IN**C**OMPREHENSIBLE
IN**C**ONTROVERTIBLE
MI**C**ROELECTRONICS
MI**C**ROENCAPSULATE
UN**C**ONSTITUTIONAL
UN**D**ERREPRESENTED
EL**E**CTROCHEMISTRY
EL**E**CTROHYDRAULIC
EL**E**CTROMAGNETISM
PI**E**ZOELECTRICITY
PR**E**STIDIGITATION
OR**G**ANOPHOSPHORUS
MU**L**TIDIMENSIONAL
MU**L**TIMILLIONAIRE
MU**L**TIPROGRAMMING
CO**M**PARTMENTALIZE
CO**N**TAINERIZATION
NO**N**PROLIFERATION
TI**N**TINNABULATION
PA**R**APROFESSIONAL
GA**S**TROENTEROLOGY
GA**S**TROINTESTINAL
MI**S**COMMUNICATION
MI**S**UNDERSTANDING
SE**S**QUICENTENNIAL
VA**S**OCONSTRICTION
AN**T**HROPOMORPHISM
AN**T**IHYPERTENSIVE
AR**T**ERIOSCLEROSIS
AU**T**OINTOXICATION
EX**T**RATERRESTRIAL
EX**T**RATERRITORIAL
IN**T**ERCONTINENTAL
IN**T**ERNATIONALISM
IN**T**ERNATIONALIZE
UL**T**RAFASHIONABLE
UL**T**RAMICROSCOPIC
CO**U**NTERCLOCKWISE
CO**U**NTERESPIONAGE
CO**U**NTEROFFENSIVE
EN**V**IRONMENTALIST

### 4th Letter

ORG**A**NOPHOSPHORUS
PAR**A**PROFESSIONAL
ELE**C**TROCHEMISTRY
ELE**C**TROHYDRAULIC
ELE**C**TROMAGNETISM
MIS**C**OMMUNICATION
ART**E**RIOSCLEROSIS
DEC**E**NTRALIZATION
INT**E**RCONTINENTAL
INT**E**RNATIONALISM
INT**E**RNATIONALIZE
UND**E**RREPRESENTED
ANT**H**ROPOMORPHISM
ANT**I**HYPERTENSIVE
ENV**I**RONMENTALIST
COU**N**TERCLOCKWISE
COU**N**TERESPIONAGE
COU**N**TEROFFENSIVE
TRA**N**SCONTINENTAL
AUT**O**INTOXICATION
INC**O**MPREHENSIBLE
INC**O**NTROVERTIBLE
UNC**O**NSTITUTIONAL
VAS**O**CONSTRICTION
COM**P**ARTMENTALIZE
NON**P**ROLIFERATION
SES**Q**UICENTENNIAL
EXT**R**ATERRESTRIAL
EXT**R**ATERRITORIAL
MIC**R**OELECTRONICS
MIC**R**OENCAPSULATE
ULT**R**AFASHIONABLE
ULT**R**AMICROSCOPIC
PRE**S**TIDIGITATION
CON**T**AINERIZATION
GAS**T**ROENTEROLOGY
GAS**T**ROINTESTINAL
MUL**T**IDIMENSIONAL
MUL**T**IMILLIONAIRE
MUL**T**IPROGRAMMING
TIN**T**INNABULATION
MIS**U**NDERSTANDING
PIE**Z**OELECTRICITY

### 5th Letter

COMP**A**RTMENTALIZE
CONT**A**INERIZATION
EXTR**A**TERRESTRIAL
EXTR**A**TERRITORIAL
ULTR**A**FASHIONABLE
ULTR**A**MICROSCOPIC
VASO**C**ONSTRICTION
ANTI**H**YPERTENSIVE
AUTO**I**NTOXICATION
MULT**I**DIMENSIONAL
MULT**I**MILLIONAIRE

MULT**I**PROGRAMMING
TINT**I**NNABULATION
INCO**M**PREHENSIBLE
DECE**N**TRALIZATION
INCO**N**TROVERTIBLE
MISU**N**DERSTANDING
ORGA**N**OPHOSPHORUS
UNCO**N**STITUTIONAL
MICR**O**ELECTRONICS
MICR**O**ENCAPSULATE
MISC**O**MMUNICATION
PIEZ**O**ELECTRICITY
PARA**P**ROFESSIONAL
ANTH**R**OPOMORPHISM
ARTE**R**IOSCLEROSIS
ENVI**R**ONMENTALIST
GAST**R**OENTEROLOGY
GAST**R**OINTESTINAL
INTE**R**CONTINENTAL
INTE**R**NATIONALISM
INTE**R**NATIONALIZE
NONP**R**OLIFERATION
UNDE**R**REPRESENTED
TRAN**S**CONTINENTAL
COUN**T**ERCLOCKWISE
COUN**T**ERESPIONAGE
COUN**T**EROFFENSIVE
ELEC**T**ROCHEMISTRY
ELEC**T**ROHYDRAULIC
ELEC**T**ROMAGNETISM
PRES**T**IDIGITATION
SESQ**U**ICENTENNIAL

## 6TH LETTER

INTER**C**ONTINENTAL
TRANS**C**ONTINENTAL
MISUN**D**ERSTANDING
MULTI**D**IMENSIONAL
COUNT**E**RCLOCKWISE
COUNT**E**RESPIONAGE
COUNT**E**ROFFENSIVE
MICRO**E**LECTRONICS
MICRO**E**NCAPSULATE
PIEZO**E**LECTRICITY
ULTRA**F**ASHIONABLE
ARTER**I**OSCLEROSIS
CONTA**I**NERIZATION
PREST**I**DIGITATION
SESQU**I**CENTENNIAL
MISCO**M**MUNICATION
MULTI**M**ILLIONAIRE
ULTRA**M**ICROSCOPIC
AUTOI**N**TOXICATION
INTER**N**ATIONALISM
INTER**N**ATIONALIZE
TINTI**N**NABULATION
ANTHR**O**POMORPHISM
ENVIR**O**NMENTALIST
GASTR**O**ENTEROLOGY
GASTR**O**INTESTINAL
NONPR**O**LIFERATION
ORGAN**O**PHOSPHORUS
VASOC**O**NSTRICTION
INCOM**P**REHENSIBLE
MULTI**P**ROGRAMMING
COMPA**R**TMENTALIZE
ELECT**R**OCHEMISTRY
ELECT**R**OHYDRAULIC
ELECT**R**OMAGNETISM
PARAP**R**OFESSIONAL
UNDER**R**EPRESENTED
UNCON**S**TITUTIONAL
DECEN**T**RALIZATION
EXTRA**T**ERRESTRIAL
EXTRA**T**ERRITORIAL
INCON**T**ROVERTIBLE
ANTIH**Y**PERTENSIVE

## 7TH LETTER

INTERN**A**TIONALISM
INTERN**A**TIONALIZE
ULTRAF**A**SHIONABLE
SESQUI**C**ENTENNIAL
PRESTI**D**IGITATION
EXTRAT**E**RRESTRIAL
EXTRAT**E**RRITORIAL
GASTRO**E**NTEROLOGY
MISUND**E**RSTANDING
UNDERR**E**PRESENTED
GASTRO**I**NTESTINAL
MULTID**I**MENSIONAL
MULTIM**I**LLIONAIRE
ULTRAM**I**CROSCOPIC
MICROE**L**ECTRONICS
NONPRO**L**IFERATION
PIEZOE**L**ECTRICITY
MISCOM**M**UNICATION
CONTAI**N**ERIZATION
ENVIRO**N**MENTALIST
MICROE**N**CAPSULATE
TINTIN**N**ABULATION
VASOCO**N**STRICTION
ARTERI**O**SCLEROSIS
ELECTR**O**CHEMISTRY
ELECTR**O**HYDRAULIC
ELECTR**O**MAGNETISM
INTERC**O**NTINENTAL
PARAPR**O**FESSIONAL
TRANSC**O**NTINENTAL
ANTHRO**P**OMORPHISM
ANTIHY**P**ERTENSIVE
ORGANO**P**HOSPHORUS
COUNTE**R**CLOCKWISE
COUNTE**R**ESPIONAGE
COUNTE**R**OFFENSIVE
DECENT**R**ALIZATION
INCOMP**R**EHENSIBLE
INCONT**R**OVERTIBLE
MULTIP**R**OGRAMMING
AUTOIN**T**OXICATION
COMPAR**T**MENTALIZE
UNCONS**T**ITUTIONAL

## 8TH LETTER

DECENTR**A**LIZATION
TINTINN**A**BULATION
COUNTER**C**LOCKWISE
ELECTRO**C**HEMISTRY
MICROEN**C**APSULATE
ULTRAMI**C**ROSCOPIC
ANTIHYP**E**RTENSIVE
CONTAIN**E**RIZATION
COUNTER**E**SPIONAGE
INCOMPR**E**HENSIBLE
MICROEL**E**CTRONICS
PIEZOEL**E**CTRICITY
SESQUIC**E**NTENNIAL
PARAPRO**F**ESSIONAL
ELECTRO**H**YDRAULIC
ORGANOP**H**OSPHORUS
NONPROL**I**FERATION
PRESTID**I**GITATION
UNCONST**I**TUTIONAL
MULTIMI**L**LIONAIRE
COMPART**M**ENTALIZE
ELECTRO**M**AGNETISM
ENVIRON**M**ENTALIST
MULTIDI**M**ENSIONAL
GASTROE**N**TEROLOGY
GASTROI**N**TESTINAL
INTERCO**N**TINENTAL
TRANSCO**N**TINENTAL
ANTHROP**O**MORPHISM
AUTOINT**O**XICATION
COUNTER**O**FFENSIVE
INCONTR**O**VERTIBLE
MULTIPR**O**GRAMMING
UNDERRE**P**RESENTED
EXTRATE**R**RESTRIAL
EXTRATE**R**RITORIAL
MISUNDE**R**STANDING
ARTERIO**S**CLEROSIS
ULTRAFA**S**HIONABLE
VASOCON**S**TRICTION
INTERNA**T**IONALISM
INTERNA**T**IONALIZE
MISCOMM**U**NICATION

## 9TH LETTER

ELECTROM**A**GNETISM
MICROENC**A**PSULATE
TINTINNA**B**ULATION
ARTERIOS**C**LEROSIS
MICROELE**C**TRONICS
PIEZOELE**C**TRICITY
COMPARTM**E**NTALIZE
ENVIRONM**E**NTALIST
MULTIDIM**E**NSIONAL
PARAPROF**E**SSIONAL
COUNTERO**F**FENSIVE
NONPROLI**F**ERATION
MULTIPRO**G**RAMMING
PRESTIDI**G**ITATION
ELECTROC**H**EMISTRY
INCOMPRE**H**ENSIBLE
ULTRAFAS**H**IONABLE
INTERNAT**I**ONALISM
INTERNAT**I**ONALIZE
COUNTERC**L**OCKWISE
DECENTRA**L**IZATION
MULTIMIL**L**IONAIRE
ANTHROPO**M**ORPHISM
MISCOMMU**N**ICATION
SESQUICE**N**TENNIAL
ORGANOPH**O**SPHORUS
ANTIHYPE**R**TENSIVE
CONTAINE**R**IZATION
EXTRATER**R**ESTRIAL
EXTRATER**R**ITORIAL
ULTRAMIC**R**OSCOPIC
UNDERREP**R**ESENTED
COUNTERE**S**PIONAGE
MISUNDER**S**TANDING
GASTROEN**T**EROLOGY
GASTROIN**T**ESTINAL
INTERCON**T**INENTAL
TRANSCON**T**INENTAL
UNCONSTI**T**UTIONAL
VASOCONS**T**RICTION
INCONTRO**V**ERTIBLE
AUTOINTO**X**ICATION
ELECTROH**Y**DRAULIC

## 10TH LETTER

ELECTROHYDRAULIC
ELECTROCHEMISTRY
EXTRATERRESTRIAL
GASTROENTEROLOGY
GASTROINTESTINAL
INCOMPREHENSIBLE
INCONTROVERTIBLE
NONPROLIFERATION
UNDERREPRESENTED
COUNTEROFFENSIVE
ELECTROMAGNETISM
AUTOINTOXICATION
CONTAINERIZATION
DECENTRALIZATION
EXTRATERRITORIAL
INTERCONTINENTAL
MISCOMMUNICATION
MULTIMILLIONAIRE
PRESTIDIGITATION
TRANSCONTINENTAL
ULTRAFASHIONABLE
ARTERIOSCLEROSIS
COMPARTMENTALIZE
ENVIRONMENTALIST
MULTIDIMENSIONAL
ANTHROPOMORPHISM
COUNTERCLOCKWISE
INTERNATIONALISM
INTERNATIONALIZE
ULTRAMICROSCOPIC
COUNTERESPIONAGE
MICROENCAPSULATE
MULTIPROGRAMMING
VASOCONSTRICTION
ORGANOPHOSPHORUS
PARAPROFESSIONAL
ANTIHYPERTENSIVE
MICROELECTRONICS
MISUNDERSTANDING
PIEZOELECTRICITY
SESQUICENTENNIAL
TINTINNABULATION
UNCONSTITUTIONAL

## 11TH LETTER

MISUNDERSTANDING
MULTIPROGRAMMING
AUTOINTOXICATION
COUNTERCLOCKWISE
MISCOMMUNICATION
ANTIHYPERTENSIVE
ARTERIOSCLEROSIS
COUNTEROFFENSIVE
SESQUICENTENNIAL
COUNTERESPIONAGE
VASOCONSTRICTION
TINTINNABULATION
ELECTROCHEMISTRY
ELECTROMAGNETISM
INCOMPREHENSIBLE
INTERCONTINENTAL
INTERNATIONALISM
INTERNATIONALIZE
TRANSCONTINENTAL
MULTIMILLIONAIRE
ULTRAFASHIONABLE
ORGANOPHOSPHORUS
ANTHROPOMORPHISM
ELECTROHYDRAULIC
GASTROENTEROLOGY
INCONTROVERTIBLE
MICROELECTRONICS
NONPROLIFERATION
PIEZOELECTRICITY
EXTRATERRESTRIAL
GASTROINTESTINAL
MICROENCAPSULATE
MULTIDIMENSIONAL
PARAPROFESSIONAL
ULTRAMICROSCOPIC
UNDERREPRESENTED
COMPARTMENTALIZE
ENVIRONMENTALIST
EXTRATERRITORIAL
PRESTIDIGITATION
UNCONSTITUTIONAL
CONTAINERIZATION
DECENTRALIZATION

## 12TH LETTER

AUTOINTOXICATION
COMPARTMENTALIZE
CONTAINERIZATION
DECENTRALIZATION
ELECTROHYDRAULIC
ENVIRONMENTALIST
INTERNATIONALISM
INTERNATIONALIZE
MISCOMMUNICATION
NONPROLIFERATION
PRESTIDIGITATION
TINTINNABULATION
ULTRAMICROSCOPIC
VASOCONSTRICTION
ELECTROMAGNETISM
INTERCONTINENTAL
TRANSCONTINENTAL
UNDERREPRESENTED
ORGANOPHOSPHORUS
ELECTROCHEMISTRY
MULTIDIMENSIONAL
PARAPROFESSIONAL
PIEZOELECTRICITY
UNCONSTITUTIONAL
COUNTERCLOCKWISE
MULTIPROGRAMMING
ANTIHYPERTENSIVE
COUNTEROFFENSIVE
MISUNDERSTANDING
MULTIMILLIONAIRE
SESQUICENTENNIAL
ULTRAFASHIONABLE
COUNTERESPIONAGE
EXTRATERRITORIAL
GASTROENTEROLOGY
MICROELECTRONICS
ANTHROPOMORPHISM
ARTERIOSCLEROSIS
INCOMPREHENSIBLE
EXTRATERRESTRIAL
GASTROINTESTINAL
INCONTROVERTIBLE
MICROENCAPSULATE

## 13TH LETTER

MULTIMILLIONAIRE
ULTRAFASHIONABLE
PIEZOELECTRICITY
MISUNDERSTANDING
ANTHROPOMORPHISM
GASTROINTESTINAL
INCOMPREHENSIBLE
INCONTROVERTIBLE
COMPARTMENTALIZE
ENVIRONMENTALIST
GASTROENTEROLOGY
INTERNATIONALISM
INTERNATIONALIZE
MICROENCAPSULATE
MULTIPROGRAMMING
COUNTERESPIONAGE
INTERCONTINENTAL
MICROELECTRONICS
SESQUICENTENNIAL
TRANSCONTINENTAL
UNDERREPRESENTED
ARTERIOSCLEROSIS
MULTIDIMENSIONAL
ORGANOPHOSPHORUS
PARAPROFESSIONAL
ULTRAMICROSCOPIC
UNCONSTITUTIONAL
EXTRATERRESTRIAL
EXTRATERRITORIAL
ANTIHYPERTENSIVE
COUNTEROFFENSIVE
ELECTROCHEMISTRY
AUTOINTOXICATION
CONTAINERIZATION
DECENTRALIZATION
ELECTROMAGNETISM
MISCOMMUNICATION
NONPROLIFERATION
PRESTIDIGITATION
TINTINNABULATION
VASOCONSTRICTION
ELECTROHYDRAULIC
COUNTERCLOCKWISE

## 14TH LETTER

COUNTERESPIONAGE
MICROENCAPSULATE
INCOMPREHENSIBLE
INCONTROVERTIBLE
ULTRAFASHIONABLE
ANTHROPOMORPHISM
ANTIHYPERTENSIVE
AUTOINTOXICATION
COMPARTMENTALIZE
CONTAINERIZATION
COUNTERCLOCKWISE
COUNTEROFFENSIVE
DECENTRALIZATION
ELECTROMAGNETISM
ENVIRONMENTALIST
EXTRATERRESTRIAL
EXTRATERRITORIAL
INTERNATIONALISM
INTERNATIONALIZE
MICROELECTRONICS
MISCOMMUNICATION
MISUNDERSTANDING
MULTIMILLIONAIRE
MULTIPROGRAMMING
NONPROLIFERATION
PIEZOELECTRICITY
PRESTIDIGITATION
SESQUICENTENNIAL
TINTINNABULATION
VASOCONSTRICTION
ELECTROHYDRAULIC
GASTROINTESTINAL
MULTIDIMENSIONAL
PARAPROFESSIONAL

UNCONSTITUTIO**N**AL
GASTROENTEROL**O**GY
ULTRAMICROSCO**P**IC
ORGANOPHOSPHO**R**US
ARTERIOSCLERO**S**IS
ELECTROCHEMIS**T**RY
INTERCONTINEN**T**AL
TRANSCONTINEN**T**AL
UNDERREPRESEN**T**ED

## 15TH LETTER

EXTRATERRESTRI**A**L
EXTRATERRITORI**A**L
GASTROINTESTIN**A**L
INTERCONTINENT**A**L
MULTIDIMENSION**A**L
PARAPROFESSION**A**L
SESQUICENTENNI**A**L
TRANSCONTINENT**A**L
UNCONSTITUTION**A**L
MICROELECTRONI**C**S
UNDERREPRESENT**E**D
COUNTERESPIONA**G**E
GASTROENTEROLO**G**Y
ARTERIOSCLEROS**I**S
ELECTROHYDRAUL**I**C
ULTRAMICROSCOP**I**C
INCOMPREHENSIB**L**E
INCONTROVERTIB**L**E
ULTRAFASHIONAB**L**E
MISUNDERSTANDI**N**G
MULTIPROGRAMMI**N**G
AUTOINTOXICATI**O**N
CONTAINERIZATI**O**N
DECENTRALIZATI**O**N
MISCOMMUNICATI**O**N
NONPROLIFERATI**O**N
PRESTIDIGITATI**O**N
TINTINNABULATI**O**N
VASOCONSTRICTI**O**N
ELECTROCHEMIST**R**Y
MULTIMILLIONAI**R**E
ANTHROPOMORPHI**S**M
COUNTERCLOCKWI**S**E
ELECTROMAGNETI**S**M
ENVIRONMENTALI**S**T
INTERNATIONALI**S**M
MICROENCAPSULA**T**E
PIEZOELECTRICI**T**Y
ORGANOPHOSPHOR**U**S
ANTIHYPERTENSI**V**E
COUNTEROFFENSI**V**E
COMPARTMENTALI**Z**E
INTERNATIONALI**Z**E

## 16TH LETTER

ELECTROHYDRAULI**C**
ULTRAMICROSCOPI**C**
UNDERREPRESENTE**D**
ANTIHYPERTENSIV**E**
COMPARTMENTALIZ**E**
COUNTERCLOCKWIS**E**
COUNTERESPIONAG**E**
COUNTEROFFENSIV**E**
INCOMPREHENSIBL**E**
INCONTROVERTIBL**E**
INTERNATIONALIZ**E**
MICROENCAPSULAT**E**
MULTIMILLIONAIR**E**
ULTRAFASHIONABL**E**
MISUNDERSTANDIN**G**
MULTIPROGRAMMIN**G**
EXTRATERRESTRIA**L**
EXTRATERRITORIA**L**
GASTROINTESTINA**L**
INTERCONTINENTA**L**
MULTIDIMENSIONA**L**
PARAPROFESSIONA**L**
SESQUICENTENNIA**L**
TRANSCONTINENTA**L**
UNCONSTITUTIONA**L**
ANTHROPOMORPHIS**M**
ELECTROMAGNETIS**M**
INTERNATIONALIS**M**
AUTOINTOXICATIO**N**
CONTAINERIZATIO**N**
DECENTRALIZATIO**N**
MISCOMMUNICATIO**N**
NONPROLIFERATIO**N**
PRESTIDIGITATIO**N**
TINTINNABULATIO**N**
VASOCONSTRICTIO**N**
ARTERIOSCLEROSI**S**
MICROELECTRONIC**S**
ORGANOPHOSPHORU**S**
ENVIRONMENTALIS**T**
ELECTROCHEMISTR**Y**
GASTROENTEROLOG**Y**
PIEZOELECTRICIT**Y**

# 17 LETTER WORDS

### 1st Letter

**C**ONGREGATIONALIST
**C**ONSTITUTIONALITY
**C**ONSUBSTANTIATION
**C**ONTRADISTINCTION
**C**OUNTERINSURGENCY
**C**OUNTERREVOLUTION
**E**LECTROCARDIOGRAM
**E**NCEPHALOMYELITIS
**I**MMUNOSUPPRESSIVE
**I**NTERDEPARTMENTAL
**I**NTERDISCIPLINARY
**I**NTERGENERATIONAL
**I**NTERGOVERNMENTAL
**M**ICROMINIATURIZED
**P**OSTIMPRESSIONISM
**S**UPERCONDUCTIVITY
**T**ELECOMMUNICATION
**T**RANSCENDENTALISM
**U**LTRACONSERVATIVE

### 2nd Letter

T**E**LECOMMUNICATION
M**I**CROMINIATURIZED
E**L**ECTROCARDIOGRAM
U**L**TRACONSERVATIVE
I**M**MUNOSUPPRESSIVE
E**N**CEPHALOMYELITIS
I**N**TERDEPARTMENTAL
I**N**TERDISCIPLINARY
I**N**TERGENERATIONAL
I**N**TERGOVERNMENTAL
C**O**NGREGATIONALIST
C**O**NSTITUTIONALITY
C**O**NSUBSTANTIATION
C**O**NTRADISTINCTION
C**O**UNTERINSURGENCY
C**O**UNTERREVOLUTION
P**O**STIMPRESSIONISM
T**R**ANSCENDENTALISM
S**U**PERCONDUCTIVITY

### 3rd Letter

TR**A**NSCENDENTALISM
EN**C**EPHALOMYELITIS
MI**C**ROMINIATURIZED
EL**E**CTROCARDIOGRAM
TE**L**ECOMMUNICATION
IM**M**UNOSUPPRESSIVE
CO**N**GREGATIONALIST
CO**N**STITUTIONALITY
CO**N**SUBSTANTIATION
CO**N**TRADISTINCTION
SU**P**ERCONDUCTIVITY
PO**S**TIMPRESSIONISM
IN**T**ERDEPARTMENTAL
IN**T**ERDISCIPLINARY
IN**T**ERGENERATIONAL
IN**T**ERGOVERNMENTAL
UL**T**RACONSERVATIVE
CO**U**NTERINSURGENCY
CO**U**NTERREVOLUTION

### 4th Letter

ELE**C**TROCARDIOGRAM
ENC**E**PHALOMYELITIS
INT**E**RDEPARTMENTAL
INT**E**RDISCIPLINARY
INT**E**RGENERATIONAL
INT**E**RGOVERNMENTAL
SUP**E**RCONDUCTIVITY
TEL**E**COMMUNICATION
CON**G**REGATIONALIST
COU**N**TERINSURGENCY
COU**N**TERREVOLUTION
TRA**N**SCENDENTALISM
MIC**R**OMINIATURIZED
ULT**R**ACONSERVATIVE
CON**S**TITUTIONALITY
CON**S**UBSTANTIATION
CON**T**RADISTINCTION
POS**T**IMPRESSIONISM
IMM**U**NOSUPPRESSIVE

### 5th Letter

ULTR**A**CONSERVATIVE
TELE**C**OMMUNICATION
POST**I**MPRESSIONISM
IMMU**N**OSUPPRESSIVE
MICR**O**MINIATURIZED
ENCE**P**HALOMYELITIS
CONG**R**EGATIONALIST
CONT**R**ADISTINCTION
INTE**R**DEPARTMENTAL
INTE**R**DISCIPLINARY
INTE**R**GENERATIONAL
INTE**R**GOVERNMENTAL
SUPE**R**CONDUCTIVITY
TRAN**S**CENDENTALISM
CONS**T**ITUTIONALITY
COUN**T**ERINSURGENCY
COUN**T**ERREVOLUTION
ELEC**T**ROCARDIOGRAM
CONS**U**BSTANTIATION

### 6th Letter

CONTR**A**DISTINCTION
CONSU**B**STANTIATION
SUPER**C**ONDUCTIVITY
TRANS**C**ENDENTALISM
ULTRA**C**ONSERVATIVE
INTER**D**EPARTMENTAL
INTER**D**ISCIPLINARY
CONGR**E**GATIONALIST
COUNT**E**RINSURGENCY
COUNT**E**RREVOLUTION
INTER**G**ENERATIONAL
INTER**G**OVERNMENTAL
ENCEP**H**ALOMYELITIS
CONST**I**TUTIONALITY
MICRO**M**INIATURIZED
POSTI**M**PRESSIONISM
IMMUN**O**SUPPRESSIVE
TELEC**O**MMUNICATION
ELECT**R**OCARDIOGRAM

### 7th Letter

ENCEPH**A**LOMYELITIS
CONTRA**D**ISTINCTION
INTERD**E**PARTMENTAL
INTERG**E**NERATIONAL
TRANSC**E**NDENTALISM
CONGRE**G**ATIONALIST
INTERD**I**SCIPLINARY
MICROM**I**NIATURIZED
TELECO**M**MUNICATION
ELECTR**O**CARDIOGRAM
INTERG**O**VERNMENTAL
SUPERC**O**NDUCTIVITY
ULTRAC**O**NSERVATIVE
POSTIM**P**RESSIONISM
COUNTE**R**INSURGENCY
COUNTE**R**REVOLUTION
CONSUB**S**TANTIATION
IMMUNO**S**UPPRESSIVE
CONSTI**T**UTIONALITY

### 8th Letter

CONGREG**A**TIONALIST
ELECTRO**C**ARDIOGRAM
CONTRAD**I**STINCTION
COUNTER**I**NSURGENCY
ENCEPHA**L**OMYELITIS
TELECOM**M**UNICATION
INTERGE**N**ERATIONAL
MICROMI**N**IATURIZED
SUPERCO**N**DUCTIVITY
TRANSCE**N**DENTALISM
ULTRACO**N**SERVATIVE
INTERDE**P**ARTMENTAL
COUNTER**R**EVOLUTION
POSTIMP**R**ESSIONISM
INTERDI**S**CIPLINARY
CONSUBS**T**ANTIATION
CONSTIT**U**TIONALITY
IMMUNOS**U**PPRESSIVE
INTERGO**V**ERNMENTAL

### 9th Letter

CONSUBST**A**NTIATION
ELECTROC**A**RDIOGRAM
INTERDEP**A**RTMENTAL
INTERDIS**C**IPLINARY
SUPERCON**D**UCTIVITY
TRANSCEN**D**ENTALISM
COUNTERR**E**VOLUTION
INTERGEN**E**RATIONAL
INTERGOV**E**RNMENTAL
POSTIMPR**E**SSIONISM
MICROMIN**I**ATURIZED

COUNTERI**N**SURGENCY
ENCEPHAL**O**MYELITIS
IMMUNOSU**P**PRESSIVE
CONTRADI**S**TINCTION
ULTRACON**S**ERVATIVE
CONGREGA**T**IONALIST
CONSTITU**T**IONALITY
TELECOMM**U**NICATION

## 10TH LETTER

MICROMINI**A**TURIZED
TRANSCEND**E**NTALISM
ULTRACONS**E**RVATIVE
CONGREGAT**I**ONALIST
CONSTITUT**I**ONALITY
INTERDISC**I**PLINARY
ENCEPHALO**M**YELITIS
CONSUBSTA**N**TIATION
TELECOMMU**N**ICATION
IMMUNOSUP**P**RESSIVE
ELECTROCA**R**DIOGRAM
INTERDEPA**R**TMENTAL
INTERGENE**R**ATIONAL
INTERGOVE**R**NMENTAL
COUNTERIN**S**URGENCY
POSTIMPRE**S**SIONISM
CONTRADIS**T**INCTION
SUPERCOND**U**CTIVITY
COUNTERRE**V**OLUTION

## 11TH LETTER

INTERGENER**A**TIONAL
SUPERCONDU**C**TIVITY
ELECTROCAR**D**IOGRAM
CONTRADIST**I**NCTION
TELECOMMUN**I**CATION
INTERGOVER**N**MENTAL
TRANSCENDE**N**TALISM
CONGREGATI**O**NALIST
CONSTITUTI**O**NALITY
COUNTERREV**O**LUTION
INTERDISCI**P**LINARY
IMMUNOSUPP**R**ESSIVE
ULTRACONSE**R**VATIVE
POSTIMPRES**S**IONISM
CONSUBSTAN**T**IATION
INTERDEPAR**T**MENTAL
MICROMINIA**T**URIZED
COUNTERINS**U**RGENCY
ENCEPHALOM**Y**ELITIS

## 12TH LETTER

TELECOMMUNI**C**ATION
ENCEPHALOMY**E**LITIS
IMMUNOSUPPR**E**SSIVE
CONSUBSTANT**I**ATION
ELECTROCARD**I**OGRAM
POSTIMPRESS**I**ONISM
COUNTERREVO**L**UTION
INTERDISCIP**L**INARY
INTERDEPART**M**ENTAL
INTERGOVERN**M**ENTAL
CONGREGATIO**N**ALIST
CONSTITUTIO**N**ALITY
CONTRADISTI**N**CTION
COUNTERINSU**R**GENCY
INTERGENERA**T**IONAL
SUPERCONDUC**T**IVITY
TRANSCENDEN**T**ALISM
MICROMINIAT**U**RIZED
ULTRACONSER**V**ATIVE

## 13TH LETTER

CONGREGATION**A**LIST
CONSTITUTION**A**LITY
CONSUBSTANTI**A**TION
TELECOMMUNIC**A**TION
TRANSCENDENT**A**LISM
ULTRACONSERV**A**TIVE
CONTRADISTIN**C**TION
INTERDEPARTM**E**NTAL
INTERGOVERNM**E**NTAL
COUNTERINSUR**G**ENCY
INTERDISCIPL**I**NARY
INTERGENERAT**I**ONAL
SUPERCONDUCT**I**VITY
ENCEPHALOMYE**L**ITIS
ELECTROCARDI**O**GRAM
POSTIMPRESSI**O**NISM
MICROMINIATU**R**IZED
IMMUNOSUPPRE**S**SIVE
COUNTERREVOL**U**TION

## 14TH LETTER

COUNTERINSURG**E**NCY
ELECTROCARDIO**G**RAM
ENCEPHALOMYEL**I**TIS
MICROMINIATUR**I**ZED
CONGREGATIONA**L**IST
CONSTITUTIONA**L**ITY
TRANSCENDENTA**L**ISM
INTERDEPARTME**N**TAL
INTERDISCIPLI**N**ARY
INTERGOVERNME**N**TAL
POSTIMPRESSIO**N**ISM
INTERGENERATI**O**NAL
IMMUNOSUPPRES**S**IVE
CONSUBSTANTIA**T**ION
CONTRADISTINC**T**ION
COUNTERREVOLU**T**ION
TELECOMMUNICA**T**ION
ULTRACONSERVA**T**IVE
SUPERCONDUCTI**V**ITY

## 15TH LETTER

INTERDISCIPLIN**A**RY
CONGREGATIONAL**I**ST
CONSTITUTIONAL**I**TY
CONSUBSTANTIAT**I**ON
CONTRADISTINCT**I**ON
COUNTERREVOLUT**I**ON
IMMUNOSUPPRESS**I**VE
POSTIMPRESSION**I**SM
SUPERCONDUCTIV**I**TY
TELECOMMUNICAT**I**ON
TRANSCENDENTAL**I**SM
ULTRACONSERVAT**I**VE
COUNTERINSURGE**N**CY
INTERGENERATIO**N**AL
ELECTROCARDIOG**R**AM
ENCEPHALOMYELI**T**IS
INTERDEPARTMEN**T**AL
INTERGOVERNMEN**T**AL
MICROMINIATURI**Z**ED

## 16TH LETTER

ELECTROCARDIOGR**A**M
INTERDEPARTMENT**A**L
INTERGENERATION**A**L
INTERGOVERNMENT**A**L
COUNTERINSURGEN**C**Y
MICROMINIATURIZ**E**D
ENCEPHALOMYELIT**I**S
CONSUBSTANTIATI**O**N
CONTRADISTINCTI**O**N
COUNTERREVOLUTI**O**N
TELECOMMUNICATI**O**N
INTERDISCIPLINA**R**Y
CONGREGATIONALI**S**T
POSTIMPRESSIONI**S**M
TRANSCENDENTALI**S**M
CONSTITUTIONALI**T**Y
SUPERCONDUCTIVI**T**Y
IMMUNOSUPPRESSI**V**E
ULTRACONSERVATI**V**E

## 17TH LETTER

MICROMINIATURIZE**D**
IMMUNOSUPPRESSIV**E**
ULTRACONSERVATIV**E**
INTERDEPARTMENTA**L**
INTERGENERATIONA**L**
INTERGOVERNMENTA**L**
ELECTROCARDIOGRA**M**
POSTIMPRESSIONIS**M**
TRANSCENDENTALIS**M**
CONSUBSTANTIATIO**N**
CONTRADISTINCTIO**N**
COUNTERREVOLUTIO**N**
TELECOMMUNICATIO**N**
ENCEPHALOMYELITI**S**
CONGREGATIONALIS**T**
CONSTITUTIONALIT**Y**
COUNTERINSURGENC**Y**
INTERDISCIPLINAR**Y**
SUPERCONDUCTIVIT**Y**

# 18 LETTER WORDS

### 1st Letter

**E**LECTROCARDIOGRAPH

**P**HOTODECOMPOSITION

**T**RANSUBSTANTIATION

### 2nd Letter

P**H**OTODECOMPOSITION

E**L**ECTROCARDIOGRAPH

T**R**ANSUBSTANTIATION

### 3rd Letter

TR**A**NSUBSTANTIATION

EL**E**CTROCARDIOGRAPH

PH**O**TODECOMPOSITION

### 4th Letter

ELE**C**TROCARDIOGRAPH

TRA**N**SUBSTANTIATION

PHO**T**ODECOMPOSITION

### 5th Letter

PHOT**O**DECOMPOSITION

TRAN**S**UBSTANTIATION

ELEC**T**ROCARDIOGRAPH

### 6th Letter

PHOTO**D**ECOMPOSITION

ELECT**R**OCARDIOGRAPH

TRANS**U**BSTANTIATION

### 7th Letter

TRANSU**B**STANTIATION

PHOTOD**E**COMPOSITION

ELECTR**O**CARDIOGRAPH

### 8th Letter

ELECTRO**C**ARDIOGRAPH

PHOTODE**C**OMPOSITION

TRANSUB**S**TANTIATION

### 9th Letter

ELECTROC**A**RDIOGRAPH

PHOTODEC**O**MPOSITION

TRANSUBS**T**ANTIATION

### 10th Letter

TRANSUBST**A**NTIATION

PHOTODECO**M**POSITION

ELECTROCA**R**DIOGRAPH

### 11th Letter

ELECTROCAR**D**IOGRAPH

TRANSUBSTA**N**TIATION

PHOTODECOM**P**OSITION

### 12th Letter

ELECTROCARD**I**OGRAPH

PHOTODECOMP**O**SITION

TRANSUBSTAN**T**IATION

### 13th Letter

TRANSUBSTANT**I**ATION

ELECTROCARDI**O**GRAPH

PHOTODECOMPO**S**ITION

### 14th Letter

TRANSUBSTANTI**A**TION

ELECTROCARDIO**G**RAPH

PHOTODECOMPOS**I**TION

### 15th Letter

ELECTROCARDIOG**R**APH

PHOTODECOMPOSI**T**ION

TRANSUBSTANTIA**T**ION

### 16th Letter

ELECTROCARDIOGR**A**PH

PHOTODECOMPOSIT**I**ON

TRANSUBSTANTIAT**I**ON

### 17th Letter

PHOTODECOMPOSITI**O**N

TRANSUBSTANTIATI**O**N

ELECTROCARDIOGRA**P**H

### 18th Letter

ELECTROCARDIOGRAP**H**

PHOTODECOMPOSITIO**N**

TRANSUBSTANTIATIO**N**

# 19 LETTER WORDS

### 1st Letter

**C**OUNTERINTELLIGENCE
**D**EINDUSTRIALIZATION
**E**XTRATERRITORIALITY
**I**NTERDENOMINATIONAL
**N**ONREPRESENTATIONAL

### 2nd Letter

D**E**INDUSTRIALIZATION
I**N**TERDENOMINATIONAL
C**O**UNTERINTELLIGENCE
N**O**NREPRESENTATIONAL
E**X**TRATERRITORIALITY

### 3rd Letter

DE**I**NDUSTRIALIZATION
NO**N**REPRESENTATIONAL
EX**T**RATERRITORIALITY
IN**T**ERDENOMINATIONAL
CO**U**NTERINTELLIGENCE

### 4th Letter

INT**E**RDENOMINATIONAL
COU**N**TERINTELLIGENCE
DEI**N**DUSTRIALIZATION
EXT**R**ATERRITORIALITY
NON**R**EPRESENTATIONAL

### 5th Letter

EXTR**A**TERRITORIALITY
DEIN**D**USTRIALIZATION
NONR**E**PRESENTATIONAL
INTE**R**DENOMINATIONAL
COUN**T**ERINTELLIGENCE

### 6th Letter

INTER**D**ENOMINATIONAL
COUNT**E**RINTELLIGENCE
NONRE**P**RESENTATIONAL
EXTRA**T**ERRITORIALITY
DEIND**U**STRIALIZATION

### 7th Letter

EXTRAT**E**RRITORIALITY
INTERD**E**NOMINATIONAL
COUNTE**R**INTELLIGENCE
NONREP**R**ESENTATIONAL
DEINDU**S**TRIALIZATION

### 8th Letter

NONREPR**E**SENTATIONAL
COUNTER**I**NTELLIGENCE
INTERDE**N**OMINATIONAL
EXTRATE**R**RITORIALITY
DEINDUS**T**RIALIZATION

### 9th Letter

COUNTERI**N**TELLIGENCE
INTERDEN**O**MINATIONAL
DEINDUST**R**IALIZATION
EXTRATER**R**ITORIALITY
NONREPRE**S**ENTATIONAL

### 10th Letter

NONREPRES**E**NTATIONAL
DEINDUSTR**I**ALIZATION
EXTRATERR**I**TORIALITY
INTERDENO**M**INATIONAL
COUNTERIN**T**ELLIGENCE

### 11th Letter

DEINDUSTRI**A**LIZATION
COUNTERINT**E**LLIGENCE
INTERDENOM**I**NATIONAL
NONREPRESE**N**TATIONAL
EXTRATERRI**T**ORIALITY

### 12th Letter

COUNTERINTE**L**LIGENCE
DEINDUSTRIA**L**IZATION
INTERDENOMI**N**ATIONAL
EXTRATERRIT**O**RIALITY
NONREPRESEN**T**ATIONAL

### 13th Letter

INTERDENOMIN**A**TIONAL
NONREPRESENT**A**TIONAL
DEINDUSTRIAL**I**ZATION
COUNTERINTEL**L**IGENCE
EXTRATERRITO**R**IALITY

### 14th Letter

COUNTERINTELL**I**GENCE
EXTRATERRITOR**I**ALITY
INTERDENOMINA**T**IONAL
NONREPRESENTA**T**IONAL
DEINDUSTRIALI**Z**ATION

### 15th Letter

DEINDUSTRIALIZ**A**TION
EXTRATERRITORI**A**LITY
COUNTERINTELLI**G**ENCE
INTERDENOMINAT**I**ONAL
NONREPRESENTAT**I**ONAL

### 16th Letter

COUNTERINTELLIG**E**NCE
EXTRATERRITORIA**L**ITY
INTERDENOMINATI**O**NAL
NONREPRESENTATI**O**NAL
DEINDUSTRIALIZA**T**ION

### 17th Letter

DEINDUSTRIALIZAT**I**ON
EXTRATERRITORIAL**I**TY
COUNTERINTELLIGE**N**CE
INTERDENOMINATIO**N**AL
NONREPRESENTATIO**N**AL

### 18th Letter

INTERDENOMINATION**A**L
NONREPRESENTATION**A**L
COUNTERINTELLIGEN**C**E
DEINDUSTRIALIZATI**O**N
EXTRATERRITORIALI**T**Y

### 19th Letter

COUNTERINTELLIGENC**E**
INTERDENOMINATIONA**L**
NONREPRESENTATIONA**L**
DEINDUSTRIALIZATIO**N**
EXTRATERRITORIALIT**Y**

# 20 LETTER WORDS

**1ST LETTER**

**E**LECTROENCEPHALOGRAM
**M**ICROMINIATURIZATION
**T**ETRAHYDROCANNABINOL

**2ND LETTER**

T**E**TRAHYDROCANNABINOL
M**I**CROMINIATURIZATION
E**L**ECTROENCEPHALOGRAM

**3RD LETTER**

MI**C**ROMINIATURIZATION
EL**E**CTROENCEPHALOGRAM
TE**T**RAHYDROCANNABINOL

**4TH LETTER**

ELE**C**TROENCEPHALOGRAM
MIC**R**OMINIATURIZATION
TET**R**AHYDROCANNABINOL

**5TH LETTER**

TETR**A**HYDROCANNABINOL
MICR**O**MINIATURIZATION
ELEC**T**ROENCEPHALOGRAM

**6TH LETTER**

TETRA**H**YDROCANNABINOL
MICRO**M**INIATURIZATION
ELECT**R**OENCEPHALOGRAM

**7TH LETTER**

MICROM**I**NIATURIZATION
ELECTR**O**ENCEPHALOGRAM
TETRAH**Y**DROCANNABINOL

**8TH LETTER**

TETRAHY**D**ROCANNABINOL
ELECTRO**E**NCEPHALOGRAM
MICROMI**N**IATURIZATION

**9TH LETTER**

MICROMIN**I**ATURIZATION
ELECTROE**N**CEPHALOGRAM
TETRAHYD**R**OCANNABINOL

**10TH LETTER**

MICROMINI**A**TURIZATION
ELECTROEN**C**EPHALOGRAM
TETRAHYDR**O**CANNABINOL

**11TH LETTER**

TETRAHYDRO**C**ANNABINOL
ELECTROENC**E**PHALOGRAM
MICROMINIA**T**URIZATION

**12TH LETTER**

TETRAHYDROC**A**NNABINOL
ELECTROENCE**P**HALOGRAM
MICROMINIAT**U**RIZATION

**13TH LETTER**

ELECTROENCEP**H**ALOGRAM
TETRAHYDROCA**N**NABINOL
MICROMINIATU**R**IZATION

**14TH LETTER**

ELECTROENCEPH**A**LOGRAM
MICROMINIATUR**I**ZATION
TETRAHYDROCAN**N**ABINOL

**15TH LETTER**

TETRAHYDROCANN**A**BINOL
ELECTROENCEPHA**L**OGRAM
MICROMINIATURI**Z**ATION

**16TH LETTER**

MICROMINIATURIZ**A**TION
TETRAHYDROCANNA**B**INOL
ELECTROENCEPHAL**O**GRAM

**17TH LETTER**

ELECTROENCEPHALO**G**RAM
TETRAHYDROCANNAB**I**NOL
MICROMINIATURIZA**T**ION

**18TH LETTER**

MICROMINIATURIZAT**I**ON
TETRAHYDROCANNABI**N**OL
ELECTROENCEPHALOG**R**AM

**19TH LETTER**

ELECTROENCEPHALOGR**A**M
MICROMINIATURIZATI**O**N
TETRAHYDROCANNABIN**O**L

**20TH LETTER**

TETRAHYDROCANNABINO**L**
ELECTROENCEPHALOGRA**M**
MICROMINIATURIZATIO**N**

# 21 LETTER WORDS

ELECTROENCEPHALOGRAPH

Since there are no other words of 21 letters, this one stands alone. At least two words of the same length are required in order to sort them alphabetically by any position.

# SECTION 2 • NAMES OF PEOPLE

## 2-14 LETTER WORDS

### 2 Letter

#### 1st Letter

AL
AN
BO
XC
ST
CS
ED
FU
HU
JO
LI
LU
MA
MO
OE
PI
SU
TI
TU
VE
WU
YA
YO
YU
ZI
ZU
JO
MO
YO
FU
HU
LU
SU
TU
WU
YU
ZU

#### 2nd Letter

MA
YA
ED
OE
VE
LI
PI
TI
ZI
AL
AN
BO

### 3 Letter

#### 1st Letter

ABU
ADI
AKE
ALF
AMY
ANN
ARP
ART
ASA
ASP
BAY
BEG
BEN
BOB
BOK
BOX
CHU
CON
COX
DAG
DAM
DAO
DAY
DEI
DEL
DON
DUD
ELI
ELY
EMI
EVA
EWA
FAY
FOX
GAY
GIG
GIL
GUS
GUY
HAL
HAN
HAO
HAR
HEY
HIN
HOE
HOU
HSI
HUI
IAN
IRA
IVO
JAN
JAY
JIA
JIM
JOE
JON
JOY
KAY
KEN
KIM
KIT
KUA
KUO
KYI
LEE
LEO
LEV
LEW
LEY
LIE
LIU
LON
LOW
LUN
MAX
MEL
MOE
MOO
NEF
ODD
OHM
OLE
ORR
PAN
PAR
PAZ
PDE
PER
POE
RAY
RED
REE
REX
RIO
RIS
ROD
ROY
SAM
SAN
SEE
SHI
SIH
SIR
SSU
STU
SUU
TED
THO
TIM
TOM
TSE
TSU
TUM
TZU
UGO
ULF
URE
UWE
VAL
VAN
VOS
WAN
WEI
XIE
YAN
YIN
YUL
ZAN
ZHI
ZOU

#### 2nd Letter

BAY
DAG
DAM
DAO
DAY
FAY
GAY
HAL
HAN
HAO
HAR
IAN
JAN
JAY
KAY
MAX
PAN
PAR
PAZ
RAY
SAM
SAN
VAL
VAN
WAN
YAN
ZAN
ABU
ADI
ODD
PDE
BEG
BEN
DEI
DEL
HEY
KEN
LEE
LEO
LEV
LEW
LEY
MEL
NEF
PER
RED
REE
REX
SEE
TED
WEI
UGO
CHU
OHM
SHI
THO
ZHI
GIG
GIL
HIN
JIA
JIM
KIM
KIT
LIE
LIU
RIO
RIS
SIH
SIR
TIM
XIE
YIN
AKE
ALF
ELI
ELY
OLE
ULF
AMY
EMI
ANN
BOB
BOK
BOX
CON
COX
DON
FOX
HOE
HOU
JOE
JON
JOY
LON
LOW
MOE
MOO
POE
ROD
ROY
TOM
VOS
ZOU
ARP
ART
IRA
ORR
URE
ASA
ASP
HSI
SSU
TSE
TSU
STU
DUD
GUS
GUY
HUI
KUA
KUO
LUN
SUU
TUM
YUL
EVA
IVO
EWA
UWE
KYI
TZU

#### 3rd Letter

ASA
EVA
EWA
IRA
JIA
KUA
BOB
DUD
ODD
RED
ROD
TED
AKE
HOE
JOE
LEE
LIE
MOE
OLE
PDE
POE
REE
SEE
TSE
URE
UWE
XIE
ALF
NEF
ULF
BEG
DAG
GIG
SIH
ADI
DEI
ELI
EMI
HSI
HUI
KYI
SHI
WEI
ZHI
BOK
DEL
GIL
HAL
MEL
VAL
YUL
DAM
JIM
KIM
OHM
SAM
TIM
TOM
TUM
ANN
BEN
CON
DON
HAN
HIN
IAN
JAN
JON
KEN
LON
LUN
PAN
SAN
VAN
WAN
YAN
YIN
ZAN
DAO
HAO
IVO
KUO
LEO
MOO
RIO
THO
UGO
ARP
ASP
HAR
ORR
PAR
PER
SIR
GUS
RIS
VOS
ART
KIT
ABU
CHU
HOU
LIU
SSU
STU
SUU
TSU
TZU
ZOU
LEV
LEW
LOW
BOX
COX
FOX
MAX
REX
AMY
BAY
DAY
ELY
FAY
GAY
GUY
HEY
JAY
JOY
KAY
LEY
RAY
ROY
PAZ

### 4 Letter

#### 1st Letter

AAGE
ABBE
ABBY
ABEL
ADAM
AGNE
AIME
AIRY
ALAN
ALCA
ALEC
ALEX
ALVA
AMES
ANDY
ANEL
ANNA
ANNE
ARNE
ARNO
AUER
AUNG
AXEL
BAKR
BARR
BART
BASS
BEAL
BEAN
BEDE
BEER
BELA
BELL
BELO
BENA
BENO
BENZ
BERG
BERN
BERT
BEST
BILL
BING
BINI
BIOT
BIRO
BLAS
BOAS
BODE
BOHR
BOIS
BOLL
BOLT
BOND
BORN
BOSE
BOSS
BOYD
BUCK
BUDD
BURL
BURT
BUSH
BYRD
CAGE
CAMP
CANN
CANO
CARL
CARO
CARR
CATO
CECH
CELA
CEVA
CHAN
CHAO
CHEN
CHER
CHEW
CHIA
CHIH
CHIU
CHOH
CHOU
CHUN
CLAY
CLEM
CODE
COHN
COKE
COLE
COLT
COOK
COPE
CORI
CORT
CRAM
CURL
DALE
DANA
DANE
DANY
DART
DAVE
DAVY
DAWN
DEAN
DEHN
DIAS
DIAZ
DICK
DIOR
DIRK
DODD
DONN
DORE
DORN
DORR
DOUG
DOVE
DOWD
DUKE
DUNN
DUNS
EADS
EARL
EDME
EDNA
EIKO
ELEK
ELIA
ELIE
ELIO
ELMO
ELSO
EMIL
EMMA
EMMY
ERIC
ERIK
EWEN
FADL
FAPP
FARR
FASH
FATH
FAYE
FELT
FINK
FITZ
FORD
FRED
FUNK
FUST
GAHN
GAIL
GALE
GALL
GARY
GAWA
GELL
GENE
GENG
GERD
GEZA
GIDE
GILE
GILL
GOLD

GRAM
GRAY
GREG
GREN
GREW
GREY
GUTH
GWEN
HAHN
HALE
HALL
HANS
HARD
HARE
HAUY
HAWN
HEAD
HEBB
HEIM
HENG
HERB
HERO
HESS
HIGH
HILL
HOCH
HOLM
HOMI
HOPE
HOWE
HOYT
HSIN
HSUN
HUGH
HUGO
HULL
HUME
HUNT
HURT
HYDE
HYOK
IGOR
ILYA
INGE
IVAN
IVAR
IVES
JAAP
JACK
JANE
JEAN
JEFF
JEON
JOAN
JOEL
JOHN
JOSE
JUAN
JUDY
JUMP
JUNG
JUST
KAHN
KALR
KANT
KARK
KARL
KARY
KEIR
KENG
KERN
KIDD
KING
KIRK
KISH
KLAS
KLUG
KNOW
KNUT
KOCH
KOPP
KORN
KOSA
KOWA
KUEI
KUHN
KUNG
KURI
KURT
LADY
LAMB
LAME
LAND
LANE
LANG
LARS
LEAH
LEAN
LECH
LEHN
LEIF
LENT
LENZ
LEON
LEVI
LFRY
LILA
LILY
LIND
LING
LINK
LISA
LISE
LIZA
LOEB
LOIS
LONG
LORD
LORY
LOUS
LOVE
LOYS
LUAN
LUCA
LUIS
LUNG
LYLE
LYNN
LYON
LYOT
MACH
MANN
MARC
MARK
MARX
MARY
MEAD
MELA
MIKE
MILL
MILO
MING
MIRA
MOHR
MOHS
MONA
MONK
MOON
MORE
MORO
MOTT
MUNI
MUSA
NEAL
NEIL
NGOR
NICK
NIEL
NILS
NING
NINO
NOAM
NOEL
OKEN
OKUN
OLAH
OLEN
OLOF
OMAR
OORT
OPIE
OPIK
ORRY
OTIS
OTTO
OWEN
PAGE
PAIS
PANE
PARE
PATI
PAUL
PECK
PERE
PERL
PHIL
PIRE
POLK
POLO
PONS
POPE
POTT
PUZO
QUTB
RABE
RABI
RADO
RAHN
RAPU
READ
REDI
REED
REES
REID
RENE
RICK
RING
RITA
ROCK
ROLF
ROME
RONA
ROOT
ROSE
ROSS
ROTH
ROUS
ROUX
RUSH
RUTH
RYAN
RYLE
SADI
SAHA
SALK
SALT
SATO
SAUL
SCOT
SEAN
SEKI
SETH
SHAO
SHAW
SHEN
SHIH
SHIN
SHOU
SNOW
STAN
STAS
SUNE
SUNG
SVEN
SWAN
TAFT
TAMM
TATE
THOM
TINA
TING
TJIO
TODD
TOLL
TONE
TONI
TONY
TREG
TSAI
TULL
TULP
TUTU
TUVE
TUZO
UHRY
ULAM
UREY
URIE
VANE
VEHE
VENN
VERA
VINE
VITO
VOCK
VOGT
WADA
WALD
WANG
WARD
WATT
WEBB
WEFA
WEIN
WEST
WEYL
WIEN
WILM
WING
WISE
WOLE
WONG
WOOD
WREN
XIEN
YAGA
YANG
YING
YUAN
YURI
YVES
ZENO
ZHOU
ZHUO
ZING
ZINN
ZUSE

## 2nd Letter

AAGE
BAKR
BARR
BART
BASS
CAGE
CAMP
CANN
CANO
CARL
CARO
CARR
CATO
DALE
DANA
DANE
DANY
DART
DAVE
DAVY
DAWN
EADS
EARL
FADL
FAPP
FARR
FASH
FATH
FAYE
GAHN
GAIL
GALE
GALL
GARY
GAWA
HAHN
HALE
HALL
HANS
HARD
HARE
HAUY
HAWN
JAAP
JACK
JANE
KAHN
KALR
KANT
KARK
KARL
KARY
LADY
LAMB
LAME
LAND
LANE
LANG
LARS
MACH
MANN
MARC
MARK
MARX
MARY
PAGE
PAIS
PANE
PARE
PATI
PAUL
RABE
RABI
RADO
RAHN
RAPU
SADI
SAHA
SALK
SALT
SATO
SAUL
TAFT
TAMM
TATE
VANE
WADA
WALD
WANG
WARD
WATT
YAGA
YANG
ABBE
ABBY
ABEL
SCOT
ADAM
EDME
EDNA
BEAL
BEAN
BEDE
BEER
BELA
BELL
BELO
BENA
BENO
BENZ
BERG
BERN
BERT
BEST
CECH
CELA
CEVA
DEAN
DEHN
FELT
GELL
GENE
GENG
GERD
GEZA
HEAD
HEBB
HEIM
HENG
HERB
HERO
HESS
JEAN
JEFF
JEON
KEIR
KENG
KERN
LEAH
LEAN
LECH
LEHN
LEIF
LENT
LENZ
LEON
LEVI
MEAD
MELA
NEAL
NEIL
PECK
PERE
PERL
READ
REDI
REED
REES
REID
RENE
SEAN
SEKI
SETH
VEHE
VENN
VERA
WEBB
WEFA
WEIN
WEST
WEYL
ZENO
LFRY
AGNE
IGOR
NGOR
CHAN
CHAO
CHEN
CHER
CHEW
CHIA
CHIH
CHIU
CHOH
CHOU
CHUN
PHIL
SHAO
SHAW
SHEN
SHIH
SHIN
SHOU
THOM
UHRY
ZHOU
ZHUO
AIME
AIRY
BILL
BING
BINI
BIOT
BIRO
DIAS
DIAZ
DICK
DIOR
DIRK
EIKO
FINK
FITZ
GIDE
GILE
GILL
HIGH
HILL
KIDD
KING
KIRK
KISH
LILA
LILY
LIND
LING
LINK
LISA
LISE
LIZA
MIKE
MILL
MILO
MING
MIRA
NICK
NIEL
NILS
NING
NINO
PIRE
RICK
RING
RITA
TINA
TING
VINE
VITO
WIEN
WILM
WING
WISE
XIEN
YING
ZING
ZINN
TJIO
OKEN
OKUN
ALAN
ALCA
ALEC
ALEX
ALVA
BLAS
CLAY
CLEM
ELEK
ELIA
ELIE
ELIO
ELMO
ELSO
ILYA
KLAS
KLUG
OLAH
OLEN
OLOF
ULAM
AMES
EMIL
EMMA
EMMY
OMAR
ANDY
ANEL
ANNA
ANNE
INGE
KNOW
KNUT
SNOW
BOAS
BODE
BOHR
BOIS
BOLL
BOLT
BOND
BORN
BOSE
BOSS
BOYD
CODE
COHN
COKE
COLE
COLT
COOK
COPE
CORI
CORT
DODD
DONN
DORE
DORN
DORR
DOUG
DOVE
DOWD
FORD
GOLD
HOCH
HOLM
HOMI
HOPE
HOWE
HOYT
JOAN
JOEL
JOHN
JOSE
KOCH
KOPP
KORN
KOSA
KOWA
LOEB
LOIS
LONG
LORD
LORY
LOUS
LOVE
LOYS
MOHR
MOHS
MONA
MONK
MOON
MORE
MORO
MOTT
NOAM
NOEL
OORT
POLK
POLO
PONS
POPE
POTT
ROCK
ROLF
ROME
RONA
ROOT
ROSE
ROSS
ROTH
ROUS
ROUX

TODD
TOLL
TONE
TONI
TONY
VOCK
VOGT
WOLE
WONG
WOOD
OPIE
OPIK
ARNE
ARNO
CRAM
ERIC
ERIK
FRED
GRAM
GRAY
GREG
GREN
GREW
GREY
ORRY
TREG
UREY
URIE
WREN
HSIN
HSUN
TSAI
OTIS
OTTO
STAN
STAS
AUER
AUNG
BUCK
BUDD
BURL
BURT
BUSH
CURL
DUKE
DUNN
DUNS
FUNK
FUST
GUTH
HUGH
HUGO
HULL
HUME
HUNT
HURT
JUAN
JUDY
JUMP
JUNG
JUST
KUEI
KUHN
KUNG
KURI
KURT
LUAN
LÜCA
LUIS
LUNG
MUNI
MUSA
PUZO
QUTB
RUSH
RUTH
SUNE
SUNG
TULL
TULP
TUTU
TUVE
TUZO
YUAN
YURI
ZUSE
IVAN
IVAR
IVES
SVEN
YVES
EWEN
GWEN
OWEN
SWAN
AXEL
BYRD
HYDE
HYOK
LYLE
LYNN
LYON
LYOT
RYAN
RYLE

**3rd Letter**

ADAM
ALAN
BEAL
BEAN
BLAS
BOAS
CHAN
CHAO
CLAY
CRAM
DEAN
DIAS
DIAZ
GRAM
GRAY
HEAD
IVAN
IVAR
JAAP
JEAN
JOAN
JUAN
KLAS
LEAH
LEAN
LUAN
MEAD
NEAL
NOAM
OLAH
OMAR
READ
RYAN
SEAN
SHAO
SHAW
STAN
STAS
SWAN
TSAI
ULAM
YUAN
ABBE
ABBY
HEBB
RABE
RABI
WEBB
ALCA
BUCK
CECH
DICK
HOCH
JACK
KOCH
LECH
LUCA
MACH
NICK
PECK
RICK
ROCK
VOCK
ANDY
BEDE
BODE
BUDD
CODE
DODD
EADS
FADL
GIDE
HYDE
JUDY
KIDD
LADY
RADO
REDI
SADI
TODD
WADA
ABEL
ALEC
ALEX
AMES
ANEL
AUER
AXEL
BEER
CHEN
CHER
CHEW
CLEM
ELEK
EWEN
FRED
GREG
GREN
GREW
GREY
GWEN
IVES
JOEL
KUEI
LOEB
NIEL
NOEL
OKEN
OLEN
OWEN
REED
REES
SHEN
SVEN
TREG
UREY
WIEN
WREN
XIEN
YVES
JEFF
TAFT
WEFA
AAGE
CAGE
HIGH
HUGH
HUGO
INGE
PAGE
VOGT
YAGA
BOHR
COHN
DEHN
GAHN
HAHN
JOHN
KAHN
KUHN
LEHN
MOHR
MOHS
RAHN
SAHA
VEHE
BOIS
CHIA
CHIH
CHIU
ELIA
ELIE
ELIO
EMIL
ERIC
ERIK
GAIL
HEIM
HSIN
KEIR
LEIF
LOIS
LUIS
NEIL
OPIE
OPIK
OTIS
PAIS
PHIL
REID
SHIH
SHIN
TJIO
URIE
WEIN
BAKR
COKE
DUKE
EIKO
MIKE
SEKI
BELA
BELL
BELO
BILL
BOLL
BOLT
CELA
COLE
COLT
DALE
FELT
GALE
GALL
GELL
GILE
GILL
GOLD
HALE
HALL
HILL
HOLM
HULL
KALR
LILA
LILY
LYLE
MELA
MILL
MILO
NILS
POLK
POLO
ROLF
RYLE
SALK
SALT
TOLL
TULL
TULP
WALD
WILM
WOLE
AIME
CAMP
EDME
ELMO
EMMA
EMMY
HOMI
HUME
JUMP
LAMB
LAME
ROME
TAMM
AGNE
ANNA
ANNE
ARNE
ARNO
AUNG
BENA
BENO
BENZ
BING
BINI
BOND
CANN
CANO
DANA
DANE
DANY
DONN
DUNN
DUNS
EDNA
FINK
FUNK
GENE
GENG
HANS
HENG
HUNT
JANE
JUNG
KANT
KENG
KING
KUNG
LAND
LANE
LANG
LENT
LENZ
LIND
LING
LINK
LONG
LUNG
LYNN
MANN
MING
MONA
MONK
MUNI
NING
NINO
PANE
PONS
RENE
RING
RONA
SUNE
SUNG
TINA
TING
TONE
TONI
TONY
VANE
VENN
VINE
WANG
WING
WONG
YANG
YING
ZENO
ZING
ZINN
BIOT
CHOH
CHOU
COOK
DIOR
HYOK
IGOR
JEON
KNOW
LEON
LYON
LYOT
MOON
NGOR
OLOF
ROOT
SCOT
SHOU
SNOW
THOM
WOOD
ZHOU
COPE
FAPP
HOPE
KOPP
POPE
RAPU
AIRY
BARR
BART
BERG
BERN
BERT
BIRO
BORN
BURL
BURT
BYRD
CARL
CARO
CARR
CORI
CORT
CURL
DART
DIRK
DORE
DORN
DORR
EARL
FARR
FORD
GARY
GERD
HARD
HARE
HERB
HERO
HURT
KARK
KARL
KARY
KERN
KIRK
KORN
KURI
KURT
LARS
LFRY
LORD
LORY
MARC
MARK
MARX
MARY
MIRA
MORE
MORO
OORT
ORRY
PARE
PERE
PERL
PIRE
UHRY
VERA
WARD
YURI
BASS
BEST
BOSE
BOSS
BUSH
ELSO
FASH
FUST
HESS
JOSE
JUST
KISH
KOSA
LISA
LISE
MUSA
ROSE
ROSS
RUSH
WEST
WISE
ZUSE
CATO
FATH
FITZ
GUTH
MOTT
OTTO
PATI
POTT
QUTB
RITA
ROTH
RUTH
SATO
SETH
TATE
TUTU
VITO
WATT
CHUN
DOUG
HAUY
HSUN
KLUG
KNUT
LOUS
OKUN
PAUL
ROUS
ROUX
SAUL
ZHUO
ALVA
CEVA
DAVE
DAVY
DOVE
LEVI
LOVE
TUVE
DAWN
DOWD
GAWA
HAWN
HOWE
KOWA
BOYD
FAYE
HOYT
ILYA
LOYS
WEYL
GEZA
LIZA
PUZO
TUZO

**4th Letter**

ALCA
ALVA
ANNA
BELA
BENA
CELA
CEVA
CHIA
DANA
EDNA
ELIA
EMMA
GAWA
GEZA
ILYA
KOSA
KOWA
LILA
LISA
LIZA
LUCA
MELA
MIRA
MONA
MUSA
RITA
RONA
SAHA
TINA
VERA
WADA
WEFA
YAGA
HEBB
HERB
LAMB
LOEB
QUTB
WEBB
ALEC
ERIC
MARC
BOND
BOYD
BUDD
BYRD
DODD
DOWD
FORD
FRED
GERD
GOLD
HARD
HEAD
KIDD
LAND
LIND
LORD
MEAD
READ
REED
REID
TODD
WALD
WARD
WOOD
AAGE
ABBE
AGNE
AIME
ANNE
ARNE
BEDE
BODE
BOSE
CAGE
CODE
COKE
COLE
COPE
DALE
DANE
DAVE
DORE
DOVE
DUKE
EDME
ELIE
FAYE
GALE
GENE
GIDE

GILE HALE HARE HOPE HOWE HUME HYDE INGE JANE JOSE LAME LANE LISE LOVE LYLE MIKE MORE OPIE PAGE PANE PARE PERE PIRE POPE RABE RENE ROME ROSE RYLE SUNE TATE TONE TUVE URIE VANE VEHE VINE WISE WOLE ZUSE JEFF LEIF OLOF ROLF AUNG BERG BING DOUG GENG GREG HENG JUNG KENG KING KLUG KUNG LANG

LING LONG LUNG MING NING RING SUNG TING TREG WANG WING WONG YANG YING ZING BUSH CECH CHIH CHOH FASH FATH GUTH HIGH HOCH HUGH KISH KOCH LEAH LECH MACH OLAH ROTH RUSH RUTH SETH SHIH BINI CORI HOMI KUEI KURI LEVI MUNI PATI RABI REDI SADI SEKI TONI TSAI YURI BUCK COOK DICK DIRK ELEK ERIK

FINK FUNK HYOK JACK KARK KIRK LINK MARK MONK NICK OPIK PECK POLK RICK ROCK SALK VOCK ABEL ANEL AXEL BEAL BELL BILL BOLL BURL CARL CURL EARL EMIL FADL GAIL GALL GELL GILL HALL HILL HULL JOEL KARL MILL NEAL NEIL NIEL NOEL PAUL PERL PHIL SAUL TOLL TULL WEYL ADAM CLEM CRAM GRAM HEIM HOLM

NOAM TAMM THOM ULAM WILM ALAN BEAN BERN BORN CANN CHAN CHEN CHUN COHN DAWN DEAN DEHN DONN DORN DUNN EWEN GAHN GREN GWEN HAHN HAWN HSIN HSUN IVAN JEAN JEON JOAN JOHN JUAN KAHN KERN KORN KUHN LEAN LEHN LEON LUAN LYNN LYON MANN MOON OKEN OKUN OLEN OWEN RAHN RYAN SEAN SHEN SHIN STAN SVEN

SWAN VENN WEIN WIEN WREN XIEN YUAN ZINN ARNO BELO BENO BIRO CANO CARO CATO CHAO EIKO ELIO ELMO ELSO HERO HUGO MILO MORO NINO OTTO POLO PUZO RADO SATO SHAO TJIO TUZO VITO ZENO ZHUO CAMP FAPP JAAP JUMP KOPP TULP AUER BAKR BARR BEER BOHR CARR CHER DIOR DORR FARR IGOR IVAR KALR KEIR MOHR

NGOR OMAR AMES BASS BLAS BOAS BOIS BOSS DIAS DUNS EADS HANS HESS IVES KLAS LARS LOIS LOUS LOYS LUIS MOHS NILS OTIS PAIS PONS REES ROSS ROUS STAS YVES BART BERT BEST BIOT BOLT BURT COLT CORT DART FELT FUST HOYT HUNT HURT JUST KANT KNUT KURT LENT LYOT MOTT OORT POTT ROOT SALT SCOT TAFT

VOGT WATT WEST CHIU CHOU RAPU SHOU TUTU ZHOU CHEW GREW KNOW SHAW SNOW ALEX MARX ROUX ABBY AIRY ANDY CLAY DANY DAVY EMMY GARY GRAY GREY HAUY JUDY KARY LADY LFRY LILY LORY MARY ORRY TONY UHRY UREY BENZ DIAZ FITZ LENZ

**5 Letter**

**1st Letter**

AARON ABDUS ABEGG ABNEY ADAIR ADAMS ADLER

ADOLF AGNON AHMAD AHMES AIKEN AKIRA ALDER ALDUS ALEXI ALICE ALICK ALLAN ALLEN ALMON ALOYS ALTER ALTON ALVAN ALVIN AMICI ANDRE ANGEL ANNIE ANTON ANWAR APIAN ARAGO ARBER ARIAS ARLEN ARVID ASAPH ASHBY ASSER ASTON ASTOR AVARY AVERY BAKER BANKS BARON BARRY BARUJ BASIL BASOV BASSI BATES BAUME BAYER BEACH BEAMS BEEBE BEERY BEGIN BELON BENGT BEPPO

BERRY BETHE BETTE BETTY BEVIS BHANU BILLY BINET BIROC BLACK BLAKE BLANE BLISS BLOCH BLOCK BLOOM BODEN BONDI BOOLE BOOTH BOREL BORIS BOSCH BOTHE BOTTA BOULE BOVET BOWEN BOYER BOYLE BOYSE BRADY BRAGG BRAHE BRAID BRAJA BRAND BRAUN BREEN BRENT BRIAN BRINK BROCA BROOK BROOM BROWN BRUCE BRUNO BRYAN BUELL BUNIN BURGI BURKE BURKS BURNS BURTT BYRAM

BYRON CABLE CAINE CAJAL CAMUS CAPEK CAPRA CAREL CARLO CAROL CECIL CELVE CERNY CESAR CHACE CHAIM CHAIN CHANG CHENG CHIAO CHIEH CHIEN CHING CHONG CHRIS CHUBB CHUCK CHUNG CLARA CLARK CLAUS CLERK CLIFF CLINE CLINT CLYDE COHEN COLIN COMER COMTE CONON CONTI COREY CORNU COSTA COTES COUCH COUNT COURT COWAN CRAIG CRICK CRISP CROSS CUKOR CURIE CYRIL

CYRUS DALEN DANBY DANNY DANTE DARBY DARIO DAVID DAVIS DAWES DEBYE DELLA DEMME DENIS DEREK DERVA DEWAR DEWEY DIANE DICKE DIELS DIRAC DIXON DOELL DOISY DOLBY DONAT DONNA DORIS DOUST DRACH DRAKE DRESS DRUDE DUBIN DUBOS DUMAS DURER DYSON EBERS EBING EDDIE EDGAR EDITH EDLEN EDWIN EEMIL EIGEN EJNAR ELERT ELIAS ELIHU ELION ELIOT ELLEN ELLET ELLIS

ELMER ELVEN ELWYN EMERT EMILE EMILY ENCKE. ENNIO ERICH ERMAN ERNST ERWIN ESAKI ETHEL EUGEN EULER EVANS EWALD EWING FABRI FABRY FALSE FAZAN FEGTE FELIX FERMI FERRO FIELD FINCH FIORE FITCH FLORY FLOYD FOCKE FONDA FOOTE FORTT FOSSE FOWLE FRANK FRANS FRANZ FREGE FREMY FRERE FREUD FRIED FRIES FRITZ FROSH FUCHS FUKUI FURSE FURST GABLE GABOR GAEDE

GALEN
GALLE
GAMOW
GARRY
GATES
GAUSS
GEBER
GEENA
GEMMA
GEORG
GERMI
GEROG
GERRY
GERTY
GIBBS
GIGER
GILES
GILKS
GLENN
GLUCK
GOBAT
GODEL
GODOY
GOERG
GOLGI
GOMPF
GOULD
GRACE
GRANT
GREEN
GREER
GREGG
GROSS
GROTE
GROVE
GUYOT
GWENN
HABER
HAIGH
HAING
HAISE
HALES
HAMAO
HANEY
HANKS
HANNO
HANNS
HARDY
HARRY
HARTZ
HAUGE
HAYES
HEBER
HECHT
HEINE
HEINZ
HELEN

HEMAN
HENCH
HENLE
HENRI
HENRY
HEROD
HERON
HERTZ
HESSE
HEYSE
HIGGS
HIRAM
HOKIN
HOLLY
HONDA
HOOKE
HOPPE
HORTA
HOUCK
HOYLE
HUANG
HUBEL
HUBER
HULSE
HYATT
HYMAN
HYMNS
HYRON
ICIRO
IGNAZ
IHNEN
ILICH
INNES
INOUE
IRENE
IRONS
IRVIN
IRWIN
ISAAC
JABIR
JACOB
JAKOB
JAMES
JANET
JANOS
JASON
JEANS
JENNY
JERNE
JESSE
JIMMY
JODIE
JOHAN
JOHNS
JONAS
JONES
JOOST

JORIE
JOSEF
JOSIE
JOULE
JUDAH
JULES
JULIA
JULIE
JUNGE
JURAN
KAMAL
KAMEN
KANIN
KAREL
KARLE
KATHY
KAZAN
KEIKE
KEITH
KELLY
KEOGH
KERST
KEVIN
KIRSH
KLAUS
KLEBS
KLEIN
KLINE
KOLBE
KOLFF
KORDA
KOSMA
KOWAL
KRAMS
KREBS
KRESS
KROGH
KROTO
KRUPP
KUHNE
KUNDT
KUNIO
KURTZ
KUSCH
LAING
LAMAR
LAMAS
LANDE
LANGE
LARRY
LAURA
LAWES
LAZLO
LEBON
LECOQ
LEDER
LEGER

LEIGH
LEONE
LEVAN
LEVEN
LEWIS
LIANG
LIBBY
LINDA
LINDE
LINUS
LIZZY
LLOYD
LOCKE
LODGE
LOEWI
LOGIE
LOREN
LORNE
LOTKA
LOUIS
LOWER
LOWIG
LOYAL
LUCAS
LUCIO
LUIGI
LUISE
LUKAS
LULLY
LUNDH
LURIA
LUSKE
LUZZI
LWOFF
LYELL
LYMAN
LYNDS
LYNEN
MABEL
MAEVE
MALEY
MALUS
MARCH
MARCO
MAREY
MARIA
MARIE
MARIK
MARIN
MARIO
MARKO
MARSH
MASON
MAURY
MAXIM
MAYER
MAYOW

MCKAY
MENES
MERAY
MERLE
MERYL
METON
METTY
MEYER
MILES
MILLS
MILNE
MILOS
MINOS
MINOT
MOLLO
MONGE
MONIZ
MONOD
MOORE
MORSE
MOSES
MOTTE
MOULD
MOYER
MPILO
MUREN
NAMBU
NANCY
NASIR
NATTA
NEELY
NEHER
NEILL
NELLY
NEVIL
NICOL
NIELS
NILES
NIVEN
NIXON
NOBEL
NOBLE
NORMA
NORTH
NUFER
NUNES
NUNEZ
OCHOA
OGAWA
OGDEN
OLSON
ONNES
ORBOM
ORSON
OSCAR
OSKAR
OSLER

OWENS
PABLO
PABST
PACKE
PADDY
PAGET
PANUM
PAOLO
PAPIN
PARRY
PASCH
PASSY
PATTY
PAULI
PAVEL
PAYEN
PAYNE
PEANO
PEARL
PEARY
PEDRO
PEGGY
PERCY
PERES
PEREY
PEREZ
PERSE
PESCI
PETER
PETIT
PFAFF
PIERO
PINEL
PIXII
PLATO
PLATT
PLAUT
PLINY
POPOV
PORTA
PREGL
PROUT
PUPIN
PYOTR
QUEEN
QUICK
RABIN
RAINE
RALPH
RAMAN
RAMON
RAMOS
RAMUS
RAOUL
REBER
REESE
REGAN

REICH
REISS
REMAK
RENIE
RHIND
RHINE
RICCI
RIGHI
RINIO
ROALD
ROBIN
ROCHE
ROGER
ROLLE
ROMER
ROOKE
ROSSE
ROSSI
ROUSE
ROWAN
ROYDS
RUBEL
RUBIN
RUEHL
RUNGE
RUSKA
SABIN
SACHS
SAGAN
SAINT
SAKEL
SALAM
SALLY
SANDY
SANZO
SARAH
SAYED
SCOTT
SEGRE
SELMA
SELYE
SETON
SHARP
SHENG
SHORT
SHULL
SIMIC
SIMON
SISSY
SKALL
SMALL
SMITH
SNELL
SODDY
SOLON
SONYA
SORBY

SOREN
SPIES
SPORN
SSUMA
STAIN
STARK
STEEN
STENO
STERN
STEVE
STOCK
STOLL
STONE
STOUT
STRHL
SUESS
SUGER
SULLY
SUSAN
SYNGE
SZENT
TAIEB
TALLY
TALVA
TAMBI
TANDY
TATUM
TAUBE
TEMIN
TESLA
THAER
THEON
THIEL
TIBOR
TITOV
TOLDY
TOMEI
TOMMY
TOWNE
TRACY
TRETZ
TRYON
TSENG
TSUNG
TULLY
TUROK
TWORT
TYCHO
TYLER
TYLOR
TYTUS
ULUGH
UMEKI
VASCO
VERNA
VESTO
VIETA

VITUS
VOGEL
VOLTA
WAAGE
WALAS
WALDO
WALSH
WAYNE
WEBER
WEISS
WELLS
WENDY
WHITE
WHYTT
WIARD
WIEST
WILDT
WILES
WILEY
WILLY
WIRTH
WOLFF
WOODY
WUNDT
WURTZ
WYLER
WYMAN
YALOW
YEATS
YOSEF
YOUNG
YUANG
YUSEF
ZENER
ZHANG

## 2nd Letter

AARON
BAKER
BANKS
BARON
BARRY
BARUJ
BASIL
BASOV
BASSI
BATES
BAUME
BAYER
CABLE
CAINE
CAJAL
CAMUS
CAPEK
CAPRA
CAREL
CARLO
CAROL
DALEN
DANBY
DANNY
DANTE
DARBY
DARIO
DAVID
DAVIS
DAWES
FABRI
FABRY
FALSE
FAZAN
GABLE
GABOR
GAEDE
GALEN
GALLE
GAMOW
GARRY
GATES
GAUSS
HABER
HAIGH
HAING
HAISE
HALES
HAMAO
HANEY
HANKS
HANNO
HANNS
HARDY
HARRY
HARTZ
HAUGE
HAYES
JABIR
JACOB
JAKOB
JAMES
JANET
JANOS
JASON
KAMAL
KAMEN
KANIN
KAREL
KARLE
KATHY
KAZAN
LAING
LAMAR
LAMAS
LANDE
LANGE
LARRY
LAURA
LAWES
LAZLO
MABEL
MAEVE
MALEY
MALUS
MARCH
MARCO
MAREY
MARIA
MARIE
MARIK
MARIN
MARIO
MARKO
MARSH
MASON
MAURY
MAXIM
MAYER
MAYOW
NAMBU
NANCY
NASIR
NATTA
PABLO
PABST
PACKE
PADDY
PAGET
PANUM
PAOLO
PAPIN
PARRY
PASCH
PASSY
PATTY
PAULI
PAVEL
PAYEN
PAYNE
RABIN
RAINE
RALPH
RAMAN
RAMON
RAMOS
RAMUS
RAOUL
SABIN
SACHS
SAGAN
SAINT
SAKEL
SALAM
SALLY
SANDY
SANZO
SARAH
SAYED
TAIEB
TALLY
TALVA
TAMBI
TANDY
TATUM
TAUBE
VASCO
WAAGE
WALAS
WALDO
WALSH
WAYNE
YALOW
ABDUS
ABEGG
ABNEY
EBERS
EBING
ICIRO
MCKAY
OCHOA
SCOTT
ADAIR
ADAMS
ADLER
ADOLF
EDDIE
EDGAR
EDITH
EDLEN
EDWIN
BEACH
BEAMS
BEEBE
BEERY
BEGIN
BELON
BENGT
BEPPO
BERRY
BETHE
BETTE
BETTY
BEVIS
CECIL
CELVE
CERNY
CESAR

DEBYE
DELLA
DEMME
DENIS
DEREK
DERVA
DEWAR
DEWEY
EEMIL
FEGTE
FELIX
FERMI
FERRO
GEBER
GEENA
GEMMA
GEORG
GERMI
GEROG
GERRY
GERTY
HEBER
HECHT
HEINE
HEINZ
HELEN
HEMAN
HENCH
HENLE
HENRI
HENRY
HEROD
HERON
HERTZ
HESSE
HEYSE
JEANS
JENNY
JERNE
JESSE
KEIKE
KEITH
KELLY
KEOGH
KERST
KEVIN
LEBON
LECOQ
LEDER
LEGER
LEIGH
LEONE
LEVAN
LEVEN
LEWIS
MENES
MERAY
MERLE
MERYL
METON
METTY
MEYER
NEELY
NEHER
NEILL
NELLY
NEVIL
PEANO
PEARL
PEARY
PEDRO
PEGGY
PERCY
PERES
PEREY
PEREZ
PERSE
PESCI
PETER
PETIT
REBER
REESE
REGAN
REICH
REISS
REMAK
RENIE
SEGRE
SELMA
SELYE
SETON
TEMIN
TESLA
VERNA
VESTO
WEBER
WEISS
WELLS
WENDY
YEATS
ZENER
PFAFF
AGNON
IGNAZ
OGAWA
OGDEN
AHMAD
AHMES
BHANU
CHACE
CHAIM
CHAIN
CHANG
CHENG
CHIAO
CHIEH
CHIEN
CHING
CHONG
CHRIS
CHUBB
CHUCK
CHUNG
IHNEN
RHIND
RHINE
SHARP
SHENG
SHORT
SHULL
THAER
THEON
THIEL
WHITE
WHYTT
ZHANG
AIKEN
BILLY
BINET
BIROC
DIANE
DICKE
DIELS
DIRAC
DIXON
EIGEN
FIELD
FINCH
FIORE
FITCH
GIBBS
GIGER
GILES
GILKS
HIGGS
HIRAM
JIMMY
KIRSH
LIANG
LIBBY
LINDA
LINDE
LINUS
LIZZY
MILES
MILLS
MILNE
MILOS
MINOS
MINOT
NICOL
NIELS
NILES
NIVEN
NIXON
PIERO
PINEL
PIXII
RICCI
RIGHI
RINIO
SIMIC
SIMON
SISSY
TIBOR
TITOV
VIETA
VITUS
WIARD
WIEST
WILDT
WILES
WILEY
WILLY
WIRTH
EJNAR
AKIRA
SKALL
ALDER
ALDUS
ALEXI
ALICE
ALICK
ALLAN
ALLEN
ALMON
ALOYS
ALTER
ALTON
ALVAN
ALVIN
BLACK
BLAKE
BLANE
BLISS
BLOCH
BLOCK
BLOOM
CLARA
CLARK
CLAUS
CLERK
CLIFF
CLINE
CLINT
CLYDE
ELERT
ELIAS
ELIHU
ELION
ELIOT
ELLEN
ELLET
ELLIS
ELMER
ELVEN
ELWYN
FLORY
FLOYD
GLENN
GLUCK
ILICH
KLAUS
KLEBS
KLEIN
KLINE
LLOYD
OLSON
PLATO
PLATT
PLAUT
PLINY
ULUGH
AMICI
EMERT
EMILE
EMILY
SMALL
SMITH
UMEKI
ANDRE
ANGEL
ANNIE
ANTON
ANWAR
ENCKE
ENNIO
INNES
INOUE
ONNES
SNELL
BODEN
BONDI
BOOLE
BOOTH
BOREL
BORIS
BOSCH
BOTHE
BOTTA
BOULE
BOVET
BOWEN
BOYER
BOYLE
BOYSE
COHEN
COLIN
COMER
COMTE
CONON
CONTI
COREY
CORNU
COSTA
COTES
COUCH
COUNT
COURT
COWAN
DOELL
DOISY
DOLBY
DONAT
DONNA
DORIS
DOUST
FOCKE
FONDA
FOOTE
FORTT
FOSSE
FOWLE
GOBAT
GODEL
GODOY
GOERG
GOLGI
GOMPF
GOULD
HOKIN
HOLLY
HONDA
HOOKE
HOPPE
HORTA
HOUCK
HOYLE
JODIE
JOHAN
JOHNS
JONAS
JONES
JOOST
JORIE
JOSEF
JOSIE
JOULE
KOLBE
KOLFF
KORDA
KOSMA
KOWAL
LOCKE
LODGE
LOEWI
LOGIE
LOREN
LORNE
LOTKA
LOUIS
LOWER
LOWIG
LOYAL
MOLLO
MONGE
MONIZ
MONOD
MOORE
MORSE
MOSES
MOTTE
MOULD
MOYER
NOBEL
NOBLE
NORMA
NORTH
POPOV
PORTA
ROALD
ROBIN
ROCHE
ROGER
ROLLE
ROMER
ROOKE
ROSSE
ROSSI
ROUSE
ROWAN
ROYDS
SODDY
SOLON
SONYA
SORBY
SOREN
TOLDY
TOMEI
TOMMY
TOWNE
VOGEL
VOLTA
WOLFF
WOODY
YOSEF
YOUNG
APIAN
MPILO
SPIES
SPORN
ARAGO
ARBER
ARIAS
ARLEN
ARVID
BRADY
BRAGG
BRAHE
BRAID
BRAJA
BRAND
BRAUN
BREEN
BRENT
BRIAN
BRINK
BROCA
BROOK
BROOM
BROWN
BRUCE
BRUNO
BRYAN
CRAIG
CRICK
CRISP
CROSS
DRACH
DRAKE
DRESS
DRUDE
ERICH
ERMAN
ERNST
ERWIN
FRANK
FRANS
FRANZ
FREGE
FREMY
FRERE
FREUD
FRIED
FRIES
FRITZ
FROSH
GRACE
GRANT
GREEN
GREER
GREGG
GROSS
GROTE
GROVE
IRENE
IRONS
IRVIN
IRWIN
KRAMS
KREBS
KRESS
KROGH
KROTO
KRUPP
ORBOM
ORSON
PREGL
PROUT
TRACY
TRETZ
TRYON
ASAPH
ASHBY
ASSER
ASTON
ASTOR
ESAKI
ISAAC
OSCAR
OSKAR
OSLER
SSUMA
TSENG
TSUNG
ETHEL
STAIN
STARK
STEEN
STENO
STERN
STEVE
STOCK
STOLL
STONE
STOUT
STRHL
BUELL
BUNIN
BURGI
BURKE
BURKS
BURNS
BURTT
CUKOR
CURIE
DUBIN
DUBOS
DUMAS
DURER
EUGEN
EULER
FUCHS
FUKUI
FURSE
FURST
GUYOT
HUANG
HUBEL
HUBER
HULSE
JUDAH
JULES
JULIA
JULIE
JUNGE
JURAN
KUHNE
KUNDT
KUNIO
KURTZ
KUSCH
LUCAS
LUCIO
LUIGI
LUISE
LUKAS
LULLY
LUNDH
LURIA
LUSKE
LUZZI
MUREN
NUFER
NUNES
NUNEZ
PUPIN
QUEEN
QUICK
RUBEL
RUBIN
RUEHL
RUNGE
RUSKA
SUESS
SUGER
SULLY
SUSAN
TULLY
TUROK
WUNDT
WURTZ
YUANG
YUSEF
AVARY
AVERY
EVANS
EWALD
EWING
GWENN
LWOFF
OWENS
TWORT
BYRAM
BYRON
CYRIL
CYRUS
DYSON
HYATT
HYMAN
HYMNS
HYRON
LYELL
LYMAN
LYNDS
LYNEN
PYOTR
SYNGE
TYCHO
TYLER
TYLOR
TYTUS
WYLER
WYMAN
SZENT

### 3rd Letter

ADAIR
ADAMS
ARAGO
ASAPH
AVARY
BEACH
BEAMS
BHANU
BLACK
BLAKE
BLANE
BRADY
BRAGG
BRAHE
BRAID
BRAJA
BRAND
BRAUN
CHACE
CHAIM
CHAIN
CHANG
CLARA
CLARK
CLAUS
CRAIG
DIANE
DRACH
DRAKE
ESAKI
EVANS
EWALD
FRANK
FRANS
FRANZ
GRACE
GRANT
HUANG
HYATT
ISAAC
JEANS
KLAUS
KRAMS
LIANG
OGAWA
PEANO
PEARL
PEARY
PFAFF
PLATO
PLATT
PLAUT
ROALD
SHARP
SKALL
SMALL
STAIN
STARK
THAER
TRACY
WAAGE
WIARD
YEATS
YUANG
ZHANG
ARBER
CABLE
DEBYE
DUBIN
DUBOS
FABRI
FABRY
GABLE
GABOR
GEBER
GIBBS
GOBAT
HABER
HEBER
HUBEL
HUBER
JABIR
LEBON
LIBBY

| MABEL | CLERK | GIGER | HEINE | GALLE | DEMME | HANNS | BROOK | BURNS | MARIE | SUSAN | PAULI |
|---|---|---|---|---|---|---|---|---|---|---|---|
| NOBEL | DIELS | HIGGS | HEINZ | GILES | DUMAS | HENCH | BROOM | BURTT | MARIK | TESLA | ROUSE |
| NOBLE | DOELL | LEGER | ICIRO | GILKS | EEMIL | HENLE | BROWN | BYRAM | MARIN | VASCO | SHULL |
| ORBOM | DRESS | LOGIE | ILICH | GOLGI | ELMER | HENRI | CHONG | BYRON | MARIO | VESTO | SSUMA |
| PABLO | EBERS | PAGET | KEIKE | HALES | ERMAN | HENRY | CROSS | CAREL | MARKO | YOSEF | TAUBE |
| PABST | ELERT | PEGGY | KEITH | HELEN | GAMOW | HONDA | FIORE | CARLO | MARSH | YUSEF | TSUNG |
| RABIN | EMERT | REGAN | KLINE | HOLLY | GEMMA | IGNAZ | FLORY | CAROL | MERAY | ALTER | ULUGH |
| REBER | FIELD | RIGHI | LAING | HULSE | GOMPF | IHNEN | FLOYD | CERNY | MERLE | ALTON | YOUNG |
| ROBIN | FREGE | ROGER | LEIGH | JULES | HAMAO | INNES | FOOTE | CHRIS | MERYL | ANTON | ALVAN |
| RUBEL | FREMY | SAGAN | LUIGI | JULIA | HEMAN | JANET | FROSH | COREY | MORSE | ASTON | ALVIN |
| RUBIN | FRERE | SEGRE | LUISE | JULIE | HYMAN | JANOS | GEORG | CORNU | MUREN | ASTOR | ARVID |
| SABIN | FREUD | SUGER | MPILO | KELLY | HYMNS | JENNY | GROSS | CURIE | NORMA | BATES | BEVIS |
| TIBOR | GAEDE | VOGEL | NEILL | KOLBE | JAMES | JONAS | GROTE | CYRIL | NORTH | BETHE | BOVET |
| WEBER | GEENA | ASHBY | PLINY | KOLFF | JIMMY | JONES | GROVE | CYRUS | PARRY | BETTE | DAVID |
| CECIL | GLENN | COHEN | QUICK | LULLY | KAMAL | JUNGE | HOOKE | DARBY | PERCY | BETTY | DAVIS |
| DICKE | GOERG | ETHEL | RAINE | MALEY | KAMEN | KANIN | INOUE | DARIO | PERES | BOTHE | ELVEN |
| ENCKE | GREEN | JOHAN | REICH | MALUS | LAMAR | KUNDT | IRONS | DEREK | PEREY | BOTTA | IRVIN |
| FOCKE | GREER | JOHNS | REISS | MILES | LAMAS | KUNIO | JOOST | DERVA | PEREZ | COTES | KEVIN |
| FUCHS | GREGG | KUHNE | RHIND | MILLS | LYMAN | LANDE | KEOGH | DIRAC | PERSE | FITCH | LEVAN |
| HECHT | GWENN | NEHER | RHINE | MILNE | NAMBU | LANGE | KROGH | DORIS | PORTA | GATES | LEVEN |
| JACOB | IRENE | OCHOA | SAINT | MILOS | RAMAN | LINDA | KROTO | DURER | SARAH | KATHY | NEVIL |
| LECOQ | KLEBS | AKIRA | SMITH | MOLLO | RAMON | LINDE | LEONE | FERMI | SORBY | LOTKA | NIVEN |
| LOCKE | KLEIN | ALICE | SPIES | NELLY | RAMOS | LINUS | LLOYD | FERRO | SOREN | METON | PAVEL |
| LUCAS | KREBS | ALICK | TAIEB | NILES | RAMUS | LUNDH | LWOFF | FORTT | STRHL | METTY | ANWAR |
| LUCIO | KRESS | AMICI | THIEL | OSLER | REMAK | LYNDS | MOORE | FURSE | TUROK | MOTTE | BOWEN |
| NICOL | LOEWI | APIAN | WEISS | RALPH | ROMER | LYNEN | PAOLO | FURST | VERNA | NATTA | COWAN |
| OSCAR | LYELL | ARIAS | WHITE | ROLLE | SIMIC | MENES | PROUT | GARRY | WIRTH | PATTY | DAWES |
| PACKE | MAEVE | BLISS | CAJAL | SALAM | SIMON | MINOS | PYOTR | GERMI | WURTZ | PETER | DEWAR |
| RICCI | NEELY | BRIAN | AIKEN | SALLY | TAMBI | MINOT | RAOUL | GEROG | ASSER | PETIT | DEWEY |
| ROCHE | NIELS | BRINK | BAKER | SELMA | TEMIN | MONGE | ROOKE | GERRY | BASIL | SETON | EDWIN |
| SACHS | OWENS | CAINE | CUKOR | SELYE | TOMEI | MONIZ | SCOTT | GERTY | BASOV | TATUM | ELWYN |
| TYCHO | PIERO | CHIAO | FUKUI | SOLON | TOMMY | MONOD | SHORT | HARDY | BASSI | TITOV | ERWIN |
| ABDUS | PREGL | CHIEH | HOKIN | SULLY | WYMAN | NANCY | SPORN | HARRY | BOSCH | TYTUS | FOWLE |
| ALDER | QUEEN | CHIEN | JAKOB | TALLY | ABNEY | NUNES | STOCK | HARTZ | CESAR | VITUS | IRWIN |
| ALDUS | REESE | CHING | LUKAS | TALVA | AGNON | NUNEZ | STOLL | HEROD | COSTA | BAUME | KOWAL |
| ANDRE | RUEHL | CLIFF | MCKAY | TOLDY | ANNIE | ONNES | STONE | HERON | DYSON | BOULE | LAWES |
| BODEN | SHENG | CLINE | OSKAR | TULLY | BANKS | PANUM | STOUT | HERTZ | FOSSE | BRUCE | LEWIS |
| EDDIE | SNELL | CLINT | SAKEL | TYLER | BENGT | PINEL | TWORT | HIRAM | HESSE | BRUNO | LOWER |
| GODEL | STEEN | CRICK | ADLER | TYLOR | BINET | RENIE | WOODY | HORTA | JASON | CHUBB | LOWIG |
| GODOY | STENO | CRISP | ALLAN | VOLTA | BONDI | RINIO | BEPPO | HYRON | JESSE | CHUCK | ROWAN |
| JODIE | STERN | DOISY | ALLEN | WALAS | BUNIN | RUNGE | CAPEK | JERNE | JOSEF | CHUNG | TOWNE |
| JUDAH | STEVE | EBING | ARLEN | WALDO | CONON | SANDY | CAPRA | JORIE | JOSIE | COUCH | DIXON |
| LEDER | SUESS | EDITH | BELON | WALSH | CONTI | SANZO | HOPPE | JURAN | KOSMA | COUNT | MAXIM |
| LODGE | SZENT | ELIAS | BILLY | WELLS | DANBY | SONYA | PAPIN | KAREL | KUSCH | COURT | NIXON |
| OGDEN | THEON | ELIHU | CELVE | WILDT | DANNY | SYNGE | POPOV | KARLE | LUSKE | DOUST | PIXII |
| PADDY | TRETZ | ELION | COLIN | WILES | DANTE | TANDY | PUPIN | KERST | MASON | DRUDE | BAYER |
| PEDRO | TSENG | ELIOT | DALEN | WILEY | DENIS | WENDY | AARON | KIRSH | MOSES | GAUSS | BOYER |
| SODDY | UMEKI | EMILE | DELLA | WILLY | DONAT | WUNDT | BARON | KORDA | NASIR | GLUCK | BOYLE |
| ABEGG | VIETA | EMILY | DOLBY | WOLFF | DONNA | ZENER | BARRY | KURTZ | OLSON | GOULD | BOYSE |
| ALEXI | WIEST | ERICH | EDLEN | WYLER | EJNAR | ADOLF | BARUJ | LARRY | ORSON | HAUGE | BRYAN |
| AVERY | NUFER | EWING | ELLEN | YALOW | ENNIO | ALOYS | BERRY | LOREN | PASCH | HOUCK | CLYDE |
| BEEBE | ANGEL | FRIED | ELLET | AHMAD | ERNST | BLOCH | BIROC | LORNE | PASSY | JOULE | GUYOT |
| BEERY | BEGIN | FRIES | ELLIS | AHMES | FINCH | BLOCK | BOREL | LURIA | PESCI | KRUPP | HAYES |
| BREEN | EDGAR | FRITZ | EULER | ALMON | FONDA | BLOOM | BORIS | MARCH | ROSSE | LAURA | HEYSE |
| BRENT | EIGEN | HAIGH | FALSE | CAMUS | HANEY | BOOLE | BURGI | MARCO | ROSSI | LOUIS | HOYLE |
| BUELL | EUGEN | HAING | FELIX | COMER | HANKS | BOOTH | BURKE | MAREY | RUSKA | MAURY | LOYAL |
| CHENG | FEGTE | HAISE | GALEN | COMTE | HANNO | BROCA | BURKS | MARIA | SISSY | MOULD | MAYER |

MAYOW
MEYER
MOYER
PAYEN
PAYNE
ROYDS
SAYED
TRYON
WAYNE
WHYTT
FAZAN
KAZAN
LAZLO
LIZZY
LUZZI

## 4th Letter

AHMAD
ALLAN
ALVAN
ANWAR
APIAN
ARIAS
BRIAN
BRYAN
BYRAM
CAJAL
CESAR
CHIAO
COWAN
DEWAR
DIRAC
DONAT
DUMAS
EDGAR
EJNAR
ELIAS
ERMAN
FAZAN
GOBAT
HAMAO
HEMAN
HIRAM
HYMAN
IGNAZ
ISAAC
JOHAN
JONAS
JUDAH
JURAN
KAMAL
KAZAN
KOWAL
LAMAR
LAMAS
LEVAN
LOYAL
LUCAS
LUKAS
LYMAN
MCKAY
MERAY
OSCAR
OSKAR
RAMAN
REGAN
REMAK
ROWAN
SAGAN
SALAM
SARAH
SUSAN
WALAS
WYMAN
ASHBY
BEEBE
CHUBB
DANBY
DARBY
DOLBY
GIBBS
KLEBS
KOLBE
KREBS
LIBBY
NAMBU
SORBY
TAMBI
TAUBE
ALICE
ALICK
AMICI
BEACH
BLACK
BLOCH
BLOCK
BOSCH
BROCA
BRUCE
CHACE
CHUCK
COUCH
CRICK
DRACH
ERICH
FINCH
FITCH
GLUCK
GRACE
HENCH
HOUCK
ILICH
KUSCH
MARCH
MARCO
NANCY
PASCH
PERCY
PESCI
QUICK
REICH
RICCI
STOCK
TRACY
VASCO
BONDI
BRADY
CLYDE
DRUDE
FONDA
GAEDE
HARDY
HONDA
KORDA
KUNDT
LANDE
LINDA
LINDE
LUNDH
LYNDS
PADDY
ROYDS
SANDY
SODDY
TANDY
TOLDY
WALDO
WENDY
WILDT
WOODY
WUNDT
ABNEY
ADLER
AHMES
AIKEN
ALDER
ALLEN
ALTER
ANGEL
ARBER
ARLEN
ASSER
BAKER
BATES
BAYER
BINET
BODEN
BOREL
BOVET
BOWEN
BOYER
BREEN
CAPEK
CAREL
CHIEH
CHIEN
COHEN
COMER
COREY
COTES
DALEN
DAWES
DEREK
DEWEY
DURER
EDLEN
EIGEN
ELLEN
ELLET
ELMER
ELVEN
ETHEL
EUGEN
EULER
FRIED
FRIES
GALEN
GATES
GEBER
GIGER
GILES
GODEL
GREEN
GREER
HABER
HALES
HANEY
HAYES
HEBER
HELEN
HUBEL
HUBER
IHNEN
INNES
JAMES
JANET
JONES
JOSEF
JULES
KAMEN
KAREL
LAWES
LEDER
LEGER
LEVEN
LOREN
LOWER
LYNEN
MABEL
MALEY
MAREY
MAYER
MENES
MEYER
MILES
MOSES
MOYER
MUREN
NEHER
NILES
NIVEN
NOBEL
NUFER
NUNES
NUNEZ
OGDEN
ONNES
OSLER
PAGET
PAVEL
PAYEN
PERES
PEREY
PEREZ
PETER
PINEL
QUEEN
REBER
ROGER
ROMER
RUBEL
SAKEL
SAYED
SOREN
SPIES
STEEN
SUGER
TAIEB
THAER
THIEL
TOMEI
TYLER
VOGEL
WEBER
WILES
WILEY
WYLER
YOSEF
YUSEF
ZENER
CLIFF
KOLFF
LWOFF
PFAFF
WOLFF
ABEGG
ARAGO
BENGT
BRAGG
BURGI
FREGE
GOLGI
GREGG
HAIGH
HAUGE
HIGGS
JUNGE
KEOGH
KROGH
LANGE
LEIGH
LODGE
LUIGI
MONGE
PEGGY
PREGL
RUNGE
SYNGE
ULUGH
WAAGE
BETHE
BOTHE
BRAHE
ELIHU
FUCHS
HECHT
KATHY
RIGHI
ROCHE
RUEHL
SACHS
STRHL
TYCHO
ADAIR
ALVIN
ANNIE
ARVID
BASIL
BEGIN
BEVIS
BORIS
BRAID
BUNIN
CECIL
CHAIM
CHAIN
CHRIS
COLIN
CRAIG
CURIE
CYRIL
DARIO
DAVID
DAVIS
DENIS
DORIS
DUBIN
EDDIE
EDWIN
EEMIL
ELLIS
ENNIO
ERWIN
FELIX
HOKIN
IRVIN
IRWIN
JABIR
JODIE
JORIE
JOSIE
JULIA
JULIE
KANIN
KEVIN
KLEIN
KUNIO
LEWIS
LOGIE
LOUIS
LOWIG
LUCIO
LURIA
MARIA
MARIE
MARIK
MARIN
MARIO
MAXIM
MONIZ
NASIR
NEVIL
PAPIN
PETIT
PIXII
PUPIN
RABIN
RENIE
RINIO
ROBIN
RUBIN
SABIN
SIMIC
STAIN
TEMIN
BRAJA
BANKS
BLAKE
BURKE
BURKS
DICKE
DRAKE
ENCKE
ESAKI
FOCKE
GILKS
HANKS
HOOKE
KEIKE
LOCKE
LOTKA
LUSKE
MARKO
PACKE
ROOKE
RUSKA
UMEKI
ADOLF
BILLY
BOOLE
BOULE
BOYLE
BUELL
CABLE
CARLO
DELLA
DIELS
DOELL
EMILE
EMILY
EWALD
FIELD
FOWLE
GABLE
GALLE
GOULD
HENLE
HOLLY
HOYLE
JOULE
KARLE
KELLY
LAZLO
LULLY
LYELL
MERLE
MILLS
MOLLO
MOULD
MPILO
NEELY
NEILL
NELLY
NIELS
NOBLE
PABLO
PAOLO
PAULI
ROALD
ROLLE
SALLY
SHULL
SKALL
SMALL
SNELL
STOLL
SULLY
TALLY
TESLA
TULLY
WELLS
WILLY
ADAMS
BAUME
BEAMS
DEMME
FERMI
FREMY
GEMMA
GERMI
JIMMY
KOSMA
KRAMS
NORMA
SELMA
SSUMA
TOMMY
BHANU
BLANE
BRAND
BRENT
BRINK
BRUNO
BURNS
CAINE
CERNY
CHANG
CHENG
CHING
CHONG
CHUNG
CLINE
CLINT
CORNU
COUNT
DANNY
DIANE
DONNA
EBING
EVANS
EWING
FRANK
FRANS
FRANZ
GEENA
GLENN
GRANT
GWENN
HAING
HANNO
HANNS
HEINE
HEINZ
HUANG
HYMNS
IRENE
IRONS
JEANS
JENNY
JERNE
JOHNS
KLINE
KUHNE
LAING
LEONE
LIANG
LORNE
MILNE
OWENS
PAYNE
PEANO
PLINY
RAINE
RHIND
RHINE
SAINT
SHENG
STENO
STONE
SZENT
TOWNE
TSENG
TSUNG
VERNA
WAYNE
YOUNG
YUANG
ZHANG
AARON
AGNON
ALMON
ALTON
ANTON
ASTON
ASTOR
BARON
BASOV
BELON
BIROC
BLOOM
BROOK
BROOM
BYRON
CAROL
CONON
CUKOR
DIXON
DUBOS
DYSON
ELION
ELIOT
GABOR
GAMOW
GEROG
GODOY
GUYOT
HEROD
HERON
HYRON
JACOB
JAKOB
JANOS
JASON
LEBON
LECOQ
MASON
MAYOW
METON
MILOS
MINOS
MINOT
MONOD
NICOL
NIXON
OCHOA
OLSON
ORBOM
ORSON
POPOV
RAMON
RAMOS
SETON
SIMON
SOLON
THEON
TIBOR
TITOV
TRYON
TUROK
TYLOR
YALOW
ASAPH
BEPPO
GOMPF
HOPPE
KRUPP
RALPH
AKIRA
ANDRE
AVARY
AVERY
BARRY
BEERY
BERRY
CAPRA
CLARA
CLARK
CLERK
COURT
EBERS
ELERT
EMERT
FABRI
FABRY
FERRO
FIORE
FLORY
FRERE
GARRY
GEORG
GERRY
GOERG
HARRY
HENRI
HENRY
ICIRO
LARRY
LAURA
MAURY
MOORE
PARRY
PEARL
PEARY
PEDRO
PIERO
SEGRE
SHARP
SHORT
SPORN
STARK
STERN
TWORT
WIARD
BASSI
BLISS
BOYSE
CRISP
CROSS
DOISY
DOUST
DRESS

ERNST
FALSE
FOSSE
FROSH
FURSE
FURST
GAUSS
GROSS
HAISE
HESSE
HEYSE
HULSE
JESSE
JOOST
KERST
KIRSH
KRESS
LUISE
MARSH
MORSE
PABST
PASSY
PERSE
REESE
REISS
ROSSE
ROSSI
ROUSE
SISSY
SUESS
WALSH
WEISS
WIEST
BETTE
BETTY
BOOTH
BOTTA
BURTT
COMTE
CONTI
COSTA
DANTE
EDITH
FEGTE
FOOTE
FORTT
FRITZ
GERTY
GROTE
HARTZ
HERTZ
HORTA
HYATT
KEITH
KROTO
KURTZ
METTY
MOTTE
NATTA
NORTH
PATTY
PLATO
PLATT
PORTA
PYOTR
SCOTT
SMITH
TRETZ
VESTO
VIETA
VOLTA
WHITE
WHYTT
WIRTH
WURTZ
YEATS
ABDUS
ALDUS
BARUJ
BRAUN
CAMUS
CLAUS
CYRUS
FREUD
FUKUI
INOUE
KLAUS
LINUS
MALUS
PANUM
PLAUT
PROUT
RAMUS
RAOUL
STOUT
TATUM
TYTUS
VITUS
CELVE
DERVA
GROVE
MAEVE
STEVE
TALVA
BROWN
LOEWI
OGAWA
ALEXI
ALOYS
DEBYE
ELWYN
FLOYD
LLOYD
MERYL
SELYE
SONYA
LIZZY
LUZZI
SANZO

## 5th Letter

AKIRA
BOTTA
BRAJA
BROCA
CAPRA
CLARA
COSTA
DELLA
DERVA
DONNA
FONDA
GEENA
GEMMA
HONDA
HORTA
JULIA
KORDA
KOSMA
LAURA
LINDA
LOTKA
LURIA
MARIA
NATTA
NORMA
OCHOA
OGAWA
PORTA
RUSKA
SELMA
SONYA
SSUMA
TALVA
TESLA
VERNA
VIETA
VOLTA
CHUBB
JACOB
JAKOB
TAIEB
BIROC
DIRAC
ISAAC
SIMIC
AHMAD
ARVID
BRAID
BRAND
DAVID
EWALD
FIELD
FLOYD
FREUD
FRIED
GOULD
HEROD
LLOYD
MONOD
MOULD
RHIND
ROALD
SAYED
WIARD
ALICE
ANDRE
ANNIE
BAUME
BEEBE
BETHE
BETTE
BLAKE
BLANE
BOOLE
BOTHE
BOULE
BOYLE
BOYSE
BRAHE
BRUCE
BURKE
CABLE
CAINE
CELVE
CHACE
CLINE
CLYDE
COMTE
CURIE
DANTE
DEBYE
DEMME
DIANE
DICKE
DRAKE
DRUDE
EDDIE
EMILE
ENCKE
FALSE
FEGTE
FIORE
FOCKE
FOOTE
FOSSE
FOWLE
FREGE
FRERE
FURSE
GABLE
GAEDE
GALLE
GRACE
GROTE
GROVE
HAISE
HAUGE
HEINE
HENLE
HESSE
HEYSE
HOOKE
HOPPE
HOYLE
HULSE
INOUE
IRENE
JERNE
JESSE
JODIE
JORIE
JOSIE
JOULE
JULIE
JUNGE
KARLE
KEIKE
KLINE
KOLBE
KUHNE
LANDE
LANGE
LEONE
LINDE
LOCKE
LODGE
LOGIE
LORNE
LUISE
LUSKE
MAEVE
MARIE
MERLE
MILNE
MONGE
MOORE
MORSE
MOTTE
NOBLE
PACKE
PAYNE
PERSE
RAINE
REESE
RENIE
RHINE
ROCHE
ROLLE
ROOKE
ROSSE
ROUSE
RUNGE
SEGRE
SELYE
STEVE
STONE
SYNGE
TAUBE
TOWNE
WAAGE
WAYNE
WHITE
ADOLF
CLIFF
GOMPF
JOSEF
KOLFF
LWOFF
PFAFF
WOLFF
YOSEF
YUSEF
ABEGG
BRAGG
CHANG
CHENG
CHING
CHONG
CHUNG
CRAIG
EBING
EWING
GEORG
GEROG
GOERG
GREGG
HAING
HUANG
LAING
LIANG
LOWIG
SHENG
TSENG
TSUNG
YOUNG
YUANG
ZHANG
ASAPH
BEACH
BLOCH
BOOTH
BOSCH
CHIEH
COUCH
DRACH
EDITH
ERICH
FINCH
FITCH
FROSH
HAIGH
HENCH
ILICH
JUDAH
KEITH
KEOGH
KIRSH
KROGH
KUSCH
LEIGH
LUNDH
MARCH
MARSH
NORTH
PASCH
RALPH
REICH
SARAH
SMITH
ULUGH
WALSH
WIRTH
ALEXI
AMICI
BASSI
BONDI
BURGI
CONTI
ESAKI
FABRI
FERMI
FUKUI
GERMI
GOLGI
HENRI
LOEWI
LUIGI
LUZZI
PAULI
PESCI
PIXII
RICCI
RIGHI
ROSSI
TAMBI
TOMEI
UMEKI
BARUJ
ALICK
BLACK
BLOCK
BRINK
BROOK
CAPEK
CHUCK
CLARK
CLERK
CRICK
DEREK
FRANK
GLUCK
HOUCK
MARIK
QUICK
REMAK
STARK
STOCK
TUROK
ANGEL
BASIL
BOREL
BUELL
CAJAL
CAREL
CAROL
CECIL
CYRIL
DOELL
EEMIL
ETHEL
GODEL
HUBEL
KAMAL
KAREL
KOWAL
LOYAL
LYELL
MABEL
MERYL
NEILL
NEVIL
NICOL
NOBEL
PAVEL
PEARL
PINEL
PREGL
RAOUL
RUBEL
RUEHL
SAKEL
SHULL
SKALL
SMALL
SNELL
STOLL
STRHL
THIEL
VOGEL
BLOOM
BROOM
BYRAM
CHAIM
HIRAM
MAXIM
ORBOM
PANUM
SALAM
TATUM
AARON
AGNON
AIKEN
ALLAN
ALLEN
ALMON
ALTON
ALVAN
ALVIN
ANTON
APIAN
ARLEN
ASTON
BARON
BEGIN
BELON
BODEN
BOWEN
BRAUN
BREEN
BRIAN
BROWN
BRYAN
BUNIN
BYRON
CHAIN
CHIEN
COHEN
COLIN
CONON
COWAN
DALEN
DIXON
DUBIN
DYSON
EDLEN
EDWIN
EIGEN
ELION
ELLEN
ELVEN
ELWYN
ERMAN
ERWIN
EUGEN
FAZAN
GALEN
GLENN
GREEN
GWENN
HELEN
HEMAN
HERON
HOKIN
HYMAN
HYRON
IHNEN
IRVIN
IRWIN
JASON
JOHAN
JURAN
KAMEN
KANIN
KAZAN
KEVIN
KLEIN
LEBON
LEVAN
LEVEN
LOREN
LYMAN
LYNEN
MARIN
MASON
METON
MUREN
NIVEN
NIXON
OGDEN
OLSON
ORSON
PAPIN
PAYEN
PUPIN
QUEEN
RABIN
RAMAN
RAMON
REGAN
ROBIN
ROWAN
RUBIN
SABIN
SAGAN
SETON
SIMON
SOLON
SOREN
SPORN
STAIN
STEEN
STERN
SUSAN
TEMIN
THEON
TRYON
WYMAN
ARAGO
BEPPO
BRUNO
CARLO
CHIAO
DARIO
ENNIO
FERRO
HAMAO
HANNO
ICIRO
KROTO
KUNIO
LAZLO
LUCIO
MARCO
MARIO
MARKO
MOLLO
MPILO
PABLO
PAOLO
PEANO
PEDRO
PIERO
PLATO
RINIO
SANZO
STENO
TYCHO
VASCO
VESTO
WALDO
CRISP
KRUPP
SHARP
LECOQ
ADAIR
ADLER
ALDER
ALTER
ANWAR
ARBER
ASSER
ASTOR
BAKER
BAYER
BOYER
CESAR
COMER
CUKOR
DEWAR
DURER
EDGAR
EJNAR
ELMER
EULER
GABOR
GEBER
GIGER
GREER
HABER
HEBER
HUBER
JABIR
LAMAR
LEDER
LEGER
LOWER
MAYER
MEYER
MOYER
NASIR
NEHER
NUFER
OSCAR
OSKAR
OSLER
PETER
PYOTR
REBER
ROGER
ROMER
SUGER
THAER
TIBOR
TYLER
TYLOR
WEBER
WYLER
ZENER
ABDUS
ADAMS
AHMES
ALDUS
ALOYS
ARIAS
BANKS
BATES
BEAMS
BEVIS
BLISS
BORIS

BURKS
BURNS
CAMUS
CHRIS
CLAUS
COTES
CROSS
CYRUS
DAVIS
DAWES
DENIS
DIELS
DORIS
DRESS
DUBOS
DUMAS
EBERS
ELIAS
ELLIS
EVANS
FRANS
FRIES
FUCHS
GATES
GAUSS
GIBBS
GILES
GILKS
GROSS
HALES
HANKS
HANNS
HAYES
HIGGS
HYMNS
INNES
IRONS
JAMES
JANOS
JEANS
JOHNS
JONAS
JONES
JULES
KLAUS
KLEBS
KRAMS
KREBS
KRESS
LAMAS
LAWES
LEWIS
LINUS
LOUIS
LUCAS
LUKAS

LYNDS
MALUS
MENES
MILES
MILLS
MILOS
MINOS
MOSES
NIELS
NILES
NUNES
ONNES
OWENS
PERES
RAMOS
RAMUS
REISS
ROYDS
SACHS
SPIES
SUESS
TYTUS
VITUS
WALAS
WEISS
WELLS
WILES
YEATS
BENGT
BINET
BOVET
BRENT
BURTT
CLINT
COUNT
COURT
DONAT
DOUST
ELERT
ELIOT
ELLET
EMERT
ERNST
FORTT
FURST
GOBAT
GRANT
GUYOT
HECHT
HYATT
JANET
JOOST
KERST
KUNDT
MINOT
PABST

PAGET
PETIT
PLATT
PLAUT
PROUT
SAINT
SCOTT
SHORT
STOUT
SZENT
TWORT
WHYTT
WIEST
WILDT
WUNDT
BHANU
CORNU
ELIHU
NAMBU
BASOV
POPOV
TITOV
GAMOW
MAYOW
YALOW
FELIX
ABNEY
ASHBY
AVARY
AVERY
BARRY
BEERY
BERRY
BETTY
BILLY
BRADY
CERNY
COREY
DANBY
DANNY
DARBY
DEWEY
DOISY
DOLBY
EMILY
FABRY
FLORY
FREMY
GARRY
GERRY
GERTY
GODOY
HANEY
HARDY
HARRY
HENRY

HOLLY
JENNY
JIMMY
KATHY
KELLY
LARRY
LIBBY
LIZZY
LULLY
MALEY
MAREY
MAURY
MCKAY
MERAY
METTY
NANCY
NEELY
NELLY
PADDY
PARRY
PASSY
PATTY
PEARY
PEGGY
PERCY
PEREY
PLINY
SALLY
SANDY
SISSY
SODDY
SORBY
SULLY
TALLY
TANDY
TOLDY
TOMMY
TRACY
TULLY
WENDY
WILEY
WILLY
WOODY
FRANZ
FRITZ
HARTZ
HEINZ
HERTZ
IGNAZ
KURTZ
MONIZ
NUNEZ
PEREZ
TRETZ
WURTZ

## 6 LETTER

### 1ST LETTER

ABBOTT
ADDAMS
ADOLFO
ADOLPH
ADRIAN
ADRIEN
AGNETA
AITKEN
ALARIC
ALBERT
ALCOCK
ALCOTT
ALCUIN
ALDRIN
ALEXIS
ALFRED
ALFVEN
ALISON
ALLDER
ALLVAR
ALONZO
ALPHER
ALPINI
ALTMAN
AMAGAT
AMDAHL
AMECHE
AMEDEO
AMPERE
AMTHOR
ANDERS
ANDREA
ANDREI
ANDRES
ANDREW
ANDREY
ANDRIC
ANGELL
ANGELO
ANHALT
ANNING
ANTONY
APPERT
APPOLT
ARAFAT
ARCHER
ARCHIE
ARDREY
ARGAND
ARLING
ARLISS
ARMAND

ARNAUD
ARNOLD
ARREST
ARTEDI
ARTHUR
ASHKIN
ASPDIN
ATWOOD
AUBREY
AUDREY
AUGUST
AUSTEN
AUSTIN
AUZOUT
AYLING
AYLMER
AYMAND
BAINES
BANACH
BARANY
BARBER
BARBRA
BARKLA
BARNES
BARNEY
BARROW
BARTON
BARUCH
BASEVI
BAUHIN
BAWDEN
BAXTER
BEADLE
BEATON
BEATTY
BEAVAN
BECHER
BECKET
BEGLEY
BEGUIN
BEHAIM
BELLOW
BENDER
BENITO
BENNET
BENOIT
BENSON
BENTON
BERGER
BERING
BERMAN
BERNAL
BEROZA
BERTHA
BERTIL
BESLER

BESSEL
BHABHA
BICHAT
BIDDEL
BINNIG
BISHOP
BIZIOU
BLAAUW
BLAISE
BLATTY
BODMER
BOGART
BOHLIN
BOLTON
BOLYAI
BONNER
BONNET
BONNOT
BORDEN
BORDET
BORDEU
BORMAN
BOUGHN
BOULLE
BOVERI
BOWLES
BRAMAH
BRANCA
BRANDO
BRANDT
BRENDA
BREUER
BRIAND
BRIDGE
BRIGGS
BRIGHT
BRILEY
BROOKE
BROOKS
BRUNEL
BRUTUS
BUDDHA
BULLEN
BUNCHE
BUNSEN
BURALI
BURNET
BURTON
BUSSEY
BUSTER
BUTLER
CABRAL
CAESAR
CAGNEY
CALLIE
CALVIN

CANNOM
CANNON
CANTIN
CANTON
CANTOR
CAPMAN
CARAKA
CARBON
CARLOS
CARMEN
CARNEY
CARNOT
CARREL
CARSON
CARTAN
CARTER
CARVER
CASKEY
CASPAR
CASSIN
CASTEL
CAUCHY
CAVETT
CAXTON
CAYLEY
CEDRIC
CELSUS
CERNAN
CERRAF
CESARE
CESARI
CHABRY
CHANCE
CHAPPE
CHEOPS
CHEYNE
CHIANG
CHURCH
CIMINO
CIVITA
CLAIRE
CLARKE
CLAUDE
CLORIS
CLOVIS
COATES
COBURN
COCKER
COFFIN
COLLIP
COLMAN
CONRAD
CONRAT
COOLEY
COOPER
COPLEY

CORDUS
CORNER
CORTES
COSTER
COTTON
COUPER
COWLES
CRAFTS
CRAGOE
CRAMER
CRANCH
CRELLE
CREMER
CRONIN
CROSBY
CUGNOT
CULLEN
CURTIS
CURTIZ
CUVIER
CYRANO
DAFFOS
DALTON
DANIEL
DANILO
DARWIN
DAVIES
DAWSON
DAYTON
DECUIR
DELANO
DELANY
DENJOY
DENNIS
DENTON
DENZEL
DERHAM
DESIRE
DIANNE
DIBBLE
DIESEL
DIETER
DIGGES
DILLEY
DILLON
DINTIS
DMITRI
DOMAGK
DONALD
DONATI
DONATO
DORIAN
DRAPER
DREIER
DREYER
DUDLEY

DUFOUR
DUGGAR
DULONG
DUNANT
DUNBAR
DUNCAN
DUNHAM
DUNLOP
DUPUIS
DUSTIN
DUTTON
DUVALL
DWIGHT
EAGLER
ECCLES
ECKERT
EDISON
EDLUND
EDMOND
EDUARD
EDWARD
EIFFEL
EILEEN
EISAKU
EISELE
ELISHA
ELLERY
ELLIOT
ELOISE
ELSTER
ELYTIS
EMERIC
EMILIE
EMILIO
ENDERS
ENGELS
ENRICO
ERCKER
ERLICH
ERNEST
ETIENE
EUCKEN
EUCLID
EUGENE
EVARTS
EVELYN
EYVIND
FABIAN
FAIRLY
FAJANS
FARADY
FARFAX
FARMAN
FARMER
FAROUK
FARRAR

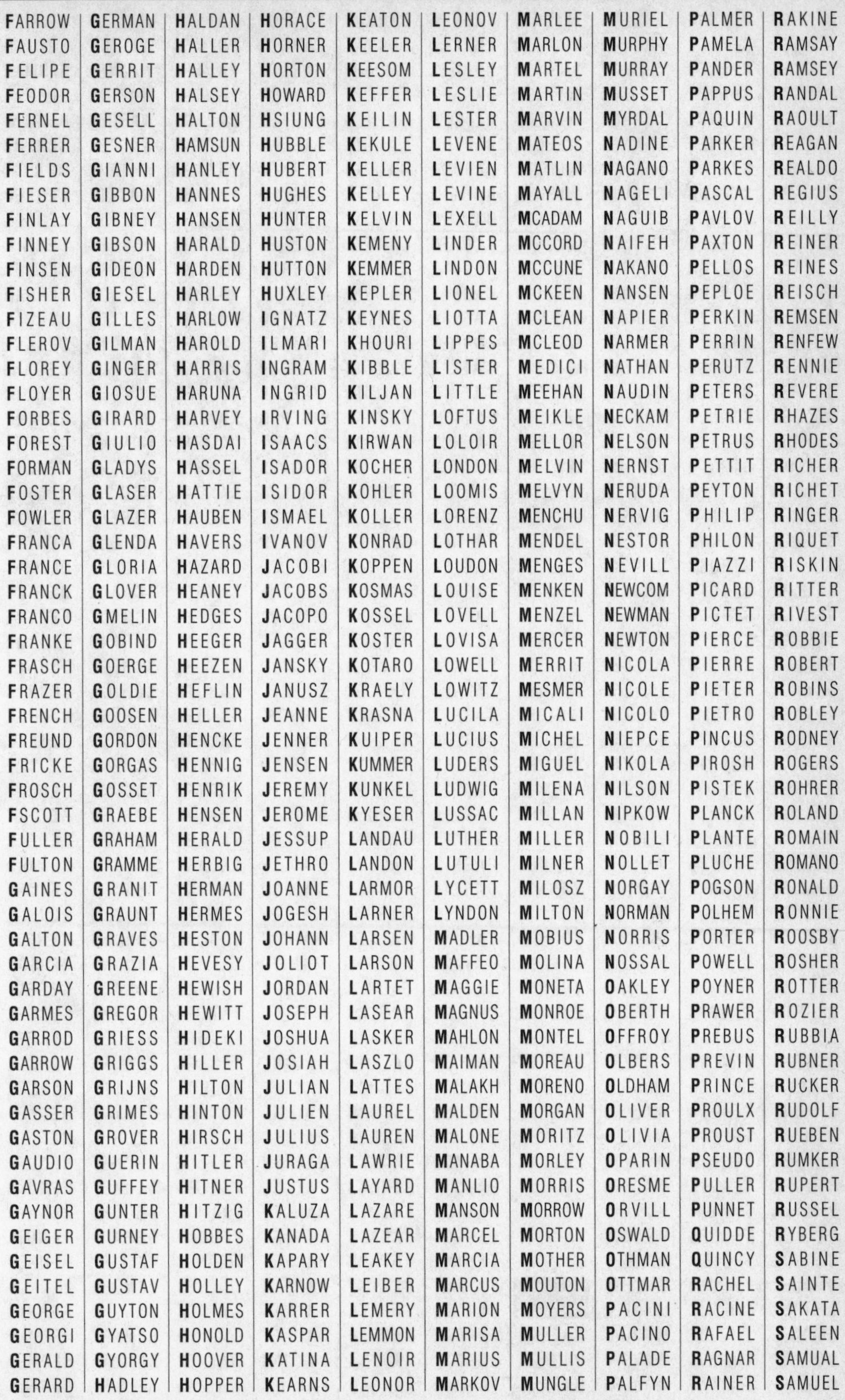

FARROW
FAUSTO
FELIPE
FEODOR
FERNEL
FERRER
FIELDS
FIESER
FINLAY
FINNEY
FINSEN
FISHER
FIZEAU
FLEROV
FLOREY
FLOYER
FORBES
FOREST
FORMAN
FOSTER
FOWLER
FRANCA
FRANCE
FRANCK
FRANCO
FRANKE
FRASCH
FRAZER
FRENCH
FREUND
FRICKE
FROSCH
FSCOTT
FULLER
FULTON
GAINES
GALOIS
GALTON
GARCIA
GARDAY
GARMES
GARROD
GARROW
GARSON
GASSER
GASTON
GAUDIO
GAVRAS
GAYNOR
GEIGER
GEISEL
GEITEL
GEORGE
GEORGI
GERALD
GERARD
GERMAN
GEROGE
GERRIT
GERSON
GESELL
GESNER
GIANNI
GIBBON
GIBNEY
GIBSON
GIDEON
GIESEL
GILLES
GILMAN
GINGER
GIOSUE
GIRARD
GIULIO
GLADYS
GLASER
GLAZER
GLENDA
GLORIA
GLOVER
GMELIN
GOBIND
GOERGE
GOLDIE
GOOSEN
GORDON
GORGAS
GOSSET
GRAEBE
GRAHAM
GRAMME
GRANIT
GRAUNT
GRAVES
GRAZIA
GREENE
GREGOR
GRIESS
GRIGGS
GRIJNS
GRIMES
GROVER
GUERIN
GUFFEY
GUNTER
GURNEY
GUSTAF
GUSTAV
GUYTON
GYATSO
GYORGY
HADLEY
HALDAN
HALLER
HALLEY
HALSEY
HALTON
HAMSUN
HANLEY
HANNES
HANSEN
HARALD
HARDEN
HARLEY
HARLOW
HAROLD
HARRIS
HARUNA
HARVEY
HASDAI
HASSEL
HATTIE
HAUBEN
HAVERS
HAZARD
HEANEY
HEDGES
HEEGER
HEEZEN
HEFLIN
HELLER
HENCKE
HENNIG
HENRIK
HENSEN
HERALD
HERBIG
HERMAN
HERMES
HESTON
HEVESY
HEWISH
HEWITT
HIDEKI
HILLER
HILTON
HINTON
HIRSCH
HITLER
HITNER
HITZIG
HOBBES
HOLDEN
HOLLEY
HOLMES
HONOLD
HOOVER
HOPPER
HORACE
HORNER
HORTON
HOWARD
HSIUNG
HUBBLE
HUBERT
HUGHES
HUNTER
HUSTON
HUTTON
HUXLEY
IGNATZ
ILMARI
INGRAM
INGRID
IRVING
ISAACS
ISADOR
ISIDOR
ISMAEL
IVANOV
JACOBI
JACOBS
JACOPO
JAGGER
JANSKY
JANUSZ
JEANNE
JENNER
JENSEN
JEREMY
JEROME
JESSUP
JETHRO
JOANNE
JOGESH
JOHANN
JOLIOT
JORDAN
JOSEPH
JOSHUA
JOSIAH
JULIAN
JULIEN
JULIUS
JURAGA
JUSTUS
KALUZA
KANADA
KAPARY
KARNOW
KARRER
KASPAR
KATINA
KEARNS
KEATON
KEELER
KEESOM
KEFFER
KEILIN
KEKULE
KELLER
KELLEY
KELVIN
KEMENY
KEMMER
KEPLER
KEYNES
KHOURI
KIBBLE
KILJAN
KINSKY
KIRWAN
KOCHER
KOHLER
KOLLER
KONRAD
KOPPEN
KOSMAS
KOSSEL
KOSTER
KOTARO
KRAELY
KRASNA
KUIPER
KUMMER
KUNKEL
KYESER
LANDAU
LANDON
LARMOR
LARNER
LARSEN
LARSON
LARTET
LASEAR
LASKER
LASZLO
LATTES
LAUREL
LAUREN
LAWRIE
LAYARD
LAZARE
LAZEAR
LEAKEY
LEIBER
LEMERY
LEMMON
LENOIR
LEONOR
LEONOV
LERNER
LESLEY
LESLIE
LESTER
LEVENE
LEVIEN
LEVINE
LEXELL
LINDER
LINDON
LIONEL
LIOTTA
LIPPES
LISTER
LITTLE
LOFTUS
LOLOIR
LONDON
LOOMIS
LORENZ
LOTHAR
LOUDON
LOUISE
LOVELL
LOVISA
LOWELL
LOWITZ
LUCILA
LUCIUS
LUDERS
LUDWIG
LUSSAC
LUTHER
LUTULI
LYCETT
LYNDON
MADLER
MAFFEO
MAGGIE
MAGNUS
MAHLON
MAIMAN
MALAKH
MALDEN
MALONE
MANABA
MANLIO
MANSON
MARCEL
MARCIA
MARCUS
MARION
MARISA
MARIUS
MARKOV
MARLEE
MARLON
MARTEL
MARTIN
MARVIN
MATEOS
MATLIN
MAYALL
MCADAM
MCCORD
MCCUNE
MCKEEN
MCLEAN
MCLEOD
MEDICI
MEEHAN
MEIKLE
MELLOR
MELVIN
MELVYN
MENCHU
MENDEL
MENGES
MENKEN
MENZEL
MERCER
MERRIT
MESMER
MICALI
MICHEL
MIGUEL
MILENA
MILLAN
MILLER
MILNER
MILOSZ
MILTON
MOBIUS
MOLINA
MONETA
MONROE
MONTEL
MOREAU
MORENO
MORGAN
MORITZ
MORLEY
MORRIS
MORROW
MORTON
MOTHER
MOUTON
MOYERS
MULLER
MULLIS
MUNGLE
MURIEL
MURPHY
MURRAY
MUSSET
MYRDAL
NADINE
NAGANO
NAGELI
NAGUIB
NAIFEH
NAKANO
NANSEN
NAPIER
NARMER
NATHAN
NAUDIN
NECKAM
NELSON
NERNST
NERUDA
NERVIG
NESTOR
NEVILL
NEWCOM
NEWMAN
NEWTON
NICOLA
NICOLE
NICOLO
NIEPCE
NIKOLA
NILSON
NIPKOW
NOBILI
NOLLET
NORGAY
NORMAN
NORRIS
NOSSAL
OAKLEY
OBERTH
OFFROY
OLBERS
OLDHAM
OLIVER
OLIVIA
OPARIN
ORESME
ORVILL
OSWALD
OTHMAN
OTTMAR
PACINI
PACINO
PALADE
PALFYN
PALMER
PAMELA
PANDER
PAPPUS
PAQUIN
PARKER
PARKES
PASCAL
PAVLOV
PAXTON
PELLOS
PEPLOE
PERKIN
PERRIN
PERUTZ
PETERS
PETRIE
PETRUS
PETTIT
PEYTON
PHILIP
PHILON
PIAZZI
PICARD
PICTET
PIERCE
PIERRE
PIETER
PIETRO
PINCUS
PIROSH
PISTEK
PLANCK
PLANTE
PLUCHE
POGSON
POLHEM
PORTER
POWELL
POYNER
PRAWER
PREBUS
PREVIN
PRINCE
PROULX
PROUST
PSEUDO
PULLER
PUNNET
QUIDDE
QUINCY
RACHEL
RACINE
RAFAEL
RAGNAR
RAINER
RAKINE
RAMSAY
RAMSEY
RANDAL
RAOULT
REAGAN
REALDO
REGIUS
REILLY
REINER
REINES
REISCH
REMSEN
RENFEW
RENNIE
REVERE
RHAZES
RHODES
RICHER
RICHET
RINGER
RIQUET
RISKIN
RITTER
RIVEST
ROBBIE
ROBERT
ROBINS
ROBLEY
RODNEY
ROGERS
ROHRER
ROLAND
ROMAIN
ROMANO
RONALD
RONNIE
ROOSBY
ROSHER
ROTTER
ROZIER
RUBBIA
RUBNER
RUCKER
RUDOLF
RUEBEN
RUMKER
RUPERT
RUSSEL
RYBERG
SABINE
SAINTE
SAKATA
SALEEN
SAMUAL
SAMUEL

SANGER
SANTEL
SAPPHO
SARGON
SARTRE
SAURIA
SAVAGE
SAVARY
SAVERY
SCARPA
SCHACK
SCHARY
SCHELL
SCHICK
SCHNEE
SCOPES
SCOTUS
SEAMUS
SEATON
SECCHI
SEGALL
SELMAN
SEMJON
SEMLER
SENECA
SERSEN
SEVERO
SEWALL
SEYLER
SHAMIR
SHANKS
SHARPE
SHEMIN
SHIMON
SHIUNG
SHMUEL
SHOVEL
SHUKEN
SIBLEY
SIDNEY
SIGRID
SILVIO
SIMEON
SIMOND
SIMONE
SIMONI
SIMONS
SINGER
SKOTAK
SLIFER
SLOANE
SMAUEL
SMILEY
SMYTHE
SOLVAY
SOPHIA
SOPHIE
SOPHUS
SPACEK
SPACEY
SPENCE
SPERRY
SQUIER
STALIN
STEARN
STEARS
STEELE
STEFAN
STEVEN
STIFEL
STILES
STOCKE
STOKES
STONEY
STRABO
STRATO
STREEP
STREET
STRONG
STRUSS
STRUTT
STRUVE
STUART
STUMPF
SUMNER
SUSUME
SUSUMU
SUTTON
SUZUKI
SVANTE
SYDNEY
TADDEO
TAGORE
TALBOT
TANAKA
TARSKI
TASMAN
TAUBES
TAUROG
TAYLOR
TELLER
TEODOR
TERESA
TESICH
TEWFIK
THABIT
THALES
THELMA
THEONI
THIOUT
THOLDE
THOMAS
TIMONI
TITIUS
TOBIAS
TOLAND
TOLMAN
TOPHAM
TORREY
TOWNES
TRAJAN
TRAVIS
TREVOR
TROFIM
TROTTI
TRUMAN
TRUMBO
TSVETT
TULLIO
TUMMEL
TURING
ULISSE
ULPIUS
ULRICH
UNDSET
UNSOLD
UPDIKE
URBAIN
USSHER
VALENS
VALLEE
VALLES
VARMUS
VAUBAN
VENETZ
VENING
VERNER
VERNON
VERTES
VICTOR
VIKTOR
VILMOS
VIRGIL
VIVIAN
VIVIEN
VOIGHT
VOISIN
WAGNER
WALDEN
WALESA
WALKEN
WALKER
WALLIS
WALSON
WALTER
WALTON
WANKEL
WARING
WARNER
WARREN
WATERS
WATKIN
WATSON
WEAVER
WEINER
WELLER
WELLES
WENZEL
WERNER
WESLEY
WESSEL
WEXLER
WHOOPI
WIENER
WIESEL
WIGNER
WILBER
WILCKE
WILDER
WILKES
WILLEM
WILLIS
WILSON
WILTER
WINSOR
WINTON
WITELO
WITTIG
WOHLER
WOLSKY
WOOLEY
WRIGHT
WYDNER
YASSER
YERGIN
YERKES
YERSIN
YOICHI
YORDAN
YUKAWA
YVONNE
ZARNKE
ZAVIER
ZAVITZ
ZEEMAN
ZENOBE
ZINNER
ZOLTAN
ZWICKY

**2nd Letter**

BAINES
BANACH
BARANY
BARBER
BARBRA
BARKLA
BARNES
BARNEY
BARROW
BARTON
BARUCH
BASEVI
BAUHIN
BAWDEN
BAXTER
CABRAL
CAESAR
CAGNEY
CALLIE
CALVIN
CANNOM
CANNON
CANTIN
CANTON
CANTOR
CAPMAN
CARAKA
CARBON
CARLOS
CARMEN
CARNEY
CARNOT
CARREL
CARSON
CARTAN
CARTER
CARVER
CASKEY
CASPAR
CASSIN
CASTEL
CAUCHY
CAVETT
CAXTON
CAYLEY
DAFFOS
DALTON
DANIEL
DANILO
DARWIN
DAVIES
DAWSON
DAYTON
EAGLER
FABIAN
FAIRLY
FAJANS
FARADY
FARFAX
FARMAN
FARMER
FAROUK
FARRAR
FARROW
FAUSTO
GAINES
GALOIS
GALTON
GARCIA
GARDAY
GARMES
GARROD
GARROW
GARSON
GASSER
GASTON
GAUDIO
GAVRAS
GAYNOR
HADLEY
HALDAN
HALLER
HALLEY
HALSEY
HALTON
HAMSUN
HANLEY
HANNES
HANSEN
HARALD
HARDEN
HARLEY
HARLOW
HAROLD
HARRIS
HARUNA
HARVEY
HASDAI
HASSEL
HATTIE
HAUBEN
HAVERS
HAZARD
JACOBI
JACOBS
JACOPO
JAGGER
JANSKY
JANUSZ
KALUZA
KANADA
KAPARY
KARNOW
KARRER
KASPAR
KATINA
LANDAU
LANDON
LARMOR
LARNER
LARSEN
LARSON
LARTET
LASEAR
LASKER
LASZLO
LATTES
LAUREL
LAUREN
LAWRIE
LAYARD
LAZARE
LAZEAR
MADLER
MAFFEO
MAGGIE
MAGNUS
MAHLON
MAIMAN
MALAKH
MALDEN
MALONE
MANABA
MANLIO
MANSON
MARCEL
MARCIA
MARCUS
MARION
MARISA
MARIUS
MARKOV
MARLEE
MARLON
MARTEL
MARTIN
MARVIN
MATEOS
MATLIN
MAYALL
NADINE
NAGANO
NAGELI
NAGUIB
NAIFEH
NAKANO
NANSEN
NAPIER
NARMER
NATHAN
NAUDIN
OAKLEY
PACINI
PACINO
PALADE
PALFYN
PALMER
PAMELA
PANDER
PAPPUS
PAQUIN
PARKER
PARKES
PASCAL
PAVLOV
PAXTON
RACHEL
RACINE
RAFAEL
RAGNAR
RAINER
RAKINE
RAMSAY
RAMSEY
RANDAL
RAOULT
SABINE
SAINTE
SAKATA
SALEEN
SAMUAL
SAMUEL
SANGER
SANTEL
SAPPHO
SARGON
SARTRE
SAURIA
SAVAGE
SAVARY
SAVERY
TADDEO
TAGORE
TALBOT
TANAKA
TARSKI
TASMAN
TAUBES
TAUROG
TAYLOR
VALENS
VALLEE
VALLES
VARMUS
VAUBAN
WAGNER
WALDEN
WALESA
WALKEN
WALKER
WALLIS
WALSON
WALTER
WALTON
WANKEL
WARING
WARNER
WARREN
WATERS
WATKIN
WATSON
YASSER
ZARNKE
ZAVIER
ZAVITZ
ABBOTT
OBERTH
ECCLES
ECKERT
MCADAM
MCCORD
MCCUNE
MCKEEN
MCLEAN
MCLEOD
SCARPA
SCHACK
SCHARY
SCHELL
SCHICK
SCHNEE
SCOPES
SCOTUS
ADDAMS
ADOLFO
ADOLPH
ADRIAN
ADRIEN
EDISON
EDLUND
EDMOND
EDUARD
EDWARD
BEADLE
BEATON
BEATTY
BEAVAN
BECHER
BECKET
BEGLEY
BEGUIN
BEHAIM
BELLOW
BENDER
BENITO
BENNET
BENOIT
BENSON
BENTON
BERGER
BERING
BERMAN
BERNAL
BEROZA
BERTHA
BERTIL
BESLER
BESSEL
CEDRIC
CELSUS
CERNAN
CERRAF
CESARE
CESARI
DECUIR
DELANO
DELANY
DENJOY
DENNIS
DENTON
DENZEL
DERHAM
DESIRE
FELIPE
FEODOR
FERNEL
FERRER
GEIGER
GEISEL
GEITEL
GEORGE
GEORGI
GERALD
GERARD
GERMAN
GEROGE
GERRIT
GERSON
GESELL
GESNER
HEANEY
HEDGES
HEEGER
HEEZEN
HEFLIN
HELLER
HENCKE
HENNIG
HENRIK
HENSEN
HERALD
HERBIG
HERMAN
HERMES
HESTON
HEVESY

HEWISH
HEWITT
JEANNE
JENNER
JENSEN
JEREMY
JEROME
JESSUP
JETHRO
KEARNS
KEATON
KEELER
KEESOM
KEFFER
KEILIN
KEKULE
KELLER
KELLEY
KELVIN
KEMENY
KEMMER
KEPLER
KEYNES
LEAKEY
LEIBER
LEMERY
LEMMON
LENOIR
LEONOR
LEONOV
LERNER
LESLEY
LESLIE
LESTER
LEVENE
LEVIEN
LEVINE
LEXELL
MEDICI
MEEHAN
MEIKLE
MELLOR
MELVIN
MELVYN
MENCHU
MENDEL
MENGES
MENKEN
MENZEL
MERCER
MERRIT
MESMER
NECKAM
NELSON
NERNST
NERUDA
NERVIG

NESTOR
NEVILL
NEWCOM
NEWMAN
NEWTON
PELLOS
PEPLOE
PERKIN
PERRIN
PERUTZ
PETERS
PETRIE
PETRUS
PETTIT
PEYTON
REAGAN
REALDO
REGIUS
REILLY
REINER
REINES
REISCH
REMSEN
RENFEW
RENNIE
REVERE
SEAMUS
SEATON
SECCHI
SEGALL
SELMAN
SEMJON
SEMLER
SENECA
SERSEN
SEVERO
SEWALL
SEYLER
TELLER
TEODOR
TERESA
TESICH
TEWFIK
VENETZ
VENING
VERNER
VERNON
VERTES
WEAVER
WEINER
WELLER
WELLES
WENZEL
WERNER
WESLEY
WESSEL
WEXLER

YERGIN
YERKES
YERSIN
ZEEMAN
ZENOBE
OFFROY
AGNETA
IGNATZ
BHABHA
CHABRY
CHANCE
CHAPPE
CHEOPS
CHEYNE
CHIANG
CHURCH
KHOURI
PHILIP
PHILON
RHAZES
RHODES
SHAMIR
SHANKS
SHARPE
SHEMIN
SHIMON
SHIUNG
SHMUEL
SHOVEL
SHUKEN
THABIT
THALES
THELMA
THEONI
THIOUT
THOLDE
THOMAS
WHOOPI
AITKEN
BICHAT
BIDDEL
BINNIG
BISHOP
BIZIOU
CIMINO
CIVITA
DIANNE
DIBBLE
DIESEL
DIETER
DIGGES
DILLEY
DILLON
DINTIS
EIFFEL
EILEEN
EISAKU

EISELE
FIELDS
FIESER
FINLAY
FINNEY
FINSEN
FISHER
FIZEAU
GIANNI
GIBBON
GIBNEY
GIBSON
GIDEON
GIESEL
GILLES
GILMAN
GINGER
GIOSUE
GIRARD
GIULIO
HIDEKI
HILLER
HILTON
HINTON
HIRSCH
HITLER
HITNER
HITZIG
KIBBLE
KILJAN
KINSKY
KIRWAN
LINDER
LINDON
LIONEL
LIOTTA
LIPPES
LISTER
LITTLE
MICALI
MICHEL
MIGUEL
MILENA
MILLAN
MILLER
MILNER
MILOSZ
MILTON
NICOLA
NICOLE
NICOLO
NIEPCE
NIKOLA
NILSON
NIPKOW
PIAZZI
PICARD

PICTET
PIERCE
PIERRE
PIETER
PIETRO
PINCUS
PIROSH
PISTEK
RICHER
RICHET
RINGER
RIQUET
RISKIN
RITTER
RIVEST
SIBLEY
SIDNEY
SIGRID
SILVIO
SIMEON
SIMOND
SIMONE
SIMONI
SIMONS
SINGER
TIMONI
TITIUS
VICTOR
VIKTOR
VILMOS
VIRGIL
VIVIAN
VIVIEN
WIENER
WIESEL
WIGNER
WILBER
WILCKE
WILDER
WILKES
WILLEM
WILLIS
WILSON
WILTER
WINSOR
WINTON
WITELO
WITTIG
ZINNER
SKOTAK
ALARIC
ALBERT
ALCOCK
ALCOTT
ALCUIN
ALDRIN
ALEXIS

ALFRED
ALFVEN
ALISON
ALLDER
ALLVAR
ALONZO
ALPHER
ALPINI
ALTMAN
BLAAUW
BLAISE
BLATTY
CLAIRE
CLARKE
CLAUDE
CLORIS
CLOVIS
ELISHA
ELLERY
ELLIOT
ELOISE
ELSTER
ELYTIS
FLEROV
FLOREY
FLOYER
GLADYS
GLASER
GLAZER
GLENDA
GLORIA
GLOVER
ILMARI
OLBERS
OLDHAM
OLIVER
OLIVIA
PLANCK
PLANTE
PLUCHE
SLIFER
SLOANE
ULISSE
ULPIUS
ULRICH
AMAGAT
AMDAHL
AMECHE
AMEDEO
AMPERE
AMTHOR
DMITRI
EMERIC
EMILIE
EMILIO
GMELIN
SMAUEL

SMILEY
SMYTHE
ANDERS
ANDREA
ANDREI
ANDRES
ANDREW
ANDREY
ANDRIC
ANGELL
ANGELO
ANHALT
ANNING
ANTONY
ENDERS
ENGELS
ENRICO
INGRAM
INGRID
UNDSET
UNSOLD
BODMER
BOGART
BOHLIN
BOLTON
BOLYAI
BONNER
BONNET
BONNOT
BORDEN
BORDET
BORDEU
BORMAN
BOUGHN
BOULLE
BOVERI
BOWLES
COATES
COBURN
COCKER
COFFIN
COLLIP
COLMAN
CONRAD
CONRAT
COOLEY
COOPER
COPLEY
CORDUS
CORNER
CORTES
COSTER
COTTON
COUPER
COWLES
DOMAGK
DONALD

DONATI
DONATO
DORIAN
FORBES
FOREST
FORMAN
FOSTER
FOWLER
GOBIND
GOERGE
GOLDIE
GOOSEN
GORDON
GORGAS
GOSSET
HOBBES
HOLDEN
HOLLEY
HOLMES
HONOLD
HOOVER
HOPPER
HORACE
HORNER
HORTON
HOWARD
JOANNE
JOGESH
JOHANN
JOLIOT
JORDAN
JOSEPH
JOSHUA
JOSIAH
KOCHER
KOHLER
KOLLER
KONRAD
KOPPEN
KOSMAS
KOSSEL
KOSTER
KOTARO
LOFTUS
LOLOIR
LONDON
LOOMIS
LORENZ
LOTHAR
LOUDON
LOUISE
LOVELL
LOVISA
LOWELL
LOWITZ
MOBIUS
MOLINA

MONETA
MONROE
MONTEL
MOREAU
MORENO
MORGAN
MORITZ
MORLEY
MORRIS
MORROW
MORTON
MOTHER
MOUTON
MOYERS
NOBILI
NOLLET
NORGAY
NORMAN
NORRIS
NOSSAL
POGSON
POLHEM
PORTER
POWELL
POYNER
ROBBIE
ROBERT
ROBINS
ROBLEY
RODNEY
ROGERS
ROHRER
ROLAND
ROMAIN
ROMANO
RONALD
RONNIE
ROOSBY
ROSHER
ROTTER
ROZIER
SOLVAY
SOPHIA
SOPHIE
SOPHUS
TOBIAS
TOLAND
TOLMAN
TOPHAM
TORREY
TOWNES
VOIGHT
VOISIN
WOHLER
WOLSKY
WOOLEY
YOICHI

YORDAN
ZOLTAN
APPERT
APPOLT
OPARIN
SPACEK
SPACEY
SPENCE
SPERRY
UPDIKE
SQUIER
ARAFAT
ARCHER
ARCHIE
ARDREY
ARGAND
ARLING
ARLISS
ARMAND
ARNAUD
ARNOLD
ARREST
ARTEDI
ARTHUR
BRAMAH
BRANCA
BRANDO
BRANDT
BRENDA
BREUER
BRIAND
BRIDGE
BRIGGS
BRIGHT
BRILEY
BROOKE
BROOKS
BRUNEL
BRUTUS
CRAFTS
CRAGOE
CRAMER
CRANCH
CRELLE
CREMER
CRONIN
CROSBY
DRAPER
DREIER
DREYER
ERCKER
ERLICH
ERNEST
FRANCA
FRANCE
FRANCK
FRANCO

FRANKE
FRASCH
FRAZER
FRENCH
FREUND
FRICKE
FROSCH
GRAEBE
GRAHAM
GRAMME
GRANIT
GRAUNT
GRAVES
GRAZIA
GREENE
GREGOR
GRIESS
GRIGGS
GRIJNS
GRIMES
GROVER
IRVING
KRAELY
KRASNA
ORESME
ORVILL
PRAWER
PREBUS
PREVIN
PRINCE
PROULX
PROUST
TRAJAN
TRAVIS
TREVOR
TROFIM
TROTTI
TRUMAN
TRUMBO
URBAIN
WRIGHT
ASHKIN
ASPDIN
FSCOTT
HSIUNG
ISAACS
ISADOR
ISIDOR
ISMAEL
OSWALD
PSEUDO
TSVETT
USSHER
ATWOOD
ETIENE
OTHMAN
OTTMAR
STALIN
STEARN
STEARS
STEELE
STEFAN
STEVEN
STIFEL
STILES
STOCKE
STOKES
STONEY
STRABO
STRATO
STREEP
STREET
STRONG
STRUSS
STRUTT
STRUVE
STUART
STUMPF
AUBREY
AUDREY
AUGUST
AUSTEN
AUSTIN
AUZOUT
BUDDHA
BULLEN
BUNCHE
BUNSEN
BURALI
BURNET
BURTON
BUSSEY
BUSTER
BUTLER
CUGNOT
CULLEN
CURTIS
CURTIZ
CUVIER
DUDLEY
DUFOUR
DUGGAR
DULONG
DUNANT
DUNBAR
DUNCAN
DUNHAM
DUNLOP
DUPUIS
DUSTIN
DUTTON
DUVALL
EUCKEN
EUCLID
EUGENE
FULLER
FULTON
GUERIN
GUFFEY
GUNTER
GURNEY
GUSTAF
GUSTAV
GUYTON
HUBBLE
HUBERT
HUGHES
HUNTER
HUSTON
HUTTON
HUXLEY
JULIAN
JULIEN
JULIUS
JURAGA
JUSTUS
KUIPER
KUMMER
KUNKEL
LUCILA
LUCIUS
LUDERS
LUDWIG
LUSSAC
LUTHER
LUTULI
MULLER
MULLIS
MUNGLE
MURIEL
MURPHY
MURRAY
MUSSET
PULLER
PUNNET
QUIDDE
QUINCY
RUBBIA
RUBNER
RUCKER
RUDOLF
RUEBEN
RUMKER
RUPERT
RUSSEL
SUMNER
SUSUME
SUSUMU
SUTTON
SUZUKI
TULLIO
TUMMEL
TURING
YUKAWA
EVARTS
EVELYN
IVANOV
SVANTE
YVONNE
DWIGHT
ZWICKY
AYLING
AYLMER
AYMAND
CYRANO
EYVIND
GYATSO
GYORGY
KYESER
LYCETT
LYNDON
MYRDAL
RYBERG
SYDNEY
WYDNER

### 3rd Letter

ALARIC
AMAGAT
ARAFAT
BEADLE
BEATON
BEATTY
BEAVAN
BHABHA
BLAAUW
BLAISE
BLATTY
BRAMAH
BRANCA
BRANDO
BRANDT
CHABRY
CHANCE
CHAPPE
CLAIRE
CLARKE
CLAUDE
COATES
CRAFTS
CRAGOE
CRAMER
CRANCH
DIANNE
DRAPER
EVARTS
FRANCA
FRANCE
FRANCK
FRANCO
FRANKE
FRASCH
FRAZER
GIANNI
GLADYS
GLASER
GLAZER
GRAEBE
GRAHAM
GRAMME
GRANIT
GRAUNT
GRAVES
GRAZIA
GYATSO
HEANEY
ISAACS
ISADOR
IVANOV
JEANNE
JOANNE
KEARNS
KEATON
KRAELY
KRASNA
LEAKEY
MCADAM
OPARIN
PIAZZI
PLANCK
PLANTE
PRAWER
REAGAN
REALDO
RHAZES
SCARPA
SEAMUS
SEATON
SHAMIR
SHANKS
SHARPE
SMAUEL
SPACEK
SPACEY
STALIN
SVANTE
THABIT
THALES
TRAJAN
TRAVIS
WEAVER
ABBOTT
ALBERT
AUBREY
CABRAL
COBURN
DIBBLE
FABIAN
GIBBON
GIBNEY
GIBSON
GOBIND
HOBBES
HUBBLE
HUBERT
KIBBLE
MOBIUS
NOBILI
OLBERS
ROBBIE
ROBERT
ROBINS
ROBLEY
RUBBIA
RUBNER
RYBERG
SABINE
SIBLEY
TOBIAS
URBAIN
ALCOCK
ALCOTT
ALCUIN
ARCHER
ARCHIE
BECHER
BECKET
BICHAT
COCKER
DECUIR
ECCLES
ERCKER
EUCKEN
EUCLID
FSCOTT
JACOBI
JACOBS
JACOPO
KOCHER
LUCILA
LUCIUS
LYCETT
MCCORD
MCCUNE
MICALI
MICHEL
NECKAM
NICOLA
NICOLE
NICOLO
PACINI
PACINO
PICARD
PICTET
RACHEL
RACINE
RICHER
RICHET
RUCKER
SECCHI
VICTOR
ADDAMS
ALDRIN
AMDAHL
ANDERS
ANDREA
ANDREI
ANDRES
ANDREW
ANDREY
ANDRIC
ARDREY
AUDREY
BIDDEL
BODMER
BUDDHA
CEDRIC
DUDLEY
ENDERS
GIDEON
HADLEY
HEDGES
HIDEKI
LUDERS
LUDWIG
MADLER
MEDICI
NADINE
OLDHAM
RODNEY
RUDOLF
SIDNEY
SYDNEY
TADDEO
UNDSET
UPDIKE
WYDNER
ALEXIS
AMECHE
AMEDEO
BRENDA
BREUER
CAESAR
CHEOPS
CHEYNE
CRELLE
CREMER
DIESEL
DIETER
DREIER
DREYER
EMERIC
EVELYN
FIELDS
FIESER
FLEROV
FRENCH
FREUND
GIESEL
GLENDA
GMELIN
GOERGE
GREENE
GREGOR
GUERIN
HEEGER
HEEZEN
KEELER
KEESOM
KYESER
MEEHAN
NIEPCE
OBERTH
ORESME
PIERCE
PIERRE
PIETER
PIETRO
PREBUS
PREVIN
PSEUDO
RUEBEN
SHEMIN
SPENCE
SPERRY
STEARN
STEARS
STEELE
STEFAN
STEVEN
THELMA
THEONI
TREVOR
WIENER
WIESEL
ZEEMAN
ALFRED
ALFVEN
COFFIN
DAFFOS
DUFOUR
EIFFEL
GUFFEY
HEFLIN
KEFFER
LOFTUS
MAFFEO
OFFROY
RAFAEL
ANGELL
ANGELO
ARGAND
AUGUST
BEGLEY
BEGUIN
BOGART
CAGNEY
CUGNOT
DIGGES
DUGGAR
EAGLER
ENGELS
EUGENE
HUGHES
INGRAM
INGRID
JAGGER
JOGESH
MAGGIE
MAGNUS
MIGUEL
NAGANO
NAGELI
NAGUIB
POGSON
RAGNAR
REGIUS
ROGERS
SEGALL
SIGRID
TAGORE
WAGNER
WIGNER
ANHALT
ASHKIN
BEHAIM
BOHLIN
JOHANN
KOHLER
MAHLON
OTHMAN
ROHRER
SCHACK
SCHARY
SCHELL
SCHICK
SCHNEE
WOHLER
ALISON
BAINES
BRIAND
BRIDGE
BRIGGS
BRIGHT
BRILEY
CHIANG
DMITRI
DWIGHT
EDISON
ELISHA
EMILIE
EMILIO
ETIENE
FAIRLY
FRICKE
GAINES
GEIGER
GEISEL
GEITEL
GRIESS
GRIGGS
GRIJNS
GRIMES
HSIUNG
ISIDOR
KEILIN
KUIPER
LEIBER
MAIMAN
MEIKLE
NAIFEH
OLIVER
OLIVIA
PHILIP
PHILON
PRINCE
QUIDDE
QUINCY
RAINER
REILLY
REINER
REINES
REISCH
SAINTE
SHIMON
SHIUNG
SLIFER
SMILEY
STIFEL
STILES
THIOUT
ULISSE
VOIGHT
VOISIN
WEINER
WRIGHT
YOICHI

ZW**I**CKY
FA**J**ANS
EC**K**ERT
KE**K**ULE
MC**K**EEN
NA**K**ANO
NI**K**OLA
OA**K**LEY
RA**K**INE
SA**K**ATA
VI**K**TOR
YU**K**AWA
AL**L**DER
AL**L**VAR
AR**L**ING
AR**L**ISS
AY**L**ING
AY**L**MER
BE**L**LOW
BO**L**TON
BO**L**YAI
BU**L**LEN
CA**L**LIE
CA**L**VIN
CE**L**SUS
CO**L**LIP
CO**L**MAN
CU**L**LEN
DA**L**TON
DE**L**ANO
DE**L**ANY
DI**L**LEY
DI**L**LON
DU**L**ONG
ED**L**UND
EI**L**EEN
EL**L**ERY
EL**L**IOT
ER**L**ICH
FE**L**IPE
FU**L**LER
FU**L**TON
GA**L**OIS
GA**L**TON
GI**L**LES
GI**L**MAN
GO**L**DIE
HA**L**DAN
HA**L**LER
HA**L**LEY
HA**L**SEY
HA**L**TON
HE**L**LER
HI**L**LER
HI**L**TON
HO**L**DEN
HO**L**LEY

HO**L**MES
JO**L**IOT
JU**L**IAN
JU**L**IEN
JU**L**IUS
KA**L**UZA
KE**L**LER
KE**L**LEY
KE**L**VIN
KI**L**JAN
KO**L**LER
LO**L**OIR
MA**L**AKH
MA**L**DEN
MA**L**ONE
MC**L**EAN
MC**L**EOD
ME**L**LOR
ME**L**VIN
ME**L**VYN
MI**L**ENA
MI**L**LAN
MI**L**LER
MI**L**NER
MI**L**OSZ
MI**L**TON
MO**L**INA
MU**L**LER
MU**L**LIS
NE**L**SON
NI**L**SON
NO**L**LET
PA**L**ADE
PA**L**FYN
PA**L**MER
PE**L**LOS
PO**L**HEM
PU**L**LER
RO**L**AND
SA**L**EEN
SE**L**MAN
SI**L**VIO
SO**L**VAY
TA**L**BOT
TE**L**LER
TO**L**AND
TO**L**MAN
TU**L**LIO
VA**L**ENS
VA**L**LEE
VA**L**LES
VI**L**MOS
WA**L**DEN
WA**L**ESA
WA**L**KEN
WA**L**KER
WA**L**LIS

WA**L**SON
WA**L**TER
WA**L**TON
WE**L**LER
WE**L**LES
WI**L**BER
WI**L**CKE
WI**L**DER
WI**L**KES
WI**L**LEM
WI**L**LIS
WI**L**SON
WI**L**TER
WO**L**SKY
ZO**L**TAN
AR**M**AND
AY**M**AND
CI**M**INO
DO**M**AGK
ED**M**OND
HA**M**SUN
IL**M**ARI
IS**M**AEL
KE**M**ENY
KE**M**MER
KU**M**MER
LE**M**ERY
LE**M**MON
PA**M**ELA
RA**M**SAY
RA**M**SEY
RE**M**SEN
RO**M**AIN
RO**M**ANO
RU**M**KER
SA**M**UAL
SA**M**UEL
SE**M**JON
SE**M**LER
SH**M**UEL
SI**M**EON
SI**M**OND
SI**M**ONE
SI**M**ONI
SI**M**ONS
SU**M**NER
TI**M**ONI
TU**M**MEL
AG**N**ETA
AN**N**ING
AR**N**AUD
AR**N**OLD
BA**N**ACH
BE**N**DER
BE**N**ITO
BE**N**NET
BE**N**OIT

BE**N**SON
BE**N**TON
BI**N**NIG
BO**N**NER
BO**N**NET
BO**N**NOT
BU**N**CHE
BU**N**SEN
CA**N**NOM
CA**N**NON
CA**N**TIN
CA**N**TON
CA**N**TOR
CO**N**RAD
CO**N**RAT
DA**N**IEL
DA**N**ILO
DE**N**JOY
DE**N**NIS
DE**N**TON
DE**N**ZEL
DI**N**TIS
DO**N**ALD
DO**N**ATI
DO**N**ATO
DU**N**ANT
DU**N**BAR
DU**N**CAN
DU**N**HAM
DU**N**LOP
ER**N**EST
FI**N**LAY
FI**N**NEY
FI**N**SEN
GI**N**GER
GU**N**TER
HA**N**LEY
HA**N**NES
HA**N**SEN
HE**N**CKE
HE**N**NIG
HE**N**RIK
HE**N**SEN
HI**N**TON
HO**N**OLD
HU**N**TER
IG**N**ATZ
JA**N**SKY
JA**N**USZ
JE**N**NER
JE**N**SEN
KA**N**ADA
KI**N**SKY
KO**N**RAD
KU**N**KEL
LA**N**DAU
LA**N**DON

LE**N**OIR
LI**N**DER
LI**N**DON
LO**N**DON
LY**N**DON
MA**N**ABA
MA**N**LIO
MA**N**SON
ME**N**CHU
ME**N**DEL
ME**N**GES
ME**N**KEN
ME**N**ZEL
MO**N**ETA
MO**N**ROE
MO**N**TEL
MU**N**GLE
NA**N**SEN
PA**N**DER
PI**N**CUS
PU**N**NET
RA**N**DAL
RE**N**FEW
RE**N**NIE
RI**N**GER
RO**N**ALD
RO**N**NIE
SA**N**GER
SA**N**TEL
SE**N**ECA
SI**N**GER
TA**N**AKA
VE**N**ETZ
VE**N**ING
WA**N**KEL
WE**N**ZEL
WI**N**SOR
WI**N**TON
ZE**N**OBE
ZI**N**NER
AD**O**LFO
AD**O**LPH
AL**O**NZO
BR**O**OKE
BR**O**OKS
CL**O**RIS
CL**O**VIS
CO**O**LEY
CO**O**PER
CR**O**NIN
CR**O**SBY
EL**O**ISE
FE**O**DOR
FL**O**REY
FL**O**YER
FR**O**SCH
GE**O**RGE

GE**O**RGI
GI**O**SUE
GL**O**RIA
GL**O**VER
GO**O**SEN
GR**O**VER
GY**O**RGY
HO**O**VER
KH**O**URI
LE**O**NOR
LE**O**NOV
LI**O**NEL
LI**O**TTA
LO**O**MIS
PR**O**ULX
PR**O**UST
RA**O**ULT
RH**O**DES
RO**O**SBY
SC**O**PES
SC**O**TUS
SH**O**VEL
SK**O**TAK
SL**O**ANE
ST**O**CKE
ST**O**KES
ST**O**NEY
TE**O**DOR
TH**O**LDE
TH**O**MAS
TR**O**FIM
TR**O**TTI
WH**O**OPI
WO**O**LEY
YV**O**NNE
AL**P**HER
AL**P**INI
AM**P**ERE
AP**P**ERT
AP**P**OLT
AS**P**DIN
CA**P**MAN
CO**P**LEY
DU**P**UIS
HO**P**PER
KA**P**ARY
KE**P**LER
KO**P**PEN
LI**P**PES
NA**P**IER
NI**P**KOW
PA**P**PUS
PE**P**LOE
RU**P**ERT
SA**P**PHO
SO**P**HIA
SO**P**HIE

SO**P**HUS
TO**P**HAM
UL**P**IUS
PA**Q**UIN
RI**Q**UET
AD**R**IAN
AD**R**IEN
AR**R**EST
BA**R**ANY
BA**R**BER
BA**R**BRA
BA**R**KLA
BA**R**NES
BA**R**NEY
BA**R**ROW
BA**R**TON
BA**R**UCH
BE**R**GER
BE**R**ING
BE**R**MAN
BE**R**NAL
BE**R**OZA
BE**R**THA
BE**R**TIL
BO**R**DEN
BO**R**DET
BO**R**DEU
BO**R**MAN
BU**R**ALI
BU**R**NET
BU**R**TON
CA**R**AKA
CA**R**BON
CA**R**LOS
CA**R**MEN
CA**R**NEY
CA**R**NOT
CA**R**REL
CA**R**SON
CA**R**TAN
CA**R**TER
CA**R**VER
CE**R**NAN
CE**R**RAF
CO**R**DUS
CO**R**NER
CO**R**TES
CU**R**TIS
CU**R**TIZ
CY**R**ANO
DA**R**WIN
DE**R**HAM
DO**R**IAN
EN**R**ICO
FA**R**ADY
FA**R**FAX
FA**R**MAN

FA**R**MER
FA**R**OUK
FA**R**RAR
FA**R**ROW
FE**R**NEL
FE**R**RER
FO**R**BES
FO**R**EST
FO**R**MAN
GA**R**CIA
GA**R**DAY
GA**R**MES
GA**R**ROD
GA**R**ROW
GA**R**SON
GE**R**ALD
GE**R**ARD
GE**R**MAN
GE**R**OGE
GE**R**RIT
GE**R**SON
GI**R**ARD
GO**R**DON
GO**R**GAS
GU**R**NEY
HA**R**ALD
HA**R**DEN
HA**R**LEY
HA**R**LOW
HA**R**OLD
HA**R**RIS
HA**R**UNA
HA**R**VEY
HE**R**ALD
HE**R**BIG
HE**R**MAN
HE**R**MES
HI**R**SCH
HO**R**ACE
HO**R**NER
HO**R**TON
JE**R**EMY
JE**R**OME
JO**R**DAN
JU**R**AGA
KA**R**NOW
KA**R**RER
KI**R**WAN
LA**R**MOR
LA**R**NER
LA**R**SEN
LA**R**SON
LA**R**TET
LE**R**NER
LO**R**ENZ
MA**R**CEL
MA**R**CIA

MA**R**CUS
MA**R**ION
MA**R**ISA
MA**R**IUS
MA**R**KOV
MA**R**LEE
MA**R**LON
MA**R**TEL
MA**R**TIN
MA**R**VIN
ME**R**CER
ME**R**RIT
MO**R**EAU
MO**R**ENO
MO**R**GAN
MO**R**ITZ
MO**R**LEY
MO**R**RIS
MO**R**ROW
MO**R**TON
MU**R**IEL
MU**R**PHY
MU**R**RAY
MY**R**DAL
NA**R**MER
NE**R**NST
NE**R**UDA
NE**R**VIG
NO**R**GAY
NO**R**MAN
NO**R**RIS
PA**R**KER
PA**R**KES
PE**R**KIN
PE**R**RIN
PE**R**UTZ
PI**R**OSH
PO**R**TER
SA**R**GON
SA**R**TRE
SE**R**SEN
ST**R**ABO
ST**R**ATO
ST**R**EEP
ST**R**EET
ST**R**ONG
ST**R**USS
ST**R**UTT
ST**R**UVE
TA**R**SKI
TE**R**ESA
TO**R**REY
TU**R**ING
UL**R**ICH
VA**R**MUS
VE**R**NER
VE**R**NON

VE**R**TES
VI**R**GIL
WA**R**ING
WA**R**NER
WA**R**REN
WE**R**NER
YE**R**GIN
YE**R**KES
YE**R**SIN
YO**R**DAN
ZA**R**NKE
AU**S**TEN
AU**S**TIN
BA**S**EVI
BE**S**LER
BE**S**SEL
BI**S**HOP
BU**S**SEY
BU**S**TER
CA**S**KEY
CA**S**PAR
CA**S**SIN
CA**S**TEL
CE**S**ARE
CE**S**ARI
CO**S**TER
DE**S**IRE
DU**S**TIN
EI**S**AKU
EI**S**ELE
EL**S**TER
FI**S**HER
FO**S**TER
GA**S**SER
GA**S**TON
GE**S**ELL
GE**S**NER
GO**S**SET
GU**S**TAF
GU**S**TAV
HA**S**DAI
HA**S**SEL
HE**S**TON
HU**S**TON
JE**S**SUP
JO**S**EPH
JO**S**HUA
JO**S**IAH
JU**S**TUS
KA**S**PAR
KO**S**MAS
KO**S**SEL
KO**S**TER
LA**S**EAR
LA**S**KER
LA**S**ZLO
LE**S**LEY

LESLIE
LESTER
LISTER
LUSSAC
MESMER
MUSSET
NESTOR
NOSSAL
PASCAL
PISTEK
RISKIN
ROSHER
RUSSEL
SUSUME
SUSUMU
TASMAN
TESICH
UNSOLD
USSHER
WESLEY
WESSEL
YASSER
AITKEN
ALTMAN
AMTHOR
ANTONY
ARTEDI
ARTHUR
BUTLER
COTTON
DUTTON
HATTIE
HITLER
HITNER
HITZIG
HUTTON
JETHRO
KATINA
KOTARO
LATTES
LITTLE
LOTHAR
LUTHER
LUTULI
MATEOS
MATLIN
MOTHER
NATHAN
OTTMAR
PETERS
PETRIE
PETRUS
PETTIT
RITTER
ROTTER
SUTTON
TITIUS

WATERS
WATKIN
WATSON
WITELO
WITTIG
BAUHIN
BOUGHN
BOULLE
BRUNEL
BRUTUS
CAUCHY
CHURCH
COUPER
EDUARD
FAUSTO
GAUDIO
GIULIO
HAUBEN
LAUREL
LAUREN
LOUDON
LOUISE
MOUTON
NAUDIN
PLUCHE
SAURIA
SHUKEN
SQUIER
STUART
STUMPF
TAUBES
TAUROG
TRUMAN
TRUMBO
VAUBAN
BOVERI
CAVETT
CIVITA
CUVIER
DAVIES
DUVALL
EYVIND
GAVRAS
HAVERS
HEVESY
IRVING
LEVENE
LEVIEN
LEVINE
LOVELL
LOVISA
NEVILL
ORVILL
PAVLOV
REVERE
RIVEST
SAVAGE

SAVARY
SAVERY
SEVERO
TSVETT
VIVIAN
VIVIEN
ZAVIER
ZAVITZ
ATWOOD
BAWDEN
BOWLES
COWLES
DAWSON
EDWARD
FOWLER
HEWISH
HEWITT
HOWARD
LAWRIE
LOWELL
LOWITZ
NEWCOM
NEWMAN
NEWTON
OSWALD
POWELL
SEWALL
TEWFIK
TOWNES
BAXTER
CAXTON
HUXLEY
LEXELL
PAXTON
WEXLER
CAYLEY
DAYTON
ELYTIS
GAYNOR
GUYTON
KEYNES
LAYARD
MAYALL
MOYERS
PEYTON
POYNER
SEYLER
SMYTHE
TAYLOR
AUZOUT
BIZIOU
FIZEAU
HAZARD
LAZARE
LAZEAR
ROZIER
SUZUKI

## 4TH LETTER

ADDAMS
AMDAHL
ANHALT
ARGAND
ARMAND
ARNAUD
AYMAND
BANACH
BARANY
BEHAIM
BLAAUW
BOGART
BRIAND
BURALI
CARAKA
CESARE
CESARI
CHIANG
CYRANO
DELANO
DELANY
DOMAGK
DONALD
DONATI
DONATO
DUNANT
DUVALL
EDUARD
EDWARD
EISAKU
FAJANS
FARADY
GERALD
GERARD
GIRARD
HARALD
HAZARD
HERALD
HORACE
HOWARD
IGNATZ
ILMARI
ISAACS
ISMAEL
JOHANN
JURAGA
KANADA
KAPARY
KOTARO
LAYARD
LAZARE
MALAKH
MANABA
MAYALL
MICALI

NAGANO
NAKANO
OSWALD
PALADE
PICARD
RAFAEL
ROLAND
ROMAIN
ROMANO
RONALD
SAKATA
SAVAGE
SAVARY
SCHACK
SCHARY
SEGALL
SEWALL
SLOANE
STEARN
STEARS
STRABO
STRATO
STUART
TANAKA
TOLAND
URBAIN
YUKAWA
BARBER
BARBRA
BHABHA
CARBON
CHABRY
DIBBLE
DUNBAR
FORBES
GIBBON
HAUBEN
HERBIG
HOBBES
HUBBLE
KIBBLE
LEIBER
PREBUS
ROBBIE
RUBBIA
RUEBEN
TALBOT
TAUBES
THABIT
VAUBAN
WILBER
AMECHE
BUNCHE
CAUCHY
DUNCAN
FRICKE
GARCIA

HENCKE
MARCEL
MARCIA
MARCUS
MENCHU
MERCER
NEWCOM
PASCAL
PINCUS
PLUCHE
SECCHI
SPACEK
SPACEY
STOCKE
WILCKE
YOICHI
ZWICKY
ALLDER
AMEDEO
ASPDIN
BAWDEN
BEADLE
BENDER
BIDDEL
BORDEN
BORDET
BORDEU
BRIDGE
BUDDHA
CORDUS
FEODOR
GARDAY
GAUDIO
GLADYS
GOLDIE
GORDON
HALDAN
HARDEN
HASDAI
HOLDEN
ISADOR
ISIDOR
JORDAN
LANDAU
LANDON
LINDER
LINDON
LONDON
LOUDON
LYNDON
MALDEN
MCADAM
MENDEL
MYRDAL
NAUDIN
PANDER
QUIDDE

RANDAL
RHODES
TADDEO
TEODOR
WALDEN
WILDER
YORDAN
AGNETA
ALBERT
AMPERE
ANDERS
ANGELL
ANGELO
APPERT
ARREST
ARTEDI
BASEVI
BOVERI
CAVETT
ECKERT
EILEEN
EISELE
ELLERY
ENDERS
ENGELS
ERNEST
ETIENE
EUGENE
FIZEAU
FOREST
GESELL
GIDEON
GRAEBE
GREENE
GRIESS
HAVERS
HEVESY
HIDEKI
HUBERT
JEREMY
JOGESH
JOSEPH
KEMENY
KRAELY
LASEAR
LAZEAR
LEMERY
LEVENE
LEXELL
LORENZ
LOVELL
LOWELL
LUDERS
LYCETT
MATEOS
MCKEEN
MCLEAN

MCLEOD
MILENA
MONETA
MOREAU
MORENO
MOYERS
NAGELI
OLBERS
PAMELA
PETERS
POWELL
REVERE
RIVEST
ROBERT
ROGERS
RUPERT
RYBERG
SALEEN
SAVERY
SCHELL
SENECA
SEVERO
SIMEON
STEELE
STREEP
STREET
TERESA
TSVETT
VALENS
VENETZ
WALESA
WATERS
WITELO
ARAFAT
COFFIN
CRAFTS
DAFFOS
EIFFEL
FARFAX
GUFFEY
KEFFER
MAFFEO
NAIFEH
PALFYN
RENFEW
SLIFER
STEFAN
STIFEL
TEWFIK
TROFIM
AMAGAT
BERGER
BOUGHN
BRIGGS
BRIGHT
CRAGOE
DIGGES

DUGGAR
DWIGHT
GEIGER
GINGER
GORGAS
GREGOR
GRIGGS
HEDGES
HEEGER
JAGGER
MAGGIE
MENGES
MORGAN
MUNGLE
NORGAY
REAGAN
RINGER
SANGER
SARGON
SINGER
VIRGIL
VOIGHT
WRIGHT
YERGIN
ALPHER
AMTHOR
ARCHER
ARCHIE
ARTHUR
BAUHIN
BECHER
BICHAT
BISHOP
DERHAM
DUNHAM
FISHER
GRAHAM
HUGHES
JETHRO
JOSHUA
KOCHER
LOTHAR
LUTHER
MEEHAN
MICHEL
MOTHER
NATHAN
OLDHAM
POLHEM
RACHEL
RICHER
RICHET
ROSHER
SOPHIA
SOPHIE
SOPHUS
TOPHAM

USSHER
ADRIAN
ADRIEN
ALPINI
ANNING
ARLING
ARLISS
AYLING
BENITO
BERING
BIZIOU
BLAISE
CIMINO
CIVITA
CLAIRE
CUVIER
DANIEL
DANILO
DAVIES
DESIRE
DORIAN
DREIER
ELLIOT
ELOISE
ENRICO
ERLICH
EYVIND
FABIAN
FELIPE
GOBIND
HEWISH
HEWITT
IRVING
JOLIOT
JOSIAH
JULIAN
JULIEN
JULIUS
KATINA
LEVIEN
LEVINE
LOUISE
LOVISA
LOWITZ
LUCILA
LUCIUS
MARION
MARISA
MARIUS
MEDICI
MOBIUS
MOLINA
MORITZ
MURIEL
NADINE
NAPIER
NEVILL

NOBILI
ORVILL
PACINI
PACINO
RACINE
RAKINE
REGIUS
ROBINS
ROZIER
SABINE
SCHICK
SQUIER
TESICH
TITIUS
TOBIAS
TURING
ULPIUS
ULRICH
UPDIKE
VENING
VIVIAN
VIVIEN
WARING
ZAVIER
ZAVITZ
DENJOY
GRIJNS
KILJAN
SEMJON
TRAJAN
AITKEN
ASHKIN
BARKLA
BECKET
CASKEY
COCKER
ERCKER
EUCKEN
KUNKEL
LASKER
LEAKEY
MARKOV
MEIKLE
MENKEN
NECKAM
NIPKOW
PARKER
PARKES
PERKIN
RISKIN
RUCKER
RUMKER
SHUKEN
STOKES
WALKEN
WALKER
WANKEL

WATKIN
WILKES
YERKES
ADOLFO
ADOLPH
BEGLEY
BELLOW
BESLER
BOHLIN
BOULLE
BOWLES
BRILEY
BULLEN
BUTLER
CALLIE
CARLOS
CAYLEY
COLLIP
COOLEY
COPLEY
COWLES
CRELLE
CULLEN
DILLEY
DILLON
DUDLEY
DUNLOP
EAGLER
ECCLES
EMILIE
EMILIO
EUCLID
EVELYN
FIELDS
FINLAY
FOWLER
FULLER
GILLES
GIULIO
GMELIN
HADLEY
HALLER
HALLEY
HANLEY
HARLEY
HARLOW
HEFLIN
HELLER
HILLER
HITLER
HOLLEY
HUXLEY
KEELER
KEILIN
KELLER
KELLEY
KEPLER

KOHLER
KOLLER
LESLEY
LESLIE
MADLER
MAHLON
MANLIO
MARLEE
MARLON
MATLIN
MELLOR
MILLAN
MILLER
MORLEY
MULLER
MULLIS
NOLLET
OAKLEY
PAVLOV
PELLOS
PEPLOE
PHILIP
PHILON
PULLER
REALDO
REILLY
ROBLEY
SEMLER
SEYLER
SIBLEY
SMILEY
STALIN
STILES
TAYLOR
TELLER
THALES
THELMA
THOLDE
TULLIO
VALLEE
VALLES
WALLIS
WELLER
WELLES
WESLEY
WEXLER
WILLEM
WILLIS
WOHLER
WOOLEY
ALTMAN
AYLMER
BERMAN
BODMER
BORMAN
BRAMAH
CAPMAN

CARMEN
COLMAN
CRAMER
CREMER
FARMAN
FARMER
FORMAN
GARMES
GERMAN
GILMAN
GRAMME
GRIMES
HERMAN
HERMES
HOLMES
KEMMER
KOSMAS
KUMMER
LARMOR
LEMMON
LOOMIS
MAIMAN
MESMER
NARMER
NEWMAN
NORMAN
OTHMAN
OTTMAR
PALMER
SEAMUS
SELMAN
SHAMIR
SHEMIN
SHIMON
STUMPF
TASMAN
THOMAS
TOLMAN
TRUMAN
TRUMBO
TUMMEL
VARMUS
VILMOS
ZEEMAN
ALONZO
BAINES
BARNES
BARNEY
BENNET
BERNAL
BINNIG
BONNER
BONNET
BONNOT
BRANCA
BRANDO
BRANDT

BRENDA
BRUNEL
BURNET
CAGNEY
CANNOM
CANNON
CARNEY
CARNOT
CERNAN
CHANCE
CORNER
CRANCH
CRONIN
CUGNOT
DENNIS
DIANNE
FERNEL
FINNEY
FRANCA
FRANCE
FRANCK
FRANCO
FRANKE
FRENCH
GAINES
GAYNOR
GESNER
GIANNI
GIBNEY
GLENDA
GRANIT
GURNEY
HANNES
HEANEY
HENNIG
HITNER
HORNER
IVANOV
JEANNE
JENNER
JOANNE
KARNOW
KEYNES
LARNER
LEONOR
LEONOV
LERNER
LIONEL
MAGNUS
MILNER
NERNST
PLANCK
PLANTE
POYNER
PRINCE
PUNNET
QUINCY

RAGNAR
RAINER
REINER
REINES
RENNIE
RODNEY
RONNIE
RUBNER
SAINTE
SCHNEE
SHANKS
SIDNEY
SPENCE
STONEY
SUMNER
SVANTE
SYDNEY
TOWNES
VERNER
VERNON
WAGNER
WARNER
WEINER
WERNER
WIENER
WIGNER
WYDNER
YVONNE
ZARNKE
ZINNER
ABBOTT
ALCOCK
ALCOTT
ANTONY
APPOLT
ARNOLD
ATWOOD
AUZOUT
BENOIT
BEROZA
BROOKE
BROOKS
CHEOPS
DUFOUR
DULONG
EDMOND
FAROUK
FSCOTT
GALOIS
GEROGE
HAROLD
HONOLD
JACOBI
JACOBS
JACOPO
JEROME
LENOIR

LOLOIR
MALONE
MCCORD
MILOSZ
NICOLA
NICOLE
NICOLO
NIKOLA
PIROSH
RUDOLF
SIMOND
SIMONE
SIMONI
SIMONS
STRONG
TAGORE
THEONI
THIOUT
TIMONI
UNSOLD
WHOOPI
ZENOBE
CASPAR
CHAPPE
COOPER
COUPER
DRAPER
HOPPER
KASPAR
KOPPEN
KUIPER
LIPPES
MURPHY
NIEPCE
PAPPUS
SAPPHO
SCOPES
ALARIC
ALDRIN
ALFRED
ANDREA
ANDREI
ANDRES
ANDREW
ANDREY
ANDRIC
ARDREY
AUBREY
AUDREY
BARROW
CABRAL
CARREL
CEDRIC
CERRAF
CHURCH
CLARKE
CLORIS

CONRAD
CONRAT
EMERIC
EVARTS
FAIRLY
FARRAR
FARROW
FERRER
FLEROV
FLOREY
GARROD
GARROW
GAVRAS
GEORGE
GEORGI
GERRIT
GLORIA
GOERGE
GUERIN
GYORGY
HARRIS
HENRIK
INGRAM
INGRID
KARRER
KEARNS
KONRAD
LAUREL
LAUREN
LAWRIE
MERRIT
MONROE
MORRIS
MORROW
MURRAY
NORRIS
OBERTH
OFFROY
OPARIN
PERRIN
PETRIE
PETRUS
PIERCE
PIERRE
ROHRER
SAURIA
SCARPA
SHARPE
SIGRID
SPERRY
TAUROG
TORREY
WARREN
ALISON
BENSON
BESSEL
BUNSEN

BUSSEY
CAESAR
CARSON
CASSIN
CELSUS
CROSBY
DAWSON
DIESEL
EDISON
ELISHA
FAUSTO
FIESER
FINSEN
FRASCH
FROSCH
GARSON
GASSER
GEISEL
GERSON
GIBSON
GIESEL
GIOSUE
GLASER
GOOSEN
GOSSET
HALSEY
HAMSUN
HANSEN
HASSEL
HENSEN
HIRSCH
JANSKY
JENSEN
JESSUP
KEESOM
KINSKY
KOSSEL
KRASNA
KYESER
LARSEN
LARSON
LUSSAC
MANSON
MUSSET
NANSEN
NELSON
NILSON
NOSSAL
ORESME
POGSON
RAMSAY
RAMSEY
REISCH
REMSEN
ROOSBY
RUSSEL
SERSEN

TARSKI
ULISSE
UNDSET
VOISIN
WALSON
WATSON
WESSEL
WIESEL
WILSON
WINSOR
WOLSKY
YASSER
YERSIN
AUSTEN
AUSTIN
BARTON
BAXTER
BEATON
BEATTY
BENTON
BERTHA
BERTIL
BLATTY
BOLTON
BRUTUS
BURTON
BUSTER
CANTIN
CANTON
CANTOR
CARTAN
CARTER
CASTEL
CAXTON
COATES
CORTES
COSTER
COTTON
CURTIS
CURTIZ
DALTON
DAYTON
DENTON
DIETER
DINTIS
DMITRI
DUSTIN
DUTTON
ELSTER
ELYTIS
FOSTER
FULTON
GALTON
GASTON
GEITEL
GUNTER
GUSTAF

GUSTAV
GUYTON
GYATSO
HALTON
HATTIE
HESTON
HILTON
HINTON
HORTON
HUNTER
HUSTON
HUTTON
JUSTUS
KEATON
KOSTER
LARTET
LATTES
LESTER
LIOTTA
LISTER
LITTLE
LOFTUS
MARTEL
MARTIN
MILTON
MONTEL
MORTON
MOUTON
NESTOR
NEWTON
PAXTON
PETTIT
PEYTON
PICTET
PIETER
PIETRO
PISTEK
PORTER
RITTER
ROTTER
SANTEL
SARTRE
SCOTUS
SEATON
SKOTAK
SMYTHE
SUTTON
TROTTI
VERTES
VICTOR
VIKTOR
WALTER
WALTON
WILTER
WINTON
WITTIG
ZOLTAN
ALCUIN
AUGUST
BARUCH
BEGUIN
BREUER
CLAUDE
COBURN
DECUIR
DUPUIS
EDLUND
FREUND
GRAUNT
HARUNA
HSIUNG
JANUSZ
KALUZA
KEKULE
KHOURI
LUTULI
MCCUNE
MIGUEL
NAGUIB
NERUDA
PAQUIN
PERUTZ
PROULX
PROUST
PSEUDO
RAOULT
RIQUET
SAMUAL
SAMUEL
SHIUNG
SHMUEL
SMAUEL
STRUSS
STRUTT
STRUVE
SUSUME
SUSUMU
SUZUKI
ALFVEN
ALLVAR
BEAVAN
CALVIN
CARVER
CLOVIS
GLOVER
GRAVES
GROVER
HARVEY
HOOVER
KELVIN
MARVIN
MELVIN
MELVYN
NERVIG
OLIVER
OLIVIA
PREVIN
SHOVEL
SILVIO
SOLVAY
STEVEN
TRAVIS
TREVOR
WEAVER
DARWIN
KIRWAN
LUDWIG
PRAWER
ALEXIS
BOLYAI
CHEYNE
DREYER
FLOYER
DENZEL
FRAZER
GLAZER
GRAZIA
HEEZEN
HITZIG
LASZLO
MENZEL
PIAZZI
RHAZES
WENZEL

**5th Letter**

ADRIAN
ALLVAR
ALTMAN
AMAGAT
ARAFAT
BEAVAN
BERMAN
BERNAL
BICHAT
BOLYAI
BORMAN
BRAMAH
CABRAL
CAESAR
CAPMAN
CARTAN
CASPAR
CERNAN
CERRAF
COLMAN
CONRAD
CONRAT
DERHAM
DORIAN
DUGGAR
DUNBAR
DUNCAN
DUNHAM
FABIAN
FARFAX
FARMAN
FARRAR
FINLAY
FIZEAU
FORMAN
GARDAY
GAVRAS
GERMAN
GILMAN
GORGAS
GRAHAM
GUSTAF
GUSTAV
HALDAN
HASDAI
HERMAN
INGRAM
JORDAN
JOSIAH
JULIAN
KASPAR
KILJAN
KIRWAN
KONRAD
KOSMAS
LANDAU
LASEAR
LAZEAR
LOTHAR
LUSSAC
MAIMAN
MCADAM
MCLEAN
MEEHAN
MILLAN
MOREAU
MORGAN
MURRAY
MYRDAL
NATHAN
NECKAM
NEWMAN
NORGAY
NORMAN
NOSSAL
OLDHAM
OTHMAN
OTTMAR
PASCAL
RAGNAR
RAMSAY
RANDAL
REAGAN
SAMUAL
SELMAN
SKOTAK
SOLVAY
STEFAN
TASMAN
THOMAS
TOBIAS
TOLMAN
TOPHAM
TRAJAN
TRUMAN
VAUBAN
VIVIAN
YORDAN
ZEEMAN
ZOLTAN
CROSBY
GRAEBE
JACOBI
JACOBS
MANABA
ROOSBY
STRABO
TRUMBO
ZENOBE
ALCOCK
BANACH
BARUCH
BRANCA
CHANCE
CHURCH
CRANCH
ENRICO
ERLICH
FRANCA
FRANCE
FRANCK
FRANCO
FRASCH
FRENCH
FROSCH
HIRSCH
HORACE
ISAACS
MEDICI
NIEPCE
PIERCE
PLANCK
PRINCE
QUINCY
REISCH
SCHACK
SCHICK
SENECA
SPENCE
TESICH
ULRICH
ARTEDI
BRANDO
BRANDT
BRENDA
CLAUDE
FARADY
FIELDS
GLENDA
KANADA
NERUDA
PALADE
PSEUDO
QUIDDE
REALDO
THOLDE
ADRIEN
AITKEN
ALFRED
ALFVEN
ALLDER
ALPHER
AMEDEO
ANDREA
ANDREI
ANDRES
ANDREW
ANDREY
ARCHER
ARDREY
AUBREY
AUDREY
AUSTEN
AYLMER
BAINES
BARBER
BARNES
BARNEY
BAWDEN
BAXTER
BECHER
BECKET
BEGLEY
BENDER
BENNET
BERGER
BESLER
BESSEL
BIDDEL
BODMER
BONNER
BONNET
BORDEN
BORDET
BORDEU
BOWLES
BREUER
BRILEY
BRUNEL
BULLEN
BUNSEN
BURNET
BUSSEY
BUSTER
BUTLER
CAGNEY
CARMEN
CARNEY
CARREL
CARTER
CARVER
CASKEY
CASTEL
CAYLEY
COATES
COCKER
COOLEY
COOPER
COPLEY
CORNER
CORTES
COSTER
COUPER
COWLES
CRAMER
CREMER
CULLEN
CUVIER
DANIEL
DAVIES
DENZEL
DIESEL
DIETER
DIGGES
DILLEY
DRAPER
DREIER
DREYER
DUDLEY
EAGLER
ECCLES
EIFFEL
EILEEN
ELSTER
ERCKER
EUCKEN
FARMER
FERNEL
FERRER
FIESER
FINNEY
FINSEN
FISHER
FLOREY
FLOYER
FORBES
FOSTER
FOWLER
FRAZER
FULLER
GAINES
GARMES
GASSER
GEIGER
GEISEL
GEITEL
GESNER
GIBNEY
GIESEL
GILLES
GINGER
GLASER
GLAZER
GLOVER
GOOSEN
GOSSET
GRAVES
GRIMES
GROVER
GUFFEY
GUNTER
GURNEY
HADLEY
HALLER
HALLEY
HALSEY
HANLEY
HANNES
HANSEN
HARDEN
HARLEY
HARVEY
HASSEL
HAUBEN
HEANEY
HEDGES
HEEGER
HEEZEN
HELLER
HENSEN
HERMES
HILLER
HITLER
HITNER
HOBBES
HOLDEN
HOLLEY
HOLMES
HOOVER
HOPPER
HORNER
HUGHES
HUNTER
HUXLEY
ISMAEL
JAGGER
JENNER
JENSEN
JULIEN
KARRER
KEELER
KEFFER
KELLER
KELLEY
KEMMER
KEPLER
KEYNES
KOCHER
KOHLER
KOLLER
KOPPEN
KOSSEL
KOSTER
KUIPER
KUMMER
KUNKEL
KYESER
LARNER
LARSEN
LARTET
LASKER
LATTES
LAUREL
LAUREN
LEAKEY
LEIBER
LERNER
LESLEY
LESTER
LEVIEN
LINDER
LIONEL
LIPPES
LISTER
LUTHER
MADLER
MAFFEO
MALDEN
MARCEL
MARLEE
MARTEL
MCKEEN
MENDEL
MENGES
MENKEN
MENZEL
MERCER
MESMER
MICHEL
MIGUEL
MILLER
MILNER
MONTEL
MORLEY
MOTHER
MULLER
MURIEL
MUSSET
NAIFEH
NANSEN
NAPIER
NARMER
NOLLET
OAKLEY
OLIVER
PALMER
PANDER
PARKER
PARKES
PICTET
PIETER
PISTEK
POLHEM
PORTER
POYNER
PRAWER
PULLER
PUNNET
RACHEL
RAFAEL
RAINER
RAMSEY
REINER
REINES
REMSEN
RENFEW
RHAZES
RHODES
RICHER
RICHET
RINGER
RIQUET
RITTER
ROBLEY
RODNEY
ROHRER
ROSHER
ROTTER
ROZIER
RUBNER
RUCKER

RUEBEN
RUMKER
RUSSEL
SALEEN
SAMUEL
SANGER
SANTEL
SCHNEE
SCOPES
SEMLER
SERSEN
SEYLER
SHMUEL
SHOVEL
SHUKEN
SIBLEY
SIDNEY
SINGER
SLIFER
SMAUEL
SMILEY
SPACEK
SPACEY
SQUIER
STEVEN
STIFEL
STILES
STOKES
STONEY
STREEP
STREET
SUMNER
SYDNEY
TADDEO
TAUBES
TELLER
THALES
TORREY
TOWNES
TUMMEL
UNDSET
USSHER
VALLEE
VALLES
VERNER
VERTES
VIVIEN
WAGNER
WALDEN
WALKEN
WALKER
WALTER
WANKEL
WARNER
WARREN
WEAVER
WEINER
WELLER
WELLES
WENZEL
WERNER
WESLEY
WESSEL
WEXLER
WIENER
WIESEL
WIGNER
WILBER
WILDER
WILKES
WILLEM
WILTER
WOHLER
WOOLEY
WYDNER
YASSER
YERKES
ZAVIER
ZINNER
ADOLFO
BRIDGE
BRIGGS
DOMAGK
GEORGE
GEORGI
GEROGE
GOERGE
GRIGGS
GYORGY
JURAGA
SAVAGE
AMDAHL
AMECHE
BERTHA
BHABHA
BOUGHN
BRIGHT
BUDDHA
BUNCHE
CAUCHY
DWIGHT
ELISHA
MENCHU
MURPHY
PLUCHE
SAPPHO
SECCHI
SMYTHE
VOIGHT
WRIGHT
YOICHI
ALARIC
ALCUIN
ALDRIN
ALEXIS
ANDRIC
ARCHIE
ASHKIN
ASPDIN
AUSTIN
BAUHIN
BEGUIN
BEHAIM
BENOIT
BERTIL
BINNIG
BOHLIN
CALLIE
CALVIN
CANTIN
CASSIN
CEDRIC
CLORIS
CLOVIS
COFFIN
COLLIP
CRONIN
CURTIS
CURTIZ
DARWIN
DECUIR
DENNIS
DINTIS
DUPUIS
DUSTIN
ELYTIS
EMERIC
EMILIE
EMILIO
EUCLID
GALOIS
GARCIA
GAUDIO
GERRIT
GIULIO
GLORIA
GMELIN
GOLDIE
GRANIT
GRAZIA
GUERIN
HARRIS
HATTIE
HEFLIN
HENNIG
HENRIK
HERBIG
HITZIG
INGRID
KEILIN
KELVIN
LAWRIE
LENOIR
LESLIE
LOLOIR
LOOMIS
LUDWIG
MAGGIE
MANLIO
MARCIA
MARTIN
MARVIN
MATLIN
MELVIN
MERRIT
MORRIS
MULLIS
NAGUIB
NAUDIN
NERVIG
NORRIS
OLIVIA
OPARIN
PAQUIN
PERKIN
PERRIN
PETRIE
PETTIT
PHILIP
PREVIN
RENNIE
RISKIN
ROBBIE
ROMAIN
RONNIE
RUBBIA
SAURIA
SHAMIR
SHEMIN
SIGRID
SILVIO
SOPHIA
SOPHIE
STALIN
TEWFIK
THABIT
TRAVIS
TROFIM
TULLIO
URBAIN
VIRGIL
VOISIN
WALLIS
WATKIN
WILLIS
WITTIG
YERGIN
YERSIN
BROOKE
BROOKS
CARAKA
CLARKE
EISAKU
FRANKE
FRICKE
HENCKE
HIDEKI
JANSKY
KINSKY
MALAKH
SHANKS
STOCKE
SUZUKI
TANAKA
TARSKI
UPDIKE
WILCKE
WOLSKY
ZARNKE
ZWICKY
ANGELL
ANGELO
ANHALT
APPOLT
ARNOLD
BARKLA
BEADLE
BOULLE
BURALI
CRELLE
DANILO
DIBBLE
DONALD
DUVALL
EISELE
ENGELS
FAIRLY
GERALD
GESELL
HARALD
HAROLD
HERALD
HONOLD
HUBBLE
KEKULE
KIBBLE
KRAELY
LASZLO
LEXELL
LITTLE
LOVELL
LOWELL
LUCILA
LUTULI
MAYALL
MEIKLE
MICALI
MUNGLE
NAGELI
NEVILL
NICOLA
NICOLE
NICOLO
NIKOLA
NOBILI
ORVILL
OSWALD
PAMELA
POWELL
PROULX
RAOULT
REILLY
RONALD
RUDOLF
SCHELL
SEGALL
SEWALL
STEELE
UNSOLD
WITELO
ADDAMS
GRAMME
JEREMY
JEROME
ORESME
SUSUME
SUSUMU
THELMA
ALPINI
ANNING
ANTONY
ARGAND
ARLING
ARMAND
AYLING
AYMAND
BARANY
BERING
BRIAND
CHEYNE
CHIANG
CIMINO
CYRANO
DELANO
DELANY
DIANNE
DULONG
DUNANT
EDLUND
EDMOND
ETIENE
EUGENE
EYVIND
FAJANS
FREUND
GIANNI
GOBIND
GRAUNT
GREENE
GRIJNS
HARUNA
HSIUNG
IRVING
JEANNE
JOANNE
JOHANN
KATINA
KEARNS
KEMENY
KRASNA
LEVENE
LEVINE
LORENZ
MALONE
MCCUNE
MILENA
MOLINA
MORENO
NADINE
NAGANO
NAKANO
PACINI
PACINO
RACINE
RAKINE
ROBINS
ROLAND
ROMANO
SABINE
SHIUNG
SIMOND
SIMONE
SIMONI
SIMONS
SLOANE
STRONG
THEONI
TIMONI
TOLAND
TURING
VALENS
VENING
WARING
YVONNE
ALISON
AMTHOR
ATWOOD
BARROW
BARTON
BEATON
BELLOW
BENSON
BENTON
BISHOP
BIZIOU
BOLTON
BONNOT
BURTON
CANNOM
CANNON
CANTON
CANTOR
CARBON
CARLOS
CARNOT
CARSON
CAXTON
COTTON
CRAGOE
CUGNOT
DAFFOS
DALTON
DAWSON
DAYTON
DENJOY
DENTON
DILLON
DUNLOP
DUTTON
EDISON
ELLIOT
FARROW
FEODOR
FLEROV
FULTON
GALTON
GARROD
GARROW
GARSON
GASTON
GAYNOR
GERSON
GIBBON
GIBSON
GIDEON
GORDON
GREGOR
GUYTON
HALTON
HARLOW
HESTON
HILTON
HINTON
HORTON
HUSTON
HUTTON
ISADOR
ISIDOR
IVANOV
JOLIOT
KARNOW
KEATON
KEESOM
LANDON
LARMOR
LARSON
LEMMON
LEONOR
LEONOV
LINDON
LONDON
LOUDON
LYNDON
MAHLON
MANSON
MARION
MARKOV
MARLON
MATEOS
MCLEOD
MELLOR
MILTON
MONROE
MORROW
MORTON
MOUTON
NELSON
NESTOR
NEWCOM
NEWTON
NILSON
NIPKOW
OFFROY
PAVLOV
PAXTON
PELLOS
PEPLOE
PEYTON
PHILON
POGSON
SARGON
SEATON
SEMJON
SHIMON
SIMEON
SUTTON
TALBOT
TAUROG
TAYLOR
TEODOR
TREVOR
VERNON
VICTOR
VIKTOR
VILMOS
WALSON
WALTON
WATSON
WILSON
WINSOR
WINTON
ADOLPH
CHAPPE
CHEOPS
FELIPE
JACOPO
JOSEPH
SCARPA
SHARPE
STUMPF
WHOOPI
ALBERT
AMPERE
ANDERS
APPERT
BARBRA
BOGART
BOVERI
CESARE
CESARI
CHABRY
CLAIRE
COBURN
DESIRE
DMITRI
ECKERT
EDUARD
EDWARD
ELLERY
ENDERS
GERARD
GIRARD
HAVERS
HAZARD
HOWARD
HUBERT
ILMARI
JETHRO
KAPARY
KHOURI
KOTARO
LAYARD
LAZARE
LEMERY
LUDERS
MCCORD
MOYERS
OLBERS
PETERS
PICARD

PIERRE
PIETRO
REVERE
ROBERT
ROGERS
RUPERT
RYBERG
SARTRE
SAVARY
SAVERY
SCHARY
SEVERO
SPERRY
STEARN
STEARS
STUART
TAGORE
WATERS
ARLISS
ARREST
AUGUST
BLAISE
ELOISE
ERNEST
FOREST
GRIESS
GYATSO
HEVESY
HEWISH
JANUSZ
JOGESH
LOUISE
LOVISA
MARISA
MILOSZ
NERNST
PIROSH
PROUST
RIVEST
STRUSS
TERESA
ULISSE
WALESA
ABBOTT
AGNETA
ALCOTT
BEATTY
BENITO
BLATTY
CAVETT
CIVITA
CRAFTS
DONATI
DONATO
EVARTS
FAUSTO
FSCOTT

HEWITT
IGNATZ
LIOTTA
LOWITZ
LYCETT
MONETA
MORITZ
OBERTH
PERUTZ
PLANTE
SAINTE
SAKATA
STRATO
STRUTT
SVANTE
TROTTI
TSVETT
VENETZ
ZAVITZ
ARNAUD
ARTHUR
AUZOUT
BLAAUW
BRUTUS
CELSUS
CORDUS
DUFOUR
FAROUK
GIOSUE
HAMSUN
JESSUP
JOSHUA
JULIUS
JUSTUS
LOFTUS
LUCIUS
MAGNUS
MARCUS
MARIUS
MOBIUS
PAPPUS
PETRUS
PINCUS
PREBUS
REGIUS
SCOTUS
SEAMUS
SOPHUS
THIOUT
TITIUS
ULPIUS
VARMUS
BASEVI
STRUVE
YUKAWA
EVELYN
GLADYS

MELVYN
PALFYN
ALONZO
BEROZA
KALUZA
PIAZZI

**6th Letter**

AGNETA
ANDREA
BARBRA
BARKLA
BEROZA
BERTHA
BHABHA
BRANCA
BRENDA
BUDDHA
CARAKA
CIVITA
ELISHA
FRANCA
GARCIA
GLENDA
GLORIA
GRAZIA
HARUNA
JOSHUA
JURAGA
KALUZA
KANADA
KATINA
KRASNA
LIOTTA
LOVISA
LUCILA
MANABA
MARCIA
MARISA
MILENA
MOLINA
MONETA
NERUDA
NICOLA
NIKOLA
OLIVIA
PAMELA
RUBBIA
SAKATA
SAURIA
SCARPA
SENECA
SOPHIA
TANAKA

TERESA
THELMA
WALESA
YUKAWA
NAGUIB
ALARIC
ANDRIC
CEDRIC
EMERIC
LUSSAC
ALFRED
ARGAND
ARMAND
ARNAUD
ARNOLD
ATWOOD
AYMAND
BRIAND
CONRAD
DONALD
EDLUND
EDMOND
EDUARD
EDWARD
EUCLID
EYVIND
FREUND
GARROD
GERALD
GERARD
GIRARD
GOBIND
HARALD
HAROLD
HAZARD
HERALD
HONOLD
HOWARD
INGRID
KONRAD
LAYARD
MCCORD
MCLEOD
OSWALD
PICARD
ROLAND
RONALD
SIGRID
SIMOND
TOLAND
UNSOLD
AMECHE
AMPERE
ARCHIE
BEADLE
BLAISE
BOULLE

BRIDGE
BROOKE
BUNCHE
CALLIE
CESARE
CHANCE
CHAPPE
CHEYNE
CLAIRE
CLARKE
CLAUDE
CRAGOE
CRELLE
DESIRE
DIANNE
DIBBLE
EISELE
ELOISE
EMILIE
ETIENE
EUGENE
FELIPE
FRANCE
FRANKE
FRICKE
GEORGE
GEROGE
GIOSUE
GOERGE
GOLDIE
GRAEBE
GRAMME
GREENE
HATTIE
HENCKE
HORACE
HUBBLE
JEANNE
JEROME
JOANNE
KEKULE
KIBBLE
LAWRIE
LAZARE
LESLIE
LEVENE
LEVINE
LITTLE
LOUISE
MAGGIE
MALONE
MARLEE
MCCUNE
MEIKLE
MONROE
MUNGLE
NADINE

NICOLE
NIEPCE
ORESME
PALADE
PEPLOE
PETRIE
PIERCE
PIERRE
PLANTE
PLUCHE
PRINCE
QUIDDE
RACINE
RAKINE
RENNIE
REVERE
ROBBIE
RONNIE
SABINE
SAINTE
SARTRE
SAVAGE
SCHNEE
SHARPE
SIMONE
SLOANE
SMYTHE
SOPHIE
SPENCE
STEELE
STOCKE
STRUVE
SUSUME
SVANTE
TAGORE
THOLDE
ULISSE
UPDIKE
VALLEE
WILCKE
YVONNE
ZARNKE
ZENOBE
CERRAF
GUSTAF
RUDOLF
STUMPF
ANNING
ARLING
AYLING
BERING
BINNIG
CHIANG
DULONG
HENNIG
HERBIG
HITZIG

HSIUNG
IRVING
LUDWIG
NERVIG
RYBERG
SHIUNG
STRONG
TAUROG
TURING
VENING
WARING
WITTIG
ADOLPH
BANACH
BARUCH
BRAMAH
CHURCH
CRANCH
ERLICH
FRASCH
FRENCH
FROSCH
HEWISH
HIRSCH
JOGESH
JOSEPH
JOSIAH
MALAKH
NAIFEH
OBERTH
PIROSH
REISCH
TESICH
ULRICH
ALPINI
ANDREI
ARTEDI
BASEVI
BOLYAI
BOVERI
BURALI
CESARI
DMITRI
DONATI
GEORGI
GIANNI
HASDAI
HIDEKI
ILMARI
JACOBI
KHOURI
LUTULI
MEDICI
MICALI
NAGELI
NOBILI
PACINI

PIAZZI
SECCHI
SIMONI
SUZUKI
TARSKI
THEONI
TIMONI
TROTTI
WHOOPI
YOICHI
ALCOCK
DOMAGK
FAROUK
FRANCK
HENRIK
PISTEK
PLANCK
SCHACK
SCHICK
SKOTAK
SPACEK
TEWFIK
AMDAHL
ANGELL
BERNAL
BERTIL
BESSEL
BIDDEL
BRUNEL
CABRAL
CARREL
CASTEL
DANIEL
DENZEL
DIESEL
DUVALL
EIFFEL
FERNEL
GEISEL
GEITEL
GESELL
GIESEL
HASSEL
ISMAEL
KOSSEL
KUNKEL
LAUREL
LEXELL
LIONEL
LOVELL
LOWELL
MARCEL
MARTEL
MAYALL
MENDEL
MENZEL
MICHEL

MIGUEL
MONTEL
MURIEL
MYRDAL
NEVILL
NOSSAL
ORVILL
PASCAL
POWELL
RACHEL
RAFAEL
RANDAL
RUSSEL
SAMUAL
SAMUEL
SANTEL
SCHELL
SEGALL
SEWALL
SHMUEL
SHOVEL
SMAUEL
STIFEL
TUMMEL
VIRGIL
WANKEL
WENZEL
WESSEL
WIESEL
BEHAIM
CANNOM
DERHAM
DUNHAM
GRAHAM
INGRAM
KEESOM
MCADAM
NECKAM
NEWCOM
OLDHAM
POLHEM
TOPHAM
TROFIM
WILLEM
ADRIAN
ADRIEN
AITKEN
ALCUIN
ALDRIN
ALFVEN
ALISON
ALTMAN
ASHKIN
ASPDIN
AUSTEN
AUSTIN
BARTON

BAUHIN
BAWDEN
BEATON
BEAVAN
BEGUIN
BENSON
BENTON
BERMAN
BOHLIN
BOLTON
BORDEN
BORMAN
BOUGHN
BULLEN
BUNSEN
BURTON
CALVIN
CANNON
CANTIN
CANTON
CAPMAN
CARBON
CARMEN
CARSON
CARTAN
CASSIN
CAXTON
CERNAN
COBURN
COFFIN
COLMAN
COTTON
CRONIN
CULLEN
DALTON
DARWIN
DAWSON
DAYTON
DENTON
DILLON
DORIAN
DUNCAN
DUSTIN
DUTTON
EDISON
EILEEN
EUCKEN
EVELYN
FABIAN
FARMAN
FINSEN
FORMAN
FULTON
GALTON
GARSON
GASTON
GERMAN

GERSON
GIBBON
GIBSON
GIDEON
GILMAN
GMELIN
GOOSEN
GORDON
GUERIN
GUYTON
HALDAN
HALTON
HAMSUN
HANSEN
HARDEN
HAUBEN
HEEZEN
HEFLIN
HENSEN
HERMAN
HESTON
HILTON
HINTON
HOLDEN
HORTON
HUSTON
HUTTON
JENSEN
JOHANN
JORDAN
JULIAN
JULIEN
KEATON
KEILIN
KELVIN
KILJAN
KIRWAN
KOPPEN
LANDON
LARSEN
LARSON
LAUREN
LEMMON
LEVIEN
LINDON
LONDON
LOUDON
LYNDON
MAHLON
MAIMAN
MALDEN
MANSON
MARION
MARLON
MARTIN
MARVIN
MATLIN
MCKEEN
MCLEAN
MEEHAN
MELVIN
MELVYN
MENKEN
MILLAN
MILTON
MORGAN
MORTON
MOUTON
NANSEN
NATHAN
NAUDIN
NELSON
NEWMAN
NEWTON
NILSON
NORMAN
OPARIN
OTHMAN
PALFYN
PAQUIN
PAXTON
PERKIN
PERRIN
PEYTON
PHILON
POGSON
PREVIN
REAGAN
REMSEN
RISKIN
ROMAIN
RUEBEN
SALEEN
SARGON
SEATON
SELMAN
SEMJON
SERSEN
SHEMIN
SHIMON
SHUKEN
SIMEON
STALIN
STEARN
STEFAN
STEVEN
SUTTON
TASMAN
TOLMAN
TRAJAN
TRUMAN
URBAIN
VAUBAN
VERNON
VIVIAN
VIVIEN
VOISIN
WALDEN
WALKEN
WALSON
WALTON
WARREN
WATKIN
WATSON
WILSON
WINTON
YERGIN
YERSIN
YORDAN
ZEEMAN
ZOLTAN
ADOLFO
ALONZO
AMEDEO
ANGELO
BENITO
BRANDO
CIMINO
CYRANO
DANILO
DELANO
DONATO
EMILIO
ENRICO
FAUSTO
FRANCO
GAUDIO
GIULIO
GYATSO
JACOPO
JETHRO
KOTARO
LASZLO
MAFFEO
MANLIO
MORENO
NAGANO
NAKANO
NICOLO
PACINO
PIETRO
PSEUDO
REALDO
ROMANO
SAPPHO
SEVERO
SILVIO
STRABO
STRATO
TADDEO
TRUMBO
TULLIO
WITELO
BISHOP
COLLIP
DUNLOP
JESSUP
PHILIP
STREEP
ALLDER
ALLVAR
ALPHER
AMTHOR
ARCHER
ARTHUR
AYLMER
BARBER
BAXTER
BECHER
BENDER
BERGER
BESLER
BODMER
BONNER
BREUER
BUSTER
BUTLER
CAESAR
CANTOR
CARTER
CARVER
CASPAR
COCKER
COOPER
CORNER
COSTER
COUPER
CRAMER
CREMER
CUVIER
DECUIR
DIETER
DRAPER
DREIER
DREYER
DUFOUR
DUGGAR
DUNBAR
EAGLER
ELSTER
ERCKER
FARMER
FARRAR
FEODOR
FERRER
FIESER
FISHER
FLOYER
FOSTER
FOWLER
FRAZER
FULLER
GASSER
GAYNOR
GEIGER
GESNER
GINGER
GLASER
GLAZER
GLOVER
GREGOR
GROVER
GUNTER
HALLER
HEEGER
HELLER
HILLER
HITLER
HITNER
HOOVER
HOPPER
HORNER
HUNTER
ISADOR
ISIDOR
JAGGER
JENNER
KARRER
KASPAR
KEELER
KEFFER
KELLER
KEMMER
KEPLER
KOCHER
KOHLER
KOLLER
KOSTER
KUIPER
KUMMER
KYESER
LARMOR
LARNER
LASEAR
LASKER
LAZEAR
LEIBER
LENOIR
LEONOR
LERNER
LESTER
LINDER
LISTER
LOLOIR
LOTHAR
LUTHER
MADLER
MELLOR
MERCER
MESMER
MILLER
MILNER
MOTHER
MULLER
NAPIER
NARMER
NESTOR
OLIVER
OTTMAR
PALMER
PANDER
PARKER
PIETER
PORTER
POYNER
PRAWER
PULLER
RAGNAR
RAINER
REINER
RICHER
RINGER
RITTER
ROHRER
ROSHER
ROTTER
ROZIER
RUBNER
RUCKER
RUMKER
SANGER
SEMLER
SEYLER
SHAMIR
SINGER
SLIFER
SQUIER
SUMNER
TAYLOR
TELLER
TEODOR
TREVOR
USSHER
VERNER
VICTOR
VIKTOR
WAGNER
WALKER
WALTER
WARNER
WEAVER
WEINER
WELLER
WERNER
WEXLER
WIENER
WIGNER
WILBER
WILDER
WILTER
WINSOR
WOHLER
WYDNER
YASSER
ZAVIER
ZINNER
ADDAMS
ALEXIS
ANDERS
ANDRES
ARLISS
BAINES
BARNES
BOWLES
BRIGGS
BROOKS
BRUTUS
CARLOS
CELSUS
CHEOPS
CLORIS
CLOVIS
COATES
CORDUS
CORTES
COWLES
CRAFTS
CURTIS
DAFFOS
DAVIES
DENNIS
DIGGES
DINTIS
DUPUIS
ECCLES
ELYTIS
ENDERS
ENGELS
EVARTS
FAJANS
FIELDS
FORBES
GAINES
GALOIS
GARMES
GAVRAS
GILLES
GLADYS
GORGAS
GRAVES
GRIESS
GRIGGS
GRIJNS
GRIMES
HANNES
HARRIS
HAVERS
HEDGES
HERMES
HOBBES
HOLMES
HUGHES
ISAACS
JACOBS
JULIUS
JUSTUS
KEARNS
KEYNES
KOSMAS
LATTES
LIPPES
LOFTUS
LOOMIS
LUCIUS
LUDERS
MAGNUS
MARCUS
MARIUS
MATEOS
MENGES
MOBIUS
MORRIS
MOYERS
MULLIS
NORRIS
OLBERS
PAPPUS
PARKES
PELLOS
PETERS
PETRUS
PINCUS
PREBUS
REGIUS
REINES
RHAZES
RHODES
ROBINS
ROGERS
SCOPES
SCOTUS
SEAMUS
SHANKS
SIMONS
SOPHUS
STEARS
STILES
STOKES
STRUSS
TAUBES
THALES
THOMAS
TITIUS
TOBIAS
TOWNES
TRAVIS
ULPIUS
VALENS
VALLES
VARMUS
VERTES
VILMOS
WALLIS
WATERS
WELLES
WILKES
WILLIS
YERKES
ABBOTT
ALBERT
ALCOTT
AMAGAT
ANHALT
APPERT
APPOLT
ARAFAT
ARREST
AUGUST
AUZOUT
BECKET
BENNET
BENOIT
BICHAT
BOGART
BONNET
BONNOT
BORDET
BRANDT
BRIGHT
BURNET
CARNOT
CAVETT
CONRAT
CUGNOT
DUNANT
DWIGHT
ECKERT
ELLIOT
ERNEST
FOREST
FSCOTT
GERRIT
GOSSET
GRANIT
GRAUNT
HEWITT
HUBERT
JOLIOT
LARTET
LYCETT
MERRIT
MUSSET
NERNST
NOLLET
PETTIT
PICTET
PROUST
PUNNET
RAOULT
RICHET
RIQUET
RIVEST
ROBERT
RUPERT
STREET
STRUTT
STUART
TALBOT
THABIT
THIOUT
TSVETT
UNDSET
VOIGHT
WRIGHT
BIZIOU
BORDEU
EISAKU
FIZEAU
LANDAU
MENCHU
MOREAU
SUSUMU
FLEROV
GUSTAV
IVANOV
LEONOV
MARKOV
PAVLOV
ANDREW
BARROW
BELLOW
BLAAUW
FARROW
GARROW
HARLOW
KARNOW
MORROW
NIPKOW
RENFEW
FARFAX

PROULX
ANDREY
ANTONY
ARDREY
AUBREY
AUDREY
BARANY
BARNEY
BEATTY
BEGLEY
BLATTY
BRILEY
BUSSEY
CAGNEY
CARNEY
CASKEY
CAUCHY
CAYLEY
CHABRY
COOLEY
COPLEY
CROSBY
DELANY
DENJOY
DILLEY
DUDLEY
ELLERY
FAIRLY
FARADY
FINLAY
FINNEY
FLOREY
GARDAY
GIBNEY
GUFFEY
GURNEY
GYORGY
HADLEY
HALLEY
HALSEY
HANLEY
HARLEY
HARVEY
HEANEY
HEVESY
HOLLEY
HUXLEY
JANSKY
JEREMY
KAPARY
KELLEY
KEMENY
KINSKY
KRAELY
LEAKEY
LEMERY
LESLEY
MORLEY
MURPHY
MURRAY
NORGAY
OAKLEY
OFFROY
QUINCY
RAMSAY
RAMSEY
REILLY
ROBLEY
RODNEY
ROOSBY
SAVARY
SAVERY
SCHARY
SIBLEY
SIDNEY
SMILEY
SOLVAY
SPACEY
SPERRY
STONEY
SYDNEY
TORREY
WESLEY
WOLSKY
WOOLEY
ZWICKY
CURTIZ
IGNATZ
JANUSZ
LORENZ
LOWITZ
MILOSZ
MORITZ
PERUTZ
VENETZ
ZAVITZ

## 7 LETTER

### 1ST LETTER

ABELARD
ABELSON
ABRAHAM
ACHESON
ACHILLE
ACKLAND
ACTINUS
ADDISON
ADELARD
ADLEMAN
ADOLPHE
ADOLPHO
ADRIAAN
ADRIAEN
AEPINUS
AGASSIZ
AGRIPPA
AIKICHI
ALBERTI
ALBINUS
ALCAEUS
ALFONSO
ALFREDO
ALHAZEN
ALLBUTT
ALVAREZ
AMBROSE
ANATOLE
ANDREAS
ANDREWS
ANDRIJA
ANGELOS
ANNAEUS
ANSELME
ANTHONY
ANTOINE
ANTONIO
APTHROP
AQUINAS
AROBLES
ARRIGHI
ARTTURI
ASHMOLE
ASTBURY
ATHAIYA
AUDUBON
AUGUSTE
AUGUSTO
AXELROD
BAKHUIS
BANGHAM
BANTING
BARBARA
BARDEEN
BARNARD
BARNETT
BATESON
BATFOUR
BAUMANN
BECKETT
BECKLIN
BECKMAN
BEDDOES
BEDNARZ
BEDNORZ
BEECHER
BEGUYER
BELKNAP
BELLINI
BELZONI
BENNETT
BENTHAM
BERGIUS
BERGMAN
BERGSON
BERNARD
BERTRAM
BERWICK
BEYRICH
BIGELOW
BINGHAM
BITTNER
BJORKEN
BJORNST
BLAGDEN
BLALACK
BLALOCK
BLERIOT
BOEHMER
BOLZANO
BORDERS
BORELLI
BORLAUG
BORZAGE
BOTTGER
BOUCHER
BOUGUER
BOULTON
BOURATT
BOUVARD
BRADLEY
BRANDES
BRANTON
BRENNAN
BRENNER
BRETTON
BRIDGES
BRITTON
BROADUS
BRODSKY
BROUWER
BRUGSCH
BRUNHES
BRYNNER
BUCHMAN
BUCHNER
BUISSON
BULLOCK
BURBANK
BURIDAN
BURNELL
BURNETT
BURROWS
BURSTYN
BURWELL
BUTTONS
CABAEUS
CABIBBO
CABRERA
CAMERON
CAMILLE
CAMILLO
CAMPION
CANETTI
CARDANO
CARDIFF
CARLSON
CARLYLE
CAROLUS
CAROLYN
CARRERE
CARRIER
CARROLL
CASIMIR
CASSINI
CASTELI
CASTNER
CATALDI
CATESBY
CATLETT
CATTELL
CECELIA
CELESTE
CELSIUS
CERLUTI
CHAFFEE
CHAPMAN
CHAPPEL
CHAPTAL
CHARCOT
CHARLES
CHARNAY
CHARPAK
CHASLES
CHAUCER
CHELPIN
CHESTER
CHLADNI
CHOMSKY
CHRISTY
CHUQUET
CLAVIUS
CLAYTON
CLEMENS
CLEMENT
CLEWALL
CLINTON
CLOPTON
CLOQUET
CLOUSER
COLBERT
COLDITZ
COLLINS
COLOMBO
COLUMBO
COMPTON
CONNERY
CONYERS
COPPOLA
CORDELL
CORLISS
CORMACK
CORRENS
COSTNER
COTTELL
COULTER
COULUMB
CREMMER
CRESCAS
CRETIEN
CRIPPEN
CROOKES
CRUTZEN
CUMMING
CURTISS
CUSHING
CZESLAW
DAIMLER
DANGEAU
DANIELE
DANIELL
DANIELS
DARLING
DARWELL
DAUBREE
DAUSSET
DEHMELT
DELBERT
DELEDDA
DELIGNE
DELISLE
DENISON
DESAULT
DESMOND
DEVILLE
DEVRIES
DIAMOND
DICKSON
DIDERIK
DIDEROT
DIOCLES
DOHERTY
DOLLOND
DOMINGO
DONDERS
DONNALL
DOPPLER
DOROTHY
DOUGLAS
DREBBEL
DREXLER
DRINKER
DUHAMEL
DUILLER
DUKAKIS
DUNAWAY
DUNNING
DYKSTRA
EASTMAN
EDELMAN
EDEMANN
EDOUARD
EDOUART
EHRLICH
EIJKMAN
EINHORN
EKEBERG
ELLIOTT
ELLMANN
EMANUAL
EMANUEL
EMERSON
EMPEROR
EPHRAIM
EPSTEIN
ERASMUS
ERNESTO
ESTELLE
ETIENNE
EUDEMUS
EUDOXUS
EUGENIO
EUSTACE
EXIGUUS
EZEKIEL
FARACHI
FARCIOT
FARNHAM
FECHNER
FERNAND
FERRARI
FERRIER
FEYNMAN
FIBIGER
FILIPPO
FISCHER
FITZROY
FLEMING
FLOWERS
FOLKERS
FOLKMAN
FONTANA
FOREMAN
FORREST
FOURIER
FRANCES
FRANCIS
FRECHET
FREDDIE
FREDRIC
FREDRIK
FREEMAN
FRESNEL
FRICKER
FRIEDEL
FRISIUS
FRITIOF
FRITSCH
GABRIEL
GADOLIN
GAGARIN
GALILEO
GALVANI
GARBETT
GARDNER
GARMIRE
GASPARD
GASSNER
GATLING
GAUSMAN
GEHRING
GELFAND
GELLERT
GEMINUS
GEORGES
GEORGII
GERBERT
GERHARD
GERHART
GERMAIN
GERSTAD
GHIORSO
GIACOMO
GIAUQUE
GIBBONS
GIELGUD
GIFFARD
GILBERT
GIORGOS
GIOVANI
GLAEVER
GLASHOW
GLAUBER
GLAUCUS
GLEASON
GLISSON
GODDARD
GODFREY
GOERGES
GOLDING
GOLDMAN
GOMBERG
GONZALO

GOODHUE
GOODMAN
GOODWIN
GOOSSON
GORGIAS
GOSSAGE
GOSSETT
GOTTLOB
GRAHAME
GREGORY
GRESHAM
GRIFFIN
GRISSOM
GROESSE
GUFFROY
GUILLET
GUSELLA
GUSTAVE
GUTHRIE
GYORGYI
HACKMAN
HADDOCK
HAECKEL
HAFSTAD
HAGEMAN
HALDANE
HALLDOR
HALPERN
HALSTED
HAMMANN
HAMMOND
HAMPSON
HAMPTON
HANTARO
HARBURG
HARDING
HARKINS
HARLING
HARRIOT
HARTLEY
HARTMAN
HARTMUT
HASKELL
HATTORI
HAVLICK
HAWKING
HAWKINS
HAWORTH
HAYFORD
HAYWARD
HECKART
HEDRICK
HEERMAN
HEITLER
HENDRIK
HENLEIN
HENNESY
HENRICK
HEPBURN
HERBERT
HERCZEG
HERMANN
HERMITE
HEROULT
HERRING
HERSHEY
HEYMANS
HICKMAN
HIGUCHI
HILAIRE
HILBERT
HILLARY
HILLIER
HILYARD
HIPPIAS
HIROSHI
HITTORF
HJALMAR
HODGKIN
HOFFMAN
HOFMANN
HOKFELT
HOMBERG
HOMEYER
HOPKINS
HOPWOOD
HORNING
HORSLEY
HOUSSAY
HUGGINS
HUMASON
HUMPHRY
HUYGENS
HYPATIA
ICHBIAH
IGNACIO
IMHOTEP
ISADORE
ISHIOKA
ISIDORE
JACINTO
JACKSON
JACOBUS
JACQUES
JAHRAUS
JANSSEN
JARCHUS
JEAKINS
JEFFERY
JEMISON
JENKINS
JENSSON
JESSICA
JIMENEZ
JOACHIM
JOCELYN
JODOCUS
JOHNSON
JOKICHI
JOUHAUX
JUERGEN
KAEMPFE
KAPITZA
KAPTEYN
KASIMIR
KASTLER
KAUFMAN
KAZAKOV
KEDROVA
KELLOGG
KENDALL
KENDREW
KENICHI
KENNEDY
KENNETH
KHAYYAM
KHORANA
KIDDINU
KIEBACH
KINGDOM
KIPLING
KIPPING
KIRCHER
KIYOSHI
KNIFTON
KOLSTER
KOMAROV
KOZYREV
KRAMERS
KRASKER
KRASNER
KROEKEL
KUBRICK
KUNCKEL
LAENNEC
LAMBERT
LAMRACK
LANCISI
LANGLEY
LANSTON
LAPLACE
LAPORTE
LARDNER
LASSELL
LAURENT
LAVERAN
LAXNESS
LAZARUS
LAZZARO
LEAVITT
LEBEDEV
LEBLANC
LECLERC
LEHMANN
LEIBNIZ
LEIPOLD
LELOUCH
LEONARD
LEOPOLD
LEUPOLD
LINACRE
LINCOLN
LIPMANN
LOCKYER
LOFFLER
LORENTZ
LORENZO
LORETTA
LORIMER
LORRAIN
LUCIANA
LUEDTKE
LUITZEN
LUMIERE
LUNARDI
LURSSEN
LYSENKO
MAARTEN
MACAVIN
MACLURE
MACQUER
MADISON
MADRAZO
MAELZEL
MAGNANI
MAHFOUZ
MAIREAD
MALCOLM
MALLAND
MALLORY
MALTHUS
MANDELA
MANDELL
MANFRED
MANTELL
MARALDI
MARCONI
MARQUEZ
MARQUIS
MARSHAK
MARTINE
MASASHI
MATTHAU
MATTHEW
MAUCHLY
MAUMONT
MAUNDER
MAUREEN
MAURIAC
MAURICE
MAXSTED
MAXWELL
MAYNARD
MCCAREY
MCCLUNG
MEGHNAD
MEINESZ
MEITNER
MELLONI
MENGOLI
MENZIES
MERRIAM
MERRILL
MESSIER
MICHAEL
MICHAIL
MICHELE
MICHELL
MIDGLEY
MIKHAIL
MILFORD
MILLAND
MISTRAL
MIYOAKA
MIYOSHI
MOHAMED
MOISSAN
MOMMSEN
MONDINO
MONTAGU
MONTALE
MONZANI
MOSELEY
MOULTON
MUELLER
MUNSTER
MURDOCK
NAGAOKA
NATHANS
NEEDHAM
NEISSER
NEWCOMB
NICCOLO
NICHOLS
NICOLAS
NICOLLE
NIELSON
NIKITIN
NIKLAUS
NIKOLAI
NIKOLAY
NODDACK
NOETHER
NORBERT
NORRISH
NYKVIST
OCTAVIO
OERSTED
OLIVIER
OLMSTED
OLYMPIA
ONSAGER
ORLANDO
OSBORNE
OSTWALD
OSVALDO
OTHNIEL
OTTILIA
PACCARD
PACIOLI
PALANCE
PALISSY
PANCINI
PAOLINI
PARESCE
PARRISH
PARSONS
PASCHEN
PASTEUR
PATRICK
PAULING
PAXINOU
PEACOCK
PEARSON
PECQUET
PELIGOT
PELLING
PELTIER
PENROSE
PENZIAS
PEOPPEL
PEREIRA
PERINAL
PERNIER
PERRINE
PERTHES
PEVONAK
PFEFFER
PHIDIAS
PHILIPP
PHILIPS
PHILLIP
PHOEBUS
PHYLLIS
PICCARD
PICKARD
PIERSON
PILATRE
PILBEAM
PIZARRO
PLUCKER
POISSON
POITIER
POLANYI
POLLACK
POMEROY
PORSCHE
PORSILD
POULSEN
PRACHAR
PRANDTL
PRESPER
PRESTON
PREVOST
PROCLUS
PROCTOR
PTASHNE
PTOLEMY
PULLMAN
PURCELL
PYTHEAS
QUENTIN
RADNITZ
RAINGER
RALEIGH
RALSTON
RAMSDEN
RAPHAEL
RAYMOND
RECORDE
REDFORD
REGNIER
REIMANN
REMNICK
RENAULT
RETZIUS
REYMOND
REYMONT
RICCATI
RICHARD
RICHLIN
RICHTER
ROBARDS
ROBBINS
ROBERTO
ROBERTS
ROBINET
ROBISON
RODBELL
ROEBUCK
ROLLAND
ROMANES
ROSALYN
ROTBLAT
ROUELLE
ROWLAND
RUDBECK
RUDOLFF
RUDOLPH
RUDYARD
RUFFINI
RUMFORD
RUNNELS
RUSSELL
RUZICKA
RYDBERG
SAKMANN
SALILEI
SALOMEN
SANCHEZ
SANDAGE
SANDERS
SARGENT
SAROYAN
SAUVEUR
SAVEGAR
SCANLAN
SCHAFER
SCHALLY
SCHEELE
SCHIRRA
SCHLACK
SCHMIDT
SCHMITT
SCHONER
SCHURER
SCHWABE
SCHWANN
SEABORG
SEBOKHT
SEEBECK
SEFERIS
SEIFERT
SEIRTON
SEMENOV
SEQUARD
SERVAIS
SEVERIN
SEVERUS
SEYMOUR
SHAFFER
SHAMROY
SHANLEY
SHANNON
SHAPIRO
SHAPLEY
SHARAFF
SHEARER
SHEEHAN
SHELDON
SHELLEY
SHELTON
SHEPARD
SHERIFF
SHERMAN
SHIELDS

SHIPLER
SHIRLEY
SHOICHI
SHUFTAN
SHUNPEI
SIEMENS
SIGMUND
SIMPSON
SINATRA
SJOBERG
SKINNER
SLIPHER
SMALLEY
SMEATON
SMELLIE
SOLOMON
SOLOVAY
SORVINO
SOYINKA
SPECTOR
SPEISER
SPEMANN
SPENCER
SPINRAD
SPITZER
SPRAGUE
STANLEY
STARKEY
STARSKI
STEARNS
STEIGER
STEINER
STENDEL
STEPHAN
STEPHEN
STEPVEN
STEVENS
STEWART
STORARO
STRABEL
STURGES
SUMMERS
SURTEES
SUSANNE
SUSRATA
SUSSMAN
SUZANNE
SWIGERT
SYLBERT
SYLVIUS
SZILARD
SZOSTAK
TADASHI
TADEUSZ
TAINTER
TAKASHI
TARAGAY
TARLOFF
TEDESCO
TELESIO
TELFORD
TENNANT
TENZING
TEODORO
TERENCE
TERRILE
THADEUS
THEILER
THENARD
THEODOR
THEURER
THOMSEN
THOMSON
TIDYMAN
TIMOTHY
TIPPETT
TORBERN
TORELLO
TORSTEN
TRAUNER
TRAVERS
TYNDALL
ULYSSES
UMEZAWA
USTINOV
VALMONT
VANESSA
VAUGHAN
VAVILOV
VEKSLER
VENKATA
VENTRIS
VERNIER
VICENTE
VILHELM
VILLARD
VINCENT
VIRCHOW
VIVIANI
VOLHARD
VOLKOFF
WAKSMAN
WALCOTT
WALLACE
WALLACH
WALTHER
WANTZEL
WARBURG
WEGENER
WEIZMAN
WELLAND
WELLMAN
WENDELL
WENTZEL
WERNHER
WHARTON
WHEELER
WHEWELL
WHIPPLE
WHISTON
WHITNEY
WHITTLE
WIDMANN
WIELAND
WILCZEL
WILFRED
WILHELM
WILKINS
WILLANS
WILLARD
WILLIAM
WINDAUS
WINKLER
WINSLOW
WINSTON
WINTERS
WISLAWA
WOODGER
WOODROW
WOOLLEY
WOOSTER
WORTLEY
WOTTITZ
WUERZER
WYCKOFF
WYVILLE
XIMENES
YEATMAN
YITZHAK
YOLANDA
YOSHIDA
ZABDIEL
ZACHARY
ZANETTI
ZEIDLER
ZERMELO
ZERNIKE
ZIEGLER
ZINSSER
ZYGMUNT

## 2nd Letter

BAKHUIS
BANGHAM
BANTING
BARBARA
BARDEEN
BARNARD
BARNETT
BATESON
BATFOUR
BAUMANN
CABAEUS
CABIBBO
CABRERA
CAMERON
CAMILLE
CAMILLO
CAMPION
CANETTI
CARDANO
CARDIFF
CARLSON
CARLYLE
CAROLUS
CAROLYN
CARRERE
CARRIER
CARROLL
CASIMIR
CASSINI
CASTELI
CASTNER
CATALDI
CATESBY
CATLETT
CATTELL
DAIMLER
DANGEAU
DANIELE
DANIELL
DANIELS
DARLING
DARWELL
DAUBREE
DAUSSET
EASTMAN
FARACHI
FARCIOT
FARNHAM
GABRIEL
GADOLIN
GAGARIN
GALILEO
GALVANI
GARBETT
GARDNER
GARMIRE
GASPARD
GASSNER
GATLING
GAUSMAN
HACKMAN
HADDOCK
HAECKEL
HAFSTAD
HAGEMAN
HALDANE
HALLDOR
HALPERN
HALSTED
HAMMANN
HAMMOND
HAMPSON
HAMPTON
HANTARO
HARBURG
HARDING
HARKINS
HARLING
HARRIOT
HARTLEY
HARTMAN
HARTMUT
HASKELL
HATTORI
HAVLICK
HAWKING
HAWKINS
HAWORTH
HAYFORD
HAYWARD
JACINTO
JACKSON
JACOBUS
JACQUES
JAHRAUS
JANSSEN
JARCHUS
KAEMPFE
KAPITZA
KAPTEYN
KASIMIR
KASTLER
KAUFMAN
KAZAKOV
LAENNEC
LAMBERT
LAMRACK
LANCISI
LANGLEY
LANSTON
LAPLACE
LAPORTE
LARDNER
LASSELL
LAURENT
LAVERAN
LAXNESS
LAZARUS
LAZZARO
MAARTEN
MACAVIN
MACLURE
MACQUER
MADISON
MADRAZO
MAELZEL
MAGNANI
MAHFOUZ
MAIREAD
MALCOLM
MALLAND
MALLORY
MALTHUS
MANDELA
MANDELL
MANFRED
MANTELL
MARALDI
MARCONI
MARQUEZ
MARQUIS
MARSHAK
MARTINE
MASASHI
MATTHAU
MATTHEW
MAUCHLY
MAUMONT
MAUNDER
MAUREEN
MAURIAC
MAURICE
MAXSTED
MAXWELL
MAYNARD
NAGAOKA
NATHANS
PACCARD
PACIOLI
PALANCE
PALISSY
PANCINI
PAOLINI
PARESCE
PARRISH
PARSONS
PASCHEN
PASTEUR
PATRICK
PAULING
PAXINOU
RADNITZ
RAINGER
RALEIGH
RALSTON
RAMSDEN
RAPHAEL
RAYMOND
SAKMANN
SALILEI
SALOMEN
SANCHEZ
SANDAGE
SANDERS
SARGENT
SAROYAN
SAUVEUR
SAVEGAR
TADASHI
TADEUSZ
TAINTER
TAKASHI
TARAGAY
TARLOFF
VALMONT
VANESSA
VAUGHAN
VAVILOV
WAKSMAN
WALCOTT
WALLACE
WALLACH
WALTHER
WANTZEL
WARBURG
ZABDIEL
ZACHARY
ZANETTI
ABELARD
ABELSON
ABRAHAM
ACHESON
ACHILLE
ACKLAND
ACTINUS
ICHBIAH
MCCAREY
MCCLUNG
OCTAVIO
SCANLAN
SCHAFER
SCHALLY
SCHEELE
SCHIRRA
SCHLACK
SCHMIDT
SCHMITT
SCHONER
SCHURER
SCHWABE
SCHWANN
ADDISON
ADELARD
ADLEMAN
ADOLPHE
ADOLPHO
ADRIAAN
ADRIAEN
EDELMAN
EDEMANN
EDOUARD
EDOUART
AEPINUS
BECKETT
BECKLIN
BECKMAN
BEDDOES
BEDNARZ
BEDNORZ
BEECHER
BEGUYER
BELKNAP
BELLINI
BELZONI
BENNETT
BENTHAM
BERGIUS
BERGMAN
BERGSON
BERNARD
BERTRAM
BERWICK
BEYRICH
CECELIA
CELESTE
CELSIUS
CERLUTI
DEHMELT
DELBERT
DELEDDA
DELIGNE
DELISLE
DENISON
DESAULT
DESMOND
DEVILLE
DEVRIES
FECHNER
FERNAND
FERRARI
FERRIER
FEYNMAN
GEHRING
GELFAND
GELLERT
GEMINUS
GEORGES
GEORGII
GERBERT
GERHARD
GERHART

GERMAIN
GERSTAD
HECKART
HEDRICK
HEERMAN
HEITLER
HENDRIK
HENLEIN
HENNESY
HENRICK
HEPBURN
HERBERT
HERCZEG
HERMANN
HERMITE
HEROULT
HERRING
HERSHEY
HEYMANS
JEAKINS
JEFFERY
JEMISON
JENKINS
JENSSON
JESSICA
KEDROVA
KELLOGG
KENDALL
KENDREW
KENICHI
KENNEDY
KENNETH
LEAVITT
LEBEDEV
LEBLANC
LECLERC
LEHMANN
LEIBNIZ
LEIPOLD
LELOUCH
LEONARD
LEOPOLD
LEUPOLD
MEGHNAD
MEINESZ
MEITNER
MELLONI
MENGOLI
MENZIES
MERRIAM
MERRILL
MESSIER
NEEDHAM
NEISSER
NEWCOMB
OERSTED
PEACOCK

PEARSON
PECQUET
PELIGOT
PELLING
PELTIER
PENROSE
PENZIAS
PEOPPEL
PEREIRA
PERINAL
PERNIER
PERRINE
PERTHES
PEVONAK
RECORDE
REDFORD
REGNIER
REIMANN
REMNICK
RENAULT
RETZIUS
REYMOND
REYMONT
SEABORG
SEBOKHT
SEEBECK
SEFERIS
SEIFERT
SEIRTON
SEMENOV
SEQUARD
SERVAIS
SEVERIN
SEVERUS
SEYMOUR
TEDESCO
TELESIO
TELFORD
TENNANT
TENZING
TEODORO
TERENCE
TERRILE
VEKSLER
VENKATA
VENTRIS
VERNIER
WEGENER
WEIZMAN
WELLAND
WELLMAN
WENDELL
WENTZEL
WERNHER
YEATMAN
ZEIDLER
ZERMELO

ZERNIKE
PFEFFER
AGASSIZ
AGRIPPA
IGNACIO
CHAFFEE
CHAPMAN
CHAPPEL
CHAPTAL
CHARCOT
CHARLES
CHARNAY
CHARPAK
CHASLES
CHAUCER
CHELPIN
CHESTER
CHLADNI
CHOMSKY
CHRISTY
CHUQUET
EHRLICH
GHIORSO
KHAYYAM
KHORANA
PHIDIAS
PHILIPP
PHILIPS
PHILLIP
PHOEBUS
PHYLLIS
SHAFFER
SHAMROY
SHANLEY
SHANNON
SHAPIRO
SHAPLEY
SHARAFF
SHEARER
SHEEHAN
SHELDON
SHELLEY
SHELTON
SHEPARD
SHERIFF
SHERMAN
SHIELDS
SHIPLER
SHIRLEY
SHOICHI
SHUFTAN
SHUNPEI
THADEUS
THEILER
THENARD
THEODOR
THEURER

THOMSEN
THOMSON
WHARTON
WHEELER
WHEWELL
WHIPPLE
WHISTON
WHITNEY
WHITTLE
AIKICHI
BIGELOW
BINGHAM
BITTNER
DIAMOND
DICKSON
DIDERIK
DIDEROT
DIOCLES
EIJKMAN
EINHORN
FIBIGER
FILIPPO
FISCHER
FITZROY
GIACOMO
GIAUQUE
GIBBONS
GIELGUD
GIFFARD
GILBERT
GIORGOS
GIOVANI
HICKMAN
HIGUCHI
HILAIRE
HILBERT
HILLARY
HILLIER
HILYARD
HIPPIAS
HIROSHI
HITTORF
JIMENEZ
KIDDINU
KIEBACH
KINGDOM
KIPLING
KIPPING
KIRCHER
KIYOSHI
LINACRE
LINCOLN
LIPMANN
MICHAEL
MICHAIL
MICHELE
MICHELL

MIDGLEY
MIKHAIL
MILFORD
MILLAND
MISTRAL
MIYOAKA
MIYOSHI
NICCOLO
NICHOLS
NICOLAS
NICOLLE
NIELSON
NIKITIN
NIKLAUS
NIKOLAI
NIKOLAY
PICCARD
PICKARD
PIERSON
PILATRE
PILBEAM
PIZARRO
RICCATI
RICHARD
RICHLIN
RICHTER
SIEMENS
SIGMUND
SIMPSON
SINATRA
TIDYMAN
TIMOTHY
TIPPETT
VICENTE
VILHELM
VILLARD
VINCENT
VIRCHOW
VIVIANI
WIDMANN
WIELAND
WILCZEL
WILFRED
WILHELM
WILKINS
WILLANS
WILLARD
WILLIAM
WINDAUS
WINKLER
WINSLOW
WINSTON
WINTERS
WISLAWA
XIMENES
YITZHAK
ZIEGLER

ZINSSER
BJORKEN
BJORNST
HJALMAR
SJOBERG
EKEBERG
SKINNER
ALBERTI
ALBINUS
ALCAEUS
ALFONSO
ALFREDO
ALHAZEN
ALLBUTT
ALVAREZ
BLAGDEN
BLALACK
BLALOCK
BLERIOT
CLAVIUS
CLAYTON
CLEMENS
CLEMENT
CLEWALL
CLINTON
CLOPTON
CLOQUET
CLOUSER
ELLIOTT
ELLMANN
FLEMING
FLOWERS
GLAEVER
GLASHOW
GLAUBER
GLAUCUS
GLEASON
GLISSON
OLIVIER
OLMSTED
OLYMPIA
PLUCKER
SLIPHER
ULYSSES
AMBROSE
EMANUAL
EMANUEL
EMERSON
EMPEROR
IMHOTEP
SMALLEY
SMEATON
SMELLIE
UMEZAWA
ANATOLE
ANDREAS
ANDREWS

ANDRIJA
ANGELOS
ANNAEUS
ANSELME
ANTHONY
ANTOINE
ANTONIO
KNIFTON
ONSAGER
BOEHMER
BOLZANO
BORDERS
BORELLI
BORLAUG
BORZAGE
BOTTGER
BOUCHER
BOUGUER
BOULTON
BOURATT
BOUVARD
COLBERT
COLDITZ
COLLINS
COLOMBO
COLUMBO
COMPTON
CONNERY
CONYERS
COPPOLA
CORDELL
CORLISS
CORMACK
CORRENS
COSTNER
COTTELL
COULTER
COULUMB
DOHERTY
DOLLOND
DOMINGO
DONDERS
DONNALL
DOPPLER
DOROTHY
DOUGLAS
FOLKERS
FOLKMAN
FONTANA
FOREMAN
FORREST
FOURIER
GODDARD
GODFREY
GOERGES
GOLDING
GOLDMAN

GOMBERG
GONZALO
GOODHUE
GOODMAN
GOODWIN
GOOSSON
GORGIAS
GOSSAGE
GOSSETT
GOTTLOB
HODGKIN
HOFFMAN
HOFMANN
HOKFELT
HOMBERG
HOMEYER
HOPKINS
HOPWOOD
HORNING
HORSLEY
HOUSSAY
JOACHIM
JOCELYN
JODOCUS
JOHNSON
JOKICHI
JOUHAUX
KOLSTER
KOMAROV
KOZYREV
LOCKYER
LOFFLER
LORENTZ
LORENZO
LORETTA
LORIMER
LORRAIN
MOHAMED
MOISSAN
MOMMSEN
MONDINO
MONTAGU
MONTALE
MONZANI
MOSELEY
MOULTON
NODDACK
NOETHER
NORBERT
NORRISH
POISSON
POITIER
POLANYI
POLLACK
POMEROY
PORSCHE
PORSILD

POULSEN
ROBARDS
ROBBINS
ROBERTO
ROBERTS
ROBINET
ROBISON
RODBELL
ROEBUCK
ROLLAND
ROMANES
ROSALYN
ROTBLAT
ROUELLE
ROWLAND
SOLOMON
SOLOVAY
SORVINO
SOYINKA
TORBERN
TORELLO
TORSTEN
VOLHARD
VOLKOFF
WOODGER
WOODROW
WOOLLEY
WOOSTER
WORTLEY
WOTTITZ
YOLANDA
YOSHIDA
APTHROP
EPHRAIM
EPSTEIN
SPECTOR
SPEISER
SPEMANN
SPENCER
SPINRAD
SPITZER
SPRAGUE
AQUINAS
AROBLES
ARRIGHI
ARTTURI
BRADLEY
BRANDES
BRANTON
BRENNAN
BRENNER
BRETTON
BRIDGES
BRITTON
BROADUS
BRODSKY
BROUWER
BRUGSCH
BRUNHES
BRYNNER
CREMMER
CRESCAS
CRETIEN
CRIPPEN
CROOKES
CRUTZEN
DREBBEL
DREXLER
DRINKER
ERASMUS
ERNESTO
FRANCES
FRANCIS
FRECHET
FREDDIE
FREDRIC
FREDRIK
FREEMAN
FRESNEL
FRICKER
FRIEDEL
FRISIUS
FRITIOF
FRITSCH
GRAHAME
GREGORY
GRESHAM
GRIFFIN
GRISSOM
GROESSE
KRAMERS
KRASKER
KRASNER
KROEKEL
ORLANDO
PRACHAR
PRANDTL
PRESPER
PRESTON
PREVOST
PROCLUS
PROCTOR
TRAUNER
TRAVERS
ASHMOLE
ASTBURY
ESTELLE
ISADORE
ISHIOKA
ISIDORE
OSBORNE
OSTWALD
OSVALDO
USTINOV
ATHAIYA
ETIENNE
OTHNIEL
OTTILIA
PTASHNE
PTOLEMY
STANLEY
STARKEY
STARSKI
STEARNS
STEIGER
STEINER
STENDEL
STEPHAN
STEPHEN
STEPVEN
STEVENS
STEWART
STORARO
STRABEL
STURGES
AUDUBON
AUGUSTE
AUGUSTO
BUCHMAN
BUCHNER
BUISSON
BULLOCK
BURBANK
BURIDAN
BURNELL
BURNETT
BURROWS
BURSTYN
BURWELL
BUTTONS
CUMMING
CURTISS
CUSHING
DUHAMEL
DUILLER
DUKAKIS
DUNAWAY
DUNNING
EUDEMUS
EUDOXUS
EUGENIO
EUSTACE
GUFFROY
GUILLET
GUSELLA
GUSTAVE
GUTHRIE
HUGGINS
HUMASON
HUMPHRY
HUYGENS
JUERGEN
KUBRICK
KUNCKEL
LUCIANA
LUEDTKE
LUITZEN
LUMIERE
LUNARDI
LURSSEN
MUELLER
MUNSTER
MURDOCK
PULLMAN
PURCELL
QUENTIN
RUDBECK
RUDOLFF
RUDOLPH
RUDYARD
RUFFINI
RUMFORD
RUNNELS
RUSSELL
RUZICKA
SUMMERS
SURTEES
SUSANNE
SUSRATA
SUSSMAN
SUZANNE
WUERZER
SWIGERT
AXELROD
EXIGUUS
DYKSTRA
GYORGYI
HYPATIA
LYSENKO
NYKVIST
PYTHEAS
RYDBERG
SYLBERT
SYLVIUS
TYNDALL
WYCKOFF
WYVILLE
ZYGMUNT
CZESLAW
EZEKIEL
SZILARD
SZOSTAK

## 3rd Letter

AGASSIZ
ANATOLE
BLAGDEN
BLALACK
BLALOCK
BRADLEY
BRANDES
BRANTON
CHAFFEE
CHAPMAN
CHAPPEL
CHAPTAL
CHARCOT
CHARLES
CHARNAY
CHARPAK
CHASLES
CHAUCER
CLAVIUS
CLAYTON
DIAMOND
EMANUAL
EMANUEL
ERASMUS
FRANCES
FRANCIS
GIACOMO
GIAUQUE
GLAEVER
GLASHOW
GLAUBER
GLAUCUS
GRAHAME
HJALMAR
ISADORE
JEAKINS
JOACHIM
KHAYYAM
KRAMERS
KRASKER
KRASNER
LEAVITT
MAARTEN
PEACOCK
PEARSON
PRACHAR
PRANDTL
PTASHNE
SCANLAN
SEABORG
SHAFFER
SHAMROY
SHANLEY
SHANNON
SHAPIRO
SHAPLEY
SHARAFF
SMALLEY
STANLEY
STARKEY
STARSKI
THADEUS
TRAUNER
TRAVERS
WHARTON
YEATMAN
ALBERTI
ALBINUS
AMBROSE
CABAEUS
CABIBBO
CABRERA
FIBIGER
GABRIEL
GIBBONS
KUBRICK
LEBEDEV
LEBLANC
OSBORNE
ROBARDS
ROBBINS
ROBERTO
ROBERTS
ROBINET
ROBISON
SEBOKHT
ZABDIEL
ALCAEUS
BECKETT
BECKLIN
BECKMAN
BUCHMAN
BUCHNER
CECELIA
DICKSON
FECHNER
HACKMAN
HECKART
HICKMAN
JACINTO
JACKSON
JACOBUS
JACQUES
JOCELYN
LECLERC
LOCKYER
LUCIANA
MACAVIN
MACLURE
MACQUER
MCCAREY
MCCLUNG
MICHAEL
MICHAIL
MICHELE
MICHELL
NICCOLO
NICHOLS
NICOLAS
NICOLLE
PACCARD
PACIOLI
PECQUET
PICCARD
PICKARD
RECORDE
RICCATI
RICHARD
RICHLIN
RICHTER
VICENTE
WYCKOFF
ZACHARY
ADDISON
ANDREAS
ANDREWS
ANDRIJA
AUDUBON
BEDDOES
BEDNARZ
BEDNORZ
DIDERIK
DIDEROT
EUDEMUS
EUDOXUS
GADOLIN
GODDARD
GODFREY
HADDOCK
HEDRICK
HODGKIN
JODOCUS
KEDROVA
KIDDINU
MADISON
MADRAZO
MIDGLEY
NODDACK
RADNITZ
REDFORD
RODBELL
RUDBECK
RUDOLFF
RUDOLPH
RUDYARD
RYDBERG
TADASHI
TADEUSZ
TEDESCO
TIDYMAN
WIDMANN
ABELARD
ABELSON
ADELARD
AXELROD
BEECHER
BLERIOT
BOEHMER
BRENNAN
BRENNER
BRETTON
CHELPIN
CHESTER
CLEMENS
CLEMENT
CLEWALL
CREMMER
CRESCAS
CRETIEN
CZESLAW
DREBBEL
DREXLER
EDELMAN
EDEMANN
EKEBERG
EMERSON
EZEKIEL
FLEMING
FRECHET
FREDDIE
FREDRIC
FREDRIK
FREEMAN
FRESNEL
GIELGUD
GLEASON
GOERGES
GREGORY
GRESHAM
HAECKEL
HEERMAN
JUERGEN
KAEMPFE
KIEBACH
LAENNEC
LUEDTKE
MAELZEL
MUELLER
NEEDHAM
NIELSON
NOETHER
PFEFFER

PI**E**RSON
PR**E**SPER
PR**E**STON
PR**E**VOST
QU**E**NTIN
RO**E**BUCK
SE**E**BECK
SH**E**ARER
SH**E**EHAN
SH**E**LDON
SH**E**LLEY
SH**E**LTON
SH**E**PARD
SH**E**RIFF
SH**E**RMAN
SI**E**MENS
SM**E**ATON
SM**E**LLIE
SP**E**CTOR
SP**E**ISER
SP**E**MANN
SP**E**NCER
ST**E**ARNS
ST**E**IGER
ST**E**INER
ST**E**NDEL
ST**E**PHAN
ST**E**PHEN
ST**E**PVEN
ST**E**VENS
ST**E**WART
TH**E**ILER
TH**E**NARD
TH**E**ODOR
TH**E**URER
UM**E**ZAWA
WH**E**ELER
WH**E**WELL
WI**E**LAND
WU**E**RZER
ZI**E**GLER
AL**F**ONSO
AL**F**REDO
GI**F**FARD
GU**F**FROY
HA**F**STAD
HO**F**FMAN
HO**F**MANN
JE**F**FERY
LO**F**FLER
RU**F**FINI
SE**F**ERIS
AN**G**ELOS
AU**G**USTE
AU**G**USTO
BE**G**UYER

BI**G**ELOW
EU**G**ENIO
GA**G**ARIN
HA**G**EMAN
HI**G**UCHI
HU**G**GINS
MA**G**NANI
ME**G**HNAD
NA**G**AOKA
RE**G**NIER
SI**G**MUND
WE**G**ENER
ZY**G**MUNT
AC**H**ESON
AC**H**ILLE
AL**H**AZEN
AS**H**MOLE
AT**H**AIYA
DE**H**MELT
DO**H**ERTY
DU**H**AMEL
EP**H**RAIM
GE**H**RING
IC**H**BIAH
IM**H**OTEP
IS**H**IOKA
JA**H**RAUS
JO**H**NSON
LE**H**MANN
MA**H**FOUZ
MO**H**AMED
OT**H**NIEL
SC**H**AFER
SC**H**ALLY
SC**H**EELE
SC**H**IRRA
SC**H**LACK
SC**H**MIDT
SC**H**MITT
SC**H**ONER
SC**H**URER
SC**H**WABE
SC**H**WANN
BR**I**DGES
BR**I**TTON
BU**I**SSON
CL**I**NTON
CR**I**PPEN
DA**I**MLER
DR**I**NKER
DU**I**LLER
ET**I**ENNE
EX**I**GUUS
FR**I**CKER
FR**I**EDEL
FR**I**SIUS

FR**I**TIOF
FR**I**TSCH
GH**I**ORSO
GL**I**SSON
GR**I**FFIN
GR**I**SSOM
GU**I**LLET
HE**I**TLER
IS**I**DORE
KN**I**FTON
LE**I**BNIZ
LE**I**POLD
LU**I**TZEN
MA**I**READ
ME**I**NESZ
ME**I**TNER
MO**I**SSAN
NE**I**SSER
OL**I**VIER
PH**I**DIAS
PH**I**LIPP
PH**I**LIPS
PH**I**LLIP
PO**I**SSON
PO**I**TIER
RA**I**NGER
RE**I**MANN
SE**I**FERT
SE**I**RTON
SH**I**ELDS
SH**I**PLER
SH**I**RLEY
SK**I**NNER
SL**I**PHER
SP**I**NRAD
SP**I**TZER
SW**I**GERT
SZ**I**LARD
TA**I**NTER
WE**I**ZMAN
WH**I**PPLE
WH**I**STON
WH**I**TNEY
WH**I**TTLE
ZE**I**DLER
EI**J**KMAN
AC**K**LAND
AI**K**ICHI
BA**K**HUIS
DU**K**AKIS
DY**K**STRA
HO**K**FELT
JO**K**ICHI
MI**K**HAIL
NI**K**ITIN
NI**K**LAUS

NI**K**OLAI
NI**K**OLAY
NY**K**VIST
SA**K**MANN
TA**K**ASHI
VE**K**SLER
WA**K**SMAN
AD**L**EMAN
AL**L**BUTT
BE**L**KNAP
BE**L**LINI
BE**L**ZONI
BO**L**ZANO
BU**L**LOCK
CE**L**ESTE
CE**L**SIUS
CH**L**ADNI
CO**L**BERT
CO**L**DITZ
CO**L**LINS
CO**L**OMBO
CO**L**UMBO
DE**L**BERT
DE**L**EDDA
DE**L**IGNE
DE**L**ISLE
DO**L**LOND
EL**L**IOTT
EL**L**MANN
FI**L**IPPO
FO**L**KERS
FO**L**KMAN
GA**L**ILEO
GA**L**VANI
GE**L**FAND
GE**L**LERT
GI**L**BERT
GO**L**DING
GO**L**DMAN
HA**L**DANE
HA**L**LDOR
HA**L**PERN
HA**L**STED
HI**L**AIRE
HI**L**BERT
HI**L**LARY
HI**L**LIER
HI**L**YARD
KE**L**LOGG
KO**L**STER
LE**L**OUCH
MA**L**COLM
MA**L**LAND
MA**L**LORY
MA**L**THUS
ME**L**LONI

MI**L**FORD
MI**L**LAND
OR**L**ANDO
PA**L**ANCE
PA**L**ISSY
PE**L**IGOT
PE**L**LING
PE**L**TIER
PI**L**ATRE
PI**L**BEAM
PO**L**ANYI
PO**L**LACK
PU**L**LMAN
RA**L**EIGH
RA**L**STON
RO**L**LAND
SA**L**ILEI
SA**L**OMEN
SO**L**OMON
SO**L**OVAY
SY**L**BERT
SY**L**VIUS
TE**L**ESIO
TE**L**FORD
VA**L**MONT
VI**L**HELM
VI**L**LARD
VO**L**HARD
VO**L**KOFF
WA**L**COTT
WA**L**LACE
WA**L**LACH
WA**L**THER
WE**L**LAND
WE**L**LMAN
WI**L**CZEL
WI**L**FRED
WI**L**HELM
WI**L**KINS
WI**L**LANS
WI**L**LARD
WI**L**LIAM
YO**L**ANDA
CA**M**ERON
CA**M**ILLE
CA**M**ILLO
CA**M**PION
CO**M**PTON
CU**M**MING
DO**M**INGO
GE**M**INUS
GO**M**BERG
HA**M**MANN
HA**M**MOND
HA**M**PSON
HA**M**PTON

HO**M**BERG
HO**M**EYER
HU**M**ASON
HU**M**PHRY
JE**M**ISON
JI**M**ENEZ
KO**M**AROV
LA**M**BERT
LA**M**RACK
LU**M**IERE
MO**M**MSEN
OL**M**STED
PO**M**EROY
RA**M**SDEN
RE**M**NICK
RO**M**ANES
RU**M**FORD
SE**M**ENOV
SI**M**PSON
SU**M**MERS
TI**M**OTHY
XI**M**ENES
AN**N**AEUS
BA**N**GHAM
BA**N**TING
BE**N**NETT
BE**N**THAM
BI**N**GHAM
CA**N**ETTI
CO**N**NERY
CO**N**YERS
DA**N**GEAU
DA**N**IELE
DA**N**IELL
DA**N**IELS
DE**N**ISON
DO**N**DERS
DO**N**NALL
DU**N**AWAY
DU**N**NING
EI**N**HORN
ER**N**ESTO
FO**N**TANA
GO**N**ZALO
HA**N**TARO
HE**N**DRIK
HE**N**LEIN
HE**N**NESY
HE**N**RICK
IG**N**ACIO
JA**N**SSEN
JE**N**KINS
JE**N**SSON
KE**N**DALL
KE**N**DREW
KE**N**ICHI

KE**N**NEDY
KE**N**NETH
KI**N**GDOM
KU**N**CKEL
LA**N**CISI
LA**N**GLEY
LA**N**STON
LI**N**ACRE
LI**N**COLN
LU**N**ARDI
MA**N**DELA
MA**N**DELL
MA**N**FRED
MA**N**TELL
ME**N**GOLI
ME**N**ZIES
MO**N**DINO
MO**N**TAGU
MO**N**TALE
MO**N**ZANI
MU**N**STER
PA**N**CINI
PE**N**ROSE
PE**N**ZIAS
RE**N**AULT
RU**N**NELS
SA**N**CHEZ
SA**N**DAGE
SA**N**DERS
SI**N**ATRA
TE**N**NANT
TE**N**ZING
TY**N**DALL
VA**N**ESSA
VE**N**KATA
VE**N**TRIS
VI**N**CENT
WA**N**TZEL
WE**N**DELL
WE**N**TZEL
WI**N**DAUS
WI**N**KLER
WI**N**SLOW
WI**N**STON
WI**N**TERS
ZA**N**ETTI
ZI**N**SSER
AD**O**LPHE
AD**O**LPHO
AR**O**BLES
BJ**O**RKEN
BJ**O**RNST
BR**O**ADUS
BR**O**DSKY
BR**O**UWER
CH**O**MSKY

CL**O**PTON
CL**O**QUET
CL**O**USER
CR**O**OKES
DI**O**CLES
ED**O**UARD
ED**O**UART
FL**O**WERS
GE**O**RGES
GE**O**RGII
GI**O**RGOS
GI**O**VANI
GO**O**DHUE
GO**O**DMAN
GO**O**DWIN
GO**O**SSON
GR**O**ESSE
GY**O**RGYI
KH**O**RANA
KR**O**EKEL
LE**O**NARD
LE**O**POLD
PA**O**LINI
PE**O**PPEL
PH**O**EBUS
PR**O**CLUS
PR**O**CTOR
PT**O**LEMY
SH**O**ICHI
SJ**O**BERG
ST**O**RARO
SZ**O**STAK
TE**O**DORO
TH**O**MSEN
TH**O**MSON
WO**O**DGER
WO**O**DROW
WO**O**LLEY
WO**O**STER
AE**P**INUS
CO**P**POLA
DO**P**PLER
EM**P**EROR
HE**P**BURN
HI**P**PIAS
HO**P**KINS
HO**P**WOOD
HY**P**ATIA
KA**P**ITZA
KA**P**TEYN
KI**P**LING
KI**P**PING
LA**P**LACE
LA**P**ORTE
LI**P**MANN
RA**P**HAEL

TIPPETT
SEQUARD
ABRAHAM
ADRIAAN
ADRIAEN
AGRIPPA
ARRIGHI
BARBARA
BARDEEN
BARNARD
BARNETT
BERGIUS
BERGMAN
BERGSON
BERNARD
BERTRAM
BERWICK
BORDERS
BORELLI
BORLAUG
BORZAGE
BURBANK
BURIDAN
BURNELL
BURNETT
BURROWS
BURSTYN
BURWELL
CARDANO
CARDIFF
CARLSON
CARLYLE
CAROLUS
CAROLYN
CARRERE
CARRIER
CARROLL
CERLUTI
CHRISTY
CORDELL
CORLISS
CORMACK
CORRENS
CURTISS
DARLING
DARWELL
DOROTHY
EHRLICH
FARACHI
FARCIOT
FARNHAM
FERNAND
FERRARI
FERRIER
FOREMAN
FORREST
GARBETT
GARDNER
GARMIRE
GERBERT
GERHARD
GERHART
GERMAIN
GERSTAD
GORGIAS
HARBURG
HARDING
HARKINS
HARLING
HARRIOT
HARTLEY
HARTMAN
HARTMUT
HERBERT
HERCZEG
HERMANN
HERMITE
HEROULT
HERRING
HERSHEY
HIROSHI
HORNING
HORSLEY
JARCHUS
KIRCHER
LARDNER
LORENTZ
LORENZO
LORETTA
LORIMER
LORRAIN
LURSSEN
MARALDI
MARCONI
MARQUEZ
MARQUIS
MARSHAK
MARTINE
MERRIAM
MERRILL
MURDOCK
NORBERT
NORRISH
OERSTED
PARESCE
PARRISH
PARSONS
PEREIRA
PERINAL
PERNIER
PERRINE
PERTHES
PORSCHE
PORSILD
PURCELL
SARGENT
SAROYAN
SERVAIS
SORVINO
SPRAGUE
STRABEL
SURTEES
TARAGAY
TARLOFF
TERENCE
TERRILE
TORBERN
TORELLO
TORSTEN
VERNIER
VIRCHOW
WARBURG
WERNHER
WORTLEY
ZERMELO
ZERNIKE
ANSELME
CASIMIR
CASSINI
CASTELI
CASTNER
COSTNER
CUSHING
DESAULT
DESMOND
EASTMAN
EPSTEIN
EUSTACE
FISCHER
GASPARD
GASSNER
GOSSAGE
GOSSETT
GUSELLA
GUSTAVE
HASKELL
JESSICA
KASIMIR
KASTLER
LASSELL
LYSENKO
MASASHI
MESSIER
MISTRAL
MOSELEY
ONSAGER
PASCHEN
PASTEUR
ROSALYN
RUSSELL
SUSANNE
SUSRATA
SUSSMAN
WISLAWA
YOSHIDA
ACTINUS
ANTHONY
ANTOINE
ANTONIO
APTHROP
ARTTURI
ASTBURY
BATESON
BATFOUR
BITTNER
BOTTGER
BUTTONS
CATALDI
CATESBY
CATLETT
CATTELL
COTTELL
ESTELLE
FITZROY
GATLING
GOTTLOB
GUTHRIE
HATTORI
HITTORF
MATTHAU
MATTHEW
NATHANS
OCTAVIO
OSTWALD
OTTILIA
PATRICK
PYTHEAS
RETZIUS
ROTBLAT
USTINOV
WOTTITZ
YITZHAK
AQUINAS
BAUMANN
BOUCHER
BOUGUER
BOULTON
BOURATT
BOUVARD
BRUGSCH
BRUNHES
CHUQUET
COULTER
COULUMB
CRUTZEN
DAUBREE
DAUSSET
DOUGLAS
FOURIER
GAUSMAN
HOUSSAY
JOUHAUX
KAUFMAN
LAURENT
LEUPOLD
MAUCHLY
MAUMONT
MAUNDER
MAUREEN
MAURIAC
MAURICE
MOULTON
PAULING
PLUCKER
POULSEN
ROUELLE
SAUVEUR
SHUFTAN
SHUNPEI
STURGES
VAUGHAN
ALVAREZ
DEVILLE
DEVRIES
HAVLICK
LAVERAN
OSVALDO
PEVONAK
SAVEGAR
SEVERIN
SEVERUS
VAVILOV
VIVIANI
WYVILLE
HAWKING
HAWKINS
HAWORTH
NEWCOMB
ROWLAND
LAXNESS
MAXSTED
MAXWELL
PAXINOU
BEYRICH
BRYNNER
FEYNMAN
HAYFORD
HAYWARD
HEYMANS
HUYGENS
KIYOSHI
MAYNARD
MIYOAKA
MIYOSHI
OLYMPIA
PHYLLIS
RAYMOND
REYMOND
REYMONT
SEYMOUR
SOYINKA
ULYSSES
KAZAKOV
KOZYREV
LAZARUS
LAZZARO
PIZARRO
RUZICKA
SUZANNE

### 4th Letter

ABRAHAM
ALCAEUS
ALHAZEN
ALVAREZ
ANNAEUS
ATHAIYA
BROADUS
CABAEUS
CATALDI
CHLADNI
DESAULT
DUHAMEL
DUKAKIS
DUNAWAY
FARACHI
GAGARIN
GLEASON
HILAIRE
HUMASON
HYPATIA
IGNACIO
KAZAKOV
KOMAROV
LAZARUS
LINACRE
LUNARDI
MACAVIN
MARALDI
MASASHI
MCCAREY
MOHAMED
NAGAOKA
OCTAVIO
ONSAGER
ORLANDO
OSVALDO
PALANCE
PILATRE
PIZARRO
POLANYI
RENAULT
ROBARDS
ROMANES
ROSALYN
SCHAFER
SCHALLY
SHEARER
SINATRA
SMEATON
SPRAGUE
STEARNS
STRABEL
SUSANNE
SUZANNE
TADASHI
TAKASHI
TARAGAY
YOLANDA
ALLBUTT
AROBLES
ASTBURY
BARBARA
BURBANK
COLBERT
DAUBREE
DELBERT
DREBBEL
EKEBERG
GARBETT
GERBERT
GIBBONS
GILBERT
GOMBERG
HARBURG
HEPBURN
HERBERT
HILBERT
HOMBERG
ICHBIAH
KIEBACH
LAMBERT
LEIBNIZ
NORBERT
PILBEAM
ROBBINS
RODBELL
ROEBUCK
ROTBLAT
RUDBECK
RYDBERG
SEABORG
SEEBECK
SJOBERG
SYLBERT
TORBERN
WARBURG
BEECHER
BOUCHER
DIOCLES
FARCIOT
FISCHER
FRECHET
FRICKER
GIACOMO
HAECKEL
HERCZEG
JARCHUS
JOACHIM
KIRCHER
KUNCKEL
LANCISI
LINCOLN
MALCOLM
MARCONI
MAUCHLY
NEWCOMB
NICCOLO
PACCARD
PANCINI
PASCHEN
PEACOCK
PICCARD
PLUCKER
PRACHAR
PROCLUS
PROCTOR
PURCELL
RICCATI
SANCHEZ
SPECTOR
VINCENT
VIRCHOW
WALCOTT
WILCZEL
BARDEEN
BEDDOES
BORDERS
BRADLEY
BRIDGES
BRODSKY
CARDANO
CARDIFF
COLDITZ
CORDELL
DONDERS
FREDDIE
FREDRIC
FREDRIK
GARDNER
GODDARD
GOLDING
GOLDMAN

GOODHUE
GOODMAN
GOODWIN
HADDOCK
HALDANE
HARDING
HENDRIK
ISADORE
ISIDORE
KENDALL
KENDREW
KIDDINU
LARDNER
LUEDTKE
MANDELA
MANDELL
MONDINO
MURDOCK
NEEDHAM
NODDACK
PHIDIAS
SANDAGE
SANDERS
TEODORO
THADEUS
TYNDALL
WENDELL
WINDAUS
WOODGER
WOODROW
ZABDIEL
ZEIDLER
ACHESON
ADLEMAN
ALBERTI
ANGELOS
ANSELME
BATESON
BIGELOW
BORELLI
CAMERON
CANETTI
CATESBY
CECELIA
CELESTE
DELEDDA
DIDERIK
DIDEROT
DOHERTY
EMPEROR
ERNESTO
ESTELLE
ETIENNE
EUDEMUS
EUGENIO
FOREMAN
FREEMAN
FRIEDEL
GLAEVER
GROESSE
GUSELLA
HAGEMAN
HOMEYER
JIMENEZ
JOCELYN
KROEKEL
LAVERAN
LEBEDEV
LORENTZ
LORENZO
LORETTA
LYSENKO
MOSELEY
PARESCE
PEREIRA
PHOEBUS
POMEROY
RALEIGH
ROBERTO
ROBERTS
ROUELLE
SAVEGAR
SCHEELE
SEFERIS
SEMENOV
SEVERIN
SEVERUS
SHEEHAN
SHIELDS
TADEUSZ
TEDESCO
TELESIO
TERENCE
TORELLO
VANESSA
VICENTE
WEGENER
WHEELER
XIMENES
ZANETTI
BATFOUR
CHAFFEE
GELFAND
GIFFARD
GODFREY
GRIFFIN
GUFFROY
HAYFORD
HOFFMAN
HOKFELT
JEFFERY
KAUFMAN
KNIFTON
LOFFLER
MAHFOUZ
MANFRED
MILFORD
PFEFFER
REDFORD
RUFFINI
RUMFORD
SEIFERT
SHAFFER
SHUFTAN
TELFORD
WILFRED
BANGHAM
BERGIUS
BERGMAN
BERGSON
BINGHAM
BLAGDEN
BOUGUER
BRUGSCH
DANGEAU
DOUGLAS
EXIGUUS
GORGIAS
GREGORY
HODGKIN
HUGGINS
HUYGENS
KINGDOM
LANGLEY
MENGOLI
MIDGLEY
SARGENT
SWIGERT
VAUGHAN
ZIEGLER
ANTHONY
APTHROP
BAKHUIS
BOEHMER
BUCHMAN
BUCHNER
CUSHING
EINHORN
FECHNER
GERHARD
GERHART
GRAHAME
GUTHRIE
JOUHAUX
MEGHNAD
MICHAEL
MICHAIL
MICHELE
MICHELL
MIKHAIL
NATHANS
NICHOLS
PYTHEAS
RAPHAEL
RICHARD
RICHLIN
RICHTER
VILHELM
VOLHARD
WILHELM
YOSHIDA
ZACHARY
ACHILLE
ACTINUS
ADDISON
ADRIAAN
ADRIAEN
AEPINUS
AGRIPPA
AIKICHI
ALBINUS
AQUINAS
ARRIGHI
BURIDAN
CABIBBO
CAMILLE
CAMILLO
CASIMIR
CHRISTY
DANIELE
DANIELL
DANIELS
DELIGNE
DELISLE
DENISON
DEVILLE
DOMINGO
ELLIOTT
FIBIGER
FILIPPO
GALILEO
GEMINUS
ISHIOKA
JACINTO
JEMISON
JOKICHI
KAPITZA
KASIMIR
KENICHI
LORIMER
LUCIANA
LUMIERE
MADISON
NIKITIN
OTTILIA
PACIOLI
PALISSY
PAXINOU
PELIGOT
PERINAL
ROBINET
ROBISON
RUZICKA
SALILEI
SCHIRRA
SHOICHI
SOYINKA
SPEISER
STEIGER
STEINER
THEILER
USTINOV
VAVILOV
VIVIANI
WYVILLE
BECKETT
BECKLIN
BECKMAN
BELKNAP
DICKSON
EIJKMAN
EZEKIEL
FOLKERS
FOLKMAN
HACKMAN
HARKINS
HASKELL
HAWKING
HAWKINS
HECKART
HICKMAN
HOPKINS
JACKSON
JEAKINS
JENKINS
LOCKYER
PICKARD
VENKATA
VOLKOFF
WILKINS
WINKLER
WYCKOFF
ABELARD
ABELSON
ACKLAND
ADELARD
ADOLPHE
ADOLPHO
AXELROD
BELLINI
BLALACK
BLALOCK
BORLAUG
BOULTON
BULLOCK
CARLSON
CARLYLE
CATLETT
CERLUTI
CHELPIN
COLLINS
CORLISS
COULTER
COULUMB
DARLING
DOLLOND
DUILLER
EDELMAN
EHRLICH
GATLING
GELLERT
GIELGUD
GUILLET
HALLDOR
HARLING
HAVLICK
HENLEIN
HILLARY
HILLIER
HJALMAR
KELLOGG
KIPLING
LAPLACE
LEBLANC
LECLERC
MACLURE
MAELZEL
MALLAND
MALLORY
MCCLUNG
MELLONI
MILLAND
MOULTON
MUELLER
NIELSON
NIKLAUS
PAOLINI
PAULING
PELLING
PHILIPP
PHILIPS
PHILLIP
PHYLLIS
POLLACK
POULSEN
PTOLEMY
PULLMAN
ROLLAND
ROWLAND
SCHLACK
SHELDON
SHELLEY
SHELTON
SMALLEY
SMELLIE
SZILARD
TARLOFF
VILLARD
WALLACE
WALLACH
WELLAND
WELLMAN
WIELAND
WILLANS
WILLARD
WILLIAM
WISLAWA
WOOLLEY
ASHMOLE
BAUMANN
CHOMSKY
CLEMENS
CLEMENT
CORMACK
CREMMER
CUMMING
DAIMLER
DEHMELT
DESMOND
DIAMOND
EDEMANN
ELLMANN
FLEMING
GARMIRE
GERMAIN
HAMMANN
HAMMOND
HERMANN
HERMITE
HEYMANS
HOFMANN
KAEMPFE
KRAMERS
LEHMANN
LIPMANN
MAUMONT
MOMMSEN
OLYMPIA
RAYMOND
REIMANN
REYMOND
REYMONT
SAKMANN
SCHMIDT
SCHMITT
SEYMOUR
SHAMROY
SIEMENS
SIGMUND
SPEMANN
SUMMERS
THOMSEN
THOMSON
VALMONT
WIDMANN
ZERMELO
ZYGMUNT
BARNARD
BARNETT
BEDNARZ
BEDNORZ
BENNETT
BERNARD
BRANDES
BRANTON
BRENNAN
BRENNER
BRUNHES
BRYNNER
BURNELL
BURNETT
CLINTON
CONNERY
DONNALL
DRINKER
DUNNING
EMANUAL
EMANUEL
FARNHAM
FERNAND
FEYNMAN
FRANCES
FRANCIS
HENNESY
HORNING
JOHNSON
KENNEDY
KENNETH
LAENNEC
LAXNESS
LEONARD
MAGNANI
MAUNDER
MAYNARD
MEINESZ
OTHNIEL
PERNIER
PRANDTL
QUENTIN
RADNITZ
RAINGER
REGNIER
REMNICK
RUNNELS
SCANLAN
SHANLEY

SHANNON
SHUNPEI
SKINNER
SPENCER
SPINRAD
STANLEY
STENDEL
TAINTER
TENNANT
THENARD
VERNIER
WERNHER
ZERNIKE
ALFONSO
ANTOINE
ANTONIO
CAROLUS
CAROLYN
COLOMBO
CROOKES
DOROTHY
EUDOXUS
GADOLIN
GHIORSO
HAWORTH
HEROULT
HIROSHI
IMHOTEP
JACOBUS
JODOCUS
KIYOSHI
LAPORTE
LELOUCH
MIYOAKA
MIYOSHI
NICOLAS
NICOLLE
NIKOLAI
NIKOLAY
OSBORNE
PEVONAK
RECORDE
RUDOLFF
RUDOLPH
SALOMEN
SAROYAN
SCHONER
SEBOKHT
SOLOMON
SOLOVAY
THEODOR
TIMOTHY
CAMPION
CHAPMAN
CHAPPEL
CHAPTAL
CLOPTON
COMPTON
COPPOLA
CRIPPEN
DOPPLER
GASPARD
HALPERN
HAMPSON
HAMPTON
HIPPIAS
HUMPHRY
KIPPING
LEIPOLD
LEOPOLD
LEUPOLD
PEOPPEL
SHAPIRO
SHAPLEY
SHEPARD
SHIPLER
SIMPSON
SLIPHER
STEPHAN
STEPHEN
STEPVEN
TIPPETT
WHIPPLE
CHUQUET
CLOQUET
JACQUES
MACQUER
MARQUEZ
MARQUIS
PECQUET
ALFREDO
AMBROSE
ANDREAS
ANDREWS
ANDRIJA
BEYRICH
BJORKEN
BJORNST
BLERIOT
BOURATT
BURROWS
CABRERA
CARRERE
CARRIER
CARROLL
CHARCOT
CHARLES
CHARNAY
CHARPAK
CORRENS
DEVRIES
EMERSON
EPHRAIM
FERRARI
FERRIER
FORREST
FOURIER
GABRIEL
GEHRING
GEORGES
GEORGII
GIORGOS
GOERGES
GYORGYI
HARRIOT
HEDRICK
HEERMAN
HENRICK
HERRING
JAHRAUS
JUERGEN
KEDROVA
KHORANA
KUBRICK
LAMRACK
LAURENT
LORRAIN
MAARTEN
MADRAZO
MAIREAD
MAUREEN
MAURIAC
MAURICE
MERRIAM
MERRILL
NORRISH
PARRISH
PATRICK
PEARSON
PENROSE
PERRINE
PIERSON
SEIRTON
SHARAFF
SHERIFF
SHERMAN
SHIRLEY
STARKEY
STARSKI
STORARO
STURGES
SUSRATA
TERRILE
WHARTON
WUERZER
AGASSIZ
BUISSON
BURSTYN
CASSINI
CELSIUS
CHASLES
CHESTER
CRESCAS
CZESLAW
DAUSSET
DYKSTRA
ERASMUS
FRESNEL
FRISIUS
GASSNER
GAUSMAN
GERSTAD
GLASHOW
GLISSON
GOOSSON
GOSSAGE
GOSSETT
GRESHAM
GRISSOM
HAFSTAD
HALSTED
HERSHEY
HORSLEY
HOUSSAY
JANSSEN
JENSSON
JESSICA
KOLSTER
KRASKER
KRASNER
LANSTON
LASSELL
LURSSEN
MARSHAK
MAXSTED
MESSIER
MOISSAN
MUNSTER
NEISSER
OERSTED
OLMSTED
PARSONS
POISSON
PORSCHE
PORSILD
PRESPER
PRESTON
PTASHNE
RALSTON
RAMSDEN
RUSSELL
SUSSMAN
SZOSTAK
TORSTEN
ULYSSES
VEKSLER
WAKSMAN
WHISTON
WINSLOW
WINSTON
WOOSTER
ZINSSER
ANATOLE
ARTTURI
BANTING
BENTHAM
BERTRAM
BITTNER
BOTTGER
BRETTON
BRITTON
BUTTONS
CASTELI
CASTNER
CATTELL
COSTNER
COTTELL
CRETIEN
CRUTZEN
CURTISS
EASTMAN
EPSTEIN
EUSTACE
FONTANA
FRITIOF
FRITSCH
GOTTLOB
GUSTAVE
HANTARO
HARTLEY
HARTMAN
HARTMUT
HATTORI
HEITLER
HITTORF
KAPTEYN
KASTLER
LUITZEN
MALTHUS
MANTELL
MARTINE
MATTHAU
MATTHEW
MEITNER
MISTRAL
MONTAGU
MONTALE
NOETHER
PASTEUR
PELTIER
PERTHES
POITIER
SPITZER
SURTEES
VENTRIS
WALTHER
WANTZEL
WENTZEL
WHITNEY
WHITTLE
WINTERS
WORTLEY
WOTTITZ
YEATMAN
AUDUBON
AUGUSTE
AUGUSTO
BEGUYER
BROUWER
CHAUCER
CLOUSER
COLUMBO
EDOUARD
EDOUART
GIAUQUE
GLAUBER
GLAUCUS
HIGUCHI
SCHURER
SEQUARD
THEURER
TRAUNER
BOUVARD
CLAVIUS
GALVANI
GIOVANI
LEAVITT
NYKVIST
OLIVIER
PREVOST
SAUVEUR
SERVAIS
SORVINO
STEVENS
SYLVIUS
TRAVERS
BERWICK
BURWELL
CLEWALL
DARWELL
FLOWERS
HAYWARD
HOPWOOD
MAXWELL
OSTWALD
SCHWABE
SCHWANN
STEWART
WHEWELL
DREXLER
CLAYTON
CONYERS
HILYARD
KHAYYAM
KOZYREV
RUDYARD
TIDYMAN
BELZONI
BOLZANO
BORZAGE
FITZROY
GONZALO
LAZZARO
MENZIES
MONZANI
PENZIAS
RETZIUS
TENZING
UMEZAWA
WEIZMAN
YITZHAK

## 5th Letter

ABELARD
ACKLAND
ADELARD
ADRIAAN
ADRIAEN
BARBARA
BARNARD
BAUMANN
BEDNARZ
BERNARD
BLALACK
BOLZANO
BORLAUG
BORZAGE
BOURATT
BOUVARD
BURBANK
CARDANO
CLEWALL
CORMACK
DONNALL
EDEMANN
EDOUARD
EDOUART
ELLMANN
EPHRAIM
EUSTACE
FERNAND
FERRARI
FONTANA
GALVANI
GASPARD
GELFAND
GERHARD
GERHART
GERMAIN
GIFFARD
GIOVANI
GODDARD
GONZALO
GOSSAGE
GRAHAME
GUSTAVE
HALDANE
HAMMANN
HANTARO
HAYWARD
HECKART
HERMANN
HEYMANS
HILLARY
HILYARD
HOFMANN
JAHRAUS
JOUHAUX
KENDALL
KHORANA
KIEBACH
LAMRACK
LAPLACE
LAZZARO
LEBLANC
LEHMANN
LEONARD
LIPMANN
LORRAIN
LUCIANA
MADRAZO
MAGNANI
MALLAND
MAYNARD
MICHAEL
MICHAIL
MIKHAIL
MILLAND
MIYOAKA
MONTAGU
MONTALE
MONZANI
NATHANS
NIKLAUS
NODDACK
OSTWALD
PACCARD
PICCARD
PICKARD
POLLACK
RAPHAEL
REIMANN
RICCATI

RICHARD
ROLLAND
ROWLAND
RUDYARD
SAKMANN
SANDAGE
SCHLACK
SCHWABE
SCHWANN
SEQUARD
SERVAIS
SHARAFF
SHEPARD
SPEMANN
STEWART
STORARO
SUSRATA
SZILARD
TENNANT
THENARD
TYNDALL
UMEZAWA
VENKATA
VILLARD
VIVIANI
VOLHARD
WALLACE
WALLACH
WELLAND
WIDMANN
WIELAND
WILLANS
WILLARD
WINDAUS
WISLAWA
ZACHARY
AUDUBON
CABIBBO
DREBBEL
GLAUBER
JACOBUS
PHOEBUS
STRABEL
AIKICHI
CHARCOT
CHAUCER
CRESCAS
FARACHI
FRANCES
FRANCIS
GLAUCUS
HIGUCHI
IGNACIO
JODOCUS
JOKICHI
KENICHI
LINACRE
PORSCHE
RUZICKA
SHOICHI
SPENCER
BLAGDEN
BRANDES
BROADUS
BURIDAN
CHLADNI
DELEDDA
FREDDIE
FRIEDEL
HALLDOR
KINGDOM
LEBEDEV
MAUNDER
PRANDTL
RAMSDEN
SHELDON
STENDEL
THEODOR
ALCAEUS
ALFREDO
ANDREAS
ANDREWS
ANNAEUS
BARDEEN
BARNETT
BECKETT
BENNETT
BORDERS
BURNELL
BURNETT
BURWELL
CABAEUS
CABRERA
CARRERE
CASTELI
CATLETT
CATTELL
CLEMENS
CLEMENT
COLBERT
CONNERY
CONYERS
CORDELL
CORRENS
COTTELL
DANGEAU
DANIELE
DANIELL
DANIELS
DARWELL
DEHMELT
DELBERT
DONDERS
EKEBERG
EPSTEIN
FLOWERS
FOLKERS
FORREST
GARBETT
GELLERT
GERBERT
GILBERT
GOMBERG
GOSSETT
HALPERN
HASKELL
HENLEIN
HENNESY
HERBERT
HILBERT
HOKFELT
HOMBERG
HUYGENS
JEFFERY
KAPTEYN
KENNEDY
KENNETH
KRAMERS
LAMBERT
LASSELL
LAURENT
LAXNESS
LECLERC
LUMIERE
MAIREAD
MANDELA
MANDELL
MANTELL
MAUREEN
MAXWELL
MEINESZ
MICHELE
MICHELL
NORBERT
PASTEUR
PILBEAM
PTOLEMY
PURCELL
PYTHEAS
RODBELL
RUDBECK
RUNNELS
RUSSELL
RYDBERG
SANDERS
SARGENT
SAUVEUR
SCHEELE
SEEBECK
SEIFERT
SIEMENS
SJOBERG
STEVENS
SUMMERS
SURTEES
SWIGERT
SYLBERT
THADEUS
TIPPETT
TORBERN
TRAVERS
VILHELM
VINCENT
WENDELL
WHEWELL
WILHELM
WINTERS
ZERMELO
CHAFFEE
GRIFFIN
PFEFFER
SCHAFER
SHAFFER
ARRIGHI
BOTTGER
BRIDGES
DELIGNE
FIBIGER
GEORGES
GEORGII
GIELGUD
GIORGOS
GOERGES
GYORGYI
JUERGEN
ONSAGER
PELIGOT
RAINGER
SAVEGAR
SPRAGUE
STEIGER
STURGES
TARAGAY
WOODGER
ABRAHAM
BANGHAM
BEECHER
BENTHAM
BINGHAM
BOUCHER
BRUNHES
FARNHAM
FISCHER
FRECHET
GLASHOW
GOODHUE
GRESHAM
HERSHEY
HUMPHRY
JARCHUS
JOACHIM
KIRCHER
MALTHUS
MARSHAK
MATTHAU
MATTHEW
MAUCHLY
NEEDHAM
NOETHER
PASCHEN
PERTHES
PRACHAR
PTASHNE
SANCHEZ
SHEEHAN
SLIPHER
STEPHAN
STEPHEN
VAUGHAN
VIRCHOW
WALTHER
WERNHER
YITZHAK
ANDRIJA
ANTOINE
ATHAIYA
BANTING
BELLINI
BERGIUS
BERWICK
BEYRICH
BLERIOT
CAMPION
CARDIFF
CARRIER
CASSINI
CELSIUS
CLAVIUS
COLDITZ
COLLINS
CORLISS
CRETIEN
CUMMING
CURTISS
CUSHING
DARLING
DEVRIES
DUNNING
EHRLICH
EZEKIEL
FARCIOT
FERRIER
FLEMING
FOURIER
FRISIUS
FRITIOF
GABRIEL
GARMIRE
GATLING
GEHRING
GOLDING
GORGIAS
HARDING
HARKINS
HARLING
HARRIOT
HAVLICK
HAWKING
HAWKINS
HEDRICK
HENRICK
HERMITE
HERRING
HILAIRE
HILLIER
HIPPIAS
HOPKINS
HORNING
HUGGINS
ICHBIAH
JEAKINS
JENKINS
JESSICA
KIDDINU
KIPLING
KIPPING
KUBRICK
LANCISI
LEAVITT
MARTINE
MAURIAC
MAURICE
MENZIES
MERRIAM
MERRILL
MESSIER
MONDINO
NORRISH
NYKVIST
OLIVIER
OTHNIEL
PANCINI
PAOLINI
PARRISH
PATRICK
PAULING
PELLING
PELTIER
PENZIAS
PEREIRA
PERNIER
PERRINE
PHIDIAS
PHILIPP
PHILIPS
POITIER
PORSILD
RADNITZ
RALEIGH
REGNIER
REMNICK
RETZIUS
ROBBINS
RUFFINI
SCHMIDT
SCHMITT
SHAPIRO
SHERIFF
SORVINO
SYLVIUS
TENZING
TERRILE
VERNIER
WILKINS
WILLIAM
WOTTITZ
YOSHIDA
ZABDIEL
ZERNIKE
BJORKEN
CROOKES
DRINKER
DUKAKIS
FRICKER
HAECKEL
HODGKIN
KAZAKOV
KRASKER
KROEKEL
KUNCKEL
PLUCKER
SEBOKHT
STARKEY
ACHILLE
ANGELOS
ANSELME
AROBLES
BECKLIN
BIGELOW
BORELLI
BRADLEY
CAMILLE
CAMILLO
CAROLUS
CAROLYN
CATALDI
CECELIA
CHARLES
CHASLES
CZESLAW
DAIMLER
DEVILLE
DIOCLES
DOPPLER
DOUGLAS
DREXLER
DUILLER
ESTELLE
GADOLIN
GALILEO
GOTTLOB
GUILLET
GUSELLA
HARTLEY
HEITLER
HORSLEY
JOCELYN
KASTLER
LANGLEY
LOFFLER
MARALDI
MIDGLEY
MOSELEY
MUELLER
NICOLAS
NICOLLE
NIKOLAI
NIKOLAY
OSVALDO
OTTILIA
PHILLIP
PHYLLIS
PROCLUS
RICHLIN
ROSALYN
ROTBLAT
ROUELLE
RUDOLFF
RUDOLPH
SALILEI
SCANLAN
SCHALLY
SHANLEY
SHAPLEY
SHELLEY
SHIELDS
SHIPLER
SHIRLEY
SMALLEY
SMELLIE
STANLEY
THEILER
TORELLO
VAVILOV
VEKSLER
WHEELER

WINKLER
WINSLOW
WOOLLEY
WORTLEY
WYVILLE
ZEIDLER
ZIEGLER
ADLEMAN
BECKMAN
BERGMAN
BOEHMER
BUCHMAN
CASIMIR
CHAPMAN
COLOMBO
COLUMBO
CREMMER
DUHAMEL
EASTMAN
EDELMAN
EIJKMAN
ERASMUS
EUDEMUS
FEYNMAN
FOLKMAN
FOREMAN
FREEMAN
GAUSMAN
GOLDMAN
GOODMAN
HACKMAN
HAGEMAN
HARTMAN
HARTMUT
HEERMAN
HICKMAN
HJALMAR
HOFFMAN
KASIMIR
KAUFMAN
LORIMER
MOHAMED
PULLMAN
SALOMEN
SHERMAN
SOLOMON
SUSSMAN
TIDYMAN
WAKSMAN
WEIZMAN
WELLMAN
YEATMAN
ACTINUS
AEPINUS
ALBINUS
ALFONSO
ANTONIO

AQUINAS
BELKNAP
BITTNER
BJORNST
BRENNAN
BRENNER
BRYNNER
BUCHNER
CASTNER
CHARNAY
COSTNER
DOMINGO
ETIENNE
EUGENIO
FECHNER
FRESNEL
GARDNER
GASSNER
GEMINUS
JACINTO
JIMENEZ
KRASNER
LAENNEC
LARDNER
LEIBNIZ
LORENTZ
LORENZO
LYSENKO
MEGHNAD
MEITNER
ORLANDO
PALANCE
PAXINOU
PERINAL
PEVONAK
POLANYI
ROBINET
ROMANES
SCHONER
SEMENOV
SHANNON
SKINNER
SOYINKA
STEINER
SUSANNE
SUZANNE
TERENCE
TRAUNER
USTINOV
VICENTE
WEGENER
WHITNEY
XIMENES
YOLANDA
AMBROSE
ANATOLE
ANTHONY

ASHMOLE
BATFOUR
BEDDOES
BEDNORZ
BELZONI
BLALOCK
BULLOCK
BURROWS
BUTTONS
CARROLL
COPPOLA
DESMOND
DIAMOND
DOLLOND
EINHORN
ELLIOTT
GIACOMO
GIBBONS
GREGORY
HADDOCK
HAMMOND
HATTORI
HAYFORD
HITTORF
HOPWOOD
ISADORE
ISHIOKA
ISIDORE
KEDROVA
KELLOGG
LEIPOLD
LEOPOLD
LEUPOLD
LINCOLN
MAHFOUZ
MALCOLM
MALLORY
MARCONI
MAUMONT
MELLONI
MENGOLI
MILFORD
MURDOCK
NAGAOKA
NEWCOMB
NICCOLO
NICHOLS
PACIOLI
PARSONS
PEACOCK
PENROSE
PREVOST
RAYMOND
REDFORD
REYMOND
REYMONT
RUMFORD

SEABORG
SEYMOUR
TARLOFF
TELFORD
TEODORO
VALMONT
VOLKOFF
WALCOTT
WYCKOFF
ADOLPHE
ADOLPHO
AGRIPPA
CHAPPEL
CHARPAK
CHELPIN
CRIPPEN
FILIPPO
KAEMPFE
OLYMPIA
PEOPPEL
PRESPER
SHUNPEI
WHIPPLE
GIAUQUE
ALBERTI
ALVAREZ
APTHROP
AXELROD
BERTRAM
CAMERON
DAUBREE
DIDERIK
DIDEROT
DOHERTY
EMPEROR
FITZROY
FREDRIC
FREDRIK
GAGARIN
GHIORSO
GODFREY
GUFFROY
GUTHRIE
HAWORTH
HENDRIK
KENDREW
KOMAROV
KOZYREV
LAPORTE
LAVERAN
LAZARUS
LUNARDI
MANFRED
MCCAREY
MISTRAL
OSBORNE
PIZARRO

POMEROY
RECORDE
ROBARDS
ROBERTO
ROBERTS
SCHIRRA
SCHURER
SEFERIS
SEVERIN
SEVERUS
SHAMROY
SHEARER
SPINRAD
STEARNS
THEURER
VENTRIS
WILFRED
WOODROW
ABELSON
ACHESON
ADDISON
AGASSIZ
AUGUSTE
AUGUSTO
BATESON
BERGSON
BRODSKY
BRUGSCH
BUISSON
CARLSON
CATESBY
CELESTE
CHOMSKY
CHRISTY
CLOUSER
DAUSSET
DELISLE
DENISON
DICKSON
EMERSON
ERNESTO
FRITSCH
GLEASON
GLISSON
GOOSSON
GRISSOM
GROESSE
HAMPSON
HIROSHI
HOUSSAY
HUMASON
JACKSON
JANSSEN
JEMISON
JENSSON
JOHNSON
KIYOSHI

LURSSEN
MADISON
MASASHI
MIYOSHI
MOISSAN
MOMMSEN
NEISSER
NIELSON
PALISSY
PARESCE
PEARSON
PIERSON
POISSON
POULSEN
ROBISON
SIMPSON
SPEISER
STARSKI
TADASHI
TAKASHI
TEDESCO
TELESIO
THOMSEN
THOMSON
ULYSSES
VANESSA
ZINSSER
BOULTON
BRANTON
BRETTON
BRITTON
BURSTYN
CANETTI
CHAPTAL
CHESTER
CLAYTON
CLINTON
CLOPTON
COMPTON
COULTER
DOROTHY
DYKSTRA
GERSTAD
HAFSTAD
HALSTED
HAMPTON
HYPATIA
IMHOTEP
KAPITZA
KNIFTON
KOLSTER
LANSTON
LORETTA
LUEDTKE
MAARTEN
MAXSTED
MOULTON

MUNSTER
NIKITIN
OERSTED
OLMSTED
PILATRE
PRESTON
PROCTOR
QUENTIN
RALSTON
RICHTER
SEIRTON
SHELTON
SHUFTAN
SINATRA
SMEATON
SPECTOR
SZOSTAK
TAINTER
TIMOTHY
TORSTEN
WHARTON
WHISTON
WHITTLE
WINSTON
WOOSTER
ZANETTI
ALLBUTT
ARTTURI
ASTBURY
BAKHUIS
BOUGUER
CERLUTI
CHUQUET
CLOQUET
COULUMB
DESAULT
EMANUAL
EMANUEL
EXIGUUS
HARBURG
HEPBURN
HEROULT
JACQUES
LELOUCH
MACLURE
MACQUER
MARQUEZ
MARQUIS
MCCLUNG
PECQUET
RENAULT
ROEBUCK
SIGMUND
TADEUSZ
WARBURG
ZYGMUNT
GLAEVER

MACAVIN
OCTAVIO
SOLOVAY
STEPVEN
BROUWER
DUNAWAY
GOODWIN
EUDOXUS
BEGUYER
CARLYLE
HOMEYER
KHAYYAM
LOCKYER
SAROYAN
ALHAZEN
CRUTZEN
HERCZEG
LUITZEN
MAELZEL
SPITZER
WANTZEL
WENTZEL
WILCZEL
WUERZER

## 6th Letter

ABRAHAM
ADLEMAN
ADRIAAN
ANDREAS
AQUINAS
BANGHAM
BECKMAN
BELKNAP
BENTHAM
BERGMAN
BERTRAM
BINGHAM
BRENNAN
BUCHMAN
BURIDAN
CHAPMAN
CHAPTAL
CHARNAY
CHARPAK
CRESCAS
CZESLAW
DANGEAU
DOUGLAS
DUNAWAY
EASTMAN
EDELMAN
EIJKMAN
EMANUAL

FARNHAM
FEYNMAN
FOLKMAN
FOREMAN
FREEMAN
GAUSMAN
GERSTAD
GOLDMAN
GOODMAN
GORGIAS
GRESHAM
HACKMAN
HAFSTAD
HAGEMAN
HARTMAN
HEERMAN
HICKMAN
HIPPIAS
HJALMAR
HOFFMAN
HOUSSAY
ICHBIAH
KAUFMAN
KHAYYAM
LAVERAN
MAIREAD
MARSHAK
MATTHAU
MAURIAC
MEGHNAD
MERRIAM
MISTRAL
MOISSAN
NEEDHAM
NICOLAS
NIKOLAI
NIKOLAY
PENZIAS
PERINAL
PEVONAK
PHIDIAS
PILBEAM
PRACHAR
PULLMAN
PYTHEAS
ROTBLAT
SAROYAN
SAVEGAR
SCANLAN
SHEEHAN
SHERMAN
SHUFTAN
SOLOVAY
SPINRAD
STEPHAN
SUSSMAN
SZOSTAK

TARAGAY
TIDYMAN
VAUGHAN
WAKSMAN
WEIZMAN
WELLMAN
WILLIAM
YEATMAN
YITZHAK
CABIBBO
CATESBY
COLOMBO
COLUMBO
SCHWABE
BERWICK
BEYRICH
BLALACK
BLALOCK
BRUGSCH
BULLOCK
CORMACK
EHRLICH
EUSTACE
FRITSCH
HADDOCK
HAVLICK
HEDRICK
HENRICK
JESSICA
KIEBACH
KUBRICK
LAMRACK
LAPLACE
LELOUCH
MAURICE
MURDOCK
NODDACK
PALANCE
PARESCE
PATRICK
PEACOCK
POLLACK
REMNICK
ROEBUCK
RUDBECK
SCHLACK
SEEBECK
TEDESCO
TERENCE
WALLACE
WALLACH
ALFREDO
CATALDI
DELEDDA
KENNEDY
LUNARDI
MARALDI

ORLANDO
OSVALDO
RECORDE
ROBARDS
SCHMIDT
SHIELDS
YOLANDA
YOSHIDA
ADRIAEN
ALHAZEN
ALVAREZ
AROBLES
BARDEEN
BEDDOES
BEECHER
BEGUYER
BITTNER
BJORKEN
BLAGDEN
BOEHMER
BOTTGER
BOUCHER
BOUGUER
BRADLEY
BRANDES
BRENNER
BRIDGES
BROUWER
BRUNHES
BRYNNER
BUCHNER
CARRIER
CASTNER
CHAFFEE
CHAPPEL
CHARLES
CHASLES
CHAUCER
CHESTER
CHUQUET
CLOQUET
CLOUSER
COSTNER
COULTER
CREMMER
CRETIEN
CRIPPEN
CROOKES
CRUTZEN
DAIMLER
DAUBREE
DAUSSET
DEVRIES
DIOCLES
DOPPLER
DREBBEL
DREXLER

DRINKER
DUHAMEL
DUILLER
EMANUEL
EZEKIEL
FECHNER
FERRIER
FIBIGER
FISCHER
FOURIER
FRANCES
FRECHET
FRESNEL
FRICKER
FRIEDEL
GABRIEL
GALILEO
GARDNER
GASSNER
GEORGES
GLAEVER
GLAUBER
GODFREY
GOERGES
GUILLET
HAECKEL
HALSTED
HARTLEY
HEITLER
HERCZEG
HERSHEY
HILLIER
HOMEYER
HORSLEY
IMHOTEP
JACQUES
JANSSEN
JIMENEZ
JUERGEN
KASTLER
KENDREW
KIRCHER
KOLSTER
KOZYREV
KRASKER
KRASNER
KROEKEL
KUNCKEL
LAENNEC
LANGLEY
LARDNER
LEBEDEV
LOCKYER
LOFFLER
LORIMER
LUITZEN
LURSSEN

MAARTEN
MACQUER
MAELZEL
MANFRED
MARQUEZ
MATTHEW
MAUNDER
MAUREEN
MAXSTED
MCCAREY
MEITNER
MENZIES
MESSIER
MICHAEL
MIDGLEY
MOHAMED
MOMMSEN
MOSELEY
MUELLER
MUNSTER
NEISSER
NOETHER
OERSTED
OLIVIER
OLMSTED
ONSAGER
OTHNIEL
PASCHEN
PECQUET
PELTIER
PEOPPEL
PERNIER
PERTHES
PFEFFER
PLUCKER
POITIER
POULSEN
PRESPER
RAINGER
RAMSDEN
RAPHAEL
REGNIER
RICHTER
ROBINET
ROMANES
SALILEI
SALOMEN
SANCHEZ
SCHAFER
SCHONER
SCHURER
SHAFFER
SHANLEY
SHAPLEY
SHEARER
SHELLEY
SHIPLER

SHIRLEY
SHUNPEI
SKINNER
SLIPHER
SMALLEY
SPEISER
SPENCER
SPITZER
STANLEY
STARKEY
STEIGER
STEINER
STENDEL
STEPHEN
STEPVEN
STRABEL
STURGES
SURTEES
TAINTER
THEILER
THEURER
THOMSEN
TORSTEN
TRAUNER
ULYSSES
VEKSLER
VERNIER
WALTHER
WANTZEL
WEGENER
WENTZEL
WERNHER
WHEELER
WHITNEY
WILCZEL
WILFRED
WINKLER
WOODGER
WOOLLEY
WOOSTER
WORTLEY
WUERZER
XIMENES
ZABDIEL
ZEIDLER
ZIEGLER
ZINSSER
CARDIFF
KAEMPFE
RUDOLFF
SHARAFF
SHERIFF
TARLOFF
VOLKOFF
WYCKOFF
BORZAGE
DOMINGO

GOSSAGE
KELLOGG
MONTAGU
RALEIGH
SANDAGE
ADOLPHE
ADOLPHO
AIKICHI
ARRIGHI
DOROTHY
FARACHI
HIGUCHI
HIROSHI
JOKICHI
KENICHI
KIYOSHI
MASASHI
MIYOSHI
PORSCHE
SEBOKHT
SHOICHI
TADASHI
TAKASHI
TIMOTHY
AGASSIZ
ANTONIO
BAKHUIS
BECKLIN
CASIMIR
CECELIA
CHELPIN
DIDERIK
DUKAKIS
EPHRAIM
EPSTEIN
EUGENIO
FRANCIS
FREDDIE
FREDRIC
FREDRIK
GADOLIN
GAGARIN
GEORGII
GERMAIN
GOODWIN
GRIFFIN
GUTHRIE
HENDRIK
HENLEIN
HODGKIN
HYPATIA
IGNACIO
JOACHIM
KASIMIR
LEIBNIZ
LORRAIN
MACAVIN

MARQUIS
MICHAIL
MIKHAIL
NIKITIN
OCTAVIO
OLYMPIA
OTTILIA
PHILLIP
PHYLLIS
QUENTIN
RICHLIN
SEFERIS
SERVAIS
SEVERIN
SMELLIE
TELESIO
VENTRIS
ANDRIJA
BRODSKY
CHOMSKY
ISHIOKA
LUEDTKE
LYSENKO
MIYOAKA
NAGAOKA
RUZICKA
SOYINKA
STARSKI
ZERNIKE
ACHILLE
ANATOLE
ASHMOLE
BORELLI
BURNELL
BURWELL
CAMILLE
CAMILLO
CARLYLE
CARROLL
CASTELI
CATTELL
CLEWALL
COPPOLA
CORDELL
COTTELL
DANIELE
DANIELL
DANIELS
DARWELL
DEHMELT
DELISLE
DESAULT
DEVILLE
DONNALL
ESTELLE
GONZALO
GUSELLA

| | | | | | | | |
|---|---|---|---|---|---|---|---|
| HASKE**L**L | BELZO**N**I | LIPMA**N**N | AXELR**O**D | POMER**O**Y | GASPA**R**D | SHAPI**R**O | ELLIO**T**T |
| HEROU**L**T | BOLZA**N**O | LUCIA**N**A | BATES**O**N | PREST**O**N | GELLE**R**T | SHEPA**R**D | ERNES**T**O |
| HOKFE**L**T | BURBA**N**K | MAGNA**N**I | BERGS**O**N | PROCT**O**R | GERBE**R**T | SINAT**R**A | GARBE**T**T |
| KENDA**L**L | BUTTO**N**S | MALLA**N**D | BIGEL**O**W | RALST**O**N | GERHA**R**D | SJOBE**R**G | GOSSE**T**T |
| LASSE**L**L | CARDA**N**O | MARCO**N**I | BLERI**O**T | ROBIS**O**N | GERHA**R**T | STEWA**R**T | HAWOR**T**H |
| LEIPO**L**D | CASSI**N**I | MARTI**N**E | BOULT**O**N | SEIRT**O**N | GIFFA**R**D | STORA**R**O | HERMI**T**E |
| LEOPO**L**D | CHLAD**N**I | MAUMO**N**T | BRANT**O**N | SEMEN**O**V | GILBE**R**T | SUMME**R**S | JACIN**T**O |
| LEUPO**L**D | CLEME**N**S | MCCLU**N**G | BRETT**O**N | SHAMR**O**Y | GODDA**R**D | SWIGE**R**T | KENNE**T**H |
| LINCO**L**N | CLEME**N**T | MELLO**N**I | BRITT**O**N | SHANN**O**N | GOMBE**R**G | SYLBE**R**T | LAPOR**T**E |
| MALCO**L**M | COLLI**N**S | MILLA**N**D | BUISS**O**N | SHELD**O**N | GREGO**R**Y | SZILA**R**D | LEAVI**T**T |
| MANDE**L**A | CORRE**N**S | MONDI**N**O | CAMER**O**N | SHELT**O**N | HALPE**R**N | TELFO**R**D | LOREN**T**Z |
| MANDE**L**L | CUMMI**N**G | MONZA**N**I | CAMPI**O**N | SIMPS**O**N | HANTA**R**O | TEODO**R**O | LORET**T**A |
| MANTE**L**L | CUSHI**N**G | NATHA**N**S | CARLS**O**N | SMEAT**O**N | HARBU**R**G | THENA**R**D | PRAND**T**L |
| MAUCH**L**Y | DARLI**N**G | OSBOR**N**E | CHARC**O**T | SOLOM**O**N | HATTO**R**I | TORBE**R**N | RADNI**T**Z |
| MAXWE**L**L | DELIG**N**E | PANCI**N**I | CLAYT**O**N | SPECT**O**R | HAYFO**R**D | TRAVE**R**S | RICCA**T**I |
| MENGO**L**I | DESMO**N**D | PAOLI**N**I | CLINT**O**N | THEOD**O**R | HAYWA**R**D | VILLA**R**D | ROBER**T**O |
| MERRI**L**L | DIAMO**N**D | PARSO**N**S | CLOPT**O**N | THOMS**O**N | HECKA**R**T | VOLHA**R**D | ROBER**T**S |
| MICHE**L**E | DOLLO**N**D | PAULI**N**G | COMPT**O**N | USTIN**O**V | HEPBU**R**N | WARBU**R**G | SCHMI**T**T |
| MICHE**L**L | DUNNI**N**G | PELLI**N**G | DENIS**O**N | VAVIL**O**V | HERBE**R**T | WILLA**R**D | SUSRA**T**A |
| MONTA**L**E | EDEMA**N**N | PERRI**N**E | DICKS**O**N | VIRCH**O**W | HILAI**R**E | WINTE**R**S | TIPPE**T**T |
| NICCO**L**O | ELLMA**N**N | PTASH**N**E | DIDER**O**T | WHART**O**N | HILBE**R**T | ZACHA**R**Y | VENKA**T**A |
| NICHO**L**S | ETIEN**N**E | RAYMO**N**D | EMERS**O**N | WHIST**O**N | HILLA**R**Y | ALFON**S**O | VICEN**T**E |
| NICOL**L**E | FERNA**N**D | REIMA**N**N | EMPER**O**R | WINSL**O**W | HILYA**R**D | AMBRO**S**E | WALCO**T**T |
| OSTWA**L**D | FLEMI**N**G | REYMO**N**D | FARCI**O**T | WINST**O**N | HITTO**R**F | BJORN**S**T | WOTTI**T**Z |
| PACIO**L**I | FONTA**N**A | REYMO**N**T | FITZR**O**Y | WOODR**O**W | HOMBE**R**G | CORLI**S**S | ZANET**T**I |
| PORSI**L**D | GALVA**N**I | ROBBI**N**S | FRITI**O**F | AGRIP**P**A | HUMPH**R**Y | CURTI**S**S | ACTIN**U**S |
| PURCE**L**L | GATLI**N**G | ROLLA**N**D | GIORG**O**S | FILIP**P**O | ISADO**R**E | FORRE**S**T | AEPIN**U**S |
| RENAU**L**T | GEHRI**N**G | ROWLA**N**D | GLASH**O**W | PHILI**P**P | ISIDO**R**E | GHIOR**S**O | ALBIN**U**S |
| RODBE**L**L | GELFA**N**D | RUFFI**N**I | GLEAS**O**N | PHILI**P**S | JEFFE**R**Y | GROES**S**E | ALCAE**U**S |
| ROUEL**L**E | GIBBO**N**S | SAKMA**N**N | GLISS**O**N | RUDOL**P**H | KRAME**R**S | HENNE**S**Y | ANNAE**U**S |
| RUNNE**L**S | GIOVA**N**I | SARGE**N**T | GOOSS**O**N | ABELA**R**D | LAMBE**R**T | LANCI**S**I | BATFO**U**R |
| RUSSE**L**L | GOLDI**N**G | SCHWA**N**N | GOTTL**O**B | ADELA**R**D | LAZZA**R**O | LAXNE**S**S | BERGI**U**S |
| SCHAL**L**Y | HALDA**N**E | SIEME**N**S | GRISS**O**M | ARTTU**R**I | LECLE**R**C | MEINE**S**Z | BORLA**U**G |
| SCHEE**L**E | HAMMA**N**N | SIGMU**N**D | GUFFR**O**Y | ASTBU**R**Y | LEONA**R**D | NORRI**S**H | BROAD**U**S |
| TERRI**L**E | HAMMO**N**D | SORVI**N**O | HALLD**O**R | BARBA**R**A | LINAC**R**E | NYKVI**S**T | CABAE**U**S |
| TOREL**L**O | HARDI**N**G | SPEMA**N**N | HAMPS**O**N | BARNA**R**D | LUMIE**R**E | PALIS**S**Y | CAROL**U**S |
| TYNDA**L**L | HARKI**N**S | STEAR**N**S | HAMPT**O**N | BEDNA**R**Z | MACLU**R**E | PARRI**S**H | CELSI**U**S |
| VILHE**L**M | HARLI**N**G | STEVE**N**S | HARRI**O**T | BEDNO**R**Z | MALLO**R**Y | PENRO**S**E | CLAVI**U**S |
| WENDE**L**L | HAWKI**N**G | SUSAN**N**E | HOPWO**O**D | BERNA**R**D | MAYNA**R**D | PREVO**S**T | ERASM**U**S |
| WHEWE**L**L | HAWKI**N**S | SUZAN**N**E | HUMAS**O**N | BORDE**R**S | MILFO**R**D | TADEU**S**Z | EUDEM**U**S |
| WHIPP**L**E | HERMA**N**N | TENNA**N**T | JACKS**O**N | BOUVA**R**D | NORBE**R**T | VANES**S**A | EUDOX**U**S |
| WHITT**L**E | HERRI**N**G | TENZI**N**G | JEMIS**O**N | CABRE**R**A | PACCA**R**D | ALBER**T**I | EXIGU**U**S |
| WILHE**L**M | HEYMA**N**S | VALMO**N**T | JENSS**O**N | CARRE**R**E | PEREI**R**A | ALLBU**T**T | FRISI**U**S |
| WYVIL**L**E | HOFMA**N**N | VINCE**N**T | JOHNS**O**N | COLBE**R**T | PICCA**R**D | AUGUS**T**E | GEMIN**U**S |
| ZERME**L**O | HOPKI**N**S | VIVIA**N**I | KAZAK**O**V | CONNE**R**Y | PICKA**R**D | AUGUS**T**O | GIAUQ**U**E |
| ANSEL**M**E | HORNI**N**G | WELLA**N**D | KINGD**O**M | CONYE**R**S | PILAT**R**E | BARNE**T**T | GIELG**U**D |
| COULU**M**B | HUGGI**N**S | WIDMA**N**N | KNIFT**O**N | DELBE**R**T | PIZAR**R**O | BECKE**T**T | GLAUC**U**S |
| GIACO**M**O | HUYGE**N**S | WIELA**N**D | KOMAR**O**V | DONDE**R**S | REDFO**R**D | BENNE**T**T | GOODH**U**E |
| GRAHA**M**E | JEAKI**N**S | WILKI**N**S | LANST**O**N | DYKST**R**A | RICHA**R**D | BOURA**T**T | HARTM**U**T |
| NEWCO**M**B | JENKI**N**S | WILLA**N**S | MADIS**O**N | EDOUA**R**D | RUDYA**R**D | BURNE**T**T | JACOB**U**S |
| PTOLE**M**Y | KHORA**N**A | ZYGMU**N**T | MOULT**O**N | EDOUA**R**T | RUMFO**R**D | CANET**T**I | JAHRA**U**S |
| ACKLA**N**D | KIDDI**N**U | ABELS**O**N | NIELS**O**N | EINHO**R**N | RYDBE**R**G | CATLE**T**T | JARCH**U**S |
| ANTHO**N**Y | KIPLI**N**G | ACHES**O**N | PAXIN**O**U | EKEBE**R**G | SANDE**R**S | CELES**T**E | JODOC**U**S |
| ANTOI**N**E | KIPPI**N**G | ADDIS**O**N | PEARS**O**N | FERRA**R**I | SCHIR**R**A | CERLU**T**I | JOUHA**U**X |
| BANTI**N**G | LAURE**N**T | ANGEL**O**S | PELIG**O**T | FLOWE**R**S | SEABO**R**G | CHRIS**T**Y | LAZAR**U**S |
| BAUMA**N**N | LEBLA**N**C | APTHR**O**P | PIERS**O**N | FOLKE**R**S | SEIFE**R**T | COLDI**T**Z | MAHFO**U**Z |
| BELLI**N**I | LEHMA**N**N | AUDUB**O**N | POISS**O**N | GARMI**R**E | SEQUA**R**D | DOHER**T**Y | MALTH**U**S |

NIKLAUS
PASTEUR
PHOEBUS
PROCLUS
RETZIUS
SAUVEUR
SEVERUS
SEYMOUR
SPRAGUE
SYLVIUS
THADEUS
WINDAUS
GUSTAVE
KEDROVA
ANDREWS
BURROWS
UMEZAWA
WISLAWA
ATHAIYA
BURSTYN
CAROLYN
GYORGYI
JOCELYN
KAPTEYN
POLANYI
ROSALYN
KAPITZA
LORENZO
MADRAZO

## 7TH LETTER

AGRIPPA
ANDRIJA
ATHAIYA
BARBARA
CABRERA
CECELIA
COPPOLA
DELEDDA
DYKSTRA
FONTANA
GUSELLA
HYPATIA
ISHIOKA
JESSICA
KAPITZA
KEDROVA
KHORANA
LORETTA
LUCIANA
MANDELA
MIYOAKA
NAGAOKA
OLYMPIA
OTTILIA
PEREIRA
RUZICKA
SCHIRRA
SINATRA
SOYINKA
SUSRATA
UMEZAWA
VANESSA
VENKATA
WISLAWA
YOLANDA
YOSHIDA
COULUMB
GOTTLOB
NEWCOMB
FREDRIC
LAENNEC
LEBLANC
LECLERC
MAURIAC
ABELARD
ACKLAND
ADELARD
AXELROD
BARNARD
BERNARD
BOUVARD
DESMOND
DIAMOND
DOLLOND
EDOUARD
FERNAND
GASPARD
GELFAND
GERHARD
GERSTAD
GIELGUD
GIFFARD
GODDARD
HAFSTAD
HALSTED
HAMMOND
HAYFORD
HAYWARD
HILYARD
HOPWOOD
LEIPOLD
LEONARD
LEOPOLD
LEUPOLD
MAIREAD
MALLAND
MANFRED
MAXSTED
MAYNARD
MEGHNAD
MILFORD
MILLAND
MOHAMED
OERSTED
OLMSTED
OSTWALD
PACCARD
PICCARD
PICKARD
PORSILD
RAYMOND
REDFORD
REYMOND
RICHARD
ROLLAND
ROWLAND
RUDYARD
RUMFORD
SEQUARD
SHEPARD
SIGMUND
SPINRAD
SZILARD
TELFORD
THENARD
VILLARD
VOLHARD
WELLAND
WIELAND
WILFRED
WILLARD
ACHILLE
ADOLPHE
AMBROSE
ANATOLE
ANSELME
ANTOINE
ASHMOLE
AUGUSTE
BORZAGE
CAMILLE
CARLYLE
CARRERE
CELESTE
CHAFFEE
DANIELE
DAUBREE
DELIGNE
DELISLE
DEVILLE
ESTELLE
ETIENNE
EUSTACE
FREDDIE
GARMIRE
GIAUQUE
GOODHUE
GOSSAGE
GRAHAME
GROESSE
GUSTAVE
GUTHRIE
HALDANE
HERMITE
HILAIRE
ISADORE
ISIDORE
KAEMPFE
LAPLACE
LAPORTE
LINACRE
LUEDTKE
LUMIERE
MACLURE
MARTINE
MAURICE
MICHELE
MONTALE
NICOLLE
OSBORNE
PALANCE
PARESCE
PENROSE
PERRINE
PILATRE
PORSCHE
PTASHNE
RECORDE
ROUELLE
SANDAGE
SCHEELE
SCHWABE
SMELLIE
SPRAGUE
SUSANNE
SUZANNE
TERENCE
TERRILE
VICENTE
WALLACE
WHIPPLE
WHITTLE
WYVILLE
ZERNIKE
CARDIFF
FRITIOF
HITTORF
RUDOLFF
SHARAFF
SHERIFF
TARLOFF
VOLKOFF
WYCKOFF
BANTING
BORLAUG
CUMMING
CUSHING
DARLING
DUNNING
EKEBERG
FLEMING
GATLING
GEHRING
GOLDING
GOMBERG
HARBURG
HARDING
HARLING
HAWKING
HERCZEG
HERRING
HOMBERG
HORNING
KELLOGG
KIPLING
KIPPING
MCCLUNG
PAULING
PELLING
RYDBERG
SEABORG
SJOBERG
TENZING
WARBURG
BEYRICH
BRUGSCH
EHRLICH
FRITSCH
HAWORTH
ICHBIAH
KENNETH
KIEBACH
LELOUCH
NORRISH
PARRISH
RALEIGH
RUDOLPH
WALLACH
AIKICHI
ALBERTI
ARRIGHI
ARTTURI
BELLINI
BELZONI
BORELLI
CANETTI
CASSINI
CASTELI
CATALDI
CERLUTI
CHLADNI
FARACHI
FERRARI
GALVANI
GEORGII
GIOVANI
GYORGYI
HATTORI
HIGUCHI
HIROSHI
JOKICHI
KENICHI
KIYOSHI
LANCISI
LUNARDI
MAGNANI
MARALDI
MARCONI
MASASHI
MELLONI
MENGOLI
MIYOSHI
MONZANI
NIKOLAI
PACIOLI
PANCINI
PAOLINI
POLANYI
RICCATI
RUFFINI
SALILEI
SHOICHI
SHUNPEI
STARSKI
TADASHI
TAKASHI
VIVIANI
ZANETTI
BERWICK
BLALACK
BLALOCK
BULLOCK
BURBANK
CHARPAK
CORMACK
DIDERIK
FREDRIK
HADDOCK
HAVLICK
HEDRICK
HENDRIK
HENRICK
KUBRICK
LAMRACK
MARSHAK
MURDOCK
NODDACK
PATRICK
PEACOCK
PEVONAK
POLLACK
REMNICK
ROEBUCK
RUDBECK
SCHLACK
SEEBECK
SZOSTAK
YITZHAK
BURNELL
BURWELL
CARROLL
CATTELL
CHAPPEL
CHAPTAL
CLEWALL
CORDELL
COTTELL
DANIELL
DARWELL
DONNALL
DREBBEL
DUHAMEL
EMANUAL
EMANUEL
EZEKIEL
FRESNEL
FRIEDEL
GABRIEL
HAECKEL
HASKELL
KENDALL
KROEKEL
KUNCKEL
LASSELL
MAELZEL
MANDELL
MANTELL
MAXWELL
MERRILL
MICHAEL
MICHAIL
MICHELL
MIKHAIL
MISTRAL
OTHNIEL
PEOPPEL
PERINAL
PRANDTL
PURCELL
RAPHAEL
RODBELL
RUSSELL
STENDEL
STRABEL
TYNDALL
WANTZEL
WENDELL
WENTZEL
WHEWELL
WILCZEL
ZABDIEL
ABRAHAM
BANGHAM
BENTHAM
BERTRAM
BINGHAM
EPHRAIM
FARNHAM
GRESHAM
GRISSOM
JOACHIM
KHAYYAM
KINGDOM
MALCOLM
MERRIAM
NEEDHAM
PILBEAM
VILHELM
WILHELM
WILLIAM
ABELSON
ACHESON
ADDISON
ADLEMAN
ADRIAAN
ADRIAEN
ALHAZEN
AUDUBON
BARDEEN
BATESON
BAUMANN
BECKLIN
BECKMAN
BERGMAN
BERGSON
BJORKEN
BLAGDEN
BOULTON
BRANTON
BRENNAN
BRETTON
BRITTON
BUCHMAN
BUISSON
BURIDAN
BURSTYN
CAMERON
CAMPION
CARLSON
CAROLYN
CHAPMAN
CHELPIN

CLAYTON
CLINTON
CLOPTON
COMPTON
CRETIEN
CRIPPEN
CRUTZEN
DENISON
DICKSON
EASTMAN
EDELMAN
EDEMANN
EIJKMAN
EINHORN
ELLMANN
EMERSON
EPSTEIN
FEYNMAN
FOLKMAN
FOREMAN
FREEMAN
GADOLIN
GAGARIN
GAUSMAN
GERMAIN
GLEASON
GLISSON
GOLDMAN
GOODMAN
GOODWIN
GOOSSON
GRIFFIN
HACKMAN
HAGEMAN
HALPERN
HAMMANN
HAMPSON
HAMPTON
HARTMAN
HEERMAN
HENLEIN
HEPBURN
HERMANN
HICKMAN
HODGKIN
HOFFMAN
HOFMANN
HUMASON
JACKSON
JANSSEN
JEMISON
JENSSON
JOCELYN
JOHNSON
JUERGEN
KAPTEYN
KAUFMAN

KNIFTON
LANSTON
LAVERAN
LEHMANN
LINCOLN
LIPMANN
LORRAIN
LUITZEN
LURSSEN
MAARTEN
MACAVIN
MADISON
MAUREEN
MOISSAN
MOMMSEN
MOULTON
NIELSON
NIKITIN
PASCHEN
PEARSON
PIERSON
POISSON
POULSEN
PRESTON
PULLMAN
QUENTIN
RALSTON
RAMSDEN
REIMANN
RICHLIN
ROBISON
ROSALYN
SAKMANN
SALOMEN
SAROYAN
SCANLAN
SCHWANN
SEIRTON
SEVERIN
SHANNON
SHEEHAN
SHELDON
SHELTON
SHERMAN
SHUFTAN
SIMPSON
SMEATON
SOLOMON
SPEMANN
STEPHAN
STEPHEN
STEPVEN
SUSSMAN
THOMSEN
THOMSON
TIDYMAN
TORBERN

TORSTEN
VAUGHAN
WAKSMAN
WEIZMAN
WELLMAN
WHARTON
WHISTON
WIDMANN
WINSTON
YEATMAN
ADOLPHO
ALFONSO
ALFREDO
ANTONIO
AUGUSTO
BOLZANO
CABIBBO
CAMILLO
CARDANO
COLOMBO
COLUMBO
DOMINGO
ERNESTO
EUGENIO
FILIPPO
GALILEO
GHIORSO
GIACOMO
GONZALO
HANTARO
IGNACIO
JACINTO
LAZZARO
LORENZO
LYSENKO
MADRAZO
MONDINO
NICCOLO
OCTAVIO
ORLANDO
OSVALDO
PIZARRO
ROBERTO
SHAPIRO
SORVINO
STORARO
TEDESCO
TELESIO
TEODORO
TORELLO
ZERMELO
APTHROP
BELKNAP
IMHOTEP
PHILIPP
PHILLIP
BATFOUR

BEECHER
BEGUYER
BITTNER
BOEHMER
BOTTGER
BOUCHER
BOUGUER
BRENNER
BROUWER
BRYNNER
BUCHNER
CARRIER
CASIMIR
CASTNER
CHAUCER
CHESTER
CLOUSER
COSTNER
COULTER
CREMMER
DAIMLER
DOPPLER
DREXLER
DRINKER
DUILLER
EMPEROR
FECHNER
FERRIER
FIBIGER
FISCHER
FOURIER
FRICKER
GARDNER
GASSNER
GLAEVER
GLAUBER
HALLDOR
HEITLER
HILLIER
HJALMAR
HOMEYER
KASIMIR
KASTLER
KIRCHER
KOLSTER
KRASKER
KRASNER
LARDNER
LOCKYER
LOFFLER
LORIMER
MACQUER
MAUNDER
MEITNER
MESSIER
MUELLER
MUNSTER

NEISSER
NOETHER
OLIVIER
ONSAGER
PASTEUR
PELTIER
PERNIER
PFEFFER
PLUCKER
POITIER
PRACHAR
PRESPER
PROCTOR
RAINGER
REGNIER
RICHTER
SAUVEUR
SAVEGAR
SCHAFER
SCHONER
SCHURER
SEYMOUR
SHAFFER
SHEARER
SHIPLER
SKINNER
SLIPHER
SPECTOR
SPEISER
SPENCER
SPITZER
STEIGER
STEINER
TAINTER
THEILER
THEODOR
THEURER
TRAUNER
VEKSLER
VERNIER
WALTHER
WEGENER
WERNHER
WHEELER
WINKLER
WOODGER
WOOSTER
WUERZER
ZEIDLER
ZIEGLER
ZINSSER
ACTINUS
AEPINUS
ALBINUS
ALCAEUS
ANDREAS
ANDREWS

ANGELOS
ANNAEUS
AQUINAS
AROBLES
BAKHUIS
BEDDOES
BERGIUS
BORDERS
BRANDES
BRIDGES
BROADUS
BRUNHES
BURROWS
BUTTONS
CABAEUS
CAROLUS
CELSIUS
CHARLES
CHASLES
CLAVIUS
CLEMENS
COLLINS
CONYERS
CORLISS
CORRENS
CRESCAS
CROOKES
CURTISS
DANIELS
DEVRIES
DIOCLES
DONDERS
DOUGLAS
DUKAKIS
ERASMUS
EUDEMUS
EUDOXUS
EXIGUUS
FLOWERS
FOLKERS
FRANCES
FRANCIS
FRISIUS
GEMINUS
GEORGES
GIBBONS
GIORGOS
GLAUCUS
GOERGES
GORGIAS
HARKINS
HAWKINS
HEYMANS
HIPPIAS
HOPKINS
HUGGINS
HUYGENS

JACOBUS
JACQUES
JAHRAUS
JARCHUS
JEAKINS
JENKINS
JODOCUS
KRAMERS
LAXNESS
LAZARUS
MALTHUS
MARQUIS
MENZIES
NATHANS
NICHOLS
NICOLAS
NIKLAUS
PARSONS
PENZIAS
PERTHES
PHIDIAS
PHILIPS
PHOEBUS
PHYLLIS
PROCLUS
PYTHEAS
RETZIUS
ROBARDS
ROBBINS
ROBERTS
ROMANES
RUNNELS
SANDERS
SEFERIS
SERVAIS
SEVERUS
SHIELDS
SIEMENS
STEARNS
STEVENS
STURGES
SUMMERS
SURTEES
SYLVIUS
THADEUS
TRAVERS
ULYSSES
VENTRIS
WILKINS
WILLANS
WINDAUS
WINTERS
XIMENES
ALLBUTT
BARNETT
BECKETT
BENNETT

BJORNST
BLERIOT
BOURATT
BURNETT
CATLETT
CHARCOT
CHUQUET
CLEMENT
CLOQUET
COLBERT
DAUSSET
DEHMELT
DELBERT
DESAULT
DIDEROT
EDOUART
ELLIOTT
FARCIOT
FORREST
FRECHET
GARBETT
GELLERT
GERBERT
GERHART
GILBERT
GOSSETT
GUILLET
HARRIOT
HARTMUT
HECKART
HERBERT
HEROULT
HILBERT
HOKFELT
LAMBERT
LAURENT
LEAVITT
MAUMONT
NORBERT
NYKVIST
PECQUET
PELIGOT
PREVOST
RENAULT
REYMONT
ROBINET
ROTBLAT
SARGENT
SCHMIDT
SCHMITT
SEBOKHT
SEIFERT
STEWART
SWIGERT
SYLBERT
TENNANT
TIPPETT

VALMONT
VINCENT
WALCOTT
ZYGMUNT
DANGEAU
KIDDINU
MATTHAU
MONTAGU
PAXINOU
KAZAKOV
KOMAROV
KOZYREV
LEBEDEV
SEMENOV
USTINOV
VAVILOV
BIGELOW
CZESLAW
GLASHOW
KENDREW
MATTHEW
VIRCHOW
WINSLOW
WOODROW
JOUHAUX
ANTHONY
ASTBURY
BRADLEY
BRODSKY
CATESBY
CHARNAY
CHOMSKY
CHRISTY
CONNERY
DOHERTY
DOROTHY
DUNAWAY
FITZROY
GODFREY
GREGORY
GUFFROY
HARTLEY
HENNESY
HERSHEY
HILLARY
HORSLEY
HOUSSAY
HUMPHRY
JEFFERY
KENNEDY
LANGLEY
MALLORY
MAUCHLY
MCCAREY
MIDGLEY
MOSELEY
NIKOLAY
PALISSY
POMEROY
PTOLEMY
SCHALLY
SHAMROY
SHANLEY
SHAPLEY
SHELLEY
SHIRLEY
SMALLEY
SOLOVAY
STANLEY
STARKEY
TARAGAY
TIMOTHY
WHITNEY
WOOLLEY
WORTLEY
ZACHARY
AGASSIZ
ALVAREZ
BEDNARZ
BEDNORZ
COLDITZ
JIMENEZ
LEIBNIZ
LORENTZ
MAHFOUZ
MARQUEZ
MEINESZ
RADNITZ
SANCHEZ
TADEUSZ
WOTTITZ

## 8 Letter
## 1st Letter

ADELBERT
ADOVASIO
ADRIENNE
AECHYLUS
AFANASSI
AGOSTINO
AGRICOLA
AHLQUIST
ALBERTUS
ALBRECHT
ALCMAEON
ALDREDGE
ALGERNON
ALISTAIR
AMBROISE
AMERICUS
AMONTONS
AMUNDSEN
ANDERSON
ANFINSEN
ANGSTROM
ANJELICA
ANSCHUTZ
ANTIONIO
APPLETON
ARCHYTAS
ARISTIDE
ARZACHEL
ASHCROFT
ASTURIAS
AUGUSTIN
AUGUSTUS
AURELIUS
AVERROES
AVICENNA
AVILDSEN
AVOGADRO
BANCROFT
BAPTISTA
BAPTISTE
BARONESS
BARTHOUD
BARTLETT
BASHEVIS
BASILIUS
BATTISTA
BAUCHENS
BEATRICE
BEAUMONT
BECCARIA
BECKWITH
BEECKMAN
BELTRAMI
BENEDICT
BENJAMIN
BENNETTI
BERKELEY
BERLINER
BERNARDO
BERNHARD
BEROULLI
BERTRAND
BESSEMER
BILLINGS
BIRDSEYE
BIRKHOFF
BJERKNES
BJORNSON
BLACKETT
BLANFORD
BLUMBERG
BOETHIUS
BOLTWOOD
BOMBELLI
BORGNINE
BOTSTEIN
BOULLIAU
BOURBAKI
BOURGOIN
BOWDITCH
BOYLSTON
BRACKETT
BRADFORD
BRAMANTE
BRANTING
BRATTAIN
BRENTANO
BREWSTER
BRICKMAN
BRIDGMAN
BRINDLEY
BRONSTED
BRUNFELS
BUCHANAN
BUCKLAND
BUMSTEAD
BUSCHING
BUSHNELL
BUSTILLO
BUTLEROV
CAGLIONE
CALANDRI
CALLAHAN
CALMETTE
CAMPANUS
CAMPBELL
CANONERO
CAPELLER
CARADINI
CARDUCCI
CARFAGNO
CARLETON
CARLISLE
CARNEGIE
CAROLINE
CASTILLO
CHADWICK
CHAKIRIS
CHALONGE
CHAMBERS
CHANDLER
CHANNING
CHARGAFF
CHARLIER
CHARLTON
CHATELET
CHEVREUL
CHIRIKOV
CHISHOLM
CHRISTIE
CHROWDER
CLAIRAUT
CLARENCE
CLAUDINE
CLAUDIUS
CLAUSIUS
CLEMENCE
CLIFFORD
COBLENTZ
COLLINGS
COLUMBUS
CONVERSI
COOLIDGE
CORNELIS
CORONADO
CORRIGAN
COTTRELL
COUNTESS
COURNAND
COURTOIS
COUSTEAU
CRAWFORD
CRISTIAN
CROMPTON
CROWFOOT
CUTHBERT
DAGUERRE
DAREVSKY
DAVIDSON
DAVISSON
DEBIERNE
DEDEKIND
DELAMBRE
DELBRUCK
DEMARCAY
DEMPSTER
DESHNJOV
DESIDERI
DESORMES
DILLEHAY
DOMENICO
DOUGLASS
DRESSLER
DREYFUSS
DRUMMOND
DUCOMMUN
DUJARDIN
EASTWOOD
EBERHARD
EGBERTUS
EILHARDT
EINSTEIN
ELDREDGE
ELEANORE
ELLICOTT
ELSASSER
ELVEHJEM
EMMANUEL
EPALINUS
EPICURUS
ERICKSON
ERICSSON
ERLANGER
ESQUIVEL
EUGENIUS
EUTOCIUS
EVARISTE
FAHLBERG
FAUCHARD
FAULKNER
FAVALORO
FEILDING
FELICITA
FILLMORE
FISHBACH
FLANNERY
FLEMMING
FLETCHER
FLINDERS
FLORENCE
FLOURENS
FONTAINE
FOUCAULT
FOURCROY
FOURNIER
FRAENKEL
FRAMPTON
FRANCOIS
FRANKLIN
FREDERIC
FREDHOLM
FREDRICH
FREEDMAN
FRENICLE
FRIDTJOF
FRIEDKIN
FRIEDMAN
FRUEHAUF
GABRIELA
GAERTNER
GAJDUSEK
GAMALIEL
GANGELIN
GARDINER
GARFIELD
GARNERIN
GASCOYNE
GASSENDI
GEISSLER
GEOFFORY
GEOFFREY
GEORGIUS
GERARDUS
GERGONNE
GERHARDT
GERTRUDE
GHERARDI
GHISLAIN
GIACCONI
GILLETTE
GIORDANO
GIOVANNI
GIROLAMO
GIUSEPPE
GODEFROY
GOEPPERT
GOLDBACH
GOLDBERG
GOLDMARK
GOLITZEN
GOODRICH
GOODYEAR
GORDIMER
GOTTLIEB
GOUDSMIT
GRANTLEY
GREENHAM
GRIFFITH
GRIGNARD
GRIMALDI
GROTRIAN
GUETTARD
GUINNESS
GUISEPPE
GULDBERG
HADAMARD
HADFIELD
HAFFKINE
HAGGERTY
HALLBERG
HAMILTON
HANNIBAL
HARCOURT
HARKNESS
HARRISON
HARTLINE
HARTMANN
HATCHETT
HAUKSBEE
HAUPTMAN
HAVELOCK
HEINEMAN
HEINRICH
HEMPHREY
HENDRICK
HENRICUS
HERANADO
HERSCHEL
HERZBERG
HEVELIUS
HIJUELOS
HILDYARD
HIPPACOS
HIPPALUS
HIPPASUS
HIRAYAMA
HISINGER
HOAGLAND
HOFFMANN
HOLLIDAY
HOLWARDA
HORNBECK
HORROCKS
HORSFALL
HOUSEMAN
HOUTGAST
HUFELAND
HUMPHREY
HUNTSMAN
HURLBERT
HUTSHING
IMMANUEL
INGEBORG
IPATIEFF
ISAEVICH
ISAMBARD
JACOBSON
JACQUARD
JAENISCH
JANNINGS
JAROSLAV
JEANETTE
JEDEDIAH
JEFFREYS
JEFFRIES
JENNIFER
JENNINGS
JENNISON
JEREMIAH
JEREMIAS
JHABVALA
JOHANNES
JOHANSON
JOHNSTON
JONATHAN
JORDANUS
JOUFFROY
JUNGHANS
KAMINSKI
KAMMERER
KANELLOS
KAUFMANN
KAWABATA
KAZUHIKO
KENNELLY
KINGSLEY
KIRCHHOF
KIRKWOOD

KITASATO
KJELDAHL
KLAPROTH
KORNBERG
KORNGOLD
KUBOYAMA
LAGERLOF
LAGRANGE
LANGEVIN
LANGMUIR
LANTIERI
LAPWORTH
LASHELLE
LASSALLY
LASSETER
LAUGHTON
LAURENCE
LAWRENCE
LEACHMAN
LEBESGUE
LEDERMAN
LEGENDRE
LEISHMAN
LEMAITRE
LEMELSON
LEONARDO
LEONHARD
LEOPOLDO
LEUCKART
LEVINSON
LIBAVIUS
LINDBLAD
LINDHEIM
LINNAEUS
LIPPMANN
LIPSCOMB
LJAPUNOW
LOBASHOV
LUNDBERG
MACBRIDE
MACLAINE
MACQUORN
MADESANI
MAGELLAN
MAGENDIE
MAGIDSON
MAITLAND
MALPIGHI
MANUTIUS
MARCELIN
MARCELLO
MARGARET
MARGGRAF
MARIOTTE
MARJORIE
MARSHALL
MARSHMAN
MARSIGLI
MARTINUS
MATHISON
MATTHIAS
MATUYAMA
MAUDSLAY
MCCARTHY
MCCLEARY
MCCOLLUM
MCDANIEL
MCDIVITT
MCEVILLY
MCKINLEY
MCLAGLEN
MCLELLAN
MCMILLAN
MCMURTRY
MEISSNER
MELCHIOR
MELLANBY
MENACHEM
MENELAUS
MENGHINI
MERCATOR
MERCEDES
MEREDITH
MERSENNE
MESENKOP
MEYERHOF
MIESCHER
MILLIKAN
MILSTEIN
MINNAERT
MINNELLI
MITCHELL
MOHAMMED
MONNARTZ
MORGAGNI
MORRISON
MOSANDER
MUHAMMAD
MULLIKEN
NAARMANN
NAPOLEON
NARINDER
NEHEMIAH
NEWCOMBE
NEWCOMEN
NEWLANDS
NICHOLAS
NICKOLAI
NICOLAAS
NICOLASS
NICOLAUS
NIKOLASS
NIKOLAUS
NOBUYUKI
NORDHEIM
NORTHROP
NOVARESE
NUSSLEIN
ODYSSEUS
OLIPHANT
OSHEROFF
OSIANDER
OUGHTRED
PAGANINI
PALITZSH
PALMIERI
PARRONDO
PATERSON
PATRICIA
PATRIZIA
PATTISON
PEDERSEN
PEDERSON
PERCIVAL
PERELMAN
PERICLES
PERRAULT
PERSONNE
PESCUCCI
PETERSON
PETRUCCI
PHILIPPE
PHILLIPE
PICKFORD
PIERPONT
PITISCUS
PLASKETT
PLAYFAIR
PLUNKETT
POINCARE
POLIDORE
POLITZER
POLYKARP
PONCELET
PRESCOTT
PROSPERO
PURKINJE
PYLARINI
QUARANTA
QUETELET
RAMBALDI
RAYLEIGH
REDFIELD
REDGRAVE
REGINALD
REGNAULT
REINHOLD
REITSEMA
RENNAHAN
REYNOLDS
RHETICUS
RICCARDO
RICCIOLI
RICHARDS
RICHMANN
RICHMOND
RICKETTS
RICKOVER
ROBERTUS
ROBINSON
RODERICK
ROEBLING
ROENTGEN
ROSALIND
ROUSSEAU
RUDOLPHE
RUGGIERO
RUTLEDGE
RYDSTROM
SAAVEDRA
SABATIER
SACCHERI
SAKHAROV
SALVADOR
SANTIAGO
SANTILLO
SARANDON
SAUNDERS
SAUTUOLA
SCALIGER
SCHAEFER
SCHALLER
SCHAWLOW
SCHEINER
SCHIMMEL
SCHIMPER
SCHROTER
SCHULMAN
SCHULTES
SCHULTZE
SCHUSTER
SCHWARTZ
SCIPIONE
SCOFIELD
SEDGWICK
SEFSTROM
SELEUCUS
SEPKOSKI
SERVETUS
SHEARMAN
SHERIDAN
SHERWOOD
SHOCKLEY
SHRAPNEL
SIEGBAHN
SIGNORET
SIKORSKI
SILLIMAN
SINCLAIR
SKOLNICK
SMITHSON
SOCRATES
SORENSEN
SOUFFLOT
SOUTHERN
SPEDDING
SPITTLER
SPRECKER
SPRENGEL
STAFFORD
STANFORD
STARLING
STAUFFER
STEINITZ
STEINORE
STEPHENS
STEVINUS
STIRLING
STOTHART
STRAIGHT
STROWGER
STURGEON
SULEIMAN
SULLIVAN
SUNDMANN
SVEDBERG
SYDENHAM
TAKAMINE
TARADASH
TERENIUS
THATCHER
THEEUWES
THEOBALD
THEODORE
THEORELL
THEVENET
THIBAULT
THIMOTHY
THOMPSON
THUNBERG
TISELIUS
TOMBAUGH
TOMMASON
TOMONAGA
TONEGAWA
TOWNSEND
TRAJANUS
TREMBLEY
TRUMPLER
TRUSCOTT
UNSWORTH
VALDEMAR
VALENTIN
VALERIUS
VALSALVA
VANNEVAR
VASSILIS
VESALIUS
VILLEMIN
VINCENTE
VINCENZO
VIRTANEN
VITTORIO
VLADIMIR
VOLTAIRE
VOLTERRA
VONNEGUT
WAKELING
WALDEMAR
WALDEYER
WANSTALL
WATANABE
WATERMAN
WECHSLER
WEHINGER
WEINBERG
WEISMANN
WELSBACH
WENDELIN
WESTMORE
WHISTLER
WHITFORD
WIECHERT
WILLHELM
WILLIAMS
WIMPERIS
WINTHROP
WOLFGANG
WOODBURY
WOODRUFF
WOODWARD
YAMAMOTO
YAMAZAKE
YAMAZAKI
YANOFSKY
YASUMASA
YASUNARI
YOICHIRO
ZAILLIAN
ZEMECKIS
ZEPPELIN
ZSIGMOND
ZWORYKIN

## 2ND LETTER

BANCROFT
BAPTISTA
BAPTISTE
BARONESS
BARTHOUD
BARTLETT
BASHEVIS
BASILIUS
BATTISTA
BAUCHENS
CAGLIONE
CALANDRI
CALLAHAN
CALMETTE
CAMPANUS
CAMPBELL
CANONERO
CAPELLER
CARADINI
CARDUCCI
CARFAGNO
CARLETON
CARLISLE
CARNEGIE
CAROLINE
CASTILLO
DAGUERRE
DAREVSKY
DAVIDSON
DAVISSON
EASTWOOD
FAHLBERG
FAUCHARD
FAULKNER
FAVALORO
GABRIELA
GAERTNER
GAJDUSEK
GAMALIEL
GANGELIN
GARDINER
GARFIELD
GARNERIN
GASCOYNE
GASSENDI
HADAMARD
HADFIELD
HAFFKINE
HAGGERTY
HALLBERG
HAMILTON
HANNIBAL
HARCOURT
HARKNESS
HARRISON
HARTLINE
HARTMANN
HATCHETT
HAUKSBEE
HAUPTMAN
HAVELOCK
JACOBSON
JACQUARD
JAENISCH
JANNINGS
JAROSLAV
KAMINSKI
KAMMERER
KANELLOS
KAUFMANN
KAWABATA
KAZUHIKO
LAGERLOF
LAGRANGE
LANGEVIN
LANGMUIR
LANTIERI
LAPWORTH
LASHELLE
LASSALLY
LASSETER
LAUGHTON
LAURENCE
LAWRENCE
MACBRIDE
MACLAINE
MACQUORN
MADESANI
MAGELLAN
MAGENDIE
MAGIDSON
MAITLAND
MALPIGHI
MANUTIUS
MARCELIN
MARCELLO
MARGARET
MARGGRAF
MARIOTTE
MARJORIE
MARSHALL
MARSHMAN
MARSIGLI
MARTINUS
MATHISON
MATTHIAS
MATUYAMA
MAUDSLAY
NAARMANN
NAPOLEON
NARINDER
PAGANINI
PALITZSH
PALMIERI
PARRONDO
PATERSON
PATRICIA
PATRIZIA

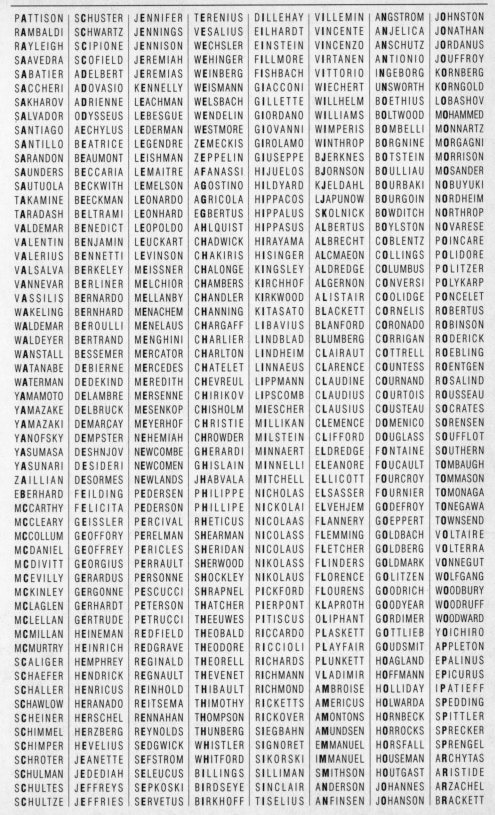

P**A**TTISON
R**A**MBALDI
R**A**YLEIGH
S**A**AVEDRA
S**A**BATIER
S**A**CCHERI
S**A**KHAROV
S**A**LVADOR
S**A**NTIAGO
S**A**NTILLO
S**A**RANDON
S**A**UNDERS
S**A**UTUOLA
T**A**KAMINE
T**A**RADASH
V**A**LDEMAR
V**A**LENTIN
V**A**LERIUS
V**A**LSALVA
V**A**NNEVAR
V**A**SSILIS
W**A**KELING
W**A**LDEMAR
W**A**LDEYER
W**A**NSTALL
W**A**TANABE
W**A**TERMAN
Y**A**MAMOTO
Y**A**MAZAKE
Y**A**MAZAKI
Y**A**NOFSKY
Y**A**SUMASA
Y**A**SUNARI
Z**A**ILLIAN
E**B**ERHARD
M**C**CARTHY
M**C**CLEARY
M**C**COLLUM
M**C**DANIEL
M**C**DIVITT
M**C**EVILLY
M**C**KINLEY
M**C**LAGLEN
M**C**LELLAN
M**C**MILLAN
M**C**MURTRY
S**C**ALIGER
S**C**HAEFER
S**C**HALLER
S**C**HAWLOW
S**C**HEINER
S**C**HIMMEL
S**C**HIMPER
S**C**HROTER
S**C**HULMAN
S**C**HULTES
S**C**HULTZE
S**C**HUSTER
S**C**HWARTZ
S**C**IPIONE
S**C**OFIELD
A**D**ELBERT
A**D**OVASIO
A**D**RIENNE
O**D**YSSEUS
A**E**CHYLUS
B**E**ATRICE
B**E**AUMONT
B**E**CCARIA
B**E**CKWITH
B**E**ECKMAN
B**E**LTRAMI
B**E**NEDICT
B**E**NJAMIN
B**E**NNETTI
B**E**RKELEY
B**E**RLINER
B**E**RNARDO
B**E**RNHARD
B**E**ROULLI
B**E**RTRAND
B**E**SSEMER
D**E**BIERNE
D**E**DEKIND
D**E**LAMBRE
D**E**LBRUCK
D**E**MARCAY
D**E**MPSTER
D**E**SHNJOV
D**E**SIDERI
D**E**SORMES
F**E**ILDING
F**E**LICITA
G**E**ISSLER
G**E**OFFORY
G**E**OFFREY
G**E**ORGIUS
G**E**RARDUS
G**E**RGONNE
G**E**RHARDT
G**E**RTRUDE
H**E**INEMAN
H**E**INRICH
H**E**MPHREY
H**E**NDRICK
H**E**NRICUS
H**E**RANADO
H**E**RSCHEL
H**E**RZBERG
H**E**VELIUS
J**E**ANETTE
J**E**DEDIAH
J**E**FFREYS
J**E**FFRIES
J**E**NNIFER
J**E**NNINGS
J**E**NNISON
J**E**REMIAH
J**E**REMIAS
K**E**NNELLY
L**E**ACHMAN
L**E**BESGUE
L**E**DERMAN
L**E**GENDRE
L**E**ISHMAN
L**E**MAITRE
L**E**MELSON
L**E**ONARDO
L**E**ONHARD
L**E**OPOLDO
L**E**UCKART
L**E**VINSON
M**E**ISSNER
M**E**LCHIOR
M**E**LLANBY
M**E**NACHEM
M**E**NELAUS
M**E**NGHINI
M**E**RCATOR
M**E**RCEDES
M**E**REDITH
M**E**RSENNE
M**E**SENKOP
M**E**YERHOF
N**E**HEMIAH
N**E**WCOMBE
N**E**WCOMEN
N**E**WLANDS
P**E**DERSEN
P**E**DERSON
P**E**RCIVAL
P**E**RELMAN
P**E**RICLES
P**E**RRAULT
P**E**RSONNE
P**E**SCUCCI
P**E**TERSON
P**E**TRUCCI
R**E**DFIELD
R**E**DGRAVE
R**E**GINALD
R**E**GNAULT
R**E**INHOLD
R**E**ITSEMA
R**E**NNAHAN
R**E**YNOLDS
S**E**DGWICK
S**E**FSTROM
S**E**LEUCUS
S**E**PKOSKI
S**E**RVETUS
T**E**RENIUS
V**E**SALIUS
W**E**CHSLER
W**E**HINGER
W**E**INBERG
W**E**ISMANN
W**E**LSBACH
W**E**NDELIN
W**E**STMORE
Z**E**MECKIS
Z**E**PPELIN
A**F**ANASSI
A**G**OSTINO
A**G**RICOLA
E**G**BERTUS
A**H**LQUIST
C**H**ADWICK
C**H**AKIRIS
C**H**ALONGE
C**H**AMBERS
C**H**ANDLER
C**H**ANNING
C**H**ARGAFF
C**H**ARLIER
C**H**ARLTON
C**H**ATELET
C**H**EVREUL
C**H**IRIKOV
C**H**ISHOLM
C**H**RISTIE
C**H**ROWDER
G**H**ERARDI
G**H**ISLAIN
J**H**ABVALA
P**H**ILIPPE
P**H**ILLIPE
R**H**ETICUS
S**H**EARMAN
S**H**ERIDAN
S**H**ERWOOD
S**H**OCKLEY
S**H**RAPNEL
T**H**ATCHER
T**H**EEUWES
T**H**EOBALD
T**H**EODORE
T**H**EORELL
T**H**EVENET
T**H**IBAULT
T**H**IMOTHY
T**H**OMPSON
T**H**UNBERG
W**H**ISTLER
W**H**ITFORD
B**I**LLINGS
B**I**RDSEYE
B**I**RKHOFF
D**I**LLEHAY
E**I**LHARDT
E**I**NSTEIN
F**I**LLMORE
F**I**SHBACH
G**I**ACCONI
G**I**LLETTE
G**I**ORDANO
G**I**OVANNI
G**I**ROLAMO
G**I**USEPPE
H**I**JUELOS
H**I**LDYARD
H**I**PPACOS
H**I**PPALUS
H**I**PPASUS
H**I**RAYAMA
H**I**SINGER
K**I**NGSLEY
K**I**RCHHOF
K**I**RKWOOD
K**I**TASATO
L**I**BAVIUS
L**I**NDBLAD
L**I**NDHEIM
L**I**NNAEUS
L**I**PPMANN
L**I**PSCOMB
M**I**ESCHER
M**I**LLIKAN
M**I**LSTEIN
M**I**NNAERT
M**I**NNELLI
M**I**TCHELL
N**I**CHOLAS
N**I**CKOLAI
N**I**COLAAS
N**I**COLASS
N**I**COLAUS
N**I**KOLASS
N**I**KOLAUS
P**I**CKFORD
P**I**ERPONT
P**I**TISCUS
R**I**CCARDO
R**I**CCIOLI
R**I**CHARDS
R**I**CHMANN
R**I**CHMOND
R**I**CKETTS
R**I**CKOVER
S**I**EGBAHN
S**I**GNORET
S**I**KORSKI
S**I**LLIMAN
S**I**NCLAIR
T**I**SELIUS
V**I**LLEMIN
V**I**NCENTE
V**I**NCENZO
V**I**RTANEN
V**I**TTORIO
W**I**ECHERT
W**I**LLHELM
W**I**LLIAMS
W**I**MPERIS
W**I**NTHROP
B**J**ERKNES
B**J**ORNSON
K**J**ELDAHL
L**J**APUNOW
S**K**OLNICK
A**L**BERTUS
A**L**BRECHT
A**L**CMAEON
A**L**DREDGE
A**L**GERNON
A**L**ISTAIR
B**L**ACKETT
B**L**ANFORD
B**L**UMBERG
C**L**AIRAUT
C**L**ARENCE
C**L**AUDINE
C**L**AUDIUS
C**L**AUSIUS
C**L**EMENCE
C**L**IFFORD
E**L**DREDGE
E**L**EANORE
E**L**LICOTT
E**L**SASSER
E**L**VEHJEM
F**L**ANNERY
F**L**EMMING
F**L**ETCHER
F**L**INDERS
F**L**ORENCE
F**L**OURENS
K**L**APROTH
O**L**IPHANT
P**L**ASKETT
P**L**AYFAIR
P**L**UNKETT
V**L**ADIMIR
A**M**BROISE
A**M**ERICUS
A**M**ONTONS
A**M**UNDSEN
E**M**MANUEL
I**M**MANUEL
S**M**ITHSON
A**N**DERSON
A**N**FINSEN
A**N**GSTROM
A**N**JELICA
A**N**SCHUTZ
A**N**TIONIO
I**N**GEBORG
U**N**SWORTH
B**O**ETHIUS
B**O**LTWOOD
B**O**MBELLI
B**O**RGNINE
B**O**TSTEIN
B**O**ULLIAU
B**O**URBAKI
B**O**URGOIN
B**O**WDITCH
B**O**YLSTON
C**O**BLENTZ
C**O**LLINGS
C**O**LUMBUS
C**O**NVERSI
C**O**OLIDGE
C**O**RNELIS
C**O**RONADO
C**O**RRIGAN
C**O**TTRELL
C**O**UNTESS
C**O**URNAND
C**O**URTOIS
C**O**USTEAU
D**O**MENICO
D**O**UGLASS
F**O**NTAINE
F**O**UCAULT
F**O**URCROY
F**O**URNIER
G**O**DEFROY
G**O**EPPERT
G**O**LDBACH
G**O**LDBERG
G**O**LDMARK
G**O**LITZEN
G**O**ODRICH
G**O**ODYEAR
G**O**RDIMER
G**O**TTLIEB
G**O**UDSMIT
H**O**AGLAND
H**O**FFMANN
H**O**LLIDAY
H**O**LWARDA
H**O**RNBECK
H**O**RROCKS
H**O**RSFALL
H**O**USEMAN
H**O**UTGAST
J**O**HANNES
J**O**HANSON
J**O**HNSTON
J**O**NATHAN
J**O**RDANUS
J**O**UFFROY
K**O**RNBERG
K**O**RNGOLD
L**O**BASHOV
M**O**HAMMED
M**O**NNARTZ
M**O**RGAGNI
M**O**RRISON
M**O**SANDER
N**O**BUYUKI
N**O**RDHEIM
N**O**RTHROP
N**O**VARESE
P**O**INCARE
P**O**LIDORE
P**O**LITZER
P**O**LYKARP
P**O**NCELET
R**O**BERTUS
R**O**BINSON
R**O**DERICK
R**O**EBLING
R**O**ENTGEN
R**O**SALIND
R**O**USSEAU
S**O**CRATES
S**O**RENSEN
S**O**UFFLOT
S**O**UTHERN
T**O**MBAUGH
T**O**MMASON
T**O**MONAGA
T**O**NEGAWA
T**O**WNSEND
V**O**LTAIRE
V**O**LTERRA
V**O**NNEGUT
W**O**LFGANG
W**O**ODBURY
W**O**ODRUFF
W**O**ODWARD
Y**O**ICHIRO
A**P**PLETON
E**P**ALINUS
E**P**ICURUS
I**P**ATIEFF
S**P**EDDING
S**P**ITTLER
S**P**RECKER
S**P**RENGEL
A**R**CHYTAS
A**R**ISTIDE
A**R**ZACHEL
B**R**ACKETT

BRADFORD
BRAMANTE
BRANTING
BRATTAIN
BRENTANO
BREWSTER
BRICKMAN
BRIDGMAN
BRINDLEY
BRONSTED
BRUNFELS
CRAWFORD
CRISTIAN
CROMPTON
CROWFOOT
DRESSLER
DREYFUSS
DRUMMOND
ERICKSON
ERICSSON
ERLANGER
FRAENKEL
FRAMPTON
FRANCOIS
FRANKLIN
FREDERIC
FREDHOLM
FREDRICH
FREEDMAN
FRENICLE
FRIDTJOF
FRIEDKIN
FRIEDMAN
FRUEHAUF
GRANTLEY
GREENHAM
GRIFFITH
GRIGNARD
GRIMALDI
GROTRIAN
PRESCOTT
PROSPERO
TRAJANUS
TREMBLEY
TRUMPLER
TRUSCOTT
ASHCROFT
ASTURIAS
ESQUIVEL
ISAEVICH
ISAMBARD
OSHEROFF
OSIANDER
ZSIGMOND
STAFFORD
STANFORD
STARLING
STAUFFER
STEINITZ
STEINORE
STEPHENS
STEVINUS
STIRLING
STOTHART
STRAIGHT
STROWGER
STURGEON
AUGUSTIN
AUGUSTUS
AURELIUS
BUCHANAN
BUCKLAND
BUMSTEAD
BUSCHING
BUSHNELL
BUSTILLO
BUTLEROV
CUTHBERT
DUCOMMUN
DUJARDIN
EUGENIUS
EUTOCIUS
GUETTARD
GUINNESS
GUISEPPE
GULDBERG
HUFELAND
HUMPHREY
HUNTSMAN
HURLBERT
HUTSHING
JUNGHANS
KUBOYAMA
LUNDBERG
MUHAMMAD
MULLIKEN
NUSSLEIN
OUGHTRED
PURKINJE
QUARANTA
QUETELET
RUDOLPHE
RUGGIERO
RUTLEDGE
SULEIMAN
SULLIVAN
SUNDMANN
AVERROES
AVICENNA
AVILDSEN
AVOGADRO
EVARISTE
SVEDBERG
ZWORYKIN
PYLARINI
RYDSTROM
SYDENHAM

### 3rd Letter

AFANASSI
BEATRICE
BEAUMONT
BLACKETT
BLANFORD
BRACKETT
BRADFORD
BRAMANTE
BRANTING
BRATTAIN
CHADWICK
CHAKIRIS
CHALONGE
CHAMBERS
CHANDLER
CHANNING
CHARGAFF
CHARLIER
CHARLTON
CHATELET
CLAIRAUT
CLARENCE
CLAUDINE
CLAUDIUS
CLAUSIUS
CRAWFORD
EPALINUS
EVARISTE
FLANNERY
FRAENKEL
FRAMPTON
FRANCOIS
FRANKLIN
GIACCONI
GRANTLEY
HOAGLAND
IPATIEFF
ISAEVICH
ISAMBARD
JEANETTE
JHABVALA
KLAPROTH
LEACHMAN
LJAPUNOW
NAARMANN
PLASKETT
PLAYFAIR
QUARANTA
SAAVEDRA
SCALIGER
STAFFORD
STANFORD
STARLING
STAUFFER
THATCHER
TRAJANUS
VLADIMIR
ALBERTUS
ALBRECHT
AMBROISE
COBLENTZ
DEBIERNE
EGBERTUS
GABRIELA
KUBOYAMA
LEBESGUE
LIBAVIUS
LOBASHOV
NOBUYUKI
ROBERTUS
ROBINSON
SABATIER
AECHYLUS
ALCMAEON
ARCHYTAS
BECCARIA
BECKWITH
BUCHANAN
BUCKLAND
DUCOMMUN
JACOBSON
JACQUARD
MACBRIDE
MACLAINE
MACQUORN
MCCARTHY
MCCLEARY
MCCOLLUM
NICHOLAS
NICKOLAI
NICOLAAS
NICOLASS
NICOLAUS
PICKFORD
RICCARDO
RICCIOLI
RICHARDS
RICHMANN
RICHMOND
RICKETTS
RICKOVER
SACCHERI
SOCRATES
WECHSLER
ALDREDGE
ANDERSON
DEDEKIND
ELDREDGE
GODEFROY
HADAMARD
HADFIELD
JEDEDIAH
LEDERMAN
MADESANI
MCDANIEL
MCDIVITT
PEDERSEN
PEDERSON
REDFIELD
REDGRAVE
RODERICK
RUDOLPHE
RYDSTROM
SEDGWICK
SYDENHAM
ADELBERT
AMERICUS
AVERROES
BEECKMAN
BJERKNES
BOETHIUS
BRENTANO
BREWSTER
CHEVREUL
CLEMENCE
DRESSLER
DREYFUSS
EBERHARD
ELEANORE
FLEMMING
FLETCHER
FREDERIC
FREDHOLM
FREDRICH
FREEDMAN
FRENICLE
GAERTNER
GHERARDI
GOEPPERT
GREENHAM
GUETTARD
JAENISCH
KJELDAHL
MCEVILLY
MIESCHER
PIERPONT
PRESCOTT
QUETELET
RHETICUS
ROEBLING
ROENTGEN
SHEARMAN
SHERIDAN
SHERWOOD
SIEGBAHN
SPEDDING
STEINITZ
STEINORE
STEPHENS
STEVINUS
SVEDBERG
THEEUWES
THEOBALD
THEODORE
THEORELL
THEVENET
TREMBLEY
WIECHERT
ANFINSEN
HAFFKINE
HOFFMANN
HUFELAND
JEFFREYS
JEFFRIES
SEFSTROM
ALGERNON
ANGSTROM
AUGUSTIN
AUGUSTUS
CAGLIONE
DAGUERRE
EUGENIUS
HAGGERTY
INGEBORG
LAGERLOF
LAGRANGE
LEGENDRE
MAGELLAN
MAGENDIE
MAGIDSON
OUGHTRED
PAGANINI
REGINALD
REGNAULT
RUGGIERO
SIGNORET
ASHCROFT
FAHLBERG
JOHANNES
JOHANSON
JOHNSTON
MOHAMMED
MUHAMMAD
NEHEMIAH
OSHEROFF
SCHAEFER
SCHALLER
SCHAWLOW
SCHEINER
SCHIMMEL
SCHIMPER
SCHROTER
SCHULMAN
SCHULTES
SCHULTZE
SCHUSTER
SCHWARTZ
WEHINGER
ALISTAIR
ARISTIDE
AVICENNA
AVILDSEN
BRICKMAN
BRIDGMAN
BRINDLEY
CHIRIKOV
CHISHOLM
CLIFFORD
CRISTIAN
EPICURUS
ERICKSON
ERICSSON
FEILDING
FLINDERS
FRIDTJOF
FRIEDKIN
FRIEDMAN
GEISSLER
GHISLAIN
GRIFFITH
GRIGNARD
GRIMALDI
GUINNESS
GUISEPPE
HEINEMAN
HEINRICH
LEISHMAN
MAITLAND
MEISSNER
OLIPHANT
OSIANDER
PHILIPPE
PHILLIPE
POINCARE
REINHOLD
REITSEMA
SCIPIONE
SMITHSON
SPITTLER
STIRLING
THIBAULT
THIMOTHY
WEINBERG
WEISMANN
WHISTLER
WHITFORD
YOICHIRO
ZAILLIAN
ZSIGMOND
ANJELICA
DUJARDIN
GAJDUSEK
HIJUELOS
MCKINLEY
NIKOLASS
NIKOLAUS
SAKHAROV
SIKORSKI
TAKAMINE
WAKELING
AHLQUIST
BELTRAMI
BILLINGS
BOLTWOOD
CALANDRI
CALLAHAN
CALMETTE
COLLINGS
COLUMBUS
DELAMBRE
DELBRUCK
DILLEHAY
EILHARDT
ELLICOTT
ERLANGER
FELICITA
FILLMORE
GILLETTE
GOLDBACH
GOLDBERG
GOLDMARK
GOLITZEN
GULDBERG
HALLBERG
HILDYARD
HOLLIDAY
HOLWARDA
MALPIGHI
MCLAGLEN
MCLELLAN
MELCHIOR
MELLANBY
MILLIKAN
MILSTEIN
MULLIKEN
PALITZSH
PALMIERI
POLIDORE
POLITZER
POLYKARP
PYLARINI
SALVADOR
SELEUCUS
SILLIMAN

SULEIMAN
SULLIVAN
VALDEMAR
VALENTIN
VALERIUS
VALSALVA
VILLEMIN
VOLTAIRE
VOLTERRA
WALDEMAR
WALDEYER
WELSBACH
WILLHELM
WILLIAMS
WOLFGANG
BOMBELLI
BUMSTEAD
CAMPANUS
CAMPBELL
DEMARCAY
DEMPSTER
DOMENICO
EMMANUEL
GAMALIEL
HAMILTON
HEMPHREY
HUMPHREY
IMMANUEL
KAMINSKI
KAMMERER
LEMAITRE
LEMELSON
MCMILLAN
MCMURTRY
RAMBALDI
TOMBAUGH
TOMMASON
TOMONAGA
WIMPERIS
YAMAMOTO
YAMAZAKE
YAMAZAKI
ZEMECKIS
BANCROFT
BENEDICT
BENJAMIN
BENNETTI
CANONERO
CONVERSI
EINSTEIN
FONTAINE
GANGELIN
HANNIBAL
HENDRICK
HENRICUS
HUNTSMAN
JANNINGS
JENNIFER
JENNINGS
JENNISON
JONATHAN
JUNGHANS
KANELLOS
KENNELLY
KINGSLEY
LANGEVIN
LANGMUIR
LANTIERI
LINDBLAD
LINDHEIM
LINNAEUS
LUNDBERG
MANUTIUS
MENACHEM
MENELAUS
MENGHINI
MINNAERT
MINNELLI
MONNARTZ
PONCELET
RENNAHAN
SANTIAGO
SANTILLO
SINCLAIR
SUNDMANN
TONEGAWA
VANNEVAR
VINCENTE
VINCENZO
VONNEGUT
WANSTALL
WENDELIN
WINTHROP
YANOFSKY
ADOVASIO
AGOSTINO
AMONTONS
AVOGADRO
BJORNSON
BRONSTED
COOLIDGE
CROMPTON
CROWFOOT
FLORENCE
FLOURENS
GEOFFORY
GEOFFREY
GEORGIUS
GIORDANO
GIOVANNI
GOODRICH
GOODYEAR
GROTRIAN
LEONARDO
LEONHARD
LEOPOLDO
PROSPERO
SCOFIELD
SHOCKLEY
SKOLNICK
STOTHART
THOMPSON
WOODBURY
WOODRUFF
WOODWARD
ZWORYKIN
APPLETON
BAPTISTA
BAPTISTE
CAPELLER
HIPPACOS
HIPPALUS
HIPPASUS
LAPWORTH
LIPPMANN
LIPSCOMB
NAPOLEON
SEPKOSKI
ZEPPELIN
ESQUIVEL
ADRIENNE
AGRICOLA
AURELIUS
BARONESS
BARTHOUD
BARTLETT
BERKELEY
BERLINER
BERNARDO
BERNHARD
BEROULLI
BERTRAND
BIRDSEYE
BIRKHOFF
BORGNINE
CARADINI
CARDUCCI
CARFAGNO
CARLETON
CARLISLE
CARNEGIE
CAROLINE
CHRISTIE
CHROWDER
CORNELIS
CORONADO
CORRIGAN
DAREVSKY
GARDINER
GARFIELD
GARNERIN
GERARDUS
GERGONNE
GERHARDT
GERTRUDE
GIROLAMO
GORDIMER
HARCOURT
HARKNESS
HARRISON
HARTLINE
HARTMANN
HERANADO
HERSCHEL
HERZBERG
HIRAYAMA
HORNBECK
HORROCKS
HORSFALL
HURLBERT
JAROSLAV
JEREMIAH
JEREMIAS
JORDANUS
KIRCHHOF
KIRKWOOD
KORNBERG
KORNGOLD
MARCELIN
MARCELLO
MARGARET
MARGGRAF
MARIOTTE
MARJORIE
MARSHALL
MARSHMAN
MARSIGLI
MARTINUS
MERCATOR
MERCEDES
MEREDITH
MERSENNE
MORGAGNI
MORRISON
NARINDER
NORDHEIM
NORTHROP
PARRONDO
PERCIVAL
PERELMAN
PERICLES
PERRAULT
PERSONNE
PURKINJE
SARANDON
SERVETUS
SHRAPNEL
SORENSEN
SPRECKER
SPRENGEL
STRAIGHT
STROWGER
TARADASH
TERENIUS
VIRTANEN
ANSCHUTZ
BASHEVIS
BASILIUS
BESSEMER
BUSCHING
BUSHNELL
BUSTILLO
CASTILLO
DESHNJOV
DESIDERI
DESORMES
EASTWOOD
ELSASSER
FISHBACH
GASCOYNE
GASSENDI
HISINGER
LASHELLE
LASSALLY
LASSETER
MESENKOP
MOSANDER
NUSSLEIN
PESCUCCI
ROSALIND
TISELIUS
UNSWORTH
VASSILIS
VESALIUS
WESTMORE
YASUMASA
YASUNARI
ANTIONIO
ASTURIAS
BATTISTA
BOTSTEIN
BUTLEROV
COTTRELL
CUTHBERT
EUTOCIUS
GOTTLIEB
HATCHETT
HUTSHING
KITASATO
MATHISON
MATTHIAS
MATUYAMA
MITCHELL
PATERSON
PATRICIA
PATRIZIA
PATTISON
PETERSON
PETRUCCI
PITISCUS
RUTLEDGE
VITTORIO
WATANABE
WATERMAN
AMUNDSEN
BAUCHENS
BLUMBERG
BOULLIAU
BOURBAKI
BOURGOIN
BRUNFELS
COUNTESS
COURNAND
COURTOIS
COUSTEAU
DOUGLASS
DRUMMOND
FAUCHARD
FAULKNER
FOUCAULT
FOURCROY
FOURNIER
FRUEHAUF
GIUSEPPE
GOUDSMIT
HAUKSBEE
HAUPTMAN
HOUSEMAN
HOUTGAST
JOUFFROY
KAUFMANN
LAUGHTON
LAURENCE
LEUCKART
MAUDSLAY
PLUNKETT
ROUSSEAU
SAUNDERS
SAUTUOLA
SOUFFLOT
SOUTHERN
STURGEON
THUNBERG
TRUMPLER
TRUSCOTT
DAVIDSON
DAVISSON
ELVEHJEM
FAVALORO
HAVELOCK
HEVELIUS
LEVINSON
NOVARESE
BOWDITCH
KAWABATA
LAWRENCE
NEWCOMBE
NEWCOMEN
NEWLANDS
TOWNSEND
BOYLSTON
MEYERHOF
ODYSSEUS
RAYLEIGH
REYNOLDS
ARZACHEL
KAZUHIKO

## 4th Letter

ARZACHEL
CALANDRI
CARADINI
DELAMBRE
DEMARCAY
DUJARDIN
ELEANORE
ELSASSER
EMMANUEL
ERLANGER
FAVALORO
GAMALIEL
GERARDUS
HADAMARD
HERANADO
HIRAYAMA
IMMANUEL
JOHANNES
JOHANSON
JONATHAN
KAWABATA
KITASATO
LEMAITRE
LIBAVIUS
LOBASHOV
MCCARTHY
MCDANIEL
MCLAGLEN
MENACHEM
MOHAMMED
MOSANDER
MUHAMMAD
NOVARESE
OSIANDER
PAGANINI
PYLARINI
ROSALIND
SABATIER
SARANDON
SCHAEFER
SCHALLER
SCHAWLOW
SHEARMAN
SHRAPNEL
STRAIGHT
TAKAMINE
TARADASH
VESALIUS
WATANABE
YAMAMOTO
YAMAZAKE
YAMAZAKI
BOMBELLI
DELBRUCK
JHABVALA
MACBRIDE
RAMBALDI
ROEBLING
THIBAULT
TOMBAUGH
ANSCHUTZ
ASHCROFT
AVICENNA
BANCROFT
BAUCHENS
BECCARIA
BEECKMAN
BLACKETT
BRACKETT
BRICKMAN
BUSCHING
EPICURUS
ERICKSON
ERICSSON
FAUCHARD
FOUCAULT
GASCOYNE
GIACCONI
HARCOURT
HATCHETT
KIRCHHOF
LEACHMAN
LEUCKART
MARCELIN
MARCELLO
MELCHIOR
MERCATOR
MERCEDES
MITCHELL
NEWCOMBE
NEWCOMEN
PERCIVAL
PESCUCCI
PONCELET

RIC**C**ARDO
RIC**C**IOLI
SAC**C**HERI
SHO**C**KLEY
SIN**C**LAIR
VIN**C**ENTE
VIN**C**ENZO
WIE**C**HERT
YOI**C**HIRO
BIR**D**SEYE
BOW**D**ITCH
BRA**D**FORD
BRI**D**GMAN
CAR**D**UCCI
CHA**D**WICK
FRE**D**ERIC
FRE**D**HOLM
FRE**D**RICH
FRI**D**TJOF
GAJ**D**USEK
GAR**D**INER
GOL**D**BACH
GOL**D**BERG
GOL**D**MARK
GOO**D**RICH
GOO**D**YEAR
GOR**D**IMER
GOU**D**SMIT
GUL**D**BERG
HEN**D**RICK
HIL**D**YARD
JOR**D**ANUS
LIN**D**BLAD
LIN**D**HEIM
LUN**D**BERG
MAU**D**SLAY
NOR**D**HEIM
SPE**D**DING
SUN**D**MANN
SVE**D**BERG
VAL**D**EMAR
VLA**D**IMIR
WAL**D**EMAR
WAL**D**EYER
WEN**D**ELIN
WOO**D**BURY
WOO**D**RUFF
WOO**D**WARD
ALB**E**RTUS
ALG**E**RNON
AND**E**RSON
ANJ**E**LICA
AUR**E**LIUS
BEN**E**DICT
CAP**E**LLER
DAR**E**VSKY
DED**E**KIND
DOM**E**NICO
EGB**E**RTUS
ELV**E**HJEM
EUG**E**NIUS
FRA**E**NKEL
FRE**E**DMAN
FRI**E**DKIN
FRI**E**DMAN
FRU**E**HAUF
GOD**E**FROY
GRE**E**NHAM
HAV**E**LOCK
HEV**E**LIUS
HUF**E**LAND
ING**E**BORG
ISA**E**VICH
JED**E**DIAH
JER**E**MIAH
JER**E**MIAS
KAN**E**LLOS
LAG**E**RLOF
LEB**E**SGUE
LED**E**RMAN
LEG**E**NDRE
LEM**E**LSON
MAD**E**SANI
MAG**E**LLAN
MAG**E**NDIE
MCL**E**LLAN
MEN**E**LAUS
MER**E**DITH
MES**E**NKOP
MEY**E**RHOF
NEH**E**MIAH
OSH**E**ROFF
PAT**E**RSON
PED**E**RSEN
PED**E**RSON
PER**E**LMAN
PET**E**RSON
ROB**E**RTUS
ROD**E**RICK
SCH**E**INER
SEL**E**UCUS
SOR**E**NSEN
SPR**E**CKER
SPR**E**NGEL
SUL**E**IMAN
SYD**E**NHAM
TER**E**NIUS
THE**E**UWES
TIS**E**LIUS
TON**E**GAWA
VAL**E**NTIN
VAL**E**RIUS
WAK**E**LING
WAT**E**RMAN
ZEM**E**CKIS
CAR**F**AGNO
CLI**F**FORD
GAR**F**IELD
GEO**F**FORY
GEO**F**FREY
GRI**F**FITH
HAD**F**IELD
HAF**F**KINE
HOF**F**MANN
JEF**F**REYS
JEF**F**RIES
JOU**F**FROY
KAU**F**MANN
RED**F**IELD
SCO**F**IELD
SOU**F**FLOT
STA**F**FORD
WOL**F**GANG
AVO**G**ADRO
BOR**G**NINE
DOU**G**LASS
GAN**G**ELIN
GER**G**ONNE
GRI**G**NARD
HAG**G**ERTY
HOA**G**LAND
JUN**G**HANS
KIN**G**SLEY
LAN**G**EVIN
LAN**G**MUIR
LAU**G**HTON
MAR**G**ARET
MAR**G**GRAF
MEN**G**HINI
MOR**G**AGNI
RED**G**RAVE
RUG**G**IERO
SED**G**WICK
SIE**G**BAHN
ZSI**G**MOND
AEC**H**YLUS
ARC**H**YTAS
BAS**H**EVIS
BUC**H**ANAN
BUS**H**NELL
CUT**H**BERT
DES**H**NJOV
EIL**H**ARDT
FIS**H**BACH
GER**H**ARDT
LAS**H**ELLE
MAT**H**ISON
NIC**H**OLAS
OUG**H**TRED
RIC**H**ARDS
RIC**H**MANN
RIC**H**MOND
SAK**H**AROV
WEC**H**SLER
ADR**I**ENNE
AGR**I**COLA
ANF**I**NSEN
ANT**I**ONIO
BAS**I**LIUS
CHR**I**STIE
CLA**I**RAUT
DAV**I**DSON
DAV**I**SSON
DEB**I**ERNE
DES**I**DERI
ELL**I**COTT
FEL**I**CITA
GOL**I**TZEN
HAM**I**LTON
HIS**I**NGER
KAM**I**NSKI
LEV**I**NSON
MAG**I**DSON
MAR**I**OTTE
MCD**I**VITT
MCK**I**NLEY
MCM**I**LLAN
NAR**I**NDER
PAL**I**TZSH
PER**I**CLES
PIT**I**SCUS
POL**I**DORE
POL**I**TZER
REG**I**NALD
ROB**I**NSON
SCH**I**MMEL
SCH**I**MPER
STE**I**NITZ
STE**I**NORE
WEH**I**NGER
BEN**J**AMIN
MAR**J**ORIE
TRA**J**ANUS
BEC**K**WITH
BER**K**ELEY
BIR**K**HOFF
BUC**K**LAND
CHA**K**IRIS
HAR**K**NESS
HAU**K**SBEE
KIR**K**WOOD
NIC**K**OLAI
PIC**K**FORD
PUR**K**INJE
RIC**K**ETTS
RIC**K**OVER
SEP**K**OSKI
ADE**L**BERT
APP**L**ETON
AVI**L**DSEN
BER**L**INER
BIL**L**INGS
BOU**L**LIAU
BOY**L**STON
BUT**L**EROV
CAG**L**IONE
CAL**L**AHAN
CAR**L**ETON
CAR**L**ISLE
CHA**L**ONGE
COB**L**ENTZ
COL**L**INGS
COO**L**IDGE
DIL**L**EHAY
EPA**L**INUS
FAH**L**BERG
FAU**L**KNER
FEI**L**DING
FIL**L**MORE
GIL**L**ETTE
HAL**L**BERG
HOL**L**IDAY
HUR**L**BERT
KJE**L**DAHL
MAC**L**AINE
MCC**L**EARY
MEL**L**ANBY
MIL**L**IKAN
MUL**L**IKEN
NEW**L**ANDS
PHI**L**IPPE
PHI**L**LIPE
RAY**L**EIGH
RUT**L**EDGE
SCA**L**IGER
SIL**L**IMAN
SKO**L**NICK
SUL**L**IVAN
VIL**L**EMIN
WIL**L**HELM
WIL**L**IAMS
ZAI**L**LIAN
ALC**M**AEON
BLU**M**BERG
BRA**M**ANTE
CAL**M**ETTE
CHA**M**BERS
CLE**M**ENCE
CRO**M**PTON
DRU**M**MOND
FLE**M**MING
FRA**M**PTON
GRI**M**ALDI
ISA**M**BARD
KAM**M**ERER
PAL**M**IERI
THI**M**OTHY
THO**M**PSON
TOM**M**ASON
TRE**M**BLEY
TRU**M**PLER
AFA**N**ASSI
AMO**N**TONS
AMU**N**DSEN
BEN**N**ETTI
BER**N**ARDO
BER**N**HARD
BLA**N**FORD
BRA**N**TING
BRE**N**TANO
BRI**N**DLEY
BRO**N**STED
BRU**N**FELS
CAR**N**EGIE
CHA**N**DLER
CHA**N**NING
COR**N**ELIS
COU**N**TESS
FLA**N**NERY
FLI**N**DERS
FRA**N**COIS
FRA**N**KLIN
FRE**N**ICLE
GAR**N**ERIN
GRA**N**TLEY
GUI**N**NESS
HAN**N**IBAL
HEI**N**EMAN
HEI**N**RICH
HOR**N**BECK
JAE**N**ISCH
JAN**N**INGS
JEA**N**ETTE
JEN**N**IFER
JEN**N**INGS
JEN**N**ISON
JOH**N**STON
KEN**N**ELLY
KOR**N**BERG
KOR**N**GOLD
LEO**N**ARDO
LEO**N**HARD
LIN**N**AEUS
MIN**N**AERT
MIN**N**ELLI
MON**N**ARTZ
PLU**N**KETT
POI**N**CARE
REG**N**AULT
REI**N**HOLD
REN**N**AHAN
REY**N**OLDS
ROE**N**TGEN
SAU**N**DERS
SIG**N**ORET
STA**N**FORD
THU**N**BERG
TOW**N**SEND
VAN**N**EVAR
VON**N**EGUT
WEI**N**BERG
BAR**O**NESS
BER**O**ULLI
CAN**O**NERO
CAR**O**LINE
CHR**O**WDER
COR**O**NADO
DES**O**RMES
DUC**O**MMUN
EUT**O**CIUS
GIR**O**LAMO
JAC**O**BSON
JAR**O**SLAV
KUB**O**YAMA
MCC**O**LLUM
NAP**O**LEON
NIC**O**LAAS
NIC**O**LASS
NIC**O**LAUS
NIK**O**LASS
NIK**O**LAUS
RUD**O**LPHE
SIK**O**RSKI
STR**O**WGER
THE**O**BALD
THE**O**DORE
THE**O**RELL
TOM**O**NAGA
YAN**O**FSKY
CAM**P**ANUS
CAM**P**BELL
DEM**P**STER
GOE**P**PERT
HAU**P**TMAN
HEM**P**HREY
HIP**P**ACOS
HIP**P**ALUS
HIP**P**ASUS
HUM**P**HREY
KLA**P**ROTH
LEO**P**OLDO
LIP**P**MANN
LJA**P**UNOW
MAL**P**IGHI
OLI**P**HANT
SCI**P**IONE
STE**P**HENS
WIM**P**ERIS
ZEP**P**ELIN
AHL**Q**UIST
JAC**Q**UARD
MAC**Q**UORN
ALB**R**ECHT
ALD**R**EDGE
AMB**R**OISE
AME**R**ICUS
AVE**R**ROES
BJE**R**KNES
BJO**R**NSON
BOU**R**BAKI
BOU**R**GOIN
CHA**R**GAFF
CHA**R**LIER
CHA**R**LTON
CHI**R**IKOV
CLA**R**ENCE
COR**R**IGAN
COU**R**NAND
COU**R**TOIS
EBE**R**HARD
ELD**R**EDGE
EVA**R**ISTE
FLO**R**ENCE
FOU**R**CROY
FOU**R**NIER
GAB**R**IELA
GAE**R**TNER
GEO**R**GIUS
GHE**R**ARDI
GIO**R**DANO
HAR**R**ISON
HEN**R**ICUS
HOR**R**OCKS
LAG**R**ANGE
LAU**R**ENCE
LAW**R**ENCE
MOR**R**ISON
NAA**R**MANN
PAR**R**ONDO
PAT**R**ICIA
PAT**R**IZIA
PER**R**AULT
PET**R**UCCI
PIE**R**PONT
QUA**R**ANTA
SCH**R**OTER
SHE**R**IDAN
SHE**R**WOOD
SOC**R**ATES
STA**R**LING
STI**R**LING
STU**R**GEON
ZWO**R**YKIN
AGO**S**TINO
ALI**S**TAIR
ANG**S**TROM

ARI**S**TIDE
BES**S**EMER
BOT**S**TEIN
BUM**S**TEAD
CHI**S**HOLM
COU**S**TEAU
CRI**S**TIAN
DRE**S**SLER
EIN**S**TEIN
GAS**S**ENDI
GEI**S**SLER
GHI**S**LAIN
GIU**S**EPPE
HER**S**CHEL
HOR**S**FALL
HOU**S**EMAN
HUT**S**HING
LAS**S**ALLY
LAS**S**ETER
LEI**S**HMAN
LIP**S**COMB
MAR**S**HALL
MAR**S**HMAN
MAR**S**IGLI
MEI**S**SNER
MER**S**ENNE
MIE**S**CHER
MIL**S**TEIN
NUS**S**LEIN
ODY**S**SEUS
PER**S**ONNE
PLA**S**KETT
PRE**S**COTT
PRO**S**PERO
ROU**S**SEAU
RYD**S**TROM
SEF**S**TROM
TRU**S**COTT
VAL**S**ALVA
VAS**S**ILIS
WAN**S**TALL
WEI**S**MANN
WEL**S**BACH
WHI**S**TLER
BAP**T**ISTA
BAP**T**ISTE
BAR**T**HOUD
BAR**T**LETT
BAT**T**ISTA
BEA**T**RICE
BEL**T**RAMI
BER**T**RAND
BOE**T**HIUS
BOL**T**WOOD
BRA**T**TAIN
BUS**T**ILLO
CAS**T**ILLO
CHA**T**ELET
COT**T**RELL
EAS**T**WOOD
FLE**T**CHER
FON**T**AINE
GER**T**RUDE
GOT**T**LIEB
GRO**T**RIAN
GUE**T**TARD
HAR**T**LINE
HAR**T**MANN
HOU**T**GAST
HUN**T**SMAN
IPA**T**IEFF
LAN**T**IERI
MAI**T**LAND
MAR**T**INUS
MAT**T**HIAS
NOR**T**HROP
PAT**T**ISON
QUE**T**ELET
REI**T**SEMA
RHE**T**ICUS
SAN**T**IAGO
SAN**T**ILLO
SAU**T**UOLA
SMI**T**HSON
SOU**T**HERN
SPI**T**TLER
STO**T**HART
THA**T**CHER
VIR**T**ANEN
VIT**T**ORIO
VOL**T**AIRE
VOL**T**ERRA
WES**T**MORE
WHI**T**FORD
WIN**T**HROP
AST**U**RIAS
AUG**U**STIN
AUG**U**STUS
BEA**U**MONT
CLA**U**DINE
CLA**U**DIUS
CLA**U**SIUS
COL**U**MBUS
DAG**U**ERRE
ESQ**U**IVEL
FLO**U**RENS
HIJ**U**ELOS
KAZ**U**HIKO
MAN**U**TIUS
MAT**U**YAMA
MCM**U**RTRY
NOB**U**YUKI
SCH**U**LMAN
SCH**U**LTES
SCH**U**LTZE
SCH**U**STER
STA**U**FFER
YAS**U**MASA
YAS**U**NARI
ADO**V**ASIO
CHE**V**REUL
CON**V**ERSI
GIO**V**ANNI
MCE**V**ILLY
SAA**V**EDRA
SAL**V**ADOR
SER**V**ETUS
STE**V**INUS
THE**V**ENET
BRE**W**STER
CRA**W**FORD
CRO**W**FOOT
HOL**W**ARDA
LAP**W**ORTH
SCH**W**ARTZ
UNS**W**ORTH
DRE**Y**FUSS
PLA**Y**FAIR
POL**Y**KARP
HER**Z**BERG

**5th Letter**

ADOV**A**SIO
AFAN**A**SSI
ALCM**A**EON
AVOG**A**DRO
BECC**A**RIA
BENJ**A**MIN
BERN**A**RDO
BRAM**A**NTE
BUCH**A**NAN
CALL**A**HAN
CAMP**A**NUS
CARF**A**GNO
EILH**A**RDT
FONT**A**INE
FOUC**A**ULT
GERH**A**RDT
GHER**A**RDI
GIOV**A**NNI
GRIM**A**LDI
HIPP**A**COS
HIPP**A**LUS
HIPP**A**SUS
HOLW**A**RDA
JORD**A**NUS
LAGR**A**NGE
LASS**A**LLY
LEON**A**RDO
LINN**A**EUS
MACL**A**INE
MARG**A**RET
MELL**A**NBY
MERC**A**TOR
MINN**A**ERT
MONN**A**RTZ
MORG**A**GNI
NEWL**A**NDS
PERR**A**ULT
QUAR**A**NTA
RAMB**A**LDI
REGN**A**ULT
RENN**A**HAN
RICC**A**RDO
RICH**A**RDS
SAKH**A**ROV
SALV**A**DOR
SCHW**A**RTZ
SOCR**A**TES
THIB**A**ULT
TOMB**A**UGH
TOMM**A**SON
TRAJ**A**NUS
VALS**A**LVA
VIRT**A**NEN
VOLT**A**IRE
ADEL**B**ERT
BLUM**B**ERG
BOUR**B**AKI
CAMP**B**ELL
CHAM**B**ERS
CUTH**B**ERT
FAHL**B**ERG
FISH**B**ACH
GOLD**B**ACH
GOLD**B**ERG
GULD**B**ERG
HALL**B**ERG
HERZ**B**ERG
HORN**B**ECK
HURL**B**ERT
INGE**B**ORG
ISAM**B**ARD
JACO**B**SON
KAWA**B**ATA
KORN**B**ERG
LIND**B**LAD
LUND**B**ERG
SIEG**B**AHN
SVED**B**ERG
THEO**B**ALD
THUN**B**ERG
TREM**B**LEY
WEIN**B**ERG
WELS**B**ACH
WOOD**B**URY
AGRI**C**OLA
ARZA**C**HEL
ELLI**C**OTT
EUTO**C**IUS
FELI**C**ITA
FLET**C**HER
FOUR**C**ROY
FRAN**C**OIS
GIAC**C**ONI
HERS**C**HEL
LIPS**C**OMB
MENA**C**HEM
MIES**C**HER
PERI**C**LES
POIN**C**ARE
PRES**C**OTT
SPRE**C**KER
THAT**C**HER
TRUS**C**OTT
ZEME**C**KIS
AMUN**D**SEN
AVIL**D**SEN
BENE**D**ICT
BRIN**D**LEY
CARA**D**INI
CHAN**D**LER
CLAU**D**INE
CLAU**D**IUS
DAVI**D**SON
DESI**D**ERI
FEIL**D**ING
FLIN**D**ERS
FREE**D**MAN
FRIE**D**KIN
FRIE**D**MAN
GIOR**D**ANO
JEDE**D**IAH
KJEL**D**AHL
MAGI**D**SON
MERE**D**ITH
POLI**D**ORE
SAUN**D**ERS
SPED**D**ING
TARA**D**ASH
THEO**D**ORE
ADRI**E**NNE
ALBR**E**CHT
ALDR**E**DGE
APPL**E**TON
AVIC**E**NNA
BASH**E**VIS
BENN**E**TTI
BERK**E**LEY
BESS**E**MER
BOMB**E**LLI
BUTL**E**ROV
CALM**E**TTE
CARL**E**TON
CARN**E**GIE
CHAT**E**LET
CLAR**E**NCE
CLEM**E**NCE
COBL**E**NTZ
CONV**E**RSI
CORN**E**LIS
DAGU**E**RRE
DEBI**E**RNE
DILL**E**HAY
ELDR**E**DGE
FLOR**E**NCE
FRED**E**RIC
GANG**E**LIN
GARN**E**RIN
GASS**E**NDI
GILL**E**TTE
GIUS**E**PPE
HAGG**E**RTY
HEIN**E**MAN
HIJU**E**LOS
HOUS**E**MAN
JEAN**E**TTE
KAMM**E**RER
KENN**E**LLY
LANG**E**VIN
LASH**E**LLE
LASS**E**TER
LAUR**E**NCE
LAWR**E**NCE
MARC**E**LIN
MARC**E**LLO
MCCL**E**ARY
MERC**E**DES
MERS**E**NNE
MINN**E**LLI
PONC**E**LET
QUET**E**LET
RAYL**E**IGH
RICK**E**TTS
RUTL**E**DGE
SAAV**E**DRA
SCHA**E**FER
SERV**E**TUS
THEV**E**NET
VALD**E**MAR
VANN**E**VAR
VILL**E**MIN
VINC**E**NTE
VINC**E**NZO
VOLT**E**RRA
VONN**E**GUT
WALD**E**MAR
WALD**E**YER
WEND**E**LIN
WIMP**E**RIS
ZEPP**E**LIN
BLAN**F**ORD
BRAD**F**ORD
BRUN**F**ELS
CLIF**F**ORD
CRAW**F**ORD
CROW**F**OOT
DREY**F**USS
GEOF**F**ORY
GEOF**F**REY
GODE**F**ROY
GRIF**F**ITH
HORS**F**ALL
JOUF**F**ROY
PICK**F**ORD
PLAY**F**AIR
SOUF**F**LOT
STAF**F**ORD
STAN**F**ORD
STAU**F**FER
WHIT**F**ORD
YANO**F**SKY
BOUR**G**OIN
BRID**G**MAN
CHAR**G**AFF
GEOR**G**IUS
HOUT**G**AST
KORN**G**OLD
MARG**G**RAF
MCLA**G**LEN
STUR**G**EON
TONE**G**AWA
WOLF**G**ANG
ANSC**H**UTZ
BART**H**OUD
BAUC**H**ENS
BERN**H**ARD
BIRK**H**OFF
BOET**H**IUS
BUSC**H**ING
CHIS**H**OLM
EBER**H**ARD
ELVE**H**JEM
FAUC**H**ARD
FRED**H**OLM
FRUE**H**AUF
HATC**H**ETT
HEMP**H**REY
HUMP**H**REY
HUTS**H**ING
JUNG**H**ANS
KAZU**H**IKO
KIRC**H**HOF
LAUG**H**TON
LEAC**H**MAN
LEIS**H**MAN
LEON**H**ARD
LIND**H**EIM
MARS**H**ALL
MARS**H**MAN
MATT**H**IAS
MELC**H**IOR
MENG**H**INI
MITC**H**ELL
NORD**H**EIM
NORT**H**ROP
OLIP**H**ANT
REIN**H**OLD
SACC**H**ERI
SMIT**H**SON
SOUT**H**ERN
STEP**H**ENS
STOT**H**ART
WIEC**H**ERT
WILL**H**ELM
WINT**H**ROP
YOIC**H**IRO
AMER**I**CUS
BAPT**I**STA
BAPT**I**STE
BATT**I**STA
BERL**I**NER
BILL**I**NGS
BOWD**I**TCH
BUST**I**LLO
CAGL**I**ONE
CARL**I**SLE
CAST**I**LLO
CHAK**I**RIS
CHIR**I**KOV
COLL**I**NGS
COOL**I**DGE
CORR**I**GAN
EPAL**I**NUS
ESQU**I**VEL
EVAR**I**STE
FREN**I**CLE
GABR**I**ELA
GARD**I**NER
GARF**I**ELD
GORD**I**MER
HADF**I**ELD
HANN**I**BAL
HARR**I**SON
HENR**I**CUS
HOLL**I**DAY
IPAT**I**EFF
JAEN**I**SCH
JANN**I**NGS
JENN**I**FER
JENN**I**NGS
JENN**I**SON
LANT**I**ERI

LEMAITRE
MALPIGHI
MARSIGLI
MARTINUS
MATHISON
MCEVILLY
MILLIKAN
MORRISON
MULLIKEN
PALMIERI
PATRICIA
PATRIZIA
PATTISON
PERCIVAL
PHILIPPE
PURKINJE
REDFIELD
RHETICUS
RICCIOLI
RUGGIERO
SANTIAGO
SANTILLO
SCALIGER
SCHEINER
SCIPIONE
SCOFIELD
SHERIDAN
SILLIMAN
STEVINUS
STRAIGHT
SULEIMAN
SULLIVAN
VASSILIS
VLADIMIR
WILLIAMS
BEECKMAN
BJERKNES
BLACKETT
BRACKETT
BRICKMAN
DEDEKIND
ERICKSON
FAULKNER
FRANKLIN
HAFFKINE
LEUCKART
PLASKETT
PLUNKETT
POLYKARP
SHOCKLEY
ANJELICA
AURELIUS
BARTLETT
BASILIUS
BOULLIAU
BUCKLAND
CAPELLER
CAROLINE
CHARLIER
CHARLTON
DOUGLASS
FAVALORO
GAMALIEL
GHISLAIN
GIROLAMO
GOTTLIEB
HAMILTON
HARTLINE
HAVELOCK
HEVELIUS
HOAGLAND
HUFELAND
KANELLOS
LEMELSON
MAGELLAN
MAITLAND
MCCOLLUM
MCLELLAN
MCMILLAN
MENELAUS
NAPOLEON
NICOLAAS
NICOLASS
NICOLAUS
NIKOLASS
NIKOLAUS
NUSSLEIN
PERELMAN
PHILLIPE
ROEBLING
ROSALIND
RUDOLPHE
SCHALLER
SCHULMAN
SCHULTES
SCHULTZE
SINCLAIR
STARLING
STIRLING
TISELIUS
VESALIUS
WAKELING
ZAILLIAN
BEAUMONT
COLUMBUS
DELAMBRE
DRUMMOND
DUCOMMUN
FILLMORE
FLEMMING
GOLDMARK
HADAMARD
HARTMANN
HOFFMANN
JEREMIAH
JEREMIAS
KAUFMANN
LANGMUIR
LIPPMANN
MOHAMMED
MUHAMMAD
NAARMANN
NEHEMIAH
RICHMANN
RICHMOND
SCHIMMEL
SCHIMPER
SUNDMANN
TAKAMINE
WEISMANN
WESTMORE
YAMAMOTO
YASUMASA
ZSIGMOND
ANFINSEN
BARONESS
BJORNSON
BORGNINE
BUSHNELL
CALANDRI
CANONERO
CHANNING
CORONADO
COURNAND
DESHNJOV
DOMENICO
ELEANORE
EMMANUEL
ERLANGER
EUGENIUS
FLANNERY
FOURNIER
FRAENKEL
GREENHAM
GRIGNARD
GUINNESS
HARKNESS
HERANADO
HISINGER
IMMANUEL
JOHANNES
JOHANSON
KAMINSKI
LEGENDRE
LEVINSON
MAGENDIE
MCDANIEL
MCKINLEY
MESENKOP
MOSANDER
NARINDER
OSIANDER
PAGANINI
REGINALD
ROBINSON
SARANDON
SKOLNICK
SORENSEN
SPRENGEL
STEINITZ
STEINORE
SYDENHAM
TERENIUS
TOMONAGA
VALENTIN
WATANABE
WEHINGER
YASUNARI
AMBROISE
ANTIONIO
CHALONGE
GASCOYNE
GERGONNE
HARCOURT
HORROCKS
LAPWORTH
LEOPOLDO
MARIOTTE
MARJORIE
NEWCOMBE
NEWCOMEN
NICHOLAS
NICKOLAI
PARRONDO
PERSONNE
REYNOLDS
RICKOVER
SCHROTER
SEPKOSKI
SIGNORET
THIMOTHY
UNSWORTH
VITTORIO
CROMPTON
FRAMPTON
GOEPPERT
PIERPONT
PROSPERO
SHRAPNEL
THOMPSON
TRUMPLER
ALBERTUS
ALGERNON
ANDERSON
ASHCROFT
ASTURIAS
AVERROES
BANCROFT
BEATRICE
BELTRAMI
BERTRAND
CHEVREUL
CLAIRAUT
COTTRELL
DELBRUCK
DEMARCAY
DESORMES
DUJARDIN
EGBERTUS
FLOURENS
FREDRICH
GERARDUS
GERTRUDE
GOODRICH
GROTRIAN
HEINRICH
HENDRICK
JEFFREYS
JEFFRIES
KLAPROTH
LAGERLOF
LEDERMAN
MACBRIDE
MCCARTHY
MCMURTRY
MEYERHOF
NOVARESE
OSHEROFF
PATERSON
PEDERSEN
PEDERSON
PETERSON
PYLARINI
REDGRAVE
ROBERTUS
RODERICK
SHEARMAN
SIKORSKI
THEORELL
VALERIUS
WATERMAN
WOODRUFF
AUGUSTIN
AUGUSTUS
BIRDSEYE
BOYLSTON
BREWSTER
BRONSTED
CHRISTIE
CLAUSIUS
DAVISSON
DEMPSTER
DRESSLER
ELSASSER
ERICSSON
GEISSLER
GOUDSMIT
HAUKSBEE
HUNTSMAN
JAROSLAV
JOHNSTON
KINGSLEY
KITASATO
LEBESGUE
LOBASHOV
MADESANI
MAUDSLAY
MEISSNER
ODYSSEUS
PITISCUS
REITSEMA
ROUSSEAU
SCHUSTER
TOWNSEND
WECHSLER
AGOSTINO
ALISTAIR
AMONTONS
ANGSTROM
ARISTIDE
BOTSTEIN
BRANTING
BRATTAIN
BRENTANO
BUMSTEAD
COUNTESS
COURTOIS
COUSTEAU
CRISTIAN
EINSTEIN
FRIDTJOF
GAERTNER
GOLITZEN
GRANTLEY
GUETTARD
HAUPTMAN
JONATHAN
MANUTIUS
MILSTEIN
OUGHTRED
PALITZSH
POLITZER
ROENTGEN
RYDSTROM
SABATIER
SEFSTROM
SPITTLER
WANSTALL
WHISTLER
AHLQUIST
BEROULLI
CARDUCCI
EPICURUS
GAJDUSEK
JACQUARD
LJAPUNOW
MACQUORN
PESCUCCI
PETRUCCI
SAUTUOLA
SELEUCUS
THEEUWES
DAREVSKY
ISAEVICH
JHABVALA
LIBAVIUS
MCDIVITT
BECKWITH
BOLTWOOD
CHADWICK
CHROWDER
EASTWOOD
KIRKWOOD
SCHAWLOW
SEDGWICK
SHERWOOD
STROWGER
WOODWARD
AECHYLUS
ARCHYTAS
GOODYEAR
HILDYARD
HIRAYAMA
KUBOYAMA
MATUYAMA
NOBUYUKI
ZWORYKIN
YAMAZAKE
YAMAZAKI

## 6th Letter

ALISTAIR
BELTRAMI
BERNHARD
BERTRAND
BOURBAKI
BRATTAIN
BRENTANO
BUCKLAND
CHARGAFF
CLAIRAUT
CORONADO
COURNAND
DOUGLASS
EBERHARD
FAUCHARD
FISHBACH
FRUEHAUF
GHISLAIN
GIORDANO
GIROLAMO
GOLDBACH
GOLDMARK
GRIGNARD
GUETTARD
HADAMARD
HARTMANN
HERANADO
HILDYARD
HIRAYAMA
HOAGLAND
HOFFMANN
HORSFALL
HOUTGAST
HUFELAND
ISAMBARD
JACQUARD
JHABVALA
JUNGHANS
KAUFMANN
KAWABATA
KITASATO
KJELDAHL
KUBOYAMA
LEONHARD
LEUCKART
LIPPMANN
MADESANI
MAITLAND
MARSHALL
MATUYAMA
MCCLEARY
MENELAUS
NAARMANN
NICOLAAS
NICOLASS
NICOLAUS
NIKOLASS
NIKOLAUS
OLIPHANT
PLAYFAIR
POINCARE
POLYKARP
REDGRAVE
REGINALD
RICHMANN
SANTIAGO
SIEGBAHN
SINCLAIR
STOTHART
SUNDMANN
TARADASH
THEOBALD

TOMONAGA
TONEGAWA
WANSTALL
WATANABE
WEISMANN
WELSBACH
WILLIAMS
WOLFGANG
WOODWARD
YAMAZAKE
YAMAZAKI
YASUMASA
YASUNARI
COLUMBUS
DELAMBRE
HANNIBAL
HAUKSBEE
ALBRECHT
AMERICUS
CARDUCCI
DEMARCAY
FRENICLE
HENRICUS
HIPPACOS
HORROCKS
PATRICIA
PESCUCCI
PETRUCCI
PITISCUS
RHETICUS
SELEUCUS
ALDREDGE
AVOGADRO
CALANDRI
CHROWDER
COOLIDGE
DUJARDIN
ELDREDGE
GERARDUS
HOLLIDAY
LEGENDRE
MAGENDIE
MERCEDES
MOSANDER
NARINDER
OSIANDER
RUTLEDGE
SAAVEDRA
SALVADOR
SARANDON
SHERIDAN
ADELBERT
ALCMAEON
BARONESS
BARTLETT
BAUCHENS
BIRDSEYE
BLACKETT
BLUMBERG
BOTSTEIN
BRACKETT
BRUNFELS
BUMSTEAD
BUSHNELL
CAMPBELL
CANONERO
CHAMBERS
CHEVREUL
COTTRELL
COUNTESS
COUSTEAU
CUTHBERT
DESIDERI
EINSTEIN
FAHLBERG
FLANNERY
FLINDERS
FLOURENS
GABRIELA
GARFIELD
GOEPPERT
GOLDBERG
GOODYEAR
GUINNESS
GULDBERG
HADFIELD
HALLBERG
HARKNESS
HATCHETT
HERZBERG
HORNBECK
HURLBERT
IPATIEFF
JEFFREYS
KORNBERG
LANTIERI
LINDHEIM
LINNAEUS
LUNDBERG
MILSTEIN
MINNAERT
MITCHELL
NAPOLEON
NORDHEIM
NOVARESE
NUSSLEIN
ODYSSEUS
PALMIERI
PLASKETT
PLUNKETT
PROSPERO
REDFIELD
REITSEMA
ROUSSEAU
RUGGIERO
SACCHERI
SAUNDERS
SCOFIELD
SOUTHERN
STEPHENS
STURGEON
SVEDBERG
THEORELL
THUNBERG
TOWNSEND
WEINBERG
WIECHERT
WILLHELM
JENNIFER
SCHAEFER
STAUFFER
CARFAGNO
CARNEGIE
CORRIGAN
ERLANGER
HISINGER
LEBESGUE
MALPIGHI
MARSIGLI
MORGAGNI
ROENTGEN
SCALIGER
SPRENGEL
STRAIGHT
STROWGER
VONNEGUT
WEHINGER
ARZACHEL
CALLAHAN
DILLEHAY
FLETCHER
GREENHAM
HERSCHEL
JONATHAN
KIRCHHOF
LOBASHOV
MENACHEM
MEYERHOF
MIESCHER
RENNAHAN
SYDENHAM
THATCHER
AGOSTINO
AHLQUIST
AMBROISE
ANJELICA
ARISTIDE
ASTURIAS
AURELIUS
BASILIUS
BEATRICE
BECKWITH
BENEDICT
BOETHIUS
BORGNINE
BOULLIAU
BRANTING
BUSCHING
CARADINI
CAROLINE
CHADWICK
CHANNING
CHARLIER
CLAUDINE
CLAUDIUS
CLAUSIUS
CRISTIAN
DEDEKIND
DOMENICO
EUGENIUS
EUTOCIUS
FEILDING
FELICITA
FLEMMING
FONTAINE
FOURNIER
FREDRICH
GAMALIEL
GEORGIUS
GOODRICH
GOTTLIEB
GRIFFITH
GROTRIAN
HAFFKINE
HARTLINE
HEINRICH
HENDRICK
HEVELIUS
HUTSHING
ISAEVICH
JEDEDIAH
JEFFRIES
JEREMIAH
JEREMIAS
KAZUHIKO
LIBAVIUS
MACBRIDE
MACLAINE
MANUTIUS
MATTHIAS
MCDANIEL
MCDIVITT
MELCHIOR
MENGHINI
MEREDITH
NEHEMIAH
PAGANINI
PHILLIPE
PYLARINI
RAYLEIGH
RODERICK
ROEBLING
ROSALIND
SABATIER
SEDGWICK
SKOLNICK
SPEDDING
STARLING
STEINITZ
STIRLING
TAKAMINE
TERENIUS
TISELIUS
VALERIUS
VESALIUS
VOLTAIRE
WAKELING
YOICHIRO
ZAILLIAN
DESHNJOV
ELVEHJEM
FRIDTJOF
CHIRIKOV
FRAENKEL
FRIEDKIN
MESENKOP
MILLIKAN
MULLIKEN
SPRECKER
ZEMECKIS
ZWORYKIN
AECHYLUS
BERKELEY
BEROULLI
BOMBELLI
BRINDLEY
BUSTILLO
CAPELLER
CASTILLO
CHANDLER
CHATELET
CORNELIS
DRESSLER
FRANKLIN
GANGELIN
GEISSLER
GRANTLEY
GRIMALDI
HIJUELOS
HIPPALUS
JAROSLAV
KANELLOS
KENNELLY
KINGSLEY
LAGERLOF
LASHELLE
LASSALLY
LEOPOLDO
LINDBLAD
MAGELLAN
MARCELIN
MARCELLO
MAUDSLAY
MCCOLLUM
MCEVILLY
MCKINLEY
MCLAGLEN
MCLELLAN
MCMILLAN
MINNELLI
NICHOLAS
NICKOLAI
PERICLES
PONCELET
QUETELET
RAMBALDI
REYNOLDS
SANTILLO
SCHALLER
SCHAWLOW
SHOCKLEY
SOUFFLOT
SPITTLER
TREMBLEY
TRUMPLER
VALSALVA
VASSILIS
WECHSLER
WENDELIN
WHISTLER
ZEPPELIN
BEECKMAN
BENJAMIN
BESSEMER
BRICKMAN
BRIDGMAN
DESORMES
DUCOMMUN
FREEDMAN
FRIEDMAN
GORDIMER
GOUDSMIT
HAUPTMAN
HEINEMAN
HOUSEMAN
HUNTSMAN
LEACHMAN
LEDERMAN
LEISHMAN
MARSHMAN
MOHAMMED
MUHAMMAD
NEWCOMBE
NEWCOMEN
PERELMAN
SCHIMMEL
SCHULMAN
SHEARMAN
SILLIMAN
SULEIMAN
VALDEMAR
VILLEMIN
VLADIMIR
WALDEMAR
WATERMAN
ADRIENNE
ALGERNON
ANTIONIO
AVICENNA
BERLINER
BILLINGS
BJERKNES
BRAMANTE
BUCHANAN
CAMPANUS
CHALONGE
CLARENCE
CLEMENCE
COBLENTZ
COLLINGS
EPALINUS
FAULKNER
FLORENCE
GAERTNER
GARDINER
GASSENDI
GERGONNE
GIOVANNI
JANNINGS
JENNINGS
JOHANNES
JORDANUS
LAGRANGE
LAURENCE
LAWRENCE
LJAPUNOW
MARTINUS
MEISSNER
MELLANBY
MERSENNE
NEWLANDS
PARRONDO
PERSONNE
PURKINJE
QUARANTA
SCHEINER
SHRAPNEL
STEVINUS
THEVENET
TRAJANUS
VINCENTE
VINCENZO
VIRTANEN
AGRICOLA
AMONTONS
ASHCROFT
AVERROES
BANCROFT
BARTHOUD
BEAUMONT
BIRKHOFF
BLANFORD
BOLTWOOD
BOURGOIN
BRADFORD
CAGLIONE
CHISHOLM
CLIFFORD
COURTOIS
CRAWFORD
CROWFOOT
DRUMMOND
EASTWOOD
ELEANORE
ELLICOTT
FAVALORO
FILLMORE
FRANCOIS
FREDHOLM
GEOFFORY
GIACCONI
HAVELOCK
INGEBORG
KIRKWOOD
KLAPROTH
KORNGOLD
LIPSCOMB
MACQUORN
OSHEROFF
PICKFORD
PIERPONT
POLIDORE
PRESCOTT
REINHOLD
RICCIOLI
RICHMOND
SAUTUOLA
SCIPIONE
SHERWOOD
STAFFORD
STANFORD
STEINORE
THEODORE
TRUSCOTT
WESTMORE
WHITFORD

YAMAMOTO
ZSIGMOND
GIUSEPPE
PHILIPPE
RUDOLPHE
SCHIMPER
ANGSTROM
BECCARIA
BERNARDO
BUTLEROV
CHAKIRIS
CONVERSI
DAGUERRE
DEBIERNE
EILHARDT
EPICURUS
FOURCROY
FREDERIC
GARNERIN
GEOFFREY
GERHARDT
GHERARDI
GODEFROY
HAGGERTY
HEMPHREY
HOLWARDA
HUMPHREY
JOUFFROY
KAMMERER
LAPWORTH
LEONARDO
MARGARET
MARGGRAF
MARJORIE
MONNARTZ
NORTHROP
OUGHTRED
RICCARDO
RICHARDS
RYDSTROM
SAKHAROV
SCHWARTZ
SEFSTROM
SIGNORET
UNSWORTH
VITTORIO
VOLTERRA
WIMPERIS
WINTHROP
ADOVASIO
AFANASSI
AMUNDSEN
ANDERSON
ANFINSEN
AVILDSEN
BAPTISTA
BAPTISTE
BATTISTA
BJORNSON
CARLISLE
DAREVSKY
DAVIDSON
DAVISSON
ELSASSER
ERICKSON
ERICSSON
EVARISTE
GAJDUSEK
HARRISON
HIPPASUS
JACOBSON
JAENISCH
JENNISON
JOHANSON
KAMINSKI
LEMELSON
LEVINSON
MAGIDSON
MATHISON
MORRISON
PATERSON
PATTISON
PEDERSEN
PEDERSON
PETERSON
ROBINSON
SEPKOSKI
SIKORSKI
SMITHSON
SORENSEN
THOMPSON
TOMMASON
YANOFSKY
ALBERTUS
APPLETON
ARCHYTAS
AUGUSTIN
AUGUSTUS
BENNETTI
BOWDITCH
BOYLSTON
BREWSTER
BRONSTED
CALMETTE
CARLETON
CHARLTON
CHRISTIE
CROMPTON
DEMPSTER
EGBERTUS
FRAMPTON
GILLETTE
HAMILTON
JEANETTE
JOHNSTON
LASSETER
LAUGHTON
LEMAITRE
MARIOTTE
MCCARTHY
MCMURTRY
MERCATOR
RICKETTS
ROBERTUS
SCHROTER
SCHULTES
SCHULTZE
SCHUSTER
SERVETUS
SOCRATES
THIMOTHY
VALENTIN
ANSCHUTZ
DELBRUCK
DREYFUSS
EMMANUEL
FOUCAULT
GERTRUDE
HARCOURT
IMMANUEL
LANGMUIR
NOBUYUKI
PERRAULT
REGNAULT
THIBAULT
TOMBAUGH
WOODBURY
WOODRUFF
BASHEVIS
ESQUIVEL
LANGEVIN
PERCIVAL
RICKOVER
SULLIVAN
VANNEVAR
THEEUWES
GASCOYNE
WALDEYER
GOLITZEN
PALITZSH
PATRIZIA
POLITZER

## 7th Letter

ARCHYTAS
ASTURIAS
BEECKMAN
BOULLIAU
BRICKMAN
BRIDGMAN
BUCHANAN
BUMSTEAD
CALLAHAN
CORRIGAN
COUSTEAU
CRISTIAN
DEMARCAY
DILLEHAY
FREEDMAN
FRIEDMAN
GOODYEAR
GREENHAM
GROTRIAN
HANNIBAL
HAUPTMAN
HEINEMAN
HOLLIDAY
HOUSEMAN
HUNTSMAN
JAROSLAV
JEDEDIAH
JEREMIAH
JEREMIAS
JONATHAN
LEACHMAN
LEDERMAN
LEISHMAN
LINDBLAD
MAGELLAN
MARGGRAF
MARSHMAN
MATTHIAS
MAUDSLAY
MCLELLAN
MCMILLAN
MILLIKAN
MUHAMMAD
NEHEMIAH
NICHOLAS
NICKOLAI
NICOLAAS
PERCIVAL
PERELMAN
RENNAHAN
ROUSSEAU
SCHULMAN
SHEARMAN
SHERIDAN
SILLIMAN
SULEIMAN
SULLIVAN
SYDENHAM
VALDEMAR
VANNEVAR
WALDEMAR
WATERMAN
ZAILLIAN
MELLANBY
NEWCOMBE
WATANABE
ANJELICA
BEATRICE
BENEDICT
BOWDITCH
CARDUCCI
CHADWICK
CLARENCE
CLEMENCE
DELBRUCK
DOMENICO
FISHBACH
FLORENCE
FREDRICH
GOLDBACH
GOODRICH
HAVELOCK
HEINRICH
HENDRICK
HORNBECK
ISAEVICH
JAENISCH
LAURENCE
LAWRENCE
PESCUCCI
PETRUCCI
RODERICK
SEDGWICK
SKOLNICK
WELSBACH
ARISTIDE
BERNARDO
CORONADO
EILHARDT
GASSENDI
GERHARDT
GERTRUDE
GHERARDI
GRIMALDI
HERANADO
HOLWARDA
LEONARDO
LEOPOLDO
MACBRIDE
NEWLANDS
PARRONDO
RAMBALDI
REYNOLDS
RICCARDO
RICHARDS
AMUNDSEN
ANFINSEN
ARZACHEL
AVERROES
AVILDSEN
BERKELEY
BERLINER
BESSEMER
BJERKNES
BREWSTER
BRINDLEY
BRONSTED
CAPELLER
CHANDLER
CHARLIER
CHATELET
CHROWDER
DEMPSTER
DESORMES
DRESSLER
ELSASSER
ELVEHJEM
EMMANUEL
ERLANGER
ESQUIVEL
FAULKNER
FLETCHER
FOURNIER
FRAENKEL
GAERTNER
GAJDUSEK
GAMALIEL
GARDINER
GEISSLER
GEOFFREY
GOLITZEN
GORDIMER
GOTTLIEB
GRANTLEY
HAUKSBEE
HEMPHREY
HERSCHEL
HISINGER
HUMPHREY
IMMANUEL
JEFFRIES
JENNIFER
JOHANNES
KAMMERER
KINGSLEY
LASSETER
MARGARET
MCDANIEL
MCKINLEY
MCLAGLEN
MEISSNER
MENACHEM
MERCEDES
MIESCHER
MOHAMMED
MOSANDER
MULLIKEN
NARINDER
NEWCOMEN
OSIANDER
OUGHTRED
PEDERSEN
PERICLES
POLITZER
PONCELET
QUETELET
RICKOVER
ROENTGEN
SABATIER
SCALIGER
SCHAEFER
SCHALLER
SCHEINER
SCHIMMEL
SCHIMPER
SCHROTER
SCHULTES
SCHUSTER
SHOCKLEY
SHRAPNEL
SIGNORET
SOCRATES
SORENSEN
SPITTLER
SPRECKER
SPRENGEL
STAUFFER
STROWGER
THATCHER
THEEUWES
THEVENET
TREMBLEY
TRUMPLER
VIRTANEN
WALDEYER
WECHSLER
WEHINGER
WHISTLER
ASHCROFT
BANCROFT
BIRKHOFF
CHARGAFF
IPATIEFF
OSHEROFF
WOODRUFF
ALDREDGE
BILLINGS
CHALONGE
COLLINGS
COOLIDGE
ELDREDGE
JANNINGS
JENNINGS
LAGRANGE
RAYLEIGH
RUTLEDGE
SANTIAGO
TOMBAUGH
TOMONAGA
ALBRECHT
KJELDAHL
MALPIGHI
MCCARTHY
RUDOLPHE
SIEGBAHN
STRAIGHT
THIMOTHY
ADOVASIO
ALISTAIR
ANTIONIO
AUGUSTIN
BASHEVIS
BECCARIA
BENJAMIN
BOTSTEIN
BOURGOIN
BRATTAIN
CARNEGIE
CHAKIRIS
CHRISTIE
CORNELIS
COURTOIS
DUJARDIN
EINSTEIN
FRANCOIS
FRANKLIN
FREDERIC
FRIEDKIN
GANGELIN
GARNERIN
GHISLAIN
GOUDSMIT
LANGEVIN
LANGMUIR
LINDHEIM
MAGENDIE
MARCELIN
MARJORIE
MILSTEIN
NORDHEIM
NUSSLEIN
PATRICIA
PATRIZIA
PLAYFAIR
SINCLAIR
VALENTIN
VASSILIS
VILLEMIN
VITTORIO

VLADIMIR
WENDELIN
WIMPERIS
ZEMECKIS
ZEPPELIN
ZWORYKIN
PURKINJE
BOURBAKI
DAREVSKY
HORROCKS
KAMINSKI
KAZUHIKO
NOBUYUKI
SEPKOSKI
SIKORSKI
YAMAZAKE
YAMAZAKI
YANOFSKY
AGRICOLA
BEROULLI
BOMBELLI
BRUNFELS
BUSHNELL
BUSTILLO
CAMPBELL
CARLISLE
CASTILLO
CHISHOLM
COTTRELL
FOUCAULT
FREDHOLM
FRENICLE
GABRIELA
GARFIELD
HADFIELD
HORSFALL
JHABVALA
KENNELLY
KORNGOLD
LASHELLE
LASSALLY
MARCELLO
MARSHALL
MARSIGLI
MCEVILLY
MINNELLI
MITCHELL
PERRAULT
REDFIELD
REGINALD
REGNAULT
REINHOLD
RICCIOLI
SANTILLO
SAUTUOLA
SCOFIELD
THEOBALD
THEORELL
THIBAULT
WANSTALL
WILLHELM
BELTRAMI
GIROLAMO
HIRAYAMA
KUBOYAMA
LIPSCOMB
MATUYAMA
REITSEMA
WILLIAMS
ADRIENNE
AGOSTINO
AMONTONS
AVICENNA
BAUCHENS
BEAUMONT
BERTRAND
BORGNINE
BRANTING
BRENTANO
BUCKLAND
BUSCHING
CAGLIONE
CARADINI
CARFAGNO
CAROLINE
CHANNING
CLAUDINE
COURNAND
DEBIERNE
DEDEKIND
DRUMMOND
FEILDING
FLEMMING
FLOURENS
FONTAINE
GASCOYNE
GERGONNE
GIACCONI
GIORDANO
GIOVANNI
HAFFKINE
HARTLINE
HARTMANN
HOAGLAND
HOFFMANN
HUFELAND
HUTSHING
JUNGHANS
KAUFMANN
LIPPMANN
MACLAINE
MADESANI
MAITLAND
MENGHINI
MERSENNE
MORGAGNI
NAARMANN
OLIPHANT
PAGANINI
PERSONNE
PIERPONT
PYLARINI
RICHMANN
RICHMOND
ROEBLING
ROSALIND
SCIPIONE
SPEDDING
STARLING
STEPHENS
STIRLING
SUNDMANN
TAKAMINE
TOWNSEND
WAKELING
WEISMANN
WOLFGANG
ZSIGMOND
ALCMAEON
ALGERNON
ANDERSON
ANGSTROM
APPLETON
BJORNSON
BOLTWOOD
BOYLSTON
BUTLEROV
CARLETON
CHARLTON
CHIRIKOV
CROMPTON
CROWFOOT
DAVIDSON
DAVISSON
DESHNJOV
EASTWOOD
ERICKSON
ERICSSON
FOURCROY
FRAMPTON
FRIDTJOF
GODEFROY
HAMILTON
HARRISON
HIJUELOS
HIPPACOS
JACOBSON
JENNISON
JOHANSON
JOHNSTON
JOUFFROY
KANELLOS
KIRCHHOF
KIRKWOOD
LAGERLOF
LAUGHTON
LEMELSON
LEVINSON
LJAPUNOW
LOBASHOV
MAGIDSON
MATHISON
MELCHIOR
MERCATOR
MESENKOP
MEYERHOF
MORRISON
NAPOLEON
NORTHROP
PATERSON
PATTISON
PEDERSON
PETERSON
ROBINSON
RYDSTROM
SAKHAROV
SALVADOR
SARANDON
SCHAWLOW
SEFSTROM
SHERWOOD
SMITHSON
SOUFFLOT
STURGEON
THOMPSON
TOMMASON
WINTHROP
GIUSEPPE
PHILIPPE
PHILLIPE
ADELBERT
AVOGADRO
BERNHARD
BLANFORD
BLUMBERG
BRADFORD
CALANDRI
CANONERO
CHAMBERS
CLIFFORD
CRAWFORD
CUTHBERT
DAGUERRE
DELAMBRE
DESIDERI
EBERHARD
ELEANORE
FAHLBERG
FAUCHARD
FAVALORO
FILLMORE
FLANNERY
FLINDERS
GEOFFORY
GOEPPERT
GOLDBERG
GOLDMARK
GRIGNARD
GUETTARD
GULDBERG
HADAMARD
HALLBERG
HARCOURT
HERZBERG
HILDYARD
HURLBERT
INGEBORG
ISAMBARD
JACQUARD
KORNBERG
LANTIERI
LEGENDRE
LEMAITRE
LEONHARD
LEUCKART
LUNDBERG
MACQUORN
MCCLEARY
MCMURTRY
MINNAERT
PALMIERI
PICKFORD
POINCARE
POLIDORE
POLYKARP
PROSPERO
RUGGIERO
SAAVEDRA
SACCHERI
SAUNDERS
SOUTHERN
STAFFORD
STANFORD
STEINORE
STOTHART
SVEDBERG
THEODORE
THUNBERG
VOLTAIRE
VOLTERRA
WEINBERG
WESTMORE
WHITFORD
WIECHERT
WOODBURY
WOODWARD
YASUNARI
YOICHIRO
AFANASSI
AHLQUIST
AMBROISE
BARONESS
CONVERSI
COUNTESS
DOUGLASS
DREYFUSS
GUINNESS
HARKNESS
HOUTGAST
NICOLASS
NIKOLASS
NOVARESE
PALITZSH
TARADASH
YASUMASA
ANSCHUTZ
BAPTISTA
BAPTISTE
BARTLETT
BATTISTA
BECKWITH
BENNETTI
BLACKETT
BRACKETT
BRAMANTE
CALMETTE
COBLENTZ
ELLICOTT
EVARISTE
FELICITA
GILLETTE
GRIFFITH
HAGGERTY
HATCHETT
JEANETTE
KAWABATA
KITASATO
KLAPROTH
LAPWORTH
MARIOTTE
MCDIVITT
MEREDITH
MONNARTZ
PLASKETT
PLUNKETT
PRESCOTT
QUARANTA
RICKETTS
SCHWARTZ
STEINITZ
TRUSCOTT
UNSWORTH
VINCENTE
YAMAMOTO
AECHYLUS
ALBERTUS
AMERICUS
AUGUSTUS
AURELIUS
BARTHOUD
BASILIUS
BOETHIUS
CAMPANUS
CHEVREUL
CLAIRAUT
CLAUDIUS
CLAUSIUS
COLUMBUS
DUCOMMUN
EGBERTUS
EPALINUS
EPICURUS
EUGENIUS
EUTOCIUS
FRUEHAUF
GEORGIUS
GERARDUS
HENRICUS
HEVELIUS
HIPPALUS
HIPPASUS
JORDANUS
LEBESGUE
LIBAVIUS
LINNAEUS
MANUTIUS
MARTINUS
MCCOLLUM
MENELAUS
NICOLAUS
NIKOLAUS
ODYSSEUS
PITISCUS
RHETICUS
ROBERTUS
SELEUCUS
SERVETUS
STEVINUS
TERENIUS
TISELIUS
TRAJANUS
VALERIUS
VESALIUS
VONNEGUT
REDGRAVE
VALSALVA
TONEGAWA
BIRDSEYE
JEFFREYS
SCHULTZE
VINCENZO

## 8th Letter

AGRICOLA
ANJELICA
AVICENNA
BAPTISTA
BATTISTA
BECCARIA
FELICITA
GABRIELA
HIRAYAMA
HOLWARDA
JHABVALA
KAWABATA
KUBOYAMA
MATUYAMA
PATRICIA
PATRIZIA
QUARANTA
REITSEMA
SAAVEDRA
SAUTUOLA
TOMONAGA
TONEGAWA
VALSALVA
VOLTERRA
YASUMASA
GOTTLIEB
LIPSCOMB
FREDERIC
BARTHOUD
BERNHARD
BERTRAND
BLANFORD
BOLTWOOD
BRADFORD
BRONSTED
BUCKLAND
BUMSTEAD
CLIFFORD
COURNAND
CRAWFORD
DEDEKIND
DRUMMOND
EASTWOOD
EBERHARD
FAUCHARD
GARFIELD
GRIGNARD
GUETTARD
HADAMARD
HADFIELD

| | | | | | | | |
|---|---|---|---|---|---|---|---|
| HILDYARD | FRENICLE | BUSCHING | GIACCONI | WANSTALL | HARTMANN | SULEIMAN | DEMPSTER |
| HOAGLAND | GASCOYNE | CHANNING | GIOVANNI | ANGSTROM | HAUPTMAN | SULLIVAN | DRESSLER |
| HUFELAND | GERGONNE | FAHLBERG | GRIMALDI | CHISHOLM | HEINEMAN | SUNDMANN | ELSASSER |
| ISAMBARD | GERTRUDE | FEILDING | KAMINSKI | ELVEHJEM | HOFFMANN | THOMPSON | ERLANGER |
| JACQUARD | GILLETTE | FLEMMING | LANTIERI | FREDHOLM | HOUSEMAN | TOMMASON | FAULKNER |
| KIRKWOOD | GIUSEPPE | GOLDBERG | MADESANI | GREENHAM | HUNTSMAN | VALENTIN | FLETCHER |
| KORNGOLD | HAFFKINE | GULDBERG | MALPIGHI | LINDHEIM | JACOBSON | VILLEMIN | FOURNIER |
| LEONHARD | HARTLINE | HALLBERG | MARSIGLI | MCCOLLUM | JENNISON | VIRTANEN | GAERTNER |
| LINDBLAD | HAUKSBEE | HERZBERG | MENGHINI | MENACHEM | JOHANSON | WATERMAN | GARDINER |
| MAITLAND | JEANETTE | HUTSHING | MINNELLI | NORDHEIM | JOHNSTON | WEISMANN | GEISSLER |
| MOHAMMED | LAGRANGE | INGEBORG | MORGAGNI | RYDSTROM | JONATHAN | WENDELIN | GOODYEAR |
| MUHAMMAD | LASHELLE | KORNBERG | NICKOLAI | SEFSTROM | KAUFMANN | ZAILLIAN | GORDIMER |
| OUGHTRED | LAURENCE | LUNDBERG | NOBUYUKI | SYDENHAM | LANGEVIN | ZEPPELIN | HISINGER |
| PICKFORD | LAWRENCE | ROEBLING | PAGANINI | WILLHELM | LAUGHTON | ZWORYKIN | JENNIFER |
| REDFIELD | LEBESGUE | SPEDDING | PALMIERI | ALCMAEON | LEACHMAN | ADOVASIO | KAMMERER |
| REGINALD | LEGENDRE | STARLING | PESCUCCI | ALGERNON | LEDERMAN | AGOSTINO | LANGMUIR |
| REINHOLD | LEMAITRE | STIRLING | PETRUCCI | AMUNDSEN | LEISHMAN | ANTIONIO | LASSETER |
| RICHMOND | MACBRIDE | SVEDBERG | PYLARINI | ANDERSON | LEMELSON | AVOGADRO | MEISSNER |
| ROSALIND | MACLAINE | THUNBERG | RAMBALDI | ANFINSEN | LEVINSON | BERNARDO | MELCHIOR |
| SCOFIELD | MAGENDIE | WAKELING | RICCIOLI | APPLETON | LIPPMANN | BRENTANO | MERCATOR |
| SHERWOOD | MARIOTTE | WEINBERG | SACCHERI | AUGUSTIN | MACQUORN | BUSTILLO | MIESCHER |
| STAFFORD | MARJORIE | WOLFGANG | SEPKOSKI | AVILDSEN | MAGELLAN | CANONERO | MOSANDER |
| STANFORD | MERSENNE | BECKWITH | SIKORSKI | BEECKMAN | MAGIDSON | CARFAGNO | NARINDER |
| THEOBALD | NEWCOMBE | BOWDITCH | YAMAZAKI | BENJAMIN | MARCELIN | CASTILLO | OSIANDER |
| TOWNSEND | NOVARESE | FISHBACH | YASUNARI | BJORNSON | MARSHMAN | CORONADO | PLAYFAIR |
| WHITFORD | PERSONNE | FREDRICH | CHADWICK | BOTSTEIN | MATHISON | DOMENICO | POLITZER |
| WOODWARD | PHILIPPE | GOLDBACH | DELBRUCK | BOURGOIN | MCLAGLEN | FAVALORO | RICKOVER |
| ZSIGMOND | PHILLIPE | GOODRICH | GAJDUSEK | BOYLSTON | MCLELLAN | GIORDANO | SABATIER |
| ADRIENNE | POINCARE | GRIFFITH | GOLDMARK | BRATTAIN | MCMILLAN | GIROLAMO | SALVADOR |
| ALDREDGE | POLIDORE | HEINRICH | HAVELOCK | BRICKMAN | MILLIKAN | HERANADO | SCALIGER |
| AMBROISE | PURKINJE | ISAEVICH | HENDRICK | BRIDGMAN | MILSTEIN | KAZUHIKO | SCHAEFER |
| ARISTIDE | REDGRAVE | JAENISCH | HORNBECK | BUCHANAN | MORRISON | KITASATO | SCHALLER |
| BAPTISTE | RUDOLPHE | JEDEDIAH | RODERICK | CALLAHAN | MULLIKEN | LEONARDO | SCHEINER |
| BEATRICE | RUTLEDGE | JEREMIAH | SEDGWICK | CARLETON | NAARMANN | LEOPOLDO | SCHIMPER |
| BIRDSEYE | SCHULTZE | KLAPROTH | SKOLNICK | CHARLTON | NAPOLEON | MARCELLO | SCHROTER |
| BORGNINE | SCIPIONE | LAPWORTH | ARZACHEL | CORRIGAN | NEWCOMEN | PARRONDO | SCHUSTER |
| BRAMANTE | STEINORE | MEREDITH | BUSHNELL | CRISTIAN | NUSSLEIN | PROSPERO | SINCLAIR |
| CAGLIONE | TAKAMINE | NEHEMIAH | CAMPBELL | CROMPTON | PATERSON | RICCARDO | SPITTLER |
| CALMETTE | THEODORE | PALITZSH | CHEVREUL | DAVIDSON | PATTISON | RUGGIERO | SPRECKER |
| CARLISLE | VINCENTE | RAYLEIGH | COTTRELL | DAVISSON | PEDERSEN | SANTIAGO | STAUFFER |
| CARNEGIE | VOLTAIRE | TARADASH | EMMANUEL | DUCOMMUN | PEDERSON | SANTILLO | STROWGER |
| CAROLINE | WATANABE | TOMBAUGH | ESQUIVEL | DUJARDIN | PERELMAN | VINCENZO | THATCHER |
| CHALONGE | WESTMORE | UNSWORTH | FRAENKEL | EINSTEIN | PETERSON | VITTORIO | TRUMPLER |
| CHRISTIE | YAMAZAKE | WELSBACH | GAMALIEL | ERICKSON | RENNAHAN | YAMAMOTO | VALDEMAR |
| CLARENCE | BIRKHOFF | AFANASSI | HANNIBAL | ERICSSON | RICHMANN | YOICHIRO | VANNEVAR |
| CLAUDINE | CHARGAFF | BELTRAMI | HERSCHEL | FRAMPTON | ROBINSON | MESENKOP | VLADIMIR |
| CLEMENCE | FRIDTJOF | BENNETTI | HORSFALL | FRANKLIN | ROENTGEN | NORTHROP | WALDEMAR |
| COOLIDGE | FRUEHAUF | BEROULLI | IMMANUEL | FREEDMAN | SARANDON | POLYKARP | WALDEYER |
| DAGUERRE | IPATIEFF | BOMBELLI | KJELDAHL | FRIEDKIN | SCHULMAN | WINTHROP | WECHSLER |
| DEBIERNE | KIRCHHOF | BOURBAKI | MARSHALL | FRIEDMAN | SHEARMAN | ALISTAIR | WEHINGER |
| DELAMBRE | LAGERLOF | CALANDRI | MCDANIEL | GANGELIN | SHERIDAN | BERLINER | WHISTLER |
| ELDREDGE | MARGGRAF | CARADINI | MITCHELL | GARNERIN | SIEGBAHN | BESSEMER | AECHYLUS |
| ELEANORE | MEYERHOF | CARDUCCI | PERCIVAL | GHISLAIN | SILLIMAN | BREWSTER | ALBERTUS |
| EVARISTE | OSHEROFF | CONVERSI | SCHIMMEL | GOLITZEN | SMITHSON | CAPELLER | AMERICUS |
| FILLMORE | WOODRUFF | DESIDERI | SHRAPNEL | GROTRIAN | SORENSEN | CHANDLER | AMONTONS |
| FLORENCE | BLUMBERG | GASSENDI | SPRENGEL | HAMILTON | SOUTHERN | CHARLIER | ARCHYTAS |
| FONTAINE | BRANTING | GHERARDI | THEORELL | HARRISON | STURGEON | CHROWDER | ASTURIAS |

AUGUSTUS
AURELIUS
AVERROES
BARONESS
BASHEVIS
BASILIUS
BAUCHENS
BILLINGS
BJERKNES
BOETHIUS
BRUNFELS
CAMPANUS
CHAKIRIS
CHAMBERS
CLAUDIUS
CLAUSIUS
COLLINGS
COLUMBUS
CORNELIS
COUNTESS
COURTOIS
DESORMES
DOUGLASS
DREYFUSS
EGBERTUS
EPALINUS
EPICURUS
EUGENIUS
EUTOCIUS
FLINDERS
FLOURENS
FRANCOIS
GEORGIUS
GERARDUS
GUINNESS
HARKNESS
HENRICUS
HEVELIUS
HIJUELOS
HIPPACOS
HIPPALUS
HIPPASUS
HORROCKS
JANNINGS
JEFFREYS
JEFFRIES
JENNINGS
JEREMIAS
JOHANNES
JORDANUS
JUNGHANS
KANELLOS
LIBAVIUS
LINNAEUS
MANUTIUS
MARTINUS
MATTHIAS
MENELAUS
MERCEDES
NEWLANDS
NICHOLAS
NICOLAAS
NICOLASS
NICOLAUS
NIKOLASS
NIKOLAUS
ODYSSEUS
PERICLES
PITISCUS
REYNOLDS
RHETICUS
RICHARDS
RICKETTS
ROBERTUS
SAUNDERS
SCHULTES
SELEUCUS
SERVETUS
SOCRATES
STEPHENS
STEVINUS
TERENIUS
THEEUWES
TISELIUS
TRAJANUS
VALERIUS
VASSILIS
VESALIUS
WILLIAMS
WIMPERIS
ZEMECKIS
ADELBERT
AHLQUIST
ALBRECHT
ASHCROFT
BANCROFT
BARTLETT
BEAUMONT
BENEDICT
BLACKETT
BRACKETT
CHATELET
CLAIRAUT
CROWFOOT
CUTHBERT
EILHARDT
ELLICOTT
FOUCAULT
GERHARDT
GOEPPERT
GOUDSMIT
HARCOURT
HATCHETT
HOUTGAST
HURLBERT
LEUCKART
MARGARET
MCDIVITT
MINNAERT
OLIPHANT
PERRAULT
PIERPONT
PLASKETT
PLUNKETT
PONCELET
PRESCOTT
QUETELET
REGNAULT
SIGNORET
SOUFFLOT
STOTHART
STRAIGHT
THEVENET
THIBAULT
TRUSCOTT
VONNEGUT
WIECHERT
BOULLIAU
COUSTEAU
ROUSSEAU
BUTLEROV
CHIRIKOV
DESHNJOV
JAROSLAV
LOBASHOV
SAKHAROV
LJAPUNOW
SCHAWLOW
BERKELEY
BRINDLEY
DAREVSKY
DEMARCAY
DILLEHAY
FLANNERY
FOURCROY
GEOFFORY
GEOFFREY
GODEFROY
GRANTLEY
HAGGERTY
HEMPHREY
HOLLIDAY
HUMPHREY
JOUFFROY
KENNELLY
KINGSLEY
LASSALLY
MAUDSLAY
MCCARTHY
MCCLEARY
MCEVILLY
MCKINLEY
MCMURTRY
MELLANBY
SHOCKLEY
THIMOTHY
TREMBLEY
WOODBURY
YANOFSKY
ANSCHUTZ
COBLENTZ
MONNARTZ
SCHWARTZ
STEINITZ

## 9 Letter

### 1st Letter

AFRAGAMUS
AGRAMONTE
ALBERTSON
ALDEROTTI
ALEKSANDR
ALEXANDER
ALEXANDRE
ALGAROTTI
ALMENDROS
ALTRAMURA
AMMERMANN
ANACHARIS
ARBUTHNOT
ARCHIBALD
ARFWEDSON
ARISTIDES
ARISTOTLE
ARKWRIGHT
ARMSTRONG
ARNOLDSON
ARRHENIUS
ARYABHATA
ASERINSKY
ATANASOFF
AULENBACK
BALTIMORE
BAMBERGER
BARGHOORN
BARRINGER
BARRYMORE
BARTHOLIN
BATAILLON
BEAUCHAMP
BECQUEREL
BEERNAERT
BEILSTEIN
BEKTHEREV
BENAVENTE
BENEDETTO
BENEDICKS
BENZELIUS
BERGSTROM
BERNIGAUD
BERNOULLI
BERNSTEIN
BERTHELOT
BERZELIUS
BESSARION
BIANCHINI
BIRKELAND
BJORKHOLM
BLAKESLEE
BLANCHARD
BOCCACCIO
BOERHAAVE
BOLTZMANN
BORNSTEIN
BOSCOVICH
BOURGEOIS
BRACEWELL
BRACONNOT
BRODERICK
BROUNCKER
BURGUNDIO
BURKHARDT
BURROUGHS
BUTENANDT
CAILLETET
CALLENDAR
CALLIPPUS
CAROTHERS
CARPENTER
CASCARDIO
CASSERIUS
CAVALIERI
CAVENDISH
CESALPINO
CHAYEFSKY
CHERENKOV
CHRISTAIN
CHRISTIAN
CHRISTINE
CHRISTOFF
CHRISTOPH
CHURCHILL
CLAPEYRON
CLAUDETTE
CLEOPATRA
CLEVELAND
COCKCROFT
COCKERELL
CONDORCET
CONYBEARE
CORNEILLE
CORNELIUS
CORNFORTH
CRESWICKE
CRISTIANI
CRONSTEDT
CTESIBIUS
DALRYMPLE
DAMOISEAU
DAUBENTON
DECONCINI
DELEZENNE
DEMESTRAL
DESARGUES
DESCARTES
DESMAREST
DICKINSON
DIEUDONNE
DIONYSIUS
DIRICHLET
DOMINIQUE
DONALDSON
DUNALDSON
DUTROCHET
ECHEGARAY
EDDINGTON
EHRENBERG
EILENBERG
EINTHOVEN
ELIZABETH
ELLENSHAW
ESTABROOK
EUPALINUS
EURIPIDES
EUSTACHIO
FABRICIUS
FAIRBAIRN
FALLOPIUS
FERCHAULT
FERDINAND
FESSENDEN
FEUERBACH
FIBONACCI
FLAMSTEED
FLORIMOND
FORLANINI
FORSSMANN
FRANCESCO
FRANCISCO
FRANCOISE
FRANKLAND
FREDERICK
FRIEDMANN
FRIEDRICH
FROESCHEL
FRONTINUS
FRUCHTMAN
FULLERTON
GABRIELLA
GABRIELLE
GANSWINDT
GASCOIGNE
GAZZANIGA
GEGENBAUR
GEMINIANO
GERALDINE
GIANNETTI
GILLESPIE
GJELLERUP
GLADSTONE
GOLDHABER
GOLDSTEIN
GOLDSTINE
GOLDSTONE
GOODRICKE
GORBACHEV
GOTTFRIED
GRANVILLE
GRASSMANN
GREENBERG
GREENWOOD
GROTEFEND
GROTTHUSS
GRUENTZIG
GUGLIELMO
GUILLAUME
GUILLEMIN
GUSTAFSON
GUTENBERG
HAFFENDEN
HAHNEMANN
HAMMURABI
HASBROUCK
HAUPTMANN
HAUSDORFF
HEAVISIDE
HECATAEUS
HELVETIUS
HEMINGWAY
HENDERSON
HENRIETTA
HERODOTUS
HEYROVSKY
HIPPOLYTE
HITCHINGS
HOLLERITH
HORODYSKY
HUTCHINGS
HUTCHISON
HYACINTHE
IVANOVICH
IVANOVSKY
JARNOWSKY
JEFFERSON
JOHANNSEN
JOHNSTONE
JORGENSEN
JORGENSON
JOSEPHINE
JOSEPHSON
JUSTINIAN
KARDASHEV
KARLFELDT
KATHARINE
KENZABURO
KETTERING
KIRCHHOFF
KISSINGER
KOBREUTER
KOENEKAMP
KOLREUTER
KRAUSHAAR
KRONECKER
KURCHATOV
LAMORISSE
LANCASTER
LATREILLE
LAVOISIER
LECLANCHE
LEDERBERG
LEMONOSOV
LENORMAND
LEUCIPPUS
LEVERRIER
LINDBERGH
LIOUVILLE
LLEWELLYN
LOMONOSOV
LOSCHMIDT
LUCRETIUS
MACARTHUR
MACDONALD
MACEDONIO
MACMILLAN
MAHARIDGE
MARTINSON
MASKELYNE
MAUROLICO
MCALISTER
MCCONNELL
MCCORMICK
MCDOUGALL
MCPHERSON
MCQUARRIE
MECHNIKOV
MEHRINGER
MENDELEEV
MICHAELIS
MICHELSON
MIELZINER
MILESTONE
MINKOWSKI

MONTANARI
MORTILLET
MOSSBAUER
MURCHISON
MUSSOLINI
NATHANAEL
NATHANIEL
NEETHLING
NICEPHORE
NICHOLSON
NICKERSON
NICOLAIER
NIEUWLAND
NIRENBERG
NISHIJIMA
OENOPIDES
OLDENBURG
PARKINSON
PASTERNAK
PELLETIER
PERCIVALL
PETROSIAN
PHILIPPUS
PHILOLAUS
PICKERING
POLLENDER
PRIESTLEY
PRIGOGINE
PRITCHARD
PROKHOROV
PRUDHOMME
QUASIMODO
RAINWATER
RAMANUJAN
RAWLINSON
REVEILLON
RIGOBERTA
ROBERTSON
ROCCHETTI
ROCHESTER
ROGGEVEEN
ROMANENKO
ROOSEVELT
ROOZEBOOM
RORSCHACH
ROSENBAUM
ROSENBERG
ROUSSELOT
RUHMKORFF
SABASTIAN
SALVATORE
SCAEBERLE
SCHAFFNER
SCHAUDINN
SCHLEIDEN
SCHOEFFER
SCHONBEIN
SCHONLEIN
SCHULBERG
SCHWEIZER
SCHWINGER
SEBASTIAN
SEMIRAMIS
SERTURNER
SHECHTMAN
SHOLOKHOV
SIEGFRIED
SILLANPAA
SODERBLOM
SOMERFELD
SOPHOCLES
SOSIGENES
SOUBEIRAN
SOUTHGATE
SPIELBERG
SPITTELER
SRINIVASA
STANISLAO
STANISLAW
STAPLETON
STEENBERG
STEENBOCK
STEINBECK
STEINKAMP
STEINMETZ
STEVENSON
STOICHEFF
STONEHILL
STRADLING
STRASSMAN
STREISAND
STROMGREN
SUSSMILCH
SYLVESTER
TACHENIUS
TAKAHASHI
TANIGUCHI
TARANTINO
TARTAGLIA
THEODORIC
THEODORUS
THEOPHILE
THORNDIKE
TINBERGEN
TITCHENER
TOUSSIENG
TSCHERMAK
TUNNSTALL
UHLENBECK
VALENTINA
VALENTINE
VANNOCCIO
VAUQUELIN
VERNADSKY
VESPASIAN
VESPUSIUS
VIEUSSENS
VINCENZIO
VITRUVIUS
WAHLSTROM
WARBURTON
WASSERMAN
WEDGEWOOD
WEISSKOPF
WEISSMANN
WETHERALD
WHINFIELD
WHITEHEAD
WHITTAKER
WHITWORTH
WIESCHAUS
WILKINSON
WILLADSEN
WILLUGHBY
WITHERING
WLADYSLAW
WOLFSKEHL
WOLLASTON
ZACHERIAS
ZINNEMANN
ZSIGMONDY

## 2nd Letter

BALTIMORE
BAMBERGER
BARGHOORN
BARRINGER
BARRYMORE
BARTHOLIN
BATAILLON
CAILLETET
CALLENDAR
CALLIPPUS
CAROTHERS
CARPENTER
CASCARDIO
CASSERIUS
CAVALIERI
CAVENDISH
DALRYMPLE
DAMOISEAU
DAUBENTON
FABRICIUS
FAIRBAIRN
FALLOPIUS
GABRIELLA
GABRIELLE
GANSWINDT
GASCOIGNE
GAZZANIGA
HAFFENDEN
HAHNEMANN
HAMMURABI
HASBROUCK
HAUPTMANN
HAUSDORFF
JARNOWSKY
KARDASHEV
KARLFELDT
KATHARINE
LAMORISSE
LANCASTER
LATREILLE
LAVOISIER
MACARTHUR
MACDONALD
MACEDONIO
MACMILLAN
MAHARIDGE
MARTINSON
MASKELYNE
MAUROLICO
NATHANAEL
NATHANIEL
PARKINSON
PASTERNAK
RAINWATER
RAMANUJAN
RAWLINSON
SABASTIAN
SALVATORE
TACHENIUS
TAKAHASHI
TANIGUCHI
TARANTINO
TARTAGLIA
VALENTINA
VALENTINE
VANNOCCIO
VAUQUELIN
WAHLSTROM
WARBURTON
WASSERMAN
ZACHERIAS
ECHEGARAY
MCALISTER
MCCONNELL
MCCORMICK
MCDOUGALL
MCPHERSON
MCQUARRIE
SCAEBERLE
SCHAFFNER
SCHAUDINN
SCHLEIDEN
SCHOEFFER
SCHONBEIN
SCHONLEIN
SCHULBERG
SCHWEIZER
SCHWINGER
EDDINGTON
BEAUCHAMP
BECQUEREL
BEERNAERT
BEILSTEIN
BEKTHEREV
BENAVENTE
BENEDETTO
BENEDICKS
BENZELIUS
BERGSTROM
BERNIGAUD
BERNOULLI
BERNSTEIN
BERTHELOT
BERZELIUS
BESSARION
CESALPINO
DECONCINI
DELEZENNE
DEMESTRAL
DESARGUES
DESCARTES
DESMAREST
FERCHAULT
FERDINAND
FESSENDEN
FEUERBACH
GEGENBAUR
GEMINIANO
GERALDINE
HEAVISIDE
HECATAEUS
HELVETIUS
HEMINGWAY
HENDERSON
HENRIETTA
HERODOTUS
HEYROVSKY
JEFFERSON
KENZABURO
KETTERING
LECLANCHE
LEDERBERG
LEMONOSOV
LENORMAND
LEUCIPPUS
LEVERRIER
MECHNIKOV
MEHRINGER
MENDELEEV
NEETHLING
OENOPIDES
PELLETIER
PERCIVALL
PETROSIAN
REVEILLON
SEBASTIAN
SEMIRAMIS
SERTURNER
VERNADSKY
VESPASIAN
VESPUSIUS
WEDGEWOOD
WEISSKOPF
WEISSMANN
WETHERALD
AFRAGAMUS
AGRAMONTE
CHAYEFSKY
CHERENKOV
CHRISTAIN
CHRISTIAN
CHRISTINE
CHRISTOFF
CHRISTOPH
CHURCHILL
EHRENBERG
PHILIPPUS
PHILOLAUS
SHECHTMAN
SHOLOKHOV
THEODORIC
THEODORUS
THEOPHILE
THORNDIKE
UHLENBECK
WHINFIELD
WHITEHEAD
WHITTAKER
WHITWORTH
BIANCHINI
BIRKELAND
DICKINSON
DIEUDONNE
DIONYSIUS
DIRICHLET
EILENBERG
EINTHOVEN
FIBONACCI
GIANNETTI
GILLESPIE
HIPPOLYTE
HITCHINGS
KIRCHHOFF
KISSINGER
LINDBERGH
LIOUVILLE
MICHAELIS
MICHELSON
MIELZINER
MILESTONE
MINKOWSKI
NICEPHORE
NICHOLSON
NICKERSON
NICOLAIER
NIEUWLAND
NIRENBERG
NISHIJIMA
PICKERING
RIGOBERTA
SIEGFRIED
SILLANPAA
TINBERGEN
TITCHENER
VIEUSSENS
VINCENZIO
VITRUVIUS
WIESCHAUS
WILKINSON
WILLADSEN
WILLUGHBY
WITHERING
ZINNEMANN
BJORKHOLM
GJELLERUP
ALBERTSON
ALDEROTTI
ALEKSANDR
ALEXANDER
ALEXANDRE
ALGAROTTI
ALMENDROS
ALTRAMURA
BLAKESLEE
BLANCHARD
CLAPEYRON
CLAUDETTE
CLEOPATRA
CLEVELAND
ELIZABETH
ELLENSHAW
FLAMSTEED
FLORIMOND
GLADSTONE
LLEWELLYN
OLDENBURG
WLADYSLAW
AMMERMANN
ANACHARIS
BOCCACCIO
BOERHAAVE
BOLTZMANN
BORNSTEIN
BOSCOVICH
BOURGEOIS
COCKCROFT
COCKERELL
CONDORCET
CONYBEARE
CORNEILLE
CORNELIUS
CORNFORTH
DOMINIQUE
DONALDSON
FORLANINI
FORSSMANN
GOLDHABER
GOLDSTEIN
GOLDSTINE
GOLDSTONE
GOODRICKE
GORBACHEV
GOTTFRIED
HOLLERITH
HORODYSKY
JOHANNSEN
JOHNSTONE
JORGENSEN
JORGENSON
JOSEPHINE
JOSEPHSON
KOBREUTER
KOENEKAMP
KOLREUTER
LOMONOSOV
LOSCHMIDT
MONTANARI
MORTILLET
MOSSBAUER
POLLENDER
ROBERTSON
ROCCHETTI
ROCHESTER
ROGGEVEEN
ROMANENKO
ROOSEVELT
ROOZEBOOM
RORSCHACH
ROSENBAUM
ROSENBERG
ROUSSELOT
SODERBLOM
SOMERFELD
SOPHOCLES
SOSIGENES
SOUBEIRAN
SOUTHGATE
TOUSSIENG
WOLFSKEHL
WOLLASTON

SPIELBERG
SPITTELER
ARBUTHNOT
ARCHIBALD
ARFWEDSON
ARISTIDES
ARISTOTLE
ARKWRIGHT
ARMSTRONG
ARNOLDSON
ARRHENIUS
ARYABHATA
BRACEWELL
BRACONNOT
BRODERICK
BROUNCKER
CRESWICKE
CRISTIANI
CRONSTEDT
FRANCESCO
FRANCISCO
FRANCOISE
FRANKLAND
FREDERICK
FRIEDMANN
FRIEDRICH
FROESCHEL
FRONTINUS
FRUCHTMAN
GRANVILLE
GRASSMANN
GREENBERG
GREENWOOD
GROTEFEND
GROTTHUSS
GRUENTZIG
KRAUSHAAR
KRONECKER
PRIESTLEY
PRIGOGINE
PRITCHARD
PROKHOROV
PRUDHOMME
SRINIVASA
ASERINSKY
ESTABROOK
TSCHERMAK
ZSIGMONDY
ATANASOFF
CTESIBIUS
STANISLAO
STANISLAW
STAPLETON
STEENBERG
STEENBOCK
STEINBECK
STEINKAMP
STEINMETZ
STEVENSON
STOICHEFF
STONEHILL
STRADLING
STRASSMAN
STREISAND
STROMGREN
AULENBACK
BURGUNDIO
BURKHARDT
BURROUGHS
BUTENANDT
DUNALDSON
DUTROCHET
EUPALINUS
EURIPIDES
EUSTACHIO
FULLERTON
GUGLIELMO
GUILLAUME
GUILLEMIN
GUSTAFSON
GUTENBERG
HUTCHINGS
HUTCHISON
JUSTINIAN
KURCHATOV
LUCRETIUS
MURCHISON
MUSSOLINI
QUASIMODO
RUHMKORFF
SUSSMILCH
TUNNSTALL
IVANOVICH
IVANOVSKY
HYACINTHE
SYLVESTER

## 3rd Letter

ANACHARIS
ATANASOFF
BEAUCHAMP
BIANCHINI
BLAKESLEE
BLANCHARD
BRACEWELL
BRACONNOT
CHAYEFSKY
CLAPEYRON
CLAUDETTE
FLAMSTEED
FRANCESCO
FRANCISCO
FRANCOISE
FRANKLAND
GIANNETTI
GLADSTONE
GRANVILLE
GRASSMANN
HEAVISIDE
HYACINTHE
IVANOVICH
IVANOVSKY
KRAUSHAAR
MCALISTER
QUASIMODO
SCAEBERLE
STANISLAO
STANISLAW
STAPLETON
WLADYSLAW
ALBERTSON
ARBUTHNOT
FABRICIUS
FIBONACCI
GABRIELLA
GABRIELLE
KOBREUTER
ROBERTSON
SABASTIAN
SEBASTIAN
ARCHIBALD
BECQUEREL
BOCCACCIO
COCKCROFT
COCKERELL
DECONCINI
DICKINSON
HECATAEUS
LECLANCHE
LUCRETIUS
MACARTHUR
MACDONALD
MACEDONIO
MACMILLAN
MCCONNELL
MCCORMICK
MECHNIKOV
MICHAELIS
MICHELSON
NICEPHORE
NICHOLSON
NICKERSON
NICOLAIER
PICKERING
ROCCHETTI
ROCHESTER
TACHENIUS
TSCHERMAK
ZACHERIAS
ALDEROTTI
EDDINGTON
LEDERBERG
MCDOUGALL
OLDENBURG
SODERBLOM
WEDGEWOOD
ALEKSANDR
ALEXANDER
ALEXANDRE
ASERINSKY
BEERNAERT
BOERHAAVE
CHERENKOV
CLEOPATRA
CLEVELAND
CRESWICKE
CTESIBIUS
DIEUDONNE
FREDERICK
GJELLERUP
GREENBERG
GREENWOOD
KOENEKAMP
LLEWELLYN
MIELZINER
NEETHLING
NIEUWLAND
SHECHTMAN
SIEGFRIED
STEENBERG
STEENBOCK
STEINBECK
STEINKAMP
STEINMETZ
STEVENSON
THEODORIC
THEODORUS
THEOPHILE
VIEUSSENS
WIESCHAUS
ARFWEDSON
HAFFENDEN
JEFFERSON
ALGAROTTI
GEGENBAUR
GUGLIELMO
RIGOBERTA
ROGGEVEEN
ECHEGARAY
HAHNEMANN
JOHANNSEN
JOHNSTONE
MAHARIDGE
MEHRINGER
RUHMKORFF
SCHAFFNER
SCHAUDINN
SCHLEIDEN
SCHOEFFER
SCHONBEIN
SCHONLEIN
SCHULBERG
SCHWEIZER
SCHWINGER
WAHLSTROM
ARISTIDES
ARISTOTLE
BEILSTEIN
CAILLETET
CRISTIANI
ELIZABETH
FAIRBAIRN
FRIEDMANN
FRIEDRICH
GUILLAUME
GUILLEMIN
PHILIPPUS
PHILOLAUS
PRIESTLEY
PRIGOGINE
PRITCHARD
RAINWATER
SPIELBERG
SPITTELER
SRINIVASA
WEISSKOPF
WEISSMANN
WHINFIELD
WHITEHEAD
WHITTAKER
WHITWORTH
ZSIGMONDY
ARKWRIGHT
BEKTHEREV
TAKAHASHI
AULENBACK
BALTIMORE
BOLTZMANN
CALLENDAR
CALLIPPUS
DALRYMPLE
DELEZENNE
EILENBERG
ELLENSHAW
FALLOPIUS
FULLERTON
GILLESPIE
GOLDHABER
GOLDSTEIN
GOLDSTINE
GOLDSTONE
HELVETIUS
HOLLERITH
KOLREUTER
MILESTONE
PELLETIER
POLLENDER
SALVATORE
SILLANPAA
SYLVESTER
UHLENBECK
VALENTINA
VALENTINE
WILKINSON
WILLADSEN
WILLUGHBY
WOLFSKEHL
WOLLASTON
ALMENDROS
AMMERMANN
ARMSTRONG
BAMBERGER
DAMOISEAU
DEMESTRAL
DOMINIQUE
GEMINIANO
HAMMURABI
HEMINGWAY
LAMORISSE
LEMONOSOV
LOMONOSOV
RAMANUJAN
ROMANENKO
SEMIRAMIS
SOMERFELD
ARNOLDSON
BENAVENTE
BENEDETTO
BENEDICKS
BENZELIUS
CONDORCET
CONYBEARE
DONALDSON
DUNALDSON
EINTHOVEN
GANSWINDT
HENDERSON
HENRIETTA
KENZABURO
LANCASTER
LENORMAND
LINDBERGH
MENDELEEV
MINKOWSKI
MONTANARI
OENOPIDES
TANIGUCHI
TINBERGEN
TUNNSTALL
VANNOCCIO
VINCENZIO
ZINNEMANN
BJORKHOLM
BRODERICK
BROUNCKER
CRONSTEDT
DIONYSIUS
FLORIMOND
FROESCHEL
FRONTINUS
GOODRICKE
GROTEFEND
GROTTHUSS
KRONECKER
LIOUVILLE
PROKHOROV
ROOSEVELT
ROOZEBOOM
SHOLOKHOV
STOICHEFF
STONEHILL
THORNDIKE
EUPALINUS
HIPPOLYTE
MCPHERSON
SOPHOCLES
MCQUARRIE
AFRAGAMUS
AGRAMONTE
ARRHENIUS
BARGHOORN
BARRINGER
BARRYMORE
BARTHOLIN
BERGSTROM
BERNIGAUD
BERNOULLI
BERNSTEIN
BERTHELOT
BERZELIUS
BIRKELAND
BORNSTEIN
BURGUNDIO
BURKHARDT
BURROUGHS
CAROTHERS
CARPENTER
CHRISTAIN
CHRISTIAN
CHRISTINE
CHRISTOFF
CHRISTOPH
CORNEILLE
CORNELIUS
CORNFORTH
DIRICHLET
EHRENBERG
EURIPIDES
FERCHAULT
FERDINAND
FORLANINI
FORSSMANN
GERALDINE
GORBACHEV
HERODOTUS
HORODYSKY
JARNOWSKY
JORGENSEN
JORGENSON
KARDASHEV
KARLFELDT
KIRCHHOFF
KURCHATOV
MARTINSON
MORTILLET
MURCHISON
NIRENBERG
PARKINSON
PERCIVALL
RORSCHACH
SERTURNER
STRADLING
STRASSMAN
STREISAND
STROMGREN
TARANTINO
TARTAGLIA
VERNADSKY
WARBURTON
BESSARION
BOSCOVICH
CASCARDIO
CASSERIUS
CESALPINO
DESARGUES
DESCARTES
DESMAREST
EUSTACHIO
FESSENDEN
GASCOIGNE
GUSTAFSON
HASBROUCK
JOSEPHINE
JOSEPHSON
JUSTINIAN
KISSINGER
LOSCHMIDT
MASKELYNE
MOSSBAUER
MUSSOLINI
NISHIJIMA
PASTERNAK
ROSENBAUM

ROSENBERG
SOSIGENES
SUSSMILCH
VESPASIAN
VESPUSIUS
WASSERMAN
ALTRAMURA
BATAILLON
BUTENANDT
DUTROCHET
ESTABROOK
GOTTFRIED
GUTENBERG
HITCHINGS
HUTCHINGS
HUTCHISON
KATHARINE
KETTERING
LATREILLE
NATHANAEL
NATHANIEL
PETROSIAN
TITCHENER
VITRUVIUS
WETHERALD
WITHERING
BOURGEOIS
CHURCHILL
DAUBENTON
FEUERBACH
FRUCHTMAN
GRUENTZIG
HAUPTMANN
HAUSDORFF
LEUCIPPUS
MAUROLICO
PRUDHOMME
ROUSSELOT
SOUBEIRAN
SOUTHGATE
TOUSSIENG
VAUQUELIN
CAVALIERI
CAVENDISH
LAVOISIER
LEVERRIER
REVEILLON
RAWLINSON
ARYABHATA
HEYROVSKY
GAZZANIGA

## 4TH LETTER

AFRAGAMUS
AGRAMONTE
ALGAROTTI
ARYABHATA
BATAILLON
BENAVENTE
CAVALIERI
CESALPINO
DESARGUES
DONALDSON
DUNALDSON
ESTABROOK
EUPALINUS
GERALDINE
HECATAEUS
JOHANNSEN
MACARTHUR
MAHARIDGE
RAMANUJAN
ROMANENKO
SABASTIAN
SCHAFFNER
SCHAUDINN
SEBASTIAN
STRADLING
STRASSMAN
TAKAHASHI
TARANTINO
BAMBERGER
DAUBENTON
GORBACHEV
HASBROUCK
SOUBEIRAN
TINBERGEN
WARBURTON
ANACHARIS
BOCCACCIO
BOSCOVICH
BRACEWELL
BRACONNOT
CASCARDIO
DESCARTES
FERCHAULT
FRUCHTMAN
GASCOIGNE
HITCHINGS
HUTCHINGS
HUTCHISON
HYACINTHE
KIRCHHOFF
KURCHATOV
LANCASTER
LEUCIPPUS
LOSCHMIDT
MURCHISON
PERCIVALL
ROCCHETTI
SHECHTMAN
TITCHENER
VINCENZIO
BRODERICK
CONDORCET
FERDINAND
FREDERICK
GLADSTONE
GOLDHABER
GOLDSTEIN
GOLDSTINE
GOLDSTONE
GOODRICKE
HENDERSON
KARDASHEV
LINDBERGH
MACDONALD
MENDELEEV
PRUDHOMME
WLADYSLAW
ALBERTSON
ALDEROTTI
ALMENDROS
AMMERMANN
AULENBACK
BENEDETTO
BENEDICKS
BUTENANDT
CAVENDISH
DELEZENNE
DEMESTRAL
ECHEGARAY
EHRENBERG
EILENBERG
ELLENSHAW
FEUERBACH
FRIEDMANN
FRIEDRICH
FROESCHEL
GEGENBAUR
GREENBERG
GREENWOOD
GRUENTZIG
GUTENBERG
JOSEPHINE
JOSEPHSON
LEDERBERG
LEVERRIER
MACEDONIO
MILESTONE
NICEPHORE
NIRENBERG
OLDENBURG
PRIESTLEY
REVEILLON
ROBERTSON
ROSENBAUM
ROSENBERG
SCAEBERLE
SODERBLOM
SOMERFELD
SPIELBERG
STEENBERG
STEENBOCK
STREISAND
UHLENBECK
VALENTINA
VALENTINE
HAFFENDEN
JEFFERSON
WOLFSKEHL
BARGHOORN
BERGSTROM
BURGUNDIO
JORGENSEN
JORGENSON
PRIGOGINE
ROGGEVEEN
SIEGFRIED
WEDGEWOOD
ZSIGMONDY
ARCHIBALD
ARRHENIUS
KATHARINE
MCPHERSON
MECHNIKOV
MICHAELIS
MICHELSON
NATHANAEL
NATHANIEL
NICHOLSON
NISHIJIMA
ROCHESTER
SOPHOCLES
TACHENIUS
TSCHERMAK
WETHERALD
WITHERING
ZACHERIAS
CHRISTAIN
CHRISTIAN
CHRISTINE
CHRISTOFF
CHRISTOPH
DIRICHLET
DOMINIQUE
EDDINGTON
EURIPIDES
GEMINIANO
HEMINGWAY
SEMIRAMIS
SOSIGENES
STEINBECK
STEINKAMP
STEINMETZ
STOICHEFF
TANIGUCHI
ALEKSANDR
BIRKELAND
BLAKESLEE
BURKHARDT
COCKCROFT
COCKERELL
DICKINSON
MASKELYNE
MINKOWSKI
NICKERSON
PARKINSON
PICKERING
PROKHOROV
WILKINSON
BEILSTEIN
CAILLETET
CALLENDAR
CALLIPPUS
FALLOPIUS
FORLANINI
FULLERTON
GILLESPIE
GJELLERUP
GUGLIELMO
GUILLAUME
GUILLEMIN
HOLLERITH
KARLFELDT
LECLANCHE
MCALISTER
MIELZINER
PELLETIER
PHILIPPUS
PHILOLAUS
POLLENDER
RAWLINSON
SCHLEIDEN
SHOLOKHOV
SILLANPAA
WAHLSTROM
WILLADSEN
WILLUGHBY
WOLLASTON
DESMAREST
FLAMSTEED
HAMMURABI
MACMILLAN
RUHMKORFF
ATANASOFF
BERNIGAUD
BERNOULLI
BERNSTEIN
BIANCHINI
BLANCHARD
BORNSTEIN
CORNEILLE
CORNELIUS
CORNFORTH
CRONSTEDT
DIONYSIUS
FRANCESCO
FRANCISCO
FRANCOISE
FRANKLAND
FRONTINUS
GIANNETTI
GRANVILLE
HAHNEMANN
IVANOVICH
IVANOVSKY
JARNOWSKY
JOHNSTONE
KOENEKAMP
KRONECKER
RAINWATER
SRINIVASA
STANISLAO
STANISLAW
STONEHILL
TUNNSTALL
VANNOCCIO
VERNADSKY
WHINFIELD
ZINNEMANN
ARNOLDSON
CAROTHERS
CLEOPATRA
DAMOISEAU
DECONCINI
FIBONACCI
HERODOTUS
HORODYSKY
LAMORISSE
LAVOISIER
LEMONOSOV
LENORMAND
LOMONOSOV
MCCONNELL
MCCORMICK
MCDOUGALL
NICOLAIER
OENOPIDES
RIGOBERTA
SCHOEFFER
SCHONBEIN
SCHONLEIN
STROMGREN
THEODORIC
THEODORUS
THEOPHILE
CARPENTER
CLAPEYRON
HAUPTMANN
HIPPOLYTE
STAPLETON
VESPASIAN
VESPUSIUS
BECQUEREL
VAUQUELIN
ALTRAMURA
ASERINSKY
BARRINGER
BARRYMORE
BEERNAERT
BJORKHOLM
BOERHAAVE
BOURGEOIS
BURROUGHS
CHERENKOV
CHURCHILL
DALRYMPLE
DUTROCHET
FABRICIUS
FAIRBAIRN
FLORIMOND
GABRIELLA
GABRIELLE
HENRIETTA
HEYROVSKY
KOBREUTER
KOLREUTER
LATREILLE
LUCRETIUS
MAUROLICO
MEHRINGER
PETROSIAN
THORNDIKE
VITRUVIUS
ARISTIDES
ARISTOTLE
ARMSTRONG
BESSARION
CASSERIUS
CRESWICKE
CRISTIANI
CTESIBIUS
FESSENDEN
FORSSMANN
GANSWINDT
GRASSMANN
HAUSDORFF
KISSINGER
MOSSBAUER
MUSSOLINI
QUASIMODO
ROOSEVELT
RORSCHACH
ROUSSELOT
SUSSMILCH
TOUSSIENG
WASSERMAN
WEISSKOPF
WEISSMANN
WIESCHAUS
BALTIMORE
BARTHOLIN
BEKTHEREV
BERTHELOT
BOLTZMANN
EINTHOVEN
EUSTACHIO
GOTTFRIED
GROTEFEND
GROTTHUSS
GUSTAFSON
JUSTINIAN
KETTERING
MARTINSON
MONTANARI
MORTILLET
NEETHLING
PASTERNAK
PRITCHARD
SERTURNER
SOUTHGATE
SPITTELER
TARTAGLIA
WHITEHEAD
WHITTAKER
WHITWORTH
ARBUTHNOT
BEAUCHAMP
BROUNCKER
CLAUDETTE
DIEUDONNE
KRAUSHAAR
LIOUVILLE
MCQUARRIE
NIEUWLAND
SCHULBERG
VIEUSSENS
CLEVELAND
HEAVISIDE
HELVETIUS
SALVATORE
STEVENSON
SYLVESTER
ARFWEDSON
ARKWRIGHT
LLEWELLYN
SCHWEIZER
SCHWINGER
ALEXANDER
ALEXANDRE
CHAYEFSKY
CONYBEARE
BENZELIUS

BER**Z**ELIUS
ELI**Z**ABETH
GAZ**Z**ANIGA
KEN**Z**ABURO
ROO**Z**EBOOM

### 5th Letter

ALEX**A**NDER
ALEX**A**NDRE
ALTR**A**MURA
ATAN**A**SOFF
BESS**A**RION
BOCC**A**CCIO
CASC**A**RDIO
DESC**A**RTES
DESM**A**REST
ELIZ**A**BETH
EUST**A**CHIO
FORL**A**NINI
GAZZ**A**NIGA
GORB**A**CHEV
GUST**A**FSON
KARD**A**SHEV
KATH**A**RINE
KENZ**A**BURO
LANC**A**STER
LECL**A**NCHE
MCQU**A**RRIE
MICH**A**ELIS
MONT**A**NARI
NATH**A**NAEL
NATH**A**NIEL
SALV**A**TORE
SILL**A**NPAA
TART**A**GLIA
VERN**A**DSKY
VESP**A**SIAN
WILL**A**DSEN
WOLL**A**STON
ARYA**B**HATA
CONY**B**EARE
ESTA**B**ROOK
FAIR**B**AIRN
LIND**B**ERGH
MOSS**B**AUER
RIGO**B**ERTA
SCAE**B**ERLE
BEAU**C**HAMP
BIAN**C**HINI
BLAN**C**HARD
CHUR**C**HILL
COCK**C**ROFT
DIRI**C**HLET
FRAN**C**ESCO
FRAN**C**ISCO
FRAN**C**OISE
PRIT**C**HARD
RORS**C**HACH
STOI**C**HEFF
WIES**C**HAUS
BENE**D**ETTO
BENE**D**ICKS
CLAU**D**ETTE
DIEU**D**ONNE
FRIE**D**MANN
FRIE**D**RICH
HAUS**D**ORFF
HERO**D**OTUS
HORO**D**YSKY
MACE**D**ONIO
STRA**D**LING
THEO**D**ORIC
THEO**D**ORUS
ARFW**E**DSON
ARRH**E**NIUS
BAMB**E**RGER
BENZ**E**LIUS
BERZ**E**LIUS
BIRK**E**LAND
BLAK**E**SLEE
BRAC**E**WELL
BROD**E**RICK
CALL**E**NDAR
CARP**E**NTER
CASS**E**RIUS
CHAY**E**FSKY
CHER**E**NKOV
CLAP**E**YRON
CLEV**E**LAND
COCK**E**RELL
CORN**E**ILLE
CORN**E**LIUS
DAUB**E**NTON
FESS**E**NDEN
FRED**E**RICK
FULL**E**RTON
GILL**E**SPIE
GROT**E**FEND
HAFF**E**NDEN
HAHN**E**MANN
HELV**E**TIUS
HEND**E**RSON
HOLL**E**RITH
JEFF**E**RSON
JORG**E**NSEN
JORG**E**NSON
KETT**E**RING
KOBR**E**UTER
KOEN**E**KAMP
KOLR**E**UTER
KRON**E**CKER
LATR**E**ILLE
LLEW**E**LLYN
LUCR**E**TIUS
MASK**E**LYNE
MCPH**E**RSON
MEND**E**LEEV
MICH**E**LSON
NICK**E**RSON
PAST**E**RNAK
PELL**E**TIER
PICK**E**RING
POLL**E**NDER
ROCH**E**STER
ROGG**E**VEEN
ROOS**E**VELT
ROOZ**E**BOOM
SCHL**E**IDEN
SCHO**E**FFER
SCHW**E**IZER
SOUB**E**IRAN
STEV**E**NSON
STON**E**HILL
SYLV**E**STER
TACH**E**NIUS
TINB**E**RGEN
TSCH**E**RMAK
VINC**E**NZIO
WASS**E**RMAN
WEDG**E**WOOD
WETH**E**RALD
WHIT**E**HEAD
WITH**E**RING
ZACH**E**RIAS
ZINN**E**MANN
CORN**F**ORTH
GOTT**F**RIED
KARL**F**ELDT
SCHA**F**FNER
SIEG**F**RIED
WHIN**F**IELD
AFRA**G**AMUS
BOUR**G**EOIS
ECHE**G**ARAY
SOSI**G**ENES
TANI**G**UCHI
ANAC**H**ARIS
BARG**H**OORN
BART**H**OLIN
BEKT**H**EREV
BERT**H**ELOT
BOER**H**AAVE
BURK**H**ARDT
EINT**H**OVEN
FERC**H**AULT
FRUC**H**TMAN
GOLD**H**ABER
HITC**H**INGS
HUTC**H**INGS
HUTC**H**ISON
KIRC**H**HOFF
KURC**H**ATOV
LOSC**H**MIDT
MURC**H**ISON
NEET**H**LING
PROK**H**OROV
PRUD**H**OMME
ROCC**H**ETTI
SHEC**H**TMAN
SOUT**H**GATE
TAKA**H**ASHI
TITC**H**ENER
ARCH**I**BALD
ASER**I**NSKY
BALT**I**MORE
BARR**I**NGER
BATA**I**LLON
BERN**I**GAUD
CALL**I**PPUS
CTES**I**BIUS
DAMO**I**SEAU
DICK**I**NSON
FABR**I**CIUS
FERD**I**NAND
FLOR**I**MOND
GABR**I**ELLA
GABR**I**ELLE
GUGL**I**ELMO
HEAV**I**SIDE
HENR**I**ETTA
HYAC**I**NTHE
JUST**I**NIAN
KISS**I**NGER
LAVO**I**SIER
LEUC**I**PPUS
MACM**I**LLAN
MART**I**NSON
MCAL**I**STER
MEHR**I**NGER
MORT**I**LLET
NISH**I**JIMA
PARK**I**NSON
PERC**I**VALL
PHIL**I**PPUS
QUAS**I**MODO
RAWL**I**NSON
REVE**I**LLON
SCHW**I**NGER
SRIN**I**VASA
STAN**I**SLAO
STAN**I**SLAW
STRE**I**SAND
WILK**I**NSON
BJOR**K**HOLM
FRAN**K**LAND
RUHM**K**ORFF
ARNO**L**DSON
CAIL**L**ETET
CAVA**L**IERI
CESA**L**PINO
DONA**L**DSON
DUNA**L**DSON
EUPA**L**INUS
GERA**L**DINE
GJEL**L**ERUP
GUIL**L**AUME
GUIL**L**EMIN
NICO**L**AIER
SCHU**L**BERG
SPIE**L**BERG
STAP**L**ETON
AGRA**M**ONTE
STRO**M**GREN
SUSS**M**ILCH
ZSIG**M**ONDY
ALME**N**DROS
AULE**N**BACK
BEER**N**AERT
BROU**N**CKER
BUTE**N**ANDT
CAVE**N**DISH
DECO**N**CINI
DOMI**N**IQUE
EDDI**N**GTON
EHRE**N**BERG
EILE**N**BERG
ELLE**N**SHAW
FIBO**N**ACCI
GEGE**N**BAUR
GEMI**N**IANO
GIAN**N**ETTI
GREE**N**BERG
GREE**N**WOOD
GRUE**N**TZIG
GUTE**N**BERG
HEMI**N**GWAY
JOHA**N**NSEN
LEMO**N**OSOV
LOMO**N**OSOV
MCCO**N**NELL
MECH**N**IKOV
NIRE**N**BERG
OLDE**N**BURG
RAMA**N**UJAN
ROMA**N**ENKO
ROSE**N**BAUM
ROSE**N**BERG
SCHO**N**BEIN
SCHO**N**LEIN
STEE**N**BERG
STEE**N**BOCK
STEI**N**BECK
STEI**N**KAMP
STEI**N**METZ
TARA**N**TINO
THOR**N**DIKE
UHLE**N**BECK
VALE**N**TINA
VALE**N**TINE
BERN**O**ULLI
BOSC**O**VICH
BRAC**O**NNOT
BURR**O**UGHS
COND**O**RCET
DUTR**O**CHET
FALL**O**PIUS
GASC**O**IGNE
HEYR**O**VSKY
HIPP**O**LYTE
IVAN**O**VICH
IVAN**O**VSKY
JARN**O**WSKY
MACD**O**NALD
MAUR**O**LICO
MINK**O**WSKI
MUSS**O**LINI
NICH**O**LSON
PETR**O**SIAN
PHIL**O**LAUS
PRIG**O**GINE
SHOL**O**KHOV
SOPH**O**CLES
VANN**O**CCIO
CLEO**P**ATRA
EURI**P**IDES
JOSE**P**HINE
JOSE**P**HSON
NICE**P**HORE
OENO**P**IDES
THEO**P**HILE
ALBE**R**TSON
ALDE**R**OTTI
ALGA**R**OTTI
AMME**R**MANN
ARKW**R**IGHT
DESA**R**GUES
FEUE**R**BACH
GOOD**R**ICKE
HASB**R**OUCK
LAMO**R**ISSE
LEDE**R**BERG
LENO**R**MAND
LEVE**R**RIER
MACA**R**THUR
MAHA**R**IDGE
MCCO**R**MICK
ROBE**R**TSON
SEMI**R**AMIS
SODE**R**BLOM
SOME**R**FELD
ALEK**S**ANDR
BEIL**S**TEIN
BERG**S**TROM
BERN**S**TEIN
BORN**S**TEIN
CHRI**S**TAIN
CHRI**S**TIAN
CHRI**S**TINE
CHRI**S**TOFF
CHRI**S**TOPH
CRON**S**TEDT
DEME**S**TRAL
FLAM**S**TEED
FORS**S**MANN
FROE**S**CHEL
GLAD**S**TONE
GOLD**S**TEIN
GOLD**S**TINE
GOLD**S**TONE
GRAS**S**MANN
JOHN**S**TONE
KRAU**S**HAAR
MILE**S**TONE
PRIE**S**TLEY
ROUS**S**ELOT
SABA**S**TIAN
SEBA**S**TIAN
STRA**S**SMAN
TOUS**S**IENG
TUNN**S**TALL
VIEU**S**SENS
WAHL**S**TROM
WEIS**S**KOPF
WEIS**S**MANN
WOLF**S**KEHL
ARBU**T**HNOT
ARIS**T**IDES
ARIS**T**OTLE
ARMS**T**RONG
CARO**T**HERS
CRIS**T**IANI
FRON**T**INUS
GROT**T**HUSS
HAUP**T**MANN
HECA**T**AEUS
SPIT**T**ELER
WHIT**T**AKER
BECQ**U**EREL
BURG**U**NDIO
HAMM**U**RABI
MCDO**U**GALL
SCHA**U**DINN
SERT**U**RNER
VAUQ**U**ELIN
VESP**U**SIUS
VITR**U**VIUS
WARB**U**RTON
WILL**U**GHBY
BENA**V**ENTE
GRAN**V**ILLE
LIOU**V**ILLE
CRES**W**ICKE
GANS**W**INDT
NIEU**W**LAND
RAIN**W**ATER
WHIT**W**ORTH
BARR**Y**MORE
DALR**Y**MPLE
DION**Y**SIUS
WLAD**Y**SLAW
BOLT**Z**MANN
DELE**Z**ENNE
MIEL**Z**INER

### 6th Letter

AFRAG**A**MUS
ALEKS**A**NDR
ANACH**A**RIS
BEERN**A**ERT
BOERH**A**AVE
BURKH**A**RDT
BUTEN**A**NDT
CLEOP**A**TRA
ECHEG**A**RAY
FAIRB**A**IRN
FERCH**A**ULT
FIBON**A**CCI
GOLDH**A**BER
GUILL**A**UME
HECAT**A**EUS
KURCH**A**TOV
MOSSB**A**UER
NICOL**A**IER
RAINW**A**TER
SEMIR**A**MIS
TAKAH**A**SHI
WHITT**A**KER
ARCHI**B**ALD
AULEN**B**ACK
CTESI**B**IUS
EHREN**B**ERG
EILEN**B**ERG
ELIZA**B**ETH
FEUER**B**ACH
GEGEN**B**AUR
GREEN**B**ERG
GUTEN**B**ERG
KENZA**B**URO
LEDER**B**ERG
NIREN**B**ERG

OLDENBURG
ROOZEBOOM
ROSENBAUM
ROSENBERG
SCHONBEIN
SCHULBERG
SODERBLOM
SPIELBERG
STEENBERG
STEENBOCK
STEINBECK
UHLENBECK
BOCCACCIO
BROUNCKER
DECONCINI
DUTROCHET
EUSTACHIO
FABRICIUS
FROESCHEL
GORBACHEV
KRONECKER
SOPHOCLES
VANNOCCIO
ALMENDROS
ARFWEDSON
ARNOLDSON
CAVENDISH
DONALDSON
DUNALDSON
GERALDINE
SCHAUDINN
THORNDIKE
VERNADSKY
WILLADSEN
BECQUEREL
BEKTHEREV
BENAVENTE
BENEDETTO
BERTHELOT
BOURGEOIS
CAILLETET
CLAUDETTE
CONYBEARE
DELEZENNE
FRANCESCO
GABRIELLA
GABRIELLE
GIANNETTI
GJELLERUP
GUGLIELMO
GUILLEMIN
HENRIETTA
KARLFELDT
LINDBERGH
MICHAELIS
RIGOBERTA
ROCCHETTI

ROMANENKO
ROUSSELOT
SCAEBERLE
SOSIGENES
SPITTELER
STAPLETON
TITCHENER
VAUQUELIN
CHAYEFSKY
GROTEFEND
GUSTAFSON
SCHAFFNER
SCHOEFFER
SOMERFELD
BERNIGAUD
DESARGUES
EDDINGTON
HEMINGWAY
MCDOUGALL
PRIGOGINE
SOUTHGATE
STROMGREN
TARTAGLIA
WILLUGHBY
ARBUTHNOT
ARYABHATA
BEAUCHAMP
BIANCHINI
BJORKHOLM
BLANCHARD
CAROTHERS
CHURCHILL
DIRICHLET
GROTTHUSS
JOSEPHINE
JOSEPHSON
KIRCHHOFF
KRAUSHAAR
NICEPHORE
PRITCHARD
RORSCHACH
STOICHEFF
STONEHILL
THEOPHILE
WHITEHEAD
WIESCHAUS
ARISTIDES
ARKWRIGHT
BENEDICKS
CAVALIERI
CORNEILLE
CRESWICKE
CRISTIANI
DOMINIQUE
EUPALINUS
EURIPIDES
FRANCISCO

FRONTINUS
GANSWINDT
GASCOIGNE
GEMINIANO
GOODRICKE
GRANVILLE
HITCHINGS
HUTCHINGS
HUTCHISON
LAMORISSE
LATREILLE
LIOUVILLE
MAHARIDGE
MECHNIKOV
MIELZINER
MURCHISON
OENOPIDES
SCHLEIDEN
SCHWEIZER
SOUBEIRAN
SUSSMILCH
TOUSSIENG
WHINFIELD
NISHIJIMA
KOENEKAMP
SHOLOKHOV
STEINKAMP
WEISSKOPF
WOLFSKEHL
BATAILLON
BENZELIUS
BERZELIUS
BIRKELAND
CLEVELAND
CORNELIUS
FRANKLAND
HIPPOLYTE
LLEWELLYN
MACMILLAN
MASKELYNE
MAUROLICO
MENDELEEV
MICHELSON
MORTILLET
MUSSOLINI
NEETHLING
NICHOLSON
NIEUWLAND
PHILOLAUS
REVEILLON
SCHONLEIN
STRADLING
ALTRAMURA
AMMERMANN
BALTIMORE
BARRYMORE
BOLTZMANN

DALRYMPLE
FLORIMOND
FORSSMANN
FRIEDMANN
GRASSMANN
HAHNEMANN
HAUPTMANN
LENORMAND
LOSCHMIDT
MCCORMICK
QUASIMODO
STEINMETZ
WEISSMANN
ZINNEMANN
ALEXANDER
ALEXANDRE
ARRHENIUS
ASERINSKY
BARRINGER
BRACONNOT
BURGUNDIO
CALLENDAR
CARPENTER
CHERENKOV
DAUBENTON
DICKINSON
FERDINAND
FESSENDEN
FORLANINI
GAZZANIGA
HAFFENDEN
HYACINTHE
JOHANNSEN
JORGENSEN
JORGENSON
JUSTINIAN
KISSINGER
LECLANCHE
MACDONALD
MARTINSON
MCCONNELL
MEHRINGER
MONTANARI
NATHANAEL
NATHANIEL
PARKINSON
POLLENDER
RAWLINSON
SCHWINGER
SILLANPAA
STEVENSON
TACHENIUS
VINCENZIO
WILKINSON
AGRAMONTE
ALDEROTTI
ALGAROTTI

ARISTOTLE
BARGHOORN
BARTHOLIN
CORNFORTH
DIEUDONNE
EINTHOVEN
FRANCOISE
HASBROUCK
HAUSDORFF
HERODOTUS
LEMONOSOV
LOMONOSOV
MACEDONIO
PROKHOROV
PRUDHOMME
RUHMKORFF
THEODORIC
THEODORUS
WHITWORTH
ZSIGMONDY
CALLIPPUS
CESALPINO
FALLOPIUS
LEUCIPPUS
PHILIPPUS
ARMSTRONG
BAMBERGER
BESSARION
BRODERICK
CASCARDIO
CASSERIUS
COCKCROFT
COCKERELL
CONDORCET
DESCARTES
DESMAREST
ESTABROOK
FREDERICK
FRIEDRICH
FULLERTON
GOTTFRIED
HAMMURABI
HENDERSON
HOLLERITH
JEFFERSON
KATHARINE
KETTERING
LEVERRIER
MCPHERSON
MCQUARRIE
NICKERSON
PASTERNAK
PICKERING
SERTURNER
SIEGFRIED
TINBERGEN
TSCHERMAK

WARBURTON
WASSERMAN
WETHERALD
WITHERING
ZACHERIAS
ATANASOFF
BLAKESLEE
DAMOISEAU
DIONYSIUS
ELLENSHAW
GILLESPIE
HEAVISIDE
KARDASHEV
LANCASTER
LAVOISIER
MCALISTER
PETROSIAN
ROCHESTER
STANISLAO
STANISLAW
STRASSMAN
STREISAND
SYLVESTER
VESPASIAN
VESPUSIUS
VIEUSSENS
WLADYSLAW
WOLLASTON
ALBERTSON
BEILSTEIN
BERGSTROM
BERNSTEIN
BORNSTEIN
CHRISTAIN
CHRISTIAN
CHRISTINE
CHRISTOFF
CHRISTOPH
CRONSTEDT
DEMESTRAL
FLAMSTEED
FRUCHTMAN
GLADSTONE
GOLDSTEIN
GOLDSTINE
GOLDSTONE
GRUENTZIG
HELVETIUS
JOHNSTONE
LUCRETIUS
MACARTHUR
MILESTONE
PELLETIER
PRIESTLEY
ROBERTSON
SABASTIAN
SALVATORE

SEBASTIAN
SHECHTMAN
TARANTINO
TUNNSTALL
VALENTINA
VALENTINE
WAHLSTROM
BERNOULLI
BURROUGHS
KOBREUTER
KOLREUTER
RAMANUJAN
TANIGUCHI
BOSCOVICH
HEYROVSKY
IVANOVICH
IVANOVSKY
PERCIVALL
ROGGEVEEN
ROOSEVELT
SRINIVASA
VITRUVIUS
BRACEWELL
GREENWOOD
JARNOWSKY
MINKOWSKI
WEDGEWOOD
CLAPEYRON
HORODYSKY

## 7TH LETTER

AMMERMANN
ARCHIBALD
ARYABHATA
AULENBACK
BEAUCHAMP
BERNIGAUD
BIRKELAND
BLANCHARD
BOERHAAVE
BOLTZMANN
CHRISTAIN
CLEVELAND
CONYBEARE
CRISTIANI
FERDINAND
FEUERBACH
FORSSMANN
FRANKLAND
FRIEDMANN
GEGENBAUR
GEMINIANO
GRASSMANN
HAHNEMANN

HAMMURABI
HAUPTMANN
KOENEKAMP
KRAUSHAAR
LENORMAND
MACDONALD
MCDOUGALL
MONTANARI
NATHANAEL
NIEUWLAND
PERCIVALL
PHILOLAUS
PRITCHARD
RORSCHACH
ROSENBAUM
SOUTHGATE
SRINIVASA
STEINKAMP
STREISAND
TUNNSTALL
WEISSMANN
WETHERALD
WIESCHAUS
ZINNEMANN
GOLDHABER
BENEDICKS
BOCCACCIO
CONDORCET
CRESWICKE
FIBONACCI
GOODRICKE
LECLANCHE
TANIGUCHI
VANNOCCIO
ALEXANDER
ALEXANDRE
ARISTIDES
BURGUNDIO
CALLENDAR
CASCARDIO
EURIPIDES
FESSENDEN
HAFFENDEN
MAHARIDGE
OENOPIDES
POLLENDER
SCHLEIDEN
BEERNAERT
BEILSTEIN
BERNSTEIN
BORNSTEIN
BRACEWELL
CAROTHERS
CAVALIERI
COCKERELL
CRONSTEDT
DAMOISEAU

DESMAREST
EHRENBERG
EILENBERG
ELIZABETH
FLAMSTEED
GOLDSTEIN
GREENBERG
GROTEFEND
GUTENBERG
HECATAEUS
LEDERBERG
MCCONNELL
MENDELEEV
NIRENBERG
ROGGEVEEN
ROOSEVELT
ROSENBERG
SCHONBEIN
SCHONLEIN
SCHULBERG
SOMERFELD
SPIELBERG
STEENBERG
STEINBECK
STEINMETZ
STOICHEFF
TOUSSIENG
UHLENBECK
VIEUSSENS
WHINFIELD
WHITEHEAD
WOLFSKEHL
SCHOEFFER
ARKWRIGHT
BAMBERGER
BARRINGER
BURROUGHS
GASCOIGNE
KISSINGER
MEHRINGER
SCHWINGER
TINBERGEN
DUTROCHET
ELLENSHAW
EUSTACHIO
FROESCHEL
GORBACHEV
KARDASHEV
MACARTHUR
SHOLOKHOV
WILLUGHBY
ARRHENIUS
BENZELIUS
BERZELIUS
BESSARION
BIANCHINI
BOSCOVICH

BRODERICK
CASSERIUS
CAVENDISH
CESALPINO
CHRISTIAN
CHRISTINE
CHURCHILL
CORNELIUS
CTESIBIUS
DECONCINI
DIONYSIUS
FABRICIUS
FAIRBAIRN
FALLOPIUS
FORLANINI
FRANCOISE
FREDERICK
FRIEDRICH
GAZZANIGA
GERALDINE
GOLDSTINE
GOTTFRIED
HEAVISIDE
HELVETIUS
HOLLERITH
IVANOVICH
JOSEPHINE
JUSTINIAN
KATHARINE
KETTERING
LAVOISIER
LEVERRIER
LOSCHMIDT
LUCRETIUS
MAUROLICO
MCCORMICK
MUSSOLINI
NATHANIEL
NEETHLING
NICOLAIER
NISHIJIMA
PELLETIER
PETROSIAN
PICKERING
PRIGOGINE
SABASTIAN
SCHAUDINN
SEBASTIAN
SIEGFRIED
STONEHILL
STRADLING
TACHENIUS
TARANTINO
THEOPHILE
THORNDIKE
VALENTINA
VALENTINE

VESPASIAN
VESPUSIUS
VITRUVIUS
WITHERING
ZACHERIAS
RAMANUJAN
BROUNCKER
CHERENKOV
KRONECKER
MECHNIKOV
WHITTAKER
BARTHOLIN
BATAILLON
BERNOULLI
BERTHELOT
BLAKESLEE
CORNEILLE
DIRICHLET
GABRIELLA
GABRIELLE
GRANVILLE
GUGLIELMO
KARLFELDT
LATREILLE
LIOUVILLE
LLEWELLYN
MACMILLAN
MICHAELIS
MORTILLET
PRIESTLEY
REVEILLON
ROUSSELOT
SODERBLOM
SOPHOCLES
SPITTELER
STANISLAO
STANISLAW
SUSSMILCH
TARTAGLIA
VAUQUELIN
WLADYSLAW
AFRAGAMUS
FRUCHTMAN
GUILLEMIN
PRUDHOMME
SEMIRAMIS
SHECHTMAN
STRASSMAN
TSCHERMAK
WASSERMAN
AGRAMONTE
ALEKSANDR
ARBUTHNOT
BENAVENTE
BRACONNOT
BUTENANDT
DELEZENNE

DIEUDONNE
EUPALINUS
FRONTINUS
GANSWINDT
HITCHINGS
HUTCHINGS
MACEDONIO
MIELZINER
PASTERNAK
ROMANENKO
SCHAFFNER
SERTURNER
SOSIGENES
TITCHENER
ZSIGMONDY
ARMSTRONG
ATANASOFF
BALTIMORE
BARGHOORN
BARRYMORE
BJORKHOLM
BOURGEOIS
CHRISTOFF
CHRISTOPH
COCKCROFT
ESTABROOK
FLORIMOND
GLADSTONE
GOLDSTONE
GREENWOOD
JOHNSTONE
KIRCHHOFF
MILESTONE
NICEPHORE
QUASIMODO
ROOZEBOOM
SALVATORE
STEENBOCK
WEDGEWOOD
WEISSKOPF
CALLIPPUS
DALRYMPLE
GILLESPIE
LEUCIPPUS
PHILIPPUS
SILLANPAA
DOMINIQUE
ALMENDROS
ANACHARIS
BECQUEREL
BEKTHEREV
BERGSTROM
BURKHARDT
CLAPEYRON
CORNFORTH
DEMESTRAL
ECHEGARAY

GJELLERUP
HAUSDORFF
LINDBERGH
MCQUARRIE
PROKHOROV
RIGOBERTA
RUHMKORFF
SCAEBERLE
SOUBEIRAN
STROMGREN
THEODORIC
THEODORUS
WAHLSTROM
WHITWORTH
ALBERTSON
ARFWEDSON
ARNOLDSON
ASERINSKY
CHAYEFSKY
DICKINSON
DONALDSON
DUNALDSON
FRANCESCO
FRANCISCO
GUSTAFSON
HENDERSON
HEYROVSKY
HORODYSKY
HUTCHISON
IVANOVSKY
JARNOWSKY
JEFFERSON
JOHANNSEN
JORGENSEN
JORGENSON
JOSEPHSON
LAMORISSE
LEMONOSOV
LOMONOSOV
MARTINSON
MCPHERSON
MICHELSON
MINKOWSKI
MURCHISON
NICHOLSON
NICKERSON
PARKINSON
RAWLINSON
ROBERTSON
STEVENSON
TAKAHASHI
VERNADSKY
WILKINSON
WILLADSEN
ALDEROTTI
ALGAROTTI
ARISTOTLE

BENEDETTO
CAILLETET
CARPENTER
CLAUDETTE
CLEOPATRA
DAUBENTON
DESCARTES
EDDINGTON
FULLERTON
GIANNETTI
HENRIETTA
HERODOTUS
HYACINTHE
KOBREUTER
KOLREUTER
KURCHATOV
LANCASTER
MCALISTER
RAINWATER
ROCCHETTI
ROCHESTER
STAPLETON
SYLVESTER
WARBURTON
WOLLASTON
ALTRAMURA
DESARGUES
FERCHAULT
GROTTHUSS
GUILLAUME
HASBROUCK
KENZABURO
MOSSBAUER
OLDENBURG
EINTHOVEN
HEMINGWAY
HIPPOLYTE
MASKELYNE
GRUENTZIG
SCHWEIZER
VINCENZIO

### 8th Letter

CALLENDAR
CHRISTIAN
DAMOISEAU
DEMESTRAL
ECHEGARAY
ELLENSHAW
FRUCHTMAN
HEMINGWAY
JUSTINIAN
KRAUSHAAR
MACMILLAN

PASTERNAK
PETROSIAN
RAMANUJAN
SABASTIAN
SEBASTIAN
SHECHTMAN
SILLANPAA
SOUBEIRAN
STANISLAO
STANISLAW
STRASSMAN
TSCHERMAK
VESPASIAN
WASSERMAN
WHITEHEAD
WLADYSLAW
ZACHERIAS
HAMMURABI
WILLUGHBY
AULENBACK
BOSCOVICH
BRODERICK
FEUERBACH
FIBONACCI
FRANCESCO
FRANCISCO
FREDERICK
FRIEDRICH
HASBROUCK
IVANOVICH
MAUROLICO
MCCORMICK
RORSCHACH
STEENBOCK
STEINBECK
SUSSMILCH
UHLENBECK
ALEKSANDR
BURKHARDT
BUTENANDT
CRONSTEDT
GANSWINDT
HEAVISIDE
KARLFELDT
LOSCHMIDT
QUASIMODO
ZSIGMONDY
ALEXANDER
ARISTIDES
BAMBERGER
BARRINGER
BECQUEREL
BEKTHEREV
BLAKESLEE
BROUNCKER
CAILLETET
CARPENTER

CONDORCET
DESARGUES
DESCARTES
DIRICHLET
DUTROCHET
EINTHOVEN
EURIPIDES
FESSENDEN
FLAMSTEED
FROESCHEL
GOLDHABER
GORBACHEV
GOTTFRIED
HAFFENDEN
JOHANNSEN
JORGENSEN
KARDASHEV
KISSINGER
KOBREUTER
KOLREUTER
KRONECKER
LANCASTER
LAVOISIER
LEVERRIER
MCALISTER
MEHRINGER
MENDELEEV
MIELZINER
MORTILLET
MOSSBAUER
NATHANAEL
NATHANIEL
NICOLAIER
OENOPIDES
PELLETIER
POLLENDER
PRIESTLEY
RAINWATER
ROCHESTER
ROGGEVEEN
SCHAFFNER
SCHLEIDEN
SCHOEFFER
SCHWEIZER
SCHWINGER
SERTURNER
SIEGFRIED
SOPHOCLES
SOSIGENES
SPITTELER
STROMGREN
SYLVESTER
TINBERGEN
TITCHENER
WHITTAKER
WILLADSEN
ATANASOFF

CHRISTOFF
COCKCROFT
HAUSDORFF
KIRCHHOFF
RUHMKORFF
STOICHEFF
GAZZANIGA
HITCHINGS
HUTCHINGS
LINDBERGH
MAHARIDGE
ARKWRIGHT
BURROUGHS
HYACINTHE
LECLANCHE
TAKAHASHI
TANIGUCHI
WOLFSKEHL
ANACHARIS
BARTHOLIN
BEILSTEIN
BERNSTEIN
BOCCACCIO
BORNSTEIN
BOURGEOIS
BURGUNDIO
CASCARDIO
CHRISTAIN
EUSTACHIO
GILLESPIE
GOLDSTEIN
GRUENTZIG
GUILLEMIN
MACEDONIO
MCQUARRIE
MICHAELIS
SCHONBEIN
SCHONLEIN
SEMIRAMIS
TARTAGLIA
THEODORIC
VANNOCCIO
VAUQUELIN
VINCENZIO
ASERINSKY
BENEDICKS
CHAYEFSKY
CRESWICKE
GOODRICKE
HEYROVSKY
HORODYSKY
IVANOVSKY
JARNOWSKY
MINKOWSKI
ROMANENKO
THORNDIKE
VERNADSKY

ARCHIBALD
ARISTOTLE
BERNOULLI
BJORKHOLM
BRACEWELL
CHURCHILL
COCKERELL
CORNEILLE
DALRYMPLE
FERCHAULT
GABRIELLA
GABRIELLE
GRANVILLE
LATREILLE
LIOUVILLE
MACDONALD
MCCONNELL
MCDOUGALL
PERCIVALL
ROOSEVELT
SCAEBERLE
SOMERFELD
STONEHILL
THEOPHILE
TUNNSTALL
WETHERALD
WHINFIELD
BEAUCHAMP
GUGLIELMO
GUILLAUME
KOENEKAMP
NISHIJIMA
PRUDHOMME
STEINKAMP
AMMERMANN
ARMSTRONG
BIANCHINI
BIRKELAND
BOLTZMANN
CESALPINO
CHRISTINE
CLEVELAND
CRISTIANI
DECONCINI
DELEZENNE
DIEUDONNE
FERDINAND
FLORIMOND
FORLANINI
FORSSMANN
FRANKLAND
FRIEDMANN
GASCOIGNE
GEMINIANO
GERALDINE
GLADSTONE
GOLDSTINE

GOLDSTONE
GRASSMANN
GROTEFEND
HAHNEMANN
HAUPTMANN
JOHNSTONE
JOSEPHINE
KATHARINE
KETTERING
LENORMAND
MASKELYNE
MILESTONE
MUSSOLINI
NEETHLING
NIEUWLAND
PICKERING
PRIGOGÍNE
SCHAUDINN
STRADLING
STREISAND
TARANTINO
TOUSSIENG
VALENTINA
VALENTINE
VIEUSSENS
WEISSMANN
WITHERING
ZINNEMANN
ALBERTSON
ALMENDROS
ARBUTHNOT
ARFWEDSON
ARNOLDSON
BATAILLON
BERGSTROM
BERTHELOT
BESSARION
BRACONNOT
CHERENKOV
CLAPEYRON
DAUBENTON
DICKINSON
DONALDSON
DUNALDSON
EDDINGTON
ESTABROOK
FULLERTON
GREENWOOD
GUSTAFSON
HENDERSON
HUTCHISON
JEFFERSON
JORGENSON
JOSEPHSON
KURCHATOV
LEMONOSOV
LOMONOSOV

MARTINSON
MCPHERSON
MECHNIKOV
MICHELSON
MURCHISON
NICHOLSON
NICKERSON
PARKINSON
PROKHOROV
RAWLINSON
REVEILLON
ROBERTSON
ROOZEBOOM
ROUSSELOT
SHOLOKHOV
SODERBLOM
STAPLETON
STEVENSON
WAHLSTROM
WARBURTON
WEDGEWOOD
WILKINSON
WOLLASTON
CHRISTOPH
WEISSKOPF
ALEXANDRE
ALTRAMURA
BALTIMORE
BARGHOORN
BARRYMORE
BEERNAERT
BLANCHARD
CAROTHERS
CAVALIERI
CLEOPATRA
CONYBEARE
EHRENBERG
EILENBERG
FAIRBAIRN
GREENBERG
GUTENBERG
KENZABURO
LEDERBERG
MONTANARI
NICEPHORE
NIRENBERG
OLDENBURG
PRITCHARD
ROSENBERG
SALVATORE
SCHULBERG
SPIELBERG
STEENBERG
CAVENDISH
DESMAREST
FRANCOISE
GROTTHUSS

LAMORISSE
SRINIVASA
AGRAMONTE
ALDEROTTI
ALGAROTTI
ARYABHATA
BENAVENTE
BENEDETTO
CLAUDETTE
CORNFORTH
ELIZABETH
GIANNETTI
HENRIETTA
HIPPOLYTE
HOLLERITH
RIGOBERTA
ROCCHETTI
SOUTHGATE
STEINMETZ
WHITWORTH
AFRAGAMUS
ARRHENIUS
BENZELIUS
BERNIGAUD
BERZELIUS
CALLIPPUS
CASSERIUS
CORNELIUS
CTESIBIUS
DIONYSIUS
DOMINIQUE
EUPALINUS
FABRICIUS
FALLOPIUS
FRONTINUS
GEGENBAUR
GJELLERUP
HECATAEUS
HELVETIUS
HERODOTUS
LEUCIPPUS
LUCRETIUS
MACARTHUR
PHILIPPUS
PHILOLAUS
ROSENBAUM
TACHENIUS
THEODORUS
VESPUSIUS
VITRUVIUS
WIESCHAUS
BOERHAAVE
LLEWELLYN

## 9th Letter

ALTRAMURA
ARYABHATA
CLEOPATRA
GABRIELLA
GAZZANIGA
HENRIETTA
NISHIJIMA
RIGOBERTA
SILLANPAA
SRINIVASA
TARTAGLIA
VALENTINA
THEODORIC
ARCHIBALD
BERNIGAUD
BIRKELAND
BLANCHARD
CLEVELAND
FERDINAND
FLAMSTEED
FLORIMOND
FRANKLAND
GOTTFRIED
GREENWOOD
GROTEFEND
LENORMAND
MACDONALD
NIEUWLAND
PRITCHARD
SIEGFRIED
SOMERFELD
STREISAND
WEDGEWOOD
WETHERALD
WHINFIELD
WHITEHEAD
AGRAMONTE
ALEXANDRE
ARISTOTLE
BALTIMORE
BARRYMORE
BENAVENTE
BLAKESLEE
BOERHAAVE
CHRISTINE
CLAUDETTE
CONYBEARE
CORNEILLE
CRESWICKE
DALRYMPLE
DELEZENNE
DIEUDONNE
DOMINIQUE
FRANCOISE
GABRIELLE

GASCOIGNE
GERALDINE
GILLESPIE
GLADSTONE
GOLDSTINE
GOLDSTONE
GOODRICKE
GRANVILLE
GUILLAUME
HEAVISIDE
HIPPOLYTE
HYACINTHE
JOHNSTONE
JOSEPHINE
KATHARINE
LAMORISSE
LATREILLE
LECLANCHE
LIOUVILLE
MAHARIDGE
MASKELYNE
MCQUARRIE
MILESTONE
NICEPHORE
PRIGOGINE
PRUDHOMME
SALVATORE
SCAEBERLE
SOUTHGATE
THEOPHILE
THORNDIKE
VALENTINE
ATANASOFF
CHRISTOFF
HAUSDORFF
KIRCHHOFF
RUHMKORFF
STOICHEFF
WEISSKOPF
ARMSTRONG
EHRENBERG
EILENBERG
GREENBERG
GRUENTZIG
GUTENBERG
KETTERING
LEDERBERG
NEETHLING
NIRENBERG
OLDENBURG
PICKERING
ROSENBERG
SCHULBERG
SPIELBERG
STEENBERG
STRADLING
TOUSSIENG

WITHERING
BOSCOVICH
CAVENDISH
CHRISTOPH
CORNFORTH
ELIZABETH
FEUERBACH
FRIEDRICH
HOLLERITH
IVANOVICH
LINDBERGH
RORSCHACH
SUSSMILCH
WHITWORTH
ALDEROTTI
ALGAROTTI
BERNOULLI
BIANCHINI
CAVALIERI
CRISTIANI
DECONCINI
FIBONACCI
FORLANINI
GIANNETTI
HAMMURABI
MINKOWSKI
MONTANARI
MUSSOLINI
ROCCHETTI
TAKAHASHI
TANIGUCHI
AULENBACK
BRODERICK
ESTABROOK
FREDERICK
HASBROUCK
MCCORMICK
PASTERNAK
STEENBOCK
STEINBECK
TSCHERMAK
UHLENBECK
BECQUEREL
BRACEWELL
CHURCHILL
COCKERELL
DEMESTRAL
FROESCHEL
MCCONNELL
MCDOUGALL
NATHANAEL
NATHANIEL
PERCIVALL
STONEHILL
TUNNSTALL
WOLFSKEHL
BERGSTROM

BJORKHOLM
ROOZEBOOM
ROSENBAUM
SODERBLOM
WAHLSTROM
ALBERTSON
AMMERMANN
ARFWEDSON
ARNOLDSON
BARGHOORN
BARTHOLIN
BATAILLON
BEILSTEIN
BERNSTEIN
BESSARION
BOLTZMANN
BORNSTEIN
CHRISTAIN
CHRISTIAN
CLAPEYRON
DAUBENTON
DICKINSON
DONALDSON
DUNALDSON
EDDINGTON
EINTHOVEN
FAIRBAIRN
FESSENDEN
FORSSMANN
FRIEDMANN
FRUCHTMAN
FULLERTON
GOLDSTEIN
GRASSMANN
GUILLEMIN
GUSTAFSON
HAFFENDEN
HAHNEMANN
HAUPTMANN
HENDERSON
HUTCHISON
JEFFERSON
JOHANNSEN
JORGENSEN
JORGENSON
JOSEPHSON
JUSTINIAN
LLEWELLYN
MACMILLAN
MARTINSON
MCPHERSON
MICHELSON
MURCHISON
NICHOLSON
NICKERSON
PARKINSON
PETROSIAN
RAMANUJAN
RAWLINSON
REVEILLON
ROBERTSON
ROGGEVEEN
SABASTIAN
SCHAUDINN
SCHLEIDEN
SCHONBEIN
SCHONLEIN
SEBASTIAN
SHECHTMAN
SOUBEIRAN
STAPLETON
STEVENSON
STRASSMAN
STROMGREN
TINBERGEN
VAUQUELIN
VESPASIAN
WARBURTON
WASSERMAN
WEISSMANN
WILKINSON
WILLADSEN
WOLLASTON
ZINNEMANN
BENEDETTO
BOCCACCIO
BURGUNDIO
CASCARDIO
CESALPINO
EUSTACHIO
FRANCESCO
FRANCISCO
GEMINIANO
GUGLIELMO
KENZABURO
MACEDONIO
MAUROLICO
QUASIMODO
ROMANENKO
STANISLAO
TARANTINO
VANNOCCIO
VINCENZIO
BEAUCHAMP
GJELLERUP
KOENEKAMP
STEINKAMP
ALEKSANDR
ALEXANDER
BAMBERGER
BARRINGER
BROUNCKER
CALLENDAR
CARPENTER
GEGENBAUR
GOLDHABER
KISSINGER
KOBREUTER
KOLREUTER
KRAUSHAAR
KRONECKER
LANCASTER
LAVOISIER
LEVERRIER
MACARTHUR
MCALISTER
MEHRINGER
MIELZINER
MOSSBAUER
NICOLAIER
PELLETIER
POLLENDER
RAINWATER
ROCHESTER
SCHAFFNER
SCHOEFFER
SCHWEIZER
SCHWINGER
SERTURNER
SPITTELER
SYLVESTER
TITCHENER
WHITTAKER
AFRAGAMUS
ALMENDROS
ANACHARIS
ARISTIDES
ARRHENIUS
BENEDICKS
BENZELIUS
BERZELIUS
BOURGEOIS
BURROUGHS
CALLIPPUS
CAROTHERS
CASSERIUS
CORNELIUS
CTESIBIUS
DESARGUES
DESCARTES
DIONYSIUS
EUPALINUS
EURIPIDES
FABRICIUS
FALLOPIUS
FRONTINUS
GROTTHUSS
HECATAEUS
HELVETIUS
HERODOTUS
HITCHINGS
HUTCHINGS
LEUCIPPUS
LUCRETIUS
MICHAELIS
OENOPIDES
PHILIPPUS
PHILOLAUS
SEMIRAMIS
SOPHOCLES
SOSIGENES
TACHENIUS
THEODORUS
VESPUSIUS
VIEUSSENS
VITRUVIUS
WIESCHAUS
ZACHERIAS
ARBUTHNOT
ARKWRIGHT
BEERNAERT
BERTHELOT
BRACONNOT
BURKHARDT
BUTENANDT
CAILLETET
COCKCROFT
CONDORCET
CRONSTEDT
DESMAREST
DIRICHLET
DUTROCHET
FERCHAULT
GANSWINDT
KARLFELDT
LOSCHMIDT
MORTILLET
ROOSEVELT
ROUSSELOT
DAMOISEAU
BEKTHEREV
CHERENKOV
GORBACHEV
KARDASHEV
KURCHATOV
LEMONOSOV
LOMONOSOV
MECHNIKOV
MENDELEEV
PROKHOROV
SHOLOKHOV
ELLENSHAW
STANISLAW
WLADYSLAW
ASERINSKY
CHAYEFSKY
ECHEGARAY
HEMINGWAY
HEYROVSKY
HORODYSKY
IVANOVSKY
JARNOWSKY
PRIESTLEY
VERNADSKY
WILLUGHBY
ZSIGMONDY
STEINMETZ

## 10 Letter
### 1st Letter

ALDROVANDI
ALEIXANDRE
ALESSANDRO
ALLESANDRO
ANAXAGORAS
ANAXIMENES
ANDREEVICH
ANDRONIKOS
APOLLONIUS
ARCHDEACON
ARCHIMEDES
ARGELANDER
ARISTIPPUS
ATHANASIUS
BARKHAUSEN
BARTOLEMEO
BARTOLOMEU
BEIJERINCK
BELOZERSKY
BENZENBERG
BERNARDINO
BERTHOLLET
BERTOLUCCI
BIGELEISEN
BLUMENBACH
BLUMENTHAL
BODENSTEIN
BRANSFIELD
BRETHERTON
BRETONNEAU
BROCKHOUSE
CALLINICUS
CAMERARIUS
CAMPANELLA
CANNIZZARO
CARMICHAEL
CARRINGTON
CARTWRIGHT
CASSEGRAIN
CASSINELLI
CATHERWOOD
CAVANILLES
CHAMBERLIN
CHARDONNET
CHRISTIAAN
CHRISTIANE
CHRISTOPHE
CLATWORTHY
CLOUDESLEY
COPERNICUS
COURCHESNE
CRUIKSHANK
CUNNINGHAM
DEMOCRITUS
DESIDERIUS
DIOPHANTUS
DOBEREINER
DOBZHANSKY
DORNBERGER
EBBINGHAUS
EHRENFRIED
EISENHOWER
EIZAGUIRRE
EMPEDOCLES
ENGELBREGT
ERLENMEYER
FAHRENHEIT
FEIGENBAUM
FERDINANDO
FITZGERALD
FOETTINGER
FOTHERGILL
FOTOPOULOS
FRACASTORO
FRANCISCUS
FRIEDERICH
GALSWORTHY
GELLIBRAND
GIORDMAINE
GOLDBERGER
GREENSTEIN
GULLSTRAND
HARGREAVES
HARRINGTON
HEISENBERG
HELLRIEGEL
HERACLITUS
HEROPHILUS
HERSCHBACH
HEYDENBERG
HIERONYMUS
HIPPARCHUS
HOFMESITER
HOFSTADTER
HOLLDOBLER
HOUNSFIELD
INGENHOUSZ
IOSIFOVICH
KAMERLINGH
KLEBESADEL
KOMUNYAKAA
KONSTANTIN
KOURGANOFF
KOVALEVSKI
KOVALEVSKY
KRETSCHMER
LAGERKVIST
LAMBERTSON
LANGERHANS
LAURENTINE
LILIENTHAL
LIPPERSHEY
MACFARLANE
MAIMONIDES
MANCHESTER
MANDELBROT
MANKIEWICZ
MARGUERITE
MASCHERONI
MAXIMILIAN
MCCLINTOCK
MCCULLOUGH
MENAECHMUS
MERRIFIELD
MONTALCINI
MOOKHERJEE
MUGGLESTON
NEMORARIUS
NEUGEBAUER
NIKOLAYEVA
OTTAVIOANO
PACHACUTEC
PARACELSUS
PARMENIDES
PASQUALINO
PHILOPONUS
PIRANDELLO
POCAHONTAS
POGGENDORF
POISEUILLE
PRAXAGORAS
PRINGSHEIM
PROTAGORAS
PYTHAGORAS
RAMMAZZINI
REICHSTEIN
RICHARDSON
ROKITANSKY
RUTHERFORD
RUTTENBERG
SACROBOSCO
SAMUELSSON
SANCTORIUS
SCARFIOTTI
SCHEUCHZER

SCHICKARDT
SCHLIEMANN
SCHRIEFFER
SCHUMACHER
SCHWEIGGER
SCHWEITZER
SEFERIADIS
SEMENOVICH
SENEFELDER
SHINGLETON
SHKLOVSKII
SILLIPHANT
SKLODOWSKA
SKOBELTZYN
SOMERVILLE
SOMMEILLER
SONNENBERG
SPIEGELMAN
STAHLECKER
STAUDINGER
STEINHARDT
STEPHENSON
STRESEMANN
STROHMEYER
STROMINGER
STURTEVANT
SUTHERLAND
SWAMMERDAM
SWEDENBORG
SZYMBORSKA
TAVOULARIS
TEISSERENC
TERESHKOVA
THEAETETUS
THEODOSIUS
THUCYDIDES
TISSANDIER
TORRICELLI
TOSCANELLI
TREVITHICK
TRUTFETTER
TSCHIRIKOV
VERROCCHIO
VINOGRADOV
WARRINGTON
WATERHOUSE
WEATHERWAX
WEIZSACKER
WETHERHILL
WHEATSTONE
WILLEBRORD
WILLIAMSON
WISLICENUS
WROBLEWSKI
WUNDERLICH
XENOPHANES
ZEHETBAUER

### 2nd Letter

BARKHAUSEN
BARTOLEMEO
BARTOLOMEU
CALLINICUS
CAMERARIUS
CAMPANELLA
CANNIZZARO
CARMICHAEL
CARRINGTON
CARTWRIGHT
CASSEGRAIN
CASSINELLI
CATHERWOOD
CAVANILLES
FAHRENHEIT
GALSWORTHY
HARGREAVES
HARRINGTON
KAMERLINGH
LAGERKVIST
LAMBERTSON
LANGERHANS
LAURENTINE
MACFARLANE
MAIMONIDES
MANCHESTER
MANDELBROT
MANKIEWICZ
MARGUERITE
MASCHERONI
MAXIMILIAN
PACHACUTEC
PARACELSUS
PARMENIDES
PASQUALINO
RAMMAZZINI
SACROBOSCO
SAMUELSSON
SANCTORIUS
TAVOULARIS
WARRINGTON
WATERHOUSE
EBBINGHAUS
MCCLINTOCK
MCCULLOUGH
SCARFIOTTI
SCHEUCHZER
SCHICKARDT
SCHLIEMANN
SCHRIEFFER
SCHUMACHER
SCHWEIGGER
SCHWEITZER
BEIJERINCK
BELOZERSKY
BENZENBERG
BERNARDINO
BERTHOLLET
BERTOLUCCI
DEMOCRITUS
DESIDERIUS
FEIGENBAUM
FERDINANDO
GELLIBRAND
HEISENBERG
HELLRIEGEL
HERACLITUS
HEROPHILUS
HERSCHBACH
HEYDENBERG
MENAECHMUS
MERRIFIELD
NEMORARIUS
NEUGEBAUER
REICHSTEIN
SEFERIADIS
SEMENOVICH
SENEFELDER
TEISSERENC
TERESHKOVA
VERROCCHIO
WEATHERWAX
WEIZSACKER
WETHERHILL
XENOPHANES
ZEHETBAUER
CHAMBERLIN
CHARDONNET
CHRISTIAAN
CHRISTIANE
CHRISTOPHE
EHRENFRIED
PHILOPONUS
SHINGLETON
SHKLOVSKII
THEAETETUS
THEODOSIUS
THUCYDIDES
WHEATSTONE
BIGELEISEN
DIOPHANTUS
EISENHOWER
EIZAGUIRRE
FITZGERALD
GIORDMAINE
HIERONYMUS
HIPPARCHUS
LILIENTHAL
LIPPERSHEY
NIKOLAYEVA
PIRANDELLO
RICHARDSON
SILLIPHANT
TISSANDIER
VINOGRADOV
WILLEBRORD
WILLIAMSON
WISLICENUS
SKLODOWSKA
SKOBELTZYN
ALDROVANDI
ALEIXANDRE
ALESSANDRO
ALLESANDRO
BLUMENBACH
BLUMENTHAL
CLATWORTHY
CLOUDESLEY
KLEBESADEL
EMPEDOCLES
ANAXAGORAS
ANAXIMENES
ANDREEVICH
ANDRONIKOS
ENGELBREGT
INGENHOUSZ
BODENSTEIN
COPERNICUS
COURCHESNE
DOBEREINER
DOBZHANSKY
DORNBERGER
FOETTINGER
FOTHERGILL
FOTOPOULOS
GOLDBERGER
HOFMESITER
HOFSTADTER
HOLLDOBLER
HOUNSFIELD
IOSIFOVICH
KOMUNYAKAA
KONSTANTIN
KOURGANOFF
KOVALEVSKI
KOVALEVSKY
MONTALCINI
MOOKHERJEE
POCAHONTAS
POGGENDORF
POISEUILLE
ROKITANSKY
SOMERVILLE
SOMMEILLER
SONNENBERG
TORRICELLI
TOSCANELLI
APOLLONIUS
SPIEGELMAN
ARCHDEACON
ARCHIMEDES
ARGELANDER
ARISTIPPUS
BRANSFIELD
BRETHERTON
BRETONNEAU
BROCKHOUSE
CRUIKSHANK
ERLENMEYER
FRACASTORO
FRANCISCUS
FRIEDERICH
GREENSTEIN
KRETSCHMER
PRAXAGORAS
PRINGSHEIM
PROTAGORAS
TREVITHICK
TRUTFETTER
WROBLEWSKI
TSCHIRIKOV
ATHANASIUS
OTTAVIOANO
STAHLECKER
STAUDINGER
STEINHARDT
STEPHENSON
STRESEMANN
STROHMEYER
STROMINGER
STURTEVANT
CUNNINGHAM
GULLSTRAND
MUGGLESTON
RUTHERFORD
RUTTENBERG
SUTHERLAND
WUNDERLICH
SWAMMERDAM
SWEDENBORG
PYTHAGORAS
SZYMBORSKA

### 3rd Letter

ANAXAGORAS
ANAXIMENES
BRANSFIELD
CHAMBERLIN
CHARDONNET
CLATWORTHY
FRACASTORO
FRANCISCUS
PRAXAGORAS
SCARFIOTTI
STAHLECKER
STAUDINGER
SWAMMERDAM
WEATHERWAX
DOBEREINER
DOBZHANSKY
EBBINGHAUS
ARCHDEACON
ARCHIMEDES
MACFARLANE
MCCLINTOCK
MCCULLOUGH
PACHACUTEC
POCAHONTAS
RICHARDSON
SACROBOSCO
TSCHIRIKOV
ALDROVANDI
ANDREEVICH
ANDRONIKOS
BODENSTEIN
ALEIXANDRE
ALESSANDRO
BRETHERTON
BRETONNEAU
FOETTINGER
GREENSTEIN
HIERONYMUS
KLEBESADEL
KRETSCHMER
STEINHARDT
STEPHENSON
SWEDENBORG
THEAETETUS
THEODOSIUS
TREVITHICK
WHEATSTONE
HOFMESITER
HOFSTADTER
SEFERIADIS
ARGELANDER
BIGELEISEN
ENGELBREGT
INGENHOUSZ
LAGERKVIST
MUGGLESTON
POGGENDORF
ATHANASIUS
FAHRENHEIT
SCHEUCHZER
SCHICKARDT
SCHLIEMANN
SCHRIEFFER
SCHUMACHER
SCHWEIGGER
SCHWEITZER
ZEHETBAUER
ARISTIPPUS
BEIJERINCK
FEIGENBAUM
FRIEDERICH
HEISENBERG
MAIMONIDES
PHILOPONUS
POISEUILLE
PRINGSHEIM
REICHSTEIN
SHINGLETON
SPIEGELMAN
TEISSERENC
WEIZSACKER
NIKOLAYEVA
ROKITANSKY
SHKLOVSKII
ALLESANDRO
BELOZERSKY
CALLINICUS
ERLENMEYER
GALSWORTHY
GELLIBRAND
GOLDBERGER
GULLSTRAND
HELLRIEGEL
HOLLDOBLER
LILIENTHAL
SILLIPHANT
SKLODOWSKA
WILLEBRORD
WILLIAMSON
CAMERARIUS
CAMPANELLA
DEMOCRITUS
KAMERLINGH
KOMUNYAKAA
LAMBERTSON
NEMORARIUS
RAMMAZZINI
SAMUELSSON
SEMENOVICH
SOMERVILLE
SOMMEILLER
BENZENBERG
CANNIZZARO
CUNNINGHAM
KONSTANTIN
LANGERHANS
MANCHESTER
MANDELBROT
MANKIEWICZ
MENAECHMUS
MONTALCINI
SANCTORIUS
SENEFELDER

SO**N**NENBERG
VI**N**OGRADOV
WU**N**DERLICH
XE**N**OPHANES
AP**O**LLONIUS
BR**O**CKHOUSE
CL**O**UDESLEY
DI**O**PHANTUS
GI**O**RDMAINE
MO**O**KHERJEE
PR**O**TAGORAS
SK**O**BELTZYN
WR**O**BLEWSKI
CO**P**ERNICUS
EM**P**EDOCLES
HI**P**PARCHUS
LI**P**PERSHEY
BA**R**KHAUSEN
BA**R**TOLEMEO
BA**R**TOLOMEU
BE**R**NARDINO
BE**R**THOLLET
BE**R**TOLUCCI
CA**R**MICHAEL
CA**R**RINGTON
CA**R**TWRIGHT
CH**R**ISTIAAN
CH**R**ISTIANE
CH**R**ISTOPHE
DO**R**NBERGER
EH**R**ENFRIED
FE**R**DINANDO
HA**R**GREAVES
HA**R**RINGTON
HE**R**ACLITUS
HE**R**OPHILUS
HE**R**SCHBACH
MA**R**GUERITE
ME**R**RIFIELD
PA**R**ACELSUS
PA**R**MENIDES
PI**R**ANDELLO
ST**R**ESEMANN
ST**R**OHMEYER
ST**R**OMINGER
TE**R**ESHKOVA
TO**R**RICELLI
VE**R**ROCCHIO
WA**R**RINGTON
CA**S**SEGRAIN
CA**S**SINELLI
DE**S**IDERIUS
EI**S**ENHOWER
IO**S**IFOVICH
MA**S**CHERONI
PA**S**QUALINO
TI**S**SANDIER
TO**S**CANELLI
WI**S**LICENUS
CA**T**HERWOOD
FI**T**ZGERALD
FO**T**HERGILL
FO**T**OPOULOS
OT**T**AVIOANO
PY**T**HAGORAS
RU**T**HERFORD
RU**T**TENBERG
SU**T**HERLAND
WA**T**ERHOUSE
WE**T**HERHILL
BL**U**MENBACH
BL**U**MENTHAL
CO**U**RCHESNE
CR**U**IKSHANK
HO**U**NSFIELD
KO**U**RGANOFF
LA**U**RENTINE
NE**U**GEBAUER
ST**U**RTEVANT
TH**U**CYDIDES
TR**U**TFETTER
CA**V**ANILLES
KO**V**ALEVSKJ
KO**V**ALEVSKY
TA**V**OULARIS
MA**X**IMILIAN
HE**Y**DENBERG
SZ**Y**MBORSKA
EI**Z**AGUIRRE

## 4th Letter

ATH**A**NASIUS
CAV**A**NILLES
EIZ**A**GUIRRE
HER**A**CLITUS
KOV**A**LEVSKI
KOV**A**LEVSKY
MEN**A**ECHMUS
OTT**A**VIOANO
PAR**A**CELSUS
PIR**A**NDELLO
POC**A**HONTAS
THE**A**ETETUS
WHE**A**TSTONE
KLE**B**ESADEL
LAM**B**ERTSON
SKO**B**ELTZYN
WRO**B**LEWSKI
BRO**C**KHOUSE
FRA**C**ASTORO
MAN**C**HESTER
MAS**C**HERONI
REI**C**HSTEIN
SAN**C**TORIUS
THU**C**YDIDES
TOS**C**ANELLI
FER**D**INANDO
GOL**D**BERGER
HEY**D**ENBERG
MAN**D**ELBROT
SWE**D**ENBORG
WUN**D**ERLICH
ALL**E**SANDRO
ARG**E**LANDER
BIG**E**LEISEN
BOD**E**NSTEIN
CAM**E**RARIUS
COP**E**RNICUS
DOB**E**REINER
EHR**E**NFRIED
EIS**E**NHOWER
EMP**E**DOCLES
ENG**E**LBREGT
ERL**E**NMEYER
FRI**E**DERICH
GRE**E**NSTEIN
ING**E**NHOUSZ
KAM**E**RLINGH
LAG**E**RKVIST
SCH**E**UCHZER
SEF**E**RIADIS
SEM**E**NOVICH
SEN**E**FELDER
SOM**E**RVILLE
SPI**E**GELMAN
STR**E**SEMANN
TER**E**SHKOVA
WAT**E**RHOUSE
ZEH**E**TBAUER
MAC**F**ARLANE
FEI**G**ENBAUM
HAR**G**REAVES
LAN**G**ERHANS
MAR**G**UERITE
MUG**G**LESTON
NEU**G**EBAUER
POG**G**ENDORF
ARC**H**DEACON
ARC**H**IMEDES
CAT**H**ERWOOD
FOT**H**ERGILL
PAC**H**ACUTEC
PYT**H**AGORAS
RIC**H**ARDSON
RUT**H**ERFORD
STA**H**LECKER
SUT**H**ERLAND
TSC**H**IRIKOV
WET**H**ERHILL
ALE**I**XANDRE
CHR**I**STIAAN
CHR**I**STIANE
CHR**I**STOPHE
CRU**I**KSHANK
DES**I**DERIUS
EBB**I**NGHAUS
IOS**I**FOVICH
LIL**I**ENTHAL
MAX**I**MILIAN
ROK**I**TANSKY
SCH**I**CKARDT
STE**I**NHARDT
BEI**J**ERINCK
BAR**K**HAUSEN
MAN**K**IEWICZ
MOO**K**HERJEE
APO**L**LONIUS
CAL**L**INICUS
GEL**L**IBRAND
GUL**L**STRAND
HEL**L**RIEGEL
HOL**L**DOBLER
MCC**L**INTOCK
PHI**L**OPONUS
SCH**L**IEMANN
SHK**L**OVSKII
SIL**L**IPHANT
WIL**L**EBRORD
WIL**L**IAMSON
WIS**L**ICENUS
BLU**M**ENBACH
BLU**M**ENTHAL
CAR**M**ICHAEL
CHA**M**BERLIN
HOF**M**ESITER
MAI**M**ONIDES
PAR**M**ENIDES
RAM**M**AZZINI
SOM**M**EILLER
SWA**M**MERDAM
SZY**M**BORSKA
BER**N**ARDINO
BRA**N**SFIELD
CAN**N**IZZARO
CUN**N**INGHAM
DOR**N**BERGER
FRA**N**CISCUS
HOU**N**SFIELD
PRI**N**GSHEIM
SHI**N**GLETON
SON**N**ENBERG
BEL**O**ZERSKY
DEM**O**CRITUS
FOT**O**POULOS
HER**O**PHILUS
NEM**O**RARIUS
NIK**O**LAYEVA
SKL**O**DOWSKA
STR**O**HMEYER
STR**O**MINGER
TAV**O**ULARIS
THE**O**DOSIUS
VIN**O**GRADOV
XEN**O**PHANES
CAM**P**ANELLA
DIO**P**HANTUS
HIP**P**ARCHUS
LIP**P**ERSHEY
STE**P**HENSON
PAS**Q**UALINO
ALD**R**OVANDI
AND**R**EEVICH
AND**R**ONIKOS
CAR**R**INGTON
CHA**R**DONNET
COU**R**CHESNE
FAH**R**ENHEIT
GIO**R**DMAINE
HAR**R**INGTON
HIE**R**ONYMUS
KOU**R**GANOFF
LAU**R**ENTINE
MER**R**IFIELD
SAC**R**OBOSCO
SCA**R**FIOTTI
SCH**R**IEFFER
STU**R**TEVANT
TOR**R**ICELLI
VER**R**OCCHIO
WAR**R**INGTON
ALE**S**SANDRO
ARI**S**TIPPUS
CAS**S**EGRAIN
CAS**S**INELLI
GAL**S**WORTHY
HEI**S**ENBERG
HER**S**CHBACH
HOF**S**TADTER
KON**S**TANTIN
POI**S**EUILLE
TEI**S**SERENC
TIS**S**ANDIER
BAR**T**OLEMEO
BAR**T**OLOMEU
BER**T**HOLLET
BER**T**OLUCCI
BRE**T**HERTON
BRE**T**ONNEAU
CAR**T**WRIGHT
CLA**T**WORTHY
FOE**T**TINGER
KRE**T**SCHMER
MON**T**ALCINI
PRO**T**AGORAS
RUT**T**ENBERG
TRU**T**FETTER
WEA**T**HERWAX
CLO**U**DESLEY
KOM**U**NYAKAA
MCC**U**LLOUGH
SAM**U**ELSSON
SCH**U**MACHER
STA**U**DINGER
TRE**V**ITHICK
SCH**W**EIGGER
SCH**W**EITZER
ANA**X**AGORAS
ANA**X**IMENES
PRA**X**AGORAS
BEN**Z**ENBERG
DOB**Z**HANSKY
FIT**Z**GERALD
WEI**Z**SACKER

## 5th Letter

ANAX**A**GORAS
BERN**A**RDINO
CAMP**A**NELLA
FRAC**A**STORO
HIPP**A**RCHUS
MACF**A**RLANE
MONT**A**LCINI
PACH**A**CUTEC
PRAX**A**GORAS
PROT**A**GORAS
PYTH**A**GORAS
RAMM**A**ZZINI
RICH**A**RDSON
TISS**A**NDIER
TOSC**A**NELLI
CHAM**B**ERLIN
DORN**B**ERGER
GOLD**B**ERGER
SZYM**B**ORSKA
COUR**C**HESNE
DEMO**C**RITUS
FRAN**C**ISCUS
HERA**C**LITUS
HERS**C**HBACH
PARA**C**ELSUS
SCHI**C**KARDT
ARCH**D**EACON
CHAR**D**ONNET
CLOU**D**ESLEY
DESI**D**ERIUS
EMPE**D**OCLES
FRIE**D**ERICH
GIOR**D**MAINE
HOLL**D**OBLER
SKLO**D**OWSKA
STAU**D**INGER
THEO**D**OSIUS
ANDR**E**EVICH
BEIJ**E**RINCK
BENZ**E**NBERG
BLUM**E**NBACH
BLUM**E**NTHAL
CASS**E**GRAIN
CATH**E**RWOOD
FAHR**E**NHEIT
FEIG**E**NBAUM
FOTH**E**RGILL
HEIS**E**NBERG
HEYD**E**NBERG
HOFM**E**SITER
KLEB**E**SADEL
LAMB**E**RTSON
LANG**E**RHANS
LAUR**E**NTINE
LILI**E**NTHAL
LIPP**E**RSHEY
MAND**E**LBROT
MENA**E**CHMUS
NEUG**E**BAUER
PARM**E**NIDES
POGG**E**NDORF
POIS**E**UILLE
RUTH**E**RFORD
RUTT**E**NBERG
SAMU**E**LSSON
SCHW**E**IGGER
SCHW**E**ITZER
SKOB**E**LTZYN
SOMM**E**ILLER
SONN**E**NBERG
SUTH**E**RLAND
SWED**E**NBORG
THEA**E**TETUS
WETH**E**RHILL
WILL**E**BRORD
WUND**E**RLICH
IOSI**F**OVICH
SCAR**F**IOTTI
SENE**F**ELDER
TRUT**F**ETTER
EIZA**G**UIRRE
FITZ**G**ERALD
KOUR**G**ANOFF
PRIN**G**SHEIM
SHIN**G**LETON
SPIE**G**ELMAN
VINO**G**RADOV
BARK**H**AUSEN

BERT**H**OLLET
BRET**H**ERTON
DIOP**H**ANTUS
DOBZ**H**ANSKY
MANC**H**ESTER
MASC**H**ERONI
MOOK**H**ERJEE
POCA**H**ONTAS
REIC**H**STEIN
STEP**H**ENSON
STRO**H**MEYER
WEAT**H**ERWAX
ANAX**I**MENES
ARCH**I**MEDES
CALL**I**NICUS
CANN**I**ZZARO
CARM**I**CHAEL
CARR**I**NGTON
CASS**I**NELLI
CUNN**I**NGHAM
FERD**I**NANDO
GELL**I**BRAND
HARR**I**NGTON
MANK**I**EWICZ
MCCL**I**NTOCK
MERR**I**FIELD
SCHL**I**EMANN
SCHR**I**EFFER
SILL**I**PHANT
TORR**I**CELLI
TREV**I**THICK
TSCH**I**RIKOV
WARR**I**NGTON
WILL**I**AMSON
WISL**I**CENUS
BROC**K**HOUSE
CRUI**K**SHANK
APOL**L**ONIUS
ARGE**L**ANDER
BIGE**L**EISEN
ENGE**L**BREGT
KOVA**L**EVSKI
KOVA**L**EVSKY
MCCU**L**LOUGH
MUGG**L**ESTON
NIKO**L**AYEVA
STAH**L**ECKER
WROB**L**EWSKI
MAXI**M**ILIAN
SCHU**M**ACHER
STRO**M**INGER
SWAM**M**ERDAM
ATHA**N**ASIUS
BODE**N**STEIN
CAVA**N**ILLES
EBBI**N**GHAUS
EHRE**N**FRIED
EISE**N**HOWER
ERLE**N**MEYER
GREE**N**STEIN
INGE**N**HOUSZ
KOMU**N**YAKAA
PIRA**N**DELLO
SEME**N**OVICH
STEI**N**HARDT
ALDR**O**VANDI
ANDR**O**NIKOS
BART**O**LEMEO
BART**O**LOMEU
BERT**O**LUCCI
BRET**O**NNEAU
HIER**O**NYMUS
MAIM**O**NIDES
PHIL**O**PONUS
SACR**O**BOSCO
SHKL**O**VSKII
VERR**O**CCHIO
FOTO**P**OULOS
HERO**P**HILUS
XENO**P**HANES
CAME**R**ARIUS
COPE**R**NICUS
DOBE**R**EINER
HARG**R**EAVES
HELL**R**IEGEL
KAME**R**LINGH
LAGE**R**KVIST
NEMO**R**ARIUS
SEFE**R**IADIS
SOME**R**VILLE
WATE**R**HOUSE
ALES**S**ANDRO
ALLE**S**ANDRO
BRAN**S**FIELD
CHRI**S**TIAAN
CHRI**S**TIANE
CHRI**S**TOPHE
GULL**S**TRAND
HOUN**S**FIELD
KRET**S**CHMER
STRE**S**EMANN
TEIS**S**ERENC
TERE**S**HKOVA
WEIZ**S**ACKER
ARIS**T**IPPUS
FOET**T**INGER
HOFS**T**ADTER
KONS**T**ANTIN
ROKI**T**ANSKY
SANC**T**ORIUS
STUR**T**EVANT
WHEA**T**STONE
ZEHE**T**BAUER
MARG**U**ERITE
PASQ**U**ALINO
SCHE**U**CHZER
TAVO**U**LARIS
OTTA**V**IOANO
CART**W**RIGHT
CLAT**W**ORTHY
GALS**W**ORTHY
ALEI**X**ANDRE
THUC**Y**DIDES
BELO**Z**ERSKY

### 6th Letter

ALEIX**A**NDRE
ALESS**A**NDRO
ALLES**A**NDRO
ARGEL**A**NDER
ATHAN**A**SIUS
BARKH**A**USEN
CAMER**A**RIUS
DIOPH**A**NTUS
DOBZH**A**NSKY
HOFST**A**DTER
KONST**A**NTIN
KOURG**A**NOFF
NEMOR**A**RIUS
NIKOL**A**YEVA
PASQU**A**LINO
ROKIT**A**NSKY
SCHUM**A**CHER
WEIZS**A**CKER
WILLI**A**MSON
ENGEL**B**REGT
GELLI**B**RAND
NEUGE**B**AUER
SACRO**B**OSCO
WILLE**B**RORD
ZEHET**B**AUER
CARMI**C**HAEL
KRETS**C**HMER
MENAE**C**HMUS
PACHA**C**UTEC
SCHEU**C**HZER
TORRI**C**ELLI
VERRO**C**CHIO
WISLI**C**ENUS
PIRAN**D**ELLO
THUCY**D**IDES
ANDRE**E**VICH
ARCHD**E**ACON
BELOZ**E**RSKY
BIGEL**E**ISEN
BRETH**E**RTON
CHAMB**E**RLIN
CLOUD**E**SLEY
DESID**E**RIUS
DOBER**E**INER
DORNB**E**RGER
FITZG**E**RALD
FRIED**E**RICH
GOLDB**E**RGER
HARGR**E**AVES
KOVAL**E**VSKI
KOVAL**E**VSKY
MANCH**E**STER
MANKI**E**WICZ
MARGU**E**RITE
MASCH**E**RONI
MOOKH**E**RJEE
MUGGL**E**STON
PARAC**E**LSUS
SCHLI**E**MANN
SCHRI**E**FFER
SENEF**E**LDER
SPIEG**E**LMAN
STAHL**E**CKER
STEPH**E**NSON
STRES**E**MANN
STURT**E**VANT
SWAMM**E**RDAM
TEISS**E**RENC
TRUTF**E**TTER
WEATH**E**RWAX
WROBL**E**WSKI
BRANS**F**IELD
EHREN**F**RIED
HOUNS**F**IELD
MERRI**F**IELD
ANAXA**G**ORAS
CASSE**G**RAIN
EBBIN**G**HAUS
PRAXA**G**ORAS
PROTA**G**ORAS
PYTHA**G**ORAS
BROCK**H**OUSE
COURC**H**ESNE
EISEN**H**OWER
HEROP**H**ILUS
HERSC**H**BACH
INGEN**H**OUSZ
STEIN**H**ARDT
TERES**H**KOVA
WATER**H**OUSE
XENOP**H**ANES
ARIST**I**PPUS
CAVAN**I**LLES
FOETT**I**NGER
FRANC**I**SCUS
HELLR**I**EGEL
MAXIM**I**LIAN
OTTAV**I**OANO
SCARF**I**OTTI
SCHWE**I**GGER
SCHWE**I**TZER
SEFER**I**ADIS
SOMME**I**LLER
STAUD**I**NGER
STROM**I**NGER
LAGER**K**VIST
SCHIC**K**ARDT
BARTO**L**EMEO
BARTO**L**OMEU
BERTO**L**UCCI
HERAC**L**ITUS
KAMER**L**INGH
MANDE**L**BROT
MCCUL**L**OUGH
MONTA**L**CINI
SAMUE**L**SSON
SHING**L**ETON
SKOBE**L**TZYN
TAVOU**L**ARIS
ANAXI**M**ENES
ARCHI**M**EDES
ERLEN**M**EYER
GIORD**M**AINE
STROH**M**EYER
ANDRO**N**IKOS
BENZE**N**BERG
BLUME**N**BACH
BLUME**N**THAL
BRETO**N**NEAU
CALLI**N**ICUS
CAMPA**N**ELLA
CARRI**N**GTON
CASSI**N**ELLI
COPER**N**ICUS
CUNNI**N**GHAM
FAHRE**N**HEIT
FEIGE**N**BAUM
FERDI**N**ANDO
HARRI**N**GTON
HEISE**N**BERG
HEYDE**N**BERG
HIERO**N**YMUS
LAURE**N**TINE
LILIE**N**THAL
MAIMO**N**IDES
MCCLI**N**TOCK
PARME**N**IDES
POGGE**N**DORF
RUTTE**N**BERG
SONNE**N**BERG
SWEDE**N**BORG
TISSA**N**DIER
TOSCA**N**ELLI
WARRI**N**GTON
APOLL**O**NIUS
BERTH**O**LLET
CHARD**O**NNET
CLATW**O**RTHY
EMPED**O**CLES
FOTOP**O**ULOS
GALSW**O**RTHY
HOLLD**O**BLER
IOSIF**O**VICH
POCAH**O**NTAS
SANCT**O**RIUS
SEMEN**O**VICH
SKLOD**O**WSKA
SZYMB**O**RSKA
THEOD**O**SIUS
PHILO**P**ONUS
SILLI**P**HANT
BEIJE**R**INCK
BERNA**R**DINO
CARTW**R**IGHT
CATHE**R**WOOD
DEMOC**R**ITUS
FOTHE**R**GILL
HIPPA**R**CHUS
LAMBE**R**TSON
LANGE**R**HANS
LIPPE**R**SHEY
MACFA**R**LANE
RICHA**R**DSON
RUTHE**R**FORD
SUTHE**R**LAND
TSCHI**R**IKOV
VINOG**R**ADOV
WETHE**R**HILL
WUNDE**R**LICH
BODEN**S**TEIN
CRUIK**S**HANK
FRACA**S**TORO
GREEN**S**TEIN
HOFME**S**ITER
KLEBE**S**ADEL
PRING**S**HEIM
REICH**S**TEIN
WHEAT**S**TONE
CHRIS**T**IAAN
CHRIS**T**IANE
CHRIS**T**OPHE
GULLS**T**RAND
THEAE**T**ETUS
TREVI**T**HICK
EIZAG**U**IRRE
POISE**U**ILLE
ALDRO**V**ANDI
SHKLO**V**SKII
SOMER**V**ILLE
KOMUN**Y**AKAA
CANNI**Z**ZARO
RAMMA**Z**ZINI

### 7th Letter

ALDROV**A**NDI
ARCHDE**A**CON
FERDIN**A**NDO
GIORDM**A**INE
HARGRE**A**VES
KLEBES**A**DEL
KOMUNY**A**KAA
NEUGEB**A**UER
SCHICK**A**RDT
SEFERI**A**DIS
STEINH**A**RDT
TAVOUL**A**RIS
VINOGR**A**DOV
XENOPH**A**NES
ZEHETB**A**UER
BENZEN**B**ERG
BLUMEN**B**ACH
FEIGEN**B**AUM
HEISEN**B**ERG
HERSCH**B**ACH
HEYDEN**B**ERG
HOLLDO**B**LER
MANDEL**B**ROT
RUTTEN**B**ERG
SONNEN**B**ERG
SWEDEN**B**ORG
EMPEDO**C**LES
HIPPAR**C**HUS
MONTAL**C**INI
SCHUMA**C**HER
STAHLE**C**KER
VERROC**C**HIO
WEIZSA**C**KER
BERNAR**D**INO
HOFSTA**D**TER
POGGEN**D**ORF
RICHAR**D**SON
TISSAN**D**IER
ANAXIM**E**NES
ARCHIM**E**DES
BARTOL**E**MEO
CAMPAN**E**LLA
CASSIN**E**LLI
COURCH**E**SNE
ERLENM**E**YER
HELLRI**E**GEL
PIRAND**E**LLO
SHINGL**E**TON
STROHM**E**YER
THEAET**E**TUS
TORRIC**E**LLI
TOSCAN**E**LLI
WISLIC**E**NUS
RUTHER**F**ORD
SCHRIE**F**FER

CARRINGTON
CUNNINGHAM
FOTHERGILL
HARRINGTON
SCHWEIGGER
WARRINGTON
CARMICHAEL
CRUIKSHANK
EBBINGHAUS
FAHRENHEIT
KRETSCHMER
LANGERHANS
MENAECHMUS
PRINGSHEIM
SCHEUCHZER
SILLIPHANT
TREVITHICK
WETHERHILL
ANDRONIKOS
BEIJERINCK
BIGELEISEN
BRANSFIELD
CALLINICUS
CARTWRIGHT
CHRISTIAAN
CHRISTIANE
COPERNICUS
DEMOCRITUS
DOBEREINER
EIZAGUIRRE
HERACLITUS
HEROPHILUS
HOFMESITER
HOUNSFIELD
KAMERLINGH
MAIMONIDES
MERRIFIELD
PARMENIDES
POISEUILLE
SOMERVILLE
THUCYDIDES
TSCHIRIKOV
TERESHKOVA
BERTHOLLET
CAVANILLES
MACFARLANE
MAXIMILIAN
PARACELSUS
PASQUALINO
SENEFELDER
SOMMEILLER
SPIEGELMAN
SUTHERLAND
WUNDERLICH
SCHLIEMANN
STRESEMANN
WILLIAMSON
ALEIXANDRE
ALESSANDRO
ALLESANDRO
APOLLONIUS
ARGELANDER
BRETONNEAU
CHARDONNET
DIOPHANTUS
DOBZHANSKY
FOETTINGER
KONSTANTIN
KOURGANOFF
POCAHONTAS
ROKITANSKY
STAUDINGER
STEPHENSON
STROMINGER
ANAXAGORAS
BARTOLOMEU
BROCKHOUSE
CHRISTOPHE
EISENHOWER
INGENHOUSZ
MCCULLOUGH
OTTAVIOANO
PHILOPONUS
PRAXAGORAS
PROTAGORAS
PYTHAGORAS
SACROBOSCO
SCARFIOTTI
WATERHOUSE
ARISTIPPUS
BELOZERSKY
BRETHERTON
CAMERARIUS
CASSEGRAIN
CHAMBERLIN
CLATWORTHY
DESIDERIUS
DORNBERGER
EHRENFRIED
ENGELBREGT
FITZGERALD
FRIEDERICH
GALSWORTHY
GELLIBRAND
GOLDBERGER
GULLSTRAND
MARGUERITE
MASCHERONI
MOOKHERJEE
NEMORARIUS
SANCTORIUS
SWAMMERDAM
SZYMBORSKA
TEISSERENC
WEATHERWAX
WILLEBRORD
ATHANASIUS
CLOUDESLEY
FRANCISCUS
LIPPERSHEY
MANCHESTER
MUGGLESTON
SAMUELSSON
SHKLOVSKII
THEODOSIUS
BLUMENTHAL
BODENSTEIN
FRACASTORO
GREENSTEIN
LAMBERTSON
LAURENTINE
LILIENTHAL
MCCLINTOCK
REICHSTEIN
SCHWEITZER
SKOBELTZYN
TRUTFETTER
WHEATSTONE
BARKHAUSEN
BERTOLUCCI
FOTOPOULOS
PACHACUTEC
ANDREEVICH
IOSIFOVICH
KOVALEVSKI
KOVALEVSKY
LAGERKVIST
SEMENOVICH
STURTEVANT
CATHERWOOD
MANKIEWICZ
SKLODOWSKA
WROBLEWSKI
HIERONYMUS
NIKOLAYEVA
CANNIZZARO
RAMMAZZINI

### 8th Letter

BLUMENBACH
CANNIZZARO
CARMICHAEL
CASSEGRAIN
CHRISTIAAN
CHRISTIANE
CRUIKSHANK
EBBINGHAUS
FEIGENBAUM
FITZGERALD
GELLIBRAND
GULLSTRAND
HERSCHBACH
LANGERHANS
MACFARLANE
OTTAVIOANO
SCHLIEMANN
SILLIPHANT
STRESEMANN
STURTEVANT
SUTHERLAND
ARCHDEACON
BERTOLUCCI
CALLINICUS
COPERNICUS
FRANCISCUS
ALEIXANDRE
ALESSANDRO
ALLESANDRO
ARCHIMEDES
ARGELANDER
KLEBESADEL
MAIMONIDES
PARMENIDES
SEFERIADIS
SENEFELDER
SWAMMERDAM
THUCYDIDES
VINOGRADOV
BENZENBERG
BODENSTEIN
BRANSFIELD
BRETONNEAU
ENGELBREGT
FAHRENHEIT
GREENSTEIN
HEISENBERG
HEYDENBERG
HOUNSFIELD
MERRIFIELD
NIKOLAYEVA
PRINGSHEIM
REICHSTEIN
RUTTENBERG
SONNENBERG
TEISSERENC
SCHRIEFFER
CARTWRIGHT
DORNBERGER
FOETTINGER
GOLDBERGER
HELLRIEGEL
SCHWEIGGER
STAUDINGER
STROMINGER
BLUMENTHAL
CUNNINGHAM
HIPPARCHUS
LILIENTHAL
LIPPERSHEY
SCHUMACHER
VERROCCHIO
ANDREEVICH
APOLLONIUS
ATHANASIUS
BERNARDINO
CAMERARIUS
DESIDERIUS
EHRENFRIED
FOTHERGILL
FRIEDERICH
GIORDMAINE
IOSIFOVICH
LAGERKVIST
LAURENTINE
MANKIEWICZ
MARGUERITE
MAXIMILIAN
MONTALCINI
NEMORARIUS
PASQUALINO
RAMMAZZINI
SANCTORIUS
SEMENOVICH
THEODOSIUS
TISSANDIER
TREVITHICK
WETHERHILL
WUNDERLICH
MOOKHERJEE
ANDRONIKOS
KOMUNYAKAA
SHKLOVSKII
STAHLECKER
TSCHIRIKOV
WEIZSACKER
BERTHOLLET
CAMPANELLA
CASSINELLI
CAVANILLES
CHAMBERLIN
CLOUDESLEY
EMPEDOCLES
FOTOPOULOS
HEROPHILUS
HOLLDOBLER
PIRANDELLO
POISEUILLE
SOMERVILLE
SOMMEILLER
TORRICELLI
TOSCANELLI
BARTOLEMEO
BARTOLOMEU
HIERONYMUS
KRETSCHMER
MENAECHMUS
SPIEGELMAN
ALDROVANDI
ANAXIMENES
BEIJERINCK
CHARDONNET
DOBEREINER
FERDINANDO
KAMERLINGH
PHILOPONUS
WISLICENUS
XENOPHANES
CATHERWOOD
FRACASTORO
KOURGANOFF
MASCHERONI
MCCLINTOCK
POGGENDORF
RUTHERFORD
SWEDENBORG
TERESHKOVA
WHEATSTONE
WILLEBRORD
ARISTIPPUS
CHRISTOPHE
ANAXAGORAS
EIZAGUIRRE
MANDELBROT
PRAXAGORAS
PROTAGORAS
PYTHAGORAS
SCHICKARDT
STEINHARDT
TAVOULARIS
BARKHAUSEN
BELOZERSKY
BIGELEISEN
COURCHESNE
DOBZHANSKY
KOVALEVSKI
KOVALEVSKY
LAMBERTSON
PARACELSUS
RICHARDSON
ROKITANSKY
SACROBOSCO
SAMUELSSON
SKLODOWSKA
STEPHENSON
SZYMBORSKA
WILLIAMSON
WROBLEWSKI
BRETHERTON
CARRINGTON
CLATWORTHY
DEMOCRITUS
DIOPHANTUS
GALSWORTHY
HARRINGTON
HERACLITUS
HOFMESITER
HOFSTADTER
KONSTANTIN
MANCHESTER
MUGGLESTON
PACHACUTEC
POCAHONTAS
SCARFIOTTI
SHINGLETON
THEAETETUS
TRUTFETTER
WARRINGTON
BROCKHOUSE
INGENHOUSZ
MCCULLOUGH
NEUGEBAUER
WATERHOUSE
ZEHETBAUER
HARGREAVES
EISENHOWER
WEATHERWAX
ERLENMEYER
STROHMEYER
SCHEUCHZER
SCHWEITZER
SKOBELTZYN

### 9th Letter

ANAXAGORAS
BLUMENTHAL
BRETONNEAU
CHRISTIAAN
CUNNINGHAM
KOMUNYAKAA
LILIENTHAL
MAXIMILIAN
POCAHONTAS
PRAXAGORAS
PROTAGORAS
PYTHAGORAS
SPIEGELMAN
SWAMMERDAM
WEATHERWAX
ANDREEVICH
BEIJERINCK
BERTOLUCCI
BLUMENBACH
FRIEDERICH

HERSCHBACH
IOSIFOVICH
MANKIEWICZ
MCCLINTOCK
SACROBOSCO
SEMENOVICH
TREVITHICK
WUNDERLICH
ALDROVANDI
FERDINANDO
SCHICKARDT
STEINHARDT
ANAXIMENES
ARCHIMEDES
ARGELANDER
BARKHAUSEN
BARTOLEMEO
BARTOLOMEU
BERTHOLLET
BIGELEISEN
CARMICHAEL
CAVANILLES
CHARDONNET
CLOUDESLEY
DOBEREINER
DORNBERGER
EHRENFRIED
EISENHOWER
EMPEDOCLES
ERLENMEYER
FOETTINGER
GOLDBERGER
HARGREAVES
HELLRIEGEL
HOFMESITER
HOFSTADTER
HOLLDOBLER
KLEBESADEL
KRETSCHMER
LIPPERSHEY
MAIMONIDES
MANCHESTER
MOOKHERJEE
NEUGEBAUER
PACHACUTEC
PARMENIDES
SCHEUCHZER
SCHRIEFFER
SCHUMACHER
SCHWEIGGER
SCHWEITZER
SENEFELDER
SOMMEILLER
STAHLECKER
STAUDINGER
STROHMEYER
STROMINGER

THUCYDIDES
TISSANDIER
TRUTFETTER
WEIZSACKER
XENOPHANES
ZEHETBAUER
KOURGANOFF
ENGELBREGT
KAMERLINGH
MCCULLOUGH
CARTWRIGHT
CHRISTOPHE
CLATWORTHY
GALSWORTHY
BODENSTEIN
CASSEGRAIN
CHAMBERLIN
FAHRENHEIT
GREENSTEIN
KONSTANTIN
PRINGSHEIM
REICHSTEIN
SEFERIADIS
SHKLOVSKII
TAVOULARIS
VERROCCHIO
BELOZERSKY
DOBZHANSKY
KOVALEVSKI
KOVALEVSKY
ROKITANSKY
SKLODOWSKA
SZYMBORSKA
WROBLEWSKI
BRANSFIELD
CAMPANELLA
CASSINELLI
FITZGERALD
FOTHERGILL
HOUNSFIELD
MERRIFIELD
PIRANDELLO
POISEUILLE
SOMERVILLE
TORRICELLI
TOSCANELLI
WETHERHILL
BERNARDINO
CHRISTIANE
COURCHESNE
CRUIKSHANK
GELLIBRAND
GIORDMAINE
GULLSTRAND
LANGERHANS
LAURENTINE
MACFARLANE

MASCHERONI
MONTALCINI
OTTAVIOANO
PASQUALINO
RAMMAZZINI
SCHLIEMANN
SILLIPHANT
STRESEMANN
STURTEVANT
SUTHERLAND
TEISSERENC
WHEATSTONE
ANDRONIKOS
ARCHDEACON
BRETHERTON
CARRINGTON
CATHERWOOD
FOTOPOULOS
HARRINGTON
LAMBERTSON
MANDELBROT
MUGGLESTON
RICHARDSON
SAMUELSSON
SHINGLETON
STEPHENSON
TSCHIRIKOV
VINOGRADOV
WARRINGTON
WILLIAMSON
ALEIXANDRE
ALESSANDRO
ALLESANDRO
BENZENBERG
CANNIZZARO
EIZAGUIRRE
FRACASTORO
HEISENBERG
HEYDENBERG
POGGENDORF
RUTHERFORD
RUTTENBERG
SONNENBERG
SWEDENBORG
WILLEBRORD
BROCKHOUSE
INGENHOUSZ
LAGERKVIST
WATERHOUSE
MARGUERITE
SCARFIOTTI
APOLLONIUS
ARISTIPPUS
ATHANASIUS
CALLINICUS
CAMERARIUS
COPERNICUS

DEMOCRITUS
DESIDERIUS
DIOPHANTUS
EBBINGHAUS
FEIGENBAUM
FRANCISCUS
HERACLITUS
HEROPHILUS
HIERONYMUS
HIPPARCHUS
MENAECHMUS
NEMORARIUS
PARACELSUS
PHILOPONUS
SANCTORIUS
THEAETETUS
THEODOSIUS
WISLICENUS
NIKOLAYEVA
TERESHKOVA
SKOBELTZYN

## 10th Letter

CAMPANELLA
KOMUNYAKAA
NIKOLAYEVA
SKLODOWSKA
SZYMBORSKA
TERESHKOVA
PACHACUTEC
TEISSERENC
BRANSFIELD
CATHERWOOD
EHRENFRIED
FITZGERALD
GELLIBRAND
GULLSTRAND
HOUNSFIELD
MERRIFIELD
RUTHERFORD
SUTHERLAND
WILLEBRORD
ALEIXANDRE
BROCKHOUSE
CHRISTIANE
CHRISTOPHE
COURCHESNE
EIZAGUIRRE
GIORDMAINE
LAURENTINE
MACFARLANE
MARGUERITE
MOOKHERJEE
POISEUILLE

SOMERVILLE
WATERHOUSE
WHEATSTONE
KOURGANOFF
POGGENDORF
BENZENBERG
HEISENBERG
HEYDENBERG
RUTTENBERG
SONNENBERG
SWEDENBORG
ANDREEVICH
BLUMENBACH
FRIEDERICH
HERSCHBACH
IOSIFOVICH
KAMERLINGH
MCCULLOUGH
SEMENOVICH
WUNDERLICH
ALDROVANDI
BERTOLUCCI
CASSINELLI
KOVALEVSKI
MASCHERONI
MONTALCINI
RAMMAZZINI
SCARFIOTTI
SHKLOVSKII
TORRICELLI
TOSCANELLI
WROBLEWSKI
BEIJERINCK
CRUIKSHANK
MCCLINTOCK
TREVITHICK
BLUMENTHAL
CARMICHAEL
FOTHERGILL
HELLRIEGEL
KLEBESADEL
LILIENTHAL
WETHERHILL
CUNNINGHAM
FEIGENBAUM
PRINGSHEIM
SWAMMERDAM
ARCHDEACON
BARKHAUSEN
BIGELEISEN
BODENSTEIN
BRETHERTON
CARRINGTON
CASSEGRAIN
CHAMBERLIN
CHRISTIAAN
GREENSTEIN

HARRINGTON
KONSTANTIN
LAMBERTSON
MAXIMILIAN
MUGGLESTON
REICHSTEIN
RICHARDSON
SAMUELSSON
SCHLIEMANN
SHINGLETON
SKOBELTZYN
SPIEGELMAN
STEPHENSON
STRESEMANN
WARRINGTON
WILLIAMSON
ALESSANDRO
ALLESANDRO
BARTOLEMEO
BERNARDINO
CANNIZZARO
FERDINANDO
FRACASTORO
OTTAVIOANO
PASQUALINO
PIRANDELLO
SACROBOSCO
VERROCCHIO
ARGELANDER
DOBEREINER
DORNBERGER
EISENHOWER
ERLENMEYER
FOETTINGER
GOLDBERGER
HOFMESITER
HOFSTADTER
HOLLDOBLER
KRETSCHMER
MANCHESTER
NEUGEBAUER
SCHEUCHZER
SCHRIEFFER
SCHUMACHER
SCHWEIGGER
SCHWEITZER
SENEFELDER
SOMMEILLER
STAHLECKER
STAUDINGER
STROHMEYER
STROMINGER
TISSANDIER
TRUTFETTER
WEIZSACKER
ZEHETBAUER
ANAXAGORAS

ANAXIMENES
ANDRONIKOS
APOLLONIUS
ARCHIMEDES
ARISTIPPUS
ATHANASIUS
CALLINICUS
CAMERARIUS
CAVANILLES
COPERNICUS
DEMOCRITUS
DESIDERIUS
DIOPHANTUS
EBBINGHAUS
EMPEDOCLES
FOTOPOULOS
FRANCISCUS
HARGREAVES
HERACLITUS
HEROPHILUS
HIERONYMUS
HIPPARCHUS
LANGERHANS
MAIMONIDES
MENAECHMUS
NEMORARIUS
PARACELSUS
PARMENIDES
PHILOPONUS
POCAHONTAS
PRAXAGORAS
PROTAGORAS
PYTHAGORAS
SANCTORIUS
SEFERIADIS
TAVOULARIS
THEAETETUS
THEODOSIUS
THUCYDIDES
WISLICENUS
XENOPHANES
BERTHOLLET
CARTWRIGHT
CHARDONNET
ENGELBREGT
FAHRENHEIT
LAGERKVIST
MANDELBROT
SCHICKARDT
SILLIPHANT
STEINHARDT
STURTEVANT
BARTOLOMEU
BRETONNEAU
TSCHIRIKOV
VINOGRADOV
WEATHERWAX

BELOZERSKY
CLATWORTHY
CLOUDESLEY
DOBZHANSKY
GALSWORTHY
KOVALEVSKY
LIPPERSHEY
ROKITANSKY
INGENHOUSZ
MANKIEWICZ

### 11 Letter

#### 1st Letter

ALBATEGNIUS
ANAXIMANDER
ARISTARCHUS
ARTSIMOVICH
ASCLEPIADES
AUENBRUGGER
BARTHOLOMEW
BIRINGUCCIO
BLOEMBERGEN
BOEKELHEIDE
BONAVENTURA
BRADWARDINE
BRAHMAGUPTA
BRUNSCHWYGK
BUCKMINSTER
CAESALPINUS
CALLICRATES
CHAMBERLAIN
CHAMBERLAND
CHAMPOLLION
CHARLEMAGNE
CHRISTOFFEL
CHRISTOPHER
CRUICKSHANK
DEISENHOFER
DESAGULIERS
DICAEARCHUS
DIOSCORIDES
DMITRIEVICH
EVANGELISTA
GIAMBATISTA
GOLDSCHMIDT
GOODPASTURE
GROSSETESTE
HASELBERGER
HATZIDHAKIS
HERACLEIDES
HERTZSPRUNG
HINSHELWOOD
HIPPOCRATES
HUDALRICHUS
JABLOCHKOFF
KIBALCHITCH
LANDSTEINER
LEONIDOVICH
LOBACHEVSKI
MACHIAVELLI
MAETERLINCK
MARKOVNIKOV
MCCAMBRIDGE
MOHNOROVCIC
MONTGOLFIER
MORGENSTERN
NEDDERMEYER
NICHOMACHUS
NIGHTINGALE
NUSSENZWEIG
OPPENHEIMER
PAPANICOLAU
PHOCYCLIDES
PICCOLOMINI
PONTOPPIDAN
POSEIDONIUS
PRESSBURGER
PRZHEVALSKY
REICHENBACH
SCHILDKRAUT
SCHLESINGER
SCHNIRELMAN
SCHOONMAKER
SCHRODINGER
SCHWEICKART
SEMMELWEISS
SENNACHERIB
SERGEYEVICH
SHAKESPEARE
SHERRINGTON
SHIBASABURO
SIENKIEWICZ
SONDERGAARD
SPALLANZANI
STEENBURGEN
STEINBERGER
STERRENBERG
STRASBURGER
TSIOLKOVKSY
UNVERDORBEN
WEIERSTRASS
WILLSTATTER
ZINKERNAGEL

#### 2nd Letter

BARTHOLOMEW
CAESALPINUS
CALLICRATES
HASELBERGER
HATZIDHAKIS
JABLOCHKOFF
LANDSTEINER
MACHIAVELLI
MAETERLINCK
MARKOVNIKOV
PAPANICOLAU
MCCAMBRIDGE
SCHILDKRAUT
SCHLESINGER
SCHNIRELMAN
SCHOONMAKER
SCHRODINGER
SCHWEICKART
DEISENHOFER
DESAGULIERS
HERACLEIDES
HERTZSPRUNG
LEONIDOVICH
NEDDERMEYER
REICHENBACH
SEMMELWEISS
SENNACHERIB
SERGEYEVICH
WEIERSTRASS
CHAMBERLAIN
CHAMBERLAND
CHAMPOLLION
CHARLEMAGNE
CHRISTOFFEL
CHRISTOPHER
PHOCYCLIDES
SHAKESPEARE
SHERRINGTON
SHIBASABURO
BIRINGUCCIO
DICAEARCHUS
DIOSCORIDES
GIAMBATISTA
HINSHELWOOD
HIPPOCRATES
KIBALCHITCH
NICHOMACHUS
NIGHTINGALE
PICCOLOMINI
SIENKIEWICZ
WILLSTATTER
ZINKERNAGEL
ALBATEGNIUS
BLOEMBERGEN
DMITRIEVICH
ANAXIMANDER
UNVERDORBEN
BOEKELHEIDE
BONAVENTURA
GOLDSCHMIDT
GOODPASTURE
LOBACHEVSKI
MOHNOROVCIC
MONTGOLFIER
MORGENSTERN
PONTOPPIDAN
POSEIDONIUS
SONDERGAARD
OPPENHEIMER
SPALLANZANI
ARISTARCHUS
ARTSIMOVICH
BRADWARDINE
BRAHMAGUPTA
BRUNSCHWYGK
CRUICKSHANK
GROSSETESTE
PRESSBURGER
PRZHEVALSKY
ASCLEPIADES
TSIOLKOVKSY
STEENBURGEN
STEINBERGER
STERRENBERG
STRASBURGER
AUENBRUGGER
BUCKMINSTER
HUDALRICHUS
NUSSENZWEIG
EVANGELISTA

#### 3rd Letter

ANAXIMANDER
BRADWARDINE
BRAHMAGUPTA
CHAMBERLAIN
CHAMBERLAND
CHAMPOLLION
CHARLEMAGNE
EVANGELISTA
GIAMBATISTA
SHAKESPEARE
SPALLANZANI
ALBATEGNIUS
JABLOCHKOFF
KIBALCHITCH
LOBACHEVSKI
ASCLEPIADES
BUCKMINSTER
DICAEARCHUS
MACHIAVELLI
MCCAMBRIDGE
NICHOMACHUS
PICCOLOMINI
HUDALRICHUS
NEDDERMEYER
AUENBRUGGER
BOEKELHEIDE
CAESALPINUS
MAETERLINCK
PRESSBURGER
SHERRINGTON
SIENKIEWICZ
STEENBURGEN
STEINBERGER
STERRENBERG
NIGHTINGALE
MOHNOROVCIC
SCHILDKRAUT
SCHLESINGER
SCHNIRELMAN
SCHOONMAKER
SCHRODINGER
SCHWEICKART
ARISTARCHUS
DEISENHOFER
DMITRIEVICH
REICHENBACH
SHIBASABURO
TSIOLKOVKSY
WEIERSTRASS
CALLICRATES
GOLDSCHMIDT
WILLSTATTER
SEMMELWEISS
BONAVENTURA
HINSHELWOOD
LANDSTEINER
MONTGOLFIER
PONTOPPIDAN
SENNACHERIB
SONDERGAARD
ZINKERNAGEL
BLOEMBERGEN
DIOSCORIDES
GOODPASTURE
GROSSETESTE
LEONIDOVICH
PHOCYCLIDES
HIPPOCRATES
OPPENHEIMER
PAPANICOLAU
BARTHOLOMEW
BIRINGUCCIO
CHRISTOFFEL
CHRISTOPHER
HERACLEIDES
HERTZSPRUNG
MARKOVNIKOV
MORGENSTERN
SERGEYEVICH
STRASBURGER
DESAGULIERS
HASELBERGER
NUSSENZWEIG
POSEIDONIUS
ARTSIMOVICH
HATZIDHAKIS
BRUNSCHWYGK
CRUICKSHANK
UNVERDORBEN
PRZHEVALSKY

#### 4th Letter

ALBATEGNIUS
BONAVENTURA
DESAGULIERS
DICAEARCHUS
HERACLEIDES
HUDALRICHUS
KIBALCHITCH
LOBACHEVSKI
MCCAMBRIDGE
PAPANICOLAU
STRASBURGER
SHIBASABURO
PHOCYCLIDES
PICCOLOMINI
REICHENBACH
BRADWARDINE
GOLDSCHMIDT
GOODPASTURE
LANDSTEINER
NEDDERMEYER
SONDERGAARD
BLOEMBERGEN
HASELBERGER
OPPENHEIMER
POSEIDONIUS
STEENBURGEN
UNVERDORBEN
WEIERSTRASS
MORGENSTERN
SERGEYEVICH
BRAHMAGUPTA
MACHIAVELLI
NICHOMACHUS
NIGHTINGALE
PRZHEVALSKY
BIRINGUCCIO
CHRISTOFFEL
CHRISTOPHER
CRUICKSHANK
SCHILDKRAUT
STEINBERGER
BOEKELHEIDE
BUCKMINSTER
MARKOVNIKOV
SHAKESPEARE
ZINKERNAGEL
ASCLEPIADES
CALLICRATES
JABLOCHKOFF
SCHLESINGER
SPALLANZANI
WILLSTATTER
CHAMBERLAIN
CHAMBERLAND
CHAMPOLLION
GIAMBATISTA
SEMMELWEISS
AUENBRUGGER
BRUNSCHWYGK
EVANGELISTA
LEONIDOVICH
MOHNOROVCIC
SCHNIRELMAN
SENNACHERIB
SIENKIEWICZ
SCHOONMAKER
TSIOLKOVKSY
HIPPOCRATES
CHARLEMAGNE
SCHRODINGER
SHERRINGTON
STERRENBERG
ARISTARCHUS
ARTSIMOVICH
CAESALPINUS
DEISENHOFER
DIOSCORIDES
GROSSETESTE
HINSHELWOOD
NUSSENZWEIG
PRESSBURGER
BARTHOLOMEW
DMITRIEVICH
HERTZSPRUNG
MAETERLINCK
MONTGOLFIER
PONTOPPIDAN
SCHWEICKART
ANAXIMANDER
HATZIDHAKIS

#### 5th Letter

CAESALPINUS
SENNACHERIB

SHIB**A**SABURO
AUEN**B**RUGGER
CHAM**B**ERLAIN
CHAM**B**ERLAND
GIAM**B**ATISTA
CRUI**C**KSHANK
DIOS**C**ORIDES
HERA**C**LEIDES
LOBA**C**HEVSKI
ASCL**E**PIADES
BOEK**E**LHEIDE
DEIS**E**NHOFER
DICA**E**ARCHUS
MAET**E**RLINCK
MORG**E**NSTERN
NEDD**E**RMEYER
NUSS**E**NZWEIG
PRZH**E**VALSKY
SCHL**E**SINGER
SCHW**E**ICKART
SEMM**E**LWEISS
SERG**E**YEVICH
SHAK**E**SPEARE
SOND**E**RGAARD
ZINK**E**RNAGEL
DESA**G**ULIERS
EVAN**G**ELISTA
MONT**G**OLFIER
BART**H**OLOMEW
HINS**H**ELWOOD
REIC**H**ENBACH
ANAX**I**MANDER
ARTS**I**MOVICH
CALL**I**CRATES
HATZ**I**DHAKIS
LEON**I**DOVICH
MACH**I**AVELLI
POSE**I**DONIUS
SCHN**I**RELMAN
SIEN**K**IEWICZ
CHAR**L**EMAGNE
HASE**L**BERGER
HUDA**L**RICHUS
KIBA**L**CHITCH
SCHI**L**DKRAUT
SPAL**L**ANZANI
TSIO**L**KOVKSY
BLOE**M**BERGEN
BRAH**M**AGUPTA
BUCK**M**INSTER
MCCA**M**BRIDGE
BIRI**N**GUCCIO
OPPE**N**HEIMER
PAPA**N**ICOLAU
STEE**N**BURGEN
STEI**N**BERGER
HIPP**O**CRATES
JABL**O**CHKOFF
MARK**O**VNIKOV
MOHN**O**ROVCIC
NICH**O**MACHUS
PICC**O**LOMINI
PONT**O**PPIDAN
SCHO**O**NMAKER
SCHR**O**DINGER
CHAM**P**OLLION
GOOD**P**ASTURE
DMIT**R**IEVICH
SHER**R**INGTON
STER**R**ENBERG
UNVE**R**DORBEN
WEIE**R**STRASS
BRUN**S**CHWYGK
CHRI**S**TOFFEL
CHRI**S**TOPHER
GOLD**S**CHMIDT
GROS**S**ETESTE
LAND**S**TEINER
PRES**S**BURGER
STRA**S**BURGER
WILL**S**TATTER
ALBA**T**EGNIUS
ARIS**T**ARCHUS
NIGH**T**INGALE
BONA**V**ENTURA
BRAD**W**ARDINE
PHOC**Y**CLIDES
HERT**Z**SPRUNG

### 6th Letter

ARIST**A**RCHUS
BRADW**A**RDINE
BRAHM**A**GUPTA
DICAE**A**RCHUS
GIAMB**A**TISTA
GOODP**A**STURE
MACHI**A**VELLI
SPALL**A**NZANI
BLOEM**B**ERGEN
HASEL**B**ERGER
MCCAM**B**RIDGE
PRESS**B**URGER
STEEN**B**URGEN
STEIN**B**ERGER
STRAS**B**URGER
BRUNS**C**HWYGK
CALLI**C**RATES
GOLDS**C**HMIDT
HIPPO**C**RATES
JABLO**C**HKOFF
KIBAL**C**HITCH
PHOCY**C**LIDES
SENNA**C**HERIB
HATZI**D**HAKIS
LEONI**D**OVICH
POSEI**D**ONIUS
SCHIL**D**KRAUT
SCHRO**D**INGER
UNVER**D**ORBEN
ALBAT**E**GNIUS
BONAV**E**NTURA
CHAMB**E**RLAIN
CHAMB**E**RLAND
CHARL**E**MAGNE
EVANG**E**LISTA
GROSS**E**TESTE
HINSH**E**LWOOD
REICH**E**NBACH
STERR**E**NBERG
BIRIN**G**UCCIO
LOBAC**H**EVSKI
OPPEN**H**EIMER
BUCKM**I**NSTER
DMITR**I**EVICH
NIGHT**I**NGALE
PAPAN**I**COLAU
SCHWE**I**CKART
SHERR**I**NGTON
SIENK**I**EWICZ
CRUIC**K**SHANK
TSIOL**K**OVKSY
BOEKE**L**HEIDE
CAESA**L**PINUS
HERAC**L**EIDES
PICCO**L**OMINI
SEMME**L**WEISS
ANAXI**M**ANDER
ARTSI**M**OVICH
NICHO**M**ACHUS
DEISE**N**HOFER
MORGE**N**STERN
NUSSE**N**ZWEIG
SCHOO**N**MAKER
BARTH**O**LOMEW
CHAMP**O**LLION
DIOSC**O**RIDES
MONTG**O**LFIER
ASCLE**P**IADES
PONTO**P**PIDAN
AUENB**R**UGGER
HUDAL**R**ICHUS
MAETE**R**LINCK
MOHNO**R**OVCIC
NEDDE**R**MEYER
SCHNI**R**ELMAN
SONDE**R**GAARD
ZINKE**R**NAGEL
HERTZ**S**PRUNG
SCHLE**S**INGER
SHAKE**S**PEARE
SHIBA**S**ABURO
WEIER**S**TRASS
CHRIS**T**OFFEL
CHRIS**T**OPHER
LANDS**T**EINER
WILLS**T**ATTER
DESAG**U**LIERS
MARKO**V**NIKOV
PRZHE**V**ALSKY
SERGE**Y**EVICH

### 7th Letter

ANAXIM**A**NDER
NICHOM**A**CHUS
PRZHEV**A**LSKY
SHIBAS**A**BURO
WILLST**A**TTER
PAPANI**C**OLAU
SCHWEI**C**KART
BLOEMB**E**RGEN
DMITRI**E**VICH
HASELB**E**RGER
HERACL**E**IDES
LANDST**E**INER
LOBACH**E**VSKI
OPPENH**E**IMER
SCHNIR**E**LMAN
SERGEY**E**VICH
SIENKI**E**WICZ
STEINB**E**RGER
ALBATE**G**NIUS
BRAHMA**G**UPTA
SONDER**G**AARD
BOEKEL**H**EIDE
BRUNSC**H**WYGK
DEISEN**H**OFER
GOLDSC**H**MIDT
HATZID**H**AKIS
JABLOC**H**KOFF
KIBALC**H**ITCH
SENNAC**H**ERIB
ASCLEP**I**ADES
HUDALR**I**CHUS
SCHLES**I**NGER
SCHROD**I**NGER
SCHILD**K**RAUT
BARTHO**L**OMEW
CHAMPO**L**LION
DESAGU**L**IERS
EVANGE**L**ISTA
HINSHE**L**WOOD
MAETER**L**INCK
MONTGO**L**FIER
PHOCYC**L**IDES
CHARLE**M**AGNE
NEDDER**M**EYER
SCHOON**M**AKER
BONAVE**N**TURA
BUCKMI**N**STER
MARKOV**N**IKOV
NIGHTI**N**GALE
REICHE**N**BACH
SHERRI**N**GTON
SPALLA**N**ZANI
STERRE**N**BERG
ZINKER**N**AGEL
ARTSIM**O**VICH
CHRIST**O**FFEL
CHRIST**O**PHER
LEONID**O**VICH
MOHNOR**O**VCIC
PICCOL**O**MINI
POSEID**O**NIUS
TSIOLK**O**VKSY
UNVERD**O**RBEN
CAESAL**P**INUS
HERTZS**P**RUNG
PONTOP**P**IDAN
SHAKES**P**EARE
ARISTA**R**CHUS
BRADWA**R**DINE
CALLIC**R**ATES
CHAMBE**R**LAIN
CHAMBE**R**LAND
DICAEA**R**CHUS
DIOSCO**R**IDES
HIPPOC**R**ATES
MCCAMB**R**IDGE
CRUICK**S**HANK
GOODPA**S**TURE
MORGEN**S**TERN
GIAMBA**T**ISTA
GROSSE**T**ESTE
WEIERS**T**RASS
AUENBR**U**GGER
BIRING**U**CCIO
PRESSB**U**RGER
STEENB**U**RGEN
STRASB**U**RGER
MACHIA**V**ELLI
SEMMEL**W**EISS
NUSSEN**Z**WEIG

### 8th Letter

ASCLEPI**A**DES
CALLICR**A**TES
CHARLEM**A**GNE
HATZIDH**A**KIS
HIPPOCR**A**TES
SCHOONM**A**KER
SONDERG**A**ARD
ZINKERN**A**GEL
REICHEN**B**ACH
SHIBASA**B**URO
STERREN**B**ERG
ARISTAR**C**HUS
BIRINGU**C**CIO
DICAEAR**C**HUS
HUDALRI**C**HUS
NICHOMA**C**HUS
BRADWAR**D**INE
BOEKELH**E**IDE
GROSSET**E**STE
MACHIAV**E**LLI
NEDDERM**E**YER
SEMMELW**E**ISS
SENNACH**E**RIB
SHAKESP**E**ARE
CHRISTO**F**FEL
MONTGOL**F**IER
AUENBRU**G**GER
NIGHTIN**G**ALE
SHERRIN**G**TON
CRUICKS**H**ANK
CAESALP**I**NUS
DESAGUL**I**ERS
DIOSCOR**I**DES
EVANGEL**I**STA
GIAMBAT**I**STA
HERACLE**I**DES
KIBALCH**I**TCH
LANDSTE**I**NER
MAETERL**I**NCK
MARKOVN**I**KOV
MCCAMBR**I**DGE
OPPENHE**I**MER
PHOCYCL**I**DES
PONTOPP**I**DAN
JABLOCH**K**OFF
SCHWEIC**K**ART
CHAMBER**L**AIN
CHAMBER**L**AND
CHAMPOL**L**ION
PRZHEVA**L**SKY
SCHNIRE**L**MAN
GOLDSCH**M**IDT
PICCOLO**M**INI
ALBATEG**N**IUS
ANAXIMA**N**DER
POSEIDO**N**IUS
SCHLESI**N**GER
SCHRODI**N**GER
BARTHOL**O**MEW
DEISENH**O**FER
PAPANIC**O**LAU
CHRISTO**P**HER
BLOEMBE**R**GEN
HASELBE**R**GER
HERTZSP**R**UNG
PRESSBU**R**GER
SCHILDK**R**AUT
STEENBU**R**GEN
STEINBE**R**GER
STRASBU**R**GER
UNVERDO**R**BEN
WEIERST**R**ASS
BUCKMIN**S**TER
BONAVEN**T**URA
GOODPAS**T**URE
MORGENS**T**ERN
WILLSTA**T**TER
BRAHMAG**U**PTA
ARTSIMO**V**ICH
DMITRIE**V**ICH
LEONIDO**V**ICH
LOBACHE**V**SKI
MOHNORO**V**CIC
SERGEYE**V**ICH
TSIOLKO**V**KSY
BRUNSCH**W**YGK
HINSHEL**W**OOD
NUSSENZ**W**EIG
SIENKIE**W**ICZ
SPALLAN**Z**ANI

### 9th Letter

CHAMBERL**A**IN
CHAMBERL**A**ND
CRUICKSH**A**NK
NIGHTING**A**LE
REICHENB**A**CH
SCHILDKR**A**UT
SCHWEICK**A**RT
SHAKESPE**A**RE
SONDERGA**A**RD
SPALLANZ**A**NI
WEIERSTR**A**SS
UNVERDOR**B**EN
BIRINGUC**C**IO
MOHNOROV**C**IC
ANAXIMAN**D**ER
ASCLEPIA**D**ES
DIOSCORI**D**ES
HERACLEI**D**ES
MCCAMBRI**D**GE
PHOCYCLI**D**ES
PONTOPPI**D**AN

DESAGULIERS
MORGENSTERN
NUSSENZWEIG
STERRENBERG
CHRISTOFFEL
DEISENHOFER
AUENBRUGGER
BLOEMBERGEN
CHARLEMAGNE
HASELBERGER
PRESSBURGER
SCHLESINGER
SCHRODINGER
STEENBURGEN
STEINBERGER
STRASBURGER
ZINKERNAGEL
ARISTARCHUS
CHRISTOPHER
DICAEARCHUS
HUDALRICHUS
NICHOMACHUS
ALBATEGNIUS
ARTSIMOVICH
BOEKELHEIDE
BRADWARDINE
CHAMPOLLION
DMITRIEVICH
GOLDSCHMIDT
LEONIDOVICH
MONTGOLFIER
PICCOLOMINI
POSEIDONIUS
SEMMELWEISS
SERGEYEVICH
SIENKIEWICZ
HATZIDHAKIS
MARKOVNIKOV
SCHOONMAKER
TSIOLKOVKSY
MACHIAVELLI
PAPANICOLAU
BARTHOLOMEW
OPPENHEIMER
SCHNIRELMAN
CAESALPINUS
LANDSTEINER
MAETERLINCK
HINSHELWOOD
JABLOCHKOFF
BRAHMAGUPTA
SENNACHERIB
EVANGELISTA
GIAMBATISTA
GROSSETESTE
LOBACHEVSKI
PRZHEVALSKY
BUCKMINSTER
CALLICRATES
HIPPOCRATES
KIBALCHITCH
SHERRINGTON
WILLSTATTER
BONAVENTURA
GOODPASTURE
HERTZSPRUNG
SHIBASABURO
BRUNSCHWYGK
NEDDERMEYER

### 10th Letter

PAPANICOLAU
PONTOPPIDAN
SCHNIRELMAN
ARTSIMOVICH
DMITRIEVICH
KIBALCHITCH
LEONIDOVICH
MAETERLINCK
REICHENBACH
SERGEYEVICH
SIENKIEWICZ
BOEKELHEIDE
GOLDSCHMIDT
ANAXIMANDER
ASCLEPIADES
AUENBRUGGER
BARTHOLOMEW
BLOEMBERGEN
BUCKMINSTER
CALLICRATES
CHRISTOFFEL
CHRISTOPHER
DEISENHOFER
DIOSCORIDES
HASELBERGER
HERACLEIDES
HIPPOCRATES
LANDSTEINER
MONTGOLFIER
NEDDERMEYER
OPPENHEIMER
PHOCYCLIDES
PRESSBURGER
SCHLESINGER
SCHOONMAKER
SCHRODINGER
STEENBURGEN
STEINBERGER
STRASBURGER
UNVERDORBEN
WILLSTATTER
ZINKERNAGEL
JABLOCHKOFF
BRUNSCHWYGK
MCCAMBRIDGE
BIRINGUCCIO
CHAMBERLAIN
HATZIDHAKIS
MOHNOROVCIC
NUSSENZWEIG
SENNACHERIB
LOBACHEVSKI
PRZHEVALSKY
MACHIAVELLI
NIGHTINGALE
BRADWARDINE
CHAMBERLAND
CHARLEMAGNE
CRUICKSHANK
HERTZSPRUNG
PICCOLOMINI
SPALLANZANI
CHAMPOLLION
HINSHELWOOD
MARKOVNIKOV
SHERRINGTON
BONAVENTURA
DESAGULIERS
GOODPASTURE
MORGENSTERN
SCHWEICKART
SHAKESPEARE
SHIBASABURO
SONDERGAARD
STERRENBERG
SEMMELWEISS
TSIOLKOVKSY
WEIERSTRASS
BRAHMAGUPTA
EVANGELISTA
GIAMBATISTA
GROSSETESTE
ALBATEGNIUS
ARISTARCHUS
CAESALPINUS
DICAEARCHUS
HUDALRICHUS
NICHOMACHUS
POSEIDONIUS
SCHILDKRAUT

### 11th Letter

BONAVENTURA
BRAHMAGUPTA
EVANGELISTA
GIAMBATISTA
SENNACHERIB
MOHNOROVCIC
CHAMBERLAND
HINSHELWOOD
SONDERGAARD
BOEKELHEIDE
BRADWARDINE
CHARLEMAGNE
GOODPASTURE
GROSSETESTE
MCCAMBRIDGE
NIGHTINGALE
SHAKESPEARE
JABLOCHKOFF
HERTZSPRUNG
NUSSENZWEIG
STERRENBERG
ARTSIMOVICH
DMITRIEVICH
KIBALCHITCH
LEONIDOVICH
REICHENBACH
SERGEYEVICH
LOBACHEVSKI
MACHIAVELLI
PICCOLOMINI
SPALLANZANI
BRUNSCHWYGK
CRUICKSHANK
MAETERLINCK
CHRISTOFFEL
ZINKERNAGEL
BLOEMBERGEN
CHAMBERLAIN
CHAMPOLLION
MORGENSTERN
PONTOPPIDAN
SCHNIRELMAN
SHERRINGTON
STEENBURGEN
UNVERDORBEN
BIRINGUCCIO
SHIBASABURO
ANAXIMANDER
AUENBRUGGER
BUCKMINSTER
CHRISTOPHER
DEISENHOFER
HASELBERGER
LANDSTEINER
MONTGOLFIER
NEDDERMEYER
OPPENHEIMER
PRESSBURGER
SCHLESINGER
SCHOONMAKER
SCHRODINGER
STEINBERGER
STRASBURGER
WILLSTATTER
ALBATEGNIUS
ARISTARCHUS
ASCLEPIADES
CAESALPINUS
CALLICRATES
DESAGULIERS
DICAEARCHUS
DIOSCORIDES
HATZIDHAKIS
HERACLEIDES
HIPPOCRATES
HUDALRICHUS
NICHOMACHUS
PHOCYCLIDES
POSEIDONIUS
SEMMELWEISS
WEIERSTRASS
GOLDSCHMIDT
SCHILDKRAUT
SCHWEICKART
PAPANICOLAU
MARKOVNIKOV
BARTHOLOMEW
PRZHEVALSKY
TSIOLKOVKSY
SIENKIEWICZ

## 12 Letter

### 1st Letter

ALEKSEYEVICH
ALEPOUDHELIS
AMAZASPOVICH
AMBARTSUMIAN
ANTHONISZOON
ATTENBOROUGH
BOUSSINGAULT
COLLINGRIDGE
DESHOUILLERS
ERASISTRATUS
ERATOSTHENES
GALANOPOULOS
HAMMARSKJOLD
HOLLINGSHEAD
HULDSCHINSKY
KLEINSCHMIDT
MERGENTHALER
MICHELANGELO
MITSCHERLICH
NIKOLAEVITCH
NORDENSKIOLD
OSTROGRADSKI
RABINDRANATH
RAMACHANDRAN
SATYENDRANTH
SCHERTZINGER
SCHIAPARELLI
SCHOENHEIMER
SOLZHENITSYN
SQUARCIAPINO
SUBRAHMANYAN
THEOPHRASTUS
UYTTERHOEVEN
WEINDENREICH
WESTINGHOUSE

### 2nd Letter

GALANOPOULOS
HAMMARSKJOLD
RABINDRANATH
RAMACHANDRAN
SATYENDRANTH
SCHERTZINGER
SCHIAPARELLI
SCHOENHEIMER
DESHOUILLERS
MERGENTHALER
WEINDENREICH
WESTINGHOUSE
THEOPHRASTUS
MICHELANGELO
MITSCHERLICH
NIKOLAEVITCH
ALEKSEYEVICH
ALEPOUDHELIS
KLEINSCHMIDT
AMAZASPOVICH
AMBARTSUMIAN
ANTHONISZOON
BOUSSINGAULT
COLLINGRIDGE
HOLLINGSHEAD
NORDENSKIOLD
SOLZHENITSYN
SQUARCIAPINO
ERASISTRATUS
ERATOSTHENES
OSTROGRADSKI
ATTENBOROUGH
HULDSCHINSKY
SUBRAHMANYAN
UYTTERHOEVEN

### 3rd Letter

AMAZASPOVICH
ERASISTRATUS
ERATOSTHENES
AMBARTSUMIAN
RABINDRANATH
SUBRAHMANYAN
MICHELANGELO
ALEKSEYEVICH
ALEPOUDHELIS
KLEINSCHMIDT
THEOPHRASTUS
SCHERTZINGER
SCHIAPARELLI
SCHOENHEIMER
WEINDENREICH
NIKOLAEVITCH
COLLINGRIDGE
GALANOPOULOS
HOLLINGSHEAD
HULDSCHINSKY
SOLZHENITSYN
HAMMARSKJOLD
RAMACHANDRAN
MERGENTHALER
NORDENSKIOLD
DESHOUILLERS
WESTINGHOUSE
ANTHONISZOON
ATTENBOROUGH
MITSCHERLICH
OSTROGRADSKI
SATYENDRANTH
UYTTERHOEVEN
BOUSSINGAULT
SQUARCIAPINO

### 4th Letter

AMBARTSUMIAN
GALANOPOULOS
RAMACHANDRAN
SQUARCIAPINO
HULDSCHINSKY
NORDENSKIOLD
ATTENBOROUGH
SCHERTZINGER
MERGENTHALER
ANTHONISZOON
DESHOUILLERS
MICHELANGELO
KLEINSCHMIDT
RABINDRANATH
SCHIAPARELLI
ALEKSEYEVICH
COLLINGRIDGE
HOLLINGSHEAD
HAMMARSKJOLD
WEINDENREICH
NIKOLAEVITCH
SCHOENHEIMER
THEOPHRASTUS
ALEPOUDHELIS
OSTROGRADSKI
SUBRAHMANYAN
BOUSSINGAULT
ERASISTRATUS
MITSCHERLICH
ERATOSTHENES
UYTTERHOEVEN
WESTINGHOUSE
SATYENDRANTH
AMAZASPOVICH
SOLZHENITSYN

### 5th Letter

AMAZASPOVICH
HAMMARSKJOLD
SCHIAPARELLI
SUBRAHMANYAN
MITSCHERLICH
RAMACHANDRAN
WEINDENREICH
MERGENTHALER
MICHELANGELO
NORDENSKIOLD
SATYENDRANTH
SCHOENHEIMER
UYTTERHOEVEN
SOLZHENITSYN
COLLINGRIDGE
ERASISTRATUS
HOLLINGSHEAD
WESTINGHOUSE
NIKOLAEVITCH
ATTENBOROUGH
GALANOPOULOS
KLEINSCHMIDT
RABINDRANATH
ALEPOUDHELIS
ANTHONISZOON
DESHOUILLERS
ERATOSTHENES
OSTROGRADSKI
THEOPHRASTUS
AMBARTSUMIAN
SCHERTZINGER
SQUARCIAPINO
ALEKSEYEVICH
BOUSSINGAULT
HULDSCHINSKY

### 6th Letter

NIKOLAEVITCH
ATTENBOROUGH
HULDSCHINSKY
SQUARCIAPINO
RABINDRANATH
ALEKSEYEVICH
SOLZHENITSYN
WEINDENREICH
OSTROGRADSKI
MITSCHERLICH
RAMACHANDRAN
SUBRAHMANYAN
THEOPHRASTUS
BOUSSINGAULT
MICHELANGELO
ANTHONISZOON
COLLINGRIDGE
HOLLINGSHEAD
MERGENTHALER
NORDENSKIOLD
SATYENDRANTH
SCHOENHEIMER
WESTINGHOUSE
GALANOPOULOS
SCHIAPARELLI
HAMMARSKJOLD
UYTTERHOEVEN
AMAZASPOVICH
ERASISTRATUS
ERATOSTHENES
KLEINSCHMIDT
AMBARTSUMIAN
SCHERTZINGER
ALEPOUDHELIS
DESHOUILLERS

### 7th Letter

MICHELANGELO
RAMACHANDRAN
SCHIAPARELLI
KLEINSCHMIDT
ALEPOUDHELIS
SATYENDRANTH
MITSCHERLICH
NIKOLAEVITCH
COLLINGRIDGE
HOLLINGSHEAD
WESTINGHOUSE
HULDSCHINSKY
SCHOENHEIMER
UYTTERHOEVEN
ANTHONISZOON
DESHOUILLERS
SQUARCIAPINO
SUBRAHMANYAN
BOUSSINGAULT
SOLZHENITSYN
WEINDENREICH
ATTENBOROUGH
AMAZASPOVICH
GALANOPOULOS
OSTROGRADSKI
RABINDRANATH
THEOPHRASTUS
AMBARTSUMIAN
HAMMARSKJOLD
NORDENSKIOLD
ERASISTRATUS
ERATOSTHENES
MERGENTHALER
ALEKSEYEVICH
SCHERTZINGER

### 8th Letter

OSTROGRADSKI
RABINDRANATH
SQUARCIAPINO
SUBRAHMANYAN
THEOPHRASTUS
ALEKSEYEVICH
SCHOENHEIMER
BOUSSINGAULT
ALEPOUDHELIS
ERATOSTHENES
KLEINSCHMIDT
MERGENTHALER
WESTINGHOUSE
HULDSCHINSKY
SCHERTZINGER
SOLZHENITSYN
HAMMARSKJOLD
NORDENSKIOLD
DESHOUILLERS
MICHELANGELO
RAMACHANDRAN
AMAZASPOVICH
GALANOPOULOS
UYTTERHOEVEN
ATTENBOROUGH
COLLINGRIDGE
ERASISTRATUS
MITSCHERLICH
SATYENDRANTH
SCHIAPARELLI
WEINDENREICH
ANTHONISZOON
HOLLINGSHEAD
AMBARTSUMIAN
NIKOLAEVITCH

### 9th Letter

BOUSSINGAULT
ERASISTRATUS
MERGENTHALER
SATYENDRANTH
OSTROGRADSKI
RAMACHANDRAN
ALEPOUDHELIS
ERATOSTHENES
SCHIAPARELLI
UYTTERHOEVEN
WEINDENREICH
MICHELANGELO
HOLLINGSHEAD
COLLINGRIDGE
NIKOLAEVITCH
NORDENSKIOLD
SCHOENHEIMER
HAMMARSKJOLD
DESHOUILLERS
MITSCHERLICH
AMBARTSUMIAN
KLEINSCHMIDT
HULDSCHINSKY
RABINDRANATH
SCHERTZINGER
SUBRAHMANYAN
ATTENBOROUGH
WESTINGHOUSE
SQUARCIAPINO
THEOPHRASTUS
SOLZHENITSYN
GALANOPOULOS
ALEKSEYEVICH
AMAZASPOVICH
ANTHONISZOON

### 10th Letter

RABINDRANATH
COLLINGRIDGE
DESHOUILLERS
HOLLINGSHEAD
MICHELANGELO
SCHERTZINGER
ALEKSEYEVICH
AMAZASPOVICH
AMBARTSUMIAN
KLEINSCHMIDT
MITSCHERLICH
SQUARCIAPINO
WEINDENREICH
ALEPOUDHELIS
GALANOPOULOS
MERGENTHALER
SCHIAPARELLI
SCHOENHEIMER
ERATOSTHENES
SATYENDRANTH
ANTHONISZOON
HAMMARSKJOLD
NORDENSKIOLD
RAMACHANDRAN
HULDSCHINSKY
OSTROGRADSKI
SOLZHENITSYN
ERASISTRATUS
NIKOLAEVITCH
THEOPHRASTUS
ATTENBOROUGH
BOUSSINGAULT
WESTINGHOUSE
UYTTERHOEVEN
SUBRAHMANYAN

### 11th Letter

AMBARTSUMIAN
HOLLINGSHEAD
RAMACHANDRAN
SUBRAHMANYAN
ALEKSEYEVICH
AMAZASPOVICH
MITSCHERLICH
NIKOLAEVITCH
WEINDENREICH
KLEINSCHMIDT
ERATOSTHENES
MERGENTHALER
SCHERTZINGER
SCHOENHEIMER
UYTTERHOEVEN
ATTENBOROUGH
COLLINGRIDGE
ALEPOUDHELIS
HULDSCHINSKY
OSTROGRADSKI

BOUSSINGAU**L**T
HAMMARSKJO**L**D
MICHELANGE**L**O
NORDENSKIO**L**D
SCHIAPAREL**L**I
SQUARCIAPI**N**O
ANTHONISZO**O**N
GALANOPOUL**O**S
DESHOUILLE**R**S
WESTINGHOU**S**E
RABINDRANA**T**H
SATYENDRAN**T**H
ERASISTRAT**U**S
THEOPHRAST**U**S
SOLZHENITS**Y**N

### 12th Letter

HAMMARSKJOL**D**
HOLLINGSHEA**D**
NORDENSKIOL**D**
COLLINGRIDG**E**
WESTINGHOUS**E**
ALEKSEYEVIC**H**
AMAZASPOVIC**H**
ATTENBOROUG**H**
MITSCHERLIC**H**
NIKOLAEVITC**H**
RABINDRANAT**H**
SATYENDRANT**H**
WEINDENREIC**H**
OSTROGRADSK**I**
SCHIAPARELL**I**
AMBARTSUMIA**N**
ANTHONISZOO**N**
RAMACHANDRA**N**
SOLZHENITSY**N**
SUBRAHMANYA**N**
UYTTERHOEVE**N**
MICHELANGEL**O**
SQUARCIAPIN**O**
MERGENTHALE**R**
SCHERTZINGE**R**
SCHOENHEIME**R**
ALEPOUDHELI**S**
DESHOUILLER**S**
ERASISTRATU**S**
ERATOSTHENE**S**
GALANOPOULO**S**
THEOPHRASTU**S**
BOUSSINGAUL**T**
KLEINSCHMID**T**
HULDSCHINSK**Y**

## 13 Letter

### 1st Letter

**B**ARTHOLOMAEUS
**B**HATTACHARYYA
**B**RANDENBURGER
**C**HANDRASEKHAR
**K**ANELLOPOULOS
**R**EGIOMONTANUS
**R**EICHELDERFER
**S**CHWARZSCHILD
**W**ALDSEEMULLER

### 2nd Letter

B**A**RTHOLOMAEUS
K**A**NELLOPOULOS
W**A**LDSEEMULLER
S**C**HWARZSCHILD
R**E**GIOMONTANUS
R**E**ICHELDERFER
B**H**ATTACHARYYA
C**H**ANDRASEKHAR
B**R**ANDENBURGER

### 3rd Letter

BH**A**TTACHARYYA
BR**A**NDENBURGER
CH**A**NDRASEKHAR
RE**G**IOMONTANUS
SC**H**WARZSCHILD
RE**I**CHELDERFER
WA**L**DSEEMULLER
KA**N**ELLOPOULOS
BA**R**THOLOMAEUS

### 4th Letter

REI**C**HELDERFER
WAL**D**SEEMULLER
KAN**E**LLOPOULOS
REG**I**OMONTANUS
BRA**N**DENBURGER
CHA**N**DRASEKHAR
BAR**T**HOLOMAEUS
BHA**T**TACHARYYA
SCH**W**ARZSCHILD

### 5th Letter

SCHW**A**RZSCHILD
BRAN**D**ENBURGER
CHAN**D**RASEKHAR
BART**H**OLOMAEUS
REIC**H**ELDERFER
KANE**L**LOPOULOS
REGI**O**MONTANUS
WALD**S**EEMULLER
BHAT**T**ACHARYYA

### 6th Letter

BHATT**A**CHARYYA
BRAND**E**NBURGER
REICH**E**LDERFER
WALDS**E**EMULLER
KANEL**L**OPOULOS
REGIO**M**ONTANUS
BARTH**O**LOMAEUS
CHAND**R**ASEKHAR
SCHWA**R**ZSCHILD

### 7th Letter

CHANDR**A**SEKHAR
BHATTA**C**HARYYA
WALDSE**E**MULLER
BARTHO**L**OMAEUS
REICHE**L**DERFER
BRANDE**N**BURGER
KANELL**O**POULOS
REGIOM**O**NTANUS
SCHWAR**Z**SCHILD

### 8th Letter

BRANDEN**B**URGER
REICHEL**D**ERFER
BHATTAC**H**ARYYA
WALDSEE**M**ULLER
REGIOMO**N**TANUS
BARTHOL**O**MAEUS
KANELLO**P**OULOS
CHANDRA**S**EKHAR
SCHWARZ**S**CHILD

### 9th Letter

BHATTACH**A**RYYA
SCHWARZS**C**HILD
CHANDRAS**E**KHAR
REICHELD**E**RFER
BARTHOLO**M**AEUS
KANELLOP**O**ULOS
REGIOMON**T**ANUS
BRANDENB**U**RGER
WALDSEEM**U**LLER

### 10th Letter

BARTHOLOM**A**EUS
REGIOMONT**A**NUS
SCHWARZSC**H**ILD
CHANDRASE**K**HAR
WALDSEEMU**L**LER
BHATTACHA**R**YYA
BRANDENBU**R**GER
REICHELDE**R**FER
KANELLOPO**U**LOS

### 11th Letter

BARTHOLOMA**E**US
REICHELDER**F**ER
BRANDENBUR**G**ER
CHANDRASEK**H**AR
SCHWARZSCH**I**LD
KANELLOPOU**L**OS
WALDSEEMUL**L**ER
REGIOMONTA**N**US
BHATTACHAR**Y**YA

### 12th Letter

CHANDRASEKH**A**R
BRANDENBURG**E**R
REICHELDERF**E**R
WALDSEEMULL**E**R
SCHWARZSCHI**L**D
KANELLOPOUL**O**S
BARTHOLOMAE**U**S
REGIOMONTAN**U**S
BHATTACHARY**Y**A

### 13th Letter

BHATTACHARYY**A**
SCHWARZSCHIL**D**
BRANDENBURGE**R**
CHANDRASEKHA**R**
REICHELDERFE**R**
WALDSEEMULLE**R**
BARTHOLOMAEU**S**
KANELLOPOULO**S**
REGIOMONTANU**S**

## 14 Letter

### 1st Letter

**A**LEKSANDROVICH
**C**HANDRASEKHARA
**J**AGADISCHANDRA
**K**LINGENSTIERNA
**S**CHALLENBERGER

### 2nd Letter

J**A**GADISCHANDRA
S**C**HALLENBERGER
C**H**ANDRASEKHARA
A**L**EKSANDROVICH
K**L**INGENSTIERNA

### 3rd Letter

CH**A**NDRASEKHARA
AL**E**KSANDROVICH
JA**G**ADISCHANDRA
SC**H**ALLENBERGER
KL**I**NGENSTIERNA

### 4th Letter

JAG**A**DISCHANDRA
SCH**A**LLENBERGER
ALE**K**SANDROVICH
CHA**N**DRASEKHARA
KLI**N**GENSTIERNA

### 5th Letter

CHAN**D**RASEKHARA
JAGA**D**ISCHANDRA
KLIN**G**ENSTIERNA
SCHA**L**LENBERGER
ALEK**S**ANDROVICH

### 6th Letter

ALEKS**A**NDROVICH
KLING**E**NSTIERNA
JAGAD**I**SCHANDRA
SCHAL**L**ENBERGER
CHAND**R**ASEKHARA

### 7th Letter

CHANDR**A**SEKHARA
SCHALL**E**NBERGER
ALEKSA**N**DROVICH
KLINGE**N**STIERNA
JAGADI**S**CHANDRA

### 8th Letter

JAGADIS**C**HANDRA
ALEKSAN**D**ROVICH
SCHALLE**N**BERGER
CHANDRA**S**EKHARA
KLINGEN**S**TIERNA

### 9th Letter

SCHALLEN**B**ERGER
CHANDRAS**E**KHARA
JAGADISC**H**ANDRA
ALEKSAND**R**OVICH
KLINGENS**T**IERNA

### 10th Letter

JAGADISCH**A**NDRA
SCHALLENB**E**RGER
KLINGENST**I**ERNA
CHANDRASE**K**HARA
ALEKSANDR**O**VICH

**11th Letter**

KLINGENSTI**E**RNA
CHANDRASEK**H**ARA
JAGADISCHA**N**DRA
SCHALLENBE**R**GER
ALEKSANDRO**V**ICH

**12th Letter**

CHANDRASEKH**A**RA
JAGADISCHAN**D**RA
SCHALLENBER**G**ER
ALEKSANDROV**I**CH
KLINGENSTIE**R**NA

**13th Letter**

ALEKSANDROVI**C**H
SCHALLENBERG**E**R
KLINGENSTIER**N**A
CHANDRASEKHA**R**A
JAGADISCHAND**R**A

**14th Letter**

CHANDRASEKHAR**A**
JAGADISCHANDR**A**
KLINGENSTIERN**A**
ALEKSANDROVIC**H**
SCHALLENBERGE**R**

# SECTION 3 • GEOGRAPHIC NAMES

## 2-13 LETTER WORDS

**2 LETTER**
**1ST LETTER**

AD AE AF AG AI AK AL AM AN AO AQ AR AS AT AU AW AZ BA BB BD BE BF BG BH BI BJ BM BN BO BR BS BT BV BW BY BZ CA CC CF CG CH CI

CK CL CM CN CO CR CT CU CV CX CY CZ DA DC DE DJ DK DM DO DZ EC EE EG EH EL ER ES ET FE FI FJ FK FL FM FO FR GA GD GE GF GG GH GI GL GM GN

GP GQ GR GS GT GU GW GY HI HK HM HN HR HT HU IA ID IE IL IM IN IO IQ IR IS IT JE JM JO JP KE KG KH KI KM KN KP KR KS KW KY KZ LA LB LC LI

LK LR LS LT LU LV LY MA MC MD ME MG MH MI MK ML MN MO MP MQ MR MS MT MU MV MW MX MY MZ NA NC ND NE NF NG NH NI NJ NL NM NO NP NR NU NV NY

NZ OF OH OK OM OR PA PE PF PG PH PK PL PM PN PR PT PW PY QA RE RI RO RU RW SA SB SC SD SE SG SH SI SJ SK SL SM SN SO SP SR ST SV SY SZ TC

TD TF TG TH TJ TK TM TN TO TR TT TW TX TZ UA UG UK UM US UT UY UZ VA VC VE VG VI VN VT VU WA WF WI WS WV WY YE YT YU ZA ZM ZR ZW

**2ND LETTER**

BA CA DA GA IA LA MA NA PA QA SA UA VA WA ZA BB LB SB CC DC EC LC MC NC SC TC VC AD BD GD ID MD ND SD TD AE BE DE EE FE GE IE JE KE

ME NE PE RE SE VE YE AF BF CF GF NF OF PF TF WF AG BG CG EG GG KG MG NG PG SG TG UG VG BH CH EH GH KH MH NH OH PH SH TH AI BI CI FI GI HI

KI LI MI NI RI SI VI WI BJ DJ FJ NJ SJ TJ AK CK DK FK HK LK MK OK PK SK TK UK AL CL EL FL GL IL ML NL PL SL AM BM CM DM FM GM HM IM JM KM

NM OM PM SM TM UM ZM AN BN CN GN HN IN KN MN PN SN TN VN AO BO CO DO FO IO JO MO NO RO SO TO GP JP KP MP NP SP AQ GQ IQ MQ AR BR CR ER FR

GR HR IR KR LR MR NR OR PR SR TR ZR AS BS ES GS IS KS LS MS US WS AT BT CT ET GT HT IT LT MT PT ST TT UT VT YT AU CU GU HU LU MU NU RU VU

YU BV CV LV MV NV SV WV AW BW GW KW MW PW RW TW ZW CX MX TX BY CY GY KY LY MY NY PY SY UY WY AZ BZ CZ DZ KZ MZ NZ SZ TZ UZ

**3 LETTER**
**1ST LETTER**

ABU AND BAY DES INO JAN MAN NEW PAZ RED SAN SAO SEA SRI THE

**2ND LETTER**

BAY JAN MAN PAZ SAN SAO ABU DES NEW RED SEA THE AND INO SRI

**3RD LETTER**

SEA AND RED THE SRI JAN MAN SAN INO SAO DES ABU NEW BAY PAZ

**4 LETTER**
**1ST LETTER**

ADEN APAN APIA ARAB ARAL AVES BAKU BASS BEAR BERN CAPE CHAD CITY COOK CUBA DEAD EAST ERIE FIJI FOXE GUAM GULF HONG IOWA IRAN IRAQ

JAVA JOSE JUAN KANE KARA KIEV KONG LAGO LAKE LAOS LIMA LINE LOME MALE MALI MAUD MAUI NIUE NOVO NUKU OHIO OMAN OSLO PAGO PAUL PENH PERU PORT REEF RICA RICO RIGA ROAD ROCK ROME ROSS SALT SERI SULU SUVA TOGO TOME TOWN TURK ULAN UTAH VILA WAKE WEST YORK

**2nd Letter**

BAKU BASS CAPE EAST JAVA KANE KARA LAGO LAKE LAOS MALE MALI MAUD MAUI PAGO PAUL SALT WAKE ADEN BEAR BERN DEAD PENH PERU REEF SERI WEST CHAD OHIO CITY FIJI KIEV LIMA LINE NIUE RICA RICO RIGA VILA ULAN OMAN COOK FOXE HONG IOWA JOSE KONG LOME NOVO PORT ROAD ROCK ROME ROSS TOGO TOME TOWN YORK APAN APIA ARAB ARAL ERIE IRAN IRAQ OSLO UTAH CUBA GUAM GULF JUAN NUKU SULU SUVA TURK AVES

**3rd Letter**

APAN ARAB ARAL BEAR CHAD DEAD GUAM IRAN IRAQ JUAN OMAN ROAD ULAN UTAH CUBA RICA RICO ROCK ADEN AVES KIEV REEF LAGO PAGO RIGA TOGO APIA ERIE OHIO FIJI BAKU LAKE NUKU WAKE GULF MALE MALI OSLO SALT SULU VILA LIMA LOME ROME TOME HONG KANE KONG LINE PENH COOK LAOS CAPE BERN KARA PERU PORT SERI TURK YORK BASS EAST JOSE ROSS WEST CITY MAUD MAUI NIUE PAUL JAVA NOVO SUVA IOWA TOWN FOXE

**4th Letter**

APIA CUBA IOWA JAVA KARA LIMA RICA RIGA SUVA VILA ARAB CHAD DEAD MAUD ROAD CAPE ERIE FOXE JOSE KANE LAKE LINE LOME MALE NIUE ROME TOME WAKE GULF REEF HONG KONG PENH UTAH FIJI MALI MAUI SERI COOK ROCK TURK YORK ARAL PAUL GUAM ADEN APAN BERN IRAN JUAN OMAN TOWN ULAN LAGO NOVO OHIO OSLO PAGO RICO TOGO IRAQ BEAR AVES BASS LAOS ROSS EAST PORT SALT WEST BAKU NUKU PERU SULU KIEV CITY

**5 Letter**

**1st Letter**

ABABA ABUJA ACCRA ADDIS AGANA AIRES ALAND ALGER ALOFA ALOFI AMMAN ARUBA ATOLL BANDA BASIN BASSE BATON BATOR BENIN BIGHT BLACK BOISE CAIRO CEUTA CHILE CHINA COAST COCOS CONGO CORAL COSTA CUNHA CZECH DAKAR DAVIS DELHI DENIS DHABI DHAKA DOVER EGYPT FAROE FUNDI GABON GHANA GRAND GREAT HAITI HANOI HEARD HURON IDAHO INDIA IRISH ITALY IVORY JAPAN JOHNS KABUL KENYA KITTS KOREA KUALA LANKA LEONE LIBYA LOUIS LUCIA MACAO MAINE MALTA MAYEN MINSK NAURU NEPAL NEVIS NIGER NORTH OCEAN PALAU PAPUA PARIS PEARY PHNOM PORTO PRAIA QATAR QUEEN QUITO RABAT RHODE ROUGE SAINT SALEM SAMOA SANAA SANTA SANTO SAUDI SEOUL SIDRA SLAVE SMITH SOFIA SOUND SOUTH SPAIN SUDAN SYRIA TERRE TEXAS TIMOR TONGA TOYKO TUNIS TURKS VADUZ VELLA VERDE WALES WHITE YAREN YEMEN ZAIRE

**2nd Letter**

BANDA BASIN BASSE BATON BATOR CAIRO DAKAR DAVIS FAROE GABON HAITI HANOI JAPAN KABUL LANKA MACAO MAINE MALTA MAYEN NAURU PALAU PAPUA PARIS QATAR RABAT SAINT SALEM SAMOA SANAA SANTA SANTO SAUDI VADUZ WALES YAREN ZAIRE ABABA ABUJA ACCRA OCEAN ADDIS IDAHO BENIN CEUTA DELHI DENIS HEARD KENYA LEONE NEPAL NEVIS PEARY SEOUL TERRE TEXAS VELLA VERDE YEMEN AGANA EGYPT CHILE CHINA DHABI DHAKA GHANA PHNOM RHODE WHITE AIRES BIGHT KITTS LIBYA MINSK NIGER SIDRA TIMOR ALAND ALGER ALOFA ALOFI BLACK SLAVE AMMAN SMITH INDIA BOISE COAST COCOS CONGO CORAL COSTA DOVER JOHNS KOREA LOUIS NORTH PORTO ROUGE SOFIA SOUND SOUTH TONGA TOYKO SPAIN ARUBA GRAND GREAT IRISH PRAIA ATOLL ITALY CUNHA FUNDI HURON KUALA LUCIA QUEEN QUITO SUDAN TUNIS TURKS IVORY SYRIA CZECH

**3rd Letter**

ABABA AGANA ALAND BLACK COAST DHABI DHAKA GHANA GRAND HEARD IDAHO ITALY KUALA PEARY PRAIA SLAVE SPAIN GABON KABUL LIBYA RABAT ACCRA COCOS LUCIA MACAO ADDIS INDIA SIDRA SUDAN VADUZ CZECH GREAT OCEAN QUEEN SOFIA ALGER BIGHT NIGER JOHNS BOISE CAIRO CHILE CHINA HAITI IRISH MAINE QUITO SAINT SMITH WHITE ZAIRE DAKAR DELHI MALTA PALAU SALEM VELLA WALES AMMAN SAMOA TIMOR YEMEN BANDA BENIN CONGO CUNHA DENIS FUNDI HANOI KENYA LANKA MINSK PHNOM SANAA SANTA SANTO TONGA TUNIS ALOFA ALOFI ATOLL IVORY LEONE RHODE SEOUL JAPAN NEPAL PAPUA AIRES CORAL FAROE HURON KOREA NORTH PARIS PORTO SYRIA TERRE TURKS VERDE YAREN BASIN BASSE COSTA BATON BATOR KITTS QATAR ABUJA ARUBA CEUTA LOUIS NAURU ROUGE SAUDI SOUND SOUTH DAVIS DOVER NEVIS TEXAS EGYPT

MAYEN
TOYKO

**4th Letter**

AMMAN
CORAL
DAKAR
GREAT
JAPAN
MACAO
NEPAL
OCEAN
PALAU
QATAR
RABAT
SANAA
SUDAN
TEXAS
ABABA
ARUBA
DHABI
BLACK
CZECH
BANDA
FUNDI
RHODE
SAUDI
VERDE
AIRES
ALGER
DOVER
KOREA
MAYEN
NIGER
QUEEN
SALEM
WALES
YAREN
YEMEN
ALOFA
ALOFI
CONGO
ROUGE
TONGA
BIGHT
CUNHA
DELHI
IDAHO
ADDIS
BASIN
BENIN
DAVIS
DENIS
INDIA
LOUIS
LUCIA
NEVIS
PARIS
PRAIA
SOFIA
SPAIN
SYRIA
TUNIS
ABUJA
DHAKA
LANKA
TOYKO
TURKS
ATOLL
CHILE
ITALY
KUALA
VELLA
AGANA
ALAND
CHINA
GHANA
GRAND
JOHNS
LEONE
MAINE
SAINT
SOUND
BATON
BATOR
COCOS
FAROE
GABON
HANOI
HURON
PHNOM
SAMOA
TIMOR
EGYPT
ACCRA
CAIRO
HEARD
IVORY
NAURU
PEARY
SIDRA
TERRE
ZAIRE
BASSE
BOISE
COAST
IRISH
MINSK
CEUTA
COSTA
HAITI
KITTS
MALTA
NORTH
PORTO
QUITO
SANTA
SANTO
SMITH
SOUTH
WHITE
KABUL
PAPUA
SEOUL
VADUZ
SLAVE
KENYA
LIBYA

**5th Letter**

ABABA
ABUJA
ACCRA
AGANA
ALOFA
ARUBA
BANDA
CEUTA
CHINA
COSTA
CUNHA
DHAKA
GHANA
INDIA
KENYA
KOREA
KUALA
LANKA
LIBYA
LUCIA
MALTA
PAPUA
PRAIA
SAMOA
SANAA
SANTA
SIDRA
SOFIA
SYRIA
TONGA
VELLA
ALAND
GRAND
HEARD
SOUND
BASSE
BOISE
CHILE
FAROE
LEONE
MAINE
RHODE
ROUGE
SLAVE
TERRE
VERDE
WHITE
ZAIRE
CZECH
IRISH
NORTH
SMITH
SOUTH
ALOFI
DELHI
DHABI
FUNDI
HAITI
HANOI
SAUDI
BLACK
MINSK
ATOLL
CORAL
KABUL
NEPAL
SEOUL
PHNOM
SALEM
AMMAN
BASIN
BATON
BENIN
GABON
HURON
JAPAN
MAYEN
OCEAN
QUEEN
SPAIN
SUDAN
YAREN
YEMEN
CAIRO
CONGO
IDAHO
MACAO
PORTO
QUITO
SANTO
TOYKO
ALGER
BATOR
DAKAR
DOVER
NIGER
QATAR
TIMOR
ADDIS
AIRES
COCOS
DAVIS
DENIS
JOHNS
KITTS
LOUIS
NEVIS
PARIS
TEXAS
TUNIS
TURKS
WALES
BIGHT
COAST
EGYPT
GREAT
RABAT
SAINT
NAURU
PALAU
ITALY
IVORY
PEARY
VADUZ

**6 Letter**

**1st Letter**

AEGEAN
AFRICA
ALASKA
ALBANY
ALBERT
ALMATY
AMALIE
ANGOLA
ANKARA
ARABIA
ASMARA
ATHENS
AUSTIN
AZORES
BAFFIN
BAGDAD
BAIKAL
BALTIC
BAMAKO
BANABA
BANDAR
BANGUI
BANJUL
BEIRUT
BELIZE
BENGAL
BERING
BERLIN
BHUTAN
BISCAY
BISSAU
BOGOTA
BOSNIA
BOSTON
BOUVET
BRAZIL
BRUNEI
BUENOS
CAICOS
CANADA
CANARY
CARSON
CAYMAN
CELTIC
CROZET
CYPRUS
DAKOTA
DAWHAH
DENVER
DODOMA
DUBLIN
EASTER
EDWARD
FRANCE
FRENCH
FUTANA
GAMBIA
GEORGE
GIGEDO
GREECE
GUIANA
GUINEA
GUYANA
HARARE
HAVANA
HAWAII
HECATE
HELENA
HORMUZ
HUDSON
INDIAN
ISLAND
ISRAEL
JALUIT
JERSEY
JORDAN
JUNEAU
KANSAS
KIGALI
KUWAIT
LADOGA
LAPTEV
LATVIA
LISBON
LITTLE
LONDON
LUANDA
LUMPUR
LUSAKA
MADRID
MALABO
MALAWI
MANAMA
MANILA
MAPUTO
MARINO
MARTIN
MASERU
MEXICO
MIDWAY
MINAMI
MOINES
MONACO
MORONI
MOSCOW
MUSCAT
NANSEN
NASSAU
NEVADA
NIAMEY
NORWAY
NOUMEA
OREGON
OTTAWA
PANAMA
PIERRE
POLAND
PRAGUE
PRINCE
PUERTO
RIYADH
ROSEAU
RUSSIA
RWANDA
SAHARA
SCOTIA
SERBIA
SIERRA
STATES
STRAIT
SWEDEN
TAIWAN
TARAWA
TASMAN
TEHRAN
THIMBU
TIRANA
TOBAGO
TONKIN
TOPEKA
TURKEY
UGANDA
UNGAVA
UNITED
VALLEY
VIENNA
VIRGIN
WALLIS
WARSAW
YANGON
YELLOW
ZAGREB
ZAMBIA

**2nd Letter**

BAFFIN
BAGDAD
BAIKAL
BALTIC
BAMAKO
BANABA
BANDAR
BANGUI
BANJUL
CAICOS
CANADA
CANARY
CARSON
CAYMAN
DAKOTA
DAWHAH
EASTER
GAMBIA
HARARE
HAVANA
HAWAII
JALUIT
KANSAS
LADOGA
LAPTEV
LATVIA
MADRID
MALABO
MALAWI
MANAMA
MANILA
MAPUTO
MARINO
MARTIN
MASERU
NANSEN
NASSAU
PANAMA
SAHARA
TAIWAN
TARAWA
TASMAN
VALLEY
WALLIS
WARSAW
YANGON
ZAGREB
ZAMBIA
SCOTIA
EDWARD
AEGEAN
BEIRUT
BELIZE
BENGAL
BERING
BERLIN
CELTIC
DENVER
GEORGE
HECATE
HELENA
JERSEY
MEXICO
NEVADA
SERBIA
TEHRAN
YELLOW
AFRICA
UGANDA
BHUTAN
THIMBU
BISCAY
BISSAU
GIGEDO
KIGALI
LISBON
LITTLE
MIDWAY
MINAMI
NIAMEY
PIERRE
RIYADH
SIERRA
TIRANA
VIENNA
VIRGIN
ALASKA
ALBANY
ALBERT
ALMATY
AMALIE
ANGOLA
ANKARA
INDIAN
UNGAVA
UNITED
BOGOTA
BOSNIA
BOSTON
BOUVET
DODOMA
HORMUZ
JORDAN
LONDON
MOINES
MONACO
MORONI
MOSCOW
NORWAY
NOUMEA
POLAND
ROSEAU
TOBAGO
TONKIN
TOPEKA
ARABIA
BRAZIL
BRUNEI
CROZET
FRANCE
FRENCH
GREECE
OREGON
PRAGUE
PRINCE
ASMARA
ISLAND
ISRAEL
ATHENS
OTTAWA
STATES
STRAIT
AUSTIN
BUENOS
DUBLIN
FUTANA
GUIANA
GUINEA
GUYANA
HUDSON
JUNEAU
KUWAIT
LUANDA
LUMPUR
LUSAKA

MUSCAT
PUERTO
RUSSIA
TURKEY
RWANDA
SWEDEN
CYPRUS
AZORES
BEIRUT
CAICOS
GUIANA
GUINEA
MOINES
PRINCE
TAIWAN
THIMBU
UNITED
ANKARA
DAKOTA

### 3rd Letter

ALASKA
AMALIE
ARABIA
BRAZIL
FRANCE
LUANDA
NIAMEY
PRAGUE
RWANDA
STATES
UGANDA
ALBANY
ALBERT
DUBLIN
TOBAGO
HECATE
DODOMA
HUDSON
INDIAN
LADOGA
MADRID
MIDWAY
BUENOS
FRENCH
GREECE
OREGON
PIERRE
PUERTO
SIERRA
SWEDEN
VIENNA
BAFFIN
AEGEAN
ANGOLA
BAGDAD
BOGOTA
GIGEDO
KIGALI
UNGAVA
ZAGREB
ATHENS
SAHARA
TEHRAN
BAIKAL
BALTIC
BELIZE
CELTIC
HELENA
ISLAND
JALUIT
MALABO
MALAWI
POLAND
VALLEY
WALLIS
YELLOW
ALMATY
ASMARA
BAMAKO
GAMBIA
LUMPUR
ZAMBIA
BANABA
BANDAR
BANGUI
BANJUL
BENGAL
CANADA
CANARY
DENVER
JUNEAU
KANSAS
LONDON
MANAMA
MANILA
MINAMI
MONACO
NANSEN
PANAMA
TONKIN
YANGON
AZORES
CROZET
GEORGE
SCOTIA
CYPRUS
LAPTEV
MAPUTO
TOPEKA
AFRICA
BERING
BERLIN
CARSON
HARARE
HORMUZ
ISRAEL
JERSEY
JORDAN
MARINO
MARTIN
MORONI
NORWAY
SERBIA
STRAIT
TARAWA
TIRANA
TURKEY
VIRGIN
WARSAW
AUSTIN
BISCAY
BISSAU
BOSNIA
BOSTON
EASTER
LISBON
LUSAKA
MASERU
MOSCOW
MUSCAT
NASSAU
ROSEAU
RUSSIA
TASMAN
FUTANA
LATVIA
LITTLE
OTTAWA
BHUTAN
BOUVET
BRUNEI
NOUMEA
HAVANA
NEVADA
DAWHAH
EDWARD
HAWAII
KUWAIT
MEXICO
CAYMAN
GUYANA
RIYADH

### 4th Letter

ALBANY
ALMATY
ANKARA
ASMARA
BAMAKO
BANABA
CANADA
CANARY
EDWARD
FUTANA
GUIANA
GUYANA
HARARE
HAVANA
HAWAII
HECATE
ISLAND
ISRAEL
KIGALI
KUWAIT
LUSAKA
MALABO
MALAWI
MANAMA
MINAMI
MONACO
NEVADA
OTTAWA
PANAMA
POLAND
RIYADH
SAHARA
STRAIT
TARAWA
TIRANA
TOBAGO
UNGAVA
ARABIA
GAMBIA
LISBON
SERBIA
ZAMBIA
BISCAY
CAICOS
MOSCOW
MUSCAT
BAGDAD
BANDAR
JORDAN
LONDON
SWEDEN
AEGEAN
ALBERT
ATHENS
GIGEDO
GREECE
HELENA
JUNEAU
MASERU
ROSEAU
TOPEKA
BAFFIN
BANGUI
BENGAL
OREGON
PRAGUE
VIRGIN
YANGON
DAWHAH
AFRICA
BELIZE
BERING
INDIAN
MANILA
MARINO
MEXICO
BANJUL
BAIKAL
TONKIN
TURKEY
AMALIE
BERLIN
DUBLIN
VALLEY
WALLIS
YELLOW
CAYMAN
HORMUZ
NIAMEY
NOUMEA
TASMAN
THIMBU
BOSNIA
BRUNEI
BUENOS
FRANCE
FRENCH
GUINEA
LUANDA
MOINES
PRINCE
RWANDA
UGANDA
VIENNA
ANGOLA
BOGOTA
DAKOTA
DODOMA
LADOGA
MORONI
LUMPUR
AZORES
BEIRUT
CYPRUS
GEORGE
MADRID
PIERRE
PUERTO
SIERRA
TEHRAN
ZAGREB
ALASKA
BISSAU
CARSON
HUDSON
JERSEY
KANSAS
NANSEN
NASSAU
RUSSIA
WARSAW
AUSTIN
BALTIC
BHUTAN
BOSTON
CELTIC
EASTER
LAPTEV
LITTLE
MARTIN
SCOTIA
STATES
UNITED
JALUIT
MAPUTO
BOUVET
DENVER
LATVIA
MIDWAY
NORWAY
TAIWAN
BRAZIL
CROZET

### 5th Letter

AEGEAN
BAGDAD
BAIKAL
BANDAR
BENGAL
BHUTAN
BISCAY
BISSAU
CAYMAN
DAWHAH
INDIAN
JORDAN
JUNEAU
KANSAS
MIDWAY
MUSCAT
NASSAU
NORWAY
ROSEAU
TAIWAN
TASMAN
TEHRAN
WARSAW
BANABA
MALABO
THIMBU
AFRICA
FRANCE
FRENCH
GREECE
MEXICO
MONACO
PRINCE
CANADA
GIGEDO
LUANDA
NEVADA
RIYADH
RWANDA
UGANDA
AZORES
BOUVET
BRUNEI
CROZET
DENVER
EASTER
GUINEA
ISRAEL
JERSEY
LAPTEV
MOINES
NANSEN
NIAMEY
NOUMEA
STATES
SWEDEN
TURKEY
UNITED
VALLEY
ZAGREB
GEORGE
LADOGA
TOBAGO
AMALIE
ARABIA
AUSTIN
BAFFIN
BALTIC
BERLIN
BOSNIA
BRAZIL
CELTIC
DUBLIN
GAMBIA
HAWAII
JALUIT
KUWAIT
LATVIA
MADRID
MARTIN
RUSSIA
SCOTIA
SERBIA
STRAIT
TONKIN
VIRGIN
WALLIS
ZAMBIA
ALASKA
BAMAKO
LUSAKA
TOPEKA
ANGOLA
KIGALI
LITTLE
MANILA
DODOMA
MANAMA
MINAMI
PANAMA
ALBANY
ATHENS
BERING
FUTANA
GUIANA
GUYANA
HAVANA
HELENA
ISLAND
MARINO
MORONI
POLAND
TIRANA
VIENNA
BOSTON
BUENOS
CAICOS
CARSON
HUDSON
LISBON
LONDON
MOSCOW
OREGON
YANGON
YELLOW
ALBERT
ANKARA
ASMARA
CANARY
EDWARD
HARARE
MASERU
PIERRE
SAHARA
SIERRA
ALMATY
BOGOTA
DAKOTA
HECATE
MAPUTO
PUERTO
BANGUI
BANJUL
BEIRUT
CYPRUS
HORMUZ
LUMPUR
PRAGUE
UNGAVA
MALAWI
OTTAWA
TARAWA
BELIZE

### 6th Letter

AFRICA
ALASKA
ANGOLA
ANKARA
ARABIA
ASMARA
BANABA
BOGOTA
BOSNIA
CANADA
DAKOTA
DODOMA
FUTANA
GAMBIA
GUIANA
GUINEA
GUYANA
HAVANA
HELENA
LADOGA
LATVIA
LUANDA
LUSAKA
MANAMA
MANILA
NEVADA
NOUMEA
OTTAWA
PANAMA
RUSSIA
RWANDA
SAHARA
SCOTIA
SERBIA
SIERRA
TARAWA
TIRANA
TOPEKA
UGANDA
UNGAVA
VIENNA
ZAMBIA
ZAGREB
BALTIC
CELTIC
BAGDAD
EDWARD
ISLAND
MADRID
POLAND
UNITED
AMALIE
BELIZE
FRANCE
GEORGE
GREECE
HARARE
HECATE
LITTLE
PIERRE
PRAGUE
PRINCE
BERING
DAWHAH
FRENCH
RIYADH
BANGUI
BRUNEI
HAWAII
KIGALI
MALAWI
MINAMI
MORONI
BAIKAL
BANJUL
BENGAL
BRAZIL
ISRAEL
AEGEAN
AUSTIN
BAFFIN

BERLIN
BHUTAN
BOSTON
CARSON
CAYMAN
DUBLIN
HUDSON
INDIAN
JORDAN
LISBON
LONDON
MARTIN
NANSEN
OREGON
SWEDEN
TAIWAN
TONKIN
TASMAN
TEHRAN
VIRGIN
YANGON
BAMAKO
GIGEDO
MALABO
MAPUTO
MARINO
MEXICO
MONACO
PUERTO
TOBAGO
BANDAR
DENVER
EASTER
LUMPUR
ATHENS
AZORES
BUENOS
CAICOS
CYPRUS
KANSAS
MOINES
STATES
WALLIS
ALBERT
BEIRUT
BOUVET
CROZET
JALUIT
KUWAIT
MUSCAT
STRAIT
BISSAU
JUNEAU
MASERU
NASSAU
ROSEAU
THIMBU
LAPTEV
MOSCOW
WARSAW
YELLOW
ALBANY
ALMATY
BISCAY
CANARY
JERSEY
MIDWAY
NIAMEY
NORWAY
TURKEY
VALLEY
HORMUZ

## 7 Letter

### 1st Letter

ABIDJAN
AFRICAN
AGULHAS
ALABAMA
ALBANIA
ALGERIA
AMERICA
ANDAMAN
ANDORRA
ANDREAS
ANNOBON
ANTIGUA
ARABIAN
ARAFURA
ARIZONA
ARMENIA
ATLANTA
AUGUSTA
AUSTRIA
BAHAMAS
BAHRAIN
BANGKOK
BARBUDA
BARENTS
BEGAWAN
BEIJING
BELARUS
BELGIUM
BERMUDA
BISHKEK
BOLIVIA
BOOTHIA
BRISTOL
BRITISH
BURKINA
BURUNDI
CARACAS
CASPIAN
CAYENNE
CELEBES
CENTRAL
CHANNEL
CHATHAM
CHUKCHI
COLOMBO
COMOROS
CONAKRY
CONCORD
CROATIA
DENMARK
DOMINGO
ECUADOR
ENGLAND
ENGLISH
ERITREA
ESTONIA
FINLAND
FLORIDA
GEORGES
GEORGIA
GERMANY
GODTHAR
GRENADA
HONIARA
HOWLAND
HUNGARY
ICELAND
INDIANA
IRELAND
ISLANDS
JACKSON
JAKARTA
JAMAICA
KINGDOM
KINGMAN
KOLONIA
LANSING
LEBANON
LESOTHO
LIBERIA
LINCOLN
MAARTEN
MADEIRA
MADISON
MAKAROV
MALPELO
MANAGUA
MARIANA
MAYOTTE
MBABANE
MELILLA
MOLDOVA
MONTANA
MORESBY
MOROCCO
MYANMAR
NAIROBI
NAMIBIA
NAVASSA
NICOSIA
NIGERIA
NORFOLK
NORONHA
OKHOTSK
OLYMPIA
ONTARIO
PACIFIC
PAPEETE
PEOPLES
PERSIAN
PHOENIX
RALEIGH
REUNION
REVILLA
ROMANIA
SENEGAL
SOLOMON
SOMALIA
SPENCER
STANLEY
STRAITS
SURINAM
TALLINN
TBILISI
THIMPHU
TOKELAU
TORTOLA
TRENTON
TRIPOLI
TRISTAN
TUNISIA
UKRAINE
URAGUAY
VANUATU
VATICAN
VERMONT
VIETNAM
VILNIUS
VINCENT
WEDDELL
WESTERN
WHARTON
WYOMING
YAOUNDE
YEREVAN
ZEALAND

### 2nd Letter

BAHAMAS
BAHRAIN
BANGKOK
BARBUDA
BARENTS
CARACAS
CASPIAN
CAYENNE
JACKSON
JAKARTA
JAMAICA
LANSING
MAARTEN
MADEIRA
MADISON
MAKAROV
MALPELO
MANAGUA
MARIANA
MAYOTTE
NAIROBI
NAMIBIA
NAVASSA
PACIFIC
PAPEETE
RALEIGH
TALLINN
VANUATU
VATICAN
YAOUNDE
ABIDJAN
MBABANE
TBILISI
ECUADOR
ICELAND
BEGAWAN
BEIJING
BELARUS
BELGIUM
BERMUDA
CELEBES
CENTRAL
DENMARK
GEORGES
GEORGIA
GERMANY
LEBANON
LESOTHO
MELILLA
PEOPLES
PERSIAN
REUNION
REVILLA
SENEGAL
VERMONT
WEDDELL
WESTERN
YEREVAN
ZEALAND
AFRICAN
AGULHAS
CHANNEL
CHATHAM
CHUKCHI
PHOENIX
THIMPHU
WHARTON
BISHKEK
FINLAND
KINGDOM
KINGMAN
LIBERIA
LINCOLN
NICOSIA
NIGERIA
VIETNAM
VILNIUS
VINCENT
OKHOTSK
UKRAINE
ALABAMA
ALBANIA
ALGERIA
FLORIDA
OLYMPIA
AMERICA
ANDAMAN
ANDORRA
ANDREAS
ANNOBON
ANTIGUA
ENGLAND
ENGLISH
INDIANA
ONTARIO
BOLIVIA
BOOTHIA
COLOMBO
COMOROS
CONAKRY
CONCORD
DOMINGO
GODTHAR
HONIARA
HOWLAND
KOLONIA
MOLDOVA
MONTANA
MORESBY
MOROCCO
NORFOLK
NORONHA
ROMANIA
SOLOMON
SOMALIA
TOKELAU
TORTOLA
SPENCER
ARABIAN
ARAFURA
ARIZONA
ARMENIA
BRISTOL
BRITISH
CROATIA
ERITREA
GRENADA
IRELAND
TRENTON
TRIPOLI
TRISTAN
URAGUAY
ESTONIA
ISLANDS
ATLANTA
STANLEY
STRAITS
AUGUSTA
AUSTRIA
BURKINA
BURUNDI
HUNGARY
SURINAM
TUNISIA
MYANMAR
WYOMING

### 3rd Letter

ALABAMA
ARABIAN
ARAFURA
CHANNEL
CHATHAM
MAARTEN
MBABANE
MYANMAR
STANLEY
URAGUAY
WHARTON
ZEALAND
ALBANIA
LEBANON
LIBERIA
JACKSON
NICOSIA
PACIFIC
ANDAMAN
ANDORRA
ANDREAS
INDIANA
MADEIRA
MADISON
WEDDELL
AMERICA
GRENADA
ICELAND
IRELAND
SPENCER
TRENTON
VIETNAM
ALGERIA
AUGUSTA
BEGAWAN
ENGLAND
ENGLISH
NIGERIA
BAHAMAS
BAHRAIN
OKHOTSK
ABIDJAN
ARIZONA
BEIJING
BRISTOL
BRITISH
ERITREA
NAIROBI
TBILISI
THIMPHU
TRIPOLI
TRISTAN
JAKARTA
MAKAROV
TOKELAU
ATLANTA
BELARUS
BELGIUM
BOLIVIA
CELEBES
COLOMBO
ISLANDS
KOLONIA
MALPELO
MELILLA
MOLDOVA
RALEIGH
SOLOMON
TALLINN
VILNIUS
ARMENIA
COMOROS
DOMINGO
JAMAICA
NAMIBIA

ROMANIA
SOMALIA
ANNOBON
BANGKOK
CENTRAL
CONAKRY
CONCORD
DENMARK
FINLAND
HONIARA
HUNGARY
KINGDOM
KINGMAN
LANSING
LINCOLN
MANAGUA
MONTANA
SENEGAL
TUNISIA
VANUATU
VINCENT
BOOTHIA
CROATIA
FLORIDA
GEORGES
GEORGIA
PEOPLES
PHOENIX
WYOMING
YAOUNDE
PAPEETE
AFRICAN
BARBUDA
BARENTS
BERMUDA
BURKINA
BURUNDI
CARACAS
GERMANY
MARIANA
MORESBY
MOROCCO
NORFOLK
NORONHA
PERSIAN
STRAITS
SURINAM
TORTOLA
UKRAINE
VERMONT
YEREVAN
AUSTRIA
BISHKEK
CASPIAN
LESOTHO
WESTERN
ANTIGUA
ESTONIA
ONTARIO
VATICAN
AGULHAS
CHUKCHI
ECUADOR
REUNION
NAVASSA
REVILLA
HOWLAND
CAYENNE
MAYOTTE
OLYMPIA

## 4th Letter

ALBANIA
ANDAMAN
ATLANTA
BAHAMAS
BEGAWAN
BELARUS
CARACAS
CONAKRY
CROATIA
ECUADOR
ISLANDS
JAKARTA
JAMAICA
LEBANON
MAKAROV
MANAGUA
NAVASSA
ONTARIO
ROMANIA
SOMALIA
STRAITS
UKRAINE
ALABAMA
ARABIAN
BARBUDA
MBABANE
CONCORD
LINCOLN
VINCENT
ABIDJAN
MOLDOVA
WEDDELL
ALGERIA
ARMENIA
BARENTS
CAYENNE
CELEBES
LIBERIA
MADEIRA
MORESBY
NIGERIA
PAPEETE
PHOENIX
RALEIGH
SENEGAL
TOKELAU
YEREVAN
ARAFURA
NORFOLK
BANGKOK
BELGIUM
HUNGARY
KINGDOM
KINGMAN
URAGUAY
BISHKEK
AFRICAN
ANTIGUA
BOLIVIA
DOMINGO
HONIARA
INDIANA
MADISON
MARIANA
MELILLA
NAMIBIA
PACIFIC
REVILLA
SURINAM
TUNISIA
VATICAN
BEIJING
BURKINA
CHUKCHI
JACKSON
AGULHAS
ENGLAND
ENGLISH
FINLAND
HOWLAND
ICELAND
IRELAND
TALLINN
TBILISI
ZEALAND
BERMUDA
DENMARK
GERMANY
OLYMPIA
THIMPHU
VERMONT
WYOMING
CHANNEL
GRENADA
MYANMAR
REUNION
SPENCER
STANLEY
TRENTON
VILNIUS
ANDORRA
ANNOBON
COLOMBO
COMOROS
ESTONIA
KOLONIA
LESOTHO
MAYOTTE
MOROCCO
NICOSIA
NORONHA
OKHOTSK
SOLOMON
CASPIAN
MALPELO
PEOPLES
TRIPOLI
AMERICA
ANDREAS
BAHRAIN
FLORIDA
GEORGES
GEORGIA
MAARTEN
NAIROBI
WHARTON
BRISTOL
LANSING
PERSIAN
TRISTAN
AUSTRIA
BOOTHIA
BRITISH
CENTRAL
CHATHAM
ERITREA
GODTHAR
MONTANA
TORTOLA
VIETNAM
WESTERN
AUGUSTA
BURUNDI
VANUATU
YAOUNDE
ARIZONA

## 5th Letter

ALABAMA
BAHRAIN
DENMARK
ENGLAND
FINLAND
GERMANY
GRENADA
HONIARA
HOWLAND
HUNGARY
ICELAND
INDIANA
IRELAND
MARIANA
MBABANE
MONTANA
VANUATU
ZEALAND
ANNOBON
CELEBES
NAMIBIA
AFRICAN
CARACAS
CHUKCHI
MOROCCO
SPENCER
VATICAN
ECUADOR
KINGDOM
ANDREAS
MALPELO
PAPEETE
VINCENT
WEDDELL
WESTERN
PACIFIC
ANTIGUA
GEORGES
GEORGIA
MANAGUA
SENEGAL
AGULHAS
BOOTHIA
CHATHAM
GODTHAR
AMERICA
ARABIAN
BEIJING
BELGIUM
BRITISH
BURKINA
CASPIAN
ENGLISH
FLORIDA
JAMAICA
LANSING
MADEIRA
PERSIAN
RALEIGH
REUNION
STRAITS
TALLINN
TBILISI
UKRAINE
VILNIUS
WYOMING
ABIDJAN
BANGKOK
BISHKEK
CONAKRY
MELILLA
PEOPLES
REVILLA
SOMALIA
STANLEY
TOKELAU
ANDAMAN
BAHAMAS
COLOMBO
KINGMAN
MYANMAR
SOLOMON
ALBANIA
ARMENIA
ATLANTA
BARENTS
BURUNDI
CAYENNE
CHANNEL
DOMINGO
ESTONIA
ISLANDS
KOLONIA
LEBANON
NORONHA
PHOENIX
ROMANIA
SURINAM
VIETNAM
YAOUNDE
ARIZONA
CONCORD
LINCOLN
MOLDOVA
NAIROBI
NORFOLK
TORTOLA
TRIPOLI
VERMONT
OLYMPIA
THIMPHU
ALGERIA
ANDORRA
AUSTRIA
BELARUS
CENTRAL
COMOROS
ERITREA
JAKARTA
LIBERIA
MAKAROV
NIGERIA
ONTARIO
AUGUSTA
JACKSON
MADISON
MORESBY
NAVASSA
NICOSIA
TUNISIA
BRISTOL
CROATIA
LESOTHO
MAARTEN
MAYOTTE
OKHOTSK
TRENTON
TRISTAN
WHARTON
ARAFURA
BARBUDA
BERMUDA
URAGUAY
BOLIVIA
YEREVAN
BEGAWAN

## 6th Letter

ABIDJAN
AFRICAN
AGULHAS
ANDAMAN
ANDREAS
ARABIAN
BAHAMAS
BEGAWAN
CARACAS
CASPIAN
CENTRAL
CHATHAM
GODTHAR
KINGMAN
MYANMAR
PERSIAN
SENEGAL
SURINAM
TOKELAU
TRISTAN
URAGUAY
VATICAN
VIETNAM
YEREVAN
COLOMBO
MORESBY
NAIROBI
AMERICA
JAMAICA
MOROCCO
BARBUDA
BERMUDA
BURUNDI
FLORIDA
GRENADA
ISLANDS
YAOUNDE
BISHKEK
CELEBES
CHANNEL
ERITREA
GEORGES
MAARTEN
PEOPLES
SPENCER
STANLEY
DOMINGO
RALEIGH
CHUKCHI
LESOTHO
NORONHA
THIMPHU
ALBANIA
ALGERIA
ARMENIA
AUSTRIA
BAHRAIN
BOLIVIA
BOOTHIA
CROATIA
ESTONIA
GEORGIA
KOLONIA
LIBERIA
NAMIBIA
NICOSIA
NIGERIA
OLYMPIA
ONTARIO
PACIFIC
PHOENIX
ROMANIA
SOMALIA
TUNISIA
LINCOLN
MALPELO
MELILLA
NORFOLK
REVILLA

TORTOLA
TRIPOLI
WEDDELL
ALABAMA
ARIZONA
BEIJING
BURKINA
CAYENNE
ENGLAND
FINLAND
GERMANY
HOWLAND
ICELAND
INDIANA
IRELAND
LANSING
MARIANA
MBABANE
MONTANA
TALLINN
UKRAINE
VERMONT
VINCENT
WYOMING
ZEALAND
ANNOBON
BANGKOK
BRISTOL
COMOROS
ECUADOR
JACKSON
KINGDOM
LEBANON
MADISON
MAKAROV
REUNION
SOLOMON
TRENTON
WHARTON
ANDORRA
ARAFURA
CONAKRY
CONCORD
DENMARK
HONIARA
HUNGARY
MADEIRA
WESTERN
BRITISH
ENGLISH
NAVASSA
OKHOTSK
TBILISI
ATLANTA
AUGUSTA
BARENTS
JAKARTA
MAYOTTE
PAPEETE
STRAITS
VANUATU
ANTIGUA
BELARUS
BELGIUM
MANAGUA
VILNIUS
MOLDOVA

**7th Letter**

ALABAMA
ALBANIA
ALGERIA
AMERICA
ANDORRA
ANTIGUA
ARAFURA
ARIZONA
ARMENIA
ATLANTA
AUGUSTA
AUSTRIA
BARBUDA
BERMUDA
BOLIVIA
BOOTHIA
BURKINA
CROATIA
ERITREA
ESTONIA
FLORIDA
GEORGIA
GRENADA
HONIARA
INDIANA
JAKARTA
JAMAICA
KOLONIA
LIBERIA
MADEIRA
MANAGUA
MARIANA
MELILLA
MOLDOVA
MONTANA
NAMIBIA
NAVASSA
NICOSIA
NIGERIA
NORONHA
OLYMPIA
REVILLA
ROMANIA
SOMALIA
TORTOLA
TUNISIA
PACIFIC
CONCORD
ENGLAND
FINLAND
HOWLAND
ICELAND
IRELAND
ZEALAND
CAYENNE
MAYOTTE
MBABANE
PAPEETE
UKRAINE
YAOUNDE
BEIJING
LANSING
WYOMING
BRITISH
ENGLISH
RALEIGH
BURUNDI
CHUKCHI
NAIROBI
TBILISI
TRIPOLI
BANGKOK
BISHKEK
DENMARK
NORFOLK
OKHOTSK
BRISTOL
CENTRAL
CHANNEL
SENEGAL
WEDDELL
BELGIUM
CHATHAM
KINGDOM
SURINAM
VIETNAM
ABIDJAN
AFRICAN
ANDAMAN
ANNOBON
ARABIAN
BAHRAIN
BEGAWAN
CASPIAN
JACKSON
KINGMAN
LEBANON
LINCOLN
MAARTEN
MADISON
PERSIAN
REUNION
SOLOMON
TALLINN
TRENTON
TRISTAN
VATICAN
WESTERN
WHARTON
YEREVAN
COLOMBO
DOMINGO
LESOTHO
MALPELO
MOROCCO
ONTARIO
ECUADOR
GODTHAR
MYANMAR
SPENCER
AGULHAS
ANDREAS
BAHAMAS
BARENTS
BELARUS
CARACAS
CELEBES
COMOROS
GEORGES
ISLANDS
PEOPLES
STRAITS
VILNIUS
VERMONT
VINCENT
THIMPHU
TOKELAU
VANUATU
MAKAROV
PHOENIX
CONAKRY
GERMANY
HUNGARY
MORESBY
STANLEY
URAGUAY

**8 Letter**

**1st Letter**

ADRIATIC
ALEUTIAN
AMERICAN
AMUNDSEN
ANGUILLA
ANTILLES
ARKANSAS
ASHGABAT
ASUNCION
ATLANTIC
BALKHASH
BARBADOS
BEAUFORD
BELGRADE
BELMOPAN
BISMARCK
BOTSWANA
BRASILIA
BRUSSELS
BUDAPEST
BULGARIA
CAMBODIA
CAMEROON
CANBERRA
CAROLINA
CAROLINE
CASTRIES
CHEYENNE
COCKBURN
COLOMBIA
COLORADO
COLUMBIA
COLUMBUS
DAMASCUS
DELAWARE
DJIBOUTI
DOMINICA
DUSHANBE
EMIRATES
ETHIOPIA
FALKLAND
FERNANDO
FREETOWN
GABORONE
GODTHAAB
GUERNSEY
HAMILTON
HARTFORD
HELSINKI
HONDURAS
HONOLULU
ILLINOIS
JOHNSTON
KENTUCKY
KHARTOUM
KINGSTON
KINSHASA
KIRIBATI
KISHINEV
LABRADOR
LAWRENCE
LILONGWE
LONGYEAR
MAGELLAN
MALAYSIA
MALDIVES
MARSHALL
MARYLAND
MCDONALD
MELVILLE
MICHIGAN
MIQUELON
MISSOURI
MONGOLIA
MONROVIA
NEBRASKA
NORTHERN
OKLAHOMA
PAKISTAN
PARAGUAY
PITCAIRN
PLYMOUTH
PORTUGAL
PRINCIPE
PROVEDEN
REINDEER
REPUBLIC
RICHMOND
SALVADOR
SANTIAGO
SCORESBY
SCOTLAND
SIBERIAN
SLOVAKIA
SLOVENIA
SOUTHERN
SUPERIOR
SVALBARD
TANZANIA
TASHKENT
THAILAND
TITICACA
TRINIDAD
VALLETTA
VICTORIA
VIRGINIA
VISCOUNT
WINDHOEK
WINNIPEG
ZANZIBAR
ZIMBABWE

**2nd Letter**

BALKHASH
BARBADOS
CAMBODIA
CAMEROON
CANBERRA
CAROLINA
CAROLINE
CASTRIES
DAMASCUS
FALKLAND
GABORONE
HAMILTON
HARTFORD
LABRADOR
LAWRENCE
MAGELLAN
MALAYSIA
MALDIVES
MARSHALL
MARYLAND
PAKISTAN
PARAGUAY
SALVADOR
SANTIAGO
TANZANIA
TASHKENT
VALLETTA
ZANZIBAR
MCDONALD
SCORESBY
SCOTLAND
ADRIATIC
BEAUFORD
BELGRADE
BELMOPAN
DELAWARE
FERNANDO
HELSINKI
KENTUCKY
MELVILLE
NEBRASKA
REINDEER
REPUBLIC
CHEYENNE
KHARTOUM
THAILAND
BISMARCK
KINGSTON
KINSHASA
KIRIBATI
KISHINEV
LILONGWE
MICHIGAN
MIQUELON
MISSOURI
PITCAIRN
RICHMOND
SIBERIAN
TITICACA
VICTORIA
VIRGINIA
VISCOUNT
WINDHOEK
WINNIPEG
ZIMBABWE
DJIBOUTI
OKLAHOMA
ALEUTIAN
ILLINOIS
PLYMOUTH
SLOVAKIA
SLOVENIA
AMERICAN
AMUNDSEN
EMIRATES
ANGUILLA
ANTILLES
BOTSWANA
COCKBURN
COLOMBIA
COLORADO
COLUMBIA
COLUMBUS
DOMINICA
GODTHAAB
HONDURAS
HONOLULU
JOHNSTON
LONGYEAR
MONGOLIA
MONROVIA
NORTHERN
PORTUGAL
SOUTHERN
ARKANSAS
BRASILIA
BRUSSELS
FREETOWN
PRINCIPE
PROVEDEN
TRINIDAD
ASHGABAT
ASUNCION
ATLANTIC
ETHIOPIA
BUDAPEST
BULGARIA
DUSHANBE
GUERNSEY
SUPERIOR
SVALBARD

### 3rd Letter

BE**A**UFORD
BR**A**SILIA
KH**A**RTOUM
SV**A**LBARD
TH**A**ILAND
GA**B**ORONE
LA**B**RADOR
NE**B**RASKA
SI**B**ERIAN
CO**C**KBURN
MI**C**HIGAN
RI**C**HMOND
VI**C**TORIA
BU**D**APEST
GO**D**THAAB
MC**D**ONALD
AL**E**UTIAN
AM**E**RICAN
CH**E**YENNE
FR**E**ETOWN
GU**E**RNSEY
AN**G**UILLA
MA**G**ELLAN
AS**H**GABAT
ET**H**IOPIA
JO**H**NSTON
DJ**I**BOUTI
EM**I**RATES
PR**I**NCIPE
RE**I**NDEER
TR**I**NIDAD
AR**K**ANSAS
PA**K**ISTAN
AT**L**ANTIC
BA**L**KHASH
BE**L**GRADE
BE**L**MOPAN
BU**L**GARIA
CO**L**OMBIA
CO**L**ORADO
CO**L**UMBIA
CO**L**UMBUS
DE**L**AWARE
FA**L**KLAND
HE**L**SINKI
IL**L**INOIS
LI**L**ONGWE
MA**L**AYSIA
MA**L**DIVES
ME**L**VILLE
OK**L**AHOMA
SA**L**VADOR
VA**L**LETTA
CA**M**BODIA
CA**M**EROON
DA**M**ASCUS
DO**M**INICA
HA**M**ILTON
ZI**M**BABWE
CA**N**BERRA
HO**N**DURAS
HO**N**OLULU
KE**N**TUCKY
KI**N**GSTON
KI**N**SHASA
LO**N**GYEAR
MO**N**GOLIA
MO**N**ROVIA
SA**N**TIAGO
TA**N**ZANIA
WI**N**DHOEK
WI**N**NIPEG
ZA**N**ZIBAR
PR**O**VEDEN
SC**O**RESBY
SC**O**TLAND
SL**O**VAKIA
SL**O**VENIA
RE**P**UBLIC
SU**P**ERIOR
MI**Q**UELON
AD**R**IATIC
BA**R**BADOS
CA**R**OLINA
CA**R**OLINE
FE**R**NANDO
HA**R**TFORD
KI**R**IBATI
MA**R**SHALL
MA**R**YLAND
NO**R**THERN
PA**R**AGUAY
PO**R**TUGAL
VI**R**GINIA
BI**S**MARCK
CA**S**TRIES
DU**S**HANBE
KI**S**HINEV
MI**S**SOURI
TA**S**HKENT
VI**S**COUNT
AN**T**ILLES
BO**T**SWANA
PI**T**CAIRN
TI**T**ICACA
AM**U**NDSEN
AS**U**NCION
BR**U**SSELS
SO**U**THERN
LA**W**RENCE
PL**Y**MOUTH

### 4th Letter

ARK**A**NSAS
ATL**A**NTIC
BUD**A**PEST
DAM**A**SCUS
DEL**A**WARE
MAL**A**YSIA
OKL**A**HOMA
PAR**A**GUAY
BAR**B**ADOS
CAM**B**ODIA
CAN**B**ERRA
DJI**B**OUTI
ZIM**B**ABWE
PIT**C**AIRN
VIS**C**OUNT
HON**D**URAS
MAL**D**IVES
WIN**D**HOEK
CAM**E**ROON
FRE**E**TOWN
MAG**E**LLAN
SIB**E**RIAN
SUP**E**RIOR
ASH**G**ABAT
BEL**G**RADE
BUL**G**ARIA
KIN**G**STON
LON**G**YEAR
MON**G**OLIA
VIR**G**INIA
DUS**H**ANBE
KIS**H**INEV
MIC**H**IGAN
RIC**H**MOND
TAS**H**KENT
ADR**I**ATIC
ANT**I**LLES
DOM**I**NICA
ETH**I**OPIA
HAM**I**LTON
ILL**I**NOIS
KIR**I**BATI
PAK**I**STAN
THA**I**LAND
TIT**I**CACA
BAL**K**HASH
COC**K**BURN
FAL**K**LAND
SVA**L**BARD
VAL**L**ETTA
BEL**M**OPAN
BIS**M**ARCK
PLY**M**OUTH
AMU**N**DSEN
ASU**N**CION
FER**N**ANDO
JOH**N**STON
PRI**N**CIPE
REI**N**DEER
TRI**N**IDAD
WIN**N**IPEG
CAR**O**LINA
CAR**O**LINE
COL**O**MBIA
COL**O**RADO
GAB**O**RONE
HON**O**LULU
LIL**O**NGWE
MCD**O**NALD
AME**R**ICAN
EMI**R**ATES
GUE**R**NSEY
KHA**R**TOUM
LAB**R**ADOR
LAW**R**ENCE
MON**R**OVIA
NEB**R**ASKA
SCO**R**ESBY
BOT**S**WANA
BRA**S**ILIA
BRU**S**SELS
HEL**S**INKI
KIN**S**HASA
MAR**S**HALL
MIS**S**OURI
CAS**T**RIES
GOD**T**HAAB
HAR**T**FORD
KEN**T**UCKY
NOR**T**HERN
POR**T**UGAL
SAN**T**IAGO
SCO**T**LAND
SOU**T**HERN
VIC**T**ORIA
ALE**U**TIAN
ANG**U**ILLA
BEA**U**FORD
COL**U**MBIA
COL**U**MBUS
MIQ**U**ELON
REP**U**BLIC
MEL**V**ILLE
PRO**V**EDEN
SAL**V**ADOR
SLO**V**AKIA
SLO**V**ENIA
CHE**Y**ENNE
MAR**Y**LAND
TAN**Z**ANIA
ZAN**Z**IBAR

### 5th Letter

ADRI**A**TIC
ASHG**A**BAT
BARB**A**DOS
BISM**A**RCK
BULG**A**RIA
DUSH**A**NBE
EMIR**A**TES
FERN**A**NDO
LABR**A**DOR
NEBR**A**SKA
PITC**A**IRN
SALV**A**DOR
SLOV**A**KIA
TANZ**A**NIA
ZIMB**A**BWE
COCK**B**URN
KIRI**B**ATI
REPU**B**LIC
SVAL**B**ARD
ASUN**C**ION
PRIN**C**IPE
TITI**C**ACA
AMUN**D**SEN
REIN**D**EER
CANB**E**RRA
CHEY**E**NNE
LAWR**E**NCE
MIQU**E**LON
PROV**E**DEN
SCOR**E**SBY
SLOV**E**NIA
VALL**E**TTA
BEAU**F**ORD
HART**F**ORD
PARA**G**UAY
BALK**H**ASH
GODT**H**AAB
KINS**H**ASA
MARS**H**ALL
NORT**H**ERN
OKLA**H**OMA
SOUT**H**ERN
WIND**H**OEK
AMER**I**CAN
ANGU**I**LLA
BRAS**I**LIA
HELS**I**NKI
KISH**I**NEV
MALD**I**VES
MELV**I**LLE
MICH**I**GAN
SANT**I**AGO
TRIN**I**DAD
VIRG**I**NIA
WINN**I**PEG
ZANZ**I**BAR
TASH**K**ENT
ANTI**L**LES
CARO**L**INA
CARO**L**INE
FALK**L**AND
HAMI**L**TON
HONO**L**ULU
MAGE**L**LAN
MARY**L**AND
SCOT**L**AND
THAI**L**AND
COLO**M**BIA
COLU**M**BIA
COLU**M**BUS
RICH**M**OND
ARKA**N**SAS
ATLA**N**TIC
DOMI**N**ICA
GUER**N**SEY
ILLI**N**OIS
LILO**N**GWE
MCDO**N**ALD
BELM**O**PAN
CAMB**O**DIA
DJIB**O**UTI
ETHI**O**PIA
MISS**O**URI
MONG**O**LIA
MONR**O**VIA
PLYM**O**UTH
VICT**O**RIA
VISC**O**UNT
BUDA**P**EST
BELG**R**ADE
CAME**R**OON
CAST**R**IES
COLO**R**ADO
GABO**R**ONE
SIBE**R**IAN
SUPE**R**IOR
BRUS**S**ELS
DAMA**S**CUS
JOHN**S**TON
KING**S**TON
PAKI**S**TAN
ALEU**T**IAN
FREE**T**OWN
KHAR**T**OUM
HOND**U**RAS
KENT**U**CKY
PORT**U**GAL
BOTS**W**ANA
DELA**W**ARE
LONG**Y**EAR
MALA**Y**SIA

### 6th Letter

BALKH**A**SH
BELGR**A**DE
BOTSW**A**NA
COLOR**A**DO
DELAW**A**RE
FALKL**A**ND
GODTH**A**AB
KINSH**A**SA
KIRIB**A**TI
MARSH**A**LL
MARYL**A**ND
MCDON**A**LD
SANTI**A**GO
SCOTL**A**ND
SVALB**A**RD
THAIL**A**ND
TITIC**A**CA
ASHGA**B**AT
COLOM**B**IA
COLUM**B**IA
COLUM**B**US
ZANZI**B**AR
ZIMBA**B**WE
AMERI**C**AN
DAMAS**C**US
KENTU**C**KY
BARBA**D**OS
CAMBO**D**IA
LABRA**D**OR
PROVE**D**EN
SALVA**D**OR
TRINI**D**AD
BRUSS**E**LS
BUDAP**E**ST
LONGY**E**AR
NORTH**E**RN
REIND**E**ER
SOUTH**E**RN
TASHK**E**NT
LILON**G**WE
MICHI**G**AN
PORTU**G**AL
ALEUT**I**AN
ASUNC**I**ON
CAROL**I**NA
CAROL**I**NE
CASTR**I**ES
DOMIN**I**CA
PITCA**I**RN
PRINC**I**PE
SIBER**I**AN
SUPER**I**OR
SLOVA**K**IA
ANGUI**L**LA
ANTIL**L**ES
BRASI**L**IA
MAGEL**L**AN
MELVI**L**LE
MIQUE**L**ON
MONGO**L**IA
REPUB**L**IC
CHEYE**N**NE
DUSHA**N**BE
FERNA**N**DO
HELSI**N**KI
KISHI**N**EV
LAWRE**N**CE
SLOVE**N**IA
TANZA**N**IA
VIRGI**N**IA
BEAUF**O**RD
CAMER**O**ON
FREET**O**WN
GABOR**O**NE
HARTF**O**RD
ILLIN**O**IS
KHART**O**UM
OKLAH**O**MA
RICHM**O**ND
WINDH**O**EK
BELMO**P**AN
ETHIO**P**IA
WINNI**P**EG
BISMA**R**CK
BULGA**R**IA
CANBE**R**RA
HONDU**R**AS
VICTO**R**IA
AMUND**S**EN
ARKAN**S**AS
GUERN**S**EY
MALAY**S**IA
NEBRA**S**KA
SCORE**S**BY
ADRIA**T**IC
ATLAN**T**IC
EMIRA**T**ES
HAMIL**T**ON
JOHNS**T**ON
KINGS**T**ON
PAKIS**T**AN
VALLE**T**TA
COCKB**U**RN
DJIBO**U**TI
HONOL**U**LU
MISSO**U**RI
PARAG**U**AY
PLYMO**U**TH
VISCO**U**NT
MALDI**V**ES
MONRO**V**IA

### 7th Letter

ALEUTIAN
AMERICAN
ARKANSAS
ASHGABAT
BELMOPAN
GODTHAAB
HONDURAS
LONGYEAR
MAGELLAN
MICHIGAN
PAKISTAN
PARAGUAY
PORTUGAL
SIBERIAN
TRINIDAD
ZANZIBAR
DUSHANBE
SCORESBY
BISMARCK
DOMINICA
LAWRENCE
TITICACA
BELGRADE
COLORADO
FERNANDO
AMUNDSEN
ANTILLES
CASTRIES
EMIRATES
GUERNSEY
KISHINEV
MALDIVES
PROVEDEN
REINDEER
WINDHOEK
WINNIPEG
SANTIAGO
ADRIATIC
ATLANTIC
BRASILIA
BULGARIA
CAMBODIA
COLOMBIA
COLUMBIA
ETHIOPIA
ILLINOIS
MALAYSIA
MONGOLIA
MONROVIA
REPUBLIC
SLOVAKIA
SLOVENIA
TANZANIA
VICTORIA
VIRGINIA
HELSINKI
KENTUCKY
NEBRASKA
ANGUILLA
BRUSSELS
HONOLULU
MARSHALL
MCDONALD
MELVILLE
OKLAHOMA
BOTSWANA
CAROLINA
CAROLINE
CHEYENNE
FALKLAND
GABORONE
MARYLAND
RICHMOND
SCOTLAND
TASHKENT
THAILAND
VISCOUNT
ASUNCION
BARBADOS
CAMEROON
HAMILTON
JOHNSTON
KINGSTON
LABRADOR
MIQUELON
SALVADOR
SUPERIOR
PRINCIPE
BEAUFORD
CANBERRA
COCKBURN
DELAWARE
HARTFORD
MISSOURI
NORTHERN
PITCAIRN
SOUTHERN
SVALBARD
BALKHASH
BUDAPEST
KINSHASA
DJIBOUTI
KIRIBATI
PLYMOUTH
VALLETTA
COLUMBUS
DAMASCUS
KHARTOUM
FREETOWN
LILONGWE
ZIMBABWE

### 8th Letter

ANGUILLA
BOTSWANA
BRASILIA
BULGARIA
CAMBODIA
CANBERRA
CAROLINA
COLOMBIA
COLUMBIA
DOMINICA
ETHIOPIA
KINSHASA
MALAYSIA
MONGOLIA
MONROVIA
NEBRASKA
OKLAHOMA
SLOVAKIA
SLOVENIA
TANZANIA
TITICACA
VALLETTA
VICTORIA
VIRGINIA
GODTHAAB
ADRIATIC
ATLANTIC
REPUBLIC
BEAUFORD
FALKLAND
HARTFORD
MARYLAND
MCDONALD
RICHMOND
SCOTLAND
SVALBARD
THAILAND
TRINIDAD
BELGRADE
CAROLINE
CHEYENNE
DELAWARE
DUSHANBE
GABORONE
LAWRENCE
LILONGWE
MELVILLE
PRINCIPE
ZIMBABWE
WINNIPEG
BALKHASH
PLYMOUTH
DJIBOUTI
HELSINKI
KIRIBATI
MISSOURI
BISMARCK
WINDHOEK
MARSHALL
PORTUGAL
KHARTOUM
ALEUTIAN
AMERICAN
AMUNDSEN
ASUNCION
BELMOPAN
CAMEROON
COCKBURN
FREETOWN
HAMILTON
JOHNSTON
KINGSTON
MAGELLAN
MICHIGAN
MIQUELON
NORTHERN
PAKISTAN
PITCAIRN
PROVEDEN
SIBERIAN
SOUTHERN
COLORADO
FERNANDO
SANTIAGO
LABRADOR
LONGYEAR
REINDEER
SALVADOR
SUPERIOR
ZANZIBAR
ANTILLES
ARKANSAS
BARBADOS
BRUSSELS
CASTRIES
COLUMBUS
DAMASCUS
EMIRATES
HONDURAS
ILLINOIS
MALDIVES
ASHGABAT
BUDAPEST
TASHKENT
VISCOUNT
HONOLULU
KISHINEV
GUERNSEY
KENTUCKY
PARAGUAY
SCORESBY

## 9 Letter

### 1st Letter

AMSTERDAM
ANNAPOLIS
ARGENTINA
ARGENTINE
ASCENSION
ASHKHABAD
ATHABASCA
AUSTRALIA
BAILIWICK
BUCHAREST
BUJUMBURA
CALEDONIA
CARIBBEAN
CHARLOTTE
CHRISTMAS
CHURCHILL
DOMINICAN
FRANKFORT
GALAPAGOS
GIBRALTAR
GREENLAND
GUATEMALA
HAMPSHIRE
INDONESIA
ISLAMABAD
JAMESTOWN
JEFFERSON
JERUSALEM
KATHMANDU
KERGUELEN
KINGSTOWN
KUSKOKWIM
KYRGYSTAN
LANCASTER
LITHUANIA
LJUBLJANA
LOUISIANA
MACEDONIA
MACQUARIE
MASCARENE
MAURITIUS
MINNESOTA
MOGADISHU
NASHVILLE
NICARAGUA
NORTHWEST
NORWEGIAN
OGASAWARA
POLYNESIA
RAROTONGA
REYKJAVIK
RODRIGUES
SHELIKHOV
SINGAPORE
STOCKHOLM
SWAZILAND
TENNESSEE
TERRITORY
THORSHAVN
TORISHIMA
VENEZUELA
VIENTIANE
WISCONSIN

### 2nd Letter

BAILIWICK
CALEDONIA
CARIBBEAN
GALAPAGOS
HAMPSHIRE
JAMESTOWN
KATHMANDU
LANCASTER
MACEDONIA
MACQUARIE
MASCARENE
MAURITIUS
NASHVILLE
RAROTONGA
JEFFERSON
JERUSALEM
KERGUELEN
REYKJAVIK
TENNESSEE
TERRITORY
VENEZUELA
OGASAWARA
CHARLOTTE
CHRISTMAS
CHURCHILL
SHELIKHOV
THORSHAVN
GIBRALTAR
KINGSTOWN
LITHUANIA
MINNESOTA
NICARAGUA
SINGAPORE
VIENTIANE
WISCONSIN
LJUBLJANA
AMSTERDAM
ANNAPOLIS
INDONESIA
DOMINICAN
LOUISIANA
MOGADISHU
NORTHWEST
NORWEGIAN
POLYNESIA
RODRIGUES
TORISHIMA
ARGENTINA
ARGENTINE
FRANKFORT
GREENLAND
ASCENSION
ASHKHABAD
ISLAMABAD
ATHABASCA
STOCKHOLM
AUSTRALIA
BUCHAREST
BUJUMBURA
GUATEMALA
KUSKOKWIM
SWAZILAND
KYRGYSTAN

### 3rd Letter

CHARLOTTE
FRANKFORT
GUATEMALA
OGASAWARA
SWAZILAND
GIBRALTAR
ASCENSION
BUCHAREST
MACEDONIA
MACQUARIE
NICARAGUA
INDONESIA
RODRIGUES
GREENLAND
SHELIKHOV
VIENTIANE
JEFFERSON
ARGENTINA
ARGENTINE
MOGADISHU
ASHKHABAD
ATHABASCA
BAILIWICK
BUJUMBURA
CALEDONIA
GALAPAGOS
ISLAMABAD
POLYNESIA
DOMINICAN
HAMPSHIRE
JAMESTOWN
ANNAPOLIS
KINGSTOWN
LANCASTER
MINNESOTA
SINGAPORE
TENNESSEE
VENEZUELA
STOCKHOLM
THORSHAVN
CARIBBEAN
CHRISTMAS
JERUSALEM
KERGUELEN
KYRGYSTAN
NORTHWEST
NORWEGIAN
RAROTONGA
TERRITORY
TORISHIMA
AMSTERDAM
AUSTRALIA
KUSKOKWIM
MASCARENE
NASHVILLE
WISCONSIN
KATHMANDU
LITHUANIA
CHURCHILL
LJUBLJANA
LOUISIANA
MAURITIUS
REYKJAVIK

### 4th Letter

ANNAPOLIS
ATHABASCA
GALAPAGOS
ISLAMABAD
MOGADISHU
NICARAGUA
LJUBLJANA
LANCASTER
MASCARENE
STOCKHOLM
WISCONSIN
ARGENTINA
ARGENTINE
ASCENSION
CALEDONIA
GREENLAND
JAMESTOWN
MACEDONIA
VENEZUELA
JEFFERSON

KER**G**UELEN
KIN**G**STOWN
KYR**G**YSTAN
SIN**G**APORE
BUC**H**AREST
KAT**H**MANDU
LIT**H**UANIA
NAS**H**VILLE
CAR**I**BBEAN
CHR**I**STMAS
DOM**I**NICAN
LOU**I**SIANA
TOR**I**SHIMA
ASH**K**HABAD
KUS**K**OKWIM
REY**K**JAVIK
BAI**L**IWICK
SHE**L**IKHOV
FRA**N**KFORT
MIN**N**ESOTA
TEN**N**ESSEE
IND**O**NESIA
RAR**O**TONGA
HAM**P**SHIRE
MAC**Q**UARIE
CHA**R**LOTTE
CHU**R**CHILL
GIB**R**ALTAR
MAU**R**ITIUS
ROD**R**IGUES
TER**R**ITORY
THO**R**SHAVN
OGA**S**AWARA
AMS**T**ERDAM
AUS**T**RALIA
GUA**T**EMALA
NOR**T**HWEST
BUJ**U**MBURA
JER**U**SALEM
NOR**W**EGIAN
POL**Y**NESIA
SWA**Z**ILAND

### 5th Letter

BUCH**A**REST
GIBR**A**LTAR
LANC**A**STER
MASC**A**RENE
OGAS**A**WARA
SING**A**PORE
ATHA**B**ASCA
CARI**B**BEAN
CHUR**C**HILL
CALE**D**ONIA
MACE**D**ONIA
MOGA**D**ISHU
AMST**E**RDAM
GUAT**E**MALA
JEFF**E**RSON
MINN**E**SOTA
NORW**E**GIAN
TENN**E**SSEE
ASHK**H**ABAD
NORT**H**WEST
BAIL**I**WICK
MAUR**I**TIUS
RODR**I**GUES
SHEL**I**KHOV
SWAZ**I**LAND
TERR**I**TORY
REYK**J**AVIK
FRAN**K**FORT
STOC**K**HOLM
CHAR**L**OTTE
LJUB**L**JANA
BUJU**M**BURA
ISLA**M**ABAD
KATH**M**ANDU
ARGE**N**TINA
ARGE**N**TINE
ASCE**N**SION
DOMI**N**ICAN
GREE**N**LAND
INDO**N**ESIA
POLY**N**ESIA
KUSK**O**KWIM
WISC**O**NSIN
ANNA**P**OLIS
GALA**P**AGOS
AUST**R**ALIA
NICA**R**AGUA
CHRI**S**TMAS
HAMP**S**HIRE
JAME**S**TOWN
JERU**S**ALEM
KING**S**TOWN
LOUI**S**IANA
THOR**S**HAVN
TORI**S**HIMA
RARO**T**ONGA
VIEN**T**IANE
KERG**U**ELEN
LITH**U**ANIA
MACQ**U**ARIE
NASH**V**ILLE
KYRG**Y**STAN
VENE**Z**UELA

### 6th Letter

ASHKH**A**BAD
ATHAB**A**SCA
AUSTR**A**LIA
GALAP**A**GOS
ISLAM**A**BAD
JERUS**A**LEM
KATHM**A**NDU
LITHU**A**NIA
MACQU**A**RIE
NICAR**A**GUA
REYKJ**A**VIK
BUJUM**B**URA
CARIB**B**EAN
INDON**E**SIA
KERGU**E**LEN
POLYN**E**SIA
FRANK**F**ORT
NORWE**G**IAN
RODRI**G**UES
CHURC**H**ILL
HAMPS**H**IRE
STOCK**H**OLM
THORS**H**AVN
TORIS**H**IMA
DOMIN**I**CAN
LOUIS**I**ANA
MOGAD**I**SHU
NASHV**I**LLE
VIENT**I**ANE
LJUBL**J**ANA
KUSKO**K**WIM
SHELI**K**HOV
GIBRA**L**TER
GREEN**L**AND
SWAZI**L**AND
GUATE**M**ALA
WISCO**N**SIN
ANNAP**O**LIS
CALED**O**NIA
CHARL**O**TTE
MACED**O**NIA
RAROT**O**NGA
SINGA**P**ORE
AMSTE**R**DAM
BUCHA**R**EST
JEFFE**R**SON
MASCA**R**ENE
ASCEN**S**ION
KYRGY**S**TAN
LANCA**S**TER
MINNE**S**OTA
TENNE**S**SEE
ARGEN**T**INA
ARGEN**T**INE
CHRIS**T**MAS
JAMES**T**OWN
KINGS**T**OWN
MAURI**T**IUS
TERRI**T**ORY
VENEZ**U**ELA
BAILI**W**ICK
NORTH**W**EST
OGASA**W**ARA

### 7th Letter

GREENL**A**ND
GUATEM**A**LA
LJUBLJ**A**NA
LOUISI**A**NA
OGASAW**A**RA
THORSH**A**VN
SWAZIL**A**ND
VIENTI**A**NE
ASHKHA**B**AD
ISLAMA**B**AD
DOMINI**C**AN
AMSTER**D**AM
BUCHAR**E**ST
CARIBB**E**AN
MASCAR**E**NE
NORTHW**E**ST
VENEZU**E**LA
GALAPA**G**OS
NICARA**G**UA
SHELIK**H**OV
ARGENT**I**NA
ARGENT**I**NE
ASCENS**I**ON
BAILIW**I**CK
CHURCH**I**LL
HAMPSH**I**RE
MAURIT**I**US
NORWEG**I**AN
TORISH**I**MA
ANNAPO**L**IS
AUSTRA**L**IA
JERUSA**L**EM
KERGUE**L**EN
NASHVI**L**LE
CHRIST**M**AS
CALEDO**N**IA
KATHMA**N**DU
LITHUA**N**IA
MACEDO**N**IA
RAROTO**N**GA
FRANKF**O**RT
JAMEST**O**WN
KINGST**O**WN
MINNES**O**TA
SINGAP**O**RE
STOCKH**O**LM
TERRIT**O**RY
MACQUA**R**IE
ATHABA**S**CA
INDONE**S**IA
JEFFER**S**ON
MOGADI**S**HU
POLYNE**S**IA
TENNES**S**EE
WISCON**S**IN
CHARLO**T**TE
GIBRAL**T**AR
KYRGYS**T**AN
LANCAS**T**ER
BUJUMB**U**RA
RODRIG**U**ES
REYKJA**V**IK
KUSKOK**W**IM

### 8th Letter

AMSTERD**A**M
ASKHAB**A**D
CARIBBE**A**N
CHRISTM**A**S
DOMINIC**A**N
GIBRALT**A**R
ISLAMAB**A**D
KYRGYST**A**N
NORWEGI**A**N
ATHABAS**C**A
BAILIWI**C**K
KATHMAN**D**U
JERUSAL**E**M
KERGUEL**E**N
LANCAST**E**R
RODRIGU**E**S
TENNESS**E**E
RAROTON**G**A
MOGADIS**H**U
ANNAPOL**I**S
AUSTRAL**I**A
CALEDON**I**A
INDONES**I**A
KUSKOKW**I**M
LITHUAN**I**A
MACEDON**I**A
MACQUAR**I**E
POLYNES**I**A
REYKJAV**I**K
WISCONS**I**N
CHURCHI**L**L
GUATEMA**L**A
NASHVIL**L**E
STOCKHO**L**M
VENEZUE**L**A
TORISHI**M**A
ARGENTI**N**A
ARGENTI**N**E
GREENLA**N**D
LJUBLJA**N**A
LOUISIA**N**A
MASCARE**N**E
SWAZILA**N**D
VIENTIA**N**E
ASCENSI**O**N
GALAPAG**O**S
JEFFERS**O**N
SHELIKH**O**V
BUJUMBU**R**A
FRANKFO**R**T
HAMPSHI**R**E
OGASAWA**R**A
SINGAPO**R**E
TERRITO**R**Y
BUCHARE**S**T
NORTHWE**S**T
CHARLOT**T**E
MINNESO**T**A
MAURITI**U**S
NICARAG**U**A
THORSHA**V**N
JAMESTO**W**N
KINGSTO**W**N

### 9th Letter

ARGENTIN**A**
ATHABASC**A**
AUSTRALI**A**
BUJUMBUR**A**
CALEDONI**A**
GUATEMAL**A**
INDONESI**A**
LITHUANI**A**
LJUBLJAN**A**
LOUISIAN**A**
MACEDONI**A**
MINNESOT**A**
NICARAGU**A**
OGASAWAR**A**
POLYNESI**A**
RAROTONG**A**
TORISHIM**A**
VENEZUEL**A**
ASHKHABA**D**
GREENLAN**D**
ISLAMABA**D**
SWAZILAN**D**
ARGENTIN**E**
CHARLOTT**E**
HAMPSHIR**E**
MACQUARI**E**
MASCAREN**E**
NASHVILL**E**
SINGAPOR**E**
TENNESSE**E**
VIENTIAN**E**
BAILIWIC**K**
REYKJAVI**K**
CHURCHIL**L**
AMSTERDA**M**
JERUSALE**M**
KUSKOKWI**M**
STOCKHOL**M**
ASCENSIO**N**
CARIBBEA**N**
DOMINICA**N**
JAMESTOW**N**
JEFFERSO**N**
KERGUELE**N**
KINGSTOW**N**
KYRGYSTA**N**
NORWEGIA**N**
THORSHAV**N**
WISCONSI**N**
GIBRALTA**R**
LANCASTE**R**
ANNAPOLI**S**
CHRISTMA**S**
GALAPAGO**S**
MAURITIU**S**
RODRIGUE**S**
BUCHARES**T**
FRANKFOR**T**
NORTHWES**T**
KATHMAND**U**
MOGADISH**U**
SHELIKHO**V**
TERRITOR**Y**

## 10 Letter

### 1st Letter

**A**NTARCTICA
**A**USTRALIAN
**A**ZERBAIJAN
**B**ANGLADESH
**B**ASSETERRE
**B**RATISLAVA
**B**RIDGETOWN
**C**ALIFORNIA
**C**HARLESTON

CLIPPERTON
COPENHAGEN
CORONATION
DARUSSALAM
DEMOCRATIC
EQUATORIAL
GEORGETOWN
GRENADINES
GUADELOUPE
HARRISBURG
KAZAKHSTAN
LIBREVILLE
LUXEMBOURG
MADAGASCAR
MARTINIQUE
MAURITANIA
MICRONESIA
MONTENEGRO
MONTEVIDEO
MONTGOMERY
MONTPELIER
MONTSERRAT
MOZAMBIQUE
NOUAKCHOTT
ORANJESTAD
PARAMARIBO
PHILIPPINE
PROVIDENCE
SACRAMENTO
SEYCHELLES
TAJIKISTAN
TANGANYIKA
TYRRHENIAN
UZBEKISTAN
WASHINGTON
WELLINGTON
WILLEMSTAD
YUGOSLAVIA

## 2nd Letter

BANGLADESH
BASSETERRE
CALIFORNIA
DARUSSALAM
HARRISBURG
KAZAKHSTAN
MADAGASCAR
MARTINIQUE
MAURITANIA
PARAMARIBO
SACRAMENTO
TAJIKISTAN
TANGANYIKA
WASHINGTON
DEMOCRATIC
GEORGETOWN
SEYCHELLES
WELLINGTON
CHARLESTON
PHILIPPINE
LIBREVILLE
MICRONESIA
WILLEMSTAD
CLIPPERTON
ANTARCTICA
COPENHAGEN
CORONATION
MONTENEGRO
MONTEVIDEO
MONTGOMERY
MONTPELIER
MONTSERRAT
MOZAMBIQUE
NOUAKCHOTT
EQUATORIAL
BRATISLAVA
BRIDGETOWN
GRENADINES
ORANJESTAD
PROVIDENCE
AUSTRALIAN
GUADELOUPE
LUXEMBOURG
YUGOSLAVIA
TYRRHENIAN
AZERBAIJAN
UZBEKISTAN

## 3rd Letter

BRATISLAVA
CHARLESTON
GUADELOUPE
ORANJESTAD
LIBREVILLE
UZBEKISTAN
MICRONESIA
SACRAMENTO
MADAGASCAR
AZERBAIJAN
GRENADINES
YUGOSLAVIA
BRIDGETOWN
CLIPPERTON
PHILIPPINE
TAJIKISTAN
CALIFORNIA
WELLINGTON
WILLEMSTAD
DEMOCRATIC
BANGLADESH
MONTENEGRO
MONTEVIDEO
MONTGOMERY
MONTPELIER
MONTSERRAT
TANGANYIKA
GEORGETOWN
PROVIDENCE
COPENHAGEN
CORONATION
DARUSSALAM
HARRISBURG
MARTINIQUE
PARAMARIBO
TYRRHENIAN
AUSTRALIAN
BASSETERRE
WASHINGTON
ANTARCTICA
EQUATORIAL
MAURITANIA
NOUAKCHOTT
LUXEMBOURG
SEYCHELLES
KAZAKHSTAN
MOZAMBIQUE

## 4th Letter

ANTARCTICA
EQUATORIAL
KAZAKHSTAN
MADAGASCAR
MOZAMBIQUE
NOUAKCHOTT
PARAMARIBO
SEYCHELLES
BRIDGETOWN
GUADELOUPE
COPENHAGEN
LUXEMBOURG
UZBEKISTAN
BANGLADESH
TANGANYIKA
WASHINGTON
CALIFORNIA
TAJIKISTAN
PHILIPPINE
WELLINGTON
WILLEMSTAD
GRENADINES
ORANJESTAD
CORONATION
DEMOCRATIC
YUGOSLAVIA
CLIPPERTON
AZERBAIJAN
CHARLESTON
GEORGETOWN
HARRISBURG
LIBREVILLE
MAURITANIA
MICRONESIA
SACRAMENTO
TYRRHENIAN
BASSETERRE
AUSTRALIAN
BRATISLAVA
MARTINIQUE
MONTENEGRO
MONTEVIDEO
MONTGOMERY
MONTPELIER
MONTSERRAT
DARUSSALAM
PROVIDENCE

## 5th Letter

GRENADINES
SACRAMENTO
TANGANYIKA
AZERBAIJAN
DEMOCRATIC
BASSETERRE
GUADELOUPE
LIBREVILLE
MONTENEGRO
MONTEVIDEO
WILLEMSTAD
CALIFORNIA
BRIDGETOWN
GEORGETOWN
MADAGASCAR
MONTGOMERY
SEYCHELLES
TYRRHENIAN
BRATISLAVA
HARRISBURG
MARTINIQUE
MAURITANIA
PHILIPPINE
PROVIDENCE
WASHINGTON
WELLINGTON
ORANJESTAD
KAZAKHSTAN
NOUAKCHOTT
TAJIKISTAN
UZBEKISTAN
BANGLADESH
CHARLESTON
LUXEMBOURG
MOZAMBIQUE
PARAMARIBO
COPENHAGEN
CORONATION
MICRONESIA
CLIPPERTON
MONTPELIER
ANTARCTICA
AUSTRALIAN
DARUSSALAM
MONTSERRAT
YUGOSLAVIA
EQUATORIAL

## 6th Letter

AUSTRALIAN
AZERBAIJAN
BANGLADESH
CORONATION
MADAGASCAR
PARAMARIBO
LUXEMBOURG
MOZAMBIQUE
ANTARCTICA
NOUAKCHOTT
GRENADINES
PROVIDENCE
BRIDGETOWN
CHARLESTON
CLIPPERTON
GEORGETOWN
MONTSERRAT
MONTPELIER
ORANJESTAD
SEYCHELLES
TYRRHENIAN
COPENHAGEN
KAZAKHSTAN
TAJIKISTAN
UZBEKISTAN
GUADELOUPE
YUGOSLAVIA
SACRAMENTO
WILLEMSTAD
MARTINIQUE
MICRONESIA
MONTENEGRO
TANGANYIKA
WASHINGTON
WELLINGTON
CALIFORNIA
EQUATORIAL
MONTGOMERY
PHILIPPINE
DEMOCRATIC
BRATISLAVA
DARUSSALAM
HARRISBURG
BASSETERRE
MAURITANIA
LIBREVILLE
MONTEVIDEO

## 7th Letter

COPENHAGEN
DARUSSALAM
DEMOCRATIC
MAURITANIA
YUGOSLAVIA
HARRISBURG
BANGLADESH
BASSETERRE
MICRONESIA
MONTENEGRO
PROVIDENCE
SACRAMENTO
WASHINGTON
WELLINGTON
NOUAKCHOTT
AZERBAIJAN
GRENADINES
LIBREVILLE
MARTINIQUE
MONTEVIDEO
MOZAMBIQUE
AUSTRALIAN
BRATISLAVA
MONTPELIER
SEYCHELLES
MONTGOMERY
TYRRHENIAN
GUADELOUPE
LUXEMBOURG
PHILIPPINE
CALIFORNIA
CLIPPERTON
EQUATORIAL
MONTSERRAT
PARAMARIBO
CHARLESTON
KAZAKHSTAN
MADAGASCAR
ORANJESTAD
TAJIKISTAN
UZBEKISTAN
WILLEMSTAD
ANTARCTICA
BRIDGETOWN
CORONATION
GEORGETOWN
TANGANYIKA

## 8th Letter

BRATISLAVA
MADAGASCAR
MONTEVIDEO
BANGLADESH
MONTGOMERY
COPENHAGEN
MONTENEGRO
ANTARCTICA
AUSTRALIAN
CORONATION
EQUATORIAL
MONTPELIER
PARAMARIBO
PHILIPPINE
TANGANYIKA
TYRRHENIAN
AZERBAIJAN
DARUSSALAM
LIBREVILLE
SEYCHELLES
CALIFORNIA
GRENADINES
MAURITANIA
PROVIDENCE
SACRAMENTO
BRIDGETOWN
GEORGETOWN
NOUAKCHOTT
MARTINIQUE
MOZAMBIQUE
BASSETERRE
MONTSERRAT
MICRONESIA
CHARLESTON
CLIPPERTON
DEMOCRATIC
KAZAKHSTAN
ORANJESTAD
TAJIKISTAN
UZBEKISTAN
WASHINGTON
WELLINGTON
WILLEMSTAD
GUADELOUPE

HARRISB**U**RG
LUXEMBO**U**RG
YUGOSLA**V**IA

### 9th Letter

AUSTRALI**A**N
AZERBAIJ**A**N
DARUSSAL**A**M
EQUATORI**A**L
KAZAKHST**A**N
MADAGASC**A**R
MONTSERR**A**T
ORANJEST**A**D
TAJIKIST**A**N
TYRRHENI**A**N
UZBEKIST**A**N
WILLEMST**A**D
PARAMARI**B**O
ANTARCTI**C**A
PROVIDEN**C**E
COPENHAG**E**N
GRENADIN**E**S
MONTEVID**E**O
MONTPELI**E**R
SEYCHELL**E**S
CALIFORN**I**A
DEMOCRAT**I**C
MAURITAN**I**A
MICRONES**I**A
YUGOSLAV**I**A
TANGANYI**K**A
LIBREVIL**L**E
PHILIPPI**N**E
CHARLEST**O**N
CLIPPERT**O**N
CORONATI**O**N
WASHINGT**O**N
WELLINGT**O**N
GUADELOU**P**E
BASSETER**R**E
HARRISBU**R**G
LUXEMBOU**R**G
MONTENEG**R**O
MONTGOME**R**Y
BANGLADE**S**H
NOUAKCHO**T**T
SACRAMEN**T**O
MARTINIQ**U**E
MOZAMBIQ**U**E
BRATISLA**V**A
BRIDGETO**W**N
GEORGETO**W**N

### 10th Letter

ANTARCTIC**A**
BRATISLAV**A**
CALIFORNI**A**
MAURITANI**A**
MICRONESI**A**
TANGANYIK**A**
YUGOSLAVI**A**
DEMOCRATI**C**
ORANJESTA**D**
WILLEMSTA**D**
BASSETERR**E**
GUADELOUP**E**
LIBREVILL**E**
MARTINIQU**E**
MOZAMBIQU**E**
PHILIPPIN**E**
PROVIDENC**E**
HARRISBUR**G**
LUXEMBOUR**G**
BANGLADES**H**
EQUATORIA**L**
DARUSSALA**M**
AUSTRALIA**N**
AZERBAIJA**N**
BRIDGETOW**N**
CHARLESTO**N**
CLIPPERTO**N**
COPENHAGE**N**
CORONATIO**N**
GEORGETOW**N**
KAZAKHSTA**N**
TAJIKISTA**N**
TYRRHENIA**N**
UZBEKISTA**N**
WASHINGTO**N**
WELLINGTO**N**
MONTENEGR**O**
MONTEVIDE**O**
PARAMARIB**O**
SACRAMENT**O**
MADAGASCA**R**
MONTPELIE**R**
GRENADINE**S**
SEYCHELLE**S**
MONTSERRA**T**
NOUAKCHOT**T**
MONTGOMER**Y**

## 11 Letter

### 1st Letter

**A**FGHANISTAN
**B**RAZZAVILLE
**C**ARPENTARIA
**C**HRISTOPHER
**C**ONNECTICUT
**H**ERZEGOVINA
**L**AKSHADWEEP
**M**ISSISSIPPI
**M**ONTPELLIER
**N**ETHERLANDS
**O**UAGADOUGOU
**P**HILIPPINES
**S**PRINGFIELD
**S**WITZERLAND
**T**ALLAHASSEE
**T**EGUCIGALPA
**T**ERRITORIES

### 2nd Letter

C**A**RPENTARIA
L**A**KSHADWEEP
T**A**LLAHASSEE
H**E**RZEGOVINA
N**E**THERLANDS
T**E**GUCIGALPA
T**E**RRITORIES
A**F**GHANISTAN
C**H**RISTOPHER
P**H**ILIPPINES
M**I**SSISSIPPI
C**O**NNECTICUT
M**O**NTPELLIER
S**P**RINGFIELD
B**R**AZZAVILLE
O**U**AGADOUGOU
S**W**ITZERLAND

### 3rd Letter

BR**A**ZZAVILLE
OU**A**GADOUGOU
AF**G**HANISTAN
TE**G**UCIGALPA
PH**I**LIPPINES
SW**I**TZERLAND
LA**K**SHADWEEP
TA**L**LAHASSEE
CO**N**NECTICUT
MO**N**TPELLIER
CA**R**PENTARIA
CH**R**ISTOPHER
HE**R**ZEGOVINA
SP**R**INGFIELD
TE**R**RITORIES
MI**S**SISSIPPI
NE**T**HERLANDS

### 4th Letter

OUA**G**ADOUGOU
AFG**H**ANISTAN
NET**H**ERLANDS
CHR**I**STOPHER
SPR**I**NGFIELD
PHI**L**IPPINES
TAL**L**AHASSEE
CON**N**ECTICUT
CAR**P**ENTARIA
TER**R**ITORIES
LAK**S**HADWEEP
MIS**S**ISSIPPI
MON**T**PELLIER
SWI**T**ZERLAND
TEG**U**CIGALPA
BRA**Z**ZAVILLE
HER**Z**EGOVINA

### 5th Letter

AFGH**A**NISTAN
OUAG**A**DOUGOU
TALL**A**HASSEE
TEGU**C**IGALPA
CARP**E**NTARIA
CONN**E**CTICUT
HERZ**E**GOVINA
NETH**E**RLANDS
LAKS**H**ADWEEP
MISS**I**SSIPPI
PHIL**I**PPINES
TERR**I**TORIES
SPRI**N**GFIELD
MONT**P**ELLIER
CHRI**S**TOPHER
BRAZ**Z**AVILLE
SWIT**Z**ERLAND

### 6th Letter

BRAZZ**A**VILLE
LAKSH**A**DWEEP
CONNE**C**TICUT
OUAGA**D**OUGOU
MONTP**E**LLIER
SWITZ**E**RLAND
HERZE**G**OVINA
SPRIN**G**FIELD
TALLA**H**ASSEE
TEGUC**I**GALPA
AFGHA**N**ISTAN
CARPE**N**TARIA
PHILI**P**PINES
NETHE**R**LANDS
MISSI**S**SIPPI
CHRIS**T**OPHER
TERRI**T**ORIES

### 7th Letter

TALLAH**A**SSEE
LAKSHA**D**WEEP
SPRING**F**IELD
TEGUCI**G**ALPA
AFGHAN**I**STAN
MONTPE**L**LIER
NETHER**L**ANDS
CHRIST**O**PHER
HERZEG**O**VINA
OUAGAD**O**UGOU
TERRIT**O**RIES
PHILIP**P**INES
SWITZE**R**LAND
MISSIS**S**IPPI
CARPEN**T**ARIA
CONNEC**T**ICUT
BRAZZA**V**ILLE

### 8th Letter

CARPENT**A**RIA
NETHERL**A**NDS
TEGUCIG**A**LPA
BRAZZAV**I**LLE
CONNECT**I**CUT
MISSISS**I**PPI
PHILIPP**I**NES
SPRINGF**I**ELD
MONTPEL**L**IER
SWITZER**L**AND
CHRISTO**P**HER
TERRITO**R**IES
AFGHANI**S**TAN
TALLAHA**S**SEE
OUAGADO**U**GOU
HERZEGO**V**INA
LAKSHAD**W**EEP

### 9th Letter

SWITZERL**A**ND
CONNECTI**C**UT
LAKSHADW**E**EP
SPRINGFI**E**LD
OUAGADOU**G**OU
CHRISTOP**H**ER
HERZEGOV**I**NA
MONTPELL**I**ER
TERRITOR**I**ES
BRAZZAVI**L**LE
TEGUCIGA**L**PA
NETHERLA**N**DS
PHILIPPI**N**ES
MISSISSI**P**PI
CARPENTA**R**IA
TALLAHAS**S**EE
AFGHANIS**T**AN

### 10th Letter

AFGHANIST**A**N
NETHERLAN**D**S
CHRISTOPH**E**R
LAKSHADWE**E**P
MONTPELLI**E**R
PHILIPPIN**E**S
TALLAHASS**E**E
TERRITORI**E**S
CARPENTAR**I**A
BRAZZAVIL**L**E
SPRINGFIE**L**D
HERZEGOVI**N**A
SWITZERLA**N**D
OUAGADOUG**O**U
MISSISSIP**P**I
TEGUCIGAL**P**A
CONNECTIC**U**T

### 11th Letter

CARPENTARI**A**
HERZEGOVIN**A**

TEGUCIGALP**A**
SPRINGFIEL**D**
SWITZERLAN**D**
BRAZZAVILL**E**
TALLAHASSE**E**
MISSISSIPP**I**
AFGHANISTA**N**
LAKSHADWEE**P**
CHRISTOPHE**R**
MONTPELLIE**R**
NETHERLAND**S**
PHILIPPINE**S**
TERRITORIE**S**
CONNECTICU**T**
OUAGADOUGO**U**

## 12 Letter

### 1st Letter

**A**NTANANARIVO
**F**ORTDEFRANCE
**I**NDIANAPOLIS
**P**ENNSYLVANIA
**T**URKMENISTAN
**Y**AMOUSSOUKRO

### 2nd Letter

Y**A**MOUSSOUKRO
P**E**NNSYLVANIA
A**N**TANANARIVO
I**N**DIANAPOLIS
F**O**RTDEFRANCE
T**U**RKMENISTAN

### 3rd Letter

IN**D**IANAPOLIS
YA**M**OUSSOUKRO
PE**N**NSYLVANIA
FO**R**TDEFRANCE
TU**R**KMENISTAN
AN**T**ANANARIVO

### 4th Letter

ANT**A**NANARIVO
IND**I**ANAPOLIS
TUR**K**MENISTAN
PEN**N**SYLVANIA
YAM**O**USSOUKRO
FOR**T**DEFRANCE

### 5th Letter

INDI**A**NAPOLIS
FORT**D**EFRANCE
TURK**M**ENISTAN
ANTA**N**ANARIVO
PENN**S**YLVANIA
YAMO**U**SSOUKRO

### 6th Letter

ANTAN**A**NARIVO
FORTD**E**FRANCE
TURKM**E**NISTAN
INDIA**N**APOLIS
YAMOU**S**SOUKRO
PENNS**Y**LVANIA

### 7th Letter

INDIAN**A**POLIS
FORTDE**F**RANCE
PENNSY**L**VANIA
ANTANA**N**ARIVO
TURKME**N**ISTAN
YAMOUS**S**OUKRO

### 8th Letter

ANTANAN**A**RIVO
TURKMEN**I**STAN
YAMOUSS**O**UKRO
INDIANA**P**OLIS
FORTDEF**R**ANCE
PENNSYL**V**ANIA

### 9th Letter

FORTDEFR**A**NCE
PENNSYLV**A**NIA
INDIANAP**O**LIS
ANTANANA**R**IVO
TURKMENI**S**TAN
YAMOUSSO**U**KRO

### 10th Letter

ANTANANAR**I**VO
YAMOUSSOU**K**RO
INDIANAPO**L**IS
FORTDEFRA**N**CE
PENNSYLVA**N**IA
TURKMENIS**T**AN

### 11th Letter

TURKMENIST**A**N
FORTDEFRAN**C**E
INDIANAPOL**I**S
PENNSYLVAN**I**A
YAMOUSSOUK**R**O
ANTANANARI**V**O

### 12th Letter

PENNSYLVANI**A**
FORTDEFRANC**E**
TURKMENISTA**N**
ANTANANARIV**O**
YAMOUSSOUKR**O**
INDIANAPOLI**S**

## 13 Letter

### 1st Letter

**L**IECHTENSTEIN
**M**ASSACHUSETTS
**M**EDITERRANEAN

### 2nd Letter

M**A**SSACHUSETTS
M**E**DITERRANEAN
L**I**ECHTENSTEIN

### 3rd Letter

ME**D**ITERRANEAN
LI**E**CHTENSTEIN
MA**S**SACHUSETTS

### 4th Letter

LIE**C**HTENSTEIN
MED**I**TERRANEAN
MAS**S**ACHUSETTS

### 5th Letter

MASS**A**CHUSETTS
MEDI**T**ERRANEAN
LIEC**H**TENSTEIN

### 6th Letter

MEDIT**E**RRANEAN
MASSA**C**HUSETTS
LIECH**T**ENSTEIN

### 7th Letter

LIECHT**E**NSTEIN
MASSAC**H**USETTS
MEDITE**R**RANEAN

### 8th Letter

LIECHTE**N**STEIN
MEDITER**R**ANEAN
MASSACH**U**SETTS

### 9th Letter

MEDITERR**A**NEAN
LIECHTEN**S**TEIN
MASSACHU**S**ETTS

### 10th Letter

MASSACHUS**E**TTS
MEDITERRA**N**EAN
LIECHTENS**T**EIN

### 11th Letter

LIECHTENST**E**IN
MEDITERRAN**E**AN
MASSACHUSE**T**TS

### 12th Letter

MEDITERRANE**A**N
LIECHTENSTE**I**N
MASSACHUSET**T**S

### 13th Letter

LIECHTENSTEI**N**
MEDITERRANEA**N**
MASSACHUSETT**S**

# TABLE OF COUNTRIES, WITH ABBREVIATIONS AND CAPITAL CITIES

| COUNTRY | ABBR. | CAPITAL |
|---|---|---|
| AFGHANISTAN | AF | KABUL |
| ALAND ISLANDS | — | —— |
| ALBANIA | AL | TIRANA |
| ALGERIA | DZ | ALGER |
| AMERICAN SAMOA | AS | PAGO PAGO |
| AMSTERDAM ISLANDS | — | —— |
| ANDORRA | AD | ANDORRA LA VELLA |
| ANGOLA | AO | LUANDA |
| ANGUILLA | AI | THE VALLEY |
| ANDAMAN ISLANDS | US | —— |
| ANNOBON ISLAND | IT | —— |
| ANTARCTICA | AQ | —— |
| ANTIGUA | AG | SAINT JOHNS |
| ARGENTINA | AR | BUENOS AIRES |
| ARMENIA | AM | YEREVAN |
| ARUBA | AW | ORANJESTAD |
| ASCENSION ISLAND | UK | —— |
| AUSTRALIA | AU | CANBERRA |
| AUSTRIA | AT | VIENNA |
| AVES ISLAND | IT | —— |
| AZERBAIJAN | AZ | BAKU |
| AZORES ISLANDS | PT | —— |
| BAHAMAS | BS | NASSAU |
| BAHRAIN | BH | MANAMA |
| BAILIWICK OF JERSEY | JE | —— |
| BANABA ISLAND | JP | —— |
| BANGLADESH | BD | DHAKA |
| BARBADOS | BB | BRIDGETOWN |
| BARBUDA | AG | SAINT JOHN'S |
| BELARUS | BY | MINSK |
| BELGIUM | BE | BRUSSELS |
| BELIZE | BZ | BELMOPAN |
| BENIN | BJ | PORTO NOVO |
| BERMUDA | BM | HAMILTON |
| BHUTAN | BT | THIMPHU (THIMBU) |
| BOLIVIA | BO | LA PAZ |
| BOSNIA | BA | —— |
| BOTSWANA | BW | GABORONE |
| BOUVET ISLAND | BV | —— |
| BRAZIL | BR | BRASILIA |
| BRITISH INDIAN OCEAN TERRITORY | IO | —— |
| BRITISH VIRGIN ISLANDS | VG | ROAD TOWN, TORTOLA |
| BRUNEI DARUSSALAM | BN | BANDAR SERI BEGAWAN |
| BULGARIA | BG | SOFIA |
| BURKINA FASO | BF | OUAGADOUGOU |
| BURUNDI | BI | BUJUMBURA |
| CAICOS ISLANDS | TC | COCKBURN TOWN, GRANDTURK |
| CAMBODIA | KH | PHNOM PENH |
| CAMEROON | CM | YAOUNDE |
| CANADA | CA | OTTAWA |
| CANARY ISLANDS | ES | —— |
| CAPE VERDE | CV | PRAIA |
| CAYMAN ISLANDS | KY | GEORGE TOWN |
| CENTRAL AFRICAN REPUBLIC | CF | BANGUI |
| CEUTA ISLAND | ES | —— |
| CHAD | TD | N'DJAMENA |
| CHATHAM ISLAND | IT | —— |
| CHILE | CL | SANTIAGO |
| CHINA | CN | BEIJING |
| CHRISTMAS ISLAND | CX | —— |
| CLIPPERTON ISLAND | IT | —— |
| COCOS ISLANDS | CC | —— |
| COLOMBIA | CO | BOGOTA |
| COMOROS | KM | MORONI |
| CONGO | CG | BRAZZAVILLE |
| COOK ISLANDS | CK | RAROTONGA |
| COSTA RICA | CR | SAN JOSE |
| CROATIA | HR | ZAGREB |
| CROZET | | —— |
| CUBA | CU | HAVANA |
| CYPRUS | CY | NICOSIA |
| CZECH REPUBLIC | CZ | PRAGUE |
| DEMOCRATIC PEOPLE'S REPUBLIC OF KOREA | KP | P'YONGYANG |
| DEMOCRATIC REPUBLIC OF CONGO (ZAIRE) | | KINSHASA |
| DENMARK | DK | COPENHAGEN |
| DJIBOUTI | DJ | DJIBOUTI |
| DOMINICA | DM | ROSEAU |
| DOMINICAN REPUBLIC | DO | SANTO DOMINGO |
| EASTER ISLAND | US | —— |
| EAST TIMOR | TP | —— |
| ECUADOR | EC | QUITO |
| EGYPT | EG | CAIRO |
| EL SALVADOR | SV | SAN SALVADOR |
| ENGLAND | EN | LONDON |
| EQUATORIAL GUINEA | GQ | MALABO |

| COUNTRY | ABBR. | CAPITAL | COUNTRY | ABBR. | CAPITAL | COUNTRY | ABBR. | CAPITAL |
|---|---|---|---|---|---|---|---|---|
| ERITREA | ER | ASMARA | HERZEGOVINA | BA | —— | LITHUANIA | LT | VILNIUS |
| ESTONIA | EE | TALLINN | HONDURAS | HN | TEGUCIGALPA | LUXEMBOURG | LU | LUXEMBOURG |
| ETHIOPIA | ET | ADDIS ABABA | HONG KONG | HK | VICTORIA | **M**ACAO | MO | MACAO |
| **F**AEROE ISLANDS | FO | THORSHAVN | HOWLAND ISLAND | UM | —— | MACEDONIA | MK | —— |
| FALKLAND ISLANDS | FK | STANLEY | HUNGARY | HU | BUDAPEST | MACQUARIE ISLAND | NF | —— |
| FERNANDO | | | **I**CELAND | IS | REYKJAVIK | MADAGASCAR | MG | ANTANA- |
| DE NORONHA | | | ISLAND OF MAN | IM | —— | | | NARIVO |
| ISLAND | BR | —— | INDIA | IN | NEW DELHI | MADEIRA ISLANDS | PT | —— |
| FIJI | FJ | SUVA | INDONESIA | ID | JAKARTA | MALAWI | MW | LILONGWE |
| FINLAND | FI | HELSINKI | IRAN | IR | TEHRAN | MALAYSIA | MY | KUALA |
| FRANCE | FR | PARIS | IRAQ | IQ | BAGDAD | | | LUMPUR |
| FRENCH GUIANA | GF | CAYENNE | IRELAND | IE | DUBLIN | MALDIVES | MV | MALE |
| FRENCH POLYNESIA | PF | PAPEETE | ISRAEL | IL | JERUSALEM | MALI | ML | BAMAKO |
| FRENCH | | | ITALY | IT | ROME | MALPELO PACIFIC | | |
| SOUTHERN | | | IVORY COAST | CI | ABIDJAN | ISLAND | IT | —— |
| TERRITORIES | TF | —— | **J**AMAICA | JM | KINGSTON | MALTA | MT | VALLETTA |
| FUTANA ISLANDS | WF | —— | JAN MAYEN ISLANDS | SJ | —— | MARIANA ISLANDS | MP | —— |
| **G**ABON | GA | LIBREVILLE | JAPAN | JP | TOYKO | MARSHALL ISLANDS | MH | JALUIT |
| GALAPAGOS ISLANDS | EC | —— | JOHNSTON ATOLL | UM | —— | MARTINIQUE | MQ | FORT-DE- |
| GAMBIA | GM | BANJUL | JORDAN | JO | AMMAN | | | FRANCE |
| GEORGIA | GE | TBILISI | **K**AZAKHSTAN | KZ | ALMATY | MAURITANIA | MR | NOUAKCHOTT |
| GERMANY | DE | BERLIN | KENYA | KE | NAIROBI | MAURITIUS | MU | PORT LOUIS |
| GHANA | GH | ACCRA | KERGUELEN ISLANDS | FR | —— | MAYOTTE | YT | —— |
| GIBRALTAR | GI | GIBRALTER | KINGMAN REEF | | | MCDONALD ISLANDS | HM | —— |
| GREECE | GR | ATHENS | ISLAND | UM | —— | MELILLA ISLAND | ES | —— |
| GREENLAND | GL | GODTHAR | KIRIBATI | KI | TARAWA | MEXICO | MX | MEXICO |
| GRENADA | GD | SAINT | KUWAIT | KW | KUWAIT CITY | | | CITY |
| | | GEORGE'S | KYRGYSTAN | KG | BISHKEK | MICRONESIA | FM | KOLONIA |
| GRENADINES | VC | —— | **L**AKSHADWEEP | | | MIDWAY ISLANDS | UM | —— |
| GUADELOUPE | GP | BASSE TERRE | ISLAND | CA | —— | MINAMI TORISHIMA | | |
| GUAM | GU | AGANA | LAOS DEMOCRATIC | | | ISLAND | SP | —— |
| GUATEMALA | GT | GUATEMALA | REPUBLIC | LA | VIENTIANE | MOLDOVA | MD | KISHINEV |
| GUERNSEY | GG | —— | LATVIA | LV | RIGA | MONACO | MC | MONACO |
| GUINEA | GN | CONAKRY | LEBANON | LB | BEIRUT | MONGOLIA | MN | ULAN BATOR |
| GUINEA-BISSAU | GW | BISSAU | LESOTHO | LS | MASERU | MONTENEGRO | YU | —— |
| GUYANA | GY | GEORGETOWN | LIBERIA | LR | MONROVIA | MONTSERRAT | MS | PLYMOUTH |
| **H**AITI | HT | PORT- | LIBYA | LY | TRIPOLI | MOROCCO | MA | RABAT |
| | | AU-PRINCE | LIECHTENSTEIN | LI | VADUZ | MOZAMBIQUE | MZ | MAPUTO |
| HEARD ISLANDS | HM | —— | LINE ISLANDS | JP | —— | MYANMAR | BM | YANGON |

| COUNTRY | ABBR. | CAPITAL |
|---|---|---|
| NAMIBIA | NA | WINDHOEK |
| NAURU | NR | YAREN |
| NAVASSA ISLAND | UM | — |
| NEPAL | NP | KATHMANDU |
| NETHERLANDS | NL | AMSTERDAM |
| NETHERLANDS ANTILLES | AN | WILLEMSTAD |
| NEW CALEDONIA | NC | NOUMEA |
| NEW ZEALAND | NZ | WELLINGTON |
| NICARAGUA | NI | MANAGUA |
| NIGER | NE | NIAMEY |
| NIGERIA | NG | ABUJA |
| NIUE | NU | ALOFI |
| NORFOLK ISLAND | NF | — |
| NORTHERN MARIANA ISLANDS | NP | — |
| NORWAY | NO | OSLO |
| OGASAWARA ISLAND | US | — |
| OMAN | OM | MUSCAT |
| PAKISTAN | PK | ISLAMABAD |
| PALAU | PW | — |
| PANAMA | PA | PANAMA |
| PAPUA NEW GUINEA | PG | PORT MORESBY |
| PARAGUAY | PY | ASUNCION |
| PERU | PE | LIMA |
| PHILIPPINES | PH | MANILA |
| PITCAIRN | PN | — |
| POLAND | PL | WARSAW |
| PORTUGAL | PT | LISBON |
| PRINCE EDWARD ISLAND | UK | — |
| PROVEDEN ISLAND | CO | — |
| PUERTO RICO | PR | SAN JUAN |
| QATAR | QA | AD DAWHAH |
| REPUBLIC OF KOREA | KR | SEOUL |
| REUNION | RE | SAINT-DENIS |
| REVILLA GIGEDO ISLANDS | US | — |
| RODRIGUES ISLAND | US | — |
| ROMANIA | RO | BUCHAREST |
| RUSSIA | RU | MOSCOW |
| RWANDA | RW | KIGALI |
| SAINT CHRISTOPHER ISLAND | KN | — |
| SAINT HELENA | SH | JAMESTOWN |
| SAINT KITTS | KN | BASSETERRE |
| SAINT LUCIA | LC | CASTRIES |
| SAINT MAARTEN | SM | — |
| SAINT MARTIN | SM | — |
| SAINT MIQUELON | PM | — |
| SAINT NEVIS | KN | BASSETERRE |
| SAINT PAUL | — | — |
| SAINT PIERRE | PM | — |
| SAINT VINCENT | VC | KINGSTOWN |
| SAMOA | WS | APIA |
| SAN INO | SM | — |
| SAN MARINO | SM | SAN MARINO |
| SAN ANDREAS ISLAND | CO | |
| SAO TOME AND PRINCIPE | ST | SAO TOME |
| SAUDI ARABIA | SA | RIYADH |
| SCOTLAND | UK | — |
| SENEGAL | SN | DAKAR |
| SERBIA | YU | — |
| SEYCHELLES | SC | VICTORIA |
| SIERRA LEONE | SL | FREETOWN |
| SINGAPORE | SG | SINGAPORE |
| SLOVAKIA | SK | BRATISLAVA |
| SLOVENIA | SI | LJUBLJANA |
| SOLOMON ISLANDS | SB | HONIARA |
| SOMALIA | SO | MOGADISHU |
| SOUTH AFRICA | ZA | CAPE TOWN |
| SOUTH GEORGIA | GS | — |
| SPAIN | ES | MADRID |
| SRI LANKA | LK | COLOMBO |
| SUDAN | SD | KHARTOUM |
| SURINAM | SR | PARAMARIBO |
| SVALBARD ISLANDS | SJ | LONGYEAR CITY |
| SWAZILAND | SZ | MBABANE |
| SWEDEN | SE | STOCKHOLM |
| SWITZERLAND | CH | BERN |
| SYRIA | SY | DAMASCUS |
| TAIWAN | TW | T'AI-PEI |
| TAJIKISTAN | TJ | DUSHANBE |
| TANZANIA | TZ | DODOMA |
| THAILAND | TH | BANGKOK |
| TOBAGO | TT | PORT OF SPAIN |
| TOGO | TG | LOME |
| TOKELAU | TK | — |
| TONGA | TO | NUKUALOFA |
| TRINIDAD | TT | PORT OF SPAIN |
| TRISTAN DA CUNHA ISLAND | UK | — |
| TUNISIA | TN | TUNIS |
| TURKEY | TR | ANKARA |
| TURKMENISTAN | TM | ASHGABAT |
| TURKS ISLANDS | TC | — |
| UGANDA | UG | KAMPALA |
| UKRAINE | UA | KIEV |
| UNITED ARAB EMIRATES | AE | ABU DHABI |
| UNITED KINGDOM | UK | LONDON |
| UNITED STATES OF AMERICA | US | WASHINGTON |
| URAGUAY | UY | MONTEVIDEO |
| US VIRGIN ISLANDS | VI | CHARLOTTE AMALIE |
| UZBEKISTAN | UZ | TASHKENT |

| COUNTRY | ABBR. | CAPITAL |
|---|---|---|
| **V**ANUATU | VU | VILA |
| VATICAN CITY | VA | VATICAN CITY |
| VENEZUELA | VE | CARACAS |
| VIETNAM | VN | HANOI |
| VIRGIN ISLANDS | VI | —— |
| WAKE ISLAND | UM | —— |
| WALES | UK | —— |
| WALLIS ISLANDS | WF | —— |
| WESTERN SAHARA | EH | —— |
| **Y**EMEN | YE | SANAA |
| YUGOSLAVIA | YU | BELGRADE |
| ZAMBIA | ZM | LUSAKA |
| ZANZIBAR | US | —— |
| ZIMBABWE | ZW | HARARE |

# TABLE OF STATES, WITH ABBREVIATIONS AND CAPITAL CITIES

| STATE | ABBR. | CAPITAL |
|---|---|---|
| **A**LABAMA | AL | MONTGOMERY |
| ALASKA | AK | JUNEAU |
| ARIZONA | AZ | PHOENIX |
| ARKANSAS | AR | LITTLE ROCK |
| **C**ALIFORNIA | CA | SACRAMENTO |
| COLORADO | CO | DENVER |
| CONNECTICUT | CT | HARTFORD |
| **D**ELAWARE | DE | DOVER |
| **F**LORIDA | FL | TALLAHASSEE |
| **G**EORGIA | GA | ATLANTA |
| **H**AWAII | HI | HONOLULU |
| **I**DAHO | ID | BOISE |
| ILLINOIS | IL | SPRINGFIELD |
| INDIANA | IN | INDIANAPOLIS |
| IOWA | IA | DES MOINES |
| **K**ANSAS | KS | TOPEKA |
| KENTUCKY | KY | FRANKFORT |
| **L**OUISIANA | LA | BATON ROUGE |
| **M**AINE | ME | AUGUSTA |
| MARYLAND | MD | ANNAPOLIS |
| MASSACHUSETTS | MA | BOSTON |
| MICHIGAN | MI | LANSING |
| MINNESOTA | MN | SAINT PAUL |
| MISSISSIPPI | MS | JACKSON |
| MISSOURI | MO | JEFFERSON CITY |
| MONTANA | MT | HELENA |
| **N**EBRASKA | NE | LINCOLN |
| NEVADA | NV | CARSON CITY |
| NEW HAMPSHIRE | NH | CONCORD |
| NEW JERSEY | NJ | TRENTON |
| NEW MEXICO | NM | SANTA FE |
| NEW YORK | NY | ALBANY |
| NORTH CAROLINA | NC | RALEIGH |
| NORTH DAKOTA | ND | BISMARCK |
| **O**HIO | OH | COLUMBUS |
| OKLAHOMA | OK | OKLAHOMA CITY |
| OREGON | OR | SALEM |
| **P**ENNSYLVANIA | PA | HARRISBURG |
| **R**HODE ISLAND | RI | PROVIDENCE |
| **S**OUTH CAROLINA | SC | COLUMBIA |
| SOUTH DAKOTA | SD | PIERRE |
| **T**ENNESSEE | TN | NASHVILLE |
| TEXAS | TX | AUSTIN |
| **U**TAH | UT | SALT LAKE CITY |
| **V**ERMONT | VT | MONTPELIER |
| VIRGINIA | VA | RICHMOND |
| **W**ASHINGTON | WA | OLYMPIA |
| WEST VIRGINIA | WV | CHARLESTON |
| WISCONSIN | WI | MADISON |
| WYOMING | WY | CHEYENNE |

# MAJOR BODIES OF WATER

ADRIATIC SEA
AEGEAN SEA
AGULHAS BASIN
ALEUTIAN BASIN
ALEUTIAN ISLANDS
AMUNDSEN GULF
ARABIAN SEA
ARAFURA SEA
ARAL SEA
ARGENTINE BASIN
ATLANTIC OCEAN
ATLANTIC-INDIAN BASIN
BAFFIN BAY
BALTIC SEA
BANDA SEA
BARENTS SEA
BASS STRAIT
BAY OF BENGAL
BAY OF BISCAY
BAY OF FUNDI
BEAUFORD SEA
BERING SEA
BERING STRAIT
BLACK SEA
BRAZIL BASIN
BRISTOL BAY
CANADA BASIN
CARIBBEAN SEA
CASPIAN SEA
CELEBES SEA
CELTIC SEA
CENTRAL PACIFIC BASIN
CHUKCHI SEA
CHURCHILL LAKE
CORAL SEA
CORONATION GULF
CROZET BASIN
DAVIS STRAIT
DEAD SEA
DENMARK STRAIT
EAST CAROLINE BASIN
EAST CHINA SEA
EAST MARIANA BASIN
EAST SIBERIAN SEA
ENGLISH CHANNEL
FOXE CHANNEL
FOXE BASIN
GREAT AUSTRALIAN BIGHT
GREAT BEAR LAKE
GREAT SALT LAKE
GREAT SLAVE LAKE
GUINEA BASIN
GULF OF ADEN
GULF OF BAHRAIN
GULF OF BOOTHIA
GULF OF CALIFORNIA
GULF OF CARPENTARIA
GULF OF FINLAND
GULF OF GUINEA
GULF OF MEXICO
GULF OF PANAMA
GULF OF SAINT LAWRENCE
GULF OF SIDRA
GULF OF TONKIN
GULF OF THAILAND
HECATE STRAIT
HUDSON BAY
HUDSON STRAIT
INDIAN OCEAN
IRISH SEA
JAVA SEA
KANE BASIN
KARA SEA
KOREA STRAIT
KUSKOKWIM BAY
LABRADOR SEA
LAKE ALBERT
LAKE ATHABASCA
LAKE BAIKAL
LAKE BALKHASH
LAKE EDWARD
LAKE ERIE
LAKE HURON
LAKE LADOGA
LAKE MALAWI
LAKE MICHIGAN
LAKE ONTARIO
LAKE SUPERIOR
LAKE TANGANYIKA
LAKE TITICACA
LAKE VICTORIA
LAKE WINNIPEG
LANCASTER SOUND
LAPTEV SEA
LINCOLN SEA
M'CLINTOCK CHANNEL
M'CLURE STRAIT
MADAGASCAR BASIN
MAKAROV BASIN
MASCARENE BASIN
MEDITERRANEAN SEA
MOZAMBIQUE CHANNEL
NANSEN BASIN
NORTH AMERICAN BASIN
NORTH SEA
NORTHWEST PACIFIC BASIN
NORWEGIAN SEA
NORWEGIAN BAY
PACIFIC OCEAN
PEARY CHANNEL
PERSIAN GULF
PERU BASIN
PHILIPPINE SEA
QUEEN CHARLOTTE SOUND
QUEEN MAUD GULF
RED SEA
REINDEER LAKE
ROSS SEA
SCORESBY SOUND
SCOTIA SEA
SEA OF JAPAN
SEA OF OKHOTSK
SHELIKHOV GULF
SIERRA LEONE BASIN
SMITH BAY
SOLOMON SEA
SOUTH CHINA SEA
SPENCER GULF
STRAIT OF HORMUZ
STRAIT OF MAGELLAN
STRAITS OF FLORIDA
SULU SEA
TAIWAN STRAIT
TASMAN SEA
TIMOR SEA
TYRRHENIAN SEA
UNGAVA BAY
VISCOUNT MELVILLE SOUND
WEDDELL SEA
WEST CAROLINE BASIN
WHARTON BASIN
WHITE SEA
YELLOW SEA